TORAH

THE FIVE BOOKS *of* MOSES

WITH COMPLETE HAFTARAH CYCLE

THE FIVE BOOKS *of* MOSES
TORAH
WITH COMPLETE HAFTARAH CYCLE

with reflections and inspirations compiled by
RABBI CHAIM MILLER
from hundreds of Jewish thinkers, ancient to contemporary

The SLAGER EDITION

THE GUTNICK LIBRARY
of JEWISH CLASSICS

First Edition
First impression . . . . November 2011

TORAH — THE FIVE BOOKS OF MOSES
WITH COMPLETE HAFTARAH CYCLE

with reflections and inspirations compiled by Rabbi Chaim Miller
from hundreds of Jewish thinkers, ancient to contemporary

ISBN 13: 978-1-934152-26-3
ISBN 10: 1-934152-26-9

Library of Congress Control Number: 2011920491

© Copyright 2011 by Chaim Miller
Printed in China

All rights reserved. No part of this book may be reproduced in any manner whatsoever without written permission from the copyright holder, except in the case of brief quotations in reviews for inclusion in a magazine, newspaper or broadcast.

We gratefully acknowledge the assistance of Gefen Publishing House
in the preparation of parts of the Hebrew text.

TABLE *of* CONTENTS

Introduction	xi
Transliteration rules	xxi
Blessings on reading the Torah	xxiii
Blessings on reading the Haftarah	1286
References	1481
Bibliography	1495

GENESIS בראשית

	PARASHAH	HAFTARAH
Bere'shit	2	1288
Noah	36	1291
Lekh Lekha	62	1293
Va-Yera'	88	1295
Ḥayyei Sarah	120	1298
Toledot	142	1301
Va-Yetze'	166	1303
Va-Yishlaḥ	198	1307
Va-Yeshev	228	1310
Mikketz	252	1311
Va-Yiggash	282	1313
Va-Yeḥi	304	1315

EXODUS שמות

	PARASHAH	HAFTARAH
Shemot	328	1316
Va-'Era'	354	1319
Bo'	380	1322
Be-Shallaḥ	406	1323
Yitro	432	1328
Mishpatim	456	1330
Terumah	480	1332
Tetzavveh	498	1334
Ki Tissa'	518	1336
Va-Yakhel	550	1340
Pekudei	572	1342

LEVITICUS ויקרא

	PARASHAH	HAFTARAH
Va-Yikra'	590	1344
Tzav	618	1347
Shemini	638	1349
Tazria‘	660	1353
Metzora‘	676	1356
'Aḥarei Mot	696	1358
Kedoshim	716	1359
'Emor	734	1363
Be-Har	760	1365
Be-Ḥukkotai	774	1367

NUMBERS במדבר

	PARASHAH	HAFTARAH
Be-Midbar	794	1369
Naso'	820	1371
Be-Ha‘alotekha	852	1373
Shelaḥ-Lekha	882	1376
Koraḥ	908	1378
Ḥukkat	930	1381
Balak	954	1384
Pinḥas	978	1386
Mattot	1010	1388
Mase'ei	1032	1390

DEUTERONOMY דברים

	PARASHAH	HAFTARAH
Devarim	1056	1394
Va-'Etḥannan	1080	1396
‘Ekev	1106	1398
Re'eh	1132	1401
Shofetim	1160	1402
Ki Tetze'	1184	1404
Ki Tavo'	1210	1405
Nitzavim	1234	1407
Va-Yelekh	1246	1409
Ha'azinu	1256	1412
Ve-Zo't Ha-Berakhah	1270	1476

INDEX of SPECIAL TORAH READINGS

TORAH READING	MAFTIR	Occasion	HAFTARAH
WEEKLY PARASHAH		Shabbat Erev Rosh Ḥodesh	P. 1415
NUMBERS 28:1–15 P. 998		Rosh Ḥodesh	
WEEKLY PARASHAH	NUMBERS 28:9–15 P. 1000	Shabbat Rosh Ḥodesh	P. 1417
GENESIS 21:1–34 P. 106	NUMBERS 29:1–6 P. 1004	Rosh Ha-Shanah I	P. 1457
GENESIS 22:1–24 P. 112	NUMBERS 29:1–6 P. 1004	Rosh Ha-Shanah II	P. 1460
EXODUS 32:11–14; 34:1–10 P. 530		Fast of Gedaliah [1]	P. 1455
LEVITICUS 16:1–34 P. 698	NUMBERS 29:7–11 P. 1004	Yom Kippur morning	P. 1462
LEVITICUS 18:1–30 P. 710		Yom Kippur afternoon	P. 1464
LEVITICUS 22:26–23:44 P. 744	NUMBERS 29:12–16 P. 1006	Sukkot I	P. 1469
LEVITICUS 22:26–23:44 P. 744	NUMBERS 29:12–16 P. 1006	Sukkot II	P. 1471
NUMBERS 29:17–25 P. 1006		Sukkot intermediate day I	
NUMBERS 29:20–28 P. 1006		Sukkot intermediate day II	
NUMBERS 29:23–31 P. 1006		Sukkot intermediate day III	
NUMBERS 29:26–34 P. 1006		Sukkot intermediate day IV	
EXODUS 33:12–34:26 P. 540	SEE NOTE 2	Sukkot intermediate Shabbat	P. 1472
NUMBERS 29:26–34 P. 1006		Hoshana Raba	
DEUTERONOMY 14:22–16:17 P. 1148	NUMBERS 29:35–30:1 P. 1008	Shemini Atzeret	P. 1474
DEUT. 33:1–34:12; GEN. 1:1–2:3 P. 1272; 4	NUMBERS 29:35–30:1 P. 1008	Simhat Torah	P. 1476
NUMBERS 7:1–17 P. 840		Ḥanukkah I	
NUMBERS 7:18–29 P. 844		Ḥanukkah II	
NUMBERS 7:24–35 P. 844		Ḥanukkah III	
NUMBERS 7:30–41 P. 844		Ḥanukkah IV	
NUMBERS 7:36–47 P. 844		Ḥanukkah V	
NUMBERS 28:1–15; 7:42–47 P. 998; 846		Ḥanukkah VI (Rosh Ḥodesh)	
NUMBERS 7:48–59 P. 846		Ḥanukkah VII	
NUMBERS 28:1–15; 7:48–53 P. 998; 846		Ḥanukkah VII (Rosh Ḥodesh)	

1. On these days the *Torah* is read during both morning services and afternoon services. The *Haftarah* is read during afternoon services only.

2. Intermediate **Day One**—Numbers 29:17–22 (p. 1006); **Day Three**—ibid. 23–28 (p. 1006); **Day Four**—ibid. 26–31 (p. 1006).

3. **Day One**—Numbers 7:1–17 (p. 840); **Day Two**—ibid. 18–23 (p. 844); **Day Three**—ibid. 24–29 (p. 844); **Day Four**—ibid. 30–35 (p. 844); **Day Six**—six *aliyyot* are read from the weekly *Parashah*, the seventh *aliyah* is read from Numbers 28:9–15 (p. 1000), and *Maftir* from ibid. 7:42–47 (p. 846); **Day Seven**—ibid. 48–53 (p. 846); **Day Eight**—ibid. 54–8:4 (p. 846).

INDEX of SPECIAL TORAH READINGS

HAFTARAH	Occasion	MAFTIR	TORAH READING
	Ḥanukkah VIII		NUMBERS 7:54–8:4 P. 846
P. 1420; 1423	Shabbat Hanukkah (I and II)	SEE NOTE 3	WEEKLY PARASHAH
P. 1455	Tenth of Tevet [1]		EXODUS 32:11–14; 34:1–10 P. 530
P. 1424	Parashat Shekalim	EXODUS 30:11–16 P. 520	WEEKLY PARASHAH [4]
P. 1427	Parashat Zakhor	DEUT. 25:17–19 P. 1208	WEEKLY PARASHAH
P. 1455	Fast of Esther [1]		EXODUS 32:11–14; 34:1–10 P. 530
	Purim		EXODUS 17:8–16 P. 428
P. 1431	Parashat Parah	NUMBERS 19:1–22 P. 932	WEEKLY PARASHAH
P. 1433	Parashat Ha-Ḥodesh	EXODUS 12:1–20 P. 392	WEEKLY PARASHAH [4]
P. 1437	Shabbat Ha-Gadol	WEEKLY MAFTIR	WEEKLY PARASHAH
P. 1439	Pesaḥ I	NUMBERS 28:16–25 P. 1002	EXODUS 12:21–51 P. 396
P. 1441	Pesaḥ II	NUMBERS 28:16–25 P. 1002	LEVITICUS 22:26–23:44 P. 744
	Pesaḥ intermediate day I		EX. 13:1–16; NUM. 28:19–25 P. 402; 1002
	Pesaḥ intermediate day II [5]		EX. 22:24–23:19; NUM. 28:19–25 P. 468, 1002
	Pesaḥ intermediate day III [6]		EX. 34:1–26; NUM. 28:19–25 P. 542; 1002
	Pesaḥ intermediate day IV		NUMBERS 9:1–14; 28:19–25 P. 860; 1002
P. 1443	Pesaḥ intermediate Shabbat	NUM. 28:19–25 P. 1002	EXODUS 33:12–34:26 P. 540
P. 1445	Pesaḥ VII	NUM. 28:19–25 P. 1002	EXODUS 13:17–15:26 P. 408
P. 1445	Pesaḥ VIII (weekday)	NUM. 28:19–25 P. 1002	DEUTERONOMY 15:19–16:17 P. 1154
P. 1445	Pesaḥ VIII (Shabbat)	NUM. 28:19–25 P. 1002	DEUTERONOMY 14:22–16:17 P. 1148
P. 1447	Shavuot I	NUM. 28:26–31 P. 1002	EXODUS 19:1–20:23 P. 440
P. 1450	Shavuot II (weekday)	NUM. 28:26–31 P. 1002	DEUTERONOMY 15:19–16:17 P. 1154
P. 1450	Shavuot II (Shabbat)	NUM. 28:26–31 P. 1002	DEUTERONOMY 14:22–16:17 P. 1148
P. 1455	Seventeenth of Tammuz [1]		EXODUS 32:11–14; 34:1–10 P. 530
P. 1452	Ninth of Av morning		DEUTERONOMY 4:25–40 P. 1088
P. 1455	Ninth of Av afternoon		EXODUS 32:11–14; 34:1–10 P. 530

4. When Parashat Shekalim or Ha-Ḥodesh occurs on Rosh Ḥodesh, six aliyyot are read from the weekly Parashah, the seventh aliyah is read from Numbers 28:9-15 (p. 1000).

5. If the first intermediate day occurs on Shabbat, we read the portion for the first intermediate day (p. 402) on the second day.

6. If the first intermediate day occurs on Shabbat, we read the portion for the second intermediate day (p. 468) on the third day

INTRODUCTION

In my childhood and teenage years the Torah's doors had not yet opened for me. I found the Torah reading in synagogue thoroughly boring and devoid of meaning. I didn't understand Hebrew, and the antiquated translation and commentary available to me were really quite disturbing. Something *was* tugging at me, probably a sense of family and peoplehood; but why did our customs seem to be so weird and incomprehensible? And why did *nothing* in the synagogue actually make me feel accomplished and adequate? It all seemed so burdensome.

I never dreamt that the Torah could be a powerful tool of personal transformation, and that it could calm the worries of my body, mind, heart and soul on a daily basis. I had no idea that the text which appeared to me so boring would, in fact, *relieve* much of the existential boredom of my adult life and infuse it with meaning.

There is a reason why the Torah—the Five Books of Moses—is the oldest sacred text in western civilization that has been in constant use: *Because the Torah reflects your own life back to you.*

The Torah is not a story about some other people and it is not about some other time. It is a guide to your inner self, which, if read properly, can illuminate every possible human experience.

This book will prime you to read the Torah as a guide to life. You will learn to appreciate every line, perhaps every word, of the Torah as a set of tools that empower you to expand consciousness, to discover your humanity, and to cultivate your inner life.

These pages don't contain any of my own ideas. I have merely collected teachings of the great Rabbinic minds of the past two thousand years, rendering them in a contemporary voice. But you will probably find it different from any Torah commentary you have read before, because I have chosen to emphasize things that others have generally overlooked.

You see, most commentaries presume that the reader is extremely interested in the text, that he or she wants to pore over multiple possible translations, delve into the nuances of the Hebrew language, uncover inconsistencies and fix them, or be exposed to as many interpretations as possible. I'm presuming that you're not especially interested in that kind of stuff. I've included some of it—probably accounting for around ten to twenty percent of the commentary—just so that you get a "balanced diet," but I have mainly looked for something else. My key criterion for selecting comments has been *relevancy*. When selecting a passage I repeatedly asked myself: Is this insightful? Is it life-enhancing? Does this open new possibilities for self-transformation? Is it refreshing?

In other words, I'm presuming that you're turning to this book primarily for guidance in your life, to enhance your stay on this planet, and not to become the world's next great Biblical scholar.

Are we betraying the Torah's sanctity by turning it into some sort of "self-help" book?

Absolutely not. In fact, we betray the Torah by *not* doing so. "Torah" is usually translated as "law," but in Hebrew it is also derived from the word *hora'ah*, meaning "lesson" or "guidance." If you study the Torah in a mood of personal detachment, you fail to capture its essence and spirit. The Torah is meant to engage you.

And when I say "guidance" I am not talking here about Jewish law (*halakhah*). The Five Books of Moses are the source text for an enormous body of civil, criminal and ritual law which was codified in the Talmud, and subsequently in the 16th century Code of Rabbi Joseph Caro, the *Shulḥan Arukh* ("Set Table"). While this is extremely important, it has not been my focus here, and is amply dealt with in other works.

I want you to experience the Torah as a guide to inner life, as a tremendous blessing which simply needs to be unwrapped like a gift. I want the Torah to be a *revelation* which flows forth to you in the present moment. I want you to read each Torah portion as your spiritual homework for the week, helping you to reach the fullness of your humanity—something that heals your soul, and thereby *the world*.

All of this is to be found in the Torah and its vast ocean of classic commentaries. I have spent the last fifteen years of my life learning how to read the Torah as a book of *hora'ah*, insight and guidance, and this book is a humble offering to you of some of the lessons I have gathered.

If you want the Torah to be a blessing in your life, it's crucial that you have the right attitude towards reading and studying it. The emphasis should be on savoring every word and allowing it to penetrate you. Sacred energy is gushing forth when the Torah is read in the synagogue, or even when you read the text in the privacy of your own home, and you need to surrender to its power so that it can begin to transform you.

Don't be concerned if this kind of language is unfamiliar to you. As with anything, you will come to it with time. While volumes could be filled with this topic, I'd like to give you just a few basic pointers as to how to open yourself to the Torah's transformational and healing properties.

There are several phases to this process, which could be briefly summed-up as: *awakening, self-realization, growth* and *healing*.

- First, you must *awaken* from the constraints of your narrow consciousness. That's a fancy way of saying that you need to expose the faulty thought patterns that have led you to unhealthy or dysfunctional behavior.
- *Self-realization* is the difficult task of acknowledging your resistance to healing and becoming convinced that you have a problem that needs fixing.
- Then you need to *grow,* by repeatedly meditating on the Torah insight which initially brought about your awakening, affirming its truth over an extended period of time so that it gradually becomes your new perception of reality.
- Once this elevated perspective of life becomes the norm, you will begin to *heal,* over a period of weeks, months, or perhaps, years.

You've probably realized by now that surrendering to the Torah's power is far from a passive experience. Surrendering doesn't mean sitting back and doing nothing while the Torah does its work. It's an arduous process of releasing your attachment to unhealthy mind patterns that you mistakenly thought were a source of stability and security, and replacing them with attitudes that are truer to your real self and essence.

And this brings me to another point. What determines whether a thought pattern is dysfunctional or healthy?

It's often very difficult to tell, since we are all such masters of self-deception when it comes to these things, but I'm going to give you a couple of very important rules which will help you navigate the turbulent waters of personal transformation and healing.

The arrows of growth always point in the direction of interconnectedness and love, and away from separation and fear.

From a very young age, you learned that this world is a dangerous place. If you hit your knee on a table, it hurt. There were times when you were distressed and nobody really understood. People were nasty towards you because they wanted to gain something for themselves. So you slowly developed a scarcity mentality, imagining that the pleasurable stuff of this life is in short supply and nobody except "yours truly" is going to ensure that you get your fair share (or more than your fair share). These kinds of thoughts fuel an outlook of separation and fear. The result is that you desperately cling to whatever you think is going to provide you with the security and bounty that you need in this lonely, dangerous world.

The Torah teaches that this kind of attitude is incorrect and dysfunctional. Your trust in mankind, and in God, might have been tested by some unpleasant experiences, but goodness is going to come your way by expanding your mind, not by narrowing it. If you can learn to love and identify with all of God's creatures, by training your eye to see the spark of goodness in everything and the utter sacredness hidden just below the surface of mundane acts, then you will feel safe enough to start shedding your dysfunctional attitudes of fear and isolation. These emotions suffocate your spirit and dim your light, because your mind is not made to function in a state of constriction. Daily, we are told in the Torah to leave Egypt (*mitzrayim*): we are to depart from the mind-set of narrowness and constriction (*metzarim*).

How can you tell if you are succeeding in this journey of *tikkun*, healing yourself and, ultimately, the universe?

You will notice a gradual shift from *resentment* to *wonder*.

When you look at the world through the narrow lens of fear and separation, you are always angry at something. You don't have enough of what you need. Somebody is wronging you or treating you unfairly. If only your boss, or *your spouse*, or your kids would change, then everything would be okay. So much seems to be in the hand of circumstances beyond your control.

As you heal, you begin to look at this world in wonder and gratitude. Every person you meet, all the details of the natural world, and even—yes, even the difficulties of life, are all enriching encounters with the all-pervasive Divine presence. You come to know that you are the universe in microcosm. Everything you see or hear teaches you something about yourself. And it works the other way too: as you heal yourself, you are making the universe a better place.

You realize that *everything* is in your hands. The more positive you'll be, the more you'll cheer up your surroundings, engendering more healthy relationships at work and at home. Instead of worrying about what you don't have and what might soon go wrong, you are overwhelmed by encountering God's presence in all the people you meet, all the events of your life and the words of Torah that you read—embracing it all in radical amazement. As you shift from anger to wonder, you will attract wholesome people and experiences to your life, and negative things will either depart or they will be reframed in a different light. You'll realize that they were only there because you had invited them in.

I have not completed this journey, but I am on my way and I know which directions the arrows face. This book will, I hope, be a great blessing to your life, igniting and fanning your inner flame for many years to come.

If your perception of the Torah is only as a book of law, then you will read the numerous instructions in this book as "commandments"—an ethical and religious code of conduct. But the word *mitzvah*, has another, extremely important connotation; it also means "connection."

A mitzvah is a connection ritual, a sacred technology that brings you closer to God.

If you observe a *mitzvah* purely out of a sense of fear, or to feel good, or to appear religious (to yourself or to others), or to please your parents, or your spouse, or your rabbi—then you have missed the most important point. A *mitzvah* is a powerful act of connection which slices through the myriad layers of "white noise" that separate you from the Power of the universe. But for it to be fully effective *you need to be conscious of what you are doing*. Like any spiritual practice, the *mitzvah* requires a focused intention and awareness for it to be a fully transformational force.

To appreciate this book and to harness its powers of personal healing, you need to go beyond just reading, thinking and talking about it; you need to start *doing* it. Regardless of your current level of observance, I recommend that you begin by focusing on a handful of *mitzvot*—and it doesn't matter in the slightest whether these are *mitzvot* which you observe already, have observed in the past and now lapsed, or have never observed at all. These will become your spiritual work, your primary connection rituals.

You know that when your mind is narrow, fear and separation rule supreme. Your special *mitzvot* will connect you to God, expanding the boundaries of your soul and warming your heart; they will stimulate that part of you which is never judgmental, always connected, and gushing with love. As you practice your special *mitzvot* regularly, you will deepen and refine the experience over time.

A few words about the translation and commentary. The Torah, of course, was written in ancient Hebrew, which is really quite impossible to translate into English. That's because the two tongues differ so radically: Hebrew is a *pregnant* language, as opposed to English, which is a *precise* tongue. A single Hebrew word lends itself to multiple interpretations; it is pregnant with meaning. In fact, it may have many different possible translations, and since the Torah text in its original source contains no vowels or punctuation, it could literally have a host of renditions.

English, on the other hand, is extremely precise. There are a host of different words to say the same thing, each differing slightly in nuance and implication. So by its very nature, an English word carries a certain connotation and level of emphasis which is just not present in biblical Hebrew.

Any English translation of the Torah is only able to bring to light one facet of the multiple meanings and implications that are present in the Hebrew original. In other words, *the translation really is a commentary*. It must take a particular approach to decoding the source text.

Since this fact is disconcerting—an honest translator wishes to render the text *as it is* from one language to another—most translations of the Torah try to hide their inevitable exegetical bias. They present commentary and interpretation as if it were straight translation (although to minimize the problem they usually follow the most straightforward and simple commentaries).

I have taken a more open approach. I figure that if my "translation" has *to be* a very particular interpretation/commentary then this fact needs to be obvious. So I have placed anything that is "interpretive" in nature in parentheses, to distinguish it from the rest of the text which is a more or less "pure" translation.

Another courageous leap is that I have stuck exclusively to one particular interpretation of the text. It is always easier for the translator to pick and choose which interpretation to follow on a verse-by-verse basis. While the result may be clearer, it is exegetically disjointed. One phrase may be rendered from an interpretative viewpoint which is at odds with the next one.

So I have opted for consistency, following the interpretation of Rabbi Solomon Yitzhaki (known by the acronym of his Hebrew name, *Rashi*), the 11th century French commentator of Bible and Talmud. Avoiding this approach might have made my task as translator—and yours as reader— a lot easier. But *Rashi* is the most popular, most printed and most loved of all the Torah commentaries; and, I believe, even his more "alarming" interpretations are motivated by a rigorous internal consistency. So by following *Rashi*, and highlighting his exegetical comments in parentheses, I hope to have rendered a translation which is thoroughly transparent to its biases and historically consistent with the way the Torah has popularly been taught and read for the past nine hundred years, or so.

A small final point—which is kind of obvious but I will state it in any case—is that any part of the text which seems to be intended as an instruction (command) as opposed to narrative, has been presented as a bulleted list, for the sake of clarity and an easier read.

I've already told you my criteria for choosing and adapting the commentaries presented on each page, so I won't repeat them here. But a word or two is in order about the highlighted features which are swimming inside the commentary: *Kabbalah Bites*, *Spiritual Vitamins* and *Food for Thought*.

Kabbalah is Jewish esotericism. It seeks to *open* and *expose* classical texts, rather than to merely understand and explain them. Its teachings, the most important of which are found in the *Zohar* (*Book of Radiance*) and the writings of Rabbi Isaac Luria (16th century), offer a bold transformation of the scriptural understanding of God and the universe.

In the Bible, the relationship between us and God seems largely covenantal: we enter into an agreement with God to observe certain ethical and ritual practices, and this pleases Him. When God is happy, He directs the events of our lives, and of history in general, for the good.

According to the Kabbalah, these same ethical and ritual deeds are perceived as having a strikingly different role. God and the world are linked in a *causal system*. Through the correct actions and intentions we somehow "activate" the Godhead, harmonize Divine emanations, and cause them to flow into the world, bringing the desired positive results.

That does not mean to say that we have stripped God of His will, or that man is now controlling God, because in the Kabbalistic system man can only influence God's *emanations*, not His infinite, unknowable *essence*. By drawing this important distinction, we preserve God's utter aloofness and oneness, while at the same time rendering Him extremely accessible and even subject to human influence. Most of the Kabbalah is devoted to a discussion of these complex and dynamic Divine emanations, the core of which are called the ten *sefirot*.

The origins of the Kabbalah are extremely obscure because any public teaching of this wisdom violated the basic rule of esotericism: secrecy. Besides the obvious fear of error (the doctrine of the *sefirot* treads extremely close to a heretical pluralism), Kabbalists felt that popularizing such intimate secrets about the Godhead was simply inappropriate; this was for the eyes of a few enlightened souls only. So while the Zohar, for example, only began to emerge in the thirteenth century, the Kabbalah was in the hands of an elite few for many centuries prior to that. Some see it as being as old as Judaism itself—or even older, attributing Kabbalistic knowledge to Adam, the first man.

But what is undisputed is that since the sixteenth century and on, Kabbalistic ideas have become irreversibly enmeshed in the beliefs and observances of Judaism. And in today's postmodern climate, interest in the Kabbalah has flourished more than ever.

Kabbalah comes from the root *k b l*, which means "receive," to stress that it was not the figment of human imagination, but was actually received from a higher source. This is especially important to stress in the case of esoteric wisdom, because, unlike the exoteric law which follows strictly defined rules of exegesis, there is no critique which can be applied to test the validity of a proposed esoteric teaching. Either you accept it *because it comes from a reliable source*, or you reject it. It cannot be evaluated by any revealed, traditional system.

What *does the Kabbalah* discuss? In addition to dealing with conventional theological topics such as creation, God's emanations, man's soul, the meaning of the commandments, the problem of evil, and the afterlife, *Kabbalistic* wisdom also includes fascinating discussions of more obscure topics, such as demonology, reincarnation (*gilgul*) and astrology.

The *"Kabbalah Bites"* presented here do little justice to this fascinating and immense body of Jewish esoteric wisdom. But for the vast majority of people who are intrigued by the *Kabbalah* but have never tasted from it, these insights will provide an excellent primer. No background knowledge should be required to understand them, other than what I have written here. (Sources for each "bite" are found in the back of this volume.)

The *"Spiritual Vitamins"* interspersed throughout this book are based on traditional, Rabbinic Judaism. They are novel in the sense that they are not actually a commentary on the Torah at all. I placed them here out of the conviction that you might often read the Torah on a weekly or even daily basis looking for suggestions or ideas of how to bring the teachings of Judaism directly and practically into your life. I wanted to make sure that you always find inspirational teachings of healing, awareness and well-being without having to look too hard, wading through scripture, commentary and super-commentary. I hope you find these "vitamins" gentle and affirming, and that they help to make your day more fulfilling, less stressful and a little happier.

Each weekly Torah reading provides plenty of material for stimulating discussion—in the classroom, or around the family table—about a broad range of ethical, personal and behavioral issues. The Torah and its commentaries are not only meant to impart you with wisdom as a passive receiver, they should also stimulate your mind and get you thinking. So I have included here some points for discussion and contemplation, under the heading *"Food for Thought."* No answers are given, of course, because that would defy the point. Some parts of the learning experience cannot be spoon-fed.

My favorite part of writing a book is the acknowledgments. Unlike a regular "thank you" which easily gets lost in the wind, a written, published acknowledgement is eternal, and that thought is awesome.

First and foremost I would like to thank David Slager whose tireless support of my work has made this book possible. David is an outstandingly generous man, and his philanthropy to countless causes around the globe has been an inspiration to thousands of people. Thank you, David, for your friendship, for your support, and for believing so strongly in what I do. May God bless you, Lara and your precious daughters Hannah and Sara Malka, both physically and spiritually.

My partner in publishing for close to a decade has been my dear friend Rabbi Meyer Gutnick. Meyer is a person who simply takes pleasure in helping people and in getting things done. I was unbelievably fortunate that he chose to support my writing career, not only financially but also with so much of his time and energy. Not many people get to write a Torah commentary in their lifetime, and I have now the merit of writing two. Thanks to Meyer, the first was a resounding success, and it is a privilege to have him behind this project too. Thank you, Meyer, for your love, support and dedication, and for being patient with me and giving me the space and peace of mind to work freely and productively. May God bless you, Shaindy and all your wonderful family forever.

Putting a work like this together is a formidable task, and would not have been possible without the dedicated assistance of many. First, the loyal team in my office who have really made this project a labor of love. I thank you all for tolerating me and for working so hard on this project: Rabbis Itzik Yarmush, Mendy Angyalfi, Yaakov Paley, Yossi Barber, Menachem Kirschenbaum and Chani Telsner. I also thank the following for their significant contributions: Rabbi Mendy Lent, Rabbi Shmuel Rabin, Chaviva Galatz, Nancy Rosenbaum, Chana Boteach, Chaya Sara Cantor, Yehudis Homnick, Sarah Yarmush, Ya'akovah Weber, Sarah Lehat, Boruch Ezagui, Mendel Katzman, Yehuda Kirsh, Zushe Greisman and Raphael Freeman. I extend a special thanks to Yossi Belkin for designing the beautiful front cover and for his tireless assistance with much of the interior design.

May God bless my wife, Chani, and our wonderful children, Leah, Mendel, Mushka, Levi and Esther Miriam, with a vibrancy of spirit and a sincerity of heart, to aspire to goodness all their lives and to live with the Torah.

Rabbi Chaim Miller
Rosh Ḥodesh Nisan 5771

TRANSLITERATION RULES

Name of Letter	Hebrew Character	English Transliteration
alef	א	ʾ —generally not transliterated
bet	בּ	b
vet	ב	v
gimmel	ג	g
dalet	ד	d
he	ה	h
vav	ו	v —when not a vowel
zayin	ז	z
het	ח	ḥ
tet	ט	t
yod	י	y
—	—	i —when a vowel or at end of words [1]
kaf	כּ	k
khaf	כ	kh
lamed	ל	l
mem	מ	m
nun	נ	n
samekh	ס	s
ayin	ע	ʿ —generally not transliterated
pe	פּ	p
fe	פ	f [2]
tzadi (tzaddik)	צ	tz
kof	ק	k
resh	ר	r
shin	שׁ	sh
sin	שׂ	s
tav	תּ	t
tav (sav)	ת	t —as per Sephardic pronunciation [3]

Name of Vowel	Hebrew Vowels	English Transliteration
kametz	אָ	a
pataḥ	אַ	a
tzere	אֵ	e
tzere + yod	אֵי	e —biblical
—	—	ei —non-biblical
segol	אֶ	e
sheva	אְ	e —only sheva na is transliterated
ḥirek	אִ	i
ḥirek + yod	אִי	i
ḥolem	אֹ, וֹ	o
kibbutz, shurek	אֻ, וּ	u

[1] Occasionally, y is used to emphasize the letter yod. [2] Or ph to emphasize association with pe in a related word. [3] In Ashkenazic pronunciation—s.

טעמי המקרא
CANTILLATION NOTES

פַּשְׁטָא֙ מֻנַּ֣ח זַרְקָ֘א מֻנַּ֒ח סֶגּוֹל֒ מֻנַּ֣ח ׀ מֻנַּ֨ח רְבִ֗יעִי
מַהְפַּ֤ךְ פַּשְׁטָא֙ זָקֵ֔ף קָטֹ֔ן זָקֵֽף־גָּד֕וֹל מֵרְכָ֥א טִפְחָ֖א
מֻנַּ֣ח אֶתְנַחְתָּ֑א פָּזֵ֡ר תְּלִישָֽׁא־קְטַנָּ֩ה
תְּלִישָֽׁא־גְד֠וֹלָה קַדְמָ֨א וְאַזְלָ֜א אַזְלָא־גֵּ֜רֶשׁ גֵּרְשַׁ֞יִם
דַּרְגָּ֧א תְּבִ֛יר יְתִ֞יב פְּסִ֓יק ׀ סוֹף־פָּסֽוּק׃ שַׁלְשֶׁ֓לֶת
קַרְנֵי־פָרָ֟ה מֵרְכָֽא־כְּפוּלָ֦ה יֶ֝רַח־בֶּן־יוֹמ֗וֹ׃

NOTE on PAGE FLOW

For ease of use, the English commentaries on each page-spread flow from left-to-right. That means, for example, that the English commentaries that begin on page 23 continue on page 22.

← PAGES GO THIS WAY ←

ENGLISH COMMENTARIES → FLOW THIS WAY →

ברכות לעולה לתורה
BLESSINGS ON READING *the* TORAH

The Reader indicates the section in the Torah scroll about to be read.

The one called to the Torah touches the text of the scroll at the place indicated with a corner of his *tallit*, *tefillin* strap, or the belt/mantle of the Torah, which he then kisses.

Holding the handles of the Torah scroll, he begins the blessing.

בָּרְכוּ אֶת יְיָ הַמְבֹרָךְ.

Congregation responds:

בָּרוּךְ יְיָ הַמְבֹרָךְ לְעוֹלָם וָעֶד.

The one called to the Torah continues:

בָּרוּךְ יְיָ הַמְבֹרָךְ לְעוֹלָם וָעֶד:

בָּרוּךְ אַתָּה יְיָ אֱלֹהֵינוּ מֶלֶךְ הָעוֹלָם, אֲשֶׁר בָּחַר בָּנוּ מִכָּל הָעַמִּים, וְנָתַן לָנוּ אֶת תּוֹרָתוֹ. בָּרוּךְ אַתָּה יְיָ, נוֹתֵן הַתּוֹרָה:

After the Torah is read, the one called to the Torah concludes:

בָּרוּךְ אַתָּה יְיָ אֱלֹהֵינוּ מֶלֶךְ הָעוֹלָם, אֲשֶׁר נָתַן לָנוּ תּוֹרַת אֱמֶת, וְחַיֵּי עוֹלָם נָטַע בְּתוֹכֵנוּ. בָּרוּךְ אַתָּה יְיָ, נוֹתֵן הַתּוֹרָה:

ספר בראשית

THE BOOK *of* GENESIS

You can experience **Creation** by contemplating the fact that **God recreates** the world continually. Focus your consciousness on the **present moment,** to receive, in **radical amazement,** the creative energy within the **now.**

BERE'SHIT
בראשית

CREATION	1:1 – 2:24
SIN OF THE TREE OF KNOWLEDGE	2:25 – 3:24
CAIN AND ABEL	4:1–26
OFFSPRING OF ADAM	5:1–32
BIRTH OF NOAH	5:28–29
MORAL CORRUPTION OF MAN	6:1–8

NAME
Bere'shit

MEANING
"In the beginning"

LINES IN TORAH SCROLL
241

PARASHIYYOT
10 open; 12 closed

VERSES
146

WORDS
1931

LETTERS
7235

DATE
0 – 1556

LOCATION
Garden of Eden, country of Nod

KEY PEOPLE
Adam, Eve, the Serpent, Cain, Abel, Seth, Enoch, Noah

MASORETIC FEATURES
The letter *bet* of the word *bere'shit* is oversized (1:1).

MITZVOT
1 positive

NOTE
Read the Sabbath following *Simhat Torah*.

CHARACTER PROFILE

NAME
Eve ("mother of all life")

HUSBAND
Adam

CHILDREN
Cain, Abel and Seth

BURIAL PLACE
Cave of Machpelah in Hebron

ACHIEVEMENTS
Formed by God out of Adam's thirteenth rib; was created fully developed as a twenty-year-old

KNOWN FOR
Was extremely beautiful; influenced by the serpent to first touch the Tree of Knowledge and then to eat from its fruit, together with her husband; cursed that women would have pain in childbirth

CREATION

God created the world with the intention that we should sanctify the mundane, making a "home" for Him down below. God constantly recreates the world, keeping us in existence for this purpose (1:1).

TIME

God finished working exactly as the Sabbath began. Every single moment is important and you should endeavor to not misuse or waste even a second (2:2).

WHERE ARE YOU?

God knew where Adam was, but He still asked him, "Where are you?" Every day God says to you, "Where are you?"—how are you using your capabilities and talents to make the world a better place? (3:9).

בראשית א:א-ו

א **בְּרֵאשִׁית** בָּרָא אֱלֹהִים אֵת הַשָּׁמַיִם וְאֵת הָאָרֶץ: 2 וְהָאָרֶץ הָיְתָה תֹהוּ וָבֹהוּ וְחֹשֶׁךְ עַל־פְּנֵי תְהוֹם וְרוּחַ אֱלֹהִים מְרַחֶפֶת עַל־פְּנֵי הַמָּיִם: 3 וַיֹּאמֶר אֱלֹהִים יְהִי אוֹר וַיְהִי־אוֹר: 4 וַיַּרְא אֱלֹהִים אֶת־הָאוֹר כִּי־טוֹב וַיַּבְדֵּל אֱלֹהִים בֵּין הָאוֹר וּבֵין הַחֹשֶׁךְ: 5 וַיִּקְרָא אֱלֹהִים | לָאוֹר יוֹם וְלַחֹשֶׁךְ קָרָא לָיְלָה וַיְהִי־עֶרֶב וַיְהִי־בֹקֶר יוֹם אֶחָד: פ 6 וַיֹּאמֶר אֱלֹהִים יְהִי רָקִיעַ בְּתוֹךְ

But this enormous love would have completely overwhelmed the Creation, bringing about its annihilation, so it had to be restrained. God therefore looked at the future deeds of the wicked, and His powers of severity were aroused. This is what made it possible to create the world (*Rabbi Gedaliah b. Isaac of Lunietz, 18th century*).

2. Astoundingly desolate. God desires a "home" in the *lowest* realms (*Midrash Tanḥuma*).

The world began with utter desolation—the lowest of all existence—into which light and the Torah were then added (*Rabbi Alexander Zusya ha-Kohen, 19th century*).

God's breath. This "breath" refers to the spirit of the Messiah (*Genesis Rabbah*).

The concept of the Messiah is even more primal than that of light, for the spirit of the Messiah *preceded* the creation of light (*Rabbi Moses Aryeh Leib Lits-Rosenbaum, 19th century*).

Hovered. Kabbalah teaches that the purpose of Creation is to elevate two hundred and eighty-eight Godly "sparks" which are trapped in the physical world. This number is hinted to by the word "hovered," *meraḥefet*, whose root letters *resh-pe-ḥet* have the numerical equivalent of two hundred and eighty-eight (*Rabbi Ḥayyim b. Joseph Vital, 16th–17th century*).

4. God separated the light from the darkness. God saw that this primordial light was good and it was not proper for the wicked to use it, so He put it away for the righteous in the future (*Rashi, 11th century*).

The light which was created on the first day had two properties: (a) its superficial quality of physical illumination; and (b) an inner, deeper "goodness" that was detached (*Rabbi Judah Loew b. Bezalel of Prague, 16th century*).

The *form* of the light was altered. In its original form it had such a potent spirituality that it negated man's free choice, giving him no opportunity to sin. By revealing truth, the inner purpose of every object was plainly evident.

In its altered state, the spirituality of the light was "separated" for all future generations, with the provision that people obtain it through their own efforts in genuine worship. Men who use their free choice unwisely do not receive it at all (*Rabbi Israel Friedman of Ruzhin, 19th century*).

> **kabbalah bites**
>
> **1:1** Before God created this world He created other, spiritual worlds, *but He was not happy with them, so He destroyed them.* The problem with all those worlds is that they lacked empathy; they were worlds of *tohu* (chaos) because their constituent forces could not tolerate each other. Our world, which God favored, is called *tikkun* (corrected), because every element of this world has the capability to appreciate everything else.

genesis 1:1–6 — bere'shit

parashat bere'shit

Creation: The First Day—Light and Darkness

1 ¹ In the beginning of God's creation of the heavens and the earth (and their contents), ² when the earth was astoundingly desolate, darkness was on the surface of the deep (waters that covered the land), and the (throne of) God('s glory) hovered over the water (at the command of God's) breath, ³ God said, "Let there be light!"—and there was light.

⁴ God saw that the light was good, and God separated the (times of) light from the (times of) darkness (in the following manner:) ⁵ God called out to the light (and assigned it to the) day, and He called out to the darkness (and assigned it to) the night.

It became evening and it became morning—one day.

The Second Day—Separation of Waters

⁶ God said, "Let the firmament (materialize) between the waters, and let it separate between (the upper) waters and (the lower) waters."

1:1 In the beginning (*bere'shit*) of God's creation. What is the significance of the Torah beginning with the *second* letter of the Hebrew alphabet, *bet*? Why did it not start with the first letter, *alef*?

Bet is the first letter of the word *berakhah*, "blessing," whereas *alef* is the first letter of the word *'arur*, "curse." God said, "I will not create the world with an *alef*, so that people should not say, 'How can you expect the world to endure if it was created with a letter of curses?' Instead, I will create the world with the letter *bet* that suggests blessing—and I wish that it will endure" (*Jerusalem Talmud, Ḥagigah* 2:1).

The Torah begins with the second letter of the Hebrew alphabet, *bet*, which has a numerical value of two, alluding to the creation of two worlds: this world and the afterlife (*Rabbi Jacob b. Asher, 13ᵗʰ–14ᵗʰ century*).

A foundation of Torah is the belief that God created the universe *ex nihilo*. The phrase *"In the beginning"* should not be understood in terms of time, for time itself is a creation. Time is dependent upon the movement of the heavenly bodies, and they too were created (*Maimonides, 12ᵗʰ century*).

Just as God renews the Creation every day, you too must make some innovation in this world every single day (*Rabbi Aaron b. Jacob of Karlin, 18ᵗʰ century*).

When God foresaw the future deeds of the righteous, it aroused in Him a very great longing to bestow good upon them, and this is what prompted Him to create the world.

---

food for thought

1. *"In the beginning of God's creation"*—why do you think we exist?

2. *"It was good"*—how often do you contemplate the beauty of Creation?

3. *"Let there be light!"*—what light have you brought to your surroundings?

בראשית א:ו-יד בראשית

הַמַּיִם וַיְהִי מַבְדִּיל בֵּין מַיִם לָמָיִם: 7 וַיַּעַשׂ אֱלֹהִים אֶת־הָרָקִיעַ וַיַּבְדֵּל בֵּין הַמַּיִם אֲשֶׁר מִתַּחַת לָרָקִיעַ וּבֵין הַמַּיִם אֲשֶׁר מֵעַל לָרָקִיעַ וַיְהִי־כֵן: 8 וַיִּקְרָא אֱלֹהִים לָרָקִיעַ שָׁמָיִם וַיְהִי־עֶרֶב וַיְהִי־בֹקֶר יוֹם שֵׁנִי: פ 9 וַיֹּאמֶר אֱלֹהִים יִקָּווּ הַמַּיִם מִתַּחַת הַשָּׁמַיִם אֶל־מָקוֹם אֶחָד וְתֵרָאֶה הַיַּבָּשָׁה וַיְהִי־כֵן: 10 וַיִּקְרָא אֱלֹהִים | לַיַּבָּשָׁה אֶרֶץ וּלְמִקְוֵה הַמַּיִם קָרָא יַמִּים וַיַּרְא אֱלֹהִים כִּי־טוֹב: 11 וַיֹּאמֶר אֱלֹהִים תַּדְשֵׁא הָאָרֶץ דֶּשֶׁא עֵשֶׂב מַזְרִיעַ זֶרַע עֵץ פְּרִי עֹשֶׂה פְּרִי לְמִינוֹ אֲשֶׁר זַרְעוֹ־בוֹ עַל־הָאָרֶץ וַיְהִי־כֵן: 12 וַתּוֹצֵא הָאָרֶץ דֶּשֶׁא עֵשֶׂב מַזְרִיעַ זֶרַע לְמִינֵהוּ וְעֵץ עֹשֶׂה־פְּרִי אֲשֶׁר זַרְעוֹ־בוֹ לְמִינֵהוּ וַיַּרְא אֱלֹהִים כִּי־טוֹב: 13 וַיְהִי־עֶרֶב וַיְהִי־בֹקֶר יוֹם שְׁלִישִׁי: פ 14 וַיֹּאמֶר אֱלֹהִים יְהִי מְאֹרֹת בִּרְקִיעַ

heavens to grant them life. For if the letters were to depart even for an instant, God forbid, and return to their source, all the heavens would revert to absolute nothingness, and it would be as though they had never existed at all (*Rabbi Israel Ba'al Shem Tov, 18th century*).

10. God called the dry land "earth" ('aretz). After a while, the habitual pleasures of life begin to lose their appeal. One thing, however, which is always a great source of pleasure to man is the ability to give to others, so that they can enjoy life.

The same is true with God, so to speak. His greatest pleasure is not to receive, but to provide. "*God called the dry land 'aretz*"—dry land gave Him the greatest pleasure, because it satisfied His desire to give, making human life possible. Therefore He named it *'aretz*, which also means "desire" (*Rabbi Abraham Joshua Heschel of Apta, 18th century*).

11. Let the earth be covered with ... trees (with edible bark that tastes like its) fruit. God instructed that the tree should taste like the fruit, but the earth did not comply. Therefore, when man was cursed because of his sin, the earth too was punished for its sin (*Rashi, 11th century*).

Obviously the earth, which has no free choice, did not sin in the literal sense. Rather, what *Rashi* is pointing to here is an intrinsic metaphysical flaw in all earthly, physical things.

The physical world is situated at the end of countless worlds of emanation, so it is, by definition, a *recipient*. Because of this, a recipient mentality plagues the earth and everything that was created from it—an overstated desire to receive and a reluctance to give. This is ultimately the cause of all our sins.

Here, at the beginning of Creation, this flaw first began to manifest itself with the creation of the fruit tree. Mirroring the physical and

food for thought

1. Why did God create unintelligent creatures?

2. What does the universe's vastness mean to you?

3. When the sun rises daily, is it natural, or a miracle?

genesis 1:7–14 — bere'shit

⁷ God made the firmament (fixed in its position). He separated between the waters that were below the firmament and the waters that were above the firmament (by suspending the upper waters in mid-air), and it remained that way. ⁸ God called the firmament "sky."

It became evening and it became morning—a second day.

The Third Day—Land and Vegetation

⁹ God said, "Let the water that is below the skies gather into one location, and let the dry land appear!"—and that is what happened.

¹⁰ God called the dry land "earth," and He called the gathering of the waters "seas." God saw that (the work) was good.

¹¹ God said, "Let the earth be covered with vegetation, plants that reproduce by seed, and trees (with edible bark that tastes like its) fruit, which produce fruit of their own species containing their own seed, over the earth!"—and that is what happened. ¹² The earth germinated vegetation, plants that reproduce by seed of their own species, and fruit-producing trees, in which seeds of its own species are found.

God saw that it was good.

¹³ It became evening and it became morning—a third day.

The Fourth Day—Sun, Moon and Stars

¹⁴ God said, "The luminaries shall be positioned in the firmament of the skies to separate between the day and the night! They will serve as omens (of bad events,

6. Let the firmament (materialize) between the waters. These words of God's original utterance, *"Let the firmament (materialize) between the waters, etc.,"* are *constantly* found within the

spiritual vitamin

> When you get hold of a printed book of hundreds of pages, containing a connected story, or philosophy, you cannot by any stretch of the imagination assume that a bottle of ink has been spilled and has accidentally produced the book. Still less, and infinitely so, is it possible that our universe, with its infinite number of atoms, molecules and particles, all arranged in perfect order and harmony, could have come into existence by accident. Obviously there is a Creator and Architect, who arranges and relates all the various parts of the universe in perfect unity and harmony.

בראשית א:יד-כו

הַשָּׁמַיִם לְהַבְדִּיל בֵּין הַיּוֹם וּבֵין הַלָּיְלָה וְהָיוּ לְאֹתֹת וּלְמוֹעֲדִים וּלְיָמִים וְשָׁנִים: 15 וְהָיוּ לִמְאוֹרֹת בִּרְקִיעַ הַשָּׁמַיִם לְהָאִיר עַל־הָאָרֶץ וַיְהִי־כֵן: 16 וַיַּעַשׂ אֱלֹהִים אֶת־שְׁנֵי הַמְּאֹרֹת הַגְּדֹלִים אֶת־הַמָּאוֹר הַגָּדֹל לְמֶמְשֶׁלֶת הַיּוֹם וְאֶת־הַמָּאוֹר הַקָּטֹן לְמֶמְשֶׁלֶת הַלַּיְלָה וְאֵת הַכּוֹכָבִים: 17 וַיִּתֵּן אֹתָם אֱלֹהִים בִּרְקִיעַ הַשָּׁמָיִם לְהָאִיר עַל־הָאָרֶץ: 18 וְלִמְשֹׁל בַּיּוֹם וּבַלַּיְלָה וּלֲהַבְדִּיל בֵּין הָאוֹר וּבֵין הַחֹשֶׁךְ וַיַּרְא אֱלֹהִים כִּי־טוֹב: 19 וַיְהִי־עֶרֶב וַיְהִי־בֹקֶר יוֹם רְבִיעִי: פ 20 וַיֹּאמֶר אֱלֹהִים יִשְׁרְצוּ הַמַּיִם שֶׁרֶץ נֶפֶשׁ חַיָּה וְעוֹף יְעוֹפֵף עַל־הָאָרֶץ עַל־פְּנֵי רְקִיעַ הַשָּׁמָיִם: 21 וַיִּבְרָא אֱלֹהִים אֶת־הַתַּנִּינִם הַגְּדֹלִים וְאֵת כָּל־נֶפֶשׁ הַחַיָּה | הָרֹמֶשֶׂת אֲשֶׁר שָׁרְצוּ הַמַּיִם לְמִינֵהֶם וְאֵת כָּל־עוֹף כָּנָף לְמִינֵהוּ וַיַּרְא אֱלֹהִים כִּי־טוֹב: 22 וַיְבָרֶךְ אֹתָם אֱלֹהִים לֵאמֹר פְּרוּ וּרְבוּ וּמִלְאוּ אֶת־הַמַּיִם בַּיַּמִּים וְהָעוֹף יִרֶב בָּאָרֶץ: 23 וַיְהִי־עֶרֶב וַיְהִי־בֹקֶר יוֹם חֲמִישִׁי: פ 24 וַיֹּאמֶר אֱלֹהִים תּוֹצֵא הָאָרֶץ נֶפֶשׁ חַיָּה לְמִינָהּ בְּהֵמָה וָרֶמֶשׂ וְחַיְתוֹ־אֶרֶץ לְמִינָהּ וַיְהִי־כֵן: 25 וַיַּעַשׂ אֱלֹהִים אֶת־חַיַּת הָאָרֶץ לְמִינָהּ וְאֶת־הַבְּהֵמָה לְמִינָהּ וְאֵת כָּל־רֶמֶשׂ הָאֲדָמָה לְמִינֵהוּ וַיַּרְא אֱלֹהִים כִּי־טוֹב: 26 וַיֹּאמֶר אֱלֹהִים נַעֲשֶׂה אָדָם בְּצַלְמֵנוּ כִּדְמוּתֵנוּ וְיִרְדּוּ בִדְגַת

impart flavor to the tree, it could not do so, because, as a *recipient*, the earth was metaphysically inferior to the tree—a *provider*.

Man, who was created from the earth, also inherited the recipient mentality. *He was therefore attracted to the fruit which possessed the same flaw as himself.* His sin was that he detached the fruit from the tree—he made receiving primary and giving secondary (*Rabbi Judah Loew b. Bezalel of Prague, 16th century*).

26. God (consulted the Heavenly Court and) said, "Let us make man in our mold." The Torah's term for "man," *'adam*, comes from the term *domeh*, "comparison."

Once God had finished the work of Creation, He desired that His handiwork could appreciate His work and marvel at the complexity of the universe. Until that point, only fish, birds, and mammals had been created—creatures that understand things according to their own limited context.

So God created *'adam*, the "creature of comparison." Combining elements of the spiritual and physical realms—a clay body and a Godly soul—resulted in a creature with the exclusively

when there is an eclipse, and will determine the times of the) festivals, (and the sun and moon will define) the days and years! ¹⁵ They will (also) act as luminaries in the firmament of the skies to shed light upon the earth!"—and that is what happened.

¹⁶ God made two large luminaries (but since they clashed, He reduced one in size. Thus,) the large luminary was to rule over the day and the small luminary was to rule over the night, and (He made) the stars (in order to appease the moon). ¹⁷ God placed them in the firmament of the skies to shed light upon the earth, ¹⁸ to rule over the day and over the night, and to separate between the light and between the darkness.

God saw that it was good.

¹⁹ It became evening and it became morning—a fourth day.

The Fifth Day—Small Creatures, Fish and Birds

²⁰ God said, "Let the waters produce swarms of (small) living creatures, and let birds fly over the earth, across the firmament of the skies!"

²¹ God created the large sea fish, all the creeping living creatures that the waters produced in swarms, according to their species, and all the winged birds according to their species.

God saw that it was good.

²² God blessed them, saying, "Be fruitful and multiply, and fill the waters of the seas, and let the birds multiply upon the earth!"

²³ It became evening and it became morning—a fifth day.

The Sixth Day—Animals and Man

²⁴ God said, "Let the earth produce living creatures according to their (various) species, cattle, creeping things and wild animals of the earth according to their (various) species!"—and that is what happened.

²⁵ God made the wild animals of the earth according to their (various) species, the cattle according to their (various) species, and all the creeping things of the ground according to their (various) species.

God saw that it was good.

²⁶ God (consulted the Heavenly Court and) said, "Let us make man ['*adam*] in our mold, (intellectually endowed) like us, and (if he is worthy) let him rule over

---

spiritual worlds, the fruit and its tree are in a *recipient-provider* relationship: the tree provides nourishment from the ground, which the fruit absorbs and stores. When God told the earth to

בראשית א:כו-ל

הַיָּם וּבְעוֹף הַשָּׁמַיִם וּבַבְּהֵמָה וּבְכָל־הָאָרֶץ וּבְכָל־הָרֶמֶשׂ הָרֹמֵשׂ עַל־הָאָרֶץ:
27 וַיִּבְרָא אֱלֹהִים | אֶת־הָאָדָם בְּצַלְמוֹ בְּצֶלֶם אֱלֹהִים בָּרָא אֹתוֹ זָכָר וּנְקֵבָה בָּרָא אֹתָם:
28 וַיְבָרֶךְ אֹתָם אֱלֹהִים וַיֹּאמֶר לָהֶם אֱלֹהִים פְּרוּ וּרְבוּ וּמִלְאוּ אֶת־הָאָרֶץ וְכִבְשֻׁהָ וּרְדוּ בִּדְגַת הַיָּם וּבְעוֹף הַשָּׁמַיִם וּבְכָל־חַיָּה הָרֹמֶשֶׂת עַל־הָאָרֶץ:
29 וַיֹּאמֶר אֱלֹהִים הִנֵּה נָתַתִּי לָכֶם אֶת־כָּל־עֵשֶׂב | זֹרֵעַ זֶרַע אֲשֶׁר עַל־פְּנֵי כָל־הָאָרֶץ וְאֶת־כָּל־הָעֵץ אֲשֶׁר־בּוֹ פְרִי־עֵץ זֹרֵעַ זָרַע לָכֶם יִהְיֶה לְאָכְלָה:
30 וּלְכָל־חַיַּת הָאָרֶץ וּלְכָל־עוֹף הַשָּׁמַיִם וּלְכֹל | רוֹמֵשׂ עַל־הָאָרֶץ אֲשֶׁר־בּוֹ

entirely populated with dishonest and quarrelsome people? Surely it was obvious that there would be a mixture of temperaments?

The opposing angels' argument was that, in many instances, life will place man in a situation of irresolvable dilemma. If he follows the path of truth, he will offend his fellow; if he follows the path of peace, he will be guilty of dishonesty. Neither group of angels saw mankind as entirely untruthful or entirely disharmonious, but *collectively* they saw a world where truth *and* peace would be inviable.

"What did God do? He took 'truth' and threw it to the ground." He gave us the Torah here on earth ("the ground"), a teaching which guides us, in every area of life, in how to balance the sensitivities of truth and peace (*Rabbi Ḥayyim Soloveichik, 19th–20th century*).

28. Be fruitful and multiply. Technically according to Jewish law, the responsibility to *"be fruitful and multiply"* rests on the man, and not the woman. This, however, points to the spiritual superiority of women. Knowing that men are inclined to deviate from their primary mission in this world, to rear the next generation in a functional family unit, God *commanded* them to do so by the force of the law. Women, who are more instinctively attuned to this God-given mission, do not need the law to tell them what they know already to be true.

Thus, the stronger legal emphasis on the man is, paradoxically, suggestive of an inferior spiritual status (*Rabbi Menahem Mendel Schneerson, 20th century*).

29. Plants … fruit … shall be food for you. God did not allow Adam and his wife to kill a creature and to eat its flesh. They were only permitted to eat the vegetation, as were the animals. Later, He permitted the sons of Noah to eat flesh (see *Genesis 9:3; Rashi, 11th century*).

spiritual vitamin

> The world is a well-coordinated system created by God, in which there is nothing superfluous and nothing lacking.

the fish of the sea, over the birds of the skies, over the cattle, over all the earth and over all the creeping things that creep upon the earth!"

²⁷ God created man (by hand) in (the) mold (which was made for) him. The mold (which He used) to create him (resembled the image of) God. (On that day,) He created (both) male and female.

²⁸ God blessed them. God said to them, "Be fruitful and multiply, and fill the earth! Take control of it! Rule over the fish of the sea, the birds of the skies and over all the wild animals that move upon the earth!"

²⁹ God said, "I have hereby given you every plant that reproduces by seed that is upon the surface of the entire earth, and every tree that has seed-bearing fruit! They shall be food for you, ³⁰ for all the wild animals of the earth, for all the birds of the skies, and for everything which moves upon the earth that is alive! The food (for humans and animals) shall be plant vegetation (only)!"—and that is what happened.

---

human ability to contrast and compare, observe and ponder all of Creation. 'Adam could envision spiritual concepts with his mind, and, at the same time, experience physical phenomena with his body. The ability to see this "bigger picture" is God's exclusive gift to mankind (*Rabbi Simhah Bunem of Przysucha, 18ᵗʰ–19ᵗʰ century*).

Man's name—Adam—reflects his gift of free choice. Adam can either mean "comparable" (*domeh*) or it can refer to the earth (*'adamah*). If man chooses good, then he is comparable to the Divine; if he chooses evil he is like the animals who were formed from the earth. The choice is his (*Rabbi Menahem Azariah da Fano, 16ᵗʰ–17ᵗʰ century*).

This statement, *"Let us,"* is phrased in the plural. The Sages teach that when God was about to create man, He consulted with His ministering angels. However, with the creation of woman, God consulted no one.

Therefore, women recite the blessing each morning, *"Blessed are You, Lord our God, King of the universe, who has made me according to His will,"* because God created woman as He willed, without consulting others (*Rabbi Jacob Meshullam Ornstein of Lvov, 19ᵗʰ century*).

When God came to create man, the angels split into groups. The angels of kindness and angels of righteousness were in favor of man who, they argued, would perform kind and charitable acts. But the angels of truth and angels of peace opposed man's creation, arguing that humanity would be torn apart with lies and quarrels.

What did God do? He took "truth" and threw it to the ground (*Genesis Rabbah*).

The angels' arguments are puzzling. Why did the angels of kindness assume that mankind would be *entirely* charitable? And why did the other angels assume that the world would be

---

food for thought

1. Are humans better off, or do animals have easier lives?

2. In which ways do we reflect "the image of God"?

3. Have we become tyrants in our charge to *"rule over ... all the earth"*?

בראשית א:ל – ב:ה

נֶ֣פֶשׁ חַיָּ֔ה אֶֽת־כָּל־יֶ֥רֶק עֵ֖שֶׂב לְאָכְלָ֑ה וַֽיְהִי־כֵֽן׃ 31 וַיַּ֨רְא אֱלֹהִ֜ים אֶת־כָּל־אֲשֶׁ֣ר עָשָׂ֗ה וְהִנֵּה־ט֖וֹב מְאֹ֑ד וַֽיְהִי־עֶ֥רֶב וַֽיְהִי־בֹ֖קֶר י֥וֹם הַשִּׁשִּֽׁי׃ פ

ב 1 וַיְכֻלּ֛וּ הַשָּׁמַ֥יִם וְהָאָ֖רֶץ וְכָל־צְבָאָֽם׃ 2 וַיְכַ֤ל אֱלֹהִים֙ בַּיּ֣וֹם הַשְּׁבִיעִ֔י מְלַאכְתּ֖וֹ אֲשֶׁ֣ר עָשָׂ֑ה וַיִּשְׁבֹּת֙ בַּיּ֣וֹם הַשְּׁבִיעִ֔י מִכָּל־מְלַאכְתּ֖וֹ אֲשֶׁ֥ר עָשָֽׂה׃ 3 וַיְבָ֤רֶךְ אֱלֹהִים֙ אֶת־י֣וֹם הַשְּׁבִיעִ֔י וַיְקַדֵּ֖שׁ אֹת֑וֹ כִּ֣י ב֤וֹ שָׁבַת֙ מִכָּל־מְלַאכְתּ֔וֹ אֲשֶׁר־בָּרָ֥א אֱלֹהִ֖ים לַעֲשֽׂוֹת׃ פ [SECOND READING] 4 אֵ֣לֶּה תוֹלְד֧וֹת הַשָּׁמַ֛יִם וְהָאָ֖רֶץ בְּהִבָּֽרְאָ֑ם בְּי֗וֹם עֲשׂ֛וֹת יְהֹוָ֥ה אֱלֹהִ֖ים אֶ֥רֶץ וְשָׁמָֽיִם׃ 5 וְכֹ֣ל ׀ שִׂ֣יחַ הַשָּׂדֶ֗ה טֶ֚רֶם יִֽהְיֶ֣ה בָאָ֔רֶץ וְכָל־עֵ֥שֶׂב הַשָּׂדֶ֖ה טֶ֣רֶם יִצְמָ֑ח כִּי֩ לֹ֨א הִמְטִ֜יר יְהֹוָ֤ה אֱלֹהִים֙ עַל־

utmost fervor! What could this lowly generation possibly achieve beyond the accomplishments of our illustrious ancestors?

The answer to this question can be derived from God's conduct when creating the world. Just as we see that every moment was precious to God, to the extent that He continued working to the very last opportunity, likewise, the final work of the very last generations is of paramount importance (*Rabbi Menahem Mendel Schneerson, 20th century*).

On the seventh day, He rested. What is the Sabbath? It is the name of God (*Zohar*).

God's very name is Sabbath or "rest," because movement cannot be attributed to Him. Movement is only possible for an entity that exists within time and space. But God does not move from place to place, nor is He limited by time (*Rabbi Israel Ba'al Shem Tov, 18th century*).

3. God blessed the seventh day. The peace and pleasure that your soul finds on the Sabbath is so great that it is as if you have been given an additional soul. When this condition ceases at the end of the Sabbath, and you re-enter the period of hard work and stress, it is as if this additional soul has departed from you, and you become weakened (*Rabbi Solomon b. Abraham Adret, 13th century*).

spiritual vitamin

> One of the foundations of our faith and way of life is the firm conviction that God's Providence extends to everyone individually, and that He is the essence of goodness, and does only good, as the Torah states, *"God saw everything that He had made, and—look!—it was very good"* (1:31).

genesis 1:31 – 2:5   bere'shit

³¹ God saw everything that He had made, and—look!—it was very good.

It became evening and it became morning—the sixth day.

The Seventh Day—God Rests from Work

2 ¹ The skies, the earth and all their numerous components were completed.
² On the seventh day, God completed His work that He had made. On the seventh day, He rested from all His work that He had done.

³ God blessed the seventh day (so that a double portion of manna should descend in its honor) and He sanctified it (so that no manna should descend on the Sabbath itself), because on that (day) God rested from all His work that He had created, (for the remaining work which was left) to be done (on the Sabbath, He carried out on Friday instead, by doubling His workload).

[SECOND READING] ⁴ These (above-mentioned details) are the chronology of the skies and the earth when they were created, on the (first) day when God, Almighty God, made earth and skies, (and the subsequent days, when He materialized the creations).

Details of the Creation of Man and Woman

(The Torah now adds further details concerning the creation of man and woman, mentioned above, 1:27.)

⁵ (The vegetation had only germinated within the ground, but) none of the trees of the field were yet (sprouting) on the (surface of the) earth, nor had any

---

31. The sixth day. You will notice that the other days of creation are described simply as *"a third day"* or *"a fourth day,"* unlike *"the sixth day."*

The article *the* hints to the unique "sixth day" made eternally famous in another context, namely, the sixth day of the month of *Sivan*, the day that the Torah was given at Sinai. By linking the conclusion of Creation with the event at Sinai, the Torah informs you that one was conditional upon the other. God stipulated with the works of Creation, "If Israel accepts the Torah, you will continue to exist. If not, I will return you to primordial nothingness!" (*Babylonian Talmud, Shabbat* 88a).

2:2 On the seventh day, God completed. How was Creation *completed* on the seventh day, when God merely rested? God continued working all the way up to the Sabbath and entered the Sabbath "by a hairsbreadth."

Another answer: The world was lacking one thing—rest. When the Sabbath came, rest came. The work of Creation was then completed and finished (*Rashi, 11th century*).

Rashi explains that God worked until the last possible moment. What was gained by this feat of precision? God was teaching a lesson to mankind about the preciousness of time: So long as you have the opportunity to carry out your Divinely ordained mission in this world, you should utilize every moment in order to realize your fullest potential, pushing every allocation of time to its utmost limits.

Also, you might bemoan the fact that you are living in a spiritually desensitized generation. Gone are the days of the prophets and Talmudic sages, when the people served God with the

הָאָרֶץ וְאָדָם אַיִן לַעֲבֹד אֶת־הָאֲדָמָה: 6 וְאֵד יַעֲלֶה מִן־הָאָרֶץ וְהִשְׁקָה אֶת־כָּל־פְּנֵי הָאֲדָמָה: 7 וַיִּיצֶר יְהֹוָה אֱלֹהִים אֶת־הָאָדָם עָפָר מִן־הָאֲדָמָה וַיִּפַּח בְּאַפָּיו נִשְׁמַת חַיִּים וַיְהִי הָאָדָם לְנֶפֶשׁ חַיָּה: 8 וַיִּטַּע יְהֹוָה אֱלֹהִים גַּן־בְּעֵדֶן מִקֶּדֶם וַיָּשֶׂם שָׁם אֶת־הָאָדָם אֲשֶׁר יָצָר: 9 וַיַּצְמַח יְהֹוָה אֱלֹהִים מִן־הָאֲדָמָה כָּל־עֵץ נֶחְמָד לְמַרְאֶה וְטוֹב לְמַאֲכָל וְעֵץ הַחַיִּים בְּתוֹךְ הַגָּן וְעֵץ הַדַּעַת טוֹב וָרָע: 10 וְנָהָר יֹצֵא מֵעֵדֶן לְהַשְׁקוֹת אֶת־הַגָּן וּמִשָּׁם יִפָּרֵד וְהָיָה לְאַרְבָּעָה רָאשִׁים: 11 שֵׁם הָאֶחָד פִּישׁוֹן הוּא הַסֹּבֵב אֵת כָּל־אֶרֶץ הַחֲוִילָה אֲשֶׁר־שָׁם הַזָּהָב: 12 וּזְהַב הָאָרֶץ הַהִוא טוֹב שָׁם הַבְּדֹלַח וְאֶבֶן הַשֹּׁהַם: 13 וְשֵׁם־הַנָּהָר

and not the *"Why?"* For him, dignity—"Divine image"—is translated as control: *"Fill the earth and take control of it."*

Adam the second asks *"Why?"* The living soul breathed into his nostrils by God indicates his primary concern with the spiritual and the Divine. He is not a practical, creative being, but one interested in introspection and self-discovery.

Contemporary man has failed to take notice of the duality in Adam. The creative enterprises of our civilization have led us to deny that Adam the second exists. Man's ties to religion are not motivated by a desire for introspection and redemption, but to furthering his sense of dignity and success. For this reason, contemporary majestic man stands as an incomplete being (*Rabbi Joseph B. Soloveitchik, 20th century*).

8. God planted a garden in Eden.
God did not initially create man within the Garden of Eden, rather, He placed him there afterwards. This was in order that man should see how unpleasant the world was, so that he should not imagine that the entire world was as beautiful as Eden (*Rabbi Hezekiah b. Manoah, 13th century*).

As a result of being brought into Eden from the outside, man would recognize the kindness God had performed for him by placing him in Eden (*Rabbi David Kimḥi, 12th–13th century*).

---

kabbalah bites

2:6 When you pray to God, it is not merely that God "listens" to your prayers from above and responds accordingly. The process of prayer itself *refines* you spiritually, rendering you a suitable receptacle for additional Divine blessings. The receipt of a blessing is the *direct outcome* of sincere, focused prayer.

This process is mirrored in the physical world by the method in which rain is formed. Rain is not a new entity that is formed in heaven, but rather, the same "mist" that ascends from the ground, forms clouds and eventually condenses into rain which showers back down onto the earth.

genesis 2:5–13 — bere'shit

vegetation of the field yet grown, because God, Almighty God, had not brought rain upon the earth (since) there was no man to (appreciate the rain and) work the soil.

⁶ (God caused) a mist to ascend from the earth (moistening the clouds in order to) soak the entire surface of the ground (so that man should be created from moist earth). ⁷ God, Almighty God, formed man out of soil from (the four corners of) the earth. He blew into his nostrils a living soul, and man became a living, (thinking and speaking) being.

⁸ God, Almighty God, planted a garden in Eden to the east, and placed there the man that He had formed. ⁹ (In the garden) God, Almighty God, made every tree that is pleasant to look at and good to eat grow out from the ground. The Tree of Life (grew) in the middle of the garden, and the Tree of Knowledge of good and evil (also grew in the garden).

¹⁰ A river flowed out of Eden to water the garden, and from there it separated and became the source of four riverheads. ¹¹ The name of one is Pishon (the Nile), which surrounds the entire land of Havilah, where there is gold. ¹² The gold of that land is good. Crystal and onyx (are found) there. ¹³ The name of the second river is

---

6. (God caused) a mist to ascend from the earth. This first rain came in response to man's prayer (*Rashi, 11th century*).

7. God formed man out of soil from the earth. In creating man, God gathered soil from the entire earth, from all four directions, so that wherever man would die, the earth would accept him for burial (*Rashi*).

He blew into his nostrils a living soul. This scriptural analogy illustrates that the soul contains a deeper manifestation of Divinity than the rest of the world, since it was "blown" out from God's "innards," rather than the more "superficial" creative method of Divine "speech." When you blow, you exhale from deep inside your body (*Nahmanides, 13th century*).

In the case of animals and plants God created the soul and body together as a single unit. In creating man, God first created a lifeless body into which He *later* infused a "soul of life." The soul of man is simply so high in comparison to the body that it could not reasonably be formed as a single unit. Rather, a separate act of God was required to achieve the astounding union between them (*Rabbi Shneur Zalman of Lyady, 18th century*).

In the first account of Adam's creation (*Genesis* 1:27), we are told that man was made "in the image of God," but we are not informed *how* his body was fashioned, only *why* he was created: *"Be fruitful and multiply. Fill the earth and take control of it"* (ibid. 28). Here, in the second account of Adam's creation, this emphasis on controlling the world is lacking. Instead, we find a greater insight into the *interior* workings of man: *"He blew into his nostrils a living soul."*

These two accounts speak of two distinct "types" of men that exist within us all. Adam the first is a creator. He expresses his "Divine image" through practical activity in the world. Adam the first is not busy with the metaphysical questions of life; he is concerned only with the *"How"*

בראשית ב:יג-כב

הַשֵּׁנִי גִּיחוֹן הוּא הַסּוֹבֵב אֵת כָּל־אֶרֶץ כּוּשׁ: 14 וְשֵׁם הַנָּהָר הַשְּׁלִישִׁי חִדֶּקֶל הוּא הַהֹלֵךְ קִדְמַת אַשּׁוּר וְהַנָּהָר הָרְבִיעִי הוּא פְרָת: 15 וַיִּקַּח יְהֹוָה אֱלֹהִים אֶת־הָאָדָם וַיַּנִּחֵהוּ בְגַן־עֵדֶן לְעָבְדָהּ וּלְשָׁמְרָהּ: 16 וַיְצַו יְהֹוָה אֱלֹהִים עַל־הָאָדָם לֵאמֹר מִכֹּל עֵץ־הַגָּן אָכֹל תֹּאכֵל: 17 וּמֵעֵץ הַדַּעַת טוֹב וָרָע לֹא תֹאכַל מִמֶּנּוּ כִּי בְּיוֹם אֲכָלְךָ מִמֶּנּוּ מוֹת תָּמוּת: 18 וַיֹּאמֶר יְהֹוָה אֱלֹהִים לֹא־טוֹב הֱיוֹת הָאָדָם לְבַדּוֹ אֶעֱשֶׂה־לּוֹ עֵזֶר כְּנֶגְדּוֹ: 19 וַיִּצֶר יְהֹוָה אֱלֹהִים מִן־הָאֲדָמָה כָּל־חַיַּת הַשָּׂדֶה וְאֵת כָּל־עוֹף הַשָּׁמַיִם וַיָּבֵא אֶל־הָאָדָם לִרְאוֹת מַה־יִּקְרָא־לוֹ וְכֹל אֲשֶׁר יִקְרָא־לוֹ הָאָדָם נֶפֶשׁ חַיָּה הוּא שְׁמוֹ: 20 [THIRD READING] וַיִּקְרָא הָאָדָם שֵׁמוֹת לְכָל־הַבְּהֵמָה וּלְעוֹף הַשָּׁמַיִם וּלְכֹל חַיַּת הַשָּׂדֶה וּלְאָדָם לֹא־מָצָא עֵזֶר כְּנֶגְדּוֹ: 21 וַיַּפֵּל יְהֹוָה אֱלֹהִים | תַּרְדֵּמָה עַל־הָאָדָם וַיִּישָׁן וַיִּקַּח אַחַת מִצַּלְעֹתָיו וַיִּסְגֹּר בָּשָׂר תַּחְתֶּנָּה: 22 וַיִּבֶן יְהֹוָה אֱלֹהִים | אֶת־הַצֵּלָע אֲשֶׁר־לָקַח מִן־הָאָדָם

19. Whatever the man called each living thing (remained) its name (forever). A Hebrew name tells you something about an entity's essential qualities. In his great wisdom, Adam was able to discern the correct name for each species through observing its nature (*Rabbi Abraham Menahem Rapa of Porto, 16th century*).

spiritual vitamin

> Adam was placed in the Garden of Eden *"to cultivate it and to guard it"* (v. 15), and only after that did God tell him, *"You may eat freely from every tree of the Garden"* (v. 16).
>
> Do not strive towards a state of life in which you can enjoy the maximum pleasure with the minimum effort. Human nature is such that you derive true pleasure only if you are a partner in its attainment, through your own exertion. If you receive it entirely *gratis* it is degrading to you, as though you were receiving charity, "bread of shame."
>
> And the harder the work, the sweeter tastes the fruit of achievement.

Gihon, which surrounds the entire land of Cush. [14] The name of the third river is Hiddekel (the Tigris), which flows to the east of Asshur (Assyria), and the fourth river is Pras (the Euphrates).

[15] God, Almighty God, (persuaded) the man (to enter the garden), and settled him in the Garden of Eden to cultivate it and to guard it.

[16] God, Almighty God, commanded man, saying, "You may eat freely from every tree of the Garden, [17] but you must not eat from the Tree of Knowledge of good and evil. For on the day that you will eat from it you will certainly die."

[18] God, Almighty God, said, "It is not good that man is alone. I will make him a helpmate opposite him."

[19] God, Almighty God, formed from the earth every beast of the field and every bird of the skies, and He brought (each species straightaway as it was formed) to man to see what he would call it. Whatever the man called each living thing (remained) its name (forever).

[THIRD READING] [20] Man named all the cattle and the birds of the skies and all the beasts of the field (and saw that each had a male and female partner). Man, however, did not find any helpmate opposite him (so he complained to God).

[21] God, Almighty God, caused a deep sleep to fall upon man, and he slept. He took (a piece from) one of his sides, and He sealed the flesh in its place. [22] God,

kabbalah bites

2:22 The *Zohar* teaches that a man and his wife are, in essence, two halves of the same body. So, according to the Kabbalah, it would not be correct to say that women are "exempt" from some of the commandments incumbent on men. Rather, as Rabbi Isaac Luria writes, "Once the man has observed the commandment, there is *no need* for the woman to do it separately, for she was already included with him when he carried out the command."

15. And settled him in the Garden of Eden. God enticed him with pleasant words and persuaded him to enter (*Rashi, 11th century*).

18. It is not good that man is alone. People might mistakenly assume, "There are two dominions! God alone rules over the upper worlds and He has no partner, and man is the sole ruler of the lower worlds, and he has no partner!" (*Rashi, 11th century*).

The creation of man differed from the creation of other living species in that man was created as a single individual, unlike the other living creatures, which were created in pairs. *It was God's design that the human race, all humans everywhere and at all times, should know that we all descend from the one and the same single progenitor, a fully developed human being created in the image of God, so that no human being could claim superior ancestral origin* (see *Mishnah, Sanhedrin* 4:5). This would make it easier to cultivate a real feeling of kinship in all interhuman relationships (*Rabbi Menahem Mendel Schneerson, 20th century*).

I will make him a helpmate opposite him. If he is worthy, she will be a helpmate. If he is not worthy, she will be against him, to fight him (*Rashi, 11th century*).

בראשית ב:כב - ג:ו

לְאִשָּׁה וַיְבִאֶהָ אֶל־הָאָדָם: 23 וַיֹּאמֶר הָאָדָם זֹאת הַפַּעַם עֶצֶם מֵעֲצָמַי וּבָשָׂר מִבְּשָׂרִי לְזֹאת יִקָּרֵא אִשָּׁה כִּי מֵאִישׁ לֻקֳחָה־זֹּאת: 24 עַל־כֵּן יַעֲזָב־אִישׁ אֶת־אָבִיו וְאֶת־אִמּוֹ וְדָבַק בְּאִשְׁתּוֹ וְהָיוּ לְבָשָׂר אֶחָד: 25 וַיִּהְיוּ שְׁנֵיהֶם עֲרוּמִּים הָאָדָם וְאִשְׁתּוֹ וְלֹא יִתְבֹּשָׁשׁוּ:

ג 1 וְהַנָּחָשׁ הָיָה עָרוּם מִכֹּל חַיַּת הַשָּׂדֶה אֲשֶׁר עָשָׂה יְהֹוָה אֱלֹהִים וַיֹּאמֶר אֶל־הָאִשָּׁה אַף כִּי־אָמַר אֱלֹהִים לֹא תֹאכְלוּ מִכֹּל עֵץ הַגָּן: 2 וַתֹּאמֶר הָאִשָּׁה אֶל־הַנָּחָשׁ מִפְּרִי עֵץ־הַגָּן נֹאכֵל: 3 וּמִפְּרִי הָעֵץ אֲשֶׁר בְּתוֹךְ־הַגָּן אָמַר אֱלֹהִים לֹא תֹאכְלוּ מִמֶּנּוּ וְלֹא תִגְּעוּ בּוֹ פֶּן־תְּמֻתוּן: 4 וַיֹּאמֶר הַנָּחָשׁ אֶל־הָאִשָּׁה לֹא־מוֹת תְּמֻתוּן: 5 כִּי יֹדֵעַ אֱלֹהִים כִּי בְּיוֹם אֲכָלְכֶם מִמֶּנּוּ וְנִפְקְחוּ עֵינֵיכֶם וִהְיִיתֶם כֵּאלֹהִים יֹדְעֵי טוֹב וָרָע: 6 וַתֵּרֶא הָאִשָּׁה כִּי טוֹב הָעֵץ לְמַאֲכָל וְכִי

kabbalah bites

2:23 In the supernal realms, both *Din* (severity) and *Hesed* (love) are always a good thing. Down here, however, the world cannot always tolerate severity, unless it has undergone *tikkun* (spiritual healing).

The Kabbalah teaches that Adam had a first wife, Lilith, who was rooted in *Din*. She soon passed away as the young, fresh world was not yet ready for harshness. Eve—Adam's second wife—was rooted in *Hesed*.

The two wives are alluded to here: the hard *"bone from my bones"*—Lilith; and the softer *"flesh from my flesh"*—Eve. And *"this"*—second wife, Eve—*"shall be called woman."*

"Did God perhaps say?" Is it really so terrible if you do not listen to Him?

Simply minimizing the importance of the Torah can lead you to become lax in observing it (*Rabbi Isaac Meir Alter of Gur, 19th century*).

4. Your eyes will be opened and you will be like God (with the ability to create worlds and) knowing good and evil. The Kabbalah teaches that all of our souls were included in the "universal soul" of Adam. This means, presumably, that we were also there at the moment Adam sinned and ate from the Tree of Knowledge. Why, then, did we not stop him from eating?

We had to let him eat the fruit, because, otherwise, the serpent's lie would have remained unrefuted. The serpent had promised, "Your eyes will be opened and you will be like God, *with the ability to create worlds and knowing good and evil*," so Adam had to eat the fruit to prove that he would remain a human being and no more (*Rabbi Elimelech of Lyzhansk, 18th century*).

Almighty God, built the side that He had taken from man into a woman, and He brought her to man. ²³ Man said, "(After searching for a mate among all the animals and failing,) this time (I have found the) bone from my bones, and flesh from my flesh. This shall be called *'ishah* (woman) because she was taken from *'ish* (man)." ²⁴ Therefore, a man shall leave his father and his mother, and cling to his wife, and they shall become one flesh (through their children).

The Sin of the Tree of Knowledge

They were both naked, the man and his wife, and they were not ashamed (since they had no evil inclination, but their nakedness aroused the interest of the serpent).

3 ¹ The serpent was cunning, more than all the beasts of the field that God, Almighty God, had made. It said to the woman, "Did God perhaps say, 'You shall not eat from any of the trees of the garden'?"

² The woman said to the serpent, "We may eat from the fruit of the trees of the garden, ³ but from the fruit of the tree that is in the middle of the garden, God has said, "You shall not eat of it, and you shall not touch it, lest you die.'"

⁴ The serpent said to the woman, "You will surely not die. ⁵ God (told you not to eat it, because He) knows that on the day that you eat from it, your eyes will be opened, and you will be like God (with the ability to create worlds, and) knowing good and evil."

⁶ The woman (believed the serpent) that the tree was good food (that would make a person like God), that it was desirable to the eyes (for it would open them), and that the tree was desirable to make one wise (knowing good and evil). She took of its fruit and she ate (it), and she also gave (some to the cattle and wild animals, and fearing that she would die and that her husband would remarry, she gave some) to her husband (who was) with her, and he ate (it).

Through merely seeing the physical animal, Adam was able to determine its spiritual source (*Rabbi Isaiah Horowitz, 16ᵗʰ–17ᵗʰ century*).

Man's naming of the animals *connected* the spiritual source of each creature with its existence on the physical plane (*Rabbi Shneur Zalman of Lyady, 18ᵗʰ century*).

22. God, Almighty God, built the side that He had taken from man into a woman. *"Understanding"* (*binah*, spelled: *bet-yod-nun-he*) has the same etymology as the term *"God built"* (*yiven*, spelled: *yod-bet-nun*), implying that He granted women understanding. This teaches you that God has endowed women with more understanding than men (*Babylonian Talmud, Niddah* 45b).

3:1 Did God perhaps say? The serpent's question is written with a dismissive tone, minimizing the significance of God's command and denigrating the consequence of transgressing it.

בראשית ג:ו-יד

תַאֲוָה־הוּא לָעֵינַיִם וְנֶחְמָד הָעֵץ לְהַשְׂכִּיל וַתִּקַּח מִפִּרְיוֹ וַתֹּאכַל וַתִּתֵּן גַּם־לְאִישָׁהּ עִמָּהּ וַיֹּאכַל: 7 וַתִּפָּקַחְנָה עֵינֵי שְׁנֵיהֶם וַיֵּדְעוּ כִּי עֵירֻמִּם הֵם וַיִּתְפְּרוּ עֲלֵה תְאֵנָה וַיַּעֲשׂוּ לָהֶם חֲגֹרֹת: 8 וַיִּשְׁמְעוּ אֶת־קוֹל יְהוָה אֱלֹהִים מִתְהַלֵּךְ בַּגָּן לְרוּחַ הַיּוֹם וַיִּתְחַבֵּא הָאָדָם וְאִשְׁתּוֹ מִפְּנֵי יְהוָה אֱלֹהִים בְּתוֹךְ עֵץ הַגָּן: 9 וַיִּקְרָא יְהוָה אֱלֹהִים אֶל־הָאָדָם וַיֹּאמֶר לוֹ אַיֶּכָּה: 10 וַיֹּאמֶר אֶת־קֹלְךָ שָׁמַעְתִּי בַּגָּן וָאִירָא כִּי־עֵירֹם אָנֹכִי וָאֵחָבֵא: 11 וַיֹּאמֶר מִי הִגִּיד לְךָ כִּי עֵירֹם אָתָּה הֲמִן־הָעֵץ אֲשֶׁר צִוִּיתִיךָ לְבִלְתִּי אֲכָל־מִמֶּנּוּ אָכָלְתָּ: 12 וַיֹּאמֶר הָאָדָם הָאִשָּׁה אֲשֶׁר נָתַתָּה עִמָּדִי הִוא נָתְנָה־לִּי מִן־הָעֵץ וָאֹכֵל: 13 וַיֹּאמֶר יְהוָה אֱלֹהִים לָאִשָּׁה מַה־זֹּאת עָשִׂית וַתֹּאמֶר הָאִשָּׁה הַנָּחָשׁ הִשִּׁיאַנִי וָאֹכֵל: 14 וַיֹּאמֶר יְהוָה אֱלֹהִים | אֶל־הַנָּחָשׁ כִּי עָשִׂיתָ זֹּאת אָרוּר אַתָּה מִכָּל־הַבְּהֵמָה וּמִכֹּל חַיַּת הַשָּׂדֶה עַל־גְּחֹנְךָ

14. God, Almighty God said to the serpent, "Because you have done this, you are (now) cursed, etc." Whoever sets his eyes on something that does not belong to him will not obtain what he desires, and what he already has will be taken away from him.

The serpent in the Garden of Eden craved something that was out of bounds—it lusted after Eve—so the thing it wanted it did not get, and what it already had was taken away from it. God said, "Originally, I said that the serpent should be the king of all animals, but, *'You are now cursed more than all the cattle and more than all the wild animals of the field!'* I said that the serpent should walk with an erect posture, but now, *'You shall go on your belly.'* I said that it should eat the same food as man eats, but now it will eat dust. The serpent had planned to kill Adam and wed Eve, but now, God said, *"I shall place hatred between you and between the woman and between your descendants and between her descendants'"* (v. 14-15; *Babylonian Talmud, Sotah* 9b).

You shall eat soil all the days of your life! How is this a curse? Soil is found almost everywhere, so it seems as if the snake is being blessed, as he never will lack nourishment.

Being surrounded by his sustenance will ensure that the snake never has to ask God to provide for him. Unlike the other animals who pray to God, as described by King David, *"He gives the beast his food and to the young ravens who cry"* (*Psalms* 147:9), the snake is given everything he needs. This is the curse: being cast out and sent away from God's Presence (*Rabbi Simḥah Bunem of Przysucha, 18ᵗʰ–19ᵗʰ century*).

kabbalah bites

3:7 After the sin, the serpent caused a spiritual pollutant, called *zuhama'*, to enter Eve's soul. This pollutant would plague all the souls of her children until it was finally eradicated when the Torah was given at Sinai.

But when the people sinned with the Golden Calf, it returned, and we will only rid ourselves of it completely when the New Era finally comes.

genesis 3:7–14 — bere'shit

⁷ The (intellectual) "eyes" of both of them were opened, and they realized that they were naked (of Divine commandments, having ignored the only command they had been given by God). They sewed together fig leaves (from the tree) and made themselves loincloths.

⁸ They heard the sound of God, Almighty God, walking in the garden in the direction (which the sun sets every) day. The man and his wife hid from God, Almighty God, among the trees of the garden.

⁹ God, Almighty God, called to the man, and said to him, "Where are you?" (to engage him in conversation).

¹⁰ (Man) said, "I heard Your sound in the garden, and I was afraid because I am naked, so I hid."

¹¹ (God) said, "Who told you that you are naked? Have you eaten from the tree from which I commanded you not to eat?"

¹² The man said, "The woman whom You gave (to be) with me gave me from the tree, and I ate."

¹³ God, Almighty God, said to the woman, "What is this that you have done?"

The woman said, "The serpent misled me, and I ate."

¹⁴ God, Almighty God, said to the serpent, "Because you have done this, you are (now) cursed more than all the cattle and more than all the wild animals of

---

7. They sewed together fig leaves (from the tree) and made themselves loincloths. Rabbi Nehemiah said, "The tree from which Adam and Eve ate was a fig tree, for it is logical that the thing with which they sinned—the fig—became the means through which the damage was repaired, when *'they sewed together fig leaves'* as clothing" (*Babylonian Talmud, Sanhedrin* 70b).

13. The serpent misled me, and I ate. Everything in the world contains holy "sparks." Nothing is devoid of these sparks, even wood and stones. In all of man's actions, even in a sin he commits, there are sparks.

What are the sparks in a sin? Repentance. When repenting for the sin, you elevate the sparks contained within it to the Supernal World. This is the inner meaning of *"Is my sin too great to bear?"* (4:13)—lit. "to carry," i.e., to be raised and elevated on high (*Rabbi Israel Ba'al Shem Tov, 18th century*).

spiritual vitamin

> When Adam committed the sin, he experienced a Divine call demanding, *"Where are you?"* (3:9). Do you realize what you have done and what you are supposed to do? From time to time you should also ask yourself, "Where am I?" Take a moment of introspection and soul-searching to find yourself again.

בראשית ג:יד-כד

תֵלֵךְ וְעָפָר תֹּאכַל כָּל־יְמֵי חַיֶּיךָ: 15 וְאֵיבָה | אָשִׁית בֵּינְךָ וּבֵין הָאִשָּׁה וּבֵין זַרְעֲךָ וּבֵין זַרְעָהּ הוּא יְשׁוּפְךָ רֹאשׁ וְאַתָּה תְּשׁוּפֶנּוּ עָקֵב: ס 16 אֶל־הָאִשָּׁה אָמַר הַרְבָּה אַרְבֶּה עִצְּבוֹנֵךְ וְהֵרֹנֵךְ בְּעֶצֶב תֵּלְדִי בָנִים וְאֶל־אִישֵׁךְ תְּשׁוּקָתֵךְ וְהוּא יִמְשָׁל־בָּךְ: ס 17 וּלְאָדָם אָמַר כִּי שָׁמַעְתָּ לְקוֹל אִשְׁתֶּךָ וַתֹּאכַל מִן־הָעֵץ אֲשֶׁר צִוִּיתִיךָ לֵאמֹר לֹא תֹאכַל מִמֶּנּוּ אֲרוּרָה הָאֲדָמָה בַּעֲבוּרֶךָ בְּעִצָּבוֹן תֹּאכֲלֶנָּה כֹּל יְמֵי חַיֶּיךָ: 18 וְקוֹץ וְדַרְדַּר תַּצְמִיחַ לָךְ וְאָכַלְתָּ אֶת־עֵשֶׂב הַשָּׂדֶה: 19 בְּזֵעַת אַפֶּיךָ תֹּאכַל לֶחֶם עַד שׁוּבְךָ אֶל־הָאֲדָמָה כִּי מִמֶּנָּה לֻקָּחְתָּ כִּי־עָפָר אַתָּה וְאֶל־עָפָר תָּשׁוּב: 20 וַיִּקְרָא הָאָדָם שֵׁם אִשְׁתּוֹ חַוָּה כִּי הִוא הָיְתָה אֵם כָּל־חָי: 21 וַיַּעַשׂ יְהוָה אֱלֹהִים לְאָדָם וּלְאִשְׁתּוֹ כָּתְנוֹת עוֹר וַיַּלְבִּשֵׁם: פ [FOURTH READING] 22 וַיֹּאמֶר | יְהוָה אֱלֹהִים הֵן הָאָדָם הָיָה כְּאַחַד מִמֶּנּוּ לָדַעַת טוֹב וָרָע וְעַתָּה | פֶּן־יִשְׁלַח יָדוֹ וְלָקַח גַּם מֵעֵץ הַחַיִּים וְאָכַל וָחַי לְעֹלָם: 23 וַיְשַׁלְּחֵהוּ יְהוָה אֱלֹהִים מִגַּן־עֵדֶן לַעֲבֹד אֶת־הָאֲדָמָה אֲשֶׁר לֻקַּח מִשָּׁם: 24 וַיְגָרֶשׁ אֶת־הָאָדָם וַיַּשְׁכֵּן מִקֶּדֶם לְגַן־עֵדֶן אֶת־הַכְּרֻבִים וְאֵת לַהַט הַחֶרֶב הַמִּתְהַפֶּכֶת לִשְׁמֹר אֶת־דֶּרֶךְ עֵץ הַחַיִּים: ס

18. Thorns and thistles will grow (with) your (crops). When God said to Adam, *"Thorns and thistles will grow with your crops and you will eat the herbs of the field,"* tears flowed from Adam's eyes. He cried to God, "Master of the universe! Will my donkey and I eat from the same trough? Being confined to a donkey's diet, will we humans be reduced to having the same nature and intelligence as a donkey?"

When God said to him, *"With the sweat of your face … will you eat bread"* (3:19), assuring him of a uniquely human food that stimulates intelligence, he was relieved (*Babylonian Talmud, Pesaḥim* 118a, according to *Rabbi Samuel Edels, 16th–17th century*).

21. He clothed them. The Torah begins with an act of kindness and ends with an act of kindness. It begins with kindness, as the verse states, *"God, Almighty God, made for Adam and for his wife skintight garments and He clothed them."* It ends with kindness, as the verse states, *"(God) buried him in the valley"* (Deuteronomy 34:6; *Babylonian Talmud, Sotah* 14a).

the field! You (will have your legs cut off so that you) shall go on your belly, and you shall eat soil all the days of your life! ¹⁵ I shall place hatred between you and between the woman (you desired), and between your descendants and between her descendants. (Man) will crush you (on the) head, and you will bite his heel."

¹⁶ To the woman He said, "I will greatly increase your anguish (of rearing children) and your (labor pains of) pregnancy. You will give birth to children in pain. You will desire (to be with) your husband but he will rule over you (to be with you when he desires)."

¹⁷ To man He said, "Since you listened to your wife's voice, and you ate from the tree about which I commanded you, saying, 'Do not eat from it,' the ground will be cursed because of you (producing loathsome insects), and you will toil to eat from it all the days of your life. ¹⁸ (When you sow seeds, then artichokes and cardoons that have) thorns and thistles will grow (with) your (crops), and you will eat the(se artichokes, cardoons and other) herbs of the field (that take a long time to prepare, due to lack of an alternative. ¹⁹ Only) with the sweat of your face (after much toil) will you eat bread, until you go back to the earth from where you were taken. For you are (from the) soil, and to soil you will return."

(The narrative now returns to the subject of giving names, mentioned above, 2:19-20.)

²⁰ The man named his wife Eve [*ḤAVvah*], because she was the mother of all life [*ḤAI*].

²¹ God, Almighty God, made for Adam and for his wife skintight garments (alternatively: garments of animal skins), and He clothed them.

Expulsion from the Garden of Eden

[FOURTH READING] ²² God, Almighty God, said, "Look! Man has become unique in the (lower) world by himself (since, unlike the animals,) he has the ability of knowing good and evil. Now, (there is a fear that) perhaps he will stretch out his hand and take also from the Tree of Life and eat (from it, and he will) live forever (and is likely to lead others astray, as they will think he is a god)."

²³ God, Almighty God, sent him out of the Garden of Eden to cultivate the earth from which he had been taken. ²⁴ He drove the man out, and to the east (side) of the Garden of Eden He stationed angels (of destruction) and the flame (alternatively: blade) of the revolving sword, to guard the way to the Tree of Life.

---

food for thought

1. Have you been talked into something you greatly regretted later on?

2. Are you swayed by emotional arguments or by rational ones?

3. Do you have a strategy for ignoring an inappropriate urge or enticement?

א ‎1 וְהָאָדָם יָדַע אֶת־חַוָּה אִשְׁתּוֹ וַתַּהַר וַתֵּלֶד אֶת־קַיִן וַתֹּאמֶר קָנִיתִי אִישׁ
אֶת־יְהוָה: ‎2 וַתֹּסֶף לָלֶדֶת אֶת־אָחִיו אֶת־הָבֶל וַיְהִי־הֶבֶל רֹעֵה צֹאן וְקַיִן
הָיָה עֹבֵד אֲדָמָה: ‎3 וַיְהִי מִקֵּץ יָמִים וַיָּבֵא קַיִן מִפְּרִי הָאֲדָמָה מִנְחָה לַיהוָה:
‎4 וְהֶבֶל הֵבִיא גַם־הוּא מִבְּכֹרוֹת צֹאנוֹ וּמֵחֶלְבֵהֶן וַיִּשַׁע יְהוָה אֶל־הֶבֶל וְאֶל־
מִנְחָתוֹ: ‎5 וְאֶל־קַיִן וְאֶל־מִנְחָתוֹ לֹא שָׁעָה וַיִּחַר לְקַיִן מְאֹד וַיִּפְּלוּ פָּנָיו: ‎6 וַיֹּאמֶר
יְהוָה אֶל־קָיִן לָמָּה חָרָה לָךְ וְלָמָּה נָפְלוּ פָנֶיךָ: ‎7 הֲלוֹא אִם־תֵּיטִיב שְׂאֵת וְאִם
לֹא תֵיטִיב לַפֶּתַח חַטָּאת רֹבֵץ וְאֵלֶיךָ תְּשׁוּקָתוֹ וְאַתָּה תִּמְשָׁל־בּוֹ: ‎8 וַיֹּאמֶר
קַיִן אֶל־הֶבֶל אָחִיו וַיְהִי בִּהְיוֹתָם בַּשָּׂדֶה וַיָּקָם קַיִן אֶל־הֶבֶל אָחִיו וַיַּהַרְגֵהוּ:
‎9 וַיֹּאמֶר יְהוָה אֶל־קַיִן אֵי הֶבֶל אָחִיךָ וַיֹּאמֶר לֹא יָדַעְתִּי הֲשֹׁמֵר אָחִי אָנֹכִי:

Abel and his offering, but to Cain and his offering He did not turn" (v. 4-5). Was it necessary to ask him, *"Why is your face dejected"*?

God was actually asking Cain a more subtle question: What is the main reason motivating your anger and dejection? Is it because your sacrifice was rejected, or because your brother's sacrifice was accepted? Which was more painful to you? (*Rabbi Ḥayyim Soloveichik, 19th–20th century*).

7. Surely, if you improve yourself you will be forgiven, etc. God said to the Jewish people: I created the evil impulse and I created the Torah as its antidote. If you study the Torah, you will not be won over by the evil impulse, as it is written, *"Surely, if you improve yourself you will be forgiven."* But if you do not study the Torah, you will be caught by the evil impulse, as the verse continues, *"sin is crouching in wait."* Furthermore, the evil impulse spends all his energy trying to make you sin, as it is written, *"It is longing to entice you."* But if you desire, you can overpower it by learning Torah, as the passage concludes, *"but you can rule over it"* (*Babylonian Talmud, Kiddushin* 30b).

(Your) sin is crouching (in wait) at the entrance. It is far easier to hold fast to your values when you are within your comfort zone than when you are outside it. "Sin is crouching (in wait) *at the entrance*"—the evil impulse waits for you to emerge from your comfort zone to introduce obstacles and challenges (*Rabbi Abraham Samuel Benjamin Sofer, 19th century*).

9. God said to Cain, "Where is Abel your brother?" He said, "I don't know. Am I my brother's guardian?" In this conversation, God and Cain were discussing who was responsible for Abel's death. God asked Cain, *"Where is Abel your brother?"*

---

food for thought

1. How would you react if you were a victim of jealousy?

2. To what extent are you able to rejoice at others' success?

3. What would you do to show God great appreciation?

genesis 4:1–9   bere'shit

Cain and Abel

4 ¹ The man knew his wife Eve (before the sin), and she conceived and bore Cain (together with a twin girl. When he was born) she said, "I have acquired [*KaNiti*] a man (as a partner) with God." ² She gave birth again, to his brother Abel (together with two girls).

Abel was a shepherd of flocks (because he did not want to work with the land, which was cursed), and Cain was a worker of the land.

³ It was at the end of (a number of) days, that Cain brought some of the (worst) fruit of the land as an offering to God. ⁴ Abel also offered from the firstborn of his flocks, from their fattest ones.

God turned to Abel and to his offering (and it was consumed by a fire from heaven), ⁵ but to Cain and to his offering He did not turn. Cain became very angry, and his face grew dejected.

⁶ God said to Cain, "Why are you angry, and why is your face dejected? ⁷ Surely, if you improve yourself you will be forgiven? If you do not improve yourself, however, then (your) sin is crouching (in wait) at the entrance (of your grave. The evil inclination) is longing (to entice you), but you can rule over it (if you want)."

⁸ Cain (started an argument) with Abel his brother (to find a pretext to kill him). Then, when they were in the field, Cain assaulted Abel his brother and killed him.

⁹ God said to Cain, "Where is Abel your brother?"

He said, "I don't know. Am I my brother's guardian?"

---

kabbalah bites

4:1-2 After the sin, the forces of good and evil became inextricably bound together. Abel's soul was *primarily* good, with a little evil mixed in; and Cain's soul was *primarily* evil, with a kernel of good. In fact, that kernel of good in Cain's soul was of the highest quality, as he was the firstborn.

4:3-4 It was at the end of days, that Cain brought … Abel also offered from the firstborn of his flocks. Cain came to offer sacrifices to God "at the *end* of days" when he was old and anticipating death. Abel, however, had served God even when he was young and full of vigor. That was why God accepted Abel's offering (*Rabbi Simḥah Bunem of Przysucha, 18th–19th century*).

Of his flocks. Abel brought an offering from sheep, the most inferior type of cattle, demonstrating his lack of interest in worldly matters (*Rabbi Baḥya b. Asher, 13th century*).

From their fattest ones. This teaches you that when serving God you should always choose the best. In addition to choosing the best animals for sacrifices, your houses of worship should be more beautiful than your own houses, the food that you offer to the hungry should be better than your own and the clothes with which you clothe the poor should be finer than your own (*Maimonides, 12th century*).

6. Why is your face dejected? The Torah seems to make patently clear the reason for Cain's dejection: *"God turned to*

בראשית ד:י-יח

10 וַיֹּ֖אמֶר מֶ֣ה עָשִׂ֑יתָ ק֚וֹל דְּמֵ֣י אָחִ֔יךָ צֹעֲקִ֥ים אֵלַ֖י מִן־הָֽאֲדָמָֽה: 11 וְעַתָּ֖ה אָר֣וּר אָ֑תָּה מִן־הָֽאֲדָמָה֙ אֲשֶׁ֣ר פָּצְתָ֣ה אֶת־פִּ֔יהָ לָקַ֛חַת אֶת־דְּמֵ֥י אָחִ֖יךָ מִיָּדֶֽךָ: 12 כִּ֤י תַֽעֲבֹד֙ אֶת־הָ֣אֲדָמָ֔ה לֹֽא־תֹסֵ֥ף תֵּת־כֹּחָ֖הּ לָ֑ךְ נָ֥ע וָנָ֖ד תִּֽהְיֶ֥ה בָאָֽרֶץ: 13 וַיֹּ֥אמֶר קַ֖יִן אֶל־יְהֹוָ֑ה גָּד֥וֹל עֲוֹנִ֖י מִנְּשֹֽׂא: 14 הֵן֩ גֵּרַ֨שְׁתָּ אֹתִ֜י הַיּ֗וֹם מֵעַל֙ פְּנֵ֣י הָֽאֲדָמָ֔ה וּמִפָּנֶ֖יךָ אֶסָּתֵ֑ר וְהָיִ֜יתִי נָ֤ע וָנָד֙ בָּאָ֔רֶץ וְהָיָ֥ה כָל־מֹֽצְאִ֖י יַֽהַרְגֵֽנִי: 15 וַיֹּ֧אמֶר ל֣וֹ יְהֹוָ֗ה לָכֵן֙ כָּל־הֹרֵ֣ג קַ֔יִן שִׁבְעָתַ֖יִם יֻקָּ֑ם וַיָּ֨שֶׂם יְהֹוָ֤ה לְקַ֨יִן֙ א֔וֹת לְבִלְתִּ֥י הַכּוֹת־אֹת֖וֹ כָּל־מֹֽצְאֽוֹ: 16 וַיֵּ֥צֵא קַ֖יִן מִלִּפְנֵ֣י יְהֹוָ֑ה וַיֵּ֥שֶׁב בְּאֶֽרֶץ־נ֖וֹד קִדְמַת־עֵֽדֶן: 17 וַיֵּ֤דַע קַ֨יִן֙ אֶת־אִשְׁתּ֔וֹ וַתַּ֖הַר וַתֵּ֣לֶד אֶת־חֲנ֑וֹךְ וַֽיְהִי֙ בֹּ֣נֶה עִ֔יר וַיִּקְרָא֙ שֵׁ֣ם הָעִ֔יר כְּשֵׁ֖ם בְּנ֥וֹ חֲנֽוֹךְ: 18 וַיִּוָּלֵ֤ד לַֽחֲנוֹךְ֙ אֶת־עִירָ֔ד וְעִירָ֕ד יָלַ֖ד אֶת־מְחֽוּיָאֵ֑ל וּמְחִיָּיאֵ֗ל יָלַ֤ד

10. Your brother's blood (and the blood of his would-be descendants) is crying out. In monetary cases, if a witness testifies falsely, it is sinful. However, he can still pay compensation to the person who suffered a loss through the false testimony, and the sin is forgiven.

With capital cases, however, the false witness cannot correct his wrong. He is held responsible for the blood of the man who was executed through his false testimony and for the blood of the victim's lost descendants that would have been born (*Babylonian Talmud, Sanhedrin* 37a).

13. Is my sin too great to bear? Cain was the first person to repent before God. God set him as an example for all future penitents (*Genesis Rabbah*).

Cain's repentance consisted of three practical phases.

(1) Confession—Cain declared to God, *"My sin is too great to bear."* (2) Exile—*"He dwelt in the land of the wanderers"* (v. 16).

(3) Rebound into positive action—There is a tremendous temptation for the penitent to remain low-spirited for the rest of his days. The mere thought of his past deeds, which cannot be erased from his mind, is sufficient to plague him with feelings of inferiority. Obviously, in the midst of such a mood he will find it difficult to be active within the world, as he will be constantly wondering, "Who am I to carry out a holy activity like this?"

The challenge of the penitent is that when his repentance is complete, he must propel himself "outwards" into the world. He must free himself from his feelings of inadequacy and start to contribute constructively to the world in the most expansive manner possible.

> **kabbalah bites**
>
> **4:15** The Hebrew term used in reference to Cain's vengeance is *YuKaM*. This alludes to Cain's future reincarnations: *Yitro* (Jethro), *Korah* and *Mitzri*, the Egyptian whom Moses killed. (See: *Exodus* 2:11, 18:1; *Numbers* 16:1.)

genesis 4:10–18 — bere'shit

¹⁰ (God) said, "What have you done? Your brother's blood (and the blood of his would-be descendants) is crying out to Me from the earth! ¹¹ Now, you are (going to be) even more cursed than the ground, which opened its mouth to take your brother's blood from your hand! ¹² (Therefore) when you work the soil, it will no longer give its strength to you! You will be a wanderer over the earth."

¹³ Cain said to God, "Is my sin too great to bear (for You, God, who carries the burden of the upper and lower worlds)? ¹⁴ You have already driven me today off the face of the earth! (Is it possible) to hide from Your face? I will be a wanderer in the land, and then whoever finds me will kill me!"

¹⁵ God said to him, "In that case, whoever kills Cain (will be punished. Abel will only be) avenged after seven generations (when Lamech will kill Cain)." God placed a letter (of His name) on Cain('s forehead) so that he should not be killed by anyone who would find him.

¹⁶ Cain left God's presence (humbly), and he dwelt in the land of the wanderers, to the east of Eden (where his father had been expelled after his sin).

(The seven generations—mentioned in verse 15—occurred as follows:)

¹⁷ Cain knew his wife. She conceived and gave birth to Enoch. (Cain) was building a city, and he named the city like his son's name, Enoch. ¹⁸ Irad was born to Enoch, Irad fathered Mehujael, Mehujael fathered Methusael, and Methusael fathered Lamech.

What have you done! You had a choice between killing him and allowing him to live and you chose to kill him. Clearly, you are responsible for his death.

Cain, on the other hand, shifted the responsibility to God, replying in the spirit of the Talmudic teaching that *"No man on earth so much as strikes his finger unless it is ordained from heaven"* (*Babylonian Talmud, Ḥullin* 7b). He felt that since Abel's death was part of God's plan, he was only the messenger. Therefore he replied, *"Am I my brother's guardian?"* It is You, God, who is in charge of the world. Therefore I should not be liable to punishment.

However, this logic is clearly flawed. Our freedom to choose between good or evil is absolute, and we are held responsible for all of our deeds (*Rabbi Simḥah Bunem of Przysucha, 18ᵗʰ–19ᵗʰ century*).

spiritual vitamin

> Repentance is effective in every case and whatever the transgression, for repentance is one of God's commandments, and God does not require of us the impossible.

בראשית ד:יח-כו

אֶת־מְתוּשָׁאֵ֑ל וּמְתֽוּשָׁאֵ֖ל יָלַ֥ד אֶת־לָֽמֶךְ׃ [FIFTH READING] 19 וַיִּֽקַּֽח־ל֥וֹ לֶ֖מֶךְ שְׁתֵּ֣י נָשִׁ֑ים שֵׁ֤ם הָֽאַחַת֙ עָדָ֔ה וְשֵׁ֥ם הַשֵּׁנִ֖ית צִלָּֽה׃ 20 וַתֵּ֥לֶד עָדָ֖ה אֶת־יָבָ֑ל ה֣וּא הָיָ֔ה אֲבִ֕י יֹשֵׁ֥ב אֹ֖הֶל וּמִקְנֶֽה׃ 21 וְשֵׁ֥ם אָחִ֖יו יוּבָ֑ל ה֣וּא הָיָ֔ה אֲבִ֕י כָּל־תֹּפֵ֥שׂ כִּנּ֖וֹר וְעוּגָֽב׃ 22 וְצִלָּ֣ה גַם־הִ֗וא יָֽלְדָה֙ אֶת־תּ֣וּבַל קַ֔יִן לֹטֵ֕שׁ כָּל־חֹרֵ֥שׁ נְחֹ֖שֶׁת וּבַרְזֶ֑ל וַֽאֲח֥וֹת תּֽוּבַל־קַ֖יִן נַֽעֲמָֽה׃ 23 וַיֹּ֨אמֶר לֶ֜מֶךְ לְנָשָׁ֗יו עָדָ֤ה וְצִלָּה֙ שְׁמַ֣עַן קוֹלִ֔י נְשֵׁ֣י לֶ֔מֶךְ הַֽאְזֵ֖נָּה [SIXTH READING] אִמְרָתִ֑י כִּ֣י אִ֤ישׁ הָרַ֨גְתִּי֙ לְפִצְעִ֔י וְיֶ֖לֶד לְחַבֻּֽרָתִֽי׃ 24 כִּ֥י שִׁבְעָתַ֖יִם יֻקַּם־קָ֑יִן וְלֶ֖מֶךְ שִׁבְעִ֥ים וְשִׁבְעָֽה׃ 25 וַיֵּ֨דַע אָדָ֥ם עוֹד֙ אֶת־אִשְׁתּ֔וֹ וַתֵּ֣לֶד בֵּ֔ן וַתִּקְרָ֥א אֶת־שְׁמ֖וֹ שֵׁ֑ת כִּ֣י שָֽׁת־לִ֤י אֱלֹהִים֙ זֶ֣רַע אַחֵ֔ר תַּ֣חַת הֶ֔בֶל כִּ֥י הֲרָג֖וֹ קָֽיִן׃ 26 וּלְשֵׁ֤ת גַּם־הוּא֙ יֻלַּד־בֵּ֔ן וַיִּקְרָ֥א אֶת־שְׁמ֖וֹ אֱנ֑וֹשׁ אָ֣ז הוּחַ֔ל לִקְרֹ֖א בְּשֵׁ֥ם יְהוָֽה׃ ס

---

existence of God by saying that only such-and-such a star exists.

However, after some time, false prophets arose and began to claim that God had come to them in prophecy and insisted that people worship a certain star. They would bring sacrifices to it and prostrate themselves before it, until they formed figures in temples in the stars' likeness.

Eventually, the people were taught to believe that it was the star that brought about good and evil and that it was fitting to serve and fear it. They were assured that with service and worship would come great wealth and success. Through the passage of time, the honored name of God was forgotten by all of nature and people recognized only their forms of wood and stone. There was not a single person that acknowledged God except for famed individuals, such as Enoch, Methuselah, Noah, Shem, and Eber. Things continued in this manner until Abraham arrived (*Maimonides, 12th century*).

kabbalah bites

4:26 *"Calling by the name of God."* This was the first abuse of the Kabbalah, through which it is possible to manipulate the flow of Divine energy to the world by chanting various Hebrew names of God. Through this technique, the people were able to channel Divine light into their idols to make them effective.

Calling humans and idols by the name of God. Not only is there no deity or power other than God, but in fact, *there is no true existence at all outside God*. The fact that we see a physical world is only due to our inability to see the Godly energy which enlivens it. In truth, however, we are totally subsumed within the absolute oneness of God (*Rabbi Shneur Zalman of Lyady, 18th century*).

genesis 4:19–26 — bere'shit

[FIFTH READING] ¹⁹ Lamech took for himself two wives: one was named Adah, and the other was named Zillah. ²⁰ Adah bore Jabal. He was the father of nomadic cattle rearing. ²¹ His brother's name was Jubal. He was the father of those who play harp and flute (for idol-worship). ²² Zillah also gave birth, to Tubal-cain, who would sharpen all crafting tools for copper and iron (making weapons). Tubal-cain's sister was Naamah.

[SIXTH READING] ²³ Lamech (accidentally killed Cain and Tubal-cain, and his wives separated from him. He) said to his wives, "Adah and Zillah, listen to my voice (and accept me back)! Wives of Lamech, incline your ears to my words! (Did) I slay a man by wounding (him intentionally), or a child by hitting (him intentionally)? ²⁴ If Cain (who killed intentionally) was avenged after seven generations, then Lamech (who killed unintentionally) shall be (avenged after) seventy-seven (generations)!"

²⁵ Adam knew his wife again, and she bore a son. She named him Seth, (saying), "For God has given [ShaT] me other seed, instead of Abel, for Cain killed him." ²⁶ Seth also fathered a son, and he named him Enosh.

Then, (God's name) became profaned, by (people) calling (humans and idols) by the name of God.

Thus, we find that after repenting, Cain propelled himself back into the world: (a) He fathered a son, Enoch. (b) He built a city—an ambitious project aimed at repairing the world that he had damaged. (c) *"He named the city after his son's name, Enoch"* (v. 17). Not only did he free himself from feelings of lowliness, he went to the opposite extreme and *publicized* his achievements boldly to the entire world (*Rabbi Menahem Mendel Schneerson, 20ᵗʰ century*).

26. Then (God's name) became profaned, by (people) calling (humans and idols) by the name of God. In the days of Enosh, people made a serious mistake. They erroneously reasoned that since God created the skies and spheres as part of nature and placed them on high, giving them dignity; and since the skies and spheres are servants who serve Him—it would be appropriate to laud, glorify and honor them in the same way that a king wants to honor the servants who serve him. This is the fundamental basis of idolatry. Yet, they did not deny the

kabbalah bites

4:25 *Adam knew his wife again, and she bore a son. She named him Seth.* Abel's soul was mainly good with a little evil (See above, 4:1-2). The good from Abel's soul was passed onto Seth, whereas the evil was diverted to Balaam's soul.

Later, Abel's soul, which had now achieved its full *tikkun* (spiritual healing) would be reincarnated into Moses (*Mosheh*). Thus the three letters of the word *MoSHeH* are an acronym for **M**osheh, **SH**et (Seth) and **H**evel (Abel).

א זֶה סֵפֶר תּוֹלְדֹת אָדָם בְּיוֹם בְּרֹא אֱלֹהִים אָדָם בִּדְמוּת אֱלֹהִים עָשָׂה אֹתוֹ: 2 זָכָר וּנְקֵבָה בְּרָאָם וַיְבָרֶךְ אֹתָם וַיִּקְרָא אֶת־שְׁמָם אָדָם בְּיוֹם הִבָּרְאָם: 3 וַיְחִי אָדָם שְׁלֹשִׁים וּמְאַת שָׁנָה וַיּוֹלֶד בִּדְמוּתוֹ כְּצַלְמוֹ וַיִּקְרָא אֶת־שְׁמוֹ שֵׁת: 4 וַיִּהְיוּ יְמֵי־אָדָם אַחֲרֵי הוֹלִידוֹ אֶת־שֵׁת שְׁמֹנֶה מֵאֹת שָׁנָה וַיּוֹלֶד בָּנִים וּבָנוֹת: 5 וַיִּהְיוּ כָּל־יְמֵי אָדָם אֲשֶׁר־חַי תְּשַׁע מֵאוֹת שָׁנָה וּשְׁלֹשִׁים שָׁנָה וַיָּמֹת: ס 6 וַיְחִי־שֵׁת חָמֵשׁ שָׁנִים וּמְאַת שָׁנָה וַיּוֹלֶד אֶת־אֱנוֹשׁ: 7 וַיְחִי־שֵׁת אַחֲרֵי הוֹלִידוֹ אֶת־אֱנוֹשׁ שֶׁבַע שָׁנִים וּשְׁמֹנֶה מֵאוֹת שָׁנָה וַיּוֹלֶד בָּנִים וּבָנוֹת: 8 וַיִּהְיוּ כָּל־יְמֵי־שֵׁת שְׁתֵּים עֶשְׂרֵה שָׁנָה וּתְשַׁע מֵאוֹת שָׁנָה וַיָּמֹת: ס 9 וַיְחִי אֱנוֹשׁ תִּשְׁעִים שָׁנָה וַיּוֹלֶד אֶת־קֵינָן: 10 וַיְחִי אֱנוֹשׁ אַחֲרֵי הוֹלִידוֹ אֶת־קֵינָן חֲמֵשׁ עֶשְׂרֵה שָׁנָה וּשְׁמֹנֶה מֵאוֹת שָׁנָה וַיּוֹלֶד בָּנִים וּבָנוֹת: 11 וַיִּהְיוּ כָּל־יְמֵי

so God acted mercifully and took him away before his time (*Rashi* to v. 24). And yet he was a descendent of Seth, the *founder* of humanity!

But this, precisely, is the point. The quality of Seth within us—the outwardness and the ambition—should harbor within it the quality of Enoch—inwardness and piety. We should study Torah expansively, aiming to acquire vast amounts of knowledge, but at least occasionally we should study without any ulterior motive at all. We should observe the commandments to make ourselves better people, but sometimes we should observe a commandment simply because it is God's will. In that way, we ensure that the Seth within us gives birth to the occasional Enoch (*Rabbi Menahem Mendel Schneerson, 20th century*).

He created him with a resemblance (*demut*) to God. Here man is described as being in the "resemblance," *demut*, of God, but elsewhere he is described as being in God's "mold," *tzelem* (above 1:24). What inner significance do these two terms carry?

spiritual vitamin

> Godliness is the actual reality of all things, except that it was God's will that the spiritual should be hidden in a material frame. Through mindfulness you can reveal the spiritual by concentrating on the predominance of form over matter, the spiritual over the material, the soul over the body, until you perceive how the material is being constantly brought into existence as in the six days of creation.

genesis 5:1–11 — bere'shit

The Offspring of Adam

5 ¹ This is the account of Adam's offspring:

On the day that God created man (he fathered children). He created him with a resemblance to God. ² He created them male and female, and He blessed them. He named them man ['*adam*] on the day they were created.

³ Adam lived one hundred and thirty years, and he fathered (a son) resembling himself and with his form, and he named him Seth. ⁴ After he had fathered Seth, Adam lived for eight hundred years and he fathered sons and daughters. ⁵ Adam lived a total of nine hundred and thirty years, and he died.

⁶ Seth lived one hundred and five years, and then he fathered Enosh. ⁷ After he had fathered Enosh, Seth lived eight hundred and seven years, and he fathered sons and daughters. ⁸ Seth lived a total of nine hundred and twelve years, and he died.

⁹ Enosh lived ninety years, and then he fathered Kenan. ¹⁰ After he had fathered Kenan, Enosh lived eight hundred and fifteen years, and he fathered sons and daughters. ¹¹ Enosh lived a total of nine hundred and five years, and he died.

kabbalah bites

5:3 In his efforts of atonement after the sin, Adam separated from his wife for one hundred and thirty years; but this act of piety inadvertently led to far-reaching, catastrophic results. From Adam's involuntary sins, deeply dysfunctional souls came into being.

Every soul must have a male and female element, which is normally derived from the pleasure of each of the parents during conception. In this case, however, in the absence of Adam's partner, the female component of these souls was substituted with forces from *kelippah* (the demonic realm). The result, over such a prolonged period, was a host of lofty souls so deeply dysfunctional that they would take many generations of reincarnation to heal, as we shall later see. (See below, 6:12; 11:5; 13:13; 41:55; 47:9; *Exodus* 7:7; 12:38; 15:25; 18:21; 21:37.)

5:1 Adam's offspring. The "generations of man" are all descended from Adam's son Seth, whereas the descendants of Cain died out. Seth represents man's quality of building, propagating, and healing the world. Cain, on the other hand, is indicative of man's tendency to struggle within himself, toiling with his own darker side in a search for personal perfection. Seth was world-orientated; Cain was self-orientated.

Which is the correct approach?

Presumably, Seth was correct, since we see that the descendants of Seth prevailed whereas those of Cain did not.

However, the outward, world-orientated approach of Seth was not *entirely* correct. For even a person whose goals are to cultivate the world around him still needs to strive for personal perfection in his own life. His worldliness needs to be tempered with inwardness; his productivity coupled with piety.

So, even Seth—the pioneer of all civilization—had a descendent, Enoch, who was a total isolationist. In fact Enoch was so detached from the world that he would have become corrupted with the slightest exposure to humanity,

בראשית ה:יא-ל

אֱנ֕וֹשׁ חָמֵ֣שׁ שָׁנִ֔ים וּתְשַׁ֥ע מֵא֖וֹת שָׁנָ֑ה וַיָּמֹֽת׃ ס 12 וַיְחִ֣י קֵינָ֔ן שִׁבְעִ֖ים שָׁנָ֑ה וַיּ֖וֹלֶד אֶֽת־מַֽהֲלַלְאֵֽל׃ 13 וַיְחִ֣י קֵינָ֗ן אַֽחֲרֵי֙ הוֹלִיד֣וֹ אֶת־מַֽהֲלַלְאֵ֔ל אַרְבָּעִ֣ים שָׁנָ֔ה וּשְׁמֹנֶ֥ה מֵא֖וֹת שָׁנָ֑ה וַיּ֥וֹלֶד בָּנִ֖ים וּבָנֽוֹת׃ 14 וַיִּֽהְיוּ֙ כָּל־יְמֵ֣י קֵינָ֔ן עֶ֣שֶׂר שָׁנִ֔ים וּתְשַׁ֥ע מֵא֖וֹת שָׁנָ֑ה וַיָּמֹֽת׃ ס 15 וַיְחִ֣י מַֽהֲלַלְאֵ֔ל חָמֵ֥שׁ שָׁנִ֖ים וְשִׁשִּׁ֣ים שָׁנָ֑ה וַיּ֖וֹלֶד אֶת־יָֽרֶד׃ 16 וַיְחִ֣י מַֽהֲלַלְאֵ֗ל אַֽחֲרֵי֙ הוֹלִיד֣וֹ אֶת־יֶ֔רֶד שְׁלֹשִׁ֣ים שָׁנָ֔ה וּשְׁמֹנֶ֥ה מֵא֖וֹת שָׁנָ֑ה וַיּ֥וֹלֶד בָּנִ֖ים וּבָנֽוֹת׃ 17 וַיִּֽהְיוּ֙ כָּל־יְמֵ֣י מַֽהֲלַלְאֵ֔ל חָמֵ֤שׁ וְתִשְׁעִים֙ שָׁנָ֔ה וּשְׁמֹנֶ֥ה מֵא֖וֹת שָׁנָ֑ה וַיָּמֹֽת׃ ס 18 וַֽיְחִי־יֶ֔רֶד שְׁתַּ֧יִם וְשִׁשִּׁ֛ים שָׁנָ֖ה וּמְאַ֣ת שָׁנָ֑ה וַיּ֖וֹלֶד אֶת־חֲנֽוֹךְ׃ 19 וַֽיְחִי־יֶ֗רֶד אַֽחֲרֵי֙ הוֹלִיד֣וֹ אֶת־חֲנ֔וֹךְ שְׁמֹנֶ֥ה מֵא֖וֹת שָׁנָ֑ה וַיּ֥וֹלֶד בָּנִ֖ים וּבָנֽוֹת׃ 20 וַיִּֽהְיוּ֙ כָּל־יְמֵי־יֶ֔רֶד שְׁתַּ֤יִם וְשִׁשִּׁים֙ שָׁנָ֔ה וּתְשַׁ֥ע מֵא֖וֹת שָׁנָ֑ה וַיָּמֹֽת׃ ס 21 וַיְחִ֣י חֲנ֔וֹךְ חָמֵ֥שׁ וְשִׁשִּׁ֖ים שָׁנָ֑ה וַיּ֖וֹלֶד אֶת־מְתוּשָֽׁלַח׃ 22 וַיִּתְהַלֵּ֨ךְ חֲנ֜וֹךְ אֶת־הָֽאֱלֹהִ֗ים אַֽחֲרֵי֙ הוֹלִיד֣וֹ אֶת־מְתוּשֶׁ֔לַח שְׁלֹ֥שׁ מֵא֖וֹת שָׁנָ֑ה וַיּ֥וֹלֶד בָּנִ֖ים וּבָנֽוֹת׃ 23 וַיְהִ֖י כָּל־יְמֵ֣י חֲנ֑וֹךְ חָמֵ֤שׁ וְשִׁשִּׁים֙ שָׁנָ֔ה וּשְׁלֹ֥שׁ מֵא֖וֹת שָׁנָֽה׃ 24 וַיִּתְהַלֵּ֥ךְ חֲנ֖וֹךְ אֶת־הָֽאֱלֹהִ֑ים וְאֵינֶ֕נּוּ כִּֽי־לָקַ֥ח אֹת֖וֹ אֱלֹהִֽים׃ ס [SEVENTH READING] 25 וַיְחִ֣י מְתוּשֶׁ֔לַח שֶׁ֧בַע וּשְׁמֹנִ֛ים שָׁנָ֖ה וּמְאַ֣ת שָׁנָ֑ה וַיּ֖וֹלֶד אֶת־לָֽמֶךְ׃ 26 וַיְחִ֣י מְתוּשֶׁ֗לַח אַֽחֲרֵי֙ הוֹלִיד֣וֹ אֶת־לֶ֔מֶךְ שְׁתַּ֤יִם וּשְׁמוֹנִים֙ שָׁנָ֔ה וּשְׁבַ֥ע מֵא֖וֹת שָׁנָ֑ה וַיּ֥וֹלֶד בָּנִ֖ים וּבָנֽוֹת׃ 27 וַיִּֽהְיוּ֙ כָּל־יְמֵ֣י מְתוּשֶׁ֔לַח תֵּ֤שַׁע וְשִׁשִּׁים֙ שָׁנָ֔ה וּתְשַׁ֥ע מֵא֖וֹת שָׁנָ֑ה וַיָּמֹֽת׃ ס 28 וַֽיְחִי־לֶ֔מֶךְ שְׁתַּ֧יִם וּשְׁמֹנִ֛ים שָׁנָ֖ה וּמְאַ֣ת שָׁנָ֑ה וַיּ֖וֹלֶד בֵּֽן׃ 29 וַיִּקְרָ֧א אֶת־שְׁמ֛וֹ נֹ֖חַ לֵאמֹ֑ר זֶ֠֞ה יְנַֽחֲמֵ֤נוּ מִֽמַּֽעֲשֵׂ֨נוּ֙ וּמֵֽעִצְּב֣וֹן יָדֵ֔ינוּ מִן־הָ֣אֲדָמָ֔ה אֲשֶׁ֥ר אֵֽרְרָ֖הּ יְהֹוָֽה׃ 30 וַֽיְחִי־לֶ֗מֶךְ אַֽחֲרֵי֙ הוֹלִיד֣וֹ אֶת־נֹ֔חַ חָמֵ֤שׁ וְתִשְׁעִים֙ שָׁנָ֔ה וַֽחֲמֵ֥שׁ

Consequently, even though Enoch *"followed God,"* as soon as he left the world, *"he was no longer around"*—his memory did not live on, for he had left no one to follow in his path. But Abraham's efforts in outreach assured that his memory and message remain alive for eternity (*Rabbi Abraham Samuel Benjamin Sofer, 19th century*).

genesis 5:12–30 — bere'shit

[12] Kenan lived seventy years, and then he fathered Mahalalel. [13] After he had fathered Mahalalel, Kenan lived eight hundred and forty years, and he fathered sons and daughters. [14] Kenan lived a total of nine hundred and ten years, and he died.

[15] Mahalalel lived sixty-five years, and then he fathered Jared. [16] After he had fathered Jared, Mahalalel lived eight hundred and thirty years, and he fathered sons and daughters. [17] Mahalalel lived a total of eight hundred and ninety-five years, and he died.

[18] Jared lived one hundred and sixty-two years, and then he fathered Enoch. [19] After he had fathered Enoch, Jared lived eight hundred years, and he fathered sons and daughters. [20] Jared lived a total of nine hundred and sixty-two years, and he died.

[21] Enoch lived sixty-five years, and he fathered Methuselah. [22] After he had fathered Methuselah, Enoch followed God for three hundred years, and he fathered sons and daughters. [23] Enoch lived a total of three hundred and sixty-five years. [24] Enoch followed God (but he could easily be misled, so God saved him by taking him away before his time), and he was no longer (around), for God had taken him.

[SEVENTH READING] [25] Methuselah lived one hundred and eighty-seven years, and he fathered Lamech. [26] After he had fathered Lamech, Methuselah lived seven hundred and eighty-two years, and he fathered sons and daughters. [27] Methuselah lived a total of nine hundred and sixty-nine years, and he died.

[28] Lamech lived one hundred and eighty-two years, and he fathered a son (from whom the world was rebuilt). [29] He named him Noah [*No'AḤ*], saying, "This one will give us rest [*yeNAḤamenu*] from our work and from the toil of our hands from the ground which God has cursed" (because he was to invent agricultural tools). [30] After he had fathered Noah, Lamech lived five hundred and ninety-five

---

Tzelem refers to the expressionless body, like an infant who is just born. Afterwards, when your desires gradually expand you adopt what we call a *demut*. The same process is mirrored in your spiritual life: The first drop of Torah that enters into you is your *tzelem*, and the desire with which you yearn for further words of Torah is your *demut*.

Our verse teaches, *"On the day that God created man, He created him with a demut to God"*—the main point in creating you was in order that you should desire to grow spiritually through increasing your Torah knowledge. And *"this is the account of Adam's offspring"*—if your *demut* will be stimulated and developed with Torah study then you will count many years and generations of offspring (*Rabbi Mordecai Joseph Leiner of Izbica, 19th century*).

24. Enoch followed God ... and he was no longer (around), for God had taken him. Enoch followed God, but he did not concern himself too much with the other people in his generation. Abraham, on the other hand, dedicated much effort to draw his generation closer to God.

מְאַת שָׁנָה וַיּוֹלֶד בָּנִים וּבָנוֹת: 31 וַיְהִי כָּל־יְמֵי־לֶמֶךְ שֶׁבַע וְשִׁבְעִים שָׁנָה וּשְׁבַע מֵאוֹת שָׁנָה וַיָּמֹת: ס 32 וַיְהִי־נֹחַ בֶּן־חֲמֵשׁ מֵאוֹת שָׁנָה וַיּוֹלֶד נֹחַ אֶת־שֵׁם אֶת־חָם וְאֶת־יָפֶת:

ו 1 וַיְהִי כִּי־הֵחֵל הָאָדָם לָרֹב עַל־פְּנֵי הָאֲדָמָה וּבָנוֹת יֻלְּדוּ לָהֶם: 2 וַיִּרְאוּ בְנֵי־הָאֱלֹהִים אֶת־בְּנוֹת הָאָדָם כִּי טֹבֹת הֵנָּה וַיִּקְחוּ לָהֶם נָשִׁים מִכֹּל אֲשֶׁר בָּחָרוּ: 3 וַיֹּאמֶר יְהֹוָה לֹא־יָדוֹן רוּחִי בָאָדָם לְעֹלָם בְּשַׁגַּם הוּא בָשָׂר וְהָיוּ יָמָיו מֵאָה וְעֶשְׂרִים שָׁנָה: 4 הַנְּפִלִים הָיוּ בָאָרֶץ בַּיָּמִים הָהֵם וְגַם אַחֲרֵי־כֵן אֲשֶׁר יָבֹאוּ בְּנֵי הָאֱלֹהִים אֶל־בְּנוֹת הָאָדָם וְיָלְדוּ לָהֶם הֵמָּה הַגִּבֹּרִים אֲשֶׁר מֵעוֹלָם אַנְשֵׁי הַשֵּׁם: פ 5 [MAFTIR] וַיַּרְא יְהֹוָה כִּי רַבָּה רָעַת הָאָדָם בָּאָרֶץ וְכָל־יֵצֶר מַחְשְׁבֹת לִבּוֹ רַק רַע כָּל־הַיּוֹם: 6 וַיִּנָּחֶם יְהֹוָה כִּי־עָשָׂה אֶת־הָאָדָם בָּאָרֶץ וַיִּתְעַצֵּב אֶל־לִבּוֹ: 7 וַיֹּאמֶר יְהֹוָה אֶמְחֶה אֶת־הָאָדָם אֲשֶׁר־בָּרָאתִי מֵעַל פְּנֵי הָאֲדָמָה מֵאָדָם עַד־בְּהֵמָה עַד־רֶמֶשׂ וְעַד־עוֹף הַשָּׁמָיִם כִּי נִחַמְתִּי כִּי עֲשִׂיתִם:

8 וְנֹחַ מָצָא חֵן בְּעֵינֵי יְהֹוָה: פ פ פ

קמ"ו פסוקים, אמצי"ה סימן, יחזקיה"ו סימן.

6:6 God was consoled (by the fact) that He had made man upon the earth. God was consoled by the fact that he had made man *from* the earth, which had imparted him with a tendency to laziness and depression, like the heavy earth. If God had not included such a significant earthy component in man, he would not have become so corrupt (*Rabbi Phinehas Menahem Eleazar Justman, 20th century*).

7. God said, "I will wash away man, whom I created, from upon the face of the earth, man as well as cattle, creeping things and birds of the skies." Why were all the animals destroyed? Because the only way to save the animals from the Flood would have been through a miracle, since they inhabited the earth along with man (*Rabbi David Kimḥi, 12th–13th century*).

8. But Noah found favor in the eyes of God. We all have at least one spark within us through which we will find favor in God's eyes. That spark is the secret of man's continued existence (*Rabbi Isaac Meir Alter of Gur, 19th century*).

years, and he fathered sons and daughters. ³¹ Lamech lived a total of seven hundred and seventy-seven years, and he died.

³² (After) Noah was five hundred years old, Noah fathered Shem, Ham, and Japheth.

Moral Corruption of Man

6 ¹ Then, when man began to multiply upon the face of the earth and daughters were born to them, ² the sons of nobility (violated) the daughters of (common) people when they were beautifying themselves (for their weddings). They took for themselves wives from whomever they chose (even married women, males and animals).

³ God said, "My Spirit will not remain in conflict over (whether to destroy) man for a long time! Furthermore, he is (only) flesh (and yet he does not humble himself before Me! I will give him) one hundred and twenty years to live (and if he does not repent, I will destroy him with a flood)!"

⁴ There were giants on the earth in the days of (Enosh and Cain, when God brought a flood that destroyed a third of the world's population due to their wickedness), and (despite witnessing Divine punishment, they continued their evil) afterwards as well, when the sons of the (giant) nobles would (violate) the daughters of (common) people, and they would bear (giant) children for them. They were the greatest (rebels of all) men who ever existed, men who were (mentioned above) by name(s which hinted to their later destruction).

[MAFTIR] ⁵ God saw that man's wickedness on earth was increasing, and every thought that came from his heart throughout the day was purely evil. ⁶ God was consoled (by the fact) that He had made man upon the earth (and not in heaven, where he would have caused the angels to rebel. God decided) in His heart (to cause man) pain.

food for thought

1. How has corruption impacted your life?

2. Is the moral character of contemporary society shifting?

3. How would you remain principled in power?

⁷ God said, "I will wash away man, whom I created, from upon the face of the earth, man as well as cattle, creeping things and birds of the skies, for I have reckoned (what to do) about (the fact that) I made them."

⁸ But Noah found favor in the eyes of God.

Haftarot: Bere'shit—page 1288.   *Erev Rosh Ḥodesh*—page 1415.

> The **Flood waters** had a spiritually **cleansing effect** on the world. After the Flood, the world and all its inhabitants had a greater **conscience** and a greater **appreciation of God.** This in turn brought a greater **peace** and **serenity** to the world.

NOAH
נחַ

OFFSPRING OF NOAH	6:9–10
THE FLOOD	6:11 – 8:22
NOAH COMMANDED TO POPULATE THE WORLD	9:1–7
GOD ESTABLISHES COVENANT WITH MANKIND	9:8–17
HAM ASSAULTS NOAH	9:18–29
DESCENDANTS OF NOAH	10:1–32
TOWER OF BABEL	11:1–9
DESCENDANTS OF SHEM	11:10–26
DESCENDANTS OF TERAH	11:27–32

NAME
Noah

MEANING
"Serenity"

LINES IN TORAH SCROLL
230

PARASHIYYOT
5 open; 13 closed

VERSES
153

WORDS
1861

LETTERS
6907

DATE
1556 – 2083

LOCATION
Ur of the Chaldeans, Mount Ararat, Haran

KEY PEOPLE
Noah, Shem, Ham, Japheth, Terah, Abram

MASORETIC FEATURES
Final *nun* of *be-haran* (11:32) is inverted

MITZVOT
None

NOTE
Follows the first full "working" week of the year, after the festivals of *Tishri*

CHARACTER PROFILE

NAME
Noah

FATHER
Lamech

GRANDFATHER
Methuselah

WIFE
Naamah

CHILDREN
Shem, Ham, Japheth

LIFE SPAN
950 years

ACHIEVEMENTS
Understood the languages of all creatures; compiled a book of cures that he heard from Angel Raphael; invented farming tools

KNOWN FOR
Spent 120 years building the ark; cared for the animals in the ark at great personal sacrifice; was promised by God that the world would never be destroyed again by a flood; planted a vineyard and became drunk; cursed Ham and Canaan for their misconduct

REAL CARE

Although he encouraged them to repent, Noah did not pray for his generation; he only felt responsible for himself. This is in contrast to Abraham who prayed for Sodom to be saved.

NEGATIVE SPEECH

When describing the animals that Noah should take into the ark, the Torah states, "Those that are not pure," to avoid the negative term *tame'* (impure). Negative speech is so undesirable that the Torah is careful not to disparage even an animal (7:8).

BLESSING OF UNITY

Noah's generation worked against each other while those that built the Tower of Babel worked together in unity. Therefore God did not destroy them (11:9).

אֵ֚לֶּה תּוֹלְדֹ֣ת נֹ֔חַ נֹ֗חַ אִ֥ישׁ צַדִּ֛יק תָּמִ֥ים הָיָ֖ה בְּדֹֽרֹתָ֑יו אֶת־הָֽאֱלֹהִ֖ים הִֽתְהַלֶּךְ־נֹֽחַ: 10 וַיּ֥וֹלֶד נֹ֖חַ שְׁלֹשָׁ֣ה בָנִ֑ים אֶת־שֵׁ֖ם אֶת־חָ֥ם וְאֶת־יָֽפֶת: 11 וַתִּשָּׁחֵ֥ת הָאָ֖רֶץ לִפְנֵ֣י הָֽאֱלֹהִ֑ים וַתִּמָּלֵ֥א הָאָ֖רֶץ חָמָֽס: 12 וַיַּ֧רְא אֱלֹהִ֛ים אֶת־הָאָ֖רֶץ וְהִנֵּ֣ה נִשְׁחָ֑תָה כִּֽי־הִשְׁחִ֧ית כָּל־בָּשָׂ֛ר אֶת־דַּרְכּ֖וֹ עַל־הָאָֽרֶץ: ס 13 וַיֹּ֨אמֶר אֱלֹהִ֜ים לְנֹ֗חַ קֵ֤ץ כָּל־בָּשָׂר֙ בָּ֣א לְפָנַ֔י כִּֽי־מָלְאָ֥ה הָאָ֖רֶץ חָמָ֣ס מִפְּנֵיהֶ֑ם וְהִנְנִ֥י מַשְׁחִיתָ֖ם אֶת־הָאָֽרֶץ:

Rabbi Judah said, "Moses asked for forgiveness in the merit of the Patriarchs, but Noah, who had no such merits, was unable to do so."

Rabbi Isaac said, "Notwithstanding this impediment, Noah should have prayed for his generation" (*Zohar*).

We are taught to *"judge every person favorably"* (*Avot* 1:6). Why, then, did some of the Sages interpret Noah's actions *derogatorily*?

To repudiate the notion that Noah's behavior—of saving himself alone—was acceptable. By expressing their discontent, the Sages sent the message that you must always accept responsibility for the people around you, both physically and spiritually.

In actual fact, Noah *did* involve himself with his contemporaries, and spent one hundred and twenty years rebuking them to repentance (*Rashi* to v. 14). However, his efforts were not considered genuine for a man of his piety. Noah rebuked the generation *only because he was commanded to do so*, to discharge the obligation which God had given him. It did not bother him sufficiently whether his generation would actually repent, *and it was his lack of sincerity that caused his lack of success.*

Contrast this with Moses, who demonstrated self-sacrifice when his people were in jeopardy, pleading to God, *"If You forgive their sin (then well and good), but if not, please erase me from Your Book (the Torah)!"* (Exodus 32:32; Rabbi Menahem Mendel Schneerson, 20th century).

10. Noah fathered three sons: Shem, Ham, and Japheth. His sons' names hint to Noah's own good deeds (mentioned in the previous verse). Shem, meaning "name," reflects on Noah's efforts to glorify the name of God through his deeds. Ham, meaning "warmth," symbolizes Noah's warmth and enthusiasm for God's commandments. Japheth, meaning "beauty," suggests that Noah's deeds brought honor and glory to God (Rabbi Tzevi Hirsch of Rymanow, 18th–19th century).

13. The earth has become full of robbery. Their sin consisted of lewdness and immorality, but their fate was sealed only on account of the robbery they committed (*Rashi*, 11th century).

kabbalah bites

6:12 The Generation of the Flood was the first incarnation of the "dysfunctional souls" which Adam had brought into being during the 130 years he separated from Eve (see *Genesis* 5:3). Since these souls had been formed through wasted seed, their obsessive-compulsive sin was to spill their own seed on the ground (*hishḥit ... 'al ha-'aretz*, lit., "wasted on the ground"; cf. ibid., 38:9).

God thus said *"I will wash away man (Adam)"* (6:7), because Adam himself was directly responsible for these souls.

genesis 6:9–13 — noah

parashat noaḥ

The Offspring of Noah

⁹ These are the offspring of Noah.

Noah was a righteous man. He was perfect(ly righteous) in (relation to) his generation. Noah walked (only) with (the support of) God.

¹⁰ Noah fathered three sons: Shem, Ham, and Japheth.

News of the Flood—Noah Builds the Ark

¹¹ The earth became depraved (and idolatrous) before God, and the earth became full of robbery. ¹² God saw the earth, and—look!—it had become depraved, for all (human and animal) flesh had depraved its nature upon the earth.

¹³ God said to Noah, "The end of all flesh has come before Me, as the earth has become full of robbery because of them. I am going to destroy them from the earth (alternatively: with the earth).

6:9 These are the offspring of Noah. Noah was a righteous man. Since the Torah mentions him, it tells his praise, in the spirit of the verse, *"The mention of a righteous man is for blessing"* (*Proverbs* 10:7). Alternatively, the Torah is teaching us that the main "offspring" of the righteous are their good deeds (*Rashi, 11th century*).

A righteous man ... perfect in his generation. Noah walked with God. There are four levels alluded to in this verse: (1) *"man"*—a regular person; (2) *"righteous"*—in all his deeds; (3) *"perfect"*—a man who is perfect in his character and serves God sincerely; and (4) *"walked with God"*—a man whose life always is focused on the Creator (*Rabbi Bahya b. Asher, 13th century*).

He was *righteous* because he resisted the wicked and violent tendencies of the generation of the Flood. He was *perfect* because he resisted the intellectual corruption of the generation of Dispersion, who built the Tower of Babel (*Rabbi Joseph b. Ephraim Caro, 16th century*).

He was perfect in his generation. Some of our Sages interpret this positively, explaining that if he had lived in a generation of righteous people he would have been even more righteous. Others interpret it derogatorily, explaining that Noah was righteous only relatively, but if he had lived in Abraham's generation he would not have been considered especially righteous at all (*Rashi, 11th century*).

God told Noah that He was going to bring a flood and wipe out mankind. But since Noah was told that he and his family would be saved, he did not pray to God for the salvation of the rest of the world, and they were destroyed. Contrast this with Moses, who prayed for the Jewish people when they worshiped the Golden Calf, and they were saved.

---

food for thought

1. Are all your heroes righteous people?

2. What does it mean to "walk with God"? Can anyone do it?

3. Why are we so easily influenced by the moral standing of our neighbors?

בראשית ו:יד – ז:ב

14 עֲשֵׂה לְךָ תֵּבַת עֲצֵי־גֹפֶר קִנִּים תַּעֲשֶׂה אֶת־הַתֵּבָה וְכָפַרְתָּ אֹתָהּ מִבַּיִת וּמִחוּץ בַּכֹּפֶר: 15 וְזֶה אֲשֶׁר תַּעֲשֶׂה אֹתָהּ שְׁלֹשׁ מֵאוֹת אַמָּה אֹרֶךְ הַתֵּבָה חֲמִשִּׁים אַמָּה רָחְבָּהּ וּשְׁלֹשִׁים אַמָּה קוֹמָתָהּ: 16 צֹהַר ׀ תַּעֲשֶׂה לַתֵּבָה וְאֶל־אַמָּה תְּכַלֶנָּה מִלְמַעְלָה וּפֶתַח הַתֵּבָה בְּצִדָּהּ תָּשִׂים תַּחְתִּיִּם שְׁנִיִּם וּשְׁלִשִׁים תַּעֲשֶׂהָ: 17 וַאֲנִי הִנְנִי מֵבִיא אֶת־הַמַּבּוּל מַיִם עַל־הָאָרֶץ לְשַׁחֵת כָּל־בָּשָׂר אֲשֶׁר־בּוֹ רוּחַ חַיִּים מִתַּחַת הַשָּׁמָיִם כֹּל אֲשֶׁר־בָּאָרֶץ יִגְוָע: 18 וַהֲקִמֹתִי אֶת־בְּרִיתִי אִתָּךְ וּבָאתָ אֶל־הַתֵּבָה אַתָּה וּבָנֶיךָ וְאִשְׁתְּךָ וּנְשֵׁי־בָנֶיךָ אִתָּךְ: 19 וּמִכָּל־הָחַי מִכָּל־בָּשָׂר שְׁנַיִם מִכֹּל תָּבִיא אֶל־הַתֵּבָה לְהַחֲיֹת אִתָּךְ זָכָר וּנְקֵבָה יִהְיוּ: 20 מֵהָעוֹף לְמִינֵהוּ וּמִן־הַבְּהֵמָה לְמִינָהּ מִכֹּל רֶמֶשׂ הָאֲדָמָה לְמִינֵהוּ שְׁנַיִם מִכֹּל יָבֹאוּ אֵלֶיךָ לְהַחֲיוֹת: 21 וְאַתָּה קַח־לְךָ מִכָּל־מַאֲכָל אֲשֶׁר יֵאָכֵל וְאָסַפְתָּ אֵלֶיךָ וְהָיָה לְךָ וְלָהֶם לְאָכְלָה: 22 וַיַּעַשׂ נֹחַ כְּכֹל אֲשֶׁר צִוָּה אֹתוֹ אֱלֹהִים כֵּן עָשָׂה:

1 וַיֹּאמֶר יְהֹוָה לְנֹחַ בֹּא־אַתָּה וְכָל־בֵּיתְךָ אֶל־הַתֵּבָה כִּי־אֹתְךָ רָאִיתִי צַדִּיק לְפָנַי בַּדּוֹר הַזֶּה: 2 מִכֹּל ׀ הַבְּהֵמָה הַטְּהוֹרָה תִּקַּח־לְךָ שִׁבְעָה שִׁבְעָה [SECOND READING]

the construction for one hundred and twenty years and ask him, "Why do you need this?" Noah would then inform him, "God is going to bring a flood upon the world," and perhaps they would repent (*Rashi, 11th century*).

A light for the ark. Noah's mission was to take a world of misery and transform it into a world of light. God told him to make a light, *tzohar* (spelled: *tzadi-he-resh*), which has the same letters as the Hebrew word for "misery," *tzarah* (spelled: *tzadi-resh-he*)—replacing misery with light (*Rabbi Israel Ba'al Shem Tov, 18th century*).

17. I am ready to bring a flood of water upon the earth. The people of Noah's generation only became arrogant because of the goodness that God lavished on them. They said, "Do we need

spiritual vitamin

" By attaching ourselves to God we can sometimes defy the laws of nature. "

¹⁴ "You should make an ark of gopher wood. You should make the ark with compartments. You should coat both inside and outside with tar.

¹⁵ "This is how you should make it: the length of the ark—three hundred cubits, its breadth—fifty cubits, and its height—thirty cubits.

¹⁶ "You should make a light for the ark. You should finish it (slanting) a cubit (high) at the top. You should place the entrance of the ark at its side. You shall make it with a bottom, second and third storey.

¹⁷ "I am ready to (consent to man's destruction and) bring a flood of water upon the earth, to destroy all flesh beneath the skies in which there is the spirit of life. All that is upon the earth will perish.

¹⁸ "I will set up My covenant with you, and you will come into the ark, you, your sons, your wife and your sons' wives with you. ¹⁹ From every living (demon), and from all flesh, you should bring two of each (species) into the ark to keep alive with you; they shall be male and female. ²⁰ From the birds (which had only bred with) their own species, from the animals (which had only bred with) their own species, and from every creeping thing on the ground (which had only bred with) its own species, two of each will come to you (of their own accord) to be kept alive.

²¹ "As for you, take for yourself from every edible food and bring it in with you. It will be for you and for them to eat."

²² Noah made (the ark). He did everything that God had commanded him.

Noah Enters the Ark

7 [SECOND READING] ¹ God said to Noah, "Come into the ark, you and all your household, for I have seen you as a righteous man before Me in this generation. ² From all the (species of) animals that are pure (in Jewish law) you should take for your-

---

See how far-reaching are the consequences of robbery! The people of Noah's generation transgressed all seven universal "Noachide" laws, including prohibitions against idol worship, blasphemy, murder, forbidden relations, robbery, cruelty to animals, and the command to administer justice. Nevertheless, the decree of their punishment through the Flood was not sealed until they engaged in robbery, as God proclaimed, "The earth has become full of *robbery* ... I am going to destroy them" (*Babylonian Talmud, Sanhedrin* 108a; *Code of Maimonides, Laws of Kings and Their Wars* 9:1).

The reason why the Torah contains the three accounts of (a) Cain and Abel (b) the generation of the Flood, and (c) the generation of Dispersion (below, ch. 11), is because we all need to rid ourselves of the three undesirable traits which these stories highlight: (a) jealousy (b) lust and (c) honor (*Rabbi Israel Hapstein of Kozienice, 18th century*).

14. Make an ark. God has many ways at His disposal with which to bring relief and salvation. He burdened Noah with constructing an ark in order that the masses should see him busy with

בראשית ז:ב-יב

אִישׁ וְאִשְׁתּוֹ וּמִן־הַבְּהֵמָה אֲשֶׁר לֹא טְהֹרָה הִוא שְׁנַיִם אִישׁ וְאִשְׁתּוֹ: 3 גַּם מֵעוֹף הַשָּׁמַיִם שִׁבְעָה שִׁבְעָה זָכָר וּנְקֵבָה לְחַיּוֹת זֶרַע עַל־פְּנֵי כָל־הָאָרֶץ: 4 כִּי לְיָמִים עוֹד שִׁבְעָה אָנֹכִי מַמְטִיר עַל־הָאָרֶץ אַרְבָּעִים יוֹם וְאַרְבָּעִים לָיְלָה וּמָחִיתִי אֶת־כָּל־הַיְקוּם אֲשֶׁר עָשִׂיתִי מֵעַל פְּנֵי הָאֲדָמָה: 5 וַיַּעַשׂ נֹחַ כְּכֹל אֲשֶׁר־צִוָּהוּ יְהוָֹה: 6 וְנֹחַ בֶּן־שֵׁשׁ מֵאוֹת שָׁנָה וְהַמַּבּוּל הָיָה מַיִם עַל־הָאָרֶץ: 7 וַיָּבֹא נֹחַ וּבָנָיו וְאִשְׁתּוֹ וּנְשֵׁי־בָנָיו אִתּוֹ אֶל־הַתֵּבָה מִפְּנֵי מֵי הַמַּבּוּל: 8 מִן־הַבְּהֵמָה הַטְּהוֹרָה וּמִן־הַבְּהֵמָה אֲשֶׁר אֵינֶנָּה טְהֹרָה וּמִן־הָעוֹף וְכֹל אֲשֶׁר־רֹמֵשׂ עַל־הָאֲדָמָה: 9 שְׁנַיִם שְׁנַיִם בָּאוּ אֶל־נֹחַ אֶל־הַתֵּבָה זָכָר וּנְקֵבָה כַּאֲשֶׁר צִוָּה אֱלֹהִים אֶת־נֹחַ: 10 וַיְהִי לְשִׁבְעַת הַיָּמִים וּמֵי הַמַּבּוּל הָיוּ עַל־הָאָרֶץ: 11 בִּשְׁנַת שֵׁשׁ־מֵאוֹת שָׁנָה לְחַיֵּי־נֹחַ בַּחֹדֶשׁ הַשֵּׁנִי בְּשִׁבְעָה־עָשָׂר יוֹם לַחֹדֶשׁ בַּיּוֹם הַזֶּה נִבְקְעוּ כָּל־מַעְיְנֹת תְּהוֹם רַבָּה וַאֲרֻבֹּת הַשָּׁמַיִם נִפְתָּחוּ: 12 וַיְהִי הַגֶּשֶׁם עַל־

---

impure animals," it employs a roundabout phrase, "the animals *that are not pure*." This teaches you that you should go out of your way to avoid distasteful speech (*Babylonian Talmud, Pesahim* 3a).

11. All the wellsprings of the great depths burst forth. In the six hundredth year of the sixth millennium (=1840CE), there will be an opening of the "supernal gates" of (mystical) wisdom and the "lower wellsprings" of (secular) wisdom, preparing the world for the seventh millennium—like a person who begins to prepare himself for the Sabbath on Friday, when the sun heads downwards. This is indicated by the verse, *"In the six hundredth year of Noah's life ... all the wellsprings of the great depths burst forth, and the apertures of the skies opened up"* (*Zohar*).

12. There was rain on the earth. Here the verse states, "There *was* rain on the earth for forty days and nights," suggesting that there was only comparatively harmless "rain," and yet the Torah sends a different message later: "The *Flood* was on the earth for forty days" (v. 17), indicating a much stronger downfall.

We can resolve this contradiction by explaining that when God brought the rains down, He initially brought them down with mercy, so that if the people would repent, they would be rains of blessing (v. 12). When they failed to repent, the rains became a flood (v. 17; *Rashi, 11th century*).

---

food for thought

1. Imagine how survivors must have felt after the pogroms of history.

2. What do you think motivated survivors to live from one day to the next?

3. How were survivors' children influenced by their parents' experiences?

self seven pairs of male and female, and from the (species of) animals that are not pure (in Jewish law), two (animals), a male and female. ³ Also, from the birds of the skies (that are pure, take) seven pairs, male and female, to keep (their) seed alive upon the face of the earth. ⁴ For, in another seven days, I will make it rain upon the earth for forty days and forty nights, and I will wash away from the face of the earth all existence that I have made."

⁵ Noah obeyed (the call to enter the ark), according to all that God had commanded him.

⁶ Noah was six hundred years old when the floodwater came upon the earth.

⁷ Noah, his sons, his wife and his sons' wives with him, (eventually) went into the ark, (when they were forced) because of the floodwaters. ⁸ From the pure animals and from the animals that are not pure, from the birds, and from all that creeps upon the earth, ⁹ two by two they came to Noah into the ark, male and female, as God had commanded Noah. ¹⁰ And then, after seven days, the floodwaters were upon the earth.

The Flood Destroys Human and Animal Life

¹¹ In the six hundredth year of Noah's life, in the second month, on the seventeenth day of the month, on that day, all the wellsprings of the great depths burst forth, and the apertures of the skies opened up. ¹² There was rain on the earth for forty days and forty nights.

the Almighty for anything more than a drop of rain? Actually, we do not even need Him for that! We have rivers and streams from which to sustain ourselves."

God said, "With the very goodness that I gave them they provoke Me! Well, with that same abundance I will punish them." Immediately, God informed Noah, *"I am ready to bring a flood of water upon the earth"* (*Babylonian Talmud, Sanhedrin* 108a).

7:8 From the animals that are not pure. The Torah uses eight Hebrew letters more than necessary in an effort to avoid using a unpleasant term. For instead of simply referring to "the

spiritual vitamin

> The core of Jewish vitality and indestructibility is pure faith in God; not in some kind of an abstract Deity, hidden somewhere in the heavenly spheres, who regards this world from a distance; but absolute faith in a very personal God, who is the very life and existence of each of us and who permeates every aspect of existence. When you have such faith, there is no room for fear or anxiety, as the Psalmist says, *"I fear no evil, for You are with me"* (*Psalms* 23:4).

הָאָ֖רֶץ אַרְבָּעִ֣ים י֑וֹם וְאַרְבָּעִ֖ים לָֽיְלָה: 13 בְּעֶ֨צֶם הַיּ֤וֹם הַזֶּה֙ בָּ֣א נֹ֔חַ וְשֵֽׁם־וְחָ֥ם וָיֶ֖פֶת בְּנֵי־נֹ֑חַ וְאֵ֣שֶׁת נֹ֗חַ וּשְׁלֹ֧שֶׁת נְשֵֽׁי־בָנָ֛יו אִתָּ֖ם אֶל־הַתֵּבָֽה: 14 הֵ֜מָּה וְכָל־הַֽחַיָּ֣ה לְמִינָ֗הּ וְכָל־הַבְּהֵמָה֙ לְמִינָ֔הּ וְכָל־הָרֶ֛מֶשׂ הָרֹמֵ֥שׂ עַל־הָאָ֖רֶץ לְמִינֵ֑הוּ וְכָל־הָע֣וֹף לְמִינֵ֔הוּ כֹּ֖ל צִפּ֥וֹר כָּל־כָּנָֽף: 15 וַיָּבֹ֥אוּ אֶל־נֹ֖חַ אֶל־הַתֵּבָ֑ה שְׁנַ֤יִם שְׁנַ֨יִם֙ מִכָּל־הַבָּשָׂ֔ר אֲשֶׁר־בּ֖וֹ ר֥וּחַ חַיִּֽים: 16 וְהַבָּאִ֗ים זָכָ֨ר וּנְקֵבָ֤ה מִכָּל־בָּשָׂר֙ בָּ֔אוּ כַּֽאֲשֶׁ֛ר צִוָּ֥ה אֹת֖וֹ אֱלֹהִ֑ים וַיִּסְגֹּ֥ר יְהוָ֖ה בַּֽעֲדֽוֹ: [THIRD READING] 17 וַיְהִ֧י הַמַּבּ֛וּל אַרְבָּעִ֥ים י֖וֹם עַל־הָאָ֑רֶץ וַיִּרְבּ֣וּ הַמַּ֗יִם וַיִּשְׂאוּ֙ אֶת־הַתֵּבָ֔ה וַתָּ֖רָם מֵעַ֥ל הָאָֽרֶץ: 18 וַיִּגְבְּר֥וּ הַמַּ֛יִם וַיִּרְבּ֥וּ מְאֹ֖ד עַל־הָאָ֑רֶץ וַתֵּ֥לֶךְ הַתֵּבָ֖ה עַל־פְּנֵ֥י הַמָּֽיִם: 19 וְהַמַּ֗יִם גָּבְר֛וּ מְאֹ֥ד מְאֹ֖ד עַל־הָאָ֑רֶץ וַיְכֻסּ֗וּ כָּל־הֶֽהָרִים֙ הַגְּבֹהִ֔ים אֲשֶׁר־תַּ֖חַת כָּל־הַשָּׁמָֽיִם: 20 חֲמֵ֨שׁ עֶשְׂרֵ֤ה אַמָּה֙ מִלְמַ֔עְלָה גָּבְר֖וּ הַמָּ֑יִם וַיְכֻסּ֖וּ הֶֽהָרִֽים: 21 וַיִּגְוַ֞ע כָּל־בָּשָׂ֣ר | הָֽרֹמֵ֣שׂ עַל־הָאָ֗רֶץ בָּע֤וֹף וּבַבְּהֵמָה֙ וּבַ֣חַיָּ֔ה וּבְכָל־הַשֶּׁ֖רֶץ הַשֹּׁרֵ֣ץ עַל־הָאָ֑רֶץ וְכֹ֖ל הָֽאָדָֽם: 22 כֹּ֡ל אֲשֶׁר֩ נִשְׁמַת־ר֨וּחַ חַיִּ֜ים בְּאַפָּ֗יו מִכֹּ֛ל אֲשֶׁ֥ר בֶּחָֽרָבָ֖ה מֵֽתוּ: 23 וַיִּ֜מַח אֶת־כָּל־הַיְק֣וּם | אֲשֶׁ֣ר | עַל־פְּנֵ֣י הָֽאֲדָמָ֗ה מֵֽאָדָ֤ם עַד־בְּהֵמָה֙ עַד־רֶ֨מֶשׂ֙ וְעַד־ע֣וֹף הַשָּׁמַ֔יִם וַיִּמָּח֖וּ מִן־הָאָ֑רֶץ וַיִּשָּׁ֧אֶר אַךְ־נֹ֛חַ וַֽאֲשֶׁ֥ר אִתּ֖וֹ בַּתֵּבָֽה: 24 וַיִּגְבְּר֥וּ הַמַּ֖יִם עַל־הָאָ֑רֶץ חֲמִשִּׁ֥ים וּמְאַ֖ת יֽוֹם:

ח 1 וַיִּזְכֹּ֤ר אֱלֹהִים֙ אֶת־נֹ֔חַ וְאֵ֤ת כָּל־הַֽחַיָּה֙ וְאֶת־כָּל־הַבְּהֵמָ֔ה אֲשֶׁ֥ר אִתּ֖וֹ בַּתֵּבָ֑ה וַיַּֽעֲבֵ֨ר אֱלֹהִ֥ים ר֨וּחַ֙ עַל־הָאָ֔רֶץ וַיָּשֹׁ֖כּוּ הַמָּֽיִם: 2 וַיִּסָּֽכְרוּ֙ מַעְיְנֹ֣ת

kabbalah bites

7:23 Noah's failure to pray for his generation (see above, 6:9), later achieved *tikkun* (spiritual healing) when he was reincarnated as Moses. Here God *"washed away (yiMaH) all existence"* as a result of Noah's error. To correct this Moses requested from God that if He would not forgive the Jewish people, *"please erase me (MeHeni) from Your Book"* (Exodus 32:32).

¹³ On that very day (in full view of the wicked generation), Noah came into the ark, with Shem, Ham and Japheth—Noah's sons—together with Noah's wife and his sons' three wives. ¹⁴ They (came) with every wild animal (which had only bred with) its own species, every domesticated animal (which had only bred with) its own species, every creeping thing that creeps on the earth (which had only bred with) its own species, every bird (which had bred only with) its own species, and every winged creature (i.e. grasshoppers). ¹⁵ From all flesh in which there is the spirit of life, they came to Noah, to the ark, two by two. ¹⁶ From all flesh they came, male and female, as God had commanded him. God closed off (the ark with bears and lions for protection) in front of him.

[THIRD READING] ¹⁷ The Flood was on the earth for forty days. The waters increased, they lifted the ark, and it rose off the earth. ¹⁸ The waters surged, and they increased very much upon the earth, and the ark moved upon the waters. ¹⁹ The waters became extremely powerful upon the earth, and all the tall mountains that were under the skies were covered up. ²⁰ The mountains were totally covered by fifteen cubits of water above. ²¹ All flesh that moved upon the earth perished, among the birds, the domesticated animals, the wild animals, all creeping creatures that creep upon the earth, and all mankind. ²² Everything from upon the dry land that had the breath of the spirit of life in its nostrils died. ²³ He washed away all existence that was on the face of the earth, from man to animal to creeping thing and to the birds of the skies, and they were washed out from the earth. Only Noah and those with him in the ark survived. ²⁴ The waters surged on the earth for one hundred and fifty days.

The Flood Subsides

8 ¹ God remembered (the prayers of) Noah and (the decent behavior of) all the wild animals and all the domesticated animals that were with him in the ark. God caused a spirit (of consolation and relief) to pass over the earth, and the waters subsided. ² The wellsprings of the depths and the apertures of the skies

Forty days and forty nights. *The Flood came to purify the earth.* The earth had become filled with robbery and corruption to the extreme and required purification. It was for this reason that the floodwaters came for forty days, like a ritual pool (*mikveh*) which must contain a minimum of forty *se'ah* (approx. 87 gallons) of rainwater if it is to purify the ritually unclean (*Rabbi Shneur Zalman of Lyady, 18ᵗʰ century*).

8:1 God caused a spirit (of consolation and relief) to pass over the earth, and the waters subsided. Although this verse is speaking about an act of Divine *mercy*, it uses the Divine name *Elokim*, which represents God's attribute of justice. This suggests that the prayers of the righteous Noah were effective in transforming justice to mercy.

Conversely, wicked people transform God's attribute of mercy (indicated by the Tetragrammaton, *Havayah*) to justice, as the verse states, "God saw that man's wickedness on earth was

בראשית ח:ב-יד

תְּהוֹם וַאֲרֻבֹּת הַשָּׁמָיִם וַיִּכָּלֵא הַגֶּשֶׁם מִן־הַשָּׁמָיִם: 3 וַיָּשֻׁבוּ הַמַּיִם מֵעַל הָאָרֶץ הָלוֹךְ וָשׁוֹב וַיַּחְסְרוּ הַמַּיִם מִקְצֵה חֲמִשִּׁים וּמְאַת יוֹם: 4 וַתָּנַח הַתֵּבָה בַּחֹדֶשׁ הַשְּׁבִיעִי בְּשִׁבְעָה־עָשָׂר יוֹם לַחֹדֶשׁ עַל הָרֵי אֲרָרָט: 5 וְהַמַּיִם הָיוּ הָלוֹךְ וְחָסוֹר עַד הַחֹדֶשׁ הָעֲשִׂירִי בָּעֲשִׂירִי בְּאֶחָד לַחֹדֶשׁ נִרְאוּ רָאשֵׁי הֶהָרִים: 6 וַיְהִי מִקֵּץ אַרְבָּעִים יוֹם וַיִּפְתַּח נֹחַ אֶת־חַלּוֹן הַתֵּבָה אֲשֶׁר עָשָׂה: 7 וַיְשַׁלַּח אֶת־הָעֹרֵב וַיֵּצֵא יָצוֹא וָשׁוֹב עַד־יְבֹשֶׁת הַמַּיִם מֵעַל הָאָרֶץ: 8 וַיְשַׁלַּח אֶת־הַיּוֹנָה מֵאִתּוֹ לִרְאוֹת הֲקַלּוּ הַמַּיִם מֵעַל פְּנֵי הָאֲדָמָה: 9 וְלֹא־מָצְאָה הַיּוֹנָה מָנוֹחַ לְכַף־רַגְלָהּ וַתָּשָׁב אֵלָיו אֶל־הַתֵּבָה כִּי־מַיִם עַל־פְּנֵי כָל־הָאָרֶץ וַיִּשְׁלַח יָדוֹ וַיִּקָּחֶהָ וַיָּבֵא אֹתָהּ אֵלָיו אֶל־הַתֵּבָה: 10 וַיָּחֶל עוֹד שִׁבְעַת יָמִים אֲחֵרִים וַיֹּסֶף שַׁלַּח אֶת־הַיּוֹנָה מִן־הַתֵּבָה: 11 וַתָּבֹא אֵלָיו הַיּוֹנָה לְעֵת עֶרֶב וְהִנֵּה עֲלֵה־זַיִת טָרָף בְּפִיהָ וַיֵּדַע נֹחַ כִּי־קַלּוּ הַמַּיִם מֵעַל הָאָרֶץ: 12 וַיִּיָּחֶל עוֹד שִׁבְעַת יָמִים אֲחֵרִים וַיְשַׁלַּח אֶת־הַיּוֹנָה וְלֹא־יָסְפָה שׁוּב־אֵלָיו עוֹד: 13 וַיְהִי בְּאַחַת וְשֵׁשׁ־מֵאוֹת שָׁנָה בָּרִאשׁוֹן בְּאֶחָד לַחֹדֶשׁ חָרְבוּ הַמַּיִם מֵעַל הָאָרֶץ וַיָּסַר נֹחַ אֶת־מִכְסֵה הַתֵּבָה וַיַּרְא וְהִנֵּה חָרְבוּ פְּנֵי הָאֲדָמָה: 14 וּבַחֹדֶשׁ הַשֵּׁנִי בְּשִׁבְעָה וְעֶשְׂרִים

7. He sent out the raven, but it circled. The raven alludes to anger. Noah wanted anger to be gone from the world, but God sent him a message that, for the time being, this emotion is still needed. *Sometimes, when you are gripped by an inappropriate passion, the only way of conquering it is by getting angry at yourself.*

But the raven only circled (anger is only necessary), *"until the waters dried up off the earth"*— until the future era when man's lusts will be eradicated (*Rabbi Mordecai Joseph Leiner of Izbica, 19th century*).

11. The dove returned to him ... a torn olive leaf in its mouth. The dove exclaimed to God, "Master of the universe! I would rather my food be as bitter as an olive but from God's hand, than sweet as honey but reliant upon man" (*Babylonian Talmud, Eruvin* 18b).

A torn olive leaf. Where did the dove find an intact olive tree with leaves so soon after the Flood? The dove got its leaf from the Mount of Olives, since the floodwaters did not fall in the land of Israel.

Alternatively, the gates of the Garden of Eden were opened for the dove, and it brought the leaf from there (*Genesis Rabbah*).

genesis 8:2–14   noah

were closed, and the rain from the skies was held back. ³ The waters continued progressively to recede from the earth and, at the end of one hundred and fifty days, the waters diminished.

⁴ The (base of the) ark (which was still submerged) came to rest on the Ararat mountains in the seventh month (*Sivan*), on the seventeenth day of the month.

⁵ The waters constantly diminished until the tenth month. In the tenth (month), on the first of the month, the mountain peaks appeared.

⁶ Then, after forty (more) days, Noah opened the window of the ark that he had made. ⁷ He sent out the raven, but it (refused to go on its mission and just) circled (the ark) until the waters dried up off the earth.

⁸ (Seven days later) he sent out the dove from (being) with him, to see whether the waters had gone down from the earth's surface. ⁹ But the dove could not find a resting place for the sole of its foot because there was water upon the entire surface of the earth, so it returned to him, to the ark. He stretched out his hand and took it, and brought it to him, to the ark.

¹⁰ He waited again another seven days, and he sent out the dove from the ark again. ¹¹ The dove returned to him in the evening, and—look!—it had a torn olive leaf in its mouth. So Noah knew that the water had gone down from the surface of the earth.

¹² He made himself wait again for another seven days, and he sent out the dove, and it did not return to him any more.

¹³ It was in the six hundredth and first year, in the first (month), on the first of the month, that the waters dried up from the surface of the earth (leaving a hard crust). Noah removed the covering of the ark. He gazed, and—look!—the surface of the ground had dried up.

¹⁴ In the second month, on the twenty-seventh day of the month, the earth was (properly) dry.

---

increasing ... God (Havayah) said, 'I will wash away man, whom I created'" (v. 5-7). Even though the verse speaks of destruction (justice), the Tetragrammaton is used, indicating that the attribute of mercy was transformed to justice through man's wickedness (*Rashi, 11ᵗʰ century*).

spiritual vitamin

> There are no "random" occurrences in the world. Even the painful episodes of life are part of a Divine plan, a system which encompasses you and your family and every other person, thing and event.

בראשית ח:יד - ט:ג

יוֹם לַחֹדֶשׁ יָבְשָׁה הָאָרֶץ: ס 15 [FOURTH READING] וַיְדַבֵּר אֱלֹהִים אֶל־נֹחַ לֵאמֹר: 16 צֵא מִן־הַתֵּבָה אַתָּה וְאִשְׁתְּךָ וּבָנֶיךָ וּנְשֵׁי־בָנֶיךָ אִתָּךְ: 17 כָּל־הַחַיָּה אֲשֶׁר־אִתְּךָ מִכָּל־בָּשָׂר בָּעוֹף וּבַבְּהֵמָה וּבְכָל־הָרֶמֶשׂ הָרֹמֵשׂ עַל־הָאָרֶץ [הוצא כ׳] הַיְצֵא אִתָּךְ וְשָׁרְצוּ בָאָרֶץ וּפָרוּ וְרָבוּ עַל־הָאָרֶץ: 18 וַיֵּצֵא־נֹחַ וּבָנָיו וְאִשְׁתּוֹ וּנְשֵׁי־בָנָיו אִתּוֹ: 19 כָּל־הַחַיָּה כָּל־הָרֶמֶשׂ וְכָל־הָעוֹף כֹּל רוֹמֵשׂ עַל־הָאָרֶץ לְמִשְׁפְּחֹתֵיהֶם יָצְאוּ מִן־הַתֵּבָה: 20 וַיִּבֶן נֹחַ מִזְבֵּחַ לַיהֹוָה וַיִּקַּח מִכֹּל | הַבְּהֵמָה הַטְּהֹרָה וּמִכֹּל הָעוֹף הַטָּהוֹר וַיַּעַל עֹלֹת בַּמִּזְבֵּחַ: 21 וַיָּרַח יְהֹוָה אֶת־רֵיחַ הַנִּיחֹחַ וַיֹּאמֶר יְהֹוָה אֶל־לִבּוֹ לֹא אֹסִף לְקַלֵּל עוֹד אֶת־הָאֲדָמָה בַּעֲבוּר הָאָדָם כִּי יֵצֶר לֵב הָאָדָם רַע מִנְּעֻרָיו וְלֹא־אֹסִף עוֹד לְהַכּוֹת אֶת־כָּל־חַי כַּאֲשֶׁר עָשִׂיתִי: 22 עֹד כָּל־יְמֵי הָאָרֶץ זֶרַע וְקָצִיר וְקֹר וָחֹם וְקַיִץ וָחֹרֶף וְיוֹם וָלַיְלָה לֹא יִשְׁבֹּתוּ:

ט 1 וַיְבָרֶךְ אֱלֹהִים אֶת־נֹחַ וְאֶת־בָּנָיו וַיֹּאמֶר לָהֶם פְּרוּ וּרְבוּ וּמִלְאוּ אֶת־הָאָרֶץ: 2 וּמוֹרַאֲכֶם וְחִתְּכֶם יִהְיֶה עַל כָּל־חַיַּת הָאָרֶץ וְעַל כָּל־עוֹף הַשָּׁמָיִם בְּכֹל אֲשֶׁר תִּרְמֹשׂ הָאֲדָמָה וּבְכָל־דְּגֵי הַיָּם בְּיֶדְכֶם נִתָּנוּ: 3 כָּל־רֶמֶשׂ

To ensure that this scenario would not repeat itself, God altered the agricultural cycle after the Flood, requiring man to work incessantly day and night. Now he would simply be too busy to sin (*Midrash Tanhuma*).

spiritual vitamin

> It was the Creator's will that your soul—which is a *"part of the Divine Above"* (*Job* 31:2), should descend into the physical and coarse world and be confined within, and united with, your physical body for scores of years, in a state which is absolutely abhorrent to its very nature. All this, for the purpose of a Divine mission which your soul has to fulfil: to purify and "spiritualize" your physical body and the surrounding physical environment by permeating them with the light of God, so as to make this world an abode for the *Shekhinah* (Divine Presence).

Noah and His Family Leave the Ark

[FOURTH READING] ¹⁵ God spoke to Noah, saying: ¹⁶ "Go out of the ark, you, your wife, your sons, and your sons' wives with you. ¹⁷ Bring out with you every living thing, all flesh that is with you, from the birds, animals and from all the creeping things that creep on the earth. They shall swarm upon the earth, and they shall be fruitful and multiply upon the earth."

¹⁸ So Noah went out, his sons, his wife and his sons' wives with him. ¹⁹ Every wild animal, every creeping thing, all birds, and everything that moves upon the earth went out from the ark, (vowing to mate only) with their own species.

²⁰ Noah built an altar to God. He took from all the pure animals and from all the pure birds and brought up burnt-offerings on the altar. ²¹ God smelled the pleasant aroma, and God said to Himself, "I will no longer curse the earth because of man, for the imagination of man's heart is evil from his (first) stirring (in the womb). I will never again kill all living things as I have done. ²² So long as the earth exists there will not cease (six seasons of) seedtime, harvest, cold, heat, summer and winter, and day and night."

God Commands Noah to Populate the World

9 ¹ God blessed Noah and his sons, and He said to them: "(May you) be fruitful and multiply and fill the earth! ² Fear and dread of you will be upon all the animals of the earth, all the birds of the skies, everything that creeps upon the ground and all the fish of the sea. They have been given into your hand. ³ Every moving thing that lives shall be yours to eat. Like the green vegetation (which was

---

16. Go out of the ark. Since he only entered the ark according to God's instruction, Noah waited for God's command to leave (*Midrash Tanḥuma*).

Noah and his family enjoyed in the ark a taste of the Messianic Era, when animals will coexist in peace (see *Isaiah* 11:6-9), which explains why he was reluctant to leave.

But God told Noah to leave the ark, since his mission in life was not to isolate himself in an atmosphere of holiness, but rather, to *"be fruitful and multiply and fill the earth!"* (9:1).

You might be tempted to lock yourself away in an "ark" of personal spirituality. The Torah, however, teaches you that you must "go out of the ark" and take responsibility for the world around you (*Rabbi Menahem Mendel Schneerson, 20th century*).

21. For the imagination of man's heart is evil from his (first) stirrings (in the womb). The impulse to evil is fully present at birth. The impulse to good enters you slowly as you develop and perfect your mind (*Maimonides, 12th century*).

22. There will not cease ... day and night. The corruption of the pre-Flood generation had come about because man's life was too easy. The land had required sowing only once to produce crops for forty harvests. With little demands on his time, man's moral caliber soon declined.

בראשית ט:ג-טז

אֲשֶׁר הוּא־חַ֔י לָכֶ֥ם יִהְיֶ֖ה לְאָכְלָ֑ה כְּיֶ֣רֶק עֵ֔שֶׂב נָתַ֥תִּי לָכֶ֖ם אֶת־כֹּֽל׃ 4 אַךְ־בָּשָׂ֕ר בְּנַפְשׁ֥וֹ דָמ֖וֹ לֹ֥א תֹאכֵֽלוּ׃ 5 וְאַ֨ךְ אֶת־דִּמְכֶ֤ם לְנַפְשֹֽׁתֵיכֶם֙ אֶדְרֹ֔שׁ מִיַּ֥ד כָּל־חַיָּ֖ה אֶדְרְשֶׁ֑נּוּ וּמִיַּ֣ד הָֽאָדָ֗ם מִיַּד֙ אִ֣ישׁ אָחִ֔יו אֶדְרֹ֖שׁ אֶת־נֶ֥פֶשׁ הָֽאָדָֽם׃ 6 שֹׁפֵךְ֙ דַּ֣ם הָֽאָדָ֔ם בָּֽאָדָ֖ם דָּמ֣וֹ יִשָּׁפֵ֑ךְ כִּ֚י בְּצֶ֣לֶם אֱלֹהִ֔ים עָשָׂ֖ה אֶת־הָאָדָֽם׃ 7 וְאַתֶּ֖ם פְּר֣וּ וּרְב֑וּ שִׁרְצ֥וּ בָאָ֖רֶץ וּרְבוּ־בָֽהּ׃ ס 8 [FIFTH READING] וַיֹּ֤אמֶר אֱלֹהִים֙ אֶל־נֹ֔חַ וְאֶל־בָּנָ֥יו אִתּ֖וֹ לֵאמֹֽר׃ 9 וַאֲנִ֕י הִנְנִ֥י מֵקִ֛ים אֶת־בְּרִיתִ֖י אִתְּכֶ֑ם וְאֶֽת־זַרְעֲכֶ֖ם אַֽחֲרֵיכֶֽם׃ 10 וְאֵ֨ת כָּל־נֶ֤פֶשׁ הַֽחַיָּה֙ אֲשֶׁ֣ר אִתְּכֶ֔ם בָּע֧וֹף בַּבְּהֵמָ֛ה וּֽבְכָל־חַיַּ֥ת הָאָ֖רֶץ אִתְּכֶ֑ם מִכֹּל֙ יֹצְאֵ֣י הַתֵּבָ֔ה לְכֹ֖ל חַיַּ֥ת הָאָֽרֶץ׃ 11 וַהֲקִֽמֹתִ֤י אֶת־בְּרִיתִי֙ אִתְּכֶ֔ם וְלֹֽא־יִכָּרֵ֧ת כָּל־בָּשָׂ֛ר ע֖וֹד מִמֵּ֣י הַמַּבּ֑וּל וְלֹֽא־יִהְיֶ֥ה ע֛וֹד מַבּ֖וּל לְשַׁחֵ֥ת הָאָֽרֶץ׃ 12 וַיֹּ֣אמֶר אֱלֹהִ֗ים זֹ֤את אֽוֹת־הַבְּרִית֙ אֲשֶׁר־אֲנִ֣י נֹתֵ֗ן בֵּינִי֙ וּבֵ֣ינֵיכֶ֔ם וּבֵ֛ין כָּל־נֶ֥פֶשׁ חַיָּ֖ה אֲשֶׁ֣ר אִתְּכֶ֑ם לְדֹרֹ֖ת עוֹלָֽם׃ 13 אֶת־קַשְׁתִּ֕י נָתַ֖תִּי בֶּֽעָנָ֑ן וְהָֽיְתָה֙ לְא֣וֹת בְּרִ֔ית בֵּינִ֖י וּבֵ֥ין הָאָֽרֶץ׃ 14 וְהָיָ֕ה בְּעַֽנְנִ֥י עָנָ֖ן עַל־הָאָ֑רֶץ וְנִרְאֲתָ֥ה הַקֶּ֖שֶׁת בֶּעָנָֽן׃ 15 וְזָֽכַרְתִּ֣י אֶת־בְּרִיתִ֗י אֲשֶׁ֤ר בֵּינִי֙ וּבֵ֣ינֵיכֶ֔ם וּבֵ֛ין כָּל־נֶ֥פֶשׁ חַיָּ֖ה בְּכָל־בָּשָׂ֑ר וְלֹֽא־יִֽהְיֶ֨ה ע֤וֹד הַמַּ֨יִם֙ לְמַבּ֔וּל לְשַׁחֵ֖ת כָּל־בָּשָֽׂר׃ 16 וְהָיְתָ֥ה הַקֶּ֖שֶׁת בֶּֽעָנָ֑ן וּרְאִיתִ֗יהָ לִזְכֹּר֙ בְּרִ֣ית עוֹלָ֔ם

9:13 I have placed my rainbow in the cloud. If God had made the rainbow with its ends in the sky, it would resemble a giant archery bow, arching towards earth as if arrows were being shot at the earth from heaven. Instead, its ends face downward as a sign of peace. This also makes it more obvious that it is a bow lacking a string, from which arrows cannot be fired (*Naḥmanides, 13th century*).

14. When I (will consider) causing clouds (of darkness and destruction) to come upon the earth, the rainbow will appear in the cloud. God shows the rainbow when it arises in His mind to bring darkness and destruction to the world (*Rashi, 11th century*).

The rainbow does not appear on every cloudy day or on any occasion that it rains, but only when the generation deserves destruction, to indicate that God is guarding His promise (*Rabbi Bahya b. Asher, 13th century*).

16. Everlasting covenant between God and every living creature. Hasidic thought teaches that before the Flood, God sustained the world *despite* its low spiritual standing, due to His attribute of kindness. There was a limit, however, to how long God was willing to sustain a world without merit—hence the Flood.

genesis 9:3–16 noaḥ

all that man could eat before,) I have (now) given you everything. ⁴ But you shall not eat flesh (detached from an animal) or its blood, while it is still alive.

⁵ "But I will demand (an account) for your blood (if you take) your own lives (through suicide)."

"I will demand (the same) from every animal (that takes a human life)."

"From a man (who intentionally kills another man, or) a man (who unintentionally kills another man whom he loves like) his brother, I will demand the man's life."

⁶ "Whoever spills human blood (by killing a person, and is witnessed) by men shall have his own blood spilled, for in the image of God (the Creator) made man."

⁷ "As for you, (I am commanding you to) be fruitful and multiply! Populate the earth and become numerous on it!"

God Establishes a Covenant with Mankind

[FIFTH READING] ⁸ God (saw that Noah was afraid to have children, so He) said to Noah and to his sons (who were) with him, ⁹ "Look! I am setting up My covenant with you and with your seed after you, ¹⁰ and with every living creature that is with you, among the birds, the domesticated animals, all the wild animals of the earth that (walk) with you, all those (loathsome insects and reptiles) who came out of the ark, all the living creatures of the earth. ¹¹ I will confirm My covenant with you that never again will all flesh be wiped out by the floodwaters, and there will never again be a flood to destroy the earth."

¹² God said: "This is the sign of the (confirmation of the) covenant, which I am placing between Me and you, and every living soul that is with you, for all generations. ¹³ I have placed my rainbow in the cloud, and it will be a sign of a covenant between Myself and the earth. ¹⁴ Then, when I (will consider) causing clouds (of darkness and destruction) to come upon the earth, the rainbow will appear in the cloud, ¹⁵ and I will remember My covenant, which is between Me and you, and every living creature among all flesh, and the water will no longer become a flood to destroy all flesh. ¹⁶ The rainbow will be in the cloud, and I will look at it to remember the everlasting covenant between God('s attribute of judgment) and every living creature among all flesh that is on the earth."

food for thought

1. Why do people attempt suicide?

2. Why don't we have the right to kill ourselves?

3. Have you ever had extremely pessimistic thoughts?

בְּין אֱלֹהִים וּבֵין כָּל־נֶפֶשׁ חַיָּה בְּכָל־בָּשָׂר אֲשֶׁר עַל־הָאָרֶץ: 17 וַיֹּאמֶר אֱלֹהִים אֶל־נֹחַ זֹאת אוֹת־הַבְּרִית אֲשֶׁר הֲקִמֹתִי בֵּינִי וּבֵין כָּל־בָּשָׂר אֲשֶׁר עַל־הָאָרֶץ: פ

18 [SIXTH READING] וַיִּהְיוּ בְנֵי־נֹחַ הַיֹּצְאִים מִן־הַתֵּבָה שֵׁם וְחָם וָיָפֶת וְחָם הוּא אֲבִי כְנָעַן: 19 שְׁלֹשָׁה אֵלֶּה בְּנֵי־נֹחַ וּמֵאֵלֶּה נָפְצָה כָל־הָאָרֶץ: 20 וַיָּחֶל נֹחַ אִישׁ הָאֲדָמָה וַיִּטַּע כָּרֶם: 21 וַיֵּשְׁתְּ מִן־הַיַּיִן וַיִּשְׁכָּר וַיִּתְגַּל בְּתוֹךְ אָהֳלֹה: 22 וַיַּרְא חָם אֲבִי כְנַעַן אֵת עֶרְוַת אָבִיו וַיַּגֵּד לִשְׁנֵי־אֶחָיו בַּחוּץ: 23 וַיִּקַּח שֵׁם וָיֶפֶת אֶת־הַשִּׂמְלָה וַיָּשִׂימוּ עַל־שְׁכֶם שְׁנֵיהֶם וַיֵּלְכוּ אֲחֹרַנִּית וַיְכַסּוּ אֵת עֶרְוַת אֲבִיהֶם וּפְנֵיהֶם אֲחֹרַנִּית וְעֶרְוַת אֲבִיהֶם לֹא רָאוּ: 24 וַיִּיקֶץ נֹחַ מִיֵּינוֹ וַיֵּדַע אֵת אֲשֶׁר־עָשָׂה לוֹ בְּנוֹ הַקָּטָן: 25 וַיֹּאמֶר אָרוּר כְּנָעַן עֶבֶד עֲבָדִים יִהְיֶה לְאֶחָיו: 26 וַיֹּאמֶר בָּרוּךְ יְהֹוָה אֱלֹהֵי שֵׁם וִיהִי כְנַעַן עֶבֶד לָמוֹ: 27 יַפְתְּ אֱלֹהִים לְיֶפֶת וְיִשְׁכֹּן בְּאָהֳלֵי־שֵׁם וִיהִי כְנַעַן עֶבֶד לָמוֹ: 28 וַיְחִי־נֹחַ אַחַר הַמַּבּוּל שְׁלֹשׁ מֵאוֹת שָׁנָה וַחֲמִשִּׁים שָׁנָה: 29 וַיִּהְיוּ כָּל־יְמֵי־נֹחַ תְּשַׁע מֵאוֹת שָׁנָה וַחֲמִשִּׁים שָׁנָה וַיָּמֹת: פ

not only a "*sign*" of God's promise not to destroy the world, it was also *a physical consequence* of the refinement of the world that ensured its permanent existence (*Rabbi Menahem Mendel Schneerson, 20th century*).

21. He drank of the wine, became drunk, and uncovered himself in his tent. Noah's misconduct with wine was spiritually "corrected" by Joseph, who, says the *Babylonian Talmud* (*Shabbat* 139a), refrained from drinking wine for the entire period he was separated from his brothers (*Rabbi Menahem Azariah da Fano, 16th–17th century*).

23. They did not see their father's nakedness. If you are unclean then you tend to see, and become frustrated by, the uncleanliness of others. A pure person sees only that his fellow is in need of help (*Rabbi Israel Ba'al Shem Tov, 18th century*).

spiritual vitamin

> One of the basic elements of the Divine Design, as revealed in the Torah, is that God desires it to be carried out *by choice and not out of compulsion*. You have, therefore, the free will to live in accordance with God's will, or in defiance of it.

¹⁷ (Showing him a rainbow,) God said to Noah: "This is the sign of the covenant that I have set up, between Myself and all flesh that is on the earth."

Noah is Assaulted by Ham

[SIXTH READING] ¹⁸ The sons of Noah who came out of the ark were Shem, Ham, and Japheth. Ham was the father of Canaan. ¹⁹ These three were the sons of Noah. From them, the entire earth was populated. ²⁰ Noah, a master of the soil, degraded himself by planting a vineyard (first of all). ²¹ He drank of the wine, became drunk, and uncovered himself in his tent. ²² (Canaan told his father what had happened, and) Ham, the father of Canaan, looked at his father's nakedness (and assaulted him). He publicly related (the incident) to his two brothers.

²³ Shem and Japheth took a garment and placed it on both of their shoulders. They walked backwards, and covered their father's nakedness. (Even when they had to turn themselves around to cover him) their faces were turned backwards, so that they did not see their father's nakedness.

²⁴ Noah woke up from his wine, and he realized what his youngest son had done to him. ²⁵ He said, "Cursed be Canaan! He shall be a slave among slaves to his brethren!"

²⁶ He said, "Blessed be God, the God of Shem, and may Canaan be a (subjugated) slave to them! ²⁷ May God make Japheth spread out, may He dwell in the tents of Shem, and may Canaan be a slave to them (even after Shem is exiled)!"

²⁸ Noah lived three hundred and fifty years after the Flood. ²⁹ Noah lived a total of nine hundred and fifty years, and he died.

The waters of the Flood were not merely a punishment. They purified the world, making physicality in general more refined and spiritually attuned. Consequently, in the post-Flood era, people were more disposed to repentance. This ensured that God would always sustain the world—not despite of, but *because* of its spiritual standing. Even if man would become corrupt, people would inevitably repent, ensuring that the world *itself* would have sufficient merits for its continued existence.

With this in mind, we can explain the following details:

1. Noah was unaware of the above, so he was afraid to repopulate the world, fearing it would be destroyed again. Therefore, God had to *re-command* him to *"be fruitful and multiply"* (9:1).

2. The inner reason why Noah's generation failed to repent was because, before the Flood, the world was spiritually insensitive.

3. Meat is an extremely coarse food that can lead a person to excessive physicality. Thus, it was only permitted to the more spiritually-attuned post-Flood generation (above, v. 3).

4. Before the Flood, people had extremely long life spans because the world was sustained by God's kindness, which was bestowed *disproportionately* to people's merits.

5. Before the Flood, physicality was more coarse. This was true in a literal sense, to the extent that the clouds were too thick to refract light, so a rainbow never appeared. After the Flood, physicality became more refined, so the clouds began to refract light. Thus, the rainbow was

בראשית י:א-כד

1 וְאֵ֙לֶּה֙ תּוֹלְדֹ֣ת בְּנֵי־נֹ֔חַ שֵׁ֖ם חָ֣ם וָיָ֑פֶת וַיִּוָּלְד֧וּ לָהֶ֛ם בָּנִ֖ים אַחַ֥ר הַמַּבּֽוּל: 2 בְּנֵ֣י יֶ֔פֶת גֹּ֣מֶר וּמָג֔וֹג וּמָדַ֖י וְיָוָ֣ן וְתֻבָ֑ל וּמֶ֖שֶׁךְ וְתִירָֽס: 3 וּבְנֵ֖י גֹּ֑מֶר אַשְׁכְּנַ֥ז וְרִיפַ֖ת וְתֹגַרְמָֽה: 4 וּבְנֵ֥י יָוָ֖ן אֱלִישָׁ֣ה וְתַרְשִׁ֑ישׁ כִּתִּ֖ים וְדֹדָנִֽים: 5 מֵ֠אֵ֠לֶּה נִפְרְד֞וּ אִיֵּ֤י הַגּוֹיִם֙ בְּאַרְצֹתָ֔ם אִ֖ישׁ לִלְשֹׁנ֑וֹ לְמִשְׁפְּחֹתָ֖ם בְּגוֹיֵהֶֽם: 6 וּבְנֵ֖י חָ֑ם כּ֥וּשׁ וּמִצְרַ֖יִם וּפ֥וּט וּכְנָֽעַן: 7 וּבְנֵ֣י כ֔וּשׁ סְבָא֙ וַחֲוִילָ֔ה וְסַבְתָּ֥ה וְרַעְמָ֖ה וְסַבְתְּכָ֑א וּבְנֵ֥י רַעְמָ֖ה שְׁבָ֥א וּדְדָֽן: 8 וְכ֖וּשׁ יָלַ֣ד אֶת־נִמְרֹ֑ד ה֣וּא הֵחֵ֔ל לִֽהְי֥וֹת גִּבֹּ֖ר בָּאָֽרֶץ: 9 הֽוּא־הָיָ֥ה גִבֹּֽר־צַ֖יִד לִפְנֵ֣י יְהֹוָ֑ה עַל־כֵּן֙ יֵֽאָמַ֔ר כְּנִמְרֹ֛ד גִּבּ֥וֹר צַ֖יִד לִפְנֵ֥י יְהֹוָֽה: 10 וַתְּהִ֨י רֵאשִׁ֤ית מַמְלַכְתּוֹ֙ בָּבֶ֔ל וְאֶ֖רֶךְ וְאַכַּ֣ד וְכַלְנֵ֑ה בְּאֶ֖רֶץ שִׁנְעָֽר: 11 מִן־הָאָ֥רֶץ הַהִ֖וא יָצָ֣א אַשּׁ֑וּר וַיִּ֙בֶן֙ אֶת־נִ֣ינְוֵ֔ה וְאֶת־רְחֹבֹ֥ת עִ֖יר וְאֶת־כָּֽלַח: 12 וְֽאֶת־רֶ֔סֶן בֵּ֥ין נִֽינְוֵ֖ה וּבֵ֣ין כָּ֑לַח הִ֖וא הָעִ֥יר הַגְּדֹלָֽה: 13 וּמִצְרַ֡יִם יָלַ֞ד אֶת־לוּדִ֧ים וְאֶת־עֲנָמִ֛ים וְאֶת־לְהָבִ֖ים וְאֶת־נַפְתֻּחִֽים: 14 וְֽאֶת־פַּתְרֻסִ֞ים וְאֶת־כַּסְלֻחִ֗ים אֲשֶׁ֨ר יָצְא֥וּ מִשָּׁ֛ם פְּלִשְׁתִּ֖ים וְאֶת־כַּפְתֹּרִֽים: ס 15 וּכְנַ֗עַן יָלַ֛ד אֶת־צִידֹ֥ן בְּכֹר֖וֹ וְאֶת־חֵֽת: 16 וְאֶת־הַיְבוּסִי֙ וְאֶת־הָ֣אֱמֹרִ֔י וְאֵ֖ת הַגִּרְגָּשִֽׁי: 17 וְאֶת־הַֽחִוִּ֥י וְאֶת־הַֽעַרְקִ֖י וְאֶת־הַסִּינִֽי: 18 וְאֶת־הָֽאַרְוָדִ֥י וְאֶת־הַצְּמָרִ֖י וְאֶת־הַֽחֲמָתִ֑י וְאַחַ֣ר נָפֹ֔צוּ מִשְׁפְּח֖וֹת הַֽכְּנַעֲנִֽי: 19 וַֽיְהִ֞י גְּב֤וּל הַֽכְּנַעֲנִי֙ מִצִּידֹ֔ן בֹּאֲכָ֥ה גְרָ֖רָה עַד־עַזָּ֑ה בֹּאֲכָ֞ה סְדֹ֧מָה וַֽעֲמֹרָ֛ה וְאַדְמָ֥ה וּצְבֹיִ֖ם עַד־לָֽשַׁע: 20 אֵ֣לֶּה בְנֵי־חָ֔ם לְמִשְׁפְּחֹתָ֖ם לִלְשֹֽׁנֹתָ֑ם בְּאַרְצֹתָ֖ם בְּגוֹיֵהֶֽם: ס 21 וּלְשֵׁ֥ם יֻלַּ֖ד גַּם־ה֑וּא אֲבִי֙ כָּל־בְּנֵי־עֵ֔בֶר אֲחִ֖י יֶ֥פֶת הַגָּדֽוֹל: 22 בְּנֵ֖י שֵׁ֑ם עֵילָ֣ם וְאַשּׁ֔וּר וְאַרְפַּכְשַׁ֖ד וְל֥וּד וַֽאֲרָֽם: 23 וּבְנֵ֖י אֲרָ֑ם ע֥וּץ וְח֖וּל וְגֶ֥תֶר וָמַֽשׁ: 24 וְאַרְפַּכְשַׁ֖ד יָלַ֣ד אֶת־שָׁ֑לַח

spiritual vitamin

> When we invest in our children the original capital not only yields the highest dividends, but the dividends themselves become investment capital of the highest yield.

The Descendants of Noah

10 ¹ These are the offspring of the sons of Noah: Shem, Ham, and Japheth. Sons were born to them after the Flood.

² The sons of Japheth were Gomer, Magog, Madai, Javan, Tubal, Meshech and Tiras.

³ The sons of Gomer were Ashkenaz, Riphath and Togarmah.

⁴ The sons of Javan were Elishah, Tarshish, Kittim, and Dodanim. ⁵ They were dispersed into the islands of the nations in their (various) lands, each one with its own language, according to their local and national identity.

⁶ The sons of Ham were Cush, Mizraim, Put and Canaan.

⁷ The sons of Cush were Seba, Havilah, Sabtah, Raamah and Sabteca.

The sons of Raamah were Sheba and Dedan.

⁸ Cush fathered Nimrod. He started to be a rebel (against God) in the land. ⁹ He was a powerful trapper (of people's minds, turning them) against God. Therefore it is said (about rebellious people, that they are), "like Nimrod, a powerful trapper against God." ¹⁰ The beginning of his kingdom was Babylon, Erech, Accad and Calneh, in the land of Shinar. ¹¹ Asshur left that land (due to Nimrod), and he built Nineveh, Rehoboth-ir, Calah, ¹² and Resen, between Nineveh—which is the great city—and Calah.

¹³ Mizraim fathered Ludim, Anamim, Lehabim, Naphtuhim, ¹⁴ Pathrusim, Casluhim—from whom the Philistines were descended—and Caphtorim.

¹⁵ Canaan fathered Sidon—his firstborn—and Heth, ¹⁶ the Jebusites, the Amorites, the Girgashites, ¹⁷ the Hivites, the Arkites, the Sinites, ¹⁸ the Arvadites, the Zemarites and the Hamathites. From them, the families of the Canaanites were dispersed. ¹⁹ The border of the Canaanites was from Sidon as you come to Gerar, as far as Gaza reaching Sodom, Gomorrah, Admah and Zeboiim, until Lasha.

²⁰ The (above) are the descendants of Ham according to their families, and their languages, by their lands and their nations.

²¹ Children were also born to Shem, the father of all those who lived on the other side (of the river), the brother of Japheth, the eldest.

²² The sons of Shem were Elam, Asshur, Arpachshad, Lud and Aram.

²³ The sons of Aram were Uz, Hul, Gether and Mash.

²⁴ Arpachshad fathered Shelah, and Shelah fathered Eber.

בראשית י:כד - יא:ו

וְשָׁלַח יָלַד אֶת־עֵבֶר: 25 וּלְעֵבֶר יֻלַּד שְׁנֵי בָנִים שֵׁם הָאֶחָד פֶּלֶג כִּי בְיָמָיו נִפְלְגָה הָאָרֶץ וְשֵׁם אָחִיו יָקְטָן: 26 וְיָקְטָן יָלַד אֶת־אַלְמוֹדָד וְאֶת־שֶׁלֶף וְאֶת־חֲצַרְמָוֶת וְאֶת־יָרַח: 27 וְאֶת־הֲדוֹרָם וְאֶת־אוּזָל וְאֶת־דִּקְלָה: 28 וְאֶת־עוֹבָל וְאֶת־אֲבִימָאֵל וְאֶת־שְׁבָא: 29 וְאֶת־אוֹפִר וְאֶת־חֲוִילָה וְאֶת־יוֹבָב כָּל־אֵלֶּה בְּנֵי יָקְטָן: 30 וַיְהִי מוֹשָׁבָם מִמֵּשָׁא בֹּאֲכָה סְפָרָה הַר הַקֶּדֶם: 31 אֵלֶּה בְנֵי־שֵׁם לְמִשְׁפְּחֹתָם לִלְשֹׁנֹתָם בְּאַרְצֹתָם לְגוֹיֵהֶם: 32 אֵלֶּה מִשְׁפְּחֹת בְּנֵי־נֹחַ לְתוֹלְדֹתָם בְּגוֹיֵהֶם וּמֵאֵלֶּה נִפְרְדוּ הַגּוֹיִם בָּאָרֶץ אַחַר הַמַּבּוּל: פ

יא 1 וַיְהִי כָל־הָאָרֶץ שָׂפָה אֶחָת וּדְבָרִים אֲחָדִים: 2 וַיְהִי בְּנָסְעָם [SEVENTH READING] מִקֶּדֶם וַיִּמְצְאוּ בִקְעָה בְּאֶרֶץ שִׁנְעָר וַיֵּשְׁבוּ שָׁם: 3 וַיֹּאמְרוּ אִישׁ אֶל־רֵעֵהוּ הָבָה נִלְבְּנָה לְבֵנִים וְנִשְׂרְפָה לִשְׂרֵפָה וַתְּהִי לָהֶם הַלְּבֵנָה לְאָבֶן וְהַחֵמָר הָיָה לָהֶם לַחֹמֶר: 4 וַיֹּאמְרוּ הָבָה | נִבְנֶה־לָּנוּ עִיר וּמִגְדָּל וְרֹאשׁוֹ בַשָּׁמַיִם וְנַעֲשֶׂה־לָּנוּ שֵׁם פֶּן־נָפוּץ עַל־פְּנֵי כָל־הָאָרֶץ: 5 וַיֵּרֶד יְהֹוָה לִרְאֹת אֶת־הָעִיר וְאֶת־הַמִּגְדָּל אֲשֶׁר בָּנוּ בְּנֵי הָאָדָם: 6 וַיֹּאמֶר יְהֹוָה הֵן עַם אֶחָד

kabbalah bites

11:5 *"The tower that the descendants of Adam (bene Adam) had built."* These were *bene Adam* (children of Adam), more literally than you might imagine. According to Rabbi Isaac Luria, the souls of this generation represented the second reincarnation of the "dysfunctional souls" which Adam brought into being during the 130 years he separated from his wife (see *Genesis 5:3*). These souls were literally fathered by Adam himself, which is why they are referred to here as his "children."

bring down sufficient Divine energy to grant them physical blessings of prosperity. Therefore, their primary fear was that of being *scattered*, for the destruction of their community would stop the flow of "easy" blessings from heaven.

The key to their unity was the language that they spoke—Hebrew. Being the language of the Torah and the language with which God created the world, the Holy Tongue provided them with a powerful tool to unify themselves.

To thwart their plan, God took away the power that was unifying them—*"Let us descend and confuse their language, so that they will not understand each other's language"* (v. 7; *Rabbi Dov Baer Schneuri of Lubavitch, 19th century*).

genesis 10:25 – 11:6 — noaḥ

²⁵ Eber fathered two sons: one was named Peleg, because in his days the earth was split [*niPHLeGah*] (by languages), and the name of his brother was Joktan.

²⁶ Joktan fathered Almodad, Sheleph, Hazarmaveth, Jerah, ²⁷ Hadoram, Uzal, Diklah, ²⁸ Obal, Abimael, Sheba, ²⁹ Ophir, Havilah and Jobab. All these were the sons of Joktan. ³⁰ Their place of settlement extended from Mesha, towards Sephar, the mountain of the east.

³¹ The (above) are the sons of Shem according to their families, and their languages, by their lands and their nations.

³² The (above) are the families of the sons of Noah, according to their generations, by their nations. From them the nations were dispersed on the earth after the Flood.

Nations Unite to Build a Giant Tower

11 [SEVENTH READING] ¹ The whole earth spoke one language (Hebrew), and had a united cause (against God). ² Then, when they migrated from the east (to find a new, larger home, big enough for them all), they (only) found a valley in the land of Shinar, and they settled there.

³ Each (nation) said to the other, "Prepare yourselves! Let us mold bricks and fire them!" (since they had no stones in the valley). So the bricks were like stones for them, and they used clay for plastering.

⁴ They said, "Prepare yourselves! Let us build ourselves a city with a tower whose top is in the skies! Let us make ourselves a name, so we do not become scattered upon the face of the entire earth."

⁵ God descended to see the city and the tower that the descendants of Adam had built.

⁶ God said, "(Despite the fact) that they are one people, and they all have one language, this is what they have begun to do! Shouldn't they be stopped from

---

11:3 The bricks were like stones for them. When they would bring up the bricks they would climb from the east, and they would go down from the west. If a man fell down and died they did not pay any attention. But if a brick fell down they stopped working and cried, saying, "Woe to us! When will another brick be brought in its place?" (*Pirkei de-Rabbi Eliezer*).

4. So we do not become scattered upon the face of the entire earth. Why was the so-called "generation of Dispersion," who built the Tower of Babel, so afraid of becoming *"scattered upon the face of the entire earth"*? What would be the problem with inhabiting the world at large?

The people of that generation wanted to draw down God's blessings without following God's will. They understood that Divine energy will always flow into a place of peace and harmony, so they figured that by keeping together, in one giant harmonious community, they would

בראשית יא:ו-כג

וְשָׂפָה אַחַת לְכֻלָּם וְזֶה הַחִלָּם לַעֲשׂוֹת וְעַתָּה לֹא־יִבָּצֵר מֵהֶם כֹּל אֲשֶׁר יָזְמוּ לַעֲשׂוֹת: 7 הָבָה נֵרְדָה וְנָבְלָה שָׁם שְׂפָתָם אֲשֶׁר לֹא יִשְׁמְעוּ אִישׁ שְׂפַת רֵעֵהוּ: 8 וַיָּפֶץ יְהֹוָה אֹתָם מִשָּׁם עַל־פְּנֵי כָל־הָאָרֶץ וַיַּחְדְּלוּ לִבְנֹת הָעִיר: 9 עַל־כֵּן קָרָא שְׁמָהּ בָּבֶל כִּי־שָׁם בָּלַל יְהֹוָה שְׂפַת כָּל־הָאָרֶץ וּמִשָּׁם הֱפִיצָם יְהֹוָה עַל־פְּנֵי כָּל־הָאָרֶץ: פ 10 אֵלֶּה תּוֹלְדֹת שֵׁם שֵׁם בֶּן־מְאַת שָׁנָה וַיּוֹלֶד אֶת־אַרְפַּכְשָׁד שְׁנָתַיִם אַחַר הַמַּבּוּל: 11 וַיְחִי־שֵׁם אַחֲרֵי הוֹלִידוֹ אֶת־אַרְפַּכְשָׁד חֲמֵשׁ מֵאוֹת שָׁנָה וַיּוֹלֶד בָּנִים וּבָנוֹת: ס 12 וְאַרְפַּכְשַׁד חַי חָמֵשׁ וּשְׁלֹשִׁים שָׁנָה וַיּוֹלֶד אֶת־שָׁלַח: 13 וַיְחִי אַרְפַּכְשַׁד אַחֲרֵי הוֹלִידוֹ אֶת־שֶׁלַח שָׁלֹשׁ שָׁנִים וְאַרְבַּע מֵאוֹת שָׁנָה וַיּוֹלֶד בָּנִים וּבָנוֹת: ס 14 וְשֶׁלַח חַי שְׁלֹשִׁים שָׁנָה וַיּוֹלֶד אֶת־עֵבֶר: 15 וַיְחִי־שֶׁלַח אַחֲרֵי הוֹלִידוֹ אֶת־עֵבֶר שָׁלֹשׁ שָׁנִים וְאַרְבַּע מֵאוֹת שָׁנָה וַיּוֹלֶד בָּנִים וּבָנוֹת: ס 16 וַיְחִי־עֵבֶר אַרְבַּע וּשְׁלֹשִׁים שָׁנָה וַיּוֹלֶד אֶת־פָּלֶג: 17 וַיְחִי־עֵבֶר אַחֲרֵי הוֹלִידוֹ אֶת־פֶּלֶג שְׁלֹשִׁים שָׁנָה וְאַרְבַּע מֵאוֹת שָׁנָה וַיּוֹלֶד בָּנִים וּבָנוֹת: ס 18 וַיְחִי־פֶלֶג שְׁלֹשִׁים שָׁנָה וַיּוֹלֶד אֶת־רְעוּ: 19 וַיְחִי־פֶלֶג אַחֲרֵי הוֹלִידוֹ אֶת־רְעוּ תֵּשַׁע שָׁנִים וּמָאתַיִם שָׁנָה וַיּוֹלֶד בָּנִים וּבָנוֹת: ס 20 וַיְחִי רְעוּ שְׁתַּיִם וּשְׁלֹשִׁים שָׁנָה וַיּוֹלֶד אֶת־שְׂרוּג: 21 וַיְחִי רְעוּ אַחֲרֵי הוֹלִידוֹ אֶת־שְׂרוּג שֶׁבַע שָׁנִים וּמָאתַיִם שָׁנָה וַיּוֹלֶד בָּנִים וּבָנוֹת: ס 22 וַיְחִי שְׂרוּג שְׁלֹשִׁים שָׁנָה וַיּוֹלֶד אֶת־נָחוֹר: 23 וַיְחִי שְׂרוּג אַחֲרֵי

9. God confused the language of the entire earth. Even after God "confused" all the languages, something of the holy tongue remains in every language. Every language contains at least a few words of Torah. That is the inner reason why the Jewish people have been exiled

spiritual vitamin

> The human mind is so inconsistent that you might readily overlook the most glaring and evident truths that bar the way to the gratification of your lusts.

everything they have planned to do? ⁷ Prepare yourselves! Let us descend and confuse their language, so that they will not understand each other's language."

⁸ God dispersed them from there over the face of the entire earth, and they stopped building the city.

⁹ Therefore, He named it Babel, for there God confused [*BaLal*] the language of the entire earth, and from there God dispersed them upon the face of the entire earth.

Descendants of Shem

¹⁰ These are the offspring of Shem:

Shem was one hundred years old, and he fathered Arpachshad, two years after the Flood. ¹¹ After he had fathered Arpachshad, Shem lived five hundred years, and he fathered sons and daughters.

¹² Arpachshad lived thirty-five years, and then he fathered Shelah. ¹³ After he had fathered Shelah, Arpachshad lived four hundred and three years, and he fathered sons and daughters.

¹⁴ Shelah lived thirty years, and then he fathered Eber. ¹⁵ After he had fathered Eber, Shelah lived four hundred and three years, and he fathered sons and daughters.

¹⁶ Eber lived thirty-four years, and then he fathered Peleg. ¹⁷ After he had fathered Peleg, Eber lived four hundred and thirty years, and he fathered sons and daughters.

¹⁸ Peleg lived thirty years, and then he fathered Reu. ¹⁹ After he had fathered Reu, Peleg lived two hundred and nine years, and he fathered sons and daughters.

²⁰ Reu lived thirty-two years, and then he fathered Serug. ²¹ After he had fathered Serug, Reu lived two hundred and seven years, and he fathered sons and daughters.

²² Serug lived thirty years, and then he fathered Nahor. ²³ After he had fathered Nahor, Serug lived two hundred years, and he fathered sons and daughters.

8. God dispersed them. Whose sins were worse, those of the generation of the Flood or those of the generation of the Dispersion? Seemingly, the generation of Dispersion, for the former did not antagonize God intentionally, unlike the latter who waged war against Him. Nevertheless, the former were drowned, while the latter did not perish from the world!

This is because Noah's generation were thieves and lived in strife, and therefore they were destroyed. But the generation of the Dispersion behaved with love and friendship among themselves.

From this you can learn just how hateful is discord, and how very great is peace (*Rashi, 11ᵗʰ century*).

בראשית יא:כג-לב

הוֹלִידוֹ אֶת־נָחוֹר מָאתַיִם שָׁנָה וַיּוֹלֶד בָּנִים וּבָנוֹת: ס 24 וַיְחִי נָחוֹר תֵּשַׁע וְעֶשְׂרִים שָׁנָה וַיּוֹלֶד אֶת־תָּרַח: 25 וַיְחִי נָחוֹר אַחֲרֵי הוֹלִידוֹ אֶת־תֶּרַח תְּשַׁע־עֶשְׂרֵה שָׁנָה וּמְאַת שָׁנָה וַיּוֹלֶד בָּנִים וּבָנוֹת: ס 26 וַיְחִי־תֶרַח שִׁבְעִים שָׁנָה וַיּוֹלֶד אֶת־אַבְרָם אֶת־נָחוֹר וְאֶת־הָרָן: 27 וְאֵלֶּה תּוֹלְדֹת תֶּרַח תֶּרַח הוֹלִיד אֶת־אַבְרָם אֶת־נָחוֹר וְאֶת־הָרָן וְהָרָן הוֹלִיד אֶת־לוֹט: 28 וַיָּמָת הָרָן עַל־פְּנֵי תֶּרַח אָבִיו בְּאֶרֶץ מוֹלַדְתּוֹ בְּאוּר כַּשְׂדִּים: 29 [MAFTIR] וַיִּקַּח אַבְרָם וְנָחוֹר לָהֶם נָשִׁים שֵׁם אֵשֶׁת־אַבְרָם שָׂרָי וְשֵׁם אֵשֶׁת־נָחוֹר מִלְכָּה בַּת־הָרָן אֲבִי־מִלְכָּה וַאֲבִי יִסְכָּה: 30 וַתְּהִי שָׂרַי עֲקָרָה אֵין לָהּ וָלָד: 31 וַיִּקַּח תֶּרַח אֶת־אַבְרָם בְּנוֹ וְאֶת־לוֹט בֶּן־הָרָן בֶּן־בְּנוֹ וְאֵת שָׂרַי כַּלָּתוֹ אֵשֶׁת אַבְרָם בְּנוֹ וַיֵּצְאוּ אִתָּם מֵאוּר כַּשְׂדִּים לָלֶכֶת אַרְצָה כְּנַעַן וַיָּבֹאוּ עַד־חָרָן וַיֵּשְׁבוּ שָׁם: 32 וַיִּהְיוּ יְמֵי־תֶרַח חָמֵשׁ שָׁנִים וּמָאתַיִם שָׁנָה וַיָּמָת תֶּרַח בְּחָרָן: פ פ פ

קנ"ג פסוקים, בצלא"ל סימן, אב"י יסכ"ה לו"ט סימן.

---

30. Sarai was barren, she had no child. Surely it is obvious that one who is barren has no child? Rather, the Torah is implying that she did not even have a womb—the potential to have a child (*Babylonian Talmud, Yevamot* 64b).

31. They reached as far as Haran and settled there. It is relatively easy to *embark* on a spiritual journey, the difficulty lies in *completing* it. Even ordinary people, of no special religious caliber, will often have an awakening, inspiring them to change radically; but somewhere along the line their spirits become stifled and their plans thwarted. Contrast Terah, who set out *"to go to the land of Canaan,"* with good intentions, but only *"reached as far as Haran,"* with Abram, who persisted and completed his mission to journey to the land (*Rabbi Moses Grünwald of Huszt, 19th century*).

kabbalah bites

11:30 From the words *"Sarai was barren,"* we know already that she had no children. Why does the verse need to add *"she had no child"*?

Even if a union of two bodies fails to produce a child in this world, it definitely gives rise to souls in the upper world—souls of those who are destined to convert to Judaism.

So while Sarai *"had no child"* in this world, she *did* give birth to many souls in heaven—*"the souls that they made in Haran"* (literal translation of 12:5).

²⁴ Nahor lived twenty-nine years, and then he fathered Terah. ²⁵ After he had fathered Terah, Nahor lived one hundred and nineteen years, and he fathered sons and daughters.

²⁶ Terah lived seventy years, and he fathered Abram, Nahor, and Haran.

Descendants of Terah

²⁷ These are the offspring of Terah:

Terah fathered Abram, Nahor, and Haran.

Haran fathered Lot. ²⁸ Haran died during the lifetime of his father Terah, in the land of his birth, Ur of the Chaldeans.

[MAFTIR] ²⁹ Abram and Nahor took themselves wives. The name of Abram's wife was Sarai, and the name of Nahor's wife was Milcah, the daughter of Haran, who was the father of Milcah and Iscah (=Sarai).

³⁰ Sarai was barren, she had no child.

³¹ Terah took his son Abram, Lot—the son of his grandson Haran—and his daughter-in-law Sarai, the wife of his son Abram—and they (Terah and Abram) went out with them (Lot and Sarai) from Ur of the Chaldeans to go to the land of Canaan. They reached as far as Haran and settled there.

³² Terah lived a total of two hundred and five years. Terah died in Haran.

Haftarot: Noaḥ—page 1291. Rosh Ḥodesh—page 1417.
Maftir: Rosh Ḥodesh—p. 1000 (28:9–15).

kabbalah bites

11:27 Abraham and Haran came to this world to achieve a *tikkun* (spiritual healing) for Adam's sin of worshipping idols (see below, 21:9). Abraham, who rejected idol-worship and affirmed belief in one God, achieved this successfully, but Haran did not. After Haran died in Nimrod's fiery furnace, he was reincarnated as Aaron to achieve *tikkun* (see *Exodus* 32:1).

among all the nations: to elevate, in the course of their discussions in the various languages, the holy letters of the Torah which became mixed in them (*Rabbi Menahem Nahum of Chernobyl, 18th century*).

28. Haran died during the lifetime of his father Terah. By pointing out that Haran died in his father's lifetime, the Torah alludes to the fact that Haran died as a direct result of his father's actions.

Terah complained to King Nimrod that Abram had crushed his idols, so Nimrod cast Abram into a fiery furnace. Haran sat and thought, "If Abram is victorious, I will be on his side, and if Nimrod is victorious, I will be on his side."

When Abram was saved, Haran was asked, "Whose side are you on?"

Haran replied, "I am on Abram's side!"

He was cast into the fiery furnace and he was burned (*Genesis Rabbah*).

When God spoke to **Abraham** for the first time, the era of **human/Divine cooperation** began— a precursor of the future **Sinaitic revelation.** God told Abraham to leave his prior value systems and become a **"partner" with God** in enacting the Divine plan of Creation.

LEKH LEKHA
לך לך

ABRAM'S TESTS	12:1-20
ABRAM AND LOT PART COMPANY	13:1-18
WAR BETWEEN FIVE KINGS AND FOUR KINGS	14:1-24
ABRAM PROMISED CHILDREN	15:1-6
COVENANT OF THE PARTS	15:7-21
HAGAR GIVEN TO ABRAM	16:1-16
NAME CHANGE TO ABRAHAM	17:1-8
CIRCUMCISION	17:9-14
SARAI'S NAME IS CHANGED	17:15-22
ABRAHAM CIRCUMCISES HIS HOUSEHOLD	17:23-27

NAME
Lekh Lekha

MEANING
"Go for yourself"

LINES IN TORAH SCROLL
208

PARASHIYYOT
3 open; 4 closed

VERSES
126

WORDS
1686

LETTERS
6336

DATE
2023–2047

LOCATION
Haran, Canaan, Egypt, Plains of Mamre

KEY PEOPLE
Abraham, Sarah, Lot, Pharaoh, King of Sodom, Hagar, Ishmael

MITZVOT
1 positive

MASORETIC FEATURES
Dot on *yod* of the word *u-ve-neykha* (16:5)

CHARACTER PROFILE

NAME
Abraham

PARENTS
Terah and Amatlai

WIVES
Sarah, Hagar (Keturah)

LIFE SPAN
175 years

CHILDREN
Isaac, Ishmael, Zimran, Jokshan, Medan, Midian, Ishbak and Shuah

BURIAL PLACE
Cave of Machpelah

ACHIEVEMENTS
Recognized the existence of God at the age of three; passed ten tests from God; kept all the commandments before they were given; pleaded for the people of Sodom even though they were very wicked

KNOWN FOR
Thrown into a furnace by Nimrod and miraculously survived; encouraged all his guests to thank God for food; excelled in welcoming guests; was willing to sacrifice his son to fulfil the will of God

FINANCIAL INTEGRITY

Abraham was careful to muzzle his animals so that they should not graze in fields which did not belong to him (13:7).

NAMES

Your Hebrew name does not merely label you, it reflects your inner essence. God changed Abraham and Sarah's names, making Abraham "the father of a multitude of nations" and Sarah, "a princess to all mankind" (17:5,15,16).

MITZVAH

Although Abraham observed all the commandments, he waited for God to command him personally before circumcising. The highest form of worshiping God is by following His explicit commands in the Torah. Everything else is somewhat subjective (17:9-10).

בראשית יב:א-ה | לך לך

יב 1 וַיֹּאמֶר יְהֹוָה אֶל־אַבְרָם לֶךְ־לְךָ מֵאַרְצְךָ וּמִמּוֹלַדְתְּךָ וּמִבֵּית אָבִיךָ אֶל־הָאָרֶץ אֲשֶׁר אַרְאֶךָּ: 2 וְאֶעֶשְׂךָ לְגוֹי גָּדוֹל וַאֲבָרֶכְךָ וַאֲגַדְּלָה שְׁמֶךָ וֶהְיֵה בְּרָכָה: 3 וַאֲבָרֲכָה מְבָרְכֶיךָ וּמְקַלֶּלְךָ אָאֹר וְנִבְרְכוּ בְךָ כֹּל מִשְׁפְּחֹת הָאֲדָמָה: 4 וַיֵּלֶךְ אַבְרָם כַּאֲשֶׁר דִּבֶּר אֵלָיו יְהֹוָה וַיֵּלֶךְ אִתּוֹ לוֹט וְאַבְרָם בֶּן־חָמֵשׁ שָׁנִים וְשִׁבְעִים שָׁנָה בְּצֵאתוֹ מֵחָרָן: 5 וַיִּקַּח אַבְרָם אֶת־שָׂרַי אִשְׁתּוֹ וְאֶת־לוֹט

whether, after all these promises of reward, he would be able to follow God's command with purity—"as God had told him"—without mixing in thoughts of future benefits (*Rabbi Abraham Joshua Heschel of Apta, 18th century*).

This could also be rendered as "go *to* yourself." Reveal your true identity as a Jew (*Zohar*).

"From your *land*," means go away from your worldliness, from your physical desires ('*aretz*, "land," sharing the same root as *ratzon*, "desire").

"From your *birthplace*," means that you should not fulfil the commandments by rote, as a habitual routine with which you were brought up.

"From your *father's house*," indicates wisdom, which is referred to as "father" in the *Kabbalah*. The "father" alluded to in this verse is the wisdom of the evil impulse. The Torah tells us, "Go away from your 'father!'" Don't be a "wise guy" when it comes to God's laws. Don't rationalize them away.

It is through putting the above steps into practice that you come *"to the land which I will show you."* God will lead you to, and reveal to you, the true spirituality of God's supernal "land" (*Rabbi Shalom Dov Baer Schneersohn of Lubavitch, 19th–20th century*).

3. I will bless those who bless you, etc. The literal translation reads, "*I will bless those who bless you, and any person who curses you I will curse.*"

Notice that the Torah placed the phrase *"I will bless"* before *"those who bless you,"* indicating that those who intend to bless Abram will receive God's blessing *even before* they articulate their actual blessing. God counts a good intention as if the deed was performed.

Conversely, the passage concludes, *"any person who curses you I will curse,"* indicating that Abram's detractors will be cursed by God only *after* they actually have fulfilled their intention to curse him. God does not consider a bad intention as if a misdeed were performed (*Rabbi Ephraim of Luntshits, 16th–17th century*).

4. Abram left, as God had told him. Our father Abraham was tested with ten trials:

1. Influential people seek to murder the infant Abraham and he is hidden in an underground cave for thirteen years.

kabbalah bites

12:1-2 The soul has three levels, *nefesh* (soul), *ru'ah* (spirit) and *neshamah* (pneuma). Each soul must pass through at least three incarnations to achieve fulfillment on each of these levels. This is alluded to by God's threefold command here: *"from your land (nefesh), your birthplace (ru'ah) and your father's house (neshamah)."*

Nevertheless, on each occasion, *"Lot went with him"* (v. 4)—our inner demons accompany us to make each life a meaningful challenge.

genesis 12:1–5   lekh lekha

parashat lekh lekha

Abram Asked to Leave His Home

12 ¹ God said to Abram, "Go (further) away—for your (own benefit)—from your land, your birthplace and your father's house, to the land which I will show you. ² (There), I will make you into a great nation. I will bless you (with money). I will make your name great (by adding a letter to it), and you will (have the power of) blessing (other people). ³ I will bless those who bless you. I will curse (any person) who curses you. All the families of the earth will bless (their children to be like) you."

⁴ Abram left, as God had told him, and Lot went with him.

Abram was seventy-five years old when he left Haran.

⁵ Abram took Sarai, his wife, and Lot, his brother's son, all the possessions which they had acquired, and the people they had (converted) in Haran, and they departed, heading for the land of Canaan.

They arrived at the land of Canaan.

12:1 Go … from your land, your birthplace and your father's house. Abram was not commanded merely to leave his physical homeland but also to "depart" from the undesirable habits he had acquired there. In fact, God's command implied a *sequential* removal of bad habits: First, the removal of superficial habits, those that come from your surroundings and habitat ("go from your *land*"); and subsequently the more deeply ingrained habits, like those formed in your childhood by your family members ("your *birthplace* and your *father's house*"). Since the latter are entrenched deeply in the psyche, more effort is required to remove them (*Rabbi Hananiah Yom Tov Lipa Teitelbaum, 19th century*).

Go for your own benefit and for your own good (*Rashi, 11th century*).

If God promised Abram that this journey would be for his own benefit and good, as *Rashi* suggests, then why is this considered one of Abram's "Ten Trials"? What great test is there in doing something for your own benefit?

We soon discover, however, that Abram departed solely because of God's command, and not out of the desire for personal gain: "Abram left *as God had told him*" (v. 4). His test, then, was

spiritual vitamin

> God's call to Abraham to leave his land and birthplace, in order to begin a new life in the Promised Land is also, symbolically speaking, the call and challenge to you not to be swayed by inborn temptations, acquired habits, or common daily routine.

בראשית יב:ה-יב | לך לך

בֶּן־אָחִ֑יו וְאֶת־כָּל־רְכוּשָׁם֙ אֲשֶׁ֣ר רָכָ֔שׁוּ וְאֶת־הַנֶּ֖פֶשׁ אֲשֶׁר־עָשׂ֣וּ בְחָרָ֑ן וַיֵּצְא֗וּ לָלֶ֙כֶת֙ אַ֣רְצָה כְּנַ֔עַן וַיָּבֹ֖אוּ אַ֥רְצָה כְּנָֽעַן: 6 וַיַּעֲבֹ֤ר אַבְרָם֙ בָּאָ֔רֶץ עַ֚ד מְק֣וֹם שְׁכֶ֔ם עַ֖ד אֵל֣וֹן מוֹרֶ֑ה וְהַֽכְּנַעֲנִ֖י אָ֥ז בָּאָֽרֶץ: 7 וַיֵּרָ֤א יְהֹוָה֙ אֶל־אַבְרָ֔ם וַיֹּ֕אמֶר לְזַ֨רְעֲךָ֔ אֶתֵּ֖ן אֶת־הָאָ֣רֶץ הַזֹּ֑את וַיִּ֤בֶן שָׁם֙ מִזְבֵּ֔חַ לַיהֹוָ֖ה הַנִּרְאֶ֥ה אֵלָֽיו: 8 וַיַּעְתֵּ֨ק מִשָּׁ֜ם הָהָ֗רָה מִקֶּ֛דֶם לְבֵֽית־אֵ֖ל וַיֵּ֣ט אָהֳלֹ֑ה בֵּֽית־אֵ֤ל מִיָּם֙ וְהָעַ֣י מִקֶּ֔דֶם וַיִּֽבֶן־שָׁ֤ם מִזְבֵּ֙חַ֙ לַֽיהֹוָ֔ה וַיִּקְרָ֖א בְּשֵׁ֥ם יְהֹוָֽה: 9 וַיִּסַּ֣ע אַבְרָ֔ם הָל֥וֹךְ וְנָס֖וֹעַ הַנֶּֽגְבָּה: פ 10 וַיְהִ֥י רָעָ֖ב בָּאָ֑רֶץ וַיֵּ֨רֶד אַבְרָ֤ם מִצְרַ֙יְמָה֙ לָג֣וּר שָׁ֔ם כִּֽי־כָבֵ֥ד הָרָעָ֖ב בָּאָֽרֶץ: 11 וַיְהִ֕י כַּאֲשֶׁ֥ר הִקְרִ֖יב לָב֣וֹא מִצְרָ֑יְמָה וַיֹּ֙אמֶר֙ אֶל־שָׂרַ֣י אִשְׁתּ֔וֹ הִנֵּה־נָ֣א יָדַ֔עְתִּי כִּ֛י אִשָּׁ֥ה יְפַת־מַרְאֶ֖ה אָֽתְּ: 12 וְהָיָ֗ה כִּֽי־יִרְא֤וּ אֹתָךְ֙ הַמִּצְרִ֔ים וְאָמְר֖וּ אִשְׁתּ֣וֹ זֹ֑את וְהָרְג֥וּ אֹתִ֖י וְאֹתָ֥ךְ יְחַיּֽוּ:

66

10. Abram went down to Egypt. Abram and Sarai's descent into Egypt was a precursor of the Egyptian exile. Abram's escape from Egypt as a wealthy man (13:1-2) opened the spiritual "channels" of redemption that enabled his children to leave Egypt laden with gold and silver.

Similarly, Sarai's extreme caution against becoming defiled by Pharaoh (v. 17) later empowered her descendants, the Jewish women in Egypt, with the strength to remain faithful to their families (*Genesis Rabbah*; *Rabbi Abraham b. Jacob Saba, 15th century*).

Human love is rooted in the world of supreme *hesed* (Divine kindness), but when man receives the *hesed* it contains a mixture of good and evil—it is a "fallen" love. *The purpose of our worship is to purify this love and to raise it back up to God.*

To do this, you must learn to "manage" bad love. When a negative form of love comes to you, causing you to desire something forbidden, say to yourself: "This love has fallen from the World of Love, from the love of God. It is my task to raise it back up. *How could I possibly do the evil act that is tempting me to do, causing it to fall still further?*"

Also, tell yourself: "If my love has been aroused by this negative desire for this fallen material object, then how much greater should my love be for God and His Torah, through which all being was created!"

Abram mastered the emotion of love to the extent he was called *"Abraham My lover"* (Isaiah 41:8). God wanted Abram to go down to the nations of the world, whose qualities were in a very fallen state, especially in Egypt, and to elevate the love that had fallen there. Thus, *"Abram went down into Egypt."*

But he did so with great trepidation, so as not to emulate their failings, ensuring that this descent was for the sake of ascent (*Rabbi Menahem Nahum Twersky of Chernobyl, 18th century*).

1. Is it right to sever family ties for a spiritual quest?

2. Do you "owe" anything to the land in which you were raised?

3. Have you ever made a sudden break from a comfortable position?

food for thought

genesis 12:6–12 · lekh lekha

⁶ Abram traveled through the land, as far as the area of Shechem, (which is in) the plain of Moreh. At that time, the Canaanites were in (the process of conquering) the land (from the descendants of Shem). ⁷ God appeared to Abram, and He said, "I will give this land to your descendants!" (Abram) built an altar there to God, who had appeared to him.

⁸ He moved (his tent) from there to the mountain which is to the east of Bethel, where he pitched his (wife's tent first and then his own) tent. Bethel was to the west and Ai was to the east. He built an altar there to God, and he (prayed) in the name of God.

⁹ Abram traveled (periodically), always traveling southward (towards Jerusalem).

Famine in Canaan and Capture of Sarai

¹⁰ There was a famine in the land (of Canaan). Abram went down to Egypt to settle there temporarily, because the famine was severe in the land (of Canaan). ¹¹ Then, when he approached Egypt, he said to Sarai his wife, "(Until now, I had not noticed, but) now I realize that you are an attractive woman. ¹² When the Egyptians will see you, they will say, 'It's his wife!' They will kill me and keep you alive!

---

2. Abraham is imprisoned for ten years, after which he is cast into a fiery furnace.

3. Abraham is told to migrate to Canaan, away from his father's house and birthplace (v. 1)—and migration is harder for a man than for any other creature.

4. A famine—the first since the creation of the world—drives Abraham to Egypt (v. 10).

5. Pharaoh seizes Abraham's wife Sarah to be his wife (v. 15). Is there any man, who seeing his wife taken by another man, would not tear his garments in mourning? But Abraham trusted that God would not allow Pharaoh to touch her.

6. Abraham battles a group of kings who had captured Lot (14:13-15).

7. Abraham sees in a vision that his descendants were to be enslaved. He carries out the Covenant of the Parts (15:1*ff.*).

8. Abraham is circumcised at the age of ninety-nine (17:24).

9. Ishmael, who was an archer (21:20), shoots an arrow at Isaac, attempting to kill him. This forced Abraham to send away Hagar and her son—from this world and from the world to come—which *"disturbed Abraham greatly,"* more than all the other misfortunes which he suffered (ibid., 11).

10. God asks Abraham to sacrifice Isaac on an altar (22:1; *Pirkei de-Rabbi Eliezer*).

---

kabbalah bites

12:12 Why were Abraham and Isaac confronted with challenges over their wives, something Jacob was spared from, even though he had four wives?

Only Abraham and Isaac sought to teach the nations of the world the Kabbalistic secrets of monotheism, whereas Jacob did not. Abraham's contemporaries thus posed questions to him about the Kabbalah: "Is Sarai your wife or your sister?" meaning to say, "Do the male and female elements of Divinity (*"Ze'eir 'Anpin"* and *"Malkhut"*) enjoy a vertical relationship or a horizontal one?

בראשית יב:יג - יג:ד

לך לך

13 [SECOND READING] אִמְרִי־נָ֖א אֲחֹ֣תִי אָ֑תְּ לְמַ֨עַן֙ יִֽיטַב־לִ֣י בַעֲבוּרֵ֔ךְ וְחָיְתָ֥ה נַפְשִׁ֖י בִּגְלָלֵֽךְ׃
14 וַיְהִ֕י כְּב֥וֹא אַבְרָ֖ם מִצְרָ֑יְמָה וַיִּרְא֤וּ הַמִּצְרִים֙ אֶת־הָ֣אִשָּׁ֔ה כִּֽי־יָפָ֥ה הִ֖וא מְאֹֽד׃
15 וַיִּרְא֤וּ אֹתָהּ֙ שָׂרֵ֣י פַרְעֹ֔ה וַיְהַֽלְל֥וּ אֹתָ֖הּ אֶל־פַּרְעֹ֑ה וַתֻּקַּ֥ח הָאִשָּׁ֖ה בֵּ֥ית פַּרְעֹֽה׃
16 וּלְאַבְרָ֥ם הֵיטִ֖יב בַּעֲבוּרָ֑הּ וַֽיְהִי־ל֤וֹ צֹאן־וּבָקָר֙ וַחֲמֹרִ֔ים וַעֲבָדִים֙ וּשְׁפָחֹ֔ת וַאֲתֹנֹ֖ת וּגְמַלִּֽים׃ 17 וַיְנַגַּ֨ע יְהֹוָ֧ה ׀ אֶת־פַּרְעֹ֛ה נְגָעִ֥ים גְּדֹלִ֖ים וְאֶת־בֵּית֑וֹ עַל־דְּבַ֥ר שָׂרַ֖י אֵ֥שֶׁת אַבְרָֽם׃ 18 וַיִּקְרָ֤א פַרְעֹה֙ לְאַבְרָ֔ם וַיֹּ֕אמֶר מַה־זֹּ֖את עָשִׂ֣יתָ לִּ֑י לָ֚מָּה לֹא־הִגַּ֣דְתָּ לִּ֔י כִּ֥י אִשְׁתְּךָ֖ הִֽוא׃ 19 לָמָ֤ה אָמַ֙רְתָּ֙ אֲחֹ֣תִי הִ֔וא וָאֶקַּ֥ח אֹתָ֛הּ לִ֖י לְאִשָּׁ֑ה וְעַתָּ֕ה הִנֵּ֥ה אִשְׁתְּךָ֖ קַ֥ח וָלֵֽךְ׃ 20 וַיְצַ֥ו עָלָ֛יו פַּרְעֹ֖ה אֲנָשִׁ֑ים וַֽיְשַׁלְּח֥וּ אֹת֛וֹ וְאֶת־אִשְׁתּ֖וֹ וְאֶת־כָּל־אֲשֶׁר־לֽוֹ׃

יג 1 וַיַּ֩עַל֩ אַבְרָ֨ם מִמִּצְרַ֜יִם ה֠וּא וְאִשְׁתּ֧וֹ וְכָל־אֲשֶׁר־ל֛וֹ וְל֥וֹט עִמּ֖וֹ הַנֶּֽגְבָּה׃
2 וְאַבְרָ֖ם כָּבֵ֣ד מְאֹ֑ד בַּמִּקְנֶ֕ה בַּכֶּ֖סֶף וּבַזָּהָֽב׃ 3 וַיֵּ֙לֶךְ֙ לְמַסָּעָ֔יו מִנֶּ֖גֶב וְעַד־בֵּֽית־אֵ֑ל עַד־הַמָּק֗וֹם אֲשֶׁר־הָ֨יָה שָׁ֤ם אׇֽהֳלֹה֙ בַּתְּחִלָּ֔ה בֵּ֥ין בֵּֽית־אֵ֖ל וּבֵ֥ין הָעָֽי׃
4 אֶל־מְקוֹם֙ הַמִּזְבֵּ֔חַ אֲשֶׁר־עָ֥שָׂה שָׁ֖ם בָּרִאשֹׁנָ֑ה וַיִּקְרָ֥א שָׁ֛ם אַבְרָ֖ם בְּשֵׁ֥ם יְהֹוָֽה׃

13. Please say that you are my sister, so that they will favor me because of you, and my life will be spared thanks to you. This verse is problematic. Would Abram, who feared God and was loved by God, say that about his wife for his own benefit?

Even though Abram feared God, he did not rely on his own merit. He did not ask God to save Sarai in his own merit, but rather, in hers. He knew that it was through her merit that he would accumulate wealth from the other nations, since *a person acquires money in the merit of his wife*. Abram went to Egypt to obtain food from the other nations in her merit. He relied on her merit that he would not be hurt and she would not be touched, and so he was not afraid to say, *"she is my sister"* (Zohar).

16. Flocks, cattle, donkeys, menservants, maidservants, she-donkeys and camels. The Torah enumerates a total of seven items here, alluding to the idea that Abram embodied *ḥesed* (love), the highest of the soul's seven emotional attributes.

food for thought

1. Why do relatives sometimes quarrel more than friends?

2. Would you protest immoral actions carried out by a close relative?

3. Today, make peace with a relative with whom you had a misunderstanding.

¹³ "Please say that you are my sister, so that they will favor me because of you, and my life will be spared thanks to you."

[SECOND READING] ¹⁴ And so it happened, that when Abram came to Egypt, the Egyptians saw that the lady was very attractive. ¹⁵ Pharaoh's ministers saw her, and they praised her (among themselves, saying that she was fit for) Pharaoh.

The lady was taken to the house of Pharaoh. ¹⁶ He (bestowed gifts) on Abram because of her. So, (Abram) had flocks, cattle, donkeys, menservants, maidservants, she-donkeys and camels.

¹⁷ God afflicted Pharaoh and his household with a severe disease because Sarai, Abram's wife, (told an angel to do so).

¹⁸ Pharaoh summoned Abram, and he said, "What have you done to me? Why didn't you tell me that she was your wife? ¹⁹ Why did you say, 'She is my sister,' (causing) me to take her as a wife for myself? Look! Here is your wife. Take (her) and go!"

²⁰ Pharaoh gave men orders (to protect Abram). They escorted him and his wife and all their possessions.

Abram and Lot Part Company

13 ¹ Abram went up from Egypt to the south (of the land of Canaan)—both he, his wife and all their possessions, together with Lot. ² Abram was heavily (laden) with cattle, silver, and gold. ³ He journeyed (retracing the same route and the same lodgings), from the south (i.e. Egypt), passing Bethel, until reaching the place where his tent had been previously, between Bethel and Ai, ⁴ at the site of the altar which he had made there to start with. Abram (prayed) there in the name of God.

spiritual vitamin

> Abraham received a command from God, to set out on a journey whose purpose was the spreading of God's name in the world. But since he might have thought that giving of himself to others may personally deprive him in some way, God assured him at once that he would be blessed with extraordinary success, materially and spiritually.
>
> By giving of yourself to others who are in need of your teachings and inspiration, far from losing anything through the process, you will gain much more in terms of personal success.

בראשית י״ג:ה׳-י״ד

5 [THIRD READING] וְגַם־לְל֔וֹט הַהֹלֵ֖ךְ אֶת־אַבְרָ֑ם הָיָ֥ה צֹאן־וּבָקָ֖ר וְאֹהָלִֽים: 6 וְלֹא־נָשָׂ֥א אֹתָ֛ם הָאָ֖רֶץ לָשֶׁ֣בֶת יַחְדָּ֑ו כִּֽי־הָיָ֤ה רְכוּשָׁם֙ רָ֔ב וְלֹ֥א יָֽכְל֖וּ לָשֶׁ֥בֶת יַחְדָּֽו: 7 וַֽיְהִי־רִ֗יב בֵּ֚ין רֹעֵ֣י מִקְנֵֽה־אַבְרָ֔ם וּבֵ֖ין רֹעֵ֣י מִקְנֵה־ל֑וֹט וְהַֽכְּנַעֲנִי֙ וְהַפְּרִזִּ֔י אָ֖ז יֹשֵׁ֥ב בָּאָֽרֶץ: 8 וַיֹּ֨אמֶר אַבְרָ֜ם אֶל־ל֗וֹט אַל־נָ֨א תְהִ֤י מְרִיבָה֙ בֵּינִ֣י וּבֵינֶ֔ךָ וּבֵ֥ין רֹעַ֖י וּבֵ֣ין רֹעֶ֑יךָ כִּֽי־אֲנָשִׁ֥ים אַחִ֖ים אֲנָֽחְנוּ: 9 הֲלֹ֤א כָל־הָאָ֙רֶץ֙ לְפָנֶ֔יךָ הִפָּ֥רֶד נָ֖א מֵעָלָ֑י אִם־הַשְּׂמֹ֣אל וְאֵימִ֔נָה וְאִם־הַיָּמִ֖ין וְאַשְׂמְאִֽילָה: 10 וַיִּשָּׂא־ל֣וֹט אֶת־עֵינָ֗יו וַיַּרְא֙ אֶת־כָּל־כִּכַּ֣ר הַיַּרְדֵּ֔ן כִּ֥י כֻלָּ֖הּ מַשְׁקֶ֑ה לִפְנֵ֣י | שַׁחֵ֣ת יְהֹוָ֗ה אֶת־סְדֹם֙ וְאֶת־עֲמֹרָ֔ה כְּגַן־יְהֹוָה֙ כְּאֶ֣רֶץ מִצְרַ֔יִם בֹּאֲכָ֖ה צֹֽעַר: 11 וַיִּבְחַר־ל֣וֹ ל֗וֹט אֵ֚ת כָּל־כִּכַּ֣ר הַיַּרְדֵּ֔ן וַיִּסַּ֥ע ל֖וֹט מִקֶּ֑דֶם וַיִּפָּ֣רְד֔וּ אִ֖ישׁ מֵעַ֥ל אָחִֽיו: 12 אַבְרָ֖ם יָשַׁ֣ב בְּאֶֽרֶץ־כְּנָ֑עַן וְל֗וֹט יָשַׁב֙ בְּעָרֵ֣י הַכִּכָּ֔ר וַיֶּאֱהַ֖ל עַד־סְדֹֽם: 13 וְאַנְשֵׁ֣י סְדֹ֔ם רָעִ֖ים וְחַטָּאִ֑ים לַיהֹוָ֖ה מְאֹֽד: 14 וַֽיהֹוָ֞ה אָמַ֣ר אֶל־אַבְרָ֗ם אַֽחֲרֵי֙ הִפָּֽרֶד־ל֣וֹט מֵֽעִמּ֔וֹ שָׂ֣א נָ֥א עֵינֶ֖יךָ וּרְאֵ֗ה

14. God said to Abram, after Lot had parted. As long as the wicked Lot was in Abram's company, God did not speak to him (*Rashi, 11th century*).

The Torah tells us Lot's story, not to inform us of his wickedness, but to teach us that Abram's goal was that even a wicked person such as Lot should come to appreciate God and display self-sacrifice to fulfil God's will. When it became necessary for Abram to send Lot away, Abram still kept a strong connection with him, saying, *"Wherever you live, I will not distance myself from you, and I will stand by you as a protector and a helper"* (*Rashi* to v. 9). Abram's commitment to Lot was so strong that he was willing to risk his life to fight a war against the four kings to save Lot (below, ch. 14), and it was this that finally convinced Lot of the greatness of Abram and the truth of his teachings.

We find that even though Lot remained wicked and dwelled in Sodom, he was nevertheless inspired by Abram's self-sacrifice, to the extent that he too risked his own life in order to welcome guests (below, chapter 19; *Rabbi Menahem Mendel Schneerson, 20th century*).

kabbalah bites

13:13 *"The people of Sodom were perverted and corrupt to God, to the extreme."* The people of Sodom were the third incarnation of the "dysfunctional souls" which Adam brought into being during the 130 years he separated from his wife (see *Genesis* 5:3; 6:12; 11:5).

"God does all these things to a man twice, even three times" (*Job* 33:29). This was the third and last failed incarnation of these souls. When they next reappear, they will be reincarnated into the Jewish people in Egypt. And then, finally, they will attain their *tikkun*, their spiritual healing.

genesis 13:5–14   lekh lekha

[THIRD READING] ⁵ Lot, who went with Abram, also had flocks and cattle and tents. ⁶ The (pasture of the) land was insufficient for them to live together, for they possessed many (cattle that needed to graze), so they failed to live together. ⁷ A quarrel erupted between the herdsmen of Abram's cattle, (who rebuked) the herdsmen of Lot's cattle (for grazing on other people's property. Lot's herdsman argued that Lot would inherit the whole land someday in any case; but in truth, it was theft, because) the Canaanites and the Perizzites inhabited the land at that time.

⁸ Abram said to Lot, "Please don't let there be a quarrel between me and you, between my herdsmen and your herdsmen, for we are relatives. ⁹ Don't you have the whole land in front of you (to choose from)? Please part from me. If you go left, I will go (not too far) to the right (to support you), and if you go right, I will go (not too far) to the left (to support you)."

¹⁰ Lot surveyed (the land), and he saw the entire plain of the Jordan until Zoar, which was well irrigated—before God destroyed Sodom and Gomorrah—(with trees) like the garden of God, and (fertile) like the land of Egypt. ¹¹ So, Lot chose for himself the entire plain of the Jordan.

Lot traveled from the east (westward), and they parted from one another.

¹² Abram dwelt in the land of Canaan. Lot dwelt in the cities of the plain, and he pitched tent(s for) his (shepherds and cattle) as far as Sodom.

¹³ The people of Sodom were (intentionally) perverted and corrupt to God, to the extreme.

God Promises the Land to Abram

¹⁴ God said to Abram, after Lot had parted from him, "Please raise your eyes and, from the place where you are positioned, look northward, southward, eastward

---

kabbalah bites

13:8-9 By saying, *"We are relatives,"* Abraham alluded to the fact that both he and Lot were reincarnations of different portions of Adam's soul. But unlike Abraham's soul, Lot's had become entangled in the *kelippot* (demonic forces) as a result of Adam's sin. Therefore Abraham requested, *"Please part from me."*

In reference to Isaac, six details of his property are mentioned, *"He had flocks of sheep, flocks of cattle and many enterprises"* (below, 26:14), alluding to his trait of *gevurah* (fear), the sixth highest emotion.

In the case of Jacob, five items are specified, *"I possess oxen, donkeys, flocks, servants and maids"* (32:5), alluding to his predominant trait of *tiferet* (harmony), the fifth highest emotional attribute of the soul (*Rabbi Menahem Azariah da Fano, 16ᵗʰ–17ᵗʰ century*).

13:11 Lot traveled from the east. Journeying away from the "east," *kedem*, alludes to Lot deliberately distancing himself from *Kadmon*, the "One Who Preceded" the universe.

Lot declared, "I don't want Abram or his God!" (*Rashi, 11ᵗʰ century*).

בראשית יג:יד - יד:י

מִן־הַמָּקוֹם אֲשֶׁר־אַתָּה שָׁם צָפֹנָה וָנֶגְבָּה וָקֵדְמָה וָיָמָּה: 15 כִּי אֶת־כָּל־הָאָרֶץ אֲשֶׁר־אַתָּה רֹאֶה לְךָ אֶתְּנֶנָּה וּלְזַרְעֲךָ עַד־עוֹלָם: 16 וְשַׂמְתִּי אֶת־זַרְעֲךָ כַּעֲפַר הָאָרֶץ אֲשֶׁר | אִם־יוּכַל אִישׁ לִמְנוֹת אֶת־עֲפַר הָאָרֶץ גַּם־זַרְעֲךָ יִמָּנֶה: 17 קוּם הִתְהַלֵּךְ בָּאָרֶץ לְאָרְכָּהּ וּלְרָחְבָּהּ כִּי לְךָ אֶתְּנֶנָּה: 18 וַיֶּאֱהַל אַבְרָם וַיָּבֹא וַיֵּשֶׁב בְּאֵלֹנֵי מַמְרֵא אֲשֶׁר בְּחֶבְרוֹן וַיִּבֶן־שָׁם מִזְבֵּחַ לַיהוָה: פ

יד 1 וַיְהִי בִּימֵי אַמְרָפֶל מֶלֶךְ־שִׁנְעָר אַרְיוֹךְ מֶלֶךְ אֶלָּסָר כְּדָרְלָעֹמֶר [FOURTH READING] מֶלֶךְ עֵילָם וְתִדְעָל מֶלֶךְ גּוֹיִם: 2 עָשׂוּ מִלְחָמָה אֶת־בֶּרַע מֶלֶךְ סְדֹם וְאֶת־בִּרְשַׁע מֶלֶךְ עֲמֹרָה שִׁנְאָב | מֶלֶךְ אַדְמָה וְשֶׁמְאֵבֶר מֶלֶךְ [צביים כ׳] צְבוֹיִים וּמֶלֶךְ בֶּלַע הִיא־צֹעַר: 3 כָּל־אֵלֶּה חָבְרוּ אֶל־עֵמֶק הַשִּׂדִּים הוּא יָם הַמֶּלַח: 4 שְׁתֵּים עֶשְׂרֵה שָׁנָה עָבְדוּ אֶת־כְּדָרְלָעֹמֶר וּשְׁלֹשׁ־עֶשְׂרֵה שָׁנָה מָרָדוּ: 5 וּבְאַרְבַּע עֶשְׂרֵה שָׁנָה בָּא כְדָרְלָעֹמֶר וְהַמְּלָכִים אֲשֶׁר אִתּוֹ וַיַּכּוּ אֶת־רְפָאִים בְּעַשְׁתְּרֹת קַרְנַיִם וְאֶת־הַזּוּזִים בְּהָם וְאֵת הָאֵימִים בְּשָׁוֵה קִרְיָתָיִם: 6 וְאֶת־הַחֹרִי בְּהַרְרָם שֵׂעִיר עַד אֵיל פָּארָן אֲשֶׁר עַל־הַמִּדְבָּר: 7 וַיָּשֻׁבוּ וַיָּבֹאוּ אֶל־עֵין מִשְׁפָּט הִוא קָדֵשׁ וַיַּכּוּ אֶת־כָּל־שְׂדֵה הָעֲמָלֵקִי וְגַם אֶת־הָאֱמֹרִי הַיֹּשֵׁב בְּחַצְצֹן תָּמָר: 8 וַיֵּצֵא מֶלֶךְ־סְדֹם וּמֶלֶךְ עֲמֹרָה וּמֶלֶךְ אַדְמָה וּמֶלֶךְ [צביים כ׳] צְבוֹיִים וּמֶלֶךְ בֶּלַע הִוא־צֹעַר וַיַּעַרְכוּ אִתָּם מִלְחָמָה בְּעֵמֶק הַשִּׂדִּים: 9 אֵת כְּדָרְלָעֹמֶר מֶלֶךְ עֵילָם וְתִדְעָל מֶלֶךְ גּוֹיִם וְאַמְרָפֶל מֶלֶךְ שִׁנְעָר וְאַרְיוֹךְ מֶלֶךְ אֶלָּסָר אַרְבָּעָה מְלָכִים אֶת־הַחֲמִשָּׁה: 10 וְעֵמֶק הַשִּׂדִּים בֶּאֱרֹת בֶּאֱרֹת חֵמָר וַיָּנֻסוּ מֶלֶךְ־סְדֹם וַעֲמֹרָה

14-15. Raise your eyes … I will give all the land that you see to you and to your descendants for eternity. When God promised Abram that his descendants would inherit the land of Israel, the Canaanites were still living there. God told him, "*Raise your eyes*," so that Abram would look beyond the physical land and see its inherent spirituality. This inherent holiness is always present (*Rabbi Meir Simḥah of Dvinsk, 19th–20th century*).

14:7 En-mishpat. The Torah calls the place En-mishpat, meaning "spring of judgment" with reference to a future event: Moses and Aaron would later be judged there because of the

and westward. ¹⁵ Because, I will give all the land that you see to you and to your descendants for eternity. ¹⁶ I will make your descendants like the soil of the earth. (Just as) a man is (not) able to count the soil (particles) of the earth, so too your descendants will (not) be (able to be) counted. ¹⁷ Get up and walk through the land, across its length and its breadth, for I am going to give it to you."

¹⁸ Abram pitched his tent (with Sarai, since he had now been promised children), and he settled in the plain of Mamre, which is in Hebron. He built an altar to God there.

War Between the Five Kings and the Four Kings

14 [FOURTH READING] ¹ It happened in the days of King Amraphel of Shinar, King Arioch of Ellasar, King Chedorlaomer of Elam, and King Tidal of Goiim, ² that they waged war with King Bera of Sodom, King Birsha of Gomorrah, King Shinab of Admah, King Shemeber of Zeboiim, and the king of Bela, which is (now) Zoar. ³ These (five latter kings) had joined (Chedorlaomer) in the valley of Siddim, which is (now) the Dead Sea. ⁴ For twelve years they served Chedorlaomer, and for thirteen years they rebelled.

⁵ In the fourteenth year (of their rebellion), Chedorlaomer came, with the (three) kings who were his allies, and they struck the Rephaim in Ashteroth-karnaim, the Zuzim in Ham, the Emim in Shaveh-kiriathaim, ⁶ and the Horites at their mountain of Seir, until the plain of Paran, which is alongside the desert. ⁷ They returned and came to En-mishpat, which is (now) Kadesh, and they smote the entire area (which was later to be inhabited by) the Amalekites, and also the Amorites, who dwelt in Hazazon-tamar.

⁸ The king of Sodom, the king of Gomorrah, the king of Admah, the king of Zeboiim, and the king of Bela, which is (now) Zoar, came forth, and they fought a battle in the valley of Siddim, ⁹ with King Chedorlaomer of Elam, King Tidal of Goiim, King Amraphel of Shinar, and King Arioch of Ellasar—four kings against the five (and yet, the minority prevailed).

¹⁰ The valley of Siddim had many clay mines. The kings of Sodom and Gomorrah fled and fell into them. The survivors fled to a mountain.

spiritual vitamin

> Never become discouraged and never think the battle lost, but keep on fighting. Be on guard to overcome a bad habit as soon as it seems to tempt you.

בראשית יד:י-כג　לך לך

וַיִּפְּלוּ־שָׁמָּה וְהַנִּשְׁאָרִים הֶרָה נָּסוּ: 11 וַיִּקְחוּ אֶת־כָּל־רְכֻשׁ סְדֹם וַעֲמֹרָה וְאֶת־כָּל־אָכְלָם וַיֵּלֵכוּ: 12 וַיִּקְחוּ אֶת־לוֹט וְאֶת־רְכֻשׁוֹ בֶּן־אֲחִי אַבְרָם וַיֵּלֵכוּ וְהוּא יֹשֵׁב בִּסְדֹם: 13 וַיָּבֹא הַפָּלִיט וַיַּגֵּד לְאַבְרָם הָעִבְרִי וְהוּא שֹׁכֵן בְּאֵלֹנֵי מַמְרֵא הָאֱמֹרִי אֲחִי אֶשְׁכֹּל וַאֲחִי עָנֵר וְהֵם בַּעֲלֵי בְרִית־אַבְרָם: 14 וַיִּשְׁמַע אַבְרָם כִּי נִשְׁבָּה אָחִיו וַיָּרֶק אֶת־חֲנִיכָיו יְלִידֵי בֵיתוֹ שְׁמֹנָה עָשָׂר וּשְׁלֹשׁ מֵאוֹת וַיִּרְדֹּף עַד־דָּן: 15 וַיֵּחָלֵק עֲלֵיהֶם | לַיְלָה הוּא וַעֲבָדָיו וַיַּכֵּם וַיִּרְדְּפֵם עַד־חוֹבָה אֲשֶׁר מִשְּׂמֹאל לְדַמָּשֶׂק: 16 וַיָּשֶׁב אֵת כָּל־הָרְכֻשׁ וְגַם אֶת־לוֹט אָחִיו וּרְכֻשׁוֹ הֵשִׁיב וְגַם אֶת־הַנָּשִׁים וְאֶת־הָעָם: 17 וַיֵּצֵא מֶלֶךְ־סְדֹם לִקְרָאתוֹ אַחֲרֵי שׁוּבוֹ מֵהַכּוֹת אֶת־כְּדָר־לָעֹמֶר וְאֶת־הַמְּלָכִים אֲשֶׁר אִתּוֹ אֶל־עֵמֶק שָׁוֵה הוּא עֵמֶק הַמֶּלֶךְ: 18 וּמַלְכִּי־צֶדֶק מֶלֶךְ שָׁלֵם הוֹצִיא לֶחֶם וָיָיִן וְהוּא כֹהֵן לְאֵל עֶלְיוֹן: 19 וַיְבָרְכֵהוּ וַיֹּאמַר בָּרוּךְ אַבְרָם לְאֵל עֶלְיוֹן קֹנֵה שָׁמַיִם וָאָרֶץ: 20 וּבָרוּךְ אֵל עֶלְיוֹן אֲשֶׁר־מִגֵּן צָרֶיךָ בְּיָדֶךָ וַיִּתֶּן־לוֹ מַעֲשֵׂר מִכֹּל: [FIFTH READING] 21 וַיֹּאמֶר מֶלֶךְ־סְדֹם אֶל־אַבְרָם תֶּן־לִי הַנֶּפֶשׁ וְהָרְכֻשׁ קַח־לָךְ: 22 וַיֹּאמֶר אַבְרָם אֶל־מֶלֶךְ סְדֹם הֲרִמֹתִי יָדִי אֶל־יְהֹוָה אֵל עֶלְיוֹן קֹנֵה שָׁמַיִם וָאָרֶץ: 23 אִם־מִחוּט וְעַד שְׂרוֹךְ־נַעַל וְאִם־

---

blemish. That is how Shem, Noah's son, was appointed as *"a priest to the supreme God"* (*Rabbi Menahem Azariah da Fano, 16th–17th century*).

22. I raise my hand (in an oath) to God. Abram attested that his victory was not a result of his own effort but rather a miracle from God. This is the mark of a great person, for others would have perceived the victory as the result of Abram's strength. Abram therefore publicly praised and thanked God for the miracle. This was also Abram's reason for refusing to take any reward from the spoils (*Rabbi Meir Simḥah of Dvinsk, 19th–20th century*).

23. I will not take from the spoils even a thread or a shoelace. As a reward for refusing to take spoils—*"even a thread or a shoelace"*—from the King of Sodom, Abraham's descendants were given two commandments: the blue thread of the *tzitzit* (ritual fringes) and the straps of the *tefillin* (phylacteries) (*Babylonian Talmud, Sotah* 17a).

---

food for thought

1. Would you risk your life to save someone? To what extent?

2. Have you ever turned down a reward?

3. Does accepting a reward diminish the altruism of a deed?

¹¹ The (four kings) took all the possessions of Sodom and Gomorrah, and all their food, and they left. ¹² (Since) he was residing in Sodom, they took Lot, the son of Abram's brother, and his possessions, and they left.

Abram Fights to Rescue Lot

¹³ A runaway came and informed Abram, the Hebrew. He was living in the plains of Mamre the Amorite—the brother of Eshkol and the brother of Aner, who had all made a covenant with Abram.

¹⁴ When Abram heard that his relative had been taken captive, he armed three hundred and eighteen trained men who were born in his household, and he pursued them as far as Dan. ¹⁵ He and his servants divided themselves (to pursue the enemy) through the night, and smote them, and pursued them as far as Hobah (i.e. Dan), which is to the left of Damascus.

¹⁶ He brought back all the possessions, and he also restored his relative Lot and his possessions, as well as the women and the people.

Abram Refuses the Spoils of War

¹⁷ After his return from smiting Chedorlaomer and the kings who were (allied) with him, the king of Sodom went out to meet him at the valley of Shaveh, in the king('s private recreation) grounds. ¹⁸ King Melchizedek of Salem (who was, in fact, Shem son of Noah) brought out bread and wine (to show that he was not angry with Abram for killing the people of Elam, his descendants). He was a priest to the supreme God. ¹⁹ He blessed him, saying, "Blessed be Abram to the supreme God, who possesses heaven and earth! ²⁰ Blessed be the supreme God, who has delivered your enemies into your hand!"

(Abram) gave him a tenth from everything (he owned).

[FIFTH READING] ²¹ The king of Sodom said to Abram, "Give me the people (of my kingdom whom you captured), and take the possessions for yourself."

²² Abram said to the king of Sodom, "I raise my hand (in an oath) to God, the supreme God, who possesses heaven and earth, ²³ that (I will not take from the spoils) even a thread or a shoelace, nor will I take (payment) from whatever

happenings at that spring, which was subsequently referred to as *"the waters of strife"* (*Numbers* 20:13; *Rashi, 11th century*).

18. King Melchizedek of Salem (who was, in fact, Shem son of Noah) ... was a priest to the supreme God. After Noah left the ark, he desired to offer sacrifices to God. However, since Noah had been bitten by a lion in the ark (*Midrash Tanḥuma*), he was disqualified from doing so, since the law states that sacrifices may only be offered by a person who is devoid of bodily

בראשית יד:כג - טו:ח   לך לך

אֶקַּ֖ח מִכָּל־אֲשֶׁר־לָ֑ךְ וְלֹ֣א תֹאמַ֔ר אֲנִ֖י הֶעֱשַׁ֥רְתִּי אֶת־אַבְרָֽם: 24 בִּלְעָדַ֗י רַ֚ק אֲשֶׁ֣ר אָכְל֣וּ הַנְּעָרִ֔ים וְחֵ֨לֶק֙ הָֽאֲנָשִׁ֔ים אֲשֶׁ֥ר הָלְכ֖וּ אִתִּ֑י עָנֵר֙ אֶשְׁכֹּ֣ל וּמַמְרֵ֔א הֵ֖ם יִקְח֥וּ חֶלְקָֽם: ס

טו 1 אַחַ֣ר | הַדְּבָרִ֣ים הָאֵ֗לֶּה הָיָ֤ה דְבַר־יְהֹוָה֙ אֶל־אַבְרָ֔ם בַּֽמַּחֲזֶ֖ה לֵאמֹ֑ר אַל־תִּירָ֣א אַבְרָ֗ם אָֽנֹכִי֙ מָגֵ֣ן לָ֔ךְ שְׂכָרְךָ֖ הַרְבֵּ֥ה מְאֹֽד: 2 וַיֹּ֣אמֶר אַבְרָ֗ם אֲדֹנָ֤י יֱהֹוִה֙ מַה־תִּתֶּן־לִ֔י וְאָֽנֹכִ֖י הוֹלֵ֣ךְ עֲרִירִ֑י וּבֶן־מֶ֣שֶׁק בֵּיתִ֔י ה֖וּא דַּמֶּ֥שֶׂק אֱלִיעֶֽזֶר: 3 וַיֹּ֣אמֶר אַבְרָ֔ם הֵ֣ן לִ֔י לֹ֥א נָתַ֖תָּה זָ֑רַע וְהִנֵּ֥ה בֶן־בֵּיתִ֖י יוֹרֵ֥שׁ אֹתִֽי: 4 וְהִנֵּ֨ה דְבַר־יְהֹוָ֤ה אֵלָיו֙ לֵאמֹ֔ר לֹ֥א יִֽירָשְׁךָ֖ זֶ֑ה כִּי־אִם֙ אֲשֶׁ֣ר יֵצֵ֣א מִמֵּעֶ֔יךָ ה֖וּא יִֽירָשֶֽׁךָ: 5 וַיּוֹצֵ֨א אֹת֜וֹ הַח֗וּצָה וַיֹּ֨אמֶר֙ הַבֶּט־נָ֣א הַשָּׁמַ֔יְמָה וּסְפֹר֙ הַכּ֣וֹכָבִ֔ים אִם־תּוּכַ֖ל לִסְפֹּ֣ר אֹתָ֑ם וַיֹּ֣אמֶר ל֔וֹ כֹּ֥ה יִהְיֶ֖ה זַרְעֶֽךָ: 6 וְהֶֽאֱמִ֖ן בַּֽיהֹוָ֑ה וַיַּחְשְׁבֶ֥הָ לּ֖וֹ צְדָקָֽה: 7 [SIXTH READING] וַיֹּ֖אמֶר אֵלָ֑יו אֲנִ֣י יְהֹוָ֗ה אֲשֶׁ֤ר הֽוֹצֵאתִ֨יךָ֙ מֵא֣וּר כַּשְׂדִּ֔ים לָ֧תֶת לְךָ֛ אֶת־הָאָ֥רֶץ הַזֹּ֖את לְרִשְׁתָּֽהּ: 8 וַיֹּאמַ֑ר אֲדֹנָ֣י יֱהֹוִ֔ה בַּמָּ֥ה אֵדַ֖ע כִּ֥י אִֽירָשֶֽׁנָּה:

24. Except for what the lads (my servants who went with me) ate, and the share of the men who went with me. Abram refused to take any reward for himself, but he did not force this stringency on his colleagues. They deserved their share of the spoils.

There is an important lesson to be learned here. Be especially critical of your own actions, but not when it comes to those of other people (*Rabbi Israel Meir Kagan, 19th–20th century*).

15:5 He took him outside. Abram said to God, "Looking at my destiny in the stars, I see that I am not going to father a son."

God replied, "Step *outside*, away from the stars. Your people are not governed by astrology. You will have a child!" (*Babylonian Talmud, Shabbat 156a*).

Please look heavenward and count the stars. That is how your descendants will be. Before you attempt to count the stars, you know that it is impossible, but you still gaze heavenward and try. *"That is how your descendants will be"*—they will also reach for achievements far beyond natural limits (*Rabbi Meir Shapira of Lublin, 20th century*).

The stars look small and insignificant when viewed from earth, but in the heavens they are great. God said to Abram, this will be the destiny of your descendants, treated as small and insignificant down

food for thought

1. Why does suffering sometimes precede kindness and blessing?

2. Have you endured suffering that was followed by great blessing?

3. What blessings have the Jewish people enjoyed since the Holocaust?

genesis 14:23 – 15:8   lekh lekha

(treasure) you possess—so that you will not say, 'I have made Abram wealthy' (for God Himself promised to make me rich)—²⁴ except for what the lads (my servants who went with me) ate, and the share of the men who went with me. Aner, Eshkol, and Mamre (who stayed with our equipment to guard it,) will take their share."

God Promises Abram Children

15 ¹ After the words (of Abram, who verbalized his worries about losing his future reward), the word of God came to Abram in a vision, saying, "Don't be afraid, Abram! I am your shield (to protect you from being punished for the people you killed in battle). Your reward is extremely great!"

² Abram said, "God, Almighty God, what could You possibly give me? For I am childless, and the steward of my household is (not my own son but) Eliezer of Damascus." ³ Abram said, "Look! You have given me no children (so there is no point in rewarding me), as a member of my household will inherit me!"

⁴ Then, the word of God came to him, saying, "He will not be your heir. Rather, you will be inherited by someone who comes out from within you."

⁵ He took him outside (his tent), and He said, "Please look heavenward and count the stars, if you are able to count them." He said to him, "That is how (numerous) your descendants will be."

⁶ He believed in God (without asking for a sign), and (God) considered this an act of righteousness.

Vision of Exile at the Covenant of the Parts

[SIXTH READING] ⁷ He said to him, "I am God, who brought you out from Ur of the Chaldeans, to give you this land as an inheritance."

⁸ He (Abram) said, "God, Almighty God, (give me a sign) through which I can know that I will inherit it."

spiritual vitamin

> Life, in general, is divided into two spheres: your personal life and your contribution to the world. In both of these there is the spiritual life and the physical life. Your challenge is to "liberate" everything in these two spheres from bondage to freedom, that is to say, to take all things out of their limitations and "elevate" them to spirituality, until every detail of your daily life is made into an instrument of service to God.

בראשית טו:ט-יט

9 וַיֹּאמֶר אֵלָיו קְחָה לִי עֶגְלָה מְשֻׁלֶּשֶׁת וְעֵז מְשֻׁלֶּשֶׁת וְאַיִל מְשֻׁלָּשׁ וְתֹר וְגוֹזָל: 10 וַיִּקַּח־לוֹ אֶת־כָּל־אֵלֶּה וַיְבַתֵּר אֹתָם בַּתָּוֶךְ וַיִּתֵּן אִישׁ־בִּתְרוֹ לִקְרַאת רֵעֵהוּ וְאֶת־הַצִּפֹּר לֹא בָתָר: 11 וַיֵּרֶד הָעַיִט עַל־הַפְּגָרִים וַיַּשֵּׁב אֹתָם אַבְרָם: 12 וַיְהִי הַשֶּׁמֶשׁ לָבוֹא וְתַרְדֵּמָה נָפְלָה עַל־אַבְרָם וְהִנֵּה אֵימָה חֲשֵׁכָה גְדֹלָה נֹפֶלֶת עָלָיו: 13 וַיֹּאמֶר לְאַבְרָם יָדֹעַ תֵּדַע כִּי־גֵר | יִהְיֶה זַרְעֲךָ בְּאֶרֶץ לֹא לָהֶם וַעֲבָדוּם וְעִנּוּ אֹתָם אַרְבַּע מֵאוֹת שָׁנָה: 14 וְגַם אֶת־הַגּוֹי אֲשֶׁר יַעֲבֹדוּ דָּן אָנֹכִי וְאַחֲרֵי־כֵן יֵצְאוּ בִּרְכֻשׁ גָּדוֹל: 15 וְאַתָּה תָּבוֹא אֶל־אֲבֹתֶיךָ בְּשָׁלוֹם תִּקָּבֵר בְּשֵׂיבָה טוֹבָה: 16 וְדוֹר רְבִיעִי יָשׁוּבוּ הֵנָּה כִּי לֹא־שָׁלֵם עֲוֺן הָאֱמֹרִי עַד־הֵנָּה: 17 וַיְהִי הַשֶּׁמֶשׁ בָּאָה וַעֲלָטָה הָיָה וְהִנֵּה תַנּוּר עָשָׁן וְלַפִּיד אֵשׁ אֲשֶׁר עָבַר בֵּין הַגְּזָרִים הָאֵלֶּה: 18 בַּיּוֹם הַהוּא כָּרַת יְהֹוָה אֶת־אַבְרָם בְּרִית לֵאמֹר לְזַרְעֲךָ נָתַתִּי אֶת־הָאָרֶץ הַזֹּאת מִנְּהַר מִצְרַיִם עַד־הַנָּהָר הַגָּדֹל נְהַר־פְּרָת: 19 אֶת־הַקֵּינִי וְאֶת־הַקְּנִזִּי

---

it. So the miracles that will occur at the time of the future redemption will surely be many times greater than those of the Egyptian exodus (*Rabbi Saadiah b. Joseph Gaon, 10th century*).

They will leave with substantial wealth. This indicates that amassing wealth was one of the purposes of Egyptian exile. For this to be achieved, it was necessary for Joseph to become the ruler of Egypt and gather wealth from all the other lands (see 47:14—*Zohar*).

18. I have given this land. Earlier, God told Abram, "*Get up and walk through the land, across its length and its breadth, for I am going to give it to you*" (13:17). Through this procedure, Abram made a legal acquisition of the land of Israel. Therefore, God now told him, "I have *given* this land to your descendants," using the *past* tense, because by that time Abram had already acquired the land legally (*Rabbi Ḥayyim ibn Attar, 18th century*).

19. The land of the Kenites. Ten nations are listed in this passage. However, God gave the

---

kabbalah bites

15:15 *"You will come to your forefathers in peace"*—Here God informed Abraham that his father, Teraḥ, would merit the afterlife (*Genesis Rabbah*).

What is the connection between Abraham's vision of the Egyptian exile, in verses 13-14, and the announcement here that his father would merit the afterlife?

Teraḥ was reincarnated as Job, who, according to tradition, convinced Pharaoh to enslave the Israelites. As a result of the suffering which Job brought upon himself through this advice, he ultimately repented and merited the afterlife. So it was the Egyptian exile that ultimately caused Teraḥ's soul to achieve *tikkun* (spiritual healing).

genesis 15:9–19 — lekh lekha

⁹ He said to him, "Take for Me three heifers, three goats, three rams, a turtledove and a young bird."

¹⁰ (Abram) took all these (animals) for (God), and he cut (each one) in the middle (into two parts). He placed each part opposite the other, but he did not divide the birds (which represented the Jewish people). ¹¹ Birds of prey descended upon the (sections of the) carcasses, but Abram drove them away.

¹² Then, when the sun was ready to set, a deep sleep fell upon Abram, and—look!—a great, frightening darkness was falling upon him (alluding to the exiles of the Jewish people).

¹³ He said to Abram, "You should know that your descendants will be strangers in a land that is not theirs. They will enslave them and oppress them, for four hundred years! ¹⁴ I will also pronounce judgment (bringing ten plagues) on the nation that they will serve, and afterwards, they will leave with substantial wealth."

¹⁵ "(Before any of this happens,) you will come to your forefathers in peace, and you will be buried in a good old age. ¹⁶ (After three generations of exile in Egypt,) the fourth generation will return here (to this land), for the Amorites (who currently inhabit the land) will not be completely sinful (deserving eviction) until then."

¹⁷ Then, when the sun had set and it became dark, and—look!—a smoking furnace with a fiery torch passed between these parts.

¹⁸ On that day, God struck a covenant with Abram, saying, "I have given this land to your descendants, from the river of Egypt until the great river, the river Euphrates, ¹⁹ (the land of the) Kenites, the Kenizzites, the Kadmonites,

---

here on earth, but from heaven, they will be considered great and noble (*Rabbi Joseph Saul Nathanson, 19th century*).

12. A great, frightening darkness was falling upon him. This alludes to the hardships and darkness of the exiles endured by the Jewish nation throughout history (*Rashi, 11th century*).

13. They will enslave them and oppress them, for four hundred years! Why were the Egyptians punished if the enslavement of the Jewish people was a Divine decree?

God's promise here did not obligate any *individual* Egyptian to oppress an Israelite. Each Egyptian had a choice as to whether God's decree would be fulfilled through him or through another Egyptian. Therefore those who chose to oppress and enslave the Israelites were fully liable for their actions (*Maimonides, 12th century*).

14. I will also pronounce judgment on the nation they will serve. God promised that when the time would come to redeem the children of Israel from Egypt, He would *"pronounce judgment"* on the Egyptians for their oppression of the Jewish people. The many miracles and wonders of the exodus from Egypt were the result of this promise.

God also has promised that He will redeem the Jewish people from their current exile. The future redemption is mentioned numerous times in Scripture with entire chapters devoted to

בראשית טו:יט - טז:ח

וְאֶת־הַקַּדְמֹנִי: 20 וְאֶת־הַחִתִּי וְאֶת־הַפְּרִזִּי וְאֶת־הָרְפָאִים: 21 וְאֶת־הָאֱמֹרִי וְאֶת־הַכְּנַעֲנִי וְאֶת־הַגִּרְגָּשִׁי וְאֶת־הַיְבוּסִי: ס

טז 1 וְשָׂרַי אֵשֶׁת אַבְרָם לֹא יָלְדָה לוֹ וְלָהּ שִׁפְחָה מִצְרִית וּשְׁמָהּ הָגָר: 2 וַתֹּאמֶר שָׂרַי אֶל־אַבְרָם הִנֵּה־נָא עֲצָרַנִי יְהֹוָה מִלֶּדֶת בֹּא־נָא אֶל־שִׁפְחָתִי אוּלַי אִבָּנֶה מִמֶּנָּה וַיִּשְׁמַע אַבְרָם לְקוֹל שָׂרָי: 3 וַתִּקַּח שָׂרַי אֵשֶׁת־אַבְרָם אֶת־הָגָר הַמִּצְרִית שִׁפְחָתָהּ מִקֵּץ עֶשֶׂר שָׁנִים לְשֶׁבֶת אַבְרָם בְּאֶרֶץ כְּנָעַן וַתִּתֵּן אֹתָהּ לְאַבְרָם אִישָׁהּ לוֹ לְאִשָּׁה: 4 וַיָּבֹא אֶל־הָגָר וַתַּהַר וַתֵּרֶא כִּי הָרָתָה וַתֵּקַל גְּבִרְתָּהּ בְּעֵינֶיהָ: 5 וַתֹּאמֶר שָׂרַי אֶל־אַבְרָם חֲמָסִי עָלֶיךָ אָנֹכִי נָתַתִּי שִׁפְחָתִי בְּחֵיקֶךָ וַתֵּרֶא כִּי הָרָתָה וָאֵקַל בְּעֵינֶיהָ יִשְׁפֹּט יְהֹוָה בֵּינִי וּבֵינֶיךָ: 6 וַיֹּאמֶר אַבְרָם אֶל־שָׂרַי הִנֵּה שִׁפְחָתֵךְ בְּיָדֵךְ עֲשִׂי־לָהּ הַטּוֹב בְּעֵינָיִךְ וַתְּעַנֶּהָ שָׂרַי וַתִּבְרַח מִפָּנֶיהָ: 7 וַיִּמְצָאָהּ מַלְאַךְ יְהֹוָה עַל־עֵין הַמַּיִם בַּמִּדְבָּר עַל־הָעַיִן בְּדֶרֶךְ שׁוּר: 8 וַיֹּאמַר הָגָר שִׁפְחַת שָׂרַי אֵי־מִזֶּה בָאת וְאָנָה תֵלֵכִי וַתֹּאמֶר

kabbalah bites

16:6 If you are constantly at loggerheads with a relative or friend, it might be because your souls both derive from the same root, and each is vying to get more spiritual sustenance than the other. If you would only realize that you are both two halves of the same whole then you would be happy for the other's success.

birth would she reach true fulfillment and perfection. Only through a child would she perpetuate herself, causing her "building" to remain standing through the generations (*Rabbi Meir Benjamin Menahem Danon, 19th century*).

4. Her mistress became unimportant in her eyes. Hagar thought, "Sarai's inner character is not the same as what she presents. She appears to be righteous, but she is obviously not—the proof being that in all these years she has not merited to become pregnant from Abram, whereas I became pregnant from him right away" (*Rashi, 11th century*).

6-9. Sarai mistreated her. Sarai was not, God forbid, taking revenge and afflicting Hagar for libeling her. Rather, her actions were intended as a course of character refinement.

When something goes out of shape, often the only course of action is to bend it the other way. Once Sarai

genesis 15:20 – 16:8 lekh lekha

[20] the Hittites, the Perizzites, the Rephaim, [21] the Amorites, the Canaanites, the Girgashites and the Jebusites."

Sarai Gives Her Handmaid to Abram

16 [1] Sarai, Abram's wife, had not borne him children.

She had an Egyptian handmaid named Hagar. [2] Sarai said to Abram, "Now look, God has kept me from bearing children. Please come to my handmaid. Perhaps, through her, I will become established."

Abram listened to Sarai's (prophetic) voice. [3] At the end of ten years of Abram's dwelling in the land of Canaan, Abram's wife Sarai persuaded Hagar the Egyptian, her handmaid (to consent), and she gave her to Abram her husband for a wife.

[4] He came to Hagar, and she conceived (immediately). When (Hagar) noticed that she was pregnant, her mistress (who had failed to become pregnant) became unimportant in her eyes. (Sarai cast the "evil eye" on her, causing her to miscarry).

[5] Sarai said to Abram, "May (the punishment) for wronging me (by praying only for yourself) be upon you! I gave my handmaid into your bosom, and when she saw that she had become pregnant, I became unimportant in her eyes (and you were silent). Let God judge between me and you!"

[6] Abram said to Sarai, "Here is your handmaid. Treat her as you see fit!"

Sarai mistreated her, and she ran away from her.

[7] An angel of God found her by a water fountain in the desert, by the fountain on the road to Shur.

[8] He said, "Hagar, maid of Sarai, where are you coming from? And where are you going to?"

She said, "I am running away from Sarai, my mistress."

---

children of Israel only seven nations. The remaining three lands of Edom, Moab, and Ammon—referred to in this verse as the Kenites, Kenizzites, and Kadmonites—are destined to be our heritage in the future.

The seven lands that the children of Israel conquered represent the pre-Messianic task of refining our *emotional* attributes which, according to the Kabbalah, are seven in number. Only in the future era will we receive the additional three lands, alluding to a new-found *cognitive* clarity—since, Kabbalistically, the powers of the brain are three in number (*Rabbi Ḥayyim b. Joseph Vital, 16th–17th century*).

16:2 Perhaps, through her, I will become established. You would expect Sarai to have said, "Through her I will merit having a child of my own." Rather, she used the expression *'ibbaneh*, literally, "I will be *built.*"

Sarai was rejecting the outlook that giving birth and raising children causes a woman to lose her physical build and appearance. She appreciated the deeper truth that only by giving

בראשית טז:ח - יז:ג

מִפְּנֵ֥י שָׂרַ֖י גְּבִרְתִּ֑י אָנֹכִ֖י בֹּרַֽחַת: ט וַיֹּ֤אמֶר לָהּ֙ מַלְאַ֣ךְ יְהֹוָ֔ה שׁ֖וּבִי אֶל־גְּבִרְתֵּ֑ךְ וְהִתְעַנִּ֖י תַּ֥חַת יָדֶֽיהָ: י וַיֹּ֤אמֶר לָהּ֙ מַלְאַ֣ךְ יְהֹוָ֔ה הַרְבָּ֥ה אַרְבֶּ֖ה אֶת־זַרְעֵ֑ךְ וְלֹ֥א יִסָּפֵ֖ר מֵרֹֽב: יא וַיֹּ֤אמֶר לָהּ֙ מַלְאַ֣ךְ יְהֹוָ֔ה הִנָּ֥ךְ הָרָ֖ה וְיֹלַ֣דְתְּ בֵּ֑ן וְקָרָ֤את שְׁמוֹ֙ יִשְׁמָעֵ֔אל כִּֽי־שָׁמַ֥ע יְהֹוָ֖ה אֶל־עָנְיֵֽךְ: יב וְה֤וּא יִֽהְיֶה֙ פֶּ֣רֶא אָדָ֔ם יָד֣וֹ בַכֹּ֔ל וְיַ֥ד כֹּ֖ל בּ֑וֹ וְעַל־פְּנֵ֥י כָל־אֶחָ֖יו יִשְׁכֹּֽן: יג וַתִּקְרָ֤א שֵׁם־יְהֹוָה֙ הַדֹּבֵ֣ר אֵלֶ֔יהָ אַתָּ֖ה אֵ֣ל רֳאִ֑י כִּ֣י אָֽמְרָ֗ה הֲגַ֥ם הֲלֹ֛ם רָאִ֖יתִי אַחֲרֵ֥י רֹאִֽי: יד עַל־כֵּן֙ קָרָ֣א לַבְּאֵ֔ר בְּאֵ֥ר לַחַ֖י רֹאִ֑י הִנֵּ֥ה בֵין־קָדֵ֖שׁ וּבֵ֥ין בָּֽרֶד: טו וַתֵּ֧לֶד הָגָ֛ר לְאַבְרָ֖ם בֵּ֑ן וַיִּקְרָ֨א אַבְרָ֤ם שֶׁם־בְּנ֛וֹ אֲשֶׁר־יָלְדָ֥ה הָגָ֖ר יִשְׁמָעֵֽאל: טז וְאַבְרָ֕ם בֶּן־שְׁמֹנִ֥ים שָׁנָ֖ה וְשֵׁ֣שׁ שָׁנִ֑ים בְּלֶֽדֶת־הָגָ֥ר אֶת־יִשְׁמָעֵ֖אל לְאַבְרָֽם: ס

יז א וַיְהִ֣י אַבְרָ֔ם בֶּן־תִּשְׁעִ֥ים שָׁנָ֖ה וְתֵ֣שַׁע שָׁנִ֑ים וַיֵּרָ֨א יְהֹוָ֜ה אֶל־אַבְרָ֗ם וַיֹּ֤אמֶר אֵלָיו֙ אֲנִי־אֵ֣ל שַׁדַּ֔י הִתְהַלֵּ֥ךְ לְפָנַ֖י וֶהְיֵ֥ה תָמִֽים: ב וְאֶתְּנָ֥ה בְרִיתִ֖י בֵּינִ֣י וּבֵינֶ֑ךָ וְאַרְבֶּ֥ה אוֹתְךָ֖ בִּמְאֹ֥ד מְאֹֽד: ג וַיִּפֹּ֥ל אַבְרָ֖ם עַל־פָּנָ֑יו וַיְדַבֵּ֥ר אִתּ֖וֹ

How does circumcision bring you to "perfection"? Perfection is reached when you diminish yourself and annihilate your ego before God. Your very existence "flows" from God, so—paradoxically—it is only by surrendering your ego to Him that you can sustain your existence in the most complete sense.

That is why the precept of circumcision is assigned to this particular organ, where the power of reproduction lies—the most potent of all human powers. Right here, there needs to be an indication that man is inherently deficient and that he is reliant on God in order to be whole (*Rabbi Judah Aryeh Leib Alter of Gur, 19th century*).

spiritual vitamin

> Democracy and freedom should not be a cauldron of assimilation, but rather the contrary: they offer the possibility for you to take your place, enjoy your rights and live according to your faith one hundred percent.

⁹ (Another) angel of God said to her, "Return to your mistress, and allow yourself to be subjugated under her hands."

¹⁰ (Another) angel of God said to her, "I will greatly multiply your descendants, so that they will not be (able to be) counted due to (their) great number."

¹¹ (Another) angel of God said to her, "Look! (When you return) you will conceive and bear a son. You shall name him Ishmael, for God has heard [*SHaMAʿ*] your affliction. ¹² He will be an outdoor man (who loves hunting. He will be a bandit) whose hand will be upon everyone. Everyone (will hate him and put their) hands upon him (to attack him). He will live among his (numerous) descendants."

¹³ She called in the name of God, who had spoken to her, "You are the God of Vision [*ʾEL-roʾi*] (who has seen my humiliation)!"

Because she said, "I may have seen (angels in Abram's house), but would I have expected (them) here too?" ¹⁴ Therefore the well was called Beer-lahai-roi ("the well at which the living (angel) appeared"). It is found between Kadesh and Bered.

¹⁵ Hagar bore a son to Abram. Abram (prophetically) named his son, whom Hagar had borne, Ishmael. ¹⁶ Abram was eighty-six years old when Hagar bore Ishmael to Abram.

Abram's Name Is Changed to Abraham

17 ¹ When Abram was ninety-nine years old, God appeared to Abram, and said to him, "I am the Almighty God! Come close to Me in worship and be perfect. ² I will place My covenant between Me and you, and I will multiply you very greatly."

³ Abram fell upon his face (in awe of the Divine Presence).

---

saw that Hagar had lost focus and stepped out of line by maligning her mistress, she felt it necessary to employ a "tough love" approach.

Hagar did not respond well—she ran away, not wanting to face the fact that she needed to change. It took an angel to tell her that her ego was getting in the way of her success, *"Return to your mistress, and allow yourself to be subjugated under her hands."*

The angel told her: Only when you understand and accept who you are, and who you are not, will you be successful. When you will return with a refocused mind, you will conceive a child who will grow into a great nation (*Rabbi Isaac Abravanel, 15th century*).

17:1 Come close to Me in worship and be perfect. While no one occupied himself with God's will as much as our patriarch Abram, it is only after his circumcision that the Torah refers to him as "*perfect*." From here we see the tremendous importance of circumcision (*Babylonian Talmud, Nedarim 32a*).

בראשית יז:ג-יד | לך לך

אֱלֹהִ֖ים לֵאמֹֽר׃ 4 אֲנִ֕י הִנֵּ֥ה בְרִיתִ֖י אִתָּ֑ךְ וְהָיִ֕יתָ לְאַ֖ב הֲמ֥וֹן גּוֹיִֽם׃ 5 וְלֹא־יִקָּרֵ֥א ע֛וֹד אֶת־שִׁמְךָ֖ אַבְרָ֑ם וְהָיָ֤ה שִׁמְךָ֙ אַבְרָהָ֔ם כִּ֛י אַב־הֲמ֥וֹן גּוֹיִ֖ם נְתַתִּֽיךָ׃ 6 וְהִפְרֵתִ֤י אֹֽתְךָ֙ בִּמְאֹ֣ד מְאֹ֔ד וּנְתַתִּ֖יךָ לְגוֹיִ֑ם וּמְלָכִ֖ים מִמְּךָ֥ יֵצֵֽאוּ׃ [SEVENTH READING] 7 וַהֲקִמֹתִ֨י אֶת־בְּרִיתִ֜י בֵּינִ֣י וּבֵינֶ֗ךָ וּבֵ֨ין זַרְעֲךָ֧ אַחֲרֶ֛יךָ לְדֹרֹתָ֖ם לִבְרִ֣ית עוֹלָ֑ם לִהְי֤וֹת לְךָ֙ לֵֽאלֹהִ֔ים וּֽלְזַרְעֲךָ֖ אַחֲרֶֽיךָ׃ 8 וְנָתַתִּ֣י לְ֠ךָ֠ וּלְזַרְעֲךָ֨ אַחֲרֶ֜יךָ אֵ֣ת ׀ אֶ֣רֶץ מְגֻרֶ֗יךָ אֵ֚ת כָּל־אֶ֣רֶץ כְּנַ֔עַן לַאֲחֻזַּ֖ת עוֹלָ֑ם וְהָיִ֥יתִי לָהֶ֖ם לֵאלֹהִֽים׃ 9 וַיֹּ֤אמֶר אֱלֹהִים֙ אֶל־אַבְרָהָ֔ם וְאַתָּ֖ה אֶת־בְּרִיתִ֣י תִשְׁמֹ֑ר אַתָּ֛ה וְזַרְעֲךָ֥ אַֽחֲרֶ֖יךָ לְדֹרֹתָֽם׃ 10 זֹ֣את בְּרִיתִ֞י אֲשֶׁ֣ר תִּשְׁמְר֗וּ בֵּינִי֙ וּבֵ֣ינֵיכֶ֔ם וּבֵ֥ין זַרְעֲךָ֖ אַחֲרֶ֑יךָ הִמּ֥וֹל לָכֶ֖ם כָּל־זָכָֽר׃ 11 וּנְמַלְתֶּ֕ם אֵ֖ת בְּשַׂ֣ר עָרְלַתְכֶ֑ם וְהָיָה֙ לְא֣וֹת בְּרִ֔ית בֵּינִ֖י וּבֵינֵיכֶֽם׃ 12 וּבֶן־שְׁמֹנַ֣ת יָמִ֗ים יִמּ֥וֹל לָכֶ֛ם כָּל־זָכָ֖ר לְדֹרֹתֵיכֶ֑ם יְלִ֣יד בָּ֔יִת וּמִקְנַת־כֶּ֨סֶף֙ מִכֹּ֣ל בֶּן־נֵכָ֔ר אֲשֶׁ֛ר לֹ֥א מִֽזַּרְעֲךָ֖ הֽוּא׃ 13 הִמּ֧וֹל ׀ יִמּ֛וֹל יְלִ֥יד בֵּיתְךָ֖ וּמִקְנַ֣ת כַּסְפֶּ֑ךָ וְהָיְתָ֧ה בְרִיתִ֛י בִּבְשַׂרְכֶ֖ם לִבְרִ֥ית עוֹלָֽם׃ 14 וְעָרֵ֣ל ׀ זָכָ֗ר אֲשֶׁ֤ר לֹֽא־יִמּוֹל֙ אֶת־בְּשַׂ֣ר עָרְלָת֔וֹ וְנִכְרְתָ֛ה הַנֶּ֥פֶשׁ הַהִ֖וא

explicitly commanded, in the understanding that this was a superior form of worship. However, he did so on the basis that after being commanded by God to observe the precept, he would *continue* to do so and receive the additional merit of "fulfilling a mandatory commandment." Circumcision, however, can be performed only *once*, making this approach impossible (*Rabbi Israel Hapstein of Kozienice, 18th century*).

kabbalah bites

17:5 *The greatest virtue is to reveal the Divine in everything. The greatest crime is to conceal it.*

"Abram" ('av-ram) means "lofty wisdom," suggesting a mastery of the monotheistic idea. Through changing his name, God gave AbraHam the gift of communication, signified by the addition of the Hebrew letter *he*. The full width and height of the *he* (ה) signifies the ability to take an idea and flesh it out in all directions, rendering it clear and engaging to the intended audience.

Therefore, "one who refers to Abraham as Abram commits a sin" (*Babylonian Talmud, Berakhot* 13a), because our most sacred task is to *communicate* the mystically inspired message of pure monotheism.

God spoke with him, saying, [4] "As for Me, this is My covenant with you: you shall become the father of a multitude of nations. [5] Your name shall no longer be called Abram, but your name shall be Abraham [*AVraHAM*], for I have made you the father of a multitude [*AV-HAMon*] of nations. [6] I will make you extremely fruitful. I will make you into the nations (of Israel and Edom), and kings will emerge from you. [SEVENTH READING] [7] I will establish My covenant between Me and between you and between your descendants after you throughout their generations as an everlasting covenant, to be to you for a God and to your descendants after you. [8] I will give you, and your descendants after you, the land in which you live, the entire land of Canaan, as an everlasting possession. I will be God to the (inhabitants of the land)."

The Covenant of Circumcision

[9] God said to Abraham, "As for you, you should keep My covenant, you and your descendants after you, throughout their generations. [10] This is My covenant, which you should observe between Me and you, and your seed after you: that every male among you should be circumcised.

- ❖ [11] You should circumcise the flesh of your foreskin, and it will be the sign of a covenant between Me and you.

- ❖ [12] At the age of eight days, every male shall be circumcised to you, throughout your generations, one that is born in the house (to a slavewoman), or one that is purchased with money (after he is born) from any foreigner, who is not of your seed. [13] Those born in your house and those purchased with your money shall be circumcised, and My covenant shall be in your flesh as an everlasting covenant.

- ❖ [14] (As for) an uncircumcised male who does not circumcise the flesh of his foreskin, (when he reaches the age of liability,) that soul will be cut off from its people (so that he remains childless, and dies before his time). He has broken My covenant."

5. Your name shall be Abraham, for I have made you the father of a multitude of nations. The name Abraham (*'av-ra-ham*) is formed from the first part of the phrase *"father of a multitude of nations"* (*'av-hamon-goyim*), with the addition of the letter *resh*, which Abraham carried over from his original name, Abram.

The meaning of his original title, Abram, is "father of Aram" (*'av-[A]ram*), for at that point he was only a patriarchal figure in his native region of Aram. Now, however, God promised that Abraham would become a father to all humanity (*Rashi, 11th century*).

10. Every male among you should be circumcised. Abraham fulfilled the commandment of circumcision only after God's direct command, despite having fulfilled all of the remaining commandments on his own volition without being commanded. Why?

"One who fulfils a mandatory commandment is superior to one who acts voluntarily" (*Babylonian Talmud, Kiddushin* 31a). Abraham fulfilled the other precepts without being

בראשית יז:יד-כז

מֵעַמֶּיהָ אֶת־בְּרִיתִי הֵפַר: ס 15 וַיֹּאמֶר אֱלֹהִים אֶל־אַבְרָהָם שָׂרַי אִשְׁתְּךָ לֹא־תִקְרָא אֶת־שְׁמָהּ שָׂרָי כִּי שָׂרָה שְׁמָהּ: 16 וּבֵרַכְתִּי אֹתָהּ וְגַם נָתַתִּי מִמֶּנָּה לְךָ בֵּן וּבֵרַכְתִּיהָ וְהָיְתָה לְגוֹיִם מַלְכֵי עַמִּים מִמֶּנָּה יִהְיוּ: 17 וַיִּפֹּל אַבְרָהָם עַל־פָּנָיו וַיִּצְחָק וַיֹּאמֶר בְּלִבּוֹ הַלְּבֶן מֵאָה־שָׁנָה יִוָּלֵד וְאִם־שָׂרָה הֲבַת־תִּשְׁעִים שָׁנָה תֵּלֵד: 18 וַיֹּאמֶר אַבְרָהָם אֶל־הָאֱלֹהִים לוּ יִשְׁמָעֵאל יִחְיֶה לְפָנֶיךָ: 19 וַיֹּאמֶר אֱלֹהִים אֲבָל שָׂרָה אִשְׁתְּךָ יֹלֶדֶת לְךָ בֵּן וְקָרָאתָ אֶת־שְׁמוֹ יִצְחָק וַהֲקִמֹתִי אֶת־בְּרִיתִי אִתּוֹ לִבְרִית עוֹלָם לְזַרְעוֹ אַחֲרָיו: 20 וּלְיִשְׁמָעֵאל שְׁמַעְתִּיךָ הִנֵּה | בֵּרַכְתִּי אֹתוֹ וְהִפְרֵיתִי אֹתוֹ וְהִרְבֵּיתִי אֹתוֹ בִּמְאֹד מְאֹד שְׁנֵים־עָשָׂר נְשִׂיאִם יוֹלִיד וּנְתַתִּיו לְגוֹי גָּדוֹל: 21 וְאֶת־בְּרִיתִי אָקִים אֶת־יִצְחָק אֲשֶׁר תֵּלֵד לְךָ שָׂרָה לַמּוֹעֵד הַזֶּה בַּשָּׁנָה הָאַחֶרֶת: 22 וַיְכַל לְדַבֵּר אִתּוֹ וַיַּעַל אֱלֹהִים מֵעַל אַבְרָהָם: 23 וַיִּקַּח אַבְרָהָם אֶת־יִשְׁמָעֵאל בְּנוֹ וְאֵת כָּל־יְלִידֵי בֵיתוֹ וְאֵת כָּל־מִקְנַת כַּסְפּוֹ כָּל־זָכָר בְּאַנְשֵׁי בֵּית אַבְרָהָם וַיָּמָל אֶת־בְּשַׂר עָרְלָתָם בְּעֶצֶם הַיּוֹם הַזֶּה כַּאֲשֶׁר דִּבֶּר אִתּוֹ אֱלֹהִים: 24 [MAFTIR] וְאַבְרָהָם בֶּן־תִּשְׁעִים וָתֵשַׁע שָׁנָה בְּהִמֹּלוֹ בְּשַׂר עָרְלָתוֹ: 25 וְיִשְׁמָעֵאל בְּנוֹ בֶּן־שְׁלֹשׁ עֶשְׂרֵה שָׁנָה בְּהִמֹּלוֹ אֵת בְּשַׂר עָרְלָתוֹ: 26 בְּעֶצֶם הַיּוֹם הַזֶּה נִמּוֹל אַבְרָהָם וְיִשְׁמָעֵאל בְּנוֹ: 27 וְכָל־אַנְשֵׁי בֵיתוֹ יְלִיד בָּיִת וּמִקְנַת־כֶּסֶף מֵאֵת בֶּן־נֵכָר נִמֹּלוּ אִתּוֹ: פ פ פ

קכ"ו פסוקים, נמל"ו סימן, מכנדי"ב סימן.

The Torah emphasizes the *effect* of undergoing a circumcision, the most obvious and immediate effect being considerable pain. Abraham felt substantial pain from his circumcision, in order that God should double his reward (*Genesis Rabbah*).

The verse states, "My covenant shall be *in your flesh*" (above, 17:13), which suggests that the *flesh itself* should feel the effects of the covenant. The sensation of pain is actually a fundamental part of the commandment of circumcision, and a failure to feel pain would mean that God's covenant had not properly penetrated the body.

Consequently, if Abraham would not have felt pain while, and as a result of, circumcising himself, then he would not have been observing the commandment properly. Therefore, despite his great joy and spiritual elation at fulfilling this great precept, Abraham *forced himself* to be aware of the natural pain which his body was experiencing, so that God's covenant should penetrate his physical body (*Rabbi Meir b. Aaron Judah Arik, 19th century*).

genesis 17:15–27 — lekh lekha

Sarai's Name is Changed—She is Promised a Child

¹⁵ God said to Abraham, "As for your wife Sarai, you shall not call her by the name Sarai, for Sarah is now her name. ¹⁶ I will bless her (so that she can produce milk), and I will also give you a son from her. I will bless her, and she will become (a mother of) nations. Kings of nations will come from her."

¹⁷ Abraham fell on his face and rejoiced. He said to himself, "Could (anyone be so fortunate as I,) that a child be born to a person who is a hundred years old? Could (anyone be so fortunate as) Sarah, who, at ninety years old, (will have the merit) of giving birth?"

¹⁸ Abraham said to God, "If only Ishmael will live (in fear of) You, (that would be sufficient)!"

¹⁹ God said, "Indeed, your wife Sarah will bear you a son, and you will name him Isaac. I will establish My covenant with him as an everlasting covenant for his descendants after him. ²⁰ Regarding Ishmael, I have heard you. Look! I have blessed him, I will make him fruitful, and extremely numerous. He will father twelve princes, and I will make him into a great nation. ²¹ But I will establish My covenant with Isaac, whom Sarah will bear to you at this time next year."

²² He finished speaking with him, and God ascended from Abraham.

Abraham Circumcises Himself and His Household

²³ Abraham took Ishmael his son, all those born in his house and all those purchased with his money—every male of the people of Abraham's household—and he circumcised the flesh of their foreskins on that very day, as God had told him.

[MAFTIR] ²⁴ Abraham was ninety-nine years old, when the flesh of his foreskin was circumcised.

²⁵ Ishmael his son was thirteen years old, when he had the flesh of his foreskin circumcised. ²⁶ On that very day, Abraham was circumcised, and (so was) Ishmael his son. ²⁷ All the people of his household, those born in his house and those bought with money from foreigners, were circumcised with him.

The Haftarah for Lekh Lekha is on page 1293.

---

15. For Sarah is now her name. The meaning of the name Sarah is the same as Sarai—"princess." The difference is that Sarai translates as *"my* princess," indicating that initially she was a sovereign only of her own people. Sarah, on the other hand, simply means "princess," without limiting her to a particular nation or region. This indicates an expanded, universal influence (*Babylonian Talmud, Berakhot* 13a).

26. On that very day, Abraham was circumcised. Why does the Torah use the *passive* phrase, "Abraham *was* circumcised," when the previous verses indicate that Abraham actively circumcised himself?

> Just as **God** revealed Himself to Abraham, He also **reveals Himself to you.** But you need to learn how to discern the more subtle, **contemporary forms of revelation,** and to constantly **beseech** God that His revelations to you should be more **overt.**

VA-YERA'
וירא

THREE ANGELS VISIT ABRAHAM	18:1–15
DESTRUCTION OF SODOM AND GOMORRAH	18:16 – 19:38
ABIMELECH SEIZES SARAH	20:1–18
BIRTH OF ISAAC	21:1–8
EXPULSION OF HAGAR AND ISHMAEL	21:9–21
ABIMELECH MAKES COVENANT WITH ABRAHAM	21:22–34
THE BINDING OF ISAAC	22:1–19
BIRTH OF REBEKAH	22:20–24

NAME
Va-Yera'

MEANING
"And He appeared"

LINES IN TORAH SCROLL
252

PARASHIYYOT
4 open; 2 closed

VERSES
147

WORDS
2085

LETTERS
7862

DATE
2047–2085

LOCATION
Plains of Mamre, Sodom, Zoar, Gerar (land of the Philistines), Desert of Beer-sheba, Mount Moriah, Hebron

KEY PEOPLE
Abraham, three angels, Sarah, Lot and his family, Abimelech, Isaac, Ishmael, Hagar

MASORETIC FEATURES
The word 'elayv (18:9) has three dots above it.

CHARACTER PROFILE

NAME
Isaac

PARENTS
Abraham and Sarah

GRANDFATHERS
Terah, Haran

WIFE
Rebekah

CHILDREN
Jacob and Esau

LIFE SPAN
180 years

BURIAL PLACE
Cave of Machpelah

ACHIEVEMENTS
At the age of 37, he was ready to offer himself up as a sacrifice to fulfil the word of God; dug wells

KNOWN FOR
A visitation of angels announced his conception; was childless for 20 years before having Jacob and Esau; bore a strong resemblance to Abraham; became blind; died by a "kiss" from the Divine Presence

HOSPITALITY

When the three angels appeared, Abraham jumped up and ran towards them, interrupting his conversation with God. From this we learn that "welcoming guests is greater than welcoming the Divine Presence" (18:2).

MIRACLES

Sarah was ninety years old, physically unable to bear children. Yet God reversed nature and she gave birth to Isaac. Look for God's miracles daily. Your life is full of them (21:1).

PRAYER

Abraham pleaded for Sodom, even though God's decree had already been sealed. Always continue to beseech God to answer your prayers, even when it seems that all hope is lost (18:23–33).

בראשית יח:א-ו | וירא

יח 1 וַיֵּרָ֤א אֵלָיו֙ יְהֹוָ֔ה בְּאֵלֹנֵ֖י מַמְרֵ֑א וְה֛וּא יֹשֵׁ֥ב פֶּֽתַח־הָאֹ֖הֶל כְּחֹ֥ם הַיּֽוֹם: 2 וַיִּשָּׂ֤א עֵינָיו֙ וַיַּ֔רְא וְהִנֵּה֙ שְׁלֹשָׁ֣ה אֲנָשִׁ֔ים נִצָּבִ֖ים עָלָ֑יו וַיַּ֗רְא וַיָּ֤רָץ לִקְרָאתָם֙ מִפֶּ֣תַח הָאֹ֔הֶל וַיִּשְׁתַּ֖חוּ אָֽרְצָה: 3 וַיֹּאמַ֑ר אֲדֹנָ֗י אִם־נָ֨א מָצָ֤אתִי חֵן֙ בְּעֵינֶ֔יךָ אַל־נָ֥א תַעֲבֹ֖ר מֵעַ֥ל עַבְדֶּֽךָ: 4 יֻקַּֽח־נָ֣א מְעַט־מַ֔יִם וְרַחֲצ֖וּ רַגְלֵיכֶ֑ם וְהִֽשָּׁעֲנ֖וּ תַּ֥חַת הָעֵֽץ: 5 וְאֶקְחָ֨ה פַת־לֶ֜חֶם וְסַעֲד֤וּ לִבְּכֶם֙ אַחַ֣ר תַּעֲבֹ֔רוּ כִּֽי־עַל־כֵּ֥ן עֲבַרְתֶּ֖ם עַל־עַבְדְּכֶ֑ם וַיֹּ֣אמְר֔וּ כֵּ֥ן תַּעֲשֶׂ֖ה כַּאֲשֶׁ֥ר דִּבַּֽרְתָּ: 6 וַיְמַהֵ֧ר אַבְרָהָ֛ם הָאֹ֖הֱלָה אֶל־שָׂרָ֑ה וַיֹּ֗אמֶר מַהֲרִ֞י שְׁלֹ֤שׁ סְאִים֙ קֶ֣מַח סֹ֔לֶת ל֖וּשִׁי וַעֲשִׂ֥י עֻגֽוֹת:

"And—look!—three men were standing there"—the *Zohar* teaches that these three "men" were the embodiment of Abraham himself, Isaac, and Jacob. When "God appears to you," each day, your instant reaction is to remember the sanctity of your ancestors, the Patriarchs, to "run towards them" and say, "When will my deeds equal theirs?" (*Rabbi Menahem Nahum of Chernobyl, 18th century*).

2. Three (angels, in the form of) men were standing in front of him. There are many different levels of prophecy, largely depending on the quality of prophet. When the angels appeared to Abraham, who had reached a very high spiritual standing, they appeared as fellow men. To Lot, whose spiritual caliber was much inferior, they appeared as angels; and he perceived them as frightening and terrifying (*Maimonides, 12th century*).

4. Please, let some water be brought. In reward for Abraham's three acts of hospitality to wayfarers, his descendants merited three Divine favors while wandering through the Sinai Desert. As a reward for the cream and milk he served to strangers (v. 8), his descendants received the manna. As a reward for standing over them like a waiter (ibid.), they received a pillar of cloud that escorted them through the wilderness. And as a reward for Abraham's command, *"Let some water be brought,"* they merited the Well of Miriam, which accompanied them on their travels, supplying them with water (*Babylonian Talmud, Bava Metzia* 86b).

6. Abraham rushed to Sarah's tent. Here we see the importance of acting quickly for your guests, especially when they are poor (*Rabbi Alexander Zusya Friedman, 20th century*).

kabbalah bites

18:2 The two millennia of *tohu* (chaos), during which mankind had demonstrated highly dysfunctional behavior patterns, was drawing to a close. Now God was to send souls of *tikkun* (spiritual repair), through Abraham and his seed, who would eventually heal the world and usher in the New Era of the Messiah.

All *"three (angels in the form of) men"* were necessary to signal this juncture of history: Angel Michael brought news of Isaac's imminent birth, the beginning of the souls of *tikkun*; Angel Gabriel overturned Sodom, where the soul of the Messiah was trapped; and Angel Raphael rescued Lot, ancestor of King David and, ultimately, the Messiah.

genesis 18:1–6 — va-yera'

parashat va-yera'

Three Angels Visit Abraham

18 ¹ God appeared to (Abraham) in the plains of Mamre (three days after his circumcision), while he was sitting at the entrance of the tent (looking for passersby to welcome), in the heat of the day.

² He looked around and saw—look!—three (angels, in the form of) men were standing in front of him. (He realized that they did not wish to trouble him,) so he ran toward them from the entrance of the tent, and he prostrated himself on the ground.

³ He said, "My lords! If I have found favor in your eyes, please do not go away from your servant!"

⁴ "Please, let some water be brought (by my staff) so you can bathe your feet and recline under the tree. ⁵ I will get some bread for you to satisfy your hearts. Afterwards, you may continue on. (I ask this of you) because you have (honored me by) visiting your servant."

They said, "Do what you have suggested."

⁶ Abraham rushed to Sarah's tent, and he said, "Quickly, get three *se'ah* of sifted flour, knead them and make loaves!"

---

food for thought

1. Is having guests a joy or a burden for you?

2. How much would you inconvenience yourself to help a stranger?

3. To what extent, if any, should you neglect your own needs to help others?

18:1 God appeared. God revealed Himself in order to visit the sick. It was the third day from Abraham's circumcision, and God came to inquire about his welfare (*Rashi, 11th century*).

When God revealed Himself to Abraham, this healed him. The Divine revelation was a cure for the sickness caused by his circumcision, as the verse states, *"In the light of the King's countenance there is life"* (*Proverbs 16:15; Naḥmanides, 12th century*).

The Kabbalah speaks of "fifty gates" of spiritual understanding, forty-nine of which can be achieved by a person as a result of his own initiative. The final, fiftieth gate is then granted by God from above.

When Abraham had circumcised himself, he had reached the greatest degree of spiritual perfection that he could possibly achieve as a human being—the forty-ninth gate—and he became "sick" yearning for the fiftieth gate. This is alluded to by the fact that the Hebrew term for a sick person, *ḥoleh*, has the numerical value of forty-nine (*Rabbi Menaḥem Mendel Schneerson, 20th century*).

God appeared ... and—look!—three men were standing there. *"God appeared to him"*—God manifests Himself within every person. Every day, you will experience an awakening as He "appears" to you with thoughts of returning closer to Him.

בראשית יח:ז-י · וירא

7 וְאֶל־הַבָּקָר רָץ אַבְרָהָם וַיִּקַּח בֶּן־בָּקָר רַךְ וָטוֹב וַיִּתֵּן אֶל־הַנַּעַר וַיְמַהֵר לַעֲשׂוֹת אֹתוֹ: 8 וַיִּקַּח חֶמְאָה וְחָלָב וּבֶן־הַבָּקָר אֲשֶׁר עָשָׂה וַיִּתֵּן לִפְנֵיהֶם וְהוּא־עֹמֵד עֲלֵיהֶם תַּחַת הָעֵץ וַיֹּאכֵלוּ: 9 וַיֹּאמְרוּ אֵלָיו אַיֵּה שָׂרָה אִשְׁתֶּךָ וַיֹּאמֶר הִנֵּה בָאֹהֶל: 10 וַיֹּאמֶר שׁוֹב אָשׁוּב אֵלֶיךָ כָּעֵת חַיָּה וְהִנֵּה־בֵן לְשָׂרָה אִשְׁתֶּךָ וְשָׂרָה

God had appeared to Abraham (v. 1), but when Abraham noticed some potential guests approaching, he exclaimed, *"My Lord!—referring to God—Please do not go away from Your servant"* (v. 3), asking God to wait while he attended to the guests. This teaches you that attending to guests is greater than welcoming the Divine Presence (*Babylonian Talmud, Shabbat* 127a).

You might have thought that attending to guests is *not* greater than welcoming the Divine Presence, because sometimes hosting guests leads you to neglect the study of Torah or to inadvertently utter words of gossip. The Talmud therefore informs you that, despite these valid concerns, attending to guests is greater (*Rabbi Israel Ba'al Shem Tov, 18th century*).

With the above words, the Ba'al Shem Tov was addressing an unspoken question on the Talmud's teaching. If the performance of any Biblical command draws the Divine Presence into our midst, then surely this is achieved by attending to guests too? If so, why does the Talmud present the idea of hosting guests as an alternative to welcoming the Divine Presence when, in practice, both will be achieved at the same time?

The *Ba'al Shem Tov* answered that sometimes when we entertain, we fail to draw down the Divine Presence, due to gossip, etc. Nevertheless, even in such a situation the Talmud informs us that attending to guests is greater than welcoming the Divine Presence (*Rabbi Israel Hager of Vizhnitz, 19th century*).

9. They said to him, "Where is Sarah your wife?" The Hebrew word *"to him," 'elayv*, is spelled *alef-lamed-yod-vav*. In the Torah scroll, dots are inscribed above three of these letters: *alef-yod-vov*, which taken on their own spell the word *'ayyo, "Where is he?"* This hints to the fact that, in addition to asking Abraham as to Sarah's whereabouts, the angels also questioned Sarah, "Where is Abraham?" From here you learn that a person should always inquire from his host about his hostess, and from his hostess about his host (*Rashi, 11th century*).

The ministering angels knew where Sarah was to be found. Nevertheless, they inquired as to her whereabouts to emphasize her modesty to Abraham, in order to endear her to her husband.

Rabbi Yose son of Ḥanina taught that the angels asked after Sarah in order to send her wine from the "cup of blessing" over which the Grace After Meals had been recited (*Babylonian Talmud, Bava Metzia* 87a).

If Sarah was very modest, then why did she accept wine from strange men? It would appear somewhat inappropriate for Sarah to drink from their cup?

Consider, however, that the author of this teaching, Rabbi Yose son of Ḥanina, is also the author of another, better-known teaching: *"A woman recognizes the nature of her guests more than a man"* (*Babylonian Talmud, Berakhot* 10b). Sarah would have recognized, more than Abraham, that her guests were actually angels. It was thus not immodest of her to accept their cup of blessing, since she was aware of their true identity (*Rabbi Menahem Mendel Schneerson, 20th century*).

genesis 18:7–10 — va-yera'

⁷ Abraham ran to the cattle, took (three) tender and good calves, and he gave (them) to the young lad (Ishmael), and he hurried to prepare (three cooked tongues with mustard).

⁸ He took cream, milk and the calves that he had prepared, and placed them in front of (the angels). He stood over them, under the tree, as they (pretended) to eat.

⁹ They said to him, "Where is Sarah your wife?"

He said, "Here, in the tent."

¹⁰ (One angel) said (on behalf of God), "I will be returning to you at this time next year, and then, your wife Sarah will have a son."

---

8. Cream, milk and the calves. Abraham served them little by little. As each item was prepared, he immediately brought it to them (*Rashi, 11th century*).

Abraham served them both dairy and meat—*"cream, milk and the calves."* However, since he did not serve them everything at once (as *Rashi* explains), he avoided serving them meat and milk together, which is forbidden by the Torah. Abraham served milk and then *afterwards* meat, which is permissible (*The Tosafists, 12th–14th centuries*).

He offered each of the angels either milk *or* meat. Abraham prepared *"three calves' tongues"* to give each of the guests the option of eating meat. However, he then "took the cream, milk and the calves that he had prepared, and *placed it in front of the angels"* so that they could choose either dairy or meat. This was done in order to fulfil the sacred duty of hosting guests in the best possible fashion. No guest, however, was served milk and meat simultaneously (*Rabbi Jacob Culi, 18th century*).

The angels who visited Abraham were polar opposites, spiritually speaking. Michael was from the "right side" of *ḥesed*, kindness, and Gabriel from the "left side" of *gevurah*, severity (*Zohar*). Abraham's task was to bring harmony between them and to temper their characteristics. Therefore, he served them milk and meat—milk has an affinity to *ḥesed*, which gave him the opportunity to speak to them about the esoteric meaning of milk and the concept of *ḥesed*. Afterwards, he served them meat, which has an affinity to *gevurah*, and he provided them with an explanation about the esoteric meaning of meat. Using this approach, he was successful in harmonizing the angels and tempering their traits (*Rabbi Menahem Mendel of Rymanow, 18th century*).

As they (pretended) to eat. The angels pretended to eat like men. From here we learn that you should not deviate from the local custom (*Rashi, 11th century*).

spiritual vitamin

> Abraham's actions always exceeded his words, and he always did a great deal more than he promised. It befits us, who are called the children of Abraham, to follow in his footsteps.

בראשית יח:י-כא / וירא

שֹׁמַעַת פֶּתַח הָאֹהֶל וְהוּא אַחֲרָיו: 11 וְאַבְרָהָם וְשָׂרָה זְקֵנִים בָּאִים בַּיָּמִים חָדַל לִהְיוֹת לְשָׂרָה אֹרַח כַּנָּשִׁים: 12 וַתִּצְחַק שָׂרָה בְּקִרְבָּהּ לֵאמֹר אַחֲרֵי בְלֹתִי הָיְתָה־לִּי עֶדְנָה וַאדֹנִי זָקֵן: 13 וַיֹּאמֶר יְהוָה אֶל־אַבְרָהָם לָמָּה זֶּה צָחֲקָה שָׂרָה לֵאמֹר הַאַף אֻמְנָם אֵלֵד וַאֲנִי זָקַנְתִּי: 14 הֲיִפָּלֵא מֵיְהוָה דָּבָר לַמּוֹעֵד אָשׁוּב אֵלֶיךָ כָּעֵת חַיָּה וּלְשָׂרָה בֵן: 15 [SECOND READING] וַתְּכַחֵשׁ שָׂרָה | לֵאמֹר לֹא צָחַקְתִּי כִּי | יָרֵאָה וַיֹּאמֶר | לֹא כִּי צָחָקְתְּ: 16 וַיָּקֻמוּ מִשָּׁם הָאֲנָשִׁים וַיַּשְׁקִפוּ עַל־פְּנֵי סְדֹם וְאַבְרָהָם הֹלֵךְ עִמָּם לְשַׁלְּחָם: 17 וַיהוָה אָמָר הַמֲכַסֶּה אֲנִי מֵאַבְרָהָם אֲשֶׁר אֲנִי עֹשֶׂה: 18 וְאַבְרָהָם הָיוֹ יִהְיֶה לְגוֹי גָּדוֹל וְעָצוּם וְנִבְרְכוּ־בוֹ כֹּל גּוֹיֵי הָאָרֶץ: 19 כִּי יְדַעְתִּיו לְמַעַן אֲשֶׁר יְצַוֶּה אֶת־בָּנָיו וְאֶת־בֵּיתוֹ אַחֲרָיו וְשָׁמְרוּ דֶּרֶךְ יְהוָה לַעֲשׂוֹת צְדָקָה וּמִשְׁפָּט לְמַעַן הָבִיא יְהוָה עַל־אַבְרָהָם אֵת אֲשֶׁר־דִּבֶּר עָלָיו: 20 וַיֹּאמֶר יְהוָה זַעֲקַת סְדֹם וַעֲמֹרָה כִּי־רָבָּה וְחַטָּאתָם כִּי כָבְדָה מְאֹד: 21 אֵרֲדָה־נָּא וְאֶרְאֶה הַכְּצַעֲקָתָהּ הַבָּאָה אֵלַי עָשׂוּ | כָּלָה וְאִם־לֹא אֵדָעָה:

---

12. Sarah laughed. Sarah laughed, but Abraham rejoiced (v. 17). Abraham believed and rejoiced, but Sarah did not believe and she ridiculed. For this reason God was angry with Sarah (v. 13), but He was not angry with Abraham (*Rashi, 11th century*).

13. Is it really true (*ha-'af 'umnam*) that I will give birth? Why should Sarah, a prophetess of God, have been so surprised at the prospect of God enacting a miracle?

The answer lies in the word *'af*, which can also mean "anger." Sarah's disbelief was: At a time when there is so much anger in the world, how could God shine such Divine illumination on us? (*Rabbi Menahem Nahum Twersky of Chernobyl, 18th century*).

20. The outcry of Sodom. There was a certain girl who would bring bread out to the poor when nobody was looking, hiding it in her pitcher when she went to draw water. Eventually, her secret was discovered, and they smeared her with honey and placed her on top of the city wall. Bees came and devoured her. It was her cries in particular to which God referred in deciding the fate of Sodom (*Babylonian Talmud, Sanhedrin* 109b and *Rashi*, ibid.).

21. I will descend now and see: if they have actually caused the outcry which has reached Me. Many have asked the question: Why did the omniscient God have to "descend" to Sodom to see if His judgment had been correct?

There are two types of Divine judgment for an inappropriate action: *individual* judgment and *cultural-contextual* judgment. In the case of individual judgment, each deed is measured on its own merits according to the values of the Torah, and, "*He who commits even a single transgression acquires for himself a single accuser*" (*Avot* 4:11).

Sarah heard from the entrance of the tent, which was right behind (the angel).

¹¹ Abraham and Sarah were old, (but still) immersed in daily life. Sarah had stopped having a woman's cycle. ¹² (Looking at) her bodily organs, Sarah laughed, saying, "After I have withered, will I (now) have smooth skin? And my husband is old!"

¹³ God said to Abraham, "Why did Sarah laugh, saying, 'Is it really true that I will give birth, even though I am old'? ¹⁴ Is anything hidden from God? I will return to you at the time (which we have just) fixed, this time next year, and Sarah will have a son."

¹⁵ Sarah denied it, saying, "I didn't laugh," because she was afraid.

He said, "No. You did laugh."

Abraham Pleads for Sodom and Gomorrah

[SECOND READING] ¹⁶ The (angels) got up from there, and gazed (disparagingly) upon Sodom. Abraham went with them to escort them.

¹⁷ God said, "(How) could I conceal from Abraham what I am doing (to Sodom, in the very land I promised to give to him)?" ¹⁸ (Since Abraham was mentioned by God, He blessed him:) "Abraham will become a great and powerful nation, and all the nations of the world will be blessed through him. ¹⁹ For I have known (and cherished) him because he instructs his sons and his household after him to keep the way of God, acting with charity and justice. (He instructs them to do so) in order that God will bring upon Abraham everything He had said (He would do for) him."

²⁰ (Keeping to His word,) God said (to Abraham), "Since the outcry of Sodom and Gomorrah has become great, and since their sin has become very grave, ²¹ I will descend now and see: if they have actually caused the outcry which has reached Me, then (there will be) destruction! If not, I will know (how to punish them)."

---

11. Abraham and Sarah were old, (but still) immersed in daily life. Their days were whole, and not lacking. Not a day passed when they did not worship God (*Zohar*).

spiritual vitamin

> "*Judge every person favorably*" (*Avot* 1:6). If you meet a person who has not yet attained the standards of religion and morality which you hold dear, the approach must still be that of respect and affection.

ויראבראשית יח:כב-ל

22 וַיִּפְנ֤וּ מִשָּׁם֙ הָֽאֲנָשִׁ֔ים וַיֵּלְכ֖וּ סְדֹ֑מָה וְאַ֨בְרָהָ֔ם עוֹדֶ֥נּוּ עֹמֵ֖ד לִפְנֵ֥י יְהֹוָֽה: 23 וַיִּגַּ֥שׁ אַבְרָהָ֖ם וַיֹּאמַ֑ר הַאַ֣ף תִּסְפֶּ֔ה צַדִּ֖יק עִם־רָשָֽׁע: 24 אוּלַ֛י יֵ֛שׁ חֲמִשִּׁ֥ים צַדִּיקִ֖ם בְּת֣וֹךְ הָעִ֑יר הַאַ֤ף תִּסְפֶּה֙ וְלֹא־תִשָּׂ֣א לַמָּק֔וֹם לְמַ֛עַן חֲמִשִּׁ֥ים הַצַּדִּיקִ֖ם אֲשֶׁ֥ר בְּקִרְבָּֽהּ: 25 חָלִ֨לָה לְּךָ֜ מֵעֲשֹׂ֣ת ׀ כַּדָּבָ֣ר הַזֶּ֗ה לְהָמִ֤ית צַדִּיק֙ עִם־רָשָׁ֔ע וְהָיָ֥ה כַצַּדִּ֖יק כָּרָשָׁ֑ע חָלִ֣לָה לָּ֔ךְ הֲשֹׁפֵט֙ כָּל־הָאָ֔רֶץ לֹ֥א יַעֲשֶׂ֖ה מִשְׁפָּֽט: 26 וַיֹּ֣אמֶר יְהֹוָ֔ה אִם־אֶמְצָ֥א בִסְדֹ֛ם חֲמִשִּׁ֥ים צַדִּיקִ֖ם בְּת֣וֹךְ הָעִ֑יר וְנָשָׂ֥אתִי לְכָל־הַמָּק֖וֹם בַּעֲבוּרָֽם: 27 וַיַּ֥עַן אַבְרָהָ֖ם וַיֹּאמַ֑ר הִנֵּה־נָ֤א הוֹאַ֙לְתִּי֙ לְדַבֵּ֣ר אֶל־אֲדֹנָ֔י וְאָנֹכִ֖י עָפָ֥ר וָאֵֽפֶר: 28 אוּלַ֠י יַחְסְר֞וּן חֲמִשִּׁ֤ים הַצַּדִּיקִם֙ חֲמִשָּׁ֔ה הֲתַשְׁחִ֥ית בַּחֲמִשָּׁ֖ה אֶת־כָּל־הָעִ֑יר וַיֹּ֙אמֶר֙ לֹ֣א אַשְׁחִ֔ית אִם־אֶמְצָ֣א שָׁ֔ם אַרְבָּעִ֖ים וַחֲמִשָּֽׁה: 29 וַיֹּ֨סֶף ע֜וֹד לְדַבֵּ֤ר אֵלָיו֙ וַיֹּאמַ֔ר אוּלַ֛י יִמָּצְא֥וּן שָׁ֖ם אַרְבָּעִ֑ים וַיֹּ֙אמֶר֙ לֹ֣א אֶֽעֱשֶׂ֔ה בַּעֲב֖וּר הָאַרְבָּעִֽים: 30 וַ֠יֹּאמֶר אַל־נָ֞א יִ֤חַר לַֽאדֹנָי֙ וַאֲדַבֵּ֔רָה אוּלַ֛י יִמָּצְא֥וּן שָׁ֖ם שְׁלֹשִׁ֑ים

This teaches you that, when faced with the task of saving a life, you must be prepared to overcome your natural disposition and take radical action. Abraham, whose nature was to be only kind and polite, managed to gather the courage to act harshly and severely, in an attempt to save lives.

This also applies to the *spiritual* life of others. If you see somebody "drowning" spiritually, you must make every effort to help that person—even if it entails an act which is out of character with your personality (*Rabbi Menahem Mendel Schneerson, 20th century*).

24. Perhaps there are fifty righteous men in the midst of the city. Abraham stressed "in the midst of the city," because a righteous man who involves himself with others is far greater than the recluse who shuts himself away (*Rabbi Menahem Mendel Morgensztern of Kotsk, 19th century*).

27. I would be dust (*'afar*) and ashes (*'efer*). Abraham possessed the soul of Adam, who was formed from the "dust" of the earth. Adam's soul was blemished from the sin of the Tree of Knowledge, but Abraham did much to heal it when he willingly jumped into a fiery furnace at Ur of the Chaldeans, resisting idol-worship. Here Abraham hinted to his achievement, "I received the soul of Adam—dust—which I healed with the 'ashes' of the fiery furnace" (*Rabbi Menahem Azariah da Fano, 16th–17th century*).

> **kabbalah bites**
>
> **18:27** Abraham's confession of utter humility, comparing himself to "dust and ashes," was later hinted to by Job: *"I am comforted over dust and ashes"* (Job 32:2). This is not surprising when we consider that Job possessed the soul of Abraham's father, Terah, which was reincarnated to achieve *tikkun* (spiritual healing) for Terah's idolatrous ways.

genesis 18:22–30 — va-yera'

²² The (angels) turned from there (where Abraham had escorted them) and went to Sodom. (God) was still present before (Abraham). ²³ Abraham approached (God) and said, "Will You also destroy the righteous with the wicked? ²⁴ Perhaps there are fifty righteous men in the midst of the city. Will You still destroy it, and not spare the place for the sake of the fifty righteous people who are in it? ²⁵ To do such a thing as this, to put to death the righteous with the wicked, equating the innocent and the guilty, would desecrate (people's perception of) You (in this world and it would desecrate You in the next world). Would the Judge of the entire earth not perform (true) justice?"

²⁶ God said, "If I find in Sodom fifty righteous men within the city, I will forgive the entire (region of five cities) for their sake."

²⁷ Abraham responded and said, "I wish to speak with God! I (would be) dust and ashes (were it not for You)! ²⁸ What if the fifty righteous men will be missing five? Will You destroy the entire city because of the five?"

He said, "I will not destroy it if I find there forty-five."

²⁹ (Abraham) continued to speak to Him. He said, "What if forty will be found there?"

He said, "I will not do it for the sake of the forty."

³⁰ (Abraham) said, "Please don't let God's anger be kindled, and let me speak: What if thirty will be found there?"

---

food for thought

1. When is "arguing" with God a virtue, and when is it disrespectful?

2. Does God stand outside morality or is He the primary exemplar of it?

3. Is Judaism strictly heteronomous, or is there room for autonomy too?

With *cultural-contextual* judgment, God takes into consideration a person's deeds in relation to the surrounding environment. If there is a transgression which the Torah considers severe, but in the person's locality everybody treats the matter lightly, then, in this scheme of judgment the person might be viewed with compassion.

Therefore, in the case of Sodom, God said, *"I will descend now and see, etc."*—I have judged their sins *individually* and their crimes are heinous. Now I must "descend" into their culture to see, perhaps, when viewed *contextually*, their transgressions could be pardoned (*Rabbi Menahem Mendel of Rymanow, 18th century*).

23. Abraham approached. We find the expression "approaching" used in the context of war—*"Joab approached to do battle"* (II Samuel 10:13); "approaching" in the context of placating—*"Judah approached him and said 'Please, my master, etc.'"* (below, 44:18); and "approaching" in the context of prayer—*"Elijah the prophet approached and said, 'God of Abraham, Isaac and Jacob, etc.'"* (I Kings 18:36).

Abraham employed each of these three methods: speaking harshly, attempting to appease, and offering prayerful pleas (*Rashi, 11th century*).

Since Abraham excelled in the attribute of kindness, it is somewhat surprising to find that he "spoke harshly" with God, arguing aggressively for the salvation of Sodom.

בראשית יח:ל - יט:ט

וַיֹּאמֶר לֹא אֶעֱשֶׂה אִם־אֶמְצָא שָׁם שְׁלֹשִׁים: 31 וַיֹּאמֶר הִנֵּה־נָא הוֹאַלְתִּי לְדַבֵּר אֶל־אֲדֹנָי אוּלַי יִמָּצְאוּן שָׁם עֶשְׂרִים וַיֹּאמֶר לֹא אַשְׁחִית בַּעֲבוּר הָעֶשְׂרִים: 32 וַיֹּאמֶר אַל־נָא יִחַר לַאדֹנָי וַאֲדַבְּרָה אַךְ־הַפַּעַם אוּלַי יִמָּצְאוּן שָׁם עֲשָׂרָה וַיֹּאמֶר לֹא אַשְׁחִית בַּעֲבוּר הָעֲשָׂרָה: 33 וַיֵּלֶךְ יְהֹוָה כַּאֲשֶׁר כִּלָּה לְדַבֵּר אֶל־אַבְרָהָם וְאַבְרָהָם שָׁב לִמְקֹמוֹ:

יט [THIRD READING] 1 וַיָּבֹאוּ שְׁנֵי הַמַּלְאָכִים סְדֹמָה בָּעֶרֶב וְלוֹט יֹשֵׁב בְּשַׁעַר־סְדֹם וַיַּרְא־לוֹט וַיָּקָם לִקְרָאתָם וַיִּשְׁתַּחוּ אַפַּיִם אָרְצָה: 2 וַיֹּאמֶר הִנֶּה נָּא־אֲדֹנַי סוּרוּ נָא אֶל־בֵּית עַבְדְּכֶם וְלִינוּ וְרַחֲצוּ רַגְלֵיכֶם וְהִשְׁכַּמְתֶּם וַהֲלַכְתֶּם לְדַרְכְּכֶם וַיֹּאמְרוּ לֹּא כִּי בָרְחוֹב נָלִין: 3 וַיִּפְצַר־בָּם מְאֹד וַיָּסֻרוּ אֵלָיו וַיָּבֹאוּ אֶל־בֵּיתוֹ וַיַּעַשׂ לָהֶם מִשְׁתֶּה וּמַצּוֹת אָפָה וַיֹּאכֵלוּ: 4 טֶרֶם יִשְׁכָּבוּ וְאַנְשֵׁי הָעִיר אַנְשֵׁי סְדֹם נָסַבּוּ עַל־הַבַּיִת מִנַּעַר וְעַד־זָקֵן כָּל־הָעָם מִקָּצֶה: 5 וַיִּקְרְאוּ אֶל־לוֹט וַיֹּאמְרוּ לוֹ אַיֵּה הָאֲנָשִׁים אֲשֶׁר־בָּאוּ אֵלֶיךָ הַלָּיְלָה הוֹצִיאֵם אֵלֵינוּ וְנֵדְעָה אֹתָם: 6 וַיֵּצֵא אֲלֵהֶם לוֹט הַפֶּתְחָה וְהַדֶּלֶת סָגַר אַחֲרָיו: 7 וַיֹּאמַר אַל־נָא אַחַי תָּרֵעוּ: 8 הִנֵּה־נָא לִי שְׁתֵּי בָנוֹת אֲשֶׁר לֹא־יָדְעוּ אִישׁ אוֹצִיאָה־נָּא אֶתְהֶן אֲלֵיכֶם וַעֲשׂוּ לָהֶן כַּטּוֹב בְּעֵינֵיכֶם רַק לָאֲנָשִׁים הָאֵל אַל־תַּעֲשׂוּ דָבָר כִּי־עַל־כֵּן בָּאוּ בְּצֵל קֹרָתִי: 9 וַיֹּאמְרוּ | גֶּשׁ־הָלְאָה וַיֹּאמְרוּ הָאֶחָד בָּא־לָגוּר

spiritual vitamin

> The history of mankind has continuously demonstrated that human life can make no real progress where the imperatives of morality and ethics are not based on the authority of the Supreme Being, but are human inventions that can be changed and modified to suit the proclivities of the age.

He said, "I will not do it if I find thirty there."

³¹ (Abraham) said, "Please! I want to speak to God! What if twenty will be found there?"

He said, "I will not destroy it for the sake of the twenty."

³² (Abraham) said, "Please don't let God's anger be kindled, and let me speak once more: what if ten will be found there?"

He said, "I will not destroy it for the sake of the ten."

³³ When He had finished speaking to Abraham, God (the Judge) departed. Abraham (the advocate) returned home. (But the prosecution remained.)

Angels Arrive to Destroy Sodom and Save Lot

19 [THIRD READING] ¹ The two angels came to Sodom in the evening: (one to destroy, and one to save Lot. That day,) Lot was (appointed to be the chief judge) at the gate of Sodom.

Lot (always looked for guests, so he) saw them (arrive). He went up to greet them, and prostrated himself, face to the ground. ² He said, "Look now my lords, please (go inconspicuously) to your servant's house. Stay overnight, wash your feet, and you can get up early and go on your way."

They said, "No. We will stay overnight in the street."

³ He urged them strongly, so they (went inconspicuously) towards his (house).

When they came to his house, he made them a feast and he baked unleavened bread (since it was Passover), and they ate. ⁴ Before they went to bed (they discussed the wickedness of) the people of the city.

The people of Sodom surrounded the house, both young and old, the entire population from every end (of the city, without exception). ⁵ They called out to Lot, saying to him, "Where are the men who came to you tonight? Bring them out to us, and let us (sodomize) them!"

⁶ Lot came out to them at the entrance, and he shut the door behind him. ⁷ He said, "My brothers! Please don't act wickedly. ⁸ Look! I have two daughters who have never known a man. I will bring them out to you, and you can do to them as you see fit. But don't do anything to these men, because they have come under the shelter of my roof."

⁹ They said, "Get out of the way!"

In each of my two pockets I carry a different teaching. In one pocket it is written, *"The world was created for my sake"* (Babylonian Talmud, Sanhedrin 37a), and in the other, *"I would be dust and ashes."* It takes a mature soul to know when to draw on the Torah's bold endorsement of man's adequacy, and when to remind yourself of Abraham's declaration of our inherent inadequacy before God (*Rabbi Simḥah Bunem of Przysucha, 18ᵗʰ–19ᵗʰ century*).

וַיִּשְׁפֹּט שָׁפוֹט עַתָּה נָרַע לְךָ מֵהֶם וַיִּפְצְרוּ בָאִישׁ בְּלוֹט מְאֹד וַיִּגְּשׁוּ לִשְׁבֹּר הַדָּלֶת: 10 וַיִּשְׁלְחוּ הָאֲנָשִׁים אֶת־יָדָם וַיָּבִיאוּ אֶת־לוֹט אֲלֵיהֶם הַבָּיְתָה וְאֶת־הַדֶּלֶת סָגָרוּ: 11 וְאֶת־הָאֲנָשִׁים אֲשֶׁר־פֶּתַח הַבַּיִת הִכּוּ בַּסַּנְוֵרִים מִקָּטֹן וְעַד־גָּדוֹל וַיִּלְאוּ לִמְצֹא הַפָּתַח: 12 וַיֹּאמְרוּ הָאֲנָשִׁים אֶל־לוֹט עֹד מִי־לְךָ פֹה חָתָן וּבָנֶיךָ וּבְנֹתֶיךָ וְכֹל אֲשֶׁר־לְךָ בָּעִיר הוֹצֵא מִן־הַמָּקוֹם: 13 כִּי־מַשְׁחִתִים אֲנַחְנוּ אֶת־הַמָּקוֹם הַזֶּה כִּי־גָדְלָה צַעֲקָתָם אֶת־פְּנֵי יְהֹוָה וַיְשַׁלְּחֵנוּ יְהֹוָה לְשַׁחֲתָהּ: 14 וַיֵּצֵא לוֹט וַיְדַבֵּר | אֶל־חֲתָנָיו | לֹקְחֵי בְנֹתָיו וַיֹּאמֶר קוּמוּ צְּאוּ מִן־הַמָּקוֹם הַזֶּה כִּי־מַשְׁחִית יְהֹוָה אֶת־הָעִיר וַיְהִי כִמְצַחֵק בְּעֵינֵי חֲתָנָיו: 15 וּכְמוֹ הַשַּׁחַר עָלָה וַיָּאִיצוּ הַמַּלְאָכִים בְּלוֹט לֵאמֹר קוּם קַח אֶת־אִשְׁתְּךָ וְאֶת־שְׁתֵּי בְנֹתֶיךָ הַנִּמְצָאֹת פֶּן־תִּסָּפֶה בַּעֲוֹן הָעִיר: 16 וַיִּתְמַהְמָהּ | וַיַּחֲזִיקוּ הָאֲנָשִׁים בְּיָדוֹ וּבְיַד־אִשְׁתּוֹ וּבְיַד שְׁתֵּי בְנֹתָיו בְּחֶמְלַת יְהֹוָה עָלָיו וַיֹּצִאֻהוּ וַיַּנִּחֻהוּ מִחוּץ לָעִיר: 17 וַיְהִי כְהוֹצִיאָם אֹתָם הַחוּצָה וַיֹּאמֶר הִמָּלֵט עַל־נַפְשֶׁךָ אַל־תַּבִּיט אַחֲרֶיךָ וְאַל־תַּעֲמֹד בְּכָל־הַכִּכָּר הָהָרָה הִמָּלֵט פֶּן־תִּסָּפֶה: 18 וַיֹּאמֶר לוֹט אֲלֵהֶם אַל־נָא אֲדֹנָי: 19 הִנֵּה־נָא מָצָא עַבְדְּךָ חֵן בְּעֵינֶיךָ וַתַּגְדֵּל חַסְדְּךָ אֲשֶׁר עָשִׂיתָ עִמָּדִי לְהַחֲיוֹת אֶת־נַפְשִׁי וְאָנֹכִי לֹא אוּכַל לְהִמָּלֵט הָהָרָה פֶּן־תִּדְבָּקַנִי הָרָעָה וָמַתִּי: 20 הִנֵּה־נָא הָעִיר הַזֹּאת קְרֹבָה לָנוּס שָׁמָּה וְהִיא מִצְעָר אִמָּלְטָה נָּא שָׁמָּה הֲלֹא מִצְעָר הִוא וּתְחִי נַפְשִׁי: [FOURTH READING] 21 וַיֹּאמֶר אֵלָיו הִנֵּה נָשָׂאתִי פָנֶיךָ גַּם לַדָּבָר הַזֶּה לְבִלְתִּי הָפְכִּי אֶת־הָעִיר אֲשֶׁר דִּבַּרְתָּ: 22 מַהֵר הִמָּלֵט שָׁמָּה כִּי לֹא אוּכַל

19:14 He seemed like a comedian in the eyes of his sons-in-law. Why did they not believe him? Had they not seen with their own eyes how all the people of the city had become blind and that they had toiled in vain to find the entrance to Lot's house? That miracle alone should have made them aware that God had the power to destroy the city.

However, they, too, were struck by blindness—a spiritual blindness that made them unable to connect the miracle they had witnessed to their own predicament (*Rabbi Samuel Bornstein of Sochaczew, 19th century*).

genesis 19:9–22 — va-yera'

(In response to his protection of the visitors,) they said, "(You are) one (single person) who has come (from foreign parts) to live here, and now (you are) rebuking us! Now, we'll treat you worse than them!" They pushed hard on the man, on Lot, and they came forward to break the door.

¹⁰ The (angels) stretched their hands out, brought Lot to them in the house, and they shut the door. ¹¹ They struck the men who were at the entrance of the house with (a plague of) blindness—young and old alike—who toiled in vain to find the entrance.

¹² The (angels) said to Lot, "Who else do you have here? A son-in-law? Your own sons? Your daughters? Get anyone you have in the city out of the area! ¹³ For we are going to destroy this place, since the (people's) outcry is great before God. God has sent us to destroy it."

¹⁴ So Lot went and spoke to his (two) sons-in-law (and) the fiancés of his daughters. He said, "Get moving and get out of here! God is destroying the city!"—but he seemed like a comedian in the eyes of his sons-in-law.

Lot is Saved—Sodom and Gomorrah are Destroyed

¹⁵ As the dawn was breaking, the angels hurried Lot, saying, "Get up and take your wife, and your two daughters who (are willing to come), so that you won't be wiped out because of the city's sins!"

¹⁶ (In trying to save his money,) he was delayed. Out of God's pity for him, (the angels) took hold of his hand, his wife's hand, and the hands of his two daughters, and they took him out, placing him outside the city.

¹⁷ Then, when they took them outside, (one of the angels) said, "(Don't worry about your money,) flee for your life! Don't look behind you (as you don't deserve to see their punishment)! Don't stand in the entire plain (of Jordan). Flee to (Abraham, who is on) the mountain, so that you won't be wiped out."

¹⁸ Lot said to them, "Please, my God, don't (tell me to flee to the mountain)! ¹⁹ Right now, Your servant has found favor in Your eyes, and Your kindness that You did in saving my life was great. But I cannot flee to the mountain, in case (I will be considered) evil (in comparison to Abraham) and I will die. ²⁰ Now here, there is a city to which I can flee, which (is recently inhabited) and (its sins are) small. Please let me flee there and live! (After all), doesn't it have (only a) few (sins)?"

[FOURTH READING] ²¹ (One of the angels) said to him (on God's behalf), "Look! I am giving you a special dispensation that (not only will you be saved), but I will not overturn the city that you have mentioned. ²² Hurry and flee there, for I will not be able to do anything until you arrive there."

וירא   בראשית יט:כב-לג

לַעֲשׂ֣וֹת דָּבָ֔ר עַד־בֹּאֲךָ֖ שָׁ֑מָּה עַל־כֵּ֛ן קָרָ֥א שֵׁם־הָעִ֖יר צֽוֹעַר: 23 הַשֶּׁ֖מֶשׁ יָצָ֣א עַל־הָאָ֑רֶץ וְל֖וֹט בָּ֥א צֹֽעֲרָה: 24 וַֽיהֹוָ֗ה הִמְטִ֧יר עַל־סְדֹ֛ם וְעַל־עֲמֹרָ֖ה גָּפְרִ֣ית וָאֵ֑שׁ מֵאֵ֥ת יְהֹוָ֖ה מִן־הַשָּׁמָֽיִם: 25 וַֽיַּהֲפֹךְ֙ אֶת־הֶעָרִ֣ים הָאֵ֔ל וְאֵ֖ת כָּל־הַכִּכָּ֑ר וְאֵת֙ כָּל־יֹשְׁבֵ֣י הֶֽעָרִ֔ים וְצֶ֖מַח הָאֲדָמָֽה: 26 וַתַּבֵּ֥ט אִשְׁתּ֖וֹ מֵאַחֲרָ֑יו וַתְּהִ֖י נְצִ֥יב מֶֽלַח: 27 וַיַּשְׁכֵּ֥ם אַבְרָהָ֖ם בַּבֹּ֑קֶר אֶל־הַ֙מָּקוֹם֙ אֲשֶׁר־עָ֥מַד שָׁ֖ם אֶת־פְּנֵ֥י יְהֹוָֽה: 28 וַיַּשְׁקֵ֗ף עַל־פְּנֵ֤י סְדֹם֙ וַֽעֲמֹרָ֔ה וְעַֽל־כָּל־פְּנֵ֖י אֶ֣רֶץ הַכִּכָּ֑ר וַיַּ֗רְא וְהִנֵּ֤ה עָלָה֙ קִיטֹ֣ר הָאָ֔רֶץ כְּקִיטֹ֖ר הַכִּבְשָֽׁן: 29 וַיְהִ֗י בְּשַׁחֵ֤ת אֱלֹהִים֙ אֶת־עָרֵ֣י הַכִּכָּ֔ר וַיִּזְכֹּ֥ר אֱלֹהִ֖ים אֶת־אַבְרָהָ֑ם וַיְשַׁלַּ֤ח אֶת־לוֹט֙ מִתּ֣וֹךְ הַהֲפֵכָ֔ה בַּהֲפֹךְ֙ אֶת־הֶ֣עָרִ֔ים אֲשֶׁר־יָשַׁ֥ב בָּהֵ֖ן לֽוֹט: 30 וַיַּ֩עַל֩ ל֨וֹט מִצּ֜וֹעַר וַיֵּ֣שֶׁב בָּהָ֗ר וּשְׁתֵּ֤י בְנֹתָיו֙ עִמּ֔וֹ כִּ֥י יָרֵ֖א לָשֶׁ֣בֶת בְּצ֑וֹעַר וַיֵּ֙שֶׁב֙ בַּמְּעָרָ֔ה ה֖וּא וּשְׁתֵּ֥י בְנֹתָֽיו: 31 וַתֹּ֧אמֶר הַבְּכִירָ֛ה אֶל־הַצְּעִירָ֖ה אָבִ֣ינוּ זָקֵ֑ן וְאִ֨ישׁ אֵ֤ין בָּאָ֙רֶץ֙ לָב֣וֹא עָלֵ֔ינוּ כְּדֶ֖רֶךְ כָּל־הָאָֽרֶץ: 32 לְכָ֨ה נַשְׁקֶ֧ה אֶת־אָבִ֛ינוּ יַ֖יִן וְנִשְׁכְּבָ֣ה עִמּ֑וֹ וּנְחַיֶּ֥ה מֵאָבִ֖ינוּ זָֽרַע: 33 וַתַּשְׁקֶ֧יןָ אֶת־אֲבִיהֶ֛ן יַ֖יִן בַּלַּ֣יְלָה ה֑וּא וַתָּבֹ֤א הַבְּכִירָה֙ וַתִּשְׁכַּ֣ב אֶת־אָבִ֔יהָ וְלֹֽא־יָדַ֥ע בְּשִׁכְבָ֖הּ וּבְקוּמָֽהּ:

Sodom was a physical manifestation of the failed world of *tohu*. The city was destroyed because its citizens were free-radicals who refused to pay attention to anybody else but themselves (*Rabbi Shneur Zalman of Lyady, 18th century*).

31-32. There is no man on earth .... We'll produce offspring through our father. Lot's daughters imagined—incorrectly—that the world was utterly desolate and that their actions were necessary to save mankind. But their words did have prophetic overtones. The Messiah, who *will* save mankind, is destined to come from King David, whose ancestry can be traced to this fateful act of Lot's daughter (*Rabbi Menahem Azariah da Fano, 16th–17th century*).

33. He wasn't aware of her lying down or of her getting up. The scribal marking above the letter *vav* on the word *u-ve-kumah* ("or of her getting up") alludes to the notion that God was secretly assisting the event, for the Messiah was destined to materialize from this union. (The Messiah will be a descendant of King David, whose great-grandmother Ruth was descended from Moab, the son produced from Lot's union with his older daughter.) When the verse states that Lot "wasn't aware," it means that he was not aware that the Messiah was destined to come from this union (*Zohar*).

The city was therefore named Zoar (meaning, "small").

²³ As the sun rose over the earth, Lot came to Zoar.

²⁴ God (and His court) caused it to rain down upon Sodom and Gomorrah (first rain and then fiery) sulfur. It came from God, from the sky. ²⁵ (God) turned over (the bedrock on which) these (four) cities (were situated) and the entire plain, with all the inhabitants of the cities, and the earth's vegetation.

²⁶ (Lot's) wife looked (backwards) from behind where (Lot stood), and she became a pillar of salt (as a punishment for withholding salt from guests).

²⁷ Abraham got up early in the morning, (and returned) to the place where he had stood before God (in prayer). ²⁸ He gazed at the site of Sodom and Gomorrah, and over the entire area of the plain, and he saw that—look!—(a pillar of) smoke from the earth had risen like the smoke from a lime-kiln.

²⁹ When God had destroyed the cities of the plain, God had remembered (how Lot kept secret that Sarah was not) Abraham('s sister). Thus, when He overturned the cities in which Lot had lived, He sent Lot from the midst of the destruction.

Lot has Children from his Daughters

³⁰ Lot left Zoar, and he settled in the mountain with his two daughters, since he was afraid to live in Zoar (as it was so close to Sodom). He lived in a cave, (just) he and his two daughters.

³¹ (The daughters thought that the whole world had been obliterated, as it had been with the Flood, so) the older one said to the younger one, "Our father is old (and who knows how much longer he will be able to father children)? There is no man on earth to marry us in the usual fashion. ³² Come, let's give our father wine to drink, and let's lie with him. We'll produce offspring through our father."

³³ They gave their father wine to drink on that night, and the older one came and lay with her father, and he wasn't aware of her lying down or of her getting up.

---

25. God turned over these four cities and the entire plain. *"I have found David, My servant (i.e. the Messiah)" (Psalms 89:21). Where did I find him? In Sodom (Genesis Rabbah).*

The prophet Ezekiel declared that in the Messianic Era the city of Sodom will be re-inhabited, *"I shall bring back their exiles, the exiles of Sodom and her daughters" (Ezekiel 16:53).* Abraham made a tremendous effort to save the city of Sodom because he was aware of its future significance (*Rabbi Isaiah Horowitz, 16th–17th century*).

Before the world was created, God created another spiritual world—referred to in *Kabbalah* as the world of "chaos," or *tohu* (as in *Genesis* 1:2)—that collapsed because its components were highly charged free-radicals that would not interact. In *principle*, that intensity was good, for it was a powerhouse of spirituality. In practice however, it failed.

בראשית י"ט:ל"ד - כ':ח

וירא

34 וַיְהִי מִמָּחֳרָת וַתֹּאמֶר הַבְּכִירָה אֶל־הַצְּעִירָה הֵן־שָׁכַבְתִּי אֶמֶשׁ אֶת־אָבִי נַשְׁקֶנּוּ יַיִן גַּם־הַלַּיְלָה וּבֹאִי שִׁכְבִי עִמּוֹ וּנְחַיֶּה מֵאָבִינוּ זָרַע: 35 וַתַּשְׁקֶיןָ גַּם בַּלַּיְלָה הַהוּא אֶת־אֲבִיהֶן יָיִן וַתָּקָם הַצְּעִירָה וַתִּשְׁכַּב עִמּוֹ וְלֹא־יָדַע בְּשִׁכְבָהּ וּבְקֻמָהּ: 36 וַתַּהֲרֶיןָ שְׁתֵּי בְנוֹת־לוֹט מֵאֲבִיהֶן: 37 וַתֵּלֶד הַבְּכִירָה בֵּן וַתִּקְרָא שְׁמוֹ מוֹאָב הוּא אֲבִי־מוֹאָב עַד־הַיּוֹם: 38 וְהַצְּעִירָה גַם־הִוא יָלְדָה בֵּן וַתִּקְרָא שְׁמוֹ בֶּן־עַמִּי הוּא אֲבִי בְנֵי־עַמּוֹן עַד־הַיּוֹם: ס

כ

1 וַיִּסַּע מִשָּׁם אַבְרָהָם אַרְצָה הַנֶּגֶב וַיֵּשֶׁב בֵּין־קָדֵשׁ וּבֵין שׁוּר וַיָּגָר בִּגְרָר: 2 וַיֹּאמֶר אַבְרָהָם אֶל־שָׂרָה אִשְׁתּוֹ אֲחֹתִי הִוא וַיִּשְׁלַח אֲבִימֶלֶךְ מֶלֶךְ גְּרָר וַיִּקַּח אֶת־שָׂרָה: 3 וַיָּבֹא אֱלֹהִים אֶל־אֲבִימֶלֶךְ בַּחֲלוֹם הַלָּיְלָה וַיֹּאמֶר לוֹ הִנְּךָ מֵת עַל־הָאִשָּׁה אֲשֶׁר־לָקַחְתָּ וְהִוא בְּעֻלַת בָּעַל: 4 וַאֲבִימֶלֶךְ לֹא קָרַב אֵלֶיהָ וַיֹּאמַר אֲדֹנָי הֲגוֹי גַּם־צַדִּיק תַּהֲרֹג: 5 הֲלֹא הוּא אָמַר־לִי אֲחֹתִי הִוא וְהִיא־גַם־הִוא אָמְרָה אָחִי הוּא בְּתָם־לְבָבִי וּבְנִקְיֹן כַּפַּי עָשִׂיתִי זֹאת: 6 וַיֹּאמֶר אֵלָיו הָאֱלֹהִים בַּחֲלֹם גַּם אָנֹכִי יָדַעְתִּי כִּי בְתָם־לְבָבְךָ עָשִׂיתָ זֹּאת וָאֶחְשֹׂךְ גַּם־אָנֹכִי אוֹתְךָ מֵחֲטוֹ־לִי עַל־כֵּן לֹא־נְתַתִּיךָ לִנְגֹּעַ אֵלֶיהָ: 7 וְעַתָּה הָשֵׁב אֵשֶׁת־הָאִישׁ כִּי־נָבִיא הוּא וְיִתְפַּלֵּל בַּעַדְךָ וֶחְיֵה וְאִם־אֵינְךָ מֵשִׁיב דַּע כִּי־מוֹת תָּמוּת אַתָּה וְכָל־אֲשֶׁר־לָךְ: 8 וַיַּשְׁכֵּם אֲבִימֶלֶךְ בַּבֹּקֶר וַיִּקְרָא לְכָל־עֲבָדָיו וַיְדַבֵּר אֶת־כָּל־הַדְּבָרִים הָאֵלֶּה בְּאָזְנֵיהֶם וַיִּירְאוּ הָאֲנָשִׁים מְאֹד:

Why should the Messianic line enter the world in such an undignified manner?

When a very lofty soul is about to descend into the world, the demonic forces oppose the soul's descent vehemently. Sometimes, however, the forces will consent to the soul's descent if it occurs through a particularly sinful act. Thus we find that from this undesirable act, the ancestor of the Messiah was born (*Rabbi Moses b. Jacob Cordovero, 16th century*).

20:8 The men were very frightened. They knew that Sodom had been completely obliterated, and they feared that the angels who had destroyed Sodom were returning to wreak destruction upon them (*Genesis Rabbah*).

³⁴ Then, on the next day, the older one said to the younger one, "Look! Last night I lay with my father. Let's give him wine to drink tonight too, and you'll come and lie with him, and we'll produce offspring through our father."

³⁵ So they gave their father to drink on that night as well, and the younger one got up and lay with him, and he wasn't aware of her lying down or of her getting up.

³⁶ Lot's two daughters conceived from their father. ³⁷ The older one bore a son, and she named him Moab (lit. "from the father"). He is the father of (the people of) Moab (which continues) to this day. ³⁸ The younger one also bore a son, and she named him Ben-ammi (lit. "son of my people"). He is the father of the people of Ammon (which continues) to this day.

Abimelech Seizes Sarah

20 ¹ Abraham traveled away from the area (since he was unable to find guests after the destruction of Sodom) to the land of the Negeb, and he settled between Kadesh and Shur, living in Gerar. ² (Without her consent) Abraham said about his wife Sarah that "she is my sister."

King Abimelech of Gerar sent for and took Sarah.

³ God came to Abimelech in a dream at night. He said to him, "Look! You are going to die because of the woman whom you have taken, for she is a married woman!"

⁴ Abimelech had not come near to her, so he said, "God! Would you kill even a righteous nation? ⁵ Didn't he say to me, 'She is my sister'? And she also said, 'He is my brother,' (and so did her staff) too. I have done this with the innocence of my heart and with the purity of my hands (for I haven't touched her)!"

⁶ God said to him in the dream, "I know that you did this with the innocence of your heart (but you do not have 'pure hands.') I have prevented you from sinning against Me, and that is why I did not give you (the strength) to touch her. ⁷ Now, return the man's wife (and do not worry that he will hate you), because he is a prophet (and will know that you did not touch her). He will pray for you and you will live. But if you do not return (her), know that you will surely die, both you and all that is yours."

⁸ Abimelech got up early in the morning, and he summoned all his servants, and he spoke about all these occurrences into their ears. The men were very frightened.

food for thought

1. Have you ever told a "white lie" that badly backfired?

2. How can we better protect women in our society?

3. Why is misconduct so rampant among those in power?

בראשית כ:ט - כא:ב

9 וַיִּקְרָ֨א אֲבִימֶ֜לֶךְ לְאַבְרָהָ֗ם וַיֹּ֨אמֶר ל֜וֹ מֶֽה־עָשִׂ֤יתָ לָּ֨נוּ֙ וּמֶֽה־חָטָ֣אתִי לָ֔ךְ כִּֽי־הֵבֵ֧אתָ עָלַ֛י וְעַל־מַמְלַכְתִּ֖י חֲטָאָ֣ה גְדֹלָ֑ה מַעֲשִׂים֙ אֲשֶׁ֣ר לֹא־יֵֽעָשׂ֔וּ עָשִׂ֖יתָ עִמָּדִֽי: 10 וַיֹּ֥אמֶר אֲבִימֶ֖לֶךְ אֶל־אַבְרָהָ֑ם מָ֣ה רָאִ֔יתָ כִּ֥י עָשִׂ֖יתָ אֶת־הַדָּבָ֥ר הַזֶּֽה: 11 וַיֹּ֨אמֶר֙ אַבְרָהָ֔ם כִּ֣י אָמַ֗רְתִּי רַ֚ק אֵין־יִרְאַ֣ת אֱלֹהִ֔ים בַּמָּק֖וֹם הַזֶּ֑ה וַהֲרָג֖וּנִי עַל־דְּבַ֥ר אִשְׁתִּֽי: 12 וְגַם־אָמְנָ֗ה אֲחֹתִ֤י בַת־אָבִי֙ הִ֔וא אַ֖ךְ לֹ֣א בַת־אִמִּ֑י וַתְּהִי־לִ֖י לְאִשָּֽׁה: 13 וַיְהִ֞י כַּאֲשֶׁ֧ר הִתְע֣וּ אֹתִ֗י אֱלֹהִים֮ מִבֵּ֣ית אָבִי֒ וָאֹמַ֣ר לָ֔הּ זֶ֣ה חַסְדֵּ֔ךְ אֲשֶׁ֥ר תַּעֲשִׂ֖י עִמָּדִ֑י אֶ֤ל כָּל־הַמָּקוֹם֙ אֲשֶׁ֣ר נָב֣וֹא שָׁ֔מָּה אִמְרִי־לִ֖י אָחִ֥י הֽוּא: 14 וַיִּקַּ֨ח אֲבִימֶ֜לֶךְ צֹ֣אן וּבָקָ֗ר וַעֲבָדִים֙ וּשְׁפָחֹ֔ת וַיִּתֵּ֖ן לְאַבְרָהָ֑ם וַיָּ֣שֶׁב ל֔וֹ אֵ֖ת שָׂרָ֥ה אִשְׁתּֽוֹ: 15 וַיֹּ֣אמֶר אֲבִימֶ֔לֶךְ הִנֵּ֥ה אַרְצִ֖י לְפָנֶ֑יךָ בַּטּ֥וֹב בְּעֵינֶ֖יךָ שֵֽׁב: 16 וּלְשָׂרָ֣ה אָמַ֗ר הִנֵּ֨ה נָתַ֜תִּי אֶ֤לֶף כֶּ֨סֶף֙ לְאָחִ֔יךְ הִנֵּ֤ה הוּא־לָךְ֙ כְּס֣וּת עֵינַ֔יִם לְכֹ֖ל אֲשֶׁ֣ר אִתָּ֑ךְ וְאֵ֥ת כֹּ֖ל וְנֹכָֽחַת: 17 וַיִּתְפַּלֵּ֥ל אַבְרָהָ֖ם אֶל־הָאֱלֹהִ֑ים וַיִּרְפָּ֨א אֱלֹהִ֜ים אֶת־אֲבִימֶ֧לֶךְ וְאֶת־אִשְׁתּ֛וֹ וְאַמְהֹתָ֖יו וַיֵּלֵֽדוּ: 18 כִּֽי־עָצֹ֤ר עָצַר֙ יְהֹוָ֔ה בְּעַ֥ד כָּל־רֶ֖חֶם לְבֵ֣ית אֲבִימֶ֑לֶךְ עַל־דְּבַ֥ר שָׂרָ֖ה אֵ֥שֶׁת אַבְרָהָֽם: ס

כא

1 וַֽיהֹוָ֛ה פָּקַ֥ד אֶת־שָׂרָ֖ה כַּאֲשֶׁ֣ר אָמָ֑ר וַיַּ֧עַשׂ יְהֹוָ֛ה לְשָׂרָ֖ה כַּאֲשֶׁ֥ר דִּבֵּֽר: 2 וַתַּהַר֩ וַתֵּ֨לֶד שָׂרָ֧ה לְאַבְרָהָ֛ם בֵּ֖ן לִזְקֻנָ֑יו לַמּוֹעֵ֕ד אֲשֶׁר־דִּבֶּ֥ר

21:1 God remembered (His promise of pregnancy to) Sarah. The Torah placed the account of Sarah's pregnancy immediately following the account of Abraham's prayer on behalf of

spiritual vitamin

> The difficulties, trials, and tests of life are themselves the means by which we are to attain our ultimate *objective*—that the soul achieve the lofty spiritual level it once possessed before it descended into the body. The purpose of life is for the soul to regain that status and even transcend it.

⁹ Abimelech summoned Abraham and said to him, "What have you done to us? What have I sinned against you, that you have brought upon me and upon my kingdom a great sin? You have caused me (to get a disease) which never happens (where every bodily orifice becomes blocked)!"

¹⁰ "What led you to do this thing?" Abimelech said to Abraham.

¹¹ Abraham said, "(It was) because I said, 'Surely, there is no fear of God in this place, and they will kill me because of my wife. ¹² Besides, she really is my sister—my father's (grand)daughter (which is like a daughter), but not my mother's daughter—and she became my wife. ¹³ Then, when God caused me to wander from my father's house (among wicked people), I said to her, 'Do me a favor! Whichever place we come to, say about me, 'He is my brother.'"

¹⁴ Abimelech took flocks, cattle, servants and maids, and he gave (them) to Abraham (to appease him, so that he should pray for him), and he restored his wife Sarah to him.

¹⁵ Abimelech said, "Here is my land before you! You may settle wherever you like."

¹⁶ To Sarah he said, "Look! I have given a thousand pieces of silver to (Abraham, who you said was) your brother. (If anyone suspects you of being abused by me and then discarded, the money) will be a veil (to divert the suspicion from) you and all those who are with you. You can prove (your innocence) to everybody."

¹⁷ Abraham prayed to God. God healed Abimelech, his wife and his handmaids, and they were relieved. ¹⁸ For God had shut every (orifice) of Abimelech's household, because of Sarah, Abraham's wife.

The Birth of Isaac

21 ¹ God remembered (His promise of pregnancy) to Sarah as He had said (when the angels visited Abraham). God made Sarah (pregnant) as He had told (Abraham, at the Covenant of the Parts). ² Sarah conceived and bore

16. I have given a thousand pieces of silver (*kesef*) to (Abraham). Abraham and Sarah had failed to conceive a child because their intimacy lacked an element of physical desire which is necessary for conception. Even when they were together, their minds remained transfixed on spiritual matters and they were unable to be drawn to the pleasures of this world. The incident with Abimelech, however, changed all of this, since they were inevitably influenced—albeit subtly—through their interactions with him, and were subsequently able to derive pleasure from their intimate relations. The Torah hints to this here as the word *kesef* ("silver") can also mean "desire" (see below, 31:30). Abimelech said, "It is I who have given you desire" (*Rabbi Moses Ḥayyim Ephraim of Sudylkow, 18ᵗʰ century*).

בראשית כא:ב - יד | וירא

3 וַיִּקְרָא אַבְרָהָם אֶת־שֶׁם־בְּנוֹ הַנּוֹלַד־לוֹ אֲשֶׁר־יָלְדָה־לּוֹ שָׂרָה אֹתוֹ אֱלֹהִים: 4 וַיָּמָל אַבְרָהָם אֶת־יִצְחָק בְּנוֹ בֶּן־שְׁמֹנַת יָמִים כַּאֲשֶׁר צִוָּה אֹתוֹ יִצְחָק: אֱלֹהִים: 5 וְאַבְרָהָם בֶּן־מְאַת שָׁנָה בְּהִוָּלֶד לוֹ אֵת יִצְחָק בְּנוֹ: [FIFTH READING] 6 וַתֹּאמֶר שָׂרָה צְחֹק עָשָׂה לִי אֱלֹהִים כָּל־הַשֹּׁמֵעַ יִצְחַק־לִי: 7 וַתֹּאמֶר מִי מִלֵּל לְאַבְרָהָם הֵינִיקָה בָנִים שָׂרָה כִּי־יָלַדְתִּי בֵן לִזְקֻנָיו: 8 וַיִּגְדַּל הַיֶּלֶד וַיִּגָּמַל וַיַּעַשׂ אַבְרָהָם מִשְׁתֶּה גָדוֹל בְּיוֹם הִגָּמֵל אֶת־יִצְחָק: 9 וַתֵּרֶא שָׂרָה אֶת־בֶּן־הָגָר הַמִּצְרִית אֲשֶׁר־יָלְדָה לְאַבְרָהָם מְצַחֵק: 10 וַתֹּאמֶר לְאַבְרָהָם גָּרֵשׁ הָאָמָה הַזֹּאת וְאֶת־בְּנָהּ כִּי לֹא יִירַשׁ בֶּן־הָאָמָה הַזֹּאת עִם־בְּנִי עִם־יִצְחָק: 11 וַיֵּרַע הַדָּבָר מְאֹד בְּעֵינֵי אַבְרָהָם עַל אוֹדֹת בְּנוֹ: 12 וַיֹּאמֶר אֱלֹהִים אֶל־אַבְרָהָם אַל־יֵרַע בְּעֵינֶיךָ עַל־הַנַּעַר וְעַל־אֲמָתֶךָ כֹּל אֲשֶׁר תֹּאמַר אֵלֶיךָ שָׂרָה שְׁמַע בְּקֹלָהּ כִּי בְיִצְחָק יִקָּרֵא לְךָ זָרַע: 13 וְגַם אֶת־בֶּן־הָאָמָה לְגוֹי אֲשִׂימֶנּוּ כִּי זַרְעֲךָ הוּא: 14 וַיַּשְׁכֵּם אַבְרָהָם | בַּבֹּקֶר וַיִּקַּח־לֶחֶם וְחֵמַת מַיִם וַיִּתֵּן אֶל־הָגָר שָׂם עַל־שִׁכְמָהּ וְאֶת־

Thus, *"Abraham prayed to God"* (v. 17) is immediately followed by *"God remembered (His promise of pregnancy to) Sarah,"* the precise Hebrew suggesting that "God had already remembered" Sarah. She became pregnant before Abimelech was healed (*Rashi, 11th century; Rabbi Judah Loew b. Bezalel of Prague, 16th century*).

When a person prays for another and sweetens a Divine judgment, the flow of blessing descends downwards into the soul of the one who prayed, and from there the blessing spreads to other souls. Therefore, if the person who prayed is in need of the very same blessing as the one he is praying for, he will inevitably receive the blessing first, as his soul was the channel through which the blessing entered the world (*Rabbi Ḥanokh Zundel b. Joseph of Bialystok, 19th century*).

11. His son's (idol-worship) disturbed Abraham greatly. Abraham was unsettled by the fact that Ishmael had begun wicked ways.

The simple meaning is that Abraham was disturbed by Sarah's request (v. 10) to send Ishmael away (*Rashi, 11th century*).

kabbalah bites

21:9 Adam's sin was tantamount to the three cardinal sins of idol-worship, murder and infidelity. To achieve *tikkun* (spiritual healing) for this he was reincarnated into all three Patriarchs: Abraham, Isaac and Jacob.

Abraham achieved *tikkun* for the sin of idol-worship by entering Nimrod's furnace (since idols are destroyed by fire—see Deuteronomy 12:3). The idolatrous spark departed from him and entered the soul of Ishmael. That is why Ishmael had *"become depraved."*

a son to Abraham in his old age, at the time of which God had told him (through the angels). ³ Abraham named his son who had been born to him—whom Sarah had borne to him—Isaac. ⁴ Abraham circumcised his son Isaac when he was eight days old, as God had commanded him. [FIFTH READING] ⁵ Abraham was a hundred years old, when his son Isaac was born to him.

⁶ Sarah said, "God has made me happy! Whoever hears (about this) will be happy for me."

⁷ She said, "How (awesome is God,) who said to Abraham that Sarah would nurse children, for I have borne a son in his old age!"

⁸ The child grew and was weaned (at twenty-four months). On the day that Isaac was weaned, Abraham made a feast (inviting all the) great (people of the generation).

Abraham's Ninth Test: Expulsion of Hagar and Ishmael

⁹ Sarah saw the son of Hagar the Egyptian—whom she had borne to Abraham—become depraved (worshipping idols). ¹⁰ Sarah said to Abraham, "Get rid of this handmaid and her son! The son of this handmaid (is not worthy) to share an inheritance with (anyone who is) my son, (or) with (anyone as righteous as) Isaac."

¹¹ His son's (idol-worship) disturbed Abraham greatly. ¹² God said to Abraham, "Don't be disturbed about the boy and about your handmaid. Whatever Sarah tells you, listen to her (prophetic) voice, because your (true) descendants will be through Isaac. ¹³ I will also make the son of the handmaid into a nation, because he is your (physical) descendant."

¹⁴ Abraham got up early in the morning, and he took bread and a leather pouch of water, and he gave them to Hagar. He placed them on her shoulder with the boy, and he sent her away.

Abimelech. This teaches us that if you pray for your friend, when you yourself need that very thing you are praying for, you will be answered first.

kabbalah bites

21:3 Isaac was a reincarnation of Adam's soul, particularly as that soul had taken expression through Abel, his son. This is hinted to here by the words *beno ha-nolad lo* ("*his son who had been born to him*"), whose first letters spell Abel's Hebrew name, HeBeL. Thus the sacrifice of Isaac did not take place until his thirty-seventh year, which is the *gematria* (numerical value) of the word HeBeL.

בראשית כא:יד-כו | וירא

הַיֶּלֶד וַיְשַׁלְּחֶהָ וַתֵּלֶךְ וַתֵּתַע בְּמִדְבַּר בְּאֵר שָׁבַע: 15 וַיִּכְלוּ הַמַּיִם מִן־הַחֵמֶת וַתַּשְׁלֵךְ אֶת־הַיֶּלֶד תַּחַת אַחַד הַשִּׂיחִם: 16 וַתֵּלֶךְ וַתֵּשֶׁב לָהּ מִנֶּגֶד הַרְחֵק כִּמְטַחֲוֵי קֶשֶׁת כִּי אָמְרָה אַל־אֶרְאֶה בְּמוֹת הַיָּלֶד וַתֵּשֶׁב מִנֶּגֶד וַתִּשָּׂא אֶת־קֹלָהּ וַתֵּבְךְּ: 17 וַיִּשְׁמַע אֱלֹהִים אֶת־קוֹל הַנַּעַר וַיִּקְרָא מַלְאַךְ אֱלֹהִים | אֶל־הָגָר מִן־הַשָּׁמַיִם וַיֹּאמֶר לָהּ מַה־לָּךְ הָגָר אַל־תִּירְאִי כִּי־שָׁמַע אֱלֹהִים אֶל־קוֹל הַנַּעַר בַּאֲשֶׁר הוּא־שָׁם: 18 קוּמִי שְׂאִי אֶת־הַנַּעַר וְהַחֲזִיקִי אֶת־יָדֵךְ בּוֹ כִּי־לְגוֹי גָּדוֹל אֲשִׂימֶנּוּ: 19 וַיִּפְקַח אֱלֹהִים אֶת־עֵינֶיהָ וַתֵּרֶא בְּאֵר מָיִם וַתֵּלֶךְ וַתְּמַלֵּא אֶת־הַחֵמֶת מַיִם וַתַּשְׁקְ אֶת־הַנָּעַר: 20 וַיְהִי אֱלֹהִים אֶת־הַנַּעַר וַיִּגְדָּל וַיֵּשֶׁב בַּמִּדְבָּר וַיְהִי רֹבֶה קַשָּׁת: 21 וַיֵּשֶׁב בְּמִדְבַּר פָּארָן וַתִּקַּח־לוֹ אִמּוֹ אִשָּׁה מֵאֶרֶץ מִצְרָיִם: פ 22 [SIXTH READING] וַיְהִי בָּעֵת הַהִוא וַיֹּאמֶר אֲבִימֶלֶךְ וּפִיכֹל שַׂר־צְבָאוֹ אֶל־אַבְרָהָם לֵאמֹר אֱלֹהִים עִמְּךָ בְּכֹל אֲשֶׁר־אַתָּה עֹשֶׂה: 23 וְעַתָּה הִשָּׁבְעָה לִּי בֵאלֹהִים הֵנָּה אִם־תִּשְׁקֹר לִי וּלְנִינִי וּלְנֶכְדִּי כַּחֶסֶד אֲשֶׁר־עָשִׂיתִי עִמְּךָ תַּעֲשֶׂה עִמָּדִי וְעִם־הָאָרֶץ אֲשֶׁר־גַּרְתָּה בָּהּ: 24 וַיֹּאמֶר אַבְרָהָם אָנֹכִי אִשָּׁבֵעַ: 25 וְהוֹכִחַ אַבְרָהָם אֶת־אֲבִימֶלֶךְ עַל־אֹדוֹת בְּאֵר הַמַּיִם אֲשֶׁר גָּזְלוּ עַבְדֵי אֲבִימֶלֶךְ: 26 וַיֹּאמֶר אֲבִימֶלֶךְ לֹא יָדַעְתִּי מִי עָשָׂה אֶת־הַדָּבָר הַזֶּה וְגַם־אַתָּה

spiritual vitamin

> When a problem arose about Isaac's development, due to the undesirable influence by his half-brother, Ishmael, both Sarah and Abraham found it necessary to suppress their natural kindness for the sake of Isaac's healthy upbringing and development. This teaches you how vital the education of children is: that parents must be prepared to make sacrifices in terms of emotional strain and suppressing natural feelings, not to mention financial strain, in order to ensure maximum possible advantages for their children's education.

genesis 21:14–26   va-yera'

She went (back to idolatry) and wandered in the desert of Beer-sheba.

¹⁵ (Ishmael became ill and drank a lot of water.) When the water was depleted from the leather pouch, she cast the child under one of the bushes. ¹⁶ She went and sat down some distance away—approximately two bow-shots—as she said, "I don't want to see the boy die." She sat from afar, and she cried loudly and wept.

¹⁷ God heard the boy's cry. An angel of God called to Hagar from heaven, and said to her, "What's the matter, Hagar? Don't be afraid, because God has heard the boy's cry (and judged him) where he is. ¹⁸ Get up and pick up the boy and grasp hold of him, because I will make him into a great nation."

¹⁹ God opened her eyes, and she saw a well of water. She went and filled the pouch with water and gave the boy to drink.

²⁰ God was with the boy. He grew up and he lived in the desert, and he became an archer. ²¹ He settled in the desert of Paran, and his mother found him a wife from the land of Egypt (where she came from originally).

Abimelech Makes a Covenant with Abraham

[SIXTH READING] ²² Around that time, Abimelech—and Phicol, his army general—said to Abraham, "(Judging by your miraculous salvation from Sodom, victory in war and fatherhood at old age,) God is with you in all that you do. ²³ Now, swear to me here by God, that you will not deceive me, or my son, or my grandson. In the same way that I have been kind to you (by offering you the pick of my whole land), do the same to me, and to the land where you have lived."

²⁴ Abraham said, "I will swear."

²⁵ Abraham argued with Abimelech about the well of water that the servants of Abimelech had seized. ²⁶ Abimelech said, "I don't know who did this thing. You never told me about it, and I never heard about it until today."

Sarah perceived through Divine inspiration that Ishmael was evil. Abraham, however, loved Ishmael his son, and being weaker in prophecy than Sarah (*Rashi* to v. 12), he was not able to perceive Ishmael's future. Thus Abraham became very surprised and disturbed when he discovered that Ishmael had begun to follow evil ways, since he was unaware of Ishmael's destiny. Sarah, however, perceived Ishmael's future regression, and told Abraham to expel him, along with his mother (*Rabbi Meir Benjamin Menahem Danon, 19th century*).

17. God has heard the boy's cry where he is. God judged him according to his current circumstances and not according to what he was destined to do (*Rashi, 11th century*).

Rashi's explanation would not be acceptable to the *Midrash*, which maintained that, even at this age, Ishmael was guilty of adultery, idol-worship and murder (*Genesis Rabbah*). A more universally acceptable interpretation would be to translate the end of the verse as referring to God. God judged Ishmael "where *He* is," in the Heavenly Court, where man is only liable

וירא / בראשית כא:כו - כב:ב

לֹא־הִגַּ֣דְתָּ לִּ֔י וְגַ֧ם אָנֹכִ֛י לֹ֥א שָׁמַ֖עְתִּי בִּלְתִּ֥י הַיּֽוֹם׃ 27 וַיִּקַּ֤ח אַבְרָהָם֙ צֹ֣אן וּבָקָ֔ר וַיִּתֵּ֖ן לַאֲבִימֶ֑לֶךְ וַיִּכְרְת֥וּ שְׁנֵיהֶ֖ם בְּרִֽית׃ 28 וַיַּצֵּ֣ב אַבְרָהָ֗ם אֶת־שֶׁ֛בַע כִּבְשֹׂ֥ת הַצֹּ֖אן לְבַדְּהֶֽן׃ 29 וַיֹּ֥אמֶר אֲבִימֶ֖לֶךְ אֶל־אַבְרָהָ֑ם מָ֣ה הֵ֗נָּה שֶׁ֤בַע כְּבָשֹׂת֙ הָאֵ֔לֶּה אֲשֶׁ֥ר הִצַּ֖בְתָּ לְבַדָּֽנָה׃ 30 וַיֹּ֕אמֶר כִּ֚י אֶת־שֶׁ֣בַע כְּבָשֹׂ֔ת תִּקַּ֖ח מִיָּדִ֑י בַּעֲבוּר֙ תִּֽהְיֶה־לִּ֣י לְעֵדָ֔ה כִּ֥י חָפַ֖רְתִּי אֶת־הַבְּאֵ֥ר הַזֹּֽאת׃ 31 עַל־כֵּ֗ן קָרָ֛א לַמָּק֥וֹם הַה֖וּא בְּאֵ֣ר שָׁ֑בַע כִּ֛י שָׁ֥ם נִשְׁבְּע֖וּ שְׁנֵיהֶֽם׃ 32 וַיִּכְרְת֥וּ בְרִ֖ית בִּבְאֵ֣ר שָׁ֑בַע וַיָּ֣קָם אֲבִימֶ֗לֶךְ וּפִיכֹל֙ שַׂר־צְבָא֔וֹ וַיָּשֻׁ֖בוּ אֶל־אֶ֥רֶץ פְּלִשְׁתִּֽים׃ 33 וַיִּטַּ֥ע אֶ֖שֶׁל בִּבְאֵ֣ר שָׁ֑בַע וַיִּ֨קְרָא־שָׁ֔ם בְּשֵׁ֥ם יְהוָ֖ה אֵ֥ל עוֹלָֽם׃ 34 וַיָּ֧גָר אַבְרָהָ֛ם בְּאֶ֥רֶץ פְּלִשְׁתִּ֖ים יָמִ֥ים רַבִּֽים׃ פ

כב 1 [SEVENTH READING] וַיְהִ֗י אַחַר֙ הַדְּבָרִ֣ים הָאֵ֔לֶּה וְהָ֣אֱלֹהִ֔ים נִסָּ֖ה אֶת־אַבְרָהָ֑ם וַיֹּ֣אמֶר אֵלָ֗יו אַבְרָהָם֙ וַיֹּ֥אמֶר הִנֵּֽנִי׃ 2 וַיֹּ֡אמֶר קַח־נָ֠א אֶת־בִּנְךָ֨ אֶת־

for guests during their meal. The other sage said that it was an inn for lodging, in which there were all sorts of fruits (*Rashi, 11th century*).

Since he had a well, Abraham wanted to plant an orchard which could be nurtured from the well-water. Abraham's main intention was to benefit guests with the fruit, as the verse continues, *"He (encouraged all guests) there to proclaim the name of God, the God of the world"* (*Rabbi Baḥya b. Asher, 13th century*).

According to *Midrash Tehillim*, *'eshel* (*alef-shin-lamed*) is an acronym for *'akhilah* (eating), *shetiyyah* (drinking), and *levayah* (escorting). Abraham wished to correct the sins of earlier generations: Adam had sinned through *eating*, Noah through *drinking*, and Sodom through their treatment of *guests* (*Rabbi Elijah of Vilna, 18th century*).

He (encouraged all the guests) there to proclaim the name of God. By means of that *'eshel*, God was called "God of the whole world." After the guests would eat and drink, (Abraham) would say to them, "Bless the One of whose food you have eaten! Do you think that you've eaten *my* food? It belongs to the One who spoke and the world came into being!" (*Rashi, 11th century*).

22:1 God tested Abraham. When God tests a person, it is for the benefit of the one being tested. Every person has the potential to do great things, to fulfil God's will or do good deeds. In order to actualize this potential, God tests the person by providing him with a challenge, hoping that through the power of free choice to accomplish the deed, the person's potential will be realized.

God tests the righteous in order to bestow blessings on them as a reward for passing His test. However, God does not usually test errant individuals that do not obey Him, and they remain unable to actualize their potential (*Naḥmanides, 13th century*).

genesis 21:27 – 22:2   va-yera'

²⁷ Abraham took flocks and cattle, and gave them to Abimelech, and they both formed a covenant.

²⁸ Abraham placed seven female lambs by themselves. ²⁹ Abimelech said to Abraham, "What are these seven female lambs, which you have placed by themselves?"

³⁰ He said, "You are going to take these seven female lambs from my hand, as a proof that I dug this well."

³¹ The place was therefore named Beer-sheba ("well of the oath"), because the two of them took an oath. ³² They formed a covenant in Beer-sheba.

Abimelech and his army general Phicol got up and they returned to the land of the Philistines.

³³ (Abraham) planted an orchard (alternatively: established an inn) in Beer-sheba, and he (encouraged all guests) there to proclaim the name of God, the God of the world (after they finished eating).

³⁴ Abraham dwelt in the land of the Philistines for (twenty-six years,) several days (more than the twenty-five years he lived in Hebron).

Abraham's Tenth Test: the Binding of Isaac

22 [SEVENTH READING] ¹ What happened was, after the words (of the Satan, who accused Abraham of not offering a sacrifice to God at his celebratory feast), God tested Abraham.

He said to him, "Abraham!"

(Abraham) said, "I'm here (for You)!"

² He said, "Please take your son, your only one, whom you love, Isaac, and go

---

for punishment from the age of twenty (*Jerusalem Talmud, Bikkurim* 2:1)—and, at that time, Ishmael was just seventeen years old (*Rabbi Menahem Azariah da Fano, 16ᵗʰ–17ᵗʰ century*).

30. As proof that I dug this well. Quoting the verse, *"as a proof that I dug this well"* (v. 30), the *Zohar* refers, rather strangely, to *"Isaac's well."* Why is the well dug by Abraham accredited to Isaac?

Abraham embodied the attribute of love of God, whereas Isaac represented the fear of God. In general, you should endeavor to be in Abraham's positive mode of loving God, continuing always in joyful Divine worship. However, if you possess *only* love of God, and no fear, then your worship will not prevail, for inevitably your love of God will become narcissistic and degenerate into a love for other things. Fear of God is required to *preserve* your love of God.

The well which Abraham dug did not prevail. It was filled in by the Philistines, until, eventually, Isaac redug it. So, the *Zohar* refers even to the original well as *"Isaac's well,"* since it was Isaac's fear that perpetuated Abraham's love (*Rabbi Menahem Mendel Schneerson, 20ᵗʰ century*).

33. Abraham planted an orchard ('eshel). The meaning of the term *'eshel* was disputed between Rav and Samuel. One sage said that it was an orchard from which fruits were brought

בראשית כב:ב-ה

וירא

יְחִידְךָ֤ אֲשֶׁר־אָהַ֙בְתָּ֙ אֶת־יִצְחָ֔ק וְלֶךְ־לְךָ֔ אֶל־אֶ֖רֶץ הַמֹּרִיָּ֑ה וְהַעֲלֵ֤הוּ שָׁם֙ לְעֹלָ֔ה עַ֚ל אַחַ֣ד הֶֽהָרִ֔ים אֲשֶׁ֖ר אֹמַ֥ר אֵלֶֽיךָ׃ 3 וַיַּשְׁכֵּ֨ם אַבְרָהָ֜ם בַּבֹּ֗קֶר וַֽיַּחֲבֹשׁ֙ אֶת־חֲמֹר֔וֹ וַיִּקַּ֞ח אֶת־שְׁנֵ֤י נְעָרָיו֙ אִתּ֔וֹ וְאֵ֖ת יִצְחָ֣ק בְּנ֑וֹ וַיְבַקַּע֙ עֲצֵ֣י עֹלָ֔ה וַיָּ֣קָם וַיֵּ֔לֶךְ אֶל־הַמָּק֖וֹם אֲשֶׁר־אָֽמַר־ל֥וֹ הָאֱלֹהִֽים׃ 4 בַּיּ֣וֹם הַשְּׁלִישִׁ֗י וַיִּשָּׂ֨א אַבְרָהָ֧ם אֶת־עֵינָ֛יו וַיַּ֥רְא אֶת־הַמָּק֖וֹם מֵרָחֹֽק׃ 5 וַיֹּ֨אמֶר אַבְרָהָ֜ם אֶל־נְעָרָ֗יו שְׁבוּ־לָכֶ֥ם פֹּה֙ עִם־

Abraham responded, "This one is the only son of his mother, and that one is the only son of his mother."

God added, "The one whom you love."

"But I love both of them," Abraham insisted.

Finally, God specified, "Isaac."

Why was all of this necessary? Why did God not say in the first place, "Take Isaac"?

So that Abraham would be spared the shock of a sudden demand to sacrifice his son (*Babylonian Talmud, Sanhedrin* 89b).

Please take. God said to him, "I beg you! Pass this test for Me, so that people will not say that the first nine tests were totally insignificant" (*Rashi, 11th century*).

The binding of Isaac was the ultimate test, since Abraham, who had devoted his life to promote awareness of the One God in the world, was asked to execute the only person who could continue this cause after him. This test would prove whether Abraham had promoted the awareness of God in the world for God's sake, or for his own.

Abraham's earlier tests did not fully clarify this point, since it could be argued that even allowing himself to be burned in the fiery furnace at Ur of the Chaldeans was ultimately an act which would have furthered his life's mission. Abraham knew that giving up his life *in public* would have made a tremendous impression on all those present, and would possibly be recorded as an act of true martyrdom for all time. While it *appeared* to be an act of total self-sacrifice, we could not rule out the possibility that Abraham desired to be a martyr, and he entered the furnace because it suited him to do so, at least partially.

Only at the binding of Isaac, where Abraham was asked to perform an act which was (a) contrary to everything that he desired; and (b) in total privacy, could it be proven without doubt that all Abraham's earlier trials were done out of an unquestioning submission to God's will (*Rabbi Menahem Mendel Schneerson, 20th century*).

3. He saddled his donkey (personally). Out of a love of God and eagerness to obey His command, Abraham disregarded his personal stature and insisted on saddling the donkey himself. This shows that intense love leads a person to disregard all formalities (*Babylonian Talmud, Sanhedrin* 105b).

4. On the third day, Abraham looked around and he saw from afar. Even on "the third day" his fervor had not diminished. After all the ordeal of travel and its delays, the fire in his heart and the power of his will still had not waned. *"Abraham looked around"* (lit., "lifted up his eyes")—he was still in a mood of elevation (*Rabbi Menahem Mendel Morgensztern of Kotsk, 19th century*).

away to the land of Moriah (Jerusalem) and bring him up there for a burnt-offering on one of the mountains, where I will tell you."

³ Abraham got up early in the morning (to perform God's command), and he saddled his donkey (personally). He took his two young men (Ishmael and Eliezer) with him (so at least one of them would be with him all the time) and Isaac his son. He cut wood for a burnt-offering, departed, and went to the place of which God had told him.

⁴ On the third day, Abraham looked around and he saw from afar (one particular mountain with a cloud on it).

⁵ Abraham said to his young men, "Stay here with the donkey, while I and the boy will go (a little) further (to our destination). We will prostrate ourselves and return to you."

What was the point of God's testing Abraham, if God already knew that Abraham would pass the test? It was certainly not a demonstration of Abraham's faith to others, since not even the two lads who accompanied Abraham were present at the time. Rather, the purpose of the test was to inspire later generations of Jewish people who would follow in Abraham's footsteps (*Rabbi David Kimḥi, 12ᵗʰ–13ᵗʰ century*).

To perform a new type of act which you have never done before, a spiritual "channel" needs to be opened, allowing the reserves of potential in your soul to spread through your body. In a more general sense this applies on a global scale. A person who commits a spiritually unprecedented act in the world becomes a pioneer, who actually makes it possible for others to follow in his footsteps. He opens a new "channel," breaking down barriers not only for himself, but for his descendants and followers.

The binding of Isaac was not merely an inspiring historical event from which we can learn. It made an indelible mark on the Jewish personality, enabling Abraham's outstanding subordination to God to be duplicated by any of us who will rise to the challenge (*Rabbi Shalom Dov Baer Schneersohn of Lubavitch, 19ᵗʰ–20ᵗʰ century*).

2. Please take your son, your only one, whom you love, Isaac. God said to Abraham, "Take your son."

Abraham replied, "I have two sons, Isaac and Ishmael. Which one should I take?"

"Your only one," God said.

spiritual vitamin

> Of course there are times when things do not go as expected or as desired. But the Torah has already forewarned us to regard such times as temporary trials and tests of our faith in God. As a matter of fact, the stronger your faith in God remains even under adverse circumstances, the sooner it will become clear it was all a matter of a test.

בראשית כב:ו-יב · וירא

הַחֲמוֹר וַאֲנִי וְהַנַּעַר נֵלְכָה עַד-כֹּה וְנִשְׁתַּחֲוֶה וְנָשׁוּבָה אֲלֵיכֶם: ⁶ וַיִּקַּח אַבְרָהָם אֶת-עֲצֵי הָעֹלָה וַיָּשֶׂם עַל-יִצְחָק בְּנוֹ וַיִּקַּח בְּיָדוֹ אֶת-הָאֵשׁ וְאֶת-הַמַּאֲכֶלֶת וַיֵּלְכוּ שְׁנֵיהֶם יַחְדָּו: ⁷ וַיֹּאמֶר יִצְחָק אֶל-אַבְרָהָם אָבִיו וַיֹּאמֶר אָבִי וַיֹּאמֶר הִנֶּנִּי בְנִי וַיֹּאמֶר הִנֵּה הָאֵשׁ וְהָעֵצִים וְאַיֵּה הַשֶּׂה לְעֹלָה: ⁸ וַיֹּאמֶר אַבְרָהָם אֱלֹהִים יִרְאֶה-לּוֹ הַשֶּׂה לְעֹלָה בְּנִי וַיֵּלְכוּ שְׁנֵיהֶם יַחְדָּו: ⁹ וַיָּבֹאוּ אֶל-הַמָּקוֹם אֲשֶׁר אָמַר-לוֹ הָאֱלֹהִים וַיִּבֶן שָׁם אַבְרָהָם אֶת-הַמִּזְבֵּחַ וַיַּעֲרֹךְ אֶת-הָעֵצִים וַיַּעֲקֹד אֶת-יִצְחָק בְּנוֹ וַיָּשֶׂם אֹתוֹ עַל-הַמִּזְבֵּחַ מִמַּעַל לָעֵצִים: ¹⁰ וַיִּשְׁלַח אַבְרָהָם אֶת-יָדוֹ וַיִּקַּח אֶת-הַמַּאֲכֶלֶת לִשְׁחֹט אֶת-בְּנוֹ: ¹¹ וַיִּקְרָא אֵלָיו מַלְאַךְ יְהֹוָה מִן-הַשָּׁמַיִם וַיֹּאמֶר אַבְרָהָם | אַבְרָהָם וַיֹּאמֶר הִנֵּנִי: ¹² וַיֹּאמֶר אַל-תִּשְׁלַח יָדְךָ אֶל-הַנַּעַר וְאַל-תַּעַשׂ לוֹ מְאוּמָה כִּי | עַתָּה יָדַעְתִּי כִּי-יְרֵא אֱלֹהִים אַתָּה וְלֹא

take your son, etc." I did not alter the utterance of My lips! I never said to you, *"slaughter him,"* but rather, *"bring him up."* You have brought him up. Now, take him down (*Rashi, 11ᵗʰ century*).

Now I know that you are a God-fearing man. Abraham was known for his tremendous love of God. Why was he awarded the title here of "God-fearing"?

Let us answer this question with another question. Why was the binding of Isaac an especially difficult trial for Abraham. We are speaking here of a man who was already willing to cast his *own self* into a fiery furnace, rather than transgress the will of God. Surely, then, he would be willing to sacrifice his child?

While Abraham did not know that this was only a test, he nevertheless felt something was lacking. Since it was not, in fact, God's will that Isaac should be slaughtered, Abraham failed to establish his normal sense of connectedness and attachment to God through this command. On the other hand, it was an explicit order from God and he had to obey it.

So for the first time, Abraham was forced to serve God entirely out of fear. There was no opportunity for positive feelings of love and connectedness in this emotionally "empty" deed; only fear and obedience. This was entirely against Abraham's nature and his usual mode of worship, and it presented a formidable test for him. So, upon passing the test,

kabbalah bites

22:7 Adam's sin was tantamount to the three cardinal sins of idol-worship, murder, and infidelity. To achieve *tikkun* (spiritual healing) for this he was reincarnated into all three Patriarchs: Abraham, Isaac and Jacob.

Isaac offered his life as a burnt-offering upon the altar to be slaughtered because his reincarnation was to achieve *tikkun* for the sin of murder. But since this murderous spark was not Isaac's sin, but Adam's, he was spared, and a ram was offered in his stead.

genesis 22:6–12 va-yera'

⁶ Abraham took the wood for the burnt-offering, and he placed it upon his son Isaac. He took the fire and the knife in his hand, and they both went together.

⁷ Isaac spoke to Abraham his father, saying, "My father!"

He said, "I'm here (for you), my son."

(Isaac) said, "Here is the fire and the wood, but where is the lamb for the burnt-offering?"

⁸ Abraham said, "God will provide for Himself the lamb for the burnt-offering, my son," and they both went together.

⁹ They came to the place which God had told him about. Abraham built the altar there and arranged the wood, and he tied (the hands and feet of) his son Isaac (behind him) and placed him on the altar, upon the wood.

¹⁰ Abraham stretched out his hand and took the knife, to slaughter his son.

¹¹ An angel of God called to him from heaven and said, "Abraham! Abraham!"

He said, "I'm here!"

¹² (The angel) said, "Do not stretch out your hand to (slaughter) the boy, or do the slightest thing to him, for now I know (evidence to answer the Satan) that you are a God-fearing man and that you did not withhold your son, your only one, from Me."

---

7. Here is the fire and the wood, but where is the lamb for the burnt-offering? Why did Isaac speak of "*the* fire and *the* wood," as if he were referring to a certain fire and wood in particular?

When God commanded Abraham to *"Please take your son, your only one, whom you love, Isaac, and go away to the land of Moriah and bring him up there for a burnt-offering"* (v. 2), Abraham's heart burned with fire to fulfil God's will. He was aware, however, that this enthusiasm was likely to wane during the course of a three-day journey to the land of Moriah. So Abraham decided to act immediately, chopping some wood right away, to ensure that his intense emotions would be put into action while they were still strong.

Isaac therefore asked: *"Here is the fire and the wood"*—This wood proves that you have a fiery passion to fulfil God's will. *"But where is the lamb?"*—Why, then, do you need to offer me? Your dedication to God has already been proven. A lamb should now suffice! (*Rabbi Elimelech of Lyzhansk, 18th century*)

12. Now I know. Abraham said to God: I will explain my grievance before You: Beforehand, You said to me, *"Your (true) descendants will be through Isaac"* (above, 21:12), and then You retracted and said, *"Please take your son ... and bring him up there for a burnt-offering"* (v. 2). Now, You are saying to me, *"Do not stretch out your hand to (slaughter) the boy!"*

God said to him: *"I shall not profane My covenant, nor shall I alter the utterance of My lips"* (Psalms 89:35). From when I said to you, *"Please*

---

food for thought

1. Why is *fear*—and not *love*—the foundation of our relationship with God?

2. Are you ready to demonstrate why and how you are a follower of God?

3. Do your spiritual beliefs inform your human relations at a very fundamental level?

בראשית כב:יב-כד — וירא

חָשַׂ֖כְתָּ אֶת־בִּנְךָ֣ אֶת־יְחִידְךָ֑ מִמֶּֽנִּי: 13 וַיִּשָּׂ֨א אַבְרָהָ֜ם אֶת־עֵינָ֗יו וַיַּרְא֙ וְהִנֵּה־אַ֔יִל אַחַ֕ר נֶאֱחַ֥ז בַּסְּבַ֖ךְ בְּקַרְנָ֑יו וַיֵּ֤לֶךְ אַבְרָהָם֙ וַיִּקַּ֣ח אֶת־הָאַ֔יִל וַיַּעֲלֵ֥הוּ לְעֹלָ֖ה תַּ֥חַת בְּנֽוֹ: 14 וַיִּקְרָ֧א אַבְרָהָ֛ם שֵֽׁם־הַמָּק֥וֹם הַה֖וּא יְהֹוָ֣ה | יִרְאֶ֑ה אֲשֶׁר֙ יֵאָמֵ֣ר הַיּ֔וֹם בְּהַ֥ר יְהֹוָ֖ה יֵרָאֶֽה: 15 וַיִּקְרָ֛א מַלְאַ֥ךְ יְהֹוָ֖ה אֶל־אַבְרָהָ֑ם שֵׁנִ֖ית מִן־הַשָּׁמָֽיִם: 16 וַיֹּ֕אמֶר בִּ֥י נִשְׁבַּ֖עְתִּי נְאֻם־יְהֹוָ֑ה כִּ֗י יַ֚עַן אֲשֶׁ֤ר עָשִׂ֨יתָ֙ אֶת־הַדָּבָ֣ר הַזֶּ֔ה וְלֹ֥א חָשַׂ֖כְתָּ אֶת־בִּנְךָ֥ אֶת־יְחִידֶֽךָ: 17 כִּֽי־בָרֵ֣ךְ אֲבָרֶכְךָ֗ וְהַרְבָּ֨ה אַרְבֶּ֤ה אֶת־זַרְעֲךָ֙ כְּכוֹכְבֵ֣י הַשָּׁמַ֔יִם וְכַח֕וֹל אֲשֶׁ֖ר עַל־שְׂפַ֣ת הַיָּ֑ם וְיִרַ֣שׁ זַרְעֲךָ֔ אֵ֖ת שַׁ֥עַר אֹיְבָֽיו: 18 וְהִתְבָּרֲכ֣וּ בְזַרְעֲךָ֔ כֹּ֖ל גּוֹיֵ֣י הָאָ֑רֶץ עֵ֕קֶב אֲשֶׁ֥ר שָׁמַ֖עְתָּ בְּקֹלִֽי: 19 וַיָּ֤שָׁב אַבְרָהָם֙ אֶל־נְעָרָ֔יו וַיָּקֻ֛מוּ וַיֵּלְכ֥וּ יַחְדָּ֖ו אֶל־בְּאֵ֣ר שָׁ֑בַע וַיֵּ֥שֶׁב אַבְרָהָ֖ם בִּבְאֵ֥ר שָֽׁבַע: פ 20 [MAFTIR] וַיְהִ֗י אַחֲרֵי֙ הַדְּבָרִ֣ים הָאֵ֔לֶּה וַיֻּגַּ֥ד לְאַבְרָהָ֖ם לֵאמֹ֑ר הִ֠נֵּ֠ה יָלְדָ֨ה מִלְכָּ֥ה גַם־הִ֛וא בָּנִ֖ים לְנָח֥וֹר אָחִֽיךָ: 21 אֶת־ע֥וּץ בְּכֹר֖וֹ וְאֶת־בּ֣וּז אָחִ֑יו וְאֶת־קְמוּאֵ֖ל אֲבִ֥י אֲרָֽם: 22 וְאֶת־כֶּ֣שֶׂד וְאֶת־חֲז֔וֹ וְאֶת־פִּלְדָּ֖שׁ וְאֶת־יִדְלָ֑ף וְאֵ֖ת בְּתוּאֵֽל: 23 וּבְתוּאֵ֖ל יָלַ֣ד אֶת־רִבְקָ֑ה שְׁמֹנָ֤ה אֵ֨לֶּה֙ יָלְדָ֣ה מִלְכָּ֔ה לְנָח֖וֹר אֲחִ֥י אַבְרָהָֽם: 24 וּפִֽילַגְשׁ֖וֹ וּשְׁמָ֣הּ רְאוּמָ֑ה וַתֵּ֤לֶד גַּם־הִוא֙ אֶת־טֶ֣בַח וְאֶת־גַּ֔חַם וְאֶת־תַּ֖חַשׁ וְאֶֽת־מַעֲכָֽה: פ פ פ

קמ"ז פסוקים, אמנו"ן סימן.

of Abraham. This had the effect of containing his unbounded love, enabling all of us to receive it (*Rabbi Menahem Nahum Twersky of Chernobyl, 18th century*).

15. A second time. Abraham was sure that the angel who said, *"Do not stretch out your hand to slaughter the boy"* (v. 12), had come to trick him, and that God really *did* want him to slaughter Isaac. Therefore, it was necessary for God to call out to Abraham a second time to confirm that he had acted correctly (*Rabbi Abraham b. Jacob Saba, 15th century*).

In this second calling, God promised that He would *"multiply your descendants (and your son's) like the stars of the heavens and like the sand that is on the seashore, and your descendants will inherit the cities of their enemies"* (v. 17). But surely He had already promised this to Abraham before (above, 15:5)?

In fact, however, God had merely *promised* that he would multiply Abraham's descendants, but the promise could have been retracted if Abraham's descendants would have sinned. Here however, God *swore* that he would keep His promise, regardless of whether the Jewish people sinned or not. This constitutes the Divine assurance of the redemption which is destined to come in the future (*Nahmanides, 13th century*).

genesis 22:13–24 — va-yera'

¹³ Abraham looked around to see and—look!—there was a ram. (Abraham saw it) after (the angel spoke to him, noticing that) it was caught in a tree by its horns. Abraham went and took the ram and offered it up as a burnt-offering instead of his son.

¹⁴ Abraham named that place Adonai-yireh ("God will select"). To this day it is the mountain (associated with) God's revelation.

¹⁵ An angel of God called to Abraham a second time from heaven. ¹⁶ He said, "'I Myself have sworn,' says God, 'that because you have done this thing and you did not withhold your son, your only one, ¹⁷ I will bless you (and your son), and I will multiply your descendants (and your son's) like the stars of the heavens and like the sand that is on the seashore, and your descendants will inherit the cities of their enemies. ¹⁸ All the nations of the world will be blessed through your children, because you listened to My voice.'"

¹⁹ Abraham returned to his young men, and they got up and went together to Beer-sheba. Abraham stayed in Beer-sheba (for a while, before returning to Hebron, where he had already lived for twelve years after leaving Beer-sheba).

The Birth of Rebekah

[MAFTIR] ²⁰ Then, after the words (of Abraham, who expressed his view that Isaac should marry and have children,) Abraham was told (by God about the birth of Rebekah), "Milcah has given birth to sons from your brother Nahor and she too (has eight boys in the family, just like your future grandson Jacob will have from his main wives. Milcah's sons are:) ²¹ Uz the first born, Buz his brother, Kemuel the father of Aram, ²² Chesed, Hazo, Pildash, Jidlaph, and Bethuel. ²³ Bethuel fathered Rebekah." Milcah bore these eight to Nahor, Abraham's brother.

²⁴ His concubine, whose name was Reumah, had also given birth to (four boys, just as Jacob would have from his concubines. Reumah's sons were): Tebah, Gaham, Tahash and Maacah.

The Haftarah for Va-Yera' is on page 1295.

---

his primary achievement was highlighted: "Now I know that you are a God-*fearing* man" (*Rabbi Judah Aryeh Leib Alter of Gur, 19th century*).

Abraham brought down love to his generation from Above, which is why he is referred to in Scripture as *"Abraham My lover"* (*Isaiah 41:8*). The love, however, was so intense, it was debilitating. Therefore *gevurah* (severity)—*"the fear of Isaac"* (below, 31:42)—also had to be brought into the world, through Isaac, so that the deeds of love started by Abraham would endure. *The fear of Isaac contained the love of Abraham so that all future recipients could withstand it.*

It was necessary, then, for the two of them, the love and the fear, to be commingled; and that was why Abraham was commanded to perform the binding of Isaac. When Abraham was forced to arouse cruelty from within his own self, he had to draw on the "fear of Isaac" for the sake of his love of God, and this resulted in the quality of Isaac becoming subsumed within that

Although this portion describes events **after Sarah's passing,** it is called "the **life** of Sarah" for **purpose** in life now unfolded—**her son** married, the **land of Israel** began to be acquired. You are truly "alive" when your **achievements** are **immortalized.**

ḤAYYEI SARAH
חיי שרה

SARAH'S PASSING	23:1–20
ELIEZER IS SENT TO FIND ISAAC A WIFE	24:1–67
ABRAHAM REMARRIES HAGAR	4:1–26
OFFSPRING OF ABRAHAM	25:1–6
ABRAHAM'S PASSING	25:7–11
ISHMAEL'S DESCENDANTS	25:12–18

NAME
Ḥayyei Sarah

MEANING
"Life of Sarah"

LINES IN TORAH SCROLL
171

PARASHIYYOT
3 open; 1 closed

VERSES
105

WORDS
1402

LETTERS
5314

DATE
2085–2123

LOCATION
Hebron (Kiriath-arba), Aram-naharaim, Beer-lahai-roi

KEY PEOPLE
Sarah, Abraham, Ephron the Hittite, Eliezer, Rebekah, Bethuel, Laban, Isaac, Hagar

MITZVOT
None

MASORETIC FEATURES
The word *va-yo'mar* (24:12) has an unusual cantillation note, the *shalshelet* (֓).

CHARACTER PROFILE

NAME
Sarah (Iscah)

FATHER
Haran

HUSBAND
Abraham

SISTER
Milcah

CHILD
Isaac

LIFE SPAN
127 years

BURIAL PLACE
Cave of Machpelah

ACHIEVEMENTS
Only prophetess that God spoke to directly; greater in prophecy than Abraham.

KNOWN FOR
Her beauty; her lack of sin; was kidnapped by both Abimelech and Pharaoh and miraculously saved; gave birth at 90 years of age; when Sarah conceived, many other barren women were also healed and many sick people were cured.

HONORING THE DEAD

Abraham's purchase of a plot for his wife is the first reference in the Bible to burial. Respecting the dead and ensuring prompt and proper burial is central to Jewish values (23:3–20).

CARE OF ANIMALS

Eliezer was assured that Rebekah was the correct wife for Isaac when, in addition to offering him water, she offered to give his camels water to drink. Judaism prohibits the mistreatment of animals; we are even commanded to feed our animals before we feed ourselves (24:19).

LOVE

The Torah states that Isaac began to love Rebekah only *after* he had married her. Genuine love must be accompanied by commitment and care, otherwise it is nothing more than a self-gratifying infatuation. A lover is as eager to give as he or she is to receive, and every healthy loving relationship needs to be nurtured constantly with increased trust and openness (24:67).

חיי שרה | בראשית כג:א-ג

כג

1 וַיִּהְיוּ֙ חַיֵּ֣י שָׂרָ֔ה מֵאָ֥ה שָׁנָ֛ה וְעֶשְׂרִ֥ים שָׁנָ֖ה וְשֶׁ֣בַע שָׁנִ֑ים שְׁנֵ֖י חַיֵּ֥י שָׂרָֽה: 2 וַתָּ֣מָת שָׂרָ֗ה בְּקִרְיַ֥ת אַרְבַּ֛ע הִ֥וא חֶבְר֖וֹן בְּאֶ֣רֶץ כְּנָ֑עַן וַיָּבֹא֙ אַבְרָהָ֔ם לִסְפֹּ֥ד לְשָׂרָ֖ה וְלִבְכֹּתָֽהּ: 3 וַיָּ֙קָם֙ אַבְרָהָ֔ם מֵעַ֖ל פְּנֵ֣י מֵת֑וֹ וַיְדַבֵּ֥ר אֶל־בְּנֵי־

Then, the *Midrash* describes type "b": *"'God knows the days of the perfect ones'—this refers to Sarah, who was perfect in her actions. Rabbi Johanan said, 'like a perfect calf,'"* i.e., her actions *as a whole* were perfect (*Rabbi Menahem Mendel Schneerson, 20th century*).

The years of Sarah's life (were all equally good). Among Sarah's misfortunes, she suffered exile, abduction, and ninety years of infertility—experiences that crush the spirit, making it hard to remain righteous. But Sarah did not allow these setbacks to ruffle her fine character and dedication to God; she always remained strong in her belief in God's providence. In her eyes, all her years were "equally good" (*Rabbi Aaron Lewin of Rzeszow, 20th century*).

2. Sarah died. The account of Sarah's passing was recorded after the binding of Isaac, because upon hearing that her son was prepared for slaughter and was almost slaughtered, her soul departed from her, and she died (*Rashi, 11th century*).

In the Torah of Moses, faithful shepherd of the Jewish people, these two events—the death of Sarah and the binding of Isaac—are placed side by side as an argument in our defense. The suggestion is that, while it may be true that *"suffering purifies a person"* (*Babylonian Talmud, Berakhot* 5a), it is also true that we are damaged by excessive suffering. To be purified by suffering, it must be doled out mercifully, bearing in mind the person's ability to cope. If the pain is, God forbid, unbearable, death can result. If Sarah, who was of such great stature, could not withstand extreme anguish, how much less so can the rest of us cope!

Sarah died for the good of the Jewish people. *She died to show God that we should not be expected to suffer unreasonable levels of pain.* You might tend to judge Sarah as having sinned against the remainder of her years, because if she had not taken the binding of Isaac so much to heart, she would have lived longer. But, since this was done for the good of the Jewish people, the years Sarah might have lived beyond her one hundred and twenty-seven years were not wasted at all (*Rabbi Kalonymous Kalman Shapira, 20th century*).

Sarah died in Kiriath-arba, which is Hebron, in the land of Canaan. The literal translation of Kiriath-arba is the "city of four." Why does the Torah refer to Hebron in this way?

Because of the four couples that were eventually buried there: Adam and Eve; Abraham and Sarah; Isaac and Rebekah; and Jacob and Leah (*Rashi, 11th century*).

To eulogize Sarah and to weep over her. Surely, weeping comes before a eulogy? However, when Abraham arrived, the household had already wept for Sarah and were already eulogizing her. Therefore, Abraham joined in the eulogy first, and then wept for her later (*Rabbi Judah b. Eliezer, 13th century*).

The feeling of loss, which normally weakens with time, actually grew stronger after Sarah's passing. Thus, the weeping continued long after the eulogies (*Rabbi Ephraim of Luntshits, 16th–17th century*).

food for thought

1. Why is aging so difficult for us?

2. Can old age really be "equally good" as youth?

3. Have you ever lied about your age? If so, why?

parashat ḥayyei sarah

Sarah Passes Away

23 ¹ Sarah's lifetime was (a total of) one hundred years, twenty years and seven years. The years of Sarah's life (were all equally good).

² Sarah died in Kiriath-arba, which is Hebron, in the land of Canaan. Abraham came (from Beer-sheba, immediately after the binding of Isaac, the shock of which had caused her death) to eulogize Sarah and to weep over her.

Abraham Purchases the Cave of Machpelah

³ Abraham got up from in front of his deceased (wife).

23:1 One hundred years, twenty years and seven years. *"God knows the days of the perfect ones, and their inheritance shall be forever"* (*Psalms* 37:18)—just as their days are perfect, their years are perfect too. At twenty, Sarah was as beautiful as at seven. At one hundred, she was as free from sin as at twenty.

An alternative explanation: *"God knows the days of the perfect ones"*—this refers to Sarah, who was perfect in her actions. Rabbi Johanan said, "like a perfect calf" (*Genesis Rabbah*).

The perfection of Sarah's entire lifetime could be understood in two different ways:

(a) Perfection in every detail—each day of her life was perfect.

(b) Her life *as a whole* was perfect—an overall perfection.

A practical difference between these two approaches is illustrated by the case of a penitent. Clearly, the penitent does not possess the perfection of type "a," where every detail in his life is perfect, for there was a period when he had erred. But he could claim to have perfection of type "b" (overall perfection), since his repentance atones for the past, and we look at his former life in the context of his present repentance.

Thus, perfection of type "a" is greater than type 'b', since a person possessing perfection of type "a" has perfect days *literally*. Type "b" perfection—the penitent—takes a more holistic approach, which perceives *retrospectively* the positive quality even within imperfect days.

The *Midrash* deemed it appropriate to attribute both types of perfection to Sarah. First we read, *"Just as their days are perfect, so are their years perfect. At twenty, she (Sarah) was as beautiful as at seven, etc.,"* i.e., the perfection of each individual day and year in its own right (type "a").

spiritual vitamin

" Sarah's passing reflected a subtle weakness on her part, that she was not capable of containing the joy of Isaac being saved from slaughter and "her soul departed from her, and she died."

True worship of God requires you to channel moments of joy into further activity, and not to allow yourself to be carried away by them. "

חיי שרה • בראשית כג:ג-טו

4 חֵת לֵאמֹר: גֵּר־וְתוֹשָׁב אָנֹכִי עִמָּכֶם תְּנוּ לִי אֲחֻזַּת־קֶבֶר עִמָּכֶם וְאֶקְבְּרָה מֵתִי מִלְּפָנָי: 5 וַיַּעֲנוּ בְנֵי־חֵת אֶת־אַבְרָהָם לֵאמֹר לוֹ: 6 שְׁמָעֵנוּ ׀ אֲדֹנִי נְשִׂיא אֱלֹהִים אַתָּה בְּתוֹכֵנוּ בְּמִבְחַר קְבָרֵינוּ קְבֹר אֶת־מֵתֶךָ אִישׁ מִמֶּנּוּ אֶת־קִבְרוֹ לֹא־יִכְלֶה מִמְּךָ מִקְּבֹר מֵתֶךָ: 7 וַיָּקָם אַבְרָהָם וַיִּשְׁתַּחוּ לְעַם־הָאָרֶץ לִבְנֵי־חֵת: 8 וַיְדַבֵּר אִתָּם לֵאמֹר אִם־יֵשׁ אֶת־נַפְשְׁכֶם לִקְבֹּר אֶת־מֵתִי מִלְּפָנַי שְׁמָעוּנִי וּפִגְעוּ־לִי בְּעֶפְרוֹן בֶּן־צֹחַר: 9 וְיִתֶּן־לִי אֶת־מְעָרַת הַמַּכְפֵּלָה אֲשֶׁר־לוֹ אֲשֶׁר בִּקְצֵה שָׂדֵהוּ בְּכֶסֶף מָלֵא יִתְּנֶנָּה לִי בְּתוֹכְכֶם לַאֲחֻזַּת־קָבֶר: 10 וְעֶפְרוֹן יֹשֵׁב בְּתוֹךְ בְּנֵי־חֵת וַיַּעַן עֶפְרוֹן הַחִתִּי אֶת־אַבְרָהָם בְּאָזְנֵי בְנֵי־חֵת לְכֹל בָּאֵי שַׁעַר־עִירוֹ לֵאמֹר: 11 לֹא־אֲדֹנִי שְׁמָעֵנִי הַשָּׂדֶה נָתַתִּי לָךְ וְהַמְּעָרָה אֲשֶׁר־בּוֹ לְךָ נְתַתִּיהָ לְעֵינֵי בְנֵי־עַמִּי נְתַתִּיהָ לָּךְ קְבֹר מֵתֶךָ: 12 וַיִּשְׁתַּחוּ אַבְרָהָם לִפְנֵי עַם־הָאָרֶץ: 13 וַיְדַבֵּר אֶל־עֶפְרוֹן בְּאָזְנֵי עַם־הָאָרֶץ לֵאמֹר אַךְ אִם־אַתָּה לוּ שְׁמָעֵנִי נָתַתִּי כֶּסֶף הַשָּׂדֶה קַח מִמֶּנִּי וְאֶקְבְּרָה אֶת־מֵתִי שָׁמָּה: 14 וַיַּעַן עֶפְרוֹן אֶת־אַבְרָהָם לֵאמֹר לוֹ: 15 אֲדֹנִי שְׁמָעֵנִי אֶרֶץ אַרְבַּע מֵאֹת שֶׁקֶל־כֶּסֶף בֵּינִי וּבֵינְךָ מַה־הִוא

me, 'I will give this land to your descendants'" (above, 12:7; *Rashi, 11th century*).

5. The people of Het answered. The people of Het said to Abraham, "We know that in the future God is going to give all these lands to you and your descendants. Strike a covenant with us that the Jewish people will only inherit the city of the Jebusites with the consent of the Jebusite people" (who were descendants of Het). Abraham struck the covenant with them and purchased the cave of Machpelah (*Pirkei de-Rabbi Eliezer*).

9. The cave of Machpelah. The cave was called *Machpelah*, meaning "double," because it was doubled for couples. Four couples were buried there: Adam and Eve, Abraham and Sarah, Isaac and Rebekah, Jacob and Leah (*Rashi, 11th century*).

kabbalah bites

23:9 "*Its full price.*" Why is it so tempting when we are offered something for free?

The *Zohar* teaches that things which are "free" come from the *sitra 'ahara'*, the demonic realm. Everything that is connected with your true destiny is connected with effort, but the demonic forces try to derail you with countless "free" offers.

So when Abraham acquired the holy cave of Machpelah he was careful to pay "*its full price.*"

He spoke to the people of Het, saying, [4] "I am an immigrant and a resident among you. Let me have some land for a burial ground with you, so that I may bury my dead from in front of me."

[5] The people of Het answered Abraham, saying to him, [6] "Listen to us, sir! You are a prince of God in our midst. You may bury your dead in the choicest of our burial places. Not one of us will hold back his burial place from you to bury your dead."

[7] Abraham got up and prostrated himself to the people of the land, the people of Het.

[8] He said to them, "If you wish me to bury my dead from in front of me, listen to me and ask Ephron son of Zohar [9] to give me his cave of Machpelah, which is at the end of his field. Let him give it to me for its full price, as land for a burial plot in your midst."

[10] (Due to Abraham's importance,) Ephron sat (in a high position) among the people of Het.

Ephron the Hittite responded to Abraham in (front of) an audience of the people of Het—who had all (stopped work and) come to the gate of the city (in honor of Sarah)—saying, [11] "No, sir, (I will not accept your money). Listen to me! I have given you the field, and I have given you the cave which is in it. I have given it to you, in the presence of my people, to bury your dead."

[12] Abraham threw himself to the ground in front of the local people. [13] He spoke to Ephron, in (front of) the (gathered) audience of local people, saying, "But if only you would listen to me! I have the money (ready) for the field. Take it from me, and I will bury my dead there."

[14] Ephron replied to Abraham, saying to him, [15] "Sir, listen to me! What is a (piece of) land worth four hundred shekels of silver between (friends like) me and you? (Forget about the money) and bury your dead!"

4. I am an immigrant and a resident among you. According to the *Midrash*, he was saying, "If you wish to sell me a burial site then I am like an immigrant and will purchase it from you for a good price. But, if not, I will be a resident and will take it by rights, since God said to

spiritual vitamin

> Your life is just long enough for you to fulfil your purpose on this earth; it is not a day too short, nor is it a day too long. If you let a single day, or week, let alone months, to pass by without fulfilling your purpose it is an irretrievable loss both for you and for the universe at large.

בראשית כג:טז - כד:ז   חיי שרה

וְאֶת־מֵתְךָ֖ קְבֹֽר׃ 16 וַיִּשְׁמַ֣ע אַבְרָהָם֮ אֶל־עֶפְרוֹן֒ וַיִּשְׁקֹ֤ל אַבְרָהָם֙ לְעֶפְרֹ֔ן אֶת־הַכֶּ֕סֶף אֲשֶׁ֥ר דִּבֶּ֖ר בְּאָזְנֵ֣י בְנֵי־חֵ֑ת אַרְבַּ֤ע מֵאוֹת֙ שֶׁ֣קֶל כֶּ֔סֶף עֹבֵ֖ר לַסֹּחֵֽר׃ [SECOND READING]

17 וַיָּ֣קָם ׀ שְׂדֵ֣ה עֶפְר֗וֹן אֲשֶׁר֙ בַּמַּכְפֵּלָ֔ה אֲשֶׁ֖ר לִפְנֵ֣י מַמְרֵ֑א הַשָּׂדֶה֙ וְהַמְּעָרָ֣ה אֲשֶׁר־בּ֔וֹ וְכָל־הָעֵץ֙ אֲשֶׁ֣ר בַּשָּׂדֶ֔ה אֲשֶׁ֥ר בְּכָל־גְּבֻל֖וֹ סָבִֽיב׃ 18 לְאַבְרָהָ֥ם לְמִקְנָ֖ה לְעֵינֵ֣י בְנֵי־חֵ֑ת בְּכֹ֖ל בָּאֵ֥י שַֽׁעַר־עִירֽוֹ׃ 19 וְאַחֲרֵי־כֵן֩ קָבַ֨ר אַבְרָהָ֜ם אֶת־שָׂרָ֣ה אִשְׁתּ֗וֹ אֶל־מְעָרַ֞ת שְׂדֵ֧ה הַמַּכְפֵּלָ֛ה עַל־פְּנֵ֥י מַמְרֵ֖א הִ֣וא חֶבְר֑וֹן בְּאֶ֖רֶץ כְּנָֽעַן׃ 20 וַיָּ֨קָם הַשָּׂדֶ֜ה וְהַמְּעָרָ֧ה אֲשֶׁר־בּ֛וֹ לְאַבְרָהָ֖ם לַאֲחֻזַּת־קָ֑בֶר מֵאֵ֖ת בְּנֵי־חֵֽת׃ ס

כד 1 וְאַבְרָהָ֣ם זָקֵ֔ן בָּ֖א בַּיָּמִ֑ים וַֽיהוָ֛ה בֵּרַ֥ךְ אֶת־אַבְרָהָ֖ם בַּכֹּֽל׃ 2 וַיֹּ֣אמֶר אַבְרָהָ֗ם אֶל־עַבְדּוֹ֙ זְקַ֣ן בֵּית֔וֹ הַמֹּשֵׁ֖ל בְּכָל־אֲשֶׁר־ל֑וֹ שִֽׂים־נָ֥א יָדְךָ֖ תַּ֥חַת יְרֵכִֽי׃ 3 וְאַשְׁבִּ֣יעֲךָ֔ בַּֽיהוָה֙ אֱלֹהֵ֣י הַשָּׁמַ֔יִם וֵֽאלֹהֵ֖י הָאָ֑רֶץ אֲשֶׁ֨ר לֹֽא־תִקַּ֤ח אִשָּׁה֙ לִבְנִ֔י מִבְּנוֹת֙ הַֽכְּנַעֲנִ֔י אֲשֶׁ֥ר אָנֹכִ֖י יוֹשֵׁ֥ב בְּקִרְבּֽוֹ׃ 4 כִּ֧י אֶל־אַרְצִ֛י וְאֶל־מֽוֹלַדְתִּ֖י תֵּלֵ֑ךְ וְלָקַחְתָּ֥ אִשָּׁ֖ה לִבְנִ֥י לְיִצְחָֽק׃ 5 וַיֹּ֤אמֶר אֵלָיו֙ הָעֶ֔בֶד אוּלַי֙ לֹֽא־תֹאבֶ֣ה הָֽאִשָּׁ֔ה לָלֶ֥כֶת אַחֲרַ֖י אֶל־הָאָ֣רֶץ הַזֹּ֑את הֶֽהָשֵׁ֤ב אָשִׁיב֙ אֶת־בִּנְךָ֔ אֶל־הָאָ֖רֶץ אֲשֶׁר־יָצָ֥אתָ מִשָּֽׁם׃ 6 וַיֹּ֥אמֶר אֵלָ֖יו אַבְרָהָ֑ם הִשָּׁ֣מֶר לְךָ֔ פֶּן־תָּשִׁ֥יב אֶת־בְּנִ֖י שָֽׁמָּה׃ 7 יְהוָ֣ה ׀ אֱלֹהֵ֣י הַשָּׁמַ֗יִם אֲשֶׁ֨ר לְקָחַ֜נִי מִבֵּ֤ית אָבִי֙ וּמֵאֶ֣רֶץ מֽוֹלַדְתִּ֔י

---

6. Be insistent not to take my son back there. Abraham did not want Isaac to marry a girl from Canaan (v. 3), for the local people had a disposition towards self-indulgent desires. The family of Laban and Bethuel did not possess this predisposition but, on the other hand, they were idol-worshipers.

Idol-worship, however, is not an inherited quality, but a cultural phenomenon. Therefore, Abraham requested that (a) Isaac's wife should not be from Canaan but from *"my birthplace,"* so that she should be of good disposition; and (b) he insisted *"not to take my son back there,"* i.e., the girl must be removed from the idol-worshiping culture and brought to Isaac, and not the other way around (*Rabbi Ephraim of Luntshits, 16th–17th century*).

7. God of the heavens. He did not say, "and the God of the earth," as he had said above, *"I will make you swear by God, the God of the heavens and the God of the earth"* (v. 3). Abraham said to him, *"now* he is the God of the heavens and the God of the earth, because I have made it habitual for creatures to mention him. But when he took me from my father's house, he was the

[SECOND READING] ¹⁶ Abraham listened to Ephron. Abraham weighed to Ephron the (amount of) silver that he had mentioned in the presence of the people of Het: four hundred shekels of silver in standard currency (and he accepted it).

¹⁷ The field of Ephron which was in Machpelah, facing Mamre, was established (as Abraham's possession. This included) the field and the cave which was in it, all the trees that were in the field, which were within its entire border around. ¹⁸ (It became) Abraham's as a possession in the presence of the people of Het, who had come to the gate of his city.

¹⁹ Afterwards, Abraham buried Sarah his wife in the cave in the field of Machpelah, facing Mamre, which is Hebron, in the land of Canaan. ²⁰ The field and the cave within it were established as Abraham's burial plot, (purchased) from the people of Het.

Abraham Sends Eliezer to Find a Wife for Isaac

24 ¹ Abraham was old, (but still) immersed in daily life. God had blessed Abraham with everything (including a son). ² Abraham said to his servant, the senior member of his house, who was in charge of everything he had, "Please place your hand under my thigh (to swear an oath). ³ I will make you swear by God, the God of the heavens and the God of the earth, that you will not take a wife for my son from the daughters of the Canaanites, among whom I live. ⁴ Rather, you should go to my land, to my birthplace, and you will take a wife for my son, for Isaac."

⁵ The servant said to him, "What if the woman will not want to follow me to this land? Shall I take your son back to the land from where you came?"

⁶ Abraham said to him, "Be insistent not to take my son back there. ⁷ God, the God of the heavens—who took me from my father's house (in Haran) and from the land (Ur of the Chaldeans) where I was born; who spoke to me (about my

24:1 God had blessed Abraham with everything. Abraham was blessed with the attitude of being satisfied with his lot, never feeling that he was missing anything. If you crave nothing then you have "everything" (*Rabbi Eliezer b. Elijah Ashkenazi, 16ᵗʰ century*).

spiritual vitamin

❝ Abraham—the first of the Patriarchs, the first Jew—demonstrated the goal of a Jew: that wherever you may find yourself, and in whatever company you may be, the focus of everyday life is to spread awareness of God, such that all those around you see that God is "God of the heavens" *and* "God of the earth" (v. 3). ❞

בראשית כד:ז-טו

וַאֲשֶׁר דִּבֶּר־לִי וַאֲשֶׁר נִשְׁבַּע־לִי לֵאמֹר לְזַרְעֲךָ אֶתֵּן אֶת־הָאָרֶץ הַזֹּאת הוּא יִשְׁלַח מַלְאָכוֹ לְפָנֶיךָ וְלָקַחְתָּ אִשָּׁה לִבְנִי מִשָּׁם: 8 וְאִם־לֹא תֹאבֶה הָאִשָּׁה לָלֶכֶת אַחֲרֶיךָ וְנִקִּיתָ מִשְּׁבֻעָתִי זֹאת רַק אֶת־בְּנִי לֹא תָשֵׁב שָׁמָּה: 9 וַיָּשֶׂם הָעֶבֶד אֶת־יָדוֹ תַּחַת יֶרֶךְ אַבְרָהָם אֲדֹנָיו וַיִּשָּׁבַע לוֹ עַל־הַדָּבָר הַזֶּה: [THIRD READING]

10 וַיִּקַּח הָעֶבֶד עֲשָׂרָה גְמַלִּים מִגְּמַלֵּי אֲדֹנָיו וַיֵּלֶךְ וְכָל־טוּב אֲדֹנָיו בְּיָדוֹ וַיָּקָם וַיֵּלֶךְ אֶל־אֲרַם נַהֲרַיִם אֶל־עִיר נָחוֹר: 11 וַיַּבְרֵךְ הַגְּמַלִּים מִחוּץ לָעִיר אֶל־בְּאֵר הַמָּיִם לְעֵת עֶרֶב לְעֵת צֵאת הַשֹּׁאֲבֹת: 12 וַיֹּאמַר | יְהֹוָה אֱלֹהֵי אֲדֹנִי אַבְרָהָם הַקְרֵה־נָא לְפָנַי הַיּוֹם וַעֲשֵׂה־חֶסֶד עִם אֲדֹנִי אַבְרָהָם: 13 הִנֵּה אָנֹכִי נִצָּב עַל־עֵין הַמָּיִם וּבְנוֹת אַנְשֵׁי הָעִיר יֹצְאֹת לִשְׁאֹב מָיִם: 14 וְהָיָה הַנַּעֲרָ אֲשֶׁר אֹמַר אֵלֶיהָ הַטִּי־נָא כַדֵּךְ וְאֶשְׁתֶּה וְאָמְרָה שְׁתֵה וְגַם־גְּמַלֶּיךָ אַשְׁקֶה אֹתָהּ הֹכַחְתָּ לְעַבְדְּךָ לְיִצְחָק וּבָהּ אֵדַע כִּי־עָשִׂיתָ חֶסֶד עִם־אֲדֹנִי: 15 וַיְהִי־הוּא טֶרֶם כִּלָּה לְדַבֵּר וְהִנֵּה רִבְקָה יֹצֵאת אֲשֶׁר יֻלְּדָה לִבְתוּאֵל בֶּן־מִלְכָּה אֵשֶׁת נָחוֹר אֲחִי

Some parents think that when a child reaches the age of twenty, the obligations of parenthood end. The son or daughter is now a mature adult who can, and must, learn to fend for his or herself.

However, we can learn from the conduct of Abraham that education *never* ceases. At this point, Isaac was thirty-seven years old, and Abraham could have quite reasonably taken a "back seat," allowing Isaac to make his own choices about where to live and whom to marry.

If fact, Abraham did precisely the opposite. Instead of relaxing and enjoying his own life, he relinquished *his life's savings and all his possessions*, giving them to Isaac in an attempt to help him find an appropriate wife.

From this we can learn that parenthood never ends. Even when children become mature adults, parents should be willing to sacrifice *everything* that they have for their child's benefit (*Rabbi Menahem Mendel Schneerson, 20th century*).

food for thought

1. Have you ever had your prayers answered instantly?

2. When a prayer goes unanswered, is God ignoring you?

3. When were you last impressed by an outstanding act of kindness?

15. He had not yet finished speaking. Three people were answered while their words were still upon their tongues: Abraham's servant Eliezer, Moses and Solomon. Regarding Eliezer, the verse states, *"He had not yet finished speaking, and—look!—*

needs), and swore to me (at the Covenant of the Parts), saying, 'I will give this land to your descendants'—He will send His angel ahead of you, and you will take a wife for my son from there. ⁸ If the woman doesn't want to follow you, then you will be absolved of this oath of mine. But don't take my son back there!"

⁹ The servant placed his hand under the thigh of Abraham, his master, and made him this oath.

Eliezer's Successful Trip

[THIRD READING] ¹⁰ The servant took ten camels from his master's (stock of muzzled) camels, and he left. In his hand were all of his master's belongings.

He set out, and went to Aram-naharaim, Nahor's city.

¹¹ He made the camels lie down outside the city, beside the well of water, towards the evening time when the girls go out to draw water.

¹² He said, "O God! The God of my master Abraham, please let something happen to me today and do kindness to my master, Abraham. ¹³ Look, I am standing by the water well. The daughters of this city's residents are coming out to draw water. ¹⁴ If I say to a girl, 'Please tilt down your pitcher and let me drink,' and she says, 'Drink, and I will also give your camels to drink,' (she will be fit to) be chosen by You for Your servant, for Isaac (since she performs acts of kindness. If she is from the right family and shows kindness) I will know that through her You have acted kindly with my master."

¹⁵ He had not yet finished speaking, and—look!—Rebekah, the daughter of Bethuel son of Milcah, who was the wife of Abraham's brother Nahor, came out,

---

God of the heavens but *not* the God of the earth, because mankind did not acknowledge Him, and His name was not commonplace on the earth" (*Rashi, 11th century*).

10. In his hand were all his master's belongings. How did Eliezer carry *"all* his master's belongings"?

Abraham wrote a deed stating that he had given everything he owned to Isaac as a gift, so that they would jump at the chance to send him their daughter (*Rashi, 11th century*).

spiritual vitamin

> It is a fundamental principle of science that material things never become obliterated completely. How much more so everlasting spiritual things, including hereditary qualities of the spirit and character, which come down from generations of fine ancestors.

בראשית כד:טז-ל

אַבְרָהָ֔ם וְכַדָּ֖הּ עַל־שִׁכְמָֽהּ׃ ¹⁶ וְהַֽנַּעֲרָ֗ טֹבַ֤ת מַרְאֶה֙ מְאֹ֔ד בְּתוּלָ֕ה וְאִ֖ישׁ לֹ֣א יְדָעָ֑הּ וַתֵּ֣רֶד הָעַ֔יְנָה וַתְּמַלֵּ֥א כַדָּ֖הּ וַתָּֽעַל׃ ¹⁷ וַיָּ֥רָץ הָעֶ֖בֶד לִקְרָאתָ֑הּ וַיֹּ֕אמֶר הַגְמִיאִ֥ינִי נָ֛א מְעַט־מַ֖יִם מִכַּדֵּֽךְ׃ ¹⁸ וַתֹּ֖אמֶר שְׁתֵ֣ה אֲדֹנִ֑י וַתְּמַהֵ֗ר וַתֹּ֧רֶד כַּדָּ֛הּ עַל־יָדָ֖הּ וַתַּשְׁקֵֽהוּ׃ ¹⁹ וַתְּכַ֖ל לְהַשְׁקֹת֑וֹ וַתֹּ֗אמֶר גַּ֤ם לִגְמַלֶּ֙יךָ֙ אֶשְׁאָ֔ב עַ֥ד אִם־כִּלּ֖וּ לִשְׁתֹּֽת׃ ²⁰ וַתְּמַהֵ֗ר וַתְּעַ֤ר כַּדָּהּ֙ אֶל־הַשֹּׁ֔קֶת וַתָּ֥רָץ ע֛וֹד אֶֽל־הַבְּאֵ֖ר לִשְׁאֹ֑ב וַתִּשְׁאַ֖ב לְכׇל־גְּמַלָּֽיו׃ ²¹ וְהָאִ֥ישׁ מִשְׁתָּאֵ֖ה לָ֑הּ מַחֲרִ֕ישׁ לָדַ֗עַת הַֽהִצְלִ֧יחַ יְהֹוָ֛ה דַּרְכּ֖וֹ אִם־לֹֽא׃ ²² וַיְהִ֗י כַּאֲשֶׁ֨ר כִּלּ֤וּ הַגְּמַלִּים֙ לִשְׁתּ֔וֹת וַיִּקַּ֤ח הָאִישׁ֙ נֶ֣זֶם זָהָ֔ב בֶּ֖קַע מִשְׁקָל֑וֹ וּשְׁנֵ֤י צְמִידִים֙ עַל־יָדֶ֔יהָ עֲשָׂרָ֥ה זָהָ֖ב מִשְׁקָלָֽם׃ ²³ וַיֹּ֙אמֶר֙ בַּת־מִ֣י אַ֔תְּ הַגִּ֥ידִי נָ֖א לִ֑י הֲיֵ֧שׁ בֵּית־אָבִ֛יךְ מָק֥וֹם לָ֖נוּ לָלִֽין׃ ²⁴ וַתֹּ֣אמֶר אֵלָ֔יו בַּת־בְּתוּאֵ֖ל אָנֹ֑כִי בֶּן־מִלְכָּ֕ה אֲשֶׁ֥ר יָלְדָ֖ה לְנָחֽוֹר׃ ²⁵ וַתֹּ֣אמֶר אֵלָ֔יו גַּם־תֶּ֥בֶן גַּם־מִסְפּ֖וֹא רַ֣ב עִמָּ֑נוּ גַּם־מָק֖וֹם לָלֽוּן׃ ²⁶ וַיִּקֹּ֣ד הָאִ֔ישׁ וַיִּשְׁתַּ֖חוּ לַֽיהֹוָֽה׃ [FOURTH READING] ²⁷ וַיֹּ֗אמֶר בָּר֤וּךְ יְהֹוָה֙ אֱלֹהֵי֙ אֲדֹנִ֣י אַבְרָהָ֔ם אֲ֠שֶׁ֠ר לֹֽא־עָזַ֥ב חַסְדּ֛וֹ וַאֲמִתּ֖וֹ מֵעִ֣ם אֲדֹנִ֑י אָנֹכִ֗י בַּדֶּ֙רֶךְ֙ נָחַ֣נִי יְהֹוָ֔ה בֵּ֖ית אֲחֵ֥י אֲדֹנִֽי׃ ²⁸ וַתָּ֙רׇץ֙ הַֽנַּעֲרָ֔ וַתַּגֵּ֖ד לְבֵ֣ית אִמָּ֑הּ כַּדְּבָרִ֖ים הָאֵֽלֶּה׃ ²⁹ וּלְרִבְקָ֥ה אָ֖ח וּשְׁמ֣וֹ לָבָ֑ן וַיָּ֨רׇץ לָבָ֧ן אֶל־הָאִ֛ישׁ הַח֖וּצָה אֶל־הָעָֽיִן׃ ³⁰ וַיְהִ֣י ׀ כִּרְאֹ֣ת אֶת־הַנֶּ֗זֶם

18. She said, "I will also draw water for your camels." *"You must not eat before first feeding your animal"* (*Babylonian Talmud, Berakhot* 40a). How does the Talmud's ruling square with Rebekah's actions here, giving Eliezer to drink *before* his camels?

kabbalah bites

24:24 The story of Rebekah and Isaac's union is associated with numerous miracles, and it is repeated in all its detail (v. 38ff). Why?

Because this union is the story of the Torah itself: the marriage of the higher (Isaac's lineage) and the lower (Rebekah's lineage). Isaac was born in holiness, never left the Holy Land and was all but offered as a sacrifice on an altar. Rebekah, on the other hand, stemmed from an idol-worshiping family outside the land of Israel.

In our own lives this represents the marriage of good *intention* (higher) and good *action* (lower). Each on their own is noble and fine, but only when they are wedded together do we fulfil our destiny.

and her pitcher was on her shoulder. ¹⁶ The girl was very pretty, a virgin, and no man had known her.

She went down to the spring, filled her pitcher and came back up.

¹⁷ (When he saw that the water rose from the well towards her,) the servant ran toward her, and said, "Please let me sip a little water from your pitcher."

¹⁸ She said, "Drink, sir." She quickly took down her pitcher (from her shoulder) into her hand, and gave him a drink. ¹⁹ When she finished giving him a drink, she said, "I will also draw (water) for your camels, until they have finished drinking."

²⁰ She quickly emptied her pitcher into the trough and ran to the well again to draw water. She drew (water) for all his camels. ²¹ The man was amazed by her. He (observed her) silently to know whether God had led his way to success or not.

²² Then, when the camels had finished drinking, the man took a golden nose ring, weighing a *beka'*, and two bracelets, weighing ten gold (shekels), for her hands. ²³ (After giving her the presents,) he said, "Whose daughter are you? Please tell me if there is place for us to stay in your father's house?"

²⁴ She said to him, "I am the daughter of Bethuel, the son born to Milcah and Nahor." ²⁵ (In response to the second question,) she said to him, "We have plenty of straw and fodder and also a place to stay."

²⁶ The man knelt and prostrated himself to God.

[FOURTH READING] ²⁷ He said, "Blessed is God, the God of my master, Abraham, who has not withheld His loving-kindness and His truth from my master. God has led me on the path to the house of my master's brothers!"

Eliezer Recounts the Story

²⁸ The girl ran, and she told her mother, (who was sitting in her work-)house, what had happened. ²⁹ Rebekah had a brother whose name was Laban. Laban ran to the man outside by the fountain (because) ³⁰ he saw the nose ring and the bracelets on his sister's hands, and he heard his sister Rebekah say, "This is what the man said to me..." (so he set his eyes on the money).

Rebekah ... came out" (v. 15). Regarding Moses, the verse states (after his authority had been challenged by Korah), *"As soon as he finished speaking all these words, the earth beneath them split open"* (*Numbers* 16:31). Regarding Solomon, the verse states that at the inauguration of the Holy Temple, *"When Solomon finished speaking to God, the fire descended from heaven"* (*II Chronicles* 7:1).

In fact, it appears that Eliezer's prayer was even greater than that of Moses or Solomon, since they were only answered *after* finishing speaking, whereas Eliezer "had *not yet* finished speaking," when Rebekah came out with a pitcher on her shoulder (*Midrash Sekhel Tov*).

בראשית כד:ל-מד חיי שרה

וְאֶת־הַצְּמִדִים֮ עַל־יְדֵ֣י אֲחֹתוֹ֒ וּכְשָׁמְע֗וֹ אֶת־דִּבְרֵ֞י רִבְקָ֤ה אֲחֹתוֹ֙ לֵאמֹ֔ר כֹּֽה־דִבֶּ֥ר אֵלַ֖י הָאִ֑ישׁ וַיָּבֹא֙ אֶל־הָאִ֔ישׁ וְהִנֵּ֛ה עֹמֵ֥ד עַל־הַגְּמַלִּ֖ים עַל־הָעָֽיִן: 31 וַיֹּ֕אמֶר בּ֕וֹא בְּר֖וּךְ יְהֹוָ֑ה לָ֤מָּה תַעֲמֹד֙ בַּח֔וּץ וְאָנֹכִי֙ פִּנִּ֣יתִי הַבַּ֔יִת וּמָק֖וֹם לַגְּמַלִּֽים: 32 וַיָּבֹ֤א הָאִישׁ֙ הַבַּ֔יְתָה וַיְפַתַּ֖ח הַגְּמַלִּ֑ים וַיִּתֵּ֨ן תֶּ֤בֶן וּמִסְפּוֹא֙ לַגְּמַלִּ֔ים וּמַ֕יִם לִרְחֹ֣ץ רַגְלָ֔יו וְרַגְלֵ֥י הָאֲנָשִׁ֖ים אֲשֶׁ֥ר אִתּֽוֹ: 33 [וייש״כ] וַיּוּשַׂ֤ם לְפָנָיו֙ לֶֽאֱכֹ֔ל וַיֹּ֕אמֶר לֹ֣א אֹכַ֔ל עַ֥ד אִם־דִּבַּ֖רְתִּי דְּבָרָ֑י וַיֹּ֖אמֶר דַּבֵּֽר: 34 וַיֹּאמַ֑ר עֶ֥בֶד אַבְרָהָ֖ם אָנֹֽכִי: 35 וַֽיהֹוָ֞ה בֵּרַ֧ךְ אֶת־אֲדֹנִ֛י מְאֹ֖ד וַיִּגְדָּ֑ל וַיִּתֶּן־ל֞וֹ צֹ֤אן וּבָקָר֙ וְכֶ֣סֶף וְזָהָ֔ב וַעֲבָדִם֙ וּשְׁפָחֹ֔ת וּגְמַלִּ֖ים וַחֲמֹרִֽים: 36 וַתֵּ֡לֶד שָׂרָה֩ אֵ֨שֶׁת אֲדֹנִ֥י בֵן֙ לַֽאדֹנִ֔י אַחֲרֵ֖י זִקְנָתָ֑הּ וַיִּתֶּן־ל֖וֹ אֶת־כָּל־אֲשֶׁר־לֽוֹ: 37 וַיַּשְׁבִּעֵ֥נִי אֲדֹנִ֖י לֵאמֹ֑ר לֹא־תִקַּ֤ח אִשָּׁה֙ לִבְנִ֔י מִבְּנוֹת֙ הַֽכְּנַעֲנִ֔י אֲשֶׁ֥ר אָנֹכִ֖י יֹשֵׁ֥ב בְּאַרְצֽוֹ: 38 אִם־לֹ֧א אֶל־בֵּית־אָבִ֛י תֵּלֵ֖ךְ וְאֶל־מִשְׁפַּחְתִּ֑י וְלָקַחְתָּ֥ אִשָּׁ֖ה לִבְנִֽי: 39 וָאֹמַ֖ר אֶל־אֲדֹנִ֑י אֻלַ֛י לֹא־תֵלֵ֥ךְ הָאִשָּׁ֖ה אַחֲרָֽי: 40 וַיֹּ֖אמֶר אֵלָ֑י יְהֹוָ֞ה אֲשֶׁר־הִתְהַלַּ֣כְתִּי לְפָנָ֗יו יִשְׁלַ֨ח מַלְאָכ֤וֹ אִתָּךְ֙ וְהִצְלִ֣יחַ דַּרְכֶּ֔ךָ וְלָקַחְתָּ֤ אִשָּׁה֙ לִבְנִ֔י מִמִּשְׁפַּחְתִּ֖י וּמִבֵּ֥ית אָבִֽי: 41 אָ֤ז תִּנָּקֶה֙ מֵאָ֣לָתִ֔י כִּ֥י תָב֖וֹא אֶל־מִשְׁפַּחְתִּ֑י וְאִם־לֹ֤א יִתְּנוּ֙ לָ֔ךְ וְהָיִ֥יתָ נָקִ֖י מֵאָלָתִֽי: 42 וָאָבֹ֥א הַיּ֖וֹם אֶל־הָעָ֑יִן וָאֹמַ֗ר יְהֹוָה֙ אֱלֹהֵי֙ אֲדֹנִ֣י אַבְרָהָ֔ם אִם־יֶשְׁךָ־נָּ֛א מַצְלִ֥יחַ דַּרְכִּ֖י אֲשֶׁ֥ר אָנֹכִ֖י הֹלֵ֥ךְ עָלֶֽיהָ: 43 הִנֵּ֛ה אָנֹכִ֥י נִצָּ֖ב עַל־עֵ֣ין הַמָּ֑יִם וְהָיָ֤ה הָֽעַלְמָה֙ הַיֹּצֵ֣את לִשְׁאֹ֔ב וְאָמַרְתִּ֣י אֵלֶ֔יהָ הַשְׁקִֽינִי־נָ֥א מְעַט־מַ֖יִם מִכַּדֵּֽךְ: 44 וְאָמְרָ֣ה אֵלַ֗י גַּם־אַתָּ֣ה שְׁתֵ֔ה וְגַ֥ם

however, forfeited this right because of his sins—God no longer feeds man because of his rightful claim, but simply as an act of charity.

Animals, on the other hand, never lost their right to be fed without effort, since they do not sin. You must therefore feed your animal before yourself, *since the animal has a stronger claim to the food than you*.

However, this distinction is only applicable when applied to yourself, for every man knows that he is not without sin. But when it comes to feeding others, then a man takes priority over his animal, *because we must give our fellow the benefit of the doubt and assume he is without sin*. Therefore Rebekah gave Eliezer to drink before his camels (*Rabbi Joseph B. Soloveitchik, 20th century*).

genesis 24:30–44 — ḥayyei sarah

So, he came to the man, and—look!—he was standing over the camels at the well. [31] He said, "Come, you who are blessed by God! Why should you stand outside, when I have cleared the house (of idols), and made a place for the camels?"

[32] So the man came to the house and unmuzzled the camels. (Laban) gave straw and fodder to the camels and water (to Eliezer) to wash his feet, and the feet of the men who accompanied him. [33] Food was placed before him, but he said, "I will not eat until I have spoken my words."

"Speak," said (the host).

[34] He said, "I am Abraham's servant. [35] God blessed my master tremendously, and he became great. (God) gave him sheep, cattle, silver, gold, menservants, maidservants, camels and donkeys. [36] After she had become old, Sarah, my master's wife, gave birth to a son for my master. (My master) has given him all that he possesses.

[37] "My master made me swear, saying, 'Do not take a wife for my son from the daughters of the Canaanites, in whose land I dwell. [38] Instead, you must go to my father's house, to my family, and take a wife for my son.'

[39] "I said to my master, 'What if the woman will not want to follow me?'

[40] "He replied, 'God, before whom I walked, will send His angel with you and lead your way to success. You should take a wife for my son from my family, from my father's house. [41] You will then be absolved from my oath. When you come to my family, if they do not give her to you, you will be absolved from my oath.'

[42] "So, I came today to the well, and I said, 'God, God of my master Abraham, please lead my way to success! [43] Look, I am standing by the well. When a girl comes out to draw (water), I will say to her, 'Please, give me a little water to drink from your pitcher.' [44] If she says to me, 'You (and your men) too can drink, and I will also draw water for your camels,' she is the woman whom God has designated for my master's son.'

The requirement to feed your animal before yourself stems from the differing claims to food by animals and by man. Ideally, all of creation would have a rightful claim to find sustenance through minimal effort, because the One who gives life ought to provide sustenance too. Man,

kabbalah bites

24:31 Eliezer's lineage is described as "cursed" because his soul was trapped among the *kelipot* (demonic forces); but through his outstanding dedication to Abraham, Eliezer's soul was redeemed from "cursed" to "blessed." Nevertheless, this redemption was not complete until Laban—the human embodiment of the *kelipot*—openly declared to Eliezer, *"Come, you who are blessed by God."*

In the merit of redeeming Eliezer's soul, Laban would later be reincarnated as Caleb.

בראשית כד:מד-ס

לְגְמַלֶּיךָ אִשְׁאָב הִוא הָאִשָּׁה אֲשֶׁר־הֹכִיחַ יהוה לְבֶן־אֲדֹנִי: 45 אֲנִי֩ טֶ֨רֶם אֲכַלֶּ֜ה לְדַבֵּ֣ר אֶל־לִבִּ֗י וְהִנֵּ֨ה רִבְקָ֤ה יֹצֵאת֙ וְכַדָּ֣הּ עַל־שִׁכְמָ֔הּ וַתֵּ֥רֶד הָעַ֖יְנָה וַתִּשְׁאָ֑ב וָאֹמַ֥ר אֵלֶ֖יהָ הַשְׁקִ֥ינִי נָֽא: 46 וַתְּמַהֵ֗ר וַתּ֤וֹרֶד כַּדָּהּ֙ מֵֽעָלֶ֔יהָ וַתֹּ֣אמֶר שְׁתֵ֔ה וְגַם־גְּמַלֶּ֖יךָ אַשְׁקֶ֑ה וָאֵ֕שְׁתְּ וְגַ֥ם הַגְּמַלִּ֖ים הִשְׁקָֽתָה: 47 וָאֶשְׁאַ֣ל אֹתָ֗הּ וָאֹמַר֮ בַּת־מִ֣י אַ֒תְּ֒ וַתֹּ֗אמֶר בַּת־בְּתוּאֵל֙ בֶּן־נָח֔וֹר אֲשֶׁ֥ר יָֽלְדָה־לּ֖וֹ מִלְכָּ֑ה וָאָשִׂ֤ם הַנֶּ֨זֶם֙ עַל־אַפָּ֔הּ וְהַצְּמִידִ֖ים עַל־יָדֶֽיהָ: 48 וָאֶקֹּ֥ד וָֽאֶשְׁתַּחֲוֶ֖ה לַיהוה וָאֲבָרֵ֗ךְ אֶת־יהוה אֱלֹהֵי֙ אֲדֹנִ֣י אַבְרָהָ֔ם אֲשֶׁ֤ר הִנְחַ֨נִי֙ בְּדֶ֣רֶךְ אֱמֶ֔ת לָקַ֛חַת אֶת־בַּת־אֲחִ֥י אֲדֹנִ֖י לִבְנֽוֹ: 49 וְ֠עַתָּה אִם־יֶשְׁכֶ֨ם עֹשִׂ֜ים חֶ֧סֶד וֶֽאֱמֶ֛ת אֶת־אֲדֹנִ֖י הַגִּ֣ידוּ לִ֑י וְאִם־לֹ֕א הַגִּ֣ידוּ לִ֔י וְאֶפְנֶ֥ה עַל־יָמִ֖ין א֥וֹ עַל־שְׂמֹֽאל: 50 וַיַּ֨עַן לָבָ֤ן וּבְתוּאֵל֙ וַיֹּ֣אמְר֔וּ מֵיהוה יָצָ֣א הַדָּבָ֑ר לֹ֥א נוּכַ֛ל דַּבֵּ֥ר אֵלֶ֖יךָ רַ֥ע אוֹ־טֽוֹב: 51 הִנֵּֽה־רִבְקָ֥ה לְפָנֶ֖יךָ קַ֣ח וָלֵ֑ךְ וּתְהִ֤י אִשָּׁה֙ לְבֶן־אֲדֹנֶ֔יךָ כַּאֲשֶׁ֖ר דִּבֶּ֥ר יהוה: 52 וַיְהִ֕י כַּאֲשֶׁ֥ר שָׁמַ֛ע עֶ֥בֶד אַבְרָהָ֖ם אֶת־דִּבְרֵיהֶ֑ם וַיִּשְׁתַּ֥חוּ אַ֖רְצָה לַֽיהוה: 53 [FIFTH READING] וַיּוֹצֵ֨א הָעֶ֜בֶד כְּלֵי־כֶ֨סֶף וּכְלֵ֤י זָהָב֙ וּבְגָדִ֔ים וַיִּתֵּ֖ן לְרִבְקָ֑ה וּמִ֨גְדָּנֹ֔ת נָתַ֥ן לְאָחִ֖יהָ וּלְאִמָּֽהּ: 54 וַיֹּאכְל֣וּ וַיִּשְׁתּ֗וּ ה֧וּא וְהָאֲנָשִׁ֛ים אֲשֶׁר־עִמּ֖וֹ וַיָּלִ֑ינוּ וַיָּק֣וּמוּ בַבֹּ֔קֶר וַיֹּ֖אמֶר שַׁלְּחֻ֥נִי לַֽאדֹנִֽי: 55 וַיֹּ֤אמֶר אָחִ֨יהָ֙ וְאִמָּ֔הּ תֵּשֵׁ֨ב הַנַּעֲרָ֥ אִתָּ֛נוּ יָמִ֖ים א֣וֹ עָשׂ֑וֹר אַחַ֖ר תֵּלֵֽךְ: 56 וַיֹּ֤אמֶר אֲלֵהֶם֙ אַל־תְּאַחֲר֣וּ אֹתִ֔י וַיהוה הִצְלִ֣יחַ דַּרְכִּ֑י שַׁלְּח֕וּנִי וְאֵלְכָ֖ה לַֽאדֹנִֽי: 57 וַיֹּאמְר֖וּ נִקְרָ֣א לַֽנַּעֲרָ֑ וְנִשְׁאֲלָ֖ה אֶת־פִּֽיהָ: 58 וַיִּקְרְא֤וּ לְרִבְקָה֙ וַיֹּאמְר֣וּ אֵלֶ֔יהָ הֲתֵלְכִ֖י עִם־הָאִ֣ישׁ הַזֶּ֑ה וַתֹּ֖אמֶר אֵלֵֽךְ: 59 וַֽיְשַׁלְּח֛וּ אֶת־רִבְקָ֥ה אֲחֹתָ֖ם וְאֶת־מֵנִקְתָּ֑הּ וְאֶת־עֶ֥בֶד אַבְרָהָ֖ם וְאֶת־אֲנָשָֽׁיו: 60 וַיְבָרְכ֤וּ אֶת־רִבְקָה֙ וַיֹּ֣אמְרוּ לָ֔הּ אֲחֹתֵ֕נוּ אַ֥תְּ הֲיִ֖י

57. Let us call the girl and ask her. From here we learn that one may not marry off a woman without her consent (*Rashi, 11th century*).

Earlier, in verse 51, Rebekah's family was ready to consent to her immediate departure, declaring, "*Rebekah is now yours. Take her and leave.*" In the present verse, however, they revert to indecisiveness and decide to ask her for her opinion. What sparked the sudden change?

genesis 24:45–60 / ḥayyei sarah

⁴⁵ "I had not yet finished speaking to myself, and Rebekah suddenly came out with her pitcher on her shoulder, went down to the well and drew water. I said to her, 'Please give me a drink.' ⁴⁶ She quickly lowered her pitcher from her (shoulder), and said, 'Drink, and I will give your camels to drink too!' I drank, and she gave the camels to drink.

⁴⁷ "I questioned her and said, 'Whose daughter are you?'

"She replied, 'The daughter of Bethuel, the son born to Milcah and Nahor.' I then placed the ring on her nose and the bracelets on her hands.

⁴⁸ "I knelt and prostrated myself to God, and I blessed God, the God of my master Abraham, who led me on the true path, to take the daughter of my master's brother for his son.

⁴⁹ "Now, if you want to be kind and truthful to my master, tell me. If not, say so, and I will turn to the right (and find a girl from the daughters of Ishmael), or to the left (and find a girl from the daughters of Lot)."

The Consent

⁵⁰ Laban and Bethuel replied, saying, "This thing has come from God! We cannot refuse you (for any reason) either bad or good. ⁵¹ Rebekah is now yours. Take her and leave, and let her be a wife for your master's son, as God has spoken."

⁵² When Abraham's servant heard their words, he prostrated himself on the ground to God.

[FIFTH READING] ⁵³ (Later, when he saw Rebekah), the servant took out silver and gold items and pieces of clothing, and he gave them to Rebekah. He gave delicious (fruits from the land of Canaan) to her brother and her mother. ⁵⁴ Both (Eliezer) and the men who accompanied him ate and drank, and they stayed overnight.

When they got up in the morning, (Eliezer) said, "Send me away to my master."

⁵⁵ (Rebekah's) brother and mother said, "Let the girl stay with us a year or ten (months). Afterwards, she will go."

⁵⁶ He said to them, "Do not delay me now that God has made my trip successful. Send me away, and I will go to my master."

⁵⁷ They said, "Let us call the girl and ask her."

⁵⁸ They called Rebekah, and said to her, "Will you go with this man?"

She said, "I will go (whether you like it or not)!"

⁵⁹ So they sent away their sister Rebekah with her nurse, Abraham's servant and his men. ⁶⁰ They blessed Rebekah, saying to her, "Our sister! May you come to be thousands of myriads, and may your descendants inherit the cities of their enemies (as God blessed Abraham)."

בראשית כד:ס-סז　　חיי שרה

לְאַלְפֵ֖י רְבָבָ֑ה וְיִירַ֣שׁ זַרְעֵ֔ךְ אֵ֖ת שַׁ֥עַר שֹׂנְאָֽיו: 61 וַתָּ֨קָם רִבְקָ֜ה וְנַעֲרֹתֶ֗יהָ וַתִּרְכַּ֨בְנָה֙ עַל־הַגְּמַלִּ֔ים וַתֵּלַ֖כְנָה אַחֲרֵ֣י הָאִ֑ישׁ וַיִּקַּ֥ח הָעֶ֛בֶד אֶת־רִבְקָ֖ה וַיֵּלַֽךְ: 62 וְיִצְחָק֙ בָּ֣א מִבּ֔וֹא בְּאֵ֥ר לַחַ֖י רֹאִ֑י וְה֥וּא יוֹשֵׁ֖ב בְּאֶ֥רֶץ הַנֶּֽגֶב: 63 וַיֵּצֵ֥א יִצְחָ֛ק לָשׂ֥וּחַ בַּשָּׂדֶ֖ה לִפְנ֣וֹת עָ֑רֶב וַיִּשָּׂ֤א עֵינָיו֙ וַיַּ֔רְא וְהִנֵּ֥ה גְמַלִּ֖ים בָּאִֽים: 64 וַתִּשָּׂ֤א רִבְקָה֙ אֶת־עֵינֶ֔יהָ וַתֵּ֖רֶא אֶת־יִצְחָ֑ק וַתִּפֹּ֖ל מֵעַ֥ל הַגָּמָֽל: 65 וַתֹּ֣אמֶר אֶל־הָעֶ֗בֶד מִֽי־הָאִ֤ישׁ הַלָּזֶה֙ הַהֹלֵ֤ךְ בַּשָּׂדֶה֙ לִקְרָאתֵ֔נוּ וַיֹּ֥אמֶר הָעֶ֖בֶד ה֣וּא אֲדֹנִ֑י וַתִּקַּ֥ח הַצָּעִ֖יף וַתִּתְכָּֽס: 66 וַיְסַפֵּ֥ר הָעֶ֖בֶד לְיִצְחָ֑ק אֵ֥ת כָּל־הַדְּבָרִ֖ים אֲשֶׁ֥ר עָשָֽׂה: 67 וַיְבִאֶ֣הָ יִצְחָ֗ק הָאֹ֨הֱלָה֙ שָׂרָ֣ה אִמּ֔וֹ וַיִּקַּ֧ח אֶת־רִבְקָ֛ה וַתְּהִי־ל֥וֹ לְאִשָּׁ֖ה וַיֶּאֱהָבֶ֑הָ וַיִּנָּחֵ֥ם יִצְחָ֖ק אַחֲרֵ֥י אִמּֽוֹ: פ

primary responsibility: Separating a portion of dough (*hallah*), lighting the Sabbath candles, and the laws of family purity (symbolized by the cloud fixed to the tent). Since the fourth practice mentioned in the *Midrash* had no special significance, *Rashi* omitted it (*Rabbi Judah Loew b. Bezalel of Prague, 16th century*).

In recent years the custom for girls to light Sabbath candles before their marriage has re-emerged. This is actually an ancient practice which is indicated by *Rashi's* comment to verse 67. Here we see that Rebekah lit candles before she was married, for only after Isaac had taken her into "the tent of Sarah his mother" and witnessed her Sabbath candles burning for the entire week, did he take her to be his wife. If fact, it was primarily the observance of this commandment that proved to Isaac the suitability of Rebekah as a spouse, and a mother in Israel (*Rabbi Menahem Mendel Schneerson, 20th century*).

spiritual vitamin

> Divine Providence is continuously active, every day and in every detail of your life. *Supernatural (miraculous) Divine Providence is not limited to revealed miracles, but also in ordinary daily life there is miraculous intervention, except that "the one to whom a miracle occurs does not recognize his miracle"* (*Babylonian Talmud, Niddah* 30b).

⁶¹ Rebekah and her maidens set off, riding on camels, following the man. The servant took Rebekah and left.

The Marriage of Isaac and Rebekah

⁶² Isaac had returned (from escorting Hagar) from Beer-lahai-roi (to Abraham, so that he could marry her), he was living in the southern part of the land. ⁶³ Isaac went out to pray in the field towards evening. He looked up and saw—look!—camels were approaching.

⁶⁴ Rebekah looked up and saw Isaac (and she was stunned by his splendid appearance). She lowered herself from the camel, ⁶⁵ and said to the servant, "Who is that man walking in the field towards us?"

The servant said, "He is my master." She took the veil and covered herself.

⁶⁶ The servant told Isaac about all the (miraculous) things that had been done (for him).

⁶⁷ Isaac brought her to the tent of his mother Sarah. He took Rebekah, she became his wife, and he loved her. Isaac was comforted for (the loss of) his mother.

When Eliezer first arrived at their house, laden with gold and silver vessels, Rebekah's family assumed that they would receive a portion of the gold and silver; their greed accelerated their consent and overrode any concern for their sister's welfare. Now that Eliezer had given all the gold and silver to Rebekah (v. 53), while they received mere gifts of fruits, they quickly changed their minds. It was in their interest to keep their now wealthy sister under their roof for as long as possible, and they raised the issue of Rebekah's consent as an excuse for their hesitance (*Rabbi Moses Alshekh, 16ᵗʰ century*).

58. I will go. She said, "I will go of my own accord, even if you do not desire it" (*Rashi, 11ᵗʰ century*).

66. The servant told Isaac, etc. Eliezer revealed to him the miracles which had occurred: that his journey had been shortened and that Rebekah had appeared during his prayer (*Rashi, 11ᵗʰ century*).

67. Isaac was comforted for (the loss of) his mother. The verse states that *"Isaac brought her to the tent of his mother Sarah,"* suggesting that *"He brought her to the tent, and—look!—it was Sarah his mother,"* i.e., she became the likeness of Sarah his mother. For, as long as Sarah was alive, a candle burned from one Sabbath eve to the next, the dough would be blessed, and a cloud was attached to the tent. When she died these things ceased; but when Rebekah arrived, they resumed (*Rashi, 11ᵗʰ century*).

Rashi based his comments on the *Midrash*. However, he ignored the fourth practice mentioned there, that Sarah's doors were always open wide for the poor. For *Rashi* brought only the three miracles that correspond to the three commandments for which women take the

בראשית כה:א-יא

חיי שרה

[SIXTH READING] **כה** 1 וַיֹּ֧סֶף אַבְרָהָ֛ם וַיִּקַּ֥ח אִשָּׁ֖ה וּשְׁמָ֥הּ קְטוּרָֽה: 2 וַתֵּ֣לֶד ל֗וֹ אֶת־זִמְרָן֙ וְאֶת־יָקְשָׁ֔ן וְאֶת־מְדָ֖ן וְאֶת־מִדְיָ֑ן וְאֶת־יִשְׁבָּ֖ק וְאֶת־שֽׁוּחַ: 3 וְיָקְשָׁ֣ן יָלַ֔ד אֶת־שְׁבָ֖א וְאֶת־דְּדָ֑ן וּבְנֵ֣י דְדָ֗ן הָי֛וּ אַשּׁוּרִ֥ם וּלְטוּשִׁ֖ם וּלְאֻמִּֽים: 4 וּבְנֵ֣י מִדְיָ֗ן עֵיפָ֤ה וָעֵ֨פֶר֙ וַחֲנֹ֔ךְ וַאֲבִידָ֖ע וְאֶלְדָּעָ֑ה כָּל־אֵ֖לֶּה בְּנֵ֥י קְטוּרָֽה: 5 וַיִּתֵּ֧ן אַבְרָהָ֛ם אֶת־כָּל־אֲשֶׁר־ל֖וֹ לְיִצְחָֽק: 6 וְלִבְנֵ֤י הַפִּֽילַגְשִׁים֙ אֲשֶׁ֣ר לְאַבְרָהָ֔ם נָתַ֥ן אַבְרָהָ֖ם מַתָּנֹ֑ת וַֽיְשַׁלְּחֵ֞ם מֵעַ֨ל יִצְחָ֤ק בְּנוֹ֙ בְּעוֹדֶ֣נּוּ חַ֔י קֵ֖דְמָה אֶל־אֶ֥רֶץ קֶֽדֶם: 7 וְאֵ֗לֶּה יְמֵ֛י שְׁנֵֽי־חַיֵּ֥י אַבְרָהָ֖ם אֲשֶׁר־חָ֑י מְאַ֥ת שָׁנָ֛ה וְשִׁבְעִ֥ים שָׁנָ֖ה וְחָמֵ֥שׁ שָׁנִֽים: 8 וַיִּגְוַ֨ע וַיָּ֧מָת אַבְרָהָ֛ם בְּשֵׂיבָ֥ה טוֹבָ֖ה זָקֵ֣ן וְשָׂבֵ֑עַ וַיֵּאָ֖סֶף אֶל־עַמָּֽיו: 9 וַיִּקְבְּר֨וּ אֹת֜וֹ יִצְחָ֤ק וְיִשְׁמָעֵאל֙ בָּנָ֔יו אֶל־מְעָרַ֖ת הַמַּכְפֵּלָ֑ה אֶל־שְׂדֵ֞ה עֶפְרֹ֤ן בֶּן־צֹ֨חַר֙ הַֽחִתִּ֔י אֲשֶׁ֖ר עַל־פְּנֵ֥י מַמְרֵֽא: 10 הַשָּׂדֶ֛ה אֲשֶׁר־קָנָ֥ה אַבְרָהָ֖ם מֵאֵ֣ת בְּנֵי־חֵ֑ת שָׁ֛מָּה קֻבַּ֥ר אַבְרָהָ֖ם וְשָׂרָ֥ה אִשְׁתּֽוֹ: 11 וַיְהִ֗י אַחֲרֵי֙ מ֣וֹת אַבְרָהָ֔ם וַיְבָ֥רֶךְ אֱלֹהִ֖ים

Abraham possessed both qualities. Therefore when he died, he was eulogized by "all the leaders of the world" (*Rabbi Judah Leib Ginsburg, 20th century*).

9. His sons Isaac and Ishmael buried him. Isaac is mentioned before his older brother Ishmael. From here we learn that Ishmael repented and allowed Isaac to go before him (*Rashi, 11th century*).

11. After Abraham died, God blessed Isaac his son. God came to console Isaac with words of comfort that are offered to mourners. From here we learn that comforting the bereaved is one of the attributes of God, which we are expected to emulate when the occasion demands it (*Babylonian Talmud, Sotah 14a*).

kabbalah bites

25:8 Until the time of Abraham, a man's hair did not whiten with old age (*Babylonian Talmud, Bava Metzia 87a*). The abstractness of the color white represents the transcendent.

Abraham was the first to draw a revelation of the transcendent into the world, which is the inner reason why his beard was the first to whiten.

genesis 25:1–11 — ḥayyei sarah

Abraham Remarries

25 [SIXTH READING] ¹ Abraham took another wife and her name was Keturah (also known as Hagar). ² She bore him Zimran, Jokshan, Medan, Midian, Ishbak and Shuah.

³ Jokshan fathered Sheba and Dedan.

The sons of Dedan were Asshurim, Letushim, and Leummim.

⁴ The sons of Midyan were Ephah, Epher, Enoch, Abida and Eldaah.

All these were Keturah's descendants.

⁵ Abraham gave all (the power of blessing) that he possessed to Isaac. ⁶ To the sons of Abraham's concubine (Hagar, also known as Keturah), Abraham gave gifts. He sent them away eastward from his son Isaac while he (Abraham) was still alive, to the land of the East.

Abraham Passes Away

This is the total of the years of Abraham's life that he lived: one hundred years, seventy years and five years.

⁸ Abraham breathed his last and died at a good age, old and satisfied, and his (soul) was gathered to (be with the souls of) his people. ⁹ His sons Isaac and Ishmael buried him in the cave of Machpelah, in the field of Ephron—the son of Zohar the Hittite—which faces Mamre, ¹⁰ the field that Abraham had bought from the sons of Het. Abraham and his wife Sarah were buried there.

¹¹ After Abraham died, God blessed Isaac his son. Isaac lived near Beer-lahai-roi.

25:1 Her name was Keturah. This is Hagar. She was called Keturah because her deeds were as pleasant as incense—*ketoret* (*Rashi, 11th century*).

How could Hagar be described as a person whose "deeds were as pleasant as incense" when, after Abraham sent her away, she returned to idol-worship (*Rashi* to 21:14)? She must have repented before Abraham took her for the second time, and the Torah therefore calls her Keturah due to the sweet "aroma" of her repentance (*Rabbi Hezekiah b. Manoah, 13th century*).

8. Abraham breathed his last and died. On the day that Abraham died, all the leaders of the world stood and said, "Woe to the world that has lost its leader, and woe to the ship that has lost its captain!" (*Babylonian Talmud, Bava Batra* 91b).

Some people are natural leaders during a time of peace. They excel in a calm environment, but when war strikes they fail to stand out as leaders. For others, the opposite is the case: their leadership qualities and greatness only emerge during a crisis, like a captain guiding a storm-tossed ship. When things calm down, however, they no longer shine.

בראשית כה:יא-יח | חיי שרה

אֶת־יִצְחָ֣ק בְּנ֑וֹ וַיֵּ֣שֶׁב יִצְחָ֔ק עִם־בְּאֵ֥ר לַחַ֖י רֹאִֽי׃ פ [SEVENTH READING] 12 וְאֵ֛לֶּה תֹּלְדֹ֥ת יִשְׁמָעֵ֖אל בֶּן־אַבְרָהָ֑ם אֲשֶׁ֨ר יָלְדָ֜ה הָגָ֧ר הַמִּצְרִ֛ית שִׁפְחַ֥ת שָׂרָ֖ה לְאַבְרָהָֽם׃ 13 וְאֵ֗לֶּה שְׁמוֹת֙ בְּנֵ֣י יִשְׁמָעֵ֔אל בִּשְׁמֹתָ֖ם לְתוֹלְדֹתָ֑ם בְּכֹ֤ר יִשְׁמָעֵאל֙ נְבָיֹ֔ת וְקֵדָ֥ר וְאַדְבְּאֵ֖ל וּמִבְשָֽׂם׃ 14 וּמִשְׁמָ֥ע וְדוּמָ֖ה וּמַשָּֽׂא׃ 15 חֲדַ֣ד וְתֵימָ֔א יְט֥וּר נָפִ֖ישׁ וָקֵֽדְמָה׃ 16 [MAFTIR] אֵ֣לֶּה הֵ֞ם בְּנֵ֤י יִשְׁמָעֵאל֙ וְאֵ֣לֶּה שְׁמֹתָ֔ם בְּחַצְרֵיהֶ֖ם וּבְטִֽירֹתָ֑ם שְׁנֵים־עָשָׂ֥ר נְשִׂיאִ֖ם לְאֻמֹּתָֽם׃ 17 וְאֵ֗לֶּה שְׁנֵי֙ חַיֵּ֣י יִשְׁמָעֵ֔אל מְאַ֥ת שָׁנָ֛ה וּשְׁלֹשִׁ֥ים שָׁנָ֖ה וְשֶׁ֣בַע שָׁנִ֑ים וַיִּגְוַ֣ע וַיָּ֔מָת וַיֵּאָ֖סֶף אֶל־עַמָּֽיו׃ 18 וַיִּשְׁכְּנ֨וּ מֵֽחֲוִילָ֜ה עַד־שׁ֗וּר אֲשֶׁר֙ עַל־פְּנֵ֣י מִצְרַ֔יִם בֹּאֲכָ֖ה אַשּׁ֑וּרָה עַל־פְּנֵ֥י כָל־אֶחָ֖יו נָפָֽל׃ פ פ פ

ק"ה פסוקים, יהוד"ע סימן.

140

Ishmael's Descendants

[SEVENTH READING] ¹² The following are the descendants of Ishmael son of Abraham, whom Hagar the Egyptian—Sarah's maid—bore to Abraham:

¹³ These are the names of the sons of Ishmael, listed according to (the order of) their births: the firstborn of Ishmael was Nebaioth, then Kedar, Adbeel, Mibsam, ¹⁴ Mishma, Dumah, Massa, ¹⁵ Hadad, Tema, Jetur, Naphish, and Kedmah.

[MAFTIR] ¹⁶ These were Ishmael's sons and this is how they were called in their towns and their walled cities. There were twelve princes for their nations.

¹⁷ These were the years of Ishmael's life: (a total of) one hundred years, thirty years and seven years. He breathed his last and died, and he was gathered to his people.

¹⁸ (His descendants) lived between Havilah and Shur, which is near Egypt, towards Asshur. They dwelt (near) all their brethren.

The Haftarah for Ḥayyei Sarah is on page 1298.

spiritual vitamin

> During the soul's lifetime on earth in partnership with the body, the soul is necessarily "handicapped"—in certain respects—by the requirements of the body (such as eating and drinking, etc.). Even a *tzaddik* (pious person), whose entire life is consecrated to God, cannot escape the restraints of life in a material and physical environment. Consequently, the time that comes for the soul to return "home" is essentially a *release*, as the soul makes its ascent to a higher world, no longer restrained by a physical body and physical environment.

Connect to your **lineage** and discover the presence of your **ancestors** within you. You will receive the **merit** of all their efforts and be **empowered** to become **fully human,** as best as you can be.

TOLEDOT
תולדות

BIRTH OF JACOB AND ESAU	25:19–26
JACOB BUYS BIRTHRIGHT FROM ESAU	25:27–34
ISAAC RELOCATES TO GERAR DUE TO FAMINE	26:1–33
ESAU MARRIES	26:34–35
JACOB TAKES ESAU'S BLESSING	27:1–45
ISAAC INSTRUCTS JACOB TO MARRY	27:46 – 28:5
ESAU MARRIES ISHMAEL'S DAUGHTER	28:6–9

NAME
Toledot

MEANING
"Descendants"

LINES IN TORAH SCROLL
173

PARASHIYYOT
2 open; 2 closed

VERSES
106

WORDS
1432

LETTERS
5426

DATE
2108–2171

LOCATION
Canaan, Gerar, land of Philistines, Beer-sheba

KEY PEOPLE
Isaac, Rebekah, Jacob, Esau, Abimelech

MITZVOT
None

MASORETIC FEATURES
Kof of the word *katzti* (27:46) is undersized

CHARACTER PROFILE

NAME
Rebekah

MEANING
"Secured"

PARENTS
Bethuel and Milcah

GRANDFATHER
Nahor

BROTHER
Laban

BIRTHPLACE
Aram-naharaim

CHILDREN
Jacob and Esau

ACHIEVEMENTS
When she entered Sarah's tent, three miracles recurred; was able to maintain her integrity even when living among those who were dishonest

KNOWN FOR
Her beauty; well waters rose up to greet her when she went to draw water for Eliezer and his camels; was three years old when she left her father's home; childless for twenty years before bearing Jacob and Esau

STRUGGLE

Rebekah felt the twins within her struggling. Esau would move when she passed houses of idol-worship, while Jacob would move when she passed houses of prayer. Within you are two impulses which struggle with each other. One inclines towards the mundane while the other towards the Godly. It is your choice which impulse to follow (25:22).

PAIN

Rebekah's pregnancy was extremely painful, leading her to wonder why she wanted to have children. Pain constricts your mind, eclipses all your concerns, makes you forgetful of your sacred mission in life. If pain presents itself, remember that it is only a transient "doorway," which you need to pass through (25:22).

BLESSING CHILDREN

Before he died, Isaac wanted to bless his sons. Make a point of blessing your children, sharing your hopes and aspirations for them in a spirit of love.

תולדות

בראשית כה:יט-כג

19 וְאֵ֛לֶּה תּוֹלְדֹ֥ת יִצְחָ֖ק בֶּן־אַבְרָהָ֑ם אַבְרָהָ֖ם הוֹלִ֥יד אֶת־יִצְחָֽק: 20 וַיְהִ֤י יִצְחָק֙ בֶּן־אַרְבָּעִ֣ים שָׁנָ֔ה בְּקַחְתּ֣וֹ אֶת־רִבְקָ֗ה בַּת־בְּתוּאֵל֙ הָֽאֲרַמִּ֔י מִפַּדַּ֖ן אֲרָ֑ם אֲח֛וֹת לָבָ֥ן הָאֲרַמִּ֖י ל֥וֹ לְאִשָּֽׁה: 21 וַיֶּעְתַּ֨ר יִצְחָ֤ק לַֽיהוָֹה֙ לְנֹ֣כַח אִשְׁתּ֔וֹ כִּ֥י עֲקָרָ֖ה הִ֑וא וַיֵּעָ֤תֶר לוֹ֙ יְהוָֹ֔ה וַתַּ֖הַר רִבְקָ֥ה אִשְׁתּֽוֹ: 22 וַיִּתְרֹֽצֲצ֤וּ הַבָּנִים֙ בְּקִרְבָּ֔הּ וַתֹּ֣אמֶר אִם־כֵּ֔ן לָ֥מָּה זֶּ֖ה אָנֹ֑כִי וַתֵּ֖לֶךְ לִדְרֹ֥שׁ אֶת־יְהוָֹֽה: 23 וַיֹּ֨אמֶר יְהוָֹ֜ה לָ֗הּ שְׁנֵ֤י [גיים כ׳] גוֹיִם֙

God can either make a person's disposition naturally good or naturally bad. However, even if a person has a natural inclination to evil, that does not mean that he is evil *per se*, for a man is given free choice. The reason why he was given such an inclination was to rise to the challenge *and overcome it*. Esau was given a natural tendency to evil so that he could excel in the task of quashing the evil impulse.

Even though he failed in his task, you can nevertheless learn from Esau that if you have a strong desire to do something bad, it means that you have been given the special Divine mission of overcoming your inclination (*Rabbi Menahem Mendel Schneerson, 20th century*).

She went to ask God. Rebekah went to the Academy of Shem to ask, "What will happen in the end?" (*Rashi, 11th century*).

Rebekah was not particularly concerned with the struggle between good and evil *per se*. She was more worried about the struggle's conclusion: "What will happen in the end?

We all experience a daily tug-of-war within our hearts and minds, with selfish tendencies pitted against altruistic leanings. Such turmoil is perfectly natural, considering the dual tendencies planted within us, our good and the evil impulses, and should not be the cause of any discouragement. Taking the example of Rebekah, we ought to focus on the *conclusion* and ask ourselves, "What will be in the end?" The main thing is to guarantee that the pure voice has the last word (*Rabbi Simḥah Bunem of Przysucha, 18th–19th century*).

23. Two esteemed individuals are in your womb. Two kingdoms will separate from your innards. Why was Jacob, the most perfect of all the Patriarchs, and Esau, who was so evil, linked to each other so intimately? Why did God not, at least, bring them into the world through two different births? It is hard enough to understand how Esau could have emerged at all from the womb of the righteous Rebekah, let alone at the same time as Jacob!

> **kabbalah bites**
>
> **25:22-23** Rebekah knew that her purpose in life was to achieve *tikkun* (spiritual healing) for the sin of Adam and Eve. *Tikkun* occurs when the forces of good and evil, which have been inappropriately mingled through sin, are separated once again.
>
> But when Rebekah saw that the souls of Cain (Esau) and Abel (Jacob) were fighting in her womb in full force, with Esau seeking to kill Jacob, she feared that *tikkun* would not be achieved through her.
>
> The response given to her by Shem was that, to the contrary, in their lifetimes *tikkun* would occur: "*The elder (son) will serve the younger (son).*"

genesis 25:19–23   toledot

parashat toledot

The Birth of Jacob and Esau

¹⁹ And these are the descendants of Isaac, the son of Abraham:

(The Torah now digresses, before continuing with Isaac's descendants in verses 25-26.)

(After God gave Abram the name) Abraham, (he) fathered Isaac. ²⁰ Isaac was forty years old when he took Rebekah for himself as a wife. (Even though she was) the daughter of Bethuel the Aramean of Paddan-aram, sister of Laban the Aramean (she did not learn from their wicked ways).

²¹ Isaac prayed (repeatedly) to God (in one corner of the room) opposite his wife, because she was barren. God accepted his prayer, and his wife Rebekah conceived.

²² The children struggled inside her. She said, "If (the pain of pregnancy is) so (much) why did I (want to be like) this?" She went (to the Academy of Shem) to ask God (what was going to happen to her).

²³ (Through Shem's Divine inspiration) God said to her, "(The ancestors of) two esteemed individuals are in your womb. (Furthermore,) two kingdoms will

---

25:19 And these are the descendants of Isaac, the son of Abraham. Abraham was pure love, which was not capable of redeeming this world of its chaos. Only through the *restraint* of Isaac was Abraham's love granted continuity. Therefore, the Torah attributes the "descendants" to Isaac (i.e. continuity). But this mission itself was powered by Abraham's love—Isaac was merely "the son of Abraham" (*Rabbi Menahem Nahum Twersky of Chernobyl, 18th century*).

21. Isaac prayed to God, opposite his wife. It does not say that Isaac prayed for his wife, but that he prayed together with her. From here we see that Rebekah and Isaac were both infertile and that they both prayed to be healed.

Why did our forefathers have difficulties with fertility?

Rabbi Isaac said, "God yearns for the prayers of the righteous. That is why He initially caused them to be infertile, so that they would pray to Him for help" (*Babylonian Talmud, Yevamot 64a*).

Because she was barren. In fact, Isaac was also unable to have children. In this verse, the word for "she" is not spelled in the Torah in the usual manner, *he-yod-alef*, but rather *he-vav-alef*, which can also be read as "he," suggesting that Isaac also could not have children (*Midrash ha-Gadol*).

22. The children struggled inside her. When she passed by the entrance to the Academy of Shem and Eber, Jacob would struggle to come out. When she passed the entrance of a temple of idolatry, Esau would struggle to come out (*Rashi, 11th century*).

How could Isaac, our righteous Patriarch, have a son whose very nature *even in the womb* was inclined towards idol-worship?

בְּבִטְנֵךְ וּשְׁנֵי לְאֻמִּים מִמֵּעַיִךְ יִפָּרֵדוּ וּלְאֹם מִלְאֹם יֶאֱמָץ וְרַב יַעֲבֹד צָעִיר: 24 וַיִּמְלְאוּ יָמֶיהָ לָלֶדֶת וְהִנֵּה תוֹמִם בְּבִטְנָהּ: 25 וַיֵּצֵא הָרִאשׁוֹן אַדְמוֹנִי כֻּלּוֹ כְּאַדֶּרֶת שֵׂעָר וַיִּקְרְאוּ שְׁמוֹ עֵשָׂו: 26 וְאַחֲרֵי־כֵן יָצָא אָחִיו וְיָדוֹ אֹחֶזֶת בַּעֲקֵב עֵשָׂו וַיִּקְרָא שְׁמוֹ יַעֲקֹב וְיִצְחָק בֶּן־שִׁשִּׁים שָׁנָה בְּלֶדֶת אֹתָם: 27 וַיִּגְדְּלוּ הַנְּעָרִים וַיְהִי עֵשָׂו אִישׁ יֹדֵעַ צַיִד אִישׁ שָׂדֶה וְיַעֲקֹב אִישׁ תָּם יֹשֵׁב אֹהָלִים: 28 וַיֶּאֱהַב יִצְחָק אֶת־עֵשָׂו כִּי־צַיִד בְּפִיו וְרִבְקָה אֹהֶבֶת אֶת־יַעֲקֹב: 29 וַיָּזֶד יַעֲקֹב נָזִיד

rated from agricultural produce). This would have led Isaac to think that Esau was extremely particular in observing commandments, going beyond the letter of the law to separate tithes even in a case where there is no obligation to do so (*Rabbi Elijah Mizraḥi, 15th–16th century*).

Why did Esau pick specifically these examples, of salt and straw, in order to fool his father?

In the scheme of creation, there is a duality of *primary* versus *secondary*. For example, our world is secondary to the world to come, the six days of creation are secondary to the Sabbath; and, on a more physical plane, the peel is secondary to the fruit.

The rule is: *That which is secondary must know its place and defer to that which is primary.* In doing so, it achieves its own potential.

Esau was of secondary importance to Jacob, but Esau was too arrogant to come to terms with this fact. He would have achieved his own perfection by accepting his secondary status and deferring to his brother, but foolishly, he saw Jacob as a competitor.

This fundamental error is hinted to in Esau's question about tithing salt and straw. Both of these are inessential, secondary substances—salt merely enhances the taste of food, and straw is animal fodder. So, Esau, following his very own nature, gravitated towards things that were superficial and secondary (*Rabbi Samuel Bornstein of Sochaczew, 20th century*).

Jacob was ... dwelling in tents. While this is traditionally understood as referring to Jacob's devotion to Torah study, Scripture does not state this fact specifically. We are merely informed that he was "dwelling in tents." From here you learn that spending time in the synagogue and study hall *even without prayer and study* is a very great virtue (*Rabbi Menaḥem Azariah da Fano, 16th–17th century*).

29. Jacob was cooking a (lentil) stew (to feed his father). On that day Abraham died, prompting Jacob to prepare a lentil stew for his father Isaac.

> **kabbalah bites**
>
> **25:26** *"His hand was grasping Esau's heel."* Esau, the firstborn of Isaac, was a reincarnation of Cain, Adam's firstborn. Jacob was a reincarnation of Abel.
>
> Abel's soul was *primarily* good, with a little evil mixed in, and Cain's soul was *primarily* evil, with a kernel of good (see above, 4:1-2).
>
> Jacob, who possessed Abel's soul, sought to capture the kernel of good in Cain's soul which had been reincarnated into Esau. That is why Jacob was holding onto Esau's heel—the heel representing those lowly, demonic forces in Cain's soul that had trapped the kernel of good inside.

separate from your innards (one to wickedness, one to innocence). One kingdom will (always) become mightier than the other kingdom (for when one rises the other will fall). The elder (son) will serve the younger (son)."

[24] The term of her pregnancy was complete, and—look!—there were twins in her womb.

[25] The first one came out reddish and completely (covered in hair), like a fur coat of hair. They named him Esau. [26] Afterwards, his brother emerged, and his hand was grasping Esau's heel. (God) named him Jacob.

Isaac was sixty years old when she gave birth to them.

Jacob Buys the Birthright from Esau

[27] The boys grew up (and their differences became recognizable). Esau was a man who knew how to trap (people with his mouth), a man of the field (who enjoyed hunting). Jacob was an honest person, dwelling in tents (the Academy of Shem and Eber).

[28] Isaac loved Esau because (he provided) his mouth with game; but Rebekah loved Jacob.

[29] (On the day that Abraham died), Jacob was cooking a (lentil) stew (to feed his father), when Esau came (home) from the field, exhausted (from his murderous activities).

God, however, anticipated in His great foresight that Jacob's mission was to be the raising of holy sparks in the descendants of Esau. In order to lift something up, you have to go down to its level and grasp it. Jacob and Esau had to be in the same place at the same time *so that Jacob could lift up the holiness which lies in Esau*. Otherwise Esau would forever remain evil (*Rabbi Menahem Nahum Twersky of Chernobyl, 18th century*).

27. A man who knew how to trap. He knew how to trap and deceive his father with his mouth, asking him, "Father, how do we separate tithes from salt and straw?" This made his father think that he was punctilious in the observance of commandments (*Rashi, 11th century*).

Esau's question, "How do we separate tithes from salt and straw?" was deceptive because there is in fact no obligation in Torah law to separate tithes from salt or straw (tithes are only sepa-

spiritual vitamin

> The greater the accomplishment in the realm of the good and the holy, the greater is the opposition on the part of the "other side" (negative forces).

בראשית כה:כט – כו:ד

וַיָּבֹא עֵשָׂו מִן־הַשָּׂדֶה וְהוּא עָיֵף: 30 וַיֹּאמֶר עֵשָׂו אֶל־יַעֲקֹב הַלְעִיטֵנִי נָא מִן־הָאָדֹם הָאָדֹם הַזֶּה כִּי עָיֵף אָנֹכִי עַל־כֵּן קָרָא־שְׁמוֹ אֱדוֹם: 31 וַיֹּאמֶר יַעֲקֹב מִכְרָה כַיּוֹם אֶת־בְּכֹרָתְךָ לִי: 32 וַיֹּאמֶר עֵשָׂו הִנֵּה אָנֹכִי הוֹלֵךְ לָמוּת וְלָמָּה־זֶּה לִי בְּכֹרָה: 33 וַיֹּאמֶר יַעֲקֹב הִשָּׁבְעָה לִּי כַּיּוֹם וַיִּשָּׁבַע לוֹ וַיִּמְכֹּר אֶת־בְּכֹרָתוֹ לְיַעֲקֹב: 34 וְיַעֲקֹב נָתַן לְעֵשָׂו לֶחֶם וּנְזִיד עֲדָשִׁים וַיֹּאכַל וַיֵּשְׁתְּ וַיָּקָם וַיֵּלַךְ וַיִּבֶז עֵשָׂו אֶת־הַבְּכֹרָה: פ

כו 1 וַיְהִי רָעָב בָּאָרֶץ מִלְּבַד הָרָעָב הָרִאשׁוֹן אֲשֶׁר הָיָה בִּימֵי אַבְרָהָם וַיֵּלֶךְ יִצְחָק אֶל־אֲבִימֶלֶךְ מֶלֶךְ־פְּלִשְׁתִּים גְּרָרָה: 2 וַיֵּרָא אֵלָיו יְהֹוָה וַיֹּאמֶר אַל־תֵּרֵד מִצְרָיְמָה שְׁכֹן בָּאָרֶץ אֲשֶׁר אֹמַר אֵלֶיךָ: 3 גּוּר בָּאָרֶץ הַזֹּאת וְאֶהְיֶה עִמְּךָ וַאֲבָרְכֶךָּ כִּי־לְךָ וּלְזַרְעֲךָ אֶתֵּן אֶת־כָּל־הָאֲרָצֹת הָאֵל וַהֲקִמֹתִי אֶת־הַשְּׁבֻעָה אֲשֶׁר נִשְׁבַּעְתִּי לְאַבְרָהָם אָבִיךָ: 4 וְהִרְבֵּיתִי אֶת־זַרְעֲךָ כְּכוֹכְבֵי

Jacob" (v. 33). Why does the Torah wait all the way until this point, after Esau has finished eating and departed, to inform us of his contemptuous attitude, that *"Esau despised the birthright"*?

When Esau came home from the field tired and famished, his behavior might have been excusable—perhaps he sold the birthright because he was on the verge of starvation? Once he was satiated, however, he should have tried to undo the damage by claiming that the sale was not really valid, since he had not been thinking clearly. It is only when he simply *"got up and left,"* that we know for certain that Esau *"despised the birthright"* (*Rabbi Ḥayyim Aryeh Leib of Jedwabne, 19th century*).

Esau despised the birthright. Even though Esau's moral and spiritual standing was extremely low, to the extent that he *"despised the birthright,"* and his very disposition indicated that he was a murderous person (*Rashi* to 25:25), we still find later on that Jacob sent messengers ("angels") to inform Esau that he was at peace with him, and sought his affection (see 32:4; *Rashi* to v. 6, ibid.).

From this we can learn a powerful lesson: We should reach out and "send messengers" even to those Jews who appear to be on the level of Esau. Even such a person is your "brother" who needs to be treated in a pleasant and peace-loving manner, with love and affection. He needs to be drawn closer to the Torah with "ropes of love" (*Rabbi Menahem Mendel Schneerson, 20th century*).

26:2 Do not go down to Egypt. He had in mind to go down to Egypt, as his father had gone down in the days of the famine. God said to him, "Do not go down to Egypt! You are a perfect burnt-offering, and being outside the land of Israel is not fitting for you" (*Rashi, 11th century*).

³⁰ Esau said to Jacob, "Pour some of this red stuff [*'adom*] (down my throat) because I'm exhausted!"—he was therefore given the name Edom (meaning "red").

³¹ Jacob (thought that Esau was not fit to perform the sacrificial services carried out by the firstborn, so he) said, "Sell me your birthright (so that I own it indisputably) like day(light)."

³² Esau replied, "Look, (with my lifestyle) I am going to (be punishable by) death (if I retain the right to sacrificial services) so why do I need this birthright?"

³³ Jacob said, "Swear to me (so that I own it indisputably) like day(light)." So he swore to him, and sold his birthright to Jacob.

³⁴ Jacob gave bread and lentil stew to Esau, who ate and drank. Then he got up and left.

Esau despised (the whole idea of serving God which came with) the birthright.

Isaac Moves to Gerar Because of Famine

26 ¹ There was a famine in the land, besides the first famine that existed in the days of Abraham. Isaac went to King Abimelech of the Philistines, in Gerar.

² God appeared to him, and said, "Do not go down to Egypt! Inhabit the land which I will tell you (about). ³ Settle in this land, and I will be with you and I will bless you. For I will give all these lands to you and to your descendants, and I will uphold the oath that I swore to Abraham, your father. ⁴ I will multiply your

---

Why lentils? Just as a lentil has no "mouth" (open cleft, like other legumes), the mourner has no mouth, no words to fully express himself (*Babylonian Talmud, Bava Batra* 16b).

34. Jacob gave bread and lentil stew to Esau, who ate and drank. Then he got up and left. Esau despised the birthright. Esau sold his birthright to Jacob in return for mere bread and lentil stew. He then scorned the merit of the birthright by declaring, *"Why do I need this birthright?"* (v. 32). The Torah then confirms the sale, stating that he *"sold his birthright to*

spiritual vitamin

> In His infinite goodness, God gave you the possibility of approach and communion with Him. Through the Torah, God showed you the way a finite created being can reach beyond his inherent limitations, and commune with God, the Infinite.

בראשית כו:ד-טז   תולדות

הַשָּׁמַ֔יִם וְנָתַתִּ֣י לְזַרְעֲךָ֔ אֵ֥ת כָּל־הָאֲרָצֹ֖ת הָאֵ֑ל וְהִתְבָּרֲכ֣וּ בְזַרְעֲךָ֔ כֹּ֖ל גּוֹיֵ֥י הָאָֽרֶץ:
5 עֵ֕קֶב אֲשֶׁר־שָׁמַ֥ע אַבְרָהָ֖ם בְּקֹלִ֑י וַיִּשְׁמֹר֙ מִשְׁמַרְתִּ֔י מִצְוֺתַ֖י חֻקּוֹתַ֥י וְתוֹרֹתָֽי:
6 [SECOND READING] וַיֵּ֥שֶׁב יִצְחָ֖ק בִּגְרָֽר: 7 וַֽיִּשְׁאֲל֞וּ אַנְשֵׁ֤י הַמָּקוֹם֙ לְאִשְׁתּ֔וֹ וַיֹּ֖אמֶר אֲחֹ֣תִי
הִ֑וא כִּ֤י יָרֵא֙ לֵאמֹ֣ר אִשְׁתִּ֔י פֶּן־יַֽהַרְגֻ֜נִי אַנְשֵׁ֤י הַמָּקוֹם֙ עַל־רִבְקָ֔ה כִּֽי־טוֹבַ֥ת
מַרְאֶ֖ה הִֽוא: 8 וַיְהִ֗י כִּ֣י אָֽרְכוּ־ל֥וֹ שָׁם֙ הַיָּמִ֔ים וַיַּשְׁקֵ֗ף אֲבִימֶ֨לֶךְ֙ מֶ֣לֶךְ פְּלִשְׁתִּ֔ים
בְּעַ֖ד הַֽחַלּ֑וֹן וַיַּ֗רְא וְהִנֵּ֤ה יִצְחָק֙ מְצַחֵ֔ק אֵ֖ת רִבְקָ֥ה אִשְׁתּֽוֹ: 9 וַיִּקְרָ֨א אֲבִימֶ֜לֶךְ
לְיִצְחָ֗ק וַיֹּ֨אמֶר֙ אַ֣ךְ הִנֵּ֤ה אִשְׁתְּךָ֙ הִ֔וא וְאֵ֥יךְ אָמַ֖רְתָּ אֲחֹ֣תִי הִ֑וא וַיֹּ֤אמֶר אֵלָיו֙
יִצְחָ֔ק כִּ֣י אָמַ֔רְתִּי פֶּן־אָמ֖וּת עָלֶֽיהָ: 10 וַיֹּ֣אמֶר אֲבִימֶ֔לֶךְ מַה־זֹּ֖את עָשִׂ֣יתָ לָּ֑נוּ
כִּ֠מְעַ֠ט שָׁכַ֞ב אַחַ֤ד הָעָם֙ אֶת־אִשְׁתֶּ֔ךָ וְהֵֽבֵאתָ֥ עָלֵ֖ינוּ אָשָֽׁם: 11 וַיְצַ֤ו אֲבִימֶ֨לֶךְ֙ אֶת־
כָּל־הָעָ֖ם לֵאמֹ֑ר הַנֹּגֵ֜עַ בָּאִ֥ישׁ הַזֶּ֛ה וּבְאִשְׁתּ֖וֹ מ֥וֹת יוּמָֽת: 12 וַיִּזְרַ֤ע יִצְחָק֙ בָּאָ֣רֶץ
הַהִ֔וא וַיִּמְצָ֛א בַּשָּׁנָ֥ה הַהִ֖וא מֵאָ֣ה שְׁעָרִ֑ים וַֽיְבָרֲכֵ֖הוּ יְהֹוָֽה: 13 [THIRD READING] וַיִּגְדַּ֖ל
הָאִ֑ישׁ וַיֵּ֤לֶךְ הָלוֹךְ֙ וְגָדֵ֔ל עַ֥ד כִּֽי־גָדַ֖ל מְאֹֽד: 14 וַֽיְהִי־ל֤וֹ מִקְנֵה־צֹאן֙ וּמִקְנֵ֣ה בָקָ֔ר
וַעֲבֻדָּ֖ה רַבָּ֑ה וַיְקַנְא֥וּ אֹת֖וֹ פְּלִשְׁתִּֽים: 15 וְכָל־הַבְּאֵרֹ֗ת אֲשֶׁ֤ר חָֽפְרוּ֙ עַבְדֵ֣י אָבִ֔יו
בִּימֵ֖י אַבְרָהָ֣ם אָבִ֑יו סִתְּמ֣וּם פְּלִשְׁתִּ֔ים וַיְמַלְא֖וּם עָפָֽר: 16 וַיֹּ֥אמֶר אֲבִימֶ֖לֶךְ

15. The Philistines stopped up all the wells that his father's servants had dug in the days of Abraham, his father, and they filled them with earth. All the hard work that was carried out by Abraham's servants—people who served God with fear of heaven, educating the masses about the One God and hoping to transform them into "wells" brimming with the waters of

spiritual vitamin

> God could have established a world order, where morality and ethics would reign supreme, with little or no effort on the part of man. However, obviously, there is no comparison between something received as a gift and the same thing attained through hard effort.

descendants like the stars of the heavens, and I will give your descendants all these lands. All the nations of the earth will give blessings to each other by (comparing themselves to) your descendants. [5] (All this is) because Abraham listened to My voice (when I tested him); he guarded My (secondary prohibitions that) protect (a person from transgressing Biblical prohibitions), My rational commands, My suprarational commands, and My instructions (in the Oral Law)."

[SECOND READING] [6] So, Isaac settled in Gerar. [7] When the local men asked about his wife, he said, "She is my sister," because he was afraid to say, "(She is) my wife," (because he said to himself,) "perhaps the local men will kill me because of Rebekah, for she is pleasant-looking."

[8] Then, when he had been there for many days (he felt it was safe to stop pretending as if Rebekah was his sister), King Abimelech of the Philistines looked through the window, and he saw—look!—Isaac was courting Rebekah, his wife.

[9] Abimelech summoned Isaac, and he said, "She really is your wife! How could you have said, 'She is my sister'?"

Isaac said to him, "Because I said (to myself), 'perhaps I'll die because of her.'"

[10] "What have you done to us?" said Abimelech. "(I, the King,) the highest of the people, might easily have lain with your wife, and (if I had done so) you would have brought guilt upon us."

[11] Abimelech instructed all the people, saying, "Whoever touches this man or his wife will be put to death."

Isaac Prospers

[12] Isaac sowed (crops) in that land (which was not as fertile as the main part of the land of Canaan), and he found (even) in that year (which was a bad one for crops, that the land yielded) a hundred times (more than average)—and God blessed him.

[THIRD READING] [13] The man (Isaac) became prosperous, and he grew constantly greater until he had grown very great (even in comparison to Abimelech). [14] He had flocks of sheep, flocks of cattle and many enterprises, and the Philistines envied him. [15] The Philistines stopped up all the wells that his father's servants had dug in the days of Abraham, his father, and they filled them with earth.

[16] Abimelech said to Isaac, "Go away from us, for you have become much stronger than us."

---

food for thought

1. Do you see your wealth as your own achievement, or God's?

2. What are some of the challenges of wealth?

3. Is it inappropriate for rabbis to be wealthy?

בראשית כו:טז-כח תולדות

אֱלֵֽי־יִצְחָ֔ק לֵ֥ךְ מֵעִמָּ֑נוּ כִּֽי־עָצַ֥מְתָּ מִמֶּ֖נּוּ מְאֹֽד׃ 17 וַיֵּ֥לֶךְ מִשָּׁ֖ם יִצְחָ֑ק וַיִּ֥חַן בְּנַֽחַל־גְּרָ֖ר וַיֵּ֥שֶׁב שָֽׁם׃ 18 וַיָּ֨שָׁב יִצְחָ֜ק וַיַּחְפֹּ֣ר ׀ אֶת־בְּאֵרֹ֣ת הַמַּ֗יִם אֲשֶׁ֤ר חָֽפְרוּ֙ בִּימֵי֙ אַבְרָהָ֣ם אָבִ֔יו וַיְסַתְּמ֣וּם פְּלִשְׁתִּ֔ים אַחֲרֵ֖י מ֣וֹת אַבְרָהָ֑ם וַיִּקְרָ֤א לָהֶן֙ שֵׁמ֔וֹת כַּשֵּׁמֹ֕ת אֲשֶׁר־קָרָ֥א לָהֶ֖ן אָבִֽיו׃ 19 וַיַּחְפְּר֥וּ עַבְדֵֽי־יִצְחָ֖ק בַּנָּ֑חַל וַיִּ֨מְצְאוּ־שָׁ֔ם בְּאֵ֖ר מַ֥יִם חַיִּֽים׃ 20 וַיָּרִ֜יבוּ רֹעֵ֣י גְרָ֗ר עִם־רֹעֵ֥י יִצְחָ֛ק לֵאמֹ֖ר לָ֣נוּ הַמָּ֑יִם וַיִּקְרָ֤א שֵֽׁם־הַבְּאֵר֙ עֵ֔שֶׂק כִּ֥י הִֽתְעַשְּׂק֖וּ עִמּֽוֹ׃ 21 וַֽיַּחְפְּרוּ֙ בְּאֵ֣ר אַחֶ֔רֶת וַיָּרִ֖יבוּ גַּם־עָלֶ֑יהָ וַיִּקְרָ֥א שְׁמָ֖הּ שִׂטְנָֽה׃ 22 וַיַּעְתֵּ֣ק מִשָּׁ֗ם וַיַּחְפֹּר֙ בְּאֵ֣ר אַחֶ֔רֶת וְלֹ֥א רָב֖וּ עָלֶ֑יהָ וַיִּקְרָ֤א שְׁמָהּ֙ רְחֹב֔וֹת וַיֹּ֗אמֶר כִּֽי־עַתָּ֞ה הִרְחִ֧יב יְהֹוָ֛ה לָ֖נוּ וּפָרִ֥ינוּ בָאָֽרֶץ׃ [FOURTH READING:]
23 וַיַּ֥עַל מִשָּׁ֖ם בְּאֵ֥ר שָֽׁבַע׃ 24 וַיֵּרָ֨א אֵלָ֤יו יְהֹוָה֙ בַּלַּ֣יְלָה הַה֔וּא וַיֹּ֕אמֶר אָנֹכִ֕י אֱלֹהֵ֖י אַבְרָהָ֣ם אָבִ֑יךָ אַל־תִּירָא֙ כִּֽי־אִתְּךָ֣ אָנֹ֔כִי וּבֵֽרַכְתִּ֨יךָ֙ וְהִרְבֵּיתִ֣י אֶֽת־זַרְעֲךָ֔ בַּעֲב֖וּר אַבְרָהָ֥ם עַבְדִּֽי׃ 25 וַיִּ֤בֶן שָׁם֙ מִזְבֵּ֔חַ וַיִּקְרָ֖א בְּשֵׁ֣ם יְהֹוָ֑ה וַיֶּט־שָׁ֣ם אׇהֳל֔וֹ וַיִּכְרוּ־שָׁ֥ם עַבְדֵי־יִצְחָ֖ק בְּאֵֽר׃ 26 וַאֲבִימֶ֕לֶךְ הָלַ֥ךְ אֵלָ֖יו מִגְּרָ֑ר וַאֲחֻזַּת֙ מֵֽרֵעֵ֔הוּ וּפִיכֹ֖ל שַׂר־צְבָאֽוֹ׃ 27 וַיֹּ֤אמֶר אֲלֵהֶם֙ יִצְחָ֔ק מַדּ֖וּעַ בָּאתֶ֣ם אֵלָ֑י וְאַתֶּם֙ שְׂנֵאתֶ֣ם אֹתִ֔י וַתְּשַׁלְּח֖וּנִי מֵאִתְּכֶֽם׃ 28 וַיֹּאמְר֗וּ רָא֣וֹ רָאִ֘ינוּ֮ כִּֽי־הָיָ֣ה יְהֹוָ֣ה ׀ עִמָּךְ֒ וַנֹּ֗אמֶר תְּהִ֨י

| 152 |

Second Temple (see Ezra 4:6). The third well was called Rehoboth ("spacious"), alluding to the future Third Temple which will be built without quarrel or feud, when God will expand our borders—speedily, in our days (*Naḥmanides, 13th century*).

The analogy of digging a well precisely describes the process of building the Temple. First there is a phase of intense physical effort to dig the well, followed by the actual filling of the well with water which does not require any direct effort, it simply floods in. Similarly, the building of the Temple requires tremendous human effort, but the indwelling of the Divine Presence—which is the very purpose of building the Temple—is an effortless consequence of the Temple's construction.

This analogy appears to break down, however, in the case of the Third Temple which, according to the *Zohar*, will be built by God, and not by man. It seems at first glance that Naḥmanides' analogy for the Third Temple of *digging* a well is inappropriate.

However, even according to the *Zohar*, the Third Temple will be built through human effort too. Not through the physical effort of working with stones and mortar, but through dedicated acts of worship, in defiance of the challenges of exile. The cumulative effects of these acts are

¹⁷ Isaac went away from there, set up camp in the Gerar Valley, and settled there.

¹⁸ (However, before he left Gerar) Isaac re-dug the water wells which had been dug in the days of his father, Abraham, and were stopped up by the Philistines after Abraham's death. He gave them names; the same names that his father had given them.

¹⁹ (After settling) in the valley, Isaac's servants dug, and they found there a well of living waters. ²⁰ The shepherds of Gerar argued with Isaac's shepherds, saying, "The water is ours," so he named the well Esek ("argument"), because they had argued with him.

²¹ They dug another well, and the (shepherds) quarreled about it also, so he named it Sitnah ("harassment").

²² He moved away from there and dug another well. They did not quarrel over it, so he named it Rehoboth [*ReHoVot*]. He said, "For now God has made space [*hiRHiV*] for us, and we will be fruitful in the land."

[FOURTH READING] ²³ He went up from there to Beer-sheba. ²⁴ That night, God appeared to him and said, "I am the God of Abraham, your father. Do not be afraid, for I am with you. I will bless you and multiply your descendants for the sake of Abraham, My servant."

²⁵ He built an altar there, and he (prayed) in the name of God. He pitched his tent there, and Isaac's servants dug a well there.

Abimelech Swears an Oath with Isaac

²⁶ Abimelech came to him from Gerar with a group of his companions and Phicol, his army-general. ²⁷ Isaac said to them, "Why have you come to me, if you hate me, and you sent me away from you?"

²⁸ They said, "We see that God was with you (and) we saw (that God was with your father), so we said: Let the oath that was between us (from the days of your

---

spiritual life—was stopped by the Philistines. The Philistines filled the "wells" with "earth"—they attempted to transform Abraham's enlightened followers into materialistic "earthy" individuals, by desensitizing them to spirituality, leading them to serve God halfheartedly (*Rabbi Elimelech of Lyzhansk, 18ᵗʰ century*).

19. A well of living waters. Everywhere there is a hidden "point" of God. We only have to remove the external facade to reveal that inner point which is called *"a well of living waters"* (*Rabbi Isaac Meir Alter of Gur, 19ᵗʰ century*).

21. They dug another well. The Torah informs us that Isaac dug three wells, hinting to the three Holy Temples. The first well, named Esek ("argument"), alludes to the First Temple, which was contested by the nations who oppressed the Jewish people with wars, until they destroyed it. The second well, Sitnah ("harassment"), is a name actually used by Scripture to refer to the

בראשית כו:כח - כז:ג　　　תולדות

נָ֣א אָלָ֞ה בֵּינוֹתֵ֗ינוּ בֵּינֵ֙ינוּ֙ וּבֵינֶ֔ךָ וְנִכְרְתָ֥ה בְרִ֖ית עִמָּֽךְ: 29 אִם־תַּעֲשֵׂ֨ה עִמָּ֜נוּ רָעָ֗ה כַּאֲשֶׁר֙ לֹ֣א נְגַֽעֲנ֔וּךָ וְכַאֲשֶׁ֨ר עָשִׂ֤ינוּ עִמְּךָ֙ רַק־ט֔וֹב וַנְּשַׁלֵּֽחֲךָ֖ בְּשָׁל֑וֹם אַתָּ֥ה עַתָּ֖ה בְּר֥וּךְ יְהוָֽה: [FIFTH READING] 30 וַיַּ֤עַשׂ לָהֶם֙ מִשְׁתֶּ֔ה וַיֹּאכְל֖וּ וַיִּשְׁתּֽוּ: 31 וַיַּשְׁכִּ֣ימוּ בַבֹּ֔קֶר וַיִּשָּׁבְע֖וּ אִ֣ישׁ לְאָחִ֑יו וַיְשַׁלְּחֵ֣ם יִצְחָ֔ק וַיֵּלְכ֥וּ מֵאִתּ֖וֹ בְּשָׁלֽוֹם: 32 וַיְהִ֣י | בַּיּ֣וֹם הַה֗וּא וַיָּבֹ֙אוּ֙ עַבְדֵ֣י יִצְחָ֔ק וַיַּגִּ֣דוּ ל֔וֹ עַל־אֹד֥וֹת הַבְּאֵ֖ר אֲשֶׁ֣ר חָפָ֑רוּ וַיֹּ֥אמְרוּ ל֖וֹ מָצָ֥אנוּ מָֽיִם: 33 וַיִּקְרָ֥א אֹתָ֖הּ שִׁבְעָ֑ה עַל־כֵּ֤ן שֵׁם־הָעִיר֙ בְּאֵ֣ר שֶׁ֔בַע עַ֖ד הַיּ֥וֹם הַזֶּֽה: ס
34 וַיְהִ֤י עֵשָׂו֙ בֶּן־אַרְבָּעִ֣ים שָׁנָ֔ה וַיִּקַּ֤ח אִשָּׁה֙ אֶת־יְהוּדִ֔ית בַּת־בְּאֵרִ֖י הַֽחִתִּ֑י וְאֶת־בָּ֣שְׂמַ֔ת בַּת־אֵילֹ֖ן הַֽחִתִּֽי: 35 וַתִּהְיֶ֖יןָ מֹ֣רַת ר֑וּחַ לְיִצְחָ֖ק וּלְרִבְקָֽה: ס

כז 1 וַיְהִי֙ כִּֽי־זָקֵ֣ן יִצְחָ֔ק וַתִּכְהֶ֥יןָ עֵינָ֖יו מֵרְאֹ֑ת וַיִּקְרָ֞א אֶת־עֵשָׂ֣ו | בְּנ֣וֹ הַגָּדֹ֗ל וַיֹּ֤אמֶר אֵלָיו֙ בְּנִ֔י וַיֹּ֥אמֶר אֵלָ֖יו הִנֵּֽנִי: 2 וַיֹּ֕אמֶר הִנֵּה־נָ֖א זָקַ֑נְתִּי לֹ֥א יָדַ֖עְתִּי י֥וֹם מוֹתִֽי: 3 וְעַתָּה֙ שָׂא־נָ֣א כֵלֶ֔יךָ תֶּלְיְךָ֖ וְקַשְׁתֶּ֑ךָ וְצֵא֙ הַשָּׂדֶ֔ה וְצ֥וּדָה לִּ֖י

He summoned Esau. What could possibly have been the reason why the blessings which Isaac eventually gave to Jacob were consciously intended for Esau?

Jacob and his family were a paradigm of total unity, in contrast to Esau's family, which consisted of disparate, atomized units (see *Rashi* to 46:26, below). If Isaac had blessed Jacob directly, he would have blessed the unified Congregation of Israel, as a whole. Ironically, *this would have limited the scope of the blessing*—he would have only blessed the congregation in general and not each individual Jew, in particular.

It was the will of God that Isaac should also bless the individual. Therefore, it was orchestrated that Isaac's blessing should consciously be directed towards Esau, who epitomizes separation. In this way the blessing had both virtues, of reaching the congregation and the individual (*Rabbi Kalonymous Kalman Shapira, 20th century*).

spiritual vitamin

" Human nature is such that things that come easily are easily taken for granted, and are not so appreciated and cherished as things for which you had to fight and struggle. When you make real efforts to reach a certain level of religious observance, it permeates you more deeply and thoroughly. "

father) be between you and us. Let us form a covenant with you, ²⁹ that you do no harm to us, just as we have not touched you. And, just as we only treated you well and we sent you away in peace, you too—blessed one of God—now (do the same)."

[FIFTH READING] ³⁰ (Isaac) made a feast for them, and they ate and drank. ³¹ They got up early in the morning and swore an oath with each other. Isaac sent them off, and they went away from him in peace.

³² Then, on that same day, Isaac's servants came and told him about the well that they had dug. They said to him, "We have found water." ³³ He named it Shibah ("oath"). The city is therefore called Beer-sheba to this very day.

Esau Marries

³⁴ When Esau was forty years old he married Judith daughter of Beeri the Hittite, and Basemath daughter of Elon the Hittite. ³⁵ (Their idol-worship) tormented Isaac and Rebekah.

Jacob Takes Esau's Blessing

27 ¹ Isaac had grown old (and he wanted to bless Esau).

The vision of his eyes had dimmed. He summoned Esau, his older son, and he said to him, "My son."

"I'm here," he replied.

² "Look, now I have grown old. I don't know when I will die. ³ So now, sharpen your tools, (take) your sword and your bow, and go out to the field to hunt game

---

depicted by the *Zohar* as a "building made by God," though in fact, it is a building made by human acts that are *totally surrendered* to God.

Since the Third Temple will be built from commandments performed out of utter dedication to God, it will be eternal (*Rabbi Menahem Mendel Schneerson, 20th century*).

34. When Esau was forty years old. Esau has been compared to a pig, as the verse states, *"The pig from the forest gnaws at it"* (*Psalms* 80:14). This pig, when it lies down, stretches out its hooves, as if to say, "See, I am a kosher animal." For forty years, Esau kidnapped wives from their husbands and violated them. When he was forty years old, he said, "My father married at forty. I too will do the same" (*Rashi, 11th century*).

27:1 The vision of his eyes had dimmed. They became weakened because of the smoke of the above-mentioned wives of Esau who would burn incense in idol-worship.

Another explanation: When Isaac was bound on the altar and his father was about to slaughter him, the heavens opened and the ministering angels looked down and wept. Their tears fell on Isaac's eyes and as a result, his eyes became dim.

Another explanation: To enable Jacob to take the blessings (*Rashi, 11th century*).

בראשית כז:ג-יח תולדות

[צידה כ׳] 4 צָיִד: וַעֲשֵׂה־לִי מַטְעַמִּים כַּאֲשֶׁר אָהַבְתִּי וְהָבִיאָה לִּי וְאֹכֵלָה בַּעֲבוּר תְּבָרֶכְךָ נַפְשִׁי בְּטֶרֶם אָמוּת: 5 וְרִבְקָה שֹׁמַעַת בְּדַבֵּר יִצְחָק אֶל־עֵשָׂו בְּנוֹ וַיֵּלֶךְ עֵשָׂו הַשָּׂדֶה לָצוּד צַיִד לְהָבִיא: 6 וְרִבְקָה אָמְרָה אֶל־יַעֲקֹב בְּנָהּ לֵאמֹר הִנֵּה שָׁמַעְתִּי אֶת־אָבִיךָ מְדַבֵּר אֶל־עֵשָׂו אָחִיךָ לֵאמֹר: 7 הָבִיאָה לִּי צַיִד וַעֲשֵׂה־לִי מַטְעַמִּים וְאֹכֵלָה וַאֲבָרֶכְכָה לִפְנֵי יְהֹוָה לִפְנֵי מוֹתִי: 8 וְעַתָּה בְנִי שְׁמַע בְּקֹלִי לַאֲשֶׁר אֲנִי מְצַוָּה אֹתָךְ: 9 לֶךְ־נָא אֶל־הַצֹּאן וְקַח־לִי מִשָּׁם שְׁנֵי גְּדָיֵי עִזִּים טֹבִים וְאֶעֱשֶׂה אֹתָם מַטְעַמִּים לְאָבִיךָ כַּאֲשֶׁר אָהֵב: 10 וְהֵבֵאתָ לְאָבִיךָ וְאָכָל בַּעֲבֻר אֲשֶׁר יְבָרֶכְךָ לִפְנֵי מוֹתוֹ: 11 וַיֹּאמֶר יַעֲקֹב אֶל־רִבְקָה אִמּוֹ הֵן עֵשָׂו אָחִי אִישׁ שָׂעִר וְאָנֹכִי אִישׁ חָלָק: 12 אוּלַי יְמֻשֵּׁנִי אָבִי וְהָיִיתִי בְעֵינָיו כִּמְתַעְתֵּעַ וְהֵבֵאתִי עָלַי קְלָלָה וְלֹא בְרָכָה: 13 וַתֹּאמֶר לוֹ אִמּוֹ עָלַי קִלְלָתְךָ בְּנִי אַךְ שְׁמַע בְּקֹלִי וְלֵךְ קַח־לִי: 14 וַיֵּלֶךְ וַיִּקַּח וַיָּבֵא לְאִמּוֹ וַתַּעַשׂ אִמּוֹ מַטְעַמִּים כַּאֲשֶׁר אָהֵב אָבִיו: 15 וַתִּקַּח רִבְקָה אֶת־בִּגְדֵי עֵשָׂו בְּנָהּ הַגָּדֹל הַחֲמֻדֹת אֲשֶׁר אִתָּהּ בַּבָּיִת וַתַּלְבֵּשׁ אֶת־יַעֲקֹב בְּנָהּ הַקָּטָן: 16 וְאֵת עֹרֹת גְּדָיֵי הָעִזִּים הִלְבִּישָׁה עַל־יָדָיו וְעַל חֶלְקַת צַוָּארָיו: 17 וַתִּתֵּן אֶת־הַמַּטְעַמִּים וְאֶת־הַלֶּחֶם אֲשֶׁר עָשָׂתָה בְּיַד יַעֲקֹב בְּנָהּ: 18 וַיָּבֹא

abundance, Isaac wished to bring about joy through those very materialistic things he was blessing—food and drink (*Rabbi Bahya b. Asher, 13th century*).

5. Rebekah was listening as Isaac spoke to Esau, his son. Apparently Rebekah never told Isaac about God's prophecy, *"the elder (son) will serve the younger (son)"* (above 25:23), for how could Isaac disobey the word of God? Initially, she had not told him because of her sense of morality and modesty—*"she went to ask God (what was going to happen to her)"* (ibid., 22), and she had gone without Isaac's permission. Or perhaps she had thought, "I need not report a prophecy to a prophet, for he is greater than the one who informed me."

At this point she did not want to inform Isaac of the prophecy, fearing that out of Isaac's love for Esau he would refrain from blessing Jacob, and leave everything in God's hands (*Nahmanides, 13th century*).

kabbalah bites

27:13 Adam and Eve were reincarnated as Jacob and Rebekah to achieve *tikkun* (spiritual healing) for the sin of the Tree of Knowledge. The sin resulted from Adam listening to Eve's advice, so now the *tikkun*—to be achieved through Isaac's blessing—was to come through Jacob's heeding the words of Rebekah.

for me. ⁴ Make for me the tasty foods that I love, and bring them to me to eat. For (doing this) my soul will bless you before I die."

⁵ Rebekah was listening as Isaac spoke to Esau, his son.

Esau went to the field to hunt game. (He intended) to bring (meat from stolen animals if he was unable to trap his own).

⁶ Rebekah said to her son Jacob, "Look, I heard your father speaking to Esau your brother, saying, ⁷ 'Bring me game and make me tasty foods to eat, and I will bless you before my death, before God.' ⁸ Now, my son, listen to my voice, to what I am commanding you: ⁹ Go now to the flock, and take two of my choice kids from there, and I will make (one of) them into tasty foods for your father, (the types) that he loves (since a goat tastes like game). ¹⁰ You will bring (them) to your father to eat. For (doing this) he will bless you before he dies."

¹¹ Jacob said to Rebekah his mother, "But my brother Esau is a hairy person, and I am a smooth (skinned) person. ¹² Maybe my father will feel me, and see that I am an imposter—I will bring upon myself a curse and not a blessing."

¹³ But his mother said to him, "Let your curse be on me, my son. Listen to my voice: go and get (the goats) for me."

¹⁴ So he went, and took (the goats), and he brought (them) to his mother. His mother made tasty foods, that his father loved. ¹⁵ Rebekah took her older son Esau's clean clothing which she had in the house, and she dressed Jacob, her younger son. ¹⁶ She put the goats' skins on his hands and on the smooth part of his neck. ¹⁷ She gave the tasty foods and the bread which she had made, into the hand of Jacob, her son.

¹⁸ He came to his father and said, "My father!"

4. Make for me the tasty foods that I love, and bring them to me to eat. For (doing this) my soul will bless you before I die. Why did Isaac make his blessing of Esau dependent on eating the "tasty foods" he would prepare?

In order to bless Esau, Isaac needed to draw down the prophetic spirit, which can only be achieved when in a joyous mood. Since Esau's blessing was primarily for physical and material

kabbalah bites

27:4 "*Make for me (two) tasty foods.*" After the sin, the serpent caused a spiritual pollutant, called *zuhama'*, to enter Eve's soul, which was subsequently passed onto Cain (see 3:6). Esau was a reincarnation of Cain, and Isaac now sought to achieve *tikkun* (spiritual healing) for the sin. The serpent had tempted Eve with the duality of "*knowing good and evil*" (ibid., 5), so Isaac begged of the serpent—now in the guise of Esau—to bring him *two* tasty foods.

אֶל־אָבִיו וַיֹּאמֶר אָבִי וַיֹּאמֶר הִנֶּנִּי מִי אַתָּה בְּנִי: 19 וַיֹּאמֶר יַעֲקֹב אֶל־אָבִיו אָנֹכִי עֵשָׂו בְּכֹרֶךָ עָשִׂיתִי כַּאֲשֶׁר דִּבַּרְתָּ אֵלָי קוּם־נָא שְׁבָה וְאָכְלָה מִצֵּידִי בַּעֲבוּר תְּבָרֲכַנִּי נַפְשֶׁךָ: 20 וַיֹּאמֶר יִצְחָק אֶל־בְּנוֹ מַה־זֶּה מִהַרְתָּ לִמְצֹא בְּנִי וַיֹּאמֶר כִּי הִקְרָה יְהֹוָה אֱלֹהֶיךָ לְפָנָי: 21 וַיֹּאמֶר יִצְחָק אֶל־יַעֲקֹב גְּשָׁה־נָּא וַאֲמֻשְׁךָ בְּנִי הַאַתָּה זֶה בְּנִי עֵשָׂו אִם־לֹא: 22 וַיִּגַּשׁ יַעֲקֹב אֶל־יִצְחָק אָבִיו וַיְמֻשֵּׁהוּ וַיֹּאמֶר הַקֹּל קוֹל יַעֲקֹב וְהַיָּדַיִם יְדֵי עֵשָׂו: 23 וְלֹא הִכִּירוֹ כִּי־הָיוּ יָדָיו כִּידֵי עֵשָׂו אָחִיו שְׂעִרֹת וַיְבָרֲכֵהוּ: 24 וַיֹּאמֶר אַתָּה זֶה בְּנִי עֵשָׂו וַיֹּאמֶר אָנִי: 25 וַיֹּאמֶר הַגִּשָׁה לִּי וְאֹכְלָה מִצֵּיד בְּנִי לְמַעַן תְּבָרֶכְךָ נַפְשִׁי וַיַּגֶּשׁ־לוֹ וַיֹּאכַל וַיָּבֵא לוֹ יַיִן וַיֵּשְׁתְּ: 26 וַיֹּאמֶר אֵלָיו יִצְחָק אָבִיו גְּשָׁה־נָּא וּשְׁקָה־לִּי בְּנִי: 27 וַיִּגַּשׁ וַיִּשַּׁק־לוֹ וַיָּרַח אֶת־רֵיחַ בְּגָדָיו וַיְבָרֲכֵהוּ וַיֹּאמֶר רְאֵה רֵיחַ בְּנִי כְּרֵיחַ שָׂדֶה אֲשֶׁר בֵּרֲכוֹ יְהֹוָה: 28 [SIXTH READING] וְיִתֶּן־לְךָ הָאֱלֹהִים מִטַּל הַשָּׁמַיִם וּמִשְׁמַנֵּי הָאָרֶץ וְרֹב דָּגָן וְתִירֹשׁ:

In a sense, Isaac was correct—his blessings *did* have the power to rescue the sparks trapped in Esau. But the blessing needed to pass first *via Jacob*, because Esau was not sufficiently prepared to utilize Isaac's blessing properly (*Rabbi Shneur Zalman of Lyady, 18th century*).

27. The fragrance of my son is like the fragrance of a field. Surely there is no odor more offensive than that of goat's hair (which Jacob was wearing—see v. 16)? Here you learn that the fragrance of the Garden of Eden entered with him (and it was *this* fragrance that is referred to here). *"The fragrance of a field, which God has blessed,"* indicates it had a pleasant fragrance, that of a field of apples (*Rashi, 11th century*).

Esau's garments, which Jacob was wearing, originally belonged to Nimrod, and they were coveted (and stolen from him) by Esau. Nimrod obtained them from Adam, who wore them in the Garden of Eden (*Pirkei de-Rabbi Eliezer*).

28. May the Almighty give you, etc. Jacob's blessing was that a glimmer of God's light would accompany him in all his endeavors (*Rabbi Abraham Bornstein of Sochaczew, 19th century*).

kabbalah bites

27:27 When they were created, Adam and Eve were enclothed with garments of *light* ('*or*, אור). After the sin, this light departed, remaining in the "walls" of the Garden of Eden, and they were left only with garments of *skin* ('*or*, עור) (*Genesis* 3:21).

These skin garments passed into the possession of Nimrod, and when Esau murdered Nimrod, he took them.

When Jacob donned these garments their inner light, which had departed after the sin, returned—and, as *Rashi* writes, "*the fragrance of the Garden of Eden entered with him.*"

genesis 27:18–28   toledot

(Isaac) said, "I'm here. Who are you, my son?"

¹⁹ Jacob said to his father, "I am...Esau your firstborn. I did what you told me. Please come and sit (at the table) and eat some of my game, in order that your soul will bless me."

²⁰ Isaac said to his son, "How did you find it so quickly, my son?"

He said, "Because God, your God, brought it to me."

²¹ (When Jacob mentioned God, Isaac became suspicious, so) Isaac said to Jacob, "Please come closer, so that I may feel you, my son, to see if you are my son Esau, or not."

²² Jacob drew near to Isaac his father, and he felt him. (Isaac) said, "The voice is (polite like) the voice of Jacob, but the hands are the hands of Esau!" ²³ He did not recognize him because his hands were hairy like his brother Esau's hands, and he blessed him.

²⁴ He said, "Are you my son Esau?"

"I am," he said.

²⁵ He said, "Serve me, so that I can eat my son's game. For (doing this) my soul will bless you."

(Jacob) served him, and he ate. He brought him wine, and he drank.

²⁶ His father Isaac said to him, "Please come closer and kiss me, my son."

²⁷ (Jacob) came closer, and he kissed him. (Isaac) smelled the fragrance of (what he thought was) his garments, and he blessed him. He said, "Look, the fragrance of my son is like the fragrance of a field (of apples), which God has blessed!"

[SIXTH READING] ²⁸ "And may the Almighty give you (repeatedly) from the dew of the skies

---

19. I am... Esau your firstborn. This could also be rendered, "I *and* Esau are your firstborn." Esau was the *physical* firstborn who was conceived from Isaac's first drop of seed (*Zohar*), and had emerged first from the womb. But Jacob was Isaac's *spiritual* firstborn, whom Isaac's thoughts had been fixated upon during conception and who possessed the superior soul of the two brothers. So in suggesting that both *"I and Esau are your firstborn,"* Jacob was not, in fact, lying (*Rabbi Menahem Azariah da Fano, 16th–17th century*).

21. Come closer, so that I may feel you, my son. Isaac said, "I know that Esau doesn't mention God's name, and this man did mention it. He must be Jacob and not Esau" (*Genesis Rabbah*).

If Isaac knew that "Esau doesn't mention God's name," then why did he want to bless Esau, and not Jacob?

Isaac perceived that within Esau were holy sparks of an extremely lofty spiritual source, more so than in Jacob. Therefore, he chose to bless Esau, because Isaac understood that his blessing had the spiritual power to elevate the sparks which were trapped within Esau's unholy existence, allowing them to return to their source.

בראשית כז:כט-לח | תולדות

29 יַעַבְד֤וּךָ עַמִּים֙ וְיִשְׁתַּחֲו֣וּ [וישתחו כ׳] לְךָ֣ לְאֻמִּ֔ים הֱוֵ֤ה גְבִיר֙ לְאַחֶ֔יךָ וְיִשְׁתַּחֲו֥וּ לְךָ֖ בְּנֵ֣י אִמֶּ֑ךָ אֹרְרֶ֣יךָ אָר֔וּר וּֽמְבָרְכֶ֖יךָ בָּרֽוּךְ: 30 וַיְהִ֗י כַּאֲשֶׁ֨ר כִּלָּ֣ה יִצְחָק֮ לְבָרֵ֣ךְ אֶֽת־יַעֲקֹב֒ וַיְהִ֗י אַ֣ךְ יָצֹ֤א יָצָא֙ יַעֲקֹ֔ב מֵאֵ֥ת פְּנֵ֖י יִצְחָ֣ק אָבִ֑יו וְעֵשָׂ֣ו אָחִ֔יו בָּ֖א מִצֵּידֽוֹ: 31 וַיַּ֤עַשׂ גַּם־הוּא֙ מַטְעַמִּ֔ים וַיָּבֵ֖א לְאָבִ֑יו וַיֹּ֣אמֶר לְאָבִ֗יו יָקֻ֤ם אָבִי֙ וְיֹאכַל֙ מִצֵּ֣יד בְּנ֔וֹ בַּעֲב֖וּר תְּבָרֲכַ֥נִּי נַפְשֶֽׁךָ: 32 וַיֹּ֥אמֶר ל֛וֹ יִצְחָ֥ק אָבִ֖יו מִי־אָ֑תָּה וַיֹּ֕אמֶר אֲנִ֛י בִּנְךָ֥ בְכֹרְךָ֖ עֵשָֽׂו: 33 וַיֶּחֱרַ֨ד יִצְחָ֣ק חֲרָדָה֮ גְּדֹלָ֣ה עַד־מְאֹד֒ וַיֹּ֡אמֶר מִֽי־אֵפ֡וֹא ה֣וּא הַצָּֽד־צַ֩יִד֩ וַיָּ֨בֵא לִ֜י וָאֹכַ֥ל מִכֹּ֛ל בְּטֶ֥רֶם תָּב֖וֹא וָאֲבָרֲכֵ֑הוּ גַּם־בָּר֖וּךְ יִהְיֶֽה: 34 כִּשְׁמֹ֤עַ עֵשָׂו֙ אֶת־דִּבְרֵ֣י אָבִ֔יו וַיִּצְעַ֣ק צְעָקָ֔ה גְּדֹלָ֥ה וּמָרָ֖ה עַד־מְאֹ֑ד וַיֹּ֣אמֶר לְאָבִ֔יו בָּרֲכֵ֥נִי גַם־אָ֖נִי אָבִֽי: 35 וַיֹּ֕אמֶר בָּ֥א אָחִ֖יךָ בְּמִרְמָ֑ה וַיִּקַּ֖ח בִּרְכָתֶֽךָ: 36 וַיֹּ֡אמֶר הֲכִי֩ קָרָ֨א שְׁמ֜וֹ יַעֲקֹ֗ב וַֽיַּעְקְבֵ֨נִי֙ זֶ֣ה פַעֲמַ֔יִם אֶת־בְּכֹרָתִ֣י לָקָ֔ח וְהִנֵּ֥ה עַתָּ֖ה לָקַ֣ח בִּרְכָתִ֑י וַיֹּאמַ֕ר הֲלֹא־אָצַ֥לְתָּ לִּ֖י בְּרָכָֽה: 37 וַיַּ֨עַן יִצְחָ֜ק וַיֹּ֣אמֶר לְעֵשָׂ֗ו הֵ֣ן גְּבִ֞יר שַׂמְתִּ֥יו לָךְ֙ וְאֶת־כָּל־אֶחָ֗יו נָתַ֤תִּי לוֹ֙ לַעֲבָדִ֔ים וְדָגָ֥ן וְתִירֹ֖שׁ סְמַכְתִּ֑יו וּלְכָ֣ה אֵפ֔וֹא מָ֥ה אֶֽעֱשֶׂ֖ה בְּנִֽי: 38 וַיֹּ֨אמֶר עֵשָׂ֜ו אֶל־אָבִ֗יו הַֽבְרָכָ֨ה אַחַ֤ת הִֽוא־לְךָ֙

From the dew of the skies and from the fatness of the earth, an abundance of grain and wine. The curse inflicted on the earth through Adam's error of listening to Eve's advice (above, 3:17-19) is now transformed to blessing, through Jacob's listening to Rebekah's advice:

"The ground will be cursed because of you," becomes a blessing, *"from the fatness of the earth."*

"You will toil to eat from it," becomes a blessing, *"from the dew of the skies."*

"Thorns and thistles will grow (with) your (crops)," but now, *"an abundance of grain and wine."*

"With the sweat of your face will you eat bread," becomes, *"nations will serve you"* (Zohar).

33. Isaac was extremely bewildered. The *Midrash Tanḥuma* states: Why did Isaac become bewildered? He said, "Perhaps I am guilty of a sin, for I have blessed the younger son before the older one, and thus altered the order of the relationship."

Then, Esau began to weep, "He has already deceived me twice!"

His father said to him, "What did he do to you?"

He replied, "He took my birthright."

Isaac said, "That is why I was troubled and bewildered, for I was afraid that perhaps I had transgressed the letter of the law. But now I know that I actually blessed the firstborn, let him be blessed too" (*Rashi, 11th century*).

and from the fatness of the earth, an abundance of grain and wine. ²⁹ Nations will serve you; kingdoms will bow down to you. You will be a master over your brothers, and your mother's sons will bow down to you. Those who curse you will be cursed, and those who bless you will be blessed."

Esau Discovers that His Blessing was Given Away

³⁰ Then, when Isaac had finished blessing Jacob—just as Jacob had left his father Isaac's presence—his brother Esau came back from his hunt. ³¹ He had also made tasty foods, and he brought (them) to his father.

He said to his father, "My father should get up and eat his son's game, so that your soul will bless me."

³² His father, Isaac, said to him, "Who are you?"

He said, "I am your son, your firstborn, Esau."

³³ Isaac was extremely bewildered. He said, "Who then is the one who hunted game and brought it to me, then I ate it all before you came, and I blessed him? Let him be blessed too (in any case)."

³⁴ When Esau heard his father's words, he cried extremely loudly and bitterly. He said to his father, "Bless me too, my father!"

³⁵ (Isaac) said, "Your brother came ingeniously and took your blessing."

³⁶ (Esau) said, "Is that why he was called Jacob [*ya'AKoV*] (because he was destined to deceive me [*va-yA'KeVeni*])? He has deceived me twice! He took my birthright, and—look!—now he has taken my blessing!"

(Esau) said (to Isaac), "Haven't you saved a blessing for me?"

³⁷ Isaac answered, saying to Esau, "(Whatever blessing I give you will be of no use, because) I have already made him a master over you, given him all his brothers as servants, and I have sustained him with grain and wine. So, for you then, what shall I do, my son (if I bless you he will acquire your possessions in any case, since he is your master)?"

³⁸ Esau said to his father, "Haven't you just one blessing, my father? Bless me too, my father." Esau raised his voice and wept.

Isaac was saying: "May He give, and give again" (*Rashi, 11ᵗʰ century*).

Isaac said, *"May He give"* blessings initially, and even if you will sin, He will "give again" (*Rabbi Shabbetai b. Joseph Bass, 17ᵗʰ–18ᵗʰ century*).

The blessing is that God will give, not only when a Jewish person is visible and recognizable as a Jew, but also when he is lost. Even at such times God will "give again." God will return to search for us, find us, and give us everything that is good (*Rabbi Kalonymous Kalman Shapira, 20ᵗʰ century*).

בראשית כז:לח - כח:ד תולדות

אָבִי בָּרְכֵנִי גַם־אָנִי אָבִי וַיִּשָּׂא עֵשָׂו קֹלוֹ וַיֵּבְךְּ: 39 וַיַּעַן יִצְחָק אָבִיו וַיֹּאמֶר אֵלָיו הִנֵּה מִשְׁמַנֵּי הָאָרֶץ יִהְיֶה מוֹשָׁבֶךָ וּמִטַּל הַשָּׁמַיִם מֵעָל: 40 וְעַל־חַרְבְּךָ תִחְיֶה וְאֶת־אָחִיךָ תַּעֲבֹד וְהָיָה כַּאֲשֶׁר תָּרִיד וּפָרַקְתָּ עֻלּוֹ מֵעַל צַוָּארֶךָ: 41 וַיִּשְׂטֹם עֵשָׂו אֶת־יַעֲקֹב עַל־הַבְּרָכָה אֲשֶׁר בֵּרְכוֹ אָבִיו וַיֹּאמֶר עֵשָׂו בְּלִבּוֹ יִקְרְבוּ יְמֵי אֵבֶל אָבִי וְאַהַרְגָה אֶת־יַעֲקֹב אָחִי: 42 וַיֻּגַּד לְרִבְקָה אֶת־דִּבְרֵי עֵשָׂו בְּנָהּ הַגָּדֹל וַתִּשְׁלַח וַתִּקְרָא לְיַעֲקֹב בְּנָהּ הַקָּטָן וַתֹּאמֶר אֵלָיו הִנֵּה עֵשָׂו אָחִיךָ מִתְנַחֵם לְךָ לְהָרְגֶךָ: 43 וְעַתָּה בְנִי שְׁמַע בְּקֹלִי וְקוּם בְּרַח־לְךָ אֶל־לָבָן אָחִי חָרָנָה: 44 וְיָשַׁבְתָּ עִמּוֹ יָמִים אֲחָדִים עַד אֲשֶׁר־תָּשׁוּב חֲמַת אָחִיךָ: 45 עַד־שׁוּב אַף־אָחִיךָ מִמְּךָ וְשָׁכַח אֵת אֲשֶׁר־עָשִׂיתָ לּוֹ וְשָׁלַחְתִּי וּלְקַחְתִּיךָ מִשָּׁם לָמָה אֶשְׁכַּל גַּם־שְׁנֵיכֶם יוֹם אֶחָד: 46 וַתֹּאמֶר רִבְקָה אֶל־יִצְחָק קַצְתִּי בְחַיַּי מִפְּנֵי בְּנוֹת חֵת אִם־לֹקֵחַ יַעֲקֹב אִשָּׁה מִבְּנוֹת־חֵת כָּאֵלֶּה מִבְּנוֹת הָאָרֶץ לָמָּה לִּי חַיִּים:

כח 1 וַיִּקְרָא יִצְחָק אֶל־יַעֲקֹב וַיְבָרֶךְ אֹתוֹ וַיְצַוֵּהוּ וַיֹּאמֶר לוֹ לֹא־תִקַּח אִשָּׁה מִבְּנוֹת כְּנָעַן: 2 קוּם לֵךְ פַּדֶּנָה אֲרָם בֵּיתָה בְתוּאֵל אֲבִי אִמֶּךָ וְקַח־לְךָ מִשָּׁם אִשָּׁה מִבְּנוֹת לָבָן אֲחִי אִמֶּךָ: 3 וְאֵל שַׁדַּי יְבָרֵךְ אֹתְךָ וְיַפְרְךָ וְיַרְבֶּךָ וְהָיִיתָ לִקְהַל עַמִּים: 4 וְיִתֶּן־לְךָ אֶת־בִּרְכַּת אַבְרָהָם לְךָ וּלְזַרְעֲךָ אִתָּךְ

46. I am sick of my life. Rebekah thought it unwise to inform Isaac that Esau wanted to kill Jacob. She feared that Isaac might withhold some blessing from Jacob, so as not to further anger Esau. She therefore maintained that she had sent Jacob away, because *"I am sick of my life, etc."* (Rabbi Israel b. Pethahiah Isserlein, 15th century).

28:1 Isaac called Jacob and blessed him. He instructed him, saying to him, "You should not take a wife from the Canaanite girls." Isaac first blessed Jacob, and only then instructed him not to *"take a wife from the Canaanite girls."* When educating, it is best initially to create a pleasant atmosphere and only later to assert authority. This will ensure that the message reaching the child is one of love and care (Rabbi Israel Meir Kagan, 19th–20th century).

4. May He give you the blessing of Abraham. God said to Abraham, *"I will make you into a great nation"* (above, 12:2), and, *"all the nations of the world will be blessed through your*

³⁹ His father Isaac answered, saying, "Look, your dwelling place shall be from the fat places of the land, and from the dew of the skies from above. ⁴⁰ You will live by your sword, and you shall serve your brother. But, when you grieve (about the blessings he took, because the Jewish people will have transgressed the Torah) then you will break his yoke off your neck."

Esau Plans to Kill Jacob / Rebekah Tells Jacob to Flee

⁴¹ Esau hated Jacob because of the blessing which his father had given him. Esau said to himself, "The days of mourning for my father will soon come, and then I will kill my brother Jacob."

⁴² Rebekah was told (by Divine inspiration) the words of Esau, her older son. She sent (a message) and summoned Jacob, her younger son. She said to him, "Beware! Your brother Esau regrets (his relationship) to you (and wishes to kill you. ⁴³ Now, my son, listen to my voice! Go and run away to my brother Laban, in Haran. ⁴⁴ You can live with him for a few days until your brother's anger has calmed down, ⁴⁵ until your brother's anger against you has calmed down, and he forgets what you did to him. Then I will send (for you) and bring you from there. Why should I be bereaved from both of you on one day (for if you kill him, his sons will kill you)?"

Isaac Instructs Jacob to Marry

⁴⁶ Rebekah said to Isaac, "I am sick of my life because of the Hittite girls. If Jacob takes a wife from among the Hittite girls like these, from the daughters of this land, what use is life to me?"

28
¹ Isaac called Jacob and blessed him. He instructed him, saying to him, "You should not take a wife from the Canaanite girls. ² Go and travel to Paddan-aram, to the house of Bethuel, your mother's father, and take yourself a wife from there, from the daughters of Laban, your mother's brother. ³ May God Almighty bless you, make you fruitful and multiply, and you will become an assembly of nations. ⁴ May He give you the blessing of Abraham—to you, and to your seed with you—that you will inherit the land in which you (only) wandered (in up until now), which God gave to Abraham."

---

food for thought

1. Have you ever sought payback for an injustice against you?

2. Why do people seek revenge when it cannot change the past?

3. Is revenge ever acceptable, or perhaps necessary?

בראשית כח:ד-ט   תולדות

לְרִשְׁתְּךָ֙ אֶת־אֶ֣רֶץ מְגֻרֶ֔יךָ אֲשֶׁר־נָתַ֥ן אֱלֹהִ֖ים לְאַבְרָהָֽם: [SEVENTH READING] 5 וַיִּשְׁלַ֣ח יִצְחָ֗ק אֶֽת־יַעֲקֹב֙ וַיֵּ֣לֶךְ פַּדֶּ֣נָֽה אֲרָ֑ם אֶל־לָבָ֤ן בֶּן־בְּתוּאֵל֙ הָֽאֲרַמִּ֔י אֲחִ֣י רִבְקָ֔ה אֵ֥ם יַעֲקֹ֖ב וְעֵשָֽׂו: 6 וַיַּ֣רְא עֵשָׂ֗ו כִּֽי־בֵרַ֣ךְ יִצְחָק֮ אֶֽת־יַעֲקֹב֒ וְשִׁלַּ֤ח אֹתוֹ֙ פַּדֶּ֣נָֽה אֲרָ֔ם לָקַֽחַת־ל֥וֹ מִשָּׁ֖ם אִשָּׁ֑ה בְּבָֽרֲכ֣וֹ אֹת֔וֹ וַיְצַ֤ו עָלָיו֙ לֵאמֹ֔ר לֹֽא־תִקַּ֥ח אִשָּׁ֖ה מִבְּנ֥וֹת כְּנָֽעַן: [MAFTIR] 7 וַיִּשְׁמַ֣ע יַעֲקֹ֔ב אֶל־אָבִ֖יו וְאֶל־אִמּ֑וֹ וַיֵּ֖לֶךְ פַּדֶּ֥נָֽה אֲרָֽם: 8 וַיַּ֣רְא עֵשָׂ֔ו כִּ֥י רָע֖וֹת בְּנ֣וֹת כְּנָ֑עַן בְּעֵינֵ֖י יִצְחָ֥ק אָבִֽיו: 9 וַיֵּ֥לֶךְ עֵשָׂ֖ו אֶל־יִשְׁמָעֵ֑אל וַיִּקַּ֡ח אֶֽת־מָחֲלַ֣ת ׀ בַּת־יִשְׁמָעֵ֨אל בֶּן־אַבְרָהָ֜ם אֲח֤וֹת נְבָיוֹת֙ עַל־נָשָׁ֔יו ל֖וֹ לְאִשָּֽׁה: ס ס ס

ק"ו פסוקים, על"י סימן.

So, the Torah's description of Esau here, at the end of the Torah portion, comes to alert us to the moral corruption exemplified by Esau. We are warned to steer clear of this lowly activity: promoting ourselves as righteous while the truth is something very different indeed (*Rabbi Menahem Mendel Schneerson, 20th century*).

spiritual vitamin

> When *your faith in God is deep*, and when you reflect that God's benevolent Providence extends to each and every person, and to each and every detail, and each and every minute, you will develop a profound sense of security and confidence.

genesis 28:5–9 toledot

[SEVENTH READING] ⁵ Isaac sent Jacob off, and he went to Paddan-aram, to Laban son of Bethuel the Aramean, the brother of Rebekah, Jacob and Esau's mother.

Esau Marries Ishmael's Daughter

⁶ Esau saw that Isaac had blessed Jacob and sent him away to Paddan-aram, to take himself a wife from there, and that when he blessed him, he instructed him, saying, "You shall not take a wife from the daughters of Canaan," [MAFTIR] ⁷ (and he saw that) Jacob listened to his father and his mother, and went to Paddan-aram. ⁸ (So, since) Esau saw that the daughters of Canaan were displeasing to his father Isaac, ⁹ Esau went to Ishmael, and took for a wife, Mahalath daughter of Abraham's son Ishmael, a sister of Nebaioth—in addition to his other wives.

Haftarot: Toledot —page 1301.   *Erev Rosh Ḥodesh*—page 1415.

---

children" (22:18). May those blessings be for you. May that nation and those blessed children emerge from you (*Rashi, 11ᵗʰ century*).

That you will inherit the land in which you wandered. After giving Jacob the *"blessing of Abraham,"* only one fear might have remained in Jacob's mind: Since Esau was remaining in the land of Israel and Jacob was leaving, perhaps Esau would seize the land for himself?

To relieve Jacob from this worry, Isaac added, *"You will inherit the land in which you (only) wandered (in up until now), which God gave to Abraham"* (*Rabbi Moses Alshekh, 16ᵗʰ century*).

9. In addition to his other wives. He added wickedness upon his wickedness, in that he did not divorce the first ones (*Rashi, 11ᵗʰ century*).

Earlier, we read of Esau's deceptive acts towards his father, climaxing here at the end of the Torah portion, where he marries one of Ishmael's daughters in order to appear righteous in Isaac's eyes. However, just as he had married his first wives in an attempt to appear righteous (see above, 26:34), so too here, "he added wickedness upon wickedness," marrying once again to maintain his deceptive veil of righteousness, this time to a member of Abraham's family.

> Just as your **soul** "departed" from its **heavenly abode,** you too should not confine yourself exclusively to a spiritually and **religiously comfortable** environment. Judaism's vision of a **perfect world** cannot be fulfilled through **excessive insularity.**

VA-YETZE'
ויצא

JACOB'S JOURNEY AND DREAMS	28:10–22
JACOB MARRIES AND BUILDS A FAMILY	29:1 – 30:34
JACOB CONTINUES TO WORK FOR LABAN	30:25–43
JACOB FLEES FROM LABAN WITH HIS FAMILY	31:1–32:3

NAME
Va-Yetze'

MEANING
"And he departed"

LINES IN TORAH SCROLL
235

PARASHIYYOT
1 closed

VERSES
148

WORDS
2021

LETTERS
7512

DATE
2171–2205

LOCATION
Mount Moriah, Haran

KEY PEOPLE
Jacob, Rachel, Laban, Leah, Bilhah, Zilpah

MITZVOT
None

CHARACTER PROFILE

NAME
Jacob (Israel)

MEANING
"Heel"

PARENTS
Isaac and Rebekah

GRANDFATHERS
Bethuel, Abraham

SIBLING
Twin brother, Esau

WIVES
Rachel, Leah, Bilhah, Zilpah

CHILDREN
Reuben, Simeon, Levi, Judah, Issachar, Zebulun, Dan, Naphtali, Gad, Asher, Joseph, Benjamin, Dinah

LIFE SPAN
147 years

BURIAL PLACE
Cave of Machpelah

ACHIEVEMENTS
Studied in the Academy of Shem and Eber for fourteen years without a full night's sleep; rolled a large stone that was blocking the well in Haran with one hand; blessed Pharaoh that the famine should end

KNOWN FOR
Facial features resembled Abraham; purchased birthright from Esau; disguised himself as Esau to receive blessings from his father; wrestled with an angel

ANGELS

In Jacob's dream, he saw guardian angels ascending and descending from a ladder. Every time you observe a commandment, an angel is appointed to watch over you and protect you (28:12).

TITHING

Jacob promised God that he would give away a tenth of all his possessions (28:22). This was a precursor to the tithes given to the Levites and the poor. Are you careful to give away no less than a tenth of your earnings to charity?

SELFLESSNESS

Jacob had given Rachel signs that would identify her, since he suspected that Laban would try to trick him. Knowing that her sister would be shamed in front of the entire town, Rachel revealed the signs to Leah. Can you point to an utterly selfless act in your life which saved somebody from severe embarrassment? (29:23).

ויצא   בראשית כח:י-יא

10 וַיֵּצֵא יַעֲקֹב מִבְּאֵר שָׁבַע וַיֵּלֶךְ חָרָנָה: 11 וַיִּפְגַּע בַּמָּקוֹם וַיָּלֶן שָׁם כִּי־בָא הַשֶּׁמֶשׁ וַיִּקַּח מֵאַבְנֵי הַמָּקוֹם וַיָּשֶׂם מְרַאֲשֹׁתָיו וַיִּשְׁכַּב בַּמָּקוֹם הַהוּא:

delayed until seven generations after Isaac (*Rabbi Issachar Berman b. Naphtali ha-Kohen, 16th century*).

And went towards Haran. Jacob's descent to Haran alludes to the later descent of the Jewish people into exile (*Genesis Rabbah*).

11. He came across the place. Abraham instituted the morning prayer, as the verse states, *"Abraham got up early in the morning, to the place where he had stood before God"* (19:27), and in this context *"standing"* can refer only to prayer. Isaac instituted the afternoon prayer, as the verse states, *"Isaac went out to pray in the field towards evening"* (24:63). And Jacob instituted the evening prayer, as the verse states, *"He came across (va-yifgga') the place,"* and in this context *pegi'ah* can only refer to prayer (*Babylonian Talmud, Berakhot* 26b).

Abraham was amazed by the fact that people seemed to enjoy a very good life even though they did not, in any way, recognize God. Enamored by this tremendous kindness of God, who continued to sustain those who rebelled against Him, Abraham taught a path of worship which emphasized love with burning intensity. Therefore, Abraham enacted his unique prayer in the morning when the Divine attribute of love and kindness is aroused—*"to relate Your kindness at dawn"* (*Psalms* 92:3).

When Isaac saw the many thousands of converts that Abraham had attracted, who served God only with love, he was concerned that it would all not last. There must be, he felt, an element of fear and shame in the presence of God, accepting the yoke of His Kingdom regardless of the way in which He treats us. Therefore, Isaac prayed towards the late afternoon, when darkness approaches, which has the natural tendency to instill fear.

Jacob established his unique time of prayer in the evening, the time of sleep. Jacob's path of worship was *truth*, i.e., honesty and integrity, and a person's dreams are a disclosure of his conscience during the day, since, *"A man is shown in a dream only what is suggested by his own thoughts"* (*Babylonian Talmud, Berakhot* 55b). Also, at this junction in his life, Jacob was about to reside with Laban, a liar and charlatan. Therefore he prayed to be strengthened with the attribute of truth (*Rabbi Menahem Mendel of Rymanow, 18th century*).

He spent the night there because the sun had set (suddenly). Whenever illumination, i.e., clarity of mind, came to him, he would make it "night"—he would remind himself that the insight had come from God and not merely through his own insight (*Rabbi Elimelech of Lyzhansk, 18th century*).

He took some of the stones of the place and placed (them) around his head. In this verse it says *"stones,"* in the plural, whereas later it says, *"he took the STONE that he had placed at his head"* (28:18). How can this inconsistency, from plural to singular, be reconciled?

Rabbi Isaac taught that when Jacob lay down, all these stones gathered into one place, saying, "May the righteous man rest his head on me!" The result was that all the stones were fused into one (*Babylonian Talmud, Ḥullin* 91b).

Torah wisdom originates from the sublime and completely unified realms above; it is divided only as it enters into our universe of distinctions, the place where the souls originate. That is the how the controversies in understanding the Torah arose among the Sages.

genesis 28:10–11 va-yetze'

parashat va-yetze'

Jacob's Journey

¹⁰ Jacob left Beer-sheba, and went (towards) Haran.

¹¹ He came across the place (Mount Moriah) and spent the night there because the sun had set (suddenly). He took some of the stones of the place and placed (them) around his head (for protection from wild animals), and he lay down (to sleep) in that place.

28:10 Jacob left Beer-sheba. Scripture only needed to state, "Jacob *went* to Haran." Why did it mention his departure?

This teaches us that the departure of a righteous man (*tzaddik*) from a place makes an impression. While the righteous man is in a town, he is its aura, he is its light, and he is its honor. When he departs from there, its aura has departed, its light has departed, and its honor has departed (*Rashi, 11th century*).

The word *roshem*, "impression," shares the same letters as the word *shomer*, "watchman." When a righteous man departs from a town, it not only makes an impression, he also leaves protective energy for the place to guard it so that no misfortune should occur there (*Rabbi Menahem Mendel of Rymanow, 18th century*).

Surely Isaac and Rebekah, who were also righteous, still remained in Beer-sheba? Why, then, did Jacob's departure cause the "light" and "honor" of Beer-sheba to depart?

Rashi describes the *tzaddik's* presence in a town as having three effects: 1) *Honor*—the visible presence of the *tzaddik* makes the local inhabitants proud that their town is the place where a great person resides. 2) *Light* (*ziv*)—a *ziv* is a ray of light emitted from a light source. This depicts how the *tzaddik* "emits" inspiration for others to perform more good deeds. 3) *Aura* (*hod*)—indicates a stronger beam of light, as in the expression *"Moses' beams of splendor"* (*Rashi* to *Exodus* 34:30). This refers to his intimidating effect on others, promoting fear of God in his vicinity—as in the verse, *"the skin of his face had become radiant, and they were afraid to come near him"* (ibid.).

Obviously, in order to affect people in these three ways, the *tzaddik* must be seen visibly by others and interact with them. Thus, when Jacob left Beer-sheba, "honor," "light" and "aura" departed from the town, *since Isaac was housebound due to his blindness* (*Rashi* to 28:3, above), and he was not seen by any of the local inhabitants. Rebekah, in addition to her general modesty, would have spent virtually all of her time attending to Isaac, so she, too, would not have been seen publicly (*Rabbi Menahem Mendel Schneerson, 20th century*).

Beer-sheba. Beer-sheba means "the well of the oath." Jacob said, "I do not want Abimelech to approach me and demand, 'Swear to me, like your grandfather swore to me,' and then I would cause the rejoicing of my descendants to be delayed by seven generations," because Abraham's oath with Abimelech delayed the entry of the Jewish people into the land of Israel by seven generations (*Genesis Rabbah*).

Since Isaac also made an oath with Abimelech, we find that the full conquest of the land of Israel, including the lands of Sihon and Og, was

---

food for thought

1. At what moment in your life were you most alone and uncertain?

2. Why do we feel closest to God when our power is at its weakest?

3. Have you ever been driven to a spontaneous verbalization of God's awe?

ויצא   בראשית כח:יב-יד

12 וַיַּחֲלֹם וְהִנֵּה סֻלָּם מֻצָּב אַרְצָה וְרֹאשׁוֹ מַגִּיעַ הַשָּׁמָיְמָה וְהִנֵּה מַלְאֲכֵי אֱלֹהִים עֹלִים וְיֹרְדִים בּוֹ: 13 וְהִנֵּה יְהוָה נִצָּב עָלָיו וַיֹּאמַר אֲנִי יְהוָה אֱלֹהֵי אַבְרָהָם אָבִיךָ וֵאלֹהֵי יִצְחָק הָאָרֶץ אֲשֶׁר אַתָּה שֹׁכֵב עָלֶיהָ לְךָ אֶתְּנֶנָּה וּלְזַרְעֶךָ: 14 וְהָיָה זַרְעֲךָ כַּעֲפַר הָאָרֶץ וּפָרַצְתָּ יָמָּה וָקֵדְמָה וְצָפֹנָה וָנֶגְבָּה וְנִבְרְכוּ בְךָ כָּל־מִשְׁפְּחֹת

This explains why Jacob received his prophecy only while dreaming and not while fully awake—as the *Zohar* asks—because Jacob was not really "found" in the land of Israel, and fully conscious prophecy cannot be initiated in the Diaspora.

Why did the *Zohar* not offer this solution? Because ultimately Jacob wished to return to the land of Israel. So you cannot say that his mind was *fully* immersed in the Diaspora (*Rabbi Samuel Bornstein of Sochaczew, 19th century*).

A ladder was wedged in the ground and its top reached to heaven. The word *sullam*, "ladder," has the same numerical value as *mamon*, "money." Money is extremely materialistic, it is "wedged in the ground"; but, on the other hand, if used for the right purposes it can bring you to the greatest spiritual heights. *"Angels of God were going up and down on it"*—men, who are all angels of God, constantly rise and fall with the challenge of wealth. For some, money brings them from spiritual greatness to tragic collapse; for others, it is the ladder to heaven (*Rabbi Israel Ba'al Shem Tov, 18th century*).

Jacob foresaw that *"from the time the Temple was destroyed, the gates of prayer are locked"* (*Babylonian Talmud, Bava Metzia* 59a). He therefore sought some solution for his offspring, a way through which their prayers could ascend on high. So God showed him, *"A ladder was wedged in the ground"*—the ladder alluding to the *Shekhinah*, the Divine Presence, which is *"the gateway to God, the righteous may come through it"* (*Psalms* 118:20). It is "wedged in the ground," for even though the *Shekhinah* has departed with the Temple's destruction, there is always still some residual presence. And it is this which enables us to reach God—*"its top reached to heaven"* (*Rabbi Menahem Nahum Twersky of Chernobyl, 18th century*).

Angels of God were going up and down on it. They went up before they went down. The angels that escorted him in the land of Israel were those that do not go outside the land, so they ascended to heaven. Then, the angels assigned to the Diaspora descended to escort him (*Rashi, 11th century*).

God was standing over him, and He said, "I am God, the God of Abraham your father." God was hinting, "Even if there will come a time when you have *no merits*, I will still be the God of Abraham your father. If I cannot say to you 'I am God *your* God,' I will still be able to say, 'I am the God of *your father*.'" This is how God was "standing over him" to protect him (*Rabbi Kalonymous Kalman Shapira, 20th century*).

14. Your descendants will be (as widespread) as the dust of the earth. The children of Israel are compared to "stars," "sand," and "dust"

> **kabbalah bites**
>
> **28:12** Just as dreams are full of nonsense but always have a kernel of truth, there is no evil in this world that does not have even the tiniest glimmer of goodness within.

genesis 28:12–14 — va-yetze'

[12] He dreamt, and—look!—a ladder was wedged in the ground and its top reached to heaven, and—look!—angels of God were going up and down on it.

[13] Suddenly, God was standing over him, and He said, "I am God, the God of Abraham your father, and the God of Isaac. I will give to you and to your descendants the land on which you are lying. [14] Your descendants will be (as widespread) as the dust of the earth, and you will be strong to the west, to the east, to the north and to the south. All the families of the earth will be blessed through you and your descendants."

The twelve stones which Jacob placed around his head represent the twelve tribes—twelve general paths of understanding the Torah. Every sage's opinion follows the root of his soul, which is why he understands the Torah in his own particular way.

In their source, *"both are the words of the living God"* (*Babylonian Talmud, Eruvin* 13b), since they are all one. It is only as the Torah enters the world of distinctions that it is divided and flows through different channels. All the Sages really mean the same thing, since all of them are drawing from the same source, but in this world of separation their opinions seem divergent. When the controversy is lifted back to its root, to the world of unity, all become one again, and *"both are the words of the living God."*

The twelve stones, each representing a different tribe, were "quarreling" with each other. Each said, *"May the righteous man rest his head on me!"*—may he rely on my opinion to worship God properly and observe His commandments! Each of them aspires to the truth, for they all draw from the same source. It is only because our world is divided that they appear contradictory, but in their source *they become one stone again.* There is no dispute or conflict at all (*Rabbi Menahem Nahum Twersky of Chernobyl, 18th century*).

12-13. He dreamt, and ... suddenly, God was standing over him. How is it that to holy Jacob, the most perfect of the Patriarchs, God was revealed only in a dream?

Because: (a) Jacob was incomplete, as he was not yet married; and (b) His father, Isaac, was still alive (*Zohar*).

Where are you really located? *Wherever your mind is, that is where you are really considered to be.* Since Jacob left Beer-sheba and was focused on traveling to his uncle's house in Haran, that is where he was found, even if his physical body was on the Temple Mount. Even while he was located on the Temple Mount, mentally, Jacob had already left Israel.

spiritual vitamin

> *"You will be strong (u-faratzeta)"* (v. 14)—means breaking through barriers, even when those barriers represent good and valid limitations. For example: extending your times for Torah study; or giving more charity than Jewish law requires; or meditating on the greatness of God for extended periods before, during and even after prayer. This ability to break beyond all constraints is the inheritance of Jacob, our father.

בראשית כח:יד - כט:ב | ויצא

הָאֲדָמָ֖ה וּבְזַרְעֶֽךָ: 15 וְהִנֵּ֨ה אָנֹכִ֜י עִמָּ֗ךְ וּשְׁמַרְתִּ֨יךָ֙ בְּכֹ֣ל אֲשֶׁר־תֵּלֵ֔ךְ וַהֲשִׁ֣בֹתִ֔יךָ אֶל־הָאֲדָמָ֖ה הַזֹּ֑את כִּ֚י לֹ֣א אֶֽעֱזָבְךָ֔ עַ֚ד אֲשֶׁ֣ר אִם־עָשִׂ֔יתִי אֵ֥ת אֲשֶׁר־דִּבַּ֖רְתִּי לָֽךְ: 16 וַיִּיקַ֣ץ יַעֲקֹב֮ מִשְּׁנָתוֹ֒ וַיֹּ֕אמֶר אָכֵן֙ יֵ֣שׁ יְהֹוָ֔ה בַּמָּק֖וֹם הַזֶּ֑ה וְאָנֹכִ֖י לֹ֥א יָדָֽעְתִּי: 17 וַיִּירָא֙ וַיֹּאמַ֔ר מַה־נּוֹרָ֖א הַמָּק֣וֹם הַזֶּ֑ה אֵ֣ין זֶ֗ה כִּ֚י אִם־בֵּ֣ית אֱלֹהִ֔ים וְזֶ֖ה שַׁ֥עַר הַשָּׁמָֽיִם: 18 וַיַּשְׁכֵּ֨ם יַעֲקֹ֜ב בַּבֹּ֗קֶר וַיִּקַּ֤ח אֶת־הָאֶ֨בֶן֙ אֲשֶׁר־שָׂ֣ם מְרַֽאֲשֹׁתָ֔יו וַיָּ֥שֶׂם אֹתָ֖הּ מַצֵּבָ֑ה וַיִּצֹ֥ק שֶׁ֖מֶן עַל־רֹאשָֽׁהּ: 19 וַיִּקְרָ֛א אֶת־שֵֽׁם־הַמָּק֥וֹם הַה֖וּא בֵּֽית־אֵ֑ל וְאוּלָ֛ם ל֥וּז שֵׁם־הָעִ֖יר לָרִֽאשֹׁנָֽה: 20 וַיִּדַּ֥ר יַעֲקֹ֖ב נֶ֣דֶר לֵאמֹ֑ר אִם־יִהְיֶ֨ה אֱלֹהִ֜ים עִמָּדִ֗י וּשְׁמָרַ֨נִי֙ בַּדֶּ֤רֶךְ הַזֶּה֙ אֲשֶׁ֣ר אָנֹכִ֣י הוֹלֵ֔ךְ וְנָֽתַן־לִ֥י לֶ֛חֶם לֶאֱכֹ֖ל וּבֶ֥גֶד לִלְבֹּֽשׁ: 21 וְשַׁבְתִּ֥י בְשָׁל֖וֹם אֶל־בֵּ֣ית אָבִ֑י וְהָיָ֧ה יְהֹוָ֛ה לִ֖י לֵֽאלֹהִֽים: 22 וְהָאֶ֣בֶן הַזֹּ֗את אֲשֶׁר־שַׂ֨מְתִּי֙ מַצֵּבָ֔ה יִהְיֶ֖ה בֵּ֣ית אֱלֹהִ֑ים וְכֹל֙ אֲשֶׁ֣ר תִּתֶּן־לִ֔י עַשֵּׂ֖ר אֲעַשְּׂרֶ֥נּוּ לָֽךְ:

כט 1 וַיִּשָּׂ֥א יַעֲקֹ֖ב רַגְלָ֑יו וַיֵּ֖לֶךְ אַ֥רְצָה בְנֵי־קֶֽדֶם: [SECOND READING] 2 וַיַּ֞רְא וְהִנֵּ֧ה בְאֵ֣ר בַּשָּׂדֶ֗ה וְהִנֵּה־שָׁ֞ם שְׁלֹשָׁ֤ה עֶדְרֵי־צֹאן֙ רֹבְצִ֣ים עָלֶ֔יהָ כִּ֚י מִן־

20. Jacob made a vow. Jacob did not intend to fulfil his promise only if God would abide by the specified clauses, since a man should serve God regardless of the reward. Rather, he was saying to God, "Just as I am fulfilling my promise, I hope You will fulfil Yours" (*Rabbi Isaac b. Judah ha-Levi, 13th century*).

29:2 Look!—a well was in the field. The word "well" is mentioned seven times in this Torah section. This alludes to the seven wells which were dug by Abraham and Isaac (who dug three and four wells respectively).

kabbalah bites

28:15 After God had promised Jacob, *"I will not abandon you,"* Jacob should have trusted that God would send him a wife without having to work for the wicked Laban for seven years. He should have expected a direct solution from God, rather than succumbing to Laban's unreasonably demanding terms.

To achieve *tikkun* (spiritual healing) for this, Jacob would later be reincarnated as King David, and LaBaN as NaBaL.

That is why we find that David provided protection for Nabal's sheep (*I Samuel 25:16*), just as Jacob had tended Laban's sheep in exchange for a wife.

genesis 28:15 – 29:2   va-yetze'

¹⁵ "Look, I am with you, and I will guard you (from Esau and Laban) wherever you go. I will bring you back to this land, for I will not abandon you until I have carried out what I have spoken (to Abraham, a promise that was intended) for you (and not Esau)."

¹⁶ Jacob woke up from his sleep, and he said, "God is truly in this place, and I didn't realize (otherwise I wouldn't have slept here)!"

¹⁷ He felt frightened. He said, "How awesome is this place! This is none other than the house of God. This is the gate of heaven (through which all prayers ascend)."

¹⁸ Jacob arose early in the morning. He took the stone that he had placed at his head, set it up as a monument, and poured oil on top of it. ¹⁹ He named the place Bethel, but Luz was originally the name of the city.

²⁰ Jacob made a vow, saying, "If God will be with me (keeping His promises), and He will guard me on this route in which I am going (as He said He would), and He will give me bread to eat (as He promised not to abandon me,) and garments to wear, ²¹ and if I return in peace to my father's house (as He promised I would), and God will be my God (to prevent any of my children from going off the path— ²² then I will do the following for You:) this stone, which I have placed as a monument, will (eventually be built to) be a house of God, and I will definitely separate tithes for You from everything that You give me."

Jacob Meets Rachel by the Well

29 [SECOND READING] ¹ Jacob (found it easy to) lift his feet (after hearing the good news), and went off towards the land of the people of the East.

² He glanced, and—look!—a well was in the field, and—look!—three flocks of sheep were lying beside it, because they would give water to the flocks from that well.

(above, 13:16; 22:17). Stars are distant from one another, and they do not touch. Grains of sand are piled together, but they are not stuck together, unlike dust, which tends to stick together.

God said, *"Your descendants will be (as widespread) as the dust of the earth."* If your children live in unity, sticking together as the dust of the earth, then they will receive the following blessing: *"You will be strong to the west, to the east, to the north, and to the south"* (*Rabbi Aaron Lewin of Rzeszow, 20th century*).

16. Jacob woke up from his sleep, and he said, "God is truly in this place, and I didn't realize." According to the *Midrash*, Jacob's departure from his home and birthplace to a foreign land foretold the exile of his descendants, the Israelites (see above, commentary to v. 10). When Jacob was shown a ladder with angels climbing up and down, he understood that God would accompany his children in exile to protect them.

Jacob exclaimed, *"God is truly in this place"*—I now see that the Divine Presence will remain with my children even during exile; *"and I didn't realize"*—I had not known this before (*Rabbi Aryeh Leib Zuenz of Plotsk, 19th century*).

ויצא

בראשית כט:ב-יג

הַבְּאֵר הַהִוא יַשְׁקוּ הָעֲדָרִים וְהָאֶבֶן גְּדֹלָה עַל־פִּי הַבְּאֵר: 3 וְנֶאֶסְפוּ־שָׁמָּה כָל־הָעֲדָרִים וְגָלֲלוּ אֶת־הָאֶבֶן מֵעַל פִּי הַבְּאֵר וְהִשְׁקוּ אֶת־הַצֹּאן וְהֵשִׁיבוּ אֶת־הָאֶבֶן עַל־פִּי הַבְּאֵר לִמְקֹמָהּ: 4 וַיֹּאמֶר לָהֶם יַעֲקֹב אַחַי מֵאַיִן אַתֶּם וַיֹּאמְרוּ מֵחָרָן אֲנָחְנוּ: 5 וַיֹּאמֶר לָהֶם הַיְדַעְתֶּם אֶת־לָבָן בֶּן־נָחוֹר וַיֹּאמְרוּ יָדָעְנוּ: 6 וַיֹּאמֶר לָהֶם הֲשָׁלוֹם לוֹ וַיֹּאמְרוּ שָׁלוֹם וְהִנֵּה רָחֵל בִּתּוֹ בָּאָה עִם־הַצֹּאן: 7 וַיֹּאמֶר הֵן עוֹד הַיּוֹם גָּדוֹל לֹא־עֵת הֵאָסֵף הַמִּקְנֶה הַשְׁקוּ הַצֹּאן וּלְכוּ רְעוּ: 8 וַיֹּאמְרוּ לֹא נוּכַל עַד אֲשֶׁר יֵאָסְפוּ כָּל־הָעֲדָרִים וְגָלֲלוּ אֶת־הָאֶבֶן מֵעַל פִּי הַבְּאֵר וְהִשְׁקִינוּ הַצֹּאן: 9 עוֹדֶנּוּ מְדַבֵּר עִמָּם וְרָחֵל | בָּאָה עִם־הַצֹּאן אֲשֶׁר לְאָבִיהָ כִּי רֹעָה הִוא: 10 וַיְהִי כַּאֲשֶׁר רָאָה יַעֲקֹב אֶת־רָחֵל בַּת־לָבָן אֲחִי אִמּוֹ וְאֶת־צֹאן לָבָן אֲחִי אִמּוֹ וַיִּגַּשׁ יַעֲקֹב וַיָּגֶל אֶת־הָאֶבֶן מֵעַל פִּי הַבְּאֵר וַיַּשְׁקְ אֶת־צֹאן לָבָן אֲחִי אִמּוֹ: 11 וַיִּשַּׁק יַעֲקֹב לְרָחֵל וַיִּשָּׂא אֶת־קֹלוֹ וַיֵּבְךְּ: 12 וַיַּגֵּד יַעֲקֹב לְרָחֵל כִּי אֲחִי אָבִיהָ הוּא וְכִי בֶן־רִבְקָה הוּא וַתָּרָץ וַתַּגֵּד לְאָבִיהָ: 13 וַיְהִי כִשְׁמֹעַ לָבָן אֶת־שֵׁמַע | יַעֲקֹב בֶּן־אֲחֹתוֹ וַיָּרָץ לִקְרָאתוֹ וַיְחַבֶּק־לוֹ וַיְנַשֶּׁק־לוֹ

There was a huge rock on the mouth of the well. The huge stumbling-rock—our impulse to evil—rears its head everywhere, but at *"the mouth of the well,"* it is at its strongest. It stops us from opening our mouths in prayer (the "well"), the "service of the heart." That is why we ask God before we pray to remove the rock from the well, *"God, open my lips so that my mouth can declare Your praise" (Psalms 51:17).*

The truth is, there are no simple solutions when it comes to prayer. The more we are conscious of God in everything that we do, the better we will be able to open our mouths in prayer. That is why prayer is called the "service of the heart"—it depends on how much our hearts long for God *during the day* in all that we do. Each time we pray, we "gather the flocks" of all the moments we thought of God during that day. That is the only thing which will help us lift the rock off the well (*Rabbi Judah Aryeh Leib Alter of Gur, 19th century*).

7. It's still the middle of the day. It's not yet the time to take in the flocks. Were the shepherds not aware that it was the middle of the day? Why did Jacob need to tell them this fact?

The previous day, God had caused the sun to set suddenly so that Jacob would spend the night at the site of the future Temple. This had resulted in the shepherd's gathering their sheep together after night had fallen.

The following day, when Jacob arrived, the shepherds had already gathered their flocks, in an attempt to avoid the previous night's difficulty of gathering the sheep in the dark. Jacob there-

There was a huge rock on the mouth of the well. ³ (When) the flocks would gather there, they would roll the rock off the mouth of the well and give water to the sheep, and (then) they would return the rock onto the mouth of the well, to its place.

⁴ Jacob said to them, "Where are you from, my brothers?"

They said, "We're from Haran."

⁵ He said to them, "Do you know Laban, the (grand)son of Nahor?"

They said, "We know (him)."

⁶ He said to them, "Is he well?"

They said, "He's fine. Here is his daughter Rachel, coming with the sheep."

⁷ (Jacob saw that the flocks were lying down before the day's work had ended, so) he said, "It's still the middle of the day. It's not yet the time to take in the flocks. (Why don't you) water the sheep and then go and pasture."

⁸ They said, "We can't, until all the flocks are gathered together and they'll roll the rock off the mouth of the well. Then we'll give water to the sheep."

⁹ While he was still talking with them, Rachel came with her father's sheep, for she was a shepherdess. ¹⁰ Then, when Jacob saw Laban's daughter Rachel, his mother's brother, and the sheep of Laban, his mother's brother, Jacob stepped forward and rolled the rock off the mouth of the well (effortlessly, showing his great strength), and he watered the sheep of Laban, his mother's brother.

¹¹ Jacob kissed Rachel. (He perceived prophetically that she would not be buried with him, so) he wept loudly.

¹² Jacob told Rachel that he was her father's relative and that he was Rebekah's son. She ran and told her father (since her mother was no longer alive).

Jacob Works Seven Years for Rachel

¹³ Then, when Laban heard the news about Jacob, his sister's son, he ran towards him (thinking that he would be laden with money, like Eliezer. When he saw no

---

Jacob merited that the well that he saw possessed the spiritual greatness of all the other seven wells combined (*Rabbi Levi Isaac Schneersohn of Yekaterinoslav, 20th century*).

spiritual vitamin

> If we make a determined effort, success is Divinely assured, and the obstacles and obstructions which at first loom large, dissolve and disappear.

ויצא • בראשית כט:יג-כא

וַיְבִיאֵהוּ אֶל־בֵּיתוֹ וַיְסַפֵּר לְלָבָן אֵת כָּל־הַדְּבָרִים הָאֵלֶּה: 14 וַיֹּאמֶר לוֹ לָבָן אַךְ עַצְמִי וּבְשָׂרִי אָתָּה וַיֵּשֶׁב עִמּוֹ חֹדֶשׁ יָמִים: 15 וַיֹּאמֶר לָבָן לְיַעֲקֹב הֲכִי־אָחִי אַתָּה וַעֲבַדְתַּנִי חִנָּם הַגִּידָה לִּי מַה־מַּשְׂכֻּרְתֶּךָ: 16 וּלְלָבָן שְׁתֵּי בָנוֹת שֵׁם הַגְּדֹלָה לֵאָה וְשֵׁם הַקְּטַנָּה רָחֵל: 17 וְעֵינֵי לֵאָה רַכּוֹת וְרָחֵל הָיְתָה יְפַת־תֹּאַר וִיפַת מַרְאֶה: 18 [THIRD READING] וַיֶּאֱהַב יַעֲקֹב אֶת־רָחֵל וַיֹּאמֶר אֶעֱבָדְךָ שֶׁבַע שָׁנִים בְּרָחֵל בִּתְּךָ הַקְּטַנָּה: 19 וַיֹּאמֶר לָבָן טוֹב תִּתִּי אֹתָהּ לָךְ מִתִּתִּי אֹתָהּ לְאִישׁ אַחֵר שְׁבָה עִמָּדִי: 20 וַיַּעֲבֹד יַעֲקֹב בְּרָחֵל שֶׁבַע שָׁנִים וַיִּהְיוּ בְעֵינָיו כְּיָמִים אֲחָדִים בְּאַהֲבָתוֹ אֹתָהּ: 21 וַיֹּאמֶר יַעֲקֹב אֶל־לָבָן הָבָה אֶת־אִשְׁתִּי כִּי מָלְאוּ יָמָי וְאָבוֹאָה אֵלֶיהָ:

17. Leah's eyes were tender. Leah's eyes were tender from weeping, because she was expecting to become Esau's wife. For everyone was saying, "Rebekah has two sons, and Laban has two daughters: the older daughter is for the older son, and the younger daughter is for the younger son" (*Rashi, 11th century*).

Rachel had beautiful facial features and a beautiful complexion. Rachel represents the approach of the righteous, whose lives are utterly holy; and Leah, the approach of penitents who elevate the secular world to holiness.

Rachel was naturally attractive—"*Rachel had beautiful (facial) features and a beautiful complexion*" (v. 17)—like the righteous whose character is flawless; whereas Leah cried profusely, alluding to the process of repentance.

Jacob busied himself only with holy things—the approach of the righteous. Therefore, people said that Jacob was destined for Rachel, since their characters matched. Leah represented the path of the penitent and was therefore associated with the wicked Esau (*Rabbi Zadok ha-Kohen Rabinowitz of Lublin, 19th century*).

19. Laban said, "It's better for me to give her to you than for me to give her to another man." Laban's intentions here were not altruistic. He knew his daughter Rachel was an attractive girl. If he gave her to Jacob then perhaps Jacob would become enraptured by her beauty and lose focus in achieving his own spiritual growth (*Rabbi Simḥah Bunem of Przysucha, 18th–19th century*).

kabbalah bites

29:21 From this union, Reuben was conceived (*Rashi, Genesis* 49:3). However, Reuben's soul suffered from a spiritual blemish because Jacob was inevitably thinking about Rachel during this union, and not Leah. It was this imperfection that possibly led Reuben to err with Bilhah (ibid., 35:22).

But we see the Divine justice when, as a result of Reuben's sin, Joseph was awarded the double inheritance rights of the firstborn, in Reuben's place (see ibid., 49:3-4). Jacob's original intention was thus fulfilled: to have a firstborn with Rachel.

money) he embraced him (to feel what was in his pockets), and he kissed him (to see if pearls were hidden in his mouth).

(Laban) brought him into his house. He told Laban what had happened (with Esau, how he had run for his life without any money). ¹⁴ Laban said to him, "(Since you have no money I should really turn you away) but, you are my bone and my flesh (so you can stay)." (Jacob) stayed with him a month (and pastured Laban's sheep).

¹⁵ Laban said to Jacob, "Should you work for me for free just because you are my relative? Tell me what your wages should be!"

¹⁶ Laban had two daughters, the older one was called Leah, and the younger one was called Rachel. ¹⁷ Leah's eyes were tender, and Rachel had beautiful (facial) features and a beautiful complexion.

[THIRD READING] ¹⁸ Jacob loved Rachel, so he said, "I will work for you seven years for Rachel, your younger daughter."

¹⁹ Laban said, "It's better for me to give her to you than for me to give her to another man. Stay with me." ²⁰ So Jacob worked for Rachel seven years, but to him it felt like a few days because of his love for her.

Laban Deceptively Gives Leah to Jacob in Marriage

²¹ Jacob said to Laban, "Give me my wife, for my time is up, and let me come to her (and establish the future generations)."

---

kabbalah bites

29:18 When Adam sinned, he allowed some of the forces of *kedushah* (holiness) to pass to *kelippah* (the demonic realm), symbolized by the Serpent. As a result of this primordial error, Laban, who embodied the Serpent, was able to have control over the two holy souls of Rachel and Leah.

Jacob, who was a reincarnation of Adam, now had the mission of achieving *tikkun* (spiritual healing) for Adam's sin, by reclaiming Rachel and Leah from Laban.

fore informed them, *"It's still the middle of the day"*—don't worry, the sun will not set early again today, so, *"it's not yet the time to take in the flocks"* (*Rabbi Tzevi Hirsch Ashkenazi, 17th century*).

16. The older one was called Leah, and the younger one was called Rachel. Laban named his daughters with a profound recognition of their personality types. The name Rachel suggests *unspoken* envy and competition, *"like a sheep (raḥel) silent before her shearers"* (*Isaiah* 53:7). Rachel's envy was, of course, for the sake of heaven, as we read below, *"Rachel was jealous of her sister('s good deeds, due to which she had merited children)"* (30:1).

The name Leah is a derivative of the word *nil'ah*, "exhausted," suggesting that she was always drained from thirsting for the salvation of God (*Rabbi Mordecai Joseph Leiner of Izbica, 19th century*).

בראשית כט:כב-לב

22 וַיֶּאֱסֹף לָבָן אֶת־כָּל־אַנְשֵׁי הַמָּקוֹם וַיַּעַשׂ מִשְׁתֶּה: 23 וַיְהִי בָעֶרֶב וַיִּקַּח אֶת־לֵאָה בִתּוֹ וַיָּבֵא אֹתָהּ אֵלָיו וַיָּבֹא אֵלֶיהָ: 24 וַיִּתֵּן לָבָן לָהּ אֶת־זִלְפָּה שִׁפְחָתוֹ לְלֵאָה בִתּוֹ שִׁפְחָה: 25 וַיְהִי בַבֹּקֶר וְהִנֵּה־הִוא לֵאָה וַיֹּאמֶר אֶל־לָבָן מַה־זֹּאת עָשִׂיתָ לִּי הֲלֹא בְרָחֵל עָבַדְתִּי עִמָּךְ וְלָמָּה רִמִּיתָנִי: 26 וַיֹּאמֶר לָבָן לֹא־יֵעָשֶׂה כֵן בִּמְקוֹמֵנוּ לָתֵת הַצְּעִירָה לִפְנֵי הַבְּכִירָה: 27 מַלֵּא שְׁבֻעַ זֹאת וְנִתְּנָה לְךָ גַּם־אֶת־זֹאת בַּעֲבֹדָה אֲשֶׁר תַּעֲבֹד עִמָּדִי עוֹד שֶׁבַע־שָׁנִים אֲחֵרוֹת: 28 וַיַּעַשׂ יַעֲקֹב כֵּן וַיְמַלֵּא שְׁבֻעַ זֹאת וַיִּתֶּן־לוֹ אֶת־רָחֵל בִּתּוֹ לוֹ לְאִשָּׁה: 29 וַיִּתֵּן לָבָן לְרָחֵל בִּתּוֹ אֶת־בִּלְהָה שִׁפְחָתוֹ לָהּ לְשִׁפְחָה: 30 וַיָּבֹא גַּם אֶל־רָחֵל וַיֶּאֱהַב גַּם־אֶת־רָחֵל מִלֵּאָה וַיַּעֲבֹד עִמּוֹ עוֹד שֶׁבַע־שָׁנִים אֲחֵרוֹת: 31 וַיַּרְא יְהֹוָה כִּי־שְׂנוּאָה לֵאָה וַיִּפְתַּח אֶת־רַחְמָהּ וְרָחֵל עֲקָרָה: 32 וַתַּהַר לֵאָה וַתֵּלֶד בֵּן וַתִּקְרָא שְׁמוֹ רְאוּבֵן

such a thing, to give the younger one before the firstborn" (v. 26)—his behavior was not fraudulent because Jacob's request to marry Rachel was a breach of local practice.

However, since Jacob had promised to marry Rachel, and she had been waiting to get married for seven years, Jacob was unable to renege on his promise. Otherwise, he too would be guilty of deception.

Jacob was therefore forced to overlook his *personal stringency* of keeping the entire Torah, which does not allow a person to marry two sisters, so as not to be guilty of deception towards Rachel, which was *prohibited* by Noachide law.

From this you can learn the importance of overlooking your own spiritual *luxury* to help someone else acquire a spiritual *necessity* (*Rabbi Menahem Mendel Schneerson, 20th century*).

32. Reuben. Leah said, "See (*RE'U*) the difference between my son (*BeNi*) and my father-in-law's son (Esau), who sold the birthright to Jacob. But this son of mine did not sell his birthright to Joseph. He did not protest against Joseph when the birthright was taken from him. To the contrary, he attempted to take Joseph out of the pit" (*Rashi, 11th century*).

spiritual vitamin

> A feeling of satisfaction is commensurate only with the amount of effort exerted in a struggle, which makes the fruits of victory so much more delicious.

genesis 29:22–32 — va-yetze'

²² Laban gathered all the local people, and he made a feast. ²³ Then, in the evening (when it was dark), Laban took his daughter Leah, and brought her to (Jacob. Leah told Jacob the secret code which Rachel had divulged) and he came to her. ²⁴ Laban gave Zilpah his maid to his daughter Leah as a maid.

²⁵ Then, in the morning, (Jacob saw that)—look!—it was Leah! He said to Laban, "What's this that you've done to me? Didn't I work with you for Rachel? Why have you deceived me?"

²⁶ Laban said, "In our neighborhood, we don't do such a thing, to give the younger one before the firstborn. ²⁷ Finish the week (of feasting for) this (newlywed), and we'll give you (her sister) too (for a wife straightaway—in return) for the work that you will do for me for another seven years (after the second wedding)."

²⁸ Jacob did just that. He completed the week (of feasting for) this (newlywed), and (Laban) gave his daughter Rachel to him as a wife. ²⁹ Laban gave his maid Bilhah to his daughter Rachel as a maid. ³⁰ (Jacob) came to Rachel too. He also loved Rachel, rather than Leah.

He worked with (Laban) for another seven years.

Jacob Builds His Family

³¹ God saw that Leah was hated, so He opened her womb. Rachel was barren.

³² Leah became pregnant and gave birth to a son. She named him Reuben, because she said, "For God has seen [*Ra'Ah*] my affliction [*Be-'aNyi*], since now my husband will love me."

---

25. Then, in the morning, (Jacob saw that)—look—it was Leah! Does this mean that until the morning it was not Leah? Obviously not. However, to prevent Laban from substituting Leah for Rachel, Jacob had given Rachel a code through which he could identify her. When Rachel saw that her father was planning to have Leah take her place, Rachel gave the code to Leah to save her the embarrassment of being exposed. Because of the prearranged signs that Rachel had revealed to Leah—including the code—Jacob did not know until the morning that it had been Leah (*Babylonian Talmud, Megillah* 13b).

27. We'll give you her sister too. If the Patriarchs kept the entire Torah before it was given (*Rashi* to 26:5), how could Jacob marry two sisters, which is a Biblical prohibition (*Leviticus* 18:18)?

Abraham and his descendants were not *obligated* to observe the Torah's commandments; they did so as a personal *stringency*. On the other hand, they were bound, along with the rest of humanity, by the universal code of law which God had communicated to Noah.

After being fooled into marrying Leah, Jacob challenged Laban, *"Why have you deceived me?"* (v. 25)—Jacob accused Laban of fraud, which was obviously prohibited by Noachide law.

Laban could not merely shrug off Jacob's remark—for then he would be admitting liability for fraudulent behavior. Rather, he was forced to give a *legal* defense: *"In our land, we don't do*

בראשית כט:לב - ל:ח

כִּי אָמְרָה כִּי־רָאָה יְהֹוָה בְּעָנְיִי כִּי עַתָּה יֶאֱהָבַנִי אִישִׁי: 33 וַתַּהַר עוֹד וַתֵּלֶד בֵּן וַתֹּאמֶר כִּי־שָׁמַע יְהֹוָה כִּי־שְׂנוּאָה אָנֹכִי וַיִּתֶּן־לִי גַּם־אֶת־זֶה וַתִּקְרָא שְׁמוֹ שִׁמְעוֹן: 34 וַתַּהַר עוֹד וַתֵּלֶד בֵּן וַתֹּאמֶר עַתָּה הַפַּעַם יִלָּוֶה אִישִׁי אֵלַי כִּי־יָלַדְתִּי לוֹ שְׁלֹשָׁה בָנִים עַל־כֵּן קָרָא־שְׁמוֹ לֵוִי: 35 וַתַּהַר עוֹד וַתֵּלֶד בֵּן וַתֹּאמֶר הַפַּעַם אוֹדֶה אֶת־יְהֹוָה עַל־כֵּן קָרְאָה שְׁמוֹ יְהוּדָה וַתַּעֲמֹד מִלֶּדֶת:

ל 1 וַתֵּרֶא רָחֵל כִּי לֹא יָלְדָה לְיַעֲקֹב וַתְּקַנֵּא רָחֵל בַּאֲחֹתָהּ וַתֹּאמֶר אֶל־יַעֲקֹב הָבָה־לִּי בָנִים וְאִם־אַיִן מֵתָה אָנֹכִי: 2 וַיִּחַר־אַף יַעֲקֹב בְּרָחֵל וַיֹּאמֶר הֲתַחַת אֱלֹהִים אָנֹכִי אֲשֶׁר־מָנַע מִמֵּךְ פְּרִי־בָטֶן: 3 וַתֹּאמֶר הִנֵּה אֲמָתִי בִלְהָה בֹּא אֵלֶיהָ וְתֵלֵד עַל־בִּרְכַּי וְאִבָּנֶה גַם־אָנֹכִי מִמֶּנָּה: 4 וַתִּתֶּן־לוֹ אֶת־בִּלְהָה שִׁפְחָתָהּ לְאִשָּׁה וַיָּבֹא אֵלֶיהָ יַעֲקֹב: 5 וַתַּהַר בִּלְהָה וַתֵּלֶד לְיַעֲקֹב בֵּן: 6 וַתֹּאמֶר רָחֵל דָּנַנִּי אֱלֹהִים וְגַם שָׁמַע בְּקֹלִי וַיִּתֶּן־לִי בֵּן עַל־כֵּן קָרְאָה שְׁמוֹ דָּן: 7 וַתַּהַר עוֹד וַתֵּלֶד בִּלְהָה שִׁפְחַת רָחֵל בֵּן שֵׁנִי לְיַעֲקֹב: 8 וַתֹּאמֶר רָחֵל

The Sages taught, *"Only three may be called Patriarchs"* (*Babylonian Talmud, Berakhot* 16b)—Abraham, Isaac and Jacob—because the spiritual qualities of these three are to be found within *every* Jewish person.

The twelve tribes, on the other hand, each had their own distinct qualities, but these qualities are not found universally among *all* Jews. Thus, the Patriarchs represent the *general* source of Jewish spirituality, whereas the tribes highlight more *specific* features.

As we pass from the general to the specific, emphasis on detail becomes more important. Therefore the name of each tribe is explained in the Torah—*in contrast to the Patriarchs, whose names are not formally explained*—since the more detailed spiritual motif of each tribe requires a more specific emphasis.

And this too sheds light on the fact that it was the Matriarchs, and not Jacob, who named each tribe. For just like it is the mother who nurtures the specific features of the child in her womb, so too, the more detailed spiritual features of the Jewish nation were defined by our Matriarchs (*Rabbi Menahem Mendel Schneerson, 20th century*).

food for thought

1. Why is infertility so devastating?

2. How can an infertile person avoid guilt, blame, depression and hopelessness?

3. Does infertility strain or deepen a person's relationship with God?

³³ She became pregnant again and gave birth to a son. She said, "Since God has heard [*SHaMaʿ*] that I am hated, He gave me this one too," and she named him Simeon [*SHiMʿon*].

³⁴ She became pregnant again and gave birth to a son. She said, "Now this time my husband will be attached [*yilLaVeh*] to me, for I have borne him three sons (one quarter of the twelve tribes)." Therefore, (God) named him Levi.

³⁵ She became pregnant again and gave birth to a son. She said, "This time, I will thank [*'ODeH*] God (because I have had more than my quarter-share of the twelve tribes)." Therefore, she named him Judah [*yehUDaH*].

Then, she stopped having children.

30

¹ Rachel saw that she had not borne Jacob children. Rachel was jealous of her sister('s good deeds, due to which she had merited children). She said to Jacob, "Give me children (through your prayers), otherwise, I am (as good as) dead."

² Jacob became angry with Rachel. He said, "Am I in place of God, who has withheld the fruit of the womb from you?"

³ She said, "Here is my maid Bilhah—come to her. She will bear children whom I will raise, so that I too will be built up from her."

⁴ So she gave him Bilhah, her maid, for a wife, and Jacob came to her.

⁵ Bilhah became pregnant, and she gave birth to a son for Jacob. ⁶ Rachel said, "God has judged me [*DaNanni*] (and acquitted me). He has also listened to my voice and given me a son." Therefore she named him Dan.

⁷ Rachel's maid Bilhah became pregnant again and gave birth to a second son for Jacob. ⁸ Rachel said, "I have stubbornly offered my tortuous prayers [*NaphTuLe*]

---

34. Now this time my husband will be attached to me. Since the Matriarchs were prophetesses, they knew that twelve tribes would come from Jacob, and that he would marry four wives. Leah said, "From now on, he has no cause for complaint against me, as I have contributed my quarter share of sons" (*Rashi, 11th century*).

Leah thought, "Up until now I had two sons, whom I looked after with my two hands. Now, with the third son, I will need my husband's help" (*Rabbi Hezekiah b. Manoah, 13th century*).

When something occurs three times, it constitutes a legal precedent (*ḥazakah*). Levi's birth thus appeared to be evidence that Leah would have many more children (*Rabbi Obadiah Sforno, 16th century*).

Therefore, (God) named him Levi. In all the other cases, the Torah states, "and *she* named," whereas in this instance, the Torah states, "and *he* named." The Sages in *Deuteronomy Rabbah* state that God sent the angel Gabriel who brought the baby before Him. The angel gave the baby his name, and gave him the twenty-four priestly gifts. Because "he was accompanied"—*livvahu*—with gifts, He named him Levi (*Rashi, 11th century*).

בראשית ל:ח-ט

ויצא

נַפְתּוּלֵ֨י אֱלֹהִ֧ים ׀ נִפְתַּ֛לְתִּי עִם־אֲחֹתִ֖י גַּם־יָכֹ֑לְתִּי וַתִּקְרָ֥א שְׁמ֖וֹ נַפְתָּלִֽי׃ 9 וַתֵּ֣רֶא לֵאָ֔ה כִּ֥י עָמְדָ֖ה מִלֶּ֑דֶת וַתִּקַּח֙ אֶת־זִלְפָּ֣ה שִׁפְחָתָ֔הּ וַתִּתֵּ֥ן אֹתָ֛הּ לְיַעֲקֹ֖ב לְאִשָּֽׁה׃ 10 וַתֵּ֗לֶד זִלְפָּ֛ה שִׁפְחַ֥ת לֵאָ֖ה לְיַעֲקֹ֥ב בֵּֽן׃ 11 וַתֹּ֥אמֶר לֵאָ֖ה בָּ֣א גָ֑ד [בגד כ׳] וַתִּקְרָ֥א אֶת־שְׁמ֖וֹ גָּֽד׃ 12 וַתֵּ֗לֶד זִלְפָּה֙ שִׁפְחַ֣ת לֵאָ֔ה בֵּ֥ן שֵׁנִ֖י לְיַעֲקֹֽב׃ 13 וַתֹּ֣אמֶר לֵאָ֗ה בְּאׇשְׁרִ֕י כִּ֥י אִשְּׁר֖וּנִי בָּנ֑וֹת וַתִּקְרָ֥א אֶת־שְׁמ֖וֹ אָשֵֽׁר׃ 14 [FOURTH READING] וַיֵּ֨לֶךְ רְאוּבֵ֜ן בִּימֵ֣י קְצִיר־חִטִּ֗ים וַיִּמְצָ֤א דֽוּדָאִים֙ בַּשָּׂדֶ֔ה וַיָּבֵ֣א אֹתָ֔ם אֶל־לֵאָ֖ה אִמּ֑וֹ וַתֹּ֤אמֶר רָחֵל֙ אֶל־לֵאָ֔ה תְּנִי־נָ֣א לִ֔י מִדּוּדָאֵ֖י בְּנֵֽךְ׃ 15 וַתֹּ֣אמֶר לָ֗הּ הַמְעַט֙ קַחְתֵּ֣ךְ אֶת־אִישִׁ֔י וְלָקַ֕חַת גַּ֥ם אֶת־דּוּדָאֵ֖י בְּנִ֑י וַתֹּ֣אמֶר רָחֵ֗ל לָכֵן֙ יִשְׁכַּ֤ב עִמָּךְ֙ הַלַּ֔יְלָה תַּ֖חַת דּוּדָאֵ֥י בְנֵֽךְ׃ 16 וַיָּבֹ֨א יַעֲקֹ֣ב מִן־הַשָּׂדֶה֮ בָּעֶרֶב֒ וַתֵּצֵ֨א לֵאָ֜ה לִקְרָאת֗וֹ וַתֹּ֙אמֶר֙ אֵלַ֣י תָּב֔וֹא כִּ֚י שָׂכֹ֣ר שְׂכַרְתִּ֔יךָ בְּדוּדָאֵ֖י בְּנִ֑י וַיִּשְׁכַּ֥ב עִמָּ֖הּ בַּלַּ֥יְלָה הֽוּא׃ 17 וַיִּשְׁמַ֥ע אֱלֹהִ֖ים אֶל־לֵאָ֑ה וַתַּ֛הַר וַתֵּ֥לֶד לְיַעֲקֹ֖ב בֵּ֥ן חֲמִישִֽׁי׃ 18 וַתֹּ֣אמֶר לֵאָ֗ה נָתַ֤ן אֱלֹהִים֙ שְׂכָרִ֔י אֲשֶׁר־נָתַ֥תִּי שִׁפְחָתִ֖י לְאִישִׁ֑י וַתִּקְרָ֥א שְׁמ֖וֹ יִשָּׂשכָֽר׃ 19 וַתַּ֤הַר עוֹד֙ לֵאָ֔ה וַתֵּ֛לֶד

born on 10 *Marḥeshvan*; Asher was born on 20 *Shevat*; Issachar was born on 10 *Av*; Zebulun was born on 7 *Tishri*; Joseph was born on 1 *Tammuz*; Benjamin was born on 11 *Marḥeshvan* (*Midrash Tadshe*).

kabbalah bites

30:18 When Jacob grasped Esau's heel at birth, he had captured the kernel of good within Esau's soul (which had originated from Cain's soul—see above, 25:26; 4:25). That kernel was passed down to Issachar's soul. So Issachar effectively possessed the tiny bit of good found in Cain's soul; and since Cain was the firstborn, it was of the highest quality.

This completed Cain's *tikkun* (spiritual healing). Cain's name is suggestive of acquisition (*KaNiti*—see *Genesis* 4:1), and his *tikkun* was achieved through Issachar, born as a result of Leah's *acquiring* conjugal rights from Rachel (v. 16).

Issachar's soul was later reincarnated into Rabbi Akiva.

to God, and my prayers were accepted, as with my sister. I too have been successful," and she named him Naphtali.

⁹ When Leah saw that she had stopped having children, she took her maid Zilpah and gave her to Jacob for a wife. ¹⁰ Leah's maid Zilpah gave birth to a son for Jacob.

¹¹ Leah said, "Good fortune [*GaD*] has come," and she named him Gad.

¹² Leah's maid Zilpah gave birth to a second son for Jacob. ¹³ Leah said, "I am praised [*be-'ASHRi*], because women (now) praise me," so she named him Asher.

[FOURTH READING] ¹⁴ In the days of the wheat harvest, Reuben went and found jasmine plants in the field, and he brought them to Leah, his mother. Rachel said to Leah, "Please give me some of your son's jasmine plants."

¹⁵ "Isn't it enough that you've taken away my husband?" she said to her. "(Now you want) to take my son's jasmine plants too!"

Rachel said, "In that case, Jacob can sleep with you tonight (instead of me) as payment for your son's jasmine plants."

¹⁶ When Jacob came from the field in the evening, Leah came out towards him. She said, "You can come to me (tonight), because I have paid a fee for you (to Rachel) with my son's jasmine plants." And he slept with her on that night.

¹⁷ God listened to Leah('s prayers to have more tribes born through her). She became pregnant and gave birth to a fifth son for Jacob. ¹⁸ Leah said, "God has given (me) my reward [*SeKHaRi*] because I have given my maid to my husband," and she named him Issachar.

¹⁹ Leah became pregnant again, and she gave birth to a sixth son for Jacob.

30:9 She took her maid Zilpah and gave her to Jacob. Note how there was no discussion between Leah and Jacob about this matter first, as with Sarah, who had said to Abraham, *"Please come to my handmaid"* (above, 16:2). This suggests that Leah gave Zilpah to Jacob that night *without him realizing* (and he had imagined that Zilpah was actually Rachel). This would mean that Gad, like Reuben, was conceived while Jacob was not conscious of his partner, since Reuben had been conceived on Leah's wedding night when Laban had swapped Rachel for Leah.

This is the inner reason why the tribes of Reuben and Gad did not merit to receive a portion of the land of Israel (see *Numbers* ch. 32)—because God's *revealed* providence is present constantly over the Land, and these two tribes came into the world in a way that was *hidden* from Jacob's consciousness (*Rabbi Menahem Azariah da Fano, 16ᵗʰ–17ᵗʰ century*).

19. She gave birth. The *Midrash* informs us of the precise birthday of all of Jacob's sons: Reuben was born on 14 *Kislev*; Simeon was born on 21 *Tevet*; Levi was born on 16 *Nisan*; Judah was born on 15 *Sivan*; Dan was born on 9 *Elul*; Naphtali was born on 5 *Tishri*; Gad was

בראשית ל:ט-לב   ויצא

בֶּן־שִׁשִּׁי לְיַעֲקֹב: 20 וַתֹּאמֶר לֵאָה זְבָדַנִי אֱלֹהִים ׀ אֹתִי זֵבֶד טוֹב הַפַּעַם יִזְבְּלֵנִי אִישִׁי כִּי־יָלַדְתִּי לוֹ שִׁשָּׁה בָנִים וַתִּקְרָא אֶת־שְׁמוֹ זְבֻלוּן: 21 וְאַחַר יָלְדָה בַּת וַתִּקְרָא אֶת־שְׁמָהּ דִּינָה: 22 וַיִּזְכֹּר אֱלֹהִים אֶת־רָחֵל וַיִּשְׁמַע אֵלֶיהָ אֱלֹהִים וַיִּפְתַּח אֶת־רַחְמָהּ: 23 וַתַּהַר וַתֵּלֶד בֵּן וַתֹּאמֶר אָסַף אֱלֹהִים אֶת־חֶרְפָּתִי: 24 וַתִּקְרָא אֶת־שְׁמוֹ יוֹסֵף לֵאמֹר יֹסֵף יְהֹוָה לִי בֵּן אַחֵר: 25 וַיְהִי כַּאֲשֶׁר יָלְדָה רָחֵל אֶת־יוֹסֵף וַיֹּאמֶר יַעֲקֹב אֶל־לָבָן שַׁלְּחֵנִי וְאֵלְכָה אֶל־מְקוֹמִי וּלְאַרְצִי: 26 תְּנָה אֶת־נָשַׁי וְאֶת־יְלָדַי אֲשֶׁר עָבַדְתִּי אֹתְךָ בָּהֵן וְאֵלֵכָה כִּי אַתָּה יָדַעְתָּ אֶת־עֲבֹדָתִי אֲשֶׁר עֲבַדְתִּיךָ: 27 וַיֹּאמֶר אֵלָיו לָבָן אִם־נָא מָצָאתִי חֵן בְּעֵינֶיךָ נִחַשְׁתִּי וַיְבָרֲכֵנִי יְהֹוָה בִּגְלָלֶךָ: 28 [FIFTH READING] וַיֹּאמַר נָקְבָה שְׂכָרְךָ עָלַי וְאֶתֵּנָה: 29 וַיֹּאמֶר אֵלָיו אַתָּה יָדַעְתָּ אֵת אֲשֶׁר עֲבַדְתִּיךָ וְאֵת אֲשֶׁר־הָיָה מִקְנְךָ אִתִּי: 30 כִּי מְעַט אֲשֶׁר־הָיָה לְךָ לְפָנַי וַיִּפְרֹץ לָרֹב וַיְבָרֶךְ יְהֹוָה אֹתְךָ לְרַגְלִי וְעַתָּה מָתַי אֶעֱשֶׂה גַם־אָנֹכִי לְבֵיתִי: 31 וַיֹּאמֶר מָה אֶתֶּן־לָךְ וַיֹּאמֶר יַעֲקֹב לֹא־תִתֶּן־לִי מְאוּמָה אִם־תַּעֲשֶׂה־לִּי הַדָּבָר הַזֶּה אָשׁוּבָה אֶרְעֶה צֹאנְךָ אֶשְׁמֹר: 32 אֶעֱבֹר בְּכָל־צֹאנְךָ הַיּוֹם הָסֵר מִשָּׁם כָּל־שֶׂה ׀ נָקֹד וְטָלוּא וְכָל־שֶׂה־חוּם בַּכְּשָׂבִים

27. God has blessed me because of you. *"I have found out by divining, that God has blessed me because of you"*—Laban used magic and sorcery to see if he was blessed because of Jacob. He found that, due to Jacob, he had received an additional one hundred sheep, one hundred lambs, and one hundred male goats to his flocks every month.

Rabbi Abba said, "Jacob brought Laban an additional one thousand cattle, one thousand lambs, and one thousand male goats every month, as the verse states, *'For the few that you had before I (came) have increased extensively, and God blessed you (because of) my arrival'"* (v. 30) (*Zohar*).

Did Laban receive the blessing which God had reserved for *him*? Or, did he merit to share in a portion of *Jacob's* personal blessing? This point was disputed by the two views of the *Zohar*. The first view understood that Laban was receiving his own blessing. Therefore, he received a smaller amount (one hundred per month), and the *Zohar* quotes Laban's *own words* as proof.

But Rabbi Abba understood that Laban actually merited receiving part of *Jacob's* blessing. Thus, the blessing was greater (one thousand per month) and, to stress this point, Rabbi Abba quoted a proof from *Jacob's words* (v. 30).

The first opinion of the *Zohar* perceived the non-Jew to be secondary to the Jew. Therefore, Laban received an inferior blessing to Jacob.

genesis 30:20–32 va-yetze'

²⁰ Leah said, "God has given me a good portion. This time, my husband will live with me [*yiZBeLeNi*] (more than with his other wives), for I have borne him six sons (as many as all the other wives put together will produce)," and she named him Zebulun.

²¹ Afterwards, she gave birth to a daughter, and she named her Dinah.

²² God remembered (that) Rachel (had divulged Jacob's code to Leah to save her from Esau. She feared Jacob would divorce her for being childless, and Esau had already set his eyes on her). So, God listened to her, and opened her womb.

²³ She became pregnant and gave birth to a son. She said, "God has concealed [*aSaPH*] my disgrace." ²⁴ She named him Joseph, saying, "May God add [*YoSePH*] another son for me!"

Jacob Continues to Work for Laban and He Prospers

²⁵ Then, when Rachel had given birth to Joseph (who was destined to destroy Esau, Jacob felt safe to return). Jacob said to Laban, "Send me away! I will go to my place and to my land. ²⁶ Let me have my wives and my children, for whom I served you, and I will go—for you are aware of my services, which I have carried out for you."

²⁷ Laban said to him, "If I have found favor in your eyes, please (stay)! I have found out by divining, that God has blessed me because of you." [FIFTH READING] ²⁸ He said, "Specify (what is to be) your wage from me, and I will give (it)."

²⁹ (Jacob) said to him, "You know how I have worked for you, and how (few) your flocks were (when they first came to be) with me. ³⁰ For the few that you had before I (came) have increased extensively, and God blessed you (because of) my arrival. But now, when will I also do something for my own household?"

³¹ (Laban) said, "What can I give you?"

Jacob said, "Don't give me anything. If you'll do the following for me, I will come back, pasture your flocks (and) guard (them): ³² Let me pass throughout all your flocks today, and remove from there every spotted and patched lamb and every

---

21. Afterwards, she gave birth to a daughter, and she named her Dinah. *"Afterwards"*—What does this refer to? After Leah had passed judgment on herself, saying, "Jacob is destined to father twelve tribes. I have already produced six, and each of the handmaids has produced two, making ten. If I am carrying a boy, then my sister Rachel will not even be equal to one of the handmaids, as she will have produced one tribe, whereas the handmaids each have two."

In order to save her sister from this humiliation, Leah prayed that she should have a girl. And *"afterwards, she gave birth to a daughter, and she named her Dinah."* The name Dinah comes from the Hebrew word *din*, which means "judgment" (*Babylonian Talmud, Berakhot* 60a).

22. God listened to her, and opened her womb. Rabbi Johanan said: The key for childbirth is in the hand of God alone. It is not assigned to any spiritual agency, as the verse states, *"God listened to her and opened her womb"* (*Babylonian Talmud, Ta'anit* 2a).

בראשית ל:לב-מג

וְטָלוּא בָּעִזִּים וְהָיָה שְׂכָרִי: 33 וְעָנְתָה־בִּי צִדְקָתִי בְּיוֹם מָחָר כִּי־תָבוֹא עַל־שְׂכָרִי לְפָנֶיךָ כֹּל אֲשֶׁר־אֵינֶנּוּ נָקֹד וְטָלוּא בָּעִזִּים וְחוּם בַּכְּשָׂבִים גָּנוּב הוּא אִתִּי: 34 וַיֹּאמֶר לָבָן הֵן לוּ יְהִי כִדְבָרֶךָ: 35 וַיָּסַר בַּיּוֹם הַהוּא אֶת־הַתְּיָשִׁים הָעֲקֻדִּים וְהַטְּלֻאִים וְאֵת כָּל־הָעִזִּים הַנְּקֻדּוֹת וְהַטְּלֻאֹת כֹּל אֲשֶׁר־לָבָן בּוֹ וְכָל־חוּם בַּכְּשָׂבִים וַיִּתֵּן בְּיַד־בָּנָיו: 36 וַיָּשֶׂם דֶּרֶךְ שְׁלֹשֶׁת יָמִים בֵּינוֹ וּבֵין יַעֲקֹב וְיַעֲקֹב רֹעֶה אֶת־צֹאן לָבָן הַנּוֹתָרֹת: 37 וַיִּקַּח־לוֹ יַעֲקֹב מַקַּל לִבְנֶה לַח וְלוּז וְעַרְמוֹן וַיְפַצֵּל בָּהֵן פְּצָלוֹת לְבָנוֹת מַחְשֹׂף הַלָּבָן אֲשֶׁר עַל־הַמַּקְלוֹת: 38 וַיַּצֵּג אֶת־הַמַּקְלוֹת אֲשֶׁר פִּצֵּל בָּרֳהָטִים בְּשִׁקֲתוֹת הַמָּיִם אֲשֶׁר תָּבֹאןָ הַצֹּאן לִשְׁתּוֹת לְנֹכַח הַצֹּאן וַיֵּחַמְנָה בְּבֹאָן לִשְׁתּוֹת: 39 וַיֶּחֱמוּ הַצֹּאן אֶל־הַמַּקְלוֹת וַתֵּלַדְןָ הַצֹּאן עֲקֻדִּים נְקֻדִּים וּטְלֻאִים: 40 וְהַכְּשָׂבִים הִפְרִיד יַעֲקֹב וַיִּתֵּן פְּנֵי הַצֹּאן אֶל־עָקֹד וְכָל־חוּם בְּצֹאן לָבָן וַיָּשֶׁת לוֹ עֲדָרִים לְבַדּוֹ וְלֹא שָׁתָם עַל־צֹאן לָבָן: 41 וְהָיָה בְּכָל־יַחֵם הַצֹּאן הַמְקֻשָּׁרוֹת וְשָׂם יַעֲקֹב אֶת־הַמַּקְלוֹת לְעֵינֵי הַצֹּאן בָּרֳהָטִים לְיַחְמֵנָּה בַּמַּקְלוֹת: 42 וּבְהַעֲטִיף הַצֹּאן לֹא יָשִׂים וְהָיָה הָעֲטֻפִים לְלָבָן וְהַקְּשֻׁרִים לְיַעֲקֹב: 43 וַיִּפְרֹץ הָאִישׁ מְאֹד מְאֹד וַיְהִי־לוֹ צֹאן רַבּוֹת וּשְׁפָחוֹת וַעֲבָדִים וּגְמַלִּים וַחֲמֹרִים:

It was a phenomenal miracle, a reversal of nature (*Rabbi Ḥayyim ibn Attar, 18th century*).

43. Fertile flocks and maids, servants, camels and donkeys. He would sell his flocks at a high price and purchase all these things (*Rashi, 11th century*).

spiritual vitamin

> State of mind is a powerful factor, not only in regard to your spiritual life, but also your physical and material life. When you go about your affairs in a happy frame of mind, with faith and confidence, you are bound to be more successful.

genesis 30:32–43   va-yetze'

brown lamb, from among the sheep, and every patched and spotted one from among the goats (for your sons to guard separately, so you will not claim that I am breeding these types). My wages shall be (any spotted or patched goats, or brown sheep that are born from the remaining sheep that I guard). ³³ Thus, at a future time (when I leave), my financial integrity will be self-evident before you, (because) any non-spotted or non-patched goats or non-brown sheep in my (personal) possession will (obviously be) stolen (from you)."

³⁴ "Agreed!" said Laban. "(I) only (hope) it will be as you say (and you won't change your mind)!"

³⁵ On that day (Laban) removed the ringed and patched male goats and all the spotted and patched female goats, whichever had white (patches) on them, and all the brown ones (from) among the sheep, and he gave (them) into the hands of his sons. ³⁶ He set three days' journey between himself and Jacob, and Jacob tended (the dregs of) Laban's remaining flocks.

³⁷ Jacob took himself fresh sticks of poplar, hazel and chestnut (wood), and he peeled white streaks on them by uncovering the white that was (inside) the sticks. ³⁸ He inserted the sticks that he had peeled, into the (ground, by the) pools (into which) the watering troughs (would fill) where the flocks would come to drink, so that they faced the animals. (This caused them) to become stimulated (and mate) when they came to drink. ³⁹ The flocks became stimulated (and mated on seeing) the rods, and the flocks bore ringed, patched, and striped (young).

⁴⁰ Jacob segregated the (newborn) sheep: He made the (other) animals in Laban's flocks (into a group behind, so that) they faced the ringed ones and all the brown ones. (Jacob) separated the flocks (in the above manner) for his own (benefit). He did not place them with Laban's animals.

⁴¹ What happened was, that whenever the early-bearing flocks would become stimulated (ready to mate), Jacob would place the sticks in the troughs, before the eyes of the animals, (in order) to stimulate them (into mating) by (means of) the rods. ⁴² But when the flocks were late in bearing, he would not place (the sticks). Thus, the ones that were born late went to Laban, and the ones that were born early to Jacob.

⁴³ The man (Jacob) became exceedingly wealthy. He had extremely fertile flocks and maids, servants, camels and donkeys.

Rabbi Abba on the other hand took a deeper approach, seeing the non-Jew not merely as an assistant but as a partner in a Jew's observance of the Torah who shares some of the exclusive qualities of that status. Therefore, Laban was able to *share* a part of Jacob's *personal* blessing (*Rabbi Menahem Mendel Schneerson, 20th century*).

39. The flocks became stimulated (and mated on seeing) the rods. Jacob's technique of rods was a natural method of causing animals to mate, though it was of course by Divine Providence (*Rabbi Levi b. Gershom, 14th century*).

בראשית לא:א-יב

לא 1 וַיִּשְׁמַע אֶת־דִּבְרֵי בְנֵי־לָבָן לֵאמֹר לָקַח יַעֲקֹב אֵת כָּל־אֲשֶׁר לְאָבִינוּ וּמֵאֲשֶׁר לְאָבִינוּ עָשָׂה אֵת כָּל־הַכָּבֹד הַזֶּה: 2 וַיַּרְא יַעֲקֹב אֶת־פְּנֵי לָבָן וְהִנֵּה אֵינֶנּוּ עִמּוֹ כִּתְמוֹל שִׁלְשׁוֹם: 3 וַיֹּאמֶר יְהֹוָה אֶל־יַעֲקֹב שׁוּב אֶל־אֶרֶץ אֲבוֹתֶיךָ וּלְמוֹלַדְתֶּךָ וְאֶהְיֶה עִמָּךְ: 4 וַיִּשְׁלַח יַעֲקֹב וַיִּקְרָא לְרָחֵל וּלְלֵאָה הַשָּׂדֶה אֶל־צֹאנוֹ: 5 וַיֹּאמֶר לָהֶן רֹאֶה אָנֹכִי אֶת־פְּנֵי אֲבִיכֶן כִּי־אֵינֶנּוּ אֵלַי כִּתְמֹל שִׁלְשֹׁם וֵאלֹהֵי אָבִי הָיָה עִמָּדִי: 6 וְאַתֵּנָה יְדַעְתֶּן כִּי בְּכָל־כֹּחִי עָבַדְתִּי אֶת־אֲבִיכֶן: 7 וַאֲבִיכֶן הֵתֶל בִּי וְהֶחֱלִף אֶת־מַשְׂכֻּרְתִּי עֲשֶׂרֶת מֹנִים וְלֹא־נְתָנוֹ אֱלֹהִים לְהָרַע עִמָּדִי: 8 אִם־כֹּה יֹאמַר נְקֻדִּים יִהְיֶה שְׂכָרֶךָ וְיָלְדוּ כָל־הַצֹּאן נְקֻדִּים וְאִם־כֹּה יֹאמַר עֲקֻדִּים יִהְיֶה שְׂכָרֶךָ וְיָלְדוּ כָל־הַצֹּאן עֲקֻדִּים: 9 וַיַּצֵּל אֱלֹהִים אֶת־מִקְנֵה אֲבִיכֶם וַיִּתֶּן־לִי: 10 וַיְהִי בְּעֵת יַחֵם הַצֹּאן וָאֶשָּׂא עֵינַי וָאֵרֶא בַּחֲלוֹם וְהִנֵּה הָעַתֻּדִים הָעֹלִים עַל־הַצֹּאן עֲקֻדִּים נְקֻדִּים וּבְרֻדִּים: 11 וַיֹּאמֶר אֵלַי מַלְאַךְ הָאֱלֹהִים בַּחֲלוֹם יַעֲקֹב וָאֹמַר הִנֵּנִי: 12 וַיֹּאמֶר שָׂא־נָא עֵינֶיךָ וּרְאֵה כָּל־הָעַתֻּדִים הָעֹלִים עַל־הַצֹּאן עֲקֻדִּים נְקֻדִּים וּבְרֻדִּים כִּי רָאִיתִי אֵת כָּל־

Often the most unassuming passages actually contain the deepest of secrets. *The story of Jacob's sheep tells us how the ten sefirot, the fundamental "energy types" of the cosmos, came into being.*

Initially, the *sefirot* were "ringed" or tied together. They were so intense that they could not yet be distinguished as ten separate types of energy. Later, when the *sefirot* would be complete, each would have its own distinct "vessel," or "tool" that would collect its energy and project it downwards into our world. But here in the realm of *'akuddim*, all ten energies are lumped into a single vessel.

As we pass into the realm of *nekudim*, more spiritual evolution takes place. Now the *sefirot* are "spotted"—they are ten distinct points with their own individual identity. But they are so highly charged that they cannot function as a collective unit. The disunity in the world of *nekudim* brought about the "shattering of the vessels," the dispersion of its energy and the scattering of its "sparks" into physical reality. Much of history, according to the Kabbalists, has been devoted to the correction of this primordial catastrophe. *Nekudim* is also known as the world of *Tohu*—Chaos.

In *Beruddim* ("stripes") we mature to the point of interconnectedness. The ten *sefirot* function in harmony and share energies. This is also known as the world of *Tikkun*, Correction. God's presence can rest because there is mutual understanding and empathy in all the forces of creation (*Rabbi Ḥayyim b. Joseph Vital, 16th–17th century*).

genesis 31:1–12   va-yetze'

Jacob Flees from Laban with his Family

31 ¹ Then, he heard the words of Laban's sons, saying, "Jacob has taken everything that belonged to our father, and he has amassed this entire fortune from what belonged to our father." ² Jacob saw Laban's face, and—look!— it was not (friendly) towards him like yesterday and the day before.

³ God said to Jacob, "Return to the land of your forefathers, to your birthplace, and I will be with you."

⁴ So Jacob sent (a message) and called Rachel and Leah to the field, to his flocks. ⁵ He said to them, "I see that your father's face is not (friendly) toward me like yesterday and the day before, but (my riches came because) the God of my father was with me. ⁶ You know that I served your father with all my might. ⁷ Your father mocked me and changed my wages a hundred times, but God did not permit him to harm me. ⁸ If he would say, 'Spotted ones shall be your wages,' then all the animals would give birth to spotted ones. If he would say, 'Ringed ones shall be your wages,' then all the animals would give birth to ringed ones. ⁹ God took away your father's livestock and gave it to me. ¹⁰ Then, at the time when the animals became stimulated, I lifted my eyes and saw in a dream, that—look!—(angels were bringing) ringed, spotted, and striped he-goats (from the flocks of Laban's sons) to mate with the (female) animals.

¹¹ "In the dream, an angel of God said to me, 'Jacob!'

"I said, 'Here I am.'

¹² "He said, 'Now lift your eyes and see (that) all the he-goats mounting the animals are ringed, spotted, and striped, for I have seen all that Laban is doing

---

food for thought

1. Have you ever been mistreated at work?

2. How much injustice would you suffer in silence?

3. How could you help an employer recognize that he is being unfair or abusive?

31:10 And saw in a dream. He dreamt that although Laban had set aside all the goats, so that the animals would not conceive in their likeness, the angels were bringing them from the flock that had been transferred into the hands of Laban's sons to the flock that was in Jacob's hands (see above v. 32ff; *Rashi, 11th century*).

In the dream, God's angel told Jacob that he no longer needed to use the mating method of the sticks, for from now on the sheep would be born with the correct patterns (*Naḥmanides, 13th century*).

Striped. A white strip made of many spots encircles the body all around. The spots of the strip are disconnected but give the impression of being continuous from end to end—but I have no evidence from Scripture (*Rashi, 11th century*).

Ringed (*'akuddim*), spotted (*nekuddim*) and striped (*beruddim*) he-goats. Why did the Torah find it necessary to give so much attention to the descriptions of Jacob's sheep?

ויצא בראשית לא:יב-כג

אֲשֶׁ֥ר לָבָ֖ן עֹ֥שֶׂה לָּֽךְ׃ 13 אָנֹכִ֤י הָאֵל֙ בֵּֽית־אֵ֔ל אֲשֶׁ֨ר מָשַׁ֤חְתָּ שָּׁם֙ מַצֵּבָ֔ה אֲשֶׁ֨ר נָדַ֥רְתָּ לִּ֛י שָׁ֖ם נֶ֑דֶר עַתָּ֗ה ק֤וּם צֵא֙ מִן־הָאָ֣רֶץ הַזֹּ֔את וְשׁ֖וּב אֶל־אֶ֥רֶץ מוֹלַדְתֶּֽךָ׃ 14 וַתַּ֤עַן רָחֵל֙ וְלֵאָ֔ה וַתֹּאמַ֖רְנָה ל֑וֹ הַע֥וֹד לָ֛נוּ חֵ֥לֶק וְנַחֲלָ֖ה בְּבֵ֥ית אָבִֽינוּ׃ 15 הֲל֧וֹא נׇכְרִיּ֛וֹת נֶחְשַׁ֥בְנוּ ל֖וֹ כִּ֣י מְכָרָ֑נוּ וַיֹּ֥אכַל גַּם־אָכ֖וֹל אֶת־כַּסְפֵּֽנוּ׃ 16 כִּ֣י כׇל־הָעֹ֗שֶׁר אֲשֶׁ֨ר הִצִּ֤יל אֱלֹהִים֙ מֵֽאָבִ֔ינוּ לָ֥נוּ ה֖וּא וּלְבָנֵ֑ינוּ וְעַתָּ֗ה כֹּל֩ אֲשֶׁ֨ר אָמַ֧ר אֱלֹהִ֛ים אֵלֶ֖יךָ עֲשֵֽׂה׃ 17 [SIXTH READING] וַיָּ֖קׇם יַעֲקֹ֑ב וַיִּשָּׂ֛א אֶת־בָּנָ֥יו וְאֶת־נָשָׁ֖יו עַל־הַגְּמַלִּֽים׃ 18 וַיִּנְהַ֣ג אֶת־כׇּל־מִקְנֵ֗הוּ וְאֶת־כׇּל־רְכֻשׁוֹ֙ אֲשֶׁ֣ר רָכָ֔שׁ מִקְנֵה֙ קִנְיָנ֔וֹ אֲשֶׁ֥ר רָכַ֖שׁ בְּפַדַּ֣ן אֲרָ֑ם לָב֛וֹא אֶל־יִצְחָ֥ק אָבִ֖יו אַ֥רְצָה כְּנָֽעַן׃ 19 וְלָבָ֣ן הָלַ֔ךְ לִגְזֹ֖ז אֶת־צֹאנ֑וֹ וַתִּגְנֹ֣ב רָחֵ֔ל אֶת־הַתְּרָפִ֖ים אֲשֶׁ֥ר לְאָבִֽיהָ׃ 20 וַיִּגְנֹ֣ב יַעֲקֹ֔ב אֶת־לֵ֥ב לָבָ֖ן הָאֲרַמִּ֑י עַל־בְּלִי֙ הִגִּ֣יד ל֔וֹ כִּ֥י בֹרֵ֖חַ הֽוּא׃ 21 וַיִּבְרַ֥ח הוּא֙ וְכׇל־אֲשֶׁר־ל֔וֹ וַיָּ֖קׇם וַיַּעֲבֹ֣ר אֶת־הַנָּהָ֑ר וַיָּ֥שֶׂם אֶת־פָּנָ֖יו הַ֥ר הַגִּלְעָֽד׃ 22 וַיֻּגַּ֥ד לְלָבָ֖ן בַּיּ֣וֹם הַשְּׁלִישִׁ֑י כִּ֥י בָרַ֖ח יַעֲקֹֽב׃ 23 וַיִּקַּ֤ח אֶת־אֶחָיו֙ עִמּ֔וֹ וַיִּרְדֹּ֣ף אַחֲרָ֔יו דֶּ֖רֶךְ שִׁבְעַ֣ת יָמִ֑ים וַיַּדְבֵּ֥ק אֹת֖וֹ בְּהַ֥ר

The *teraphim* were copper items resembling a sundial, used to foretell the future. Or they may have been idols, shaped in the image of a human (*Rabbi Abraham ibn Ezra, 12th century*).

Rachel took the *teraphim* in order to protect her family. She wished to prevent Laban divining information about the fact that they had fled (*Pirkei de-Rabbi Eliezer*).

23. And pursued him. Before Jacob went to Laban there had not yet been any revelation of Torah; all was still hidden. Various spiritual "roots" of the Torah lay scattered in lowly places, and in Laban's house there were many such "roots" to be found. Jacob spent twenty years there with Laban working to bring forth and refine those "roots" of Torah from their burial deep beneath the potent demonic powers of Laban. And that is why all these narratives—about Laban's daughters, and the details of his dealings with sheep—were recorded in the Torah, *because they are the story of the Torah itself*, how its spiritual essence came to be revealed.

The current passage, where Laban pursues Jacob and confronts him, consists of those bits of Torah still hidden with Laban which Jacob had not managed to redeem. God orchestrated that Laban should run after Jacob, to bring to him that remaining part of the Torah. When Laban reached him, Jacob was able, through the conversation recorded here, to refine this last portion of Torah, so that nothing now remained with Laban (*Rabbi Menahem Nahum Twersky of Chernobyl, 18th century*).

While most of your achievements in life will come through your own conscious efforts, there will be some "super-conscious" achievements that are so lofty that they cannot occur intentionally. You are usually the one that chooses your own path in life—to find the "sparks" of

to you. ¹³ I am the God of Bethel, where you anointed a monument and where you made a vow to Me. Now, get moving, leave this land, and return to the land of your birth.'"

¹⁴ Rachel and Leah replied, saying to him, "(It's not as if) we still have a share or an inheritance in our father's house (for that will go to our brothers). ¹⁵ Aren't we considered strangers to him, for he sold us (to you in marriage without a dowry) and (when you worked for him to marry us) he totally consumed our money! ¹⁶ Rather, all the wealth that God separated from our father belongs to us and our children. So now, do everything that God said to you."

[SIXTH READING] ¹⁷ Jacob got moving. He lifted up his sons and his wives onto the camels, ¹⁸ and he led off all his livestock and all his possessions that he had acquired in Paddan-aram—purchased (through the sale of the livestock) that he owned—to come to Isaac, his father, in the land of Canaan.

¹⁹ Laban had gone to shear his sheep (which were with his sons, three days' journey away), so Rachel stole her father's idols (attempting to wean him off idol-worship).

²⁰ Jacob duped Laban the Aramean by not telling him that he was running away. ²¹ He fled, with all his belongings. He got moving, crossed the river, and headed towards Mount Gilead.

Laban Chases after Jacob and Confronts Him

²² On the third day, Laban was informed that Jacob had fled. ²³ He took his relatives with him and pursued him. (He covered) seven day's journey (in one day), and he reached (Jacob) at Mount Gilead.

---

19. Rachel stole her father's idols (*teraphim*). Why were they called *teraphim*? Because they were the product of lewdness *(ma'aseh toref)*, of impurity. How did they make them? They would take a firstborn person, slaughter him and pickle him with salts and herbs. They would write the name of an impure spirit on a golden frontlet, and place the frontlet with spells under his tongue. They would place him on the wall, kindle lights before him and bow down to him. He would then speak to them in a whisper (*Midrash Tanḥuma*).

spiritual vitamin

> Depression and gloom is, in itself, one of the strategic weapons which discourage you from serving God with joy. No matter what the past has been, it is always possible to attach yourself to God.

בראשית לא:כג-לז | ויצא

הַגִּלְעָד: 24 וַיָּבֹא אֱלֹהִים אֶל־לָבָן הָאֲרַמִּי בַּחֲלֹם הַלָּיְלָה וַיֹּאמֶר לוֹ הִשָּׁמֶר לְךָ פֶּן־תְּדַבֵּר עִם־יַעֲקֹב מִטּוֹב עַד־רָע: 25 וַיַּשֵּׂג לָבָן אֶת־יַעֲקֹב וְיַעֲקֹב תָּקַע אֶת־אָהֳלוֹ בָּהָר וְלָבָן תָּקַע אֶת־אֶחָיו בְּהַר הַגִּלְעָד: 26 וַיֹּאמֶר לָבָן לְיַעֲקֹב מֶה עָשִׂיתָ וַתִּגְנֹב אֶת־לְבָבִי וַתְּנַהֵג אֶת־בְּנֹתַי כִּשְׁבֻיוֹת חָרֶב: 27 לָמָּה נַחְבֵּאתָ לִבְרֹחַ וַתִּגְנֹב אֹתִי וְלֹא־הִגַּדְתָּ לִּי וָאֲשַׁלֵּחֲךָ בְּשִׂמְחָה וּבְשִׁרִים בְּתֹף וּבְכִנּוֹר: 28 וְלֹא נְטַשְׁתַּנִי לְנַשֵּׁק לְבָנַי וְלִבְנֹתָי עַתָּה הִסְכַּלְתָּ עֲשׂוֹ: 29 יֶשׁ־לְאֵל יָדִי לַעֲשׂוֹת עִמָּכֶם רָע וֵאלֹהֵי אֲבִיכֶם אֶמֶשׁ | אָמַר אֵלַי לֵאמֹר הִשָּׁמֶר לְךָ מִדַּבֵּר עִם־יַעֲקֹב מִטּוֹב עַד־רָע: 30 וְעַתָּה הָלֹךְ הָלַכְתָּ כִּי־נִכְסֹף נִכְסַפְתָּה לְבֵית אָבִיךָ לָמָּה גָנַבְתָּ אֶת־אֱלֹהָי: 31 וַיַּעַן יַעֲקֹב וַיֹּאמֶר לְלָבָן כִּי יָרֵאתִי כִּי אָמַרְתִּי פֶּן־תִּגְזֹל אֶת־בְּנוֹתֶיךָ מֵעִמִּי: 32 עִם אֲשֶׁר תִּמְצָא אֶת־אֱלֹהֶיךָ לֹא יִחְיֶה נֶגֶד אַחֵינוּ הַכֶּר־לְךָ מָה עִמָּדִי וְקַח־לָךְ וְלֹא־יָדַע יַעֲקֹב כִּי רָחֵל גְּנָבָתַם: 33 וַיָּבֹא לָבָן בְּאֹהֶל־יַעֲקֹב | וּבְאֹהֶל לֵאָה וּבְאֹהֶל שְׁתֵּי הָאֲמָהֹת וְלֹא מָצָא וַיֵּצֵא מֵאֹהֶל לֵאָה וַיָּבֹא בְּאֹהֶל רָחֵל: 34 וְרָחֵל לָקְחָה אֶת־הַתְּרָפִים וַתְּשִׂמֵם בְּכַר הַגָּמָל וַתֵּשֶׁב עֲלֵיהֶם וַיְמַשֵּׁשׁ לָבָן אֶת־כָּל־הָאֹהֶל וְלֹא מָצָא: 35 וַתֹּאמֶר אֶל־אָבִיהָ אַל־יִחַר בְּעֵינֵי אֲדֹנִי כִּי לוֹא אוּכַל לָקוּם מִפָּנֶיךָ כִּי־דֶרֶךְ נָשִׁים לִי וַיְחַפֵּשׂ וְלֹא מָצָא אֶת־הַתְּרָפִים: 36 וַיִּחַר לְיַעֲקֹב וַיָּרֶב בְּלָבָן וַיַּעַן יַעֲקֹב וַיֹּאמֶר לְלָבָן מַה־פִּשְׁעִי מַה חַטָּאתִי כִּי דָלַקְתָּ אַחֲרָי: 37 כִּי־מִשַּׁשְׁתָּ אֶת־כָּל־כֵּלַי מַה־מָּצָאתָ מִכֹּל כְּלֵי־בֵיתֶךָ שִׂים כֹּה נֶגֶד

27. Why did you flee secretly and deceive me? Why didn't you tell me? I would have sent you off with rejoicing, songs, drum and harp! Laban was a charlatan, devoid of honesty and fear of God. Since Jacob was in the field all day, Laban presumed that he also had no connection with God.

However, after God came to Laban in a dream and said, "Beware not to speak with Jacob either good or bad," Laban realized that Jacob was a God-fearing man. Laban asked Jacob, *"Why did you flee secretly?"*—Why were you so secretive about your righteousness?

"Why didn't you tell me?" If I would have known what a God-fearing man you were, *"I would have sent you off with rejoicing, songs, drum and harp,"* as soon as you arrived, for I have no interest in people like you (*Rabbi Levi Isaac of Berdichev, 18th century*).

genesis 31:24–37 — va-yetze'

[24] God came to Laban the Aramean in a nighttime dream. He said to him, "Beware not to speak with Jacob either good or bad (for even your 'good' is bad)."

[25] When Laban caught up to Jacob, Jacob had pitched his tent on the mountain, and Laban pitched (his tent) with his relatives on Mount Gilead.

[26] Laban said to Jacob, "What have you done? You duped me, and led away my daughters like prisoners of war! [27] Why did you flee secretly and deceive me? Why didn't you tell me? I would have sent you off with rejoicing, songs, drum and harp! [28] You didn't allow me to kiss my sons and daughters. You have now acted foolishly."

[29] "I am sufficiently strong to harm you, but the God of your father spoke to me last night, saying, 'Beware not to speak with Jacob either good or bad.'

[30] "Now, you have repeatedly (wanted) to go away, because you longed again and again for your father's house (but we worked things out sensibly and you stayed!) And why have you stolen my gods?"

[31] Jacob replied (to the questions in order). He said to Laban, "(I ran off without telling you) because I was afraid, since I said (to myself), 'perhaps you will kidnap your daughters from me.'

[32] "(In answer to your second question:) Whoever you find has your idols shall not live. In front of our relatives, identify for yourself which (of your possessions) is with me, and take (it) for yourself"—but Jacob did not know that Rachel had stolen them.

[33] Laban entered Jacob's (and Rachel's) tent, then Leah's tent and the tent of the two handmaids, but he did not find (them). When he came out of Leah's tent he (re-)entered Rachel's tent (since he was suspicious of her).

[34] Rachel had taken the idols and placed them into the camel saddle, sitting on them. Laban rummaged the entire tent, but he did not find (them).

[35] She said to her father, "I hope my master will not be annoyed that I can't get up before you, because the way of women is upon me." (Laban) searched, but did not find the idols.

[36] Jacob became angry and argued with Laban. He said to Laban, "What is my crime? What is my sin, that you have pursued me? [37] You have rummaged through all my things. Whatever you have found from among any of the utensils of your house, place it here, in front of my relatives and your relatives, and let them decide between the two of us (who is right).

---

goodness which you are destined to elevate—but sometimes your "sparks" will pursue you, because they are too sublime to be "extracted" solely by your own endeavors (*Rabbi Menahem Mendel Schneerson, 20th century*).

בראשית לא:לז-נג

אַחַי וְאַחֶיךָ וְיוֹכִיחוּ בֵּין שְׁנֵינוּ: 38 זֶה עֶשְׂרִים שָׁנָה אָנֹכִי עִמָּךְ רְחֵלֶיךָ וְעִזֶּיךָ לֹא שִׁכֵּלוּ וְאֵילֵי צֹאנְךָ לֹא אָכָלְתִּי: 39 טְרֵפָה לֹא־הֵבֵאתִי אֵלֶיךָ אָנֹכִי אֲחַטֶּנָּה מִיָּדִי תְּבַקְשֶׁנָּה גְּנֻבְתִי יוֹם וּגְנֻבְתִי לָיְלָה: 40 הָיִיתִי בַיּוֹם אֲכָלַנִי חֹרֶב וְקֶרַח בַּלָּיְלָה וַתִּדַּד שְׁנָתִי מֵעֵינָי: 41 זֶה־לִּי עֶשְׂרִים שָׁנָה בְּבֵיתֶךָ עֲבַדְתִּיךָ אַרְבַּע־עֶשְׂרֵה שָׁנָה בִּשְׁתֵּי בְנֹתֶיךָ וְשֵׁשׁ שָׁנִים בְּצֹאנֶךָ וַתַּחֲלֵף אֶת־מַשְׂכֻּרְתִּי עֲשֶׂרֶת מֹנִים: 42 לוּלֵי אֱלֹהֵי אָבִי אֱלֹהֵי אַבְרָהָם וּפַחַד יִצְחָק הָיָה לִי כִּי עַתָּה רֵיקָם שִׁלַּחְתָּנִי אֶת־עָנְיִי וְאֶת־יְגִיעַ כַּפַּי רָאָה אֱלֹהִים וַיּוֹכַח אָמֶשׁ: 43 [SEVENTH READING] וַיַּעַן לָבָן וַיֹּאמֶר אֶל־יַעֲקֹב הַבָּנוֹת בְּנֹתַי וְהַבָּנִים בָּנַי וְהַצֹּאן צֹאנִי וְכֹל אֲשֶׁר־אַתָּה רֹאֶה לִי־הוּא וְלִבְנֹתַי מָה־אֶעֱשֶׂה לָאֵלֶּה הַיּוֹם אוֹ לִבְנֵיהֶן אֲשֶׁר יָלָדוּ: 44 וְעַתָּה לְכָה נִכְרְתָה בְרִית אֲנִי וָאָתָּה וְהָיָה לְעֵד בֵּינִי וּבֵינֶךָ: 45 וַיִּקַּח יַעֲקֹב אָבֶן וַיְרִימֶהָ מַצֵּבָה: 46 וַיֹּאמֶר יַעֲקֹב לְאֶחָיו לִקְטוּ אֲבָנִים וַיִּקְחוּ אֲבָנִים וַיַּעֲשׂוּ־גָל וַיֹּאכְלוּ שָׁם עַל־הַגָּל: 47 וַיִּקְרָא־לוֹ לָבָן יְגַר שָׂהֲדוּתָא וְיַעֲקֹב קָרָא לוֹ גַּלְעֵד: 48 וַיֹּאמֶר לָבָן הַגַּל הַזֶּה עֵד בֵּינִי וּבֵינְךָ הַיּוֹם עַל־כֵּן קָרָא־שְׁמוֹ גַּלְעֵד: 49 וְהַמִּצְפָּה אֲשֶׁר אָמַר יִצֶף יְהוָה בֵּינִי וּבֵינֶךָ כִּי נִסָּתֵר אִישׁ מֵרֵעֵהוּ: 50 אִם־תְּעַנֶּה אֶת־בְּנֹתַי וְאִם־תִּקַּח נָשִׁים עַל־בְּנֹתַי אֵין אִישׁ עִמָּנוּ רְאֵה אֱלֹהִים עֵד בֵּינִי וּבֵינֶךָ: 51 וַיֹּאמֶר לָבָן לְיַעֲקֹב הִנֵּה | הַגַּל הַזֶּה וְהִנֵּה הַמַּצֵּבָה אֲשֶׁר יָרִיתִי בֵּינִי וּבֵינֶךָ: 52 עֵד הַגַּל הַזֶּה וְעֵדָה הַמַּצֵּבָה אִם־אָנִי לֹא־אֶעֱבֹר אֵלֶיךָ אֶת־הַגַּל הַזֶּה וְאִם־אַתָּה לֹא־תַעֲבֹר אֵלַי אֶת־הַגַּל הַזֶּה וְאֶת־הַמַּצֵּבָה הַזֹּאת לְרָעָה: 53 אֱלֹהֵי אַבְרָהָם וֵאלֹהֵי נָחוֹר

---

52. Nor are you to pass. Laban said, "You may not pass to do harm, but you may pass to do business" (*Rashi, 11th century*).

The "pile of stones" represents the boundary between the Jew (Jacob) and his non-Jewish surroundings (Laban). This boundary is *not* supposed to be a total barrier, where the Jew totally isolates himself from the world and wants nothing to do with his non-Jewish neighbors—or, for that matter, anything secular.

genesis 31:38–53 — va-yetze'

³⁸ "It's already twenty years that I've been with you, and your ewes and she-goats have not miscarried. I have not eaten the (newborn) rams of your flocks. ³⁹ I have not brought home to you an animal torn (by a lion or a wolf. In such a case) I would suffer its loss (because) you would demand (payment) from my hand. (I also paid for) what was stolen by day and what was stolen at night."

⁴⁰ "(Where) I was by day, the heat consumed me. At night there was frost, and my eyes were deprived of sleep.

⁴¹ "It's twenty years that I've spent in your house. I served you fourteen years for your two daughters and six years for your animals, and you changed my wages a hundred times. ⁴² If it weren't for the God of my father, the God of Abraham and the (One whom) Isaac feared, who was with me, you would now have sent me away empty-handed. God has seen my affliction and the toil of my hands, and He reprimanded (you) last night."

Laban Makes a Pact With Jacob

[SEVENTH READING] ⁴³ Laban answered Jacob and said, "The daughters are my daughters! The sons are my sons! The flocks are my flocks! All that you see is mine! As for my daughters...what (harm) would I (dream of) doing to them today? Or to the children that they have borne?

⁴⁴ "Now come! Let's make a pact—you and I. And may (God) be a witness between me and you."

⁴⁵ Jacob took a stone and set it up as a monument.

⁴⁶ Jacob said to his (sons), "Gather stones!"

They took stones and made a pile, and they ate there by the pile. ⁴⁷ Laban called it Yegar-sahadutha ("the pile is a witness," in Aramaic). Jacob called it Gal-ed (the same in its Hebrew translation).

⁴⁸ Laban said, "This pile is a witness between me and you today"—it was therefore named Gal-ed. ⁴⁹ (It is also known as) Mizpah ("watch"), because he said, "May God watch me and you when we are hidden from each other. ⁵⁰ If you neglect my daughters, or if you take wives in addition to my daughters when no one is with us—look!—God is a witness between me and you."

⁵¹ Laban said to Jacob, "Here is the pile and here is the monument which I have set up between me and you. ⁵² This pile is a witness, and this monument is a witness, that I am not to pass this pile (to go) to you, nor are you to pass this pile and this monument to (come to) me to (do) harm. ⁵³ May the God of Abraham, the god of Nahor and the god of their father judge between us."

Jacob swore by the (One whom) his father Isaac feared.

בראשית לא:נג - לב:ג | ויצא

יִשְׁפְּטוּ בֵינֵינוּ אֱלֹהֵי אֲבִיהֶם וַיִּשָּׁבַע יַעֲקֹב בְּפַחַד אָבִיו יִצְחָק: 54 וַיִּזְבַּח יַעֲקֹב זֶבַח בָּהָר וַיִּקְרָא לְאֶחָיו לֶאֱכָל־לָחֶם וַיֹּאכְלוּ לֶחֶם וַיָּלִינוּ בָּהָר:

לב [MAFTIR] 1 וַיַּשְׁכֵּם לָבָן בַּבֹּקֶר וַיְנַשֵּׁק לְבָנָיו וְלִבְנוֹתָיו וַיְבָרֶךְ אֶתְהֶם וַיֵּלֶךְ וַיָּשָׁב לָבָן לִמְקֹמוֹ: 2 וְיַעֲקֹב הָלַךְ לְדַרְכּוֹ וַיִּפְגְּעוּ־בוֹ מַלְאֲכֵי אֱלֹהִים: 3 וַיֹּאמֶר יַעֲקֹב כַּאֲשֶׁר רָאָם מַחֲנֵה אֱלֹהִים זֶה וַיִּקְרָא שֵׁם־הַמָּקוֹם הַהוּא מַחֲנָיִם: פ פ פ

קמ״ח פסוקים. חלק״י סימן. מחני״ם סימן.

spiritual vitamin

> You should always try to bring out your best and innermost self, and also influence your environment, at all times, whether or not there are any external sources of inspiration. If you take the trouble you *can* see God's miracles at every step; but even if not, this should only indicate that God regards you as sufficiently grown up and mature not to require constant "interjections" and stimulants from outside.

genesis 31:54 – 32:3 — va-yetze'

⁵⁴ Jacob slaughtered animals (for a feast) on the mountain. He invited his friends (who were with Laban) to eat a meal. They ate a meal and slept overnight on the mountain.

32 [MAFTIR] ¹ Laban got up early in the morning. He kissed his sons and daughters and blessed them, and then Laban went off and returned to his home.

Angels from the Land of Israel Greet Jacob

² Jacob went on his way, and angels of God (from the land of Israel) encountered him (to escort him to the land). ³ When he saw them, Jacob said, "This is a camp of God," and he named the place Mahanaim ("Double-Camp"—due to the two sets of angels that had escorted him from the Diaspora and that had escorted him to the land of Israel).

The Haftarah for Va-Yetze' is on page 1303.

Rather, as *Rashi* indicates, it is a "semi-permeable" interface, *"You may not pass to do harm, but you may pass to do business."* You must interact with your surroundings, but not in a way that causes you spiritual "harm." You need to "profit" spiritually from each interaction with the world, by training your eye to perceive how its physical existence is being constantly renewed at every moment by God.

Attune yourself to a level of consciousness that you are not dealing with secular matters at all, but with physical objects that are a manifestation of God. In this way you will come to fulfil the dictum (*Proverbs 3:6*), *"In all your ways know Him"*—in your own non-sacred affairs, you come to a heightened awareness of the Divine (*Rabbi Menahem Mendel Schneerson, 20th century*).

32:2 Angels of God encountered him. Angels from the land of Israel came to greet him, to escort him to the land (*Rashi, 11th century*).

The portion of *Va-Yetze'* represented the **emergence** ("going out") of the process of *tikkun 'olam*, **healing our fractured world**. *Va-Yishlaḥ* is a more **advanced** stage where: a) you **inspire others** to this sacred cause—like Jacob, who **sent angels** on his behalf; and b) even the world's most **dysfunctional elements** (Esau) are **healed**.

VA-YISHLAḤ
וישלח

JACOB'S CONFRONTATION WITH ESAU	32:4 – 33:20
DINAH'S ABDUCTION	34:1-31
JACOB'S NAME IS CHANGED	35:1-15
BENJAMIN IS BORN; RACHEL PASSES AWAY	35:16-21
JACOB'S DESCENDANTS	35:22-26
ISAAC PASSES AWAY	35:27-29
ESAU'S DESCENDANTS	36:1-43

NAME
Va-Yishlaḥ

MEANING
"And he sent"

LINES IN TORAH SCROLL
237

PARASHIYYOT
6 open; 3 closed

VERSES
153

WORDS
1976

LETTERS
7458

DATE
2205–2228

LOCATION
Land of Canaan

KEY PEOPLE
Jacob, Esau, Dinah, Shechem, Simeon, Levi, Rachel, Isaac

MITZVOT
1 prohibition

MASORETIC FEATURES
Va-yishakehu (33:4) has six dots above it

CHARACTER PROFILE

NAME
Esau (Edom)

MEANING
"Made"

PARENTS
Isaac and Rebekah

GRANDFATHERS
Bethuel, Abraham

SIBLING
His twin brother Jacob

LIFE SPAN
147 years

WIVES
Adah, Oholibamah and Basemath

CHILDREN
Eliphaz, Reuel, Jeush, Jalam and Korah

BURIAL PLACE
Cave of Machpelah (head), Mount Seir (body)

ACHIEVEMENTS
Honoring his father; was an accomplished hunter; acquired Adam's garments when he killed Nimrod

KNOWN FOR
Was born hairy and with teeth; sold the birthright to Jacob; was given Mount Seir as an inheritance

CONFRONTATION

From Jacob's preparations to meet Esau you can learn the correct approach to take when dealing with a confrontation. First, try to deal positively, as Jacob did by sending gifts, and only if that fails should you engage offensively. And always pray to God to help you (32:4).

INNER BATTLE

Before confronting his brother, Jacob wrestled all night with an angel. The difficulties of your outer life can only be addressed after addressing your own internal struggles (32:25-33).

HUMAN RIGHTS

The people of Shechem ignored the injustice of Dinah's abduction. Simeon and Levi chose an extreme response, as it seemed to be their only option (ch. 34).

וישלח | בראשית לב:ד-ט

׃ וַיִּשְׁלַ֨ח יַעֲקֹ֤ב מַלְאָכִים֙ לְפָנָ֔יו אֶל־עֵשָׂ֖ו אָחִ֑יו אַ֥רְצָה שֵׂעִ֖יר שְׂדֵ֥ה אֱדֽוֹם׃
׃ וַיְצַ֤ו אֹתָם֙ לֵאמֹ֔ר כֹּ֣ה תֹאמְר֔וּן לַֽאדֹנִ֖י לְעֵשָׂ֑ו כֹּ֤ה אָמַר֙ עַבְדְּךָ֣ יַעֲקֹ֔ב עִם־לָבָ֣ן גַּ֔רְתִּי וָאֵחַ֖ר עַד־עָֽתָּה׃ 6 וַֽיְהִי־לִי֙ שׁ֣וֹר וַחֲמ֔וֹר צֹ֖אן וְעֶ֣בֶד וְשִׁפְחָ֑ה וָֽאֶשְׁלְחָה֙ לְהַגִּ֣יד לַֽאדֹנִ֔י לִמְצֹא־חֵ֖ן בְּעֵינֶֽיךָ׃ 7 וַיָּשֻׁ֙בוּ֙ הַמַּלְאָכִ֔ים אֶֽל־יַעֲקֹ֖ב לֵאמֹ֑ר בָּ֤אנוּ אֶל־אָחִ֙יךָ֙ אֶל־עֵשָׂ֔ו וְגַם֙ הֹלֵ֣ךְ לִקְרָֽאתְךָ֔ וְאַרְבַּע־מֵא֥וֹת אִ֖ישׁ עִמּֽוֹ׃ 8 וַיִּירָ֧א יַעֲקֹ֛ב מְאֹ֖ד וַיֵּ֣צֶר ל֑וֹ וַיַּ֜חַץ אֶת־הָעָ֣ם אֲשֶׁר־אִתּ֗וֹ וְאֶת־הַצֹּ֧אן וְאֶת־הַבָּקָ֛ר וְהַגְּמַלִּ֖ים לִשְׁנֵ֥י מַחֲנֽוֹת׃ 9 וַיֹּ֕אמֶר אִם־יָב֥וֹא עֵשָׂ֛ו אֶל־הַֽמַּחֲנֶ֥ה הָאַחַ֖ת וְהִכָּ֑הוּ וְהָיָ֛ה

9. If Esau comes to one camp and strikes it down (then I will fight with him), so the remaining camp will survive. Jacob said, "The remaining camp will survive against Esau's will, for I will wage war with him" (*Rashi, 11th century*).

Jacob was not certain that the second camp would survive. He was merely expressing a hope that perhaps the second camp would flee while the first was being attacked, or that Esau's anger might become subdued after attacking one camp (*Rabbi Abraham ibn Ezra, 12th century*).

Jacob knew that, with God's help, Esau would not obliterate his family entirely. Therefore, he understood that at least one camp would be saved, containing part of his family (*Naḥmanides, 13th century*).

How was Jacob so certain that a part of his family would stay alive? Rebekah had prophesied that Jacob and Esau would die on the same day—*"Why should I be bereaved from both of you on one day?"* (below, 27:45). Jacob therefore reasoned that if Esau managed to kill him together with the first camp, Esau also would be dead by the end of the day. Since the two camps were a day's journey apart, the remaining members of Jacob's family would be free from danger (*Rabbi Abraham Joshua Heschel of Cracow, 17th century*).

Jacob prepared himself for three things: for giving a gift, for war, and for prayer. For giving a gift: *"So the gift passed on ahead of him"* (v. 22). For prayer: *"O God of my father Abraham"* (v. 10). For war: *"The remaining camp will survive"* (*Rashi, 11th century*).

kabbalah bites

32:4 Are you a person of *tohu*: passionate, spontaneous and radical? Or is your character one of *tikkun*: cautious, orderly and predictable?

The Kabbalah teaches that *tikkun* is preferable, because reliability is so crucial in life. But *tikkun* alone can be too dry and lacking in energy, so, in the ideal world, it needs to be charged with *tohu* too.

After many years of carefully building his *tikkun* personality, Jacob thought it was now time to incorporate the approach of *tohu*. So he reached out to his passionate, unpredictable brother with an invitation to join forces.

But the time was not yet ripe.

Only now, at the dawn of the New Era, are we capable of drawing the lights of *tohu* into the vessels of *tikkun*.

genesis 32:4–9 va-yishlaḥ

parashat va-yishlaḥ

Jacob Prepares to Confront Esau

⁴ Jacob sent angels ahead of him to his brother Esau, to the land of Seir, to the fields of Edom. ⁵ He instructed them, saying, "Say the following to my master, to Esau: 'This is what your servant Jacob said, "I have been living with Laban (like a stranger, so there's no need to be jealous of me), and I have been delayed until now. ⁶ I possess oxen, donkeys, flocks, servants and maids (but Father's blessing for 'dew of the heavens and fatness of the earth' has not been fulfilled). I have sent (this message) to tell this to my master (to let you know that I am coming), to find favor in your eyes (since I seek peace with you)."'"

⁷ The angels returned to Jacob, saying, "We came to your brother (but he is still behaving like the wicked) Esau. He is also heading toward you, and four hundred men are with him!"

⁸ Jacob was very worried (that he might be killed) and pained (that he may kill other people too), so he divided the people who were with him, the flocks, the cattle and the camels into two camps. ⁹ He said, "If Esau comes to one camp and strikes it down (then I will fight with him), so the remaining camp will survive."

32:4 Jacob sent angels. Jacob sent Esau actual angels (*Rashi, 11ᵗʰ century*).

Jacob sent actual angels to intimidate him. Esau would wonder, "Is my brother so powerful that he has a host of angels under his control? Surely, I will not be able to overcome him" (*Rabbi Mordecai b. Abraham Jaffe, 16ᵗʰ century*).

5. I have been living with Laban. Two types of spiritual "elevation" are demanded from us.

(a) The "elevation" of the objects found in this physical world by using them for holy purposes. This is achieved both by the observance of the Torah, and by being conscious of God *all* the time, doing everything "for the sake of heaven."

(b) The "elevation" of humanity, leading to the point where *"I will convert the peoples to a pure language that all of them call in the name of God, to worship Him of one accord"* (*Zephaniah* 3:9).

These two phases were also implicit in the life of Jacob. While in Laban's house, Jacob observed the Torah's commandments (*Rashi* to v. 5), corresponding to the first mode of elevation ("a") described above.

Then, Jacob attempted to "elevate" Esau, who represents the remainder of humanity, by sending him angels, gifts and words of appeasement—corresponding to the second kind of elevation ("b").

Only then was Jacob's spiritual mission complete, enabling him to return back to "his father's house" in the land of Israel (*Rabbi Menahem Mendel Schneerson, 20ᵗʰ century*).

7. The angels returned to Jacob. The angels failed in their mission to appease Esau. From here we can learn that all attempts to reconcile a dispute need to be made *in person*, not through messengers or representatives. Even real angels cannot carry out this task for you! (*Rabbi Baruch of Medzibezh, 18ᵗʰ century*).

בראשית לב:ט-יח · וישלח

הַמַּחֲנֶה הַנִּשְׁאָר לִפְלֵיטָה: 10 וַיֹּאמֶר יַעֲקֹב אֱלֹהֵי אָבִי אַבְרָהָם וֵאלֹהֵי אָבִי יִצְחָק יְהֹוָה הָאֹמֵר אֵלַי שׁוּב לְאַרְצְךָ וּלְמוֹלַדְתְּךָ וְאֵיטִיבָה עִמָּךְ: 11 קָטֹנְתִּי מִכֹּל הַחֲסָדִים וּמִכָּל־הָאֱמֶת אֲשֶׁר עָשִׂיתָ אֶת־עַבְדֶּךָ כִּי בְמַקְלִי עָבַרְתִּי אֶת־הַיַּרְדֵּן הַזֶּה וְעַתָּה הָיִיתִי לִשְׁנֵי מַחֲנוֹת: 12 הַצִּילֵנִי נָא מִיַּד אָחִי מִיַּד עֵשָׂו כִּי־יָרֵא אָנֹכִי אֹתוֹ פֶּן־יָבוֹא וְהִכַּנִי אֵם עַל־בָּנִים: 13 וְאַתָּה אָמַרְתָּ הֵיטֵב אֵיטִיב עִמָּךְ וְשַׂמְתִּי אֶת־זַרְעֲךָ כְּחוֹל הַיָּם אֲשֶׁר לֹא־יִסָּפֵר מֵרֹב: [SECOND READING] 14 וַיָּלֶן שָׁם בַּלַּיְלָה הַהוּא וַיִּקַּח מִן־הַבָּא בְיָדוֹ מִנְחָה לְעֵשָׂו אָחִיו: 15 עִזִּים מָאתַיִם וּתְיָשִׁים עֶשְׂרִים רְחֵלִים מָאתַיִם וְאֵילִים עֶשְׂרִים: 16 גְּמַלִּים מֵינִיקוֹת וּבְנֵיהֶם שְׁלֹשִׁים פָּרוֹת אַרְבָּעִים וּפָרִים עֲשָׂרָה אֲתֹנֹת עֶשְׂרִים וַעְיָרִם עֲשָׂרָה: 17 וַיִּתֵּן בְּיַד־עֲבָדָיו עֵדֶר עֵדֶר לְבַדּוֹ וַיֹּאמֶר אֶל־עֲבָדָיו עִבְרוּ לְפָנַי וְרֶוַח תָּשִׂימוּ בֵּין עֵדֶר וּבֵין עֵדֶר: 18 וַיְצַו אֶת־הָרִאשׁוֹן לֵאמֹר כִּי יִפְגָּשְׁךָ עֵשָׂו אָחִי וּשְׁאֵלְךָ

Why did Jacob say that he was "small"? He meant: "My merits have diminished because of all the kindness that You have done for me. I fear that perhaps I have become soiled by sin since You made those promises to me, and this will cause me to be delivered into Esau's hand" (*Rashi, 11th century*).

A perfectly pious individual is not static; he constantly grows spiritually from one level to the next. After reaching a higher level, his previous actions are spiritually deficient compared to his current standing. They are considered as "sins," metaphorically speaking (*Rabbi Ḥayyim b. Joseph Vital, 16th–17th century*).

12. Save me from the hand of my (so-called) brother, from the hand of Esau. Why did Jacob pray that God would save him from *"the hand of my brother,"* and then again, from *"the hand of Esau"*?

Jacob's meeting with Esau could have ended in one of two ways, both of which concerned Jacob. If Esau came as a "brother" and befriended Jacob's household, he could have influenced them to follow his depraved ways. If he came as "Esau" and attacked Jacob's family, there could have been many casualties. So Jacob prayed to God to save him from either scenario: *"my brother"* and *"Esau."*

God fulfilled both of Jacob's requests. Jacob's family was saved from bloodshed, and then, immediately after their encounter, *"Esau went back to Seir"* (33:16), sparing them from his negative influence (*Rabbi Joseph Baer Soloveichik of Volozhin, 19th century*).

¹⁰ Jacob said, "O God of my father Abraham and God of my father Isaac! God, who said to me, 'Return to the land of your forefathers, to your birthplace, and I will be with you'! ¹¹ (My merits) have become small due to all the acts of kindness and the true (fulfillment of all Your promises) that You have done for Your servant, (so I fear that I've lost the merit to be saved from Esau)—for (when) I crossed this (river) Jordan, I (only) had my stick, and now I have amassed two camps. ¹² Please save me from the hand of my (so-called) brother, from the hand of Esau, for I am afraid of him. He might come and strike me, (and even) a mother with (her) children. ¹³ You said, 'I will do good to you (in your own merit and) I will do good (in the merit of your forefathers), and I will make your descendants as the sands of the sea, which cannot be counted because of their great number.'"

[SECOND READING] ¹⁴ He slept there that night.

(As a further preparation) he took a gift from his possessions for his brother Esau: ¹⁵ two hundred female goats, twenty male goats, two hundred ewes and twenty rams, ¹⁶ thirty nursing camels with their young, forty cows, ten bulls, twenty female donkeys and ten male donkeys. ¹⁷ He gave each (species in its own) herd separately into the hands of his servants.

He said to his servants, "Pass on ahead of me (about one day's distance) and make a space (no more than the eye can see) between one herd and another herd (so that Esau appreciates the size of the gift)."

¹⁸ He instructed the first (group), saying, "When my brother Esau encounters you and questions you, saying, 'Whose property are you? Where are you

---

10. God of my father Isaac! God, who said to me, etc. But above, the verse states, "the (One whom) Isaac *feared*" (31:42). And why did Jacob repeat the Tetragrammaton? The verse should have stated, *"God of my father Isaac, who said to me, etc.,"* (omitting the extra word "God").

This is what Jacob said to God. You gave me two promises: First, when I left my father's house in Beer-sheba, when You said, *"I am God, the God of Abraham your father, and the God of Isaac"* (28:13), You said to me, *"I will guard you wherever you go"* (ibid., v. 15). Second, in Laban's house You said to me, *"Return to the land of your forefathers, to your birthplace, and I will be with you"* (31:3). There You revealed Yourself to me with the Tetragrammaton alone, as the verse states, *"God said to Jacob, 'Return, etc.'"*

The extra Tetragrammaton in our verse hints to this second promise. Jacob said, "With these two promises I am coming before You..." (*Rashi, 11th century*).

11. (My merits) have become small. When God shows His kindness to you, it brings you closer to God, causing your feelings of self-importance to diminish, *since everything is like nothing before God.*

It was *because* God had been so kind to Jacob, that Jacob became small in his own eyes—for the kindness brought him closer to God, so he felt that he was not worthy of God's promise to be saved (*Rabbi Shneur Zalman of Lyady, 18th century*).

בראשית לב:יח-כו · וישלח

לֵאמֹר לְמִי־אַתָּה וְאָנָה תֵלֵךְ וּלְמִי אֵלֶּה לְפָנֶיךָ: 19 וְאָמַרְתָּ לְעַבְדְּךָ לְיַעֲקֹב מִנְחָה הִוא שְׁלוּחָה לַאדֹנִי לְעֵשָׂו וְהִנֵּה גַם־הוּא אַחֲרֵינוּ: 20 וַיְצַו גַּם אֶת־הַשֵּׁנִי גַּם אֶת־הַשְּׁלִישִׁי גַּם אֶת־כָּל־הַהֹלְכִים אַחֲרֵי הָעֲדָרִים לֵאמֹר כַּדָּבָר הַזֶּה תְּדַבְּרוּן אֶל־עֵשָׂו בְּמֹצַאֲכֶם אֹתוֹ: 21 וַאֲמַרְתֶּם גַּם הִנֵּה עַבְדְּךָ יַעֲקֹב אַחֲרֵינוּ כִּי־אָמַר אֲכַפְּרָה פָנָיו בַּמִּנְחָה הַהֹלֶכֶת לְפָנָי וְאַחֲרֵי־כֵן אֶרְאֶה פָנָיו אוּלַי יִשָּׂא פָנָי: 22 וַתַּעֲבֹר הַמִּנְחָה עַל־פָּנָיו וְהוּא לָן בַּלַּיְלָה־הַהוּא בַּמַּחֲנֶה: 23 וַיָּקָם | בַּלַּיְלָה הוּא וַיִּקַּח אֶת־שְׁתֵּי נָשָׁיו וְאֶת־שְׁתֵּי שִׁפְחֹתָיו וְאֶת־אַחַד עָשָׂר יְלָדָיו וַיַּעֲבֹר אֵת מַעֲבַר יַבֹּק: 24 וַיִּקָּחֵם וַיַּעֲבִרֵם אֶת־הַנָּחַל וַיַּעֲבֵר אֶת־אֲשֶׁר־לוֹ: 25 וַיִּוָּתֵר יַעֲקֹב לְבַדּוֹ וַיֵּאָבֵק אִישׁ עִמּוֹ עַד עֲלוֹת הַשָּׁחַר: 26 וַיַּרְא כִּי לֹא יָכֹל לוֹ וַיִּגַּע בְּכַף־יְרֵכוֹ וַתֵּקַע כַּף־יֶרֶךְ יַעֲקֹב בְּהֵאָבְקוֹ עִמּוֹ:

There are other generations in which they have done to us such things as these, and even worse, but we have endured and it has passed by us. This is hinted to by the verse, *"Jacob came to the city of Shechem—which is in the land of Canaan—perfect (in health, wealth and Torah knowledge)"* (33:18; *Nahmanides, 13th century*).

The fact that Jacob was later healed *completely* indicates that when the Exile finally ends there will be no remnant *whatsoever* of Jewish suffering. In other words, the key emphasis here in Jacob's battle with the angel is not the injury that Jacob suffered, but the fact that it was only a *temporary* injury.

When we observe the prohibition against eating the sciatic nerve, our emphasis too should be a positive one. Rather than focusing on Jacob's *injury* to the sciatic nerve, we should stress the fact that later he was *totally healed*, representing the ability of a Jew to withstand all the tribulations of exile and emerge unblemished (*Rabbi Menahem Mendel Schneerson, 20th century*).

kabbalah bites

32:25 *"A man wrestled with him."* Jacob was the most perfect of the Patriarchs. Abraham and Isaac both had errant children, pointing to subtle imperfections in their own personalities, but Jacob had a "full complement" of righteous children.

Since Jacob's perfection posed the greatest threat to the *kelippot* (demonic forces), they attacked him here with full force. Jacob's near perfect holiness almost defeated the *kelippot*—but they managed to catch him on his leg, an external organ.

Later, this spiritual battle would re-emerge as the war against Amalek (*Exodus* 17:18ff.).

going? Whose property are these (animals) in front of you?' ¹⁹ You should say, '(We belong) to your servant Jacob. This is a gift sent to my master, to Esau, and—look!—(Jacob) himself is (coming right) behind us.'"

²⁰ He also instructed the second (group), the third (group), and all those who followed the herds, saying, "This is how you should speak to Esau when you meet him. ²¹ You should also say, 'Look, your servant Jacob is behind us.'" For (Jacob) said (to himself), "I'll appease his anger with the gift that is going ahead of me, and afterwards I'll see him face(-to-face). Perhaps he'll accept me."

²² So the gift passed on ahead of him, and he slept that night in the camp.

²³ (During) that night he got up, and he took his two wives, his two maids and his eleven children (together with Dinah, who was hidden in a chest), and crossed the shallow part of (the river) Jabbok. ²⁴ He took them and brought them across the stream. He (went backwards and forwards and) took across everything he had.

Jacob Fights with Esau's Guardian Angel

²⁵ Jacob (forgot some small jars, and went back for them. He) was left alone. (Esau's guardian angel, appearing as) a man, wrestled with him until the break of dawn.

²⁶ When he saw that he could not prevail against (Jacob), he touched the joint of his hip. As he wrestled with him, the socket of Jacob's hip became dislocated.

---

23. His eleven children. Where was Dinah? Jacob put her into a chest and locked her in, so that Esau would not set eyes on her.

Jacob was wrong for withholding her from his brother, for perhaps she would have made a decent person of him. That is why she ended up falling into the hands of Shechem (*Rashi, 11ᵗʰ century*).

25. (Esau's guardian angel, appearing as) a man, wrestled with him. The angel appeared to Jacob as a pagan idol-worshiper. Or perhaps the angel appeared as a Torah sage (*Babylonian Talmud, Ḥullin* 91a).

The two Talmudic views of how the guardian angel of Esau manifested itself allude to two different manifestations of the *yetzer ha-ra'* (impulse to evil). The "idol-worshiper" is the overt *yetzer ha-ra'* for physical pleasures. The "sage" represents the covert actions of the *yetzer ha-ra'* to entice a person with arguments which appear, superficially, to be legitimate (*Rabbi Abraham Bornstein of Sochaczew, 19ᵗʰ century*).

26. He touched the joint of his hip. This entire event constitutes a hint to his descendants, indicating that there will be a generation from the seed of Jacob against whom Esau will prevail, almost uprooting them. This occurred during the era of the Mishnaic sages, during the generation of Rabbi Judah son of Bava and his colleagues (117-138 c.e.).

בראשית לב:כז-לא

27 וַיֹּאמֶר שַׁלְּחֵנִי כִּי עָלָה הַשָּׁחַר וַיֹּאמֶר לֹא אֲשַׁלֵּחֲךָ כִּי אִם־בֵּרַכְתָּנִי: 28 וַיֹּאמֶר אֵלָיו מַה־שְּׁמֶךָ וַיֹּאמֶר יַעֲקֹב: 29 וַיֹּאמֶר לֹא יַעֲקֹב יֵאָמֵר עוֹד שִׁמְךָ כִּי אִם־יִשְׂרָאֵל כִּי־שָׂרִיתָ עִם־אֱלֹהִים וְעִם־אֲנָשִׁים וַתּוּכָל: 30 וַיִּשְׁאַל יַעֲקֹב וַיֹּאמֶר הַגִּידָה־נָּא שְׁמֶךָ וַיֹּאמֶר לָמָּה זֶּה תִּשְׁאַל לִשְׁמִי וַיְבָרֶךְ אֹתוֹ שָׁם: [THIRD READING]

31 וַיִּקְרָא יַעֲקֹב שֵׁם הַמָּקוֹם פְּנִיאֵל כִּי־רָאִיתִי אֱלֹהִים פָּנִים אֶל־פָּנִים וַתִּנָּצֵל

So Jacob said, "I will not let you go unless you bless me," attempting to ensure that, after the suffering, there would not only be quietude, but also, some progress and salvation from God (*Rabbi Kalonymous Kalman Shapira, 20th century*).

29. Your name will no longer be called Jacob ... but rather, Israel. Changing your name can annul an unfavorable heavenly decree. If there had been a decree that Esau would subjugate Jacob, God reassured Jacob, "since you will no longer be Jacob and your name will be Israel, you can feel safe" (*Rabbi Levi b. Gershom, 14th century*).

The names "Jacob" and "Israel," which we have all inherited, refer to the body and the soul respectively. You need to spiritually rectify your body so that the power of your soul can dwell in it. Then you deserve to be called "Israel."

The human soul is on a higher level than an angel; but an angel's "body" surpasses that of a human. Jacob had rectified his body to such a great extent that it became a direct channel which expressed the Divine—his body was like a soul. Therefore he was able to struggle with an angel *even with his physical self*.

God said, "*Your name will no longer be called Jacob*"—even though man's body is called "Jacob," in your case, it is no longer a normal, selfish body, but more like a selfless spirit (*Rabbi Judah Aryeh Leib Alter of Gur, 19th century*).

You have fought with (an angel of) God and with (Laban and Esau), and you have overcome (them). The Hebrew word here for "fought" is *sar*, which can also mean "lord." The angel was intimating: "You were a lord at the very outset, and that is why you were victorious. Before the battle had started you had already won, because you ruled over your spirits and never allowed them to fall. Even in difficult times you were still, within yourself, a lord" (*Rabbi Kalonymous Kalman Shapira, 20th century*).

31-32. Jacob named the place Peniel ... when he passed Penuel. Only Jacob *himself* called the place Peniel. Thus when the Torah mentions the place in verse 32 it changes the name to Penuel (*Rabbi Ḥayyim ibn Attar, 18th century*).

Of the different levels of angels, the tenth level is called an *'ish*, "man" (*Maimonides*). This is the term with which the Torah refers to the angel that fought with Jacob (v. 25).

In Hebrew, the difference between Peniel and Penuel is that the former contains the letter *yod* where the latter has a *vav*. When Jacob was fighting the angel, and his mind was fixed in the spiritual realms, he called the place Peniel with a *yod*, hinting to his involvement with the angel of the tenth level (*yod*=ten). However, later when he came back "down to earth" he changed the *yod* for a *vav* (=six), representing the physical world which is manifested in the six directions: north, south, west, east, up and down (*Rabbi Bahya b. Asher, 13th century*).

genesis 32:27–31 va-yishlaḥ

²⁷ (The angel) said, "Let me go, for the morning has arrived (and I must recite songs of praise)."

(Jacob) said, "I will not let you go unless you (consent to the) blessing (which Esau is grieved that my father gave) me."

²⁸ (The angel) said to him, "What is your name?"

"Jacob," he said.

²⁹ "(Please be patient!)" he said, "(God will reveal Himself to you in Bethel, and then) your name will no longer be called Jacob [*yaʿAKoV*] (which denotes trickery [*ʿAKeVah*] and deceit), but rather, Israel [*yiSRaʾel*] (suggesting that the blessings were authorized [*be-SeRarah*]), because you have fought with (an angel of) God and with (Laban and Esau), and you have overcome (them. I will be there too, and I will consent to your blessing then.)"

³⁰ Jacob questioned him and said, "Tell me your name."

He said, "Why is it that you ask for my name? (We angels simply don't have a fixed name)."

(Jacob persisted that the angel consent to his blessings. Eventually the angel conceded) and he blessed him there.

[THIRD READING] ³¹ Jacob named the place Peniel ("God's face"), "because I saw God face to face, and my soul was saved."

27. I will not let you go unless you bless me. Why did Jacob feel it so important to be blessed by a mere angel when he had a direct blessing from God Himself (above, 28:13-15)?

When the angel began to leave, Jacob said, "Can this be it? Will this be the fate of my children? When they have suffered all the pain inflicted on them, is their whole victory to be *that they survived*? Will they simply revert to the same state prior to all their suffering?"

spiritual vitamin

> Jacob was given the additional name "Israel" after he had *"fought with an angel of God and with men, and prevailed"* (v. 29). The experience of Jacob reflects Jewish experience throughout the ages, on the individual as well as communal levels.
>
> Expect to meet challenges by adversaries, whether in the guise of angels (including your inner demons) or humans, who attempt to place obstacles in Jacob's going "on *his* way" (v. 2). Far from being discouraged or sidetracked by such obstacles, you should rise to the challenge with absolute determination—and then you are assured of victory.

בראשית לב:לא - לג:ז   וישלח

32 נַפְשִׁי: וַיִּזְרַח־לוֹ הַשֶּׁמֶשׁ כַּאֲשֶׁר עָבַר אֶת־פְּנוּאֵל וְהוּא צֹלֵעַ עַל־יְרֵכוֹ:
33 עַל־כֵּן לֹא־יֹאכְלוּ בְנֵי־יִשְׂרָאֵל אֶת־גִּיד הַנָּשֶׁה אֲשֶׁר עַל־כַּף הַיָּרֵךְ עַד הַיּוֹם הַזֶּה כִּי נָגַע בְּכַף־יֶרֶךְ יַעֲקֹב בְּגִיד הַנָּשֶׁה:

לג 1 וַיִּשָּׂא יַעֲקֹב עֵינָיו וַיַּרְא וְהִנֵּה עֵשָׂו בָּא וְעִמּוֹ אַרְבַּע מֵאוֹת אִישׁ וַיַּחַץ אֶת־הַיְלָדִים עַל־לֵאָה וְעַל־רָחֵל וְעַל שְׁתֵּי הַשְּׁפָחוֹת: 2 וַיָּשֶׂם אֶת־הַשְּׁפָחוֹת וְאֶת־יַלְדֵיהֶן רִאשֹׁנָה וְאֶת־לֵאָה וִילָדֶיהָ אַחֲרֹנִים וְאֶת־רָחֵל וְאֶת־יוֹסֵף אַחֲרֹנִים: 3 וְהוּא עָבַר לִפְנֵיהֶם וַיִּשְׁתַּחוּ אַרְצָה שֶׁבַע פְּעָמִים עַד־גִּשְׁתּוֹ עַד־אָחִיו: 4 וַיָּרָץ עֵשָׂו לִקְרָאתוֹ וַיְחַבְּקֵהוּ וַיִּפֹּל עַל־צַוָּארָו וַיִּשָּׁקֵהוּ וַיִּבְכּוּ: 5 וַיִּשָּׂא אֶת־עֵינָיו וַיַּרְא אֶת־הַנָּשִׁים וְאֶת־הַיְלָדִים וַיֹּאמֶר מִי־אֵלֶּה לָּךְ וַיֹּאמַר הַיְלָדִים אֲשֶׁר־חָנַן אֱלֹהִים אֶת־עַבְדֶּךָ: 6 [FOURTH READING] וַתִּגַּשְׁןָ הַשְּׁפָחוֹת הֵנָּה וְיַלְדֵיהֶן וַתִּשְׁתַּחֲוֶיןָ: 7 וַתִּגַּשׁ גַּם־לֵאָה וִילָדֶיהָ וַיִּשְׁתַּחֲווּ וְאַחַר נִגַּשׁ

demonic forces of evil take hold, which is why they prevailed historically at this time—both first and second Temples were destroyed, Betar was defeated, and Jerusalem was ploughed over.

Its diametric opposite point in time is the Day of Atonement, the most holy and elevated day of the year, when the Satan has no power to rise in accusation (*Rabbi Menaḥem Naḥum Twersky of Chernobyl, 18th century*).

33:4 Embraced him. Esau embraced Jacob because his compassion was aroused when he saw Jacob prostrate himself all those times (*Rashi, 11th century*).

He kissed him. In the Torah scroll, there are dots over the word *va-yishakehu* ("and he kissed him"), and there is a difference of opinion about this matter in the *Midrash*. Some interpret the dots to mean that Esau did not kiss him wholeheartedly. Rabbi Simeon son of Yoḥai said, "The fact that Esau hates Jacob is obvious and incontrovertible, like a legal ruling. However, at that moment Esau's feelings of compassion were aroused, and he kissed him wholeheartedly" (*Rashi, 11th century*).

> **kabbalah bites**
>
> **32:33** *"The children of Israel may not eat…"* This phrase is followed by the Hebrew particle, *et* (*alef-tav*), an abbreviation for *Tish'ah* (9th) *be-'Av*.
>
> The Ninth of Av, when both the First and Second Temples were destroyed, is a date on which the strength of the *kelippot* (demonic forces) predominates, so it is alluded to here, when the *kelippot* had a partial victory over Jacob.

genesis 32:32 – 33:7 va-yishlaḥ

³² When he passed Penuel, the sun rose for him, and he was limping on his thigh.

❖ ³³ Consequently, to this day, the children of Israel may not eat the sciatic nerve (of an animal) which (arises) by the hip joint, because (the angel) touched the joint of Jacob's hip at the sciatic nerve.

Jacob Confronts Esau

33 ¹ Jacob looked around to see, and—look!—Esau was coming, and four hundred men were with him! So (Jacob) divided the children among Leah, Rachel and the two maids. ² He placed the maids and their children first, Leah and her children behind (because they were more cherished), and Rachel with Joseph last (because they were most cherished).

³ He went ahead of them (to protect them) and prostrated himself (progressively) on the ground seven times, until he approached his brother. ⁴ (This aroused Esau's compassion, so) Esau ran toward him and embraced him. He fell on (Jacob's) neck and kissed him, and they wept.

⁵ (Esau) looked around and saw the women and the children. He said, "How are these (people related) to you?"

(Jacob) said, "(They are) the children whom God has graciously given your servant."

[FOURTH READING] ⁶ The maids approached (Esau, both) they and their children, and they prostrated themselves. ⁷ Leah and her children approached and prostrated themselves, and afterwards, Joseph and Rachel approached and prostrated themselves.

---

32. He was limping on his thigh. Included in the original privileges of the firstborn were the duties of sacrificial service. Esau was extremely resentful at having lost this to Jacob in a moment of weakness, by selling his birthright.

That is why the angel attacked Jacob on his way to meet his brother: to injure Jacob sufficiently to disqualify him from priestly service. The sight of a now-limping Jacob, who clearly could not serve as a priest, would help to neutralize Esau's anger at their pending reunion (*Rabbi Baruch Epstein, 19th–20th century*).

33. Consequently, to this day, the children of Israel may not eat the sciatic nerve. *Earth, time,* and the human *soul* are all constituted the same way, in the image of the human body. Each of them contains the equivalent of the two hundred forty-eight "limbs" and the three hundred sixty-five "sinews" of the body. Thus, in reference to the *earth* we find such bodily expressions as the "navel" of the earth (*Ezekiel* 38:12), the "mouth" of the earth (*Numbers* 26:10), the "nakedness" of the earth (below, 42:9). In the case of *time*, each of the three hundred and sixty-five days of the year represents a particular "sinew."

Among the days of the year, it is the ninth of *Av* that corresponds to the "sciatic nerve," in the bodily representation of time (see *"Kabbalah Bites,"* opposite). This is the moment where the

בראשית לג:ז-יט
וישלח

יוֹסֵף וְרָחֵל וַיִּשְׁתַּחֲוּוּ: 8 וַיֹּאמֶר מִי לְךָ כָּל־הַמַּחֲנֶה הַזֶּה אֲשֶׁר פָּגָשְׁתִּי וַיֹּאמֶר לִמְצֹא־חֵן בְּעֵינֵי אֲדֹנִי: 9 וַיֹּאמֶר עֵשָׂו יֶשׁ־לִי רָב אָחִי יְהִי לְךָ אֲשֶׁר־לָךְ: 10 וַיֹּאמֶר יַעֲקֹב אַל־נָא אִם־נָא מָצָאתִי חֵן בְּעֵינֶיךָ וְלָקַחְתָּ מִנְחָתִי מִיָּדִי כִּי עַל־כֵּן רָאִיתִי פָנֶיךָ כִּרְאֹת פְּנֵי אֱלֹהִים וַתִּרְצֵנִי: 11 קַח־נָא אֶת־בִּרְכָתִי אֲשֶׁר הֻבָאת לָךְ כִּי־חַנַּנִי אֱלֹהִים וְכִי יֶשׁ־לִי־כֹל וַיִּפְצַר־בּוֹ וַיִּקָּח: 12 וַיֹּאמֶר נִסְעָה וְנֵלֵכָה וְאֵלְכָה לְנֶגְדֶּךָ: 13 וַיֹּאמֶר אֵלָיו אֲדֹנִי יֹדֵעַ כִּי־הַיְלָדִים רַכִּים וְהַצֹּאן וְהַבָּקָר עָלוֹת עָלָי וּדְפָקוּם יוֹם אֶחָד וָמֵתוּ כָּל־הַצֹּאן: 14 יַעֲבָר־נָא אֲדֹנִי לִפְנֵי עַבְדּוֹ וַאֲנִי אֶתְנָהֲלָה לְאִטִּי לְרֶגֶל הַמְּלָאכָה אֲשֶׁר־לְפָנַי וּלְרֶגֶל הַיְלָדִים עַד אֲשֶׁר־אָבֹא אֶל־אֲדֹנִי שֵׂעִירָה: 15 וַיֹּאמֶר עֵשָׂו אַצִּיגָה־נָּא עִמְּךָ מִן־הָעָם אֲשֶׁר אִתִּי וַיֹּאמֶר לָמָּה זֶּה אֶמְצָא־חֵן בְּעֵינֵי אֲדֹנִי: 16 וַיָּשָׁב בַּיּוֹם הַהוּא עֵשָׂו לְדַרְכּוֹ שֵׂעִירָה: 17 וְיַעֲקֹב נָסַע סֻכֹּתָה וַיִּבֶן לוֹ בָּיִת וּלְמִקְנֵהוּ עָשָׂה סֻכֹּת עַל־כֵּן קָרָא שֵׁם־הַמָּקוֹם סֻכּוֹת: ס 18 וַיָּבֹא יַעֲקֹב שָׁלֵם עִיר שְׁכֶם אֲשֶׁר בְּאֶרֶץ כְּנַעַן בְּבֹאוֹ מִפַּדַּן אֲרָם וַיִּחַן אֶת־פְּנֵי הָעִיר: 19 וַיִּקֶן אֶת־חֶלְקַת הַשָּׂדֶה

9. Esau said, "I have plenty." Here we can see a clear distinction between Jacob and Esau. Esau boasted, *"I have plenty,"* while Jacob responded, *"I have everything (I need)"* (v. 11). The wicked always lust for more and more, and the righteous are content with whatever they have (*Rabbi Ephraim of Luntshits, 16th–17th century*).

14. Please go ahead ... until I come (and meet) my master at (our final destination of) Seir. We have searched through all of Scripture and we have not found that Jacob ever went to Mount Seir! Could it be that Jacob, who was such a truthful person, deceived him?

Actually, he was truthful, for Esau will come to him in the future—*"Deliverers will go up on Mount Zion to judge the Mount of Esau"* (Obadiah 1:21; *Genesis Rabbah*).

18. Jacob came to the city of Shechem ... whole. Jacob was physically whole, for he was cured of his limp; financially whole, for he had not diminished in assets after the gift to

food for thought

1. Do you have *plenty*? Or do you have *everything* you need?

2. Why do we let our materialistic drives overcome us?

3. How much do you define your worth by material success levels?

genesis 33:8–19   va-yishlaḥ

⁸ (Esau) said, "What was your (idea of) this whole entourage that I met?"

"To find favor in my master's eyes," said Jacob.

⁹ Esau said, "I have plenty (more than I need). My brother, you can keep what is yours."

¹⁰ Jacob said, "Please don't (say that). If indeed I have now found favor in your eyes, then take my gift from my hand."

(Jacob intimidated Esau by saying, "You deserve the gift simply) because I have seen your face, which is like seeing the face of (an angel of) God, (for I have indeed seen your guardian angel)—and you have been appeased by me. ¹¹ Please take my gift, which has been brought to you (through tremendous effort), for God has favored me, and I have everything (I need)."

(Jacob) urged him, and he took it.

¹² (Esau) said, "Set off and we'll go (together). I will go alongside you (as slowly as you want)."

¹³ (Jacob) said to him, "My master knows that the children are tender. The flocks and the cattle, (which) are raising their young, depend upon me. If they push them too hard one day, all the flocks will die. ¹⁴ Let my master please go ahead (at his own pace) before his servant, and I will move at my own slow pace—according to the pace of the (animal) workforce (that I'm responsible for), and according to the pace of the children—until I come (and meet) my master at (our final destination of) Seir."

¹⁵ Esau said, "Please let me station with you some of the men that are with me."

"Why is that (necessary)?" (Jacob) said. "May I find favor in my master's eyes (and don't pay me anything)."

¹⁶ On that day, Esau went back to Seir, his usual hang-out, (alone).

¹⁷ Jacob traveled to Succoth and built himself a house. He made huts [*sukkot*] for his cattle—therefore he named the place Succoth.

¹⁸ (After eighteen months) on his way from Paddan-aram, Jacob came to the city of Shechem—which is in the land of Canaan—whole (in health, wealth and Torah knowledge), and he encamped in front of the city. ¹⁹ He bought the part of the

spiritual vitamin

> If you were perfect and had achieved everything, there would be nothing else to live for. There must remain some lack or imperfection so that you will have something to strive for tomorrow.

בראשית לג:יט - לד:יב

וישלח

אֲשֶׁר נָטָה־שָׁם אָהֳלוֹ מִיַּד בְּנֵי־חֲמוֹר אֲבִי שְׁכֶם בְּמֵאָה קְשִׂיטָה: 20 וַיַּצֶּב־שָׁם מִזְבֵּחַ וַיִּקְרָא־לוֹ אֵל אֱלֹהֵי יִשְׂרָאֵל: ס

לד

1 [FIFTH READING] וַתֵּצֵא דִינָה בַּת־לֵאָה אֲשֶׁר יָלְדָה לְיַעֲקֹב לִרְאוֹת בִּבְנוֹת הָאָרֶץ: 2 וַיַּרְא אֹתָהּ שְׁכֶם בֶּן־חֲמוֹר הַחִוִּי נְשִׂיא הָאָרֶץ וַיִּקַּח אֹתָהּ וַיִּשְׁכַּב אֹתָהּ וַיְעַנֶּהָ: 3 וַתִּדְבַּק נַפְשׁוֹ בְּדִינָה בַּת־יַעֲקֹב וַיֶּאֱהַב אֶת־הַנַּעֲרָ וַיְדַבֵּר עַל־לֵב הַנַּעֲרָ: 4 וַיֹּאמֶר שְׁכֶם אֶל־חֲמוֹר אָבִיו לֵאמֹר קַח־לִי אֶת־הַיַּלְדָּה הַזֹּאת לְאִשָּׁה: 5 וְיַעֲקֹב שָׁמַע כִּי טִמֵּא אֶת־דִּינָה בִתּוֹ וּבָנָיו הָיוּ אֶת־מִקְנֵהוּ בַּשָּׂדֶה וְהֶחֱרִשׁ יַעֲקֹב עַד־בֹּאָם: 6 וַיֵּצֵא חֲמוֹר אֲבִי־שְׁכֶם אֶל־יַעֲקֹב לְדַבֵּר אִתּוֹ: 7 וּבְנֵי יַעֲקֹב בָּאוּ מִן־הַשָּׂדֶה כְּשָׁמְעָם וַיִּתְעַצְּבוּ הָאֲנָשִׁים וַיִּחַר לָהֶם מְאֹד כִּי־נְבָלָה עָשָׂה בְיִשְׂרָאֵל לִשְׁכַּב אֶת־בַּת־יַעֲקֹב וְכֵן לֹא יֵעָשֶׂה: 8 וַיְדַבֵּר חֲמוֹר אִתָּם לֵאמֹר שְׁכֶם בְּנִי חָשְׁקָה נַפְשׁוֹ בְּבִתְּכֶם תְּנוּ נָא אֹתָהּ לוֹ לְאִשָּׁה: 9 וְהִתְחַתְּנוּ אֹתָנוּ בְּנֹתֵיכֶם תִּתְּנוּ־לָנוּ וְאֶת־בְּנֹתֵינוּ תִּקְחוּ לָכֶם: 10 וְאִתָּנוּ תֵּשֵׁבוּ וְהָאָרֶץ תִּהְיֶה לִפְנֵיכֶם שְׁבוּ וּסְחָרוּהָ וְהֵאָחֲזוּ בָּהּ: 11 וַיֹּאמֶר שְׁכֶם אֶל־אָבִיהָ וְאֶל־אַחֶיהָ אֶמְצָא־חֵן בְּעֵינֵיכֶם וַאֲשֶׁר תֹּאמְרוּ אֵלַי אֶתֵּן: 12 הַרְבּוּ עָלַי מְאֹד

guard in all matters of modesty, it is crucial that Jewish women spend time outside the home, utilizing their God-given talents for the sake of heaven (*Rabbi Menahem Mendel Schneerson, 20th century*).

kabbalah bites

34:8 *"My son Shechem's soul yearns for your daughter."* After the sin of the Tree of Knowledge, sparks of Adam's soul became trapped by the *kelippot* (demonic forces). The soul of Shechem was such a spark, which is why he yearned to be reunited with his soul-root by attaching himself to Jacob's daughter, for Jacob was a reincarnation of Adam.

When Shechem circumcised, he achieved his *tikkun* (spiritual healing), shortly before his death.

field where he had pitched his tent from the sons of Hamor, Shechem's father, for one hundred *kesitah*. ²⁰ He erected an altar there, and (to commemorate the miracle of his salvation) he named it: El-elohe-yisrael ("God (is the) God of Israel)."

Dinah and Shechem

34 [FIFTH READING] ¹ Dinah—Leah's daughter, whom she had borne to Jacob—went out to observe the daughters of the land. ² Shechem—the son of Hamor the Hivite, prince of the land—saw her. He took her, lay with her, and violated her.

³ His soul cleaved to Dinah, Jacob's daughter. He loved the girl. He spoke to the girl's heart (telling her how much wealth he had, more than Jacob).

⁴ Shechem spoke to his father, Hamor, saying, "Take this girl for me as a wife."

⁵ While his sons were with his flocks in the field, Jacob heard that (Shechem) had defiled his daughter Dinah. Jacob kept silent, (waiting) until they came (home).

⁶ Hamor, Shechem's father, went off to Jacob to speak with him.

⁷ When they heard (the news), Jacob's sons came (home) from the field. The men were distressed and extremely angry, for (Shechem) had committed a disgraceful act in Israel, to lie with a daughter of Jacob. Such (acts) were not done (even by the nations, at that time).

⁸ Hamor spoke with them, saying, "My son Shechem's soul yearns for your daughter. Please give her to him for a wife. ⁹ (Your whole family can) marry with us: give your daughters to us, and take our daughters for yourselves. ¹⁰ Live with us! The land will be (free) before you. Settle (in it), do business in it and buy property in it."

¹¹ Shechem said to (Dinah's) father and to her brothers, "May I find favor in your eyes. Whatever you tell me I will give! ¹² Impose upon me a large dowry and gifts and I'll give whatever you ask me. (Just) give me the girl for a wife."

Esau; and whole in his Torah knowledge, which he had not forgotten in Laban's house (*Rashi, 11ᵗʰ century*).

34:1 Dinah, Leah's daughter ... went out. Because she *"went out"* to observe the daughters of the land she was called "Leah's daughter," since Leah too was outgoing, as the verse states, *"Leah came out towards him"* (30:16). About her, they coined the saying, "Like mother, like daughter" (*Rashi, 11ᵗʰ century*).

From Dinah's conduct we can learn that Jewish women who are blessed with a God-given ability to influence others positively should make sure to use their talents productively outside the home as well. Of course, a Jewish woman must always maintain an air of modesty, and even when she is outside the home it should be recognizable in her actions that *"the entire glory of the king's daughter is within"* (*Psalms* 45:14). Nevertheless, while retaining the utmost

בראשית לד:יב-כט

מֹ֤הַר וּמַתָּ֗ן וְאֶתְּנָה֙ כַּאֲשֶׁ֣ר תֹּאמְר֣וּ אֵלָ֔י וּתְנוּ־לִ֥י אֶת־הַֽנַּעֲרָ֖ לְאִשָּֽׁה׃ 13 וַיַּעֲנ֨וּ בְנֵֽי־יַעֲקֹ֜ב אֶת־שְׁכֶ֨ם וְאֶת־חֲמ֥וֹר אָבִ֛יו בְּמִרְמָ֖ה וַיְדַבֵּ֑רוּ אֲשֶׁ֣ר טִמֵּ֔א אֵ֖ת דִּינָ֥ה אֲחֹתָֽם׃ 14 וַיֹּאמְר֣וּ אֲלֵיהֶ֗ם לֹ֤א נוּכַל֙ לַעֲשׂוֹת֙ הַדָּבָ֣ר הַזֶּ֔ה לָתֵת֙ אֶת־אֲחֹתֵ֔נוּ לְאִ֖ישׁ אֲשֶׁר־ל֣וֹ עָרְלָ֑ה כִּֽי־חֶרְפָּ֥ה הִ֖וא לָֽנוּ׃ 15 אַךְ־בְּזֹ֖את נֵא֣וֹת לָכֶ֑ם אִ֚ם תִּהְי֣וּ כָמֹ֔נוּ לְהִמֹּ֥ל לָכֶ֖ם כָּל־זָכָֽר׃ 16 וְנָתַ֤נּוּ אֶת־בְּנֹתֵ֙ינוּ֙ לָכֶ֔ם וְאֶת־בְּנֹתֵיכֶ֖ם נִֽקַּֽח־לָ֑נוּ וְיָשַׁ֣בְנוּ אִתְּכֶ֔ם וְהָיִ֖ינוּ לְעַ֥ם אֶחָֽד׃ 17 וְאִם־לֹ֧א תִשְׁמְע֛וּ אֵלֵ֖ינוּ לְהִמּ֑וֹל וְלָקַ֥חְנוּ אֶת־בִּתֵּ֖נוּ וְהָלָֽכְנוּ׃ 18 וַיִּֽיטְב֥וּ דִבְרֵיהֶ֖ם בְּעֵינֵ֣י חֲמ֑וֹר וּבְעֵינֵ֖י שְׁכֶ֥ם בֶּן־חֲמֽוֹר׃ 19 וְלֹֽא־אֵחַ֤ר הַנַּ֙עַר֙ לַעֲשׂ֣וֹת הַדָּבָ֔ר כִּ֥י חָפֵ֖ץ בְּבַֽת־יַעֲקֹ֑ב וְה֣וּא נִכְבָּ֔ד מִכֹּ֖ל בֵּ֥ית אָבִֽיו׃ 20 וַיָּבֹ֥א חֲמ֛וֹר וּשְׁכֶ֥ם בְּנ֖וֹ אֶל־שַׁ֣עַר עִירָ֑ם וַיְדַבְּר֛וּ אֶל־אַנְשֵׁ֥י עִירָ֖ם לֵאמֹֽר׃ 21 הָאֲנָשִׁ֨ים הָאֵ֜לֶּה שְֽׁלֵמִ֧ים הֵ֣ם אִתָּ֗נוּ וְיֵשְׁב֤וּ בָאָ֙רֶץ֙ וְיִסְחֲר֣וּ אֹתָ֔הּ וְהָאָ֛רֶץ הִנֵּ֥ה רַחֲבַֽת־יָדַ֖יִם לִפְנֵיהֶ֑ם אֶת־בְּנֹתָם֙ נִקַּֽח־לָ֣נוּ לְנָשִׁ֔ים וְאֶת־בְּנֹתֵ֖ינוּ נִתֵּ֥ן לָהֶֽם׃ 22 אַךְ־בְּ֠זֹאת יֵאֹ֨תוּ לָ֤נוּ הָאֲנָשִׁים֙ לָשֶׁ֣בֶת אִתָּ֔נוּ לִהְי֖וֹת לְעַ֣ם אֶחָ֑ד בְּהִמּ֥וֹל לָ֙נוּ֙ כָּל־זָכָ֔ר כַּאֲשֶׁ֖ר הֵ֥ם נִמֹּלִֽים׃ 23 מִקְנֵהֶ֤ם וְקִנְיָנָם֙ וְכָל־בְּהֶמְתָּ֔ם הֲל֥וֹא לָ֖נוּ הֵ֑ם אַ֚ךְ נֵא֣וֹתָה לָהֶ֔ם וְיֵשְׁב֖וּ אִתָּֽנוּ׃ 24 וַיִּשְׁמְע֤וּ אֶל־חֲמוֹר֙ וְאֶל־שְׁכֶ֣ם בְּנ֔וֹ כָּל־יֹצְאֵ֖י שַׁ֣עַר עִיר֑וֹ וַיִּמֹּ֙לוּ֙ כָּל־זָכָ֔ר כָּל־יֹצְאֵ֖י שַׁ֥עַר עִירֽוֹ׃ 25 וַיְהִי֩ בַיּ֨וֹם הַשְּׁלִישִׁ֜י בִּֽהְיוֹתָ֣ם כֹּֽאֲבִ֗ים וַיִּקְח֣וּ שְׁנֵֽי־בְנֵי־יַ֠עֲקֹב שִׁמְע֨וֹן וְלֵוִ֜י אֲחֵ֤י דִינָה֙ אִ֣ישׁ חַרְבּ֔וֹ וַיָּבֹ֥אוּ עַל־הָעִ֖יר בֶּ֑טַח וַיַּֽהַרְג֖וּ כָּל־זָכָֽר׃ 26 וְאֶת־חֲמוֹר֙ וְאֶת־שְׁכֶ֣ם בְּנ֔וֹ הָרְג֖וּ לְפִי־חָ֑רֶב וַיִּקְח֧וּ אֶת־דִּינָ֛ה מִבֵּ֥ית שְׁכֶ֖ם וַיֵּצֵֽאוּ׃ 27 בְּנֵ֣י יַעֲקֹ֗ב בָּ֚אוּ עַל־הַ֣חֲלָלִ֔ים וַיָּבֹ֖זּוּ הָעִ֑יר אֲשֶׁ֥ר טִמְּא֖וּ אֲחוֹתָֽם׃ 28 אֶת־צֹאנָ֥ם וְאֶת־בְּקָרָ֖ם וְאֶת־חֲמֹרֵיהֶ֑ם וְאֵ֧ת אֲשֶׁר־בָּעִ֛יר וְאֶת־אֲשֶׁ֥ר בַּשָּׂדֶ֖ה לָקָֽחוּ׃ 29 וְאֶת־כָּל־חֵילָ֤ם וְאֶת־כָּל־טַפָּם֙

---

25. They killed every male. One of the seven Noachide Laws, binding on all humanity, is to establish a justice system. Since the people of Shechem failed to judge Shechem for his crime against Dinah, all the people were collectively liable for the death penalty for failing to uphold justice (*Maimonides, 12th century*).

genesis 34:13–29 — va-yishlaḥ

[13] Jacob's sons responded ingeniously to Shechem and his father Hamor, and they spoke (up. Their response was not dishonest when one considers that) he had defiled their sister Dinah. [14] They said to them, "We are unable to do this thing—to give our sister to a man who has a foreskin, as to us it's a (blemish of) disqualification."

[15] "We will consent to you, however, with this (condition): if you will be like us, to have all your males circumcised. [16] Then we will give you our daughters, and we will take your daughters for ourselves. We will live with you and become one people."

[17] "But if you do not listen to us, to be circumcised, we will take our daughter and go."

[18] Hamor and Shechem, Hamor's son, were pleased with their words. [19] The young man did not delay carrying out the matter, because he desired Jacob's daughter. He was the most honored of all his father's household.

[20] Hamor and his son Shechem came to the gate of their city, and they spoke to the people of their city, saying, [21] "These men are peaceful (and sincere) with us. They're going to live in the land and do business in it. The land is clearly spacious enough for them (so there's nothing to lose). We'll take their daughters for ourselves as wives, and we'll give them our daughters."

[22] "But the men will only agree to live with us, to be one family, on this (condition): by all our males being circumcised, just as they are circumcised."

[23] "Then, won't all their flocks, their property, and all their cattle be ours? Let's consent to them, and (then) they will live with us."

[24] All the residents of his city listened to Hamor and his son Shechem, and every male that lived in his city became circumcised.

[25] And then, on the third day, when they were in pain, Jacob's two sons Simeon and Levi, Dinah's brothers, took each man a sword. They came to the city confidently (since they knew the people were weak), and they killed every male.

[26] They killed Hamor and his son Shechem with a sword. They took Dinah out of Shechem's house and left.

[27] Jacob's sons came (to strip) the corpses (of their possessions). They plundered the city that had defiled their sister: [28] They took their flocks, their cattle, their donkeys—whatever was in the city and whatever was in the field. [29] They captured and plundered all their wealth, all their infants, their wives and everything that was in the house.

food for thought

1. How can we tell if conversion is sincere?

2. How can retaliation be appropriately measured?

3. Simeon and Levi's reactions were extreme. Can you justify them?

בראשית לד:כט - לה:ח　　וישלח

וְאֶת־נְשֵׁיהֶ֥ם שָׁב֖וּ וַיָּבֹ֑זּוּ וְאֵ֖ת כָּל־אֲשֶׁ֥ר בַּבָּֽיִת: 30 וַיֹּ֨אמֶר יַעֲקֹ֜ב אֶל־שִׁמְע֣וֹן וְאֶל־לֵוִי֮ עֲכַרְתֶּ֣ם אֹתִי֒ לְהַבְאִישֵׁ֨נִי֙ בְּיֹשֵׁ֣ב הָאָ֔רֶץ בַּֽכְּנַעֲנִ֖י וּבַפְּרִזִּ֑י וַאֲנִי֙ מְתֵ֣י מִסְפָּ֔ר וְנֶאֶסְפ֤וּ עָלַי֙ וְהִכּ֔וּנִי וְנִשְׁמַדְתִּ֖י אֲנִ֥י וּבֵיתִֽי: 31 וַיֹּאמְר֑וּ הַכְזוֹנָ֕ה יַעֲשֶׂ֖ה אֶת־אֲחוֹתֵֽנוּ: פ

לה

1 וַיֹּ֤אמֶר אֱלֹהִים֙ אֶֽל־יַעֲקֹ֔ב ק֛וּם עֲלֵ֥ה בֵֽית־אֵ֖ל וְשֶׁב־שָׁ֑ם וַעֲשֵׂה־שָׁ֣ם מִזְבֵּ֔חַ לָאֵל֙ הַנִּרְאֶ֣ה אֵלֶ֔יךָ בְּבָרְחֲךָ֔ מִפְּנֵ֖י עֵשָׂ֥ו אָחִֽיךָ: 2 וַיֹּ֤אמֶר יַעֲקֹב֙ אֶל־בֵּית֔וֹ וְאֶ֖ל כָּל־אֲשֶׁ֣ר עִמּ֑וֹ הָסִ֜רוּ אֶת־אֱלֹהֵ֤י הַנֵּכָר֙ אֲשֶׁ֣ר בְּתֹכְכֶ֔ם וְהִֽטַּהֲר֔וּ וְהַחֲלִ֖יפוּ שִׂמְלֹתֵיכֶֽם: 3 וְנָק֥וּמָה וְנַעֲלֶ֖ה בֵּֽית־אֵ֑ל וְאֶֽעֱשֶׂה־שָּׁ֣ם מִזְבֵּ֗חַ לָאֵ֞ל הָעֹנֶ֤ה אֹתִי֙ בְּי֣וֹם צָֽרָתִ֔י וַיְהִי֙ עִמָּדִ֔י בַּדֶּ֖רֶךְ אֲשֶׁ֥ר הָלָֽכְתִּי: 4 וַיִּתְּנ֣וּ אֶֽל־יַעֲקֹ֗ב אֵ֣ת כָּל־אֱלֹהֵ֤י הַנֵּכָר֙ אֲשֶׁ֣ר בְּיָדָ֔ם וְאֶת־הַנְּזָמִ֖ים אֲשֶׁ֣ר בְּאָזְנֵיהֶ֑ם וַיִּטְמֹ֤ן אֹתָם֙ יַעֲקֹ֔ב תַּ֥חַת הָאֵלָ֖ה אֲשֶׁ֥ר עִם־שְׁכֶֽם: 5 וַיִּסָּ֑עוּ וַיְהִ֣י | חִתַּ֣ת אֱלֹהִ֗ים עַל־הֶֽעָרִים֙ אֲשֶׁר֙ סְבִיבֹ֣תֵיהֶ֔ם וְלֹ֣א רָֽדְפ֔וּ אַחֲרֵ֖י בְּנֵ֥י יַעֲקֹֽב: 6 וַיָּבֹ֨א יַעֲקֹ֜ב ל֗וּזָה אֲשֶׁר֙ בְּאֶ֣רֶץ כְּנַ֔עַן הִ֖וא בֵּֽית־אֵ֑ל ה֖וּא וְכָל־הָעָ֥ם אֲשֶׁר־עִמּֽוֹ: 7 וַיִּ֤בֶן שָׁם֙ מִזְבֵּ֔חַ וַיִּקְרָא֙ לַמָּק֔וֹם אֵ֖ל בֵּֽית־אֵ֑ל כִּ֣י שָׁ֗ם נִגְל֤וּ אֵלָיו֙ הָֽאֱלֹהִ֔ים בְּבָרְח֖וֹ מִפְּנֵ֥י אָחִֽיו: 8 וַתָּ֤מָת דְּבֹרָה֙ מֵינֶ֣קֶת רִבְקָ֔ה וַתִּקָּבֵ֛ר מִתַּ֥חַת לְבֵֽית־אֵ֖ל תַּ֣חַת הָֽאַלּ֑וֹן וַיִּקְרָ֥א שְׁמ֖וֹ אַלּ֥וֹן בָּכֽוּת: פ

spiritual vitamin

> Once you know that anyone can "do business" with your religion; trim it a bit here, a bit there, then whatever is left—what value can be attached to it, and what binding force can it have? At the same time, you lose your self-respect, recognizing your lack of courage and personal weakness to hold to your own belief, or the beliefs of your people, and taking instead the line of least resistance.

genesis 34:30 – 35:8 — va-yishlaḥ

³⁰ Jacob said to Simeon and to Levi, "You have made (my mind) troubled, creating hostility (between) me and the inhabitants of the land, among the Canaanites and among the Perizzites. I have only a few (men). They can gather against me and attack me, and then I and my household will be destroyed!"

³¹ (Simeon and Levi) said, "Could we (allow them) to make our sister like a harlot?"

Journey to Bethel / Jacob's Name is Changed

35 ¹ God said to Jacob, "Get going and travel up to Bethel, and settle there. Make there an altar to the God who appeared to you when you fled from your brother Esau."

² Jacob said to his household, and to all those who were with him, "Remove the foreign gods which are among you (from the booty of Shechem). Purify yourselves (from idol-worship) and change your clothes (in case they were used for idol-worship too). ³ We're setting off to go up to Bethel. I will make an altar to the God who answered me on the day of my distress, and who was with me on the way that I went."

⁴ They gave Jacob all the foreign gods that were in their possession and the earrings that were in their ears. Jacob hid them under the (non-fruit-bearing) tree that was near Shechem.

⁵ Then they journeyed. The fear of God was upon the cities that were around them, and they did not pursue the children of Jacob.

⁶ Jacob came to Luz—which is Bethel—that is in the land of Canaan—(both) he and all the people who were with him. ⁷ He built an altar there, and he called the place El-bethel ("God (is in) Bethel"), for God was revealed to him there when he was fleeing from his brother.

⁸ Rebekah's nurse Deborah (who had come to fetch Jacob from Laban's house) died. She was buried beneath Bethel, at the bottom of the plain, so he named it Allon-bacuth ("Plain of Weeping").

Establishing a justice system is a positive command, but there is no *prohibition* punishable by death against failing to uphold justice, as Maimonides argues. Rather, the people of Shechem were *already* liable for the death penalty, even before the incident with Dinah, since they were idol-worshipers. After Dinah's abduction, Simeon and Levi sought revenge based on the people's prior sins (*Naḥmanides, 13th century*).

If the people of Shechem were liable for the death penalty in any case, why did Jacob become angry with Simeon and Levi (v. 20)?

Because when the people of Shechem circumcised themselves, they actually converted to Judaism, and a convert is considered to be like a newborn baby, clean of sin (*Rabbi David b. Solomon ibn Abi Zimra, 16th century*).

בראשית לה:ט-כא | וישלח

9 וַיֵּרָא אֱלֹהִים אֶל־יַעֲקֹב עוֹד בְּבֹאוֹ מִפַּדַּן אֲרָם וַיְבָרֶךְ אֹתוֹ: 10 וַיֹּאמֶר־לוֹ אֱלֹהִים שִׁמְךָ יַעֲקֹב לֹא־יִקָּרֵא שִׁמְךָ עוֹד יַעֲקֹב כִּי אִם־יִשְׂרָאֵל יִהְיֶה שְׁמֶךָ וַיִּקְרָא אֶת־שְׁמוֹ יִשְׂרָאֵל: 11 וַיֹּאמֶר לוֹ אֱלֹהִים אֲנִי אֵל שַׁדַּי פְּרֵה וּרְבֵה גּוֹי וּקְהַל גּוֹיִם יִהְיֶה מִמֶּךָּ וּמְלָכִים מֵחֲלָצֶיךָ יֵצֵאוּ: [SIXTH READING] 12 וְאֶת־הָאָרֶץ אֲשֶׁר נָתַתִּי לְאַבְרָהָם וּלְיִצְחָק לְךָ אֶתְּנֶנָּה וּלְזַרְעֲךָ אַחֲרֶיךָ אֶתֵּן אֶת־הָאָרֶץ: 13 וַיַּעַל מֵעָלָיו אֱלֹהִים בַּמָּקוֹם אֲשֶׁר־דִּבֶּר אִתּוֹ: 14 וַיַּצֵּב יַעֲקֹב מַצֵּבָה בַּמָּקוֹם אֲשֶׁר־דִּבֶּר אִתּוֹ מַצֶּבֶת אָבֶן וַיַּסֵּךְ עָלֶיהָ נֶסֶךְ וַיִּצֹק עָלֶיהָ שָׁמֶן: 15 וַיִּקְרָא יַעֲקֹב אֶת־שֵׁם הַמָּקוֹם אֲשֶׁר דִּבֶּר אִתּוֹ שָׁם אֱלֹהִים בֵּית־אֵל: 16 וַיִּסְעוּ מִבֵּית אֵל וַיְהִי־עוֹד כִּבְרַת־הָאָרֶץ לָבוֹא אֶפְרָתָה וַתֵּלֶד רָחֵל וַתְּקַשׁ בְּלִדְתָּהּ: 17 וַיְהִי בְהַקְשֹׁתָהּ בְּלִדְתָּהּ וַתֹּאמֶר לָהּ הַמְיַלֶּדֶת אַל־תִּירְאִי כִּי־גַם־זֶה לָךְ בֵּן: 18 וַיְהִי בְּצֵאת נַפְשָׁהּ כִּי מֵתָה וַתִּקְרָא שְׁמוֹ בֶּן־אוֹנִי וְאָבִיו קָרָא־לוֹ בִנְיָמִין: 19 וַתָּמָת רָחֵל וַתִּקָּבֵר בְּדֶרֶךְ אֶפְרָתָה הִוא בֵּית לָחֶם: 20 וַיַּצֵּב יַעֲקֹב מַצֵּבָה עַל־קְבֻרָתָהּ הִוא מַצֶּבֶת קְבֻרַת־רָחֵל עַד־הַיּוֹם: 21 וַיִּסַּע יִשְׂרָאֵל וַיֵּט אָהֳלֹה מֵהָלְאָה

21. Israel journeyed, and he pitched his tent at some distance past the Tower of Eder. The *Midrash* states, *"Even after all the tribulations of Jacob, the death of Rachel was more difficult for him than all of them"* (Ruth Rabbah). The righteous do not question the ways of God, trusting that everything is for the good. This is why, after the death of Rachel, the Torah states, *"and he*

kabbalah bites

35:18 When a man and woman are intimate for the first time, part of the man's soul passes *irretrievably* to the woman. All the children they are destined to have together will inherit both a portion of their mother's soul along with part of this male soul that was "donated" by the father.

When this "additional soul" is depleted, the woman will no longer be able to have children.

In the case of Rachel, the depletion of her additional male soul coincided with her passing, since Benjamin took what remained within her.

genesis 35:9–21 — va-yishlah

⁹ God appeared again to Jacob (in the same location) as he was coming from Paddan-aram, and He blessed him. ¹⁰ God said to him, "Your name is Jacob. You will no longer be named Jacob [*ya'AKoV*] (denoting deception [*'AKeVah*]). Rather, Israel [*yiSRa'el*] shall be your name (denoting a leader [*SaR*])," and He named him Israel.

¹¹ God said to him, "I am the Almighty God (who has the power to bless). Be fruitful and multiply! A nation (through Benjamin) and a multitude of nations (through Manasseh and Ephraim) will come from you, and kings (Saul and Ish-bosheth, descended from Benjamin) shall emerge from your loins."

[SIXTH READING] ¹² "I will give you the land that I gave to Abraham and to Isaac, and I will give the land to your descendants after you."

¹³ God('s glory) ascended from him, in the place where He had spoken with him. ¹⁴ Jacob erected a monument in the place where (God) had spoken with him, a stone monument. He poured a libation on it, and then he poured oil on it.

¹⁵ Jacob named the place where God had spoken with him Bethel.

Benjamin is Born / Rachel Passes Away

¹⁶ They journeyed from Bethel, and there was still considerable distance to come to Ephrath (when) Rachel went into labor. Her labor was difficult.

¹⁷ And then, when she was having difficulty giving birth, the midwife said to her, "Do not be afraid, for this one, too, is a son for you."

¹⁸ And then, as her soul was departing, for she was dying, she named him Ben-oni ("son of my sorrow")—but his father called him Benjamin ("son of the south"), i.e., the land of Canaan).

¹⁹ Rachel died. She was buried on the road to Ephrath, which is Bethlehem. ²⁰ Jacob erected a monument on her grave, which is the monument of Rachel's grave until this day.

Reuben Moves Jacob's Bed

²¹ Israel journeyed, and he pitched his tent at some distance past the Tower of Eder.

35:10 Israel shall be your name. Jacob is a name which represents tactical wisdom (see 32:29 and *Rashi*, ibid.). This represents the ability to *tackle* the spiritual concealment of this physical world, evaluating each move to ensure that it is spiritually productive.

The name Israel was given, *"because you have fought with (an angel of) God and with (Laban and Esau), and you have overcome (them)"* (ibid.), representing the ability to *penetrate* the concealment of "angels and men" and *rise above it* (*Rabbi Shneur Zalman of Lyady, 18th century*).

וישלח   בראשית לה:כא - לו:ב

לְמִגְדַּל־עֵדֶר: 22 וַיְהִ֗י בִּשְׁכֹּ֤ן יִשְׂרָאֵל֙ בָּאָ֣רֶץ הַהִ֔וא וַיֵּ֣לֶךְ רְאוּבֵ֔ן וַיִּשְׁכַּב֙ אֶת־בִּלְהָה֙ פִּילֶ֣גֶשׁ אָבִ֔יו וַיִּשְׁמַ֖ע יִשְׂרָאֵ֑ל פ וַיִּֽהְי֥וּ בְנֵֽי־יַעֲקֹ֖ב שְׁנֵ֥ים עָשָֽׂר: 23 בְּנֵ֣י לֵאָ֔ה בְּכ֥וֹר יַעֲקֹ֖ב רְאוּבֵ֑ן וְשִׁמְעוֹן֙ וְלֵוִ֣י וִֽיהוּדָ֔ה וְיִשָּׂשכָ֖ר וּזְבֻלֽוּן: 24 בְּנֵ֣י רָחֵ֔ל יוֹסֵ֖ף וּבִנְיָמִֽן: 25 וּבְנֵ֤י בִלְהָה֙ שִׁפְחַ֣ת רָחֵ֔ל דָּ֖ן וְנַפְתָּלִֽי: 26 וּבְנֵ֥י זִלְפָּ֛ה שִׁפְחַ֥ת לֵאָ֖ה גָּ֣ד וְאָשֵׁ֑ר אֵ֚לֶּה בְּנֵ֣י יַעֲקֹ֔ב אֲשֶׁ֥ר יֻלַּד־ל֖וֹ בְּפַדַּ֥ן אֲרָֽם: 27 וַיָּבֹ֤א יַעֲקֹב֙ אֶל־יִצְחָ֣ק אָבִ֔יו מַמְרֵ֖א קִרְיַ֣ת הָֽאַרְבַּ֑ע הִ֣וא חֶבְר֔וֹן אֲשֶׁר־גָּֽר־שָׁ֥ם אַבְרָהָ֖ם וְיִצְחָֽק: 28 וַיִּֽהְי֖וּ יְמֵ֣י יִצְחָ֑ק מְאַ֥ת שָׁנָ֖ה וּשְׁמֹנִ֥ים שָׁנָֽה: 29 וַיִּגְוַ֨ע יִצְחָ֤ק וַיָּ֨מָת֙ וַיֵּאָ֣סֶף אֶל־עַמָּ֔יו זָקֵ֖ן וּשְׂבַ֣ע יָמִ֑ים וַיִּקְבְּר֣וּ אֹת֔וֹ עֵשָׂ֥ו וְיַעֲקֹ֖ב בָּנָֽיו: פ

לו 1 וְאֵ֛לֶּה תֹּלְד֥וֹת עֵשָׂ֖ו ה֥וּא אֱדֽוֹם: 2 עֵשָׂ֛ו לָקַ֥ח אֶת־נָשָׁ֖יו מִבְּנ֣וֹת כְּנָ֑עַן אֶת־עָדָ֗ה בַּת־אֵילוֹן֙ הַֽחִתִּ֔י וְאֶת־אָהֳלִֽיבָמָה֙ בַּת־עֲנָ֔ה בַּת־צִבְע֖וֹן

220

29. Isaac breathed his last. The Torah is not in chronological order. The sale of Joseph actually preceded Isaac's passing by 12 years.

— When Jacob was born, Isaac was 60 years old (25:26).

— Isaac died in Jacob's 120th year, because the verse states, *"Isaac was 60 years old when she gave birth to them"* (ibid.), and if you subtract 60 from 180 (Isaac's age at death; v. 28), you have 120 left.

— Joseph was 17 years old when he was sold, and Jacob was 108 years old. How is this so? Jacob was blessed by Isaac at the age of 63 (*Rashi* to 28:9). For 14 years he hid in the Academy of Eber, until he was 77. He worked 14 years for a wife, at the end of which time Joseph was born—as the verse states, *"Then, when Rachel had given birth to Joseph, Jacob said to Laban, 'Send me away!'"* (30:25)—totaling 91. Add to this, the 17 years until Joseph was sold, and it totals 108 (*Rashi, 11th century*).

spiritual vitamin

> The sages say that *"the experiences of the fathers are a guide for their children"* (see *Midrash Tanhuma, Lekh Lekha, par. 9*). What happened to our Patriarchs reflected events that would repeat themselves in the history of our people, both of the individual and of the nation as a whole.

²² And then, when Israel was living in that land, Reuben (moved the bed of Jacob from where it) lay with Bilhah, his father's concubine (as a protest that Jacob had not moved his bed to Leah's tent after Rachel's passing). Israel heard (about it).

Jacob's Descendants

²³ Jacob now had twelve sons (after Benjamin's birth):

²³ Leah's sons: Reuben—Jacob's firstborn—Simeon, Levi, Judah, Issachar, and Zebulun.

²⁴ Rachel's sons: Joseph and Benjamin.

²⁵ Rachel's maid Bilhah's sons: Dan and Naphtali.

²⁶ Leah's maid Zilpah's sons: Gad and Asher.

(All) these are Jacob's sons who were born to him in Paddan-aram.

Isaac Passes Away

(Isaac's passing actually occurred much later, 12 years after the sale of Joseph.)

²⁷ Jacob came to his father Isaac, at (the plain of) Mamre in Kiriath-arba, which is Hebron, where Abraham and Isaac lived.

²⁸ Isaac lived a total of one hundred and eighty years. ²⁹ Isaac breathed his last and died, and (his soul) was gathered to (be with the souls of) his people. (He was) old and satisfied with (lengthy) days. His sons Esau and Jacob buried him.

Esau's Descendants

36
¹ These are the descendants of Esau, who is (also called) Edom:

² Esau took his wives from the Canaanite girls:

Adah (also known as Basemath) daughter of Elon the Hittite; Oholibamah (also

---

pitched his tent at some distance past the Tower of Eder," suggesting that Jacob strengthened his heart to not doubt God (both "tower" and "Eder" (lit. "herd") are terms denoting strength). Jacob trusted that God must have had some deep intention with the death of Rachel, something which he could never fathom. He resigned to the fact that he would never understand why.

Afterwards, God indicated to Jacob that it *is* appropriate to ask for such secrets to be revealed. While we may not question God's ways, we should nevertheless beg Him to give us some insight into His seemingly unfathomable actions. God immediately showed Jacob a far-reaching effect of Rachel's passing: the incident with Reuben (v. 22), which resulted in Jacob's most cherished son, Joseph, rising to the status of firstborn (*Rabbi Mordecai Joseph Leiner of Izbica, 19th century*).

בראשית לו:ב-יד | וישלח

הַחֹרִ֑י: 3 וְאֶת־בָּשְׂמַ֥ת בַּת־יִשְׁמָעֵ֖אל אֲח֥וֹת נְבָיֽוֹת: 4 וַתֵּ֧לֶד עָדָ֛ה לְעֵשָׂ֖ו אֶת־אֱלִיפָ֑ז וּבָ֣שְׂמַ֔ת יָלְדָ֖ה אֶת־רְעוּאֵֽל: 5 וְאָהֳלִיבָמָ֣ה יָֽלְדָ֗ה אֶת־ [יעיש כ׳] יְע֧וּשׁ וְאֶת־יַעְלָ֖ם וְאֶת־קֹ֑רַח אֵ֚לֶּה בְּנֵ֣י עֵשָׂ֔ו אֲשֶׁ֥ר יֻלְּדוּ־ל֖וֹ בְּאֶ֥רֶץ כְּנָֽעַן: 6 וַיִּקַּ֣ח עֵשָׂ֡ו אֶת־נָ֠שָׁיו וְאֶת־בָּנָ֣יו וְאֶת־בְּנֹתָיו֮ וְאֶת־כׇּל־נַפְשׁ֣וֹת בֵּיתוֹ֒ וְאֶת־מִקְנֵ֣הוּ וְאֶת־כׇּל־בְּהֶמְתּ֗וֹ וְאֵת֙ כׇּל־קִנְיָנ֔וֹ אֲשֶׁ֥ר רָכַ֖שׁ בְּאֶ֣רֶץ כְּנָ֑עַן וַיֵּ֣לֶךְ אֶל־אֶ֔רֶץ מִפְּנֵ֖י יַעֲקֹ֥ב אָחִֽיו: 7 כִּֽי־הָיָ֧ה רְכוּשָׁ֛ם רָ֖ב מִשֶּׁ֣בֶת יַחְדָּ֑ו וְלֹ֨א יָֽכְלָ֜ה אֶ֤רֶץ מְגֽוּרֵיהֶם֙ לָשֵׂ֣את אֹתָ֔ם מִפְּנֵ֖י מִקְנֵיהֶֽם: 8 וַיֵּ֤שֶׁב עֵשָׂו֙ בְּהַ֣ר שֵׂעִ֔יר עֵשָׂ֖ו ה֥וּא אֱדֽוֹם: 9 וְאֵ֛לֶּה תֹּלְד֥וֹת עֵשָׂ֖ו אֲבִ֣י אֱד֑וֹם בְּהַ֖ר שֵׂעִֽיר: 10 אֵ֖לֶּה שְׁמ֣וֹת בְּנֵֽי־עֵשָׂ֑ו אֱלִיפַ֗ז בֶּן־עָדָה֙ אֵ֣שֶׁת עֵשָׂ֔ו רְעוּאֵ֕ל בֶּן־בָּשְׂמַ֖ת אֵ֥שֶׁת עֵשָֽׂו: 11 וַיִּהְי֖וּ בְּנֵ֣י אֱלִיפָ֑ז תֵּימָ֣ן אוֹמָ֔ר צְפ֥וֹ וְגַעְתָּ֖ם וּקְנַֽז: 12 וְתִמְנַ֣ע ׀ הָיְתָ֣ה פִילֶ֗גֶשׁ לֶֽאֱלִיפַז֙ בֶּן־עֵשָׂ֔ו וַתֵּ֥לֶד לֶאֱלִיפַ֖ז אֶת־עֲמָלֵ֑ק אֵ֕לֶּה בְּנֵ֥י עָדָ֖ה אֵ֥שֶׁת עֵשָֽׂו: 13 וְאֵ֙לֶּה֙ בְּנֵ֣י רְעוּאֵ֔ל נַ֥חַת וָזֶ֖רַח שַׁמָּ֣ה וּמִזָּ֑ה אֵ֣לֶּה הָי֔וּ בְּנֵ֥י בָשְׂמַ֖ת אֵ֥שֶׁת עֵשָֽׂו: 14 וְאֵ֣לֶּה הָי֗וּ בְּנֵ֨י אׇהֳלִיבָמָ֧ה בַת־עֲנָ֛ה בַּת־צִבְע֖וֹן אֵ֣שֶׁת עֵשָׂ֑ו וַתֵּ֣לֶד לְעֵשָׂ֔ו אֶת־ [יעיש כ׳] יְע֥וּשׁ וְאֶת־יַעְלָ֖ם וְאֶת־קֹֽרַח:

222

land, and he will return to his true home, the land of Israel, in full and total settlement (*Rabbi Menahem Mendel Schneerson, 20th century*).

kabbalah bites

36:12 *"Timna … gave birth to Amalek."* Timna was a princess who desperately wished to convert to Judaism but, rejected by Jacob, she married into Esau's family instead. The Talmud considers this to have been a grave error, resulting in the birth of Amalek, the father of a nation that would later wreak havoc on Israel (*Babylonian Talmud, Sanhedrin* 99b).

Rabbi Isaac Luria, however, considered Jacob's rejection of Timna as an act of piety, the result of which he merited to be buried in the land of Israel.

How are we to reconcile these two views? Rabbi Samuel Vital argues that Jacob *should* have married Timna. He should have attempted to refine and elevate her, *even if this would mean losing the merit of being buried in the land of Israel*. Sometimes we have to engage with the world, even if it will tarnish us slightly, for the overall good of mankind.

known as Judith), daughter of Anah and daughter of Zibeon the Hivite; ³ and Basemath (also known as Mahalath), sister of Nebaioth, daughter of Ishmael.

⁴ Adah gave birth to Eliphaz for Esau, and Basemath gave birth to Reuel. ⁵ Oholibamah gave birth to Jeush, Jalam and Korah. (All) these are the children of Esau who were born to him in the land of Canaan.

⁶ Esau took his wives, his sons, his daughters, all the people of his household, his flocks, all his animals and all his property that he had acquired in the land of Canaan, and he went to (find another) land, due to his brother Jacob, ⁷ because their possessions were too numerous for them to dwell together. The land which they inhabited could not support them because (there was not enough space) for their flocks (to graze). ⁸ So Esau settled in Mount Seir. Esau is (also known as) Edom.

⁹ These are the descendants of Esau, the father of the Edom(ites), on Mount Seir:

¹⁰ These are the names of Esau's sons: Eliphaz, son of Esau's wife Adah, and Reuel, son of Esau's wife Basemath. ¹¹ The children of Eliphaz were Teman, Omar, Zepho, Gatam, and Kenaz. ¹² Timna was a concubine to Eliphaz, Esau's son, and she gave birth to Amalek for Eliphaz. (All) these are the children of Adah, the wife of Esau.

¹³ These are the children of Reuel: Nahath, Zerah, Shammah, and Mizzah. They are the children of Basemath, the wife of Esau.

¹⁴ These are the children of Oholibamah daughter of Anah and daughter of Zibeon, Esau's wife: She gave birth to Jeush, Jalam, and Korah for Esau.

36:6 He went to (find another) land. The land in which they lived could not provide sufficient pasture for their animals.

The *Midrash* explains that Esau left *"due to his brother Jacob"* (v. 6), because of the writ of obligation which accompanied the decree on the descendants of Isaac, *"your descendants will be strangers in a land that is not theirs. They will enslave them and oppress them"* (15:13). Esau said, "I will go away from here. I want no part in the gift—this land which Isaac was given—nor in the payment of the debt."

Also, he left on account of the shame for having sold his birthright (*Rashi, 11ᵗʰ century*).

Since Esau loved Jacob, he left him the land of Canaan, knowing that Jacob desired it and that his descendants would inherit it in the future (*Rabbi Isaac Abravanel, 15ᵗʰ century*).

8. Esau settled in Mount Seir. So long as we have not reached the end of exile when the Holy Temple will be built and we will all return to the land of Israel, a Jew needs to be conscious that he is, "a stranger in a land that is not his own" (see 15:13). The fact that Jews inhabit any land other than the land of Israel is a temporary situation. It was Esau that "settled" in the Diaspora, but a Jew waits impatiently for the time when he will cease to be a "stranger" in a foreign

בראשית לו:טו-ל | וישלח

15 אֵלֶּה אַלּוּפֵי בְנֵי־עֵשָׂו בְּנֵי אֱלִיפַז בְּכוֹר עֵשָׂו אַלּוּף תֵּימָן אַלּוּף אוֹמָר אַלּוּף צְפוֹ אַלּוּף קְנַז: 16 אַלּוּף־קֹרַח אַלּוּף גַּעְתָּם אַלּוּף עֲמָלֵק אֵלֶּה אַלּוּפֵי אֱלִיפַז בְּאֶרֶץ אֱדוֹם אֵלֶּה בְּנֵי עָדָה: 17 וְאֵלֶּה בְּנֵי רְעוּאֵל בֶּן־עֵשָׂו אַלּוּף נַחַת אַלּוּף זֶרַח אַלּוּף שַׁמָּה אַלּוּף מִזָּה אֵלֶּה אַלּוּפֵי רְעוּאֵל בְּאֶרֶץ אֱדוֹם אֵלֶּה בְּנֵי בָשְׂמַת אֵשֶׁת עֵשָׂו: 18 וְאֵלֶּה בְּנֵי אָהֳלִיבָמָה אֵשֶׁת עֵשָׂו אַלּוּף יְעוּשׁ אַלּוּף יַעְלָם אַלּוּף קֹרַח אֵלֶּה אַלּוּפֵי אָהֳלִיבָמָה בַּת־עֲנָה אֵשֶׁת עֵשָׂו: 19 אֵלֶּה בְנֵי־עֵשָׂו וְאֵלֶּה אַלּוּפֵיהֶם הוּא אֱדוֹם: ס 20 [SEVENTH READING] אֵלֶּה בְנֵי־שֵׂעִיר הַחֹרִי יֹשְׁבֵי הָאָרֶץ לוֹטָן וְשׁוֹבָל וְצִבְעוֹן וַעֲנָה: 21 וְדִשׁוֹן וְאֵצֶר וְדִישָׁן אֵלֶּה אַלּוּפֵי הַחֹרִי בְּנֵי שֵׂעִיר בְּאֶרֶץ אֱדוֹם: 22 וַיִּהְיוּ בְנֵי־לוֹטָן חֹרִי וְהֵימָם וַאֲחוֹת לוֹטָן תִּמְנָע: 23 וְאֵלֶּה בְּנֵי שׁוֹבָל עַלְוָן וּמָנַחַת וְעֵיבָל שְׁפוֹ וְאוֹנָם: 24 וְאֵלֶּה בְנֵי־צִבְעוֹן וְאַיָּה וַעֲנָה הוּא עֲנָה אֲשֶׁר מָצָא אֶת־הַיֵּמִם בַּמִּדְבָּר בִּרְעֹתוֹ אֶת־הַחֲמֹרִים לְצִבְעוֹן אָבִיו: 25 וְאֵלֶּה בְנֵי־עֲנָה דִּשֹׁן וְאָהֳלִיבָמָה בַּת־עֲנָה: 26 וְאֵלֶּה בְּנֵי דִישָׁן חֶמְדָּן וְאֶשְׁבָּן וְיִתְרָן וּכְרָן: 27 אֵלֶּה בְּנֵי־אֵצֶר בִּלְהָן וְזַעֲוָן וַעֲקָן: 28 אֵלֶּה בְנֵי־דִישָׁן עוּץ וַאֲרָן: 29 אֵלֶּה אַלּוּפֵי הַחֹרִי אַלּוּף לוֹטָן אַלּוּף שׁוֹבָל אַלּוּף צִבְעוֹן אַלּוּף עֲנָה: 30 אַלּוּף דִּשֹׁן אַלּוּף אֵצֶר אַלּוּף דִּישָׁן אֵלֶּה אַלּוּפֵי הַחֹרִי לְאַלֻּפֵיהֶם בְּאֶרֶץ שֵׂעִיר: פ

20. These are the children of Seir the Horite, the inhabitants of the land. Here, the unexpected phrase, *"the inhabitants of the land,"* tells us that the Horites were experts in agriculture. They were able to accurately predict: this piece of land is best suited for planting olive trees,

spiritual vitamin

" The ways of the Torah are ways of pleasantness and peace. Nothing is more hateful than dissension and strife, and nothing is more praiseworthy than peace, which is the "vessel" for all blessings. It is in this spirit that all problems and differences should be settled. "

[SEVENTH READING indicator appears at verse 20]

¹⁵ These are the (family) heads of the children of Esau:

(From) the children of Eliphaz, Esau's firstborn: (the) head (of the) Teman (family, the) head (of the) Omar (family, the) head (of the) Zepho (family, the) head (of the) Kenaz (family), ¹⁶ (the) head (of the) Korah (family, the) head (of the) Gatam (family, the) head (of the) Amalek (family). They are the (family) heads of Eliphaz in the land of Edom. (All) these are the children of Adah.

¹⁷ These are (the family heads from) the children of Reuel, Esau's son: (the) head (of the) Nahath (family, the) head (of the) Zerah (family, the) head (of the) Shammah (family), and (the) head (of the) Mizzah (family). They are the (family) heads of Reuel in the land of Edom. (All) these are the children of Basemath, Esau's wife.

¹⁸ These are (the family heads from) the children of Oholibamah, Esau's wife: (the) head (of the) Jeush (family, the) head (of the) Jalam (family, the) head (of the) Korah (family). They are the (family) heads of Oholibamah daughter of Anah, Esau's wife.

¹⁹ These (mentioned above) are the children of Esau. (All) these are their family chiefs. (Esau is also known) as Edom.

Seir's Descendants

²⁰ These are the children of Seir the Horite, the inhabitants of the land (before Esau arrived there): Lotan, Shobal, Zibeon, Anah, ²¹ Dishon, Ezer, and Dishan. (All) these are the (family) heads of the Horites, Seir's children, in the land of Edom.

²² The children of Lotan were Hori and Hemam. The sister of Lotan was Timna.

²³ These are the children of Shobal: Alvan, Manahath, Ebal, Shepho and Onam.

²⁴ These are the children of Zibeon: Aiah and Anah. He is Anah who (crossbred) mules in the wilderness when he pastured the donkeys for his father Zibeon.

²⁵ These are the children of Anah: Dishon and Oholibamah, the daughter of Anah.

²⁶ These are the children of Dishon: Hemdan, Eshban, Ithran, and Cheran.

²⁷ These are the children of Ezer: Bilhan, Zaavan, and Akan.

²⁸ These are the children of Dishan: Uz and Aran.

²⁹ These are the (family) chiefs of the Horites: (the) head (of the) Lotan (family, the) head (of the) Shobal (family, the) head (of the) Zibeon (family, the) head (of the) Anah (family), ³⁰ (the) head (of the) Dishon (family, the) head (of the) Ezer (family), and (the) head (of the) Dishan (family. All) these are the (family) heads of the Horites according to their families in the land of Edom.

בראשית לו:לא-מג | וישלח

31 וְאֵ֙לֶּה֙ הַמְּלָכִ֔ים אֲשֶׁ֥ר מָלְכ֖וּ בְּאֶ֣רֶץ אֱד֑וֹם לִפְנֵ֥י מְלָךְ־מֶ֖לֶךְ לִבְנֵ֥י יִשְׂרָאֵֽל׃
32 וַיִּמְלֹ֣ךְ בֶּאֱד֔וֹם בֶּ֖לַע בֶּן־בְּע֑וֹר וְשֵׁ֥ם עִיר֖וֹ דִּנְהָֽבָה׃ 33 וַיָּ֖מָת בָּ֑לַע וַיִּמְלֹ֣ךְ תַּחְתָּ֔יו יוֹבָ֥ב בֶּן־זֶ֖רַח מִבָּצְרָֽה׃ 34 וַיָּ֖מָת יוֹבָ֑ב וַיִּמְלֹ֣ךְ תַּחְתָּ֔יו חֻשָׁ֖ם מֵאֶ֥רֶץ הַתֵּימָנִֽי׃
35 וַיָּ֖מָת חֻשָׁ֑ם וַיִּמְלֹ֨ךְ תַּחְתָּ֜יו הֲדַ֣ד בֶּן־בְּדַ֗ד הַמַּכֶּ֤ה אֶת־מִדְיָן֙ בִּשְׂדֵ֣ה מוֹאָ֔ב וְשֵׁ֥ם עִיר֖וֹ עֲוִֽית׃ 36 וַיָּ֖מָת הֲדָ֑ד וַיִּמְלֹ֣ךְ תַּחְתָּ֔יו שַׂמְלָ֖ה מִמַּשְׂרֵקָֽה׃ 37 וַיָּ֖מָת שַׂמְלָ֑ה וַיִּמְלֹ֣ךְ תַּחְתָּ֔יו שָׁא֖וּל מֵרְחֹב֥וֹת הַנָּהָֽר׃ 38 וַיָּ֖מָת שָׁא֑וּל וַיִּמְלֹ֣ךְ תַּחְתָּ֔יו בַּ֥עַל חָנָ֖ן בֶּן־עַכְבּֽוֹר׃ 39 וַיָּ֡מָת בַּ֣עַל חָנָן֮ בֶּן־עַכְבּוֹר֒ וַיִּמְלֹ֤ךְ תַּחְתָּיו֙ הֲדַ֔ר וְשֵׁ֥ם עִיר֖וֹ פָּ֑עוּ וְשֵׁ֨ם אִשְׁתּ֤וֹ מְהֵֽיטַבְאֵל֙ בַּת־מַטְרֵ֔ד בַּ֖ת מֵ֥י זָהָֽב׃ 40 [MAFTIR] וְ֠אֵ֠לֶּה שְׁמ֞וֹת אַלּוּפֵ֤י עֵשָׂו֙ לְמִשְׁפְּחֹתָ֔ם לִמְקֹמֹתָ֖ם בִּשְׁמֹתָ֑ם אַלּ֥וּף תִּמְנָ֛ע אַלּ֥וּף עַלְוָ֖ה אַלּ֥וּף יְתֵֽת׃ 41 אַלּ֧וּף אׇהֳלִיבָמָ֛ה אַלּ֥וּף אֵלָ֖ה אַלּ֥וּף פִּינֹֽן׃ 42 אַלּ֥וּף קְנַ֛ז אַלּ֥וּף תֵּימָ֖ן אַלּ֥וּף מִבְצָֽר׃ 43 אַלּ֥וּף מַגְדִּיאֵ֖ל אַלּ֣וּף עִירָ֑ם אֵ֣לֶּה ׀ אַלּוּפֵ֣י אֱד֗וֹם לְמֹֽשְׁבֹתָם֙ בְּאֶ֣רֶץ אֲחֻזָּתָ֔ם ה֥וּא עֵשָׂ֖ו אֲבִ֥י אֱדֽוֹם׃ פ פ פ

קנ״ד פסוקים, קלי״ט סימן.

kabbalah bites

36:31 These kings of Edom retell the story of the primordial realm of *tohu* (chaos). Despite their extraordinary energy and passion, they ruled and died one after the other.

The vessels of tohu broke and were shattered.

In *tohu* there were too many *lights* and too few *vessels*. The vessels shattered from an excess of light, which they could not contain, just like a person stammers when he cannot find the words to express an idea.

The vessels also fell and broke because they were too self-orientated. They could not have a meaningful exchange with anything outside themselves.

The rest of history is the process of finding these lost fragments of the vessels and returning them to their source. So this brief passage about the kings of Edom is, in essence, the story of the world's dysfunction—something which it is our task to heal.

genesis 36:31–43 — va-yishlaḥ

The Kings of Edom

³¹ These are the kings who reigned in the land of Edom before any king reigned over the children of Israel: ³² Bela son of Beor reigned in Edom, and the name of his city was Dinhabah.

³³ Bela died, and Jobab son of Zerah of Bozrah reigned in his place.

³⁴ Jobab died, and Husham from the land of the Temanites reigned in his place.

³⁵ Husham died, and Hadad son of Bedad—who defeated the Midian(ites) in the field of Moab—reigned in his place. The name of his city was Avith.

³⁶ Hadad died, and Samlah of Masrekah reigned in his place.

³⁷ Samlah died, and Saul of Rehoboth-on-the-river (Euphrates) reigned in his place.

³⁸ Shaul died, and Baal-hanan son of Achbor reigned in his place.

³⁹ Baal-hanan son of Achbor died, and Hadar reigned in his place. The name of his city was Pau. His wife's name was Mehetabel daughter of Matred daughter of Me-zahab.

(After Hadar died, Esau's descendants lost their autonomy over their family groups. Instead the authority structure became regional, and each place was assigned its own leader):

[MAFTIR] ⁴⁰ These are the names of the (regional) heads of Esau('s land), according to (what was previously) their families, (but now assigned by) their places, (all of which had) their (own) names:

(The) head (of the) Timna (area, the) head (of the) Alvah (area, the) head (of the) Jetheth (area), ⁴¹ (the) head (of the) Oholibamah (area, the) head (of the) Elah (area, the) head (of the) Pinon (area), ⁴² (the) head (of the) Kenaz (area, the) head (of the) Teman (area, the) head (of the) Mibzar (area), ⁴³ (the) head (of the) Magdiel (area, which is Rome, the) head (of the) Iram (area). These are the (regional) heads of Edom according to the inhabited areas in the land of their inheritance.

(Edom is also known) as Esau, father of the Edomites.

The *Haftarah* for *Va-Yishlaḥ* is on page 1307.

---

this plot is best suited for grapevines and this is best suited for fig trees. The name *"Horite"* suggests that they smelled the earth to discern its properties, for by transposing the letters of *"Horite"*—Ḥori (spelled: *ḥet-resh-yod*) we obtain the Hebrew word for "scent"—*rei'aḥ* (spelled: *resh-yod-ḥet*). By the smell of the earth they were able to tell which crop would thrive on any given piece of land (*Babylonian Talmud, Shabbat* 85a).

> Jews have **survived history** only because they were **dreamers.** Dreaming helps you to **rise above** the **limitations** of life and fulfil your **potential.**

VA-YESHEV
וישב

JOSEPH IS SOLD BY HIS BROTHERS	37:1–36
JUDAH AND TAMAR	38:1–30
JOSEPH IN EGYPT	39:1 – 40:23

NAME
Va-Yeshev

MEANING
"And he settled"

LINES IN TORAH SCROLL
190

PARASHIYYOT
3 open; 1 closed

VERSES
112

WORDS
1558

LETTERS
5972

DATE
2216–2226

LOCATION
Land of Canaan, Egypt

KEY PEOPLE
Jacob, Joseph, Judah, Reuben, Midianite merchants, Tamar, Potiphar, Potiphar's wife, chief butler, chief baker

MITZVOT
None

MASORETIC FEATURES
The word *va-yema'en* (39:8) has an unusual cantillation note, the *shalshelet* (֓).

NOTE
Often read the week before Ḥanukkah

CHARACTER PROFILE

NAME
Judah

MEANING
"God will be praised"

PARENTS
Jacob and Leah

GRANDFATHERS
Laban, Isaac

WIFE
Daughter of Shua

SIBLINGS
Reuben, Simeon, Levi, Issachar, Zebulun, Dan, Naphtali, Gad, Asher, Joseph, Benjamin, Dinah

CHILDREN
Er, Onan, Shelah, Perez and Zerah

LIFE SPAN
119 years

BIRTHDATE
15 *Nisan*

BURIAL PLACE
Near Bethlehem

ACHIEVEMENTS
Because of his great accomplishments Judaism is named after him; saved Joseph's life

KNOWN FOR
Extraordinary strength; established Torah academies in Goshen; merited rulership over Israel

PARTIALITY

Joseph's brothers' hatred was fueled, in part, by Jacob's favoritism for Joseph. Partiality is a form of injustice. If you naturally favor one of your children, make sure that this preference does not become known (37:2-3).

HATRED

Hatred is an extremely toxic emotion which, once in place, can easily blow out of proportion. When Joseph innocently related his dreams to his brothers, their perception was colored by their hatred of him (37:3-8).

SHAMING ANOTHER

Tamar did not identify Judah overtly as the father of her children so that he would not be publicly shamed. "It is better to be thrown into a fire," says the Talmud, "rather than embarrass someone in public" (38:25).

RESISTING TEMPTATION

Joseph consistently refused his master's wife's advances. From where did he get the strength? By seeing the image of his father. When faced with a struggle, looking at your illustrious roots—the Patriarchs and Matriarchs—can help you make the correct choice (39:7-12).

בראשית לז:א-ט | וישב

לז 1 וַיֵּשֶׁב יַעֲקֹב בְּאֶרֶץ מְגוּרֵי אָבִיו בְּאֶרֶץ כְּנָעַן: 2 אֵלֶּה | תֹּלְדוֹת יַעֲקֹב יוֹסֵף בֶּן־שְׁבַע־עֶשְׂרֵה שָׁנָה הָיָה רֹעֶה אֶת־אֶחָיו בַּצֹּאן וְהוּא נַעַר אֶת־בְּנֵי בִלְהָה וְאֶת־בְּנֵי זִלְפָּה נְשֵׁי אָבִיו וַיָּבֵא יוֹסֵף אֶת־דִּבָּתָם רָעָה אֶל־אֲבִיהֶם: 3 וְיִשְׂרָאֵל אָהַב אֶת־יוֹסֵף מִכָּל־בָּנָיו כִּי־בֶן־זְקֻנִים הוּא לוֹ וְעָשָׂה לוֹ כְּתֹנֶת פַּסִּים: 4 וַיִּרְאוּ אֶחָיו כִּי־אֹתוֹ אָהַב אֲבִיהֶם מִכָּל־אֶחָיו וַיִּשְׂנְאוּ אֹתוֹ וְלֹא יָכְלוּ דַּבְּרוֹ לְשָׁלֹם: 5 וַיַּחֲלֹם יוֹסֵף חֲלוֹם וַיַּגֵּד לְאֶחָיו וַיּוֹסִפוּ עוֹד שְׂנֹא אֹתוֹ: 6 וַיֹּאמֶר אֲלֵיהֶם שִׁמְעוּ־נָא הַחֲלוֹם הַזֶּה אֲשֶׁר חָלָמְתִּי: 7 וְהִנֵּה אֲנַחְנוּ מְאַלְּמִים אֲלֻמִּים בְּתוֹךְ הַשָּׂדֶה וְהִנֵּה קָמָה אֲלֻמָּתִי וְגַם־נִצָּבָה וְהִנֵּה תְסֻבֶּינָה אֲלֻמֹּתֵיכֶם וַתִּשְׁתַּחֲוֶיןָ לַאֲלֻמָּתִי: 8 וַיֹּאמְרוּ לוֹ אֶחָיו הֲמָלֹךְ תִּמְלֹךְ עָלֵינוּ אִם־מָשׁוֹל תִּמְשֹׁל בָּנוּ וַיּוֹסִפוּ עוֹד שְׂנֹא אֹתוֹ עַל־חֲלֹמֹתָיו וְעַל־דְּבָרָיו: 9 וַיַּחֲלֹם עוֹד חֲלוֹם אַחֵר וַיְסַפֵּר אֹתוֹ לְאֶחָיו וַיֹּאמֶר הִנֵּה חָלַמְתִּי חֲלוֹם עוֹד וְהִנֵּה הַשֶּׁמֶשׁ וְהַיָּרֵחַ

According to *Targum Onkelos*, however, it means "because he was a *wise son* to him"—from the alternative meaning of *zaken*, "sage." Whatever Jacob had learned from Shem and Eber, he passed on to Joseph.

A third explanation of the phrase is to see it as a contraction of the expression *ziv 'ikonin*, "facial features," indicating that Joseph's features resembled Jacob's (*Rashi, 11th century*).

4. They hated him, and they couldn't speak with him civilly. Just as Abraham had produced the errant Ishmael, and Isaac, the deviant Esau, the brothers judged Joseph to be the impure offspring of Jacob (*Rabbi Menaham Azariah da Fano, 16th–17th century*).

If they had spoken with each another, they would have made peace. The main problem in disputes is a lack of communication, specifically when one side refuses to listen to the other. If people knew how to communicate, they would see that there is no room to argue (*Rabbi Jonathan Eybeschuetz, 18th century*).

8. They hated him even more because of his dreams. Why was Joseph at fault for dreaming, and why did this bring about the hatred of his brothers?

> ### kabbalah bites
>
> **37:2** Through provoking his brothers with "evil reports" and by recounting his dreams, Joseph incited his brothers to dispose of him. So he was somewhat responsible for their sin.
>
> To achieve *tikkun* (spiritual healing) for this, Joseph was reincarnated in Rabbi Ishmael son of Elisha, the High Priest. Rabbi Ishmael died a martyr as a *tikkun* for Joseph's soul.

genesis 37:1–9 — va-yeshev

parashat va-yeshev

Joseph Angers His Brothers

37 ¹ Jacob settled in the land which his father inhabited, the land of Canaan. ² These are (the episodes of) Jacob's descendants (until they were finally settled):

Joseph was seventeen years old. (For many years previously) he would pasture the sheep with his brothers. He (would) do boy(ish things, like curling his hair and touching up his eyes to look attractive, and he spent his time) with Bilhah's sons and Zilpah's sons—(the sons of) his father's wives—(whom Leah's sons had treated disrespectfully). Joseph (used to) bring reports to their father (of all Leah's sons' behavior that he thought was) evil.

³ Israel loved Joseph more than all his sons, because he was a son (born to him in) old age, so he made him a robe of fine wool. ⁴ When his brothers saw that their father loved him more than all his brothers, they hated him, and they couldn't speak with him civilly.

⁵ Joseph had a dream and told his brothers about it, and they hated him even more. ⁶ (This is what) he said to them: "Please listen to this dream, which I have dreamed! ⁷ There we were, binding sheaves in the middle of the field, when—look!—my sheaf stood upright and it kept standing too. And then—look!—your sheaves gathered around and threw themselves down (in front of) my sheaf."

⁸ His brothers said to him, "(Does this mean that you want to) reign constantly over us, or rule us all the time?" And they hated him even more because of his dreams, and because of his (evil) reports (to their father).

⁹ (Joseph) had yet another dream, and he told his brothers about it. He said, "Here, I have dreamed another dream. Just look! The sun, the moon, and eleven stars threw themselves down before me!"

37:1 Jacob settled. When Jacob sought to settle in tranquility, Joseph's anger (against his brothers) leapt upon him. The righteous seek to settle in tranquility. God said, "Isn't it enough for the righteous to have what's prepared for them in the world to come, that they seek to settle in tranquility in this world too?" (*Rashi, 11th century*).

2. These are Jacob's descendants, Joseph. "Joseph" means "increase." If you want to have "descendants," to extend beyond the limitations of your own existence, then you must always increase your efforts in study and good deeds, worshiping God with greater passion (*Rabbi Menahem Mendel of Rymanow, 18th century*).

3. Because he was a son (born to him in) old age (*ben zekunim*). The phrase *ben zekunim* means that Joseph was born to Jacob in his old age—*zikenato*.

בראשית לז:ט-יז · וישב

וְאַחַ֤ד עָשָׂר֙ כּֽוֹכָבִ֔ים מִֽשְׁתַּחֲוִ֖ים לִֽי: 10 וַיְסַפֵּ֣ר אֶל־אָבִיו֮ וְאֶל־אֶחָיו֒ וַיִּגְעַר־בּ֣וֹ אָבִ֔יו וַיֹּ֣אמֶר ל֔וֹ מָ֛ה הַחֲל֥וֹם הַזֶּ֖ה אֲשֶׁ֣ר חָלָ֑מְתָּ הֲב֣וֹא נָב֗וֹא אֲנִי֙ וְאִמְּךָ֣ וְאַחֶ֔יךָ לְהִשְׁתַּחֲוֺ֥ת לְךָ֖ אָֽרְצָה: 11 וַיְקַנְאוּ־ב֖וֹ אֶחָ֑יו וְאָבִ֖יו שָׁמַ֥ר אֶת־הַדָּבָֽר: [SECOND READING]

12 וַיֵּלְכ֖וּ אֶחָ֑יו לִרְע֛וֹת אֶת־צֹ֥אן אֲבִיהֶ֖ם בִּשְׁכֶֽם: 13 וַיֹּ֨אמֶר יִשְׂרָאֵ֜ל אֶל־יוֹסֵ֗ף הֲל֤וֹא אַחֶ֨יךָ֙ רֹעִ֣ים בִּשְׁכֶ֔ם לְכָ֖ה וְאֶשְׁלָחֲךָ֣ אֲלֵיהֶ֑ם וַיֹּ֥אמֶר ל֖וֹ הִנֵּֽנִי: 14 וַיֹּ֣אמֶר ל֗וֹ לֶךְ־נָ֨א רְאֵ֜ה אֶת־שְׁל֤וֹם אַחֶ֨יךָ֙ וְאֶת־שְׁל֣וֹם הַצֹּ֔אן וַהֲשִׁבֵ֖נִי דָּבָ֑ר וַיִּשְׁלָחֵ֨הוּ֙ מֵעֵ֣מֶק חֶבְר֔וֹן וַיָּבֹ֖א שְׁכֶֽמָה: 15 וַיִּמְצָאֵ֣הוּ אִ֔ישׁ וְהִנֵּ֥ה תֹעֶ֖ה בַּשָּׂדֶ֑ה וַיִּשְׁאָלֵ֧הוּ הָאִ֛ישׁ לֵאמֹ֖ר מַה־תְּבַקֵּֽשׁ: 16 וַיֹּ֕אמֶר אֶת־אַחַ֖י אָנֹכִ֣י מְבַקֵּ֑שׁ הַגִּֽידָה־נָּ֣א לִ֔י אֵיפֹ֖ה הֵ֥ם רֹעִֽים: 17 וַיֹּ֤אמֶר הָאִישׁ֙ נָסְע֣וּ מִזֶּ֔ה כִּ֤י שָׁמַ֨עְתִּי֙ אֹֽמְרִ֔ים נֵלְכָ֖ה דֹּתָ֑יְנָה

Joseph, would diffuse the brothers' anger, for they would see that his superiority over them was no more than a matter of being successful *in rearing better crops*.

When Joseph had the second dream, he thought that it would definitely calm his brothers, for it demonstrated even more clearly that they had no reason to be jealous. In this dream, it was clear that Joseph was not destined to have any *physical* advantage over his brothers at all. It was only that *"the sun, the moon, and eleven stars threw themselves down before me"* (v. 9)—only the stars, representing the *mazalot* (spiritual roots) of the brothers (see *Rashi* to 15:5), were bowing down to Joseph, and not the brothers themselves.

Joseph did follow a logical path, because he expected that everybody would take his dreams literally, just as he had done. However, since hatred tends to hinder a person from being rational, the brothers did not take the dreams literally. Rather, they saw them in the light of their own prejudice against Joseph (*Rabbi Menahem Mendel Schneerson, 20th century*).

11. His father (however, believed in the dream). He waited expectantly for the dream to materialize (*Rashi, 11th century*).

17. They've left here, for I heard them saying, "Let's go to Dothan" (*nelekhah Dotaynah*). *"They've left here,"* implies, "they've parted from brotherhood." *Nelekhah dotaynah* implies, "they went to seek legal pretexts (*nikhelei datot*) to put you to death."

Dothan is also the name of an actual place, since Scripture does not depart from its literal meaning (*Rashi, 11th century*).

Rashi's interpretations were not actually said by Gabriel to Joseph, for Joseph would surely not have gone to his brothers if he knew they were planning to kill him. Rather, *Rashi* is explaining the *double entendre* of Scripture (*Nahmanides, 13th century*).

food for thought

1. Is favoritism ever appropriate?

2. Have you ever been wrongfully slandered? How did you respond?

3. Is it better to be tactful or truthful?

¹⁰ He (then) told it to his father (in the presence of) his brothers. His father rebuked him (in order to calm the brothers down). He said to (Joseph), "What is this dream that you have dreamed? How could I, your mother, and your brothers come and throw ourselves down to you on the ground (when your mother has already passed away)?" ¹¹ But his brothers (still) envied him.

His father (however, believed in the dream) and kept (waiting) for the event (to occur).

The Sale of Joseph

[SECOND READING] ¹² His brothers went to pasture their father's flocks in Shechem. ¹³ Israel said to Joseph, "Aren't your brothers pasturing in Shechem? Come, I'll send you to join them."

"I'm ready," (Joseph) said to him (even though he knew his brothers hated him).

¹⁴ (Israel) said to him, "Go now and see how your brothers are doing and how the sheep are doing, and bring me back news."

So (Israel) sent him off from the Hebron Valley, and he came to Shechem.

¹⁵ (The angel Gabriel in the guise of) a man found him, and—look!—he was lost in the field. The man questioned him, saying, "What do you want?"

¹⁶ (Joseph) said, "I am looking for my brothers. Please tell me where they are pasturing?"

¹⁷ The man said, "They've left here (they're not acting like your brothers any more), for I heard them saying, 'Let's go to Dothan (we'll find a legal pretext to kill our brother).'"

You tend to dream about the things you think about during the day. The brothers assumed that Joseph constantly thought of ruling over them, and therefore, he had dreamt about it at night. This aroused their anger (*Rabbi Ephraim of Luntshits, 16th–17th century*).

10. He then told it to his father (in the presence of his brothers). Joseph already knew that his brothers hated him, so what could have been his logic behind this entire exercise of repeating the dreams, which only provoked his brothers further?

According to Torah Law, a person is prohibited from withholding a prophecy that he receives (*Babylonian Talmud, Sanhedrin 89a*). Therefore, Joseph was obligated to relate his prophetic dream, which described how he would rule over his brothers, despite the consequences (*Rabbi Asher b. Jehiel, 13th–14th century*).

When Joseph saw that his brothers were jealous of him—because Jacob had made a special robe for him—he would have looked for a means to reduce his brothers' jealousy and diffuse their anger.

Joseph presumed that when he would tell his brothers, *"Your sheaves gathered a round and threw themselves down (in front of) my sheaf"* (v. 7), they would interpret the matter literally—that *his sheaves* would be stronger and more valuable than those of his brothers. This, thought

בראשית לז:יז-כה · וישב

וַיֵּ֤לֶךְ יוֹסֵף֙ אַחַ֣ר אֶחָ֔יו וַיִּמְצָאֵ֖ם בְּדֹתָֽן: 18 וַיִּרְא֥וּ אֹת֖וֹ מֵרָחֹ֑ק וּבְטֶ֨רֶם֙ יִקְרַ֣ב אֲלֵיהֶ֔ם וַיִּֽתְנַכְּל֥וּ אֹת֖וֹ לַהֲמִיתֽוֹ: 19 וַיֹּאמְר֖וּ אִ֣ישׁ אֶל־אָחִ֑יו הִנֵּ֗ה בַּ֛עַל הַחֲלֹמ֥וֹת הַלָּזֶ֖ה בָּֽא: 20 וְעַתָּ֣ה | לְכ֣וּ וְנַֽהַרְגֵ֗הוּ וְנַשְׁלִכֵ֨הוּ֙ בְּאַחַ֣ד הַבֹּר֔וֹת וְאָמַ֕רְנוּ חַיָּ֥ה רָעָ֖ה אֲכָלָ֑תְהוּ וְנִרְאֶ֕ה מַה־יִּהְי֖וּ חֲלֹמֹתָֽיו: 21 וַיִּשְׁמַ֣ע רְאוּבֵ֔ן וַיַּצִּלֵ֖הוּ מִיָּדָ֑ם וַיֹּ֕אמֶר לֹ֥א נַכֶּ֖נּוּ נָֽפֶשׁ: 22 וַיֹּ֨אמֶר אֲלֵהֶ֣ם | רְאוּבֵן֮ אַל־תִּשְׁפְּכוּ־דָם֒ הַשְׁלִ֣יכוּ אֹת֗וֹ אֶל־הַבּ֤וֹר הַזֶּה֙ אֲשֶׁ֣ר בַּמִּדְבָּ֔ר וְיָ֖ד אַל־תִּשְׁלְחוּ־ב֑וֹ לְמַ֗עַן הַצִּ֤יל אֹתוֹ֙ מִיָּדָ֔ם לַהֲשִׁיב֖וֹ אֶל־אָבִֽיו: 23 [THIRD READING] וַֽיְהִ֕י כַּֽאֲשֶׁר־בָּ֥א יוֹסֵ֖ף אֶל־אֶחָ֑יו וַיַּפְשִׁ֤יטוּ אֶת־יוֹסֵף֙ אֶת־כֻּתָּנְתּ֔וֹ אֶת־כְּתֹ֥נֶת הַפַּסִּ֖ים אֲשֶׁ֥ר עָלָֽיו: 24 וַיִּ֨קָּחֻ֔הוּ וַיַּשְׁלִ֥כוּ אֹת֖וֹ הַבֹּ֑רָה וְהַבּ֣וֹר רֵ֔ק אֵ֥ין בּ֖וֹ מָֽיִם: 25 וַיֵּשְׁבוּ֮ לֶֽאֱכָל־לֶחֶם֒ וַיִּשְׂא֤וּ עֵֽינֵיהֶם֙ וַיִּרְא֔וּ וְהִנֵּה֙ אֹרְחַ֣ת

---

wanted to save Joseph "from *their* hands"—from the hands of those that had free choice (*Rabbi Hayyim ibn Attar, 18th century*).

24. The pit was empty, There was no water in it. Since the verse states, *"the pit was empty,"* don't I already know that *"there was no water in it"*? Why did the Torah need to write, *"there was no water in it"*? The Torah is hinting that there was no water in it, but there were snakes and scorpions in it (*Rashi, 11th century*).

If there were snakes and scorpions in the pit why is it written of Reuben, *"(He said this only) in order to save (Joseph) from their hands, to return him to his father"* (v. 22)? Didn't Reuben fear that the snakes and scorpions would harm Joseph? If so, how did he plan to return him to his father? The verse states that his actions were "in order *to save him*."

Reuben saw that Joseph would surely come to harm in their hands, for he knew how much they hated him and wished to kill him. Reuben said, "It is better to cast him into the pit of snakes and scorpions than to deliver him to those who hate him and who have no compassion for him. For, in a place of snakes and scorpions, if a man is righteous God will perform a miracle for him and save him, or sometimes he is saved by the merit of his fathers. But once delivered into the hands of enemies, few escape."

Come and behold the piety of Reuben! He knew that Simeon and Levi were ruthless and cunning when they joined forces. When they joined against Shechem, they killed all the males. Reuben said, "If such a great city did not escape them, then if this boy falls into their hands, not a shred of flesh will remain. Therefore, it is better to save him from them" (*Zohar*).

The *Zohar's* stress on Reuben's piety appears to be perplexing: Why is it an especially impressive act of piety that he attempted to save Joseph from great danger, such that the *Zohar* declares, *"Come and behold* the piety of Reuben"? Surely it is a *basic obligation* to save a man who is in life-threatening danger, and not an exceptional act of piety?

In order to save Joseph, Reuben was forced to act deceptively (v. 22), and this was the very opposite of his nature. *Rashi* explains on the verse, *"They couldn't speak with him nicely"* (v. 4)—

genesis 37:17–25 — va-yeshev

So Joseph went after his brothers, and he found them in Dothan. ¹⁸ They saw him from a distance, and before he came near them they plotted against him to put him to death. ¹⁹ They said to each other, "Look! That dreamer is coming. ²⁰ So now, come and we'll kill him! Then we'll cast him into one of the pits, and we'll say, 'A wild beast devoured him.'"

(But God said,) "We are going to see what (indeed) will become of his dreams!"

²¹ When Reuben heard (their plan) he saved (Joseph) from their hands. He said, "Let's not give him a lethal blow.

²² "Don't shed blood!" Reuben said to them. "Throw him into this pit that's in the desert, but don't lay a hand upon him." (He said this only) in order to save (Joseph) from their hands, (and then he planned to rescue him and) return him to his father.

[THIRD READING] ²³ Then, when Joseph came to his brothers, they stripped Joseph of his tunic and the fine woolen robe which he had on. ²⁴ They took him and cast him into a pit.

The pit was empty. There was no water in it (but there were snakes and scorpions in it).

²⁵ They sat down to eat a meal. They glanced around and saw—look!—a caravan

---

18. They plotted against him to put him to death. The brothers thought that Joseph was joining them, not in an act of friendship, but to find fault in their actions. They thought he would then make a bad report to Jacob, who would curse the brothers in anger (or that God Himself would punish them), and they would die. Joseph would then remain alone, as the blessed of the sons.

The other brothers were completely pious individuals, as we find that all their names are mentioned on the High Priest's breastplate. In this case, they followed the legal principle that if a person comes to kill you, you must kill him first, in self-defense (*Babylonian Talmud, Sanhedrin* 72b; *Rabbi Obadiah Sforno, 16th century*).

21. When Reuben heard (their plan) he saved (Joseph) from their hands. Reuben's suggestion to throw Joseph into the pit was done with good intentions, as Reuben intended to rescue him later. When Reuben subsequently saw that Joseph was no longer in the pit (37:29), he was sure that his suggestion had been a foolish one. But the Torah testifies here that Reuben *had* saved Joseph from death, for if it weren't for his suggestion, Joseph would have been killed by his other brothers. *Good intentions, although not always realized, are not in vain* (*Rabbi Judah Aryeh Leib Alter of Gur, 19th century*).

22. In order to save Joseph from their hands. Since a man has free will, he is able to kill somebody whom Heaven does not hold liable for death. However, the snakes and scorpions in the pit where Joseph had been placed did not have free choice. While the brothers could have executed Joseph, the snakes and scorpions would only have been able to kill him if he actually deserved to die, by ruling of the Heavenly Court. Therefore, the verse states that Reuben

בראשית לז:כה-לג — וישב

יִשְׁמְעֵאלִים בָּאָה מִגִּלְעָד וּגְמַלֵּיהֶם נֹשְׂאִים נְכֹאת וּצְרִי וָלֹט הוֹלְכִים לְהוֹרִיד מִצְרָיְמָה: 26 וַיֹּאמֶר יְהוּדָה אֶל־אֶחָיו מַה־בֶּצַע כִּי נַהֲרֹג אֶת־אָחִינוּ וְכִסִּינוּ אֶת־דָּמוֹ: 27 לְכוּ וְנִמְכְּרֶנּוּ לַיִּשְׁמְעֵאלִים וְיָדֵנוּ אַל־תְּהִי־בוֹ כִּי־אָחִינוּ בְשָׂרֵנוּ הוּא וַיִּשְׁמְעוּ אֶחָיו: 28 וַיַּעַבְרוּ אֲנָשִׁים מִדְיָנִים סֹחֲרִים וַיִּמְשְׁכוּ וַיַּעֲלוּ אֶת־יוֹסֵף מִן־הַבּוֹר וַיִּמְכְּרוּ אֶת־יוֹסֵף לַיִּשְׁמְעֵאלִים בְּעֶשְׂרִים כָּסֶף וַיָּבִיאוּ אֶת־יוֹסֵף מִצְרָיְמָה: 29 וַיָּשָׁב רְאוּבֵן אֶל־הַבּוֹר וְהִנֵּה אֵין־יוֹסֵף בַּבּוֹר וַיִּקְרַע אֶת־בְּגָדָיו: 30 וַיָּשָׁב אֶל־אֶחָיו וַיֹּאמַר הַיֶּלֶד אֵינֶנּוּ וַאֲנִי אָנָה אֲנִי־בָא: 31 וַיִּקְחוּ אֶת־כְּתֹנֶת יוֹסֵף וַיִּשְׁחֲטוּ שְׂעִיר עִזִּים וַיִּטְבְּלוּ אֶת־הַכֻּתֹּנֶת בַּדָּם: 32 וַיְשַׁלְּחוּ אֶת־כְּתֹנֶת הַפַּסִּים וַיָּבִיאוּ אֶל־אֲבִיהֶם וַיֹּאמְרוּ זֹאת מָצָאנוּ הַכֶּר־נָא הַכְּתֹנֶת בִּנְךָ הִוא אִם־לֹא: 33 וַיַּכִּירָהּ וַיֹּאמֶר כְּתֹנֶת בְּנִי חַיָּה רָעָה אֲכָלָתְהוּ טָרֹף טֹרַף יוֹסֵף:

29. Reuben returned. When Joseph was sold, Reuben was absent, because it was his day to go and tend to his father.

Another explanation: He was busy with his sackcloth and his fasting for disturbing his father's bed (see above, 35:22; *Rashi, 11th century*).

Joseph had been tending to his father during the period before he left, so now somebody else had to replace him. Since Reuben was the firstborn, he went first (*Rabbi Mordecai ha-Kohen, 17th century*).

33. A wild beast has devoured him! Why did God not reveal to Jacob that Joseph was alive?

The brothers excommunicated and cursed anyone who would reveal it, and they included God as a partner with them.

Isaac knew that Joseph was alive, but he said, "How can I reveal it to Jacob if God does not wish to reveal it to him?" (*Rashi, 11th century*).

spiritual vitamin

> Life's trials, tragedies and difficulties actually bring us closer to our goal, our *raison d'etre*; they are part of the Divine system of toil and endeavor enabling us, finite mortals, to reach the highest levels of rewards and goodness—which can only be earned by meaningful "labor" and effort.

genesis 37:25–33 va-yeshev

of Arabs was coming from Gilead. Their camels were laden with spice mixtures, balsam, and birthwort. They were on their way to take (them) down to Egypt.

²⁶ Judah said to his brothers, "What (profit) will we gain if we kill our brother and hide his blood(y death)? ²⁷ Come, let's sell him to the Arabs, and let our own hands not (act) against him, for he is our brother, our flesh." His brothers listened (to him).

²⁸ (Meanwhile, another caravan of) Midianite men, merchants, passed by.

(The brothers) pulled Joseph and lifted him up from the pit. They sold Joseph to the Arabs for twenty silver (pieces, and the Arabs sold him to the Midianites). They brought Joseph to Egypt.

²⁹ Reuben (had been tending to his father. He) returned to the pit, and—look!—Joseph wasn't in the pit. He tore his garments. ³⁰ He returned to his brothers and said, "The boy's not there! Where can I go (to escape my father's anguish)?"

³¹ They took Joseph's robe, slaughtered a young goat, and dipped the robe into the blood. ³² They sent the fine woolen coat (with messengers who) brought it to their father. They said, "We have found this. Please could you identify if this is your son's coat or not."

³³ He recognized it, and he said, "(It's) my son's coat! A wild beast has devoured him! Joseph has been ripped apart again and again!"

"From what is stated to their discredit, we may learn something to their credit—they did not say one thing with their mouths and think differently in their hearts." Certainly, this statement included Reuben too, which indicated that he was an extremely honest person. In order to save Joseph, he was forced to *defy his nature* and act deceptively.

And this is the very definition of a pious person: one who goes beyond his natural inclinations. Therefore, the *Zohar* declared, *"Come and behold the piety of Reuben"* (*Rabbi Menahem Mendel Schneerson, 20th century*).

25. They sat down to eat a meal. The brothers sat down to eat a meal after casting Joseph into the pit because they were uncertain whether to kill him or not. Reuben had argued, "Don't shed blood!" (v. 22), and now they lacked a clear direction of how to deal with Joseph. They were questioning their earlier judgment that he deserved to be killed. Therefore, they sat down to eat a meal, hoping that through eating they would find clarity in this matter.

And this is what actually transpired—after eating the meal they decided to sell Joseph (*Rabbi Menahem Mendel of Rymanow, 18th century*).

28. They sold Joseph. By selling Joseph, the brothers rendered him as their slave, not only in a physical, but in a spiritual sense too. Since Joseph was the future viceroy of Egypt, his sale into slavery by the brothers established Egypt as "slaves" of the Jewish people.

This proved to be of benefit later on, during the Egyptian exile. Even when the Jewish people were enslaved physically, it was the *Egyptians* who were slaves spiritually. And this deeper truth *did* have some physical expression, in that it was impossible for the Egyptians to have total control over the Jewish people, even while the latter were slaves (*Zohar*).

בראשית לז:לד - לח:יד   וישב

34 וַיִּקְרַ֤ע יַעֲקֹב֙ שִׂמְלֹתָ֔יו וַיָּ֥שֶׂם שַׂ֖ק בְּמָתְנָ֑יו וַיִּתְאַבֵּ֥ל עַל־בְּנ֖וֹ יָמִ֥ים רַבִּֽים:
35 וַיָּקֻ֩מוּ֩ כָל־בָּנָ֨יו וְכָל־בְּנֹתָ֜יו לְנַחֲמ֗וֹ וַיְמָאֵן֙ לְהִתְנַחֵ֔ם וַיֹּ֕אמֶר כִּֽי־אֵרֵ֧ד אֶל־בְּנִ֛י אָבֵ֖ל שְׁאֹ֑לָה וַיֵּ֥בְךְּ אֹת֖וֹ אָבִֽיו: 36 וְהַ֨מְּדָנִ֔ים מָכְר֥וּ אֹת֖וֹ אֶל־מִצְרָ֑יִם לְפֽוֹטִיפַר֙ סְרִ֣יס פַּרְעֹ֔ה שַׂ֖ר הַטַּבָּחִֽים: פ

לח

[FOURTH READING] 1 וַֽיְהִי֙ בָּעֵ֣ת הַהִ֔וא וַיֵּ֥רֶד יְהוּדָ֖ה מֵאֵ֣ת אֶחָ֑יו וַיֵּ֛ט עַד־אִ֥ישׁ עֲדֻלָּמִ֖י וּשְׁמ֥וֹ חִירָֽה: 2 וַיַּרְא־שָׁ֧ם יְהוּדָ֛ה בַּת־אִ֥ישׁ כְּנַעֲנִ֖י וּשְׁמ֣וֹ שׁ֑וּעַ וַיִּקָּחֶ֖הָ וַיָּבֹ֥א אֵלֶֽיהָ: 3 וַתַּ֖הַר וַתֵּ֣לֶד בֵּ֑ן וַיִּקְרָ֥א אֶת־שְׁמ֖וֹ עֵֽר: 4 וַתַּ֥הַר ע֖וֹד וַתֵּ֣לֶד בֵּ֑ן וַתִּקְרָ֥א אֶת־שְׁמ֖וֹ אוֹנָֽן: 5 וַתֹּ֤סֶף עוֹד֙ וַתֵּ֣לֶד בֵּ֔ן וַתִּקְרָ֥א אֶת־שְׁמ֖וֹ שֵׁלָ֑ה וְהָיָ֥ה בִכְזִ֖יב בְּלִדְתָּ֥הּ אֹתֽוֹ: 6 וַיִּקַּ֧ח יְהוּדָ֛ה אִשָּׁ֖ה לְעֵ֣ר בְּכוֹר֑וֹ וּשְׁמָ֖הּ תָּמָֽר:
7 וַיְהִ֗י עֵ֚ר בְּכ֣וֹר יְהוּדָ֔ה רַ֖ע בְּעֵינֵ֣י יְהוָ֑ה וַיְמִתֵ֖הוּ יְהוָֽה: 8 וַיֹּ֤אמֶר יְהוּדָה֙ לְאוֹנָ֔ן בֹּ֛א אֶל־אֵ֥שֶׁת אָחִ֖יךָ וְיַבֵּ֣ם אֹתָ֑הּ וְהָקֵ֥ם זֶ֖רַע לְאָחִֽיךָ: 9 וַיֵּ֣דַע אוֹנָ֔ן כִּ֛י לֹּ֥א ל֖וֹ יִֽהְיֶ֣ה הַזָּ֑רַע וְהָיָ֞ה אִם־בָּ֨א אֶל־אֵ֤שֶׁת אָחִיו֙ וְשִׁחֵ֣ת אַ֔רְצָה לְבִלְתִּ֥י נְתָן־זֶ֖רַע לְאָחִֽיו:
10 וַיֵּ֛רַע בְּעֵינֵ֥י יְהוָ֖ה אֲשֶׁ֣ר עָשָׂ֑ה וַיָּ֖מֶת גַּם־אֹתֽוֹ: 11 וַיֹּ֣אמֶר יְהוּדָה֩ לְתָמָ֨ר כַּלָּת֜וֹ שְׁבִ֧י אַלְמָנָ֣ה בֵית־אָבִ֗יךְ עַד־יִגְדַּל֙ שֵׁלָ֣ה בְנִ֔י כִּ֣י אָמַ֔ר פֶּן־יָמ֥וּת גַּם־ה֖וּא כְּאֶחָ֑יו וַתֵּ֣לֶךְ תָּמָ֔ר וַתֵּ֖שֶׁב בֵּ֥ית אָבִֽיהָ: 12 וַיִּרְבּוּ֙ הַיָּמִ֔ים וַתָּ֖מָת בַּת־שׁ֣וּעַ אֵֽשֶׁת־יְהוּדָ֑ה וַיִּנָּ֣חֶם יְהוּדָ֗ה וַיַּ֜עַל עַל־גֹּֽזְזֵ֤י צֹאנוֹ֙ ה֗וּא וְחִירָ֛ה רֵעֵ֥הוּ הָעֲדֻלָּמִ֖י תִּמְנָֽתָה: 13 וַיֻּגַּ֥ד לְתָמָ֖ר לֵאמֹ֑ר הִנֵּ֥ה חָמִ֛יךְ עֹלֶ֥ה תִמְנָ֖תָה לָגֹ֥ז צֹאנֽוֹ: 14 וַתָּ֩סַר֩ בִּגְדֵ֨י אַלְמְנוּתָ֜הּ

38:1 It was at that time that Judah went down. Why was this section placed here, interrupting the section dealing with Joseph?

To teach you that Judah's brothers demoted him from his high position when they saw their father's distress. They said, "You told us to sell him. If you would have told us to return him to our father, we would have listened to you" (*Rashi, 11th century*).

The brothers were busy selling Joseph; Joseph was busy with his sackcloth and fasting; Reuben was busy with his sackcloth and fasting; Jacob was busy with his sackcloth and fasting; Judah was busy finding himself a wife—*and God was busy creating the light of the Messiah.* Perez, ancestor of the Messiah, was born from Judah and Tamar (*Genesis Rabbah*).

³⁴ Jacob tore his garments and tied sackcloth around his waist. He mourned many days for his son.

³⁵ All his sons and all his daughters tried to console him, but he was unable to be consoled. He said, "I will go down to my grave while I am (still) mourning for my son (for I will never be consoled)."

(Jacob's) father (Isaac) wept for him.

³⁶ The Midianites sold (Joseph) to Egypt, to Potiphar, Pharaoh's officer, chief of the butchers.

Judah and Tamar

38 [FOURTH READING] ¹ It was at that time that Judah('s level of respect) from his brothers went down (since they blamed him for not averting the entire incident with Joseph), so he turned away (from his brothers and went into partnership) with an Adullamite man, named Hirah. ² There, Judah saw the daughter of a businessman, named Shua, and he married her and came to her.

³ She conceived and gave birth to a son, and he named him Er.

⁴ She conceived again and gave birth to a son, and she named him Onan.

⁵ She bore yet another son, and she named him Shelah. (Judah) was in Chezib when she gave birth to him.

⁶ Judah took a wife named Tamar for Er, his firstborn.

⁷ Er, Judah's firstborn, was evil in the eyes of God, and God made him die. ⁸ So Judah said to Onan, "Come to your brother's wife and enter into levirate marriage [*yibbum*] with her, and raise up children in your brother('s name)."

⁹ Onan knew that the children would not (be named after) him. So, whenever he came to his brother's wife, he would waste on the ground, so as not to establish children in his brother('s name).

¹⁰ What he did was evil in the eyes of God, and He made him die too.

¹¹ Judah said to his daughter-in-law, Tamar, "Stay as a widow in your father's house until my son Shelah grows up." (Whenever she asked about Shelah, he pushed her off), for he said (to himself), "Maybe he'll die too, like his brothers." So Tamar went, and she stayed in her father's house.

¹² Many days passed and Judah's wife—Shua's daughter—died. After Judah was consoled, he went up to Timnah, both he and his Adullamite friend, (to supervise) his sheepshearers. ¹³ (Someone) reported to Tamar, saying, "Look, your father-in-law is going up to Timnah to shear his sheep."

¹⁴ She took off her widow's clothes, covered (her head) with a scarf and covered

מֵעָלֶיהָ וַתְּכַס בַּצָּעִיף וַתִּתְעַלָּף וַתֵּשֶׁב בְּפֶתַח עֵינַיִם אֲשֶׁר עַל־דֶּרֶךְ תִּמְנָתָה כִּי רָאֲתָה כִּי־גָדַל שֵׁלָה וְהִוא לֹא־נִתְּנָה לוֹ לְאִשָּׁה: 15 וַיִּרְאֶהָ יְהוּדָה וַיַּחְשְׁבֶהָ לְזוֹנָה כִּי כִסְּתָה פָּנֶיהָ: 16 וַיֵּט אֵלֶיהָ אֶל־הַדֶּרֶךְ וַיֹּאמֶר הָבָה־נָּא אָבוֹא אֵלַיִךְ כִּי לֹא יָדַע כִּי כַלָּתוֹ הִוא וַתֹּאמֶר מַה־תִּתֶּן־לִי כִּי תָבוֹא אֵלָי: 17 וַיֹּאמֶר אָנֹכִי אֲשַׁלַּח גְּדִי־עִזִּים מִן־הַצֹּאן וַתֹּאמֶר אִם־תִּתֵּן עֵרָבוֹן עַד שָׁלְחֶךָ: 18 וַיֹּאמֶר מָה הָעֵרָבוֹן אֲשֶׁר אֶתֶּן־לָךְ וַתֹּאמֶר חֹתָמְךָ וּפְתִילֶךָ וּמַטְּךָ אֲשֶׁר בְּיָדֶךָ וַיִּתֶּן־ לָהּ וַיָּבֹא אֵלֶיהָ וַתַּהַר לוֹ: 19 וַתָּקָם וַתֵּלֶךְ וַתָּסַר צְעִיפָהּ מֵעָלֶיהָ וַתִּלְבַּשׁ בִּגְדֵי אַלְמְנוּתָהּ: 20 וַיִּשְׁלַח יְהוּדָה אֶת־גְּדִי הָעִזִּים בְּיַד רֵעֵהוּ הָעֲדֻלָּמִי לָקַחַת הָעֵרָבוֹן מִיַּד הָאִשָּׁה וְלֹא מְצָאָהּ: 21 וַיִּשְׁאַל אֶת־אַנְשֵׁי מְקֹמָהּ לֵאמֹר אַיֵּה הַקְּדֵשָׁה הִוא בָעֵינַיִם עַל־הַדָּרֶךְ וַיֹּאמְרוּ לֹא־הָיְתָה בָזֶה קְדֵשָׁה: 22 וַיָּשָׁב אֶל־ יְהוּדָה וַיֹּאמֶר לֹא מְצָאתִיהָ וְגַם אַנְשֵׁי הַמָּקוֹם אָמְרוּ לֹא־הָיְתָה בָזֶה קְדֵשָׁה: 23 וַיֹּאמֶר יְהוּדָה תִּקַּח־לָהּ פֶּן נִהְיֶה לָבוּז הִנֵּה שָׁלַחְתִּי הַגְּדִי הַזֶּה וְאַתָּה לֹא מְצָאתָהּ: 24 וַיְהִי | כְּמִשְׁלֹשׁ חֳדָשִׁים וַיֻּגַּד לִיהוּדָה לֵאמֹר זָנְתָה תָּמָר כַּלָּתֶךָ וְגַם הִנֵּה הָרָה לִזְנוּנִים וַיֹּאמֶר יְהוּדָה הוֹצִיאוּהָ וְתִשָּׂרֵף: 25 הִוא מוּצֵאת וְהִיא

assistant in this matter would have been sufficient to shame him as well (*Rabbi Ezra b. Elijah Tarab, 19th century*).

24. Take her out and let her be burned. The *Zohar* teaches that the words, "*Take her out and let her be burned*" (v. 24), refer to the soul in the times of exile. Even though the soul has been "taken out" of its natural habitat of being close to God, it still "burns" with the love for God (*Rabbi Shneur Zalman of Lyady, 18th century*).

kabbalah bites

38:16 The Messiah, descended from King David, traces his lineage back to the union between Judah and Tamar.

Why did the line of God's illustrious anointed one enter the world in such a distasteful manner? Because the demonic forces of *kelippah* refused to allow the Messiah's appearance in this world. They only consented because his entry was enshrouded in *kelippah*.

her face. She sat down at the crossroads which is on the way to Timnah (in order to offer herself to Judah). For she saw that Shelah had grown up, and she had not been given to him as a wife (and she desired to have children from Judah).

¹⁵ When Judah saw her, he thought she was a harlot (because she was sitting by the crossroads, and he did not recognize her) because she had covered her face. ¹⁶ He turned off (the road on which he was traveling) to the road (where) she (was). He said, "Get ready please, let me come to you," for he did not know that she was his daughter-in-law.

She said, "What will you give me if you come to me?"

¹⁷ He said, "I will send a young goat from the herd."

"(Only) if you give me some collateral until you send it," she said.

¹⁸ "What collateral should I give you?" he said.

She said, "Your signet ring, your cloak, and the staff that's in your hand."

He gave them to her, and he came to her. She conceived from him (men of similar might and righteousness as Judah).

¹⁹ She got up and went off. She removed her scarf, and put on her widow's clothing. ²⁰ Judah sent the young goat through his Adullamite friend to take the collateral from the woman's hand, but he did not find her. ²¹ So he asked the people of her locality, saying, "Where is the harlot who was at the crossroads on the way?"

They said, "There was no harlot here."

²² He returned to Judah, and he said, "I have not found her, and the people of the place also said, 'No harlot was here.'"

²³ Judah said, "Let her keep them for herself, otherwise we'll be put to shame (if everyone finds out, and I've made every effort to pay her, for) look, I sent this young goat, but you did not find her."

²⁴ Then, after nearly three months, (someone) reported to Judah, saying, "Your daughter-in-law Tamar has acted as a harlot, and—look!—she is pregnant from harlotry!"

Judah said, "Take her out and let her be burned!"

²⁵ She was taken out (to be burned). She sent (a message) to her father-in-law,

---

14. She sat down at the crossroads (*petah 'enayim*). *Petah 'enayim* literally means "entranceway of the eyes." Tamar looked towards the entranceway *"to which all eyes expectantly gaze"* (*Psalms* 145:15), and prayed for heaven's assistance—"Please, O God, do not let me leave here empty-handed!" (*Genesis Rabbah*).

23. Otherwise we'll be put to shame. Judah included his friend Hirah in the shame, even though Hirah had not actively participated in anything dishonorable. Merely acting as Judah's

וישב   בראשית לד:כה - לט:ג

שָׁלְחָה אֶל־חָמִיהָ לֵאמֹר לְאִישׁ אֲשֶׁר־אֵלֶּה לּוֹ אָנֹכִי הָרָה וַתֹּאמֶר הַכֶּר־נָא לְמִי הַחֹתֶמֶת וְהַפְּתִילִים וְהַמַּטֶּה הָאֵלֶּה: 26 וַיַּכֵּר יְהוּדָה וַיֹּאמֶר צָדְקָה מִמֶּנִּי כִּי־עַל־כֵּן לֹא־נְתַתִּיהָ לְשֵׁלָה בְנִי וְלֹא־יָסַף עוֹד לְדַעְתָּהּ: 27 וַיְהִי בְּעֵת לִדְתָּהּ וְהִנֵּה תְאוֹמִים בְּבִטְנָהּ: 28 וַיְהִי בְלִדְתָּהּ וַיִּתֶּן־יָד וַתִּקַּח הַמְיַלֶּדֶת וַתִּקְשֹׁר עַל־יָדוֹ שָׁנִי לֵאמֹר זֶה יָצָא רִאשֹׁנָה: 29 וַיְהִי | כְּמֵשִׁיב יָדוֹ וְהִנֵּה יָצָא אָחִיו וַתֹּאמֶר מַה־פָּרַצְתָּ עָלֶיךָ פָּרֶץ וַיִּקְרָא שְׁמוֹ פָּרֶץ: 30 וְאַחַר יָצָא אָחִיו אֲשֶׁר עַל־יָדוֹ הַשָּׁנִי וַיִּקְרָא שְׁמוֹ זָרַח: ס

לט

1 [FIFTH READING] וְיוֹסֵף הוּרַד מִצְרָיְמָה וַיִּקְנֵהוּ פּוֹטִיפַר סְרִיס פַּרְעֹה שַׂר הַטַּבָּחִים אִישׁ מִצְרִי מִיַּד הַיִּשְׁמְעֵאלִים אֲשֶׁר הוֹרִדֻהוּ שָׁמָּה: 2 וַיְהִי יְהוָה אֶת־יוֹסֵף וַיְהִי אִישׁ מַצְלִיחַ וַיְהִי בְּבֵית אֲדֹנָיו הַמִּצְרִי: 3 וַיַּרְא

all well and good. If not, she would rather be burned than publicly shame him (*Babylonian Talmud, Sotah* 10b).

39:1 Joseph had been brought down to Egypt. Scripture juxtaposed the incident of Potiphar's wife with the incident of Tamar, to teach you that just as Tamar's intentions were for the sake of heaven, Potiphar's wife's intentions were also for the sake of heaven. She saw through astrology that she was destined to raise children from Joseph, but she did not know whether they would be from her or from her daughter (*Rashi, 11th century*).

2. God was with Joseph, and he became a successful person (while) he was in the house of his Egyptian master. It is easy for man to attribute his success to hard work and effort and only when he is not successful to acknowledge God's role. Joseph, however, recognized and publicized that all of his accomplishments and successes were through God's help (*Rabbi Simḥah Bunem Sofer, 19th century*).

There are those who serve God diligently as a pauper, only to reject the commandments once their fortune changes. The opposite also can happen. Joseph, however, remained consistent in his loyalty to God, both when *"he became a successful person,"* and as a slave *"in the house of his Egyptian master"* (*Rabbi Moses ha-Levi Pollak, 19th century*).

food for thought

1. Would you publicly acknowledge your sins?

2. Why is moral courage so crucial to leadership?

3. Whose leadership qualities impress you more: Judah's or Joseph's?

saying, "I am pregnant from the man to whom these belong." She said, "Please identify whose signet ring, cloak, and staff are these?"

²⁶ Judah recognized (them). He said, "She's right (in what she says. She became pregnant) from me (justifiably), because I did not give her to my son Shelah." But he didn't continue to be intimate with her anymore (alternatively: he did continue).

The Birth of Perez and Zerah

²⁷ Then, when she was giving birth—look!—there were twins in her womb.

²⁸ What happened was, when she was giving birth (one baby) stretched out his hand. The midwife took a crimson thread and tied it on his hand, saying, "This one came out first." ²⁹ Then, after (the baby) brought his hand (back inside)—look!—his brother emerged.

She said, "With such strength [*PaReTZ*] you have forced yourself!" So he (Judah) named him Perez.

³⁰ Afterwards, his brother emerged, the one who had the crimson thread on his hand, and he named him Zerah [*ZaRaḤ*] (because of the shining appearance [*ZeRiḤah*] of the crimson).

Joseph in Potiphar's House

39 [FIFTH READING] ¹ Joseph had been brought down to Egypt, and Potiphar—Pharaoh's officer, chief of the butchers, a native Egyptian—purchased him from the Arabs who had brought him down there.

² God was with Joseph, and he became a successful person (while) he was in the house of his Egyptian master. ³ His master saw that (the name of) God was

---

25. I am pregnant from the man to whom these belong. Why did she speak in such a veiled fashion? She could have said, "Judah, you are the father of my child, and here are your possessions to prove it!"

From Tamar we learn that *it is better to cast yourself into a fiery furnace than publicly shame another person.* She simply showed the items to Judah. If he would admit that he was the father,

spiritual vitamin

> When you succumb to temptation and commit a sin, if you are honest and courageous, you will recognize the act for what it is: a failure, as well as a breach of your own true will and conscience.

בראשית לט:ג–יב · וישב

אֲדֹנָיו כִּי יְהוָה אִתּוֹ וְכֹל אֲשֶׁר־הוּא עֹשֶׂה יְהוָה מַצְלִיחַ בְּיָדוֹ: 4 וַיִּמְצָא יוֹסֵף חֵן בְּעֵינָיו וַיְשָׁרֶת אֹתוֹ וַיַּפְקִדֵהוּ עַל־בֵּיתוֹ וְכָל־יֶשׁ־לוֹ נָתַן בְּיָדוֹ: 5 וַיְהִי מֵאָז הִפְקִיד אֹתוֹ בְּבֵיתוֹ וְעַל כָּל־אֲשֶׁר יֶשׁ־לוֹ וַיְבָרֶךְ יְהוָה אֶת־בֵּית הַמִּצְרִי בִּגְלַל יוֹסֵף וַיְהִי בִּרְכַּת יְהוָה בְּכָל־אֲשֶׁר יֶשׁ־לוֹ בַּבַּיִת וּבַשָּׂדֶה: 6 וַיַּעֲזֹב כָּל־אֲשֶׁר־לוֹ בְּיַד־יוֹסֵף וְלֹא־יָדַע אִתּוֹ מְאוּמָה כִּי אִם־הַלֶּחֶם אֲשֶׁר־הוּא אוֹכֵל וַיְהִי יוֹסֵף יְפֵה־תֹאַר וִיפֵה מַרְאֶה: [SIXTH READING] 7 וַיְהִי אַחַר הַדְּבָרִים הָאֵלֶּה וַתִּשָּׂא אֵשֶׁת־אֲדֹנָיו אֶת־עֵינֶיהָ אֶל־יוֹסֵף וַתֹּאמֶר שִׁכְבָה עִמִּי: 8 וַיְמָאֵן | וַיֹּאמֶר אֶל־אֵשֶׁת אֲדֹנָיו הֵן אֲדֹנִי לֹא־יָדַע אִתִּי מַה־בַּבָּיִת וְכֹל אֲשֶׁר־יֶשׁ־לוֹ נָתַן בְּיָדִי: 9 אֵינֶנּוּ גָדוֹל בַּבַּיִת הַזֶּה מִמֶּנִּי וְלֹא־חָשַׂךְ מִמֶּנִּי מְאוּמָה כִּי אִם־אוֹתָךְ בַּאֲשֶׁר אַתְּ־אִשְׁתּוֹ וְאֵיךְ אֶעֱשֶׂה הָרָעָה הַגְּדֹלָה הַזֹּאת וְחָטָאתִי לֵאלֹהִים: 10 וַיְהִי כְּדַבְּרָהּ אֶל־יוֹסֵף יוֹם | יוֹם וְלֹא־שָׁמַע אֵלֶיהָ לִשְׁכַּב אֶצְלָהּ לִהְיוֹת עִמָּהּ: 11 וַיְהִי כְּהַיּוֹם הַזֶּה וַיָּבֹא הַבַּיְתָה לַעֲשׂוֹת מְלַאכְתּוֹ וְאֵין אִישׁ מֵאַנְשֵׁי הַבַּיִת שָׁם בַּבָּיִת: 12 וַתִּתְפְּשֵׂהוּ בְּבִגְדוֹ לֵאמֹר שִׁכְבָה עִמִּי וַיַּעֲזֹב בִּגְדוֹ בְּיָדָהּ וַיָּנָס וַיֵּצֵא הַחוּצָה:

Are you willing, for the sake of just a moment's pleasure, to have your name erased from the holy breastplate worn before God?" (*Babylonian Talmud, Sotah* 36b).

When encouraged to sin, your immediate reaction must be to completely reject the thought. Only *after* you have refused, may you then begin to explain your rationale for refusing. This is precisely what Joseph did: Only after *"he refused,"* did he make an effort to clarify his reasoning, *"He has given everything that's his into my hand … he has not withheld anything from me … so how could I do this extremely wicked (act)?"* (*Rabbi Judah Aryeh Leib Alter of Gur, 19th century*).

12. She grabbed him by his clothes. "Clothes" are often employed by Scripture as a metaphor for our external behavior patterns. Joseph had become too vain in his own eyes—he used to beautify himself with attractive hairstyles. It was through these "clothes" that Potiphar was able to grab hold of him.

Joseph realized what had happened, and he understood that this represented Potiphar's power over him. So he *"dashed off and went*

food for thought

1. Does beauty invite others to judge you for the wrong reasons?

2. Are beautiful people inevitably more vain?

3. At what point would you say that unwanted advances are "incited"?

(always) on his (lips), and that whatever he put his hand to, God made successful. ⁴ Joseph found favor in his (master's) eyes, and he attended to him (personally. Potiphar) appointed him over his house, and he gave everything he had into (Joseph's) hand.

⁵ What happened was, that from the time that he appointed (Joseph) over his house and over everything he had, God blessed the house of the Egyptian because of Joseph. God's blessing was (found) in everything he had, in the house and in the field. ⁶ He left everything he had in Joseph's hand, and he didn't (care to) know about anything of his, except the crumpet that he ate. (Since Joseph was in control, he pampered himself so that) Joseph had handsome features and a beautiful complexion. (God said, "You are pampering yourself while your father mourns! I will incite Potiphar's wife against you!")

[SIXTH READING] ⁷ Then, after these words (of God), his master's wife cast her eyes on Joseph, and she said, "Sleep with me!"

⁸ But he refused. He said to his master's wife, "Look, my master doesn't (care to) know about any of my (affairs) in the house, and he has given everything that's his into my hand. ⁹ In this house there's no one greater than me, and he has not withheld anything from me except you, since you're his wife. So how could I do this extremely wicked (act), and sin against God?"

¹⁰ When she would speak to Joseph day in and day out, he would not listen to her, (even) to lie (in the same bed as) her (or) to be with her.

¹¹ Then, when a certain (religious holi)day arrived, (Joseph) came to the house to do his business, and none of the members of the house were there in the house (since they had all gone to the temple of idolatry). ¹² She grabbed him by his clothes, saying, "Sleep with me!"

Joseph dashed off and went outside, leaving his clothes in her hand.

8-9. He refused. He said ... how could I do this extremely wicked (act)? Joseph had a vision in which the image of his father, Jacob, appeared. He heard his father saying, "Joseph! The names of my sons are destined to be engraved on the breastplate worn by the High Priest.

kabbalah bites

39:6 Joseph was a reincarnation of Enoch. Enoch, a direct descendant of Adam (*above*, 5:18), merited to receive an extremely lofty portion of Adam's soul.

Even the appearance of your physical body is a reflection of your soul. "*Joseph had handsome features and a beautiful complexion,*" because he possessed the beauty of Adam himself.

Later this soul was reincarnated into Rabbi Ishmael son of Elisha the High Priest, who was also known for his beauty.

בראשית לט:יג - מ:ד | וישב

13 וַיְהִי כִּרְאוֹתָהּ כִּי־עָזַב בִּגְדוֹ בְּיָדָהּ וַיָּנָס הַחוּצָה: 14 וַתִּקְרָא לְאַנְשֵׁי בֵיתָהּ וַתֹּאמֶר לָהֶם לֵאמֹר רְאוּ הֵבִיא לָנוּ אִישׁ עִבְרִי לְצַחֶק בָּנוּ בָּא אֵלַי לִשְׁכַּב עִמִּי וָאֶקְרָא בְּקוֹל גָּדוֹל: 15 וַיְהִי כְשָׁמְעוֹ כִּי־הֲרִימֹתִי קוֹלִי וָאֶקְרָא וַיַּעֲזֹב בִּגְדוֹ אֶצְלִי וַיָּנָס וַיֵּצֵא הַחוּצָה: 16 וַתַּנַּח בִּגְדוֹ אֶצְלָהּ עַד־בּוֹא אֲדֹנָיו אֶל־בֵּיתוֹ:
17 וַתְּדַבֵּר אֵלָיו כַּדְּבָרִים הָאֵלֶּה לֵאמֹר בָּא אֵלַי הָעֶבֶד הָעִבְרִי אֲשֶׁר־הֵבֵאתָ לָּנוּ לְצַחֶק בִּי: 18 וַיְהִי כַּהֲרִימִי קוֹלִי וָאֶקְרָא וַיַּעֲזֹב בִּגְדוֹ אֶצְלִי וַיָּנָס הַחוּצָה:
19 וַיְהִי כִשְׁמֹעַ אֲדֹנָיו אֶת־דִּבְרֵי אִשְׁתּוֹ אֲשֶׁר דִּבְּרָה אֵלָיו לֵאמֹר כַּדְּבָרִים הָאֵלֶּה עָשָׂה לִי עַבְדֶּךָ וַיִּחַר אַפּוֹ: 20 וַיִּקַּח אֲדֹנֵי יוֹסֵף אֹתוֹ וַיִּתְּנֵהוּ אֶל־בֵּית הַסֹּהַר מְקוֹם אֲשֶׁר־[אסורי כ׳] אֲסִירֵי הַמֶּלֶךְ אֲסוּרִים וַיְהִי־שָׁם בְּבֵית הַסֹּהַר:
21 וַיְהִי יְהֹוָה אֶת־יוֹסֵף וַיֵּט אֵלָיו חָסֶד וַיִּתֵּן חִנּוֹ בְּעֵינֵי שַׂר בֵּית־הַסֹּהַר: 22 וַיִּתֵּן שַׂר בֵּית־הַסֹּהַר בְּיַד־יוֹסֵף אֵת כָּל־הָאֲסִירִם אֲשֶׁר בְּבֵית הַסֹּהַר וְאֵת כָּל־אֲשֶׁר עֹשִׂים שָׁם הוּא הָיָה עֹשֶׂה: 23 אֵין | שַׂר בֵּית־הַסֹּהַר רֹאֶה אֶת־כָּל־מְאוּמָה בְּיָדוֹ בַּאֲשֶׁר יְהֹוָה אִתּוֹ וַאֲשֶׁר־הוּא עֹשֶׂה יְהֹוָה מַצְלִיחַ: פ

מ 1 [SEVENTH READING] וַיְהִי אַחַר הַדְּבָרִים הָאֵלֶּה חָטְאוּ מַשְׁקֵה מֶלֶךְ־מִצְרַיִם וְהָאֹפֶה לַאֲדֹנֵיהֶם לְמֶלֶךְ מִצְרָיִם: 2 וַיִּקְצֹף פַּרְעֹה עַל שְׁנֵי סָרִיסָיו עַל שַׂר הַמַּשְׁקִים וְעַל שַׂר הָאוֹפִים: 3 וַיִּתֵּן אֹתָם בְּמִשְׁמַר בֵּית שַׂר הַטַּבָּחִים אֶל־בֵּית הַסֹּהַר מְקוֹם אֲשֶׁר יוֹסֵף אָסוּר שָׁם: 4 וַיִּפְקֹד שַׂר הַטַּבָּחִים אֶת־

40:1 The king of Egypt's butler and baker committed an offense. Why does this section follow the account of Potiphar's wife?

Since that accursed woman had accustomed everybody to talk badly about Joseph the righteous one, God brought to the Egyptians the sin of these men, the butler and the baker, so that the Egyptians would turn their attention to them and not to Joseph. And furthermore, so that relief would come through them to Joseph, the righteous one (*Rashi, 11th century*).

¹³ Then, when she saw that he had left his clothes in her hand and had dashed outside, ¹⁴ she called the members of her house, and spoke to them, saying, "See! (My husband) brought us a Hebrew man to deprave us! He came to me, to lie with me, but I called loudly, ¹⁵ and so when he heard that I raised my voice and screamed, he left his clothes with me, and dashed off outside."

¹⁶ She left his clothes beside her, until (Joseph's) master came home. ¹⁷ Then she told him the same thing, saying, "The Hebrew slave that you brought us came to me to deprave me. ¹⁸ And then, when I raised my voice and screamed, he left his clothes with me, and dashed off outside."

¹⁹ Then, when (Joseph's) master heard his wife's report which she told him, saying, "Your slave did things like this to me," he became furious. ²⁰ Joseph's master took him and put him into prison, the place where the king's prisoners were imprisoned.

(While) he was in the prison, ²¹ God was with Joseph, and He granted him a favor(able image), and granted him favor in the eyes of the prison's warden. ²² So, the prison's warden delivered all the captives that were in the prison into Joseph's hand, and everything that was done there was done through his (command). ²³ The prison's warden did not see (fault) in anything that was in (Joseph's) hands, because God was with him. God made whatever he did successful.

Joseph Interprets Dreams in Prison

40 [SEVENTH READING] ¹ Then, after these words (of Potiphar's wife, who bad-mouthed Joseph throughout Egypt, the attention was taken away from Joseph when), the king of Egypt's butler and baker committed an offense against their master, the king of Egypt. ² Pharaoh became furious at his two officers, the chief butler and the chief baker, ³ and he placed them into the custody of the chief butcher's house, in the prison where Joseph was held. ⁴ The chief butcher

---

outside, leaving his clothes in her hand" (v. 13). He removed his spiritually unclean "clothing" and returned to God (*Rabbi Menahem Nahum Twersky of Chernobyl, 18th century*).

spiritual vitamin

❝ *"I demand only according to their capacity"* (*Numbers Rabbah*). God, your Creator, declares in the Torah what He requests and demands of you, and He will not exceed your capacity. All that is needed is your firm determination to carry out God's request. ❞

בראשית מ:ד-יז　　וישב

יוֹסֵ֥ף אִתָּ֖ם וַיְשָׁ֣רֶת אֹתָ֑ם וַיִּהְי֥וּ יָמִ֖ים בְּמִשְׁמָֽר: 5 וַיַּֽחַלְמוּ֩ חֲל֨וֹם שְׁנֵיהֶ֜ם אִ֤ישׁ חֲלֹמוֹ֙ בְּלַ֣יְלָה אֶחָ֔ד אִ֖ישׁ כְּפִתְר֣וֹן חֲלֹמ֑וֹ הַמַּשְׁקֶ֣ה וְהָאֹפֶ֗ה אֲשֶׁר֙ לְמֶ֣לֶךְ מִצְרַ֔יִם אֲשֶׁ֥ר אֲסוּרִ֖ים בְּבֵ֥ית הַסֹּֽהַר: 6 וַיָּבֹ֧א אֲלֵיהֶ֛ם יוֹסֵ֖ף בַּבֹּ֑קֶר וַיַּ֣רְא אֹתָ֔ם וְהִנָּ֖ם זֹֽעֲפִֽים: 7 וַיִּשְׁאַ֞ל אֶת־סְרִיסֵ֣י פַרְעֹ֗ה אֲשֶׁ֨ר אִתּ֧וֹ בְמִשְׁמַ֛ר בֵּ֥ית אֲדֹנָ֖יו לֵאמֹ֑ר מַדּ֛וּעַ פְּנֵיכֶ֥ם רָעִ֖ים הַיּֽוֹם: 8 וַיֹּאמְר֣וּ אֵלָ֔יו חֲל֣וֹם חָלַ֔מְנוּ וּפֹתֵ֖ר אֵ֣ין אֹת֑וֹ וַיֹּ֨אמֶר אֲלֵהֶ֜ם יוֹסֵ֗ף הֲל֤וֹא לֵֽאלֹהִים֙ פִּתְרֹנִ֔ים סַפְּרוּ־נָ֖א לִֽי: 9 וַיְסַפֵּ֧ר שַֽׂר־הַמַּשְׁקִ֛ים אֶת־חֲלֹמ֖וֹ לְיוֹסֵ֑ף וַיֹּ֣אמֶר ל֔וֹ בַּֽחֲלוֹמִ֕י וְהִנֵּה־גֶ֖פֶן לְפָנָֽי: 10 וּבַגֶּ֖פֶן שְׁלֹשָׁ֣ה שָֽׂרִיגִ֑ם וְהִ֤יא כְפֹרַ֨חַת֙ עָֽלְתָ֣ה נִצָּ֔הּ הִבְשִׁ֥ילוּ אַשְׁכְּלֹתֶ֖יהָ עֲנָבִֽים: 11 וְכ֥וֹס פַּרְעֹ֖ה בְּיָדִ֑י וָֽאֶקַּ֣ח אֶת־הָֽעֲנָבִ֗ים וָֽאֶשְׂחַ֤ט אֹתָם֙ אֶל־כּ֣וֹס פַּרְעֹ֔ה וָֽאֶתֵּ֥ן אֶת־הַכּ֖וֹס עַל־כַּ֥ף פַּרְעֹֽה: 12 וַיֹּ֤אמֶר לוֹ֙ יוֹסֵ֔ף זֶ֖ה פִּתְרֹנ֑וֹ שְׁלֹ֨שֶׁת֙ הַשָּׂ֣רִגִ֔ים שְׁלֹ֥שֶׁת יָמִ֖ים הֵֽם: 13 בְּע֣וֹד ׀ שְׁלֹ֣שֶׁת יָמִ֗ים יִשָּׂ֤א פַרְעֹה֙ אֶת־רֹאשֶׁ֔ךָ וַֽהֲשִֽׁיבְךָ֖ עַל־כַּנֶּ֑ךָ וְנָֽתַתָּ֤ כוֹס־פַּרְעֹה֙ בְּיָד֔וֹ כַּמִּשְׁפָּט֙ הָֽרִאשׁ֔וֹן אֲשֶׁ֥ר הָיִ֖יתָ מַשְׁקֵֽהוּ: 14 כִּ֧י אִם־זְכַרְתַּ֣נִי אִתְּךָ֗ כַּֽאֲשֶׁר֙ יִ֣יטַב לָ֔ךְ וְעָשִֽׂיתָ־נָּ֥א עִמָּדִ֖י חָ֑סֶד וְהִזְכַּרְתַּ֨נִי֙ אֶל־פַּרְעֹ֔ה וְהֽוֹצֵאתַ֖נִי מִן־הַבַּ֥יִת הַזֶּֽה: 15 כִּֽי־גֻנֹּ֣ב גֻּנַּ֔בְתִּי מֵאֶ֖רֶץ הָֽעִבְרִ֑ים וְגַם־פֹּה֙ לֹֽא־עָשִׂ֣יתִי מְא֔וּמָה כִּֽי־שָׂמ֥וּ אֹתִ֖י בַּבּֽוֹר: 16 וַיַּ֥רְא שַֽׂר־הָֽאֹפִ֖ים כִּ֣י ט֣וֹב פָּתָ֑ר וַיֹּ֨אמֶר֙ אֶל־יוֹסֵ֔ף אַף־אֲנִי֙ בַּֽחֲלוֹמִ֔י וְהִנֵּ֗ה שְׁלֹשָׁ֛ה סַלֵּ֥י חֹרִ֖י עַל־רֹאשִֽׁי: 17 וּבַסַּ֣ל הָֽעֶלְי֔וֹן מִכֹּ֛ל מַֽאֲכַ֥ל

248

In hindsight, we see that *from this single act of kindness Joseph was eventually saved, leading him to save the entire Egyptian people from starvation!*

This teaches us: (a) the extreme importance of caring for others; and (b) never to underestimate the power of one single good deed. Joseph's sensitivity to another's distress, a person whom he had every right to despise, led to the salvation of Egypt (*Rabbi Menahem Mendel Schneerson, 20th century*).

16. The chief baker saw that he had interpreted well. How did he know that Joseph's interpretation was correct? The chief butler and the chief baker dreamed their own dreams, and then each one also dreamed the interpretation of his colleague's dream (*Babylonian Talmud, Berakhot* 55b).

genesis 40:4–17   va-yeshev

assigned Joseph (to be) with them, and he attended to them. They were in custody for (many) days, (a whole year).

⁵ Both of them—the king of Egypt's butler and baker, who were confined in the prison—had a dream. Each person had his dream on the same night (as the other), and each person dreamed his own destiny.

⁶ Joseph came to them in the morning. He saw them and—look!—they were depressed. ⁷ So he asked (these) officers of Pharaoh, who were with him in custody (in) his master's house's, saying, "Why do your faces (look) so down today?"

⁸ They said to him, "We've had a dream, but there is no one to interpret it."

Joseph said to them, "Don't (dream) interpretations come from God? Please tell me (your dreams)."

⁹ The chief butler told his dream to Joseph. He said to him, "In my dream—look!—a vine was before me. ¹⁰ On the vine were three tendrils. It seemed to be blossoming, and its buds came out. (Then) its clusters ripened into grapes."

¹¹ "Pharaoh's cup was in my hand, and I took the grapes and squeezed them into Pharaoh's cup. I placed the cup on Pharaoh's palm."

¹² Joseph said to him, "This is its interpretation: the three tendrils are three days. ¹³ In another three days, Pharaoh will (count his officers to serve him at a meal and) he will count your head, and restore you to your position. Then, you will place Pharaoh's cup into his hand, just like when you were his butler in the first instance."

¹⁴ "If you would then remember me, alongside you, when things go well for you, please, do me a favor and mention me to Pharaoh, and get me out of this prison. ¹⁵ For I was kidnapped from the land of the Hebrews, and I haven't done anything (wrong) here either, for them to have put me into prison."

¹⁶ The chief baker saw that he had interpreted well. So, he said to Joseph, "In my dream, I too (was there) and—look!—there were three wicker baskets on my head. ¹⁷ In the upper basket was a selection of all Pharaoh's foods, made by a baker, and the birds were eating them from the basket on top of my head."

---

7. Why do your faces (look) so down today? The natural reaction for Joseph, after being wrongly imprisoned, would be utter contempt for Egypt and its government. When Joseph was joined by the chief butler and chief baker—two of Pharaoh's high-ranking ministers—it would only have been natural for Joseph to shun them and hate them.

But Joseph did the very opposite. Not only did he bear no grudge against Pharaoh's ministers, who were key members of the corrupt regime that had wrongfully imprisoned him, he took an active interest in their welfare. In fact, he was even sensitive enough to notice that they had been troubled by their dreams, inquiring, *"Why do your faces (look) so down today?"*

בראשית מ:יז-כג ׀ וישב

פַּרְעֹה מַעֲשֵׂה אֹפֶה וְהָעוֹף אֹכֵל אֹתָם מִן־הַסַּל מֵעַל רֹאשִׁי: 18 וַיַּעַן יוֹסֵף וַיֹּאמֶר זֶה פִּתְרֹנוֹ שְׁלֹשֶׁת הַסַּלִּים שְׁלֹשֶׁת יָמִים הֵם: 19 בְּעוֹד ׀ שְׁלֹשֶׁת יָמִים יִשָּׂא פַרְעֹה אֶת־רֹאשְׁךָ מֵעָלֶיךָ וְתָלָה אוֹתְךָ עַל־עֵץ וְאָכַל הָעוֹף אֶת־בְּשָׂרְךָ מֵעָלֶיךָ: [MAFTIR] 20 וַיְהִי ׀ בַּיּוֹם הַשְּׁלִישִׁי יוֹם הֻלֶּדֶת אֶת־פַּרְעֹה וַיַּעַשׂ מִשְׁתֶּה לְכָל־עֲבָדָיו וַיִּשָּׂא אֶת־רֹאשׁ ׀ שַׂר הַמַּשְׁקִים וְאֶת־רֹאשׁ שַׂר הָאֹפִים בְּתוֹךְ עֲבָדָיו: 21 וַיָּשֶׁב אֶת־שַׂר הַמַּשְׁקִים עַל־מַשְׁקֵהוּ וַיִּתֵּן הַכּוֹס עַל־כַּף פַּרְעֹה: 22 וְאֵת שַׂר הָאֹפִים תָּלָה כַּאֲשֶׁר פָּתַר לָהֶם יוֹסֵף: 23 וְלֹא־זָכַר שַׂר־הַמַּשְׁקִים אֶת־יוֹסֵף וַיִּשְׁכָּחֵהוּ: פ פ פ

קנ"ב פסוקים, יב"ק סימן.

to "write the script" on God's behalf. Instead of relying on God to save him *via the butler*, Joseph should have depended on God to save him *in whichever way God deemed fit*, while realizing that there was a distinct possibility that it might be through the butler (*Rabbi Menahem Mendel Schneerson, 20th century*).

spiritual vitamin

> On your birthday, your *mazal* is renewed. The *mazal* is the "root" of your soul, which remains attached to its Source on high, while only an extension of your soul descends into your body and vitalizes it. When your birthday comes you experience a strengthening of the very root of your soul, and, naturally, the change is felt also in the "lower" aspects of your soul that vitalize your physical body.

genesis 40:18–23 — va-yeshev

¹⁸ Joseph replied and said, "This is its interpretation: The three baskets are three days. ¹⁹ In another three days, Pharaoh will remove your head from you and hang you on a gallows, and the birds will eat your flesh off you."

[MAFTIR] ²⁰ And so it happened, that on the third day, (it was) Pharaoh's birthday. Pharaoh made a banquet for all his servants and he counted the chief butler and chief baker among his servants. ²¹ He restored the chief butler to his (position as) butler, and (the butler) placed the cup on Pharaoh's palm. ²² And, just as Joseph had predicted, he hanged the chief baker.

²³ But, (that day) the chief butler did not remember Joseph. And he forgot him (later on too).

The *Haftarah* for *Va-Yeshev* is on page 1310.

On *Shabbat Ḥanukkah:*
Maftir: **Day One**—*Numbers* 7:1–17 (p. 840); **Day Two**—ibid. 18–23 (p. 844).
The *Haftarah* for *Ḥanukkah (first Shabbat)* is on page 1420.

---

23. He forgot him. Because Joseph relied on the butler to remember him, he was compelled to be confined for two years, in the spirit of the verse, *"Happy is the man who trusts in God and did not turn to the arrogant"* (*Psalms* 40:5; *Rashi, 11th century*).

In his commentary to verse 1, *Rashi* writes that Pharaoh's butler and baker were imprisoned, *"so that relief would come through them to Joseph, the righteous one."* This begs the question: If God's intent in sending the butler and the baker to be imprisoned with Joseph was "so that relief would come through them to him," why was Joseph wrong to have "relied on the butler to remember him"?

While it is true that God sent the butler and baker to jail as a means of saving Joseph, Joseph nevertheless made a subtle miscalculation concerning the significance of their arrival. Joseph's mistake was that he saw his newfound relationship with the butler and the baker as the *certain* way out of jail, rather than *a possible* means by which God would send salvation. Thus, *Rashi* stresses, "Because Joseph *relied on* the butler to remember him, he was compelled to be confined for two years." Joseph should have relied directly upon God, who can send help in any possible manner imaginable, rather than relying on what *he thought* was God's chosen route of salvation.

Of course, Joseph was not wrong in attempting to find a natural, logical route by which God might save him. He merely erred in the *significance* that he attached to that route, attempting

Mikketz tells the story behind our **enslavement in Egypt.** Spiritually speaking, "enslavement" is the complete **identification of ego** with the physical world; a loss of **your connection** with the **limitless.**

MIKKETZ
מקץ

JOSEPH INTERPRETS PHARAOH'S DREAMS	41:1-38
JOSEPH APPOINTED RULER OVER EGYPT	41:39-57
BROTHERS' JOURNEY TO EGYPT	42:1 - 44:17

NAME
Mikketz

MEANING
"At the end"

LINES IN TORAH SCROLL
255

PARASHIYYOT
1 open; 0 closed

VERSES
146

WORDS
2022

LETTERS
7914

DATE
2228–2236

LOCATION
Egypt, Canaan

KEY PEOPLE
Joseph, Pharaoh, Jacob (Israel), Reuben, Judah, Benjamin

MITZVOT
None

NOTE
Usually read during the festival of Ḥanukkah

CHARACTER PROFILE

NAME
Joseph

MEANING
"Add"

PARENTS
Jacob and Rachel

GRANDFATHERS
Isaac, Laban

SIBLINGS
Reuben, Simeon, Levi, Judah, Issachar, Zebulun, Dan, Naphtali, Gad, Asher, Benjamin, Dinah

WIFE
Asenath

CHILDREN
Manasseh, Ephraim

LIFE SPAN
110 years

BURIAL PLACE
Shechem

ACHIEVEMENTS
Merited instead of Reuben the firstborn's double portion; successfully interpreted dreams; appointed viceroy of Egypt; ensured his father was buried in Israel

KNOWN FOR
Born after his mother was childless for seven years; born circumcised; was given a colored garment by his father; his dreams; sold by his brothers into slavery; his bones were carried through the desert by the Jewish people and eventually buried in the land of Israel

LISTENING

Joseph's success in interpreting dreams is attributed to his ability to "listen" to all the relevant details. God gave you two ears and just one tongue, teaching you to spend more time listening than talking (41:15).

CONFESSION

After the brothers admitted their mistake, Joseph turned aside and wept. He realized that they had completely repented for their former actions. In order for a sin to be corrected there must be a verbal admittance of wrongdoing (42:21-24).

RESPONSIBILITY

When Jacob refused to let Benjamin travel to Egypt to collect more grain, Judah took responsibility for his younger brother and guaranteed his safe return (43:9).

מא

1 וַיְהִ֕י מִקֵּ֖ץ שְׁנָתַ֣יִם יָמִ֑ים וּפַרְעֹ֣ה חֹלֵ֔ם וְהִנֵּ֖ה עֹמֵ֥ד עַל־הַיְאֹֽר׃
2 וְהִנֵּ֣ה מִן־הַיְאֹ֗ר עֹלֹת֙ שֶׁ֣בַע פָּר֔וֹת יְפ֥וֹת מַרְאֶ֖ה וּבְרִיאֹ֣ת בָּשָׂ֑ר וַתִּרְעֶ֖ינָה בָּאָֽחוּ׃
3 וְהִנֵּ֞ה שֶׁ֧בַע פָּר֣וֹת אֲחֵר֗וֹת עֹל֤וֹת אַחֲרֵיהֶן֙ מִן־הַיְאֹ֔ר רָע֥וֹת מַרְאֶ֖ה וְדַקּ֣וֹת בָּשָׂ֑ר וַֽתַּעֲמֹ֛דְנָה אֵ֥צֶל הַפָּר֖וֹת עַל־שְׂפַ֥ת הַיְאֹֽר׃
4 וַתֹּאכַ֣לְנָה הַפָּר֗וֹת רָע֤וֹת הַמַּרְאֶה֙ וְדַקֹּ֣ת הַבָּשָׂ֔ר אֵ֚ת שֶׁ֣בַע הַפָּר֔וֹת יְפֹ֥ת הַמַּרְאֶ֖ה וְהַבְּרִיאֹ֑ת וַיִּיקַ֖ץ פַּרְעֹֽה׃
5 וַיִּישָׁ֕ן וַֽיַּחֲלֹ֖ם שֵׁנִ֑ית וְהִנֵּ֣ה ׀ שֶׁ֣בַע שִׁבֳּלִ֗ים עֹל֛וֹת בְּקָנֶ֥ה אֶחָ֖ד בְּרִיא֥וֹת וְטֹבֽוֹת׃
6 וְהִנֵּה֙ שֶׁ֣בַע שִׁבֳּלִ֔ים דַּקּ֖וֹת וּשְׁדוּפֹ֣ת קָדִ֑ים צֹמְח֖וֹת אַחֲרֵיהֶֽן׃
7 וַתִּבְלַ֨עְנָה֙ הַשִּׁבֳּלִ֣ים הַדַּקּ֔וֹת אֵ֚ת שֶׁ֣בַע הַשִּׁבֳּלִ֔ים הַבְּרִיא֖וֹת וְהַמְּלֵא֑וֹת וַיִּיקַ֥ץ פַּרְעֹ֖ה וְהִנֵּ֥ה חֲלֽוֹם׃
8 וַיְהִ֤י בַבֹּ֙קֶר֙ וַתִּפָּ֣עֶם רוּח֔וֹ וַיִּשְׁלַ֗ח וַיִּקְרָ֛א אֶת־כָּל־חַרְטֻמֵּ֥י

---

imperceptibly. These forces have no independent power other than that Divine energy. It *looks* like they have some power of their own, but it's not true.

This fact had to be shown to Pharaoh before the exile was about to begin. Even though Israel were going to be under his control, he needed to know that, in truth, there is no power that stands independent of God (*Rabbi Judah Aryeh Leib Alter of Gur, 19th century*).

6. Seven thin ears of grain … were growing up after them. When the thin ears of grain are mentioned, the verse is phrased differently from than when the healthy ears of grain are mentioned, which were *"growing on one stalk"* (41:5). The good years were all equally good ("on one stalk"), whereas the bad years were not equal. Each year was worse than the preceding one (*Rabbi Jacob b. Asher, 13th–14th century*).

kabbalah bites

41:2-3 Man's soul has seven core emotional attributes. The seven "nice-looking cows" (v. 2) allude to the positive application of these attributes in the worship of God: *Love*—love of God; *Fear*—to be in awe of Him; *Glory*—to glorify Him; *Victory*—to conquer the impulse to evil; *Gratitude*—to be grateful to God; *Bonding*—to be deeply connected with all these emotions; *Dominion*—ascribing power to God, making Him King over the world.

Then there are "seven other, ugly-looking, thin cows" (v. 3), the emotional tools of the impulse to evil:
Love—the love of money and other pleasures; *Fear*—the fear of punishment; *Glory*—the glorification of self; *Victory*—the need to defeat others; *Gratitude*—appreciating yourself alone; *Bonding*—being deeply connected with all these emotions; *Dominion*—autonomy and self-rule.

genesis 41:1–8 mikketz

parashat mikketz

Joseph Interprets Pharaoh's Dreams

41 ¹ At the end of two years, it happened that Pharaoh was dreaming, and—look!—he was standing by the Nile. ² Then, from the Nile—look!—there were seven nice-looking, well-built cows coming up, and they pastured in the marshland. ³ Then—look!—seven other, ugly-looking, thin cows were coming up after them from the Nile, and they stood beside the (other) cows on the bank of the Nile. ⁴ Then, the ugly-looking, thin cows devoured the seven nice-looking, well-built cows, and Pharaoh woke up.

⁵ He fell asleep and dreamed again, and—look!—seven healthy and good ears of grain were growing on one stalk. ⁶ And—look!—seven thin ears of grain, parched by the east wind, were growing up after them. ⁷ Then, the thin ears of grain swallowed up the seven healthy and full ears of grain.

Pharaoh woke up, and now (he had) a (complete) dream (that needed to be interpreted).

⁸ In the morning, his mind was buzzing (with agitation). So he sent (messengers)

41:1 Pharaoh was dreaming. Pharaoh's dream is the beginning of the story of Egyptian exile. The dream predicted a famine which eventually caused Jacob and his family to settle in Egypt where, a generation later, they were enslaved (*Rabbi Moses Alshekh, 16ᵗʰ century*).

In times of exile, the Jewish people are forced to withstand the fluctuation between two contradictory modes of life: love of God at the time of prayer, and then total immersion into the physical world during business and private affairs the rest of the day. Hasidic teachings compare this situation to a dream, because in a dream two opposite, contradictory phenomena can coexist simultaneously (*Rabbi Shneur Zalman of Lyady, 18ᵗʰ century*).

Joseph, a righteous person, dreamed about *working* in the field with his brothers, binding sheaves. Pharaoh, a wicked man, had a dream which involved no effort on his part at all.

This highlights the fact that everything that is good in life requires *effort*, ensuring that what we receive from God in return should not be unearned "bread of shame" (see *Jerusalem Talmud, Orlah* 1:3; *Rabbi Menahem Mendel Schneerson, 20ᵗʰ century*).

2. They pastured in the marshland. The term *'aḥu* ("reed grass") is rendered by *Targum Onkelos* as *'aḥavah*, "brotherhood"—they pastured in brotherhood.

In most instances, hatred is motivated by pride or jealousy, the feeling that "I should have received the honor which went to him or her."

If you render yourself passive, like cattle, you can love the whole world. You will have no hatred for another person (*Rabbi Menahem Nahum Twersky of Chernobyl, 18ᵗʰ century*).

4. The ugly-looking, thin cows devoured the seven nice-looking, well-built cows. The power of the "other side," the forces of evil, represented here by the thin cows, exists only because Divine energy is concealed within them—because they have "swallowed" well-built cows

בראשית מא:ח-יט

מִצְרַ֙יִם֙ וְאֶת־כָּל־חֲכָמֶ֔יהָ וַיְסַפֵּ֨ר פַּרְעֹ֤ה לָהֶם֙ אֶת־חֲלֹמ֔וֹ וְאֵין־פּוֹתֵ֥ר אוֹתָ֖ם לְפַרְעֹֽה׃ 9 וַיְדַבֵּר֙ שַׂ֣ר הַמַּשְׁקִ֔ים אֶת־פַּרְעֹ֖ה לֵאמֹ֑ר אֶת־חֲטָאַ֕י אֲנִ֖י מַזְכִּ֥יר הַיּֽוֹם׃ 10 פַּרְעֹ֖ה קָצַ֣ף עַל־עֲבָדָ֑יו וַיִּתֵּ֨ן אֹתִ֜י בְּמִשְׁמַ֗ר בֵּ֚ית שַׂ֣ר הַטַּבָּחִ֔ים אֹתִ֕י וְאֵ֖ת שַׂ֥ר הָאֹפִֽים׃ 11 וַנַּֽחַלְמָ֥ה חֲל֛וֹם בְּלַ֥יְלָה אֶחָ֖ד אֲנִ֣י וָה֑וּא אִ֛ישׁ כְּפִתְר֥וֹן חֲלֹמ֖וֹ חָלָֽמְנוּ׃ 12 וְשָׁ֨ם אִתָּ֜נוּ נַ֣עַר עִבְרִ֗י עֶ֚בֶד לְשַׂ֣ר הַטַּבָּחִ֔ים וַנְּ֨סַפֶּר־ל֔וֹ וַיִּפְתָּר־לָ֖נוּ אֶת־חֲלֹמֹתֵ֑ינוּ אִ֥ישׁ כַּחֲלֹמ֖וֹ פָּתָֽר׃ 13 וַיְהִ֛י כַּאֲשֶׁ֥ר פָּֽתַר־לָ֖נוּ כֵּ֣ן הָיָ֑ה אֹתִ֛י הֵשִׁ֥יב עַל־כַּנִּ֖י וְאֹת֥וֹ תָלָֽה׃ 14 וַיִּשְׁלַ֤ח פַּרְעֹה֙ וַיִּקְרָ֣א אֶת־יוֹסֵ֔ף וַיְרִיצֻ֖הוּ מִן־הַבּ֑וֹר וַיְגַלַּח֙ וַיְחַלֵּ֣ף שִׂמְלֹתָ֔יו וַיָּבֹ֖א אֶל־פַּרְעֹֽה׃ 15 [SECOND READING] וַיֹּ֤אמֶר פַּרְעֹה֙ אֶל־יוֹסֵ֔ף חֲל֣וֹם חָלַ֔מְתִּי וּפֹתֵ֖ר אֵ֣ין אֹת֑וֹ וַאֲנִ֗י שָׁמַ֤עְתִּי עָלֶ֙יךָ֙ לֵאמֹ֔ר תִּשְׁמַ֥ע חֲל֖וֹם לִפְתֹּ֥ר אֹתֽוֹ׃ 16 וַיַּ֨עַן יוֹסֵ֧ף אֶת־פַּרְעֹ֛ה לֵאמֹ֖ר בִּלְעָדָ֑י אֱלֹהִ֕ים יַעֲנֶ֖ה אֶת־שְׁל֥וֹם פַּרְעֹֽה׃ 17 וַיְדַבֵּ֥ר פַּרְעֹ֖ה אֶל־יוֹסֵ֑ף בַּחֲלֹמִ֕י הִנְנִ֥י עֹמֵ֖ד עַל־שְׂפַ֥ת הַיְאֹֽר׃ 18 וְהִנֵּ֣ה מִן־הַיְאֹ֗ר עֹלֹת֙ שֶׁ֣בַע פָּר֔וֹת בְּרִיא֥וֹת בָּשָׂ֖ר וִיפֹ֣ת תֹּ֑אַר וַתִּרְעֶ֖ינָה בָּאָֽחוּ׃ 19 וְהִנֵּ֞ה שֶֽׁבַע־פָּר֤וֹת אֲחֵרוֹת֙ עֹל֣וֹת אַחֲרֵיהֶ֔ן דַּלּ֨וֹת וְרָע֥וֹת תֹּ֛אַר מְאֹ֖ד וְרַקּ֣וֹת בָּשָׂ֑ר לֹא־

Egypt's advisors offered ingenious interpretations to Pharaoh's dreams. He rejected them because these solutions were only satisfactory to himself as a private person. No one, however, "interpreted them *for Pharaoh.*"

The title "Pharaoh" was not a personal name, but a generic term for the rulers of ancient Egypt; it represented his monarchy. Pharaoh presumed that his dreams held a message for the empire he controlled, and when his sorcerers offered only personal interpretations ("You will first bear seven daughters, and then bury seven daughters," etc.) he knew that they were false. Only when Joseph presented an interpretation that was essential to the survival of his entire state—then, finally, someone had "interpreted them *for Pharaoh*" (*Rabbi Ḥayyim ibn Attar, 18th century*).

15. You listen to a dream, (understand it, and are then able) to interpret it. Dreams contain a kernel of truth; the *Talmud* teaches that a dream is one-sixtieth of prophecy (*Babylonian Talmud, Berakhot* 57b). The problem is that this "kernel" is confused among heaps of useless information which is produced from your wandering thoughts during the day.

Why was Joseph so adept at interpreting dreams? Because he had succeeded in cleaning his mind of useless and lustful daytime thoughts. This enabled him to fine-tune the art of learning which elements of a dream are productive and useful (*Rabbi Zadok ha-Kohen Rabinowitz of Lublin, 19th century*).

and called all the sorcerers of Egypt and all its sages. Pharaoh related his dreams to them, but no one interpreted them (satisfactorily) for Pharaoh.

⁹ The chief butler spoke to Pharaoh, saying, "I (have to) mention my wrongdoings today! ¹⁰ When Pharaoh was angry with his servants, and he put me in prison in the house of the chief slaughterer—(both) myself and the chief baker, ¹¹ we both dreamed a dream on the same night. Each person had a dream (that clearly depicted) his destiny.

¹² "There was a Hebrew lad with us, a slave of the chief slaughterer, and we told (the dreams) to him. He interpreted our dreams for us. He gave each person a (feasible) interpretation of his dream.

¹³ "Then, things happened just as he had interpreted for us: (Pharaoh) restored me to my position, and he hanged (the chief baker)."

¹⁴ So Pharaoh sent (a messenger) and called for Joseph.

They rushed him from the dungeon. He cut his hair (especially for the king), changed his (prison) clothes, and he came to Pharaoh.

[SECOND READING] ¹⁵ Pharaoh said to Joseph, "I've had a dream, but there is no one to interpret it, but I've heard it said about you with certainty that you listen to a dream, (understand it, and are then able) to interpret it."

¹⁶ Joseph replied to Pharaoh, saying, "(The wisdom to interpret dreams) is not from me. God will put an answer that will appease Pharaoh (into my mouth)."

¹⁷ Pharaoh said to Joseph, "In my dream—look!—I was standing on the bank of the Nile. ¹⁸ Then—look!—seven well-built, nice-looking cows were coming up from the Nile, and they pastured in the marshland. ¹⁹ Then—look!—seven other cows were coming up after them, (which were) weak, very ugly-looking and thin. I have never seen such bad (cows) throughout the entire land of Egypt."

8. But no one interpreted them (satisfactorily) for Pharaoh. The Egyptian sorcerers said "The seven good cows represent seven daughters that will be born to you. The seven ugly cows mean that you will bury seven daughters. The seven good ears of grain are seven countries that you will conquer. The seven bad ears of grain are seven colonies that will rebel against you" (*Genesis Rabbah*).

spiritual vitamin

> The Sages taught: *"Life is like a turning wheel"* (*Ruth Rabbah*). When a point on the wheel reaches the lowest degree, it is bound to turn upwards again.

בראשית מא:יט-לד

רָאִ֔יתִי כָּהֵ֛נָּה בְּכָל־אֶ֥רֶץ מִצְרַ֖יִם לָרֹֽעַ׃ 20 וַתֹּאכַ֣לְנָה הַפָּר֔וֹת הָרַקּ֖וֹת וְהָרָע֑וֹת אֵ֣ת שֶׁ֧בַע הַפָּר֛וֹת הָרִאשֹׁנ֖וֹת הַבְּרִיאֹֽת׃ 21 וַתָּבֹ֣אנָה אֶל־קִרְבֶּ֗נָה וְלֹ֤א נוֹדַע֙ כִּי־בָ֣אוּ אֶל־קִרְבֶּ֔נָה וּמַרְאֵיהֶ֣ן רַ֔ע כַּאֲשֶׁ֖ר בַּתְּחִלָּ֑ה וָאִיקָֽץ׃ 22 וָאֵ֖רֶא בַּחֲלֹמִ֑י וְהִנֵּ֣ה ׀ שֶׁ֣בַע שִׁבֳּלִ֗ים עֹלֹ֛ת בְּקָנֶ֥ה אֶחָ֖ד מְלֵאֹ֥ת וְטֹבֽוֹת׃ 23 וְהִנֵּה֙ שֶׁ֣בַע שִׁבֳּלִ֔ים צְנֻמ֛וֹת דַּקּ֖וֹת שְׁדֻפ֣וֹת קָדִ֑ים צֹמְח֖וֹת אַחֲרֵיהֶֽם׃ 24 וַתִּבְלַ֣עְןָ הַשִּׁבֳּלִ֣ים הַדַּקֹּ֔ת אֵ֛ת שֶׁ֥בַע הַֽשִּׁבֳּלִ֖ים הַטֹּב֑וֹת וָֽאֹמַר֙ אֶל־הַֽחַרְטֻמִּ֔ים וְאֵ֥ין מַגִּ֖יד לִֽי׃ 25 וַיֹּ֤אמֶר יוֹסֵף֙ אֶל־פַּרְעֹ֔ה חֲל֥וֹם פַּרְעֹ֖ה אֶחָ֣ד ה֑וּא אֵ֣ת אֲשֶׁ֧ר הָאֱלֹהִ֛ים עֹשֶׂ֖ה הִגִּ֥יד לְפַרְעֹֽה׃ 26 שֶׁ֧בַע פָּרֹ֣ת הַטֹּבֹ֗ת שֶׁ֤בַע שָׁנִים֙ הֵ֔נָּה וְשֶׁ֤בַע הַֽשִּׁבֳּלִים֙ הַטֹּבֹ֔ת שֶׁ֥בַע שָׁנִ֖ים הֵ֑נָּה חֲל֖וֹם אֶחָ֥ד הֽוּא׃ 27 וְשֶׁ֣בַע הַ֠פָּרוֹת הָֽרַקּ֨וֹת וְהָרָעֹ֜ת הָעֹלֹ֣ת אַחֲרֵיהֶ֗ן שֶׁ֤בַע שָׁנִים֙ הֵ֔נָּה וְשֶׁ֤בַע הַֽשִּׁבֳּלִים֙ הָרֵק֔וֹת שְׁדֻפ֖וֹת הַקָּדִ֑ים יִהְי֕וּ שֶׁ֖בַע שְׁנֵ֥י רָעָֽב׃ 28 ה֣וּא הַדָּבָ֔ר אֲשֶׁ֥ר דִּבַּ֖רְתִּי אֶל־פַּרְעֹ֑ה אֲשֶׁ֧ר הָאֱלֹהִ֛ים עֹשֶׂ֖ה הֶרְאָ֥ה אֶת־פַּרְעֹֽה׃ 29 הִנֵּ֛ה שֶׁ֥בַע שָׁנִ֖ים בָּא֑וֹת שָׂבָ֥ע גָּד֖וֹל בְּכָל־אֶ֥רֶץ מִצְרָֽיִם׃ 30 וְ֠קָ֠מוּ שֶׁ֨בַע שְׁנֵ֤י רָעָב֙ אַחֲרֵיהֶ֔ן וְנִשְׁכַּ֥ח כָּל־הַשָּׂבָ֖ע בְּאֶ֣רֶץ מִצְרָ֑יִם וְכִלָּ֥ה הָרָעָ֖ב אֶת־הָאָֽרֶץ׃ 31 וְלֹֽא־יִוָּדַ֤ע הַשָּׂבָע֙ בָּאָ֔רֶץ מִפְּנֵ֛י הָרָעָ֥ב הַה֖וּא אַחֲרֵי־כֵ֑ן כִּֽי־כָבֵ֥ד ה֖וּא מְאֹֽד׃ 32 וְעַ֨ל הִשָּׁנ֧וֹת הַחֲל֛וֹם אֶל־פַּרְעֹ֖ה פַּעֲמָ֑יִם כִּֽי־נָכ֤וֹן הַדָּבָר֙ מֵעִ֣ם הָאֱלֹהִ֔ים וּמְמַהֵ֥ר הָאֱלֹהִ֖ים לַעֲשֹׂתֽוֹ׃ 33 וְעַתָּה֙ יֵרֶ֣א פַרְעֹ֔ה אִ֖ישׁ נָב֣וֹן וְחָכָ֑ם וִישִׁיתֵ֖הוּ עַל־אֶ֥רֶץ מִצְרָֽיִם׃ 34 יַעֲשֶׂ֣ה

32. Concerning the repetition of the dream ... this is because ... God is quickly going to carry it out. The repetition of a dream is only a sign that it will occur quickly if the dream

spiritual vitamin

> Science can never tell us, "Do this," or "Do not do that." It can only maintain that if we desire to attain B, we must first accomplish A, and if B is undesirable, then A should be avoided.

genesis 41:20–34 — mikketz

[20] "Then, the thin, ugly cows devoured the first seven healthy cows. [21] They were swallowed up inside them, but it wasn't recognizable that they'd gone inside them. They looked as ugly as they were to start with. Then I woke up."

[22] "I saw in (another of) my dream(s): Look! Seven ears of healthy and good grain were growing on one stalk. [23] And—look!—seven thin ears of dehydrated grain, parched by the east wind, were growing up after them. [24] Then, the thin ears of grain swallowed up the seven good ears of grain."

"I told (my dreams to all) the sorcerers, but no one is telling me (a satisfactory explanation)."

[25] Joseph said to Pharaoh, "Pharaoh's (two) dream(s) have a single (meaning). God has told Pharaoh what He is (planning) to do: [26] The seven good cows are seven years, and the seven good ears of grain are (the same) seven years—it's one dream. [27] The seven thin and ugly cows coming up after them are seven years, as are the seven bare ears of grain, beaten by the east wind. They will be seven years of famine.

[28] "It is as I have told Pharaoh. God has shown Pharaoh what He is about to do!

[29] "Look! Seven years of great abundance are coming throughout the entire land of Egypt. [30] (The significance of the swallowing is that) seven years of famine will follow after them, when all the abundance in the land of Egypt will be forgotten. The famine will destroy the land. [31] (The fact that it wasn't recognizable that the thin cows had swallowed the fat cows means that) the abundance will not be recognizable because of the famine that will follow, for it (will be) very severe.

[32] "Concerning the repetition of the dream to Pharaoh, this is because the matter is ready before God, and God is quickly going to carry it out.

[33] "And now, Pharaoh should select a person who is understanding and wise, and appoint him over the land of Egypt. [34] Pharaoh should enact that he appoint

kabbalah bites

41:33 God's sustenance to the world flows through the ten heavenly *Sefirot*: the upper three *intellectual Sefirot* feeding the lower seven *emotional Sefirot*. The demise of the seven fat cows hinted to a decadence in the seven lower *Sefirot*. The world was now in danger of destruction.

Joseph advised Pharaoh to seek a way of infusing the lower seven *Sefirot* with a fresh flow from the upper three: he should seek a man who is "*understanding (naBoN) and wise (ḤaKHam),*" i.e., *connected* to the upper Sefirot of *Binah* and *Ḥokhmah*. (Since few men are connected to *Keter*, the highest *Sefirah*, Joseph limited his advice to *Binah* and *Ḥokhmah* alone.)

פַרְעֹה וְיַפְקֵד פְּקִדִים עַל־הָאָרֶץ וְחִמֵּשׁ אֶת־אֶרֶץ מִצְרַיִם בְּשֶׁבַע שְׁנֵי הַשָּׂבָע׃
35 וְיִקְבְּצוּ אֶת־כָּל־אֹכֶל הַשָּׁנִים הַטֹּבוֹת הַבָּאֹת הָאֵלֶּה וְיִצְבְּרוּ־בָר תַּחַת יַד־
פַּרְעֹה אֹכֶל בֶּעָרִים וְשָׁמָרוּ׃ 36 וְהָיָה הָאֹכֶל לְפִקָּדוֹן לָאָרֶץ לְשֶׁבַע שְׁנֵי הָרָעָב
אֲשֶׁר תִּהְיֶיןָ בְּאֶרֶץ מִצְרָיִם וְלֹא־תִכָּרֵת הָאָרֶץ בָּרָעָב׃ 37 וַיִּיטַב הַדָּבָר בְּעֵינֵי
פַרְעֹה וּבְעֵינֵי כָּל־עֲבָדָיו׃ 38 וַיֹּאמֶר פַּרְעֹה אֶל־עֲבָדָיו הֲנִמְצָא כָזֶה אִישׁ אֲשֶׁר
רוּחַ אֱלֹהִים בּוֹ׃ 39 [THIRD READING] וַיֹּאמֶר פַּרְעֹה אֶל־יוֹסֵף אַחֲרֵי הוֹדִיעַ אֱלֹהִים
אוֹתְךָ אֶת־כָּל־זֹאת אֵין־נָבוֹן וְחָכָם כָּמוֹךָ׃ 40 אַתָּה תִּהְיֶה עַל־בֵּיתִי וְעַל־פִּיךָ
יִשַּׁק כָּל־עַמִּי רַק הַכִּסֵּא אֶגְדַּל מִמֶּךָּ׃ 41 וַיֹּאמֶר פַּרְעֹה אֶל־יוֹסֵף רְאֵה נָתַתִּי
אֹתְךָ עַל כָּל־אֶרֶץ מִצְרָיִם׃ 42 וַיָּסַר פַּרְעֹה אֶת־טַבַּעְתּוֹ מֵעַל יָדוֹ וַיִּתֵּן אֹתָהּ
עַל־יַד יוֹסֵף וַיַּלְבֵּשׁ אֹתוֹ בִּגְדֵי־שֵׁשׁ וַיָּשֶׂם רְבִד הַזָּהָב עַל־צַוָּארוֹ׃ 43 וַיַּרְכֵּב
אֹתוֹ בְּמִרְכֶּבֶת הַמִּשְׁנֶה אֲשֶׁר־לוֹ וַיִּקְרְאוּ לְפָנָיו אַבְרֵךְ וְנָתוֹן אֹתוֹ עַל כָּל־אֶרֶץ
מִצְרָיִם׃ 44 וַיֹּאמֶר פַּרְעֹה אֶל־יוֹסֵף אֲנִי פַרְעֹה וּבִלְעָדֶיךָ לֹא־יָרִים אִישׁ אֶת־יָדוֹ
וְאֶת־רַגְלוֹ בְּכָל־אֶרֶץ מִצְרָיִם׃ 45 וַיִּקְרָא פַרְעֹה שֵׁם־יוֹסֵף צָפְנַת פַּעְנֵחַ וַיִּתֶּן־

---

38. Would we find like this? A man who has God's spirit in him?
A *tzaddik* (righteous man) will usually be dressed tidily, but not suavely. Joseph, however, styled his hair and was very well-dressed. This led Pharaoh to exclaim, *"Would we find like this? A man who has God's spirit in him?"*—is it possible that the spirit of God would be found in such a fashionable, well-dressed young man? (*Rabbi Simḥah Bunem of Przysucha, 18th–19th century*).

45. Zaphenath-paneah. If this is an Egyptian name then we don't understand it. If it is a translation of his name into Hebrew, then we don't know Joseph's Egyptian name (*Rabbi Abraham ibn Ezra, 12th century*).

Joseph was given this name because it was the custom in Egypt to give a person a special appellation when he assumed a position of office. Thus, we find that Moses *"called Hosea son of Nun, 'Joshua'"* (Numbers 13:16), when he was appointed Moses' assistant (*Rabbi Samuel b. Meir, 12th century*).

Zaphenath-paneah means, "Explainer of Hidden Things." The word *pa'neaḥ* has no parallel in Scripture (*Rashi, 11th century*).

---

food for thought

1. Are you ready to accept wisdom even from a "lowly" person?

2. What would be your priorities if appointed vice-president today?

3. Do you think that your dreams sometimes carry a prophetic message?

officials over the land, and prepare the land of Egypt during the seven years of abundance. ³⁵ Let them collect all the food from these coming seven good years, and let them gather the grain under Pharaoh's control, food guarded in the storehouses. ³⁶ The food (that is stored) will thus remain as a reserve for the land for the seven years of famine which will be in the land of Egypt, so that the land will not be destroyed by the famine."

Joseph is Appointed Ruler of Egypt

³⁷ The matter pleased Pharaoh and all his servants.

³⁸ Pharaoh said to his servants, "(Even if we tried,) would we find (anyone else) like this? A man who has God's spirit in him?"

[THIRD READING] ³⁹ Pharaoh said to Joseph, "Since God has let you know all this (it proves that) there's no one as understanding and wise as you. ⁴⁰ You will be in charge of my household, all my people will be fed through your command. Only (by virtue of) the throne will I be greater than you."

⁴¹ Pharaoh said to Joseph, "See, I have appointed you over the entire land of Egypt!"

⁴² Pharaoh removed his ring from his hand and placed it on Joseph's hand. He had him dressed in linen robes, and placed a golden chain around his neck. ⁴³ He had (Joseph) ride in his second (royal) chariot, and they called out before him, "(This is) the king's advisor." (Pharaoh thus) gave (Joseph) authority over the entire land of Egypt.

⁴⁴ Pharaoh said to Joseph, "I am Pharaoh (king of Egypt, and I hereby decree that), without your permission, no man may raise his hand (to hold a weapon) or his foot (to ride on a horse) in the entire land of Egypt."

⁴⁵ Pharaoh named Joseph "Zaphenath-paneah" ("Explainer of Hidden Things"),

---

is repeated twice *on one night*. Joseph's dreams were also repeated (37:5-9), but they did not materialize quickly, as the two dreams occurred on different nights (*Rabbi Samuel b. Meir, 12th century*).

kabbalah bites

41:44 When Joseph woke that morning he had been impregnated with the soul of Enoch. Enoch did not die a normal death, but rather was "taken away" by God (*above* 5:24) and transformed into the angel Metatron, the "king" of seventy angels, appointed over the seventy nations. Having received these new soul powers, Joseph found that he could now understand and speak seventy languages, which would prove indispensable when his capabilities were later questioned by Pharaoh's ministers.

לוֹ אֶת־אָסְנַת בַּת־פּוֹטִי פֶרַע כֹּהֵן אֹן לְאִשָּׁה וַיֵּצֵא יוֹסֵף עַל־אֶרֶץ מִצְרָיִם: 46 וְיוֹסֵף בֶּן־שְׁלֹשִׁים שָׁנָה בְּעָמְדוֹ לִפְנֵי פַּרְעֹה מֶלֶךְ־מִצְרָיִם וַיֵּצֵא יוֹסֵף מִלִּפְנֵי פַרְעֹה וַיַּעֲבֹר בְּכָל־אֶרֶץ מִצְרָיִם: 47 וַתַּעַשׂ הָאָרֶץ בְּשֶׁבַע שְׁנֵי הַשָּׂבָע לִקְמָצִים: 48 וַיִּקְבֹּץ אֶת־כָּל־אֹכֶל | שֶׁבַע שָׁנִים אֲשֶׁר הָיוּ בְּאֶרֶץ מִצְרַיִם וַיִּתֶּן־אֹכֶל בֶּעָרִים אֹכֶל שְׂדֵה־הָעִיר אֲשֶׁר סְבִיבֹתֶיהָ נָתַן בְּתוֹכָהּ: 49 וַיִּצְבֹּר יוֹסֵף בָּר כְּחוֹל הַיָּם הַרְבֵּה מְאֹד עַד כִּי־חָדַל לִסְפֹּר כִּי־אֵין מִסְפָּר: 50 וּלְיוֹסֵף יֻלַּד שְׁנֵי בָנִים בְּטֶרֶם תָּבוֹא שְׁנַת הָרָעָב אֲשֶׁר יָלְדָה־לּוֹ אָסְנַת בַּת־פּוֹטִי פֶרַע כֹּהֵן אוֹן: 51 וַיִּקְרָא יוֹסֵף אֶת־שֵׁם הַבְּכוֹר מְנַשֶּׁה כִּי־נַשַּׁנִי אֱלֹהִים אֶת־כָּל־עֲמָלִי וְאֵת כָּל־בֵּית אָבִי: 52 וְאֵת שֵׁם הַשֵּׁנִי קָרָא אֶפְרָיִם כִּי־הִפְרַנִי אֱלֹהִים בְּאֶרֶץ עָנְיִי: 53 וַתִּכְלֶינָה שֶׁבַע שְׁנֵי הַשָּׂבָע אֲשֶׁר הָיָה בְּאֶרֶץ מִצְרָיִם: [FOURTH READING] 54 וַתְּחִלֶּינָה שֶׁבַע שְׁנֵי הָרָעָב לָבוֹא כַּאֲשֶׁר אָמַר יוֹסֵף וַיְהִי רָעָב בְּכָל־הָאֲרָצוֹת וּבְכָל־אֶרֶץ מִצְרַיִם הָיָה לָחֶם: 55 וַתִּרְעַב כָּל־אֶרֶץ מִצְרַיִם וַיִּצְעַק הָעָם אֶל־פַּרְעֹה לַלָּחֶם וַיֹּאמֶר פַּרְעֹה לְכָל־מִצְרַיִם לְכוּ אֶל־יוֹסֵף אֲשֶׁר־יֹאמַר לָכֶם תַּעֲשׂוּ:

55. The entire land of Egypt was hungry. All their grain which they had stored had rotted, except for Joseph's (*Rashi, 11th century*).

Do whatever he will tell you. Joseph would tell them to circumcise themselves. When they complained to Pharaoh, he replied to them: "Why didn't you gather grain? Didn't Joseph announce to you that years of famine were coming?"

They replied, "We gathered a lot, but it rotted."

Pharaoh replied, "If so, do everything that he will tell you. He already issued a decree upon the grain, and it rotted. He might now issue a decree upon us and we'll die!" (*Rashi, 11th century*).

Joseph saw prophetically that the Jewish people were to be exiled in Egypt. Therefore, he tried to ensure that the Egyptians would be circumcised, in order to prevent the Jewish people from abandoning the precept of circumcision through assimilation (*Rabbi Ḥanokh Zundel b. Joseph of Bialystok, 19th century*).

kabbalah bites

41:55 *Go to Joseph. Do whatever he will tell you.* Why did Joseph insist that the Egyptians who came to him for grain must circumcise themselves? What was to be gained from this forced "conversion"?

Joseph perceived prophetically that these Egyptians possessed the lofty "dysfunctional souls" which Adam had brought into being during the 130 years that he separated from Eve (see above 5:3). Seeing that their dysfunction had not yet been corrected, Joseph sought to heal them spiritually through circumcision.

and he gave him Asenath—the daughter of Poti-phera (i.e. Potiphar), the governor of On—for a wife. And Joseph went forth (as a ruler) over the land of Egypt.

⁴⁶ Joseph was thirty years old when he stood before Pharaoh, the king of Egypt. Joseph then left Pharaoh's presence, and visited the entire land of Egypt.

The Seven Years of Abundance

⁴⁷ In the seven years of abundance, (the inhabitants of) the land gradually made collections (of grain). ⁴⁸ (Joseph) collected all the (surplus) grain of the seven years (of abundance) that was in the land of Egypt, and he placed the grain in the cities. He stored the grain of the fields surrounding each city in (its adjacent city, along with some local soil as a preservative).

⁴⁹ Joseph gathered grain in large amounts, like the sands of the sea, until (they decided to) give up counting it, since the counting had no (meaning).

Birth of Manasseh and Ephraim

⁵⁰ Two sons were born to Joseph before the year that the famine set in, whom Asenath, the daughter of Poti-phera, the governor of On, bore to him. ⁵¹ Joseph named the firstborn Manasseh, because (he said), "God has caused me to forget [*NaSHani*] all my hardships and all that was in my father's house." ⁵² He named the second one Ephraim, because (he said), "God has made me fruitful [*hiPH'Rani*] in the land of my subjugation."

Onset of the Famine

[FOURTH READING] ⁵³ When the seven years of plenty that were in the land of Egypt were finished, ⁵⁴ the seven years of famine began, as Joseph had said. There was famine in all the lands, but throughout the land of Egypt there was bread. ⁵⁵ (Then all the accumulated grain rotted, except for Joseph's, so) the entire land of Egypt was hungry. (When Joseph demanded that the people become circumcised if they wanted grain) the people cried out to Pharaoh for bread, but Pharaoh said to all the Egyptians, "Go to Joseph. Do whatever he will tell you."

It is possible that Pharaoh inquired of Joseph what a respectable name would be in his own language, or that he was familiar with the language of Canaan, as it was close to Egypt. Thus we find that Pharaoh's daughter also gave Moses a Hebrew name, *"She named him Moses [MoSHeh], and she said, 'For I drew him [MeSHitihu] from the water'"* (2:10; *Naḥmanides, 13ᵗʰ century*).

50. Two sons were born to Joseph before the year that the famine set in. From here we derive the rule that it is prohibited to conceive a child during years of famine (*Rashi, 11ᵗʰ century*).

The prohibition of having children during times of famine does not apply to a person who has not yet had both a son and a daughter (*Rabbi Elijah Mizraḥi, 15ᵗʰ–16ᵗʰ century*).

We are not speaking here of an actual prohibition which existed in those days, but rather, a personal stringency of Joseph (*The Tosafists, 12ᵗʰ–14ᵗʰ centuries*).

בראשית מא:נו - מב:ו

56 וְהָרָעָב הָיָה עַל כָּל־פְּנֵי הָאָרֶץ וַיִּפְתַּח יוֹסֵף אֶת־כָּל־אֲשֶׁר בָּהֶם וַיִּשְׁבֹּר לְמִצְרַיִם וַיֶּחֱזַק הָרָעָב בְּאֶרֶץ מִצְרָיִם: 57 וְכָל־הָאָרֶץ בָּאוּ מִצְרַיְמָה לִשְׁבֹּר אֶל־יוֹסֵף כִּי־חָזַק הָרָעָב בְּכָל־הָאָרֶץ:

מב 1 וַיַּרְא יַעֲקֹב כִּי יֶשׁ־שֶׁבֶר בְּמִצְרָיִם וַיֹּאמֶר יַעֲקֹב לְבָנָיו לָמָּה תִּתְרָאוּ: 2 וַיֹּאמֶר הִנֵּה שָׁמַעְתִּי כִּי יֶשׁ־שֶׁבֶר בְּמִצְרָיִם רְדוּ־שָׁמָּה וְשִׁבְרוּ־לָנוּ מִשָּׁם וְנִחְיֶה וְלֹא נָמוּת: 3 וַיֵּרְדוּ אֲחֵי־יוֹסֵף עֲשָׂרָה לִשְׁבֹּר בָּר מִמִּצְרָיִם: 4 וְאֶת־בִּנְיָמִין אֲחִי יוֹסֵף לֹא־שָׁלַח יַעֲקֹב אֶת־אֶחָיו כִּי אָמַר פֶּן־יִקְרָאֶנּוּ אָסוֹן: 5 וַיָּבֹאוּ בְּנֵי יִשְׂרָאֵל לִשְׁבֹּר בְּתוֹךְ הַבָּאִים כִּי־הָיָה הָרָעָב בְּאֶרֶץ כְּנָעַן: 6 וְיוֹסֵף הוּא הַשַּׁלִּיט עַל־הָאָרֶץ הוּא הַמַּשְׁבִּיר לְכָל־עַם הָאָרֶץ

The sons of Ishmaelites and the sons of Esau were not even present in the land of Canaan at that time, so why would Jacob tell his sons not to show off "in front of them"?

Perhaps, the Ishmaelites and the sons of Esau passed through Canaan on their way to Egypt to buy grain. So Jacob was concerned that if his family appeared to have grain, his relatives would come to his house to eat his food (*Nahmanides, 13th century*).

Why would the Ishmaelites and children of Esau be jealous of Jacob's family more than the other peoples of Ammon and Moab? The jealousy which we are speaking about here is one that could only arise between close relatives, since a person is expected to care for his brother at a time of suffering. Therefore, Jacob feared jealousy only from the descendants of Abraham and Isaac (*Rabbi Samuel Edels, 16th–17th century*).

The children of Esau hated Jacob for taking the blessings from Isaac, and the children of Ishmael resented Abraham's preference for Isaac. Therefore, Jacob told his sons to be wary of them in particular (*Rabbi Ephraim of Luntshits, 16th–17th century*).

Jacob was afraid of jealousy from people in general and not just the Ishmaelites and the children of Esau (*Rabbi Samuel b. Meir, 12th century*).

5. Among the visitors. The brothers mingled so that they would not be recognized, because their father had commanded them not to appear all together at one entrance. Rather, each should enter through a different entrance so that the "evil eye" would have no power over them, for they were all handsome and strong (*Rashi, 11th century*).

6. Joseph was the ruler over the land. He was the one who sold grain to all the people of the land. In his empathy for the hungry, Joseph took personal charge of the grain distribution. Although, as second-in-command to Pharaoh, he had many servants who could carry out the

⁵⁶ The famine spread (even) to all the (wealthy) people of the land. Joseph opened all (the storehouses) in which there was (grain), and he sold it to the Egyptians. The famine intensified in the land of Egypt.

⁵⁷ All (the inhabitants of) the earth came to Egypt to buy grain from Joseph, because the famine had intensified throughout the whole earth.

The Brothers Appear Before Joseph

42 ¹ Jacob saw (by Divine inspiration) that there was grain being sold in Egypt. Jacob said to his sons, "Why are you showing off (that we still have grain)?"

² He said, "Look, I have heard that there is grain being sold in Egypt. Go down there and buy us (some) from there, so that we will live and not die."

³ So Joseph's brothers went down to Egypt (united in their mission) to buy grain (but split into) ten (about their decision to try and redeem Joseph). ⁴ But Jacob did not send Benjamin, Joseph's brother, with his brothers, because he said, "Perhaps a fatal (accident) will occur to him."

⁵ So the sons of Israel came to buy (grain, mingling) among the visitors, for the land of Canaan was in a state of famine.

⁶ Joseph was the ruler over the land. He was the one who sold grain to all the people of the land. So, Joseph's brothers came and threw themselves to the ground in front of him, with their faces to the ground.

Even though Joseph forced the Egyptians to circumcise themselves under duress, he hoped that later they would come to observe this commandment sincerely.

Alternatively, Joseph feared that the Egyptians might attempt to remove him from power on the basis that he was circumcised and of a different religion. Therefore, he forced the Egyptians to circumcise themselves too.

Or, perhaps, Joseph was attempting to send a covert message to his father that he was still alive. When Jacob would hear that the ruler of Egypt was forcing the nation to circumcise, he would realize that it must be Joseph (*Rabbi David Pardo, 18th century*).

42:1 Jacob saw that there was grain (*shever*) being sold in Egypt. Jacob understood that the "broken vessels" which remained from the previous worlds that God had created and destroyed, existed as fragments (*shever*) in Egypt. And this was the inner reason for the Egyptian exile, to redeem these lost fragments (*Rabbi Menahem Nahum Twersky of Chernobyl, 18th century*).

Why are you showing off? Jacob criticized his sons by saying, "Why do you show yourselves in front of the Ishmaelites and the sons of Esau as if you have plenty of grain?" For at that time they still had some grain (*Rashi, 11th century*).

בראשית מב:ו-טז

וַיָּבֹאוּ אֲחֵי יוֹסֵף וַיִּשְׁתַּחֲווּ־לוֹ אַפַּיִם אָרְצָה: 7 וַיַּרְא יוֹסֵף אֶת־אֶחָיו וַיַּכִּרֵם וַיִּתְנַכֵּר אֲלֵיהֶם וַיְדַבֵּר אִתָּם קָשׁוֹת וַיֹּאמֶר אֲלֵהֶם מֵאַיִן בָּאתֶם וַיֹּאמְרוּ מֵאֶרֶץ כְּנַעַן לִשְׁבָּר־אֹכֶל: 8 וַיַּכֵּר יוֹסֵף אֶת־אֶחָיו וְהֵם לֹא הִכִּרֻהוּ: 9 וַיִּזְכֹּר יוֹסֵף אֵת הַחֲלֹמוֹת אֲשֶׁר חָלַם לָהֶם וַיֹּאמֶר אֲלֵהֶם מְרַגְּלִים אַתֶּם לִרְאוֹת אֶת־עֶרְוַת הָאָרֶץ בָּאתֶם: 10 וַיֹּאמְרוּ אֵלָיו לֹא אֲדֹנִי וַעֲבָדֶיךָ בָּאוּ לִשְׁבָּר־אֹכֶל: 11 כֻּלָּנוּ בְּנֵי אִישׁ־אֶחָד נָחְנוּ כֵּנִים אֲנַחְנוּ לֹא־הָיוּ עֲבָדֶיךָ מְרַגְּלִים: 12 וַיֹּאמֶר אֲלֵהֶם לֹא כִּי־עֶרְוַת הָאָרֶץ בָּאתֶם לִרְאוֹת: 13 וַיֹּאמְרוּ שְׁנֵים עָשָׂר עֲבָדֶיךָ אַחִים | אֲנַחְנוּ בְּנֵי אִישׁ־אֶחָד בְּאֶרֶץ כְּנָעַן וְהִנֵּה הַקָּטֹן אֶת־אָבִינוּ הַיּוֹם וְהָאֶחָד אֵינֶנּוּ: 14 וַיֹּאמֶר אֲלֵהֶם יוֹסֵף הוּא אֲשֶׁר דִּבַּרְתִּי אֲלֵכֶם לֵאמֹר מְרַגְּלִים אַתֶּם: 15 בְּזֹאת תִּבָּחֵנוּ חֵי פַרְעֹה אִם־תֵּצְאוּ מִזֶּה כִּי אִם־בְּבוֹא אֲחִיכֶם הַקָּטֹן הֵנָּה: 16 שִׁלְחוּ מִכֶּם אֶחָד וְיִקַּח אֶת־אֲחִיכֶם וְאַתֶּם הֵאָסְרוּ וְיִבָּחֲנוּ דִּבְרֵיכֶם הַאֱמֶת אִתְּכֶם

---

tzaddik can interact with the world, at its most basic level, and yet remain totally enwrapped in Godly awareness.

Thus, the brothers who were sequestrial shepherds did not recognize Joseph who was a terrestrial governor—for they simply could not conceive how a person could be so intimately involved with the world, and yet remain a perfect *tzaddik* (*Rabbi Dov Baer Schneuri of Lubavitch, 19th century*).

10-11. Your servants have come to buy food. We are all sons of one man.
"Don't say that! Your servants have come to buy food" (*Rashi, 11th century*).

Coming to buy food was not a *proof* that they were not spies, for spies often pose as merchants. They were saying, "Don't say that! It's not true! *Rather*, your servants have come to buy food" (*Rabbi Elijah Mizrahi, 15th–16th century*).

They told him that they were brothers because it is highly unlikely that a king would pick ten spies who were all brothers (*Rabbi Obadiah Sforno, 16th century*).

12. You have come to survey the land's weak points!
In order to ensure that his brothers did not immediately discover his true identity, Joseph devised a plan. By accusing them of being spies, the brothers refrained from talking with the locals and traveling freely throughout Egypt, for they did not wish to lend support to Joseph's

---

kabbalah bites

42:9 In the days of Moses, before the twelve spies would depart to search out the land of Israel, they would be impregnated with the souls of Jacob's sons. This is alluded to here by Joseph's words: "*You are spies*"—*your souls are destined to be impregnated in the souls of the spies.*

genesis 42:7–16 — mikketz

⁷ Joseph saw his brothers, and he recognized them, but he acted like a stranger to them, and he spoke with them harshly. He said to them, "Where do you come from?"

"From the land of Canaan," they said, "to purchase food."

⁸ Joseph recognized his brothers, but they did not recognize him (because they hadn't seen him with a beard). ⁹ Joseph remembered the dreams that he had had about them (and he realized that they were being fulfilled). He said to them, "You are spies! You have come to survey the land's weak points (from where it can be attacked)!"

¹⁰ "No, my master," they said to him, "your servants have come to buy food. ¹¹ We are all sons of one man. We are (telling the) truth. Your servants were never spies."

¹² "No!" he said to them. "You have come to see the land's weak points!"

¹³ They said, "We, your servants, are twelve brothers, the sons of one man in the land of Canaan. Right now, the youngest is with our father, and one is lost (so we split up to look for him)."

¹⁴ Joseph said to them, "When I said to you, 'You are spies' I was (correct). ¹⁵ The following will be your test: By Pharaoh's life, you shall not leave this place unless your youngest brother comes here. ¹⁶ Send one of you and let him fetch your brother, and (the rest of) you will be imprisoned so that your words will be tested

---

task, Joseph wanted to ensure that proper compassion was shown to those who were begging for food (*Rabbi Mordecai ha-Kohen, 17th century*).

6-7. Joseph's brothers came and threw themselves to the ground in front of him ... but he acted like a stranger to them. This passage brings to light Joseph's compassion. The brothers would surely have felt unbearable humiliation had Joseph pointed out that they were now fulfilling his earlier dreams in bowing down to him. Many people in Joseph's position would have gleefully grabbed the opportunity for vindication, letting the oppressors taste the full bitterness of defeat. But Joseph did not use this chance to retaliate for the pain the brothers had caused him. Instead, *"he acted like a stranger,"* to ensure that they would not feel ashamed (*Rabbi Levi Isaac of Berdichev, 18th century*).

8. They did not recognize him. There are two types of *tzaddikim* (righteous individuals): the "sequestrial" *tzaddik*, and the "terrestrial" *tzaddik*.

The sequestrial *tzaddik* finds this world a distraction from his emotional union with God. The world is mundane; God is sublime. So the sequestrial *tzaddik* shies away from interaction with people and things, secluding himself in a place where he can pray, meditate and study undisturbed.

The terrestrial *tzaddik*, by contrast, is bound to God in a much stronger manner, to the extent that the world does not—and cannot—distract him from his consciousness of the Divine. This

וְאִם־לֹא חֵי פַרְעֹה כִּי מְרַגְּלִים אַתֶּם: 17 וַיֶּאֱסֹף אֹתָם אֶל־מִשְׁמָר שְׁלֹשֶׁת יָמִים: 18 וַיֹּאמֶר אֲלֵהֶם יוֹסֵף בַּיּוֹם הַשְּׁלִישִׁי זֹאת עֲשׂוּ וִחְיוּ אֶת־הָאֱלֹהִים אֲנִי יָרֵא: [FIFTH READING] 19 אִם־כֵּנִים אַתֶּם אֲחִיכֶם אֶחָד יֵאָסֵר בְּבֵית מִשְׁמַרְכֶם וְאַתֶּם לְכוּ הָבִיאוּ שֶׁבֶר רַעֲבוֹן בָּתֵּיכֶם: 20 וְאֶת־אֲחִיכֶם הַקָּטֹן תָּבִיאוּ אֵלַי וְיֵאָמְנוּ דִבְרֵיכֶם וְלֹא תָמוּתוּ וַיַּעֲשׂוּ־כֵן: 21 וַיֹּאמְרוּ אִישׁ אֶל־אָחִיו אֲבָל אֲשֵׁמִים | אֲנַחְנוּ עַל־אָחִינוּ אֲשֶׁר רָאִינוּ צָרַת נַפְשׁוֹ בְּהִתְחַנְנוֹ אֵלֵינוּ וְלֹא שָׁמָעְנוּ עַל־כֵּן בָּאָה אֵלֵינוּ הַצָּרָה הַזֹּאת: 22 וַיַּעַן רְאוּבֵן אֹתָם לֵאמֹר הֲלוֹא אָמַרְתִּי אֲלֵיכֶם | לֵאמֹר אַל־תֶּחֶטְאוּ בַיֶּלֶד וְלֹא שְׁמַעְתֶּם וְגַם־דָּמוֹ הִנֵּה נִדְרָשׁ: 23 וְהֵם לֹא יָדְעוּ כִּי שֹׁמֵעַ יוֹסֵף כִּי הַמֵּלִיץ בֵּינֹתָם: 24 וַיִּסֹּב מֵעֲלֵיהֶם וַיֵּבְךְּ וַיָּשָׁב אֲלֵהֶם וַיְדַבֵּר אֲלֵהֶם וַיִּקַּח מֵאִתָּם אֶת־שִׁמְעוֹן וַיֶּאֱסֹר אֹתוֹ לְעֵינֵיהֶם: 25 וַיְצַו יוֹסֵף וַיְמַלְאוּ

21. We are guilty for our brother. Like Joseph's brothers, a person should always see any punishment he receives as just, and search his actions in order to attribute the punishment to some bad that he has done (*Rabbi Levi b. Gershom, 14th century*).

Happy are the righteous who accept affliction with joy and declare God to be just in every way that He acts! (*Midrash ha-Gadol*).

The brothers still maintained that they were justified in attempting to kill Joseph, based on the halakhic principle that if a person comes to kill you, you should kill him first in self-defense (*Babylonian Talmud, Sanhedrin* 72b). However, now they regretted being cruel to him, and not listening to his cries for help. They understood that they were now being treated harshly as a punishment for their cruelty to Joseph.

Reuben therefore counteracted, "His blood is also being claimed"— Joseph was an *innocent* child, so we are not just being punished for being cruel to him. We are also guilty of spilling innocent blood (*Rabbi Obadiah Sforno, 16th century*).

The reaction of Joseph's brothers teaches us that when bad things *happen to a person*, he should search his deeds to ascertain the bad that he has done, and then repent, confessing to God and asking forgiveness from Him (*Rabbi David Kimḥi, 12th–13th century*).

22. Reuben responded. The brothers said, "It's true, we are guilty for our brother, because we saw his distress when he begged us, and we didn't listen. *That's why this trouble has come upon us*" (v. 21). They only began to repent because they found themselves in dire straits.

food for thought

1. What would you do if your abusers came begging for food?

2. Have you opted not to avenge a severe personal maltreatment?

3. How forgiving are you?

whether you're telling the truth. But if you don't (bring him, I swear,) as Pharaoh lives, that you are spies!"

¹⁷ He put them in prison for three days.

¹⁸ On the third day, Joseph said to them, "If you do as I say you will live. I fear the Almighty."

[FIFTH READING] ¹⁹ "If you are genuine, one of your brothers will remain imprisoned where you are now, while you go and bring back grain (which you purchased to relieve) the hunger of your households. ²⁰ Bring your youngest brother to me, so that your words may be verified, and you will not die."

They (agreed) to do so.

The Brothers Repent

²¹ They said to each other, "It's true, we are guilty for our brother, because we saw his distress when he begged us, and we didn't listen. That's why this trouble has come upon us."

²² Reuben responded to them, saying, "Didn't I warn you, saying, 'Don't sin against the lad'? But you didn't listen...and also his blood (and our father's anguish) is now being claimed!"

²³ They did not know that Joseph understood (their language), for the interpreter was between them. ²⁴ He turned away from them and wept (since he realized that they regretted selling him).

Then he returned to them, and spoke with them. He took Simeon (the one who had thrown him into the pit) from among them and imprisoned him before their eyes (until they left, when he set him free).

²⁵ Joseph commanded (his servants), and they filled (the brothers') bags with

---

claim that they had come to *"survey the land's weak points."* Restricted in their movements and interactions, they had no opportunity to inquire about the new leader's background and origins. Thus Joseph's identity could remain hidden until he was ready to reveal himself to his brothers (*Rabbi Ephraim of Luntshits, 16th–17th century*).

spiritual vitamin

> *"Everything that the Merciful One does is for the good"* (*Babylonian Talmud, Berakhot* 60b). Of course, you cannot always understand the ways of God, but you should be unshaken in your trust in God. This very faith is in itself a channel and vessel to receive God's blessings.

בראשית מב:כה-לח

אֶת־כְּלֵיהֶם בָּר וּלְהָשִׁיב כַּסְפֵּיהֶם אִישׁ אֶל־שַׂקּוֹ וְלָתֵת לָהֶם צֵדָה לַדָּרֶךְ וַיַּעַשׂ לָהֶם כֵּן: 26 וַיִּשְׂאוּ אֶת־שִׁבְרָם עַל־חֲמֹרֵיהֶם וַיֵּלְכוּ מִשָּׁם: 27 וַיִּפְתַּח הָאֶחָד אֶת־שַׂקּוֹ לָתֵת מִסְפּוֹא לַחֲמֹרוֹ בַּמָּלוֹן וַיַּרְא אֶת־כַּסְפּוֹ וְהִנֵּה־הוּא בְּפִי אַמְתַּחְתּוֹ: 28 וַיֹּאמֶר אֶל־אֶחָיו הוּשַׁב כַּסְפִּי וְגַם הִנֵּה בְאַמְתַּחְתִּי וַיֵּצֵא לִבָּם וַיֶּחֶרְדוּ אִישׁ אֶל־אָחִיו לֵאמֹר מַה־זֹּאת עָשָׂה אֱלֹהִים לָנוּ: 29 וַיָּבֹאוּ אֶל־יַעֲקֹב אֲבִיהֶם אַרְצָה כְּנָעַן וַיַּגִּידוּ לוֹ אֵת כָּל־הַקֹּרֹת אֹתָם לֵאמֹר: 30 דִּבֶּר הָאִישׁ אֲדֹנֵי הָאָרֶץ אִתָּנוּ קָשׁוֹת וַיִּתֵּן אֹתָנוּ כִּמְרַגְּלִים אֶת־הָאָרֶץ: 31 וַנֹּאמֶר אֵלָיו כֵּנִים אֲנָחְנוּ לֹא הָיִינוּ מְרַגְּלִים: 32 שְׁנֵים־עָשָׂר אֲנַחְנוּ אַחִים בְּנֵי אָבִינוּ הָאֶחָד אֵינֶנּוּ וְהַקָּטֹן הַיּוֹם אֶת־אָבִינוּ בְּאֶרֶץ כְּנָעַן: 33 וַיֹּאמֶר אֵלֵינוּ הָאִישׁ אֲדֹנֵי הָאָרֶץ בְּזֹאת אֵדַע כִּי כֵנִים אַתֶּם אֲחִיכֶם הָאֶחָד הַנִּיחוּ אִתִּי וְאֶת־רַעֲבוֹן בָּתֵּיכֶם קְחוּ וָלֵכוּ: 34 וְהָבִיאוּ אֶת־אֲחִיכֶם הַקָּטֹן אֵלַי וְאֵדְעָה כִּי לֹא מְרַגְּלִים אַתֶּם כִּי כֵנִים אַתֶּם אֶת־אֲחִיכֶם אֶתֵּן לָכֶם וְאֶת־הָאָרֶץ תִּסְחָרוּ: 35 וַיְהִי הֵם מְרִיקִים שַׂקֵּיהֶם וְהִנֵּה־אִישׁ צְרוֹר־כַּסְפּוֹ בְּשַׂקּוֹ וַיִּרְאוּ אֶת־צְרֹרוֹת כַּסְפֵּיהֶם הֵמָּה וַאֲבִיהֶם וַיִּירָאוּ: 36 וַיֹּאמֶר אֲלֵהֶם יַעֲקֹב אֲבִיהֶם אֹתִי שִׁכַּלְתֶּם יוֹסֵף אֵינֶנּוּ וְשִׁמְעוֹן אֵינֶנּוּ וְאֶת־בִּנְיָמִן תִּקָּחוּ עָלַי הָיוּ כֻלָּנָה: 37 וַיֹּאמֶר רְאוּבֵן אֶל־אָבִיו לֵאמֹר אֶת־שְׁנֵי בָנַי תָּמִית אִם־לֹא אֲבִיאֶנּוּ אֵלֶיךָ תְּנָה אֹתוֹ עַל־יָדִי וַאֲנִי אֲשִׁיבֶנּוּ אֵלֶיךָ: 38 וַיֹּאמֶר לֹא־יֵרֵד בְּנִי עִמָּכֶם כִּי־אָחִיו מֵת וְהוּא לְבַדּוֹ נִשְׁאָר וּקְרָאָהוּ אָסוֹן בַּדֶּרֶךְ אֲשֶׁר תֵּלְכוּ־בָהּ וְהוֹרַדְתֶּם אֶת־שֵׂיבָתִי בְּיָגוֹן שְׁאוֹלָה:

25. Provisions for the journey. Joseph said, "I have no intention of harming you if your words are verified." Therefore he gave them provisions for the journey, so that they would be able to bring Benjamin back to him.

While they were carrying a large amount of food already, Joseph's extra provisions were offered so that they would not have to eat from what they had purchased on their way home (*Naḥmanides, 13th century*).

grain. (He also instructed) to return their money (with which they paid for the grain) into each person's sack, and to give them provisions for the journey, which (his servants) did for them. ²⁶ They loaded their grain onto their donkeys, and departed.

²⁷ At the hotel, (Levi) opened his sack to give fodder to his donkey, and he saw his money. Look! There it was, at the top of his sack. ²⁸ He said to his brothers, "My money has been returned, and—look!—it's here in my sack!"

Their hearts sank. Trembling, they turned to one another, saying, "Why is God doing this to us?"

Jacob Refuses to Send Benjamin

²⁹ They came to Jacob their father, in the land of Canaan, and they told him everything that had happened to them: They said, ³⁰ "The man, the chief of the land, spoke to us harshly. He accused us of spying on the land. ³¹ We said to him, 'We are honest! We were never spies. ³² We are twelve brothers, the sons of our father. One is missing, and now the youngest is with our father in the land of Canaan.' ³³ The man, the chief of the land, said to us, 'With this (test) I'll know if you are honest: leave one of your brothers with me, and (what's needed for) the hunger of your households, take and leave. ³⁴ Bring your youngest brother to me, so that I will know that you are not spies, and that you are honest. (Then) I'll give you your brother, and you can do business around the land.'"

³⁵ Then, when they were emptying their sacks—look!—each person's bundle of money was in his sack. As they saw the bundles of their money, together with their father, they became frightened.

³⁶ Their father, Jacob, said to them, "You have bereaved me! Joseph is gone, and Simeon is gone, and you want to take Benjamin! All these (troubles) have come upon me!"

³⁷ Reuben spoke to his father, saying, "You may put my two sons to death if I don't bring (Benjamin) to you. Put him into my care and I will return him to you."

³⁸ (Jacob) said, "My son shall not go down with you, because his brother is dead, and he is the only one left. A fatality will occur to him on the way in which you will be going, and you will bring my old age to the grave in grief."

Therefore, Reuben—who was the first person to carry out a genuine repentance (*Genesis Rabbah*)—felt the need to make his brothers refocus on the *sin itself*, "*Didn't I warn you, saying, 'Don't sin against the lad'? But you didn't listen...*" He was telling them that it was incorrect to repent as a result of the misfortune which had befallen them. They should have striven to feel genuine remorse for what they had done because the *act itself* was evil (*Rabbi Menahem Mendel Schneerson, 20ᵗʰ century*).

בראשית מג:א-יד · מקץ

מג 1 וְהָרָעָב כָּבֵד בָּאָרֶץ: 2 וַיְהִי כַּאֲשֶׁר כִּלּוּ לֶאֱכֹל אֶת־הַשֶּׁבֶר אֲשֶׁר הֵבִיאוּ מִמִּצְרָיִם וַיֹּאמֶר אֲלֵיהֶם אֲבִיהֶם שֻׁבוּ שִׁבְרוּ־לָנוּ מְעַט־אֹכֶל: 3 וַיֹּאמֶר אֵלָיו יְהוּדָה לֵאמֹר הָעֵד הֵעִד בָּנוּ הָאִישׁ לֵאמֹר לֹא־תִרְאוּ פָנַי בִּלְתִּי אֲחִיכֶם אִתְּכֶם: 4 אִם־יֶשְׁךָ מְשַׁלֵּחַ אֶת־אָחִינוּ אִתָּנוּ נֵרְדָה וְנִשְׁבְּרָה לְךָ אֹכֶל: 5 וְאִם־אֵינְךָ מְשַׁלֵּחַ לֹא נֵרֵד כִּי־הָאִישׁ אָמַר אֵלֵינוּ לֹא־תִרְאוּ פָנַי בִּלְתִּי אֲחִיכֶם אִתְּכֶם: 6 וַיֹּאמֶר יִשְׂרָאֵל לָמָה הֲרֵעֹתֶם לִי לְהַגִּיד לָאִישׁ הַעוֹד לָכֶם אָח: 7 וַיֹּאמְרוּ שָׁאוֹל שָׁאַל־הָאִישׁ לָנוּ וּלְמוֹלַדְתֵּנוּ לֵאמֹר הַעוֹד אֲבִיכֶם חַי הֲיֵשׁ לָכֶם אָח וַנַּגֶּד־לוֹ עַל־פִּי הַדְּבָרִים הָאֵלֶּה הֲיָדוֹעַ נֵדַע כִּי יֹאמַר הוֹרִידוּ אֶת־אֲחִיכֶם: 8 וַיֹּאמֶר יְהוּדָה אֶל־יִשְׂרָאֵל אָבִיו שִׁלְחָה הַנַּעַר אִתִּי וְנָקוּמָה וְנֵלֵכָה וְנִחְיֶה וְלֹא נָמוּת גַּם־אֲנַחְנוּ גַם־אַתָּה גַּם־טַפֵּנוּ: 9 אָנֹכִי אֶעֶרְבֶנּוּ מִיָּדִי תְּבַקְשֶׁנּוּ אִם־לֹא הֲבִיאֹתִיו אֵלֶיךָ וְהִצַּגְתִּיו לְפָנֶיךָ וְחָטָאתִי לְךָ כָּל־הַיָּמִים: 10 כִּי לוּלֵא הִתְמַהְמָהְנוּ כִּי־עַתָּה שַׁבְנוּ זֶה פַעֲמָיִם: 11 וַיֹּאמֶר אֲלֵהֶם יִשְׂרָאֵל אֲבִיהֶם אִם־כֵּן | אֵפוֹא זֹאת עֲשׂוּ קְחוּ מִזִּמְרַת הָאָרֶץ בִּכְלֵיכֶם וְהוֹרִידוּ לָאִישׁ מִנְחָה מְעַט צֳרִי וּמְעַט דְּבַשׁ נְכֹאת וָלֹט בָּטְנִים וּשְׁקֵדִים: 12 וְכֶסֶף מִשְׁנֶה קְחוּ בְיֶדְכֶם וְאֶת־הַכֶּסֶף הַמּוּשָׁב בְּפִי אַמְתְּחֹתֵיכֶם תָּשִׁיבוּ בְיֶדְכֶם אוּלַי מִשְׁגֶּה הוּא: 13 וְאֶת־אֲחִיכֶם קָחוּ וְקוּמוּ שׁוּבוּ אֶל־הָאִישׁ: 14 וְאֵל שַׁדַּי יִתֵּן לָכֶם רַחֲמִים לִפְנֵי הָאִישׁ

When Joseph would eventually reveal his identity to the brothers, he wanted to be able to show that he had not been unnecessarily cruel. Therefore, he gave them provisions. He also

spiritual vitamin

> Opinions are derived from reality and not reality from opinions. No theory, however cleverly conceived, can change the facts; if it is inconsistent with the facts it can only do harm to its adherents.

genesis 43:1–14   mikketz

Jacob Acquiesces

43 ¹ The famine in the land was severe. ² So, when they finished eating the grain which they had brought from Egypt, their father said to them, "Go back and buy us a little food."

³ Judah spoke to him, saying, "The man repeatedly warned us, saying, 'You will not see my face if your brother is not with you.'"

⁴ "If you send our brother with us, we'll go down and buy food for you. ⁵ But if you won't send (him), we won't go down, because the man said to us, 'You will not see my face if your brother is not with you.'"

⁶ Israel said, "Why have you harmed me, by telling the man that you have another brother?"

⁷ They said, "The man asked about us and about our family, saying, 'Is your father still alive? Do you have a brother?' We (were forced to) tell him (that we have a father and brother) to answer his questions. Could we have known that he would say, 'Bring your brother down'?"

⁸ Judah said to Israel, his father, "Send the lad with me. Let us get going and travel. Then we'll live and we won't die (of hunger)—both we and you and our young children too. ⁹ I will guarantee his (safe return). You can demand him from my hand! If I do not bring him to you, standing up (alive) before you, I will have sinned against you forever."

¹⁰ "For if we had not delayed (due to your hesitation), we would have already returned by now twice in this (time, and you would not have been troubled all these days by Simeon's absence)."

¹¹ Israel, their father, said to them, "If in fact this is the case, then do the following: Take some of the land's most exclusive products in your bags, and bring them to the man as a gift—a little balsam, a little honey, wax, birthwort, pistachios and almonds. ¹² Take double the (previous amount of) money with you (for perhaps the prices have increased), and return the money that was given back in the top of your sacks along with you. Perhaps, it was an error.

¹³ "Take your brother, get going, and return to the man. ¹⁴ May God Almighty grant you mercy before the man, so that he will release your other brother (Simeon) and Benjamin back to you.

---

food for thought

1. Are you able to remain focused and effective in a situation of urgency?

2. When should you be firm with your parents, and when would it be disrespectful?

3. Judah was not the firstborn. Is all good leadership the result of meritocracy?

בראשית מג:יד-כג | מקץ

וְשִׁלַּ֨ח לָכֶ֧ם אֶת־אֲחִיכֶ֛ם אַחֵ֖ר וְאֶת־בִּנְיָמִ֑ין וַאֲנִ֕י כַּאֲשֶׁ֥ר שָׁכֹ֖לְתִּי שָׁכָֽלְתִּי: 15 וַיִּקְח֤וּ הָֽאֲנָשִׁים֙ אֶת־הַמִּנְחָ֣ה הַזֹּ֔את וּמִשְׁנֶה־כֶּ֛סֶף לָקְח֥וּ בְיָדָ֖ם וְאֶת־בִּנְיָמִ֑ן וַיָּקֻ֙מוּ֙ וַיֵּרְד֣וּ מִצְרַ֔יִם וַיַּֽעַמְד֖וּ לִפְנֵ֥י יוֹסֵֽף: [SIXTH READING] 16 וַיַּ֨רְא יוֹסֵ֣ף אִתָּם֮ אֶת־בִּנְיָמִין֒ וַיֹּ֙אמֶר֙ לַֽאֲשֶׁ֣ר עַל־בֵּית֔וֹ הָבֵ֥א אֶת־הָאֲנָשִׁ֖ים הַבָּ֑יְתָה וּטְבֹ֤חַ טֶ֙בַח֙ וְהָכֵ֔ן כִּ֥י אִתִּ֛י יֹאכְל֥וּ הָאֲנָשִׁ֖ים בַּֽצָּהֳרָֽיִם: 17 וַיַּ֣עַשׂ הָאִ֔ישׁ כַּֽאֲשֶׁ֖ר אָמַ֣ר יוֹסֵ֑ף וַיָּבֵ֥א הָאִ֛ישׁ אֶת־הָאֲנָשִׁ֖ים בֵּ֥יתָה יוֹסֵֽף: 18 וַיִּֽירְא֣וּ הָֽאֲנָשִׁ֗ים כִּ֣י הֽוּבְאוּ֮ בֵּ֣ית יוֹסֵף֒ וַיֹּֽאמְר֗וּ עַל־דְּבַ֤ר הַכֶּ֙סֶף֙ הַשָּׁ֣ב בְּאַמְתְּחֹתֵ֔ינוּ בַּתְּחִלָּ֖ה אֲנַ֣חְנוּ מֽוּבָאִ֑ים לְהִתְגֹּלֵ֤ל עָלֵ֙ינוּ֙ וּלְהִתְנַפֵּ֣ל עָלֵ֔ינוּ וְלָקַ֧חַת אֹתָ֛נוּ לַעֲבָדִ֖ים וְאֶת־חֲמֹרֵֽינוּ: 19 וַֽיִּגְּשׁוּ֙ אֶל־הָאִ֔ישׁ אֲשֶׁ֖ר עַל־בֵּ֣ית יוֹסֵ֑ף וַיְדַבְּר֥וּ אֵלָ֖יו פֶּ֥תַח הַבָּֽיִת: 20 וַיֹּאמְר֖וּ בִּ֣י אֲדֹנִ֑י יָרֹ֥ד יָרַ֛דְנוּ בַּתְּחִלָּ֖ה לִשְׁבָּר־אֹֽכֶל: 21 וַיְהִ֞י כִּי־בָ֣אנוּ אֶל־הַמָּל֗וֹן וַֽנִּפְתְּחָה֙ אֶת־אַמְתְּחֹתֵ֔ינוּ וְהִנֵּ֤ה כֶֽסֶף־אִישׁ֙ בְּפִ֣י אַמְתַּחְתּ֔וֹ כַּסְפֵּ֖נוּ בְּמִשְׁקָל֑וֹ וַנָּ֥שֶׁב אֹת֖וֹ בְּיָדֵֽנוּ: 22 וְכֶ֧סֶף אַחֵ֛ר הוֹרַ֥דְנוּ בְיָדֵ֖נוּ לִשְׁבָּר־אֹ֑כֶל לֹ֣א יָדַ֔עְנוּ מִי־שָׂ֥ם כַּסְפֵּ֖נוּ בְּאַמְתְּחֹתֵֽינוּ: 23 וַיֹּ֩אמֶר֩ שָׁל֨וֹם לָכֶ֜ם אַל־תִּירָ֗אוּ אֱלֹֽהֵיכֶ֞ם וֵֽאלֹהֵ֤י אֲבִיכֶם֙ נָתַ֨ן לָכֶ֤ם מַטְמוֹן֙

much danger that he will not survive an extended medical treatment, God says, "enough," and he is cured immediately. When the Jewish people cannot withstand their anguish and persecution another moment, God says "enough" and saves them instantly.

Jacob saw prophetically that, in the course of time, salvation would come through the "Egyptian man." But Jacob's suffering was already unbearable, so he said, "May *'El Shaddai* grant you mercy *before* the man"—before the man has the opportunity to grant you mercy, in the extended, natural course of events, God should say "enough" and rescue you (*Rabbi Kalonymous Kalman Shapira, 20th century*).

Judah had suggested that returning Simeon was an entirely straightforward matter that could not possibly go wrong: *"For if we had not delayed (due to your hesitation), we would have already returned by now twice in this (time and you would not have been troubled all these days by Simeon's absence)"* (v. 10). Therefore, Jacob warned his sons, "Even if it is true, as you say, that there is no danger here, you still need to pray to God. Don't just pray to God when you feel it is an emergency. You need His help for a natural plan to succeed too."

From this you can learn not only to turn to God when you feel you are lacking something. You should also ask God for things which you perceive will *inevitably* come your way. For, in

"(Until your return I will consider myself to be bereft of my children due to doubt), and like I am bereaved (of Joseph and Simeon) I am (now) bereaved (of Benjamin too)."

Joseph is Reunited with All his Brothers

¹⁵ The men took the gift, and they took double the (previous amount of) money with them, and (they persuaded) Benjamin (to come). They got going and went down to Egypt, where they stood before Joseph.

[SIXTH READING] ¹⁶ Joseph saw Benjamin with them. He said to the supervisor of his house, "Bring the men into the house and (give orders) to slaughter an animal and to prepare (a meal), for the men will eat with me at lunch."

¹⁷ The man did as Joseph had said. The man brought the men into Joseph's house.

¹⁸ The men became afraid (that they were being framed) because they had been brought to Joseph's house. They said, "We are being brought (here) on account of the money that was put in our sacks earlier on, so as to incite (a false accusation) against us which will fall upon us. (This is in order) to take us as slaves and (confiscate) our donkeys."

¹⁹ So they approached the man who supervised Joseph's house and spoke to him at the house's entrance. ²⁰ "Please sir," they said, "we originally came down to purchase food. ²¹ And then, when we came to the hotel we opened our sacks, and—look!—each person's money (with which he had paid for the grain) was (back) in the top of his sack. We've brought it back with us. ²² We brought down more money with us to purchase food. We don't know who put our money (back) into our sacks."

²³ He said, "Don't worry, everything's okay for you. (Either) your merit (or) the merit of the God of your father has brought you a hidden gift. I did receive the money that you paid."

---

gave them back their money to ensure that they would not delay in returning to Egypt due to lack of funds (*Rabbi Isaac Abravanel, 15th century*).

43:14 May God Almighty grant you mercy before the man. Jacob was saying: Now you lack nothing but prayer. I am praying for you so may God Almighty—whose mercy is sufficient, and who has it in His power to give—grant you compassion (*Rashi, 11th century*).

The name "God Almighty" (*'El Shaddai*) is explained by the *Midrash* to mean *"God who said 'enough' (dai) to the universe"* (*Genesis Rabbah*). If God had not said "enough" to the world, it would have extended infinitely. What does this mean practically? When a sick person is in so

בראשית מג:כג-לג | מקץ

בְּאַמְתְּחֹתֵיכֶם כַּסְפְּכֶם בָּא אֵלָי וַיּוֹצֵא אֲלֵהֶם אֶת־שִׁמְעוֹן: 24 וַיָּבֵא הָאִישׁ אֶת־הָאֲנָשִׁים בֵּיתָה יוֹסֵף וַיִּתֶּן־מַיִם וַיִּרְחֲצוּ רַגְלֵיהֶם וַיִּתֵּן מִסְפּוֹא לַחֲמֹרֵיהֶם: 25 וַיָּכִינוּ אֶת־הַמִּנְחָה עַד־בּוֹא יוֹסֵף בַּצָּהֳרָיִם כִּי שָׁמְעוּ כִּי־שָׁם יֹאכְלוּ לָחֶם: 26 וַיָּבֹא יוֹסֵף הַבַּיְתָה וַיָּבִיאוּ לוֹ אֶת־הַמִּנְחָה אֲשֶׁר־בְּיָדָם הַבָּיְתָה וַיִּשְׁתַּחֲווּ־לוֹ אָרְצָה: 27 וַיִּשְׁאַל לָהֶם לְשָׁלוֹם וַיֹּאמֶר הֲשָׁלוֹם אֲבִיכֶם הַזָּקֵן אֲשֶׁר אֲמַרְתֶּם הַעוֹדֶנּוּ חָי: 28 וַיֹּאמְרוּ שָׁלוֹם לְעַבְדְּךָ לְאָבִינוּ עוֹדֶנּוּ חָי וַיִּקְּדוּ [וישתחו כ'] וַיִּשְׁתַּחֲוּוּ: 29 וַיִּשָּׂא עֵינָיו וַיַּרְא אֶת־בִּנְיָמִין אָחִיו בֶּן־אִמּוֹ וַיֹּאמֶר הֲזֶה אֲחִיכֶם הַקָּטֹן אֲשֶׁר אֲמַרְתֶּם אֵלָי וַיֹּאמַר אֱלֹהִים יָחְנְךָ בְּנִי: 30 [SEVENTH READING] וַיְמַהֵר יוֹסֵף כִּי־נִכְמְרוּ רַחֲמָיו אֶל־אָחִיו וַיְבַקֵּשׁ לִבְכּוֹת וַיָּבֹא הַחַדְרָה וַיֵּבְךְּ שָׁמָּה: 31 וַיִּרְחַץ פָּנָיו וַיֵּצֵא וַיִּתְאַפַּק וַיֹּאמֶר שִׂימוּ לָחֶם: 32 וַיָּשִׂימוּ לוֹ לְבַדּוֹ וְלָהֶם לְבַדָּם וְלַמִּצְרִים הָאֹכְלִים אִתּוֹ לְבַדָּם כִּי לֹא יוּכְלוּן הַמִּצְרִים לֶאֱכֹל אֶת־הָעִבְרִים לֶחֶם כִּי־תוֹעֵבָה הִוא לְמִצְרָיִם: 33 וַיֵּשְׁבוּ לְפָנָיו הַבְּכֹר כִּבְכֹרָתוֹ וְהַצָּעִיר

30. His compassion was suddenly stirred up over his brother. Joseph asked Benjamin, "Do you have a brother from your mother's side?"

He replied, "I had a brother, but I don't know where he is."

"Do you have any sons?"

"I have ten," he replied.

"And what are their names?"

"Bela, Becher, etc.," he replied, (reciting all their names).

Joseph asked, "What is the significance of these names?"

He replied, "All of them are connected to my brother and the troubles *that* befell him. My first son was named Bela because my brother was swallowed up (from the root *bala'*) among the nations. My second son was named Bekher because my brother was the firstborn (*bekhor*) of my mother. My third son was named Ashbel because God put my brother into captivity (a contraction of *SHe-Va'o 'EL*). My fourth son was named Gera because my brother lived away (*nitGAyyeR*) from home. My fifth son was named Naaman because my brother was very

1. Why are adult men often embarrassed to express deep emotion and cry?

2. Are the effects of repressing emotions toxic?

3. How can we learn to express our feelings healthily?

He brought Simeon out to them.

²⁴ The man brought the (brothers) into Joseph's house. He gave (them) water, and they washed their feet. He gave fodder to their donkeys. ²⁵ They prepared the gift (in beautiful containers) before Joseph came for lunch, for they heard that they would be dining there.

²⁶ When Joseph came home, they brought him the gift which they had with them, into the (main chamber of the) house and they threw themselves on the ground in front of him.

²⁷ He inquired about their welfare. Then he asked them, "Is your elderly father, whom you mentioned, well? Is he still alive?"

²⁸ They said, "Your servant, our father, is well. He is still alive." They bowed (their heads) and then threw themselves to the ground (thanking him for inquiring about their welfare).

²⁹ (Joseph) looked around and saw Benjamin, his brother, his mother's son. He said, "Is this your little brother, whom you told me about?"

"May God be gracious to you, my son," (Joseph) said.

[SEVENTH READING] ³⁰ (When Joseph heard how Benjamin had named all his sons after him,) his compassion was suddenly stirred up over his brother, and he wanted to cry, so he quickly went into the (side) room and cried there.

³¹ He washed his face and came out. He restrained himself and said, "Put out the food."

³² They set for him separately and for them separately, and for the Egyptians who ate with him separately, since the Egyptians could not eat food with the Hebrews, because it is an abomination to the Egyptians (since Hebrews eat the animals which Egyptians worship).

³³ They sat before him (in age order): the firstborn (of each mother) according to his birthright (followed by the other sons from that mother down to) the youngest (who sat last) according to his young age, (and Benjamin sat next to Joseph).

---

truth, God is the only provider, whether the blessing comes naturally or supernaturally (*Rabbi Menahem Mendel Schneerson, 20th century*).

16. (Give orders) to slaughter an animal and to prepare (a meal). What is the significance of these orders? Joseph's instructions *"to slaughter an animal,"* implied: show them the place where the animal has been ritually slaughtered. And his command *"to prepare"* the animal, implied: remove the sciatic nerve in front of them, for Israelites do not eat the sciatic nerve (*Genesis 32:33; Babylonian Talmud, Ḥullin 91a*).

בראשית מג:לג - מד:י

כְּצִעֲרָתוֹ וַיִּתְמְה֥וּ הָאֲנָשִׁ֖ים אִ֥ישׁ אֶל־רֵעֵֽהוּ׃ 34 וַיִּשָּׂ֨א מַשְׂאֹ֜ת מֵאֵ֣ת פָּנָיו֮ אֲלֵהֶם֒ וַתֵּ֜רֶב מַשְׂאַ֧ת בִּנְיָמִ֛ן מִמַּשְׂאֹ֥ת כֻּלָּ֖ם חָמֵ֣שׁ יָד֑וֹת וַיִּשְׁתּ֥וּ וַֽיִּשְׁכְּר֖וּ עִמּֽוֹ׃

מד 1 וַיְצַ֞ו אֶת־אֲשֶׁ֣ר עַל־בֵּיתוֹ֮ לֵאמֹר֒ מַלֵּ֞א אֶת־אַמְתְּחֹ֤ת הָֽאֲנָשִׁים֙ אֹ֔כֶל כַּאֲשֶׁ֥ר יוּכְל֖וּן שְׂאֵ֑ת וְשִׂ֥ים כֶּֽסֶף־אִ֖ישׁ בְּפִ֥י אַמְתַּחְתּֽוֹ׃ 2 וְאֶת־גְּבִיעִ֣י גְבִ֣יעַ הַכֶּ֗סֶף תָּשִׂים֙ בְּפִי֙ אַמְתַּ֣חַת הַקָּטֹ֔ן וְאֵ֖ת כֶּ֣סֶף שִׁבְר֑וֹ וַיַּ֕עַשׂ כִּדְבַ֥ר יוֹסֵ֖ף אֲשֶׁ֥ר דִּבֵּֽר׃ 3 הַבֹּ֖קֶר א֑וֹר וְהָאֲנָשִׁ֣ים שֻׁלְּח֔וּ הֵ֖מָּה וַחֲמֹרֵיהֶֽם׃ 4 הֵ֠ם יָצְא֣וּ אֶת־הָעִיר֮ לֹ֣א הִרְחִיקוּ֒ וְיוֹסֵ֤ף אָמַר֙ לַֽאֲשֶׁ֣ר עַל־בֵּית֔וֹ ק֥וּם רְדֹ֖ף אַחֲרֵ֣י הָֽאֲנָשִׁ֑ים וְהִשַּׂגְתָּם֙ וְאָמַרְתָּ֣ אֲלֵהֶ֔ם לָ֛מָּה שִׁלַּמְתֶּ֥ם רָעָ֖ה תַּ֥חַת טוֹבָֽה׃ 5 הֲל֣וֹא זֶ֗ה אֲשֶׁ֨ר יִשְׁתֶּ֤ה אֲדֹנִי֙ בּ֔וֹ וְה֕וּא נַחֵ֥שׁ יְנַחֵ֖שׁ בּ֑וֹ הֲרֵעֹתֶ֖ם אֲשֶׁ֥ר עֲשִׂיתֶֽם׃ 6 וַֽיַּשִּׂגֵ֑ם וַיְדַבֵּ֣ר אֲלֵהֶ֔ם אֶת־הַדְּבָרִ֖ים הָאֵֽלֶּה׃ 7 וַיֹּאמְר֣וּ אֵלָ֔יו לָ֚מָּה יְדַבֵּ֣ר אֲדֹנִ֔י כַּדְּבָרִ֖ים הָאֵ֑לֶּה חָלִ֙ילָה֙ לַעֲבָדֶ֔יךָ מֵעֲשׂ֖וֹת כַּדָּבָ֥ר הַזֶּֽה׃ 8 הֵ֣ן כֶּ֗סֶף אֲשֶׁ֤ר מָצָ֙אנוּ֙ בְּפִ֣י אַמְתְּחֹתֵ֔ינוּ הֱשִׁיבֹ֥נוּ אֵלֶ֖יךָ מֵאֶ֣רֶץ כְּנָ֑עַן וְאֵ֗יךְ נִגְנֹב֙ מִבֵּ֣ית אֲדֹנֶ֔יךָ כֶּ֖סֶף א֥וֹ זָהָֽב׃ 9 אֲשֶׁ֨ר יִמָּצֵ֥א אִתּ֛וֹ מֵעֲבָדֶ֖יךָ וָמֵ֑ת וְגַם־אֲנַ֕חְנוּ נִֽהְיֶ֥ה לַֽאדֹנִ֖י לַעֲבָדִֽים׃ 10 וַיֹּ֕אמֶר

They drank (for the first time since Joseph was sold). Although they had refrained from drinking wine for the past twenty-two years, the brothers feared that if they refused to drink,

kabbalah bites

44:1 One of the effects of the *shevirah* (primordial "Breaking of the Vessels"), was that love of God degenerated into the love of physical pleasure.

"Jacob saw that there was grain (SHeVeR) being sold in Egypt" (42:1). He saw the effects of the SHeViRah, how it had caused moral attributes to degenerate into self-serving ones.

In response, Joseph *"put each man's money (kesef) into the top of his sack,"* kesef also connoting "love." Joseph wanted to send a covert message to his father that there was at least one person in Egypt who was busy gathering up the bits of love that had fallen in the *shevirah* and realigning them with their Creator.

The men (looked) in astonishment at each other. ³⁴ (Joseph) had portions brought to them from (what was laid out) before him. Benjamin's portion was five times as large as any of their portions (to include Joseph, Asenath, Manasseh and Ephraim too). They drank (for the first time since Joseph was sold) and became drunk with him.

Joseph's Goblet is Planted in Benjamin's Sack

44 ¹ He commanded the supervisor of his house, saying, "Fill the men's sacks with food, as much as they can carry, and put each man's money (which he used to pay for the grain) into the top of his sack. ² Put my goblet, the silver goblet, into the top of the youngest's sack, with his money (which he used to pay for) his grain." (The supervisor) carried out the instructions which Joseph had said.

³ When it became light the (next) morning, the men were sent (on their way), both they and their donkeys. ⁴ When they had left the city, but had not gone far, Joseph said to the supervisor of his house, "Get going and chase after the men. When you overtake them, say to them, 'Why have you repaid good with evil (stealing my master's goblet)? ⁵ This is none other than the (goblet) which my master drinks from. He (also) divines with it regularly. What you have done is evil!'"

⁶ (The supervisor) overtook them, and he said these words to them.

⁷ They said to him, "Why should my master say such words as these? Far be it from your servants to do a thing like this! ⁸ Look, (if) we (even) returned to you the money we found in the top of our sacks (all the way) from the land of Canaan, how could we (possibly) steal silver or gold from your master's house? ⁹ Whichever one of your servants is found to have (the goblet) shall die, and also, we will be slaves to my master (if it is found)."

¹⁰ He replied, "It's true as you say (that you are all collectively guilty, but I will

---

pleasant (*na'im*). My sixth and seventh sons were named Ehi and Rosh because he was my brother (*aḥi*), and he was my superior (*ro'sh*). My eighth son was named Muppim because my brother learned from the mouth of my father (*MiPPi 'avi*). My ninth son was named Huppim because my brother did not see my wedding canopy (*ḥuppah*), neither did I see his. My tenth son was named Ard because my brother descended (*yARaD*) among the nations."

Immediately, on hearing this, *"his compassion was stirred up"* (Rashi, 11ᵗʰ century).

34. Benjamin's portion was five times as large as any of their portions. Joseph favored his brother Benjamin with a gift five times the size of his other brothers' gifts, to see if they would display jealousy toward him. Joseph wanted to see whether his brothers had rid themselves of sibling-envy (*Rabbi Obadiah Sforno, 16ᵗʰ century*).

בראשית מד:י-יז / מקץ

גַּם־עַתָּה כְדִבְרֵיכֶם כֶּן־הוּא אֲשֶׁר יִמָּצֵא אִתּוֹ יִהְיֶה־לִּי עָבֶד וְאַתֶּם תִּהְיוּ נְקִיִּם: 11 וַיְמַהֲרוּ וַיּוֹרִדוּ אִישׁ אֶת־אַמְתַּחְתּוֹ אָרְצָה וַיִּפְתְּחוּ אִישׁ אַמְתַּחְתּוֹ: 12 וַיְחַפֵּשׂ בַּגָּדוֹל הֵחֵל וּבַקָּטֹן כִּלָּה וַיִּמָּצֵא הַגָּבִיעַ בְּאַמְתַּחַת בִּנְיָמִן: 13 וַיִּקְרְעוּ שִׂמְלֹתָם וַיַּעֲמֹס אִישׁ עַל־חֲמֹרוֹ וַיָּשֻׁבוּ הָעִירָה: 14 וַיָּבֹא יְהוּדָה וְאֶחָיו בֵּיתָה יוֹסֵף וְהוּא עוֹדֶנּוּ שָׁם וַיִּפְּלוּ לְפָנָיו אָרְצָה: [MAFTIR] 15 וַיֹּאמֶר לָהֶם יוֹסֵף מָה־הַמַּעֲשֶׂה הַזֶּה אֲשֶׁר עֲשִׂיתֶם הֲלוֹא יְדַעְתֶּם כִּי־נַחֵשׁ יְנַחֵשׁ אִישׁ אֲשֶׁר כָּמֹנִי: 16 וַיֹּאמֶר יְהוּדָה מַה־נֹּאמַר לַאדֹנִי מַה־נְּדַבֵּר וּמַה־נִּצְטַדָּק הָאֱלֹהִים מָצָא אֶת־עֲוֹן עֲבָדֶיךָ הִנֶּנּוּ עֲבָדִים לַאדֹנִי גַּם־אֲנַחְנוּ גַּם אֲשֶׁר־נִמְצָא הַגָּבִיעַ בְּיָדוֹ: 17 וַיֹּאמֶר חָלִילָה לִּי מֵעֲשׂוֹת זֹאת הָאִישׁ אֲשֶׁר נִמְצָא הַגָּבִיעַ בְּיָדוֹ הוּא יִהְיֶה־לִּי עָבֶד וְאַתֶּם עֲלוּ לְשָׁלוֹם אֶל־אֲבִיכֶם: ס ס ס

קמ״ו פסוקים, אמצי״ה סימן. יחזקיה״ו סימן.

He possibly had three goals. First, to atone for their sin of kidnaping of him, he rendered them suspects in a theft. In this way, they might also begin to feel shameful for their prior misdeed to him, which would lead to contrition and forgiveness.

Second, Joseph wanted to see if the brothers would be willing to defend Benjamin, even at risk to their lives. This display of extreme brotherly love would atone for their prior hatred towards Joseph.

Third, Joseph wanted to hint that he was aware of their identity, just as when he had seated them at the lunch table in the order of their ages (*Rabbi Hayyim ibn Attar, 18th century*).

spiritual vitamin

> Whenever you feel very broken and fall into despair, it is really a product of your imagination. It is not that the cause does not exist—it may indeed have some foundation. But as a reason for depression—it is false.

genesis 44:10–17 — mikketz

have mercy and only) the one with whom (the goblet) is found shall be my slave. (The rest of) you will be cleared."

¹¹ They hurried and each one lowered his sack to the ground and opened his sack. ¹² (The supervisor) searched: he started with the eldest (so they would not sense that he knew where it was) and finished with the youngest. The goblet was found in Benjamin's sack.

¹³ They tore their garments. Each one loaded up his donkey, and they returned to the city.

Benjamin is Retained and the Other Brothers Sent Home

¹⁴ Judah and his brothers came to Joseph's house, and he was still there (waiting for them). They fell on the ground in front of him.

[MAFTIR] ¹⁵ Joseph said to them, "What is this deed that you have done? Don't you know that an (important) person like me regularly practices divination (so I could figure out that you stole the goblet)?"

¹⁶ Judah said, "What shall we say to my master? How can we speak? How can we justify ourselves? (We know we have done no wrong, but) God has found your servants' guilt. Both we and the one in whose possession the goblet has been found will be (your) slaves."

¹⁷ (Joseph) said, "Far be it from me to do this! The man in whose possession the goblet was found will be my slave. You may all go in peace to your father."

The *Haftarah* for *Mikketz* is on page 1311.

On *Shabbat Ḥanukkah:*

Maftir: **Day Three**—*Numbers* 24-29 (p. 844); **Day Four**—ibid. 30-35 (p. 844); **Day Six**—six *aliyyot* are read from the weekly *Parashah*, seventh *aliyah* is read from *Numbers* 28:9-15 (p. 1000), and *Maftir* is ibid. 7:42-47 (p. 846); **Day Seven**—ibid. 48–53 (p. 846); **Day Eight**—ibid. 7:54–8:4 (p. 846).

Haftarah: First *Shabbat* (Days 3-7)—page 1420; Second *Shabbat* (Day 8)—page 1423.

Joseph would repeat his accusation that they were spies, using their refusal as proof. Joseph could easily argue that if they were innocent they would not have minded drinking wine, which inevitably leads to a lowered guard (*Rabbi Judah Loew b. Bezalel of Prague, 16th century*).

44:2 Put my goblet, the silver goblet, into the top of the youngest's sack, with his money. What was Joseph's intention in framing his brothers as thieves? His previous actions towards them seem to prove that he had already made peace with them in his heart and did not intend to cause them grief.

Judah's **impassioned words** to Joseph, the **leader** of a powerful country, were **visceral** rather than **rational**—and that is why they were **effective.** The physical and spiritual **welfare of your people** should be so **crucial** to you that you **defend** it like Judah.

VA-YIGGASH
ויגש

JUDAH CHALLENGES JOSEPH	44:18-34
JOSEPH REVEALS HIS IDENTITY	45:1-28
JACOB TRAVELS TO EGYPT WITH HIS FAMILY	46:1 - 47:12
JOSEPH ACQUIRES EGYPT FOR PHARAOH	47:13-27

NAME
Va-Yiggash

MEANING
"And he approached"

LINES IN TORAH SCROLL
178

PARASHIYYOT
0 open; 3 closed

VERSES
106

WORDS
1480

LETTERS
5680

DATE
2236–2238

LOCATION
Egypt, Canaan

KEY PEOPLE
Judah, Joseph, Pharaoh

MITZVOT
None

MASORETIC FEATURES
Does not have a gap separating it from the following portion

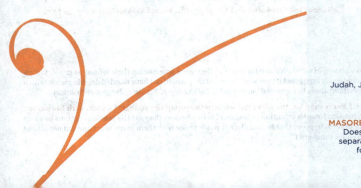

CHARACTER PROFILE

NAME
Jochebed (Shiphrah)

MEANING
"Divine splendor"
("Straighten")

HUSBAND
Amram

FATHER
Levi

GRANDFATHER
Jacob

SIBLINGS
Gershon, Kohath, and Merari

CHILDREN
Miriam, Aaron and Moses

LIFE SPAN
More than 250 years

ACHIEVEMENTS
Chief midwife of the Jews; defied Pharaoh's decree to kill all newborn baby boys; built a basket for Moses to hide in when he was put into the Nile, saving his life

KNOWN FOR
Born as Jacob and his family entered Egypt; gave birth to Moses at the age of one hundred and thirty

SPEAKING UP FOR JUSTICE

Although in no physical danger, Judah knew that the loss of Benjamin would destroy his father. Standing up for justice and people who are wronged is important even if you are not the one directly impacted (44:18).

RECONCILIATION

After twenty-two years apart from his father due to his brothers' actions, Joseph revealed himself to his family. He bore no grudge or thoughts of revenge; instead he talked to his brothers softly, with sensitivity—a powerful example of forgiveness and reconciliation (45:5-8).

NEPOTISM

Many of Pharaoh's ministers feared that they would lose their jobs to members of Joseph's newly arrived family. Nepotism has many damaging effects on organizations, such as eroding the support of non-favored employees and reducing the quality and creativity of management. Would you award a position to a friend or family member who did not compete in terms of merit? (45:17)

ויגש   בראשית מד:יח - כו

18 וַיִּגַּ֨שׁ אֵלָ֜יו יְהוּדָ֗ה וַיֹּאמֶר֮ בִּ֣י אֲדֹנִי֒ יְדַבֶּר־נָ֨א עַבְדְּךָ֤ דָבָר֙ בְּאָזְנֵ֣י אֲדֹנִ֔י וְאַל־יִ֥חַר אַפְּךָ֖ בְּעַבְדֶּ֑ךָ כִּ֥י כָמ֖וֹךָ כְּפַרְעֹֽה: 19 אֲדֹנִ֣י שָׁאַ֔ל אֶת־עֲבָדָ֖יו לֵאמֹ֑ר הֲיֵשׁ־לָכֶ֥ם אָ֖ב אוֹ־אָֽח: 20 וַנֹּ֙אמֶר֙ אֶל־אֲדֹנִ֔י יֶשׁ־לָ֖נוּ אָ֣ב זָקֵ֑ן וְיֶ֧לֶד זְקֻנִ֛ים קָטָ֖ן וְאָחִ֣יו מֵ֔ת וַיִּוָּתֵ֨ר ה֧וּא לְבַדּ֛וֹ לְאִמּ֖וֹ וְאָבִ֥יו אֲהֵבֽוֹ: 21 וַתֹּ֙אמֶר֙ אֶל־עֲבָדֶ֔יךָ הוֹרִדֻ֖הוּ אֵלָ֑י וְאָשִׂ֥ימָה עֵינִ֖י עָלָֽיו: 22 וַנֹּ֙אמֶר֙ אֶל־אֲדֹנִ֔י לֹא־יוּכַ֥ל הַנַּ֖עַר לַעֲזֹ֣ב אֶת־אָבִ֑יו וְעָזַ֥ב אֶת־אָבִ֖יו וָמֵֽת: 23 וַתֹּ֙אמֶר֙ אֶל־עֲבָדֶ֔יךָ אִם־לֹ֥א יֵרֵ֛ד אֲחִיכֶ֥ם הַקָּטֹ֖ן אִתְּכֶ֑ם לֹ֥א תֹסִפ֖וּן לִרְא֥וֹת פָּנָֽי: 24 וַיְהִי֙ כִּ֣י עָלִ֔ינוּ אֶֽל־עַבְדְּךָ֖ אָבִ֑י וַנַּ֨גֶּד־ל֔וֹ אֵ֖ת דִּבְרֵ֥י אֲדֹנִֽי: 25 וַיֹּ֖אמֶר אָבִ֑ינוּ שֻׁ֖בוּ שִׁבְרוּ־לָ֥נוּ מְעַט־אֹֽכֶל: 26 וַנֹּ֕אמֶר לֹ֥א נוּכַ֖ל לָרֶ֑דֶת אִם־יֵשׁ֩ אָחִ֨ינוּ הַקָּטֹ֤ן אִתָּ֙נוּ֙ וְיָרַ֔דְנוּ כִּי־לֹ֣א נוּכַ֗ל לִרְאוֹת֙ פְּנֵ֣י הָאִ֔ישׁ וְאָחִ֥ינוּ הַקָּטֹ֖ן

How do we muster the strength and the courage to lift ourselves from the *perceived reality* to reality? The answer is: via the *mystical reality*.

In our case, when we approach God in prayer, it reveals our inner bond with the Almighty, which gives us the ability to rise above the challenges of exile—and to succeed (*Rabbi Menahem Mendel Schneerson, 20th century*).

Please, my master! Initially Judah thought that this misfortune would lead them all to becoming slaves, as retribution for their sale of Joseph into slavery. But when he saw that Joseph was setting the rest of the brothers free and only wanted to keep Benjamin, Judah understood that this had not been caused by the sin of selling Joseph; it was an arrest based on false charges. That is when Judah spoke up to Joseph (*Rabbi Moses Alshekh, 16th century*).

19. My master interrogated his servants. Judah confronted Joseph, "Why, my master, did you interrogate us so strongly if, as you said, '*an (important) person like me regularly practices divination*'?" (44:15). If your goblet is truly able to divine our identity and purpose here, why did you ask us so many questions? All this is proof that you are trying to accuse us falsely, and your interrogation is only a pretense to pressure us to admit to your fabricated allegations" (*Rabbi Tzevi Hirsch ha-Kohen, 20th century*).

20. His brother is dead. Judah was afraid to say that his brother may be alive. He thought: "If I tell the ruler that Joseph could be alive, he will order me to bring him here" (*Rashi, 11th century*).

Judah was convinced that Joseph was no longer alive. He presumed that since Joseph had been so close to his father, he would have definitely contacted his father if he were still alive. This lack of communication convinced Judah that Joseph must be dead (*Rabbi Meir Simhah of Dvinsk, 19th–20th century*).

food for thought

1. Are you willing to speak truth to power?

2. You can't fake sincerity—but how do you achieve it?

3. What tips can you learn from Judah in effective speech making?

parashat va-yiggash

Judah Challenges Joseph

¹⁸ Then Judah approached him and said, "Please, my master! Your servant now (wants to) say something to which (I hope) my master will listen. (I'm going to be firm) so please don't get angry at your servant, for you are as (important in my eyes) as Pharaoh (himself)."

¹⁹ "(From the very first instance,) my master interrogated his servants (accusingly), saying, 'Have you a father or a brother?'

²⁰ "(Nevertheless, we held nothing back from you). We said to my master, 'We have an elderly father (who has) a baby born to him in old age. His brother is dead, so he is the only child of his mother, and his father loves him.'

²¹ "You said to your servants, 'Bring him down to me, so I can see him for myself.'

²² "We said to my master, 'The boy cannot leave his father, for if he leaves his father (we are concerned that) he will die (enroute, for his mother died while traveling).'

²³ "You said to your servants, 'If your youngest brother doesn't come down with you, you'll never see my face again!'

²⁴ "Then, when we went up to your servant, my father, and we told him the words of my master, ²⁵ our father said, 'Go back and buy us a bit of food.'

²⁶ "We said, 'We can't go down (like we did before)! We'll (only) go down if our youngest brother is with us, because the man won't let us see him if our youngest brother isn't with us.'

44:18 Judah approached him. Whom does the word "him" refer to? There are many layers of meaning here. It refers to Joseph, to Judah's own self—*Judah confronted himself*—and also to God. Judah offered nothing new in his words, nor did he have a reasonable argument to present to Joseph. Nevertheless, as he clarified the truth of the matter, salvation came to him— *"Truth grows from the earth"* (*Psalms 85:12; Rabbi Judah Aryeh Leib Alter of Gur, 19th century*).

These words describe an occurrence which took place in three different worlds:

(a) *The perceived reality*—Judah was approaching the viceroy of Egypt, who was capable of deciding the future of Judah and his entire family.

(b) *The reality*—the viceroy of Egypt was none other than Joseph, Judah's brother.

(c) *The mystical reality*—Judah approaching Joseph represents man approaching God in prayer (see *Genesis Rabbah*).

All the interpretations to any given verse must be connected. In our case, the *perceived reality* is that we are in exile, subjugated to the other nations. In truth, however, the Jewish people are impervious to exile and they have the ability to rise above it—rather like the *"reality"* in our Torah portion that Joseph, a Jew, was the *ruler* of Egypt.

בראשית מד:כז – מה:ג | ויגש

אֵינֶנּוּ אִתָּנוּ: 27 וַיֹּאמֶר עַבְדְּךָ אָבִי אֵלֵינוּ אַתֶּם יְדַעְתֶּם כִּי שְׁנַיִם יָלְדָה־לִּי אִשְׁתִּי: 28 וַיֵּצֵא הָאֶחָד מֵאִתִּי וָאֹמַר אַךְ טָרֹף טֹרָף וְלֹא רְאִיתִיו עַד־הֵנָּה: 29 וּלְקַחְתֶּם גַּם־אֶת־זֶה מֵעִם פָּנַי וְקָרָהוּ אָסוֹן וְהוֹרַדְתֶּם אֶת־שֵׂיבָתִי בְּרָעָה שְׁאֹלָה: 30 וְעַתָּה כְּבֹאִי אֶל־עַבְדְּךָ אָבִי וְהַנַּעַר אֵינֶנּוּ אִתָּנוּ וְנַפְשׁוֹ קְשׁוּרָה בְנַפְשׁוֹ: 31 [SECOND READING] וְהָיָה כִּרְאוֹתוֹ כִּי־אֵין הַנַּעַר וָמֵת וְהוֹרִידוּ עֲבָדֶיךָ אֶת־שֵׂיבַת עַבְדְּךָ אָבִינוּ בְּיָגוֹן שְׁאֹלָה: 32 כִּי עַבְדְּךָ עָרַב אֶת־הַנַּעַר מֵעִם אָבִי לֵאמֹר אִם־לֹא אֲבִיאֶנּוּ אֵלֶיךָ וְחָטָאתִי לְאָבִי כָּל־הַיָּמִים: 33 וְעַתָּה יֵשֶׁב־נָא עַבְדְּךָ תַּחַת הַנַּעַר עֶבֶד לַאדֹנִי וְהַנַּעַר יַעַל עִם־אֶחָיו: 34 כִּי־אֵיךְ אֶעֱלֶה אֶל־אָבִי וְהַנַּעַר אֵינֶנּוּ אִתִּי פֶּן אֶרְאֶה בָרָע אֲשֶׁר יִמְצָא אֶת־אָבִי:

מה 1 וְלֹא־יָכֹל יוֹסֵף לְהִתְאַפֵּק לְכֹל הַנִּצָּבִים עָלָיו וַיִּקְרָא הוֹצִיאוּ כָל־אִישׁ מֵעָלָי וְלֹא־עָמַד אִישׁ אִתּוֹ בְּהִתְוַדַּע יוֹסֵף אֶל־אֶחָיו: 2 וַיִּתֵּן אֶת־קֹלוֹ בִּבְכִי וַיִּשְׁמְעוּ מִצְרַיִם וַיִּשְׁמַע בֵּית פַּרְעֹה: 3 וַיֹּאמֶר יוֹסֵף אֶל־אֶחָיו אֲנִי יוֹסֵף הַעוֹד אָבִי חָי וְלֹא־יָכְלוּ אֶחָיו לַעֲנוֹת אֹתוֹ כִּי נִבְהֲלוּ מִפָּנָיו:

3. Is my father still alive? Joseph knew that his father was still alive. However, he thought that the brothers would be shocked when he revealed himself, so he asked them, "Is my father still alive?" to enter into a conversation. He was then planning to ask them, "How are your

kabbalah bites

45:3 *Whenever Rabbi Eleazar came to this verse he wept, exclaiming: "If the rebuke of a human being is so powerful, how much more so the rebuke of God!"* (Babylonian Talmud, Hagigah 4b).

Surely, however, there is a distinction here. The brothers genuinely *harmed* Joseph, rendering his subsequent rebuke powerful. It seems ludicrous, though, to suggest that we actually "harm" God when we sin against Him?

But, according to the Kabbalah, we can. Of course we cannot harm God's very essence, but sins do "damage" the Ten *Sefirot*, so to speak, causing God's light not to invest itself in them.

Perhaps, then, it is time for some repair?

₂₇ "Your servant, my father, said to us, 'You know that my wife (Rachel) bore me two (children). ²⁸ One of them has departed from me, and I said, "He must have been ripped apart again and again"—and I haven't seen him since. ²⁹ If you'll take this one away from me too, and a fatal (accident) occurs to him, you'll bring my old age to the grave in grief.'

³⁰ "So, if I'll come (back) now to your servant, my father, and the boy isn't with us, (being that) his soul is attached to (the boy's) soul, [SECOND READING] ³¹ he'll simply die (from grief) when he'll see that the boy is gone. Then your servants will have brought the old age of your servant, our father, to the grave in grief.

³² "Now (I am speaking out here in particular because I), your servant, assumed responsibility for the boy (when we took him) from my father, saying, 'If I don't bring him (back) to you, I will have sinned against my father forever.' ³³ So now, please let your servant stay as a slave to my master instead of the boy, and let the boy go back with his brothers. ³⁴ For how could I go back to my father if the boy is not with me? (I can't bear) to see the misery that my father would suffer!"

Joseph Reveals His Identity

45 ¹ Joseph couldn't bear (the thought that) all (the Egyptians) standing beside him (would see his brothers' shame when he revealed himself to them). So, he called out, "Take everyone away from me!" Thus, no one stood with Joseph when he revealed himself to his brothers.

² He wept so loudly that the Egyptians (who had been sent out) heard. (Soon, the whole of) Pharaoh's household heard (about it).

³ Joseph said to his brothers, "I am Joseph! Is my father still alive?"

But his brothers were unable to answer him because they were ashamed before him.

45:1 No one stood with Joseph when he revealed himself to his brothers. Joseph's spiritual path had been a secret one—his main test of integrity, with Potiphar's wife, took place when no one was present. His physical appearance also concealed his righteousness: he had an attractive, carefully modeled hair style and he dressed quite elegantly.

Judah's spiritual path, on the other hand, was a very public one. For example, he openly admitted to his guilty association with Tamar.

Each of these two paths has an indispensable quality of its own. The spirituality of Joseph's hidden righteousness is more potent; it *penetrates* the world more deeply, and it is therefore more effective in subduing the forces of evil. Judah's path is less potent, but, being revealed, it *engages* and elevates the world to a greater extent. In other words, Joseph's path *imparts* spirituality to his surroundings, but Judah's *inspires* everybody to worship God. That is why King David, who was descended from Judah, was the author of so many of our songs of praise and prayer (*Rabbi Abraham Bornstein of Sochaczew, 19th century*).

בראשית מה:ד-יג   ויגש

4 וַיֹּ֨אמֶר יוֹסֵ֤ף אֶל־אֶחָיו֙ גְּשׁוּ־נָ֣א אֵלַ֔י וַיִּגָּ֑שׁוּ וַיֹּ֗אמֶר אֲנִי֙ יוֹסֵ֣ף אֲחִיכֶ֔ם אֲשֶׁר־מְכַרְתֶּ֥ם אֹתִ֖י מִצְרָֽיְמָה: 5 וְעַתָּ֣ה | אַל־תֵּעָ֣צְב֗וּ וְאַל־יִ֙חַר֙ בְּעֵ֣ינֵיכֶ֔ם כִּֽי־מְכַרְתֶּ֥ם אֹתִ֖י הֵ֑נָּה כִּ֣י לְמִֽחְיָ֔ה שְׁלָחַ֥נִי אֱלֹהִ֖ים לִפְנֵיכֶֽם: 6 כִּי־זֶ֛ה שְׁנָתַ֥יִם הָרָעָ֖ב בְּקֶ֣רֶב הָאָ֑רֶץ וְעוֹד֙ חָמֵ֣שׁ שָׁנִ֔ים אֲשֶׁ֥ר אֵין־חָרִ֖ישׁ וְקָצִֽיר: 7 וַיִּשְׁלָחֵ֤נִי אֱלֹהִים֙ לִפְנֵיכֶ֔ם לָשׂ֥וּם לָכֶ֛ם שְׁאֵרִ֖ית בָּאָ֑רֶץ וּלְהַחֲי֣וֹת לָכֶ֔ם לִפְלֵיטָ֖ה גְּדֹלָֽה: [THIRD READING] 8 וְעַתָּ֗ה לֹֽא־אַתֶּ֞ם שְׁלַחְתֶּ֤ם אֹתִי֙ הֵ֔נָּה כִּ֖י הָאֱלֹהִ֑ים וַיְשִׂימֵ֨נִי לְאָ֜ב לְפַרְעֹ֗ה וּלְאָדוֹן֙ לְכָל־בֵּית֔וֹ וּמֹשֵׁ֖ל בְּכָל־אֶ֥רֶץ מִצְרָֽיִם: 9 מַהֲרוּ֮ וַעֲל֣וּ אֶל־אָבִי֒ וַאֲמַרְתֶּ֣ם אֵלָ֗יו כֹּ֤ה אָמַר֙ בִּנְךָ֣ יוֹסֵ֔ף שָׂמַ֧נִי אֱלֹהִ֛ים לְאָד֖וֹן לְכָל־מִצְרָ֑יִם רְדָ֥ה אֵלַ֖י אַֽל־תַּעֲמֹֽד: 10 וְיָשַׁבְתָּ֣ בְאֶֽרֶץ־גֹּ֗שֶׁן וְהָיִ֤יתָ קָרוֹב֙ אֵלַ֔י אַתָּ֕ה וּבָנֶ֖יךָ וּבְנֵ֣י בָנֶ֑יךָ וְצֹאנְךָ֥ וּבְקָרְךָ֖ וְכָל־אֲשֶׁר־לָֽךְ: 11 וְכִלְכַּלְתִּ֤י אֹֽתְךָ֙ שָׁ֔ם כִּי־ע֛וֹד חָמֵ֥שׁ שָׁנִ֖ים רָעָ֑ב פֶּן־תִּוָּרֵ֛שׁ אַתָּ֥ה וּבֵֽיתְךָ֖ וְכָל־אֲשֶׁר־לָֽךְ: 12 וְהִנֵּ֤ה עֵֽינֵיכֶם֙ רֹא֔וֹת וְעֵינֵ֖י אָחִ֣י בִנְיָמִ֑ין כִּי־פִ֖י הַֽמְדַבֵּ֥ר אֲלֵיכֶֽם: 13 וְהִגַּדְתֶּ֣ם לְאָבִ֗י אֶת־כָּל־כְּבוֹדִי֙ בְּמִצְרַ֔יִם וְאֵ֖ת כָּל־אֲשֶׁ֥ר

He was asking about Jacob's *spiritual* welfare. Joseph was saying: "Is my father's prophetic spirit still alive?" (*Rabbi Joseph b. Solomon Colon, 15th century*).

4. Please come closer to me. You can learn from the example of Joseph towards his brothers that you should never seek revenge against a person who causes you any form of distress or damage. Rather, you ought to repay even a guilty offender with kindness (*Rabbi Shneur Zalman of Lyady, 18th century*).

I am your brother Joseph, whom you sold to Egypt. Why, in this moment of reconciliation, did Joseph need to reiterate how his brothers had wronged him by selling him into slavery?

In fact, Joseph was *comforting* his brothers: "Do not fear. My journey to Egypt did not corrupt me. In fact, I have reached even a higher level of piety here in Egypt" (*Rabbi Judah Aryeh Leib Alter of Gur, 19th century*).

12. Look, you can see for yourself—and my brother Benjamin can see for himself. Joseph told his brothers: "Just as I feel no resentment against Benjamin, who was not yet born at the time when you sold me, I have no resentment against you" (*Babylonian Talmud, Megillah 16b*).

food for thought

1. Why are disputes so difficult to resolve?

2. Can belief in God's providence help you to reconcile disputes?

3. Have you openly seen God's providence in your life?

⁴ (When he saw that they were ashamed) Joseph said to his brothers, "Please come closer to me." They drew closer (and he showed them that he was circumcised).

He said, "I am your brother Joseph, whom you sold to Egypt. ⁵ But now, don't be upset or angry with yourselves that you sold me to this place, for (now we see that) God sent me ahead of you to save (your) lives ⁶ For it's two years now that there's been a famine in the land, and there won't be any plowing or harvesting for another five years. ⁷ God sent me ahead of you to ensure your survival in the land and to sustain (your families and flocks for the) great salvation (they will need, due to their substantial size).

[THIRD READING] ⁸ "Now (we can see that) it was not you who sent me here, but God. He made me an advisor to Pharaoh, a master over all his household and a ruler over the entire land of Egypt.

⁹ "Hurry and go up (to the land of Israel) to my father, and say to him, 'This is what your son Joseph said: "God has made me a master over all the Egyptians. Come down here to me! Do not delay! ¹⁰ You can dwell in the land of Goshen—you, your children, your grandchildren, your flocks, your cattle and everything that's yours—and you'll be near me. ¹¹ I will sustain you there—you, your household and everything that's yours—so you don't become poor, for there are still five years of famine."'

¹² "Look, you can see for yourself—and my brother Benjamin can see for himself—that (I really am Joseph, because I am circumcised and) my mouth is speaking to you (in Hebrew).

¹³ "You should tell my father about all the honor which I receive in Egypt and about everything that you've seen, and you should quickly bring my father down here."

families?", but the conversation could not continue, since they *"were unable to answer him because they were ashamed before him"* (*Rabbi Isaac Abravanel, 15ᵗʰ century*).

Joseph was saying, "If you are scared that I will kill you, you have nothing to be scared of, because my father is still alive. Do you think I would be worse than Esau, who refrained from killing his brother so long as his father was alive?" (*Rabbi Jonathan Eybeschuetz, 18ᵗʰ century*).

spiritual vitamin

> Sometimes, a temporary setback is just what you need in order to advance with greater vigor. When an athlete has to negotiate a hurdle, his stepping back is the means to a higher leap.

ויגש

בראשית מה:יג-כג

רְאִיתֶ֑ם וּמִֽהַרְתֶּ֛ם וְהוֹרַדְתֶּ֥ם אֶת־אָבִ֖י הֵֽנָּה: 14 וַיִּפֹּ֛ל עַל־צַוְּארֵ֥י בִנְיָמִֽן־אָחִ֖יו וַיֵּ֑בְךְּ וּבִ֨נְיָמִ֔ן בָּכָ֖ה עַל־צַוָּארָֽיו: 15 וַיְנַשֵּׁ֥ק לְכָל־אֶחָ֖יו וַיֵּ֣בְךְּ עֲלֵהֶ֑ם וְאַחֲרֵ֣י כֵ֔ן דִּבְּר֥וּ אֶחָ֖יו אִתּֽוֹ: 16 וְהַקֹּ֣ל נִשְׁמַ֗ע בֵּ֤ית פַּרְעֹה֙ לֵאמֹ֔ר בָּ֖אוּ אֲחֵ֣י יוֹסֵ֑ף וַיִּיטַב֙ בְּעֵינֵ֣י פַרְעֹ֔ה וּבְעֵינֵ֖י עֲבָדָֽיו: 17 וַיֹּ֤אמֶר פַּרְעֹה֙ אֶל־יוֹסֵ֔ף אֱמֹ֥ר אֶל־אַחֶ֖יךָ זֹ֣את עֲשׂ֑וּ טַֽעֲנוּ֙ אֶת־בְּעִ֣ירְכֶ֔ם וּלְכוּ־בֹ֖אוּ אַ֥רְצָה כְּנָֽעַן: 18 וּקְח֧וּ אֶת־אֲבִיכֶ֛ם וְאֶת־בָּתֵּיכֶ֖ם וּבֹ֣אוּ אֵלָ֑י וְאֶתְּנָ֣ה לָכֶ֗ם אֶת־טוּב֙ אֶ֣רֶץ מִצְרַ֔יִם וְאִכְל֖וּ אֶת־חֵ֥לֶב הָאָֽרֶץ: 19 וְאַתָּ֥ה צֻוֵּ֖יתָה זֹ֣את עֲשׂ֑וּ קְחוּ־לָכֶם֩ מֵאֶ֨רֶץ מִצְרַ֜יִם עֲגָל֗וֹת לְטַפְּכֶם֙ וְלִנְשֵׁיכֶ֔ם וּנְשָׂאתֶ֥ם אֶת־אֲבִיכֶ֖ם וּבָאתֶֽם: 20 וְעֵ֣ינְכֶ֔ם אַל־תָּחֹ֖ס עַל־כְּלֵיכֶ֑ם כִּי־ט֛וּב כָּל־אֶ֥רֶץ מִצְרַ֖יִם לָכֶ֥ם הֽוּא: 21 וַיַּֽעֲשׂוּ־כֵן֙ בְּנֵ֣י יִשְׂרָאֵ֔ל וַיִּתֵּ֨ן לָהֶ֥ם יוֹסֵ֛ף עֲגָל֖וֹת עַל־פִּ֣י פַרְעֹ֑ה וַיִּתֵּ֥ן לָהֶ֛ם צֵדָ֖ה לַדָּֽרֶךְ: 22 לְכֻלָּ֥ם נָתַ֛ן לָאִ֖ישׁ חֲלִפ֣וֹת שְׂמָלֹ֑ת וּלְבִנְיָמִ֣ן נָתַ֗ן שְׁלֹ֤שׁ מֵאוֹת֙ כֶּ֔סֶף וְחָמֵ֖שׁ חֲלִפֹ֥ת שְׂמָלֹֽת: 23 וּלְאָבִ֞יו שָׁלַ֤ח כְּזֹאת֙ עֲשָׂרָ֣ה

The love between Joseph and Benjamin was so strong that each one was affected by his brother's sorrow more than his own: Joseph and Benjamin each shed tears over the misfortune that was going to affect the other's descendants. Benjamin knew that for the Temple to be built in his own territory, the Sanctuary in Joseph's territory would have to be destroyed. But the thought pained him. He would rather not have the Temple built in his own territory if it required the destruction of the Sanctuary in his brother's land (*Rabbi Ezekiel Taub of Kazimierz, 19th century*).

Joseph and Benjamin cried over the sanctuaries which were to be destroyed in *each other's* territory, and not over the destruction that was to occur in *their own* territories.

Eliminating other people's problems ultimately depends on the other person's own free will. Friends can help with their prayers and advice, but the person himself must take the necessary action.

So, when Joseph and Benjamin perceived that they were *powerless* to solve each other's problems, they cried in sympathy. Nevertheless, they did not cry over the future destruction of *their own* sanctuaries, because they had the responsibility to find a solution to their own problems, and not merely to sit and cry (*Rabbi Menahem Mendel Schneerson, 20th century*).

22. He gave each one of them a set of clothes. When the goblet was found in Benjamin's sack, the brothers *"tore their garments"* (44:13). When Joseph saw that he had inadvertently been the cause of their torn garments, he *"gave each of them a set of clothes,"* thereby correcting the matter (*Rabbi Isaac b. Joseph Caro, 15th century*).

genesis 45:14-23 — va-yiggash

¹⁴ (Joseph) fell on his brother Benjamin's neck and cried, and Benjamin cried on his neck. ¹⁵ He kissed all his brothers and cried over them. After his brothers (saw that he was sincere, they) spoke with him.

Pharaoh and Joseph Send Gifts to Jacob

¹⁶ The news was heard in Pharaoh's house: (People were) saying, "Joseph's brothers have come!" (The news) pleased Pharaoh and his servants.

¹⁷ Pharaoh said to Joseph, "Tell your brothers, 'This is what you should do: Load up your animals (with grain) then go and bring them to the land of Canaan. ¹⁸ Fetch your father and (the people of) your households and come to me. I will give you (the land of Goshen which is) the best of the land of Egypt, and you will eat the finest (produce) of the land.'

¹⁹ (Pharaoh said to Joseph), "You have been commanded (by me to say to them), 'This is what you should do: Take wagons for yourselves from the land of Egypt, for your young children and for your wives. Transport your father, and come here. ²⁰ Don't worry about (bringing) your belongings, because the best of all the land of Egypt is (now) yours.'"

²¹ Israel's sons did what (they were instructed). Joseph gave them wagons by Pharaoh's orders, and he gave them provisions for the journey. ²² He gave each one of them a set of clothes, and he gave Benjamin three hundred silver pieces and five sets of clothes. ²³ He (also) sent to his father the same (amount of donkeys that Pharaoh had sent): ten male donkeys carrying Egypt's finest produce.

14. Joseph fell on his brother Benjamin's neck and cried, and Benjamin cried on his neck. Joseph fell on Benjamin's neck and wept for the two Temples which were destined to be in Benjamin's territory, that would ultimately be destroyed. Benjamin wept on Joseph's neck for the Tabernacle at Shiloh, which was destined to be in Joseph's territory, and would ultimately be destroyed (*Rashi, 11th century*).

spiritual vitamin

> Because God is good, He wants everyone to be happy. It happens, however, that with your physical eyes, you cannot see and understand His ways. But you must be firm in your faith that only good can come from the good God, and that the good will become apparent eventually.

חֲמֹרִים נְשֹׂאִים מִטּוּב מִצְרָיִם וְעֶשֶׂר אֲתֹנֹת נֹשְׂאֹת בָּר וָלֶחֶם וּמָזוֹן לְאָבִיו לַדָּרֶךְ: 24 וַיְשַׁלַּח אֶת־אֶחָיו וַיֵּלֵכוּ וַיֹּאמֶר אֲלֵהֶם אַל־תִּרְגְּזוּ בַּדָּרֶךְ: 25 וַיַּעֲלוּ מִמִּצְרָיִם וַיָּבֹאוּ אֶרֶץ כְּנַעַן אֶל־יַעֲקֹב אֲבִיהֶם: 26 וַיַּגִּדוּ לוֹ לֵאמֹר עוֹד יוֹסֵף חַי וְכִי־הוּא מֹשֵׁל בְּכָל־אֶרֶץ מִצְרָיִם וַיָּפָג לִבּוֹ כִּי לֹא־הֶאֱמִין לָהֶם: 27 וַיְדַבְּרוּ אֵלָיו אֵת כָּל־דִּבְרֵי יוֹסֵף אֲשֶׁר דִּבֶּר אֲלֵהֶם וַיַּרְא אֶת־הָעֲגָלוֹת אֲשֶׁר־שָׁלַח יוֹסֵף לָשֵׂאת אֹתוֹ וַתְּחִי רוּחַ יַעֲקֹב אֲבִיהֶם: 28 [FOURTH READING] וַיֹּאמֶר יִשְׂרָאֵל רַב עוֹד־יוֹסֵף בְּנִי חָי אֵלְכָה וְאֶרְאֶנּוּ בְּטֶרֶם אָמוּת:

מו 1 וַיִּסַּע יִשְׂרָאֵל וְכָל־אֲשֶׁר־לוֹ וַיָּבֹא בְּאֵרָה שָּׁבַע וַיִּזְבַּח זְבָחִים לֵאלֹהֵי אָבִיו יִצְחָק: 2 וַיֹּאמֶר אֱלֹהִים | לְיִשְׂרָאֵל בְּמַרְאֹת הַלַּיְלָה

292

have not been elevated because Joseph is too attached to his life; he has not surrendered himself sufficiently. *"Let me go and see him"*—this can also be read, "let me go and *show* him." I will show him the spiritual discipline of surrender. *"Before I die"*—not through actually giving up your life and dying, but through surrendering and releasing attachment to the ego while still alive (*Rabbi Menahem Mendel of Rymanow, 18th century*).

46:1 He slaughtered sacrifices to the God of his father Isaac. A person is obligated to honor his father more than his grandfather. Therefore he attributed the sacrifices to the "God of Isaac" and he did not mention Abraham (*Rashi, 11th century*).

In Hebrew, the word for sacrifice is *korban*, which implies "coming close" (*kiruv*). This term also hints to Isaac's distinctive spiritual path. Isaac embodied *fear*, and Abraham, *love*. Only fear can bring you to the total surrender of the ego that is necessary to come close to God— for all love harbors a kernel of narcissism—which is why Isaac, in particular, is associated with *korban*, coming close (*Rabbi Judah Loew b. Bezalel of Prague, 16th century*).

2. In a nighttime vision, God spoke to Israel. Jacob was the only one of the three forefathers to whom God appeared *"in a nighttime vision."* This occurred to Jacob twice, in this verse, and when he spent the night on Mount Moriah (above, 28:13).

Both times when God appeared to Jacob at night, he was traveling and leaving the land of Israel. God appeared to him when it was dark, hinting that even during the darkness of exile, when the Jewish people

food for thought

1. How have Jews retained their identity while living in foreign cultures?

2. Why is it so uncomfortable to be different?

3. How much of the surrounding culture is it appropriate for Jews to embrace?

(In addition, Joseph also sent) ten female donkeys carrying grain, bread, and delicacies for his father (to eat) on the way.

²⁴ He escorted his brothers off, and they went. (As they left) he said to them, "Don't argue on the way (about the past. It's all over now)."

²⁵ So they went up from Egypt, and came to the land of Canaan, to their father, Jacob. ²⁶ They told him (what had happened), saying, "Joseph is still alive." (They told him) that (Joseph) ruled over the entire land of Egypt, but his heart denied it, because he did not believe them.

²⁷ (However) when they told him all of Joseph's words which he had told them (including the content of the last discussion which Joseph had had with Jacob), and he saw the wagons that Joseph had sent to carry him, the spirit of their father Jacob was revived.

[FOURTH READING] ²⁸ Israel said, "(I have) a lot (to look forward to now), because my son Joseph is still alive. Let me go and see him before I die!"

Jacob Travels to Egypt with His Family

46 ¹ Israel traveled with all his possessions, and he arrived at Beer-sheba. He slaughtered sacrifices to the God of his father Isaac.

² In a nighttime vision, God spoke to Israel. He said, "Jacob, Jacob!"

---

26. His heart denied it, because he did not believe them. This is the punishment of a liar: even when he speaks the truth, no one believes him—and that is what happened to the sons of Jacob. They deceived their father when they said, *"We have found this. Please could you identify if this is your son's coat or not?"* And Jacob immediately recognized it, saying, *"My son's coat!"* (37:32-33). In the end, although they spoke the truth, he did not believe them, as the verse states, *"His heart denied it, because he did not believe them."*

He only believed them after they told him Joseph's "password," which was the last topic his father had studied with him before his abduction (*Avot de-Rabbi Nathan*).

27. The spirit of their father Jacob was revived. The prophetic inspiration that had departed from Jacob when Joseph was sold, returned to him at that moment (*Avot de-Rabbi Nathan*).

28. Israel said, "(I have) a lot (to look forward to now), because my son Joseph is still alive. Let me go and see him before I die!" The numerical value of the Hebrew word *rav* ("a lot") is two hundred and two. Jacob knew that there were two hundred and eighty-eight primordial "sparks" trapped in Egypt and that God's intention in placing Joseph there had been to elevate them. But Joseph only managed to elevate eighty-six sparks, leaving two hundred and two still enmeshed in Egypt.

Joseph was unable to elevate the remaining sparks because this required an utter surrender of the self (*mesirat nefesh*), and he lacked this quality. Realizing this, Jacob said, *"Rav"*—there are still two hundred and two sparks remaining in Egypt! *"My son Joseph is still alive"*—they

ויגש • בראשית מו:ב-יד

2 וַיֹּאמֶר יַעֲקֹב ׀ יַעֲקֹב וַיֹּאמֶר הִנֵּנִי: 3 וַיֹּאמֶר אָנֹכִי הָאֵל אֱלֹהֵי אָבִיךָ אַל־תִּירָא מֵרְדָה מִצְרַיְמָה כִּי־לְגוֹי גָּדוֹל אֲשִׂימְךָ שָׁם: 4 אָנֹכִי אֵרֵד עִמְּךָ מִצְרַיְמָה וְאָנֹכִי אַעַלְךָ גַם־עָלֹה וְיוֹסֵף יָשִׁית יָדוֹ עַל־עֵינֶיךָ: 5 וַיָּקָם יַעֲקֹב מִבְּאֵר שָׁבַע וַיִּשְׂאוּ בְנֵי־יִשְׂרָאֵל אֶת־יַעֲקֹב אֲבִיהֶם וְאֶת־טַפָּם וְאֶת־נְשֵׁיהֶם בָּעֲגָלוֹת אֲשֶׁר־שָׁלַח פַּרְעֹה לָשֵׂאת אֹתוֹ: 6 וַיִּקְחוּ אֶת־מִקְנֵיהֶם וְאֶת־רְכוּשָׁם אֲשֶׁר רָכְשׁוּ בְּאֶרֶץ כְּנַעַן וַיָּבֹאוּ מִצְרַיְמָה יַעֲקֹב וְכָל־זַרְעוֹ אִתּוֹ: 7 בָּנָיו וּבְנֵי בָנָיו אִתּוֹ בְּנֹתָיו וּבְנוֹת בָּנָיו וְכָל־זַרְעוֹ הֵבִיא אִתּוֹ מִצְרַיְמָה: ס [FIFTH READING] 8 וְאֵלֶּה שְׁמוֹת בְּנֵי־יִשְׂרָאֵל הַבָּאִים מִצְרַיְמָה יַעֲקֹב וּבָנָיו בְּכֹר יַעֲקֹב רְאוּבֵן: 9 וּבְנֵי רְאוּבֵן חֲנוֹךְ וּפַלּוּא וְחֶצְרֹן וְכַרְמִי: 10 וּבְנֵי שִׁמְעוֹן יְמוּאֵל וְיָמִין וְאֹהַד וְיָכִין וְצֹחַר וְשָׁאוּל בֶּן־הַכְּנַעֲנִית: 11 וּבְנֵי לֵוִי גֵּרְשׁוֹן קְהָת וּמְרָרִי: 12 וּבְנֵי יְהוּדָה עֵר וְאוֹנָן וְשֵׁלָה וָפֶרֶץ וָזָרַח וַיָּמָת עֵר וְאוֹנָן בְּאֶרֶץ כְּנַעַן וַיִּהְיוּ בְנֵי־פֶרֶץ חֶצְרֹן וְחָמוּל: 13 וּבְנֵי יִשָּׂשכָר תּוֹלָע וּפֻוָּה וְיוֹב וְשִׁמְרֹן: 14 וּבְנֵי זְבֻלוּן סֶרֶד וְאֵלוֹן וְיַחְלְאֵל:

The nighttime visions were a comfort to Jacob, a message that his children would never be alone, even in exile (*Rabbi Meir Simhah of Dvinsk, 19th–20th century*).

3. Do not be afraid of going down to Egypt. Jacob was pained that he was forced to go outside the land of Israel (*Rashi, 11th century*).

Jacob was saying, "Now that I'm going down to Egypt, it must be that God's words to my grandfather are soon to be fulfilled and my children will be enslaved and persecuted in a foreign land."

God replied, "Do not be afraid of going down to Egypt. For just as I warned him about what was going to happen, I am coming to you with a promise. While the days of slavery and persecution may be approaching, we are also approaching the time when the blessing that I gave to your grandfather will be fulfilled: *'I will make you into a great nation'*" (above, 12:2; *Rabbi Hezekiah b. Manoah, 13th century*).

I will make you into a great nation there. God told Jacob, "I will make you into a great nation there"—in Egypt—but God did *not* tell Jacob that he was wrong for wanting to stay

> **kabbalah bites**
>
> **46:3** Jacob and his descendants were required to be relocated to Egypt in order to rescue the many lofty souls that were trapped there.

"Here I am!" (Jacob) said.

³ He said, "I am God, the God of your father. Do not be afraid of going down to Egypt, for I will make you into a great nation there. ⁴ I will go down with you to Egypt, and I will also bring you up (and bury you in the land of Israel). Joseph (will outlive you) and he will put his hands on your eyes (after you pass away)."

⁵ Jacob got going from Beer-sheba. The sons of Israel transported their father Jacob, together with their young children and their wives, in the wagons Pharaoh had sent to carry him. ⁶ They took their livestock and their possessions that they had acquired in the land of Canaan, and they came to Egypt.

Jacob was together with all his descendants. ⁷ His sons and his grandsons were with him. He brought his daughters, his granddaughters and all his descendants with him to Egypt.

The Seventy Souls that Descended to Egypt

[FIFTH READING] ⁸ These are the names of the children of Israel, Jacob and his sons, who went down to Egypt: Jacob's firstborn was Reuben. ⁹ Reuben's sons were Enoch, Pallu, Hezron and Carmi.

¹⁰ Simeon's sons were Jemuel, Jamin, Ohad, Jachin, Zohar, and Saul, the son of (Dinah, who was called) the Canaanite woman (because she was violated by Shechem, a Canaanite).

¹¹ Levi's sons were Gershon, Kohath, and Merari.

¹² Judah's sons were Er, Onan, Shelah, Perez, and Zerah. Er and Onan died in the land of Canaan. Perez's sons were Hezron and Hamul.

¹³ Issachar's sons were Tola, Puvah, Iob, and Shimron.

¹⁴ Zebulun's sons were Sered, Elon, and Jahleel.

would be away from the land of Israel, He would always remain together with them: *"When the Jewish people were exiled to Babylon, the Divine Presence was exiled with them; when they were exiled to Egypt, the Divine Presence was exiled with them"* (*Babylonian Talmud, Megillah* 29a).

spiritual vitamin

> The way to accomplishment, even if it is intended for the community as a whole, must begin with concentration on yourself, and on the members of your family and immediate circle.

בראשית מו:טו-כט · ויגש

15 אֵ֣לֶּה ׀ בְּנֵ֣י לֵאָ֗ה אֲשֶׁ֨ר יָֽלְדָ֤ה לְיַֽעֲקֹב֙ בְּפַדַּ֣ן אֲרָ֔ם וְאֵ֖ת דִּינָ֣ה בִתּ֑וֹ כָּל־נֶ֧פֶשׁ בָּנָ֛יו וּבְנוֹתָ֖יו שְׁלֹשִׁ֥ים וְשָׁלֹֽשׁ׃ 16 וּבְנֵ֣י גָ֔ד צִפְי֥וֹן וְחַגִּ֖י שׁוּנִ֣י וְאֶצְבֹּ֑ן עֵרִ֥י וַֽאֲרוֹדִ֖י וְאַרְאֵלִֽי׃ 17 וּבְנֵ֣י אָשֵׁ֗ר יִמְנָ֧ה וְיִשְׁוָ֛ה וְיִשְׁוִ֥י וּבְרִיעָ֖ה וְשֶׂ֣רַח אֲחֹתָ֑ם וּבְנֵ֣י בְרִיעָ֔ה חֶ֖בֶר וּמַלְכִּיאֵֽל׃ 18 אֵ֚לֶּה בְּנֵ֣י זִלְפָּ֔ה אֲשֶׁר־נָתַ֥ן לָבָ֖ן לְלֵאָ֣ה בִתּ֑וֹ וַתֵּ֤לֶד אֶת־אֵ֨לֶּה֙ לְיַֽעֲקֹ֔ב שֵׁ֥שׁ עֶשְׂרֵ֖ה נָֽפֶשׁ׃ 19 בְּנֵ֤י רָחֵל֙ אֵ֣שֶׁת יַֽעֲקֹ֔ב יוֹסֵ֖ף וּבִנְיָמִֽן׃ 20 וַיִּוָּלֵ֣ד לְיוֹסֵף֮ בְּאֶ֣רֶץ מִצְרַ֒יִם֒ אֲשֶׁ֤ר יָֽלְדָה־לּוֹ֙ אָֽסְנַ֔ת בַּת־פּ֥וֹטִי פֶ֖רַע כֹּהֵ֣ן אֹ֑ן אֶת־מְנַשֶּׁ֖ה וְאֶת־אֶפְרָֽיִם׃ 21 וּבְנֵ֣י בִנְיָמִ֗ן בֶּ֤לַע וָבֶ֨כֶר֙ וְאַשְׁבֵּ֔ל גֵּרָ֥א וְנַֽעֲמָ֖ן אֵחִ֣י וָרֹ֑אשׁ מֻפִּ֥ים וְחֻפִּ֖ים וָאָֽרְדְּ׃ 22 אֵ֚לֶּה בְּנֵ֣י רָחֵ֔ל אֲשֶׁ֥ר יֻלַּ֖ד לְיַֽעֲקֹ֑ב כָּל־נֶ֖פֶשׁ אַרְבָּעָ֥ה עָשָֽׂר׃

23 וּבְנֵי־דָ֖ן חֻשִֽׁים׃ 24 וּבְנֵ֖י נַפְתָּלִ֑י יַחְצְאֵ֥ל וְגוּנִ֖י וְיֵ֥צֶר וְשִׁלֵּֽם׃ 25 אֵ֚לֶּה בְּנֵ֣י בִלְהָ֔ה אֲשֶׁר־נָתַ֥ן לָבָ֖ן לְרָחֵ֣ל בִּתּ֑וֹ וַתֵּ֧לֶד אֶת־אֵ֛לֶּה לְיַֽעֲקֹ֖ב כָּל־נֶ֥פֶשׁ שִׁבְעָֽה׃ 26 כָּל־הַ֠נֶּ֠פֶשׁ הַבָּ֨אָה לְיַֽעֲקֹ֤ב מִצְרַ֨יְמָה֙ יֹֽצְאֵ֣י יְרֵכ֔וֹ מִלְּבַ֖ד נְשֵׁ֣י בְנֵֽי־יַֽעֲקֹ֑ב כָּל־נֶ֖פֶשׁ שִׁשִּׁ֥ים וָשֵֽׁשׁ׃ 27 וּבְנֵ֥י יוֹסֵ֛ף אֲשֶׁר־יֻלַּד־ל֥וֹ בְמִצְרַ֖יִם נֶ֣פֶשׁ שְׁנָ֑יִם כָּל־הַנֶּ֧פֶשׁ לְבֵית־יַֽעֲקֹ֛ב הַבָּ֥אָה מִצְרַ֖יְמָה שִׁבְעִֽים׃ ס 28 [SIXTH READING] וְאֶת־יְהוּדָ֞ה שָׁלַ֤ח לְפָנָיו֙ אֶל־יוֹסֵ֔ף לְהוֹרֹ֥ת לְפָנָ֖יו גֹּ֑שְׁנָה וַיָּבֹ֖אוּ אַ֥רְצָה גֹּֽשֶׁן׃ 29 וַיֶּאְסֹ֤ר יוֹסֵף֙ מֶרְכַּבְתּ֔וֹ וַיַּ֛עַל לִקְרַֽאת־יִשְׂרָאֵ֥ל אָבִ֖יו גֹּ֑שְׁנָה וַיֵּרָ֣א אֵלָ֔יו וַיִּפֹּל֙ עַל־צַוָּארָ֔יו וַיֵּ֥בְךְּ עַל־צַוָּארָ֖יו

Why wasn't Joseph also reciting the *Shema?* It was not the proper time of reciting *Shema*, but when great things happen to righteous men, they immediately desire to thank God. After

kabbalah bites

46:29 "*(Joseph) appeared before his (father).*" Literally, "He revealed himself to him."

Despite the fact that he was Jacob's son, Joseph possessed a higher spiritual root.

Joseph was from *tohu* (chaos) and Jacob from *tikkun* (order). Therefore, "He revealed himself to him," Joseph's presence was, in fact, a revelation for his father.

¹⁵ The above were (from) the sons of Leah that she bore to Jacob in Paddan-aram—as well as Dinah his daughter. All his sons and daughters (from Leah) totalled thirty-three souls.

¹⁶ Gad's sons were Ziphion, Haggi, Shuni, and Ezbon, Eri, Arodi, and Areli.

¹⁷ Asher's sons were Imnah, Ishvah, Ishvi, and Beriah, and their sister was Serah. Beriah's sons were Heber and Malchiel.

¹⁸ The above were (from) the sons of Zilpah, whom Laban gave to his daughter Leah. She bore these sixteen souls to Jacob.

¹⁹ The sons of Rachel, Jacob's (main) wife, were Joseph and Benjamin. ²⁰ In the land of Egypt, Joseph fathered Manasseh and Ephraim, whom Asenath—the daughter of Poti-phera, the governor of On—bore to him.

²¹ The sons of Benjamin were Bela, Becher, Ashbel, Gera, Naaman, Ehi, Rosh, Muppim, Huppim, and Ard.

²² The above were (from) the sons of Rachel, who were born to Jacob, a total of fourteen souls.

²³ Dan's sons were Hushim.

²⁴ Naphtali's sons were Jahzeel, Guni, Jezer, and Shillem.

²⁵ The above were from the sons of Bilhah, whom Laban had given to his daughter Rachel, and she bore a total of seven souls to Jacob.

²⁶ The total number of people coming to Egypt with Jacob, his offspring, excluding Jacob's sons' wives was sixty-six souls. ²⁷ Joseph's sons, who were born to him in Egypt, were two souls (plus Joseph himself made sixty-nine, and Jochebed was born to Levi while entering Egypt). Thus, on entering Egypt, the house of Jacob totalled seventy souls.

Jacob is Reunited with Joseph

[SIXTH READING] ²⁸ He sent Judah ahead of him to Joseph, to direct him to Goshen, and they came to the land of Goshen.

²⁹ Joseph harnessed his chariot, and he went up to Goshen to meet Israel his father. When (Joseph) appeared before his (father), he fell on his neck, and he wept on his neck profusely.

---

in the land of Israel. This teaches you that even when successful in times of exile, you ought to always feel the deep pain and remorse that you are still in exile, away from your homeland (*Rabbi Menahem Mendel Schneerson, 20th century*).

29. (Joseph) appeared before his (father), he fell on his neck, and he wept on his neck profusely. Jacob did not fall on Joseph's neck and did not kiss him, because he was reciting the *Shema* [an affirmation of faith from *Deuteronomy* 6:4-9] (*Rashi, 11th century*).

בראשית מו:כט - מז:ו

30 וַיֹּאמֶר יִשְׂרָאֵל אֶל־יוֹסֵף אָמוּתָה הַפָּעַם אַחֲרֵי רְאוֹתִי אֶת־פָּנֶיךָ כִּי עוֹדְךָ חָי: 31 וַיֹּאמֶר יוֹסֵף אֶל־אֶחָיו וְאֶל־בֵּית אָבִיו אֶעֱלֶה וְאַגִּידָה לְפַרְעֹה וְאֹמְרָה אֵלָיו אַחַי וּבֵית־אָבִי אֲשֶׁר בְּאֶרֶץ־כְּנַעַן בָּאוּ אֵלָי: 32 וְהָאֲנָשִׁים רֹעֵי צֹאן כִּי־אַנְשֵׁי מִקְנֶה הָיוּ וְצֹאנָם וּבְקָרָם וְכָל־אֲשֶׁר לָהֶם הֵבִיאוּ: 33 וְהָיָה כִּי־יִקְרָא לָכֶם פַּרְעֹה וְאָמַר מַה־מַּעֲשֵׂיכֶם: 34 וַאֲמַרְתֶּם אַנְשֵׁי מִקְנֶה הָיוּ עֲבָדֶיךָ מִנְּעוּרֵינוּ וְעַד־עַתָּה גַּם־אֲנַחְנוּ גַּם־אֲבֹתֵינוּ בַּעֲבוּר תֵּשְׁבוּ בְּאֶרֶץ גֹּשֶׁן כִּי־תוֹעֲבַת מִצְרַיִם כָּל־רֹעֵה צֹאן:

מז

1 וַיָּבֹא יוֹסֵף וַיַּגֵּד לְפַרְעֹה וַיֹּאמֶר אָבִי וְאַחַי וְצֹאנָם וּבְקָרָם וְכָל־אֲשֶׁר לָהֶם בָּאוּ מֵאֶרֶץ כְּנָעַן וְהִנָּם בְּאֶרֶץ גֹּשֶׁן: 2 וּמִקְצֵה אֶחָיו לָקַח חֲמִשָּׁה אֲנָשִׁים וַיַּצִּגֵם לִפְנֵי פַרְעֹה: 3 וַיֹּאמֶר פַּרְעֹה אֶל־אֶחָיו מַה־מַּעֲשֵׂיכֶם וַיֹּאמְרוּ אֶל־פַּרְעֹה רֹעֵה צֹאן עֲבָדֶיךָ גַּם־אֲנַחְנוּ גַּם־אֲבוֹתֵינוּ: 4 וַיֹּאמְרוּ אֶל־פַּרְעֹה לָגוּר בָּאָרֶץ בָּאנוּ כִּי־אֵין מִרְעֶה לַצֹּאן אֲשֶׁר לַעֲבָדֶיךָ כִּי־כָבֵד הָרָעָב בְּאֶרֶץ כְּנָעַן וְעַתָּה יֵשְׁבוּ־נָא עֲבָדֶיךָ בְּאֶרֶץ גֹּשֶׁן: 5 וַיֹּאמֶר פַּרְעֹה אֶל־יוֹסֵף לֵאמֹר אָבִיךָ וְאַחֶיךָ בָּאוּ אֵלֶיךָ: 6 אֶרֶץ מִצְרַיִם לְפָנֶיךָ הִוא בְּמֵיטַב הָאָרֶץ הוֹשֵׁב אֶת־אָבִיךָ וְאֶת־אַחֶיךָ יֵשְׁבוּ בְּאֶרֶץ גֹּשֶׁן וְאִם־יָדַעְתָּ וְיֶשׁ־בָּם אַנְשֵׁי־חַיִל וְשַׂמְתָּם שָׂרֵי

kabbalah bites

46:29-30 Why was Jacob only comforted upon *seeing* Joseph, when he had already been informed that Joseph was alive and he *believed the report?*

Joseph wept profusely on Jacob's neck because he saw that the Holy Temple was to be destroyed. It is only when Jacob saw this and realized that his son was not merely physically alive, but had remained spiritually sensitive after all his years of political life in Egypt, that Jacob was finally comforted.

Make it your business to ensure that your children live on spiritually, and not just physically.

genesis 46:30 – 47:6 va-yiggash

³⁰ Israel said to Joseph, "(If) I would die this time (I would be comforted), since I have seen your face, that you are still alive!"

³¹ Joseph said to his brothers and to his father's household, "I will go up and inform Pharaoh, and I'll say to him, 'My brothers and my father's household who were in the land of Canaan have come to me.' ³² (I'll also tell him), 'The men are shepherds, and they've (always) been owners of livestock, so they've brought their flocks and their cattle and all their possessions.' ³³ So if Pharaoh summons you and asks you, 'What is your occupation?' ³⁴ Say, 'Your servants have been owners of livestock from our youth until now, both we and our ancestors.' (You should do this in order) to live in the land of Goshen, because all shepherds are abhorrent to the Egyptians (since they worship the sheep)."

Pharaoh Meets Joseph's Family

47 ¹ Joseph came and informed Pharaoh. He said, "My father and my brothers have come from the land of Canaan with their flocks, their cattle and their possessions, and now they are in the land of Goshen."

² (Joseph) took five (of the weakest) men from among his brothers, and he presented them to Pharaoh (hoping that Pharaoh would not enlist them as warriors).

³ Pharaoh said to (Joseph's) brothers, "What is your occupation?"

They said to Pharaoh, "Your servants are shepherds, both we and our forefathers." ⁴ They said to Pharaoh, "We have come to sojourn in the land, for your servants' flocks have no pasture, since the famine is severe in the land of Canaan. Now, please let your servants settle in the land of Goshen."

⁵ Pharaoh spoke to Joseph, saying, "Your father and your brothers have come to you. ⁶ The land of Egypt is (open) before you. Settle your father and your brothers in the best of the land—let them dwell in the land of Goshen. If you know that there are capable men among them (who are good at their occupation of tending sheep), then make them livestock officers over my (sheep)."

---

meeting Joseph and seeing he was the ruler in Egypt, as well as all the rewards that God had given him, it brought out in Jacob a desire to recite the *Shema* (*Rabbi Judah Loew b. Bezalel of Prague, 16th century*).

47:2 Joseph took five men from among his brothers. Joseph presented to Pharaoh the weakest among them, for if Pharaoh would see that they were strong he might enlist them into his army. The five picked were: Reuben, Simeon, Levi, Issachar and Benjamin (*Genesis Rabbah*).

בראשית מז:ו–יח ויגש

מִקְנֶה עַל־אֲשֶׁר־לִי: 7 וַיָּבֵא יוֹסֵף אֶת־יַעֲקֹב אָבִיו וַיַּעֲמִדֵהוּ לִפְנֵי פַרְעֹה וַיְבָרֶךְ יַעֲקֹב אֶת־פַּרְעֹה: 8 וַיֹּאמֶר פַּרְעֹה אֶל־יַעֲקֹב כַּמָּה יְמֵי שְׁנֵי חַיֶּיךָ: 9 וַיֹּאמֶר יַעֲקֹב אֶל־פַּרְעֹה יְמֵי שְׁנֵי מְגוּרַי שְׁלֹשִׁים וּמְאַת שָׁנָה מְעַט וְרָעִים הָיוּ יְמֵי שְׁנֵי חַיַּי וְלֹא הִשִּׂיגוּ אֶת־יְמֵי שְׁנֵי חַיֵּי אֲבֹתַי בִּימֵי מְגוּרֵיהֶם: 10 וַיְבָרֶךְ יַעֲקֹב אֶת־פַּרְעֹה וַיֵּצֵא מִלִּפְנֵי פַרְעֹה: [SEVENTH READING] 11 וַיּוֹשֵׁב יוֹסֵף אֶת־אָבִיו וְאֶת־אֶחָיו וַיִּתֵּן לָהֶם אֲחֻזָּה בְּאֶרֶץ מִצְרַיִם בְּמֵיטַב הָאָרֶץ בְּאֶרֶץ רַעְמְסֵס כַּאֲשֶׁר צִוָּה פַרְעֹה: 12 וַיְכַלְכֵּל יוֹסֵף אֶת־אָבִיו וְאֶת־אֶחָיו וְאֵת כָּל־בֵּית אָבִיו לֶחֶם לְפִי הַטָּף: 13 וְלֶחֶם אֵין בְּכָל־הָאָרֶץ כִּי־כָבֵד הָרָעָב מְאֹד וַתֵּלַהּ אֶרֶץ מִצְרַיִם וְאֶרֶץ כְּנַעַן מִפְּנֵי הָרָעָב: 14 וַיְלַקֵּט יוֹסֵף אֶת־כָּל־הַכֶּסֶף הַנִּמְצָא בְאֶרֶץ־מִצְרַיִם וּבְאֶרֶץ כְּנַעַן בַּשֶּׁבֶר אֲשֶׁר־הֵם שֹׁבְרִים וַיָּבֵא יוֹסֵף אֶת־הַכֶּסֶף בֵּיתָה פַרְעֹה: 15 וַיִּתֹּם הַכֶּסֶף מֵאֶרֶץ מִצְרַיִם וּמֵאֶרֶץ כְּנַעַן וַיָּבֹאוּ כָל־מִצְרַיִם אֶל־יוֹסֵף לֵאמֹר הָבָה־לָּנוּ לֶחֶם וְלָמָּה נָמוּת נֶגְדֶּךָ כִּי אָפֵס כָּסֶף: 16 וַיֹּאמֶר יוֹסֵף הָבוּ מִקְנֵיכֶם וְאֶתְּנָה לָכֶם בְּמִקְנֵיכֶם אִם־אָפֵס כָּסֶף: 17 וַיָּבִיאוּ אֶת־מִקְנֵיהֶם אֶל־יוֹסֵף וַיִּתֵּן לָהֶם יוֹסֵף לֶחֶם בַּסּוּסִים וּבְמִקְנֵה הַצֹּאן וּבְמִקְנֵה הַבָּקָר וּבַחֲמֹרִים וַיְנַהֲלֵם בַּלֶּחֶם בְּכָל־מִקְנֵהֶם בַּשָּׁנָה הַהִוא: 18 וַתִּתֹּם הַשָּׁנָה הַהִוא וַיָּבֹאוּ אֵלָיו בַּשָּׁנָה הַשֵּׁנִית וַיֹּאמְרוּ לוֹ לֹא־נְכַחֵד מֵאֲדֹנִי כִּי אִם־תַּם הַכֶּסֶף וּמִקְנֵה הַבְּהֵמָה אֶל־אֲדֹנִי לֹא

kabbalah bites

47:9 Jacob was a reincarnation of Adam to achieve *tikkun* (spiritual healing) for Adam's soul. Adam had sinned for one hundred and thirty years (see above 5:3), which was healed by Jacob's "few and miserable" one hundred and thirty years of wandering and exile.

At this point *tikkun* was achieved. He then lived a further seventeen years (v. 28), which is the numerical value of the word *tov* (good), hinting to the fact that these were post-*tikkun* years, when the good in his soul had been redeemed.

genesis 47:7–18 va-yiggash

⁷ Joseph brought Jacob his father and stood him before Pharaoh, and Jacob greeted Pharaoh.

⁸ Pharaoh said to Jacob, "How many years have you been alive?"

⁹ Jacob said to Pharaoh, "I've been wandering around for a hundred and thirty years. (Compared to) my fathers' lifetimes, when they were wandering around, the days of my life have been few and miserable. (Even ignoring the miseries that I've had, my days) have not been (as good as theirs)."

¹⁰ Jacob blessed Pharaoh (that the Nile should irrigate the land) and he left Pharaoh's presence.

[SEVENTH READING] ¹¹ Joseph settled his father and his brothers, and he gave them property in the land of Egypt in the best of the land, in the district of Rameses (within the area of Goshen), as Pharaoh had commanded.

¹² Joseph sustained his father, his brothers and his father's entire household (with an excess of) bread (as if they were) young children (who need to be given extra food, as they waste so much).

Joseph Acquires the Land of Egypt for Pharaoh

(The following occurred at the beginning of the famine, two years before Jacob's arrival in Egypt:)

¹³ There was no food in the entire land, for the famine had grown exceedingly severe. The land of Egypt and the land of Canaan were exhausted because of the famine. ¹⁴ Joseph collected all the money that was to be found in the land of Egypt and in the land of Canaan through the (purchase of) grain that they were buying, and Joseph brought the money into Pharaoh's house.

¹⁵ When the money was depleted from the land of Egypt and from the land of Canaan, all the Egyptians came to Joseph, saying, "Give us food! Why should we die in front of you because the money has run out?"

¹⁶ Joseph said, "If the money has run out, give (me) your livestock, and I will give you (food in return) for your livestock." ¹⁷ So they brought their livestock to Joseph, and Joseph gave them food (in return) for horses, flocks of sheep (and goats), herds of cattle and donkeys. He provided them with food that (entire) year (by exchanging) bread for all their livestock.

¹⁸ When that year ended, they came to him in the second year (of the famine), and said to him, "We are

food for thought

1. To what extent does a government "own" its citizens?

2. How can we improve our efforts to eliminate starvation?

3. Do today's governments have too much power, or too little?

בראשית מז:יח-כז | ויגש

נִשְׁאַר לִפְנֵי אֲדֹנִי בִּלְתִּי אִם־גְּוִיָּתֵנוּ וְאַדְמָתֵנוּ: 19 לָמָּה נָמוּת לְעֵינֶיךָ גַּם־אֲנַחְנוּ גַּם־אַדְמָתֵנוּ קְנֵה־אֹתָנוּ וְאֶת־אַדְמָתֵנוּ בַּלָּחֶם וְנִהְיֶה אֲנַחְנוּ וְאַדְמָתֵנוּ עֲבָדִים לְפַרְעֹה וְתֶן־זֶרַע וְנִחְיֶה וְלֹא נָמוּת וְהָאֲדָמָה לֹא תֵשָׁם: 20 וַיִּקֶן יוֹסֵף אֶת־כָּל־אַדְמַת מִצְרַיִם לְפַרְעֹה כִּי־מָכְרוּ מִצְרַיִם אִישׁ שָׂדֵהוּ כִּי־חָזַק עֲלֵהֶם הָרָעָב וַתְּהִי הָאָרֶץ לְפַרְעֹה: 21 וְאֶת־הָעָם הֶעֱבִיר אֹתוֹ לֶעָרִים מִקְצֵה גְבוּל־מִצְרַיִם וְעַד־קָצֵהוּ: 22 רַק אַדְמַת הַכֹּהֲנִים לֹא קָנָה כִּי חֹק לַכֹּהֲנִים מֵאֵת פַּרְעֹה וְאָכְלוּ אֶת־חֻקָּם אֲשֶׁר נָתַן לָהֶם פַּרְעֹה עַל־כֵּן לֹא מָכְרוּ אֶת־אַדְמָתָם: 23 וַיֹּאמֶר יוֹסֵף אֶל־הָעָם הֵן קָנִיתִי אֶתְכֶם הַיּוֹם וְאֶת־אַדְמַתְכֶם לְפַרְעֹה הֵא־לָכֶם זֶרַע וּזְרַעְתֶּם אֶת־הָאֲדָמָה: 24 וְהָיָה בַּתְּבוּאֹת וּנְתַתֶּם חֲמִישִׁית לְפַרְעֹה וְאַרְבַּע הַיָּדֹת יִהְיֶה לָכֶם לְזֶרַע הַשָּׂדֶה וּלְאָכְלְכֶם וְלַאֲשֶׁר בְּבָתֵּיכֶם וְלֶאֱכֹל לְטַפְּכֶם: 25 [MAFTIR] וַיֹּאמְרוּ הֶחֱיִתָנוּ נִמְצָא־חֵן בְּעֵינֵי אֲדֹנִי וְהָיִינוּ עֲבָדִים לְפַרְעֹה: 26 וַיָּשֶׂם אֹתָהּ יוֹסֵף לְחֹק עַד־הַיּוֹם הַזֶּה עַל־אַדְמַת מִצְרַיִם לְפַרְעֹה לַחֹמֶשׁ רַק אַדְמַת הַכֹּהֲנִים לְבַדָּם לֹא הָיְתָה לְפַרְעֹה: 27 וַיֵּשֶׁב יִשְׂרָאֵל בְּאֶרֶץ מִצְרַיִם בְּאֶרֶץ גֹּשֶׁן וַיֵּאָחֲזוּ בָהּ וַיִּפְרוּ וַיִּרְבּוּ מְאֹד:

ק״ו פסוקים, יהללא״ל סימן.

spiritual vitamin

> You have a so-called "animal soul," connected with the material body, which is often a source of confusion and distraction, leading you from the right path, and robbing you of your peace of mind, etc. On the other hand, you also have a Divine soul, which makes it possible to overcome all these distractions. And the Sages taught, *"Anyone who is determined to purify himself receives aid from on high"* (Babylonian Talmud, Yoma 38b).

genesis 47:18–27 — va-yiggash

not withholding anything from our master! Since the money and the herds of animals have been depleted (and come) into (the hands of) our master, there's nothing left (to give to) our master except our bodies and our farmland. ¹⁹ Why should we die before your eyes, (eliminating) us and (leaving) our farmland (desolate)? Buy us and our farmland (in exchange) for food, let us and our land become subjugated to Pharaoh. Just give (us) seed (to sow the earth), so that we will live and not die, and the farmland will not be desolate."

²⁰ So Joseph bought all the farmland of the Egyptians for Pharaoh, since each one of the Egyptians sold his field because the famine had become too strong for them. Thus, the land became Pharaoh's.

²¹ (Joseph) transferred the people (from city) to city, from (one) end of the boundary of Egypt to its (other) end (to remind them that they no longer owned the land). ²² The only land which he did not buy was that of the priests, for the priests were given a (daily) allotment (of bread) from Pharaoh. Since they (were able) to eat their allotment which Pharaoh had given them, they did not sell their land.

²³ Joseph said to the people, "Since I have now bought you and your land for Pharaoh—look!—here is grain-seed for you. Sow the farmland. ²⁴ When the harvest (is gathered in) you must give one fifth to Pharaoh, and the (remaining) four parts of grain-seed will be yours—for (your) field(s), for your food, for the members of your households, and for your young children to eat."

[MAFTIR] ²⁵ "You have saved our lives!" they replied. "Just let us find favor in our master's eyes, and we will be subservient to Pharaoh (paying him the tax every year)."

²⁶ So Joseph instituted a law, (that is in force) until today, that one-fifth of (whatever grows on) Egyptian farmland belonged to Pharaoh. The only (exception was that) the priests' land did not belong to Pharaoh.

²⁷ The Jewish people settled in Egypt, in the district of Goshen, and they acquired property there. They were fertile, and their population increased very rapidly.

The *Haftarah* for *Va-Yiggash* is on page 1313.

---

27. They acquired property there. The verse states *va-ye'aḥazu vah*, which means "they acquired property in it (Goshen)" (*Rashi, 11th century*).

Ye'aḥazu vah means that the land grasped them, like a person who is grabbed against his will (*Midrash Tadshe*).

This Torah portion, which describes **Jacob's passing,** is nevertheless named "and he **lived,"** because Jacob **lives on within you.** He is constantly **whispering** to you: Do you want to know how to be **fully human?** Look here in **the Torah.**

VA-YEḤI
ויחי

JOSEPH SWEARS TO BURY JACOB IN CANAAN	47:28–31
JACOB'S FINAL BLESSINGS	48:1 – 49:28
JACOB PASSES AWAY	49:29 – 50:14
JOSEPH'S RELATIONSHIP WITH HIS BROTHERS	50:15–21
JOSEPH PASSES AWAY	50:22–26

NAME
Va-Yehi

MEANING
"And he lived"

LINES IN TORAH SCROLL
148

PARASHIYYOT
7 open; 5 closed

VERSES
85

WORDS
1158

LETTERS
4448

DATE
2238–2309

LOCATION
Egypt, Canaan

KEY PEOPLE
Jacob, Jacob's sons, Ephraim, Manasseh

MITZVOT
None

CHARACTER PROFILE

NAME
Benjamin, (Ben-oni)

MEANING
"Son of right", ("Son of my sorrow")

PARENTS
Jacob and Rachel

GRANDFATHERS
Laban, Isaac

SIBLINGS
Reuben, Simeon, Levi, Judah, Issachar, Zebulun, Dan, Naphtali, Gad, Asher, Joseph, Dinah

WIVES
Mechalia, the daughter of Aram (Terah's grandson); Aribath, daughter of Zimran (Abraham's son)

CHILDREN
From Mechalia:
Bela, Becher, Ashbel, Gera, Naaman; from Aribath:
Ehi, Rosh, Muppim, Huppim, Ard

LIFE SPAN
115 years

BURIAL PLACE
Jerusalem, opposite the Jebusite city

ACHIEVEMENTS
Did not participate in the sale of Joseph; did not reveal to his father that Joseph had been sold

KNOWN FOR
The only one of Jacob's children born in the land of Canaan; closely resembled Rachel, named all his children in memory of Joseph

BUSINESS

Zebulun was blessed that he would live by the sea coast and engage in business; he would provide food for the tribe of Issachar, who would engage in Torah study. But these roles are not mutually exclusive. The businessman must still pray and study Torah to the best of his ability, and the Torah scholar must also be charitable (49:13).

CULTURE

Jacob's years in Egypt are described as "the best of his life," although he lived in a corrupt, immoral culture. So long as there is the right determination, it is not the place that affects the man, it is man who affects the place (47:28).

LEADERSHIP QUALITIES

When Jacob reprimanded his sons before passing away, it is Judah who emerged as the leader. Jacob praised Judah for bravery, steadiness, dependability, determination and acceptance by his peers. The other brothers were disqualified for a variety of reasons such as instability, use of violence, lack of concern and lack of respect from others (49:1-28).

ויחי • בראשית מז:כח - מח:ד

28 וַיְחִ֤י יַעֲקֹב֙ בְּאֶ֣רֶץ מִצְרַ֔יִם שְׁבַ֥ע עֶשְׂרֵ֖ה שָׁנָ֑ה וַיְהִ֤י יְמֵֽי־יַעֲקֹב֙ שְׁנֵ֣י חַיָּ֔יו שֶׁ֣בַע שָׁנִ֔ים וְאַרְבָּעִ֥ים וּמְאַ֖ת שָׁנָֽה: 29 וַיִּקְרְב֣וּ יְמֵֽי־יִשְׂרָאֵל֮ לָמוּת֒ וַיִּקְרָ֣א | לִבְנ֣וֹ לְיוֹסֵ֗ף וַיֹּ֤אמֶר לוֹ֙ אִם־נָ֨א מָצָ֤אתִי חֵן֙ בְּעֵינֶ֔יךָ שִֽׂים־נָ֥א יָדְךָ֖ תַּ֣חַת יְרֵכִ֑י וְעָשִׂ֤יתָ עִמָּדִי֙ חֶ֣סֶד וֶאֱמֶ֔ת אַל־נָ֥א תִקְבְּרֵ֖נִי בְּמִצְרָֽיִם: 30 וְשָֽׁכַבְתִּי֙ עִם־אֲבֹתַ֔י וּנְשָׂאתַ֨נִי֙ מִמִּצְרַ֔יִם וּקְבַרְתַּ֖נִי בִּקְבֻֽרָתָ֑ם וַיֹּאמַ֕ר אָנֹכִ֖י אֶעֱשֶׂ֥ה כִדְבָרֶֽךָ: 31 וַיֹּ֗אמֶר הִשָּֽׁבְעָה֙ לִ֔י וַיִּשָּׁבַ֖ע ל֑וֹ וַיִּשְׁתַּ֥חוּ יִשְׂרָאֵ֖ל עַל־רֹ֥אשׁ הַמִּטָּֽה: פ

מח

1 וַיְהִ֗י אַחֲרֵי֙ הַדְּבָרִ֣ים הָאֵ֔לֶּה וַיֹּ֣אמֶר לְיוֹסֵ֔ף הִנֵּ֥ה אָבִ֖יךָ חֹלֶ֑ה וַיִּקַּ֞ח אֶת־שְׁנֵ֤י בָנָיו֙ עִמּ֔וֹ אֶת־מְנַשֶּׁ֖ה וְאֶת־אֶפְרָֽיִם: 2 וַיַּגֵּ֣ד לְיַעֲקֹ֔ב וַיֹּ֕אמֶר הִנֵּ֛ה בִּנְךָ֥ יוֹסֵ֖ף בָּ֣א אֵלֶ֑יךָ וַיִּתְחַזֵּק֙ יִשְׂרָאֵ֔ל וַיֵּ֖שֶׁב עַל־הַמִּטָּֽה: 3 וַיֹּ֤אמֶר יַעֲקֹב֙ אֶל־יוֹסֵ֔ף אֵ֥ל שַׁדַּ֛י נִרְאָֽה־אֵלַ֥י בְּל֖וּז בְּאֶ֣רֶץ כְּנָ֑עַן וַיְבָ֖רֶךְ אֹתִֽי: 4 וַיֹּ֣אמֶר

---

29. That you will do for me true kindness. When you perform an act of kindness for a living person, you usually help him only in a material way, so the kindness itself is not considered complete "truth." But the kindness that you perform for the dead is purely for their spiritual benefit—this is true kindness (*Rabbi Abraham Samuel Benjamin Sofer, 19th century*).

Please don't let me be buried in Egypt. Jacob asked not to be buried in Egypt so that the Egyptians would not make a deity of him (*Rashi, 11th century*).

31. Swear to me. Jacob did not suspect that his righteous and beloved son would disobey him. Jacob only made Joseph swear an oath so that his wish to be buried in the land of Israel would be respected *by Pharaoh*, who may not have given Joseph permission to leave Egypt. Or, Pharaoh might want such a saintly person as Jacob to be buried in his country, as an honor to the nation. But Jacob knew that Pharaoh would not make Joseph violate an oath that he had sworn to his father, as we find later that Pharaoh said, "Go and bury your father, *as he had you swear*" (50:6; *Nahmanides, 13th century*).

---

kabbalah bites

47:31 Jacob's bowing of the head is an allusion that he had achieved the spiritual level of *tefillin* (leather phylacteries), which are placed on the head.

Jacob's life work achieved *tikkun* (spiritual healing) for the damage caused to the universe by Adam. Originally, Adam had worn garments of light; when he sinned, they were replaced with leather garments (see above 3:21). Jacob's *tikkun* ensured that wearing *tefillin* of leather would now become a mark of distinction rather than a reminder of man's disgrace.

And the twelve stitches with which the housings of the *tefillin* are sewn hint to the assistance Jacob received from his twelve sons in carrying out this *tikkun*.

genesis 47:28 – 48:4   va-yeḥi

parashat va-yeḥi

Joseph Swears Not to Bury Jacob in Egypt

²⁸ Jacob lived in the land of Egypt for seventeen years. (The total of) Jacob's days, the years of his life, were a hundred and forty-seven years.

²⁹ When the time drew near for Israel to die, he called his son Joseph and said to him, "If I have now found favor in your eyes, please place your hand beneath my thigh (and swear an oath) that you will do for me true kindness: please don't let me be buried in Egypt. ³⁰ Let me lie with my fathers. Carry me out of Egypt, and bury me in their grave."

"I will do as you say," said (Joseph).

³¹ (Jacob) said, "Swear to me," and he swore to him. Then Israel bowed down to (Joseph, turning towards the Divine Presence which was) at the top of the bed.

Jacob Blesses Ephraim and Manasseh

48 ¹ Then, after these words (had been exchanged between Jacob and Joseph, a messenger) said to Joseph, "Beware, your father is sick!" He took his two sons Manasseh and Ephraim with him (to Jacob to bless them before he passed away).

² (A messenger) came to inform Jacob and said, "Look! Your son Joseph is coming to (visit) you."

Israel summoned his strength and sat up on the bed (since Joseph was a king).

³ Jacob said to Joseph, "God Almighty appeared to me in Luz, in the land of Canaan, and He blessed me. ⁴ He said to me, 'Look, I will make you fruitful and

---

47:28 Jacob lived in the land of Egypt for seventeen years. Usually, in the Torah scroll, there is a space between two Torah portions. However, between the portions of *Va-Yiggash* and *Va-Yeḥi* there is no space—it is "closed."

This alludes to the fact that Jacob wished to reveal the End of Days, when the Messiah would come, but the information was "closed" (concealed) from him (*Rashi, 11th century*).

Why did Jacob want to reveal this information to his sons? Jacob wanted to teach that there is Godliness hidden within the mundane world, making the Exile easier to endure. But God wanted us to come to this realization on our own. Therefore, He concealed Jacob's vision (*Rabbi Judah Aryeh Leib Alter of Gur, 19th century*).

Jacob lived in the land of Egypt for seventeen years. "Jacob *lived* in the land"—during these years, Jacob's life was content. His prior years could not be considered real living (*Zohar*).

When Joseph was separated from his father, Joseph was seventeen years old. Now, Jacob was repaid for his earlier parental support: Jacob had supported Joseph for his first seventeen years, so he was worthy that Joseph should support him in dignity for his final seventeen years (*Rabbi Bahya b. Asher, 13th century*).

בראשית מח:ד-יג ויחי

אֵלַ֔י הִנְנִ֣י מַפְרְךָ֗ וְהִרְבִּיתִ֙ךָ֙ וּנְתַתִּ֖יךָ לִקְהַ֣ל עַמִּ֑ים וְנָתַתִּ֞י אֶת־הָאָ֤רֶץ הַזֹּאת֙ לְזַרְעֲךָ֣ אַחֲרֶ֔יךָ אֲחֻזַּ֖ת עוֹלָֽם׃ 5 וְעַתָּ֡ה שְׁנֵֽי־בָנֶיךָ֩ הַנּוֹלָדִ֨ים לְךָ֜ בְּאֶ֣רֶץ מִצְרַ֗יִם עַד־בֹּאִ֥י אֵלֶ֛יךָ מִצְרַ֖יְמָה לִי־הֵ֑ם אֶפְרַ֙יִם֙ וּמְנַשֶּׁ֔ה כִּרְאוּבֵ֥ן וְשִׁמְע֖וֹן יִֽהְיוּ־לִֽי׃ 6 וּמוֹלַדְתְּךָ֛ אֲשֶׁר־הוֹלַ֥דְתָּ אַחֲרֵיהֶ֖ם לְךָ֣ יִֽהְי֑וּ עַ֣ל שֵׁ֧ם אֲחֵיהֶ֛ם יִקָּרְא֖וּ בְּנַחֲלָתָֽם׃ 7 וַאֲנִ֣י ׀ בְּבֹאִ֣י מִפַּדָּ֗ן מֵ֩תָה֩ עָלַ֨י רָחֵ֜ל בְּאֶ֤רֶץ כְּנַ֙עַן֙ בַּדֶּ֔רֶךְ בְּע֥וֹד כִּבְרַת־אֶ֖רֶץ לָבֹ֣א אֶפְרָ֑תָה וָאֶקְבְּרֶ֤הָ שָּׁם֙ בְּדֶ֣רֶךְ אֶפְרָ֔ת הִ֖וא בֵּ֥ית לָֽחֶם׃ 8 וַיַּ֥רְא יִשְׂרָאֵ֖ל אֶת־בְּנֵ֣י יוֹסֵ֑ף וַיֹּ֖אמֶר מִי־אֵֽלֶּה׃ 9 וַיֹּ֤אמֶר יוֹסֵף֙ אֶל־אָבִ֔יו בָּנַ֣י הֵ֔ם אֲשֶׁר־נָֽתַן־לִ֥י אֱלֹהִ֖ים בָּזֶ֑ה וַיֹּאמַ֕ר קָֽחֶם־נָ֥א אֵלַ֖י וַאֲבָרֲכֵֽם׃ 10 [SECOND READING] וְעֵינֵ֤י יִשְׂרָאֵל֙ כָּבְד֣וּ מִזֹּ֔קֶן לֹ֥א יוּכַ֖ל לִרְא֑וֹת וַיַּגֵּ֤שׁ אֹתָם֙ אֵלָ֔יו וַיִּשַּׁ֥ק לָהֶ֖ם וַיְחַבֵּ֥ק לָהֶֽם׃ 11 וַיֹּ֤אמֶר יִשְׂרָאֵל֙ אֶל־יוֹסֵ֔ף רְאֹ֥ה פָנֶ֖יךָ לֹ֣א פִלָּ֑לְתִּי וְהִנֵּ֨ה הֶרְאָ֥ה אֹתִ֛י אֱלֹהִ֖ים גַּ֥ם אֶת־זַרְעֶֽךָ׃ 12 וַיּוֹצֵ֥א יוֹסֵ֛ף אֹתָ֖ם מֵעִ֣ם בִּרְכָּ֑יו וַיִּשְׁתַּ֥חוּ לְאַפָּ֖יו אָֽרְצָה׃ 13 וַיִּקַּ֣ח יוֹסֵף֮ אֶת־שְׁנֵיהֶם֒ אֶת־אֶפְרַ֤יִם בִּֽימִינוֹ֙ מִשְּׂמֹ֣אל יִשְׂרָאֵ֔ל וְאֶת־מְנַשֶּׁ֥ה בִשְׂמֹאל֖וֹ מִימִ֣ין יִשְׂרָאֵ֑ל

But Joseph chose to allow his casket to remain in Egypt, wishing to remain *with* his people as they were exiled.

Since Jacob understood that he and his son differed in their opinion as to where a Jewish leader should remain, he made Joseph swear an oath that he would bury his father outside the land of Egypt (*Rabbi Menahem Mendel Schneerson, 20th century*).

48:7 Rachel died on me. Jacob said "Although I am burdening you to bury me in the land of Canaan, which I did not do for your mother, for she died near Bethlehem, and I did not even carry her to Bethlehem in order to bring her to a settled land, and I know that you have it in your heart against me—"

"But you should know that it was by the word of God that I buried her there, so that she might help her descendants. For when Nebuzaradan will send them into exile and they will pass by way of her grave, Rachel will emerge from her grave. She will cry and beseech mercy from God for them, as the verse states, *"A voice is heard in Ramah, Rachel is weeping for her children..."* and God answers her, *"'There is reward for your action,' says God, 'for your children will return to their borders'"* (*Jeremiah 31:15-17; Rashi, 11th century*).

food for thought

1. How much do you fear your own mortality?

2. What acts have you done in your life that will immortalize you?

3. In Judaism, is death always associated with sin?

cause you to multiply, and I will make you into a multitude of peoples, and I will give this land to your descendants after you for an everlasting inheritance.'"

⁵ "And now, your two sons—who were born to you in the land of Egypt, before I came to you (here) in Egypt—(will be counted as) mine (to receive a share in the land of Israel): Ephraim and Manasseh will be mine, like Reuben and Simeon. ⁶ But (if) you have more children after them, they will be (counted as) your own (and not as separate tribes). Regarding their inheritance, they will (not be tribes unto themselves, but rather) classified according to their brothers' names."

⁷ "I (know that you are angry with me because) when I was coming from Paddan (and) Rachel died on me—while traveling through the land of Canaan, when there was still (about) a (half-a-mile) stretch of land to reach Ephrath—and (you're upset that) I buried her there on the way to Ephrath, in Bethlehem (but you shouldn't be upset, because God told me to bury her there)."

⁸ Israel saw Joseph's sons. (When he tried to bless them, the Divine Presence departed, so) he said, "(From) where were these (boys born, who are not worthy of being blessed)?"

⁹ (Producing his betrothal and marriage contracts) Joseph said to his father, "They are my sons, whom God gave through (a marriage certified by) this (documentation)."

(When the Divine spirit returned, Jacob) said, "Bring them near to me, and I'll bless them."

[SECOND READING] ¹⁰ Israel's eyes had become heavy with age (and) he could not see, so (Joseph) brought (the boys) near to him, and he kissed them and hugged them. ¹¹ Israel said to Joseph, "I didn't (even) expect to see your face, and—look!—God has shown me your children too!"

¹² (After Jacob kissed the boys) Joseph took them from (Jacob's) lap (and placed one child to his right and one to his left, so that he could rest his hands on them and bless them. Joseph stepped back and) threw himself down on the ground. ¹³ Joseph then took them both: Ephraim on his right, to Israel's left, and Manasseh (the firstborn) on his left, to Israel's right (so that he would place his right hand on the firstborn), and he brought (them) close to him.

"A prisoner cannot free himself from jail" (*Babylonian Talmud, Berakhot* 5b). The solution to escape from a particular confinement cannot come from within the confinement itself. It has to be an *external* solution.

The inner reason why Jacob did not want to be buried in Egypt is because he wished to provide the external (spiritual) solution for the Jewish people to leave exile. Being buried outside Egypt meant that Jacob remained higher than the Egyptian exile, empowering his children with the spiritual potential to rise above their confinement, and eventually escape.

בראשית מח:יג-כ | ויחי

14 וַיִּגַּשׁ אֵלָיו: וַיִּשְׁלַח יִשְׂרָאֵל אֶת־יְמִינוֹ וַיָּשֶׁת עַל־רֹאשׁ אֶפְרַיִם וְהוּא הַצָּעִיר וְאֶת־שְׂמֹאלוֹ עַל־רֹאשׁ מְנַשֶּׁה שִׂכֵּל אֶת־יָדָיו כִּי מְנַשֶּׁה הַבְּכוֹר: 15 וַיְבָרֶךְ אֶת־יוֹסֵף וַיֹּאמַר הָאֱלֹהִים אֲשֶׁר הִתְהַלְּכוּ אֲבֹתַי לְפָנָיו אַבְרָהָם וְיִצְחָק הָאֱלֹהִים הָרֹעֶה אֹתִי מֵעוֹדִי עַד־הַיּוֹם הַזֶּה: 16 הַמַּלְאָךְ הַגֹּאֵל אֹתִי מִכָּל־רָע יְבָרֵךְ אֶת־הַנְּעָרִים וְיִקָּרֵא בָהֶם שְׁמִי וְשֵׁם אֲבֹתַי אַבְרָהָם וְיִצְחָק וְיִדְגּוּ לָרֹב בְּקֶרֶב הָאָרֶץ: 17 [THIRD READING] וַיַּרְא יוֹסֵף כִּי־יָשִׁית אָבִיו יַד־יְמִינוֹ עַל־רֹאשׁ אֶפְרַיִם וַיֵּרַע בְּעֵינָיו וַיִּתְמֹךְ יַד־אָבִיו לְהָסִיר אֹתָהּ מֵעַל רֹאשׁ־אֶפְרַיִם עַל־רֹאשׁ מְנַשֶּׁה: 18 וַיֹּאמֶר יוֹסֵף אֶל־אָבִיו לֹא־כֵן אָבִי כִּי־זֶה הַבְּכֹר שִׂים יְמִינְךָ עַל־רֹאשׁוֹ: 19 וַיְמָאֵן אָבִיו וַיֹּאמֶר יָדַעְתִּי בְנִי יָדַעְתִּי גַּם־הוּא יִהְיֶה־לְּעָם וְגַם־הוּא יִגְדָּל וְאוּלָם אָחִיו הַקָּטֹן יִגְדַּל מִמֶּנּוּ וְזַרְעוֹ יִהְיֶה מְלֹא־הַגּוֹיִם: 20 וַיְבָרֲכֵם בַּיּוֹם הַהוּא לֵאמוֹר בְּךָ יְבָרֵךְ יִשְׂרָאֵל לֵאמֹר יְשִׂמְךָ אֱלֹהִים כְּאֶפְרַיִם וְכִמְנַשֶּׁה

Manasseh by "demoting" him to the lesser position on Jacob's left. Therefore, Jacob employed the more subtle and sensitive approach of switching his own hands (*Rabbi Elimelech of Lyzhansk, 18th century*).

15-16. He blessed Joseph and said ... "Bless these lads!" In the following verses, Jacob only blesses Joseph's two sons, Manasseh and Ephraim. Why does the verse state "He blessed *Joseph*?"

The biggest blessing for a father is that his children will be successful. So Jacob's blessing to Manasseh and Ephraim, *"May the angel whom (You always sent) to redeem me from all harm bless these lads!"* was really a blessing for Joseph as well (*Naḥmanides, 13th century*).

19. His children('s fame) will spread throughout the nations. When did Ephraim's descendants become famous throughout the nations? When Joshua, who was descended from Ephraim, said, *"Sun, stand still at Gibeon, and moon, in the valley of Aijalon"* (Joshua 10:12). When the sun stood still, Joshua's fame spread to all the nations (*Babylonian Talmud, Avodah Zarah 25a*).

20. May God make you like Ephraim and Manasseh. Jacob blessed the children of Israel with strength to flourish in exile when their spirituality would be

> **kabbalah bites**
>
> **48:14** Joseph's wife, Asenath, was the child produced from Shechem's unlawful union with Dinah (above 34:2; she was later adopted by Potiphar). Asenath was thus half *kedushah* (holiness), from her innocent mother, and half *kelippah* (evil), from her father.
>
> Her *kelippah* was passed onto her firstborn, Manasseh, whereas Ephraim, her second child, inherited her *kedushah*. Recognizing this spiritual blemish, Jacob switched hands to give preference to Ephraim.

genesis 48:14–20 — va-yehi

¹⁴ But Israel stretched out his right hand and placed it on Ephraim's head, although he was the younger, and (he placed) his left hand on Manasseh's head. He guided his hands deliberately (in full awareness) that Manasseh was the firstborn.

¹⁵ He blessed Joseph and said, "O God, before whom my fathers Abraham and Isaac walked! O God, who has looked after me from my birth to this day! ¹⁶ May the angel whom (You always sent) to redeem me from all harm bless these lads! May they be called by my name and the name of my fathers, Abraham and Isaac, and may they increase in the land like fish!"

[THIRD READING] ¹⁷ When Joseph saw that his father was placing his right hand on Ephraim's head, he became upset. So he lifted up his father's hand, removing it from upon Ephraim's head (in order to place it) on Manasseh's head. ¹⁸ Joseph said to his father, "Father, that's not right! This one is the firstborn. Put your right hand on his head!"

¹⁹ But his father refused. He said, "I know, my son (that he is the firstborn), I know. He too will father a nation, and he too will be great. But his younger brother will be greater than him, and his children('s fame) will spread throughout the nations."

²⁰ He blessed them on that day, saying, "(The children of) Israel will (always) bless (their children) with your (names), saying, 'May God make you like Ephraim and Manasseh.'" He placed Ephraim before Manasseh (in his blessing, to indicate that he would take precedence in the order of tribes).

---

14. His right hand and placed it on Ephraim's head … and his left hand on Manasseh's head. Manasseh—*Menasheh*, in Hebrew—received his name because, *"God has caused me to forget (NaSHani) all my hardships and all that was in my father's house"* (41:51). This expressed how Joseph was pained to find himself in a place which made him forget his father's house. Ephraim was named, because *"God has made me fruitful (hiPH'Rani) in the land of my subjugation"* (ibid., v. 52), expressing how Joseph had succeeded in Egypt.

Manasseh and Ephraim represent two approaches to the Exile. One approach is *transcendence*, to long to leave the Exile and return to your "father's house." The other is *action*, to realize that there is a mission to be carried out there and to toil to succeed.

Manasseh was the firstborn because *first of all* you need to feel "out of place" in exile, to ensure that you do not become seduced by it. But the primary purpose of being in exile is to *succeed* in your spiritual mission here—which is why Jacob wished to bless Ephraim first (*Rabbi Elimelech of Lyzhansk, 18ᵗʰ century*).

He guided his hands deliberately (in full awareness) that Manasseh was the firstborn. Rendered literally, the verse reads, "He switched his hands *because* Manasseh was the firstborn." The logic seems inverted here: the verse should have said that he switched his hands *despite the fact* that Manasseh was older.

But the Torah wishes to teach us a lesson in respectful behavior. Jacob could have easily *moved the boys themselves* into the desired positions, but this would have embarrassed

בראשית מח:כ - מט:ד / ויחי

וַיָּשֶׂם אֶת־אֶפְרַיִם לִפְנֵי מְנַשֶּׁה: 21 וַיֹּאמֶר יִשְׂרָאֵל אֶל־יוֹסֵף הִנֵּה אָנֹכִי מֵת וְהָיָה אֱלֹהִים עִמָּכֶם וְהֵשִׁיב אֶתְכֶם אֶל־אֶרֶץ אֲבֹתֵיכֶם: 22 וַאֲנִי נָתַתִּי לְךָ שְׁכֶם אַחַד עַל־אַחֶיךָ אֲשֶׁר לָקַחְתִּי מִיַּד הָאֱמֹרִי בְּחַרְבִּי וּבְקַשְׁתִּי: פ

מט 1 וַיִּקְרָא יַעֲקֹב אֶל־בָּנָיו וַיֹּאמֶר הֵאָסְפוּ וְאַגִּידָה לָכֶם [FOURTH READING] אֵת אֲשֶׁר־יִקְרָא אֶתְכֶם בְּאַחֲרִית הַיָּמִים: הִקָּבְצוּ וְשִׁמְעוּ בְּנֵי יַעֲקֹב וְשִׁמְעוּ אֶל־יִשְׂרָאֵל אֲבִיכֶם: 3 רְאוּבֵן בְּכֹרִי אַתָּה כֹּחִי וְרֵאשִׁית אוֹנִי יֶתֶר שְׂאֵת וְיֶתֶר עָז: 4 פַּחַז כַּמַּיִם אַל־תּוֹתַר כִּי עָלִיתָ מִשְׁכְּבֵי אָבִיךָ אָז חִלַּלְתָּ

with the words *"And this is the blessing"* (Deuteronomy 33:1), because it was clear to him at the outset what he was going to say.)

The Torah only states that Jacob "blessed them" *after* he finished speaking (v. 28), when it was clear to him that all the blessings were from God (*Rabbi Mordecai Joseph Leiner of Izbica, 19th century*).

Gather round and I will tell you what will happen to you at the End of Days. Jacob wanted to disclose to his sons the "End of Days," when the Messiah would come, but the *Shekhinah* (Divine Presence) departed from him, so he began to speak about other things (*Rashi, 11th century*).

When Jacob perceived the terrible persecution that his descendants would have to suffer before the Messiah would eventually come, he became deeply dejected. That is why the *Shekhinah* departed from him, because a prophetic spirit will not dwell amid sadness and depression (*Rabbi Naphtali Zevi Horowitz of Ropczyce, 18th century*).

Jacob asked his sons to *"gather round,"* to unite together. Through this you will merit *"the End of Days"* (*Rabbi Judah Aryeh Leib Alter of Gur, 19th century*).

3-4. Reuben ... you will not be privileged. You were fit to be superior over your brothers with the priesthood and with kingship, but you hastened to display your anger—similar to water which hastens on its course. Therefore *"you will not be privileged"*—you will no longer receive all these superior positions that were fit for you.

What was the restlessness that you exhibited? You interfered with your father's bed (above, 35:22). You profaned the *Shekhinah* (Divine Presence), which would rest on my bed (*Rashi, 11th century*).

Reuben's error was the aggressive and hostile manner in which he carried out his plan, which offended his father. This proved that he was unfit for the privileges of royalty, which demand a sensitivity to the feelings of other people (*Rabbi Isaac Abravanel, 15th century*).

312

> **kabbalah bites**
>
> **49:1** There were three who erred in attempting to predict the End of Days: Jacob, Samuel (*I Samuel 16:6*), and Rabbi Akiva, who deemed Bar Kokhba to be the Messiah. (Thus *'AKYVa'* and *Ya'AKoV* (Jacob) share the same Hebrew letters.) They all needed to be reincarnated to achieve *tikkun* (spiritual healing) for this mistake.

²¹ Israel said to Joseph, "Look, I'm going to die. God will be with you, and He will bring you back to the land of your fathers. ²² (Since you are taking the trouble to bury me) I have given you one portion more than your brothers, (the city) of Shechem, which I took from the hand of the Amorites with my sword and with my bow (when they waged war against us after Simeon and Levi killed the people of Shechem)."

Jacob Blesses His Sons Before Passing Away

49 [FOURTH READING] ¹ Jacob called for his sons and said, "Gather round and I will tell you what will happen to you at the End of Days" (but Jacob found himself unable to reveal the time when the Messiah would come, so he changed the subject).

² (He said,) "Sons of Jacob, gather round and listen. Listen to Israel, your father!

³ "Reuben, you are my firstborn, my strength, (conceived from) my first (drop) of vigor. (You were worthy of being) privileged with priesthood and privileged with kingship. ⁴ (But because of your reckless) haste (which was) like (running) water,

---

challenged. He blessed that they should have the qualities of Ephraim and Manasseh who were born, raised and educated in exile and nevertheless remained loyal to Jacob's ways (*Rabbi Zalman b. Ben-Zion Sorotzkin, 20th century*).

When Jacob blessed his grandchildren, he placed his hand on Ephraim first, even though Ephraim was younger than Manasseh. This prompted the two brothers to display their exemplary qualities: Manasseh did not become envious of his brother, and Ephraim showed no feelings of pride or superiority. On seeing this, Jacob blessed his children that all their descendants should emulate these traits, conducting themselves without envy or arrogance (*Rabbi Tzvi Elimelech of Dynow, 19th century*).

49:1 Jacob called for his sons. Though Jacob wanted to bless his sons, he was doubtful whether he should bless them after the pain they had caused him through the sale of Joseph. Therefore the verse states that he "called," implying a longing of the heart. He surrendered his heart to God and simply said whatever God put in his mouth.

Thus the verse does not say "Jacob called for his sons *to bless them*," because it was not yet clear to him what he was going to say. (Moses, on the other hand, did begin his final speech

spiritual vitamin

> Good teaching starts a chain reaction. Eventually the students themselves become sources of influence, whether as teachers or in other active capacities, with the same enthusiasm and inspiration.

בראשית מט:ד-י

יְצוּעִי עָלָה: פ 5 שִׁמְעוֹן וְלֵוִי אַחִים כְּלֵי חָמָס מְכֵרֹתֵיהֶם: 6 בְּסֹדָם אַל־תָּבֹא נַפְשִׁי בִּקְהָלָם אַל־תֵּחַד כְּבֹדִי כִּי בְאַפָּם הָרְגוּ אִישׁ וּבִרְצֹנָם עִקְּרוּ־שׁוֹר: 7 אָרוּר אַפָּם כִּי עָז וְעֶבְרָתָם כִּי קָשָׁתָה אֲחַלְּקֵם בְּיַעֲקֹב וַאֲפִיצֵם בְּיִשְׂרָאֵל: פ 8 יְהוּדָה אַתָּה יוֹדוּךָ אַחֶיךָ יָדְךָ בְּעֹרֶף אֹיְבֶיךָ יִשְׁתַּחֲווּ לְךָ בְּנֵי אָבִיךָ: 9 גּוּר אַרְיֵה יְהוּדָה מִטֶּרֶף בְּנִי עָלִיתָ כָּרַע רָבַץ כְּאַרְיֵה וּכְלָבִיא מִי יְקִימֶנּוּ: 10 לֹא־יָסוּר שֵׁבֶט מִיהוּדָה וּמְחֹקֵק מִבֵּין רַגְלָיו עַד כִּי־יָבֹא שִׁילֹה וְלוֹ יִקְּהַת עַמִּים:

7. Cursed be their wrath, for it is powerful, and their rage, for it is callous. Both Simeon and Levi had acted with the very best of intentions when eliminating the inhabitants of Shechem—they were defending the honor of their sister Dinah. But despite their good will, Jacob now condemned their anger. Learn to calm your anger even if you think you have the very best of intentions (*Rabbi Samson Raphael Hirsch, 19th century*).

9. You withdrew yourself. "You withdrew yourself and said, *"What will we gain if we kill our brother and hide his blood?"* (37:26). Also, in the case of Tamar's execution, he confessed, *"She's right (in what she says). She became pregnant) from me (justifiably)"* (38:26; *Rashi, 11th century*).

While *on a personal level* Reuben's attempts to save Joseph (see 37:21-22) and the intensity of his repentance were more impressive than Judah's (see *Rashi* to 37:29)—nevertheless, with regards to the effect on *other people,* Judah's efforts were vastly superior.

Judah *actually saved Joseph's life,* whereas Reuben did not. And Judah's few seconds of repentance saved Tamar's life, whereas Reuben's nine years of repentance did not bring benefit to anybody but himself. In fact, if Reuben would not have been so "busy with his sackcloth and fasting," *he might have been able to save Joseph* while the brothers were busy eating a meal (37:25).

Consequently, when Reuben was denied the privileges of priesthood and royalty for his insensitivity to others, royalty was granted to Judah. For Judah had demonstrated, more than all the other brothers, an ability to actually help other people (*Rabbi Menahem Mendel Schneerson, 20th century*).

kabbalah bites

49:8 According to the teachings of the Kabbalah:

Reuben = *spiritual hunger;*

Simeon = *recoiling in terror from sensing awesomeness;*

Levi = *attachment through reading sacred texts;*

Judah = *submission, release from the ego.*

"Judah! Your brothers will acknowledge you"—the spiritual mode of Judah is superior to that of your brothers.

when you interfered with your father's bed, you will not be privileged. (For) then, you desecrated (the Divine Presence which) rested above my bed.

⁵ "Simeon and Levi are (the) brothers (who plotted against Shechem and against Joseph too. Their murderous use of) weapons has been stolen (from Esau).

⁶ "(When the tribe of Simeon will conspire against Moses), do not let my own (name) be mentioned with their conspiracy!

"(When Levi's great-grandson Korah and his colleagues will rebel against Moses) do not let my honorable (name) be associated with their (rebellious) congregation!

(Simeon and Levi) killed (every) man (in Shechem) to vent their anger, and they willingly (attempted) to maim (Joseph who is like) an ox, (the king of animals). ⁷ Cursed be their wrath, for it is powerful, and their rage, for it is callous. I will separate them (by denying Levi a share in the land, like the other sons) of Jacob, and I will scatter (both of) them throughout Israel (since the tribe of Levi will be searching for tithes, and the tribe of Simeon's source of income will cause them to spread out)."

⁸ (When Judah saw that Jacob was rebuking his sons he drew back, so Jacob called out to him), "Judah! You (are not like them)! Your brothers will acknowledge you (as their leader). Your hand will be on the neck of your enemies. Your father's sons will bow down to you. ⁹ (From) Judah (King David will emerge, first as) a lion cub (during Saul's reign, and then a fully grown) lion (when he becomes king for himself).

"(Even though I suspected you of the plot) to tear (Joseph like) prey, you withdrew yourself (from the plot), my son, (and you refrained from killing Tamar. Therefore, your descendant King Solomon will) crouch, and rest like a lion (while the Jewish people dwell in safety. No nation) will dare intimidate him, as if (he were) a lion.

¹⁰ "(The) stick (of authority) will never leave Judah, nor scholars from the feet (of his descendants), until the coming (of the Messiah)—to whom (kingship) belongs. He will gather the people.

kabbalah bites

49:5 Jacob did not bless Simeon and Levi because they were from the side of *Gevurah* (severity), and if these forces would be intensified the world could not endure them. Rather, Jacob joined these *Gevurot* with the left side of the *Shekhinah* (Divine Presence) so as to soften and sweeten them.

What parts of your personality come from *Gevurah*? Can your world endure them? How might you be able to sweeten them?

ויחי   בראשית מט:יא-כד

11 אֹסְרִ֤י לַגֶּ֙פֶן֙ עִיר֔וֹ וְלַשֹּׂרֵקָ֖ה בְּנִ֣י אֲתֹנ֑וֹ כִּבֵּ֤ס בַּיַּ֙יִן֙ לְבֻשׁ֔וֹ וּבְדַם־עֲנָבִ֖ים סוּתֹֽה: 12 חַכְלִילִ֥י עֵינַ֖יִם מִיָּ֑יִן וּלְבֶן־שִׁנַּ֖יִם מֵחָלָֽב: פ 13 זְבוּלֻ֕ן לְח֥וֹף יַמִּ֖ים יִשְׁכֹּ֑ן וְהוּא֙ לְח֣וֹף אֳנִיּ֔וֹת וְיַרְכָת֖וֹ עַל־צִידֹֽן: פ 14 יִשָּׂשכָ֖ר חֲמֹ֣ר גָּ֑רֶם רֹבֵ֖ץ בֵּ֥ין הַֽמִּשְׁפְּתָֽיִם: 15 וַיַּ֤רְא מְנֻחָה֙ כִּ֣י ט֔וֹב וְאֶת־הָאָ֖רֶץ כִּ֣י נָעֵ֑מָה וַיֵּ֤ט שִׁכְמוֹ֙ לִסְבֹּ֔ל וַיְהִ֖י לְמַס־עֹבֵֽד: ס 16 דָּ֖ן יָדִ֣ין עַמּ֑וֹ כְּאַחַ֖ד שִׁבְטֵ֥י יִשְׂרָאֵֽל: 17 יְהִי־דָן֙ נָחָ֣שׁ עֲלֵי־דֶ֔רֶךְ שְׁפִיפֹ֖ן עֲלֵי־אֹ֑רַח הַנֹּשֵׁךְ֙ עִקְּבֵי־ס֔וּס וַיִּפֹּ֥ל רֹֽכְב֖וֹ אָחֽוֹר: 18 לִֽישׁוּעָתְךָ֖ קִוִּ֥יתִי יְהוָֽה: ס 19 [FIFTH READING] גָּ֖ד גְּד֣וּד יְגוּדֶ֑נּוּ וְה֖וּא יָגֻ֥ד עָקֵֽב: ס 20 מֵאָשֵׁ֖ר שְׁמֵנָ֣ה לַחְמ֑וֹ וְה֥וּא יִתֵּ֖ן מַֽעֲדַנֵּי־מֶֽלֶךְ: ס 21 נַפְתָּלִ֖י אַיָּלָ֣ה שְׁלֻחָ֑ה הַנֹּתֵ֖ן אִמְרֵי־שָֽׁפֶר: ס 22 בֵּ֤ן פֹּרָת֙ יוֹסֵ֔ף בֵּ֥ן פֹּרָ֖ת עֲלֵי־עָ֑יִן בָּנ֕וֹת צָעֲדָ֖ה עֲלֵי־שֽׁוּר: 23 וַֽיְמָרֲרֻ֖הוּ וָרֹ֑בּוּ וַֽיִּשְׂטְמֻ֖הוּ בַּעֲלֵ֥י חִצִּֽים: 24 וַתֵּ֤שֶׁב בְּאֵיתָן֙ קַשְׁתּ֔וֹ וַיָּפֹ֖זּוּ זְרֹעֵ֣י יָדָ֑יו מִידֵי֙ אֲבִ֣יר יַעֲקֹ֔ב מִשָּׁ֥ם

13. Zebulun will live (in his territory) by the sea coast. Zebulun is mentioned first, even though his brother and partner, Issachar, was older. The two brothers had a partnership where Issachar studied Torah for both of them, and Zebulun supported both of them. By blessing Zebulun first, Jacob hinted that supporting those who study Torah carries a greater reward than studying it (*Rabbi Isaac b. Joseph Caro, 15th century*).

The majority of the Jewish people fall into the category of Zebulun, rather than Issachar. Since this state of affairs is Divinely orchestrated, it follows that God's plan for creation must be carried out to a greater extent by the businessman than the Torah scholar—for otherwise, God would have made a world with more Torah scholars than businessmen. This is because the ultimate purpose of creation is that *"God desired a home in the lowest realms"* (*Midrash Tanḥuma*), and it is predominantly the businessman who works in those "lowest realms," with the intention of elevating them to a higher purpose (*Rabbi Menaḥem Mendel Schneerson, 20th century*).

16. Dan will enact vengeance for his people. The tribe of Dan was well populated, and they traveled in convoy. If anyone lost property, they would return it (*Rashi, 11th century*).

spiritual vitamin

> You come into this world with a certain spiritual heritage that you received from your people. The perpetuation of this heritage is not a matter of pure benevolence or philanthropy, but the discharge of a debt and an obligation.

¹¹ "(In Judah's territory, wine will flow like a fountain such that) a man will harness his donkey to a (single) vine, or a young donkey to a (single) vine branch (and it will already be loaded to capacity). (There will be so much wine that a person could) wash his clothes with wine, and his robe with grape juice. ¹² (People will be) red-eyed from wine and white-toothed from (the abundance of) milk.

¹³ "Zebulun will live (in his territory) by the sea coast. He (will be) at the ships' port (doing business). The end of his territory will be at Zidon.

¹⁴ "Issachar is (like) a donkey with strong bones (because he bears the yoke of Torah. Like a donkey that journeys day and night) resting (temporarily) between the city borders (the Torah scholar cannot rest day or night from Torah study).

¹⁵ "(Issachar) will see that his portion (in the land of Israel) is good, and that the land is fertile (so he will not have to work hard. Consequently), he will bend his shoulders down to bear (the yoke of Torah) and he will pay his dues by serving (the rest of the Jewish people, teaching Torah Law).

¹⁶ "Dan will exact vengeance for his people (against the Philistines) and the tribes of Israel will be as one (with him). ¹⁷ Samson, a descendant of) Dan will be a serpent on the road, a viper on the path, who bites the horse's heels, so its rider falls backwards (without even having to fight with the rider). ¹⁸ (But when Samson will be overcome by his enemies, he will say) 'I hope for your salvation, O God!'

[FIFTH READING] ¹⁹ "(As for) Gad, troops will troop forth from him (over the Jordan river to conquer the land). They will troop back in their own tracks (to the lands of their inheritance on the other side of the Jordan, and not one man will be missing from them).

²⁰ "From Asher('s land) will come rich food, and he will provide royal delicacies.

²¹ "Naphtali('s land) will yield fruit like) a gazelle (that has just been freed and) runs quickly, for which (the people) will give thanks and blessing.

²² "Joseph is a charming son, a son whose charm impresses the eye (that sees him. Egyptian) girls would step (along a wall) to gaze at his (beauty. ²³ His brothers) made him bitter, quarreled with him and hated him. (They were) men (with tongues) like arrows. ²⁴ But (in spite of that) his power was firmly established and (a golden ring) was placed on his finger, through the hands of (God), the Mighty One of Jacob, and from there (he rose) to royalty (and was) the provider of Israel.

---

food for thought

1. How often do you bless your children?

2. What would you like future generations to inherit from you?

3. Why does the Torah lend such importance to giving and receiving blessings?

בראשית מט:כד - נ:ד | ויחי

רֹעֶה אֶבֶן יִשְׂרָאֵל: 25 מֵאֵל אָבִיךָ וְיַעְזְרֶךָּ וְאֵת שַׁדַּי וִיבָרֲכֶךָּ בִּרְכֹת שָׁמַיִם מֵעָל בִּרְכֹת תְּהוֹם רֹבֶצֶת תָּחַת בִּרְכֹת שָׁדַיִם וָרָחַם: 26 בִּרְכֹת אָבִיךָ גָּבְרוּ עַל־בִּרְכֹת הוֹרַי עַד־תַּאֲוַת גִּבְעֹת עוֹלָם תִּהְיֶיןָ לְרֹאשׁ יוֹסֵף וּלְקָדְקֹד נְזִיר אֶחָיו: פ

[SIXTH READING] 27 בִּנְיָמִין זְאֵב יִטְרָף בַּבֹּקֶר יֹאכַל עַד וְלָעֶרֶב יְחַלֵּק שָׁלָל: 28 כָּל־אֵלֶּה שִׁבְטֵי יִשְׂרָאֵל שְׁנֵים עָשָׂר וְזֹאת אֲשֶׁר־דִּבֶּר לָהֶם אֲבִיהֶם וַיְבָרֶךְ אוֹתָם אִישׁ אֲשֶׁר כְּבִרְכָתוֹ בֵּרַךְ אֹתָם: 29 וַיְצַו אוֹתָם וַיֹּאמֶר אֲלֵהֶם אֲנִי נֶאֱסָף אֶל־עַמִּי קִבְרוּ אֹתִי אֶל־אֲבֹתָי אֶל־הַמְּעָרָה אֲשֶׁר בִּשְׂדֵה עֶפְרוֹן הַחִתִּי: 30 בַּמְּעָרָה אֲשֶׁר בִּשְׂדֵה הַמַּכְפֵּלָה אֲשֶׁר־עַל־פְּנֵי־מַמְרֵא בְּאֶרֶץ כְּנַעַן אֲשֶׁר קָנָה אַבְרָהָם אֶת־הַשָּׂדֶה מֵאֵת עֶפְרֹן הַחִתִּי לַאֲחֻזַּת־קָבֶר: 31 שָׁמָּה קָבְרוּ אֶת־אַבְרָהָם וְאֵת שָׂרָה אִשְׁתּוֹ שָׁמָּה קָבְרוּ אֶת־יִצְחָק וְאֵת רִבְקָה אִשְׁתּוֹ וְשָׁמָּה קָבַרְתִּי אֶת־לֵאָה: 32 מִקְנֵה הַשָּׂדֶה וְהַמְּעָרָה אֲשֶׁר־בּוֹ מֵאֵת בְּנֵי־חֵת: 33 וַיְכַל יַעֲקֹב לְצַוֹּת אֶת־בָּנָיו וַיֶּאֱסֹף רַגְלָיו אֶל־הַמִּטָּה וַיִּגְוַע וַיֵּאָסֶף אֶל־עַמָּיו:

נ 1 וַיִּפֹּל יוֹסֵף עַל־פְּנֵי אָבִיו וַיֵּבְךְּ עָלָיו וַיִּשַּׁק־לוֹ: 2 וַיְצַו יוֹסֵף אֶת־עֲבָדָיו אֶת־הָרֹפְאִים לַחֲנֹט אֶת־אָבִיו וַיַּחַנְטוּ הָרֹפְאִים אֶת־יִשְׂרָאֵל: 3 וַיִּמְלְאוּ־לוֹ אַרְבָּעִים יוֹם כִּי כֵּן יִמְלְאוּ יְמֵי הַחֲנֻטִים וַיִּבְכּוּ אֹתוֹ מִצְרַיִם שִׁבְעִים יוֹם: 4 וַיַּעַבְרוּ

27. Benjamin is a wolf. A *tzaddik* (righteous person) causes God to be revealed in this world. Generally speaking, there are two possible ways of achieving this goal: One approach is for the *tzaddik* to act as a holy "channel" through which Godly revelation is brought *into* the world from the heavens above. A second approach is for the *tzaddik* to work *with* the lower realms, transforming and elevating them.

This is the key distinction between Rachel's two sons, Joseph and Benjamin. Both were *tzaddikim* who brought revelation to the world. But Joseph was the "upper *tzaddik*" who channeled that revelation from heaven to earth, whereas Benjamin was the "lower *tzaddik*" who worked to render the earth itself receptive to spirituality (*Zohar*).

33. Jacob … breathed his last, and he was gathered into his people. The Torah makes no mention of Jacob's actual "death" (*Rashi*, 11th century).

Rabbi Johanan said, "Jacob our father never died!"

Rabbi Naḥman asked, "Was it for nothing that they eulogized, embalmed, and buried him?"

²⁵ "(All this came to you) from the God of your father, and He will (continue to) help you. (Your heart was) with God (when you refused to listen to Potiphar's wife, and therefore) He will bless you (with) the blessings of the heavens above, and the blessings of the depths that lie below, the blessings that fathers and mothers (need).

²⁶ "The blessings (which God gave) to your father surpassed the blessings (which He gave) to my parents, (for He gave me an unlimited blessing, reaching) to the end of the world's hills. May (all these blessings) be on Joseph's head, the man who was separated from his brothers.

[SIXTH READING] ²⁷ "Benjamin('s descendants will be 'grabbers,' like) a wolf that (grabs and) tears his prey. (From him, Saul will arise) in the morning (of Israel's history and) he will devour plunder. In the evening (of Israel's history, Benjamin's descendants, Mordecai and Esther) will divide the spoil (of Haman)."

²⁸ These are all the twelve tribes of Israel, and this is what their father spoke to them.

(In addition to rebuking Reuben, Simeon and Levi,) he blessed them (too. He blessed each son) with the blessing (that befitted) him, (and) he (also) blessed (all of his sons with all of the blessings, in general).

Jacob Passes Away

²⁹ He instructed them, saying to them, "I (will soon die and my soul) will be gathered in to (be with the souls of) my people. Bury me with my fathers in the cave which is in Ephron the Hittite's field, ³⁰ in the cave that's in the field of Machpelah, facing Mamre in the land of Canaan—the field which Abraham bought from Ephron the Hittite as a burial plot. ³¹ They buried Abraham and his wife Sarah there, they buried Isaac and his wife Rebekah there, and I buried Leah there. ³² The purchase of the field, and its cave, from the sons of Het (still stands)."

³³ As Jacob finished commanding his sons, he gathered his legs onto the bed, breathed his last, and his (soul) was gathered in to (be with the souls of) his people.

Jacob's Burial

50
¹ Joseph fell on his father's face, wept over him and kissed him.

² Joseph commanded his staff of physicians to embalm his father, and the physicians embalmed Israel (with spices). ³ After forty days—which is how long embalming takes—the Egyptians mourned him for (a further thirty days, totaling) seventy days.

⁴ When the period of mourning for him had passed, Joseph spoke to Pharaoh's

בראשית נ:ד-יד

יְמֵי בְכִיתוֹ וַיְדַבֵּר יוֹסֵף אֶל־בֵּית פַּרְעֹה לֵאמֹר אִם־נָא מָצָאתִי חֵן בְּעֵינֵיכֶם דַּבְּרוּ־נָא בְּאָזְנֵי פַרְעֹה לֵאמֹר: 5 אָבִי הִשְׁבִּיעַנִי לֵאמֹר הִנֵּה אָנֹכִי מֵת בְּקִבְרִי אֲשֶׁר כָּרִיתִי לִי בְּאֶרֶץ כְּנַעַן שָׁמָּה תִּקְבְּרֵנִי וְעַתָּה אֶעֱלֶה־נָּא וְאֶקְבְּרָה אֶת־אָבִי וְאָשׁוּבָה: 6 וַיֹּאמֶר פַּרְעֹה עֲלֵה וּקְבֹר אֶת־אָבִיךָ כַּאֲשֶׁר הִשְׁבִּיעֶךָ: 7 וַיַּעַל יוֹסֵף לִקְבֹּר אֶת־אָבִיו וַיַּעֲלוּ אִתּוֹ כָּל־עַבְדֵי פַרְעֹה זִקְנֵי בֵיתוֹ וְכֹל זִקְנֵי אֶרֶץ־מִצְרָיִם: 8 וְכֹל בֵּית יוֹסֵף וְאֶחָיו וּבֵית אָבִיו רַק טַפָּם וְצֹאנָם וּבְקָרָם עָזְבוּ בְּאֶרֶץ גֹּשֶׁן: 9 וַיַּעַל עִמּוֹ גַּם־רֶכֶב גַּם־פָּרָשִׁים וַיְהִי הַמַּחֲנֶה כָּבֵד מְאֹד: 10 וַיָּבֹאוּ עַד־גֹּרֶן הָאָטָד אֲשֶׁר בְּעֵבֶר הַיַּרְדֵּן וַיִּסְפְּדוּ־שָׁם מִסְפֵּד גָּדוֹל וְכָבֵד מְאֹד וַיַּעַשׂ לְאָבִיו אֵבֶל שִׁבְעַת יָמִים: 11 וַיַּרְא יוֹשֵׁב הָאָרֶץ הַכְּנַעֲנִי אֶת־הָאֵבֶל בְּגֹרֶן הָאָטָד וַיֹּאמְרוּ אֵבֶל־כָּבֵד זֶה לְמִצְרָיִם עַל־כֵּן קָרָא שְׁמָהּ אָבֵל מִצְרַיִם אֲשֶׁר בְּעֵבֶר הַיַּרְדֵּן: 12 וַיַּעֲשׂוּ בָנָיו לוֹ כֵּן כַּאֲשֶׁר צִוָּם: 13 וַיִּשְׂאוּ אֹתוֹ בָנָיו אַרְצָה כְּנַעַן וַיִּקְבְּרוּ אֹתוֹ בִּמְעָרַת שְׂדֵה הַמַּכְפֵּלָה אֲשֶׁר קָנָה אַבְרָהָם אֶת־הַשָּׂדֶה לַאֲחֻזַּת־קֶבֶר מֵאֵת עֶפְרֹן הַחִתִּי עַל־פְּנֵי מַמְרֵא: 14 וַיָּשָׁב יוֹסֵף מִצְרַיְמָה הוּא וְאֶחָיו וְכָל־

50:5 My father bound me by an oath, saying, "Look, I am (soon) going to die. You should bury me in my grave which I dug for myself in the land of Canaan." An Egyptian monarch was required to know all the languages of the world. When Joseph was appointed viceroy of Egypt, he had already mastered every language, and, surprisingly, when he addressed Pharaoh in Hebrew, Pharaoh did not understand. Pharaoh made Joseph swear not to reveal this secret to anyone, as it would disqualify him from being the ruler of Egypt.

Years later, when Joseph asked Pharaoh for temporary leave to take his father's remains to the land of Israel, saying, *"My father bound me by an oath,"* Pharaoh retorted, "Go and ask the Sages to release you from your oath!"

"In that case," Joseph responded, "I will also ask to be released from my oath not to reveal your ignorance of Hebrew."

Hearing this, Pharaoh conceded, *"Go and bury your father, as he had you swear"* (50:6; *Babylonian Talmud, Sotah* 36b).

13. His sons carried him. Not all of Jacob's sons carried his coffin. Jacob ordered, "Levi shall not carry it because he (i.e. his tribe), is destined to carry the ark. Joseph shall not carry it because he is a king. Manasseh and Ephraim shall carry it instead of them" (*Rashi, 11th century*).

household, saying, "If I have now found favor in your eyes, speak now directly to Pharaoh and tell him, ⁵ (that) my father bound me by an oath, saying, 'Look, I am (soon) going to die. You should bury me in my grave which I dug for myself in the land of Canaan.' So now, please let me go and bury my father, then I'll return."

⁶ "Go and bury your father," Pharaoh said, "as he had you swear."

⁷ So Joseph went to bury his father. All Pharaoh's servants, the senior members of his house, and all the senior (ministers) of the land of Egypt went with him, ⁸ together with Joseph's entire household, his brothers and his father's household. They only left behind their young children, flocks and cattle in the land of Goshen. ⁹ Chariots and horsemen also went along, so the entourage was very large.

¹⁰ When they reached Goren ha-Atad, which is on the other side of the Jordan, they made a very grandiose and intense eulogy there. Then (Joseph) designated a mourning period of seven days for his father.

¹¹ When the Canaanites, the local inhabitants, saw the mourning at Goren ha-Atad they said, "This is an intense mourning for the Egyptians." Therefore, they named (the place), which is on the other side of the Jordan, Abel-mizraim ("Mourning of Egypt").

¹² (Jacob's) sons did for him exactly as he had instructed them (not to allow any Egyptian or even one of Jacob's grandsons to carry him). ¹³ His sons carried him to the land of Canaan, and they buried him in the cave that is in the field of Machpelah, facing Mamre—the field which Abraham had bought for a burial plot from Ephron the Hittite.

¹⁴ After he had buried his father, Joseph returned to Egypt—both he, his brothers, and all those who had gone with him to bury his father.

Rabbi Isaac replied, "I derive it from Scripture: *'But you have no fear, My servant Jacob ... I will deliver you from far away and your children from the land of captivity'* (*Jeremiah* 30:10). The verse equates Jacob with his children, the Jewish people. Just as his children are alive, so too, he is alive (*Babylonian Talmud, Ta'anit* 5b).

spiritual vitamin

> The descent of your soul is for the purpose of ascent. There is no other way to obtain this goal except through your soul's descent to live on this earth. If there were an easier way, God would not compel your soul to descend from the sublime heights of the Seat of Glory down to this, the lowest of all worlds.

בראשית נ:יד-כה

הָעֹלִים אִתּוֹ לִקְבֹּר אֶת־אָבִיו אַחֲרֵי קָבְרוֹ אֶת־אָבִיו: 15 וַיִּרְאוּ אֲחֵי־יוֹסֵף כִּי־מֵת אֲבִיהֶם וַיֹּאמְרוּ לוּ יִשְׂטְמֵנוּ יוֹסֵף וְהָשֵׁב יָשִׁיב לָנוּ אֵת כָּל־הָרָעָה אֲשֶׁר גָּמַלְנוּ אֹתוֹ: 16 וַיְצַוּוּ אֶל־יוֹסֵף לֵאמֹר אָבִיךָ צִוָּה לִפְנֵי מוֹתוֹ לֵאמֹר: 17 כֹּה־תֹאמְרוּ לְיוֹסֵף אָנָּא שָׂא נָא פֶּשַׁע אַחֶיךָ וְחַטָּאתָם כִּי־רָעָה גְמָלוּךָ וְעַתָּה שָׂא נָא לְפֶשַׁע עַבְדֵי אֱלֹהֵי אָבִיךָ וַיֵּבְךְּ יוֹסֵף בְּדַבְּרָם אֵלָיו: 18 וַיֵּלְכוּ גַּם־אֶחָיו וַיִּפְּלוּ לְפָנָיו וַיֹּאמְרוּ הִנֶּנּוּ לְךָ לַעֲבָדִים: 19 וַיֹּאמֶר אֲלֵהֶם יוֹסֵף אַל־תִּירָאוּ כִּי הֲתַחַת אֱלֹהִים אָנִי: 20 וְאַתֶּם חֲשַׁבְתֶּם עָלַי רָעָה אֱלֹהִים חֲשָׁבָהּ לְטֹבָה לְמַעַן עֲשֹׂה כַּיּוֹם הַזֶּה לְהַחֲיֹת עַם־רָב: [SEVENTH READING] 21 וְעַתָּה אַל־תִּירָאוּ אָנֹכִי אֲכַלְכֵּל אֶתְכֶם וְאֶת־טַפְּכֶם וַיְנַחֵם אוֹתָם וַיְדַבֵּר עַל־לִבָּם: 22 וַיֵּשֶׁב יוֹסֵף בְּמִצְרַיִם הוּא וּבֵית אָבִיו וַיְחִי יוֹסֵף מֵאָה וָעֶשֶׂר שָׁנִים: [MAFTIR] 23 וַיַּרְא יוֹסֵף לְאֶפְרַיִם בְּנֵי שִׁלֵּשִׁים גַּם בְּנֵי מָכִיר בֶּן־מְנַשֶּׁה יֻלְּדוּ עַל־בִּרְכֵּי יוֹסֵף: 24 וַיֹּאמֶר יוֹסֵף אֶל־אֶחָיו אָנֹכִי מֵת וֵאלֹהִים פָּקֹד יִפְקֹד אֶתְכֶם וְהֶעֱלָה אֶתְכֶם מִן־הָאָרֶץ הַזֹּאת אֶל־הָאָרֶץ אֲשֶׁר נִשְׁבַּע לְאַבְרָהָם לְיִצְחָק וּלְיַעֲקֹב: 25 וַיַּשְׁבַּע יוֹסֵף אֶת־בְּנֵי יִשְׂרָאֵל

was able to remain strongly connected with God and, at the same time, be heavily involved in the running of a country.

When the brothers came to Egypt, they were no longer able to live a life of total seclusion, and they were forced to have more involvement with worldly matters. Consequently, their relationship with Joseph became crucial, as only Joseph was able to teach them how to live in the world without losing their spiritual sensitivities.

In this light we can see the split between Joseph and his brothers was actually the cause of the ensuing exile. For without the support of Joseph, the brothers eventually found themselves unable to harmonize their spiritual and physical lives.

From this you can learn how crucial it is that your moments of Torah study and prayer have a direct effect on everyday life—harnessing that inspiration towards the goal of spiritual-physical integration (*Rabbi Menahem Mendel Schneerson, 20th century*).

21. He (continued to) comfort them and spoke (more words of encouragement) to their hearts. Joseph told his brothers "If ten lights could not extinguish one light," i.e, the actions of the ten of you could not hurt me—on the contrary, you preempted my rise to power—"how can one light extinguish ten?" If ten brothers could not harm one, one will definitely not harm ten (*Babylonian Talmud, Megillah* 16b).

Joseph and his Brothers after Jacob's Passing

¹⁵ Joseph's brothers saw (a change for the worse in Joseph's conduct with them after) their father had died. They said, "Maybe Joseph will (start to) hate us and pay us back for all the bad things that we did to him." ¹⁶ So they (fabricated a plan and) instructed (messengers to go) to Joseph and say, "Your father instructed us before his death, saying, ¹⁷ 'This is what you should say to Joseph, "Please, will you now forgive the wrongdoing of your brothers and their sin, that they did evil things to you." So, please will you now forgive the wrongdoing of the servants of the God of your father (for even though your father died, his God is alive).'"

When the (messengers) spoke to him, Joseph wept.

¹⁸ (In addition to sending messengers) his brothers also went (to Joseph). They fell down in front of him, and said, "Look! We are your slaves!"

¹⁹ Joseph said to them, "Don't be afraid, for (God only desires the good for you). Am I instead of God?"

²⁰ "You planned to do bad things to me, (but) God (had already) intended (that what you did to me should happen) for good (reasons)—in order to make things as they are today, (where I am) keeping a great number of people alive."

[SEVENTH READING] ²¹ "So don't be afraid now. I will provide for you and your children." He (continued to) comfort them and spoke (more words of encouragement) to their hearts.

Joseph Passes Away

²² Joseph lived in Egypt—both he and his father's household—and Joseph lived a hundred and ten years. [MAFTIR] ²³ Joseph saw children of a third generation (born) to Ephraim. The sons of Machir, Manasseh's son, were born (and) Joseph (raised them) on his knee.

²⁴ Joseph said to his brothers, "I am (soon) going to die. God will surely remember you and take you out of this land, to the land that He swore to Abraham, Isaac, and Jacob."

²⁵ Joseph made the children of Israel swear, saying, "God will surely remember you, and you should (then) take my bones out of here."

15. Joseph's brothers saw their father had died. What does it mean that "they saw their father had died"? They recognized Jacob's death in Joseph. They used to dine at Joseph's table, and he was friendly towards them out of respect for his father. But after Jacob died, he ceased to be friendly toward them (*Rashi, 11ᵗʰ century*).

Joseph's brothers were all shepherds who enjoyed isolation because they found the world a distraction from their primary interests of Torah study and prayer. Joseph, on the other hand,

בראשית נ:כה-כו | ויחי

לֵאמֹר פָּקֹד יִפְקֹד אֱלֹהִים אֶתְכֶם וְהַעֲלִתֶם אֶת־עַצְמֹתַי מִזֶּה: 26 וַיָּמָת יוֹסֵף בֶּן־מֵאָה וָעֶשֶׂר שָׁנִים וַיַּחַנְטוּ אֹתוֹ וַיִּישֶׂם בָּאָרוֹן בְּמִצְרָיִם:

חֲזַק חֲזַק וְנִתְחַזֵּק

פ"ה פסוקים, פ"ה אל פה סימן. סכום פסוקי דספר בראשית אלף וחמש מאות ושלשים וארבעה א"ך ל"ד סימן. וחציו ועל חרבך תחיה. ופרשיותיו י"ב ו"ה שמי לעלם סימן. וסדריו מ"ג ידידי"ה סימן. ופרקיו נ' ה' חננו ל"ך קוינו סימן: מנין הפתוחות מ"ג והסתומות מ"ח. הכל צ"א פרשיות צ"א אתה וכל העם אשר ברגליך סימן:

324

spiritual vitamin

❝ God's Providence extends to you, in every aspect of your life. If you reflect upon this frequently and deeply, all anxiety and worry will be dispelled at once. ❞

²⁶ Joseph died at the age of one hundred and ten years. They embalmed him and he was placed into a coffin in Egypt.

The congregation, followed by the reader, proclaims:

Be strong! Be strong! And may we be strengthened!

The *Haftarah* for *Va-Yeḥi* is on page 1315.

ספר שמות

THE BOOK *of* EXODUS

The **Israelites** were **enslaved** in Egypt for **generations,** but it is only when they **cried** to God in **anguish** that the process of **redemption** was set in motion. God is waiting for your cry—**a plea to be freed** from your **downtroddenness** and **narrow vision** of yourself.

SHEMOT
שמות

BEGINNING OF THE EGYPTIAN EXILE	1:1–22
THE BIRTH OF MOSES	2:1–10
MOSES FLEES TO MIDIAN	2:11–22
GOD REMEMBERS HIS COVENANT	2:23 – 4:17
MOSES EMBARKS ON HIS MISSION TO EGYPT	4:18 – 6:1

NAME
Shemot

MEANING
"Names"

LINES IN TORAH SCROLL
215

PARASHIYYOT
6 open; 1 closed

VERSES
124

WORDS
1763

LETTERS
6762

DATE
2238–2447

LOCATION
Egypt, Midian, Mount Sinai

KEY PEOPLE
Pharaoh, Jochebed (Shiphrah), Miriam (Puah), Moses, Bithiah, Jethro, Zipporah, Aaron

MITZVOT
None

CHARACTER PROFILE

NAME
Bithiah (Bityah/Batyah)

MEANING
"Daughter of God"

FATHER
Pharaoh

HUSBAND
Caleb (Mered)

CHILDREN
Jered, Heber, Yekuthiel

ACHIEVEMENTS
Went to the Nile to cleanse herself of idolatry; gave Moses his name; raised Moses as her own son; converted to Judaism; left Egypt with the Jewish people; is counted among the twenty-two "women of valor"

KNOWN FOR
Her hand miraculously extended so that she could reach Moses' basket; was cured of leprosy when she touched Moses' basket; was not affected by the Ten Plagues

ANTI-SEMITISM

Pharaoh, like other anti-Semitic tyrants throughout history, hated Jews. What inspired his hatred? Why have the Jews been despised by so many? (1:9–10).

RIGHTEOUS DESCENDANTS

For their defiance, the Jewish midwives were rewarded with the promise of "houses." This was a reference to righteous descendants: priests, Levites and kings. Righteous descendants are the greatest reward with which you can be blessed. Pray for them (1:21).

RELUCTANCE

Even when asked personally by God to lead the Jewish people, Moses initially declined. Are you eager to accept positions of honor and leadership? Or do you question whether you are really qualified and deserving? (3:11).

שמות

שמות א:א–יד

א וְאֵלֶּה שְׁמוֹת בְּנֵי יִשְׂרָאֵל הַבָּאִים מִצְרָיְמָה אֵת יַעֲקֹב אִישׁ וּבֵיתוֹ בָּאוּ: 2 רְאוּבֵן שִׁמְעוֹן לֵוִי וִיהוּדָה: 3 יִשָּׂשכָר זְבוּלֻן וּבִנְיָמִן: 4 דָּן וְנַפְתָּלִי גָּד וְאָשֵׁר: 5 וַיְהִי כָּל־נֶפֶשׁ יֹצְאֵי יֶרֶךְ־יַעֲקֹב שִׁבְעִים נָפֶשׁ וְיוֹסֵף הָיָה בְמִצְרָיִם: 6 וַיָּמָת יוֹסֵף וְכָל־אֶחָיו וְכֹל הַדּוֹר הַהוּא: 7 וּבְנֵי יִשְׂרָאֵל פָּרוּ וַיִּשְׁרְצוּ וַיִּרְבּוּ וַיַּעַצְמוּ בִּמְאֹד מְאֹד וַתִּמָּלֵא הָאָרֶץ אֹתָם: פ 8 וַיָּקָם מֶלֶךְ־חָדָשׁ עַל־מִצְרָיִם אֲשֶׁר לֹא־יָדַע אֶת־יוֹסֵף: 9 וַיֹּאמֶר אֶל־עַמּוֹ הִנֵּה עַם בְּנֵי יִשְׂרָאֵל רַב וְעָצוּם מִמֶּנּוּ: 10 הָבָה נִתְחַכְּמָה לוֹ פֶּן־יִרְבֶּה וְהָיָה כִּי־תִקְרֶאנָה מִלְחָמָה וְנוֹסַף גַּם־הוּא עַל־שֹׂנְאֵינוּ וְנִלְחַם־בָּנוּ וְעָלָה מִן־הָאָרֶץ: 11 וַיָּשִׂימוּ עָלָיו שָׂרֵי מִסִּים לְמַעַן עַנֹּתוֹ בְּסִבְלֹתָם וַיִּבֶן עָרֵי מִסְכְּנוֹת לְפַרְעֹה אֶת־פִּתֹם וְאֶת־רַעַמְסֵס: 12 וְכַאֲשֶׁר יְעַנּוּ אֹתוֹ כֵּן יִרְבֶּה וְכֵן יִפְרֹץ וַיָּקֻצוּ מִפְּנֵי בְּנֵי יִשְׂרָאֵל: 13 וַיַּעֲבִדוּ מִצְרַיִם אֶת־בְּנֵי יִשְׂרָאֵל בְּפָרֶךְ: 14 וַיְמָרְרוּ אֶת־חַיֵּיהֶם בַּעֲבֹדָה קָשָׁה בְּחֹמֶר וּבִלְבֵנִים וּבְכָל־עֲבֹדָה בַּשָּׂדֶה אֵת כָּל־עֲבֹדָתָם אֲשֶׁר־עָבְדוּ בָהֶם בְּפָרֶךְ:

8. A new king arose, who did not know Joseph. The Talmudic sages Rav and Samuel disagreed about the meaning of this verse. One said that it was actually a new king. But the other said that it was the same king, but that he issued new decrees. According to this second opinion, verse 8 (that Pharaoh *"did not know Joseph"*) means that he *made himself* as if he did not know Joseph (*Rashi, 11th century*).

10. Come, let us deal shrewdly with them (lit. "him"). Why is the verse written in the singular, "let us deal shrewdly *with him*"? Rabbi Ḥama son of Rabbi Ḥanina said: Pharaoh meant to say, "Let's deal shrewdly with God, the Savior of Israel. God always responds measure for measure, so if we afflict Israel with fire, God will send us fire. If we afflict them with the sword, He will bring the sword on us. Let us afflict them with water, casting every newborn boy into the Nile, and God won't be able to respond, since He swore that He would never again bring a flood upon the world."

Pharaoh was unaware, however, that God could flood just one nation, nor did he realize that water need not come to the Egyptians to drown them; they could go and fall into the water. And that is exactly what happened: *"The Egyptians fled towards (the water). God stirred the Egyptians in the sea"* (below, 14:27; *Babylonian Talmud, Sotah* 11a).

14. They embittered their lives with hard labor, with mortar and with bricks. *"They embittered their lives with hard (kashah) labor"*—This alludes to the Talmudic-style question, *kashya*; *"with mortar (homer)"*—the *a fortiori* argument, *kal-va-ḥomer*; *"and with bricks (levenim)"*—the legislative process, *libbun halakhah* (*Zohar*).

exodus 1:1–14 — shemot

parashat shemot

Beginning of the Egyptian Exile

1 ¹ These are the names of the children of Israel, who came to Egypt with Jacob, each man came with his household: ² Reuben, Simeon, Levi, and Judah. ³ Issachar, Zebulun, and Benjamin. ⁴ Dan and Naphtali, Gad and Asher.

⁵ All the people who emerged from Jacob's loins were seventy souls, and Joseph was in Egypt.

⁶ Joseph died, as well as all his brothers and all of that generation. ⁷ The children of Israel were fruitful and swarmed and increased and became extremely strong. The land became filled with them.

⁸ A new king arose over Egypt, who did not know Joseph. ⁹ He said to his people, "Look!—the nation of Israel's descendants are more numerous and stronger than we are! ¹⁰ Come, let us deal shrewdly with them, lest they increase. For if a war will occur, they will join our enemies, fight against us, and depart from the land."

¹¹ So they appointed over them tax collectors to afflict them with their burdens, and (the Jewish people) built storage cities for Pharaoh, namely Pithom and Raamses. ¹² But as much as they would (set their hearts to) afflict them, so did they multiply and so did they spread. (The Egyptians) were disgusted because of the children of Israel.

¹³ The Egyptians enslaved the children of Israel with crushing labor. ¹⁴ They embittered their lives with hard labor, with mortar and with bricks and with all kinds of labor in the fields. All their work that they made them do was crushing labor.

1:1 These are the names of the children of Israel. Although God counted them by their names in their lifetime, He counted them again after they died, to teach us how precious they were to Him.

This is analogous to the stars, of which it is written (*Isaiah* 40:26): *"He who takes out their hosts by number, calls them all by name"* (*Rashi, 11th century*).

A parent can show love to a child through a gift, or through words of affection, or through physical embrace. Why did God show His affection to the tribes through repetition of their names?

These other signs of affection are all relative to the situation at hand. For example, what might be a generous gift for one child would be an insult to another. Similarly, words of affection must be specific for a particular child at his level. And while a hug may always seem appropriate, it requires the presence of the child and his alertness. Only the calling of a name breaks through these barriers and is applicable in *all* circumstances.

Consequently, when the Jewish people were immersed in the idolatrous culture of Egypt, they had few merits, and so the only possible sign of affection was to repeat their names. This teaches us that God's love for us is unconditional (*Rabbi Menahem Mendel Schneerson, 20th century*).

שמות א:טו-כב

15 וַיֹּ֙אמֶר֙ מֶ֣לֶךְ מִצְרַ֔יִם לַֽמְיַלְּדֹ֖ת הָֽעִבְרִיֹּ֑ת אֲשֶׁ֨ר שֵׁ֤ם הָֽאַחַת֙ שִׁפְרָ֔ה וְשֵׁ֥ם הַשֵּׁנִ֖ית פּוּעָֽה: 16 וַיֹּ֗אמֶר בְּיַלֶּדְכֶן֙ אֶת־הָ֣עִבְרִיּ֔וֹת וּרְאִיתֶ֖ן עַל־הָאָבְנָ֑יִם אִם־בֵּ֥ן הוּא֙ וַהֲמִתֶּ֣ן אֹת֔וֹ וְאִם־בַּ֥ת הִ֖וא וָחָֽיָה: 17 וַתִּירֶ֤אןָ הַֽמְיַלְּדֹת֙ אֶת־הָ֣אֱלֹהִ֔ים וְלֹ֣א עָשׂ֔וּ כַּאֲשֶׁ֛ר דִּבֶּ֥ר אֲלֵיהֶ֖ן מֶ֣לֶךְ מִצְרָ֑יִם וַתְּחַיֶּ֖יןָ אֶת־הַיְלָדִֽים: [SECOND READING] 18 וַיִּקְרָ֤א מֶֽלֶךְ־מִצְרַ֙יִם֙ לַֽמְיַלְּדֹ֔ת וַיֹּ֣אמֶר לָהֶ֔ן מַדּ֥וּעַ עֲשִׂיתֶ֖ן הַדָּבָ֣ר הַזֶּ֑ה וַתְּחַיֶּ֖יןָ אֶת־הַיְלָדִֽים: 19 וַתֹּאמַ֤רְןָ הַֽמְיַלְּדֹת֙ אֶל־פַּרְעֹ֔ה כִּ֣י לֹ֧א כַנָּשִׁ֛ים הַמִּצְרִיֹּ֖ת הָֽעִבְרִיֹּ֑ת כִּֽי־חָי֣וֹת הֵ֔נָּה בְּטֶ֨רֶם תָּב֧וֹא אֲלֵהֶ֛ן הַמְיַלֶּ֖דֶת וְיָלָֽדוּ: 20 וַיֵּ֥יטֶב אֱלֹהִ֖ים לַֽמְיַלְּדֹ֑ת וַיִּ֧רֶב הָעָ֛ם וַיַּֽעַצְמ֖וּ מְאֹֽד: 21 וַיְהִ֕י כִּֽי־יָֽרְא֥וּ הַֽמְיַלְּדֹ֖ת אֶת־הָאֱלֹהִ֑ים וַיַּ֥עַשׂ לָהֶ֖ם בָּתִּֽים: 22 וַיְצַ֣ו פַּרְעֹ֔ה לְכָל־עַמּ֖וֹ לֵאמֹ֑ר כָּל־הַבֵּ֣ן הַיִּלּ֗וֹד הַיְאֹ֙רָה֙ תַּשְׁלִיכֻ֔הוּ וְכָל־הַבַּ֖ת תְּחַיּֽוּן: פ

---

redeemed, and the heart always follows the mind. Fill your head with words of Torah and it will ease the struggle in your heart (*Rabbi Menahem Nahum Twersky of Chernobyl, 18th century*).

15. One who was named Shiphrah, and the second who was named Puah. "Shiphrah" actually refers to Jochebed, the mother of Moses. She was called Shiphrah, which implies that she prettified (groomed) children at birth. Likewise, "Puah" actually refers to Miriam (Moses' sister), since she was effective at cooing to children when they cried (*Rashi, 11th century*).

20-21. It was because the midwives feared God that He made them into houses. This does not mean "houses" in the literal sense. It refers to the exclusive tribe of Levi, which was descended from Jochebed, and the house of royalty through King David, a descendant of Miriam. This is the implication of the words, *"God was good to the midwives"* (*Rashi, 11th century*).

Fear is a negative emotion. It is toxic to your system and deprives you of inner peace. But that is only if you fear man and man-made systems. Fear of God, on the other hand, is constructive and empowering. It builds your confidence and self-worth. *"It was because the midwives feared God that He made them into houses"*—when you fear God, you become a "house": mentally organized, settled, and structured (*Rabbi Mordecai Joseph Leiner of Izbica, 19th century*).

22. Every son who is born you shall cast into the Nile. Pharaoh's astrologers saw that God was destined to punish the redeemer of Israel with water, so they decreed, *"Every son who is born, you shall cast into*

Food for thought

1. Would you have the courage to disobey the law if you felt it was immoral?

2. The Torah names the midwives. Name two heroic women that you admire.

3. Have you ever acted heroically due to fear of God?

exodus 1:15–22 — shemot

Jewish Midwives Defy Pharaoh

15 The king of Egypt spoke to the Hebrew midwives, one who was named Shiphrah, and the second who was named Puah. 16 He said, "When you help the Hebrew women give birth, and you look on the birthstool, if it is a son, you shall put him to death, but if it is a daughter, she may live." 17 The midwives, however, feared God and they did not do what the king of Egypt had told them. They kept the boys alive.

[SECOND READING] 18 The king of Egypt summoned the midwives and said to them, "Why have you done this thing, that you have let the boys live?"

19 The midwives said to Pharaoh, "Because the Hebrew women are not like the Egyptian women, for they are skilled as midwives. Before the midwife comes to them, they have already given birth."

20 God was good to the midwives, and the people multiplied and became very strong.

21 It was because the midwives feared God that He made them (into) houses (of royalty and priesthood).

22 Pharaoh commanded all his people, saying, "Every son who is born you shall cast into the Nile, and every daughter you shall allow to live."

What was the *Zohar's* intention in finding allusions to future methods of Talmudic study in the persecutions of the Egyptian exile?

Exile is a state of spiritual dormancy. It is an eclipse of God, a time when man's ability to connect to his Creator is compromised. *The Egyptian exile was an eclipse of the mind.* The people found it terribly difficult to understand how there could be one God, so they lapsed into thoughts of idol-worship. The Torah, which connects our minds with God, was in exile; it was unavailable to the people. That is what the *Zohar* wishes to teach us.

Our current exile is an eclipse of the heart, the character of man. Compared to the days of Pharaoh, it is now relatively easy to come to an awareness of God, and the Torah is accessible to us—but we are greatly challenged by a war of temperament: bad love, misguided fear, and inappropriate pride tempt us all. So "remember the day you left Egypt": knowledge has been

spiritual vitamin

> Our generation is confused and perplexed by the shattering events of the twentieth century, as a result of which many thinking people have become completely disillusioned by the ideas and ideologies which they had held in the past, and are now earnestly searching for true spirituality.

שמות ב:א-ז

1 וַיֵּלֶךְ אִישׁ מִבֵּית לֵוִי וַיִּקַּח אֶת־בַּת־לֵוִי: 2 וַתַּהַר הָאִשָּׁה וַתֵּלֶד בֵּן וַתֵּרֶא אֹתוֹ כִּי־טוֹב הוּא וַתִּצְפְּנֵהוּ שְׁלֹשָׁה יְרָחִים: 3 וְלֹא־יָכְלָה עוֹד הַצְּפִינוֹ וַתִּקַּח־לוֹ תֵּבַת גֹּמֶא וַתַּחְמְרָה בַחֵמָר וּבַזָּפֶת וַתָּשֶׂם בָּהּ אֶת־הַיֶּלֶד וַתָּשֶׂם בַּסּוּף עַל־שְׂפַת הַיְאֹר: 4 וַתֵּתַצַּב אֲחֹתוֹ מֵרָחֹק לְדֵעָה מַה־יֵּעָשֶׂה לוֹ: 5 וַתֵּרֶד בַּת־פַּרְעֹה לִרְחֹץ עַל־הַיְאֹר וְנַעֲרֹתֶיהָ הֹלְכֹת עַל־יַד הַיְאֹר וַתֵּרֶא אֶת־הַתֵּבָה בְּתוֹךְ הַסּוּף וַתִּשְׁלַח אֶת־אֲמָתָהּ וַתִּקָּחֶהָ: 6 וַתִּפְתַּח וַתִּרְאֵהוּ אֶת־הַיֶּלֶד וְהִנֵּה־נַעַר בֹּכֶה וַתַּחְמֹל עָלָיו וַתֹּאמֶר מִיַּלְדֵי הָעִבְרִים זֶה: 7 וַתֹּאמֶר אֲחֹתוֹ אֶל־בַּת־פַּרְעֹה הַאֵלֵךְ וְקָרָאתִי לָךְ אִשָּׁה מֵינֶקֶת מִן הָעִבְרִיֹּת וְתֵינִק לָךְ אֶת־

---

two extraordinary occurrences would both seem to be signs of his future greatness. Being born circumcised is a sign of exceptionally *personal* holiness and purity; the house filling with light indicated the ability of Moses to impart holiness to the *outside* world.

Therefore, the two opinions of the *Talmud* were arguing: What was Moses' primary leadership talent? His unique personal connection with God, or his ability to provide illumination for others? (*Rabbi Menachem Mendel Schneerson, 20th century*).

3. She could no longer hide him. Whenever the Egyptians discovered that a woman had given birth, they would bring one of their babies there. When the Jewish baby would hear the Egyptian baby cry, he too would start crying, for a baby tends to cry when it hears the cries of others (*Babylonian Talmud, Sotah* 12a).

She placed it among the reeds at the Nile's edge. Jochebed hid Moses by the side of the river in such a way that he was not visible to those walking on the riverbank itself. Only a person who was actually bathing in the river could see the basket. This explains why Pharaoh's daughter, who bathed in the river, saw Moses, whereas her maidens, who were on the riverbank, did not (see v. 5; *Rabbi Samuel b. Meir, 12th century*).

Since the Nile was worshiped in Egypt as an idol, Jochebed did not want to put Moses in it, as it is forbidden to make use of an object of idol-worship, even to save a life. So, she left him by the riverside.

When Pharaoh's daughter came to wash in the river, she did so in order to "wash herself of her father's idols" (*Babylonian Talmud, Sotah* 12b), an act of rejecting her father's idolatry. In this way, she annulled the idolatrous nature of the Nile. At this point, Moses' basket moved into the river, *and she found it*. This explains why she found the basket *"in the river"* (v. 5), even though Jochebed placed it by the riverside (*Rabbi Joseph Rozin of Rogachov, 19th–20th century*).

5. She sent her maidservant (*amatah*), and she took it. The Sages interpreted *'amatah* as "her hand," which increased in length miraculously, enabling her to reach the basket (*Rashi, 11th century*).

Pharaoh's daughter extended her hand to take the basket immediately upon seeing it at a distance, not knowing that a miracle would take place, enabling her to reach the basket.

exodus 2:1–7   shemot

The Birth of Moses

2 ¹ A man of the house of Levi went and took (remarried) a daughter of Levi. ² The woman became pregnant and gave birth to a son. She saw that he was good and she hid him for three months. ³ She could no longer hide him, so she took for him a reed basket, smeared it with clay and tar, put the child into it, and placed it amongst the reeds at the Nile's edge. ⁴ His sister stood from afar, in order to know what would happen to him.

⁵ Pharaoh's daughter went down to bathe in the Nile, and her maidens were walking along the Nile, and she saw the basket among the reeds, and she sent her maidservant, and she took it. ⁶ She opened it, and she saw him, the child. And—look!—a youth was crying! She had compassion on him, and she said, "This is one of the Hebrew boys."

⁷ (Moses') sister said to Pharaoh's daughter, "Shall I go and call for you a wet-nurse from the Hebrew women to nurse the child for you?"

---

the Nile." After Moses had been thrown into the Nile, the astrologers said, "We no longer see that sign," because their prediction had partially come true, so Pharaoh withdrew his decree. They did not know that Moses was to be punished through the *"waters of strife"* (Numbers 20:13), and this was what they had really foreseen (*Babylonian Talmud, Sotah* 12b).

2:1 A man from the house of Levi went. Where did he go? Rabbi Judah son of Zevina said: He went and acted on the advice of his daughter. Amram was the greatest in his generation; when he heard Pharaoh's decree, that every newborn boy must be cast into the Nile, he said to himself, "Our efforts to have children are in vain," and he divorced his wife. Following his example, all the men of Israel divorced their wives too.

His daughter, Miriam, said to him, "Father, your decree is more harsh than Pharaoh's. He only decreed against the males, whereas you decreed against males and females! He only denied children life in this world, but you prevent them from being born altogether, denying them this world and the hereafter!

"And if the wicked Pharaoh makes a decree, it will not necessarily be carried out. But you are a righteous man, and your decree will surely be fulfilled!"

Hearing this, Amram remarried his wife, and all the others remarried their wives (*Babylonian Talmud, Sotah* 12a).

2. She saw that he was good. She saw that he was born circumcised, indicating his greatness. According to another opinion, when he was born the entire house was filled with light, which is why "she *saw* that he was good" (*Babylonian Talmud, Sotah* 12a).

It could be argued that *both* of these events actually occurred. The sages of the *Talmud* were only arguing about which of these two occurrences was the *most important*.

Since the *Midrash* (*Exodus Rabbah*) states that all the leadership talents that Moses possessed were inherent at birth, these

---

kabbalah bites

2:2 To solve a problem, you need to rise above it, think "out of the box," and not be bound by its constraints. Moses received his redemptive powers from his mother, Jochebed, who was conceived *outside* Egypt (*Bava Batra* 120a), and was intrinsically free from its spiritually constraining influences.

שמות ב:ז-יט

הַיָּלֶד: 8 וַתֹּאמֶר־לָהּ בַּת־פַּרְעֹה לֵכִי וַתֵּלֶךְ הָעַלְמָה וַתִּקְרָא אֶת־אֵם הַיָּלֶד: 9 וַתֹּאמֶר לָהּ בַּת־פַּרְעֹה הֵילִיכִי אֶת־הַיֶּלֶד הַזֶּה וְהֵינִקִהוּ לִי וַאֲנִי אֶתֵּן אֶת־שְׂכָרֵךְ וַתִּקַּח הָאִשָּׁה הַיֶּלֶד וַתְּנִיקֵהוּ: 10 וַיִּגְדַּל הַיֶּלֶד וַתְּבִאֵהוּ לְבַת־פַּרְעֹה וַיְהִי־לָהּ לְבֵן וַתִּקְרָא שְׁמוֹ מֹשֶׁה וַתֹּאמֶר כִּי מִן־הַמַּיִם מְשִׁיתִהוּ: [THIRD READING] 11 וַיְהִי | בַּיָּמִים הָהֵם וַיִּגְדַּל מֹשֶׁה וַיֵּצֵא אֶל־אֶחָיו וַיַּרְא בְּסִבְלֹתָם וַיַּרְא אִישׁ מִצְרִי מַכֶּה אִישׁ־עִבְרִי מֵאֶחָיו: 12 וַיִּפֶן כֹּה וָכֹה וַיַּרְא כִּי אֵין אִישׁ וַיַּךְ אֶת־הַמִּצְרִי וַיִּטְמְנֵהוּ בַּחוֹל: 13 וַיֵּצֵא בַּיּוֹם הַשֵּׁנִי וְהִנֵּה שְׁנֵי־אֲנָשִׁים עִבְרִים נִצִּים וַיֹּאמֶר לָרָשָׁע לָמָּה תַכֶּה רֵעֶךָ: 14 וַיֹּאמֶר מִי שָׂמְךָ לְאִישׁ שַׂר וְשֹׁפֵט עָלֵינוּ הַלְהָרְגֵנִי אַתָּה אֹמֵר כַּאֲשֶׁר הָרַגְתָּ אֶת־הַמִּצְרִי וַיִּירָא מֹשֶׁה וַיֹּאמַר אָכֵן נוֹדַע הַדָּבָר: 15 וַיִּשְׁמַע פַּרְעֹה אֶת־הַדָּבָר הַזֶּה וַיְבַקֵּשׁ לַהֲרֹג אֶת־מֹשֶׁה וַיִּבְרַח מֹשֶׁה מִפְּנֵי פַרְעֹה וַיֵּשֶׁב בְּאֶרֶץ־מִדְיָן וַיֵּשֶׁב עַל־הַבְּאֵר: 16 וּלְכֹהֵן מִדְיָן שֶׁבַע בָּנוֹת וַתָּבֹאנָה וַתִּדְלֶנָה וַתְּמַלֶּאנָה אֶת־הָרְהָטִים לְהַשְׁקוֹת צֹאן אֲבִיהֶן: 17 וַיָּבֹאוּ הָרֹעִים וַיְגָרְשׁוּם וַיָּקָם מֹשֶׁה וַיּוֹשִׁעָן וַיַּשְׁקְ אֶת־צֹאנָם: 18 וַתָּבֹאנָה אֶל־רְעוּאֵל אֲבִיהֶן וַיֹּאמֶר מַדּוּעַ מִהַרְתֶּן בֹּא הַיּוֹם: 19 וַתֹּאמַרְןָ אִישׁ מִצְרִי הִצִּילָנוּ מִיַּד

11. He went out to his brothers and he saw their burdens. The righteous feel the pain of exile so greatly that they deserve to taste from the light of redemption while it is still on its way. Moses "saw their burdens" and empathized with his brothers so profoundly that God showed him the hidden light that was to come out of all this suffering. The people were only able to see it after the redemption actually took place, but Moses saw it *within the thornbush* (below 3:2), during the exile itself (*Rabbi Judah Aryeh Leib Alter of Gur, 19th century*).

12. He turned this way and that way, and he saw that no man was there. Moses used his prophetic vision to see there would be no righteous descendant destined to be born from the Egyptian (*Zohar*).

19. An Egyptian man rescued us. Without realizing it, they spoke prophetically. It was because Moses was fleeing from killing an Egyptian man, that he had encountered them and saved them (*Zohar*).

Food for thought

1. What can we learn from Moses' reaction to human injustice?

2. How did you react last time you saw something unjust?

3. Is there anybody in your community who is being treated wrongly?

⁸ Pharaoh's daughter said to her, "Go!"

So the girl went and called the child's mother. ⁹ Pharaoh's daughter said to her, "Take this child and nurse him for me, and I will give you your wages." So the woman took the boy and nursed him. ¹⁰ The child grew up, and she brought him to Pharaoh's daughter, and he became like her son. She named him Moses [*MoSHeh*], and she said, "For I drew him [*MeSHitihu*] from the water."

Moses Grows Up

[THIRD READING] ¹¹ It was in those days that Moses grew up, and he went out to his brothers and he saw their burdens. He saw an Egyptian man striking a Hebrew man, one of his brothers. ¹² He turned this way and that way, and he saw that no man was there, so he struck the Egyptian and hid him in the sand.

¹³ He went out on the second day, and—look!—two Hebrew men were quarreling. He said to the wicked one, "Why would you strike your friend?"

¹⁴ He replied, "Who made you a man, a prince, and a judge over us? Do you plan to slay me, as you have slain the Egyptian?" Moses became frightened and said, "Indeed, the matter has become known!"

¹⁵ Pharaoh heard of this incident, and he attempted to kill Moses. Moses fled from Pharaoh and he settled in the land of Midian. He sat down by the well.

¹⁶ The governor of Midian had seven daughters. They came and drew water, and they filled troughs to water their father's flock. ¹⁷ But the shepherds came and drove them away. Moses got up and rescued them and watered their flock.

¹⁸ They came to their father Reuel. He said, "Why have you come so quickly today?"

¹⁹ They said, "An Egyptian man rescued us from the hands of the shepherds, and he also drew water for us and watered the flock."

Always do what you can without making calculations whether the result is possible. If you have the desire, a miracle will come about by itself (*Rabbi Menahem Mendel Morgensztern of Kotsk, 19ᵗʰ century*).

kabbalah bites

2:10 Moses' name highlights the bridge between water and dry land—"*For I drew him from the water.*" Water hides what is beneath the surface, representing *Gevurah*, the power to restrain and conceal. Dry land leaves everything exposed, representing *Hesed*, the tendency to give and reveal. It is not too difficult to be indiscriminately free and giving, or to always hold back. What takes maturity and discernment from deeper soul powers is to bridge the two: when to exercise *Hesed* and when to opt for *Gevurah*.

שמות ב:כ - ג:ד

הָרֹעִים וְגַם־דָּלֹה דָלָה לָנוּ וַיַּשְׁקְ אֶת־הַצֹּאן: 20 וַיֹּאמֶר אֶל־בְּנֹתָיו וְאַיּוֹ לָמָּה זֶּה עֲזַבְתֶּן אֶת־הָאִישׁ קִרְאֶן לוֹ וְיֹאכַל לָחֶם: 21 וַיּוֹאֶל מֹשֶׁה לָשֶׁבֶת אֶת־הָאִישׁ וַיִּתֵּן אֶת־צִפֹּרָה בִתּוֹ לְמֹשֶׁה: 22 וַתֵּלֶד בֵּן וַיִּקְרָא אֶת־שְׁמוֹ גֵּרְשֹׁם כִּי אָמַר גֵּר הָיִיתִי בְּאֶרֶץ נָכְרִיָּה: פ 23 וַיְהִי בַיָּמִים הָרַבִּים הָהֵם וַיָּמָת מֶלֶךְ מִצְרַיִם וַיֵּאָנְחוּ בְנֵי־יִשְׂרָאֵל מִן־הָעֲבֹדָה וַיִּזְעָקוּ וַתַּעַל שַׁוְעָתָם אֶל־הָאֱלֹהִים מִן־הָעֲבֹדָה: 24 וַיִּשְׁמַע אֱלֹהִים אֶת־נַאֲקָתָם וַיִּזְכֹּר אֱלֹהִים אֶת־בְּרִיתוֹ אֶת־אַבְרָהָם אֶת־יִצְחָק וְאֶת־יַעֲקֹב: 25 וַיַּרְא אֱלֹהִים אֶת־בְּנֵי יִשְׂרָאֵל וַיֵּדַע אֱלֹהִים: ס

ג 1 וּמֹשֶׁה הָיָה רֹעֶה אֶת־צֹאן יִתְרוֹ חֹתְנוֹ כֹּהֵן מִדְיָן וַיִּנְהַג אֶת־הַצֹּאן [FOURTH READING] אַחַר הַמִּדְבָּר וַיָּבֹא אֶל־הַר הָאֱלֹהִים חֹרֵבָה: 2 וַיֵּרָא מַלְאַךְ יְהֹוָה אֵלָיו בְּלַבַּת־אֵשׁ מִתּוֹךְ הַסְּנֶה וַיַּרְא וְהִנֵּה הַסְּנֶה בֹּעֵר בָּאֵשׁ וְהַסְּנֶה אֵינֶנּוּ אֻכָּל: 3 וַיֹּאמֶר מֹשֶׁה אָסֻרָה־נָּא וְאֶרְאֶה אֶת־הַמַּרְאֶה הַגָּדֹל הַזֶּה מַדּוּעַ לֹא־יִבְעַר הַסְּנֶה: 4 וַיַּרְא יְהֹוָה כִּי סָר לִרְאוֹת וַיִּקְרָא אֵלָיו אֱלֹהִים מִתּוֹךְ הַסְּנֶה וַיֹּאמֶר

| 338 |

tually reached water and began to drink. When Moses found the sheep he said, *"I didn't realize that you were running away because you were thirsty. You must be tired!"* So, Moses lifted the sheep onto his shoulders and walked back.

God said to Himself, *"You have such compassion for the sheep of a mere human being! You are going to shepherd My sheep, the Jewish people"* (Exodus Rabbah).

2. From within the thornbush. The Angel of God revealed himself to Moses specifically through a thornbush rather than another type of tree, in the spirit of the verse, *"I [God] am with him in distress"* (Psalms 91:15; Rashi, 11th century).

The thornbush was not being consumed. The Torah scholar might eventually become self-satisfied with his knowledge, and his "fire" to become more connected to God could become extinguished. But the simple Jew—represented by the humble thornbush—has a devotion that never wanes (*Rabbi Israel Ba'al Shem Tov, 18th century*).

Food for thought

1. Have you ever "cried out" to God and been answered?

2. If God knows everything, why do we share our anguish with Him?

3. Why is it important to remind God of His covenant with us?

exodus 2:20 – 3:4 shemot

²⁰ He said to his daughters, "So where is he? Why have you left the man? Invite him, and let him eat bread!"

²¹ Moses agreed to live with the man, and (the man) gave his daughter Zipporah to Moses. ²² She bore a son, whom he named Gershom, for he said, "I was a stranger [*ger*] in a foreign land."

God Remembers His Covenant

²³ After many days had passed, the king of Egypt died. The children of Israel groaned from the hard work, and they cried out. Their cries, caused by the hard work, went up to God. ²⁴ God heard their cry, and God remembered His covenant with Abraham, with Isaac, and with Jacob. ²⁵ God saw the children of Israel, and God knew (i.e. He took their cries to heart).

The Burning Bush

3 [FOURTH READING] ¹ Moses was pasturing the flocks of Jethro, his father-in-law, the governor of Midian. He led the flocks into the desert, and he came to the mountain of God, at Horeb.

² An angel of God appeared to him in a flame of fire from within the thornbush. (Moses) gazed, and—look!—the thornbush was burning with fire, but the thornbush was not being consumed. ³ Moses said, "Let me turn now and see this great spectacle! Why will the thornbush not burn?"

⁴ God saw that he had turned to see, and God called to him from within the thornbush, and He said, "Moses, Moses!"

---

23. The king of Egypt died. The children of Israel groaned from the hard work. Pharaoh did not actually die. Rather, he was afflicted with *tzara'at* (leprosy), and he used to slaughter Jewish children and bathe in their blood for a cure (*Rashi, 11ᵗʰ century*).

3:1 Moses was pasturing the flocks. God tests righteous individuals to see if they are fit to lead His people, through first observing how they tend to sheep. When Moses was tending the sheep of Jethro in the desert, one sheep ran off and Moses chased after it. The sheep even-

---

spiritual vitamin

> In sending difficulties and trials, God also provides the capacity to overcome them. Far from being discouraged by such difficulties, you should consider them as challenges to be overcome, in order to reap the benefits that are inherent.

שמות ג:ד-יג

מֹשֶׁה מֹשֶׁה וַיֹּאמֶר הִנֵּנִי: 5 וַיֹּאמֶר אַל־תִּקְרַב הֲלֹם שַׁל־נְעָלֶיךָ מֵעַל רַגְלֶיךָ כִּי הַמָּקוֹם אֲשֶׁר אַתָּה עוֹמֵד עָלָיו אַדְמַת־קֹדֶשׁ הוּא: 6 וַיֹּאמֶר אָנֹכִי אֱלֹהֵי אָבִיךָ אֱלֹהֵי אַבְרָהָם אֱלֹהֵי יִצְחָק וֵאלֹהֵי יַעֲקֹב וַיַּסְתֵּר מֹשֶׁה פָּנָיו כִּי יָרֵא מֵהַבִּיט אֶל־הָאֱלֹהִים: 7 וַיֹּאמֶר יְהוָה רָאֹה רָאִיתִי אֶת־עֳנִי עַמִּי אֲשֶׁר בְּמִצְרָיִם וְאֶת־צַעֲקָתָם שָׁמַעְתִּי מִפְּנֵי נֹגְשָׂיו כִּי יָדַעְתִּי אֶת־מַכְאֹבָיו: 8 וָאֵרֵד לְהַצִּילוֹ | מִיַּד מִצְרַיִם וּלְהַעֲלֹתוֹ מִן־הָאָרֶץ הַהִוא אֶל־אֶרֶץ טוֹבָה וּרְחָבָה אֶל־אֶרֶץ זָבַת חָלָב וּדְבָשׁ אֶל־מְקוֹם הַכְּנַעֲנִי וְהַחִתִּי וְהָאֱמֹרִי וְהַפְּרִזִּי וְהַחִוִּי וְהַיְבוּסִי: 9 וְעַתָּה הִנֵּה צַעֲקַת בְּנֵי־יִשְׂרָאֵל בָּאָה אֵלָי וְגַם־רָאִיתִי אֶת־הַלַּחַץ אֲשֶׁר מִצְרַיִם לֹחֲצִים אֹתָם: 10 וְעַתָּה לְכָה וְאֶשְׁלָחֲךָ אֶל־פַּרְעֹה וְהוֹצֵא אֶת־עַמִּי בְנֵי־יִשְׂרָאֵל מִמִּצְרָיִם: 11 וַיֹּאמֶר מֹשֶׁה אֶל־הָאֱלֹהִים מִי אָנֹכִי כִּי אֵלֵךְ אֶל־פַּרְעֹה וְכִי אוֹצִיא אֶת־בְּנֵי יִשְׂרָאֵל מִמִּצְרָיִם: 12 וַיֹּאמֶר כִּי־אֶהְיֶה עִמָּךְ וְזֶה־לְּךָ הָאוֹת כִּי אָנֹכִי שְׁלַחְתִּיךָ בְּהוֹצִיאֲךָ אֶת־הָעָם מִמִּצְרַיִם תַּעַבְדוּן אֶת־הָאֱלֹהִים עַל הָהָר הַזֶּה: 13 וַיֹּאמֶר מֹשֶׁה אֶל־הָאֱלֹהִים הִנֵּה אָנֹכִי בָא אֶל־בְּנֵי יִשְׂרָאֵל

and lift them up to a higher rung of holiness. And subsequently, *"the cry of the children of Israel has come to Me"* (v. 9; *Rabbi Elimelech of Lyzhansk, 18th century*).

spiritual vitamin

> *"When you take the people out of Egypt, you will worship God on this mountain"* (v.12). The Exodus itself was an act of Heavenly grace, and in a manner of wonderful and obvious miracles. But, it was conditioned from the start on *serving* God. And as with the nation as a whole, so it is with the individual: Your striving should be to act and to achieve results; and not merely to act, but to do so with exertion.

exodus 3:4–13 shemot

He said, "Here I am!"

⁵ (God) said, "Do not draw near here. Take your shoes off your feet, because the place upon which you stand is holy soil." ⁶ He said, "I am the God of your father, the God of Abraham, the God of Isaac, and the God of Jacob."

Moses hid his face because he was afraid to look at God.

⁷ God said, "I have truly seen the suffering of My nation which is in Egypt, and I have heard its cries caused by its slave-drivers, for I know its pains. ⁸ I shall descend to rescue it from the hands of the Egyptians and to bring it up from that land, to a good and spacious land, to a land flowing with milk and honey, to the place of the Canaanites, the Hittites, the Amorites, the Perizzites, the Hivites, and the Jebusites.

⁹ "Now, behold, the cry of the children of Israel has come to Me, and I have also seen the oppression with which the Egyptians are persecuting them. ¹⁰ Now, go, and I will send you to Pharaoh, and you will take My nation, the children of Israel, out of Egypt."

Moses Declines God's Mission

¹¹ Moses said to God, "Who am I that I should go to Pharaoh, and that I should take the children of Israel out of Egypt?"

¹² He said, "For I will be with you, and this (burning thornbush) is a sign for you that you have been sent by Me (and that you will succeed). When you take the people out of Egypt, you will worship God on this mountain."

¹³ Moses said to God, "When I come to the children of Israel, and I say to them,

---

5. Take your shoes off your feet. God told Moses to remove his shoes as a preparation for Divine Revelation. God was hinting to Moses that in the same way a shoe is an external covering for the foot, the physical body is a covering for the soul. In order to attain Divine Revelation, you must rid yourself of your physicality, your human desires, so as to access your soul within (*Rabbi Bahya b. Asher, 13th century*).

When you wear shoes, small stones and other items are barely felt beneath your feet, unlike when barefooted, you feel every tiny pebble and thorn. The lesson here is that you ought to heighten your sensitivity to God's will, so that you do not come to trample on the seemingly minor details of the Torah (*Rabbi Ephraim of Luntshits, 16th–17th century*).

8. I shall descend to rescue it from the hands of the Egyptians. If a person has not uncluttered his mind and it is filled with too many superficial thoughts of this physical world, it is very hard for his prayers to reach God.

When the Jewish people were exiled in Egypt, a land of impurity, they became corrupted and it was impossible for their prayers to reach God. So God said, *"I shall descend"*—I will go down

שמות ג:יג-כב

וְאָמַרְתִּי לָהֶם אֱלֹהֵי אֲבוֹתֵיכֶם שְׁלָחַנִי אֲלֵיכֶם וְאָמְרוּ־לִי מַה־שְּׁמוֹ מָה אֹמַר אֲלֵהֶם: 14 וַיֹּאמֶר אֱלֹהִים אֶל־מֹשֶׁה אֶהְיֶה אֲשֶׁר אֶהְיֶה וַיֹּאמֶר כֹּה תֹאמַר לִבְנֵי יִשְׂרָאֵל אֶהְיֶה שְׁלָחַנִי אֲלֵיכֶם: 15 וַיֹּאמֶר עוֹד אֱלֹהִים אֶל־מֹשֶׁה כֹּה־תֹאמַר אֶל־בְּנֵי יִשְׂרָאֵל יְהֹוָה אֱלֹהֵי אֲבֹתֵיכֶם אֱלֹהֵי אַבְרָהָם אֱלֹהֵי יִצְחָק וֵאלֹהֵי יַעֲקֹב שְׁלָחַנִי אֲלֵיכֶם זֶה־שְּׁמִי לְעֹלָם וְזֶה זִכְרִי לְדֹר דֹּר: 16 [FIFTH READING] לֵךְ וְאָסַפְתָּ אֶת־זִקְנֵי יִשְׂרָאֵל וְאָמַרְתָּ אֲלֵהֶם יְהֹוָה אֱלֹהֵי אֲבֹתֵיכֶם נִרְאָה אֵלַי אֱלֹהֵי אַבְרָהָם יִצְחָק וְיַעֲקֹב לֵאמֹר פָּקֹד פָּקַדְתִּי אֶתְכֶם וְאֶת־הֶעָשׂוּי לָכֶם בְּמִצְרָיִם: 17 וָאֹמַר אַעֲלֶה אֶתְכֶם מֵעֳנִי מִצְרַיִם אֶל־אֶרֶץ הַכְּנַעֲנִי וְהַחִתִּי וְהָאֱמֹרִי וְהַפְּרִזִּי וְהַחִוִּי וְהַיְבוּסִי אֶל־אֶרֶץ זָבַת חָלָב וּדְבָשׁ: 18 וְשָׁמְעוּ לְקֹלֶךָ וּבָאתָ אַתָּה וְזִקְנֵי יִשְׂרָאֵל אֶל־מֶלֶךְ מִצְרַיִם וַאֲמַרְתֶּם אֵלָיו יְהֹוָה אֱלֹהֵי הָעִבְרִיִּים נִקְרָה עָלֵינוּ וְעַתָּה נֵלֲכָה־נָּא דֶּרֶךְ שְׁלֹשֶׁת יָמִים בַּמִּדְבָּר וְנִזְבְּחָה לַיהֹוָה אֱלֹהֵינוּ: 19 וַאֲנִי יָדַעְתִּי כִּי לֹא־יִתֵּן אֶתְכֶם מֶלֶךְ מִצְרַיִם לַהֲלֹךְ וְלֹא בְּיָד חֲזָקָה: 20 וְשָׁלַחְתִּי אֶת־יָדִי וְהִכֵּיתִי אֶת־מִצְרַיִם בְּכֹל נִפְלְאֹתַי אֲשֶׁר אֶעֱשֶׂה בְּקִרְבּוֹ וְאַחֲרֵי־כֵן יְשַׁלַּח אֶתְכֶם: 21 וְנָתַתִּי אֶת־חֵן הָעָם־הַזֶּה בְּעֵינֵי מִצְרָיִם וְהָיָה כִּי תֵלֵכוּן לֹא תֵלְכוּ רֵיקָם: 22 וְשָׁאֲלָה אִשָּׁה מִשְּׁכֶנְתָּהּ וּמִגָּרַת בֵּיתָהּ כְּלֵי־כֶסֶף וּכְלֵי זָהָב וּשְׂמָלֹת וְשַׂמְתֶּם עַל־בְּנֵיכֶם וְעַל־בְּנֹתֵיכֶם וְנִצַּלְתֶּם אֶת־מִצְרָיִם:

cries caused by its slave-drivers, for I know its pains' (v. 7-9)—then why did He put us in this situation in the first place?"

They would ask, *"What is His name?"* What kind of "name" does He have if He listens to us only after harsh labor and the murder of our children? Therefore, Moses said to God, *"What shall I say to them?"* for he felt that they had a justified complaint.

Consequently, Rashi explains that God answered, *"I will be with them in their time of need."* It is not the case that God overlooks the suffering of the Jewish people. Rather, He empathizes with their pain, as the verse states, *"All their pain is pain for Him too"* (Isaiah 63:9; *Rabbi Menahem Mendel Schneerson, 20th century*).

22. Each woman shall request from her neighbor ... silver and gold objects. God would not permit fraudulent behavior, namely, that the Jewish people should borrow the gold and silver vessels and not return them. Rather, the Egyptians gave them willingly as gifts (*Rabbi Hananel b. Ḥushi'el, 11th century*).

'The God of your fathers has sent me to you,' and they say to me, 'What is His name?'—what shall I say to them?"

¹⁴ God said to Moses, "*'Ehyeh-'Asher-'Ehyeh*" (lit., "I-Will-Be-What-I-Will-Be"), and He said, "So shall you say to the children of Israel: *'Ehyeh* ('I-Will-Be') has sent me to you."

¹⁵ God also said to Moses, "So shall you say to the children of Israel, 'God, the God of your forefathers, the God of Abraham, the God of Isaac, and the God of Jacob has sent me to you.' This is My eternal name, and this is how I should be recalled in every generation.'"

[FIFTH READING] ¹⁶ "Go and assemble the elders of Israel, and say to them, 'God, the God of your forefathers, has appeared to me; the God of Abraham, Isaac, and Jacob, saying, "I have truly remembered you and what is being done to you in Egypt."' ¹⁷ I have said, 'I will bring you out from the affliction of Egypt, to the land of the Canaanites, the Hittites, the Amorites, the Perizzites, the Hivites, and the Jebusites, to a land flowing with milk and honey.'"

¹⁸ "They will listen to your voice. You and the elders of Israel shall come to the king of Egypt, and say to him, 'God, the God of the Hebrews, has come upon us. Now, let us go for a three-day journey in the desert and offer up sacrifices to God, our God.'"

¹⁹ "I (already) know that the king of Egypt will not permit you to go, unless (I show him) a mighty hand. ²⁰ So, I will send forth My hand and I will smite the Egyptians with all My miracles which I will perform inside their land. Afterwards, he will send you out."

²¹ "I shall grant this people favor in the eyes of the Egyptians, so that when you (eventually) leave, you will not go empty-handed. ²² Each woman shall request from her neighbor and from (a woman) living in her house silver and gold objects, and clothing. You shall put them on your sons and on your daughters, and you shall empty Egypt (of its wealth)."

13-14. "'What is His name?'—what shall I say to them?" ... "I Will Be What I Will Be." The meaning of God's response is that He will be with them in their present time of need, just as He will be with them at the time of future persecutions (*Rashi, 11th century*).

It seems strange to imagine that the Jewish people did not know God's name, when in this verse, Moses says, "When I come to the children of Israel, and I say to them, *the God of your fathers* has sent me to you..." Obviously, if they were aware of the existence of God, they must have referred to Him by a particular name, especially when addressing Him in prayer.

Therefore, *Rashi* writes that God's answer, *"I-Will-Be-What-I-Will-Be,"* cannot be just His name, but rather, the answer to a deeper concern about which Moses was worried the Jewish people might challenge him. Having suffered harsh slave labor and the slaughter of thousands of Jewish children, they would have a serious complaint: "If God cares about us so much, and He is saying, *'I have truly seen the suffering of My nation which is in Egypt, and I have heard its*

שמות ד:א-י

א וַיַּעַן מֹשֶׁה וַיֹּאמֶר וְהֵן לֹא־יַאֲמִינוּ לִי וְלֹא יִשְׁמְעוּ בְּקֹלִי כִּי יֹאמְרוּ לֹא־נִרְאָה אֵלֶיךָ יְהֹוָה: ב וַיֹּאמֶר אֵלָיו יְהֹוָה [מזה כ׳] מַזֶּה בְיָדֶךָ וַיֹּאמֶר מַטֶּה: ג וַיֹּאמֶר הַשְׁלִיכֵהוּ אַרְצָה וַיַּשְׁלִכֵהוּ אַרְצָה וַיְהִי לְנָחָשׁ וַיָּנָס מֹשֶׁה מִפָּנָיו: ד וַיֹּאמֶר יְהֹוָה אֶל־מֹשֶׁה שְׁלַח יָדְךָ וֶאֱחֹז בִּזְנָבוֹ וַיִּשְׁלַח יָדוֹ וַיַּחֲזֶק בּוֹ וַיְהִי לְמַטֶּה בְּכַפּוֹ: ה לְמַעַן יַאֲמִינוּ כִּי־נִרְאָה אֵלֶיךָ יְהֹוָה אֱלֹהֵי אֲבֹתָם אֱלֹהֵי אַבְרָהָם אֱלֹהֵי יִצְחָק וֵאלֹהֵי יַעֲקֹב: ו וַיֹּאמֶר יְהֹוָה לוֹ עוֹד הָבֵא־נָא יָדְךָ בְּחֵיקֶךָ וַיָּבֵא יָדוֹ בְּחֵיקוֹ וַיּוֹצִאָהּ וְהִנֵּה יָדוֹ מְצֹרַעַת כַּשָּׁלֶג: ז וַיֹּאמֶר הָשֵׁב יָדְךָ אֶל־חֵיקֶךָ וַיָּשֶׁב יָדוֹ אֶל־חֵיקוֹ וַיּוֹצִאָהּ מֵחֵיקוֹ וְהִנֵּה־שָׁבָה כִּבְשָׂרוֹ: ח וְהָיָה אִם־לֹא יַאֲמִינוּ לָךְ וְלֹא יִשְׁמְעוּ לְקֹל הָאֹת הָרִאשׁוֹן וְהֶאֱמִינוּ לְקֹל הָאֹת הָאַחֲרוֹן: ט וְהָיָה אִם־לֹא יַאֲמִינוּ גַּם לִשְׁנֵי הָאֹתוֹת הָאֵלֶּה וְלֹא יִשְׁמְעוּן לְקֹלֶךָ וְלָקַחְתָּ מִמֵּימֵי הַיְאֹר וְשָׁפַכְתָּ הַיַּבָּשָׁה וְהָיוּ הַמַּיִם אֲשֶׁר תִּקַּח מִן־הַיְאֹר וְהָיוּ לְדָם בַּיַּבָּשֶׁת: י וַיֹּאמֶר מֹשֶׁה אֶל־יְהֹוָה בִּי אֲדֹנָי לֹא אִישׁ דְּבָרִים אָנֹכִי גַּם מִתְּמוֹל

sign: through the *gevurah* of Isaac, Egypt was destined to be destroyed permanently (*Rabbi Samuel Bornstein of Sochaczew, 20th century*).

kabbalah bites

4:1 Moses trusted that the people would believe in God, but he doubted if they would believe *in him* ("they will not believe *in me*").

Moses embodied the attribute of *din* (judgment), since Moses was one with the Torah and all legal systems must be based on strict justice. Moses feared that if the Exodus were to take place with him as redeemer it would be too *din* oriented. This could have undesirable effects for the Jewish people, since many of them needed to improve their ways and a very strict redemption might pose questions about whether these Jews deserved to be redeemed. So Moses complained to God, "I have too much *din* to be the redeemer for this less-than-perfect people."

God's response was to add Aaron to Moses' mission (below, v. 14-17). Aaron, being rooted in *Hesed* (kindness), would "sweeten" the harsher side of Moses' *din*.

Moses Questions God

4 ¹ Moses responded and said, "They will not believe me, and they will not listen to my voice, for they will say, 'God did not appear to you.'"

² God said to him, "What is this in your hand?"

(Moses) said, "A staff."

³ (God) said, "Cast it to the ground," and he cast it to the ground and it became a serpent, and Moses ran away from it. ⁴ God said to Moses, "Stretch out your hand and take hold of its tail." Moses stretched out his hand and grasped it, and it became a staff in his palm.

⁵ "This is in order that they believe that God, the God of their forefathers, has appeared to you; the God of Abraham, the God of Isaac, and the God of Jacob."

⁶ God then said to him, "Please place your hand on your chest." (Moses) placed his hand on his chest. He then removed it and his hand was leprous like snow.

⁷ (God) said, "Place your hand back on your chest." (Moses) placed his hand back on his chest, and when he took it out from his chest, it had returned to be like his flesh.

⁸ "Then, if they do not believe you, and they do not heed the voice of the first sign, they will believe the voice of the latter sign. ⁹ And then, if they do not believe either of these two signs, and they do not listen to your voice, you shall take some water from the Nile and spill it on the ground. The water that you take from the Nile will become blood on the ground."

¹⁰ Moses said to God, "I beg You, my Master! I am not a man of words, not

---

4:3-6 It became a serpent ... his hand was leprous like snow. God turned Moses' staff into a serpent, hinting to him that he had spoken disparagingly about the Jewish people and had thus adopted the ways of a serpent. His hand was afflicted with *tzara'at* (leprosy), for the same reason (*Rashi, 11th century*).

8-9. If they do not believe you, and they do not heed the voice of the first sign, they will believe the voice of the latter sign. And then, if they do not believe either of these two signs ... you shall take some water from the Nile and spill it on the ground. The water that you take from the Nile will become blood on the ground. Why was this last sign more powerful than the previous two signs, of a staff turning into a serpent (v. 3) and a hand turning leprous (v. 7)?

The three signs correspond to the three Patriarchs. The first sign hints to Jacob, who is depicted by the Kabbalah as a serpent, due to his cunning opposition to Esau.

The second sign hints to Abraham—the white leprous hand alluding to *ḥesed* (kindness), the predominant character trait of Abraham.

And the third sign, red blood, hints to *gevurah* (severity), the predominant character trait of Isaac. Unlike Moses' staff and hand, which returned to their former states, the blood did not return to water, and was swallowed up by the earth. This, therefore, was the most powerful

שמות ד:י-כ

גַּם מִשִּׁלְשֹׁם גַּם מֵאָז דַּבֶּרְךָ אֶל־עַבְדֶּךָ כִּי כְבַד־פֶּה וּכְבַד לָשׁוֹן אָנֹכִי: 11 וַיֹּאמֶר יְהֹוָה אֵלָיו מִי שָׂם פֶּה לָאָדָם אוֹ מִי־יָשׂוּם אִלֵּם אוֹ חֵרֵשׁ אוֹ פִקֵּחַ אוֹ עִוֵּר הֲלֹא אָנֹכִי יְהֹוָה: 12 וְעַתָּה לֵךְ וְאָנֹכִי אֶהְיֶה עִם־פִּיךָ וְהוֹרֵיתִיךָ אֲשֶׁר תְּדַבֵּר: 13 וַיֹּאמֶר בִּי אֲדֹנָי שְׁלַח־נָא בְּיַד־תִּשְׁלָח: 14 וַיִּחַר־אַף יְהֹוָה בְּמֹשֶׁה וַיֹּאמֶר הֲלֹא אַהֲרֹן אָחִיךָ הַלֵּוִי יָדַעְתִּי כִּי־דַבֵּר יְדַבֵּר הוּא וְגַם הִנֵּה־הוּא יֹצֵא לִקְרָאתֶךָ וְרָאֲךָ וְשָׂמַח בְּלִבּוֹ: 15 וְדִבַּרְתָּ אֵלָיו וְשַׂמְתָּ אֶת־הַדְּבָרִים בְּפִיו וְאָנֹכִי אֶהְיֶה עִם־פִּיךָ וְעִם־פִּיהוּ וְהוֹרֵיתִי אֶתְכֶם אֵת אֲשֶׁר תַּעֲשׂוּן: 16 וְדִבֶּר־הוּא לְךָ אֶל־הָעָם וְהָיָה הוּא יִהְיֶה־לְּךָ לְפֶה וְאַתָּה תִּהְיֶה־לּוֹ לֵאלֹהִים: 17 וְאֶת־הַמַּטֶּה הַזֶּה תִּקַּח בְּיָדֶךָ אֲשֶׁר תַּעֲשֶׂה־בּוֹ אֶת־הָאֹתֹת: פ [SIXTH READING] 18 וַיֵּלֶךְ מֹשֶׁה וַיָּשָׁב | אֶל־יֶתֶר חֹתְנוֹ וַיֹּאמֶר לוֹ אֵלְכָה נָּא וְאָשׁוּבָה אֶל־אַחַי אֲשֶׁר־בְּמִצְרַיִם וְאֶרְאֶה הַעוֹדָם חַיִּים וַיֹּאמֶר יִתְרוֹ לְמֹשֶׁה לֵךְ לְשָׁלוֹם: 19 וַיֹּאמֶר יְהֹוָה אֶל־מֹשֶׁה בְּמִדְיָן לֵךְ שֻׁב מִצְרָיִם כִּי־מֵתוּ כָּל־הָאֲנָשִׁים הַמְבַקְשִׁים אֶת־נַפְשֶׁךָ: 20 וַיִּקַּח מֹשֶׁה אֶת־אִשְׁתּוֹ וְאֶת־בָּנָיו וַיַּרְכִּבֵם עַל־הַחֲמֹר וַיָּשָׁב אַרְצָה מִצְרָיִם וַיִּקַּח מֹשֶׁה

---

10. For I am heavy of mouth and heavy of tongue. Moses was "heavy of mouth and heavy of tongue" so that it would be clearly seen that the power of his leadership was not due to his own capabilities or oratory. It was the spirit of God within him that gave him the power to lead the Jewish people and transmit the Torah from God directly to them (*Rabbi Nissim b. Reuben Gerondi, 14th century*).

13. Send the one that You usually send (i.e. Aaron. Alternatively: Send the one that You will eventually send, i.e., the Messiah). God spent seven days speaking to Moses from the burning thornbush, trying to convince him to accept the mission to redeem the Jewish people. Moses objected, claiming that such an important job should be carried out by his older brother Aaron, especially as Aaron was already a prophet. Moses also complained that his verbal articulation was poor, unfit to present the case of the Jewish people before Pharaoh. Moses' final argument was that, since he was not destined to enter the land of Israel, God should send the final redeemer of the Jewish people (the Messiah) instead.

God replied to Moses (v. 14) that Aaron would not be angry with him, as he had expected.

Eventually, God became angry with Moses, and he accepted the mission upon himself (*Rashi, 11th century*).

20. Upon the (famous) donkey. Moses mounted his wife and children on a unique donkey. This was the donkey which Abraham himself prepared for the journey to sacrifice his son,

yesterday, nor the day before, nor from the very first time that You spoke to Your servant, for I am heavy of mouth and heavy of tongue."

[11] God said to him, "Who gave man a mouth, or who makes a person dumb or deaf, sighted or blind? Is it not I, God? [12] So now, go! I will be with your mouth, and I will teach you what you should say."

[13] But (Moses) said, "Please, my Master, send the one that You usually send (i.e. Aaron. Alternatively: Send the one that You will eventually send, i.e., the Messiah)."

[14] God became angry with Moses, and He said, "I know that Aaron your brother, the Levite, will surely speak (for you. When you return to Egypt you will find that) he comes to greet you, and when he sees you, he will rejoice in his heart. [15] You will speak to him, and put the words in his mouth. I will then be with your mouth and with his mouth, and I will instruct you both what you shall do. [16] He will speak on your behalf to the people. He will be your spokesman, and you will be his leader."

[17] "You shall take this staff in your hand, with which you will perform the signs."

Moses Embarks on his Mission to Egypt

[SIXTH READING] [18] Moses went and returned to Jether, his father-in-law, and he said to him, "Let me go now and return to my brothers who are in Egypt, and let me see whether they are still alive."

Jethro said to Moses, "Go in peace."

[19] God said to Moses in Midian, "Go, return to Egypt, for all the people who seek your life have died."

[20] Moses took his wife and his sons, mounted them upon the (famous) donkey, and he returned to the land of Egypt. Moses took the staff of God in his hand.

kabbalah bites

4:10 The Kabbalah teaches that our souls contain *lights* (*'orot*) and *vessels* (*kelim*). The *lights* endow us with inspiration and intellectual brilliance, whereas the *vessels* manage ideas into coherent words and messages.

Sometimes, a genius cannot express himself because his *lights* are simply too intense for his *vessels*. This was Moses' complaint: *"I am heavy of mouth and heavy of tongue."* God replied, *"I will be with your mouth"* (v. 12). He would enrich Moses' vessels so that they could contain his great light.

Pray to God that He should enrich your vessels, enabling your great light to impact the world.

שמות ד:כ - לא

אֶת־מַטֵּה הָאֱלֹהִים בְּיָדוֹ: 21 וַיֹּאמֶר יְהֹוָה אֶל־מֹשֶׁה בְּלֶכְתְּךָ לָשׁוּב מִצְרַיְמָה רְאֵה כָּל־הַמֹּפְתִים אֲשֶׁר־שַׂמְתִּי בְיָדֶךָ וַעֲשִׂיתָם לִפְנֵי פַרְעֹה וַאֲנִי אֲחַזֵּק אֶת־לִבּוֹ וְלֹא יְשַׁלַּח אֶת־הָעָם: 22 וְאָמַרְתָּ אֶל־פַּרְעֹה כֹּה אָמַר יְהֹוָה בְּנִי בְכֹרִי יִשְׂרָאֵל: 23 וָאֹמַר אֵלֶיךָ שַׁלַּח אֶת־בְּנִי וְיַעַבְדֵנִי וַתְּמָאֵן לְשַׁלְּחוֹ הִנֵּה אָנֹכִי הֹרֵג אֶת־בִּנְךָ בְּכֹרֶךָ: 24 וַיְהִי בַדֶּרֶךְ בַּמָּלוֹן וַיִּפְגְּשֵׁהוּ יְהֹוָה וַיְבַקֵּשׁ הֲמִיתוֹ: 25 וַתִּקַּח צִפֹּרָה צֹר וַתִּכְרֹת אֶת־עָרְלַת בְּנָהּ וַתַּגַּע לְרַגְלָיו וַתֹּאמֶר כִּי חֲתַן־דָּמִים אַתָּה לִי: 26 וַיִּרֶף מִמֶּנּוּ אָז אָמְרָה חֲתַן דָּמִים לַמּוּלֹת: פ 27 וַיֹּאמֶר יְהֹוָה אֶל־אַהֲרֹן לֵךְ לִקְרַאת מֹשֶׁה הַמִּדְבָּרָה וַיֵּלֶךְ וַיִּפְגְּשֵׁהוּ בְּהַר הָאֱלֹהִים וַיִּשַּׁק־לוֹ: 28 וַיַּגֵּד מֹשֶׁה לְאַהֲרֹן אֵת כָּל־דִּבְרֵי יְהֹוָה אֲשֶׁר שְׁלָחוֹ וְאֵת כָּל־הָאֹתֹת אֲשֶׁר צִוָּהוּ: 29 וַיֵּלֶךְ מֹשֶׁה וְאַהֲרֹן וַיַּאַסְפוּ אֶת־כָּל־זִקְנֵי בְּנֵי יִשְׂרָאֵל: 30 וַיְדַבֵּר אַהֲרֹן אֵת כָּל־הַדְּבָרִים אֲשֶׁר־דִּבֶּר יְהֹוָה אֶל־מֹשֶׁה וַיַּעַשׂ הָאֹתֹת לְעֵינֵי הָעָם: 31 וַיַּאֲמֵן הָעָם וַיִּשְׁמְעוּ כִּי־פָקַד יְהֹוָה אֶת־בְּנֵי יִשְׂרָאֵל וְכִי רָאָה אֶת־עָנְיָם וַיִּקְּדוּ וַיִּשְׁתַּחֲווּ:

is greater. Why don't you learn from Abraham, who did not question Me? He followed My orders right away without asking any questions, and his spirits were joyful, since He knew he was doing My will. And that was despite the inhumane act that he was asked to do!"

(b) It was the Messiah's donkey. This indicated an answer to Moses' complaint that God should send the final redeemer instead of himself, *"Please, my Master, send the one that You will eventually send"* (4:13). God was hinting to Moses, "You may think that you are in no way connected to the final redeemer. But you are wrong! The Messiah will only come because you made the entire concept of redemption a possibility. The Messiah will finish off the task that you are now starting" (*Rabbi Menahem Mendel Schneerson, 20th century*).

22. Israel is My son, My firstborn. A firstborn child transforms a man into a father. The firstborn has the earliest privilege to call his father "father" and the subsequent children follow his lead.

The Jewish People were the first to recognize God as the single creator of all humanity and master of the world. They declared God's existence to the world and referred to Him as their father, causing others to do the same. Therefore they are considered God's "firstborn" even though many nations existed before them (*Rabbi Meir Simhah of Dvinsk, 19th–20th century*).

Food for thought

1. Are you surprised that the people believed Moses?

2. Has personal suffering ever caused you to reexamine your beliefs?

3. Do you find it easy or difficult to be optimistic about other people?

exodus 4:21–31   shemot

²¹ God said to Moses, "When you go to return to Egypt, reflect upon all the miracles that I have placed in your hand, and perform them before Pharaoh. I will, however, strengthen his heart, and he will not send the people away.

²² "You shall say to Pharaoh, 'This is what God said: "Israel is My son, My firstborn."' ²³ (Therefore,) I say to you, 'Send out My son so that he may worship Me. If you refuse to send him out, I am going to slay your firstborn son.'"

²⁴ At an inn, on the way, (an angel of) God met him and wanted to kill him. ²⁵ So Zipporah took a sharp stone, cut off her son's foreskin and threw it at (Moses') feet, and she said (to her son), "You are my husband's attempted killer!"

²⁶ When he (the angel) released him, she said, "My husband would have been killed because of the matter of circumcision."

²⁷ God said to Aaron, "Go to greet Moses in the desert." He went to meet him at the mountain of God, and he kissed him. ²⁸ Moses told Aaron all the words of God with which He had sent him, and all the signs that He had commanded him.

Moses and Aaron Announce the News of Redemption

²⁹ Moses and Aaron went, and they assembled all the elders of the children of Israel. ³⁰ Aaron spoke all the words that God had spoken to Moses, and he performed the signs before the eyes of the people.

³¹ And the people believed. They heard that God had remembered the children of Israel, and that He had seen their affliction. They bowed and prostrated themselves on the ground.

Isaac. And it is the donkey on which the Messiah is going to be revealed, as the verse states that the Messiah is *"a poor man riding on a donkey"* (*Zechariah* 9:9; *Rashi, 11ᵗʰ century*).

God arranged for Moses to use this famous donkey to carry his family, as the unique qualities of this donkey indicated the answers to two questions.

(a) It was Abraham's donkey, which he used for the journey to the binding of Isaac. The Torah recounts that when Abraham was told to sacrifice his son, he did not question God and acted with the utmost haste, preparing his own donkey for the journey (*Genesis* 22:3). Thus, God was hinting to Moses, "You might not want to accept this mission, since you feel that your brother

spiritual vitamin

" The concept of being "God's children" (v.22) means, among other things, that just as God is master and ruler over the world and all that is in it, so must we rise above the material drives of life and become their master. "

שמות ה:א-יד

ה [SEVENTH READING] 1 וְאַחַ֗ר בָּ֚אוּ מֹשֶׁ֣ה וְאַהֲרֹ֔ן וַיֹּאמְר֖וּ אֶל־פַּרְעֹ֑ה כֹּֽה־אָמַ֤ר יְהוָה֙ אֱלֹהֵ֣י יִשְׂרָאֵ֔ל שַׁלַּח֙ אֶת־עַמִּ֔י וְיָחֹ֥גּוּ לִ֖י בַּמִּדְבָּֽר: 2 וַיֹּ֣אמֶר פַּרְעֹ֔ה מִ֤י יְהוָה֙ אֲשֶׁ֣ר אֶשְׁמַ֣ע בְּקֹל֔וֹ לְשַׁלַּ֖ח אֶת־יִשְׂרָאֵ֑ל לֹ֤א יָדַ֙עְתִּי֙ אֶת־יְהוָ֔ה וְגַ֥ם אֶת־יִשְׂרָאֵ֖ל לֹ֥א אֲשַׁלֵּֽחַ: 3 וַיֹּ֣אמְר֔וּ אֱלֹהֵ֥י הָעִבְרִ֖ים נִקְרָ֣א עָלֵ֑ינוּ נֵ֣לֲכָה נָּ֡א דֶּרֶךְ֩ שְׁלֹ֨שֶׁת יָמִ֜ים בַּמִּדְבָּ֗ר וְנִזְבְּחָה֙ לַיהוָ֣ה אֱלֹהֵ֔ינוּ פֶּן־יִפְגָּעֵ֔נוּ בַּדֶּ֖בֶר א֥וֹ בֶחָֽרֶב: 4 וַיֹּ֤אמֶר אֲלֵהֶם֙ מֶ֣לֶךְ מִצְרַ֔יִם לָ֚מָּה מֹשֶׁ֣ה וְאַהֲרֹ֔ן תַּפְרִ֥יעוּ אֶת־הָעָ֖ם מִֽמַּעֲשָׂ֑יו לְכ֖וּ לְסִבְלֹתֵיכֶֽם: 5 וַיֹּ֣אמֶר פַּרְעֹ֔ה הֵן־רַבִּ֥ים עַתָּ֖ה עַ֣ם הָאָ֑רֶץ וְהִשְׁבַּתֶּ֥ם אֹתָ֖ם מִסִּבְלֹתָֽם: 6 וַיְצַ֥ו פַּרְעֹ֖ה בַּיּ֣וֹם הַה֑וּא אֶת־הַנֹּגְשִׂ֣ים בָּעָ֔ם וְאֶת־שֹׁטְרָ֖יו לֵאמֹֽר: 7 לֹ֣א תֹאסִפ֞וּן לָתֵ֨ת תֶּ֧בֶן לָעָ֛ם לִלְבֹּ֥ן הַלְּבֵנִ֖ים כִּתְמ֣וֹל שִׁלְשֹׁ֑ם הֵ֚ם יֵֽלְכ֔וּ וְקֹשְׁשׁ֥וּ לָהֶ֖ם תֶּֽבֶן: 8 וְאֶת־מַתְכֹּ֨נֶת הַלְּבֵנִ֜ים אֲשֶׁ֣ר הֵם֩ עֹשִׂ֨ים תְּמ֤וֹל שִׁלְשֹׁם֙ תָּשִׂ֣ימוּ עֲלֵיהֶ֔ם לֹ֥א תִגְרְע֖וּ מִמֶּ֑נּוּ כִּֽי־נִרְפִּ֣ים הֵ֔ם עַל־כֵּ֗ן הֵ֤ם צֹֽעֲקִים֙ לֵאמֹ֔ר נֵלְכָ֖ה נִזְבְּחָ֥ה לֵאלֹהֵֽינוּ: 9 תִּכְבַּ֧ד הָעֲבֹדָ֛ה עַל־הָאֲנָשִׁ֖ים וְיַעֲשׂוּ־בָ֑הּ וְאַל־יִשְׁע֖וּ בְּדִבְרֵי־שָֽׁקֶר: 10 וַיֵּ֨צְא֜וּ נֹגְשֵׂ֤י הָעָם֙ וְשֹׁ֣טְרָ֔יו וַיֹּאמְר֥וּ אֶל־הָעָ֖ם לֵאמֹ֑ר כֹּ֚ה אָמַ֣ר פַּרְעֹ֔ה אֵינֶ֛נִּי נֹתֵ֥ן לָכֶ֖ם תֶּֽבֶן: 11 אַתֶּ֗ם לְכ֨וּ קְח֤וּ לָכֶם֙ תֶּ֔בֶן מֵאֲשֶׁ֖ר תִּמְצָ֑אוּ כִּ֣י אֵ֥ין נִגְרָ֛ע מֵעֲבֹדַתְכֶ֖ם דָּבָֽר: 12 וַיָּ֥פֶץ הָעָ֖ם בְּכָל־אֶ֣רֶץ מִצְרָ֑יִם לְקֹשֵׁ֥שׁ קַ֖שׁ לַתֶּֽבֶן: 13 וְהַנֹּגְשִׂ֖ים אָצִ֣ים לֵאמֹ֑ר כַּלּ֤וּ מַעֲשֵׂיכֶם֙ דְּבַר־י֣וֹם בְּיוֹמ֔וֹ כַּאֲשֶׁ֖ר בִּהְי֥וֹת הַתֶּֽבֶן: 14 וַיֻּכּ֗וּ שֹֽׁטְרֵי֙ בְּנֵ֣י יִשְׂרָאֵ֔ל אֲשֶׁר־שָׂ֣מוּ עֲלֵהֶ֔ם נֹגְשֵׂ֥י פַרְעֹ֖ה לֵאמֹ֑ר מַדּ֡וּעַ לֹא֩ כִלִּיתֶ֨ם חָקְכֶ֤ם

| 350

4. Go and deal with your own burdens. Pharaoh meant, "Go and do the work that has to be done in your own houses." For the entire tribe of Levi, of which Moses and Aaron were members, was exempt from the slavery. We see this from the fact that Moses and Aaron were able to enter and leave the palace without asking permission to be relieved from their labor (*Rashi, 11th century*).

7. Let them go and gather straw for themselves. Pharaoh's intention in commanding them to "gather straw for themselves" was not merely to increase their workload (he could have merely increased their daily quota). Rather, he had a more sinister intention.

With only a limited amount of straw that was not sufficient to fill all the quotas easily, Pharaoh hoped that the Jewish people's unity would erode and divisiveness would set in. This, he hoped, would delay or even stop their redemption (*Rabbi Isaac of Warka, 19th century*).

exodus 5:1–14 — shemot

5 [SEVENTH READING] ¹ Afterwards, Moses and Aaron came and said to Pharaoh, "This is what God, the God of Israel, said: 'Send out My nation, and let them sacrifice to Me in the desert.'"

² Pharaoh said, "Who is God that I should listen to His voice and let Israel out? I do not know of God, nor will I let Israel out!"

³ They said, "The God of the Hebrews has come upon us. Now let us go on a three-day journey into the desert and we will sacrifice to God, our God. Otherwise, He may strike us (i.e. a polite way of saying "you") with a plague or with a sword."

⁴ The king of Egypt said to them, "Why, Moses and Aaron, do you disturb the people from their work? Go and deal with your own burdens." ⁵ Pharaoh said, "The people of the land are now numerous, and you are suggesting that they rest from their work!"

The Situation Worsens

⁶ On that day, Pharaoh commanded the (Egyptian) taskmasters of the people and their (Jewish) guards, saying, ⁷ "You shall not continue to give straw to the people to make the bricks like yesterday and the day before. Let them go and gather straw for themselves. ⁸ You shall impose upon them the same number of bricks that they have been making yesterday and the day before. Do not reduce it, for they are becoming lazy, and that is why they cry out, saying, 'Let us go and sacrifice to our God.' ⁹ Let the labor fall heavily upon the men and let them work at it, and let them not talk about pointless matters."

¹⁰ The taskmasters of the people and their guards went out to the people, saying, "Pharaoh said, 'I am not giving you straw. ¹¹ You must go and obtain straw for yourselves from wherever you can find it, because nothing can be reduced from your workload.'"

¹² The people spread out throughout the entire land of Egypt to gather grain stalks for straw. ¹³ The taskmasters were pressing them, saying, "Finish your work, each day's amount in its day, just as when there was straw."

¹⁴ The guards of the children of Israel whom Pharaoh's taskmasters had appointed were beaten. They were told, "Why have you not completed your requirement to make bricks like the day before yesterday, neither yesterday nor today?"

5:2 Who is God? God said to the children of Israel: I love you because even when I make you great, you are still humble before Me.

I made Abraham great, yet he still said to Me, *"I am dust and ashes"* (*Genesis* 18:27). I made Moses and Aaron great, and they still said, *"Of what significance are we?"* (below, 16:8). But when I made Pharaoh great, he said, *"Who is God that I should listen to His voice?"* (*Babylonian Talmud, Ḥullin* 89a).

שמות

לִלְבֹּן כִּתְמוֹל שִׁלְשֹׁם גַּם־תְּמוֹל גַּם־הַיּוֹם: 15 וַיָּבֹאוּ שֹׁטְרֵי בְּנֵי יִשְׂרָאֵל וַיִּצְעֲקוּ אֶל־פַּרְעֹה לֵאמֹר לָמָּה תַעֲשֶׂה כֹה לַעֲבָדֶיךָ: 16 תֶּבֶן אֵין נִתָּן לַעֲבָדֶיךָ וּלְבֵנִים אֹמְרִים לָנוּ עֲשׂוּ וְהִנֵּה עֲבָדֶיךָ מֻכִּים וְחָטָאת עַמֶּךָ: 17 וַיֹּאמֶר נִרְפִּים אַתֶּם נִרְפִּים עַל־כֵּן אַתֶּם אֹמְרִים נֵלְכָה נִזְבְּחָה לַיהֹוָה: 18 וְעַתָּה לְכוּ עִבְדוּ וְתֶבֶן לֹא־יִנָּתֵן לָכֶם וְתֹכֶן לְבֵנִים תִּתֵּנוּ: 19 וַיִּרְאוּ שֹׁטְרֵי בְנֵי־יִשְׂרָאֵל אֹתָם בְּרָע לֵאמֹר לֹא־תִגְרְעוּ מִלִּבְנֵיכֶם דְּבַר־יוֹם בְּיוֹמוֹ: 20 וַיִּפְגְּעוּ אֶת־מֹשֶׁה וְאֶת־אַהֲרֹן נִצָּבִים לִקְרָאתָם בְּצֵאתָם מֵאֵת פַּרְעֹה: 21 וַיֹּאמְרוּ אֲלֵהֶם יֵרֶא יְהֹוָה עֲלֵיכֶם וְיִשְׁפֹּט אֲשֶׁר הִבְאַשְׁתֶּם אֶת־רֵיחֵנוּ בְּעֵינֵי פַרְעֹה וּבְעֵינֵי עֲבָדָיו לָתֶת־חֶרֶב בְּיָדָם לְהָרְגֵנוּ: 22 [MAFTIR] וַיָּשָׁב מֹשֶׁה אֶל־יְהֹוָה וַיֹּאמַר אֲדֹנָי לָמָה הֲרֵעֹתָה לָעָם הַזֶּה לָמָּה זֶּה שְׁלַחְתָּנִי: 23 וּמֵאָז בָּאתִי אֶל־פַּרְעֹה לְדַבֵּר בִּשְׁמֶךָ הֵרַע לָעָם הַזֶּה וְהַצֵּל לֹא־הִצַּלְתָּ אֶת־עַמֶּךָ:

ו 1 וַיֹּאמֶר יְהֹוָה אֶל־מֹשֶׁה עַתָּה תִרְאֶה אֲשֶׁר אֶעֱשֶׂה לְפַרְעֹה כִּי בְיָד חֲזָקָה יְשַׁלְּחֵם וּבְיָד חֲזָקָה יְגָרְשֵׁם מֵאַרְצוֹ: ס ס ס

קכ"ד פסוקים, וק"ח סימן, מעד"י סימן.

---

22. Why have You mistreated this people? Why have You sent me? *"Why have You mistreated this people?"*—Why did you give this people an evil impulse which caused them to have doubts when I informed them that the redemption is near? *"Why have You sent me?"*—I never doubt *You* and I find it bizarre and incomprehensible that others do. So why have You picked *me* for this mission? (*Rabbi Levi Isaac of Berdichev, 18th century*).

6:1 Now you will see what I will do to Pharaoh. God replied to Moses, *"You questioned My ways! You are not like Abraham, to whom I promised to make Isaac his heir, and then I said to offer him up as a burnt-offering. He did not question My ways."* Therefore, the verse says, *"Now you will see,"* meaning to say, *"Now* you will see the defeat of Pharaoh, but you will not see the defeat of the seven nations, when I bring the Jewish people into the land of Israel (*Rashi, 11th century*).

¹⁵ The guards of the children of Israel came and cried out to Pharaoh, saying, "Why do you do this to your servants? ¹⁶ Straw is not given to your servants, but they still tell us, 'Make bricks.' Your servants are being beaten, and it is bringing sin upon your people."

¹⁷ He said, "You are lazy, simply lazy! That is why you say, 'Let us go, let us sacrifice to God.'

¹⁸ "Now, go and work, but you will not be given straw. Nevertheless, you must produce the same number of bricks."

¹⁹ The guards of the children of Israel saw them in distress, when they said, "Do not reduce the number of your bricks, each day's requirement in its day."

²⁰ When they came out from Pharaoh's presence, (a group of Jewish people) met Moses and Aaron, waiting to meet them. ²¹ They said to them (Moses and Aaron), "May God look upon you and judge, for you have made our scent abhorrent in the eyes of Pharaoh and in the eyes of his servants. You have placed a sword into their hands to kill us."

Moses Complains to God

[MAFTIR] ²² Moses returned to God and said, "O God! Why have You mistreated this people? Why have You sent me? ²³ Since I have come to Pharaoh to speak in Your name, he has mistreated this people, and You have not saved Your people."

6 ¹ God said to Moses, "Now you will see what I will do to Pharaoh! For with a mighty hand he will send them out, and with a mighty hand he will drive them out of his land."

The *Haftarah* for *Shemot* is on page 1316.

spiritual vitamin

> It is certainly not surprising that a human being does not understand the ways of God, for a created and finite being surely cannot understand the Infinite. The opposite would rather be surprising, and it is only due to God's infinite kindness that He has revealed to man certain aspects of His Divine Providence.

> "They did **not listen** to Moses due to **shortness of breath** and **hard labor**" (6:9). To hear God's messages you need to **declutter** your mind. Take a **pause** from life's pressures and invite in a **moment of stillness**.

VA-'ERA'
וארא

GOD AND MOSES: FURTHER DIALOGUE	6:2 – 7:7
MOSES AND AARON COME BEFORE PHARAOH	7:8–13
THE PLAGUES	7:14 – 9:35

NAME
Va-'Era'

MEANING
"And I appeared"

LINES IN TORAH SCROLL
222

PARASHIYYOT
8 open; 8 closed

VERSES
121

WORDS
1748

LETTERS
6701

DATE
2447–8

LOCATION
Egypt

KEY PEOPLE
Moses, Aaron, Pharaoh, Pharaoh's sorcerers, Egyptian people

MITZVOT
None

CHARACTER PROFILE

NAME
Amram

MEANING
"High people"—a lofty people issued from him

FATHER
Kohath

GRANDFATHER
Levi

SIBLINGS
Izhar, Hebron, and Uzziel

WIFE
Jochebed (his aunt)

CHILDREN
Miriam, Aaron, Moses

LIFE SPAN
137 years

ACHIEVEMENTS
Considered one of the greatest men of his generation; a leading legal decisor; brought the Divine Presence from the second heaven to the first; saw his great-grandfather Jacob and lived to see his own great-grandchildren; one of four men in history to die free of sin

KNOWN FOR
Divorced his wife to avert Pharaoh's decree and later remarried her after a sharp critique from his daughter, Miriam

KNOWING GOD

God is known through many different names. The truth of His existence can be confirmed by family tradition, seeing God's miracles and through philosophic investigation. Are all of these necessary? Which is your path to God? (6:2-3).

REPAYMENT OF GOOD

Since the Nile had saved Moses as a baby, he did not smite it to begin the first two plagues. Never bite the hand that fed you! (7:19).

SOUL NUMBING

From Pharaoh we learn that every evil act numbs and "hardens" the heart of man, leading him to be more stubbornly persistent in his actions. But the reverse is also true: every good act you perform "softens" your heart, and invigorates you (9:12).

וארא   שמות ו:ב-ו

2 וַיְדַבֵּ֥ר אֱלֹהִ֖ים אֶל־מֹשֶׁ֑ה וַיֹּ֥אמֶר אֵלָ֖יו אֲנִ֥י יְהוָֽה: 3 וָאֵרָ֗א אֶל־אַבְרָהָ֛ם אֶל־יִצְחָ֥ק וְאֶֽל־יַעֲקֹ֖ב בְּאֵ֣ל שַׁדָּ֑י וּשְׁמִ֣י יְהוָ֔ה לֹ֥א נוֹדַ֖עְתִּי לָהֶֽם: 4 וְגַ֨ם הֲקִמֹ֤תִי אֶת־בְּרִיתִי֙ אִתָּ֔ם לָתֵ֥ת לָהֶ֖ם אֶת־אֶ֣רֶץ כְּנָ֑עַן אֵ֛ת אֶ֥רֶץ מְגֻרֵיהֶ֖ם אֲשֶׁר־גָּ֥רוּ בָֽהּ: 5 וְגַ֣ם | אֲנִ֣י שָׁמַ֗עְתִּי אֶֽת־נַאֲקַת֙ בְּנֵ֣י יִשְׂרָאֵ֔ל אֲשֶׁ֥ר מִצְרַ֖יִם מַעֲבִדִ֣ים אֹתָ֑ם וָאֶזְכֹּ֖ר אֶת־בְּרִיתִֽי: 6 לָכֵ֞ן אֱמֹ֥ר לִבְנֵֽי־יִשְׂרָאֵל֮ אֲנִ֣י יְהוָה֒ וְהוֹצֵאתִ֣י אֶתְכֶ֗ם מִתַּ֙חַת֙ סִבְלֹ֣ת מִצְרַ֔יִם וְהִצַּלְתִּ֥י אֶתְכֶ֖ם מֵעֲבֹדָתָ֑ם וְגָאַלְתִּ֤י אֶתְכֶם֙ בִּזְר֣וֹעַ נְטוּיָ֔ה

the Torah—God's wisdom—was transmitted through him. The Patriarchs, on the other hand, served God primarily through *emotion*. Since the primary emphasis of the Patriarchs' Divine service was not intellectual, they never found a need to question God or challenge Him for an explanation of His actions. Only Moses, whose focus was intellectual, demanded to know, *"Why have You mistreated this people?"* (5:22).

Moses' question was not inappropriate. An inability to understand God's actions would have weakened Moses' intellectual bond with his Maker. Moses questioned God, not as a challenge, but rather, in an attempt to come closer to God.

God replied, *"With My (true) name 'ADONAI ("Havayah"), I did not become known to them."* The Tetragrammaton, *"Havayah,"* transcends all limitations. God was intimating to Moses, "Do not serve Me with intellect *alone*. Temper your intellect with emotion and faith, so that you serve Me without limitation" (*Rabbi Menahem Mendel Schneerson, 20th century*).

4. I also established My covenant with them, to give them the land of Canaan. Here we find an allusion to the resurrection of the dead. When God mentions His covenant with Abraham, Isaac, and Jacob, regarding the land of Canaan, the verse does not say, *"to give you,"* i.e., to the children of Israel, but rather, *"to give them"*—the Patriarchs. The implication is that the Patriarchs *themselves* will one day inherit the land of Canaan. Since they are no longer alive, this promise can only be fulfilled when they will be resurrected (*Babylonian Talmud, Sanhedrin* 90b).

6. I will take you out from under the burdens (sivlot) of Egypt. The word *sivlot*, "burdens," is related to the term *savlanut*, "tolerance." God said, "I will take you out from your tolerance of this exile. How can you expect to be redeemed if you are comfortable with your situation?" The main difficulty of leaving the exile is that you become accustomed to it and eventually come to like it (*Rabbi Isaac Meir Alter of Gur, 19th century*).

> ### kabbalah bites
>
> **6:2** *"Elokim spoke to Moses and said, 'I am HaVaYaH (the Tetragrammaton).'"* When God feels close to us and we can relate to Him, we refer to Him as *Elokim*. When He is distant, He is called *Havayah*.
>
> Moses already knew that God can manifest Himself as *either* close *or* distant. Here he was taught a deeper insight: *"Elokim said, 'I am Havayah.'"* Even when God feels close, He remains above and beyond. And even when He may sometimes appear distant and indifferent to your life, He is close to you at that moment too.

exodus 6:2–6 — va-ʾeraʾ

parashat va-ʾeraʾ

Continued Dialogue Between God and Moses

² God spoke to Moses and said to him, "I am God. ³ I revealed Myself to Abraham, to Isaac, and to Jacob with the name *ʾEl Shaddai* (Almighty God), but with My (true) name *ʾAdonai* ("*Havayah*"), I did not become known to them.

⁴ "I also established My covenant with them to give them the land of Canaan, the land of their temporary residence in which they lived as strangers. ⁵ I also heard the moans of the children of Israel, whom the Egyptians are holding as slaves, and I remembered My covenant. ⁶ Therefore, say to the children of Israel, 'I am God, and I will take you out from under the burdens of Egypt, and I will save you from their labor, and I will redeem you with an outstretched arm and with great acts

---

6:2 God spoke to Moses. God spoke to Moses sternly, because Moses had spoken to God sternly, saying, *"Why have You mistreated this people?"* (5:22; *Rashi, 11th century*).

God (*Elokim*) spoke to Moses and said to him, "I am God (*Havayah*)." If God is infinite and the world is finite, how can He really be found in the world?

The answer: God *contracts* Himself, so to speak, in a way that the world can bear. This is what the Talmud means, *"You shall love God very much, with every measure that He metes out for you"* (*Babylonian Talmud, Berakhot* 54a). God "measures" Himself, so to speak, allowing a perfect amount of His light to reach the world, so that you don't get "burned."

This "measure" of God's presence varies at different times in your life. And it is always exact: *At any given time it is impossible for you to receive more of the Divine Presence than is flowing to you at that moment.* When you know and appreciate this fact, you will rejoice in the precise "measure" of God's presence that is coming right now, thanking Him for giving you the exact amount that you are capable of receiving—no more, no less.

When you accept whatever "measure" God gives you—whether He seems to act with mercy or with judgment—you succeed in "unifying" the names *Havayah* (representing mercy) and *ʾElokim* (representing judgment). You declare, "All the events in my life manifest the kindness of the One God, who acts with me in different ways at different times so that I am able to perceive His presence at all times. I accept that His justice is also a form of kindness. It's the right 'measure' for that day."

Now we can understand the verse, *"God (ʾElokim) spoke to Moses and said to him, 'I am God (Havayah).'"* Moses had just complained to God, "Why have You mistreated this people?" (5:22) God now responds that He had not mistreated them at all. *ʾElokim* said, "I really am *Havayah*"—*My attribute of justice is, in reality, merciful*. It is what God's unfathomable wisdom has decreed to be the precise "measure" of emanation that was called for in that particular instant (*Rabbi Menahem Nahum Twersky of Chernobyl, 18th century*).

With My (true) name *ʾAdonai* ("*Havayah*"), I did not become known to them. Moses served God primarily through *intellect*, which is why

---

Food for thought

1. Have you ever pondered the nature of your personal, Divine calling?

2. Do you ever ignore what you know is God's message?

3. Can you perceive the hand of God in current world events?

וארא / שמות ו:א-טז

וּבִשְׁפָטִ֖ים גְּדֹלִֽים׃ 7 וְלָקַחְתִּ֨י אֶתְכֶ֥ם לִי֙ לְעָ֔ם וְהָיִ֥יתִי לָכֶ֖ם לֵֽאלֹהִ֑ים וִֽידַעְתֶּ֗ם כִּ֣י אֲנִ֤י יְהֹוָה֙ אֱלֹ֣הֵיכֶ֔ם הַמּוֹצִ֣יא אֶתְכֶ֔ם מִתַּ֖חַת סִבְל֥וֹת מִצְרָֽיִם׃ 8 וְהֵבֵאתִ֤י אֶתְכֶם֙ אֶל־הָאָ֔רֶץ אֲשֶׁ֤ר נָשָׂ֙אתִי֙ אֶת־יָדִ֔י לָתֵ֣ת אֹתָ֔הּ לְאַבְרָהָ֥ם לְיִצְחָ֖ק וּֽלְיַעֲקֹ֑ב וְנָתַתִּ֨י אֹתָ֥הּ לָכֶ֛ם מוֹרָשָׁ֖ה אֲנִ֥י יְהֹוָֽה׃ 9 וַיְדַבֵּ֥ר מֹשֶׁ֛ה כֵּ֖ן אֶל־בְּנֵ֣י יִשְׂרָאֵ֑ל וְלֹ֤א שָֽׁמְעוּ֙ אֶל־מֹשֶׁ֔ה מִקֹּ֣צֶר ר֔וּחַ וּמֵעֲבֹדָ֖ה קָשָֽׁה׃ פ 10 וַיְדַבֵּ֥ר יְהֹוָ֖ה אֶל־מֹשֶׁ֥ה לֵּאמֹֽר׃ 11 בֹּ֣א דַבֵּ֔ר אֶל־פַּרְעֹ֖ה מֶ֣לֶךְ מִצְרָ֑יִם וִֽישַׁלַּ֥ח אֶת־בְּנֵֽי־יִשְׂרָאֵ֖ל מֵאַרְצֽוֹ׃ 12 וַיְדַבֵּ֣ר מֹשֶׁ֔ה לִפְנֵ֥י יְהֹוָ֖ה לֵאמֹ֑ר הֵ֤ן בְּנֵֽי־יִשְׂרָאֵל֙ לֹא־שָׁמְע֣וּ אֵלַ֔י וְאֵיךְ֙ יִשְׁמָעֵ֣נִי פַרְעֹ֔ה וַאֲנִ֖י עֲרַ֥ל שְׂפָתָֽיִם׃ פ 13 וַיְדַבֵּ֣ר יְהֹוָה֮ אֶל־מֹשֶׁ֣ה וְאֶֽל־אַהֲרֹן֒ וַיְצַוֵּם֙ אֶל־בְּנֵ֣י יִשְׂרָאֵ֔ל וְאֶל־פַּרְעֹ֖ה מֶ֣לֶךְ מִצְרָ֑יִם לְהוֹצִ֥יא אֶת־בְּנֵֽי־יִשְׂרָאֵ֖ל מֵאֶ֥רֶץ מִצְרָֽיִם׃ ס 14 [SECOND READING] אֵ֖לֶּה רָאשֵׁ֣י בֵית־אֲבֹתָ֑ם בְּנֵ֨י רְאוּבֵ֜ן בְּכֹ֣ר יִשְׂרָאֵ֗ל חֲנ֤וֹךְ וּפַלּוּא֙ חֶצְר֣וֹן וְכַרְמִ֔י אֵ֖לֶּה מִשְׁפְּחֹ֥ת רְאוּבֵֽן׃ 15 וּבְנֵ֣י שִׁמְע֗וֹן יְמוּאֵ֨ל וְיָמִ֤ין וְאֹ֙הַד֙ וְיָכִ֣ין וְצֹ֔חַר וְשָׁא֖וּל בֶּן־הַֽכְּנַעֲנִ֑ית אֵ֖לֶּה מִשְׁפְּחֹ֥ת שִׁמְעֽוֹן׃ 16 וְאֵ֛לֶּה שְׁמ֥וֹת בְּנֵֽי־לֵוִ֖י

Rabbi Nehemiah said that all the tribes worshiped idols in Egypt, while the tribes of Reuben, Simeon, and Levi did not.

The other Rabbis said that the rest of the tribes did not have a position of leadership in Egypt, while Reuben, Simeon, and Levi did have one (*Midrash Rabbah*).

Why were these three tribes not burdened with slavery equally with the other tribes? Because when Jacob blessed his sons before his passing, Reuben, Simeon, and Levi received no blessings and were rebuked instead (*Genesis* 49:3-7). This clouded their outlook for the future with an element of pessimism. God therefore spared them from a slavery which may have proven to be a test too great for them (*Rabbi Meir Simhah of Dvinsk, 19th–20th century*).

16. These are the names of Levi's sons. The Torah uses the phrase "the *names* of" only when discussing the Levites. This hints to the idea that, while the tribe of Levi were not enslaved, they gave their children names with exile themes out of empathy for their brothers' hardships.

— *Gershon* is derived from the word *ger* (stranger), since they were living in a foreign land (*Genesis* 15:13).

— *Kohath* is derived from *kehot*, as in the expression "their teeth were *set on edge*," suggesting a state of great agitation (see *Jeremiah* 31:28).

— *Merari* is derived from "they *embittered* (*mareru*) their lives with hard labor" (1:14).

By emphasizing that "*these are the names of Levi's sons*," the Torah teaches us an important lesson in empathy (*Rabbi Isaiah Horowitz, 16th–17th century*).

of judgment. ⁷ I will take you as a people for Myself, and I will be a God to you, and you will know that I am God, your God, who is taking you out from under the burdens of Egypt. ⁸ I will bring you to the land, regarding which I raised My hand (swearing) to give it to Abraham, to Isaac, and to Jacob, and I will give it to you as a heritage; I am God.'"

⁹ Moses related this to the children of Israel, but they did not listen to Moses due to shortness of breath and hard labor.

¹⁰ God spoke to Moses, saying, ¹¹ "Come, speak to Pharaoh, the king of Egypt, that he should send the children of Israel from his land."

¹² Moses spoke before God, saying, "If the children of Israel did not listen to me, then how will Pharaoh listen to me? I have sealed lips!"

Moses and Aaron are Appointed as Redeemers

¹³ God spoke to Moses and to Aaron, and He commanded them about the children of Israel and about Pharaoh, the king of Egypt, to take the children of Israel out of the land of Egypt. ¹⁴ The following are the heads of their fathers' families:

[SECOND READING] ¹⁴ The sons of Reuben, Israel's firstborn: Enoch, Pallu, Hezron, and Carmi, these are the families of Reuben. ¹⁵ The sons of Simeon: Jemuel, Jamin, Ohad, Jachin, Zohar and Saul, the son of the Canaanite woman. These are the families of Simeon. ¹⁶ These are the names of Levi's sons in order of their birth: Gershon,

---

12. If the children of Israel did not listen to me, then how will Pharaoh listen to me? I have sealed lips! With humility, Moses defended the children of Israel's disbelief of his message by deflecting their shortcoming onto himself. It is not that they doubted God's message of deliverance; they felt Pharaoh would not be moved by Moses, since he lacked the oratory skills required for such a task (*Rabbi Aaron Lewin of Rzeszow, 20ᵗʰ century*).

A prophet is empowered by his listeners. It was *because* the Jewish people had refused to listen that Moses suffered from "sealed lips."

This actually delayed the giving of the Ten Commandments. God's word was in exile for a long time, as the future recipients of the Torah had not yet prepared themselves to hear it. Even if they were not actually worshiping idols, they were attached to ideas that were foreign to true spirituality. If they had been ready to hear God's word, they would have been redeemed immediately.

To be able to listen, your mind must be still. This is our problem today, too—we cannot release ourselves from the world's pleasures; we cannot clear our hearts to hear God's word without any distractions. And that is why we mention the Exodus every day, because it empowers us to rid the mind of distraction (*Rabbi Judah Aryeh Leib Alter of Gur, 19ᵗʰ century*).

14-16. The sons of Reuben ... The sons of Simeon ... These are the names of Levi's sons.... Why does the Torah count the tribes of Reuben, Simeon, and Levi here without counting the other tribes?

Rabbi Judah said that all the other tribes did not preserve their genealogical purity in Egypt, while the tribes of Reuben, Simeon, and Levi did.

לְתֹלְדֹתָם גֵּרְשׁוֹן וּקְהָת וּמְרָרִי וּשְׁנֵי חַיֵּי לֵוִי שֶׁבַע וּשְׁלֹשִׁים וּמְאַת שָׁנָה: 17 בְּנֵי גֵרְשׁוֹן לִבְנִי וְשִׁמְעִי לְמִשְׁפְּחֹתָם: 18 וּבְנֵי קְהָת עַמְרָם וְיִצְהָר וְחֶבְרוֹן וְעֻזִּיאֵל וּשְׁנֵי חַיֵּי קְהָת שָׁלֹשׁ וּשְׁלֹשִׁים וּמְאַת שָׁנָה: 19 וּבְנֵי מְרָרִי מַחְלִי וּמוּשִׁי אֵלֶּה מִשְׁפְּחֹת הַלֵּוִי לְתֹלְדֹתָם: 20 וַיִּקַּח עַמְרָם אֶת־יוֹכֶבֶד דֹּדָתוֹ לוֹ לְאִשָּׁה וַתֵּלֶד לוֹ אֶת־אַהֲרֹן וְאֶת־מֹשֶׁה וּשְׁנֵי חַיֵּי עַמְרָם שֶׁבַע וּשְׁלֹשִׁים וּמְאַת שָׁנָה: 21 וּבְנֵי יִצְהָר קֹרַח וָנֶפֶג וְזִכְרִי: 22 וּבְנֵי עֻזִּיאֵל מִישָׁאֵל וְאֶלְצָפָן וְסִתְרִי: 23 וַיִּקַּח אַהֲרֹן אֶת־אֱלִישֶׁבַע בַּת־עַמִּינָדָב אֲחוֹת נַחְשׁוֹן לוֹ לְאִשָּׁה וַתֵּלֶד לוֹ אֶת־נָדָב וְאֶת־אֲבִיהוּא אֶת־אֶלְעָזָר וְאֶת־אִיתָמָר: 24 וּבְנֵי קֹרַח אַסִּיר וְאֶלְקָנָה וַאֲבִיאָסָף אֵלֶּה מִשְׁפְּחֹת הַקָּרְחִי: 25 וְאֶלְעָזָר בֶּן־אַהֲרֹן לָקַח־לוֹ מִבְּנוֹת פּוּטִיאֵל לוֹ לְאִשָּׁה וַתֵּלֶד לוֹ אֶת־פִּינְחָס אֵלֶּה רָאשֵׁי אֲבוֹת הַלְוִיִּם לְמִשְׁפְּחֹתָם: 26 הוּא אַהֲרֹן וּמֹשֶׁה אֲשֶׁר אָמַר יְהֹוָה לָהֶם הוֹצִיאוּ אֶת־בְּנֵי יִשְׂרָאֵל מֵאֶרֶץ מִצְרַיִם עַל־צִבְאֹתָם: 27 הֵם הַמְדַבְּרִים אֶל־פַּרְעֹה מֶלֶךְ־מִצְרַיִם לְהוֹצִיא אֶת־בְּנֵי־יִשְׂרָאֵל מִמִּצְרָיִם הוּא מֹשֶׁה וְאַהֲרֹן: 28 וַיְהִי בְּיוֹם דִּבֶּר יְהֹוָה אֶל־מֹשֶׁה בְּאֶרֶץ מִצְרָיִם: ס 29 [THIRD READING] וַיְדַבֵּר יְהֹוָה אֶל־מֹשֶׁה לֵּאמֹר אֲנִי יְהֹוָה דַּבֵּר אֶל־פַּרְעֹה מֶלֶךְ מִצְרַיִם אֵת כָּל־אֲשֶׁר אֲנִי דֹּבֵר אֵלֶיךָ: 30 וַיֹּאמֶר מֹשֶׁה לִפְנֵי יְהֹוָה הֵן אֲנִי עֲרַל שְׂפָתַיִם וְאֵיךְ יִשְׁמַע אֵלַי פַּרְעֹה: פ

Moses and Aaron were certainly not the same, yet the Torah considers them equal. This is because the goal of connecting the people with God was accomplished through their combined efforts. Moses brought the word of God to the people, while Aaron, the High Priest, atoned for their sins, making it possible for the Divine Presence to rest among them.

The same holds true for all generations: There is always the "Moses," who dedicates himself to teaching God's word to the masses, and the "Aaron," who reconciles the people with God, inspiring them to lead more sanctified lives. Both are equally important (*Rabbi Jacob Isaac ha-Hozeh of Lublin, 18th–19th century*).

27. They are the ones who (followed their instructions to) speak to Pharaoh, the king of Egypt ... both Moses and Aaron. Even after standing in Pharaoh's presence, engulfed by corruption and impurity, Moses and Aaron upheld their spiritual preeminence. Uninfluenced

Kohath, and Merari. The years of Levi's life were one hundred and thirty-seven years. ¹⁷ The sons of Gershon were Libni and Shimei according to their families. ¹⁸ The sons of Kohath were Amram, Izhar, Hebron, and Uzziel. The years of Kohath's life were one hundred and thirty-three years. ¹⁹ The sons of Merari were Mahli and Mushi.

These are the families of the Levites in order of their birth. ²⁰ Amram took Jochebed, his aunt, as a wife for himself, and she bore him Aaron and Moses. The years of Amram's life were one hundred and thirty-seven years. ²¹ The sons of Izhar were Korah, Nepheg and Zichri. ²² The sons of Uzziel were Mishael, Elzaphan, and Sithri. ²³ Aaron took Elisheba, the daughter of Amminadab, the sister of Nahshon, as a wife for himself. She bore him Nadab and Abihu, Eleazar and Ithamar. ²⁴ The sons of Korah were Assir, Elkanah and Abiasaph. These are the families of the Korahites. ²⁵ Eleazar son of Aaron took one of the daughters of Putiel for himself as a wife, and she bore him Phinehas. The above are the heads of the fathers of the Levites, according to their families.

²⁶ It was (the above-mentioned) Aaron and Moses to whom God said, "Take the children of Israel out of the land of Egypt according to their (tribal) legions." ²⁷ They are the ones who (followed their instructions to) speak to Pharaoh, the king of Egypt, to take out the children of Israel from Egypt. Both Moses and Aaron (together completed this mission).

²⁸ It was on the day when God spoke to Moses in the land of Egypt.

[THIRD READING] ²⁹ God spoke to Moses, saying, "I am God. Tell over to Pharaoh everything that I speak to you."

God Promises to Harden Pharaoh's Heart

³⁰ Moses said before God, "But I have sealed lips! How will Pharaoh possibly listen to me?"

---

26. Aaron and Moses. Sometimes Aaron is mentioned before Moses, and sometimes Moses is mentioned before Aaron. This teaches us that they were equal (*Rashi, 11ᵗʰ century*).

spiritual vitamin

> For reasons best known to God Himself, He wished that there should be many nations in the world, but only one Jewish people, a people who should be separated and different from all the other nations, with a destiny and function of its own.

וארא   שמות ז:א-ו

א וַיֹּאמֶר יְהֹוָה אֶל־מֹשֶׁה רְאֵה נְתַתִּיךָ אֱלֹהִים לְפַרְעֹה וְאַהֲרֹן אָחִיךָ יִהְיֶה נְבִיאֶךָ: ב אַתָּה תְדַבֵּר אֵת כָּל־אֲשֶׁר אֲצַוֶּךָּ וְאַהֲרֹן אָחִיךָ יְדַבֵּר אֶל־פַּרְעֹה וְשִׁלַּח אֶת־בְּנֵי־יִשְׂרָאֵל מֵאַרְצוֹ: ג וַאֲנִי אַקְשֶׁה אֶת־לֵב פַּרְעֹה וְהִרְבֵּיתִי אֶת־אֹתֹתַי וְאֶת־מוֹפְתַי בְּאֶרֶץ מִצְרָיִם: ד וְלֹא־יִשְׁמַע אֲלֵכֶם פַּרְעֹה וְנָתַתִּי אֶת־יָדִי בְּמִצְרָיִם וְהוֹצֵאתִי אֶת־צִבְאֹתַי אֶת־עַמִּי בְנֵי־יִשְׂרָאֵל מֵאֶרֶץ מִצְרַיִם בִּשְׁפָטִים גְּדֹלִים: ה וְיָדְעוּ מִצְרַיִם כִּי־אֲנִי יְהֹוָה בִּנְטֹתִי אֶת־יָדִי עַל־מִצְרָיִם וְהוֹצֵאתִי אֶת־בְּנֵי־יִשְׂרָאֵל מִתּוֹכָם: ו וַיַּעַשׂ מֹשֶׁה וְאַהֲרֹן כַּאֲשֶׁר צִוָּה יְהֹוָה אֹתָם כֵּן עָשׂוּ:

5. The Egyptians shall know that I am God. The Torah stresses repeatedly that the Ten Plagues were enacted so that *"The Egyptians shall know that I am God"* (7:5. See also ibid. 17; 8:6, 18; 9:14, 29; 11:7; 14:4, 18). In other words, the goal of the plagues was to bring the Egyptian nation, which believed in the many gods of nature and chance, to an appreciation that there is in fact one God who rules this world.

Viewed from this angle, the plagues were not so much a form of Divine oppression against Egypt but rather, something that was intended for their benefit, to teach them a valuable religious truth. The harshness of the plagues was only necessary because the Egyptians were highly resistant to the message. They were such devout polytheists—a belief in which their ego was heavily invested—that it would take a series of national catastrophes to prove the truth of monotheism to them. But in theory, at least, they could have learned the same lesson much more easily.

If the Egyptian exodus had been a perfect one, the nations would have come to "know that I am God," without the havoc and destruction of the plagues. In fact, God saw it as tragic that the Egyptians had to be destroyed, rather than learn their lesson: *"My handiwork is drowning in the sea,"* said God to the angels, when they requested permission to sing, *'and you want to sing praise!'"* (*Babylonian Talmud, Megillah* 10b). But, sadly, the Egyptians had proven to be too obstinate and, as human beings with free choice, they refused to accept the truth of one God. The time had clearly not yet come for complete redemption, and at this point in history, God's plan could only be furthered, unfortunately, through destruction.

But regardless of the approach—destruction through plagues, as it was in the past, or "repair" through the Messiah, as it will be in our days—the theme remains the same. Our task as Jews is to act as a source of genuine ethics and spirituality for the entire world, so that all nations "shall know that I am God." And then, *"God will be King over the entire earth. On that day, God will be One and His name will be One"* (*Zechariah* 14:9; *Rabbi Menahem Mendel Schneerson, 20th century*).

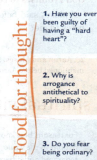

Food for thought

1. Have you ever been guilty of having a "hard heart"?

2. Why is arrogance antithetical to spirituality?

3. Do you fear being ordinary?

exodus 7:1–6 — va-ʾeraʾ

7 ¹ God said to Moses, "See, I have made you a master (of plagues and torture) over Pharaoh. Aaron your brother will be your interpreter. ² You should first say all My commands (to Pharaoh), and Aaron, your brother, will then explain to Pharaoh that he should send the children of Israel out of his land."

³ "I will harden Pharaoh's heart (in order that) I should increase My miracles and wonders in the land of Egypt. ⁴ Pharaoh will not listen to you. I will lay My hand upon Egypt (to strike them), and I will take My legions, My people, the children of Israel, out of Egypt with great acts of judgment. ⁵ When I stretch forth My hand over Egypt, the Egyptians shall know that I am God, and I will take the children of Israel out from among them."

⁶ Moses and Aaron did this. They did what God commanded them.

---

by their surroundings, they continued to receive Divine prophecy, exactly as before (*Rabbi Ḥayyim of Tchernowitz, 18th century*).

7:1 See, I have made you a master (*'Elokim*) over Pharaoh. This could also be rendered, "See, I have made you a *god* over Pharaoh." Pharaoh claimed that he was a god (*Rashi* to v. 15), and sometimes negative forces can only be disarmed through imitation. God said to Moses, "I have made you like a god over Pharaoh. You will perform miracles before him—things of a Divine nature—to put an end to his ridiculous claims that he is a god. Instead, he is going to think that *you* are a god."

Obviously, when God asks you to "play god" it can strain your sense of humility. So Moshe was warned, *"See..."* Watch out! For this mission you must always be especially conscious of who you really are (*Rabbi Elimelech of Lyzhansk, 18th century*).

3. I will harden Pharaoh's heart. Pharaoh was punished with the removal of his free choice as a punishment for his prior enslavement of the Jewish people.

But, if God had already decreed that the Jewish people would be enslaved (see *Genesis* 15:13), why were the Egyptians punished? Surely, they were carrying out God's will?

God only decreed that a *nation* was destined to enslave the Jewish people. Each individual Egyptian was free do as he chose, and was punished accordingly if he chose to harm the Israelites (*Maimonides, 12th century*).

It was decreed by God that the Egyptians would enslave the Jewish people. However, the Egyptians themselves did not enslave the Jewish people in order to carry out God's will, but to satisfy their own inhumane desires. Therefore, they were punished (*Rabbi Yom Tov Lipmann Heller, 17th century*).

---

kabbalah bites

7:1 If everything is ultimately from God, how can evil exist? The Kabbalah explains that evil is really a form of *chaos*, where we simply cannot fathom what is going on; and good could really be defined as *order*. *Chaos* brings you stress and causes you to fragment; *order* is conducive to mental, emotional and physical wellbeing.

"*God said to Moses, 'I have made you a master over Pharaoh.'*" God empowers you with the ability to overcome Pharaoh (chaos) and master your life with order. Every time you make a decision, ask yourself: Am I mastering Pharaoh? Am I inviting chaos, or bringing harmony and order?

שמות ז:ז - טו | וארא

7 וּמֹשֶׁה בֶּן־שְׁמֹנִים שָׁנָה וְאַהֲרֹן בֶּן־שָׁלֹשׁ וּשְׁמֹנִים שָׁנָה בְּדַבְּרָם אֶל־פַּרְעֹה: פ
8 [FOURTH READING] וַיֹּאמֶר יְהֹוָה אֶל־מֹשֶׁה וְאֶל־אַהֲרֹן לֵאמֹר: 9 כִּי יְדַבֵּר אֲלֵכֶם פַּרְעֹה לֵאמֹר תְּנוּ לָכֶם מוֹפֵת וְאָמַרְתָּ אֶל־אַהֲרֹן קַח אֶת־מַטְּךָ וְהַשְׁלֵךְ לִפְנֵי־פַרְעֹה יְהִי לְתַנִּין: 10 וַיָּבֹא מֹשֶׁה וְאַהֲרֹן אֶל־פַּרְעֹה וַיַּעֲשׂוּ כֵן כַּאֲשֶׁר צִוָּה יְהֹוָה וַיַּשְׁלֵךְ אַהֲרֹן אֶת־מַטֵּהוּ לִפְנֵי פַרְעֹה וְלִפְנֵי עֲבָדָיו וַיְהִי לְתַנִּין: 11 וַיִּקְרָא גַּם־פַּרְעֹה לַחֲכָמִים וְלַמְכַשְּׁפִים וַיַּעֲשׂוּ גַם־הֵם חַרְטֻמֵּי מִצְרַיִם בְּלַהֲטֵיהֶם כֵּן: 12 וַיַּשְׁלִיכוּ אִישׁ מַטֵּהוּ וַיִּהְיוּ לְתַנִּינִם וַיִּבְלַע מַטֵּה־אַהֲרֹן אֶת־מַטֹּתָם: 13 וַיֶּחֱזַק לֵב פַּרְעֹה וְלֹא שָׁמַע אֲלֵהֶם כַּאֲשֶׁר דִּבֶּר יְהֹוָה: ס 14 וַיֹּאמֶר יְהֹוָה אֶל־מֹשֶׁה כָּבֵד לֵב פַּרְעֹה מֵאֵן לְשַׁלַּח הָעָם: 15 לֵךְ אֶל־פַּרְעֹה בַּבֹּקֶר הִנֵּה יֹצֵא הַמַּיְמָה וְנִצַּבְתָּ לִקְרָאתוֹ עַל־שְׂפַת הַיְאֹר וְהַמַּטֶּה אֲשֶׁר־נֶהְפַּךְ לְנָחָשׁ תִּקַּח בְּיָדֶךָ:

---

and upright people. They had been negatively influenced by the local culture but could soon return to their former level of morality. All that was needed was to remove them from their corrupt surroundings.

Moses illustrated the point graphically with "the staff of God" (4:20). When it was thrown to the ground, entering Pharaoh's immediate surroundings, it became a poisonous snake. Once Moses retrieved it back to his own domain, it quickly reverted to "a staff of God" (*Rabbi Meir Shapira of Lublin, 20th century*).

12. Aaron's staff swallowed their staffs. Generally, you should draw others closer only by showering them with love and care. But sometimes it's necessary to speak some stronger words, to "swallow up" your friend.

Then, you should remember, (a) that "swallowing" is to be done *with the staff of Aaron*, who was renowned for his boundless love of mankind. Even in a moment of necessary rebuke, you must be extremely careful not to mix in any personal anger. The "swallowing" must be only what is necessary for the benefit of the recipient.

(b) The swallowing must not be done while the staff is a snake, i.e., not through venomous anger, but with the solid resolve ("staff") of a responsible educator (*Rabbi Menahem Mendel Schneerson, 20th century*).

---

kabbalah bites

7:14 "*God has set one against the other*" (Ecclesiastes 7:14). The Kabbalah teaches that every negative energy has a corresponding positive energy. What is the spiritual mirror-image of Pharaoh's hardened heart? Being stubborn in upholding your values and not melting in the face of pressure.

Aaron Performs a Miracle for Pharaoh

[FOURTH READING] 7 Moses was eighty years old, and Aaron was eighty-three years old, when they spoke to Pharaoh.

8 God spoke to Moses and Aaron, saying, 9 "When Pharaoh speaks to you, saying, 'Prove yourselves (as emissaries of a higher power) with a miracle,' you shall say to Aaron, 'Take your staff, and cast it in front of Pharaoh.' It will become a snake."

10 Moses and Aaron came to Pharaoh, and they did exactly as God had commanded. Aaron cast his staff in front of Pharaoh and in front of his servants, and it became a snake.

11 Pharaoh also summoned sages and magicians and they, the sorcerers of Egypt, did the same thing with their spells. 12 Each one of them cast down his staff, and they became snakes. Aaron's staff (then reverted back from a snake to a staff and) swallowed their staffs.

13 Pharaoh's heart became hardened, and he did not listen to them, just as God had said.

The First Plague—The Nile Turns into Blood

14 God said to Moses, "Pharaoh's heart is heavy. He refuses to send the people out. 15 Go to Pharaoh in the morning, when he goes out to the water, and stand

---

kabbalah bites

7:7 *"Moses was eighty years old,"* when the 210-year Egyptian exile ended, from which it follows that he was born in the 130th year of the exile. According to the Kabbalah this is highly significant.

The "dysfunctional souls" which Adam brought into being during the 130 years he separated from his wife (see *Genesis 5:3*), were reincarnated into the children of Israel in Egypt. Mirroring Adam's 130 sinful years, these souls took 130 years to heal. At the moment the healing was complete, Moses, their redeemer, was born.

---

9. When Pharaoh speaks to you, saying, "Prove yourselves with a miracle." Rendered literally, the verse reads, "Show yourselves a miracle." One would, of course, have expected Pharaoh to say, "Show *me* a miracle." What does "show yourselves a miracle" mean?

God said to Moses, "Perform something that will be wondrous and novel *even for you*. Pharaoh will be convinced when he sees something that is amazing even in your eyes" (*Rabbi Elimelech of Lyzhansk, 18th century*).

Take your staff, and cast it in front of Pharaoh. It will become a snake. We are all influenced by our surroundings. Bad people can be influenced by decent neighbors just as good people can become corrupt when they are surrounded by dishonesty.

Moses wanted Pharaoh to understand that the Israelites were, at their core, a noble

וארא · שמות ז:טז-כה

16 וְאָמַרְתָּ֣ אֵלָ֗יו יְהֹוָ֞ה אֱלֹהֵ֤י הָעִבְרִים֙ שְׁלָחַ֣נִי אֵלֶ֣יךָ לֵאמֹ֔ר שַׁלַּח֙ אֶת־עַמִּ֔י וְיַֽעַבְדֻ֖נִי בַּמִּדְבָּ֑ר וְהִנֵּ֥ה לֹֽא־שָׁמַ֖עְתָּ עַד־כֹּֽה: 17 כֹּ֚ה אָמַ֣ר יְהֹוָ֔ה בְּזֹ֣את תֵּדַ֔ע כִּ֖י אֲנִ֣י יְהֹוָ֑ה הִנֵּ֨ה אָנֹכִ֜י מַכֶּ֣ה ׀ בַּמַּטֶּ֣ה אֲשֶׁר־בְּיָדִ֗י עַל־הַמַּ֛יִם אֲשֶׁ֥ר בַּיְאֹ֖ר וְנֶהֶפְכ֥וּ לְדָֽם: 18 וְהַדָּגָ֧ה אֲשֶׁר־בַּיְאֹ֛ר תָּמ֖וּת וּבָאַ֣שׁ הַיְאֹ֑ר וְנִלְא֣וּ מִצְרַ֔יִם לִשְׁתּ֥וֹת מַ֖יִם מִן־הַיְאֹֽר: ס 19 וַיֹּ֨אמֶר יְהֹוָ֜ה אֶל־מֹשֶׁ֗ה אֱמֹ֣ר אֶל־אַהֲרֹ֡ן קַ֣ח מַטְּךָ֣ וּנְטֵה־יָדְךָ֩ עַל־מֵימֵ֨י מִצְרַ֜יִם עַל־נַהֲרֹתָ֣ם ׀ עַל־יְאֹרֵיהֶ֣ם וְעַל־אַגְמֵיהֶ֗ם וְעַ֛ל כָּל־מִקְוֵ֥ה מֵימֵיהֶ֖ם וְיִֽהְיוּ־דָ֑ם וְהָ֤יָה דָם֙ בְּכָל־אֶ֣רֶץ מִצְרַ֔יִם וּבָעֵצִ֖ים וּבָאֲבָנִֽים: 20 וַיַּֽעֲשׂוּ־ כֵן֩ מֹשֶׁ֨ה וְאַהֲרֹ֜ן כַּאֲשֶׁ֣ר ׀ צִוָּ֣ה יְהֹוָ֗ה וַיָּ֤רֶם בַּמַּטֶּה֙ וַיַּ֤ךְ אֶת־הַמַּ֨יִם֙ אֲשֶׁ֣ר בַּיְאֹ֔ר לְעֵינֵ֣י פַרְעֹ֔ה וּלְעֵינֵ֖י עֲבָדָ֑יו וַיֵּהָ֥פְכ֛וּ כָּל־הַמַּ֥יִם אֲשֶׁר־בַּיְאֹ֖ר לְדָֽם: 21 וְהַדָּגָ֨ה אֲשֶׁר־בַּיְאֹ֥ר מֵ֨תָה֙ וַיִּבְאַ֣שׁ הַיְאֹ֔ר וְלֹא־יָכְל֣וּ מִצְרַ֔יִם לִשְׁתּ֥וֹת מַ֖יִם מִן־הַיְאֹ֑ר וַיְהִ֥י הַדָּ֖ם בְּכָל־אֶ֥רֶץ מִצְרָֽיִם: 22 וַיַּֽעֲשׂוּ־כֵ֛ן חַרְטֻמֵּ֥י מִצְרַ֖יִם בְּלָטֵיהֶ֑ם וַיֶּחֱזַ֤ק לֵב־פַּרְעֹה֙ וְלֹא־שָׁמַ֣ע אֲלֵהֶ֔ם כַּאֲשֶׁ֖ר דִּבֶּ֥ר יְהֹוָֽה: 23 וַיִּ֣פֶן פַּרְעֹ֔ה וַיָּבֹ֖א אֶל־בֵּית֑וֹ וְלֹא־שָׁ֥ת לִבּ֖וֹ גַּם־לָזֹֽאת: 24 וַיַּחְפְּר֧וּ כָל־מִצְרַ֛יִם סְבִיבֹ֥ת הַיְאֹ֖ר מַ֣יִם לִשְׁתּ֑וֹת כִּ֣י לֹ֤א יָֽכְלוּ֙ לִשְׁתֹּ֔ת מִמֵּימֵ֖י הַיְאֹֽר: 25 וַיִּמָּלֵ֖א שִׁבְעַ֣ת יָמִ֑ים אַחֲרֵ֥י הַכּוֹת־יְהֹוָ֖ה

"I can't do that," said Moses. "Does a person who drinks water from a well throw a stone into it?"

God said, "Let Aaron go and turn it to blood." So Aaron went and struck the Nile, and it turned to blood.

Why did Moses not strike it? He said, "I was cast into it, and it did not harm me." Therefore, Aaron struck it (*Exodus Rabbah*).

24. The Egyptians dug around the Nile ... since they could not drink from the water of the Nile. The Jewish people were unaffected by the plague. When the Egyptians would draw from barrels of water owned by Jews, the part that they took miraculously turned into blood. Even if a Jew held a cup of water and allowed an Egyptian to drink water from it, the water turned into blood. Even when they drank together from the same dish, the Jew drank water and the Egyptian drank blood. However, if an Egyptian *paid* the Jew for some water, it did not turn into blood (*Exodus Rabbah*).

The miraculous transformation of blood into water in the hands of the Jewish people is not mentioned at all in the Torah. We are therefore given to understand that the first three plagues

opposite him on the bank of the Nile. Take in your hand the staff that turned into a snake. ¹⁶ Say to him, 'God, the God of the Hebrews, sent me to you, saying, "Send away My people, so that they may serve Me in the desert."

"Up to this point, you have not listened. ¹⁷ So God is (now) saying, 'With this you will know that I am God.' With the staff that is in my hand I am going to hit the water that is in the Nile, and it will turn to blood. ¹⁸ The fish that are in the Nile will die, and the Nile will become foul smelling. The Egyptians will become weary from trying (to find a way) to drink water from the Nile.'"

¹⁹ God said to Moses, "Say to Aaron, 'Take your staff and extend your hand over the waters of Egypt, over their rivers, over their canals, over their ponds, and over all their bodies of water, and they will become blood. There will be blood throughout the entire land of Egypt, even in wood (vessels) and in stone (vessels).'"

²⁰ Moses and Aaron did exactly as God had commanded. He raised the staff and struck the water that was in the Nile, before the eyes of Pharaoh and before the eyes of his servants, and all the water that was in the Nile turned to blood. ²¹ The fish-life that was in the Nile died, and the Nile stank. The Egyptians could not drink water from the Nile. There was blood throughout the entire land of Egypt.

²² The sorcerers of Egypt did the same thing with their spells. (This caused) Pharaoh's heart to become hardened, and he did not listen to them, as God had said.

²³ Pharaoh turned around and went home. He didn't take (either miracle) to heart.

²⁴ All the Egyptians dug around the Nile for water to drink, since they could not drink from the water of the Nile.

²⁵ Seven days were completed after God had struck the Nile.

19. Take your staff and extend your hand over the waters of Egypt ... and they will become blood. God said to Moses, "Where do the Egyptians get their drinking water?"

"From the Nile," answered Moses.

God said, "Turn it into blood."

spiritual vitamin

> The exodus from Egypt represents the release of the Divine soul from its corporeal imprisonment, and it must be experienced every day, constantly, in order to enjoy true freedom—freedom from enslavement, freedom from pain—in both the material as well as the spiritual sense.

שמות ז:כו - ח:ד | וארא

אֶת־הַיְאֹֽר: פ ²⁶ וַיֹּ֤אמֶר יְהֹוָה֙ אֶל־מֹשֶׁ֔ה בֹּ֖א אֶל־פַּרְעֹ֑ה וְאָמַרְתָּ֣ אֵלָ֗יו כֹּ֚ה אָמַ֣ר יְהֹוָ֔ה שַׁלַּ֥ח אֶת־עַמִּ֖י וְיַֽעַבְדֻֽנִי: ²⁷ וְאִם־מָאֵ֥ן אַתָּ֖ה לְשַׁלֵּ֑חַ הִנֵּ֣ה אָֽנֹכִ֗י נֹגֵ֛ף אֶת־כׇּל־גְּבֽוּלְךָ֖ בַּֽצְפַרְדְּעִֽים: ²⁸ וְשָׁרַ֣ץ הַיְאֹר֮ צְפַרְדְּעִים֒ וְעָלוּ֙ וּבָ֣אוּ בְּבֵיתֶ֔ךָ וּבַחֲדַ֥ר מִשְׁכָּבְךָ֖ וְעַל־מִטָּתֶ֑ךָ וּבְבֵ֤ית עֲבָדֶ֙יךָ֙ וּבְעַמֶּ֔ךָ וּבְתַנּוּרֶ֖יךָ וּבְמִשְׁאֲרוֹתֶֽיךָ: ²⁹ וּבְכָ֥ה וּבְעַמְּךָ֖ וּבְכׇל־עֲבָדֶ֑יךָ יַעֲל֖וּ הַֽצְפַרְדְּעִֽים:

ח ¹ וַיֹּ֣אמֶר יְהֹוָה֮ אֶל־מֹשֶׁה֒ אֱמֹ֣ר אֶֽל־אַהֲרֹ֗ן נְטֵ֤ה אֶת־יָדְךָ֙ בְּמַטֶּ֔ךָ עַל־הַ֨נְּהָרֹ֔ת עַל־הַיְאֹרִ֖ים וְעַל־הָאֲגַמִּ֑ים וְהַ֥עַל אֶת־הַֽצְפַרְדְּעִ֖ים עַל־אֶ֥רֶץ מִצְרָֽיִם: ² וַיֵּ֤ט אַהֲרֹן֙ אֶת־יָד֔וֹ עַ֖ל מֵימֵ֣י מִצְרָ֑יִם וַתַּ֙עַל֙ הַצְּפַרְדֵּ֔עַ וַתְּכַ֖ס אֶת־אֶ֥רֶץ מִצְרָֽיִם: ³ וַיַּֽעֲשׂוּ־כֵ֥ן הַֽחַרְטֻמִּ֖ים בְּלָטֵיהֶ֑ם וַיַּעֲל֥וּ אֶת־הַֽצְפַרְדְּעִ֖ים עַל־אֶ֥רֶץ מִצְרָֽיִם: ⁴ וַיִּקְרָ֨א פַרְעֹ֜ה לְמֹשֶׁ֣ה וּֽלְאַהֲרֹ֗ן וַיֹּ֙אמֶר֙ הַעְתִּ֣ירוּ אֶל־יְהֹוָ֔ה

---

the Nile along with its waters that had been diverted into canals or stored in containers (see v.19) turned to blood, but that the water beneath the ground was unaffected. To the contrary, if any water other than the Nile-waters had been affected, then it would not have been clear to Pharaoh that his deity was being targeted *specifically*.

In fact, the greatest embarrassment for Pharaoh was not only that his deity was struck by the plague, but that the water immediately *adjacent* to his deity was totally unaffected (*Rabbi Menahem Mendel Schneerson, 20th century*).

28. Into your ovens and into your kneading bowls. The kneading bowl is found near the oven at the time of baking, when the oven is hot. So when the frogs jumped into the ovens, they knew that they would be burned, yet they did not hesitate. This was exceptionally wondrous, since a frog's natural habitat is the water, where it is cool. By jumping into the hot ovens, they went against their nature to fulfil the will of God (*Babylonian Talmud, Pesaḥim 53b, according to Rabbi Samuel Edels, 16th–17th century*).

8:2 The frog came up. When the Torah states that *"the frog came up"* it means that there was one frog initially. They hit it and it streamed out swarms of frogs (*Rashi, 11th century*).

After first hitting the frog, the Egyptians should have realized that continuing to hit it was only to their detriment, as it continued multiplying. Yet, in their anger they did not think of the consequences of their actions, continuing to smite the lone frog until frogs *"covered the land of Egypt."*

All arguments begin with one person "hitting" the other. If the victim remains silent the likelihood of the argument subsiding is good. But if the victim retaliates, "hitting" back, the cycle continues and it becomes difficult to stop as the conflict escalates (*Rabbi Jacob Israel Kanievsky, 20th century*).

exodus 7:26 – 8:4 va-'era'

The Second Plague—Infestation of Frogs

²⁶ God said to Moses, "Come to Pharaoh, and say to him, 'This is what God said: Let My people go, so that they may serve Me. ²⁷ But if you refuse to let them go, I will strike all your territories with frogs. ²⁸ The Nile will swarm with frogs, and they will go up (from the river) and come into your house, into your bedroom, upon your bed, into the house of your servants and of your people, into your ovens, and into your kneading bowls. ²⁹ The frogs will go up into (the intestines of) yourself, your people, and all your servants.'"

8 ¹ God said to Moses, "Say to Aaron, 'Stretch out your hand with your staff over the rivers, over the canals, and over the ponds, and make the frogs come up over the land of Egypt.'"

² Aaron stretched out his hand over the waters of Egypt, and the frog came up, (and then multiplied) and covered the land of Egypt.

³ The sorcerers did the same thing with their spells, and they brought up the frogs over the land of Egypt.

⁴ Pharaoh summoned Moses and Aaron, and said, "Plead to God that He remove the frogs away from me and from my people, and I will send out the people of Israel so that they may sacrifice to God."

---

of blood, frogs and lice affected both the Egyptians and the Jews. When it came to the fourth plague of wild beasts, which was more severe, God saved the Jewish people from being affected. Thus, in addition to the Egyptians' digging for water, the Jewish people were also forced to dig for water (*Rabbi Abraham ibn Ezra, 12ᵗʰ century*).

The Nile was Pharaoh's deity. Consequently, God first struck Pharaoh's deity, with the plague of blood (and later frogs), and then He struck the Egyptian people with the other plagues. Therefore, although the Jewish people also suffered from the plague of blood, the fact that Pharaoh's *god* was afflicted sent an extremely powerful message to Pharaoh.

Since the key threat here to Pharaoh was that his god (the Nile) was afflicted, it follows that if any part of the Nile was unaffected (such as in the Jewish district of Goshen), then Pharaoh could come to the conclusion that at least *part* of his deity was mightier than God. Thus, it was crucial that all of the Nile, even the parts used exclusively by the Jewish people, should be afflicted.

The above interpretation also explains why the Egyptians were able to obtain fresh water through digging. Since the point of the plague was that Pharaoh's god should be afflicted, it follows that *only* the water within

kabbalah bites

7:28 The plague of blood was on the trajectory of cold to hot: cold water was transformed to warm blood. The plague of frogs worked in the reverse direction: hot ovens were cooled down by hoards of cold-blooded frogs.

Do you sometimes find yourself to be "hot" and enthusiastic when you should be "cool," and indifferent; or "cool" when you should be "hot"? It's one of the tricks of our inner opponent. Beware!

ואראשמות ח:ד-טז

וְיָסֵר הַצְפַרְדְּעִים מִמֶּנִּי וּמֵעַמִּי וַאֲשַׁלְּחָה אֶת־הָעָם וְיִזְבְּחוּ לַיהוָה: 5 וַיֹּאמֶר מֹשֶׁה לְפַרְעֹה הִתְפָּאֵר עָלַי לְמָתַי ׀ אַעְתִּיר לְךָ וְלַעֲבָדֶיךָ וּלְעַמְּךָ לְהַכְרִית הַצְפַרְדְּעִים מִמְּךָ וּמִבָּתֶּיךָ רַק בַּיְאֹר תִּשָּׁאַרְנָה: 6 וַיֹּאמֶר לְמָחָר וַיֹּאמֶר כִּדְבָרְךָ לְמַעַן תֵּדַע כִּי־אֵין כַּיהוָה אֱלֹהֵינוּ: [FIFTH READING] 7 וְסָרוּ הַצְפַרְדְּעִים מִמְּךָ וּמִבָּתֶּיךָ וּמֵעֲבָדֶיךָ וּמֵעַמֶּךָ רַק בַּיְאֹר תִּשָּׁאַרְנָה: 8 וַיֵּצֵא מֹשֶׁה וְאַהֲרֹן מֵעִם פַּרְעֹה וַיִּצְעַק מֹשֶׁה אֶל־יְהוָה עַל־דְּבַר הַצְפַרְדְּעִים אֲשֶׁר־שָׂם לְפַרְעֹה: 9 וַיַּעַשׂ יְהוָה כִּדְבַר מֹשֶׁה וַיָּמֻתוּ הַצְפַרְדְּעִים מִן־הַבָּתִּים מִן־הַחֲצֵרֹת וּמִן־הַשָּׂדֹת: 10 וַיִּצְבְּרוּ אֹתָם חֳמָרִם חֳמָרִם וַתִּבְאַשׁ הָאָרֶץ: 11 וַיַּרְא פַּרְעֹה כִּי הָיְתָה הָרְוָחָה וְהַכְבֵּד אֶת־לִבּוֹ וְלֹא שָׁמַע אֲלֵהֶם כַּאֲשֶׁר דִּבֶּר יְהוָה: ס 12 וַיֹּאמֶר יְהוָה אֶל־מֹשֶׁה אֱמֹר אֶל־אַהֲרֹן נְטֵה אֶת־מַטְּךָ וְהַךְ אֶת־עֲפַר הָאָרֶץ וְהָיָה לְכִנִּם בְּכָל־אֶרֶץ מִצְרָיִם: 13 וַיַּעֲשׂוּ־כֵן וַיֵּט אַהֲרֹן אֶת־יָדוֹ בְמַטֵּהוּ וַיַּךְ אֶת־עֲפַר הָאָרֶץ וַתְּהִי הַכִּנָּם בָּאָדָם וּבַבְּהֵמָה כָּל־עֲפַר הָאָרֶץ הָיָה כִנִּים בְּכָל־אֶרֶץ מִצְרָיִם: 14 וַיַּעֲשׂוּ־כֵן הַחַרְטֻמִּים בְּלָטֵיהֶם לְהוֹצִיא אֶת־הַכִּנִּים וְלֹא יָכֹלוּ וַתְּהִי הַכִּנָּם בָּאָדָם וּבַבְּהֵמָה: 15 וַיֹּאמְרוּ הַחַרְטֻמִּם אֶל־פַּרְעֹה אֶצְבַּע אֱלֹהִים הִוא וַיֶּחֱזַק לֵב־פַּרְעֹה וְלֹא־שָׁמַע אֲלֵהֶם כַּאֲשֶׁר דִּבֶּר יְהוָה: ס 16 וַיֹּאמֶר יְהוָה

kabbalah bites

8:15 God's "fingers" are the ten *Sefirot*, the Godly lights which He emanated in order to conduct the world. As God's tools of implementation they are referred to as "fingers," in a similar way that your fingers enable you to grasp and tackle that which is outside yourself.

Man was created in the image of God: *The reason why you have ten fingers is because there are ten Sefirot.*

So it's not that God does something that metaphorically resembles your fingers—on the contrary, your fingers are the metaphor for something which God does.

exodus 8:5–16   va-'era'

⁵ Moses said to Pharaoh, "Give me a challenge. Tell me when I should plead for you, for your servants, and for your people, for the frogs to be eliminated from you and from your houses, leaving them only in the Nile?"

⁶ Pharaoh said, "(Plead today for the frogs to be eliminated) tomorrow."

He (Moses) said, "(It will be) as you say, in order that you should know that there is none like God, our God. [FIFTH READING] ⁷ The frogs will depart from you and from your houses and from your servants and from your people. They will remain only in the Nile."

⁸ Moses and Aaron went out from Pharaoh's presence, and (immediately,) Moses cried out to God about the frogs that He had brought upon Pharaoh.

⁹ God acted according to Moses' word, and the frogs within the houses, the courtyards, and the fields died. ¹⁰ They gathered them into many heaps, and the land stank.

¹¹ Pharaoh saw that there was relief. He continued to harden his heart, and he did not listen to them, as God had said.

The Third Plague—Lice Infestation

¹² God said to Moses, "Say to Aaron, 'Stretch out your staff and hit the earth of the land, and it will become lice throughout the entire land of Egypt.'"

¹³ They did this. Aaron stretched forth his hand with his staff and struck the earth of the land, and the (creeping mass of) lice was upon man and beast. Throughout all Egypt the earth of the land turned into lice.

¹⁴ The sorcerers did the same thing with their spells, trying to create lice (from another place), but they were unable to do so. The lice were upon man and beast. ¹⁵ The sorcerers said to Pharaoh, "It is the finger of God (and not witchcraft)!" However, Pharaoh's heart became hardened, and he did not listen to them, as God had said.

The Fourth Plague—Wild Animals Wreak Havoc

¹⁶ God said to Moses, "Get up early in the morning and stand yourself before

8. Moses cried out to God about the frogs that He had brought upon Pharaoh. The seemingly superfluous phrase, "that He had brought upon Pharaoh," instructs us how to pray to God—*our requests to God should pertain to even the minor details of our lives*. In the same way that Moses detailed his request, we should specify exactly what we want from God and not be content with the thought that "God knows what I need and desire, so there is no point in my specifying my requests" (*Rabbi Ḥayyim ibn Attar, 18th century*).

14. The sorcerers did the same thing ... trying to create lice, but they were unable to do so. The Egyptian sorcerers were not able to perform sorcery on objects smaller than a barleycorn. Thus, they were unable to create lice of their own (*Rashi, 11th century*).

וארא
שמות ח:טז-כג

אֶל־מֹשֶׁה הַשְׁכֵּם בַּבֹּקֶר וְהִתְיַצֵּב לִפְנֵי פַרְעֹה הִנֵּה יוֹצֵא הַמָּיְמָה וְאָמַרְתָּ אֵלָיו כֹּה אָמַר יְהֹוָה שַׁלַּח עַמִּי וְיַעַבְדֻנִי: 17 כִּי אִם־אֵינְךָ מְשַׁלֵּחַ אֶת־עַמִּי הִנְנִי מַשְׁלִיחַ בְּךָ וּבַעֲבָדֶיךָ וּבְעַמְּךָ וּבְבָתֶּיךָ אֶת־הֶעָרֹב וּמָלְאוּ בָּתֵּי מִצְרַיִם אֶת־הֶעָרֹב וְגַם הָאֲדָמָה אֲשֶׁר־הֵם עָלֶיהָ: 18 וְהִפְלֵיתִי בַיּוֹם הַהוּא אֶת־אֶרֶץ גֹּשֶׁן אֲשֶׁר עַמִּי עֹמֵד עָלֶיהָ לְבִלְתִּי הֱיוֹת־שָׁם עָרֹב לְמַעַן תֵּדַע כִּי אֲנִי יְהֹוָה בְּקֶרֶב הָאָרֶץ: 19 [SIXTH READING] וְשַׂמְתִּי פְדֻת בֵּין עַמִּי וּבֵין עַמֶּךָ לְמָחָר יִהְיֶה הָאֹת הַזֶּה: 20 וַיַּעַשׂ יְהֹוָה כֵּן וַיָּבֹא עָרֹב כָּבֵד בֵּיתָה פַרְעֹה וּבֵית עֲבָדָיו וּבְכָל־אֶרֶץ מִצְרַיִם תִּשָּׁחֵת הָאָרֶץ מִפְּנֵי הֶעָרֹב: 21 וַיִּקְרָא פַרְעֹה אֶל־מֹשֶׁה וּלְאַהֲרֹן וַיֹּאמֶר לְכוּ זִבְחוּ לֵאלֹהֵיכֶם בָּאָרֶץ: 22 וַיֹּאמֶר מֹשֶׁה לֹא נָכוֹן לַעֲשׂוֹת כֵּן כִּי תּוֹעֲבַת מִצְרַיִם נִזְבַּח לַיהֹוָה אֱלֹהֵינוּ הֵן נִזְבַּח אֶת־תּוֹעֲבַת מִצְרַיִם לְעֵינֵיהֶם וְלֹא יִסְקְלֻנוּ: 23 דֶּרֶךְ שְׁלֹשֶׁת יָמִים נֵלֵךְ בַּמִּדְבָּר וְזָבַחְנוּ לַיהֹוָה אֱלֹהֵינוּ כַּאֲשֶׁר

"I will set apart the land of Goshen where My people remain, so that there will not be any harmful beast there"—the wild animals spread throughout the land of Egypt, attacking all Egyptian areas, but avoided places where the Israelites lived. Similarly, with the plague of pestilence, we find a clear act of Divine Providence, *"God will separate between the cattle of Israel and the cattle of Egypt"* (9:4). And with the boils, even though there was "dust upon the *entire* land of Egypt" only the Egyptians were smitten.

This verse, then, (*"In order that you know that I am God on earth"*) is an introduction to the following three plagues, which serve as a lesson that God not only exists in the heavens but He also controls every detail of that which occurs on earth (*Rabbi Ephraim of Luntshits, 16th–17th century*).

19. I will bring about salvation which will set apart My people ('ammi) and your people ('ammekha). The difference in the numerical value of the two words 'ammi (120) and 'ammekha (130) is ten. This hints to the fact that the Israelites, who were currently Pharaoh's people ('ammekha), were soon to become Moses' people ('ammi), and this was to be achieved through the Ten Plagues (*Rabbi Joseph Ḥayyim b. Elijah Al-Ḥakam of Baghdad, 19th century*).

22. We will be sacrificing the deity of the Egyptians. The Egyptian god was shaped in the form of a ram, since they understood that Aries, the ram, was the astrological sign that ruled over Egypt.

The Egyptians were, in fact, vegans—they refrained from eating meat, milk, blood, fish or eggs, or anything from a living creature. They did not allow meat-eating people into their country, and they despised the profession of shepherding. They did, however, own many cattle and livestock for the purposes of carrying burdens—riding, plowing—and they kept sheep for wool (*Rabbi Abraham ibn Ezra, 12th century*).

exodus 8:16–23

va-'era'

Pharaoh when he goes out to the water. Say to him, 'This is what God said, "Let My people go out and serve Me. [17] For if you do not let My people go, then I will incite a mixture (of harmful beasts, snakes and scorpions) against yourself, your servants, your people, and your houses. The houses of Egypt, and the land on which they stand, will be filled with a mixture (of harmful beasts, snakes and scorpions). [18] On that day, I will set apart the land of Goshen where My people remain, so that there will not be any harmful beast there, in order that you know that I am God (and My decrees are upheld) on earth. [SIXTH READING] [19] I will bring about salvation (from this plague for My people), which will set apart My people and your people. This miracle will occur tomorrow."

[20] God did this, and a heavy mixture (of harmful beasts, snakes and scorpions) came to Pharaoh's house and his servants' homes and throughout the entire land of Egypt. The land was destroyed because of the mixture (of harmful beasts, snakes and scorpions).

[21] Pharaoh summoned Moses and Aaron, and he said, "Go and slaughter to your God, (but do it) in this land."

[22] Moses said, "It would not be appropriate to do that, for we will be sacrificing the deity of the Egyptians to our God! As if we could sacrifice the deity of the Egyptians before their eyes, and they wouldn't stone us? [23] Let us go for a three-day journey into the desert and sacrifice to God, our God, as He is going to tell us."

18. I will set apart the land of Goshen where My people remain, so that there will not be any harmful beast there, in order that you know that I am God on earth. The first three plagues—blood, frogs and lice—had largely been aimed at proving the basic fact of the *existence* of God. This had been achieved by first demonstrating the powerlessness of Pharaoh's god (the Nile), with the plague of blood; then Pharaoh had witnessed the willingness of the frogs to sacrifice their lives for God; and finally the lice led him to the realization that *"it is the finger of God"* (8:15).

Now that Pharaoh was aware that God *existed*, the next three plagues were aimed at demonstrating God's *providence*—that "I am God *on earth*." This point was to be made clear when

spiritual vitamin

> In order to achieve fullest productivity, you must often begin by breaking your outer shell or crust (formed by habits, natural dispositions, environmental influences, etc.). This will release your tremendous inner powers and resources, which are infinitely greater than those on the surface, and, more importantly, are infinitely more stable and durable, since they are closer to your self and are anchored in the essence of your soul.

שמות ח:כג - ט:י

וארא

יֹאמַר אֵלֵינוּ: 24 וַיֹּאמֶר פַּרְעֹה אָנֹכִי אֲשַׁלַּח אֶתְכֶם וּזְבַחְתֶּם לַיהוָה אֱלֹהֵיכֶם בַּמִּדְבָּר רַק הַרְחֵק לֹא־תַרְחִיקוּ לָלֶכֶת הַעְתִּירוּ בַּעֲדִי: 25 וַיֹּאמֶר מֹשֶׁה הִנֵּה אָנֹכִי יוֹצֵא מֵעִמָּךְ וְהַעְתַּרְתִּי אֶל־יְהוָה וְסָר הֶעָרֹב מִפַּרְעֹה מֵעֲבָדָיו וּמֵעַמּוֹ מָחָר רַק אַל־יֹסֵף פַּרְעֹה הָתֵל לְבִלְתִּי שַׁלַּח אֶת־הָעָם לִזְבֹּחַ לַיהוָה: 26 וַיֵּצֵא מֹשֶׁה מֵעִם פַּרְעֹה וַיֶּעְתַּר אֶל־יְהוָה: 27 וַיַּעַשׂ יְהוָה כִּדְבַר מֹשֶׁה וַיָּסַר הֶעָרֹב מִפַּרְעֹה מֵעֲבָדָיו וּמֵעַמּוֹ לֹא נִשְׁאַר אֶחָד: 28 וַיַּכְבֵּד פַּרְעֹה אֶת־לִבּוֹ גַּם בַּפַּעַם הַזֹּאת וְלֹא שִׁלַּח אֶת־הָעָם: פ

ט 1 וַיֹּאמֶר יְהוָה אֶל־מֹשֶׁה בֹּא אֶל־פַּרְעֹה וְדִבַּרְתָּ אֵלָיו כֹּה־אָמַר יְהוָה אֱלֹהֵי הָעִבְרִים שַׁלַּח אֶת־עַמִּי וְיַעַבְדֻנִי: 2 כִּי אִם־מָאֵן אַתָּה לְשַׁלֵּחַ וְעוֹדְךָ מַחֲזִיק בָּם: 3 הִנֵּה יַד־יְהוָה הוֹיָה בְּמִקְנְךָ אֲשֶׁר בַּשָּׂדֶה בַּסּוּסִים בַּחֲמֹרִים בַּגְּמַלִּים בַּבָּקָר וּבַצֹּאן דֶּבֶר כָּבֵד מְאֹד: 4 וְהִפְלָה יְהוָה בֵּין מִקְנֵה יִשְׂרָאֵל וּבֵין מִקְנֵה מִצְרָיִם וְלֹא יָמוּת מִכָּל־לִבְנֵי יִשְׂרָאֵל דָּבָר: 5 וַיָּשֶׂם יְהוָה מוֹעֵד לֵאמֹר מָחָר יַעֲשֶׂה יְהוָה הַדָּבָר הַזֶּה בָּאָרֶץ: 6 וַיַּעַשׂ יְהוָה אֶת־הַדָּבָר הַזֶּה מִמָּחֳרָת וַיָּמָת כֹּל מִקְנֵה מִצְרָיִם וּמִמִּקְנֵה בְנֵי־יִשְׂרָאֵל לֹא־מֵת אֶחָד: 7 וַיִּשְׁלַח פַּרְעֹה וְהִנֵּה לֹא־מֵת מִמִּקְנֵה יִשְׂרָאֵל עַד־אֶחָד וַיִּכְבַּד לֵב פַּרְעֹה וְלֹא שִׁלַּח אֶת־הָעָם: פ 8 וַיֹּאמֶר יְהוָה אֶל־מֹשֶׁה וְאֶל־אַהֲרֹן קְחוּ לָכֶם מְלֹא חָפְנֵיכֶם פִּיחַ כִּבְשָׁן וּזְרָקוֹ מֹשֶׁה הַשָּׁמַיְמָה לְעֵינֵי פַרְעֹה: 9 וְהָיָה לְאָבָק עַל כָּל־אֶרֶץ מִצְרָיִם וְהָיָה עַל־הָאָדָם וְעַל־הַבְּהֵמָה לִשְׁחִין פֹּרֵחַ אֲבַעְבֻּעֹת בְּכָל־אֶרֶץ מִצְרָיִם: 10 וַיִּקְחוּ אֶת־פִּיחַ הַכִּבְשָׁן וַיַּעַמְדוּ לִפְנֵי פַרְעֹה וַיִּזְרֹק אֹתוֹ מֹשֶׁה הַשָּׁמָיְמָה וַיְהִי שְׁחִין אֲבַעְבֻּעֹת פֹּרֵחַ בָּאָדָם וּבַבְּהֵמָה:

The soot was extremely hot, and it spread throughout the entire land of Egypt. Consequently, when it touched a person's skin it had the effect of erupting boils naturally. Alternatively, we could argue that when the soot reached the air, God transformed the nature of the air so that it caused boils to erupt (*Naḥmanides, 13th century*).

²⁴ Pharaoh said, "I will send you out in order to sacrifice to God, your God, in the desert, on the condition that you do not go too far away. Plead with Him on my behalf!"

²⁵ Moses said, " I am going away from you, and I will plead with God. The mixture of harmful beasts will depart from Pharaoh, from his servants, and from his people tomorrow. Only Pharaoh should not continue to (act in a manner of) ridicule, by not sending the people to go and sacrifice to God."

²⁶ Moses left Pharaoh's presence and pleaded with God.

²⁷ God acted in accordance with Moses' word. He removed the mixture (of harmful beasts) from Pharaoh, from his servants, and from his people. Not a single one remained.

²⁸ Pharaoh hardened his heart this time too, and he did not send the people away.

The Fifth Plague—Death of Cattle through Disease

9 ¹ God said to Moses, "Come to Pharaoh and say to him, 'This is what God, the God of the Hebrews, said, "Let My people go, that they may serve Me. ² For if you refuse to let them go, and you continue to hold onto them, ³ behold, the hand of God will place a very severe epidemic upon your livestock that is in the field—upon the horses, upon the donkeys, upon the camels, upon the cattle, and upon the sheep. ⁴ God will separate between the cattle of Israel and the cattle of Egypt, and not one (animal) belonging to a Jew will die." ⁵ God set an appointed time, saying, "Tomorrow, God will do this thing in the land."

⁶ The following day, God did this thing, and all the livestock of the Egyptians died, but from the cattle of the children of Israel not one died.

⁷ Pharaoh sent (messengers), and lo and behold, not even one of the cattle of Israel had died.

Pharaoh's heart became hardened, and he did not send the people away.

The Sixth Plague—Infestation of Boils

⁸ God said to Moses and to Aaron, "Take for yourselves a double handful of furnace soot, and Moses shall throw it towards heaven in front of Pharaoh's eyes. ⁹ It will become dust upon the entire land of Egypt, and it will become boils, breaking out into blisters upon man and upon beast, throughout the entire land of Egypt."

¹⁰ They took furnace soot, and they stood before Pharaoh. Moses threw it towards heaven, and then boils broke out into blisters on man and beast.

9:10 Boils broke out into blisters. The fact that a small amount of soot managed to spread throughout the entire land of Egypt was miraculous. The plague itself was also miraculous, for when the soot reached the skin of the Egyptians it erupted into boils (*Rabbi Bahya b. Asher, 13ᵗʰ century*).

שמות ט:יא-כא | וארא

11 וְלֹא־יָכְל֣וּ הַֽחַרְטֻמִּ֗ים לַעֲמֹ֛ד לִפְנֵ֥י מֹשֶׁ֖ה מִפְּנֵ֣י הַשְּׁחִ֑ין כִּֽי־הָיָ֣ה הַשְּׁחִ֔ין בַּֽחֲרְטֻמִּ֖ם וּבְכׇל־מִצְרָֽיִם: 12 וַיְחַזֵּ֤ק יְהֹוָה֙ אֶת־לֵ֣ב פַּרְעֹ֔ה וְלֹ֥א שָׁמַ֖ע אֲלֵהֶ֑ם כַּאֲשֶׁ֛ר דִּבֶּ֥ר יְהֹוָ֖ה אֶל־מֹשֶֽׁה: ס 13 וַיֹּ֨אמֶר יְהֹוָ֜ה אֶל־מֹשֶׁ֗ה הַשְׁכֵּ֣ם בַּבֹּ֘קֶר֘ וְהִתְיַצֵּ֣ב לִפְנֵ֣י פַרְעֹה֒ וְאָמַרְתָּ֣ אֵלָ֗יו כֹּֽה־אָמַ֤ר יְהֹוָה֙ אֱלֹהֵ֣י הָֽעִבְרִ֔ים שַׁלַּ֥ח אֶת־עַמִּ֖י וְיַֽעַבְדֻֽנִי: 14 כִּ֣י ׀ בַּפַּ֣עַם הַזֹּ֗את אֲנִ֨י שֹׁלֵ֜חַ אֶת־כׇּל־מַגֵּפֹתַי֙ אֶֽל־לִבְּךָ֔ וּבַעֲבָדֶ֖יךָ וּבְעַמֶּ֑ךָ בַּעֲב֣וּר תֵּדַ֔ע כִּ֛י אֵ֥ין כָּמֹ֖נִי בְּכׇל־הָאָֽרֶץ: 15 כִּ֤י עַתָּה֙ שָׁלַ֣חְתִּי אֶת־יָדִ֔י וָאַ֥ךְ אֽוֹתְךָ֛ וְאֶֽת־עַמְּךָ֖ בַּדָּ֑בֶר וַתִּכָּחֵ֖ד מִן־הָאָֽרֶץ: 16 וְאוּלָ֗ם בַּעֲב֥וּר זֹאת֙ הֶעֱמַדְתִּ֔יךָ בַּעֲב֖וּר הַרְאֹתְךָ֣ אֶת־כֹּחִ֑י וּלְמַ֛עַן סַפֵּ֥ר שְׁמִ֖י בְּכׇל־הָאָֽרֶץ: [SEVENTH READING] 17 עוֹדְךָ֖ מִסְתּוֹלֵ֣ל בְּעַמִּ֑י לְבִלְתִּ֖י שַׁלְּחָֽם: 18 הִנְנִ֤י מַמְטִיר֙ כָּעֵ֣ת מָחָ֔ר בָּרָ֖ד כָּבֵ֣ד מְאֹ֑ד אֲשֶׁ֨ר לֹא־הָיָ֤ה כָמֹ֙הוּ֙ בְּמִצְרַ֔יִם לְמִן־הַיּ֥וֹם הִוָּסְדָ֖ה וְעַד־עָֽתָּה: 19 וְעַתָּ֗ה שְׁלַ֤ח הָעֵז֙ אֶֽת־מִקְנְךָ֔ וְאֵ֛ת כׇּל־אֲשֶׁ֥ר לְךָ֖ בַּשָּׂדֶ֑ה כׇּל־הָאָדָ֨ם וְהַבְּהֵמָ֜ה אֲשֶֽׁר־יִמָּצֵ֣א בַשָּׂדֶ֗ה וְלֹ֤א יֵֽאָסֵף֙ הַבַּ֔יְתָה וְיָרַ֧ד עֲלֵהֶ֛ם הַבָּרָ֖ד וָמֵֽתוּ: 20 הַיָּרֵא֙ אֶת־דְּבַ֣ר יְהֹוָ֔ה מֵֽעַבְדֵ֖י פַּרְעֹ֑ה הֵנִ֛יס אֶת־עֲבָדָ֥יו וְאֶת־מִקְנֵ֖הוּ אֶל־הַבָּתִּֽים: 21 וַאֲשֶׁ֥ר לֹא־שָׂ֛ם

18. I am going to rain down a very heavy hail (*barad*). Since the Egyptians did not return to God and repent after the cattle disease (*dever*), those very same letters switched positions and returned, killing all those who remained—*dever* (*dalet-bet-resh*) returned as *barad* (*resh-bet-dalet*). What is the difference between them? One comes gently, the other with great fury (*Zohar*).

20. Whoever feared the word of God among Pharaoh's servants drove his servants and his livestock into the houses. Pharaoh sent his servants with an announcement that all Egyptians were to disregard Moses' warning. However, there were some Egyptians who feared God and listened to Moses' warning. ("Among Pharaoh's servants" can also be rendered as *"more* than Pharaoh's servants"—the Egyptians who feared God more than Pharaoh's servants were protected from the hail.) Moses later hinted to this point to Pharaoh: He stated that although there were some Egyptians who feared God, "I know that *you and your servants* still do not fear God" (v. 30; *Rabbi Meir Simḥah of Dvinsk, 19th-20th century*).

Food for thought

1. Are natural disasters a form of Divine rebuke?

2. Why does tragedy tend to move people closer to God?

3. Do difficulties generally weaken or deepen your commitment?

exodus 9:11–21 — va-'era'

¹¹ The sorcerers could not stand before Moses due to the boils, for the boils were upon the sorcerers and on all of Egypt.

¹² God strengthened Pharaoh's heart, and he did not listen to them, as God had said to Moses.

The Seventh Plague—Hail Kills Humans and Animals

¹³ God said to Moses, "Rise early in the morning and stand in front of Pharaoh, and say to him, 'This is what God, the God of the Hebrews, said, "Let My people go so that they may worship Me. ¹⁴ Because this time, I am sending (a plague equivalent to) all My plagues upon your heart, upon your servants and your people, in order that you know that there is none like Me in the entire earth. ¹⁵ For now I could have stretched out My hand and smitten you and your people with an epidemic, and you would have been annihilated from the earth. ¹⁶ But, for the following reason I have kept you alive: In order to show you My strength and thus declare My name all over the earth."'

[SEVENTH READING] ¹⁷ "If you still tread upon My people, not sending them out, ¹⁸ then I am going to rain down a very heavy hail at this time tomorrow, the likes of which have never occurred in Egypt from the day it was founded until now.

¹⁹ "Now, send, gather in your livestock and all that you have in the field. The hail shall fall on any man or beast that is found in the field and not brought into the house, and they will die."

²⁰ Whoever feared the word of God among Pharaoh's servants drove his servants and his livestock into the houses. ²¹ But whoever did not pay attention to the word of God left his servants and his livestock in the field.

Surely, God would not change nature unnecessarily and allow a small amount of soot to fill the entire land of Egypt? Rather, we must conclude that Moses and Aaron merely initiated this plague, and that the boils themselves erupted miraculously, independently of the soot (*Rabbi Hezekiah b. Manoah, 13ᵗʰ century*).

spiritual vitamin

> It is not surprising that you cannot understand the ways of God; on the contrary, it is quite easy to see why a human being should *not* be able to understand the ways of God, for how could a created being understand the Creator? You need to be strong in your trust in God and let nothing discourage you or cause any depression, God forbid.

שמות ט:כא-לה ואראל

לִבּ֔וֹ אֶל־דְּבַ֣ר יְהֹוָ֑ה וַֽיַּעֲזֹ֛ב אֶת־עֲבָדָ֥יו וְאֶת־מִקְנֵ֖הוּ בַּשָּׂדֶֽה: פ 22 וַיֹּ֨אמֶר יְהֹוָ֜ה אֶל־מֹשֶׁ֗ה נְטֵ֤ה אֶת־יָֽדְךָ֙ עַל־הַשָּׁמַ֔יִם וִיהִ֥י בָרָ֖ד בְּכָל־אֶ֣רֶץ מִצְרָ֑יִם עַל־הָ֣אָדָ֔ם וְעַל־הַבְּהֵמָ֔ה וְעַ֛ל כָּל־עֵ֥שֶׂב הַשָּׂדֶ֖ה בְּאֶ֥רֶץ מִצְרָֽיִם: 23 וַיֵּ֨ט מֹשֶׁ֣ה אֶת־מַטֵּ֘הוּ֮ עַל־הַשָּׁמַ֒יִם֒ וַֽיהֹוָ֗ה נָתַ֤ן קֹלֹת֙ וּבָרָ֔ד וַתִּ֥הֲלַךְ אֵ֖שׁ אָ֑רְצָה וַיַּמְטֵ֧ר יְהֹוָ֛ה בָּרָ֖ד עַל־אֶ֥רֶץ מִצְרָֽיִם: 24 וַיְהִ֣י בָרָ֔ד וְאֵ֕שׁ מִתְלַקַּ֖חַת בְּת֣וֹךְ הַבָּרָ֑ד כָּבֵ֣ד מְאֹ֔ד אֲשֶׁ֨ר לֹֽא־הָיָ֤ה כָמֹ֙הוּ֙ בְּכָל־אֶ֣רֶץ מִצְרַ֔יִם מֵאָ֖ז הָיְתָ֥ה לְגֽוֹי: 25 וַיַּ֨ךְ הַבָּרָ֜ד בְּכָל־אֶ֣רֶץ מִצְרַ֗יִם אֵ֚ת כָּל־אֲשֶׁ֣ר בַּשָּׂדֶ֔ה מֵאָדָ֖ם וְעַד־בְּהֵמָ֑ה וְאֵ֨ת כָּל־עֵ֤שֶׂב הַשָּׂדֶה֙ הִכָּ֣ה הַבָּרָ֔ד וְאֶת־כָּל־עֵ֥ץ הַשָּׂדֶ֖ה שִׁבֵּֽר: 26 רַ֚ק בְּאֶ֣רֶץ גֹּ֔שֶׁן אֲשֶׁר־שָׁ֖ם בְּנֵ֣י יִשְׂרָאֵ֑ל לֹ֥א הָיָ֖ה בָּרָֽד: 27 וַיִּשְׁלַ֣ח פַּרְעֹ֗ה וַיִּקְרָא֙ לְמֹשֶׁ֣ה וּֽלְאַהֲרֹ֔ן וַיֹּ֥אמֶר אֲלֵהֶ֖ם חָטָ֣אתִי הַפָּ֑עַם יְהֹוָה֙ הַצַּדִּ֔יק וַאֲנִ֥י וְעַמִּ֖י הָרְשָׁעִֽים: 28 הַעְתִּ֙ירוּ֙ אֶל־יְהֹוָ֔ה וְרַ֕ב מִֽהְיֹ֛ת קֹלֹ֥ת אֱלֹהִ֖ים וּבָרָ֑ד וַאֲשַׁלְּחָ֣ה אֶתְכֶ֔ם וְלֹ֥א תֹסִפ֖וּן לַעֲמֹֽד: 29 וַיֹּ֤אמֶר אֵלָיו֙ מֹשֶׁ֔ה כְּצֵאתִי֙ אֶת־הָעִ֔יר אֶפְרֹ֥שׂ אֶת־כַּפַּ֖י אֶל־יְהֹוָ֑ה הַקֹּל֣וֹת יֶחְדָּל֗וּן וְהַבָּרָד֙ לֹ֣א יִֽהְיֶה־ע֔וֹד לְמַ֣עַן תֵּדַ֔ע כִּ֥י לַֽיהֹוָ֖ה הָאָֽרֶץ: 30 וְאַתָּ֖ה וַעֲבָדֶ֑יךָ יָדַ֕עְתִּי כִּ֚י טֶ֣רֶם תִּֽירְא֔וּן מִפְּנֵ֖י יְהֹוָ֥ה אֱלֹהִֽים: 31 וְהַפִּשְׁתָּ֥ה וְהַשְּׂעֹרָ֖ה נֻכָּ֑תָה כִּ֤י הַשְּׂעֹרָה֙ אָבִ֔יב וְהַפִּשְׁתָּ֖ה גִּבְעֹֽל: 32 וְהַחִטָּ֥ה וְהַכֻּסֶּ֖מֶת לֹ֣א נֻכּ֑וּ כִּ֥י אֲפִילֹ֖ת הֵֽנָּה: [MAFTIR] 33 וַיֵּצֵ֨א מֹשֶׁ֜ה מֵעִ֤ם פַּרְעֹה֙ אֶת־הָעִ֔יר וַיִּפְרֹ֥שׂ כַּפָּ֖יו אֶל־יְהֹוָ֑ה וַֽיַּחְדְּל֤וּ הַקֹּלוֹת֙ וְהַבָּרָ֔ד וּמָטָ֖ר לֹא־נִתַּ֥ךְ אָֽרְצָה: 34 וַיַּ֣רְא פַּרְעֹ֗ה כִּֽי־חָדַ֨ל הַמָּטָ֧ר וְהַבָּרָ֛ד וְהַקֹּלֹ֖ת וַיֹּ֣סֶף לַחֲטֹ֑א וַיַּכְבֵּ֥ד לִבּ֖וֹ ה֥וּא וַעֲבָדָֽיו: 35 וַֽיֶּחֱזַק֙ לֵ֣ב פַּרְעֹ֔ה וְלֹ֥א שִׁלַּ֖ח אֶת־בְּנֵ֣י יִשְׂרָאֵ֑ל כַּאֲשֶׁ֛ר דִּבֶּ֥ר יְהֹוָ֖ה בְּיַד־מֹשֶֽׁה: פ פ פ

קכ״א פסוקים, גיבעו״ל סימן, יעיא״ל סימן.

This was Moses' response to Pharaoh here: You claim to have oppressed the Jews because of God's decree, but *"I know that you and your servants still do not fear God."* God knows the thoughts of man and He can discern that you and your servants acted out of sheer malice (*Rabbi Moses Sofer, 18th–19th century*).

²² God said to Moses, "Stretch out your hand towards heaven, and hail will be upon the entire land of Egypt, upon man, beast, and all the vegetation of the field in the land of Egypt."

²³ So Moses stretched forth his staff towards heaven, and God gave forth thunder and hail, and fire came down to the earth, and God rained down hail upon the land of Egypt. ²⁴ There was hail, and fire blazing inside the hail. (It was) very heavy, the likes of which had never been throughout the entire land of Egypt since it had become a nation. ²⁵ Throughout the entire land of Egypt the hail struck all that was in the field, man and beast, all the vegetation of the field, and it broke all the trees of the field.

²⁶ Only in the land of Goshen, where the children of Israel were, there was no hail.

²⁷ Pharaoh sent (messengers) and summoned Moses and Aaron. He said to them, "I have sinned this time. God is the righteous One. I and my people are the wicked ones. ²⁸ Plead with God, and let God's thunder and hail (which He has already sent down) be enough. I will send you away, and you shall not continue to remain (here)."

²⁹ Moses said to him, "When I leave the city, I will spread my hands to God. The thunder will cease, and there will be no more hail, in order that you should know that the land belongs to God. ³⁰ I know that you and your servants still do not fear God, the Almighty God. ³¹ The flax and the barley have been broken, since the barley was ripe, and the flax was (hard) in its stalk. ³² But the wheat and the spelt, however, have not been broken, because they ripen late."

[MAFTIR] ³³ Moses went away from Pharaoh, out of the city, and he spread out his hands to God. The thunder and the hail ceased, and rain did not reach the earth.

³⁴ Pharaoh saw that the rain, the hail, and the thunder had ceased. He continued to sin, and hardened his heart, both he and his servants. ³⁵ Pharaoh's heart became strong, and he did not let the children of Israel go out, as God had said through Moses.

Haftarot: Va-'Era'—page 1319.   *Rosh Ḥodesh*—page 1417.

Maftir: Rosh Ḥodesh—page 1000 (28:9–15).

---

30. I know that you and your servants still do not fear God. The commentaries explain that even though God had decreed that the Israelites were to be oppressed (*Genesis* 15:13), the Egyptians were fully culpable for their actions, since they acted out of cruelty and hatred and not out of a desire to follow the word of God (see commentary to 7:3).

Daily, we are told in the Torah, we must **leave Egypt** (*mitzrayim*): we are to **depart** from the mindset of **narrowness** and **constriction** (*metzarim*).

BO'
בא

FINAL PLAGUES	10:1 – 11:10
THE NEW MOON AND PASSOVER	12:1–28
DEATH OF THE FIRSTBORN	12:29–42
ADDITIONAL LAWS	12:43 – 13:16

NAME
Bo'

MEANING
"Come"

LINES IN TORAH SCROLL
207

PARASHIYYOT
8 open; 6 closed

VERSES
106

WORDS
1655

LETTERS
6149

DATE
2448 *Shevat-Nisan*

LOCATION
Egypt, Succoth

KEY PEOPLE
Moses, Aaron, Pharaoh

MITZVOT
9 positive; 11 prohibitions

CHARACTER PROFILE

NAME
Moses

MEANING
"Draw out"

OTHER NAMES
Tobiah, Abi-gedor, Jered, Heber, Abi-soco, Yekuthiel, Abi-zanoah, Shemaiah son of Nethanel

PARENTS
Amram and Jochebed

GRANDFATHERS
Levi, Kohath

SIBLINGS
Miriam, Aaron

WIFE
Zipporah

FATHER-IN-LAW
Jethro

CHILDREN
Gershom, Eliezer

LIFE SPAN
120 years

BURIAL PLACE
Mount Nebo

ACHIEVEMENTS
Led the Jews to freedom; split the sea; received the Torah for the Jewish people; smashed the tablets; was the greatest prophet who ever lived; was extremely humble

KNOWN FOR
Was born circumcised; house filled with light at his birth; killed an Egyptian taskmaster; took Joseph's bones out of Egypt; his face shone with rays of light; composed some of Psalms; enacted weekly Torah reading; was denied entry into the land of Israel although he prayed 515 times; requested to die by Divine kiss; was buried by God and no man knows his burial place

FINANCIAL INTEGRITY

For three days during the plague of darkness, the Egyptians were helpless, and their precious valuables were easily accessible. The Jews proved their outstanding financial integrity by not taking any of Egypt's treasures at this time (10:23).

NEW MOON

The Jewish calendar follows the moon's cycle. The waning and waxing of the moon is a fitting metaphor for the Jewish people, who at times are downtrodden yet are assured that they will rise again (12:2).

PASSOVER SACRIFICE

The Egyptians worshiped sheep as one of their gods. Taking a lamb as the Pascal sacrifice showed the Jewish people's complete rejection and separation from their captors and former idolatrous ways (12:6).

TRANSMISSION

The memory of the Exodus is kept alive by repeating the story to our children on Passover (13:14).

1 וַיֹּ֤אמֶר יְהֹוָה֙ אֶל־מֹשֶׁ֔ה בֹּ֖א אֶל־פַּרְעֹ֑ה כִּֽי־אֲנִ֞י הִכְבַּ֤דְתִּי אֶת־לִבּוֹ֙ וְאֶת־לֵ֣ב עֲבָדָ֔יו לְמַ֗עַן שִׁתִ֛י אֹתֹתַ֥י אֵ֖לֶּה בְּקִרְבּֽוֹ: 2 וּלְמַ֡עַן תְּסַפֵּר֩ בְּאׇזְנֵ֨י בִנְךָ֜ וּבֶן־בִּנְךָ֗ אֵ֣ת אֲשֶׁ֤ר הִתְעַלַּ֙לְתִּי֙ בְּמִצְרַ֔יִם וְאֶת־אֹתֹתַ֖י אֲשֶׁר־שַׂ֣מְתִּי בָ֑ם וִֽידַעְתֶּ֖ם כִּֽי־אֲנִ֥י יְהֹוָֽה: 3 וַיָּבֹ֨א מֹשֶׁ֤ה וְאַֽהֲרֹן֙ אֶל־פַּרְעֹ֔ה וַיֹּֽאמְר֣וּ אֵלָ֗יו כֹּֽה־אָמַ֤ר יְהֹוָה֙ אֱלֹהֵ֣י הָֽעִבְרִ֔ים עַד־מָתַ֣י מֵאַ֔נְתָּ לֵֽעָנֹ֖ת מִפָּנָ֑י שַׁלַּ֥ח עַמִּ֖י וְיַֽעַבְדֻֽנִי: 4 כִּ֛י אִם־מָאֵ֥ן אַתָּ֖ה לְשַׁלֵּ֣חַ אֶת־עַמִּ֑י הִנְנִ֨י מֵבִ֥יא מָחָ֛ר אַרְבֶּ֖ה בִּגְבֻלֶֽךָ: 5 וְכִסָּה֙ אֶת־עֵ֣ין הָאָ֔רֶץ וְלֹ֥א יוּכַ֖ל לִרְאֹ֣ת אֶת־הָאָ֑רֶץ וְאָכַ֣ל | אֶת־יֶ֣תֶר הַפְּלֵטָ֗ה הַנִּשְׁאֶ֤רֶת לָכֶם֙ מִן־הַבָּרָ֔ד וְאָכַל֙ אֶת־כׇּל־הָעֵ֔ץ הַצֹּמֵ֥חַ לָכֶ֖ם מִן־הַשָּׂדֶֽה: 6 וּמָלְא֨וּ בָתֶּ֜יךָ וּבָתֵּ֣י כׇל־עֲבָדֶ֘יךָ֮ וּבָתֵּ֣י כׇל־מִצְרַ֒יִם֒ אֲשֶׁ֨ר לֹֽא־רָא֤וּ אֲבֹתֶ֙יךָ֙ וַֽאֲב֣וֹת אֲבֹתֶ֔יךָ מִיּ֗וֹם הֱיוֹתָם֙ עַל־

miracles of the Ten Plagues, he would have been unable to withstand the pressure and his decisions would have been forced through supernatural means. God therefore denied Pharaoh the ability to be moved by the miraculous events that he witnessed (*Rabbi Obadiah Sforno, 16th century*).

In order that I may put these miracles of Mine in his midst. Judaism rejects the dualistic notion that evil possesses an independent power base of its own, separate from God. Ultimately, the forces of evil must somehow nurture themselves from holy emanations, like parasites sucking off a host. The key to uprooting and eliminating evil, therefore, is to identify where the demonic forces have anchored their "point of attachment" and to disconnect them. This, in brief, was the goal of the Ten Plagues—to "detach" the root of Pharaoh's spiritual nourishment.

Pharaoh's demonic power was nurtured from an offshoot of the Divine name *'Elokim*. This five-lettered Hebrew word has one hundred and twenty possible anagrams, each alluding to a measure of energy flowing forth from the name, a potential parasitic source for the demonic forces. (The name *itself* is too holy for any demonic-parasitic attachment.)

Of the one hundred and twenty measures of energy, Pharaoh succeeded in nurturing from the lowest forty-eight—exactly two-fifths of the name, i.e., the last two letters, *mem* and *yod*. (Therefore Pharaoh had said, *"Who (MiY) is God that I should listen to His voice?"*—the word *MiY*, consisting of a *mem* and a *yod*, indicating the power of Pharaoh's heretical existence.)

The plagues took place through a disclosure of the first three letters of the name *'Elokim* (*alef-lamed-he*), from which Pharaoh had no sustenance. This is hinted to here, as the plagues are referred to as "these (*elleh*, spelled: *alef-lamed-he*) miracles" (*Rabbi Ḥayyim b. Joseph Vital, 16th–17th century*).

kabbalah bites

10:2 "In order that you relate (*tesapper*) in the ears of your son." The purpose of the Ten Plagues was to reveal the full power of the ten *Sefirot*, each plague corresponding to its own *Sefirah*. Thus Pharaoh's heart was hardened here, "in order *teSaPpeR*," for the sake of the *SePhiRot*.

parashat bo'

The Eighth Plague—Locusts

10 ¹ God said to Moses: "Come to Pharaoh (and warn him), for I have hardened his heart and the heart of his servants, in order that I may put these miracles of Mine in his midst, ² and in order that you relate in the ears of your son and your grandson how I toyed around with the Egyptians, and about the miraculous signs which I performed among them. You will then know that I am God."

³ Moses and Aaron came to Pharaoh and said to him, "This is what God, the God of the Hebrews, said, 'How long will you refuse to humble yourself before Me? Let My people go, so that they can worship Me! ⁴ For if you refuse to let them go, then tomorrow I am going to bring a swarm of locusts into your border. ⁵ It will obscure the view of the earth, and no one will be able to see the earth. It will consume everything of yours that remains from the hail, and it will eat all of your trees that grow from the field. ⁶ They will fill your houses, your servants' houses and the houses of all the Egyptians, in a way which your fathers and grandfathers have not seen since the day they came onto the earth until today.'"

kabbalah bites

10:1 *"Come to Pharaoh."* What is the symbolism of the ominous "Great Snake" which the Zohar identifies with Pharaoh? Rabbi Ḥayyim Vital teaches that the snake represents *our irrational attachment to the pleasures of this world*. Moses felt that he could successfully battle with the desire for pleasure so long as it remained rational, but he feared that the irrational impulse was invincible—until God offered to "hold his hand," saying "Come to Pharaoh with Me."

What was the result of this affair? It means that now, through reading the Five Books of Moses, we are spiritually empowered with the self-control to contain our most powerful, irrational desires.

10:1 Come to Pharaoh. Notice that God did not say *"Go* to Pharaoh," because you cannot go away from God—He is everywhere. God said to Moses, "Come *with Me* to Pharaoh. I am with you wherever you go, and you will not be alone" (*Rabbi Menahem Mendel Morgensztern of Kotsk, 19ᵗʰ century*).

Surely God should have told Moses to "*go* to Pharaoh." Why did He tell him to "come"? Due to the supreme power of the demonic force associated with Pharaoh, "the great snake," in his palace, Moses was afraid to go there. Therefore, God did not say *"Go to Pharaoh,"* but rather *"Come to Pharaoh."* God offered to accompany Moses on this treacherous journey. God would take Moses to the very essence of the demonic force, to neutralize it (*Zohar*).

I have hardened his heart. The plague of hail was horrific, and yet it failed to bring a change of heart in Pharaoh. This weakened Moses' spirits, so God now said to Moses, "It is still worth coming to Pharaoh to inform him of the next plague. He did not free you last time, only because I had hardened his heart. When I remove the hardness from his heart, he will let you go" (*Rabbi Ḥayyim ibn Attar, 18ᵗʰ century*).

God hardened Pharaoh's heart to *preserve* his free will. If Pharaoh had been objectively influenced by the

שמות י:ו-טו

הָאֲדָמָ֔ה עַ֖ד הַיּ֣וֹם הַזֶּ֑ה וַיִּ֥פֶן וַיֵּצֵ֖א מֵעִ֥ם פַּרְעֹֽה: 7 וַיֹּאמְרוּ֩ עַבְדֵ֨י פַרְעֹ֜ה אֵלָ֗יו עַד־מָתַי֙ יִהְיֶ֨ה זֶ֥ה לָ֨נוּ֙ לְמוֹקֵ֔שׁ שַׁלַּח֙ אֶת־הָ֣אֲנָשִׁ֔ים וְיַֽעַבְד֖וּ אֶת־יְהֹוָ֣ה אֱלֹהֵיהֶ֑ם הֲטֶ֣רֶם תֵּדַ֔ע כִּ֥י אָבְדָ֖ה מִצְרָֽיִם: 8 וַיּוּשַׁ֞ב אֶת־מֹשֶׁ֤ה וְאֶֽת־אַהֲרֹן֙ אֶל־פַּרְעֹ֔ה וַיֹּ֣אמֶר אֲלֵהֶ֔ם לְכ֥וּ עִבְד֖וּ אֶת־יְהֹוָ֣ה אֱלֹהֵיכֶ֑ם מִ֥י וָמִ֖י הַהֹלְכִֽים: 9 וַיֹּ֣אמֶר מֹשֶׁ֔ה בִּנְעָרֵ֥ינוּ וּבִזְקֵנֵ֖ינוּ נֵלֵ֑ךְ בְּבָנֵ֨ינוּ וּבִבְנוֹתֵ֜נוּ בְּצֹאנֵ֤נוּ וּבִבְקָרֵ֨נוּ֙ נֵלֵ֔ךְ כִּ֥י חַג־יְהֹוָ֖ה לָֽנוּ:

10 וַיֹּ֣אמֶר אֲלֵהֶ֗ם יְהִ֨י כֵ֤ן יְהֹוָה֙ עִמָּכֶ֔ם כַּאֲשֶׁ֛ר אֲשַׁלַּ֥ח אֶתְכֶ֖ם וְאֶֽת־טַפְּכֶ֑ם רְא֕וּ כִּ֥י רָעָ֖ה נֶ֥גֶד פְּנֵיכֶֽם: 11 לֹ֣א כֵ֗ן לְכֽוּ־נָ֤א הַגְּבָרִים֙ וְעִבְד֣וּ אֶת־יְהֹוָ֔ה כִּ֥י אֹתָ֖הּ אַתֶּ֣ם מְבַקְשִׁ֑ים וַיְגָ֣רֶשׁ אֹתָ֔ם מֵאֵ֖ת פְּנֵ֥י פַרְעֹֽה: ס 12 [SECOND READING] וַיֹּ֨אמֶר יְהֹוָ֜ה אֶל־מֹשֶׁ֗ה נְטֵ֨ה יָדְךָ֜ עַל־אֶ֤רֶץ מִצְרַ֨יִם֙ בָּֽאַרְבֶּ֔ה וְיַ֖עַל עַל־אֶ֣רֶץ מִצְרָ֑יִם וְיֹאכַל֙ אֶת־כָּל־עֵ֣שֶׂב הָאָ֔רֶץ אֵ֛ת כָּל־אֲשֶׁ֥ר הִשְׁאִ֖יר הַבָּרָֽד: 13 וַיֵּ֨ט מֹשֶׁ֣ה אֶת־מַטֵּהוּ֮ עַל־אֶ֣רֶץ מִצְרַיִם֒ וַֽיהֹוָ֗ה נִהַ֤ג ר֣וּחַ קָדִים֙ בָּאָ֔רֶץ כָּל־הַיּ֥וֹם הַה֖וּא וְכָל־הַלָּ֑יְלָה הַבֹּ֣קֶר הָיָ֔ה וְר֨וּחַ֙ הַקָּדִ֔ים נָשָׂ֖א אֶת־הָאַרְבֶּֽה: 14 וַיַּ֣עַל הָֽאַרְבֶּ֗ה עַ֚ל כָּל־אֶ֣רֶץ מִצְרַ֔יִם וַיָּ֕נַח בְּכֹ֖ל גְּב֣וּל מִצְרָ֑יִם כָּבֵ֣ד מְאֹ֔ד לְ֠פָנָ֠יו לֹא־הָ֨יָה כֵ֤ן אַרְבֶּה֙ כָּמֹ֔הוּ וְאַחֲרָ֖יו לֹ֥א יִֽהְיֶה־כֵּֽן:

15 וַיְכַ֞ס אֶת־עֵ֣ין כָּל־הָאָרֶץ֮ וַתֶּחְשַׁ֣ךְ הָאָרֶץ֒ וַיֹּ֜אכַל אֶת־כָּל־עֵ֣שֶׂב הָאָ֗רֶץ וְאֵת֙ כָּל־פְּרִ֣י הָעֵ֔ץ אֲשֶׁ֥ר הוֹתִ֖יר הַבָּרָ֑ד וְלֹא־נוֹתַ֨ר כָּל־יֶ֧רֶק בָּעֵ֛ץ וּבְעֵ֥שֶׂב הַשָּׂדֶ֖ה

384

kabbalah bites

10:8-11 Pharaoh said, "*Exactly who will be going?*"—Exactly which *Sefirot* are going to be revealed? "*Moses said, 'With our youth and with our elders'*"—All of them, from the lowest to the highest!

Pharaoh immediately realized that this would signify a complete obliteration of the forces of evil (*sitra' 'ahara*). He replied, "*See that the evil turns back at you*"—This will not transpire. You will see that evil will prevail!

"*They were then driven out from Pharaoh's presence,*" as Pharaoh desperately attempted to protect his demonic forces from the revelation associated with Moses.

exodus 10:6–15   bo'

He turned away, and left Pharaoh.

⁷ Pharaoh's servants said to him, "How long will this one be a stumbling block to us? Let the people go and they will worship their God. Don't you know yet that Egypt is lost?"

⁸ Moses and Aaron were brought back to Pharaoh (by a messenger). He said to them, "Go, worship God, your God. But exactly who will be going?"

⁹ Moses said, "With our youth and with our elders we will go! With our sons and with our daughters, with our flocks and with our cattle we will go, for it is a festival of God for us!"

¹⁰ He said to them, "(You will need) God to be with you (even if) I will send (only) you and your children (all the more so if I send the cattle too). See that the evil (which you intend to commit) turns back at you. ¹¹ Not so! (I will not allow you to take the children as you are requesting now. Rather,) just the men can go and serve God, for that is what you have requested (in the past)." They were then driven out from Pharaoh's presence.

¹² God said to Moses, "Stretch out your hand over the land of Egypt (to bring about the plague of) locusts. It will pass up over the land of Egypt, and eat all the vegetation of the earth that was spared by the hail."

¹³ Moses stretched forth his staff over the land of Egypt, and God caused an east wind to blow upon the land all of that day and all night. By the time it was morning, the east wind was carrying the swarm of locusts. ¹⁴ The swarm of locusts went up over the entire land of Egypt, and rested within all the borders of Egypt in a very severe manner. Before it, there was never such a locust swarm, and after it, there will never be one like it. ¹⁵ It obscured the view of all the earth, and the land became dark. It ate all the vegetation of the earth and all the fruits of the trees which were spared by the hail. No greenery in the trees or vegetation in the fields remained throughout the entire land of Egypt.

13. God caused an east wind to blow upon the land, all of that day and all night. By the time it was morning, the east wind was carrying the swarm of locusts. God, in His mercy waits to administer punishment, although His kindness is quick in coming. In this verse, God *"caused an east wind to blow on the land, all of that day and all night,"* before the locusts came. Compare this to when, in an instant, *"God turned back a very strong west wind. It carried the swarm of locusts and plunged them into the Sea of Reeds"* (*Exodus* 10:19; *Rabbi Moses b. Gershom Gentili, 17th century*).

14. The swarm of locusts went up over the entire land of Egypt. God brought the plague of locusts upon the Egyptians, because the Egyptians forced the children of Israel to plant wheat, barley, and various kinds of beans for them, just so the Israelite men would be away from home and would have fewer children. The locusts swallowed up all that had been planted (*Tanna de-Vei Eliyahu*).

שמות י:טו-כד

בְּכָל־אֶרֶץ מִצְרָיִם: 16 וַיְמַהֵר פַּרְעֹה לִקְרֹא לְמֹשֶׁה וּלְאַהֲרֹן וַיֹּאמֶר חָטָאתִי לַיהוָה אֱלֹהֵיכֶם וְלָכֶם: 17 וְעַתָּה שָׂא נָא חַטָּאתִי אַךְ הַפַּעַם וְהַעְתִּירוּ לַיהוָה אֱלֹהֵיכֶם וְיָסֵר מֵעָלַי רַק אֶת־הַמָּוֶת הַזֶּה: 18 וַיֵּצֵא מֵעִם פַּרְעֹה וַיֶּעְתַּר אֶל־יְהוָה: 19 וַיַּהֲפֹךְ יְהוָה רוּחַ־יָם חָזָק מְאֹד וַיִּשָּׂא אֶת־הָאַרְבֶּה וַיִּתְקָעֵהוּ יָמָּה סּוּף לֹא נִשְׁאַר אַרְבֶּה אֶחָד בְּכֹל גְּבוּל מִצְרָיִם: 20 וַיְחַזֵּק יְהוָה אֶת־לֵב פַּרְעֹה וְלֹא שִׁלַּח אֶת־בְּנֵי יִשְׂרָאֵל: פ 21 וַיֹּאמֶר יְהוָה אֶל־מֹשֶׁה נְטֵה יָדְךָ עַל־הַשָּׁמַיִם וִיהִי חֹשֶׁךְ עַל־אֶרֶץ מִצְרָיִם וְיָמֵשׁ חֹשֶׁךְ: 22 וַיֵּט מֹשֶׁה אֶת־יָדוֹ עַל־הַשָּׁמָיִם וַיְהִי חֹשֶׁךְ־אֲפֵלָה בְּכָל־אֶרֶץ מִצְרַיִם שְׁלֹשֶׁת יָמִים: 23 לֹא־רָאוּ אִישׁ אֶת־אָחִיו וְלֹא־קָמוּ אִישׁ מִתַּחְתָּיו שְׁלֹשֶׁת יָמִים וּלְכָל־בְּנֵי יִשְׂרָאֵל הָיָה אוֹר בְּמוֹשְׁבֹתָם: 24 [THIRD READING] וַיִּקְרָא פַרְעֹה אֶל־מֹשֶׁה וַיֹּאמֶר לְכוּ עִבְדוּ אֶת־יְהוָה

23. No person could see his brother, nor could any person rise from his place. The blindness that occurs when you cannot "see your brother," to recognize and appreciate another person's virtues, is extremely far-reaching. So long as you fail to "see your brother," you cannot "rise from your place"—you will be unable to grow and refine your character (*Rabbi Isaac Meir Alter of Gur, 19th century*).

The children of Israel had light in all their homes. In the land of Goshen, where the Jewish people lived, there was light. Supernatural light also entered any place that a Jew would come, revealing the contents of barrels and storage boxes, as well as buried treasures (*Genesis Rabbah*).

While many Jews died during these days of darkness, because they did not deserve to be redeemed (see commentary to v. 22), nevertheless, even those errant souls expired amid thoughts of penitence and spiritual yearning. Due to this they merited the afterlife in *Gan Eden* (heaven).

Consequently, those who survived had physical light in their earthly abodes, whereas those

kabbalah bites

10:23 "*The children of Israel had light in all their homes.*" God is a single infinite Light, but He projects Himself through different *vessels* to achieve different effects. It's rather like looking at white light through different-colored glasses: we see a variety of colors, but really it's all one light.

Bringing the plague of darkness for the Egyptians while the Israelites enjoyed light was aimed to prove that God is *both* master of light and darkness. The Egyptians only understood the idea of vessels, so they imagined that "the god of light did not create darkness." They did not focus on the light that was behind the vessels.

You, too, can train yourself to see everything in this world as being translucent to the single Light which is behind it.

¹⁶ Pharaoh quickly summoned Moses and Aaron and he said, "I have sinned against God, your God, and against you. ¹⁷ Now, please forgive my sin just this time and entreat God, your God! Let him take away just this death from me."

¹⁸ He left Pharaoh and pleaded with God. ¹⁹ God turned back a very strong west wind. It carried the swarm of locusts and plunged them into the Sea of Reeds. Not one locust remained within the entire border of Egypt.

²⁰ God strengthened Pharaoh's heart, and he did not send the children of Israel away.

The Ninth Plague—Darkness

²¹ God said to Moses, "Stretch out your hand towards the heaven, and there will be darkness over the land of Egypt. The darkness will become more intense (than normal darkness)." ²² Moses stretched out his hand towards the heaven, and there was thick darkness over the entire land of Egypt for three days. ²³ No person could see his brother, nor could any person rise from his place for three days. (However), the children of Israel had light in all their homes.

[THIRD READING] ²⁴ Pharaoh summoned Moses and said, "Go and worship God! But your flocks and your cattle must remain. Your children may also go with you."

21. There will be darkness over the land of Egypt. The darkness will become more intense (than normal darkness). The darkness in Egypt differed from ordinary nighttime darkness in that it could be felt, and not merely seen. Ordinary darkness is the mere absence of light, and can be dispelled by the introduction of light. In this case, however, the darkness was a tangible substance that could not be driven away by shining a light (*Rabbi Obadiah Sforno, 16th century*).

22. There was thick darkness. Why did God bring darkness upon the Egyptians? Because there were wicked people among the children of Israel in that generation, who did not want to leave Egypt. They died during the three days of darkness, so that the Egyptians would not see their downfall and say, "The Jews are being struck by the plagues just like us!" (*Rashi, 11th century*).

There were many other wicked people among the children of Israel—informants and even idol-worshipers—who *did* leave Egypt. Only "those who did not want to leave Egypt" died in the plague of darkness, and not the other wicked people.

This phenomenon could be understood in light of the principle that the Day of Atonement atones for all sins, except for the desecration of the actual Day of Atonement (*Babylonian Talmud, Shevu'ot* 13a). On this holy day, a Jew's intrinsic connection to God is illuminated, which wipes away sin. Sinning on the Day of Atonement itself inhibits this revelation, preventing the day from having its effect.

Similarly, those who did not wish to leave Egypt *forfeited the merit which was the key to their redemption*.

With the true and final redemption, however, every single Jew will be redeemed. This is because, at the giving of the Torah, God *chose* the Jewish people, forging an intrinsic connection which can never become totally "blocked." Therefore, the final redemption, which occurs after the giving of the Torah, will be for all Jews (*Rabbi Menahem Mendel Schneerson, 20th century*).

שמות י:כד - יא:ב

רַק צֹאנְכֶם וּבְקַרְכֶם יֻצָּג גַּם־טַפְּכֶם יֵלֵךְ עִמָּכֶם: 25 וַיֹּאמֶר מֹשֶׁה גַּם־אַתָּה תִּתֵּן בְּיָדֵנוּ זְבָחִים וְעֹלֹת וְעָשִׂינוּ לַיהֹוָה אֱלֹהֵינוּ: 26 וְגַם־מִקְנֵנוּ יֵלֵךְ עִמָּנוּ לֹא תִשָּׁאֵר פַּרְסָה כִּי מִמֶּנּוּ נִקַּח לַעֲבֹד אֶת־יְהֹוָה אֱלֹהֵינוּ וַאֲנַחְנוּ לֹא־נֵדַע מַה־נַּעֲבֹד אֶת־יְהֹוָה עַד־בֹּאֵנוּ שָׁמָּה: 27 וַיְחַזֵּק יְהֹוָה אֶת־לֵב פַּרְעֹה וְלֹא אָבָה לְשַׁלְּחָם: 28 וַיֹּאמֶר־לוֹ פַרְעֹה לֵךְ מֵעָלָי הִשָּׁמֶר לְךָ אַל־תֹּסֶף רְאוֹת פָּנַי כִּי בְּיוֹם רְאֹתְךָ פָנַי תָּמוּת: 29 וַיֹּאמֶר מֹשֶׁה כֵּן דִּבַּרְתָּ לֹא־אֹסִף עוֹד רְאוֹת פָּנֶיךָ: פ

יא 1 וַיֹּאמֶר יְהֹוָה אֶל־מֹשֶׁה עוֹד נֶגַע אֶחָד אָבִיא עַל־פַּרְעֹה וְעַל־מִצְרַיִם אַחֲרֵי־כֵן יְשַׁלַּח אֶתְכֶם מִזֶּה כְּשַׁלְּחוֹ כָּלָה גָּרֵשׁ יְגָרֵשׁ אֶתְכֶם מִזֶּה: 2 דַּבֶּר־נָא בְּאָזְנֵי הָעָם וְיִשְׁאֲלוּ אִישׁ | מֵאֵת רֵעֵהוּ וְאִשָּׁה מֵאֵת רְעוּתָהּ כְּלֵי־

with the land of Egypt. So God ensured that Pharaoh would drive the Jews out of Egypt, making a complete break between the children of Israel and the land of Egypt— *"When he sends you out, he will drive you out of here completely."* The children of Israel could then become a *"legion of God"* (below, 12:41; *Rabbi Judah Aryeh Leib Alter of Gur, 19th century*).

2. Please speak in the ears of the people and tell each man to request from his friend, and each woman from her friend, silver vessels and golden vessels. God requested this so that the righteous Abraham would not have a grievance against Him: "You fulfilled the promise that the Egyptians *'will enslave them and oppress them',* but You did not fulfil the other part of that promise, *'afterwards, they will leave with substantial wealth'"* (Genesis 15:13-14; *Babylonian Talmud, Berakhot* 9a).

Did God make this request only so that Abraham would not have *grievances*? God surely was bound to keep His promise regardless of Abraham's sentiments.

God knew that the children of Israel sought only redemption. They were willing to forgo the wealth, and this released God from his "obligation."

God nevertheless upheld it, "so that Abraham would not have a grievance." Abraham could argue that the children of Israel had not wanted the first part of the promise, that the Egyptians *"will enslave them and afflict them,"* yet God had fulfilled it. In the same way, although they did not seek the second part of the promise *"afterwards, they will leave with substantial wealth,"* God should fulfil it! (*Rabbi Jehiel Meir Lifschits of Gostynin, 19th–20th century*).

God could have fulfilled his promise that *"afterwards they will leave Egypt with substantial wealth,"* with only a spiritual form of wealth—the Torah.

However, again, Abraham would have a complaint: "The first clause of God's promise, that the Egyptians *'will enslave them and oppress them,'* was fulfilled literally and physically, so the second clause, that *'afterwards, they will leave with substantial wealth'* must also be fulfilled literally and physically!" (*Rabbi Ḥayyim Aryeh Leib of Jedwabne, 19th century*).

²⁵ Moses said, "(Not only will we take our own cattle but) you will also provide us with (animals for) sacrifices and burnt-offerings, and we will offer them for God, our God. ²⁶ Our cattle will also go with us—not a single hoof will remain—for we will take (sacrifices) from it to worship God, our God, and we do not know how much worship will be (required by) God until we arrive there."

²⁷ God hardened Pharaoh's heart, and he did not wish to send them out. ²⁸ Pharaoh said to him, "Go away from me! Beware not to look at my face again, for on the day that you see my face, you shall die!"

²⁹ Moses said, "Well said! I will never see your face again!"

The Tenth Plague—Death of Firstborn Egyptians

11 ¹ God said to Moses (while he was standing in Pharaoh's presence), "I will bring one more plague upon Pharaoh and upon Egypt, and afterwards he will send you away from here. When he sends you out, he will drive you out of here completely. ² Please speak in the ears of the people and tell each man to request from his friend, and each woman from her friend, silver vessels and golden vessels."

---

who died had spiritual illumination in heaven. So it was correct to say that "the children of Israel had light in *all* their homes"—either in this world or the next (*Rabbi Menahem Azariah da Fano, 16ᵗʰ–17ᵗʰ century*).

26. We do not know how much worship will be (required by) God until we arrive there. Until *"we arrive there,"* we do not know how many miracles and wonders God will perform for us. Therefore we do not know how many sacrifices we will need to offer in thanks.

The previous verse can also be explained in a similar vein. *"You will also provide us with (animals for) sacrifices and burnt-offerings."* It is *because* of Pharaoh's wickedness and terrible decrees that God performed even more miracles for the children of Israel, which in turn caused them to offer more sacrifices as thanks (*Rabbi Abraham Samuel Benjamin Sofer, 19ᵗʰ century*).

11:1 When he sends you out, he will drive you out of here completely. The children of Israel, after living in Egypt for so many years, had absorbed many of its negative influences. When God took them out, He wanted them to reject all traces of the Egyptian culture and become *"a kingdom of ministers and a holy nation"* (19:6). This would only be possible if they cut all ties

spiritual vitamin

" It is faith that carried the Jews through the ages, an insignificant physical minority in the midst of a hostile world, a spot of light threatened by an overwhelming darkness. It is this absolute faith in God that we need nowadays more than ever before. "

שמות י״א:ב׳-י׳

כֶּסֶף וּכְלֵי זָהָב: 3 וַיִּתֵּ֧ן יְהֹוָ֛ה אֶת־חֵ֥ן הָעָ֖ם בְּעֵינֵ֣י מִצְרָ֑יִם גַּ֣ם ׀ הָאִ֣ישׁ מֹשֶׁ֗ה גָּד֤וֹל מְאֹד֙ בְּאֶ֣רֶץ מִצְרַ֔יִם בְּעֵינֵ֥י עַבְדֵֽי־פַרְעֹ֖ה וּבְעֵינֵ֥י הָעָֽם: ס 4 וַיֹּ֣אמֶר מֹשֶׁ֔ה [FOURTH READING] כֹּ֥ה אָמַ֖ר יְהֹוָ֑ה כַּחֲצֹ֣ת הַלַּ֔יְלָה אֲנִ֥י יוֹצֵ֖א בְּת֥וֹךְ מִצְרָֽיִם: 5 וּמֵ֣ת כׇּל־בְּכוֹר֮ בְּאֶ֣רֶץ מִצְרַ֒יִם֒ מִבְּכ֤וֹר פַּרְעֹה֙ הַיֹּשֵׁ֣ב עַל־כִּסְא֔וֹ עַ֚ד בְּכ֣וֹר הַשִּׁפְחָ֔ה אֲשֶׁ֖ר אַחַ֣ר הָרֵחָ֑יִם וְכֹ֖ל בְּכ֥וֹר בְּהֵמָֽה: 6 וְהָ֥יְתָ֛ה צְעָקָ֥ה גְדֹלָ֖ה בְּכׇל־אֶ֣רֶץ מִצְרָ֑יִם אֲשֶׁ֤ר כָּמֹ֙הוּ֙ לֹ֣א נִהְיָ֔תָה וְכָמֹ֖הוּ לֹ֥א תֹסִֽף: 7 וּלְכֹ֣ל ׀ בְּנֵ֣י יִשְׂרָאֵ֗ל לֹ֤א יֶחֱרַץ־כֶּ֙לֶב֙ לְשֹׁנ֔וֹ לְמֵאִ֖ישׁ וְעַד־בְּהֵמָ֑ה לְמַ֙עַן֙ תֵּֽדְע֔וּן אֲשֶׁר֙ יַפְלֶ֣ה יְהֹוָ֔ה בֵּ֥ין מִצְרַ֖יִם וּבֵ֥ין יִשְׂרָאֵֽל: 8 וְיָרְד֣וּ כׇל־עֲבָדֶ֩יךָ֩ אֵ֨לֶּה אֵלַ֜י וְהִשְׁתַּחֲווּ־לִ֣י לֵאמֹ֗ר צֵ֤א אַתָּה֙ וְכׇל־הָעָ֣ם אֲשֶׁר־בְּרַגְלֶ֔יךָ וְאַחֲרֵי־כֵ֖ן אֵצֵ֑א וַיֵּצֵ֥א מֵֽעִם־פַּרְעֹ֖ה בׇּחֳרִי־אָֽף: ס 9 וַיֹּ֤אמֶר יְהֹוָה֙ אֶל־מֹשֶׁ֔ה לֹא־יִשְׁמַ֥ע אֲלֵיכֶ֖ם פַּרְעֹ֑ה לְמַ֛עַן רְב֥וֹת מוֹפְתַ֖י בְּאֶ֥רֶץ מִצְרָֽיִם: 10 וּמֹשֶׁ֣ה וְאַהֲרֹ֗ן עָשׂ֛וּ אֶת־כׇּל־הַמֹּפְתִ֥ים הָאֵ֖לֶּה לִפְנֵ֣י פַרְעֹ֑ה וַיְחַזֵּ֤ק יְהֹוָה֙ אֶת־לֵ֣ב פַּרְעֹ֔ה וְלֹֽא־שִׁלַּ֥ח אֶת־בְּנֵֽי־יִשְׂרָאֵ֖ל מֵאַרְצֽוֹ: ס

390

Doubt is the "midnight" of your mind. Midnight is that exact point which separates the first part of the night from the second—and when you are in doubt, you can see equal opportunities in two different directions. At that moment, *"I will go out into the midst of Egypt"*—God will come to you to enlighten you (*Rabbi Israel Ba'al Shem Tov, 18th century*).

7. Not one dog will bark ferociously at any man or animal. What was the need for this extra miracle, preventing the Egyptian dogs from barking even at the Jewish people's cattle? The answer is self-understood from Moses' statement earlier, "With our youth and with our elders we will go! With our sons and with our daughters, *with our flocks and with our cattle we will go; for it is a festival of God to us!*" (10:9) and, *"our cattle will go with us—not a single hoof will remain"* (ibid. 26). In order for this promise to be fulfilled, it was crucial that the Egyptian dogs should not scare off even one animal belonging to the Jewish people (*Rabbi Menahem Mendel Schneerson, 20th century*).

8. All these servants of yours will come down to me and throw themselves down in front of me. Moses told Pharaoh, *"All your servants will come and bow down to me,"* but out of respect for the monarchy, he did not say to Pharaoh, *"You will come and bow down to me"*—even though this is what transpired (*Babylonian Talmud, Zevaḥim* 102a).

9. Pharaoh will not listen to you. God told Moses and Aaron explicitly that Pharaoh would not listen to them, and that their efforts would

Food for thought

1. How do you cope with temporary setbacks?

2. Can you always see the "light at the end of the tunnel"?

3. Do you believe that every setback will ultimately lead to progress?

exodus 11:3-10 — bo'

³ God granted the people favor in the eyes of the Egyptians. Moses was also a highly respected person in the eyes of Pharaoh's servants and in the eyes of the people.

[FOURTH READING] ⁴ Moses said (to Pharaoh), "This is what God said, 'At the dividing point of the night, I will go out into the midst of Egypt, ⁵ and every firstborn in the land of Egypt will die, from the firstborn of Pharaoh who sits on his throne to the firstborn of the slave woman who is behind the millstones, and the firstborn animals too. ⁶ There will be a great cry throughout the entire land of Egypt, like which there never has been before, and like which there will never be again. ⁷ Not one dog will bark ferociously at any man or animal of all the children of Israel, so that you will know that God will have distinguished between the Egyptians and Israel. ⁸ All these servants of yours will come down to me and throw themselves down in front of me, saying, "Go away! You and all your followers!" Afterwards, I will leave (your land together with the entire people).'"

He (Moses) then left Pharaoh in a very angry state.

⁹ God said to Moses, "Pharaoh will not listen to you, so that My miracles in the land of Egypt will be increased."

¹⁰ Moses and Aaron had performed all these miracles before Pharaoh, but God strengthened Pharaoh's heart, and he did not send the children of Israel out from his land.

Why was it a praiseworthy act on the part of the Israelites to request the Egyptians' silver and gold? Was it not motivated out of self-interest? Yet below, the Torah states proudly, *"They emptied out Egypt"* (v. 36).

Logically, the Israelites should have taken every precaution to ensure there was no reason to ever see the Egyptians ever again, ensuring that they would not have to return to Egypt. Moses' directive, to borrow silver and gold utensils, was fraught with danger—it meant that the Egyptians were much more likely to pursue the Israelites to get their treasured possessions back. The fact that the Israelites loyally obeyed the directive despite these considerations was especially impressive (*Rabbi Menahem Mendel of Rymanow, 18th century*).

3. Moses was also a highly respected person in the eyes of Pharaoh's servants and in the eyes of the people. Moses was respected by all classes in Egyptian society, both the upper class, *"Pharaoh's servants,"* and the ordinary *"people."* Usually a person is respected by one segment of society and disregarded or even despised by a lower or higher class. The fact that Moses was respected by the nobility and the masses attests to his exceptional personality (*Rabbi Aaron Lewin of Rzeszow, 20th century*).

4. At the dividing point of the night (lit. around midnight) I will go out into the midst of Egypt. God told Moses that the plague would start at precisely midnight, but Moses decided not to tell this fact to Pharaoh. He feared that the Egyptian astrologers might err in their calculations of the exact moment of midnight. Then, when the plague failed to come at the time they had expected, the astrologers would conclude that Moses had spoken falsely. Therefore, Moses told Pharaoh that the plague would start at *"around"* midnight (*Rashi, 11th century*).

שמות יב:א-ט

יב １ וַיֹּאמֶר יְהֹוָה אֶל־מֹשֶׁה וְאֶל־אַהֲרֹן בְּאֶרֶץ מִצְרַיִם לֵאמֹר: ２ הַחֹדֶשׁ הַזֶּה לָכֶם רֹאשׁ חֳדָשִׁים רִאשׁוֹן הוּא לָכֶם לְחָדְשֵׁי הַשָּׁנָה: ３ דַּבְּרוּ אֶל־כָּל־עֲדַת יִשְׂרָאֵל לֵאמֹר בֶּעָשֹׂר לַחֹדֶשׁ הַזֶּה וְיִקְחוּ לָהֶם אִישׁ שֶׂה לְבֵית־אָבֹת שֶׂה לַבָּיִת: ４ וְאִם־יִמְעַט הַבַּיִת מִהְיוֹת מִשֶּׂה וְלָקַח הוּא וּשְׁכֵנוֹ הַקָּרֹב אֶל־בֵּיתוֹ בְּמִכְסַת נְפָשֹׁת אִישׁ לְפִי אָכְלוֹ תָּכֹסּוּ עַל־הַשֶּׂה: ５ שֶׂה תָמִים זָכָר בֶּן־שָׁנָה יִהְיֶה לָכֶם מִן־הַכְּבָשִׂים וּמִן־הָעִזִּים תִּקָּחוּ: ６ וְהָיָה לָכֶם לְמִשְׁמֶרֶת עַד אַרְבָּעָה עָשָׂר יוֹם לַחֹדֶשׁ הַזֶּה וְשָׁחֲטוּ אֹתוֹ כֹּל קְהַל עֲדַת־יִשְׂרָאֵל בֵּין הָעַרְבָּיִם: ７ וְלָקְחוּ מִן־הַדָּם וְנָתְנוּ עַל־שְׁתֵּי הַמְּזוּזֹת וְעַל־הַמַּשְׁקוֹף עַל הַבָּתִּים אֲשֶׁר־יֹאכְלוּ אֹתוֹ בָּהֶם: ８ וְאָכְלוּ אֶת־הַבָּשָׂר בַּלַּיְלָה הַזֶּה צְלִי־אֵשׁ וּמַצּוֹת עַל־מְרֹרִים יֹאכְלֻהוּ: ９ אַל־תֹּאכְלוּ מִמֶּנּוּ נָא וּבָשֵׁל מְבֻשָּׁל בַּמָּיִם כִּי אִם־צְלִי־אֵשׁ

12:2 This month shall be the head of the months for you. Why is the precept of *Rosh Ḥodesh* (determining the new month) the first commandment recorded in the Torah?

When learning of the first precept, a person will immediately be struck by the question: Where are the practical details of this law? The verse states only, *"This month shall be the head of the months for you. It shall be the first of the months of the year for you"* (v. 2). No mention is made of the requirements of a Jewish court to establish the new month, the need for witnesses who have spotted the new moon, etc., which are all crucial components of the commandment.

From this you learn at the very outset, when embarking on your study of the very first *precept of the Torah*, that Scripture can only be understood by means of the Oral Law. Right at the beginning of the legal segment of the Torah, a foundation is laid down that the Written and Oral traditions are indispensable to each other (*Rabbi Abraham ibn Ezra, 12th century*).

---

kabbalah bites

12:2 *"This month shall be for you, etc."* The Torah should really have begun here, with its first actual command, the Sages suggested, and not with the story of Creation.

Why? Because the Torah's purpose is to reveal the Endless Light of God; and this can only take place through a *direct command from God to man*. Creation, on the other hand, however wondrous it might seem, was a process of *tzimtzum*—a *concealment* of the Endless Light, to make room for the world. So starting the Torah with concealment is a little misleading, because this book is all about Light.

exodus 12:1–9 — bo'

12 The New Moon and Passover

¹ God spoke to Moses and to Aaron in the land of Egypt, saying:

- ² "This month shall be the head of the months for you. It shall be the first of the months of the year for you.

³ "Speak to the entire community of Israel, saying:

- "On the tenth of this month they should take for themselves: one lamb (or kid) for one extended family, one lamb (or kid) for each household.

- ⁴ "But if the household is too small (to eat a whole) lamb (or kid), then he should take one with a neighbor of his, who is near to his house, according to the number of people involved. Each person should be counted for the lamb (or kid) according to his ability to eat.

- ⁵ "You must have a perfect (unblemished) male lamb (or kid), in its first year;

- "You may take either sheep or goats.

- ⁶ "You should hold it for inspection until the fourteenth day of this month. Then, the entire congregation of the community of Israel shall have it slaughtered in the afternoon.

- ⁷ "They shall take some of its blood and put it on the two doorposts and on the lintel of the houses in which they will be eating it.

- ⁸ "On that night, they shall eat the meat. They should eat it roasted over fire, together with unleavened bread and bitter herbs.

- ⁹ "Do not eat it under-cooked, or boiled in water, only roasted over the fire (in one piece), its head with its legs and with its innards.

be futile. Nevertheless, they did as God instructed, *"Moses and Aaron had performed all these miracles before Pharaoh"* (v. 10). There is an important lesson here: you should fulfil the commandments even when you do not recognize their tangible effects (*Rabbi Phinehas Zalman Horowitz, 19th century*).

spiritual vitamin

By ordaining the Jewish people to count all the months of the year from *Nisan* (v.2), the month of revealed Divine miracles, the Torah teaches us that *this is the essence of the Divine conduct of the universe throughout all the months of the year*—whether through revealed miracles, or in miracles which are dressed in "natural" garments.

שמות יב:ט-כ

רֹאשׁ֥וֹ עַל־כְּרָעָ֖יו וְעַל־קִרְבּֽוֹ׃ 10 וְלֹא־תוֹתִ֥ירוּ מִמֶּ֖נּוּ עַד־בֹּ֑קֶר וְהַנֹּתָ֥ר מִמֶּ֛נּוּ עַד־בֹּ֖קֶר בָּאֵ֥שׁ תִּשְׂרֹֽפוּ׃ 11 וְכָ֘כָה֮ תֹּאכְל֣וּ אֹתוֹ֒ מָתְנֵיכֶ֣ם חֲגֻרִ֔ים נַֽעֲלֵיכֶם֙ בְּרַגְלֵיכֶ֔ם וּמַקֶּלְכֶ֖ם בְּיֶדְכֶ֑ם וַאֲכַלְתֶּ֤ם אֹתוֹ֙ בְּחִפָּז֔וֹן פֶּ֥סַח ה֖וּא לַיהוָֽה׃ 12 וְעָבַרְתִּ֣י בְאֶֽרֶץ־מִצְרַ֘יִם֮ בַּלַּ֣יְלָה הַזֶּה֒ וְהִכֵּיתִ֤י כָל־בְּכוֹר֙ בְּאֶ֣רֶץ מִצְרַ֔יִם מֵאָדָ֖ם וְעַד־בְּהֵמָ֑ה וּבְכָל־אֱלֹהֵ֥י מִצְרַ֛יִם אֶעֱשֶׂ֥ה שְׁפָטִ֖ים אֲנִ֥י יְהוָֽה׃ 13 וְהָיָה֩ הַדָּ֨ם לָכֶ֜ם לְאֹ֗ת עַ֤ל הַבָּתִּים֙ אֲשֶׁ֣ר אַתֶּ֣ם שָׁ֔ם וְרָאִ֙יתִי֙ אֶת־הַדָּ֔ם וּפָסַחְתִּ֖י עֲלֵכֶ֑ם וְלֹֽא־יִֽהְיֶ֨ה בָכֶ֥ם נֶ֙גֶף֙ לְמַשְׁחִ֔ית בְּהַכֹּתִ֖י בְּאֶ֥רֶץ מִצְרָֽיִם׃ 14 וְהָיָה֩ הַיּ֨וֹם הַזֶּ֤ה לָכֶם֙ לְזִכָּר֔וֹן וְחַגֹּתֶ֥ם אֹת֖וֹ חַ֣ג לַֽיהוָ֑ה לְדֹרֹ֣תֵיכֶ֔ם חֻקַּ֥ת עוֹלָ֖ם תְּחָגֻּֽהוּ׃ 15 שִׁבְעַ֤ת יָמִים֙ מַצּ֣וֹת תֹּאכֵ֔לוּ אַ֚ךְ בַּיּ֣וֹם הָרִאשׁ֔וֹן תַּשְׁבִּ֥יתוּ שְּׂאֹ֖ר מִבָּתֵּיכֶ֑ם כִּ֣י ׀ כָּל־אֹכֵ֣ל חָמֵ֗ץ וְנִכְרְתָ֞ה הַנֶּ֤פֶשׁ הַהִוא֙ מִיִּשְׂרָאֵ֔ל מִיּ֥וֹם הָרִאשֹׁ֖ן עַד־י֥וֹם הַשְּׁבִעִֽי׃ 16 וּבַיּ֤וֹם הָרִאשׁוֹן֙ מִקְרָא־קֹ֔דֶשׁ וּבַיּוֹם֙ הַשְּׁבִיעִ֔י מִקְרָא־קֹ֖דֶשׁ יִהְיֶ֣ה לָכֶ֑ם כָּל־מְלָאכָה֙ לֹא־יֵעָשֶׂ֣ה בָהֶ֔ם אַ֚ךְ אֲשֶׁ֣ר יֵאָכֵ֣ל לְכָל־נֶ֔פֶשׁ ה֖וּא לְבַדּ֥וֹ יֵעָשֶׂ֥ה לָכֶֽם׃ 17 וּשְׁמַרְתֶּם֮ אֶת־הַמַּצּוֹת֒ כִּ֗י בְּעֶ֙צֶם֙ הַיּ֣וֹם הַזֶּ֔ה הוֹצֵ֥אתִי אֶת־צִבְאוֹתֵיכֶ֖ם מֵאֶ֣רֶץ מִצְרָ֑יִם וּשְׁמַרְתֶּ֞ם אֶת־הַיּ֥וֹם הַזֶּ֛ה לְדֹרֹתֵיכֶ֖ם חֻקַּ֥ת עוֹלָֽם׃ 18 בָּרִאשֹׁ֡ן בְּאַרְבָּעָה֩ עָשָׂ֨ר י֤וֹם לַחֹ֙דֶשׁ֙ בָּעֶ֔רֶב תֹּאכְל֖וּ מַצֹּ֑ת עַ֠ד י֣וֹם הָאֶחָ֧ד וְעֶשְׂרִ֛ים לַחֹ֖דֶשׁ בָּעָֽרֶב׃ 19 שִׁבְעַ֣ת יָמִ֔ים שְׂאֹ֕ר לֹ֥א יִמָּצֵ֖א בְּבָתֵּיכֶ֑ם כִּ֣י ׀ כָּל־אֹכֵ֣ל מַחְמֶ֗צֶת וְנִכְרְתָ֞ה הַנֶּ֤פֶשׁ הַהִוא֙ מֵעֲדַ֣ת יִשְׂרָאֵ֔ל בַּגֵּ֖ר וּבְאֶזְרַ֥ח הָאָֽרֶץ׃ 20 כָּל־מַחְמֶ֖צֶת לֹ֣א תֹאכֵ֑לוּ בְּכֹל֙ מוֹשְׁבֹ֣תֵיכֶ֔ם

14. You shall celebrate it as a festival for God. For all generations shall you celebrate it, as an eternal statute. Why do we continue celebrating the exodus from Egypt at Passover when the Jewish people are now once again in exile, often oppressed by the nations of the world?

We still celebrate a *"festival for God"*—a time when the Jewish people became a nation; a time when God led us out of slavery to make us His own. That can never be undone. No matter how many physical oppressors we have, we will always remain His nation. We can *"celebrate it as an eternal statute,"* even in the worst periods of exile (*Rabbi Meir Simhah of Dvinsk, 19th–20th century*).

- 10 "You shall not leave over any of it until morning.

- "Any part of it that is left over until morning should be burned in fire.

- 11 "This is how you shall eat it: your waist should be belted (i.e. you should be ready to travel), your shoes on your feet, and your staff in your hand. You should eat it quickly. It is (called) a Passover [*pesaḥ*] to (commemorate how) God (passed over [*pasaḥ*] the Jewish houses in Egypt).

- 12 "I will pass through the land of Egypt on this night, and I will smite every firstborn in the land of Egypt, both man and beast, and upon all the gods of Egypt I will perform acts of judgment. I, God, (will do this personally).

- 13 "The blood will be for you as a sign upon the houses where you are. I will see the blood and skip over you. There will be no plague to destroy you when I strike in the land of Egypt.

- 14 "This day shall be for you as a memorial, and you shall celebrate it as a festival for God. For all generations shall you celebrate it as an eternal statute.

- 15 "For seven days you shall eat unleavened bread, but on the preceding day you shall eliminate all leaven from your houses. For whoever eats leaven from the first day until the seventh day will have his soul cut off from Israel.

- 16 "On the first day, there shall be a sacred holiday, and on the seventh day, you shall have a sacred holiday. But the only work that you may do is that which is needed to provide food for (Jewish people or their cattle).

- 17 "You shall guard the unleavened bread, for on this very day I have taken your legions out of the land of Egypt. You shall observe this day throughout your generations, as an eternal statute.

- 18 "In the first month, on the fourteenth day of the month, in the evening, you shall eat unleavened bread, until the twenty-first day of the month, in the evening.

- 19 "For seven days, leaven shall not be found in your houses. If any person eats a leavening substance, his soul will be cut off from the community of Israel. (This applies to both) the convert and the native-born of the land.

- 20 "You shall not eat any leavening substance. Throughout all the places where you live, you shall eat unleavened bread."

13. The blood will be for you as a sign upon the houses. What was the purpose of this "sign"? Surely God would know which houses belonged to the Israelites without the need for any visual identification?

By displaying blood on their doorposts, the Israelites demonstrated their absolute trust in God, and it was *in the merit of this trust that God saved them* (*Rabbi Isaac Abravanel, 15th century*).

שמות יב:כ-ל

תֹּאכְל֖וּ מַצּֽוֹת׃ פ [FIFTH READING] 21 וַיִּקְרָ֥א מֹשֶׁ֛ה לְכׇל־זִקְנֵ֥י יִשְׂרָאֵ֖ל וַיֹּ֣אמֶר אֲלֵהֶ֑ם מִֽשְׁכ֗וּ וּקְח֨וּ לָכֶ֥ם צֹ֛אן לְמִשְׁפְּחֹתֵיכֶ֖ם וְשַׁחֲט֥וּ הַפָּֽסַח׃ 22 וּלְקַחְתֶּ֞ם אֲגֻדַּ֣ת אֵז֗וֹב וּטְבַלְתֶּם֮ בַּדָּ֣ם אֲשֶׁר־בַּסַּף֒ וְהִגַּעְתֶּ֤ם אֶל־הַמַּשְׁקוֹף֙ וְאֶל־שְׁתֵּ֣י הַמְּזוּזֹ֔ת מִן־הַדָּ֖ם אֲשֶׁ֣ר בַּסָּ֑ף וְאַתֶּ֗ם לֹ֥א תֵצְא֛וּ אִ֥ישׁ מִפֶּֽתַח־בֵּית֖וֹ עַד־בֹּֽקֶר׃ 23 וְעָבַ֣ר יְהֹוָה֮ לִנְגֹּ֣ף אֶת־מִצְרַ֒יִם֒ וְרָאָ֤ה אֶת־הַדָּם֙ עַל־הַמַּשְׁק֔וֹף וְעַ֖ל שְׁתֵּ֣י הַמְּזוּזֹ֑ת וּפָסַ֤ח יְהֹוָה֙ עַל־הַפֶּ֔תַח וְלֹ֤א יִתֵּן֙ הַמַּשְׁחִ֔ית לָבֹ֥א אֶל־בָּתֵּיכֶ֖ם לִנְגֹּֽף׃ 24 וּשְׁמַרְתֶּ֖ם אֶת־הַדָּבָ֣ר הַזֶּ֑ה לְחׇק־לְךָ֥ וּלְבָנֶ֖יךָ עַד־עוֹלָֽם׃ 25 וְהָיָ֞ה כִּֽי־תָבֹ֣אוּ אֶל־הָאָ֗רֶץ אֲשֶׁ֨ר יִתֵּ֧ן יְהֹוָ֛ה לָכֶ֖ם כַּאֲשֶׁ֣ר דִּבֵּ֑ר וּשְׁמַרְתֶּ֖ם אֶת־הָעֲבֹדָ֥ה הַזֹּֽאת׃ 26 וְהָיָ֕ה כִּֽי־יֹאמְר֥וּ אֲלֵיכֶ֖ם בְּנֵיכֶ֑ם מָ֛ה הָעֲבֹדָ֥ה הַזֹּ֖את לָכֶֽם׃ 27 וַאֲמַרְתֶּ֡ם זֶֽבַח־פֶּ֨סַח ה֜וּא לַֽיהֹוָ֗ה אֲשֶׁ֣ר פָּ֠סַ֠ח עַל־בָּתֵּ֤י בְנֵֽי־יִשְׂרָאֵל֙ בְּמִצְרַ֔יִם בְּנׇגְפּ֥וֹ אֶת־מִצְרַ֖יִם וְאֶת־בָּתֵּ֣ינוּ הִצִּ֑יל וַיִּקֹּ֥ד הָעָ֖ם וַיִּֽשְׁתַּחֲוֽוּ׃ 28 וַיֵּלְכ֥וּ וַיַּעֲשׂ֖וּ בְּנֵ֣י יִשְׂרָאֵ֑ל כַּאֲשֶׁ֨ר צִוָּ֧ה יְהֹוָ֛ה אֶת־מֹשֶׁ֥ה וְאַהֲרֹ֖ן כֵּ֥ן עָשֽׂוּ׃ ס 29 [SIXTH READING] וַיְהִ֣י ׀ בַּחֲצִ֣י הַלַּ֗יְלָה וַֽיהֹוָה֮ הִכָּ֣ה כׇל־בְּכוֹר֮ בְּאֶ֣רֶץ מִצְרַ֒יִם֒ מִבְּכֹ֤ר פַּרְעֹה֙ הַיֹּשֵׁ֣ב עַל־כִּסְא֔וֹ עַ֚ד בְּכ֣וֹר הַשְּׁבִ֔י אֲשֶׁ֖ר בְּבֵ֣ית הַבּ֑וֹר וְכֹ֖ל בְּכ֥וֹר בְּהֵמָֽה׃ 30 וַיָּ֨קׇם פַּרְעֹ֜ה לַ֗יְלָה ה֤וּא וְכׇל־עֲבָדָיו֙ וְכׇל־מִצְרַ֔יִם וַתְּהִ֛י צְעָקָ֥ה גְדֹלָ֖ה

defined, the distinction between Jew and Egyptian was framed somewhat differently, because in terms of *culpability* for sins, the Jews were not too different from their Egyptian neighbors. *Who could say that a Jew was better than an Egyptian?*

So now it was crucial for the Jewish people to make a sign on the doorposts, and not leave their houses until the morning, for when the prosecuting angel comes to the streets or to unmarked houses, he will punish anybody for their sins.

Why was this seemingly minor "sign" sufficient to save the Jewish people if they were indeed guilty? Is it rational or fair that one sinful nation should be punished while another is saved?

The answer is no, it is not rational at all. But God's commitment to the Jewish people is suprarational, *it defies and transcends logic.* He simply loves us, like a parent loves a child.

But to evoke that love *we have to remind Him of it.* We need to demonstrate our suprarational commitment to God. The blood of the Paschal Lamb required the ultimate suprarational commitment from the Jewish people—to endanger their lives by slaughtering a lamb, the deity of Egypt, merely to perform a religious ritual.

Love evokes love. The Jewish people's irrational commitment to God, despite their low standing, aroused a similar sentiment above, and God saved His people whom He loves so dearly (*Rabbi Menahem Mendel Schneerson, 20th century*).

exodus 12:21–30   bo'

[FIFTH READING] ²¹ Moses summoned all the elders of Israel and said to them:

- "Draw (from your own flock) or buy for yourselves sheep for your families and slaughter the Passover sacrifice.

- ²² "You shall take a bunch of hyssop and immerse it in blood that is in a basin. You shall touch the lintel and the two doorposts with some of the blood that is in the basin.

- "Not a single one of you shall go out from the entrance of his house until morning.

- ²³ "God will pass through to strike the Egyptians, and He will see the blood that is on the lintel and the two doorposts. God will skip over the entrance and He will not permit the force of destruction to enter your houses and strike.

- ²⁴ "You shall keep this matter as a statute for you and for your children forever.

- ²⁵ "You will (only) have to keep this ritual service when you enter the land that God is going to give you, as He promised.

- ²⁶ When your children say to you, 'What is this ritual service to you?' ²⁷ You should say, 'It is a Passover [*pesah*] slaughter (required by) God, because He skipped over [*pasah*] the houses of the children of Israel in Egypt when He struck the Egyptians, and He saved our houses.'"

The people bowed and prostrated themselves (on hearing this news). ²⁸ The children of Israel went and did (exactly) what God commanded Moses and Aaron. (Moses and Aaron also) did so.

Death of Firstborn—Jewish People Leave Egypt

[SIXTH READING] ²⁹ It was at midnight that God (and His court) struck every firstborn in the land of Egypt, from the firstborn of Pharaoh sitting on his throne to the firstborn of the prisoner in the dungeon, and every firstborn animal. ³⁰ Pharaoh arose at night (from his bed), both he and all his servants and all Egypt. There was a great outcry in Egypt, for there was no house devoid of a corpse.

22. You shall take a bunch of hyssop ... touch the lintel. We may seem as lowly as the hyssop, which grows close to the ground—but as long as we remain united and bound together, we will be able to "*touch the lintel*," attaining great heights (*Rabbi Ezekiel Taub of Kazimierz, 19*th *century*).

In all previous cases, the primary purpose of the plagues was to teach *the Egyptians* about God, "*Egypt shall know that I am God*" (7:5; see also 8:6, 18; 9:14, 29; 14:4, 18). The Jewish people, however, already believed in God (since *"the people believed"*—4:21), and there was no need for them to be taught a lesson of faith.

With the death of the firstborn, however, the goal was clearly one of punishment rather than education. (Once a person is dead he can no longer learn.) With the purpose of the plague re-

שמות יב:ל-מא

בְּמִצְרַיִם כִּי־אֵין בַּיִת אֲשֶׁר אֵין־שָׁם מֵת: 31 וַיִּקְרָא לְמֹשֶׁה וּלְאַהֲרֹן לַיְלָה וַיֹּאמֶר קוּמוּ צְּאוּ מִתּוֹךְ עַמִּי גַּם־אַתֶּם גַּם־בְּנֵי יִשְׂרָאֵל וּלְכוּ עִבְדוּ אֶת־יְהֹוָה כְּדַבֶּרְכֶם: 32 גַּם־צֹאנְכֶם גַּם־בְּקַרְכֶם קְחוּ כַּאֲשֶׁר דִּבַּרְתֶּם וָלֵכוּ וּבֵרַכְתֶּם גַּם־אֹתִי: 33 וַתֶּחֱזַק מִצְרַיִם עַל־הָעָם לְמַהֵר לְשַׁלְּחָם מִן־הָאָרֶץ כִּי אָמְרוּ כֻּלָּנוּ מֵתִים: 34 וַיִּשָּׂא הָעָם אֶת־בְּצֵקוֹ טֶרֶם יֶחְמָץ מִשְׁאֲרֹתָם צְרֻרֹת בְּשִׂמְלֹתָם עַל־שִׁכְמָם: 35 וּבְנֵי־יִשְׂרָאֵל עָשׂוּ כִּדְבַר מֹשֶׁה וַיִּשְׁאֲלוּ מִמִּצְרַיִם כְּלֵי־כֶסֶף וּכְלֵי זָהָב וּשְׂמָלֹת: 36 וַיהֹוָה נָתַן אֶת־חֵן הָעָם בְּעֵינֵי מִצְרַיִם וַיַּשְׁאִלוּם וַיְנַצְּלוּ אֶת־מִצְרָיִם: פ 37 וַיִּסְעוּ בְנֵי־יִשְׂרָאֵל מֵרַעְמְסֵס סֻכֹּתָה כְּשֵׁשׁ־מֵאוֹת אֶלֶף רַגְלִי הַגְּבָרִים לְבַד מִטָּף: 38 וְגַם־עֵרֶב רַב עָלָה אִתָּם וְצֹאן וּבָקָר מִקְנֶה כָּבֵד מְאֹד: 39 וַיֹּאפוּ אֶת־הַבָּצֵק אֲשֶׁר הוֹצִיאוּ מִמִּצְרַיִם עֻגֹת מַצּוֹת כִּי לֹא חָמֵץ כִּי־גֹרְשׁוּ מִמִּצְרַיִם וְלֹא יָכְלוּ לְהִתְמַהְמֵהַּ וְגַם־צֵדָה לֹא־עָשׂוּ לָהֶם: 40 וּמוֹשַׁב בְּנֵי יִשְׂרָאֵל אֲשֶׁר יָשְׁבוּ בְּמִצְרָיִם שְׁלֹשִׁים שָׁנָה וְאַרְבַּע מֵאוֹת שָׁנָה: 41 וַיְהִי

Later, however, God's objection against Moses was vindicated, because it was the mixed multitude who were responsible for making the Golden Calf (*Zohar*).

kabbalah bites

12:38 The children of Israel in Egypt *and* the "mixed multitude" (*'erev rav*) were a reincarnation of the "dysfunctional souls" which Adam brought into being during the 130 years he separated from his wife (see Genesis 5:3).

These "dysfunctional souls" were, in fact, derivatives of Abel's soul. And since Moses was a reincarnation of Abel himself, we can appreciate why he had a strong urge to redeem the mixed multitude, even when God warned him to the contrary.

Also, Moses' lofty soul was from the level of *Da'at* (knowledge), and so were the souls of the *'erev rav*.

Thus the Hebrew words *Da'at* and *'erev rav* share the same *gematria* (numerical value).

exodus 12:31–41 — bo'

³¹ He called (personally) for Moses and Aaron at night, and he said, "Get up and go out from among my people, both you and the children of Israel! Go and worship God, as you said. ³² Take also your flocks and your cattle, as you said, and go. Bless me too (that I should not die, as I am a firstborn)."

³³ The Egyptians urged the people to send them speedily from the land, because they said, "We are all dying!"

³⁴ The people picked up their dough when it was not yet leavened. Their leftovers (of unleavened bread and bitter herbs) were wrapped in their robes on their shoulders.

³⁵ The children of Israel followed the order of Moses, and they requested from the Egyptians silver objects, golden objects, and robes. ³⁶ God granted the people favor in the eyes of the Egyptians, and they granted their request. They emptied out Egypt.

³⁷ The children of Israel journeyed (a large distance miraculously) from Raamses to Succoth, about six hundred thousand men on foot, besides the young children. ³⁸ Also, a great mixed multitude (of converts from other nations) went up with them, as well as flocks and cattle, a huge amount of livestock.

³⁹ They baked the dough that they had taken out of Egypt into cakes of unleavened bread, for it had not leavened, since they were driven out of Egypt, and they could not delay. Furthermore, they had not made provisions for themselves.

⁴⁰ The children of Israel had inhabited Egypt for four hundred and thirty years. ⁴¹ It was at the end of four hundred and thirty years, on that very day, that all the

---

Food for thought

1. Can financial compensation be made for *any* wrongdoing?

2. To what extent does financial compensation confer dignity?

3. Was it correct to accept reparations from Germany after World War II?

---

34. Their leftovers (of unleavened bread and bitter herbs) were wrapped in their robes on their shoulders. They had animals to carry the unleavened bread—*"flocks and cattle, a huge amount of livestock"* (v. 38). Nevertheless, they carried the leftover bread and herbs personally, on their shoulders, out of great love for God's commandment (*Mekhilta*).

38. A great mixed multitude went up with them. The mixed multitude included all the magicians and sorcerers of Egypt. Originally, they attempted to stand up against the miracles of God, but when they saw what Moses performed in Egypt they sided with Moses.

God said to Moses, "Do not accept them."

Moses replied, "Master of the universe! They saw Your mighty deeds, and they want to convert. Let them see Your mighty deeds every day, and they will know that there is no God besides You!" And Moses accepted them.

שמות יב:מא-מח

מִקֵּץ שְׁלֹשִׁים שָׁנָה וְאַרְבַּע מֵאוֹת שָׁנָה וַיְהִי בְּעֶצֶם הַיּוֹם הַזֶּה יָצְאוּ כָּל־צִבְאוֹת יְהֹוָה מֵאֶרֶץ מִצְרָיִם: 42 לֵיל שִׁמֻּרִים הוּא לַיהֹוָה לְהוֹצִיאָם מֵאֶרֶץ מִצְרָיִם הוּא־הַלַּיְלָה הַזֶּה לַיהֹוָה שִׁמֻּרִים לְכָל־בְּנֵי יִשְׂרָאֵל לְדֹרֹתָם: פ 43 וַיֹּאמֶר יְהֹוָה אֶל־מֹשֶׁה וְאַהֲרֹן זֹאת חֻקַּת הַפָּסַח כָּל־בֶּן־נֵכָר לֹא־יֹאכַל בּוֹ: 44 וְכָל־עֶבֶד אִישׁ מִקְנַת־כָּסֶף וּמַלְתָּה אֹתוֹ אָז יֹאכַל בּוֹ: 45 תּוֹשָׁב וְשָׂכִיר לֹא־יֹאכַל בּוֹ: 46 בְּבַיִת אֶחָד יֵאָכֵל לֹא־תוֹצִיא מִן־הַבַּיִת מִן־הַבָּשָׂר חוּצָה וְעֶצֶם לֹא תִשְׁבְּרוּ־בוֹ: 47 כָּל־עֲדַת יִשְׂרָאֵל יַעֲשׂוּ אֹתוֹ: 48 וְכִי־יָגוּר אִתְּךָ גֵּר וְעָשָׂה פֶסַח לַיהֹוָה הִמּוֹל לוֹ כָל־זָכָר וְאָז יִקְרַב לַעֲשֹׂתוֹ וְהָיָה כְּאֶזְרַח הָאָרֶץ וְכָל־עָרֵל לֹא־יֹאכַל בּוֹ:

Most of the laws of the Passover sacrifice were given on the first day of *Nisan* (12:3-11). However, in order to encourage the Jewish people further, God gave these additional laws at the last moment, on the fourteenth (*Rabbi David Pardo, 18th century*).

These additional laws contain the requirement that the Passover sacrifice be eaten only by a circumcised person. Since God wanted the Jewish people to circumcise themselves on the fourteenth of *Nisan*—so that the blood of sacrifice and the blood of circumcision would coincide—He gave them these laws at the last moment (*Rabbi Judah Loew b. Bezalel of Prague, 16th century*).

This is the law (*ḥok*). Both the Passover sacrifice and the Red Heifer (*Numbers* 19:2) are referred to as a *ḥok*—a "statute," or supranational command. So we do not initially know which is greater than the other.

It is like the case of two ladies who were walking side by side together, apparently on equal footing. Who is greater? The lady who is being accompanied to her house by her friend, because the other lady is really following her.

Similarly, the Passover is called a *ḥok* and the Red Heifer is called a *ḥok*. Which is greater? The Red Heifer—because those who eat the Passover sacrifice require the purifying ashes of the Red Heifer first (*Exodus Rabbah*).

These two great statutes correspond to the first two commandments of the Decalogue—the Passover sacrifice corresponds to *"I am God"* (below, 20:2), and the Red Heifer correlates to *"You shall not (possess an idol) of other deities"* (ibid. 3). Just as the purifying ashes of the Red Heifer must be used before the Passover sacrifice may be eaten, we would have expected that the second commandment, to rid ourselves of foreign gods, would have preceded the first, to believe in God. Surely we would have to reject all incorrect ideas about God before embracing the correct one? But in His great compassion, God reversed the order and allowed us to come close to Him even if we have not yet fully purified ourselves (*Rabbi Mordecai Joseph Leiner of Izbica, 19th century*).

46. You must not break any of its bones. We are prohibited from breaking the bones to extract the marrow because the children of Israel are considered royalty on Passover, for whom such

legions of God went out of the land of Egypt. ⁴² It is a night which God (had been) keeping (in mind) to take them out of the land of Egypt. This is the night (about) which God (told Abraham that He would redeem his children), and it is guarded (against harmful forces) for all the children of Israel throughout their generations.

Additional Laws of the Passover Sacrifice

⁴³ God said to Moses and Aaron, "This is the law of the Passover sacrifice:

- ❖ "No stranger (non-Jew or apostate Jew) may eat from it.

- ❖ ⁴⁴ "Any slave belonging to a person that was purchased for money shall be circumcised, and then he will be permitted to eat from it.

- ❖ ⁴⁵ "A resident (alien) or a (circumcised non-Jewish) hired worker may not eat from it.

- ❖ ⁴⁶ "It must be eaten within one house (i.e. one group). You must not take any of the meat outside the house (group).

- ❖ "You must not break any of its bones.

- ❖ ⁴⁷ "The entire community of Israel shall make it.

- ❖ ⁴⁸ "When a convert joins you, he should make a Passover sacrifice to God. In order for him to offer it, all his male family members shall be circumcised. Then he will be like a native of the land (bringing the sacrifice in its prescribed time).

- ❖ "No uncircumcised male may eat from it.

43. This is the law of the Passover sacrifice. Even though they were written here, these laws were actually given on the fourteenth of *Nisan*, before the Jewish people offered the Passover sacrifice (*Rashi, 11ᵗʰ century*).

The Torah did not wish to interrupt its narrative of the departure from Egypt to mention these additional laws. Therefore, they were written at this point, even though they were given earlier, on the fourteenth (*Naḥmanides, 13ᵗʰ century*).

spiritual vitamin

> Although God's commandments must be observed for their own sake, the Creator also revealed to us that each commandment has a particular significance of its own, which is connected with the spiritual and physical well-being of the person fulfilling it.

שמות יב:מט - יג:ט

בא

49 תּוֹרָה אַחַת יִהְיֶה לָאֶזְרָח וְלַגֵּר הַגָּר בְּתוֹכְכֶם: 50 וַיַּעֲשׂוּ כָּל־בְּנֵי יִשְׂרָאֵל כַּאֲשֶׁר צִוָּה יְהֹוָה אֶת־מֹשֶׁה וְאֶת־אַהֲרֹן כֵּן עָשׂוּ: ס 51 וַיְהִי בְּעֶצֶם הַיּוֹם הַזֶּה הוֹצִיא יְהֹוָה אֶת־בְּנֵי יִשְׂרָאֵל מֵאֶרֶץ מִצְרַיִם עַל־צִבְאֹתָם: פ

יג 1 וַיְדַבֵּר יְהֹוָה אֶל־מֹשֶׁה לֵּאמֹר: 2 קַדֶּשׁ־לִי כָל־בְּכוֹר פֶּטֶר [SEVENTH READING] כָּל־רֶחֶם בִּבְנֵי יִשְׂרָאֵל בָּאָדָם וּבַבְּהֵמָה לִי הוּא: 3 וַיֹּאמֶר מֹשֶׁה אֶל־הָעָם זָכוֹר אֶת־הַיּוֹם הַזֶּה אֲשֶׁר יְצָאתֶם מִמִּצְרַיִם מִבֵּית עֲבָדִים כִּי בְּחֹזֶק יָד הוֹצִיא יְהֹוָה אֶתְכֶם מִזֶּה וְלֹא יֵאָכֵל חָמֵץ: 4 הַיּוֹם אַתֶּם יֹצְאִים בְּחֹדֶשׁ הָאָבִיב: 5 וְהָיָה כִי־יְבִיאֲךָ יְהֹוָה אֶל־אֶרֶץ הַכְּנַעֲנִי וְהַחִתִּי וְהָאֱמֹרִי וְהַחִוִּי וְהַיְבוּסִי אֲשֶׁר נִשְׁבַּע לַאֲבֹתֶיךָ לָתֶת לָךְ אֶרֶץ זָבַת חָלָב וּדְבָשׁ וְעָבַדְתָּ אֶת־הָעֲבֹדָה הַזֹּאת בַּחֹדֶשׁ הַזֶּה: 6 שִׁבְעַת יָמִים תֹּאכַל מַצֹּת וּבַיּוֹם הַשְּׁבִיעִי חַג לַיהֹוָה: 7 מַצּוֹת יֵאָכֵל אֵת שִׁבְעַת הַיָּמִים וְלֹא־יֵרָאֶה לְךָ חָמֵץ וְלֹא־יֵרָאֶה לְךָ שְׂאֹר בְּכָל־גְּבֻלֶךָ: 8 וְהִגַּדְתָּ לְבִנְךָ בַּיּוֹם הַהוּא לֵאמֹר בַּעֲבוּר זֶה עָשָׂה יְהֹוָה לִי בְּצֵאתִי מִמִּצְרָיִם: 9 וְהָיָה לְךָ לְאוֹת עַל־יָדְךָ וּלְזִכָּרוֹן בֵּין עֵינֶיךָ לְמַעַן תִּהְיֶה תּוֹרַת יְהֹוָה בְּפִיךָ

15:13). In truth, the Jewish people left Egypt far earlier than planned. This is because their level of morality had degenerated to such an extent that if they had stayed any longer, they would have been unworthy of redemption. In order to hint to this point, Moses discussed the laws of

spiritual vitamin

> *"In every generation, a person must see himself as though he had that day been liberated from Egypt"* (Babylonian Talmud, Pesahim 116b). "Liberation from Egypt" means attaining freedom from the obstacles and limitations which you encounter on your way to self-fulfillment, hindering you from reaching your destiny and from accomplishing what you must. That is why the freedom which you experienced yesterday does not hold good for your position and state of today, and your attainment today will prove inadequate tomorrow.

exodus 12:49 – 13:9   bo'

- ❖ ⁴⁹ The native (born Jew) and the convert who joins you share the same law (for all the commandments of the Torah as well)."

⁵⁰ All the children of Israel did as God had commanded Moses and Aaron. They did it exactly.

⁵¹ It happened on that very day, that God took the children of Israel out of the land of Egypt in their legions.

13 Remembering the Departure from Egypt

[SEVENTH READING] ¹ God spoke to Moses, saying:

- ❖ "Sanctify to Me every firstborn. The first of each womb among the children of Israel, of humans and animals, is Mine."

³ Moses said to the people:

- ❖ "Remember this day, when you went out of Egypt, from the house of bondage, for with a mighty hand God took you out of here.

- ❖ "(Therefore) leaven should not be eaten.

- ❖ ⁴ "Today you are going out, in the month of Abib (i.e. a spring month when the weather is mild). ⁵ When God will bring you into the land of the Canaanites, the Hittites, the Amorites, the Hivites, and the Jebusites, which He swore to your forefathers to give you—a land flowing with milk and honey—you shall perform this ritual (Passover) service in this month.

- ❖ ⁶ "For seven days you shall eat unleavened bread.

- ❖ "The seventh day is a festival for God.

- ❖ ⁷ "Unleavened bread shall be eaten during the seven days, and no leavened bread that belongs to you shall be seen in your possession. No leaven that belongs to you shall be seen throughout your borders.

- ❖ ⁸ "You shall tell your son on that day, saying, 'Because of this (i.e. these commandments of Passover, unleavened bread, and bitter herbs,) God did this for me when I went out of Egypt.'

- ❖ ⁹ "(The exodus from Egypt) shall be for you as a sign upon your hand and as a remembrance between your eyes, so that the Torah of God shall be in your mouth, for with a mighty hand God took you out of Egypt.

behavior is inappropriate. Each year, we remember how, in an instant, we were elevated from slaves to kings (*Rabbi Aaron ha-Levi (Ḥinnukh), 13th century*).

13:1-13 God spoke to Moses, saying, "Sanctify to Me every firstborn…" Moses said to the people … "leaven should not be eaten … you should redeem every firstborn." The Jewish people thought that the plague of the firstborn and the subsequent exodus had occurred solely in fulfillment of God's oath to Abraham that the Jewish people would leave Egypt (*Genesis*

שמות יג:ט-טז

10 כִּי בְּיָד חֲזָקָה הוֹצִאֲךָ יְהֹוָה מִמִּצְרָיִם: וְשָׁמַרְתָּ אֶת־הַחֻקָּה הַזֹּאת לְמוֹעֲדָהּ מִיָּמִים יָמִימָה: פ 11 וְהָיָה כִּי־יְבִאֲךָ יְהֹוָה אֶל־אֶרֶץ הַכְּנַעֲנִי כַּאֲשֶׁר נִשְׁבַּע לְךָ וְלַאֲבֹתֶיךָ וּנְתָנָהּ לָךְ: 12 וְהַעֲבַרְתָּ כָל־פֶּטֶר־רֶחֶם לַיהֹוָה וְכָל־פֶּטֶר | שֶׁגֶר בְּהֵמָה אֲשֶׁר יִהְיֶה לְךָ הַזְּכָרִים לַיהֹוָה: 13 וְכָל־פֶּטֶר חֲמֹר תִּפְדֶּה בְשֶׂה וְאִם־לֹא תִפְדֶּה וַעֲרַפְתּוֹ וְכֹל בְּכוֹר אָדָם בְּבָנֶיךָ תִּפְדֶּה: [MAFTIR] 14 וְהָיָה כִּי־יִשְׁאָלְךָ בִנְךָ מָחָר לֵאמֹר מַה־זֹּאת וְאָמַרְתָּ אֵלָיו בְּחֹזֶק יָד הוֹצִיאָנוּ יְהֹוָה מִמִּצְרַיִם מִבֵּית עֲבָדִים: 15 וַיְהִי כִּי־הִקְשָׁה פַרְעֹה לְשַׁלְּחֵנוּ וַיַּהֲרֹג יְהֹוָה כָּל־בְּכוֹר בְּאֶרֶץ מִצְרַיִם מִבְּכֹר אָדָם וְעַד־בְּכוֹר בְּהֵמָה עַל־כֵּן אֲנִי זֹבֵחַ לַיהֹוָה כָּל־פֶּטֶר רֶחֶם הַזְּכָרִים וְכָל־בְּכוֹר בָּנַי אֶפְדֶּה: 16 וְהָיָה לְאוֹת עַל־יָדְכָה וּלְטוֹטָפֹת בֵּין עֵינֶיךָ כִּי בְּחֹזֶק יָד הוֹצִיאָנוּ יְהֹוָה מִמִּצְרָיִם: ס ס ס

ק״ה פסוקים, ימנ״ה סימן.

---

passages inside the *tefillin* corresponds to one of the four letters of the Tetragrammaton, the name of the Holy King. Two of those passages are written here.

The first portion, *"Sanctify to Me every firstborn"* (v. 1-10), corresponds to the *yod* (י) of God's name. This passage speaks of the opening of the womb, alluding to *Ḥokhmah* (inspiration), the initial disclosure of the Divine—the opening of the Divine "womb," so to speak.

The second portion, *"There will come a time when God will bring you into the land"* (v. 11-16), corresponds to the *he* (ה) of God's name. The letter *he* is the "palace"—the womb that was opened by the *yod*. It contains a full disclosure of the fifty gates of *Binah* (cognition).

Binah is the Divine *"shofar"* through which all supernal lights are disclosed. Thus the Exodus is mentioned in this portion, since the Israelites went forth from Egypt with the sounding of the *shofar*—as they are destined to do once again at the end of days (*Zohar*).

Food for thought

1. Have you ever felt compelled to express overwhelming gratitude?

2. What is the significance of recalling ancient Divine benevolence?

3. Why does God insist on tangible symbols of His deliverance?

❖ ¹⁰ "You shall keep this statute at its appointed time, from year to year.

❖ ¹¹ "There will come a time when God will bring you into the land of the Canaanites, as He swore to you and to your forefathers, and then (you should consider that) He has given it to you (on that day, not as an inheritance from your ancestors). ¹² You shall (then) set aside for God the first of every womb. The males belong to God from every miscarriage which emerges first from the womb (from an animal) that belongs to you.

❖ ¹³ "You should redeem every firstborn donkey with a lamb (or kid).

❖ "If you do not redeem it, you must break the back of its neck with an ax.

❖ "You should redeem every firstborn person among your sons (for five shekels).

❖ [MAFTIR] ¹⁴ "It will come to pass that if your son asks you in the future, saying, 'What is this?'—you shall say to him: 'With a mighty hand God took us out of Egypt, out of the house of slavery. ¹⁵ When Pharaoh stubbornly refused to send us out, God slew every firstborn in the land of Egypt, both the firstborn of people and animals. Therefore, I am slaughtering to God all males that come out of the womb first, and I will redeem every one of my firstborn sons.'

❖ ¹⁶ "It shall be for a sign upon your arm and *totafot* (phylacteries/*tefillin*) between your eyes, for God took us out of Egypt with a mighty hand."

The Haftarah for Bo' is on page 1322.

---

leavened and unleavened bread before introducing the law of sanctifying the firstborn. The message was subtle: Just as it takes just a few minutes to turn an unleavened product into leaven, so too, had the Jewish people remained just a short while longer in Egypt, they would never have been able to leave (*Rabbi Moses Alshekh, 16th century*).

13. You should redeem every firstborn donkey with a lamb (or kid). Only the firstborn of a donkey must be redeemed, not the firstborn of any other non-kosher animal. The donkeys helped the children of Israel carry the cumbersome treasures of gold and silver out of Egypt, and God wanted to reward them. Anyone who performs kindness is not forgotten by God (*Babylonian Talmud, Bekhorot* 5b).

16. It shall be for a sign upon your arm and *totafot* (phylacteries/*tefillin*) between your eyes. When you put on *tefillin,* you perfect yourself in the image of God. Each of the four Torah

When the **Reed Sea split,** every person witnessed **Divine revelation** without first entering into a **transcendental** state. This will occur again in the **future era** when "I will pour out **My spirit** on all flesh, and your sons and daughters will **prophesy**" (*Joel* 3:1).

BE-SHALLAḤ
בשלח

JOURNEY ON A ROUNDABOUT ROUTE	13:17–22
PHARAOH HAS A CHANGE OF HEART	14:1–20
THE SEA SPLITS	14:21–31
MOSES LEADS THE "SONG AT THE SEA"	15:1–21
COMPLAINTS AND REBUKE IN THE DESERT	15:22 – 17:16

NAME
Be-Shallaḥ

MEANING
"When he sent"

LINES IN TORAH SCROLL
216

PARASHIYYOT
9 open; 5 closed

VERSES
116

WORDS
1681

LETTERS
6423

DATE
2448
15 *Nisan*–end of *Iyyar*

LOCATION
Succoth, Etham, Reed Sea, Desert of Shur, Marah, Elim, Desert of Sin, Rephidim

KEY PEOPLE
Moses, Aaron, Pharaoh, Miriam, Joshua, Hur, Amalek

MITZVOT
1 prohibition

MASORETIC FEATURES
"Song at the Sea" is written in a special format of exactly 30 lines.

CHARACTER PROFILE

NAME
Dathan and Abiram

MEANING
"(Transgressed) law"; "fortified (his heart not to repent)."

FATHER
Eliab

TRIBE
Reuben

PLACE OF DEATH
Were swallowed up by the ground for participation in the revolt of Korah

KNOWN FOR
Informed Pharaoh that Moses had killed an Egyptian and that he was not, in fact, Pharaoh's grandson; twice incited the Jews to return to Egypt: at the Reed Sea and after the spies returned; kept the manna overnight after Moses had forbidden doing so; two of the leaders of Korah's revolt; spoke disrespectfully to Moses

EMERGENCY

Standing at the edge of the Reed Sea with the Egyptian army in pursuit, the Jewish people cried out to God. In times of trouble or hardship your natural instinct should be to pray. Recognize that everything comes from Him; ask for salvation from trouble (14:10).

LIVELIHOOD

Moses preserved a jug of manna for future generations, to teach us that God alone is responsible for our sustenance. Later, Jeremiah brought the jug out to emphasize this point to his generation (16:33).

SYMBOLS OF FAITH

Miriam's faith, and that of the other women, was so strong that they had prepared musical instruments in advance to accompany their songs of thanks for salvation (15:20).

שמות יג:יז-כא · בשלח

יז וַיְהִ֗י בְּשַׁלַּ֣ח פַּרְעֹה֮ אֶת־הָעָם֒ וְלֹא־נָחָ֣ם אֱלֹהִ֗ים דֶּ֚רֶךְ אֶ֣רֶץ פְּלִשְׁתִּ֔ים כִּ֥י קָר֖וֹב ה֑וּא כִּ֣י ׀ אָמַ֣ר אֱלֹהִ֗ים פֶּן־יִנָּחֵ֥ם הָעָ֛ם בִּרְאֹתָ֥ם מִלְחָמָ֖ה וְשָׁ֥בוּ מִצְרָֽיְמָה: יח וַיַּסֵּ֨ב אֱלֹהִ֧ים ׀ אֶת־הָעָ֛ם דֶּ֥רֶךְ הַמִּדְבָּ֖ר יַם־ס֑וּף וַחֲמֻשִׁ֛ים עָל֥וּ בְנֵֽי־יִשְׂרָאֵ֖ל מֵאֶ֥רֶץ מִצְרָֽיִם: יט וַיִּקַּ֥ח מֹשֶׁ֛ה אֶת־עַצְמ֥וֹת יוֹסֵ֖ף עִמּ֑וֹ כִּי֩ הַשְׁבֵּ֨עַ הִשְׁבִּ֜יעַ אֶת־בְּנֵ֤י יִשְׂרָאֵל֙ לֵאמֹ֔ר פָּקֹ֨ד יִפְקֹ֤ד אֱלֹהִים֙ אֶתְכֶ֔ם וְהַעֲלִיתֶ֧ם אֶת־עַצְמֹתַ֛י מִזֶּ֖ה אִתְּכֶֽם: כ וַיִּסְע֖וּ מִסֻּכֹּ֑ת וַיַּחֲנ֣וּ בְאֵתָ֔ם בִּקְצֵ֖ה הַמִּדְבָּֽר: כא וַֽיהֹוָ֞ה הֹלֵ֨ךְ לִפְנֵיהֶ֤ם

114:3) in honor of Joseph, who *"fled"* from sin in Potiphar's house (*Genesis* 39:12; *Rabbi Solomon ha-Levi Alkabetz, 16th century*).

Moses took Joseph's bones. This verse teaches us that a person is rewarded reciprocally for a good deed. Moses looked after the remains of Joseph, and, in return, God Himself took care of Moses' burial, as the verse states, *"He (God) buried him in the valley"* (*Deuteronomy* 34:6; *Babylonian Talmud, Sotah* 9b).

When Joseph was born, the Torah states: *"She named him Joseph, saying, 'May God add another son for me'"* (*Genesis* 30:24). The Hebrew word *'aher*, "another," can also refer to things that are profane. Thus we find that evil is often termed the "other" side (*sitra' 'ahara'*).

In this vein, the verse is suggesting that Joseph was blessed with the power to transform "another" into a "son," i.e., an estranged person into a pious one. In fact, Joseph was unique among the forefathers in his ability to live in the secular world and yet remain a pious Jew, and he passed on this ability to his descendants.

With this we can understand why the Torah mentions Joseph here. The Torah tells us that the Jewish people did not travel directly to the land of Israel, but that rather, *"God led the people on a roundabout route through the desert."* This caused them to be confronted with numerous trials and challenges (as we will read in the coming passages).

Therefore, it was crucial that *"Moses took Joseph's bones with him,"* for these challenges could only be overcome successfully through the power that Joseph had bequeathed to the Jewish people (*Rabbi Menahem Mendel Schneerson, 20th century*).

---

kabbalah bites

13:17 From Egypt to the land of Israel is a journey of eleven days, but God led them through the desert for forty years (*Exodus Rabbah* 20:13).

Eleven (ten plus one) hints to the "One without number," who is manifested through the ten *Sefirot*. The real purpose of God's delaying an eleven-day journey for so long was in order for the Israelites to *internalize* the message of One God (symbolized by the number eleven).

True spirituality cannot be acquired in shallow waters of superficiality. Many years must pass before the truths we have learned become our very flesh. Real transformation takes hard work, patience, and a helping hand from God.

parashat be-shallaḥ

Jewish People Follow a Roundabout Route

¹⁷ When Pharaoh sent the people away, God did not lead them through the land of the Philistines, because it was (too) close. This is because God said, "When the people see a war they may regret (leaving) and return to Egypt." ¹⁸ God led the people on a roundabout route through the desert to the Sea of Reeds.

The children of Israel were armed when they went up out of Egypt.

¹⁹ Moses took Joseph's bones with him, because he (Joseph) had made (his brothers) swear that they would make (their children) swear (to do so), saying, "God will surely remember you, and you shall bring up my bones from here with you."

²⁰ (On the second day) they traveled from Succoth, and they encamped in Etham, at the edge of the desert.

²¹ God went before them by day in a pillar of cloud to guide them along their route, and at night in a pillar of fire to give them light, so that they could travel day

---

13:17 The people ... may regret (leaving) and return to Egypt. The Jewish people were not yet fit to receive the Torah, because their faith in Moses was not complete. It is only later, after the sea had split and the Egyptians had perished, that *"they believed in God and in Moses, His servant"* (14:31). God now led the Jewish people on a circuitous route so that they would come to a higher level of belief through seeing His miracles (*Rabbi Ephraim of Luntshits, 16th–17th century*).

18-19. The children of Israel were armed when they went up out of Egypt. Moses took Joseph's bones with him. Their "weapons" were none other than Joseph's bones, since the merits of the righteous have protective power. Joseph's merit was especially significant in connection with the splitting of the sea, as the *Midrash* relates that *"the sea saw and fled"* (Psalms

---

spiritual vitamin

> God's Providence is a benevolent providence. God is the essence of goodness and desires to do good, for, *"It is in the nature of the good to do good."* Therefore, it is easy to see how right King David was in the holy Psalms when he said, *"God is with me, I shall not fear"* (118:6), *"God is my shepherd, I shall not want"* (23:1). Reflect upon this frequently and deeply, and all anxiety and worry will be dispelled at once.

שמות יג:כא - יד:יג · בשלח

יוֹמָם בְּעַמּוּד עָנָן לַנְחֹתָם הַדֶּרֶךְ וְלַיְלָה בְּעַמּוּד אֵשׁ לְהָאִיר לָהֶם לָלֶכֶת יוֹמָם וָלָיְלָה: 22 לֹא־יָמִישׁ עַמּוּד הֶעָנָן יוֹמָם וְעַמּוּד הָאֵשׁ לָיְלָה לִפְנֵי הָעָם: פ

יד 1 וַיְדַבֵּר יְהֹוָה אֶל־מֹשֶׁה לֵּאמֹר: 2 דַּבֵּר אֶל־בְּנֵי יִשְׂרָאֵל וְיָשֻׁבוּ וְיַחֲנוּ לִפְנֵי פִּי הַחִירֹת בֵּין מִגְדֹּל וּבֵין הַיָּם לִפְנֵי בַּעַל צְפֹן נִכְחוֹ תַחֲנוּ עַל־הַיָּם: 3 וְאָמַר פַּרְעֹה לִבְנֵי יִשְׂרָאֵל נְבֻכִים הֵם בָּאָרֶץ סָגַר עֲלֵיהֶם הַמִּדְבָּר: 4 וְחִזַּקְתִּי אֶת־לֵב־פַּרְעֹה וְרָדַף אַחֲרֵיהֶם וְאִכָּבְדָה בְּפַרְעֹה וּבְכָל־חֵילוֹ וְיָדְעוּ מִצְרַיִם כִּי־אֲנִי יְהֹוָה וַיַּעֲשׂוּ־כֵן: 5 וַיֻּגַּד לְמֶלֶךְ מִצְרַיִם כִּי בָרַח הָעָם וַיֵּהָפֵךְ לְבַב פַּרְעֹה וַעֲבָדָיו אֶל־הָעָם וַיֹּאמְרוּ מַה־זֹּאת עָשִׂינוּ כִּי־שִׁלַּחְנוּ אֶת־יִשְׂרָאֵל מֵעָבְדֵנוּ: 6 וַיֶּאְסֹר אֶת־רִכְבּוֹ וְאֶת־עַמּוֹ לָקַח עִמּוֹ: 7 וַיִּקַּח שֵׁשׁ־מֵאוֹת רֶכֶב בָּחוּר וְכֹל רֶכֶב מִצְרָיִם וְשָׁלִשִׁם עַל־כֻּלּוֹ: 8 וַיְחַזֵּק יְהֹוָה אֶת־לֵב פַּרְעֹה מֶלֶךְ מִצְרַיִם וַיִּרְדֹּף אַחֲרֵי בְּנֵי יִשְׂרָאֵל וּבְנֵי יִשְׂרָאֵל יֹצְאִים בְּיָד רָמָה: [SECOND READING] 9 וַיִּרְדְּפוּ מִצְרַיִם אַחֲרֵיהֶם וַיַּשִּׂיגוּ אוֹתָם חֹנִים עַל־הַיָּם כָּל־סוּס רֶכֶב פַּרְעֹה וּפָרָשָׁיו וְחֵילוֹ עַל־פִּי הַחִירֹת לִפְנֵי בַּעַל צְפֹן: 10 וּפַרְעֹה הִקְרִיב וַיִּשְׂאוּ בְנֵי־יִשְׂרָאֵל אֶת־עֵינֵיהֶם וְהִנֵּה מִצְרַיִם | נֹסֵעַ אַחֲרֵיהֶם וַיִּירְאוּ מְאֹד וַיִּצְעֲקוּ בְנֵי־יִשְׂרָאֵל אֶל־יְהֹוָה: 11 וַיֹּאמְרוּ אֶל־מֹשֶׁה הֲמִבְּלִי אֵין־קְבָרִים בְּמִצְרַיִם לְקַחְתָּנוּ לָמוּת בַּמִּדְבָּר מַה־זֹּאת עָשִׂיתָ לָּנוּ לְהוֹצִיאָנוּ מִמִּצְרָיִם: 12 הֲלֹא־זֶה הַדָּבָר אֲשֶׁר דִּבַּרְנוּ אֵלֶיךָ בְמִצְרַיִם לֵאמֹר חֲדַל מִמֶּנּוּ וְנַעַבְדָה אֶת־מִצְרָיִם כִּי טוֹב לָנוּ עֲבֹד אֶת־מִצְרַיִם מִמֻּתֵנוּ בַּמִּדְבָּר: 13 וַיֹּאמֶר מֹשֶׁה אֶל־הָעָם אַל־תִּירָאוּ

14:10 The children of Israel cried out to God. They prayed to God, practicing the profession of their ancestors. For we find that Abraham prayed, as the verse states, *"Abraham got up early in the morning, to the place where he had stood before God"* (Genesis 19:27). Isaac prayed, as the verse states, *"Isaac went out to pray in the field"* (ibid., 24:63). Jacob prayed, as the verse states, *"He came across the place"* (ibid., 28:11; Rashi, 11th century).

and night. ²² He did not move away the pillar of cloud by day (until the pillar of fire was fully illuminated, nor did He move) the pillar of fire at night from before the people (until the pillar of cloud had risen fully).

Pharaoh Has a Change of Heart

14 ¹ God spoke to Moses, saying: ² "Speak to the children of Israel, and let them turn back (in order to confuse Pharaoh) and encamp in front of the Mouth of the Rocks (Pithom), between Migdol and the sea. You should encamp opposite the (Egyptian deity) of Baal-zephon by the sea (in order to confuse the Egyptians further). ³ Pharaoh will say about the children of Israel, 'They are trapped in the land. The desert has closed in upon them.' ⁴ I will harden Pharaoh's heart, and he will pursue them. I will be glorified through (wreaking vengeance on) Pharaoh and his whole army, and Egypt will know that I am God." (The children of Israel) did so (as they had been commanded).

⁵ (On the fourth day) it was reported to the king of Egypt that the people had fled. Pharaoh and his servants had a change of heart towards the people, and they said, "What have we done, that we have sent away Israel from serving us?"

⁶ So he harnessed his chariot, and persuaded his people to come with him. ⁷ He took six hundred select chariots and all the (remaining) chariots of Egypt, with officers over them all.

Egypt Pursues—The Jewish People Cry to God

⁸ God hardened the heart of Pharaoh, the king of Egypt (because he was having second thoughts), and he chased after the children of Israel. The children of Israel were going out triumphantly. [SECOND READING] ⁹ The Egyptians chased after them and overtook them while they were encamped by the sea. Every horse of Pharaoh's chariots, his horsemen, and his army were there, by the Mouth of the Rocks, opposite Baal-zephon.

¹⁰ Pharaoh advanced (ahead of his troops). The children of Israel raised their eyes, and—look!—the Egyptians were advancing after them (in total unity). They were very frightened, so the children of Israel cried out to God.

¹¹ They said to Moses, "Is it because there was a shortage of graves in Egypt that you took us to die in the desert? What is this (that) you have done to us, in taking us out of Egypt? ¹² Aren't these the words that we spoke to you in Egypt, saying, 'Leave us alone, and we will serve the Egyptians, because we would rather serve the Egyptians than die in the desert'?"

¹³ Moses said to the people, "Don't be afraid! Stand firm and see God's salvation that He will perform for you today!

Food for thought

1. Has your spiritual journey elicited external opposition?

2. Why does life present an unrelenting series of challenges?

3. Do you tend to avoid life's obstacles or tackle them directly?

שמות יד:יג-כג | בשלח

הִתְיַצְּב֗וּ וּרְאוּ֙ אֶת־יְשׁוּעַ֣ת יְהוָ֔ה אֲשֶׁר־יַעֲשֶׂ֥ה לָכֶ֖ם הַיּ֑וֹם כִּ֗י אֲשֶׁ֨ר רְאִיתֶ֤ם אֶת־מִצְרַ֙יִם֙ הַיּ֔וֹם לֹ֥א תֹסִ֛פוּ לִרְאֹתָ֥ם ע֖וֹד עַד־עוֹלָֽם: 14 יְהוָ֖ה יִלָּחֵ֣ם לָכֶ֑ם וְאַתֶּ֖ם תַּחֲרִשֽׁוּן: פ [THIRD READING] 15 וַיֹּ֤אמֶר יְהוָה֙ אֶל־מֹשֶׁ֔ה מַה־תִּצְעַ֖ק אֵלָ֑י דַּבֵּ֥ר אֶל־בְּנֵֽי־יִשְׂרָאֵ֖ל וְיִסָּֽעוּ: 16 וְאַתָּ֞ה הָרֵ֣ם אֶֽת־מַטְּךָ֗ וּנְטֵ֧ה אֶת־יָדְךָ֛ עַל־הַיָּ֖ם וּבְקָעֵ֑הוּ וְיָבֹ֧אוּ בְנֵֽי־יִשְׂרָאֵ֛ל בְּת֥וֹךְ הַיָּ֖ם בַּיַּבָּשָֽׁה: 17 וַאֲנִ֗י הִנְנִ֤י מְחַזֵּק֙ אֶת־לֵ֣ב מִצְרַ֔יִם וְיָבֹ֖אוּ אַחֲרֵיהֶ֑ם וְאִכָּבְדָ֤ה בְּפַרְעֹה֙ וּבְכָל־חֵיל֔וֹ בְּרִכְבּ֖וֹ וּבְפָרָשָֽׁיו: 18 וְיָדְע֥וּ מִצְרַ֖יִם כִּֽי־אֲנִ֣י יְהוָ֑ה בְּהִכָּבְדִ֣י בְּפַרְעֹ֔ה בְּרִכְבּ֖וֹ וּבְפָרָשָֽׁיו: 19 וַיִּסַּ֞ע מַלְאַ֤ךְ הָאֱלֹהִים֙ הַהֹלֵךְ֙ לִפְנֵי֙ מַחֲנֵ֣ה יִשְׂרָאֵ֔ל וַיֵּ֖לֶךְ מֵאַחֲרֵיהֶ֑ם וַיִּסַּ֞ע עַמּ֤וּד הֶֽעָנָן֙ מִפְּנֵיהֶ֔ם וַיַּֽעֲמֹ֖ד מֵאַחֲרֵיהֶֽם: 20 וַיָּבֹ֞א בֵּ֣ין ׀ מַחֲנֵ֣ה מִצְרַ֗יִם וּבֵין֙ מַחֲנֵ֣ה יִשְׂרָאֵ֔ל וַיְהִ֤י הֶֽעָנָן֙ וְהַחֹ֔שֶׁךְ וַיָּ֖אֶר אֶת־הַלָּ֑יְלָה וְלֹא־קָרַ֥ב זֶ֛ה אֶל־זֶ֖ה כָּל־הַלָּֽיְלָה: 21 וַיֵּ֨ט מֹשֶׁ֣ה אֶת־יָדוֹ֮ עַל־הַיָּם֒ וַיּ֣וֹלֶךְ יְהוָ֣ה ׀ אֶת־הַ֠יָּם בְּר֨וּחַ קָדִ֤ים עַזָּה֙ כָּל־הַלַּ֔יְלָה וַיָּ֥שֶׂם אֶת־הַיָּ֖ם לֶחָרָבָ֑ה וַיִּבָּקְע֖וּ הַמָּֽיִם: 22 וַיָּבֹ֧אוּ בְנֵֽי־יִשְׂרָאֵ֛ל בְּת֥וֹךְ הַיָּ֖ם בַּיַּבָּשָׁ֑ה וְהַמַּ֤יִם לָהֶם֙ חוֹמָ֔ה מִֽימִינָ֖ם וּמִשְּׂמֹאלָֽם: 23 וַיִּרְדְּפ֤וּ מִצְרַ֙יִם֙ וַיָּבֹ֣אוּ אַחֲרֵיהֶ֔ם

14. God will fight for you, but you must remain silent! "Not only will He fight for you right now, but for all eternity God will wage war for you against your enemies" (*Mekhilta*).

God will wage war for you even when *"you must remain silent."* Even when you have no significant claim to God's help, He will nevertheless defend you against those who attack you (*Rabbi Meir Simḥah of Dvinsk, 19th–20th century*).

16. You should lift your staff. Ten miracles occurred at the Sea of Reeds for the children of Israel:

(1) The sea split; (2) the sea became a canopy over their heads, so that they were walking through a tunnel of water; (3) the seabed became dry; (4) the dried seabed became clay that trapped the Egyptians; (5) the water was like uniformly shaped bricks in a wall; (6) the water became hard as stone, which later crushed the Egyptians; (7) the sea divided into twelve paths; (8) the water became transparent, so that the Israelites, walking along the twelve paths, could see one another; (9) sweet

Food for thought

1. How responsible are you for what you do when under great duress?

2. To what extent do you place your destiny in God's hands?

3. Have you ever experienced paralyzing fear? Where was God at that moment?

You may be seeing the Egyptians today, but you will never see them again! ¹⁴ God will fight for you, but you must remain silent!"

[THIRD READING] ¹⁵ (Moses stood praying to God, but) God said to Moses, "Why do you cry out to Me? Speak to the children of Israel and (tell them that all they have to do is) travel. ¹⁶ You should lift your staff and stretch out your hand over the sea and split it. The children of Israel will come into the sea on dry land."

¹⁷ Look! I will harden the hearts of the Egyptians, and they will come after them. I will be glorified (by wreaking vengeance on) Pharaoh, his entire army, his chariots, and his horsemen. ¹⁸ The Egyptians will know that I am God, when I will be glorified through (wreaking vengeance on) Pharaoh, his chariots, and his horsemen."

Miraculous Protection—Splitting of the Sea

¹⁹ The angel of God, who had been going in front of the Israelite camp, moved and went behind them (to intercept the arrows and catapult stones of Egypt. At night,) the pillar of cloud moved away from in front of them and stood behind them (instead of disappearing, as it usually did). ²⁰ It came between the camp of Egypt and the camp of Israel. Thus, the cloud and the darkness were there (for the Egyptians, but the children of Israel had the pillar of fire) which illuminated the night. So, one (camp) did not approach the other all night.

²¹ Moses stretched out his hand over the sea, and God moved the sea with a strong east wind throughout the entire night. He made the sea into dry land, and the water split (miraculously, throughout the entire world).

²² Then the children of Israel came into the sea on dry land. The water acted for them as a wall on their right and on their left.

²³ The Egyptians pursued and came after them. Every horse of Pharaoh, his chariots and his horsemen came into the sea.

kabbalah bites

14:21 *"He made the sea into dry land."* The splitting of the sea was a result of *full disclosure of the Divine.*

Within the worlds of the spirit, there is both an elusive, subconscious realm (*'alema' de-'itkasseya'*), as well as more defined, conscious forms of emanation (*'alema' de-'itggalleya'*). As mortal, limited creatures, we of course cannot access the *'alema' de-'itkasseya'*, as this would represent a fatal clash of being and non-being.

But at the splitting of the sea this is exactly what occurred. Subconscious emanation—represented by the sea, which hides its contents—was fully disclosed; it was rendered into open, naked land. Why, then, did a fatal clash not occur? Because when God's *essence* is at play, even the impossible is possible.

שמות יד:כד - טו:א | בשלח

כָּל־ס֤וּס פַּרְעֹה֙ רִכְבּ֣וֹ וּפָרָשָׁ֔יו אֶל־תּ֖וֹךְ הַיָּֽם: 24 וַֽיְהִי֙ בְּאַשְׁמֹ֣רֶת הַבֹּ֔קֶר וַיַּשְׁקֵ֤ף יְהֹוָה֙ אֶל־מַחֲנֵ֣ה מִצְרַ֔יִם בְּעַמּ֥וּד אֵ֖שׁ וְעָנָ֑ן וַיָּ֕הָם אֵ֖ת מַחֲנֵ֥ה מִצְרָֽיִם: 25 וַיָּ֗סַר אֵ֚ת אֹפַ֣ן מַרְכְּבֹתָ֔יו וַֽיְנַהֲגֵ֖הוּ בִּכְבֵדֻ֑ת וַיֹּ֣אמֶר מִצְרַ֗יִם אָנ֨וּסָה֙ מִפְּנֵ֣י יִשְׂרָאֵ֔ל כִּ֣י יְהֹוָ֔ה נִלְחָ֥ם לָהֶ֖ם בְּמִצְרָֽיִם: פ [FOURTH READING] 26 וַיֹּ֤אמֶר יְהֹוָה֙ אֶל־מֹשֶׁ֔ה נְטֵ֥ה אֶת־יָדְךָ֖ עַל־הַיָּ֑ם וְיָשֻׁ֤בוּ הַמַּ֨יִם֙ עַל־מִצְרַ֔יִם עַל־רִכְבּ֖וֹ וְעַל־פָּרָשָֽׁיו: 27 וַיֵּט֩ מֹשֶׁ֨ה אֶת־יָד֜וֹ עַל־הַיָּ֗ם וַיָּ֨שָׁב הַיָּ֜ם לִפְנ֥וֹת בֹּ֨קֶר֙ לְאֵ֣יתָנ֔וֹ וּמִצְרַ֖יִם נָסִ֣ים לִקְרָאת֑וֹ וַיְנַעֵ֧ר יְהֹוָ֛ה אֶת־מִצְרַ֖יִם בְּת֥וֹךְ הַיָּֽם: 28 וַיָּשֻׁ֣בוּ הַמַּ֗יִם וַיְכַסּ֤וּ אֶת־הָרֶ֨כֶב֙ וְאֶת־הַפָּ֣רָשִׁ֔ים לְכֹל֙ חֵ֣יל פַּרְעֹ֔ה הַבָּאִ֥ים אַחֲרֵיהֶ֖ם בַּיָּ֑ם לֹֽא־נִשְׁאַ֥ר בָּהֶ֖ם עַד־אֶחָֽד: 29 וּבְנֵ֧י יִשְׂרָאֵ֛ל הָלְכ֥וּ בַיַּבָּשָׁ֖ה בְּת֣וֹךְ הַיָּ֑ם וְהַמַּ֤יִם לָהֶם֙ חֹמָ֔ה מִֽימִינָ֖ם וּמִשְּׂמֹאלָֽם: 30 וַיּ֨וֹשַׁע יְהֹוָ֜ה בַּיּ֥וֹם הַה֛וּא אֶת־יִשְׂרָאֵ֖ל מִיַּ֣ד מִצְרָ֑יִם וַיַּ֤רְא יִשְׂרָאֵל֙ אֶת־מִצְרַ֔יִם מֵ֖ת עַל־שְׂפַ֥ת הַיָּֽם: 31 וַיַּ֨רְא יִשְׂרָאֵ֜ל אֶת־הַיָּ֣ד הַגְּדֹלָ֗ה אֲשֶׁ֨ר עָשָׂ֤ה יְהֹוָה֙ בְּמִצְרַ֔יִם וַיִּֽירְא֥וּ הָעָ֖ם אֶת־יְהֹוָ֑ה וַֽיַּאֲמִ֨ינוּ֙ בַּֽיהֹוָ֔ה וּבְמֹשֶׁ֖ה עַבְדּֽוֹ: פ

טו 1 אָ֣ז יָשִֽׁיר־מֹשֶׁה֩ וּבְנֵ֨י יִשְׂרָאֵ֜ל אֶת־הַשִּׁירָ֤ה הַזֹּאת֙ לַֽיהֹוָ֔ה וַיֹּאמְר֖וּ לֵאמֹ֑ר אָשִׁ֣ירָה לַּֽיהֹוָה֙ כִּֽי־גָאֹ֣ה גָּאָ֔ה ס֥וּס וְרֹכְב֖וֹ רָמָ֥ה בַיָּֽם:

However, the Tenth Song of the Messiah will be chanted amid a feeling that God is *already* close and found openly in our midst (*Rabbi Shneur Zalman of Lyady, 18th century*).

I will sing. The Jewish people sang this song in a state of wondrous unity, without any division between them whatsoever, as if they were just one person.

spiritual vitamin

> The great rise from the abyss of Egypt to the sublime height of Sinai was attained by pure and simple faith in God, from the day when parents and children, adults and infants, several million souls in all, set out on the trek through the desert, undaunted by the irrationality of it, but simply obeying the Divine call with absolute trust.

²⁴ It was (in the latter third of the night,) towards the morning, that God looked down on the Egyptian camp with a pillar of cloud. (He turned the seabed into mud,) and with a pillar of fire (He boiled the mud, causing the hooves of Egypt's horses to come off). He threw the Egyptian camp into confusion. ²⁵ He removed the wheels of their chariots (with the fire, causing their passengers' limbs to dislocate), and He treated them harshly. Egypt said, "Let me run away from the Israelites, because God is fighting for them against the Egyptians."

[FOURTH READING] ²⁶ God said to Moses, "Stretch out your hand over the sea, and the water will revert (from being a wall) onto Egypt, onto its chariots and horsemen."

²⁷ Moses stretched out his hand over the sea, and in the early morning, the sea returned to its (original) strength. The Egyptians (were so confused that they) fled towards (the water). God stirred the Egyptians in the sea, (mixing them up and down). ²⁸ The waters returned and covered the chariots, horsemen, and the entire army of Pharaoh who were coming after them into the sea. Not even one of them remained.

²⁹ The children of Israel went on dry land in the midst of the sea, and the water was for them as a wall on their right and on their left.

³⁰ On that day, God saved Israel from the hands of the Egyptians. Israel saw the Egyptians dead on the seashore.

³¹ Israel saw the great might which God had enacted upon the Egyptians, and the people feared God. They believed in God and in Moses, His servant.

Moses Leads the "Song at the Sea"

15 ¹ Then, (upon seeing the miracle), Moses (led) the children of Israel in this song to God. They said as follows:

freshwater streamed out for them to drink; (10) the remnants of this water were heaped into mounds (*Midrash Tanḥuma*).

29. The children of Israel went on dry land in the midst of the sea. Normally, people are only impressed when they see overtly miraculous events. They fail to take note that nature itself is an outstanding miracle through which the wonders of God can be observed on a daily basis.

The Israelites, however, did not make this mistake. As they *"walked on dry land in the midst of the sea,"* they were cognizant that walking on dry land is no less miraculous than walking through the sea (*Rabbi Elimelech of Lyzhansk, 18th century*).

15:1 Moses (led) the children of Israel in this song to God. The *Mekhilta* speaks of "Ten Songs": the First was the "Song at the Sea" led by Moses, and the last and Tenth Song will be sung with the Messiah. All the (nine) songs mentioned in Scripture are written in the feminine (*shirah*), since their rejoicing was followed by ("gave birth to") further servitude. The Tenth Song of the Messiah, however, is written in the masculine (*shir*) to indicate that it is permanent.

Ḥasidic teachings explain that the first nine songs emphasize a desire to come closer to God from a distance, like feminine energy which longs to come closer to the masculine.

שמות טו:ב-יא — בשלח

2 עָזִּ֤י וְזִמְרָת֙ יָ֔הּ וַֽיְהִי־לִ֖י לִֽישׁוּעָ֑ה זֶ֤ה אֵלִי֙ וְאַנְוֵ֔הוּ אֱלֹהֵ֥י אָבִ֖י וַאֲרֹמְמֶֽנְהוּ: 3 יְהֹוָ֖ה אִ֣ישׁ מִלְחָמָ֑ה יְהֹוָ֖ה שְׁמֽוֹ: 4 מַרְכְּבֹ֥ת פַּרְעֹ֛ה וְחֵיל֖וֹ יָרָ֣ה בַיָּ֑ם וּמִבְחַ֥ר שָֽׁלִשָׁ֖יו טֻבְּע֥וּ בְיַם־סֽוּף: 5 תְּהֹמֹ֖ת יְכַסְיֻ֑מוּ יָרְד֥וּ בִמְצוֹלֹ֖ת כְּמוֹ־אָֽבֶן: 6 יְמִֽינְךָ֣ יְהֹוָ֔ה נֶאְדָּרִ֖י בַּכֹּ֑חַ יְמִֽינְךָ֥ יְהֹוָ֖ה תִּרְעַ֥ץ אוֹיֵֽב: 7 וּבְרֹ֥ב גְּאוֹנְךָ֖ תַּהֲרֹ֣ס קָמֶ֑יךָ תְּשַׁלַּח֙ חֲרֹ֣נְךָ֔ יֹאכְלֵ֖מוֹ כַּקַּֽשׁ: 8 וּבְר֤וּחַ אַפֶּ֨יךָ֙ נֶ֣עֶרְמוּ מַ֔יִם נִצְּב֥וּ כְמוֹ־נֵ֖ד נֹזְלִ֑ים קָֽפְא֥וּ תְהֹמֹ֖ת בְּלֶב־יָֽם: 9 אָמַ֥ר אוֹיֵ֛ב אֶרְדֹּ֥ף אַשִּׂ֖יג אֲחַלֵּ֣ק שָׁלָ֑ל תִּמְלָאֵ֣מוֹ נַפְשִׁ֔י אָרִ֣יק חַרְבִּ֔י תּוֹרִישֵׁ֖מוֹ יָדִֽי: 10 נָשַׁ֥פְתָּ בְרוּחֲךָ֖ כִּסָּ֣מוֹ יָ֑ם צָֽלְלוּ֙ כַּֽעוֹפֶ֔רֶת בְּמַ֖יִם אַדִּירִֽים: 11 מִֽי־כָמֹ֤כָה בָּֽאֵלִם֙ יְהֹוָ֔ה מִ֥י כָּמֹ֖כָה נֶאְדָּ֣ר בַּקֹּ֑דֶשׁ נוֹרָ֥א תְהִלֹּ֖ת עֹ֥שֵׂה פֶֽלֶא:

8. The deep waters congealed in the heart of the sea. Where is a man's heart located? It is just above two thirds of his height. Similarly, the water congealed over them at two thirds of its depth.

The sea had no heart, but a heart was attributed to it. A terebinth tree has no heart, but a heart was attributed to it—as the verse states, *"while he was still alive in the heart of the terebinth"* (*II Samuel* 18:14). The heavens have no heart, but a heart was attributed to them—as the verse states, *"the mountain was burning with fire up to the heart of the heavens"* (*Deuteronomy* 4:11).

The sea, which had no heart, and to which He ascribed a heart, should come and punish the Egyptians who possessed hearts, but who had nevertheless persecuted the Israelites. The terebinth which has no heart, and to which He ascribed a heart, should punish Absalom, who had a heart, because he had deceived three hearts: his father's, the court's, and that of the men of Israel. And the heavens which have no heart, and to which He ascribed a heart, should come and send down manna to Israel, who possess a heart, accept the Torah with all their heart, and love their Creator with all their heart (*Midrash Tanhuma*).

kabbalah bites

15:1-19 The problem with revelations and epiphanies is that they tend to evaporate rather quickly. The consolidation of a revelation occurs when ideas are put into words—or, in the Kabbalistic metaphor, when "light" enters "vessels."

Moses' song was his attempt to ensure that the great revelation of the splitting of the sea should enter vessels and be consolidated.

This is hinted to by the introductory word *'az* ("then"), which is the combination of the letters *alef* (1) and *zayin* (7). Moses sought to consolidate all the revelation from the very first of God's attributes (*sefirot*) down to the seventh and lowest emotional attribute.

Make sure that your inspirational moments do not evaporate. Write them down and consolidate them with firm resolutions.

I will sing to God, for very exalted is He, horse and its rider He cast into the sea. ² God's strength and vengeance were my salvation. This is my God, and I will build Him a Sanctuary, the God of my father, and I will exalt Him.

³ God is the Master of War. God (uses) His name (to do battle).

⁴ He cast Pharaoh's chariots and army into the sea, his elite officers sank in (the mud of) the Sea of Reeds, ⁵ (so that) the deep waters would (return and) cover them. The (average ones) descended into the depths (quickly) like stone.

⁶ Your right hand, O God, is most powerful (and saves Israel. When Israel follows Your will, Your punishing left hand becomes like) Your right hand, O God, and (constantly) crushes the enemy.

⁷ (And that is merely Your hand, but when You reveal) Your great majesty, then Your opponents are devastated. (And that is merely Your majesty, but) when You send forth Your burning wrath, the (most wicked of them) are consumed like straw.

⁸ With the (angry) breath of Your nostrils, the waters were heaped up. The running water stood erect like a wall. The deep waters congealed in the heart of the sea.

⁹ The enemy said, "I will pursue, I will overtake, I will divide spoils! My desire will be filled from them. I will draw my sword, my hand will impoverish them."

¹⁰ You blew with Your wind, the sea covered them.

The (decent ones) sank like lead in the powerful waters.

¹¹ Who is like You among the mighty, O God?

Who is like You, powerful in holiness, too awesome for praises, Performer of Wonders?

To hint to this point, the verse uses the expression, *"I* will sing," conjugated in the singular; and not, *"we* will sing," in the plural (*Rabbi Ḥayyim ibn Attar, 18ᵗʰ century*).

spiritual vitamin

> All creation is derived from "the word of God" which brings matter into being and sustains it every instant continuously. However, a parallel Godly force of contraction and concealment obscures the Divine creative force; as a result, all you can see is the external form of the physical. Your task is to "bring to the surface" the Godliness inherent in everything in our lives, and to remove as much as possible the mask of physical externality obscuring the inner Godliness.

בשלח · שמות טו:יב-כד

12 נָטִ֙יתָ֙ יְמִ֣ינְךָ֔ תִּבְלָעֵ֖מוֹ אָֽרֶץ׃ 13 נָחִ֥יתָ בְחַסְדְּךָ֖ עַם־ז֣וּ גָּאָ֑לְתָּ נֵהַ֥לְתָּ בְעׇזְּךָ֖ אֶל־נְוֵ֥ה קׇדְשֶֽׁךָ׃ 14 שָֽׁמְע֥וּ עַמִּ֖ים יִרְגָּז֑וּן חִ֣יל אָחַ֔ז יֹשְׁבֵ֖י פְּלָֽשֶׁת׃ 15 אָ֤ז נִבְהֲלוּ֙ אַלּוּפֵ֣י אֱד֔וֹם אֵילֵ֣י מוֹאָ֔ב יֹֽאחֲזֵ֖מוֹ רָ֑עַד נָמֹ֕גוּ כֹּ֖ל יֹשְׁבֵ֥י כְנָֽעַן׃ 16 תִּפֹּ֨ל עֲלֵיהֶ֤ם אֵימָ֙תָה֙ וָפַ֔חַד בִּגְדֹ֥ל זְרוֹעֲךָ֖ יִדְּמ֣וּ כָּאָ֑בֶן עַד־יַעֲבֹ֤ר עַמְּךָ֙ יְהֹוָ֔ה עַֽד־יַעֲבֹ֖ר עַם־ז֥וּ קָנִֽיתָ׃ 17 תְּבִאֵ֗מוֹ וְתִטָּעֵ֙מוֹ֙ בְּהַ֣ר נַחֲלָֽתְךָ֔ מָכ֧וֹן לְשִׁבְתְּךָ֛ פָּעַ֖לְתָּ יְהֹוָ֑ה מִקְּדָ֕שׁ אֲדֹנָ֖י כּוֹנְנ֥וּ יָדֶֽיךָ׃ 18 יְהֹוָ֥ה ׀ יִמְלֹ֖ךְ לְעֹלָ֥ם וָעֶֽד׃ 19 כִּ֣י בָא֩ ס֨וּס פַּרְעֹ֜ה בְּרִכְבּ֤וֹ וּבְפָרָשָׁיו֙ בַּיָּ֔ם וַיָּ֧שֶׁב יְהֹוָ֛ה עֲלֵהֶ֖ם אֶת־מֵ֣י הַיָּ֑ם וּבְנֵ֧י יִשְׂרָאֵ֛ל הָלְכ֥וּ בַיַּבָּשָׁ֖ה בְּת֥וֹךְ הַיָּֽם׃ פ 20 וַתִּקַּח֩ מִרְיָ֨ם הַנְּבִיאָ֜ה אֲח֤וֹת אַהֲרֹן֙ אֶת־הַתֹּ֣ף בְּיָדָ֑הּ וַתֵּצֶ֤אןָ כׇל־הַנָּשִׁים֙ אַחֲרֶ֔יהָ בְּתֻפִּ֖ים וּבִמְחֹלֹֽת׃ 21 וַתַּ֥עַן לָהֶ֖ם מִרְיָ֑ם שִׁ֤ירוּ לַֽיהֹוָה֙ כִּֽי־גָאֹ֣ה גָּאָ֔ה ס֥וּס וְרֹכְב֖וֹ רָמָ֥ה בַיָּֽם׃ ס 22 וַיַּסַּ֨ע מֹשֶׁ֤ה אֶת־יִשְׂרָאֵל֙ מִיַּם־ס֔וּף וַיֵּצְא֖וּ אֶל־מִדְבַּר־שׁ֑וּר וַיֵּלְכ֧וּ שְׁלֹֽשֶׁת־יָמִ֛ים בַּמִּדְבָּ֖ר וְלֹא־מָ֥צְאוּ מָֽיִם׃ 23 וַיָּבֹ֣אוּ מָרָ֔תָה וְלֹ֣א יָֽכְל֗וּ לִשְׁתֹּ֥ת מַ֙יִם֙ מִמָּרָ֔ה כִּ֥י מָרִ֖ים הֵ֑ם עַל־כֵּ֥ן קָרָֽא־שְׁמָ֖הּ מָרָֽה׃ 24 וַיִּלֹּ֧נוּ

17. A foundation for Your dwelling place ... the Sanctuary. This refers to the first Temple, which the Jewish people built after entering the land of Israel (*Rabbi Obadiah Sforno, 16th century*).

This refers to the final Temple, which will be built in the Messianic Era (*Rashi, 11th century*).

Had the Jewish people merited, the true and final (Messianic) redemption would have occurred immediately upon their entering the land of Israel for the first time (*Zohar*).

20. All the women came out ... with tambourines. The righteous women of that generation were certain that God would perform miracles for them, so they took tambourines out of Egypt (*Rashi, 11th century*).

kabbalah bites

15:23 You can only appreciate sweetness if you have tasted something bitter. You only appreciate light because you have seen darkness. So evil is really a "flavor enhancer" for good.

exodus 15:12–24   be-shallaḥ

¹² You tilted Your right hand, the earth swallowed them up.

¹³ With Your loving kindness, You led the people You redeemed. You led with Your might to Your holy abode.

¹⁴ People heard, they trembled. A shudder seized the inhabitants of Philistia.

¹⁵ Then the chieftains of Edom were confounded. Trembling gripped the powerful men of Moab. All the inhabitants of Canaan melted.

¹⁶ May dread fall upon (the distant ones) and fear upon (the near ones). At the greatness of Your arm, may they become as still as a stone, until Your people cross over (the stream of Arnon), O God, until this nation that You have cherished, crosses over (the Jordan).

¹⁷ You shall bring them and plant them on the mount of Your heritage, a foundation for Your dwelling place that You made, O God, the Sanctuary, O God, which Your hands founded.

¹⁸ God will reign to all eternity.

¹⁹ When Pharaoh's horse came with his chariots and his horsemen into the sea, God brought the waters of the sea back upon them, and the children of Israel walked on dry land in the midst of the sea.

Miriam Leads the Women in Song

²⁰ Miriam, (who was) a prophetess (when she was) Aaron's sister (even before Moses was born) took a tambourine in her hand, and all the women came out after her with tambourines and with dancing.

²¹ Miriam called out to the (women, leading them in the above song): "Sing to God, for very exalted is He, horse and its rider He cast into the sea (etc.)."

The First Complaint: Bitter Waters

²² Moses moved Israel on (against their will) from the Reed Sea (since they were busy collecting the spoils of Egypt). They went out into the desert of Shur. They traveled for three days in the desert without finding water.

²³ They came to Marah, but they could not drink water from Marah because it was bitter. Therefore, they named it Marah ("bitter").

²⁴ The people complained to Moses, saying, "What shall we drink?"

Food for thought

1. What role does music play in your relationship with God?

2. Are you willing to sing about religious ideas you have difficulty believing in?

3. In what way is music the "pen of the soul"?

בשלח / שמות טו:כד - טז:א

הָעָ֛ם עַל־מֹשֶׁ֥ה לֵּאמֹ֖ר מַה־נִּשְׁתֶּֽה׃ 25 וַיִּצְעַ֣ק אֶל־יְהֹוָ֗ה וַיּוֹרֵ֤הוּ יְהֹוָה֙ עֵ֔ץ וַיַּשְׁלֵךְ֙ אֶל־הַמַּ֔יִם וַֽיִּמְתְּק֖וּ הַמָּ֑יִם שָׁ֣ם שָׂ֥ם ל֛וֹ חֹ֥ק וּמִשְׁפָּ֖ט וְשָׁ֥ם נִסָּֽהוּ׃ 26 וַיֹּ֩אמֶר֩ אִם־שָׁמ֨וֹעַ תִּשְׁמַ֜ע לְק֣וֹל ׀ יְהֹוָ֣ה אֱלֹהֶ֗יךָ וְהַיָּשָׁ֤ר בְּעֵינָיו֙ תַּעֲשֶׂ֔ה וְהַֽאֲזַנְתָּ֙ לְמִצְוֺתָ֔יו וְשָׁמַרְתָּ֖ כָּל־חֻקָּ֑יו כָּֽל־הַמַּחֲלָ֞ה אֲשֶׁר־שַׂ֤מְתִּי בְמִצְרַ֨יִם֙ לֹא־אָשִׂ֣ים עָלֶ֔יךָ כִּ֛י אֲנִ֥י יְהֹוָ֖ה רֹפְאֶֽךָ׃ ס 27 [FIFTH READING] וַיָּבֹ֣אוּ אֵילִ֔מָה וְשָׁ֗ם שְׁתֵּ֥ים עֶשְׂרֵ֛ה עֵינֹ֥ת מַ֖יִם וְשִׁבְעִ֣ים תְּמָרִ֑ים וַיַּחֲנוּ־שָׁ֖ם עַל־הַמָּֽיִם׃

טז 1 וַיִּסְעוּ֙ מֵֽאֵילִ֔ם וַיָּבֹ֜אוּ כָּל־עֲדַ֤ת בְּנֵֽי־יִשְׂרָאֵל֙ אֶל־מִדְבַּר־סִ֔ין אֲשֶׁ֥ר בֵּין־אֵילִ֖ם וּבֵ֣ין סִינָ֑י בַּחֲמִשָּׁ֨ה עָשָׂ֥ר יוֹם֙ לַחֹ֣דֶשׁ הַשֵּׁנִ֔י לְצֵאתָ֖ם מֵאֶ֥רֶץ

(a) Combatting ("diluting") evil with good; (b) revealing a much greater good that makes evil fade away; or (c) teaching the evil how bad it is, so that it no longer wishes to be evil.

The last method (c) is the approach of the penitents, who realize that they are distant from God, and abandon their former lifestyles for the better (*Rabbi Menahem Mendel Schneerson, 20th century*).

There (at Marah, God) gave them the commandments and the laws. He tested the people. At Marah, God gave the Jewish people some sections of the Torah with which to busy themselves, namely, the laws governing the Sabbath, the Red Heifer, and laws of monetary claims (*Rashi, 11th century*).

26. All the sicknesses that I have placed upon Egypt, I will not place upon you, for I am God, your Healer. At first glance, there seems to be a certain redundancy here. If God is going to save the Jewish people from all sicknesses, then surely they will not be in need of any healing?

Even if God finds it necessary to afflict the children of Israel, it is only because He is their Healer, who wishes to restore their spiritual health. Like a doctor, His incision is part of the healing process, and before lifting the scalpel, He prepares all the medications, *"for I am God, your Healer"* (*Rabbi Meir Loeb Weisser, 19th century*).

More than simply stating that God is our Healer, this verse implies that faith in God itself can bring about remedial effects. *"I am God"*—the very belief that God is the life-force of creation, is *"your Healer"* (*Rabbi Moses Polier of Kobrin, 19th century*).

---

kabbalah bites

15:25 The generation that left Egypt had experienced three prior incarnations: 1. the generation of the Flood, 2. the generation of Dispersion, and 3. the inhabitants of Sodom (see *Genesis 6:12; 11:5; 13:13*). Generally speaking, all this had achieved its *tikkun* (spiritual healing) through the Egyptian exile, but a tiny residue of spiritual filth still remained from each incarnation.

Now, the children of Israel were given the laws of Sabbath to achieve full *tikkun* for their second incarnation, in the generation of Dispersion. Sabbath, which brings to light how God created the world was a *tikkun* for their earlier denial of God through building the Tower of Babel. (For the other *tikkunim*, see below, 18:21; 21:37.)

²⁵ He cried out to God, and God instructed him about a (type of) wood. He threw it into the water, and the water became sweetened.

The First Rebuke: Acceptance of the Commandments

There (at Marah, God) gave them the commandments (of the Sabbath and the Red Heifer) and the laws (of monetary claims). He tested (the people by denying them water, to see how they would treat Moses). ²⁶ He said, "If you will (accept upon yourselves) to listen to the voice of God, your God, and you will (actually) perform (the commandments) which are just in His eyes, and you observe His commandments (with precision), and observe all His statutes (which defy logic)—then all the sicknesses that I have placed upon Egypt I will not place upon you, for I am God, your Healer.

[FIFTH READING] ²⁷ They came to Elim, where there were twelve water fountains and seventy date-palms. They encamped there by the water.

The Second Complaint and Rebuke

16 ¹ They journeyed from Elim, and the entire community of the children of Israel came to the desert of Sin—which is between Elim and Sinai—on the fifteenth day of the second month after their departure from the land of Egypt.

25. God instructed him about a (type of) wood. He threw it into the water, and the water became sweetened. There are three ways of sweetening bitter waters: (a) *Dilution* with a large amount of fresh water. (This method was not used here, according to all opinions.)

(b) *Transforming* the bitter flavor into a sweet one, by adding an extremely powerful agent that is capable of transforming a bitter flavor into a sweet one. This is the opinion of the *Zohar*, that a piece of the Tree of Life was used to overwhelm the waters.

(c) *Self-realization*. Making the bitter waters "realize" how bad it is to be bitter, so that they become sweet of their own accord. This is the opinion of Rabbi Joshua son of Korḥa (*Mekhilta*), that the waters were sweetened by adding *bitter* wood.

These three approaches correspond to three methods of eliminating evil:

spiritual vitamin

> Medicine has two general aspects: cure and prevention. At first glance, the accomplishment of the physician in curing the sick seems more impressive by its dramatic results, than preventative medicine, where there could be some delusion that sickness would be somehow avoided. In truth, however, it is better to be certain of immunity to sickness. The latter is the way of God, as the verse states: *"All the sicknesses … I will not place upon you, for I am God, your Healer"* (v. 26).

שמות ט״ז:א-י״ב — בשלח

מִצְרָיִם: [וילונו כ׳] 2 וַיִּלּוֹנוּ כָּל־עֲדַת בְּנֵי־יִשְׂרָאֵל עַל־מֹשֶׁה וְעַל־אַהֲרֹן בַּמִּדְבָּר: 3 וַיֹּאמְרוּ אֲלֵהֶם בְּנֵי יִשְׂרָאֵל מִי־יִתֵּן מוּתֵנוּ בְיַד־יְהֹוָה בְּאֶרֶץ מִצְרַיִם בְּשִׁבְתֵּנוּ עַל־סִיר הַבָּשָׂר בְּאָכְלֵנוּ לֶחֶם לָשֹׂבַע כִּי־הוֹצֵאתֶם אֹתָנוּ אֶל־הַמִּדְבָּר הַזֶּה לְהָמִית אֶת־כָּל־הַקָּהָל הַזֶּה בָּרָעָב: ס 4 וַיֹּאמֶר יְהֹוָה אֶל־מֹשֶׁה הִנְנִי מַמְטִיר לָכֶם לֶחֶם מִן־הַשָּׁמָיִם וְיָצָא הָעָם וְלָקְטוּ דְּבַר־יוֹם בְּיוֹמוֹ לְמַעַן אֲנַסֶּנּוּ הֲיֵלֵךְ בְּתוֹרָתִי אִם־לֹא: 5 וְהָיָה בַּיּוֹם הַשִּׁשִּׁי וְהֵכִינוּ אֵת אֲשֶׁר־יָבִיאוּ וְהָיָה מִשְׁנֶה עַל אֲשֶׁר־יִלְקְטוּ יוֹם | יוֹם: 6 וַיֹּאמֶר מֹשֶׁה וְאַהֲרֹן אֶל־כָּל־בְּנֵי יִשְׂרָאֵל עֶרֶב וִידַעְתֶּם כִּי יְהֹוָה הוֹצִיא אֶתְכֶם מֵאֶרֶץ מִצְרָיִם: 7 וּבֹקֶר וּרְאִיתֶם אֶת־כְּבוֹד יְהֹוָה בְּשָׁמְעוֹ אֶת־תְּלֻנֹּתֵיכֶם עַל־יְהֹוָה וְנַחְנוּ מָה כִּי [תלונו כ׳] תַלִּינוּ עָלֵינוּ: 8 וַיֹּאמֶר מֹשֶׁה בְּתֵת יְהֹוָה לָכֶם בָּעֶרֶב בָּשָׂר לֶאֱכֹל וְלֶחֶם בַּבֹּקֶר לִשְׂבֹּעַ בִּשְׁמֹעַ יְהֹוָה אֶת־תְּלֻנֹּתֵיכֶם אֲשֶׁר־אַתֶּם מַלִּינִם עָלָיו וְנַחְנוּ מָה לֹא־עָלֵינוּ תְלֻנֹּתֵיכֶם כִּי עַל־יְהֹוָה: 9 וַיֹּאמֶר מֹשֶׁה אֶל־אַהֲרֹן אֱמֹר אֶל־כָּל־עֲדַת בְּנֵי יִשְׂרָאֵל קִרְבוּ לִפְנֵי יְהֹוָה כִּי שָׁמַע אֵת תְּלֻנֹּתֵיכֶם: 10 וַיְהִי כְּדַבֵּר אַהֲרֹן אֶל־כָּל־עֲדַת בְּנֵי־יִשְׂרָאֵל וַיִּפְנוּ אֶל־הַמִּדְבָּר וְהִנֵּה כְּבוֹד יְהֹוָה נִרְאָה בֶּעָנָן: פ [SIXTH READING] 11 וַיְדַבֵּר יְהֹוָה אֶל־מֹשֶׁה לֵּאמֹר: 12 שָׁמַעְתִּי אֶת־תְּלוּנֹּת בְּנֵי יִשְׂרָאֵל דַּבֵּר אֲלֵהֶם לֵאמֹר בֵּין הָעַרְבַּיִם תֹּאכְלוּ בָשָׂר וּבַבֹּקֶר תִּשְׂבְּעוּ־לָחֶם וִידַעְתֶּם כִּי אֲנִי

16:8 God will give you meat to eat in the evening, and bread in the morning, to fill up. Meat is a fatty food. It represents the mystical parts of Torah, which are not crucial to Torah observance, but add inspiration, rather like fat, which adds richness of flavor to food.

Bread is a staple food. It thus represents the scriptural and legal ("revealed") parts of Torah, which must be studied in order for a person to know how to observe the commandments. For this reason, the request for bread was considered to be appropriate, as the scriptural and legal parts of Judaism are the staple diet of the Jew.

The request for mysticism (meat), however, was considered inappropriate *at that time*, since before the giving of the Torah, it was simply unnecessary to reveal such secrets.

Now, however, the mystical teachings of Kabbalah and Ḥasidism have become a welcome supplement to the staple diet of Scripture and Talmud (*Rabbi Menahem Mendel Schneerson, 20th century*).

² The entire community of the children of Israel complained against Moses and against Aaron in the desert (because their supplies of bread had run out). ³ The children of Israel said to them, "If only we had died by the hand of God in the land of Egypt, when we sat by pots of meat, when we ate bread to our fill! For you have brought us out into this desert, to starve the entire congregation to death!"

Meat and Manna Arrive

⁴ God said to Moses, "Look! I am going to rain down for you bread from heaven. (Every day) the people will go out and gather what is needed for that day, so that I can test them (to see) whether or not they will follow My Torah. ⁵ On Friday, when they are preparing what to bring home, they will gather (the same amount as usual, but when they measure it, they will find that it is) double the amount that they gather every day."

⁶ Moses and Aaron said to all the children of Israel:

"In the evening, you will realize that (it is not us, but) God who brought you out of the land of Egypt (because He will deliver you quails to satisfy your desires. But He will not give it to you gracefully, since you asked for it improperly).

⁷ "In the morning, you will see God's glory (in the beautiful way that he delivers you bread, indicating that) God has heard your (properly delivered) complaints against Him (about the lack of bread).

"But of what significance are we, that you make the people complain against us?"

⁸ Moses said, "God will give you meat to eat in the evening and bread in the morning to fill up. God hears your complaints, which you are causing (people to) complain against Him. But of what significance are we? Your complaints are not against us but against God."

⁹ Moses said to Aaron, "Say to the entire community of the children of Israel, 'Draw near before (the cloud of glory where) God (will descend), for He has heard your complaints.'"

¹⁰ When Aaron spoke to the entire community of the children of Israel, they turned toward the desert, and—look!—the glory of God appeared in the cloud.

[SIXTH READING] ¹¹ God spoke to Moses, saying, ¹² "I have heard the complaints of the children of Israel. Speak to them and say, 'In the afternoon you shall eat meat, and in the morning you shall be full with bread, and you will know that I am God, your God.'"

Food for thought

1. How well do you resist the temptation to complain?

2. Does complaining imply a denial of God's power?

3. When are complaints valid?

שמות טז:יב-כג | בשלח

יְהוָה אֱלֹהֵיכֶם: 13 וַיְהִי בָעֶרֶב וַתַּעַל הַשְּׂלָו וַתְּכַס אֶת־הַמַּחֲנֶה וּבַבֹּקֶר הָיְתָה שִׁכְבַת הַטָּל סָבִיב לַמַּחֲנֶה: 14 וַתַּעַל שִׁכְבַת הַטָּל וְהִנֵּה עַל־פְּנֵי הַמִּדְבָּר דַּק מְחֻסְפָּס דַּק כַּכְּפֹר עַל־הָאָרֶץ: 15 וַיִּרְאוּ בְנֵי־יִשְׂרָאֵל וַיֹּאמְרוּ אִישׁ אֶל־אָחִיו מָן הוּא כִּי לֹא יָדְעוּ מַה־הוּא וַיֹּאמֶר מֹשֶׁה אֲלֵהֶם הוּא הַלֶּחֶם אֲשֶׁר נָתַן יְהוָה לָכֶם לְאָכְלָה: 16 זֶה הַדָּבָר אֲשֶׁר צִוָּה יְהוָה לִקְטוּ מִמֶּנּוּ אִישׁ לְפִי אָכְלוֹ עֹמֶר לַגֻּלְגֹּלֶת מִסְפַּר נַפְשֹׁתֵיכֶם אִישׁ לַאֲשֶׁר בְּאָהֳלוֹ תִּקָּחוּ: 17 וַיַּעֲשׂוּ־כֵן בְּנֵי יִשְׂרָאֵל וַיִּלְקְטוּ הַמַּרְבֶּה וְהַמַּמְעִיט: 18 וַיָּמֹדּוּ בָעֹמֶר וְלֹא הֶעְדִּיף הַמַּרְבֶּה וְהַמַּמְעִיט לֹא הֶחְסִיר אִישׁ לְפִי־אָכְלוֹ לָקָטוּ: 19 וַיֹּאמֶר מֹשֶׁה אֲלֵהֶם אִישׁ אַל־יוֹתֵר מִמֶּנּוּ עַד־בֹּקֶר: 20 וְלֹא־שָׁמְעוּ אֶל־מֹשֶׁה וַיּוֹתִרוּ אֲנָשִׁים מִמֶּנּוּ עַד־בֹּקֶר וַיָּרֻם תּוֹלָעִים וַיִּבְאַשׁ וַיִּקְצֹף עֲלֵהֶם מֹשֶׁה: 21 וַיִּלְקְטוּ אֹתוֹ בַּבֹּקֶר בַּבֹּקֶר אִישׁ כְּפִי אָכְלוֹ וְחַם הַשֶּׁמֶשׁ וְנָמָס: 22 וַיְהִי | בַּיּוֹם הַשִּׁשִּׁי לָקְטוּ לֶחֶם מִשְׁנֶה שְׁנֵי הָעֹמֶר לָאֶחָד וַיָּבֹאוּ כָּל־נְשִׂיאֵי הָעֵדָה וַיַּגִּידוּ לְמֹשֶׁה: 23 וַיֹּאמֶר אֲלֵהֶם הוּא אֲשֶׁר דִּבֶּר יְהוָה שַׁבָּתוֹן שַׁבַּת־קֹדֶשׁ לַיהוָה מָחָר אֵת אֲשֶׁר־תֹּאפוּ אֵפוּ וְאֵת אֲשֶׁר־תְּבַשְּׁלוּ בַּשֵּׁלוּ וְאֵת כָּל־הָעֹדֵף הַנִּיחוּ לָכֶם לְמִשְׁמֶרֶת עַד־הַבֹּקֶר:

Rather than overexert yourself in business for nothing, devote extra time to more important concerns (*Rabbi Meir Loeb Weisser, 19th century*).

spiritual vitamin

> If you are not afraid to be exposed to a test or trial, know that the Sages who knew well human nature, strongly cautioned against such overconfidence. When King David, God's anointed, in a moment of great spiritual elation said, *"Examine me, O God … test me"* (Psalms 139:23), it brought him into trouble.

¹³ That evening, quails came up and covered the camp.

In the morning, there was a layer of dew around the camp. ¹⁴ The layer of dew evaporated, and—look!—on the surface of the desert, there was a fine substance as fine as frost, uncovered on the ground.

¹⁵ When the children of Israel saw it, they said to one another, "It is a prepared food [*man*]," because they did not know what it was (to call it by its correct name).

Moses said to them, "It is the bread which God has given you to eat. ¹⁶ This is what God has commanded: each person should gather as much as he needs to eat, i.e., an *'omer* (measure) for each person. You should take (one *'omer*) for every person in your tent."

¹⁷ The children of Israel did so. There were those that gathered too much, and those that gathered too little. ¹⁸ (When they came home and) measured it with an *'omer*-measure (they found that, miraculously), whoever had gathered too much did not have more (than an *'omer* per person), and whoever gathered too little did not have less. Each one had gathered exactly what he needed to eat.

¹⁹ Moses said to them, "Let no man leave any of it over until morning."

²⁰ (Dathan and Abiram) did not listen to Moses, and they left some of it over until morning. It became foul-smelling and bred worms, and Moses became angry with them.

²¹ They gathered it morning by morning, according to what each person could eat. When the sun grew hot, (the manna remaining in the fields) melted.

Double Portion of Manna for the Sabbath

²² On Friday, they gathered (what they later discovered to be) a double portion of bread, two *'omer*s for each person. The heads of the community came and reported it to Moses (because Moses had not yet informed them about the precept of the Sabbath, which God commanded him earlier to give over).

²³ He said to them, "This is what God said, 'Tomorrow is a rest day, a holy Sabbath to God. Bake whatever you wish to bake (today), and cook whatever you wish to cook (today). Whatever is left over, put aside for storage until morning."

18. Whoever had gathered too much did not have more (than an *'omer* per person), and whoever gathered too little did not have less. Some people intentionally gathered less than an *'omer*, while others deliberately gathered more. Nevertheless, upon measuring, they discovered that they had exactly an *'omer* for each family member. Those who were weak in their trust of God and gathered more than they should have did not gain by their extra effort. On the other hand, people who gathered less than an *'omer did* gain because they spent less time gathering their food, freeing their schedule for other pursuits. The lesson here is that *our sustenance does not ultimately depend on the extent of our efforts but upon what God has decreed that we will earn.*

24 וַיַּנִּ֤יחוּ אֹתוֹ֙ עַד־הַבֹּ֔קֶר כַּאֲשֶׁ֖ר צִוָּ֣ה מֹשֶׁ֑ה וְלֹ֣א הִבְאִ֔ישׁ וְרִמָּ֖ה לֹא־הָ֥יְתָה בּֽוֹ: 25 וַיֹּ֤אמֶר מֹשֶׁה֙ אִכְלֻ֣הוּ הַיּ֔וֹם כִּֽי־שַׁבָּ֥ת הַיּ֖וֹם לַיהוָ֑ה הַיּ֕וֹם לֹ֥א תִמְצָאֻ֖הוּ בַּשָּׂדֶֽה: 26 שֵׁ֥שֶׁת יָמִ֖ים תִּלְקְטֻ֑הוּ וּבַיּ֧וֹם הַשְּׁבִיעִ֛י שַׁבָּ֖ת לֹ֥א יִֽהְיֶה־בּֽוֹ: 27 וַֽיְהִי֙ בַּיּ֣וֹם הַשְּׁבִיעִ֔י יָצְא֥וּ מִן־הָעָ֖ם לִלְקֹ֑ט וְלֹ֖א מָצָֽאוּ: ס 28 וַיֹּ֥אמֶר יְהוָ֖ה אֶל־מֹשֶׁ֑ה עַד־אָ֙נָה֙ מֵֽאַנְתֶּ֔ם לִשְׁמֹ֥ר מִצְוֹתַ֖י וְתוֹרֹתָֽי: 29 רְא֗וּ כִּֽי־יְהוָה֮ נָתַ֣ן לָכֶ֣ם הַשַּׁבָּת֒ עַל־כֵּ֠ן ה֣וּא נֹתֵ֥ן לָכֶ֛ם בַּיּ֥וֹם הַשִּׁשִּׁ֖י לֶ֣חֶם יוֹמָ֑יִם שְׁב֣וּ | אִ֣ישׁ תַּחְתָּ֗יו אַל־יֵ֥צֵא אִ֛ישׁ מִמְּקֹמ֖וֹ בַּיּ֥וֹם הַשְּׁבִיעִֽי: 30 וַיִּשְׁבְּת֥וּ הָעָ֖ם בַּיּ֥וֹם הַשְּׁבִעִֽי: 31 וַיִּקְרְא֧וּ בֵֽית־יִשְׂרָאֵ֛ל אֶת־שְׁמ֖וֹ מָ֑ן וְה֗וּא כְּזֶ֤רַע גַּד֙ לָבָ֔ן וְטַעְמ֖וֹ כְּצַפִּיחִ֥ת בִּדְבָֽשׁ: 32 וַיֹּ֣אמֶר מֹשֶׁ֗ה זֶ֤ה הַדָּבָר֙ אֲשֶׁ֣ר צִוָּ֣ה יְהוָ֔ה מְלֹ֤א הָעֹ֙מֶר֙ מִמֶּ֔נּוּ לְמִשְׁמֶ֖רֶת לְדֹרֹתֵיכֶ֑ם לְמַ֣עַן | יִרְא֣וּ אֶת־הַלֶּ֗חֶם אֲשֶׁ֨ר הֶאֱכַ֤לְתִּי אֶתְכֶם֙ בַּמִּדְבָּ֔ר בְּהוֹצִיאִ֥י אֶתְכֶ֖ם מֵאֶ֥רֶץ מִצְרָֽיִם: 33 וַיֹּ֨אמֶר מֹשֶׁ֜ה אֶֽל־אַהֲרֹ֗ן קַ֚ח צִנְצֶ֣נֶת אַחַ֔ת וְתֶן־שָׁ֥מָּה מְלֹֽא־הָעֹ֖מֶר מָ֑ן וְהַנַּ֤ח אֹתוֹ֙ לִפְנֵ֣י יְהוָ֔ה לְמִשְׁמֶ֖רֶת לְדֹרֹתֵיכֶֽם: 34 כַּאֲשֶׁ֛ר צִוָּ֥ה יְהוָ֖ה אֶל־מֹשֶׁ֑ה וַיַּנִּיחֵ֧הוּ אַהֲרֹ֛ן לִפְנֵ֥י הָעֵדֻ֖ת לְמִשְׁמָֽרֶת: 35 וּבְנֵ֣י יִשְׂרָאֵ֗ל אָֽכְל֤וּ אֶת־הַמָּן֙ אַרְבָּעִ֣ים שָׁנָ֔ה עַד־בֹּאָ֖ם אֶל־אֶ֣רֶץ נוֹשָׁ֑בֶת אֶת־הַמָּן֙ אָֽכְל֔וּ עַד־בֹּאָ֕ם אֶל־קְצֵ֖ה אֶ֥רֶץ כְּנָֽעַן: 36 וְהָעֹ֕מֶר עֲשִׂרִ֥ית הָאֵיפָ֖ה הֽוּא: פ

יז 1 [SEVENTH READING] וַ֠יִּסְע֞וּ כָּל־עֲדַ֨ת בְּנֵֽי־יִשְׂרָאֵ֧ל מִמִּדְבַּר־סִ֛ין לְמַסְעֵיהֶ֖ם עַל־פִּ֣י יְהוָ֑ה וַֽיַּחֲנוּ֙ בִּרְפִידִ֔ים וְאֵ֥ין מַ֖יִם לִשְׁתֹּ֥ת הָעָֽם: 2 וַיָּ֤רֶב הָעָם֙ עִם־מֹשֶׁ֔ה וַיֹּ֣אמְר֔וּ תְּנוּ־לָ֥נוּ מַ֖יִם וְנִשְׁתֶּ֑ה וַיֹּ֤אמֶר לָהֶם֙ מֹשֶׁ֔ה מַה־תְּרִיבוּן֙ עִמָּדִ֔י מַה־

35. The children of Israel ate the manna for (almost) forty years. The children of Israel were able to taste in the manna any taste that they desired. But poor people who had never tasted respectable food simply did not know what to think when eating the manna. The wealthy people therefore advised the poor what to think of: delicious meat and fish rather than onions and hard bread. In this way the wealthy were able to fulfil, to a certain extent, the precept of charity (*Rabbi Aaron Roke'ah of Belz, 20th century*).

²⁴ They put it away until the morning, as Moses had commanded, and it did not become foul-smelling or worm-infested.

²⁵ Moses said, "Eat it today, for today is a Sabbath to God. Today you will not find it in the field. ²⁶ Six days you will gather it, but on (the Day of Atonement and the festivals,) there will not be any."

²⁷ On the seventh day, some of the people went out to gather manna, but they did not find any.

²⁸ God said to Moses, "How long will you refuse to observe My commandments and My teachings? ²⁹ You can see (with your own eyes) that God has given you the Sabbath (because a miracle occurs) on the Friday, and He gives you enough bread for two days.

"Let each person remain in his place. Nobody should leave his place on the seventh day." ³⁰ So the people rested on the seventh day.

Manna is Named—Jug of Manna is Preserved

³¹ The House of Israel named it (the food) "manna." It was (round) like coriander seed, (but) it was white. It tasted like dough fried in honey.

³² Moses said, "This is what God has commanded: 'A full *'omer* of it should be stored away for your generations to come, in order that they see the bread that I fed you in the desert, when I took you out of the land of Egypt.'"

(The following verse was actually said after the Tent of Meeting was built, but it was included here:)

³³ Moses said to Aaron, "Take an (earthenware) jug and put a full *'omer* of manna into it. You should place it before (the ark of) God, to be preserved for your generations to come." ³⁴ As God had commanded Moses, Aaron deposited it in front of the ark, to be preserved.

³⁵ The children of Israel ate the manna for (almost) forty years until they came to an inhabited land (after crossing the Jordan. However,) the manna (only descended) until they came to (the plains of Moab at) the border of the land of Canaan (where Moses passed away, before they crossed the Jordan. After that, they ate from the manna which they had stored up on that day).

³⁶ The *'omer* is one-tenth of an *'ephah*.

The Third Complaint: No Water

17 [SEVENTH READING] ¹ The whole community of the children of Israel journeyed from the desert of Sin, traveling according to God's instructions. They camped in Rephidim and there was no water for the people to drink. ² The people quarreled with Moses, and they said, "Give us water so we can drink."

שמות יז:ב-י • בשלח

תְּנַסּוּן אֶת־יְהוָה: 3 וַיִּצְמָא שָׁם הָעָם לַמַּיִם וַיָּלֶן הָעָם עַל־מֹשֶׁה וַיֹּאמֶר לָמָּה זֶּה הֶעֱלִיתָנוּ מִמִּצְרַיִם לְהָמִית אֹתִי וְאֶת־בָּנַי וְאֶת־מִקְנַי בַּצָּמָא: 4 וַיִּצְעַק מֹשֶׁה אֶל־יְהוָה לֵאמֹר מָה אֶעֱשֶׂה לָעָם הַזֶּה עוֹד מְעַט וּסְקָלֻנִי: 5 וַיֹּאמֶר יְהוָה אֶל־מֹשֶׁה עֲבֹר לִפְנֵי הָעָם וְקַח אִתְּךָ מִזִּקְנֵי יִשְׂרָאֵל וּמַטְּךָ אֲשֶׁר הִכִּיתָ בּוֹ אֶת־הַיְאֹר קַח בְּיָדְךָ וְהָלָכְתָּ: 6 הִנְנִי עֹמֵד לְפָנֶיךָ שָּׁם | עַל־הַצּוּר בְּחֹרֵב וְהִכִּיתָ בַצּוּר וְיָצְאוּ מִמֶּנּוּ מַיִם וְשָׁתָה הָעָם וַיַּעַשׂ כֵּן מֹשֶׁה לְעֵינֵי זִקְנֵי יִשְׂרָאֵל: 7 וַיִּקְרָא שֵׁם הַמָּקוֹם מַסָּה וּמְרִיבָה עַל־רִיב | בְּנֵי יִשְׂרָאֵל וְעַל נַסֹּתָם אֶת־יְהוָה לֵאמֹר הֲיֵשׁ יְהוָה בְּקִרְבֵּנוּ אִם־אָיִן: פ 8 וַיָּבֹא עֲמָלֵק וַיִּלָּחֶם עִם־יִשְׂרָאֵל בִּרְפִידִם: 9 וַיֹּאמֶר מֹשֶׁה אֶל־יְהוֹשֻׁעַ בְּחַר־לָנוּ אֲנָשִׁים וְצֵא הִלָּחֵם בַּעֲמָלֵק מָחָר אָנֹכִי נִצָּב עַל־רֹאשׁ הַגִּבְעָה וּמַטֵּה הָאֱלֹהִים בְּיָדִי: 10 וַיַּעַשׂ יְהוֹשֻׁעַ כַּאֲשֶׁר אָמַר־לוֹ מֹשֶׁה לְהִלָּחֵם בַּעֲמָלֵק וּמֹשֶׁה אַהֲרֹן וְחוּר עָלוּ רֹאשׁ הַגִּבְעָה:

among us or not?' By your life! A dog will come and bite you, and you will cry out to Me, and then you will know where I am."

This can be compared to a man who mounted his son on his shoulder and set out on the road. Whenever his son saw something, he would say, "Father, take that thing and give it to me," and the father would give it to him. This happened a second time, and then a third time.

Then they met a man, and the son said to him, "Have you seen my father anywhere?"

His father said to him, "Don't you know where I am?"

He threw his son down off him, and a dog came and bit him (*Rashi, 11th century*).

Amalek. The character of Amalek refers to coldness in the service of God. On the verse, *"Remember what Amalek did to you ... on your journey out of Egypt; how they surprised you (korekha) on the road..."* (*Deuteronomy* 25:17-18), the Hebrew word *korekha* could also be interpreted as "he cooled you off." Similarly, the Rabbis have noted the numerical equivalence (*gematria*) between Amalek and the word *safek*, meaning "doubt."

Amalek represents the doubts that are raised in our minds, cooling off our excitement after witnessing the miracles that accompany our personal exodus from Egypt. It deadens our sensitivity to the providence with which God controls our

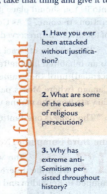

Food for thought

1. Have you ever been attacked without justification?

2. What are some of the causes of religious persecution?

3. Why has extreme anti-Semitism persisted throughout history?

Moses said to them, "Why are you quarreling with me? Why are you trying to test God (to see if He can give water in a dry land)?"

³ The people thirsted there for water. The people complained to Moses and said, "Why have you brought us up from Egypt to make me and my children and my livestock die of thirst?"

⁴ Moses cried out to God, saying, "What shall I do for this people? (If I wait) a bit longer they will stone me!"

⁵ God said to Moses, "Pass before the people (and you will see that your words were unfounded, as they will not stone you). Bring with you some of the elders of Israel (as witnesses), and take in your hand your staff, with which you struck the Nile, and go. ⁶ I will stand before you there on the rock at Horeb. You shall strike into the rock (and split it), and water will come out of it, and the people will drink."

Moses did so before the eyes of the elders of Israel.

⁷ He named the place Massah and Meribah ("testing and quarreling") because of the children of Israel's quarreling and because they tested God, saying, "Is God among us, or not?"

The Third Rebuke—Attack of Amalek

⁸ (As a punishment for doubting God, the following occurred): Amalek came and fought with Israel in Rephidim.

⁹ Moses said to Joshua, "Choose (strong and God-fearing) men for us, and go out (from the protection of the cloud of glory), and fight against Amalek. Tomorrow, (during the battle,) I will stand on top of the hill with the staff of God in my hand."

¹⁰ Joshua followed Moses' instruction to fight against Amalek. Moses, Aaron, and

17:7-8 "Is God among us, or not?" Amalek came and fought. The section about Amalek was placed straight after the verse, *"Is God among us, or not?"* to suggest God's response: "I am always among you, and I am always prepared for all your necessities, and yet you say, 'Is God

spiritual vitamin

> The difficulties and obstacles which you encounter are really intended to evoke in you untapped powers, to reinforce your determination and stimulate further efforts to the maximum degree.

שמות יז:יא-טז — בשלח

11 וְהָיָ֗ה כַּאֲשֶׁ֨ר יָרִ֥ים מֹשֶׁ֛ה יָד֖וֹ וְגָבַ֣ר יִשְׂרָאֵ֑ל וְכַאֲשֶׁ֥ר יָנִ֛יחַ יָד֖וֹ וְגָבַ֥ר עֲמָלֵֽק׃
12 וִידֵ֤י מֹשֶׁה֙ כְּבֵדִ֔ים וַיִּקְחוּ־אֶ֛בֶן וַיָּשִׂ֥ימוּ תַחְתָּ֖יו וַיֵּ֣שֶׁב עָלֶ֑יהָ וְאַהֲרֹ֨ן וְח֜וּר תָּֽמְכ֣וּ בְיָדָ֗יו מִזֶּ֤ה אֶחָד֙ וּמִזֶּ֣ה אֶחָ֔ד וַיְהִ֥י יָדָ֛יו אֱמוּנָ֖ה עַד־בֹּ֥א הַשָּֽׁמֶשׁ׃
13 וַיַּחֲלֹ֧שׁ יְהוֹשֻׁ֛עַ אֶת־עֲמָלֵ֥ק וְאֶת־עַמּ֖וֹ לְפִי־חָֽרֶב׃ פ [MAFTIR]
14 וַיֹּ֨אמֶר יְהוָ֜ה אֶל־מֹשֶׁ֗ה כְּתֹ֨ב זֹ֤את זִכָּרוֹן֙ בַּסֵּ֔פֶר וְשִׂ֖ים בְּאָזְנֵ֣י יְהוֹשֻׁ֑עַ כִּֽי־מָחֹ֤ה אֶמְחֶה֙ אֶת־זֵ֣כֶר עֲמָלֵ֔ק מִתַּ֖חַת הַשָּׁמָֽיִם׃
15 וַיִּ֥בֶן מֹשֶׁ֖ה מִזְבֵּ֑חַ וַיִּקְרָ֥א שְׁמ֖וֹ יְהוָ֥ה ׀ נִסִּֽי׃
16 וַיֹּ֗אמֶר כִּֽי־יָד֙ עַל־כֵּ֣ס יָ֔הּ מִלְחָמָ֥ה לַיהוָ֖ה בַּֽעֲמָלֵ֑ק מִדֹּ֖ר דֹּֽר׃ פ פ פ

קי"ו פסוקים. י"ד אמונ"ה סימן. סנא"ה סימן.

---

11. When Moses raised his hand, Israel would prevail. Did Moses' hands decide the battle? Obviously not. Rather, the Torah teaches us here that so long as the children of Israel looked towards heaven in prayer and aligned their hearts to God, they would prevail. When they failed to do so, they began to lose (*Babylonian Talmud, Rosh Ha-Shanah* 29a).

12. Moses' hands grew heavy. Because he was lax in performing the commandment to wage war against Amalek, and had appointed someone else in his place, his hands became heavy (*Rashi, 11th century*).

(Aaron and Hur) took a stone and placed it under him, and he sat (directly) on it. Did Moses have to sit on a bare stone? Did he not have a cushion or a pillow? Moses said, "I insist on sitting on a stone. Since the children of Israel are in anguish and under attack by Amalek, I will share their anguish with them" (*Babylonian Talmud, Ta'anit* 11a). A righteous person shares in the lot of the masses, even if he had no part in the failings that brought on the calamity (*Rabbi Aḥai Gaon of Shabḥa, 8th century*).

Hur (Miriam's son) ascended to the top of the hill. ¹¹ It happened, that when Moses raised his hand, Israel would prevail, and when he lowered his hand, Amalek would prevail.

¹² Moses' hands grew heavy (because he was lax with his duty, discharging it to Joshua). (Aaron and Hur) took a stone and placed it under him, and he sat (directly) on it. Aaron and Hur supported his hands; one from this side, and one from that side. His hands were (spread heavenward) in faith (and prayer) until sunset.

¹³ Joshua weakened Amalek and his people (by decapitating their key warriors) with the edge of the sword (but he allowed the others to live).

[MAFTIR] ¹⁴ God said to Moses, "Inscribe (the story of how Amalek attacked Israel before all the other nations) as a memorial in the book. Recite it in the ears of Joshua (who will bring the Jewish people into the land of Israel) because I will surely obliterate the remembrance of Amalek from beneath the heavens."

¹⁵ Then Moses built an altar, and named it Adonai-nissi ("God is my Miracle"). ¹⁶ He said, "For there is a hand on the throne of God (which swears) that there shall be a war of God against Amalek from generation to generation."

The Haftarah for Be-Shallaḥ is on page 1323.

lives. Therefore, for God's sovereignty to be revealed, Amalek must be nullified (*Rabbi Shneur Zalman of Lyady, 18ᵗʰ century*).

kabbalah bites

17:14 The destruction of Amalek is a prelude to rebuilding the Temple (*Babylonian Talmud, Sanhedrin* 20b). This is hinted to in the Kabbalistic practice of reading the word "remembrance" (זכר), twice with different *nikkud* (vowels): once with a *segol* (*zekher*), and once with a *tzere* (*zeikher*).

The triad of points in the *segol* (ֶ) alludes to: 1. The Tabernacle, 2. The First Temple, and 3. The Second Temple.

This is then followed by the two-pointed *tzere* (ֵ) representing the transition from a temporal (historic) structure to a permanent (messianic) one.

> The people **did not believe** in Moses on account of the **wonders** he performed. For when our **faith** is **based on miracles** alone, **doubt** always lingers. Rather, it was the **event at Sinai,** when we saw revelation **with our own eyes** and heard **with our own ears.**

YITRO
יתרו

JETHRO COMES TO THE DESERT	18:1–12
JETHRO ADVISES MOSES TO APPOINT JUDGES	18:13–27
GIVING OF THE TORAH AT SINAI	19:1 – 20:23

NAME
Yitro

LINES IN TORAH SCROLL
138

PARASHIYYOT
4 open; 11 closed

VERSES
75

WORDS
1105

LETTERS
4022

DATE
Iyyar – 6 Sivan, 2448

LOCATION
Sinai Desert

KEY PEOPLE
Moses, Jethro

MITZVOT
3 positive; 14 prohibitions

MASORETIC FEATURES
There is a distinct set of cantillation notes for the public Torah reading of the Ten Commandments.

CHARACTER PROFILE

NAME
Jethro (Yitro)

MEANING
"Addition"

OTHER NAMES
Reuel, Jether, Hobab, Heber, Keni, Putiel

CHILDREN
Zipporah (Moses' wife), and six other daughters

RESIDENCE
Midian

ACHIEVEMENTS
Was an advisor to Pharaoh; fled to Midian after he opposed the genocidal policy against Jewish boys; was the High Priest of Midian before renouncing idol-worship; was a genuine convert to Judaism; first to utter a blessing to God for the wonders performed for the Israelites; brought about the adding of a portion of the Torah (hence his name)

KNOWN FOR
Advised Moses on the reorganization of the judicial system; departed for home before the revelation at Sinai

CONVERSION

The decision of Jethro to reject his own culture and wisdom, and follow the Jewish people to the desert, was a crucial preparation for the giving of the Torah. With this expression of commitment, he elevated all his occult and secular knowledge, for which he was world-renowned, to the Torah (18:1).

SHARING AUTHORITY

Jethro saw that Moses was suffering physical strain in an attempt to judge all the cases himself. He suggested that Moses delegate some of his duties to others who were worthy (18:13-24).

REVELATION

At Mount Sinai, God revealed Himself. This broke down a certain barrier between the physical and the spiritual, forging a greater connection between man and God through the commandments observed after Sinai (19:20).

SUBMISSION

When Moses asked the Jewish people if they wanted to accept the Torah, they replied, "We will do." They were willing to accept God on *His* terms, not as colored by their own perception (19:8).

שמות יח:א-י · יתרו

יח

1 וַיִּשְׁמַ֞ע יִתְר֨וֹ כֹהֵ֤ן מִדְיָן֙ חֹתֵ֣ן מֹשֶׁ֔ה אֵת֩ כָּל־אֲשֶׁ֨ר עָשָׂ֤ה אֱלֹהִים֙ לְמֹשֶׁ֔ה וּלְיִשְׂרָאֵ֖ל עַמּ֑וֹ כִּֽי־הוֹצִ֧יא יְהֹוָ֛ה אֶת־יִשְׂרָאֵ֖ל מִמִּצְרָֽיִם: 2 וַיִּקַּ֗ח יִתְרוֹ֙ חֹתֵ֣ן מֹשֶׁ֔ה אֶת־צִפֹּרָ֖ה אֵ֣שֶׁת מֹשֶׁ֑ה אַחַ֖ר שִׁלּוּחֶֽיהָ: 3 וְאֵ֖ת שְׁנֵ֣י בָנֶ֑יהָ אֲשֶׁ֨ר שֵׁ֤ם הָֽאֶחָד֙ גֵּֽרְשֹׁ֔ם כִּ֣י אָמַ֔ר גֵּ֣ר הָיִ֔יתִי בְּאֶ֖רֶץ נָכְרִיָּֽה: 4 וְשֵׁ֥ם הָאֶחָ֖ד אֱלִיעֶ֑זֶר כִּֽי־אֱלֹהֵ֤י אָבִי֙ בְּעֶזְרִ֔י וַיַּצִּלֵ֖נִי מֵחֶ֥רֶב פַּרְעֹֽה: 5 וַיָּבֹ֞א יִתְר֨וֹ חֹתֵ֥ן מֹשֶׁ֛ה וּבָנָ֥יו וְאִשְׁתּ֖וֹ אֶל־מֹשֶׁ֑ה אֶל־הַמִּדְבָּ֗ר אֲשֶׁ֨ר ה֥וּא חֹנֶ֛ה שָׁ֖ם הַ֥ר הָאֱלֹהִֽים: 6 וַיֹּ֙אמֶר֙ אֶל־מֹשֶׁ֔ה אֲנִ֛י חֹתֶנְךָ֥ יִתְר֖וֹ בָּ֣א אֵלֶ֑יךָ וְאִ֨שְׁתְּךָ֔ וּשְׁנֵ֥י בָנֶ֖יהָ עִמָּֽהּ: 7 וַיֵּצֵ֨א מֹשֶׁ֜ה לִקְרַ֣את חֹֽתְנ֗וֹ וַיִּשְׁתַּ֙חוּ֙ וַיִּשַּׁק־ל֔וֹ וַיִּשְׁאֲל֥וּ אִישׁ־לְרֵעֵ֖הוּ לְשָׁל֑וֹם וַיָּבֹ֖אוּ הָאֹֽהֱלָה: 8 וַיְסַפֵּ֤ר מֹשֶׁה֙ לְחֹ֣תְנ֔וֹ אֵת֩ כָּל־אֲשֶׁ֨ר עָשָׂ֤ה יְהֹוָה֙ לְפַרְעֹ֣ה וּלְמִצְרַ֔יִם עַ֖ל אוֹדֹ֣ת יִשְׂרָאֵ֑ל אֵ֤ת כָּל־הַתְּלָאָה֙ אֲשֶׁ֣ר מְצָאָ֣תַם בַּדֶּ֔רֶךְ וַיַּצִּלֵ֖ם יְהֹוָֽה: 9 וַיִּ֣חַדְּ יִתְר֔וֹ עַ֚ל כָּל־הַטּוֹבָ֔ה אֲשֶׁר־עָשָׂ֥ה יְהֹוָ֖ה לְיִשְׂרָאֵ֑ל אֲשֶׁ֥ר הִצִּיל֖וֹ מִיַּ֥ד מִצְרָֽיִם: 10 וַיֹּ֘אמֶר֘ יִתְרוֹ֒ בָּר֣וּךְ יְהֹוָ֔ה אֲשֶׁ֨ר הִצִּ֥יל אֶתְכֶ֛ם מִיַּ֥ד מִצְרַ֖יִם וּמִיַּ֣ד פַּרְעֹ֑ה אֲשֶׁ֤ר הִצִּיל֙ אֶת־הָעָ֔ם מִתַּ֖חַת

---

into a desert to be with Moses and the Jewish people. Through this act he raised the esteem of the Jewish people in the eyes of the nations (*Rabbi Ḥayyim ibn Attar, 18th century*).

4. One was named Eliezer, because ... rescued me from Pharaoh's sword. The Pharaoh who had sought Moses' life died before the birth of Eliezer, and it was only then that Moses felt "rescued from his sword." Until that point he never felt secure, always concerned that his whereabouts could become known to Pharaoh (*Rabbi Obadiah Sforno, 16th century*).

6. Your wife and her two sons. Were they not Moses' sons, as well? Why did Jethro refer to them as *"her* two sons"?

This hints to the fact that Moses did not come to this world for his own sake. He only came to sweeten the judgments of this world so it should not be destroyed (*Rabbi Menahem Azariah da Fano, 16th–17th century*).

kabbalah bites

18:1 Jethro—also known as *Keini* (see *Rashi*)—was a reincarnation of Cain's soul, after it had undergone *tikkun* (spiritual healing). Initially, Cain's soul, which had been severely damaged by the sin of the Tree of Knowledge, was reincarnated as the Egyptian whom Moses killed (above 2:12). Moses was a reincarnation of Abel and deeply yearned for Cain's soul to achieve *tikkun*. He achieved this goal by killing the Egyptian with God's ineffable name.

At that point, the good from Cain's soul entered Jethro, which is what inspired him to convert to Judaism.

parashat yitro

Jethro Comes to Moses in the Desert

18 ¹ Jethro, the priest of Midian, father-in-law of Moses, heard (about the splitting of the Sea of Reeds and the war with Amalek and) all that God had done for Moses and for Israel, His people, (providing them with manna and water in the desert and, most importantly,) that God had taken Israel out of Egypt.

² Jethro, Moses' father-in-law, took with him Zipporah, Moses' wife, who had been sent away (back home by Moses, to save her from entering Egypt), ³ and her two sons. One of them was named Gershom, because he (Moses) had said, "I was a stranger [*GeR*] in a foreign land," ⁴ and one was named Eliezer, because, "The God of my father came to my aid [*ʾELohe ʾavI be-ʿEZRi*] and rescued me from Pharaoh's sword."

⁵ Jethro, Moses' father-in-law, came with his (Moses') sons and his wife to Moses, to the desert where he was encamped by the mountain of God. ⁶ He (sent a message) to Moses, "I, Jethro, your father-in-law, am coming to you, and so is your wife, and her two sons with her."

⁷ Moses (together with Aaron, Nadab and Abihu, and a huge welcoming committee,) went out to greet his father-in-law, and he (Moses) bowed down and kissed him. They asked about each other's welfare, and they entered the tent.

⁸ Moses told his father-in-law about all that God had done to Pharaoh and to the Egyptians for Israel's sake, and about all the hardships that had befallen them on the way (with the sea and with Amalek), and that God had saved them.

⁹ Jethro rejoiced (alternatively: his flesh became prickly with unease) about all the good that God had done for Israel (in sending them manna; but most of all, because) He had rescued them from the hand of Egypt (since no slave had ever escaped from there before). ¹⁰ Jethro said, "Blessed is God, who has rescued you from the hand of Egypt (a mighty nation), and from the hand of Pharaoh (a mighty

---

18:1 Jethro. Jethro's arrival is juxtaposed with the war with Amalek (17:8-16) to contrast their different attitudes towards Israel. Amalek acted viciously towards them; whereas Jethro acted benevolently, advising Moses how to set up a court system and guiding the Israelites in the desert (*Rabbi Abraham ibn Ezra, 12th century*).

The priest of Midian. Why does the Torah speak derogatorily of Moses' father-in-law, emphasizing that Jethro was *"the priest of Midian,"* a master of idol-worship?

This, however, points to his greatness. Jethro had reached a senior rank of idol-worship for which he was highly respected in society, but he nevertheless abandoned his position, *traveling*

שמות יח:י-יח / יתרו

יַד־מִצְרָיִם: 11 עַתָּה יָדַעְתִּי כִּי־גָדוֹל יְהוָה מִכָּל־הָאֱלֹהִים כִּי בַדָּבָר אֲשֶׁר זָדוּ עֲלֵיהֶם: 12 וַיִּקַּח יִתְרוֹ חֹתֵן מֹשֶׁה עֹלָה וּזְבָחִים לֵאלֹהִים וַיָּבֹא אַהֲרֹן וְכֹל | זִקְנֵי יִשְׂרָאֵל לֶאֱכָל־לֶחֶם עִם־חֹתֵן מֹשֶׁה לִפְנֵי הָאֱלֹהִים: 13 [SECOND READING] וַיְהִי מִמָּחֳרָת וַיֵּשֶׁב מֹשֶׁה לִשְׁפֹּט אֶת־הָעָם וַיַּעֲמֹד הָעָם עַל־מֹשֶׁה מִן־הַבֹּקֶר עַד־הָעָרֶב: 14 וַיַּרְא חֹתֵן מֹשֶׁה אֵת כָּל־אֲשֶׁר־הוּא עֹשֶׂה לָעָם וַיֹּאמֶר מָה־הַדָּבָר הַזֶּה אֲשֶׁר אַתָּה עֹשֶׂה לָעָם מַדּוּעַ אַתָּה יוֹשֵׁב לְבַדֶּךָ וְכָל־הָעָם נִצָּב עָלֶיךָ מִן־בֹּקֶר עַד־עָרֶב: 15 וַיֹּאמֶר מֹשֶׁה לְחֹתְנוֹ כִּי־יָבֹא אֵלַי הָעָם לִדְרֹשׁ אֱלֹהִים: 16 כִּי־יִהְיֶה לָהֶם דָּבָר בָּא אֵלַי וְשָׁפַטְתִּי בֵּין אִישׁ וּבֵין רֵעֵהוּ וְהוֹדַעְתִּי אֶת־חֻקֵּי הָאֱלֹהִים וְאֶת־תּוֹרֹתָיו: 17 וַיֹּאמֶר חֹתֵן מֹשֶׁה אֵלָיו לֹא־טוֹב הַדָּבָר אֲשֶׁר אַתָּה עֹשֶׂה: 18 נָבֹל תִּבֹּל גַּם־אַתָּה גַּם־הָעָם הַזֶּה אֲשֶׁר עִמָּךְ כִּי־כָבֵד מִמְּךָ הַדָּבָר לֹא־תוּכַל

With the same thing that they plotted, God punished them. The Egyptians were punished by drowning because they had plotted to drown all newborn males, exceeding God's decree that Abraham's descendants will be afflicted with slavery (*Nahmanides, 13th century*).

15-16. The people come to me to seek God. If any of them has a claim, he comes to me, and I judge between a man and his fellow. I make known the statutes of God and His teachings. Moses explained that there were three general reasons for which the people waited to see him:

1) So that he would pray for them—*"The people come to me to seek God;"* 2) To settle monetary disputes—*"If any of them has a claim, he comes to me;"* and 3) to teach them Torah—*"I make known the statutes of God and His teachings."*

Since Moses was the only person fulfilling these responsibilities, the Jewish people had to wait *"from morning until evening"* (v.14) to see him (*Nahmanides, 13th century*).

18. The matter is too heavy for you. Moses was not mistaken in his judgment. He *was* capable of carrying out this job singlehandedly, and the people would not become weary waiting all day to speak with him. Through Moses' holy presence and gaze upon the Jewish people *he raised them up* to the level where they could stand *"from morning until the evening"* (v.14) without becoming weary.

So when Jethro asked Moses why he alone was acting as judge, Moses replied, *"Because the people come to me to seek God"* (v.15). Moses argued that through learning from him, it was as if the people were learning directly from God, and that was irreplaceable.

Food for thought

1. Are you able to accept constructive criticism?

2. What mental barriers must be overcome to delegate responsibility to others?

3. What impact has friendly advice had on your life?

king); who has rescued the people from (the tyranny of) Egypt. ¹¹ (Even before this, I believed in God; but) now I know that God is greater than all the deities (that I have worshiped in the past), for with the same thing that they plotted (i.e. to drown Jewish babies in water, God punished them, by drowning the Egyptians in the sea)."

¹² Jethro, Moses' father-in-law, sacrificed burnt-offerings and peace-offerings to God. Aaron and all the elders of Israel came to dine with Moses' father-in-law, before God; (and Moses personally served the meal).

Jethro Advises Moses to Appoint Judges

[SECOND READING] ¹³ On the day after (the Day of Atonement, when Moses came down from Mount Sinai with the second set of tablets), Moses sat down to judge the people. The people stood before Moses from the morning until the evening.

¹⁴ Moses' father-in-law saw what he was doing to the people, and he said, "What is this thing that you are doing to the people? Why do you sit by yourself, while all the people stand before you from morning until evening?"

¹⁵ Moses said to his father-in-law, "Because the people come to me to seek God('s teachings). ¹⁶ If any of them has a claim, he comes to me, and I judge between a man and his fellow. I make known the statutes of God and His teachings."

¹⁷ Moses' father-in-law said to him, "The thing that you are doing is not good. ¹⁸ You will surely wear yourself out, along with (Aaron, Hur and) this nation that is with you! For the matter is too heavy for you. You cannot do it alone!"

kabbalah bites

18:14 Why did the suggestion to appoint judges come from Jethro and not directly from God?

Jethro was a reincarnation of Cain, who had killed his brother, Abel, saying, *"There is no law and no judge"* (*Targum Jonathan, Genesis* 4:8). To achieve *tikkun* (spiritual healing) for this error, the idea of an effective judicial system came from Jethro.

11. Now I know that God is greater than all the deities (that I have worshiped in the past). Now Jethro recognized God's superiority over all other gods. Previously, he had only recognized God's power, not His absolute superiority (*Rabbi Elijah Mizraḥi, 15th–16th century*).

It was only after Jethro came and acknowledged God by saying, *"Now I know that God is greater than all the deities"* that God rose in glory above and below. Only then could the Torah be given in full, expressing God's sovereignty over everything (*Zohar*).

The revelations that had occurred at the splitting of the Reed Sea had all been lofty Divine revelations. In order that the Torah be able to sanctify even the realm of the mundane, it was crucial that an event occur where the forces of impurity and evil would be "handed over" to the side of holiness. This occurred through the conversion of Jethro, whose history of expertise in idol-worship was elevated to holiness when he converted. Now it was possible for the Torah to penetrate even the profane (*Rabbi Menahem Mendel Schneerson, 20th century*).

שמות יח:יח-כז
יתרו

19. עֲשֵׂהוּ לְבַדֶּךָ: עַתָּה שְׁמַע בְּקֹלִי אִיעָצְךָ וִיהִי אֱלֹהִים עִמָּךְ הֱיֵה אַתָּה לָעָם מוּל הָאֱלֹהִים וְהֵבֵאתָ אַתָּה אֶת־הַדְּבָרִים אֶל־הָאֱלֹהִים: 20. וְהִזְהַרְתָּה אֶתְהֶם אֶת־הַחֻקִּים וְאֶת־הַתּוֹרֹת וְהוֹדַעְתָּ לָהֶם אֶת־הַדֶּרֶךְ יֵלְכוּ בָהּ וְאֶת־הַמַּעֲשֶׂה אֲשֶׁר יַעֲשׂוּן: 21. וְאַתָּה תֶחֱזֶה מִכָּל־הָעָם אַנְשֵׁי־חַיִל יִרְאֵי אֱלֹהִים אַנְשֵׁי אֱמֶת שֹׂנְאֵי בָצַע וְשַׂמְתָּ עֲלֵהֶם שָׂרֵי אֲלָפִים שָׂרֵי מֵאוֹת שָׂרֵי חֲמִשִּׁים וְשָׂרֵי עֲשָׂרֹת: 22. וְשָׁפְטוּ אֶת־הָעָם בְּכָל־עֵת וְהָיָה כָּל־הַדָּבָר הַגָּדֹל יָבִיאוּ אֵלֶיךָ וְכָל־הַדָּבָר הַקָּטֹן יִשְׁפְּטוּ־הֵם וְהָקֵל מֵעָלֶיךָ וְנָשְׂאוּ אִתָּךְ: 23. אִם אֶת־הַדָּבָר הַזֶּה תַּעֲשֶׂה וְצִוְּךָ אֱלֹהִים וְיָכָלְתָּ עֲמֹד וְגַם כָּל־הָעָם הַזֶּה עַל־מְקֹמוֹ יָבֹא בְשָׁלוֹם: [THIRD READING] 24. וַיִּשְׁמַע מֹשֶׁה לְקוֹל חֹתְנוֹ וַיַּעַשׂ כֹּל אֲשֶׁר אָמָר: 25. וַיִּבְחַר מֹשֶׁה אַנְשֵׁי־חַיִל מִכָּל־יִשְׂרָאֵל וַיִּתֵּן אֹתָם רָאשִׁים עַל־הָעָם שָׂרֵי אֲלָפִים שָׂרֵי מֵאוֹת שָׂרֵי חֲמִשִּׁים וְשָׂרֵי עֲשָׂרֹת: 26. וְשָׁפְטוּ אֶת־הָעָם בְּכָל־עֵת אֶת־הַדָּבָר הַקָּשֶׁה יְבִיאוּן אֶל־מֹשֶׁה וְכָל־הַדָּבָר הַקָּטֹן יִשְׁפּוּטוּ הֵם: 27. וַיְשַׁלַּח מֹשֶׁה אֶת־חֹתְנוֹ וַיֵּלֶךְ לוֹ אֶל־אַרְצוֹ: פ

Jethro argued that the Jewish people needed to be prepared for a time when Moses would be away—up on the mountain, or after Moses' death—when the people would need guidance.

Why did this insight come from Jethro? Because, coming from the outside, Jethro had many different religious experiences on his spiritual journey, so he was fully aware of the regressive state that could occur without Moses' direct guidance (*Rabbi Menahem Mendel Schneerson, 20th century*).

26. They would bring any difficult case to Moses. Notice the difference in wording between this verse and Jethro's earlier suggestion, *"When any major matter arises, they will bring it*

spiritual vitamin

> Torah means *instruction*, or *guidance*, because the Torah is your guide in life. The Torah makes you constantly aware of your duties in life; it gives you a true definition of your life's purpose, and it shows you the ways and means of attaining this goal.

¹⁹ "Now, listen to me. I will advise you, but let God be (in agreement) with you (on this matter). You (should represent) the people before God, and you will bring (their disputes) to God. ²⁰ You will caution them about the statutes and the teachings, and you will show them the path to follow and the things that they must do."

²¹ "(But, using Divine inspiration,) you should seek out from among all the people, (financially independent) men who fear God, men of truth (whose words are reliable,) and who hate monetary gain (through litigation). You should appoint them over (the people with differing levels of responsibility:) leaders of thousands, leaders of hundreds, leaders of fifties, and leaders of tens."

²² "They will judge the people on a fulltime basis. When any major matter arises, they will bring it to you, but the minor matters they will judge for themselves. This will make it easier for you, for they will bear the burden with you."

²³ "(Now consult God about this suggestion,) and if (He consents, and) you do this thing, you will be able to remain firm. Furthermore, (Aaron, Nadab, Abihu, and the seventy elders, who are also becoming worn out,) will come to their destination in peace."

[THIRD READING] ²⁴ Moses listened to his father-in-law, and did all that he said. ²⁵ Moses chose (financially independent) men from among all Israel and appointed them as heads over the people: leaders of thousands, leaders of hundreds, leaders of fifties, and leaders of tens. ²⁶ They judged the people on a fulltime basis. They would bring any difficult case to Moses, and they judged the minor cases themselves.

²⁷ Moses saw his father-in-law off, and he went away to his land (to convert his family).

Jethro perceived the Jews in a different light (not how they existed once Moses had elevated them to his own level, but rather), how they existed by themselves, while Moses was in a different realm or a different place.

kabbalah bites

18:21 The generation that left Egypt had experienced three prior incarnations: 1. the generation of the Flood, 2. the generation of Dispersion, and 3. the inhabitants of Sodom (see *Genesis* 6:12; 11:5; 13:13).

Generally speaking, all this had achieved its *tikkun* (spiritual healing) through the Egyptian exile, but a tiny residue of spiritual filth remained from each incarnation.

Now the children of Israel were given the laws of fair judgment to achieve full *tikkun* for their third incarnation in the people of Sodom, who had rejected all forms of fair trial and justice (see also 15:25 and 21:37).

שמות יט:א-ד

יתרו

יט 1 [FOURTH READING] בַּחֹ֙דֶשׁ֙ הַשְּׁלִישִׁ֔י לְצֵ֥את בְּנֵֽי־יִשְׂרָאֵ֖ל מֵאֶ֣רֶץ מִצְרָ֑יִם בַּיּ֣וֹם הַזֶּ֔ה בָּ֖אוּ מִדְבַּ֥ר סִינָֽי: 2 וַיִּסְע֣וּ מֵרְפִידִ֗ים וַיָּבֹ֙אוּ֙ מִדְבַּ֣ר סִינַ֔י וַֽיַּחֲנ֖וּ בַּמִּדְבָּ֑ר וַיִּֽחַן־שָׁ֥ם יִשְׂרָאֵ֖ל נֶ֥גֶד הָהָֽר: 3 וּמֹשֶׁ֥ה עָלָ֖ה אֶל־הָאֱלֹהִ֑ים וַיִּקְרָ֙א אֵלָ֤יו יְהֹוָה֙ מִן־הָהָ֣ר לֵאמֹ֔ר כֹּ֤ה תֹאמַר֙ לְבֵ֣ית יַעֲקֹ֔ב וְתַגֵּ֖יד לִבְנֵ֥י יִשְׂרָאֵֽל: 4 אַתֶּ֣ם רְאִיתֶ֔ם אֲשֶׁ֥ר עָשִׂ֖יתִי לְמִצְרָ֑יִם וָאֶשָּׂ֤א אֶתְכֶם֙ עַל־כַּנְפֵ֣י נְשָׁרִ֔ים וָאָבִ֥א אֶתְכֶ֖ם

"Israel encamped there"—The peculiar use of the singular (lit. "he encamped" rather than "they encamped") led the Sages to declare that they were "like one man with one heart." *They were in a state of communal harmony* (Rabbi Ḥayyim ibn Attar, 18th century).

3. Moses ascended to God. When Moses ascended on high, the ministering angels said before God, "Master of the world! What is someone born of a woman doing among us?"

"He has come to receive the Torah," God said.

They said, "This coveted treasure which was secreted with You before the creation of the world—how could You give it to a man of flesh and blood?"

"Give them an answer!" God said to Moses.

"Master of the universe," Moses replied, "this Torah which You are giving to me, what is written in it? *'I am God, the God of every one of you, who took you out of the land of Egypt'* (20: 2)." Turning to the angels, he said, "Did *you* go down to Egypt? Were *you* enslaved to Pharaoh? Why, then, should the Torah be yours?

"What else is written in it? *'You shall not possess an idol of other deities'* (ibid. 3). Do you live among nations that worship idols?

"What else is written in it? *'Remember the Sabbath day to sanctify it'* (ibid. 8). Do you do any work from which you would need to rest?

"What else is written in it? *'Honor your father and your mother'* (ibid. 12). Do you have a father or mother?

"What else is written in it? *'You shall not murder,' 'You shall not commit adultery,' 'You shall not steal'* (ibid. 13). Are you capable of envy? Do you have an evil inclination?"

Without further ado, the angels conceded to God (*Babylonian Talmud, Shabbat* 88b).

You should say the following to the House of Jacob (i.e. the women), and tell (the same thing) to the sons of Israel. If God had commanded Moses to address the men before the women, the women could have later excused themselves from observing the Torah, claiming

spiritual vitamin

> Before giving the Torah to the whole people of Israel, God told Moses to first approach the women, and then the men. This emphasizes the primary role of the Jewish woman in preserving the Torah.

The Jewish People Camp by Mount Sinai

19 [FOURTH READING] ¹ On (the first day of) the third month after the children of Israel's departure from Egypt, they arrived at the desert of Sinai. ² They had departed from Rephidim (in a state of repentance) and they arrived at the desert of Sinai (in a state of repentance). They encamped in the desert. Israel encamped there, (towards the east side of) the mountain (in a state of total unity, as if they were one single person with one heart).

God Chooses the Jewish People as His Own

³ Moses ascended to God (on the second day of the month, early in the morning). God called to him from the mountain, saying, "You should say the following to the House of Jacob (i.e. the women) and tell (the same thing in a more explicit manner, stressing the punishments and fine details) to the sons of Israel (i.e. the men):

⁴ 'You have seen what I did to the Egyptians, and how I gathered (you together in a short period of time, and I protected you through the angel of God, as if you

---

to you" (v. 22). Jethro judged a case's importance by the amount of money at stake—he determined if it was a *"major* matter." Torah law, however, treats all cases equally, regardless of the sums involved. So Moses commanded the judges to bring "any *difficult* case" to him to judge. To Moses, the amount of money at stake was not important; his expertise was required to resolve difficult and complicated matters of the law (*Rabbi Jacob Kattina, 19th century*).

19:1 On the third month. Why was the Torah given in the third month? Because that month's astrological sign is "twins" (Gemini), and it was in that month that God and the Jewish people became twins (*Midrash*).

God said, "See which month I gave the Torah—the third month, whose sign is 'twins' (Gemini). If the wicked Esau, Jacob's twin, would decide to convert, repent and come to study Torah, let him come and study and I will accept him!" That is why He gave it in the third month (*Pesikta de-Rav Kahana*).

2. Israel encamped there. The singular conjugation of "encamped" is used here suggesting that every Jewish soul until the end of time was present at this moment. Since the souls derive from a single source, the verse chose not to use the plural (*Rabbi Moses Prisco, 19th century*).

They had departed from Rephidim and they arrived at the desert of Sinai ... Israel encamped there. Here we have a hint to three prerequisites for receiving the Torah: *enthusiasm, humility* and *communal harmony*.

"They had departed from Rephidim"—Rephidim suggesting *rafu yedeihem*, a slackening of the hands, i.e., a loss of enthusiasm in worship (*Babylonian Talmud, Sanhedrin* 106a). This had been the cause of Amalek's attack. But now they "had departed" from this. *They were full of enthusiasm.*

"They arrived at the desert"—The Sages taught, "If you make yourself entirely humble like the desert you will attain the Torah as a gift from God" (ibid., *Eruvin* 54a). *They were submissive and humble.*

שמות יט:ד-יג   יתרו

אֵלָֽי: 5 וְעַתָּ֗ה אִם־שָׁמ֤וֹעַ תִּשְׁמְעוּ֙ בְּקֹלִ֔י וּשְׁמַרְתֶּ֖ם אֶת־בְּרִיתִ֑י וִהְיִ֨יתֶם לִ֤י סְגֻלָּה֙ מִכָּל־הָ֣עַמִּ֔ים כִּי־לִ֖י כָּל־הָאָֽרֶץ: 6 וְאַתֶּ֧ם תִּֽהְיוּ־לִ֛י מַמְלֶ֥כֶת כֹּהֲנִ֖ים וְג֣וֹי קָד֑וֹשׁ אֵ֚לֶּה הַדְּבָרִ֔ים אֲשֶׁ֥ר תְּדַבֵּ֖ר אֶל־בְּנֵ֥י יִשְׂרָאֵֽל: [FIFTH READING] 7 וַיָּבֹ֣א מֹשֶׁ֔ה וַיִּקְרָ֖א לְזִקְנֵ֣י הָעָ֑ם וַיָּ֣שֶׂם לִפְנֵיהֶ֗ם אֵ֚ת כָּל־הַדְּבָרִ֣ים הָאֵ֔לֶּה אֲשֶׁ֥ר צִוָּ֖הוּ יְהוָֽה: 8 וַיַּעֲנ֨וּ כָל־הָעָ֤ם יַחְדָּו֙ וַיֹּ֣אמְר֔וּ כֹּ֛ל אֲשֶׁר־דִּבֶּ֥ר יְהוָ֖ה נַעֲשֶׂ֑ה וַיָּ֤שֶׁב מֹשֶׁה֙ אֶת־דִּבְרֵ֥י הָעָ֖ם אֶל־יְהוָֽה: 9 וַיֹּ֨אמֶר יְהוָ֜ה אֶל־מֹשֶׁ֗ה הִנֵּ֨ה אָנֹכִ֜י בָּ֣א אֵלֶיךָ֮ בְּעַ֣ב הֶֽעָנָן֒ בַּעֲב֞וּר יִשְׁמַ֤ע הָעָם֙ בְּדַבְּרִ֣י עִמָּ֔ךְ וְגַם־בְּךָ֖ יַאֲמִ֣ינוּ לְעוֹלָ֑ם וַיַּגֵּ֥ד מֹשֶׁ֛ה אֶת־דִּבְרֵ֥י הָעָ֖ם אֶל־יְהוָֽה: 10 וַיֹּ֨אמֶר יְהוָ֤ה אֶל־מֹשֶׁה֙ לֵ֣ךְ אֶל־הָעָ֔ם וְקִדַּשְׁתָּ֥ם הַיּ֖וֹם וּמָחָ֑ר וְכִבְּס֖וּ שִׂמְלֹתָֽם: 11 וְהָי֥וּ נְכֹנִ֖ים לַיּ֣וֹם הַשְּׁלִישִׁ֑י כִּ֣י | בַּיּ֣וֹם הַשְּׁלִשִׁ֗י יֵרֵ֧ד יְהוָ֛ה לְעֵינֵ֥י כָל־הָעָ֖ם עַל־הַ֥ר סִינָֽי: 12 וְהִגְבַּלְתָּ֤ אֶת־הָעָם֙ סָבִ֣יב לֵאמֹ֔ר הִשָּׁמְר֥וּ לָכֶ֛ם עֲל֥וֹת בָּהָ֖ר וּנְגֹ֣עַ בְּקָצֵ֑הוּ כָּל־הַנֹּגֵ֥עַ בָּהָ֖ר מ֥וֹת יוּמָֽת: 13 לֹא־תִגַּ֨ע

8. All the people replied in unison and said, "Everything that God has said we shall do!" Why did they respond, "Everything that God *has said* we shall do," in the past tense? God had not yet spoken to them!

A simple answer would be to argue that they were referring to the few laws given to them in advance of Sinai, while encamped at Marah (above, 15:25).

But the inner meaning is that they were referring to the Torah that their souls had heard even before coming into the world (see *Babylonian Talmud, Niddah* 20b). *"Everything that God has said"*—to our souls, before we entered the world—*"we shall do!"* (*Rabbi Joseph b. Ephraim Caro, 16th century*).

Moses conveyed the words of the people back to God. When Moses contemplated the Jewish people's response, that they had willingly accepted the Torah even before hearing what laws it contained, he realized that this was something wondrous that human beings could not possibly have done without Divine assistance. Moses understood that this must have been nothing other than the spirit of God speaking through them! So now *"Moses conveyed the words of the people back to God"*—he attributed the people's response to God (*Rabbi Levi Isaac of Berdichev, 18th century*).

Food for thought

1. What does it mean to be "a kingdom of ministers and a holy nation"? (v. 6)

2. How do you relate to the idea of "chosenness"?

3. Where do you draw the line between pride and bigotry?

exodus 19:4–13 — yitro

were carried) on eagles' wings, and I brought you to My (service). ⁵ Now, if you listen to Me and keep My covenant (through observing the Torah), you will be a precious treasure to Me among all the peoples, for the whole earth is Mine (and yet the other nations are like nothing to Me). ⁶ You shall be to Me a kingdom of ministers and a holy nation.'

"These are the words that you shall speak to the children of Israel (no more and no less)."

[FIFTH READING] ⁷ Moses returned and summoned the elders of Israel and placed before them all these words that God had commanded him.

⁸ All the people replied in unison and said, "Everything that God has said we shall do!"

(On the third day,) Moses (ascended the mountain once again and) conveyed the words of the people back to God.

⁹ God said to Moses, "Look! I am going to come (down) to you in a fog (within its deepest part), in order that the people hear when I speak to you, and they will also believe in you (and the prophets that follow you) forever."

Moses (returned to relay God's words and, on the fourth day, he ascended to) relay the people's reply to God (that they did not wish merely to overhear God speaking to Moses, but they wanted to hear God directly).

Preparations for the Giving of the Torah

¹⁰ God said to Moses, "(If the people want to hear Me directly, then) go to the people and make them ready, today and tomorrow. They should wash their garments. ¹¹ They should be prepared for the third day (having separated from their wives), for on the third day (from today, i.e., the sixth of the month), God will descend before the eyes of all the people on Mount Sinai.

¹² "You should set boundaries around (the mountain) for the people around, which say, 'Beware of ascending the mountain or touching its edge! Whoever touches the mountain shall surely be put to death!' ¹³ No hand shall touch it, for

---

that they had only accepted it to please their husbands. Therefore, God commanded Moses to address the women first (*Rabbi Natan Ashkenazi Shapira of Grodno, 16ᵗʰ century*).

5. You will be a precious treasure to Me among all the peoples, for the whole earth is Mine. Do not get the wrong idea! When a woman is her husband's precious treasure, she might seclude herself from everyone but him. When a son is his father's precious treasure, he might seclude himself from everyone but his father. Does that mean that the Jewish people should seclude themselves from the other nations of the world?

To refute this notion, the verse states, *"for the whole earth is mine"* (*Mekhilta de-Rabbi Simeon ben Yoḥai*).

שמות יט:יג-כב · יתרו

בוֹ יָד כִּי־סָקוֹל יִסָּקֵל אוֹ־יָרֹה יִיָּרֶה אִם־בְּהֵמָה אִם־אִישׁ לֹא יִחְיֶה בִּמְשֹׁךְ הַיֹּבֵל הֵמָּה יַעֲלוּ בָהָר: 14 וַיֵּרֶד מֹשֶׁה מִן־הָהָר אֶל־הָעָם וַיְקַדֵּשׁ אֶת־הָעָם וַיְכַבְּסוּ שִׂמְלֹתָם: 15 וַיֹּאמֶר אֶל־הָעָם הֱיוּ נְכֹנִים לִשְׁלֹשֶׁת יָמִים אַל־תִּגְּשׁוּ אֶל־אִשָּׁה: 16 וַיְהִי בַיּוֹם הַשְּׁלִישִׁי בִּהְיֹת הַבֹּקֶר וַיְהִי קֹלֹת וּבְרָקִים וְעָנָן כָּבֵד עַל־הָהָר וְקֹל שֹׁפָר חָזָק מְאֹד וַיֶּחֱרַד כָּל־הָעָם אֲשֶׁר בַּמַּחֲנֶה: 17 וַיּוֹצֵא מֹשֶׁה אֶת־הָעָם לִקְרַאת הָאֱלֹהִים מִן־הַמַּחֲנֶה וַיִּתְיַצְּבוּ בְּתַחְתִּית הָהָר: 18 וְהַר סִינַי עָשַׁן כֻּלּוֹ מִפְּנֵי אֲשֶׁר יָרַד עָלָיו יְהֹוָה בָּאֵשׁ וַיַּעַל עֲשָׁנוֹ כְּעֶשֶׁן הַכִּבְשָׁן וַיֶּחֱרַד כָּל־הָהָר מְאֹד: 19 וַיְהִי קוֹל הַשֹּׁפָר הוֹלֵךְ וְחָזֵק מְאֹד מֹשֶׁה יְדַבֵּר וְהָאֱלֹהִים יַעֲנֶנּוּ בְקוֹל: [SIXTH READING] 20 וַיֵּרֶד יְהֹוָה עַל־הַר סִינַי אֶל־רֹאשׁ הָהָר וַיִּקְרָא יְהֹוָה לְמֹשֶׁה אֶל־רֹאשׁ הָהָר וַיַּעַל מֹשֶׁה: 21 וַיֹּאמֶר יְהֹוָה אֶל־מֹשֶׁה רֵד הָעֵד בָּעָם פֶּן־יֶהֶרְסוּ אֶל־יְהֹוָה לִרְאוֹת וְנָפַל מִמֶּנּוּ רָב: 22 וְגַם הַכֹּהֲנִים הַנִּגָּשִׁים אֶל־יְהֹוָה

the mountain, *"No hand shall touch it, for he shall be stoned or cast down."* When God's presence departed, everyone was allowed to climb the mountain (*Mekhilta*).

14. Moses went down from the mountain to the people. Rather than first taking care of his own affairs, Moses went directly from the mountain to the people, placing them before himself (*Rashi, 11th century*).

20. God descended onto Mount Sinai. Man can only accurately describe man. When describing creatures lower than himself or forces higher than himself, he is forced to employ metaphors from the human experience. Clearly, when the verse states that God "descended" on Mount Sinai, it is simply a metaphor to assist the reader in understanding as much as the mortal mind can comprehend (*Rabbi Abraham ibn Ezra, 12th century*).

You might think that He actually descended upon it. To counteract this notion the Torah states: *"You have seen that from the heavens I have spoken with you"* (20:19). This teaches that He bent down the upper heavens and the lower heavens and spread them upon the mountain like a sheet on a bed, and that God's Throne of Glory descended upon them (*Rashi, 11th century*).

22. The (firstborn) priests, (despite the fact that) they (usually) go near to God (to offer sacrifices). There were separate boundaries at various levels of Mount Sinai, for Moses, Aaron, and the priests (*Mekhilta*).

Although they were closer than the rest of the nation, the priests still were forbidden from going beyond their designated position (*Rabbi Ḥayyim ibn Attar, 18th century*).

he shall be stoned or cast down; whether man or beast, he shall not live. When the ram's horn sounds a long, drawn out blast, (God's presence will depart and) they may ascend the mountain."

¹⁴ Moses went down from the mountain, (directly) to the people. He prepared the people, and they washed their clothing. ¹⁵ He said to the people, "Prepare yourselves for three days (alternatively: "for the third day"). Do not come close to your wives."

¹⁶ On the third day, when it was becoming morning, (before the people arrived), there were thunder claps and lightning flashes—a thick cloud was upon the mountain—and a very powerful blast of a ram's horn. The entire nation that was in the camp shuddered.

¹⁷ Moses brought the people out from the camp, towards the Divine Presence (which approached them), and they stood at the bottom of the mountain.

¹⁸ The whole of Mount Sinai smoked, because God had descended upon it in fire. Its smoke ascended like the smoke of a limekiln, and the entire mountain shook violently.

¹⁹ The sound of the ram's horn grew increasingly stronger.

(Since God only spoke the first two commandments, and Moses said the rest, the following method was used:)

Moses would speak and (in order to make him be heard), God would respond by (amplifying) his (Moses') voice.

[SIXTH READING] ²⁰ God descended onto Mount Sinai, to the peak of the mountain. God summoned Moses to the peak of the mountain, and Moses ascended.

²¹ God said to Moses, "Go down, warn the people (not to come up the mountain), lest they break (from their present position due to their desire to go nearer) to God, to see (His revelation), and if (any) of them will fall, (it will be as tragic as if) many (had fallen). ²² Also, the (firstborn) priests, (despite the fact that) they (usually) go near to God (to offer sacrifices, they should not consider themselves important

---

13. Cast down. The person who touches the mountain should be put to death *from a distance*, by stoning or being shot with arrows, but not by having others approach the mountain (*Rabbi Samuel b. Meir, 12ᵗʰ century*).

Ram's horn *(yovel)*. *Yovel* is a *shofar* (horn) of a ram, for in Arabia, they call a ram *yovela'*. This particular *shofar* came from the ram that Abraham had sacrificed in the place of Isaac (see *Genesis 22:13; Rashi, 11ᵗʰ century*).

(God's presence will depart and) they may ascend the mountain. It is not the place that honors the man, but the man who honors the place. So long as God's presence remained upon

שמות יט:כב - כ:ד | יתרו

יִתְקַדְּשׁ֔וּ פֶּן־יִפְרֹ֥ץ בָּהֶ֖ם יְהֹוָֽה: 23 וַיֹּ֤אמֶר מֹשֶׁה֙ אֶל־יְהֹוָ֔ה לֹא־יוּכַ֣ל הָעָ֔ם לַעֲלֹ֖ת אֶל־הַ֣ר סִינָ֑י כִּֽי־אַתָּ֞ה הַעֵדֹ֤תָה בָּ֨נוּ֙ לֵאמֹ֔ר הַגְבֵּ֥ל אֶת־הָהָ֖ר וְקִדַּשְׁתּֽוֹ: 24 וַיֹּ֨אמֶר אֵלָ֤יו יְהֹוָה֙ לֶךְ־רֵ֔ד וְעָלִ֥יתָ אַתָּ֖ה וְאַהֲרֹ֣ן עִמָּ֑ךְ וְהַכֹּהֲנִ֣ים וְהָעָ֗ם אַל־יֶֽהֶרְס֛וּ לַעֲלֹ֥ת אֶל־יְהֹוָ֖ה פֶּן־יִפְרָץ־בָּֽם: 25 וַיֵּ֥רֶד מֹשֶׁ֖ה אֶל־הָעָ֑ם וַיֹּ֖אמֶר אֲלֵהֶֽם: ס

כ 1 וַיְדַבֵּ֣ר אֱלֹהִ֔ים אֵ֛ת כָּל־הַדְּבָרִ֥ים הָאֵ֖לֶּה לֵאמֹֽר: ס 2 אָֽנֹכִ֖י֙ יְהֹוָ֣ה אֱלֹהֶ֑֔יךָ אֲשֶׁ֧ר הֽוֹצֵאתִ֛יךָ מֵאֶ֥רֶץ מִצְרַ֖יִם מִבֵּ֣֥ית עֲבָדִ֑֔ים: 3 לֹֽ֣א־יִהְיֶֽה־לְךָ֛֩ אֱלֹהִ֥֨ים אֲחֵרִ֖֜ים עַל־פָּנָֽ֗יַ: 4 לֹֽ֣א־תַֽעֲשֶׂ֨ה־לְךָ֥֣ פֶ֣֨סֶל֙ וְכָל־תְּמוּנָ֔֡ה אֲשֶׁ֤֣ר בַּשָּׁמַ֣֨יִם֙ מִמַּ֡֔עַל

*Cantillation notes for public reading on page 1282.

Imagination is addressed by the first and last command—*"I am God"* is the source of our positive imaginations; *"You shall not covet"* addresses the negative.

Contemplation is addressed by the second and third commandments, not to think of any other gods, and not to take God's name in vain, i.e., not to discard anything in the world—which contains a spark of God—as unnecessary or useless.

Will is addressed by the sixth and seventh commandments, not to kill or commit adultery.

Speech is addressed by the eighth and ninth commandments, not to steal or bear false witness. Withholding oral teaching from others is a form of "stealing" (*Babylonian Talmud, Sanhedrin* 91b); by the same reasoning "bearing false witness," means speaking too much.

Action is addressed by the fourth and fifth commandments, to observe the Sabbath and to honor your parents (*Rabbi Mordecai Joseph Leiner of Izbica, 19th century*).

(The) God (of every one) of you. *"Three rings are interlocked together: Israel, the Torah and God. All are on different planes, one higher than the other, partly hidden, partly revealed* (*Zohar*). The "revealed" qualities of Israel include the unique intelligence and natural character of the Jew. The hidden qualities of Israel include the pure, simple and refined faith in God found in every Jew's heart.

As for the Torah, the "revealed" part is the logical interpretation of all the various subjects of the Torah, which discuss man's life on this earth, as well as how the world came into being. The "hidden" part of the Torah is its Divine intellect which differs essentially from human intellect and cannot be properly grasped by man.

In the case of God, there are also "revealed" or conceivable attributes, and "hidden" or inconceivable attributes. What is conceivable about God is that

446

kabbalah bites

20:1 Rendered literally, the verse reads: *"God spoke all these words saying."* The final word, *"saying,"* is superfluous here. Every member of the children of Israel was present at the time, as well as all the souls of future generations, so who else did God's message need to be "said" to?

The Maggid of Mezhirech answered that the extra word is a warning against dissonance, that our spiritual side should always "speak to" and inform our physical lives. Or, as the Maggid himself put it: *"We must draw the Ten Commandments into the Ten Utterances of Genesis with which God created the world."*

enough to ascend the mountain. Rather,) they shall be ready to stand in their positions. Failing that, God will make a breach (by destroying some of) them."

²³ Moses said to God, "(I do not need to warn them, since) the people cannot ascend to Mount Sinai, for You (have already) warned us, saying, 'Set boundaries for the mountain and sanctify it.'"

²⁴ God said to him, "Go down (and warn them a second time). Then, you should ascend (to the highest level), Aaron should come with you (but to a lower level), and the priests (can come up, but to a lower level still). But the people must not break from their position to ascend to God, for failing that, He will make a breach against them."

²⁵ Moses went down to the people and said this (warning) to them.

The Ten Commandments

20 ¹ God spoke all (the Ten Commandments in one single utterance. He then went back, and specified each one individually).

(The Jewish people) responded ("Yes" to the positive commands and "No" to the prohibitions):

- ² "I am God, (the) God (of every one) of you, Who took you out of the land of Egypt, out of the house of bondage.

- ³ "You shall not (possess an idol) of other deities (so long as I exist). ⁴ You shall not make for yourself a sculptured image or any picture of that which is in the heavens

23-24. You (have already) warned us, saying, "Set boundaries for the mountain and sanctify it." God said to him, "Go down (and warn them a second time)." Moses could simply not imagine how it would be possible to sin after having been instructed not to by God. So God told him, *"Go down!"* Climb down from your lofty perch because the rest of the people are not like you. They need another warning (*Rabbi Levi Isaac of Berdichev, 18th century*).

20:1 God spoke. If Israel sanctify themselves they will always merit to hear the voice of God speaking to them, as He did at Sinai (*Rabbi Isaac Judah Jehiel Safrin of Komarno, 19th century*).

2. I am God. All that the Jewish people heard directly from the mouth of God was the letter *alef*, enunciated with the vowel *kametz*—that is, the first letter of the word *'anokhi*, *"I"* (*Rabbi Menahem Mendel of Rymanow, 18th century*).

What does this mean? The entire message of the Torah is contained in this one letter, *kametz–alef. Alef ('a-l-ph)* is an acronym for *'ozen* (ear), *lev* (heart) and *peh* (mouth). Added together these words have the numerical equivalence of the word *'einayim* (eyes). *Kametz* means to "contain." The entire Torah depends on "containing" our ears, heart, mouth and eyes, ensuring that they are only fed with appropriate content (*Rabbi Asher Isaiah of Ropczyce, 19th century*).

The Ten Commandments address the five core faculties of man: *imagination, contemplation, will, speech* and *action*. Two commandments are dedicated to each faculty.

וַאֲשֶׁ֣ר בָּאָ֔רֶץ מִתַּ֖חַת וַאֲשֶׁ֥ר בַּמַּ֖יִם ׀ מִתַּ֣חַת לָאָֽרֶץ׃ 5 לֹֽא־תִשְׁתַּחֲוֶ֥ה לָהֶ֖ם וְלֹ֣א תׇעׇבְדֵ֑ם כִּ֣י אָֽנֹכִ֞י יְהֹוָ֤ה אֱלֹהֶ֙יךָ֙ אֵ֣ל קַנָּ֔א פֹּ֠קֵ֠ד עֲוֺ֨ן אָבֹ֧ת עַל־בָּנִ֛ים עַל־שִׁלֵּשִׁ֥ים וְעַל־רִבֵּעִ֖ים לְשֹׂנְאָֽי׃ 6 וְעֹ֥שֶׂה חֶ֖סֶד לַאֲלָפִ֑ים לְאֹהֲבַ֖י וּלְשֹׁמְרֵ֥י מִצְוֺתָֽי׃ ס 7 לֹ֥א תִשָּׂ֛א אֶת־שֵֽׁם־יְהֹוָ֥ה אֱלֹהֶ֖יךָ לַשָּׁ֑וְא כִּ֣י לֹ֤א יְנַקֶּה֙ יְהֹוָ֔ה אֵ֛ת אֲשֶׁר־יִשָּׂ֥א אֶת־שְׁמ֖וֹ לַשָּֽׁוְא׃ פ 8 זָכ֛וֹר֩ אֶת־י֥֨וֹם הַשַּׁבָּ֖֜ת לְקַדְּשֽׁ֗וֹ׃ 9 שֵׁ֤֣שֶׁת יָמִ֣ים֙ תַּֽעֲבֹ֔ד֮ וְעָשִׂ֖֣יתָ כׇּל־מְלַאכְתֶּֽךָ֒׃ 10 וְי֨וֹם֙ הַשְּׁבִיעִ֔֜י שַׁבָּ֖֣ת ׀ לַיהֹוָ֣ה אֱלֹהֶ֑֗יךָ לֹֽ֣א־תַעֲשֶׂ֣ה כׇל־מְלָאכָ֡ה אַתָּ֣ה ׀ וּבִנְךָ֣ וּ֠בִתֶּ֗ךָ עַבְדְּךָ֤ וַאֲמָֽתְךָ֙ וּבְהֶמְתֶּ֔ךָ וְגֵרְךָ֖ אֲשֶׁ֥ר בִּשְׁעָרֶֽיךָ׃ 11 כִּ֣י שֵֽׁשֶׁת־יָמִים֩ עָשָׂ֨ה יְהֹוָ֜ה אֶת־הַשָּׁמַ֣יִם וְאֶת־הָאָ֗רֶץ אֶת־הַיָּם֙ וְאֶת־כׇּל־אֲשֶׁר־בָּ֔ם וַיָּ֖נַח

7. You shall not take the name of God, your God, in vain. This includes swearing by the hallowed name of God unnecessarily. For example, a person swears about something *that is true* but self-evident—that the pillar is made of marble and he is standing by it, and everyone can see that this is the case (*Naḥmanides, 13th century*).

Falsely representing yourself as a pious, God-fearing person is, in a subtle way, taking the name of God in vain, as it creates a false impression (*Rabbi Ḥayyim ibn Attar, 18th century*).

"When God said at Sinai, 'You shall not take the name of God, your God, in vain,' the entire world trembled" (*Babylonian Talmud, Shevu'ot* 39a). Why did the world tremble with this command in particular? Because God's name gives life to the entire world, and by taking His name in vain you disturb the life force to the world, causing it to tremble (*Rabbi Ephraim of Luntshits, 16th–17th century*).

8. Remember the Sabbath day to sanctify it. Here, the Torah uses the expression *"remember the Sabbath."* In the repetition of the Ten Commandments in *Deuteronomy* (5:12) it states *"guard the Sabbath."* In fact, God pronounced both expressions in one simultaneous utterance (*Rashi, 11th century*).

9-10. Six days you may work and perform all your labor, but the seventh day is a Sabbath to God, your God. You shall perform no labor. All our prayers and good deeds in this world are aimed at purifying and elevating fallen "sparks" of sublime holiness. Since these "sparks" are trapped in even the most material aspects of the world, all sorts of physical work can be employed for a *mitzvah* (commandment), thereby elevating sparks. For example, when you go to plow the ground, *"You may not plow with an ox and donkey together"* (*Deuteronomy* 22:10); and when you go to plant, *"You may not sow your vineyard with a mixture of seeds"* (ibid. 9).

To accomplish all this, man requires assistance from above. So the upper worlds descend down here on weekdays to assist man in elevating the fallen sparks. Or, to be precise, the seven lower *sefirot* (Divine emanations) descend and become infused in the seven days of the week.

However only six of the seven *sefirot* have sufficient energy to successfully power this elevation—which is why there are only six workdays. The Sabbath corresponds to the final

above, which is on the earth below, or which is in the water beneath the earth. ⁵ You shall not bow down before them, nor worship them, for I, God, your God, am a God who is zealous (to exact punishment), who visits the iniquity of the fathers upon the sons, upon the third and the fourth generation of those who (continue in their fathers' ways to) hate Me. ⁶ But I act kindly to those who love Me and to those who keep My commandments, for two thousand generations.

❖ ⁷ "You shall not take the name of God, your God, in vain, for God will not absolve anyone who takes His name in vain.

❖ ⁸ "Remember the Sabbath day to sanctify it. ⁹ Six days you may work and perform all your labor, ¹⁰ but the seventh day is a Sabbath to God, your God. You shall perform no labor, neither you, your son, your daughter, your manservant, your maidservant, your beast, nor your convert who is within your gates. ¹¹ For in six days God made the heavens, the earth and the sea—and all that is in them—and

He creates and forms the world and its contents from nothingness and He constantly infuses them with vitality. What is inconceivable about God is His true essence and identity—that which lies beyond His involvement with the world. Nevertheless, the realization of God's greatness as He transcends the world should move us to a longing and yearning to cleave to Him.

All three "rings" are connected—*The revealed qualities of Israel unite with the revealed attributes of God, by means of the revealed part of the Torah; the hidden qualities of Israel unite with the hidden attributes of God, by means of the hidden part of the Torah* (*Rabbi Joseph Isaac Schneersohn of Lubavitch, 20th century*).

5. You shall not bow down before them, nor worship them. Idol-worship may seem a concept that is foreign to our modern lives, but in truth, a mistake not dissimilar from that of the idol-worshipers can easily be made in our business activities. Men of old may have worshiped the sun and the moon, but do we "worship" our jobs and our clients and make the mistake of seeing "market forces" as being independent from God?

Just as then there was a need to see the sun and the moon as mere tools of God, *"an axe in the hand of the chopper"* (after *Isaiah* 10:15), we should see the marketplace as nothing other than a Divine tool by which God—and God alone—provides our sustenance. Our business efforts do not bring us wealth; they merely make a "vessel" into which God may channel His blessings (*Rabbi Shalom Dov Baer Schneersohn of Lubavitch, 19th–20th century*).

Even the idol-worshipers receive their spiritual sustenance in this world from God's holiness, as the verse states, *"You sustain them all"* (*Nehemiah* 9:6). Through God's abundant patience, His kindness flows even to a place which conceals holiness.

The reason why they enjoy so much wealth and glory which they do not deserve, is that their spiritual sustenance comes from a very lofty Godly energy *which is concealed from them* and that is why they deny God and arrogantly perceive themselves as independent of Him (*Rabbi Shneur Zalman of Lyady, 18th century*).

6. To those who love Me and to those who keep My commandments. *"Those who keep My commandments"* refers to the majority of righteous people who maintain their faith. *"Those who love Me"* refers to the martyrs who let themselves be slain for the sanctification of God's name* (*Naḥmanides, 13th century*).

בַּיּוֹם הַשְּׁבִיעִי עַל־כֵּן בֵּרַךְ יְהֹוָה אֶת־יוֹם הַשַּׁבָּת וַיְקַדְּשֵׁהוּ: ס 12 כַּבֵּד אֶת־אָבִיךָ וְאֶת־אִמֶּךָ לְמַעַן יַאֲרִכוּן יָמֶיךָ עַל הָאֲדָמָה אֲשֶׁר־יְהֹוָה אֱלֹהֶיךָ נֹתֵן לָךְ: ס 13 לֹא תִּרְצָח ס לֹא תִּנְאָף ס לֹא תִּגְנֹב ס לֹא־תַעֲנֶה בְרֵעֲךָ עֵד שָׁקֶר: ס 14 לֹא תַחְמֹד בֵּית רֵעֶךָ ס לֹא־תַחְמֹד אֵשֶׁת רֵעֶךָ וְעַבְדּוֹ וַאֲמָתוֹ וְשׁוֹרוֹ וַחֲמֹרוֹ

nevertheless appropriate to honor your parents, in the spirit of the saying, *"Though the wine belongs to the owner, the thanks are given to the butler"* (*Babylonian Talmud, Bava Kamma* 92b). The butler may only be delivering the master's wine, but he had the choice whether or not to do so; consequently, he needs to be thanked too.

However, praising the sun, moon and stars, etc., is inappropriate since they possess no free will at all (*Rabbi Menahem Mendel Schneersohn of Lubavitch, 19th century*).

13. You shall not murder. The first five commandments correspond to the second five. *"I am God"* (v. 2), corresponds to *"You shall not murder,"* since they both comprise one, single principle. One who murders diminishes the Divine image, because man was created in the image of God (*Genesis 9:6; Zohar*).

You shall not murder. You shall not commit adultery. You shall not steal. With all these three commandments the word *lo'* ("*shall not*") has a cantillation note instructing it to be chanted in a drawn out fashion, making an interruption. This transforms the meaning of each phrase, suggesting that, in certain circumstances, acts resembling murder, adultery and theft *are* permissible.

"You shall not murder"—Without the interruptive note you would not be permitted to enact capital punishment and there would be no social order. But since the note is there, the act is both forbidden and permitted.

"You shall not commit adultery"—Without the interruptive note you would not be permitted to procreate or delight with your wife. But since the note is there, the act is both prohibited and permissible.

"You shall not steal"—Without the interruptive note you would not be permitted to make personal use of your teacher's wisdom; or feast at a Torah scholar's enlightened face. And a judge would be forbidden to expose a defendant's lies by questioning him deceptively. But since the note is there, the act is both prohibited and permissible.

But when it comes to *"You shall not bear false witness against your neighbor,"* there is no interruptive note. This act, then, is totally forbidden (*Zohar*).

14. You shall not covet. It *is* possible for you not to desire a beautiful object if you are wise, if you realize that you can only acquire that which is willed to you by God. Whatever God did not choose for you, you will be unable to attain by your own devices (*Rabbi Abraham ibn Ezra, 12th century*).

Food for thought

1. Why is envy self-destructive?

2. Can envy be reduced or eliminated through spiritual teachings and meditation?

3. For how long did your last purchase make you happy?

> He rested (so to speak) on the seventh day. Therefore, God blessed the Sabbath day (by causing a double portion of manna to fall on Friday) and sanctified it (by not bringing the manna on the Sabbath).

- ❖ ¹² "Honor your father and your mother, in order that your days will be lengthened on the land that God, your God, is giving you.
- ❖ ¹³ "You shall not murder.
- ❖ "You shall not commit adultery.
- ❖ "You shall not steal (people, i.e., kidnap).
- ❖ "You shall not bear false witness against your neighbor.
- ❖ ¹⁴ "You shall not covet your neighbor's house. You shall not covet your neighbor's wife, his manservant, his maidservant, his ox, his donkey, or whatever belongs to your neighbor."

emanation, *malchut* (sovereignty), which, being the weakest of all, is unable to empower us to elevate any "sparks."

So what happens is, on the Sabbath, all the six higher *sefirot* that were infused in our world during the six workdays, return and ascend to their original heavenly location.

On the weekday we DRAW Divine energy into the world, by performing work. On the Sabbath, we allow that energy to RETURN, by refraining from work.

What do these energies do on the Sabbath once they have been restored to their natural habitat? They couple with each other and reenergize themselves. That is why, on the Sabbath, physical coupling is encouraged, too, down here (*Babylonian Talmud, Ketubbot* 62b), because the lower is a reflection of the upper (*Rabbi Isaac Luria, 16th century*).

12. Honor your father and your mother. There are three partners in your formation: God, your father, and your mother. When you honor your father and your mother, God says, "I consider it as if I lived with them and they honored Me." By honoring your parents, you honor God (*Babylonian Talmud, Kiddushin* 30b).

A person should recognize and act kindly towards anyone who has been kind to him. He should take to heart that his father and mother are the cause of his presence in the world and therefore it is genuinely appropriate for him to honor them and assist them in whichever way he is able. For they brought him to the world and toiled greatly with his needs when he was a child.

By adopting this trait, he will come to recognize the kindness of God, who is the cause of both the person and all his ancestors back to the time of the first man (*Rabbi Aaron ha-Levi (Ḥinnukh) 13th century*).

The Torah prohibits lending importance to or honoring any intermediary. The sun gives you light and warmth, on which your very life depends, yet you are forbidden to honor it. Why, then, may you honor your parents?

Because your parents were given the *free choice* whether to have children or not and whether to act kindly towards you or not. Therefore, even though God is the source of all good, it is

שמות כ:יד-כ

וְכֹל אֲשֶׁר לְרֵעֶךָ׃ פ 15 [SEVENTH READING] וְכָל־הָעָם רֹאִים אֶת־הַקּוֹלֹת וְאֶת־הַלַּפִּידִם וְאֵת קוֹל הַשֹּׁפָר וְאֶת־הָהָר עָשֵׁן וַיַּרְא הָעָם וַיָּנֻעוּ וַיַּעַמְדוּ מֵרָחֹק׃ 16 וַיֹּאמְרוּ אֶל־מֹשֶׁה דַּבֵּר־אַתָּה עִמָּנוּ וְנִשְׁמָעָה וְאַל־יְדַבֵּר עִמָּנוּ אֱלֹהִים פֶּן־נָמוּת׃ 17 וַיֹּאמֶר מֹשֶׁה אֶל־הָעָם אַל־תִּירָאוּ כִּי לְבַעֲבוּר נַסּוֹת אֶתְכֶם בָּא הָאֱלֹהִים וּבַעֲבוּר תִּהְיֶה יִרְאָתוֹ עַל־פְּנֵיכֶם לְבִלְתִּי תֶחֱטָאוּ׃ 18 וַיַּעֲמֹד הָעָם מֵרָחֹק וּמֹשֶׁה נִגַּשׁ אֶל־הָעֲרָפֶל אֲשֶׁר־שָׁם הָאֱלֹהִים׃ ס 19 [MAFTIR] וַיֹּאמֶר יְהוָה אֶל־מֹשֶׁה כֹּה תֹאמַר אֶל־בְּנֵי יִשְׂרָאֵל אַתֶּם רְאִיתֶם כִּי מִן־הַשָּׁמַיִם דִּבַּרְתִּי עִמָּכֶם׃ 20 לֹא תַעֲשׂוּן אִתִּי

Because God's initial utterance was the contraction of His Divine Presence into all the holy letters of the Torah, both the Written and Oral Law. It also filled the whole world with His glory. Once this was achieved, it is now the task of man to uncover the Divine light that is implanted within the letters and the world.

So there had to be one full disclosure of the Divine, even if we did not fully appreciate it at the time, to sow the seeds of spirit into the world which we could then dedicate our lives to cultivating (*Rabbi Menahem Nahum Twersky of Chernobyl, 18th century*).

If the Jewish people had not requested from Moses, *"You speak to us,"* but had heard all the commandments directly from God, they would have totally lost their evil impulse and would never have sinned from then on. Through saying "You speak to us," they brought about all their own future sins. Hearing the commandments from the righteous Moses was a very great thing, but he was a mere mortal. To have heard them from God would have been a different experience altogether (*Rabbi Moses Ḥayyim Ephraim of Sudylkow, 18th century*).

18. The people remained a long way off. Scripture repeats this to contrast the people's deeds with Moses' deeds. These people stood from afar, while Moses drew near to the opaque darkness (*Rabbi Abraham ibn Ezra, 12th century*).

20-21. You should not make for yourselves gods of silver or gods of gold … You shall make for Me an altar (attached to) the earth. The very first command that was given after the Jewish people received the Torah was something negative: not to make idols of silver and gold. This was followed by

kabbalah bites

20:18 *"The people remained a long way off. Moses drew near to the fog, where God was."* When an obstacle, a "fog," obstructs your path of spiritual development, you should know that God is hiding within the obstacle. The fog scared the people away and they remained "a long way off," but Moses knew that God was within, so "he drew near."

[SEVENTH READING] ¹⁵ All the people could see the sounds (which God spoke), the torches, the sound of the ram's horn, and the smoking mountain. The people saw and they trembled and they withdrew backwards (the full length of the camp).

¹⁶ They said to Moses, "You speak to us, and we will listen; but do not let God speak to us, lest we die!"

¹⁷ Moses said to the people, "Fear not, for God has come in order to promote your (reputation throughout the world), and in order that (having seen) His awe (you will know there is no other than Him), so that you shall not sin."

¹⁸ The people remained a long way off. Moses drew near (first through the darkness, then to the cloud, and deeper still,) to the fog, where God was.

Additional Commandments Are Given

[MAFTIR] ¹⁹ God said to Moses, "Say the following to the children of Israel:

You have seen that from the skies I have spoken with you (and I have shown My fire and might down on earth).

- ²⁰ You shall not make images of any (of My spiritual servants) that are with Me.

- (You should not make the cherubim) from silver, (thus rendering them as false) gods. (Rather, they must be made of gold.)

- (You should not make more than two cherubim, and if you do I will consider them as false) gods of gold.

Alternatively, one might argue that this commandment *is* beyond your immediate control. *"You shall not covet"* is not a command but a *promise:* If you carefully observe the first nine commandments you are assured by the Torah that you will not covet (*Rabbi Jehiel Mikhel of Zloczow, 18th century*).

15. All the people could see the sounds. Every person saw the root of his own life-force and, with his own eyes, he saw the Godly soul that we all possess. They didn't need to *believe* in the commandments because they could actually "see the sounds." That's the way it is when God speaks (*Rabbi Judah Aryeh Leib Alter of Gur, 19th century*).

The people saw and they trembled and they withdrew backwards. It is possible for a man to witness everything, to tremble and to be shocked, yet he draws backwards and stands at a distance (*Rabbi Menahem Mendel Morgensztern of Kotsk, 19th century*).

16. You speak to us, and we will listen; but do not let God speak to us, lest we die! Afterwards God spoke through Moses, filtering His words through Moses' voice in order to be compatible with mortals.

But God surely knew that the people would not be able to receive the Torah directly from Him unless His words would be filtered through Moses, so why did He say them first in an incompatible way?

שמות כ:כ-כג — יתרו

אֱלֹהֵי כֶסֶף וֵאלֹהֵי זָהָב לֹא תַעֲשׂוּ לָכֶם: 21 מִזְבַּח אֲדָמָה תַּעֲשֶׂה־לִּי וְזָבַחְתָּ עָלָיו אֶת־עֹלֹתֶיךָ וְאֶת־שְׁלָמֶיךָ אֶת־צֹאנְךָ וְאֶת־בְּקָרֶךָ בְּכָל־הַמָּקוֹם אֲשֶׁר אַזְכִּיר אֶת־שְׁמִי אָבוֹא אֵלֶיךָ וּבֵרַכְתִּיךָ: 22 וְאִם־מִזְבַּח אֲבָנִים תַּעֲשֶׂה־לִּי לֹא־תִבְנֶה אֶתְהֶן גָּזִית כִּי חַרְבְּךָ הֵנַפְתָּ עָלֶיהָ וַתְּחַלְלֶהָ: 23 וְלֹא־תַעֲלֶה בְמַעֲלֹת עַל־מִזְבְּחִי אֲשֶׁר לֹא־תִגָּלֶה עֶרְוָתְךָ עָלָיו: פ פ פ

ע"ב פסוקים, יונד"ב סימן.

spiritual vitamin

" After their liberation from enslavement in Egypt, the Jewish people reached, in a comparatively very short time, the highest spiritual level which is humanly possible to attain, making them all, men, women and children, fit for Divine revelation at Mount Sinai. You, too, can rise from the lowest depths to the loftiest spiritual heights in a comparatively short time, provided you have the sincere will and desire to do so. "

- You should not make for yourselves (a replica of the cherubim in your own synagogues).
- ²¹ You shall make for Me an altar (attached to) the earth (alternatively: filled with earth), and you shall slaughter near it your burnt-offerings and your peace-offerings, (which come from) your sheep and your cattle.
- Wherever I allow My name to be mentioned (i.e. only in the Holy Temple, by the priests), I will come to you and bless you.
- ²² When you make for Me an altar of stones, you shall not build them of cut stones, lest you wield your sword upon it and desecrate it (by using an object of death to form the altar, which is an object of life).
- ²³ (When you build a ramp) to My altar, do not (make it) ascend with steps, so that it will not (look as if) your nakedness is exposed upon it."

The *Haftarah* for *Yitro* is on page 1328.

the command to construct the earthen altar which, while being a positive commandment, also has a negative connotation, since "earth" is something which everybody tramples upon. This teaches you that the first stage of spiritual growth must be "negative." You need to release your personal desires and whims if you are to become close to God. This acts as a spiritual "vacuum" which allows the holiness of the Torah to penetrate (*Rabbi Menahem Mendel Schneerson, 20th century*).

23. To My altar, do not ascend with steps. All the hearts of Israel are "My altar." *To My altar, do not ascend.* Do not think you are greater than any other soul in Israel! (*Rabbi Mordecai Joseph Leiner of Izbica, 19th century*).

Mishpatim begins with the word "And," **connecting** it with the previous Torah portion, the **revelation at Sinai.** Even these laws, which are **rationally dictated** by the human mind, ought to be **observed** because they are **God's commands.** It is only that God also wanted these commands to be **understood by man.**

MISHPATIM
משפטים

LAWS OF SLAVES	21:1–11
LAWS OF ASSAULT AND KIDNAPPING	21:12–27
LAWS OF NEGLIGENCE AND THEFT	21:28 – 22:14
ILLICIT AND IDOLATROUS BEHAVIOR	22:15–19
HELPING THE UNFORTUNATE	22:20–27
AGRICULTURAL OFFERINGS	22:28–30
JUDICIAL LAWS AND AVOIDING PREJUDICE	23:1–9
SABBATH; FESTIVALS; MENTIONING IDOLS	23:10–19
CONQUEST OF THE LAND	23:20–33
THE PEOPLE ENTER COVENANT WITH GOD	24:1–11
MOSES ASCENDS MOUNTAIN FOR FORTY DAYS	24:12–18

NAME
Mishpatim

MEANING
"Laws"

LINES IN TORAH SCROLL
185

PARASHIYYOT
6 open; 27 closed

VERSES
118

WORDS
1462

LETTERS
5313

DATE
4 *Sivan* – 17 *Tammuz*, 2448

LOCATION
Mount Sinai

KEY PEOPLE
Moses, Joshua

MITZVOT
23 positive;
30 prohibitions

CHARACTER PROFILE

NAME
Hur

PARENTS
Caleb and Miriam

GRANDFATHERS
Amram, Jephunneh

CHILD
Uri

DESCENDANTS
Bezalel

PLACE OF DEATH
Beside Mount Sinai

ACHIEVEMENTS
Was a prophet; in charge of judicial matters when Moses went up Mount Sinai to receive the tablets; was murdered for his opposition to the Golden Calf; ranks among the martyred prophets of Israel and the seven righteous men of the world

KNOWN FOR
Supporting Moses' left hand during the war with Amalek

NEGLIGENCE

The Torah details many laws of negligence. At all times you must be conscious of your actions and what could result from them (21:33,34).

COMPASSION

Although we ought to extend compassion to everyone, the Torah stresses our obligation to be mindful of the feelings of widows and orphans. Their loss and constant pain makes any additional hardship harder to bear (22:21).

HEARSAY

The Torah warns judges, "Do not listen to a false report." Only eyewitness testimony may decide a person's fate. Believing rumors about others can destroy friendships and even lives. When hearing something negative about another, make sure you verify the information before you act on it (23:1).

משפטים — שמות כא:א-ו

כא 1 וְאֵ֨לֶּה֙ הַמִּשְׁפָּטִ֔ים אֲשֶׁ֥ר תָּשִׂ֖ים לִפְנֵיהֶֽם: 2 כִּ֤י תִקְנֶה֙ עֶ֣בֶד עִבְרִ֔י שֵׁ֥שׁ שָׁנִ֖ים יַעֲבֹ֑ד וּבַ֨שְּׁבִעִ֔ת יֵצֵ֥א לַֽחָפְשִׁ֖י חִנָּֽם: 3 אִם־בְּגַפּ֥וֹ יָבֹ֖א בְּגַפּ֣וֹ יֵצֵ֑א אִם־בַּ֤עַל אִשָּׁה֙ ה֔וּא וְיָצְאָ֥ה אִשְׁתּ֖וֹ עִמּֽוֹ: 4 אִם־אֲדֹנָיו֙ יִתֶּן־ל֣וֹ אִשָּׁ֔ה וְיָלְדָה־ל֥וֹ בָנִ֖ים א֣וֹ בָנ֑וֹת הָאִשָּׁ֣ה וִילָדֶ֗יהָ תִּהְיֶה֙ לַֽאדֹנֶ֔יהָ וְה֖וּא יֵצֵ֥א בְגַפּֽוֹ: 5 וְאִם־אָמֹ֤ר יֹאמַר֙ הָעֶ֔בֶד אָהַ֨בְתִּי֙ אֶת־אֲדֹנִ֔י אֶת־אִשְׁתִּ֖י וְאֶת־בָּנָ֑י לֹ֥א אֵצֵ֖א חָפְשִֽׁי: 6 וְהִגִּישׁ֤וֹ אֲדֹנָיו֙ אֶל־הָ֣אֱלֹהִ֔ים וְהִגִּישׁוֹ֙ אֶל־הַדֶּ֔לֶת א֖וֹ אֶל־הַמְּזוּזָ֑ה

The highest level of Divine service is symbolized by the *Hebrew maidservant*. One of the goals of the Hebrew maidservant is her eventual marriage, unity with a spouse (*Maimonides, 12th century*). Similarly, when the soul is sent on its earthly journey into a body, the ultimate goal is a total unity (marriage) with God. Thus, the Hebrew maidservant represents the person whose desire for worldly pleasures has been completely sublimated and transformed to desire only Godliness (*Rabbi Menahem Mendel Schneerson, 20th century*).

6. Standing (the slave) next to a door (which is attached to) a doorpost. The piercing was done against the doorpost because of its significant role in the exodus from Egypt: *"God will pass through to strike the Egyptians, and He will see the blood that is on the lintel and the two doorposts. God will skip over the entrance and He will not permit the force of destruction to enter your houses"* (above, 12:23). God used the doorposts as witnesses to freeing us from slavery. At that time, He declared that *"the children of Israel are slaves to Me"* (*Leviticus* 25:55). They are God's slaves, not the slaves of slaves. Yet this person defied this declaration witnessed by the doorpost and acquired a different master for himself. Therefore, the piercing was done in the presence of the doorpost (*Babylonian Talmud, Kiddushin* 22b).

The piercing was not done as soon as he committed the offense of becoming a slave, since a man is not given two punishments at once—the slave labor is considered punishment enough. However, when the seventh year arrives and he does not want to be set free, claiming, *"I love my master,"* he clearly does not consider his enslavement to have been a punishment. Consequently, a second punishment was carried out, *"and his master shall pierce his right ear with a pointed tool"* (*Rabbi Ephraim of Luntshits, 16th–17th century*).

kabbalah bites

21:1 "A Hebrew slave (who is sold … because he was a thief)." What an anticlimax! After the awesomeness of the Sinaitic event *we now turn to the story of a thief who got caught?*

There is, however, a profound lesson here. After every epiphany, those moments of spiritual elation where you feel connected and inspired, there is the danger of an immediate and substantial regression as soon as the moment passes. After feeling God's presence, His subsequent absence is all the more marked. So when inspiration passes, leaving you in a vacuum, you might be tempted like the thief, who acts selfishly because he thinks no one is watching.

Therefore, the first spiritual malady that the Torah addresses after the revelation at Sinai is the thief who got caught.

exodus 21:1–6 — mishpatim

parashat mishpatim

21 The Laws of Slaves

¹ And these are the laws that you should set before them:

- ² If you buy a Hebrew slave (who is sold into slavery by the court because he could not repay his theft), he shall work for six years. But, in the seventh year, he is to be released without liability.

- ³ If he was unmarried when he entered (service, he may not marry a non-Jewish slave-woman during his period of service). He shall be released unmarried.

- If he is married to a (Jewish) woman (when he enters service, the master must provide food for the wife and children until) he is released with his wife.

- ⁴ If his master gives him a (non-Jewish slave-woman for a) wife, and she bears him sons or daughters, then (when it is time to dismiss the Hebrew slave,) the woman and her children will remain her master's property, and he is dismissed alone.

- ⁵ If the slave says, "I love my master, my (non-Jewish) wife, and my children. I will not go free," ⁶ his master shall bring him to the judges (of the Jewish court that sold him as a slave in the first place). Standing (the slave) next to a door (which is attached to) a doorpost, his master shall pierce his (right) ear with a pointed tool. He must then serve (his master) "forever," (i.e. until the Jubilee year).

21:1 These are the laws that you should set before them. The phrase *"set before them"* implies that we must set the Divine laws before ourselves. God's laws take precedence over our personal needs; we must set aside ourselves—our wants and desires—to fulfil these laws (*Rabbi Simḥah Bunem of Przysucha, 18th–19th century*).

2. If you buy a Hebrew slave. Why did the Torah record the laws pertaining to slaves before all other civil laws?

There is nothing in the world more difficult for a human being to bear than to be under the control of another human being. The Torah therefore began with the law of slaves: the slave is in the most disheartening of circumstances, so his needs are addressed first (*Rabbi Abraham ibn Ezra, 12th century*).

The slave's freedom is reminiscent of both the exodus from Egypt and the Sabbath, since the slave works for six years and rests on the seventh. Since this law alludes to matters of paramount religious importance, it was recorded first (*Nahmanides, 13th century*).

The *Zohar* teaches that the laws of servitude are symbolic of the descent of the soul into the body:

The *Canaanite slave* refers to the initial stages of man's worship, when he must overcome the influence of the animalistic impulse that lusts for worldly pleasures. This is accomplished with fear of the Master and acceptance of His yoke. The person coerces his animalistic impulse to conform to the wishes of the Master, at least on the practical level.

The *Hebrew slave* has reached a higher level. In him, the Divine attributes of his Godly soul illuminate his animal side, influencing it to feel some desire for Godliness. Nevertheless, the worldly desires of the animal instinct have not been completely quieted or subdued.

משפטים   שמות כא:ו-כ

וְרָצַע אֲדֹנָיו אֶת־אָזְנוֹ בַּמַּרְצֵעַ וַעֲבָדוֹ לְעֹלָם: ס 7 וְכִי־יִמְכֹּר אִישׁ אֶת־בִּתּוֹ לְאָמָה לֹא תֵצֵא כְּצֵאת הָעֲבָדִים: 8 אִם־רָעָה בְּעֵינֵי אֲדֹנֶיהָ אֲשֶׁר [לֹא כ׳] לוֹ יְעָדָהּ וְהֶפְדָּהּ לְעַם נָכְרִי לֹא־יִמְשֹׁל לְמָכְרָהּ בְּבִגְדוֹ־בָהּ: 9 וְאִם־לִבְנוֹ יִיעָדֶנָּה כְּמִשְׁפַּט הַבָּנוֹת יַעֲשֶׂה־לָּהּ: 10 אִם־אַחֶרֶת יִקַּח־לוֹ שְׁאֵרָהּ כְּסוּתָהּ וְעֹנָתָהּ לֹא יִגְרָע: 11 וְאִם־שְׁלָשׁ־אֵלֶּה לֹא יַעֲשֶׂה לָהּ וְיָצְאָה חִנָּם אֵין כָּסֶף: ס 12 מַכֵּה אִישׁ וָמֵת מוֹת יוּמָת: 13 וַאֲשֶׁר לֹא צָדָה וְהָאֱלֹהִים אִנָּה לְיָדוֹ וְשַׂמְתִּי לְךָ מָקוֹם אֲשֶׁר יָנוּס שָׁמָּה: ס 14 וְכִי־יָזִד אִישׁ עַל־רֵעֵהוּ לְהָרְגוֹ בְעָרְמָה מֵעִם מִזְבְּחִי תִּקָּחֶנּוּ לָמוּת: ס 15 וּמַכֵּה אָבִיו וְאִמּוֹ מוֹת יוּמָת: ס 16 וְגֹנֵב אִישׁ וּמְכָרוֹ וְנִמְצָא בְיָדוֹ מוֹת יוּמָת: ס 17 וּמְקַלֵּל אָבִיו וְאִמּוֹ מוֹת יוּמָת: ס 18 וְכִי־יְרִיבֻן אֲנָשִׁים וְהִכָּה־אִישׁ אֶת־רֵעֵהוּ בְּאֶבֶן אוֹ בְאֶגְרֹף וְלֹא יָמוּת וְנָפַל לְמִשְׁכָּב: 19 אִם־יָקוּם וְהִתְהַלֵּךְ בַּחוּץ עַל־מִשְׁעַנְתּוֹ וְנִקָּה הַמַּכֶּה רַק שִׁבְתּוֹ יִתֵּן וְרַפֹּא יְרַפֵּא: ס [SECOND READING] 20 וְכִי־יַכֶּה אִישׁ אֶת־עַבְדּוֹ אוֹ אֶת־אֲמָתוֹ בַּשֵּׁבֶט וּמֵת

His master shall pierce his (right) ear. Why was the ear chosen out of all the organs of the body to be pierced? The ear that heard on Mount Sinai, *"You shall not steal"* (above, 20:13), and then went and stole, shall be pierced. If the slave sold himself into servitude voluntarily (and not due to theft), the reason that the ear is pierced is because it is the ear that heard, *"For the children of Israel are slaves to Me"* (Leviticus 25:55), and nevertheless went and acquired a master for himself (*Rashi, 11th century*).

16. If a person kidnaps. Why is the prohibition of kidnapping placed in between the prohibitions of hitting and cursing parents (v. 15 and 17)? Generally speaking, it is children who are kidnapped and not adults. The children then grow up away from their parents and do not recognize them or form a close relationship with them. This presents the possibility of a child cursing or hurting his parent, which otherwise would be unthinkable (*Rabbi Saadiah b. Joseph Gaon, 10th century*).

19. He must (pay all) his medical (fees). If God chooses to strike a person with disease, on what basis may the physician attempt to reverse God's decree and cure him?

The Sages find the answer in this verse. *"He must (pay all) his medical (fees),"* teaches us that a physician is permitted to administer treatment (*Babylonian Talmud, Bava Kamma 85a*).

Food for thought

1. How do you view the connection between the ritual and ethical commandments?

2. Do you find the ritual laws more religiously appealing than the ethical ones?

3. Why do we sometimes fail to perceive ethical actions as "religious"?

exodus 21:7-20 — mishpatim

- ⁷ If a man sells his daughter as a (child) maidservant, she shall not be freed the same way that (non-Jewish) male slaves are released, (i.e. through the loss of a tooth or an eye. Rather she must work for six years, or until the Jubilee year, or until she shows signs of puberty—whichever comes first).

- ⁸ If she is displeasing to her master (and he decides) not to designate her for himself (as a future wife, an act which the Torah recommends), then he must let her be redeemed. If he does betray her (by not designating her as his future wife), he does not have the right to sell her to another (person).

- ⁹ If (the master chooses instead to) designate her for his son, he must treat her like any other girl (providing for her food, clothing and marital relations).

- ¹⁰ If (he keeps the maidservant as a wife and) then he takes another wife for himself, he may not diminish (from the maidservant) her sustenance, her clothing, or her times (of marital relations).

- ¹¹ If he does not do these three things (designating her for himself, or for his son, or redeeming her), she shall be released without liability or payment (if she shows signs of puberty).

Laws of Assault and Kidnapping

- ¹² A person who strikes another man is (only) put to death if (the victim) dies.

- ¹³ If a person did not ambush (another, and he did not intend to kill him,) but God orchestrated it to happen to him, then I will make a place for you where he can find refuge.

- ¹⁴ (Only) if a man plots deliberately against (another Jew) to kill him (and his strike is intended to kill), should he be put to death. (This applies even to a priest who wishes to serve) on My altar.

- ¹⁵ If a person strikes his father (or) his mother, (causing a bruise,) he must be put to death (through strangulation).

- ¹⁶ If a person kidnaps a man, and (witnesses) found him in his possession (before he was sold,) he shall be put to death (by strangulation).

- ¹⁷ A person who curses his father or mother shall be put to death (through stoning).

- ¹⁸ If two men quarrel, and one strikes the other with a stone or with a fist, and he does not die but is confined to his bed, ¹⁹ (then the aggressor is put in jail, until it is determined if the victim will survive). If he gets up and walks about outside unaided, then the aggressor is acquitted. He need only give compensation for (the victim's) inability to work, and he must (pay all) his medical (fees).

- [SECOND READING] ²⁰ If a man strikes his male or female (non-Jewish) slave with a rod (that is capable of inflicting a fatal wound), and (the slave) dies under his hand (within 24 hours, the slave's death) must be avenged (i.e. the killer is executed by the

שמות כא:כ-לג משפטים

תַּחַת יָדוֹ נָקֹם יִנָּקֵם: 21 אַךְ אִם־יוֹם אוֹ יוֹמַיִם יַעֲמֹד לֹא יֻקַּם כִּי כַסְפּוֹ הוּא: ס 22 וְכִי־יִנָּצוּ אֲנָשִׁים וְנָגְפוּ אִשָּׁה הָרָה וְיָצְאוּ יְלָדֶיהָ וְלֹא יִהְיֶה אָסוֹן עָנוֹשׁ יֵעָנֵשׁ כַּאֲשֶׁר יָשִׁית עָלָיו בַּעַל הָאִשָּׁה וְנָתַן בִּפְלִלִים: 23 וְאִם־אָסוֹן יִהְיֶה וְנָתַתָּה נֶפֶשׁ תַּחַת נָפֶשׁ: 24 עַיִן תַּחַת עַיִן שֵׁן תַּחַת שֵׁן יָד תַּחַת יָד רֶגֶל תַּחַת רָגֶל: 25 כְּוִיָּה תַּחַת כְּוִיָּה פֶּצַע תַּחַת פָּצַע חַבּוּרָה תַּחַת חַבּוּרָה: ס 26 וְכִי־יַכֶּה אִישׁ אֶת־עֵין עַבְדּוֹ אוֹ־אֶת־עֵין אֲמָתוֹ וְשִׁחֲתָהּ לַחָפְשִׁי יְשַׁלְּחֶנּוּ תַּחַת עֵינוֹ: 27 וְאִם־שֵׁן עַבְדּוֹ אוֹ־שֵׁן אֲמָתוֹ יַפִּיל לַחָפְשִׁי יְשַׁלְּחֶנּוּ תַּחַת שִׁנּוֹ: פ 28 וְכִי־יִגַּח שׁוֹר אֶת־אִישׁ אוֹ אֶת־אִשָּׁה וָמֵת סָקוֹל יִסָּקֵל הַשּׁוֹר וְלֹא יֵאָכֵל אֶת־בְּשָׂרוֹ וּבַעַל הַשּׁוֹר נָקִי: 29 וְאִם שׁוֹר נַגָּח הוּא מִתְּמֹל שִׁלְשֹׁם וְהוּעַד בִּבְעָלָיו וְלֹא יִשְׁמְרֶנּוּ וְהֵמִית אִישׁ אוֹ אִשָּׁה הַשּׁוֹר יִסָּקֵל וְגַם־בְּעָלָיו יוּמָת: 30 אִם־כֹּפֶר יוּשַׁת עָלָיו וְנָתַן פִּדְיֹן נַפְשׁוֹ כְּכֹל אֲשֶׁר־יוּשַׁת עָלָיו: 31 אוֹ־בֵן יִגָּח אוֹ־בַת יִגָּח כַּמִּשְׁפָּט הַזֶּה יֵעָשֶׂה לּוֹ: 32 אִם־עֶבֶד יִגַּח הַשּׁוֹר אוֹ אָמָה כֶּסֶף | שְׁלֹשִׁים שְׁקָלִים יִתֵּן לַאדֹנָיו וְהַשּׁוֹר יִסָּקֵל: ס 33 וְכִי־יִפְתַּח אִישׁ בּוֹר אוֹ כִּי־יִכְרֶה אִישׁ בֹּר וְלֹא יְכַסֶּנּוּ וְנָפַל־שָׁמָּה שּׁוֹר אוֹ חֲמוֹר:

kabbalah bites

21:24 *"An eye for an eye."* According to the Oral Tradition this means that if a person injures an eye, he must give compensation to *the value* of an eye.

But why does the Torah appear to mislead us? Read at face value, the verse seems to suggest that a victim may seek vengeance and gouge his aggressor's eye. Why could the Written Law not have been more clear?

Because our verse wishes to teach us a powerful secret: *Man truly is created in the image of God.*

Every human limb teaches us something about the Divine. So it is really the case that "an eye is for an eye"—our eye is a reflection of God's.

sword). ²¹ However, if (the slave) survives for a day or two (i.e. 24 hours), he shall not be avenged, because he is his (master's) property.

- ❖ ²² If two men quarrel (with each other) and (accidentally) hit a pregnant woman, and she miscarries, but (the woman) does not suffer fatal injury, (the assailant) must (pay) a penalty. When the woman's husband (takes him to court and) makes demands of him, then he must give (compensation) according to the judges' orders.

- ❖ ²³ If there is a fatal injury (to the woman), you shall give a life for a life (alternatively: full compensation for her life).

- ❖ ²⁴ (Compensation must be paid: The value of) an eye for an eye (injury, the value of) a tooth for a tooth (injury, the value of) a hand for a hand (injury, and the value of) a foot for a foot (injury).

- ❖ ²⁵ (Compensation must be paid for pain suffered in the following cases: The value of) a burn for a burn, (the value of) a wound for a wound, (plus compensation for loss of income, healing, embarrassment where appropriate, and the value of) a bruise for a bruise.

- ❖ ²⁶ If a man strikes the eye of his male (non-Jewish) slave or the eye of his female (non-Jewish) slave and destroys it, he shall set him free in compensation for his eye. ²⁷ If he knocks out the tooth of his male (non-Jewish) slave or the tooth of his female (non-Jewish) slave, he shall set him free in return for his tooth (etc.).

Laws of Negligence and Theft

- ❖ ²⁸ If an ox (or any other animal) gores and kills a man or a woman, the ox must be stoned. (After the ox is sentenced, even if it is slaughtered, and not stoned,) its flesh may not be eaten (nor may benefit be derived from it). The owner of the ox is innocent.

- ❖ ²⁹ If it is a habitually goring ox, both yesterday and the day before (i.e. on three occasions), and its owner had been warned (in the presence of witnesses), but he did not guard (the ox properly) and it kills a man or a woman, then the ox shall be stoned.

- ❖ Also, its owner is (punished) with death (through the hands of heaven). ³⁰ (Therefore,) an atonement fine must be imposed upon him. He must give whatever is assessed against him, in order to redeem his soul. ³¹ This law is (also) applied to (a person whose animal) gores a young boy or a young girl.

- ❖ ³² If an ox gores a (non-Jewish) male slave or female slave, (the owner of the ox) must give (a fixed penalty) of thirty shekels of silver to (the slave's) master. The bull is stoned.

- ❖ ³³ If a person opens (the cover of) a pit, or if a person digs (an existing) pit (making it larger) and does not cover it, and then an ox or a donkey (or any other animal)

שמות כא:לד - כב:ו משפטים

34 בַּעַל הַבּוֹר יְשַׁלֵּם כֶּסֶף יָשִׁיב לִבְעָלָיו וְהַמֵּת יִהְיֶה־לּוֹ: ס 35 וְכִי־יִגֹּף שׁוֹר־אִישׁ אֶת־שׁוֹר רֵעֵהוּ וָמֵת וּמָכְרוּ אֶת־הַשּׁוֹר הַחַי וְחָצוּ אֶת־כַּסְפּוֹ וְגַם אֶת־הַמֵּת יֶחֱצוּן: 36 אוֹ נוֹדַע כִּי שׁוֹר נַגָּח הוּא מִתְּמוֹל שִׁלְשֹׁם וְלֹא יִשְׁמְרֶנּוּ בְּעָלָיו שַׁלֵּם יְשַׁלֵּם שׁוֹר תַּחַת הַשּׁוֹר וְהַמֵּת יִהְיֶה־לּוֹ: ס 37 כִּי יִגְנֹב־אִישׁ שׁוֹר אוֹ־שֶׂה וּטְבָחוֹ אוֹ מְכָרוֹ חֲמִשָּׁה בָקָר יְשַׁלֵּם תַּחַת הַשּׁוֹר וְאַרְבַּע־צֹאן תַּחַת הַשֶּׂה:

כב

1 אִם־בַּמַּחְתֶּרֶת יִמָּצֵא הַגַּנָּב וְהֻכָּה וָמֵת אֵין לוֹ דָּמִים: 2 אִם־זָרְחָה הַשֶּׁמֶשׁ עָלָיו דָּמִים לוֹ שַׁלֵּם יְשַׁלֵּם אִם־אֵין לוֹ וְנִמְכַּר בִּגְנֵבָתוֹ: 3 אִם־הִמָּצֵא תִמָּצֵא בְיָדוֹ הַגְּנֵבָה מִשּׁוֹר עַד־חֲמוֹר עַד־שֶׂה חַיִּים שְׁנַיִם יְשַׁלֵּם: ס [THIRD READING] 4 כִּי יַבְעֶר־אִישׁ שָׂדֶה אוֹ־כֶרֶם וְשִׁלַּח אֶת־בְּעִירֹה וּבִעֵר בִּשְׂדֵה אַחֵר מֵיטַב שָׂדֵהוּ וּמֵיטַב כַּרְמוֹ יְשַׁלֵּם: ס 5 כִּי־תֵצֵא אֵשׁ וּמָצְאָה קֹצִים וְנֶאֱכַל גָּדִישׁ אוֹ הַקָּמָה אוֹ הַשָּׂדֶה שַׁלֵּם יְשַׁלֵּם הַמַּבְעִר אֶת־הַבְּעֵרָה: ס 6 כִּי־יִתֵּן אִישׁ אֶל־רֵעֵהוּ כֶּסֶף אוֹ־כֵלִים לִשְׁמֹר וְגֻנַּב מִבֵּית הָאִישׁ אִם־יִמָּצֵא

double." He gives back what he has taken, and adds to it the exact same amount of his own property, so that, besides restoring what he took, he also ends up losing what he intended to steal (*Maimonides, 12th century*).

6-14. If a person gives his friend money or articles for safekeeping. The Torah describes four guardians: the unpaid guardian (v. 6-8), the borrower (v. 13-14), the paid guardian (v. 9-10), and

kabbalah bites

21:37 The generation that left Egypt had experienced three prior incarnations:

1. The generation of the Flood (see *Genesis* 6:12);
2. The generation of Dispersion (ibid. 11:5);
3. The inhabitants of Sodom (ibid. 13:13).

Generally speaking, all this had achieved its *tikkun* (spiritual healing) through the Egyptian exile, but a tiny residue of spiritual filth remained from each incarnation. Now, the children of Israel were given the laws of theft to achieve full *tikkun* for their first incarnation, the generation of the Flood, since the Flood was decreed by God in response to the sin of theft (see *Genesis* 6:11; for the other *tikkunim*, see above, 15:25; 18:21).

falls into it, ³⁴ the one responsible for the pit must pay (compensation, either) giving money (or any produce of value) to its owner. The dead (animal) belongs to (its original owner).

- ³⁵ If a man's ox strikes his fellow's ox and it dies, (the owner of the attacking ox pays half the value of the loss, up to the value of the attacking ox. Thus if both oxen are of equal value) they (could settle) by selling the live bull and dividing the money received for it, and dividing the (value of the) carcass.

- ³⁶ Alternatively, if it was known to be a habitually goring ox, since yesterday and the day before (i.e. it gored three times), and its owner does not watch it, he must pay (full compensation) an ox for an ox. The dead (animal) belongs to (its original owner).

- ³⁷ If a man steals an ox or a lamb and slaughters it or sells it, he must repay five oxen for the ox or four sheep for the lamb. (This only applies to oxen and sheep.)

22

- ¹ If (a person) strikes and kills a thief who is discovered tunneling (into his house) it is not considered bloodshed (i.e. he is not guilty of murder). ² If the sun shone upon him (i.e. it is obvious that the thief did not intend to kill) it is considered bloodshed.

- (The thief) must pay (full compensation for what he stole). If he has no money, he shall be sold (to slavery) for his theft.

- ³ If the stolen article is found in his possession, whether a live ox, a donkey, or a lamb (or any other object) he must pay double.

- [THIRD READING] ⁴ If a man leads his animal into a field or a vineyard, whether he lets his animal loose (and it tramples crops) or it eats in another's field, he must pay (compensation with land from) the best of his field or the best of his vineyard.

- ⁵ If a fire goes forth (even by itself) and (spreads through) thorns to destroy a stack of grain or standing grain, or (it scorched a plowed) field, (requiring it to be plowed again) the one who ignited the fire must pay (compensation, even though he lit the fire in his own property).

The Four Guardians

- ⁶ If a person gives his friend money or articles for safekeeping (and does not pay him for his services) and they are stolen from the man's house, then if the thief is found, he must pay twofold (to the owner).

22:3 If the stolen article is found in his possession ... he must pay double. The punishments for crimes against another person generally follow the principle of reciprocity: If a man causes damage, he must suffer personally. In our case, if someone steals the property of another, he must lose a corresponding amount of his own property, as the verse states, *"he must pay*

שמות כב:ו-יט משפטים

הַגַּנָּב יְשַׁלֵּם שְׁנָיִם: 7 אִם־לֹא יִמָּצֵא הַגַּנָּב וְנִקְרַב בַּעַל־הַבַּיִת אֶל־הָאֱלֹהִים אִם־לֹא שָׁלַח יָדוֹ בִּמְלֶאכֶת רֵעֵהוּ: 8 עַל־כָּל־דְּבַר־פֶּשַׁע עַל־שׁוֹר עַל־חֲמוֹר עַל־שֶׂה עַל־שַׂלְמָה עַל־כָּל־אֲבֵדָה אֲשֶׁר יֹאמַר כִּי־הוּא זֶה עַד הָאֱלֹהִים יָבֹא דְּבַר־שְׁנֵיהֶם אֲשֶׁר יַרְשִׁיעֻן אֱלֹהִים יְשַׁלֵּם שְׁנַיִם לְרֵעֵהוּ: ס 9 כִּי־יִתֵּן אִישׁ אֶל־רֵעֵהוּ חֲמוֹר אוֹ־שׁוֹר אוֹ־שֶׂה וְכָל־בְּהֵמָה לִשְׁמֹר וּמֵת אוֹ־נִשְׁבַּר אוֹ־נִשְׁבָּה אֵין רֹאֶה: 10 שְׁבֻעַת יְהוָה תִּהְיֶה בֵּין שְׁנֵיהֶם אִם־לֹא שָׁלַח יָדוֹ בִּמְלֶאכֶת רֵעֵהוּ וְלָקַח בְּעָלָיו וְלֹא יְשַׁלֵּם: 11 וְאִם־גָּנֹב יִגָּנֵב מֵעִמּוֹ יְשַׁלֵּם לִבְעָלָיו: 12 אִם־טָרֹף יִטָּרֵף יְבִאֵהוּ עֵד הַטְּרֵפָה לֹא יְשַׁלֵּם: פ 13 וְכִי־יִשְׁאַל אִישׁ מֵעִם רֵעֵהוּ וְנִשְׁבַּר אוֹ־מֵת בְּעָלָיו אֵין־עִמּוֹ שַׁלֵּם יְשַׁלֵּם: 14 אִם־בְּעָלָיו עִמּוֹ לֹא יְשַׁלֵּם אִם־שָׂכִיר הוּא בָּא בִּשְׂכָרוֹ: ס 15 וְכִי־יְפַתֶּה אִישׁ בְּתוּלָה אֲשֶׁר לֹא־אֹרָשָׂה וְשָׁכַב עִמָּהּ מָהֹר יִמְהָרֶנָּה לּוֹ לְאִשָּׁה: 16 אִם־מָאֵן יְמָאֵן אָבִיהָ לְתִתָּהּ לוֹ כֶּסֶף יִשְׁקֹל כְּמֹהַר הַבְּתוּלֹת: ס 17 מְכַשֵּׁפָה לֹא תְחַיֶּה: 18 כָּל־שֹׁכֵב עִם־בְּהֵמָה מוֹת יוּמָת: 19 זֹבֵחַ לָאֱלֹהִים יָחֳרָם בִּלְתִּי לַיהוָה לְבַדּוֹ:

The *unpaid guardian* represents the man who feels that he was created only to serve God. He sees his life and possessions as Divine "property" which has been placed in his trust, and he does not feel that God owes him anything in "compensation" for his efforts.

The *borrower* benefits from what he borrows, and the owner enjoys no benefit. This represents the man who seeks self-fulfillment alone. He does not feel that he owes anything for the use of life's blessings, even though he may acknowledge who the ultimate owner is.

The *renter* resembles the borrower in that he prioritizes the fulfillment and enhancement of self, but nevertheless, he feels that he ought to earn this privilege by "also" serving his Creator.

The *paid guardian* is like the unpaid guardian in that he sees the fulfillment of God's will as the ultimate purpose of life. He differs only in that he reserves for himself a level of self-interest, feeling that he also deserves some independence in return for his work as a guardian of God's property (*Rabbi Isaiah Horowitz, 16th–17th century*).

15. If a man seduces a virgin. After the Torah finishes detailing the laws regarding the theft of money, it begins to discuss the laws regarding theft of the *heart*, namely the seducer (*Rabbi Hezekiah b. Manoah, 13th century*).

- ❖ ⁷ If the thief is not found, the homeowner must approach the judges (if he is challenged by the owner, to swear an oath) that he has not laid his hand upon his friend's property (and then he is exempt from compensation, since he was not paid for his services).

- ❖ ⁸ In every case of dishonesty (when swearing an oath, whether it is) about an ox, about a donkey, about a lamb, about a garment, or about any lost article, if (a witness) will say that "This thing here (is the very thing which you swore about, saying that it was not in your possession)!"—then the claims of both parties shall come to the judges, and whoever the judges declare guilty must pay twofold to his friend.

- ❖ ⁹ If a man gives his friend a donkey, an ox, a lamb, or any animal for safekeeping (and pays him for his services), and it dies, breaks a limb, or is captured without witnesses, ¹⁰ (then the dispute) between the two of them (is decided by the guardian swearing) an oath to God that he did not lay his hand upon his friend's property (to use it for himself). Its owner must accept (the oath), and (the guardian) does not pay. ¹¹ (However), if it is stolen from him, he must pay its owner.

- ❖ ¹² If it (the animal) is torn apart (by a wild beast), he may bring witness(es to prove that he was not negligent) with it, and then he does not have to pay compensation for the torn (animal, so long as he could not possibly have saved it).

- ❖ ¹³ If a person borrows an animal from his friend and it breaks a limb or dies, and its owner is not (working for the borrower), he must pay compensation. ¹⁴ If its owner is (working for the borrower), he shall not pay.

- ❖ If the article was hired, it came (into his possession) for its hiring fee.

Illicit and Idolatrous Behavior

- ❖ ¹⁵ If a man seduces a virgin who is not married and sleeps with her, he must pay a dowry and must marry her. ¹⁶ If her father refuses to give her to him in marriage, he must pay (a fixed) weight of (50) silver (shekels, which is) the usual dowry money for virgins.

- ❖ ¹⁷ Do not allow a sorceress (or sorcerer) to live.

- ❖ ¹⁸ Any person who sleeps with an animal must be put to death (by stoning).

- ❖ ¹⁹ Whoever slaughters to gods other than God alone must be destroyed, (i.e. put to death).

---

the renter (v. 14). In a case of loss, the unpaid guardian swears on all losses and is absolved; the borrower pays for everything; and the paid guardian and the renter swear in the case of breakage, robbery, and death, and pay for loss and theft (*Babylonian Talmud, Bava Metzia* 93a).

שמות כב:כ - כג:ב   משפטים

20 וְגֵ֖ר לֹא־תוֹנֶ֣ה וְלֹ֣א תִלְחָצֶ֑נּוּ כִּֽי־גֵרִ֥ים הֱיִיתֶ֖ם בְּאֶ֥רֶץ מִצְרָֽיִם: 21 כָּל־אַלְמָנָ֥ה וְיָת֖וֹם לֹ֥א תְעַנּֽוּן: 22 אִם־עַנֵּ֥ה תְעַנֶּ֖ה אֹת֑וֹ כִּ֣י אִם־צָעֹ֤ק יִצְעַק֙ אֵלַ֔י שָׁמֹ֥עַ אֶשְׁמַ֖ע צַעֲקָתֽוֹ: 23 וְחָרָ֣ה אַפִּ֔י וְהָרַגְתִּ֥י אֶתְכֶ֖ם בֶּחָ֑רֶב וְהָי֤וּ נְשֵׁיכֶם֙ אַלְמָנ֔וֹת וּבְנֵיכֶ֖ם יְתֹמִֽים: פ 24 אִם־כֶּ֣סֶף | תַּלְוֶ֣ה אֶת־עַמִּ֗י אֶת־הֶֽעָנִי֙ עִמָּ֔ךְ לֹא־תִהְיֶ֥ה ל֖וֹ כְּנֹשֶׁ֑ה לֹֽא־תְשִׂימ֥וּן עָלָ֖יו נֶֽשֶׁךְ: 25 אִם־חָבֹ֥ל תַּחְבֹּ֖ל שַׂלְמַ֣ת רֵעֶ֑ךָ עַד־בֹּ֥א הַשֶּׁ֖מֶשׁ תְּשִׁיבֶ֥נּוּ לֽוֹ: 26 כִּ֣י הִ֤וא כְסוּתֹה֙ לְבַדָּ֔הּ הִ֥וא שִׂמְלָת֖וֹ לְעֹר֑וֹ בַּמֶּ֣ה יִשְׁכָּ֔ב וְהָיָה֙ כִּֽי־יִצְעַ֣ק אֵלַ֔י וְשָׁמַעְתִּ֖י כִּֽי־חַנּ֥וּן אָֽנִי: ס [FOURTH READING] 27 אֱלֹהִ֖ים לֹ֣א תְקַלֵּ֑ל וְנָשִׂ֥יא בְעַמְּךָ֖ לֹ֥א תָאֹֽר: 28 מְלֵאָתְךָ֥ וְדִמְעֲךָ֖ לֹ֣א תְאַחֵ֑ר בְּכ֥וֹר בָּנֶ֖יךָ תִּתֶּן־לִֽי: 29 כֵּֽן־תַּעֲשֶׂ֥ה לְשֹׁרְךָ֖ לְצֹאנֶ֑ךָ שִׁבְעַ֤ת יָמִים֙ יִהְיֶ֣ה עִם־אִמּ֔וֹ בַּיּ֥וֹם הַשְּׁמִינִ֖י תִּתְּנוֹ־לִֽי: 30 וְאַנְשֵׁי־קֹ֖דֶשׁ תִּהְי֣וּן לִ֑י וּבָשָׂ֨ר בַּשָּׂדֶ֤ה טְרֵפָה֙ לֹ֣א תֹאכֵ֔לוּ לַכֶּ֖לֶב תַּשְׁלִכ֥וּן אֹתֽוֹ: ס

כג 1 לֹ֥א תִשָּׂ֖א שֵׁ֣מַע שָׁ֑וְא אַל־תָּ֤שֶׁת יָֽדְךָ֙ עִם־רָשָׁ֔ע לִהְיֹ֖ת עֵ֥ד חָמָֽס:
2 לֹֽא־תִהְיֶ֥ה אַחֲרֵֽי־רַבִּ֖ים לְרָעֹ֑ת וְלֹא־תַעֲנֶ֣ה עַל־רִ֗ב לִנְטֹ֛ת אַחֲרֵ֥י רַבִּ֖ים

21. You shall not oppress (any person, especially) a widow or orphan. Although the subsequent verse discusses the case of one who oppresses, and is written in the *singular*, this warning, *"You should not oppress,"* is written in the *plural*. This suggests that not only will the one who torments the widow and orphan be punished, but so will those who fail to intervene on their behalf. They will be considered to have shared in the tormenting (*Rabbi Abraham ibn Ezra, 12th century*).

30. If you will be holy men, you will be Mine. The turn of phrase *"holy men"* implies that you shall be holy, but as *men*—sanctifying your human, mundane lives. God has plenty of angels in heaven (*Rabbi Menahem Mendel Morgensztern of Kotsk, 19th century*).

23:2 By the majority. Every commandment that God gave to Moses our Teacher, peace unto him, was given along with its explanation. God would tell him the commandment, and then He would clarify its meaning and significance.

And when Moses died, peace unto him, after he bequeathed to Joshua the explanation he had received from Above, Joshua and his contemporaries subjected it to a thorough analysis. *But there was no discussion or debate over what he or any of the Sages had heard explicitly from Moses.*

Food for thought

1. Do memories of oppression prevent a person from oppressing others?

2. If the "abused become abusers," how can we break family heirlooms of dysfunction?

3. In your values system, how important is being sensitive to others?

Helping the Unfortunate and Respecting Leaders

- ❖ ²⁰ You should not verbally harass a foreigner (i.e. a convert), nor oppress him (by robbing his property), because you were foreigners in the land of Egypt.

- ❖ ²¹ You shall not oppress (any person, especially) a widow or orphan. ²² If you do oppress him, (beware!)—for if he cries out to Me, I will hear his cry, ²³ and My anger will be kindled, and I will kill you with the sword. (Furthermore, there will not be witnesses to your death, so) your wives will be (chained) widows, and your orphaned children (will be unable to inherit your property).

- ❖ ²⁴ When you lend money, (prioritize first) My people (i.e. Jews), the poor person, and (the inhabitant of your city) who is with you.

- ❖ (If you know he cannot yet repay your loan,) do not behave towards him as a lender (claiming your money forcibly), and do not place interest payments upon him.

- ❖ ²⁵ If (he fails to pay the loan on time and) you take your friend's (daytime) garment as security, you must return it to him (for the entire day), until the sun sets.

- ❖ ²⁶ (You must also return his night garments by night,) for it is his only covering; it is his garment for his skin. With what shall he sleep? If he cries out to Me, I will listen, because I am compassionate.

- ❖ [FOURTH READING] ²⁷ Do not curse a judge.

- ❖ Do not curse a leader among your people.

Agricultural Offerings

- ❖ ²⁸ Do not delay your offering (of first fruit) when it ripens, or your offering of *terumah*.

- ❖ You must present Me the firstborn of your sons (to be redeemed by the priest after thirty days).

- ❖ ²⁹ You must do likewise with your ox and with your sheep (i.e. redeem it after thirty days. But at the very minimum,) for seven days it shall be with its mother, and on the eighth day you may give it to Me.

- ❖ ³⁰ (If) you will be holy men, you will be Mine. Do not eat flesh that is torn off in the field (or any other place). Throw it to the dogs (or sell it to a non-Jew).

23 Judicial Laws and Avoiding Prejudice

- ❖ ¹ Do not listen to a false report.

- ❖ Do not associate with a wicked person (who is making a false claim) to be a corrupt witness.

- ❖ ² Do not conform to the majority who are perverting justice. Do not condone a lawsuit (in which justice was perverted) by the majority.

שמות כג:ב-יג   משפטים

לְהַטֹּֽת׃ 3 וְדָ֕ל לֹ֥א תֶהְדַּ֖ר בְּרִיבֽוֹ׃ ס 4 כִּ֣י תִפְגַּ֞ע שׁ֧וֹר אֹֽיִבְךָ֛ א֥וֹ חֲמֹר֖וֹ תֹּעֶ֑ה הָשֵׁ֥ב תְּשִׁיבֶ֖נּוּ לֽוֹ׃ ס 5 כִּֽי־תִרְאֶ֞ה חֲמ֣וֹר שֹׂנַאֲךָ֗ רֹבֵץ֙ תַּ֣חַת מַשָּׂא֔וֹ וְחָדַלְתָּ֖ מֵעֲזֹ֣ב ל֑וֹ עָזֹ֥ב תַּעֲזֹ֖ב עִמּֽוֹ׃ ס 6 [FIFTH READING] לֹ֥א תַטֶּ֛ה מִשְׁפַּ֥ט אֶבְיֹנְךָ֖ בְּרִיבֽוֹ׃ 7 מִדְּבַר־שֶׁ֖קֶר תִּרְחָ֑ק וְנָקִ֤י וְצַדִּיק֙ אַֽל־תַּהֲרֹ֔ג כִּ֥י לֹא־אַצְדִּ֖יק רָשָֽׁע׃ 8 וְשֹׁ֖חַד לֹ֣א תִקָּ֑ח כִּ֤י הַשֹּׁ֨חַד֙ יְעַוֵּ֣ר פִּקְחִ֔ים וִֽיסַלֵּ֖ף דִּבְרֵ֥י צַדִּיקִֽים׃ 9 וְגֵ֖ר לֹ֣א תִלְחָ֑ץ וְאַתֶּ֗ם יְדַעְתֶּם֙ אֶת־נֶ֣פֶשׁ הַגֵּ֔ר כִּֽי־גֵרִ֥ים הֱיִיתֶ֖ם בְּאֶ֥רֶץ מִצְרָֽיִם׃ 10 וְשֵׁ֥שׁ שָׁנִ֖ים תִּזְרַ֣ע אֶת־אַרְצֶ֑ךָ וְאָסַפְתָּ֖ אֶת־תְּבוּאָתָֽהּ׃ 11 וְהַשְּׁבִיעִ֞ת תִּשְׁמְטֶ֣נָּה וּנְטַשְׁתָּ֗הּ וְאָֽכְלוּ֙ אֶבְיֹנֵ֣י עַמֶּ֔ךָ וְיִתְרָ֕ם תֹּאכַ֖ל חַיַּ֣ת הַשָּׂדֶ֑ה כֵּֽן־תַּעֲשֶׂ֥ה לְכַרְמְךָ֖ לְזֵיתֶֽךָ׃ 12 שֵׁ֤שֶׁת יָמִים֙ תַּעֲשֶׂ֣ה מַעֲשֶׂ֔יךָ וּבַיּ֥וֹם הַשְּׁבִיעִ֖י תִּשְׁבֹּ֑ת לְמַ֣עַן יָנ֗וּחַ שֽׁוֹרְךָ֙ וַחֲמֹרֶ֔ךָ וְיִנָּפֵ֥שׁ בֶּן־אֲמָתְךָ֖ וְהַגֵּֽר׃ 13 וּבְכֹ֛ל אֲשֶׁר־אָמַ֥רְתִּי אֲלֵיכֶ֖ם תִּשָּׁמֵ֑רוּ וְשֵׁ֨ם אֱלֹהִ֤ים אֲחֵרִים֙

When a person is charitable, he weakens the poor man's claim against God. On the other hand, when a person refrains from giving charity, the poor man's arguments are strengthened. Thus, we are commanded not to reinforce the poor man's claim, but to extend a helping hand (*Rabbi Ḥayyim ibn Attar, 18th century*).

5. If you see your enemy's donkey (*ḥamor*) lying under its load. When you carefully examine your *ḥomer* ("matter"), your material, bodily existence, you will see *"your enemy"*—that your *ḥomer* hates your soul. Furthermore, your body is *"lying under its load,"* placed upon it, i.e., the burden of overcoming laziness and achieving personal refinement through the Torah.

It may then occur to you that *"you would (want to) refrain from helping him"*— you will follow a path of asceticism to crush the body.

Know that this is not the way of the Torah! Rather, *"you must help him"*—purify the body. Work with it, but do not punish it (*Rabbi Israel Ba'al Shem Tov, 18th century*).

12. On the seventh day you must rest. You should not reason that since the entire year is a kind of "Sabbath" (v. 11), the weekly Sabbath need not be observed in it. The weekly Sabbath, which commemorates God's act of Creation, is never uprooted (*Rashi, 11th century*).

The Sabbatical year and the weekly Sabbath have the same purpose, to remind us of how God refrained from work on the seventh day when creating the world. Therefore, we might reason that since the very nature of a Sabbatical year is to remind us of the Divine act of creation, it follows that the further sign of the weekly Sabbath is unnecessary. This could be compared to the law that the *tefillin* (phylacteries), worn on the head and arm as a sign of the covenant between the Jewish people and God, are not worn on the Sabbath, since the day of Sabbath is, in any case, such a "sign."

- ❖ ³ Do not accord honor (i.e. be biased towards) a poor man in his lawsuit.

- ❖ ⁴ If you come across your enemy's ox or his stray donkey, you must return it to him.

- ❖ ⁵ (Perhaps,) if you see your enemy's donkey lying under its load you would (want to) refrain from helping him. (However,) you must help him (unload).

- ❖ [FIFTH READING] ⁶ Do not pervert the judgment of your poor man in his lawsuit.

- ❖ ⁷ Distance yourself from anything false.

- ❖ Do not kill a (convicted person, if fresh evidence arises before his execution suggesting that he is innocent); or one who has been vindicated (by the court, even if fresh evidence arises suggesting that he is guilty), for I will not let a guilty person escape punishment.

- ❖ ⁸ Do not accept a bribe, for a bribe blinds the eyes of those who can see (i.e. Torah scholars,) and corrupts righteous words.

- ❖ ⁹ Do not oppress a foreigner (convert), for you know the feelings of the foreigner, since you were foreigners in the land of Egypt.

The Sabbath and the Festivals—Mentioning Idols

- ❖ ¹⁰ Six years you may sow your land and gather in its produce, ¹¹ but in the seventh year you shall cease to work in it and refrain from (eating its fruit). The poor among your people shall eat from it (without separating tithes), and what they leave over will be eaten by the beasts of the field. This also applies to your vineyard and to your olive grove.

- ❖ ¹² Six days you may do your work, but on the seventh day you must rest (even in the seventh year), in order that your ox and your donkey shall rest (in the field), and your maidservant's son and the resident alien shall be refreshed.

- ❖ ¹³ You should be careful to keep everything that I have said to you.

- ❖ Do not mention the name of the gods of others.

Further ramifications of these laws which were not explicitly heard from the Prophet's lips, in those areas in which no information was received, were derived logically using the *Thirteen Principles of Torah Interpretation* given at Mount Sinai.

Some of the laws derived in this manner evoked no controversy and were unanimously agreed upon. But some of them were subject to a difference of opinion, and they would follow the majority opinion, as the Torah states, *"...by the majority"* (*Maimonides, 12ᵗʰ century*).

3. Do not accord honor (i.e. be biased toward) a poor man in his lawsuit. These words hint at the complaint or *"lawsuit"* that the poor man raises against God. He argues, "Why does God provide sustenance for others, while I remain destitute and starving?"

שמות כג:יג-יט • משפטים

לֹא תַזְכִּירוּ לֹא יִשָּׁמַע עַל־פִּיךָ: 14 שָׁלֹשׁ רְגָלִים תָּחֹג לִי בַּשָּׁנָה: 15 אֶת־חַג הַמַּצּוֹת תִּשְׁמֹר שִׁבְעַת יָמִים תֹּאכַל מַצּוֹת כַּאֲשֶׁר צִוִּיתִךָ לְמוֹעֵד חֹדֶשׁ הָאָבִיב כִּי־בוֹ יָצָאתָ מִמִּצְרָיִם וְלֹא־יֵרָאוּ פָנַי רֵיקָם: 16 וְחַג הַקָּצִיר בִּכּוּרֵי מַעֲשֶׂיךָ אֲשֶׁר תִּזְרַע בַּשָּׂדֶה וְחַג הָאָסִף בְּצֵאת הַשָּׁנָה בְּאָסְפְּךָ אֶת־מַעֲשֶׂיךָ מִן־הַשָּׂדֶה: 17 שָׁלֹשׁ פְּעָמִים בַּשָּׁנָה יֵרָאֶה כָּל־זְכוּרְךָ אֶל־פְּנֵי הָאָדֹן ׀ יְהֹוָה: 18 לֹא־תִזְבַּח עַל־חָמֵץ דַּם־זִבְחִי וְלֹא־יָלִין חֵלֶב־חַגִּי עַד־בֹּקֶר: 19 רֵאשִׁית בִּכּוּרֵי אַדְמָתְךָ תָּבִיא בֵּית יְהֹוָה אֱלֹהֶיךָ לֹא־תְבַשֵּׁל גְּדִי בַּחֲלֵב אִמּוֹ: פ

The prohibition is written in three places in the Torah, each repetition coming to teach another aspect of the law: once for the prohibition of *eating* meat with milk, once for the prohibition of *deriving benefit* from meat with milk, and once for the prohibition of *cooking* meat with milk (*Rashi, 11th century*).

It is an act of moral insensitivity to eat a kid which was cooked in its own mother's milk. Even though this prohibition applies even if an animal is cooked in milk that does not come from its mother, nevertheless, the concept of eating meat cooked in milk is considered insensitive, as it resembles the above act (*Nahmanides, 13th century*).

Both milk and meat represent certain spiritual entities. Just as both milk and meat when kept separate are permitted substances but are prohibited when combined, likewise the spiritual entities which they represent ought to be kept distinct.

Our Sages taught that in the future God will reveal to the Jewish people the reason why milk with meat is prohibited. In the current era, people are plagued by the evil inclination and are unable to relate to the subtleties of the mystical secrets (*Rabbi Bahya b. Asher, 13th century*).

Meat is red, alluding to the spiritual forces of Divine judgment and severity, and milk represents Divine kindness. Mixing milk and meat thus causes an inappropriate mixing of spiritual forces which can have negative consequences (*Rabbi Isaiah Horowitz, 16th–17th century*).

kabbalah bites

23:19 The prohibition of eating meat cooked in milk is a *hok*, a command that partially transcends logic. Why was it included here amid a long list of *mishpatim*, laws which appeal to the rational mind?

Without some measure of sacrifice for the greater good, "spiritual growth" can eventually become just another form of self-indulgence. Therefore, after a long list of rationally satisfying and morally invigorating laws we are given here something rather uncomfortable, in that it defies logic, to remind us of the dangers of spiritual narcissism.

exodus 23:13–19 mishpatim

- You should not cause (a non-Jew) to make heard (the name of his idol) through your mouth.

¹⁴ Three times you shall celebrate for Me during the year:

- ¹⁵ Observe the Festival of Unleavened Bread. Eat unleavened bread for seven days, as I have commanded you, at the appointed time of the month of springtime, since this is when you left Egypt.

- (When the Jewish people come to be seen before Me on the festivals,) they shall not appear before Me empty-handed. (Rather, they must come with a burnt-offering.)

- ¹⁶ And the Festival of the Harvest (i.e. the Festival of Weeks, which is the time of bringing first) fruits of your crops which you will sow in the field.

- And the Festival of the Ingathering (i.e. the Festival of Tabernacles), at the end of the year, when you gather your produce from the field (into the house before the rain starts).

- ¹⁷ Three times during the year, all your males must appear before the Lord God.

- ¹⁸ Do not slaughter the blood of My (Passover) sacrifice (until you destroy any) leavened bread (that is in your possession).

- The fat of My festive sacrifice must not be left overnight until morning.

- ¹⁹ Bring to the House of God, your God, the choicest of the first fruits of your soil (even in the seventh year).

- Do not cook a tender young animal in its mother's milk.

To counteract this notion, *Rashi* informs us that even during the Sabbatical year, the weekly Sabbath still applies (*Rabbi Baruch Epstein, 19th–20th century*).

14. Three times you shall celebrate for Me during the year. The Hebrew term for festivals, *regalim*, is a derivative of the word *regel*, meaning "foot." This alludes to a level of profound commitment to God where you are not merely serving your Maker for rational reasons, or due to your spiritual sentiments, but out of simple obedience, like a "foot soldier."

On the other hand, the festivals are also associated with *joy*, where your personal feelings towards God take outward expression.

What is the connection between obedience and joy?

The answer is hinted to by the fact that the Torah fixed the festivals according to the agricultural cycle. In order for a seed to grow, it must first shed its outer shell, and only through this shedding is the seed able to grow many hundreds of times in size. When you will put aside ("shed") your superficial preconceptions ("shell") about Judaism and observe all the commandments with absolute loyalty, you will experience an enormous spiritual growth.

And if you serve God with joy, which "breaks all boundaries," you will also experience an unrestrained spiritual growth (*Rabbi Menahem Mendel Schneerson, 20th century*).

19. Do not cook a tender young animal in its mother's milk. The Hebrew term *gedi* is translated mostly as "kid." However, *gedi* actually means a tender young animal. Therefore, not only kid goats, but also a calf and a lamb are included in this prohibition.

משפטים שמות כג:כ-לג

20 [SIXTH READING] הִנֵּ֨ה אָנֹכִ֜י שֹׁלֵ֤חַ מַלְאָךְ֙ לְפָנֶ֔יךָ לִשְׁמָרְךָ֖ בַּדָּ֑רֶךְ וְלַהֲבִ֣יאֲךָ֔ אֶל־הַמָּק֖וֹם אֲשֶׁ֥ר הֲכִנֹֽתִי: 21 הִשָּׁ֧מֶר מִפָּנָ֛יו וּשְׁמַ֥ע בְּקֹל֖וֹ אַל־תַּמֵּ֣ר בּ֑וֹ כִּ֣י לֹ֤א יִשָּׂא֙ לְפִשְׁעֲכֶ֔ם כִּ֥י שְׁמִ֖י בְּקִרְבּֽוֹ: 22 כִּ֣י אִם־שָׁמ֤וֹעַ תִּשְׁמַע֙ בְּקֹל֔וֹ וְעָשִׂ֕יתָ כֹּ֖ל אֲשֶׁ֣ר אֲדַבֵּ֑ר וְאָֽיַבְתִּי֙ אֶת־אֹ֣יְבֶ֔יךָ וְצַרְתִּ֖י אֶת־צֹרְרֶֽיךָ: 23 כִּֽי־יֵלֵ֣ךְ מַלְאָכִי֮ לְפָנֶיךָ֒ וֶהֱבִֽיאֲךָ֗ אֶל־הָֽאֱמֹרִי֙ וְהַ֣חִתִּ֔י וְהַפְּרִזִּי֙ וְהַֽכְּנַעֲנִ֔י הַחִוִּ֖י וְהַיְבוּסִ֑י וְהִכְחַדְתִּֽיו: 24 לֹֽא־תִשְׁתַּחֲוֶ֤ה לֵאלֹֽהֵיהֶם֙ וְלֹ֣א תָֽעָבְדֵ֔ם וְלֹ֥א תַעֲשֶׂ֖ה כְּמַעֲשֵׂיהֶ֑ם כִּ֤י הָרֵס֙ תְּהָ֣רְסֵ֔ם וְשַׁבֵּ֥ר תְּשַׁבֵּ֖ר מַצֵּבֹתֵיהֶֽם: 25 וַעֲבַדְתֶּ֗ם אֵ֚ת יְהֹוָ֣ה אֱלֹֽהֵיכֶ֔ם וּבֵרַ֥ךְ אֶֽת־לַחְמְךָ֖ וְאֶת־מֵימֶ֑יךָ וַהֲסִרֹתִ֥י מַחֲלָ֖ה מִקִּרְבֶּֽךָ: ס 26 [SEVENTH READING] לֹ֥א תִֽהְיֶ֛ה מְשַׁכֵּלָ֥ה וַעֲקָרָ֖ה בְּאַרְצֶ֑ךָ אֶת־מִסְפַּ֥ר יָמֶ֖יךָ אֲמַלֵּֽא: 27 אֶת־אֵֽימָתִי֙ אֲשַׁלַּ֣ח לְפָנֶ֔יךָ וְהַמֹּתִי֙ אֶת־כׇּל־הָעָ֔ם אֲשֶׁ֥ר תָּבֹ֖א בָּהֶ֑ם וְנָתַתִּ֛י אֶת־כׇּל־אֹיְבֶ֥יךָ אֵלֶ֖יךָ עֹֽרֶף: 28 וְשָׁלַחְתִּ֥י אֶת־הַצִּרְעָ֖ה לְפָנֶ֑יךָ וְגֵרְשָׁ֗ה אֶת־הַחִוִּ֧י אֶת־הַֽכְּנַעֲנִ֛י וְאֶת־הַחִתִּ֖י מִלְּפָנֶֽיךָ: 29 לֹ֧א אֲגָרְשֶׁ֛נּוּ מִפָּנֶ֖יךָ בְּשָׁנָ֣ה אֶחָ֑ת פֶּן־תִּהְיֶ֤ה הָאָ֙רֶץ֙ שְׁמָמָ֔ה וְרַבָּ֥ה עָלֶ֖יךָ חַיַּ֥ת הַשָּׂדֶֽה: 30 מְעַ֥ט מְעַ֛ט אֲגָרְשֶׁ֖נּוּ מִפָּנֶ֑יךָ עַ֚ד אֲשֶׁ֣ר תִּפְרֶ֔ה וְנָחַלְתָּ֖ אֶת־הָאָֽרֶץ: 31 וְשַׁתִּ֣י אֶת־גְּבֻלְךָ֗ מִיַּם־סוּף֙ וְעַד־יָ֣ם פְּלִשְׁתִּ֔ים וּמִמִּדְבָּ֖ר עַד־הַנָּהָ֑ר כִּ֣י ׀ אֶתֵּ֣ן בְּיֶדְכֶ֗ם אֵ֚ת יֹשְׁבֵ֣י הָאָ֔רֶץ וְגֵרַשְׁתָּ֖מוֹ מִפָּנֶֽיךָ: 32 לֹֽא־תִכְרֹ֥ת לָהֶ֛ם וְלֵאלֹֽהֵיהֶ֖ם בְּרִֽית: 33 לֹ֤א יֵשְׁבוּ֙ בְּאַרְצְךָ֔ פֶּן־יַחֲטִ֥יאוּ אֹתְךָ֖ לִ֑י כִּ֤י תַעֲבֹד֙ אֶת־אֱלֹ֣הֵיהֶ֔ם כִּֽי־יִהְיֶ֥ה לְךָ֖ לְמוֹקֵֽשׁ: פ

spiritual vitamin

> The conquest of the promised Holy Land was to take place in stages (v. 30), and the same applies, in a deeper sense, to the personal conquest of the self. The best method is usually through gradual advancement step by step, and stage by stage, rather than through drastic change.

exodus 23:20–33   mishpatim

Dispersion of Enemies and Conquest of the Land

[SIXTH READING] 20 (When you will sin with the Golden Calf, My Divine Presence will not accompany you personally. Rather,) I will send an angel before you to guard you on the way and to bring you to the place that I have prepared (to give you). 21 Beware of him and listen to him, for My name is associated with him. Do not rebel against him, for he will not forgive your transgression (since he never sins himself). 22 But, if you listen to his voice and do all that I say, I will be the enemy of your enemies and I will oppress your oppressors. 23 For My angel will go before you, and bring you to the Amorites, the Hittites, the Perizzites, the Canaanites, the Hivites, and the Jebusites, and I will destroy them.

24 Do not bow down to their gods. Do not worship them, and do not follow their practices. Rather, you should demolish (their gods) and completely shatter their stones (which they stand on so as to bow down to them). 25 You shall worship God, your God, and He will bless your food and your drink. I will banish illness from among you.

[SEVENTH READING] 26 (If you obey My will,) then there will not be a woman who miscarries or a barren woman in your land. I will cause the days (of your lives) to be full. 27 I will send My terror ahead of you, and I will throw into confusion all the people among whom you will come. I will make all your enemies turn their backs (and flee from) you.

28 I will send swarms of hornets before you (that will strike your enemies in the eyes and inject venom into them) and they will drive out the Hivites, the Canaanites, and the Hittites from before you. 29 I will not drive them away from you in one year, lest the land become depopulated and the beasts of the field become too many for you (to contend with). 30 Little by little, I will drive them away from you, until you have increased and can occupy the land.

31 I will set your borders from the Sea of Reeds to the Sea of Philistia, and from the desert to the river (Euphrates), for I will deliver the inhabitants of the land into your hands, and you will drive them away from you.

32 Do not make a covenant with them or with their gods. 33 Do not let them live in your land, since they may cause you to sin against Me, in that you will worship their gods, which will be a trap for you.

---

20. The place that I have prepared. The simple meaning of this Hebrew phrase is "the place that I (God) have designated to give to you." In its deeper, homiletical interpretation, God is informing us that "My Presence is *already* aligned opposite this place." This is one of the verses which indicates that the heavenly Temple is aligned directly opposite the earthly Temple (*Rashi, 11th century*).

משפטים / שמות כד:א-יא

כד 1 וְאֶל־מֹשֶׁה אָמַר עֲלֵה אֶל־יְהֹוָה אַתָּה וְאַהֲרֹן נָדָב וַאֲבִיהוּא וְשִׁבְעִים מִזִּקְנֵי יִשְׂרָאֵל וְהִשְׁתַּחֲוִיתֶם מֵרָחֹק: 2 וְנִגַּשׁ מֹשֶׁה לְבַדּוֹ אֶל־יְהֹוָה וְהֵם לֹא יִגָּשׁוּ וְהָעָם לֹא יַעֲלוּ עִמּוֹ: 3 וַיָּבֹא מֹשֶׁה וַיְסַפֵּר לָעָם אֵת כָּל־דִּבְרֵי יְהֹוָה וְאֵת כָּל־הַמִּשְׁפָּטִים וַיַּעַן כָּל־הָעָם קוֹל אֶחָד וַיֹּאמְרוּ כָּל־הַדְּבָרִים אֲשֶׁר־דִּבֶּר יְהֹוָה נַעֲשֶׂה: 4 וַיִּכְתֹּב מֹשֶׁה אֵת כָּל־דִּבְרֵי יְהֹוָה וַיַּשְׁכֵּם בַּבֹּקֶר וַיִּבֶן מִזְבֵּחַ תַּחַת הָהָר וּשְׁתֵּים עֶשְׂרֵה מַצֵּבָה לִשְׁנֵים עָשָׂר שִׁבְטֵי יִשְׂרָאֵל: 5 וַיִּשְׁלַח אֶת־נַעֲרֵי בְּנֵי יִשְׂרָאֵל וַיַּעֲלוּ עֹלֹת וַיִּזְבְּחוּ זְבָחִים שְׁלָמִים לַיהֹוָה פָּרִים: 6 וַיִּקַּח מֹשֶׁה חֲצִי הַדָּם וַיָּשֶׂם בָּאַגָּנֹת וַחֲצִי הַדָּם זָרַק עַל־הַמִּזְבֵּחַ: 7 וַיִּקַּח סֵפֶר הַבְּרִית וַיִּקְרָא בְּאָזְנֵי הָעָם וַיֹּאמְרוּ כֹּל אֲשֶׁר־דִּבֶּר יְהֹוָה נַעֲשֶׂה וְנִשְׁמָע: 8 וַיִּקַּח מֹשֶׁה אֶת־הַדָּם וַיִּזְרֹק עַל־הָעָם וַיֹּאמֶר הִנֵּה דַם־הַבְּרִית אֲשֶׁר כָּרַת יְהֹוָה עִמָּכֶם עַל כָּל־הַדְּבָרִים הָאֵלֶּה: 9 וַיַּעַל מֹשֶׁה וְאַהֲרֹן נָדָב וַאֲבִיהוּא וְשִׁבְעִים מִזִּקְנֵי יִשְׂרָאֵל: 10 וַיִּרְאוּ אֵת אֱלֹהֵי יִשְׂרָאֵל וְתַחַת רַגְלָיו כְּמַעֲשֵׂה לִבְנַת הַסַּפִּיר וּכְעֶצֶם הַשָּׁמַיִם לָטֹהַר: 11 וְאֶל־אֲצִילֵי

blood of the sacrifice on the altar—for there is a law that one may not sprinkle blood unless immersion has preceded it (*Rashi, 11th century*).

Two basins. It is an ancient custom that when two parties enter into a covenant, they divide an animal into parts and pass between them—as in the case of Abraham's covenant with God

spiritual vitamin

> The first word of acceptance of the Torah by all the people, in complete unanimity, was *na'aseh*—"we will do" (v. 7). The fact that it was said at a moment of the greatest spiritual elation makes it all the more significant. It is a clear instruction not to let yourself be carried away by enthusiasm alone, but to immediately translate it into the reality of tangible deeds.

exodus 24:1–11   mishpatim

The Jewish People Enter into Covenant with God

(The following was said by God on the fourth of Sivan, before the giving of the Torah:)

24 ¹ To Moses, He said, "Go up to God—you and Aaron, Nadab and Abihu, and seventy elders of Israel—and bow down from afar. ² Moses alone shall approach (the fog where) God (is), but they shall not approach, and the people shall not go up with him."

³ (On the same day,) Moses came and told the people all the words of God (about separating from their wives and making a boundary around the mountain), and all the laws (of the Noachide code, and the laws of the Sabbath, honoring parents, the Red Heifer, and the civil laws which were given at Marah). All the people answered in unison and said, "All the words that God has spoken, we will do."

⁴ Moses wrote down all of God's words (from the beginning of *Genesis* until the giving of the Torah).

(On the fifth of *Sivan*,) he arose early in the morning and built an altar at the foot of the mountain and twelve stone monuments for the twelve tribes of Israel. ⁵ He sent the (firstborn of the) children of Israel, and they offered up burnt-offerings, and they slaughtered bulls as peace-offerings to God. ⁶ Moses took half the blood and put it into (two) basins, and half the blood he cast onto the altar.

⁷ He took the Book of the Covenant (i.e. from the beginning of *Genesis* to the giving of the Torah, plus the commandments they were given at Marah), and read it aloud so the people could hear, and they said, "We will do and we will hear everything that God has said."

⁸ Moses took the blood and sprinkled it on the people, and he said, "This is the blood of the covenant, which God has made with you regarding all these words."

⁹ Moses and Aaron, Nadab and Abihu, and seventy of the elders of Israel went up, ¹⁰ and they saw the God of Israel, and beneath His feet was something like a sapphire brick (that God had placed before Him to remember the pain of Israel's enslavement), which was as clear as the heavens (shining light which signified that the Jewish people had been redeemed). ¹¹ Upon (Nadab and Abihu and the elders,) the nobles of the children of Israel He did not lay His hand (even though they deserved it for looking directly at God). They looked at God (while) they ate and drank.

24:6 Moses took half the blood and put it into (two) basins. Two basins were used, one for half of the blood of the burnt-offering and one for half of the blood of the peace-offering, in order to sprinkle the blood on the people. From here the Sages learned that our ancestors entered the covenant with circumcision, immersion in a ritual pool (*mikveh*), and the sprinkling of the

שמות כד:יא-יח · משפטים

12 בְּנֵי יִשְׂרָאֵל לֹא שָׁלַח יָדוֹ וַיֶּחֱזוּ אֶת־הָאֱלֹהִים וַיֹּאכְלוּ וַיִּשְׁתּוּ: ס וַיֹּאמֶר יְהֹוָה אֶל־מֹשֶׁה עֲלֵה אֵלַי הָהָרָה וֶהְיֵה־שָׁם וְאֶתְּנָה לְךָ אֶת־לֻחֹת הָאֶבֶן וְהַתּוֹרָה וְהַמִּצְוָה אֲשֶׁר כָּתַבְתִּי לְהוֹרֹתָם: 13 וַיָּקָם מֹשֶׁה וִיהוֹשֻׁעַ מְשָׁרְתוֹ וַיַּעַל מֹשֶׁה אֶל־הַר הָאֱלֹהִים: 14 וְאֶל־הַזְּקֵנִים אָמַר שְׁבוּ־לָנוּ בָזֶה עַד אֲשֶׁר־נָשׁוּב אֲלֵיכֶם וְהִנֵּה אַהֲרֹן וְחוּר עִמָּכֶם מִי־בַעַל דְּבָרִים יִגַּשׁ אֲלֵהֶם: [MAFTIR] 15 וַיַּעַל מֹשֶׁה אֶל־הָהָר וַיְכַס הֶעָנָן אֶת־הָהָר: 16 וַיִּשְׁכֹּן כְּבוֹד־יְהֹוָה עַל־הַר סִינַי וַיְכַסֵּהוּ הֶעָנָן שֵׁשֶׁת יָמִים וַיִּקְרָא אֶל־מֹשֶׁה בַּיּוֹם הַשְּׁבִיעִי מִתּוֹךְ הֶעָנָן: 17 וּמַרְאֵה כְּבוֹד יְהֹוָה כְּאֵשׁ אֹכֶלֶת בְּרֹאשׁ הָהָר לְעֵינֵי בְּנֵי יִשְׂרָאֵל: 18 וַיָּבֹא מֹשֶׁה בְּתוֹךְ הֶעָנָן וַיַּעַל אֶל־הָהָר וַיְהִי מֹשֶׁה בָּהָר אַרְבָּעִים יוֹם וְאַרְבָּעִים לָיְלָה: פ פ פ

קי"ח פסוקים, עזיא"ל סימן, חנני"י סימן.

Smoke represents the burning desire of man to escape the confines of corporeal existence and ascend upwards to become one with his Creator.

Normally, smoke can be made only when there is some fuel present, be it animal or mineral. But, at Mount Sinai, God made a "consuming fire" which emanated from the mountain itself—fire from a rock.

This teaches you the need to bring enthusiasm even to the dreary, "inanimate" parts of your life. You may think that excitement—love and fear of God—are to be reserved for the synagogue or for Torah study. But when it comes to petty chores and simple, mundane acts, these are totally disconnected from any higher purpose.

Not so! Remember that at Mount Sinai, even the rock burned. Even the most dull and monotonous acts can be brought alive with the fire and energy of spiritual inspiration (*Rabbi Menahem Mendel Schneerson, 20th century*).

Moses was upon the mountain forty days and forty nights. Every new insight that a Torah scholar was destined to introduce was already given to Moses at Sinai (*Babylonian Talmud, Megillah* 19b).

Is it possible that Moses was taught the entire Torah? Scripture states, *"Its measure is longer than the earth, and broader than the sea"* (*Job* 11:9). Is it possible that in forty days Moses learned all of this? Obviously, God taught him only the general principles (*Exodus Rabbah*).

It is not feasible that the Torah would have been given in a comprehensive manner, suitable for every generation, because new types of human interaction and conduct arise constantly and they are too vast in scope to be included in a book. Therefore, Moses was given at Sinai the general principles, hinted to briefly in the Torah, from which the sages of each generation would be able to innovate further points of law (*Rabbi Joseph Albo, 15th century*).

Moses Ascends the Mountain for Forty Days

¹² God said to Moses, "Come up to Me to the mountain and remain there, and I will give you the stone tablets (which incorporate the entire) Torah and Commandment, which I have written to instruct them."

¹³ Moses arose with Joshua his servant (to the boundary. Since Joshua could go no further, he pitched his tent there). Moses went up to the mountain of God. ¹⁴ (As he left the camp,) he said to the elders, "Wait for us here (and be ready to judge any dispute) until we return to you. Look! Aaron and Hur (son of Miriam and Caleb) are with you. Whoever has a (legal) case should approach them."

[MAFTIR] ¹⁵ Moses ascended the mountain, and the cloud covered the mountain. ¹⁶ The glory of God rested on Mount Sinai, and the cloud covered (the mountain) for six days. He called to Moses on the seventh day from within the cloud (to say the Ten Commandments).

¹⁷ The appearance of the glory of God was like a consuming fire on top of the mountain, before the eyes of the children of Israel.

¹⁸ Moses came (into a path) within the cloud, and he went up to the mountain.

Moses was upon the mountain forty days and forty nights.

Haftarot: Mishpatim—page 1330. *Shekalim*—page 1424. *Erev Rosh Ḥodesh*—page 1415.
Rosh Ḥodesh—page 1417.

Maftir: Shekalim—page 520 (30:11–16). *Rosh Ḥodesh*—page 1000 (28:9–15).

(*Genesis* 15:17). Here, however, the covenant was made by dividing blood and not animal parts. God was hinting to the Jewish people that if any of the conditions of the covenant were to be breached, then blood would be spilled, as the verse states, *"If you do not listen to My voice ... I will bring a sword upon you, avenging the vengeance of the covenant"* (*Leviticus* 26:21, 25; *Rabbi Hezekiah b. Manoah, 13th century*).

18. Within the cloud. This cloud was like smoke, and God made a path within it for Moses (*Rashi, 11th century*).

kabbalah bites

24:17 Why is God's presence described in the Torah as a *"consuming fire"*?

The light of God only enters where you let it in. Arrogance and ego act as an obstacle to the light. When the ego is softened with submissiveness and humility the light is drawn in.

The analogy of fire offers a physical illustration of this point: Hard, impervious substances such as stone will not burn; soft matter, like straw, is consumed in an instant.

So to embrace the "consuming fire" of God, you need to make yourself combustible by cracking that rock-hard ego.

> Although the Tabernacle was a **temporary structure** which was later **superseded** by the **Temple in Jerusalem,** it possessed an **advantage** which the Temple did not have. It was built in the **desert,** in the farthest of places, teaching of the need to bring **Judaism** to the most **distant places.**

TERUMAH
תרומה

CONTRIBUTIONS TO THE TABERNACLE	25:1–9
VESSELS OF THE TABERNACLE	25:10–40
COVERINGS OF THE TABERNACLE	26:1–14
WALLS OF THE TABERNACLE	26:15–33
CONTENTS OF THE TABERNACLE	26:34–37
THE COPPER ALTAR	27:1–8
THE COURTYARD OF THE TABERNACLE	27:9–19

NAME
Terumah

MEANING
"Contribution"

LINES IN TORAH SCROLL
155

PARASHIYYOT
4 open; 5 closed

VERSES
96

WORDS
1145

LETTERS
4692

DATE
10 Tishri, 2448

LOCATION
Mount Sinai

KEY PEOPLE
Moses

MITZVOT
2 positive; 1 prohibition

CHARACTER PROFILE

NAME
Zipporah

MEANING
"Bird," "look and see"

FATHER
Jethro

SIBLINGS
Six younger sisters

HUSBAND
Moses

CHILDREN
Gershom, Eliezer

ACHIEVEMENTS
Her fame did not change her: she was lovely in her youth and lovely in her old age; she circumcised her son while on the journey to Egypt to save her husband's life; raised two sons on her own

KNOWN FOR
Her exceptional beauty; her love for Moses—she ran after him like a bird; she was the topic of Miriam's gossip about Moses, for which Miriam was stricken with leprosy; Moses separated from her by God's command, to achieve higher levels of prophecy.

NON-COERCION

The donations to the Tabernacle were to be taken *"from every person whose heart inspires him"* (v. 25:20). Religious observance ought to be spontaneous and willing, not coerced and dry.

WEALTH

The Tabernacle, God's "home" in this world, was made of gold and silver and other materials. Riches are not to be shunned. They were created for a purpose—to be utilized in the service of God (25:3-7).

SANCTUARY

The Tabernacle was a tangible, visible assurance that God had entered into an eternal covenant with Israel, a presence that would accompany them on all their travels (25:8).

תרומה | שמות כה:א-י

כה ‎1 וַיְדַבֵּר יְהֹוָה אֶל־מֹשֶׁה לֵּאמֹר: ‎2 דַּבֵּר אֶל־בְּנֵי יִשְׂרָאֵל וְיִקְחוּ־לִי תְּרוּמָה מֵאֵת כָּל־אִישׁ אֲשֶׁר יִדְּבֶנּוּ לִבּוֹ תִּקְחוּ אֶת־תְּרוּמָתִי: ‎3 וְזֹאת הַתְּרוּמָה אֲשֶׁר תִּקְחוּ מֵאִתָּם זָהָב וָכֶסֶף וּנְחֹשֶׁת: ‎4 וּתְכֵלֶת וְאַרְגָּמָן וְתוֹלַעַת שָׁנִי וְשֵׁשׁ וְעִזִּים: ‎5 וְעֹרֹת אֵילִם מְאָדָּמִים וְעֹרֹת תְּחָשִׁים וַעֲצֵי שִׁטִּים: ‎6 שֶׁמֶן לַמָּאֹר בְּשָׂמִים לְשֶׁמֶן הַמִּשְׁחָה וְלִקְטֹרֶת הַסַּמִּים: ‎7 אַבְנֵי־שֹׁהַם וְאַבְנֵי מִלֻּאִים לָאֵפֹד וְלַחֹשֶׁן: ‎8 וְעָשׂוּ לִי מִקְדָּשׁ וְשָׁכַנְתִּי בְּתוֹכָם: ‎9 כְּכֹל אֲשֶׁר אֲנִי מַרְאֶה אוֹתְךָ אֵת תַּבְנִית הַמִּשְׁכָּן וְאֵת תַּבְנִית כָּל־כֵּלָיו וְכֵן תַּעֲשׂוּ: ס ‎10 וְעָשׂוּ אֲרוֹן עֲצֵי שִׁטִּים אַמָּתַיִם וָחֵצִי אָרְכּוֹ וְאַמָּה וָחֵצִי רָחְבּוֹ וְאַמָּה וָחֵצִי קֹמָתוֹ:

482

build a Tabernacle in the desert, so he brought acacia trees to Egypt and planted them. He commanded his children to take the trees with them when they left Egypt (*Rashi, 11th century*).

8. They should make a Sanctuary (dedicated) to Me and I will dwell among them. It would seem more accurate for the text to read "and I will dwell in *it*," in the singular, referring to the Sanctuary.

"*Them*," refers to the children of Israel, charging them with creating a dwelling within their hearts for God, inviting God to *"dwell among them"* (*Rabbi Moses Alshekh, 16th century*).

Rashi (v. 9) notes that the obligation to build a Sanctuary applies for future generations as well. This means, metaphorically speaking, that the people of *every* generation have the obligation and the ability to cultivate their hearts and minds as inner sanctuaries dedicated to the Divine (*Rabbi Meir Loeb Weisser, 19th century*).

10. An ark of acacia wood, two and a half cubits in its length. The three dimensions of the ark that housed the tablets, the essence of the Torah, are not whole numbers but fractions of one-half. These fractions teach you that a Torah scholar ought to be humble and contrite, seeing

kabbalah bites

25:10 If something is a logical absurdity, such as making a "square circle," can God still do it? Jewish philosophers, such as Maimonides, said, no, He cannot. The inability to do something which is utter nonsense does not reflect any weakness on God's part.

Kabbalists, however, disagreed. God, they argued, is not limited to the confines of the intellect. Just because *we* can't understand something doesn't mean that *He* can't do it.

Where is the proof? From the ark. While the ark always measured 2½ x 1½ cubits of space, through some awesome Divine intervention it took up no space in the Holy of Holies (*Babylonian Talmud, Yoma* 21a).

At the same time that it took up a fixed space it also took up no space. That is a logical absurdity, and yet God still made it happen.

parashat terumah

Contributions to the Tabernacle

25 ¹ God spoke to Moses, saying: ² Speak to the children of Israel, and have them (dedicate) to Me a contribution. Take My offering from every person whose heart inspires him to generosity. ³ These are the (types of) contribution that you shall collect from them:

Gold, silver, and copper; ⁴ turquoise, purple, and crimson wool; linen and goats' hair; ⁵ rams' skin dyed red, (multicolored) *taḥash* skins, and acacia wood; ⁶ oil for the (eternal) lamp; spices for the anointing oil and for the incense fumes; ⁷ *shoham* stones and filling stones for the apron and for the breastplate.

⁸ They should make a Sanctuary (dedicated) to Me and I will dwell among them.

⁹ You should make the Tabernacle and the design of all its vessels according to all that I show you.

The Ark

¹⁰ They should make an ark of acacia wood, two and a half cubits in its length, a cubit and a half in its width, and a cubit and a half in its height.

---

kabbalah bites

25:3 *"Gold, silver, and copper."* If you are awakened to your essential true nature you will recognize that same essence in all other people. When you sense the Divine essence in every person, however lowly he or she may be, you will recognize it as one with your own essence and love it as yourself.

So the Tabernacle had to include not only gold (spiritual giants) and silver (the righteous), it also contained copper, alluding to the wicked and unredeemed. (Copper, *NeHoSHet*, is suggestive of the evil *NaHaSH*, the primordial Serpent.)

At the level of essence, we are all one.

25:1 Have them (dedicate) [lit. take] to Me a contribution. The contributions to the Tabernacle had two dimensions: (a) the act of *donation*—which *removed* the contribution from the owner's private possession, the realm of the mundane; and (b) the act of *collection*—which *elevated* the contribution to become the sacred property of the Tabernacle.

This represents two modes of worship: (a) *refraining from evil*—by which you *remove* undesirable habits and actions from yourself; and (b) *doing good*—through which you *elevate* this world towards the perfection for which it was originally intended.

In practice, the act of donation did not have to be accompanied by holy intentions, whereas the act of collection did. The lesson here is that when you refrain from doing bad, the purity of your intentions is not of paramount importance; but when you do good deeds and commandments, thereby making a "home" for God in this world, pure intentions are of the utmost importance (*Rabbi Menahem Mendel Schneerson, 20th century*).

5. Acacia wood. Rabbi Tanḥuma states that Jacob saw prophetically that the Jewish people were destined to

שמות כה:יא-כא — תרומה

11 וְצִפִּיתָ אֹתוֹ זָהָב טָהוֹר מִבַּיִת וּמִחוּץ תְּצַפֶּנּוּ וְעָשִׂיתָ עָלָיו זֵר זָהָב סָבִיב:
12 וְיָצַקְתָּ לּוֹ אַרְבַּע טַבְּעֹת זָהָב וְנָתַתָּה עַל אַרְבַּע פַּעֲמֹתָיו וּשְׁתֵּי טַבָּעֹת עַל־צַלְעוֹ הָאֶחָת וּשְׁתֵּי טַבָּעֹת עַל־צַלְעוֹ הַשֵּׁנִית:
13 וְעָשִׂיתָ בַדֵּי עֲצֵי שִׁטִּים וְצִפִּיתָ אֹתָם זָהָב:
14 וְהֵבֵאתָ אֶת־הַבַּדִּים בַּטַּבָּעֹת עַל צַלְעֹת הָאָרֹן לָשֵׂאת אֶת־הָאָרֹן בָּהֶם:
15 בְּטַבְּעֹת הָאָרֹן יִהְיוּ הַבַּדִּים לֹא יָסֻרוּ מִמֶּנּוּ:
16 וְנָתַתָּ אֶל־הָאָרֹן אֵת הָעֵדֻת אֲשֶׁר אֶתֵּן אֵלֶיךָ: [SECOND READING]
17 וְעָשִׂיתָ כַפֹּרֶת זָהָב טָהוֹר אַמָּתַיִם וָחֵצִי אָרְכָּהּ וְאַמָּה וָחֵצִי רָחְבָּהּ:
18 וְעָשִׂיתָ שְׁנַיִם כְּרֻבִים זָהָב מִקְשָׁה תַּעֲשֶׂה אֹתָם מִשְּׁנֵי קְצוֹת הַכַּפֹּרֶת:
19 וַעֲשֵׂה כְּרוּב אֶחָד מִקָּצָה מִזֶּה וּכְרוּב־אֶחָד מִקָּצָה מִזֶּה מִן־הַכַּפֹּרֶת תַּעֲשׂוּ אֶת־הַכְּרֻבִים עַל־שְׁנֵי קְצוֹתָיו:
20 וְהָיוּ הַכְּרֻבִים פֹּרְשֵׂי כְנָפַיִם לְמַעְלָה סֹכְכִים בְּכַנְפֵיהֶם עַל־הַכַּפֹּרֶת וּפְנֵיהֶם אִישׁ אֶל־אָחִיו אֶל־הַכַּפֹּרֶת יִהְיוּ פְּנֵי הַכְּרֻבִים:
21 וְנָתַתָּ אֶת־הַכַּפֹּרֶת עַל־הָאָרֹן מִלְמָעְלָה

This was an expression of God's love for His people, in the spirit of the verse, *"From when Israel was a child I have loved him"* (*Hosea* 11:1; *Rabbi Jacob b. Asher, 13th–14th century*).

In addition, the cherubim on the ark containing the Torah served to remind those engaging in Torah study that they ought to study the Torah like a child who is pure, innocent of sin and accepting of authority (*Rabbi Hayyim Joseph David Azulai, 18th century*).

20. The cherubim should have their wings spread upwards, sheltering the lid with their wings. The world survives in the merit of children studying Torah (*Babylonian Talmud, Shabbat 119b*). This Talmudic dictum is implied by the verse, *"Out of the mouths of babes and sucklings have You established strength"* (*Psalms* 8:3). From the conclusion of the same verse, *"...so that You might silence the enemy and the avenger,"* we can glean that children's Torah study also shields us from negative forces.

This protective quality is reflected in the description of the cherubim on the ark, which contained the Torah. The cherubim, whose faces resembled youths, spread their wings in a sheltering posture, indicating that the Torah study of youngsters serves as a protection for the entire community (*Rabbi Abraham b. Jacob Saba, 15th century*).

Their faces toward one another. In contrast to the description here of cherubim facing each other, the cherubim in Solomon's Temple are described as *"standing up, facing the House"* (*II Chronicles* 3:13), so that their faces were pointed *away* from each other, eastward.

In our verse the cherubim face each other, suggesting the loving relationship between God and His people when Israel obeyed the will of God. The second verse, where the cherubim are turned away from each other, refers to a time when Israel did not obey the will of God (*Babylonian Talmud, Bava Batra* 99a).

exodus 25:11–21 — terumah

¹¹ You should coat it with pure gold, coating it inside and out, and you should make upon it a golden-rimmed edge all around.

¹² You should cast four golden rings for it, and you should place them upon its four corners: two rings on its first side, and two rings on its other side.

¹³ You should make poles of acacia wood and you should coat them with gold.

¹⁴ You should bring the poles into the rings on the sides of the ark, to carry the ark with them. ¹⁵ The poles of the ark should remain in the rings. They must (never) be removed from it.

¹⁶ You should place into the ark, the (Tablets of) Testimony which I will give you.

[SECOND READING] ¹⁷ You should make a lid (for the ark) of pure gold, two and a half cubits in its length and a cubit and a half in its width. ¹⁸ You should make two golden cherubim (each with the face of a child). Make them from (the same piece of metal) hammered out from the two ends of the lid. ¹⁹ Make one cherub from one end and the other cherub from the other end. Make (one of) the cherubim at each of the two ends of the lid (from the same piece of metal). ²⁰ The cherubim should have their wings spread upwards, sheltering the lid with their wings, their faces toward one another. The faces of the cherubim should be turned towards the lid. ²¹ You should place the lid on the ark from above.

---

himself as having achieved only half his goals in Torah study and devotion to God (*Rabbi Jacob b. Asher, 13th–14th century*).

15. The poles of the ark should remain in the rings. They must (never) be removed. The reason for this requirement can be understood by a comparison with the kindling of the candelabrum.

Maimonides maintained that the candelabrum in the Temple was lit even in daytime. This is consistent with the rabbinic teaching that the candelabrum was not used for illumination (see *Babylonian Talmud, Shabbat* 22b). In order to *demonstrate* that the candelabrum was not meant as a source of light, the Torah commanded that it be kindled during the daytime—the understanding being that even at night the candelabrum is not meant as a source of light.

Similarly, the Torah commands that the poles remain in the rings of the ark, never to be removed. The implication is that the poles were not needed to transport the ark, since "the ark carries itself" (*Babylonian Talmud, Sotah* 35a). Just as the poles in the rings were not needed when the ark was at rest, they also were not needed when the ark was being moved (*Rabbi Meir Simhah of Dvinsk, 19th–20th century*).

18. Two golden cherubim. The facial features of the cherubim resembled a child's face. Indeed, the term "cherub" means "like a child" (*ke-ruv*), as in the Aramaic word for a child: *ravya'* (*Babylonian Talmud, Sukkah* 5b; *Rashi, 11th century*).

Food for thought

1. Why did God request a physical house?

2. How have you made your own home inviting for God's presence?

3. How do you feel when asked to donate to a sacred cause?

שמות כה:כא-לב | תרומה

וְאֶל־הָאָרֹן תִּתֵּן אֶת־הָעֵדֻת אֲשֶׁר אֶתֵּן אֵלֶיךָ: 22 וְנוֹעַדְתִּי לְךָ שָׁם וְדִבַּרְתִּי אִתְּךָ מֵעַל הַכַּפֹּרֶת מִבֵּין שְׁנֵי הַכְּרֻבִים אֲשֶׁר עַל־אֲרוֹן הָעֵדֻת אֵת כָּל־אֲשֶׁר אֲצַוֶּה אוֹתְךָ אֶל־בְּנֵי יִשְׂרָאֵל: פ 23 וְעָשִׂיתָ שֻׁלְחָן עֲצֵי שִׁטִּים אַמָּתַיִם אָרְכּוֹ וְאַמָּה רָחְבּוֹ וְאַמָּה וָחֵצִי קֹמָתוֹ: 24 וְצִפִּיתָ אֹתוֹ זָהָב טָהוֹר וְעָשִׂיתָ לּוֹ זֵר זָהָב סָבִיב: 25 וְעָשִׂיתָ לּוֹ מִסְגֶּרֶת טֹפַח סָבִיב וְעָשִׂיתָ זֵר־זָהָב לְמִסְגַּרְתּוֹ סָבִיב: 26 וְעָשִׂיתָ לּוֹ אַרְבַּע טַבְּעֹת זָהָב וְנָתַתָּ אֶת־הַטַּבָּעֹת עַל אַרְבַּע הַפֵּאֹת אֲשֶׁר לְאַרְבַּע רַגְלָיו: 27 לְעֻמַּת הַמִּסְגֶּרֶת תִּהְיֶיןָ הַטַּבָּעֹת לְבָתִּים לְבַדִּים לָשֵׂאת אֶת־הַשֻּׁלְחָן: 28 וְעָשִׂיתָ אֶת־הַבַּדִּים עֲצֵי שִׁטִּים וְצִפִּיתָ אֹתָם זָהָב וְנִשָּׂא־בָם אֶת־הַשֻּׁלְחָן: 29 וְעָשִׂיתָ קְּעָרֹתָיו וְכַפֹּתָיו וּקְשׂוֹתָיו וּמְנַקִּיֹּתָיו אֲשֶׁר יֻסַּךְ בָּהֵן זָהָב טָהוֹר תַּעֲשֶׂה אֹתָם: 30 וְנָתַתָּ עַל־הַשֻּׁלְחָן לֶחֶם פָּנִים לְפָנַי תָּמִיד: פ 31 וְעָשִׂיתָ מְנֹרַת זָהָב טָהוֹר מִקְשָׁה תֵּיעָשֶׂה הַמְּנוֹרָה יְרֵכָהּ וְקָנָהּ [THIRD READING] גְּבִיעֶיהָ כַּפְתֹּרֶיהָ וּפְרָחֶיהָ מִמֶּנָּה יִהְיוּ: 32 וְשִׁשָּׁה קָנִים יֹצְאִים מִצִּדֶּיהָ שְׁלֹשָׁה |

22. I will arrange My meetings with you there. I will speak with you from above the lid between the two cherubim. This was one of the ways in which Moses' prophecy differed from that of the other prophets. Moses heard God communicate with him *directly*, from above the lid between the two cherubim, without any intermediary: *"It was I who told him mouth to mouth"* (Numbers 12:8; Maimonides, 12th century).

23. Make a table. The verses describing the table immediately follow the verses describing the ark that contained the Torah, alluding to the Sages' statement, *"When three people eat at the same table and discuss Torah, it is as if they have eaten from the table of God"* (Mishnah, Avot 3:3; Rabbi Ephraim b. Isaac of Regensburg, 12th century).

32. Six branches should be coming out of its sides (diagonally). Unlike the popular misconception that the branches are curved—as on the Arch of Titus in Rome—the recent discovery of Maimonides' handwritten diagram proves that the image of the vessels of the Temple on the Arch of Titus is inaccurate. Maimonides clearly depicts them as straight, diagonal branches (as is also clearly the opinion of *Rashi* to this verse).

Food for thought

1. Are diversity ("branches") and unity ("common base") mutually exclusive?

2. How can we promote the sense that we are branches of the same *menorah*?

3. In which ways are you a "source of light" to others?

You should place the (Tablets of) Testimony which I will give you into the ark. ²² I will arrange My meetings with you there. I will speak with you from above the lid, between the two cherubim that are upon the Ark of the Testimony, and (what I speak to you there is) all that I will command you to tell the children of Israel.

The Table

²³ You should make a table of acacia wood, two cubits in its length, one cubit in its width, and a cubit and a half in its height. ²⁴ You should coat it with pure gold, and you should make for it a golden-rimmed edge all around.

²⁵ You should make for it a frame one handbreadth in width all around. You should make a golden-rimmed edge for its frame all around.

²⁶ You should make for it (the table) four golden rings, and you should place the rings on the four corners of its four legs. ²⁷ The rings should be (attached to the legs) adjacent to the frame, as holders for the poles with which to carry the table.

²⁸ You should make the poles of acacia wood, and you should coat them with gold. The table should be carried with them.

²⁹ You should make its (i.e. the table's) bread-molds, its spoons, its separating bars—which will cover (the breads, and allow ventilation)—and its supporting bars. You should make them from pure gold.

³⁰ You should place on the table multisurface bread before Me at all times.

The Candelabrum

[THIRD READING] ³¹ You should make a candelabrum of pure gold. The candelabrum should be made (from a single metal block that is then) hammered. Its base and its stem, its (ornamental) cups, spheres, and flowers should all come from (the same piece of metal and not be made separately).

³² Six branches should be coming out of its sides (diagonally): three candelabrum

kabbalah bites

25:31 *"The candelabrum should be made hammered (from a single piece of metal)."* The seven branches of the candelabrum represented the complete range of Divine emotional attributes (*Sefirot*): *Ḥesed* (kindness), *Gevurah* (severity), *Tiferet* (beauty), *Netzaḥ* (victory), *Hod* (splendor), *Yesod* (connection) and *Malkhut* (humility).

One of the dangers of studying the Kabbalah is that you might take these metaphors too literally. As much as the *Sefirot* are real and distinct, you need to remember that they are all absorbed in God's absolute oneness. Therefore, the candelabrum, which alludes to the *Sefirot*, was made of *"a single piece of metal."*

שמות כה:לב - כו:ג | תרומה

קְנֵי מְנֹרָה מִצִּדָּהּ הָאֶחָד וּשְׁלֹשָׁה קְנֵי מְנֹרָה מִצִּדָּהּ הַשֵּׁנִי: 33 שְׁלֹשָׁה גְבִעִים מְשֻׁקָּדִים בַּקָּנֶה הָאֶחָד כַּפְתֹּר וָפֶרַח וּשְׁלֹשָׁה גְבִעִים מְשֻׁקָּדִים בַּקָּנֶה הָאֶחָד כַּפְתֹּר וָפָרַח כֵּן לְשֵׁשֶׁת הַקָּנִים הַיֹּצְאִים מִן־הַמְּנֹרָה: 34 וּבַמְּנֹרָה אַרְבָּעָה גְבִעִים מְשֻׁקָּדִים כַּפְתֹּרֶיהָ וּפְרָחֶיהָ: 35 וְכַפְתֹּר תַּחַת שְׁנֵי הַקָּנִים מִמֶּנָּה וְכַפְתֹּר תַּחַת שְׁנֵי הַקָּנִים מִמֶּנָּה וְכַפְתֹּר תַּחַת־שְׁנֵי הַקָּנִים מִמֶּנָּה לְשֵׁשֶׁת הַקָּנִים הַיֹּצְאִים מִן־הַמְּנֹרָה: 36 כַּפְתֹּרֵיהֶם וּקְנֹתָם מִמֶּנָּה יִהְיוּ כֻּלָּהּ מִקְשָׁה אַחַת זָהָב טָהוֹר: 37 וְעָשִׂיתָ אֶת־נֵרֹתֶיהָ שִׁבְעָה וְהֶעֱלָה אֶת־נֵרֹתֶיהָ וְהֵאִיר עַל־עֵבֶר פָּנֶיהָ: 38 וּמַלְקָחֶיהָ וּמַחְתֹּתֶיהָ זָהָב טָהוֹר: 39 כִּכַּר זָהָב טָהוֹר יַעֲשֶׂה אֹתָהּ אֵת כָּל־הַכֵּלִים הָאֵלֶּה: 40 וּרְאֵה וַעֲשֵׂה בְּתַבְנִיתָם אֲשֶׁר־אַתָּה מָרְאֶה בָּהָר: ס

כו 1 וְאֶת־הַמִּשְׁכָּן תַּעֲשֶׂה עֶשֶׂר יְרִיעֹת שֵׁשׁ מָשְׁזָר וּתְכֵלֶת וְאַרְגָּמָן וְתֹלַעַת שָׁנִי כְּרֻבִים מַעֲשֵׂה חֹשֵׁב תַּעֲשֶׂה אֹתָם: 2 אֹרֶךְ | הַיְרִיעָה הָאַחַת שְׁמֹנֶה וְעֶשְׂרִים בָּאַמָּה וְרֹחַב אַרְבַּע בָּאַמָּה הַיְרִיעָה הָאֶחָת מִדָּה אַחַת לְכָל־הַיְרִיעֹת: 3 חֲמֵשׁ הַיְרִיעֹת תִּהְיֶיןָ חֹבְרֹת אִשָּׁה אֶל־אֲחֹתָהּ וְחָמֵשׁ יְרִיעֹת חֹבְרֹת אִשָּׁה אֶל־

33. Three decorated cups. The general purpose of the candelabrum is to "spill out" spiritual light and holiness throughout the entire world. In fact, we also find that the windows of the Temple are wide on the outside and narrow within (the reverse of common practice), indicating that light flows outwards from the Temple (*Babylonian Talmud, Menahot* 86b; and *Rashi*, ibid.).

kabbalah bites

26:1 When God created the world, He covered Himself with primordial light and used it to create the heavens.

Light and darkness were not together, because light is from the right side and darkness is from the left side. What did God do? He joined them together and created the heaven from them.

What are "heavens" (SHaMAYIM)? 'ESH (fire) and MAYIM (water). He joined them together and made peace between them.

And when they were joined together, He expanded them and spread them like a curtain. And this is the meaning of the verse: *"You should make the Tabernacle from ten tapestries."*

branches from one of its sides and three candelabrum branches from its second side.

³³ On one branch, put three decorated cups, a sphere and a flower. On the next branch, put three decorated cups, a sphere and a flower. So too for all six branches that come out of the candelabrum.

³⁴ On (the stem of) the candelabrum, there should be four decorated cups: (one below the point where the branches emerge, and three at the top), together with its spheres and its flowers.

³⁵ There should be a sphere (on the stem) where the (first) two branches come out of it, a sphere where the (next) two branches come out of it, and a sphere where the (last) two branches come out of it. (This covers) all six branches that come out of the candelabrum.

³⁶ Its spheres and branches should all be (formed) from it. All of it should be one hammered mass of pure gold.

³⁷ You should make seven lamps for it, and (the mouths of the lamps should be arranged so that when) he kindles its lamps, they shed light toward its center.

³⁸ Its wick-tongs and its ash-scoops should be of pure gold.

³⁹ It should be made from (exactly) a *kikkar* of pure gold, including all these utensils.

⁴⁰ Observe their design which you are being shown on the mountain, and construct accordingly.

Coverings of the Tabernacle

26 ¹ You should make the (roof of the) Tabernacle from ten tapestries made of fine linen thread twisted with turquoise, purple, and crimson wool thread. Animal designs should be professionally woven into them (on both sides).

² The length of each tapestry should be twenty-eight cubits, and the width of each tapestry should be four cubits. The same measurements apply to all the tapestries.

³ Five of these tapestries should be stitched to one another, and the other five tapestries should also be stitched to one another.

There are several possible reasons for this mistake: (a) perhaps the artist did not attempt to make a precise image; (b) Titus may never have discovered the original candelabrum, as many of the holy vessels were hidden in anticipation of the Temple's prophesied destruction; or (c) the artist may have attempted to depict a different candelabrum altogether.

Whatever the reason may be, the drawing is inaccurate and ought not to be copied in publications or in our *menorahs* used on Ḥanukkah (*Rabbi Menahem Mendel Schneerson, 20th century*).

שמות כו:ג-יז — תרומה

אֶחָֽתָה׃ 4 וְעָשִׂ֜יתָ לֻֽלְאֹ֣ת תְּכֵ֗לֶת עַ֣ל שְׂפַ֤ת הַיְרִיעָה֙ הָאֶחָ֔ת מִקָּצָ֖ה בַּחֹבָ֑רֶת וְכֵ֤ן תַּעֲשֶׂה֙ בִּשְׂפַ֣ת הַיְרִיעָ֔ה הַקִּ֣יצוֹנָ֔ה בַּמַּחְבֶּ֖רֶת הַשֵּׁנִֽית׃ 5 חֲמִשִּׁ֣ים לֻֽלָאֹ֗ת תַּעֲשֶׂה֮ בַּיְרִיעָ֣ה הָאֶחָת֒ וַחֲמִשִּׁ֣ים לֻֽלָאֹ֗ת תַּעֲשֶׂה֙ בִּקְצֵ֣ה הַיְרִיעָ֔ה אֲשֶׁ֖ר בַּמַּחְבֶּ֣רֶת הַשֵּׁנִ֑ית מַקְבִּילֹת֙ הַלֻּ֣לָאֹ֔ת אִשָּׁ֖ה אֶל־אֲחֹתָֽהּ׃ 6 וְעָשִׂ֕יתָ חֲמִשִּׁ֖ים קַרְסֵ֣י זָהָ֑ב וְחִבַּרְתָּ֨ אֶת־הַיְרִיעֹ֜ת אִשָּׁ֤ה אֶל־אֲחֹתָהּ֙ בַּקְּרָסִ֔ים וְהָיָ֥ה הַמִּשְׁכָּ֖ן אֶחָֽד׃ 7 וְעָשִׂ֙יתָ֙ יְרִיעֹ֣ת עִזִּ֔ים לְאֹ֖הֶל עַל־הַמִּשְׁכָּ֑ן עַשְׁתֵּי־עֶשְׂרֵ֥ה יְרִיעֹ֖ת תַּעֲשֶׂ֥ה אֹתָֽם׃ 8 אֹ֣רֶךְ ׀ הַיְרִיעָ֣ה הָאַחַ֗ת שְׁלֹשִׁים֙ בָּֽאַמָּ֔ה וְרֹ֙חַב֙ אַרְבַּ֣ע בָּֽאַמָּ֔ה הַיְרִיעָ֖ה הָאֶחָ֑ת מִדָּ֣ה אַחַ֔ת לְעַשְׁתֵּ֥י עֶשְׂרֵ֖ה יְרִיעֹֽת׃ 9 וְחִבַּרְתָּ֞ אֶת־חֲמֵ֤שׁ הַיְרִיעֹת֙ לְבָ֔ד וְאֶת־שֵׁ֥שׁ הַיְרִיעֹ֖ת לְבָ֑ד וְכָפַלְתָּ֙ אֶת־הַיְרִיעָ֣ה הַשִּׁשִּׁ֔ית אֶל־מ֖וּל פְּנֵ֥י הָאֹֽהֶל׃ 10 וְעָשִׂ֜יתָ חֲמִשִּׁ֣ים לֻֽלָאֹ֗ת עַ֣ל שְׂפַ֤ת הַיְרִיעָה֙ הָֽאֶחָ֔ת הַקִּֽיצֹנָ֖ה בַּחֹבָ֑רֶת וַחֲמִשִּׁ֣ים לֻֽלָאֹ֗ת עַ֚ל שְׂפַ֣ת הַיְרִיעָ֔ה הַחֹבֶ֖רֶת הַשֵּׁנִֽית׃ 11 וְעָשִׂ֛יתָ קַרְסֵ֥י נְחֹ֖שֶׁת חֲמִשִּׁ֑ים וְהֵבֵאתָ֤ אֶת־הַקְּרָסִים֙ בַּלֻּ֣לָאֹ֔ת וְחִבַּרְתָּ֥ אֶת־הָאֹ֖הֶל וְהָיָ֥ה אֶחָֽד׃ 12 וְסֶ֙רַח֙ הָעֹדֵ֔ף בִּירִיעֹ֖ת הָאֹ֑הֶל חֲצִ֤י הַיְרִיעָה֙ הָעֹדֶ֔פֶת תִּסְרַ֕ח עַ֖ל אֲחֹרֵ֥י הַמִּשְׁכָּֽן׃ 13 וְהָאַמָּ֨ה מִזֶּ֜ה וְהָאַמָּ֤ה מִזֶּה֙ בָּעֹדֵ֔ף בְּאֹ֖רֶךְ יְרִיעֹ֣ת הָאֹ֑הֶל יִהְיֶ֨ה סָר֜וּחַ עַל־צִדֵּ֧י הַמִּשְׁכָּ֛ן מִזֶּ֥ה וּמִזֶּ֖ה לְכַסֹּתֽוֹ׃ 14 וְעָשִׂ֤יתָ מִכְסֶה֙ לָאֹ֔הֶל עֹרֹ֥ת אֵילִ֖ם מְאָדָּמִ֑ים וּמִכְסֵ֛ה עֹרֹ֥ת תְּחָשִׁ֖ים מִלְמָֽעְלָה׃ פ [FOURTH READING] 15 וְעָשִׂ֥יתָ אֶת־הַקְּרָשִׁ֖ים לַמִּשְׁכָּ֑ן עֲצֵ֥י שִׁטִּ֖ים עֹמְדִֽים׃ 16 עֶ֥שֶׂר אַמּ֖וֹת אֹ֣רֶךְ הַקָּ֑רֶשׁ וְאַמָּה֙ וַחֲצִ֣י הָֽאַמָּ֔ה רֹ֖חַב הַקֶּ֥רֶשׁ הָאֶחָֽד׃ 17 שְׁתֵּ֣י יָד֗וֹת לַקֶּ֙רֶשׁ֙ הָֽאֶחָ֔ד מְשֻׁלָּבֹ֔ת אִשָּׁ֖ה

Folly can take two forms of expression: A lack of reasoning that causes a person to act in a foolish manner. In this vein, the *Talmud* describes every sin as an act of folly, since, inherently, a Jewish person wants to observe the Torah, and it is only a "spirit of folly" that convinces him to sin.

A second form of folly stems from, not the lack of reason, but the ability to *transcend* reason when necessary.

Devotion to God demands this second type of "folly," which enables you to recognize and accept a higher Being who transcends the limited human mind (*Rabbi Samuel Schneersohn of Lubavitch, 19th century*).

exodus 26:4–17   terumah

⁴ You should make loops of turquoise wool on the edge of the tapestry which is at the end of the first group (of five tapestries), and you should do the same on the edge of the end tapestry of the second group (of five tapestries). ⁵ You should make fifty loops on the edge of the first tapestry, and you should make fifty loops on the edge of the tapestry from the second group. The loops (on the two different tapestries) should be aligned opposite one another.

⁶ You should make fifty golden clasps, and you should fasten the (two groups of) tapestries to one another with the clasps, so that the (roof of the) Tabernacle will become one.

⁷ You should make sheets of goats' hair for a covering over the Tabernacle. You should make eleven sheets. ⁸ The length of each sheet should be thirty cubits, and the width of each sheet four cubits. The same dimensions apply for the eleven sheets.

⁹ You should join five sheets by themselves, and the (other) six sheets by themselves. You should fold (half of) the sixth sheet over the entrance of the tent.

¹⁰ You should make fifty loops on the edge of the first sheet, at the end of one group, and fifty loops on the edge of the (end) sheet of the second set.

¹¹ You should make fifty copper clasps. You should bring the clasps into the loops, and you should fasten the tent together so that it will become one.

¹² (There will be an) overhanging excess in the sheets of the tent (since the sheets are bigger than the tapestries). Half of the extra sheets should hang over the rear (i.e. west side) of the Tabernacle (where the tapestries leave two cubits of beams exposed). ¹³ The (extra) cubit from one side and the cubit from the other side from the excess in the length of the sheets of the tent should hang over the (north and south) sides of the Tabernacle, on both sides, to cover it.

¹⁴ You should make a (further) covering for the (goats' hair) tent, made of rams' skin dyed red, and a covering of *taḥash* skins should be made above.

Walls and Contents of the Tabernacle

[FOURTH READING] ¹⁵ You should make the beams for the Tabernacle of acacia wood, standing upright. ¹⁶ The length of each beam should be ten cubits, and the width of each beam should be a cubit and a half. ¹⁷ Each beam should have two square pegs

---

The cups on the candelabrum represent receptacles that collect spiritual energy from the upper realms and then spill them out into the world at large, irrigating it with positive influence (*Rabbi Baḥya b. Asher, 13th century*).

26:15 Make the beams of the Tabernacle of acacia wood. The beams of the Tabernacle were made from acacia wood—*shittim*, in Hebrew, which is related to the word *shetut*, meaning "folly" (*Midrash Tanḥuma*).

שמות כו:יז-ל | תרומה

אֶל־אֲחֹתָ֑הּ כֵּ֣ן תַּעֲשֶׂ֔ה לְכֹ֖ל קַרְשֵׁ֥י הַמִּשְׁכָּֽן: 18 וְעָשִׂ֥יתָ אֶת־הַקְּרָשִׁ֖ים לַמִּשְׁכָּ֑ן עֶשְׂרִ֣ים קֶ֔רֶשׁ לִפְאַ֖ת נֶ֥גְבָּה תֵימָֽנָה: 19 וְאַרְבָּעִ֞ים אַדְנֵי־כֶ֗סֶף תַּעֲשֶׂ֔ה תַּ֖חַת עֶשְׂרִ֣ים הַקָּ֑רֶשׁ שְׁנֵ֣י אֲדָנִ֗ים תַּֽחַת־הַקֶּ֤רֶשׁ הָֽאֶחָד֙ לִשְׁתֵּ֣י יְדֹתָ֔יו וּשְׁנֵ֣י אֲדָנִ֗ים תַּֽחַת־הַקֶּ֥רֶשׁ הָֽאֶחָ֖ד לִשְׁתֵּ֥י יְדֹתָֽיו: 20 וּלְצֶ֧לַע הַמִּשְׁכָּ֛ן הַשֵּׁנִ֖ית לִפְאַ֣ת צָפ֑וֹן עֶשְׂרִ֖ים קָֽרֶשׁ: 21 וְאַרְבָּעִ֥ים אַדְנֵיהֶ֖ם כָּ֑סֶף שְׁנֵ֣י אֲדָנִ֗ים תַּ֚חַת הַקֶּ֣רֶשׁ הָֽאֶחָ֔ד וּשְׁנֵ֣י אֲדָנִ֔ים תַּ֖חַת הַקֶּ֥רֶשׁ הָאֶחָֽד: 22 וּֽלְיַרְכְּתֵ֥י הַמִּשְׁכָּ֖ן יָ֑מָּה תַּעֲשֶׂ֖ה שִׁשָּׁ֥ה קְרָשִֽׁים: 23 וּשְׁנֵ֤י קְרָשִׁים֙ תַּעֲשֶׂ֔ה לִמְקֻצְעֹ֖ת הַמִּשְׁכָּ֑ן בַּיַּרְכָתָֽיִם: 24 וְיִֽהְי֣וּ תֹֽאֲמִם֮ מִלְּמַטָּה֒ וְיַחְדָּ֗ו יִהְי֤וּ תַמִּים֙ עַל־רֹאשׁ֔וֹ אֶל־הַטַּבַּ֖עַת הָאֶחָ֑ת כֵּ֚ן יִהְיֶ֣ה לִשְׁנֵיהֶ֔ם לִשְׁנֵ֥י הַמִּקְצֹעֹ֖ת יִהְיֽוּ: 25 וְהָיוּ֙ שְׁמֹנָ֣ה קְרָשִׁ֔ים וְאַדְנֵיהֶ֣ם כֶּ֔סֶף שִׁשָּׁ֥ה עָשָׂ֖ר אֲדָנִ֑ים שְׁנֵ֣י אֲדָנִ֗ים תַּ֚חַת הַקֶּ֣רֶשׁ הָֽאֶחָ֔ד וּשְׁנֵ֣י אֲדָנִ֔ים תַּ֖חַת הַקֶּ֥רֶשׁ הָאֶחָֽד: 26 וְעָשִׂ֥יתָ בְרִיחִ֖ם עֲצֵ֣י שִׁטִּ֑ים חֲמִשָּׁ֕ה לְקַרְשֵׁ֥י צֶֽלַע־הַמִּשְׁכָּ֖ן הָאֶחָֽד: 27 וַחֲמִשָּׁ֣ה בְרִיחִ֗ם לְקַרְשֵׁי֙ צֶֽלַע־הַמִּשְׁכָּ֔ן הַשֵּׁנִ֑ית וַחֲמִשָּׁ֣ה בְרִיחִ֗ם לְקַרְשֵׁי֙ צֶ֣לַע הַמִּשְׁכָּ֔ן לַיַּרְכָתַ֖יִם יָֽמָּה: 28 וְהַבְּרִ֥יחַ הַתִּיכֹ֖ן בְּת֣וֹךְ הַקְּרָשִׁ֑ים מַבְרִ֕חַ מִן־הַקָּצֶ֖ה אֶל־הַקָּצֶֽה: 29 וְֽאֶת־הַקְּרָשִׁ֞ים תְּצַפֶּ֣ה זָהָ֗ב וְאֶת־טַבְּעֹתֵיהֶם֙ תַּעֲשֶׂ֣ה זָהָ֔ב בָּתִּ֖ים לַבְּרִיחִ֑ם וְצִפִּיתָ֥ אֶת־הַבְּרִיחִ֖ם זָהָֽב: 30 וַהֲקֵמֹתָ֖ אֶת־הַמִּשְׁכָּ֑ן כְּמִ֨שְׁפָּט֔וֹ אֲשֶׁ֥ר הָרְאֵ֖יתָ בָּהָֽר: ס

kabbalah bites

26:19 *"Silver sockets."* One would have expected the main structure of the Tabernacle to make use of precious metal, and the foundational supports to be something more functional and practical. Yet we find it was the other way around: The foundations were made of silver and the main structure from wood. Why?

Sometimes, the connection is more important than the structure.

Your body structure is mainly bones and muscle, but it is those little tendons that join muscle to bone which make movement possible.

God already made the physical and the spiritual. It is our precious task to connect them. So in the Tabernacle, which was the model of God's plans for creation, the connecting pieces were made of precious metal.

(carved at the bottom, separated) like rungs, aligned opposite each other. In this way you should make all the beams of the Tabernacle.

¹⁸ You should make the beams for the Tabernacle (as follows): twenty beams for the southern side. ¹⁹ You should make forty silver sockets under the twenty beams: two sockets under one beam, for its two square pegs, and two sockets under the next beam, for its two square pegs (etc.).

²⁰ For the second side of the Tabernacle, on the northern side: twenty beams, ²¹ their forty silver sockets, two sockets under one beam and two sockets under the next beam.

²² For the western end of the Tabernacle, you should make six beams. ²³ You should make two (further) beams at the (northwestern and southwestern) corners of the Tabernacle, at the end.

²⁴ (All the beams) should fit closely next to each other at the bottom. They should fit together closely at the top and be connected (to each other) by a ring (which slots into grooves carved into the beam). So too for both of the two (beams) at the two corners.

²⁵ (Thus, on the western side,) there should be eight beams and their silver sockets—sixteen sockets—two sockets under one beam and two sockets under the next beam.

²⁶ You should make crossbars of acacia wood: five for the beams of one side of the Tabernacle, ²⁷ five crossbars for the beams of the second side of the Tabernacle, and five crossbars for the beams of the rear side of the Tabernacle, on the western end. ²⁸ The middle bar goes inside the beams and extends from one end to the other end.

²⁹ You should coat the beams with gold. You should make rings (on the beams) of gold as holders for the crossbars, and you should coat the crossbars with gold.

³⁰ (After constructing its components separately,) you should erect the Tabernacle correctly, as you will have been shown on the mountain.

spiritual vitamin

> Divine Providence is the basis of true monotheism, a concept that to us means not only that God is one, but also is the Master, continually supervising every detail of His handiwork. *There cannot be a single point in the whole order of the world that is separated from the Supreme Being, or in any way not subject to His control.*

שמות כו:לא - כז:ה — תרומה

31 וְעָשִׂיתָ פָרֹכֶת תְּכֵלֶת וְאַרְגָּמָן וְתוֹלַעַת שָׁנִי וְשֵׁשׁ מָשְׁזָר מַעֲשֵׂה [FIFTH READING]
חֹשֵׁב יַעֲשֶׂה אֹתָהּ כְּרֻבִים: 32 וְנָתַתָּה אֹתָהּ עַל־אַרְבָּעָה עַמּוּדֵי שִׁטִּים מְצֻפִּים
זָהָב וָוֵיהֶם זָהָב עַל־אַרְבָּעָה אַדְנֵי־כָסֶף: 33 וְנָתַתָּה אֶת־הַפָּרֹכֶת תַּחַת הַקְּרָסִים
וְהֵבֵאתָ שָׁמָּה מִבֵּית לַפָּרֹכֶת אֵת אֲרוֹן הָעֵדוּת וְהִבְדִּילָה הַפָּרֹכֶת לָכֶם בֵּין
הַקֹּדֶשׁ וּבֵין קֹדֶשׁ הַקֳּדָשִׁים: 34 וְנָתַתָּ אֶת־הַכַּפֹּרֶת עַל אֲרוֹן הָעֵדֻת בְּקֹדֶשׁ
הַקֳּדָשִׁים: 35 וְשַׂמְתָּ אֶת־הַשֻּׁלְחָן מִחוּץ לַפָּרֹכֶת וְאֶת־הַמְּנֹרָה נֹכַח הַשֻּׁלְחָן עַל
צֶלַע הַמִּשְׁכָּן תֵּימָנָה וְהַשֻּׁלְחָן תִּתֵּן עַל־צֶלַע צָפוֹן: 36 וְעָשִׂיתָ מָסָךְ לְפֶתַח הָאֹהֶל
תְּכֵלֶת וְאַרְגָּמָן וְתוֹלַעַת שָׁנִי וְשֵׁשׁ מָשְׁזָר מַעֲשֵׂה רֹקֵם: 37 וְעָשִׂיתָ לַמָּסָךְ חֲמִשָּׁה
עַמּוּדֵי שִׁטִּים וְצִפִּיתָ אֹתָם זָהָב וָוֵיהֶם זָהָב וְיָצַקְתָּ לָהֶם חֲמִשָּׁה אַדְנֵי נְחֹשֶׁת: ס

494

כז 1 וְעָשִׂיתָ אֶת־הַמִּזְבֵּחַ עֲצֵי שִׁטִּים חָמֵשׁ אַמּוֹת אֹרֶךְ וְחָמֵשׁ [SIXTH READING]
אַמּוֹת רֹחַב רָבוּעַ יִהְיֶה הַמִּזְבֵּחַ וְשָׁלֹשׁ אַמּוֹת קֹמָתוֹ: 2 וְעָשִׂיתָ קַרְנֹתָיו
עַל אַרְבַּע פִּנֹּתָיו מִמֶּנּוּ תִּהְיֶיןָ קַרְנֹתָיו וְצִפִּיתָ אֹתוֹ נְחֹשֶׁת: 3 וְעָשִׂיתָ סִּירֹתָיו
לְדַשְּׁנוֹ וְיָעָיו וּמִזְרְקֹתָיו וּמִזְלְגֹתָיו וּמַחְתֹּתָיו לְכָל־כֵּלָיו תַּעֲשֶׂה נְחֹשֶׁת: 4 וְעָשִׂיתָ
לּוֹ מִכְבָּר מַעֲשֵׂה רֶשֶׁת נְחֹשֶׁת וְעָשִׂיתָ עַל־הָרֶשֶׁת אַרְבַּע טַבְּעֹת נְחֹשֶׁת עַל
אַרְבַּע קְצוֹתָיו: 5 וְנָתַתָּה אֹתָהּ תַּחַת כַּרְכֹּב הַמִּזְבֵּחַ מִלְּמָטָּה וְהָיְתָה הָרֶשֶׁת

spiritual vitamin

" The word *terumah* has two meanings; in the plain sense it means a contribution to a sacred cause. In a deeper sense, *terumah* means "elevation." Both meanings go hand in hand.

By making a contribution to a sacred cause you elevate the money from its material state to a higher spiritual plain. You also elevate your whole being, including all the energy and effort that went into earning the money which you donated. "

[FIFTH READING] ³¹ You should make a partition of turquoise, purple, and crimson wool thread, twisted with fine linen thread. Animal designs should be professionally woven into it (on both sides).

³² You should place it on four pillars of acacia wood, coated with gold—with gold hooks (to hold the partition)—inserted into four silver sockets. ³³ You should place the partition under the hooks.

You should bring the Ark of the Testimony there, to the inner side of the partition. The partition should separate for you between the Sanctuary and the Holy of Holies.

³⁴ You should place the lid over the Ark of the Testimony in the Holy of Holies.

³⁵ You should place the table on the outer side of the partition, and the candelabrum opposite the table, on the southern side of the Tabernacle. You should place the table on the northern side.

³⁶ You should make a curtain for the entrance of the tent, of turquoise, purple, and crimson wool thread, twisted with fine linen thread, professionally woven (with images on both sides). ³⁷ You should make for the curtain five pillars of acacia wood and coat them with gold. Their hooks should be gold. You should cast for them five copper sockets.

The Copper Altar

27 [SIXTH READING] ¹ You should make the altar of acacia wood, five cubits long and five cubits wide. The altar should be square, and its height should be three cubits. ² You should make protrusions on its four corners. Its protrusions should be from (the same single piece of wood). You should coat it with copper.

³ You should make for it pots to remove its ashes, shovels, sacrificial basins, flesh-hooks and fire-pans. You should make all its utensils from copper.

⁴ You should make for it a lattice of copper netting, and you should make on the netting four copper rings on its four ends. ⁵ You should place it (the lattice) beneath the decorative border of the altar, downwards. The lattice should extend downward until the middle of the altar.

27:1-2 Make the altar of acacia wood ... coat it with copper. Moses asked God, "You instructed me to build an altar of wood and plate it with a very thin coating of copper. The fire, which must burn day and night (see *Leviticus* 6:6), will inevitably burn through the copper plate and char the wood!"

God answered, "The heavenly fire that will descend upon the altar does not have the same properties as ordinary fire. It is a burning flame, but it does not consume."

This can be seen from Moses' own experience, when he *"drew near to ... where God was"* (20:18). Although Scripture describes God as a *"consuming fire"* (4:24), nevertheless, Moses was not burned, since he approached for the sake of God's honor (*Midrash Tanḥuma*).

שמות כז:ה-יט | תרומה

עַד חֲצִי הַמִּזְבֵּחַ: 6 וְעָשִׂיתָ בַדִּים לַמִּזְבֵּחַ בַּדֵּי עֲצֵי שִׁטִּים וְצִפִּיתָ אֹתָם נְחֹשֶׁת: 7 וְהוּבָא אֶת־בַּדָּיו בַּטַּבָּעֹת וְהָיוּ הַבַּדִּים עַל־שְׁתֵּי צַלְעֹת הַמִּזְבֵּחַ בִּשְׂאֵת אֹתוֹ: 8 נְבוּב לֻחֹת תַּעֲשֶׂה אֹתוֹ כַּאֲשֶׁר הֶרְאָה אֹתְךָ בָּהָר כֵּן יַעֲשׂוּ: ס [SEVENTH READING] 9 וְעָשִׂיתָ אֵת חֲצַר הַמִּשְׁכָּן לִפְאַת נֶגֶב־תֵּימָנָה קְלָעִים לֶחָצֵר שֵׁשׁ מָשְׁזָר מֵאָה בָאַמָּה אֹרֶךְ לַפֵּאָה הָאֶחָת: 10 וְעַמֻּדָיו עֶשְׂרִים וְאַדְנֵיהֶם עֶשְׂרִים נְחֹשֶׁת וָוֵי הָעַמֻּדִים וַחֲשֻׁקֵיהֶם כָּסֶף: 11 וְכֵן לִפְאַת צָפוֹן בָּאֹרֶךְ קְלָעִים מֵאָה אֹרֶךְ וְעַמֻּדָו עֶשְׂרִים וְאַדְנֵיהֶם עֶשְׂרִים נְחֹשֶׁת וָוֵי הָעַמֻּדִים וַחֲשֻׁקֵיהֶם כָּסֶף: 12 וְרֹחַב הֶחָצֵר לִפְאַת־יָם קְלָעִים חֲמִשִּׁים אַמָּה עַמֻּדֵיהֶם עֲשָׂרָה וְאַדְנֵיהֶם עֲשָׂרָה: 13 וְרֹחַב הֶחָצֵר לִפְאַת קֵדְמָה מִזְרָחָה חֲמִשִּׁים אַמָּה: 14 וַחֲמֵשׁ עֶשְׂרֵה אַמָּה קְלָעִים לַכָּתֵף עַמֻּדֵיהֶם שְׁלֹשָׁה וְאַדְנֵיהֶם שְׁלֹשָׁה: 15 וְלַכָּתֵף הַשֵּׁנִית חֲמֵשׁ עֶשְׂרֵה קְלָעִים עַמֻּדֵיהֶם שְׁלֹשָׁה וְאַדְנֵיהֶם שְׁלֹשָׁה: 16 וּלְשַׁעַר הֶחָצֵר מָסָךְ | עֶשְׂרִים אַמָּה תְּכֵלֶת וְאַרְגָּמָן וְתוֹלַעַת שָׁנִי וְשֵׁשׁ מָשְׁזָר מַעֲשֵׂה רֹקֵם עַמֻּדֵיהֶם אַרְבָּעָה וְאַדְנֵיהֶם אַרְבָּעָה: [MAFTIR] 17 כָּל־עַמּוּדֵי הֶחָצֵר סָבִיב מְחֻשָּׁקִים כֶּסֶף וָוֵיהֶם כָּסֶף וְאַדְנֵיהֶם נְחֹשֶׁת: 18 אֹרֶךְ הֶחָצֵר מֵאָה בָאַמָּה וְרֹחַב | חֲמִשִּׁים בַּחֲמִשִּׁים וְקֹמָה חָמֵשׁ אַמּוֹת שֵׁשׁ מָשְׁזָר וְאַדְנֵיהֶם נְחֹשֶׁת: 19 לְכֹל כְּלֵי הַמִּשְׁכָּן בְּכֹל עֲבֹדָתוֹ וְכָל־יְתֵדֹתָיו וְכָל־יִתְדֹת הֶחָצֵר נְחֹשֶׁת: ס ס ס

צ"ו פסוקים, יעי"ו סימן, סל"ו סימן.

spiritual vitamin

" Although, at this time, the Sanctuary, the Holy Temple, is not in existence, the sanctuary which is within your heart is always there. *Cultivate it and make it effective in sanctifying all of your life.* "

exodus 27:6–19 — terumah

⁶ You should make poles for the altar, poles of acacia wood. You should coat them with copper. ⁷ Its poles should be inserted into the rings, and the poles should be on both sides of the altar when it is carried.

⁸ You should make it (the altar) hollow, out of panels.

Just as you were shown on the mountain, so should they do.

The Courtyard of the Tabernacle

[SEVENTH READING] ⁹ You should make the courtyard of the Tabernacle (as follows): On the southern side there should be (perforated) curtains for the courtyard of twisted linen, one hundred cubits long on one side. ¹⁰ It should have twenty pillars and twenty sockets of copper. The hooks of the pillars and their belts should be of silver. ¹¹ So too for the length of the northern side: curtains one hundred cubits long, twenty pillars, and twenty sockets for them made of copper, the hooks of the pillars and their silver belts.

¹² For the width of the courtyard on the western side: curtains fifty cubits (long), ten pillars and ten sockets for them.

¹³ The width of the courtyard on the eastern side: fifty cubits (consisting of an entrance of twenty cubits and a fifteen cubit "shoulder" curtain on each side). ¹⁴ The curtains on one shoulder should be fifteen cubits, with three pillars and three sockets. ¹⁵ On the second shoulder there should be fifteen curtains, with three pillars and three sockets. ¹⁶ At the entrance of the courtyard should be a professionally woven tapestry of twenty cubits, made of turquoise, purple, and crimson wool thread, twisted with linen thread. (The tapestry should be supported by) four pillars and sockets.

[MAFTIR] ¹⁷ All the pillars around the courtyard (including the east and west sides) should have silver bands, silver hooks, and copper sockets.

¹⁸ The length of the courtyard should be one hundred cubits, and the width, fifty. (The space within the courtyard to the east of the Sanctuary is fifty) by fifty cubits. The height of the curtains should be five cubits, made of twisted fine linen, and their sockets should be of copper.

¹⁹ All the equipment (used to assemble and dismantle) the Tabernacle for all its service, and all its pegs (used to tie the curtains to the ground), and all the pegs of the courtyard, should be made from copper.

Food for thought

1. Why does the Torah pay so much attention to the details of the Tabernacle?

2. Do you have a special area in your home devoted to heightened spirituality?

3. What "resources" have you devoted to your inner "sanctuary"?

Haftarot: Terumah—page 1332. *Shekalim*—page 1424. *Zakhor*—page 1427. *Rosh Ḥodesh*—page 1417.
Maftir: Shekalim—page 520 (30:11–16). *Zakhor*—page 1208 (25:17–19).
Rosh Ḥodesh—page 1000 (28:9–15).

> In the Tabernacle **God communicated** to us through the Urim and Thummim, in **the High-Priest's breastplate.** Now God speaks through **your inner voice** and conscience. He is saying: "Just do a **little bit more** for Me today."

TETZAVVEH
תצוה

OIL FOR THE CANDELABRUM	27:20–21
APPOINTMENT OF PRIESTS; PRIESTLY GARMENTS	28:1–43
INAUGURATION OF AARON AND HIS SONS	29:1–46
THE GOLDEN INCENSE ALTAR	30:1–10

NAME
Tetzavveh

MEANING
"You should command"

LINES IN TORAH SCROLL
179

PARASHIYYOT
2 open; 8 closed

VERSES
101

WORDS
1412

LETTERS
5430

DATE
10 *Tishri*, 2449

LOCATION
Mount Sinai

KEY PEOPLE
Moses, Aaron, Nadab, Abihu, Eleazar, Ithamar

MITZVOT
4 positive; 3 prohibitions

CHARACTER PROFILE

NAME
Nadab and Abihu

MEANING
Nadab ("[God] has been generous"); Abihu ("He is my Father")

PARENTS
Aaron and Elisheba

GRANDFATHERS
Amram, Amminadab

SIBLINGS
Eleazar and Ithamar

ACHIEVEMENTS
Were deputy high priests; were mourned by the whole Jewish people

KNOWN FOR
Never married; entered the Holy of Holies and offered an unauthorized fire; desired so strongly to connect with God that their souls left their physical bodies and did not return; their physical bodies were kept intact and they were pulled from the Holy of Holies by their clothing and then buried

LIGHT

The western lamp in the Tabernacle burned continually; the Jewish people are charged to be a "light unto the nations," spreading light and goodness to the whole world (27:20).

BEAUTY

The priestly garments were made from the most lavish materials and put together by skilled artists. Make sure that all the rituals that you perform are done in the most beautiful way possible, and then you will honor God (28:2).

INNER DEVOTION

There were two altars in the Tabernacle: a copper altar outside in the courtyard, and a golden altar within the Sanctuary. Worshiping God has two elements: the public service of action and then the inner service of the heart and its feelings for God (30:6).

שמות כז:כ - כח:ג   תצוה

20 וְאַתָּ֞ה תְּצַוֶּ֣ה | אֶת־בְּנֵ֣י יִשְׂרָאֵ֗ל וְיִקְח֨וּ אֵלֶ֜יךָ שֶׁ֣מֶן זַ֥יִת זָ֛ךְ כָּתִ֖ית לַמָּא֑וֹר לְהַעֲלֹ֥ת
נֵ֖ר תָּמִֽיד: 21 בְּאֹ֣הֶל מוֹעֵד֩ מִח֨וּץ לַפָּרֹ֜כֶת אֲשֶׁ֣ר עַל־הָעֵדֻ֗ת יַעֲרֹךְ֩ אֹת֨וֹ אַהֲרֹ֧ן וּבָנָ֛יו
מֵעֶ֥רֶב עַד־בֹּ֖קֶר לִפְנֵ֣י יְהֹוָ֑ה חֻקַּ֤ת עוֹלָם֙ לְדֹ֣רֹתָ֔ם מֵאֵ֖ת בְּנֵ֥י יִשְׂרָאֵֽל: ס

כח 1 וְאַתָּ֡ה הַקְרֵ֣ב אֵלֶיךָ֩ אֶת־אַהֲרֹ֨ן אָחִ֜יךָ וְאֶת־בָּנָ֣יו אִתּ֔וֹ מִתּ֛וֹךְ
בְּנֵ֥י יִשְׂרָאֵ֖ל לְכַהֲנוֹ־לִ֑י אַהֲרֹ֕ן נָדָ֧ב וַאֲבִיה֛וּא אֶלְעָזָ֥ר וְאִיתָמָ֖ר בְּנֵ֥י
אַהֲרֹֽן: 2 וְעָשִׂ֥יתָ בִגְדֵי־קֹ֖דֶשׁ לְאַהֲרֹ֣ן אָחִ֑יךָ לְכָב֖וֹד וּלְתִפְאָֽרֶת: 3 וְאַתָּ֗ה תְּדַבֵּר֙
אֶל־כָּל־חַכְמֵי־לֵ֔ב אֲשֶׁ֥ר מִלֵּאתִ֖יו ר֣וּחַ חָכְמָ֑ה וְעָשׂ֞וּ אֶת־בִּגְדֵ֧י אַהֲרֹ֛ן לְקַדְּשׁ֖וֹ

Also, oil does not mix with other liquids; it always remains on top (*Exodus Rabbah*). Throughout history it has been astonishing that, despite their hardships, Israel has remained above its tormentors, neither intermingling with them nor imitating their way of life (*Rabbi Abraham b. Jacob Saba, 15th century*).

They should bring to you. Normally, when the Torah issues a command about the construction of the Tabernacle and its contents, we find that the expression "You should *make*" is used. Here, however, this would be inappropriate, since the Jewish people would not have had any fresh olives with them in the desert from which olive oil could be produced. So how could they be told to "make" olive oil?

Rather, the command to donate olive oil must have been fulfilled using olive oil which the Jewish people *already* had with them—oil which they took out of Egypt. Therefore, the verse says, "They should *bring* to you clear olive oil," since it was the *existing* olive oil that needed to be collected and passed before Moses for inspection, to see if it was of sufficient quality (*Naḥmanides, 13th century*).

28:1 Draw Aaron your brother close. God chose Aaron as an intermediary between Himself and the Jewish people, to teach them how to serve Him, just as Moses had acted as an intermediary through which God had been given the Torah on earth.

In other words, Moses was the intermediary through which Divine service *descended* into the world, and Aaron was to be the intermediary through which Divine service would be carried out on earth, causing it to *ascend* heavenward. Therefore, it was necessary for Moses to bring Aaron "close" to himself, elevating Aaron to his own level (*Rabbi Meir Loeb Weisser, 19th century*).

> **kabbalah bites**
>
> **28:1** Every sacrifice must involve the three divisions of Israel: Priests, who perform the sacrificial ritual; Levites, who accompany the sacrifice with song; and the Israelite, who offers the sacrifice.
>
> All three are necessary as they reflect the triad of essential Divine attributes: Priest=*Ḥesed* (kindness), Levite=*Gevurah* (severity) and Israelite=*Raḥamim* (mercy).
>
> But if the Levites are *Gevurah* how could Aaron and his sons have originated from the Levite clan, which is their polar opposite? Because that is the way of God: He can bring water from fire and fire from water.

exodus 27:20 – 28:3 tetzavveh

parashat tetzavveh

Oil for the Candelabrum

²⁰ And you should command the children of Israel that they should bring to you clear olive oil, crushed for lighting, to ignite the lamp (until it burns) continually. ²¹ In the Tent of Meeting, outside the partition that is in front of the (Ark of) Testimony, Aaron and his sons should arrange that it (has sufficient oil to burn) from evening to morning before God. This is an eternal law for the children of Israel.

Appointment of Priests—Priestly Garments

28 ¹ (When the Tabernacle is built,) you should draw Aaron your brother close to you, together with his sons, (separating them) from the children of Israel, to serve Me as priests, i.e., Aaron, and Nadab, Abihu, Eleazar and Ithamar, Aaron's sons.

² You should make holy garments for your brother Aaron, for honor and splendor.

³ You shall speak to all the wise-hearted people, whom I have filled with the spirit of wisdom, and they shall make Aaron's garments to consecrate him, so that he can serve Me as a priest.

27:20 You should command. When the Jews sinned with the Golden Calf, Moses exclaimed to God that if He would not forgive the Jewish people then, *"Please erase me from Your Book (the Torah) which You have written!"* (32:32).

There is a principle that the request of a saintly person (*tzaddik*) is always fulfilled unconditionally, regardless of any clauses that the *tzaddik* himself may attach to the request. In our case, even though the Jewish people were ultimately pardoned by God, Moses' request to be erased from the Torah still had to be fulfilled in some way.

For this reason, Moses' name is not mentioned in this entire Torah portion, so that in a subtle way, it could be said that he was "erased" from the Torah. Therefore, this portion begins, "And *you* should command," avoiding any reference to Moses' name directly (*Rabbi Jacob b. Asher, 14th century*).

Clear olive oil. The olive oil had to be pure and free of sediment (*Rashi, 11th century*).

The olives themselves had to be pure. If they were decayed or partially eaten (by birds) they could not be used for oil production (*Rabbi Abraham ibn Ezra, 12th century*).

Olive oil, crushed for lighting. The children of Israel are compared to an olive since olive oil is produced only when the olive is crushed, and the children of Israel reveal their innermost and strongest values when they are "crushed" with suffering (*Babylonian Talmud, Menaḥot* 53b).

Food for thought

1. Why is light often used as a metaphor for spirituality?

2. Have you had a "crushing" experience that proved to be illuminating?

3. "God's lamp is man's soul"; how often do you provide it with "fuel"?

תצוה
שמות כח:ג-טו

לְכַהֲנוֹ-לִי: 4 וְאֵלֶּה הַבְּגָדִים אֲשֶׁר יַעֲשׂוּ חֹשֶׁן וְאֵפוֹד וּמְעִיל וּכְתֹנֶת תַּשְׁבֵּץ מִצְנֶפֶת וְאַבְנֵט וְעָשׂוּ בִגְדֵי-קֹדֶשׁ לְאַהֲרֹן אָחִיךָ וּלְבָנָיו לְכַהֲנוֹ-לִי: 5 וְהֵם יִקְחוּ אֶת-הַזָּהָב וְאֶת-הַתְּכֵלֶת וְאֶת-הָאַרְגָּמָן וְאֶת-תּוֹלַעַת הַשָּׁנִי וְאֶת-הַשֵּׁשׁ: פ 6 וְעָשׂוּ אֶת-הָאֵפֹד זָהָב תְּכֵלֶת וְאַרְגָּמָן תּוֹלַעַת שָׁנִי וְשֵׁשׁ מָשְׁזָר מַעֲשֵׂה חֹשֵׁב: 7 שְׁתֵּי כְתֵפֹת חֹבְרֹת יִהְיֶה-לּוֹ אֶל-שְׁנֵי קְצוֹתָיו וְחֻבָּר: 8 וְחֵשֶׁב אֲפֻדָּתוֹ אֲשֶׁר עָלָיו כְּמַעֲשֵׂהוּ מִמֶּנּוּ יִהְיֶה זָהָב תְּכֵלֶת וְאַרְגָּמָן וְתוֹלַעַת שָׁנִי וְשֵׁשׁ מָשְׁזָר: 9 וְלָקַחְתָּ אֶת-שְׁתֵּי אַבְנֵי-שֹׁהַם וּפִתַּחְתָּ עֲלֵיהֶם שְׁמוֹת בְּנֵי יִשְׂרָאֵל: 10 שִׁשָּׁה מִשְּׁמֹתָם עַל הָאֶבֶן הָאֶחָת וְאֶת-שְׁמוֹת הַשִּׁשָּׁה הַנּוֹתָרִים עַל-הָאֶבֶן הַשֵּׁנִית כְּתוֹלְדֹתָם: 11 מַעֲשֵׂה חָרַשׁ אֶבֶן פִּתּוּחֵי חֹתָם תְּפַתַּח אֶת-שְׁתֵּי הָאֲבָנִים עַל-שְׁמֹת בְּנֵי יִשְׂרָאֵל מֻסַבֹּת מִשְׁבְּצוֹת זָהָב תַּעֲשֶׂה אֹתָם: 12 וְשַׂמְתָּ אֶת-שְׁתֵּי הָאֲבָנִים עַל כִּתְפֹת הָאֵפֹד אַבְנֵי זִכָּרֹן לִבְנֵי יִשְׂרָאֵל וְנָשָׂא אַהֲרֹן אֶת-שְׁמוֹתָם לִפְנֵי יְהֹוָה עַל-שְׁתֵּי כְתֵפָיו לְזִכָּרֹן: ס [SECOND READING] 13 וְעָשִׂיתָ מִשְׁבְּצֹת זָהָב: 14 וּשְׁתֵּי שַׁרְשְׁרֹת זָהָב טָהוֹר מִגְבָּלֹת תַּעֲשֶׂה אֹתָם מַעֲשֵׂה עֲבֹת וְנָתַתָּה אֶת-שַׁרְשְׁרֹת הָעֲבֹתֹת עַל-הַמִּשְׁבְּצֹת: ס 15 וְעָשִׂיתָ חֹשֶׁן מִשְׁפָּט מַעֲשֵׂה חֹשֵׁב כְּמַעֲשֵׂה אֵפֹד תַּעֲשֶׂנּוּ זָהָב תְּכֵלֶת וְאַרְגָּמָן וְתוֹלַעַת שָׁנִי וְשֵׁשׁ מָשְׁזָר

which he would gird himself, was an indication of his trust in God which always supported him. And the *robe* was a sign of his great fear of God, since it was made entirely of turquoise wool (a reminder of the heavens) (*Rabbi Mordecai Joseph Leiner of Izbica, 19th century*).

12. Aaron should bear their names upon his two shoulders before God as a remembrance. Aaron was commanded to *"bear their names upon his shoulders,"* as if he was carrying the children of Israel on his shoulders, protecting them from danger. This requirement reflects an important function of the High Priest: to pray for the children of Israel and protect them with his merit (*Rabbi Ḥayyim of Tchernowitz, 18th century*).

15. You should make a breastplate of judgment. *Rashi* writes that the breastplate served as atonement for the incorrect rulings of the Jewish courts. Of the stones in the breastplate, some were rare, and others were more common. This combination is intended as a lesson to judges: each individual case, small or large, must be treated equally (*Rabbi Isaac b. Moses Arama, 15th century*).

exodus 28:4–15   tetzavveh

⁴ These are the garments that they should make:

A breastplate, an apron, a robe, a checkered tunic, a turban, and a sash.

They should make holy garments (from the materials which were consecrated to God) for your brother Aaron and for his sons, to serve Me as priests. ⁵ The (ones who make the garments) shall take (donations of) the gold, the turquoise, purple, and crimson wool, and the linen.

The Apron

⁶ They should make the apron of gold (thread), turquoise, purple, and crimson wool, and twisted fine linen, the work of a professional weaver.

⁷ It should have two connected shoulder straps at both of its ends. (The straps should first be woven separately and then) connected to it.

⁸ Its decorative belt, which is above it, should be made from it (woven professionally as one single piece, out of) gold (thread), turquoise, purple, and crimson wool, and twisted fine linen.

⁹ You should take two *shoham* stones and engrave upon them the names of the sons of Israel: ¹⁰ six of their names on one stone and the names of the remaining six on the second stone, in the order of their birth.

¹¹ Through a craftsman, you should engrave the two stones with the names of the sons of Israel in (clear script, as is used on) a signet ring. You should make them surrounded by gold settings. ¹² You should put the two stones on the shoulder straps of the apron, as stones of remembrance for the children of Israel. Aaron should bear their names upon his two shoulders before God, as a remembrance (of the righteousness of the tribes).

The Settings and the Breastplate

[SECOND READING] ¹³ You should make settings of gold (for the breastplate), ¹⁴ and two cables of pure gold for the edges (of the breastplate). You should make them from braided metal. (When you assemble the breastplate,) you will (need to) place the cables on the settings.

¹⁵ Through a professional weaver, you should make a breastplate of judgment. You should make it in a similar fashion to the apron, (i.e.) you should make it from gold (thread), turquoise, purple, and crimson wool, and twisted fine linen.

4. A breastplate, an apron, a robe. The garments reflected precious qualities in the soul of Aaron the priest which God desired. The *forehead-plate* (below, v. 36), showed that his mind was constantly attached heavenward, as the words "Holy unto God" were engraved on the plate, placed next on his head. The *breastplate* suggested that he harbored no hatred for any soul of Israel in his heart, since the names of all the tribes were engraved on his heart. The *apron*, with

תצוה

שמות כח:טז-ל

תַּעֲשֶׂה אֹתוֹ: 16 רָבוּעַ יִהְיֶה כָּפוּל זֶרֶת אָרְכּוֹ וְזֶרֶת רָחְבּוֹ: 17 וּמִלֵּאתָ בוֹ מִלֻּאַת אֶבֶן אַרְבָּעָה טוּרִים אָבֶן טוּר אֹדֶם פִּטְדָה וּבָרֶקֶת הַטּוּר הָאֶחָד: 18 וְהַטּוּר הַשֵּׁנִי נֹפֶךְ סַפִּיר וְיָהֲלֹם: 19 וְהַטּוּר הַשְּׁלִישִׁי לֶשֶׁם שְׁבוֹ וְאַחְלָמָה: 20 וְהַטּוּר הָרְבִיעִי תַּרְשִׁישׁ וְשֹׁהַם וְיָשְׁפֵה מְשֻׁבָּצִים זָהָב יִהְיוּ בְּמִלּוּאֹתָם: 21 וְהָאֲבָנִים תִּהְיֶיןָ עַל־שְׁמֹת בְּנֵי־יִשְׂרָאֵל שְׁתֵּים עֶשְׂרֵה עַל־שְׁמֹתָם פִּתּוּחֵי חוֹתָם אִישׁ עַל־שְׁמוֹ תִּהְיֶיןָ לִשְׁנֵי עָשָׂר שָׁבֶט: 22 וְעָשִׂיתָ עַל־הַחֹשֶׁן שַׁרְשֹׁת גַּבְלֻת מַעֲשֵׂה עֲבֹת זָהָב טָהוֹר: 23 וְעָשִׂיתָ עַל־הַחֹשֶׁן שְׁתֵּי טַבְּעוֹת זָהָב וְנָתַתָּ אֶת־שְׁתֵּי הַטַּבָּעוֹת עַל־שְׁנֵי קְצוֹת הַחֹשֶׁן: 24 וְנָתַתָּה אֶת־שְׁתֵּי עֲבֹתֹת הַזָּהָב עַל־שְׁתֵּי הַטַּבָּעֹת אֶל־קְצוֹת הַחֹשֶׁן: 25 וְאֵת שְׁתֵּי קְצוֹת שְׁתֵּי הָעֲבֹתֹת תִּתֵּן עַל־שְׁתֵּי הַמִּשְׁבְּצוֹת וְנָתַתָּה עַל־כִּתְפוֹת הָאֵפֹד אֶל־מוּל פָּנָיו: 26 וְעָשִׂיתָ שְׁתֵּי טַבְּעוֹת זָהָב וְשַׂמְתָּ אֹתָם עַל־שְׁנֵי קְצוֹת הַחֹשֶׁן עַל־שְׂפָתוֹ אֲשֶׁר אֶל־עֵבֶר הָאֵפוֹד בָּיְתָה: 27 וְעָשִׂיתָ שְׁתֵּי טַבְּעוֹת זָהָב וְנָתַתָּה אֹתָם עַל־שְׁתֵּי כִתְפוֹת הָאֵפוֹד מִלְּמַטָּה מִמּוּל פָּנָיו לְעֻמַּת מַחְבַּרְתּוֹ מִמַּעַל לְחֵשֶׁב הָאֵפוֹד: 28 וְיִרְכְּסוּ אֶת־הַחֹשֶׁן מִטַּבְּעֹתָו אֶל־טַבְּעֹת הָאֵפוֹד בִּפְתִיל תְּכֵלֶת לִהְיוֹת עַל־חֵשֶׁב הָאֵפוֹד וְלֹא־יִזַּח הַחֹשֶׁן מֵעַל הָאֵפוֹד: 29 וְנָשָׂא אַהֲרֹן אֶת־שְׁמוֹת בְּנֵי־יִשְׂרָאֵל בְּחֹשֶׁן הַמִּשְׁפָּט עַל־לִבּוֹ בְּבֹאוֹ אֶל־הַקֹּדֶשׁ לְזִכָּרֹן לִפְנֵי־יְהֹוָה תָּמִיד: 30 וְנָתַתָּ אֶל־חֹשֶׁן הַמִּשְׁפָּט אֶת־הָאוּרִים וְאֶת־הַתֻּמִּים וְהָיוּ עַל־לֵב אַהֲרֹן בְּבֹאוֹ לִפְנֵי יְהֹוָה

kabbalah bites

28:28 *"The breastplate will not move off the apron."* To move the breastplate off the apron represents a violation of one of the 613 commandments of the Torah. Why is this matter so serious?

The apron (*'efod*) has the *gematria*, numerical value, of 85, which spells *peh*, mouth. Moving the apron off the breastplate, which was positioned opposite the heart, represents a dissonance between what you feel (heart) and what you say (mouth). This is, in essence, a prohibition against duplicity.

¹⁶ When folded (and ready to be worn by the High Priest), it should be square, one span (half a cubit) in its length and one span in its width.

¹⁷ You should set it with precious gems, four rows of stones.

One row should be a row of red quartz, emerald, and yellow quartz.

¹⁸ The second row: ruby, sapphire, and beryl (blue-green gem).

¹⁹ The third row: red zirconium, striped quartz, and (violet) amethyst.

²⁰ The fourth row: yellow-green olivine, onyx, and jasper (opaque quartz).

They should be inlaid in gold in their settings.

²¹ The names of the children of Israel should be on the stones, twelve names in all. The names of the twelve tribes should be engraved according to (the order of their birth) in (clear script, as is used on) a signet ring.

²² You should make chains for the breastplate at the edges, of braided, pure gold. ²³ You should make two golden rings for the breastplate and you should place the two rings on the two ends of the breastplate, ²⁴ and you should place the two golden cables on the two rings, at the ends of the breastplate. ²⁵ You should place the two ends of the two cables upon the two settings, and these you should place on the shoulder straps of the apron, on its front part. ²⁶ You should make two golden rings, and you should place them on the two ends of the breastplate, on its edge that is toward the inner side of the apron. ²⁷ You should make two golden rings and place them on the two shoulder straps of the apron, from below, toward its front, adjacent to its seam, above the band of the apron. ²⁸ They should fasten the breastplate by its rings to the rings of the apron with a turquoise cord, so as to be upon the band of the apron, and the breastplate will not move off the apron.

²⁹ Aaron should carry the names of the sons of Israel in the breastplate of judgment over his heart when he enters the Holy Place, as a remembrance before God at all times.

³⁰ You should place the Urim and Thummim (a parchment containing God's name) into the (fold of the) breastplate of judgment, so that it will be over Aaron's heart when he comes before God.

kabbalah bites

28:17 Why did the breastplate have exactly twelve stones? Because there were twelve tribes.

And why were there twelve tribes—twelve fundamental soul paths of our people?

Because God's four-letter ineffable name, the Tetragrammaton, has twelve possible permutations. Everything flows into this world through one of those expressions of His name.

שמות כח:ל-לט תצוה

וְנָשָׂא אַהֲרֹן אֶת־מִשְׁפַּט בְּנֵי־יִשְׂרָאֵל עַל־לִבּוֹ לִפְנֵי יְהֹוָה תָּמִיד: ס [THIRD READING]
31 וְעָשִׂיתָ אֶת־מְעִיל הָאֵפוֹד כְּלִיל תְּכֵלֶת: 32 וְהָיָה פִי־רֹאשׁוֹ בְּתוֹכוֹ שָׂפָה יִהְיֶה לְפִיו סָבִיב מַעֲשֵׂה אֹרֵג כְּפִי תַחְרָא יִהְיֶה־לּוֹ לֹא יִקָּרֵעַ: 33 וְעָשִׂיתָ עַל־שׁוּלָיו רִמֹּנֵי תְּכֵלֶת וְאַרְגָּמָן וְתוֹלַעַת שָׁנִי עַל־שׁוּלָיו סָבִיב וּפַעֲמֹנֵי זָהָב בְּתוֹכָם סָבִיב: 34 פַּעֲמֹן זָהָב וְרִמּוֹן פַּעֲמֹן זָהָב וְרִמּוֹן עַל־שׁוּלֵי הַמְּעִיל סָבִיב: 35 וְהָיָה עַל־אַהֲרֹן לְשָׁרֵת וְנִשְׁמַע קוֹלוֹ בְּבֹאוֹ אֶל־הַקֹּדֶשׁ לִפְנֵי יְהֹוָה וּבְצֵאתוֹ וְלֹא יָמוּת: ס 36 וְעָשִׂיתָ צִּיץ זָהָב טָהוֹר וּפִתַּחְתָּ עָלָיו פִּתּוּחֵי חֹתָם קֹדֶשׁ לַיהֹוָה: 37 וְשַׂמְתָּ אֹתוֹ עַל־פְּתִיל תְּכֵלֶת וְהָיָה עַל־הַמִּצְנָפֶת אֶל־מוּל פְּנֵי־הַמִּצְנֶפֶת יִהְיֶה: 38 וְהָיָה עַל־מֵצַח אַהֲרֹן וְנָשָׂא אַהֲרֹן אֶת־עֲוֹן הַקֳּדָשִׁים אֲשֶׁר יַקְדִּישׁוּ בְּנֵי יִשְׂרָאֵל לְכָל־מַתְּנֹת קָדְשֵׁיהֶם וְהָיָה עַל־מִצְחוֹ תָּמִיד לְרָצוֹן לָהֶם לִפְנֵי יְהֹוָה: 39 וְשִׁבַּצְתָּ הַכְּתֹנֶת שֵׁשׁ וְעָשִׂיתָ מִצְנֶפֶת שֵׁשׁ וְאַבְנֵט תַּעֲשֶׂה מַעֲשֵׂה

is generally an admirable trait, but in a leadership position, you must speak forcefully. Your voice *"should be heard,"* so that the people will be inspired by your words (*Rabbi Aaron Lewin of Rzeszow, 20th century*).

39. A sash. All of the priestly garments had a specific purpose, except the sash. At first glance it seems that the sash was intended merely to hold the checkered tunic close to the body. However, the sash was 32 cubits (approx. 48ft.) long and was wound around the priest many times (*Code of Maimonides*), so if it was merely required to hold down the checkered tunic, a considerably shorter sash could have been used.

spiritual vitamin

> When carrying out activities which are connected with the physical and material aspects of life (i.e. most of your time) you should know that those material aspects are not an end in themselves. They are, and must serve as, the means to attain the higher, spiritual realm of life. Make sure you permeate all those materialistic-physical aspects with spiritual content, and utilize them for spiritual purpose.

Aaron will carry the (tool of) judgment of the children of Israel over his heart before God at all times.

The Robe

[THIRD READING] ³¹ You should make the robe (worn under) the apron entirely of turquoise wool. ³² Its collar at the top should be hemmed inside, the work of a professional weaver, like the collar of a coat of armor. It must not be torn.

³³ On its bottom edge, you should make pomegranate shapes of turquoise, purple, and crimson wool, all around the edge, and golden bells among them all around. ³⁴ A golden bell (should be followed by) a pomegranate, (which is followed by) a golden bell and (then another) pomegranate, (and so on), on the bottom edge of the robe, all around.

³⁵ It should be on Aaron when he performs the service, and its sound should be heard when he enters the Holy Place before God, and when he leaves, so that he will not die.

The Forehead-Plate

³⁶ You should make a forehead-plate of pure gold, and you should engrave on it in (clear script, as is used on) a signet ring, (the words), "Holy to God." ³⁷ You should place it upon a ribbon of turquoise wool, and it(s ribbons) should go over the turban. It should be on (the forehead to the) front of the turban. ³⁸ It should be upon Aaron's forehead, and (with it) Aaron will obtain (forgiveness for) the sin of sacrifices consecrated and all the holy gifts offered by the Jewish people (in a state of impurity). It should be upon his forehead at all times (when carrying out service in the Temple) to make them favorable before God.

The Tunic, Turban, Sash and Pants

³⁹ You should make the checkered tunic from linen (to be worn under the robe). You should make a linen turban.

You should make a sash, the work of a professional embroiderer.

---

30. Aaron will carry the (tool of) judgment of the children of Israel over his heart before God at all times. The breastplate atoned for "judgment," the incorrect rulings of the courts. Why did the breastplate have to be placed upon Aaron's *heart*?

The High Priest symbolized the emotional core ("heart") of the Jewish people. By carrying the "tool of judgment" over his heart, the High Priest demonstrated his commitment to pray to God to alleviate the suffering of the children of Israel caused by the incorrect rulings (*Rabbi Ḥayyim of Tchernowitz, 18ᵗʰ century*).

35. Its sound should be heard. This verse is a lesson to those in a leadership role. Sometimes leaders are inappropriately reserved and reticent, reluctant to raise their voices. Humility

שמות כח:לט - כט:ד

רִקְמָה: מ וְלִבְנֵי אַהֲרֹן תַּעֲשֶׂה כֻתֳּנֹת וְעָשִׂיתָ לָהֶם אַבְנֵטִים וּמִגְבָּעוֹת תַּעֲשֶׂה לָהֶם לְכָבוֹד וּלְתִפְאָרֶת: מא וְהִלְבַּשְׁתָּ אֹתָם אֶת־אַהֲרֹן אָחִיךָ וְאֶת־בָּנָיו אִתּוֹ וּמָשַׁחְתָּ אֹתָם וּמִלֵּאתָ אֶת־יָדָם וְקִדַּשְׁתָּ אֹתָם וְכִהֲנוּ לִי: מב וַעֲשֵׂה לָהֶם מִכְנְסֵי־בָד לְכַסּוֹת בְּשַׂר עֶרְוָה מִמָּתְנַיִם וְעַד־יְרֵכַיִם יִהְיוּ: מג וְהָיוּ עַל־אַהֲרֹן וְעַל־בָּנָיו בְּבֹאָם | אֶל־אֹהֶל מוֹעֵד אוֹ בְגִשְׁתָּם אֶל־הַמִּזְבֵּחַ לְשָׁרֵת בַּקֹּדֶשׁ וְלֹא־יִשְׂאוּ עָוֹן וָמֵתוּ חֻקַּת עוֹלָם לוֹ וּלְזַרְעוֹ אַחֲרָיו: ס

כט

[FOURTH READING] א וְזֶה הַדָּבָר אֲשֶׁר תַּעֲשֶׂה לָהֶם לְקַדֵּשׁ אֹתָם לְכַהֵן לִי לְקַח פַּר אֶחָד בֶּן־בָּקָר וְאֵילִם שְׁנַיִם תְּמִימִם: ב וְלֶחֶם מַצּוֹת וְחַלֹּת מַצֹּת בְּלוּלֹת בַּשֶּׁמֶן וּרְקִיקֵי מַצּוֹת מְשֻׁחִים בַּשָּׁמֶן סֹלֶת חִטִּים תַּעֲשֶׂה אֹתָם: ג וְנָתַתָּ אוֹתָם עַל־סַל אֶחָד וְהִקְרַבְתָּ אֹתָם בַּסָּל וְאֶת־הַפָּר וְאֵת שְׁנֵי הָאֵילִם: ד וְאֶת־אַהֲרֹן וְאֶת־בָּנָיו תַּקְרִיב אֶל־פֶּתַח אֹהֶל מוֹעֵד וְרָחַצְתָּ אֹתָם

- The *linen pants* atone for illicit relations—"Make for them linen pants *to cover the flesh of their nakedness*" (28:42).
- The *turban* atones for arrogance, as Rabbi Ḥanina said, "Let an article perched high atop the head atone for haughtiness."
- The *sash* atones for immoral thoughts of the heart—the priest wears it around his chest, just below his heart.
- The *breastplate* atones for neglect of civil laws—"You should make a breastplate of *judgment*" (28:15).
- The *apron* (ephod) atones for idolatry—"There is no ephod and, (as a result, there is) the sin of teraphim (idol-worship)" (Hosea 3:4).
- The *robe* to which the bells were attached atones for slander, as Rabbi Ḥanina said, "Let sound atone for the sinful 'sound' of slander."
- The *forehead-plate* atones for brazenness—"You had the *forehead* of a harlot" (Jeremiah 3:3; Babylonian Talmud, Arakhin 16a).

kabbalah bites

29:1 Why were there seven days of inaugurating the Tabernacle?

Because the Tabernacle was God's house, the pinnacle of creation. At this moment the world had returned to its absolute perfection prior to the sin of the Tree of Knowledge. So the seven days of inauguration represented the seven days of creation all over again, which had left us with a pure world.

exodus 28:40 – 29:4   tetzavveh

⁴⁰ For Aaron's sons (only four garments should be made). You should make tunics. You should make them sashes. You should make them high hats (i.e. turbans) for honor and glory (and make them pants, as mentioned below).

⁴¹ With the (eight garments described above) you should clothe Aaron, your brother, and his sons along with him (with four garments).

You should anoint (Aaron and his sons), inaugurate them (in office) and sanctify them so that they may serve Me as priests.

⁴² Make for them linen pants to cover the flesh of their nakedness. They should reach from the waist down to the thighs.

⁴³ The (appropriate garments) should be worn by Aaron and by his sons when they enter the Tent of Meeting (Tabernacle, or Holy Temple), or when they approach the altar to serve in holiness, so they will not bear a sin and die. It should be an eternal law for him and for his descendants after him.

Inauguration of Aaron and his Sons

29 [FOURTH READING] ¹ This is what you should do for them in order to sanctify them to serve Me as priests: Take one young bull and two rams, perfect ones (without blemish), ² unleavened bread (which has been boiled and fried), unleavened loaves mixed with oil (before baking,) and unleavened wafers anointed with oil (after baking), all of which you should make from fine wheat flour. ³ You should place them in a basket, and you should bring them in the basket, and the bull and the two rams.

⁴ You should bring Aaron and his sons near the entrance of the Tent of Meeting, and you should (immerse them totally) in water.

Food for thought

1. Why must the priest's attire be resplendent and beautiful?

2. Is there any part of Judaism that you observe especially beautifully?

3. Do you focus enough on the beauty and joy of the commandments?

Rather, the uniqueness of the sash is expressed precisely in the fact that it has no *specific* function. It thus represented the *general* readiness of the priest to perform God's service, in the spirit of the verse, *"Prepare to greet your God, O Israel"* (*Amos* 4:12). The multiple winding of the sash around the body prepared the priest mentally with a total readiness to stand before God in service (*Rabbi Menahem Mendel Schneerson, 20th century*).

29:1 This is what you should do for them in order to sanctify them to serve Me as priests: Take one young bull and two rams. The passage about the priestly garments is followed by the inaugural sacrifices of the priests. These texts are positioned in sequence to teach you that, just as the sacrifices atone, so do the priestly garments atone.

➤ The *tunic* atones for the spilling of blood, as alluded to in the verse, "They took Joseph's robe, slaughtered a young goat and dipped the *robe* into the *blood*" (*Genesis* 37:31).

שמות כט:ד-כ
תצוה

בַּמָּיִם: 5 וְלָקַחְתָּ אֶת־הַבְּגָדִים וְהִלְבַּשְׁתָּ אֶת־אַהֲרֹן אֶת־הַכֻּתֹּנֶת וְאֵת מְעִיל הָאֵפֹד וְאֶת־הָאֵפֹד וְאֶת־הַחֹשֶׁן וְאָפַדְתָּ לוֹ בְּחֵשֶׁב הָאֵפֹד: 6 וְשַׂמְתָּ הַמִּצְנֶפֶת עַל־רֹאשׁוֹ וְנָתַתָּ אֶת־נֵזֶר הַקֹּדֶשׁ עַל־הַמִּצְנָפֶת: 7 וְלָקַחְתָּ אֶת־שֶׁמֶן הַמִּשְׁחָה וְיָצַקְתָּ עַל־רֹאשׁוֹ וּמָשַׁחְתָּ אֹתוֹ: 8 וְאֶת־בָּנָיו תַּקְרִיב וְהִלְבַּשְׁתָּם כֻּתֳּנֹת: 9 וְחָגַרְתָּ אֹתָם אַבְנֵט אַהֲרֹן וּבָנָיו וְחָבַשְׁתָּ לָהֶם מִגְבָּעֹת וְהָיְתָה לָהֶם כְּהֻנָּה לְחֻקַּת עוֹלָם וּמִלֵּאתָ יַד־אַהֲרֹן וְיַד־בָּנָיו: 10 וְהִקְרַבְתָּ אֶת־הַפָּר לִפְנֵי אֹהֶל מוֹעֵד וְסָמַךְ אַהֲרֹן וּבָנָיו אֶת־יְדֵיהֶם עַל־רֹאשׁ הַפָּר: 11 וְשָׁחַטְתָּ אֶת־הַפָּר לִפְנֵי יְהֹוָה פֶּתַח אֹהֶל מוֹעֵד: 12 וְלָקַחְתָּ מִדַּם הַפָּר וְנָתַתָּה עַל־קַרְנֹת הַמִּזְבֵּחַ בְּאֶצְבָּעֶךָ וְאֶת־כָּל־הַדָּם תִּשְׁפֹּךְ אֶל־יְסוֹד הַמִּזְבֵּחַ: 13 וְלָקַחְתָּ אֶת־כָּל־הַחֵלֶב הַמְכַסֶּה אֶת־הַקֶּרֶב וְאֵת הַיֹּתֶרֶת עַל־הַכָּבֵד וְאֵת שְׁתֵּי הַכְּלָיֹת וְאֶת־הַחֵלֶב אֲשֶׁר עֲלֵיהֶן וְהִקְטַרְתָּ הַמִּזְבֵּחָה: 14 וְאֶת־בְּשַׂר הַפָּר וְאֶת־עֹרוֹ וְאֶת־פִּרְשׁוֹ תִּשְׂרֹף בָּאֵשׁ מִחוּץ לַמַּחֲנֶה חַטָּאת הוּא: 15 וְאֶת־הָאַיִל הָאֶחָד תִּקָּח וְסָמְכוּ אַהֲרֹן וּבָנָיו אֶת־יְדֵיהֶם עַל־רֹאשׁ הָאָיִל: 16 וְשָׁחַטְתָּ אֶת־הָאָיִל וְלָקַחְתָּ אֶת־דָּמוֹ וְזָרַקְתָּ עַל־הַמִּזְבֵּחַ סָבִיב: 17 וְאֶת־הָאַיִל תְּנַתֵּחַ לִנְתָחָיו וְרָחַצְתָּ קִרְבּוֹ וּכְרָעָיו וְנָתַתָּ עַל־נְתָחָיו וְעַל־רֹאשׁוֹ: 18 וְהִקְטַרְתָּ אֶת־כָּל־הָאַיִל הַמִּזְבֵּחָה עֹלָה הוּא לַיהֹוָה רֵיחַ נִיחוֹחַ אִשֶּׁה לַיהֹוָה הוּא: [FIFTH READING] 19 וְלָקַחְתָּ אֵת הָאַיִל הַשֵּׁנִי וְסָמַךְ אַהֲרֹן וּבָנָיו אֶת־יְדֵיהֶם עַל־רֹאשׁ הָאָיִל: 20 וְשָׁחַטְתָּ אֶת־הָאַיִל וְלָקַחְתָּ מִדָּמוֹ וְנָתַתָּה עַל־תְּנוּךְ אֹזֶן אַהֲרֹן וְעַל־תְּנוּךְ אֹזֶן בָּנָיו הַיְמָנִית וְעַל־

kabbalah bites

29:10, 16, 20 All phases of sacrificial ritual are the exclusive domain of the priest, except slaughter. Why is this the case?

Because a priest manifests Divine *Hesed* (kindness) and slaughter is a form of *Din* (judgment). So we cannot demand that the priest do something which is the opposite of his Divine energy.

exodus 29:5–20   tetzavveh

⁵ You should take the garments and clothe Aaron with the tunic, with the robe (worn under) the apron, with the apron, and with the breastplate, and you should adorn him with the decorative belt of the apron. ⁶ You should place the turban upon his head and place the holy crown (i.e. the forehead-plate) on his (forehead, tightening the ribbons over) the turban.

⁷ You should take the anointing oil and pour it on his head and anoint him.

⁸ You should bring his sons near, and you should clothe them with tunics. ⁹ You should gird them—Aaron and his sons—with sashes, and you should dress them with high hats (turbans).

The priesthood will be an eternal law for them. (By means of all these things) you will inaugurate Aaron and his sons into office.

¹⁰ You should bring the bull to the front of the Tent of Meeting. Aaron and his sons should lean their hands upon the head of the bull. ¹¹ You should then slaughter the bull before God (in the courtyard of the Tabernacle), at the entrance of the Tent of Meeting. ¹² You should take some of the blood of the bull and apply it on the horns of the altar with your finger, and you should pour out all the (remaining) blood onto the (protruding) base of the altar.

¹³ You should then take all the fat covering the stomach, the diaphragm (together with some of) the liver, the two kidneys and the fat which is on them, and make them go up in smoke upon the altar.

¹⁴ You should burn the flesh of the bull, its hide and its dung in fire outside the camp. It is a sin-offering.

¹⁵ You should take the ram, and Aaron and his sons should lean their hands on the ram's head. ¹⁶ You should slaughter the ram, and you should take its blood and sprinkle it on (two diagonally opposite horns of the) altar, (so it is visible) all around. ¹⁷ You should dissect the ram into its parts. You should wash its innards and its legs and put them with its (other) parts and with its head, ¹⁸ and you should make the entire ram go up in smoke upon the altar. It is a burnt-offering made to God, a pleasing fragrance (to Him). It is a fire-offering for God.

[FIFTH READING] ¹⁹ You should take the second ram, and Aaron and his sons should lean their hands upon the ram's head. ²⁰ You should slaughter the ram, take some of its blood and put it on the cartilage of Aaron's right ear and on the cartilage of Aaron's sons' right ears, on the thumbs of their right hands, and on the big toes

20. Put it on the cartilage of Aaron's right ear. Putting the ram's blood on the ear, hand, and foot of Aaron and his sons in the inauguration process served as an important lesson. We ought to dedicate our senses and our ability to act, represented by these body parts, to be used only for the service of God (*Rabbi Judah b. Joseph Muscato, 16ᵗʰ century*).

שמות כט:כ-לג | תצוה

בְּהֹ֤ן יָדָם֙ הַיְמָנִ֔ית וְעַל־בֹּ֥הֶן רַגְלָ֖ם הַיְמָנִ֑ית וְזָרַקְתָּ֧ אֶת־הַדָּ֛ם עַל־הַמִּזְבֵּ֖חַ סָבִֽיב:

21 וְלָקַחְתָּ֞ מִן־הַדָּ֨ם אֲשֶׁ֥ר עַֽל־הַמִּזְבֵּחַ֮ וּמִשֶּׁ֣מֶן הַמִּשְׁחָה֒ וְהִזֵּיתָ֤ עַֽל־אַהֲרֹן֙ וְעַל־בְּגָדָ֔יו וְעַל־בָּנָ֛יו וְעַל־בִּגְדֵ֥י בָנָ֖יו אִתּ֑וֹ וְקָדַ֥שׁ ה֛וּא וּבְגָדָ֖יו וּבָנָ֥יו וּבִגְדֵ֥י בָנָ֖יו אִתּֽוֹ:

22 וְלָקַחְתָּ֣ מִן־הָ֠אַ֠יִל הַחֵ֨לֶב וְהָֽאַלְיָ֜ה וְאֶת־הַחֵ֣לֶב ׀ הַֽמְכַסֶּ֣ה אֶת־הַקֶּ֗רֶב וְאֵ֨ת יֹתֶ֤רֶת הַכָּבֵד֙ וְאֵ֣ת ׀ שְׁתֵּ֣י הַכְּלָיֹ֗ת וְאֶת־הַחֵ֙לֶב֙ אֲשֶׁ֣ר עֲלֵיהֶ֔ן וְאֵ֖ת שׁ֣וֹק הַיָּמִ֑ין כִּ֛י אֵ֥יל מִלֻּאִ֖ים הֽוּא:

23 וְכִכַּ֨ר לֶ֜חֶם אַחַ֗ת וְֽחַלַּ֨ת לֶ֥חֶם שֶׁ֛מֶן אַחַ֖ת וְרָקִ֣יק אֶחָ֑ד מִסַּל֙ הַמַּצּ֔וֹת אֲשֶׁ֖ר לִפְנֵ֥י יְהֹוָֽה:

24 וְשַׂמְתָּ֣ הַכֹּ֔ל עַ֚ל כַּפֵּ֣י אַהֲרֹ֔ן וְעַ֖ל כַּפֵּ֣י בָנָ֑יו וְהֵנַפְתָּ֥ אֹתָ֛ם תְּנוּפָ֖ה לִפְנֵ֥י יְהֹוָֽה:

25 וְלָקַחְתָּ֤ אֹתָם֙ מִיָּדָ֔ם וְהִקְטַרְתָּ֥ הַמִּזְבֵּ֖חָה עַל־הָעֹלָ֑ה לְרֵ֤יחַ נִיחוֹחַ֙ לִפְנֵ֣י יְהֹוָ֔ה אִשֶּׁ֥ה ה֖וּא לַיהֹוָֽה:

26 וְלָקַחְתָּ֣ אֶת־הֶֽחָזֶ֗ה מֵאֵ֤יל הַמִּלֻּאִים֙ אֲשֶׁ֣ר לְאַהֲרֹ֔ן וְהֵנַפְתָּ֥ אֹת֛וֹ תְּנוּפָ֖ה לִפְנֵ֣י יְהֹוָ֑ה וְהָיָ֥ה לְךָ֖ לְמָנָֽה:

27 וְקִדַּשְׁתָּ֞ אֵ֣ת ׀ חֲזֵ֣ה הַתְּנוּפָ֗ה וְאֵת֙ שׁ֣וֹק הַתְּרוּמָ֔ה אֲשֶׁ֥ר הוּנַ֖ף וַאֲשֶׁ֣ר הוּרָ֑ם מֵאֵיל֙ הַמִּלֻּאִ֔ים מֵאֲשֶׁ֥ר לְאַהֲרֹ֖ן וּמֵאֲשֶׁ֥ר לְבָנָֽיו:

28 וְהָיָה֩ לְאַהֲרֹ֨ן וּלְבָנָ֜יו לְחָק־עוֹלָ֗ם מֵאֵת֙ בְּנֵ֣י יִשְׂרָאֵ֔ל כִּ֥י תְרוּמָ֖ה ה֑וּא וּתְרוּמָ֨ה יִהְיֶ֜ה מֵאֵ֤ת בְּנֵֽי־יִשְׂרָאֵל֙ מִזִּבְחֵ֣י שַׁלְמֵיהֶ֔ם תְּרוּמָתָ֖ם לַיהֹוָֽה:

29 וּבִגְדֵ֤י הַקֹּ֙דֶשׁ֙ אֲשֶׁ֣ר לְאַהֲרֹ֔ן יִהְי֥וּ לְבָנָ֖יו אַחֲרָ֑יו לְמָשְׁחָ֣ה בָהֶ֔ם וּלְמַלֵּא־בָ֖ם אֶת־יָדָֽם:

30 שִׁבְעַ֣ת יָמִ֗ים יִלְבָּשָׁ֧ם הַכֹּהֵ֛ן תַּחְתָּ֖יו מִבָּנָ֑יו אֲשֶׁ֥ר יָבֹ֛א אֶל־אֹ֥הֶל מוֹעֵ֖ד לְשָׁרֵ֥ת בַּקֹּֽדֶשׁ:

31 וְאֵ֛ת אֵ֥יל הַמִּלֻּאִ֖ים תִּקָּ֑ח וּבִשַּׁלְתָּ֥ אֶת־בְּשָׂר֖וֹ בְּמָקֹ֥ם קָדֹֽשׁ:

32 וְאָכַ֨ל אַהֲרֹ֤ן וּבָנָיו֙ אֶת־בְּשַׂ֣ר הָאַ֔יִל וְאֶת־הַלֶּ֖חֶם אֲשֶׁ֣ר בַּסָּ֑ל פֶּ֖תַח אֹ֥הֶל מוֹעֵֽד:

33 וְאָכְל֤וּ אֹתָם֙ אֲשֶׁ֣ר

---

33. They should eat those things ... A non-priest may not eat of them, because they are (extremely) sacred. Everything carried out with the offerings is in order to focus our thoughts and intentions positively and to calm the craving spirit within us. That is why all matters of the Temple and the offerings are conducted with nobility, grandeur and honor, to inspire in us awe, humility and lowliness of spirit. The respectful treatment of an offering is that it should be eaten by the ministers themselves and they should not give it to their servants and dogs, or sell it to a buyer (*Rabbi Aaron ha-Levi (Ḥinnukh), 13th century*).

of their right feet. You should sprinkle the blood upon the altar all around. ²¹ You should then take some of the blood that is upon the altar and some of the anointing oil, and sprinkle it on Aaron and on his garments, on his sons and on his sons' garments with him. He will become consecrated along with his garments, and his sons and their garments, with him.

²² You should take out of the ram the (abdominal) fat, the tail-piece, the fat that covers the innards, the diaphragm of the liver, the two kidneys along with the fat that is upon them, and the right thigh—for it is a ram of perfection—²³ one (unleavened) loaf, one (unleavened) loaf (which is boiled and fried in) oil, and one wafer, (a total of one tenth) of the basket of unleavened bread that stands before God. ²⁴ You should place it all upon Aaron's palms and upon his sons' palms, and you (Moses) should wave the(ir hands together with them from underneath) as a waving before God.

²⁵ You should then take (the breads) from their hands and make them go up in smoke upon the altar with the burnt-offering as a pleasurable fragrance before God. It is a fire-offering for God('s sake).

²⁶ You should take the breast of Aaron's ram of perfection, and wave it as a waving before God, and it will become your portion.

²⁷ (On future occasions, follow a different procedure:) you should consecrate the breast of the wave-offering through waving (horizontally) and the thigh of the raised-offering by raising (vertically), from the ram of perfection, (giving it to) Aaron and his sons (to eat). ²⁸ This (donation of the breast and thigh) from the Jewish people will be an eternal law for Aaron and his sons, for it is a donation, and it should remain an offering from the children of Israel from their peace-offerings. It is their donation to God.

²⁹ Aaron's holy garments should be (passed on to his successor as High Priest among) his sons after him, to be exalted through them and inaugurated into office through them. ³⁰ The (unique) one of his sons (who will succeed him as High) Priest in his place, who will enter the Tent of Meeting to serve in the Holy Place, should wear them (first) for seven (consecutive) days.

³¹ You should take the (remainder of the) ram of perfection and cook its flesh in a holy place (i.e. in the courtyard of the Tent of Meeting). ³² Aaron and his sons should eat the flesh of the ram and the bread that is in the basket, at the entrance of the Tent of Meeting. ³³ They should eat those things that cleansed them (of their

25. A pleasurable fragrance before God. If you understand the secret of man's soul, you will understand why the Torah employs anthropomorphic language. (A human being cannot speak of things above or below him without the use of human frames of reference.) (*Rabbi Abraham ibn Ezra, 12ᵗʰ century*).

שמות כט:לג-מו | תצוה

כִּפֶּר בָּהֶם לְמַלֵּא אֶת־יָדָם לְקַדֵּשׁ אֹתָם וְזָר לֹא־יֹאכַל כִּי־קֹדֶשׁ הֵם: 34 וְאִם־יִוָּתֵר מִבְּשַׂר הַמִּלֻּאִים וּמִן־הַלֶּחֶם עַד־הַבֹּקֶר וְשָׂרַפְתָּ אֶת־הַנּוֹתָר בָּאֵשׁ לֹא יֵאָכֵל כִּי־קֹדֶשׁ הוּא: 35 וְעָשִׂיתָ לְאַהֲרֹן וּלְבָנָיו כָּכָה כְּכֹל אֲשֶׁר־צִוִּיתִי אֹתָכָה שִׁבְעַת יָמִים תְּמַלֵּא יָדָם: 36 וּפַר חַטָּאת תַּעֲשֶׂה לַיּוֹם עַל־הַכִּפֻּרִים וְחִטֵּאתָ עַל־הַמִּזְבֵּחַ בְּכַפֶּרְךָ עָלָיו וּמָשַׁחְתָּ אֹתוֹ לְקַדְּשׁוֹ: 37 שִׁבְעַת יָמִים תְּכַפֵּר עַל־הַמִּזְבֵּחַ וְקִדַּשְׁתָּ אֹתוֹ וְהָיָה הַמִּזְבֵּחַ קֹדֶשׁ קָדָשִׁים כָּל־הַנֹּגֵעַ בַּמִּזְבֵּחַ יִקְדָּשׁ: ס

38 [SIXTH READING] וְזֶה אֲשֶׁר תַּעֲשֶׂה עַל־הַמִּזְבֵּחַ כְּבָשִׂים בְּנֵי־שָׁנָה שְׁנַיִם לַיּוֹם תָּמִיד: 39 אֶת־הַכֶּבֶשׂ הָאֶחָד תַּעֲשֶׂה בַבֹּקֶר וְאֵת הַכֶּבֶשׂ הַשֵּׁנִי תַּעֲשֶׂה בֵּין הָעַרְבָּיִם: 40 וְעִשָּׂרֹן סֹלֶת בָּלוּל בְּשֶׁמֶן כָּתִית רֶבַע הַהִין וְנֵסֶךְ רְבִיעִת הַהִין יָיִן לַכֶּבֶשׂ הָאֶחָד: 41 וְאֵת הַכֶּבֶשׂ הַשֵּׁנִי תַּעֲשֶׂה בֵּין הָעַרְבָּיִם כְּמִנְחַת הַבֹּקֶר וּכְנִסְכָּהּ תַּעֲשֶׂה־לָּהּ לְרֵיחַ נִיחֹחַ אִשֶּׁה לַיהוָה: 42 עֹלַת תָּמִיד לְדֹרֹתֵיכֶם פֶּתַח אֹהֶל־מוֹעֵד לִפְנֵי יְהוָה אֲשֶׁר אִוָּעֵד לָכֶם שָׁמָּה לְדַבֵּר אֵלֶיךָ שָׁם: 43 וְנֹעַדְתִּי שָׁמָּה לִבְנֵי יִשְׂרָאֵל וְנִקְדַּשׁ בִּכְבֹדִי: 44 וְקִדַּשְׁתִּי אֶת־אֹהֶל מוֹעֵד וְאֶת־הַמִּזְבֵּחַ וְאֶת־אַהֲרֹן וְאֶת־בָּנָיו אֲקַדֵּשׁ לְכַהֵן לִי: 45 וְשָׁכַנְתִּי בְּתוֹךְ בְּנֵי יִשְׂרָאֵל וְהָיִיתִי לָהֶם לֵאלֹהִים: 46 וְיָדְעוּ כִּי אֲנִי יְהוָה אֱלֹהֵיהֶם אֲשֶׁר הוֹצֵאתִי אֹתָם מֵאֶרֶץ מִצְרַיִם לְשָׁכְנִי בְתוֹכָם אֲנִי יְהוָה אֱלֹהֵיהֶם: פ

spiritual vitamin

> Everything and every person has its own purpose or task, and this does not make anyone any more or less important, for everyone is important in the totality of things, just as every limb or organ of a body is important. If one person would wish to change his or her function, it would not only disturb his or her own personal harmony, but would also disturb the total harmony.

non-priestly status) in order to inaugurate them into office. A non-priest may not eat of them, because they are (extremely) sacred.

³⁴ If any of the flesh of the perfection-offering or any of the bread is left over until the next morning, you should burn the leftovers in fire. It may not be eaten, because it is a sacred thing.

³⁵ You should do everything (without exception) that I have commanded you to Aaron and his sons. Their inauguration will take seven days (and you should carry out the same procedures on each day). ³⁶ Each day, you should offer up a bull as a sin-offering to cleanse (the altar from its previous state of profanity). You should apply blood to the altar to cleanse (it), and you should anoint it, in order to consecrate it. ³⁷ For seven days, you should perform (this) cleansing on the altar and sanctify it. Then, the altar will be a holy of holies. (Even an invalid offering which) touches the altar will become holy.

[SIXTH READING] ³⁸ This is what you should offer on the altar: lambs in their first year, two a day, regularly. ³⁹ One lamb you should offer up in the morning and the other lamb you should offer up in the afternoon.

⁴⁰ With the first lamb, offer one tenth of fine flour, thoroughly mixed with a quarter of a *hin* of crushed olive oil, and a libation of one quarter of a *hin* of wine. ⁴¹ You should offer up the second lamb in the afternoon. You should offer with it the same flour-offering as the morning and its libation. (The flour-offering is) a pleasurable fragrance, a fire-offering to God. ⁴² It should be a regular burnt-offering for your generations, at the entrance of the Tent of Meeting before God, where I will arrange meetings with you, to speak to you there. ⁴³ There I will arrange meetings with the children of Israel, and (the Tabernacle) will be sanctified by My Presence. ⁴⁴ I will sanctify the Tent of Meeting and the altar, and I will sanctify Aaron and his sons to serve Me as priests. ⁴⁵ I will dwell in the midst of the children of Israel and I will be their God. ⁴⁶ They will know that I, God, am their God, who brought them out of the land of Egypt (in order) to dwell among them. I am God, their God.

39. One lamb you should offer up in the morning and the other lamb you should offer up in the afternoon. The morning sacrifice symbolizes the years of our youth, the morning of our lives. The afternoon sacrifice symbolizes the years toward the end of our lives. Offering two sacrifices each day reminds us that we ought to dedicate ourselves to worshiping God both when we are young and healthy, and in our twilight years (*Rabbi Aaron Lewin of Rzeszow, 20ᵗʰ century*).

45. I will dwell in the midst of the children of Israel and I will be their God. In this verse, the Torah uses a Divine name that implies strict justice (*'Elokim*), rather than a name implying mercy. God says that He will *"dwell in the midst of the children of Israel,"* loving them as a father loves his children, and yet by using the attribute of *'Elokim*, His quality of strict justice, He will punish those who seek to harm His children (*Rabbi Eliezer Horowitz of Tarnogrod, 18ᵗʰ century*).

שמות ל:א-י · תצוה

ל

[SEVENTH READING] 1 וְעָשִׂ֥יתָ מִזְבֵּ֖חַ מִקְטַ֣ר קְטֹ֑רֶת עֲצֵ֥י שִׁטִּ֖ים תַּעֲשֶׂ֥ה אֹתֽוֹ: 2 אַמָּ֨ה אָרְכּ֜וֹ וְאַמָּ֤ה רָחְבּוֹ֙ רָב֣וּעַ יִהְיֶ֔ה וְאַמָּתַ֖יִם קֹמָת֑וֹ מִמֶּ֖נּוּ קַרְנֹתָֽיו: 3 וְצִפִּיתָ֨ אֹת֜וֹ זָהָ֣ב טָה֗וֹר אֶת־גַּגּ֧וֹ וְאֶת־קִירֹתָ֛יו סָבִ֖יב וְאֶת־קַרְנֹתָ֑יו וְעָשִׂ֥יתָ לּ֛וֹ זֵ֥ר זָהָ֖ב סָבִֽיב: 4 וּשְׁתֵּי֩ טַבְּעֹ֨ת זָהָ֜ב תַּֽעֲשֶׂה־לּ֣וֹ ׀ מִתַּ֣חַת לְזֵר֗וֹ עַ֚ל שְׁתֵּ֣י צַלְעֹתָ֔יו תַּעֲשֶׂ֖ה עַל־שְׁנֵ֣י צִדָּ֑יו וְהָיָה֙ לְבָתִּ֣ים לְבַדִּ֔ים לָשֵׂ֥את אֹת֖וֹ בָּהֵֽמָּה: 5 וְעָשִׂ֥יתָ אֶת־הַבַּדִּ֖ים עֲצֵ֣י שִׁטִּ֑ים וְצִפִּיתָ֥ אֹתָ֖ם זָהָֽב: 6 וְנָתַתָּ֤ה אֹתוֹ֙ לִפְנֵ֣י הַפָּרֹ֔כֶת אֲשֶׁ֖ר עַל־אֲרֹ֣ן הָעֵדֻ֑ת לִפְנֵ֣י הַכַּפֹּ֗רֶת אֲשֶׁר֙ עַל־הָ֣עֵדֻ֔ת אֲשֶׁ֛ר אִוָּעֵ֥ד לְךָ֖ שָֽׁמָּה: 7 וְהִקְטִ֥יר עָלָ֛יו אַהֲרֹ֖ן קְטֹ֣רֶת סַמִּ֑ים בַּבֹּ֣קֶר בַּבֹּ֗קֶר בְּהֵיטִיב֛וֹ אֶת־הַנֵּרֹ֖ת יַקְטִירֶֽנָּה: [MAFTIR] 8 וּבְהַעֲלֹ֨ת אַהֲרֹ֧ן אֶת־הַנֵּרֹ֛ת בֵּ֥ין הָעַרְבַּ֖יִם יַקְטִירֶ֑נָּה קְטֹ֧רֶת תָּמִ֛יד לִפְנֵ֥י יְהוָֹ֖ה לְדֹרֹתֵיכֶֽם: 9 לֹא־תַעֲל֥וּ עָלָ֛יו קְטֹ֥רֶת זָרָ֖ה וְעֹלָ֣ה וּמִנְחָ֑ה וְנֵ֕סֶךְ לֹ֥א תִסְּכ֖וּ עָלָֽיו: 10 וְכִפֶּ֤ר אַהֲרֹן֙ עַל־קַרְנֹתָ֔יו אַחַ֖ת בַּשָּׁנָ֑ה מִדַּ֞ם חַטַּ֣את הַכִּפֻּרִ֗ים אַחַ֤ת בַּשָּׁנָה֙ יְכַפֵּ֤ר עָלָיו֙ לְדֹרֹ֣תֵיכֶ֔ם קֹֽדֶשׁ־קָֽדָשִׁ֥ים ה֖וּא לַיהוָֹֽה: פ פ פ

ק"א פסוקים, מיכא"ל סימן.

This is indicated by the Hebrew term for "incense," *ketoret*, which suggests "connecting" (as in *keter*, the Aramaic translation of the Hebrew word *kesher*, meaning "knot" or "connection"). We are not speaking of two separate entities which have become close, but rather, of two entities that have become *one* (*Rabbi Dov Baer Schneuri of Lubavitch, 19th century*).

spiritual vitamin

" From time to time, whether it be on a Saturday, Sunday or Wednesday—we sometimes feel that we have accomplished more than our own natural capabilities would allow; this extra "power" is a form of God's revelation within us. "

exodus 30:1–10   tetzavveh

The Golden Incense Altar

30 [SEVENTH READING] ¹ You should make an altar for bringing incense up in smoke. You should make it out of acacia wood. ² It should be one cubit long and one cubit wide, a square, and two cubits high. Its horns should be one piece with it. ³ You should coat it with pure gold, its top, its walls all around, and its horns, and you should make for it a golden-rimmed edge all around.

⁴ You should make for it two golden rings underneath its rimmed edge on its two sides. You should make them on its two sides, so that they should serve as holders for poles with which to carry it. ⁵ You should make the poles out of acacia wood and coat them with gold.

⁶ You should place it in front of the partition, which is in front of the Ark of Testimony, in front of the ark's lid, which is on the testimony, where I will arrange to meet with you.

⁷ Aaron should make incense of spices go up in smoke upon it. Every morning, when he cleans the lamps (of the candelabrum,) he should make it go up in smoke. [MAFTIR] ⁸ When Aaron kindles the lights in the afternoon, he should make incense go up in smoke. It is an eternal incense before God, for all generations. ⁹ You should not offer up on it unauthorized incense, a burnt-offering or a flour-offering. You should not pour any libation on it.

¹⁰ Once a year (on the Day of Atonement), Aaron should (pour blood) on its horns to achieve atonement. He should achieve atonement once a year with the blood of the atonement sacrifice, for all generations. It is holy of holies to God.

Haftarot: Tetzavveh page 1334.   Zakhor—page 1427.

Maftir: Zakhor—page 1208 (25:17–19).

30:1 Make an altar for bringing incense up in smoke. Why is the command to build the incense altar recorded here, and not along with instructions regarding the other apparatus (above, ch. 25-27)?

The Tabernacle, together with its apparatus, caused the Divine Presence to dwell within it, and the offering of sacrifices then brought God's glory to the Tabernacle. The incense, however, had a different function. Namely, that *after* the duties involving all of the Tabernacle's apparatus had been put to use in sacrificial and other duties, the incense was burned *to appease God*, so that He should find all the service that had been carried out acceptable. The incense altar is therefore mentioned separately, after all other apparatus and priestly clothing has been described (*Rabbi Obadiah Sforno, 16th century*).

The command to build the incense altar was recorded here, because although the Tabernacle had been erected, the priests inaugurated and God's Presence rested in the Tabernacle (ch. 25-29), nevertheless, God was only *close* to the Jewish people, and not *one* with them until the incense was offered (*Rabbi Abraham b. Jacob Saba, 15th century*).

This Torah portion, which tells the **tragic story** of the **Golden Calf**, is nevertheless named *Ki Tissa*, "when you will **raise up**," because even the **darkest moments** of Jewish history have been **orchestrated** by God as a pathway to **growth** and **redemption**.

KI TISSA'
כי תשא

METHOD OF COUNTING THE JEWISH PEOPLE	30:11-16
THE TABERNACLE	30:17-38
BEZALEL AND OHOLIAB	31:1-11
THE SABBATH	31:12-17
THE GOLDEN CALF	31:18 – 33:6
MOSES' TENT	33:7-11
MOSES ASKS TO KNOW THE WAYS OF GOD	33:12-23
THE SECOND TABLETS	34:1-4
THIRTEEN ATTRIBUTES OF MERCY	34:5-10
NATIONAL IDENTITY	34:11-16
OTHER COMMANDS	34:17-26
MOSES DESCENDS WITH SECOND TABLETS	34:27-35

NAME
Ki Tissa'

MEANING
"When you raise up"

LINES IN TORAH SCROLL
245

PARASHIYYOT
10 open; 4 closed

VERSES
139

WORDS
2002

LETTERS
7424

LOCATION
Sinai Desert

DATE
17 *Tammuz*, 2448 –
10 *Tishri*, 2449

KEY PEOPLE
Moses, Aaron and his sons, Bezalel, Oholiab, Levites

MITZVOT
4 positive; 5 prohibitions

MASORETIC FEATURES
Nun of *notzer* (34:7) and *resh* of *aher* (34:14) are oversized

CHARACTER PROFILE

NAME
Bezalel

MEANING
"In the shadow of God"

FATHER
Uri

GRANDFATHER
Hur

OTHER NAMES
Reaiah ("the seer"), Shobal ("builder of the dovecote"), Jahath ("the dreadful"), Ahumai ("unifier of Israel"), and Lahad ("one who beautified Israel")

ACHIEVEMENTS
Appointed builder of the Tabernacle at the age of thirteen; personally constructed the ark; an expert in metalwork, stonecutting, and woodcarving; knew how to manipulate the Hebrew letters with which heaven and earth were created

KNOWN FOR
His wisdom

HALF-SHEKEL

The half-shekel donation reminds us all of our inter-dependency. We must all construct this holy Tabernacle together. Everyone's contribution is equal (30:16).

FAITHFUL SHEPHERD

Moses heroically put the needs of the people before his own. After the Golden Calf, when God offered Moses to *"make you into a great nation instead,"* Moses replied, *"if You forgive their sin, then well and good, but if not, please erase me from Your Book, which You have written"* (32:32).

EMULATING GOD

God's "Thirteen Attributes" outlined here are ways in which you can emulate the Divine. If you are consistently slow to anger and compassionate, then you are beginning to behave like God (34:6-7).

שמות ל:יא-טו · כי תשא

11 וַיְדַבֵּ֥ר יְהֹוָ֖ה אֶל־מֹשֶׁ֥ה לֵּאמֹֽר: 12 כִּ֣י תִשָּׂ֞א אֶת־רֹ֥אשׁ בְּנֵֽי־יִשְׂרָאֵל֮ לִפְקֻדֵיהֶם֒ וְנָ֨תְנ֜וּ אִ֣ישׁ כֹּ֧פֶר נַפְשׁ֛וֹ לַיהֹוָ֖ה בִּפְקֹ֣ד אֹתָ֑ם וְלֹא־יִהְיֶ֥ה בָהֶ֛ם נֶ֖גֶף בִּפְקֹ֥ד אֹתָֽם: 13 זֶ֣ה ׀ יִתְּנ֗וּ כׇּל־הָעֹבֵר֙ עַל־הַפְּקֻדִ֔ים מַחֲצִ֥ית הַשֶּׁ֖קֶל בְּשֶׁ֣קֶל הַקֹּ֑דֶשׁ עֶשְׂרִ֤ים גֵּרָה֙ הַשֶּׁ֔קֶל מַחֲצִ֣ית הַשֶּׁ֔קֶל תְּרוּמָ֖ה לַֽיהֹוָֽה: 14 כֹּ֗ל הָעֹבֵר֙ עַל־הַפְּקֻדִ֔ים מִבֶּ֛ן עֶשְׂרִ֥ים שָׁנָ֖ה וָמָ֑עְלָה יִתֵּ֖ן תְּרוּמַ֥ת יְהֹוָֽה: 15 הֶֽעָשִׁ֣יר לֹֽא־יַרְבֶּ֗ה וְהַדַּל֙ לֹ֣א יַמְעִ֔יט מִֽמַּחֲצִ֖ית הַשָּׁ֑קֶל לָתֵת֙ אֶת־תְּרוּמַ֣ת יְהֹוָ֔ה לְכַפֵּ֖ר עַל־נַפְשֹׁתֵיכֶֽם:

took a *coin of fire* from beneath His Throne of Glory and showed it to Moses, saying, "They should give one like this" (*Midrash Tanḥuma; The Tosafists, 12th–14th centuries*).

It is not the coin, it is the fire and enthusiasm with which you give it that will bring atonement (*Rabbi Menaḥem Mendel Morgensztern of Kotsk, 19th century*).

By showing Moses a fiery coin from heaven, God was indicating that money, like a fire, can be used for two contrasting purposes. When used wisely, fire can sustain life; when left unchecked, it can destroy and kill. Money can be used to aid good causes, such as feeding the hungry and healing the sick; but money can also be used to fund extortion and wars. Be sure that the fire generated by your coin is a heavenly one (*Rabbi Elimelech of Lyzhansk, 18th century*).

Fire differs from all other elements on this earth, in that it gravitates upwards, reaching ever higher, dancing and flickering, until finally it frees itself of its chains when the wick burns out and it unites with its source. Fire is the paradigm of self-effacement, having no distinct shape or form of its own.

A coin, on the other hand, is hewed from the depths of the earth, the lowest of the four elements. The antithesis of fire, the heavy coin falls ever downward, and it is clearly defined in its shape and form. Fire represents the transcendence of the spiritual; a coin represents the crassness of the physical.

It was not *despite* the sharp contrast between them, but specifically *because* of it, that God showed Moses a coin of fire. God taught Moses that the coarse and the unrefined is not necessarily the antithesis of the most holy and pure. The physical does not have to repel the spiritual, but rather, they can work in harmony, until they reach absolute unity, as represented by a coin made of fire.

On a practical level, God taught Moses that even coarse human beings who are naturally driven by selfish motives, self-love being their basic instinct, can also serve the Divine with the most noble of services, as represented by the complete selflessness of fire (*Rabbi Menaḥem Mendel Schneerson, 20th century*).

15. A half-shekel ... to atone for your souls. This half-shekel donation formed a fund from which communal sacrifices were

kabbalah bites

30:13 Why was a *half-shekel* given to atone for the sin of the Golden Calf?

According to the Kabbalah every soul has both a male and a female component. Since women did not participate in the sin of the Golden Calf, only the masculine part of each of our souls requires atonement. Thus each person need give only a half-shekel.

exodus 30:11–15   ki tissa'

parashat ki-tissa'

Prohibition Against Counting the Jewish People Directly

(The following occurred after the incident with the Golden Calf:)

¹¹ God spoke to Moses, saying: ¹² "When you (wish to) take the sum of the children of Israel to determine their numbers, count them by letting each man give to God an atonement for his soul. (Avoid counting them directly,) then there will be no plague among them when they are counted.

Donation of a Half-Shekel

¹³ "This is what they should give—everyone who goes through the counting (system)—a half-shekel according to the shekel (measurement system which is used for) sanctified (items, as follows:) Twenty *gerah* equal one shekel. The contribution to God should be a half-shekel.

¹⁴ "Everyone who goes through the counting (system), from the age of twenty years and upward, should give a contribution to God. ¹⁵ The rich should give no more, and the poor should give no less than a half-shekel when giving the offering to God, to atone for your souls.

30:12 When you take the sum. The word *tissa'* ("*you take*") could also be translated as "you lift up." This would be referring to the uplifting quality of donating the half-shekel which came after the spiritual regression of the sin of the Golden Calf (*Midrash Tanḥuma*).

Count them by letting each man give to God an atonement for his soul. The Hebrew word used here for "give" (ונתנו) is a palindrome—it reads the same backwards and forwards. The message is: Your funds will not be diminished by the charity you give. The amount you offer as charity will eventually come back to you (*Rabbi Jacob b. Asher, 14th century*).

13. This is what they should give … a half-shekel. When Moses found it difficult to understand how the half-shekel donation could achieve atonement for the children of Israel, God

spiritual vitamin

> The law of the half-shekel teaches us, among other things, that human effort, provided it is sincere and resolute, is "met halfway" by Divine Grace. Even though the goal may, at first glance, seem too ambitious or even beyond reach, you are not limited to your own human resources, since your initial effort evokes a reciprocal "impulse" from On High which assures the attainment of even the "unattainable."

שמות ל:טז-כג

כי תשא

16 וְלָקַחְתָּ אֶת־כֶּסֶף הַכִּפֻּרִים מֵאֵת בְּנֵי יִשְׂרָאֵל וְנָתַתָּ אֹתוֹ עַל־עֲבֹדַת אֹהֶל מוֹעֵד וְהָיָה לִבְנֵי יִשְׂרָאֵל לְזִכָּרוֹן לִפְנֵי יְהֹוָה לְכַפֵּר עַל־נַפְשֹׁתֵיכֶם: פ 17 וַיְדַבֵּר יְהֹוָה אֶל־מֹשֶׁה לֵּאמֹר: 18 וְעָשִׂיתָ כִּיּוֹר נְחֹשֶׁת וְכַנּוֹ נְחֹשֶׁת לְרָחְצָה וְנָתַתָּ אֹתוֹ בֵּין־אֹהֶל מוֹעֵד וּבֵין הַמִּזְבֵּחַ וְנָתַתָּ שָׁמָּה מָיִם: 19 וְרָחֲצוּ אַהֲרֹן וּבָנָיו מִמֶּנּוּ אֶת־יְדֵיהֶם וְאֶת־רַגְלֵיהֶם: 20 בְּבֹאָם אֶל־אֹהֶל מוֹעֵד יִרְחֲצוּ־מַיִם וְלֹא יָמֻתוּ אוֹ בְגִשְׁתָּם אֶל־הַמִּזְבֵּחַ לְשָׁרֵת לְהַקְטִיר אִשֶּׁה לַיהֹוָה: 21 וְרָחֲצוּ יְדֵיהֶם וְרַגְלֵיהֶם וְלֹא יָמֻתוּ וְהָיְתָה לָהֶם חָק־עוֹלָם לוֹ וּלְזַרְעוֹ לְדֹרֹתָם: פ 22 וַיְדַבֵּר יְהֹוָה אֶל־מֹשֶׁה לֵּאמֹר: 23 וְאַתָּה קַח־לְךָ בְּשָׂמִים רֹאשׁ מָר־דְּרוֹר חֲמֵשׁ מֵאוֹת וְקִנְּמָן־בֶּשֶׂם מַחֲצִיתוֹ חֲמִשִּׁים וּמָאתָיִם וּקְנֵה־בֹשֶׂם חֲמִשִּׁים

19. Aaron and his sons should wash their hands and feet. Any cleansing process is the removal of impurity. Here the "impurity" which the priest fears is any inappropriate motives that might creep into his worship. Through the act of washing, the priest surrenders himself to God with the intention that he will only do that which God desires.

This is the very same purpose of our ritual washing every morning upon awakening, and before eating bread. When we begin to fulfil the needs of the body we pray to God that if our dealings with the world bring us into contact with something which God does not want, He should remove ("wash away") any desire we might have to do that inappropriate action. When we eat food, which gives us energy, we pray that we will use that energy only to do good in this world.

So our ritual washing is a kind of prayer to God that from every experience we wish to receive only the good that is found in it (*Rabbi Mordecai Joseph Leiner of Izbica, 19th century*).

23-25. Spices ... oil for holy anointment. The sages of Israel disputed how the anointing oil was produced from the specified herbs.

Rabbi Meir said "They boiled the roots (of the spices) in the oil." Rabbi Judah said to him, "Surely the amount of oil specified by the Torah did not suffice even to smear the roots, never mind boil them? Rather, they soaked the roots in water so that they would not absorb the oil, and then poured the oil on them until it absorbed the scent, and then they wiped the oil off the roots" (*Rashi, 11th century*).

> **kabbalah bites**
>
> **30:19** God made a covenant between the fingers of the hands and the toes of the feet that they would both hint to the reason for the existence of the body found between them—to emulate God's attributes, the ten *Sefirot*.
>
> Water, which is crucial for all life, alludes to *Hesed* (kindness). Thus, before service in the Tabernacle the ten *Sefirot* are flooded with *Hesed*.

exodus 30:16–23   ki tissa'

¹⁶ "You should take the atonement silver from the children of Israel and use it for making (sockets of) the Tent of Meeting. It will be a reminder for the children of Israel before God, to atone for your souls."

The Urn

¹⁷ God spoke to Moses, saying: ¹⁸ "You should make an urn of copper to be used for washing and a base for it from copper. You should place it (in the area) between the Tent of Meeting and the altar (to one side), and you should put water in it.

¹⁹ "Aaron and his sons should wash their hands and feet (simultaneously) from it. ²⁰ When they enter the Tent of Meeting, they should wash with water, otherwise they will die. Or, when they approach the altar to serve, to make a fire-offering rise up in smoke to God, ²¹ they should wash their hands and feet, otherwise they will die. This should be for them an eternal statute—for him (Aaron) and for his descendants, for all their generations."

The Anointing Oil

²² God spoke to Moses, saying: ²³ "You should take for yourself (high quality) spices: 500 (shekels) of common myrrh, (two) half portions (each consisting) of

---

purchased. Since these sacrifices achieved atonement for the community, the verse states, *"to atone for your souls"* (*Rashi, 11ᵗʰ century*).

18. An urn of copper. The copper came from the mirrors of the women who had given birth to legions of children in Egypt. The Israelite women owned mirrors, which they would use to adorn themselves for their husbands. And they did not withhold even their personal mirrors when contributing towards the Tabernacle.

But Moses rejected them, because they had been used to inspire lustful thoughts.

God said to him, "Accept them! They are more precious to Me than anything else, because through them the women set up legions in Egypt" (*Rashi, 11ᵗʰ century*).

Moses was known as the great "lover of the Jewish people" (*Babylonian Talmud, Menahot* 65a) and was aware that the Jewish women had used the mirrors with good intentions. If so, why did he reject them?

There are two types of holy acts: (a) spiritually *transparent* acts, which are totally pure and holy; and (b) spiritually *opaque* acts, which are mundane or potentially profane, but have been carried out with good motives, rendering them holy. The superiority of the "transparent" act is that its sanctity is more apparent. Moses felt that the materials used for God's Tabernacle should be totally "transparent" and that the women's mirrors, harboring spirituality of the "opaque" form, were out of place in God's revealed Presence.

"Accept them! They are more precious to Me than anything else," replied God. For the "opaque" act, while less obviously holy, is more effective in achieving God's desire to "be found in the lowest realms" (*Midrash Tanḥuma*). Its more profound, albeit less apparent, spirituality is the more precious of the two kinds of acts, in the eyes of God (*Rabbi Samuel Schneersohn of Lubavitch, 19ᵗʰ century*).

שמות ל:כג - לא:ה

וּמָאתָ֑יִם 24 וְקִדָּ֛ה חֲמֵ֥שׁ מֵא֖וֹת בְּשֶׁ֣קֶל הַקֹּ֑דֶשׁ וְשֶׁ֥מֶן זַ֖יִת הִֽין׃ 25 וְעָשִׂ֣יתָ אֹת֗וֹ שֶׁ֚מֶן מִשְׁחַת־קֹ֔דֶשׁ רֹ֥קַח מִרְקַ֖חַת מַעֲשֵׂ֣ה רֹקֵ֑חַ שֶׁ֥מֶן מִשְׁחַת־קֹ֖דֶשׁ יִהְיֶֽה׃ 26 וּמָשַׁחְתָּ֥ ב֖וֹ אֶת־אֹ֣הֶל מוֹעֵ֑ד וְאֵ֖ת אֲר֥וֹן הָעֵדֻֽת׃ 27 וְאֶת־הַשֻּׁלְחָן֙ וְאֶת־כָּל־כֵּלָ֔יו וְאֶת־הַמְּנֹרָ֖ה וְאֶת־כֵּלֶ֑יהָ וְאֵ֖ת מִזְבַּ֥ח הַקְּטֹֽרֶת׃ 28 וְאֶת־מִזְבַּ֥ח הָעֹלָ֖ה וְאֶת־כָּל־כֵּלָ֑יו וְאֶת־הַכִּיֹּ֖ר וְאֶת־כַּנּֽוֹ׃ 29 וְקִדַּשְׁתָּ֣ אֹתָ֔ם וְהָי֖וּ קֹ֣דֶשׁ קָֽדָשִׁ֑ים כָּל־הַנֹּגֵ֥עַ בָּהֶ֖ם יִקְדָּֽשׁ׃ 30 וְאֶֽת־אַהֲרֹ֥ן וְאֶת־בָּנָ֖יו תִּמְשָׁ֑ח וְקִדַּשְׁתָּ֥ אֹתָ֖ם לְכַהֵ֥ן לִֽי׃ 31 וְאֶל־בְּנֵ֥י יִשְׂרָאֵ֖ל תְּדַבֵּ֣ר לֵאמֹ֑ר שֶׁ֠מֶן מִשְׁחַת־קֹ֨דֶשׁ יִהְיֶ֥ה זֶ֛ה לִ֖י לְדֹרֹתֵיכֶֽם׃ 32 עַל־בְּשַׂ֤ר אָדָם֙ לֹ֣א יִיסָ֔ךְ וּבְמַ֨תְכֻּנְתּ֔וֹ לֹ֥א תַעֲשׂ֖וּ כָּמֹ֑הוּ קֹ֣דֶשׁ ה֔וּא קֹ֖דֶשׁ יִהְיֶ֥ה לָכֶֽם׃ 33 אִ֚ישׁ אֲשֶׁ֣ר יִרְקַ֣ח כָּמֹ֔הוּ וַאֲשֶׁ֥ר יִתֵּ֛ן מִמֶּ֖נּוּ עַל־זָ֑ר וְנִכְרַ֖ת מֵעַמָּֽיו׃ ס 34 וַיֹּאמֶר֩ יְהֹוָ֨ה אֶל־מֹשֶׁ֜ה קַח־לְךָ֣ סַמִּ֗ים נָטָ֤ף ׀ וּשְׁחֵ֙לֶת֙ וְחֶלְבְּנָ֔ה סַמִּ֖ים וּלְבֹנָ֣ה זַכָּ֑ה בַּ֥ד בְּבַ֖ד יִהְיֶֽה׃ 35 וְעָשִׂ֤יתָ אֹתָהּ֙ קְטֹ֔רֶת רֹ֖קַח מַעֲשֵׂ֣ה רוֹקֵ֑חַ מְמֻלָּ֖ח טָה֥וֹר קֹֽדֶשׁ׃ 36 וְשָׁחַקְתָּ֣ מִמֶּ֘נָּה֮ הָדֵק֒ וְנָתַתָּ֨ה מִמֶּ֜נָּה לִפְנֵ֤י הָעֵדֻת֙ בְּאֹ֣הֶל מוֹעֵ֔ד אֲשֶׁ֛ר אִוָּעֵ֥ד לְךָ֖ שָׁ֑מָּה קֹ֥דֶשׁ קָֽדָשִׁ֖ים תִּהְיֶ֥ה לָכֶֽם׃ 37 וְהַקְּטֹ֙רֶת֙ אֲשֶׁ֣ר תַּעֲשֶׂ֔ה בְּמַ֨תְכֻּנְתָּ֔הּ לֹ֥א תַעֲשׂ֖וּ לָכֶ֑ם קֹ֛דֶשׁ תִּהְיֶ֥ה לְךָ֖ לַיהֹוָֽה׃ 38 אִ֛ישׁ אֲשֶׁר־יַעֲשֶׂ֥ה כָמ֖וֹהָ לְהָרִ֣יחַ בָּ֑הּ וְנִכְרַ֖ת מֵעַמָּֽיו׃ ס

לא

1 וַיְדַבֵּ֥ר יְהֹוָ֖ה אֶל־מֹשֶׁ֥ה לֵּאמֹֽר׃ 2 רְאֵ֖ה קָרָ֣אתִֽי בְשֵׁ֑ם בְּצַלְאֵ֛ל בֶּן־אוּרִ֥י בֶן־ח֖וּר לְמַטֵּ֥ה יְהוּדָֽה׃ 3 וָאֲמַלֵּ֥א אֹת֖וֹ ר֣וּחַ אֱלֹהִ֑ים בְּחָכְמָ֛ה וּבִתְבוּנָ֥ה וּבְדַ֖עַת וּבְכָל־מְלָאכָֽה׃ 4 לַחְשֹׁ֖ב מַחֲשָׁבֹ֑ת לַעֲשׂ֛וֹת בַּזָּהָ֥ב וּבַכֶּ֖סֶף וּבַנְּחֹֽשֶׁת׃ 5 וּבַחֲרֹ֥שֶׁת אֶ֙בֶן֙ לְמַלֹּ֔את וּבַחֲרֹ֥שֶׁת עֵ֖ץ לַעֲשׂ֥וֹת בְּכָל־מְלָאכָֽה׃

31:4 To do master weaving. An alternative translation of this phrase is *to interpret thoughts.* Bezalel decided how donations brought for the Tabernacle would be used, and he made these decisions by intuiting the donor's intentions. If a person contributed solely for God, his gift was used for the holiest components, such as the holy ark. If he harbored ulterior motives, it was

exodus 30:23 – 31:5 ki tissa'

250 (shekels) of fragrant cinnamon, 250 (shekels) of aromatic cane, ²⁴ 500 (shekels) of cassia herb—according to the shekel (measurement system which is used for) sanctified (items), and one *hin* of olive oil.

²⁵ "You should make this into an oil for holy anointment, a professional mixture, made by a professional perfumer. It will be oil for holy anointment."

²⁶ "You should use it to anoint the Tent of Meeting and the Ark of Testimony, ²⁷ the table and all its utensils, the candelabrum and its utensils, the incense altar, ²⁸ the sacrificial altar and all its utensils, the urn and its base. ²⁹ (The anointing) consecrates them so that they become holy of holies. Whatever touches them will become holy."

³⁰ "You should anoint Aaron and his sons and consecrate them to serve Me as priests."

³¹ "You should speak to the children of Israel, saying: 'This will be oil of holy anointment to Me for all your generations. ³² It should not be poured upon human flesh. You must not use the same formula to make anything that is like it. It is holy. It will be holy to you. ³³ Any person who makes a mixture like it, or puts any of (the mixture made by Moses) on an unauthorized person, will be cut off from his people.'"

The Incense

³⁴ God said to Moses: "Take for yourself spices: balsam sap, onycha and galbanum, (other) spices, and pure frankincense. They should be of equal weight. ³⁵ You should make this into incense, a professionally mixed compound that is finely blended, pure, and holy.

³⁶ "You should grind some of it finely, and you should set some of it (daily) before the (Ark of) Testimony in the Tent of Meeting, where I will arrange meetings with you. It shall be holy of holies to you. ³⁷ The incense that you will make should not be duplicated for personal use. It will be holy to you for God. ³⁸ Any person who makes anything like it, to smell its fragrance, will be cut off from his people."

Food for thought

1. How does artistic talent reflect the Divine?

2. Does an artist mimic the Divine power to breathe life into the lifeless?

3. What role does aesthetic beauty play in Judaism?

Appointment of Bezalel and Oholiab

31 ¹ God spoke to Moses, saying: ² "See, I have appointed (to work for Me) Bezalel son of Uri son of Hur of the tribe of Judah, ³ and I have filled him with the spirit of God, with wisdom, with insight, with Divine inspiration, and with the ability for all types of work: ⁴ to do master weaving; to work with gold; with silver, and with copper; ⁵ with the craft of setting gems; and with the craft of wood, to do all kinds of work.

שמות לא:ו-טו · כי תשא

6 וַאֲנִ֞י הִנֵּ֧ה נָתַ֣תִּי אִתּ֗וֹ אֵ֣ת אָהֳלִיאָ֞ב בֶּן־אֲחִֽיסָמָךְ֙ לְמַטֵּה־דָ֔ן וּבְלֵ֥ב כָּל־חֲכַם־לֵ֖ב נָתַ֣תִּי חָכְמָ֑ה וְעָשׂ֕וּ אֵ֖ת כָּל־אֲשֶׁ֥ר צִוִּיתִֽךָ: 7 אֵ֣ת ׀ אֹ֣הֶל מוֹעֵ֗ד וְאֶת־הָֽאָרֹן֙ לָֽעֵדֻ֔ת וְאֶת־הַכַּפֹּ֖רֶת אֲשֶׁ֣ר עָלָ֑יו וְאֵ֖ת כָּל־כְּלֵ֥י הָאֹֽהֶל: 8 וְאֶת־הַשֻּׁלְחָן֙ וְאֶת־כֵּלָ֔יו וְאֶת־הַמְּנֹרָ֥ה הַטְּהֹרָ֖ה וְאֶת־כָּל־כֵּלֶ֑יהָ וְאֵ֖ת מִזְבַּ֥ח הַקְּטֹֽרֶת: 9 וְאֶת־מִזְבַּ֥ח הָעֹלָ֖ה וְאֶת־כָּל־כֵּלָ֑יו וְאֶת־הַכִּיּ֖וֹר וְאֶת־כַּנּֽוֹ: 10 וְאֵ֖ת בִּגְדֵ֣י הַשְּׂרָ֑ד וְאֶת־בִּגְדֵ֤י הַקֹּ֨דֶשׁ֙ לְאַהֲרֹ֣ן הַכֹּהֵ֔ן וְאֶת־בִּגְדֵ֥י בָנָ֖יו לְכַהֵֽן: 11 וְאֵ֨ת שֶׁ֤מֶן הַמִּשְׁחָה֙ וְאֶת־קְטֹ֣רֶת הַסַּמִּ֔ים לַקֹּ֑דֶשׁ כְּכֹ֥ל אֲשֶׁר־צִוִּיתִ֖ךָ יַעֲשֽׂוּ: פ 12 וַיֹּ֥אמֶר יְהֹוָ֖ה אֶל־מֹשֶׁ֥ה לֵּאמֹֽר:

13 וְאַתָּ֞ה דַּבֵּ֨ר אֶל־בְּנֵ֤י יִשְׂרָאֵל֙ לֵאמֹ֔ר אַ֥ךְ אֶת־שַׁבְּתֹתַ֖י תִּשְׁמֹ֑רוּ כִּי֩ א֨וֹת הִ֜וא בֵּינִ֣י וּבֵֽינֵיכֶ֗ם לְדֹרֹ֣תֵיכֶ֔ם לָדַ֕עַת כִּ֛י אֲנִ֥י יְהֹוָ֖ה מְקַדִּשְׁכֶֽם: 14 וּשְׁמַרְתֶּם֙ אֶת־הַשַּׁבָּ֔ת כִּ֛י קֹ֥דֶשׁ הִ֖וא לָכֶ֑ם מְחַֽלְלֶ֨יהָ֙ מ֣וֹת יוּמָ֔ת כִּ֗י כָּל־הָעֹשֶׂ֥ה בָהּ֙ מְלָאכָ֔ה וְנִכְרְתָ֛ה הַנֶּ֥פֶשׁ הַהִ֖וא מִקֶּ֥רֶב עַמֶּֽיהָ: 15 שֵׁ֣שֶׁת יָמִים֮ יֵעָשֶׂ֣ה מְלָאכָה֒ וּבַיּ֣וֹם

Why might you come to the conclusion that the construction of the Tabernacle would override the Sabbath? Since the Torah commands you to waive the laws of the Sabbath for the sake of offering sacrifices, you might think that they should be set aside also for the building of the Tabernacle in which the sacrifices are offered. Therefore you must be warned to the contrary (*Rabbi Elijah Mizrahi, 15th–16th century*).

"*What is the Sabbath? It is the name of the blessed Holy One, which is complete from all sides*" (*Zohar*). The "completeness" of the Sabbath suggests the absence of any lack or deficiency. This is the very opposite of labor, which we perform when its results are needed. On the Sabbath, which is associated with God's name, nothing is lacking, so no work is needed. Godliness flows to us effortlessly. (This is, of course, provided that we do not violate the Sabbath, indicating that we do not wish to be part of it.)

In this verse, we learn that the restrictions of the Sabbath apply even to the construction of the Tabernacle. On a personal level, this "construction" means repairing our ethical and religious imperfections so as to become a worthy dwelling place for the Divine—a human "Tabernacle." Even this, we are told, is outlawed on the Sabbath! All we need do is observe the Sabbath and rejoice in the presence of God, for on this day He will dwell among us regardless of our inadequacies (*Rabbi Menahem Nahum Twersky of Chernobyl, 18th century*).

14. Keep the Sabbath. Our observance of the Sabbath, commemorating God's resting after six days of creation, proclaims our belief in creation *ex nihilo*. Repeating this declaration weekly ensures that it will be remembered for all generations (*Maimonides, 12th century*).

It is a sacred thing for you. What is the distinction between the Sabbath day and a Festival day? The festivals are "*proclaimed*" holy (see above, 12:16), since we "proclaim" holiness upon

exodus 31:6–15 — ki tissa'

⁶ "I have also given him Oholiab son of Ahisamach of the tribe of Dan. Into all the (other) wise-hearted (men among you) I have (also) instilled the wisdom to make everything that I have commanded you:

⁷ "The Tent of Meeting, and the ark (which holds the Tablets of) Testimony, as well as the lid which goes on it, all the tent equipment, ⁸ the table and its implements, the pure candelabrum and all its utensils, the incense altar, ⁹ the sacrificial altar and all its utensils, the urn and its base, ¹⁰ the meshwork cloths (used to pack the Tabernacle's utensils during transport), the sacred garments for Aaron the priest, and the garments of his sons in which to serve as priests, ¹¹ the anointing oil, and the incense (used to raise smoke which is) holy.

"They should do everything that I have commanded you."

Observance of the Sabbath

¹² God spoke to Moses, saying: ¹³ "You should speak to the children of Israel and say: 'But keep My Sabbath (even when you are building the Tabernacle)! For it is a sign between Me and you for all your generations (that I chose you, and so that the nations should) know that I, God, am making you holy. ¹⁴ Keep the Sabbath, for it is a sacred thing for you. Those who desecrate it should be put to death (if witnesses were present, but if no witnesses were present, then) anyone who performs work on it will have his soul cut off from among his people. ¹⁵ Six days

---

spent on components of lesser degrees of sanctity, such as the Tabernacle's outer beams (*Rabbi Abraham Lichtstein, 18th–19th century*).

13. But keep My Sabbath (even when you are building the Tabernacle)! God was saying, "Although you will be eager and enthusiastic in the work of the Tabernacle, the Sabbath should not be set aside because of it" (*Rashi, 11th century*).

spiritual vitamin

> Sabbath (Shabbat) lights have to do with the practical reason of lighting up the house so that no one will stumble in darkness and get hurt, God forbid. But in a deeper sense, the Shabbat candles light up the house and every member of the family with the light of Torah, to walk safely through the path of life, which is full of dangerous pitfalls. In addition, lighting a candle in honor of Shabbat and the Festivals represents the lighting up of your *mazal* (fortunes), to be blessed by God also in material needs.

שמות לא:טו - לב:ג   כי תשא

הַשְּׁבִיעִ֗י שַׁבַּ֧ת שַׁבָּת֛וֹן קֹ֖דֶשׁ לַיהֹוָ֑ה כָּל־הָעֹשֶׂ֧ה מְלָאכָ֛ה בְּי֥וֹם הַשַּׁבָּ֖ת מ֥וֹת יוּמָֽת: 16 וְשָׁמְר֥וּ בְנֵֽי־יִשְׂרָאֵ֖ל אֶת־הַשַּׁבָּ֑ת לַעֲשׂ֧וֹת אֶת־הַשַּׁבָּ֛ת לְדֹרֹתָ֖ם בְּרִ֥ית עוֹלָֽם: 17 בֵּינִ֗י וּבֵין֙ בְּנֵ֣י יִשְׂרָאֵ֔ל א֥וֹת הִ֖וא לְעֹלָ֑ם כִּי־שֵׁ֣שֶׁת יָמִ֗ים עָשָׂ֤ה יְהֹוָה֙ אֶת־הַשָּׁמַ֣יִם וְאֶת־הָאָ֔רֶץ וּבַיּוֹם֙ הַשְּׁבִיעִ֔י שָׁבַ֖ת וַיִּנָּפַֽשׁ: ס 18 [SECOND READING] וַיִּתֵּ֣ן אֶל־מֹשֶׁ֗ה כְּכַלֹּתוֹ֙ לְדַבֵּ֤ר אִתּוֹ֙ בְּהַ֣ר סִינַ֔י שְׁנֵ֖י לֻחֹ֣ת הָעֵדֻ֑ת לֻחֹת֙ אֶ֔בֶן כְּתֻבִ֖ים בְּאֶצְבַּ֥ע אֱלֹהִֽים:

לב 1 וַיַּ֣רְא הָעָ֔ם כִּֽי־בֹשֵׁ֥שׁ מֹשֶׁ֖ה לָרֶ֣דֶת מִן־הָהָ֑ר וַיִּקָּהֵ֨ל הָעָ֜ם עַֽל־אַהֲרֹ֗ן וַיֹּאמְר֤וּ אֵלָיו֙ ק֣וּם ׀ עֲשֵׂה־לָ֣נוּ אֱלֹהִ֗ים אֲשֶׁ֤ר יֵֽלְכוּ֙ לְפָנֵ֔ינוּ כִּי־זֶ֣ה ׀ מֹשֶׁ֣ה הָאִ֗ישׁ אֲשֶׁ֤ר הֶֽעֱלָ֙נוּ֙ מֵאֶ֣רֶץ מִצְרַ֔יִם לֹ֥א יָדַ֖עְנוּ מֶה־הָ֥יָה לֽוֹ: 2 וַיֹּ֤אמֶר אֲלֵהֶם֙ אַהֲרֹ֔ן פָּֽרְקוּ֙ נִזְמֵ֣י הַזָּהָ֔ב אֲשֶׁר֙ בְּאָזְנֵ֣י נְשֵׁיכֶ֔ם בְּנֵיכֶ֖ם וּבְנֹתֵיכֶ֑ם וְהָבִ֖יאוּ אֵלָֽי: 3 וַיִּתְפָּֽרְקוּ֙ כָּל־הָעָ֔ם אֶת־נִזְמֵ֥י הַזָּהָ֖ב אֲשֶׁ֣ר בְּאָזְנֵיהֶ֑ם וַיָּבִ֖יאוּ אֶֽל־אַהֲרֹֽן:

and excitement of a bride and groom at their wedding (*Rabbi Menahem Nahum Twersky of Chernobyl, 18th century*).

He gave Moses the two Tablets of the Testimony. The Ten Commandments were written on two tablets: The first tablet contained five laws pertaining to man's relationship to God; the second tablet contained an additional five laws relating to man's relationship with his fellow man. *Rashi* states that the two tablets were "equal," suggesting that we ought to attach equal importance to both types of commandments, not differentiating between those relating to God and those relating to our fellow (*Rabbi Simḥah Bunem Ehrenfeld, 19th–20th century*).

32:3 All the people stripped themselves of the golden earrings. The women did not give their gold for the making of the Golden Calf; the husbands donated their own gold. Here we see that monotheistic belief was stronger with the women than with the men (*Midrash Tanḥuma*).

kabbalah bites

32:1 Aaron was a reincarnation of Haran, Abraham's brother. Abraham and Haran came to this world to achieve *tikkun* (spiritual healing) for Adam's sin of worshiping idols. Abraham, who rejected idol-worship and believed in one God, achieved this successfully, but Haran did not (see *Genesis 11:27*).

Aaron saw that the perpetrators of the Golden Calf would kill him if he did not consent to their plan, just as they had killed Hur, his nephew (*Rashi* to v. 5). Really he should have given his life, which would have achieved *tikkun* for Haran's soul. But he imagined that this *tikkun* had already been achieved through Hur's death.

work may be done, but on the seventh day, (it) is a Sabbath of complete rest, (with the intention of being) holy to God. Whoever performs work on the Sabbath day should be put to death. ¹⁶ The children of Israel should observe the Sabbath, to make the Sabbath throughout their generations as an everlasting covenant. ¹⁷ It is an eternal sign between Me and the children of Israel that in six days God created the heaven and the earth, and on the seventh day He ceased and rested.'"

The Sin of the Golden Calf

(The following occurred before the construction of the Tabernacle:)

[SECOND READING] ¹⁸ When He had finished speaking with him on Mount Sinai (telling him the laws that are found in *Parashat Mishpatim*), He gave Moses the two Tablets of the Testimony, stone tablets, written with the finger of God.

32 ¹ The people saw that Moses was delayed in coming down from the mountain.

The people gathered against Aaron, and they said to him: "Come on! Make us gods that will go before us (and lead us), because (as for) this man Moses, who brought us up from the land of Egypt, we don't know what has become of him."

² Aaron said to them, "Take the golden earrings off the ears of your wives, your sons, and your daughters and bring them to me (hoping to delay them until Moses came down)."

³ All the people stripped themselves of the golden earrings that were on their

---

them, sanctifying the day. The Sabbath, by contrast, is *intrinsically* holy, as the verse stresses, "It *is* a sacred thing for you" (*Zohar*).

Since the Sabbath is *intrinsically* holy there is no special symbolic commandment to observe on the Sabbath itself. On the Festivals, by contrast, special commandments are required—such as the ram's horn or four species—to *proclaim* the day holy (*Rabbi Kalonymous Kalman Shapira, 20th century*)

16. The children of Israel should observe the Sabbath. The word *shameru*, translated here as *"observe,"* has an alternative translation, as seen in *Genesis* 37:11, where *Rashi* describes Jacob as *"enthusiastically waiting"* (*shamar*) for the fulfillment of Joseph's dreams. The verse could therefore be interpreted as follows: Rather than viewing the Sabbath as a burdensome day of restrictions, we are commanded to *eagerly anticipate it* (*Rabbi Ḥayyim ibn Attar, 18th century*).

18. When He had finished (ke-khalloto) speaking with him on Mount Sinai. Moses kept studying the Torah and forgetting it, until God gave it to him as a gift, like a bride (*kallah*) to a bridegroom" (*Babylonian Talmud, Nedarim* 38a).

This does not mean that Moses forgot the factual information that he had been taught by God. Rather he lost the sense of joy experienced with something new, since any pleasurable experience eventually becomes boring. So God granted him the gift of Torah "like a bride to a bridegroom." Moses was given the power to experience the Torah each day with the joy

שמות לב:ד-יא | כי תשא

4 וַיִּקַּח מִיָּדָם וַיָּצַר אֹתוֹ בַּחֶרֶט וַיַּעֲשֵׂהוּ עֵגֶל מַסֵּכָה וַיֹּאמְרוּ אֵלֶּה אֱלֹהֶיךָ יִשְׂרָאֵל אֲשֶׁר הֶעֱלוּךָ מֵאֶרֶץ מִצְרָיִם: 5 וַיַּרְא אַהֲרֹן וַיִּבֶן מִזְבֵּחַ לְפָנָיו וַיִּקְרָא אַהֲרֹן וַיֹּאמַר חַג לַיהוָה מָחָר: 6 וַיַּשְׁכִּימוּ מִמָּחֳרָת וַיַּעֲלוּ עֹלֹת וַיַּגִּשׁוּ שְׁלָמִים וַיֵּשֶׁב הָעָם לֶאֱכֹל וְשָׁתוֹ וַיָּקֻמוּ לְצַחֵק: פ 7 וַיְדַבֵּר יְהוָה אֶל־מֹשֶׁה לֶךְ־רֵד כִּי שִׁחֵת עַמְּךָ אֲשֶׁר הֶעֱלֵיתָ מֵאֶרֶץ מִצְרָיִם: 8 סָרוּ מַהֵר מִן־הַדֶּרֶךְ אֲשֶׁר צִוִּיתִם עָשׂוּ לָהֶם עֵגֶל מַסֵּכָה וַיִּשְׁתַּחֲווּ־לוֹ וַיִּזְבְּחוּ־לוֹ וַיֹּאמְרוּ אֵלֶּה אֱלֹהֶיךָ יִשְׂרָאֵל אֲשֶׁר הֶעֱלוּךָ מֵאֶרֶץ מִצְרָיִם: 9 וַיֹּאמֶר יְהוָה אֶל־מֹשֶׁה רָאִיתִי אֶת־הָעָם הַזֶּה וְהִנֵּה עַם־קְשֵׁה־עֹרֶף הוּא: 10 וְעַתָּה הַנִּיחָה לִּי וְיִחַר־אַפִּי בָהֶם וַאֲכַלֵּם וְאֶעֱשֶׂה אוֹתְךָ לְגוֹי גָּדוֹל: 11 וַיְחַל מֹשֶׁה אֶת־פְּנֵי יְהוָה אֱלֹהָיו וַיֹּאמֶר

However, instead of making cherubim with the face of a human child, as God had intended for the Tabernacle, they chose instead the face of a calf. This is because the face of an ox appeared on the left-hand side of the celestial chariot (in Ezekiel's vision), whereas Moses is associated with God's "right side," as the verse states, *"He led at Moses' right, the arm of His glory"* (*Isaiah 63:12*). When Moses departed, leaving Aaron in charge, they presumed that God was no longer channeling His blessings through the right-hand side of the chariot, but rather through the left, via Aaron. Therefore, they made cherubim with the face of a calf (*Rabbi Jonathan Eybeschuetz, 18th century*).

7. Go down, for your people ... have become corrupt. Only three thousand individuals were actively involved in the sin of the Golden Calf (see verse 28), which was a comparatively small percentage of the Jewish population of a few million. Nevertheless, God told Moses to *"go down,"* which the Sages interpret, as *"descend from your high position. I gave you this high position only for their sake"* (see *Rashi*).

From this we see the disproportionate significance that even a comparatively small number of Jews can generate, to the extent that they can affect the spiritual status of Moses himself, despite his being absent during their sin.

From the negative, we can also learn the positive—how greatly significant the good deeds of even a small number of people can be for benefit of the entire Jewish population (*Rabbi Menahem Mendel Schneerson, 20th century*).

10. I will make you into a great nation. When God said into Moses, *"Now leave Me alone, etc.,"* Moses answered, "Master of the universe! If a three-legged stool—a nation supported by the merits of three Patriarchs—cannot stand before You,

> **kabbalah bites**
>
> **32:4** We are a reincarnation of the generation of the Golden Calf. In those days it was the women who had the spiritual upper hand: unlike their husbands, they refused to participate in the construction of the calf. And so it is in our day it is the women who are spiritually superior to their husbands and consequently able to dominate them.

exodus 32:3-11 — ki tissa'

ears (immediately) and brought them to Aaron. ⁴ He took (the rings) from their hands, tied it up in a cloth, and (then sorcerers from the mixed multitude) made it into a molten calf. They (the mixed multitude) said: "These are your gods, O Israel, who have brought you up from the land of Egypt!"

⁵ When Aaron saw (that the Golden Calf had life in it), he built an altar in front of it (to push them off further). Aaron called out and said: "Tomorrow should be a festival to God (for he was sure that Moses would come down by then)."

⁶ On the next day, they arose early, offered up burnt-offerings and brought peace-offerings, and the people sat down to eat and to drink, and they became depraved.

Moses Calms God's Anger

⁷ God said (sternly) to Moses: "Go down, for your people that you have brought up from the land of Egypt have become corrupt. ⁸ They have rapidly abandoned the way which I commanded them. They made themselves a molten calf, they bowed down to it, slaughtered sacrifices to it, and said: 'These are your gods, O Israel, who have brought you up from the land of Egypt.'"

⁹ God said to Moses: "I have observed this people and—look!—they are a stiff-necked people (who do not like being rebuked). ¹⁰ Now leave Me alone, and My anger will be kindled against them and I will annihilate them. I will make you into a great nation (instead)."

¹¹ Moses pleaded before God, his God, and said: "Why, O God, should Your anger

---

4. A molten calf. Aaron wanted to test the Jewish people to see if they would actually worship idols, so he pretended to go along with their plan. But since he did not execute the idol-worshipers immediately when they stumbled, God became angry with Aaron as well (*Rabbi Saadiah b. Joseph Gaon, 10th century*).

The Jewish people did not intend to worship idols, God forbid. Rather, in Moses' absence, they were seeking a concrete form of Divine service. The calf was thus intended to be an object through which they worshiped *God*, as Aaron said explicitly, "Tomorrow should be a festival *to God*" (v. 5; *Rabbi Abraham ibn Ezra, 12th century; Rabbi Judah Halevi, 12th century*).

Rather than seeking an idol, the Jewish people merely sought a replacement for Moses, who had disappeared, to guide them in serving God. Aaron chose a calf, since in God's celestial chariot (as described in *Ezekiel* 1:10) the face of an ox can be seen to the left side, representing God's strength (*Naḥmanides, 13th century*).

The Jewish people were split into three groups: (a) Some were merely looking for a new leader; (b) others wished to worship idols; while (c) the tribe of Levi remained totally loyal to God (below, v. 26; *the Tosafists, 12th–14th centuries*).

The Jewish people knew that if Moses had not disappeared, the Tabernacle would have been built and God would have spoken to Moses from between the two cherubim (see 25:22). When they saw that Moses had departed, they decided to make the cherubim themselves so that God would speak to them. Thus, they told Aaron, "Make us *gods* that will go before us" (v. 1), in the *plural* since they intended to make *two* cherubim.

שמות לב:יא-יח   כי תשא

לָמָה יְהֹוָה יֶחֱרֶה אַפְּךָ בְּעַמֶּךָ אֲשֶׁר הוֹצֵאתָ מֵאֶרֶץ מִצְרַיִם בְּכֹחַ גָּדוֹל וּבְיָד חֲזָקָה: 12 לָמָּה יֹאמְרוּ מִצְרַיִם לֵאמֹר בְּרָעָה הוֹצִיאָם לַהֲרֹג אֹתָם בֶּהָרִים וּלְכַלֹּתָם מֵעַל פְּנֵי הָאֲדָמָה שׁוּב מֵחֲרוֹן אַפֶּךָ וְהִנָּחֵם עַל־הָרָעָה לְעַמֶּךָ: 13 זְכֹר לְאַבְרָהָם לְיִצְחָק וּלְיִשְׂרָאֵל עֲבָדֶיךָ אֲשֶׁר נִשְׁבַּעְתָּ לָהֶם בָּךְ וַתְּדַבֵּר אֲלֵהֶם אַרְבֶּה אֶת־זַרְעֲכֶם כְּכוֹכְבֵי הַשָּׁמָיִם וְכָל־הָאָרֶץ הַזֹּאת אֲשֶׁר אָמַרְתִּי אֶתֵּן לְזַרְעֲכֶם וְנָחֲלוּ לְעֹלָם: 14 וַיִּנָּחֶם יְהֹוָה עַל־הָרָעָה אֲשֶׁר דִּבֶּר לַעֲשׂוֹת לְעַמּוֹ: פ

15 וַיִּפֶן וַיֵּרֶד מֹשֶׁה מִן־הָהָר וּשְׁנֵי לֻחֹת הָעֵדֻת בְּיָדוֹ לֻחֹת כְּתֻבִים מִשְּׁנֵי עֶבְרֵיהֶם מִזֶּה וּמִזֶּה הֵם כְּתֻבִים: 16 וְהַלֻּחֹת מַעֲשֵׂה אֱלֹהִים הֵמָּה וְהַמִּכְתָּב מִכְתַּב אֱלֹהִים הוּא חָרוּת עַל־הַלֻּחֹת: 17 וַיִּשְׁמַע יְהוֹשֻׁעַ אֶת־קוֹל הָעָם בְּרֵעֹה וַיֹּאמֶר אֶל־מֹשֶׁה קוֹל מִלְחָמָה בַּמַּחֲנֶה: 18 וַיֹּאמֶר אֵין קוֹל עֲנוֹת גְּבוּרָה וְאֵין

not the Jewish people who are at fault here, but the mixed multitudes (*Rabbi Ḥayyim ibn Attar, 18th century*).

14. God changed His mind about the evil that He said He would do to His people. Why did God forgive the Israelites for the sin of the Golden Calf, when they had not repented—and yet for the sin of the spies, for which they *did* repent, He refused to forgive them?

The sin of the Golden Calf harbored a certain spirituality, a thirst for a higher power, *"Make us gods"* (v. 1). The sin of the spies, on the other hand, was nothing more than a desire for the material, *"See what kind of land it is"* (Numbers 13:18; *Rabbi Menaḥem Mendel Morgensztern of Kotsk, 19th century*).

15. Two Tablets of the Testimony. The tablets were each 6 by 6 handbreadths in size, and together they filled the ark, leaving no empty space (*Babylonian Talmud, Bava Batra* 14a).

spiritual vitamin

> Human nature is such that once you accept the principle of compromise in matters of faith, there is bound to be steady erosion, every time with a lighter mind and fewer qualms.

be kindled against Your people whom You have brought up from the land of Egypt with great power and with a strong hand? ¹² Why should the Egyptians say, 'He brought them out with evil intent: to kill them in the mountains and to annihilate them from upon the face of the earth'?

"Withdraw from the heat of Your anger and change Your mind about doing evil to Your people! ¹³ Remember Abraham, Isaac, and Israel, Your servants, to whom You Yourself swore when You said to them: 'I will multiply your seed like the stars of the heavens, and all this land which I promised you I will give to your descendants and they will possess it forever.'"

¹⁴ God changed His mind about the evil that He had said He would do to His people.

Moses Descends and Smashes the Tablets

¹⁵ Moses turned and came down from the mountain bearing the two Tablets of the Testimony in his hand, tablets inscribed (so that the letters could miraculously be read) from both their sides. They were inscribed on both sides. ¹⁶ The tablets were the work of God, and the writing was the writing of God, engraved on the tablets.

¹⁷ When Joshua heard the noise of the people shouting (rejoicing and laughing), he said to Moses: "It sounds like a battle in the camp!"

¹⁸ Moses said: "It is neither a voice shouting victory, nor a voice shouting defeat. It is a voice of blasphemy that I hear."

---

certainly a one-legged stool will not! And I will be put to shame before my ancestors. They will say, 'Look at this leader they appointed! He seeks glory for himself but does not bother to ask for mercy for them.'" (*Babylonian Talmud, Berakhot* 32a).

11. Why, O God, should Your anger be kindled against Your people whom You have brought up from the land of Egypt. Moses evoked the memory of Egypt, pleading: Take into account from where Your people have just emerged. Please remember that You have only recently removed them from a breeding ground of immorality, lust, and iniquity. In their moment of vulnerability, they have relapsed to the familiar habits that surrounded them for centuries (*Exodus Rabbah*).

Moses attempted to diffuse God's anger, rationalizing, "Is a wise man jealous of anyone but another wise man? Or is a strong man jealous of anyone but another strong man? Why then, O God, should Your anger be kindled?" (*Rashi, 11th century*).

Surely Moses should have prayed to God respectfully, and remorsefully, rather than challenging Him, "Why are You angry?" Moses was saying to God, "Why have You directed Your attribute of fierce judgment *'against Your people'*? Save that for their enemies!" (*Nahmanides, 13th century*).

The sin of the Golden Calf was orchestrated by the "mixed multitudes" of Egyptian converts who had joined the Jewish people. Moses told God, "Do not be angry at *Your people*," since it is

שמות לב:יח-כז | כי תשא

קוֹל עֲנוֹת חֲלוּשָׁה קוֹל עַנּוֹת אָנֹכִי שֹׁמֵעַ: 19 וַיְהִי כַּאֲשֶׁר קָרַב אֶל־הַמַּחֲנֶה וַיַּרְא אֶת־הָעֵגֶל וּמְחֹלֹת וַיִּחַר־אַף מֹשֶׁה וַיַּשְׁלֵךְ מִיָּדָו אֶת־הַלֻּחֹת וַיְשַׁבֵּר אֹתָם תַּחַת הָהָר: 20 וַיִּקַּח אֶת־הָעֵגֶל אֲשֶׁר עָשׂוּ וַיִּשְׂרֹף בָּאֵשׁ וַיִּטְחַן עַד אֲשֶׁר־דָּק וַיִּזֶר עַל־פְּנֵי הַמַּיִם וַיַּשְׁקְ אֶת־בְּנֵי יִשְׂרָאֵל: 21 וַיֹּאמֶר מֹשֶׁה אֶל־אַהֲרֹן מֶה־עָשָׂה לְךָ הָעָם הַזֶּה כִּי־הֵבֵאתָ עָלָיו חֲטָאָה גְדֹלָה: 22 וַיֹּאמֶר אַהֲרֹן אַל־יִחַר אַף אֲדֹנִי אַתָּה יָדַעְתָּ אֶת־הָעָם כִּי בְרָע הוּא: 23 וַיֹּאמְרוּ לִי עֲשֵׂה־לָנוּ אֱלֹהִים אֲשֶׁר יֵלְכוּ לְפָנֵינוּ כִּי־זֶה | מֹשֶׁה הָאִישׁ אֲשֶׁר הֶעֱלָנוּ מֵאֶרֶץ מִצְרַיִם לֹא יָדַעְנוּ מֶה־הָיָה לוֹ: 24 וָאֹמַר לָהֶם לְמִי זָהָב הִתְפָּרָקוּ וַיִּתְּנוּ־לִי וָאַשְׁלִכֵהוּ בָאֵשׁ וַיֵּצֵא הָעֵגֶל הַזֶּה: 25 וַיַּרְא מֹשֶׁה אֶת־הָעָם כִּי פָרֻעַ הוּא כִּי־פְרָעֹה אַהֲרֹן לְשִׁמְצָה בְּקָמֵיהֶם: 26 וַיַּעֲמֹד מֹשֶׁה בְּשַׁעַר הַמַּחֲנֶה וַיֹּאמֶר מִי לַיהוָה אֵלָי וַיֵּאָסְפוּ אֵלָיו כָּל־בְּנֵי לֵוִי: 27 וַיֹּאמֶר לָהֶם כֹּה־אָמַר יְהוָה אֱלֹהֵי יִשְׂרָאֵל שִׂימוּ אִישׁ־חַרְבּוֹ עַל־יְרֵכוֹ עִבְרוּ וָשׁוּבוּ מִשַּׁעַר לָשַׁעַר בַּמַּחֲנֶה וְהִרְגוּ אִישׁ־אֶת־אָחִיו וְאִישׁ

534

The status of the Torah is dependent, to a very great extent, on the readiness of the Jewish people to receive it. That is why the letters flew off the tablets when the people sinned. Moses, however, had not sinned and he still retained the power to hold onto the Torah, as God had said to him, *"I will make you into a great nation (instead)"* (v. 10).

But instead, Moses gave over his life for the Jewish people, refusing to separate himself from them. Moses loved the community of Israel even more than he loved the tablets, for he knew that in God's eyes, the people themselves were more precious than anything. And it was only when Moses joined himself with the Jewish people, relinquishing his hold on the Torah, that the tablets lost all their potential and the letters actually flew off them.

By joining himself with Israel, Moses healed them spiritually. Once he and they were bonded in this way, they were redeemed of their sin (*Rabbi Judah Aryeh Leib Alter of Gur, 19th century*).

And shattered them. God approved, exclaiming, "Well done for breaking them!" (*Babylonian Talmud, Shabbat* 87a).

When Moses was concerned at having broken the tablets, God consoled him, "Don't be pained! The first set of tablets contained only the Ten Commandments, but in the second set that I will give you I will

Food for thought

1. How can you be sure that your worship of God is not, in fact, self-worship?

2. How can we, as humans, relate to God if we may possess no image of Him?

3. Which is religiously inferior: idolatry or atheism?

exodus 32:19–27   ki tissa'

[19] When he drew closer to the camp and saw the calf and the dances, Moses became angry, and he threw the tablets from his hands and shattered them at the foot of the mountain.

Perpetrators of the Calf Are Punished

[20] He took the calf they had made, burned it in fire, ground it to fine powder, scattered it upon the surface of the water, and gave it to the children of Israel to drink.

[21] Moses said to Aaron: "What (torture) did this people do to you that you brought such a grave sin on them?"

[22] Aaron replied: "Do not be angry, my lord. You know that the people are always going off the tracks. [23] They said to me, 'Make us gods that will go before us (and lead us), because as for this man Moses, who brought us up from the land of Egypt, we don't know what has become of him.' [24] I (only) said to them, 'Who has gold?' and they took it off (quickly) and gave it to me. I threw it into the fire and, (to my surprise,) out came this calf."

[25] Moses saw that people had been exposed, for Aaron had exposed them to disgrace before their enemies.

[26] Moses stood in the gate of the camp and said: "Whoever is for God, (let him come) to me!" All the Levites gathered around him. [27] He said to them: "This is what God, the God of Israel, said: '(Any person who worships idols should be put to death. Therefore,) let every man place his sword upon his thigh and pass back and forth from one gate to the other in the camp, and let every man kill his (half-)brother, his friend, and his relative.'"

---

19. When he drew closer to the camp and saw the calf and the dances ... he threw the tablets from his hands and shattered them. Although Moses had been informed by God of the sin of the Golden Calf, he did not shatter the tablets until actually seeing the idol and the dancing. This teaches you that you should not judge on the basis of guesswork or, in this case, on the basis of hearsay (*Jerusalem Talmud, Ta'anit* 4:5).

He threw the tablets from his hands. Was it not disrespectful of Moses to break the tablets inscribed by God? If he did not feel that the Jewish people merited them, he could have buried them.

The tablets were extremely heavy and Moses could only walk slowly with them. When he saw the Jewish people worshiping the calf, he wanted to stop them immediately and, in order to reach the people more quickly, he let go of the tablets, which fell and shattered instantly (*The Tosafists, 12th-14th centuries*).

As Moses descended the mountain, the letters on the tablets flew off, indicating that the Jewish people were not worthy of receiving them. When the Divine content of the tablets had gone, Moses saw no objection to breaking them.

Or perhaps Moses felt so physically drained when he saw the calf-worship, he was unable to bear the immense weight of the tablets (*Rabbi Baḥya b. Asher, 13th century*).

שמות לב:כז - לג:א | כי תשא

אֶת־רֵעֵ֖הוּ וְאִ֥ישׁ אֶת־קְרֹבֽוֹ׃ 28 וַיַּעֲשׂ֥וּ בְנֵֽי־לֵוִ֖י כִּדְבַ֣ר מֹשֶׁ֑ה וַיִּפֹּ֤ל מִן־הָעָם֙ בַּיּ֣וֹם הַה֔וּא כִּשְׁלֹ֥שֶׁת אַלְפֵ֖י אִֽישׁ׃ 29 וַיֹּ֣אמֶר מֹשֶׁ֗ה מִלְא֨וּ יֶדְכֶ֤ם הַיּוֹם֙ לַֽיהֹוָ֔ה כִּ֛י אִ֥ישׁ בִּבְנ֖וֹ וּבְאָחִ֑יו וְלָתֵ֧ת עֲלֵיכֶ֛ם הַיּ֖וֹם בְּרָכָֽה׃ 30 וַֽיְהִי֙ מִֽמׇּחֳרָ֔ת וַיֹּ֤אמֶר מֹשֶׁה֙ אֶל־הָעָ֔ם אַתֶּ֥ם חֲטָאתֶ֖ם חֲטָאָ֣ה גְדֹלָ֑ה וְעַתָּה֙ אֶֽעֱלֶ֣ה אֶל־יְהֹוָ֔ה אוּלַ֥י אֲכַפְּרָ֖ה בְּעַ֥ד חַטַּאתְכֶֽם׃ 31 וַיָּ֧שׇׁב מֹשֶׁ֛ה אֶל־יְהֹוָ֖ה וַיֹּאמַ֑ר אָ֣נָּ֗א חָטָ֞א הָעָ֤ם הַזֶּה֙ חֲטָאָ֣ה גְדֹלָ֔ה וַיַּעֲשׂ֥וּ לָהֶ֖ם אֱלֹהֵ֥י זָהָֽב׃ 32 וְעַתָּ֖ה אִם־תִּשָּׂ֣א חַטָּאתָ֑ם וְאִם־אַ֕יִן מְחֵ֣נִי נָ֔א מִֽסִּפְרְךָ֖ אֲשֶׁ֥ר כָּתָֽבְתָּ׃ 33 וַיֹּ֥אמֶר יְהֹוָ֖ה אֶל־מֹשֶׁ֑ה מִ֚י אֲשֶׁ֣ר חָֽטָא־לִ֔י אֶמְחֶ֖נּוּ מִסִּפְרִֽי׃ 34 וְעַתָּ֞ה לֵ֣ךְ ׀ נְחֵ֣ה אֶת־הָעָ֗ם אֶ֤ל אֲשֶׁר־דִּבַּ֙רְתִּי֙ לָ֔ךְ הִנֵּ֥ה מַלְאָכִ֖י יֵלֵ֣ךְ לְפָנֶ֑יךָ וּבְי֣וֹם פׇּקְדִ֔י וּפָקַדְתִּ֥י עֲלֵיהֶ֖ם חַטָּאתָֽם׃ 35 וַיִּגֹּ֥ף יְהֹוָ֖ה אֶת־הָעָ֑ם עַ֚ל אֲשֶׁ֣ר עָשׂ֣וּ אֶת־הָעֵ֔גֶל אֲשֶׁ֥ר עָשָׂ֖ה אַהֲרֹֽן׃ ס

 1 וַיְדַבֵּ֨ר יְהֹוָ֜ה אֶל־מֹשֶׁ֗ה לֵ֣ךְ עֲלֵ֤ה מִזֶּה֙ אַתָּ֣ה וְהָעָ֔ם אֲשֶׁ֥ר הֶעֱלִ֖יתָ מֵאֶ֣רֶץ מִצְרָ֑יִם אֶל־הָאָ֗רֶץ אֲשֶׁ֣ר נִ֠שְׁבַּ֠עְתִּי לְאַבְרָהָ֨ם לְיִצְחָ֤ק וּֽלְיַעֲקֹב֙

Moses acknowledged the terrible nature of their sin in order to emphasize their remorse and ensure their forgiveness—because the true test of a person's repentance *is when he accepts full responsibility for his actions.*

When God confronted Adam with his sin in the Garden of Eden, Adam immediately excused his behavior, *"The woman whom You gave (to be) with me…"* (*Genesis* 3:12). This showed that he was not genuinely remorseful.

Moses, on the other hand, wishing for his people's repentance to be complete and accepted by God, stated clearly, *"This people has committed a terrible sin."* They are taking full responsibility for their actions and are ashamed of what they have done. They recognize the magnitude of their sin, without justification or excuses. Therefore, O God, they are worthy of Your forgiveness (*Rabbi Ezekiel Taub of Kazimierz, 19th century*).

They have made themselves a god of gold. Moses *detailed* the transgression of the children of Israel. When repenting, you should follow his example, listing and describing the sins for which you seek atonement (*Maimonides, 12th century*).

32. If You forgive their sin (then well and good), but if not, please erase me from Your Book (the Torah). Moses was saying, "In either case, erase me from Your Book. If You are willing to forgive them on the condition that they have someone to suffer for their sins, then I am willing to serve as their instrument of atonement. Erase me so that they can survive. If, on the other

exodus 32:28 – 33:1 ki tissa'

[28] The sons of Levi followed Moses' word. On that day some three thousand men fell from among the people.

[29] Moses said: "Today you can be ordained (to be priests) for God with a blessing, for each man (was even willing to kill) his son and his brother."

[30] On the next day, Moses said to the people: "You have committed a terrible sin. Now I will go up to God. Perhaps I will obtain atonement for your sin."

[31] Moses returned to God, and he said: "Please! This people has committed a terrible sin. They have made themselves a god of gold. [32] Now, if You forgive their sin (then well and good), but if not, please erase me from Your Book (the Torah), which You have written."

[33] God said to Moses: " I will erase from My Book whoever has sinned against Me!"

[34] "Now, go and lead the people to the place which I told you about. My angel (and not I) will go before you. When I bring punishment for their sins (in the future, I will always take the Golden Calf into consideration)."

[35] Then God struck the people with a plague, because they had made the calf which Aaron brought about.

33

[1] God spoke to Moses: "Go, up from here, you and the people you have brought up from the land of Egypt, to the land that I swore to Abraham,

add legal instruction (*Halakhah*) as well as exegetical and homiletical teachings (*Midrash* and *Aggadah*)" (*Exodus Rabbah*).

Why did God not include these additional qualities of Oral Law (*Halakhah, Midrash* and *Aggadah*) in the first set of tablets to begin with? Then Moses would not have needed to break the first set, only in order to be encouraged by God that the second set would be better.

In a sense, the Written Law is limited, since it cannot be added to or detracted from. The Oral Law, on the other hand, is infinite in scope, as there is no limit to the number of innovations it can inspire. *The infinite proportion of the Oral Law is an expression of God's infinitude.*

When the Torah was given, the Jewish people were at a spiritually heightened state. Ironically, this posed a certain disadvantage: the awareness of their own spiritual greatness made it difficult for them to feel humble.

God's infinitude can only be appreciated by a truly humble person. So, since the Jewish people were somewhat lacking in humility at the giving of the Torah, they were not suitable receptacles for the Oral Law whose infinite proportion is an expression of God's infinity.

Only through the humbling experience of the Golden Calf, and the subsequent reconciliation with God, did the Jewish people become sufficiently broken in their own eyes to be receptacles for the *Halakhah, Midrash* and *Aggadah*. The breaking of the first tablets witnessed the humbling of the Jewish people, which was the key to their later greatness (*Rabbi Menahem Mendel Schneerson, 20th century*).

31. Moses returned to God, and he said: "Please! This people has committed a terrible sin."
If Moses' intention was to pray to God so that He should forgive the people, why did he emphasize the extent of their betrayal?

שמות לג:א-יא · כי תשא

לֵאמֹר לְזַרְעֲךָ אֶתְּנֶנָּה: ² וְשָׁלַחְתִּי לְפָנֶיךָ מַלְאָךְ וְגֵרַשְׁתִּי אֶת־הַכְּנַעֲנִי הָאֱמֹרִי וְהַחִתִּי וְהַפְּרִזִּי הַחִוִּי וְהַיְבוּסִי: ³ אֶל־אֶרֶץ זָבַת חָלָב וּדְבָשׁ כִּי לֹא אֶעֱלֶה בְּקִרְבְּךָ כִּי עַם־קְשֵׁה־עֹרֶף אַתָּה פֶּן־אֲכֶלְךָ בַּדָּרֶךְ: ⁴ וַיִּשְׁמַע הָעָם אֶת־הַדָּבָר הָרָע הַזֶּה וַיִּתְאַבָּלוּ וְלֹא־שָׁתוּ אִישׁ עֶדְיוֹ עָלָיו: ⁵ וַיֹּאמֶר יְהֹוָה אֶל־מֹשֶׁה אֱמֹר אֶל־בְּנֵי־יִשְׂרָאֵל אַתֶּם עַם־קְשֵׁה־עֹרֶף רֶגַע אֶחָד אֶעֱלֶה בְקִרְבְּךָ וְכִלִּיתִיךָ וְעַתָּה הוֹרֵד עֶדְיְךָ מֵעָלֶיךָ וְאֵדְעָה מָה אֶעֱשֶׂה־לָּךְ: ⁶ וַיִּתְנַצְּלוּ בְנֵי־יִשְׂרָאֵל אֶת־עֶדְיָם מֵהַר חוֹרֵב: ⁷ וּמֹשֶׁה יִקַּח אֶת־הָאֹהֶל וְנָטָה־לוֹ | מִחוּץ לַמַּחֲנֶה הַרְחֵק מִן־הַמַּחֲנֶה וְקָרָא לוֹ אֹהֶל מוֹעֵד וְהָיָה כָּל־מְבַקֵּשׁ יְהֹוָה יֵצֵא אֶל־אֹהֶל מוֹעֵד אֲשֶׁר מִחוּץ לַמַּחֲנֶה: ⁸ וְהָיָה כְּצֵאת מֹשֶׁה אֶל־הָאֹהֶל יָקוּמוּ כָּל־הָעָם וְנִצְּבוּ אִישׁ פֶּתַח אָהֳלוֹ וְהִבִּיטוּ אַחֲרֵי מֹשֶׁה עַד־בֹּאוֹ הָאֹהֱלָה: ⁹ וְהָיָה כְּבֹא מֹשֶׁה הָאֹהֱלָה יֵרֵד עַמּוּד הֶעָנָן וְעָמַד פֶּתַח הָאֹהֶל וְדִבֶּר עִם־מֹשֶׁה: ¹⁰ וְרָאָה כָל־הָעָם אֶת־עַמּוּד הֶעָנָן עֹמֵד פֶּתַח הָאֹהֶל וְקָם כָּל־הָעָם וְהִשְׁתַּחֲוּוּ אִישׁ פֶּתַח אָהֳלוֹ: ¹¹ וְדִבֶּר יְהֹוָה אֶל־מֹשֶׁה פָּנִים אֶל־פָּנִים כַּאֲשֶׁר יְדַבֵּר אִישׁ אֶל־רֵעֵהוּ וְשָׁב אֶל־הַמַּחֲנֶה וּמְשָׁרְתוֹ יְהוֹשֻׁעַ בִּן־נוּן נַעַר לֹא יָמִישׁ מִתּוֹךְ הָאֹהֶל: פ

—On 17 *Tammuz*, the tablets were broken;

—On 18 *Tammuz*, he burned the calf and judged the sinners;

—On 19 *Tammuz*, he ascended Mount Sinai and spent forty days there;

—On *Rosh Ḥodesh Elul*, he ascended Mount Sinai to receive the second tablets;

—On 10 *Tishri*, God gave him the second tablets, and he came down, and God began to command him about the Tabernacle.

—On *Rosh Ḥodesh Nisan*, the Tabernacle was constructed and God no longer spoke with Moses, except from the Tent of Meeting (*Rashi, 11th century*).

Rashi maintained that God only instructed the Jewish people to build the Tabernacle after the sin of the Golden Calf. This implies that *if it were not for the sin there would not have been a Tabernacle*. The first tablets would simply have been in Israel's midst, without an ark or Tabernacle.

The ideal scenario is that the Israelites would have connected to God without the need for any physical focus of worship. It is only that, through the sin, they became somewhat disconnected from God, and the solution to bring them close again was through the Tabernacle and its vessels (*Rabbi Judah Aryeh Leib Alter of Gur, 19th century*).

exodus 33:1–11   ki tissa'

Isaac, and Jacob, saying: 'I will give it to your descendants.' ² I will send an angel before you, and I will drive out the Canaanites, the Amorites, the Hittites, the Perizzites, the Hivites, and the Jebusites. ³ (You should take them up) to a land flowing with milk and honey. (I am sending an angel,) because I (personally) will not go up with you, since you are a stiff-necked people, and I may destroy you on the way."

⁴ When the people heard this bad news (that the Divine Presence would not accompany them), they mourned, and no man put on his crown.

⁵ God said to Moses: "Say to the children of Israel: 'You are a stiff-necked people. If (instead of sending My angel,) I go up with you (and then you rebel against Me, I will become angry) in one moment, and I will destroy you.'"

"Now (you will be punished immediately in that) you take off your crowns, and (as for the rest of the punishment,) I know what (I intend) to do to you."

⁶ So the children of Israel stripped themselves of their crowns from Mount Horeb.

Moses' Private Tent of Meeting

⁷ Moses would take the tent (from then on until the Tabernacle was erected, since the Divine Presence was banished from the camp), and pitch it for himself outside the camp, distancing it (two thousand cubits) from the camp. He called it the Tent of Meeting. Thus, anyone seeking God would go out to the Tent of Meeting, which was outside the camp.

⁸ It would be that when Moses would go out (from the camp) to the tent, all the people would stand up, and remain standing (until he was out of sight), each one at the entrance of his tent, and they would gaze at Moses until he went into the tent.

⁹ It would be that when Moses entered the tent, a pillar of cloud would descend and stand at the entrance of the tent, and He (God) would speak with Moses. ¹⁰ When all the people would see the pillar of cloud standing at the entrance of the tent, all the people would stand up and bow down (to the Divine Presence), each one at the entrance of his tent.

¹¹ God would speak to Moses face to face, as a man would speak to his friend. (Afterwards,) he would return to the camp (to teach the elders what he had learned); but his attendant, a lad, Joshua son of Nun, would not depart from the tent.

hand, You are unwilling to forgive them, then erase me along with them, because I cannot bear to witness the end of my people" (*Rabbi Ephraim of Luntshits, 16ᵗʰ–17ᵗʰ century*).

33:11 God would speak to Moses face to face, as a man would speak to his friend. (Afterwards,) he would return to the camp (to teach the elders what he had learned). Moses did this from the Day of Atonement until the Tabernacle was erected, but no longer.

שמות לג:יב-כג | כי תשא

12 [THIRD READING] וַיֹּאמֶר מֹשֶׁה אֶל־יְהֹוָה רְאֵה אַתָּה אֹמֵר אֵלַי הַעַל אֶת־הָעָם הַזֶּה וְאַתָּה לֹא הוֹדַעְתַּנִי אֵת אֲשֶׁר־תִּשְׁלַח עִמִּי וְאַתָּה אָמַרְתָּ יְדַעְתִּיךָ בְשֵׁם וְגַם־מָצָאתָ חֵן בְּעֵינָי: 13 וְעַתָּה אִם־נָא מָצָאתִי חֵן בְּעֵינֶיךָ הוֹדִעֵנִי נָא אֶת־דְּרָכֶךָ וְאֵדָעֲךָ לְמַעַן אֶמְצָא־חֵן בְּעֵינֶיךָ וּרְאֵה כִּי עַמְּךָ הַגּוֹי הַזֶּה: 14 וַיֹּאמַר פָּנַי יֵלֵכוּ וַהֲנִחֹתִי לָךְ: 15 וַיֹּאמֶר אֵלָיו אִם־אֵין פָּנֶיךָ הֹלְכִים אַל־תַּעֲלֵנוּ מִזֶּה: 16 וּבַמֶּה | יִוָּדַע אֵפוֹא כִּי־מָצָאתִי חֵן בְּעֵינֶיךָ אֲנִי וְעַמֶּךָ הֲלוֹא בְּלֶכְתְּךָ עִמָּנוּ וְנִפְלֵינוּ אֲנִי וְעַמְּךָ מִכָּל־הָעָם אֲשֶׁר עַל־פְּנֵי הָאֲדָמָה: פ 17 [FOURTH READING] וַיֹּאמֶר יְהֹוָה אֶל־מֹשֶׁה גַּם אֶת־הַדָּבָר הַזֶּה אֲשֶׁר דִּבַּרְתָּ אֶעֱשֶׂה כִּי־מָצָאתָ חֵן בְּעֵינַי וָאֵדָעֲךָ בְּשֵׁם: 18 וַיֹּאמַר הַרְאֵנִי נָא אֶת־כְּבֹדֶךָ: 19 וַיֹּאמֶר אֲנִי אַעֲבִיר כָּל־טוּבִי עַל־פָּנֶיךָ וְקָרָאתִי בְשֵׁם יְהֹוָה לְפָנֶיךָ וְחַנֹּתִי אֶת־אֲשֶׁר אָחֹן וְרִחַמְתִּי אֶת־אֲשֶׁר אֲרַחֵם: 20 וַיֹּאמֶר לֹא תוּכַל לִרְאֹת אֶת־פָּנָי כִּי לֹא־יִרְאַנִי הָאָדָם וָחָי: 21 וַיֹּאמֶר יְהֹוָה הִנֵּה מָקוֹם אִתִּי וְנִצַּבְתָּ עַל־הַצּוּר: 22 וְהָיָה בַּעֲבֹר כְּבֹדִי וְשַׂמְתִּיךָ בְּנִקְרַת הַצּוּר וְשַׂכֹּתִי כַפִּי עָלֶיךָ עַד־עָבְרִי: 23 וַהֲסִרֹתִי אֶת־כַּפִּי וְרָאִיתָ אֶת־אֲחֹרָי וּפָנַי לֹא יֵרָאוּ: פ

21–22. There is a place for Me and you should stand on the rock. When My glory passes by, I will place you into the cleft of the rock. There are times to speak up forcefully, without reservation. Then there are issues to address discreetly, with great subtlety. A good leader will be able to discern the approach that best fits the occasion.

The general rule is that when *"there is a place for Me,"* when the matter concerns God's honor, *"you should stand on the rock"*—proud and unyielding as a rock. However, *"when My glory passes by,"* and the issue at hand is no longer God's glory, but private affairs, then *"I will place you into the cleft of the rock"*—you should act discreetly (*Rabbi Meir Shapira of Lublin, 20th century*).

23. You will see My back, but My face will not be seen. This verse cannot be understood literally. Rather, it figuratively expresses our understanding of God's role in world events.

The beginning of the verse, *"You will see My back,"* implies that only after an event has transpired and we view its *"back"*

Food for thought

1. Would knowing the reward for your actions lessen life's challenges?

2. Have you ever prayed for insight into God's ways?

3. If you were "God for an hour," would you change the way things are?

exodus 33:12–23 — ki tissa'

Moses Asks to Know the Ways of God

[THIRD READING] ¹² Moses said to God: "Look, You say to me: 'Bring this people up!' But You have not informed me whom You will send with me (besides the angel, whom I do not desire), and yet You said: 'I have distinguished you (from all other people) by (a special) name and you have also found favor in My eyes.'

¹³ "Now, if I have indeed found favor in Your eyes, please let me know Your methods (of reward) so that I may know (what) You(r rewards are) and I (can appreciate what) finding favor in Your eyes (means). (My reward will be through) this nation, Your people (and not through a new nation)."

¹⁴ He (God) said, "(Instead of an angel), My Presence will go (with you), and I will give you rest (from your enemies)."

¹⁵ He (Moses) said to Him, "If Your Presence does not go with us, do not take us onwards from here. ¹⁶ For how else will it be known that I have found favor in Your eyes, I and Your people? Is it not by Your going with us? Then I and Your people will be distinguished from every other nation on the face of the earth."

[FOURTH READING] ¹⁷ God said to Moses: "Even this thing that you have spoken (that the Divine Presence should not rest on the nations), I will do, for you have found favor in My eyes, and I will distinguish you by name (of importance)."

¹⁸ (Since Moses perceived that the time was opportune,) he said: "Show me, please, Your glory!"

¹⁹ He said: "I will let all My goodness pass before you. I will proclaim the name of God before you, (but I will still) favor whomever I wish to favor, and I will have compassion for whomever I wish to have compassion." ²⁰ He said, "You will not be able to see My face, for no man can see Me and live." ²¹ God said: "Here there is a place (ready for) Me (to hide you, so that you will not be harmed by My Presence), and you should stand on the rock. ²² When My glory passes by, I will place you into the cleft of the rock, and I will cover you with My hand until I have passed by. ²³ Then I will remove My hand, and you will see My back, but My face will not be seen."

kabbalah bites

33:13 *Now, if I have indeed found favor in Your eyes.* Moses knew that he was a reincarnation of Seth and Abel, as these were alluded to in his name [*MoSHeH* (Moses) is an acronym for **M**osheh, **SH**et (Seth) and **H**evel (Abel)—see *Genesis* 4:25]. What he was unsure about was whether he was also a reincarnation of Noah.

So now he asked God: "*If I have indeed found favor* (*matza'ti ḥen*)": Am I an incarnation of Noah, who *found favor* in Your eyes (*Genesis* 6:8)? (*HeN* is also an anagram of *NoaH*).

God replied: "*You have found favor in My eyes*" (below, v. 17): Yes, you are indeed a reincarnation of Noah.

שמות לד:א-ז · כי תשא

לֵךְ [FIFTH READING] 1 וַיֹּאמֶר יְהֹוָה אֶל־מֹשֶׁה פְּסָל־לְךָ שְׁנֵי־לֻחֹת אֲבָנִים כָּרִאשֹׁנִים וְכָתַבְתִּי עַל־הַלֻּחֹת אֶת־הַדְּבָרִים אֲשֶׁר הָיוּ עַל־הַלֻּחֹת הָרִאשֹׁנִים אֲשֶׁר שִׁבַּרְתָּ: 2 וֶהְיֵה נָכוֹן לַבֹּקֶר וְעָלִיתָ בַבֹּקֶר אֶל־הַר סִינַי וְנִצַּבְתָּ לִי שָׁם עַל־רֹאשׁ הָהָר: 3 וְאִישׁ לֹא־יַעֲלֶה עִמָּךְ וְגַם־אִישׁ אַל־יֵרָא בְּכָל־הָהָר גַּם־הַצֹּאן וְהַבָּקָר אַל־יִרְעוּ אֶל־מוּל הָהָר הַהוּא: 4 וַיִּפְסֹל שְׁנֵי־לֻחֹת אֲבָנִים כָּרִאשֹׁנִים וַיַּשְׁכֵּם מֹשֶׁה בַבֹּקֶר וַיַּעַל אֶל־הַר סִינַי כַּאֲשֶׁר צִוָּה יְהֹוָה אֹתוֹ וַיִּקַּח בְּיָדוֹ שְׁנֵי לֻחֹת אֲבָנִים: 5 וַיֵּרֶד יְהֹוָה בֶּעָנָן וַיִּתְיַצֵּב עִמּוֹ שָׁם וַיִּקְרָא בְשֵׁם יְהֹוָה: 6 וַיַּעֲבֹר יְהֹוָה | עַל־פָּנָיו וַיִּקְרָא יְהֹוָה | יְהֹוָה אֵל רַחוּם וְחַנּוּן אֶרֶךְ אַפַּיִם וְרַב־חֶסֶד וֶאֱמֶת: 7 נֹצֵר חֶסֶד לָאֲלָפִים נֹשֵׂא עָוֺן וָפֶשַׁע וְחַטָּאָה וְנַקֵּה לֹא יְנַקֶּה

542

influence the Heavenly realms, but they remain an important key with which to open the gates of mercy in every generation (*Rabbi Bahya b. Asher, 13th century*).

kabbalah bites

34:6-7 In *The Palm Tree of Deborah*, Kabbalist Rabbi Moses Cordovero, teaches us how to emulate God's *Thirteen Attributes of Mercy* in our relationships. Try using the following affirmations on a regular basis:

1. *I always give, even if the recipients will use what I give them to spite me.*

2. *I am tolerant of everyone—however long it takes—until they awaken.*

3. *I will help others to heal themselves. Their healing matters to me.*

4. *I feel for other people's suffering like my own.*

5. *I will dissolve my anger when it is hurting a relationship.*

6. *I will always focus on the good in others.*

7. *I always make sure that a fixed relationship is better than it was before it broke.*

8. *I have already overcome the human tendency towards negativity. I see only good in others.*

9. *I do not rejoice even in the suffering of the very wicked. I try to find compassion for them.*

10. *I do not judge others because I can never know their limitations. Instead, I have compassion for all God's children.*

11. *I treasure people of exceptional piety and go out of my way to help them.*

12. *When I cannot see good in a person, I remember the good done by his ancestors.*

13. *If I cannot find any merits in a person's ancestors, I imagine him at the time he was an innocent baby and have mercy on him.*

exodus 34:1–7 — ki tissa'

The Second Tablets

34 [FIFTH READING] ¹ God said to Moses: "Carve for yourself two stone tablets like the first ones, and I will write upon the tablets the words that were on the first tablets, which you broke. ² Be ready in the morning. Go up Mount Sinai in the morning and stand before Me there on the top of the mountain. ³ No man should ascend with you, neither should anyone be seen anywhere on the mountain. Also, the sheep and cattle should not graze facing that mountain."

⁴ So he carved two stone tablets like the first ones, and Moses arose early in the morning and ascended Mount Sinai, as God had commanded him, and he took two stone tablets in his hand.

God Proclaims His Thirteen Attributes of Mercy

⁵ God descended in the cloud and stood with him there, and He (God) called with the name of God. ⁶ God passed before him and called out: God (of the sinner), God (of the penitent, the merciful) God, who is compassionate and gracious, slow to anger, abundant in loving kindness and true (to reward), ⁷ preserving kindness (that people do) for two thousand (generations), forgiving intentional sin and rebellion, and unintentional sin, who absolves, but not all at once. He visits the sins of parents upon the children, and the children's children, to the third and fourth generations."

---

can we *"see"* and recognize the Divine hand apparent in it. Similarly, the ending of the verse, *"but My face will not be seen,"* implies that during the event, when it is *"facing"* us, we fail to comprehend the rationale for God's actions—it cannot be *"seen"* (*Rabbi Moses Sofer, 18th–19th century*).

Food for thought

1. How easily do you forgive when somebody has wronged you?

2. What makes you hold onto grudges?

3. At what point do you believe that God has forgiven you for a sin?

34:1 Two stone tablets like the first ones. Only the first tablets possessed the quality of *"the writing of God, engraved on the tablets"* (above, 32:16), which would have caused the words to be forever engraved in Israel's heart and never forgotten (*Babylonian Talmud, Eruvin* 54a; and *Rashi*, ibid.).

When they received the first tablets, the Jewish people were saintly, whereas the second tablets were given to a nation of penitents (*Rabbi Judah Aryeh Leib Alter of Gur, 19th century*).

6. God (of the sinner). God informed Moses that whenever the Jewish people would sin in the future, they should recite these Thirteen Attributes, and He would forgive them. A covenant exists concerning these Thirteen Attributes, guaranteeing their effectiveness forever (*Babylonian Talmud, Rosh Ha-Shanah* 17b).

Today we are without the Holy Temple, without a High Priest, and without the sacrifices to assist us in atoning for our sins. But we can invoke these Thirteen Attributes of Divine mercy in our prayers. We may not understand the full implication of these words or how they

שמות לד:ז-כ   כי תשא

פֹּקֵ֣ד ׀ עֲוֺ֣ן אָב֗וֹת עַל־בָּנִים֙ וְעַל־בְּנֵ֣י בָנִ֔ים עַל־שִׁלֵּשִׁ֖ים וְעַל־רִבֵּעִֽים: 8 וַיְמַהֵ֖ר מֹשֶׁ֑ה וַיִּקֹּ֥ד אַ֖רְצָה וַיִּשְׁתָּֽחוּ: 9 וַיֹּ֡אמֶר אִם־נָא֩ מָצָ֨אתִי חֵ֤ן בְּעֵינֶ֙יךָ֙ אֲדֹנָ֔י יֵֽלֶךְ־נָ֥א אֲדֹנָ֖י בְּקִרְבֵּ֑נוּ כִּ֤י עַם־קְשֵׁה־עֹ֙רֶף֙ ה֔וּא וְסָלַחְתָּ֛ לַעֲוֺנֵ֥נוּ וּלְחַטָּאתֵ֖נוּ וּנְחַלְתָּֽנוּ: 10 וַיֹּ֗אמֶר הִנֵּ֣ה אָנֹכִי֮ כֹּרֵ֣ת בְּרִית֒ נֶ֤גֶד כָּֽל־עַמְּךָ֙ אֶעֱשֶׂ֣ה נִפְלָאֹ֔ת אֲשֶׁ֛ר לֹֽא־נִבְרְא֥וּ בְכָל־הָאָ֖רֶץ וּבְכָל־הַגּוֹיִ֑ם וְרָאָ֣ה כָל־הָ֠עָם אֲשֶׁר־אַתָּ֨ה בְקִרְבּ֜וֹ אֶת־מַעֲשֵׂ֤ה יְהֹוָה֙ כִּֽי־נוֹרָ֣א ה֔וּא אֲשֶׁ֥ר אֲנִ֖י עֹשֶׂ֥ה עִמָּֽךְ: 11 שְׁמָר־לְךָ֔ אֵ֛ת אֲשֶׁ֥ר אָנֹכִ֖י מְצַוְּךָ֣ הַיּ֑וֹם הִנְנִ֧י גֹרֵ֣שׁ מִפָּנֶ֗יךָ אֶת־הָאֱמֹרִי֙ וְהַֽכְּנַעֲנִ֔י וְהַחִתִּי֙ וְהַפְּרִזִּ֔י וְהַחִוִּ֖י וְהַיְבוּסִֽי: 12 הִשָּׁ֣מֶר לְךָ֗ פֶּן־תִּכְרֹ֤ת בְּרִית֙ לְיוֹשֵׁ֣ב הָאָ֔רֶץ אֲשֶׁ֥ר אַתָּ֖ה בָּ֣א עָלֶ֑יהָ פֶּן־יִהְיֶ֥ה לְמוֹקֵ֖שׁ בְּקִרְבֶּֽךָ: 13 כִּ֤י אֶת־מִזְבְּחֹתָם֙ תִּתֹּצ֔וּן וְאֶת־מַצֵּבֹתָ֖ם תְּשַׁבֵּר֑וּן וְאֶת־אֲשֵׁרָ֖יו תִּכְרֹתֽוּן: 14 כִּ֛י לֹ֥א תִשְׁתַּחֲוֶ֖ה לְאֵ֣ל אַחֵ֑ר כִּ֤י יְהֹוָה֙ קַנָּ֣א שְׁמ֔וֹ אֵ֥ל קַנָּ֖א הֽוּא: 15 פֶּן־תִּכְרֹ֥ת בְּרִ֖ית לְיוֹשֵׁ֣ב הָאָ֑רֶץ וְזָנ֣וּ ׀ אַחֲרֵ֣י אֱלֹֽהֵיהֶ֗ם וְזָבְחוּ֙ לֵאלֹ֣הֵיהֶ֔ם וְקָרָ֣א לְךָ֔ וְאָכַלְתָּ֖ מִזִּבְחֽוֹ: 16 וְלָקַחְתָּ֥ מִבְּנֹתָ֖יו לְבָנֶ֑יךָ וְזָנ֣וּ בְנֹתָ֗יו אַחֲרֵי֙ אֱלֹ֣הֵיהֶ֔ן וְהִזְנוּ֙ אֶת־בָּנֶ֔יךָ אַחֲרֵ֖י אֱלֹהֵיהֶֽן: 17 אֱלֹהֵ֥י מַסֵּכָ֖ה לֹ֥א תַעֲשֶׂה־לָּֽךְ: 18 אֶת־חַ֣ג הַמַּצּוֹת֮ תִּשְׁמֹר֒ שִׁבְעַ֨ת יָמִ֜ים תֹּאכַ֤ל מַצּוֹת֙ אֲשֶׁ֣ר צִוִּיתִ֔ךָ לְמוֹעֵ֖ד חֹ֣דֶשׁ הָאָבִ֑יב כִּ֚י בְּחֹ֣דֶשׁ הָֽאָבִ֔יב יָצָ֖אתָ מִמִּצְרָֽיִם: 19 כָּל־פֶּ֥טֶר רֶ֖חֶם לִ֑י וְכָֽל־מִקְנְךָ֙ תִּזָּכָ֔ר פֶּ֖טֶר שׁ֥וֹר וָשֶֽׂה: 20 וּפֶ֤טֶר חֲמוֹר֙ תִּפְדֶּ֣ה בְשֶׂ֔ה וְאִם־לֹ֥א תִפְדֶּ֖ה וַעֲרַפְתּ֑וֹ כֹּ֣ל בְּכ֤וֹר בָּנֶ֙יךָ֙ תִּפְדֶּ֔ה וְלֹֽא־יֵרָא֥וּ פָנַ֖י רֵיקָֽם:

spiritual vitamin

> Never entertain a thought of despair that any sin cannot be corrected or forgiven. For God is the essence of goodness and of mercy and never rejects repentance carried out at the proper time and in the proper way.

exodus 34:8–20 — ki tissa'

⁸ Moses hurried, bowed his head to the ground, and prostrated himself.

⁹ He (Moses) said: "If I have now found favor in Your eyes, O God, let God go now with us (as You promised,) even if they are a stiff-necked people, and You should forgive our intentional and unintentional sins and make us Your own."

[SIXTH READING] ¹⁰ He (God) said: "Look! I will form a covenant (about this). In the presence of all your people, I will make distinctions (between you and the nations), the likes of which have never been created on all the earth, among all the nations. Then all the people, among whom you dwell, will see the work of God, how that which I will do for you is awesome.

Not to Strike a Covenant with the Nations

¹¹ "Keep carefully what I am commanding you today. Behold, I will drive out from before you the Amorites and the Canaanites, the Hittites and the Perizzites, the Hivites and the Jebusites. ¹² Beware not to make a covenant with the inhabitants of the land into which you are coming, so that it does not become a trap in your midst. ¹³ But you should demolish their altars, shatter their monuments, and cut down their sacred trees. ¹⁴ For you should not bow down before another god, because God's name is Zealous One, for He is a God who is zealous (to exact payment).

¹⁵ "(Be careful) not to form a covenant with the inhabitants of the land, for when they go astray after their gods, and they offer sacrifices to their gods, and they invite you, you will eat of their slaughtering, ¹⁶ and you will take from their daughters for your sons. Then their daughters will go astray after their gods and lead your sons astray after their gods.

Prohibition of Idolatry and Other Commands

- ¹⁷ "You should not make cast metal gods for yourself.

- ¹⁸ "You should observe the Festival of Unleavened Bread. For seven days you should eat unleavened bread, as I have commanded you, at the appointed time of the month of the early ripening, for in the month of the early ripening you went out of Egypt.

- ¹⁹ "Every (human male) who is the first of the womb is Mine, as well as all your livestock who gives birth to a male, the firstborn of an ox or lamb (shall be Mine).

- ²⁰ "You should redeem a firstborn donkey with a lamb.

- "If you do not redeem it, you should break its neck.

- "You should redeem every firstborn of your sons.

- "(When they go up to Jerusalem for a festival,) they should not appear before Me empty of (a sacrifice).

שמות לד:כא-לד

כי תשא

21 שֵׁ֤שֶׁת יָמִים֙ תַּֽעֲבֹ֔ד וּבַיּ֥וֹם הַשְּׁבִיעִ֖י תִּשְׁבֹּ֑ת בֶּחָרִ֥ישׁ וּבַקָּצִ֖יר תִּשְׁבֹּֽת: 22 וְחַ֤ג שָֽׁבֻעֹת֙ תַּעֲשֶׂ֣ה לְךָ֔ בִּכּוּרֵ֖י קְצִ֣יר חִטִּ֑ים וְחַג֙ הָֽאָסִ֔יף תְּקוּפַ֖ת הַשָּׁנָֽה: 23 שָׁלֹ֥שׁ פְּעָמִ֖ים בַּשָּׁנָ֑ה יֵֽרָאֶה֙ כָּל־זְכ֣וּרְךָ֔ אֶת־פְּנֵ֛י הָֽאָדֹ֥ן ׀ יְהֹוָ֖ה אֱלֹהֵ֥י יִשְׂרָאֵֽל: 24 כִּֽי־ אוֹרִ֤ישׁ גּוֹיִם֙ מִפָּנֶ֔יךָ וְהִרְחַבְתִּ֖י אֶת־גְּבֻלֶ֑ךָ וְלֹא־יַחְמֹ֥ד אִישׁ֙ אֶת־אַרְצְךָ֔ בַּעֲלֹֽתְךָ֗ לֵֽרָאוֹת֙ אֶת־פְּנֵי֙ יְהֹוָ֣ה אֱלֹהֶ֔יךָ שָׁלֹ֥שׁ פְּעָמִ֖ים בַּשָּׁנָֽה: 25 לֹֽא־תִשְׁחַ֥ט עַל־חָמֵ֖ץ דַּם־זִבְחִ֑י וְלֹֽא־יָלִ֣ין לַבֹּ֔קֶר זֶ֖בַח חַ֥ג הַפָּֽסַח: 26 רֵאשִׁ֗ית בִּכּוּרֵי֙ אַדְמָ֣תְךָ֔ תָּבִ֕יא בֵּ֖ית יְהֹוָ֣ה אֱלֹהֶ֑יךָ לֹֽא־תְבַשֵּׁ֥ל גְּדִ֖י בַּחֲלֵ֥ב אִמּֽוֹ: פ 27 [SEVENTH READING] וַיֹּ֤אמֶר יְהֹוָה֙ אֶל־ מֹשֶׁ֔ה כְּתָב־לְךָ֖ אֶת־הַדְּבָרִ֣ים הָאֵ֑לֶּה כִּ֞י עַל־פִּ֣י ׀ הַדְּבָרִ֣ים הָאֵ֗לֶּה כָּרַ֧תִּי אִתְּךָ֛ בְּרִ֖ית וְאֶת־יִשְׂרָאֵֽל: 28 וַֽיְהִי־שָׁ֣ם עִם־יְהֹוָ֗ה אַרְבָּעִ֥ים יוֹם֙ וְאַרְבָּעִ֣ים לַ֔יְלָה לֶ֚חֶם לֹ֣א אָכַ֔ל וּמַ֖יִם לֹ֣א שָׁתָ֑ה וַיִּכְתֹּ֣ב עַל־הַלֻּחֹ֗ת אֵ֚ת דִּבְרֵ֣י הַבְּרִ֔ית עֲשֶׂ֖רֶת הַדְּבָרִֽים: 29 וַיְהִ֗י בְּרֶ֤דֶת מֹשֶׁה֙ מֵהַ֣ר סִינַ֔י וּשְׁנֵ֨י לֻחֹ֤ת הָעֵדֻת֙ בְּיַד־מֹשֶׁ֔ה בְּרִדְתּ֖וֹ מִן־הָהָ֑ר וּמֹשֶׁ֣ה לֹֽא־יָדַ֗ע כִּ֥י קָרַ֛ן ע֥וֹר פָּנָ֖יו בְּדַבְּר֥וֹ אִתּֽוֹ: 30 וַיַּ֨רְא אַהֲרֹ֜ן וְכָל־בְּנֵ֤י יִשְׂרָאֵל֙ אֶת־מֹשֶׁ֔ה וְהִנֵּ֥ה קָרַ֖ן ע֣וֹר פָּנָ֑יו וַיִּֽירְא֖וּ מִגֶּ֥שֶׁת אֵלָֽיו: 31 וַיִּקְרָ֤א אֲלֵהֶם֙ מֹשֶׁ֔ה וַיָּשֻׁ֧בוּ אֵלָ֛יו אַהֲרֹ֥ן וְכָל־הַנְּשִׂאִ֖ים בָּעֵדָ֑ה וַיְדַבֵּ֥ר מֹשֶׁ֖ה אֲלֵהֶֽם: 32 וְאַחֲרֵי־כֵ֥ן נִגְּשׁ֖וּ כָּל־בְּנֵ֣י יִשְׂרָאֵ֑ל וַיְצַוֵּ֕ם אֵת֩ כָּל־אֲשֶׁ֨ר דִּבֶּ֧ר יְהֹוָ֛ה אִתּ֖וֹ בְּהַ֥ר סִינָֽי: [MAFTIR] 33 וַיְכַ֣ל מֹשֶׁ֔ה מִדַּבֵּ֖ר אִתָּ֑ם וַיִּתֵּ֥ן עַל־פָּנָ֖יו מַסְוֶֽה: 34 וּבְבֹ֨א מֹשֶׁ֜ה לִפְנֵ֤י יְהֹוָה֙

28-29. He ate no bread and drank no water .... The skin of his face had become radiant. A person should never dishonor a local custom, for Moses went up on high and he did not eat or drink. Similarly, when the angels came to visit Abraham (*Genesis 18:2ff.*), do you think they ate or drank? Rather, they merely appeared as if they were eating (*Babylonian Talmud, Bava Metzia* 86b).

Moses initially went up the mountain to receive the first set of tablets, which were *"the work of God"* (32:16), i.e., totally supernatural. Since Moses went to receive something miraculous, it follows that, on this occasion, his own ability to manage without eating and drinking would have also been miraculous.

The second occasion that Moses went up the mountain was to seek forgiveness for the sin of the Golden Calf. At that time God was angry, so we can presume that He withheld the use of all

exodus 34:21–34 — ki tissa'

- ²¹ "Six days you may work, and on the seventh day you should rest. You should rest from plowing and harvesting.

- ²² "You should make the Festival of Weeks for yourself, with the first fruits of the wheat harvest (making them into two loaves), and the Festival of the Harvest after the year turns.

- ²³ "Three times during the year all your males should appear directly before the Master, God, the God of Israel. ²⁴ (You will only be able to come three times a year,) because I will drive out nations from before you and I will widen your border (so you will live far away). No one will covet your land when you go up, to appear before God, your God, three times each year.

- ²⁵ "While anything leavened is in your possession, you should not slaughter or sprinkle the blood of My (Passover) slaughter.

- "The (parts of the) Passover slaughter should not remain overnight until the morning.

- ²⁶ "You should bring the first fruits of your land to the house of God, your God.

- "Do not cook a tender young animal in its mother's milk."

Moses Descends with the Second Tablets

[SEVENTH READING] ²⁷ God said to Moses: "Write these words (but not the Oral Law) for yourself, for according to these words I have formed a covenant with you and with Israel."

²⁸ He was there with God for forty days and forty nights. He ate no bread and drank no water. He inscribed upon the tablets the words of the Covenant, the Ten Commandments.

²⁹ (On the Day of Atonement,) Moses came down from Mount Sinai, and the two Tablets of the Testimony were in Moses' hand when he came down from the mountain. Moses did not know that the skin of his face had become radiant while He (God) had spoken with him. ³⁰ Aaron and all the children of Israel saw Moses and—look!—The skin of his face had become radiant, and they were afraid to come near him.

(The following system was used by Moses to convey God's words:)

³¹ Moses called to them, and Aaron and all the leaders of the community returned to him, and Moses would speak to them (telling them God's words). ³² Afterwards all the children of Israel would draw near, and he would command them everything that God had spoken with him on Mount Sinai.

[MAFTIR] ³³ When Moses had finished speaking with them, he placed a covering over his face. ³⁴ When Moses would come before God to speak with Him, he would

שמות לד:לד-לה

לְדַבֵּ֣ר אִתּ֔וֹ יָסִ֥יר אֶת־הַמַּסְוֶ֖ה עַד־צֵאת֑וֹ וְיָצָ֗א וְדִבֶּר֙ אֶל־בְּנֵ֣י יִשְׂרָאֵ֔ל אֵ֖ת אֲשֶׁ֥ר יְצֻוֶּֽה: 35 וְרָא֤וּ בְנֵֽי־יִשְׂרָאֵל֙ אֶת־פְּנֵ֣י מֹשֶׁ֔ה כִּ֣י קָרַ֔ן ע֖וֹר פְּנֵ֣י מֹשֶׁ֑ה וְהֵשִׁ֨יב מֹשֶׁ֤ה אֶת־הַמַּסְוֶה֙ עַל־פָּנָ֔יו עַד־בֹּא֖וֹ לְדַבֵּ֥ר אִתּֽוֹ: ס ס ס

קל"ט פסוקים, חננא"ל סימן.

spiritual vitamin

> Through the medium of the Torah, God "descends" on Mount Sinai, and we ascend to God. Your soul is released from all the fetters which tie it down to earthly things, and on the "wings" of fear of God and love of God, it unites with the Creator in complete communion.

remove the covering until he left. He would then leave and speak to the children of Israel that which had been commanded. ³⁵ Then the children of Israel would see Moses' face, that the skin of Moses' face had become radiant, and then Moses would replace the covering over his face until he would come again to speak with Him.

Haftarot: Ki-Tissa'—page 1336.   *Parah*—page 1431.

Maftir: Parah—page 932 (19:1–22).

supernatural activity. On the second trip, then, Moses' ability to go without eating would have been natural, i.e., he simply forgot to eat and did not feel hungry.

Moses ascended the mountain a final time to receive the second tablets. These were a fusion of the natural and the supernatural, since they were given by God and yet they were made by Moses (above, v. 1). Therefore we can presume that Moses' ability not to eat or drink on this occasion was also a fusion of the natural and supernatural—he (miraculously) became like an angel and subsequently it was natural for him not to eat.

This explains why Moses' face only shone with light when he came down from the mountain for the third time, with the second tablets. For, on this occasion his *natural physical functioning* had been elevated to that of an angel, and so the light of his soul was no longer obstructed by his body (*Rabbi Menahem Mendel Schneerson, 20th century*).

Va-Yakhel teaches the importance of **the whole over its constituent parts.** The components of the Tabernacle only attained their **unique status** when they were assembled as a whole. And however **important** you may be as a person, your worth will become all the more apparent when you **identify with your people.**

VA-YAKHEL
ויקהל

COMMAND TO BUILD THE TABERNACLE	35:1–29
APPOINTMENT OF BEZALEL AND OHOLIAB	35:30–35
CONSTRUCTION OF TABERNACLE BEGINS	36:1 – 38:20

NAME
Va-Yakhel

MEANING
"And he assembled"

LINES IN TORAH SCROLL
211

PARASHIYYOT
7 open; 6 closed

VERSES
122

WORDS
1558

LETTERS
6181

DATE
11 *Tishri–Kislev*, 2449

LOCATION
Sinai Desert

KEY PEOPLE
Moses, Bezalel, Oholiab

MITZVOT
1 prohibition

NOTE
Often read together with the portion of *Pekudei*

CHARACTER PROFILE

NAME
Oholiab

MEANING
"Tent (for) my Father"

FATHER
Ahisamach

ACHIEVEMENTS
Worked together with Bezalel to lead the construction of the Tabernacle; inspired his fellow tribe members to participate in the construction when they saw that although from a less esteemed tribe, Bezalel had worked with him

KNOWN FOR
He was a craftsman, an artistic weaver and an embroiderer of turquoise, purple and crimson wool and linen.

SANCTITY OF THE SABBATH

Moses began with the laws of the Sabbath, emphasizing that their observance takes precedence over building the Tabernacle. The Sabbath is an integral part of our lives, and safeguarding its sanctity comes before any other work (35:2).

GENEROUS DONATIONS

The Jewish people eagerly gave contributions of their possessions to the Tabernacle. So much was donated, in fact, that Moses had to send messengers to the entire camp, informing them that no more contributions were needed (36:5).

TALENTS

Virtually every talent can be used to worship God. There were those who were able to spin goat's hair while it was still on the animal and those whose wisdom instructed the craftsmen (35:26-33).

שמות לה:א-ז | ויקהל

לה 1 וַיַּקְהֵ֣ל מֹשֶׁ֗ה אֶֽת־כָּל־עֲדַ֛ת בְּנֵ֥י יִשְׂרָאֵ֖ל וַיֹּ֣אמֶר אֲלֵהֶ֑ם אֵ֚לֶּה הַדְּבָרִ֔ים אֲשֶׁר־צִוָּ֥ה יְהֹוָ֖ה לַעֲשֹׂ֥ת אֹתָֽם: 2 שֵׁ֣שֶׁת יָמִים֮ תֵּעָשֶׂ֣ה מְלָאכָה֒ וּבַיּ֣וֹם הַשְּׁבִיעִ֗י יִהְיֶ֨ה לָכֶ֥ם קֹ֛דֶשׁ שַׁבַּ֥ת שַׁבָּת֖וֹן לַיהֹוָ֑ה כָּל־הָעֹשֶׂ֥ה ב֛וֹ מְלָאכָ֖ה יוּמָֽת: 3 לֹא־תְבַעֲר֣וּ אֵ֔שׁ בְּכֹ֖ל מֹשְׁבֹֽתֵיכֶ֑ם בְּי֖וֹם הַשַּׁבָּֽת: פ 4 וַיֹּ֣אמֶר מֹשֶׁ֗ה אֶל־כָּל־עֲדַ֛ת בְּנֵֽי־יִשְׂרָאֵ֖ל לֵאמֹ֑ר זֶ֣ה הַדָּבָ֔ר אֲשֶׁר־צִוָּ֥ה יְהֹוָ֖ה לֵאמֹֽר: 5 קְח֨וּ מֵֽאִתְּכֶ֤ם תְּרוּמָה֙ לַֽיהֹוָ֔ה כֹּ֚ל נְדִ֣יב לִבּ֔וֹ יְבִיאֶ֕הָ אֵ֖ת תְּרוּמַ֣ת יְהֹוָ֑ה זָהָ֥ב וָכֶ֖סֶף וּנְחֹֽשֶׁת: 6 וּתְכֵ֧לֶת וְאַרְגָּמָ֛ן וְתוֹלַ֥עַת שָׁנִ֖י וְשֵׁ֥שׁ וְעִזִּֽים: 7 וְעֹרֹ֨ת אֵילִ֥ם

(d) The assembly was made by Moses, since every one of us has a "spark" of Moses, and it is through revealing this spark that the people are brought to a state of unity.

(e) Moses mentioned, first of all, the commandment of the Sabbath, since Sabbath observance is based on the belief that God provides a person with his sustenance, a belief which also prevents financial disputes between man and his fellow (*Rabbi Menahem Mendel Schneerson, 20th century*).

2. For six days work may be done, but the seventh day should be holy for you. Moses prefaced the commandment to construct the Tabernacle with the warning not to transgress the Sabbath, in order to indicate that its construction does not override the prohibitions of the Sabbath (*Rashi, 11th century*).

The children of Israel were forbidden to desecrate the Sabbath by building the Tabernacle, which was a testament to God's glory. By contrast, Jewish law obligates us to desecrate the Sabbath if a life is in danger. This distinction illustrates the sanctity of the people, that they are more precious to God than the construction of the Tabernacle. God's presence rests primarily in the soul, even more so than in the Holy Temple (*Rabbi Moses Sofer, 18th–19th century*).

5. Collect from among yourselves a contribution-offering for God. Every person whose heart inspires him to generosity should bring the contribution for God (lit. "God's contribution"). There appears to be a contradiction in this verse. It begins, *"Collect* from among yourselves a contribution-offering for God," suggesting that we are speaking of a compulsory donation which was "collected." However, the verse concludes, "Every person *whose heart inspires him to generosity should bring* the contribution for God," suggesting a voluntary type of contribution, which depended on the feelings of the giver. From this we see that there were in fact two types of contributions: compulsory and voluntary.

There are two possible attitudes to the acquisition of wealth. Some see their financial gains as the result of their own effort and skill, and so they find it very difficult to part with their money. Regarding these people, the command came to forcibly *collect* materials for the Tabernacle, transferring it from their ownership to God's.

Food for thought

1. What does the Sabbath mean to you personally?

2. How has Sabbath observance changed you?

3. Are you good at resting? If not, why?

exodus 35:1–7 — va-yakhel

parashat va-yakhel

Moses Assembles the Jewish People

35 ¹ Moses caused the whole community of the children of Israel to assemble (on the day after the Day of Atonement), and he said to them: "These are the things that God commanded to be done. ² For six days work may be done, but the seventh day should be holy for you, a day of complete rest to God. Whoever does work on it should be put to death. ³ You should not kindle fire in any of your dwelling places on the Sabbath day."

⁴ Moses spoke to the entire community of the children of Israel, saying: "This is the thing which God has commanded (me) to say (to you): ⁵ Collect from among yourselves a contribution-offering for God. Every person whose heart inspires him to generosity should bring the (following) contribution for God: gold, silver, and copper; turquoise, purple, and crimson wool; linen and goats' hair; ⁷ rams' skin

---

35:1 Moses caused the whole community of the children of Israel to assemble. He came down from the mountain on the Day of Atonement, and gathered the Jewish people the following day (*Rashi, 11th century*).

Rashi concluded that Moses gathered the Jewish people *the first day* after descending the mountain, based on the principle that *"enthusiastic people will perform a commandment at the earliest opportunity"* (*Babylonian Talmud, Pesaḥim* 4a; *Rabbi Elijah Mizraḥi, 15th–16th century*).

When the Torah was given at Sinai, the Jewish people were awarded the privilege of causing God's presence to dwell on earth. However, this did not actually happen until the Tabernacle was built, as the *Midrash* states, *"When did the Divine Presence dwell on earth? On the day that the Tabernacle was erected"* (*Numbers Rabbah*). The building of the Tabernacle was, in effect, the "practical application" of the giving of the Torah.

Just as the event at Sinai had been preceded by a state of total unity among the nation, having encamped *"as one person with one heart"* (*Rashi* to 19:2, above), similarly, the practical construction of the Tabernacle was preceded by an assembly of unity, as described in this passage. In fact, this assembly was superior to the unity at Sinai, in that the latter was a unity of *intention* (to accept the Torah), whereas this assembly was a unity of *action* (to construct the Tabernacle).

This sheds light on a number of details:

(a) Money is one of the greatest causes of dispute. Here, however, the people willingly gave of their possessions for the construction of the Tabernacle.

(b) The assembly occurred on the day after the *Day of Atonement*, a day of friendship, unity and forgiving.

(c) The assembly occurred on the day *after* the Day of Atonement, indicating that the spirit of the holy day was being channeled into the mundane weekdays.

---

kabbalah bites

35:1 According to the Kabbalah, when we sin, it "damages" the *Sefirot*, so to speak, disturbing the flow of Divine energy from entering this world. So after the sin of the Golden Calf, the first thing that Moses did was *"to assemble"*— to regather the disoriented *Sefirot* and put them back in order.

שמות לה:ז-כג | ויקהל

מְאָדָּמִים וְעֹרֹת תְּחָשִׁים וַעֲצֵי שִׁטִּים: 8 וְשֶׁמֶן לַמָּאוֹר וּבְשָׂמִים לְשֶׁמֶן הַמִּשְׁחָה וְלִקְטֹרֶת הַסַּמִּים: 9 וְאַבְנֵי־שֹׁהַם וְאַבְנֵי מִלֻּאִים לָאֵפוֹד וְלַחֹשֶׁן: 10 וְכָל־חֲכַם־לֵב בָּכֶם יָבֹאוּ וְיַעֲשׂוּ אֵת כָּל־אֲשֶׁר צִוָּה יְהֹוָה: 11 אֶת־הַמִּשְׁכָּן אֶת־אָהֳלוֹ וְאֶת־מִכְסֵהוּ אֶת־קְרָסָיו וְאֶת־קְרָשָׁיו אֶת־בְּרִיחָו אֶת־עַמֻּדָיו וְאֶת־אֲדָנָיו: 12 אֶת־הָאָרֹן וְאֶת־בַּדָּיו אֶת־הַכַּפֹּרֶת וְאֵת פָּרֹכֶת הַמָּסָךְ: 13 אֶת־הַשֻּׁלְחָן וְאֶת־בַּדָּיו וְאֶת־כָּל־כֵּלָיו וְאֵת לֶחֶם הַפָּנִים: 14 וְאֶת־מְנֹרַת הַמָּאוֹר וְאֶת־כֵּלֶיהָ וְאֶת־נֵרֹתֶיהָ וְאֵת שֶׁמֶן הַמָּאוֹר: 15 וְאֶת־מִזְבַּח הַקְּטֹרֶת וְאֶת־בַּדָּיו וְאֵת שֶׁמֶן הַמִּשְׁחָה וְאֵת קְטֹרֶת הַסַּמִּים וְאֶת־מָסַךְ הַפֶּתַח לְפֶתַח הַמִּשְׁכָּן: 16 אֵת | מִזְבַּח הָעֹלָה וְאֶת־מִכְבַּר הַנְּחֹשֶׁת אֲשֶׁר־לוֹ אֶת־בַּדָּיו וְאֶת־כָּל־כֵּלָיו אֶת־הַכִּיֹּר וְאֶת־כַּנּוֹ: 17 אֵת קַלְעֵי הֶחָצֵר אֶת־עַמֻּדָיו וְאֶת־אֲדָנֶיהָ וְאֵת מָסַךְ שַׁעַר הֶחָצֵר: 18 אֶת־יִתְדֹת הַמִּשְׁכָּן וְאֶת־יִתְדֹת הֶחָצֵר וְאֶת־מֵיתְרֵיהֶם: 19 אֶת־בִּגְדֵי הַשְּׂרָד לְשָׁרֵת בַּקֹּדֶשׁ אֶת־בִּגְדֵי הַקֹּדֶשׁ לְאַהֲרֹן הַכֹּהֵן וְאֶת־בִּגְדֵי בָנָיו לְכַהֵן: 20 וַיֵּצְאוּ כָּל־עֲדַת בְּנֵי־יִשְׂרָאֵל מִלִּפְנֵי מֹשֶׁה: [SECOND READING] 21 וַיָּבֹאוּ כָּל־אִישׁ אֲשֶׁר־נְשָׂאוֹ לִבּוֹ וְכֹל אֲשֶׁר נָדְבָה רוּחוֹ אֹתוֹ הֵבִיאוּ אֶת־תְּרוּמַת יְהֹוָה לִמְלֶאכֶת אֹהֶל מוֹעֵד וּלְכָל־עֲבֹדָתוֹ וּלְבִגְדֵי הַקֹּדֶשׁ: 22 וַיָּבֹאוּ הָאֲנָשִׁים עַל־הַנָּשִׁים כֹּל | נְדִיב לֵב הֵבִיאוּ חָח וָנֶזֶם וְטַבַּעַת וְכוּמָז כָּל־כְּלִי זָהָב וְכָל־אִישׁ אֲשֶׁר הֵנִיף תְּנוּפַת זָהָב לַיהֹוָה: 23 וְכָל־אִישׁ אֲשֶׁר־נִמְצָא אִתּוֹ תְּכֵלֶת וְאַרְגָּמָן

spiritual vitamin

> A person who excels in his individual area of endeavor will generally be limited, or even useless, in another area. Who can say which is more important, which individual contributes the most? Only a harmonious partnership and the use of all human resources will contribute to the overall good of society.

exodus 35:7–23 — va-yakhel

dyed red, (multicolored) *taḥash* skins, and acacia wood; ⁸ oil for the (eternal) lamp; spices for the anointing oil and for the incense fumes; ⁹ *shoham* stones and filling stones for the apron and for the breastplate.

¹⁰ "Every wise-hearted person among you should come, and they should make everything which God has commanded:

¹¹ "The Tabernacle, its roof and its cover, its clasps and its beams, its crossbars, its pillars, and its sockets, ¹² the ark and its poles, the lid and the partition, ¹³ the table and its poles and all its utensils, and the multisurface bread, ¹⁴ the candelabrum for lighting, its utensils and its lamps, and oil for lighting, ¹⁵ the incense altar, its poles, the anointing oil, the incense of spices, the curtain for the entrance of the Tabernacle, ¹⁶ the sacrificial altar, its copper netting, its poles and all its utensils, the urn and its base, ¹⁷ the curtains of the courtyard, its pillars, and its sockets, and the curtain for the entrance of the courtyard, ¹⁸ the pegs of the Tabernacle and the pegs of the courtyard, and their ropes, ¹⁹ the meshwork cloths which are used in the holy (Sanctuary to cover the apparatus during transportation), the holy garments for Aaron the High Priest, and the garments of his sons worn for service."

²⁰ The entire community left Moses' presence.

[SECOND READING] ²¹ Every person whose heart inspired him came, and everyone whose generous spirit inspired him brought the contribution for God, for the work of the Tent of Meeting, for all its necessities, and for the holy garments:

²² The men came together with the women (next to them). Everyone whose heart inspired him to generosity brought bracelets, earrings, rings and body ornaments, all kinds of golden objects—every man who donated an offering of gold to God. ²³ Everyone who had turquoise, purple, or crimson wool, linen, goats' hair,

Food for thought

1. How significant are the motives for which people give charitable donations?

2. How important a cause is giving to a synagogue?

3. Do you ever attach conditions to your donations or use them to gain control?

Others, however, were aware that everything belongs to God and that even their earned wealth is not really their own. Hearing that materials were needed for the Tabernacle, their hearts inspired them to donate even before the collectors arrived. Parting with their wealth for a good cause came naturally to them, for they saw it as giving to God what was always His—as the verse states that they brought, *"God's contribution"* (*Rabbi Ephraim of Luntshits, 16th–17th century*).

The construction of the Tabernacle was a commandment which God gave to the Jewish people to achieve atonement for making the Golden Calf.

Practically speaking, we see that this atonement was achieved by the donations of the Jewish people to the Tabernacle. Previously they had given their gold enthusiastically to build an idol; now they gave with even greater enthusiasm for the sake of God. The people brought *"much more than (is needed) to do the work which God has commanded"* (below, 36:5; *Exodus Rabbah*; *Rabbi Samuel Jaffe Ashkenazi, 16th century*).

שמות לה:כג-לא | ויקהל

וְתוֹלַעַת שָׁנִי וְשֵׁשׁ וְעִזִּים וְעֹרֹת אֵילִם מְאָדָּמִים וְעֹרֹת תְּחָשִׁים הֵבִיאוּ: 24 כָּל־מֵרִים תְּרוּמַת כֶּסֶף וּנְחֹשֶׁת הֵבִיאוּ אֵת תְּרוּמַת יְהוָה וְכֹל אֲשֶׁר נִמְצָא אִתּוֹ עֲצֵי שִׁטִּים לְכָל־מְלֶאכֶת הָעֲבֹדָה הֵבִיאוּ: 25 וְכָל־אִשָּׁה חַכְמַת־לֵב בְּיָדֶיהָ טָווּ וַיָּבִיאוּ מַטְוֶה אֶת־הַתְּכֵלֶת וְאֶת־הָאַרְגָּמָן אֶת־תּוֹלַעַת הַשָּׁנִי וְאֶת־הַשֵּׁשׁ: 26 וְכָל־הַנָּשִׁים אֲשֶׁר נָשָׂא לִבָּן אֹתָנָה בְּחָכְמָה טָווּ אֶת־הָעִזִּים: 27 וְהַנְּשִׂאִם הֵבִיאוּ אֵת אַבְנֵי הַשֹּׁהַם וְאֵת אַבְנֵי הַמִּלֻּאִים לָאֵפוֹד וְלַחֹשֶׁן: 28 וְאֶת־הַבֹּשֶׂם וְאֶת־הַשָּׁמֶן לְמָאוֹר וּלְשֶׁמֶן הַמִּשְׁחָה וְלִקְטֹרֶת הַסַּמִּים: 29 כָּל־אִישׁ וְאִשָּׁה אֲשֶׁר נָדַב לִבָּם אֹתָם לְהָבִיא לְכָל־הַמְּלָאכָה אֲשֶׁר צִוָּה יְהוָה לַעֲשׂוֹת בְּיַד־מֹשֶׁה הֵבִיאוּ בְנֵי־יִשְׂרָאֵל נְדָבָה לַיהוָה: פ 30 [THIRD READING / SECOND WHEN JOINED] וַיֹּאמֶר מֹשֶׁה אֶל־בְּנֵי יִשְׂרָאֵל רְאוּ קָרָא יְהוָה בְּשֵׁם בְּצַלְאֵל בֶּן־אוּרִי בֶן־חוּר לְמַטֵּה יְהוּדָה: 31 וַיְמַלֵּא אֹתוֹ רוּחַ אֱלֹהִים בְּחָכְמָה בִּתְבוּנָה וּבְדַעַת וּבְכָל־מְלָאכָה:

God said, "Nevertheless, go and speak to the people, and see what they have to say."

Moses went and asked Israel, "Do you consider Bezalel fit?"

They replied, "If God and you consider him fit, then we definitely consider him fit!"

Here you learn not to appoint a leader without first consulting the community (*Babylonian Talmud, Berakhot* 55a).

Bezalel son of Uri son of Hur of the tribe of Judah. Hur, Bezalel's grandfather, was killed by the Israelites when he rebuked them for making the Golden Calf (*Exodus Rabbah*). If God, two generations later, was now appointing a descendent of the martyred Hur to lead the construction of the Tabernacle, then their sin must have been forgiven. If this were not so, Hur would have acted as their prosecutor in heaven rather than their defender. So from Bezalel's lineage here we can learn that the sin of the Golden Calf had already been atoned for at this point, through the donations of the Jewish people (*Rabbi Isaac Luria, 16th century*).

31. He has filled him with the spirit of God, with wisdom, with insight, with Divine inspiration. Bezalel received Divine inspiration as a reward for the self-sacrifice of his ancestors. The leader of his tribe of Judah, Nahshon son of Amminadab, had been the first to follow God's command and wade into the Reed Sea, even before it had split. In addition, his grandfather Hur had fought with the perpetrators of the Golden Calf and ultimately was killed by them. In this merit, they were blessed with a brilliant grandson filled with wisdom

kabbalah bites

35:30 Through his knowledge of the ancient Kabbalistic text *Sefer Yetzirah*, Bezalel knew how to manipulate and combine the primordial letters with which God created the world.

rams' skin dyed red, or *taḥash* skins, brought them. ²⁴ Everyone who set aside a donation of silver or copper brought the donation for God. Everyone who had acacia wood for all the work that needed to be done brought it. ²⁵ Every wise-hearted woman spun with her hands, and they brought spun thread: turquoise, purple, and crimson wool, and linen. ²⁶ All the women whose hearts inspired them with wisdom spun the goats' hair. ²⁷ The leaders brought the *shoham* stones and filling stones for the apron and for the breastplate, ²⁸ the spice, the oil for lighting, for the anointing oil, and for the incense.

²⁹ Every man and woman whose heart inspired them to generosity to bring (a donation) for any of the work that God had commanded them through Moses to make was brought by the children of Israel as a gift for God.

Appointment of Bezalel and Oholiab

[THIRD READING / SECOND WHEN JOINED] ³⁰ Moses said to the children of Israel: "See, God has appointed Bezalel son of Uri son of Hur of the tribe of Judah. ³¹ He has filled him with the spirit of God, with wisdom, with insight, with Divine inspiration, and with the

---

26. All the women whose heart inspired them with wisdom spun the goats' hair. This demanded exceptional craftsmanship, since they spun the goats' hair while it was still attached to the back of the goats (*Rashi, 11ᵗʰ century*).

The women wished not only to dedicate the materials, and hours of work, to God's Tabernacle, but also to offer the highest quality gift possible. Spinning the hair while it is attached to the goats ensured that it remained fresh and shiny, because after being detached from the animal it would gradually deteriorate (*Rabbi Obadiah Sforno, 16ᵗʰ century*).

An animal offering is superior to a vegetable offering, as we find that Cain brought an offering to God of flax, whereas Abel brought animal offerings, and God accepted the latter (*Genesis 4:3ff.*). By contributing goats' hair that was spun while attached to the goats, the women had the advantage of involving a live animal in their offering to the Tabernacle, rather than a mere animal *product*. For this reason, the Jewish women inconvenienced themselves considerably to spin the goats' hair while it was still attached to the goats (*Rabbi Menahem Mendel Schneerson, 20ᵗʰ century*).

27. The leaders brought. What prompted the leaders to donate first for the dedication of the altar, and not for the construction of the Tabernacle? They said, "Let the community donate what they will donate, and whatever they are missing we will complete."

However, the community donated everything, as the Torah declares, *"The work was sufficient"* (36:7). The leaders then wondered, "What are we to do?" So they brought the precious *shoham* stones. Subsequently, when it came time to bring donations for the dedication of the altar, they made certain to donate first. Nevertheless, since they were idle in the first instance, a letter is missing from their name in the Torah, and וְהַנְּשִׂאִים (*"the leaders"*) is written missing the letter *yod*—וְהַנְּשִׂאם (*Rashi, 11ᵗʰ century*).

30. God has appointed Bezalel. "Moses!" asked God, "Do you consider Bezalel fit for this task?"

Moses replied, "Master of the universe! If You consider Bezalel fit, then I certainly consider him fit!"

שמות לה:לב - לו:ו ויקהל

32 וְלַחְשֹׁ֖ב מַחֲשָׁבֹ֑ת לַעֲשֹׂ֛ת בַּזָּהָ֥ב וּבַכֶּ֖סֶף וּבַנְּחֹֽשֶׁת: 33 וּבַחֲרֹ֥שֶׁת אֶ֛בֶן לְמַלֹּ֖את וּבַחֲרֹ֣שֶׁת עֵ֑ץ לַעֲשׂ֖וֹת בְּכָל־מְלֶ֥אכֶת מַחֲשָֽׁבֶת: 34 וּלְהוֹרֹ֖ת נָתַ֣ן בְּלִבּ֑וֹ ה֕וּא וְאָֽהֳלִיאָ֥ב בֶּן־אֲחִֽיסָמָ֖ךְ לְמַטֵּה־דָֽן: 35 מִלֵּ֨א אֹתָ֜ם חָכְמַת־לֵ֗ב לַעֲשׂוֹת֮ כָּל־מְלֶ֣אכֶת חָרָ֣שׁ | וְחֹשֵׁב֒ וְרֹקֵ֗ם בַּתְּכֵ֙לֶת֙ וּבָֽאַרְגָּמָ֔ן בְּתוֹלַ֥עַת הַשָּׁנִ֖י וּבַשֵּׁ֑שׁ וְאֹרֵג֒ עֹשֵׂי֙ כָּל־מְלָאכָ֔ה וְחֹשְׁבֵ֖י מַחֲשָׁבֹֽת:

לו

וְעָשָׂה֩ בְצַלְאֵ֨ל וְאָהֳלִיאָ֜ב וְכֹ֣ל | אִ֣ישׁ חֲכַם־לֵ֗ב אֲשֶׁר֩ נָתַ֨ן יְהֹוָ֜ה חָכְמָ֤ה וּתְבוּנָה֙ בָּהֵ֔מָּה לָדַ֣עַת לַעֲשֹׂ֔ת אֶֽת־כָּל־מְלֶ֖אכֶת עֲבֹדַ֣ת הַקֹּ֑דֶשׁ לְכֹ֥ל אֲשֶׁר־צִוָּ֖ה יְהֹוָֽה: 2 וַיִּקְרָ֣א מֹשֶׁ֗ה אֶל־בְּצַלְאֵל֮ וְאֶל־אָֽהֳלִיאָב֒ וְאֶל֙ כָּל־אִ֣ישׁ חֲכַם־לֵ֔ב אֲשֶׁ֨ר נָתַ֧ן יְהֹוָ֛ה חָכְמָ֖ה בְּלִבּ֑וֹ כֹּ֚ל אֲשֶׁ֣ר נְשָׂא֣וֹ לִבּ֔וֹ לְקָרְבָ֥ה אֶל־הַמְּלָאכָ֖ה לַעֲשֹׂ֥ת אֹתָֽהּ: 3 וַיִּקְח֞וּ מִלִּפְנֵ֣י מֹשֶׁ֗ה אֵ֤ת כָּל־הַתְּרוּמָה֙ אֲשֶׁ֨ר הֵבִ֜יאוּ בְּנֵ֣י יִשְׂרָאֵ֗ל לִמְלֶ֛אכֶת עֲבֹדַ֥ת הַקֹּ֖דֶשׁ לַעֲשֹׂ֣ת אֹתָ֑הּ וְ֠הֵ֠ם הֵבִ֨יאוּ אֵלָ֥יו ע֛וֹד נְדָבָ֖ה בַּבֹּ֥קֶר בַּבֹּֽקֶר: 4 וַיָּבֹ֙אוּ֙ כָּל־הַ֣חֲכָמִ֔ים הָעֹשִׂ֕ים אֵ֖ת כָּל־מְלֶ֣אכֶת הַקֹּ֑דֶשׁ אִֽישׁ־אִ֥ישׁ מִמְּלַאכְתּ֖וֹ אֲשֶׁר־הֵ֥מָּה עֹשִֽׂים: 5 וַיֹּאמְרוּ֙ אֶל־מֹשֶׁ֣ה לֵּאמֹ֔ר מַרְבִּ֥ים הָעָ֖ם לְהָבִ֑יא מִדֵּ֤י הָֽעֲבֹדָה֙ לַמְּלָאכָ֔ה אֲשֶׁר־צִוָּ֥ה יְהֹוָ֖ה לַעֲשֹׂ֥ת אֹתָֽהּ: 6 וַיְצַ֣ו מֹשֶׁ֗ה וַיַּעֲבִ֨ירוּ ק֥וֹל בַּֽמַּחֲנֶה֮ לֵאמֹר֒ אִ֣ישׁ וְאִשָּׁ֗ה אַל־יַעֲשׂוּ־ע֛וֹד מְלָאכָ֖ה לִתְרוּמַ֣ת

36:6 Moses issued a command, and an announcement was made in the camp, saying: "No man or woman should do any more work." The Tabernacle was not yet complete so why did Moses instruct *the artisans* to stop working? If sufficient materials had been donated then surely he should have announced *to the Israelites* that they should cease bringing more?

spiritual vitamin

> When you take part of your hard-earned money and dedicate it to a sacred cause in fulfillment of God's will, you also dedicate the considerable physical and mental efforts that went into earning the money.

ability for all types of work: ³² to do master weaving; to work with gold, silver, and copper; ³³ with the craft of setting gems; and with the craft of wood, to do all kinds of skilled work.

³⁴ (God) gave both him (Bezalel) and Oholiab son of Ahisamach of the tribe of Dan the ability to teach (others). ³⁵ He instilled within them the wisdom of heart required to perform all the skills of a craftsman, an artistic weaver, an embroiderer, and a weaver, using turquoise, purple, and crimson wool and linen. (They are able) to do all kinds of work and weave professionally.

36 ¹ "Bezalel and Oholiab should do (all the work) together with every wise-hearted man into whom God had instilled wisdom and insight to know how to do all the work of the holy (Sanctuary), in accordance with everything which God has commanded."

² Moses called Bezalel and Oholiab and every wise-hearted man into whose heart God had instilled wisdom, everyone whose heart inspired him to dedicate himself to do the work. ³ They took before Moses all the contributions which the children of Israel had offered for the work of the holy (Sanctuary). They continued to bring him more donations every morning.

Contributions Are Completed and Construction Begins

⁴ All the wise men that were doing the work of the holy (Sanctuary) came. Each one of them (left) the work which he had been doing. ⁵ They spoke to Moses, saying: "The people are bringing a lot, much more than (is needed) to do the work which God has commanded to do."

⁶ Moses issued a command, and an announcement was made in the camp, saying: "No man or woman should do any more work for donations to the holy

---

and Divine inspiration, who would oversee the construction of God's Tabernacle (*Rabbi Meir Simhah of Dvinsk, 19th–20th century*).

34. (God) gave both him (Bezalel) and Oholiab ... the ability to teach. Some scholars have wisdom but keep it to themselves, because they are either unwilling or unable to pass on their knowledge to others. Bezalel and Oholiab were endowed with both the ability and the will "to teach," communicating their knowledge to their disciples (*Rabbi Abraham ibn Ezra, 12th century*).

Oholiab. Hur was the son of Miriam, sister of Moses. Oholiab was from the tribe of Dan, of the lowest of the tribes, from Jacob's concubines. Yet God put him on par with Bezalel for the work of the Tabernacle—even though Bezalel was from one of the greatest tribes (Judah)—in the spirit of the verse, *"a prince is not recognized before a pauper"* (*Job 34:19; Rashi, 11th century*).

This encouraged the poorer members of the community, who could not afford to make large donations, that their contributions were as meaningful to God as those of a rich man (*Rabbi Menahem Mendel Schneerson, 20th century*).

שמות לו:ו-יט · ויקהל

הַקֹּדֶשׁ וַיִּכָּלֵא הָעָם מֵהָבִיא: ⁷ וְהַמְּלָאכָה הָיְתָה דַיָּם לְכָל־הַמְּלָאכָה לַעֲשׂוֹת אֹתָהּ וְהוֹתֵר: ס ⁸ [FOURTH READING] וַיַּעֲשׂוּ כָל־חֲכַם־לֵב בְּעֹשֵׂי הַמְּלָאכָה אֶת־הַמִּשְׁכָּן עֶשֶׂר יְרִיעֹת שֵׁשׁ מָשְׁזָר וּתְכֵלֶת וְאַרְגָּמָן וְתוֹלַעַת שָׁנִי כְּרֻבִים מַעֲשֵׂה חֹשֵׁב עָשָׂה אֹתָם: ⁹ אֹרֶךְ הַיְרִיעָה הָאַחַת שְׁמֹנֶה וְעֶשְׂרִים בָּאַמָּה וְרֹחַב אַרְבַּע בָּאַמָּה הַיְרִיעָה הָאֶחָת מִדָּה אַחַת לְכָל־הַיְרִיעֹת: ¹⁰ וַיְחַבֵּר אֶת־חֲמֵשׁ הַיְרִיעֹת אַחַת אֶל־אֶחָת וְחָמֵשׁ יְרִיעֹת חִבַּר אַחַת אֶל־אֶחָת: ¹¹ וַיַּעַשׂ לֻלְאֹת תְּכֵלֶת עַל שְׂפַת הַיְרִיעָה הָאֶחָת מִקָּצָה בַּמַּחְבָּרֶת כֵּן עָשָׂה בִּשְׂפַת הַיְרִיעָה הַקִּיצוֹנָה בַּמַּחְבֶּרֶת הַשֵּׁנִית: ¹² חֲמִשִּׁים לֻלָאֹת עָשָׂה בַּיְרִיעָה הָאֶחָת וַחֲמִשִּׁים לֻלָאֹת עָשָׂה בִּקְצֵה הַיְרִיעָה אֲשֶׁר בַּמַּחְבֶּרֶת הַשֵּׁנִית מַקְבִּילֹת הַלֻּלָאֹת אַחַת אֶל־אֶחָת: ¹³ וַיַּעַשׂ חֲמִשִּׁים קַרְסֵי זָהָב וַיְחַבֵּר אֶת־הַיְרִיעֹת אַחַת אֶל־אַחַת בַּקְּרָסִים וַיְהִי הַמִּשְׁכָּן אֶחָד: פ ¹⁴ וַיַּעַשׂ יְרִיעֹת עִזִּים לְאֹהֶל עַל־הַמִּשְׁכָּן עַשְׁתֵּי־עֶשְׂרֵה יְרִיעֹת עָשָׂה אֹתָם: ¹⁵ אֹרֶךְ הַיְרִיעָה הָאַחַת שְׁלֹשִׁים בָּאַמָּה וְאַרְבַּע אַמּוֹת רֹחַב הַיְרִיעָה הָאֶחָת מִדָּה אַחַת לְעַשְׁתֵּי עֶשְׂרֵה יְרִיעֹת: ¹⁶ וַיְחַבֵּר אֶת־חֲמֵשׁ הַיְרִיעֹת לְבָד וְאֶת־שֵׁשׁ הַיְרִיעֹת לְבָד: ¹⁷ וַיַּעַשׂ לֻלָאֹת חֲמִשִּׁים עַל שְׂפַת הַיְרִיעָה הַקִּיצֹנָה בַּמַּחְבָּרֶת וַחֲמִשִּׁים לֻלָאֹת עָשָׂה עַל־שְׂפַת הַיְרִיעָה הַחֹבֶרֶת הַשֵּׁנִית: ¹⁸ וַיַּעַשׂ קַרְסֵי נְחֹשֶׁת חֲמִשִּׁים לְחַבֵּר אֶת־הָאֹהֶל לִהְיֹת אֶחָד: ¹⁹ וַיַּעַשׂ מִכְסֶה לָאֹהֶל

---

a different sequence to that which God transmitted to Moses (see *Rashi* to 38:22). When the reader notices this point, he may suspect that, in addition to changing the order of construction, perhaps further changes were made. Therefore, the Torah repeated the construction process in intricate detail to show that only the order was changed, whereas all the measurements and weights were preserved (*Rabbi Isaac Abravanel, 15th century*).

The Torah repeats all the details of construction here, following its tendency to repeat things which are cherished and beloved. A precedent for this approach is the Torah's repetition of Eliezer's account of finding a marriage partner for Isaac which was repeated due to its cherished nature (see *Rashi to Genesis 24:42; Rabbi Ḥayyim ibn Attar, 18th century*).

The Tabernacle is a model of how God bestows His beneficence upon us, which is why each piece of apparatus must be made with precise measurements. These physical items correspond

(Sanctuary)," and the people stopped bringing. ⁷ The work (which people had done to bring the donations) was sufficient for (those who built the Tabernacle) to do all the necessary (construction) work, and to leave a surplus.

[FOURTH READING] ⁸ Then every wise-hearted person among those doing the work made the Tabernacle out of ten tapestries made from fine linen thread twisted with turquoise, purple, and crimson wool. He made them with animal designs, the work of a professional weaver.

⁹ The length of each tapestry was twenty-eight cubits, and the width of each tapestry was four cubits. The same measurements applied for all the tapestries.

¹⁰ He stitched five of these tapestries to one another, and the other five tapestries he also stitched to one another.

¹¹ He made loops of turquoise wool on the edge of the tapestry which is at the end of the first group (of five tapestries), and he did the same on the edge of the end curtain of the second group (of five tapestries). ¹² He made fifty loops on the edge of the first tapestry, and he made fifty loops on the edge of the tapestry from the second group. The loops (on the two different tapestries) corresponded to one another.

¹³ He made fifty golden clasps, and he fastened the (two groups of) tapestries to one another with the clasps, so that (the roof of) the Tabernacle became one.

¹⁴ He made sheets of goats' hair for a covering over the Tabernacle. He made eleven sheets. ¹⁵ The length of each sheet was thirty cubits, and the width of each sheet was four cubits. The dimensions applied for the eleven sheets.

¹⁶ He joined the five sheets by themselves, and the (other) six sheets by themselves.

¹⁷ He made fifty loops on the edge of the first sheet, at the end of one group, and fifty loops on the edge of the (end) sheet of the second set.

¹⁸ He made fifty copper clasps to fasten the tent together so that it became one.

¹⁹ He made a (further) covering for the (goats' hair) tent, of rams' skin dyed red and a covering of *taḥash* skins above.

The artisans carried out their work with such a spirit of holiness that it warmed the hearts of all the Israelites, arousing in them a fervent desire to participate. This had motivated all of the donations. Moses knew that as soon as the noise of work would stop, the enthusiasm for generous donations would soon dissipate—and very soon, *"the people stopped bringing"* (*Rabbi Menahem Mendel of Rymanow, 18th century*).

8. Then every wise-hearted person among those doing the work made the Tabernacle. Why did the Torah see fit to repeat all the details of the Tabernacle's construction after having described it all earlier (ch. 25*ff*.)? The Tabernacle was actually constructed by Bezalel in

שמות לו:יט-לו | ויקהל

עֹרֹת אֵילִם מְאָדָּמִים וּמִכְסֵה עֹרֹת תְּחָשִׁים מִלְמָעְלָה: ס [FIFTH READING] 20 וַיַּעַשׂ אֶת־הַקְּרָשִׁים לַמִּשְׁכָּן עֲצֵי שִׁטִּים עֹמְדִים: 21 עֶשֶׂר אַמֹּת אֹרֶךְ הַקָּרֶשׁ וְאַמָּה וַחֲצִי הָאַמָּה רֹחַב הַקֶּרֶשׁ הָאֶחָד: 22 שְׁתֵּי יָדֹת לַקֶּרֶשׁ הָאֶחָד מְשֻׁלָּבֹת אַחַת אֶל־אֶחָת כֵּן עָשָׂה לְכֹל קַרְשֵׁי הַמִּשְׁכָּן: 23 וַיַּעַשׂ אֶת־הַקְּרָשִׁים לַמִּשְׁכָּן עֶשְׂרִים קְרָשִׁים לִפְאַת נֶגֶב תֵּימָנָה: 24 וְאַרְבָּעִים אַדְנֵי־כֶסֶף עָשָׂה תַּחַת עֶשְׂרִים הַקְּרָשִׁים שְׁנֵי אֲדָנִים תַּחַת־הַקֶּרֶשׁ הָאֶחָד לִשְׁתֵּי יְדֹתָיו וּשְׁנֵי אֲדָנִים תַּחַת־הַקֶּרֶשׁ הָאֶחָד לִשְׁתֵּי יְדֹתָיו: 25 וּלְצֶלַע הַמִּשְׁכָּן הַשֵּׁנִית לִפְאַת צָפוֹן עָשָׂה עֶשְׂרִים קְרָשִׁים: 26 וְאַרְבָּעִים אַדְנֵיהֶם כָּסֶף שְׁנֵי אֲדָנִים תַּחַת הַקֶּרֶשׁ הָאֶחָד וּשְׁנֵי אֲדָנִים תַּחַת הַקֶּרֶשׁ הָאֶחָד: 27 וּלְיַרְכְּתֵי הַמִּשְׁכָּן יָמָּה עָשָׂה שִׁשָּׁה קְרָשִׁים: 28 וּשְׁנֵי קְרָשִׁים עָשָׂה לִמְקֻצְעֹת הַמִּשְׁכָּן בַּיַּרְכָתָיִם: 29 וְהָיוּ תוֹאֲמִם מִלְּמַטָּה וְיַחְדָּו יִהְיוּ תַמִּים אֶל־רֹאשׁוֹ אֶל־הַטַּבַּעַת הָאֶחָת כֵּן עָשָׂה לִשְׁנֵיהֶם לִשְׁנֵי הַמִּקְצֹעֹת: 30 וְהָיוּ שְׁמֹנָה קְרָשִׁים וְאַדְנֵיהֶם כֶּסֶף שִׁשָּׁה עָשָׂר אֲדָנִים שְׁנֵי אֲדָנִים שְׁנֵי אֲדָנִים תַּחַת הַקֶּרֶשׁ הָאֶחָד: 31 וַיַּעַשׂ בְּרִיחֵי עֲצֵי שִׁטִּים חֲמִשָּׁה לְקַרְשֵׁי צֶלַע־הַמִּשְׁכָּן הָאֶחָת: 32 וַחֲמִשָּׁה בְרִיחִם לְקַרְשֵׁי צֶלַע־הַמִּשְׁכָּן הַשֵּׁנִית וַחֲמִשָּׁה בְרִיחִם לְקַרְשֵׁי הַמִּשְׁכָּן לַיַּרְכָתַיִם יָמָּה: 33 וַיַּעַשׂ אֶת־הַבְּרִיחַ הַתִּיכֹן לִבְרֹחַ בְּתוֹךְ הַקְּרָשִׁים מִן־הַקָּצֶה אֶל־הַקָּצֶה: 34 וְאֶת־הַקְּרָשִׁים צִפָּה זָהָב וְאֶת־טַבְּעֹתָם עָשָׂה זָהָב בָּתִּים לַבְּרִיחִם וַיְצַף אֶת־הַבְּרִיחִם זָהָב: 35 וַיַּעַשׂ אֶת־הַפָּרֹכֶת תְּכֵלֶת וְאַרְגָּמָן וְתוֹלַעַת שָׁנִי וְשֵׁשׁ מָשְׁזָר מַעֲשֵׂה חֹשֵׁב עָשָׂה אֹתָהּ כְּרֻבִים: 36 וַיַּעַשׂ לָהּ אַרְבָּעָה עַמּוּדֵי שִׁטִּים וַיְצַפֵּם זָהָב וָוֵיהֶם זָהָב

Although the Torah depicts the Divine Presence as dwelling in the Tabernacle, its primary resting place is in man. Therefore, when the Torah speaks of the Tabernacle, we ought to understand it as if it is speaking about man himself (*Rabbi Abraham Joshua Heschel of Apta, 18th century*).

exodus 36:20–36 — va-yakhel

The Walls of the Tabernacle Are Constructed

[FIFTH READING] [20] He made the beams for the Tabernacle of acacia wood, standing upright. [21] The length of each beam was ten cubits, and the width of each beam was a cubit and a half. [22] Each beam had two square pegs (carved at the bottom, separated) like rungs, aligned opposite each other. In this way he made all the beams of the Tabernacle.

[23] He made the beams for the Tabernacle (as follows): twenty beams for the southern side. [24] He made forty silver sockets under the twenty beams, two sockets under one beam for its two square pegs, and two sockets under the next beam for its two square pegs (etc.).

[25] For the second side of the Tabernacle, on the northern side, he made twenty beams, [26] and their forty silver sockets: two sockets under one beam and two sockets under the next beam.

[27] For the western end of the Tabernacle he made six beams. [28] He made two (further) beams at the (northwestern and southwestern) corners of the Tabernacle, at the end.

[29] (All the beams) fit closely next to each other at the bottom. They fit together closely at the top and were connected (to each other) by a ring (which slots into grooves carved into the beam). So too for both of the two (beams) at the two corners.

[30] (Thus, on the western side,) there were eight beams and their silver sockets—sixteen sockets—two sockets under one beam and two sockets under the next beam.

[31] He made crossbars of acacia wood, five for the beams of one side of the Tabernacle, [32] five crossbars for the beams of the second side of the Tabernacle, and five crossbars for the beams of the rear side of the Tabernacle, on the western end. [33] He made the middle bar to go inside the beams, extending from one end to the other end.

[34] He coated the beams with gold. He made rings (on the beams) of gold as holders for the crossbars, and he coated the bars with gold.

[35] He made a partition of turquoise, purple, and crimson wool thread twisted with fine linen thread, the work of an artistic weaver. Animal designs were professionally woven into it (on both sides).

[36] He made for it four pillars of acacia wood, coated with gold—with gold hooks (to hold the partition)—inserted into four silver sockets.

---

to spiritual "vessels"—limitations, strict judgments—through which we are able to receive the infinite love of God.

שמות לו:לו - לז:יב / ויקהל

וַיִּצֹ֥ק לָהֶ֖ם אַרְבָּעָ֣ה אַדְנֵי־כָֽסֶף׃ 37 וַיַּ֤עַשׂ מָסָךְ֙ לְפֶ֣תַח הָאֹ֔הֶל תְּכֵ֥לֶת וְאַרְגָּמָ֖ן וְתוֹלַ֣עַת שָׁנִ֑י וְשֵׁ֥שׁ מָשְׁזָ֖ר מַעֲשֵׂ֥ה רֹקֵֽם׃ 38 וְאֶת־עַמּוּדָ֣יו חֲמִשָּׁה֮ וְאֶת־וָוֵיהֶם֒ וְצִפָּ֧ה רָאשֵׁיהֶ֛ם וַחֲשֻׁקֵיהֶ֖ם זָהָ֑ב וְאַדְנֵיהֶ֥ם חֲמִשָּׁ֖ה נְחֹֽשֶׁת׃ פ

לז 1 וַיַּ֧עַשׂ בְּצַלְאֵ֛ל אֶת־הָאָרֹ֖ן עֲצֵ֣י שִׁטִּ֑ים אַמָּתַ֨יִם וָחֵ֜צִי אָרְכּ֗וֹ וְאַמָּ֤ה וָחֵ֙צִי֙ רָחְבּ֔וֹ וְאַמָּ֥ה וָחֵ֖צִי קֹמָתֽוֹ׃ 2 וַיְצַפֵּ֛הוּ זָהָ֥ב טָה֖וֹר מִבַּ֣יִת וּמִח֑וּץ וַיַּ֥עַשׂ ל֛וֹ זֵ֥ר זָהָ֖ב סָבִֽיב׃ 3 וַיִּצֹ֣ק ל֗וֹ אַרְבַּע֙ טַבְּעֹ֣ת זָהָ֔ב עַ֖ל אַרְבַּ֣ע פַּעֲמֹתָ֑יו וּשְׁתֵּ֣י טַבָּעֹ֗ת עַל־צַלְעוֹ֙ הָֽאֶחָ֔ת וּשְׁתֵּי֙ טַבָּעֹ֔ת עַל־צַלְע֖וֹ הַשֵּׁנִֽית׃ 4 וַיַּ֥עַשׂ בַּדֵּ֖י עֲצֵ֣י שִׁטִּ֑ים וַיְצַ֥ף אֹתָ֖ם זָהָֽב׃ 5 וַיָּבֵ֤א אֶת־הַבַּדִּים֙ בַּטַּבָּעֹ֔ת עַ֖ל צַלְעֹ֣ת הָאָרֹ֑ן לָשֵׂ֖את אֶת־הָאָרֹֽן׃ 6 וַיַּ֥עַשׂ כַּפֹּ֖רֶת זָהָ֣ב טָה֑וֹר אַמָּתַ֤יִם וָחֵ֙צִי֙ אָרְכָּ֔הּ וְאַמָּ֥ה וָחֵ֖צִי רָחְבָּֽהּ׃ 7 וַיַּ֛עַשׂ שְׁנֵ֥י כְרֻבִ֖ים זָהָ֑ב מִקְשָׁה֙ עָשָׂ֣ה אֹתָ֔ם מִשְּׁנֵ֖י קְצ֥וֹת הַכַּפֹּֽרֶת׃ 8 כְּרוּב־אֶחָ֤ד מִקָּצָה֙ מִזֶּ֔ה וּכְרוּב־אֶחָ֥ד מִקָּצָ֖ה מִזֶּ֑ה מִן־הַכַּפֹּ֛רֶת עָשָׂ֥ה אֶת־הַכְּרֻבִ֖ים מִשְּׁנֵ֥י [קצוותיו כ'] קְצוֹתָֽיו׃ 9 וַיִּהְי֣וּ הַכְּרֻבִים֩ פֹּרְשֵׂ֨י כְנָפַ֜יִם לְמַ֗עְלָה סֹֽכְכִ֤ים בְּכַנְפֵיהֶם֙ עַל־הַכַּפֹּ֔רֶת וּפְנֵיהֶ֖ם אִ֣ישׁ אֶל־אָחִ֑יו אֶ֨ל־הַכַּפֹּ֔רֶת הָי֖וּ פְּנֵ֥י הַכְּרֻבִֽים׃ פ 10 וַיַּ֥עַשׂ אֶת־הַשֻּׁלְחָ֖ן עֲצֵ֣י שִׁטִּ֑ים אַמָּתַ֤יִם אָרְכּוֹ֙ וְאַמָּ֣ה רָחְבּ֔וֹ וְאַמָּ֥ה וָחֵ֖צִי קֹמָתֽוֹ׃ 11 וַיְצַ֥ף אֹת֖וֹ זָהָ֣ב טָה֑וֹר וַיַּ֥עַשׂ ל֛וֹ זֵ֥ר זָהָ֖ב סָבִֽיב׃ 12 וַיַּ֨עַשׂ ל֤וֹ מִסְגֶּ֙רֶת֙ טֹ֔פַח

6, He made a lid (for the ark) of pure gold. All the Tabernacle apparatus was made of acacia wood inlaid with gold, except for the *lid* covering for the holy ark, and the *candelabrum*, which were both made from pure gold.

spiritual vitamin

> A human being may be compared to an ark. The body, which consists of tissue, bone, etc., is physical, but it houses the soul, which is spiritual, sacred and pure. Consequently, the body, too, must be kept holy, just as the ark itself is revered.

³⁷ He made a curtain for the entrance of the tent of turquoise, purple, and crimson wool thread twisted with fine linen thread, the work of an embroiderer (with images on both sides), ³⁸ its five pillars and their hooks. He coated their tops and their decorative bands with gold, and their five sockets were made from copper.

The Tabernacle's Apparatus Is Made

37 ¹ Bezalel (and his assistants) made the ark of acacia wood, two and a half cubits in its length, a cubit and a half in its width, and a cubit and a half in its height. ² He coated it with pure gold, coating it inside and out, and he made upon it a golden-rimmed edge all around.

³ He cast four golden rings for it, on its four corners, two rings on one of its sides and two rings on its other side. ⁴ He made poles of acacia wood and coated them with gold. ⁵ He inserted the poles into the rings on the sides of the ark, to carry the ark.

⁶ He made a lid (for the ark) of pure gold, two and a half cubits in its length and a cubit and a half in its width. ⁷ He made two golden cherubim (each with the face of a child). He made them (from the same piece of metal) hammered out from the two ends of the lid. ⁸ He made one cherub from one end and the other cherub from the other end. He made (one of) the cherubim at each of the two ends of the lid (from the same piece of metal). ⁹ The cherubim had their wings spread upwards, sheltering the lid with their wings, their faces toward one another. The faces of the cherubim were turned towards the lid.

¹⁰ He made a table of acacia wood, two cubits in its length, one cubit in its width, and a cubit and a half in its height. ¹¹ He coated it with pure gold, and he made for it a golden-rimmed edge all around.

¹² He made for it a frame one handbreadth in width all around. He made a golden-rimmed edge for its frame all around.

37:1 Bezalel made the ark. All the apparatus of the Tabernacle built in the Sinai Desert was rebuilt for the first and second Temples in Jerusalem, with the exception of the ark, which was preserved. The original ark of the Tabernacle was the same one used in the first Temple. And in anticipation of the prophesied destruction of the first Temple, King Josiah hid the ark away to be used in the future third Temple (*Babylonian Talmud, Yoma* 52b).

This course of events was prophetically alluded to here, where the Torah stresses that *"Bezalel made"* the ark, in contrast to all the other holy apparatus, regarding which the Torah states nondescriptly, "and *he* made." The architect of all the other items is not referred to personally, as they were later to be replicated by other architects. By contrast, the Torah emphasizes that *"Bezalel made the ark,"* for the only Temple ark in history was that which "Bezalel made" (*Rabbi Meir Simḥah of Dvinsk, 19ᵗʰ–20ᵗʰ century*).

שמות לז:יב-כו | ויקהל

סָבִ֑יב וַיַּ֧עַשׂ זֵר־זָהָ֛ב לְמִסְגַּרְתּ֖וֹ סָבִֽיב׃ 13 וַיִּצֹ֣ק ל֔וֹ אַרְבַּ֖ע טַבְּעֹ֣ת זָהָ֑ב וַיִּתֵּן֙ אֶת־הַטַּבָּעֹ֔ת עַ֚ל אַרְבַּ֣ע הַפֵּאֹ֔ת אֲשֶׁ֖ר לְאַרְבַּ֥ע רַגְלָֽיו׃ 14 לְעֻמַּת֙ הַמִּסְגֶּ֔רֶת הָי֖וּ הַטַּבָּעֹ֑ת בָּתִּים֙ לַבַּדִּ֔ים לָשֵׂ֖את אֶת־הַשֻּׁלְחָֽן׃ 15 וַיַּ֤עַשׂ אֶת־הַבַּדִּים֙ עֲצֵ֣י שִׁטִּ֔ים וַיְצַ֥ף אֹתָ֖ם זָהָ֑ב לָשֵׂ֖את אֶת־הַשֻּׁלְחָֽן׃ 16 וַיַּ֜עַשׂ אֶת־הַכֵּלִ֣ים ׀ אֲשֶׁ֣ר עַל־הַשֻּׁלְחָ֗ן אֶת־קְעָרֹתָ֤יו וְאֶת־כַּפֹּתָיו֙ וְאֵת֙ מְנַקִּיֹּתָ֔יו וְאֶת־הַקְּשָׂוֺ֔ת אֲשֶׁ֥ר יֻסַּ֖ךְ בָּהֵ֑ן זָהָ֥ב טָהֽוֹר׃ פ

17 **SIXTH READING** **THIRD WHEN JOINED** וַיַּ֥עַשׂ אֶת־הַמְּנֹרָ֖ה זָהָ֣ב טָה֑וֹר מִקְשָׁ֞ה עָשָׂ֤ה אֶת־הַמְּנֹרָה֙ יְרֵכָ֣הּ וְקָנָ֔הּ גְּבִיעֶ֛יהָ כַּפְתֹּרֶ֥יהָ וּפְרָחֶ֖יהָ מִמֶּ֥נָּה הָיֽוּ׃ 18 וְשִׁשָּׁ֣ה קָנִ֔ים יֹצְאִ֖ים מִצִּדֶּ֑יהָ שְׁלֹשָׁ֣ה ׀ קְנֵ֣י מְנֹרָ֗ה מִצִּדָּהּ֙ הָֽאֶחָ֔ד וּשְׁלֹשָׁה֙ קְנֵ֣י מְנֹרָ֔ה מִצִּדָּ֖הּ הַשֵּׁנִֽי׃ 19 שְׁלֹשָׁ֣ה גְ֠בִעִים מְֽשֻׁקָּדִ֞ים בַּקָּנֶ֣ה הָאֶחָד֮ כַּפְתֹּ֣ר וָפֶרַח֒ וּשְׁלֹשָׁ֣ה גְבִעִ֗ים מְשֻׁקָּדִ֛ים בְּקָנֶ֥ה אֶחָ֖ד כַּפְתֹּ֣ר וָפָ֑רַח כֵּ֚ן לְשֵׁ֣שֶׁת הַקָּנִ֔ים הַיֹּצְאִ֖ים מִן־הַמְּנֹרָֽה׃ 20 וּבַמְּנֹרָ֖ה אַרְבָּעָ֣ה גְבִעִ֑ים מְ֠שֻׁקָּדִים כַּפְתֹּרֶ֖יהָ וּפְרָחֶֽיהָ׃ 21 וְכַפְתֹּ֡ר תַּ֩חַת֩ שְׁנֵ֨י הַקָּנִ֜ים מִמֶּ֗נָּה וְכַפְתֹּר֙ תַּ֣חַת שְׁנֵ֤י הַקָּנִים֙ מִמֶּ֔נָּה וְכַפְתֹּ֕ר תַּֽחַת־שְׁנֵ֥י הַקָּנִ֖ים מִמֶּ֑נָּה לְשֵׁ֙שֶׁת֙ הַקָּנִ֔ים הַיֹּצְאִ֖ים מִמֶּֽנָּה׃ 22 כַּפְתֹּרֵיהֶ֥ם וּקְנֹתָ֖ם מִמֶּ֣נָּה הָי֑וּ כֻּלָּ֛הּ מִקְשָׁ֥ה אַחַ֖ת זָהָ֥ב טָהֽוֹר׃ 23 וַיַּ֥עַשׂ אֶת־נֵרֹתֶ֖יהָ שִׁבְעָ֑ה וּמַלְקָחֶ֥יהָ וּמַחְתֹּתֶ֖יהָ זָהָ֥ב טָהֽוֹר׃ 24 כִּכָּ֛ר זָהָ֥ב טָה֖וֹר עָשָׂ֣ה אֹתָ֑הּ וְאֵ֖ת כָּל־כֵּלֶֽיהָ׃ פ 25 וַיַּ֛עַשׂ אֶת־מִזְבַּ֥ח הַקְּטֹ֖רֶת עֲצֵ֣י שִׁטִּ֑ים אַמָּ֣ה אָרְכּוֹ֩ וְאַמָּ֨ה רָחְבּ֜וֹ רָב֗וּעַ וְאַמָּתַ֙יִם֙ קֹֽמָת֔וֹ מִמֶּ֖נּוּ הָי֥וּ קַרְנֹתָֽיו׃ 26 וַיְצַ֨ף אֹת֜וֹ זָהָ֣ב טָה֗וֹר אֶת־גַּגּ֧וֹ וְאֶת־קִירֹתָ֛יו סָבִ֖יב וְאֶת־קַרְנֹתָ֑יו

566

spiritual vitamin

" Souls are also called "lights," as the verse states, *"The soul of man is the candle of God"* (Proverbs 20:27). They are lights which God has sent to earth to light up the darkness of this world. "

exodus 37:13–26 — va-yakhel

¹³ He made for it (the table) four golden rings, and he placed the rings on the four corners of its four legs. ¹⁴ The rings were (attached to the legs) adjacent to the frame as holders for the poles with which to carry the table.

¹⁵ He made the poles of acacia wood, and he coated them with gold. The table was carried with them.

¹⁶ He made the table's utensils from pure gold: its bread-molds, its spoons, its supporting bars and its separating bars, which covered (the breads, and allowed ventilation).

[SIXTH READING / THIRD WHEN JOINED] ¹⁷ He made the candelabrum of pure gold. The candelabrum was made hammered (from a single piece of metal). Its base and its stem, its (ornamental) cups, spheres, and flowers were all from (the same piece of metal and not made separately). ¹⁸ Six branches were coming out of its sides (diagonally), three candelabrum branches from one of its sides and three candelabrum branches from its second side.

¹⁹ On one branch were three decorated cups, a sphere and a flower. On the next branch were three decorated cups, a sphere and a flower. So too for all six branches that came out of the candelabrum.

²⁰ On (the stem of) the candelabrum there were four decorated cups (one below the point where the branches emerge and three at the top), together with its spheres and its flowers.

²¹ There was a sphere (on the stem) where the (first) two branches came out of it, a sphere where the (next) two branches came out of it, and a sphere where the (last) two branches came out of it. (This covered) all six branches that come out of the candelabrum.

²² Its spheres and branches were all (formed) from it. All of it was one hammered mass of pure gold.

²³ He made its seven lamps, and its wick-tongs and its ash-scoops from pure gold.

²⁴ He made it from (exactly) a *kikkar* of pure gold, including all these utensils.

²⁵ He made the incense altar out of acacia wood, one cubit in its length and one cubit in its width, a square, and two cubits in its height. Its horns were (formed) from it. ²⁶ He coated it with pure gold, its top, its walls all around, and its horns, and he made for it a golden-rimmed edge all around.

The Tabernacle and its apparatus were modeled on the human body, each structural element corresponding to a different limb—the lid corresponding to the heart, and the candelabrum, to the eyes. *Both of these must be especially pure, and not corrupted.*

With the other limbs we say, "Eventually you will act for the sake of heaven. Keep trying." But with the eyes and heart you have to be especially careful, always (*Rabbi Mordecai Joseph Leiner of Izbica, 19th century*).

שמות לז:כו - לח:טו | ויקהל

וַיַּעַשׂ לוֹ זֵר זָהָב סָבִיב: 27 וּשְׁתֵּי טַבְּעֹת זָהָב עָשָׂה־לוֹ | מִתַּחַת לְזֵרוֹ עַל שְׁתֵּי
צַלְעֹתָיו עַל שְׁנֵי צִדָּיו לְבָתִּים לְבַדִּים לָשֵׂאת אֹתוֹ בָּהֶם: 28 וַיַּעַשׂ אֶת־הַבַּדִּים
עֲצֵי שִׁטִּים וַיְצַף אֹתָם זָהָב: 29 וַיַּעַשׂ אֶת־שֶׁמֶן הַמִּשְׁחָה קֹדֶשׁ וְאֶת־קְטֹרֶת
הַסַּמִּים טָהוֹר מַעֲשֵׂה רֹקֵחַ: ס

לח

[SEVENTH READING / FOURTH WHEN JOINED]

1 וַיַּעַשׂ אֶת־מִזְבַּח הָעֹלָה עֲצֵי שִׁטִּים חָמֵשׁ
אַמּוֹת אָרְכּוֹ וְחָמֵשׁ־אַמּוֹת רָחְבּוֹ רָבוּעַ וְשָׁלֹשׁ אַמּוֹת קֹמָתוֹ:
2 וַיַּעַשׂ קַרְנֹתָיו עַל אַרְבַּע פִּנֹּתָיו מִמֶּנּוּ הָיוּ קַרְנֹתָיו וַיְצַף אֹתוֹ נְחֹשֶׁת: 3 וַיַּעַשׂ
אֶת־כָּל־כְּלֵי הַמִּזְבֵּחַ אֶת־הַסִּירֹת וְאֶת־הַיָּעִים וְאֶת־הַמִּזְרָקֹת אֶת־הַמִּזְלָגֹת
וְאֶת־הַמַּחְתֹּת כָּל־כֵּלָיו עָשָׂה נְחֹשֶׁת: 4 וַיַּעַשׂ לַמִּזְבֵּחַ מִכְבָּר מַעֲשֵׂה רֶשֶׁת
נְחֹשֶׁת תַּחַת כַּרְכֻּבּוֹ מִלְּמַטָּה עַד־חֶצְיוֹ: 5 וַיִּצֹק אַרְבַּע טַבָּעֹת בְּאַרְבַּע הַקְּצָוֹת
לְמִכְבַּר הַנְּחֹשֶׁת בָּתִּים לַבַּדִּים: 6 וַיַּעַשׂ אֶת־הַבַּדִּים עֲצֵי שִׁטִּים וַיְצַף אֹתָם
נְחֹשֶׁת: 7 וַיָּבֵא אֶת־הַבַּדִּים בַּטַּבָּעֹת עַל צַלְעֹת הַמִּזְבֵּחַ לָשֵׂאת אֹתוֹ בָּהֶם
נְבוּב לֻחֹת עָשָׂה אֹתוֹ: ס 8 וַיַּעַשׂ אֵת הַכִּיּוֹר נְחֹשֶׁת וְאֵת כַּנּוֹ נְחֹשֶׁת בְּמַרְאֹת
הַצֹּבְאֹת אֲשֶׁר צָבְאוּ פֶּתַח אֹהֶל מוֹעֵד: ס 9 וַיַּעַשׂ אֶת־הֶחָצֵר לִפְאַת | נֶגֶב
תֵּימָנָה קַלְעֵי הֶחָצֵר שֵׁשׁ מָשְׁזָר מֵאָה בָּאַמָּה: 10 עַמּוּדֵיהֶם עֶשְׂרִים וְאַדְנֵיהֶם
עֶשְׂרִים נְחֹשֶׁת וָוֵי הָעַמּוּדִים וַחֲשֻׁקֵיהֶם כָּסֶף: 11 וְלִפְאַת צָפוֹן מֵאָה בָאַמָּה
עַמּוּדֵיהֶם עֶשְׂרִים וְאַדְנֵיהֶם עֶשְׂרִים נְחֹשֶׁת וָוֵי הָעַמּוּדִים וַחֲשֻׁקֵיהֶם כָּסֶף:
12 וְלִפְאַת־יָם קְלָעִים חֲמִשִּׁים בָּאַמָּה עַמּוּדֵיהֶם עֲשָׂרָה וְאַדְנֵיהֶם עֲשָׂרָה וָוֵי
הָעַמֻּדִים וַחֲשׁוּקֵיהֶם כָּסֶף: 13 וְלִפְאַת קֵדְמָה מִזְרָחָה חֲמִשִּׁים אַמָּה: 14 קְלָעִים
חֲמֵשׁ־עֶשְׂרֵה אַמָּה אֶל־הַכָּתֵף עַמּוּדֵיהֶם שְׁלֹשָׁה וְאַדְנֵיהֶם שְׁלֹשָׁה: 15 וְלַכָּתֵף
הַשֵּׁנִית מִזֶּה וּמִזֶּה לְשַׁעַר הֶחָצֵר קְלָעִים חֲמֵשׁ עֶשְׂרֵה אַמָּה עַמֻּדֵיהֶם שְׁלֹשָׁה

27 He made two golden rings for it underneath its rimmed edge on its two corners. He made them on its two sides, so that they should serve as holders for poles with which to carry it. 28 He made the poles out of acacia wood and coated them with gold.

29 He made the holy anointing oil and the pure incense, professionally mixed.

The Courtyard and Its Apparatus Are Made

38 [SEVENTH READING / FOURTH WHEN JOINED] 1 He made the altar for burnt-offerings of acacia wood, five cubits long and five cubits wide. (The altar was) square, and its height was three cubits. 2 He made protrusions on its four corners. Its protrusions were from (the same single piece of wood). He coated it with copper.

3 He made all the utensils of the altar, the pots, the shovels, the sacrificial basins, the flesh hooks and the fire pans. He made all its utensils from copper.

4 He made for the altar a lattice of copper netting beneath its decorative border, extending downwards until the middle of the altar. 5 He cast four rings on the four ends of the copper netting, as holders for the poles.

6 He made the poles of acacia wood, and he coated them with copper. 7 He inserted the poles into the rings on the sides of the altar in order to carry it with them.

He made (the altar) hollow, out of panels.

8 He made the copper urn and its copper base from the mirrors of the women who had (borne) legions (of children in Egypt), who congregated at the entrance of the tent of meeting (to give their contribution).

9 He made the courtyard (as follows): On the southern side there were (perforated) curtains for the courtyard of twisted linen, one hundred cubits long. 10 It had twenty pillars and twenty sockets of copper. The hooks of the pillars and their belts were silver.

11 The northern side was one hundred cubits. There were twenty copper pillars, and their twenty copper sockets for them. The hooks of the pillars and their belts were silver.

12 The western side had fifty cubits of curtains, ten pillars and ten sockets for them. The hooks of the pillars and their belts were silver.

13 The eastern end was fifty cubits (consisting of an entrance of twenty cubits and a fifteen cubit "shoulder" curtain on each side). 14 There were fifteen cubits of curtains on one shoulder, with their three pillars and their three sockets. 15 So too on the second shoulder, so that on either side of the gate of the courtyard there were curtains of fifteen cubits, with their three pillars and their three sockets.

שמות לח:טז-כ • ויקהל

וְאַדְנֵיהֶם שְׁלֹשָׁה: 16 כָּל־קַלְעֵי הֶחָצֵר סָבִיב שֵׁשׁ מָשְׁזָר: 17 וְהָאֲדָנִים לָעַמֻּדִים נְחֹשֶׁת וָוֵי הָעַמּוּדִים וַחֲשׁוּקֵיהֶם כֶּסֶף וְצִפּוּי רָאשֵׁיהֶם כָּסֶף וְהֵם מְחֻשָּׁקִים כֶּסֶף כֹּל עַמֻּדֵי הֶחָצֵר: [MAFTIR] 18 וּמָסַךְ שַׁעַר הֶחָצֵר מַעֲשֵׂה רֹקֵם תְּכֵלֶת וְאַרְגָּמָן וְתוֹלַעַת שָׁנִי וְשֵׁשׁ מָשְׁזָר וְעֶשְׂרִים אַמָּה אֹרֶךְ וְקוֹמָה בְרֹחַב חָמֵשׁ אַמּוֹת לְעֻמַּת קַלְעֵי הֶחָצֵר: 19 וְעַמֻּדֵיהֶם אַרְבָּעָה וְאַדְנֵיהֶם אַרְבָּעָה נְחֹשֶׁת וָוֵיהֶם כֶּסֶף וְצִפּוּי רָאשֵׁיהֶם וַחֲשֻׁקֵיהֶם כָּסֶף: 20 וְכָל־הַיְתֵדֹת לַמִּשְׁכָּן וְלֶחָצֵר סָבִיב נְחֹשֶׁת: ס ס ס

קכ"ב פסוקים, סנוא"ה סימן.

exodus 38:16–20 — va-yakhel

¹⁶ All the curtains that surrounded the courtyard were made from twisted fine linen. ¹⁷ The sockets for the pillars were made from copper. The hooks of the pillars and their belts were made from silver, and their covering on the tops was silver. All the pillars of the courtyard had belts of silver.

[MAFTIR] ¹⁸ At the entrance of the courtyard was a professionally woven tapestry made of turquoise, purple, and crimson wool thread twisted with linen thread, twenty cubits high and five cubits wide, the same (height) as the hangings of the courtyard. ¹⁹ It had four pillars, and four sockets, made from copper. Their hooks were silver, and the coverings on their tops and their belts were silver. ²⁰ All the pegs of the Tabernacle and of the courtyard all around were made from copper.

Haftarot: Va-Yakhel—page 1340. *Shekalim*—page 1424. *Parah*—page 1431.

Maftir: Shekalim—page 520 (30:11–16). *Parah*—page 932 (19:1–22).

spiritual vitamin

" If you feel that no one seems interested in your work, remember that God, whose knowledge and providence extends to everyone individually, knows and is interested in what you are doing. "

Pekudei teaches us the advantage of the **practical** and **this-worldly** over the **theoretical** and **heavenly.** God prefers the earthly Tabernacle, built by **imperfect people** such as ourselves, to a heavenly palace of angels. You are **never inadequate** in the eyes of God.

PEKUDEI
פקודי

ACCOUNT OF THE TABERNACLE	38:21
MATERIALS OF THE TABERNACLE ARE AUDITED	38:22–31
MAKING OF THE PRIESTLY GARMENTS	39:1–31
THE TABERNACLE IS COMPLETED AND ERECTED	39:32 – 40:38

NAME
Pekudei

MEANING
"Accounts"

LINES IN TORAH SCROLL
159

PARASHIYYOT
6 open; 14 closed

VERSES
92

WORDS
1182

LETTERS
4432

DATE
11 *Tishri* – 1 *Nisan*, 2449

LOCATION
Mount Sinai

KEY PEOPLE
Moses, Ithamar, Bezalel, Oholiab, Aaron and his sons

MITZVOT
None

NOTE
Is often read together with the preceding portion *Va-Yakhel*

CHARACTER PROFILE

NAME
Ithamar ("speaking")

GRANDFATHERS
Amram and Amminadab

PARENTS
Aaron and Elisheba

SIBLINGS
Nadab, Abihu, Eleazar

ACHIEVEMENTS
Served as High Priest after his brother Eleazar died; was third in the chain of Torah transmission in the desert after Moses and Aaron; was a leader of the Levites and officer over the Gershonites and Merarites

KNOWN FOR
Served as priest during the inauguration of the Tabernacle

ACCOUNTABILITY

Moses gave a complete reckoning to the Jewish people of what their donations had been used for. Financial transparency is essential for all organizations and especially those that are supported by the community (38:21–31).

GOD'S HELP

The Jewish people brought the beams of the Tabernacle to Moses since they were unable to erect it. Moses too was unable to erect it, but a miracle occurred and the beams "erected themselves" through Moses' efforts. In life sometimes all that God is waiting for is our effort. Then He helps us with our challenges (39:33, 40:17).

GOD'S PRESENCE

When the Tabernacle was erected, God's glory "filled" it. This was a sign that the Jewish people had been forgiven for the Golden Calf. Today we do not have a Tabernacle or Temple. Instead, God's glory is revealed by our good actions (40:34).

21 אֵ֣לֶּה פְקוּדֵ֤י הַמִּשְׁכָּן֙ מִשְׁכַּ֣ן הָעֵדֻ֔ת אֲשֶׁ֥ר פֻּקַּ֖ד עַל־פִּ֣י מֹשֶׁ֑ה עֲבֹדַת֙ הַלְוִיִּ֔ם בְּיַד֙ אִֽיתָמָ֔ר בֶּֽן־אַהֲרֹ֖ן הַכֹּהֵֽן: 22 וּבְצַלְאֵ֛ל בֶּן־אוּרִ֥י בֶן־ח֖וּר לְמַטֵּ֣ה יְהוּדָ֑ה עָשָׂ֕ה אֵ֛ת כָּל־אֲשֶׁר־צִוָּ֥ה יְהֹוָ֖ה אֶת־מֹשֶֽׁה: 23 וְאִתּ֗וֹ אׇהֳלִיאָ֞ב בֶּן־אֲחִיסָמָ֛ךְ לְמַטֵּה־דָ֖ן חָרָ֣שׁ וְחֹשֵׁ֑ב וְרֹקֵ֗ם בַּתְּכֵ֙לֶת֙ וּבָֽאַרְגָּמָ֔ן וּבְתוֹלַ֥עַת הַשָּׁנִ֖י וּבַשֵּֽׁשׁ: ס 24 כָּל־הַזָּהָ֗ב הֶֽעָשׂוּי֙ לַמְּלָאכָ֔ה בְּכֹ֖ל מְלֶ֣אכֶת הַקֹּ֑דֶשׁ וַיְהִ֣י ׀ זְהַ֣ב הַתְּנוּפָ֗ה תֵּ֤שַׁע וְעֶשְׂרִים֙ כִּכָּ֔ר וּשְׁבַ֨ע מֵא֧וֹת וּשְׁלֹשִׁ֛ים שֶׁ֖קֶל בְּשֶׁ֥קֶל הַקֹּֽדֶשׁ: 25 וְכֶ֛סֶף פְּקוּדֵ֥י הָעֵדָ֖ה מְאַ֣ת כִּכָּ֑ר וְאֶ֩לֶף֩ וּשְׁבַ֨ע מֵא֜וֹת וַחֲמִשָּׁ֧ה וְשִׁבְעִ֛ים שֶׁ֖קֶל בְּשֶׁ֥קֶל הַקֹּֽדֶשׁ: 26 בֶּ֚קַע לַגֻּלְגֹּ֔לֶת מַחֲצִ֥ית הַשֶּׁ֖קֶל בְּשֶׁ֣קֶל הַקֹּ֑דֶשׁ לְכֹ֨ל הָעֹבֵ֜ר עַל־הַפְּקֻדִ֗ים מִבֶּ֨ן עֶשְׂרִ֤ים שָׁנָה֙

But with the Tabernacle this was not a concern. The Tabernacle was so deeply connected to God, through Moses, that nothing could disconnect it from its source (*Rabbi Abraham Joshua Heschel of Apta, 18th century*).

The Testimony. This was a testimony to the Jewish people that God had genuinely forgiven them for worshiping the Golden Calf, since now He was making His presence dwell among them (*Rashi, 11th century*).

Why did they need this? Because the people had been so shamed by sin they needed a clear indication—a "testimony"—to strengthen their hearts that the damage caused by their sin had been repaired. They needed to be free of guilt so that they could worship God properly.

Every year, after the Day of Atonement, we do the same thing. We build a miniature Tabernacle—a *sukkah* (booth)—where God's presence dwells, to strengthen our resolve that He has forgiven us for our sins and that we are now worthy for Him to rest in our midst (*Rabbi Judah Aryeh Leib Alter of Gur, 19th century*).

At Moses' command. Throughout this entire portion of the Torah, why is it written repeatedly, *"as God had commanded Moses,"* after each detail of the Tabernacle's construction? Could this fact not have been mentioned once, at the conclusion?

Every commandment we observe must be accompanied with the appropriate *kavvanah* (mystical intention), and constructing the Tabernacle was no exception. In this case, it was important for all the participants to be conscious that *"as the Tabernacle was erected below, so it was erected Above"* (*Midrash Tanḥuma; Zohar*). But since not all the construction staff were mystics, and they lacked an understanding of the Heavenly Tabernacle, many simply fulfilled their obligation by saying, "Our *kavvanah* is whatever God commanded Moses."

That is why we find this phrase repeated in every instance—the people were fulfilling their basic requirement to infuse each act with *kavvanah* (*Rabbi Jacob Joseph of Polonnoye, 18th century*).

22. Bezalel … made all that God had commanded Moses. It does not say that Bezalel carried out "all that Moses had commanded him," but rather "all that God had commanded Moses." This teaches us that Bezalel correctly intuited what Moses had been told by God on Mount Sinai, even in those instances where Bezalel did not hear these instructions from his teacher.

exodus 38:21–26   pekudei

parashat pekudei

Appointments of the Tabernacle

²¹ These are the accounts of the Tabernacle, the Tabernacle of the Testimony, which were counted at Moses' command. (All these items) were serviced by the Levites under the direction of Ithamar, son of Aaron the priest.

Accounting of the Tabernacle Materials

²² Bezalel son of Uri son of Hur of the tribe of Judah had made all that God had commanded Moses. ²³ With him was Oholiab son of Ahisamach of the tribe of Dan, a craftsman, an artistic weaver and an embroiderer of turquoise, purple, and crimson wool and linen.

²⁴ All the gold that had been used for work in all the work of the holy (Sanctuary), which was the gold donated, (was) twenty-nine *kikkar*, seven hundred and thirty shekels, according to the shekel (measurement system which is used for) sanctified (items).

²⁵ The silver census money from the community was 100 *kikkar* and 1775 shekels, according to the shekel (measurement system which is used for) sanctified (items). ²⁶ (This consisted of) one *bekaʿ* per head, i.e., a half-shekel according to the shekel (measurement system which is used for) sanctified (items), for each person who went through the counting (system), from the age of twenty years and upward (which totaled) 603,550 (people).

38:21 These are the accounts of the Tabernacle, the Tabernacle of the Testimony. The Divine Presence resting in the Tabernacle testified that all the donations had been allocated correctly and that no funds had been misappropriated. Had there been any dishonesty, the Divine Presence would not have rested there. As the verse states, *"I am God ... who hates theft in a burnt-offering"* (Isaiah 61:8; Rabbi Meir Loeb Weisser, 19th century).

The accounts. Judaism praises the virtues of private accomplishments that are not broadcast for all to see—*"A blessing does not rest on something unless it is hidden from the eyes"* (Babylonian Talmud, Ta'anit 8b).

Why, then, did Moses make the details of the Tabernacle so public?

The discouragement of public attention is based on a fear of *'ayin ha-raʿ*, the "evil eye." What does this mean? If a person looks at an item in a very physical, lustful way it can cause damage by severing the item's tie with its spiritual source. If the desirous look is very strong, only the physical portion of the item will remain and its inner essence will be severed from its roots.

Food for thought

1. Do you need to know exactly how your charitable donations are spent?

2. What lesson do you take from the Torah's financial transparency?

3. Is financial secrecy ever necessary?

שמות לח:כו - לט:ח

פקודי

27 וַיְהִי וָמַעְלָה לְשֵׁשׁ־מֵאוֹת אֶלֶף וּשְׁלֹשֶׁת אֲלָפִים וַחֲמֵשׁ מֵאוֹת וַחֲמִשִּׁים: וַיְהִי מְאַת כִּכַּר הַכֶּסֶף לָצֶקֶת אֵת אַדְנֵי הַקֹּדֶשׁ וְאֵת אַדְנֵי הַפָּרֹכֶת מְאַת אֲדָנִים לִמְאַת הַכִּכָּר כִּכָּר לָאָדֶן: 28 וְאֶת־הָאֶלֶף וּשְׁבַע הַמֵּאוֹת וַחֲמִשָּׁה וְשִׁבְעִים עָשָׂה וָוִים לָעַמּוּדִים וְצִפָּה רָאשֵׁיהֶם וְחִשַּׁק אֹתָם: 29 וּנְחֹשֶׁת הַתְּנוּפָה שִׁבְעִים כִּכָּר וְאַלְפַּיִם וְאַרְבַּע־מֵאוֹת שָׁקֶל: 30 וַיַּעַשׂ בָּהּ אֶת־אַדְנֵי פֶּתַח אֹהֶל מוֹעֵד וְאֵת מִזְבַּח הַנְּחֹשֶׁת וְאֶת־מִכְבַּר הַנְּחֹשֶׁת אֲשֶׁר־לוֹ וְאֵת כָּל־כְּלֵי הַמִּזְבֵּחַ: 31 וְאֶת־אַדְנֵי הֶחָצֵר סָבִיב וְאֶת־אַדְנֵי שַׁעַר הֶחָצֵר וְאֵת כָּל־יִתְדֹת הַמִּשְׁכָּן וְאֶת־כָּל־יִתְדֹת הֶחָצֵר סָבִיב:

לט

1 וּמִן־הַתְּכֵלֶת וְהָאַרְגָּמָן וְתוֹלַעַת הַשָּׁנִי עָשׂוּ בִגְדֵי־שְׂרָד לְשָׁרֵת בַּקֹּדֶשׁ וַיַּעֲשׂוּ אֶת־בִּגְדֵי הַקֹּדֶשׁ אֲשֶׁר לְאַהֲרֹן כַּאֲשֶׁר צִוָּה יְהוָה אֶת־מֹשֶׁה: פ [SECOND READING / FIFTH WHEN JOINED] 2 וַיַּעַשׂ אֶת־הָאֵפֹד זָהָב תְּכֵלֶת וְאַרְגָּמָן וְתוֹלַעַת שָׁנִי וְשֵׁשׁ מָשְׁזָר: 3 וַיְרַקְּעוּ אֶת־פַּחֵי הַזָּהָב וְקִצֵּץ פְּתִילִם לַעֲשׂוֹת בְּתוֹךְ הַתְּכֵלֶת וּבְתוֹךְ הָאַרְגָּמָן וּבְתוֹךְ תּוֹלַעַת הַשָּׁנִי וּבְתוֹךְ הַשֵּׁשׁ מַעֲשֵׂה חֹשֵׁב: 4 כְּתֵפֹת עָשׂוּ־לוֹ חֹבְרֹת עַל־שְׁנֵי [קצוותיו כ׳] קְצוֹתָיו חֻבָּר: 5 וְחֵשֶׁב אֲפֻדָּתוֹ אֲשֶׁר עָלָיו מִמֶּנּוּ הוּא כְּמַעֲשֵׂהוּ זָהָב תְּכֵלֶת וְאַרְגָּמָן וְתוֹלַעַת שָׁנִי וְשֵׁשׁ מָשְׁזָר כַּאֲשֶׁר צִוָּה יְהוָה אֶת־מֹשֶׁה: ס 6 וַיַּעֲשׂוּ אֶת־אַבְנֵי הַשֹּׁהַם מֻסַבֹּת מִשְׁבְּצֹת זָהָב מְפֻתָּחֹת פִּתּוּחֵי חוֹתָם עַל־שְׁמוֹת בְּנֵי יִשְׂרָאֵל: 7 וַיָּשֶׂם אֹתָם עַל כִּתְפֹת הָאֵפֹד אַבְנֵי זִכָּרוֹן לִבְנֵי יִשְׂרָאֵל כַּאֲשֶׁר צִוָּה יְהוָה אֶת־מֹשֶׁה: פ 8 וַיַּעַשׂ אֶת־הַחֹשֶׁן מַעֲשֵׂה חֹשֵׁב כְּמַעֲשֵׂה אֵפֹד זָהָב תְּכֵלֶת וְאַרְגָּמָן וְתוֹלַעַת

27. One hundred sockets were made from one hundred *kikkar*, one *kikkar* for each socket.
The one hundred sockets used in the Tabernacle correspond to the one hundred blessings that we are encouraged to make every day (*Rabbi Jacob ben Asher, 14th century*).

exodus 38:27 – 39:8   pekudei

[27] The 100 *kikkar* of silver was used for casting the sockets of the holy (Tabernacle) and the sockets of the partition. One hundred sockets were made from one hundred *kikkar*, one *kikkar* for each socket. [28] From the 1775 shekels he made hooks for the pillars, and he covered their tops and put belts on them.

[29] The copper donated was 70 *kikkar* and 2400 shekels. [30] With it he made the sockets for the entrance to the Tent of Meeting, the copper altar, its copper netting, and all the utensils of the altar, [31] the sockets of the surrounding courtyard, and the sockets of the gate to the courtyard, all the pegs of the Tabernacle and all the pegs of the surrounding courtyard.

Making of the Priestly Garments

39 [1] From the turquoise, purple, and crimson wool they made the meshwork cloths (used to pack the Tabernacle's utensils during transport,) to serve in the holy (Sanctuary), and they made Aaron's holy garments, as God had commanded Moses.

[SECOND READING / FIFTH WHEN JOINED] [2] He made the apron of gold (thread), turquoise, purple, and crimson wool, and twisted fine linen. [3] They hammered out the sheets of gold and cut strands from them to work the gold into the turquoise wool, the purple wool, the crimson wool, and the fine linen, through the work of a professional weaver.

[4] They made connected shoulder straps at both its ends. (The straps were woven separately first and then) connected to it.

[5] Its decorative belt, which is above it, was made from it (professionally woven as one single piece, out of) gold (thread), turquoise, purple, and crimson wool, and twisted fine linen, as God had commanded Moses.

[6] They prepared the *shoham* stones surrounded in gold settings, engraved in (clear script as is used on) a signet ring, with the names of the sons of Israel. [7] He put them on the shoulder straps of the apron as stones of remembrance for the children of Israel, as God had commanded Moses.

[8] He made the breastplate, the work of a professional weaver in a similar fashion to the apron, (i.e.) from gold (thread), turquoise, purple, and crimson wool, and twisted fine linen.

For Moses had told Bezalel to make the apparatus first and the Tabernacle afterward, but Bezalel responded, "Isn't the normal thing to build the house first and then place the items inside?"

Moses answered, "Actually, that's exactly what I heard from God! Your name means 'In the shadow of God.' It is as if you were there when God commanded me."

And that is what Bezalel did—first he made the Tabernacle and then the apparatus (*Rashi, 11th century*).

שמות ל״ט:ח-כו • פקודי

שָׁנִ֥י וְשֵׁ֖שׁ מָשְׁזָֽר: 9 רָב֧וּעַ הָיָ֛ה כָּפ֖וּל עָשׂ֣וּ אֶת־הַחֹ֑שֶׁן זֶ֧רֶת אָרְכּ֛וֹ וְזֶ֥רֶת רָחְבּ֖וֹ כָּפֽוּל: 10 וַיְמַלְאוּ־ב֔וֹ אַרְבָּעָ֖ה ט֣וּרֵי אָ֑בֶן ט֗וּר אֹ֤דֶם פִּטְדָה֙ וּבָרֶ֔קֶת הַטּ֖וּר הָאֶחָֽד: 11 וְהַטּ֖וּר הַשֵּׁנִ֑י נֹ֥פֶךְ סַפִּ֖יר וְיָהֲלֹֽם: 12 וְהַטּ֖וּר הַשְּׁלִישִׁ֑י לֶ֥שֶׁם שְׁב֖וֹ וְאַחְלָֽמָה: 13 וְהַטּוּר֙ הָֽרְבִיעִ֔י תַּרְשִׁ֥ישׁ שֹׁ֖הַם וְיָֽשְׁפֵ֑ה מֽוּסַבֹּ֛ת מִשְׁבְּצֹ֥ת זָהָ֖ב בְּמִלֻּאֹתָֽם: 14 וְ֠הָאֲבָנִ֠ים עַל־שְׁמֹ֨ת בְּנֵֽי־יִשְׂרָאֵ֥ל הֵ֛נָּה שְׁתֵּ֥ים עֶשְׂרֵ֖ה עַל־שְׁמֹתָ֑ם פִּתּוּחֵ֤י חֹתָם֙ אִ֣ישׁ עַל־שְׁמ֔וֹ לִשְׁנֵ֥ים עָשָׂ֖ר שָֽׁבֶט: 15 וַיַּֽעֲשׂ֧וּ עַל־הַחֹ֛שֶׁן שַׁרְשְׁרֹ֥ת גַּבְלֻ֖ת מַֽעֲשֵׂ֣ה עֲבֹ֑ת זָהָ֖ב טָהֽוֹר: 16 וַֽיַּעֲשׂ֗וּ שְׁתֵּי֙ מִשְׁבְּצֹ֣ת זָהָ֔ב וּשְׁתֵּ֖י טַבְּעֹ֣ת זָהָ֑ב וַֽיִּתְּנ֗וּ אֶת־שְׁתֵּי֙ הַטַּבָּעֹ֔ת עַל־שְׁנֵ֖י קְצ֥וֹת הַחֹֽשֶׁן: 17 וַֽיִּתְּנ֗וּ שְׁתֵּי֙ הָֽעֲבֹתֹ֣ת הַזָּהָ֔ב עַל־שְׁתֵּ֖י הַטַּבָּעֹ֑ת עַל־קְצ֖וֹת הַחֹֽשֶׁן: 18 וְאֵ֗ת שְׁתֵּי֙ קְצ֣וֹת שְׁתֵּ֣י הָֽעֲבֹתֹ֔ת נָֽתְנ֖וּ עַל־שְׁתֵּ֣י הַֽמִּשְׁבְּצֹ֑ת וַֽיִּתְּנֻ֛ם עַל־כִּתְפֹ֥ת הָֽאֵפֹ֖ד אֶל־מ֥וּל פָּנָֽיו: 19 וַֽיַּעֲשׂ֗וּ שְׁתֵּי֙ טַבְּעֹ֣ת זָהָ֔ב וַיָּשִׂ֕ימוּ עַל־שְׁנֵ֖י קְצ֣וֹת הַחֹ֑שֶׁן עַל־שְׂפָת֕וֹ אֲשֶׁ֛ר אֶל־עֵ֥בֶר הָֽאֵפֹ֖ד בָּֽיְתָה: 20 וַֽיַּעֲשׂוּ֮ שְׁתֵּ֣י טַבְּעֹ֣ת זָהָב֒ וַֽיִּתְּנֻ֗ם עַל־שְׁתֵּ֨י כִתְפֹ֤ת הָֽאֵפֹד֙ מִלְּמַ֔טָּה מִמּ֣וּל פָּנָ֔יו לְעֻמַּ֖ת מַחְבַּרְתּ֑וֹ מִמַּ֕עַל לְחֵ֖שֶׁב הָֽאֵפֹֽד: 21 וַיִּרְכְּס֣וּ אֶת־הַחֹ֡שֶׁן מִטַּבְּעֹתָיו֩ אֶל־טַבְּעֹ֨ת הָֽאֵפֹ֜ד בִּפְתִ֣יל תְּכֵ֗לֶת לִֽהְיֹת֙ עַל־חֵ֣שֶׁב הָֽאֵפֹ֔ד וְלֹֽא־יִזַּ֣ח הַחֹ֔שֶׁן מֵעַ֖ל הָֽאֵפֹ֑ד כַּֽאֲשֶׁ֛ר צִוָּ֥ה יְהֹוָ֖ה אֶת־מֹשֶֽׁה: פ 22 [THIRD READING / SIXTH WHEN JOINED] וַיַּ֛עַשׂ אֶת־מְעִ֥יל הָֽאֵפֹ֖ד מַֽעֲשֵׂ֣ה אֹרֵ֑ג כְּלִ֖יל תְּכֵֽלֶת: 23 וּפִֽי־הַמְּעִ֥יל בְּתוֹכ֖וֹ כְּפִ֣י תַחְרָ֑א שָׂפָ֥ה לְפִ֛יו סָבִ֖יב לֹ֥א יִקָּרֵֽעַ: 24 וַֽיַּעֲשׂוּ֙ עַל־שׁוּלֵ֣י הַמְּעִ֔יל רִמּוֹנֵ֕י תְּכֵ֥לֶת וְאַרְגָּמָ֖ן וְתוֹלַ֣עַת שָׁנִ֑י מָשְׁזָֽר: 25 וַיַּֽעֲשׂ֥וּ פַֽעֲמֹנֵ֖י זָהָ֣ב טָה֑וֹר וַיִּתְּנ֤וּ אֶת־הַפַּֽעֲמֹנִים֙ בְּת֣וֹךְ הָרִמֹּנִ֔ים עַל־שׁוּלֵ֥י הַמְּעִ֖יל סָבִ֑יב בְּת֖וֹךְ הָֽרִמֹּנִֽים: 26 פַּֽעֲמֹ֤ן וְרִמֹּן֙ פַּֽעֲמֹ֣ן וְרִמֹּ֔ן

578

39:25-30 Bells of pure gold … diadem of pure gold. Why does the Torah not give a precise accounting of the gold, as it did with the silver and copper (above, 38:27-30)?

The *Midrash* states that after the Tabernacle's components had been made, Moses made an accounting together with Ithamar and the Levites, showing how the donations had been

⁹ When folded (ready to be worn by the High Priest), it was square, one span (half a cubit) in its length and one span in its width.

¹⁰ They set it with four rows of precious stones.

One row was a row of red quartz, emerald, and yellow quartz.

¹¹ The second row: ruby, sapphire, and beryl (blue-green gem).

¹² The third row: red zirconium, striped quartz, and (violet) amethyst.

¹³ The fourth row: yellow-green olivine, onyx, and jasper (opaque quartz).

They were inlaid in gold in their settings.

¹⁴ The names of the children of Israel were on the stones, twelve names in all. The names of the twelve tribes were engraved according to (the order of their birth) in (clear script, as is used on) a signet ring.

¹⁵ They made chains for the breastplate at the edges, of braided, pure gold. ¹⁶ They made two settings of gold and two golden rings, and they placed the two rings on the two ends of the breastplate, ¹⁷ and they placed the two golden cables on the two rings, at the ends of the breastplate. ¹⁸ They placed the two ends of the two cables upon the two settings, and these they placed on the shoulder straps of the apron, on its front part. ¹⁹ They made two golden rings, and they placed them on the two ends of the breastplate, on its edge that is toward the inner side of the apron. ²⁰ They made two golden rings and placed them on the two shoulder straps of the apron, from below, toward its front, adjacent to its seam, above the band of the apron. ²¹ They fastened the breastplate by its rings to the rings of the apron with a turquoise cord, so as to be upon the band of the apron, and the breastplate would then not move off the apron, as God had commanded Moses.

[THIRD READING / FIFTH WHEN JOINED] ²² He made the robe (worn under) the apron entirely of turquoise wool, through a professional weaver. ²³ Its collar at the top was hemmed inside, like the collar of a coat of armor, so that it should not be torn.

²⁴ On its bottom edge they made pomegranate shapes of twisted turquoise, purple, and crimson wool. ²⁵ They made bells of pure gold, and they placed the bells between the pomegranates on the bottom edge of the robe, all around, between the pomegranates. ²⁶ A golden bell (was followed by) a pomegranate, (which was followed by) a golden bell and (then another) pomegranate (and so on), on the bottom edge of the robe, all around. (It was thus ready) for service (in the Tabernacle), as God had commanded Moses.

The daily blessings represent the "foundations" of a spiritual outlook on life, just as the sockets were the underpinnings and base of the Tabernacle (*Rabbi Isaac Meir Alter of Gur, 19th century*).

שמות לט:כו-מ פקודי

עַל־שׁוּלֵ֥י הַמְּעִ֖יל סָבִ֑יב לְשָׁרֵ֕ת כַּאֲשֶׁ֛ר צִוָּ֥ה יְהֹוָ֖ה אֶת־מֹשֶֽׁה: ס 27 וַֽיַּעֲשׂ֛וּ אֶת־הַכָּתְנֹ֥ת שֵׁ֖שׁ מַעֲשֵׂ֣ה אֹרֵ֑ג לְאַהֲרֹ֖ן וּלְבָנָֽיו: 28 וְאֵת֙ הַמִּצְנֶ֣פֶת שֵׁ֔שׁ וְאֶת־פַּאֲרֵ֥י הַמִּגְבָּעֹ֖ת שֵׁ֑שׁ וְאֶת־מִכְנְסֵ֥י הַבָּ֖ד שֵׁ֥שׁ מָשְׁזָֽר: 29 וְאֶת־הָאַבְנֵ֞ט שֵׁ֣שׁ מָשְׁזָ֗ר וּתְכֵ֧לֶת וְאַרְגָּמָ֛ן וְתוֹלַ֥עַת שָׁנִ֖י מַעֲשֵׂ֣ה רֹקֵ֑ם כַּאֲשֶׁ֛ר צִוָּ֥ה יְהֹוָ֖ה אֶת־מֹשֶֽׁה: ס 30 וַֽיַּעֲשׂ֛וּ אֶת־צִ֥יץ נֵֽזֶר־הַקֹּ֖דֶשׁ זָהָ֣ב טָה֑וֹר וַיִּכְתְּב֣וּ עָלָ֗יו מִכְתַּב֙ פִּתּוּחֵ֣י חוֹתָ֔ם קֹ֖דֶשׁ לַיהֹוָֽה: 31 וַיִּתְּנ֤וּ עָלָיו֙ פְּתִ֣יל תְּכֵ֔לֶת לָתֵ֥ת עַל־הַמִּצְנֶ֖פֶת מִלְמָ֑עְלָה כַּאֲשֶׁ֛ר צִוָּ֥ה יְהֹוָ֖ה אֶת־מֹשֶֽׁה: ס 32 וַתֵּ֕כֶל כׇּל־עֲבֹדַ֕ת מִשְׁכַּ֖ן אֹ֣הֶל מוֹעֵ֑ד וַֽיַּעֲשׂוּ֙ בְּנֵ֣י יִשְׂרָאֵ֔ל כְּ֠כֹ֠ל אֲשֶׁ֨ר צִוָּ֧ה יְהֹוָ֛ה אֶת־מֹשֶׁ֖ה כֵּ֥ן עָשֽׂוּ: פ 33 [FOURTH READING] וַיָּבִ֤יאוּ אֶת־הַמִּשְׁכָּן֙ אֶל־מֹשֶׁ֔ה אֶת־הָאֹ֖הֶל וְאֶת־כׇּל־כֵּלָ֑יו קְרָסָ֣יו קְרָשָׁ֔יו בְּרִיחָ֖ו וְעַמֻּדָ֥יו וַאֲדָנָֽיו: 34 וְאֶת־מִכְסֵ֞ה עוֹרֹ֤ת הָֽאֵילִם֙ הַמְאׇדָּמִ֔ים וְאֶת־מִכְסֵ֖ה עֹרֹ֣ת הַתְּחָשִׁ֑ים וְאֵ֖ת פָּרֹ֥כֶת הַמָּסָֽךְ: 35 אֶת־אֲר֥וֹן הָעֵדֻ֖ת וְאֶת־בַּדָּ֑יו וְאֵ֖ת הַכַּפֹּֽרֶת: 36 אֶת־הַשֻּׁלְחָן֙ אֶת־כׇּל־כֵּלָ֔יו וְאֵ֖ת לֶ֥חֶם הַפָּנִֽים: 37 אֶת־הַמְּנֹרָ֨ה הַטְּהֹרָ֜ה אֶת־נֵרֹתֶ֗יהָ נֵרֹ֛ת הַמַּעֲרָכָ֖ה וְאֶת־כׇּל־כֵּלֶ֑יהָ וְאֵ֖ת שֶׁ֥מֶן הַמָּאֽוֹר: 38 וְאֵת֙ מִזְבַּ֣ח הַזָּהָ֔ב וְאֵת֙ שֶׁ֣מֶן הַמִּשְׁחָ֔ה וְאֵ֖ת קְטֹ֣רֶת הַסַּמִּ֑ים וְאֵ֕ת מָסַ֖ךְ פֶּ֥תַח הָאֹֽהֶל: 39 אֵ֣ת ׀ מִזְבַּ֣ח הַנְּחֹ֗שֶׁת וְאֶת־מִכְבַּ֤ר הַנְּחֹ֨שֶׁת֙ אֲשֶׁר־ל֔וֹ אֶת־בַּדָּ֖יו וְאֶת־כׇּל־כֵּלָ֑יו אֶת־הַכִּיֹּ֖ר וְאֶת־כַּנּֽוֹ: 40 אֵת֩ קַלְעֵ֨י הֶחָצֵ֜ר אֶת־עַמֻּדֶ֣יהָ וְאֶת־אֲדָנֶ֗יהָ וְאֶת־הַמָּסָךְ֙ לְשַׁ֣עַר הֶֽחָצֵ֔ר אֶת־מֵיתָרָ֖יו וִיתֵדֹתֶ֑יהָ וְאֵ֗ת כׇּל־כְּלֵ֛י עֲבֹדַ֥ת הַמִּשְׁכָּ֖ן לְאֹ֥הֶל מוֹעֵֽד:

In fact, these 1,775 shekels of silver had been used to make the hooks which were attached to the pillars of the courtyard, but this detail had been forgotten. God perceived that Moses' reputation was in danger, so He made a voice announce, "The 1,775 shekels were used for the hooks of the pillars."

Once Moses' honesty had been attested to, the Jewish people did not need any accounting for the gold. Thus, the Torah does not mention the details of how the gold was allocated (*Rabbi Ephraim of Luntshits, 16th–17th century*).

exodus 39:27–40   pekudei

²⁷ They made the checkered tunic from linen through a professional weaver, for Aaron and for his sons, ²⁸ the linen turban (for Aaron), and the beautiful linen turbans (for his sons), and the linen pants, (all from) fine twisted linen, ²⁹ the professionally embroidered sash of fine linen twisted with turquoise, purple, and crimson wool, as God had commanded Moses.

³⁰ They made the forehead-plate, the holy diadem, of pure gold, and they engraved on it in (clear script, as is used on) a signet ring (the words), "Holy to God." ³¹ They placed on it a ribbon of turquoise wool to go over the turban from above, as God had commanded Moses.

The Tabernacle Is Brought to Moses

³² All the work of the Tabernacle of the Tent of Meeting was completed. The children of Israel had done everything that God had commanded Moses. They did it (correctly).

[FOURTH READING] ³³ (When they found that the beams were too heavy to erect,) they brought the Tabernacle to Moses, the tent and all its furnishings, its clasps, its beams, its bolts, its pillars and its sockets, ³⁴ the covering of rams' skins dyed red, the covering of *taḥash* skins, and the partition, ³⁵ the Ark of the Testimony and its poles and the lid, ³⁶ the table, all its utensils and the multisurface bread, ³⁷ the pure candelabrum, its lamps—the lamps which were to be arranged (daily)—all its utensils and the oil for lighting, ³⁸ the golden altar, the anointing oil and the incense, and the curtain of the entrance to the Tent, ³⁹ the copper altar and its copper netting, its poles and all its utensils, the urn and its base, ⁴⁰ the curtains of the courtyard, its pillars and its sockets, the curtain for the gate of the courtyard, its ropes and its pegs, and all the utensils for the service of the Tabernacle,

allocated, in order to prove to the Jewish people that he was not guilty of misappropriation. However, the accounting of silver showed an unaccounted 1,775 shekels of silver.

spiritual vitamin

> The purpose of the Torah is to insure that you act consistently in the best interests of yourself and society; that you avoid groping in darkness, confused by conflicting ideas and theories around you; and that you cease to be perplexed by conflicting emotions and instincts within you, inherent in all human beings.

שמות לט:מא - מ:יד — פקודי

41 אֶת־בִּגְדֵ֥י הַשְּׂרָ֖ד לְשָׁרֵ֣ת בַּקֹּ֑דֶשׁ אֶת־בִּגְדֵ֤י הַקֹּ֙דֶשׁ֙ לְאַהֲרֹ֣ן הַכֹּהֵ֔ן וְאֶת־בִּגְדֵ֥י בָנָ֖יו לְכַהֵֽן: 42 כְּכֹ֛ל אֲשֶׁר־צִוָּ֥ה יְהֹוָ֖ה אֶת־מֹשֶׁ֑ה כֵּ֤ן עָשׂוּ֙ בְּנֵ֣י יִשְׂרָאֵ֔ל אֵ֖ת כָּל־הָעֲבֹדָֽה: 43 וַיַּ֨רְא מֹשֶׁ֜ה אֶת־כָּל־הַמְּלָאכָ֗ה וְהִנֵּה֙ עָשׂ֣וּ אֹתָ֔הּ כַּאֲשֶׁ֛ר צִוָּ֥ה יְהֹוָ֖ה כֵּ֣ן עָשׂ֑וּ וַיְבָ֥רֶךְ אֹתָ֖ם מֹשֶֽׁה: פ

מ 1 וַיְדַבֵּ֥ר יְהֹוָ֖ה אֶל־מֹשֶׁ֥ה לֵּאמֹֽר: 2 בְּיוֹם־הַחֹ֥דֶשׁ [FIFTH READING / SEVENTH WHEN JOINED] הָרִאשׁ֖וֹן בְּאֶחָ֣ד לַחֹ֑דֶשׁ תָּקִ֕ים אֶת־מִשְׁכַּ֖ן אֹ֥הֶל מוֹעֵֽד: 3 וְשַׂמְתָּ֣ שָׁ֔ם אֵ֖ת אֲר֣וֹן הָעֵד֑וּת וְסַכֹּתָ֥ עַל־הָאָרֹ֖ן אֶת־הַפָּרֹֽכֶת: 4 וְהֵבֵאתָ֙ אֶת־הַשֻּׁלְחָ֔ן וְעָרַכְתָּ֖ אֶת־עֶרְכּ֑וֹ וְהֵבֵאתָ֙ אֶת־הַמְּנֹרָ֔ה וְהַעֲלֵיתָ֖ אֶת־נֵרֹתֶֽיהָ: 5 וְנָתַתָּ֞ה אֶת־מִזְבַּ֣ח הַזָּהָ֗ב לִקְטֹ֙רֶת֙ לִפְנֵ֣י אֲר֣וֹן הָעֵדֻ֔ת וְשַׂמְתָּ֛ אֶת־מָסַ֥ךְ הַפֶּ֖תַח לַמִּשְׁכָּֽן: 6 וְנָ֣תַתָּ֔ה אֵ֖ת מִזְבַּ֣ח הָעֹלָ֑ה לִפְנֵ֕י פֶּ֖תַח מִשְׁכַּ֥ן אֹֽהֶל־מוֹעֵֽד: 7 וְנָֽתַתָּ֙ אֶת־הַכִּיֹּ֔ר בֵּֽין־אֹ֥הֶל מוֹעֵ֖ד וּבֵ֣ין הַמִּזְבֵּ֑חַ וְנָתַתָּ֥ שָׁ֖ם מָֽיִם: 8 וְשַׂמְתָּ֥ אֶת־הֶחָצֵ֖ר סָבִ֑יב וְנָ֣תַתָּ֔ אֶת־מָסַ֖ךְ שַׁ֥עַר הֶחָצֵֽר: 9 וְלָקַחְתָּ֙ אֶת־שֶׁ֣מֶן הַמִּשְׁחָ֔ה וּמָשַׁחְתָּ֥ אֶת־הַמִּשְׁכָּ֖ן וְאֶת־כָּל־אֲשֶׁר־בּ֑וֹ וְקִדַּשְׁתָּ֥ אֹת֛וֹ וְאֶת־כָּל־כֵּלָ֖יו וְהָ֥יָה קֹֽדֶשׁ: 10 וּמָשַׁחְתָּ֛ אֶת־מִזְבַּ֥ח הָעֹלָ֖ה וְאֶת־כָּל־כֵּלָ֑יו וְקִדַּשְׁתָּ֙ אֶת־הַמִּזְבֵּ֔חַ וְהָיָ֥ה הַמִּזְבֵּ֖חַ קֹ֥דֶשׁ קָֽדָשִֽׁים: 11 וּמָשַׁחְתָּ֥ אֶת־הַכִּיֹּ֖ר וְאֶת־כַּנּ֑וֹ וְקִדַּשְׁתָּ֖ אֹתֽוֹ: 12 וְהִקְרַבְתָּ֤ אֶת־אַהֲרֹן֙ וְאֶת־בָּנָ֔יו אֶל־פֶּ֖תַח אֹ֣הֶל מוֹעֵ֑ד וְרָחַצְתָּ֥ אֹתָ֖ם בַּמָּֽיִם: 13 וְהִלְבַּשְׁתָּ֙ אֶת־אַהֲרֹ֔ן אֵ֖ת בִּגְדֵ֣י הַקֹּ֑דֶשׁ וּמָשַׁחְתָּ֥ אֹת֛וֹ וְקִדַּשְׁתָּ֥ אֹת֖וֹ וְכִהֵ֥ן לִֽי: 14 וְאֶת־בָּנָ֖יו תַּקְרִ֑יב וְהִלְבַּשְׁתָּ֥ אֹתָ֖ם

When Moses realized that they had effectively balanced religious passion with careful observance, he *blessed them*—to continue always in the same fashion (*Rabbi Samson Raphael Hirsch, 19th century*).

40:2 You should set up the Tabernacle, the Tent of Meeting. Moses already had his own personal "Tabernacle," the "Tent of Meeting," which was outside the camp (above, 33:7). Therefore, he did not need to be involved in constructing the Tabernacle, which was primarily for the Divine Presence to dwell among the Jewish people. Nevertheless, God told Moses that he should be involved, and gave him the task of erecting the Tabernacle.

(i.e.) the Tent of Meeting, ⁴¹ the meshwork cloths which are used in the holy (Sanctuary to cover the apparatus during transportation), the holy garments for Aaron the High Priest, and his sons' garments for serving as priests.

⁴² The children of Israel did all the work in accordance with everything which God had commanded Moses. ⁴³ Moses saw the entire work, and—look!—they had done it as God had commanded. They had done it (correctly), and so Moses blessed them.

God Instructs Moses to Erect the Tabernacle

40 [FIFTH READING / SEVENTH WHEN JOINED] ¹ God spoke to Moses, saying: ² "On the day (of inauguration in) the first month, on the first of the month, you should set up the Tabernacle, the Tent of Meeting. ³ You should place the Ark of the Testimony there, and you should protect the ark with the partition. ⁴ You should bring in the table and set up its arrangement (of multisurface bread). You should bring in the candelabrum and kindle its lamps. ⁵ You should place the golden incense altar in front of the Ark of the Testimony, and you should put up the curtain of the entrance to the Tabernacle.

⁶ "You should place the sacrificial altar in front of the entrance of the Tabernacle of the Tent of Meeting. ⁷ You should place the urn between the Tent of Meeting and the altar, and you should put water there. ⁸ You should set up the surrounding courtyard, and you should put up the curtain for the entrance to the courtyard.

⁹ "You should take the anointing oil and anoint the Tabernacle and everything inside it. You should sanctify it and all its equipment, and it will become holy. ¹⁰ You should anoint the sacrificial altar and all its utensils. You should sanctify the altar, and the altar will become a holy of holies. ¹¹ You should anoint the urn and its base and sanctify it.

¹² "You should bring Aaron and his sons near the entrance of the Tent of Meeting, and you should bathe them in water. ¹³ You should dress Aaron with the holy garments, and you should anoint him and sanctify him so that he may serve Me as a priest. ¹⁴ You should bring his sons near and clothe them with checkered tunics.

43. Moses saw the entire work and—look!—they had done it as God had commanded. They had done it (correctly), and so Moses blessed them. There is always a danger that religious enthusiasm might lead a person beyond the scope of what his religion actually demands. Moses was impressed that, in this case, the children of Israel had managed to act enthusiastically without deviating from what needed to be done. *"They had done it"*—the entire nation, young and old, had enthusiastically devoted themselves to building the Tabernacle. And *"they had done it as God had commanded,"* keeping strictly to the precise instructions. No artisan had attempted to bring his own ideas to bear on his work.

כֻּתֳּנֹֽת: 15 וּמָשַׁחְתָּ֣ אֹתָ֗ם כַּאֲשֶׁ֤ר מָשַׁ֙חְתָּ֙ אֶת־אֲבִיהֶ֔ם וְכִהֲנ֖וּ לִ֑י וְ֠הָיְתָ֠ה לִהְיֹ֨ת לָהֶ֧ם מָשְׁחָתָ֛ם לִכְהֻנַּ֥ת עוֹלָ֖ם לְדֹרֹתָֽם: 16 וַיַּ֖עַשׂ מֹשֶׁ֑ה כְּ֠כֹל אֲשֶׁ֨ר צִוָּ֧ה יְהֹוָ֛ה אֹת֖וֹ כֵּ֥ן עָשָֽׂה: ס [SIXTH READING] 17 וַיְהִ֞י בַּחֹ֧דֶשׁ הָרִאשׁ֛וֹן בַּשָּׁנָ֥ה הַשֵּׁנִ֖ית בְּאֶחָ֣ד לַחֹ֑דֶשׁ הוּקַ֖ם הַמִּשְׁכָּֽן: 18 וַיָּ֨קֶם מֹשֶׁ֜ה אֶת־הַמִּשְׁכָּ֗ן וַיִּתֵּן֙ אֶת־אֲדָנָ֔יו וַיָּ֙שֶׂם֙ אֶת־קְרָשָׁ֔יו וַיִּתֵּ֖ן אֶת־בְּרִיחָ֑יו וַיָּ֖קֶם אֶת־עַמּוּדָֽיו: 19 וַיִּפְרֹ֤שׂ אֶת־הָאֹ֙הֶל֙ עַל־הַמִּשְׁכָּ֔ן וַיָּ֜שֶׂם אֶת־מִכְסֵ֥ה הָאֹ֛הֶל עָלָ֖יו מִלְמָ֑עְלָה כַּאֲשֶׁ֛ר צִוָּ֥ה יְהֹוָ֖ה אֶת־מֹשֶֽׁה: ס 20 וַיִּקַּ֞ח וַיִּתֵּ֤ן אֶת־הָעֵדֻת֙ אֶל־הָ֣אָרֹ֔ן וַיָּ֥שֶׂם אֶת־הַבַּדִּ֖ים עַל־הָאָרֹ֑ן וַיִּתֵּ֧ן אֶת־הַכַּפֹּ֛רֶת עַל־הָאָרֹ֖ן מִלְמָֽעְלָה: 21 וַיָּבֵ֤א אֶת־הָֽאָרֹן֙ אֶל־הַמִּשְׁכָּ֔ן וַיָּ֕שֶׂם אֵ֖ת פָּרֹ֣כֶת הַמָּסָ֑ךְ

empowered the nation to spiritually rehabilitate themselves and rebuild their Sanctuary seven times, after each was destroyed.

The same is true in our personal experience. God gives us the power to rebuild our spiritual lives and inner sanctuaries, time and again. Although we may stumble or even collapse, we are always able to rise again (*Rabbi Abraham Mordecai Alter of Gur, 20th century*).

18. Moses set up the Tabernacle. The "Tabernacle" refers specifically to the woven tapestries which covered the Tabernacle. We are informed here that these coverings were "set up" *before* the supporting beams were erected (*Rabbi Obadiah Sforno, 16th century*).

What was the necessity for this strange construction procedure? Surely it would have made more practical sense to erect the beams first and then spread the tapestries over them?

After the sin of the Golden Calf, the Jewish people were hardly ready for the great revelations of the Tabernacle, where the Divine Presence was to rest on earth. But God did not withhold the Tabernacle from them, despite their low standing. Their unreadiness, however, was hinted to by the order of construction: the tapestries, which constituted the key component of the

spiritual vitamin

> Both sanctuaries—the "sanctuary" that is within every person, and the Sanctuary which God commanded to be built as a dwelling place for Him on earth—are mentioned in the same sentence in the Torah: "*They should make a Sanctuary (dedicated) to Me and I will dwell among them*" (above, 25:8)—"Within each and every one of them," as our Sages interpret this verse. In other words, the ultimate purpose of the Sanctuary built for God is to make every heart and mind a fitting abode for God to dwell in.

Moses Erects the Tabernacle

[SIXTH READING] ¹⁶ Moses did according to all that God had commanded him. He did so (precisely). ¹⁷ It was in the first month of the second year, on the first day of the month, that the Tabernacle was set up. ¹⁸ Moses set up the Tabernacle, positioned its sockets, put up its beams, put in its bolts, and set up its pillars (with miraculous Divine assistance, as the beams were too heavy to lift). ¹⁹ He spread the (goats' hair sheet) tent over the Tabernacle, and he placed the cover of the tent over it from above, as God had commanded Moses.

²⁰ He took the (Tablets of) Testimony and placed them into the ark, put the poles on the ark, and placed the lid on the ark from above. ²¹ He brought the ark into the Tabernacle and placed the partition so that it formed a protective covering in front of the Ark of the Testimony, as God had commanded Moses.

Food for thought

1. How has reading the *Book of Exodus* over the past weeks inspired you?

2. Identify one mental or emotional constraint you have freed yourself from.

3. Identify one permanent change that it has inspired in you.

---

¹⁵ You should anoint them, as you have anointed their father, so that they may serve Me as priests. This should be done so that their anointment will confer on them an everlasting priesthood throughout their generations."

This teaches us that a person cannot only busy himself with his own spiritual development and Torah study. He needs also to be involved in helping others, in the same way that God instructed Moses to be involved in the Tabernacle: not just as a spiritual leader and mentor, but also, "with his hands" (*Rabbi Menahem Mendel Schneerson, 20th century*).

17. The Tabernacle was set up. On each of the seven days of inauguration, Moses erected and then dismantled the entire structure. Finally, on the eighth day, *"the Tabernacle was set up"* permanently.

This eerily foreshadowed the future fate of the Sanctuary, which was destined to rebuild a number of times: in Gilgal, Shiloh, Nob, and Gibeon, and twice in Jerusalem. There were seven structures in all.

Echoing Moses' seven days of constructing and dismantling the Sanctuary in the desert, each of these structures was either dismantled (for relocation) or destroyed by enemies, forcing the construction of a replacement.

God promised, however, that corresponding to the efforts of Moses on the eighth day of inauguration, a final, eighth structure—the Third Temple in Jerusalem—will eventually be built, and it will never be demolished: *"In the end of days, the mountain of God's House will be firmly established at the top of mountains and will be exalted above peaks, and all the nations will stream to it. Many nations will go, saying, 'Come, let us ascend to the Mount of God, to the House of God of Jacob, and He will teach us of His ways and we will walk in His path' ... nation will not lift up a sword against another nation and they will they no longer learn war"* (Isaiah 2:2-4; *Rabbi Samson Raphael Hirsch, 19th century*).

For seven days, Moses set up the Tabernacle all over again single-handedly, for only Moses—a man of God—was able to "resurrect" a dismantled Sanctuary. Moses' actions here

שמות מ:כא-לח • פקודי

וַיָּבֵ֤א אֶת־הָאָרֹן֙ אֶל־הַמִּשְׁכָּ֔ן וַיָּ֕שֶׂם אֵ֖ת פָּרֹ֣כֶת הַמָּסָ֑ךְ וַיָּ֕סֶךְ עַ֖ל אֲר֣וֹן הָעֵד֑וּת כַּאֲשֶׁ֛ר צִוָּ֥ה יְהֹוָ֖ה אֶת־מֹשֶֽׁה: ס 22 וַיִּתֵּ֣ן אֶת־הַשֻּׁלְחָ֗ן בְּאֹ֤הֶל מוֹעֵד֙ עַ֣ל יֶ֣רֶךְ הַמִּשְׁכָּ֖ן צָפֹ֑נָה מִח֖וּץ לַפָּרֹֽכֶת: 23 וַיַּעֲרֹ֥ךְ עָלָ֛יו עֵ֥רֶךְ לֶ֖חֶם לִפְנֵ֣י יְהֹוָ֑ה כַּאֲשֶׁ֛ר צִוָּ֥ה יְהֹוָ֖ה אֶת־מֹשֶֽׁה: ס 24 וַיָּ֤שֶׂם אֶת־הַמְּנֹרָה֙ בְּאֹ֣הֶל מוֹעֵ֔ד נֹ֖כַח הַשֻּׁלְחָ֑ן עַ֛ל יֶ֥רֶךְ הַמִּשְׁכָּ֖ן נֶֽגְבָּה: 25 וַיַּ֥עַל הַנֵּרֹ֖ת לִפְנֵ֣י יְהֹוָ֑ה כַּאֲשֶׁ֛ר צִוָּ֥ה יְהֹוָ֖ה אֶת־מֹשֶֽׁה: ס 26 וַיָּ֛שֶׂם אֶת־מִזְבַּ֥ח הַזָּהָ֖ב בְּאֹ֣הֶל מוֹעֵ֑ד לִפְנֵ֖י הַפָּרֹֽכֶת: 27 וַיַּקְטֵ֥ר עָלָ֖יו קְטֹ֣רֶת סַמִּ֑ים כַּאֲשֶׁ֛ר צִוָּ֥ה יְהֹוָ֖ה אֶת־מֹשֶֽׁה: ס [SEVENTH READING] 28 וַיָּ֛שֶׂם אֶת־מָסַ֥ךְ הַפֶּ֖תַח לַמִּשְׁכָּֽן: 29 וְאֵ֗ת מִזְבַּ֤ח הָעֹלָה֙ שָׂ֔ם פֶּ֖תַח מִשְׁכַּ֣ן אֹֽהֶל־מוֹעֵ֑ד וַיַּ֣עַל עָלָ֗יו אֶת־הָעֹלָה֙ וְאֶת־הַמִּנְחָ֔ה כַּאֲשֶׁ֛ר צִוָּ֥ה יְהֹוָ֖ה אֶת־מֹשֶֽׁה: ס 30 וַיָּ֙שֶׂם֙ אֶת־הַכִּיֹּ֔ר בֵּֽין־אֹ֥הֶל מוֹעֵ֖ד וּבֵ֣ין הַמִּזְבֵּ֑חַ וַיִּתֵּ֥ן שָׁ֛מָּה מַ֖יִם לְרָחְצָֽה: 31 וְרָחֲצ֣וּ מִמֶּ֔נּוּ מֹשֶׁ֖ה וְאַהֲרֹ֣ן וּבָנָ֑יו אֶת־יְדֵיהֶ֖ם וְאֶת־רַגְלֵיהֶֽם: 32 בְּבֹאָ֞ם אֶל־אֹ֤הֶל מוֹעֵד֙ וּבְקׇרְבָתָ֣ם אֶל־הַמִּזְבֵּ֔חַ יִרְחָ֑צוּ כַּאֲשֶׁ֛ר צִוָּ֥ה יְהֹוָ֖ה אֶת־מֹשֶֽׁה: ס 33 וַיָּ֣קֶם אֶת־הֶחָצֵ֗ר סָבִיב֙ לַמִּשְׁכָּ֣ן וְלַמִּזְבֵּ֔חַ וַיִּתֵּ֕ן אֶת־מָסַ֖ךְ שַׁ֣עַר הֶחָצֵ֑ר וַיְכַ֥ל מֹשֶׁ֖ה אֶת־הַמְּלָאכָֽה: פ [MAFTIR] 34 וַיְכַ֥ס הֶעָנָ֖ן אֶת־אֹ֣הֶל מוֹעֵ֑ד וּכְב֣וֹד יְהֹוָ֔ה מָלֵ֖א אֶת־הַמִּשְׁכָּֽן: 35 וְלֹא־יָכֹ֣ל מֹשֶׁ֗ה לָבוֹא֙ אֶל־אֹ֣הֶל מוֹעֵ֔ד כִּֽי־שָׁכַ֥ן עָלָ֖יו הֶעָנָ֑ן וּכְב֣וֹד יְהֹוָ֔ה מָלֵ֖א אֶת־הַמִּשְׁכָּֽן: 36 וּבְהֵעָל֤וֹת הֶֽעָנָן֙ מֵעַ֣ל הַמִּשְׁכָּ֔ן יִסְע֖וּ בְּנֵ֣י יִשְׂרָאֵ֑ל בְּכֹ֖ל מַסְעֵיהֶֽם: 37 וְאִם־לֹ֥א יֵעָלֶ֖ה הֶעָנָ֑ן וְלֹ֣א יִסְע֔וּ עַד־י֖וֹם הֵעָלֹתֽוֹ: 38 כִּי֩ עֲנַ֨ן יְהֹוָ֤ה עַֽל־הַמִּשְׁכָּן֙ יוֹמָ֔ם וְאֵ֕שׁ תִּהְיֶ֥ה לַ֖יְלָה בּ֑וֹ לְעֵינֵ֥י כׇל־בֵּֽית־יִשְׂרָאֵ֖ל בְּכׇל־מַסְעֵיהֶֽם:

חֲזַק חֲזַק וְנִתְחַזֵּק

צ"ב פסוקים, בלי כ"ל סימן. סכום פסוקי ספר. ואלה שמות אלף ומאתים ותשעה, אר"ט סימן, וחציו אלהים לא תקלל. ופרשיותיו י"א א"י זה בית אשר תבנו לי סימן. וסדריו כ"ט ולילה לילו יחו"ה דעת סימן, ופרקיו מ' תורת אלהיו בלב"ו סימן, מנין הפתוחות ס"ט והסתומות צ"ה. סך הכל קס"ד פרשיות ישלח עזרך מקודש ומציון יסעד"ך סימן.

²² He placed the table in the Tent of Meeting in the northern half of the Tabernacle, outside the partition. ²³ He set an arrangement of bread upon it before God, as God had commanded Moses.

²⁴ He placed the candelabrum in the Tent of Meeting, opposite the table, in the southern half of the Tabernacle. ²⁵ He kindled the lamps before God, as God had commanded Moses.

²⁶ He placed the golden altar in the Tent of Meeting in front of the partition. ²⁷ He made the incense go up in smoke on it, as God had commanded Moses.

[SEVENTH READING] ²⁸ He put up the curtain for the entrance of the Tabernacle.

²⁹ He placed the sacrificial altar in front of the entrance of the Tabernacle, the Tent of Meeting, and he offered up the (daily) burnt-offering and the (accompanying) meal-offering on it, as God had commanded Moses.

³⁰ He placed the urn between the Tent of Meeting and the altar, and he put water there for washing. ³¹ Moses, Aaron, and his sons washed their hands and their feet from it. ³² Whenever they entered the Tent of Meeting and whenever they approached the altar they would wash, as God had commanded Moses.

³³ He set up the courtyard surrounding the Tabernacle and the altar, and he put up the curtain at the entrance to the courtyard. And, (with this,) Moses completed the work.

[MAFTIR] ³⁴ The cloud covered the Tent of Meeting, and the glory of God filled the Tabernacle. ³⁵ Moses could not enter the Tent of Meeting because the cloud rested upon it and the glory of God filled the Tabernacle.

³⁶ When the cloud rose up from over the Tabernacle, the children of Israel would set out on all their journeys. ³⁷ But if the cloud did not rise up, they did not set out until the day that it rose. ³⁸ For God's cloud would remain on the Tabernacle by day, and there was fire on it at night, before the eyes of the entire house of Israel in all their encampments.

The congregation, followed by the reader, proclaims:

Be strong! Be strong! And may we be strengthened!

Haftarot: Pekudei—page 1342. *Shekalim*—page 1424. *Parah*—page 1431. *Ha-Ḥodesh*—page 1433.

Maftir: Shekalim—page 520 (30:11–16). *Parah*—page 932 (19:1–22).
Ha-Ḥodesh—page 392 (12:1–20).

Tabernacle, were spread *before* the support beams were in place, suggesting that the people were granted a revelation that they were not yet able to "support" on their own merits (*Rabbi Samuel Bornstein of Sochaczew, 20ᵗʰ century*).

ספר ויקרא

THE BOOK *of* LEVITICUS

Va-Yikra' means **"He affectionately called."** God is calling to you **intimately** to **connect** with Him, to achieve **harmony** and **balance** in your life. He wants to **free** you from your **distractions** and ensure that your life flows with His **unbounded love.**

VA-YIKRA' ויקרא

BURNT-OFFERINGS	1:1–17
MEAL-OFFERINGS	2:1–13
THE *'OMER*-OFFERING	2:14–16
PEACE-OFFERINGS	3:1–17
SIN-OFFERINGS	4:1 – 5:13
GUILT-OFFERINGS	5:14–26

NAME
Va-Yikra'

MEANING
"And He called"

LINES IN TORAH SCROLL
215

PARASHIYYOT
13 open; 8 closed

VERSES
111

WORDS
1673

LETTERS
6222

DATE
Nisan – 20 *Iyyar*, 2449

LOCATION
Sinai Desert

KEY PEOPLE
Moses, Priests

MITZVOT
11 positive; 5 prohibitions

MASORETIC FEATURES
The letter *alef* of the word *va-yikra'* (1:1) is undersized.

CHARACTER PROFILE

NAME
Nasi

MEANING
Leader; prince; president

FUNCTION
Highest-ranking member and president of the *Sanhedrin* (supreme Rabbinic Court); responsible for: determining the calendar by proclaiming the new moon and leap years, proclaiming national fast days in an emergency, ordaining rabbis and appointing judges

ACTIVE PERIOD
191 BCE – 425 CE. The last *nasi* was Gamaliel VI, executed by Emperor Theodosius II, who also terminated the office of *nasi*. There were 21 in all, including the famous Rabbi Judah the *Nasi*, author of the *Mishnah*

SACRIFICES

Korban (sacrifice) means "draw near": bringing a sacrifice draws a person closer to God. Today, prayer is used instead to strengthen our natural connection to God (1:2).

SENSITIVITY

So that the poor man would not have to feel ashamed that he was unable to afford an animal, God arranged a special sacrifice for him. In fact, the commentaries write that God considers the poor man's meal offering "as if he has sacrificed his very soul" (2:1).

LEADERSHIP

A true leader confesses his unintentional sins and seeks to rectify them. The example that he sets is one of humility and integrity, to encourage others to examine their actions and fix them (4:22).

ויקרא א:א-ה

א 1 וַיִּקְרָ֖א אֶל־מֹשֶׁ֑ה וַיְדַבֵּ֤ר יְהֹוָה֙ אֵלָ֔יו מֵאֹ֥הֶל מוֹעֵ֖ד לֵאמֹֽר: 2 דַּבֵּ֞ר אֶל־בְּנֵ֤י יִשְׂרָאֵל֙ וְאָמַרְתָּ֣ אֲלֵהֶ֔ם אָדָ֗ם כִּֽי־יַקְרִ֥יב מִכֶּ֛ם קׇרְבָּ֖ן לַֽיהֹוָ֑ה מִן־הַבְּהֵמָ֗ה מִן־הַבָּקָר֙ וּמִן־הַצֹּ֔אן תַּקְרִ֖יבוּ אֶת־קׇרְבַּנְכֶֽם: 3 אִם־עֹלָ֤ה קׇרְבָּנוֹ֙ מִן־הַבָּקָ֔ר זָכָ֥ר תָּמִ֖ים יַקְרִיבֶ֑נּוּ אֶל־פֶּ֜תַח אֹ֤הֶל מוֹעֵד֙ יַקְרִ֣יב אֹת֔וֹ לִרְצֹנ֖וֹ לִפְנֵ֥י יְהֹוָֽה: 4 וְסָמַ֣ךְ יָד֔וֹ עַ֖ל רֹ֣אשׁ הָעֹלָ֑ה וְנִרְצָ֥ה ל֖וֹ לְכַפֵּ֥ר עָלָֽיו: 5 וְשָׁחַ֛ט אֶת־בֶּ֥ן הַבָּקָ֖ר לִפְנֵ֣י יְהֹוָ֑ה וְ֠הִקְרִ֠יבוּ בְּנֵ֨י אַהֲרֹ֤ן הַכֹּֽהֲנִים֙ אֶת־הַדָּ֔ם וְזָרְק֨וּ אֶת־הַדָּ֤ם עַל־הַמִּזְבֵּ֙חַ֙ סָבִ֔יב

The point here is that greatness and humility should not be two disjointed entities. Some people are generally contrite, but when it comes to their field of expertise their feelings of humility are suspended. The Torah is teaching us here that your humility (represented by smallness) should be in the *very same area* as your greatness (represented by the *alef*). Your unique talents as special qualities themselves should lead you to feel humble, when you contemplate the fact that if another person had been given the same capabilities as you, that person would probably have surpassed your achievements (*Rabbi Menahem Mendel Schneerson, 20th century*).

God spoke to him ... saying. The word *"saying"* means that God was telling Moses to pass on the message to others.

From here you learn that when hearing something from a friend, you should not repeat it to others unless you are permitted to do so by your friend (*Babylonian Talmud, Yoma* 4b).

2. When a man from (among) you brings a (voluntary) offering to God. The verse can be read, "When a man brings an offering to God, from you." A sacrifice is not merely the offering of a physical animal, but an offering of yourself—*"from you"*—dedicating your being to God (*Rabbi Shneur Zalman of Lyadi, 18th century*).

Heaven forefend to say that God actually needs animals to be burned! Rather, the significance here is a mystical one (*Rabbi Abraham ibn Ezra, 12th century*).

Sinning involves thought, speech and action. Therefore, God decreed that atonement for sin should also be threefold: First you place your hands on the animal, an *action* of atonement. Then, you confess *verbally*. And finally, the animal's innards—symbolizing physical desire—are burned, corre-

kabbalah bites

1:1 In the Masoretic text the letter *alef* of the word *va-yikra'* ("*He called*") is written small, suggesting some sort of deficiency. The *Zohar* explains:

"When the king is sitting on his throne wearing a royal crown, he is called 'Exalted King.' When he comes down to his servants' chamber, he is called 'Small King.'

When God is transcendent, over everything, He is called Supreme King. But once He comes below and is immanent, He is King, but not supreme as before. So the alef is small" (*Zohar* 1:239a).

Only when the New Era dawns will God's transcendence fully manifest itself in this world. Then, even within the confines of time and space, we will experience that which cannot ordinarily be contained by time and space.

leviticus 1:1–5 — va-yikra'

parashat va-yikra'

1. The Voluntary Offerings

¹ He called to Moses (affectionately). God spoke to him (alone) from (within) the Tent of Meeting, saying: ² Speak to the children of Israel, and say to them:

- ❖ When a man from (among) you brings a (voluntary) offering to God, you should bring your offering from (domesticated) animals—from cattle (which have not been worshiped as an idol) or from flocks (which have not been set aside for pagan worship, and from those which have not killed people).

The Burnt-Offering from Cattle

- ❖ ³ If his offering is a burnt-offering (taken) from cattle, he should bring a perfect (unblemished) male (animal).

- ❖ (If a person fails to bring the offering that he has promised, he must be coerced until) he will bring it willingly to the entrance of the Tent of Meeting.

- ❖ (If the offering is brought) before God (i.e. in the Holy Temple, and not on a private altar), ⁴ he should lean his hands upon the head of the burnt-offering.

- ❖ (The burnt-offering) will be accepted (by God) for him, to atone for him.

- ❖ ⁵ He (is permitted) to slaughter the young bull before God (in the Temple Courtyard, even if he is not a priest, but from that point on) Aaron's descendants (must carry out all the procedures).

- ❖ The priests should catch the blood (in a receptacle) and dash the blood on (the wall of) the altar, around (the four corners of the altar) which is at the entrance of the Tent of Meeting.

1:1 He called. Why is the word *va-yikra'* ("*He called*") written scribally with a small letter *alef*? Because even though Moses spoke directly with God regularly, he remained humble in his own eyes in the presence of God, and in the presence of the people (*Rabbi Isaac b. Judah ha-Levi, 13th century*).

The small *alef* is an allusion to the custom that small children traditionally begin their studies with the Book of Leviticus. As the *Midrash* states, "Why do we initiate small children with the Torah portion which speaks of sacrifices? Because just as the sacrifices are pure, so too, the children are pure" (*Rabbi Ephraim of Luntshits, 16th–17th century*).

Being the first of the twenty-two letters of the Hebrew alphabet, *alef* is the "head" or "leader" of all the letters. This is also hinted to by the fact that *alef* is an etymological derivative of the word *'alluf* which means "leader" or "chief."

So a small *alef* is a contradiction in terms: Why is a letter which represents leadership and greatness written *small*? If the Torah wished to allude to Moses' humility, surely this could have been done by rendering another letter small, and not the *alef*?

ויקרא א:ה-י

אֲשֶׁר־פֶּתַח אֹהֶל מוֹעֵד: 6 וְהִפְשִׁיט אֶת־הָעֹלָה וְנִתַּח אֹתָהּ לִנְתָחֶיהָ: 7 וְנָתְנוּ בְּנֵי אַהֲרֹן הַכֹּהֵן אֵשׁ עַל־הַמִּזְבֵּחַ וְעָרְכוּ עֵצִים עַל־הָאֵשׁ: 8 וְעָרְכוּ בְּנֵי אַהֲרֹן הַכֹּהֲנִים אֵת הַנְּתָחִים אֶת־הָרֹאשׁ וְאֶת־הַפָּדֶר עַל־הָעֵצִים אֲשֶׁר עַל־הָאֵשׁ אֲשֶׁר עַל־הַמִּזְבֵּחַ: 9 וְקִרְבּוֹ וּכְרָעָיו יִרְחַץ בַּמָּיִם וְהִקְטִיר הַכֹּהֵן אֶת־הַכֹּל הַמִּזְבֵּחָה עֹלָה אִשֵּׁה רֵיחַ־נִיחוֹחַ לַיהֹוָה: ס 10 וְאִם־מִן־הַצֹּאן קָרְבָּנוֹ מִן־

This represents the unique quality of sacrifices, why they cause God pleasure, so to speak, more than the other commandments of the Torah: They are done simply to carry out God's will. God derives particular satisfaction, as these offerings are, by their religious definition, totally devoid of secondary motives.

Although we find many other commandments of the Torah which defy logic (*hukkim*), the *general notion* of suprarational commands does have a logic behind it. As Maimonides writes, the observance of *hukkim* is for our benefit, since the blind observance of laws, even when they do not appear to make sense, cultivates fear and subservience to God.

But in the case of sacrifices, even this reason is absent. The act of burning an animal is not carried out to promote the character traits of fear and subservience, but simply because—as *Rashi* states here—"*I spoke and My will was carried out*." This dehumanizes the commandment, stressing God's involvement, and ignoring man's participation. Although bringing sacrifices will inevitably refine the character of the person offering them, the commandment was not given to us with this purpose in mind. The sacrifices are unique in that they are intended *exclusively* for God.

Therefore, *Rashi* stresses that God's pleasure here is the *only* priority. All that matters is that *"It brings Me a spirit of contentment that I spoke and My will was carried out"* (*Rabbi Menahem Mendel Schneerson, 20th century*).

A burnt-offering. Whoever studies the laws of bringing a burnt-offering is considered to have brought a burnt-offering (*Babylonian Talmud, Menahot* 110a).

Therefore, you should study the laws of all the sacrifices in their entirety, and the laws concerning the Temple and all its apparatus, as they are explained clearly in the *Code of Maimonides*, in the *Book of Temple Service* and the *Book of Offerings* (*Rabbi Shneur Zalman of Lyady, 18th century*).

spiritual vitamin

> The Sages taught that *"It causes pleasure, so to speak, to God that He has given a commandment and His will has been done (Sifrei, Pinhas, par. 12)."* How gratifying it is to be able to please God, especially as God has also promised a generous reward both in this world and in the world to come!

- [6] He should skin the burnt-offering and cut it into its (prescribed) pieces.
- [7] The descendants of Aaron the priest should place fire on the altar and arrange wood on the fire.
- [8] Aaron's descendants, the priests, should then arrange the pieces (of the animal), the head and the fats, on top of the wood which is on the fire, upon the altar.
- [9] (Beforehand, however,) he should wash its innards and its legs with water.
- Then, the priest should make all (of the animal's parts) go up in smoke on the altar, (with the specific intent that it is) a burnt-offering (which was slaughtered specifically as) a fire-offering, a pleasant aroma for God.

The Burnt-Offering from Sheep and Goats

- [10] And if his offering is (brought) from the flocks—from sheep or from goats—as a burnt-offering, he should offer a perfect (unblemished) male (animal).

sponding to the thoughts and desires that led you to sin. The animal's blood is also spilled out, hinting that, really, your own life should have been taken away because of the sin, but that God in His mercy has accepted the life of the animal as a substitute.

The sacrifices also have great mystical significance. That is why when listing the laws of the sacrifices the Torah uses God's most exalted name, the Tetragrammaton (*Nahmanides, 13th century*).

Sacrifices cause the Divine Presence to dwell among the Jewish people, like food which causes the soul to continue dwelling in the body. Just as you cannot understand why the soul, which is spiritual, requires *physical* food to keep it attached to the body, you cannot fathom why the Divine Presence requires the physical "food" of animals on the altar, in order to remain attached to the Jewish people (*Rabbi Judah Halevi, 12th century*).

The sacrifice represents unification with God. Thus the word *korban* ("sacrifice") is etymologically related to the word *kiruv* (coming close), indicating that by offering a sacrifice you bring the attributes of your soul closer to God (*Rabbi Bahya b. Asher, 13th century*).

7. The priest should place fire on the altar. A fire would come down from heaven to consume the sacrifices, but the priest was still required to maintain a natural fire (*Babylonian Talmud, Yoma 21b*).

When a person sins, he should, in principle, be judged by both the heavenly court and the earthly court. By combining these two fires, the heavenly and the earthly, we bring atonement to spare him judgment from both courts (*Rabbi Ephraim of Luntshits, 16th–17th century*).

9. A pleasant aroma for God. God says: "It brings Me a spirit of contentment that I spoke and My will was carried out" (*Rashi, 11th century*).

With his comment, "It brings Me a spirit of contentment that I spoke and My will was carried out," *Rashi* teaches us that *there simply is no reason* why God demanded the slaughter and burning of an animal, other than for the sake of fulfilling the Divine will.

Food for thought

1. If God spoke to you directly how could you be certain that it was Him?

2. What would you feel? Love or dread?

3. Does God "converse" with all of us in some subtle way?

ויקרא א:י - ב:ב

הַכְּשָׂבִים אוֹ מִן־הָעִזִּים לְעֹלָה זָכָר תָּמִים יַקְרִיבֶנּוּ: 11 וְשָׁחַט אֹתוֹ עַל יֶרֶךְ הַמִּזְבֵּחַ צָפֹנָה לִפְנֵי יְהֹוָה וְזָרְקוּ בְּנֵי אַהֲרֹן הַכֹּהֲנִים אֶת־דָּמוֹ עַל־הַמִּזְבֵּחַ סָבִיב: 12 וְנִתַּח אֹתוֹ לִנְתָחָיו וְאֶת־רֹאשׁוֹ וְאֶת־פִּדְרוֹ וְעָרַךְ הַכֹּהֵן אֹתָם עַל־הָעֵצִים אֲשֶׁר עַל־הָאֵשׁ אֲשֶׁר עַל־הַמִּזְבֵּחַ: 13 וְהַקֶּרֶב וְהַכְּרָעַיִם יִרְחַץ בַּמָּיִם וְהִקְרִיב הַכֹּהֵן אֶת־הַכֹּל וְהִקְטִיר הַמִּזְבֵּחָה עֹלָה הוּא אִשֵּׁה רֵיחַ נִיחֹחַ לַיהֹוָה: פ 14 [SECOND READING] וְאִם מִן־הָעוֹף עֹלָה קָרְבָּנוֹ לַיהֹוָה וְהִקְרִיב מִן־הַתֹּרִים אוֹ מִן־בְּנֵי הַיּוֹנָה אֶת־קָרְבָּנוֹ: 15 וְהִקְרִיבוֹ הַכֹּהֵן אֶל־הַמִּזְבֵּחַ וּמָלַק אֶת־רֹאשׁוֹ וְהִקְטִיר הַמִּזְבֵּחָה וְנִמְצָה דָמוֹ עַל קִיר הַמִּזְבֵּחַ: 16 וְהֵסִיר אֶת־מֻרְאָתוֹ בְּנֹצָתָהּ וְהִשְׁלִיךְ אֹתָהּ אֵצֶל הַמִּזְבֵּחַ קֵדְמָה אֶל־מְקוֹם הַדָּשֶׁן: 17 וְשִׁסַּע אֹתוֹ בִכְנָפָיו לֹא יַבְדִּיל וְהִקְטִיר אֹתוֹ הַכֹּהֵן הַמִּזְבֵּחָה עַל־הָעֵצִים אֲשֶׁר עַל־הָאֵשׁ עֹלָה הוּא אִשֵּׁה רֵיחַ נִיחֹחַ לַיהֹוָה: ס

ב 1 וְנֶפֶשׁ כִּי־תַקְרִיב קָרְבַּן מִנְחָה לַיהֹוָה סֹלֶת יִהְיֶה קָרְבָּנוֹ וְיָצַק עָלֶיהָ שֶׁמֶן וְנָתַן עָלֶיהָ לְבֹנָה: 2 וֶהֱבִיאָהּ אֶל־בְּנֵי אַהֲרֹן הַכֹּהֲנִים וְקָמַץ מִשָּׁם

14. Turtledoves or from young doves. Because of the unique character of the turtledove and the young dove, they were chosen from all birds to be used as the bird offerings. The turtledove clings to one mate; when he loses his mate, he will not attach himself to another. This symbolizes the children of Israel, who cling to God, never attaching themselves to another God.

God also chose the young dove, which has not yet begun to mate and cherishes the nest in which it is raised, never abandoning it. This hints to the children of Israel, who will not exchange God or His Torah (*Nahmanides, 13th century*).

2:1 If a (poor) soul (vows to) bring a meal-offering. Regarding all the voluntary offerings, the only instance where Scripture states the word "soul" is in the case of the meal-offering. Who usually donates a meal-offering? A poor man. God says: "I consider it as if he has sacrificed his very soul!" (*Rashi, 11th century*).

Unlike a wealthy person, who is able to give voluntary offerings in the Temple from expensive animals and birds, the poor man is only able to offer flour. Nevertheless, the Torah attributes more significance to the poor man's offering, as *Rashi* writes. This is because the poor man could not possibly be proud of his meager offering, so his is the most genuine of all, dedicated to God amid feelings of humility. Of him God says, *"It is as if he has sacrificed his very soul!"* (*Rabbi Samuel Bornstein of Sochaczew, 20th century*).

leviticus 1:11 – 2:2 — va-yikra'

- ❖ ¹¹ (If the offering is brought) before God (i.e. in the Holy Temple, and not on a private altar), he should slaughter it on the northern side of the altar.

- ❖ Aaron's descendants, the priests, should dash its blood on (the wall of) the altar, around (the four corners of the altar).

- ❖ ¹² He should cut it into its (prescribed) pieces, with its head and its fats.

- ❖ The priest should arrange the (pieces) on top of the wood which is on the fire, upon the altar.

- ❖ ¹³ He should wash its innards and its legs, with water. Then, the priest should bring all (of the animal's parts) and make them go up in smoke on the altar, (with the specific intent that it is) a burnt-offering (which was slaughtered specifically as) a fire-offering, a pleasant aroma for God.

The Burnt-Offering from Birds

- ❖ [SECOND READING] ¹⁴ If his offering to God is a burnt-offering from birds, he should bring (it) from (mature) turtle doves or from young doves.

- ❖ ¹⁵ The priest should bring it near the altar and slit away its head (with his fingernail), and make it go up in smoke on the altar.

- ❖ (Before the bird is burned), its blood should be squeezed out on the wall of the altar.

- ❖ ¹⁶ He should remove its (crop which contains) waste along with its innards, and cast them away next to the altar on the east side, where the ashes are.

- ❖ ¹⁷ He should tear it apart (by hand) with its wing feathers (still attached), but he should not split it completely.

- ❖ The priest should then make it go up in smoke on the altar, on top of the wood which is on the fire, (with the specific intent that) it is a burnt-offering (which was slaughtered specifically as) a fire-offering, a pleasant aroma for God.

The Unbaked Meal-Offering

2 ¹ If a (poor) soul (vows to) bring a meal-offering to God (without specifying which type of meal-offering he wishes to bring), his offering should be of (unbaked) fine (wheat) flour.

- ❖ (Even if he is not a priest, he can carry out the requirement to) pour oil over (all of) it and place frankincense on (part of) it.

- ❖ ² He should bring it to Aaron's descendants, the priests, and right there, (even in the area where non-priests may stand, the priest) should scoop out a three-finger fistful of its fine flour and its oil, (leaving aside) all its frankincense.

מְלֹא קֻמְצוֹ מִסָּלְתָּהּ וּמִשַּׁמְנָהּ עַל כָּל־לְבֹנָתָהּ וְהִקְטִיר הַכֹּהֵן אֶת־אַזְכָּרָתָהּ הַמִּזְבֵּחָה אִשֵּׁה רֵיחַ נִיחֹחַ לַיהוָֹה: 3 וְהַנּוֹתֶרֶת מִן־הַמִּנְחָה לְאַהֲרֹן וּלְבָנָיו קֹדֶשׁ קָדָשִׁים מֵאִשֵּׁי יְהוָֹה: ס 4 וְכִי תַקְרִב קָרְבַּן מִנְחָה מַאֲפֵה תַנּוּר סֹלֶת חַלּוֹת מַצֹּת בְּלוּלֹת בַּשֶּׁמֶן וּרְקִיקֵי מַצּוֹת מְשֻׁחִים בַּשָּׁמֶן: ס 5 וְאִם־מִנְחָה עַל־הַמַּחֲבַת קָרְבָּנֶךָ סֹלֶת בְּלוּלָה בַשֶּׁמֶן מַצָּה תִהְיֶה: 6 פָּתוֹת אֹתָהּ פִּתִּים וְיָצַקְתָּ עָלֶיהָ שָׁמֶן מִנְחָה הִוא: ס 7 [THIRD READING] וְאִם־מִנְחַת מַרְחֶשֶׁת קָרְבָּנֶךָ סֹלֶת בַּשֶּׁמֶן תֵּעָשֶׂה: 8 וְהֵבֵאתָ אֶת־הַמִּנְחָה אֲשֶׁר יֵעָשֶׂה מֵאֵלֶּה לַיהוָֹה וְהִקְרִיבָהּ אֶל־הַכֹּהֵן וְהִגִּישָׁהּ אֶל־הַמִּזְבֵּחַ: 9 וְהֵרִים הַכֹּהֵן מִן־הַמִּנְחָה אֶת־אַזְכָּרָתָהּ

2. A three-finger fistful ... a pleasant aroma for God. This verse, *"A pleasant aroma for God,"* is found in the text in reference to the meal-offering, the cattle-offering (1:9), and the bird-offering (1:17). This teaches that it is not how much you dedicate to God that matters—a large bull or small meal-offering—but the fact that you direct your heart toward God in heaven (*Babylonian Talmud, Menahot* 110b).

9. The meal offering ... a pleasant aroma for God. In Temple times, if a man brought a meal-offering, he would be rewarded for bringing a meal-offering. If he brought a burnt-offering, he would be rewarded for bringing a burnt-offering. But nowadays, to the humble man, Scripture credits *every* type of sacrifice, as the verse states: *"The sacrifices of God are a broken spirit"* (*Psalms* 51:17; *Babylonian Talmud, Sanhedrin* 44b).

kabbalah bites

According to the Kabbalah, life is all about *elevation*. When you speak to somebody positively, you elevate that conversation to God. When you eat healthy, kosher food with the intention that it should give you strength to worship God, you elevate that food. And when you think good, wholesome thoughts you elevate your mind.

The epicenter of global elevation was in the Holy Temple, on the altar. The offering of a *korban* (sacrifice), was the consummate elevation of all the worlds to God. The salt on the sacrifice elevated the mineral world; the wine and oil libations, the vegetable world; the animal itself, the animal world; the confession uttered over the animal, the human world; and the intention of the priest, God's minister, the soul world.

As you go about your day, ask yourself: Did I just elevate that interaction?

leviticus 2:2–9   va-yikra'

- Then, the priest should make (the scoop and the frankincense) go up in smoke on the altar—(with the specific intent that) it is a fire-offering—(so that its owner will be) remembered (positively before God), a pleasant aroma for God.
- ³ The remainder of the meal-offering belongs to Aaron and to his descendants. (It is their) most holy (property, only after the scoop and frankincense have been placed on the altar) as fire-offerings for God.

The Baked Meal-Offering

- ⁴ If you (vow to) bring "a meal-offering baked in an oven," it should consist of (either) unleavened loaves (made) of fine flour mixed with oil, or unleavened wafers smeared with oil.

The Shallow-Fried Meal-Offering

- ⁵ If your (vow to bring an) offering is "a meal-offering (made) in a shallow pan," it should be (made) of fine flour mixed with oil, (and) it should be unleavened.
- ⁶ (Before it is scooped) break it into pieces and pour oil over it. It is a meal-offering.

The Deep-Fried Meal-Offering

- [THIRD READING] ⁷ If your (vow to bring an) offering is "a meal-offering (fried) in the deep pot (which is in the Temple)," it should be made of fine flour with oil.

Laws Pertaining to All Meal-Offerings

- ⁸ You should bring the meal-offering—which should be made from (any of) these (above-mentioned types)—to God, (i.e.) you should bring it to the priest, and (the priest) should bring it close to the altar (touching its southwestern corner).
- ⁹ The priest should separate from the meal-offering (a three-finger fistful) and should make (the scoop and the frankincense) go up in smoke on the altar (so that its owner will be) remembered (positively before God). It is a fire-offering, a pleasant aroma for God.

spiritual vitamin

> Our spirituality should be dedicated to God, and not to the cause of false ideals and ideas which, high-sounding though they may be, drag down humanity into the mire of materialistic selfishness and coarseness.

ויקרא ב:י - ג:ד

וְהִקְטִיר הַמִּזְבֵּחָה אִשֵּׁה רֵיחַ נִיחֹחַ לַיהֹוָה: 10 וְהַנּוֹתֶרֶת מִן־הַמִּנְחָה לְאַהֲרֹן וּלְבָנָיו קֹדֶשׁ קָדָשִׁים מֵאִשֵּׁי יְהֹוָה: 11 כָּל־הַמִּנְחָה אֲשֶׁר תַּקְרִיבוּ לַיהֹוָה לֹא תֵעָשֶׂה חָמֵץ כִּי כָל־שְׂאֹר וְכָל־דְּבַשׁ לֹא־תַקְטִירוּ מִמֶּנּוּ אִשֶּׁה לַיהֹוָה: 12 קָרְבַּן רֵאשִׁית תַּקְרִיבוּ אֹתָם לַיהֹוָה וְאֶל־הַמִּזְבֵּחַ לֹא־יַעֲלוּ לְרֵיחַ נִיחֹחַ: 13 וְכָל־קָרְבַּן מִנְחָתְךָ בַּמֶּלַח תִּמְלָח וְלֹא תַשְׁבִּית מֶלַח בְּרִית אֱלֹהֶיךָ מֵעַל מִנְחָתֶךָ עַל כָּל־קָרְבָּנְךָ תַּקְרִיב מֶלַח: ס 14 וְאִם־תַּקְרִיב מִנְחַת בִּכּוּרִים לַיהֹוָה אָבִיב קָלוּי בָּאֵשׁ גֶּרֶשׂ כַּרְמֶל תַּקְרִיב אֵת מִנְחַת בִּכּוּרֶיךָ: 15 וְנָתַתָּ עָלֶיהָ שֶׁמֶן וְשַׂמְתָּ עָלֶיהָ לְבֹנָה מִנְחָה הִוא: 16 וְהִקְטִיר הַכֹּהֵן אֶת־אַזְכָּרָתָהּ מִגִּרְשָׂהּ וּמִשַּׁמְנָהּ עַל כָּל־לְבֹנָתָהּ אִשֶּׁה לַיהֹוָה: פ

ג [FOURTH READING] 1 וְאִם־זֶבַח שְׁלָמִים קָרְבָּנוֹ אִם מִן־הַבָּקָר הוּא מַקְרִיב אִם־זָכָר אִם־נְקֵבָה תָּמִים יַקְרִיבֶנּוּ לִפְנֵי יְהֹוָה: 2 וְסָמַךְ יָדוֹ עַל־רֹאשׁ קָרְבָּנוֹ וּשְׁחָטוֹ פֶּתַח אֹהֶל מוֹעֵד וְזָרְקוּ בְּנֵי אַהֲרֹן הַכֹּהֲנִים אֶת־הַדָּם עַל־הַמִּזְבֵּחַ סָבִיב: 3 וְהִקְרִיב מִזֶּבַח הַשְּׁלָמִים אִשֶּׁה לַיהֹוָה אֶת־הַחֵלֶב הַמְכַסֶּה אֶת־הַקֶּרֶב וְאֵת כָּל־הַחֵלֶב אֲשֶׁר עַל־הַקֶּרֶב: 4 וְאֵת שְׁתֵּי הַכְּלָיֹת וְאֶת־הַחֵלֶב אֲשֶׁר עֲלֵהֶן אֲשֶׁר

13. Offer salt on all your (burnt-)offerings. Offering a sacrifice on the altar represents the process of offering up your Animalistic Soul—the source of all physical desires—to God. Since these desires arise from the blood, every sacrifice must be salted to signify your strong resolution to extract those desires from the Animalistic Soul, just as salt extracts blood (*Rabbi Menahem Mendel Schneersohn of Lubavitch, 19th century*).

3:1 A peace-offering (shelamim). These offerings bring perfection (*sheiemut*) everywhere, to the upper and lower worlds. They bring harmony to all the different compass directions, a total perfection from the avenues of faith. Of all the offerings, none are as precious to God as the peace-offerings, because they bring perfection to the upper and lower worlds (*Zohar*).

kabbalah bites

2:11 Why can leaven and honey not be placed on an offering?

Because they both represent extremes, and God does not like extremes. Leaven is the extreme of sourness and harshness; honey is extremely sweet and sickly. When God created the world, He sweetened judgment with kindness, indicating that the preferred path is always one of equilibrium and balance.

So when we offer to God, extremes are ruled out.

leviticus 2:10 – 3:4 — va-yikra'

- ❖ ¹⁰ The remainder of the meal-offering belongs to Aaron and to his descendants. (It is their) most holy (property, only after the scoop and frankincense have been placed on the altar) as fire-offerings for God.

- ❖ ¹¹ No meal-offering that you offer to God should be made out of (anything) leavened. For you should not make any leavening or any honey go up in smoke as a fire-offering for God.

- ❖ ¹² You (may, however,) bring (figs and dates, the source of honey,) as a first (fruit) offering to God (and you may bring leavening, as the two loaves of the Festival of Weeks), but they should not go up on the altar as a pleasant aroma to God.

- ❖ ¹³ You should season every one of your meal-offering sacrifices with salt. You should not leave out the salt from (being placed) upon your meal-offerings (because) your God (made a) covenant (during the six days of creation that salt would always be placed on the altar).

- ❖ You should offer salt on all your (burnt-)offerings (and on the parts burned on the altar from every type of offering).

The 'Omer-Offering

- ❖ ¹⁴ When you bring the meal-offering of the first ripening grains before God, you should bring the first, fresh kernels of the (barley) harvest, parched in fire (and) coarsely ground, (as) the meal-offering of your first ripening grain.

- ❖ ¹⁵ You should put oil on it, and place frankincense upon it. It is a meal-offering.

- ❖ ¹⁶ Then, the priest should make (a scoop) from its flour and its oil, as well as its frankincense, go up in smoke on the altar (so that its owner will be) remembered (positively before God). It is a fire-offering.

3 The Peace-Offering from Cattle

- ❖ [FOURTH READING] ¹ If his offering is a peace-offering, (then) if he brings it from cattle, he should bring a perfect (unblemished) male or female (animal) before God.

- ❖ ² He should lean his hands on the head of his offering and slaughter it at the entrance of the Tent of Meeting.

- ❖ Aaron's descendants, the priests, should dash the blood upon the altar, all around.

- ❖ ³ From the peace-offering, he should bring a fire-offering to God (comprised of): the fat covering the intestines, all the fat that is on the stomach, ⁴ the two kidneys,

---

Food for thought

1. When did you last "sacrifice" a pleasurable activity for a worthwhile one?

2. What kinds of activities bring you close to God?

3. How do you express gratitude to God tangibly?

ויקרא ג:ד-טו | ויקרא

עַל־הַכְּסָלִ֔ים וְאֶת־הַיֹּתֶ֙רֶת֙ עַל־הַכָּבֵ֔ד עַל־הַכְּלָי֖וֹת יְסִירֶֽנָּה: 5 וְהִקְטִ֨ירוּ אֹת֤וֹ בְנֵֽי־אַהֲרֹן֙ הַמִּזְבֵּ֔חָה עַל־הָ֣עֹלָ֔ה אֲשֶׁ֥ר עַל־הָעֵצִ֖ים אֲשֶׁ֣ר עַל־הָאֵ֑שׁ אִשֵּׁ֛ה רֵ֥יחַ נִיחֹ֖חַ לַֽיהוָֹֽה: פ 6 וְאִם־מִן־הַצֹּ֧אן קָרְבָּנ֛וֹ לְזֶ֥בַח שְׁלָמִ֖ים לַיהוָ֑ה זָכָר֙ א֣וֹ נְקֵבָ֔ה תָּמִ֖ים יַקְרִיבֶֽנּוּ: 7 אִם־כֶּ֥שֶׂב הֽוּא־מַקְרִ֖יב אֶת־קָרְבָּנ֑וֹ וְהִקְרִ֥יב אֹת֖וֹ לִפְנֵ֥י יְהוָֹֽה: 8 וְסָמַ֤ךְ אֶת־יָדוֹ֙ עַל־רֹ֣אשׁ קָרְבָּנ֔וֹ וְשָׁחַ֣ט אֹת֔וֹ לִפְנֵ֖י אֹ֣הֶל מוֹעֵ֑ד וְ֠זָרְק֠וּ בְּנֵ֨י אַהֲרֹ֧ן אֶת־דָּמ֛וֹ עַל־הַמִּזְבֵּ֖חַ סָבִֽיב: 9 וְהִקְרִ֞יב מִזֶּ֣בַח הַשְּׁלָמִ֗ים אִשֶּׁה֙ לַֽיהוָ֔ה חֶלְבּוֹ֙ הָֽאַלְיָ֣ה תְמִימָ֔ה לְעֻמַּ֥ת הֶעָצֶ֖ה יְסִירֶ֑נָּה וְאֶת־הַחֵ֨לֶב֙ הַֽמְכַסֶּ֣ה אֶת־הַקֶּ֔רֶב וְאֵת֙ כָּל־הַחֵ֔לֶב אֲשֶׁ֖ר עַל־הַקֶּֽרֶב: 10 וְאֵת֙ שְׁתֵּ֣י הַכְּלָיֹ֔ת וְאֶת־הַחֵ֙לֶב֙ אֲשֶׁ֣ר עֲלֵהֶ֔ן אֲשֶׁ֖ר עַל־הַכְּסָלִ֑ים וְאֶת־הַיֹּתֶ֙רֶת֙ עַל־הַכָּבֵ֔ד עַל־הַכְּלָיֹ֖ת יְסִירֶֽנָּה: 11 וְהִקְטִיר֥וֹ הַכֹּהֵ֖ן הַמִּזְבֵּ֑חָה לֶ֥חֶם אִשֶּׁ֖ה לַֽיהוָֹֽה: פ 12 וְאִ֥ם עֵ֖ז קָרְבָּנ֑וֹ וְהִקְרִיב֖וֹ לִפְנֵ֥י יְהוָֹֽה: 13 וְסָמַ֤ךְ אֶת־יָדוֹ֙ עַל־רֹאשׁ֔וֹ וְשָׁחַ֣ט אֹת֔וֹ לִפְנֵ֖י אֹ֣הֶל מוֹעֵ֑ד וְ֠זָרְק֠וּ בְּנֵ֨י אַהֲרֹ֧ן אֶת־דָּמ֛וֹ עַל־הַמִּזְבֵּ֖חַ סָבִֽיב: 14 וְהִקְרִ֤יב מִמֶּ֙נּוּ֙ קָרְבָּנ֔וֹ אִשֶּׁ֖ה לַֽיהוָ֑ה אֶת־הַחֵ֙לֶב֙ הַֽמְכַסֶּ֣ה אֶת־הַקֶּ֔רֶב וְאֵת֙ כָּל־הַחֵ֔לֶב אֲשֶׁ֖ר עַל־הַקֶּֽרֶב: 15 וְאֵת֙ שְׁתֵּ֣י הַכְּלָיֹ֔ת וְאֶת־הַחֵ֙לֶב֙ אֲשֶׁ֣ר עֲלֵהֶ֔ן אֲשֶׁ֖ר עַל־הַכְּסָלִ֑ים וְאֶת־הַיֹּתֶ֙רֶת֙ עַל־הַכָּבֵ֔ד עַל־הַכְּלָיֹ֖ת יְסִירֶֽנָּה:

5. A pleasant aroma for God. The aroma of a sacrifice can be detected from far away, before you even see the source of the scent. Similarly, it was not the act of slaughtering an animal itself

spiritual vitamin

> Since the Torah comes from God and His infinite wisdom, it is not subject to man's approval and selection. Human reason is necessarily limited and imperfect. Its deficiencies are obvious, since with time and study the human intellect improves and gains knowledge, and a person's opinions change. To confine God to human judgment would violate even common sense.

(together) with the fat that is on them, which is over the flanks. He should (also) remove the diaphragm, (and a bit of) the liver (which is connected) to it, (when he takes out) the kidneys.

- ⁵ Aaron's descendants should make it go up in smoke on the altar, (after placing) the burnt-offering on top of the wood that is on the fire.

It is a fire-offering, a pleasant aroma for God.

The Peace-Offering from Sheep and Goats

- ⁶ If his offering to God for a peace-offering is (taken) from the flocks, (it may be) male or female, (and he must offer) a perfect unblemished (animal).

⁷ If he brings a sheep as his offering:

- He should bring it before God. ⁸ He should lean his hands on the head of his offering and slaughter it before the Tent of Meeting.

- Aaron's descendants should dash its blood upon the altar (all) around (using a receptacle).

- ⁹ From the peace-offering, he should bring a fire-offering to God (comprised of): its choicest part—(namely) the entire tail, which he should detach (right up to) above the kidneys—the fat covering the intestines, all the fat that is on the stomach, ¹⁰ the two kidneys, (together) with the fat that is on them, which is over the flanks. He should (also) remove the diaphragm, (and a bit of) the liver (which is connected) to it, (when he removes) the kidneys.

- ¹¹ The priest should make (this) go up in smoke on the altar, as food for the fire, to God.

¹² If his offering is a goat:

- He should bring it before God. ¹³ He should lean his hands on its head and slaughter it before the Tent of Meeting.

- Aaron's descendants should dash its blood upon the altar, (all) around.

- ¹⁴ From his offering, he should bring a fire-offering to God (consisting of): the fat covering the intestines, all the fat that is on the stomach, ¹⁵ the two kidneys, (together) with the fat that is on them, which is over the flanks. He should (also) remove the diaphragm, (and a bit of) the liver (which is connected) to it, (when he removes) the kidneys.

Food for thought

1. *Shelamim* means wholeness. How do you achieve wholeness of body, mind and spirit?

2. What thoughts bring you to inner peace?

3. Are *truth* and *peace* inherently contradictory?

ויקרא ג:טז – ד:ד

16 וְהִקְטִירָם הַכֹּהֵן הַמִּזְבֵּחָה לֶחֶם אִשֶּׁה לְרֵיחַ נִיחֹחַ כָּל־חֵלֶב לַיהוָה: 17 חֻקַּת עוֹלָם לְדֹרֹתֵיכֶם בְּכֹל מוֹשְׁבֹתֵיכֶם כָּל־חֵלֶב וְכָל־דָּם לֹא תֹאכֵלוּ: פ

ד 1 וַיְדַבֵּר יְהוָה אֶל־מֹשֶׁה לֵּאמֹר: 2 דַּבֵּר אֶל־בְּנֵי יִשְׂרָאֵל לֵאמֹר [FIFTH READING] נֶפֶשׁ כִּי־תֶחֱטָא בִשְׁגָגָה מִכֹּל מִצְוֹת יְהוָה אֲשֶׁר לֹא תֵעָשֶׂינָה וְעָשָׂה מֵאַחַת מֵהֵנָּה: 3 אִם הַכֹּהֵן הַמָּשִׁיחַ יֶחֱטָא לְאַשְׁמַת הָעָם וְהִקְרִיב עַל חַטָּאתוֹ אֲשֶׁר חָטָא פַּר בֶּן־בָּקָר תָּמִים לַיהוָה לְחַטָּאת: 4 וְהֵבִיא אֶת־הַפָּר אֶל־פֶּתַח אֹהֶל מוֹעֵד לִפְנֵי יְהוָה וְסָמַךְ אֶת־יָדוֹ עַל־רֹאשׁ הַפָּר וְשָׁחַט אֶת־הַפָּר לִפְנֵי

A person is liable to bring a sin-offering for the unintentional violation of such prohibitions (*Rashi, 11th century*).

A sin-offering only achieves atonement for unintentional transgressions. If a man sins intentionally, his soul becomes so distant from God that a sacrifice alone will not help to bring him close again (*Rabbi Ḥayyim ibn Attar, 18th century*).

Unintentionally. Even if a person sinned unintentionally he is partially responsible, since the sin was ultimately caused by his subconscious mind—resulting from the strengthening of his Animalistic Soul through indulging in too much (permitted) pleasure. For that reason, the Torah requires him to bring a sin-offering (*Rabbi Shneur Zalman of Lyady, 18th century*).

3. If it is the anointed (High) Priest who sins, bringing guilt to the people. When the High Priest sins, it brings guilt to the people, because they are dependent on him to effect their atonement and to pray for them, and now he has become corrupted (*Rashi, 11th century*).

A person in a position of leadership has to be additionally careful not to commit even an inadvertent transgression. When people see that a leader has a fault, it causes them to be more lax in their commitment to the Torah, *"bringing guilt to the people"* (*Rabbi Baruch Epstein, 19th–20th century*).

> **kabbalah bites**
>
> **4:2** *Wisdom* was asked: "What is the punishment of a sinner?" It answered: *"Sinners will be prosecuted by their own vice"* (Proverbs 13:21).
>
> *Prophecy* was asked: "What is the punishment for the sinner?" It answered: *"The soul that sins, it shall die"* (Ezekiel 18:4).
>
> *The Torah* was asked: "What is the punishment for the sinner?" It answered: *"Let him bring a sacrifice, and he will be atoned"* (Yalkut Shimoni).
>
> Here we see the Torah's compassion. Other routes to transcendence, such as "prophecy" and "wisdom," can be associated with *Gevurah*, harsh consequences, when things go wrong. But the Torah is a covenant of *Ḥesed*, kindness.
>
> Through the Torah we experience God's love for humanity.

❖ ¹⁶ The priest should make (all this) go up in smoke on the altar, the food of the fire, a pleasant aroma for God.

Forbidden Fats and Blood

❖ All the (above-mentioned) fat is (sacrificed) for God. ¹⁷ (Thus) you should not eat any (such) fat or any blood. (This is) an eternal statute for all your generations, in all the places where you live.

4 The Sin-Offering

[FIFTH READING] ¹ God spoke to Moses, saying: ² Speak to the children of Israel, saying:

❖ When a person sins unintentionally (transgressing) any of God's commandments which (would be) prohibited (with the punishment of soul excision for an intentional transgression), or if he (even) does a portion of one of the(se sins), he must bring a sin-offering).

The High Priest's Sin-Offering

❖ ³ If it is the anointed (High) Priest who sins, bringing guilt to the people, then he should bring a perfect (unblemished, three-year-old) young bull as a sin-offering to God for his sin which he has committed.

❖ ⁴ He should bring the bull to the entrance of the Tent of Meeting before God, and he should lean his hands upon the bull's head and slaughter the bull before God.

---

that brought full atonement, it was the *"aroma"* of the penitent's future good deeds that was most effective (*Rabbi Eliezer b. Elijah Ashkenazi, 16ᵗʰ century*).

4:2 When a person sins. Our Rabbis explained: A sin-offering is brought only for a transgression whose prohibition is expressed in the Torah as a negative commandment, and whose willful violation would incur the penalty of *karet* (premature death by the hands of heaven).

kabbalah bites

3:16 *"All the fat is for God."* Fat is associated with pleasure because when you indulge in too many pleasures, you grow fat. Obviously, we shouldn't be overindulgent with food and other pleasures, but this verse could also be understood as a warning against a *spiritual* self-indulgence.

Our yearning for spirituality can, sometimes, be self-serving: not because we want to heal the world, but just for the thrill of it. The Torah reminds us: *"all the fat is for God."* Do not become "obese" with a narcissistic spirituality. Everything you do should be devoted to God's plan of healing the world.

ויקרא ד:ד-יח

יְהוָה: 5 וְלָקַח הַכֹּהֵן הַמָּשִׁיחַ מִדַּם הַפָּר וְהֵבִיא אֹתוֹ אֶל־אֹהֶל מוֹעֵד: 6 וְטָבַל הַכֹּהֵן אֶת־אֶצְבָּעוֹ בַּדָּם וְהִזָּה מִן־הַדָּם שֶׁבַע פְּעָמִים לִפְנֵי יְהוָה אֶת־פְּנֵי פָּרֹכֶת הַקֹּדֶשׁ: 7 וְנָתַן הַכֹּהֵן מִן־הַדָּם עַל־קַרְנוֹת מִזְבַּח קְטֹרֶת הַסַּמִּים לִפְנֵי יְהוָה אֲשֶׁר בְּאֹהֶל מוֹעֵד וְאֵת | כָּל־דַּם הַפָּר יִשְׁפֹּךְ אֶל־יְסוֹד מִזְבַּח הָעֹלָה אֲשֶׁר־פֶּתַח אֹהֶל מוֹעֵד: 8 וְאֶת־כָּל־חֵלֶב פַּר הַחַטָּאת יָרִים מִמֶּנּוּ אֶת־הַחֵלֶב הַמְכַסֶּה עַל־הַקֶּרֶב וְאֵת כָּל־הַחֵלֶב אֲשֶׁר עַל־הַקֶּרֶב: 9 וְאֵת שְׁתֵּי הַכְּלָיֹת וְאֶת־הַחֵלֶב אֲשֶׁר עֲלֵיהֶן אֲשֶׁר עַל־הַכְּסָלִים וְאֶת־הַיֹּתֶרֶת עַל־הַכָּבֵד עַל־הַכְּלָיוֹת יְסִירֶנָּה: 10 כַּאֲשֶׁר יוּרַם מִשּׁוֹר זֶבַח הַשְּׁלָמִים וְהִקְטִירָם הַכֹּהֵן עַל מִזְבַּח הָעֹלָה: 11 וְאֶת־עוֹר הַפָּר וְאֶת־כָּל־בְּשָׂרוֹ עַל־רֹאשׁוֹ וְעַל־כְּרָעָיו וְקִרְבּוֹ וּפִרְשׁוֹ: 12 וְהוֹצִיא אֶת־כָּל־הַפָּר אֶל־מִחוּץ לַמַּחֲנֶה אֶל־מָקוֹם טָהוֹר אֶל־שֶׁפֶךְ הַדֶּשֶׁן וְשָׂרַף אֹתוֹ עַל־עֵצִים בָּאֵשׁ עַל־שֶׁפֶךְ הַדֶּשֶׁן יִשָּׂרֵף: פ 13 וְאִם כָּל־עֲדַת יִשְׂרָאֵל יִשְׁגּוּ וְנֶעְלַם דָּבָר מֵעֵינֵי הַקָּהָל וְעָשׂוּ אַחַת מִכָּל־מִצְוֹת יְהוָה אֲשֶׁר לֹא־תֵעָשֶׂינָה וְאָשֵׁמוּ: 14 וְנוֹדְעָה הַחַטָּאת אֲשֶׁר חָטְאוּ עָלֶיהָ וְהִקְרִיבוּ הַקָּהָל פַּר בֶּן־בָּקָר לְחַטָּאת וְהֵבִיאוּ אֹתוֹ לִפְנֵי אֹהֶל מוֹעֵד: 15 וְסָמְכוּ זִקְנֵי הָעֵדָה אֶת־יְדֵיהֶם עַל־רֹאשׁ הַפָּר לִפְנֵי יְהוָה וְשָׁחַט אֶת־הַפָּר לִפְנֵי יְהוָה: 16 וְהֵבִיא הַכֹּהֵן הַמָּשִׁיחַ מִדַּם הַפָּר אֶל־אֹהֶל מוֹעֵד: 17 וְטָבַל הַכֹּהֵן אֶצְבָּעוֹ מִן־הַדָּם וְהִזָּה שֶׁבַע פְּעָמִים לִפְנֵי יְהוָה אֵת פְּנֵי הַפָּרֹכֶת: 18 וּמִן־הַדָּם יִתֵּן | עַל־קַרְנֹת

spiritual vitamin

> It is difficult, almost impossible, for man never to fail, and the Torah has indicated that should this happen, there is no need to be discouraged. There is always *teshuvah*—return to God and to the right path, and the very failure can be made a springboard for a leap forward and further advance.

leviticus 4:5–18   va-yikra'

- ⁵ The anointed priest should take some of the bull's blood and bring it into the Tent of Meeting. ⁶ The priest should dip his finger into the blood and sprinkle some of the blood seven times before God, in front of the partition of the Sanctuary. ⁷ The priest should place some of the blood on the horns of the incense altar which is in the Tent of Meeting, before God, and he should pour all (the rest) of the bull's blood onto the base of the altar (used) for burnt-offerings, which is at the entrance of the Tent of Meeting.

- ⁸ He should separate from the bull of the sin-offering, all its (sacrificial) fat: the fat covering the intestines, all the fat that is on the stomach, ⁹ the two kidneys, (together) with the fat that is on them, which is over the flanks. He should (also) remove the diaphragm, (and a bit of) the liver (which is connected) to it, (when he takes out) the kidneys—¹⁰ just as was separated from the bull (sacrificed as) a peace-offering. The priest should then make these (parts) go up in smoke on the altar (used) for burnt-offerings.

- ¹¹ (He should then take) the bull's skin, all its flesh, its head, its legs, its innards and its waste matter. ¹² He should take out the entire bull to a pure place outside the camp, (namely,) to the ash depository, and he should burn it in fire on wood. It should be burnt on the ash depository (even if there are no ashes there).

The Communal Sin-Offering

- ¹³ If the entire assembly of Jewish (judges, the *Sanhedrin*,) make a mistake (and rule that an act, which is in fact punishable by soul excision, is permissible), and the matter was not detected by the eyes of the congregation, and they (follow the *Sanhedrin*, and violate) any of God's commandments which are prohibited, (thereby) incurring guilt —¹⁴ then, when the sin which they have committed becomes known, the congregation should bring a young bull as a sin-offering.

- They should bring it before the Tent of Meeting. ¹⁵ The elders of the community should lean their hands on the bull's head, before God, and one (of them) should slaughter the bull before God.

- ¹⁶ The anointed priest should bring some of the bull's blood into the Tent of Meeting. ¹⁷ The priest should dip his finger into the blood, and sprinkle (it) seven times before God, before the partition. ¹⁸ He should then place some of the blood on the horns of the altar that is before God in the Tent of Meeting. Then he should pour

---

17. Before the partition. Earlier, the Torah emphasized, "The partition *of the Sanctuary"* (v. 6). This could be compared to a king against whom one of his provinces revolted. If only a minority rebels, his family will survive. But if the entire country rebels, his family will not survive.

In the same way, when the anointed priest sinned, God's holy name was still associated with the Sanctuary. But when all the people sinned, holiness departed (*Rashi, 11th century*).

ויקרא ד:יח-כח

הַמִּזְבֵּחַ אֲשֶׁר לִפְנֵי יְהֹוָה אֲשֶׁר בְּאֹהֶל מוֹעֵד וְאֵת כָּל־הַדָּם יִשְׁפֹּךְ אֶל־יְסוֹד מִזְבַּח הָעֹלָה אֲשֶׁר־פֶּתַח אֹהֶל מוֹעֵד: 19 וְאֵת כָּל־חֶלְבּוֹ יָרִים מִמֶּנּוּ וְהִקְטִיר הַמִּזְבֵּחָה: 20 וְעָשָׂה לַפָּר כַּאֲשֶׁר עָשָׂה לְפַר הַחַטָּאת כֵּן יַעֲשֶׂה־לּוֹ וְכִפֶּר עֲלֵהֶם הַכֹּהֵן וְנִסְלַח לָהֶם: 21 וְהוֹצִיא אֶת־הַפָּר אֶל־מִחוּץ לַמַּחֲנֶה וְשָׂרַף אֹתוֹ כַּאֲשֶׁר שָׂרַף אֵת הַפָּר הָרִאשׁוֹן חַטַּאת הַקָּהָל הוּא: פ 22 אֲשֶׁר נָשִׂיא יֶחֱטָא וְעָשָׂה אַחַת מִכָּל־מִצְוֹת יְהֹוָה אֱלֹהָיו אֲשֶׁר לֹא־תֵעָשֶׂינָה בִּשְׁגָגָה וְאָשֵׁם: 23 אוֹ־הוֹדַע אֵלָיו חַטָּאתוֹ אֲשֶׁר חָטָא בָּהּ וְהֵבִיא אֶת־קָרְבָּנוֹ שְׂעִיר עִזִּים זָכָר תָּמִים: 24 וְסָמַךְ יָדוֹ עַל־רֹאשׁ הַשָּׂעִיר וְשָׁחַט אֹתוֹ בִּמְקוֹם אֲשֶׁר־יִשְׁחַט אֶת־הָעֹלָה לִפְנֵי יְהֹוָה חַטָּאת הוּא: 25 וְלָקַח הַכֹּהֵן מִדַּם הַחַטָּאת בְּאֶצְבָּעוֹ וְנָתַן עַל־קַרְנֹת מִזְבַּח הָעֹלָה וְאֶת־דָּמוֹ יִשְׁפֹּךְ אֶל־יְסוֹד מִזְבַּח הָעֹלָה: 26 וְאֶת־כָּל־חֶלְבּוֹ יַקְטִיר הַמִּזְבֵּחָה כְּחֵלֶב זֶבַח הַשְּׁלָמִים וְכִפֶּר עָלָיו הַכֹּהֵן מֵחַטָּאתוֹ וְנִסְלַח לוֹ: פ 27 [SIXTH READING] וְאִם־נֶפֶשׁ אַחַת תֶּחֱטָא בִשְׁגָגָה מֵעַם הָאָרֶץ בַּעֲשֹׂתָהּ אַחַת מִמִּצְוֹת יְהֹוָה אֲשֶׁר לֹא־תֵעָשֶׂינָה וְאָשֵׁם: 28 אוֹ הוֹדַע אֵלָיו חַטָּאתוֹ אֲשֶׁר חָטָא וְהֵבִיא קָרְבָּנוֹ שְׂעִירַת עִזִּים תְּמִימָה נְקֵבָה עַל־חַטָּאתוֹ אֲשֶׁר חָטָא:

---

21. Burn it. This symbolizes that the transgression has been eradicated and erased entirely, just as the carcass itself is completely consumed. This sacrifice is unlike any other in its complete and total consumption (*Maimonides, 12th century*).

22. If ('asher) a leader sins. The word 'asher is etymologically related to the word 'ashrei, meaning "fortunate." The verse is intimating: "Fortunate is the generation whose leader takes it to heart to bring atonement for his unintentional sin. And how much more so will he feel remorseful for the sins he has committed willfully!" (*Rashi, 11th century*).

27. If an individual among the citizens of the land sins unintentionally. Seeing yourself as *"an individual among the citizens of the land,"* disconnected from the community, will lead you to sin (*Rabbi Samuel Tzevi Danziger of Aleksandrow, 19th century*).

27-28. His offering for his sin. If someone needs to bring a sin-offering (for transgressing a prohibition) and a burnt-offering (for omitting a positive commandment), why does he offer the sin-offering first?

Food for thought

1. Is it more important for leaders to admit mistakes than for ordinary citizens?

2. When a leader admits and regrets a wrong, should he be left in power?

3. Facing up to weakness takes strength; how can we cultivate that strength?

leviticus 4:18–28 — va-yikra'

- all (the rest of) the blood onto the base of the altar (used) for burnt-offerings, which is at the entrance to the Tent of Meeting.

- ⁱ⁹ He should separate all its (sacrificial) fat from it and make it go up in smoke on the altar. (Concerning the details of what should be separated): ²⁰ He should do to this bull just as one does to the bull of the sin-offering (of the High Priest). He should do (exactly) the same with it.

- Thus the priest will make an atonement for them (the community), and they will be forgiven.

- ²¹ He should take the bull outside the camp and burn it, just as one burns the first (mentioned) bull (of the anointed priest). It is a sin-offering for the congregation.

The Leader's Sin-Offering

- ²² If a (Jewish) leader sins, unintentionally violating any of God's commandments which are prohibited, (thereby) incurring guilt, ²³ he should bring a perfect (unblemished) male goat as his offering, when his sin that he has committed is made known to him.

- ²⁴ He should lean his hands on the goat's head and slaughter it before God, in the place where burnt-offerings are slaughtered. (If it is slaughtered with the specific intention of being a sin-offering, then) it is a (valid) sin-offering.

- ²⁵ The priest should take some of the blood of the sin-offering with his finger and place it on the horns of the altar (used) for burnt-offerings. Then he should pour (the remainder of) its blood onto the base of the altar (used) for burnt-offerings.

- ²⁶ He should make all its (sacrificial) fats go up in smoke on the altar, just like the fats of the peace-offering.

Thus the priest will make an atonement for his sin, and he will be forgiven.

The Citizen's Sin-Offering

- [SIXTH READING] ²⁷ If an individual among the citizens of the land sins unintentionally, by violating any of God's commandments which are prohibited, (thereby) incurring guilt—²⁸ (then) when his sin that he has committed becomes known to him, he should bring an unblemished female goat as his offering, for his sin that he has committed:

---

19. Separate all its (sacrificial) fat from it and make it go up in smoke on the altar. Although Scripture does not mention the diaphragm and the two kidneys explicitly, they are derived from verse 20: *"He should do to this bull just as one does to the bull of the sin-offering (of the High Priest)."*

Why are these details not specified here (in verse 19)? The School of Rabbi Ishmael taught: This can be compared to a king who was furious with his beloved friend (for wronging him), but he kept it quiet because he was fond of him (*Rashi, 11ᵗʰ century*).

ויקרא ד:כט - ה:ג

29 וְסָמַךְ אֶת־יָדוֹ עַל רֹאשׁ הַחַטָּאת וְשָׁחַט אֶת־הַחַטָּאת בִּמְקוֹם הָעֹלָה: 30 וְלָקַח הַכֹּהֵן מִדָּמָהּ בְּאֶצְבָּעוֹ וְנָתַן עַל־קַרְנֹת מִזְבַּח הָעֹלָה וְאֶת־כָּל־דָּמָהּ יִשְׁפֹּךְ אֶל־יְסוֹד הַמִּזְבֵּחַ: 31 וְאֶת־כָּל־חֶלְבָּהּ יָסִיר כַּאֲשֶׁר הוּסַר חֵלֶב מֵעַל זֶבַח הַשְּׁלָמִים וְהִקְטִיר הַכֹּהֵן הַמִּזְבֵּחָה לְרֵיחַ נִיחֹחַ לַיהוה וְכִפֶּר עָלָיו הַכֹּהֵן וְנִסְלַח לוֹ: פ 32 וְאִם־כֶּבֶשׂ יָבִיא קָרְבָּנוֹ לְחַטָּאת נְקֵבָה תְמִימָה יְבִיאֶנָּה: 33 וְסָמַךְ אֶת־יָדוֹ עַל רֹאשׁ הַחַטָּאת וְשָׁחַט אֹתָהּ לְחַטָּאת בִּמְקוֹם אֲשֶׁר יִשְׁחַט אֶת־הָעֹלָה: 34 וְלָקַח הַכֹּהֵן מִדַּם הַחַטָּאת בְּאֶצְבָּעוֹ וְנָתַן עַל־קַרְנֹת מִזְבַּח הָעֹלָה וְאֶת־כָּל־דָּמָהּ יִשְׁפֹּךְ אֶל־יְסוֹד הַמִּזְבֵּחַ: 35 וְאֶת־כָּל־חֶלְבָּהּ יָסִיר כַּאֲשֶׁר יוּסַר חֵלֶב־הַכֶּשֶׂב מִזֶּבַח הַשְּׁלָמִים וְהִקְטִיר הַכֹּהֵן אֹתָם הַמִּזְבֵּחָה עַל אִשֵּׁי יְהוה וְכִפֶּר עָלָיו הַכֹּהֵן עַל־חַטָּאתוֹ אֲשֶׁר־חָטָא וְנִסְלַח לוֹ: פ

ה 1 וְנֶפֶשׁ כִּי־תֶחֱטָא וְשָׁמְעָה קוֹל אָלָה וְהוּא עֵד אוֹ רָאָה אוֹ יָדָע אִם־לוֹא יַגִּיד וְנָשָׂא עֲוֺנוֹ: 2 אוֹ נֶפֶשׁ אֲשֶׁר תִּגַּע בְּכָל־דָּבָר טָמֵא אוֹ בְנִבְלַת חַיָּה טְמֵאָה אוֹ בְּנִבְלַת בְּהֵמָה טְמֵאָה אוֹ בְּנִבְלַת שֶׁרֶץ טָמֵא וְנֶעְלַם מִמֶּנּוּ וְהוּא טָמֵא וְאָשֵׁם: 3 אוֹ כִי יִגַּע בְּטֻמְאַת אָדָם לְכֹל טֻמְאָתוֹ אֲשֶׁר יִטְמָא בָּהּ

1-2. If a person sins, by accepting an oath ... or if a person touches anything that is (ritually) impure. These two sins are extremely easy to transgress. Incorrect words can easily pass through your lips, and are more likely than a sin of action. Also, the laws of ritual purity are extremely complex, making mistakes very common. Despite the seriousness of these sins, God, in His great kindness, permitted their atonement with an offering which posed less financial burden in that it was adjusted according to a person's means (*Rabbi Aaron ha-Levi (Ḥinnukh), 13th century*).

spiritual vitamin

" When you do a good thing, no matter how big or small, you "please God" and become attached to Him through the fulfillment of His commandments. "

leviticus 4:29 – 5:3 — va-yikra'

- ⁲⁹ He should lean his hands on the head of the sin-offering, and he should slaughter the sin-offering in the (same) place as the burnt-offering (is slaughtered).

- ³⁰ The priest should take some of its blood with his finger, and place it on the horns of the altar (used) for burnt-offerings. Then he should pour all of its (remaining) blood on the base of the altar.

- ³¹ He should remove all of its (sacrificial) fats, in the same way that the fats were removed from the peace-offering. The priest should then cause them to go up in smoke on the altar, a pleasant aroma for God. The priest will make an atonement for him, and he will be forgiven.

³² If he brings a sheep for his sin-offering, he should bring a perfect (unblemished) female:

- ³³ He should lean his hands on the head of the sin-offering and slaughter it in the place where the burnt-offering is slaughtered, (with the specific intent that it) is a sin-offering,

- ³⁴ The priest should take some of the blood of the sin-offering with his finger and place it on the horns of the altar (used) for burnt-offerings. Then he should pour all its (remaining) blood onto the base of the altar.

- ³⁵ He should remove all its (sacrificial) fat, in the same way that the sheep's fat is removed from the peace-offering. The priest should then cause the(se parts) to go up in smoke on the altar, upon the (piles of wood that are made as) fires for God.

Thus the priest will make an atonement for him, for his sin which he committed, and he will be forgiven.

5 The Variable Sin-Offering

- ¹ If a person sins, by accepting an oath (denying that he was witness to a certain matter) and he does not testify, (when in reality) he was a witness because he saw or knew (about it)—he will bear (the consequences of) his sin.

- ² Or if a person touches anything that is (ritually) impure—whether it is the carcass of an impure wild animal, or the carcass of an impure domestic animal, or the carcass of an impure creeping creature—and he was unaware of the fact (and he subsequently entered the Holy Temple, or ate from a sacrifice), he is guilty.

- ³ Or if he touches a human (corpse which is) impure, or any (source of) impurity through which one can become impure, and he was unaware of the fact (and he

---

This is like a negotiator who asks the king for forgiveness on behalf of his friend, and when he attains the king's pardon, the sinner follows with a gift (*Babylonian Talmud, Zevaḥim* 7b).

5:1 He was a witness. The word "he" in this verse can also refer to God. God is witness to everything that transpires, including withholding evidence (*Rabbi Baḥya b. Asher, 13th century*).

ויקרא ה:ג-יב

וְנֶעְלַ֣ם מִמֶּ֔נּוּ וְה֥וּא יָדַ֖ע וְאָשֵֽׁם: 4 א֣וֹ נֶ֡פֶשׁ כִּ֣י תִשָּׁבַע֩ לְבַטֵּ֨א בִשְׂפָתַ֜יִם לְהָרַ֣ע | א֣וֹ לְהֵיטִ֗יב לְ֠כֹל אֲשֶׁ֨ר יְבַטֵּ֧א הָאָדָ֛ם בִּשְׁבֻעָ֖ה וְנֶעְלַ֣ם מִמֶּ֑נּוּ וְהוּא־יָדַ֥ע וְאָשֵׁ֖ם לְאַחַ֥ת מֵאֵֽלֶּה: 5 וְהָיָ֥ה כִֽי־יֶאְשַׁ֖ם לְאַחַ֣ת מֵאֵ֑לֶּה וְהִ֨תְוַדָּ֔ה אֲשֶׁ֥ר חָטָ֖א עָלֶֽיהָ: 6 וְהֵבִ֣יא אֶת־אֲשָׁמ֣וֹ לַיהֹוָ֡ה עַ֣ל חַטָּאתוֹ֩ אֲשֶׁ֨ר חָטָ֜א נְקֵבָ֨ה מִן־הַצֹּ֤אן כִּשְׂבָּה֙ אֽוֹ־שְׂעִירַ֣ת עִזִּ֔ים לְחַטָּ֑את וְכִפֶּ֥ר עָלָ֛יו הַכֹּהֵ֖ן מֵחַטָּאתֽוֹ: 7 וְאִם־לֹ֨א תַגִּ֣יע יָדוֹ֮ דֵּ֣י שֶׂה֒ וְהֵבִ֨יא אֶת־אֲשָׁמ֜וֹ אֲשֶׁ֣ר חָטָ֗א שְׁתֵּ֥י תֹרִ֛ים אֽוֹ־שְׁנֵ֥י בְנֵֽי־יוֹנָ֖ה לַיהֹוָ֑ה אֶחָ֥ד לְחַטָּ֖את וְאֶחָ֥ד לְעֹלָֽה: 8 וְהֵבִ֤יא אֹתָם֙ אֶל־הַכֹּהֵ֔ן וְהִקְרִ֛יב אֶת־אֲשֶׁ֥ר לַחַטָּ֖את רִאשׁוֹנָ֑ה וּמָלַ֧ק אֶת־רֹאשׁ֛וֹ מִמּ֥וּל עָרְפּ֖וֹ וְלֹ֥א יַבְדִּֽיל: 9 וְהִזָּ֞ה מִדַּ֤ם הַֽחַטָּאת֙ עַל־קִ֣יר הַמִּזְבֵּ֔חַ וְהַנִּשְׁאָ֣ר בַּדָּ֔ם יִמָּצֵ֖ה אֶל־יְס֣וֹד הַמִּזְבֵּ֑חַ חַטָּ֖את הֽוּא: 10 וְאֶת־הַשֵּׁנִ֛י יַעֲשֶׂ֥ה עֹלָ֖ה כַּמִּשְׁפָּ֑ט וְכִפֶּ֨ר עָלָ֧יו הַכֹּהֵ֛ן מֵחַטָּאת֥וֹ אֲשֶׁר־חָטָ֖א וְנִסְלַ֥ח לֽוֹ: ס 11 [SEVENTH READING] וְאִם־לֹא֩ תַשִּׂ֨יג יָד֜וֹ לִשְׁתֵּ֣י תֹרִ֗ים אוֹ֮ לִשְׁנֵ֣י בְנֵי־יוֹנָה֒ וְהֵבִ֨יא אֶת־קׇרְבָּנ֜וֹ אֲשֶׁ֣ר חָטָ֗א עֲשִׂירִ֧ת הָאֵפָ֛ה סֹ֖לֶת לְחַטָּ֑את לֹא־יָשִׂ֨ים עָלֶ֜יהָ שֶׁ֗מֶן וְלֹא־יִתֵּ֤ן עָלֶ֙יהָ֙ לְבֹנָ֔ה כִּ֥י חַטָּ֖את הִֽוא: 12 וֶהֱבִיאָהּ֮ אֶל־הַכֹּהֵן֒ וְקָמַ֣ץ הַכֹּהֵ֣ן ׀ מִ֠מֶּ֠נָּה מְל֨וֹא קֻמְצ֜וֹ אֶת־אַזְכָּרָתָהּ֙ וְהִקְטִ֣יר הַמִּזְבֵּ֔חָה עַ֖ל אִשֵּׁ֣י יְהֹוָ֑ה חַטָּ֖את

---

5. He should confess the sin which he had committed. Rendered literally, the verse reads, "He should confess the sin which is *upon her*." This suggests that as the person becomes spiritually cleansed by the offering, the sin will rest on "her"—on the sheep (*Zohar*).

8. He should cut its head (by piercing with his nail) opposite the back of its head, but should not separate (the head from the body by severing both the esophagus and the trachea). The sin-offering from birds is the offering of the poor man. That is why this offering does not require the usual ritual slaughter, so that the priest should not have to look for a knife and examine it, while the poor man is losing valuable time from work. The message is that you should always hurry as much as possible to fulfil a poor man's need.

Also when the bird's head is not completely separated from the body it looks more dignified. The poor man's offering should look as important as possible. It is enough for him that he is poor; we need not make things worse by making his offering look unsightly (*Rabbi Aaron ha-Levi (Ḥinnukh), 13th century*).

subsequently entered the Holy Temple, or ate from a sacrifice), and then (later) he remembers—he is guilty.

- ⁴ Or if a person swears, expressing verbally to do harm (to himself) or to do good (to himself in the future, or) whatever a person may express in an oath (about the past), and he forgot about (his oath and violated) one of these (oaths), and then (later) he remembered—he is guilty.

- ⁵ What should happen is, when someone incurs guilt in any one of these cases, he should confess the sin which he had committed.

- ⁶ He should bring his guilt-offering to God for his sin which he had committed: a female (animal) from the flock, either a sheep or a goat, for a sin-offering, and the priest will make an atonement (for him) from his sin.

⁷ If he cannot afford a sheep, he should bring as his guilt-offering before God, for that sin that he had committed: two turtledoves or two young doves, one for a sin-offering, and one for a burnt-offering:—

- ⁸ He should bring them to the priest, who should first offer up that (bird) which is (designated) for the sin-offering. He should cut its head (by piercing with his nail) opposite the back of its head, but should not separate (the head from the body by severing both the esophagus and the trachea).

- ⁹ He should sprinkle some of the blood of the sin-offering (directly from the bird) on the wall of the altar, and the remainder of the blood should be squeezed out (directly from the bird) onto the base of the altar.

- (If it was offered specifically as a sin-offering then it) is a (valid) sin-offering.

- ¹⁰ He should offer up the second one as a burnt-offering, according to the law (of burnt-offerings that come from birds). Thus the priest will make an atonement for him, for his sin which he had committed, and he will be forgiven.

[SEVENTH READING] ¹¹ But if he cannot afford two turtledoves or two young doves, then he should bring as his offering for his sin one tenth of an *'ephah* of fine flour for a sin-offering:

- He should not put oil over it, nor should he place frankincense upon it, for it is a sin-offering.

- ¹² He should bring it to the priest, and the priest should scoop out a three-finger fistful (so that its owner will be) remembered (positively before God), and make it go up in smoke on the altar, upon the (piles of wood that are made as) fires for God.

- (If it was scooped and burned with the specific intention that it is a sin-offering, then it) is a (valid) sin-offering.

ויקרא ה:יב-כג

הוּא: 13 וְכִפֶּר֩ עָלָ֨יו הַכֹּהֵ֜ן עַל־חַטָּאת֧וֹ אֲשֶׁר־חָטָ֛א מֵאַחַ֥ת מֵאֵ֖לֶּה וְנִסְלַ֣ח ל֑וֹ וְהָיְתָ֥ה לַכֹּהֵ֖ן כַּמִּנְחָֽה: ס 14 וַיְדַבֵּ֥ר יְהוָ֖ה אֶל־מֹשֶׁ֥ה לֵּאמֹֽר: 15 נֶ֚פֶשׁ כִּֽי־תִמְעֹ֣ל מַ֔עַל וְחָֽטְאָה֙ בִּשְׁגָגָ֔ה מִקָּדְשֵׁ֖י יְהוָ֑ה וְהֵבִיא֩ אֶת־אֲשָׁמ֨וֹ לַיהוָ֜ה אַ֧יִל תָּמִ֣ים מִן־הַצֹּ֗אן בְּעֶרְכְּךָ֛ כֶּֽסֶף־שְׁקָלִ֥ים בְּשֶֽׁקֶל־הַקֹּ֖דֶשׁ לְאָשָֽׁם: 16 וְאֵ֣ת אֲשֶׁר֩ חָטָ֨א מִן־הַקֹּ֜דֶשׁ יְשַׁלֵּ֗ם וְאֶת־חֲמִֽישִׁתוֹ֙ יוֹסֵ֣ף עָלָ֔יו וְנָתַ֥ן אֹת֖וֹ לַכֹּהֵ֑ן וְהַכֹּהֵ֗ן יְכַפֵּ֥ר עָלָ֛יו בְּאֵ֥יל הָאָשָׁ֖ם וְנִסְלַ֥ח לֽוֹ: פ 17 וְאִם־נֶ֨פֶשׁ֙ כִּ֣י תֶֽחֱטָ֔א וְעָ֨שְׂתָ֔ה אַחַת֙ מִכָּל־מִצְוֺ֣ת יְהוָ֔ה אֲשֶׁ֖ר לֹ֣א תֵעָשֶׂ֑ינָה וְלֹֽא־יָדַ֥ע וְאָשֵׁ֖ם וְנָשָׂ֥א עֲוֺנֽוֹ: 18 וְ֠הֵבִיא אַ֣יִל תָּמִ֧ים מִן־הַצֹּ֛אן בְּעֶרְכְּךָ֥ לְאָשָׁ֖ם אֶל־הַכֹּהֵ֑ן וְכִפֶּר֩ עָלָ֨יו הַכֹּהֵ֜ן עַ֣ל שִׁגְגָת֧וֹ אֲשֶׁר־שָׁגָ֛ג וְה֥וּא לֹֽא־יָדַ֖ע וְנִסְלַ֥ח לֽוֹ: 19 אָשָׁ֖ם ה֑וּא אָשֹׁ֥ם אָשַׁ֖ם לַיהוָֽה: פ 20 וַיְדַבֵּ֥ר יְהוָ֖ה אֶל־מֹשֶׁ֥ה לֵּאמֹֽר: 21 נֶ֚פֶשׁ כִּ֣י תֶֽחֱטָ֔א וּמָעֲלָ֥ה מַ֖עַל בַּיהוָ֑ה וְכִחֵ֨שׁ בַּעֲמִית֜וֹ בְּפִקָּד֗וֹן אֽוֹ־בִתְשׂ֤וּמֶת יָד֙ א֣וֹ בְגָזֵ֔ל א֖וֹ עָשַׁ֥ק אֶת־עֲמִיתֽוֹ: 22 אֽוֹ־מָצָ֧א אֲבֵדָ֛ה וְכִ֥חֶשׁ בָּ֖הּ וְנִשְׁבַּ֣ע עַל־שָׁ֑קֶר עַל־אַחַ֗ת מִכֹּ֛ל אֲשֶׁר־יַעֲשֶׂ֥ה הָאָדָ֖ם לַחֲטֹ֥א בָהֵֽנָּה: 23 וְהָיָה֙ כִּֽי־יֶחֱטָ֣א וְאָשֵׁ֔ם וְהֵשִׁ֨יב אֶת־הַגְּזֵלָ֜ה אֲשֶׁ֣ר גָּזָ֗ל א֚וֹ אֶת־הָעֹ֙שֶׁק֙ אֲשֶׁ֣ר עָשָׁ֔ק א֖וֹ

Food for thought

1. Is abusing the natural environment "misappropriating" God's property?

2. Your body is a temple for the Divine—are you treating it appropriately?

3. Is there a correlation between your respect for God and respect for fellow humans?

The guilt-offering, brought in a case of doubt where a man is uncertain if he transgressed a commandment un-intentionally, is actually *more expensive* than a sin-offering, brought when he is sure that he transgressed (*Babylonian Talmud, Zevaḥim* 48a). This shows that *if you are uncertain if you have sinned you are in need of more atonement.*

When you know that you have sinned, you are aware that something needs correcting, which will probably lead you to act on your feelings. But if you are uncertain that you have sinned, you are likely to take the matter less seriously. Therefore a more powerful—and more expensive—atonement is needed (*Rabbi Jonah b. Abraham Gerondi, 13th century*).

21. Acts deceitfully against God. When the Torah says that you are being deceitful *"against God"* when you are dishonest about a friend who deposited an item with you for safekeeping, it is because of the following: When you give a loan or sell something, it usually is done in front of a witness or with a contract. But when you ask someone to look after something, you

- ❖ ¹³ Thus the priest will make an atonement for his sin that he committed in any one of these (three above-mentioned cases), and he will be forgiven.

- ❖ (If it was a meal-offering, then the leftovers) belong to the priest, as (with an ordinary) meal-offering.

The Guilt-Offering for Misappropriation

¹⁴ God spoke to Moses, saying:

- ❖ ¹⁵ If a person sins unintentionally by wrongfully using something that is sacred to God (i.e. Temple property), he should bring as his guilt-offering to God a perfect (unblemished, two-year-old) ram from the flock, that is worth (at least) two silver shekels, according to the shekel (measurement system which is used for) sanctified (items), for a guilt-offering.

- ❖ ¹⁶ He must repay whatever he has deprived the Sanctuary. He should add to it one fifth of its value, and give it to the priest. The priest will then make an atonement for him through the ram of the guilt-offering, and he will be forgiven.

The Guilt-Offering in a Case of Doubt

- ❖ ¹⁷ If a person is uncertain if he sinned (by transgressing) any of God's commandments which are prohibited (with the punishment of soul-excision for an intentional transgression), he is guilty and he will bear (the consequences of) his sin.

- ❖ ¹⁸ He should bring to the priest a perfect (unblemished) ram from the flock, which has the same value as that of a guilt-offering. The priest will then make an atonement for his unintentional sin which he may have committed, and he should be forgiven. ¹⁹ It is a guilt-offering, for he has become guilty before God.

The Guilt-Offering for Dishonesty

²⁰ God spoke to Moses, saying:

- ❖ ²¹ If a person sins and acts deceitfully against God by making a false denial to his fellow concerning an item deposited (for safekeeping), cash-in-hand (which was part of a business deal or loan), or (an object taken) by robbery, or he withheld wages from his fellow, ²² or he found a lost article—and then he denied (any of the above-mentioned sins) and swore falsely (that he need not return any funds). In any of these cases where a man might sin, ²³ what should happen is that when

17. If a person in uncertain if he sinned ... he is guilty. Rabbi Akiva would cry when he would read this verse, saying, "If we are held accountable for sins that we do unintentionally, how much more so are we accountable for sinning intentionally!" (*Babylonian Talmud, Kiddushin* 81b).

ויקרא ה:כג-כו

אֶת־הַפִּקָּדוֹן אֲשֶׁר הָפְקַד אִתּוֹ אוֹ אֶת־הָאֲבֵדָה אֲשֶׁר מָצָא: 24 [MAFTIR] אוֹ מִכֹּל אֲשֶׁר־יִשָּׁבַע עָלָיו לַשֶּׁקֶר וְשִׁלַּם אֹתוֹ בְּרֹאשׁוֹ וַחֲמִשִׁתָיו יֹסֵף עָלָיו לַאֲשֶׁר הוּא לוֹ יִתְּנֶנּוּ בְּיוֹם אַשְׁמָתוֹ: 25 וְאֶת־אֲשָׁמוֹ יָבִיא לַיהֹוָה אַיִל תָּמִים מִן־הַצֹּאן בְּעֶרְכְּךָ לְאָשָׁם אֶל־הַכֹּהֵן: 26 וְכִפֶּר עָלָיו הַכֹּהֵן לִפְנֵי יְהֹוָה וְנִסְלַח לוֹ עַל־אַחַת מִכֹּל אֲשֶׁר־יַעֲשֶׂה לְאַשְׁמָה בָהּ: פ פ פ

קי״א פסוקים, דעוא״ל סימן, ציו״ה סימן.

to *"return the article which he had robbed."* It is because the thief acts as though God cannot see him. The robber equates the dignity of the servant with the dignity of the Master, while the thief does not (*Midrash Tanḥuma*).

25. He should then bring his guilt-offering to God. The sacrifice will not atone unless he first returns what he has taken (*Babylonian Talmud, Bava Kama* 110a).

leviticus 5:23–26 va-yikra'

he (feels that he) has sinned and is guilty, he should return the article which he had robbed, or the funds which he had withheld, or the item which had been deposited with him, or the article which he had found, [MAFTIR] ²⁴ or anything else about which he had sworn falsely. He should pay the principal amount and add one fifth to it. He should give it to its rightful owner on the day (that the sinner repents for) his guilt.

❖ ²⁵ He should then bring his guilt-offering to God: a perfect (unblemished) ram from the flock which has the same value as (that brought) for a guilt-offering, to the priest. ²⁶ The priest will make an atonement for him before God, and he will be forgiven for any of (the above-mentioned ways) that one may commit (a sin), incurring guilt through it.

Haftarot: Va-Yikra'—p. 1344.   *Zakhor*—p. 1427.   *Ha-Ḥodesh*—p. 1433.   *Rosh Ḥodesh*—p. 1417.
Maftir: Zakhor—p. 1208 (25:17–19).   *Ha-Ḥodesh*—p. 392 (12:1–20).
Rosh Ḥodesh—p. 1000 (28:9–15).

---

usually do it discreetly and no-one knows about it except for God. Therefore, when you deny the transaction, you are acting *"deceitfully against God"* (*Rashi, 11th century*).

23. He should return the article which he had robbed. Why does the Torah deal more harshly with a thief, who acts in secrecy, than with a robber, who acts in public? The thief is required to pay double or even four- or fivefold the amount that he stole, whereas the robber simply has

You are the **guardian** of your **inner flame,** which illuminates the path to your **highest self.** Every decision you make either **feeds** your flame or causes it to **diminish.** With a **weakened** flame, you fall easily into **fear** and **worry.** With a **strong** flame your consciousness **expands** and you are **energized.** How is your flame burning today?

TZAV צו

ADDITIONAL LAWS OF THE OFFERINGS | 6:1 – 7:27
GIFTS TO THE PRIESTS | 7:28–38
INAUGURATION OF AARON AND HIS SONS | 8:1–36

NAME
Tzav

MEANING
"Command"

LINES IN TORAH SCROLL
170

PARASHIYYOT
7 open; 1 closed

VERSES
97

WORDS
1353

LETTERS
5096

DATE
23 *Adar* – 20 *Iyyar*, 2449

LOCATION
Sinai Desert

KEY PEOPLE
Moses, Aaron, Aaron's sons

MITZVOT
9 positive; 9 prohibitions

MASORETIC FEATURES
Mem in the word *mokedah* (6:2) is undersized

NOTE
Read on the Sabbath prior to Passover, during a regular year

CHARACTER PROFILE

NAME
High Priest (*ha-kohen ha-gadol*)

OTHER NAMES
Anointed Priest (*ha-kohen ha-mashiah*)

FUNCTION
Divinely appointed, sacred representative of the Jewish people; pays homage to God in the Holy Temple, the Divine earthly abode; dresses in priestly garments; consecrated by investiture; responsible for purging sins and impurities of the Temple; enters Holy of Holies once a year, on *Yom Kippur*; subject to more restrictions than ordinary priest

ACTIVE PERIOD
From the Exodus to 70 CE

PASSION

The fire on the altar had to constantly be kept burning. Never let your passion for God and the Torah become extinguished; feed it continually so that it keeps burning (6:5).

PRIESTLY GIFTS

The priests were given pieces from the sacrifices for their own benefit. This was a sign of gratitude by the Jewish people to those who served in the Temple and had no personal livelihood (7:28–38).

LOYALTY TO GOD

The entire congregation watched as Moses anointed Aaron and his sons, dressed them in their priestly garments and inaugurated the Tabernacle. They saw how Moses and Aaron followed God's word exactly, which inspired them in their own lives (8:4).

ויקרא ו:א-ו

וַיְדַבֵּ֥ר יְהֹוָ֖ה אֶל־מֹשֶׁ֥ה לֵּאמֹֽר: 2 צַ֤ו אֶֽת־אַהֲרֹן֙ וְאֶת־בָּנָ֣יו לֵאמֹ֔ר זֹ֥את תּוֹרַ֖ת הָעֹלָ֑ה הִ֣וא הָעֹלָ֡ה עַל֩ מוֹקְדָ֨ה עַל־הַמִּזְבֵּ֤חַ כָּל־הַלַּ֙יְלָה֙ עַד־הַבֹּ֔קֶר וְאֵ֥שׁ הַמִּזְבֵּ֖חַ תּ֥וּקַד בּֽוֹ: 3 וְלָבַ֨שׁ הַכֹּהֵ֜ן מִדּ֣וֹ בַ֗ד וּמִֽכְנְסֵי־בַד֮ יִלְבַּ֣שׁ עַל־בְּשָׂרוֹ֒ וְהֵרִ֣ים אֶת־הַדֶּ֗שֶׁן אֲשֶׁ֨ר תֹּאכַ֥ל הָאֵ֛שׁ אֶת־הָעֹלָ֖ה עַל־הַמִּזְבֵּ֑חַ וְשָׂמ֕וֹ אֵ֖צֶל הַמִּזְבֵּֽחַ: 4 וּפָשַׁט֙ אֶת־בְּגָדָ֔יו וְלָבַ֖שׁ בְּגָדִ֣ים אֲחֵרִ֑ים וְהוֹצִ֤יא אֶת־הַדֶּ֙שֶׁן֙ אֶל־מִח֣וּץ לַֽמַּחֲנֶ֔ה אֶל־מָק֖וֹם טָהֽוֹר: 5 וְהָאֵ֨שׁ עַל־הַמִּזְבֵּ֤חַ תּֽוּקַד־בּוֹ֙ לֹ֣א תִכְבֶּ֔ה וּבִעֵ֨ר עָלֶ֧יהָ הַכֹּהֵ֛ן עֵצִ֖ים בַּבֹּ֣קֶר בַּבֹּ֑קֶר וְעָרַ֤ךְ עָלֶ֙יהָ֙ הָֽעֹלָ֔ה וְהִקְטִ֥יר עָלֶ֖יהָ חֶלְבֵ֥י הַשְּׁלָמִֽים: 6 אֵ֗שׁ תָּמִ֛יד תּוּקַ֥ד עַל־הַמִּזְבֵּ֖חַ לֹ֥א תִכְבֶּֽה: ס

trace of his sin, and it should not be mentioned again (*Rabbi Menahem b. Moses ha-Bavli, 16th century*).

Aaron, a leader of the Jewish people, was commanded personally to *"shovel out the ashes."* A leader must retain a sense of humility, even a willingness to deal with seemingly insignificant and lowly tasks, in order to remain in touch with the everyday needs of the people (*Rabbi Moses Sofer, 18th–19th century*).

4. Take off his garments and put on other garments. This is not an obligation, but an appropriate practice, so that he should not soil the garments in which he constantly officiates, when taking out the ashes.

When a servant pours a glass of wine for his master, he should not wear the same clothes as when cooking a pot of food for his master (*Rashi, 11th century*).

5-6. It must not go out ... a continual fire should burn. If the western lamp of the candelabrum becomes extinguished, then it may only be reignited from the outer altar (*Maimonides, 12th century*).

kabbalah bites

6:6 Making yourself right and others wrong is a dysfunctional mind pattern.

When you complain, the implication is that you are right and the situation you are reacting against is wrong.

Our verse advises: *lo' tikhbeh*, which can be read, *extinguish the "no."* Dismantle your negative, dysfunctional approach.

And how do you do that? *"A continuous fire should burn upon the altar"*—by sustaining a constant state of enthusiasm ("fire"), through daily meditation on spiritual teachings.

leviticus 6:1–6 — tzav

parashat tzav

Ashes of the Burnt-Offering

6 ¹ God spoke to Moses, saying: ² Command Aaron and his sons, saying:

- This is the law of the burnt-offering: It is the burnt-offering which (may) burn on the altar all night until morning. The altar's fire should burn with it.

- ³ The priest should put on his fitted tunic, and he should put his linen pants (directly) on his skin. He should shovel out (a shovelful of) the (innermost) ashes that remain from the burnt-offering, which the fire consumed on the altar, and put them down next to the altar (on the east ramp).

- ⁴ He should (preferably) then take off his garments and put on other garments, and he should take out the ashes to a clean place outside the camp.

Fire on the Altar

- ⁵ The fire on the altar should be kept burning upon it. It must not go out.

- The priest should kindle wood upon it every morning, and upon it, he should arrange the burnt-offering and make the fats of the peace-offerings go up in smoke upon it.

- ⁶ A continuous fire should burn upon the altar. It must not go out.

6:2 Command. The expression *tzav* always denotes "urging on" to observe a precept—for the present and also for future generations.

Rabbi Simeon taught: Scripture especially needs to urge you to observe commandments that cause you a severe financial loss (*Rashi, 11th century*).

It is during times of financial crisis that we must gather strength not to waver in our commitment to God (*Rabbi Judah Aryeh Leib Alter of Gur, 19th century*).

This is the law of the burnt-offering. From here you learn that it is permitted to offer up the fats and limbs throughout the night (*Rashi, 11th century*).

"Fats" are symbolic of pleasures, as indulging in pleasures leads to the production of fat (see *Babylonian Talmud, Gittin* 56b). The Torah is telling us that an integral part of worshiping God is dedicating your "fats"—your pleasures—to God (*Rabbi Shneur Zalman of Lyady, 18th century*).

3. Shovel out (a shovelful of) the (innermost) ashes that remain from the burnt-offering. The message here is: After a sinner brings a sacrifice and repents, there is no remaining

---

Food for thought

1. What aspect of your relationship with God do you preserve, no matter what?

2. What do you do to stoke your soul's flame on a regular basis?

3. How do you keep yourself motivated when your spiritual fire dies down?

ויקרא ו:ז–יג

7 וְזֹאת תּוֹרַת הַמִּנְחָה הַקְרֵב אֹתָהּ בְּנֵי־אַהֲרֹן לִפְנֵי יְהֹוָה אֶל־פְּנֵי הַמִּזְבֵּחַ: 8 וְהֵרִים מִמֶּנּוּ בְּקֻמְצוֹ מִסֹּלֶת הַמִּנְחָה וּמִשַּׁמְנָהּ וְאֵת כָּל־הַלְּבֹנָה אֲשֶׁר עַל־הַמִּנְחָה וְהִקְטִיר הַמִּזְבֵּחַ רֵיחַ נִיחֹחַ אַזְכָּרָתָהּ לַיהֹוָה: 9 וְהַנּוֹתֶרֶת מִמֶּנָּה יֹאכְלוּ אַהֲרֹן וּבָנָיו מַצּוֹת תֵּאָכֵל בְּמָקוֹם קָדֹשׁ בַּחֲצַר אֹהֶל־מוֹעֵד יֹאכְלוּהָ: 10 לֹא תֵאָפֶה חָמֵץ חֶלְקָם נָתַתִּי אֹתָהּ מֵאִשָּׁי קֹדֶשׁ קָדָשִׁים הִוא כַּחַטָּאת וְכָאָשָׁם: 11 כָּל־זָכָר בִּבְנֵי אַהֲרֹן יֹאכֲלֶנָּה חָק־עוֹלָם לְדֹרֹתֵיכֶם מֵאִשֵּׁי יְהֹוָה כֹּל אֲשֶׁר־יִגַּע בָּהֶם יִקְדָּשׁ: פ 12 [SECOND READING] וַיְדַבֵּר יְהֹוָה אֶל־מֹשֶׁה לֵּאמֹר: 13 זֶה קָרְבַּן אַהֲרֹן וּבָנָיו אֲשֶׁר־יַקְרִיבוּ לַיהֹוָה בְּיוֹם הִמָּשַׁח אֹתוֹ עֲשִׂירִת הָאֵפָה סֹלֶת מִנְחָה

2) When the people will see the High Priest atoning for his sins, it will encourage them to do likewise.

3) The fact that the High Priest brings an offering every day makes it less embarrassing for the sinner to bring his offering.

4) Poor people who can only afford a meal-offering will be less embarrassed to bring their offering, since the High Priest himself brings a meal-offering every day.

5) The offering serves to humble the High Priest when he sees that he is bringing a mere meal-offering which is usually brought by the poor.

6) When the people see that the High Priest's sacrifice is completely burned on the altar, they will realize that the priests offer sacrifices for God's sake, and not because they want to eat the leftovers.

7) The offering is to thank God for the gifts which the Torah requires to be given to the priests.

8) Since the priests may err during the day and perform the service incorrectly, thereby stealing from the altar, this meal-offering is entirely burned on the altar as compensation.

9) In addition to the communal sacrifices which are offered every day, God desired that there should also be a daily private sacrifice, so he required the High Priest to bring an offering (*Rabbi Isaac Abravanel, 15th century*).

spiritual vitamin

" Intellect and emotions should govern and inspire your daily life in complete harmony, and in a way that the mind rules the heart. When this inner harmony prevails, all the details of your daily life, both the material and the spiritual, will be carried out properly, without conflicts, without contradictions, and without vacillations. "

leviticus 6:7–13   tzav

Additional Laws of the Meal-Offering

- ⁷ This is the law of the meal-offering: Aaron's sons should bring it before God, to the front of the altar.

- ⁸ He should take out a three-finger fistful from the fine flour of the meal-offering and from its oil. (Afterwards he should gather) all the frankincense that is on the meal-offering, and he should make (the scoop and the frankincense) go up in smoke on the altar, (so that its owner will be) remembered (positively before God), a pleasant aroma for God.

- ⁹ Aaron and his sons should eat whatever is left over from it. It should be eaten as unleavened bread in a holy place, (namely), they should eat it in the courtyard of the Tent of Meeting. ¹⁰ (The leftovers) should not be baked leavened. I have given it to them as their portion, from My fire-offerings. It is a most holy (offering).

- (The meal-offering of the sinner is) like the sin-offering (in that the three-finger fistful must be scooped with the specific intention that it is a sin-offering. But the voluntary meal-offering is) like the guilt-offering (in that the correct intention is not crucial).

- ¹¹ Any male among Aaron's sons may eat it (even if he has a blemish that disqualifies him from Temple service. This is) an eternal statute for your generations from the fire-offerings of God.

- Anything that touches (the meal offering, and absorbs part of it) will become holy (like the meal-offering and will thus be subject to the same laws).

Meal-Offerings of the Priests

[SECOND READING] ¹² God spoke to Moses, saying:

- ¹³ This is the offering of Aaron and his sons, which they should offer to God, on the day when (one of them) is anointed (and initiated into service): One tenth of an *ʾephah* of fine flour.

- (The High Priest must bring such a) meal offering (too), daily. Half of it (is offered) in the morning and half of it in the evening.

13. The offering of Aaron and his sons ... one tenth of an *ʾephah*. The High Priest acts as an agent between the Jewish people and their Father in Heaven. He prays on their behalf, and they are atoned through his prayers and the sacrifices that he offers. Therefore, it is appropriate that such a person should have his own daily sacrifice, comparable to that of the daily communal sacrifice. And just like the daily sacrifice is offered twice a day, the High Priest is required to bring his meal-offering twice a day (*Rabbi Aaron ha-Levi (Ḥinnukh), 13ᵗʰ century*).

Nine reasons could be suggested as to why the High Priest brings a daily meal-offering:

1) The High Priest needs to be free from sin in order to act on behalf of the Jewish people. Therefore he must bring an offering every day to ensure that his sins are always atoned for.

ויקרא ו:יג – ז:ג

תָּמִ֗יד מַחֲצִיתָ֤הּ בַּבֹּ֨קֶר֙ וּמַחֲצִיתָ֣הּ בָּעָ֑רֶב: 14 עַֽל־מַחֲבַ֗ת בַּשֶּׁ֛מֶן תֵּעָשֶׂ֖ה מֻרְבֶּ֑כֶת תְּבִיאֶ֑נָּה תֻּפִינֵי֙ מִנְחַ֣ת פִּתִּ֔ים תַּקְרִ֛יב רֵֽיחַ־נִיחֹ֖חַ לַיהוָֽה: 15 וְהַכֹּהֵ֨ן הַמָּשִׁ֧יחַ תַּחְתָּ֛יו מִבָּנָ֖יו יַעֲשֶׂ֣ה אֹתָ֑הּ חָק־עוֹלָ֕ם לַיהוָ֖ה כָּלִ֥יל תָּקְטָֽר: 16 וְכָל־מִנְחַ֥ת כֹּהֵ֛ן כָּלִ֥יל תִּהְיֶ֖ה לֹ֥א תֵאָכֵֽל: פ 17 וַיְדַבֵּ֥ר יְהוָ֖ה אֶל־מֹשֶׁ֥ה לֵּאמֹֽר: 18 דַּבֵּ֤ר אֶֽל־אַהֲרֹן֙ וְאֶל־בָּנָ֣יו לֵאמֹ֔ר זֹ֥את תּוֹרַ֖ת הַֽחַטָּ֑את בִּמְק֡וֹם אֲשֶׁר֩ תִּשָּׁחֵ֨ט הָעֹלָ֜ה תִּשָּׁחֵ֤ט הַֽחַטָּאת֙ לִפְנֵ֣י יְהוָ֔ה קֹ֥דֶשׁ קָֽדָשִׁ֖ים הִֽוא: 19 הַכֹּהֵ֛ן הַֽמְחַטֵּ֥א אֹתָ֖הּ יֹאכֲלֶ֑נָּה בְּמָק֤וֹם קָדֹשׁ֙ תֵּֽאָכֵ֔ל בַּחֲצַ֖ר אֹ֥הֶל מוֹעֵֽד: 20 כֹּ֛ל אֲשֶׁר־יִגַּ֥ע בִּבְשָׂרָ֖הּ יִקְדָּ֑שׁ וַאֲשֶׁ֨ר יִזֶּ֤ה מִדָּמָהּ֙ עַל־הַבֶּ֔גֶד אֲשֶׁר֙ יִזֶּ֣ה עָלֶ֔יהָ תְּכַבֵּ֖ס בְּמָק֥וֹם קָדֹֽשׁ: 21 וּכְלִי־חֶ֛רֶשׂ אֲשֶׁ֥ר תְּבֻשַּׁל־בּ֖וֹ יִשָּׁבֵ֑ר וְאִם־בִּכְלִ֤י נְחֹ֨שֶׁת֙ בֻּשָּׁ֔לָה וּמֹרַ֥ק וְשֻׁטַּ֖ף בַּמָּֽיִם: 22 כָּל־זָכָ֥ר בַּכֹּהֲנִ֖ים יֹאכַ֣ל אֹתָ֑הּ קֹ֥דֶשׁ קָֽדָשִׁ֖ים הִֽוא: 23 וְכָל־חַטָּ֡את אֲשֶׁר֩ יוּבָ֨א מִדָּמָ֜הּ אֶל־אֹ֧הֶל מוֹעֵ֛ד לְכַפֵּ֥ר בַּקֹּ֖דֶשׁ לֹ֣א תֵאָכֵ֑ל בָּאֵ֖שׁ תִּשָּׂרֵֽף: פ

ז 1 וְזֹ֥את תּוֹרַ֖ת הָאָשָׁ֑ם קֹ֥דֶשׁ קָֽדָשִׁ֖ים הֽוּא: 2 בִּמְק֗וֹם אֲשֶׁ֤ר יִשְׁחֲטוּ֙ אֶת־הָ֣עֹלָ֔ה יִשְׁחֲט֖וּ אֶת־הָאָשָׁ֑ם וְאֶת־דָּמ֛וֹ יִזְרֹ֥ק עַל־הַמִּזְבֵּ֖חַ סָבִֽיב: 3 וְאֵ֥ת כָּל־

---

18. The sin-offering should be slaughtered ... where the burnt-offering is slaughtered. This highlights the importance of not causing embarrassment to another person, particularly to a sinner. The Torah says you should slaughter the sin-offering in the same place that the burnt-offering is slaughtered, so that an onlooker will not be able to discern the difference (*Rabbi Bahya b. Asher, 13th century*).

A penitent should not feel inferior to a righteous person who has never sinned. This is hinted to by the fact that we are commanded to slaughter "the *guilt*-offering" in the same place "where they slaughter the *burnt*-offering" (*Rabbi Moses Alshekh, 16th century*).

21. An earthenware vessel ... must be broken. But if it is cooked in a copper vessel, it should be purged and rinsed with water. This is required to remove the flavor which is absorbed in the walls of the vessel. But in the case of an earthenware vessel, Scripture teaches you here that it never rids itself of its defect and must therefore be broken (*Rashi, 11th century*).

Just as an earthenware vessel that absorbs a prohibited substance must be broken, so too, if a man's body participates in a sin, God forbid, it can be atoned for when his heart becomes "broken" through true repentance (*Zohar*).

7:1 This is the law of the guilt-offering: It is a most holy (offering). The verse can be read as follows: This is the law regarding what makes a person guilty of sin—he feels that he is "most

leviticus 6:14 – 7:3 — tzav

- [14] It should be made in a shallow pan with oil. It should be brought (after being) scalded (with boiling water. It is thus) baked many times: (scalded with water, baked in the oven, then fried in the pan). You should offer (it as) a meal-offering of broken pieces (by folding it repeatedly)—a pleasant aroma to God.

- [15] (When the High Priest dies), the priest who is anointed from among his sons in his place should prepare it.

- (This is) an eternal statute for God: It should be made to go up in smoke completely. [16] (Similarly) every meal-offering of a priest should be (burned) completely. It must not be eaten.

Additional Laws of the Sin-Offering

[17] God spoke to Moses, saying: [18] Speak to Aaron and to his sons, saying:

- This is the law of the sin-offering: The sin-offering should be slaughtered before God in the place where the burnt-offering is slaughtered. It is a most holy (offering).

- [19] The priest who offers it up as a sin-offering should eat it. It should be eaten in a holy place, (namely), in the courtyard of the Tent of Meeting.

- [20] Any (food) that touches its meat (absorbing some of it) will become holy (and thus subject to the same laws).

- If any of its blood is sprinkled on a garment, you should wash (that area of the garment) on which it has been sprinkled, in a holy place (i.e. the Temple courtyard).

- [21] An earthenware vessel in which (the meat of a sin-offering) is cooked must be broken. But if it is cooked in a copper vessel, it should be purged (in boiling water, to extract the absorbed flavor) and rinsed with water.

- [22] Every male among the priests may eat it. It is a most holy (offering).

- [23] Any sin-offering (whose blood was supposed to be poured on the outer altar, and) some of its blood was brought into the Tent of Meeting, to make atonement in the Sanctuary, (is invalid and) should not be eaten. It must be burned in fire.

7 The Guilt-Offering

[1] This is the law of the guilt-offering: It is a most holy (offering).

- [2] They should slaughter the guilt-offering in the place where they slaughter the burnt-offering. Its blood should be dashed upon the altar, all around.

- [3] He should offer all of its (sacrificial) fat from it: the tail, and the fat covering the

---

15-16. It should be made to go up in smoke completely ... be (burned) completely. From the High Priest's offering, a "three-finger fistful" is not taken out so that the remainder could be eaten; rather it is all completely burned. Of a regular priest's offering, all of it must be offered equally to God on high (*Rashi*, 11th century).

ויקרא ז:ג-יג

4 חֶלְבּוֹ יַקְרִיב מִמֶּנּוּ אֵת הָאַלְיָה וְאֶת־הַחֵלֶב הַמְכַסֶּה אֶת־הַקֶּרֶב: וְאֵת שְׁתֵּי הַכְּלָיֹת וְאֶת־הַחֵלֶב אֲשֶׁר עֲלֵהֶן אֲשֶׁר עַל־הַכְּסָלִים וְאֶת־הַיֹּתֶרֶת עַל־הַכָּבֵד עַל־הַכְּלָיֹת יְסִירֶנָּה: 5 וְהִקְטִיר אֹתָם הַכֹּהֵן הַמִּזְבֵּחָה אִשֶּׁה לַיהוָֹה אָשָׁם הוּא: 6 כָּל־זָכָר בַּכֹּהֲנִים יֹאכְלֶנּוּ בְּמָקוֹם קָדוֹשׁ יֵאָכֵל קֹדֶשׁ קָדָשִׁים הוּא: 7 כַּחַטָּאת כָּאָשָׁם תּוֹרָה אַחַת לָהֶם הַכֹּהֵן אֲשֶׁר יְכַפֶּר־בּוֹ לוֹ יִהְיֶה: 8 וְהַכֹּהֵן הַמַּקְרִיב אֶת־עֹלַת אִישׁ עוֹר הָעֹלָה אֲשֶׁר הִקְרִיב לַכֹּהֵן לוֹ יִהְיֶה: 9 וְכָל־מִנְחָה אֲשֶׁר תֵּאָפֶה בַתַּנּוּר וְכָל־נַעֲשָׂה בַמַּרְחֶשֶׁת וְעַל־מַחֲבַת לַכֹּהֵן הַמַּקְרִיב אֹתָהּ לוֹ תִהְיֶה: 10 וְכָל־מִנְחָה בְלוּלָה־בַשֶּׁמֶן וַחֲרֵבָה לְכָל־בְּנֵי אַהֲרֹן תִּהְיֶה אִישׁ כְּאָחִיו: פ 11 וְזֹאת תּוֹרַת זֶבַח הַשְּׁלָמִים אֲשֶׁר יַקְרִיב לַיהוָֹה: [THIRD READING] 12 אִם עַל־תּוֹדָה יַקְרִיבֶנּוּ | וְהִקְרִיב עַל־זֶבַח הַתּוֹדָה חַלּוֹת מַצּוֹת בְּלוּלֹת בַּשֶּׁמֶן וּרְקִיקֵי מַצּוֹת מְשֻׁחִים בַּשָּׁמֶן וְסֹלֶת מֻרְבֶּכֶת חַלֹּת בְּלוּלֹת בַּשָּׁמֶן: 13 עַל־חַלֹּת לֶחֶם חָמֵץ

Food for thought

1. Does it make sense to give a gift to God for wronging Him?

2. Should you try to eliminate all thoughts of guilt?

3. When are guilty feelings a blessing? When are they not?

journey, 3) illness, 4) imprisonment—the list is in order of *frequency*, with the most common first (*The Tosafists, 12th–14th centuries*).

The "four who are required to give thanksgiving" also allude to the hazardous journey of the soul:

1) *Sick person*. When the soul leaves its source beginning its journey down into this world, the intense love for God which it experienced previously is weakened. So the soul becomes "sick" with its desire to regain its lost love.

2) *Imprisonment*. As the soul descends further downwards, it becomes affected by the progressive confinement of the spiritual and physical worlds, until it is eventually "imprisoned" in a body.

3) *Sea voyage*. While the soul is living in this world, there is the danger that it will "drown" in the turbulent waters of worldliness and physicality.

4) *Desert*. The soul may regress further, God forbid, to the point that the person lives a life devoid and barren of any spiritual meaning whatsoever.

And since these challenges are great, the soul is made to swear an oath before it leaves its source—"Be righteous and don't be wicked"—giving it the strength to prevail against all odds (*Rabbi Menahem Mendel Schneerson, 20th century*).

intestines, [4] the two kidneys, (together) with the fat that is on them, which is over the flanks. He should (also) remove the diaphragm, (and a bit of) the liver (which is connected) to it, (when he takes out) the kidneys.

- [5] The priest should make them go up in smoke on the altar as a fire-offering to God. It is a guilt-offering.

- [6] Any male among the priests may eat it. It should be eaten in a holy place. It is a most holy (offering).

Ownership of Sacrificial Remains

- [7] The guilt-offering is like the sin-offering (in that) they have the same law (in the following instance: Only) a priest who (is permitted to pour blood on the altar and thus) effect atonement through (the sacrifice) to (its owner is allowed to eat the meat, for) it is his.

- [8] (Similarly, if such a) priest offers up a person's burnt-offering, the skin of the burnt-offering which he has offered up belongs to the priest. It will be his.

- [9] Any meal-offering baked in an oven, or any that is made in a deep pan or in a shallow pan, belongs to the priest who offers it up (together with the group of priests that are officiating that day). It will be his (and theirs).

- [10] Any (voluntary) meal-offering mixed with oil or (the meal-offering of the sinner that is) dry, should belong equally to all the sons of Aaron.

The Thanksgiving-Offering

[THIRD READING] [11] This is the law of the peace-offering, which he should bring to God:

- [12] If he is bringing it as a thanksgiving-offering, he should offer, along with the thanksgiving-offering: (ten) unleavened loaves mixed with oil, (ten) unleavened wafers smeared with oil, and (ten loaves of unleavened bread baked from) flour (which is then) scalded and mixed with oil, [13] along with (ten) loaves of leavened

---

holy." If you feel that you are perfect, you are most likely to sin (*Rabbi Joseph David Rubin, 20th century*).

12. The thanksgiving-offering. This offering is brought to give thanks to God for a miracle that had happened to a person. For instance, 1) those who made a sea-voyage, or 2) journeyed in the desert, or 3) those who had been in prison, or 4) a sick person who recovered. All these are required to give thanks to God, since regarding them, the verse states, *"They will give thanks to God for His kindness and for His wonders to mankind, and they will slaughter sacrifices of thanksgiving"* (*Psalms* 107:21-22; *Rashi, 11th century*).

In *Psalms* the sequence is: 1) desert journey (verses 4-9), 2) imprisonment (verses 10-16), 3) illness (verses 17-22), 4) sea journey (verses 23-31). The list is in order of *danger*, with the most dangerous first. However, in the *Talmud* the sequence is: 1) sea journey, 2) desert

ויקרא ז:י״ג-כ״ד

יַקְרִיב קָרְבָּנוֹ עַל־זֶבַח תּוֹדַת שְׁלָמָיו: 14 וְהִקְרִיב מִמֶּנּוּ אֶחָד מִכָּל־קָרְבָּן תְּרוּמָה לַיהֹוָה לַכֹּהֵן הַזֹּרֵק אֶת־דַּם הַשְּׁלָמִים לוֹ יִהְיֶה: 15 וּבְשַׂר זֶבַח תּוֹדַת שְׁלָמָיו בְּיוֹם קָרְבָּנוֹ יֵאָכֵל לֹא־יַנִּיחַ מִמֶּנּוּ עַד־בֹּקֶר: 16 וְאִם־נֶדֶר ׀ אוֹ נְדָבָה זֶבַח קָרְבָּנוֹ בְּיוֹם הַקְרִיבוֹ אֶת־זִבְחוֹ יֵאָכֵל וּמִמָּחֳרָת וְהַנּוֹתָר מִמֶּנּוּ יֵאָכֵל: 17 וְהַנּוֹתָר מִבְּשַׂר הַזָּבַח בַּיּוֹם הַשְּׁלִישִׁי בָּאֵשׁ יִשָּׂרֵף: 18 וְאִם הֵאָכֹל יֵאָכֵל מִבְּשַׂר־זֶבַח שְׁלָמָיו בַּיּוֹם הַשְּׁלִישִׁי לֹא יֵרָצֶה הַמַּקְרִיב אֹתוֹ לֹא יֵחָשֵׁב לוֹ פִּגּוּל יִהְיֶה וְהַנֶּפֶשׁ הָאֹכֶלֶת מִמֶּנּוּ עֲוֺנָהּ תִּשָּׂא: 19 וְהַבָּשָׂר אֲשֶׁר־יִגַּע בְּכָל־טָמֵא לֹא יֵאָכֵל בָּאֵשׁ יִשָּׂרֵף וְהַבָּשָׂר כָּל־טָהוֹר יֹאכַל בָּשָׂר: 20 וְהַנֶּפֶשׁ אֲשֶׁר־תֹּאכַל בָּשָׂר מִזֶּבַח הַשְּׁלָמִים אֲשֶׁר לַיהֹוָה וְטֻמְאָתוֹ עָלָיו וְנִכְרְתָה הַנֶּפֶשׁ הַהִוא מֵעַמֶּיהָ: 21 וְנֶפֶשׁ כִּי־תִגַּע בְּכָל־טָמֵא בְּטֻמְאַת אָדָם אוֹ ׀ בִּבְהֵמָה טְמֵאָה אוֹ בְּכָל־שֶׁקֶץ טָמֵא וְאָכַל מִבְּשַׂר־זֶבַח הַשְּׁלָמִים אֲשֶׁר לַיהֹוָה וְנִכְרְתָה הַנֶּפֶשׁ הַהִוא מֵעַמֶּיהָ: 22 וַיְדַבֵּר יְהֹוָה אֶל־מֹשֶׁה לֵּאמֹר: 23 דַּבֵּר אֶל־בְּנֵי יִשְׂרָאֵל לֵאמֹר כָּל־חֵלֶב שׁוֹר וְכֶשֶׂב וָעֵז לֹא תֹאכֵלוּ: 24 וְחֵלֶב נְבֵלָה וְחֵלֶב טְרֵפָה

17. Whatever is left over from the meat of the offering must be burned. This teaches us a great lesson in faith. Just as no meat from the sacrifice is left over for the next day, you should not restrict yourself in your needs in order to "leave over" for the next day. Have trust that God will provide your everyday needs (*Rabbi Aaron ha-Levi (Ḥinnukh), 13th century*).

18. Intention. Nowadays, prayer substitutes for sacrificial offering. Therefore you need to do your utmost to ensure that your prayers are carried out with the proper concentration and not dwell on any irrelevant or inappropriate thoughts that enter your mind (*Rabbi Jacob b. Asher, 13th–14th century*).

19. Burned in fire. The Torah requires that sacrificial meat which has become ritually impure be burned, in order that another person should not accidentally come to eat it and sin. This teaches a powerful lesson: that even if you are sure that an obstacle will not lead *yourself* to sin, you should eliminate it for the sake of *your fellow* (*Rabbi Menaḥem Mendel Schneerson, 20th century*).

kabbalah bites

7:15 *"He should not leave over any of it until morning."* According to the Kabbalah, unique Divine powers are emanated each day. You are given the spiritual potential to carry out today's tasks *today*. This opportunity will never come again, so do *"not leave over any of it until morning."*

bread. He should bring his (bread) offering along with his thanksgiving peace-offering.

- ❖ ¹⁴ He should offer (to the priest) one (bread) out of each (of the four types of bread) offering, as a donation for God. (These breads) belong to the priest, who dashes the blood of the peace-offering.

- ❖ ¹⁵ (Regarding) the meat of his thanksgiving peace-offering: His sacrifice should be eaten on the day it is offered up. He should not leave any of it over until morning.

- ❖ ¹⁶ But if his offering is (not an obligatory thanksgiving-offering with bread, but rather) a vow or a voluntary donation, it may be eaten on the day he offers up his offering; and on the next day, whatever is left over from it may be eaten. ¹⁷ However, on the third day whatever is left over from the meat of the offering must be burned in fire.

- ❖ ¹⁸ If (he offers his sacrifice with the intention that) any of the meat of his peace-offering is to be eaten on the third day, it will not be accepted. It will not count for the one who offers it, for it will be rejected, and the person who eats from it will bear (the consequences of) his sin.

- ❖ ¹⁹ The meat (of a peace-offering) that touches anything (that is ritually) impure should not be eaten. It should be burned in fire. But regarding (a piece of) meat (that was removed from its designated area): anyone who is (ritually) pure may eat (the rest of the) meat (which remained inside).

- ❖ ²⁰ (If) a person eats the meat of a peace-offering of God while (a state of ritual) impurity is upon him, (his) soul will be cut off from its people.

- ❖ ²¹ (If) a person touches anything (ritually) impure—whether it is impurity from a human or an impure animal (carcass) or any impure (carcass of an) abominable creature—and then eats from the meat of a peace-offering to God, (his) soul will be cut off from its people.

Additional Laws of Forbidden Fats and Blood

²² God spoke to Moses, saying: ²³ Speak to the children of Israel, saying:

- ❖ You should not eat any (sacrificial) fat from an ox, sheep, or goat.

- ❖ ²⁴ The fat of a carcass and the fat of an animal that was torn (to death) may be used

---

15. His sacrifice should be eaten on the day it is offered up. By limiting the time to eat the meat of the thanksgiving-offering—along with the forty bread loaves that came with it—to one day, the donor is forced to invite many guests in order to consume it all. In this way, the thanksgiving for his good fortune becomes more extensive (*Rabbi Naphtali Tzevi Judah Berlin, 19th century*).

ויקרא ז:כד-לח

יֵעָשֶׂ֖ה לְכָל־מְלָאכָ֑ה וְאָכֹ֖ל לֹ֥א תֹאכְלֻֽהוּ׃ 25 כִּ֚י כָּל־אֹכֵ֣ל חֵ֔לֶב מִן־הַבְּהֵמָ֔ה אֲשֶׁ֨ר יַקְרִ֥יב מִמֶּ֛נָּה אִשֶּׁ֖ה לַיהֹוָ֑ה וְנִכְרְתָ֛ה הַנֶּ֥פֶשׁ הָאֹכֶ֖לֶת מֵעַמֶּֽיהָ׃ 26 וְכָל־דָּם֙ לֹ֣א תֹאכְל֔וּ בְּכֹ֖ל מוֹשְׁבֹתֵיכֶ֑ם לָע֖וֹף וְלַבְּהֵמָֽה׃ 27 כָּל־נֶ֖פֶשׁ אֲשֶׁר־תֹּאכַ֣ל כָּל־דָּ֑ם וְנִכְרְתָ֛ה הַנֶּ֥פֶשׁ הַהִ֖וא מֵעַמֶּֽיהָ׃ פ 28 וַיְדַבֵּ֥ר יְהֹוָ֖ה אֶל־מֹשֶׁ֥ה לֵּאמֹֽר׃ 29 דַּבֵּ֞ר אֶל־בְּנֵ֤י יִשְׂרָאֵל֙ לֵאמֹ֔ר הַמַּקְרִ֞יב אֶת־זֶ֤בַח שְׁלָמָיו֙ לַיהֹוָ֔ה יָבִ֧יא אֶת־קׇרְבָּנ֛וֹ לַיהֹוָ֖ה מִזֶּ֥בַח שְׁלָמָֽיו׃ 30 יָדָ֣יו תְּבִיאֶ֔ינָה אֵ֖ת אִשֵּׁ֣י יְהֹוָ֑ה אֶת־הַחֵ֤לֶב עַל־הֶֽחָזֶה֙ יְבִיאֶ֔נּוּ אֵ֣ת הֶחָזֶ֗ה לְהָנִ֥יף אֹת֛וֹ תְּנוּפָ֖ה לִפְנֵ֥י יְהֹוָֽה׃ 31 וְהִקְטִ֧יר הַכֹּהֵ֛ן אֶת־הַחֵ֖לֶב הַמִּזְבֵּ֑חָה וְהָיָה֙ הֶֽחָזֶ֔ה לְאַהֲרֹ֖ן וּלְבָנָֽיו׃ 32 וְאֵת֙ שׁ֣וֹק הַיָּמִ֔ין תִּתְּנ֥וּ תְרוּמָ֖ה לַכֹּהֵ֑ן מִזִּבְחֵ֖י שַׁלְמֵיכֶֽם׃ 33 הַמַּקְרִ֞יב אֶת־דַּ֧ם הַשְּׁלָמִ֛ים וְאֶת־הַחֵ֖לֶב מִבְּנֵ֣י אַהֲרֹ֑ן ל֧וֹ תִהְיֶ֛ה שׁ֥וֹק הַיָּמִ֖ין לְמָנָֽה׃ 34 כִּי֩ אֶת־חֲזֵ֨ה הַתְּנוּפָ֜ה וְאֵ֣ת ׀ שׁ֣וֹק הַתְּרוּמָ֗ה לָקַ֙חְתִּי֙ מֵאֵ֣ת בְּנֵֽי־יִשְׂרָאֵ֔ל מִזִּבְחֵ֖י שַׁלְמֵיהֶ֑ם וָאֶתֵּ֣ן אֹ֠תָ֠ם לְאַהֲרֹ֨ן הַכֹּהֵ֤ן וּלְבָנָיו֙ לְחׇק־עוֹלָ֔ם מֵאֵ֖ת בְּנֵ֥י יִשְׂרָאֵֽל׃ 35 זֹ֣את מִשְׁחַ֤ת אַהֲרֹן֙ וּמִשְׁחַ֣ת בָּנָ֔יו מֵאִשֵּׁ֖י יְהֹוָ֑ה בְּיוֹם֙ הִקְרִ֣יב אֹתָ֔ם לְכַהֵ֖ן לַיהֹוָֽה׃ 36 אֲשֶׁר֩ צִוָּ֨ה יְהֹוָ֜ה לָתֵ֣ת לָהֶ֗ם בְּי֤וֹם מׇשְׁח֣וֹ אֹתָ֔ם מֵאֵ֖ת בְּנֵ֣י יִשְׂרָאֵ֑ל חֻקַּ֥ת עוֹלָ֖ם לְדֹרֹתָֽם׃ 37 זֹ֣את הַתּוֹרָ֗ה לָֽעֹלָה֙ לַמִּנְחָ֔ה וְלַֽחַטָּ֖את וְלָאָשָׁ֑ם וְלַ֨מִּלּוּאִ֔ים וּלְזֶ֖בַח הַשְּׁלָמִֽים׃ 38 אֲשֶׁ֨ר צִוָּ֧ה יְהֹוָ֛ה אֶת־מֹשֶׁ֖ה בְּהַ֣ר סִינָ֑י בְּי֨וֹם צַוֺּת֜וֹ אֶת־בְּנֵ֣י יִשְׂרָאֵ֗ל לְהַקְרִ֧יב אֶת־קׇרְבְּנֵיהֶ֛ם לַיהֹוָ֖ה בְּמִדְבַּ֥ר סִינָֽי׃ פ

30. A waving before God. The priest would move them forward and backward, upward and downward (*Rashi, 11th century*).

"Upward and downward" represents the progressions and regressions that you experience in your personal spiritual standing. "Forward and backward" represents the spreading of morality and spirituality outwards, to other people.

The lesson here is that regardless of whether you are "upward or downward"—on a spiritual high or low—you should endeavor to go "forward and backward," to influence other people positively (*Rabbi Menahem Mendel Schneerson, 20th century*).

leviticus 7:24–38 — tzav

for any work, but you must not eat it. ²⁵ (If) anyone eats (sacrificial) fat of animals from which sacrifices are brought as fire-offerings to God, the soul (of the person) who eats it will be cut off from its people.

- ²⁶ You should not eat any blood in any of the places where you live, whether from birds or from animals, (but the blood of fish and grasshoppers is permitted).

- ²⁷ (If) any person eats any blood, the soul (of) that (person) will be cut off from its people.

Gifts to the Priests

²⁸ God spoke to Moses, saying: ²⁹ Speak to the children of Israel, saying:

- Anyone who dedicates his peace-offering to God should bring his offering to God (personally) from (the animal dedicated as) his peace-offering.

- ³⁰ His own hands should bring the fire-offerings of God. (Namely) he should bring the fat on the breast, so he can wave the breast as a waving before God.

- ³¹ The priest should make the fat to go up in smoke on the altar. The breast will belong to Aaron and his sons.

- ³² You should give (a portion of) the right leg from your peace-offering to the priest as an elevation-offering. ³³ (Anyone) of the sons of Aaron who (is fit to) offer up the blood of the peace-offering and the fat should have (a share of) the right leg. ³⁴ For I have taken the breast of the wave-offering and the thigh of the elevation-offering from the children of Israel, from their peace-offerings, and I have given them from the children of Israel to Aaron the priest and to his sons as an eternal statute.

³⁵ (All) these are the (privileges) of Aaron and his sons from the fire-offerings of God, because they are anointed—(which they received) on the day that He brought them near (to Him) to be priests for God—³⁶ that God commanded to give them on the day that He anointed them, from the children of Israel. (It is) an eternal statute for their generations.

³⁷ (All) these are the laws of the burnt-offering, the meal-offering, the sin-offering, the guilt-offering, for the (day of) inauguration (of the priesthood), and for the peace-offering, ³⁸ which God commanded Moses on Mount Sinai, on the day He commanded the children of Israel to offer up their sacrifices to God in the Sinai Desert.

---

26. You should not eat any blood. The animal, like every other object in the world, was created by God for the use and pleasure of human beings, which are the only species that can understand that there is a God. However, humans were only permitted to derive pleasure from the flesh of an animal, not from its soul, which belongs to God alone. Since *"the blood is the soul"* (*Deuteronomy* 12:23), man is not allowed to consume it (*Naḥmanides, 13ᵗʰ century*).

ויקרא ח:א-טו

[FOURTH READING] ח 1 וַיְדַבֵּ֥ר יְהֹוָ֖ה אֶל־מֹשֶׁ֥ה לֵּאמֹֽר: 2 קַ֤ח אֶֽת־אַהֲרֹן֙ וְאֶת־בָּנָ֣יו אִתּ֔וֹ וְאֵת֙ הַבְּגָדִ֔ים וְאֵ֖ת שֶׁ֣מֶן הַמִּשְׁחָ֑ה וְאֵ֣ת ׀ פַּ֣ר הַֽחַטָּ֗את וְאֵת֙ שְׁנֵ֣י הָֽאֵילִ֔ים וְאֵ֖ת סַ֥ל הַמַּצּֽוֹת: 3 וְאֵ֥ת כׇּל־הָעֵדָ֖ה הַקְהֵ֑ל אֶל־פֶּ֖תַח אֹ֥הֶל מוֹעֵֽד: 4 וַיַּ֣עַשׂ מֹשֶׁ֔ה כַּֽאֲשֶׁ֛ר צִוָּ֥ה יְהֹוָ֖ה אֹת֑וֹ וַתִּקָּהֵל֙ הָֽעֵדָ֔ה אֶל־פֶּ֖תַח אֹ֥הֶל מוֹעֵֽד: 5 וַיֹּ֥אמֶר מֹשֶׁ֖ה אֶל־הָעֵדָ֑ה זֶ֣ה הַדָּבָ֔ר אֲשֶׁר־צִוָּ֥ה יְהֹוָ֖ה לַֽעֲשֽׂוֹת: 6 וַיַּקְרֵ֣ב מֹשֶׁ֔ה אֶֽת־אַהֲרֹ֖ן וְאֶת־בָּנָ֑יו וַיִּרְחַ֥ץ אֹתָ֖ם בַּמָּֽיִם: 7 וַיִּתֵּ֨ן עָלָ֜יו אֶת־הַכֻּתֹּ֗נֶת וַיַּחְגֹּ֤ר אֹתוֹ֙ בָּֽאַבְנֵ֔ט וַיַּלְבֵּ֤שׁ אֹתוֹ֙ אֶת־הַמְּעִ֔יל וַיִּתֵּ֥ן עָלָ֖יו אֶת־הָֽאֵפֹ֑ד וַיַּחְגֹּ֣ר אֹת֗וֹ בְּחֵ֨שֶׁב֙ הָֽאֵפֹ֔ד וַיֶּאְפֹּ֥ד ל֖וֹ בּֽוֹ: 8 וַיָּ֥שֶׂם עָלָ֖יו אֶת־הַחֹ֑שֶׁן וַיִּתֵּן֙ אֶל־הַחֹ֔שֶׁן אֶת־הָאוּרִ֖ים וְאֶת־הַתֻּמִּֽים: 9 וַיָּ֥שֶׂם אֶת־הַמִּצְנֶ֖פֶת עַל־רֹאשׁ֑וֹ וַיָּ֨שֶׂם עַֽל־הַמִּצְנֶ֜פֶת אֶל־מ֣וּל פָּנָ֗יו אֵ֣ת צִ֤יץ הַזָּהָב֙ נֵ֣זֶר הַקֹּ֔דֶשׁ כַּֽאֲשֶׁ֛ר צִוָּ֥ה יְהֹוָ֖ה אֶת־מֹשֶֽׁה: 10 וַיִּקַּ֤ח מֹשֶׁה֙ אֶת־שֶׁ֣מֶן הַמִּשְׁחָ֔ה וַיִּמְשַׁ֥ח אֶת־הַמִּשְׁכָּ֖ן וְאֶת־כׇּל־אֲשֶׁר־בּ֑וֹ וַיְקַדֵּ֖שׁ אֹתָֽם: 11 וַיַּ֥ז מִמֶּ֛נּוּ עַל־הַמִּזְבֵּ֖חַ שֶׁ֣בַע פְּעָמִ֑ים וַיִּמְשַׁ֤ח אֶת־הַמִּזְבֵּ֨חַ֙ וְאֶת־כׇּל־כֵּלָ֔יו וְאֶת־הַכִּיֹּ֥ר וְאֶת־כַּנּ֖וֹ לְקַדְּשָֽׁם: 12 וַיִּצֹ֞ק מִשֶּׁ֤מֶן הַמִּשְׁחָה֙ עַ֖ל רֹ֣אשׁ אַהֲרֹ֑ן וַיִּמְשַׁ֥ח אֹת֖וֹ לְקַדְּשֽׁוֹ: 13 וַיַּקְרֵ֨ב מֹשֶׁ֜ה אֶת־בְּנֵ֣י אַֽהֲרֹ֗ן וַיַּלְבִּשֵׁ֤ם כֻּתֳּנֹת֙ וַיַּחְגֹּ֤ר אֹתָם֙ אַבְנֵ֔ט וַיַּֽחֲבֹ֥שׁ לָהֶ֖ם מִגְבָּע֑וֹת כַּֽאֲשֶׁ֛ר צִוָּ֥ה יְהֹוָ֖ה אֶת־מֹשֶֽׁה: **[FIFTH READING]** 14 וַיַּגֵּ֕שׁ אֵ֖ת פַּ֣ר הַֽחַטָּ֑את וַיִּסְמֹ֨ךְ אַֽהֲרֹ֤ן וּבָנָיו֙ אֶת־יְדֵיהֶ֔ם עַל־רֹ֖אשׁ פַּ֥ר הַֽחַטָּֽאת: 15 וַיִּשְׁחָ֗ט וַיִּקַּ֤ח מֹשֶׁה֙ אֶת־הַדָּ֔ם וַיִּתֵּ֛ן עַל־קַרְנ֥וֹת הַמִּזְבֵּ֖חַ סָבִ֑יב בְּאֶצְבָּע֔וֹ

---

to every Israelite. In the sense of dedicating ourselves to God, we are all priests (*Rabbi Solomon Kluger, 19th century*).

11. He sprinkled from (the anointing oil) upon the altar. I do not know where in Scripture he was commanded to perform these sprinklings (*Rashi, 11th century*).

Despite being a great Torah scholar and *halakhic* authority, *Rashi* was not ashamed to write "*I do not know*," teaching us that even those of a lesser stature than *Rashi* should not be embarrassed to admit their shortcomings.

In Hasidic thought, oil represents the secrets of Torah which are so sublime that they cannot be understood. This is the inner reason why *Rashi* wrote "I do not know" in the case of anointing *oil* (*Rabbi Menahem Mendel Schneerson, 20th century*).

leviticus 8:1–15   tzav

Inauguration of Aaron and His Sons

8 [FOURTH READING] ¹ God spoke to Moses, saying, ² "Take Aaron (and persuade him to come) along with his sons. (Take) the garments, the anointing oil, the sin-offering bull, the two rams, and the basket of unleavened bread, ³ and assemble the entire community at the entrance of the Tent of Meeting."

⁴ Moses did as God had commanded him. The community assembled at the entrance of the Tent of Meeting. ⁵ Moses said to the community, "These (things that I am about to perform before you) God has commanded (me) to do."

⁶ Moses brought Aaron and his sons near and (immersed) them in water. ⁷ He placed the tunic upon (Aaron), girded him with the sash, clothed him with the robe, placed the apron upon him, girded him with the decorative band of the apron, and adorned him with it. ⁸ He placed the breastplate upon him, and he inserted the Urim and Thummim into the breastplate. ⁹ He placed the turban on (Aaron's) head, and on the turban, towards his face, he placed the golden forehead-plate, the holy crown, as God had commanded Moses.

¹⁰ Moses took the anointing oil and anointed the Sanctuary and everything inside it and (thus) sanctified it. ¹¹ He sprinkled from (the anointing oil) upon the altar seven times. He anointed the altar and all its apparatus, as well as the washstand and its base, to sanctify them. ¹² He poured some of the anointing oil upon Aaron's head and anointed him, to sanctify him.

¹³ Moses brought Aaron's sons near and clothed them with tunics, girded them with sashes, and tied high hats (turbans) on them, as God had commanded Moses.

[FIFTH READING] ¹⁴ He brought the sin-offering bull close. Aaron and his sons leaned their hands upon the head of the sin-offering bull. ¹⁵ Moses slaughtered it. He took the

---

8:5 Moses said to the community. Why did Moses tell the entire Israelite community what God had commanded? After all, he was discussing the inauguration of the priesthood, which only pertained to the priests.

Because even though the physical act of bringing sacrifices was done by the priests, there was a spiritual element to serving in the Temple and bringing sacrifices, and this was applicable

kabbalah bites

8:6 *"Moses brought Aaron and his sons near."* Literally, this verse could be rendered, *"Moses offered Aaron and his sons as a sacrifice."* After this sacred inauguration, the priests had reached the level of Isaac when he was placed on the altar by his father as a sacrifice. They had reached the mystical stature of Adam himself.

ויקרא ח:טו-כט

וַיְחַטֵּא אֶת־הַמִּזְבֵּחַ וְאֶת־הַדָּם יָצַק אֶל־יְסוֹד הַמִּזְבֵּחַ וַיְקַדְּשֵׁהוּ לְכַפֵּר עָלָיו: 16 וַיִּקַּח אֶת־כָּל־הַחֵלֶב אֲשֶׁר עַל־הַקֶּרֶב וְאֵת יֹתֶרֶת הַכָּבֵד וְאֶת־שְׁתֵּי הַכְּלָיֹת וְאֶת־חֶלְבְּהֶן וַיַּקְטֵר מֹשֶׁה הַמִּזְבֵּחָה: 17 וְאֶת־הַפָּר וְאֶת־עֹרוֹ וְאֶת־בְּשָׂרוֹ וְאֶת־פִּרְשׁוֹ שָׂרַף בָּאֵשׁ מִחוּץ לַמַּחֲנֶה כַּאֲשֶׁר צִוָּה יְהֹוָה אֶת־מֹשֶׁה: 18 וַיַּקְרֵב אֵת אֵיל הָעֹלָה וַיִּסְמְכוּ אַהֲרֹן וּבָנָיו אֶת־יְדֵיהֶם עַל־רֹאשׁ הָאָיִל: 19 וַיִּשְׁחָט וַיִּזְרֹק מֹשֶׁה אֶת־הַדָּם עַל־הַמִּזְבֵּחַ סָבִיב: 20 וְאֶת־הָאַיִל נִתַּח לִנְתָחָיו וַיַּקְטֵר מֹשֶׁה אֶת־הָרֹאשׁ וְאֶת־הַנְּתָחִים וְאֶת־הַפָּדֶר: 21 וְאֶת־הַקֶּרֶב וְאֶת־הַכְּרָעַיִם רָחַץ בַּמָּיִם וַיַּקְטֵר מֹשֶׁה אֶת־כָּל־הָאַיִל הַמִּזְבֵּחָה עֹלָה הוּא לְרֵיחַ־נִיחֹחַ אִשֶּׁה הוּא לַיהֹוָה כַּאֲשֶׁר צִוָּה יְהֹוָה אֶת־מֹשֶׁה: [SIXTH READING] 22 וַיַּקְרֵב אֶת־הָאַיִל הַשֵּׁנִי אֵיל הַמִּלֻּאִים וַיִּסְמְכוּ אַהֲרֹן וּבָנָיו אֶת־יְדֵיהֶם עַל־רֹאשׁ הָאָיִל: 23 וַיִּשְׁחָט ׀ וַיִּקַּח מֹשֶׁה מִדָּמוֹ וַיִּתֵּן עַל־תְּנוּךְ אֹזֶן־אַהֲרֹן הַיְמָנִית וְעַל־בֹּהֶן יָדוֹ הַיְמָנִית וְעַל־בֹּהֶן רַגְלוֹ הַיְמָנִית: 24 וַיַּקְרֵב אֶת־בְּנֵי אַהֲרֹן וַיִּתֵּן מֹשֶׁה מִן־הַדָּם עַל־תְּנוּךְ אָזְנָם הַיְמָנִית וְעַל־בֹּהֶן יָדָם הַיְמָנִית וְעַל־בֹּהֶן רַגְלָם הַיְמָנִית וַיִּזְרֹק מֹשֶׁה אֶת־הַדָּם עַל־הַמִּזְבֵּחַ סָבִיב: 25 וַיִּקַּח אֶת־הַחֵלֶב וְאֶת־הָאַלְיָה וְאֶת־כָּל־הַחֵלֶב אֲשֶׁר עַל־הַקֶּרֶב וְאֵת יֹתֶרֶת הַכָּבֵד וְאֶת־שְׁתֵּי הַכְּלָיֹת וְאֶת־חֶלְבְּהֶן וְאֵת שׁוֹק הַיָּמִין: 26 וּמִסַּל הַמַּצּוֹת אֲשֶׁר ׀ לִפְנֵי יְהֹוָה לָקַח חַלַּת מַצָּה אַחַת וְחַלַּת לֶחֶם שֶׁמֶן אַחַת וְרָקִיק אֶחָד וַיָּשֶׂם עַל־הַחֲלָבִים וְעַל שׁוֹק הַיָּמִין: 27 וַיִּתֵּן אֶת־הַכֹּל עַל כַּפֵּי אַהֲרֹן וְעַל כַּפֵּי בָנָיו וַיָּנֶף אֹתָם תְּנוּפָה לִפְנֵי יְהֹוָה: 28 וַיִּקַּח מֹשֶׁה אֹתָם מֵעַל כַּפֵּיהֶם וַיַּקְטֵר הַמִּזְבֵּחָה עַל־הָעֹלָה מִלֻּאִים הֵם לְרֵיחַ נִיחֹחַ אִשֶּׁה הוּא לַיהֹוָה: 29 וַיִּקַּח מֹשֶׁה אֶת־הֶחָזֶה וַיְנִיפֵהוּ תְנוּפָה לִפְנֵי יְהֹוָה מֵאֵיל הַמִּלֻּאִים

---

priesthood. This final offering is referred to by the Torah as the "inauguration ram," as it completed the process of inauguration (*Naḥmanides, 13th century*).

leviticus 8:15–29   tzav

blood and placed it on the horns of the altar, all around, with his finger, and he (thus) purified the altar. He poured the (remaining) blood at the (protruding) base of the altar, and (thus) sanctified (the altar, giving it the power) to effect atonement upon it.

¹⁶ He took all the fat which was on the stomach, the diaphragm (together with some of) the liver, the two kidneys and the fat that was on them, and Moses made them go up in smoke on the altar.

¹⁷ He burned the bull, its hide, its meat, and its dung in fire outside the camp, as God had commanded Moses.

¹⁸ He brought the burnt-offering ram near. Aaron and his sons leaned their hands upon the head of the ram. ¹⁹ Moses slaughtered it and he dashed the blood on the altar, all around. ²⁰ Moses cut up the ram into its (prescribed) parts, and he made the head, the parts and the fat go up in smoke. ²¹ Moses washed the innards and the legs in water, and (after adding these parts) he made the entire ram go up in smoke on the altar. It was a burnt-offering—a pleasant aroma, a fire offering to God—as God had commanded Moses.

[SIXTH READING] ²² He brought the second ram near, the inauguration ram. Aaron and his sons leaned their hands upon the ram's head. ²³ Moses slaughtered it. He took some of its blood and placed it on the cartilage of Aaron's right ear, on the thumb of his right hand and on the big toe of his right foot. ²⁴ Moses brought Aaron's sons near, and Moses placed some of the blood on the cartilage of their right ears, on the thumbs of their right hands, and on the big toes of their right feet. Then Moses dashed the (remaining) blood on the altar, all around.

²⁵ He took the (sacrificial) fat, the tail-piece, all the fat which covers the innards, the diaphragm (together with a piece of) liver, the two kidneys together with their fat and the right thigh. ²⁶ From the basket of unleavened bread that was before God, he took one loaf of unleavened bread, and one loaf of bread (which was boiled and fried in) oil, and one wafer, and he placed them on top of the fats and the right thigh. ²⁷ Then he placed it all on Aaron's palms and on his sons' palms, and he waved them as a waving before God. ²⁸ Moses took it from their hands and made it go up in smoke on the altar along with the burnt-offering. They were inauguration-offerings—a pleasant aroma, a fire-offering to God.

²⁹ Moses took the breast and waved it as a wave-offering before God. It belonged to Moses as a portion from the inauguration ram, as God had commanded Moses.

22. The inauguration ram. The bull sin-offering (v. 14-17) was brought to atone for the altar and sanctify it. The ram burnt-offering (v. 18-21) was brought to achieve Divine favor for the priests. And the ram peace-offering (v. 22-29) was brought to thank God for the privilege of

וַיִּקְרָא ח:כט-לו

לְמֹשֶׁה הָיָה לְמָנָה כַּאֲשֶׁר צִוָּה יְהֹוָה אֶת־מֹשֶׁה: 30 [SEVENTH READING] וַיִּקַּח מֹשֶׁה מִשֶּׁמֶן הַמִּשְׁחָה וּמִן־הַדָּם אֲשֶׁר עַל־הַמִּזְבֵּחַ וַיַּז עַל־אַהֲרֹן עַל־בְּגָדָיו וְעַל־בָּנָיו וְעַל־בִּגְדֵי בָנָיו אִתּוֹ וַיְקַדֵּשׁ אֶת־אַהֲרֹן אֶת־בְּגָדָיו וְאֶת־בָּנָיו וְאֶת־בִּגְדֵי בָנָיו אִתּוֹ: 31 וַיֹּאמֶר מֹשֶׁה אֶל־אַהֲרֹן וְאֶל־בָּנָיו בַּשְּׁלוּ אֶת־הַבָּשָׂר פֶּתַח אֹהֶל מוֹעֵד וְשָׁם תֹּאכְלוּ אֹתוֹ וְאֶת־הַלֶּחֶם אֲשֶׁר בְּסַל הַמִּלֻּאִים כַּאֲשֶׁר צִוֵּיתִי לֵאמֹר אַהֲרֹן וּבָנָיו יֹאכְלֻהוּ: 32 וְהַנּוֹתָר בַּבָּשָׂר וּבַלָּחֶם בָּאֵשׁ תִּשְׂרֹפוּ: 33 [MAFTIR] וּמִפֶּתַח אֹהֶל מוֹעֵד לֹא תֵצְאוּ שִׁבְעַת יָמִים עַד יוֹם מְלֹאת יְמֵי מִלֻּאֵיכֶם כִּי שִׁבְעַת יָמִים יְמַלֵּא אֶת־יֶדְכֶם: 34 כַּאֲשֶׁר עָשָׂה בַּיּוֹם הַזֶּה צִוָּה יְהֹוָה לַעֲשֹׂת לְכַפֵּר עֲלֵיכֶם: 35 וּפֶתַח אֹהֶל מוֹעֵד תֵּשְׁבוּ יוֹמָם וָלַיְלָה שִׁבְעַת יָמִים וּשְׁמַרְתֶּם אֶת־מִשְׁמֶרֶת יְהֹוָה וְלֹא תָמוּתוּ כִּי־כֵן צֻוֵּיתִי: 36 וַיַּעַשׂ אַהֲרֹן וּבָנָיו אֵת כָּל־הַדְּבָרִים אֲשֶׁר־צִוָּה יְהֹוָה בְּיַד־מֹשֶׁה: ס ס ס

צ"ו פסוקים, צ"ו סימן.

Where do we find that God mourned for His world for seven days? The verse states, *"Then, after seven days, the floodwaters were upon the earth"* (Genesis 7:10). Since God knew that the world would be destroyed, He was able to mourn the loss before the calamity; but humans can only mourn a loss after the fact (*Jerusalem Talmud, Mo'ed Katan* 3:5).

36. Aaron and his sons did everything that God commanded through Moses. They did not veer from their instructions, to the right or to the left (*Rashi, 11th century*).

spiritual vitamin

> "Man is born for toil" (*Job 5:7*). The "toil" here is not only in order to acquire material things, but also spiritual. In other words, God expects you to serve Him constantly and with evergrowing efforts, and this is the purpose of your life.

[SEVENTH READING] ³⁰ Moses took some of the anointing oil and some of the blood that was on the altar, and he sprinkled it on Aaron and on his garments, on his sons and on his sons' garments. He (thus) sanctified Aaron, his garments, his sons and his sons' garments with him.

³¹ Moses said to Aaron and to his sons, "Cook the meat at the entrance of the Tent of Meeting and eat it there, together with the bread that is in the basket of the inauguration-offerings, as I have commanded, saying, 'Aaron and his sons should eat it.' ³² You should burn whatever is left over from the meat and the bread in fire."

[MAFTIR] ³³ "You should not leave the entrance of the Tent of Meeting for seven days, until the concluding day of your days of inauguration, because you will (now) be inaugurated for seven days. ³⁴ God has commanded that whatever was done on this day must be done (all seven days) to atone for you. ³⁵ You should stay at the entrance to the Tent of Meeting day and night for seven days, and must guard your appointed duty to God so that you will not die, for this is what I was commanded."

³⁶ Aaron and his sons did everything that God commanded through Moses.

Haftarot: Tzav—p. 1347. *Shabbat ha-Gadol* (*Erev Pesaḥ*)—p. 1437. *Zakhor*—p. 1427. *Parah*—p. 1431.
Maftir: Zakhor—p. 1208 (25:17–19). *Parah*—p. 932 (19:1–22).

33, 35. You should not leave the entrance of the Tent of Meeting for seven days ... stay at the entrance to the Tent of Meeting day and night for seven days. If the Tabernacle was dismantled at night during the seven days of inauguration, how could Aaron and his sons stay there for seven days *and nights*? Because the outer curtains of the Tabernacle were not dismantled (*Rabbi Obadiah Sforno, 16ᵗʰ century*).

The Torah does not mean that they were literally not allowed to leave the Tabernacle day and night, but rather, that any time that they were required to be there they were not permitted to leave, whether it was day or night (*Rabbi Baḥya b. Asher, 13ᵗʰ century*).

The Tabernacle remained erected all night, and at the crack of dawn it was dismantled and immediately reassembled. In this way it was possible for the priests to stay at the entrance to the Tent of Meeting day *and night* for seven days (*Naḥmanides, 13ᵗʰ century*).

35. Guard your appointed duty to God. This can be read as "you should observe the observance of God," a cryptic allusion to the seven-day mourning period. Just as God observed a seven-day mourning period for His world with the Flood, so too, you must observe a seven-day mourning period.

> Nadab and Abihu did something **extraordinarily** right: They were **ecstatic** about God. They were **intoxicated** with the Divine. Let us not judge them negatively for their excesses; let us **admire** and **emulate** their **mystical passion**.

SHEMINI
שמיני

EIGHTH DAY OF INAUGURATION	9:1–24
NADAB AND ABIHU DIE	10:1–20
LAWS OF FORBIDDEN FOODS	11:1–23
LAWS OF RITUAL IMPURITY	11:24–40
LAWS OF FORBIDDEN REPTILES AND INSECTS	11:41–47

NAME
Shemini

MEANING
"Eighth"

LINES IN TORAH SCROLL
157

PARASHIYYOT
3 open; 3 closed

VERSES
91

WORDS
1238

LETTERS
4670

DATE
Nisan - 20 Iyyar, 2449

LOCATION
Sinai Desert

KEY PEOPLE
Moses, Aaron, Eleazar, Ithamar, Nadab, Abihu, Mishael, Elzaphan

MITZVOT
6 positive; 11 prohibitions

MASORETIC FEATURES
The letter vav of the word gahon (11:42) is oversized.

CHARACTER PROFILE

NAME
Elisheba

MEANING
"My God is my oath" or "my God is my sustenance"

FATHER
Amminadab (tribe of Judah)

HUSBAND
Aaron

BROTHER
Nahshon

CHILDREN
Nadab, Abihu, Eleazar and Ithamar

BURIAL PLACE
Outskirts of Tiberias

ACHIEVEMENTS
Matriarch of the priestly clan; her life was bound up with the most distinguished families in Israel: her husband was High Priest, her children were deputy high priests, her brother was *nasi* of the tribe of Judah and her brother-in-law was Moses

KNOWN FOR
Source for the principle that a person who wishes to marry a woman must also inquire about the character of her brothers; death of her two sons, Nadab and Abihu

SOBRIETY

Aaron and his sons were commanded to refrain from drinking wine before entering the Tabernacle. This was to ensure that they would be able to "distinguish between the holy and the profane" (10:9).

KOSHER FOOD

The food that we eat becomes a part of us, sustaining us and giving us energy to serve God. Kosher food has a positive and spiritually sensitizing influence on the soul, bringing you closer to God (ch. 11).

CONNECTION

Waters in a spring never become impure, because they are connected to their source. Connection to your source—your soul—is essential to guard against impurity (11:36).

ויקרא ט׳:א-ט

ט 1 וַיְהִי֙ בַּיּ֣וֹם הַשְּׁמִינִ֔י קָרָ֣א מֹשֶׁ֔ה לְאַהֲרֹ֖ן וּלְבָנָ֑יו וּלְזִקְנֵ֖י יִשְׂרָאֵֽל: 2 וַיֹּ֣אמֶר אֶֽל־אַהֲרֹ֗ן קַח־לְ֠ךָ עֵ֣גֶל בֶּן־בָּקָ֧ר לְחַטָּ֛את וְאַ֥יִל לְעֹלָ֖ה תְּמִימִ֑ם וְהַקְרֵ֖ב לִפְנֵ֥י יְהֹוָֽה: 3 וְאֶל־בְּנֵ֥י יִשְׂרָאֵ֖ל תְּדַבֵּ֣ר לֵאמֹ֑ר קְח֤וּ שְׂעִיר־עִזִּים֙ לְחַטָּ֔את וְעֵ֨גֶל וָכֶ֧בֶשׂ בְּנֵי־שָׁנָ֛ה תְּמִימִ֖ם לְעֹלָֽה: 4 וְשׁ֨וֹר וָאַ֜יִל לִשְׁלָמִ֗ים לִזְבֹּ֙חַ֙ לִפְנֵ֣י יְהֹוָ֔ה וּמִנְחָ֖ה בְּלוּלָ֣ה בַשָּׁ֑מֶן כִּ֣י הַיּ֔וֹם יְהֹוָ֖ה נִרְאָ֥ה אֲלֵיכֶֽם: 5 וַיִּקְח֗וּ אֵ֚ת אֲשֶׁ֣ר צִוָּ֣ה מֹשֶׁ֔ה אֶל־פְּנֵ֖י אֹ֣הֶל מוֹעֵ֑ד וַֽיִּקְרְבוּ֙ כׇּל־הָ֣עֵדָ֔ה וַיַּֽעַמְד֖וּ לִפְנֵ֥י יְהֹוָֽה: 6 וַיֹּ֣אמֶר מֹשֶׁ֔ה זֶ֧ה הַדָּבָ֛ר אֲשֶׁר־צִוָּ֥ה יְהֹוָ֖ה תַּעֲשׂ֑וּ וְיֵרָ֥א אֲלֵיכֶ֖ם כְּב֥וֹד יְהֹוָֽה: 7 וַיֹּ֨אמֶר מֹשֶׁ֜ה אֶֽל־אַהֲרֹ֗ן קְרַ֤ב אֶל־הַמִּזְבֵּ֙חַ֙ וַעֲשֵׂ֞ה אֶת־חַטָּֽאתְךָ֙ וְאֶת־עֹ֣לָתֶ֔ךָ וְכַפֵּ֥ר בַּֽעַדְךָ֖ וּבְעַ֣ד הָעָ֑ם וַעֲשֵׂ֞ה אֶת־קׇרְבַּ֤ן הָעָם֙ וְכַפֵּ֣ר בַּֽעֲדָ֔ם כַּאֲשֶׁ֖ר צִוָּ֥ה יְהֹוָֽה: 8 וַיִּקְרַ֥ב אַהֲרֹ֖ן אֶל־הַמִּזְבֵּ֑חַ וַיִּשְׁחַ֛ט אֶת־עֵ֥גֶל הַחַטָּ֖את אֲשֶׁר־לֽוֹ: 9 וַ֠יַּקְרִ֠בוּ בְּנֵ֨י אַהֲרֹ֣ן אֶת־הַדָּם֮ אֵלָיו֒ וַיִּטְבֹּ֤ל אֶצְבָּעוֹ֙ בַּדָּ֔ם וַיִּתֵּ֖ן עַל־קַרְנ֣וֹת הַמִּזְבֵּ֑חַ וְאֶת־הַדָּ֣ם יָצַ֔ק אֶל־יְס֖וֹד

Moses was saying to Aaron, "It is for this humility—which you are showing by your hesitation and embarrassment, thinking that you are not worthy of this job—which makes you the most qualified person for leadership. That is why you were chosen" (*Rabbi Isaac Luria, 16th century*).

kabbalah bites

9:6 The Divine Presence (*Shekhinah*), the "Glory of God," only appeared after Aaron had completed his sacrificial rite. Moses alone did not succeed in causing the *Shekhinah* to dwell in the Tabernacle (*Rashi, v. 23*).

Moses' task was to bring revelation from the heavens down to the earth, which the *Zohar* depicts as masculine, since it was something imposed from the outside (reminiscent of the male stereotype of aggressive dominance).

Aaron, on the other hand, was famous for making communal peace, which required emphasis on the feminine principle of an inner, personal awakening, rather than one that is externally imposed.

So when it came to the dwelling of the *Shekhinah* within the Tabernacle, Aaron was the crucial player.

Is your life dominated by a "masculine," imposed religiosity, or is it something that resonates from within?

parashat shemini

The Eighth Day of Inauguration

9 ¹ It was on the eighth day (of inauguration), that Moses called for Aaron and his sons, and the elders of Israel (so that Aaron's appointment should be in their presence).

² He said to Aaron, "Take for yourself a young bull as a sin-offering (as an atonement for the Golden Calf), and a ram as a burnt-offering, (both) unblemished, and bring them close, before God."

³ "You should speak to the children of Israel and say, 'Take a he-goat as a sin-offering; and for a burnt-offering (take) a calf and a lamb, (both) in their first year, and (both) unblemished; ⁴ and for peace-offerings (take) an ox and a ram, to be slaughtered before God; and (take) a meal-offering mixed with oil—for today (the Tabernacle will be fully inaugurated and) God('s presence) is (going to) appear to you.'"

⁵ They took what Moses had commanded to the front of the Tent of Meeting, and the entire community approached and stood before God.

⁶ Moses said, "(When) this thing which God has told you to carry out (is done, then) the glory of God will appear to you!"

⁷ Moses said to Aaron, "Approach the altar and carry out your sin-offering and burnt-offering, atoning for yourself and for the people, and carry out the people's offering, atoning for them, as God has commanded."

⁸ Aaron approached the altar and slaughtered his sin-offering calf. ⁹ Aaron's sons brought the blood to him. He dipped his finger into the blood, placing (some of it) on the horns of the altar. He then poured the (remaining) blood at the base of the

---

9:1 Moses called for Aaron and his sons, and the elders of Israel. Moses called the *"Elders of Israel,"* who were not priests, to indicate that Aaron did not serve as High Priest solely on his own merit; his power came from the people, whom the elders represented (*Rabbi Joseph Grunwald of Puppa, 20th century*).

3. Take a he-goat as a sin-offering. Aaron brought a goat as a sin-offering in order to atone for the sin of selling Joseph into slavery, when the brothers slaughtered a young goat (*Genesis 37:31; Yalkut Shimoni*).

6. (When) this thing ... (is done, then) the glory of God will appear. They must rid themselves of the evil impulse, and the Divine Presence will dwell in their midst (*Targum Jonathan*).

7. Approach the altar. Aaron was hesitant to approach the altar to do his priestly duties, so Moses said, "Why are you embarrassed? Why the hesitation? It is for this that you were chosen!" (*Rashi, 11th century*).

ויקרא ט:ט-כג   שמיני

10 וְאֶת־הַחֵ֙לֶב֙ וְאֶת־הַכְּלָיֹ֔ת וְאֶת־הַיֹּתֶ֖רֶת מִן־הַכָּבֵ֑ד מִן־הַֽחַטָּ֔את הִקְטִ֖יר הַמִּזְבֵּ֑חָה כַּאֲשֶׁ֛ר צִוָּ֥ה יְהֹוָ֖ה אֶת־מֹשֶֽׁה: 11 וְאֶת־הַבָּשָׂ֖ר וְאֶת־הָע֑וֹר שָׂרַ֣ף בָּאֵ֔שׁ מִח֖וּץ לַֽמַּחֲנֶֽה: 12 וַיִּשְׁחַ֖ט אֶת־הָֽעֹלָ֑ה וַ֠יַּמְצִ֠אוּ בְּנֵ֨י אַהֲרֹ֤ן אֵלָיו֙ אֶת־הַדָּ֔ם וַיִּזְרְקֵ֥הוּ עַל־הַמִּזְבֵּ֖חַ סָבִֽיב: 13 וְאֶת־הָעֹלָ֗ה הִמְצִ֧יאוּ אֵלָ֛יו לִנְתָחֶ֖יהָ וְאֶת־הָרֹ֑אשׁ וַיַּקְטֵ֖ר עַל־הַמִּזְבֵּֽחַ: 14 וַיִּרְחַ֥ץ אֶת־הַקֶּ֖רֶב וְאֶת־הַכְּרָעָ֑יִם וַיַּקְטֵ֥ר עַל־הָעֹלָ֖ה הַמִּזְבֵּֽחָה: 15 וַיַּקְרֵ֕ב אֵ֖ת קָרְבַּ֣ן הָעָ֑ם וַיִּקַּ֞ח אֶת־שְׂעִ֤יר הַֽחַטָּאת֙ אֲשֶׁ֣ר לָעָ֔ם וַיִּשְׁחָטֵ֥הוּ וַֽיְחַטְּאֵ֖הוּ כָּרִאשֽׁוֹן: 16 וַיַּקְרֵ֖ב אֶת־הָֽעֹלָ֑ה וַֽיַּעֲשֶׂ֖הָ כַּמִּשְׁפָּֽט: 17 [SECOND READING] וַיַּקְרֵב֮ אֶת־הַמִּנְחָה֒ וַיְמַלֵּ֤א כַפּוֹ֙ מִמֶּ֔נָּה וַיַּקְטֵ֖ר עַל־הַמִּזְבֵּ֑חַ מִלְּבַ֖ד עֹלַ֥ת הַבֹּֽקֶר: 18 וַיִּשְׁחַ֤ט אֶת־הַשּׁוֹר֙ וְאֶת־הָאַ֔יִל זֶ֥בַח הַשְּׁלָמִ֖ים אֲשֶׁ֣ר לָעָ֑ם וַ֠יַּמְצִ֠אוּ בְּנֵ֨י אַהֲרֹ֤ן אֶת־הַדָּם֙ אֵלָ֔יו וַיִּזְרְקֵ֥הוּ עַל־הַמִּזְבֵּ֖חַ סָבִֽיב: 19 וְאֶת־הַחֲלָבִ֖ים מִן־הַשּׁ֑וֹר וּמִ֨ן־הָאַ֔יִל הָֽאַלְיָ֤ה וְהַֽמְכַסֶּה֙ וְהַכְּלָיֹ֔ת וְיֹתֶ֖רֶת הַכָּבֵֽד: 20 וַיָּשִׂ֥ימוּ אֶת־הַחֲלָבִ֖ים עַל־הֶֽחָז֑וֹת וַיַּקְטֵ֥ר הַחֲלָבִ֖ים הַמִּזְבֵּֽחָה: 21 וְאֵ֣ת הֶֽחָז֗וֹת וְאֵת֙ שׁ֣וֹק הַיָּמִ֔ין הֵנִ֧יף אַהֲרֹ֛ן תְּנוּפָ֖ה לִפְנֵ֣י יְהֹוָ֑ה כַּאֲשֶׁ֖ר צִוָּ֥ה מֹשֶֽׁה: 22 וַיִּשָּׂ֨א אַהֲרֹ֤ן אֶת־יָדָו֙ אֶל־הָעָ֔ם וַֽיְבָרְכֵ֑ם וַיֵּ֗רֶד מֵעֲשֹׂ֛ת הַֽחַטָּ֥את וְהָעֹלָ֖ה וְהַשְּׁלָמִֽים: 23 וַיָּבֹ֨א

Therefore, while still standing on the altar, Aaron recited the Priestly Blessing, asking God to grant complete forgiveness to the Jewish people and that the Divine Presence should enter the Tabernacle.

Aaron said: *"May God bless you, etc."*—Since the people may be wondering how Aaron, who was responsible for making the Golden Calf, could achieve atonement for it, he stressed, "May *God* bless you," i.e., that God Himself would give the blessing of atonement.

spiritual vitamin

> The function of the synagogue is to serve as a two-way link between created beings and the Creator, where man rises upward to Godliness through worship and prayer, and brings down God's blessings materially and spiritually.

altar. ¹⁰ He made the fat, the kidneys, and the diaphragm with (a piece of) the liver from the sin-offering go up in smoke on the altar, as God had commanded Moses, ¹¹ and he burned the meat and the skin in fire, outside the camp.

¹² He slaughtered the burnt-offering. Aaron's sons presented the blood to him, and he dashed it on the altar, all around. ¹³ They presented the burnt-offering to him in its (prescribed) pieces, along with the head, and he made the (pieces) go up in smoke on the altar. ¹⁴ He washed the intestines and the legs, and he made them go up in smoke on the altar, along with the burnt-offering.

¹⁵ He brought the people's offering forward: He took the people's sin-offering goat, slaughtered it, and prepared it as a sin-offering, like the first one. ¹⁶ He brought the burnt-offering forward and prepared it according to the law. [SECOND READING] ¹⁷ He brought the meal-offering forward, filled his palm with it (making a three-finger fistful), and made it go up in smoke on the altar. (All these sacrifices were offered) in addition to the morning burnt-offering (which came first).

¹⁸ He slaughtered the ox and the ram—the people's peace-offering. Aaron's sons presented the blood to him, and he dashed it on the altar, all around. ¹⁹ (They also presented) the fats from the ox and from the ram: the tail, the (fatty) covering (of the intestines), the kidneys and the diaphragm with (a piece of) the liver. ²⁰ They placed the fats on top of the breasts, and he made the fats go up in smoke on the altar. ²¹ (Before they were burned) Aaron had waved the breasts and the right thigh as a wave-offering before God, as Moses had commanded.

²² Aaron lifted up his hands towards the people and blessed them. He then came down from where he had made the sin-offering, the burnt-offering, and the peace-offering. ²³ Moses and Aaron went into the Tent of Meeting (and Moses

Food for thought

1. Why has God's glory not been visibly manifested for millennia?

2. Have you ever palpably felt God's presence?

3. Is a hidden miracle in any way greater than an overt one?

11. He burned the meat and the skin. Because the calf was brought as an offering to atone for Aaron's part in the sin of the Golden Calf (*Rashi* to v. 2), it was burned entirely, despite the fact that sin-offerings usually are not completely burned. This indicated that no trace of that sin could still be attributed to Aaron, and he was totally forgiven (*Rabbi Mordecai ha-Kohen, 17th century*).

22. Blessed them. (Aaron blessed them with) the Priestly Blessing:

Yivarekhekha—"May God bless you…" *Ya'er*—"May God make His face shine…" *Yissa'*—"May God lift His face…" (*Rashi, 11th century*).

Even though God had already forgiven the Jewish people for the Golden Calf, nevertheless, when the Tabernacle had been fully constructed and inaugurated and the Divine Presence had still not entered, it appeared that God had not yet *fully* forgiven the Jewish people.

ויקרא ט:כג - י:ג   שמיני

מֹשֶׁה וְאַהֲרֹן אֶל־אֹהֶל מוֹעֵד וַיֵּצְאוּ וַיְבָרֲכוּ אֶת־הָעָם וַיֵּרָא כְבוֹד־יְהֹוָה אֶל־כָּל־הָעָם: 24 [THIRD READING] וַתֵּצֵא אֵשׁ מִלִּפְנֵי יְהֹוָה וַתֹּאכַל עַל־הַמִּזְבֵּחַ אֶת־הָעֹלָה וְאֶת־הַחֲלָבִים וַיַּרְא כָּל־הָעָם וַיָּרֹנּוּ וַיִּפְּלוּ עַל־פְּנֵיהֶם:

י 1 וַיִּקְחוּ בְנֵי־אַהֲרֹן נָדָב וַאֲבִיהוּא אִישׁ מַחְתָּתוֹ וַיִּתְּנוּ בָהֵן אֵשׁ וַיָּשִׂימוּ עָלֶיהָ קְטֹרֶת וַיַּקְרִבוּ לִפְנֵי יְהֹוָה אֵשׁ זָרָה אֲשֶׁר לֹא צִוָּה אֹתָם: 2 וַתֵּצֵא אֵשׁ מִלִּפְנֵי יְהֹוָה וַתֹּאכַל אוֹתָם וַיָּמֻתוּ לִפְנֵי יְהֹוָה: 3 וַיֹּאמֶר מֹשֶׁה אֶל־אַהֲרֹן הוּא אֲשֶׁר־דִּבֶּר יְהֹוָה | לֵאמֹר בִּקְרֹבַי אֶקָּדֵשׁ וְעַל־פְּנֵי כָל־הָעָם אֶכָּבֵד וַיִּדֹּם

they died. But when Aaron is commanded, *"Do not drink (enough) wine to make (yourself) intoxicated"* (v. 9), we know that they only died on account of the wine (*Leviticus Rabbah*).

Being a "personal assistant" of the king, this man should have realized on his own, *without being told*, that "hanging around the entrance of taverns" was an activity displeasing to the king. Due to the fact that they were so close to God, Nadab and Abihu should have realized that it is inappropriate to enter the Sanctuary while intoxicated, even though the prohibition had not yet been stated (*Rabbi Menahem Mendel Schneerson, 20th century*).

Why did Nadab and Abihu enter the Sanctuary "while intoxicated with wine"? *They had an intoxicating desire for a heightened spiritual awareness.* Nadab and Abihu were indeed holy people, as Moses declared to Aaron after their passing, *"Now I see that they were greater than me or you!"* (*Rashi* to v. 3). They entered the Sanctuary to be close to God.

But their desire for spirituality was imbalanced. Nadab and Abihu expired because they came *so* close to God that they no longer desired a bodily existence. And while it is appropriate and admirable to have an intense yearning for God like that of Nadab and Abihu, you must be able to refocus spiritual inspiration back into everyday life (*Rabbi Shneur Zalman of Lyady, 18th century*).

3. Moses said to Aaron, "When God said, 'I will be sanctified through those whom I have chosen, and I will be glorified before all the people,' this (event) is what He was talking about." On hearing this, *"Aaron was silent."* He accepted God's decree. Later, he was rewarded for his silence, in that God spoke directly to him, and him alone, as the verse states, "God spoke *to Aaron*" (10:8; *Babylonian Talmud, Zevahim* 115b).

spiritual vitamin

> When you are engaged in Torah and its commandments, especially when the experience is permeated with inner joy and inspiration, your soul "departs" from your body, in the sense that it abandons bodily needs, lusts and inclinations.

leviticus 9:23 – 10:3   shemini

taught Aaron how to offer the incense). Then, they came out and blessed the people, and the glory of God appeared to all the people.

[THIRD READING] ²⁴ Fire came out from before God and consumed the burnt-offering and the fats upon the altar. All the people saw. They sang praises, and fell upon their faces.

The Passing of Nadab and Abihu

10 ¹ Each of Aaron's sons, Nadab and Abihu, took his own fire pan. They put fire in them and placed incense on top, and they brought an extraneous fire before God, which He had not commanded them (to bring).

² Fire came out from before God and consumed them, and they died before God.

³ Moses said to Aaron, "When God said, 'I will be sanctified through those whom I have chosen, and I will be glorified before all the people,' this (event) is what He was talking about." Aaron was silent.

"May God make His face shine upon you, etc."—that the Jewish people should be favorable in God's eyes.

"May God lift His face to you, etc."—In his commentary to this verse, *Rashi* explains: "He should calm his anger." In this context Aaron was asking God to forgive the people for making the Golden Calf (*Rabbi Menahem Mendel Schneerson, 20th century*).

23. They came out and blessed the people. Even after Aaron's blessing, it was still necessary for Moses and Aaron to give a further blessing together, since Aaron's blessing was related to a matter which concerned him *personally*, atonement for the Golden Calf. Moses and Aaron's joint words were a *general* blessing to the entire people that their work in constructing the Tabernacle should bear fruit. They said: *"'May the pleasantness of God, our God, be upon us'* (Psalms 90:17). May it be God's will that the Divine Presence will rest in the work of your hands" (*Rashi, 11th century*).

10:2 Fire came out from before God and consumed them. Rabbi Eliezer said: Aaron's sons died only because they rendered a legal decision in the presence of Moses, their teacher, that incense should be offered on the altar.

Rabbi Ishmael said: Because they entered the Sanctuary while intoxicated with wine. The proof of this is that after their death, the Torah warned the surviving priests not to enter the Sanctuary after having drunk wine (below, verses 8-11; *Rashi, 11th century*).

A king had a personal assistant, whom he found hanging around the entrance of taverns. The king severed his head without explaining why, and appointed another assistant in his place. We would not know why he put the first one to death if he had not told the second one, "You must not enter the entrance of taverns!" Now we know that it was for this same reason that he had put the first one to death.

Similarly, when the Torah states, *"Fire came out from before God and consumed them, and they died before God,"* we would not know why

---

Food for thought

1. How do Jewish traditions help a person deal with unexpected tragedy?

2. "Aaron was silent." What was he thinking?

3. What is your reaction when people "justify" tragedies, due to sin, etc.?

ויקרא י:ג-יא   שמיני

4 וַיִּקְרָ֣א מֹשֶׁ֗ה אֶל־מִֽישָׁאֵל֙ וְאֶ֣ל אֶלְצָפָ֔ן בְּנֵ֥י עֻזִּיאֵ֖ל דֹּ֣ד אַהֲרֹ֑ן וַיֹּ֣אמֶר אֲלֵהֶ֗ם קִ֠רְב֠וּ שְׂא֤וּ אֶת־אֲחֵיכֶם֙ מֵאֵ֣ת פְּנֵי־הַקֹּ֔דֶשׁ אֶל־מִח֖וּץ לַֽמַּחֲנֶֽה: 5 וַֽיִּקְרְב֗וּ וַיִּשָּׂאֻם֙ בְּכֻתֳּנֹתָ֔ם אֶל־מִח֖וּץ לַֽמַּחֲנֶ֑ה כַּאֲשֶׁ֖ר דִּבֶּ֥ר מֹשֶֽׁה: 6 וַיֹּ֣אמֶר מֹשֶׁ֣ה אֶֽל־אַהֲרֹ֡ן וּלְאֶלְעָזָר֩ וּלְאִֽיתָמָ֨ר ׀ בָּנָ֜יו רָֽאשֵׁיכֶ֥ם אַל־תִּפְרָ֣עוּ ׀ וּבִגְדֵיכֶ֤ם לֹֽא־תִפְרֹ֨מוּ֙ וְלֹ֣א תָמֻ֔תוּ וְעַ֥ל כָּל־הָעֵדָ֖ה יִקְצֹ֑ף וַֽאֲחֵיכֶם֙ כָּל־בֵּ֣ית יִשְׂרָאֵ֔ל יִבְכּוּ֙ אֶת־הַשְּׂרֵפָ֔ה אֲשֶׁ֖ר שָׂרַ֥ף יְהֹוָֽה: 7 וּמִפֶּתַח֩ אֹ֨הֶל מוֹעֵ֜ד לֹ֤א תֵֽצְאוּ֙ פֶּן־תָּמֻ֔תוּ כִּי־שֶׁ֛מֶן מִשְׁחַ֥ת יְהֹוָ֖ה עֲלֵיכֶ֑ם וַֽיַּעֲשׂ֖וּ כִּדְבַ֥ר מֹשֶֽׁה: פ 8 וַיְדַבֵּ֣ר יְהֹוָ֔ה אֶֽל־אַהֲרֹ֖ן לֵאמֹֽר: 9 יַ֣יִן וְשֵׁכָ֞ר אַל־תֵּ֣שְׁתְּ ׀ אַתָּ֣ה ׀ וּבָנֶ֣יךָ אִתָּ֗ךְ בְּבֹֽאֲכֶ֛ם אֶל־אֹ֥הֶל מוֹעֵ֖ד וְלֹ֣א תָמֻ֑תוּ חֻקַּ֥ת עוֹלָ֖ם לְדֹרֹֽתֵיכֶֽם: 10 וּֽלֲהַבְדִּ֔יל בֵּ֥ין הַקֹּ֖דֶשׁ וּבֵ֣ין הַחֹ֑ל וּבֵ֥ין הַטָּמֵ֖א וּבֵ֥ין הַטָּהֽוֹר: 11 וּלְהוֹרֹ֖ת אֶת־בְּנֵ֣י יִשְׂרָאֵ֑ל אֵ֚ת כָּל־הַ֣חֻקִּ֔ים אֲשֶׁ֨ר דִּבֶּ֧ר יְהֹוָ֛ה אֲלֵיהֶ֖ם

From here we see a remarkable ramification of the above principle: that Jewish law takes seriously into consideration the fact that it is possible for the Messiah to come, with a completed Holy Temple, within twenty-three minutes and fifty-nine seconds, thus requiring the priests to be ready for service immediately! (*Rabbi Menahem Mendel Schneerson, 20th century*).

Wine. You need to worship God with happiness. Therefore a priest is not allowed to serve in the Temple when he has an unburied relative.

The Torah warns us against using external stimulants, like wine, to achieve happiness. The way to reach a state of bliss is if you *"distinguish between the holy and the profane"* and, *"instruct the children of Israel"* (10:10-11). It is through studying and teaching the Torah that you can gain lasting happiness (*Rabbi Naphtali Tzevi Judah Berlin, 19th century*).

kabbalah bites

10:6 If the people had not worshiped the Golden Calf, Nadab and Abihu would have died a natural death for their inadvertent sin. Through worshiping the calf, the people brought about the return of the *zuhama'*, a spiritual pollutant that had plagued the soul of Adam and his descendants since the sin of the Tree of Knowledge, until Sinai (see *Genesis 3:6*).

Nadab and Abihu were a reincarnation of Cain, who literally had part of Adam's soul, so the return of the *zuhama'* affected them particularly strongly. That is why, instead of suffering a natural death, they were burned.

Since the people who had worshiped the calf were essentially culpable for this form of death, *"the entire house of Israel"* wept about the fire.

leviticus 10:4–11 — shemini

⁴ Moses summoned Mishael and Elzaphan, the sons of Uzziel, Aaron's uncle, and said to them, "Come close and carry your brothers from the Sanctuary outside the camp."

⁵ So they approached and carried them outside of the camp (as they were, dressed) in their tunics, as Moses had said.

Laws of Mourning during Priestly Service

⁶ Moses said to Aaron, and to his sons Eleazar and Ithamar:

- ❖ "Do not let your hair grow wild and do not rend your clothes (when you carry out the service in the Tabernacle), so that you will not die, and so that He will not be angry with the entire community."

"Your brothers, the entire house of Israel, will weep about the fire that God has (caused to) burn."

- ❖ ⁷ Do not go out of the entrance of the Tent of Meeting (when you are in the middle of the service), so that you will not die, because God's anointing oil is upon you."

They did according to Moses' word.

Prohibition Against Intoxication during the Priestly Service

⁸ God spoke to Aaron, saying:

- ❖ ⁹ "When you go into the Tent of Meeting do not drink (enough) wine to make (yourself) intoxicated, neither you nor your sons with you, so that you will not die. (This is) an eternal statute for your generations. ¹⁰ (This is) so that (you will be able to) distinguish between the holy and the profane and between the unclean and the clean, ¹¹ and to (be able to) instruct the children of Israel regarding all the statutes which God has told them, through Moses."

---

4. Carry your brothers. Like a person would say to his fellow: "Remove the deceased from before the bride so as not to disturb the joyous occasion" (*Rashi, 11th century*).

Why did Moses not tell Eleazar and Ithamar, the *brothers* of Nadab and Abihu, to remove the bodies? While, generally speaking, an ordinary priest may come into contact with a corpse of a close relative, on the day of his inauguration even an ordinary priest must adopt the stringency of the High Priest who may not come into contact with a corpse of a close relative. Therefore, Mishael and Elzaphan were asked to remove the bodies instead, since they were Levites and not priests (*Rabbi Jacob b. Asher, 13th–14th century*).

9. Do not drink (enough) wine to make (yourself) intoxicated. There is a view in Jewish law that even nowadays a priest may not drink a *revi'it* (86 ml.) of wine. This is sufficient to cause some degree of intoxication, and since it is feasible that the Holy Temple will be rebuilt *within* the time it takes for him to become sober, the wine would render him unfit for service.

Now, according to Jewish law, intoxication caused by a *revi'it* of wine can be removed by either a short nap, or by waiting the time it would take to walk a *mil*. (There are different views as to precisely how long this is: either eighteen or, at most, twenty-four minutes.)

ויקרא י׳:י״ב-כ׳ שמיני

בְּיַד־מֹשֶׁה׃ פ [FOURTH READING] 12 וַיְדַבֵּ֨ר מֹשֶׁ֜ה אֶֽל־אַהֲרֹ֗ן וְאֶ֣ל אֶלְעָזָר֮ וְאֶל־אִֽיתָמָר֒ | בָּנָ֣יו הַנּֽוֹתָרִ֔ים קְח֣וּ אֶת־הַמִּנְחָ֗ה הַנּוֹתֶ֙רֶת֙ מֵאִשֵּׁ֣י יְהֹוָ֔ה וְאִכְל֥וּהָ מַצּ֖וֹת אֵ֣צֶל הַמִּזְבֵּ֑חַ כִּ֛י קֹ֥דֶשׁ קׇֽדָשִׁ֖ים הִֽוא׃ 13 וַאֲכַלְתֶּ֤ם אֹתָהּ֙ בְּמָק֣וֹם קָדֹ֔שׁ כִּ֣י חׇקְךָ֤ וְחׇק־בָּנֶ֙יךָ֙ הִ֔וא מֵאִשֵּׁ֖י יְהֹוָ֑ה כִּי־כֵ֖ן צֻוֵּֽיתִי׃ 14 וְאֵת֩ חֲזֵ֨ה הַתְּנוּפָ֜ה וְאֵ֣ת | שׁ֣וֹק הַתְּרוּמָ֗ה תֹּֽאכְלוּ֙ בְּמָק֣וֹם טָה֔וֹר אַתָּ֕ה וּבָנֶ֥יךָ וּבְנֹתֶ֖יךָ אִתָּ֑ךְ כִּֽי־חׇקְךָ֤ וְחׇק־בָּנֶ֙יךָ֙ נִתְּנ֔וּ מִזִּבְחֵ֥י שַׁלְמֵ֖י בְּנֵ֥י יִשְׂרָאֵֽל׃ 15 שׁ֣וֹק הַתְּרוּמָ֞ה וַחֲזֵ֣ה הַתְּנוּפָ֗ה עַ֣ל אִשֵּׁ֤י הַחֲלָבִים֙ יָבִ֔יאוּ לְהָנִ֥יף תְּנוּפָ֖ה לִפְנֵ֣י יְהֹוָ֑ה וְהָיָ֨ה לְךָ֜ וּלְבָנֶ֤יךָ אִתְּךָ֙ לְחׇק־עוֹלָ֔ם כַּאֲשֶׁ֖ר צִוָּ֥ה יְהֹוָֽה׃ [FIFTH READING] 16 וְאֵ֣ת | שְׂעִ֣יר הַֽחַטָּ֗את דָּרֹ֥שׁ דָּרַ֛שׁ מֹשֶׁ֖ה וְהִנֵּ֣ה שֹׂרָ֑ף וַיִּקְצֹ֨ף עַל־אֶלְעָזָ֜ר וְעַל־אִ֣יתָמָ֗ר בְּנֵ֧י אַהֲרֹ֛ן הַנּוֹתָרִ֖ם לֵאמֹֽר׃ 17 מַדּ֗וּעַ לֹֽא־אֲכַלְתֶּ֤ם אֶת־הַחַטָּאת֙ בִּמְק֣וֹם הַקֹּ֔דֶשׁ כִּ֛י קֹ֥דֶשׁ קׇֽדָשִׁ֖ים הִ֑וא וְאֹתָ֣הּ | נָתַ֣ן לָכֶ֗ם לָשֵׂאת֙ אֶת־עֲוֺ֣ן הָעֵדָ֔ה לְכַפֵּ֥ר עֲלֵיהֶ֖ם לִפְנֵ֥י יְהֹוָֽה׃ 18 הֵ֚ן לֹא־הוּבָ֣א אֶת־דָּמָ֔הּ אֶל־הַקֹּ֖דֶשׁ פְּנִ֑ימָה אָכ֨וֹל תֹּאכְל֥וּ אֹתָ֛הּ בַּקֹּ֖דֶשׁ כַּאֲשֶׁ֥ר צִוֵּֽיתִי׃ 19 וַיְדַבֵּ֨ר אַהֲרֹ֜ן אֶל־מֹשֶׁ֗ה הֵ֣ן הַ֠יּ֠וֹם הִקְרִ֨יבוּ אֶת־חַטָּאתָ֤ם וְאֶת־עֹֽלָתָם֙ לִפְנֵ֣י יְהֹוָ֔ה וַתִּקְרֶ֥אנָה אֹתִ֖י כָּאֵ֑לֶּה וְאָכַ֤לְתִּי חַטָּאת֙ הַיּ֔וֹם הַיִּיטַ֖ב בְּעֵינֵ֥י יְהֹוָֽה׃ 20 וַיִּשְׁמַ֣ע מֹשֶׁ֔ה וַיִּיטַ֖ב בְּעֵינָֽיו׃ פ

spiritual vitamin

> People get involved with trying to solve problems of a global nature, considering it beneath them to deal with the so-called trivialities associated with day-to-day living. Yet, as far as global problems are concerned, you usually cannot accomplish anything, and merely waste time and energy in futility and frustration, leaving no time or attention for what are immediate personal matters, such as the way you should conduct yourself.

leviticus 10:12–20 — shemini

End of the Day's Service after Nadab and Abihu's Passing

[FOURTH READING] ¹² Moses spoke to Aaron and his surviving sons, Eleazar and Ithamar:

"(Even though you are mourners), take the meal-offering that is left over from God's fire-offerings, and eat it as unleavened loaves beside the altar, for it is a most holy (offering). ¹³ You should eat it in a holy place, because it is your portion and your sons' portion from God's fire-offerings, for (even though mourners are usually forbidden to eat offerings) that is what I have been commanded (in this case). ¹⁴ You should eat the breast of the wave-offering and the thigh of the raised-offering in a pure place (i.e. the Jewish camp)—you, your sons and your daughters with you—for they have been given from the peace-offerings of the children of Israel as your portion and your sons' portion.

¹⁵ They should bring the thigh of the raised-offering and the breast of the wave-offering on the fats for fire-offerings, to wave as a wave-offering before God. It will belong to you along with your sons as an eternal statute, as God has commanded."

[FIFTH READING] ¹⁶ Moses made two investigations about (what had happened to) the (three) sin-offering goats, and—look!—(two had been eaten correctly, but one) had been (completely) burned! So he became angry with Eleazar and Ithamar, Aaron's surviving sons, (demanding that) they respond: ¹⁷ "Why did you not eat the sin-offering? (Was it accidentally taken outside) the holy place (where it may be eaten), and being a most holy offering (it became invalidated? God) has given it to you to gain forgiveness for the sin of the community, to atone for them before God! ¹⁸ Look, its blood was not (required to be) brought inside the Sanctuary (in which case there would indeed have been an obligation to burn it), so you should have eaten it in the holy (place, even though you are in a state of mourning), as I commanded! (Did you, perhaps, sprinkle the blood of the sacrifice while you are in a state of mourning, and thus invalidate it, requiring it to be burned?)"

¹⁹ Aaron spoke (sternly) to Moses: "(Do you think) it was they who offered up the sin-offering and the burnt-offering before God today? (No, it was I who offered them! And being the High Priest, I am allowed to sprinkle the blood while in a state of mourning.) But if I had eaten the (third) sin-offering today, would it have pleased God? (For unlike the other two sin-offerings which are temporary, the third is a permanent one, for all generations, and it is not appropriate to be lenient and allow a mourner to eat from it. Even if) this (tragedy) had happened to me (not with my sons, but with other relatives, it would not have been appropriate to eat from such a sin-offering)."

²⁰ (When) Moses heard (Aaron's explanation) it pleased him, (and he was not ashamed to admit that he had been mistaken).

שמיני

ויקרא יא:א-ו

יא וַיְדַבֵּר יְהוָה אֶל־מֹשֶׁה וְאֶל־אַהֲרֹן לֵאמֹר אֲלֵהֶם: [SIXTH READING] 2 דַּבְּרוּ אֶל־בְּנֵי יִשְׂרָאֵל לֵאמֹר זֹאת הַחַיָּה אֲשֶׁר תֹּאכְלוּ מִכָּל־הַבְּהֵמָה אֲשֶׁר עַל־הָאָרֶץ: 3 כֹּל ׀ מַפְרֶסֶת פַּרְסָה וְשֹׁסַעַת שֶׁסַע פְּרָסֹת מַעֲלַת גֵּרָה בַּבְּהֵמָה אֹתָהּ תֹּאכֵלוּ: 4 אַךְ אֶת־זֶה לֹא תֹאכְלוּ מִמַּעֲלֵי הַגֵּרָה וּמִמַּפְרִיסֵי הַפַּרְסָה אֶת־הַגָּמָל כִּי־מַעֲלֵה גֵרָה הוּא וּפַרְסָה אֵינֶנּוּ מַפְרִיס טָמֵא הוּא לָכֶם: 5 וְאֶת־הַשָּׁפָן כִּי־מַעֲלֵה גֵרָה הוּא וּפַרְסָה לֹא יַפְרִיס טָמֵא הוּא לָכֶם: 6 וְאֶת־הָאַרְנֶבֶת כִּי־מַעֲלַת גֵּרָה הִוא וּפַרְסָה לֹא הִפְרִיסָה טְמֵאָה הִוא לָכֶם:

After the sin of the Golden Calf, God said that His Presence would not accompany the Jewish people to the land of Israel (see *Exodus* 33:3). Moses succeeded with his prayers that God would grant the Jewish people the privilege of building the Tabernacle, through which the Divine Presence would return to dwell among the Jewish people.

Now that this was complete, further commandments followed to continue the process of spiritual refinement of the Jewish people, such as the dietary laws and the laws of family purity (*Rabbi Obadiah Sforno, 16th century*).

4. The camel, because it chews the cud, but does not have a (completely) split hoof. The Torah is listing forbidden animals, so why does it name the animal's *kosher* characteristics and not just the non-kosher signs, which render it forbidden?

The kosher signs on these non-kosher animals allude to a bigger problem. When something is impure and all it shows is impurity, that is fine. But if an impure thing tries to show some signs of purity, then this is especially deceitful (*Rabbi Ephraim of Luntshits, 16th–17th century*).

4-7. The camel, hyrax, hare, and pig. Why are these four animals specified?

The camel (*gamal*) alludes to the Babylonian Exile, as the verse states: *"O daughter of Babylon, you are to be destroyed. Happy is the one who pays you your retributions (gemulekh) according to how you have dealt (gamalt) with us"* (*Psalms* 137:8).

kabbalah bites

11:1-23 Life is all about embracing *Hesed* (kindness; love) and escaping from *Gevurah* (judgment; resentment). The more you become a joyous, loving person the more mentally and physically healthy you become, free from many of the internal beliefs and wounds that give rise to destructive behaviors. On the other hand, harboring negative, judgmental energy will plunge you into internal chaos, paralyzing you from taking corrective actions.

The Kabbalah teaches that your food choices can subtly influence you towards *Hesed* or towards *Gevurah*. The "pure," kosher animals originate from God's *Hesed*; the "impure," non-kosher animals, from *Gevurah*. Through ingesting *Hesed*-rooted food, *Hesed* becomes part of your flesh and blood and, over time, *Hesed* life choices become gradually easier for you.

leviticus 11:1–6 — shemini

Laws of Forbidden Animals

11 [SIXTH READING] ¹ God spoke to Moses (telling him to say) to Aaron who should say to (Eleazar and Ithamar):

² (You should all) speak to the children of Israel, and say:

These are the living creatures that you may eat, from among all the animals on earth:

- ³ You may eat any animal which has a split hoof that is completely split into two hooves, if it chews the cud.

⁴ But, among those that chew the cud and those that have a cloven hoof, you must not eat these:

- The camel, because it chews the cud, but does not have a (completely) split hoof. It is impure for you.

- ⁵ The hyrax, because it chews the cud, but does not have a (completely) split hoof. It is impure for you.

- ⁶ The hare, because it chews the cud, but does not have a (completely) split hoof. It is impure for you.

11:2 (You should all) speak to the children of Israel. God made Moses, Aaron, Eleazar and Ithamar equal messengers to relay the following section, because they remained equally silent (above, 10:3), accepting God's decree against Nadab and Abihu with love (*Rashi, 11th century*).

Even a child who is studying the Torah for the first time knows that when a person is in pain, rules of etiquette are inevitably disregarded. The child knows that when his friends hurt him he reacts, even if it is not appropriate to do so, for human nature is to react *instantly* to pain.

Even though Eleazar and Ithamar had the courtesy *in general* not to speak up in the presence of their father Aaron, nevertheless, the pain of the sudden passing of their brothers Nadab and Abihu would presumably have caused them to cry out in anger, out of sheer pain, even if it was inappropriate to do so. The fact that they remained silent was proof to *Rashi* that they had accepted God's decree with love (*Rabbi Menahem Mendel Schneerson, 20th century*).

These are the living creatures that you may eat. After the Tabernacle was completed and the priests inaugurated, they were given the command not to carry out their service while intoxicated. The Torah explains, *"(This is) so that (you will be able to) distinguish between the holy and the profane and between the unclean and the clean"* (above, 10:10). So it now became necessary for God to inform Moses and Aaron which creatures were "clean" and which were "unclean."

Furthermore, since the priests were forbidden to enter the Tabernacle in a state of ritual impurity, it now became crucial for them to know which creatures would render them impure (*Rabbi Isaac Abravanel, 15th century*).

Food for thought

1. What are the benefits of training people not to eat whatever they want?

2. Do certain types of food actually affect us mentally and/or spiritually?

3. If "you are what you eat," can eating a vicious animal make you cruel?

ויקרא יא:ז-כא | שמיני

7 וְאֶת־הַחֲזִיר כִּי־מַפְרִיס פַּרְסָה הוּא וְשֹׁסַע שֶׁסַע פַּרְסָה וְהוּא גֵּרָה לֹא־יִגָּר טָמֵא הוּא לָכֶם: 8 מִבְּשָׂרָם לֹא תֹאכֵלוּ וּבְנִבְלָתָם לֹא תִגָּעוּ טְמֵאִים הֵם לָכֶם: 9 אֶת־זֶה תֹּאכְלוּ מִכֹּל אֲשֶׁר בַּמָּיִם כֹּל אֲשֶׁר־לוֹ סְנַפִּיר וְקַשְׂקֶשֶׂת בַּמַּיִם בַּיַּמִּים וּבַנְּחָלִים אֹתָם תֹּאכֵלוּ: 10 וְכֹל אֲשֶׁר אֵין־לוֹ סְנַפִּיר וְקַשְׂקֶשֶׂת בַּיַּמִּים וּבַנְּחָלִים מִכֹּל שֶׁרֶץ הַמַּיִם וּמִכֹּל נֶפֶשׁ הַחַיָּה אֲשֶׁר בַּמָּיִם שֶׁקֶץ הֵם לָכֶם: 11 וְשֶׁקֶץ יִהְיוּ לָכֶם מִבְּשָׂרָם לֹא תֹאכֵלוּ וְאֶת־נִבְלָתָם תְּשַׁקֵּצוּ: 12 כֹּל אֲשֶׁר אֵין־לוֹ סְנַפִּיר וְקַשְׂקֶשֶׂת בַּמָּיִם שֶׁקֶץ הוּא לָכֶם: 13 וְאֶת־אֵלֶּה תְּשַׁקְּצוּ מִן־הָעוֹף לֹא יֵאָכְלוּ שֶׁקֶץ הֵם אֶת־הַנֶּשֶׁר וְאֶת־הַפֶּרֶס וְאֵת הָעָזְנִיָּה: 14 וְאֶת־הַדָּאָה וְאֶת־הָאַיָּה לְמִינָהּ: 15 אֵת כָּל־עֹרֵב לְמִינוֹ: 16 וְאֵת בַּת הַיַּעֲנָה וְאֶת־הַתַּחְמָס וְאֶת־הַשַּׁחַף וְאֶת־הַנֵּץ לְמִינֵהוּ: 17 וְאֶת־הַכּוֹס וְאֶת־הַשָּׁלָךְ וְאֶת־הַיַּנְשׁוּף: 18 וְאֶת־הַתִּנְשֶׁמֶת וְאֶת־הַקָּאָת וְאֶת־הָרָחָם: 19 וְאֵת הַחֲסִידָה הָאֲנָפָה לְמִינָהּ וְאֶת־הַדּוּכִיפַת וְאֶת־הָעֲטַלֵּף: 20 כֹּל שֶׁרֶץ הָעוֹף הַהֹלֵךְ עַל־אַרְבַּע שֶׁקֶץ הוּא לָכֶם: 21 אַךְ אֶת־זֶה תֹּאכְלוּ מִכֹּל שֶׁרֶץ הָעוֹף הַהֹלֵךְ עַל־אַרְבַּע אֲשֶׁר־ [לֹא כ']

Rabbi Johanan said: "Because the pig is equal to the other three put together."

Rabbi Simeon son of Lakish said: "It is even more than that.

"Why is Rome compared to a pig? For just as the pig reclines and puts out its hooves, as if to say, 'Look! I am clean,' so too, the empire of Rome arrogantly commits violence and robbery, while pretending to enact justice" (*Leviticus Rabbah; Rabbi Issachar Berman b. Naphtali ha-Kohen, 16th century*).

14. The buzzard. One of the names for the buzzard in the Bible is *ra'ah* (*Deuteronomy* 14:13), which means "seeing." Why is it called *ra'ah*? Because it can see extremely far. It can stand in Babylonia and see carrion in the land of Israel (*Babylonian Talmud, Ḥullin* 63b).

Having good vision can be a great asset, but if it used to see "carrion," the bad and negative in others, then it is impure (*Rabbi Zalman b. Ben-Zion Sorotzkin, 20th century*).

19. The stork. The name for stork in the Bible is *ḥasidah*, which means "the kind one." Why is it called *ḥasidah*? Because it shows kindness to its fellow storks, sharing food with them (*Babylonian Talmud, Ḥullin* 63a).

If the *ḥasidah* is a kind bird, why is it not kosher? Because it shows kindness only to its own species and not to any other creature. For this reason, it cannot be deemed kosher (*Rabbi Isaac Meir Alter of Gur, 19th century*).

leviticus 11:7-21 — shemini

- ⁷ The pig, because it has a split hoof which is completely split, but does not chew the cud. It is impure for you.

- ⁸ You must not eat their flesh. You must not touch their carcasses (when you are ritually pure, during the festivals), for they are impure for you.

Laws of Permitted and Forbidden Fish

- ⁹ Among all (the creatures) that are in the water, you may eat these: You may eat any (of) those (creatures) in the water that have fins and scales, whether (they live) in the seas or in the rivers.

- ¹⁰ But any that do not have fins and scales among all the creeping creatures in the water and among all living creatures that (live) in the water, whether in the seas or in the rivers, are an abomination for you. ¹¹ (Even if they are mixed with other food) they shall be an abomination for you. You must not eat their flesh, and you should hold their dead bodies in abomination.

- ¹² Any creature in the water that does not have fins and scales is an abomination for you (but if it had fins and scales but shed them in the water, it is permissible to you).

Laws of Forbidden Birds

- ¹³ Among birds, you shall hold the following in abomination. They must not be eaten (because) they are an abomination: the griffon vulture, the bearded vulture, the osprey, ¹⁴ the kite, the buzzard family, ¹⁵ the entire raven family, ¹⁶ the ostrich, the *taḥmas,* the gull, the hawk family, ¹⁷ the *kos* owl, the cormorant, the *yanshuf* owl, ¹⁸ the barn owl, the *ka'at* owl, the roller, ¹⁹ the stork, the heron family, the hoopoe and the bat.

Laws of Forbidden and Permitted Insects

- ²⁰ Any flying insect that walks on four (legs) is an abomination for you.

- ²¹ However, among all the flying insects that walk on four (legs), you may eat (from) those that have (additional) jointed legs with which they hop on the ground, above its (regular) legs.

The hyrax alludes to the Median Exile. Just as the hyrax possesses signs of uncleanliness and signs of cleanliness, so too, Media produced a righteous man (Mordecai) as well as a wicked man (Haman).

The hare alludes to the Greek Exile, since the mother of Ptolemy was Lagos, which is the Greek word for "hare."

The pig alludes to the Roman Exile.

Why did Moses mention three animals in one verse and the last in another verse (when he repeated them in 14:7-8)?

ויקרא יא:כא-לב

לוֹ כְרָעַיִם מִמַּעַל לְרַגְלָיו לְנַתֵּר בָּהֵן עַל־הָאָרֶץ: 22 אֶת־אֵלֶּה מֵהֶם תֹּאכֵלוּ אֶת־הָאַרְבֶּה לְמִינוֹ וְאֶת־הַסָּלְעָם לְמִינֵהוּ וְאֶת־הַחַרְגֹּל לְמִינֵהוּ וְאֶת־הֶחָגָב לְמִינֵהוּ: 23 וְכֹל שֶׁרֶץ הָעוֹף אֲשֶׁר־לוֹ אַרְבַּע רַגְלָיִם שֶׁקֶץ הוּא לָכֶם: 24 וּלְאֵלֶּה תִּטַּמָּאוּ כָּל־הַנֹּגֵעַ בְּנִבְלָתָם יִטְמָא עַד־הָעָרֶב: 25 וְכָל־הַנֹּשֵׂא מִנִּבְלָתָם יְכַבֵּס בְּגָדָיו וְטָמֵא עַד־הָעָרֶב: 26 לְכָל־הַבְּהֵמָה אֲשֶׁר הִוא מַפְרֶסֶת פַּרְסָה וְשֶׁסַע | אֵינֶנָּה שֹׁסַעַת וְגֵרָה אֵינֶנָּה מַעֲלָה טְמֵאִים הֵם לָכֶם כָּל־הַנֹּגֵעַ בָּהֶם יִטְמָא: 27 וְכֹל | הוֹלֵךְ עַל־כַּפָּיו בְּכָל־הַחַיָּה הַהֹלֶכֶת עַל־אַרְבַּע טְמֵאִים הֵם לָכֶם כָּל־הַנֹּגֵעַ בְּנִבְלָתָם יִטְמָא עַד־הָעָרֶב: 28 וְהַנֹּשֵׂא אֶת־נִבְלָתָם יְכַבֵּס בְּגָדָיו וְטָמֵא עַד־הָעֶרֶב טְמֵאִים הֵמָּה לָכֶם: ס 29 וְזֶה לָכֶם הַטָּמֵא בַּשֶּׁרֶץ הַשֹּׁרֵץ עַל־הָאָרֶץ הַחֹלֶד וְהָעַכְבָּר וְהַצָּב לְמִינֵהוּ: 30 וְהָאֲנָקָה וְהַכֹּחַ וְהַלְּטָאָה וְהַחֹמֶט וְהַתִּנְשָׁמֶת: 31 אֵלֶּה הַטְּמֵאִים לָכֶם בְּכָל־הַשָּׁרֶץ כָּל־הַנֹּגֵעַ בָּהֶם בְּמֹתָם יִטְמָא עַד־הָעָרֶב: 32 וְכֹל אֲשֶׁר־יִפֹּל־עָלָיו מֵהֶם | בְּמֹתָם יִטְמָא מִכָּל־כְּלִי־עֵץ אוֹ בֶגֶד אוֹ־עוֹר אוֹ שָׂק כָּל־כְּלִי אֲשֶׁר־יֵעָשֶׂה מְלָאכָה בָּהֶם בַּמַּיִם יוּבָא וְטָמֵא עַד־הָעֶרֶב

However, during Temple times the entire Jewish people are required to become ritually pure on each festival, so that they are fit to enter the Temple and eat sacrifices.

spiritual vitamin

" While God created you in a way that you depend on food and drink for survival—you nevertheless have the power to transform this physical necessity into a new and incomparably higher function: to eat for the purpose of being able to do good, transforming the food into energy to serve God. And in the very act of eating you can serve God, because it gives you an opportunity to make a blessing before eating, and afterwards. "

leviticus 11:22–32 — shemini

- ²² From this (locust) category, you may eat the following: The red locust family, the yellow locust family, the spotted grey locust family and the white locust family.
- ²³ Any flying insect that has four legs is an abomination for you (but a five-legged flying insect is permissible).

Laws of Ritual Impurity from Non-Kosher Animals

- ²⁴ Through (contact with) the following (animals), you will become ritually impure;
- Anyone who touches (one of) their carcasses will be ritually impure until evening;
- ²⁵ Anyone who carries (one of) their carcasses (acquires a more severe form of impurity). He should immerse his garments, and he will be ritually impure until the evening;
- ²⁶ Any animal that has a split hoof which is not completely split, and that does not chew the cud, is ritually impure for you. Anyone who touches them will become ritually impure.
- ²⁷ Among all the animals that walk on four legs, any (animal) that walks on its paws (such as a dog, bear or cat) is ritually impure for you. Anyone who touches their carcass will be ritually impure until evening. ²⁸ One who carries their carcass should immerse his garments, and he will be ritually impure until evening. They are ritually impure for you.
- ²⁹ The following are ritually impure for you among creeping creatures that creep on the ground: the weasel, the mouse, the toad family, ³⁰ the hedgehog, the chameleon, the lizard, the snail, and the mole. ³¹ (All) these are the ones that are ritually impure for you, among all creeping creatures. Anyone who touches them when they are dead will be ritually impure until the evening.

Laws of Ritual Impurity of Objects and Food

- ³² If any of these dead (creatures) fall upon anything, it will become ritually impure, whether it is any type of wooden object, a garment, an (article of) leather or sackcloth. (This applies to) any object with which work is done. It should be immersed in water, but it will remain ritually impure until the evening. It will become clean (when the sun sets).

24–40. Ritually impure. There is no objection at all to actively rendering ordinary non-sacrificial food impure, once it has been made fit for ordinary consumption by the separation of *terumah* (heave-offering) and tithes. So too, a person is free to touch any ritually impure item, and become ritually impure from it. Even the priests, who are warned against becoming ritually impure, may allow themselves to become ritually impure with any type of impurity other than that of the corpse.

ויקרא יא:לב-מב / שמיני

33 [SEVENTH READING] וְטָהֵֽר׃ וְכׇל־כְּלִי־חֶ֗רֶשׂ אֲשֶׁר־יִפֹּ֥ל מֵהֶ֛ם אֶל־תּוֹכ֖וֹ כֹּ֣ל אֲשֶׁ֣ר בְּתוֹכ֣וֹ יִטְמָ֔א וְאֹת֖וֹ תִשְׁבֹּֽרוּ׃ 34 מִכׇּל־הָאֹ֜כֶל אֲשֶׁ֣ר יֵאָכֵ֗ל אֲשֶׁ֨ר יָב֥וֹא עָלָ֛יו מַ֖יִם יִטְמָ֑א וְכׇל־מַשְׁקֶה֙ אֲשֶׁ֣ר יִשָּׁתֶ֔ה בְּכׇל־כְּלִ֖י יִטְמָֽא׃ 35 וְ֠כֹ֠ל אֲשֶׁר־יִפֹּ֨ל מִנִּבְלָתָ֥ם ׀ עָלָיו֮ יִטְמָא֒ תַּנּ֧וּר וְכִירַ֛יִם יֻתָּ֖ץ טְמֵאִ֣ים הֵ֑ם וּטְמֵאִ֖ים יִהְי֥וּ לָכֶֽם׃ 36 אַ֣ךְ מַעְיָ֥ן וּב֛וֹר מִקְוֵה־מַ֖יִם יִהְיֶ֣ה טָה֑וֹר וְנֹגֵ֥עַ בְּנִבְלָתָ֖ם יִטְמָֽא׃ 37 וְכִ֤י יִפֹּל֙ מִנִּבְלָתָ֔ם עַל־כׇּל־זֶ֥רַע זֵר֖וּעַ אֲשֶׁ֣ר יִזָּרֵ֑עַ טָה֖וֹר הֽוּא׃ 38 וְכִ֤י יֻתַּן־מַ֙יִם֙ עַל־זֶ֔רַע וְנָפַ֥ל מִנִּבְלָתָ֖ם עָלָ֑יו טָמֵ֥א ה֖וּא לָכֶֽם׃ ס 39 וְכִ֣י יָמ֔וּת מִן־הַבְּהֵמָ֖ה אֲשֶׁר־הִ֣יא לָכֶ֣ם לְאׇכְלָ֑ה הַנֹּגֵ֥עַ בְּנִבְלָתָ֖הּ יִטְמָ֥א עַד־הָעָֽרֶב׃ 40 וְהָֽאֹכֵל֙ מִנִּבְלָתָ֔הּ יְכַבֵּ֥ס בְּגָדָ֖יו וְטָמֵ֣א עַד־הָעָ֑רֶב וְהַנֹּשֵׂא֙ אֶת־נִבְלָתָ֔הּ יְכַבֵּ֥ס בְּגָדָ֖יו וְטָמֵ֥א עַד־הָעָֽרֶב׃ 41 וְכׇל־הַשֶּׁ֖רֶץ הַשֹּׁרֵ֣ץ עַל־הָאָ֑רֶץ שֶׁ֥קֶץ ה֖וּא לֹ֥א יֵאָכֵֽל׃ 42 כֹּל֩ הוֹלֵ֨ךְ עַל־גָּח֜וֹן וְכֹ֣ל ׀ הוֹלֵ֣ךְ עַל־אַרְבַּ֗ע עַ֚ד כׇּל־מַרְבֵּ֣ה רַגְלַ֔יִם לְכׇל־הַשֶּׁ֖רֶץ הַשֹּׁרֵ֣ץ עַל־הָאָ֑רֶץ לֹ֥א תֹאכְל֖וּם כִּי־שֶׁ֥קֶץ הֵֽם׃

Even though a person is permitted to eat foods that are ritually impure and drink drinks that are ritually impure, the pious members of the early generations would eat even ordinary, non-sacrificial food in a state of purity, and they would steer clear of any sort of ritual impurity their entire lives. Thus, they were called "isolationists" (*perushim*). Such a lifestyle is one of additional holiness.

Being isolated leads a person to purify the body from bad deeds; purity of the body leads him to sanctify the soul from bad traits; and sanctity of the soul causes a person to resemble the Divine Presence, as the verse states: *"You should sanctify yourselves and be holy, because I am holy"* (below, v. 44 and 21:8; *Maimonides, 12th century*).

33. If any of these (dead creatures) falls into the interior of any (type of) earthenware object, whatever is inside it will become ritually impure. Because this type of vessel is made from the earth, its only worth is the fact that it is a receptacle; earth has no value in itself. Therefore it only becomes impure through its interior.

Human beings are also made from dust (*Genesis* 2:7), and so their true worth is also measured by their interior—their content—not by superficial characteristics (*Rabbi Menahem Mendel Morgensztern of Kotsk, 19th century*).

38. If water (or another liquid) is put upon seeds. Water has the tendency to fall from a high place to a lower place. It is also a binding agent which causes substances to adhere together. In practical terms, these two qualities represent a Judaism which is not "dry" and purely academic, but "moist" and vibrant. It will cause you to attract and "bind" with people who are not as knowledgeable as you, in an effort to bring them closer to Judaism.

leviticus 11:33–42   shemini

- [SEVENTH READING] ³³ If any of these (dead creatures) falls into the interior of any (type of) earthenware object, whatever is inside it will become ritually impure, (and the vessel) itself should be broken; (but if the creature falls on the outside of an earthenware object, it remains pure).

- ³⁴ (If what is inside the earthenware object is) any (kind of) food that is edible it will (only) become ritually impure (if) water has come upon it (first, at some time in the past). And any liquid that is (normally) drunk, which is in any (impure) vessel, will become ritually impure.

- ³⁵ Anything upon which any of the carcasses of these (animals) falls will become ritually impure. (Thus,) an (earthenware) oven or stove (cannot be purified) and should be demolished (because) they are ritually impure. (However, you may still possess these items, bearing in mind that) they are ritually impure for you.

- ³⁶ Only a gathering of water—(be it) a pit, or a spring—will remain ritually pure (even if it comes into contact with impurity, and it has the power to purify others. However, if a person) touches a carcass (while he is in one of these purifying waters) he will (still) become ritually impure.

- ³⁷ If part of a carcass falls upon any seed which is sown (and has never become wet), it remains ritually pure. ³⁸ But if water (or another liquid) is put upon seeds, and (then) part of a carcass falls on them, they will be ritually impure for you.

Laws of Ritual Impurity from Kosher Animals

- ³⁹ If an animal that you (are allowed to) eat dies, anyone who touches (the flesh of) its carcass will be ritually impure until evening.

- ⁴⁰ Anyone who eats (part) of a carcass (without touching it first is not) ritually impure until evening and (does not) have to immerse his clothes, (unless he also) carries (at least an olive's-bulk of) its carcass, (in which case) he should immerse his garments, and he will be ritually impure until evening (when the sun sets).

Laws of Forbidden Reptiles and Insects of the Ground

- ⁴¹ Any creeping creature that creeps on the ground is an abomination. It must not be eaten (or fed to others).

- ⁴² You must not eat: any (snake or worm) that goes on its belly, and any (scorpion) that walks on four (legs) or any (centipede) that has many legs, and all creeping creatures that creep on the ground (including the beetle family), for they are an abomination.

From Oral Tradition we know that a person who is ritually impure may eat from the same plate as one who is ritually pure.

שמיני — ויקרא יא:מג-מז

מג אַל־תְּשַׁקְּצוּ֙ אֶת־נַפְשֹׁ֣תֵיכֶ֔ם בְּכָל־הַשֶּׁ֖רֶץ הַשֹּׁרֵ֑ץ וְלֹ֤א תִטַּמְּאוּ֙ בָּהֶ֔ם וְנִטְמֵתֶ֖ם בָּֽם: מד כִּ֣י אֲנִ֤י יְהוָה֙ אֱלֹ֣הֵיכֶ֔ם וְהִתְקַדִּשְׁתֶּם֙ וִהְיִיתֶ֣ם קְדֹשִׁ֔ים כִּ֥י קָד֖וֹשׁ אָ֑נִי וְלֹ֤א תְטַמְּאוּ֙ אֶת־נַפְשֹׁ֣תֵיכֶ֔ם בְּכָל־הַשֶּׁ֖רֶץ הָרֹמֵ֥שׂ עַל־הָאָֽרֶץ: [MAFTIR] מה כִּ֣י | אֲנִ֣י יְהוָ֗ה הַֽמַּעֲלֶ֤ה אֶתְכֶם֙ מֵאֶ֣רֶץ מִצְרַ֔יִם לִהְיֹ֥ת לָכֶ֖ם לֵאלֹהִ֑ים וִהְיִיתֶ֣ם קְדֹשִׁ֔ים כִּ֥י קָד֖וֹשׁ אָֽנִי: מו זֹ֣את תּוֹרַ֤ת הַבְּהֵמָה֙ וְהָע֔וֹף וְכֹל֙ נֶ֣פֶשׁ הַֽחַיָּ֔ה הָרֹמֶ֖שֶׂת בַּמָּ֑יִם וּלְכָל־נֶ֖פֶשׁ הַשֹּׁרֶ֥צֶת עַל־הָאָֽרֶץ: מז לְהַבְדִּ֕יל בֵּ֥ין הַטָּמֵ֖א וּבֵ֣ין הַטָּהֹ֑ר וּבֵ֤ין הַֽחַיָּה֙ הַֽנֶּאֱכֶ֔לֶת וּבֵין֙ הַֽחַיָּ֔ה אֲשֶׁ֖ר לֹ֥א תֵאָכֵֽל: פ פ פ

צ"א פסוקים, עבדי"ה סימן

44-45. You should not defile yourselves through (eating) any creeping creature ... For I am God who is bringing you up from the land of Egypt. God says, "If I had brought up the Jewish people from Egypt only so that they would not defile themselves by eating creeping creatures like the other nations, it would have been a sufficient reason for them to be redeemed" (*Rashi, 11th century*).

Is their reward for this greater than the reward for obeying the precepts concerning interest, tzitzit and honest (weights), which the Torah also connects with the exodus from Egypt?

Though their reward is no greater, it is more loathsome to eat these insects than to engage in the other sins (*Babylonian Talmud, Bava Metzia* 61b).

leviticus 11:43–47 — shemini

- ❖ **43** You should not make your souls abominable (by eating) any creeping creature that creeps. You should not defile yourselves with them, so that you will become impure through them (in the world to come).

- ❖ **44** For I am God your (holy) God. You should sanctify yourselves and be holy, because I am holy, and you should not defile yourselves through (eating) any creeping creature that crawls on the ground. [MAFTIR] **45** For I am God who is bringing you up from the land of Egypt to be your God. Thus, you shall be holy, because I am holy.

46 (The above) is the law regarding animals, birds, and all living creatures that move in water and all creatures that creep on the ground, **47** to distinguish between the ritually impure and the pure; between the animal that may be eaten and the animal that may not be eaten.

Haftarot: Shemini—page 1349.   *Erev Rosh Ḥodesh*—page 1415.   *Parah*—page 1431.
Maftir: Parah—page 932 (19:1–22).

Ḥasidic thought explains that the forces of impurity are spiritual "parasites" that target specifically those areas which are potential places of holiness. This is the inner reason why food must first become wet in order to become susceptible to ritual impurity, for only a "moist" Judaism permeated with the "waters" of love and communication is a source of genuine holiness and spiritual vitality (*Rabbi Menahem Mendel Schneerson, 20th century*).

44. Sanctify yourselves and be holy. If you sanctify yourself by refraining from indulging in life's excesses, you first receive help from heaven to continue doing so, and then you become sanctified from above. Eventually, you will be sanctified in the world to come (*Babylonian Talmud, Yoma 39a; Rabbi Samuel Edels, 16th–17th century; Rabbi Jacob Reischer, 17th–18th century*).

> The **afflictions of life,** of which *tzaraʿat* is an example, are not meant to punish us, but to act as a **stimulus for personal healing.** That is why the laws of **childbirth** are also included here, suggesting the **purpose** of any affliction is the **rebirth** that follows.

TAZRIAʿ
תזריע

LAWS OF THE RITUAL IMPURITY OF CHILDBIRTH	12:1–8
LAWS OF *TZARAʿAT*	13:1–44
ISOLATION OF THE *TZARAʿAT* SUFFERER	13:45–46
LAWS OF *TZARAʿAT* ON GARMENTS	13:47–59

NAME
Tazriaʿ

MEANING
"Conceives"

LINES IN TORAH SCROLL
128

PARASHIYYOT
5 open; 4 closed

VERSES
67

WORDS
1010

LETTERS
3667

DATE
Nisan – Iyyar 20, 2449

LOCATION
Sinai Desert

KEY PEOPLE
Moses, Aaron

MITZVOT
5 positive; 2 prohibitions

MASORETIC FEATURES
The letter *gimmel* of the word *ve-hitggallah* (13:33) is oversized.

NOTE
Often read together with the portion of *Metzoraʿ*

CHARACTER PROFILE

NAME
Rachel

MEANING
"Ewe"

FATHER
Laban

GRANDFATHER
Bethuel

HUSBAND
Jacob (married at age 21)

CHILDREN
Joseph, Benjamin

DESCENDANTS
Mordecai, Esther

LIFE SPAN
36 years (died 11 Marḥeshvan)

BURIAL PLACE
On the road to Ephrath, just outside Bethlehem

ACHIEVEMENTS
Modest conduct, even in her tent; one of four matriarchs; one of the first prophetesses

KNOWN FOR
Long period of infertility, envying her sister; conceived on *Rosh Ha-Shanah;* stole her father's idols (*teraphim*); died during childbirth; intercession for her children from heaven; her tomb remains to this day

CIRCUMCISION

Carrying out a circumcision on an eight-day-old child, before he has a chance to perform his own worship, brings to light an *inherent* connection that the child has with God. It reveals his spiritual potential (12:3).

DIAGNOSIS

Only a priest could diagnose *tzara'at*. By nature the priests were known to be especially kind, so even their harsh proclamations of impurity were carried out with the individual's best interests in mind (13:2).

ISOLATION

Those afflicted with *tzara'at* were quarantined until their affliction had passed. This isolation was a remedy for the sin which causes *tzara'at*—gossip (13:46).

תזריע

ויקרא יב:א-ז

יב 1 וַיְדַבֵּ֥ר יְהֹוָ֖ה אֶל־מֹשֶׁ֥ה לֵּאמֹֽר: 2 דַּבֵּ֞ר אֶל־בְּנֵ֤י יִשְׂרָאֵל֙ לֵאמֹ֔ר אִשָּׁה֙ כִּ֣י תַזְרִ֔יעַ וְיָלְדָ֖ה זָכָ֑ר וְטָֽמְאָה֙ שִׁבְעַ֣ת יָמִ֔ים כִּימֵ֛י נִדַּ֥ת דְּוֺתָ֖הּ תִּטְמָֽא: 3 וּבַיּ֖וֹם הַשְּׁמִינִ֑י יִמּ֖וֹל בְּשַׂ֥ר עָרְלָתֽוֹ: 4 וּשְׁלֹשִׁ֥ים יוֹם֙ וּשְׁלֹ֣שֶׁת יָמִ֔ים תֵּשֵׁ֖ב בִּדְמֵ֣י טׇהֳרָ֑ה בְּכׇל־קֹ֣דֶשׁ לֹֽא־תִגָּ֗ע וְאֶל־הַמִּקְדָּשׁ֙ לֹ֣א תָבֹ֔א עַד־מְלֹ֖את יְמֵ֥י טׇהֳרָֽהּ: 5 וְאִם־נְקֵבָ֣ה תֵלֵ֔ד וְטָמְאָ֥ה שְׁבֻעַ֖יִם כְּנִדָּתָ֑הּ וְשִׁשִּׁ֥ים יוֹם֙ וְשֵׁ֣שֶׁת יָמִ֔ים תֵּשֵׁ֖ב עַל־דְּמֵ֥י טׇהֳרָֽה: 6 וּבִמְלֹ֣את ׀ יְמֵ֣י טׇהֳרָ֗הּ לְבֵן֘ א֣וֹ לְבַת֒ תָּבִ֞יא כֶּ֤בֶשׂ בֶּן־שְׁנָתוֹ֙ לְעֹלָ֔ה וּבֶן־יוֹנָ֥ה אוֹ־תֹ֖ר לְחַטָּ֑את אֶל־פֶּ֥תַח אֹֽהֶל־מוֹעֵ֖ד אֶל־הַכֹּהֵֽן: 7 וְהִקְרִיב֞וֹ לִפְנֵ֣י יְהֹוָ֗ה וְכִפֶּ֣ר עָלֶ֔יהָ וְטָהֲרָ֖ה מִמְּקֹ֣ר דָּמֶ֑יהָ זֹ֤את תּוֹרַת֙ הַיֹּלֶ֔דֶת לַזָּכָ֖ר א֥וֹ

What is the connection between the sequence of creation and the sequence of the laws in the Torah?

And why should these two different accounts follow the same order?

Because through observing the laws of the Torah you bring the world to the perfection for which it was created. Therefore their details are recorded in the same order (*Rabbi Judah Loew b. Bezalel of Prague, 16th century*).

Unlike animals, which do not possess free choice, man is capable of rebelling against his Creator. Before man has actually performed good deeds *he is on a lower level than the animals*, since he has the potential to sin, whereas they do not. If he sins then even a gnat is superior to him (*Rabbi Shneur Zalman of Lyady, 18th century*).

kabbalah bites

12:1 All souls in the upper world are both male *and* female.

When the souls come below they initially emerge as male and female; then each side separates and goes its own way.

If you merit, the two will join together again as one unit. Your marital partner will be your true soul mate. You will join together as one unit in everything, in spirit and in body.

5. If she gives birth to a female, she will be ritually impure for two weeks. Why, after giving birth to a female, must a woman wait a longer period of time to become ritually pure than for a male?

When a woman experiences the pain of birth, she swears that she will never have children again. When a boy is born she soon regrets her oath, after seven days. After a girl is born, the concern is deeper, knowing that *when the baby grows up she too will suffer the pain of childbirth*—so it takes longer for the mother to regret her oath (*Babylonian Talmud, Niddah 31b; Rabbi Samuel Edels, 16th–17th century*).

leviticus 12:1–7 — tazria‘

parashat tazria‘

12 Laws of the Ritual Impurity from Childbirth

¹ God spoke to Moses, saying: ² Speak to the children of Israel, saying:

- If a woman conceives and gives birth to a male (or miscarries), she will be ritually impure for seven days (even if no flow of blood accompanied the birth). She will be ritually impure just like during the days of her menstrual flow.

- ³ On the eighth day, the flesh of his foreskin should be circumcised.

- ⁴ (When she immerses in a ritual-pool [*mikveh*] after seven days), then for thirty-three additional days she will have a waiting period, (during which even if she sees) blood (she) is ritually pure (to her husband. Nevertheless), she should (still) not touch (or eat) any holy (*terumah*), nor may she enter the Sanctuary, until the(se additional thirty-three) days of her (total) purification have been completed.

- ⁵ If she gives birth to a female, she will be ritually impure for two weeks, just like during her menstruation (period. Then,) for sixty-six days, she will have a waiting period (during which even if she sees) blood (she) is ritually pure (to her husband).

- ⁶ When the days of (total) purification for a son or a daughter are complete, she should bring a male lamb in its first year as a burnt-offering, and a young dove or a turtledove as a sin-offering, to the priest at the entrance of the Tent of Meeting. ⁷ He should offer it up before God and atone for her, and she will be (totally) purified from (being called impure due to) the source of her blood.

The (above) is the law of a woman who gives birth to a male or to a female.

12:2 She will be ritually impure. Rabbi Simlai said: "Just as man was formed after all the animals, wild creatures and birds, man's laws are explained here after the laws of animals, wild creatures, and birds (written in the previous Torah portion)" (*Leviticus Rabbah*).

Why was Adam created last of all beings on the eve of the Sabbath? So that if a man becomes proud, he can be reminded that the gnats preceded him in the order of creation. Another answer: So that he could go straight "into the banquet," i.e., everything should be prepared for him (*Babylonian Talmud, Sanhedrin* 38a).

spiritual vitamin

> Through *taharat ha-mishpahah* (family purity) children are born in purity and holiness, with pure hearts and minds that will help them to resist temptation and avoid the pitfalls of the environment when they grow up.

תזריע ויקרא יב:ז - יג:ד

לִנְקֵבָֽה: ח וְאִם־לֹ֨א תִמְצָ֣א יָדָהּ֮ דֵּ֣י שֶׂה֒ וְלָקְחָ֣ה שְׁתֵּֽי־תֹרִ֗ים א֤וֹ שְׁנֵי֙ בְּנֵ֣י יוֹנָ֔ה אֶחָ֥ד לְעֹלָ֖ה וְאֶחָ֣ד לְחַטָּ֑את וְכִפֶּ֥ר עָלֶ֛יהָ הַכֹּהֵ֖ן וְטָהֵֽרָה׃ פ

יג 1 וַיְדַבֵּ֣ר יְהֹוָ֔ה אֶל־מֹשֶׁ֥ה וְאֶֽל־אַהֲרֹ֖ן לֵאמֹֽר׃ 2 אָדָ֗ם כִּֽי־יִהְיֶ֤ה בְעוֹר־בְּשָׂרוֹ֙ שְׂאֵ֤ת אֽוֹ־סַפַּ֨חַת֙ א֣וֹ בַהֶ֔רֶת וְהָיָ֥ה בְעוֹר־בְּשָׂר֖וֹ לְנֶ֣גַע צָרָ֑עַת וְהוּבָא֙ אֶל־אַהֲרֹ֣ן הַכֹּהֵ֔ן א֛וֹ אֶל־אַחַ֥ד מִבָּנָ֖יו הַכֹּהֲנִֽים׃ 3 וְרָאָ֣ה הַכֹּהֵ֣ן אֶת־הַנֶּ֣גַע בְּעֽוֹר־הַ֠בָּשָׂ֠ר וְשֵׂעָ֨ר בַּנֶּ֜גַע הָפַ֣ךְ ׀ לָבָ֗ן וּמַרְאֵ֤ה הַנֶּ֨גַע֙ עָמֹק֙ מֵע֣וֹר בְּשָׂר֔וֹ נֶ֥גַע צָרַ֖עַת ה֑וּא וְרָאָ֥הוּ הַכֹּהֵ֖ן וְטִמֵּ֥א אֹתֽוֹ׃ 4 וְאִם־בַּהֶ֩רֶת֩ לְבָנָ֨ה הִ֜וא בְּע֣וֹר בְּשָׂר֗וֹ וְעָמֹק֙

judgment be done out of love—so the Torah requires it to be done by a priest (*Rabbi Solomon ha-Kohen Rabinowich of Radomsko, 19th century*).

Tzara'at on the skin of his body. Why does *tzara'at* not occur nowadays? Because only when the Jewish people are in an otherwise advanced spiritual state do they merit to have the miraculous sign of *tzara'at*.

This is hinted to by the term that is used to describe the victim of *tzara'at* in the Torah (in v. 2). The Hebrew word *'adam* is the highest of four scriptural terms which can be used to describe man, an allusion to the fact that *tzara'at* only afflicts individuals who are otherwise perfect (*Rabbi Moses Alshekh, 16th century*).

Physically, *tzara'at* is a superficial affliction. This indicates that the victim is in a healthy spiritual state internally, and that he has merely erred in a superficial manner. Those who are not in a good spiritual state internally (as is the case nowadays) do not require a miraculous sign that something is wrong superficially, since there are more serious internal problems that need to be addressed first (*Rabbi Shneur Zalman of Lyady, 18th century*).

3. The priest should examine the lesion ... when the priest examines it, he should pronounce him ritually impure. The priest would not just look at the lesion and declare the man to be impure. He also would look into circumstantial factors, such as if the affected person was just married or if it was a festival, which would make it a great burden for the man to be declared impure (see *Rashi* to v. 14). This also is why the Torah repeats the requirement for the priest to carry

664

> **kabbalah bites**
>
> **13:2** *Tzara'at* is a disease of ego, the enemy of all spiritual seekers. The ego can manifest itself in three forms:
>
> *"A blotch"*—a swelling underneath the skin. This is the veiled ego which other people do not notice and is only known to you.
>
> *"A creamy blotch"*—This form of ego will make you feel superior to other people, but not over those who exceed you in wisdom or stature.
>
> *"A bright spot"*—The strong, bright spot signifies the truly untamed ego, which makes you feel more entitled than just about everyone, regardless of wealth, wisdom or stature.
>
> God detests all of these.

leviticus 12:8 – 13:4 — tazria‘

❖ ⁸ If she cannot afford a sheep, she should take two turtledoves or two young doves: one as a burnt-offering and one as a sin-offering. The priest should (offer them and thereby) atone for her, and she will become ritually pure.

13 Laws of *Tzara'at*

¹ God spoke to Moses and Aaron, saying:

❖ ² If a man has on the skin of his body: a (white) blotch, a creamy blotch, or a (bright) spot, and it forms (a suspected) lesion of *tzara'at* on the skin of his body, he should be brought to Aaron the priest, or to one of his sons, the priests (for examination).

❖ ³ The priest should examine the lesion on the skin of his body: If (at least two) hair(s) within the lesion have turned (from black to) white and the appearance of the lesion (is white, making it look) deeper than the (surrounding) skin of his body, then it is a (genuine) *tzara'at* lesion. When the priest examines it, he should pronounce him ritually impure.

Laws of the White Spot

❖ ⁴ If there is a white spot on the skin of his body, and its appearance is not deeper than the (surrounding) skin, and its hair has not turned white, then:

---

8. One as a burnt-offering and one as a sin-offering. The Torah mentions the burnt-offering first, followed by the sin-offering, even though the sin-offering is actually sacrificed first (as *Rashi* notes). The first message that children need to hear is that, like the burnt-offering which is totally burned before God, everything belongs to Him and everything that occurs is from Him (*Rabbi Moses Feinstein, 20th century*).

Food for thought

1. Why is giving birth associated with ritual impurity?

2. "Ritually impure" does not mean "sinful" or "dirty." So what *does* it mean?

3. What does the process of "purification" mean mentally for a woman?

13:2 He should be brought. Why does it say that the man is *"brought"* to the priest, and not that he *"goes to the priest"*?

The Sages teach that when God wants to rebuke a person for his misdeeds with lesions, He does not strike the body first. First, God strikes the person's house. If he does not repent, then God strikes his clothing. If he still does not repent, then God brings lesions on the body (*Leviticus Rabbah*).

When a man notices that his clothing or his house is struck with lesions, he tends to deal with the situation without the need for external motivation. But by the time the lesions strike the man himself, he is so immersed in his sins that he probably feels no need for change—it has become a way of life. Then, he must be *"brought to Aaron"* to receive help (*Rabbi Jacob Moses Kleinbaum, 20th century*).

To Aaron the priest. It is a supranational decree of Scripture that the ritual impurity and purity of lesions can only take effect through the pronouncement of a priest (*Rashi, 11th century*).

Kohanim (priests) are people of kindness. When it comes to declaring somebody as a *tzara'at* sufferer, it is imperative that this harsh

אֵין־מַרְאֶהָ מִן־הָעוֹר וּשְׂעָרָהּ לֹא־הָפַךְ לָבָן וְהִסְגִּירוֹ הַכֹּהֵן אֶת־הַנֶּגַע שִׁבְעַת יָמִים: 5 וְרָאָהוּ הַכֹּהֵן בַּיּוֹם הַשְּׁבִיעִי וְהִנֵּה הַנֶּגַע עָמַד בְּעֵינָיו לֹא־פָשָׂה הַנֶּגַע בָּעוֹר וְהִסְגִּירוֹ הַכֹּהֵן שִׁבְעַת יָמִים שֵׁנִית: 6 [SECOND READING] וְרָאָה הַכֹּהֵן אֹתוֹ בַּיּוֹם הַשְּׁבִיעִי שֵׁנִית וְהִנֵּה כֵּהָה הַנֶּגַע וְלֹא־פָשָׂה הַנֶּגַע בָּעוֹר וְטִהֲרוֹ הַכֹּהֵן מִסְפַּחַת הִוא וְכִבֶּס בְּגָדָיו וְטָהֵר: 7 וְאִם־פָּשֹׂה תִפְשֶׂה הַמִּסְפַּחַת בָּעוֹר אַחֲרֵי הֵרָאֹתוֹ אֶל־הַכֹּהֵן לְטָהֳרָתוֹ וְנִרְאָה שֵׁנִית אֶל־הַכֹּהֵן: 8 וְרָאָה הַכֹּהֵן וְהִנֵּה פָּשְׂתָה הַמִּסְפַּחַת בָּעוֹר וְטִמְּאוֹ הַכֹּהֵן צָרַעַת הִוא: פ 9 נֶגַע צָרַעַת כִּי תִהְיֶה בְּאָדָם וְהוּבָא אֶל־הַכֹּהֵן: 10 וְרָאָה הַכֹּהֵן וְהִנֵּה שְׂאֵת־לְבָנָה בָּעוֹר וְהִיא הָפְכָה שֵׂעָר לָבָן וּמִחְיַת בָּשָׂר חַי בַּשְׂאֵת: 11 צָרַעַת נוֹשֶׁנֶת הִוא בְּעוֹר בְּשָׂרוֹ וְטִמְּאוֹ הַכֹּהֵן לֹא יַסְגִּרֶנּוּ כִּי טָמֵא הוּא: 12 וְאִם־פָּרוֹחַ תִּפְרַח הַצָּרַעַת בָּעוֹר וְכִסְּתָה הַצָּרַעַת אֵת כָּל־עוֹר הַנֶּגַע מֵרֹאשׁוֹ וְעַד־רַגְלָיו לְכָל־מַרְאֵה עֵינֵי הַכֹּהֵן: 13 וְרָאָה הַכֹּהֵן וְהִנֵּה כִסְּתָה הַצָּרַעַת אֶת־כָּל־בְּשָׂרוֹ וְטִהַר אֶת־הַנָּגַע כֻּלּוֹ הָפַךְ לָבָן טָהוֹר הוּא:

10-11. If there is healthy (-looking), live skin within the white blotch ... (the person does indeed have) *tzara'at*. Some people perpetrate gross injustices, but also perform some good on the behalf of others. They justify their wrongs by focusing on their positive accomplishments. In this verse, the Torah warns against such behavior: True, you have some "healthy-looking" skin—you may have accomplished some good in your life—but that does not excuse any injustices that you have perpetrated; those actions remain a *"lesion"* that stands to be corrected (*Rabbi Moses Feinstein, 20th century*).

13. *Tzara'at* has covered all of his body, he should pronounce the lesion ritually pure. This case is like the law of the Red Heifer, a supranational decree of Scripture (*Rabbi Bahya b. Asher, 13th century*).

When *tzara'at* covers the person's entire body it has completely exited his system and is only on the exterior (*Rabbi Abraham ibn Ezra, 12th century*).

Thus the fact that it *covers his whole body* is a sign that he will soon be completely cured (*Rabbi Jacob b. Asher, 14th century*).

The Messiah will only come when every government becomes heretical. Rabbah said, "Where do we see an allusion to this in Scripture? From the verse, *'He has turned completely white, he is ritually pure'* (v. 13). Just as when the affliction has spread throughout the entire skin the person is ritually pure, so too, when all the governments have become heretical, the Redemption will come (*Babylonian Talmud, Sanhedrin 97a*).

- The priest should quarantine the (person who has the) lesion for seven days.

- ⁵ On the seventh day, the priest should examine him. (If the lesion has spread, then he should be pronounced ritually impure. But) if the lesion has remained the same in its appearance and the lesion has not spread on the skin, then the priest should quarantine him for a further seven days.

- [SECOND READING] ⁶ The priest should then examine him on the seventh day of the second (quarantine. If the lesion has remained the same in appearance, or it has spread, then he should be pronounced ritually impure. But) if he sees the lesion has faded, and the lesion has not spread on the skin, the priest should pronounce him ritually pure. It is (merely) a discoloration (which does not cause ritual impurity, and not *tzara'at*).

- (However, since the person was quarantined) he must cleanse his garments (in a ritual-pool) and then he will become ritually pure.

- ⁷ If the discoloration spreads on the skin after it had been shown to the priest to be pronounced ritually pure, then it should be shown to the priest a second time. ⁸ The priest should examine it, and if he sees the discoloration has spread on the skin, then the priest should pronounce him ritually impure, for this (discoloration) is (actually) *tzara'at*.

Laws of the White Blotch

- ⁹ If a man has a (suspected) *tzara'at* lesion, and he is brought to the priest, ¹⁰ and the priest examines it and he sees there is a white blotch on the skin, and it has turned the hair (within it) white (the priest should pronounce him ritually impure).

- Or, if there is healthy(-looking), live skin within the white blotch, ¹¹ then (one should not think that this is not *tzara'at*, for in fact) there is an old (wound underneath which is giving the appearance of healthy skin, and the person does indeed have) *tzara'at* on the skin of his body. The priest should pronounce him ritually impure and he need not quarantine him because he is ritually impure.

Laws of *Tzara'at* Covering the Entire Skin

- ¹² If the *tzara'at* has spread extensively over the skin, such that the *tzara'at* covers all the skin of the afflicted (person) from his head to his feet, wherever the eyes of the priest might see, ¹³ then the priest should examine it. If he sees that the *tzara'at* has covered all of his body, he should pronounce the lesion ritually pure. (For since the person) has turned completely white, he is ritually pure.

out the examination: It is with the second and final examination that the priest ensures he is being sympathetic to the individual's situation (*Rabbi Meir Simḥah of Dvinsk, 19ᵗʰ–20ᵗʰ century*).

ויקרא יג:יד-כד

14 וּבְיוֹם הֵרָאוֹת בּוֹ בָּשָׂר חַי יִטְמָא: 15 וְרָאָה הַכֹּהֵן אֶת־הַבָּשָׂר הַחַי וְטִמְּאוֹ הַבָּשָׂר הַחַי טָמֵא הוּא צָרַעַת הוּא: 16 אוֹ כִי יָשׁוּב הַבָּשָׂר הַחַי וְנֶהְפַּךְ לְלָבָן וּבָא אֶל־הַכֹּהֵן: 17 וְרָאָהוּ הַכֹּהֵן וְהִנֵּה נֶהְפַּךְ הַנֶּגַע לְלָבָן וְטִהַר הַכֹּהֵן אֶת־הַנֶּגַע טָהוֹר הוּא: פ 18 [THIRD READING] וּבָשָׂר כִּי־יִהְיֶה בוֹ־בְעֹרוֹ שְׁחִין וְנִרְפָּא: 19 וְהָיָה בִּמְקוֹם הַשְּׁחִין שְׂאֵת לְבָנָה אוֹ בַהֶרֶת לְבָנָה אֲדַמְדָּמֶת וְנִרְאָה אֶל־הַכֹּהֵן: 20 וְרָאָה הַכֹּהֵן וְהִנֵּה מַרְאֶהָ שָׁפָל מִן־הָעוֹר וּשְׂעָרָהּ הָפַךְ לָבָן וְטִמְּאוֹ הַכֹּהֵן נֶגַע־צָרַעַת הִוא בַּשְּׁחִין פָּרָחָה: 21 וְאִם | יִרְאֶנָּה הַכֹּהֵן וְהִנֵּה אֵין־בָּהּ שֵׂעָר לָבָן וּשְׁפָלָה אֵינֶנָּה מִן־הָעוֹר וְהִיא כֵהָה וְהִסְגִּירוֹ הַכֹּהֵן שִׁבְעַת יָמִים: 22 וְאִם־פָּשֹׂה תִפְשֶׂה בָּעוֹר וְטִמֵּא הַכֹּהֵן אֹתוֹ נֶגַע הִוא: 23 וְאִם־תַּחְתֶּיהָ תַעֲמֹד הַבַּהֶרֶת לֹא פָשָׂתָה צָרֶבֶת הַשְּׁחִין הִוא וְטִהֲרוֹ הַכֹּהֵן: ס 24 [FOURTH READING SECOND WHEN JOINED] אוֹ בָשָׂר כִּי־יִהְיֶה בְעֹרוֹ מִכְוַת־אֵשׁ וְהָיְתָה מִחְיַת הַמִּכְוָה בַּהֶרֶת לְבָנָה אֲדַמְדֶּמֶת אוֹ לְבָנָה:

---

of a Jewish person," we delay the inspection to help him. This indicates that even at his low spiritual state, his identity as a Jew remains strong. (b) His commandments are still of genuine worth, to the extent that we delay the inspection to allow him to observe the festival, or the obligation of the wedding feast (*Rabbi Menahem Mendel Schneerson, 20th century*).

Food for thought

1. How often do you find yourself judging people by their appearance?

2. How are physical and spiritual health connected?

3. If you were quarantined for a week would your behavior change? For how long?

18. If (a person has on) the skin of his body an inflammation (caused by an infection) which heals. Unlike earlier passages, that refer to *"a person"* (*'adam*), who has a lesion, this verse reads literally, "If flesh (*basar*) will have an inflammation on its skin." The passages are also dissimilar in their conclusion: Although this verse speaks of healing, earlier passages do not.

The lesson here: Healing comes only when you are humble and supple like flesh (*basar*). A person who is arrogant and rigid like the earth (*'adamah*) will not be healed (*Babylonian Talmud, Sotah* 5a).

20. The priest should examine it. A person can see all blemishes, except his own (*Mishnah, Nega'im* 2:5).

People do not see faults in themselves. If a person does something wrong, he will explain it away, saying that it is not a fault. Therefore it is important that you have close friends whom you can listen to when they point out your faults (*Rabbi Menahem b. Solomon Meiri, 13th–14th century*).

- ⁱ⁴ But on the day that healthy(-looking), live skin appears in (the lesion), he will become ritually impure. ¹⁵ When the priest sees the healthy(-looking), live skin, he should pronounce him ritually impure. The live skin is ritually impure, (for that skin) is *tzara'at*.

- ¹⁶ But, if the healthy, live skin once again turns white, he should come to the priest, ¹⁷ and the priest should examine it. If he sees that the lesion has turned white, the priest should pronounce the lesion ritually pure (and the person will thus become) ritually pure.

Laws of *Tzara'at* on an Infected Area which Healed

- [THIRD READING] ¹⁸ If (a person has on) the skin of his body an inflammation (caused by an infection) which heals, ¹⁹ and then on the place where the inflammation (was) there appears a white blotch, or a (streaked) red and white spot, it should be shown to the priest. ²⁰ The priest should examine it, and if its appearance (is white, making it look) deeper than the (surrounding) skin of his body, and its hair has turned white, then the priest should pronounce him ritually impure, (for) it is a lesion of *tzara'at* that has erupted on the (previously) inflamed area.

²¹ But if the priest looks at it, and he sees that it does not contain white hair, nor does it appear to be deeper than the (surrounding) skin, and it is faded, the priest should quarantine him for seven days. (Then):

- ²² If it spreads on the skin, the priest should pronounce him ritually impure, for it is a (*tzara'at* blotch) lesion.

- ²³ If the spot remains in its place, without spreading, then it is (merely) the scar tissue of the inflammation, and the priest should pronounce him ritually pure.

Laws of *Tzara'at* on a Burn

- [FOURTH READING / SECOND WHEN JOINED] ²⁴ If (a person has on) the skin of his body a burn caused by fire on his skin, and on the healed area of the burn there is a (streaked) red and white

14. On the day that healthy(-looking), live skin appears. This comes to teach us that there is a day on which a suspected lesion may be examined, and there is a day on which it may not be examined. From here the Sages derived that a bridegroom is exempt—himself, his garments, and his house—from having a lesion examined throughout the seven days of his wedding feast. Similarly, we are exempt from having a lesion examined throughout all the days of a festival (*Rashi, 11ᵗʰ century*).

We might be tempted to think that if a person has a very low spiritual standing, to the extent that he should be removed from the community—like a person with *tzara'at*—then his identity as a Jew has lost its significance, and that even the commandments he performs are of little worth, since they are likely to be done with inappropriate motives.

The Torah teaches us here that even if a person is struck with *tzara'at*, eventually requiring him to be exiled from the camp, nevertheless: (a) Since "the Torah cares about the possessions

ויקרא יג:כה-לד | תזריע

25 וְרָאָה אֹתָהּ הַכֹּהֵן וְהִנֵּה נֶהְפַּךְ שֵׂעָר לָבָן בַּבַּהֶרֶת וּמַרְאֶהָ עָמֹק מִן־הָעוֹר צָרַעַת הִוא בַּמִּכְוָה פָּרָחָה וְטִמֵּא אֹתוֹ הַכֹּהֵן נֶגַע צָרַעַת הִוא: 26 וְאִם ׀ יִרְאֶנָּה הַכֹּהֵן וְהִנֵּה אֵין־בַּבַּהֶרֶת שֵׂעָר לָבָן וּשְׁפָלָה אֵינֶנָּה מִן־הָעוֹר וְהִוא כֵהָה וְהִסְגִּירוֹ הַכֹּהֵן שִׁבְעַת יָמִים: 27 וְרָאָהוּ הַכֹּהֵן בַּיּוֹם הַשְּׁבִיעִי אִם־פָּשֹׂה תִפְשֶׂה בָּעוֹר וְטִמֵּא הַכֹּהֵן אֹתוֹ נֶגַע צָרַעַת הִוא: 28 וְאִם־תַּחְתֶּיהָ תַעֲמֹד הַבַּהֶרֶת לֹא־פָשְׂתָה בָעוֹר וְהִוא כֵהָה שְׂאֵת הַמִּכְוָה הִוא וְטִהֲרוֹ הַכֹּהֵן כִּי־צָרֶבֶת הַמִּכְוָה הִוא: פ [FIFTH READING] 29 וְאִישׁ אוֹ אִשָּׁה כִּי־יִהְיֶה בוֹ נָגַע בְּרֹאשׁ אוֹ בְזָקָן: 30 וְרָאָה הַכֹּהֵן אֶת־הַנֶּגַע וְהִנֵּה מַרְאֵהוּ עָמֹק מִן־הָעוֹר וּבוֹ שֵׂעָר צָהֹב דָּק וְטִמֵּא אֹתוֹ הַכֹּהֵן נֶתֶק הוּא צָרַעַת הָרֹאשׁ אוֹ הַזָּקָן הוּא: 31 וְכִי־יִרְאֶה הַכֹּהֵן אֶת־נֶגַע הַנֶּתֶק וְהִנֵּה אֵין־מַרְאֵהוּ עָמֹק מִן־הָעוֹר וְשֵׂעָר שָׁחֹר אֵין בּוֹ וְהִסְגִּיר הַכֹּהֵן אֶת־נֶגַע הַנֶּתֶק שִׁבְעַת יָמִים: 32 וְרָאָה הַכֹּהֵן אֶת־הַנֶּגַע בַּיּוֹם הַשְּׁבִיעִי וְהִנֵּה לֹא־פָשָׂה הַנֶּתֶק וְלֹא־הָיָה בוֹ שֵׂעָר צָהֹב וּמַרְאֵה הַנֶּתֶק אֵין עָמֹק מִן־הָעוֹר: 33 וְהִתְגַּלָּח וְאֶת־הַנֶּתֶק לֹא יְגַלֵּחַ וְהִסְגִּיר הַכֹּהֵן אֶת־הַנֶּתֶק שִׁבְעַת יָמִים שֵׁנִית: 34 וְרָאָה הַכֹּהֵן אֶת־הַנֶּתֶק בַּיּוֹם הַשְּׁבִיעִי וְהִנֵּה לֹא־פָשָׂה הַנֶּתֶק בָּעוֹר וּמַרְאֵהוּ אֵינֶנּוּ עָמֹק מִן־הָעוֹר וְטִהַר אֹתוֹ הַכֹּהֵן וְכִבֶּס בְּגָדָיו וְטָהֵר:

"torn away." In the case of a *netek* lesion, hair first falls away, and then golden hair grows in its place (Nahmanides, 13th century).

spiritual vitamin

> The healthier the spirit and the greater its power over the physical body, the greater its ability to correct or overcome physical shortcoming. In many cases even physical treatments, prescriptions and drugs are considerably more effective if they are accompanied by the patient's strong will and determination to cooperate.

(spot) or a white spot, ²⁵ the priest should examine it. If he sees that the hair in the spot has turned white, and if its (white) appearance (makes it look) deeper than the (surrounding) skin, then it is *tzara'at* which has erupted in the burn. The priest should pronounce him ritually impure, (for) it is a *tzara'at* lesion.

- ²⁶ But, if the priest examines it, and he sees that there is no white hair in the spot, nor does it appear to be deeper than the (surrounding) skin, and it is faded, the priest should quarantine him for seven days.

²⁷ The priest should examine it on the seventh day, and:

- If it has spread on the skin, the priest should pronounce him ritually impure, (for) it is a *tzara'at* lesion.

- ²⁸ But if the spot remains in its place, without spreading on the skin, and it is faded, then it is (merely) a white blotch caused by the burn, and the priest should pronounce him ritually pure, because it is the scar tissue of the burn.

Laws of *Tzara'at* on Skin Covered by Hair

- [FIFTH READING] ²⁹ If a man or a woman has a (suspected *tzara'at*) lesion on the head or beard (area), ³⁰ the priest should examine the lesion. If he sees that its (white) appearance (makes it look) deeper than the skin, and that the (black) hair in it (has turned) golden, the priest should pronounce him ritually impure. It is (called) a *netek* lesion, which is *tzara'at* of the head or beard (area).

- ³¹ If the priest looks at the (suspected) *netek* lesion, and he sees that its appearance is not deeper than the skin, and that there is no black hair in it (which would render it ritually pure), then the priest should quarantine (the person with) the *netek* lesion for seven days.

- ³² On the seventh day, the priest should examine the lesion and if he sees that the *netek* (has spread or that it has golden hair in it, then the priest should pronounce him ritually impure. But if it) has not spread, and there is no golden hair in it, and the appearance of the *netek* is not deeper than the skin, ³³ (then the afflicted person) should shave himself (around the *netek*), avoiding shaving the *netek* (itself, and leaving a two-hair border around the *netek* so it can be determined if it is spreading), and the priest should quarantine (the person with) the *netek* for a further seven days.

- ³⁴ The priest should then examine the *netek* on the seventh day, and if he sees that the *netek* did not spread on the skin, and that its appearance is not deeper than the skin, the priest should pronounce him ritually pure. (However, since the

30. It is (called) a *netek* lesion, which is *tzara'at* of the head or beard. *Netek* is the name of a lesion of *tzara'at* when it occurs on an area of skin where hair normally grows. *Netek* means

ויקרא יג:לה-מו · תזריע

35 וְאִם־פָּשֹׂה יִפְשֶׂה הַנֶּתֶק בָּעוֹר אַחֲרֵי טָהֳרָתוֹ: 36 וְרָאָהוּ הַכֹּהֵן וְהִנֵּה פָּשָׂה הַנֶּתֶק בָּעוֹר לֹא־יְבַקֵּר הַכֹּהֵן לַשֵּׂעָר הַצָּהֹב טָמֵא הוּא: 37 וְאִם־בְּעֵינָיו עָמַד הַנֶּתֶק וְשֵׂעָר שָׁחֹר צָמַח־בּוֹ נִרְפָּא הַנֶּתֶק טָהוֹר הוּא וְטִהֲרוֹ הַכֹּהֵן: ס 38 וְאִישׁ אוֹ־אִשָּׁה כִּי־יִהְיֶה בְעוֹר־בְּשָׂרָם בֶּהָרֹת בֶּהָרֹת לְבָנֹת: 39 וְרָאָה הַכֹּהֵן וְהִנֵּה בְעוֹר־בְּשָׂרָם בֶּהָרֹת כֵּהוֹת לְבָנֹת בֹּהַק הוּא פָּרַח בָּעוֹר טָהוֹר הוּא: ס [SIXTH READING / THIRD WHEN JOINED]

40 וְאִישׁ כִּי יִמָּרֵט רֹאשׁוֹ קֵרֵחַ הוּא טָהוֹר הוּא: 41 וְאִם מִפְּאַת פָּנָיו יִמָּרֵט רֹאשׁוֹ גִּבֵּחַ הוּא טָהוֹר הוּא: 42 וְכִי־יִהְיֶה בַקָּרַחַת אוֹ בַגַּבַּחַת נֶגַע לָבָן אֲדַמְדָּם צָרַעַת פֹּרַחַת הִוא בְּקָרַחְתּוֹ אוֹ בְגַבַּחְתּוֹ: 43 וְרָאָה אֹתוֹ הַכֹּהֵן וְהִנֵּה שְׂאֵת־הַנֶּגַע לְבָנָה אֲדַמְדֶּמֶת בְּקָרַחְתּוֹ אוֹ בְגַבַּחְתּוֹ כְּמַרְאֵה צָרַעַת עוֹר בָּשָׂר: 44 אִישׁ־צָרוּעַ הוּא טָמֵא הוּא טַמֵּא יְטַמְּאֶנּוּ הַכֹּהֵן בְּרֹאשׁוֹ נִגְעוֹ: 45 וְהַצָּרוּעַ אֲשֶׁר־בּוֹ הַנֶּגַע בְּגָדָיו יִהְיוּ פְרֻמִים וְרֹאשׁוֹ יִהְיֶה פָרוּעַ וְעַל־שָׂפָם יַעְטֶה וְטָמֵא | טָמֵא יִקְרָא: 46 כָּל־יְמֵי אֲשֶׁר הַנֶּגַע בּוֹ יִטְמָא טָמֵא הוּא בָּדָד יֵשֵׁב מִחוּץ לַמַּחֲנֶה מוֹשָׁבוֹ: ס

---

45. Call out, "(I'm) ritually impure! (I'm) ritually impure!" An impure person has to make the public aware of his impurity, in order for them to know that he can affect them negatively (*Maimonides, 12th century*).

By sharing your misfortunes with others you have the added benefit of other people praying for your well-being (*Babylonian Talmud, Shabbat 67a*).

46. He should remain isolated. He must be isolated so as not to contaminate the other people that are around him with ritual impurity (*Babylonian Talmud, Pesaḥim 67a*).

He will have to be isolated in public disgrace, until he stops occupying himself with nasty speech, mockery and gossip (*Maimonides, 12th century*).

kabbalah bites

Ch. 13-14 The three forms of *tzara'at* represent dysfunction at three different soul levels:

Tzara'at of the house—dysfunction at the level of *nefesh* (soul).

Tzara'at of the clothing—dysfunction at the level of *ru'aḥ* (spirit).

Tzara'at of the skin—dysfunction at the level of *neshamah* (pneuma).

To correct any of this, reincarnation may be necessary.

The quarantine of *tzara'at* for seven days hints to a single lifespan which, Biblically, is said to average seventy years. *Tzara'at* can require two or even three periods of quarantine, hinting to two or three reincarnations to fully heal a soul's dysfunction.

person was quarantined) he must (still) cleanse his garments (in a ritual-pool) and then he will become ritually pure.

³⁵ If the *netek* spreads on the skin (at the end of the first or second week's quarantine, or) after he has been declared ritually pure, ³⁶ the priest should examine it, and:

- If he sees that the *netek* has spread on the skin, the priest need not look for golden hair, (for) he is ritually impure.

- ³⁷ But if the appearance of the *netek* has remained the same, or if dark hair has grown in it, the *netek* has healed. He is (thus) ritually pure, and so the priest should pronounce him ritually pure.

Additional Laws of the White Spot

- ³⁸ If a man or a woman has spots on the skin of their flesh, white spots, ³⁹ the priest should examine them, and if he sees that there are (only) dull white spots on the skin of their flesh, it is (merely) a white patch (of normal skin, devoid of pigment) which has spread on the skin (and) he is ritually pure.

Laws of *Tzara'at* on a Bald Patch

- [SIXTH READING / THIRD WHEN JOINED] ⁴⁰ If a man loses the hair on (the back of) his head, he is bald, he is ritually pure.

- ⁴¹ (Likewise,) if he loses his hair on the front toward his face and he is bald at the front (and then contracts a *netek*), he is ritually pure.

- ⁴² If there is a (streaked) red and white lesion on the back or front bald area, and it is (suspected to be) a spreading *tzara'at* in his back or front bald area, ⁴³ the priest should examine it. If he sees there is (indeed) a (streaked) red and white blotch lesion on his back or front bald area, like the appearance of *tzara'at* on the skin of the body, ⁴⁴ then he is a man afflicted with *tzara'at* (and) he is ritually impure. The priest should pronounce him ritually impure (due to) his lesion on his head.

Isolation of the *Tzara'at* Sufferer

- ⁴⁵ (The following should be done to) a person with *tzara'at*, who has a (genuine) lesion: His garments should be torn, his hair should be grown long, he should wear his cloak down to his moustache (like a mourner) and call out, "(I'm) ritually impure! (I'm) ritually impure!"

- ⁴⁶ So long as the lesion is upon him, he will be ritually impure. He should remain isolated. His place should be outside the camp.

---

40. If a man loses the hair on (the back of) his head, he is bald, he is ritually pure. If a person goes bald, then we do not consider this to be the beginning of a development of a *netek* lesion, since the fact that he has gone bald over a large area indicates that this is not *tzara'at*, but natural balding (*Naḥmanides, 13ᵗʰ century*).

ויקרא יג:מז-נט / תזריע

47 וְהַבֶּ֕גֶד כִּֽי־יִהְיֶ֥ה ב֖וֹ נֶ֣גַע צָרָ֑עַת בְּבֶ֣גֶד צֶ֔מֶר א֖וֹ בְּבֶ֥גֶד פִּשְׁתִּֽים: 48 א֤וֹ בִֽשְׁתִי֙ א֣וֹ בְעֵ֔רֶב לַפִּשְׁתִּ֖ים וְלַצָּ֑מֶר א֣וֹ בְע֔וֹר א֖וֹ בְּכָל־מְלֶ֥אכֶת עֽוֹר: 49 וְהָיָ֨ה הַנֶּ֜גַע יְרַקְרַ֣ק ׀ א֣וֹ אֲדַמְדָּ֗ם בַּבֶּ֩גֶד֩ א֨וֹ בָע֜וֹר אֽוֹ־בַשְּׁתִ֤י אוֹ־בָעֵ֙רֶב֙ א֣וֹ בְכָל־כְּלִי־ע֔וֹר נֶ֥גַע צָרַ֖עַת ה֑וּא וְהָרְאָ֖ה אֶת־הַכֹּהֵֽן: 50 וְרָאָ֥ה הַכֹּהֵ֖ן אֶת־הַנָּ֑גַע וְהִסְגִּ֥יר אֶת־הַנֶּ֖גַע שִׁבְעַ֥ת יָמִֽים: 51 וְרָאָ֨ה אֶת־הַנֶּ֜גַע בַּיּ֣וֹם הַשְּׁבִיעִ֗י כִּֽי־פָשָׂ֤ה הַנֶּ֙גַע֙ בַּ֠בֶּגֶד אֽוֹ־בַשְּׁתִ֤י אֽוֹ־בָעֵ֙רֶב֙ א֣וֹ בָע֔וֹר לְכֹ֛ל אֲשֶׁר־יֵעָשֶׂ֥ה הָע֖וֹר לִמְלָאכָ֑ה צָרַ֧עַת מַמְאֶ֛רֶת הַנֶּ֖גַע טָמֵ֥א הֽוּא: 52 וְשָׂרַ֣ף אֶת־הַבֶּ֡גֶד א֣וֹ אֶֽת־הַשְּׁתִ֣י ׀ א֣וֹ אֶת־הָעֵ֡רֶב בַּצֶּ֜מֶר א֣וֹ בַפִּשְׁתִּ֗ים א֚וֹ אֶת־כָּל־כְּלִ֣י הָע֔וֹר אֲשֶׁר־יִהְיֶ֥ה ב֖וֹ הַנָּ֑גַע כִּֽי־צָרַ֤עַת מַמְאֶ֙רֶת֙ הִ֔וא בָּאֵ֖שׁ תִּשָּׂרֵֽף: 53 וְאִם֙ יִרְאֶ֣ה הַכֹּהֵ֔ן וְהִנֵּה֙ לֹא־פָשָׂ֣ה הַנֶּ֔גַע בַּבֶּ֕גֶד א֥וֹ בַשְּׁתִ֖י א֣וֹ בָעֵ֑רֶב א֖וֹ בְּכָל־כְּלִי־עֽוֹר: 54 וְצִוָּה֙ הַכֹּהֵ֔ן וְכִ֨בְּס֔וּ אֵ֥ת אֲשֶׁר־בּ֖וֹ הַנָּ֑גַע וְהִסְגִּיר֥וֹ שִׁבְעַת־יָמִ֖ים שֵׁנִֽית:

[SEVENTH READING / FOURTH WHEN JOINED] 55 וְרָאָ֨ה הַכֹּהֵ֜ן אַחֲרֵ֣י ׀ הֻכַּבֵּ֣ס אֶת־הַנֶּ֗גַע וְ֠הִנֵּ֠ה לֹֽא־הָפַ֨ךְ הַנֶּ֤גַע אֶת־עֵינוֹ֙ וְהַנֶּ֣גַע לֹֽא־פָשָׂ֔ה טָמֵ֣א ה֔וּא בָּאֵ֖שׁ תִּשְׂרְפֶ֑נּוּ פְּחֶ֣תֶת הִ֔וא בְּקָרַחְתּ֖וֹ א֥וֹ בְגַבַּחְתּֽוֹ: 56 וְאִם֩ רָאָ֨ה הַכֹּהֵ֜ן וְהִנֵּה֙ כֵּהָ֣ה הַנֶּ֔גַע אַחֲרֵ֖י הֻכַּבֵּ֣ס אֹת֑וֹ וְקָרַ֣ע אֹת֗וֹ מִן־הַבֶּ֙גֶד֙ א֣וֹ מִן־הָע֔וֹר א֥וֹ מִן־הַשְּׁתִ֖י א֥וֹ מִן־הָעֵֽרֶב: 57 [MAFTIR] וְאִם־תֵּרָאֶ֨ה ע֜וֹד בַּ֠בֶּ֠גֶד אֽוֹ־בַשְּׁתִ֤י אֽוֹ־בָעֵ֙רֶב֙ א֣וֹ בְכָל־כְּלִי־ע֔וֹר פֹּרַ֖חַת הִ֑וא בָּאֵ֣שׁ תִּשְׂרְפֶ֔נּוּ אֵ֥ת אֲשֶׁר־בּ֖וֹ הַנָּֽגַע: 58 וְהַבֶּ֡גֶד אֽוֹ־הַשְּׁתִ֨י אוֹ־הָעֵ֜רֶב אֽוֹ־כָל־כְּלִ֤י הָעוֹר֙ אֲשֶׁ֣ר תְּכַבֵּ֔ס וְסָ֥ר מֵהֶ֖ם הַנָּ֑גַע וְכֻבַּ֥ס שֵׁנִ֖ית וְטָהֵֽר: 59 זֹ֠את תּוֹרַ֨ת נֶֽגַע־צָרַ֜עַת בֶּ֥גֶד הַצֶּ֣מֶר ׀ א֣וֹ הַפִּשְׁתִּ֗ים א֤וֹ הַשְּׁתִי֙ א֣וֹ הָעֵ֔רֶב א֖וֹ כָּל־כְּלִי־ע֑וֹר לְטַהֲר֖וֹ א֥וֹ לְטַמְּאֽוֹ: פ פ פ

ס"ז פסוקים, בני"ה סימן.

can be made (unlike skin lesions which can be ruled upon immediately). God's real intention behind bringing the lesions is to inspire repentance. An afflicted garment must be burned, so if the priest would pronounce it impure immediately, the person would have no chance to repent. By allowing it a week of being in quarantine, it gives him time to think over his actions (*Rabbi Hayyim ibn Attar, 18th century*).

leviticus 13:47–59 — tazria‛

Laws of *Tzara'at* of Garments

⁴⁷ If a garment has a *tzara'at* lesion on it—be it a woolen garment, or a linen garment, ⁴⁸ or on (threads prepared for the) warp or woof of linen or wool, or on leather or on anything made from leather:

- ⁴⁹ If the lesion on the garment, the leather, the warp or woof (threads) or on the various types of leather articles is deep green or deep red, it is a lesion of *tzara'at*, and it should be shown to the priest. ⁵⁰ The priest should examine the lesion, and he should quarantine (the article with) the lesion for seven days.

- ⁵¹ On the seventh day, he should examine the lesion: If the lesion has spread on the garment, or on the warp or woof (threads), or on the leather—for whatever purpose the leather had been made—the lesion is a piercing *tzara'at* (and) it is ritually impure. ⁵² He must burn the garment, the warp or woof (threads) of wool or of linen, or the leather article which has the lesion upon it, for it is a piercing *tzara'at*. It should be burned in fire.

- ⁵³ But if the priest examines it, and sees that the lesion has not spread on the garment, the warp or woof (threads), or the leather article, ⁵⁴ the priest should instruct that (the part of the garment) which the lesion is upon should be cleansed (by washing it), and he should quarantine it for a further seven days.

- [SEVENTH READING / FOURTH WHEN JOINED] ⁵⁵ After the lesion has been cleansed (and quarantined) the priest should examine it. If he sees that the lesion has not faded in appearance, and that the lesion has not spread, then it is ritually impure. You should burn it in fire. It is a penetrating lesion on the used or new (article).

- ⁵⁶ But if the priest examines it after it has been cleansed (and quarantined), and he sees that the lesion has become dimmer, he should tear (the lesion) out of the garment, the leather, or the warp or woof (threads, and burn it).

- [MAFTIR] ⁵⁷ If it appears again on the garment, the warp or woof (threads) or the leather article, it is a recurrent growth (of the lesion). You should (therefore) burn (the entire garment) upon which the lesion is (found) in fire.

- ⁵⁸ But if the lesion disappeared from the garment, the warp or woof (threads) or the leather article which was cleansed, it should be cleansed a second time (through immersion in a ritual-pool), and it will be ritually pure.

⁵⁹ (The above) is the law of a *tzara'at* lesion on a woolen or linen garment, warp or woof threads, or any leather article, to render it ritually pure or ritually impure.

Haftarot: Tazria‛—page 1353.   Rosh Ḥodesh—page 1417.   Ha-Ḥodesh—page 1433.
Maftir: Rosh Ḥodesh—page 1000 (28:9–15).   Ha-Ḥodesh—page 392 (12:1–20).

---

50. The priest should examine the lesion, and he should quarantine (the article with) the lesion for seven days. A garment must be quarantined first before any ruling about its lesions

> Like the **quarantined** *metzoraʿ*, we all need to **retreat from our lives,** from time to time, away from the "camp," to do our **inner work.** By spending some focused time in **introspection,** the force of our **re-integration** is so much **stronger.**

METZORAʿ
מצורע

PURIFICATION OF THE *TZARAʿAT* SUFFERER | 14:1–32
THE *TZARAʿAT* OF HOUSES | 14:33–57
RITUAL IMPURITY OF THE BODY | 15:1–33

NAME
Metzoraʿ

MEANING
"Tzaraʿat sufferer"

LINES IN TORAH SCROLL
159

PARASHIYYOT
4 open; 3 closed

VERSES
90

WORDS
1274

LETTERS
4697

DATE
Nisan - 24 Iyyar, 2449

LOCATION
Sinai Desert

KEY PEOPLE
Moses, Aaron

MITZVOT
11 positive

NOTE
Often read together with the portion of *Tazriaʿ*

CHARACTER PROFILE

NAME
The *metzora*

MEANING
Tzara'at sufferer

REQUIREMENTS FOR PURIFICATION
Two birds, cedar wood, dyed crimson thread and hyssop branches

FAMOUS INCIDENTS OF *TZARA'AT*
Moses' hand was afflicted at the burning bush; Miriam was afflicted with *Tzara'at* when she gossiped about Moses to Aaron; Uzziah was smitten with *Tzara'at* for assuming the priestly duties, as retribution for improperly burning incense on the Temple's golden altar.

COMMUNITY

The sacrifices offered at the end of the *tzara'at* sufferer's purification can be brought on his behalf by another person. This emphasizes the idea that all of us comprise a "whole entity" in which each is intrinsically connected to the other (14:21).

HIDDEN GOOD

When those who found *tzara'at* on their walls were forced to destroy the walls, they found treasures hidden by the previous inhabitants. Can you find the "treasure" in each of life's afflictions? (14:33–57).

IMMERSION

Immersion in a *mikveh* (pool) of water changes the ritual status of a person or object, symbolic of the "living waters" of the Torah which revitalize us (ch. 15).

מצורע | ויקרא יד:א-ו

יד 1 וַיְדַבֵּר יְהֹוָה אֶל־מֹשֶׁה לֵּאמֹר: 2 זֹאת תִּהְיֶה תּוֹרַת הַמְּצֹרָע בְּיוֹם טָהֳרָתוֹ וְהוּבָא אֶל־הַכֹּהֵן: 3 וְיָצָא הַכֹּהֵן אֶל־מִחוּץ לַמַּחֲנֶה וְרָאָה הַכֹּהֵן וְהִנֵּה נִרְפָּא נֶגַע־הַצָּרַעַת מִן־הַצָּרוּעַ: 4 וְצִוָּה הַכֹּהֵן וְלָקַח לַמִּטַּהֵר שְׁתֵּי־צִפֳּרִים חַיּוֹת טְהֹרוֹת וְעֵץ אֶרֶז וּשְׁנִי תוֹלַעַת וְאֵזֹב: 5 וְצִוָּה הַכֹּהֵן וְשָׁחַט אֶת־הַצִּפּוֹר הָאֶחָת אֶל־כְּלִי־חֶרֶשׂ עַל־מַיִם חַיִּים: 6 אֶת־הַצִּפֹּר הַחַיָּה יִקַּח אֹתָהּ וְאֶת־עֵץ הָאֶרֶז וְאֶת־שְׁנִי הַתּוֹלַעַת וְאֶת־הָאֵזֹב וְטָבַל אוֹתָם וְאֵת | הַצִּפֹּר

read *together* teaches us that we should not perceive exile and redemption as two separate, sequential events. Rather, each commandment that we observe in exile should be *actively* infused with the knowledge that it is an act which is hastening the redemption.

(c) In earlier generations the current portion was referred to not as *Metzora'*, but as *Zo't Tih'yeh* ("This will be the law"), but more recently this name was rejected, by Jewish custom. The *inner* reason for this change is that the Jewish people became more aware (at least subconsciously) that the Messiah's coming is very close, and it is therefore inappropriate to refer to this Torah portion, which alludes to the Messiah's coming, in the *future* tense ("This *will* be").

(d) The ritual purification of the *tzara'at* sufferer is through the laws of the Torah ("*This will be the law* (lit. "Torah") *of the tzara'at sufferer*"). One of the most effective ways to accelerate the coming of the Messiah is to study the concept of the Messiah and Redemption as it is described in the Written and Oral Torah (*Rabbi Menahem Mendel Schneerson, 20th century*).

4. Two live, pure birds. "Live birds" means birds that are not *terefah* (they need to be without a disqualifying defect or injury). "Pure birds" excludes those of a non-kosher species.

This is because lesions of *tzara'at* come as a result of gossip, which is done by chattering. Therefore, this person is required to bring birds for his ritual purification, which twitter constantly with chirping sounds (*Rashi, 11th century*).

A stick of cedar wood, a strip of crimson wool, and hyssop. Lesions of *tzara'at* come due to haughtiness symbolized by the tall cedar.

What is the remedy to be healed of *tzara'at*? He must humble himself from his haughtiness, like the worm used to make crimson dye and the hyssop plant, which does not grow tall (*Rashi, 11th century*).

6. The (remaining) live bird. He who desires life can acquire it with his tongue by studying Torah. He who desires death can acquire it with his tongue by slandering and defaming others (*Babylonian Talmud, Arakhin* 15b). This idea is hinted to by the *tzara'at* sufferer's method of purification, where two birds are brought and one is slaughtered while the other is kept alive. The one that is slaughtered suggests that, with his speech, he was capable of bringing upon himself death. The bird that is kept alive suggests that it is with his tongue, if used properly, that he also can bring upon himself life (*Rabbi Samuel Edels, 16th–17th century*).

Food for thought

1. Why does God give us suprarational laws?

2. Do you have a "cleansing ritual" for your mind?

3. What was your most humbling experience? How did it change you?

leviticus 14:1–6　　　　　　　　　　　　　　　　　　　　　　　　　　metzora'

parashat metzora'

Ritual Purification of the *Tzara'at* Sufferer

14 ¹ God spoke to Moses, saying: ² This will be the law of the *tzara'at* sufferer, on the day of his ritual purification:

- His (case) should be brought to the (attention of the) priest.
- ³ The priest should go outside the camp (where the *tzara'at* sufferer was isolated).
- If the priest examines the *tzara'at* sufferer and sees that his *tzara'at* lesion has healed, ⁴ then, upon the priest's instructions, two live, pure birds, a stick of cedar wood, a strip of crimson wool, and hyssop should be taken for the person who is to be ritually purified.
- ⁵ Upon the priest's instructions, one bird should be slaughtered (allowing its blood to fall) into an earthenware vessel (containing) spring water.
- ⁶ The (remaining) live bird should then be taken, along with the stick of cedar wood, the strip of crimson wool, and the hyssop. (The stick and hyssop should be tied together with the crimson wool) and he should dip them, together with the live bird, into the blood of the slaughtered bird (which was mixed with) the spring water.

14:2 The law of the *tzara'at* sufferer. Our Sages understood the Hebrew word for *tzara'at* sufferer—*metzora'*—as a contraction of three Hebrew words, *motzi' shem ra'*, which mean "defamer." They were of the opinion that the *tzara'at* lesions afflicted people who defamed and slandered others (*Babylonian Talmud, Arakhin* 15b).

Speech is a function that elevates humans above the rest of the animal kingdom. *Targum Onkelos* translates the verse "He blew into his nostrils a *living soul*" (*Genesis* 2:7) as referring to a "speaking soul."

There is immense power vested in speech: It can perpetuate good, or be harmful and destroy. It is this abuse of speech that the Torah wishes to curtail, by writing, *"This will be the law of the defamer—the metzora' "* (Rabbi Isaac b. Moses Arama, 15ᵗʰ century).

The Talmud describes the Messiah—as he exists during the state of exile, waiting to redeem the Jewish people—as a *tzara'at* sufferer (*Babylonian Talmud, Sanhedrin* 98b). While the Messiah himself is a pure and holy individual, he nevertheless bears the suffering of the Jewish people in exile—*"In truth he has borne our sicknesses and endured our pains, yet we held him to be stricken, smitten by God, and afflicted"* (*Isaiah* 53:4, cited by *Talmud,* ibid.).

The *ritual purification* of the *tzara'at* sufferer that we read of here alludes to the true and final redemption, when the Messiah takes the Jewish people out of exile. From this we can learn:

(a) The Messiah is not a person who will spontaneously arrive with the redemption. Rather, he is found *in exile* with the Jewish people, and helps to bear their difficulties and sorrows.

(b) The previous Torah portion (*Tazria'*) contains the laws of the affliction of *tzara'at,* alluding to *exile*. The current portion (*Metzora'*), on the other hand, contains the laws of ritual purification of *tzara'at,* alluding to redemption. The fact that these two Torah portions are usually

ויקרא יד:ו-יד

הַחַיָּה בְּדַם הַצִּפֹּר הַשְּׁחֻטָה עַל הַמַּיִם הַחַיִּים: 7 וְהִזָּה עַל הַמִּטַּהֵר מִן־הַצָּרַעַת שֶׁבַע פְּעָמִים וְטִהֲרוֹ וְשִׁלַּח אֶת־הַצִּפֹּר הַחַיָּה עַל־פְּנֵי הַשָּׂדֶה: 8 וְכִבֶּס הַמִּטַּהֵר אֶת־בְּגָדָיו וְגִלַּח אֶת־כָּל־שְׂעָרוֹ וְרָחַץ בַּמַּיִם וְטָהֵר וְאַחַר יָבוֹא אֶל־הַמַּחֲנֶה וְיָשַׁב מִחוּץ לְאָהֳלוֹ שִׁבְעַת יָמִים: 9 וְהָיָה בַיּוֹם הַשְּׁבִיעִי יְגַלַּח אֶת־כָּל־שְׂעָרוֹ אֶת־רֹאשׁוֹ וְאֶת־זְקָנוֹ וְאֵת גַּבֹּת עֵינָיו וְאֶת־כָּל־שְׂעָרוֹ יְגַלֵּחַ וְכִבֶּס אֶת־בְּגָדָיו וְרָחַץ אֶת־בְּשָׂרוֹ בַּמַּיִם וְטָהֵר: 10 וּבַיּוֹם הַשְּׁמִינִי יִקַּח שְׁנֵי־כְבָשִׂים תְּמִימִם וְכַבְשָׂה אַחַת בַּת־שְׁנָתָהּ תְּמִימָה וּשְׁלֹשָׁה עֶשְׂרֹנִים סֹלֶת מִנְחָה בְּלוּלָה בַשֶּׁמֶן וְלֹג אֶחָד שָׁמֶן: 11 וְהֶעֱמִיד הַכֹּהֵן הַמְטַהֵר אֵת הָאִישׁ הַמִּטַּהֵר וְאֹתָם לִפְנֵי יְהֹוָה פֶּתַח אֹהֶל מוֹעֵד: 12 וְלָקַח הַכֹּהֵן אֶת־הַכֶּבֶשׂ הָאֶחָד וְהִקְרִיב אֹתוֹ לְאָשָׁם וְאֶת־לֹג הַשָּׁמֶן וְהֵנִיף אֹתָם תְּנוּפָה לִפְנֵי יְהֹוָה: [SECOND READING] 13 וְשָׁחַט אֶת־הַכֶּבֶשׂ בִּמְקוֹם אֲשֶׁר יִשְׁחַט אֶת־הַחַטָּאת וְאֶת־הָעֹלָה בִּמְקוֹם הַקֹּדֶשׁ כִּי כַּחַטָּאת הָאָשָׁם הוּא לַכֹּהֵן קֹדֶשׁ קָדָשִׁים הוּא: 14 וְלָקַח הַכֹּהֵן מִדַּם הָאָשָׁם וְנָתַן הַכֹּהֵן עַל־תְּנוּךְ אֹזֶן הַמִּטַּהֵר הַיְמָנִית וְעַל־בֹּהֶן יָדוֹ הַיְמָנִית וְעַל־בֹּהֶן רַגְלוֹ הַיְמָנִית:

---

three primary causes for the *tzara'at* affliction. Hair on the head represents *haughtiness*; the beard, which surrounds the mouth, represents *slander*; and *stinginess* (tzarut 'ayin, lit. "narrowness of the eyes") is symbolized by the eyebrows (*Rabbi Ephraim of Luntshits, 16th–17th century*).

11. The person who is to be ritually purified (ha-'ish ha-mittaher). This phrase can literally be read, *"he who purifies himself."* Although it is the priest who performs the actual purification process, the Torah refers to the *tzara'at* sufferer as "he who purifies *himself.*" Rather than passively relying on the purification ritual, he must be an active partner in his own purification. He needs to improve his conduct, thereby removing the spiritual cause of his affliction (*Rabbi Moses Alshekh, 16th century*).

14. The right ear ... thumb ... big toe. The *tzara'at* sufferer, when bringing this sacrifice, is striving for a more spiritually noble lifestyle. Therefore the priest places oil on the sufferer's ear, hand, and foot, symbolizing that he ought

kabbalah bites

14:8 Why does water possess the power to invigorate and cleanse, even spiritually?

Because when God created the negative spirits, He did not allow them to enter the water. Thus, in the New Era, we are promised that "the spirit of impurity will depart *the earth*" (Zechariah 13:2). It will not need to depart from the water because it was never found there.

leviticus 14:7–14 — metzora'

- ⁷ He should then sprinkle (some of the blood and water mixture) seven times upon the person being cleansed from *tzara'at*. (This is a crucial part of) his ritual purification (process).

- He should then send away the live bird into the open field.

- ⁸ The person undergoing ritual purification should then immerse his garments (in a ritual-pool).

- He should shave off all his hair and bathe in (the) water (of a ritual-pool). (This is a crucial part of) his ritual purification (process).

- After this, he may enter the camp, but he should remain "outside his tent" (i.e. separate from his wife) for seven days.

- ⁹ Then, on the seventh day, he should shave off all his hair—(not only the hair of) his head, his beard and his eyebrows, (but) he should shave off all his (other visible) hair (too).

- He should then immerse his garments and immerse his body in (the) water (of a ritual-pool), and then he becomes (partially) ritually pure.

¹⁰ On the eighth day, he should take:

- Two perfect (unblemished) male lambs (for a guilt-offering and a burnt-offering);

- One perfect (unblemished) female lamb in its first year (for a sin-offering);

- Three tenths (of an *'ephah*) of fine flour mixed with (olive) oil as a meal-offering;

- One *log* of (olive) oil.

- ¹¹ The priest who is performing the ritual purification should place the person who is to be ritually purified (together) with these (things) before God, at the entrance of the Tent of Meeting.

- ¹² The priest should take one (male) lamb and bring it as a guilt-offering, along with the *log* of oil, and wave them as a wave-offering before God.

- [SECOND READING] ¹³ He should slaughter the lamb in the place where the sin-offering and the burnt-offering are slaughtered, in the holy place (north of the altar), for this guilt-offering is like (any) sin-offering (in terms of the service performed) by the priest. It is a holy of holies.

- ¹⁴ The priest should take some of the blood of the guilt-offering, and the priest should place it above the cartilage of the right ear of the person being cleansed, on the thumb of his right hand, and on the big toe of his right foot.

9. His head, his beard and his eyebrows. Although all body hair needs to be shaved off, the Torah mentions specifically hair on the head, the beard, and eyebrows, because they symbolize

15 וְלָקַח הַכֹּהֵן מִלֹּג הַשָּׁמֶן וְיָצַק עַל־כַּף הַכֹּהֵן הַשְּׂמָאלִית: 16 וְטָבַל הַכֹּהֵן אֶת־אֶצְבָּעוֹ הַיְמָנִית מִן־הַשֶּׁמֶן אֲשֶׁר עַל־כַּפּוֹ הַשְּׂמָאלִית וְהִזָּה מִן־הַשֶּׁמֶן בְּאֶצְבָּעוֹ שֶׁבַע פְּעָמִים לִפְנֵי יְהֹוָה: 17 וּמִיֶּתֶר הַשֶּׁמֶן אֲשֶׁר עַל־כַּפּוֹ יִתֵּן הַכֹּהֵן עַל־תְּנוּךְ אֹזֶן הַמִּטַּהֵר הַיְמָנִית וְעַל־בֹּהֶן יָדוֹ הַיְמָנִית וְעַל־בֹּהֶן רַגְלוֹ הַיְמָנִית עַל דַּם הָאָשָׁם: 18 וְהַנּוֹתָר בַּשֶּׁמֶן אֲשֶׁר עַל־כַּף הַכֹּהֵן יִתֵּן עַל־רֹאשׁ הַמִּטַּהֵר וְכִפֶּר עָלָיו הַכֹּהֵן לִפְנֵי יְהֹוָה: 19 וְעָשָׂה הַכֹּהֵן אֶת־הַחַטָּאת וְכִפֶּר עַל־הַמִּטַּהֵר מִטֻּמְאָתוֹ וְאַחַר יִשְׁחַט אֶת־הָעֹלָה: 20 וְהֶעֱלָה הַכֹּהֵן אֶת־הָעֹלָה וְאֶת־הַמִּנְחָה הַמִּזְבֵּחָה וְכִפֶּר עָלָיו הַכֹּהֵן וְטָהֵר: ס 21 [THIRD READING / FIFTH WHEN JOINED] וְאִם־דַּל הוּא וְאֵין יָדוֹ מַשֶּׂגֶת וְלָקַח כֶּבֶשׂ אֶחָד אָשָׁם לִתְנוּפָה לְכַפֵּר עָלָיו וְעִשָּׂרוֹן סֹלֶת אֶחָד בָּלוּל בַּשֶּׁמֶן לְמִנְחָה וְלֹג שָׁמֶן: 22 וּשְׁתֵּי תֹרִים אוֹ שְׁנֵי בְּנֵי יוֹנָה אֲשֶׁר תַּשִּׂיג יָדוֹ וְהָיָה אֶחָד חַטָּאת וְהָאֶחָד עֹלָה: 23 וְהֵבִיא אֹתָם בַּיּוֹם הַשְּׁמִינִי לְטָהֳרָתוֹ אֶל־הַכֹּהֵן אֶל־פֶּתַח אֹהֶל־מוֹעֵד לִפְנֵי יְהֹוָה: 24 וְלָקַח הַכֹּהֵן אֶת־כֶּבֶשׂ הָאָשָׁם וְאֶת־לֹג הַשָּׁמֶן וְהֵנִיף אֹתָם הַכֹּהֵן תְּנוּפָה לִפְנֵי יְהֹוָה: 25 וְשָׁחַט אֶת־כֶּבֶשׂ הָאָשָׁם וְלָקַח הַכֹּהֵן מִדַּם הָאָשָׁם וְנָתַן עַל־תְּנוּךְ אֹזֶן־הַמִּטַּהֵר הַיְמָנִית וְעַל־בֹּהֶן יָדוֹ הַיְמָנִית וְעַל־

—the guilt-offering atones transgressions committed *before* he was afflicted with a lesion.

—the sin-offering atones for blasphemous utterances he might have made out of pain *during* the time he had the lesion.

—the burnt-offering and meal-offering, is a purification *for the future*, when he returns to his daily routine, worshiping God more carefully (*Nahmanides, 13th century*).

21. If he is poor. If a rich person says, "I will bring the sacrifices of this *tzara'at* sufferer on his behalf," and the *tzara'at* sufferer was poor, then he must bring a rich man's sacrifice, for it is within the means of the rich sponsor to bring the sacrifice.

If a poor person says, "I will bring the sacrifices of this *tzara'at* sufferer on his behalf," and the *tzara'at* sufferer was rich, then he must bring a rich man's sacrifice, for the person who is making the vow has obligated himself with the sacrifices of a rich man (*Maimonides, 12th century*).

It seems peculiar how one person could bring a sacrifice to achieve atonement for another person. After all, it is the *tzara'at* sufferer who is in need of atonement, so how could somebody else atone on his behalf?

leviticus 14:15-25 — metzora'

- **15** The priest should then take some of the *log* of oil, and pour it onto the priest's (own) left palm. **16** The priest should then dip his right index finger into some of the oil that is on his left palm, and sprinkle some oil with his index finger seven times (towards the Holy of Holies) before God.

- **17** The priest should then place some of the oil remaining in his palm on the cartilage of the right ear of the person being cleansed, on the thumb of his right hand and on the big toe of his right foot, on (top of) the blood of the guilt-offering.

- **18** The priest should place the leftover oil in his palm on the head of the person being rendered ritually pure, and (thus) the priest will atone for him, before God.

- **19** The priest should then perform (the service of) the sin-offering, to atone for the person being rendered ritually pure, from his ritual impurity.

- After this, he should slaughter the burnt-offering.

- **20** Then the priest should bring up the burnt-offering and the meal-offering to the altar.

The priest will thus atone for him, and he will be (completely) ritually pure.

Offerings of the Poor *Tzara'at* Sufferer

[THIRD READING / FIFTH WHEN JOINED] **21** If he is poor and cannot afford (the above offerings), he should take:

- One male lamb, as a guilt-offering, for a wave-offering to atone for him;

- One tenth (of an *'ephah*) of fine flour mixed with oil, as a meal-offering;

- A *log* of oil (to apply on the thumb and big toe);

- **22** Two turtledoves or two young doves, according to what he can afford: one for a sin-offering, and one for a burnt-offering.

- **23** He should bring them on the eighth day of his ritual purification to the priest at the entrance of the Tent of Meeting, before God.

- **24** The priest should take the guilt-offering lamb and the *log* of oil, and the priest should wave them as a wave-offering before God, **25** and He should slaughter the guilt-offering lamb.

- The priest should take some of the guilt-offering's blood and place it on the cartilage of the right ear of the person being rendered ritually pure, on the thumb of his right hand, and on the big toe of his right foot.

---

to make improvements to his mind (hearing and understanding), creative actions, and aspirations (advancing) (*Rabbi Samson Raphael Hirsch, 19th century*).

18. Atone. The word *"atone"* is mentioned three times in the verses discussing the sacrifices of the *tzara'at* sufferer (14:18-20). This points to three dimensions of atonement:

מצורע ויקרא יד:כה-לה

26 וּמִן־הַשֶּׁמֶן יִצֹק הַכֹּהֵן עַל־כַּף הַכֹּהֵן הַשְּׂמָאלִית: 27 וְהִזָּה הַכֹּהֵן בְּאֶצְבָּעוֹ הַיְמָנִית מִן־הַשֶּׁמֶן אֲשֶׁר עַל־כַּפּוֹ הַשְּׂמָאלִית שֶׁבַע פְּעָמִים לִפְנֵי יְהֹוָה: 28 וְנָתַן הַכֹּהֵן מִן־הַשֶּׁמֶן ׀ אֲשֶׁר עַל־כַּפּוֹ עַל־תְּנוּךְ אֹזֶן הַמִּטַּהֵר הַיְמָנִית וְעַל־בֹּהֶן יָדוֹ הַיְמָנִית וְעַל־בֹּהֶן רַגְלוֹ הַיְמָנִית עַל־מְקוֹם דַּם הָאָשָׁם: 29 וְהַנּוֹתָר מִן־הַשֶּׁמֶן אֲשֶׁר עַל־כַּף הַכֹּהֵן יִתֵּן עַל־רֹאשׁ הַמִּטַּהֵר לְכַפֵּר עָלָיו לִפְנֵי יְהֹוָה: 30 וְעָשָׂה אֶת־הָאֶחָד מִן־הַתֹּרִים אוֹ מִן־בְּנֵי הַיּוֹנָה מֵאֲשֶׁר תַּשִּׂיג יָדוֹ: 31 אֵת אֲשֶׁר־תַּשִּׂיג יָדוֹ אֶת־הָאֶחָד חַטָּאת וְאֶת־הָאֶחָד עֹלָה עַל־הַמִּנְחָה וְכִפֶּר הַכֹּהֵן עַל הַמִּטַּהֵר לִפְנֵי יְהֹוָה: 32 זֹאת תּוֹרַת אֲשֶׁר־בּוֹ נֶגַע צָרָעַת אֲשֶׁר לֹא־תַשִּׂיג יָדוֹ בְּטָהֳרָתוֹ: פ [FOURTH READING / SIXTH WHEN JOINED] 33 וַיְדַבֵּר יְהֹוָה אֶל־מֹשֶׁה וְאֶל־אַהֲרֹן לֵאמֹר: 34 כִּי תָבֹאוּ אֶל־אֶרֶץ כְּנַעַן אֲשֶׁר אֲנִי נֹתֵן לָכֶם לַאֲחֻזָּה וְנָתַתִּי נֶגַע צָרַעַת בְּבֵית אֶרֶץ אֲחֻזַּתְכֶם: 35 וּבָא אֲשֶׁר־לוֹ הַבַּיִת וְהִגִּיד לַכֹּהֵן לֵאמֹר כְּנֶגַע נִרְאָה לִי בַּבָּיִת:

visible indication that there is a great degree of goodness "locked up" in the affliction of *tzara'at*.

And this is the inner reason why the laws of the *tzara'at* of houses are recorded in a section unto themselves (unlike the laws of contamination and purification of *tzara'at* of skin and clothes which are mixed together). For since the *tzara'at* of houses openly reveals a deeper, inner good, it is utterly unique (*Rabbi Menahem Mendel Schneerson, 20th century*).

35. There appears to me to be something like a *tzara'at* lesion. Even a Torah scholar who is certain that it is a lesion should not render judgment with certainty, saying "there is a lesion." Rather, he should say, "There appears to me to be something like a lesion" (*Rashi, 11th century*).

This is because a person, even if he is a great scholar, should avoid speaking about unfortunate events, because words are extremely powerful and merely speaking something negative could help it come to fruition. If you have to speak about something unfortunate, try to refer to it euphemistically (*Rabbi Yom Tov Lipmann Heller, 17th century*).

kabbalah bites

14:34 The houses afflicted with *tzara'at* had been built in the worship of impure forces, and therefore had to be demolished. On the other hand, those very same houses contained treasures of gold which greatly enriched their owners (*Zohar III, 50a*).

Why should the *impure* houses, which required destruction, be the source of wealth and blessing?

Because, the Kabbalah teaches: *The higher something is the lower it will fall.*

Perhaps the treasures in your life are hidden somewhere in your weaknesses and failures? Sometimes the greatest gifts can be hidden in the most unlikely places.

- ❖ ²⁶ The priest should then pour some of the oil into the priest's (own) left palm. ²⁷ The priest should sprinkle some of the oil that is in his left palm with his right index finger, seven times (towards the Holy of Holies), before God.

- ❖ ²⁸ The priest should place some of the oil in his palm on the cartilage of the right ear of the person being rendered ritually pure, on the thumb of his right hand and on the big toe of his right foot, on top of the blood of the guilt-offering.

- ❖ ²⁹ The priest should place the leftover oil in his palm on the head of the person being rendered ritually pure, and (thus) the priest will atone for him, before God.

- ❖ ³⁰ (The priest) should then perform (the service of) one of the turtledoves or of the young doves, from whatever (the person) can afford: ³¹ From whichever (type of bird) he can afford—one (bird) as a sin-offering, and one (bird) as a burnt-offering, besides the meal-offering.

(Thus) the priest will atone for the person being rendered ritually pure, before God.

³² (All) this is the law of ritual purification of a person who has a *tzara'at* lesion, who cannot afford (animal sacrifices).

The *Tzara'at* of Houses

[FOURTH READING / SIXTH WHEN JOINED] ³³ God spoke to Moses and to Aaron, saying: ³⁴ When you come to the land of Canaan, which I am giving you as (your) possession, and I place *tzara'at* lesions on houses in the land (of the Amorites) which (the children of Reuben and Gad will choose) to possess:

- ❖ ³⁵ The owner of the house should inform the priest, saying, "There appears to me to be something like a (*tzara'at*) lesion in (my) house."

The fact that one person can achieve atonement on behalf of another teaches us that the entire community are truly one "body" who need to feel each other's pain and ease each other's suffering. You ought to feel that another person's problem is your *own* problem.

And the fact that a poor person must bring a rich man's offering (if he sponsors the offering on his behalf) teaches you that if you will pledge a large sum of money to charity, God will help you to fulfil your pledge, even if it is well beyond your means (*Rabbi Menahem Mendel Schneerson, 20th century*).

34. And I place *tzara'at* lesions. It is good news for them that *tzara'at* lesions are to come upon them! Throughout the entire forty years that the Jewish people were in the desert the Amorites had hidden away treasures of gold inside the walls of their houses and, as a result of the *tzara'at* lesion, a person would demolish his house (see verses 43-45) and find them (*Rashi, 11th century*).

On houses in the land. According to Hasidic thought, *tzara'at* has an extremely sublime spiritual source, which was "misdirected" and "fell down" to become the most severe of all types of ritual impurity. This idea is expressed most poignantly by the case of *tzara'at* of houses, for when the Jewish people destroyed their houses only to find hoards of Amorite gold, they had a clear,

ויקרא יד:לו-מט   מצורע

36 וְצִוָּה הַכֹּהֵן וּפִנּוּ אֶת־הַבַּיִת בְּטֶרֶם יָבֹא הַכֹּהֵן לִרְאוֹת אֶת־הַנֶּגַע וְלֹא יִטְמָא כָּל־אֲשֶׁר בַּבָּיִת וְאַחַר כֵּן יָבֹא הַכֹּהֵן לִרְאוֹת אֶת־הַבָּיִת: 37 וְרָאָה אֶת־הַנֶּגַע וְהִנֵּה הַנֶּגַע בְּקִירֹת הַבַּיִת שְׁקַעֲרוּרֹת יְרַקְרַקֹּת אוֹ אֲדַמְדַּמֹּת וּמַרְאֵיהֶן שָׁפָל מִן־הַקִּיר: 38 וְיָצָא הַכֹּהֵן מִן־הַבַּיִת אֶל־פֶּתַח הַבָּיִת וְהִסְגִּיר אֶת־הַבַּיִת שִׁבְעַת יָמִים: 39 וְשָׁב הַכֹּהֵן בַּיּוֹם הַשְּׁבִיעִי וְרָאָה וְהִנֵּה פָּשָׂה הַנֶּגַע בְּקִירֹת הַבָּיִת: 40 וְצִוָּה הַכֹּהֵן וְחִלְּצוּ אֶת־הָאֲבָנִים אֲשֶׁר בָּהֵן הַנָּגַע וְהִשְׁלִיכוּ אֶתְהֶן אֶל־מִחוּץ לָעִיר אֶל־מָקוֹם טָמֵא: 41 וְאֶת־הַבַּיִת יַקְצִעַ מִבַּיִת סָבִיב וְשָׁפְכוּ אֶת־הֶעָפָר אֲשֶׁר הִקְצוּ אֶל־מִחוּץ לָעִיר אֶל־מָקוֹם טָמֵא: 42 וְלָקְחוּ אֲבָנִים אֲחֵרוֹת וְהֵבִיאוּ אֶל־תַּחַת הָאֲבָנִים וְעָפָר אַחֵר יִקַּח וְטָח אֶת־הַבָּיִת: 43 וְאִם־יָשׁוּב הַנֶּגַע וּפָרַח בַּבַּיִת אַחַר חִלֵּץ אֶת־הָאֲבָנִים וְאַחֲרֵי הִקְצוֹת אֶת־הַבַּיִת וְאַחֲרֵי הִטּוֹחַ: 44 וּבָא הַכֹּהֵן וְרָאָה וְהִנֵּה פָּשָׂה הַנֶּגַע בַּבָּיִת צָרַעַת מַמְאֶרֶת הִוא בַּבַּיִת טָמֵא הוּא: 45 וְנָתַץ אֶת־הַבַּיִת אֶת־אֲבָנָיו וְאֶת־עֵצָיו וְאֵת כָּל־עֲפַר הַבָּיִת וְהוֹצִיא אֶל־מִחוּץ לָעִיר אֶל־מָקוֹם טָמֵא: 46 וְהַבָּא אֶל־הַבַּיִת כָּל־יְמֵי הִסְגִּיר אֹתוֹ יִטְמָא עַד־הָעָרֶב: 47 וְהַשֹּׁכֵב בַּבַּיִת יְכַבֵּס אֶת־בְּגָדָיו וְהָאֹכֵל בַּבַּיִת יְכַבֵּס אֶת־בְּגָדָיו: 48 וְאִם־בֹּא יָבֹא הַכֹּהֵן וְרָאָה וְהִנֵּה לֹא־פָשָׂה הַנֶּגַע בַּבַּיִת אַחֲרֵי הִטֹּחַ אֶת־הַבָּיִת וְטִהַר הַכֹּהֵן אֶת־הַבַּיִת כִּי נִרְפָּא הַנָּגַע: 49 וְלָקַח לְחַטֵּא

spiritual vitamin

> The Supreme Being is the essence of perfection and goodness. And although many things in the world seem imperfect, and require completion or perfection, there can be no doubt that there is a perfect order in the world. All this is necessary for the fulfillment of the good.

leviticus 14:36–49 — metzora'

- ³⁶ Upon the priest's instructions, they should clear out the house before the priest comes to inspect the lesion, so that every (earthenware vessel) in the house should not become (irreversibly) ritually impure (if the priest pronounces the house ritually impure).

- Afterwards, the priest should come to inspect the house. ³⁷ He should inspect the lesion, and if the lesion in the walls of the house consists of dark green or dark red sunken-looking stains, appearing as if they are deeper than the wall, ³⁸ then the priest should go outside the house to the entrance of the house, and he should quarantine the house for seven days.

- ³⁹ The priest should return on the seventh day. If he sees that the lesion has spread in the walls of the house, ⁴⁰ then the priest should instruct that they remove the stones with the lesion on them, and they should cast them away outside the city, to a ritually impure place.

- ⁴¹ He should scrape out the house from the inside, all around (the lesion), and they should pour out the (mortar) dust from what they scraped outside the city, to a ritually impure place.

- ⁴² They should take other stones and bring them instead of those stones. He should take other (mortar) dust and plaster the house.

⁴³ If the lesion returns and erupts in the house (at the end of the week), after he had removed the stones, scraped the part of the house (around the lesion) and plastered it, ⁴⁴ the priest should come and inspect it. If he sees that the lesion in the house has spread, it is piercing *tzara'at* in the house (and) it is ritually impure:

- ⁴⁵ He should demolish the house, its stones, its wood, and all the (mortar) dust of the house, and he should take (the rubble) outside the city, to a ritually impure place.

- ⁴⁶ Anyone who enters the house during all the days of its quarantine will become ritually impure until the evening.

- ⁴⁷ Whoever lies down in the house should immerse his garments (in a ritual-pool). Whoever eats in the house should immerse his garments (in a ritual-pool).

- ⁴⁸ But if the priest comes and comes again and looks (at the lesion), and sees that the lesion did not spread in the house after the house has been plastered, the priest should pronounce the house ritually pure, because the lesion has healed.

⁴⁹ To (ritually) purify the house:

Food for thought

1. Does your home have a soul?

2. How does the size/quality of your home affect your self-esteem?

3. When buying a home, would you consider the behavior of its past inhabitants?

ויקרא יד:מט - טו:ד

מצורע

אֶת־הַבַּ֖יִת שְׁתֵּ֣י צִפֳּרִ֑ים וְעֵ֥ץ אֶ֛רֶז וּשְׁנִ֥י תוֹלַ֖עַת וְאֵזֹֽב: 50 וְשָׁחַ֖ט אֶת־הַצִּפֹּ֣ר הָאֶחָ֑ת אֶל־כְּלִי־חֶ֖רֶשׂ עַל־מַ֥יִם חַיִּֽים: 51 וְלָקַ֣ח אֶת־עֵֽץ־הָ֠אֶ֠רֶז וְאֶת־הָ֨אֵזֹ֜ב וְאֵ֣ת ׀ שְׁנִ֣י הַתּוֹלַ֗עַת וְאֵת֮ הַצִּפֹּ֣ר הַֽחַיָּה֒ וְטָבַ֣ל אֹתָ֗ם בְּדַם֙ הַצִּפֹּ֣ר הַשְּׁחוּטָ֔ה וּבַמַּ֖יִם הַֽחַיִּ֑ים וְהִזָּ֥ה אֶל־הַבַּ֖יִת שֶׁ֥בַע פְּעָמִֽים: 52 וְחִטֵּ֣א אֶת־הַבַּ֔יִת בְּדַם֙ הַצִּפּ֔וֹר וּבַמַּ֖יִם הַֽחַיִּ֑ים וּבַצִּפֹּ֣ר הַֽחַיָּ֗ה וּבְעֵ֥ץ הָאֶ֛רֶז וּבָאֵזֹ֖ב וּבִשְׁנִ֥י הַתּוֹלָֽעַת: 53 וְשִׁלַּ֞ח אֶת־הַצִּפֹּ֧ר הַֽחַיָּ֛ה אֶל־מִח֥וּץ לָעִ֖יר אֶל־פְּנֵ֣י הַשָּׂדֶ֑ה וְכִפֶּ֥ר עַל־הַבַּ֖יִת וְטָהֵֽר: 54 [FIFTH READING] זֹ֖את הַתּוֹרָ֑ה לְכָל־נֶ֥גַע הַצָּרַ֖עַת וְלַנָּֽתֶק: 55 וּלְצָרַ֥עַת הַבֶּ֖גֶד וְלַבָּֽיִת: 56 וְלַשְׂאֵ֥ת וְלַסַּפַּ֖חַת וְלַבֶּהָֽרֶת: 57 לְהוֹרֹ֕ת בְּי֥וֹם הַטָּמֵ֖א וּבְי֣וֹם הַטָּהֹ֑ר זֹ֖את תּוֹרַ֥ת הַצָּרָֽעַת: פ

טו 1 וַיְדַבֵּ֣ר יְהֹוָ֔ה אֶל־מֹשֶׁ֥ה וְאֶֽל־אַהֲרֹ֖ן לֵאמֹֽר: 2 דַּבְּרוּ֙ אֶל־בְּנֵ֣י יִשְׂרָאֵ֔ל וַאֲמַרְתֶּ֖ם אֲלֵהֶ֑ם אִ֣ישׁ אִ֗ישׁ כִּ֤י יִהְיֶה֙ זָ֣ב מִבְּשָׂר֔וֹ זוֹב֖וֹ טָמֵ֥א הֽוּא: 3 וְזֹ֛את תִּהְיֶ֥ה טֻמְאָת֖וֹ בְּזוֹב֑וֹ רָ֣ר בְּשָׂר֞וֹ אֶת־זוֹב֗וֹ אֽוֹ־הֶחְתִּ֤ים בְּשָׂרוֹ֙ מִזּוֹב֔וֹ טֻמְאָת֖וֹ הִֽוא: 4 כׇּל־הַמִּשְׁכָּ֗ב אֲשֶׁ֨ר יִשְׁכַּ֥ב עָלָ֛יו הַזָּ֖ב יִטְמָ֑א וְכׇֽל־הַכְּלִ֛י אֲשֶׁר־יֵשֵׁ֥ב עָלָ֖יו יִטְמָֽא:

If the home was afflicted first, why are its laws mentioned in the Torah last?

Because when the children of Israel were given the laws for *tzara'at* sufferers, they inhabited the desert and did not own any houses. Since it was not a relevant commandment at that time, it was mentioned last.

It turns out, then, that when God said to Moses, *"When you come to the land of Canaan ... and I place tzara'at lesion on the houses,"* the message was actually a positive one: When you enter the land I will give you all homes, and then, when I want to reprimand you, I will start with your houses and not with your bodies (*Rabbi Ḥayyim ibn Attar, 18th century*).

15:2 Discharge. In addition to the natural "evil impulse" which God implanted into man (see *Genesis 8:21*), our tendency to evil is further strengthened by sin. This can occur at three different levels:

(a) *Primordial.* The sin of the Tree of Knowledge strengthened the evil impulse of Adam, Eve and all their descendants.

(b) *Acute.* In addition to the above, you can choose to "incite" your evil impulse to sin even more than its own tendency to do so.

(c) *Chronic.* After doing this for a period of time, the evil impulse will become "addicted" to its excessive sinful behavior, so that it no longer needs to be "incited."

leviticus 14:49 – 15:4 — metzora'

- ❖ He should take two birds, a stick of cedar wood, a strip of crimson wool, and hyssop.

- ❖ ⁵⁰ One bird should be slaughtered (allowing its blood to fall) into an earthenware vessel, (containing) spring water.

- ❖ ⁵¹ He should take the cedar stick, the hyssop, the strip of crimson wool, and the live bird, and he should dip them into the blood of the slaughtered bird (which was mixed with) the spring water and sprinkle (some of the mixture) towards the house seven times. ⁵² (Thus) he will ritually purify the house with the bird's blood, the spring water, the live bird, the cedar wood, the hyssop and the strip of crimson wool.

- ❖ ⁵³ He should then send away the live bird outside the city, into the open field.

He will thus atone for the house, and it will be ritually pure.

[FIFTH READING] ⁵⁴ (All) this is the law for every lesion of *tzara'at*, a *netek*, ⁵⁵ *tzara'at* of garments and houses, ⁵⁶ a (white) blotch, a creamy blotch and a white spot—⁵⁷ (in order) to render decisions as to (which is) a day of ritual impurity and (which is) a day of ritual purity. (All) this is the law of *tzara'at*.

The Ritual Impurity of a Man's Unhealthy Discharge

15 ¹ God spoke to Moses and to Aaron, saying: ² Speak to the children of Israel, and say to them:

- ❖ If any man has an (unhealthy, watery venereal) discharge from his body, his discharge is ritually impure.

³ This will be (the law of) his ritual impurity when he discharges—whether his ritual impurity is due to discharge running from his body, or due to discharge clogging up his body:

- ❖ ⁴ Any (item designated as) bedding upon which the man with the discharge will lie will become ritually impure. Any object (designated as a seat) upon which he will sit will become ritually impure.

51. Sprinkle (some of the mixture) toward the house. The blood is sprinkled toward the doorpost (*Sifra*).

Houses were afflicted with lesions when the owner would act miserly, not lending out his utensils (*Babylonian Talmud, Yoma* 11b). By sprinkling blood toward the doorpost, he was demonstrating that this doorpost, which previously guarded the owner's property, is now open for everyone in time of need (*Rabbi Meir Simḥah of Dvinsk, 19ᵗʰ–20ᵗʰ century*).

55. Garments and houses. The Sages teach that when God wants to rebuke a person for his misdeeds with *tzara'at* lesions, He does not strike the body first. First, God strikes the person's house; if he does not repent, then God strikes his clothing. If he still does not repent, then God brings lesions on the body (*Leviticus Rabbah*).

ויקרא טו:ה-יג

5 וְאִישׁ אֲשֶׁר יִגַּע בְּמִשְׁכָּבוֹ יְכַבֵּס בְּגָדָיו וְרָחַץ בַּמַּיִם וְטָמֵא עַד־הָעָרֶב: 6 וְהַיֹּשֵׁב עַל־הַכְּלִי אֲשֶׁר־יֵשֵׁב עָלָיו הַזָּב יְכַבֵּס בְּגָדָיו וְרָחַץ בַּמַּיִם וְטָמֵא עַד־הָעָרֶב: 7 וְהַנֹּגֵעַ בִּבְשַׂר הַזָּב יְכַבֵּס בְּגָדָיו וְרָחַץ בַּמַּיִם וְטָמֵא עַד־הָעָרֶב: 8 וְכִי־יָרֹק הַזָּב בַּטָּהוֹר וְכִבֶּס בְּגָדָיו וְרָחַץ בַּמַּיִם וְטָמֵא עַד־הָעָרֶב: 9 וְכָל־הַמֶּרְכָּב אֲשֶׁר יִרְכַּב עָלָיו הַזָּב יִטְמָא: 10 וְכָל־הַנֹּגֵעַ בְּכֹל אֲשֶׁר יִהְיֶה תַחְתָּיו יִטְמָא עַד־הָעָרֶב וְהַנּוֹשֵׂא אוֹתָם יְכַבֵּס בְּגָדָיו וְרָחַץ בַּמַּיִם וְטָמֵא עַד־הָעָרֶב: 11 וְכֹל אֲשֶׁר יִגַּע־בּוֹ הַזָּב וְיָדָיו לֹא־שָׁטַף בַּמָּיִם וְכִבֶּס בְּגָדָיו וְרָחַץ בַּמַּיִם וְטָמֵא עַד־הָעָרֶב: 12 וּכְלִי־חֶרֶשׂ אֲשֶׁר־יִגַּע־בּוֹ הַזָּב יִשָּׁבֵר וְכָל־כְּלִי־עֵץ יִשָּׁטֵף בַּמָּיִם: 13 וְכִי־יִטְהַר הַזָּב מִזּוֹבוֹ וְסָפַר לוֹ שִׁבְעַת יָמִים לְטָהֳרָתוֹ וְכִבֶּס בְּגָדָיו וְרָחַץ בְּשָׂרוֹ בְּמַיִם חַיִּים וְטָהֵר:

(b) The second discharge must, however, be intentional. This corresponds to the *acute* strengthening of the evil impulse, where a person actively incites himself to sin more.

(c) The third discharge of the *zav* could be accidental, so long as the previous two discharges were intentional. This corresponds to the *chronic* strengthening of the evil impulse, which begins intentionally but eventually causes the person to sin "addictively" even without choosing to do so.

Nevertheless, the Torah provides a means of removing even this form of ritual impurity (verses 14-15), teaching us that there is hope for *every* person to free himself from the confines of his evil impulse (*Rabbi Menahem Mendel Schneerson, 20th century*).

13. Immerse his flesh in living (spring) water. Why does an impure person become purified through immersion in water?

After immersing himself in the water, he feels as though he were just formed anew—like in the beginning of creation, when the world was entirely covered by water.

Also, immersion symbolizes to the impure person that he should cleanse his soul from sin, like water, which serves as an agent to cleanse everything it touches (*Rabbi Aaron ha-Levi (Ḥinnukh), 13th century*).

spiritual vitamin

> With health problems, physical, mental or spiritual, the cure lies not in treating the symptoms, but in attacking the cause (although the former may sometimes be necessary for relief in acute cases).

leviticus 15:5–13 — metzora'

- **5** If a person touches (the afflicted man's) bedding, he should immerse his garments and immerse himself in (the) water (of a ritual-pool) and then he will remain ritually impure until the evening.

- **6** Anyone who sits on an object upon which the man with the discharge will sit should immerse his garments and immerse himself in (the) water (of a ritual-pool), and he will remain ritually impure until the evening.

- **7** Anyone who touches the body of the man with a discharge should immerse his garments and immerse himself in water, and he will remain ritually impure until the evening.

- **8** If the man with the discharge spits upon a ritually pure person, (that person) should immerse his garments and immerse himself in (the) water (of a ritual-pool), and he will remain ritually impure until the evening.

- **9** Any riding gear upon which the man with the discharge will ride becomes ritually impure.

- **10** Whoever touches any (riding gear) which was under (that person) when he sat on it becomes ritually impure until the evening.

- Whoever lifts up (anything contaminated by a person with a discharge) should immerse his garments and immerse himself in (the) water (of a ritual-pool), and he will remain ritually impure until the evening.

- **11** Anyone whom the man with the discharge touches, without (the latter) having (previously) rinsed his hands (and immersed in a ritual-pool), should immerse his garments and immerse himself in (the) water (of a ritual-pool), and he will remain ritually impure until the evening.

- **12** An earthenware vessel which the man with the discharge will touch (inside, or move) should be broken. Any wooden vessel (that he touches or moves) should be immersed in (the) water (of a ritual-pool).

- **13** When the man with the discharge stops having discharges, he should count seven (consecutive) days (free of discharges) from (the day) when he stopped (seeing any discharge), and then immerse his garments and immerse his flesh in living (spring) water, and he will be ritually pure.

A *zav* is a person who is in a state of ritual impurity due to sickness. In spiritual terms, this corresponds to the "sickness" of increasing the natural strength of the evil impulse by sinful behavior.

More precisely, the three levels of strengthening the evil impulse described above correspond to the three types of *zav*.

(a) A person who has a single unhealthy discharge becomes a *zav* even if it was accidental. This corresponds to the *primordial* strengthening of the evil impulse which affects every person, through no fault of his own.

ויקרא טו:יד-כג

14 וּבַיּוֹם הַשְּׁמִינִי יִקַּח־לוֹ שְׁתֵּי תֹרִים אוֹ שְׁנֵי בְּנֵי יוֹנָה וּבָא ׀ לִפְנֵי יְהֹוָה אֶל־פֶּתַח אֹהֶל מוֹעֵד וּנְתָנָם אֶל־הַכֹּהֵן: 15 וְעָשָׂה אֹתָם הַכֹּהֵן אֶחָד חַטָּאת וְהָאֶחָד עֹלָה וְכִפֶּר עָלָיו הַכֹּהֵן לִפְנֵי יְהֹוָה מִזּוֹבוֹ: ס [SIXTH READING / SEVENTH WHEN JOINED] 16 וְאִישׁ כִּי־תֵצֵא מִמֶּנּוּ שִׁכְבַת־זָרַע וְרָחַץ בַּמַּיִם אֶת־כָּל־בְּשָׂרוֹ וְטָמֵא עַד־הָעָרֶב: 17 וְכָל־בֶּגֶד וְכָל־עוֹר אֲשֶׁר־יִהְיֶה עָלָיו שִׁכְבַת־זָרַע וְכֻבַּס בַּמַּיִם וְטָמֵא עַד־הָעָרֶב: 18 וְאִשָּׁה אֲשֶׁר יִשְׁכַּב אִישׁ אֹתָהּ שִׁכְבַת־זָרַע וְרָחֲצוּ בַמַּיִם וְטָמְאוּ עַד־הָעָרֶב: פ 19 וְאִשָּׁה כִּי־תִהְיֶה זָבָה דָּם יִהְיֶה זֹבָהּ בִּבְשָׂרָהּ שִׁבְעַת יָמִים תִּהְיֶה בְנִדָּתָהּ וְכָל־הַנֹּגֵעַ בָּהּ יִטְמָא עַד־הָעָרֶב: 20 וְכֹל אֲשֶׁר תִּשְׁכַּב עָלָיו בְּנִדָּתָהּ יִטְמָא וְכֹל אֲשֶׁר־תֵּשֵׁב עָלָיו יִטְמָא: 21 וְכָל־הַנֹּגֵעַ בְּמִשְׁכָּבָהּ יְכַבֵּס בְּגָדָיו וְרָחַץ בַּמַּיִם וְטָמֵא עַד־הָעָרֶב: 22 וְכָל־הַנֹּגֵעַ בְּכָל־כְּלִי אֲשֶׁר־תֵּשֵׁב עָלָיו יְכַבֵּס בְּגָדָיו וְרָחַץ בַּמַּיִם וְטָמֵא עַד־הָעָרֶב: 23 וְאִם עַל־הַמִּשְׁכָּב הוּא אוֹ עַל־הַכְּלִי אֲשֶׁר־הִוא יֹשֶׁבֶת־עָלָיו בְּנָגְעוֹ־בוֹ יִטְמָא עַד־

19. If a woman has a menstrual discharge ... she will remain in a state of *niddah* (physical separation) for seven days. Why does the Torah say that a menstruating woman is forbidden to her husband for seven days?

In order to strengthen their marriage. If he were to be allowed to be with his wife whenever he desired, he would become disenchanted with her. Therefore the Torah says, let her become forbidden to him for seven days, and that will renew and invigorate his love for her as strong as it was when they first were married (*Babylonian Talmud, Niddah* 15b).

23. The object which she is sitting on. From this verse you learn always to use dignified expressions when speaking. Earlier, in verse 9, the Torah says, *"Any riding gear upon which the man with the discharge will ride,"* but here we read, *"the object which she is sitting on."* Why does Scripture switch from "riding" to "sitting"? Because this verse is referring to a female and it is undignified to speak of a woman who *"rides,"* because it implies that her legs are apart as she sits (*Babylonian Talmud, Pesachim* 3a).

kabbalah bites

15:19 The 13th century Italian Kabbalist, Rabbi Menahem Recanati wrote:

"I am not permitted to fully disclose the reason why a mikveh must contain forty se'ah of water. The wise person will understand it from the verse, 'He was there with God for forty days and forty nights' (Exodus 34:28). Every day Moses was taught one se'ah of the flow emanating from the supernal covenant, which totals forty se'ah."

leviticus 15:14–23 metzora‛

❖ ¹⁴ On the eighth day, he should take for himself two turtledoves or two young doves, and come before God, to the entrance of the Tent of Meeting, and give them to the priest. ¹⁵ The priest should carry out (their service): one as a sin-offering and one as a burnt-offering, and thus the priest will atone for him from his discharge, before God.

The Ritual Impurity of Seminal Emission

❖ [SIXTH READING / SEVENTH WHEN JOINED] ¹⁶ If a man has an emission of semen, he should immerse all his body in (the) water (of a ritual-pool), and he will remain ritually impure until the evening.

❖ ¹⁷ Any garment or any leather (object) which has semen on it should be immersed in (the) water (of a ritual-pool), and will remain ritually impure until the evening.

❖ ¹⁸ If a woman will lie with a man and he will have a seminal emission, they should immerse themselves in (the) water (of a ritual-pool), and they will remain ritually impure until the evening.

The Ritual Impurity of Menstruation

❖ ¹⁹ If a woman has a (menstrual) discharge and her (uterus) discharges blood, she will remain in a state of *niddah* (physical separation) for seven days.

❖ Whoever touches her will become ritually impure until the evening.

❖ ²⁰ Whatever she lies upon while in the state of *niddah* will become ritually impure, and whatever she sits upon will become ritually impure.

❖ ²¹ Anyone who touches her bedding should immerse his garments and immerse (himself) in (the) water (of a ritual-pool), and he will remain ritually impure until the evening.

❖ ²² Anyone who touches any object on which she will sit should immerse his garments and immerse himself in (the) water (of a ritual-pool), and he will remain ritually impure until the evening.

❖ ²³ (This is also the case) if someone (sits or lies indirectly) on the bedding or on the object which she is sitting on (without making direct contact with it).

❖ If someone touches (riding gear which she has used) he will become ritually impure until the evening (but he does not have to immerse his garments in the ritual-pool).

Food for thought

1. Why does the Torah give us laws about marital intimacy?

2. Do you welcome religious values into your most intimate relationship?

3. Why do you think the Torah entrusted women with the laws of intimacy?

ויקרא טו:כג-לג — מצורע

24 וְאִם שָׁכֹב יִשְׁכַּב אִישׁ אֹתָהּ וּתְהִי נִדָּתָהּ עָלָיו וְטָמֵא שִׁבְעַת יָמִים וְכָל־הַמִּשְׁכָּב אֲשֶׁר־יִשְׁכַּב עָלָיו יִטְמָא: ס 25 וְאִשָּׁה כִּי־יָזוּב זוֹב דָּמָהּ יָמִים רַבִּים בְּלֹא עֶת־נִדָּתָהּ אוֹ כִי־תָזוּב עַל־נִדָּתָהּ כָּל־יְמֵי זוֹב טֻמְאָתָהּ כִּימֵי נִדָּתָהּ תִּהְיֶה טְמֵאָה הִוא: 26 כָּל־הַמִּשְׁכָּב אֲשֶׁר־תִּשְׁכַּב עָלָיו כָּל־יְמֵי זוֹבָהּ כְּמִשְׁכַּב נִדָּתָהּ יִהְיֶה־לָּהּ וְכָל־הַכְּלִי אֲשֶׁר תֵּשֵׁב עָלָיו טָמֵא יִהְיֶה כְּטֻמְאַת נִדָּתָהּ: 27 וְכָל־הַנּוֹגֵעַ בָּם יִטְמָא וְכִבֶּס בְּגָדָיו וְרָחַץ בַּמַּיִם וְטָמֵא עַד־הָעָרֶב: 28 וְאִם־טָהֲרָה מִזּוֹבָהּ וְסָפְרָה לָּהּ שִׁבְעַת יָמִים וְאַחַר תִּטְהָר: [SEVENTH READING] 29 וּבַיּוֹם הַשְּׁמִינִי תִּקַּח־לָהּ שְׁתֵּי תֹרִים אוֹ שְׁנֵי בְּנֵי יוֹנָה וְהֵבִיאָה אוֹתָם אֶל־הַכֹּהֵן אֶל־פֶּתַח אֹהֶל מוֹעֵד: 30 וְעָשָׂה הַכֹּהֵן אֶת־הָאֶחָד חַטָּאת וְאֶת־הָאֶחָד עֹלָה וְכִפֶּר עָלֶיהָ הַכֹּהֵן לִפְנֵי יְהֹוָה מִזּוֹב טֻמְאָתָהּ: 31 [MAFTIR] וְהִזַּרְתֶּם אֶת־בְּנֵי־יִשְׂרָאֵל מִטֻּמְאָתָם וְלֹא יָמֻתוּ בְּטֻמְאָתָם בְּטַמְּאָם אֶת־מִשְׁכָּנִי אֲשֶׁר בְּתוֹכָם: 32 זֹאת תּוֹרַת הַזָּב וַאֲשֶׁר תֵּצֵא מִמֶּנּוּ שִׁכְבַת־זֶרַע לְטָמְאָה־בָהּ: 33 וְהַדָּוָה בְּנִדָּתָהּ וְהַזָּב אֶת־זוֹבוֹ לַזָּכָר וְלַנְּקֵבָה וּלְאִישׁ אֲשֶׁר יִשְׁכַּב עִם־טְמֵאָה: פ פ פ

צ׳ פסוקים, עיד״ו סימן.

---

31. Ensure that the children of Israel are dissociated (*ve-hizzartem*) from their ritual impurity. *Hizzartem* ("*dissociated*") is related to the word *zar*, which means "foreign." The verse implies that "impurity should be foreign to you." Moses and Aaron are told not only to ensure that the children of Israel do not become impure, but that the very notion of impurity should become alien and foreign to them (*Zohar*).

- [24] If a man lies with her (the ritual impurity of) her menstruation will be upon him, and he will be ritually impure for seven days. Any bedding he lies upon will become ritually impure.

The Ritual Impurity of Abnormal Menstruation

- [25] If a woman has blood flowing (from her uterus) for (as) many (as three) days when it is not the time of her menstrual separation (after counting seven days from her normal period), or she has a discharge (of uterine blood for three days that occurs a day or more) after her (counting seven days from her normal) menstrual period, then (she has a more severe ritual impurity than that of normal menstruation):

- All the days she has her ritually impure discharge (of blood) she will be ritually impure just like the days of her menstrual period.

- [26] Any bedding upon which she lies during all the time of her discharge will have the same (ritual impurity) for her as the bedding of her menstruation.

- Any object upon which she will sit will become ritually impure, like her menstrual ritual impurity.

- [27] Anyone who touches them will become ritually impure. He should immerse his garments and immerse (himself) in (the) water (of a ritual-pool), and he will remain ritually impure until the evening.

- [28] When her discharge stops, she should count for herself seven (clean) days (devoid of any discharge) and after this she can become ritually pure (by immersing in a ritual-pool).

- [SEVENTH READING] [29] On the eighth day, she should take for herself two turtledoves or two young doves, and bring them to the priest, to the entrance of the Tent of Meeting. [30] The priest should carry out (their service): one as a sin-offering and one as a burnt-offering, and the priest will atone for her from her discharge, before God.

[MAFTIR] [31] You (Moses and Aaron) should ensure that the children of Israel are dissociated from their ritual impurity, so that their ritual impurity does not cause them to die if they defile My Tabernacle (that I have placed) among them.

[32] (All) this is the law for the man who has an (unhealthy, watery venereal) discharge, a man who has a seminal emission (or an apparent emission) through which he becomes ritually impure, [33] a woman who has her menstrual flow, a man or woman who has (multiple) discharge(s), and a man who lies with a ritually impure woman.

Haftarot: Metzoraʿ (and Tazriaʿ–Metzoraʿ)—page 1356. Rosh Ḥodesh—page 1417.

Maftir: Rosh Ḥodesh—page 1000 (28:9–15).

> Every day should resemble **Yom Kippur** in that you are continually **purifying** your body as a **temple to the Divine.** When you make the **right choices** with your body, what to feed it and with whom it may be intimate, **your spirit,** too, will be **enlivened.**

'AHAREI MOT
אחרי מות

PROHIBITION OF ENTERING THE HOLY OF HOLIES	16:1–2
THE SERVICE OF *YOM KIPPUR*	16:3–34
PROHIBITION OF OFFERINGS OUTSIDE TEMPLE	17:1–9
LAWS PERTAINING TO BLOOD	17:10–14
RITUAL IMPURITY OF AN UNSLAUGHTERED BIRD	17:15–16
LAWS OF FORBIDDEN RELATIONS	18:1–30

NAME
Aharei Mot

MEANING
"After the death"

LINES IN TORAH SCROLL
154

PARASHIYYOT
3 open; 12 closed

VERSES
80

WORDS
1170

LETTERS
4294

DATE
Nisan – 20 *Iyyar*, 2449

LOCATION
Sinai Desert

KEY PEOPLE
Moses, Aaron, Nadab, Abihu, Eleazar, Ithamar

MITZVOT
2 positive; 26 prohibitions

NOTE
Often read together with portion of *Kedoshim*

CHARACTER PROFILE

NAME
Uzza and Aza'el (fallen angels)

CHILDREN
The 'Anakim (giants)

MEANING
"Strength" and "God strengthens"

LOCATION
Mountains of *Kedem*

KNOWN FOR
Opposed the creation of Adam and Eve; were challenged by God to be human and not to sin, and they "fell" to earth; they are the *nephilim* mentioned in *Genesis* 6:4; sinned with many women, including Naamah, producing demons and evil spirits; taught magic, witchcraft, sorcery and celestial matters to humans, including Laban and Balaam; introduced cosmetics; were punished by being bound in iron chains by God; they produced the souls of the "mixed multitude" (*erev rav*); were consulted by King Solomon; the scapegoat of Azazel atones for their misdeeds

YOM KIPPUR

Teshuvah, usually translated as "repentance," is more accurately rendered as "return." In essence we are all good, but it is not always apparent. The purpose of *Yom Kippur* is to "return" to our innermost essence, that is, pure goodness (16:29).

DETOX

The scapegoat "for Azazel" was removed and discarded, representing a "spiritual detox" from the harmful influences we have absorbed (16:21).

SANCTITY OF MARRIAGE

By forbidding intimate relations outside marriage, the Torah hallows the crucial importance of the family in rearing the next generation of citizens (18:6-23).

ויקרא טז:א-ד | אחרי מות

טז 1 וַיְדַבֵּ֤ר יְהֹוָה֙ אֶל־מֹשֶׁ֔ה אַחֲרֵ֣י מ֔וֹת שְׁנֵ֖י בְּנֵ֣י אַהֲרֹ֑ן בְּקׇרְבָתָ֥ם לִפְנֵֽי־יְהֹוָ֖ה וַיָּמֻֽתוּ: 2 וַיֹּ֨אמֶר יְהֹוָ֜ה אֶל־מֹשֶׁ֗ה דַּבֵּר֮ אֶל־אַהֲרֹ֣ן אָחִ֒יךָ֒ וְאַל־יָבֹ֤א בְכׇל־עֵת֙ אֶל־הַקֹּ֔דֶשׁ מִבֵּ֖ית לַפָּרֹ֑כֶת אֶל־פְּנֵ֨י הַכַּפֹּ֜רֶת אֲשֶׁ֤ר עַל־הָֽאָרֹן֙ וְלֹ֣א יָמ֔וּת כִּ֚י בֶּֽעָנָ֔ן אֵרָאֶ֖ה עַל־הַכַּפֹּֽרֶת: 3 בְּזֹ֛את יָבֹ֥א אַהֲרֹ֖ן אֶל־הַקֹּ֑דֶשׁ בְּפַ֧ר בֶּן־בָּקָ֛ר לְחַטָּ֖את וְאַ֥יִל לְעֹלָֽה: 4 כְּתֹֽנֶת־בַּ֨ד קֹ֜דֶשׁ יִלְבָּ֗שׁ וּמִֽכְנְסֵי־בַד֙ יִהְי֣וּ עַל־בְּשָׂר֔וֹ

turn back from your spiritual bliss to attend to the needs of the physical world. But if your initial intention is *to follow God's will*, then even at a point of heightened spiritual arousal, you will still be willing to "return" back to the world, and carry out the mission for which you were created—*"He created (the world) not to be empty; He formed it to be inhabited"* (Isaiah 45:18; *Rabbi Shalom Dov Baer Schneersohn of Lubavitch, 19th–20th century*).

On a smaller scale, we all sometimes have a spiritual awakening—perhaps on the Sabbath or the Festivals, or especially during the Ten Days of Repentance and the Day of Atonement. At such a time, remember that whatever you experience during this special, holy moment needs to be *taken back with you* when you return to normal, everyday life. This spiritual awakening cannot be allowed to "evaporate" without having a tangible effect. It must be "harnessed" as a moment of true, lasting inspiration (*Rabbi Menahem Mendel Schneerson, 20th century*).

1-2. After the death ... he should not come at all times into the Holy (of Holies). Rabbi Eleazar son of Azariah illustrated this with a parable of a patient who was visited by a doctor. The doctor said to him, "Do not eat chilled foods, and do not lie down in a cold, damp place."

Another doctor visited him and said, "Do not eat cold foods or lie down in a cold, damp place, *so that you will not die like so-and-so died."* Clearly, this second doctor motivated the patient more effectively to follow his instructions than the first doctor.

That is why the verse states that Aaron should be warned not to enter the Holy of Holies, *"after the death of Aaron's two sons"* (*Rashi, 11th century*).

4. Linen tunic ... pants ... sash ... turban. Why does the Torah specify only four garments, when the High Priest usually wore eight garments?

kabbalah bites

16:2 *"He should not come at all times into the Holy."* Some times are favorable to come before God, to draw down blessings and to make requests. Other times are not favorable, because *din* (judgment) is in the world.

The lunar months of *Adar*, *Nisan*, *Iyyar* and *Sivan* are times of mercy. The months of *Tammuz*, *Av*, *Tevet* and *Shevat* are times of *din*. During the months of *Elul*, *Tishri*, *Marḥeshvan* and *Kislev* judgment is pending.

Also, during the first half of each lunar month, when the moon is increasing its illumination each day, it is a favorable time. During the latter half of the lunar month, when the moon is waning, it is a time of judgment.

And there are days in the week which are favorable: Sunday, Tuesday, Wednesday and Friday; whereas Monday and Thursday are days of *din*.

leviticus 16:1–4 — 'aḥarei mot

parashat 'aḥarei mot

Prohibition of Entering the Holy of Holies

16 ¹ God said to Moses, "(When you relate the following command, stress that it is) after the death of Aaron's two sons—when they came near, before God, and they died."

² God said to Moses:

- Speak to your brother Aaron, that he should not come at all times into the Holy (of Holies) inside the partition, in front of the lid which is on the ark, so that he should not die. For My (Presence always) appears (there) with a (pillar of) cloud, (so one should not go there regularly).

The Service of the Day of Atonement

- ³ Aaron should enter the Holy (of Holies only on the Day of Atonement, when he should bring) these (offerings): a young bull for a sin-offering and a ram for a burnt-offering.

⁴ He should wear:

- A linen tunic (that belongs to the) holy (Sanctuary);

- Linen pants should be on his body;

16:1 They came near, before God, and they died. God told Moses that they had died through "coming near" to God—that they came close to the supernal Godly light through their desire for holiness, and this caused their death. This is the mystical phenomenon known as "death by Divine kiss," through which the righteous pass away.

Normally, the righteous are "kissed" *by* God, causing their passing, whereas in this case, Nadab and Abihu *themselves* "kissed" God. Their love of holiness was so strong that even when they felt that they were about to die out of their closeness to God, they did not hold themselves back from attaching themselves more strongly to God in a bond of sweetness and love—to the point that their souls expired (*Rabbi Ḥayyim ibn Attar, 18th century*).

How can you expect a person at the climax of his spiritual bliss, to want to return back "down to earth," to his mundane life? If his love of God is genuine, how can he hold himself back at the height of his arousal, and reimmerse himself into the constraints of corporeal existence? From where can you acquire the vigilance not to go too far?

It depends on how you *start* your spiritual "voyage." If you start with the goal of self-satisfaction, you will not want to

---

kabbalah bites

16:1 *"After the death of Aaron's two sons."* Don't we already know that *two* sons of Aaron had died? Why does the Torah repeat their number?

Because now the souls of Nadab and Abihu ceased to be two separate entities and became one soul, which was transmigrated into Phinehas. Their duality had "died" and they had now become one.

ויקרא טז:ד-יג אחרי מות

וּבְאַבְנֵט בַּד יַחְגֹּר וּבְמִצְנֶפֶת בַּד יִצְנֹף בִּגְדֵי־קֹדֶשׁ הֵם וְרָחַץ בַּמַּיִם אֶת־בְּשָׂרוֹ
וּלְבֵשָׁם: 5 וּמֵאֵת עֲדַת בְּנֵי יִשְׂרָאֵל יִקַּח שְׁנֵי־שְׂעִירֵי עִזִּים לְחַטָּאת וְאַיִל
אֶחָד לְעֹלָה: 6 וְהִקְרִיב אַהֲרֹן אֶת־פַּר הַחַטָּאת אֲשֶׁר־לוֹ וְכִפֶּר בַּעֲדוֹ וּבְעַד
בֵּיתוֹ: 7 וְלָקַח אֶת־שְׁנֵי הַשְּׂעִירִם וְהֶעֱמִיד אֹתָם לִפְנֵי יְהֹוָה פֶּתַח אֹהֶל מוֹעֵד:
8 וְנָתַן אַהֲרֹן עַל־שְׁנֵי הַשְּׂעִירִם גֹּרָלוֹת גּוֹרָל אֶחָד לַיהֹוָה וְגוֹרָל אֶחָד לַעֲזָאזֵל:
9 וְהִקְרִיב אַהֲרֹן אֶת־הַשָּׂעִיר אֲשֶׁר עָלָה עָלָיו הַגּוֹרָל לַיהֹוָה וְעָשָׂהוּ חַטָּאת:
10 וְהַשָּׂעִיר אֲשֶׁר עָלָה עָלָיו הַגּוֹרָל לַעֲזָאזֵל יָעֳמַד־חַי לִפְנֵי יְהֹוָה לְכַפֵּר עָלָיו
לְשַׁלַּח אֹתוֹ לַעֲזָאזֵל הַמִּדְבָּרָה: 11 וְהִקְרִיב אַהֲרֹן אֶת־פַּר הַחַטָּאת אֲשֶׁר־לוֹ
וְכִפֶּר בַּעֲדוֹ וּבְעַד בֵּיתוֹ וְשָׁחַט אֶת־פַּר הַחַטָּאת אֲשֶׁר־לוֹ: 12 וְלָקַח מְלֹא־
הַמַּחְתָּה גַּחֲלֵי־אֵשׁ מֵעַל הַמִּזְבֵּחַ מִלִּפְנֵי יְהֹוָה וּמְלֹא חָפְנָיו קְטֹרֶת סַמִּים דַּקָּה
וְהֵבִיא מִבֵּית לַפָּרֹכֶת: 13 וְנָתַן אֶת־הַקְּטֹרֶת עַל־הָאֵשׁ לִפְנֵי יְהֹוָה וְכִסָּה | עֲנַן

These two types of evil impulse are symbolized by the two goats that are used for Temple service on the Day of Atonement. One goat was sacrificed to God, representing the impulse that can be channeled properly to serve God. The second one, was *sent away* into the wilderness (*Rabbi Israel b. Tzevi ha-Kohen, 19th century*).

12. A pan full of burning coals. After the High Priest finished bringing his sin-offerings and completed his confession, he prepared himself to be illuminated with the light of God's countenance. It was then that he brought the incense to enter the Holy of Holies.

In fact, anyone who makes the right preparations will merit the light of God's holy countenance to shine upon him (*Rabbi Obadiah Sforno, 16th century*).

13. Place the incense on the fire. Through offering incense in *the Holy Temple* the potency of man's "impulse to evil" was subdued (*Zohar*).

From the fact that the incense contained galbanum amongst its spices, which had a foul odor, you learn that the wicked are part of the congregation (*Babylonian Talmud, Megillah 25a*).

The incense of the rest of the year was comparable to repenting out of fear, which has the power to *wipe*

kabbalah bites

16:12-13 'ASHaN, the "smoke" of the incense offering, is an acronym for 'Olam, SHanah, Nefesh: space, time, and spirit.

When the High Priest, the holiest man in Israel, entered the Holy of Holies, the most sanctified place in the world, on the Day of Atonement, the holiest day of the year, to offer the incense—we witnessed time, space, and spirit unite at the highest possible level.

Time, space, and spirit are the barriers separating our finite existence from the spiritual absolute. But on the Day of Atonement, these boundaries dissolve, allowing us a direct intuitive link to the transcendent.

leviticus 16:4–13 — 'aḥarei mot

- He should gird himself with a linen sash;
- He should place a linen turban (on his head);
- (Since) these are holy garments, he should immerse in (the) water (of a ritual-pool before) he puts them on.
- ⁵ He should take from the community of the children of Israel: two male goats as a sin-offering, and one ram as a burnt-offering.
- ⁶ Aaron should (first) bring his own sin-offering bull, and (confess over it) atoning for himself and for his household.
- ⁷ He should take the two male (communal) goats, and place them before God at the entrance to the Tent of Meeting. ⁸ Aaron should place lots upon the two male goats: one lot "For God," and the other lot "For (casting off) a high cliff."
- ⁹ Aaron should bring the male goat upon which the lot "For God" came up, and designate it as a sin-offering. ¹⁰ The male goat upon which the lot "For (casting off) a high cliff" came up should be placed before God while it is still alive, to (confess on it) atoning (for the Jewish people—before it is) sent away to the high cliff (to its death), in the desert.
- ¹¹ Aaron should bring his own sin-offering bull, and he should (confess upon it again) atoning for himself and for his (priestly) household. Then he should slaughter his sin-offering bull.
- ¹² He should take a pan full of burning coals from upon the (outer) altar, from (the west side of the altar, which) faces (the entrance to) God('s House), and a double handful of (extra) finely ground incense, and bring it inside the partition. ¹³ He should place the incense on the fire (that is in the fire pan), before God, so that

---

Scripture is telling us that the High Priest does not perform the "inner service," i.e., service connected with the Holy of Holies, wearing the eight priestly garments with which he performs the "outer service." This is because the eight garments contain gold, which is reminiscent of the sin of the Golden Calf. The "prosecuting attorney" of the Jewish people cannot become a "defense attorney," to atone for them.

Rather, he wears four garments, like an ordinary priest. They are all made of linen (*Rashi, 11th century*).

If you wish to be involved with the "inner service" of awakening in another person an inner desire to come close to God, you must first remove your metaphorical gold garments which are *"for honor and for glory,"* and adopt an attitude of selfless dedication, symbolized by the ordinary priest's garments of plain, white linen (*Rabbi Menahem Mendel Schneerson, 20th century*).

8. Two male goats: one lot "For God," and the other lot "For (casting off) a high cliff."
There are two types of "evil impulse." One is man's natural drive for self-gratification; the other persuades him to sin merely for the sake of disobedience. The first impulse can, and should, be harnessed for worshiping God. From the second impulse, that comes only to provoke him to be defiant, he must run away.

ויקרא טז:יג-כא — אחרי מות

הַקְּטֹרֶת אֶת־הַכַּפֹּרֶת אֲשֶׁר עַל־הָעֵדוּת וְלֹא יָמוּת: 14 וְלָקַח מִדַּם הַפָּר וְהִזָּה בְאֶצְבָּעוֹ עַל־פְּנֵי הַכַּפֹּרֶת קֵדְמָה וְלִפְנֵי הַכַּפֹּרֶת יַזֶּה שֶׁבַע־פְּעָמִים מִן־הַדָּם בְּאֶצְבָּעוֹ: 15 וְשָׁחַט אֶת־שְׂעִיר הַחַטָּאת אֲשֶׁר לָעָם וְהֵבִיא אֶת־דָּמוֹ אֶל־מִבֵּית לַפָּרֹכֶת וְעָשָׂה אֶת־דָּמוֹ כַּאֲשֶׁר עָשָׂה לְדַם הַפָּר וְהִזָּה אֹתוֹ עַל־הַכַּפֹּרֶת וְלִפְנֵי הַכַּפֹּרֶת: 16 וְכִפֶּר עַל־הַקֹּדֶשׁ מִטֻּמְאֹת בְּנֵי יִשְׂרָאֵל וּמִפִּשְׁעֵיהֶם לְכָל־חַטֹּאתָם וְכֵן יַעֲשֶׂה לְאֹהֶל מוֹעֵד הַשֹּׁכֵן אִתָּם בְּתוֹךְ טֻמְאֹתָם: 17 וְכָל־אָדָם לֹא־יִהְיֶה ׀ בְּאֹהֶל מוֹעֵד בְּבֹאוֹ לְכַפֵּר בַּקֹּדֶשׁ עַד־צֵאתוֹ וְכִפֶּר בַּעֲדוֹ וּבְעַד בֵּיתוֹ וּבְעַד כָּל־קְהַל יִשְׂרָאֵל: 18 [SECOND READING] וְיָצָא אֶל־הַמִּזְבֵּחַ אֲשֶׁר לִפְנֵי־יְהוָה וְכִפֶּר עָלָיו וְלָקַח מִדַּם הַפָּר וּמִדַּם הַשָּׂעִיר וְנָתַן עַל־קַרְנוֹת הַמִּזְבֵּחַ סָבִיב: 19 וְהִזָּה עָלָיו מִן־הַדָּם בְּאֶצְבָּעוֹ שֶׁבַע פְּעָמִים וְטִהֲרוֹ וְקִדְּשׁוֹ מִטֻּמְאֹת בְּנֵי יִשְׂרָאֵל: 20 וְכִלָּה מִכַּפֵּר אֶת־הַקֹּדֶשׁ וְאֶת־אֹהֶל מוֹעֵד וְאֶת־הַמִּזְבֵּחַ וְהִקְרִיב אֶת־הַשָּׂעִיר הֶחָי: 21 וְסָמַךְ אַהֲרֹן אֶת־שְׁתֵּי יָדָו עַל־רֹאשׁ הַשָּׂעִיר הַחַי וְהִתְוַדָּה עָלָיו אֶת־כָּל־עֲוֹנֹת בְּנֵי יִשְׂרָאֵל וְאֶת־כָּל־פִּשְׁעֵיהֶם לְכָל־חַטֹּאתָם וְנָתַן אֹתָם עַל־רֹאשׁ הַשָּׂעִיר וְשִׁלַּח

The sprinkling upwards represents our profound desire for God. However, this yearning cannot remain as an inner elation; it must be followed immediately with sprinkling downwards. Our *mundane* life must be dictated by our enrapture with God (*Rabbi Samson Raphael Hirsch, 19th century*).

17. For his household. Tradition informs us that the term "household" refers specifically to the High Priest's wife. You cannot serve in the exalted office of High Priest on the Day of Atonement unless you are married (*Babylonian Talmud, Yoma* 2a).

21. All the sins of the Jewish people. The scapegoat atones for the entire people, for all transgressions of the Torah, both severe and less severe sins — those violated intentionally and those violated unintentionally, whether you were aware of your sin or not — all are atoned for by the scapegoat. But this is provided that you repent. If you do not repent, the goat atones only for less severe sins.

Which sins are considered "severe" and which are considered "less severe"? The "severe sins" are those for which a man is liable either for

Food for thought

1. What does the Day of Atonement mean to you personally?

2. What makes a day holy?

3. Atonement depends on remorse. Why is one day better than another?

leviticus 16:13–21 — 'aḥarei mot

a cloud of the incense covers the ark's lid that is above the (Tablets of) Testimony. (He must do this precisely) so that he will not die.

- ❖ **14** He should take some of the bull's blood and sprinkle it (once) with his index finger towards the top (edge) of the ark's lid (which is facing) eastwards. And he should sprinkle some blood seven times with his index finger, towards (the lower part of) the front of the ark's lid.

- ❖ **15** He should then slaughter the male goat, which (was designated by the lottery as) the people's sin-offering, and bring its blood within the partition. He should do with its blood just as he had done with the bull's blood, and he should sprinkle it towards the top (edge) of the ark's lid and towards (the lower part of) the front of the ark's lid. **16** He will (thus) make an atonement for the Holy (of Holies) from the defilements (caused by) the children of Israel who sinned intentionally or unintentionally (by entering the Temple while in a state of ritual impurity).

- ❖ He should do likewise within the Tent of Meeting, (sprinkling blood towards the partition where God's Presence) dwells with the (Jewish people, despite) their ritual impurity.

- ❖ **17** No man should be in the Tent of Meeting when (Aaron) comes to atone in the Holy (of Holies), until he comes out. He will atone for himself, for his household, and for the entire congregation of Israel.

- ❖ [SECOND READING] **18** He should then go out (of that part of the Tent of Meeting where he had sprinkled blood towards the partition) to the (Golden) altar that is before God (in another part of the Tent of Meeting) and atone upon it (as follows): He should take some of the bull's blood and the male goat's blood (mixed together), and place it on the horns of the altar (with his finger), all around. **19** He should then sprinkle some of the blood on (top of the altar) with his index finger seven times, and he will thus purify it from the ritual impurity of the Jewish people, and sanctify it (for further use).

- ❖ **20** When he is finished atoning for the Holy (of Holies), the Tent of Meeting, and the (Golden) altar, he should bring the living male goat. **21** Aaron should lean both of his hands upon the living male goat's head and confess all the sins of the Jewish

---

away the sins of the past. The incense of the Day of Atonement, however, is comparable to repenting out of love, which has the power to *transform* intentional transgressions into merits.

The incense of the Day of Atonement is not a negative service aimed at wiping away the evil inclination, but has the positive goal of elevating the Jewish people to serve God in an unlimited manner, such that even the past is transformed for the good. For this reason, the incense was burned specifically in the Holy of Holies, where God's absolute infinitude was revealed (*Rabbi Menahem Mendel Schneerson, 20th century*).

14. Sprinkle some blood seven times. The High Priest would sprinkle once upward and seven times downward (*Babylonian Talmud, Yoma* 53b).

ויקרא טז:כא-ל אחרי מות

בְּיַד־אִישׁ עִתִּי הַמִּדְבָּרָה: 22 וְנָשָׂא הַשָּׂעִיר עָלָיו אֶת־כָּל־עֲוֺנֹתָם אֶל־אֶרֶץ גְּזֵרָה וְשִׁלַּח אֶת־הַשָּׂעִיר בַּמִּדְבָּר: 23 וּבָא אַהֲרֹן אֶל־אֹהֶל מוֹעֵד וּפָשַׁט אֶת־בִּגְדֵי הַבָּד אֲשֶׁר לָבַשׁ בְּבֹאוֹ אֶל־הַקֹּדֶשׁ וְהִנִּיחָם שָׁם: 24 וְרָחַץ אֶת־בְּשָׂרוֹ בַמַּיִם בְּמָקוֹם קָדוֹשׁ וְלָבַשׁ אֶת־בְּגָדָיו וְיָצָא וְעָשָׂה אֶת־עֹלָתוֹ וְאֶת־עֹלַת הָעָם וְכִפֶּר בַּעֲדוֹ וּבְעַד הָעָם: 25 [THIRD READING / SECOND WHEN JOINED] וְאֵת חֵלֶב הַחַטָּאת יַקְטִיר הַמִּזְבֵּחָה: 26 וְהַמְשַׁלֵּחַ אֶת־הַשָּׂעִיר לַעֲזָאזֵל יְכַבֵּס בְּגָדָיו וְרָחַץ אֶת־בְּשָׂרוֹ בַּמָּיִם וְאַחֲרֵי־כֵן יָבוֹא אֶל־הַמַּחֲנֶה: 27 וְאֵת פַּר הַחַטָּאת וְאֵת ׀ שְׂעִיר הַחַטָּאת אֲשֶׁר הוּבָא אֶת־דָּמָם לְכַפֵּר בַּקֹּדֶשׁ יוֹצִיא אֶל־מִחוּץ לַמַּחֲנֶה וְשָׂרְפוּ בָאֵשׁ אֶת־עֹרֹתָם וְאֶת־בְּשָׂרָם וְאֶת־פִּרְשָׁם: 28 וְהַשֹּׂרֵף אֹתָם יְכַבֵּס בְּגָדָיו וְרָחַץ אֶת־בְּשָׂרוֹ בַּמָּיִם וְאַחֲרֵי־כֵן יָבוֹא אֶל־הַמַּחֲנֶה: 29 וְהָיְתָה לָכֶם לְחֻקַּת עוֹלָם בַּחֹדֶשׁ הַשְּׁבִיעִי בֶּעָשׂוֹר לַחֹדֶשׁ תְּעַנּוּ אֶת־נַפְשֹׁתֵיכֶם וְכָל־מְלָאכָה לֹא תַעֲשׂוּ הָאֶזְרָח וְהַגֵּר הַגָּר בְּתוֹכְכֶם: 30 כִּי־בַיּוֹם הַזֶּה יְכַפֵּר עֲלֵיכֶם לְטַהֵר אֶתְכֶם מִכֹּל חַטֹּאתֵיכֶם לִפְנֵי

Repentance has the power of *retroactivity*. Although the past is no longer under your prerogative, nevertheless, God, who transcends the categories of time and limitation, has endowed repentance with a special and wonderful quality through which you can regain mastery over your past. By means of this special power of repentance, you are able not only to render the past neutral and ineffective, you can even reverse it and turn it into something positive—as the Sages said: *"Willful wrongs become as though they were merits"* (*Babylonian Talmud, Yoma* 86b; *Rabbi Shneur Zalman of Lyady, 18th century*).

You will be cleansed from all your sins before God. From this verse we derive that the Day of Atonement atones for transgressions against God—"Your sins *before God.*" But for transgressions between man and his fellow, the Day of Atonement will not atone unless you first make amends with your fellow (*Babylonian Talmud, Yoma* 85b).

spiritual vitamin

" A feeling of depression and anxiety is not helpful to true repentance. On the contrary, true and sincere repentance is followed by a feeling of happiness and closeness to God. "

people upon it—all their intentional and unintentional sins. He will thus place the (sins) on the male goat's head and send it off to the desert with a predesignated man. [22] The male goat will thus carry upon itself all their sins to an uninhabited land. He should send off the male goat into the desert.

(The instructions within the next verse are actually carried out after verse 28:)

- ❖ [23] Aaron should (remove his golden priestly garments, immerse in a ritual-pool, wash his hands and feet, put on his linen garments and) enter the Tent of Meeting. (He should remove the ladle used to bring the incense into the Holy of Holies and the firepan.) He should then remove the linen garments that he had worn when he came into the Holy (of Holies), and he should store them away there (never to be used again).

- ❖ [24] (Before doing the above) he should immerse his body in (the) water (of a ritual-pool found) in the holy (Temple courtyard, on the roof of the Parvah Chamber) and put on his (golden priestly) garments. He should go out and offer his burnt-offering (ram) and the people's burnt-offering (ram), atoning for himself and for the people, [THIRD READING / SECOND WHEN JOINED] [25] and he should make the fat of the sin-offering go up in smoke on the (outer) altar.

- ❖ [26] The person who sent off the male goat to the high cliff should immerse his garments and immerse his body in (the) water (of a ritual-pool), and (only) after this may he come into the camp.

- ❖ [27] Someone should take the sin-offering bull and male goat of the sin-offering—whose blood was brought to atone in the Holy (of Holies)—outside the camp, and their skin, flesh, and waste matter should be burned in fire. [28] The person who burns them should immerse his garments and immerse his body in (the) water (of a ritual-pool), and (only) after this may he come into the camp.

[29] (The Day of Atonement) will be an eternal statute for you:

- ❖ In the seventh month, on the tenth of the month, you should afflict yourselves.

- ❖ You should not do any work—neither the native nor convert who lives among you. [30] For on this day (God) will atone for you, to cleanse you. You will be cleansed from all your sins before God.

---

execution by a court or soul excision (*karet*). Other prohibitions and all positive commands that are not punishable by soul excision are "less severe sins."

Now that the Temple no longer exists and there is no altar to atone, there is only repentance—and repentance atones for all sins (Maimonides, 12th century).

26. The person who sent off the male goat to the high cliff should immerse. The goat that is cast off a cliff is not impure (*Babylonian Talmud, Zevaḥim* 105a). However, the person who sends it off becomes impure once he leaves Jerusalem, and must immerse (ibid., *Yoma* 67a).

30. On this day (God) will atone for you. The day *itself* brings atonement—but it will only be effective for those who are remorseful (*Maimonides, 12th century*).

ויקרא טז:ל - יז:ח　　אחרי מות

יְהוָֹה תִּטְהָרוּ: 31 שַׁבַּת שַׁבָּתוֹן הִיא לָכֶם וְעִנִּיתֶם אֶת־נַפְשֹׁתֵיכֶם חֻקַּת עוֹלָם: 32 וְכִפֶּר הַכֹּהֵן אֲשֶׁר־יִמְשַׁח אֹתוֹ וַאֲשֶׁר יְמַלֵּא אֶת־יָדוֹ לְכַהֵן תַּחַת אָבִיו וְלָבַשׁ אֶת־בִּגְדֵי הַבָּד בִּגְדֵי הַקֹּדֶשׁ: 33 וְכִפֶּר אֶת־מִקְדַּשׁ הַקֹּדֶשׁ וְאֶת־אֹהֶל מוֹעֵד וְאֶת־הַמִּזְבֵּחַ יְכַפֵּר וְעַל הַכֹּהֲנִים וְעַל־כָּל־עַם הַקָּהָל יְכַפֵּר: 34 וְהָיְתָה־זֹּאת לָכֶם לְחֻקַּת עוֹלָם לְכַפֵּר עַל־בְּנֵי יִשְׂרָאֵל מִכָּל־חַטֹּאתָם אַחַת בַּשָּׁנָה וַיַּעַשׂ כַּאֲשֶׁר צִוָּה יְהוָֹה אֶת־מֹשֶׁה: פ

יז 1 [FOURTH READING] וַיְדַבֵּר יְהוָֹה אֶל־מֹשֶׁה לֵּאמֹר: 2 דַּבֵּר אֶל־אַהֲרֹן וְאֶל־בָּנָיו וְאֶל כָּל־בְּנֵי יִשְׂרָאֵל וְאָמַרְתָּ אֲלֵיהֶם זֶה הַדָּבָר אֲשֶׁר־צִוָּה יְהוָֹה לֵאמֹר: 3 אִישׁ אִישׁ מִבֵּית יִשְׂרָאֵל אֲשֶׁר יִשְׁחַט שׁוֹר אוֹ־כֶשֶׂב אוֹ־עֵז בַּמַּחֲנֶה אוֹ אֲשֶׁר יִשְׁחָט מִחוּץ לַמַּחֲנֶה: 4 וְאֶל־פֶּתַח אֹהֶל מוֹעֵד לֹא הֱבִיאוֹ לְהַקְרִיב קָרְבָּן לַיהוָֹה לִפְנֵי מִשְׁכַּן יְהוָֹה דָּם יֵחָשֵׁב לָאִישׁ הַהוּא דָּם שָׁפָךְ וְנִכְרַת הָאִישׁ הַהוּא מִקֶּרֶב עַמּוֹ: 5 לְמַעַן אֲשֶׁר יָבִיאוּ בְּנֵי יִשְׂרָאֵל אֶת־זִבְחֵיהֶם אֲשֶׁר הֵם זֹבְחִים עַל־פְּנֵי הַשָּׂדֶה וֶהֱבִיאֻם לַיהוָֹה אֶל־פֶּתַח אֹהֶל מוֹעֵד אֶל־הַכֹּהֵן וְזָבְחוּ זִבְחֵי שְׁלָמִים לַיהוָֹה אוֹתָם: 6 וְזָרַק הַכֹּהֵן אֶת־הַדָּם עַל־מִזְבַּח יְהוָֹה פֶּתַח אֹהֶל מוֹעֵד וְהִקְטִיר הַחֵלֶב לְרֵיחַ נִיחֹחַ לַיהוָֹה: 7 וְלֹא־יִזְבְּחוּ עוֹד אֶת־זִבְחֵיהֶם לַשְּׂעִירִם אֲשֶׁר הֵם זֹנִים אַחֲרֵיהֶם חֻקַּת עוֹלָם תִּהְיֶה־זֹּאת לָהֶם לְדֹרֹתָם: 8 [FIFTH READING / THIRD WHEN JOINED] וַאֲלֵהֶם תֹּאמַר אִישׁ אִישׁ מִבֵּית יִשְׂרָאֵל וּמִן־הַגֵּר אֲשֶׁר־

---

34. (Aaron) did what God commanded Moses. Aaron's name is not actually mentioned in the verse. This alludes to the fact that, as a genuine leader, he served his people not out of pride or his own prestige, but because he was commanded by God to do so (*Rashi, 11th century; Rabbi Meir Simhah of Dvinsk, 19th–20th century*).

17:4 In the presence of the Tabernacle of God. These words, *"in the presence of the Tabernacle of God,"* seem redundant, as the verse just stated that he *"does not bring (his offering) to the entrance of the Tent of Meeting* to offer up as an offering to God."

leviticus 16:31 – 17:8 — 'aḥarei mot

- ❖ ³¹ It is a Sabbath of rest for you, and you should afflict yourselves. It is an eternal statute.

- ❖ ³² (Only the (High) Priest who is anointed, or one who is inaugurated to serve in his father's place (as High Priest), should carry out (this) atonement. (Only) he should don the linen garments, the holy garments. ³³ (Only) he should atone for the Holy of Holies, and (only) he should atone for the Tent of Meeting and the altar. (Only) he should atone for the priests and for all the people of the congregation.

³⁴ This will be an eternal statute for you, to atone for the Jewish people, for all their sins, once a year.

(On the following Day of Atonement, Aaron) did what God had commanded Moses (in the correct order).

Prohibition of Offering Sacrifices Outside the Temple

17 [FOURTH READING] ¹ God spoke to Moses, saying: ² Speak to Aaron and to his sons, and to all the children of Israel, and say to them, "This is the thing which God has commanded (me) to say (to you)":

- ❖ ³ Any man of the house of Israel, who slaughters an ox, a lamb, or a goat (which has been sanctified as an offering) inside the camp (but outside the Temple courtyard), or one who slaughters outside the camp, ⁴ and does not bring (his offering) to the entrance of the Tent of Meeting to offer up as an offering to God, in the presence of the Tabernacle of God—this (act) will be counted for that man like (shedding the) blood (of a human being).

- ❖ (Similarly, if he sprinkles sacrificial blood outside the Temple he is punished as if) he has shed (human) blood, and that man will be cut off from among his people.

Food for thought

1. Why limit worship to a single location?

2. Have you stood at the Western Wall imagining the Temple in its full glory?

3. Has somebody gone against your wishes in a misguided effort to please you?

⁵ (This warning is) in order that the children of Israel should take their offerings which they (are in the habit of) slaughtering in the open field, and bring them to God, to the entrance of the Tent of Meeting, to the priest, and slaughter them as peace-offerings to God. ⁶ The priest will dash the blood on God's altar at the entrance of the Tent of Meeting, and he will make the fat go up in smoke, as a pleasant aroma to God. ⁷ They should no longer slaughter their sacrifices to demons after whom they stray. This should be an eternal statute for them, for (all) their generations.

[FIFTH READING / THIRD WHEN JOINED] ⁸ You should say to them:

אחרי מות ויקרא יז:ח-טו

יָגוּר בְּתוֹכָם אֲשֶׁר־יַעֲלֶה עֹלָה אוֹ־זָבַח: 9 וְאֶל־פֶּתַח אֹהֶל מוֹעֵד לֹא יְבִיאֶנּוּ לַעֲשׂוֹת אֹתוֹ לַיהוָה וְנִכְרַת הָאִישׁ הַהוּא מֵעַמָּיו: 10 וְאִישׁ אִישׁ מִבֵּית יִשְׂרָאֵל וּמִן־הַגֵּר הַגָּר בְּתוֹכָם אֲשֶׁר יֹאכַל כָּל־דָּם וְנָתַתִּי פָנַי בַּנֶּפֶשׁ הָאֹכֶלֶת אֶת־הַדָּם וְהִכְרַתִּי אֹתָהּ מִקֶּרֶב עַמָּהּ: 11 כִּי נֶפֶשׁ הַבָּשָׂר בַּדָּם הִוא וַאֲנִי נְתַתִּיו לָכֶם עַל־הַמִּזְבֵּחַ לְכַפֵּר עַל־נַפְשֹׁתֵיכֶם כִּי־הַדָּם הוּא בַּנֶּפֶשׁ יְכַפֵּר: 12 עַל־כֵּן אָמַרְתִּי לִבְנֵי יִשְׂרָאֵל כָּל־נֶפֶשׁ מִכֶּם לֹא־תֹאכַל דָּם וְהַגֵּר הַגָּר בְּתוֹכְכֶם לֹא־יֹאכַל דָּם: 13 וְאִישׁ אִישׁ מִבְּנֵי יִשְׂרָאֵל וּמִן־הַגֵּר הַגָּר בְּתוֹכָם אֲשֶׁר יָצוּד צֵיד חַיָּה אוֹ־עוֹף אֲשֶׁר יֵאָכֵל וְשָׁפַךְ אֶת־דָּמוֹ וְכִסָּהוּ בֶּעָפָר: 14 כִּי־נֶפֶשׁ כָּל־בָּשָׂר דָּמוֹ בְנַפְשׁוֹ הוּא וָאֹמַר לִבְנֵי יִשְׂרָאֵל דַּם כָּל־בָּשָׂר לֹא תֹאכֵלוּ כִּי נֶפֶשׁ כָּל־בָּשָׂר דָּמוֹ הִוא כָּל־אֹכְלָיו יִכָּרֵת: 15 וְכָל־נֶפֶשׁ אֲשֶׁר תֹּאכַל נְבֵלָה וּטְרֵפָה בָּאֶזְרָח

It is this error that our verse attempts to forewarn. Every command should be carried out amid the heightened awareness that we are *"in the presence of the Tabernacle of God"* (*Rabbi Ḥayyim of Tchernowitz, 18th century*).

12. None of you should eat blood. This is to deter Jewish people from occult practices which involve blood, such as the Chaldean practice of attempting to summon demons by using pools of blood, or drinking blood in an attempt to enhance the power of prophecy. The Torah prohibits the consumption of blood, to guide the Jewish people away from such foolishness (*Maimonides, 12th century*).

Since *"the soul of (every creature's) body (depends on its) blood"* (v. 11), if a person eats the blood of an animal he will be influenced by the animal's soul which will bestow animalistic characteristics upon him (*Naḥmanides, 13th century*).

13. He should cover (the blood) with earth. Why does the commandment of covering blood apply only to wild animals and birds, but not to cattle?

Generally speaking, wild animals and birds are not offered on the altar (except for two species of birds), whereas most species of cattle may be offered on the altar. Therefore blood from cattle is not covered, since it is a type of blood which, in the majority of cases, was used to bring atonement on the altar, for in Temple times most cattle were slaughtered for sacrificial purposes (*Naḥmanides, 13th century*).

Blood is a symbol of energy. The blood of cattle represents energy in holy matters (which are "offered on the altar"); the blood

> **kabbalah bites**
>
> **17:13-14** Blood is symbolic of *gevurah* (judgment). Since judgment is the root from which all the demonic forces draw their energy, we honor the blood by covering it. Now that *gevurah* has been honored properly, it will not "look elsewhere" for its honor.

leviticus 17:8–15 — 'aḥarei mot

- Any man from the house of Israel, or from the converts who will live among them, who offers up (the sacrificial parts of) a burnt-offering or a (peace-)offering, [9] and does not bring them to the entrance of the Tent of Meeting to be (burned) for God—that man will be cut off from his people (i.e. he will die prematurely and his children will die).

Laws Pertaining to Eating and Covering Blood

- [10] If any man from the house of Israel, or from the converts who live among them, eats any blood, I will devote My time (away from all My affairs and deal) with the soul who eats the blood, and I will cut him off from among his people. [11] Because the soul of (every creature's) body (depends on its) blood, and that is why I assigned it to you (to be placed) upon the altar, to atone for your souls, for it is the blood (of an animal) that atones for the soul (of man). [12] Therefore, I said to the children of Israel: None of you(r parents) should (allow their children to) eat blood. The convert who lives among you should not eat blood.

- [13] Any man from the children of Israel, or from the converts who live among them, who traps (or finds) trapped, a wild animal or bird (of a kosher species) that may be eaten, and sheds its blood—he should cover (the blood) with earth. [14] For the soul of the body of every (creature depends on) its blood. (Therefore) I said to the children of Israel: You should not eat the blood of any body, for the soul of every (creature's) body (depends on) its blood. Anyone who eats it will be cut off.

The Ritual Impurity from an Unslaughtered Bird

- [15] Any person, whether a native or a convert, who eats (a kosher species of bird) which died on its own (without ritual slaughter) should immerse his garments and immerse himself in (the) water (of a ritual-pool), and he will remain unclean until the evening, when he will become clean. (But if a person merely touched such a bird, he does not become ritually impure.)

People often do what they are supposed to, but they do it for their own sake. They miss a vital ingredient: they neither make God's *"presence"* felt in their actions, nor do they act because it is right.

spiritual vitamin

> The Torah and commandments are infinite, having their source in the Infinite. Whatever reasons or lessons may be attached to a commandment, it should be remembered that they do not exhaust the full meaning and content of that particular commandment.

ויקרא יז:טו - יח:ט　　אחרי מות

וְכִבֶּס בְּגָדָיו וְרָחַץ בַּמַּיִם וְטָמֵא עַד־הָעֶרֶב וְטָהֵר: 16 וְאִם לֹא יְכַבֵּס וּבְשָׂרוֹ לֹא יִרְחָץ וְנָשָׂא עֲוֹנוֹ: פ

יח 1 וַיְדַבֵּר יְהֹוָה אֶל־מֹשֶׁה לֵּאמֹר: 2 דַּבֵּר אֶל־בְּנֵי יִשְׂרָאֵל וְאָמַרְתָּ אֲלֵהֶם אֲנִי יְהֹוָה אֱלֹהֵיכֶם: 3 כְּמַעֲשֵׂה אֶרֶץ־מִצְרַיִם אֲשֶׁר יְשַׁבְתֶּם־ בָּהּ לֹא תַעֲשׂוּ וּכְמַעֲשֵׂה אֶרֶץ־כְּנַעַן אֲשֶׁר אֲנִי מֵבִיא אֶתְכֶם שָׁמָּה לֹא תַעֲשׂוּ וּבְחֻקֹּתֵיהֶם לֹא תֵלֵכוּ: 4 אֶת־מִשְׁפָּטַי תַּעֲשׂוּ וְאֶת־חֻקֹּתַי תִּשְׁמְרוּ לָלֶכֶת בָּהֶם אֲנִי יְהֹוָה אֱלֹהֵיכֶם: 5 וּשְׁמַרְתֶּם אֶת־חֻקֹּתַי וְאֶת־מִשְׁפָּטַי אֲשֶׁר יַעֲשֶׂה אֹתָם הָאָדָם וָחַי בָּהֶם אֲנִי יְהֹוָה: ס [SIXTH READING] 6 אִישׁ אִישׁ אֶל־כָּל־שְׁאֵר בְּשָׂרוֹ לֹא תִקְרְבוּ לְגַלּוֹת עֶרְוָה אֲנִי יְהֹוָה: ס 7 עֶרְוַת אָבִיךָ וְעֶרְוַת אִמְּךָ לֹא תְגַלֵּה אִמְּךָ הִוא לֹא תְגַלֶּה עֶרְוָתָהּ: ס 8 עֶרְוַת אֵשֶׁת־אָבִיךָ לֹא תְגַלֵּה עֶרְוַת אָבִיךָ הִוא: ס 9 עֶרְוַת אֲחוֹתְךָ בַת־אָבִיךָ אוֹ בַת־אִמֶּךָ מוֹלֶדֶת בַּיִת אוֹ מוֹלֶדֶת חוּץ לֹא תְגַלֶּה

3. Do not follow the practices of the land of Egypt where you lived. The *"practices"* mentioned in this verse do not refer specifically to sinful actions. Rather, the verse is talking about regular, mundane actions, which must also be done differently than the Egyptians.

Unlike the Egyptians, who ate and drank merely in pursuit of physical pleasure, Israelites are commanded to pursue spiritual advancement in each of their daily activities by imbuing them with sanctity (*Rabbi Judah Aryeh Leib Alter of Gur, 19th century*).

4. You should fulfil My rational laws, and guard My suprarational commands. When you fulfil the suprarational commands you can be sure that you will also observe the rational laws. However, when you are not so scrupulous with the suprarational commands, it indicates a lack of spiritual refinement, which can lead to neglecting *all* the commandments. Therefore the verse says, *"You should fulfil My rational laws,"* and the way to do this is by guarding *"My suprarational commands"* (*Rabbi Levi Isaac of Berdichev, 18th century*).

5. You will live by them. This can also be read, "you will bring life *into* them." Don't do a good deed because you need to, or because you ought to. Do it with an excitement that this is what you *want* to do (*Rabbi Menahem Mendel Schneersohn of Lubavitch, 19th century*).

6. I am God. If you feel that all of your actions are to serve the Creator— knowing that *"I am God"*—then you also will see your interpersonal

Food for thought

1. How do today's negative influences compare with those of Biblical Canaan?

2. How can we ward off the negative effects of society without living in a ghetto?

3. Are the sins of forbidden relations worse than other sins?

leviticus 17:15 – 18:9   'aḥarei mot

- ❖ (The unslaughtered carcass of a bird will only transmit ritual impurity through being eaten if it is from a kosher species that is susceptible to being rendered) *terefah*.

- ❖ ¹⁶ (If a person becomes ritually impure in this manner) but he does not immerse (his garments) or immerse his body (in a ritual-pool, and then he eats from a sacrifice or enters the Temple), he will bear (the consequences of) his sin.

Laws of Forbidden Relations

18 ¹ God spoke to Moses, saying: ² "Speak to the children of Israel, and say to them: 'I am God, your God.'"

³ "Do not follow the practices of the land of Egypt where you lived. And do not follow the practices of the land of Canaan, where I am bringing you (for these two nations are the most depraved of all). Do not (even) follow their customs."

⁴ "You should fulfil My rational laws, and guard My suprarational commands and (always) follow their (wisdom, and not secular wisdom). I am God, your God. ⁵ You should guard My suprarational commands and My rational laws which a man should do, and you will live by them (in the next world, for) I am God (who is faithful to pay reward)."

- ❖ [SIXTH READING] ⁶ No man (or woman) may come near to any of his (or her) close relatives, to uncover (their) nakedness (and cohabit with them). I am God (who is faithful to pay reward).

- ❖ ⁷ You must not uncover the nakedness of your father('s wife) or the nakedness of your mother (if she is not your father's wife. Since) she is your mother, you must not uncover her nakedness.

- ❖ ⁸ You must not uncover the nakedness of your father's wife (even after death, since) it is your father's (wife's) nakedness.

- ❖ ⁹ You must not uncover your sister's nakedness, (whether) she is your father's daughter or your mother's daughter, (and regardless of whether) she is born to

of birds and wild animals represents energy and enthusiasm in your mundane physical pursuits of eating, sleeping, etc.

The lesson here is that you should attempt to "cover" and reduce any signs of your energy ("blood") in mundane matters; whereas with holy pursuits, the energy and enthusiasm should be "uncovered," i.e., visible and palpable. This is achieved by covering the blood "with earth"—with a spirit of humility and dedication to God, represented by the lowly earth (*Rabbi Menaḥem Mendel Schneerson, 20th century*).

18:2 I am God, your God. I am the One who said at Sinai, *"I am God, your God"* (*Exodus* 20:2). But then you only accepted My sovereignty upon yourselves. Now, accept My decrees too! (*Rashi, 11th century*).

ויקרא יח:ט-כב — אחרי מות

10 עֶרְוַת בַּת־בִּנְךָ אוֹ בַת־בִּתְּךָ לֹא תְגַלֶּה עֶרְוָתָן כִּי עֶרְוָתְךָ הֵנָּה: ס
11 עֶרְוַת בַּת־אֵשֶׁת אָבִיךָ מוֹלֶדֶת אָבִיךָ אֲחוֹתְךָ הִוא לֹא תְגַלֶּה עֶרְוָתָהּ: ס
12 עֶרְוַת אֲחוֹת־אָבִיךָ לֹא תְגַלֵּה שְׁאֵר אָבִיךָ הִוא: ס 13 עֶרְוַת אֲחוֹת־אִמְּךָ לֹא תְגַלֵּה כִּי־שְׁאֵר אִמְּךָ הִוא: ס 14 עֶרְוַת אֲחִי־אָבִיךָ לֹא תְגַלֵּה אֶל־אִשְׁתּוֹ לֹא תִקְרָב דֹּדָתְךָ הִוא: ס 15 עֶרְוַת כַּלָּתְךָ לֹא תְגַלֵּה אֵשֶׁת בִּנְךָ הִוא לֹא תְגַלֶּה עֶרְוָתָהּ: ס 16 עֶרְוַת אֵשֶׁת־אָחִיךָ לֹא תְגַלֵּה עֶרְוַת אָחִיךָ הִוא: ס 17 עֶרְוַת אִשָּׁה וּבִתָּהּ לֹא תְגַלֵּה אֶת־בַּת־בְּנָהּ וְאֶת־בַּת־בִּתָּהּ לֹא תִקַּח לְגַלּוֹת עֶרְוָתָהּ שַׁאֲרָה הֵנָּה זִמָּה הִוא: 18 וְאִשָּׁה אֶל־אֲחֹתָהּ לֹא תִקָּח לִצְרֹר לְגַלּוֹת עֶרְוָתָהּ עָלֶיהָ בְּחַיֶּיהָ: 19 וְאֶל־אִשָּׁה בְּנִדַּת טֻמְאָתָהּ לֹא תִקְרַב לְגַלּוֹת עֶרְוָתָהּ: 20 וְאֶל־אֵשֶׁת עֲמִיתְךָ לֹא־תִתֵּן שְׁכָבְתְּךָ לְזָרַע לְטָמְאָה־בָהּ: 21 וּמִזַּרְעֲךָ לֹא־תִתֵּן לְהַעֲבִיר לַמֹּלֶךְ וְלֹא תְחַלֵּל אֶת־שֵׁם אֱלֹהֶיךָ אֲנִי יְהֹוָה: 22 וְאֶת־זָכָר [SEVENTH READING / FOURTH WHEN JOINED.]

19. You must not come near a woman during the ritual impurity of her menstruation. Through issuing Divine commands relating to marital life, God raises human intimacy from an animalistic, sensual experience to the sphere of holiness and purity (*Rabbi Samson Raphael Hirsch, 19th century*).

kabbalah bites

18:6-20 When Joseph was inclined to commit the sin of adultery with Potiphar's wife, it was "the image of his father's face appearing by the window" which finally deterred him (*Babylonian Talmud, Sotah 36b*).

Why was the face of Jacob instrumental here? And how is this relevant to us?

Adam's primordial sin was equivalent to the three cardinal sins of idol-worship, murder and adultery. Adam's soul achieved *tikkun* by being reincarnated in the three patriarchs Abraham, Isaac and Jacob respectively (*see Genesis 21:9; 22:13*).

So when Joseph saw Jacob's face—which actually resembled that of Adam (*Babylonian Talmud, Bava Metzia 84a*)—it dawned upon him that failing this test would not represent an isolated sin; it would be a reversal of the entire spiritual mission of his father's life.

As descendants of Jacob we, too, need to perceive fidelity as being central to the Jewish mission.

a woman who may remain in the home or (if she is) born to a woman who must be expelled.

- ❖ ¹⁰ You must not uncover the nakedness of the daughter of your son or daughter (who was born from a forbidden relationship), for they are (like) your own nakedness.

- ❖ ¹¹ You must not uncover the nakedness of your father's (Jewish) wife's daughter, born to your father (because) she is your sister.

- ❖ ¹² You must not uncover the nakedness of your father's sister (because) she is the close relative of your father.

- ❖ ¹³ You must not uncover the nakedness of your mother's sister, because she is the close relative of your mother.

- ❖ ¹⁴ You must not uncover the nakedness of your father's brother, (namely) you must not come near his wife, (because) she is your aunt.

- ❖ ¹⁵ You must not uncover the nakedness of your daughter-in-law. She is your son's wife (so) you must not uncover her nakedness.

- ❖ ¹⁶ You must not uncover the nakedness of your brother's wife (for she) is your brother's nakedness.

- ❖ ¹⁷ You must not uncover the nakedness of a woman (to whom you are married) and her daughter. You must not take her son's daughter or her daughter's daughter (in marriage) to uncover her nakedness. It is the advice (of the evil inclination since) they are close relatives.

- ❖ ¹⁸ You must not take a woman (in marriage) in addition to her sister, to make them rivals by uncovering one's nakedness in addition to the other's. (Even if you divorce one sister you may not marry the other one) in her lifetime.

- ❖ ¹⁹ You must not come near a woman during the ritual impurity of her menstruation, to uncover her nakedness.

- ❖ ²⁰ You must not lie carnally with your fellowman's wife, to make yourself impure with her.

- ❖ ²¹ You must not give any of your offspring (to pagan priests) to pass through (between two bonfires, in worship of the pagan deity) Molech. You must not profane the name of your God. I am God.

- ❖ [SEVENTH READING / FOURTH WHEN JOINED] ²² You must not lie down with a man, as one lies with a woman. This is an abomination.

relationships as a means of fulfilling God's commands. Consequently, you will not come to commit the grave sins of forbidden relations (*Rabbi Levi Isaac of Berdichev, 18th century*).

ויקרא יח:כב-ל אחרי מות

23 לֹ֥א תִשְׁכַּ֖ב מִשְׁכְּבֵ֣י אִשָּׁ֑ה תּוֹעֵבָ֖ה הִֽוא: וּבְכָל־בְּהֵמָ֛ה לֹא־תִתֵּ֥ן שְׁכָבְתְּךָ֖ לְטָמְאָה־בָ֑הּ וְאִשָּׁ֗ה לֹֽא־תַעֲמֹ֞ד לִפְנֵ֧י בְהֵמָ֛ה לְרִבְעָ֖הּ תֶּ֥בֶל הֽוּא: 24 אַל־תִּֽטַּמְּא֖וּ בְּכָל־אֵ֑לֶּה כִּ֤י בְכָל־אֵ֙לֶּה֙ נִטְמְא֣וּ הַגּוֹיִ֔ם אֲשֶׁר־אֲנִ֥י מְשַׁלֵּ֖חַ מִפְּנֵיכֶֽם: 25 וַתִּטְמָ֣א הָאָ֔רֶץ וָאֶפְקֹ֥ד עֲוֺנָ֖הּ עָלֶ֑יהָ וַתָּקִ֥א הָאָ֖רֶץ אֶת־יֹשְׁבֶֽיהָ: 26 וּשְׁמַרְתֶּ֣ם אַתֶּ֗ם אֶת־חֻקֹּתַי֙ וְאֶת־מִשְׁפָּטַ֔י וְלֹ֣א תַעֲשׂ֔וּ מִכֹּ֥ל הַתּוֹעֵבֹ֖ת הָאֵ֑לֶּה הָֽאֶזְרָ֔ח וְהַגֵּ֖ר הַגָּ֥ר בְּתֽוֹכְכֶֽם: 27 כִּ֚י אֶת־כָּל־הַתּוֹעֵבֹ֣ת הָאֵ֔ל עָשׂ֥וּ אַנְשֵֽׁי־הָאָ֖רֶץ אֲשֶׁ֣ר לִפְנֵיכֶ֑ם וַתִּטְמָ֖א הָאָֽרֶץ: 28 [MAFTIR] וְלֹֽא־תָקִ֤יא הָאָ֙רֶץ֙ אֶתְכֶ֔ם בְּטַֽמַּאֲכֶ֖ם אֹתָ֑הּ כַּאֲשֶׁ֥ר קָאָ֛ה אֶת־הַגּ֖וֹי אֲשֶׁ֥ר לִפְנֵיכֶֽם: 29 כִּ֚י כָּל־אֲשֶׁ֣ר יַעֲשֶׂ֔ה מִכֹּ֥ל הַתּוֹעֵבֹ֖ת הָאֵ֑לֶּה וְנִכְרְת֛וּ הַנְּפָשׁ֥וֹת הָעֹשֹׂ֖ת מִקֶּ֥רֶב עַמָּֽם: 30 וּשְׁמַרְתֶּ֣ם אֶת־מִשְׁמַרְתִּ֗י לְבִלְתִּ֣י עֲשׂ֞וֹת מֵחֻקּ֤וֹת הַתּֽוֹעֵבֹת֙ אֲשֶׁ֣ר נַעֲשׂ֣וּ לִפְנֵיכֶ֔ם וְלֹ֥א תִֽטַּמְּא֖וּ בָּהֶ֑ם אֲנִ֖י יְהֹוָ֥ה אֱלֹהֵיכֶֽם: פ פ פ

פ' פסוקים, כ"י כ"ל סימן. עד"ו סימן.

spiritual vitamin

" The real bright light in life is the ability to see the right path, and follow it faithfully, filling it with all that is bright and good, in a state of consistent inner peace and tranquility. "

leviticus 18:23–30 — ʾaḥarei mot

❖ ²³ You must not cohabit with any animal, to become impure from it. A woman must not stand in front of an animal to cohabit with it. This is depravity.

²⁴ You must not defile yourselves by any of these things, for the nations whom I am sending away from you have defiled themselves with all these things. ²⁵ The land became defiled. I remembered its sin (bringing punishment) upon it, and the land vomited out its inhabitants.

²⁶ But you will observe My suprarational commands and My rational commands, and you will not do any of these abominations—neither the native, nor the convert who lives among you.

²⁷ The people of the land, who preceded you, did all of these abominations and the land became defiled. [MAFTIR] ²⁸ Let the land not vomit you out for having defiled it, as it vomited out the nation that preceded you. ²⁹ For if anyone commits any of these abominations, (both) the people (the man and the woman) who committed (the act) will be cut off from the midst of their people.

³⁰ (The courts should) enforce My restrictions, not to commit any of the abominable practices that were done before you, and you will not become defiled by them.

(If you keep My laws then) I am God, your God.

Haftarot: ʾAḥarei Mot—page 1358.   *Erev Rosh Ḥodesh*—page 1415.
Shabbat ha-Gadol (*Erev Pesaḥ*)—page 1437.

---

27. All of these abominations. The Sages, aiming to highlight the pitfalls of arrogance, equated an arrogant man to one who has engaged in all forbidden relations. They learn this from our verse, which describes forbidden relations as an "abomination," and regarding arrogance it says, *"Every haughty person is an abomination to God"* (*Proverbs* 16:5). This common characterization, as an abomination, indicated to the Sages a relationship between the two sins (*Babylonian Talmud, Sotah* 4b).

Bring holiness into your world, into your **everyday life.** Make it the **focal point** of your consciousness. Holiness is the opposite of **your ego,** and its **antidote.**

KEDOSHIM
קדושים

CLARIFICATION OF BASIC LAWS OF THE TORAH	19:1–25
LAWS OF PERSONAL SANCTITY	19:26–31
LAWS OF HONESTY AND RESPECT FOR OTHERS	19:32–37
PENALTY FOR TRANSGRESSING PROHIBITIONS	20:1–27

NAME
Kedoshim

MEANING
"Holy"

LINES IN TORAH SCROLL
109

PARASHIYYOT
3 open; 1 closed

VERSES
64

WORDS
868

LETTERS
3229

DATE
Nisan – 20 Iyyar, 2449

LOCATION
Sinai Desert

KEY PEOPLE
Moses

MITZVOT
13 positive;
38 prohibitions

NOTE
Often read together with portion of Aharei Mot

CHARACTER PROFILE

NAME
The Convert

FIRST
Jethro—Chief Sheikh of Midian; Moses' father-in-law; originator of the idea to develop a hierarchy of judges

FAMOUS
Obadiah—an Edomite who converted and later became a prophet, saving one hundred prophets from persecution

Shemaiah and Avtalyon—descendants of King Sennacherib of Assyria; Rabbinic sages who lived in early pre-Mishnaic era

Onkelos—member of the Roman royal family, Hadrian's nephew; composed an Aramaic translation of the Torah

Ruth—Moabite princess who followed her mother-in-law to Israel after her husband died, and converted; great grandmother of King David

MITZVOT
To love the convert (*Deuteronomy* 10:19); not to pervert the judgment of a convert (ibid., 24:17)

HOLINESS

The Hebrew word for holiness literally translates as "separate." Being holy means being one with God and utilizing all your talents for Him. Even non-sacred activities should be performed for a Godly purpose (19:2).

REVENGE

Acting in revenge ensures that the cycle of discord continues indefinitely. By breaking the cycle and not taking revenge, we demonstrate willingness to live in peace and harmony with our neighbors (19:18).

PUNISHMENT

The misfortunes of life are, at their core, really blessings. We do not always realize it at the time, but everything that God sends is ultimately for our benefit (ch. 20).

ויקרא יט:א-ח — קדושים

1 וַיְדַבֵּר יְהוָה אֶל־מֹשֶׁה לֵּאמֹר: 2 דַּבֵּר אֶל־כָּל־עֲדַת בְּנֵי־יִשְׂרָאֵל וְאָמַרְתָּ אֲלֵהֶם קְדֹשִׁים תִּהְיוּ כִּי קָדוֹשׁ אֲנִי יְהוָה אֱלֹהֵיכֶם: 3 אִישׁ אִמּוֹ וְאָבִיו תִּירָאוּ וְאֶת־שַׁבְּתֹתַי תִּשְׁמֹרוּ אֲנִי יְהוָה אֱלֹהֵיכֶם: 4 אַל־תִּפְנוּ אֶל־הָאֱלִילִים וֵאלֹהֵי מַסֵּכָה לֹא תַעֲשׂוּ לָכֶם אֲנִי יְהוָה אֱלֹהֵיכֶם: 5 וְכִי תִזְבְּחוּ זֶבַח שְׁלָמִים לַיהוָה לִרְצֹנְכֶם תִּזְבָּחֻהוּ: 6 בְּיוֹם זִבְחֲכֶם יֵאָכֵל וּמִמָּחֳרָת וְהַנּוֹתָר עַד־יוֹם הַשְּׁלִישִׁי בָּאֵשׁ יִשָּׂרֵף: 7 וְאִם הֵאָכֹל יֵאָכֵל בַּיּוֹם הַשְּׁלִישִׁי פִּגּוּל הוּא לֹא יֵרָצֶה: 8 וְאֹכְלָיו עֲוֺנוֹ יִשָּׂא כִּי־אֶת־קֹדֶשׁ יְהוָה חִלֵּל וְנִכְרְתָה הַנֶּפֶשׁ הַהִוא:

You should be holy. Through refraining from forbidden relations (*Rashi, 11ᵗʰ century*).

While *Rashi* understood that the Jewish people "become holy" by refraining from forbidden relations in particular, I see this as a command to be self-restraining *in general*. Even when the Torah permits you to eat food that is kosher and to have intimate relations, it is still desirable to exercise moderation (*Naḥmanides, 13ᵗʰ century*).

There is a principle in Ḥasidic thought, "The higher something is, the lower it falls." You reach the highest levels of spiritual greatness, not through intellectual endeavors alone, but by involving yourself in the physical world, observing the commandments and helping others to do likewise.

You best fulfil the command to *"be holy"* by refraining from the lowest and most debased of acts (forbidden relations). For the route towards the highest degrees of holiness, becoming holy *like God* ("You should be holy, *because I, God your God, am holy*"), is through refraining from the *lowest* of acts—"the higher something is, the lower it falls."

This also explains why, at the afternoon prayer on the Day of Atonement, the holiest day of the year—before beginning the closing prayer (*Ne'ilah*), the climax of the day—the Torah reading discusses forbidden relations. For it is through restraint from the very lowest of acts that you reach the highest degrees of holiness (*Rabbi Menahem Mendel Schneerson, 20ᵗʰ century*).

I, God, your God, am holy. By sanctifying our lives, God considers it as if we are sanctifying Him (*Sifra*).

3. Every person should fear his mother and his father ... observe My Sabbaths. The fear you ought to have toward your parents should reach the same level as the fear you have for God. This is because there were three partners in your creation: your mother, your father, and God.

But despite the high regard in which you should hold your parents, if they tell you to desecrate the Sabbath you should not listen to them (*Babylonian Talmud, Kiddushin* 30b; *Yevamot* 5b; *Rabbi Samuel Edels, 16ᵗʰ–17ᵗʰ century*).

Food for thought

1. How do you express reverence for your parents?

2. Do you treat your parents as you wish to be treated by your own children?

3. Where do you draw the line with respecting parents?

parashat kedoshim

Clarification of Basic Laws of the Torah

19 ¹ God spoke to Moses, saying: ² (Many basic laws depend upon the following section, so) speak to the entire congregation of the children of Israel, and say to them:

- You should be holy, because I, God, your God, am holy.

- ³ (Every) person should fear his mother and his father. But you should (not listen to them if they tell you not to) observe My Sabbaths (or any other commandment), for I am God, your God (whom your parents must honor too).

- ⁴ You should not turn to the worthless idols (and worship them). You should not make molten deities for (other people, nor should they make them for) you. I am God, your God.

⁵ When you slaughter a peace-offering to God, you must slaughter it (with the correct intentions for it) to be accepted favorably for you (by God):

- ⁶ (It must be slaughtered with the intention that) it will be eaten on the day you slaughter it or on the next day, for anything left over until the third day must be burned in fire.

- ⁷ If it (was slaughtered with the intention of eating it outside its prescribed area or with the intention) of being eaten on the third day, it is repulsive (to God) and it will not be accepted favorably (by Him).

- ⁸ (If sacrificial meat is indeed left over to the third day) then whoever eats it will bear (the consequences of) his sin, for he has profaned what is holy to God, and that person will be cut off from his people.

19:2 Speak to the entire congregation of the children of Israel. This portion was said to the entire assembled congregation because most of the fundamental teachings of the Torah depend on it (*Rashi, 11th century*).

kabbalah bites

19:4 *"You should not turn to the worthless idols."* What you gaze at affects you more than you might think. Because whatever your eyes feast on clings to your soul and makes a deep impression on it.

If you are careful to look only at things that are conducive to morality, your soul will benefit immensely.

ויקרא יט:ח-יד

מֵעַמֶּֽיהָ: 9 וּֽבְקֻצְרְכֶם֙ אֶת־קְצִ֣יר אַרְצְכֶ֔ם לֹ֧א תְכַלֶּ֛ה פְּאַ֥ת שָׂדְךָ֖ לִקְצֹ֑ר וְלֶ֥קֶט קְצִֽירְךָ֖ לֹ֥א תְלַקֵּֽט: 10 וְכַרְמְךָ֙ לֹ֣א תְעוֹלֵ֔ל וּפֶ֥רֶט כַּרְמְךָ֖ לֹ֣א תְלַקֵּ֑ט לֶֽעָנִ֤י וְלַגֵּר֙ תַּעֲזֹ֣ב אֹתָ֔ם אֲנִ֖י יְהֹוָ֥ה אֱלֹהֵיכֶֽם: 11 לֹ֖א תִּגְנֹ֑בוּ וְלֹא־תְכַחֲשׁ֥וּ וְלֹֽא־תְשַׁקְּר֖וּ אִ֥ישׁ בַּעֲמִיתֽוֹ: 12 וְלֹֽא־תִשָּׁבְע֥וּ בִשְׁמִ֖י לַשָּׁ֑קֶר וְחִלַּלְתָּ֛ אֶת־שֵׁ֥ם אֱלֹהֶ֖יךָ אֲנִ֥י יְהֹוָֽה:
13 לֹא־תַעֲשֹׁ֥ק אֶת־רֵֽעֲךָ֖ וְלֹ֣א תִגְזֹ֑ל לֹֽא־תָלִ֞ין פְּעֻלַּ֥ת שָׂכִ֛יר אִתְּךָ֖ עַד־בֹּֽקֶר:
14 לֹא־תְקַלֵּ֣ל חֵרֵ֔שׁ וְלִפְנֵ֣י עִוֵּ֔ר לֹ֥א תִתֵּ֖ן מִכְשֹׁ֑ל וְיָרֵ֥אתָ מֵּאֱלֹהֶ֖יךָ אֲנִ֥י יְהֹוָֽה:

The Torah compares robbery to ending life because the act of robbery deprives the victim of some of the *inherent rights* that life brings. This is the case regardless of how much money was taken (even "a *perutah*").

When a person suffers a robbery, it is not merely that his assets have decreased as a result of an unlawful act (as is the case with theft); his rightful ownership has been *openly challenged* and taken away by force. The robber says, "I am denying you the fundamental human right of owning your own property," which, in a certain respect, is depriving a person of the privilege of being alive. Hence, "it is as if he took his life away."

With theft, which occurs secretly, there is no *outright challenge* of ownership. It is only that, at some later date, a person will discover that he does not have as many possessions as he did previously. But there was never a moment where he was confronted by another person who forcefully uprooted his ownership and "took away his life" (*Rabbi Menahem Mendel Schneerson, 20th century*).

You should not steal. Everything you see in life can teach you a lesson in how to worship God better. Even the thief can teach you a number of positive lessons: (a) He keeps to himself; (b) he is willing to place himself in danger; (c) even the smallest detail is very important to him; (d) he works extremely hard; (e) he works quickly; (f) he is confident and hopes for the best; and (g) if he does not succeed the first time, he will try again and again (*Rabbi Zusya of Hanipoli, 18th century*).

14. You should not place a stumbling block before a person who is "blind." You may not give advice that is inappropriate for a person who is "blind" regarding a certain matter. For example, do not tell a person, "Sell your field and buy a donkey," if your plan is to take advantage of him and buy the field from him (*Rashi, 11th century*).

You may not cause a blind person to be injured, thinking that this victim will not know who caused the injury (*Naḥmanides, 13th century*).

You must fear your God. I am God. It is not discernible whether the person (who gave the advice) had good or bad

---

kabbalah bites

19:13 Rabbi Isaac Luria, the most preeminent of the Kabbalists, was extraordinarily careful about paying his workers on time. He sometimes delayed his afternoon prayers past the preferred time so as to pay a worker before sunset. He would say, "How can I pray to God when such a great *mitzvah* comes my way? Can I put it off and still face God in prayer?"

leviticus 19:9–14   kedoshim

- ⁹ When you reap the harvest of your land, you should not fully reap the corner of your field (since this should be left for the poor); nor should you gather the individual stalks of your harvest (that have fallen. ¹⁰ Similarly,) you should not harvest the young grapes of your vineyard, nor should you gather the (fallen) individual grapes of your vineyard. You should leave them for the poor and for the convert. I am God, your God.

- ¹¹ You should not steal (money).

- No man (among) you should make a false denial or false oath against his fellowman.

- ¹² You should not swear falsely by (any of) My name(s), thereby profaning the name of your God. I am God.

- ¹³ You should not oppress your fellow (by withholding his wages).

- You should not rob.

- A (daily) hired worker's wage should not be withheld by you overnight, until morning.

- ¹⁴ You should not curse a deaf person (or any other living person).

- You should not place a stumbling block before a person who is "blind" (to a certain matter. Since nobody can know your true intentions, and you could always escape blame,) you must fear your God. I am God.

9. When you reap the harvest of your land, you should not fully reap the corner of your field. If a person violates a severe prohibition that carries the consequence of soul excision (*karet*), he might mistakenly assume that he can abandon the rest of the commandments, since his soul is in any case "cut off" from God. This verse tells us that *"when you reap the harvest of your land"*—if your spiritual "land" is being cut off because of a sin you committed; *"you should not fully reap the corner of your field"*—do not continue to sin and destroy the remainder of your spiritual attachment. The entire soul can never be completely severed (*Rabbi Ḥayyim ibn Attar, 18th century*).

10. You should leave them for the poor and for the convert. I am God, your God. This means, "I am a judge who exacts punishment! And for this sin, I will demand from you nothing less than your souls"—as the verse states, *"Do not rob a poor man ... for God will plead their cause"* (*Proverbs 22:22-23; Rashi, 11th century*).

11, 13. You should not steal ... You should not rob. What is the definition of a "thief"? One who *secretly* acquires the property of another person, without the owner knowing. For example, if a man puts his hand into another's pocket and discreetly takes the owner's money. However, if a man takes possession of another's property *openly* in public, by force, then he is not a "thief" but a "robber."

Any person who robs so much as a *perutah* (small coin) is considered to have taken that person's life away, as the verse states, *"So are the ways of every one who is greedy of gain; it takes away the life of its owners"* (*Proverbs 1:19; Maimonides, 12th century*).

קדושים ויקרא יט:טו-כ

[SECOND READING FIFTH WHEN JOINED] 15 לֹא־תַעֲשׂוּ עָוֶל בַּמִּשְׁפָּט לֹא־תִשָּׂא פְנֵי־דָל וְלֹא תֶהְדַּר פְּנֵי גָדוֹל בְּצֶדֶק תִּשְׁפֹּט עֲמִיתֶךָ: 16 לֹא־תֵלֵךְ רָכִיל בְּעַמֶּיךָ לֹא תַעֲמֹד עַל־דַּם רֵעֶךָ אֲנִי יְהֹוָה: 17 לֹא־תִשְׂנָא אֶת־אָחִיךָ בִּלְבָבֶךָ הוֹכֵחַ תּוֹכִיחַ אֶת־עֲמִיתֶךָ וְלֹא־תִשָּׂא עָלָיו חֵטְא: 18 לֹא־תִקֹּם וְלֹא־תִטֹּר אֶת־בְּנֵי עַמֶּךָ וְאָהַבְתָּ לְרֵעֲךָ כָּמוֹךָ אֲנִי יְהֹוָה: 19 אֶת־חֻקֹּתַי תִּשְׁמֹרוּ בְּהֶמְתְּךָ לֹא־תַרְבִּיעַ כִּלְאַיִם שָׂדְךָ לֹא־תִזְרַע כִּלְאָיִם וּבֶגֶד כִּלְאַיִם שַׁעַטְנֵז לֹא יַעֲלֶה עָלֶיךָ: 20 וְאִישׁ כִּי־יִשְׁכַּב אֶת־אִשָּׁה שִׁכְבַת־זֶרַע וְהִוא שִׁפְחָה נֶחֱרֶפֶת לְאִישׁ וְהָפְדֵּה לֹא נִפְדָּתָה אוֹ חֻפְשָׁה לֹא

16. You should not stand by your fellow's blood. *"Do not stand by,"* watching his death, if you are able to save him. For example, if he is drowning in the river and a wild animal or robbers come upon him (*Rashi, 11th century*).

The fact that *you* saw someone whose life is in danger *proves* that "you are able to save him." For the fact that God allowed you to witness this event must surely be for a practical reason—namely that you, of all people, have the ability to save this person.

Likewise, if you see a person "drowning" spiritually, it is a sign from above that you have the ability to draw that person back to the fountains of living Judaism (*Rabbi Menahem Mendel Schneerson, 20th century*).

18. You should love your fellow as (you love) yourself. Hillel said: "What is hateful to you, do not do to your fellow. This is the entire Torah—the rest is commentary" (*Babylonian Talmud, Shabbat* 31a).

Rabbi Akiva says: "This is a major principle of the Torah" (*Rashi, 11th century*).

"Love your fellow as (you love) yourself" is an interpretation and explanation of the verse, *"Love God, your God"* (Deuteronomy 6:5). If you love your fellow then you love God, because that person's soul is a "part of God above" (*Rabbi Israel Ba'al Shem Tov, 18th century*).

All of us are brothers, literally, due to the source of our souls in the One God, and it is only our bodies that divide us. Those who care for their bodies first and their souls second cannot share true brotherly love, for their love will have an ulterior motive. This is what Hillel the Elder meant when he said about this commandment, *"This is the entire Torah, the rest is commentary"*—the basis and root of the entire Torah is to prioritize the soul over the body (*Rabbi Shneur Zalman of Lyady, 18th century*).

19. You should not crossbreed your livestock with different species. God created the world with distinct species of animals and gave them the ability to reproduce in order that those species would live on. When you crossbreed two species, it is as if you are thinking, "God didn't create the world well enough. I will improve His work by creating a new type of animal" (*Nahmanides, 13th century*).

Food for thought

1. How careful are you when you criticize?

2. How do you avoid labeling and judging people?

3. Why is hatred so toxic?

leviticus 19:15–20   kedoshim

- [SECOND READING / FIFTH WHEN JOINED] **15** You, (the judge), should not commit a perversion of justice. You should not favor a poor person or respect a great man (in judgment). You should judge your fellow correctly.

- **16** You should not go around as a gossiper among your people.

- You should not stand by your fellow's blood (if his life is in danger, and you are able to save him). I am God (who is faithful to pay reward and exact punishment).

17 You should:

- Not hate your brother in your heart.

- You should continually rebuke your fellow, but you should not bear a sin (by embarrassing) him (in public).

- **18** You should neither take revenge nor bear a grudge against the members of your people.

- You should love your fellow as (you love) yourself. I am God.

19 You should observe My suprarational commands:

- You should not crossbreed your livestock with different species.

- You should not sow your field with a mixture of seeds.

- A garment which has a mixture of *sha'atnez* (wool and linen) should not come upon you.

20 If a man will lie with a woman and he will have a seminal emission, and she is a (non-Jewish) slavewoman who is partially married to a (Jewish slave) man, and she has been (allowed to partially marry this Jewish slave since she has been) redeemed (by one of

intentions. Since he can avoid blame by saying, "I meant well!" the Torah stresses, *"You must fear your God,"* for God knows your thoughts (*Rashi, 11th century*).

15. You should not favor a poor person or respect a great man (in judgment). A judge presiding over a dispute between a poor man and a rich man should not think, "Because the wealthy man is obligated to help the poor, I will rule in favor of the poor litigant." Likewise, the judge should not be concerned to rule against a wealthy or prominent person for fear of humiliating him. He must judge each case based on its own merits (*Rashi, 11th century*).

spiritual vitamin

> The first condition of receiving the Torah was the unity of the Israelite people, so that they could be receptive to the unity of God.

ויקרא יט:כ-לא — קדושים

נִתַּן־לָהּ בְּקֹרֶת תִּהְיֶה לֹא יוּמְתוּ כִּי־לֹא חֻפָּשָׁה: 21 וְהֵבִיא אֶת־אֲשָׁמוֹ לַיהוָֹה אֶל־פֶּתַח אֹהֶל מוֹעֵד אֵיל אָשָׁם: 22 וְכִפֶּר עָלָיו הַכֹּהֵן בְּאֵיל הָאָשָׁם לִפְנֵי יְהוָֹה עַל־חַטָּאתוֹ אֲשֶׁר חָטָא וְנִסְלַח לוֹ מֵחַטָּאתוֹ אֲשֶׁר חָטָא: פ

[THIRD READING]

23 וְכִי־תָבֹאוּ אֶל־הָאָרֶץ וּנְטַעְתֶּם כָּל־עֵץ מַאֲכָל וַעֲרַלְתֶּם עָרְלָתוֹ אֶת־פִּרְיוֹ שָׁלֹשׁ שָׁנִים יִהְיֶה לָכֶם עֲרֵלִים לֹא יֵאָכֵל: 24 וּבַשָּׁנָה הָרְבִיעִת יִהְיֶה כָּל־פִּרְיוֹ קֹדֶשׁ הִלּוּלִים לַיהוָֹה: 25 וּבַשָּׁנָה הַחֲמִישִׁת תֹּאכְלוּ אֶת־פִּרְיוֹ לְהוֹסִיף לָכֶם תְּבוּאָתוֹ אֲנִי יְהוָֹה אֱלֹהֵיכֶם: 26 לֹא תֹאכְלוּ עַל־הַדָּם לֹא תְנַחֲשׁוּ וְלֹא תְעוֹנֵנוּ: 27 לֹא תַקִּפוּ פְּאַת רֹאשְׁכֶם וְלֹא תַשְׁחִית אֵת פְּאַת זְקָנֶךָ: 28 וְשֶׂרֶט לָנֶפֶשׁ לֹא תִתְּנוּ בִּבְשַׂרְכֶם וּכְתֹבֶת קַעֲקַע לֹא תִתְּנוּ בָּכֶם אֲנִי יְהוָֹה: 29 אַל־תְּחַלֵּל אֶת־בִּתְּךָ לְהַזְנוֹתָהּ וְלֹא־תִזְנֶה הָאָרֶץ וּמָלְאָה הָאָרֶץ זִמָּה: 30 אֶת־שַׁבְּתֹתַי תִּשְׁמֹרוּ וּמִקְדָּשִׁי תִּירָאוּ אֲנִי יְהוָֹה: 31 אַל־תִּפְנוּ אֶל־הָאֹבֹת וְאֶל־הַיִּדְּעֹנִים

26, 30. You should not practice divination, nor act on the basis of fortuitous times ... You should revere My Sanctuary. You should observe My Sabbaths. I am God. Verse 30 offers the Torah's positive solutions to the prohibited activities of verse 26. In contrast to acting *"on the basis of fortuitous times"* (v. 26), i.e., predicting which day is an "auspicious time" to start an activity (*Babylonian Talmud, Sanhedrin* 65b), Scripture says, *"observe My Sabbaths"* (v. 30)—your activities should be based on the time cycle that *God* designated, namely the Sabbath.

In contrast to practicing *"divination"* (v. 26), i.e., deciding a "lucky time" based on random, irrelevant events, Scripture says, *"revere My Sanctuary"* (v. 30), My Torah, and do not fear those predictions.

When you do this, *"I am God"*—you will receive many blessings and be successful (*Rabbi Samson Raphael Hirsch, 19th century*).

31. You should not turn to (the sorcery of the) ʾ**ov or** *yiddeʿoni.* The word *ʾov* also can mean "desire" (from the Hebrew word *ʾavah*), and the word *yiddeʿoni* can be translated as "knowledge" (*deʿah*). *Do not turn to desire, nor should you sway to knowledge.* As much as being knowledgeable is commendable it is not everything. The final destination, the actual good deed, is the most important thing (*Rabbi Simḥah Bunem of Przysucha, 18th–19th century*).

---

kabbalah bites

19:27 Man is created in the image of God. God, too, has a "beard," metaphorically speaking: The tufts of God's beard are the channels through which His blessings flow downwards from the heavens into this world. That is why, according to the Kabbalah, you should not cut or even trim your beard, for in this way you will maximize the flow of God's blessings to your life.

leviticus 19:20–31 — kedoshim

her masters) and she has not been redeemed (by the other), or she has not been given a document of release (by just one of her masters)—then:

- There should be an investigation (to verify the above details).
- They should not be put to death, because she had not been (completely) freed (and thus she was not fully married. Rather she is given lashes).
- ²¹ He should bring his guilt-offering to God, to the entrance of the Tent of Meeting as a guilt-offering ram. ²² The priest should atone for him with the guilt-offering ram, before God, for the sin that he had committed, and he will be forgiven for the sin that he had committed.

[THIRD READING] ²³ When you come to the land (of Canaan) and you plant any (type of) food tree:

- Its fruit will be consistently restricted from you. You will be restricted from its fruit for three years, and may not eat it.
- ²⁴ In the fourth year, all its fruit should be holy (only to be eaten in Jerusalem), in praise of God.
- ²⁵ In the fifth year, you may eat its fruit.
- (Observe this law, in order) to increase (the tree's) produce for you. I am God, your (trustworthy) God.

Laws of Personal Sanctity

- ²⁶ You should not eat (sacrificial meat) when (its) blood (has not yet been sprinkled on the altar).
- You should not practice divination, nor act on the basis of fortuitous times.
- ²⁷ You should not remove (the hair from around) the circumference of your head (making the hair behind the ears level with the hair of the temples).
- You should not destroy the extremities of your beard.
- ²⁸ You should not make scratches in your flesh, (to mourn) a person (that died).
- You should not put a tattoo on yourselves. I am God.
- ²⁹ You should not defile your daughter, allowing your unmarried daughter to have relations (not for the sake of marriage. If you do) the land will become "unfaithful" (another land will produce its fruits), and the land will be filled with immorality.
- ³⁰ You should revere My Sanctuary (by not entering the Temple with your staff, shoes, money belt or dust on your feet. But despite the great importance of the Temple) you should observe My Sabbaths (rather than building the Temple on the Sabbath). I am God.
- ³¹ You should not turn to (the sorcery of the) *'ov* or *yidde'oni*. You should not seek (these, and thereby) defile yourselves through them. I am God, your God.

ויקרא יט:לא – כ:ג   קדושים

אַל־תְּבַקְשׁוּ לְטָמְאָה בָהֶם אֲנִי יְהֹוָה אֱלֹהֵיכֶם: 32 מִפְּנֵי שֵׂיבָה תָּקוּם וְהָדַרְתָּ פְּנֵי זָקֵן וְיָרֵאתָ מֵּאֱלֹהֶיךָ אֲנִי יְהֹוָה: ס 33 [FOURTH READING / SIXTH WHEN JOINED] וְכִי־יָגוּר אִתְּךָ גֵּר בְּאַרְצְכֶם לֹא תוֹנוּ אֹתוֹ: 34 כְּאֶזְרָח מִכֶּם יִהְיֶה לָכֶם הַגֵּר | הַגָּר אִתְּכֶם וְאָהַבְתָּ לוֹ כָּמוֹךָ כִּי־גֵרִים הֱיִיתֶם בְּאֶרֶץ מִצְרָיִם אֲנִי יְהֹוָה אֱלֹהֵיכֶם: 35 לֹא־תַעֲשׂוּ עָוֶל בַּמִּשְׁפָּט בַּמִּדָּה בַּמִּשְׁקָל וּבַמְּשׂוּרָה: 36 מֹאזְנֵי צֶדֶק אַבְנֵי־צֶדֶק אֵיפַת צֶדֶק וְהִין צֶדֶק יִהְיֶה לָכֶם אֲנִי יְהֹוָה אֱלֹהֵיכֶם אֲשֶׁר־הוֹצֵאתִי אֶתְכֶם מֵאֶרֶץ מִצְרָיִם: 37 וּשְׁמַרְתֶּם אֶת־כָּל־חֻקֹּתַי וְאֶת־כָּל־מִשְׁפָּטַי וַעֲשִׂיתֶם אֹתָם אֲנִי יְהֹוָה: פ

כ 1 [FIFTH READING] וַיְדַבֵּר יְהֹוָה אֶל־מֹשֶׁה לֵּאמֹר: 2 וְאֶל־בְּנֵי יִשְׂרָאֵל תֹּאמַר אִישׁ אִישׁ מִבְּנֵי יִשְׂרָאֵל וּמִן־הַגֵּר | הַגָּר בְּיִשְׂרָאֵל אֲשֶׁר יִתֵּן מִזַּרְעוֹ לַמֹּלֶךְ מוֹת יוּמָת עַם הָאָרֶץ יִרְגְּמֻהוּ בָאָבֶן: 3 וַאֲנִי אֶתֵּן אֶת־פָּנַי בָּאִישׁ הַהוּא וְהִכְרַתִּי אֹתוֹ מִקֶּרֶב עַמּוֹ כִּי מִזַּרְעוֹ נָתַן לַמֹּלֶךְ לְמַעַן טַמֵּא אֶת־מִקְדָּשִׁי וּלְחַלֵּל אֶת־

Egyptians had chosen not to harm the Jewish people, God would have found another way to carry out His decree.

This subterfuge, of appearing to be righteous while at the same time carrying out an act of wickedness, resembles the sin of having false weights and measures, as the use of false measures is an attempt to "dress up" an act of theft as an act of honesty.

Therefore, *"If you deny the precept of accurate measures, it is as if you denied the exodus from Egypt,"* since the Exodus freed us from the dishonest subterfuge which was typified by the Egyptian people (*Rabbi Menahem Mendel Schneerson, 20th century*).

20:2 In (worship of the pagan deity) Molech. Molech was worshiped by handing over a child to the priests who would pass the child through a fire. The worship was based on a heathen belief that fate rules the world. It is not that they gave their children over to idol-worship, abandoning the service of God; they saw themselves as giving up their most precious possession—their children—to the "decree of fate."

Not only did this slander God, it violated the holiness of children who are God's assets. It was a denial that a child is meant to blossom under God's providence (*Rabbi Samson Raphael Hirsch, 19th century*).

Should be put to death. The penalty was only given when a man gave *some* of his children in worship of Molech, but in the event that he gave over *all* of his children, he was not punished with his life (*Babylonian Talmud, Sanhedrin 84b*).

Food for thought

1. Does our society respect the elderly enough?

2. Why does somebody deserve your respect just for being old?

3. What is special about the elderly?

Laws of Honesty and Respect for Others

- ❖ ³² You should rise in the presence of an old person and you should honor the presence of a sage. (Do not shut your eyes to avoid doing this commandment, but rather,) you should fear your God. I am God.

- ❖ [FOURTH READING / SIXTH WHEN JOINED] ³³ When a convert lives with you in your land, you should not (verbally) harass him (by reminding him of his past). ³⁴ The convert who lives with you should be considered by you like a native among you, and you should love him as (you love) yourself. For you (too) were (once) strangers in the land of Egypt. (Just as) I am your God, (I am his) God (too).

- ❖ ³⁵ You should not commit a perversion of justice (with false) measures, weights, or liquid measures. ³⁶ You should have accurate scales, accurate weights, an accurate dry-measure, and an accurate liquid measure. I am God, your God, who brought you out of the land of Egypt (on condition that you keep accurate weights and measures).

- ❖ ³⁷ You should observe all My suprarational commands and all My rational commands, and fulfil them. I am God.

Punishments for Transgressing Prohibitions of the Torah

20 [FIFTH READING] ¹ God spoke to Moses, saying: ² You should say (the following punishments for transgressing the prohibitions of the Torah) to the children of Israel:

- ❖ Any man of the children of Israel, or from the converts who live among Israel, who gives any of his offspring in (worship of the pagan deity) Molech should be put to death (by the court). If the court does not have the power to do so) the public should (assist the court and) pelt him to death with stones.

- ❖ ³ I will devote My time (away from all My affairs and deal) with this man (individually) and I will cut him off from among his people, (even if) he gave his (grandson) to Molech, in order to defile (the assembly of Israel) which is sacred to Me, and to profane My holy name.

36. You should have accurate scales ... I am God, your God, who brought you out of the land of Egypt. If you deny the precept of accurate measures, it is as if you denied the exodus from Egypt, which was the beginning of the Torah's commandments (*Maimonides, 12ᵗʰ century*).

By sinning surreptitiously, a person who possesses inaccurate measures disregards God's supervision of all the details of this world. He is thus denying the exodus from Egypt, and its associated miracles, which proved God's providential care and direct involvement (*Rabbi Vidal Yom Tov of Tolosa, 14ᵗʰ century*).

The Egyptian persecution of the Jewish people was done under a pretense. They *appeared* to be following God's will, for God had decreed, *"They will enslave them and oppress them"* (*Genesis* 15:13). In truth, however, the Egyptians were carrying out an act of wickedness, for they *chose* to harm the Jewish people. They were not carrying out God's will at all, for if the

ויקרא כ:ג-טו　　　　　　　　　　　　　　קדושים

שֵׁם קָדְשִׁי: 4 וְאִם הַעְלֵם יַעְלִימוּ עַם הָאָרֶץ אֶת־עֵינֵיהֶם מִן־הָאִישׁ הַהוּא בְּתִתּוֹ מִזַּרְעוֹ לַמֹּלֶךְ לְבִלְתִּי הָמִית אֹתוֹ: 5 וְשַׂמְתִּי אֲנִי אֶת־פָּנַי בָּאִישׁ הַהוּא וּבְמִשְׁפַּחְתּוֹ וְהִכְרַתִּי אֹתוֹ וְאֵת | כָּל־הַזֹּנִים אַחֲרָיו לִזְנוֹת אַחֲרֵי הַמֹּלֶךְ מִקֶּרֶב עַמָּם: 6 וְהַנֶּפֶשׁ אֲשֶׁר תִּפְנֶה אֶל־הָאֹבֹת וְאֶל־הַיִּדְּעֹנִים לִזְנוֹת אַחֲרֵיהֶם וְנָתַתִּי אֶת־פָּנַי בַּנֶּפֶשׁ הַהִוא וְהִכְרַתִּי אֹתוֹ מִקֶּרֶב עַמּוֹ: 7 וְהִתְקַדִּשְׁתֶּם וִהְיִיתֶם קְדֹשִׁים כִּי אֲנִי יְהֹוָה אֱלֹהֵיכֶם: [SIXTH READING / SEVENTH WHEN JOINED] 8 וּשְׁמַרְתֶּם אֶת־חֻקֹּתַי וַעֲשִׂיתֶם אֹתָם אֲנִי יְהֹוָה מְקַדִּשְׁכֶם: 9 כִּי־אִישׁ אִישׁ אֲשֶׁר יְקַלֵּל אֶת־אָבִיו וְאֶת־אִמּוֹ מוֹת יוּמָת אָבִיו וְאִמּוֹ קִלֵּל דָּמָיו בּוֹ: 10 וְאִישׁ אֲשֶׁר יִנְאַף אֶת־אֵשֶׁת אִישׁ אֲשֶׁר יִנְאַף אֶת־אֵשֶׁת רֵעֵהוּ מוֹת־יוּמַת הַנֹּאֵף וְהַנֹּאָפֶת: 11 וְאִישׁ אֲשֶׁר יִשְׁכַּב אֶת־אֵשֶׁת אָבִיו עֶרְוַת אָבִיו גִּלָּה מוֹת־יוּמְתוּ שְׁנֵיהֶם דְּמֵיהֶם בָּם: 12 וְאִישׁ אֲשֶׁר יִשְׁכַּב אֶת־כַּלָּתוֹ מוֹת יוּמְתוּ שְׁנֵיהֶם תֶּבֶל עָשׂוּ דְּמֵיהֶם בָּם: 13 וְאִישׁ אֲשֶׁר יִשְׁכַּב אֶת־זָכָר מִשְׁכְּבֵי אִשָּׁה תּוֹעֵבָה עָשׂוּ שְׁנֵיהֶם מוֹת יוּמָתוּ דְּמֵיהֶם בָּם: 14 וְאִישׁ אֲשֶׁר יִקַּח אֶת־אִשָּׁה וְאֶת־אִמָּהּ זִמָּה הִוא בָּאֵשׁ יִשְׂרְפוּ אֹתוֹ וְאֶתְהֶן וְלֹא־תִהְיֶה זִמָּה בְּתוֹכְכֶם: 15 וְאִישׁ אֲשֶׁר יִתֵּן שְׁכָבְתּוֹ

By ignoring a violation once, you are likely to ignore it repeatedly. People will say: Why don't you ignore what I did just like you ignored it last time? (*Rabbi Ḥayyim ibn Attar, 18th century*).

7. You should sanctify yourselves (by separating from idolatry) and be holy. To receive sustenance from the forces of holiness you must strive to be in a state of surrender to a Higher Authority. Those unwilling to make this effort follow the path of idol-worship, which does not require any compromise of the ego.

A further reason why people choose to receive their sustenance by means of idol-worship is because the short-term benefits are greater. The sustenance of the forces of evil is rooted in the transcendent realm of Godliness beyond reason and logic, so energies are bestowed there even without the appropriate effort (*Rabbi Shneur Zalman of Lyady, 18th century*).

10. (If) a (grown) man commits adultery with (another grown) man's wife. God orchestrates people's lives in a way that everyone should meet the person whom they are destined to marry. When a man commits adultery, he not only betrays the woman's husband, he also denies God, who "arranged" this marriage (*Rabbi Mordecai ha-Kohen, 17th century*).

leviticus 20:4–15 — kedoshim

- ❖ ⁴ If the public consistently ignores that man, when he gives (even) his (illegitimate) offspring to Molech, not putting him to death, ⁵ then I will devote My time (away from all My affairs and deal) with this man and with his family. (But) I will (only) cut him off, and all who follow after him to go astray after Molech, from among the people, (but I will not cut off his family too).

- ❖ ⁶ (If) a person turns to *'ov* or *yidde'oni*, to go astray after them, I will set My attention upon that person, and I will cut him off from among his people.

⁷ You should sanctify yourselves (by separating from idolatry) and be holy, for I am God, your God. [SIXTH READING / SEVENTH WHEN JOINED] ⁸ You should observe My suprarational commands and fulfil them. I am God, who sanctifies you.

- ❖ ⁹ If any man curses his father or his mother, he should be put to death, (even if) he has cursed his father or his mother (after their death). His blood(y death by stoning) is his own (fault).

- ❖ ¹⁰ (If) a (grown) man commits adultery with (another grown) man's wife: (if the person he) committed adultery with (was) the wife of his fellow (Jew), the adulterer and the adulteress should both be put to death (by strangulation).

- ❖ ¹¹ A man who lies with his father's wife (is considered to) have uncovered his father's nakedness. Both of them should be put to death. Their blood(y death by stoning) is their own (fault).

- ❖ ¹² (If) a man lies with his daughter-in-law, both of them should be put to death. They have committed a shameful act. Their blood(y death by stoning) is their own (fault).

- ❖ ¹³ (If) a man lies with a man as one would with a woman, both of them have committed an abominable act. They should both be put to death. Their blood(y death by stoning) is their own (fault).

- ❖ ¹⁴ (If) a man takes a woman (who is already his mother-in-law) and her mother (in marriage, in addition to his initial wife), it is the advice (of the evil inclination). They should burn him and them in fire (but not his initial wife), so there should be no evil advice in your midst.

- ❖ ¹⁵ A man who lies with an animal should be put to death, and the animal should be killed.

The death penalty is not a punishment for the sinner, but a method for his atonement. If a person gave every one of his children to Molech, his sin was so grave that it could not even be atoned through the death penalty (*Rabbi Bahya b. Asher, 13th century*).

4. If the public consistently ignores (*ha'lem ya'limu*) that man. The verse literally reads, "Ignore, they will ignore," the double expression teaching you the importance of consistency.

ויקרא כ:טו-כב — קדושים

בִּבְהֵמָה מוֹת יוּמָת וְאֶת־הַבְּהֵמָה תַּהֲרֹגוּ: 16 וְאִשָּׁה אֲשֶׁר תִּקְרַב אֶל־כָּל־בְּהֵמָה לְרִבְעָה אֹתָהּ וְהָרַגְתָּ אֶת־הָאִשָּׁה וְאֶת־הַבְּהֵמָה מוֹת יוּמָתוּ דְּמֵיהֶם בָּם: 17 וְאִישׁ אֲשֶׁר־יִקַּח אֶת־אֲחֹתוֹ בַּת־אָבִיו אוֹ בַת־אִמּוֹ וְרָאָה אֶת־עֶרְוָתָהּ וְהִיא־תִרְאֶה אֶת־עֶרְוָתוֹ חֶסֶד הוּא וְנִכְרְתוּ לְעֵינֵי בְּנֵי עַמָּם עֶרְוַת אֲחֹתוֹ גִּלָּה עֲוֺנוֹ יִשָּׂא: 18 וְאִישׁ אֲשֶׁר־יִשְׁכַּב אֶת־אִשָּׁה דָּוָה וְגִלָּה אֶת־עֶרְוָתָהּ אֶת־מְקֹרָהּ הֶעֱרָה וְהִוא גִּלְּתָה אֶת־מְקוֹר דָּמֶיהָ וְנִכְרְתוּ שְׁנֵיהֶם מִקֶּרֶב עַמָּם: 19 וְעֶרְוַת אֲחוֹת אִמְּךָ וַאֲחוֹת אָבִיךָ לֹא תְגַלֵּה כִּי אֶת־שְׁאֵרוֹ הֶעֱרָה עֲוֺנָם יִשָּׂאוּ: 20 וְאִישׁ אֲשֶׁר יִשְׁכַּב אֶת־דֹּדָתוֹ עֶרְוַת דֹּדוֹ גִּלָּה חֶטְאָם יִשָּׂאוּ עֲרִירִים יָמֻתוּ: 21 וְאִישׁ אֲשֶׁר יִקַּח אֶת־אֵשֶׁת אָחִיו נִדָּה הִוא עֶרְוַת אָחִיו גִּלָּה עֲרִירִים יִהְיוּ: 22 וּשְׁמַרְתֶּם אֶת־כָּל־חֻקֹּתַי וְאֶת־כָּל־מִשְׁפָּטַי וַעֲשִׂיתֶם אֹתָם וְלֹא־תָקִיא

It turns out, then, that the rational and suprarational commands *both* contain rational *and* suprarational elements. Many details of the rational precepts have no reason, and even the so-called suprarational commandments also have a reason, but not a "revealed" one. So when we say that a certain precept is "rational" or "suprarational," we are referring to which aspect of the command *predominates*.

Why is there a need for both types of commandment?

Suprarational commands foster your unquestioning subservience to God, as you are told to obey a Divine decree that is incomprehensible. On the other hand, rational commands promote your enjoyment and enthusiasm in the observance of the commandments, since you can appreciate the value of observing such precepts.

Since God wishes you to fulfil each of His commands with *both* obedience and enthusiasm, He incorporated suprarational *and* rational elements into all of them (*Rabbi Menahem Mendel Schneerson, 20th century*).

My suprarational commands. A person should not say, "I find pork disgusting," or "I don't want to wear a mixture of wool and linen." Rather, he should say, "I *do* wish to, but what can I do since my Father in Heaven has imposed these decrees upon me?" (*Rashi, 11th century*).

spiritual vitamin

> *Taharat ha-mishpahah* (family purity) is a basic factor in the preservation of peace and harmony (*shalom bayit*) in the home, which is vitally strengthened by it.

leviticus 20:16–22 — kedoshim

- ❖ ¹⁶ (If) a woman comes close to any animal so that it will mate with her, you should kill the woman and the animal. They should both be put to death. Their blood(y death by stoning) is their own (fault).

- ❖ ¹⁷ If a man takes his sister (in marriage), either his father's daughter or his mother's daughter, and he sees her nakedness, and she sees his nakedness, it is a disgraceful act. They will be cut off from the sight of the members of their people, because he uncovered his sister's nakedness. He will bear (the consequences of) his sin.

- ❖ ¹⁸ (If) a man lies with a woman who is menstruating and uncovers her nakedness, he has exposed her source, and she has exposed the source of her blood. Both of them will be cut off from among their people.

- ❖ ¹⁹ You should not uncover the nakedness of your mother's sister or your father's sister, for he (who does so) has exposed his close relative. They will bear (the consequences of) their sin.

- ❖ ²⁰ (If) a man lies with his aunt, he (is considered to) have uncovered his uncle's nakedness. They will bear (the consequences of) their transgression. They will die childless.

- ❖ ²¹ (If) a man takes his brother's wife, it is a repulsive act. He (is considered to) have uncovered his brother's nakedness. They will be childless.

²² You should guard all My suprarational commands and all My rational commands, and observe them. Then the land, where I am bringing you to live, will not vomit you out.

---

17. If a man takes his sister (in marriage) ... it is a disgraceful act (ḥesed). Ḥesed means "disgraceful" in Aramaic, but in Hebrew it means "kindness."

Human love is a manifestation of God's kindness. Through forbidden relations—bad love—a man takes Divine ḥesed and drags it to the lowest realms of impurity (*Rabbi Israel Ba'al Shem Tov, 18th century*).

22. You should guard all My suprarational commands. The suprarational commandments are "decrees of the King" which have no reason (*Rashi, 11th century*).

The suprarational commandments do not have a *revealed* reason. Nevertheless, it is appropriate to meditate upon their significance, and to find explanations for them whenever possible. But we cannot say why one offering should be a lamb, while another is a ram, and why a certain number of them should be brought. Those who trouble themselves to find a cause for any of these detailed rules are, in my eyes, devoid of sense (*Maimonides, 12th century*).

In contrast to *Rashi's* view that suprarational commands are "decrees of the King which have *no reason*," Maimonides maintained that the suprarational commands *do* have reasons. It is only that they "do not have a *revealed* reason," i.e., they have a rationale, but it is too sublime for the human intellect to appreciate completely.

However, Maimonides also maintained that many *details* of the commandments do not have any rationale whatsoever. So even the totally rational commandments do possess suprarational elements, since many of the details of these commands have no explanation.

ויקרא כ:כב-כז | קדושים

אֶתְכֶם הָאָרֶץ אֲשֶׁר אֲנִי מֵבִיא אֶתְכֶם שָׁמָּה לָשֶׁבֶת בָּהּ: 23 [SEVENTH READING] וְלֹא תֵלְכוּ בְּחֻקֹּת הַגּוֹי אֲשֶׁר־אֲנִי מְשַׁלֵּחַ מִפְּנֵיכֶם כִּי אֶת־כָּל־אֵלֶּה עָשׂוּ וָאָקֻץ בָּם: 24 וָאֹמַר לָכֶם אַתֶּם תִּירְשׁוּ אֶת־אַדְמָתָם וַאֲנִי אֶתְּנֶנָּה לָכֶם לָרֶשֶׁת אֹתָהּ אֶרֶץ זָבַת חָלָב וּדְבָשׁ אֲנִי יְהֹוָה אֱלֹהֵיכֶם אֲשֶׁר־הִבְדַּלְתִּי אֶתְכֶם מִן־הָעַמִּים: 25 [MAFTIR] וְהִבְדַּלְתֶּם בֵּין־הַבְּהֵמָה הַטְּהֹרָה לַטְּמֵאָה וּבֵין־הָעוֹף הַטָּמֵא לַטָּהֹר וְלֹא־תְשַׁקְּצוּ אֶת־נַפְשֹׁתֵיכֶם בַּבְּהֵמָה וּבָעוֹף וּבְכֹל אֲשֶׁר תִּרְמֹשׂ הָאֲדָמָה אֲשֶׁר־הִבְדַּלְתִּי לָכֶם לְטַמֵּא: 26 וִהְיִיתֶם לִי קְדֹשִׁים כִּי קָדוֹשׁ אֲנִי יְהֹוָה וָאַבְדִּל אֶתְכֶם מִן־הָעַמִּים לִהְיוֹת לִי: 27 וְאִישׁ אוֹ־אִשָּׁה כִּי־יִהְיֶה בָהֶם אוֹב אוֹ יִדְּעֹנִי מוֹת יוּמָתוּ בָּאֶבֶן יִרְגְּמוּ אֹתָם דְּמֵיהֶם בָּם: פ פ פ

ס״ד פסוקים, ונג״ה סימן. מ״י זה״ב סימן.

A penitent who previously lived a non-observant life should *not* say "I do wish to transgress the commandments, but what can I do since my Father in Heaven has imposed these decrees upon me?" For since he has tasted sin, there is a danger that he may return to his former ways if he actively desires to transgress the commandments (*Rabbi Dov Baer of Mezhirech, 18th century*).

leviticus 20:23–27 — kedoshim

[SEVENTH READING] **23** You should not follow the practices of the nation that I am driving out before you, for they committed all these (sins), and I was disgusted with them. **24** That is why I said to you: You should possess their land, and I will give it to you so that you can inherit it. (It is) a land flowing with milk and honey.

I am God, your God, who has distinguished you from the nations.

- [MAFTIR] **25** You should distinguish between animals that are pure (to you, because they have been slaughtered properly) and those that are impure (to you, because they have not been slaughtered properly); between birds that are pure (to you, because they have been slaughtered properly) and those that are impure (to you, because they have not been slaughtered properly). You should not make yourselves disgusting through such animals and birds, or any (creature) which crawls on the earth, that I have distinguished for you to be impure (and thus, forbidden).

26 You should be holy to Me, for I, God, am holy, and I have distinguished you from the nations, to be Mine.

- **27** A man or a woman who practices (the sorcery of the) *'ov* or *yidde'oni* should be put to death (if witnesses were present when they sinned, and the sinners were warned not to perform the sin). They should be pelted with stones. Their blood(y death by stoning) is their own (fault).

Haftarot: Kedoshim—page 1359.   *'Aharei Mot–Kedoshim*—page 1358.   *Rosh Ḥodesh*—page 1417.

Maftir: Rosh Ḥodesh—page 1000 (28:9–15).

The rule that a person should desire to transgress the commandments, and refrain only because "my Father in Heaven has imposed these decrees upon me," only applies to suprarational commands. You should not desire to carry out the rational prohibitions, such as theft, murder and disgracing your parents (*Maimonides, 12th century*).

'Emor means, **"Speak** to the children and **educate** them." More precisely it means to **speak softly.** A teacher must **bond** with his or her students, giving them the **feeling** that here is a teacher **who cares** whether they **understand the material** or not.

'EMOR
אמור

LAWS ADDRESSED TO THE PRIESTS	21:1 – 22:31
SANCTIFYING THE NAME OF GOD	22:32-33
SABBATH AND FESTIVALS	23:1–44
THE CANDELABRUM AND MULTISURFACE BREAD	24:1–9
THE BLASPHEMER	24:10–23

NAME
'Emor

MEANING
"Speak"

LINES IN TORAH SCROLL
215

PARASHIYYOT
11 open; 6 closed

VERSES
124

WORDS
1614

LETTERS
6106

DATE
Nisan - 20 Iyyar, 2449

LOCATION
Sinai Desert

KEY PEOPLE
Moses, Aaron, the Blasphemer

MITZVOT
24 positive; 39 prohibitions

CHARACTER PROFILE

NAME
The Blasphemer

PARENTS
Shelomith daughter of Dibri and an Egyptian man

TRIBE
Dan

ACHIEVEMENTS
The laws of blasphemy were taught by God to Moses because of his actions.

KNOWN FOR
He wanted to pitch his tent in the camp of Dan (his mother's tribe) and fought with another tribesman. After the case was solved in court and he lost, he cursed God. He was placed in jail until God commanded Moses how he was to be punished. He was taken out of the camp and stoned.

PERFECT SACRIFICES

Any sacrifice offered to God had to be free of any blemish or imperfection. All things that we use to worship God ought to be as beautiful and perfect as possible (22:20).

SANCTIFYING GOD

A fundamental principle of Judaism is the commandment to sanctify God's name. This includes acting in a moral and upstanding manner and demonstrating commitment to ideals that are Godly. At the extreme, a person may be called on to sacrifice his or her life (22:32).

JOY

We are commanded to rejoice during the festivals. Joy brings you to a higher spiritual state and strengthens your connection with God (23:40).

אמור ויקרא כא:א-ט

כא 1 וַיֹּאמֶר יְהֹוָה אֶל־מֹשֶׁה אֱמֹר אֶל־הַכֹּהֲנִים בְּנֵי אַהֲרֹן וְאָמַרְתָּ אֲלֵהֶם לְנֶפֶשׁ לֹא־יִטַּמָּא בְּעַמָּיו: 2 כִּי אִם־לִשְׁאֵרוֹ הַקָּרֹב אֵלָיו לְאִמּוֹ וּלְאָבִיו וְלִבְנוֹ וּלְבִתּוֹ וּלְאָחִיו: 3 וְלַאֲחֹתוֹ הַבְּתוּלָה הַקְּרוֹבָה אֵלָיו אֲשֶׁר לֹא־הָיְתָה לְאִישׁ לָהּ יִטַּמָּא: 4 לֹא יִטַּמָּא בַּעַל בְּעַמָּיו לְהֵחַלּוֹ: 5 לֹא [יקרחה כ׳] יִקְרְחוּ קָרְחָה בְּרֹאשָׁם וּפְאַת זְקָנָם לֹא יְגַלֵּחוּ וּבִבְשָׂרָם לֹא יִשְׂרְטוּ שָׂרָטֶת: 6 קְדֹשִׁים יִהְיוּ לֵאלֹהֵיהֶם וְלֹא יְחַלְּלוּ שֵׁם אֱלֹהֵיהֶם כִּי אֶת־אִשֵּׁי יְהֹוָה לֶחֶם אֱלֹהֵיהֶם הֵם מַקְרִיבִם וְהָיוּ קֹדֶשׁ: 7 אִשָּׁה זֹנָה וַחֲלָלָה לֹא יִקָּחוּ וְאִשָּׁה גְּרוּשָׁה מֵאִישָׁהּ לֹא יִקָּחוּ כִּי־קָדֹשׁ הוּא לֵאלֹהָיו: 8 וְקִדַּשְׁתּוֹ כִּי־אֶת־לֶחֶם אֱלֹהֶיךָ הוּא מַקְרִיב קָדֹשׁ יִהְיֶה־לָּךְ כִּי קָדוֹשׁ אֲנִי יְהֹוָה מְקַדִּשְׁכֶם: 9 וּבַת אִישׁ כֹּהֵן כִּי

21:1 Speak to the priests, Aaron's sons, and say to them. The double expression, *"Speak ... and say"* means that, in addition to telling the priests to observe these precepts, Moses should also warn the adult priests about educating their children in these areas (*Rashi, 11th century*).

How do we know that the verse comes to warn the adults about educating the children? Because, normally the Torah states, "Aaron's sons, the priests," but this verse changes the order, "the priests, Aaron's sons," suggesting that the priests are required to educate their sons in these laws (*Rabbi Joel Sirkes, 16th–17th century*).

Let no (priest) become ritually impure. If a corpse is found abandoned in a desolate area and there is no one to attend to its burial, even a priest is obligated to become ritually impure to care for the corpse (*Rashi, 11th century*).

The priests are a particularly benevolent group, who devote much of their time to guiding the rest of the people on the right path. Since this requires them to rebuke the people, they are warned: *"Let no (priest) become ritually impure with a person among your people."*

When you are "among your people," giving them words of rebuke, be careful not to have any ulterior motive—because if you do, you will become "ritually impure" (*Rabbi Dov Baer of Mezhirech, 18th century*).

8. You should (force him) to be holy. The verse reads literally, "You should sanctify him, for he offers up the food-offering of your God." You learn here that a man's sanctity does not necessarily depend on his intelligence or righteousness; it comes because God gives him sacred tasks to fulfil. You respect a priest because he fulfils his mission, presenting food-offerings to God (*Rabbi Abraham Samuel Benjamin Sofer, 19th century*).

> **kabbalah bites**
>
> **21:1** *Rashi* interprets this verse as an instruction "to warn the adults about educating their children." The Hebrew word *le-hazhir* ("to warn") is related to the word *zohar*, meaning "illumination."
>
> Genuine education must be bright and brilliant. Simply telling others what to do will not suffice. Make all your words sparkle with light and they will be taken seriously.

parashat 'emor

21 Laws Addressed to the Priests

¹ God said to Moses: Speak to the priests, Aaron's sons, and say to them:

- Let no (priest) become ritually impure (through contact) with a (dead) person (when there are others) among his people (who can tend to the burial).

- ² Except for: (his wife, who is) his closest relative, his mother, his father, his son, his daughter, his brother, ³ his virgin sister, if she is still close to him (because) she was never with a man. He must make himself ritually impure (to bury) her (and all his other close relatives).

- ⁴ A husband should not make himself ritually impure for (a wife) who violated his sacred character (because, as a priest, he was forbidden to marry her. However, this is only when there are others) among his people (who can tend to her burial).

- ⁵ (The priests) should not make bald patches on their heads (as a sign of mourning).

- They should not shave the extremities of their beards.

- They should not make scratches in their flesh. (If they do, they will be liable for every) scratch.

- ⁶ (Even against their will, the court may force) them to be holy to their God (by following the above laws), so they should not desecrate their God's name. For they are the ones that offer up God's fire-offerings, the food-offering of their God, so they should be holy.

- ⁷ They may not marry an immoral woman (who has had forbidden relations), nor a woman who (was born from a union which) violated the sacred character (of the priesthood), nor may they marry a woman who is divorced from her husband, for each (priest) is holy to his God.

- ⁸ (If he wishes to marry a divorcee) you should (force him) to be holy (against his will), for he offers up the food-offering of your God.

- You should treat him as a holy (person, by honoring him first in all matters), for I am your Holy God who makes you holy.

- ⁹ If a priest's (married) daughter violates her sacred character through adultery, she violates the sacred character of her father. She should be burned in fire.

Food for thought

1. Should authority figures be answerable to a higher moral code?

2. Does power inevitably corrupt?

3. Should priests (*Kohanim*) feel special today?

ויקרא כא:ט-כג

תָּחֵל לִזְנוֹת אֶת־אָבִיהָ הִיא מְחַלֶּלֶת בָּאֵשׁ תִּשָּׂרֵף: ס 10 וְהַכֹּהֵן הַגָּדוֹל מֵאֶחָיו אֲשֶׁר־יוּצַק עַל־רֹאשׁוֹ ׀ שֶׁמֶן הַמִּשְׁחָה וּמִלֵּא אֶת־יָדוֹ לִלְבֹּשׁ אֶת־הַבְּגָדִים אֶת־רֹאשׁוֹ לֹא יִפְרָע וּבְגָדָיו לֹא יִפְרֹם: 11 וְעַל כָּל־נַפְשֹׁת מֵת לֹא יָבֹא לְאָבִיו וּלְאִמּוֹ לֹא יִטַּמָּא: 12 וּמִן־הַמִּקְדָּשׁ לֹא יֵצֵא וְלֹא יְחַלֵּל אֵת מִקְדַּשׁ אֱלֹהָיו כִּי נֵזֶר שֶׁמֶן מִשְׁחַת אֱלֹהָיו עָלָיו אֲנִי יְהֹוָה: 13 וְהוּא אִשָּׁה בִבְתוּלֶיהָ יִקָּח: 14 אַלְמָנָה וּגְרוּשָׁה וַחֲלָלָה זֹנָה אֶת־אֵלֶּה לֹא יִקָּח כִּי אִם־בְּתוּלָה מֵעַמָּיו יִקַּח אִשָּׁה: 15 וְלֹא־יְחַלֵּל זַרְעוֹ בְּעַמָּיו כִּי אֲנִי יְהֹוָה מְקַדְּשׁוֹ: ס [SECOND READING] 16 וַיְדַבֵּר יְהֹוָה אֶל־מֹשֶׁה לֵּאמֹר: 17 דַּבֵּר אֶל־אַהֲרֹן לֵאמֹר אִישׁ מִזַּרְעֲךָ לְדֹרֹתָם אֲשֶׁר יִהְיֶה בוֹ מוּם לֹא יִקְרַב לְהַקְרִיב לֶחֶם אֱלֹהָיו: 18 כִּי כָל־אִישׁ אֲשֶׁר־בּוֹ מוּם לֹא יִקְרָב אִישׁ עִוֵּר אוֹ פִסֵּחַ אוֹ חָרֻם אוֹ שָׂרוּעַ: 19 אוֹ אִישׁ אֲשֶׁר־יִהְיֶה בוֹ שֶׁבֶר רָגֶל אוֹ שֶׁבֶר יָד: 20 אוֹ־גִבֵּן אוֹ־דַק אוֹ תְּבַלֻּל בְּעֵינוֹ אוֹ גָרָב אוֹ יַלֶּפֶת אוֹ מְרוֹחַ אָשֶׁךְ: 21 כָּל־אִישׁ אֲשֶׁר־בּוֹ מוּם מִזֶּרַע אַהֲרֹן הַכֹּהֵן לֹא יִגַּשׁ לְהַקְרִיב אֶת־אִשֵּׁי יְהֹוָה מוּם בּוֹ אֵת לֶחֶם אֱלֹהָיו לֹא יִגַּשׁ לְהַקְרִיב: 22 לֶחֶם אֱלֹהָיו מִקָּדְשֵׁי הַקֳּדָשִׁים וּמִן־הַקֳּדָשִׁים יֹאכֵל: 23 אַךְ אֶל־הַפָּרֹכֶת לֹא יָבֹא וְאֶל־

15. I am God, who sanctifies him. Priesthood is not a profession that someone chooses voluntarily; it is a life mission that God assigns to a priest upon birth. A priest can shun his duties temporarily, but he will never lose the priesthood.

In a certain sense, all Jews have this priestly quality. A Jew is born a Jew and can never be stripped of that quality. Even if he has forsaken his Jewishness temporarily, he can always return to a lifestyle that is inherently his (*Rabbi Samson Raphael Hirsch, 19th century*).

spiritual vitamin

> Never give up hope. Always strive to free yourself from the influences and limitations of your environment, as well as from internal temptations.

Laws Addressed to the High Priest

[10] The (High) Priest, who is elevated above his brothers, upon whose head the anointing oil was poured and who was inaugurated to wear the (special) garments (of the High Priest must observe the following):

- (When he is in a state of mourning) he should not leave his hair uncut (for thirty days) or tear his garments.

- [11] He should not come (under the same roof) as any dead bodies.

- He should not make himself ritually impure (to bury) his father or his mother (if there are others who can tend to the matter).

- [12] He should not leave the Sanctuary (to follow the funeral procession of his parents. He may continue to carry out the service of the Sanctuary in a state of mourning, for in doing so) he will not violate the sacred character of his God's holy Sanctuary, for (being the High Priest) the crown of his God's anointing oil is upon him. I am God.

- [13] He should marry a woman who is a virgin. [14] He may not marry the following: a widow, a divorcee, a woman who (was born from a union which) violated the sacred character (of the priesthood), or an immoral woman (who has had forbidden relations). He should only take a virgin of his people as a wife, [15] and (thus) he will not violate the sacred character of his children from among his people. (All this is) because I am God, who sanctifies him.

Blemishes that Disqualify a Priest from Service

[SECOND READING] [16] God spoke to Moses, saying, [17] Speak to Aaron, saying:

Anyone among your descendants who has a blemish should not come close (in service), to offer up food for his God. [18] For (it is) not (flattering to God) that any man who has a blemish should come close (to serve):

- A blind man, or a lame one, or one with a sunken nose or with disproportionate limbs, [19] or a man who has a broken leg or a broken arm, [20] or one with unusually long eyebrows, or a cataract, or an imperfect iris, dry lesions, weeping sores, or one with crushed testicles.

- [21] Any man from among the children of Aaron the priest who has any (other) blemish should not come close to offer up God's fire-offerings.

- (So long as) there is a blemish in him, he should not come close to offer up food to his God (but if the blemish passes, he may serve).

- [22] (Even a blemished priest) may eat his God's food, (both) from the most holy (sacrifices) and from the (less) holy ones.

- [23] But he may not come to the partition (to sprinkle blood upon it), nor may he

ויקרא כא:כג - כב:י | אמור

הַמִּזְבֵּחַ לֹא יִגַּשׁ כִּי־מ֣וּם בּ֑וֹ וְלֹ֤א יְחַלֵּל֙ אֶת־מִקְדָּשַׁ֔י כִּ֛י אֲנִ֥י יְהֹוָ֖ה מְקַדְּשָֽׁם:
24 וַיְדַבֵּ֣ר מֹשֶׁ֔ה אֶֽל־אַהֲרֹ֖ן וְאֶל־בָּנָ֑יו וְאֶֽל־כׇּל־בְּנֵ֥י יִשְׂרָאֵֽל: פ

כב 1 וַיְדַבֵּ֥ר יְהֹוָ֖ה אֶל־מֹשֶׁ֥ה לֵּאמֹֽר: 2 דַּבֵּ֨ר אֶֽל־אַהֲרֹ֜ן וְאֶל־בָּנָ֗יו וְיִנָּֽזְרוּ֙ מִקׇּדְשֵׁ֣י בְנֵֽי־יִשְׂרָאֵ֔ל וְלֹ֥א יְחַלְּל֖וּ אֶת־שֵׁ֣ם קׇדְשִׁ֑י אֲשֶׁ֨ר הֵ֧ם מַקְדִּשִׁ֛ים לִ֖י אֲנִ֥י יְהֹוָֽה: 3 אֱמֹ֣ר אֲלֵהֶ֗ם לְדֹרֹ֨תֵיכֶ֜ם כׇּל־אִ֣ישׁ ׀ אֲשֶׁר־יִקְרַ֣ב מִכׇּל־זַרְעֲכֶ֗ם אֶל־הַקֳּדָשִׁים֙ אֲשֶׁ֨ר יַקְדִּ֤ישׁוּ בְנֵֽי־יִשְׂרָאֵל֙ לַֽיהֹוָ֔ה וְטֻמְאָת֖וֹ עָלָ֑יו וְנִכְרְתָ֞ה הַנֶּ֧פֶשׁ הַהִ֛וא מִלְּפָנַ֖י אֲנִ֥י יְהֹוָֽה: 4 אִ֣ישׁ אִ֞ישׁ מִזֶּ֣רַע אַהֲרֹ֗ן וְה֤וּא צָר֙וּעַ֙ א֣וֹ זָ֔ב בַּקֳּדָשִׁים֙ לֹ֣א יֹאכַ֔ל עַ֖ד אֲשֶׁ֣ר יִטְהָ֑ר וְהַנֹּגֵ֙עַ֙ בְּכׇל־טְמֵא־נֶ֔פֶשׁ א֣וֹ אִ֔ישׁ אֲשֶׁר־תֵּצֵ֥א מִמֶּ֖נּוּ שִׁכְבַת־זָֽרַע: 5 אוֹ־אִישׁ֙ אֲשֶׁ֣ר יִגַּ֔ע בְּכׇל־שֶׁ֖רֶץ אֲשֶׁ֣ר יִטְמָא־ל֑וֹ א֤וֹ בְאָדָם֙ אֲשֶׁ֣ר יִטְמָא־ל֔וֹ לְכֹ֖ל טֻמְאָתֽוֹ: 6 נֶ֚פֶשׁ אֲשֶׁ֣ר תִּגַּע־בּ֔וֹ וְטָמְאָ֖ה עַד־הָעָ֑רֶב וְלֹ֤א יֹאכַל֙ מִן־הַקֳּדָשִׁ֔ים כִּ֛י אִם־רָחַ֥ץ בְּשָׂר֖וֹ בַּמָּֽיִם: 7 וּבָ֥א הַשֶּׁ֖מֶשׁ וְטָהֵ֑ר וְאַחַר֙ יֹאכַ֣ל מִן־הַקֳּדָשִׁ֔ים כִּ֥י לַחְמ֖וֹ הֽוּא: 8 נְבֵלָ֧ה וּטְרֵפָ֛ה לֹ֥א יֹאכַ֖ל לְטׇמְאָה־בָ֑הּ אֲנִ֖י יְהֹוָֽה: 9 וְשָׁמְר֣וּ אֶת־מִשְׁמַרְתִּ֗י וְלֹֽא־יִשְׂא֤וּ עָלָיו֙ חֵ֔טְא וּמֵ֥תוּ ב֖וֹ כִּ֣י יְחַלְּלֻ֑הוּ אֲנִ֥י יְהֹוָ֖ה מְקַדְּשָֽׁם: 10 וְכׇל־זָ֖ר לֹא־יֹ֣אכַל קֹ֑דֶשׁ תּוֹשַׁ֥ב כֹּהֵ֛ן וְשָׂכִ֖יר לֹא־יֹ֥אכַל קֹֽדֶשׁ:

22:2 Speak to Aaron and to his sons. There are two types of righteous people: those who were born into a righteous family and were raised in piety all their lives, and those who have chosen the path of righteousness on their own accord. The latter is less prone to inadvertently slipping away from their way of life—they *chose* that path, and it is what they wanted for themselves. However, this is not so with the first type. They need to be cautioned not to fall into complacency.

Therefore, the Torah says, "Speak to Aaron and *to his sons.*" Say to them: True, you have an inherent greatness because you are the sons of Aaron, but it is precisely for that reason that you need more care with your holiness and purity (*Rabbi Elimelech of Lyzhansk, 18th century*).

3. The holy sacrifices which the children of Israel consecrate to God. It is not the priest who consecrates objects to God, but the ordinary Israelite. It is only that the Israelite *entrusts* his consecrated objects to the hands of the priest on his behalf.

This also is a message to the priest not to act arrogantly or condescendingly toward the "children of Israel." A priest is only entrusted to carry out holy work on behalf of the nation (*Rabbi Samson Raphael Hirsch, 19th century*).

come close to the (outer) altar, because he has a blemish, and (thus) he should not violate the sacred character of My holy things, for I am God who makes them holy.

²⁴ Moses told (this to) Aaron and his sons, and to all of the children of Israel.

Restrictions to the Consumption of Sacrifices and *Terumah* (Heave-Offering)

22 ¹ God spoke to Moses, saying: ² Speak to Aaron and to his sons, (and tell them that if they are in a state of ritual impurity) they should keep away from the holy (sacrifices) of the children of Israel, (and from sacrifices that the priests themselves) sanctify to Me, so as not to violate the sacred character of My holy name. I am God. ³ Say to them:

- ❖ Throughout your generations, (if) any man from among any of your descendants comes near to (eat) the holy sacrifices which the children of Israel consecrate to God while he is in a state of ritual impurity—that soul will be cut off from before me. I am God.

- ❖ ⁴ If any man from among Aaron's descendants who has *tzara'at*, or has had an (unhealthy, watery venereal) discharge, should not eat from the holy sacrifices, until he renders himself ritually pure (by immersing in a ritual-pool and waiting until the evening).

- ❖ (Likewise,) a person who becomes ritually impure by contact with a (dead) person, or a person who has a seminal emission, ⁵ or a person who becomes ritually impure through contact with a creeping creature, or he becomes ritually impure through touching (even part of a dead) body, (or a person) who becomes ritually impure through any other source of ritual impurity (such as one who touches a man who has an unhealthy venereal discharge, or a woman who is menstruating normally or abnormally, or a woman who has given birth) ⁶—the person who touches (such a source of ritual impurity) will remain ritually impure until the evening, and he may not eat from the holy sacrifices unless he has immersed his body in (the) water (of a ritual-pool). ⁷ Then, when the sun sets, he becomes ritually pure, and afterwards, he may eat the holy (*terumah*), which is his food.

- ❖ ⁸ He should not eat a carcass (of a kosher species) or anything that was torn (because) it will render him ritually impure (and he will not be able to eat from the sacrifices). I am God.

- ❖ ⁹ (The priests) should observe My precautions and not bear a sin by (eating *terumah* in a state of ritual impurity) and thereby die through it, since they will have violated its holy character. I am God who sanctifies them.

- ❖ ¹⁰ No non-priest may eat holy (*terumah*).

- ❖ A (slave who refused to be freed and is) resident with a priest, or his (regular Hebrew slave) who works for him, may not eat holy (*terumah*).

ויקרא כב:יא–כב אמור

11 וְכֹהֵן כִּי־יִקְנֶה נֶפֶשׁ קִנְיַן כַּסְפּוֹ הוּא יֹאכַל בּוֹ וִילִיד בֵּיתוֹ הֵם יֹאכְלוּ בְלַחְמוֹ: 12 וּבַת־כֹּהֵן כִּי תִהְיֶה לְאִישׁ זָר הִוא בִּתְרוּמַת הַקֳּדָשִׁים לֹא תֹאכֵל: 13 וּבַת־כֹּהֵן כִּי תִהְיֶה אַלְמָנָה וּגְרוּשָׁה וְזֶרַע אֵין לָהּ וְשָׁבָה אֶל־בֵּית אָבִיהָ כִּנְעוּרֶיהָ מִלֶּחֶם אָבִיהָ תֹּאכֵל וְכָל־זָר לֹא־יֹאכַל בּוֹ: 14 וְאִישׁ כִּי־יֹאכַל קֹדֶשׁ בִּשְׁגָגָה וְיָסַף חֲמִשִׁיתוֹ עָלָיו וְנָתַן לַכֹּהֵן אֶת־הַקֹּדֶשׁ: 15 וְלֹא יְחַלְּלוּ אֶת־קָדְשֵׁי בְּנֵי יִשְׂרָאֵל אֵת אֲשֶׁר־יָרִימוּ לַיהֹוָה: 16 וְהִשִּׂיאוּ אוֹתָם עֲוֺן אַשְׁמָה בְּאָכְלָם אֶת־קָדְשֵׁיהֶם כִּי אֲנִי יְהֹוָה מְקַדְּשָׁם: פ [THIRD READING] 17 וַיְדַבֵּר יְהֹוָה אֶל־מֹשֶׁה לֵּאמֹר: 18 דַּבֵּר אֶל־אַהֲרֹן וְאֶל־בָּנָיו וְאֶל כָּל־בְּנֵי יִשְׂרָאֵל וְאָמַרְתָּ אֲלֵהֶם אִישׁ אִישׁ מִבֵּית יִשְׂרָאֵל וּמִן־הַגֵּר בְּיִשְׂרָאֵל אֲשֶׁר יַקְרִיב קָרְבָּנוֹ לְכָל־נִדְרֵיהֶם וּלְכָל־נִדְבוֹתָם אֲשֶׁר־יַקְרִיבוּ לַיהֹוָה לְעֹלָה: 19 לִרְצֹנְכֶם תָּמִים זָכָר בַּבָּקָר בַּכְּשָׂבִים וּבָעִזִּים: 20 כֹּל אֲשֶׁר־בּוֹ מוּם לֹא תַקְרִיבוּ כִּי־לֹא לְרָצוֹן יִהְיֶה לָכֶם: 21 וְאִישׁ כִּי־יַקְרִיב זֶבַח־שְׁלָמִים לַיהֹוָה לְפַלֵּא־נֶדֶר אוֹ לִנְדָבָה בַּבָּקָר אוֹ בַצֹּאן תָּמִים יִהְיֶה לְרָצוֹן כָּל־מוּם לֹא יִהְיֶה־בּוֹ: 22 עַוֶּרֶת אוֹ שָׁבוּר אוֹ־חָרוּץ אוֹ־יַבֶּלֶת אוֹ

742

16. Bringing sin and guilt upon themselves … I am God who sanctifies them. When you designate an object as holy, God responds by endowing it with an eternal sanctity. Now, you cannot withdraw its sanctity, since God has established it as holy.

This is what our verse teaches: It is your action that elicits God's response, so it is you who brings "guilt upon yourself," if you later violate the holiness of the object (*Rabbi Obadiah Sforno, 16th century*).

18. To fulfil one of his vows or one of his pledges. Since "a pledge offering" is given of your own free will you should not think that whatever you contribute is good, be it blemished or not. Everything that is dedicated to God must be done as perfectly as possible (*Rabbi Obadiah Sforno, 16th century*).

21. It should be perfect. An important theme of the sacrifices is to arouse your thoughts and feelings towards God. Therefore the animal which you offer must be perfect, otherwise your inspiration will be incomplete (*Rabbi Aaron ha-Levi (Ḥinnukh), 13th century*).

It should not have any blemish in it. A blemished bird is not disqualified. However, this only applies to minor blemishes. A bird whose body is mauled, or whose eye

Food for thought

1. Have you ever received an insulting gift?

2. Do you find a half-hearted gesture more insulting than no gesture?

3. How do you give your best to God?

- [11] If a priest acquires a (non-Jewish) person (as a slave), he becomes the financial property (of his master), so he may eat (*terumah*. Likewise, the children of a non-Jewish slave-woman who were) born in his house may eat of his (*terumah*).

- [12] If a priest's daughter is married to a person who is a non-priest, she may (no longer) eat the holy *terumah*.

- [13] If the priest's daughter becomes widowed or divorced (from a non-priest) and she has no offspring (from him), she may return to her youthful status in her father's household and eat of her father's (*terumah*).

- No non-priest may eat (*terumah*, but a priest who is in a state of mourning may eat *terumah*).

- [14] If a man (who is not a priest) eats holy (*terumah*) unintentionally, he should add a fifth of it to its (value) and give the priest (fruits to this value, which will then become) holy (*terumah*).

- [15] (The priests) should not violate the sanctity of the holy (*terumah*) of the children of Israel, which they have set aside for God, [16] thereby bringing sin and guilt upon themselves when the (non-priest) eats their holy (*terumah*), for I am God who sanctifies them.

Prohibition Against Offering a Blemished Animal

[THIRD READING] [17] God spoke to Moses, saying, [18] Speak to Aaron and to his sons, and to all the children of Israel and say to them:

- If any man from the house of Israel, or from the Jewish converts (or non-Jews) brings his offering to fulfil one of his vows or one of his pledges which he (promised to) offer up to God as a burnt-offering [19] (it should be an animal which will) be accepted favorably (by God) for him, (namely, a perfect) unblemished male, from cattle, sheep or goats.

- [20] You should not (consecrate) any (animal) that has a blemish as an offering, because it will not be accepted favorably (by God) for you.

- [21] If a man brings a peace-offering to God from cattle or from flocks to fulfil a vow or a pledge, it should be perfect in order to be accepted (by God). It should not have any blemish in it.

- [22] You should not (slaughter) any of these as an offering, or place any of them on the altar as a fire-offering for God: (An animal suffering from) blindness, or

---

15. (The priests) should not violate the sanctity of the holy (*terumah*) of the children of Israel, by eating *tevel*, produce from which *terumah* and tithes have not yet been separated, which is prohibited (*Babylonian Talmud, Sanhedrin* 83a).

גָרָב אוֹ יַלֶּפֶת לֹא־תַקְרִיבוּ אֵלֶּה לַיהוָה וְאִשֶּׁה לֹא־תִתְּנוּ מֵהֶם עַל־הַמִּזְבֵּחַ לַיהוָה: 23 וְשׁוֹר וָשֶׂה שָׂרוּעַ וְקָלוּט נְדָבָה תַּעֲשֶׂה אֹתוֹ וּלְנֵדֶר לֹא יֵרָצֶה: 24 וּמָעוּךְ וְכָתוּת וְנָתוּק וְכָרוּת לֹא תַקְרִיבוּ לַיהוָה וּבְאַרְצְכֶם לֹא תַעֲשׂוּ: 25 וּמִיַּד בֶּן־נֵכָר לֹא תַקְרִיבוּ אֶת־לֶחֶם אֱלֹהֵיכֶם מִכָּל־אֵלֶּה כִּי מָשְׁחָתָם בָּהֶם מוּם בָּם לֹא יֵרָצוּ לָכֶם: ס 26 וַיְדַבֵּר יְהוָה אֶל־מֹשֶׁה לֵּאמֹר: 27 שׁוֹר אוֹ־כֶשֶׂב אוֹ־עֵז כִּי יִוָּלֵד וְהָיָה שִׁבְעַת יָמִים תַּחַת אִמּוֹ וּמִיּוֹם הַשְּׁמִינִי וָהָלְאָה יֵרָצֶה לְקָרְבַּן אִשֶּׁה לַיהוָה: 28 וְשׁוֹר אוֹ־שֶׂה אֹתוֹ וְאֶת־בְּנוֹ לֹא תִשְׁחֲטוּ בְּיוֹם אֶחָד: 29 וְכִי־תִזְבְּחוּ זֶבַח־תּוֹדָה לַיהוָה לִרְצֹנְכֶם תִּזְבָּחוּ: 30 בַּיּוֹם הַהוּא יֵאָכֵל לֹא־תוֹתִירוּ מִמֶּנּוּ עַד־בֹּקֶר אֲנִי יְהוָה: 31 וּשְׁמַרְתֶּם מִצְוֹתַי וַעֲשִׂיתֶם אֹתָם אֲנִי יְהוָה: 32 וְלֹא תְחַלְּלוּ אֶת־שֵׁם קָדְשִׁי וְנִקְדַּשְׁתִּי בְּתוֹךְ בְּנֵי יִשְׂרָאֵל אֲנִי יְהוָה מְקַדִּשְׁכֶם: 33 הַמּוֹצִיא אֶתְכֶם מֵאֶרֶץ מִצְרַיִם לִהְיוֹת לָכֶם לֵאלֹהִים אֲנִי יְהוָה: פ

29. Accepted for you (lirtzonekhem). Literally this means, "at your own will."

After a person survived a particular danger, he was required to bring a thanksgiving-offering. Despite the inevitable feeling of gratitude after escaping danger, he would still rather have not gone through the experience in the first place, so the thanksgiving-offering is not something likely to be brought "at your own will."

The verse teaches you that when you experience something dangerous, it is by Divine Providence, in order to foster a greater bond with God. You ought to see it as something beneficial—and then your thanksgiving sacrifice will be *"at your own will"* (Rabbi Abraham Samuel Benjamin Sofer, 19th century).

32. My name should be sanctified among the children of Israel. In any case where the Torah says that a person should be killed rather than transgress, and he allowed himself to be killed and did not transgress, he sanctifies God's name.

And if there were ten Jews present, then he *publicly* sanctifies God's name—like Daniel,

kabbalah bites

22:27 The ego, that darker side of you that is self-centered rather than God-centered, is really a kind of animal. Animals, like the ego, look out for themselves; their lusts and desires dictate their life.

Egos come in different shapes and sizes: the ox, the sheep and the goat.

The "ox" ego is aggressive and overtly pleasure-seeking. The "sheep" ego seeks pleasure but is less powerful in its drive to do so. And the "goat" is the most tame of the three egos. In fact, it can be so tame that you might not realize it is an ego at all, which can make it the most dangerous of the three.

Which animal would best depict your ego?

a broken (limb), or a split (eyelid or lip), or (one that has) warts, or dry lesions or weeping sores.

- ❖ ²³ You may bring an ox or sheep that has disproportionate limbs or uncloven hooves as a pledge (for the upkeep of the Sanctuary), but it will not be accepted as a vow (to be offered on the altar).

- ❖ ²⁴ You should not offer up to God (or sprinkle the blood from any animal whose testicles are) squashed, crushed, (or whose ducts have been) ripped or cut.

- ❖ You should not (castrate any animal of a species that is found) in your land (be it kosher or non-kosher).

- ❖ ²⁵ You should not offer up any of these (blemished animals) from the hand of a gentile as food for your God. For since they are injured, they have a (disqualifying) defect. They will not be accepted (by God, to atone) on your behalf.

²⁶ God spoke to Moses, saying:

- ❖ ²⁷ When an ox, a sheep or a goat is born (naturally), it should remain with its mother for seven days. Then, from the eighth day onwards, it will be accepted as a fire-offering to God.

- ❖ ²⁸ You should not slaughter a (mother) ox or sheep and her child in one day.

- ❖ ²⁹ When you slaughter a thanksgiving-offering to God, you should slaughter it in a way that it is accepted (by God) for you: ³⁰ (At the time of slaughter you should have in mind that the sacrifice) will be eaten on the same day, and that it will not be left over (uneaten) until morning. I am God.

³¹ You should keep (studying) My commandments and observe them. I am God.

Sanctifying the Name of God

³² You should not desecrate My holy name (by violating My commands intentionally).

- ❖ (You should be willing to give up your life rather than transgress My commandments so that My name) should be sanctified, (if you are challenged to transgress a commandment in the presence of witnesses) from among the children of Israel.

I am God who sanctifies you, ³³ who is taking you out of the land of Egypt to be your God (on condition that you sanctify My name). I am God.

---

or leg is missing may not be offered on the altar, since we do not offer animals that are lacking a whole limb (*Maimonides, 12th century*).

28. You should not slaughter a (mother) ox or sheep and her child in one day. The Torah teaches us extreme care when it comes to animals. Since it is a natural instinct for a mother animal to feel love toward her children, just as humans do, it is forbidden to slaughter a mother and a child in one day, in order to prevent the killing of a child in the presence of its mother (*Maimonides, 12th century*).

ויקרא כג:א-ח

כג [FOURTH READING] 1 וַיְדַבֵּר יְהֹוָה אֶל־מֹשֶׁה לֵּאמֹר: 2 דַּבֵּר אֶל־בְּנֵי יִשְׂרָאֵל וְאָמַרְתָּ אֲלֵהֶם מוֹעֲדֵי יְהֹוָה אֲשֶׁר־תִּקְרְאוּ אֹתָם מִקְרָאֵי קֹדֶשׁ אֵלֶּה הֵם מוֹעֲדָי: 3 שֵׁשֶׁת יָמִים תֵּעָשֶׂה מְלָאכָה וּבַיּוֹם הַשְּׁבִיעִי שַׁבַּת שַׁבָּתוֹן מִקְרָא־קֹדֶשׁ כָּל־מְלָאכָה לֹא תַעֲשׂוּ שַׁבָּת הִוא לַיהֹוָה בְּכֹל מוֹשְׁבֹתֵיכֶם: פ 4 אֵלֶּה מוֹעֲדֵי יְהֹוָה מִקְרָאֵי קֹדֶשׁ אֲשֶׁר־תִּקְרְאוּ אֹתָם בְּמוֹעֲדָם: 5 בַּחֹדֶשׁ הָרִאשׁוֹן בְּאַרְבָּעָה עָשָׂר לַחֹדֶשׁ בֵּין הָעַרְבָּיִם פֶּסַח לַיהֹוָה: 6 וּבַחֲמִשָּׁה עָשָׂר יוֹם לַחֹדֶשׁ הַזֶּה חַג הַמַּצּוֹת לַיהֹוָה שִׁבְעַת יָמִים מַצּוֹת תֹּאכֵלוּ: 7 בַּיּוֹם הָרִאשׁוֹן מִקְרָא־קֹדֶשׁ יִהְיֶה לָכֶם כָּל־מְלֶאכֶת עֲבֹדָה לֹא תַעֲשׂוּ: 8 וְהִקְרַבְתֶּם אִשֶּׁה לַיהֹוָה שִׁבְעַת יָמִים בַּיּוֹם הַשְּׁבִיעִי מִקְרָא־קֹדֶשׁ כָּל־מְלֶאכֶת עֲבֹדָה

---

we bring sanctity to the day, making it different than an ordinary weekday (*Nahmanides, 13th century*).

3. The seventh day is a day of complete rest. Why does Scripture begin the chapter concerning the festivals with the commandment to keep the Sabbath?

The Sabbath was given to the children of Israel to remember the creation of the world by God (*Exodus 20:9-11*). Festivals are celebrated in order to remember the miracles God performed when taking us out of Egypt, showing us that He not only created the world, He is actively involved in bringing the world to its destiny, changing nature as He sees fit. By placing the commandment of the Sabbath in the chapter dealing with the festivals, we learn that both of these beliefs are intertwined—the belief in one enhances belief in the other (*Rabbi Moses Feinstein, 20th century*).

4. Festivals of God. The three festivals—Passover (*Pesah*), the Festival of Weeks (*Shavuot*), and the Festival of Booths (*Sukkot*)—follow the agricultural cycle. *Pesah* is the time when the produce ripens, *Shavuot* is harvest time, and *Sukkot* is the completion of the harvesting season, when all the produce has been gathered in from the field (*Rabbi Bahya b. Asher, 13th century*).

6. Festival of Unleavened Bread. While the Torah refers to *"a Festival of Unleavened Bread to God,"* the festival is more commonly referred to as Passover.

In the Torah itself, God refers to the festival with a name which highlights the greatness of the *Jewish people*, "Festival of *Unleavened Bread*"—unleavened bread reminds us of how the Jewish people left Egypt, the most civilized country in the world, and headed into a desert with just a small amount of food.

Food for thought

1. Do the festivals help you to give God your undivided attention?

2. Are the festivals meant to be relaxing or invigorating?

3. Is historical consciousness important to you?

The Sabbath and the Festivals

23 [FOURTH READING] ¹ God spoke to Moses, saying, ² Speak to the children of Israel and say to them:

❖ (You should always make an effort to come to Jerusalem to celebrate) the festivals of God (because if you get delayed on the way, the High Court that fixes the calendar) which designates (the festivals) as holy celebrations (will declare a leap year, enabling you to reach Jerusalem on time).

The following are My festivals:

❖ ³ (Just as) for six days work may be performed, but the seventh day is a day of complete rest, a holy celebration (on which) you should not do any work, (so too the festivals must be observed punctiliously, as you observe) a Sabbath to God in all the places where you live.

❖ ⁴ These festivals of God are holy celebrations, which (should be) fixed in their appropriate times (by the High Court, which establishes the beginning of each month, when the moon appears).

Passover

❖ ⁵ In the first month, on the fourteenth of the month, (after the sixth hour) in the afternoon, (you should offer) the Passover-offering to God.

❖ ⁶ On the fifteenth day of that month is a Festival of Unleavened Bread to God. You should eat unleavened bread for a period of seven days.

❖ ⁷ The first day will be a holy celebration for you, (when) you should not perform any manual work.

❖ ⁸ You should bring an (additional) fire-offering to God for a period of seven days.

❖ The seventh day will be a holy celebration, (when) you should not perform any manual work.

Hananiah, Mishael and Azariah, and like Rabbi Akiva and his colleagues. Such individuals are the victims of regimes, and there is no way of achieving such greatness as theirs. Of them, the verse states, *"For Your sake we are killed all day long, we are reckoned as sheep for the slaughter"* (Psalms 44:23), and it is said of them, *"Gather My pious ones together to Me, those that have made a covenant with Me through sacrifice"* (ibid., 50:5; *Maimonides, 12th century*).

A person who *actually* surrenders his life to God is superior to one who merely *wishes* to do so. This is because the desire to surrender to God stems from the Godly Soul, and so long as the person has not actually surrendered himself, his Animalistic Soul has not been affected by this desire (*Rabbi Dov Baer Schneuri of Lubavitch, 19th century*).

23:2 Holy celebrations (*mikra'e kodesh*—lit. "holy callings"). The Torah calls the festivals "holy callings" because festivals are days that God *calls* upon the children of Israel to put on clean, festive clothing, gather together in a place of worship to pray, and to feast. In this way

אמור ויקרא כג:ח-יז

9 לֹא תַעֲשֽׂוּ: פ 10 וַיְדַבֵּ֥ר יְהֹוָ֖ה אֶל־מֹשֶׁ֥ה לֵּאמֹֽר: דַּבֵּ֞ר אֶל־בְּנֵ֤י יִשְׂרָאֵל֙ וְאָמַרְתָּ֣ אֲלֵהֶ֔ם כִּֽי־תָבֹ֣אוּ אֶל־הָאָ֗רֶץ אֲשֶׁ֤ר אֲנִי֙ נֹתֵ֣ן לָכֶ֔ם וּקְצַרְתֶּ֖ם אֶת־קְצִירָ֑הּ וַהֲבֵאתֶ֥ם אֶת־עֹ֛מֶר רֵאשִׁ֥ית קְצִֽירְכֶ֖ם אֶל־הַכֹּהֵֽן: 11 וְהֵנִ֧יף אֶת־הָעֹ֛מֶר לִפְנֵ֥י יְהֹוָ֖ה לִֽרְצֹנְכֶ֑ם מִֽמׇּחֳרַת֙ הַשַּׁבָּ֔ת יְנִיפֶ֖נּוּ הַכֹּהֵֽן: 12 וַעֲשִׂיתֶ֕ם בְּי֥וֹם הֲנִֽיפְכֶ֖ם אֶת־הָעֹ֑מֶר כֶּ֣בֶשׂ תָּמִ֧ים בֶּן־שְׁנָת֛וֹ לְעֹלָ֖ה לַיהֹוָֽה: 13 וּמִנְחָתוֹ֩ שְׁנֵ֨י עֶשְׂרֹנִ֜ים סֹ֣לֶת בְּלוּלָ֥ה בַשֶּׁ֛מֶן אִשֶּׁ֥ה לַיהֹוָ֖ה רֵ֣יחַ נִיחֹ֑חַ וְנִסְכֹּ֥ה יַ֖יִן רְבִיעִ֥ת הַהִֽין: 14 וְלֶ֩חֶם֩ וְקָלִ֨י וְכַרְמֶ֜ל לֹ֣א תֹֽאכְל֗וּ עַד־עֶ֙צֶם֙ הַיּ֣וֹם הַזֶּ֔ה עַ֚ד הֲבִ֣יאֲכֶ֔ם אֶת־קׇרְבַּ֖ן אֱלֹהֵיכֶ֑ם חֻקַּ֤ת עוֹלָם֙ לְדֹרֹ֣תֵיכֶ֔ם בְּכֹ֖ל מֹשְׁבֹֽתֵיכֶֽם: ס 15 וּסְפַרְתֶּ֤ם לָכֶם֙ מִמׇּחֳרַ֣ת הַשַּׁבָּ֔ת מִיּוֹם֙ הֲבִ֣יאֲכֶ֔ם אֶת־עֹ֖מֶר הַתְּנוּפָ֑ה שֶׁ֥בַע שַׁבָּת֖וֹת תְּמִימֹ֥ת תִּהְיֶֽינָה: 16 עַ֣ד מִֽמׇּחֳרַ֤ת הַשַּׁבָּת֙ הַשְּׁבִיעִ֔ת תִּסְפְּר֖וּ חֲמִשִּׁ֣ים י֑וֹם וְהִקְרַבְתֶּ֛ם מִנְחָ֥ה חֲדָשָׁ֖ה לַיהֹוָֽה: 17 מִמּוֹשְׁבֹ֨תֵיכֶ֜ם תָּבִ֣יאוּ ׀ לֶ֣חֶם תְּנוּפָ֗ה שְׁתַּ֙יִם֙ שְׁנֵ֣י עֶשְׂרֹנִ֔ים סֹ֣לֶת תִּהְיֶ֔ינָה חָמֵ֖ץ

748

15. Count for yourselves (sephartem) seven weeks. *Sephartem* can also refer to "brilliance" and "brightness" (*sappir*). The message here is: *Make yourself shine!* Refine your character so that it becomes radiant (*Rabbi Dov Baer of Mezhirech, 18th century*).

They should be perfect. You must begin counting in the evening, since every twenty-four hour period begins at night. Otherwise they would not be "perfect" (*Rashi, 11th century*).

17. They should be baked leavened. Leavened bread, which is puffed up with air, represents the arrogance of a puffed-up ego. Unleavened bread is symbolic of humility.

Pride is not necessarily a bad thing if it represents a healthy self-esteem in your observance of Judaism—as the verse states: *"His heart was lifted up in the ways of God"* (II Chronicles 17:6). However, such a "healthy" ego is only possible when your Judaism matures. At the outset, there is nothing yet for you to be proud about, so your ego would be destructive.

Therefore, at Passover, which celebrates the *birth* of the Jewish nation, leavened bread (ego) is forbidden. But on the Festival of Weeks (*Shavuot*), after refining the Jewish personality through counting the *'omer*,

kabbalah bites

23:15 The seven weeks of the *'omer* are a time when we carry out a "consciousness cleanse," focusing on the seven *Sefirot* of our emotional personality.

Week 1: *Hesed* (love).
Week 2: *Gevurah* (discipline).
Week 3: *Tiferet* (compassion).
Week 4: *Netzah* (determination).
Week 5: *Hod* (humility).
Week 6: *Yesod* (bonding).
Week 7: *Malkhut* (dignity).

Keep a daily notebook during the *'omer* and take ten minutes to write down each day what you have done to refine—to bring light—to your *Sefirot*.

The 'Omer-Offering

[9] God spoke to Moses, saying, [10] Speak to the children of Israel and say to them:

- When you come to the land which I am giving you, and you reap its harvest, you should bring an *'omer*-measure from the first of your reaping to the priest.

- [11] He should wave the *'omer* (backwards, forwards, upwards and downwards) before God, so that it will be accepted (by God) on your behalf. The priest should wave it on the day following the (first) rest day (of Passover).

[12] On the day that you wave the *'omer*, you should offer up (the following as its accompaniment):

- A perfect (unblemished) lamb in its first year as a burnt-offering to God.

- [13] Its (associated) meal-offering (should be) two tenths (of an *'ephah*) of fine flour mixed with oil, as a fire-offering (which causes) a pleasant aroma to God.

- Its (associated wine) libation (should be) a quarter of a *hin* of wine.

- [14] You should not eat bread, parched grain flour or parched kernels (from the new crop), until this very day, until you bring the (*'omer*-)offering for your God. (This is) an eternal statute throughout your generations, in all the places that you live.

Counting the 'Omer and the Festival of Weeks [Shavuot]

- [15] From the day following the (first) rest day (of Passover)—the day you bring the *'omer* as a wave-offering—you should count for yourselves seven weeks. (When you count them) they should be perfect.

[16] You should count up until (but not including) fifty days, (i.e.) the day following the seventh week. (On the fiftieth day) you should bring the (first) meal-offering (from the) new (crop) to God:

- [17] From the places where you live (in the land of Israel), you should bring bread that is designated (for a higher purpose): two (loaves made from) two tenths (of an *'ephah*). They should be made from fine flour, (and) they should be baked leavened, (since they are) the first (meal-)offering to God.

The Jewish people, on the other hand, refer to the festival as Passover (*Pesaḥ*), a name which highlights *God's* greatness, how He passed over the houses of the Jewish people, despite their lowly spiritual state, and redeemed them from Egypt (*Rabbi Levi Isaac of Berdichev, 18th century*).

14. In all the places that you live. The Sages of Israel were divided about this matter. Some derived from here that *ḥadash* (the prohibition of eating new crops before the *'omer* is offered) applies even outside the land of Israel. Others were of the opinion that this phrase merely teaches us that the Jewish people were only required to observe the laws of *ḥadash* after possession and settlement, i.e., after they had conquered and apportioned the land of Israel (*Rashi, 11th century*).

ויקרא כג:יז-כז | אמור

18 תָּאפֶינָה בִּכּוּרִים לַיהוָה: וְהִקְרַבְתֶּם עַל־הַלֶּחֶם שִׁבְעַת כְּבָשִׂים תְּמִימִם בְּנֵי שָׁנָה וּפַר בֶּן־בָּקָר אֶחָד וְאֵילִם שְׁנָיִם יִהְיוּ עֹלָה לַיהוָה וּמִנְחָתָם וְנִסְכֵּיהֶם אִשֵּׁה רֵיחַ־נִיחֹחַ לַיהוָה: 19 וַעֲשִׂיתֶם שְׂעִיר־עִזִּים אֶחָד לְחַטָּאת וּשְׁנֵי כְבָשִׂים בְּנֵי שָׁנָה לְזֶבַח שְׁלָמִים: 20 וְהֵנִיף הַכֹּהֵן ׀ אֹתָם עַל לֶחֶם הַבִּכֻּרִים תְּנוּפָה לִפְנֵי יְהוָה עַל־שְׁנֵי כְּבָשִׂים קֹדֶשׁ יִהְיוּ לַיהוָה לַכֹּהֵן: 21 וּקְרָאתֶם בְּעֶצֶם ׀ הַיּוֹם הַזֶּה מִקְרָא־קֹדֶשׁ יִהְיֶה לָכֶם כָּל־מְלֶאכֶת עֲבֹדָה לֹא תַעֲשׂוּ חֻקַּת עוֹלָם בְּכָל־מוֹשְׁבֹתֵיכֶם לְדֹרֹתֵיכֶם: 22 וּבְקֻצְרְכֶם אֶת־קְצִיר אַרְצְכֶם לֹא־תְכַלֶּה פְּאַת שָׂדְךָ בְּקֻצְרֶךָ וְלֶקֶט קְצִירְךָ לֹא תְלַקֵּט לֶעָנִי וְלַגֵּר תַּעֲזֹב אֹתָם אֲנִי יְהוָה אֱלֹהֵיכֶם: פ 23 [FIFTH READING] וַיְדַבֵּר יְהוָה אֶל־מֹשֶׁה לֵּאמֹר: 24 דַּבֵּר אֶל־בְּנֵי יִשְׂרָאֵל לֵאמֹר בַּחֹדֶשׁ הַשְּׁבִיעִי בְּאֶחָד לַחֹדֶשׁ יִהְיֶה לָכֶם שַׁבָּתוֹן זִכְרוֹן תְּרוּעָה מִקְרָא־קֹדֶשׁ: 25 כָּל־מְלֶאכֶת עֲבֹדָה לֹא תַעֲשׂוּ וְהִקְרַבְתֶּם אִשֶּׁה לַיהוָה: ס 26 וַיְדַבֵּר יְהוָה אֶל־מֹשֶׁה לֵּאמֹר: 27 אַךְ בֶּעָשׂוֹר לַחֹדֶשׁ הַשְּׁבִיעִי הַזֶּה יוֹם

After the Torah commands us regarding the Festival of Weeks (*Shavuot*), which is associated with the giving of the Torah, we are told immediately about the moral obligation to give charity to the poor *to stress that the Torah comprises not only suprarational decrees and spiritual matters, but also a deep sense of humanitarianism* (Rabbi Meir Simhah of Dvinsk, 19th–20th century).

24. In the seventh month, on the first of the month. The celebration of the Jewish New Year (*Rosh Ha-Shanah*) has been ordained by the Torah to take place on the anniversary of the Creation, but not on the first day of Creation. It has been made to coincide with the sixth day,

spiritual vitamin

> Judaism is a way of life that is not relegated to several days in the year, specific holy days, or even the Sabbath, but embraces our entire life each and every day. That is why the Torah is referred to as *"our life,"* indicating that it must be continuous and uninterrupted. And this is what makes the Jewish religion radically different from any other religion: it is not something additional to yourself; it is intimately part of yourself.

leviticus 23:18–27 — 'emor

- **18** You should offer in association with the bread: seven (perfect) unblemished lambs in their first year, one young bull, and two rams. These should be a burnt-offering to God, (along with) their (associated) meal-offerings and (wine) libations. It is a fire-offering (causing) a pleasant aroma to God.

- **19** You should offer up one male goat as a sin-offering, and two lambs in their first year as a peace-offering.

- **20** The priest should wave (the two lambs) with the first (meal-)offering bread as a wave-offering before God. (This should be done while) the two lambs (are still alive. Unlike a normal peace-offering which is of a lesser degree of holiness), they will be holy to God, belonging to the priest.

- **21** You should proclaim this very day as a holy celebration for you. You should not perform any manual work. (This is) an eternal statute in all the places that you live, throughout your generations.

- **22** When you reap the harvest of your land, you should not completely remove the corner of your field during your harvesting, (since this should be left for the poor); nor should you gather the individual stalks of your harvest (that have fallen). You should leave them for the poor man and the convert. I am God, your God.

The New Year [*Rosh Ha-Shanah*]

[FIFTH READING] **23** God spoke to Moses, saying, **24** Speak to the children of Israel, saying:

- In the seventh month, on the first of the month, there will be a Sabbath for you, (when you will recite verses that) recall (the binding of Isaac, and that mention the) blowing (of the ram's horn), a holy celebration.

- **25** You should not perform any manual work.

- You should offer up a fire-offering to God.

The Day of Atonement [*Yom Kippur*]

26 God spoke to Moses, saying:

- **27** On the tenth of this seventh month is a Day of Atonement, but (it will only atone for those who return to God).

---

leavened bread (self-esteem) becomes an obligation: *"They should be baked leavened"* (*Rabbi Samuel Schneersohn of Lubavitch, 19th century*).

21. Proclaim this very day as a holy celebration. Although the Festival of Weeks (*Shavuot*) coincides with the day the Torah was given, there is no mention of this in Scripture. This is because, *really, the Torah is being given anew every day* (*Rabbi Ephraim of Luntshits, 16th–17th century*).

22. Leave them for the poor man and the convert. Why does the Torah make mention of the gifts left over for the poor in the middle of detailing all the festivals?

הַכִּפֻּרִים הוּא מִקְרָא־קֹדֶשׁ יִהְיֶה לָכֶם וְעִנִּיתֶם אֶת־נַפְשֹׁתֵיכֶם וְהִקְרַבְתֶּם
אִשֶּׁה לַיהוָֹה: 28 וְכָל־מְלָאכָה לֹא תַעֲשׂוּ בְּעֶצֶם הַיּוֹם הַזֶּה כִּי יוֹם כִּפֻּרִים הוּא
לְכַפֵּר עֲלֵיכֶם לִפְנֵי יְהוָֹה אֱלֹהֵיכֶם: 29 כִּי כָל־הַנֶּפֶשׁ אֲשֶׁר לֹא־תְעֻנֶּה בְּעֶצֶם
הַיּוֹם הַזֶּה וְנִכְרְתָה מֵעַמֶּיהָ: 30 וְכָל־הַנֶּפֶשׁ אֲשֶׁר תַּעֲשֶׂה כָּל־מְלָאכָה בְּעֶצֶם
הַיּוֹם הַזֶּה וְהַאֲבַדְתִּי אֶת־הַנֶּפֶשׁ הַהִוא מִקֶּרֶב עַמָּהּ: 31 כָּל־מְלָאכָה לֹא תַעֲשׂוּ
חֻקַּת עוֹלָם לְדֹרֹתֵיכֶם בְּכֹל מֹשְׁבֹתֵיכֶם: 32 שַׁבַּת שַׁבָּתוֹן הוּא לָכֶם וְעִנִּיתֶם
אֶת־נַפְשֹׁתֵיכֶם בְּתִשְׁעָה לַחֹדֶשׁ בָּעֶרֶב מֵעֶרֶב עַד־עֶרֶב תִּשְׁבְּתוּ שַׁבַּתְּכֶם: פ
[SIXTH READING] 33 וַיְדַבֵּר יְהוָֹה אֶל־מֹשֶׁה לֵּאמֹר: 34 דַּבֵּר אֶל־בְּנֵי יִשְׂרָאֵל לֵאמֹר
בַּחֲמִשָּׁה עָשָׂר יוֹם לַחֹדֶשׁ הַשְּׁבִיעִי הַזֶּה חַג הַסֻּכּוֹת שִׁבְעַת יָמִים לַיהוָֹה:
35 בַּיּוֹם הָרִאשׁוֹן מִקְרָא־קֹדֶשׁ כָּל־מְלֶאכֶת עֲבֹדָה לֹא תַעֲשׂוּ: 36 שִׁבְעַת
יָמִים תַּקְרִיבוּ אִשֶּׁה לַיהוָֹה בַּיּוֹם הַשְּׁמִינִי מִקְרָא־קֹדֶשׁ יִהְיֶה לָכֶם וְהִקְרַבְתֶּם
אִשֶּׁה לַיהוָֹה עֲצֶרֶת הִוא כָּל־מְלֶאכֶת עֲבֹדָה לֹא תַעֲשׂוּ: 37 אֵלֶּה מוֹעֲדֵי יְהוָֹה
אֲשֶׁר־תִּקְרְאוּ אֹתָם מִקְרָאֵי קֹדֶשׁ לְהַקְרִיב אִשֶּׁה לַיהוָֹה עֹלָה וּמִנְחָה זֶבַח
וּנְסָכִים דְּבַר־יוֹם בְּיוֹמוֹ: 38 מִלְּבַד שַׁבְּתֹת יְהוָֹה וּמִלְּבַד מַתְּנוֹתֵיכֶם וּמִלְּבַד
כָּל־נִדְרֵיכֶם וּמִלְּבַד כָּל־נִדְבוֹתֵיכֶם אֲשֶׁר תִּתְּנוּ לַיהוָֹה: 39 אַךְ בַּחֲמִשָּׁה עָשָׂר
יוֹם לַחֹדֶשׁ הַשְּׁבִיעִי בְּאָסְפְּכֶם אֶת־תְּבוּאַת הָאָרֶץ תָּחֹגּוּ אֶת־חַג־יְהוָֹה
שִׁבְעַת יָמִים בַּיּוֹם הָרִאשׁוֹן שַׁבָּתוֹן וּבַיּוֹם הַשְּׁמִינִי שַׁבָּתוֹן: 40 וּלְקַחְתֶּם
לָכֶם בַּיּוֹם הָרִאשׁוֹן פְּרִי עֵץ הָדָר כַּפֹּת תְּמָרִים וַעֲנַף עֵץ־עָבֹת וְעַרְבֵי־נָחַל

32. You should afflict yourselves. (Starting from) the ninth of the month. Is it on the ninth of *Tishri* that we fast? We fast on the tenth of *Tishri*!

Scripture is teaching you that if you feast on the ninth it is considered as if you had fasted on the ninth and the tenth (*Babylonian Talmud, Berakhot* 8b).

40. Fruit of the (citron) tree ... fronds of a date palm ... branches of a (myrtle) tree ... willows of the brookside. The four species represent four types of people. A citron (*etrog*), which possesses a good taste and a pleasant smell, represents the Jew who possesses both Torah learning

leviticus 23:27–40 — 'emor

- It will be a holy celebration for you. You must afflict yourselves, and you should offer up a fire-offering to God.
- ²⁸ You should not perform any work on that very day, for it is a Day of Atonement, for you to be atoned before God, your God. ²⁹ For any person who does not afflict himself on that very day will be cut off from his people. ³⁰ (This means that) if any person will perform any work on that very day, I will destroy that person from among his people. ³¹ You should not perform any work. (This is) an eternal statute throughout your generations in all the places that you live. ³² It is a complete day of rest for you, and you should afflict yourselves. (Starting from) the ninth of the month in the evening, from evening to evening, you should observe your rest day.

The Festival of Tabernacles [*Sukkot*] and *Shemini Atzeret* (Eighth Day)

[SIXTH READING] ³³ God spoke to Moses, saying: ³⁴ Speak to the children of Israel, saying:

- On the fifteenth day of this seventh month is the Festival of Tabernacles, a period of seven days for God.
- ³⁵ The first day is a holy celebration. You should not perform any manual work.
- ³⁶ For a period of seven days, you should bring a fire-offering to God.
- The eighth day will be a holy celebration for you, and you should bring a fire-offering to God. It is a (time when God) holds back (the Jewish people to be with Him for another day). You should not perform any manual work.
- ³⁷ These are God's festivals which you should designate as holy celebrations. (On) them (you should) offer up a fire-offering to God: a burnt-offering and (its associated) meal-offering, (other) sacrifices and (their associated) libations—each day's requirement on its appropriate day. ³⁸ In addition to God's Sabbath offerings (if the festival occurs on the Sabbath), your gift-offerings, all your vows, and all your pledges that you must give to God.
- ³⁹ On the fifteenth day of the seventh month, when you gather in the produce of the land, you should celebrate the festival of God for a period of seven days (by bringing the festival peace-offerings), but (you should not bring these offerings on the Sabbath).
- The first day should be a rest day, and the eighth day should be a rest day.
- ⁴⁰ On the first day, you should take for yourselves: The fruit of the (citron) tree, (which) dwells (on its tree for an entire year, and whose wood tastes like the fruit), the fronds of a date palm, branches of a (myrtle) tree (which are plaited like) cords, and willows of the brookside.

---

when man was created. The significance lies in the fact that the new creature, man, was essentially different from the others. *It was for what man could accomplish that the world was created* (*Rabbi Isaiah Horowitz, 16ᵗʰ–17ᵗʰ century*).

אמור   ויקרא כג:מ - כד:ז

וּשְׂמַחְתֶּ֗ם לִפְנֵ֛י יְהֹוָ֥ה אֱלֹהֵיכֶ֖ם שִׁבְעַ֥ת יָמִֽים: 41 וְחַגֹּתֶ֤ם אֹתוֹ֙ חַ֣ג לַֽיהֹוָ֔ה שִׁבְעַ֥ת יָמִ֖ים בַּשָּׁנָ֑ה חֻקַּ֤ת עוֹלָם֙ לְדֹרֹ֣תֵיכֶ֔ם בַּחֹ֥דֶשׁ הַשְּׁבִיעִ֖י תָּחֹ֥גּוּ אֹתֽוֹ: 42 בַּסֻּכֹּ֥ת תֵּשְׁב֖וּ שִׁבְעַ֣ת יָמִ֑ים כׇּל־הָֽאֶזְרָח֙ בְּיִשְׂרָאֵ֔ל יֵשְׁב֖וּ בַּסֻּכֹּֽת: 43 לְמַ֘עַן֮ יֵדְע֣וּ דֹרֹֽתֵיכֶם֒ כִּ֣י בַסֻּכּ֗וֹת הוֹשַׁ֙בְתִּי֙ אֶת־בְּנֵ֣י יִשְׂרָאֵ֔ל בְּהוֹצִיאִ֥י אוֹתָ֖ם מֵאֶ֣רֶץ מִצְרָ֑יִם אֲנִ֖י יְהֹוָ֥ה אֱלֹהֵיכֶֽם: 44 וַיְדַבֵּ֣ר מֹשֶׁ֔ה אֶת־מֹֽעֲדֵ֖י יְהֹוָ֑ה אֶל־בְּנֵ֖י יִשְׂרָאֵֽל: פ

כד 1 וַיְדַבֵּ֥ר יְהֹוָ֖ה אֶל־מֹשֶׁ֥ה לֵּאמֹֽר: [SEVENTH READING] 2 צַ֞ו אֶת־בְּנֵ֣י יִשְׂרָאֵ֗ל וְיִקְח֨וּ אֵלֶ֜יךָ שֶׁ֣מֶן זַ֥יִת זָ֛ךְ כָּתִ֖ית לַמָּא֑וֹר לְהַעֲלֹ֥ת נֵ֖ר תָּמִֽיד: 3 מִחוּץ֩ לְפָרֹ֨כֶת הָעֵדֻ֜ת בְּאֹ֣הֶל מוֹעֵ֗ד יַעֲרֹךְ֩ אֹת֨וֹ אַהֲרֹ֜ן מֵעֶ֧רֶב עַד־בֹּ֛קֶר לִפְנֵ֥י יְהֹוָ֖ה תָּמִ֑יד חֻקַּ֥ת עוֹלָ֖ם לְדֹרֹֽתֵיכֶֽם: 4 עַ֚ל הַמְּנֹרָ֣ה הַטְּהֹרָ֔ה יַעֲרֹ֖ךְ אֶת־הַנֵּר֑וֹת לִפְנֵ֥י יְהֹוָ֖ה תָּמִֽיד: פ 5 וְלָקַחְתָּ֣ סֹ֔לֶת וְאָפִיתָ֣ אֹתָ֔הּ שְׁתֵּ֥ים עֶשְׂרֵ֖ה חַלּ֑וֹת שְׁנֵי֙ עֶשְׂרֹנִ֔ים יִהְיֶ֖ה הַֽחַלָּ֥ה הָאֶחָֽת: 6 וְשַׂמְתָּ֥ אוֹתָ֛ם שְׁתַּ֥יִם מַֽעֲרָכ֖וֹת שֵׁ֣שׁ הַֽמַּעֲרָ֑כֶת עַ֛ל הַשֻּׁלְחָ֥ן הַטָּהֹ֖ר לִפְנֵ֥י יְהֹוָֽה: 7 וְנָתַתָּ֥ עַל־הַֽמַּעֲרֶ֖כֶת לְבֹנָ֣ה זַכָּ֑ה וְהָיְתָ֤ה לַלֶּ֙חֶם֙ לְאַזְכָּרָ֔ה אִשֶּׁ֖ה לַֽיהֹוָֽה:

It is a religious requirement to increase in this rejoicing. However, the dancing and rejoicing in the Temple during *Sukkot* was not done by the uneducated or anyone who so desired, but rather, by the greatest sages of Israel, the heads of the academies, the *Sanhedrin* (Supreme Court), the *ḥasidim* (pious ones), the elders, and men of high caliber. The rest of the people, both men and women, would come to see and listen (*Maimonides, 12th century*).

43. Know that I caused the children of Israel to live in (clouds of glory that resemble) booths. The Festival of Booths (*Sukkot*) is observed in autumn when the weather is pleasant and produce has been gathered from the field (*Exodus* 23:16), so man is free to appreciate the festival.

This festival, when we leave the comforts of our home and dwell in booths, teaches us that, even in times of prosperity, we must remember the hard times when the Israelites had left Egypt and were in the wilderness, living in booths. By remembering hard times amid our current prosperity we develop a greater appreciation for the good that God has bestowed upon us, fostering a feeling of humility (*Maimonides, 12th century*).

24:4 Arrange the lamps (to burn) before God continually. Here the Torah tells us that we are to have the candelabrum (*menorah*) set up continually before God, and in verse 8 we are told that multisurface bread also had to be set up *"before God continually."* By having the "light" and "bread" displayed in this way, we demonstrate that it is God who bestows us with our physical and spiritual needs (*Rabbi Samson Raphael Hirsch, 19th century*).

leviticus 23:40 – 24:7   'emor

- ❖ You should rejoice before God, your God, for a period of seven days. ⁴¹ You should celebrate it as a festival to God for seven days in the year. (It is) an eternal statute throughout your generations (that) you celebrate it in the seventh month.

- ❖ ⁴² For a seven-day period you should live in booths [*sukkot*]. Every native Jew (and convert) should live in booths, ⁴³ in order that your (ensuing) generations should know that I caused the children of Israel to live in (clouds of glory that resemble) booths when I took them out of the land of Egypt. I am God, your God.

⁴⁴ Moses told the children of Israel (these laws of) God's festivals.

24 The Candelabrum [*Menorah*] and the Multisurface Bread
[SEVENTH READING] ¹ God spoke to Moses, saying:

- ❖ ² Command the children of Israel that they should bring to you clear olive oil, crushed for lighting, to ignite the lamp continually (from night to night).

- ❖ ³ Outside the partition in front of the (Ark of) Testimony in the Tent of Meeting, Aaron should arrange that it (has sufficient oil to burn) from evening to morning before God. This is an eternal statute for your generations. ⁴ Upon the candelabrum of pure (gold), he should arrange the lamps (to burn) before God continually.

- ❖ ⁵ You should take fine flour and bake it into twelve loaves. Each loaf should be (made from) two tenths (of an *'ephah* of flour).

- ❖ ⁶ You should place them in two stacks, six in each stack, upon the table of pure (gold), before God.

- ❖ ⁷ You should place pure frankincense (in a ladle) on each stack. (Unlike the bread, the frankincense will be offered on the altar) as a fire-offering to God, which will remind (God about) the bread.

and good deeds. The date-palm branch (*lulav*) has a good taste but no fragrance, signifying those who have Torah knowledge but lack sufficient good deeds. Those who possess good deeds but are lacking in Torah knowledge are represented by the myrtle (*hadasim*), which has a fragrant odor but lacks taste. The willow (*'aravot*), which is inedible and has no aroma, represents those people lacking both in Torah and good deeds (*Leviticus Rabbah*).

You should rejoice. Even though it is a commandment to rejoice on all the festivals, in the Holy Temple there was additional rejoicing on the Festival of Booths (*Sukkot*), as the verse states, "*You should rejoice before God, your God, for a period of seven days.*"

Following the daily communal afternoon sacrifice (the last sacrifice of the day), they would rejoice the rest of the day and throughout the entire night.

The flute was blown, and they played the harp, lyre, and cymbals, each person according to his talent. Those who could sing would sing. People would dance, each person according to his ability, and they would sing songs and praises. However, this rejoicing did not override the observance of the Sabbath or the festival.

ויקרא כד:ח-יח   אמור

8 בְּיוֹם הַשַּׁבָּת בְּיוֹם הַשַּׁבָּת יַעַרְכֶנּוּ לִפְנֵי יְהֹוָה תָּמִיד מֵאֵת בְּנֵי־יִשְׂרָאֵל בְּרִית עוֹלָם: 9 וְהָיְתָה לְאַהֲרֹן וּלְבָנָיו וַאֲכָלֻהוּ בְּמָקוֹם קָדֹשׁ כִּי קֹדֶשׁ קָדָשִׁים הוּא לוֹ מֵאִשֵּׁי יְהֹוָה חָק־עוֹלָם: ס 10 וַיֵּצֵא בֶּן־אִשָּׁה יִשְׂרְאֵלִית וְהוּא בֶּן־אִישׁ מִצְרִי בְּתוֹךְ בְּנֵי יִשְׂרָאֵל וַיִּנָּצוּ בַּמַּחֲנֶה בֶּן הַיִּשְׂרְאֵלִית וְאִישׁ הַיִּשְׂרְאֵלִי: 11 וַיִּקֹּב בֶּן־הָאִשָּׁה הַיִּשְׂרְאֵלִית אֶת־הַשֵּׁם וַיְקַלֵּל וַיָּבִיאוּ אֹתוֹ אֶל־מֹשֶׁה וְשֵׁם אִמּוֹ שְׁלֹמִית בַּת־דִּבְרִי לְמַטֵּה־דָן: 12 וַיַּנִּיחֻהוּ בַּמִּשְׁמָר לִפְרֹשׁ לָהֶם עַל־פִּי יְהֹוָה: פ 13 וַיְדַבֵּר יְהֹוָה אֶל־מֹשֶׁה לֵּאמֹר: 14 הוֹצֵא אֶת־הַמְקַלֵּל אֶל־מִחוּץ לַמַּחֲנֶה וְסָמְכוּ כָל־הַשֹּׁמְעִים אֶת־יְדֵיהֶם עַל־רֹאשׁוֹ וְרָגְמוּ אֹתוֹ כָּל־הָעֵדָה: 15 וְאֶל־בְּנֵי יִשְׂרָאֵל תְּדַבֵּר לֵאמֹר אִישׁ אִישׁ כִּי־יְקַלֵּל אֱלֹהָיו וְנָשָׂא חֶטְאוֹ: 16 וְנֹקֵב שֵׁם־יְהֹוָה מוֹת יוּמָת רָגוֹם יִרְגְּמוּ־בוֹ כָּל־הָעֵדָה כַּגֵּר כָּאֶזְרָח בְּנָקְבוֹ־שֵׁם יוּמָת: 17 וְאִישׁ כִּי יַכֶּה כָּל־נֶפֶשׁ אָדָם מוֹת יוּמָת: 18 וּמַכֵּה נֶפֶשׁ־בְּהֵמָה יְשַׁלְּמֶנָּה

11. His mother's name was Shelomith daughter of Dibri. To praise the Jewish people, Scripture publicizes this case, to inform us that she was the only one who had illicit relations.

Her name Shelomith indicates that she was verbose, going about saying *shelam 'alakh!*—"How are you?" She was called *bat Divri* ("daughter of Dibri"), suggesting that she was verbose (*dabbranit*), talking with every person. That is why she fell into sin (*Rashi, 11th century*).

Why does the Torah "praise the Jewish people" at the expense of incriminating Shelomith?

This could be compared to the principle that if a person repents profoundly, his *"transgressions become for him like merits"* (*Babylonian Talmud, Yoma* 86b). Since his sins made him feel distant from God, they were ultimately the inspiration for his return. Thus *retroactively* we perceive them as merits.

So too, in the case of Shelomith. When her example inspires *other* women to behave modestly, her transgression will

> **kabbalah bites**
>
> **24:16** *"One who blasphemously pronounces (nokev) the name."* The Hebrew word *nokev* literally means "to pierce." According to the Kabbalah, immoral or sinful acts are understood to "pierce" God's name, the Tetragrammaton, creating tiny pores that allow the "leakage" of light to the demonic forces. Observing the commandments is not merely a matter of ritual or tradition; it keeps the channels of God's blessings open and flowing, and prevents leakage to those forces which could disrupt your life.

- ⁸ On each Sabbath day, he should set it up before God (to be there) continuously, from the children of Israel, as an eternal covenant.
- ⁹ It will belong to Aaron and his sons, and they should eat it in a holy place, for it is a most holy offering for him among the fire-offerings of God, an eternal statute.

The Blasphemer

¹⁰ The son of a Jewish woman who was the son of the Egyptian man (that Moses killed, who converted, to be totally) among the children of Israel (wanted to pitch his tent in the camp of Dan) and this son of the Jewish woman quarreled in the camp with a Jewish man (who opposed his claim. When) he went out (of Moses' court, having lost the case), ¹¹ the son of the Jewish woman pronounced the (Divine) name and cursed.

They brought him to Moses. His mother's name was Shelomith daughter of Dibri of the tribe of Dan. ¹² They placed him under guard, (until his sentence would) be clarified to them by the word of God.

¹³ God spoke to Moses, saying: ¹⁴ Take the blasphemer outside the camp. All (the judges and the witnesses) who heard (his blasphemy) should lean their hands on his head. (Then they should) stone him (on behalf of) the entire community.

¹⁵ You should speak to the children of Israel, saying:

- Any man who blasphemes his God will bear (the consequences of) his sin (by being cut off from his people, if he was not warned beforehand).
- ¹⁶ One who blasphemously pronounces the (explicit) name of God (in a curse and was warned not to do so) should be put to death. The entire community should stone him, convert and native alike. If he pronounces the (Divine) name, he should be put to death.
- ¹⁷ If a man strikes any human being (including a woman or child, and the victim dies), he should be put to death.
- ¹⁸ One who strikes an animal fatally should pay for it. (He should pay the value of the animal's) life (as compensation) for its life (that he took).

8. On each Sabbath day, he should set it. Each Sabbath they would remove the multisurface bread which had been on the table since the previous Sabbath, and they would arrange different breads. The bread that was removed was divided between the priests who had been on duty the past week and those that were on duty for the upcoming week, together with the High Priest, and they would eat it (*Maimonides, 12th century*).

The Sabbath brings blessing to all the days of the week that follow (*Zohar*). However, it is not clear from the *Zohar* whether one Sabbath blesses the following *Sabbath* too.

From the case of the multisurface bread, however, we see clearly that it does, as the bread placed on the table on the Sabbath is not removed until the following Sabbath (*Rabbi Menahem Mendel Schneerson, 20th century*).

ויקרא כד:יח-כג — אמור

נֶ֥פֶשׁ תַּ֖חַת נָֽפֶשׁ׃ 19 וְאִ֕ישׁ כִּֽי־יִתֵּ֥ן מ֖וּם בַּעֲמִית֑וֹ כַּאֲשֶׁ֣ר עָשָׂ֔ה כֵּ֖ן יֵעָ֥שֶׂה לּֽוֹ׃ 20 שֶׁ֚בֶר תַּ֣חַת שֶׁ֔בֶר עַ֚יִן תַּ֣חַת עַ֔יִן שֵׁ֖ן תַּ֣חַת שֵׁ֑ן כַּאֲשֶׁ֨ר יִתֵּ֥ן מוּם֙ בָּֽאָדָ֔ם כֵּ֖ן יִנָּ֥תֶן בּֽוֹ׃ 21 [MAFTIR] וּמַכֵּ֥ה בְהֵמָ֖ה יְשַׁלְּמֶ֑נָּה וּמַכֵּ֥ה אָדָ֖ם יוּמָֽת׃ 22 מִשְׁפַּ֤ט אֶחָד֙ יִהְיֶ֣ה לָכֶ֔ם כַּגֵּ֥ר כָּאֶזְרָ֖ח יִהְיֶ֑ה כִּ֛י אֲנִ֥י יְהֹוָ֖ה אֱלֹהֵיכֶֽם׃ 23 וַיְדַבֵּ֣ר מֹשֶׁה֮ אֶל־בְּנֵ֣י יִשְׂרָאֵל֒ וַיּוֹצִ֣יאוּ אֶת־הַֽמְקַלֵּ֗ל אֶל־מִחוּץ֙ לַֽמַּחֲנֶ֔ה וַיִּרְגְּמ֥וּ אֹת֖וֹ אָ֑בֶן וּבְנֵֽי־יִשְׂרָאֵ֣ל עָשׂ֔וּ כַּאֲשֶׁ֛ר צִוָּ֥ה יְהֹוָ֖ה אֶת־מֹשֶֽׁה׃ פ פ פ

קכ״ד פסוקים, עוזיא״ל סימן.

spiritual vitamin

" If you have to make a choice between good intentions and good deeds, the actual good deeds must take precedence. "

leviticus 24:19–23 — 'emor

❖ ¹⁹ If a man inflicts an injury upon his fellow man, he should be penalized according to (the severity) of what he did: ²⁰ (The value of) a fracture for a fracture (injury, the value of) an eye for an eye (injury, the value of) a tooth for a tooth (injury). He should be penalized according to (the severity) of the injury which he caused to the person.

❖ [MAFTIR] ²¹ One who strikes an animal should pay (compensation) for its (injury).

❖ One who strikes (one of his parents while they are still alive, causing a bruise) should be put to death.

²² There will be one law for you, convert and native alike, for I am God, your God.

²³ Moses told (all this) to the children of Israel.

The (judges and witnesses) took the blasphemer outside the camp and threw a stone at him. The children of Israel did (the other procedures of first pushing him off a high place, then additional stoning until he died, and the hanging of the corpse. They all did) as God had commanded Moses.

The *Haftarah* for *'Emor* is on page 1363.

---

be rendered retroactively as a merit for her. Therefore, it is publicized here (*Rabbi Menahem Mendel Schneerson, 20th century*).

23. The (judges and witnesses) took the blasphemer outside the camp and threw a stone at him. Moses is told by God that the punishment for the blasphemer is death (24:14), but the execution did not occur until after Scripture named the punishments for murdering, injuring, and damaging the property of another person.

The message here: *Only through loving other people can you truly love God.* The way to show your love to God—to the extent that you want to kill the man who blasphemed God—is by first perfecting your love for your fellow man (*Rabbi Moses Feinstein, 20th century*).

> Go up on the mountain. **Be proud** of your Judaism in the **public arena**. Reach **high,** stand **magnanimously** and be a **huge example** to others.

BE-HAR
בהר

THE SABBATICAL YEAR	25:1–7
THE JUBILEE YEAR	25:8–34
PROHIBITIONS AGAINST TAKING INTEREST	25:35–38
JEWISH SLAVES OWNED BY JEWS	25:39–46
JEWISH SLAVES OWNED BY NON-JEWS	25:47 – 26:2

NAME
Be-Har

MEANING
"On the mountain"

LINES IN TORAH SCROLL
99

PARASHIYYOT
1 open; 6 closed

VERSES
57

WORDS
737

LETTERS
2817

DATE
Nisan – 20 *Iyyar*, 2449

LOCATION
Sinai Desert

KEY PEOPLE
Moses

MITZVOT
7 positive; 17 prohibitions

NOTE
Often read together with the portion of *Be-Hukkotai*

CHARACTER PROFILE

NAME
The Levite (descendant of the tribe of Levi)

DUTIES
Religious instruction; carrying the ark; singing in the Temple; receiving tithes; guarding Temple

KABBALAH
Levite souls emanate from *gevurah* (severity).

FAMOUS LEVITES
Samuel—Prophet who lived during the years 2830 and 2882; born after his mother prayed to God and promised that he would devote his life to God; Samuel was one of the Judges of the Jewish people and appointed Saul as the first Jewish king.

Ezra—Jewish leader who lived at the end of the era of the prophets; a scribe in Babylon; discouraged intermarriage; led the rebuilding of the walls of Jerusalem together with Nehemiah

TRUST

Refraining from agricultural work during the Sabbatical year demonstrates complete trust that God will provide sustenance and livelihood in return for performing this commandment (25:1–7).

VERBAL WRONGS

We may not remind a penitent of his or her former misdeeds, nor may we remind converts of their ancestry (25:17).

CARE FOR THE POOR

Never be tempted to find fault in the poor who ask for your help. Our moral duty to the less fortunate is to help them, not to judge them (25:25).

SERVANTS OF GOD

The Torah states a rule of metaphysics that you are a servant of God, and God alone. You cannot serve two masters, and if you forget the real one, it is inevitable that you will falsely bow to the other. Believing in this with a full heart, you can defy subjugation to any external forces (25:42).

ויקרא כה:א-ט

כה 1 וַיְדַבֵּר יְהֹוָה אֶל־מֹשֶׁה בְּהַר סִינַי לֵאמֹר: 2 דַּבֵּר אֶל־בְּנֵי יִשְׂרָאֵל וְאָמַרְתָּ אֲלֵהֶם כִּי תָבֹאוּ אֶל־הָאָרֶץ אֲשֶׁר אֲנִי נֹתֵן לָכֶם וְשָׁבְתָה הָאָרֶץ שַׁבָּת לַיהֹוָה: 3 שֵׁשׁ שָׁנִים תִּזְרַע שָׂדֶךָ וְשֵׁשׁ שָׁנִים תִּזְמֹר כַּרְמֶךָ וְאָסַפְתָּ אֶת־תְּבוּאָתָהּ: 4 וּבַשָּׁנָה הַשְּׁבִיעִת שַׁבַּת שַׁבָּתוֹן יִהְיֶה לָאָרֶץ שַׁבָּת לַיהֹוָה שָׂדְךָ לֹא תִזְרָע וְכַרְמְךָ לֹא תִזְמֹר: 5 אֵת סְפִיחַ קְצִירְךָ לֹא תִקְצוֹר וְאֶת־עִנְּבֵי נְזִירֶךָ לֹא תִבְצֹר שְׁנַת שַׁבָּתוֹן יִהְיֶה לָאָרֶץ: 6 וְהָיְתָה שַׁבַּת הָאָרֶץ לָכֶם לְאָכְלָה לְךָ וּלְעַבְדְּךָ וְלַאֲמָתֶךָ וְלִשְׂכִירְךָ וּלְתוֹשָׁבְךָ הַגָּרִים עִמָּךְ: 7 וְלִבְהֶמְתְּךָ וְלַחַיָּה אֲשֶׁר בְּאַרְצֶךָ תִּהְיֶה כָל־תְּבוּאָתָהּ לֶאֱכֹל: ס 8 וְסָפַרְתָּ לְךָ שֶׁבַע שַׁבְּתֹת שָׁנִים שֶׁבַע שָׁנִים שֶׁבַע פְּעָמִים וְהָיוּ לְךָ יְמֵי שֶׁבַע שַׁבְּתֹת הַשָּׁנִים תֵּשַׁע וְאַרְבָּעִים שָׁנָה: 9 וְהַעֲבַרְתָּ שׁוֹפַר תְּרוּעָה בַּחֹדֶשׁ הַשְּׁבִעִי בֶּעָשׂוֹר לַחֹדֶשׁ בְּיוֹם הַכִּפֻּרִים

2. When you come to the land that I am giving you, the land should rest a Sabbath to God. What does Scripture seek to add by saying, *"that I am giving you"*? Surely it would be sufficient to inform us that when we would come to the land of Israel, the land should rest?

Scripture is suggesting that when the Israelites conquered the land of Israel it would not be done naturally; God would miraculously deliver the land into their hands—*"I am giving you."* In recognition that it was God who gave them the land, the Israelites were commanded to demonstrate their belief by letting *"the land rest a Sabbath to God"* (*Rabbi Moses b. Joseph Schick, 19th century*).

kabbalah bites

25:1-2 On the Sabbath, the metaphysical arrows point upwards, as we spend the day in introspection, emphasizing "being" over "doing." During the rest of the week, the arrows point downwards, as we further our careers and contribution to society at large.

Judaism is all about finding a healthy *balance* and *integration* between these two poles.

Therefore, the fact that the Torah was given *"at Mount Sinai"* is stressed here, in connection with the Sabbatical year. To make one day of the week "Sabbatical" is relatively easy; but to live the *whole year* with the spirit of the Sabbath—to maintain a spiritual outlook even as we are immersed in a material life—is a different challenge indeed.

parashat be-har

The Sabbatical Year

25 ¹ God spoke to Moses (in the desert) at Mount Sinai, saying: ² Speak to the children of Israel, saying:

- When you come to the land that I am giving you, the land should rest a Sabbath to God: ³ You may sow your field for six years, and for six years you may prune your vineyard and gather in its produce, ⁴ but in the seventh year, the land should have a complete rest, a Sabbath to God. You should not sow your field, and you should not prune your vineyard.

- ⁵ You should not reap (for yourself) the aftergrowth of your (previous year's) harvest (which sprouted on its own), and you should not pick the grapes which you had set aside (for yourself), for it will be a year of rest for the land.

- ⁶ (The produce which grows on its own during) the Sabbath of the land will be (ownerless, and thus available) to you to eat (equally with everybody else)—you, your male and female slaves, your (non-Jewish) hired worker and lodger who lives with you.

- ⁷ All of its produce may (be retained in your house to) be eaten by your domestic animals, (so long as there is sufficient produce remaining) in your land for the wild animals.

The Jubilee Year

- ⁸ You should count for yourself seven Sabbatical years, seven years, seven times. The days of these seven Sabbatical years will amount to forty-nine years for you.

- ⁹ (The following year) you should announce (the Jubilee Year with) blasts of the ram's horn, in the seventh month, on the tenth of the month. On the Day of Atonement, you should sound the ram's horn throughout your land.

Food for thought

1. Why do you think the Torah was given in a desert and not in a city?

2. Why was the Torah given on a mountain and not in a valley?

3. How much detail was said at Sinai? What difference does it make?

25:1 At Mount Sinai. What is the connection between the concept of the Sabbatical year and "Mount Sinai" that the Torah stresses how this commandment was given at Sinai? Weren't all the commandments given at Sinai? This teaches us: Just as in the case of the Sabbatical year, whose general laws and details were all stated at Sinai, the general laws and details of all the other commandments were also said at Sinai (*Sifra*).

ויקרא כה:ט-יח | בהר

תַּעֲבִ֥ירוּ שׁוֹפָ֖ר בְּכָל־אַרְצְכֶֽם: 10 וְקִדַּשְׁתֶּ֗ם אֵ֣ת שְׁנַ֤ת הַחֲמִשִּׁים֙ שָׁנָ֔ה וּקְרָאתֶ֥ם
דְּר֛וֹר בָּאָ֖רֶץ לְכָל־יֹשְׁבֶ֑יהָ יוֹבֵ֥ל הִוא֙ תִּהְיֶ֣ה לָכֶ֔ם וְשַׁבְתֶּ֗ם אִ֚ישׁ אֶל־אֲחֻזָּת֔וֹ
וְאִ֥ישׁ אֶל־מִשְׁפַּחְתּ֖וֹ תָּשֻֽׁבוּ: 11 יוֹבֵ֣ל הִ֗וא שְׁנַ֛ת הַחֲמִשִּׁ֥ים שָׁנָ֖ה תִּהְיֶ֣ה לָכֶ֑ם
לֹ֣א תִזְרָ֔עוּ וְלֹ֤א תִקְצְרוּ֙ אֶת־סְפִיחֶ֔יהָ וְלֹ֥א תִבְצְר֖וּ אֶת־נְזִרֶֽיהָ: 12 כִּ֚י יוֹבֵ֣ל הִ֔וא
קֹ֖דֶשׁ תִּהְיֶ֣ה לָכֶ֑ם מִ֨ן־הַשָּׂדֶ֔ה תֹּאכְל֖וּ אֶת־תְּבוּאָתָֽהּ: 13 בִּשְׁנַ֥ת הַיּוֹבֵ֖ל הַזֹּ֑את
תָּשֻׁ֕בוּ אִ֖ישׁ אֶל־אֲחֻזָּתֽוֹ: 14 [SECOND READING] וְכִֽי־תִמְכְּר֤וּ מִמְכָּר֙ לַעֲמִיתֶ֔ךָ א֥וֹ קָנֹ֖ה מִיַּ֣ד
עֲמִיתֶ֑ךָ אַל־תּוֹנ֖וּ אִ֥ישׁ אֶת־אָחִֽיו: 15 בְּמִסְפַּ֤ר שָׁנִים֙ אַחַ֣ר הַיּוֹבֵ֔ל תִּקְנֶ֖ה מֵאֵ֣ת
עֲמִיתֶ֑ךָ בְּמִסְפַּ֥ר שְׁנֵֽי־תְבוּאֹ֖ת יִמְכָּר־לָֽךְ: 16 לְפִ֣י ׀ רֹ֣ב הַשָּׁנִ֗ים תַּרְבֶּה֙ מִקְנָת֔וֹ
וּלְפִי֙ מְעֹ֣ט הַשָּׁנִ֔ים תַּמְעִ֖יט מִקְנָת֑וֹ כִּ֚י מִסְפַּ֣ר תְּבוּאֹ֔ת ה֖וּא מֹכֵ֥ר לָֽךְ: 17 וְלֹ֤א
תוֹנוּ֙ אִ֣ישׁ אֶת־עֲמִית֔וֹ וְיָרֵ֖אתָ מֵֽאֱלֹהֶ֑יךָ כִּ֛י אֲנִ֥י יְהֹוָ֖ה אֱלֹהֵיכֶֽם: 18 וַעֲשִׂיתֶם֙
אֶת־חֻקֹּתַ֔י וְאֶת־מִשְׁפָּטַ֥י תִּשְׁמְר֖וּ וַעֲשִׂיתֶ֣ם אֹתָ֑ם וִֽישַׁבְתֶּ֥ם עַל־הָאָ֖רֶץ לָבֶֽטַח:

Therefore the Torah says: I will make a Jubilee year following a Sabbatical year, when you can neither sow nor reap your fields, causing you to turn toward heaven *like the poor* and ask, *"What will I eat?"* (25:20). Then you too will understand the lot of the poor and have compassion to help them to the best of your ability (*Rabbi Abraham b. Jacob Saba, 15th century*).

14. You should not cheat one another. You may not cheat *yourself* either. Never inflate your own worth, and never underestimate your potential (*Rabbi Simḥah Bunem of Przysucha, 18th–19th century*).

17. You must fear your God. Your income and losses for the year are allocated on the Jewish New Year (*Babylonian Talmud, Bava Batra* 10a). If you cheat your fellow in order to gain financially, God will have to take it away from you because the money was not allocated to you. Perhaps you will have unforeseen medical expenses or other misfortunes, God forbid (*Rabbi Aryeh Leib Zuenz of Plotsk, 19th century*).

18. (The Jewish people) will live on the land securely. The next verse repeats that the children of Israel will *"live upon it securely."* Why the repetition?

kabbalah bites

25:10 According to the Kabbalah, the Sabbatical year is at the level of *Malkhut* (loyal worship), and the Jubilee year at the level of *Binah* (intuitive worship). *Malkhut* is that spirit within us that coerces us to stay loyal to our religious and spiritual values even when we lack inspiration. At the level of *Binah*, on the other hand, we "get it": our actions are infused with meaning and a higher sense of purpose. That means our passions can be unleashed because they are headed in the right direction.

When we reach *Binah*, we can *"proclaim freedom"* from the ego and enjoy a pure, uninhibited expression of the spirit.

leviticus 25:10–18 — be-har

- ¹⁰ (The court) should sanctify the (entire) period of the fiftieth year, and proclaim freedom throughout the land for all (the Hebrew slaves) who live on it. It will be (called) a "Jubilee (year)" for you.

- Each person's hereditary land (allotted to his ancestors when they first entered the land of Israel) should return to his (possession, if it had been sold).

- (A Hebrew slave who chose to remain with his master indefinitely should return) to his family.

- ¹¹ This fiftieth year will be a Jubilee for you (but it may not be extended further, into the next year).

- (Just like during a Sabbatical year) you should not sow, you should not reap (for yourself) its aftergrowth or pick (its grapes) which you had set aside (for yourselves).

- ¹² Because it is a Jubilee (if you sell produce from this year) your (money) will become (restricted as if it had been dedicated to the) Holy (Temple).

- (Just like during the Sabbatical year) you may eat its produce (and retain it in your house, so long as it is still freely available for the wild animals) from the field.

- ¹³ (If) a person (sells a field from) his hereditary land (and his son then buys it from the purchaser, the property) should be returned in the Jubilee year (to the father, who is its rightful owner).

- [SECOND READING] ¹⁴ When you make a sale to your fellow Jew or make a purchase from the hand of your fellow Jew, you should not cheat one another: ¹⁵ When you buy (a field) from your fellow Jew, he should sell it to you (at a price) based on the number of years since the (last) Jubilee, (bearing in mind) the number of years of crops (that you will be able to reap from the land until you return it to him at the next Jubilee. ¹⁶ If) more years (remain), you should increase its purchase price, and if fewer years (remain), you should decrease its purchase price, because he is selling it to you (for a price based on the) number of crops (it can produce).

- ¹⁷ A person should not (verbally) harass his fellow Jew (or give him bad advice. Since nobody can know your true intentions, and you could always escape blame,) you must fear your God—for I am God, your God.

¹⁸ You should observe My suprarational commands, guard My rational commands and perform them, (but in the merit of keeping the Sabbatical and Jubilee years alone, the Jewish people) will live on the land securely.

10. Proclaim freedom, for Hebrew slaves. Whether he is one who had his ear pierced (choosing to remain after six years of service, when a slave may go free—see *Exodus* 21:6), or one who had not yet served for a full six years when the Jubilee arrives (*Rashi, 11ᵗʰ century*).

11. (Just like during a Sabbatical year) you should not sow. Because of the lavish and carefree lifestyle that rich people often lead, the plight of the poor does not always resonate deeply.

ויקרא כה:יט-כז

19 וְנָתְנָה הָאָרֶץ פִּרְיָהּ וַאֲכַלְתֶּם לָשֹׂבַע וִישַׁבְתֶּם לָבֶטַח [THIRD READING / SECOND WHEN JOINED]
עָלֶיהָ: 20 וְכִי תֹאמְרוּ מַה־נֹּאכַל בַּשָּׁנָה הַשְּׁבִיעִת הֵן לֹא נִזְרָע וְלֹא נֶאֱסֹף אֶת־
תְּבוּאָתֵנוּ: 21 וְצִוִּיתִי אֶת־בִּרְכָתִי לָכֶם בַּשָּׁנָה הַשִּׁשִּׁית וְעָשָׂת אֶת־הַתְּבוּאָה
לִשְׁלֹשׁ הַשָּׁנִים: 22 וּזְרַעְתֶּם אֵת הַשָּׁנָה הַשְּׁמִינִת וַאֲכַלְתֶּם מִן־הַתְּבוּאָה יָשָׁן
עַד | הַשָּׁנָה הַתְּשִׁיעִת עַד־בּוֹא תְּבוּאָתָהּ תֹּאכְלוּ יָשָׁן: 23 וְהָאָרֶץ לֹא תִמָּכֵר
לִצְמִתֻת כִּי־לִי הָאָרֶץ כִּי־גֵרִים וְתוֹשָׁבִים אַתֶּם עִמָּדִי: 24 וּבְכֹל אֶרֶץ אֲחֻזַּתְכֶם
גְּאֻלָּה תִּתְּנוּ לָאָרֶץ: ס 25 כִּי־יָמוּךְ אָחִיךָ וּמָכַר מֵאֲחֻזָּתוֹ וּבָא גֹאֲלוֹ [FOURTH READING]
הַקָּרֹב אֵלָיו וְגָאַל אֵת מִמְכַּר אָחִיו: 26 וְאִישׁ כִּי לֹא יִהְיֶה־לּוֹ גֹּאֵל וְהִשִּׂיגָה
יָדוֹ וּמָצָא כְּדֵי גְאֻלָּתוֹ: 27 וְחִשַּׁב אֶת־שְׁנֵי מִמְכָּרוֹ וְהֵשִׁיב אֶת־הָעֹדֵף לָאִישׁ

New Year (the seventh month, *Tishri*); the entire seventh year; and part of the eighth year, for they will sow a new crop in *Marḥeshvan* of the eighth year and reap it in *Nisan*.

Thus God's three-year blessing lasts *"until the ninth year"* (v. 22), i.e., until the Festival of Weeks (*Shavuot*) in the ninth year, when the eighth year's crop is brought into the house. For throughout the summer season, it is kept in granaries in the field, and in *Tishri* the crop is gathered into the house.

There were occasions when it would need to yield for four years. Namely, in the sixth year preceding the seventh Sabbatical year of a forty-nine year cycle, when they would refrain from doing work on the land for *two* consecutive years—the Sabbatical year and the Jubilee year. Our verse, however, refers to normal Sabbatical years where a blessing is only required for three years (*Rashi, 11th century*).

The question in verse 20 could be understood in one of two ways: A challenge: If we do not sow crops, then how will we possibly eat in the seventh year? Or, an inquiry: Since we will not be sowing crops, could you explain what our source of food will be?

At the literal level, the verse would appear to be an inquiry, like a child inquiring from his father. For if it would be a challenge from a *non-believer*, God would not reply, *"I will direct My blessing to you, etc."* (v. 21; *Rabbi Ḥayyim ibn Attar, 18th century*).

The Babylonian Talmud (*Sanhedrin* 97a) compares the six agricultural years to the six millennia of this world, and the Sabbatical year to the seventh millennium (when the Redemption will have arrived). Since the Jewish people suffer from a gradual regression in spiritual stature as the generations pass, a person might ask: How could the efforts of the spiritually weak and "infertile" sixth millennium bring the true and complete redemption? The Torah answers: It is the *suprarational* self-sacrifice and commitment to Judaism of the final generations of exile that will bring the blessings of the Redemption (*Rabbi Menahem Mendel Schneerson, 20th century*).

23. Because the land belongs to Me. Do not begrudge returning it to its rightful owner at the Jubilee, because the land does not belong to you (*Rashi, 11th century*).

leviticus 25:19-27 — be-har

[THIRD READING / SECOND WHEN JOINED] ¹⁹ (If you keep all the commandments, then your own portion of) the land will yield its fruit and you will eat to satisfaction, and live upon it securely (without fear of drought).

²⁰ When you will say: "What will we eat in the seventh year, if we will not sow, and we will not (even) gather our produce (into) the (house from the crops which grow on their own?" ²¹ You should know that) I will direct My blessing to you in the sixth year, and it will yield produce (sufficient) for three years. ²² You will sow in the eighth year, while (still) eating from the old crops until the (Festival of Tabernacles in) the ninth year. You will be eating the old (crops) until the (new) crops arrive (from the harvest).

Redemption of Hereditary Land and Property

- ²³ The land should not be sold permanently, because the land belongs to Me, since you are strangers and residents with Me.

²⁴ Throughout the land which you possess, you should redeem land (as follows):

- [FOURTH READING] ²⁵ (Only) if your fellow Jew becomes destitute (may he) sell some (but not all) of his hereditary land. (If this happens) his close relative should come as his advocate and (buy the land back from the purchaser, thus) redeeming his relative's (undesirable) sale.

- ²⁶ If a man does not have a (close relative who is able to act as) an advocate, but he (later) becomes wealthy enough to afford its redemption, ²⁷ he should calculate the number of years for which the land has been sold (causing its devaluation),

A nation that settles a land fears that when it will become a successful and prosperous nation, its neighbors will invade. It also fears that it might not be successful, which would lead to rebellion and internal conflict. Therefore the Torah states *twice* that the children of Israel will live securely (*Rabbi Abraham Samuel Benjamin Sofer, 19th century*).

20-21. "What will we eat?" ... it will yield produce (sufficient) for three years. They must last for part of the sixth year, from the first month (*Nisan*), when the crop is reaped, until the Jewish

spiritual vitamin

> The general message of the Sabbatical year is the abrogation of the notion of dualism of matter and spirit. The Torah teaches us that there must be no separation between the spiritual and the material; that there must be no area in either nature or in human life from which God can be excluded.

אֲשֶׁר־מָכַר־לוֹ וְשָׁב לַאֲחֻזָּתוֹ: 28 וְאִם לֹא־מָצְאָה יָדוֹ דֵּי הָשִׁיב לוֹ וְהָיָה מִמְכָּרוֹ בְּיַד הַקֹּנֶה אֹתוֹ עַד שְׁנַת הַיּוֹבֵל וְיָצָא בַּיֹּבֵל וְשָׁב לַאֲחֻזָּתוֹ: ס [FIFTH READING / THIRD WHEN JOINED]

29 וְאִישׁ כִּי־יִמְכֹּר בֵּית־מוֹשַׁב עִיר חוֹמָה וְהָיְתָה גְּאֻלָּתוֹ עַד־תֹּם שְׁנַת מִמְכָּרוֹ יָמִים תִּהְיֶה גְאֻלָּתוֹ: 30 וְאִם לֹא־יִגָּאֵל עַד־מְלֹאת לוֹ שָׁנָה תְמִימָה וְקָם הַבַּיִת אֲשֶׁר־בָּעִיר אֲשֶׁר־[לָאכ׳] לוֹ חֹמָה לַצְּמִיתֻת לַקֹּנֶה אֹתוֹ לְדֹרֹתָיו לֹא יֵצֵא בַּיֹּבֵל:

31 וּבָתֵּי הַחֲצֵרִים אֲשֶׁר אֵין־לָהֶם חֹמָה סָבִיב עַל־שְׂדֵה הָאָרֶץ יֵחָשֵׁב גְּאֻלָּה תִּהְיֶה־לּוֹ וּבַיֹּבֵל יֵצֵא: 32 וְעָרֵי הַלְוִיִּם בָּתֵּי עָרֵי אֲחֻזָּתָם גְּאֻלַּת עוֹלָם תִּהְיֶה לַלְוִיִּם: 33 וַאֲשֶׁר יִגְאַל מִן־הַלְוִיִּם וְיָצָא מִמְכַּר־בַּיִת וְעִיר אֲחֻזָּתוֹ בַּיֹּבֵל כִּי בָתֵּי עָרֵי הַלְוִיִּם הִוא אֲחֻזָּתָם בְּתוֹךְ בְּנֵי יִשְׂרָאֵל: 34 וּשְׂדֵה מִגְרַשׁ עָרֵיהֶם לֹא יִמָּכֵר כִּי־אֲחֻזַּת עוֹלָם הוּא לָהֶם: ס 35 וְכִי־יָמוּךְ אָחִיךָ וּמָטָה יָדוֹ עִמָּךְ וְהֶחֱזַקְתָּ בּוֹ

He vented His anger on the Temple instead, causing its destruction (*Lamentations Rabbah*). If God would have punished the people, there would be no people and no need for a Temple. By "selling" the Temple, God caused not only its redemption, but also the redemption of the Israelites (*Rabbi Ḥayyim ibn Attar, 18th century*).

34. (If a Levite consecrates) a field in the open areas of their cities, it cannot change hands, because (these cities) are their eternal inheritance. We are prohibited to use the open area, which was for public use, for agriculture or for building development (*Babylonian Talmud, Arakhin 33b*). The reason for this, as the verse continues, is "*because (these cities) are their eternal inheritance*"—each generation has equal rights over these fields; no specific generation has control over it. *It is the moral responsibility of each generation to leave the benefits that they received from their predecessors for future generations* (*Rabbi Samson Raphael Hirsch, 19th century*).

35. You should support him. Support your fellow as soon as his fortune begins to dwindle. Do not wait until he is totally bankrupt to help him with charity (*Rashi, 11th century*).

One of the greatest forms of charity is to lend money to keep a business afloat or to form a business partnership. This can *prevent* poverty in the first place (*Maimonides, 12th century*).

"*You* should support him"—do not think that there are many other people who could help (*Rabbi Moses Alshekh, 16th century*).

Food for thought

1. What do you do to help the poor?

2. Have you ever witnessed real poverty first-hand?

3. Why does God allow poverty to exist?

and give back the balance to the man to whom he sold it. He can then return to his hereditary land.

- ²⁸ If he cannot find sufficient funds to repay (the purchaser), then what he sold will remain in the possession of its purchaser until the Jubilee year (approaches. Before) the Jubilee year (begins) the hereditary land will leave (the purchaser's possession) and return to its (rightful owner).

- [FIFTH READING / THIRD WHEN JOINED] ²⁹ (Unlike hereditary land, which may not be redeemed within two years of its sale), when a man sells (hereditary property consisting of) a residential house in a walled city, it may be redeemed until one year after its sale has elapsed. Its (period of possible) redemption should be a full year. ³⁰ If it is not redeemed by the end of a complete year, then that house which is in the walled city will be transferred absolutely to its purchaser (to be passed down) to his descendants. It will not leave (his possession) in the Jubilee, (unless the Jubilee year arrives within a year of the purchase).

- ³¹ Houses in open cities which do not have a surrounding wall have a similar law to a field of the land: (such a house) may be redeemed (at any time) and will leave (the purchaser's possession) in the Jubilee year.

³² (Regarding) the (forty-eight) cities (given to) the Levites:

- The houses of their inherited cities will forever have a (right of immediate) redemption for the Levites (unlike the houses of non-Levites in walled cities which lose their right of redemption after a year).

- ³³ If one purchases from the Levite either a house or an inherited city, it will leave (the possession of the purchaser) in the Jubilee year, because (the Levites were not given land to inherit, only cities; therefore) the houses in the Levites' cities (have the same law as) hereditary land among the (other) children of Israel—(it never loses its right of redemption).

- ³⁴ (If a Levite consecrates) a field in the open areas of their cities (to the Holy Temple and it is sold by the Temple treasurer) it cannot change hands (absolutely, i.e., the Levite will always be able to redeem it), because (these cities) are their eternal inheritance.

Prohibitions against Taking Interest

- ³⁵ If your fellow among you becomes needy and his hand is wavering, you should support him (before he becomes completely destitute) so that he can live with you—even if he is a convert or a resident (non-Jewish) alien, (provided he is not

29. When a man sells a residential house in a walled city, it may be redeemed. Allegorically, the "man" refers to God and the "residential house" he "sells," hints to the destruction of the Temple. God, in His infinite mercy, did not annihilate the Israelites when they sinned.

גֵּר וְתוֹשָׁב וָחַי עִמָּךְ: 36 אַל־תִּקַּח מֵאִתּוֹ נֶשֶׁךְ וְתַרְבִּית וְיָרֵאתָ מֵאֱלֹהֶיךָ וְחֵי אָחִיךָ עִמָּךְ: 37 אֶת־כַּסְפְּךָ לֹא־תִתֵּן לוֹ בְּנֶשֶׁךְ וּבְמַרְבִּית לֹא־תִתֵּן אָכְלֶךָ: 38 אֲנִי יְהוָה אֱלֹהֵיכֶם אֲשֶׁר־הוֹצֵאתִי אֶתְכֶם מֵאֶרֶץ מִצְרָיִם לָתֵת לָכֶם אֶת־אֶרֶץ כְּנַעַן לִהְיוֹת לָכֶם לֵאלֹהִים: ס [SIXTH READING / FOURTH WHEN JOINED] 39 וְכִי־יָמוּךְ אָחִיךָ עִמָּךְ וְנִמְכַּר־לָךְ לֹא־תַעֲבֹד בּוֹ עֲבֹדַת עָבֶד: 40 כְּשָׂכִיר כְּתוֹשָׁב יִהְיֶה עִמָּךְ עַד־שְׁנַת הַיֹּבֵל יַעֲבֹד עִמָּךְ: 41 וְיָצָא מֵעִמָּךְ הוּא וּבָנָיו עִמּוֹ וְשָׁב אֶל־מִשְׁפַּחְתּוֹ וְאֶל־אֲחֻזַּת אֲבֹתָיו יָשׁוּב: 42 כִּי־עֲבָדַי הֵם אֲשֶׁר־הוֹצֵאתִי אֹתָם מֵאֶרֶץ מִצְרָיִם לֹא יִמָּכְרוּ מִמְכֶּרֶת עָבֶד: 43 לֹא־תִרְדֶּה בוֹ בְּפָרֶךְ וְיָרֵאתָ מֵאֱלֹהֶיךָ: 44 וְעַבְדְּךָ וַאֲמָתְךָ אֲשֶׁר יִהְיוּ־לָךְ מֵאֵת הַגּוֹיִם אֲשֶׁר סְבִיבֹתֵיכֶם מֵהֶם תִּקְנוּ עֶבֶד וְאָמָה: 45 וְגַם מִבְּנֵי הַתּוֹשָׁבִים הַגָּרִים עִמָּכֶם מֵהֶם תִּקְנוּ וּמִמִּשְׁפַּחְתָּם אֲשֶׁר עִמָּכֶם אֲשֶׁר הוֹלִידוּ בְּאַרְצְכֶם וְהָיוּ לָכֶם לַאֲחֻזָּה: 46 וְהִתְנַחַלְתֶּם אֹתָם לִבְנֵיכֶם אַחֲרֵיכֶם לָרֶשֶׁת אֲחֻזָּה לְעֹלָם בָּהֶם תַּעֲבֹדוּ וּבְאַחֵיכֶם בְּנֵי־יִשְׂרָאֵל אִישׁ בְּאָחִיו לֹא־תִרְדֶּה בוֹ בְּפָרֶךְ: ס [SEVENTH READING] 47 וְכִי תַשִּׂיג יַד גֵּר וְתוֹשָׁב עִמָּךְ וּמָךְ אָחִיךָ עִמּוֹ וְנִמְכַּר לְגֵר תּוֹשָׁב עִמָּךְ אוֹ לְעֵקֶר מִשְׁפַּחַת גֵּר: 48 אַחֲרֵי נִמְכַּר גְּאֻלָּה תִּהְיֶה־לּוֹ אֶחָד

"bread of shame" which we do not truly appreciate. To be meaningful, even spiritual "revenue" must be earned by *active* involvement (*Rabbi Menahem Mendel Schneerson, 20th century*).

38. To give you the land of Canaan, (and) to be a God to you. The Israelites were given the land of Canaan to establish a nation where God would be among them. This goal was realized when they established a social order where they all lived together in harmony and assisted one another in their needs (*Rabbi Obadiah Sforno, 16th century*).

39. Do not make him do demeaning labor. The human master is charged with the task of helping the slave to mend his ways and return to his roots, to the dignified status of his ancestors (*Rabbi Mordecai ha-Kohen, 17th century*).

42. For (the Jewish people) are My servants. God says: "Their contract with Me came first" (*Rashi, 11th century*).

They should not be sold as slaves. They should not be sold by public announcement, saying, "Here is a slave for sale!" Nor may you stand him on an auction block (*Rashi, 11th century*).

The two halves of the verse are connected: "They are My slaves, whom I brought out of Egypt," *on the condition that* "they should not be sold as slaves" (*Sifra*).

leviticus 25:35-48   be-har

an idol-worshiper). [36] You should not take interest from him, (for taking) interest (is a double sin. While this may be difficult for you) you should fear your God, and (help) your fellow to live with you. [37] You should not lend him your money with interest, nor should you lend your food with interest. [38] I am God, your God, who took you out of the land of Egypt, to give you the land of Canaan, (and) to be a God to you.

Laws of Jewish Slaves Owned by Jews

- [SIXTH READING / FOURTH WHEN JOINED] [39] If your fellow among you becomes needy, and he is sold to you (as a slave), do not make him do demeaning labor. [40] He should (be treated by) you like an employee or a (hired) resident.

- He should work with you (for six years or) until the Jubilee year (whichever comes first), [41] and then he should leave you. He (should leave) along with his children. He should return to his family and resume the (dignified) status of his ancestors.

- [42] For (the Jewish people) are My servants, whom I brought out of the land of Egypt. They should not be sold as slaves.

- [43] You should not burden him with (unnecessary) labor (merely to torment him), and you should fear your God.

- [44] (However) you may acquire a male or female slave from the nations that are around you(r land and work these) male or female slaves that you have (with harsh labor). [45] You may also acquire (slaves for harsh labor) from the (non-Jewish) immigrants that live among you (who came to marry Canaanite women), and from their families that (live) with you in your land, where they were born. These (slaves) will remain yours as a permanent possession. [46] You should hold onto them as an inheritance for your children after you, as acquired property, (and) they will serve you indefinitely. But (when dealing with slaves from) your brothers, the children of Israel, a person should not work his brother with harsh labor.

Laws of Jewish Slaves Owned by Non-Jews

- [SEVENTH READING] [47] If a resident (non-Jewish) alien gains wealth (by being associated) with you, and your fellow Jew becomes needy (by being associated) with him (and his non-Jewish customs), and (the Jew) is sold to a resident (non-Jewish) alien (who lives) among you, or to (the maintenance of) idols, or to an idol-worshiper— [48] (then) as soon as he is sold, he should be redeemed. One of his

36. You should not take interest from him. When a person lends money at interest, he wishes his money to work for him, to bring in revenue, without making any effort himself.

This violates the spirit of Torah and its commandments. God gave us laws which require a tremendous *effort* on the part of man, for an unearned glory is not a glory at all. Ultimately, the requirement of effort is for our own benefit, so that our achievements should not be mere

ויקרא כה:מח – כו:ב

מֵאֶחָיו יִגְאָלֶנּוּ: 49 אוֹ־דֹדוֹ אוֹ בֶן־דֹּדוֹ יִגְאָלֶנּוּ אוֹ־מִשְּׁאֵר בְּשָׂרוֹ מִמִּשְׁפַּחְתּוֹ יִגְאָלֶנּוּ אוֹ־הִשִּׂיגָה יָדוֹ וְנִגְאָל: 50 וְחִשַּׁב עִם־קֹנֵהוּ מִשְּׁנַת הִמָּכְרוֹ לוֹ עַד שְׁנַת הַיֹּבֵל וְהָיָה כֶּסֶף מִמְכָּרוֹ בְּמִסְפַּר שָׁנִים כִּימֵי שָׂכִיר יִהְיֶה עִמּוֹ: 51 אִם־עוֹד רַבּוֹת בַּשָּׁנִים לְפִיהֶן יָשִׁיב גְּאֻלָּתוֹ מִכֶּסֶף מִקְנָתוֹ: 52 וְאִם־מְעַט נִשְׁאַר בַּשָּׁנִים עַד־שְׁנַת הַיֹּבֵל וְחִשַּׁב־לוֹ כְּפִי שָׁנָיו יָשִׁיב אֶת־גְּאֻלָּתוֹ: 53 כִּשְׂכִיר שָׁנָה בְּשָׁנָה יִהְיֶה עִמּוֹ לֹא־יִרְדֶּנּוּ בְּפֶרֶךְ לְעֵינֶיךָ: 54 וְאִם־לֹא יִגָּאֵל בְּאֵלֶּה וְיָצָא בִּשְׁנַת הַיֹּבֵל הוּא וּבָנָיו עִמּוֹ: 55 [MAFTIR] כִּי־לִי בְנֵי־יִשְׂרָאֵל עֲבָדִים עֲבָדַי הֵם אֲשֶׁר־הוֹצֵאתִי אוֹתָם מֵאֶרֶץ מִצְרָיִם אֲנִי יְהֹוָה אֱלֹהֵיכֶם:

כו 1 לֹא־תַעֲשׂוּ לָכֶם אֱלִילִם וּפֶסֶל וּמַצֵּבָה לֹא־תָקִימוּ לָכֶם וְאֶבֶן מַשְׂכִּית לֹא תִתְּנוּ בְּאַרְצְכֶם לְהִשְׁתַּחֲוֹת עָלֶיהָ כִּי אֲנִי יְהֹוָה אֱלֹהֵיכֶם: 2 אֶת־שַׁבְּתֹתַי תִּשְׁמֹרוּ וּמִקְדָּשִׁי תִּירָאוּ אֲנִי יְהֹוָה: פ פ פ

נ"ז פסוקים, חטי"ל סימן.

He should not learn from his master's actions to cast off the yoke of commandments that is upon him (*Rabbi Meir Loeb Weisser, 19th century*).

The status of the Jewish people in exile is compared to being sold into slavery to non-Jewish masters. In such a difficult situation a Jew may argue: "How can I possibly keep all the commandments when I have to live in a predominantly non-Jewish world?"

Just as the Jewish slave is required to keep all the commandments even in the house of his non-Jewish master, likewise, the Jewish people have been given the strength from God not to be perturbed by the challenges of the non-Jewish world, and to observe all of the commandments with pride (*Rabbi Menahem Mendel Schneerson, 20th century*).

- fellow (Jews) should redeem him, ⁴⁹ or his uncle or his cousin should redeem him, or another close relative from his family should redeem him; or, if his own hand will acquire (wealth), he should redeem (himself).

- ⁵⁰ He should calculate with his purchaser (the period) from the year when he was sold to him until the Jubilee year (when he would have been freed). The purchase price should then be (divided) by the number of years (to arrive at a yearly cost), as if he were a hired worker on a daily basis. ⁵¹ (Thus,) if there are still many years (until the Jubilee year), the redemption money that he returns (to his master) should be in proportion to (the work that he had already carried out, deducted from) the amount for which he was (originally) sold. ⁵² If only a few years remain until the Jubilee year, he should make the (same) calculation with (his master, and) the redemption money that he returns should take into consideration the years (that he worked). ⁵³ (Thus it is as if) he was with him as an employee hired year by year.

- If you see (the non-Jewish master) making (the Jewish slave) do harsh labor (you must stop him).

- ⁵⁴ If he is not redeemed through (any of) these (ways), he will be freed in the Jubilee year, both he and his children. [MAFTIR] ⁵⁵ For the children of Israel are slaves to Me. They are My slaves, whom I took out of the land of Egypt. I am God, your God.

26

- ¹ (If you are sold into slavery with a non-Jewish master) you should not make idols for yourselves (as he does), and you should not set up a statue or a monument for yourselves (as he does), nor should you set up a pavement stone on which to prostrate yourselves in your land, for I am God, your God. ² (Unlike your non-Jewish master,) you should keep My Sabbaths and fear My Sanctuary. I am God (who promises to reward you).

The *Haftarah* for *Be-Har* is on page 1365.

---

53. Harsh labor. An Israelite is not allowed to be used for harsh labor because *"the children of Israel are slaves"* to God (25:55). Since they are to be occupied and devoted to the service of God, they are not to use all their energy in serving their human master. So, too, with any materialistic pursuit: your main energy ought to be dedicated to serving the Almighty; the pursuit of materialism should be only out of necessity (*Rabbi Moses Feinstein, 20th century*).

26:1 You should not make idols for yourselves. He should not say, "Since my master has illicit relations, I will also be like him! Since my master worships idols, I will also be like him! Since my master desecrates the Sabbath, I will also be like him!" This is why these verses are stated here (*Rashi, 11th century*).

> The world runs on **cause and effect.** Positive actions lead to **positive outcomes;** negative actions bring about **negative outcomes.** God does not usually break these laws because they were set up for **your benefit.**

BE-ḤUKKOTAI
בחקתי

BLESSINGS FOR OBSERVING TORAH LAWS	26:3–13
CONSEQUENCES OF NEGLECTING THE LAWS	26:14–46
VALUATION OF DEDICATIONS TO THE TEMPLE	27:1–29
THE SECOND AND ANIMAL TITHES	27:30–34

NAME
Be-Ḥukkotai

MEANING
"My laws"

LINES IN TORAH SCROLL
131

PARASHIYYOT
3 open; 2 closed

VERSES
78

WORDS
1013

LETTERS
3992

DATE
Nisan – 20 *Iyyar*, 2449

LOCATION
Sinai Desert

KEY PEOPLE
Moses

MITZVOT
7 positive; 5 prohibitions

NOTE
Often read together with the portion of *Be-Har*

CHARACTER PROFILE

NAME
The Priest (*kohen*);
a descendant of Aaron

DUTIES
Sacrificial service at outer altar; guardians of the Temple; blessed the people; sounded trumpets; teachers of the law; received donations and gifts from the public; wore special priestly garments

KABBALAH
Souls emanate from *hesed* (kindness)

FAMOUS PRIESTS
The Maccabees—Family of priests from the Hasmonean dynasty that lived during the Second Temple era. During the reign of Antiochus they led a revolt against the Seleucid Empire who forbade Jewish rituals. The Maccabees were successful.

REWARDS

God promises us rewards for following His commandments. Since the majority of the commandments involve physical objects, we are promised physical rewards in return (26:3).

CONFESSION

Verbally confessing your sins is not only a legal requirement, but can also aid in repentance. The outward expression surfaces your thoughts and feelings, pushing you to return to your true self (26:40).

DEDICATIONS

As soon as an animal was dedicated to the Temple it acquired a holy status. And when we dedicate our time and resources to help holy causes, we make those things holy (27:9).

ויקרא כו:ג-י בחקתי

3 אִם־בְּחֻקֹּתַ֖י תֵּלֵ֑כוּ וְאֶת־מִצְוֺתַ֣י תִּשְׁמְר֔וּ וַעֲשִׂיתֶ֖ם אֹתָֽם: 4 וְנָתַתִּ֥י גִשְׁמֵיכֶ֖ם בְּעִתָּ֑ם וְנָתְנָ֤ה הָאָ֨רֶץ֙ יְבוּלָ֔הּ וְעֵ֥ץ הַשָּׂדֶ֖ה יִתֵּ֥ן פִּרְיֽוֹ: 5 וְהִשִּׂ֨יג לָכֶ֥ם דַּ֨יִשׁ֙ אֶת־בָּצִ֔יר וּבָצִ֖יר יַשִּׂ֣יג אֶת־זָ֑רַע וַאֲכַלְתֶּ֤ם לַחְמְכֶם֙ לָשֹׂ֔בַע וִישַׁבְתֶּ֥ם לָבֶ֖טַח בְּאַרְצְכֶֽם:

6 [SECOND READING] וְנָתַתִּ֤י שָׁלוֹם֙ בָּאָ֔רֶץ וּשְׁכַבְתֶּ֖ם וְאֵ֣ין מַחֲרִ֑יד וְהִשְׁבַּתִּ֞י חַיָּ֤ה רָעָה֙ מִן־הָאָ֔רֶץ וְחֶ֖רֶב לֹא־תַעֲבֹ֥ר בְּאַרְצְכֶֽם: 7 וּרְדַפְתֶּ֖ם אֶת־אֹיְבֵיכֶ֑ם וְנָפְל֥וּ לִפְנֵיכֶ֖ם לֶחָֽרֶב: 8 וְרָדְפ֨וּ מִכֶּ֤ם חֲמִשָּׁה֙ מֵאָ֔ה וּמֵאָ֥ה מִכֶּ֖ם רְבָבָ֣ה יִרְדֹּ֑פוּ וְנָפְל֧וּ אֹיְבֵיכֶ֛ם לִפְנֵיכֶ֖ם לֶחָֽרֶב: 9 וּפָנִ֣יתִי אֲלֵיכֶ֔ם וְהִפְרֵיתִ֣י אֶתְכֶ֔ם וְהִרְבֵּיתִ֖י אֶתְכֶ֑ם וַהֲקִימֹתִ֥י אֶת־בְּרִיתִ֖י אִתְּכֶֽם:

10 [THIRD READING / FIFTH WHEN JOINED] וַאֲכַלְתֶּ֥ם יָשָׁ֖ן נוֹשָׁ֑ן וְיָשָׁ֕ן מִפְּנֵ֥י חָדָ֖שׁ

The physical rewards mentioned here, such as rain, are for the nation as a whole, since rain does not fall for each individual according to his actions, but according to the deeds of the majority. Spiritual rewards are bestowed to each individual according to his actions (4:40; *Rabbi Joseph Albo, 15th century*).

6. I will grant peace in the land. The preceding verse states, "You will live safely in *your* land," the land of Israel. This verse's blessing is a far greater one: There will be *universal* peace, not only in the land of Israel, but in the whole world (*Rabbi Ḥayyim ibn Attar, 18th century*).

I will eliminate wild animals from the land. God will eliminate the *savage instinct* from the animals of the land.

As a reward for fulfilling the command, *"If you pursue My laws,"* you will merit a blissful state where the wild beast will return to its original, peaceful nature, like it was before the sin of the Tree of Knowledge. That is why the Talmud says, *"It's not the snake that kills, it's sin that kills"* (*Babylonian Talmud, Berakhot 33a*). The snake is not inherently a killer; it is only because of the sin of Adam that animals received this nature. But in the future era, *"A baby will play at a viper's hole,"* and *"the cow and the bear will graze together, and their young will lie down together. The lion will eat straw, like an ox"* (Isaiah 11:7-8; *Naḥmanides, 13th century*).

8. Five of you(r weakest men) will be able to chase away a hundred, and a hundred of you will be able to chase away ten thousand. According to the ratio of five men chasing away one hundred men, one hundred men should be able to chase away two thousand men, not ten thousand?

---

kabbalah bites

26:4 *"The land will yield its produce."* Ha-'aReTZ, "the land," is a Kabbalistic symbol for RaTZon, "will." So this verse could be read: "Your *will* is going to yield its produce."

You're always pregnant with some brilliant plan to spiritualize your life. Make sure that your *ratzon* "yields its produce" and you put that plan into action.

parashat be-ḥukkotai

Blessings for Observing the Commandments

³ If you pursue (the study of) My laws (in order to) guard My commands and observe them, ⁴ then I will give you rain at (a convenient) time, the land will yield its produce, and, (in the future, even) the (non-fruit-bearing) trees of the field will produce fruit. ⁵ You will be (busy) with threshing until the grape harvest, and the grape harvest will keep you (busy) until the sowing season. You will be satisfied with (even a small amount of) your bread, and you will live safely in your land.

[SECOND READING] ⁶ I will grant peace in the land, and you will go to sleep with nothing frightening (you). I will eliminate wild animals from the land, and (foreign) sword(s) will not (even) pass through your land (in peace, never mind in war). ⁷ You will chase away your enemies, and (as they are running away) they will fall (dead) by the(ir own) sword(s) before you (kill them). ⁸ Five of you(r weakest men) will be able to chase away a hundred, and a hundred of you will be able to chase away ten thousand. (As they are running away) they will fall (dead) by the(ir own) sword(s) before you (despite your tiny army).

⁹ I will turn (away from all My affairs) to (reward) you, and I will make you fruitful and (into men of) stature. I will set up My covenant with you (anew).

[THIRD READING / FIFTH WHEN JOINED] ¹⁰ You will eat matured produce (which will taste better than the fresh produce), and (the storage houses will be so full that) you will clear out the old (crops to make room for) the new.

Food for thought

1. What motivates you religiously: fear of punishment or thoughts of reward?

2. Why does God tempt us with rewards? Doesn't that breed insincerity?

3. Do you look forward to the world to come?

26:3-4 Pursue (the study of) My laws ... then I will give you rain. The main reward for observing the commandments is not mentioned here at all. God is merely promising to remove physical obstacles that interfere with the observance of the commandments.

The Torah does not mention any rewards at all, since you are supposed to observe the commandments for the sake of heaven, not in order to reap reward (*Maimonides, 12th century*).

Since man cannot understand spiritual rewards, the Torah did not specify them (*Rabbi Abraham ibn Ezra, 12th century*).

The Torah specifies these rewards for the skeptic who denies that everything is orchestrated by God. For the skeptic, physical proofs are more effective (*Rabbi Judah Halevi, 12th century*).

The Torah *does* state that man is given spiritual reward for observing the commandments, below in verses 11-12 (*Rabbi Nissim b. Reuben Gerondi, 14th century*).

ויקרא כו:י-טז בחקתי

11 תּוֹצִיאוּ: וְנָתַתִּ֥י מִשְׁכָּנִ֖י בְּתוֹכְכֶ֑ם וְלֹֽא־תִגְעַ֥ל נַפְשִׁ֖י אֶתְכֶֽם: 12 וְהִתְהַלַּכְתִּי֙ בְּתֽוֹכְכֶ֔ם וְהָיִ֥יתִי לָכֶ֖ם לֵֽאלֹהִ֑ים וְאַתֶּ֖ם תִּֽהְיוּ־לִ֥י לְעָֽם: 13 אֲנִ֞י יְהֹוָ֣ה אֱלֹֽהֵיכֶ֗ם אֲשֶׁ֨ר הוֹצֵ֤אתִי אֶתְכֶם֙ מֵאֶ֣רֶץ מִצְרַ֔יִם מִֽהְיֹ֥ת לָהֶ֖ם עֲבָדִ֑ים וָֽאֶשְׁבֹּר֙ מֹטֹ֣ת עֻלְּכֶ֔ם וָֽאוֹלֵ֥ךְ אֶתְכֶ֖ם קֽוֹמְמִיּֽוּת: פ 14 וְאִם־לֹ֥א תִשְׁמְע֖וּ לִ֑י וְלֹ֣א תַֽעֲשׂ֔וּ אֵ֥ת כָּל־הַמִּצְוֹ֖ת הָאֵֽלֶּה: 15 וְאִם־בְּחֻקֹּתַ֣י תִּמְאָ֔סוּ וְאִ֥ם אֶת־מִשְׁפָּטַ֖י תִּגְעַ֣ל נַפְשְׁכֶ֑ם לְבִלְתִּ֤י עֲשׂוֹת֙ אֶת־כָּל־מִצְוֹתַ֔י לְהַפְרְכֶ֖ם אֶת־בְּרִיתִֽי: 16 אַף־אֲנִ֞י אֶֽעֱשֶׂה־זֹּ֣את לָכֶ֗ם וְהִפְקַדְתִּ֨י עֲלֵיכֶ֤ם בֶּֽהָלָה֙ אֶת־הַשַּׁחֶ֣פֶת וְאֶת־הַקַּדַּ֔חַת מְכַלּ֥וֹת עֵינַ֖יִם וּמְדִיבֹ֥ת

the Torah, at which level we read here only of blessings. Through the study of Hasidic teachings, which reveal the subconscious aspects of the soul, we can reach a sublime union with God, at which point we will be able to see through the "disguise" in which these blessings are enclosed and appreciate them for their true worth (*Rabbi Shneur Zalman of Lyady, 18th century*).

The notion that a sublime blessing may be expressed through negative language is not of uniquely Ḥasidic origin, it is found in the Babylonian Talmud (*Mo'ed Katan* 9a-b). When Rabbi Simeon son of Yoḥai sent his son, Rabbi Eleazar, to receive blessings from two of the Sages (Rabbi Jonathan son of Asmai and Rabbi Judah son of Gerim), they responded with what appeared to be a series of curses: "May it be God's will that you will sow and not reap. That what you bring in will not go out, and what you take out will not come in. That your house will be desolate and your temporary lodgings inhabited. That your table will be disturbed, and that you will not see a new year."

When Rabbi Eleazar came home and reported what had happened, his father explained:

These are all blessings! "You will sow and not reap," means that you will have children and they will not die.

"What you bring in will not go out," means that you will bring home daughters-in-law and your sons will not die, so that their wives will not leave again.

"What you take out will not come in," means that you will give your daughters in marriage and their husbands will not die, so that your daughters need not come back.

"Your house will be desolate and your temporary lodgings inhabited," because this world is your "temporary lodging" and the next world is a "home."

"Your table will be disturbed," by sons and daughters.

> **kabbalah bites**
>
> **26:13** The word *komemiyyut*, "upright," when written scribally, has two "crowns" (*tagim*) on the Hebrew letter *kof*. This, explains the Kabbalah, indicates that the truly upright person has *two* sides to him: the perfect and the imperfect.
>
> Have you ever wondered which is spiritually superior: to be good, or to correct yourself after having erred? The two crowns here teach us that each mode is indispensable. True human greatness is a seamless blend of the good and the corrected self, which is why both crowns are on the same letter.

leviticus 26:11–16 — be-ḥukkotai

¹¹ I will place My dwelling in your midst, and My spirit will not be disgusted by you.

¹² (When you go to heaven) I will stroll among you (and you will feel comfortable with Me, but) I will (still) be your God (whom you fear), and you will be My people.

¹³ (I clearly have the power to bring all these blessings, for) I am God, your God, who took you out of the land of Egypt (with great miracles, freeing you) from their slavery. I broke the pegs of your yoke and led you upright.

Consequences of Failing to Observe the Commandments

But if: [1] You do not listen to Me (by studying the Oral Law);

[2] And you do not perform all these commandments;

[3] ¹⁵ And if (this leads you to find people who keep) My laws disgusting;

[4] (And if this leads) you to hate (Torah scholars who study) My laws;

[5] (And this leads you to) stop (others from) performing (the commandments);

[6] (And you deny) that (they are in fact) My commandments at all;

[7] (And you eventually) break My covenant (by denying the principles of faith);

— ¹⁶ then I too will do the same to you. I will direct upon you: panic, inflammation, fever, and diseases that cause hopeless longing (for a cure) and anguish (to your family members, when you pass away). You will sow your seed in vain (for it

---

This teaches us that the more we unite with those who follow the ways of Torah, the more synergy there will be, and our powers will multiply. Five men can chase only one hundred, but one hundred men can chase ten thousand (*Rashi, 11ᵗʰ century*).

12. I will stroll among you. The word "stroll" denotes that God will be among the Israelites wherever they go and not limited to one specific place, the Sanctuary. *"I will stroll among you"*—God's glory will be manifest wherever His children venture (*Rabbi Obadiah Sforno, 16ᵗʰ century*).

16. I will direct upon you. When describing the misfortunes that He will bring to those who neglect His Torah, God alludes to the mercy inherent in these curses. Instead of the punishments being administered through the Divine attribute of justice, God will *"direct"* them through a messenger. This will inevitably diminish the harshness of the punishment.

These punishments were not intended as cruel acts of retribution, but rather, like a father admonishing his child for the child's benefit (*Rabbi Mordecai ha-Kohen, 17ᵗʰ century*).

Panic, inflammation, fever, and diseases. In truth, *these are nothing but blessings*. While openly, these verses speak of the very opposite of blessing, there nevertheless exists an inner, subconscious element of

---

Food for thought

1. Is calamity always the result of sin?

2. What is your religious reaction to calamity?

3. Why did God allow the Holocaust?

ויקרא כו:טז-כה   בחקתי

נֶ֖פֶשׁ וּזְרַעְתֶּ֤ם לָרִיק֙ זַרְעֲכֶ֔ם וַאֲכָלֻ֖הוּ אֹיְבֵיכֶֽם: 17 וְנָתַתִּ֤י פָנַי֙ בָּכֶ֔ם וְנִגַּפְתֶּ֖ם לִפְנֵ֣י אֹיְבֵיכֶ֑ם וְרָד֤וּ בָכֶם֙ שֹֽׂנְאֵיכֶ֔ם וְנַסְתֶּ֖ם וְאֵין־רֹדֵ֥ף אֶתְכֶֽם: 18 וְאִ֨ם־עַד־אֵ֔לֶּה לֹ֥א תִשְׁמְע֖וּ לִ֑י וְיָסַפְתִּ֤י לְיַסְּרָה֙ אֶתְכֶ֔ם שֶׁ֖בַע עַל־חַטֹּאתֵיכֶֽם: 19 וְשָׁבַרְתִּ֖י אֶת־גְּא֣וֹן עֻזְּכֶ֑ם וְנָתַתִּ֤י אֶת־שְׁמֵיכֶם֙ כַּבַּרְזֶ֔ל וְאֶת־אַרְצְכֶ֖ם כַּנְּחֻשָֽׁה: 20 וְתַ֥ם לָרִ֖יק כֹּחֲכֶ֑ם וְלֹא־תִתֵּ֤ן אַרְצְכֶם֙ אֶת־יְבוּלָ֔הּ וְעֵ֥ץ הָאָ֖רֶץ לֹ֥א יִתֵּ֥ן פִּרְיֽוֹ: 21 וְאִם־תֵּֽלְכ֤וּ עִמִּי֙ קֶ֔רִי וְלֹ֥א תֹאב֖וּ לִשְׁמֹ֣עַֽ לִ֑י וְיָסַפְתִּ֤י עֲלֵיכֶם֙ מַכָּ֔ה שֶׁ֖בַע כְּחַטֹּאתֵיכֶֽם: 22 וְהִשְׁלַחְתִּ֨י בָכֶ֜ם אֶת־חַיַּ֤ת הַשָּׂדֶה֙ וְשִׁכְּלָ֣ה אֶתְכֶ֔ם וְהִכְרִ֖יתָה֙ אֶת־בְּהֶמְתְּכֶ֔ם וְהִמְעִ֖יטָה אֶתְכֶ֑ם וְנָשַׁ֖מּוּ דַּרְכֵיכֶֽם: 23 וְאִ֨ם־בְּאֵ֔לֶּה לֹ֥א תִוָּסְר֖וּ לִ֑י וַהֲלַכְתֶּ֥ם עִמִּ֖י קֶֽרִי: 24 וְהָלַכְתִּ֧י אַף־אֲנִ֛י עִמָּכֶ֖ם בְּקֶ֑רִי וְהִכֵּיתִ֤י אֶתְכֶם֙ גַּם־אָ֔נִי שֶׁ֖בַע עַל־חַטֹּאתֵיכֶֽם: 25 וְהֵבֵאתִ֨י עֲלֵיכֶ֜ם חֶ֗רֶב נֹקֶ֙מֶת֙ נְקַם־בְּרִ֔ית וְנֶאֱסַפְתֶּ֖ם אֶל־עָרֵיכֶ֑ם

Similarly, all the verses in the admonition belie very lofty blessings—blessings so sublime that they could not be expressed straightforwardly (*Rabbi Menahem Mendel Schneersohn of Lubavitch, 19th century*).

17. I will devote My time. Amid all the harsh admonitions, God still would neither hide His face from them, nor abandon them totally, allowing their enemies to annihilate them completely. He would still devote His attention to them (*Rabbi Ḥayyim ibn Attar, 18th century*).

24. Then I too, will be offhand with you. This verse is a reaction to verse 21, *"If you treat Me offhandedly."* If you treat my actions as "chance," that is, not heeding the call for repentance when I send a calamity, then I will bring upon you more of those "chance" incidents.

Everything that God does has a message. We have to look at our actions and see what message God is sending us, and then ask: How do we need to better ourselves? (*Maimonides, 12th century*).

spiritual vitamin

> When we observe the commandments, this widens the channels to receive God's blessings, including deeper insight and understanding to cope with problems and to make the right judgments and decisions.

will not sprout), and (if it does sprout) your enemies will eat it. ¹⁷ I will devote My time (away from all My affairs and deal) with you, and you will be struck down before your enemies. Your enemies will rule over you. You will flee (out of terror) but no one will be pursuing you (since you pose no threat to them).

¹⁸ If you do not listen to Me while these (punishments are upon you), I will add a further seven punishments corresponding to your (seven above-mentioned) sins:

[1] ¹⁹ I will destroy (the Holy Temple, which is) the pride of your strength.

[2] I will make your skies (as dry as) iron (causing a drought).

[3] Your land (will exude moisture) like copper (causing its fruits to rot).

[4] ²⁰ (You will work hard on the land) but your strength will be spent in vain.

[5] Your land will not (even) yield the (amount of) produce (which you sowed into it).

[6] The earth will not give (sufficient nourishment) to the trees.

[7] (If the trees do produce fruit) they will not give their fruit (to you, for the fruits will fall on the ground and rot).

²¹ If you (still) treat My (commands) offhandedly, and you do not wish to listen to Me, I will add seven (further) punishments corresponding to your (seven above-mentioned) sins:

[1] ²² I will incite the wild animals of the field against you,

[2] (together with domesticated animals that kill),

[3] (and venomous snakes),

[4] and they will bereave you (by killing your children).

[5] They will completely destroy your livestock (that pasture outside),

[6] and diminish (the number of) you(r livestock that you keep inside).

[7] Your (major and minor) roads will become desolate.

²³ If, despite these (calamities), you will still not be (sufficiently) chastised (to return) to Me, and you treat My (commands) offhandedly, ²⁴ then I, too, will be offhand with you, and I Myself will strike you again with seven punishments for your (seven above-mentioned) sins:

[1] ²⁵ I will bring upon you an (army armed with the) sword, to avenge you (with the punishment described in the Book of Deuteronomy, where the) avenging of the covenant (is detailed).

"You will not see a new year," means that your wife will not die and so you will not have to take another wife.

ויקרא כו:כה-לו | בחקתי

וְשִׁלַּחְתִּי דֶבֶר בְּתוֹכְכֶם וְנִתַּתֶּם בְּיַד־אוֹיֵב: 26 בְּשִׁבְרִי לָכֶם מַטֵּה־לֶחֶם וְאָפוּ עֶשֶׂר נָשִׁים לַחְמְכֶם בְּתַנּוּר אֶחָד וְהֵשִׁיבוּ לַחְמְכֶם בַּמִּשְׁקָל וַאֲכַלְתֶּם וְלֹא תִשְׂבָּעוּ: ס 27 וְאִם־בְּזֹאת לֹא תִשְׁמְעוּ לִי וַהֲלַכְתֶּם עִמִּי בְּקֶרִי: 28 וְהָלַכְתִּי עִמָּכֶם בַּחֲמַת־קֶרִי וְיִסַּרְתִּי אֶתְכֶם אַף־אָנִי שֶׁבַע עַל־חַטֹּאתֵיכֶם: 29 וַאֲכַלְתֶּם בְּשַׂר בְּנֵיכֶם וּבְשַׂר בְּנֹתֵיכֶם תֹּאכֵלוּ: 30 וְהִשְׁמַדְתִּי אֶת־בָּמֹתֵיכֶם וְהִכְרַתִּי אֶת־חַמָּנֵיכֶם וְנָתַתִּי אֶת־פִּגְרֵיכֶם עַל־פִּגְרֵי גִּלּוּלֵיכֶם וְגָעֲלָה נַפְשִׁי אֶתְכֶם: 31 וְנָתַתִּי אֶת־עָרֵיכֶם חָרְבָּה וַהֲשִׁמּוֹתִי אֶת־מִקְדְּשֵׁיכֶם וְלֹא אָרִיחַ בְּרֵיחַ נִיחֹחֲכֶם: 32 וַהֲשִׁמֹּתִי אֲנִי אֶת־הָאָרֶץ וְשָׁמְמוּ עָלֶיהָ אֹיְבֵיכֶם הַיֹּשְׁבִים בָּהּ: 33 וְאֶתְכֶם אֱזָרֶה בַגּוֹיִם וַהֲרִיקֹתִי אַחֲרֵיכֶם חָרֶב וְהָיְתָה אַרְצְכֶם שְׁמָמָה וְעָרֵיכֶם יִהְיוּ חָרְבָּה: 34 אָז תִּרְצֶה הָאָרֶץ אֶת־שַׁבְּתֹתֶיהָ כֹּל יְמֵי הֳשַׁמָּה וְאַתֶּם בְּאֶרֶץ אֹיְבֵיכֶם אָז תִּשְׁבַּת הָאָרֶץ וְהִרְצָת אֶת־שַׁבְּתֹתֶיהָ: 35 כָּל־יְמֵי הֳשַׁמָּה תִּשְׁבֹּת אֵת אֲשֶׁר לֹא־שָׁבְתָה בְּשַׁבְּתֹתֵיכֶם בְּשִׁבְתְּכֶם עָלֶיהָ: 36 וְהַנִּשְׁאָרִים בָּכֶם וְהֵבֵאתִי מֹרֶךְ בִּלְבָבָם בְּאַרְצֹת אֹיְבֵיהֶם וְרָדַף אֹתָם קוֹל עָלֶה נִדָּף וְנָסוּ

26. Ten woman will bake bread in one oven. This bread, which is the basis of your physical sustenance, is an analogy for Torah, your spiritual sustenance. Just as dough needs to be baked into bread for it to become edible, so too, the Torah that you learn needs to be "baked" in a fiery love for God. Only then will the Torah be "absorbed" into your system and sustain you spiritually.

How is this baking of your spiritual bread to be achieved? The Torah teaches, *"Ten women will bake bread in one oven"*—using all ten faculties of your soul, you should meditate at length on the absolute Oneness of God, until this produces a fiery love of God in your heart.

And then, *"You will eat (bread) and not be satisfied."* However many times you review the study of a topic in the Torah, it will still be as exciting as if you were studying it for the first time, and your desire to study it again will never cease (*Rabbi Shneur Zalman of Lyady, 18th century*).

31. I will make your Holy Temple devoid of visitors. I will not smell the pleasant aroma (of your sacrifices). The Sanctuary was intended to fulfil God's "desire" that He be manifested in this world, but the Israelites' motivation for building the Temple was self-serving. Therefore *"I will make your Holy Temple devoid"*—since it is *"your* temple," devoid of My holiness, your enemies will conquer it.

The sacrifices were suppose to be offered as *"a pleasant aroma for God"* (*Leviticus* 1:9; 2:2; 3:5; 4:31), but the children of Israel brought them to fulfil their own needs. Therefore God says,

[2] You will gather into your cities (because of the siege).

[3] I will incite a plague in your midst, and you will be (forced to bury the corpses outside Jerusalem, where you will be) delivered into the enemy's hands.

[4] ²⁶ I will cut off your source of food.

[5] (Due to a shortage of wood) ten women will bake bread in one oven.

[6] (The bread will crumble in the oven) and they will bring back your bread (as crumbs measured) by weight.

[7] You will eat (bread), and not be satisfied.

²⁷ If, despite this, you do not listen to Me, and treat Me offhandedly, ²⁸ I will act with anger (against your) offhandedness, and I Myself will chastise you seven (times) for your (seven) sins:

[1] ²⁹ You will eat the flesh of your sons, and you will eat the flesh of your daughters.

[2] ³⁰ I will demolish your tall buildings, (both towers and castles, causing your rooftop) idols (that stand in the) sun to be destroyed.

[3] (When your bellies will swell from hunger, and you take your idol to kiss it) I will make (your bellies burst so that) your corpses (fall) upon your idols.

[4] My Spirit (the Divine Presence) will be disgusted by you (and will depart from you).

[5] ³¹ I will lay your cities to ruins (that nobody even passes through).

[6] I will make your (Holy) Temple devoid (of visitors).

[7] I will not smell the pleasant aroma (of your sacrifices in the Holy Temple, for they will cease).

³² I will make the land desolate (which will have the positive outcome that) it will (also) become desolate of your enemies who (now) live in it. ³³ I will scatter you among the nations, and I will unleash (armies equipped with) the sword (to pursue) after you. Your land will be desolate (for a long time), so your cities will become ruins.

³⁴ Then, during all the time that it remains desolate while you are in your enemies' land, the land will appease (God) for its (many unobserved) Sabbatical years. (When) the land will rest, (God) will be appeased for its (many unobserved) Sabbatical years. ³⁵ During all the days that it remains desolate (during the Babylonian Exile) it will rest for (the same number of years) that it had not rested during your Sabbatical years, when you lived there.

³⁶ To those who survive among you—I will bring (such) terror into their hearts in their enemies' lands that the (mere) sound of a rustling leaf will (appear to be an enemy) pursuing them, and they will flee as one flees from the sword. They will

ויקרא כו:לו–מו בחקתי

מְנֻסַת־חֶ֔רֶב וְנָפְל֖וּ וְאֵ֥ין רֹדֵֽף׃ 37 וְכָשְׁל֧וּ אִישׁ־בְּאָחִ֛יו כְּמִפְּנֵי־חֶ֖רֶב וְרֹדֵ֣ף אָ֑יִן וְלֹא־תִֽהְיֶ֤ה לָכֶם֙ תְּקוּמָ֔ה לִפְנֵ֖י אֹֽיְבֵיכֶֽם׃ 38 וַאֲבַדְתֶּ֖ם בַּגּוֹיִ֑ם וְאָכְלָ֣ה אֶתְכֶ֔ם אֶ֖רֶץ אֹיְבֵיכֶֽם׃ 39 וְהַנִּשְׁאָרִ֣ים בָּכֶ֗ם יִמַּ֙קּוּ֙ בַּעֲוֺנָ֔ם בְּאַרְצֹ֖ת אֹיְבֵיכֶ֑ם וְאַ֛ף בַּעֲוֺנֹ֥ת אֲבֹתָ֖ם אִתָּ֥ם יִמָּֽקּוּ׃ 40 וְהִתְוַדּ֤וּ אֶת־עֲוֺנָם֙ וְאֶת־עֲוֺ֣ן אֲבֹתָ֔ם בְּמַעֲלָ֖ם אֲשֶׁ֣ר מָֽעֲלוּ־בִ֑י וְאַ֕ף אֲשֶׁר־הָלְכ֥וּ עִמִּ֖י בְּקֶֽרִי׃ 41 אַף־אֲנִ֗י אֵלֵ֤ךְ עִמָּם֙ בְּקֶ֔רִי וְהֵבֵאתִ֣י אֹתָ֔ם בְּאֶ֖רֶץ אֹיְבֵיהֶ֑ם אוֹ־אָ֣ז יִכָּנַ֗ע לְבָבָם֙ הֶֽעָרֵ֔ל וְאָ֖ז יִרְצ֥וּ אֶת־עֲוֺנָֽם׃ 42 וְזָכַרְתִּ֖י אֶת־בְּרִיתִ֣י יַעֲק֑וֹב וְאַף֩ אֶת־בְּרִיתִ֨י יִצְחָ֜ק וְאַ֨ף אֶת־בְּרִיתִ֧י אַבְרָהָ֛ם אֶזְכֹּ֖ר וְהָאָ֥רֶץ אֶזְכֹּֽר׃ 43 וְהָאָ֩רֶץ֩ תֵּעָזֵ֨ב מֵהֶ֜ם וְתִ֣רֶץ אֶת־שַׁבְּתֹתֶ֗יהָ בָּהְשַׁמָּה֙ מֵהֶ֔ם וְהֵ֖ם יִרְצ֣וּ אֶת־עֲוֺנָ֑ם יַ֣עַן וּבְיַ֔עַן בְּמִשְׁפָּטַ֖י מָאָ֔סוּ וְאֶת־חֻקֹּתַ֖י גָּעֲלָ֥ה נַפְשָֽׁם׃ 44 וְאַף־גַּם־זֹ֠את בִּֽהְיוֹתָ֞ם בְּאֶ֣רֶץ אֹֽיְבֵיהֶ֗ם לֹֽא־מְאַסְתִּ֤ים וְלֹֽא־גְעַלְתִּים֙ לְכַלֹּתָ֔ם לְהָפֵ֥ר בְּרִיתִ֖י אִתָּ֑ם כִּ֛י אֲנִ֥י יְהֹוָ֖ה אֱלֹהֵיהֶֽם׃ 45 וְזָכַרְתִּ֥י לָהֶ֖ם בְּרִ֣ית רִאשֹׁנִ֑ים אֲשֶׁ֣ר הוֹצֵֽאתִי־אֹתָם֩ מֵאֶ֨רֶץ מִצְרַ֜יִם לְעֵינֵ֣י הַגּוֹיִ֗ם לִהְיֹ֥ת לָהֶ֛ם לֵאלֹהִ֖ים אֲנִ֥י יְהֹוָֽה׃ 46 אֵ֠לֶּה הַֽחֻקִּ֣ים וְהַמִּשְׁפָּטִים֮ וְהַתּוֹרֹת֒ אֲשֶׁר֙ נָתַ֣ן יְהֹוָ֔ה בֵּינ֕וֹ וּבֵ֖ין בְּנֵ֣י יִשְׂרָאֵ֑ל בְּהַ֥ר סִינַ֖י בְּיַד־מֹשֶֽׁה׃ פ

41. I will bring them to the land of their enemies. God is saying: "I Myself will bring them!" This is good for the Jewish people, so that they should not say, "Since we have been exiled among the nations, we may as well behave like them!" God replies: "I will not let them, for I will send them My prophets, and bring them back under My very wings!" As the verse states, "'*What enters your mind to be like the nations will not come about ... 'As I live' says God ... 'I will reign over you with a strong hand'*" (*Ezekiel* 20:32-33; *Rashi, 11th century*).

42. My covenant with Isaac. The word "remember" is mentioned in this verse in reference to Abraham and Jacob, but it is not repeated again in reference to Isaac. This is because Isaac's *ashes* are visible before God, heaped up and lying on the altar. "Remembrance" is only for things that are not visibly present (*Sifra*).

44. I will not despise them and become disgusted by them to (the extent that I) annihilate them, breaking My covenant with them. "*I will not despise them,*" relates to the times of the Greeks; "*and become disgusted by them,*" to the destruction of the Temple by Vespasian; "*(to the extent that I) annihilate them,*" refers to the times of Haman; and "*breaking My covenant with them,*" relates to this long exile. Even in these most dire of times, God has not forsaken us (*Babylonian Talmud, Megillah* 11b).

fall (even though) there will be no pursuer. ³⁷ (They will flee so hurriedly that) each man will stumble over his brother, (for they will always feel they are being chased) by the sword, while there is (in reality) no pursuer. You will not be able to stand up against your enemies.

³⁸ You will become lost (from each other, scattered) among the nations, and your enemies' land will consume you. ³⁹ Those of you who survive will rot away in your enemies' lands because of their sins. They will indeed rot away because their fathers' sins are still (being practiced) by them. ⁴⁰ They will confess their sins and their fathers' sins, for the treachery with which they betrayed Me, and for following Me offhandedly. ⁴¹ Then I too, will treat them offhandedly, and I will bring them to the land of their enemies, perhaps then their stubborn heart will become humbled and their sins will then be atoned.

⁴² But I will remember My covenant with Jacob, and My covenant with Isaac too. I will also remember My covenant with Abraham, and I will remember the land.

⁴³ The land, left behind by them, will have appeased (God) for its (unobserved) Sabbatical years by lying desolate without them, and they will be atoned for their sins.

(This was all) to pay them back for having despised My rational commands and to pay them back for their having been disgusted by My suprarational commands.

⁴⁴ But despite all this (above-mentioned punishment), while they are in their enemies' land, I will not despise them and become disgusted by them to (the extent that I) annihilate them, breaking My covenant that is with them, for I am God, their God. ⁴⁵ I will remember, for their sake, the covenant made with the original (tribes), whom I took out from the land of Egypt in the sight of the nations, so as to be a God to them. I am God.

⁴⁶ These are the suprarational and rational commands (from) the (Written and Oral) Laws that God gave through Moses on Mount Sinai, (as a covenant) between Himself and the children of Israel.

"I will not smell the pleasant aroma of your sacrifice"—it is a sacrifice for *your* own pleasure, so I need not smell its *"pleasant aroma"* (*Rabbi Mordecai ha-Kohen, 17th century*).

37. Each man will stumble over his brother. Man will stumble because of *the sins* of his brother. Here you learn the great responsibility that you have for your fellow (*Babylonian Talmud, Sanhedrin 27b*).

40. They will confess their sins. Their confession will not be sincere, as we see from the following verse (41) that God will continue to punish them (*Rabbi Hezekiah b. Manoah, 13th century*).

Their "confession" will merely be a recognition that they had sinned, without an accompanying feeling of remorse. It is like someone who immerses in a ritual-pool to achieve purity, while at the same time holding a ritually impure creature in his hand (*Rabbi Ephraim of Luntshits, 16th–17th century*).

ויקרא כז:א-יב / בחקתי

כז [FOURTH READING / SIXTH WHEN JOINED] 1 וַיְדַבֵּ֥ר יְהוָ֖ה אֶל־מֹשֶׁ֥ה לֵּאמֹֽר: 2 דַּבֵּ֞ר אֶל־בְּנֵ֤י יִשְׂרָאֵל֙ וְאָמַרְתָּ֣ אֲלֵהֶ֔ם אִ֕ישׁ כִּ֥י יַפְלִ֖א נֶ֑דֶר בְּעֶרְכְּךָ֥ נְפָשֹׁ֖ת לַיהוָֽה: 3 וְהָיָ֤ה עֶרְכְּךָ֙ הַזָּכָ֔ר מִבֶּן֙ עֶשְׂרִ֣ים שָׁנָ֔ה וְעַ֖ד בֶּן־שִׁשִּׁ֣ים שָׁנָ֑ה וְהָיָ֣ה עֶרְכְּךָ֗ חֲמִשִּׁ֛ים שֶׁ֥קֶל כֶּ֖סֶף בְּשֶׁ֥קֶל הַקֹּֽדֶשׁ: 4 וְאִם־נְקֵבָ֖ה הִ֑וא וְהָיָ֥ה עֶרְכְּךָ֖ שְׁלֹשִׁ֥ים שָֽׁקֶל: 5 וְאִ֨ם מִבֶּן־חָמֵ֜שׁ שָׁנִ֗ים וְעַד֙ בֶּן־עֶשְׂרִ֣ים שָׁנָ֔ה וְהָיָ֧ה עֶרְכְּךָ֛ הַזָּכָ֖ר עֶשְׂרִ֣ים שְׁקָלִ֑ים וְלַנְּקֵבָ֖ה עֲשֶׂ֥רֶת שְׁקָלִֽים: 6 וְאִ֣ם מִבֶּן־חֹ֗דֶשׁ וְעַד֙ בֶּן־חָמֵ֣שׁ שָׁנִ֔ים וְהָיָ֤ה עֶרְכְּךָ֙ הַזָּכָ֔ר חֲמִשָּׁ֥ה שְׁקָלִ֖ים כָּ֑סֶף וְלַנְּקֵבָ֣ה עֶרְכְּךָ֔ שְׁלֹ֥שֶׁת שְׁקָלִ֖ים כָּֽסֶף: 7 וְ֠אִם מִבֶּן־שִׁשִּׁ֨ים שָׁנָ֤ה וָמַ֙עְלָה֙ אִם־זָכָ֔ר וְהָיָ֣ה עֶרְכְּךָ֔ חֲמִשָּׁ֥ה עָשָׂ֖ר שָׁ֑קֶל וְלַנְּקֵבָ֖ה עֲשָׂרָ֥ה שְׁקָלִֽים: 8 וְאִם־מָ֥ךְ הוּא֙ מֵֽעֶרְכֶּ֔ךָ וְהֶֽעֱמִידוֹ֙ לִפְנֵ֣י הַכֹּהֵ֔ן וְהֶעֱרִ֥יךְ אֹת֖וֹ הַכֹּהֵ֑ן עַל־פִּ֗י אֲשֶׁ֤ר תַּשִּׂיג֙ יַ֣ד הַנֹּדֵ֔ר יַעֲרִיכֶ֖נּוּ הַכֹּהֵֽן: ס 9 וְאִ֨ם־בְּהֵמָ֔ה אֲשֶׁ֨ר יַקְרִ֧יבוּ מִמֶּ֛נָּה קָרְבָּ֖ן לַֽיהוָ֑ה כֹּל֩ אֲשֶׁ֨ר יִתֵּ֥ן מִמֶּ֛נּוּ לַיהוָ֖ה יִֽהְיֶה־קֹּֽדֶשׁ: 10 לֹ֣א יַחֲלִיפֶ֗נּוּ וְלֹֽא־יָמִ֥יר אֹת֛וֹ ט֥וֹב בְּרָ֖ע אוֹ־רַ֣ע בְּט֑וֹב וְאִם־הָמֵ֨ר יָמִ֤יר בְּהֵמָה֙ בִּבְהֵמָ֔ה וְהָֽיָה־ה֥וּא וּתְמוּרָת֖וֹ יִֽהְיֶה־קֹּֽדֶשׁ: 11 וְאִם֙ כָּל־בְּהֵמָ֣ה טְמֵאָ֔ה אֲ֠שֶׁר לֹא־יַקְרִ֧יבוּ מִמֶּ֛נָּה קָרְבָּ֖ן לַֽיהוָ֑ה וְהֶֽעֱמִ֥יד אֶת־הַבְּהֵמָ֖ה לִפְנֵ֥י הַכֹּהֵֽן: 12 וְהֶעֱרִ֤יךְ הַכֹּהֵן֙ אֹתָ֔הּ בֵּ֥ין ט֖וֹב וּבֵ֣ין רָ֑ע כְּעֶרְכְּךָ֥ הַכֹּהֵ֖ן כֵּ֥ן יִהְיֶֽה:

Value of an (adult or child's) life. After reading the admonitions, you might become disheartened and feel worthless. Therefore Scripture follows immediately with the laws of valuation, reassuring you that every single person has intrinsic value (*Rabbi Meir Shapira of Lublin, 20th century*).

6. The amount for a male will be … the amount for a female. The term "amount" or "value" (*'erkekha*) is repeated regarding a boy, and then again regarding a girl. This is because even youngsters have their own equally intrinsic worth and offer complementary contributions to society.

The true value of any soul is utterly unfathomable. Any stated worth, the Torah declares, is only *'erkekha*, "your estimation" (*Rabbi Mordecai ha-Kohen, 17th century*).

10. One should not exchange a consecrated animal. When a man offered a sacrifice at the Temple, he was to view the offering as if it were his abilities, his drive, and his activities that he was devoting to God. If he tried to exchange a consecrated animal with a non-consecrated animal, he might lose sight of this symbolism. He would see it as a living animal that was to be offered to God which could be exchanged for another living animal. He would no longer see the offering as a holy sacrifice that involved dedicating himself to God (*Rabbi Samson Raphael Hirsch, 19th century*).

Valuation of Dedications to the Temple

27 [FOURTH READING / SIXTH WHEN JOINED] ¹ God spoke to Moses, saying, ² Speak to the children of Israel and say to them:

If an adult makes a vow, (pledging the) value of an (adult or child's) life to God('s Sanctuary, then the pledge must be given according to the following fixed amounts):

- ❖ ³ Between twenty years old and sixty years old, the amount for a male will be fifty silver shekels, according to the shekel (measurement system which is used for) sanctified (items). ⁴ For a female, the amount will be thirty shekels.

- ❖ ⁵ Between five years old and twenty years old, the amount for a male will be twenty shekels, and for a female ten shekels.

- ❖ ⁶ Between one month old and five years old, the amount for a male will be five silver shekels, and for a female will be three silver shekels.

- ❖ ⁷ For sixty-year-olds and over, the amount for a male will be fifteen shekels, and for a female ten shekels.

- ❖ ⁸ If he is too poor to pay the (above fixed) amount, then (the one who made the pledge) should bring (the person whose value he pledged) to stand before the priest, and the priest should evaluate him according to how much the one who is pledging can (possibly) afford.

Consecration of Animals to the Temple

- ❖ ⁹ (If a person consecrates to the Temple even one limb) of an animal (from a species) which is suitable to be brought as an offering to God, then whatever part of it the person consecrates to God will become holy. (The animal must then be sold, and the value of the part that was consecrated is given to the Temple.)

- ❖ ¹⁰ One should not exchange (a consecrated animal for somebody else's animal) or offer a substitute for it (from his own stock, regardless of whether) one swaps a good (unblemished) one for a bad (blemished) one, or a bad one for a good one.

- ❖ If one does substitute one animal for another animal, (both) that one and its replacement will become consecrated.

¹¹ If it is a blemished animal which is not suitable to be brought as an offering to God:

- ❖ He should stand the animal before the priest, ¹² and the priest should set its value according to its good and bad (qualities).

- ❖ (If somebody other than the original owner wishes to purchase it from the Temple he should pay) at which the priest assessed it.

27:2 If an adult makes a vow. People tend to make promises to God when distressed. Therefore the laws of voluntary dedications follow the admonitions (*Rabbi Ephraim of Luntshits, 16ᵗʰ–17ᵗʰ century*).

ויקרא כז:יג-כו   בחקתי

13 וְאִם־גָּאֹל יִגְאָלֶנָּה וְיָסַף חֲמִישִׁתוֹ עַל־עֶרְכֶּךָ: 14 וְאִישׁ כִּי־יַקְדִּשׁ אֶת־בֵּיתוֹ קֹדֶשׁ לַיהֹוָה וְהֶעֱרִיכוֹ הַכֹּהֵן בֵּין טוֹב וּבֵין רָע כַּאֲשֶׁר יַעֲרִיךְ אֹתוֹ הַכֹּהֵן כֵּן יָקוּם: 15 וְאִם־הַמַּקְדִּישׁ יִגְאַל אֶת־בֵּיתוֹ וְיָסַף חֲמִישִׁית כֶּסֶף־עֶרְכְּךָ עָלָיו וְהָיָה לוֹ:

[FIFTH READING SEVENTH WHEN JOINED] 16 וְאִם | מִשְּׂדֵה אֲחֻזָּתוֹ יַקְדִּישׁ אִישׁ לַיהֹוָה וְהָיָה עֶרְכְּךָ לְפִי זַרְעוֹ זֶרַע חֹמֶר שְׂעֹרִים בַּחֲמִשִּׁים שֶׁקֶל כָּסֶף: 17 אִם־מִשְּׁנַת הַיֹּבֵל יַקְדִּישׁ שָׂדֵהוּ כְּעֶרְכְּךָ יָקוּם: 18 וְאִם־אַחַר הַיֹּבֵל יַקְדִּישׁ שָׂדֵהוּ וְחִשַּׁב־לוֹ הַכֹּהֵן אֶת־הַכֶּסֶף עַל־פִּי הַשָּׁנִים הַנּוֹתָרֹת עַד שְׁנַת הַיֹּבֵל וְנִגְרַע מֵעֶרְכֶּךָ: 19 וְאִם־גָּאֹל יִגְאַל אֶת־הַשָּׂדֶה הַמַּקְדִּישׁ אֹתוֹ וְיָסַף חֲמִשִׁית כֶּסֶף־עֶרְכְּךָ עָלָיו וְקָם לוֹ: 20 וְאִם־לֹא יִגְאַל אֶת־הַשָּׂדֶה וְאִם־מָכַר אֶת־הַשָּׂדֶה לְאִישׁ אַחֵר לֹא יִגָּאֵל עוֹד: 21 וְהָיָה הַשָּׂדֶה בְּצֵאתוֹ בַיֹּבֵל קֹדֶשׁ לַיהֹוָה כִּשְׂדֵה הַחֵרֶם לַכֹּהֵן תִּהְיֶה אֲחֻזָּתוֹ: [SIXTH READING]

22 וְאִם אֶת־שְׂדֵה מִקְנָתוֹ אֲשֶׁר לֹא מִשְּׂדֵה אֲחֻזָּתוֹ יַקְדִּישׁ לַיהֹוָה: 23 וְחִשַּׁב־לוֹ הַכֹּהֵן אֵת מִכְסַת הָעֶרְכְּךָ עַד שְׁנַת הַיֹּבֵל וְנָתַן אֶת־הָעֶרְכְּךָ בַּיּוֹם הַהוּא קֹדֶשׁ לַיהֹוָה: 24 בִּשְׁנַת הַיּוֹבֵל יָשׁוּב הַשָּׂדֶה לַאֲשֶׁר קָנָהוּ מֵאִתּוֹ לַאֲשֶׁר־לוֹ אֲחֻזַּת הָאָרֶץ: 25 וְכָל־עֶרְכְּךָ יִהְיֶה בְּשֶׁקֶל הַקֹּדֶשׁ עֶשְׂרִים גֵּרָה יִהְיֶה הַשָּׁקֶל: 26 אַךְ־בְּכוֹר אֲשֶׁר יְבֻכַּר לַיהֹוָה בִּבְהֵמָה לֹא־יַקְדִּישׁ אִישׁ אֹתוֹ אִם־שׁוֹר אִם־שֶׂה לַיהֹוָה

14. If a man consecrates his house. It is appropriate for a person to observe these precepts of consecrating and dedicating his property so as to coerce his evil impulse not to be miserly. However, a person should never consecrate or dedicate all his property. This would not be piety but foolishness, for in losing all his property he will become dependent on the assistance of others. We should not have mercy upon him. In reference to such people, our Sages said: *"A man of misguided piety is among those who destroy the world"* (Babylonian Talmud, *Sotah* 20a; *Maimonides, 12th century*).

26. A firstborn animal. By sacrificing the first of our flock to God we are showing our gratitude to Him for what He is giving us, starting with this first animal, and affirming our belief that all that we receive is a gift from God (*Rabbi Samson Raphael Hirsch, 19th century*).

leviticus 27:13–26 — be-ḥukkotai

- ❖ ¹³ But if (the original owner) redeems it, he should add its fifth to its value.

Consecration of Real Estate to the Temple

¹⁴ If a man consecrates his house to God('s Temple) to be holy:

- ❖ The priest should value it according to its good and bad (qualities), and the price will be fixed at the amount the priest values it.
- ❖ ¹⁵ If the one who consecrated it wishes to redeem his house, he should add a fifth to its fixed value, and it will become his (once again).

[FIFTH READING / SEVENTH WHEN JOINED] ¹⁶ If a person consecrates a field from his hereditary land to God('s Temple):

- ❖ The valuation should (not be according to market value, but rather) according to its sowing capacity: fifty silver shekels for each *ḥomer* of barley seed.
- ❖ ¹⁷ If he consecrates his field (immediately after) the Jubilee year, its value will stay (at the above-mentioned price). ¹⁸ But if he consecrates his field (a number of years) after the Jubilee, the priest should calculate its price according to the remaining years of (the lease which expires) the (next) Jubilee year. (The percentage of the lease which has elapsed) should be deducted from the valuation.
- ❖ ¹⁹ If the one who consecrated it redeems the field, he should add a fifth to its fixed value (based on the above calculation), and it will become his (once again).
- ❖ ²⁰ If he does not redeem the field, and (the treasurer of the Temple) sold the field to somebody else, it will no longer be redeemed (back to the possession of the original owner at the Jubilee year. ²¹ Rather,) when the field leaves (the purchaser's possession) at the Jubilee year, it will (belong to priests and) be holy to God as a segregated field. (The original owner's) hereditary property will now belong to the priests.

[SIXTH READING] ²² If (a person) consecrates to God a field that he had purchased, which is not part of his hereditary property:

- ❖ ²³ The priest should calculate the valuation price for him (based on the time remaining) until the Jubilee year. From that day, (anybody can redeem the field) by giving its valuation (to the Temple, to be) holy to God.
- ❖ ²⁴ In the Jubilee year, the field will return to the one from whom (the initial purchaser) bought it, namely the one whose hereditary property it was.

Additional Laws of Consecration

- ❖ ²⁵ Every valuation should be made according to (the measurement system which is used for) sanctified (items), whereby twenty *gerah* equal one shekel.
- ❖ ²⁶ A firstborn animal must be (sacrificed as) a firstborn to God. Nobody may consecrate it (as a different offering). Whether it is an ox or sheep, it belongs to God.

ויקרא כז:כז-לד — בחקתי

27 וְאִם בַּבְּהֵמָה הַטְּמֵאָה וּפָדָה בְעֶרְכֶּךָ וְיָסַף חֲמִשִׁתוֹ עָלָיו וְאִם־לֹא יִגָּאֵל וְנִמְכַּר בְּעֶרְכֶּךָ: 28 אַךְ כָּל־חֵרֶם אֲשֶׁר יַחֲרִם אִישׁ לַיהוָה מִכָּל־אֲשֶׁר־לוֹ מֵאָדָם וּבְהֵמָה וּמִשְּׂדֵה אֲחֻזָּתוֹ לֹא יִמָּכֵר וְלֹא יִגָּאֵל כָּל־חֵרֶם קֹדֶשׁ־קָדָשִׁים הוּא לַיהוָה: 29 [SEVENTH READING] כָּל־חֵרֶם אֲשֶׁר יָחֳרַם מִן־הָאָדָם לֹא יִפָּדֶה מוֹת יוּמָת: 30 וְכָל־מַעְשַׂר הָאָרֶץ מִזֶּרַע הָאָרֶץ מִפְּרִי הָעֵץ לַיהוָה הוּא קֹדֶשׁ לַיהוָה: 31 וְאִם־גָּאֹל יִגְאַל אִישׁ מִמַּעַשְׂרוֹ חֲמִשִׁיתוֹ יֹסֵף עָלָיו: 32 [MAFTIR] וְכָל־מַעְשַׂר בָּקָר וָצֹאן כֹּל אֲשֶׁר־יַעֲבֹר תַּחַת הַשָּׁבֶט הָעֲשִׂירִי יִהְיֶה־קֹּדֶשׁ לַיהוָה: 33 לֹא יְבַקֵּר בֵּין־טוֹב לָרַע וְלֹא יְמִירֶנּוּ וְאִם־הָמֵר יְמִירֶנּוּ וְהָיָה־הוּא וּתְמוּרָתוֹ יִהְיֶה־קֹדֶשׁ לֹא יִגָּאֵל: 34 אֵלֶּה הַמִּצְוֹת אֲשֶׁר צִוָּה יְהוָה אֶת־מֹשֶׁה אֶל־בְּנֵי יִשְׂרָאֵל בְּהַר סִינָי:

חֲזַק חֲזַק וְנִתְחַזֵּק

ע״ח פסוקים, עז״א סימן. סכום פסוקי דספר ויקרא שמנה מאות וחמשים ותשעים נט״פ סימן. וחציו והנוגע בבשר הזב. ופרשיותיו עשרה ב״א ג״ד סימן. וסדריו כ״ג ובתורתו יהג״ה יומם ולילה סימן. ופרקיו כ״ז ואה״ה עמך ואברכך סימן: מנין הפתיחות שתים וחמשים. והסתומות ששה וארבעים. הכל שמנה ותשעים פרשיות דודי צ״ח ואדום סימן:

---

animal for a poor one and claim that it is good. The Torah therefore made an unequivocal prohibition against substitution (*Maimonides, 12th century*).

You might prefer an approach to worshipping God which feels superior to the one which has been demanded of you. For example, you might feel that simple tasks can be entrusted to anyone, whereas you should be involved in loftier matters, such as the study of mysticism. On the other hand, you may feel that *you are not sufficiently worthy to study mysticism*, since your understanding is not so profound, and you should be involved with more simple tasks.

The response to such arguments: *"He should not select a good or a bad one, nor should he offer a substitute for it."* The desire to substitute your allotted task for another comes from the evil impulse. Initially it tells you to swap a more menial task for a loftier one, but it will eventually tell you to swap a good task for a bad one.

Carry out your allotted task joyously, without looking for a substitute (*Rabbi Menahem Mendel Schneerson, 20th century*).

leviticus 27:27–34 — be-ḥukkotai

- ²⁷ If (someone consecrates) a non-kosher (species of) animal (as a donation towards the upkeep of the Temple), he may redeem it by paying the valuation price, plus an additional one fifth. If it is not redeemed (by the one who consecrated it), it should be sold for the valuation price.

- ²⁸ However, anything that a man dedicates from any of his possessions as segregated property to God('s priests)—whether it be a person, an animal, or part of his inherited field—it may not be sold, nor should it be redeemed, for all segregated property is most holy to God.

- [SEVENTH READING] ²⁹ (If a person) consecrates (the value of) a person who has been condemned (by the court) to be put to death, (it is meaningless) and need not be redeemed.

Redemption of the Second Tithe

- ³⁰ (The second) tithe of the land, whether it be from the crops of the land or the fruit of the tree, belongs to God. It is holy to God.

- ³¹ If a man redeems some of his tithe, he should add one fifth of its value to it.

The Tithe of Animals

- [MAFTIR] ³² (When a person comes to tithe his animals, and they come out from an entrance, one after the other, the tenth animal) that passes under the rod (will be) the tithe of the cattle or the flock. The tenth will be holy to God (in that its blood and fats will be offered on the altar, but a non-priest may eat the meat).

- ³³ (Despite the fact that sacrifices are generally offered from the best animals) he should not select a good (unblemished animal) or a bad (blemished) one (for his tithed animal), nor should he offer a substitute for it.

- If he does substitute it, then (both) that one and its substitution become holy. It cannot be redeemed.

³⁴ These are the commandments that God commanded Moses (in the desert) at Mount Sinai for the children of Israel.

The congregation, followed by the reader, proclaims:

Be strong! Be strong! And may we be strengthened!

The *Haftarah* for *Be-Ḥukkotai* (and *Be-Har/Be-Ḥukkotai*) is on page 1367.

---

33. Nor should he offer a substitute. The Torah anticipated man's thoughts and his evil impulse. By nature, a person seeks to increase his possessions and to be sparing with his money. If he were allowed to exchange a poor animal for a good one, he might exchange the good

ספר במדבר

THE BOOK *of* NUMBERS

The Torah was given in a **barren desert,** teaching you to be **open-minded** yet **not influenced** by your surroundings when studying it.

BE-MIDBAR
במדבר

THE CENSUS	1:1–47
LEVITES' DUTIES	1:48–54
DETAILS OF ENCAMPMENT	2:1–34
AARON'S FAMILY	3:1–4
CENSUS AND APPOINTMENT OF LEVITES	3:5–39
THE MALE FIRSTBORN	3:40–51
DUTIES OF KOHATH'S DESCENDANTS	14:1–20

NAME
Be-Midbar

MEANING
"In the desert"

LINES IN TORAH SCROLL
252

PARASHIYYOT
23 open; 7 closed

VERSES
159

WORDS
1823

LETTERS
7393

LOCATION
Sinai Desert

DATE
Iyyar, 2449

KEY PEOPLE
Moses, Aaron, Levites, the firstborn

MASORETIC FEATURES
The word *ve-'aharon* ("and Aaron") has five dots, one on top of each letter (3:39).

NOTES
Usually read the week before *Shavuot*

CHARACTER PROFILE

NAME
Eleazar ("God has helped")

WIFE
Daughter of Jethro

POSITION
Head chieftain of the Levites; succeeded his father Aaron as high priest

TEACHING
No prophet may innovate a new Torah law.

ACHIEVEMENTS
Completed census with Moses; supervised division of land with Joshua; wrote part of the Book of Joshua

FAMOUS FOR
Performing first ritual of Red Heifer; teaching a law which Moses had forgotten, in his presence

BURIAL PLACE
Mount Ephraim

INDIVIDUALITY

The importance of every single person as an asset to the Jewish nation. Counting the Jewish people highlighted the significance of every member of the community (1:2).

INFLUENCE

The importance of good neighbors. Korah lived close to the tribe of Reuben and influenced many of its members during his revolt. On the other hand, living close to wholesome people can influence you for the good (3:29).

EDUCATION

Education begins at an early age. The Levites were counted from one month, suggesting service to the community (in potential) at thirty days old (3:15).

במדבר א:א-ג

א 1 וַיְדַבֵּ֨ר יְהֹוָ֧ה אֶל־מֹשֶׁ֛ה בְּמִדְבַּ֥ר סִינַ֖י בְּאֹ֣הֶל מוֹעֵ֑ד בְּאֶחָד֩ לַחֹ֨דֶשׁ הַשֵּׁנִ֜י בַּשָּׁנָ֣ה הַשֵּׁנִ֗ית לְצֵאתָ֛ם מֵאֶ֥רֶץ מִצְרַ֖יִם לֵאמֹֽר: 2 שְׂא֗וּ אֶת־רֹאשׁ֙ כָּל־עֲדַ֣ת בְּנֵֽי־יִשְׂרָאֵ֔ל לְמִשְׁפְּחֹתָ֖ם לְבֵ֣ית אֲבֹתָ֑ם בְּמִסְפַּ֣ר שֵׁמ֔וֹת כָּל־זָכָ֖ר לְגֻלְגְּלֹתָֽם: 3 מִבֶּ֨ן עֶשְׂרִ֤ים שָׁנָה֙ וָמַ֔עְלָה כָּל־יֹצֵ֥א צָבָ֖א בְּיִשְׂרָאֵ֑ל תִּפְקְד֥וּ

among them, He counted them: On the first of *Nisan*, the Tabernacle was erected, and on the first of *Iyyar* (when this verse was said), He counted them (*Rashi, 11th century*).

The *Book of Numbers* acquired its name from the census which takes place here at the opening of the Book (see *Babylonian Talmud, Yoma* 68b).

When a group of people are counted, everybody is equal. No person is counted twice, however important he or she may be, and even the most insignificant person is counted once. What, then, are we actually counting? It is not our personalities, our talents, our wealth, our knowledge or our esteem; rather, *we are counting our very identities*. When we are counted, says Ḥasidic thought, the "nucleus" of our identities (possessed by all of us equally) is stimulated and brought to the surface.

This "nucleus" of identity is responsible for the remarkable display of courage among countless Jewish people who, throughout history, were threatened with death if they refused to renounce their Judaism. For a person who had dedicated his life to the practice of Judaism, one can understand that he might sacrifice his life because Judaism is his *raison d'être*. But logic would dictate that another person, less committed to Jewish practice, would be willing to "tolerate" a momentary lapse in observance to save his life. And even a very pious person might argue that he would later mend this temporary lapse with repentance.

In fact, however, history has shown that countless Jews, from a broad cross-section of backgrounds, gave up their lives rather than transgress. Why? Because their Jewish "nucleus" is always alive; as *Rashi* writes, *"He counts them all the time."* And when this Godly spark comes to the surface, any Jew will naturally feel that his Jewish identity is so important that he is not willing to compromise it, even for a moment (*Rabbi Menahem Mendel Schneerson, 20th century*).

Take the sum of the entire congregation. The individual does not stand alone, but as part of the whole. The entire world depends on him. By being counted, he knows his place and worth to the community at large. This self-examination results in God's Divine Presence resting on the entire community (*Rabbi Isaiah Horowitz, 16th–17th century*).

A head count (*le-gulggelotam*). This choice of phrase alludes to the idea of *gilgul*, reincarnation. The verse states, *"Take the sum,"* which rendered literally reads, *"Lift up the heads."* We ought to "lift up our heads" and strive for greatness in this lifetime so as to avoid the need for reincarnation. It is better to get it right this time around (*Rabbi Menahem Nahum Twersky of Chernobyl, 18th century*).

kabbalah bites

1:1 When the Tabernacle was erected all the worlds came to perfection; all the higher and lower worlds were scented.

Now that the Tabernacle was complete, God wanted to count the troops of the Torah. *For, every item that needs to be settled in its place does not settle until it is uttered by the mouth and is counted.*

numbers 1:1–3 — be-midbar

parashat be-midbar

The Census

1 ¹ God spoke to Moses in the Sinai Desert, in the Tent of Meeting, on the first (day) of the second month, in the second year after their exodus from the land of Egypt, saying: ² Take the sum of the entire congregation of the children of Israel (to ascertain the size of each of the tribal) families. (Those born to parents of two different tribes are considered to be part of) their father's house. (Take) a head count (by counting each person's half-shekel donation and by) keeping a count of the names. ³ (Include in the census all those) from twenty years old and

1:1 In the Sinai Desert. The giving of the Torah in the desert teaches us a valuable lesson about how to approach Torah study. Even if you have studied extensively, you have hardly begun to master the Torah's infinite wisdom. Your attempts have been as successful as cultivating a desert (*Rabbi Menahem Mendel Morgensztern of Kotsk, 19th century*).

Torah was given in three settings: fire, water, and desert. How do we know in fire? *"The whole of Mount Sinai smoked, because God had descended upon it in fire"* (*Exodus* 19:18).

How do we know in water? *"The earth trembled and the heavens dropped, the clouds also dropped water ... before God, the God of Israel"* (*Judges* 5:4-5).

And how do we know in the desert? *"God spoke to Moses in the Sinai Desert."*

Why was the Torah given in these three settings? Just as these three are freely available for all the inhabitants of the earth, so too, words of Torah are freely available, as the verse states, *"Let everyone who is thirsty come to the water"* (*Isaiah* 55:1; *Numbers Rabbah*).

The three settings in which the Torah was given—fire, water and desert—hint to the best way to study Torah: with *fiery* passion; with cognitive focus (cool *water* being symbolic of objective analysis); and a willingness to *desert* some of the pleasures of this world (*Rabbi Samuel Bornstein of Sochaczew, 20th century*).

The three settings allude to the range of different times and conditions, whether as individuals or collectively, that we are to uphold the Torah. In fire—Abraham leapt into the fiery furnace for his faith; this is *the devotion of the individual*. In water—Nahshon, followed by all the children of Israel, leapt into the Sea of Reeds, representing *collective commitment*. In the desert—the children of Israel followed God for forty years, representing *sustained faithfulness* (*Rabbi Meir Shapira of Lublin, 20th century*).

The Torah was given at Sinai to teach you to be humble—God rejected the high mountains and chose Sinai, the lowest of all (*Midrash Tehillim*).

If you are too harsh on yourself with the trait of humility you might become depressed, which is highly inadvisable. The Torah tells you always to be joyous: *"the Divine spirit does not rest upon a depressed person"* (*Babylonian Talmud, Shabbat* 30b). That is why the verse concludes, *"in the Tent of Meeting (mo'ed)"*—put yourself in the tent of the *mo'ed* (lit. "holiday"), in a continual festive spirit (*Rabbi Elimelech of Lyzhansk, 18th century*).

2. Take the sum. Because the people are precious to Him, He counts them all the time. When they left Egypt, He counted them (*Exodus* 12:37). When they sinned with the Calf, He counted them to know the number of the survivors (*Exodus* 32:28). And when He rested His Presence

במדבר א:ג-כא

אֹתָם לְצִבְאֹתָם אַתָּה וְאַהֲרֹן: 4 וְאִתְּכֶם יִהְיוּ אִישׁ אִישׁ לַמַּטֶּה אִישׁ רֹאשׁ לְבֵית־אֲבֹתָיו הוּא: 5 וְאֵלֶּה שְׁמוֹת הָאֲנָשִׁים אֲשֶׁר יַעַמְדוּ אִתְּכֶם לִרְאוּבֵן אֱלִיצוּר בֶּן־שְׁדֵיאוּר: 6 לְשִׁמְעוֹן שְׁלֻמִיאֵל בֶּן־צוּרִישַׁדָּי: 7 לִיהוּדָה נַחְשׁוֹן בֶּן־עַמִּינָדָב: 8 לְיִשָּׂשכָר נְתַנְאֵל בֶּן־צוּעָר: 9 לִזְבוּלֻן אֱלִיאָב בֶּן־חֵלֹן: 10 לִבְנֵי יוֹסֵף לְאֶפְרַיִם אֱלִישָׁמָע בֶּן־עַמִּיהוּד לִמְנַשֶּׁה גַּמְלִיאֵל בֶּן־פְּדָהצוּר: 11 לְבִנְיָמִן אֲבִידָן בֶּן־גִּדְעֹנִי: 12 לְדָן אֲחִיעֶזֶר בֶּן־עַמִּישַׁדָּי: 13 לְאָשֵׁר פַּגְעִיאֵל בֶּן־עָכְרָן: 14 לְגָד אֶלְיָסָף בֶּן־דְּעוּאֵל: 15 לְנַפְתָּלִי אֲחִירַע בֶּן־עֵינָן: 16 אֵלֶּה [קריאי כ'] קְרוּאֵי הָעֵדָה נְשִׂיאֵי מַטּוֹת אֲבוֹתָם רָאשֵׁי אַלְפֵי יִשְׂרָאֵל הֵם: 17 וַיִּקַּח מֹשֶׁה וְאַהֲרֹן אֵת הָאֲנָשִׁים הָאֵלֶּה אֲשֶׁר נִקְּבוּ בְּשֵׁמוֹת: 18 וְאֵת כָּל־הָעֵדָה הִקְהִילוּ בְּאֶחָד לַחֹדֶשׁ הַשֵּׁנִי וַיִּתְיַלְדוּ עַל־מִשְׁפְּחֹתָם לְבֵית אֲבֹתָם בְּמִסְפַּר שֵׁמוֹת מִבֶּן עֶשְׂרִים שָׁנָה וָמַעְלָה לְגֻלְגְּלֹתָם: 19 כַּאֲשֶׁר צִוָּה יְהֹוָה אֶת־מֹשֶׁה וַיִּפְקְדֵם בְּמִדְבַּר סִינָי: ס 20 [SECOND READING] וַיִּהְיוּ בְנֵי־רְאוּבֵן בְּכֹר יִשְׂרָאֵל תּוֹלְדֹתָם לְמִשְׁפְּחֹתָם לְבֵית אֲבֹתָם בְּמִסְפַּר שֵׁמוֹת לְגֻלְגְּלֹתָם כָּל־זָכָר מִבֶּן עֶשְׂרִים שָׁנָה וָמַעְלָה כֹּל יֹצֵא צָבָא: 21 פְּקֻדֵיהֶם לְמַטֵּה רְאוּבֵן שִׁשָּׁה וְאַרְבָּעִים אֶלֶף

5-15. First Tribal Sequence. The tribes are listed in the following order: The children of Leah come first: Reuben, Simeon, Judah, Issachar and Zebulun, followed by Rachel's descendants, Ephraim, Manasseh (Joseph's sons) and Benjamin. Ephraim is mentioned before Manasseh, even though Manasseh was the firstborn, because Jacob blessed Ephraim first (*Genesis* 48:20). Dan follows, since he was the firstborn of Rachel's handmaid, then Asher, because in Dan's "division" Asher was adjacent to Dan (see below, 2:27). Gad follows, since he was the firstborn of Leah's handmaid; and finally, Naphtali (*Rabbi Abraham ibn Ezra, 12th century*).

20-43. Second Tribal Sequence. Reuben comes first, because he is the firstborn, followed by Simeon, who was born right after him. Then follows Gad, who was the firstborn of Leah's handmaid. These three tribes together constitute an entire "division of regiments," the "Camp of Reuben" (see below, 2:10-17). This was then followed by the other "divisions" of Judah (Judah, Issachar, Zebulun), Ephraim (Ephraim, Manasseh, Benjamin), and Dan (Dan, Asher, Naphtali) (*Rabbi Abraham ibn Ezra, 12th century*).

Since the tribes are listed here according to the sequence of their respective "divisions," one would have expected Judah to come first (see below, 2:3ff.). Therefore, the Torah deemed it necessary to explain why Reuben was chosen to be listed first on this occasion, because he was "Israel's firstborn" (v. 20; *Rabbi Meir Loeb Weisser, 19th century*).

upwards, (i.e.) all who are fit to go out to the army in Israel. You and Aaron should count them, by their regiments.

⁴ (When you count,) there should be with you a (senior) person from each tribe, one who is head of (his tribe), his father's house. ⁵ These are the names of the men who should stand with you:

For Reuben, Elizur son of Shedeur.

⁶ For Simeon, Shelumiel son of Zurishaddai.

⁷ For Judah, Nahshon son of Amminadab.

⁸ For Issachar, Nethanel son of Zuar.

⁹ For Zebulun, Eliab son of Helon.

¹⁰ For the children of Joseph: for Ephraim, Elishama son of Ammihud; for Manasseh, Gamaliel son of Pedahzur.

¹¹ For Benjamin, Abidan son of Gideoni.

¹² For Dan, Ahiezer son of Ammishaddai.

¹³ For Asher, Pagiel son of Ochran.

¹⁴ For Gad, Eliasaph son of Deuel.

¹⁵ For Naphtali, Ahira son of Enan.

¹⁶ These are the ones (to be) summoned by the congregation (for every important matter), the leaders of their fathers' tribes. They are the heads of Israel's thousands.

¹⁷ Moses and Aaron took these men, who had been indicated (by God to Moses) by (their) names. ¹⁸ They assembled the entire congregation on the first day of the second month and verified their family (tribal) lineage, according to their paternal houses, keeping a count of the names—a head count of every male from twenty years old and upward.

¹⁹ Moses counted them in the Sinai Desert, just as God had commanded him.

The Census Results

[SECOND READING] ²⁰ The (census of) Reuben's descendants, Israel's firstborn, (included) those whose family lineage had been verified according to their paternal houses, keeping a count of the names (who gave a half-shekel) per head. (This constituted) every male from twenty years and upwards, all those eligible for the army. ²¹ Those counted from the tribe of Reuben were forty-six thousand, five hundred.

Food for thought

1. How far back can you trace your ancestry?

2. Can we enjoy tribal/party affiliation without jeopardizing unity?

3. Why did God choose such a numerically disadvantaged nation?

במדבר א:כא-לו

וַחֲמֵשׁ מֵאוֹת: פ ‎22 לִבְנֵי שִׁמְעוֹן תּוֹלְדֹתָם לְמִשְׁפְּחֹתָם לְבֵית אֲבֹתָם פְּקֻדָיו בְּמִסְפַּר שֵׁמוֹת לְגֻלְגְּלֹתָם כָּל־זָכָר מִבֶּן עֶשְׂרִים שָׁנָה וָמַעְלָה כֹּל יֹצֵא צָבָא: ‎23 פְּקֻדֵיהֶם לְמַטֵּה שִׁמְעוֹן תִּשְׁעָה וַחֲמִשִּׁים אֶלֶף וּשְׁלֹשׁ מֵאוֹת: פ ‎24 לִבְנֵי גָד תּוֹלְדֹתָם לְמִשְׁפְּחֹתָם לְבֵית אֲבֹתָם בְּמִסְפַּר שֵׁמוֹת מִבֶּן עֶשְׂרִים שָׁנָה וָמַעְלָה כֹּל יֹצֵא צָבָא: ‎25 פְּקֻדֵיהֶם לְמַטֵּה גָד חֲמִשָּׁה וְאַרְבָּעִים אֶלֶף וְשֵׁשׁ מֵאוֹת וַחֲמִשִּׁים: פ ‎26 לִבְנֵי יְהוּדָה תּוֹלְדֹתָם לְמִשְׁפְּחֹתָם לְבֵית אֲבֹתָם בְּמִסְפַּר שֵׁמֹת מִבֶּן עֶשְׂרִים שָׁנָה וָמַעְלָה כֹּל יֹצֵא צָבָא: ‎27 פְּקֻדֵיהֶם לְמַטֵּה יְהוּדָה אַרְבָּעָה וְשִׁבְעִים אֶלֶף וְשֵׁשׁ מֵאוֹת: פ ‎28 לִבְנֵי יִשָּׂשכָר תּוֹלְדֹתָם לְמִשְׁפְּחֹתָם לְבֵית אֲבֹתָם בְּמִסְפַּר שֵׁמֹת מִבֶּן עֶשְׂרִים שָׁנָה וָמַעְלָה כֹּל יֹצֵא צָבָא: ‎29 פְּקֻדֵיהֶם לְמַטֵּה יִשָּׂשכָר אַרְבָּעָה וַחֲמִשִּׁים אֶלֶף וְאַרְבַּע מֵאוֹת: פ ‎30 לִבְנֵי זְבוּלֻן תּוֹלְדֹתָם לְמִשְׁפְּחֹתָם לְבֵית אֲבֹתָם בְּמִסְפַּר שֵׁמֹת מִבֶּן עֶשְׂרִים שָׁנָה וָמַעְלָה כֹּל יֹצֵא צָבָא: ‎31 פְּקֻדֵיהֶם לְמַטֵּה זְבוּלֻן שִׁבְעָה וַחֲמִשִּׁים אֶלֶף וְאַרְבַּע מֵאוֹת: פ ‎32 לִבְנֵי יוֹסֵף לִבְנֵי אֶפְרַיִם תּוֹלְדֹתָם לְמִשְׁפְּחֹתָם לְבֵית אֲבֹתָם בְּמִסְפַּר שֵׁמֹת מִבֶּן עֶשְׂרִים שָׁנָה וָמַעְלָה כֹּל יֹצֵא צָבָא: ‎33 פְּקֻדֵיהֶם לְמַטֵּה אֶפְרַיִם אַרְבָּעִים אֶלֶף וַחֲמֵשׁ מֵאוֹת: פ ‎34 לִבְנֵי מְנַשֶּׁה תּוֹלְדֹתָם לְמִשְׁפְּחֹתָם לְבֵית אֲבֹתָם בְּמִסְפַּר שֵׁמוֹת מִבֶּן עֶשְׂרִים שָׁנָה וָמַעְלָה כֹּל יֹצֵא צָבָא: ‎35 פְּקֻדֵיהֶם לְמַטֵּה מְנַשֶּׁה שְׁנַיִם וּשְׁלֹשִׁים אֶלֶף וּמָאתָיִם: פ ‎36 לִבְנֵי

spiritual vitamin

> The whole sun is reflected in each drop of water. In the same way the whole of our nation is reflected in each individual, and what is true of the nation as a whole is true of the individual.

²² For (the census of) Simeon's descendants, those whose family lineage had been verified according to their paternal houses (were included), keeping a count of the names (who gave a half-shekel) per head. (This constituted) every male from twenty years and upwards, all those eligible for the army. ²³ Those counted from the tribe of Simeon were fifty-nine thousand, three hundred.

²⁴ For (the census of) Gad's descendants, those whose family lineage had been verified according to their paternal houses (were included), keeping a count of the names. (This constituted) every male from twenty years and upwards, all those eligible for the army. ²⁵ Those counted from the tribe of Gad were forty-five thousand, six hundred and fifty.

²⁶ For (the census of) Judah's descendants, those whose family lineage had been verified according to their paternal houses (were included), keeping a count of the names. (This constituted) every male from twenty years and upwards, all those eligible for the army. ²⁷ Those counted from the tribe of Judah were seventy-four thousand, six hundred.

²⁸ For (the census of) Issachar's descendants, those whose family lineage had been verified according to their paternal houses (were included), keeping a count of the names. (This constituted) every male from twenty years and upwards, all those eligible for the army. ²⁹ Those counted from the tribe of Issachar were fifty-four thousand, four hundred.

³⁰ For (the census of) Zebulun's descendants, those whose family lineage had been verified according to their paternal houses (were included), keeping a count of the names. (This constituted) every male from twenty years and upwards, all those eligible for the army. ³¹ Those counted from the tribe of Zebulun were fifty-seven thousand, four hundred.

³² For (the census of) Joseph's descendants:

For (the census of) Ephraim's descendants, those whose family lineage had been verified according to their paternal houses (were included), keeping a count of the names. (This constituted) every male from twenty years and upwards, all those eligible for the army. ³³ Those counted from the tribe of Ephraim were forty thousand, five hundred.

³⁴ For (the census of) Manasseh's descendants, those whose family lineage had been verified according to their paternal houses (were included), keeping a count of the names. (This constituted) every male from twenty years and upwards, all those eligible for the army. ³⁵ Those counted from the tribe of Manasseh were thirty-two thousand, two hundred.

³⁶ For (the census of) Benjamin's descendants, those whose family lineage had been verified according to their paternal houses (were included), keeping a count

בִנְיָמִ֔ן תּוֹלְדֹתָ֥ם לְמִשְׁפְּחֹתָ֖ם לְבֵ֣ית אֲבֹתָ֑ם בְּמִסְפַּ֣ר שֵׁמֹ֗ת מִבֶּ֨ן עֶשְׂרִ֤ים שָׁנָה֙ וָמַ֔עְלָה כֹּ֖ל יֹצֵ֥א צָבָֽא: 37 פְּקֻדֵיהֶ֖ם לְמַטֵּ֣ה בִנְיָמִ֑ן חֲמִשָּׁ֧ה וּשְׁלֹשִׁ֛ים אֶ֖לֶף וְאַרְבַּ֥ע מֵאֽוֹת: פ 38 לִבְנֵ֣י דָ֔ן תּוֹלְדֹתָ֥ם לְמִשְׁפְּחֹתָ֖ם לְבֵ֣ית אֲבֹתָ֑ם בְּמִסְפַּ֣ר שֵׁמֹ֗ת מִבֶּ֨ן עֶשְׂרִ֤ים שָׁנָה֙ וָמַ֔עְלָה כֹּ֖ל יֹצֵ֥א צָבָֽא: 39 פְּקֻדֵיהֶ֖ם לְמַטֵּ֣ה דָ֑ן שְׁנַ֧יִם וְשִׁשִּׁ֛ים אֶ֖לֶף וּשְׁבַ֥ע מֵאֽוֹת: פ 40 לִבְנֵ֣י אָשֵׁ֔ר תּוֹלְדֹתָ֥ם לְמִשְׁפְּחֹתָ֖ם לְבֵ֣ית אֲבֹתָ֑ם בְּמִסְפַּ֣ר שֵׁמֹ֗ת מִבֶּ֨ן עֶשְׂרִ֤ים שָׁנָה֙ וָמַ֔עְלָה כֹּ֖ל יֹצֵ֥א צָבָֽא: 41 פְּקֻדֵיהֶ֖ם לְמַטֵּ֣ה אָשֵׁ֑ר אֶחָ֧ד וְאַרְבָּעִ֛ים אֶ֖לֶף וַחֲמֵ֥שׁ מֵאֽוֹת: פ 42 בְּנֵ֣י נַפְתָּלִ֔י תּוֹלְדֹתָ֥ם לְמִשְׁפְּחֹתָ֖ם לְבֵ֣ית אֲבֹתָ֑ם בְּמִסְפַּ֣ר שֵׁמֹ֗ת מִבֶּ֨ן עֶשְׂרִ֤ים שָׁנָה֙ וָמַ֔עְלָה כֹּ֖ל יֹצֵ֥א צָבָֽא: 43 פְּקֻדֵיהֶ֖ם לְמַטֵּ֣ה נַפְתָּלִ֑י שְׁלֹשָׁ֧ה וַחֲמִשִּׁ֛ים אֶ֖לֶף וְאַרְבַּ֥ע מֵאֽוֹת: פ 44 אֵ֣לֶּה הַפְּקֻדִ֡ים אֲשֶׁר֩ פָּקַ֨ד מֹשֶׁ֤ה וְאַהֲרֹן֙ וּנְשִׂיאֵ֣י יִשְׂרָאֵ֔ל שְׁנֵ֥ים עָשָׂ֖ר אִ֑ישׁ אִישׁ־אֶחָ֥ד לְבֵית־אֲבֹתָ֖יו הָיֽוּ: 45 וַיִּהְי֛וּ כָּל־פְּקוּדֵ֥י בְנֵֽי־יִשְׂרָאֵ֖ל לְבֵ֣ית אֲבֹתָ֑ם מִבֶּ֨ן עֶשְׂרִ֤ים שָׁנָה֙ וָמַ֔עְלָה כָּל־יֹצֵ֥א צָבָ֖א בְּיִשְׂרָאֵֽל: 46 וַיִּֽהְיוּ֙ כָּל־הַפְּקֻדִ֔ים שֵׁשׁ־מֵא֥וֹת אֶ֖לֶף וּשְׁלֹ֣שֶׁת אֲלָפִ֑ים וַחֲמֵ֥שׁ מֵא֖וֹת וַחֲמִשִּֽׁים: 47 וְהַלְוִיִּ֖ם לְמַטֵּ֣ה אֲבֹתָ֑ם לֹ֥א הָתְפָּקְד֖וּ בְּתוֹכָֽם: פ 48 וַיְדַבֵּ֥ר יְהֹוָ֖ה אֶל־מֹשֶׁ֥ה לֵּאמֹֽר: 49 אַ֣ךְ אֶת־מַטֵּ֤ה לֵוִי֙ לֹ֣א תִפְקֹ֔ד וְאֶת־רֹאשָׁ֖ם לֹ֣א תִשָּׂ֑א בְּת֖וֹךְ בְּנֵ֥י יִשְׂרָאֵֽל:

Jacob's family who had arrived in Egypt had multiplied to become a nation of over six hundred thousand (*Nahmanides, 13th century*).

These reasons for the census are alluded to by three different verses: *"Counted by Moses and Aaron"*—in order to receive added blessing; *"All those eligible for the army of Israel"* (v. 45)—to determine those eligible for battle; and *"Six hundred and three thousand, etc."* (v. 46)—to publicize God's mercy (*Rabbi Abraham Samuel Benjamin Sofer, 19th century*).

49. Do not count the tribe of Levi. The king's legion deserves to be counted on its own!

Another explanation: God foresaw that a decree would be passed in the future against all those counted from twenty years and upward, condemning them to die in the desert. He said, "Let these Levites not be included! They are Mine, for they did not err with the Golden Calf" (*Rashi, 11th century*).

The primary role of the Levites was Torah study—*"They were singled out to teach the public about His morally upright ways and fair laws"* (*Maimonides, 12th century*). By contrast, the spiritual path of most Jewish people is dominated by the practical observance of the commandments.

of the names. (This constituted) every male from twenty years and upwards, all those eligible for the army. ³⁷ Those counted from the tribe of Benjamin were thirty-five thousand, four hundred.

³⁸ For (the census of) Dan's descendants, those whose family lineage had been verified according to their paternal houses (were included), keeping a count of the names. (This constituted) every male from twenty years and upwards, all those eligible for the army. ³⁹ Those counted from the tribe of Dan were sixty-two thousand, seven hundred.

⁴⁰ For (the census of) Asher's descendants, those whose family lineage had been verified according to their paternal houses (were included), keeping a count of the names. (This constituted) every male from twenty years and upwards, all those eligible for the army. ⁴¹ Those counted from the tribe of Asher were forty-one thousand, five hundred.

⁴² (The census of) Naphtali's descendants (included) those whose family lineage had been verified according to their paternal houses, keeping a count of the names. (This constituted) every male from twenty years and upwards, all those eligible for the army. ⁴³ Those counted from the tribe of Naphtali were fifty-three thousand, four hundred.

⁴⁴ These were the numbers counted by Moses, Aaron and the twelve men who were leaders of Israel, one from each paternal house. ⁴⁵ Those included in the census were all the children of Israel from twenty years and upwards, all those eligible for the army of Israel, (separated) according to their paternal houses. ⁴⁶ The sum of all those who were counted was six hundred and three thousand, five hundred and fifty.

⁴⁷ But the Levites, (identified) according to their father's tribe, were not counted with them.

The Role of the Levites

⁴⁸ God spoke to Moses saying: ⁴⁹ "Only, do not count the tribe of Levi; do not calculate their number together with the children of Israel.

> **Food for thought**
>
> **1.** What are the advantages of having an "elite" class dedicated to God's service?
>
> **2.** How can we truly dedicate ourselves to God while holding down a job, etc.?
>
> **3.** Do you know someone whose lifestyle can be described as a modern "Levite"?

44. These were the numbers. There were three reasons for counting the Israelites: 1) To have the people who passed Moses and Aaron receive additional blessing; 2) To determine who was fit to go into battle; and 3) To publicize that, through God's mercy, the seventy members of

במדבר א:נ - ב:ד

50 וְאַתָּה הַפְקֵד אֶת־הַלְוִיִּם עַל־מִשְׁכַּן הָעֵדֻת וְעַל כָּל־כֵּלָיו וְעַל כָּל־אֲשֶׁר־לוֹ הֵמָּה יִשְׂאוּ אֶת־הַמִּשְׁכָּן וְאֶת־כָּל־כֵּלָיו וְהֵם יְשָׁרְתֻהוּ וְסָבִיב לַמִּשְׁכָּן יַחֲנוּ: 51 וּבִנְסֹעַ הַמִּשְׁכָּן יוֹרִידוּ אֹתוֹ הַלְוִיִּם וּבַחֲנֹת הַמִּשְׁכָּן יָקִימוּ אֹתוֹ הַלְוִיִּם וְהַזָּר הַקָּרֵב יוּמָת: 52 וְחָנוּ בְּנֵי יִשְׂרָאֵל אִישׁ עַל־מַחֲנֵהוּ וְאִישׁ עַל־דִּגְלוֹ לְצִבְאֹתָם: 53 וְהַלְוִיִּם יַחֲנוּ סָבִיב לְמִשְׁכַּן הָעֵדֻת וְלֹא־יִהְיֶה קֶצֶף עַל־עֲדַת בְּנֵי יִשְׂרָאֵל וְשָׁמְרוּ הַלְוִיִּם אֶת־מִשְׁמֶרֶת מִשְׁכַּן הָעֵדוּת: 54 וַיַּעֲשׂוּ בְּנֵי יִשְׂרָאֵל כְּכֹל אֲשֶׁר צִוָּה יְהוָה אֶת־מֹשֶׁה כֵּן עָשׂוּ: פ

ב 1 וַיְדַבֵּר יְהוָה אֶל־מֹשֶׁה וְאֶל־אַהֲרֹן לֵאמֹר: [THIRD READING] 2 אִישׁ עַל־דִּגְלוֹ בְאֹתֹת לְבֵית אֲבֹתָם יַחֲנוּ בְּנֵי יִשְׂרָאֵל מִנֶּגֶד סָבִיב לְאֹהֶל־מוֹעֵד יַחֲנוּ: 3 וְהַחֹנִים קֵדְמָה מִזְרָחָה דֶּגֶל מַחֲנֵה יְהוּדָה לְצִבְאֹתָם וְנָשִׂיא לִבְנֵי יְהוּדָה נַחְשׁוֹן בֶּן־עַמִּינָדָב: 4 וּצְבָאוֹ וּפְקֻדֵיהֶם אַרְבָּעָה וְשִׁבְעִים אֶלֶף וְשֵׁשׁ מֵאוֹת:

bring the offering, the Torah enables him to transcend this limitation, and it is "as if" the deed was done.

This explains why the Levites, whose spiritual path was Torah, were not counted. (Rather, God simply informed Moses of the Levites' number—see *Rashi* to 3:16.) *Counting is an expression of finitude and limitation*, so it was more suited to the rest of the Jewish people (*Rabbi Menahem Mendel Schneerson, 20*[th] *century*).

52. Each man should be in his own division (consisting of three tribes). Just as there were four divisions then, contemporary Jewry is divided into four main groups: Sephardi, Ashkenazi,

kabbalah bites

2:3-31 Surrounding the camp of the Shekhinah (Divine Presence), each of the four encampments represented:

a) One of the four elements;

b) One of the four supernal angels;

c) One of the four creatures in the Heavenly Chariot, seen in Ezekiel's vision;

d) One of the four Divine attributes:

Hesed (kindness), *Gevurah* (severity), *Tiferet* (harmony) and *Malkhut* (sensitivity).

For the camp of Judah: a) Element=Air; b) Angel=Uriel; c) Creature=Man; d) Attribute=*Tiferet*.

Judah encamped in the east since Judah was a ba'al teshuvah (penitent), and teshuvah is associated with the east.

- **50** "You should appoint the Levites (to be in charge) of the Tabernacle of the Testimony, over all its vessels and everything pertaining to it. They will carry the Tabernacle, they will be its ministers, and they will camp around the Tabernacle.

- **51** "When the Tabernacle is set to travel, the Levites should dismantle it, and when the Tabernacle makes a (new) encampment, the Levites should erect it. Any unauthorized person who approaches (to participate in this task) must be put to death.

- **52** "When the children of Israel encamp, each man should be regimented in his own (specific) camp (for his tribe), and (likewise) each man should be in his own (general) division (consisting of three tribes). **53** But the Levites (alone) should encamp around the Tabernacle of the Testimony, so that there will be no (Divine) anger upon the congregation of the children of Israel. The Levites (alone) will guard the Tabernacle of the Testimony."

54 The children of Israel acted in accordance with everything that God had commanded Moses. They did so (precisely).

Details of the Encampment

2 [THIRD READING] **1** God spoke to Moses and Aaron, saying: **2** The children of Israel should encamp (in such a way that) each man is in his own division (of three tribes) signposted (by a flag which contains the same color as the gemstone in the High Priest's breastplate that is identified with) his father's house. They should encamp around the Tent of Meeting, at a distance (of one *mil*).

3 Those camping to the east, (which is considered to be) the front, were the division of regiments (of three tribes, known as) "the Camp of Judah":

- The leader of Judah's descendants was Nahshon son of Amminadab. **4** The head count of his regiment was seventy-four thousand, six hundred.

The commandments were given in a fixed number (there are exactly six hundred and thirteen), and they have strict rules concerning their observance. All this suggests some sort of subtle, inner limitation. Torah, on the other hand, is unlimited, in the sense that it transcends the confines of this world. *"If a person studies the laws of a burnt-offering it is as if he sacrificed a burnt-offering"* (Babylonian Talmud, end of *Menaḥot*)—even though he did not physically

kabbalah bites

1:50 Since they were rooted in *Gevurah* (strength; severity), the Levites were appointed to surround and protect the camp of the *Shekhinah* (Divine Presence).

The powers of good and holiness tend to attract the forces of impurity which, like parasites, come to suck energy. Therefore powerful *Gevurot* are required for protection.

במדבר ב:ה-יז

5 וְהַחֹנִ֥ים עָלָ֖יו מַטֵּ֣ה יִשָּׂשכָ֑ר וְנָשִׂיא֙ לִבְנֵ֣י יִשָּׂשכָ֔ר נְתַנְאֵ֖ל בֶּן־צוּעָֽר: 6 וּצְבָא֖וֹ וּפְקֻדָ֑יו אַרְבָּעָ֧ה וַחֲמִשִּׁ֛ים אֶ֖לֶף וְאַרְבַּ֥ע מֵאֽוֹת: 7 מַטֵּ֖ה זְבוּלֻ֑ן וְנָשִׂיא֙ לִבְנֵ֣י זְבוּלֻ֔ן אֱלִיאָ֖ב בֶּן־חֵלֹֽן: 8 וּצְבָא֖וֹ וּפְקֻדָ֑יו שִׁבְעָ֧ה וַחֲמִשִּׁ֛ים אֶ֖לֶף וְאַרְבַּ֥ע מֵאֽוֹת: 9 כָּל־הַפְּקֻדִ֞ים לְמַחֲנֵ֣ה יְהוּדָ֗ה מְאַ֨ת אֶ֜לֶף וּשְׁמֹנִ֥ים אֶ֛לֶף וְשֵֽׁשֶׁת־אֲלָפִ֥ים וְאַרְבַּע־מֵא֖וֹת לְצִבְאֹתָ֑ם רִאשֹׁנָ֖ה יִסָּֽעוּ: ס 10 דֶּ֣גֶל מַחֲנֵ֧ה רְאוּבֵ֛ן תֵּימָ֖נָה לְצִבְאֹתָ֑ם וְנָשִׂיא֙ לִבְנֵ֣י רְאוּבֵ֔ן אֱלִיצ֖וּר בֶּן־שְׁדֵיאֽוּר: 11 וּצְבָא֖וֹ וּפְקֻדָ֑יו שִׁשָּׁ֧ה וְאַרְבָּעִ֛ים אֶ֖לֶף וַחֲמֵ֥שׁ מֵאֽוֹת: 12 וְהַחוֹנִ֥ם עָלָ֖יו מַטֵּ֣ה שִׁמְע֑וֹן וְנָשִׂיא֙ לִבְנֵ֣י שִׁמְע֔וֹן שְׁלֻמִיאֵ֖ל בֶּן־צוּרִֽישַׁדָּֽי: 13 וּצְבָא֖וֹ וּפְקֻדֵיהֶ֑ם תִּשְׁעָ֧ה וַחֲמִשִּׁ֛ים אֶ֖לֶף וּשְׁלֹ֥שׁ מֵאֽוֹת: 14 וּמַטֵּ֖ה גָ֑ד וְנָשִׂיא֙ לִבְנֵ֣י גָ֔ד אֶלְיָסָ֖ף בֶּן־רְעוּאֵֽל: 15 וּצְבָא֖וֹ וּפְקֻדֵיהֶ֑ם חֲמִשָּׁ֧ה וְאַרְבָּעִ֛ים אֶ֖לֶף וְשֵׁ֥שׁ מֵא֖וֹת וַחֲמִשִּֽׁים: 16 כָּל־הַפְּקֻדִ֞ים לְמַחֲנֵ֣ה רְאוּבֵ֗ן מְאַ֨ת אֶ֜לֶף וְאֶחָ֨ד וַחֲמִשִּׁ֥ים אֶ֛לֶף וְאַרְבַּע־מֵא֖וֹת וַחֲמִשִּׁ֑ים לְצִבְאֹתָ֑ם וּשְׁנִיִּ֥ם יִסָּֽעוּ: ס 17 וְנָסַ֧ע אֹֽהֶל־מוֹעֵ֛ד מַחֲנֵ֥ה הַלְוִיִּ֖ם בְּת֣וֹךְ הַֽמַּחֲנֹ֑ת כַּאֲשֶׁ֤ר יַחֲנוּ֙ כֵּ֣ן

2:17 They should travel (in the same arrangement) as they camp. How did the children of Israel travel in the desert? Among the Talmudic sages, this was a matter of dispute. One sage said, "In a boxlike formation—the Camp of Judah in the east, Reuben in the south, Ephraim in the west, and Dan in the north."

kabbalah bites

For the camp of Reuben:
- a) Element=Water;
- b) Angel=Michael;
- c) Creature=Lion;
- d) Attribute=*Ḥesed*.
  (Reuben started the efforts to save Joseph.)

Reuben encamped in the south, which is associated with Ḥesed.

For the camp of Ephraim:
- a) Element=Earth;
- b) Angel=Raphael;
- c) Creature=Eagle;
- d) Attribute=*Malkhut*.

Ephraim encamped in the west, since the west is associated with the Shekhinah (Divine Presence) which is Malkhut.

For the camp of Dan:
- a) Element=Fire;
- b) Angel=Gabriel;
- c) Creature=Ox;
- d) Attribute=*Gevurah*.

Dan encamped in the north, since the north is associated with Gevurah and negativity (see *Jeremiah* 1:14).

- [5] Camping alongside was the tribe of Issachar. The leader of Issachar's descendants was Nethanel son of Zuar. [6] The head count of his regiment was fifty-four thousand, four hundred.

- [7] (The division was completed by) the tribe of Zebulun. The leader of Zebulun's descendants was Eliab son of Helon. [8] The head count of his regiment was fifty-seven thousand, four hundred.

- [9] The total head count of regiments for the Camp of Judah was one hundred and eighty-six thousand, four hundred;

- (When all the camps travel) they should move first.

[10] To the south was the division of regiments (of three tribes, known as) "the Camp of Reuben:"

- The leader of Reuben's descendants was Elizur son of Shedeur. [11] The head count of his regiment was forty-six thousand, five hundred.

- [12] Camping alongside was the tribe of Simeon. The leader of Simeon's descendants was Shelumiel son of Zurishaddai. [13] The head count of his regiment was fifty-nine thousand, three hundred.

- [14] (The division was completed by) the tribe of Gad. The leader of Gad's descendants was Eliasaph son of Reuel. [15] The head count of his regiment was forty-five thousand, six hundred and fifty.

- [16] The total head count of regiments for the Camp of Reuben was one hundred and fifty-one thousand, four hundred and fifty;

- (When all the camps travel) they should move second.

- [17] (After the Camp of Reuben moves) then the Tent of Meeting should move, (together with) the Levite camp, in the center of the other camps. They should travel (in the same arrangement) as they camp, with each man in his place, arranged in divisions.

Catalonian, and Italian. They must all remain loyal to their "divisions," to their own unique customs, which are all holy and precious (*Rabbi Isaac Luria, 16th century*).

spiritual vitamin

> Search for the innermost and the profound within you. Seek out the inwardness of everything around you, the soul of the universe. Search for and bring to light the Godliness that animates and pervades the world!

במדבר ב:יז-לד

יִסְּע֖וּ אִ֣ישׁ עַל־יָד֑וֹ לְדִגְלֵיהֶֽם: ס 18 דֶּ֣גֶל מַחֲנֵ֥ה אֶפְרַ֛יִם לְצִבְאֹתָ֖ם יָ֑מָּה וְנָשִׂיא֙ לִבְנֵ֣י אֶפְרַ֔יִם אֱלִישָׁמָ֖ע בֶּן־עַמִּיהֽוּד: 19 וּצְבָא֖וֹ וּפְקֻדֵיהֶ֑ם אַרְבָּעִ֥ים אֶ֖לֶף וַחֲמֵ֥שׁ מֵאֽוֹת: 20 וְעָלָ֖יו מַטֵּ֣ה מְנַשֶּׁ֑ה וְנָשִׂיא֙ לִבְנֵ֣י מְנַשֶּׁ֔ה גַּמְלִיאֵ֖ל בֶּן־פְּדָהצֽוּר: 21 וּצְבָא֖וֹ וּפְקֻדֵיהֶ֑ם שְׁנַ֧יִם וּשְׁלֹשִׁ֛ים אֶ֖לֶף וּמָאתָֽיִם: 22 וּמַטֵּ֖ה בִּנְיָמִ֑ן וְנָשִׂיא֙ לִבְנֵ֣י בִנְיָמִ֔ן אֲבִידָ֖ן בֶּן־גִּדְעֹנִֽי: 23 וּצְבָא֖וֹ וּפְקֻדֵיהֶ֑ם חֲמִשָּׁ֧ה וּשְׁלֹשִׁ֛ים אֶ֖לֶף וְאַרְבַּ֥ע מֵאֽוֹת: 24 כָּֽל־הַפְּקֻדִ֞ים לְמַחֲנֵ֣ה אֶפְרַ֗יִם מְאַ֥ת אֶ֛לֶף וּשְׁמֹנַֽת־אֲלָפִ֥ים וּמֵאָ֖ה לְצִבְאֹתָ֑ם וּשְׁלִשִׁ֖ים יִסָּֽעוּ: ס 25 דֶּ֣גֶל מַחֲנֵ֥ה דָ֛ן צָפֹ֖נָה לְצִבְאֹתָ֑ם וְנָשִׂיא֙ לִבְנֵ֣י דָ֔ן אֲחִיעֶ֖זֶר בֶּן־עַמִּֽישַׁדָּֽי: 26 וּצְבָא֖וֹ וּפְקֻדֵיהֶ֑ם שְׁנַ֧יִם וְשִׁשִּׁ֛ים אֶ֖לֶף וּשְׁבַ֥ע מֵאֽוֹת: 27 וְהַחֹנִ֥ים עָלָ֖יו מַטֵּ֣ה אָשֵׁ֑ר וְנָשִׂיא֙ לִבְנֵ֣י אָשֵׁ֔ר פַּגְעִיאֵ֖ל בֶּן־עָכְרָֽן: 28 וּצְבָא֖וֹ וּפְקֻדֵיהֶ֑ם אֶחָ֧ד וְאַרְבָּעִ֛ים אֶ֖לֶף וַחֲמֵ֥שׁ מֵאֽוֹת: 29 וּמַטֵּ֖ה נַפְתָּלִ֑י וְנָשִׂיא֙ לִבְנֵ֣י נַפְתָּלִ֔י אֲחִירַ֖ע בֶּן־עֵינָֽן: 30 וּצְבָא֖וֹ וּפְקֻדֵיהֶ֑ם שְׁלֹשָׁ֧ה וַחֲמִשִּׁ֛ים אֶ֖לֶף וְאַרְבַּ֥ע מֵאֽוֹת: 31 כָּל־הַפְּקֻדִים֙ לְמַ֣חֲנֵה דָ֔ן מְאַ֣ת אֶ֗לֶף וְשִׁבְעָ֧ה וַחֲמִשִּׁ֛ים אֶ֖לֶף וְשֵׁ֣שׁ מֵא֑וֹת לָאַחֲרֹנָ֥ה יִסְע֖וּ לְדִגְלֵיהֶֽם: פ 32 אֵ֛לֶּה פְּקוּדֵ֥י בְנֵֽי־יִשְׂרָאֵ֖ל לְבֵ֣ית אֲבֹתָ֑ם כָּל־פְּקוּדֵ֤י הַֽמַּחֲנֹת֙ לְצִבְאֹתָ֔ם שֵׁשׁ־מֵא֥וֹת אֶ֙לֶף֙ וּשְׁלֹ֣שֶׁת אֲלָפִ֔ים וַחֲמֵ֥שׁ מֵא֖וֹת וַחֲמִשִּֽׁים: 33 וְהַ֨לְוִיִּ֔ם לֹ֣א הָתְפָּקְד֔וּ בְּת֖וֹךְ בְּנֵ֣י יִשְׂרָאֵ֑ל כַּאֲשֶׁ֛ר צִוָּ֥ה יְהוָ֖ה אֶת־מֹשֶֽׁה: 34 וַֽיַּעֲשׂ֖וּ בְּנֵ֣י יִשְׂרָאֵ֑ל כְּ֠כֹל אֲשֶׁר־צִוָּ֨ה יְהוָ֜ה אֶת־מֹשֶׁ֗ה כֵּֽן־חָנ֤וּ לְדִגְלֵיהֶם֙ וְכֵ֣ן נָסָ֔עוּ אִ֥ישׁ לְמִשְׁפְּחֹתָ֖יו עַל־בֵּ֥ית אֲבֹתָֽיו: פ

The sage who argued for a boxlike formation based his opinion on the verse, *"They should travel (in the same arrangement) as they camp,"* since they camped in a boxlike configuration.

The sage who argued for a straight column based his opinion on the Torah's reference to Dan as *"the collector (of lost property) for all the other camps"* (10:25), since Dan was at the end of the procession (*Jerusalem Talmud, Eruvin* 5:1).

¹⁸ To the west was the division of regiments (of three tribes, known as) "the Camp of Ephraim:"

- The leader of Ephraim's descendants was Elishama son of Ammihud. ¹⁹ The head count of his regiment was forty thousand, five hundred.

- ²⁰ Alongside was the tribe of Manasseh. The leader of Manasseh's descendants was Gamaliel son of Pedahzur. ²¹ The head count of his regiment was thirty-two thousand, two hundred.

- ²² (The division was completed by) the tribe of Benjamin. The leader of Benjamin's descendants was Abidan son of Gideoni. ²³ The head count of his regiment was thirty-five thousand, four hundred.

- ²⁴ The total head count of regiments for the Camp of Ephraim was one hundred and eight thousand, one hundred;

- (When all the camps travel) they should move third.

²⁵ To the north was the division of regiments (of three tribes, known as) "the Camp of Dan:"

- The leader of Dan's descendants was Ahiezer son of Ammishaddai. ²⁶ The head count of his regiment was sixty-two thousand, seven hundred.

- ²⁷ Camping alongside was the tribe of Asher. The leader of Asher's descendants was Pagiel son of Ochran. ²⁸ The head count of his regiment was forty-one thousand, five hundred.

- ²⁹ (The division was completed by) the tribe of Naphtali. The leader of Naphtali's descendants was Ahira son of Enan. ³⁰ The head count of his regiment was fifty-three thousand, four hundred.

- ³¹ The total head count of regiments for the Camp of Dan was one hundred and fifty-seven thousand, six hundred;

- (When all the camps travel) arranged in divisions, they should move last.

³² (The above) are the head counts of the children of Israel, according to their fathers' houses. The total head count of regiments in the camps was six hundred and three thousand, five hundred and fifty. ³³ The Levites were not counted with the rest of the children of Israel, as God commanded Moses.

³⁴ The children of Israel did everything that God had commanded Moses. They encamped accordingly by their divisions, and they traveled accordingly, so that each was with his family, and his father's house.

The other sage said, "In a straight column—the Camp of Judah, followed by Reuben, Ephraim, and Dan."

במדבר ג:א-יג

ג [FOURTH READING] ¹ וְאֵ֛לֶּה תּוֹלְדֹ֥ת אַהֲרֹ֖ן וּמֹשֶׁ֑ה בְּי֗וֹם דִּבֶּ֧ר יְהֹוָ֛ה אֶת־מֹשֶׁ֖ה בְּהַ֥ר סִינָֽי: ² וְאֵ֛לֶּה שְׁמ֥וֹת בְּנֵֽי־אַהֲרֹ֖ן הַבְּכֹ֣ר ׀ נָדָ֑ב וַאֲבִיה֕וּא אֶלְעָזָ֖ר וְאִֽיתָמָֽר: ³ אֵ֗לֶּה שְׁמוֹת֙ בְּנֵ֣י אַהֲרֹ֔ן הַכֹּהֲנִ֖ים הַמְּשֻׁחִ֑ים אֲשֶׁר־מִלֵּ֥א יָדָ֖ם לְכַהֵֽן: ⁴ וַיָּ֣מָת נָדָ֣ב וַאֲבִיה֡וּא לִפְנֵ֣י יְהֹוָ֡ה בְּֽהַקְרִבָם֩ אֵ֨שׁ זָרָ֜ה לִפְנֵ֤י יְהֹוָה֙ בְּמִדְבַּ֣ר סִינַ֔י וּבָנִ֖ים לֹא־הָי֣וּ לָהֶ֑ם וַיְכַהֵ֤ן אֶלְעָזָר֙ וְאִ֣יתָמָ֔ר עַל־פְּנֵ֖י אַהֲרֹ֥ן אֲבִיהֶֽם: פ ⁵ וַיְדַבֵּ֥ר יְהֹוָ֖ה אֶל־מֹשֶׁ֥ה לֵּאמֹֽר: ⁶ הַקְרֵב֙ אֶת־מַטֵּ֣ה לֵוִ֔י וְהַֽעֲמַדְתָּ֣ אֹת֔וֹ לִפְנֵ֖י אַהֲרֹ֣ן הַכֹּהֵ֑ן וְשֵֽׁרְת֖וּ אֹתֽוֹ: ⁷ וְשָׁמְר֣וּ אֶת־מִשְׁמַרְתּ֗וֹ וְאֶת־מִשְׁמֶ֨רֶת֙ כָּל־הָ֣עֵדָ֔ה לִפְנֵ֖י אֹ֣הֶל מוֹעֵ֑ד לַעֲבֹ֖ד אֶת־עֲבֹדַ֥ת הַמִּשְׁכָּֽן: ⁸ וְשָׁמְר֗וּ אֶֽת־כָּל־כְּלֵי֙ אֹ֣הֶל מוֹעֵ֔ד וְאֶת־מִשְׁמֶ֖רֶת בְּנֵ֣י יִשְׂרָאֵ֑ל לַעֲבֹ֖ד אֶת־עֲבֹדַ֥ת הַמִּשְׁכָּֽן: ⁹ וְנָתַתָּה֙ אֶת־הַלְוִיִּ֔ם לְאַהֲרֹ֖ן וּלְבָנָ֑יו נְתוּנִ֨ם נְתוּנִ֥ם הֵ֛מָּה ל֖וֹ מֵאֵ֥ת בְּנֵ֥י יִשְׂרָאֵֽל: ¹⁰ וְאֶת־אַהֲרֹ֤ן וְאֶת־בָּנָיו֙ תִּפְקֹ֔ד וְשָׁמְר֖וּ אֶת־כְּהֻנָּתָ֑ם וְהַזָּ֥ר הַקָּרֵ֖ב יוּמָֽת: פ ¹¹ וַיְדַבֵּ֥ר יְהֹוָ֖ה אֶל־מֹשֶׁ֥ה לֵּאמֹֽר: ¹² וַאֲנִ֞י הִנֵּ֧ה לָקַ֣חְתִּי אֶת־הַלְוִיִּ֗ם מִתּוֹךְ֙ בְּנֵ֣י יִשְׂרָאֵ֔ל תַּ֧חַת כָּל־בְּכ֛וֹר פֶּ֥טֶר רֶ֖חֶם מִבְּנֵ֣י יִשְׂרָאֵ֑ל וְהָ֥יוּ לִ֖י הַלְוִיִּֽם: ¹³ כִּ֣י לִי֘ כָּל־בְּכוֹר֒ בְּיוֹם֩ הַכֹּתִ֨י כָל־

---

were few; and even though Aaron's children had been appointed to positions of importance, two of them died for bringing *"an extraneous fire before God"* (v. 4).

Stating that the priests were few in number also serves as an introduction as to why it was necessary to appoint the Levites as assistants to the priests, as is set out in the following section (*Rabbi Isaac Abravanel, 15th century*).

6. Draw the tribe of Levi close. Thus it is written, *"The righteous man flourishes like a palm tree. He grows tall like a cedar in Lebanon"* (Psalms 92:13; Numbers Rabbah).

A person could be righteous in one of two ways: (a) A cedar is strong, tall and beautiful, but it bears no fruit. This corresponds to a person who studies Torah and observes commandments primarily for his own personal spiritual growth. or (b) A palm tree—not as tall and strong as the cedar, but which

---

kabbalah bites

3:2 Literally, the verse states: *"The firstborn: Nadab and Abihu, Eleazar and Ithamar,"* suggesting that *both* Nadab and Abihu were somehow the firstborn. This alludes to the idea that Nadab and Abihu were both reincarnations of different portions of Cain's soul, Cain being Adam's firstborn. So, in a sense, Nadab and Abihu were both the firstborn, spiritually speaking.

Later, Cain's soul would be reincarnated into Jesse, father of King David, where it would achieve its final *tikkun* (spiritual healing) from Adam's sin.

numbers 3:1–13 — be-midbar

Aaron's Descendants

3 [FOURTH READING] ¹ The following are the descendants of Aaron, (who were disciples of) Moses, on the day that God spoke to Moses at Mount Sinai:

² These are the names of Aaron's sons: Nadab, the firstborn, Abihu, Eleazar, and Ithamar. ³ These are the names of Aaron's sons, the anointed priests, whom he inaugurated to serve as priests.

⁴ Nadab and Abihu died before God when they brought an extraneous fire before God in the Sinai Desert. They had no children.

But Eleazar and Ithamar served as priests in the lifetime of Aaron, their father.

Appointment of the Levites

⁵ God spoke to Moses, saying: ⁶ "Draw the tribe of Levi close and stand them before Aaron the priest. They will serve him (by) ⁷ taking charge of (some of) his duties, and the duties of the entire community, (standing) before the Tent of Meeting to carry out the task of (guarding) the Tabernacle (against unauthorized entry). ⁸ They should guard all the vessels of the Tent of Meeting, which is the duty of the children of Israel, to carry out the service of the Tabernacle. ⁹ You should give over the Levites to Aaron and his sons (to help them). They are to be (separated) from the children of Israel (and) totally given over to him."

¹⁰ You should appoint Aaron and his sons to safeguard their priesthood. Any unauthorized person who approaches (to participate in the priestly-service) must be put to death.

¹¹ God spoke to Moses, saying: ¹² "(If you want to know why) indeed I have taken the Levites from among the (other) children of Israel? (It is because I took them) instead of all firstborn from every womb among the children of Israel (since the firstborn worshiped the Golden Calf, so I decided instead that) the Levites would be Mine. ¹³ (If you want to know why I chose the firstborn to start with, it is)

3:1 The following are the descendants of Aaron and Moses. After promising us a list of the descendants of Aaron *and* Moses we are only given the names of Aaron's sons. But they, too, are considered the "children of Moses" because he taught them Torah, and *if you teach somebody's child Torah it is as if you had fathered that child* (Rashi, 11*th* century; Babylonian Talmud, Sanhedrin 19b).

After discussing the main census of the Jewish people (chapters 1-2), the subject now turns to the tribe of Levi. Before discussing the details pertaining to the Levites themselves, the Torah mentions the heads of this tribe—the priests (Naḥmanides, 13*th* century).

After the Torah stressed how the children of Israel multiplied to form a large population, and appointed leaders, the Torah now contrasts this with the fact that Moses and Aaron's children

במדבר ג:יג-כח

בְּכוֹר בְּאֶרֶץ מִצְרַיִם הִקְדַּשְׁתִּי לִי כָל־בְּכוֹר בְּיִשְׂרָאֵל מֵאָדָם עַד־בְּהֵמָה לִי יִהְיוּ אֲנִי יְהֹוָה: פ 14 [FIFTH READING] וַיְדַבֵּר יְהֹוָה אֶל־מֹשֶׁה בְּמִדְבַּר סִינַי לֵאמֹר: 15 פְּקֹד אֶת־בְּנֵי לֵוִי לְבֵית אֲבֹתָם לְמִשְׁפְּחֹתָם כָּל־זָכָר מִבֶּן־חֹדֶשׁ וָמַעְלָה תִּפְקְדֵם: 16 וַיִּפְקֹד אֹתָם מֹשֶׁה עַל־פִּי יְהֹוָה כַּאֲשֶׁר צֻוָּה: 17 וַיִּהְיוּ־אֵלֶּה בְנֵי־לֵוִי בִּשְׁמֹתָם גֵּרְשׁוֹן וּקְהָת וּמְרָרִי: 18 וְאֵלֶּה שְׁמוֹת בְּנֵי־גֵרְשׁוֹן לְמִשְׁפְּחֹתָם לִבְנִי וְשִׁמְעִי: 19 וּבְנֵי קְהָת לְמִשְׁפְּחֹתָם עַמְרָם וְיִצְהָר חֶבְרוֹן וְעֻזִּיאֵל: 20 וּבְנֵי מְרָרִי לְמִשְׁפְּחֹתָם מַחְלִי וּמוּשִׁי אֵלֶּה הֵם מִשְׁפְּחֹת הַלֵּוִי לְבֵית אֲבֹתָם: 21 לְגֵרְשׁוֹן מִשְׁפַּחַת הַלִּבְנִי וּמִשְׁפַּחַת הַשִּׁמְעִי אֵלֶּה הֵם מִשְׁפְּחֹת הַגֵּרְשֻׁנִּי: 22 פְּקֻדֵיהֶם בְּמִסְפַּר כָּל־זָכָר מִבֶּן־חֹדֶשׁ וָמַעְלָה פְּקֻדֵיהֶם שִׁבְעַת אֲלָפִים וַחֲמֵשׁ מֵאוֹת: 23 מִשְׁפְּחֹת הַגֵּרְשֻׁנִּי אַחֲרֵי הַמִּשְׁכָּן יַחֲנוּ יָמָּה: 24 וּנְשִׂיא בֵית־אָב לַגֵּרְשֻׁנִּי אֶלְיָסָף בֶּן־לָאֵל: 25 וּמִשְׁמֶרֶת בְּנֵי־גֵרְשׁוֹן בְּאֹהֶל מוֹעֵד הַמִּשְׁכָּן וְהָאֹהֶל מִכְסֵהוּ וּמָסַךְ פֶּתַח אֹהֶל מוֹעֵד: 26 וְקַלְעֵי הֶחָצֵר וְאֶת־מָסַךְ פֶּתַח הֶחָצֵר אֲשֶׁר עַל־הַמִּשְׁכָּן וְעַל־הַמִּזְבֵּחַ סָבִיב וְאֵת מֵיתָרָיו לְכֹל עֲבֹדָתוֹ: ס 27 וְלִקְהָת מִשְׁפַּחַת הַעַמְרָמִי וּמִשְׁפַּחַת הַיִּצְהָרִי וּמִשְׁפַּחַת הַחֶבְרֹנִי וּמִשְׁפַּחַת הָעָזִּיאֵלִי אֵלֶּה הֵם מִשְׁפְּחֹת הַקְּהָתִי: 28 בְּמִסְפַּר כָּל־זָכָר מִבֶּן־חֹדֶשׁ וָמַעְלָה

15. From the age of one month and upward. As soon as a child's viability is proven, he is counted among those called "guardians of the sacred duty" (*Rashi, 11th century*).

spiritual vitamin

> If you do not fulfil your task, and do not utilize your inestimable Divine powers, it is not merely a personal loss and failure, but something that affects the destiny of the whole world.

numbers 3:13–28 — be-midbar

because all the firstborn are Mine since the day I struck all the firstborn in the land of Egypt. (Back then) I took every firstborn of Israel, both man and beast, to be holy to Me. They will (always) be Mine, I am God."

Census of the Levites

[FIFTH READING] ¹⁴ God spoke to Moses in the Sinai Desert, saying: ¹⁵ "Take a head count head count descendants of Levi, (including) those whose family (lineage had been verified) according to their paternal houses. Count all males from the age of one month and upward."

¹⁶ Moses counted them, just as he was commanded, by God's word.

¹⁷ These were the names of Levi's sons: Gershon, Kohath, and Merari.

¹⁸ The names of Gershon's sons, heading their families, were Libni and Shimei.

¹⁹ Kohath's sons, heading their families, were Amram, Izhar, Hebron and Uzziel.

²⁰ Merari's sons, heading their families, were Mahli and Mushi.

The (above) are the families of Levi according to their paternal houses.

²¹ (The head count) for Gershon (included) the Libni family and the Shimei family, (for) these are the Gershonite families:

- ²² Their total head count included every male from the age of one month and upward. Their head count was seven thousand, five hundred.

- ²³ The Gershonite families should camp behind the Tabernacle, to the west.

- ²⁴ The leader of the paternal house of the Gershonites is Eliasaph son of Lael.

- ²⁵ The duties of Gershon's descendants in the Tent of Meeting (were to care for: the tapestries of) the Tabernacle, the (goat's hair which rested above it like a) tent, (the *taḥash* skins which acted as) its cover and the curtain at the entrance to the Tent of Meeting, ²⁶ the curtains of the courtyard and the curtain for the entrance to the courtyard which surrounds the Tabernacle and the altar, the ropes (of the Tabernacle itself), and all associated tasks.

²⁷ (The head count) for Kohath (included) the Amramite family, the Izharite family, the Hebronite family, and the Uzzielite family, (for) these are the families of Kohath:

- ²⁸ The number of all males from the age of one month and upward was eight thousand six hundred.

bears sweet, delicious fruit—is analogous to a person who is willing to sacrifice some of the time which he could have used for his own personal spiritual growth, for the sake of helping others.

This second type of person brings much healing to the world, and his reward is doubled and redoubled, far beyond the first type. Make sure that your "tree" of spiritual growth always bears some fruit! (*Rabbi Israel Ba'al Shem Tov, 18th century*).

במדבר ג:כח-מא

שְׁמֹנַת אֲלָפִים וְשֵׁשׁ מֵאוֹת שֹׁמְרֵי מִשְׁמֶרֶת הַקֹּדֶשׁ: 29 מִשְׁפְּחֹת בְּנֵי־קְהָת יַחֲנוּ עַל יֶרֶךְ הַמִּשְׁכָּן תֵּימָנָה: 30 וּנְשִׂיא בֵית־אָב לְמִשְׁפְּחֹת הַקְּהָתִי אֱלִיצָפָן בֶּן־עֻזִּיאֵל: 31 וּמִשְׁמַרְתָּם הָאָרֹן וְהַשֻּׁלְחָן וְהַמְּנֹרָה וְהַמִּזְבְּחֹת וּכְלֵי הַקֹּדֶשׁ אֲשֶׁר יְשָׁרְתוּ בָּהֶם וְהַמָּסָךְ וְכֹל עֲבֹדָתוֹ: 32 וּנְשִׂיא נְשִׂיאֵי הַלֵּוִי אֶלְעָזָר בֶּן־אַהֲרֹן הַכֹּהֵן פְּקֻדַּת שֹׁמְרֵי מִשְׁמֶרֶת הַקֹּדֶשׁ: 33 לִמְרָרִי מִשְׁפַּחַת הַמַּחְלִי וּמִשְׁפַּחַת הַמּוּשִׁי אֵלֶּה הֵם מִשְׁפְּחֹת מְרָרִי: 34 וּפְקֻדֵיהֶם בְּמִסְפַּר כָּל־זָכָר מִבֶּן־חֹדֶשׁ וָמָעְלָה שֵׁשֶׁת אֲלָפִים וּמָאתָיִם: 35 וּנְשִׂיא בֵית־אָב לְמִשְׁפְּחֹת מְרָרִי צוּרִיאֵל בֶּן־אֲבִיחָיִל עַל יֶרֶךְ הַמִּשְׁכָּן יַחֲנוּ צָפֹנָה: 36 וּפְקֻדַּת מִשְׁמֶרֶת בְּנֵי מְרָרִי קַרְשֵׁי הַמִּשְׁכָּן וּבְרִיחָיו וְעַמֻּדָיו וַאֲדָנָיו וְכָל־כֵּלָיו וְכֹל עֲבֹדָתוֹ: 37 וְעַמֻּדֵי הֶחָצֵר סָבִיב וְאַדְנֵיהֶם וִיתֵדֹתָם וּמֵיתְרֵיהֶם: 38 וְהַחֹנִים לִפְנֵי הַמִּשְׁכָּן קֵדְמָה לִפְנֵי אֹהֶל־מוֹעֵד ׀ מִזְרָחָה מֹשֶׁה ׀ וְאַהֲרֹן וּבָנָיו שֹׁמְרִים מִשְׁמֶרֶת הַמִּקְדָּשׁ לְמִשְׁמֶרֶת בְּנֵי יִשְׂרָאֵל וְהַזָּר הַקָּרֵב יוּמָת: 39 כָּל־פְּקוּדֵי הַלְוִיִּם אֲשֶׁר פָּקַד מֹשֶׁה וְאַהֲרֹן עַל־פִּי יְהֹוָה לְמִשְׁפְּחֹתָם כָּל־זָכָר מִבֶּן־חֹדֶשׁ וָמַעְלָה שְׁנַיִם וְעֶשְׂרִים אָלֶף: ס 40 [SIXTH READING] וַיֹּאמֶר יְהֹוָה אֶל־מֹשֶׁה פְּקֹד כָּל־בְּכֹר זָכָר לִבְנֵי יִשְׂרָאֵל מִבֶּן־חֹדֶשׁ וָמָעְלָה וְשָׂא אֵת מִסְפַּר שְׁמֹתָם: 41 וְלָקַחְתָּ אֶת־הַלְוִיִּם לִי אֲנִי יְהֹוָה תַּחַת כָּל־בְּכֹר בִּבְנֵי יִשְׂרָאֵל וְאֵת בֶּהֱמַת הַלְוִיִּם תַּחַת כָּל־בְּכוֹר בְּבֶהֱמַת בְּנֵי יִשְׂרָאֵל:

39. The total head count of male Levites … was twenty-two thousand. The tribe of Levi was much smaller than the other tribes. Why was this the case?

In Egypt, God caused the Israelites to increase miraculously, in direct proportion to the labor imposed on them—*"As much as they would (set their hearts to) afflict them, so did they multiply"* (*Exodus* 1:12). The tribe of Levi, however, was not subject to any slavery (*Exodus Rabbah*), so they had multiplied at a natural rate. Consequently, their tribe was much smaller than all the other tribes (*Nahmanides, 13th century*).

Since the obligation of supporting the tribe of Levi was placed upon the rest of the people, God arranged that the number of Levites should be minimal, to ease the financial burden on the community (*Rabbi Meir Simhah of Dvinsk, 19th–20th century*).

numbers 3:28–41   be-midbar

— (They were) guardians, with the sacred duty (of guarding the Tabernacle vessels).

— ²⁹ The families of Kohath's descendants camped to the south side of the Tabernacle.

— ³⁰ The leader of the paternal house of the Kohath families was Elizaphan son of Uzziel.

— ³¹ Their duties (were to care for): the ark, the table, the candelabrum, the altars, the sacred utensils used with them when ministering, the partition, and all associated tasks.

— ³² The chief over all the leaders of the Levites was Eleazar son of Aaron the priest. He appointed (all) the guardians who had sacred duties.

³³ (The head count) for Merari (included) the Mahlite family and the Mushite family, (for) these are the families of Merari:

— ³⁴ Their total head count of every male from the age of one month and upward was six thousand two hundred.

— ³⁵ The leader of the paternal house of Merari's families was Zuriel son of Abihail.

— They camped on the north side of the Tabernacle.

— ³⁶ The appointed duty of Merari's descendants (was to care for): the beams of the Tabernacle, its bars, its pillars, and its sockets, all its vessels and all its associated tasks, ³⁷ the pillars of the surrounding courtyard, their sockets, their pegs, and their ropes.

³⁸ Camping in front of the Tabernacle, in front of the Tent of Meeting to the east, were Moses, Aaron and his sons, (who were) the guardians of the Sanctuary's duties, duties (which they were appointed to perform on behalf) of the children of Israel. Any unauthorized person who approaches (to participate in this task) must be put to death.

³⁹ The total head count of male Levites whose family (lineage had been verified), from the age of one month and upward, counted by Moses and Aaron by God's word was twenty-two thousand.

Census of the Firstborn

[SIXTH READING] ⁴⁰ God said to Moses: "Count every firstborn male of the children of Israel aged one month and upward, and include their names in the census. ⁴¹ But take the Levites for Me—I am God—in place of all firstborn among the children of Israel. (Take) the Levites' animals in place of all the firstborn animals of the children of Israel."

Food for thought

1. Is there a special quality to the child born first in a family?

2. Why would we honor a person for something he or she did not work to achieve?

3. Would you wish to "trade" your sibling-position in the family?

42 וַיִּפְקֹד מֹשֶׁה כַּאֲשֶׁר צִוָּה יְהֹוָה אֹתוֹ אֶת־כָּל־בְּכוֹר בִּבְנֵי יִשְׂרָאֵל: 43 וַיְהִי כָל־בְּכוֹר זָכָר בְּמִסְפַּר שֵׁמֹת מִבֶּן־חֹדֶשׁ וָמַעְלָה לִפְקֻדֵיהֶם שְׁנַיִם וְעֶשְׂרִים אֶלֶף שְׁלֹשָׁה וְשִׁבְעִים וּמָאתָיִם: 44 וַיְדַבֵּר יְהֹוָה אֶל־מֹשֶׁה לֵּאמֹר: 45 קַח אֶת־הַלְוִיִּם תַּחַת כָּל־בְּכוֹר בִּבְנֵי יִשְׂרָאֵל וְאֶת־בֶּהֱמַת הַלְוִיִּם תַּחַת בְּהֶמְתָּם וְהָיוּ־לִי הַלְוִיִּם אֲנִי יְהֹוָה: 46 וְאֵת פְּדוּיֵי הַשְּׁלֹשָׁה וְהַשִּׁבְעִים וְהַמָּאתָיִם הָעֹדְפִים עַל־הַלְוִיִּם מִבְּכוֹר בְּנֵי יִשְׂרָאֵל: 47 וְלָקַחְתָּ חֲמֵשֶׁת חֲמֵשֶׁת שְׁקָלִים לַגֻּלְגֹּלֶת בְּשֶׁקֶל הַקֹּדֶשׁ תִּקָּח עֶשְׂרִים גֵּרָה הַשָּׁקֶל: 48 וְנָתַתָּה הַכֶּסֶף לְאַהֲרֹן וּלְבָנָיו פְּדוּיֵי הָעֹדְפִים בָּהֶם: 49 וַיִּקַּח מֹשֶׁה אֵת כֶּסֶף הַפִּדְיוֹם מֵאֵת הָעֹדְפִים עַל פְּדוּיֵי הַלְוִיִּם: 50 מֵאֵת בְּכוֹר בְּנֵי יִשְׂרָאֵל לָקַח אֶת־הַכָּסֶף חֲמִשָּׁה וְשִׁשִּׁים וּשְׁלֹשׁ מֵאוֹת וָאֶלֶף בְּשֶׁקֶל הַקֹּדֶשׁ: 51 וַיִּתֵּן מֹשֶׁה אֶת־כֶּסֶף הַפְּדֻיִם לְאַהֲרֹן וּלְבָנָיו עַל־פִּי יְהֹוָה כַּאֲשֶׁר צִוָּה יְהֹוָה אֶת־מֹשֶׁה: פ

ד 1 וַיְדַבֵּר יְהֹוָה אֶל־מֹשֶׁה וְאֶל־אַהֲרֹן לֵאמֹר: [SEVENTH READING] 2 נָשֹׂא אֶת־רֹאשׁ בְּנֵי קְהָת מִתּוֹךְ בְּנֵי לֵוִי לְמִשְׁפְּחֹתָם לְבֵית אֲבֹתָם: 3 מִבֶּן שְׁלֹשִׁים שָׁנָה וָמַעְלָה וְעַד בֶּן־חֲמִשִּׁים שָׁנָה כָּל־בָּא לַצָּבָא לַעֲשׂוֹת מְלָאכָה בְּאֹהֶל מוֹעֵד: 4 זֹאת עֲבֹדַת בְּנֵי־קְהָת בְּאֹהֶל מוֹעֵד קֹדֶשׁ הַקֳּדָשִׁים: 5 וּבָא אַהֲרֹן וּבָנָיו בִּנְסֹעַ הַמַּחֲנֶה וְהוֹרִדוּ אֵת פָּרֹכֶת הַמָּסָךְ וְכִסּוּ־בָהּ אֵת אֲרֹן הָעֵדֻת: 6 וְנָתְנוּ עָלָיו כְּסוּי עוֹר תַּחַשׁ וּפָרְשׂוּ בֶגֶד־כְּלִיל תְּכֵלֶת מִלְמָעְלָה וְשָׂמוּ בַּדָּיו:

two passages? At the age of twenty-five, a Levite would study the laws pertaining to his tasks in the Temple; and at the age of thirty, he would begin to perform the service.

From here you learn that if a student does not succeed in his studies after five years, he never will (*Babylonian Talmud, Ḥullin* 24a).

6. They should place a covering of *taḥash* skin on it and then they should spread a garment of pure turquoise wool on top of that. The covering of the ark differed from all the other pieces of apparatus in that the garment of turquoise wool was placed on the outside. (With the

⁴² Moses counted every firstborn of Israel, as God had commanded him.

⁴³ The firstborn males aged one month and upward, (including) a count of the names, was twenty-two thousand, two hundred and seventy-three.

Redemption of Additional Firstborn

⁴⁴ God spoke to Moses, saying: ⁴⁵ "Take the Levites in place of all the firstborn among the children of Israel, and the Levites' animals instead of their animals. The Levites will be Mine, I am God." ⁴⁶ "(Since the number of) firstborn of the children of Israel exceeds the (number of) Levites by two hundred and seventy-three, (the extra firstborn will require) redemption. ⁴⁷ (From each firstborn) take five shekels per head, according to the shekel (measurement system which is used for) sanctified (items), in which the shekel is twenty *gerah*. ⁴⁸ Give the money to Aaron and his sons, in redemption for the firstborn who are in excess of the (Levites)."

⁴⁹ Moses took the redemption money from the (two hundred and seventy-three firstborn) who were in excess of the (twenty-two thousand firstborn) redeemed by the Levites. ⁵⁰ He took the money from the firstborn of the children of Israel: one thousand, three hundred and sixty-five shekels (according to the measurement system which is used for) sanctified (items). ⁵¹ Moses gave the money of those who were redeemed to Aaron and his sons, in accordance with the word of God, as God had commanded Moses.

Duties of Kohath's Descendants

4 [SEVENTH READING] ¹ God spoke to Moses and Aaron, saying: ² "Single out those from Kohath's descendants (who are fit to carry) from among the (other) children of Levi, verifying their family lineage, according to their paternal houses. ³ (Pick only those) from the age of thirty years until the age of fifty years, all those who (are fit to) participate in the service (of carrying), to work in the Tent of Meeting."

⁴ The following is the service of Kohath's descendants in the Tent of Meeting, the Holy of Holies:

- ⁵ When the camp is about to travel, Aaron and his sons should come and take down the partition, and they should cover the Ark of the Testimony with it. ⁶ They should place a covering of *taḥash* skin on it and then they should spread a garment of pure turquoise wool on top of that. Then they should put its poles into place.

---

47. (From each firstborn) take five shekels. This was the sale price of Joseph, twenty silver pieces (four silver pieces equals one shekel), and he was the firstborn of Rachel (*Rashi, 11ᵗʰ century*).

4:3 From the age of thirty years until the age of fifty years. Elsewhere it says, *"He is qualified to serve, etc., from the age of twenty-five years and upwards"* (8:24). How can we reconcile these

במדבר ד:ז-כ

7 וְעַ֣ל | שֻׁלְחַ֣ן הַפָּנִ֗ים יִפְרְשׂוּ֮ בֶּ֣גֶד תְּכֵ֒לֶת֒ וְנָתְנ֣וּ עָ֠לָ֠יו אֶת־הַקְּעָרֹ֤ת וְאֶת־הַכַּפֹּת֙ וְאֶת־הַמְּנַקִּיֹּ֔ת וְאֵ֖ת קְשׂ֣וֹת הַנָּ֑סֶךְ וְלֶ֥חֶם הַתָּמִ֖יד עָלָ֥יו יִהְיֶֽה: 8 וּפָרְשׂ֣וּ עֲלֵיהֶ֗ם בֶּ֚גֶד תּוֹלַ֣עַת שָׁנִ֔י וְכִסּ֣וּ אֹת֔וֹ בְּמִכְסֵ֖ה ע֣וֹר תָּ֑חַשׁ וְשָׂמ֖וּ אֶת־בַּדָּֽיו: 9 וְלָקְח֣וּ | בֶּ֣גֶד תְּכֵ֗לֶת וְכִסּ֞וּ אֶת־מְנֹרַ֤ת הַמָּאוֹר֙ וְאֶת־נֵ֣רֹתֶ֔יהָ וְאֶת־מַלְקָחֶ֖יהָ וְאֶת־מַחְתֹּתֶ֑יהָ וְאֵת֙ כָּל־כְּלֵ֣י שַׁמְנָ֔הּ אֲשֶׁ֥ר יְשָׁרְתוּ־לָ֖הּ בָּהֶֽם: 10 וְנָתְנ֤וּ אֹתָהּ֙ וְאֶת־כָּל־כֵּלֶ֔יהָ אֶל־מִכְסֵ֖ה ע֣וֹר תָּ֑חַשׁ וְנָתְנ֖וּ עַל־הַמּֽוֹט: 11 וְעַ֣ל | מִזְבַּ֣ח הַזָּהָ֗ב יִפְרְשׂוּ֙ בֶּ֣גֶד תְּכֵ֔לֶת וְכִסּ֣וּ אֹת֔וֹ בְּמִכְסֵ֖ה ע֣וֹר תָּ֑חַשׁ וְשָׂמ֖וּ אֶת־בַּדָּֽיו: 12 וְלָקְחוּ֩ אֶת־כָּל־כְּלֵ֨י הַשָּׁרֵ֜ת אֲשֶׁ֧ר יְשָֽׁרְתוּ־בָ֣ם בַּקֹּ֗דֶשׁ וְנָֽתְנוּ֙ אֶל־בֶּ֣גֶד תְּכֵ֔לֶת וְכִסּ֣וּ אוֹתָ֔ם בְּמִכְסֵ֖ה ע֣וֹר תָּ֑חַשׁ וְנָתְנ֖וּ עַל־הַמּֽוֹט: 13 וְדִשְּׁנ֖וּ אֶת־הַמִּזְבֵּ֑חַ וּפָרְשׂ֣וּ עָלָ֔יו בֶּ֖גֶד אַרְגָּמָֽן: 14 וְנָתְנ֣וּ עָ֠לָ֠יו אֶת־כָּל־כֵּלָ֞יו אֲשֶׁ֣ר יְשָֽׁרְת֧וּ עָלָ֣יו בָּהֶ֗ם אֶת־הַמַּחְתֹּ֤ת אֶת־הַמִּזְלָגֹת֙ וְאֶת־הַיָּעִ֣ים וְאֶת־הַמִּזְרָקֹ֔ת כֹּ֖ל כְּלֵ֣י הַמִּזְבֵּ֑חַ וּפָרְשׂ֣וּ עָלָ֗יו כְּס֛וּי ע֥וֹר תַּ֖חַשׁ וְשָׂמ֥וּ בַדָּֽיו: 15 וְכִלָּ֣ה אַֽהֲרֹן־וּ֠בָנָ֠יו לְכַסֹּ֨ת אֶת־הַקֹּ֜דֶשׁ וְאֶת־כָּל־כְּלֵ֣י הַקֹּ֘דֶשׁ֘ בִּנְסֹ֣עַ הַֽמַּחֲנֶה֒ וְאַֽחֲרֵי־כֵ֗ן יָבֹ֣אוּ בְנֵֽי־קְהָת֙ לָשֵׂ֔את וְלֹֽא־יִגְּע֥וּ אֶל־הַקֹּ֖דֶשׁ וָמֵ֑תוּ אֵ֛לֶּה מַשָּׂ֥א בְנֵֽי־קְהָ֖ת בְּאֹ֥הֶל מוֹעֵֽד: 16 וּפְקֻדַּ֞ת אֶלְעָזָ֣ר | בֶּן־אַֽהֲרֹ֣ן הַכֹּהֵ֗ן שֶׁ֤מֶן הַמָּאוֹר֙ וּקְטֹ֣רֶת הַסַּמִּ֔ים וּמִנְחַ֥ת הַתָּמִ֖יד וְשֶׁ֣מֶן הַמִּשְׁחָ֑ה פְּקֻדַּ֗ת כָּל־הַמִּשְׁכָּן֙ וְכָל־אֲשֶׁר־בּ֔וֹ בְּקֹ֖דֶשׁ וּבְכֵלָֽיו: פ

17 [MAFTIR] וַיְדַבֵּ֣ר יְהֹוָ֔ה אֶל־מֹשֶׁ֥ה וְאֶל־אַֽהֲרֹ֖ן לֵאמֹֽר: 18 אַל־תַּכְרִ֕יתוּ אֶת־שֵׁ֖בֶט מִשְׁפְּחֹ֣ת הַקְּהָתִ֑י מִתּ֖וֹךְ הַֽלְוִיִּֽם: 19 וְזֹ֣את | עֲשׂ֣וּ לָהֶ֗ם וְחָיוּ֙ וְלֹ֣א יָמֻ֔תוּ בְּגִשְׁתָּ֖ם אֶת־קֹ֣דֶשׁ הַקֳּדָשִׁ֑ים אַֽהֲרֹ֤ן וּבָנָיו֙ יָבֹ֔אוּ וְשָׂמ֣וּ אוֹתָ֗ם אִ֥ישׁ אִ֛ישׁ עַל־עֲבֹֽדָת֖וֹ וְאֶל־מַשָּׂאֽוֹ: 20 וְלֹא־יָבֹ֧אוּ לִרְא֛וֹת כְּבַלַּ֥ע אֶת־הַקֹּ֖דֶשׁ וָמֵֽתוּ: פ פ פ

קנ״ט פסוקים, חלקי״ה ו סימן.

---

tremendous sanctity, they were natural "magnets" for demonic forces which always try to suck energy from holy sites. It was therefore crucial that all the items of apparatus were protected with turquoise (*Rabbi Menahem Azariah da Fano, 16th–17th century*).

- ⁷ They should spread a garment of turquoise wool on the show-table and they should place on it the bread molds, spoons, its supporting bars and separating bars. The multi-surface bread may then be placed on it. ⁸ They should spread upon them a garment of crimson wool and cover that with a covering of *taḥash* skin. Then they should put its poles into place.

- ⁹ They should take a turquoise garment and cover the brilliant candelabrum and its lamps, its tongs, and its scoops, and all its oil vessels with which its service is carried out. ¹⁰ They should put it along with its vessels into a *taḥash* skin covering (bag), and attach it to a (carrying) pole. ¹¹ Over the golden altar they should spread a garment of turquoise wool, cover it with a *taḥash* skin covering, and insert its poles.

- ¹² They should then take all the vessels used in the Sanctuary, put them into a garment of turquoise wool, cover them with a *taḥash* skin covering, and attach them to a (carrying) pole.

- ¹³ They should remove the ashes from the (copper) altar and spread a garment of purple wool over it. ¹⁴ They should place on top of it all the vessels which they use when carrying out its service: the scoops, the forks, the shovels, and the basins—all the implements of the altar. Then they should spread over it a covering of *taḥash* skin and insert its poles.

- ¹⁵ When the camp is set to travel, Aaron and his sons should finish covering the holy (ark and altar) and all the other holy (vessels), and afterwards, Kohath's descendants should come to carry (the items); but they should not touch the sacred (vessels when they are uncovered), for then they will die. The above is what Kohath's descendants must carry from the Tent of Meeting.

- ¹⁶ Eleazar son of Aaron the priest is appointed (to carry): oil for lighting, the incense of spices, the continual (daily) meal-offering, and the anointing oil. (He is also) in charge of the entire Tabernacle and all its contents, the Sanctuary and its vessels.

[MAFTIR] ¹⁷ God spoke to Moses and Aaron, saying:

- ¹⁸ Do not cause the tribe of the families of Kohath to be eliminated from among the Levites. ¹⁹ Do this for them, so they should live and not die: When they approach the Holy of Holies, Aaron and his sons should first come and appoint each man individually to his task and his load. ²⁰ They must not come in to see the holy (vessels) being encapsulated, so that they will not die.

Haftarot: Be-Midbar—page 1369.   Erev Rosh Ḥodesh—page 1415.

other items, the *taḥash* skin was the outer covering.) This honored the ark with a more distinctive, lavish appearance, even while in transit.

Turquoise was nevertheless used to cover *all* the items as, according to the Kabbalah, this color has the power to deflect negative forces. Since the Tabernacle apparatus were objects of

> Torah should **not be limited** to the realm of the **academic** or even the **spiritual**. It should affect you deeply, **lifting** you to a **higher plane**.

NASO'
נשא

DUTIES OF THE LEVITES	4:21-49
SANCTITY OF THE CAMP	5:1-4
LAWS OF GUILT OFFERING FOR DISHONESTY	5:5-8
ADDITIONAL LAWS OF GIFTS TO THE PRIESTS	5:9-10
SUSPECTED ADULTERESS	5:11-31
NAZIRITE	6:1-21
PRIESTLY BLESSING	6:22-27
TRIBAL LEADERS' DONATION TO TABERNACLE	7:1-9
DEDICATION OF ALTAR	7:10-88
DIVINE COMMUNICATION WITH MOSES	7:89

NAME
Naso'

MEANING
"Lift"

LINES IN TORAH SCROLL
311

PARASHIYYOT
18 open; 8 closed

VERSES
176

WORDS
2264

LETTERS
8632

LOCATION
Sinai Desert

DATE
Nisan and *Iyyar*, 2449

KEY PEOPLE
Moses, Aaron, *sotah*, nazirite, priests, tribal leaders

MITZVOT
7 positive; 11 prohibitions

NOTES
Longest portion in the Torah; usually read the week after *Shavuot*

CHARACTER PROFILE

NAME
Nahshon

MEANING
"Surf" or "snake"

SISTER
Elisheba, wife of Aaron

FATHER
Amminadab

POSITION
Chieftain of the tribe of Judah

FAMOUS DESCENDANTS
King David, the Messiah, Daniel, Hananiah, Mishael, and Azariah

ACHIEVEMENTS
Assisted Moses with the census; first to present his offering at the dedication of the Tabernacle; first to proceed in the desert marches

FAMOUS FOR
Walking first into the Sea of Reeds, before the waters had split

RESTITUTION

Confession is important, but a person must also make restitution to those that he has wronged. Only then can he ask for God's forgiveness (5:5-8).

HARMONY

By allowing the priest to erase God's name to bring peace between husband and wife, God demonstrates the importance of harmony and the lengths you should go to achieve it (5:23).

ABSTINENCE

The nazirite refrains from activities that are permissible according to Torah. We ought to refrain from things that, although permissible, do not spiritually enhance our lives (ch. 6).

נשא

במדבר ד:כא-ל

21 וַיְדַבֵּר יְהֹוָה אֶל־מֹשֶׁה לֵּאמֹר: 22 נָשֹׂא אֶת־רֹאשׁ בְּנֵי גֵרְשׁוֹן גַּם־הֵם לְבֵית אֲבֹתָם לְמִשְׁפְּחֹתָם: 23 מִבֶּן שְׁלֹשִׁים שָׁנָה וָמַעְלָה עַד בֶּן־חֲמִשִּׁים שָׁנָה תִּפְקֹד אוֹתָם כָּל־הַבָּא לִצְבֹא צָבָא לַעֲבֹד עֲבֹדָה בְּאֹהֶל מוֹעֵד: 24 זֹאת עֲבֹדַת מִשְׁפְּחֹת הַגֵּרְשֻׁנִּי לַעֲבֹד וּלְמַשָּׂא: 25 וְנָשְׂאוּ אֶת־יְרִיעֹת הַמִּשְׁכָּן וְאֶת־אֹהֶל מוֹעֵד מִכְסֵהוּ וּמִכְסֵה הַתַּחַשׁ אֲשֶׁר־עָלָיו מִלְמָעְלָה וְאֶת־מָסַךְ פֶּתַח אֹהֶל מוֹעֵד: 26 וְאֵת קַלְעֵי הֶחָצֵר וְאֶת־מָסַךְ | פֶּתַח | שַׁעַר הֶחָצֵר אֲשֶׁר עַל־הַמִּשְׁכָּן וְעַל־הַמִּזְבֵּחַ סָבִיב וְאֵת מֵיתְרֵיהֶם וְאֶת־כָּל־כְּלֵי עֲבֹדָתָם וְאֵת כָּל־אֲשֶׁר יֵעָשֶׂה לָהֶם וְעָבָדוּ: 27 עַל־פִּי אַהֲרֹן וּבָנָיו תִּהְיֶה כָּל־עֲבֹדַת בְּנֵי הַגֵּרְשֻׁנִּי לְכָל־מַשָּׂאָם וּלְכֹל עֲבֹדָתָם וּפְקַדְתֶּם עֲלֵהֶם בְּמִשְׁמֶרֶת אֵת כָּל־מַשָּׂאָם: 28 זֹאת עֲבֹדַת מִשְׁפְּחֹת בְּנֵי הַגֵּרְשֻׁנִּי בְּאֹהֶל מוֹעֵד וּמִשְׁמַרְתָּם בְּיַד אִיתָמָר בֶּן־אַהֲרֹן הַכֹּהֵן: ס 29 [SECOND READING] בְּנֵי מְרָרִי לְמִשְׁפְּחֹתָם לְבֵית־אֲבֹתָם תִּפְקֹד אֹתָם: 30 מִבֶּן

Even though Gershon was the firstborn, and we find that Scripture always gives precedence to the firstborn, nevertheless the Torah mentions Kohath first in this case, because Kohath's descendants carried the ark, in which the Torah was placed (*Numbers Rabbah*).

29. Count Merari's descendants. In the cases of Kohath's descendents (4:1) and Gershon's descendents (ibid., v. 21), the Torah states that they were "singled out" (literally "their heads were lifted up"). God honored them in this way because Kohath carried the ark, and Gershon was the firstborn. But in the case of Merari's descendents (v. 29), who were simple people and whose task was merely to carry the beams, supporting rods, pillars and sockets, Scripture does not refer to *them as being "singled out"* (*Numbers Rabbah*).

Any relationship with God must, of course, be based on submissiveness, where you surrender your own will and choose to follow the Divine will. But once this foundation of submissiveness is established, you also need to build up your knowledge, skills and determination. For *God*

kabbalah bites

4:21 There are two aspects to the Torah: the "interior," spiritual Torah that preceded the world (the Kabbalah); and the "exterior," legal Torah given at Sinai. While both elements are indispensable, only the interior Torah has the privilege of being the "firstborn"—it preceded the exterior, legal Torah.

Kohath's descendants carried the ark which contained tablets made from God's hand, symbolizing the interior, spiritual Torah. Therefore, Kohath's appointment (4:1ff.) was mentioned before that of Gershon, despite the fact that Gershon was the physical firstborn, because, says the Midrash, *"Kohath's descendants carried the ark in which the Torah"*—the spiritual "firstborn"— *"was placed."*

numbers 4:21–30 naso'

parashat naso'

Duties of Gershon's Descendants

²¹ God spoke to Moses, saying: ²² Single out those from Gershon's descendants (who are fit for service in the Tabernacle) too (just as you were commanded with Kohath's descendants), verifying their family lineage, according to their paternal houses. ²³ Count those from the age of thirty years and upward, until the age of fifty years, (namely) all those who are fit to join the group that performs the service in the Tent of Meeting.

²⁴ The following is the service of the Gershonite families. (Their task is to) perform service and carry (parts of the Tabernacle):

- ²⁵ They should carry the tapestries of the Tabernacle and the (goat's hair covering of) the Tent of Meeting, its (ram's skin) covering and the *taḥash* skin covering placed upon it, the partition for the entrance to the Tent of Meeting, ²⁶ the curtains of the courtyard, the curtain for the entrance gate of the courtyard which is around the Tabernacle and the altar, all its ropes and sacred utensils.

- (In addition), they must perform all tasks allotted to them.

- ²⁷ All the work of Gershon's descendants will be directed by Aaron and (one of) his sons, (including) all their tasks of carrying and all their (other) work. You should allot to them as their duty all the things they must carry.

²⁸ This was the service of the families of Gershon's descendants in the Tent of Meeting, and their duties, which were under the supervision of Ithamar son of Aaron the priest.

Duties of Merari's Descendants

[SECOND READING] ²⁹ You should count Merari's descendants, verifying their family lineage, according to their paternal houses. ³⁰ Count (only) those from the age of thirty

---

4:22 Single out. The Torah uses the term "single out" (literally "lift up the head") to indicate that the Levites were counted here in a totally different and much more honorable fashion than the other tribes.

With the other tribes, all the families were counted together in one mixed bunch. But here, Kohath's descendants were first singled out and counted separately from the other Levites as an elite group. Then, Gershon's descendants were separated out from Merari's descendants and counted, leaving only Merari's descendants at the end (*Rabbi Israel b. Pethahiah Isserlein, 15th century*).

Gershon's descendants. God said: "Single out those from Gershon's descendants too, as I commanded you with Kohath's descendants (above, 4:1*ff.*), to see how many have reached the age to serve in the Tabernacle (*Rashi, 11th century*).

במדבר ד:ל-מג

שְׁלֹשִׁ֣ים שָׁנָ֤ה וָמַ֙עְלָה֙ וְעַ֣ד בֶּן־חֲמִשִּׁ֣ים שָׁנָ֔ה תִּפְקְדֵ֑ם כָּל־הַבָּא֙ לַצָּבָ֔א לַעֲבֹ֕ד אֶת־עֲבֹדַ֖ת אֹ֥הֶל מוֹעֵֽד: 31 וְזֹאת֙ מִשְׁמֶ֣רֶת מַשָּׂאָ֔ם לְכָל־עֲבֹדָתָ֖ם בְּאֹ֣הֶל מוֹעֵ֑ד קַרְשֵׁי֙ הַמִּשְׁכָּ֔ן וּבְרִיחָ֖יו וְעַמּוּדָ֥יו וַאֲדָנָֽיו: 32 וְעַמּוּדֵי֩ הֶחָצֵ֨ר סָבִ֜יב וְאַדְנֵיהֶ֗ם וִֽיתֵדֹתָם֙ וּמֵ֣יתְרֵיהֶ֔ם לְכָ֨ל־כְּלֵיהֶ֔ם וּלְכֹ֖ל עֲבֹדָתָ֑ם וּבְשֵׁמֹ֣ת תִּפְקְד֔וּ אֶת־כְּלֵ֖י מִשְׁמֶ֥רֶת מַשָּׂאָֽם: 33 זֹ֣את עֲבֹדַ֗ת מִשְׁפְּחֹת֙ בְּנֵ֣י מְרָרִ֔י לְכָל־עֲבֹדָתָ֖ם בְּאֹ֣הֶל מוֹעֵ֑ד בְּיַד֙ אִֽיתָמָ֔ר בֶּן־אַהֲרֹ֖ן הַכֹּהֵֽן: 34 וַיִּפְקֹ֨ד מֹשֶׁ֧ה וְאַהֲרֹ֛ן וּנְשִׂיאֵ֥י הָעֵדָ֖ה אֶת־בְּנֵ֣י הַקְּהָתִ֑י לְמִשְׁפְּחֹתָ֖ם וּלְבֵ֥ית אֲבֹתָֽם: 35 מִבֶּ֨ן שְׁלֹשִׁ֤ים שָׁנָה֙ וָמַ֔עְלָה וְעַ֖ד בֶּן־חֲמִשִּׁ֣ים שָׁנָ֑ה כָּל־הַבָּא֙ לַצָּבָ֔א לַעֲבֹדָ֖ה בְּאֹ֥הֶל מוֹעֵֽד: 36 וַיִּהְי֥וּ פְקֻדֵיהֶ֖ם לְמִשְׁפְּחֹתָ֑ם אַלְפַּ֕יִם שְׁבַ֥ע מֵא֖וֹת וַחֲמִשִּֽׁים: 37 אֵ֤לֶּה פְקוּדֵי֙ מִשְׁפְּחֹ֣ת הַקְּהָתִ֔י כָּל־הָעֹבֵ֖ד בְּאֹ֣הֶל מוֹעֵ֑ד אֲשֶׁ֨ר פָּקַ֥ד מֹשֶׁ֛ה וְאַהֲרֹ֖ן עַל־פִּ֥י יְהֹוָ֖ה בְּיַד־מֹשֶֽׁה: ס 38 וּפְקוּדֵ֕י בְּנֵ֥י גֵרְשׁ֖וֹן לְמִשְׁפְּחוֹתָ֑ם וּלְבֵ֥ית אֲבֹתָֽם: 39 מִבֶּ֨ן שְׁלֹשִׁ֤ים שָׁנָה֙ וָמַ֔עְלָה וְעַ֖ד בֶּן־חֲמִשִּׁ֣ים שָׁנָ֑ה כָּל־הַבָּא֙ לַצָּבָ֔א לַעֲבֹדָ֖ה בְּאֹ֥הֶל מוֹעֵֽד: 40 וַיִּֽהְיוּ֙ פְּקֻ֣דֵיהֶ֔ם לְמִשְׁפְּחֹתָ֖ם לְבֵ֣ית אֲבֹתָ֑ם אַלְפַּ֕יִם וְשֵׁ֥שׁ מֵא֖וֹת וּשְׁלֹשִֽׁים: 41 אֵ֣לֶּה פְקוּדֵ֗י מִשְׁפְּחֹת֙ בְּנֵ֣י גֵרְשׁ֔וֹן כָּל־הָעֹבֵ֖ד בְּאֹ֣הֶל מוֹעֵ֑ד אֲשֶׁ֨ר פָּקַ֥ד מֹשֶׁ֛ה וְאַהֲרֹ֖ן עַל־פִּ֥י יְהֹוָֽה: 42 וּפְקוּדֵ֕י מִשְׁפְּחֹ֖ת בְּנֵ֣י מְרָרִ֑י לְמִשְׁפְּחֹתָ֖ם לְבֵ֥ית אֲבֹתָֽם: 43 מִבֶּ֨ן

the overseeing of the Tabernacle required the combination of both these roles—teaching us that pride and simple submissiveness need to be found in *every* heart (*Rabbi Shneur Zalman of Lyady, 18th century*).

34-49. The Census of the Levites. What is the inner reason why the Torah required those Levites who were fit to work in the Tabernacle to be counted?

The answer can be understood by first addressing why the Jewish people were required to wander in the desert for forty years. We know, of course, that they had to live somewhere for those forty years as a result of the sin of the spies, when God decreed that the entire generation would not enter the land of Israel. But surely, they could have spent this time in a civilized country, rather than in the desert?

Hasidic thought explains that the Jewish people spent those forty years in the desert so that the immense holiness of the Tabernacle would be present to undermine the forces of evil which are rooted in the desert.

years and upwards, until the age of fifty years, (which includes) all those who (are fit to) participate in the service of working in the Tent of Meeting. ³¹ The following are their transportation responsibilities for all their work in the Tent of Meeting:

- The beams of the Tabernacle, its bars, its pillars, and its sockets; ³² the pillars of the surrounding courtyard, their sockets, pegs, and ropes; (and) all the utensils for all associated tasks.

- You should appoint them by name to the utensils which they are responsible to transport.

³³ These were the tasks of the families of Merari's descendants concerning all their service in the Tent of Meeting, which was under the supervision of Ithamar son of Aaron the priest.

Tally of Levites Fit to Serve in the Tabernacle

³⁴ Moses, Aaron, and the leaders of the congregation counted Kohath's descendants—verifying their family lineage, according to their paternal houses—³⁵ from those thirty years old and upwards, until fifty years old, (including) all those who (were fit to) participate in the service of working in the Tent of Meeting. ³⁶ Their total, verified according to family lineage: two thousand, seven hundred and fifty. ³⁷ This was the total of the Kohathite families, all who served in the Tent of Meeting, who were counted by Moses and Aaron, as directed by God to Moses.

³⁸ The total of Gershon's descendants was verified according to family lineage, according to their paternal houses, ³⁹ (and included) those thirty years old and upwards, until fifty years old, all those who (were fit to) participate in the service of working in the Tent of Meeting. ⁴⁰ Their total, verified according to family lineage, according to their paternal houses: two thousand, six hundred and thirty. ⁴¹ This was the total of the families of Gershon's descendants, all those who served in the Tent of Meeting, whom Moses and Aaron counted, as directed by God.

⁴² The total of the families of Merari's descendants was verified according to family lineage, according to their paternal houses, ⁴³ (and included) those thirty

---

put you in this world to transform it, and this will simply not occur unless you nurture the qualities of ambition and desire for achievement. As long as you have a firm foundation of submissiveness, your achievements will not "go to your head" and lead you to believe that your successes are to your own credit. Your ambitions will always be permeated with the awareness that *God desires you to be successful in carrying out His plan for this world,* and it is God who is continually enabling you to do so.

This healthy equilibrium of greatness and submissiveness required for worship was reflected by the role of the Levites in the Tabernacle, God's House. The descendants of Kohath and Gershon were honored with the important tasks of carrying the most holy items, whereas Merari's descendants were "simple people" who were given the more menial tasks. Nevertheless,

שְׁלֹשִׁ֣ים שָׁנָ֔ה וָמַ֕עְלָה וְעַ֖ד בֶּן־חֲמִשִּׁ֣ים שָׁנָ֑ה כָּל־הַבָּא֙ לַצָּבָ֣א לַעֲבֹדָ֔ה בְּאֹ֖הֶל מוֹעֵֽד: 44 וַיִּהְי֣וּ פְקֻדֵיהֶ֔ם לְמִשְׁפְּחֹתָ֑ם שְׁלֹ֥שֶׁת אֲלָפִ֖ים וּמָאתָֽיִם: 45 אֵ֣לֶּה פְקוּדֵ֤י מִשְׁפְּחֹת֙ בְּנֵ֣י מְרָרִ֔י אֲשֶׁ֨ר פָּקַ֥ד מֹשֶׁ֛ה וְאַהֲרֹ֖ן עַל־פִּ֥י יְהֹוָ֖ה בְּיַד־מֹשֶֽׁה: 46 כָּל־הַפְּקֻדִ֡ים אֲשֶׁר֩ פָּקַ֨ד מֹשֶׁ֧ה וְאַהֲרֹ֛ן וּנְשִׂיאֵ֥י יִשְׂרָאֵ֖ל אֶת־הַלְוִיִּ֑ם לְמִשְׁפְּחֹתָ֖ם וּלְבֵ֥ית אֲבֹתָֽם: 47 מִבֶּ֨ן שְׁלֹשִׁ֤ים שָׁנָה֙ וָמַ֔עְלָה וְעַ֖ד בֶּן־חֲמִשִּׁ֣ים שָׁנָ֑ה כָּל־הַבָּ֗א לַעֲבֹ֤ד עֲבֹדַת֙ עֲבֹדָ֔ה וַעֲבֹדַ֥ת מַשָּׂ֖א בְּאֹ֥הֶל מוֹעֵֽד: 48 וַיִּהְי֖וּ פְּקֻדֵיהֶ֑ם שְׁמֹנַ֣ת אֲלָפִ֔ים וַחֲמֵ֥שׁ מֵא֖וֹת וּשְׁמֹנִֽים: 49 עַל־פִּ֨י יְהֹוָ֜ה פָּקַ֤ד אוֹתָם֙ בְּיַד־מֹשֶׁ֔ה אִ֥ישׁ אִ֛ישׁ עַל־עֲבֹדָת֖וֹ וְעַל־מַשָּׂא֑וֹ וּפְקֻדָ֕יו אֲשֶׁר־צִוָּ֥ה יְהֹוָ֖ה אֶת־מֹשֶֽׁה: פ

ה 1 וַיְדַבֵּ֥ר יְהֹוָ֖ה אֶל־מֹשֶׁ֥ה לֵּאמֹֽר: [THIRD READING] 2 צַ֣ו אֶת־בְּנֵ֣י יִשְׂרָאֵ֗ל וִֽישַׁלְּחוּ֙ מִן־הַֽמַּחֲנֶ֔ה כָּל־צָר֖וּעַ וְכָל־זָ֑ב וְכֹ֖ל טָמֵ֥א לָנָֽפֶשׁ: 3 מִזָּכָ֤ר עַד־נְקֵבָה֙ תְּשַׁלֵּ֔חוּ אֶל־מִח֥וּץ לַמַּחֲנֶ֖ה תְּשַׁלְּח֑וּם וְלֹ֤א יְטַמְּאוּ֙ אֶת־מַ֣חֲנֵיהֶ֔ם אֲשֶׁ֥ר אֲנִ֖י שֹׁכֵ֥ן בְּתוֹכָֽם: 4 וַיַּֽעֲשׂוּ־כֵן֙ בְּנֵ֣י יִשְׂרָאֵ֔ל וַיְשַׁלְּח֣וּ אוֹתָ֔ם אֶל־מִח֖וּץ לַֽמַּחֲנֶ֑ה כַּאֲשֶׁ֨ר דִּבֶּ֤ר יְהֹוָה֙ אֶל־מֹשֶׁ֔ה כֵּ֥ן עָשׂ֖וּ בְּנֵ֥י יִשְׂרָאֵֽל: פ 5 וַיְדַבֵּ֥ר יְהֹוָ֖ה אֶל־מֹשֶׁ֥ה לֵּאמֹֽר: 6 דַּבֵּר֮ אֶל־בְּנֵ֣י יִשְׂרָאֵל֒ אִ֣ישׁ אֽוֹ־אִשָּׁ֗ה כִּ֤י יַעֲשׂוּ֙ מִכָּל־חַטֹּ֣את הָֽאָדָ֔ם לִמְעֹ֥ל

someone afflicted with lesions (*tzara'at*) will remind him of the sores to which the body is susceptible.

Seeing someone suffering from a discharge would remind him to be aware, *"from where you came, a putrid drop"* (Mishnah, Avot 3:1); and seeing someone ritually impure from contact with a dead body would remind the person to be conscious, *"where you are going—to a place of dust, worms and maggots"* (ibid.).

The repetition of this phrase stresses the children of Israel's fulfillment of both aspects of the command. Not only did they *"send them outside the camp,"* they also took to heart the intended lesson in humility (*Rabbi Azariah Figo, 17th century*).

6. If a man or woman commits any sins (of dishonesty) against (another) man, (thereby) acting treacherously against God. Rashi says that *"Acting treacherously against God"* is referring to the sin of stealing from a convert. The convert has sought shelter beneath the wings of Judaism, so this transgression is an affront against God and it causes a desecration of His name. The one who commits it is guilty of *"acting treacherously against God"* (*Rabbi Obadiah Sforno, 16th century*).

years old and upwards, until fifty years old, all those who (were fit to) participate in the service of working in the Tent of Meeting. ⁴⁴ Their total, verified according to family lineage: three thousand, two hundred. ⁴⁵ This was the total of the families of Merari's descendants, whom Moses and Aaron counted, as directed by God to Moses.

⁴⁶ The grand total of Levites counted by Moses, Aaron, and the leaders of Israel was verified according to family lineage, according to their paternal houses, ⁴⁷ (and included) those thirty years old and upwards, until fifty years old, all those who (were fit to) participate in the service of (playing cymbals and harps during) the service and the service of carrying in the Tent of Meeting. ⁴⁸ Their total: eight thousand, five hundred and eighty. ⁴⁹ They were counted as directed by God. Each man was appointed by Moses to his service and his carrying duties. They were counted as God had commanded Moses.

Sanctity of the Camp

5 [THIRD READING] ¹ God spoke to Moses (on the day the Tabernacle was erected), saying: ² Command the children of Israel to send out from the camp:

❖ All those afflicted with *tzara'at*, all those who have had an (unhealthy, watery venereal) discharge and all those ritually impure through (contact with) the dead.

❖ ³ You should send out both male and female.

Send them outside the camp so that they do not defile their camps, where I dwell among them.

⁴ The children of Israel did so and sent them outside the camp. The children of Israel did exactly what God told Moses.

Additional Laws of the Guilt-Offering for Dishonesty

⁵ God spoke to Moses, saying: ⁶ Tell the children of Israel: If a man or woman commits any sins (of dishonesty) against (another) man, (thereby) acting treacherously against God, and that person is (found) guilty:

That is why the Levites, who were responsible for the Tabernacle, were counted. For counting a person is a means of conferring importance on him, and, in a spiritual sense, this was a way of strengthening the Levites for their "war" against the forces of evil (*Rabbi Menahem Mendel Schneerson, 20th century*).

5:4 The children of Israel did so. Further on in this same verse the Torah repeats, *"The children of Israel did exactly what God told Moses."*

The command to remove impure individuals from the camp was intended as a lesson in humility. A person should never allow himself to become vain because of his superior physical appearance or abilities, by always considering the degeneracy of his bodily existence. Seeing

מַעַל בַּיהוָה וְאָשְׁמָה הַנֶּפֶשׁ הַהִוא: 7 וְהִתְוַדּוּ אֶת־חַטָּאתָם אֲשֶׁר עָשׂוּ וְהֵשִׁיב אֶת־אֲשָׁמוֹ בְּרֹאשׁוֹ וַחֲמִישִׁתוֹ יֹסֵף עָלָיו וְנָתַן לַאֲשֶׁר אָשַׁם לוֹ: 8 וְאִם־אֵין לָאִישׁ גֹּאֵל לְהָשִׁיב הָאָשָׁם אֵלָיו הָאָשָׁם הַמּוּשָׁב לַיהוָה לַכֹּהֵן מִלְּבַד אֵיל הַכִּפֻּרִים אֲשֶׁר יְכַפֶּר־בּוֹ עָלָיו: 9 וְכָל־תְּרוּמָה לְכָל־קָדְשֵׁי בְנֵי־יִשְׂרָאֵל אֲשֶׁר־יַקְרִיבוּ לַכֹּהֵן לוֹ יִהְיֶה: 10 וְאִישׁ אֶת־קֳדָשָׁיו לוֹ יִהְיוּ אִישׁ אֲשֶׁר־יִתֵּן לַכֹּהֵן לוֹ יִהְיֶה: פ 11 וַיְדַבֵּר יְהוָה אֶל־מֹשֶׁה לֵּאמֹר: **[FOURTH READING]** 12 דַּבֵּר אֶל־בְּנֵי יִשְׂרָאֵל וְאָמַרְתָּ אֲלֵהֶם אִישׁ אִישׁ כִּי־תִשְׂטֶה אִשְׁתּוֹ וּמָעֲלָה בוֹ מָעַל: 13 וְשָׁכַב אִישׁ אֹתָהּ שִׁכְבַת־זֶרַע וְנֶעְלַם מֵעֵינֵי אִישָׁהּ וְנִסְתְּרָה וְהִיא נִטְמָאָה וְעֵד אֵין בָּהּ

One is required to confess with one's lips and state verbally those things which one has resolved in one's heart.

If a person confesses verbally, but has not resolved in his heart to repent, it is like immersing in a ritual pool while holding a *sheretz* (creature that causes ritual impurity)—the immersion will not be effective until the *sheretz* is cast away (*Maimonides, 12th century*).

Through verbal confession of sin, the sinner reveals his thoughts and feelings; his belief that all his deeds are revealed and known before God, and that he will not act as if the "Eye that sees" does not see. By mentioning the sin specifically, he will feel remorseful about it, and he will be more careful on another occasion not to stumble in the same way again (*Rabbi Aaron ha-Levi (Ḥinnukh), 13th century*).

Why is the requirement to *"confess the sin"* mentioned only in regard to the sin of stealing?

Man's physical, emotional and intellectual abilities were granted to him by God for good purposes. By sinning, he is misusing these talents in areas that he was never granted permission. In essence, then, *every time a person sins he is stealing*—he is stealing the use of his talents from God for an unintended purpose. Therefore, the requirement to confess guilt is written in connection with the sin of robbery (*Rabbi Isaac Meir Alter of Gur, 19th century*).

10. A person's holy gifts are his own. Some people believe the money in their possession is *theirs*, while the money they give away to charity is gone. Actually, the opposite is true. Only those possessions given away for noble purposes, such as those given as charity or to the priests and scholars, remain the merit of the original owner forever. The possessions acquired for your own enjoyment will not remain in your possession for longer than a fleeting moment (*Rabbi Azariah Figo, 17th century*).

12. If any man's wife goes astray. Our Sages taught: *"A person does not commit a sin, unless he is overcome by a spirit of foolishness"* (*Babylonian Talmud, Sotah* 3a). Even an adulterous woman, who lacks self-control, would have disciplined her temptations if not for her foolish spirit. This mood obscures the hidden love of her Godly soul that adheres to faith in God, to His unity and oneness.

- ❖ ⁷ They should confess the sin they committed.

- ❖ (The person) should pay back the amount he is guilty of, and add a fifth to it, giving it to the one against whom he was guilty.

- ❖ ⁸ But if the man (dies and) has no relative to whom (the offender) can pay back the debt, then the debt is to be returned "to God," (i.e.) to the priest.

- ❖ (This is, of course,) besides the atonement ram (which is brought to the priest in any case), through which he is atoned.

Additional Laws of Gifts to the Priests

- ❖ ⁹ Every offering from all the children of Israel's holy (first fruits) brought to the priest will belong to (the priest).

- ❖ ¹⁰ (The prerogative of precisely which priest or Levite) a person (chooses to give) his holy (gifts) is his own. (But) whatever a man gives to the priest is then (the priest's).

The Suspected Adulteress [*Sotah*]

[FOURTH READING] ¹¹ God spoke to Moses, saying: ¹² Speak to the children of Israel and say to them: If any man's wife goes astray (from the ways of modesty, arousing her husband's suspicion that) she had acted treacherously towards him ¹³ (and had allowed) a man to lie with her and have a seminal emission, but (the alleged act) was not seen by her husband—(Then if):

— She was secluded (with the suspected adulterer for a sufficient time to actually commit adultery);

— And there was no witness against her (to confirm that she had actually committed adultery);

— And she was not forced (by the alleged adulterer against her will);

"God loves the righteous; God preserves the proselytes" (*Psalms* 146:8). God says, "I love those who love Me." Why does God love the righteous? Because their worth is due neither to heritage nor to family. If someone desires to be a priest, he cannot be one. If he desires to be a Levite, he cannot be one. Why? Because his father was neither a priest nor a Levite. But if any man, Jew or gentile, desires to be righteous, he can be so, because the righteous do not constitute a paternal house. Therefore God loves them (*Numbers Rabbah*).

7. They should confess. If a person transgresses any of the commandments of the Torah, be it a positive command or a prohibition, either intentionally or unintentionally, he is required to confess before God when he repents and returns from his sin—as the verse states, *"If a man or woman commits any sins ... they should confess the sin they committed,"* which refers to a verbal confession. This confession is a positive command from the Torah.

במדבר ה׳:י״ג-י״ט   נשא

וְהִוא לֹא נִתְפָּשָׂה: 14 וְעָבַר עָלָיו רוּחַ־קִנְאָה וְקִנֵּא אֶת־אִשְׁתּוֹ וְהִוא נִטְמָאָה אוֹ־עָבַר עָלָיו רוּחַ־קִנְאָה וְקִנֵּא אֶת־אִשְׁתּוֹ וְהִיא לֹא נִטְמָאָה: 15 וְהֵבִיא הָאִישׁ אֶת־אִשְׁתּוֹ אֶל־הַכֹּהֵן וְהֵבִיא אֶת־קָרְבָּנָהּ עָלֶיהָ עֲשִׂירִת הָאֵיפָה קֶמַח שְׂעֹרִים לֹא־יִצֹק עָלָיו שֶׁמֶן וְלֹא־יִתֵּן עָלָיו לְבֹנָה כִּי־מִנְחַת קְנָאֹת הוּא מִנְחַת זִכָּרוֹן מַזְכֶּרֶת עָוֹן: 16 וְהִקְרִיב אֹתָהּ הַכֹּהֵן וְהֶעֱמִדָהּ לִפְנֵי יְהוָֹה: 17 וְלָקַח הַכֹּהֵן מַיִם קְדֹשִׁים בִּכְלִי־חָרֶשׂ וּמִן־הֶעָפָר אֲשֶׁר יִהְיֶה בְּקַרְקַע הַמִּשְׁכָּן יִקַּח הַכֹּהֵן וְנָתַן אֶל־הַמָּיִם: 18 וְהֶעֱמִיד הַכֹּהֵן אֶת־הָאִשָּׁה לִפְנֵי יְהוָֹה וּפָרַע אֶת־רֹאשׁ הָאִשָּׁה וְנָתַן עַל־כַּפֶּיהָ אֵת מִנְחַת הַזִּכָּרוֹן מִנְחַת קְנָאֹת הִוא וּבְיַד הַכֹּהֵן יִהְיוּ מֵי הַמָּרִים הַמְאָרֲרִים: 19 וְהִשְׁבִּיעַ אֹתָהּ הַכֹּהֵן וְאָמַר אֶל־הָאִשָּׁה אִם־לֹא שָׁכַב אִישׁ אֹתָךְ וְאִם־לֹא שָׂטִית טֻמְאָה תַּחַת אִישֵׁךְ הִנָּקִי מִמֵּי הַמָּרִים

The solution to this problem is to *"bring an offering ... of barley flour"* (v. 15), which is referred to by the Sages as "animal fodder" (ibid., 14a). In other words, the person needs to humble himself with the awareness that, compared to God, he is poor in knowledge, like an animal (*Rabbi Menahem Mendel Schneerson, 20th century*).

15. A reminder of sin. Why is this offering called a *"reminder of sin,"* when it is not yet known whether or not the woman actually sinned?

Because *someone* in this situation was in the wrong—either the woman had an adulterous relationship, or her husband falsely accused her (*Rabbi Hezekiah b. Manoah, 13th century*).

17. The priest should take holy water ... the priest should take some earth from the Tabernacle floor and put it into the water. When a person comes to *"the priest,"* the Torah scholar, seeking healing for the soul, and requires *"water,"* i.e., words of Torah and admonition—the priest must *"take some earth and put it into the water,"* he must deliver his words of rebuke with humility. That way his words will be received properly (*Rabbi Israel Ba'al Shem Tov, 18th century*).

18. He should uncover (the hair on) the head of the woman. If a woman covers her hair, her children will be superior, her husband will be blessed with spiritual and material blessings, with wealth, children and grandchildren (*Zohar*).

spiritual vitamin

> The greatest concealment of God is caused by lack of peace in the home.

numbers 5:14–19 naso'

- [14] (And this is a case where before the seclusion took place) a desire to warn (her) had come upon (her husband) and he warned his wife (not to be secluded with the man), and she (may have indeed) been defiled. But (it may be the case that) a desire to warn (her) had come upon him and he warned his wife (not to be secluded with the man), but she was (in fact) not defiled.

(In order to resolve this doubt the following should be carried out:)

- ❖ [15] The man should bring his wife to the priest and bring an offering for her, one-tenth of an *'ephah* of barley flour.

- ❖ He should not pour oil over it or put frankincense on it, for it is a meal-offering of (Divine and human) anger, a meal-offering (not of atonement but) of remembrance, a reminder of sin.

- ❖ [16] The priest should bring her near and present her before God.

- ❖ [17] The priest should take holy water (from the urn) in an earthenware vessel, and the priest should take some earth from the Tabernacle floor and put it into the water.

- ❖ [18] Then the priest should (move the woman from place to place, to tire her out, and) stand the woman up before God (at Nicanor's Gate).

- ❖ He should uncover (the hair on) the head of the woman.

- ❖ He should place the remembrance meal-offering, which is a meal-offering of anger, into her hands while the afflictive waters, (which will bring her) bitter (end), are in the priest's hand.

- ❖ [19] The priest should then place her under oath, saying to the woman: "If a man has not slept with you and you have not gone astray to become defiled (to another) in place of your husband, then (you will) be absolved through these "bitter," afflictive

---

Consider that she would be willing to give her life to avoid the mere act of bowing down to an idol, even though it would be totally devoid of any belief in the idol at all in her heart. All the more so, then, could she discipline her evil impulse and temptation for adultery, which is a sacrifice far less than death.

At any time whatsoever a person has the ability and power to cast away his mood of foolishness and forgetfulness; to remember and arouse his love for the One God which is most definitely hidden in his heart, without any doubt (*Rabbi Shneur Zalman of Lyady, 18th century*).

14. He warned his wife. God warned His "wife"—the Jewish people—not to be secluded with another "man," when He said the words: *"You shall not (possess an idol) of other deities (so long as I exist)"* (*Exodus* 20:3).

But how could you possibly become "secluded" from God, whose glory fills the entire earth? The answer is: by being arrogant. Of the arrogant person, the Sages taught: *"God says, 'He and I cannot dwell in the same place'"* (*Babylonian Talmud, Sotah* 5a)—in other words, arrogance conceals a person from God.

הַמְאָרֲרִים הָאֵלֶּה: 20 וְאַתְּ כִּי שָׂטִית תַּחַת אִישֵׁךְ וְכִי נִטְמֵאת וַיִּתֵּן אִישׁ בָּךְ אֶת־שְׁכָבְתּוֹ מִבַּלְעֲדֵי אִישֵׁךְ: 21 וְהִשְׁבִּיעַ הַכֹּהֵן אֶת־הָאִשָּׁה בִּשְׁבֻעַת הָאָלָה וְאָמַר הַכֹּהֵן לָאִשָּׁה יִתֵּן יְהֹוָה אוֹתָךְ לְאָלָה וְלִשְׁבֻעָה בְּתוֹךְ עַמֵּךְ בְּתֵת יְהֹוָה אֶת־יְרֵכֵךְ נֹפֶלֶת וְאֶת־בִּטְנֵךְ צָבָה: 22 וּבָאוּ הַמַּיִם הַמְאָרֲרִים הָאֵלֶּה בְּמֵעַיִךְ לַצְבּוֹת בֶּטֶן וְלַנְפִּל יָרֵךְ וְאָמְרָה הָאִשָּׁה אָמֵן | אָמֵן: 23 וְכָתַב אֶת־הָאָלֹת הָאֵלֶּה הַכֹּהֵן בַּסֵּפֶר וּמָחָה אֶל־מֵי הַמָּרִים: 24 וְהִשְׁקָה אֶת־הָאִשָּׁה אֶת־מֵי הַמָּרִים הַמְאָרֲרִים וּבָאוּ בָהּ הַמַּיִם הַמְאָרֲרִים לְמָרִים: 25 וְלָקַח הַכֹּהֵן מִיַּד הָאִשָּׁה אֵת מִנְחַת הַקְּנָאֹת וְהֵנִיף אֶת־הַמִּנְחָה לִפְנֵי יְהֹוָה וְהִקְרִיב אֹתָהּ אֶל־הַמִּזְבֵּחַ: 26 וְקָמַץ הַכֹּהֵן מִן־הַמִּנְחָה אֶת־אַזְכָּרָתָהּ וְהִקְטִיר הַמִּזְבֵּחָה וְאַחַר יַשְׁקֶה אֶת־הָאִשָּׁה אֶת־הַמָּיִם:

27 וְהִשְׁקָהּ אֶת־הַמַּיִם וְהָיְתָה אִם־נִטְמְאָה וַתִּמְעֹל מַעַל בְּאִישָׁהּ וּבָאוּ בָהּ הַמַּיִם הַמְאָרֲרִים לְמָרִים וְצָבְתָה בִטְנָהּ וְנָפְלָה יְרֵכָהּ וְהָיְתָה הָאִשָּׁה לְאָלָה בְּקֶרֶב עַמָּהּ: 28 וְאִם־לֹא נִטְמְאָה הָאִשָּׁה וּטְהֹרָה הִוא וְנִקְּתָה וְנִזְרְעָה זָרַע:

23. Erase it in the "bitter" waters. Great is peace between husband and wife, for the Torah states that the name of God, written in holiness, should be erased in the water given to the suspected wife (*Babylonian Talmud, Ḥullin* 141a).

God allowed His name to be erased—something that is usually forbidden—so that a woman could prove her innocence, restoring peace between husband and wife. This, in turn, causes the Divine Presence to rest upon the couple, as it is said, "Husband and wife, if they are worthy (by maintaining a peaceful relationship), then the Divine Presence rests between them" (*Babylonian Talmud, Sotah* 17a; *Rabbi Jacob Reischer, 17th–18th century*).

28. She will be proven innocent (by the waters) and she will bear children. "'*She will be proven innocent and she will bear children,*' means that if she was barren she will become pregnant"—these are the words of Rabbi Akiva.

Rabbi Ishmael said to him: "If so, then all the barren women in the world will seclude themselves with other men, but not commit adultery, and then become pregnant from drinking the bitter waters. Any woman who did not seclude herself with another man will be the loser!

> **kabbalah bites**
>
> **5:23** At Marah, we were tested with "bitter waters" (*Exodus* 15:23), like a *sotah*. And when we will be redeemed, finally entering the New Era, we will again be tested. But those who study the *Zohar*, the Tree of Life, will not require a test. So by encouraging others to study the *Zohar*, we will leave the Exile with mercy.

numbers 5:19–28 — naso'

waters. ²⁰ But if you have indeed gone astray (to another) instead of your husband and have become defiled, and you have allowed another man besides your husband to sleep with you (then you will choke!)"

- ²¹ The priest should then make the woman swear an oath (that contains) a curse. The priest should say to the woman: "May God make you (an example of) a curse (uttered within) an oath among your people, when God causes your thigh to rupture and your belly to swell. ²² For these 'bitter,' afflictive waters will enter your innards, causing (also) the belly (of your adulterous partner) to swell and the thigh (of your partner) to rupture!"

- The woman should say, "Amen! Amen!" (to accept the oath).

- ²³ Then the priest should write these curses on a scroll and erase it in the "bitter" waters.

— ²⁴ (When the priest will later) give the "bitter," afflictive waters to the woman to drink, the afflictive waters will enter (all of) her (body) to (bring a) bitter (end upon every part of her).—

- ²⁵ The priest should take the meal-offering of anger (with) the woman's hand, wave the meal-offering before God (together with her), and bring it to (the southwestern corner of) the altar.

- ²⁶ The priest should take a three-finger fistful out from the meal-offering, as a "reminder" (to God), and burn it upon the altar.

- Then he should give the woman the water to drink.

- ²⁷ (If she refuses to drink) he should make her drink the water (by force, unless she confesses guilt).

What will happen is, if she had been defiled and was unfaithful to her husband, the afflictive waters will enter (all of) her (body to bring a) bitter (end upon her. First,) her belly will swell, and (eventually) her thigh will rupture. The woman will be (an example used in) curse(s) among her people.

²⁸ But if the woman had not become defiled (with the alleged adulterer) and she is clean (from any other adulterous acts of which she had not been accused), she will be proven innocent (by the waters) and she will bear children (easily).

22. Causing (also) the belly (of your adulterous partner) to swell and the thigh (of your partner) to rupture. This verse must be referring to her suspected partner in adultery, because the previous verse already says regarding her, *"Your thigh to rupture and your belly to swell"* (*Rashi, 11th century*).

Just as the waters test her, they also test her suspected partner. If they are guilty, the waters will cause him to die in the same manner—his belly will swell and his thigh will rupture (*Babylonian Talmud, Sotah* 28a).

במדבר ה:כט - ו:ז

29 זֹאת תּוֹרַת הַקְּנָאֹת אֲשֶׁר תִּשְׂטֶה אִשָּׁה תַּחַת אִישָׁהּ וְנִטְמָאָה: 30 אוֹ אִישׁ אֲשֶׁר תַּעֲבֹר עָלָיו רוּחַ קִנְאָה וְקִנֵּא אֶת־אִשְׁתּוֹ וְהֶעֱמִיד אֶת־הָאִשָּׁה לִפְנֵי יְהֹוָה וְעָשָׂה לָהּ הַכֹּהֵן אֵת כָּל־הַתּוֹרָה הַזֹּאת: 31 וְנִקָּה הָאִישׁ מֵעָוֹן וְהָאִשָּׁה הַהִוא תִּשָּׂא אֶת־עֲוֺנָהּ: פ

ו 1 וַיְדַבֵּר יְהֹוָה אֶל־מֹשֶׁה לֵּאמֹר: 2 דַּבֵּר אֶל־בְּנֵי יִשְׂרָאֵל וְאָמַרְתָּ אֲלֵהֶם אִישׁ אוֹ־אִשָּׁה כִּי יַפְלִא לִנְדֹּר נֶדֶר נָזִיר לְהַזִּיר לַיהֹוָה: 3 מִיַּיִן וְשֵׁכָר יַזִּיר חֹמֶץ יַיִן וְחֹמֶץ שֵׁכָר לֹא יִשְׁתֶּה וְכָל־מִשְׁרַת עֲנָבִים לֹא יִשְׁתֶּה וַעֲנָבִים לַחִים וִיבֵשִׁים לֹא יֹאכֵל: 4 כֹּל יְמֵי נִזְרוֹ מִכֹּל אֲשֶׁר יֵעָשֶׂה מִגֶּפֶן הַיַּיִן מֵחַרְצַנִּים וְעַד־זָג לֹא יֹאכֵל: 5 כָּל־יְמֵי נֶדֶר נִזְרוֹ תַּעַר לֹא־יַעֲבֹר עַל־רֹאשׁוֹ עַד־מְלֹאת הַיָּמִם אֲשֶׁר־יַזִּיר לַיהֹוָה קָדֹשׁ יִהְיֶה גַּדֵּל פֶּרַע שְׂעַר רֹאשׁוֹ: 6 כָּל־יְמֵי הַזִּירוֹ לַיהֹוָה עַל־נֶפֶשׁ מֵת לֹא יָבֹא: 7 לְאָבִיו וּלְאִמּוֹ לְאָחִיו וּלְאַחֹתוֹ לֹא־יִטַּמָּא לָהֶם בְּמֹתָם כִּי נֵזֶר אֱלֹהָיו עַל־רֹאשׁוֹ:

---

pletely from them to the extent that I eat no meat, drink no wine, do not marry, do not live in a comfortable home or wear decent clothes"—this is a bad path which is forbidden to follow. Our Sages commanded a person to deny himself only the things denied him by the Torah. He should not inflict on himself vows of abstinence on things permitted to him. As our Sages said, *"Is what the Torah has forbidden you not enough that you wish to forbid yourself more things?"* (*Jerusalem Talmud Nedarim* 9:1; *Maimonides, 12th century*).

Spiritual healing mirrors the same physical process—you need to avoid extremes and adopt a middle path. The reason why the nazirite follows a path of abstinence is because he realizes that he has a weakness for worldly pleasures. Therefore, he must go to the other extreme, in order that he will eventually reach the golden mean (*Rabbi Moses b. Israel Isserles, 16th century*).

7. The "crown (*nezer*) of God" is on his head. The term nazirite comes from the term *nezer*, "crown." Most people are slaves to worldly desires. The nazirite is the "king" who has freed himself from these desires and is privileged to wear the "crown" (*Rabbi Abraham ibn Ezra, 12th century*).

---

kabbalah bites

6:3-5 The nazirite mentioned here is connected to the priest, who was the focus of the previous passage. Both the nazirite and the priest are rooted in *Ḥesed* (Divine kindness), which is why both are forbidden to drink wine (see *Leviticus* 10:9), which is rooted in *Gevurah* (severity).

Likewise, the nazirite may not shave his hair because the constant sprouting of hair represents God's continuous emanation of *Ḥesed*.

²⁹ This (concludes) the law of warnings when a woman goes astray to someone other than her husband and is defiled. ³⁰ If a desire to warn (her) comes over a man, and he warns his wife, and he presents the woman before God, then the priest should carry out all these laws with her. ³¹ (If she dies) the man will be absolved of guilt (on his part, for causing her death), since the woman will be responsible for her own sin.

The Nazirite

6 ¹ God spoke to Moses, saying: ² Speak to the children of Israel, and say to them: If a man or woman sets himself apart by making a nazirite vow to abstain for the sake of God:

- ³ He must abstain from new wine and intoxicating (aged) wine.
- He may not drink (even) vinegar made from new wine or intoxicating (aged) wine.
- He may not drink anything in which grapes have been soaked.
- He may not eat fresh grapes or dried ones.
- ⁴ All the days of his nazirite (vow) he may not eat any product of the grapevine, from its seeds to its skins.
- ⁵ All the days of his nazirite vow, no razor may pass over his head, until the completion of the period that he abstains for the sake of God. (His hair) will be sacred, and he should allow the hair on his head to grow wild.
- ⁶ All the days of his nazirite vow for God, he may not come into contact with the dead. ⁷ (Even if) his father, his mother, his brother, or his sister dies he may not allow himself to become ritually impure (through contact with them), for the "crown

---

Food for thought

1. Why is unfaithfulness in marriage so abhorrent to God?

2. How can we encourage faithful relationships?

3. Does the stigma of false accusation dissipate after being proven innocent?

"Rather the verse teaches us that if she used to have painful births, she will now have easy births. If she used to give birth to short children, she will now give birth to tall ones. And if she used to give birth to dull-faced children, she will now give birth to bright-faced ones" (*Babylonian Talmud, Sotah* 26a).

31. The man will be absolved of guilt. If the husband is free from illicit relations, the waters will test his wife effectively. If not, the waters will not test his wife. Therefore, when adultery became widespread, the bitter waters were discontinued (*Babylonian Talmud, Sotah* 47b).

6:2 A nazirite vow. Why is the section dealing with the nazirite placed next to the section of the *sotah* ("suspected wife")? To teach you that whoever sees a *sotah* in her disgrace will make a nazirite vow to abstain from wine, for drinking wine leads a person to adultery (*Rashi, 11ᵗʰ century*).

To abstain for the sake of God. If a person should argue, "Since envy, passion, and pride are evil, I will remove and separate myself com-

במדבר ו:ח-יט

8 כֹּל יְמֵי נִזְרוֹ קָדֹשׁ הוּא לַיהוָה: 9 וְכִי־יָמוּת מֵת עָלָיו בְּפֶתַע פִּתְאֹם וְטִמֵּא רֹאשׁ נִזְרוֹ וְגִלַּח רֹאשׁוֹ בְּיוֹם טָהֳרָתוֹ בַּיּוֹם הַשְּׁבִיעִי יְגַלְּחֶנּוּ: 10 וּבַיּוֹם הַשְּׁמִינִי יָבִא שְׁתֵּי תֹרִים אוֹ שְׁנֵי בְּנֵי יוֹנָה אֶל־הַכֹּהֵן אֶל־פֶּתַח אֹהֶל מוֹעֵד: 11 וְעָשָׂה הַכֹּהֵן אֶחָד לְחַטָּאת וְאֶחָד לְעֹלָה וְכִפֶּר עָלָיו מֵאֲשֶׁר חָטָא עַל־הַנָּפֶשׁ וְקִדַּשׁ אֶת־רֹאשׁוֹ בַּיּוֹם הַהוּא: 12 וְהִזִּיר לַיהוָה אֶת־יְמֵי נִזְרוֹ וְהֵבִיא כֶּבֶשׂ בֶּן־שְׁנָתוֹ לְאָשָׁם וְהַיָּמִים הָרִאשֹׁנִים יִפְּלוּ כִּי טָמֵא נִזְרוֹ: 13 וְזֹאת תּוֹרַת הַנָּזִיר בְּיוֹם מְלֹאת יְמֵי נִזְרוֹ יָבִיא אֹתוֹ אֶל־פֶּתַח אֹהֶל מוֹעֵד: 14 וְהִקְרִיב אֶת־קָרְבָּנוֹ לַיהוָה כֶּבֶשׂ בֶּן־שְׁנָתוֹ תָמִים אֶחָד לְעֹלָה וְכַבְשָׂה אַחַת בַּת־שְׁנָתָהּ תְּמִימָה לְחַטָּאת וְאַיִל־אֶחָד תָּמִים לִשְׁלָמִים: 15 וְסַל מַצּוֹת סֹלֶת חַלֹּת בְּלוּלֹת בַּשֶּׁמֶן וּרְקִיקֵי מַצּוֹת מְשֻׁחִים בַּשָּׁמֶן וּמִנְחָתָם וְנִסְכֵּיהֶם: 16 וְהִקְרִיב הַכֹּהֵן לִפְנֵי יְהוָה וְעָשָׂה אֶת־חַטָּאתוֹ וְאֶת־עֹלָתוֹ: 17 וְאֶת־הָאַיִל יַעֲשֶׂה זֶבַח שְׁלָמִים לַיהוָה עַל סַל הַמַּצּוֹת וְעָשָׂה הַכֹּהֵן אֶת־מִנְחָתוֹ וְאֶת־נִסְכּוֹ: 18 וְגִלַּח הַנָּזִיר פֶּתַח אֹהֶל מוֹעֵד אֶת־רֹאשׁ נִזְרוֹ וְלָקַח אֶת־שְׂעַר רֹאשׁ נִזְרוֹ וְנָתַן עַל־הָאֵשׁ אֲשֶׁר־תַּחַת זֶבַח הַשְּׁלָמִים: 19 וְלָקַח הַכֹּהֵן אֶת־הַזְּרֹעַ בְּשֵׁלָה מִן־הָאַיִל וְחַלַּת מַצָּה אַחַת מִן־הַסַּל וּרְקִיק מַצָּה אֶחָד וְנָתַן עַל־כַּפֵּי הַנָּזִיר אַחַר הִתְגַּלְּחוֹ אֶת־נִזְרוֹ:

14. He should bring his offering to God. When the nazirite forsakes his vows of abstinence he sins against himself. He had separated himself to be holy to God and he should have

spiritual vitamin

> The Torah and its commandments are endless, since they originate from God, who is Infinite. Consequently, there is no limit to the devotion and joy with which you can fulfil God's will. That is why there is always room for growth in all matters of goodness and holiness in the daily experience of Torah.

of his God" is upon his head. ⁸ All the days of his nazirite vow, he (may not become ritually impure because his body) is holy to God.

⁹ If someone in his presence (in the same building) dies unexpectedly (due to circumstances beyond his control) or suddenly (due to negligence), causing the (holy hair of his) nazirite head to become ritually impure:

- On the day when he (is sprinkled with the water of) ritual purification, he should shave off (the hair from) his head, (i.e.) he should shave it off on the seventh day.

- ¹⁰ (Some time from) the eighth day (onwards), he should bring two turtledoves or two young pigeons to the priest, at the entrance to the Tent of Meeting. ¹¹ The priest should offer one as a sin-offering and one as a burnt-offering, and atone on his behalf for sinning by (becoming ritually impure from a person whose) soul (had departed).

- On that day, he should (begin to) sanctify (the hair of) his head (by abstaining for the term of his vow, once again). ¹² When he has completed all the days of his nazirite vow to God, he should bring a lamb in its first year as a guilt-offering. The first days (before he became ritually impure) are excluded because his status as a nazir was defiled through ritual impurity.

¹³ This is the law of the nazirite on the day the period of his nazirite vow is completed:

- He should present himself at the entrance to the Tent of Meeting.

¹⁴ He should bring his offering to God:

- One perfect (unblemished) male lamb in its first year as a burnt-offering.

- One perfect (unblemished) female lamb in its first year, as a sin-offering.

- One perfect (unblemished) ram, as a peace-offering.

- ¹⁵ A basket of unleavened bread.

- (Ten) loaves of fine flour mixed with oil.

- (Ten) unleavened wafers anointed with oil.

- The meal-offerings and libations (associated with the burnt- and peace-offerings).

- ¹⁶ The priest should present (them) before God, and perform the service of the sin-offering and burnt-offering. ¹⁷ He should bring the ram as a peace-offering to God, along with the basket of unleavened bread, and the priest should perform the service of its meal-offering with its libation.

- ¹⁸ (After the peace-offering has been slaughtered) at the entrance to the Tent of Meeting, the nazirite should shave the (hair from) his nazirite head. He should take the hair of his nazirite head and place it on the fire, under the peace-offering.

- ¹⁹ The priest should then take the cooked foreleg of the ram, one unleavened loaf from the basket and one unleavened wafer, and place them on the hands of the

במדבר ו:כ-כז

נשא

20 וְהֵנִיף אוֹתָם הַכֹּהֵן ׀ תְּנוּפָה לִפְנֵי יְהֹוָה קֹדֶשׁ הוּא לַכֹּהֵן עַל חֲזֵה הַתְּנוּפָה וְעַל שׁוֹק הַתְּרוּמָה וְאַחַר יִשְׁתֶּה הַנָּזִיר יָיִן: 21 זֹאת תּוֹרַת הַנָּזִיר אֲשֶׁר יִדֹּר קָרְבָּנוֹ לַיהֹוָה עַל־נִזְרוֹ מִלְּבַד אֲשֶׁר־תַּשִּׂיג יָדוֹ כְּפִי נִדְרוֹ אֲשֶׁר יִדֹּר כֵּן יַעֲשֶׂה עַל תּוֹרַת נִזְרוֹ: פ 22 וַיְדַבֵּר יְהֹוָה אֶל־מֹשֶׁה לֵּאמֹר: 23 דַּבֵּר אֶל־אַהֲרֹן וְאֶל־בָּנָיו לֵאמֹר כֹּה תְבָרְכוּ אֶת־בְּנֵי יִשְׂרָאֵל אָמוֹר לָהֶם: ס 24 יְבָרֶכְךָ יְהֹוָה וְיִשְׁמְרֶךָ: ס 25 יָאֵר יְהֹוָה ׀ פָּנָיו אֵלֶיךָ וִיחֻנֶּךָּ: ס 26 יִשָּׂא יְהֹוָה ׀ פָּנָיו אֵלֶיךָ וְיָשֵׂם לְךָ שָׁלוֹם: ס 27 וְשָׂמוּ אֶת־שְׁמִי עַל־בְּנֵי יִשְׂרָאֵל וַאֲנִי אֲבָרֲכֵם: ס

---

a man and his fellow man, and between a husband and his wife. God, who knows the thoughts of a man, said to Aaron, "You always strove to make peace between Israel and My great name. Therefore I will bring forth from you sons who will make atonement for the children of Israel every year, and they will entreat peace for them every day, by saying, 'May God bless you, etc.'" (*Tanna de-Vei Eliyahu*).

"May He bless you"—that your possessions will be blessed. *"And guard you"*—that a gang of robbers will not attack you and steal your money. For if a person gives his servant a gift and cannot guard it from all other people, what benefit does he have from the gift? But God is both giver and guardian (*Rashi, 11th century*).

"May He bless you"—with the blessing stated explicitly in the Torah: *"All these blessings will come upon you and overtake you, if you listen to the voice of God, your God: You will be blessed in the city, and blessed in the field, etc., your fruits and your dough will be blessed, etc."* (*Deuteronomy 28:2-6; Sifrei*).

Since the Torah has already promised a person virtually every possible blessing in *Parashat Be-Ḥukkotai* (and later in *Parashat Ki Tavo'*), what additional blessings could possibly be added here?

Rashi concluded that *"May God bless you"* means, "that your possessions will be blessed," i.e. that the possessions that a person already has, as a result of the earlier blessings recorded in the Torah, will enjoy supernatural growth.

In other words, the blessings in *Parashat Be-Ḥukkotai* promise you an abundance of possessions. Here, with the Priestly Blessing, you are promised that, having acquired those possessions, they will flourish in a supernatural manner (*Rabbi Menaḥem Mendel Schneerson, 20th century*).

25. Favor you. Let Him favor you by granting your requests, as it says, *"I will favor whomever I wish to favor"* (*Exodus 33:19*).

An alternative view: Let Him grant you favor in the eyes of man, as it says, *"God was with Joseph ... and granted him favor in the eyes of the prison's warden"* (*Genesis 39:21; Sifrei*).

Food for thought

1. Can a blessing change what has been preordained for you?

2. How do you feel after verbally blessing another person?

3. Does wishing good things on others make you a better person?

nazirite—after he has shaven off his nazirite hair. [20] The priest should wave them as a wave-offering before God (and then they remain) set aside for the priest, along with (the usual parts given to the priest from any offering), the breast that is waved and the thigh that is lifted up.

- After this, the (former) nazirite may drink wine.

[21] This is the law of a nazirite who vows (additional burnt- or peace-) offering(s) to God for his nazirite vow in addition to that which he is required:

- He must do in accordance with the vow that he vows, in addition to the basic requirement of his nazirite vow.

The Priestly Blessing

[22] God spoke to Moses, saying: [23] Speak to Aaron and his sons, saying:

- This is how you should bless the children of Israel, by saying (the following) to them (in a way that they can all hear):

[24] "May God bless you (that your possessions should be blessed) and guard you (against robbers).

[25] "May God cause His face to shine upon you and favor you.

[26] "May God raise His face towards you (suppressing His anger) and grant you peace."

- [27] (The priests) should use My (explicit) name (when blessing) the children of Israel, and I will fulfil (their) blessings.

---

kabbalah bites

6:22-26 Why may we not look at the priests when they issue the priestly blessing?

The ten fingers of man correspond to the ten heavenly *Sefirot* (attributes) with which God guides this world. When the priest lifts his ten fingers upwards during the blessing, his intention is to draw down a flow of Divine influence through the ten *Sefirot*/fingers. Since God's *Shekhinah* (presence) is resting on the priest's fingers at that moment, it is disrespectful to look at them.

continued to live a life of holiness and separation to God. Now that he returns to defile himself with the passions of the world, he is in need of atonement (*Naḥmanides, 13th century*).

23. Speak to Aaron and his sons, saying: This is how you should bless the children of Israel, by saying (the following) to them. If the children of Israel receive blessings, the priests will also benefit, since they will receive more priestly gifts. As a result, when the priests bless their fellow Israelites, they might think of their own gain. Therefore, the Torah cautions, *"saying to them"*—your thoughts should be on them (*Rabbi Abraham Samuel Benjamin Sofer, 19th century*).

24. May God bless you and guard you. How does a man come to earn the favor of God? By continually seeking to emulate God by making peace. To emulate God, Aaron strove to make peace between the Israelites and their Father in heaven, between the Israelites and the Sages, between one sage and another sage, between

במדבר ז:א-יא נשא

1 [FIFTH READING] וַיְהִ֡י בְּיוֹם֩ כַּלּ֨וֹת מֹשֶׁ֜ה לְהָקִ֣ים אֶת־הַמִּשְׁכָּ֗ן וַיִּמְשַׁ֨ח אֹת֜וֹ וַיְקַדֵּ֤שׁ אֹתוֹ֙ וְאֶת־כָּל־כֵּלָ֔יו וְאֶת־הַמִּזְבֵּ֖חַ וְאֶת־כָּל־כֵּלָ֑יו וַיִּמְשָׁחֵ֖ם וַיְקַדֵּ֥שׁ אֹתָֽם: **2** וַיַּקְרִ֙יבוּ֙ נְשִׂיאֵ֣י יִשְׂרָאֵ֔ל רָאשֵׁ֖י בֵּ֣ית אֲבֹתָ֑ם הֵ֚ם נְשִׂיאֵ֣י הַמַּטֹּ֔ת הֵ֥ם הָעֹמְדִ֖ים עַל־הַפְּקֻדִֽים: **3** וַיָּבִ֨יאוּ אֶת־קָרְבָּנָ֜ם לִפְנֵ֣י יְהֹוָ֗ה שֵׁשׁ־עֶגְלֹ֥ת צָב֙ וּשְׁנֵ֣י עָשָׂ֣ר בָּקָ֔ר עֲגָלָ֛ה עַל־שְׁנֵ֥י הַנְּשִׂאִ֖ים וְשׁ֣וֹר לְאֶחָ֑ד וַיַּקְרִ֥יבוּ אוֹתָ֖ם לִפְנֵ֥י הַמִּשְׁכָּֽן: **4** וַיֹּ֥אמֶר יְהֹוָ֖ה אֶל־מֹשֶׁ֥ה לֵּאמֹֽר: **5** קַ֚ח מֵֽאִתָּ֔ם וְהָי֕וּ לַֽעֲבֹ֕ד אֶת־עֲבֹדַ֖ת אֹ֣הֶל מוֹעֵ֑ד וְנָֽתַתָּ֤ה אוֹתָם֙ אֶל־הַֽלְוִיִּ֔ם אִ֖ישׁ כְּפִ֥י עֲבֹֽדָתֽוֹ: **6** וַיִּקַּ֣ח מֹשֶׁ֔ה אֶת־הָעֲגָלֹ֖ת וְאֶת־הַבָּקָ֑ר וַיִּתֵּ֥ן אוֹתָ֖ם אֶל־הַֽלְוִיִּֽם: **7** אֵ֣ת | שְׁתֵּ֣י הָעֲגָל֗וֹת וְאֵת֙ אַרְבַּ֣עַת הַבָּקָ֔ר נָתַ֖ן לִבְנֵ֣י גֵֽרְשׁ֑וֹן כְּפִ֖י עֲבֹֽדָתָֽם: **8** וְאֵ֣ת | אַרְבַּ֣ע הָעֲגָלֹ֗ת וְאֵת֙ שְׁמֹנַ֣ת הַבָּקָ֔ר נָתַ֖ן לִבְנֵ֣י מְרָרִ֑י כְּפִי֙ עֲבֹ֣דָתָ֔ם בְּיַד֙ אִֽיתָמָ֔ר בֶּֽן־אַֽהֲרֹ֖ן הַכֹּהֵֽן: **9** וְלִבְנֵ֥י קְהָ֖ת לֹ֣א נָתָ֑ן כִּֽי־עֲבֹדַ֤ת הַקֹּ֙דֶשׁ֙ עֲלֵהֶ֔ם בַּכָּתֵ֖ף יִשָּֽׂאוּ: **10** וַיַּקְרִ֣יבוּ הַנְּשִׂאִ֗ים אֵ֚ת חֲנֻכַּ֣ת הַמִּזְבֵּ֔חַ בְּי֖וֹם הִמָּשַׁ֣ח אֹת֑וֹ וַיַּקְרִ֧יבוּ הַנְּשִׂיאִ֛ם אֶת־קָרְבָּנָ֖ם לִפְנֵ֥י הַמִּזְבֵּֽחַ: **11** וַיֹּ֥אמֶר יְהֹוָ֖ה אֶל־מֹשֶׁ֑ה נָשִׂ֨יא אֶחָ֜ד לַיּ֗וֹם נָשִׂ֤יא אֶחָד֙ לַיּ֔וֹם יַקְרִ֙יבוּ֙ אֶת־קָרְבָּנָ֔ם לַחֲנֻכַּ֖ת

(7:10 ff.). The lesson here is: If you wish God to answer your own prayers, petition God first for the needs of all your brethren before mentioning your own needs.

For this reason, Rabbi Shneur Zalman of Lyady writes that before prayer you should say, "I accept upon myself the commandment, *'Love your fellow as yourself'*"—because your personal petitions are more likely to be granted if they are prefaced with a sensitivity for the needs of others (*Rabbi Menahem Mendel Schneerson, 20th century*).

11. One leader each day. Why did the leaders see fit to bring these particular offerings? The Sages said: Even though they all made the same offerings, each had a different intention.

- The leader of Judah brought his offerings to commemorate royalty, since Judah was a king over his brothers.
- The leader of Issachar brought his offerings to commemorate Torah, because they loved Torah more than any of the other tribes.
- The leader of Zebulun brought his offerings on the third day because his tribe loved Torah and they extended their hands to provide ample funds for Issachar, so Issachar would not need to earn a living and would be free to study the Torah. Therefore Zebulun merited to be their partner in Torah, and so they offered after him.

numbers 7:1–11   naso'

The Tribal Leaders' Donation to the Tabernacle

7 [FIFTH READING] ¹ It was (the first of *Nisan*), the day that Moses finished erecting the Tabernacle, when he anointed it, sanctified it, along with all its utensils, together with the altar and all its utensils. ² The leaders of Israel, the heads of their paternal houses, brought their offerings. They were the leaders of the tribes (back in Egypt and) they were the ones who were present during the census. ³ They brought their offering before God: Six covered wagons and twelve oxen—one wagon for two leaders, and an ox for each one. They presented them in front of the Tabernacle (but Moses did not accept their offerings, since he had not received an instruction from God to do so).

⁴ God spoke to Moses, saying: ⁵ "Take (the gifts) from them, and let them be used in the service of the Tent of Meeting. You should give them to the Levites, (dividing them) according to each man's work."

⁶ Moses took the wagons and the cattle and gave them to the Levites:

- ⁷ He gave two wagons and four oxen to Gershon's descendants, commensurate with their work.

- ⁸ He gave four wagons and eight oxen to Merari's descendants, commensurate with their (heavier) work(load of carrying the beams, pillars and sockets)—under the direction of Ithamar son of Aaron the priest.

- ⁹ He gave nothing to Kohath's descendants, because their work involved the holy (equipment), which they had to carry on their shoulders.

Dedication of the Altar

¹⁰ The leaders' (charitable mood led them to) bring (offerings for) the dedication of the altar on the day it was anointed. The leaders presented their offerings in front of the altar (but Moses did not accept their offerings, since he had not received an instruction from God to do so).

¹¹ God said to Moses: "One leader each day! One leader each day should present his offering for the dedication of the altar."

7:3 Six covered wagons. Six, corresponding to the six days in which the world was created. Six, corresponding to the six orders of the Mishnah. Six, corresponding to the Matriarchs: Sarah, Rebekah, Rachel, Leah, Bilhah and Zilpah (*Numbers Rabbah*).

Why did the twelve leaders only donate six wagons? They brought one wagon between two leaders to show the brotherly love between them, in which merit the Divine Presence would dwell among them (*Rabbi Obadiah Sforno, 16th century*).

10. The leaders presented their offerings. The leaders first gave gifts to the Tabernacle on behalf of the entire Jewish community (7:1-9), before offering gifts on behalf of their own tribes

במדבר ז:י״א-י״ז

נשא

הַמִּזְבֵּחַ: ס 12 וַיְהִי הַמַּקְרִיב בַּיּוֹם הָרִאשׁוֹן אֶת־קָרְבָּנוֹ נַחְשׁוֹן בֶּן־עַמִּינָדָב לְמַטֵּה יְהוּדָה: 13 וְקָרְבָּנוֹ קַעֲרַת־כֶּסֶף אַחַת שְׁלֹשִׁים וּמֵאָה מִשְׁקָלָהּ מִזְרָק אֶחָד כֶּסֶף שִׁבְעִים שֶׁקֶל בְּשֶׁקֶל הַקֹּדֶשׁ שְׁנֵיהֶם | מְלֵאִים סֹלֶת בְּלוּלָה בַשֶּׁמֶן לְמִנְחָה: 14 כַּף אַחַת עֲשָׂרָה זָהָב מְלֵאָה קְטֹרֶת: 15 פַּר אֶחָד בֶּן־בָּקָר אַיִל אֶחָד כֶּבֶשׂ־אֶחָד בֶּן־שְׁנָתוֹ לְעֹלָה: 16 שְׂעִיר־עִזִּים אֶחָד לְחַטָּאת: 17 וּלְזֶבַח הַשְּׁלָמִים בָּקָר שְׁנַיִם אֵילִם חֲמִשָּׁה עַתּוּדִים חֲמִשָּׁה כְּבָשִׂים בְּנֵי־שָׁנָה חֲמִשָּׁה

years old, and representing the twenty years that the Flood had been decreed before his children were born (see ibid. 6:3).

(Weighing) seventy shekels. Corresponding to the seventy nations which emerged from Noah's sons.

One spoon. Corresponding to the Torah, which was given by the hand of God. In Hebrew, the word *kaf* means both "spoon" and "palm," alluding here to the "hand" or "palm" of God.

(Weighing) ten gold (shekels). Corresponding to the Ten Commandments.

Filled with incense. The numerical value of *ketoret*, "incense," corresponds to the six hundred and thirteen commandments, (provided that you convert the *kof* into a *dalet* with the system known as *'at bash* in which the first and last letters of the alphabet are interchangeable, etc. Thus *ketoret* is: *dalet* = four (exchanged), *tet* = nine, *resh* = two hundred, *taf* = four hundred, a total of six hundred and thirteen).

One (outstanding) young bull. Corresponding to Abraham, about whom the verse states, *"He took a young bull"* (ibid. 18:7).

One ram. Corresponding to Isaac, of whom the verse states, *"Abraham went and took the ram and offered it up as a burnt-offering instead of his son"* (ibid. 22:13).

One lamb. Corresponding to Jacob, of whom the verse states, *"Jacob separated the flocks"* (ibid. 30:40).

One young male goat. To atone for the sale of Joseph, of whom the verse states, *"His brothers slaughtered a young goat"* (ibid. 37:31).

For a peace-offering: two oxen. Corresponding to Moses and Aaron, who made peace between Israel and their Father in Heaven.

Five rams, five male goats, and five lambs. Three types, corresponding to priests, Levites, and Israelites; and corresponding to the Torah, the Prophets, and the Holy Writings.

> **kabbalah bites**
>
> **7:12** The first day's offering was from the tribe of Judah, who represented *Malkhut* (sovereignty). Only then, on the second day, was the offering from the tribe of Issachar, who represented Torah.
>
> This teaches you that in order to connect to the spiritual core of Torah you first need to develop a deep sense of inner submission to *Malkhut de-'Ein-Sof*, the sovereignty of God's infinite light.

numbers 7:12–17 — naso'

¹² The one who brought his offering on the first day was Nahshon son of Amminadab of the tribe of Judah. ¹³ His offering was:

- One silver bowl weighing one hundred and thirty (shekels),
- One silver sprinkling basin (weighing) seventy shekels, according to the shekel (measurement used for) holy (items).
- Both (bowls were) filled with fine flour mixed with olive oil for a meal-offering.
- ¹⁴ One spoon (weighing) ten gold (shekels) filled with incense;
- ¹⁵ One (outstanding) young bull, one ram and one lamb in its first year for a burnt-offering;
- ¹⁶ One young male goat for a sin-offering;
- ¹⁷ For a peace-offering: two oxen, five rams, five male goats and five lambs in their first year.

- The leader of Reuben brought his offerings to commemorate Reuben's attempts to save Joseph from being sold.
- The leader of Simeon brought his offerings to commemorate the construction of the Tabernacle, because Simeon avenged the abduction of Dinah, and the Tabernacle brought the downfall of adulterers and *sotahs* (see above, 5:11*ff*).
- The leader of Gad brought his offerings to commemorate the exodus from Egypt, since Gad was destined to lead the Jewish people across the Jordan, into the land of Israel.
- The leader of Ephraim brought his offerings to commemorate Jacob, because Jacob blessed Ephraim before Manasseh, even though Ephraim was the younger brother.
- The leader of Manasseh brought his offerings to commemorate Jacob and Manasseh.
- The leader of Benjamin brought his offerings to commemorate Rachel, the mother of Benjamin and Joseph.
- The leader of Dan brought his offerings to commemorate Samson the nazirite, who was to emerge from the tribe of Dan.
- The leader of Asher brought his offerings to commemorate the fact that God had happily chosen the Jewish people as His own.
- The leader of Naphtali brought his offerings to commemorate the Patriarchs and Matriarchs (*Numbers Rabbah*).

13-17. One silver bowl. The numerical value of the letters of this phrase (*ka'arat kesef*) is nine hundred and thirty, corresponding to the years of Adam, the first man (*Genesis* 5:5).

Weighing one hundred and thirty (shekels). When Adam began to establish a family to perpetuate the world, he was one hundred and thirty, as the verse states, *"Adam lived one hundred and thirty years, and he fathered, etc."* (*Genesis* 5:3).

One silver sprinkling basin. The numerical value of this phrase (*mizrak 'eḥad*) is five hundred and twenty, representing Noah, who began to establish a family when he was five hundred

זֶה קָרְבַּ֖ן נַחְשׁ֥וֹן בֶּן־עַמִּינָדָֽב׃ פ 18 בַּיּוֹם֙ הַשֵּׁנִ֔י הִקְרִ֖יב נְתַנְאֵ֣ל בֶּן־צוּעָ֑ר נְשִׂ֖יא יִשָּׂשכָֽר׃ 19 הִקְרִ֨ב אֶת־קָרְבָּנ֜וֹ קַֽעֲרַת־כֶּ֣סֶף אַחַ֗ת שְׁלֹשִׁ֣ים וּמֵאָה֮ מִשְׁקָלָהּ֒ מִזְרָ֣ק אֶחָ֗ד כֶּ֛סֶף שִׁבְעִ֥ים שֶׁ֖קֶל בְּשֶׁ֣קֶל הַקֹּ֑דֶשׁ שְׁנֵיהֶ֣ם ׀ מְלֵאִ֗ים סֹ֛לֶת בְּלוּלָ֥ה בַשֶּׁ֖מֶן לְמִנְחָֽה׃ 20 כַּ֥ף אַחַ֛ת עֲשָׂרָ֥ה זָהָ֖ב מְלֵאָ֥ה קְטֹֽרֶת׃ 21 פַּ֣ר אֶחָ֞ד בֶּן־בָּקָ֗ר אַ֧יִל אֶחָ֛ד כֶּֽבֶשׂ־אֶחָ֥ד בֶּן־שְׁנָת֖וֹ לְעֹלָֽה׃ 22 שְׂעִיר־עִזִּ֥ים אֶחָ֖ד לְחַטָּֽאת׃ 23 וּלְזֶ֣בַח הַשְּׁלָמִים֮ בָּקָ֣ר שְׁנַ֒יִם֒ אֵילִ֤ם חֲמִשָּׁה֙ עַתּוּדִ֣ים חֲמִשָּׁ֔ה כְּבָשִׂ֥ים בְּנֵֽי־שָׁנָ֖ה חֲמִשָּׁ֑ה זֶ֛ה קָרְבַּ֥ן נְתַנְאֵ֖ל בֶּן־צוּעָֽר׃ פ 24 בַּיּוֹם֙ הַשְּׁלִישִׁ֔י נָשִׂ֖יא לִבְנֵ֣י זְבוּלֻ֑ן אֱלִיאָ֖ב בֶּן־חֵלֹֽן׃ 25 קָרְבָּנ֞וֹ קַֽעֲרַת־כֶּ֣סֶף אַחַ֗ת שְׁלֹשִׁ֣ים וּמֵאָה֮ מִשְׁקָלָהּ֒ מִזְרָ֣ק אֶחָ֗ד כֶּ֛סֶף שִׁבְעִ֥ים שֶׁ֖קֶל בְּשֶׁ֣קֶל הַקֹּ֑דֶשׁ שְׁנֵיהֶ֣ם ׀ מְלֵאִ֗ים סֹ֛לֶת בְּלוּלָ֥ה בַשֶּׁ֖מֶן לְמִנְחָֽה׃ 26 כַּ֥ף אַחַ֛ת עֲשָׂרָ֥ה זָהָ֖ב מְלֵאָ֥ה קְטֹֽרֶת׃ 27 פַּ֣ר אֶחָ֞ד בֶּן־בָּקָ֗ר אַ֧יִל אֶחָ֛ד כֶּֽבֶשׂ־אֶחָ֥ד בֶּן־שְׁנָת֖וֹ לְעֹלָֽה׃ 28 שְׂעִיר־עִזִּ֥ים אֶחָ֖ד לְחַטָּֽאת׃ 29 וּלְזֶ֣בַח הַשְּׁלָמִים֮ בָּקָ֣ר שְׁנַ֒יִם֒ אֵילִ֤ם חֲמִשָּׁה֙ עַתּוּדִ֣ים חֲמִשָּׁ֔ה כְּבָשִׂ֥ים בְּנֵֽי־שָׁנָ֖ה חֲמִשָּׁ֑ה זֶ֛ה קָרְבַּ֥ן אֱלִיאָ֖ב בֶּן־חֵלֹֽן׃ פ 30 בַּיּוֹם֙ הָרְבִיעִ֔י נָשִׂ֖יא לִבְנֵ֣י רְאוּבֵ֑ן אֱלִיצ֖וּר בֶּן־שְׁדֵיאֽוּר׃ 31 קָרְבָּנ֞וֹ קַֽעֲרַת־כֶּ֣סֶף אַחַ֗ת שְׁלֹשִׁ֣ים וּמֵאָה֮ מִשְׁקָלָהּ֒ מִזְרָ֣ק אֶחָ֗ד כֶּ֛סֶף שִׁבְעִ֥ים שֶׁ֖קֶל בְּשֶׁ֣קֶל הַקֹּ֑דֶשׁ שְׁנֵיהֶ֣ם ׀ מְלֵאִ֗ים סֹ֛לֶת בְּלוּלָ֥ה בַשֶּׁ֖מֶן לְמִנְחָֽה׃ 32 כַּ֥ף אַחַ֛ת עֲשָׂרָ֥ה זָהָ֖ב מְלֵאָ֥ה קְטֹֽרֶת׃ 33 פַּ֣ר אֶחָ֞ד בֶּן־בָּקָ֗ר אַ֧יִל אֶחָ֛ד כֶּֽבֶשׂ־אֶחָ֥ד בֶּן־שְׁנָת֖וֹ לְעֹלָֽה׃ 34 שְׂעִיר־עִזִּ֥ים אֶחָ֖ד לְחַטָּֽאת׃ 35 וּלְזֶ֣בַח הַשְּׁלָמִים֮ בָּקָ֣ר שְׁנַ֒יִם֒ אֵילִ֤ם חֲמִשָּׁה֙ עַתּוּדִ֣ים חֲמִשָּׁ֔ה כְּבָשִׂ֥ים בְּנֵֽי־שָׁנָ֖ה חֲמִשָּׁ֑ה זֶ֛ה קָרְבַּ֥ן אֱלִיצ֖וּר בֶּן־שְׁדֵיאֽוּר׃ פ 36 בַּיּוֹם֙ הַֽחֲמִישִׁ֔י נָשִׂ֖יא לִבְנֵ֣י שִׁמְע֑וֹן שְׁלֻֽמִיאֵ֖ל בֶּן־צוּרִֽישַׁדָּֽי׃ 37 קָרְבָּנ֞וֹ קַֽעֲרַת־כֶּ֣סֶף אַחַ֗ת שְׁלֹשִׁ֣ים וּמֵאָה֮

---

likewise, each on his day," for this would have diminished the honor of the others (*Naḥmanides, 13th century*).

Seeing that the offerings of the leaders were all identical and in the same amounts, why does the Torah mention them all separately? Because each of them brought his offering of his own accord, not in order to copy the others, but solely out of his own free will (*Rabbi Simḥah Bunem of Przysucha, 18th–19th century*).

This was the offering of Nahshon son of Amminadab.

[18] On the second day, Nethanel son of Zuar, the leader of Issachar, brought his offering. [19] He brought his offering of one silver bowl weighing one hundred and thirty (shekels), one silver sprinkling basin (weighing) seventy shekels, according to the shekel (measurement used for) holy (items), both filled with fine flour mixed with olive oil for a meal-offering; [20] one spoon (weighing) ten gold (shekels) filled with incense; [21] one (outstanding) young bull, one ram and one lamb in its first year for a burnt-offering; [22] one young male goat for a sin-offering. [23] For a peace-offering: two oxen, five rams, five male goats, and five lambs in their first year. This was the offering of Nethanel son of Zuar.

[24] On the third day, was the leader of Zebulun's descendants, Eliab son of Helon. [25] His offering was one silver bowl weighing one hundred and thirty (shekels), one silver sprinkling basin (weighing) seventy shekels, according to the shekel (measurement used for) holy (items), both filled with fine flour mixed with olive oil for a meal-offering; [26] one spoon (weighing) ten gold (shekels) filled with incense; [27] one (outstanding) young bull, one ram and one lamb in its first year for a burnt-offering; [28] one young male goat for a sin-offering. [29] For a peace-offering: two oxen, five rams, five male goats, and five lambs in their first year. This was the offering of Eliab son of Helon.

[30] On the fourth day, was the leader of Reuben's descendants, Elizur son of Shedeur. [31] His offering was one silver bowl weighing one hundred and thirty (shekels), one silver sprinkling basin (weighing) seventy shekels, according to the shekel (measurement used for) holy (items), both filled with fine flour mixed with olive oil for a meal-offering; [32] one spoon (weighing) ten gold (shekels) filled with incense; [33] one (outstanding) young bull, one ram and one lamb in its first year for a burnt-offering; [34] one young male goat for a sin-offering. [35] For a peace-offering: two oxen, five rams, five male goats, and five lambs in their first year. This was the offering of Elizur son of Shedeur.

[36] On the fifth day, was the leader of Simeon's descendants, Shelumiel son of Zurishaddai. [37] His offering was one silver bowl weighing one hundred and thirty (shekels), one silver sprinkling basin (weighing) seventy shekels, according to the shekel (measurement used for) holy (items), both filled with fine flour mixed with

---

Five were brought of each of the three types, corresponding to the five books of the Pentateuch, to the five commandments inscribed on the first tablet, and the five commandments inscribed on the second tablet (*Rashi, 11th century*).

18-19. Nethanel son of Zuar, the leader of Issachar, brought his offering ... he brought his offering. God wished to mention them all by name and specify their offerings, and to mention the day for each one, not that He state only the first one and then say "and all the others offered

נשא   במדבר ז:לז-נט

מִשְׁקָלָהּ מִזְרָק אֶחָד כֶּסֶף שִׁבְעִים שֶׁקֶל בְּשֶׁקֶל הַקֹּדֶשׁ שְׁנֵיהֶם | מְלֵאִים סֹלֶת בְּלוּלָה בַשֶּׁמֶן לְמִנְחָה: 38 כַּף אַחַת עֲשָׂרָה זָהָב מְלֵאָה קְטֹרֶת: 39 פַּר אֶחָד בֶּן־בָּקָר אַיִל אֶחָד כֶּבֶשׂ־אֶחָד בֶּן־שְׁנָתוֹ לְעֹלָה: 40 שְׂעִיר־עִזִּים אֶחָד לְחַטָּאת: 41 וּלְזֶבַח הַשְּׁלָמִים בָּקָר שְׁנַיִם אֵילִם חֲמִשָּׁה עַתּוּדִים חֲמִשָּׁה כְּבָשִׂים בְּנֵי־שָׁנָה חֲמִשָּׁה זֶה קָרְבַּן שְׁלֻמִיאֵל בֶּן־צוּרִישַׁדָּי: פ 42 [SIXTH READING] בַּיּוֹם הַשִּׁשִּׁי נָשִׂיא לִבְנֵי גָד אֶלְיָסָף בֶּן־דְּעוּאֵל: 43 קָרְבָּנוֹ קַעֲרַת־כֶּסֶף אַחַת שְׁלֹשִׁים וּמֵאָה מִשְׁקָלָהּ מִזְרָק אֶחָד כֶּסֶף שִׁבְעִים שֶׁקֶל בְּשֶׁקֶל הַקֹּדֶשׁ שְׁנֵיהֶם | מְלֵאִים סֹלֶת בְּלוּלָה בַשֶּׁמֶן לְמִנְחָה: 44 כַּף אַחַת עֲשָׂרָה זָהָב מְלֵאָה קְטֹרֶת: 45 פַּר אֶחָד בֶּן־בָּקָר אַיִל אֶחָד כֶּבֶשׂ־אֶחָד בֶּן־שְׁנָתוֹ לְעֹלָה: 46 שְׂעִיר־עִזִּים אֶחָד לְחַטָּאת: 47 וּלְזֶבַח הַשְּׁלָמִים בָּקָר שְׁנַיִם אֵילִם חֲמִשָּׁה עַתֻּדִים חֲמִשָּׁה כְּבָשִׂים בְּנֵי־שָׁנָה חֲמִשָּׁה זֶה קָרְבַּן אֶלְיָסָף בֶּן־דְּעוּאֵל: פ 48 בַּיּוֹם הַשְּׁבִיעִי נָשִׂיא לִבְנֵי אֶפְרָיִם אֱלִישָׁמָע בֶּן־עַמִּיהוּד: 49 קָרְבָּנוֹ קַעֲרַת־כֶּסֶף אַחַת שְׁלֹשִׁים וּמֵאָה מִשְׁקָלָהּ מִזְרָק אֶחָד כֶּסֶף שִׁבְעִים שֶׁקֶל בְּשֶׁקֶל הַקֹּדֶשׁ שְׁנֵיהֶם | מְלֵאִים סֹלֶת בְּלוּלָה בַשֶּׁמֶן לְמִנְחָה: 50 כַּף אַחַת עֲשָׂרָה זָהָב מְלֵאָה קְטֹרֶת: 51 פַּר אֶחָד בֶּן־בָּקָר אַיִל אֶחָד כֶּבֶשׂ־אֶחָד בֶּן־שְׁנָתוֹ לְעֹלָה: 52 שְׂעִיר־עִזִּים אֶחָד לְחַטָּאת: 53 וּלְזֶבַח הַשְּׁלָמִים בָּקָר שְׁנַיִם אֵילִם חֲמִשָּׁה עַתֻּדִים חֲמִשָּׁה כְּבָשִׂים בְּנֵי־שָׁנָה חֲמִשָּׁה זֶה קָרְבַּן אֱלִישָׁמָע בֶּן־עַמִּיהוּד: פ 54 בַּיּוֹם הַשְּׁמִינִי נָשִׂיא לִבְנֵי מְנַשֶּׁה גַּמְלִיאֵל בֶּן־פְּדָהצוּר: 55 קָרְבָּנוֹ קַעֲרַת־כֶּסֶף אַחַת שְׁלֹשִׁים וּמֵאָה מִשְׁקָלָהּ מִזְרָק אֶחָד כֶּסֶף שִׁבְעִים שֶׁקֶל בְּשֶׁקֶל הַקֹּדֶשׁ שְׁנֵיהֶם | מְלֵאִים סֹלֶת בְּלוּלָה בַשֶּׁמֶן לְמִנְחָה: 56 כַּף אַחַת עֲשָׂרָה זָהָב מְלֵאָה קְטֹרֶת: 57 פַּר אֶחָד בֶּן־בָּקָר אַיִל אֶחָד כֶּבֶשׂ־אֶחָד בֶּן־שְׁנָתוֹ לְעֹלָה: 58 שְׂעִיר־עִזִּים אֶחָד לְחַטָּאת: 59 וּלְזֶבַח הַשְּׁלָמִים בָּקָר שְׁנַיִם אֵילִם חֲמִשָּׁה עַתֻּדִים

olive oil for a meal-offering; ³⁸ one spoon (weighing) ten gold (shekels) filled with incense; ³⁹ one (outstanding) young bull, one ram and one lamb in its first year for a burnt-offering; ⁴⁰ one young male goat for a sin-offering. ⁴¹ For a peace-offering: two oxen, five rams, five male goats, and five lambs in their first year. This was the offering of Shelumiel son of Zurishaddai.

[SIXTH READING] ⁴² On the sixth day, was the leader of Gad's descendants, Eliasaph son of Deuel. ⁴³ His offering was one silver bowl weighing one hundred and thirty (shekels), one silver sprinkling basin (weighing) seventy shekels, according to the shekel (measurement used for) holy (items), both filled with fine flour mixed with olive oil for a meal-offering; ⁴⁴ one spoon (weighing) ten gold (shekels) filled with incense, ⁴⁵ one (outstanding) young bull, one ram and one lamb in its first year for a burnt-offering; ⁴⁶ one young male goat for a sin-offering. ⁴⁷ For a peace-offering: two oxen, five rams, five male goats, and five lambs in their first year. This was the offering of Eliasaph son of Deuel.

⁴⁸ On the seventh day, was the leader of Ephraim's descendants, Elishama son of Ammihud. ⁴⁹ His offering was one silver bowl weighing one hundred and thirty (shekels), one silver sprinkling basin (weighing) seventy shekels, according to the shekel (measurement used for) holy (items), both filled with fine flour mixed with olive oil for a meal-offering; ⁵⁰ one spoon (weighing) ten gold (shekels) filled with incense; ⁵¹ one (outstanding) young bull, one ram and one lamb in its first year for a burnt-offering; ⁵² one young male goat for a sin-offering. ⁵³ For a peace-offering: two oxen, five rams, five male goats, and five lambs in their first year. This was the offering of Elishama son of Ammihud.

⁵⁴ On the eighth day, was the leader of Manasseh's descendants, Gamaliel son of Pedahzur. ⁵⁵ His offering was one silver bowl weighing one hundred and thirty (shekels), one silver sprinkling basin (weighing) seventy shekels, according to the shekel (measurement used for) holy (items), both filled with fine flour mixed with olive oil for a meal-offering; ⁵⁶ one spoon (weighing) ten gold (shekels) filled with incense; ⁵⁷ one (outstanding) young bull, one ram and one lamb in its first year for a burnt-offering; ⁵⁸ one young male goat for a sin-offering. ⁵⁹ For a peace-offering:

spiritual vitamin

> "*The more the knowledge, the more the pain*" (*Ecclesiastes* 1:18). For, when it comes to the knowledge of the Torah, which represents the infinite wisdom of God, the more you learn, the more you become painfully aware of the distance which is still to be covered, a distance which is indeed infinite.

חֲמִשָּׁה כְּבָשִׂים בְּנֵי־שָׁנָה חֲמִשָּׁה זֶה קָרְבַּן גַּמְלִיאֵל בֶּן־פְּדָהצֽוּר׃ פ 60 בַּיּוֹם֙ הַתְּשִׁיעִ֔י נָשִׂ֖יא לִבְנֵ֣י בִנְיָמִ֑ן אֲבִידָ֖ן בֶּן־גִּדְעֹנִֽי׃ 61 קָרְבָּנ֞וֹ קַֽעֲרַת־כֶּ֣סֶף אַחַ֗ת שְׁלֹשִׁ֣ים וּמֵאָה֮ מִשְׁקָלָהּ֒ מִזְרָ֤ק אֶחָד֙ כֶּ֔סֶף שִׁבְעִ֥ים שֶׁ֖קֶל בְּשֶׁ֣קֶל הַקֹּ֑דֶשׁ שְׁנֵיהֶ֣ם ׀ מְלֵאִ֗ים סֹ֛לֶת בְּלוּלָ֥ה בַשֶּׁ֖מֶן לְמִנְחָֽה׃ 62 כַּ֥ף אַחַ֛ת עֲשָׂרָ֥ה זָהָ֖ב מְלֵאָ֥ה קְטֹֽרֶת׃ 63 פַּ֣ר אֶחָ֞ד בֶּן־בָּקָ֗ר אַ֧יִל אֶחָ֛ד כֶּֽבֶשׂ־אֶחָ֥ד בֶּן־שְׁנָת֖וֹ לְעֹלָֽה׃ 64 שְׂעִיר־עִזִּ֥ים אֶחָ֖ד לְחַטָּֽאת׃ 65 וּלְזֶ֣בַח הַשְּׁלָמִים֮ בָּקָ֣ר שְׁנַ֒יִם֒ אֵילִ֤ם חֲמִשָּׁה֙ עַתּוּדִ֣ים חֲמִשָּׁ֔ה כְּבָשִׂ֥ים בְּנֵֽי־שָׁנָ֖ה חֲמִשָּׁ֑ה זֶ֛ה קָרְבַּ֥ן אֲבִידָ֖ן בֶּן־גִּדְעֹנִֽי׃ פ 66 בַּיּוֹם֙ הָעֲשִׂירִ֔י נָשִׂ֖יא לִבְנֵ֣י דָ֑ן אֲחִיעֶ֖זֶר בֶּן־עַמִּישַׁדָּֽי׃ 67 קָרְבָּנ֞וֹ קַעֲרַת־כֶּ֣סֶף אַחַ֗ת שְׁלֹשִׁ֣ים וּמֵאָה֮ מִשְׁקָלָהּ֒ מִזְרָ֤ק אֶחָד֙ כֶּ֔סֶף שִׁבְעִ֥ים שֶׁ֖קֶל בְּשֶׁ֣קֶל הַקֹּ֑דֶשׁ שְׁנֵיהֶ֣ם ׀ מְלֵאִ֗ים סֹ֛לֶת בְּלוּלָ֥ה בַשֶּׁ֖מֶן לְמִנְחָֽה׃ 68 כַּ֥ף אַחַ֛ת עֲשָׂרָ֥ה זָהָ֖ב מְלֵאָ֥ה קְטֹֽרֶת׃ 69 פַּ֣ר אֶחָ֞ד בֶּן־בָּקָ֗ר אַ֧יִל אֶחָ֛ד כֶּֽבֶשׂ־אֶחָ֥ד בֶּן־שְׁנָת֖וֹ לְעֹלָֽה׃ 70 שְׂעִיר־עִזִּ֥ים אֶחָ֖ד לְחַטָּֽאת׃ 71 וּלְזֶ֣בַח הַשְּׁלָמִים֮ בָּקָ֣ר שְׁנַ֒יִם֒ אֵילִ֤ם חֲמִשָּׁה֙ עַתֻּדִ֣ים חֲמִשָּׁ֔ה כְּבָשִׂ֥ים בְּנֵֽי־שָׁנָ֖ה חֲמִשָּׁ֑ה זֶ֛ה קָרְבַּ֥ן אֲחִיעֶ֖זֶר בֶּן־עַמִּישַׁדָּֽי׃ פ 72 בְּיוֹם֙ עַשְׁתֵּ֣י עָשָׂ֣ר י֔וֹם נָשִׂ֖יא לִבְנֵ֣י אָשֵׁ֑ר פַּגְעִיאֵ֖ל בֶּן־עָכְרָֽן׃ 73 קָרְבָּנ֞וֹ קַעֲרַת־כֶּ֣סֶף אַחַ֗ת שְׁלֹשִׁ֣ים וּמֵאָה֮ מִשְׁקָלָהּ֒ מִזְרָ֤ק אֶחָד֙ כֶּ֔סֶף שִׁבְעִ֥ים שֶׁ֖קֶל בְּשֶׁ֣קֶל הַקֹּ֑דֶשׁ שְׁנֵיהֶ֣ם ׀ מְלֵאִ֗ים סֹ֛לֶת בְּלוּלָ֥ה בַשֶּׁ֖מֶן לְמִנְחָֽה׃ 74 כַּ֥ף אַחַ֛ת עֲשָׂרָ֥ה זָהָ֖ב מְלֵאָ֥ה קְטֹֽרֶת׃ 75 פַּ֣ר אֶחָ֞ד בֶּן־בָּקָ֗ר אַ֧יִל אֶחָ֛ד כֶּֽבֶשׂ־אֶחָ֥ד בֶּן־שְׁנָת֖וֹ לְעֹלָֽה׃ 76 שְׂעִיר־עִזִּ֥ים אֶחָ֖ד לְחַטָּֽאת׃ 77 וּלְזֶ֣בַח הַשְּׁלָמִים֮ בָּקָ֣ר שְׁנַ֒יִם֒ אֵילִ֤ם חֲמִשָּׁה֙ עַתֻּדִ֣ים חֲמִשָּׁ֔ה כְּבָשִׂ֥ים בְּנֵֽי־שָׁנָ֖ה חֲמִשָּׁ֑ה זֶ֛ה קָרְבַּ֥ן פַּגְעִיאֵ֖ל בֶּן־עָכְרָֽן׃ פ 78 בְּיוֹם֙ שְׁנֵ֣ים עָשָׂ֣ר י֔וֹם נָשִׂ֖יא לִבְנֵ֣י נַפְתָּלִ֑י אֲחִירַ֖ע בֶּן־עֵינָֽן׃ 79 קָרְבָּנ֞וֹ קַעֲרַת־כֶּ֣סֶף אַחַ֗ת שְׁלֹשִׁ֣ים וּמֵאָה֮ מִשְׁקָלָהּ֒ מִזְרָ֤ק אֶחָד֙ כֶּ֔סֶף שִׁבְעִ֥ים שֶׁ֖קֶל בְּשֶׁ֣קֶל הַקֹּ֑דֶשׁ שְׁנֵיהֶ֣ם ׀ מְלֵאִ֗ים סֹ֛לֶת בְּלוּלָ֥ה בַשֶּׁ֖מֶן לְמִנְחָֽה׃ 80 כַּ֥ף אַחַ֛ת עֲשָׂרָ֥ה זָהָ֖ב מְלֵאָ֥ה

two oxen, five rams, five male goats, and five lambs in their first year. This was the offering of Gamaliel son of Pedahzur.

⁶⁰ On the ninth day, was the leader of Benjamin's descendants, Abidan son of Gideoni. ⁶¹ His offering was one silver bowl weighing one hundred and thirty (shekels), one silver sprinkling basin (weighing) seventy shekels, according to the shekel (measurement used for) holy (items), both filled with fine flour mixed with olive oil for a meal-offering; ⁶² one spoon (weighing) ten gold (shekels) filled with incense; ⁶³ one (outstanding) young bull, one ram and one lamb in its first year for a burnt-offering; ⁶⁴ one young male goat for a sin-offering. ⁶⁵ For a peace-offering: two oxen, five rams, five male goats, and five lambs in their first year. This was the offering of Abidan son of Gideoni.

⁶⁶ On the tenth day, was the leader of Dan's descendants, Ahiezer son of Ammishaddai. ⁶⁷ His offering was one silver bowl weighing one hundred and thirty (shekels), one silver sprinkling basin (weighing) seventy shekels, according to the shekel (measurement used for) holy (items), both filled with fine flour mixed with olive oil for a meal-offering; ⁶⁸ one spoon (weighing) ten gold (shekels) filled with incense; ⁶⁹ one (outstanding) young bull, one ram and one lamb in its first year for a burnt-offering; ⁷⁰ one young male goat for a sin-offering. ⁷¹ For a peace-offering: two oxen, five rams, five male goats, and five lambs in their first year. This was the offering of Ahiezer son of Ammishaddai.

⁷² On the eleventh day, was the leader of Asher's descendants, Pagiel son of Ochran. ⁷³ His offering was one silver bowl weighing one hundred and thirty (shekels), one silver sprinkling basin (weighing) seventy shekels, according to the shekel (measurement used for) holy (items), both filled with fine flour mixed with olive oil for a meal-offering; ⁷⁴ one spoon (weighing) ten gold (shekels) filled with incense; ⁷⁵ one (outstanding) young bull, one ram and one lamb in its first year for a burnt-offering; ⁷⁶ one young male goat for a sin-offering. ⁷⁷ For a peace-offering: two oxen, five rams, five male goats, and five lambs in their first year. This was the offering of Pagiel son of Ochran.

⁷⁸ On the twelfth day, was the leader of Naphtali's descendants, Ahira son of Enan. ⁷⁹ His offering was one silver bowl weighing one hundred and thirty (shekels); one silver sprinkling basin (weighing) seventy shekels, according to the shekel (measurement used for) holy (items), both filled with fine flour mixed with olive oil for a meal-offering; ⁸⁰ one spoon (weighing) ten gold (shekels) filled with

נשא   במדבר ז:פ-פט

81 קָטֹרֶת: פַּ֣ר אֶחָ֞ד בֶּן־בָּקָ֗ר אַ֧יִל אֶחָ֛ד כֶּֽבֶשׂ־אֶחָ֥ד בֶּן־שְׁנָת֖וֹ לְעֹלָֽה: 82 שְׂעִיר־עִזִּ֥ים אֶחָ֖ד לְחַטָּֽאת: 83 וּלְזֶ֣בַח הַשְּׁלָמִים֮ בָּקָ֣ר שְׁנַ֒יִם֒ אֵילִ֤ם חֲמִשָּׁה֙ עַתּוּדִ֣ים חֲמִשָּׁ֔ה כְּבָשִׂ֥ים בְּנֵֽי־שָׁנָ֖ה חֲמִשָּׁ֑ה זֶ֛ה קָרְבַּ֥ן אֲחִירַ֖ע בֶּן־עֵינָֽן: פ [SEVENTH READING] 84 זֹ֣את ׀ חֲנֻכַּ֣ת הַמִּזְבֵּ֗חַ בְּיוֹם֙ הִמָּשַׁ֣ח אֹת֔וֹ מֵאֵ֖ת נְשִׂיאֵ֣י יִשְׂרָאֵ֑ל קַעֲרֹ֨ת כֶּ֜סֶף שְׁתֵּ֣ים עֶשְׂרֵ֗ה מִֽזְרְקֵי־כֶ֙סֶף֙ שְׁנֵ֣ים עָשָׂ֔ר כַּפּ֥וֹת זָהָ֖ב שְׁתֵּ֥ים עֶשְׂרֵֽה: 85 שְׁלֹשִׁ֣ים וּמֵאָ֗ה הַקְּעָרָ֤ה הָֽאַחַת֙ כֶּ֔סֶף וְשִׁבְעִ֖ים הַמִּזְרָ֣ק הָאֶחָ֑ד כֹּ֚ל כֶּ֣סֶף הַכֵּלִ֔ים אַלְפַּ֥יִם וְאַרְבַּע־מֵא֖וֹת בְּשֶׁ֥קֶל הַקֹּֽדֶשׁ: 86 כַּפּוֹת֩ זָהָ֨ב שְׁתֵּים־עֶשְׂרֵ֜ה מְלֵאֹ֣ת קְטֹ֗רֶת עֲשָׂרָ֧ה עֲשָׂרָ֛ה הַכַּ֖ף בְּשֶׁ֣קֶל הַקֹּ֑דֶשׁ כָּל־זְהַ֥ב הַכַּפּ֖וֹת עֶשְׂרִ֥ים וּמֵאָֽה: 87 [MAFTIR] כָּל־הַבָּקָ֨ר לָעֹלָ֜ה שְׁנֵ֧ים עָשָׂ֣ר פָּרִ֗ים אֵילִ֤ם שְׁנֵים־עָשָׂר֙ כְּבָשִׂ֧ים בְּנֵֽי־שָׁנָ֛ה שְׁנֵ֥ים עָשָׂ֖ר וּמִנְחָתָ֑ם וּשְׂעִירֵ֥י עִזִּ֛ים שְׁנֵ֥ים עָשָׂ֖ר לְחַטָּֽאת: 88 וְכֹ֞ל בְּקַ֣ר ׀ זֶ֣בַח הַשְּׁלָמִ֗ים עֶשְׂרִ֣ים וְאַרְבָּעָה֮ פָּרִים֒ אֵילִ֤ם שִׁשִּׁים֙ עַתֻּדִ֣ים שִׁשִּׁ֔ים כְּבָשִׂ֥ים בְּנֵי־שָׁנָ֖ה שִׁשִּׁ֑ים זֹ֚את חֲנֻכַּ֣ת הַמִּזְבֵּ֔חַ אַחֲרֵ֖י הִמָּשַׁ֥ח אֹתֽוֹ: 89 וּבְבֹ֨א מֹשֶׁ֜ה אֶל־אֹ֣הֶל מוֹעֵד֮ לְדַבֵּ֣ר אִתּוֹ֒ וַיִּשְׁמַ֨ע אֶת־הַקּ֜וֹל מִדַּבֵּ֣ר אֵלָ֗יו מֵעַ֤ל הַכַּפֹּ֙רֶת֙ אֲשֶׁר֙ עַל־אֲרֹ֣ן הָעֵדֻ֔ת מִבֵּ֖ין שְׁנֵ֣י הַכְּרֻבִ֑ים וַיְדַבֵּ֖ר אֵלָֽיו: פ פ פ

קע"ו פסוקים, עמו"ס סימן. עמינד"ב סימן.

---

89. He would hear the voice. This was one of the differences between the prophecy of Moses and the other prophets. Others received prophecy in a dream or vision, but Moses would prophesy while he was awake and standing, as the verse says, *"When Moses would come into the Tent of Meeting to speak with (God), he would hear the voice speaking to him"* (Maimonides, 12th century).

He spoke to him. After stating, *"He would hear the voice speaking to him,"* why does the verse repeat, *"He spoke to him"*?

The words *"He spoke to him"* (i.e. to Moses) indicate that Aaron was excluded from hearing the Divine voice.

From the words, *"He would hear the voice,"* one might think it was a soft voice. Therefore, Scripture stresses that it was *"the voice,"* the same voice which spoke with him at Sinai. But when it reached the entrance, it stopped and did not go outside the Tent of Meeting (Rashi, 11th century).

numbers 7:80–89 naso'

incense; [81] one (outstanding) young bull, one ram and one lamb in its first year for a burnt-offering; [82] one young male goat for a sin-offering. [83] For a peace-offering: two oxen, five rams, five male goats, and five lambs in their first year. This was the offering of Ahira son of Enan.

[SEVENTH READING] [84] This was the (total) dedication-offering of the altar from the leaders, on the day it was anointed:

— (There were) twelve silver bowls, twelve silver basins and twelve gold spoons. [85] The weight of each silver bowl was one hundred and thirty (shekels), and that of each basin was seventy (shekels). All the silver of the items weighed in total: two thousand, four hundred (shekels), according to the shekel (measurement used for) holy (items).

— [86] (There were) twelve gold spoons filled with incense, each spoon weighing ten (shekels), according to the shekel (measurement used for) holy (items). All the gold spoons totaled one hundred and twenty shekels.

— [MAFTIR] [87] The total of the cattle for the burnt-offerings was twelve bulls, twelve rams, and twelve lambs in their first year with their meal-offerings.

— (There were) twelve young male goats for sin-offerings.

— [88] The total of cattle for the peace-offerings was twenty four-oxen, sixty rams, sixty male goats, and sixty lambs in their first year.

This was the (total) dedication offering for the altar, (brought) after it was anointed.

Divine Communication with Moses

[89] When Moses would come into the Tent of Meeting to speak with (God), he would hear the (same) voice (he heard at Sinai) speaking to him from between the two cherubim, above the covering which was over the Ark of Testimony. (In this fashion) He spoke to him.

The *Haftarah* for *Naso'* is on page 1371.

---

84. On the day it was anointed. Rabbi Yudan said, "Surely only one bowl, one basin and one spoon were offered *'on the day* it was anointed' (the first of *Nisan*)? Why does the Torah state that there were *'Twelve* silver bowls, *twelve* silver basins and *twelve* gold spoons' offered on this day? Because Scripture considers it as if they had all offered on the first day, and they had all offered on the last day" (*Numbers Rabbah*).

On the last day the altar became dedicated in *actual fact*, so we might think that since only one of the tribes merited to bring their offerings on the last day, only one of the twelve spiritual paths which the tribes represent is really relevant in the actual worship of God. To counteract this notion, the *Midrash* states, *"It was as if they had all offered on the last day."* We cannot relegate any of the tribes' motifs to the theoretical or purely spiritual (*Rabbi Menahem Mendel Schneerson, 20th century*).

Firing up the lamps represents finding the **switch** or **button** within every one of us—igniting the **fiery love** of God which lies **dormant** in the soul, to become a self-sufficient **powerhouse** of **enthusiasm for Judaism.**

BE-HA'ALOTEKHA
בהעלותך

KINDLING OF CANDELABRUM	8:1-4
INAUGURATION OF LEVITES	8:5-26
PASSOVER OFFERING	9:1-14
METHOD OF DESERT JOURNEYS	9:15 - 10:36
COMPLAINTS AND REBUKE	11:1-35
MIRIAM'S CRITICISM OF MOSES	12:1-16

NAME
Be-Ha'alotekha

MEANING
"When you fire up"

LINES IN TORAH SCROLL
240

PARASHIYYOT
11 open; 5 closed

VERSES
136

WORDS
1840

LETTERS
7055

MITZVOT
3 positive; 2 prohibitions

DATE
Nisan-Sivan, 2449

LOCATION
Sinai Desert, desert of Paran, Taberah, Kibroth-hattaavah and Hazeroth

KEY PEOPLE
Moses, Aaron, Miriam, Jethro, Elders, Levites, Eldad, Medad

MASORETIC FEATURES
10:35-36 is "book-ended" by two backward letter *nun*s

CHARACTER PROFILE

NAME
Miriam ("bitterness")

PARENTS
Amram and Jochebed

HUSBAND
Caleb

SIBLINGS
Moses and Aaron

CHILDREN
Hur

LIFE SPAN
around 126 years

DATE OF PASSING
10 *Nisan*

ACHIEVEMENTS
Prophesied birth of the redeemer (Moses); defied Pharaoh's order to kill Jewish boys; watched over Moses when he was in the Nile; wellspring in the desert flowed in her merit

KNOWN FOR
Leading the Jewish women in song and dance after the splitting of the Reed Sea; the camp waited for her to recover for seven days before traveling

BURIAL PLACE
Kadesh in the desert of Zin

SECOND CHANCE

It is never too late to change. Although there were people who were ritually impure at the correct time to offer the Passover sacrifice, God gave them a second chance, enabling them to fulfil the commandment one month later (9:6-14).

FOLLOWING GOD

During their sojourn in the desert, the people traveled "according to the word of God." Whether a short or long journey or encampment, they followed the cloud without complaint (9:23).

GOSSIP

Miriam spoke out of love for her brother, but she was still punished. Talking about others is very harmful, especially when it is intended derogatorily (12:1-16).

במדבר ח:א-ו | בהעלותך

ח 1 וַיְדַבֵּר יְהֹוָה אֶל־מֹשֶׁה לֵּאמֹר: 2 דַּבֵּר אֶל־אַהֲרֹן וְאָמַרְתָּ אֵלָיו בְּהַעֲלֹתְךָ אֶת־הַנֵּרֹת אֶל־מוּל פְּנֵי הַמְּנוֹרָה יָאִירוּ שִׁבְעַת הַנֵּרוֹת: 3 וַיַּעַשׂ כֵּן אַהֲרֹן אֶל־מוּל פְּנֵי הַמְּנוֹרָה הֶעֱלָה נֵרֹתֶיהָ כַּאֲשֶׁר צִוָּה יְהֹוָה אֶת־מֹשֶׁה: 4 וְזֶה מַעֲשֵׂה הַמְּנֹרָה מִקְשָׁה זָהָב עַד־יְרֵכָהּ עַד־פִּרְחָהּ מִקְשָׁה הִוא כַּמַּרְאֶה אֲשֶׁר הֶרְאָה יְהֹוָה אֶת־מֹשֶׁה כֵּן עָשָׂה אֶת־הַמְּנֹרָה: פ 5 וַיְדַבֵּר יְהֹוָה אֶל־מֹשֶׁה לֵּאמֹר: 6 קַח אֶת־הַלְוִיִּם מִתּוֹךְ בְּנֵי יִשְׂרָאֵל וְטִהַרְתָּ אֹתָם:

This we can also learn from Aaron's kindling of the lamps, which had to be *"until the flame rises by itself"* (*Rashi* to v. 2). In other words, we should continue to be an inspiration until each individual becomes a self-sufficient "powerhouse" of enthusiasm for himself (*Rabbi Menahem Mendel Schneerson, 20th century*).

3. Aaron did so. This tells the praise of Aaron, that he did not change anything he had heard from God (*Rashi, 11th century*).

Why is it important to emphasize that Aaron did as he was commanded when lighting the candelabrum? Would anyone think that a righteous man like Aaron would disrespect God's command?

Usually, a person who does a commandment for the first time is very enthusiastic, but after much repetition his enthusiasm may wane. The Torah praises Aaron because, throughout the many years that he performed the service, *his level of enthusiasm did not change.* Aaron's holy service never became routine; he performed it consistently, albeit with the same intensity as a first-time commandment (*Rabbi Judah Aryeh Leib Alter of Gur, 19th century*).

"He did not change." The fact that Aaron had become great did not change his character for the worse. He remained humble and modest, as before (*Rabbi Simḥah Bunem of Przysucha, 18th–19th century*).

4. This is the construction method of the candelabrum: (It is) a hammered work of gold (from a single piece of metal). The candelabrum was actually fashioned by God Himself. Moses cast a block of gold into the fire and a candelabrum emerged (*Midrash Tanḥuma*).

Moses had difficulty with the candelabrum, so God showed an image of it to him, pointing with His finger. That is why the verse states, *"This is the construction method"* (*Sifrei*).

God wants all of His work to include some participation on the part of man. The candelabrum was completed by God only after Moses had banged it with a hammer. Therefore it was necessary for Moses to understand its design, so he would know precisely where to hammer (*Rabbi Judah Loew b. Bezalel of Prague, 16th century*).

6. Persuade the Levites ... purify them. Why does the inauguration of the Levites follow the kindling of the candelabrum?

We find that twelve tribes offered sacrifices to dedicate the altar (7:10ff.), but the tribe of Levi offered nothing at all. So they were pained, and they said, "Why have we been excluded from bringing offerings to dedicate the altar?"

parashat be-haʿalotekha

Kindling of the Candelabrum

8 ¹ God spoke to Moses, saying: ² Speak to Aaron and say to him: "When you fire up the lamps (of the candelabrum, the wicks should be angled so that) the seven lamps cast their light towards the center (lamp) of the candelabrum." ³ Aaron did so (precisely). He fired up the lamps (so their wicks were) towards the center (lamp) of the candelabrum, as God had commanded Moses.

⁴ This is the construction method of the candelabrum: (It is) a hammered work of gold (from a single piece of metal). It is a (single) hammered piece from its (large) base to its (delicate) flowers.

He constructed the candelabrum resembling the vision that God had shown Moses (on Mount Sinai).

Inauguration of the Levites

⁵ God spoke to Moses, saying: ⁶ "Persuade the Levites (by telling them how fortunate they are to have been chosen as God's attendants) from among (all) the

---

8:2 When you fire up. *"Man's soul is a lamp of God"* (*Proverbs* 20:27)—the soul is a part of and is connected with God. But in order to enjoy its great benefits, the correct "switch" must be found, or the proper "button" pushed.

This message is conveyed by the opening of our Torah portion, where God instructs Aaron to *"Fire up the lamps."* Firing up the lamps represents finding the "switch" or "button" within every one of us, igniting the fiery love of God which lies dormant in the soul. And Aaron the priest represents the spiritual leaders of every generation who are empowered by God with special talents to find the "switch" in each person to help that person become connected with his or her own internal spiritual "powerhouse."

While it was the High Priest who would traditionally light the candelabrum, the act would nevertheless be valid if done by a non-priest (*Babylonian Talmud, Yoma* 24b). From this we learn that the task of igniting the "lamp" within others cannot be left to the leaders alone. Every person (even a "non-priest") has a responsibility to try to find the "switch" in the soul of his or her fellow. We can never know what will make the connection—perhaps just one word will open up the well or inner fountain of the soul.

How long must we continue to "ignite" another's soul, once the person appears already to be inspired?

---

kabbalah bites

8:2 In this world we suffer from a spiritual moodiness which the Kabbalists called *"ratzo' va-shov"* (*"running*, followed by *returning"*— after *Ezekiel* 1:14).

Due to their close proximity to the Divine, the inhabitants of the upper worlds are capable of receiving emanation uninterruptedly. But down here, the flow is constantly interrupted, pulsating like blood through our arteries, so there is a constant need to refresh ourselves with renewed illumination and vitality.

This is the inner meaning of the command to kindle the candelabrum regularly.

במדבר ח:ז-יח

בהעלותך

7 וְכֹה־תַעֲשֶׂה לָהֶם לְטַהֲרָם הַזֵּה עֲלֵיהֶם מֵי חַטָּאת וְהֶעֱבִירוּ תַעַר עַל־כָּל־בְּשָׂרָם וְכִבְּסוּ בִגְדֵיהֶם וְהִטֶּהָרוּ: 8 וְלָקְחוּ פַּר בֶּן־בָּקָר וּמִנְחָתוֹ סֹלֶת בְּלוּלָה בַשָּׁמֶן וּפַר־שֵׁנִי בֶן־בָּקָר תִּקַּח לְחַטָּאת: 9 וְהִקְרַבְתָּ אֶת־הַלְוִיִּם לִפְנֵי אֹהֶל מוֹעֵד וְהִקְהַלְתָּ אֶת־כָּל־עֲדַת בְּנֵי יִשְׂרָאֵל: 10 וְהִקְרַבְתָּ אֶת־הַלְוִיִּם לִפְנֵי יְהֹוָה וְסָמְכוּ בְנֵי־יִשְׂרָאֵל אֶת־יְדֵיהֶם עַל־הַלְוִיִּם: 11 וְהֵנִיף אַהֲרֹן אֶת־הַלְוִיִּם תְּנוּפָה לִפְנֵי יְהֹוָה מֵאֵת בְּנֵי יִשְׂרָאֵל וְהָיוּ לַעֲבֹד אֶת־עֲבֹדַת יְהֹוָה: 12 וְהַלְוִיִּם יִסְמְכוּ אֶת־יְדֵיהֶם עַל רֹאשׁ הַפָּרִים וַעֲשֵׂה אֶת־הָאֶחָד חַטָּאת וְאֶת־הָאֶחָד עֹלָה לַיהֹוָה לְכַפֵּר עַל־הַלְוִיִּם: 13 וְהַעֲמַדְתָּ אֶת־הַלְוִיִּם לִפְנֵי אַהֲרֹן וְלִפְנֵי בָנָיו וְהֵנַפְתָּ אֹתָם תְּנוּפָה לַיהֹוָה: 14 וְהִבְדַּלְתָּ אֶת־הַלְוִיִּם מִתּוֹךְ בְּנֵי יִשְׂרָאֵל וְהָיוּ לִי הַלְוִיִּם: 15 [SECOND READING] וְאַחֲרֵי־כֵן יָבֹאוּ הַלְוִיִּם לַעֲבֹד אֶת־אֹהֶל מוֹעֵד וְטִהַרְתָּ אֹתָם וְהֵנַפְתָּ אֹתָם תְּנוּפָה: 16 כִּי נְתֻנִים נְתֻנִים הֵמָּה לִי מִתּוֹךְ בְּנֵי יִשְׂרָאֵל תַּחַת פִּטְרַת כָּל־רֶחֶם בְּכוֹר כֹּל מִבְּנֵי יִשְׂרָאֵל לָקַחְתִּי אֹתָם לִי: 17 כִּי לִי כָל־בְּכוֹר בִּבְנֵי יִשְׂרָאֵל בָּאָדָם וּבַבְּהֵמָה בְּיוֹם הַכֹּתִי כָל־בְּכוֹר בְּאֶרֶץ מִצְרַיִם הִקְדַּשְׁתִּי אֹתָם לִי: 18 וָאֶקַּח אֶת־הַלְוִיִּם תַּחַת כָּל־בְּכוֹר בִּבְנֵי יִשְׂרָאֵל:

---

more than the others, but the king did not invite him with the others. The person was pained, and he said, "Perhaps I have no place in the king's heart at all, for he did not invite me to even one of these feasts."

After the days of feasting were over, the king called his beloved one and said to him, "I made a feast for all the people of my country. Now I am making a feast for you alone. Why? Because you are my beloved!"

Likewise with God, the King of kings, we find that the twelve tribes offered sacrifices to dedicate the altar, and that God accepted them all—as the verse states, *"Take (the gifts) from them!"* (7:5)—but the tribe of Levi did not offer. After the dedication of the altar was over, God said to Aaron and his sons, "All the tribes made a dedication, but your tribe did not!" Therefore, the Torah continues, *"Speak to Aaron and say to him: 'When you fire up the lamps, etc.'"* (v. 1-2), and afterwards, *"Persuade the Levites, etc."* (v. 6). This was the exclusive "feast" for the tribe of Levi (*Numbers Rabbah*).

numbers 8:6–18   be-ha'alotekha

children of Israel." Then you should purify them (from the ritual impurity which comes through contact with the dead). ⁷ This is what you should do to them to purify them:

- Sprinkle them with the purifying water (of the ashes of the Red Heifer), pass a razor over their entire body and they should wash their clothes. Then they will be purified.

(They should then be inaugurated as follows:)

- ⁸ They should take a young bull (as a burnt-offering, to atone for the communal idol-worship of the Golden Calf in which the Levites did not participate), with its (accompanying) meal-offering of fine flour mixed with oil.

- Take a second (offering to atone for the same sin), a young bull as a sin-offering.

- ⁹ Bring the Levites in front of the Tent of Meeting and gather the entire congregation of the children of Israel.

- ¹⁰ You should bring the Levites before God, and the children of Israel should lay their hands upon the Levites (because the Levites are like an "offering" of atonement for the entire community).

- ¹¹ Aaron should wave the Levites (from the family of Kohath) as a wave-offering before God on behalf of the children of Israel, so that they may perform God's service (of carrying the holy items).

- ¹² The Levites should lay their hands on the bulls' heads. Then one should be offered as a sin-offering and one as a burnt-offering to God, to atone for the Levites.

- ¹³ You should present the Levites (from the family of Gershon) before Aaron and his sons, and wave them as a wave-offering before God (since they will carry parts of the Tabernacle).

¹⁴ (In this way) you will set apart the Levites from among the children of Israel, and the Levites will become Mine. [SECOND READING] ¹⁵ Following this, the Levites will come to serve in the Tent of Meeting.

- You should (also) purify (the family of Merari) and wave them as a wave-offering.

¹⁶ For they are dedicated to Me from among the children of Israel (to carry the Tabernacle, and) dedicated (to sing in the Tabernacle). I have taken them for Myself instead of the firstborn of Israel, those who emerge first from the womb. ¹⁷ For all the firstborn among the children of Israel, (both) people and animals, (were originally chosen as) Mine on the day I killed all the firstborn in the land of Egypt. (At that time) I sanctified them for Myself. ¹⁸ But (now) I took the Levites

We can understand this by way of the following analogy. There was once a king who made a banquet, and he invited different groups of people. There was one person that he loved much

במדבר ח:יט-כו | בהעלותך

19 וָאֶתְּנָ֨ה אֶת־הַלְוִיִּ֜ם נְתֻנִ֣ים ׀ לְאַהֲרֹ֣ן וּלְבָנָ֗יו מִתּוֹךְ֮ בְּנֵ֣י יִשְׂרָאֵל֒ לַעֲבֹ֞ד אֶת־עֲבֹדַ֤ת בְּנֵֽי־יִשְׂרָאֵל֙ בְּאֹ֣הֶל מוֹעֵ֔ד וּלְכַפֵּ֖ר עַל־בְּנֵ֣י יִשְׂרָאֵ֑ל וְלֹ֨א יִהְיֶ֜ה בִּבְנֵ֤י יִשְׂרָאֵל֙ נֶ֔גֶף בְּגֶ֥שֶׁת בְּנֵֽי־יִשְׂרָאֵ֖ל אֶל־הַקֹּֽדֶשׁ׃ 20 וַיַּ֨עַשׂ מֹשֶׁ֧ה וְאַהֲרֹ֛ן וְכׇל־עֲדַ֥ת בְּנֵי־יִשְׂרָאֵ֖ל לַלְוִיִּ֑ם כְּ֠כֹ֠ל אֲשֶׁר־צִוָּ֨ה יְהֹוָ֤ה אֶת־מֹשֶׁה֙ לַלְוִיִּ֔ם כֵּן־עָשׂ֥וּ לָהֶ֖ם בְּנֵ֥י יִשְׂרָאֵֽל׃ 21 וַיִּֽתְחַטְּא֣וּ הַלְוִיִּ֗ם וַֽיְכַבְּסוּ֙ בִּגְדֵיהֶ֔ם וַיָּ֨נֶף אַהֲרֹ֥ן אֹתָ֛ם תְּנוּפָ֖ה לִפְנֵ֣י יְהֹוָ֑ה וַיְכַפֵּ֧ר עֲלֵיהֶ֛ם אַהֲרֹ֖ן לְטַהֲרָֽם׃ 22 וְאַחֲרֵי־כֵ֞ן בָּ֣אוּ הַלְוִיִּ֗ם לַעֲבֹ֤ד אֶת־עֲבֹֽדָתָם֙ בְּאֹ֣הֶל מוֹעֵ֔ד לִפְנֵ֥י אַהֲרֹ֖ן וְלִפְנֵ֣י בָנָ֑יו כַּאֲשֶׁר֩ צִוָּ֨ה יְהֹוָ֤ה אֶת־מֹשֶׁה֙ עַל־הַלְוִיִּ֔ם כֵּ֖ן עָשׂ֥וּ לָהֶֽם׃ ס 23 וַיְדַבֵּ֥ר יְהֹוָ֖ה אֶל־מֹשֶׁ֥ה לֵּאמֹֽר׃ 24 זֹ֖את אֲשֶׁ֣ר לַלְוִיִּ֑ם מִבֶּן֩ חָמֵ֨שׁ וְעֶשְׂרִ֤ים שָׁנָה֙ וָמַ֔עְלָה יָבוֹא֙ לִצְבֹ֣א צָבָ֔א בַּעֲבֹדַ֖ת אֹ֥הֶל מוֹעֵֽד׃ 25 וּמִבֶּן֙ חֲמִשִּׁ֣ים שָׁנָ֔ה יָשׁ֖וּב מִצְּבָ֣א הָעֲבֹדָ֑ה וְלֹ֥א יַעֲבֹ֖ד עֽוֹד׃ 26 וְשֵׁרֵ֨ת אֶת־אֶחָ֜יו בְּאֹ֤הֶל מוֹעֵד֙ לִשְׁמֹ֣ר מִשְׁמֶ֔רֶת וַעֲבֹדָ֖ה לֹ֣א יַעֲבֹ֑ד כָּ֛כָה תַּעֲשֶׂ֥ה לַלְוִיִּ֖ם בְּמִשְׁמְרֹתָֽם׃ פ

But plague and tragedy ought not be the only inspiration of prayer. They should pray to God and give charity at all times. In fact, the subject of their prayers should be that they should never need to *"approach the Sanctuary"* in distress (*Rabbi Meir Horowitz of Dzieckowitz, 19th century*).

spiritual vitamin

> Education, in general, should not be limited to the acquisition of knowledge and preparation for a career, or in common parlance, "to make a better living." We must think in terms of a "better life," not only for the individual, but also for society as a whole.
>
> The educational system must, therefore, pay more attention, indeed, the main attention, to the building of character, with emphasis on moral and ethical values.

numbers 8:18–26 — be-haʿalotekha

instead of all the firstborn of the children of Israel (because the firstborn worshiped the Golden Calf).

[19] I have given the Levites, from among the children of Israel, as a gift to Aaron and his sons, to carry out the service in the Tent of Meeting for the children of Israel, and to atone on behalf of the children of Israel. The children of Israel will (thus not need to) approach the Sanctuary (and consequently) they will not be afflicted by a plague."

[20] Moses, Aaron, and the entire congregation of Israel did this to the Levites. The children of Israel did all that God had instructed Moses regarding the Levites:

[21] The Levites cleansed themselves and washed their clothes. Aaron waved them as a wave-offering before God. Aaron atoned for them (with the sin-offering) which purified them. [22] After that, the Levites came to perform their service in the Tent of Meeting, in the presence of Aaron and his sons. Whatever God had commanded Moses regarding the Levites they (willingly) did to them.

Disqualifications of the Levites

[23] God spoke to Moses, saying: [24] This is (the rule of disqualification) for the Levites:

- He is qualified to serve in the Tent of Meeting from the age of twenty-five years and upwards.

- [25] He is withdrawn from those qualified to work from the age of fifty, and he may serve no longer. [26] (At this age) he may (position himself around) the Tent of Meeting to help his brothers guard the duty (of erecting and dismantling the Tent), but he may not perform the service.

This is (the law of how) the Levites should carry out their duties.

---

19. I have given the Levites. The words *"The children of Israel"* are written five times in this verse, making known God's affection for them—they are repeated in one verse five times corresponding to the five books of the Torah (*Rashi, 11th century*).

Since the Levites were the only ones chosen to perform the service in the Tabernacle, the rest of the people may have been distressed at not having been selected. To avert such a sentiment, the Torah emphasizes here the affection in which all the children of Israel are held (*Rabbi Isaac Meir Alter of Gur, 19th century*).

Just as each book of the Torah is its own independent unit, joined together to form one, indivisible Torah, so too, the children of Israel, although divided into priests, Levites, and Israelites, are one cohesive, indivisible nation (*Rabbi Alexander Zusya Friedman, 20th century*).

The children of Israel will approach the Sanctuary and they will not be afflicted by a plague. If tragedy or disease struck, people would *"approach the Sanctuary"* in prayer, give generously to charity, and improve their actions.

במדבר ט:א-ז — בהעלותך

א וַיְדַבֵּ֣ר יְהֹוָ֣ה אֶל־מֹשֶׁ֣ה בְמִדְבַּר־סִ֠ינַ֠י בַּשָּׁנָ֨ה הַשֵּׁנִ֜ית לְצֵאתָ֨ם מֵאֶ֧רֶץ מִצְרַ֛יִם בַּחֹ֥דֶשׁ הָרִאשׁ֖וֹן לֵאמֹֽר: ב וְיַעֲשׂ֧וּ בְנֵֽי־יִשְׂרָאֵ֛ל אֶת־הַפָּ֖סַח בְּמֽוֹעֲדֽוֹ: ג בְּאַרְבָּעָ֣ה עָשָׂר־י֠וֹם בַּחֹ֨דֶשׁ הַזֶּ֜ה בֵּ֧ין הָֽעַרְבַּ֛יִם תַּעֲשׂ֥וּ אֹת֖וֹ בְּמֹֽעֲד֑וֹ כְּכׇל־חֻקֹּתָ֥יו וּכְכׇל־מִשְׁפָּטָ֖יו תַּעֲשׂ֥וּ אֹתֽוֹ: ד וַיְדַבֵּ֥ר מֹשֶׁ֛ה אֶל־בְּנֵ֥י יִשְׂרָאֵ֖ל לַעֲשֹׂ֥ת הַפָּֽסַח: ה וַיַּעֲשׂ֣וּ אֶת־הַפֶּ֡סַח בָּרִאשׁ֡וֹן בְּאַרְבָּעָה֩ עָשָׂ֨ר י֥וֹם לַחֹ֛דֶשׁ בֵּ֥ין הָעַרְבַּ֖יִם בְּמִדְבַּ֣ר סִינָ֑י כְּ֠כֹ֠ל אֲשֶׁ֨ר צִוָּ֤ה יְהֹוָה֙ אֶת־מֹשֶׁ֔ה כֵּ֥ן עָשׂ֖וּ בְּנֵ֥י יִשְׂרָאֵֽל: ו וַיְהִ֣י אֲנָשִׁ֗ים אֲשֶׁ֨ר הָי֤וּ טְמֵאִים֙ לְנֶ֣פֶשׁ אָדָ֔ם וְלֹא־יָכְל֥וּ לַעֲשֹׂת־הַפֶּ֖סַח בַּיּ֣וֹם הַה֑וּא וַיִּקְרְב֞וּ לִפְנֵ֥י מֹשֶׁ֛ה וְלִפְנֵ֥י אַהֲרֹ֖ן בַּיּ֥וֹם הַהֽוּא: ז וַיֹּ֠אמְר֠וּ הָאֲנָשִׁ֤ים הָהֵ֙מָּה֙ אֵלָ֔יו אֲנַ֣חְנוּ טְמֵאִ֔ים לְנֶ֖פֶשׁ אָדָ֑ם לָ֣מָּה נִגָּרַ֗ע לְבִלְתִּ֨י הַקְרִ֜ב

---

2. The children of Israel should make the Passover (lamb) in its appointed time. At the time the children of Israel were commanded to offer this sacrifice, they numbered six hundred thousand men over the age of twenty.

In comparison, there were only three priests: Aaron and his two sons (Nadab and Abihu had already died). Without any outside help, these three priests had to offer up tens of thousands of sacrifices within a very short time frame—a single afternoon.

To draw our attention to this accomplishment, the Torah states that the correct time for the Paschal lamb was *"on the afternoon of the fourteenth"* (v. 3), and then repeats this information again: *"They made the Passover (lamb) ... on the afternoon of the fourteenth"* (v. 5), emphasizing the incredible feat (*Rabbi Meir Simḥah of Dvinsk, 19th–20th century*).

7. Why should we be the losers? The people were so pained at their inability to perform the Passover-offering that they cried out to Moses, begging for a chance to fulfil this special rite. They were so deeply saddened even after missing the opportunity a single time.

How much more so, now that nearly two millennia have passed since the Temple was destroyed and we have been unable to offer sacrifices, must we cry out with all our might,

---

kabbalah bites

9:7 Who were these men? They were Mishael and Elzaphan, who had become ritually impure as a result of burying Nadab and Abihu. (*Babylonian Talmud, Sukkah* 25b; see *Leviticus* 10:4 ff.)

As mentioned above (3:2), Nadab and Abihu were a reincarnation of Cain, who had the lowest part of Adam's soul, the *nefesh*. Mishael and Elzaphan hinted to this in their complaint: "We are ritually impure from a dead person (*nefesh Adam*)," i.e., we became ritually impure through attending to people who possessed the *nefesh* of Adam (see above, *Leviticus* 10:6).

numbers 9:1–7 — be-haʿalotekha

The Passover-Offering in the Desert

9 [THIRD READING] ¹ God spoke to Moses in the Sinai Desert, in the second year of their exodus from the land of Egypt, in the first month, saying:

❖ ² "The children of Israel should make the Passover (lamb) in its appointed time, ³ on the afternoon of the fourteenth of this month."

"You should make it in its appointed time (even if this coincides with the Sabbath, and even if the majority of people or the priests themselves are in a state of ritual impurity)."

❖ "Make it in accordance with all its laws (of preparation) and all its (accompanying) laws."

⁴ Moses spoke to the children of Israel (instructing them) to make the Passover (lamb). ⁵ They made the Passover (lamb) in the first month, on the afternoon of the fourteenth day of the month, in the Sinai Desert, in accordance with everything that God had commanded Moses. The children of Israel did so (precisely).

The Second Passover-Offering

⁶ There were men who were ritually impure (due to contact with) a dead person, and could not make the Passover (lamb) on that day, so they came before Moses and before Aaron on that day. ⁷ Those men said to him, "We are ritually impure (due to contact with) a dead person. Why should we be the losers? We've been prevented from offering God's sacrifice in its appointed time, with all the children of Israel!

Food for thought

1. How ready are you to listen to people's complaints?

2. Have you ever suffered the pain of exclusion?

3. Is there a spiritual experience at which you would desire a second chance?

9:1 In the first month. The passage at the beginning of this book was not said until *Iyyar*, the second month. From this you learn that the Torah does not follow a chronological order.

Why did the *Book of Numbers* not open with this passage? Because it is a disgrace that throughout the forty years the children of Israel were in the desert, they only brought this one Passover sacrifice (*Rashi, 11th century*).

The disgrace for the Jewish people was their inability to offer the Passover sacrifice in the desert because they were uncircumcised, and the law states that an uncircumcised person may not bring the Passover-offering (*Exodus* 12:48). The reason why they were uncircumcised was, as the Talmud states, the difficult climatic conditions in the desert that made circumcision prohibitive, due to the risk to life involved (*Babylonian Talmud, Yevamot* 72a; *Rabbi Obadiah b. Abraham of Bertinoro, 15th century*).

אֶת־קָרְבַּן יְהֹוָה בְּמֹעֲדוֹ בְּתוֹךְ בְּנֵי יִשְׂרָאֵל: 8 וַיֹּאמֶר אֲלֵהֶם מֹשֶׁה עִמְדוּ וְאֶשְׁמְעָה מַה־יְצַוֶּה יְהֹוָה לָכֶם: פ 9 וַיְדַבֵּר יְהֹוָה אֶל־מֹשֶׁה לֵּאמֹר: 10 דַּבֵּר אֶל־בְּנֵי יִשְׂרָאֵל לֵאמֹר אִישׁ אִישׁ כִּי־יִהְיֶה טָמֵא | לָנֶפֶשׁ אוֹ בְדֶרֶךְ רְחֹקָה לָכֶם אוֹ לְדֹרֹתֵיכֶם וְעָשָׂה פֶסַח לַיהֹוָה: 11 בַּחֹדֶשׁ הַשֵּׁנִי בְּאַרְבָּעָה עָשָׂר יוֹם בֵּין הָעַרְבַּיִם יַעֲשׂוּ אֹתוֹ עַל־מַצּוֹת וּמְרֹרִים יֹאכְלֻהוּ: 12 לֹא־יַשְׁאִירוּ מִמֶּנּוּ עַד־בֹּקֶר וְעֶצֶם לֹא יִשְׁבְּרוּ־בוֹ כְּכָל־חֻקַּת הַפֶּסַח יַעֲשׂוּ אֹתוֹ: 13 וְהָאִישׁ אֲשֶׁר־הוּא טָהוֹר וּבְדֶרֶךְ לֹא־הָיָה וְחָדַל לַעֲשׂוֹת הַפֶּסַח וְנִכְרְתָה הַנֶּפֶשׁ הַהִוא מֵעַמֶּיהָ כִּי | קָרְבַּן יְהֹוָה לֹא הִקְרִיב בְּמֹעֲדוֹ חֶטְאוֹ יִשָּׂא הָאִישׁ הַהוּא: 14 וְכִי־יָגוּר אִתְּכֶם גֵּר וְעָשָׂה פֶסַח לַיהֹוָה כְּחֻקַּת הַפֶּסַח וּכְמִשְׁפָּטוֹ כֵּן יַעֲשֶׂה חֻקָּה אַחַת יִהְיֶה לָכֶם וְלַגֵּר וּלְאֶזְרַח הָאָרֶץ: ס 15 [FOURTH READING] וּבְיוֹם הָקִים אֶת־הַמִּשְׁכָּן כִּסָּה הֶעָנָן אֶת־הַמִּשְׁכָּן לְאֹהֶל הָעֵדֻת וּבָעֶרֶב יִהְיֶה עַל־הַמִּשְׁכָּן כְּמַרְאֵה־אֵשׁ עַד־

The Second Passover, which is a compensation or correction for a prior shortcoming, represents *the path of repentance*.

Repentance is unique in two respects. (a) Through observing a commandment, you spiritually elevate and refine the physical world with which you come into contact, but you are only able to elevate the permissible and not the forbidden. Through repentance, however, even your *"intentional transgressions are transformed to merits"* (Babylonian Talmud, Yoma 86b).

(b) The spiritual effect of normative observance is gradual and cumulative—it takes many years of persistent effort and loyal adherence to elevate yourself to great spiritual heights. On the other hand, repentance is an instantaneous spiritual "leap" of quantum proportions,

spiritual vitamin

> *"God made man straight, but they sought many accounts"* (Ecclesiastes 7:29). Man often confuses himself with delving, unnecessarily, into inquiries and accounts of things which should be taken for granted and which do not really present any problems. The more intellectual a person is, the more he is inclined to seek "accounts" and, consequently, the more apt he is to get confused.

numbers 9:8–15 — be-ha'alotekha

⁸ Moses said to them, "Wait, and I will hear what God instructs concerning you."

⁹ God spoke to Moses saying: ¹⁰ Speak to the children of Israel, saying:

- Any person who becomes unclean from (contact with) the dead, or is far away, either among you or in future generations, should make a Passover (offering) for God (at a later date).

- ¹¹ They should make it in the second month, on the fourteenth day, in the afternoon.

- They should eat it with unleavened bread and bitter herbs.

- ¹² They should not leave over any (meat) from it until the next morning.

- They should not break any of its bones.

- They should offer it in accordance with all the laws connected with the (regular) Passover (lamb).

- ¹³ But if a man was ritually pure and was not on a journey, yet refrained from making the Passover (lamb), his soul will be cut off from his people, because he did not bring God's offering in its appointed time. That person will bear (the consequence of) his sin.

- ¹⁴ If a convert lives with you, and he makes a Passover (lamb) for God, he should make it in accordance with the laws (of preparation) of the Passover (lamb) and its (accompanying) laws.

- (When a person converts, he does not make a Passover lamb immediately. Rather) you (both) have the same law (concerning when a Passover lamb may be brought, both) the convert and the native-born citizen.

The Divine Signals to Journey and Encamp

[FOURTH READING] ¹⁵ On the day the Tabernacle was erected, the cloud covered the Tabernacle—which was a tent for (the Tablets of) Testimony—and at night, there

---

imploring God for immediate redemption! (*Rabbi Solomon ha-Kohen Rabinowich of Radomsko, 19th century*).

11. They should make it in the second month. One of the significant lessons of the Second Passover is never to despair, even when you have not attained the spiritual heights of others. While all the people are celebrating the Passover at its proper time, and you find yourself "far away," or otherwise unfit to enter the Sanctuary, you are told: Do not despair! Begin your journey towards the Sanctuary, come closer and closer; for you have a special opportunity to celebrate the Second Passover, if you try hard enough (*Rabbi Joseph Isaac Schneersohn of Lubavitch, 20th century*).

They should eat it with unleavened bread and bitter herbs. On the Second Passover you may keep both leavened foods and unleavened bread in the home (*Rashi, 11th century*).

בְּמִדְבַּר ט:ט״ו-כג — בְּהַעֲלֹתְךָ

בֹּקֶר: 16 כֵּן יִהְיֶה תָמִיד הֶעָנָן יְכַסֶּנּוּ וּמַרְאֵה־אֵשׁ לָיְלָה: 17 וּלְפִי הֵעָלֹת הֶעָנָן מֵעַל הָאֹהֶל וְאַחֲרֵי כֵן יִסְעוּ בְּנֵי יִשְׂרָאֵל וּבִמְקוֹם אֲשֶׁר יִשְׁכָּן־שָׁם הֶעָנָן שָׁם יַחֲנוּ בְּנֵי יִשְׂרָאֵל: 18 עַל־פִּי יְהֹוָה יִסְעוּ בְּנֵי יִשְׂרָאֵל וְעַל־פִּי יְהֹוָה יַחֲנוּ כָּל־יְמֵי אֲשֶׁר יִשְׁכֹּן הֶעָנָן עַל־הַמִּשְׁכָּן יַחֲנוּ: 19 וּבְהַאֲרִיךְ הֶעָנָן עַל־הַמִּשְׁכָּן יָמִים רַבִּים וְשָׁמְרוּ בְנֵי־יִשְׂרָאֵל אֶת־מִשְׁמֶרֶת יְהֹוָה וְלֹא יִסָּעוּ: 20 וְיֵשׁ אֲשֶׁר יִהְיֶה הֶעָנָן יָמִים מִסְפָּר עַל־הַמִּשְׁכָּן עַל־פִּי יְהֹוָה יַחֲנוּ וְעַל־פִּי יְהֹוָה יִסָּעוּ: 21 וְיֵשׁ אֲשֶׁר יִהְיֶה הֶעָנָן מֵעֶרֶב עַד־בֹּקֶר וְנַעֲלָה הֶעָנָן בַּבֹּקֶר וְנָסָעוּ אוֹ יוֹמָם וָלַיְלָה וְנַעֲלָה הֶעָנָן וְנָסָעוּ: 22 אוֹ־יֹמַיִם אוֹ־חֹדֶשׁ אוֹ־יָמִים בְּהַאֲרִיךְ הֶעָנָן עַל־הַמִּשְׁכָּן לִשְׁכֹּן עָלָיו יַחֲנוּ בְנֵי־יִשְׂרָאֵל וְלֹא יִסָּעוּ וּבְהֵעָלֹתוֹ יִסָּעוּ: 23 עַל־פִּי יְהֹוָה וְעַל־פִּי יְהֹוָה יִסָּעוּ אֶת־מִשְׁמֶרֶת יְהֹוָה שָׁמָרוּ עַל־פִּי יְהֹוָה בְּיַד־מֹשֶׁה: פ

18. The children of Israel traveled by the word of God, and they encamped by the word of God. This verse is reiterated later in the reverse order, *"They encamped by the word of God and they traveled by the word of God"* (v. 23).

There is a valuable lesson here. You should always mention God's name when talking about what you are doing. Say, "thank God," "with the help of God," "if God wills," etc.

And mention His name when you are about to travel—*"they traveled"*—and when you get to your destination—*"they encamped"* (*Rabbi Isaiah Horowitz, 16th–17th century*).

20. Sometimes, the cloud remained for (just) a few days. It would have been sufficient to say, "When the cloud lingered the people encamped, and when it rose they traveled." The duration of the encampments seems inconsequential.

The purpose of recording the duration of the encampments is to highlight the children of Israel's devotion to God while traveling in the desert. Sometimes the cloud would remain for a long time, but none of the people became impatient and complained. Then there were times when the cloud would lift immediately after they encamped, indicating that they must again resume traveling, yet they did not complain. The people were devoted to following God's lead throughout their journey in the desert, no matter how much inconvenience it caused them (*Rabbi Isaac Abravanel, 15th century*).

22. Whether it was for two days, a month, or a year. Since we are expecting global redemption at every moment, how can we possibly immerse ourselves in the drudgery of everyday life and even make plans for the future?

The answer to this question can be found in the way that the Tabernacle was dismantled and erected in the desert. Often, the Jewish people would stay encamped in one place for a considerable period of time—as much as nineteen years (*Rashi to Deuteronomy* 1:46)— so the need for fully erecting the Tabernacle, with all the labor involved, was understood.

was something that looked like fire over the Tabernacle, until morning. ¹⁶ This was always the case: The cloud covered it (by day) and there was something that looked like fire at night.

¹⁷ When the cloud rose up from over the Tent, the children of Israel would then travel. Wherever the cloud settled, that is where the children of Israel would encamp. ¹⁸ (Thus) the children of Israel traveled by the word of God, and they encamped by the word of God. They remained encamped so long as the cloud rested over the Tabernacle.

¹⁹ If the cloud lingered over the Tabernacle for many days, the children of Israel were careful to observe their duty to God and they did not travel. ²⁰ Sometimes, the cloud remained for (just) a few days above the Tabernacle, and they (continued) to encamp by the word of God and travel by the word of God. ²¹ And sometimes the cloud remained from night until morning, and when the cloud rose in the morning, they traveled. Or (sometimes) the cloud remained for a day and a night, and (still) when the cloud rose, they traveled. ²² Whether it was for two days, a month, or a year that the cloud lingered to hover over the Tabernacle, the children of Israel would encamp and not travel. (Only) when it rose did they travel.

²³ They encamped by the word of God, and they traveled by the word of God. They were careful to observe their duty to God, according to the word of God (transmitted) through Moses.

---

through which you can undergo a complete transformation in just one moment: *"There are those that acquire their afterlife in many years, and there are those that acquire it in one moment"* (ibid., *Avodah Zarah* 17a).

These two qualities of repentance are reflected in the differences between the second Passover and the first. (a) Leavened food represents the evil and the forbidden. But during the Second Passover, *"you may keep both leavened food and unleavened bread in the home,"* alluding to the fact that repentance can spiritually elevate your past forbidden acts.

(b) The first Passover spans an entire week, suggesting a gradual spiritual ascent through the course of time. But the Second Passover lasts just one day, alluding to the power of repentance to transform you in a single instant (*Rabbi Menahem Mendel Schneerson, 20th century*).

spiritual vitamin

> Throughout their long history, whether the Jewish people were in a state of restfulness and peace and prosperity, or in a state of exile and wandering, driven from place to place, the Jews always knew that it was *"by the word of God"* (v.18, 23).

במדבר י:א-יב | בהעלותך

א וַיְדַבֵּ֥ר יְהֹוָ֖ה אֶל־מֹשֶׁ֥ה לֵּאמֹֽר׃ ב עֲשֵׂ֣ה לְךָ֗ שְׁתֵּי֙ חֲצֽוֹצְרֹ֣ת כֶּ֔סֶף מִקְשָׁ֖ה תַּעֲשֶׂ֣ה אֹתָ֑ם וְהָי֤וּ לְךָ֙ לְמִקְרָ֣א הָֽעֵדָ֔ה וּלְמַסַּ֖ע אֶת־הַֽמַּחֲנֽוֹת׃ ג וְתָקְע֖וּ בָּהֵ֑ן וְנֽוֹעֲד֤וּ אֵלֶ֙יךָ֙ כׇּל־הָ֣עֵדָ֔ה אֶל־פֶּ֖תַח אֹ֥הֶל מוֹעֵֽד׃ ד וְאִם־בְּאַחַ֖ת יִתְקָ֑עוּ וְנֽוֹעֲד֤וּ אֵלֶ֙יךָ֙ הַנְּשִׂיאִ֔ים רָאשֵׁ֖י אַלְפֵ֥י יִשְׂרָאֵֽל׃ ה וּתְקַעְתֶּ֖ם תְּרוּעָ֑ה וְנָֽסְעוּ֙ הַֽמַּחֲנ֔וֹת הַחֹנִ֖ים קֵֽדְמָה׃ ו וּתְקַעְתֶּ֤ם תְּרוּעָה֙ שֵׁנִ֔ית וְנָֽסְעוּ֙ הַֽמַּחֲנ֔וֹת הַחֹנִ֖ים תֵּימָ֑נָה תְּרוּעָ֥ה יִתְקְע֖וּ לְמַסְעֵיהֶֽם׃ ז וּבְהַקְהִ֖יל אֶת־הַקָּהָ֑ל תִּתְקְע֖וּ וְלֹ֥א תָרִֽיעוּ׃ ח וּבְנֵ֤י אַהֲרֹן֙ הַכֹּ֣הֲנִ֔ים יִתְקְע֖וּ בַּחֲצֹֽצְר֑וֹת וְהָי֥וּ לָכֶ֛ם לְחֻקַּ֥ת עוֹלָ֖ם לְדֹרֹתֵיכֶֽם׃ ט וְכִֽי־תָבֹ֨אוּ מִלְחָמָ֜ה בְּאַרְצְכֶ֗ם עַל־הַצַּר֙ הַצֹּרֵ֣ר אֶתְכֶ֔ם וַהֲרֵעֹתֶ֖ם בַּחֲצֹֽצְרֹ֑ת וְנִזְכַּרְתֶּ֗ם לִפְנֵי֙ יְהֹוָ֣ה אֱלֹֽהֵיכֶ֔ם וְנֽוֹשַׁעְתֶּ֖ם מֵאֹיְבֵיכֶֽם׃ י וּבְי֨וֹם שִׂמְחַתְכֶ֥ם וּֽבְמ֖וֹעֲדֵיכֶם֮ וּבְרָאשֵׁ֣י חׇדְשֵׁיכֶם֒ וּתְקַעְתֶּ֣ם בַּחֲצֹֽצְרֹ֗ת עַ֚ל עֹלֹ֣תֵיכֶ֔ם וְעַ֖ל זִבְחֵ֣י שַׁלְמֵיכֶ֑ם וְהָי֨וּ לָכֶ֤ם לְזִכָּרוֹן֙ לִפְנֵ֣י אֱלֹֽהֵיכֶ֔ם אֲנִ֖י יְהֹוָ֥ה אֱלֹֽהֵיכֶֽם׃ פ

[FIFTH READING]

יא וַיְהִ֞י בַּשָּׁנָ֧ה הַשֵּׁנִ֛ית בַּחֹ֥דֶשׁ הַשֵּׁנִ֖י בְּעֶשְׂרִ֣ים בַּחֹ֑דֶשׁ נַעֲלָה֙ הֶֽעָנָ֔ן מֵעַ֖ל מִשְׁכַּ֥ן הָעֵדֻֽת׃ יב וַיִּסְע֧וּ בְנֵֽי־יִשְׂרָאֵ֛ל לְמַסְעֵיהֶ֖ם מִמִּדְבַּ֣ר סִינָ֑י וַיִּשְׁכֹּ֥ן הֶעָנָ֖ן בְּמִדְבַּ֥ר

10:9 If you go to war against an enemy that oppresses you. This alludes to the war against the evil impulse, your greatest enemy.

"Blow a long blast with the trumpets"—arouse your feelings of submissiveness to God, petitioning Him to help you fight the evil impulse.

"On the days of your rejoicing ... you should blow on the trumpets"—you might think that when you have enjoyed some degree of success and you are joyous, you do not need to constantly arouse feelings of humility before God. To counteract this notion, the Torah states that even *"on the days of your rejoicing,"* you must still *"blow on the trumpets!"* (Rabbi Isaiah Horowitz, 16th–17th century).

Blow a long blast with the trumpets. During times of crisis we must pray to God. It reinforces our belief that God is fully conscious of our plight, and that He has the ability to relieve our troubles (Maimonides, 12th century).

---

kabbalah bites

10:3-7 The calm, long blast was a sign of *Raḥamim* (Divine mercy). The more urgent shorter blasts signified *Din* (severity).

When the people encamped peacefully they blew trumpets of mercy. When they traveled, the *Shekhinah* passed ahead of them to protect them from their enemies, which was heralded by trumpets of *Din*.

numbers 10:1–12 · be-ha'alotekha

The Trumpets

10 ¹ God spoke to Moses, saying: ² Make two silver trumpets for yourself. Make them hammered (from one piece of metal). They should be used by you to summon the congregation and (to announce) the departure of the camps:

- ³ When a long blast is blown on both of them, the entire congregation should gather to you, at the entrance to the Tent of Meeting.

- ⁴ When a long blast is blown on one of them, the leaders, the heads of Israel's thousands, should gather to you.

- ⁵ When short blasts are blown, the camps encamped to the east should travel.

- ⁶ When short blasts are blown for a second time, the camps encamped to the south should travel.

- The short blasts are blown (only) for traveling, ⁷ but when gathering the congregation, you should blow a long blast and not short blasts.

- ⁸ Aaron's descendants, the priests, are to blow the trumpets. This is an eternal law for all time.

- ⁹ While in your land, if you go to war against an enemy that oppresses you, you should blow a long blast with the trumpets so as to be remembered before God, your God, and you will be saved from your enemies.

- ¹⁰ And on the days of your rejoicing, on your festivals and on your new-moon celebrations, you should blow on the trumpets (when bringing) your (communal) burnt-offerings and your peace-sacrifices. This will be a remembrance before your God—I am God, your God.

The First Journey

[FIFTH READING] ¹¹ On the twentieth of the second month in the second year, the cloud rose up from over the Tabernacle of the Testimony. ¹² The children of Israel traveled from the Sinai Desert (in accordance with all the laws concerning) their

---

But *"sometimes, the cloud remained for (just) a few days ... and sometimes the cloud remained from night until morning, and when the cloud rose in the morning, they traveled"* (verses 20-21). What was the point of the hundreds of man-hours involved in erecting the Tabernacle, if it was to be dismantled soon afterwards, sometimes the following day?

"They encamped by the word of God, and they traveled by the word of God" (v. 23)—each encampment was not considered to be transitory in nature, because *the direct Divine command to camp at that point conferred it with the importance of a permanent settlement.*

Likewise, while it is true that our current work is transitory in nature, for the Redemption is about to arrive at any moment, nevertheless, since in our daily work we are following *"the word of God,"* we should view what we are doing as having the utmost importance and be enthusiastic in carrying out the tiniest detail (*Rabbi Joseph Isaac Schneersohn of Lubavitch, 20th century*).

במדבר י:יב-לב — בהעלותך

13 וַיִּסְעוּ בָּרִאשֹׁנָה עַל־פִּי יְהֹוָה בְּיַד־מֹשֶׁה: 14 וַיִּסַּע דֶּגֶל מַחֲנֵה בְנֵי־ פָארָן: יְהוּדָה בָּרִאשֹׁנָה לְצִבְאֹתָם וְעַל־צְבָאוֹ נַחְשׁוֹן בֶּן־עַמִּינָדָב: 15 וְעַל־צְבָא מַטֵּה בְּנֵי יִשָּׂשכָר נְתַנְאֵל בֶּן־צוּעָר: 16 וְעַל־צְבָא מַטֵּה בְּנֵי זְבוּלֻן אֱלִיאָב בֶּן־חֵלֹן: 17 וְהוּרַד הַמִּשְׁכָּן וְנָסְעוּ בְנֵי־גֵרְשׁוֹן וּבְנֵי מְרָרִי נֹשְׂאֵי הַמִּשְׁכָּן: 18 וְנָסַע דֶּגֶל מַחֲנֵה רְאוּבֵן לְצִבְאֹתָם וְעַל־צְבָאוֹ אֱלִיצוּר בֶּן־שְׁדֵיאוּר: 19 וְעַל־צְבָא מַטֵּה בְּנֵי שִׁמְעוֹן שְׁלֻמִיאֵל בֶּן־צוּרִישַׁדָּי: 20 וְעַל־צְבָא מַטֵּה בְנֵי־גָד אֶלְיָסָף בֶּן־ דְּעוּאֵל: 21 וְנָסְעוּ הַקְּהָתִים נֹשְׂאֵי הַמִּקְדָּשׁ וְהֵקִימוּ אֶת־הַמִּשְׁכָּן עַד־בֹּאָם: 22 וְנָסַע דֶּגֶל מַחֲנֵה בְנֵי־אֶפְרַיִם לְצִבְאֹתָם וְעַל־צְבָאוֹ אֱלִישָׁמָע בֶּן־עַמִּיהוּד: 23 וְעַל־צְבָא מַטֵּה בְּנֵי מְנַשֶּׁה גַּמְלִיאֵל בֶּן־פְּדָהצוּר: 24 וְעַל־צְבָא מַטֵּה בְּנֵי בִנְיָמִן אֲבִידָן בֶּן־גִּדְעוֹנִי: 25 וְנָסַע דֶּגֶל מַחֲנֵה בְנֵי־דָן מְאַסֵּף לְכָל־הַמַּחֲנֹת לְצִבְאֹתָם וְעַל־צְבָאוֹ אֲחִיעֶזֶר בֶּן־עַמִּישַׁדָּי: 26 וְעַל־צְבָא מַטֵּה בְּנֵי אָשֵׁר פַּגְעִיאֵל בֶּן־עָכְרָן: 27 וְעַל־צְבָא מַטֵּה בְּנֵי נַפְתָּלִי אֲחִירַע בֶּן־עֵינָן: 28 אֵלֶּה מַסְעֵי בְנֵי־יִשְׂרָאֵל לְצִבְאֹתָם וַיִּסָּעוּ: ס 29 וַיֹּאמֶר מֹשֶׁה לְחֹבָב בֶּן־רְעוּאֵל הַמִּדְיָנִי חֹתֵן מֹשֶׁה נֹסְעִים | אֲנַחְנוּ אֶל־הַמָּקוֹם אֲשֶׁר אָמַר יְהֹוָה אֹתוֹ אֶתֵּן לָכֶם לְכָה אִתָּנוּ וְהֵטַבְנוּ לָךְ כִּי־יְהֹוָה דִּבֶּר־טוֹב עַל־יִשְׂרָאֵל: 30 וַיֹּאמֶר אֵלָיו לֹא אֵלֵךְ כִּי אִם־אֶל־אַרְצִי וְאֶל־מוֹלַדְתִּי אֵלֵךְ: 31 וַיֹּאמֶר אַל־נָא תַּעֲזֹב אֹתָנוּ כִּי | עַל־כֵּן יָדַעְתָּ חֲנֹתֵנוּ בַּמִּדְבָּר וְהָיִיתָ לָּנוּ לְעֵינָיִם: 32 וְהָיָה כִּי־תֵלֵךְ עִמָּנוּ וְהָיָה |

spiritual vitamin

> From the moment of birth to the last breath, we all undergo a variety of "journeys" both in our physical and spiritual development, and the "Ark of the Covenant"—the Torah—goes before us, to guide us.

journeys, and the cloud settled (in Kibroth-hattaavah) in the desert of Paran. ¹³ This was the first journey by God's word, through Moses.

¹⁴ The division of regiments (of three tribes, known as) "the Camp of Judah's descendants" traveled first: Heading the regiment was Nahshon son of Amminadab. ¹⁵ Heading the regiment of the tribe of Issachar's descendants was Nethanel son of Zuar. ¹⁶ Heading the regiment of the tribe of Zebulun's descendants was Eliab son of Helon.

¹⁷ The Tabernacle was then dismantled. Then Gershon's descendants and Merari's descendants, who carried the Tabernacle, traveled.

¹⁸ Then the division of regiments (of three tribes, known as) "the Camp of Reuben" set out according to their regiments: Heading its regiment was Elizur son of Shedeur. ¹⁹ Heading the regiment of the tribe of Simeon's descendants was Shelumiel son of Zurishaddai. ²⁰ Heading the regiment of the tribe of Gad's descendants was Eliasaph son of Deuel.

²¹ The descendants of Kohath, who carried the holy (vessels), then traveled. (In this way, when they came to encamp, they would find) the Tabernacle already erected before they arrived (by the descendants of Gershon and Merari, who traveled ahead).

²² Then the division of regiments (of three tribes, known as) "the Camp of Ephraim" set out, according to its regiments: Heading its regiment was Elishama son of Ammihud. ²³ Heading the regiment of the tribe of Manasseh's descendants was Gamaliel son of Pedahzur. ²⁴ Heading the regiment of the tribe of Benjamin's descendants was Abidan son of Gideoni.

²⁵ Then the division of regiments (of three tribes, known as) "the Camp of Dan"—the collector (of lost property) for all the other camps—set out, according to its regiments: Heading its regiment was Ahiezer son of Ammishaddai. ²⁶ Heading the regiment of the tribe of Asher's descendants was Pagiel son of Achran. ²⁷ Heading the regiment of the tribe of Naphtali's descendants was Ahira son of Enan.

²⁸ These were the journey arrangements of the children of Israel, according to their regiments.

They traveled (on that day).

—²⁹ Moses said to Hobab son of Reuel the Midianite, Moses' father-in-law (Jethro), "We are traveling (very soon) to the place about which God said, 'I will give it to you.' Come with us and we will treat you well, for God has spoken of good (things) for Israel." ³⁰ He said to him, "I'm not going. Rather, I shall go to my land and my birthplace." ³¹ (Moses) said, "Please don't leave us! For you know (all the miracles associated with) our encampments in the desert to which you have been an eyewitness. ³² If you go with us, then we will grant you (use of part of) the good (land) which God is granting us."—

במדבר י:לב - יא:ה | בהעלותך

הַטּוֹב הַהוּא אֲשֶׁר יֵיטִיב יְהֹוָה עִמָּנוּ וְהֵטַבְנוּ לָךְ: 33 וַיִּסְעוּ מֵהַר יְהֹוָה דֶּרֶךְ שְׁלֹשֶׁת יָמִים וַאֲרוֹן בְּרִית־יְהֹוָה נֹסֵעַ לִפְנֵיהֶם דֶּרֶךְ שְׁלֹשֶׁת יָמִים לָתוּר לָהֶם מְנוּחָה: 34 וַעֲנַן יְהֹוָה עֲלֵיהֶם יוֹמָם בְּנָסְעָם מִן־הַמַּחֲנֶה: ס [SIXTH READING] 35 וַיְהִי בִּנְסֹעַ הָאָרֹן וַיֹּאמֶר מֹשֶׁה קוּמָה | יְהֹוָה וְיָפֻצוּ אֹיְבֶיךָ וְיָנֻסוּ מְשַׂנְאֶיךָ מִפָּנֶיךָ: 36 וּבְנֻחֹה יֹאמַר שׁוּבָה יְהֹוָה רִבְבוֹת אַלְפֵי יִשְׂרָאֵל: ׆ פ

יא 1 וַיְהִי הָעָם כְּמִתְאֹנְנִים רַע בְּאָזְנֵי יְהֹוָה וַיִּשְׁמַע יְהֹוָה וַיִּחַר אַפּוֹ וַתִּבְעַר־בָּם אֵשׁ יְהֹוָה וַתֹּאכַל בִּקְצֵה הַמַּחֲנֶה: 2 וַיִּצְעַק הָעָם אֶל־מֹשֶׁה וַיִּתְפַּלֵּל מֹשֶׁה אֶל־יְהֹוָה וַתִּשְׁקַע הָאֵשׁ: 3 וַיִּקְרָא שֵׁם־הַמָּקוֹם הַהוּא תַּבְעֵרָה כִּי־בָעֲרָה בָם אֵשׁ יְהֹוָה: 4 וְהָאסַפְסֻף אֲשֶׁר בְּקִרְבּוֹ הִתְאַוּוּ תַּאֲוָה וַיָּשֻׁבוּ וַיִּבְכּוּ גַּם בְּנֵי יִשְׂרָאֵל וַיֹּאמְרוּ מִי יַאֲכִלֵנוּ בָּשָׂר: 5 זָכַרְנוּ אֶת־הַדָּגָה אֲשֶׁר־נֹאכַל בְּמִצְרַיִם חִנָּם אֵת הַקִּשֻּׁאִים וְאֵת הָאֲבַטִּחִים וְאֶת־הֶחָצִיר

And this is the message expressed by the verse, *"Moses would say, etc."* Within you there is a "spark" of Moses, which is capable of sustaining your enthusiasm for Torah even under the most adverse conditions. The removal of the Torah from the ark awakens this kernel of identity, to the extent that it starts to speak to you ("Moses would *say*").

"Arise, O God, may Your enemies be scattered"—and once the "spark" is awake, it begins to strengthen your commitment to Judaism in all areas, both in the growth of positive deeds for God (*"Arise, O God"*), and the withdrawal from negative things (*"May Your enemies be scattered"*).

A further blessing granted by God when the Torah scroll is taken out is that you should be able to earn a living comfortably. The Ark of the Covenant, represented by the Torah scroll, was buried along with a container of manna (*Exodus* 16:32-33), which represents how God provides sustenance without man's having to make much effort. So, when you take out the Torah scroll, God not only empowers you to serve Him better, He also blesses you that you should earn a living comfortably, enabling you to observe the Torah free from worry and concern (*Rabbi Menahem Mendel Schneerson, 20th century*).

11:4 The mob among them had strong cravings (lit. "craved a craving") ... They said, "Who will give us meat to eat?" Actually, the people craved both for meat and for the women who had recently been forbidden to them through the laws of forbidden relations (*Leviticus*, ch. 20). Since this craving was illegitimate, they could not openly express it. But the Torah hints to it by the double use of the word "craving"—*"they craved a craving."* But what they actually mentioned was only the meat (*Rabbi Moses Alshekh, 16th century*).

5. The fish that we ate in Egypt for free. If you want to say that the Egyptians gave them fish for free, has Scripture not already stated, *"You will not be given straw"* (*Exodus* 5:18)? Now, if

³³ They traveled from the mountain of God a distance of three days (in just one day, because God wanted to bring them to the land immediately). The Ark of God's Covenant traveled three days ahead of them to seek a resting place for them. ³⁴ The cloud of God was above them by day, when they traveled from their (original place of) encampment.

[SIXTH READING] ³⁵ What happened was, whenever the ark set out, Moses would say, "Arise, O God, may Your enemies be scattered and may those who hate You flee from You." ³⁶ When it came to rest he would say, "Rest (here) O God, among the myriads of thousands of Israel."

The First Complaint and Rebuke

11 ¹ The people were acting like complainers (who seek to say something) that is evil in God's ears (so as to express their dissatisfaction with the difficulties of the journey). God heard and became angry (because He was hurrying the journey for their benefit, to enter the land quickly).

A fire from God burned among them, consuming (those at) the edge of the camp. ² The people cried out to Moses. Moses prayed to God, and the fire died down.

³ He named that place Taberah ("blaze"), because the fire of God had blazed against them.

The Second Complaint and Rebuke

⁴ The mob (of Egyptian converts) among them (who had left Egypt with the Jewish people) had strong cravings. The children of Israel were also influenced, and began to cry (with them). They said, "Who will give us meat to eat? ⁵ We remember the fish that we ate in Egypt for free, the cucumbers, the watermelons,

---

35. Whenever the ark set out. According to Jewish custom, this verse is recited by the congregation whenever the Torah scroll is removed from the ark. Taking out the Torah scroll is not merely a ceremony, it is a moment when God actually instills you with the spirit of resilience and dedication required to "take out" the values of the Torah and apply them to your everyday life.

spiritual vitamin

> Most of the "conformists" in social and conventional aspects of life are to be found among older people. Young people, filled with energy, determination and faith are not naturally inclined to compromise in any field, much less in the higher values of life.

וְאֵת־הַבְּצָלִים וְאֶת־הַשּׁוּמִים: 6 וְעַתָּה נַפְשֵׁנוּ יְבֵשָׁה אֵין כֹּל בִּלְתִּי אֶל־הַמָּן עֵינֵינוּ: 7 וְהַמָּן כִּזְרַע־גַּד הוּא וְעֵינוֹ כְּעֵין הַבְּדֹלַח: 8 שָׁטוּ הָעָם וְלָקְטוּ וְטָחֲנוּ בָרֵחַיִם אוֹ דָכוּ בַּמְּדֹכָה וּבִשְּׁלוּ בַּפָּרוּר וְעָשׂוּ אֹתוֹ עֻגוֹת וְהָיָה טַעְמוֹ כְּטַעַם לְשַׁד הַשָּׁמֶן: 9 וּבְרֶדֶת הַטַּל עַל־הַמַּחֲנֶה לָיְלָה יֵרֵד הַמָּן עָלָיו: 10 וַיִּשְׁמַע מֹשֶׁה אֶת־הָעָם בֹּכֶה לְמִשְׁפְּחֹתָיו אִישׁ לְפֶתַח אָהֳלוֹ וַיִּחַר־אַף יְהֹוָה מְאֹד וּבְעֵינֵי מֹשֶׁה רָע: 11 וַיֹּאמֶר מֹשֶׁה אֶל־יְהֹוָה לָמָה הֲרֵעֹתָ לְעַבְדֶּךָ וְלָמָּה לֹא־מָצָתִי חֵן בְּעֵינֶיךָ לָשׂוּם אֶת־מַשָּׂא כָּל־הָעָם הַזֶּה עָלָי: 12 הֶאָנֹכִי הָרִיתִי אֵת כָּל־הָעָם הַזֶּה אִם־אָנֹכִי יְלִדְתִּיהוּ כִּי־תֹאמַר אֵלַי שָׂאֵהוּ בְחֵיקֶךָ כַּאֲשֶׁר יִשָּׂא הָאֹמֵן אֶת־הַיֹּנֵק עַל הָאֲדָמָה אֲשֶׁר נִשְׁבַּעְתָּ לַאֲבֹתָיו: 13 מֵאַיִן לִי בָּשָׂר לָתֵת לְכָל־הָעָם הַזֶּה כִּי־יִבְכּוּ עָלַי לֵאמֹר תְּנָה־לָּנוּ בָשָׂר וְנֹאכֵלָה: 14 לֹא־אוּכַל אָנֹכִי לְבַדִּי לָשֵׂאת אֶת־כָּל־הָעָם הַזֶּה כִּי כָבֵד מִמֶּנִּי: 15 וְאִם־כָּכָה | אַתְּ־עֹשָׂה לִּי הָרְגֵנִי נָא הָרֹג אִם־מָצָאתִי חֵן בְּעֵינֶיךָ וְאַל־אֶרְאֶה בְּרָעָתִי: פ

this since his role was that of the teacher and educator (in contrast to Aaron who was the diplomat and negotiator). But the craving for meat—and the other unspoken lusts—was not an error of ideology, but something much more basic and crude. To heal this, Moses felt, was not the task of a teacher, but a nurse: *"You tell me, 'Embrace them like a nurse carries a baby'"* (v. 12).

kabbalah bites

11:15 *"Please kill me … so that I do not see my misfortune."*

Shouldn't Moses have said, "so I do not see *their* misfortune"?

The current rebellion had been orchestrated by the *'erev rav* (mixed multitude), "dysfunctional souls" that were derivatives of Abel's soul. Since Moses was a reincarnation of Abel himself, he had a strong urge to redeem the mixed multitude, which is why he took them out of Egypt even when God warned him to the contrary (see *Exodus* 12:38).

Since both the *'erev rav* and Moses were from the same soul root, he saw himself in them. That is why he said, "If this is the way you treat *me*," and, "so that I do not see *my* misfortune," even when referring to *their* souls.

numbers 11:5–15 — be-ha'alotekha

the leeks, the onions, and the garlic! ⁶ But now, our souls are parched, for there is nothing, except the manna before our eyes (morning and evening)."

⁷ (In truth, however,) the manna (was a delicacy). It was (round) like coriander seed, and it looked like crystal. ⁸ The people would (merely have to) stroll around (without any exertion) and gather it. (It would taste of anything one desired, like something) ground in a mill, crushed in a mortar, cooked in a pot or made into cakes. It tasted as moist as oil. ⁹ When the dew came down on the camp at night, the manna came down upon it.

¹⁰ Moses heard the people weeping with their families (making as much noise as possible). Each person was at the entrance of his tent. God became very angry, and Moses was disgusted.

¹¹ Moses said to God, "Why have You mistreated Your servant? Why have I not found favor in Your eyes, in that You place the burden of this entire people upon me? ¹² Did I conceive this entire people? Did I give birth to them? (So why did You) tell me, 'Embrace them like a nurse carries a baby,' (and lead them) to the land You promised their forefathers? ¹³ Where do I have meat to give all these people? For they are crying to me, saying, 'Give us meat to eat.' ¹⁴ I cannot bear this entire people alone, as it's too hard for me."

(When Moses saw a vision of the punishments due to the Jewish people for their complaints, he said), ¹⁵ "If this is the way You treat me, please kill me—if I have found favor in Your eyes— so that I do not see my misfortune."

---

straw was not given for free, would they have given them fish for free." So what does "for free" mean? Free from commandments (*Rashi, 11ᵗʰ century*).

7. The manna. This verse comes in response to the complaints regarding the manna, for, actually, it had many good qualities. The manna was like *"coriander seed,"* which is simple to collect; it was also very noticeable, since *"it was white."* The manna could be eaten without any extra preparation, or they could *"grind it in mills"* and *"make cakes"* from it (v. 8). Also, they could *"beat it in mortars"* and *"cook it in pots."* It tasted like food *"moist with oil."* And when the manna fell, it came down *"after the dew,"* descending on a freshly cleaned place (*Rabbi Abraham ibn Ezra, 12ᵗʰ century*).

11-14. Moses said to God, "Why have You mistreated Your servant? Why have I not found favor in Your eyes, in that You place the burden of this entire people upon me? Did I conceive this entire people? Did I give birth to them? ... I cannot bear this entire people alone, as it's too hard for me." It is quite unlike Moses to become so despondent and to condemn the people. Never before had he uttered such words, even though the Israelites had rebelled on many occasions. Why did this sin evoke such an extreme reaction from Moses? Becoming overwhelmed with a desire for meat seems like a relatively minor sin compared with the more serious crime of worshiping the Golden Calf, for which Moses ardently defended the people.

The difference is that with the Golden Calf, the Jews had essentially made a theological mistake which could be corrected, over time, through education. Moses was comfortable with

במדבר יא:טז-כה   בהעלותך

16 וַיֹּ֨אמֶר יְהֹוָ֜ה אֶל־מֹשֶׁ֗ה אֶסְפָה־לִּ֞י שִׁבְעִ֣ים אִישׁ֮ מִזִּקְנֵ֣י יִשְׂרָאֵל֒ אֲשֶׁ֣ר יָדַ֔עְתָּ כִּי־הֵ֛ם זִקְנֵ֥י הָעָ֖ם וְשֹׁטְרָ֑יו וְלָקַחְתָּ֤ אֹתָם֙ אֶל־אֹ֣הֶל מוֹעֵ֔ד וְהִֽתְיַצְּב֥וּ שָׁ֖ם עִמָּֽךְ:

17 וְיָרַדְתִּ֗י וְדִבַּרְתִּ֣י עִמְּךָ֮ שָׁם֒ וְאָצַלְתִּ֗י מִן־הָר֛וּחַ אֲשֶׁ֥ר עָלֶ֖יךָ וְשַׂמְתִּ֣י עֲלֵיהֶ֑ם וְנָשְׂא֤וּ אִתְּךָ֙ בְּמַשָּׂ֣א הָעָ֔ם וְלֹא־תִשָּׂ֥א אַתָּ֖ה לְבַדֶּֽךָ:

18 וְאֶל־הָעָ֨ם תֹּאמַ֜ר הִתְקַדְּשׁ֣וּ לְמָחָר֮ וַאֲכַלְתֶּ֣ם בָּשָׂר֒ כִּ֡י בְּכִיתֶם֩ בְּאׇזְנֵ֨י יְהֹוָ֜ה לֵאמֹ֗ר מִ֤י יַאֲכִלֵ֙נוּ֙ בָּשָׂ֔ר כִּי־ט֥וֹב לָ֖נוּ בְּמִצְרָ֑יִם וְנָתַ֨ן יְהֹוָ֥ה לָכֶ֛ם בָּשָׂ֖ר וַאֲכַלְתֶּֽם:

19 לֹ֣א י֥וֹם אֶחָ֛ד תֹּאכְל֖וּן וְלֹ֣א | חֲמִשָּׁ֣ה יָמִ֑ים וְלֹא֙ עֲשָׂרָ֣ה יָמִ֔ים וְלֹ֖א עֶשְׂרִ֥ים יֽוֹם:

20 עַ֣ד | חֹ֣דֶשׁ יָמִ֗ים עַ֤ד אֲשֶׁר־יֵצֵא֙ מֵֽאַפְּכֶ֔ם וְהָיָ֥ה לָכֶ֖ם לְזָרָ֑א יַ֗עַן כִּֽי־מְאַסְתֶּ֤ם אֶת־יְהֹוָה֙ אֲשֶׁ֣ר בְּקִרְבְּכֶ֔ם וַתִּבְכּ֤וּ לְפָנָיו֙ לֵאמֹ֔ר לָ֥מָּה זֶּ֖ה יָצָ֥אנוּ מִמִּצְרָֽיִם:

21 וַיֹּ֘אמֶר֮ מֹשֶׁה֒ שֵׁשׁ־מֵא֥וֹת אֶ֙לֶף֙ רַגְלִ֔י הָעָ֕ם אֲשֶׁ֥ר אָנֹכִ֖י בְּקִרְבּ֑וֹ וְאַתָּ֣ה אָמַ֗רְתָּ בָּשָׂר֙ אֶתֵּ֣ן לָהֶ֔ם וְאָכְל֖וּ חֹ֥דֶשׁ יָמִֽים:

22 הֲצֹ֧אן וּבָקָ֛ר יִשָּׁחֵ֥ט לָהֶ֖ם וּמָצָ֣א לָהֶ֑ם אִ֣ם אֶת־כׇּל־דְּגֵ֥י הַיָּ֛ם יֵאָסֵ֥ף לָהֶ֖ם וּמָ֥צָא לָהֶֽם: פ

23 וַיֹּ֤אמֶר יְהֹוָה֙ אֶל־מֹשֶׁ֔ה הֲיַ֥ד יְהֹוָ֖ה תִּקְצָ֑ר עַתָּ֥ה תִרְאֶ֛ה הֲיִקְרְךָ֥ דְבָרִ֖י אִם־לֹֽא:

24 וַיֵּצֵ֣א מֹשֶׁ֗ה וַיְדַבֵּר֙ אֶל־הָעָ֔ם אֵ֖ת דִּבְרֵ֣י יְהֹוָ֑ה וַיֶּאֱסֹ֞ף שִׁבְעִ֥ים אִישׁ֙ מִזִּקְנֵ֣י הָעָ֔ם וַֽיַּעֲמֵ֥ד אֹתָ֖ם סְבִיבֹ֥ת הָאֹֽהֶל:

25 וַיֵּ֨רֶד יְהֹוָ֥ה | בֶּעָנָן֮ וַיְדַבֵּ֣ר אֵלָיו֒ וַיָּ֗אצֶל מִן־הָר֙וּחַ֙ אֲשֶׁ֣ר עָלָ֔יו וַיִּתֵּ֕ן עַל־שִׁבְעִ֥ים

874

in itself is something he felt simply unable to do, so how would he feel able to represent the people as their leader in this respect?

In response, God offered Moses the assistance of the elders, for they were not as removed as Moses from the notion of enjoying a physical experience. They would be able to lead the people with regard to their physical needs (*Rabbi Shneur Zalman of Lyady, 18th century*).

21. A people of six hundred thousand on foot whom I am among. Moses and the Jewish people are like "head" and "foot," as the verse states, *"A people of six hundred thousand on foot whom I am among."* For all the Jewish people are like the "feet" of Moses, and Moses is like their "head." And just like a person's feet take his head to places that the head would not be able to reach on its own, Moses achieves additional spiritual greatness through the Jewish people— his "feet" (*Rabbi Shneur Zalman of Lyady, 18th century*).

24. He assembled seventy men. All of them were written down, mentioned specifically by name, and chosen by lot. This is because the number of seventy candidates split into twelve

¹⁶ God said to Moses, "(As for your complaint that you cannot bear the people alone,) assemble for Me seventy men of the elders of Israel, the ones that you know were the people's elders and officers (back in Egypt). Persuade them to (come to) the Tent of Meeting, and have them stand there with You. ¹⁷ I will come down and speak with you there. I will magnify the spirit which is upon you and place (some of) it upon them (without reducing what you have). Then they will bear the burden of the people with you, so that you do not have to bear it alone."

¹⁸ "You should say to the people, 'Prepare yourselves for (punishment) tomorrow when you will eat meat, because you have cried into God's ears, saying, "Who will give us meat to eat? We had it better in Egypt!" God will give you meat, and you will eat. ¹⁹ You will eat it not one day, not two days, not five days, not ten days, and not twenty days, ²⁰ but for a whole month, until it comes out of your nose and makes you sick. For you have despised God, who is among you, and you cried before Him, saying, "'Why did we leave Egypt?"'"

²¹ Moses said, "It is a people of six hundred thousand on foot whom I am among, and You're saying, 'I'll give them meat to eat for a whole month'! ²² Could enough sheep and cattle possibly be slaughtered for them? If all the fish of the sea were gathered for them, would it be enough for them?"

²³ God said to Moses, "Is God's hand too short? You'll see if My word will be fulfilled for you, or not!"

²⁴ Moses went out and told the people what God had said (but they did not listen to him).

(To carry out God's first instruction), he assembled seventy men of the people's elders, and stood them around the Tent. ²⁵ God came down in a cloud and spoke

---

This role Moses never sought, and he now found it thrust upon him as the people succumbed to childlike impulses of unrestrained cravings and complaining.

Unlike a teacher, who always retains his own identity, a mother must surrender all of her own needs to her child, allowing the child to take precedence over her own life. Moses now became aware that being a teacher was not sufficient for a leader of Israel—and this was his complaint to God. Now he would have to nurture the people through their national infancy, with patient, sympathetic understanding. His personal needs and pleasures would have to be put aside.

The "teacher" role may have been sufficient in past generations to counter the temptations of other thought systems and religions, but the pleasure-seeking culture of our day also requires the "nursing-father" role. We need the warm embrace as much as the brilliant idea (*Rabbi Joseph B. Soloveitchik, 20ᵗʰ century*).

17. I will magnify the spirit which is upon you. Moses' awareness of God's presence never lapsed even for a moment. For Moses, no experience, even that of eating or sleeping, could be entirely physical, devoid of Divine consciousness.

So when the people complained to Moses that they were craving meat, Moses turned to God in exasperation and cried, "Where do *I* have meat?" (v. 13). Craving physical pleasure as an end

אִישׁ הַזְּקֵנִים וַיְהִי כְּנוֹחַ עֲלֵיהֶם הָרוּחַ וַיִּתְנַבְּאוּ וְלֹא יָסָפוּ: 26 וַיִּשָּׁאֲרוּ שְׁנֵי־אֲנָשִׁים | בַּמַּחֲנֶה שֵׁם הָאֶחָד | אֶלְדָּד וְשֵׁם הַשֵּׁנִי מֵידָד וַתָּנַח עֲלֵיהֶם הָרוּחַ וְהֵמָּה בַּכְּתֻבִים וְלֹא יָצְאוּ הָאֹהֱלָה וַיִּתְנַבְּאוּ בַּמַּחֲנֶה: 27 וַיָּרָץ הַנַּעַר וַיַּגֵּד לְמֹשֶׁה וַיֹּאמַר אֶלְדָּד וּמֵידָד מִתְנַבְּאִים בַּמַּחֲנֶה: 28 וַיַּעַן יְהוֹשֻׁעַ בִּן־נוּן מְשָׁרֵת מֹשֶׁה מִבְּחֻרָיו וַיֹּאמַר אֲדֹנִי מֹשֶׁה כְּלָאֵם: 29 וַיֹּאמֶר לוֹ מֹשֶׁה הַמְקַנֵּא אַתָּה לִי וּמִי יִתֵּן כָּל־עַם יְהוָה נְבִיאִים כִּי־יִתֵּן יְהוָה אֶת־רוּחוֹ עֲלֵיהֶם: 30 [SEVENTH READING] וַיֵּאָסֵף מֹשֶׁה אֶל־הַמַּחֲנֶה הוּא וְזִקְנֵי יִשְׂרָאֵל: 31 וְרוּחַ נָסַע | מֵאֵת יְהוָה וַיָּגָז שַׂלְוִים מִן־הַיָּם וַיִּטֹּשׁ עַל־הַמַּחֲנֶה כְּדֶרֶךְ יוֹם כֹּה וּכְדֶרֶךְ יוֹם כֹּה סְבִיבוֹת הַמַּחֲנֶה וּכְאַמָּתַיִם עַל־פְּנֵי הָאָרֶץ: 32 וַיָּקָם הָעָם כָּל־הַיּוֹם הַהוּא וְכָל־הַלַּיְלָה וְכֹל | יוֹם הַמָּחֳרָת וַיַּאַסְפוּ אֶת־הַשְּׂלָו הַמַּמְעִיט אָסַף עֲשָׂרָה חֳמָרִים וַיִּשְׁטְחוּ לָהֶם שָׁטוֹחַ סְבִיבוֹת הַמַּחֲנֶה: 33 הַבָּשָׂר עוֹדֶנּוּ בֵּין שִׁנֵּיהֶם טֶרֶם יִכָּרֵת וְאַף יְהוָה חָרָה בָעָם וַיַּךְ יְהוָה בָּעָם מַכָּה רַבָּה מְאֹד: 34 וַיִּקְרָא אֶת־שֵׁם־הַמָּקוֹם הַהוּא

One was called Eldad and the other Medad. Because Eldad and Medad were so humble, God said, "They will be made greater than all the others." Their distinction was apparent in five ways.

1. They prophesied what would take place forty years later, including the fact that Moses would die and Joshua would take the children of Israel into the land.
2. The other elders did not enter the land of Israel, but Eldad and Medad did.
3. The names of the other elders are not given in the Torah, but their names are specified.
4. The prophecy of the other elders eventually ceased, but Eldad and Medad retained their prophetic powers.
5. The prophecy of the other elders was a result of the spirit of Moses that was bestowed upon them, whereas their prophetic spirit came directly from God (*Midrash Tanḥuma*).

29. Moses said to him, "Are you being jealous on my behalf? If only all God's people were prophets!" Moses' words here are a spectacular example of humility. Apart from not envying his disciples, whom he himself reared, he sincerely desired that all the people should be prophets and that God should bestow His spirit upon them without him. This is something that any other man would be jealous of, but he did not show any jealousy (*Rabbi Isaac b. Moses Arama, 15th century*).

34. He named that place Kibroth-hattaavah, for there they buried the people who craved. The place name Kibroth-hattaavah means Graves of Craving. However, it was those who had

to him. He magnified the spirit that was upon him and placed (some of) it upon the seventy elders. When the spirit rested upon them, they became prophets, but it did not last (more than a day).

²⁶ (Meanwhile,) two men (of the nominated elders) had remained in the camp (because they felt that they were unworthy of greatness). One was called Eldad and the other Medad. The spirit (of prophecy nevertheless) rested upon them. They were among those written (in the nomination lottery), but they did not go out to the Tent (with the others). Thus, they became prophets while in the camp.

²⁷ The lad (Gershom, Moses' son) ran to inform Moses and said, "Eldad and Medad are saying prophecy in the camp!"

²⁸ Joshua son of Nun, Moses' servant from his youth, spoke up and said, "Moses, my master, stop them!"

²⁹ Moses said to him, "Are you being jealous on my behalf? If only all God's people were prophets, and God would place His spirit upon them!"

[SEVENTH READING] ³⁰ Moses (left the Tent of Meeting), entered the camp (and went to his private tent). He and the elders of Israel (did the same). ³¹ God made a wind blow which made quails fly from the sea and (soon) they were spread all over the camp, (the distance of) a day's journey this way and a day's journey that way, around the camp. (They were flying at a height of) around two cubits above the ground (to make catching them easy). ³² The people were busy all that day, all night, and the next day, gathering the quails. (Even) the one who gathered the fewest collected ten *ḥomer*. They spread them around the camp in numerous layers.

³³ The meat was still between their teeth and had not yet disappeared, when God's anger raged against the people, and God struck the people with a very severe plague.

³⁴ He named that place Kibroth-hattaavah ("Graves of Craving"), for there they buried the people who craved.

---

tribes came to six per tribe, with the exception of two tribes who would receive only five each. Moses said, "No tribe will listen to me to deduct an elder from its tribe."

What did he do? He took seventy-two lots and wrote on seventy of them "elder" and two of them he left blank. He chose six men from each tribe, a total of seventy-two, and he said to them, "Draw your lots from the box" (*Rashi, 11th century*).

26. Two men (of the nominated elders) had remained in the camp. Why did Eldad and Medad "remain in the camp"? They feared failure and did not want to pick a blank lot, so they did not participate in the lottery.

Rabbi Simeon said that they felt they were not worthy of greatness, so even after winning the lottery they did not go to the Tent to be appointed by Moses (*Babylonian Talmud*, Sanhedrin 17a, according to *Rashi*).

במדבר יא:לד – יב:ו — בהעלותך

קִבְר֥וֹת הַֽתַּאֲוָ֖ה כִּי־שָׁ֣ם קָֽבְר֔וּ אֶת־הָעָ֖ם הַמִּתְאַוִּֽים׃ 35 מִקִּבְר֧וֹת הַֽתַּאֲוָ֛ה נָסְע֥וּ הָעָ֖ם חֲצֵר֑וֹת וַיִּהְי֖וּ בַּחֲצֵרֽוֹת׃ פ

יב 1 וַתְּדַבֵּ֨ר מִרְיָ֤ם וְאַהֲרֹן֙ בְּמֹשֶׁ֔ה עַל־אֹד֛וֹת הָאִשָּׁ֥ה הַכֻּשִׁ֖ית אֲשֶׁ֣ר לָקָ֑ח כִּֽי־אִשָּׁ֥ה כֻשִׁ֖ית לָקָֽח׃ 2 וַיֹּאמְר֗וּ הֲרַ֤ק אַךְ־בְּמֹשֶׁה֙ דִּבֶּ֣ר יְהֹוָ֔ה הֲלֹ֖א גַּם־בָּ֣נוּ דִבֵּ֑ר וַיִּשְׁמַ֖ע יְהֹוָֽה׃ 3 וְהָאִ֥ישׁ מֹשֶׁ֖ה ענו מְאֹ֑ד מִכֹּל֙ הָֽאָדָ֔ם אֲשֶׁ֖ר עַל־פְּנֵ֥י הָאֲדָמָֽה׃ ס 4 וַיֹּ֨אמֶר יְהֹוָ֜ה פִּתְאֹ֗ם אֶל־מֹשֶׁ֤ה וְאֶֽל־אַהֲרֹן֙ וְאֶל־מִרְיָ֔ם צְא֥וּ שְׁלָשְׁתְּכֶ֖ם אֶל־אֹ֣הֶל מוֹעֵ֑ד וַיֵּצְא֖וּ שְׁלָשְׁתָּֽם׃ 5 וַיֵּ֤רֶד יְהֹוָה֙ בְּעַמּ֣וּד עָנָ֔ן וַֽיַּעֲמֹ֖ד פֶּ֣תַח הָאֹ֑הֶל וַיִּקְרָא֙ אַהֲרֹ֣ן וּמִרְיָ֔ם וַיֵּצְא֖וּ שְׁנֵיהֶֽם׃ 6 וַיֹּ֖אמֶר שִׁמְעוּ־נָ֣א דְבָרָ֑י

His servants raised Moses to the office of king, and they gave him the wife of Nikanos. But Moses remembered the covenant of God and did not come close to her. He placed a sword in the bed between himself and her, and he did not sin with her.

After Moses successfully reconquered Cush, he ruled as king over Cush for forty years. One day the queen said to the officials, "This ruler has never come close to me. Please install over you a descendant of Nikanos. Do not let a stranger rule over you!"

They said to Moses, "Pick out for yourself some riches and goods and depart from us and return to your homeland in peace." So Moses left for the land of Midian (*Midrash*).

3. The man, Moses, was extremely humble. God rests His presence only on a person who is strong, wealthy, wise, and humble. Moses is the primary example of someone who possessed these qualities and was thus worthy of the Divine Presence resting on him (*Babylonian Talmud, Nedarim* 38a).

Why are strength and wealth requirements for prophecy? Actually, they are prerequisites for humility. Being humble when you are lowly and poor is not difficult, but remaining humble when you have something to boast about is a sign of greatness. Moses had many exceptional qualities, and despite them, he was *"extremely humble"* (*Rabbi Baruch Epstein, 19th–20th century*).

The Sages pointed to many fine qualities that Moses possessed, but the Torah praises him only for his humility. Here you learn that the trait of humility is the equivalent of all the others (*Maimonides, 12th century*).

Even though Moses was fully aware of his own greatness, which surpassed that of every other human being, he was the most humble of all men. This is because he knew that the qualities he possessed, with which he surpassed everybody else, were given to him by God and not through his own personal accomplishment (*Rabbi Shneur Zalman of Lyady, 18th century*).

Food for thought

1. Should the private life of a public figure remain private?

2. How do your critics misunderstand you?

3. Do you ever attack someone's character rather than face the real issue?

numbers 11:35 – 12:6 — be-ha'alotekha

³⁵ From Kibroth-hattaavah the people traveled to Hazeroth, and they stayed in Hazeroth.

Miriam's Criticism of Moses

12 ¹ Miriam and Aaron spoke critically about Moses regarding (his divorce) from the woman of renowned beauty that he had married, for he had married a woman of renowned beauty. ² They said, "Has God only spoken to Moses? Hasn't He spoken to us too (yet we continue our marriages normally)?" And God heard.

³ The man, Moses, was extremely humble, more so than any person on the face of the earth.

⁴ God (appeared) suddenly to Moses, Aaron and Miriam, and said "Go out, all three of you, to the Tent of Meeting!" and the three of them went out.

⁵ God came down in a pillar of cloud and stood at the entrance of the Tent. He called out, "Aaron! Miriam!" and they both went away (from Moses, towards the entrance). ⁶ He said (to them privately, so that Moses should not hear words of praise about himself), "Please listen to My words. When someone among you experiences prophecy, (I), God, will make Myself known to him (only) in a vision,

---

craved that were buried there, not the cravings themselves. Shouldn't the name have been Graves of Those Who Craved?

It happened that the people who remained alive and witnessed the demise of those who had craved were so deeply moved that all their own cravings vanished. So it turned out this *was* a place in which "cravings" were buried (*Rabbi Azariah Figo, 17th century*).

12:1 Miriam and Aaron spoke critically about Moses. Aaron said nothing. Either he agreed with Miriam, or at the very least, his failure to rebuke her was considered a tacit approval (*Rabbi Abraham ibn Ezra, 12th century*).

For he had married a woman of renowned beauty (lit. "a Cushite woman"). It was as obvious that she was beautiful as the fact that a Cushite's skin is black (*Rashi, 11th century*).

Zipporah was a Midianite, and the Midianites are Ishmaelites who live in tents. Due to exposure to the sun their skin has no whiteness at all. So Zipporah was black, like a Cushite.

Miriam rejected the idea that Moses had separated from his wife to achieve prophecy, for both she and Aaron were prophets and yet enjoyed a marital relationship. So Miriam "spoke critically about Moses," insinuating that he had really refrained from being with her because she was unattractive to him (*Rabbi Abraham ibn Ezra, 12th century*).

Moses had fled from Egypt during a nine-year siege when King Nikanos was attempting to regain control of Cush, his own territory, which Balaam had usurped in his absence of war. Moses found favor in their eyes—the king, all of the officers, and the whole military force adored him. The king was very fond of him and appointed him commander over the army. Moses remained there for a long time, until King Nikanos contracted an illness and died.

במדבר יב:ו-טז · בהעלתך

אִם־יִהְיֶה֙ נְבִיאֲכֶ֔ם יְהֹוָ֔ה בַּמַּרְאָה֙ אֵלָ֣יו אֶתְוַדָּ֔ע בַּחֲל֖וֹם אֲדַבֶּר־בּֽוֹ: 7 לֹא־כֵ֖ן עַבְדִּ֣י מֹשֶׁ֑ה בְּכָל־בֵּיתִ֖י נֶאֱמָ֥ן הֽוּא: 8 פֶּ֣ה אֶל־פֶּ֞ה אֲדַבֶּר־בּ֗וֹ וּמַרְאֶה֙ וְלֹ֣א בְחִידֹ֔ת וּתְמֻנַ֥ת יְהֹוָ֖ה יַבִּ֑יט וּמַדּ֨וּעַ֙ לֹ֣א יְרֵאתֶ֔ם לְדַבֵּ֖ר בְּעַבְדִּ֥י בְמֹשֶֽׁה: 9 וַיִּֽחַר־אַ֧ף יְהֹוָ֛ה בָּ֖ם וַיֵּלַֽךְ: 10 וְהֶעָנָ֗ן סָ֚ר מֵעַ֣ל הָאֹ֔הֶל וְהִנֵּ֥ה מִרְיָ֖ם מְצֹרַ֣עַת כַּשָּׁ֑לֶג וַיִּ֧פֶן אַהֲרֹ֛ן אֶל־מִרְיָ֖ם וְהִנֵּ֥ה מְצֹרָֽעַת: 11 וַיֹּ֥אמֶר אַהֲרֹ֖ן אֶל־מֹשֶׁ֑ה בִּ֣י אֲדֹנִ֔י אַל־נָ֨א תָשֵׁ֤ת עָלֵ֙ינוּ֙ חַטָּ֔את אֲשֶׁ֥ר נוֹאַ֖לְנוּ וַאֲשֶׁ֥ר חָטָֽאנוּ: 12 אַל־נָ֥א תְהִ֖י כַּמֵּ֑ת אֲשֶׁ֤ר בְּצֵאתוֹ֙ מֵרֶ֣חֶם אִמּ֔וֹ וַיֵּאָכֵ֖ל חֲצִ֥י בְשָׂרֽוֹ: 13 וַיִּצְעַ֣ק מֹשֶׁ֔ה אֶל־יְהֹוָ֖ה לֵאמֹ֑ר אֵ֕ל נָ֛א רְפָ֥א נָ֖א לָֽהּ: [מפטיר] 14 וַיֹּ֨אמֶר יְהֹוָ֜ה אֶל־מֹשֶׁ֗ה וְאָבִ֙יהָ֙ יָרֹ֤ק יָרַק֙ בְּפָנֶ֔יהָ הֲלֹ֥א תִכָּלֵ֖ם שִׁבְעַ֣ת יָמִ֑ים תִּסָּגֵ֞ר שִׁבְעַ֤ת יָמִים֙ מִח֣וּץ לַֽמַּחֲנֶ֔ה וְאַחַ֖ר תֵּאָסֵֽף: 15 וַתִּסָּגֵ֥ר מִרְיָ֛ם מִח֥וּץ לַֽמַּחֲנֶ֖ה שִׁבְעַ֣ת יָמִ֑ים וְהָעָם֙ לֹ֣א נָסַ֔ע עַד־הֵאָסֵ֖ף מִרְיָֽם: 16 וְאַחַ֛ר נָסְע֥וּ הָעָ֖ם מֵחֲצֵר֑וֹת וַֽיַּחֲנ֖וּ בְּמִדְבַּ֥ר פָּארָֽן: פ פ פ

קל"ו פסוקים, מהלל"אל סימן.

arrogance or falsehood, or habit, resulting from a bad upbringing or a negative environment. If you can't identify the specific location of the illness, you cannot begin to cure it.

Most importantly "the patient" needs to know two things: a) *he is ill*, and wishes to be cured; and b) he *can* be cured. And he needs to have hope and absolute trust that, with God's help, he *will* be cured of his sickness (*Rabbi Joseph Isaac Schneersohn of Lubavitch, 20th century*).

15. The people did not travel until Miriam was brought back. This honor was accorded her by God because of the time she remained with Moses when he was cast into the river, as the verse states, *"His sister stood by from afar, etc."* (*Exodus 2:4; Rashi, 11th century*).

spiritual vitamin

> Because the soul is trapped in a physical body, it sometimes happens that the Divine signals which are sent to the soul are either not received at all or are received in distortion by the physical "static." But the signals are there. They are buried in the subconscious, and from there, impulses, thoughts and stimuli beg to be admitted into the conscious state.

numbers 12:6–16 — be-ha'alotekha

or I will speak to him (merely) in a dream. [7] But this is not the case with My servant Moses! Among my entire household, he is (the most) trusted. [8] It was I who told him, mouth to mouth (to separate from his wife), in a vision (of clarity, where every word was made known) and not in riddles. (When I speak to him) he gazes at the image of God (from behind). So why were you not afraid to speak about My servant, about Moses?" [9] Then God became angry with them, and He left.

[10] The cloud rose from above the Tent, and—look!—Miriam was afflicted with *tzara'at*, (as white) as snow. Then Aaron turned to Miriam and—look!—she was afflicted with *tzara'at*.

[11] Aaron said to Moses, "Please, master, do not count it as a sin against us, for we sinned out of foolishness. [12] Don't let her (remain a *tzara'at* sufferer, who is a source of ritual impurity) like the dead! (When a person's sister, who) comes out of his mother's womb, (is afflicted) half his (own) flesh is consumed!"

[13] Moses cried out to God, saying, "Please, God! Please heal her!"

[MAFTIR] [14] God said to Moses, "If her father were to spit in her face (angrily), wouldn't she be humiliated (and not show herself) for seven days? (All the more so now that God has become angry with her) let her be quarantined outside the camp for seven days. Afterwards, she may be brought back."

[15] Miriam was quarantined outside the camp for seven days.

The people did not travel until Miriam was brought back. [16] Then the people departed from Hazeroth, and they camped in the desert of Paran.

The Haftarah for Be-Ha'alotekha is on page 1373.

He thought that if another person had been given such abilities, he too would have reached the same degree of greatness. In fact, Moses thought, if another person had been given these talents, that person would have *definitely* put them to even better use (*Rabbi Shalom Dov Baer Schneersohn of Lubavitch, 19th–20th century*).

7. This is not the case with My servant Moses. The other prophets received their prophecies in a dream or supernatural vision, whereas Moses received his prophecy while awake and standing.

The other prophets received their prophecies by means of an angel, and therefore what they saw was a parable and riddle. But *"God would speak to Moses face to face"* (*Exodus* 33:11).

The other prophets were gripped by fear and terror when they received their prophecies, but Moses was not—*"God would speak to Moses ... as a man would speak to his friend"* (ibid.).

None of the other prophets were able to receive prophecy whenever they wanted to, which was not the case with Moses. His mind was always connected with God, the Eternal Rock, and God's glory never left him at all. His face emanated light, and he was as holy as the angels (*Maimonides, 12th century*).

13. Please God! Please heal her! *Healing the soul is just like the healing body.* The first step is to identify the "location" of the illness, whether it is caused by undesirable traits such as

> The spies failed to realize that **God's command** includes an **assurance** that **you will be able** to fulfil it. Remember that **God grants** you the **ability to fulfil** all of His ethical and ritual commandments.

SHELAḤ-LEKHA
שלח לך

EPISODE OF THE SPIES	13:1 – 14:45
ADDITIONAL LAWS OF SACRIFICES	15:1–31
FIRST SABBATH DESECRATION	15:32–36
THE COMMANDMENT OF *TZITZIT*	15:37–41

NAME
Shelaḥ-Lekha

MEANING
"Send for yourself"

LINES IN TORAH SCROLL
198

PARASHIYYOT
7 open; 3 closed

VERSES
119

WORDS
1540

LETTERS
5820

LOCATION
Sinai Desert, desert of Paran, Kadesh-barnea

DATE
Sivan–Elul, 2449

KEY PEOPLE
Moses, Aaron, Caleb, Hosea, the Spies

MITZVOT
2 positive; 1 prohibition

MASORETIC FEATURES
Enlarged letter *yod* in the word *yiggdal* (14:17)

NOTES
Usually read on the Sabbath preceding the new moon of *Tammuz*

CHARACTER PROFILE

NAME
Caleb ("devotion")

WIFE
Miriam (Ephrath)

FATHER
Jephunneh

CHILD
Hur

GRANDSON
Uri son of Hur

GREAT-GRANDSON
Bezalel son of Uri

POSITION
Leader of the tribe of Judah; Joshua's spokesman

ACHIEVEMENTS
Was chosen as a spy by both Moses and Joshua; received the city of Hebron as a reward for not being swayed by the other spies

FAMOUS FOR
Standing up in support of Moses when the spies returned

ELEVATING THE PHYSICAL

The spies did not want to leave the desert, a place geared to spiritual life, and enter a land where they would be forced to engage with the physical reality. God, however, does want you to engage with the physical world and elevate it through your actions (ch. 13).

ASSOCIATION WITH DISHONEST PEOPLE

Caleb and Joshua did not join the spies in carrying the massive fruits. The spies' intention was to mislead the Jews and, since their intention was wrong, Caleb and Joshua did not participate (13:23).

CHARITY

Only after you have separated *hallah* from dough can you use it for yourself. This applies to all your income: you should first give to charity the part that belongs to God, before using your money (15:17-21).

במדבר יג:א-יז　　　　שלח לך

יג 1 וַיְדַבֵּ֥ר יְהֹוָ֖ה אֶל־מֹשֶׁ֥ה לֵּאמֹֽר: 2 שְׁלַח־לְךָ֣ אֲנָשִׁ֗ים וְיָתֻ֙רוּ֙ אֶת־אֶ֣רֶץ כְּנַ֔עַן אֲשֶׁר־אֲנִ֥י נֹתֵ֖ן לִבְנֵ֣י יִשְׂרָאֵ֑ל אִ֣ישׁ אֶחָד֩ אִ֨ישׁ אֶחָ֜ד לְמַטֵּ֤ה אֲבֹתָיו֙ תִּשְׁלָ֔חוּ כֹּ֖ל נָשִׂ֥יא בָהֶֽם: 3 וַיִּשְׁלַ֨ח אֹתָ֥ם מֹשֶׁ֛ה מִמִּדְבַּ֥ר פָּארָ֖ן עַל־פִּ֣י יְהֹוָ֑ה כֻּלָּ֣ם אֲנָשִׁ֔ים רָאשֵׁ֥י בְנֵֽי־יִשְׂרָאֵ֖ל הֵֽמָּה: 4 וְאֵ֖לֶּה שְׁמוֹתָ֑ם לְמַטֵּ֣ה רְאוּבֵ֔ן שַׁמּ֖וּעַ בֶּן־זַכּֽוּר: 5 לְמַטֵּ֣ה שִׁמְע֔וֹן שָׁפָ֖ט בֶּן־חוֹרִֽי: 6 לְמַטֵּ֣ה יְהוּדָ֔ה כָּלֵ֖ב בֶּן־יְפֻנֶּֽה: 7 לְמַטֵּ֣ה יִשָּׂשכָ֔ר יִגְאָ֖ל בֶּן־יוֹסֵֽף: 8 לְמַטֵּ֥ה אֶפְרָ֖יִם הוֹשֵׁ֥עַ בִּן־נֽוּן: 9 לְמַטֵּ֣ה בִנְיָמִ֔ן פַּלְטִ֖י בֶּן־רָפֽוּא: 10 לְמַטֵּ֣ה זְבוּלֻ֔ן גַּדִּיאֵ֖ל בֶּן־סוֹדִֽי: 11 לְמַטֵּ֥ה יוֹסֵ֖ף לְמַטֵּ֣ה מְנַשֶּׁ֑ה גַּדִּ֖י בֶּן־סוּסִֽי: 12 לְמַטֵּ֣ה דָ֔ן עַמִּיאֵ֖ל בֶּן־גְּמַלִּֽי: 13 לְמַטֵּ֣ה אָשֵׁ֔ר סְת֖וּר בֶּן־מִיכָאֵֽל: 14 לְמַטֵּ֣ה נַפְתָּלִ֔י נַחְבִּ֖י בֶּן־וׇפְסִֽי: 15 לְמַטֵּ֣ה גָ֔ד גְּאוּאֵ֖ל בֶּן־מָכִֽי: 16 אֵ֚לֶּה שְׁמ֣וֹת הָֽאֲנָשִׁ֔ים אֲשֶׁר־שָׁלַ֥ח מֹשֶׁ֖ה לָת֣וּר אֶת־הָאָ֑רֶץ וַיִּקְרָ֥א מֹשֶׁ֛ה לְהוֹשֵׁ֥עַ בִּן־נ֖וּן יְהוֹשֻֽׁעַ: 17 וַיִּשְׁלַ֤ח אֹתָם֙ מֹשֶׁ֔ה לָת֖וּר אֶת־אֶ֣רֶץ כְּנָ֑עַן וַיֹּ֣אמֶר אֲלֵהֶ֔ם עֲל֥וּ זֶ֖ה

Nevertheless they were sent, "by the *word of God*" (v. 3), with His consent. He did not stop it (*Rashi*, 11th century).

The men expressed contempt for the land, saying, *"Let's appoint a leader and return to Egypt!"* (14:4), whereas the women adored the land, saying, *"Give us a portion"* in it (27:4; *Yalkut Shimoni*). God said to Moses, "In my opinion—for I know the future—it would be better to send women as spies, since they adore the land and they would never speak badly of it. But in your opinion, these spies are respectable, and you feel that they love the land. So send men."

"Follow your own opinion and send them," says God, "but in My opinion, you should send women" (*Rabbi Ephraim of Luntshits*, 16th–17th century).

4. These were their names. The names of each of the spies is chanted with the cantillation note *tippeḥa*, which has a prolonged tone, suggestive of interruption or disconnection. This alludes to the fact that the spies had already at this time disconnected themselves from their *spiritual root*.

The only exception is Joshua (v. 8), whose cantillation note, *merkha*, is a tone which flows more swiftly into the next word, indicating that he had retained his connection (*Rabbi Menahem Azariah da Fano*, 16th–17th century).

16. Moses called Hosea son of Nun, "Joshua." Moses added the letter *yod* to Joshua's name so it now began with the letters *yod* and *he*,

Food for thought

1. How do we balance living in the natural order with trust in God's aid?

2. Have you ever been "forced" to use deception?

3. Is it ever impossible to do God's will?

parashat shelaḥ-lekha

Moses Sends Spies to Inspect the Land

13 ¹ God spoke to Moses, saying, ² "Send out men for yourself to explore the land of Canaan, which I am giving to the children of Israel. Send one man for each paternal tribe. Each one should be a leader among them."

³ Moses sent them, by the word of God, from the desert of Paran. All of them were men of distinction. They were the heads of the children of Israel. ⁴ These were their names:

For the tribe of Reuben, Shammua son of Zaccur.

⁵ For the tribe of Simeon, Shaphat son of Hori.

⁶ For the tribe of Judah, Caleb son of Jephunneh.

⁷ For the tribe of Issachar, Igal son of Joseph.

⁸ For the tribe of Ephraim, Hosea son of Nun.

⁹ For the tribe of Benjamin, Palti son of Rafu.

¹⁰ For the tribe of Zebulun, Gaddiel son of Sodi.

¹¹ For the tribe of Joseph, the tribe of Manasseh, Gaddi son of Susi.

¹² For the tribe of Dan, Ammiel son of Gemalli.

¹³ For the tribe of Asher, Sethur son of Michael.

¹⁴ For the tribe of Naphtali, Nahbi son of Vophsi.

¹⁵ For the tribe of Gad, Geuel son of Machi.

¹⁶ These were the names of the men Moses sent to explore the land.

Moses called Hosea son of Nun, "Joshua."

¹⁷ Moses sent them to explore the land of Canaan. He said to them, "Go up this way along the south (border until you reach the sea), and then go up (the west

---

13:2 Send out men. When you arrive in a place and begin to worship God there, all the "sparks" of holiness that are found in the place become embarrassed of you, because you reveal the purpose of Creation. Once the sparks are embarrassed, you can easily conquer them.

That is why Moses sent out spies—he wanted to embarrass the sparks found in the land, making them easier to conquer.

But for the sparks to become embarrassed, you have to divest yourself, as much as possible from physicality. Only then can you conquer them. This is hinted to by the word *shelaḥ* "send," which can also mean to "strip off," as in *"they stripped (yafshitu) Joseph of his tunic,"* which is rendered by *Targum Onkelos* as *'ashlaḥu* (Genesis 37:23; *Rabbi Levi Isaac of Berdichev, 18th century*).

Send out men for yourself. God was saying, "Follow your own opinion and send them. I am not commanding you—but if you wish, you may send."

במדבר יג:יז‑כג　שלח לך

בַּנֶּגֶב וַעֲלִיתֶם אֶת־הָהָר: 18 וּרְאִיתֶם אֶת־הָאָרֶץ מַה־הִוא וְאֶת־הָעָם הַיֹּשֵׁב עָלֶיהָ הֶחָזָק הוּא הֲרָפֶה הַמְעַט הוּא אִם־רָב: 19 וּמָה הָאָרֶץ אֲשֶׁר־הוּא יֹשֵׁב בָּהּ הֲטוֹבָה הִוא אִם־רָעָה וּמָה הֶעָרִים אֲשֶׁר־הוּא יוֹשֵׁב בָּהֵנָּה הַבְּמַחֲנִים אִם בְּמִבְצָרִים: 20 וּמָה הָאָרֶץ הַשְּׁמֵנָה הִוא אִם־רָזָה הֲיֵשׁ־בָּהּ עֵץ אִם־אַיִן וְהִתְחַזַּקְתֶּם וּלְקַחְתֶּם מִפְּרִי הָאָרֶץ וְהַיָּמִים יְמֵי בִּכּוּרֵי עֲנָבִים: [SECOND READING] 21 וַיַּעֲלוּ וַיָּתֻרוּ אֶת־הָאָרֶץ מִמִּדְבַּר־צִן עַד־רְחֹב לְבֹא חֲמָת: 22 וַיַּעֲלוּ בַנֶּגֶב וַיָּבֹא עַד־חֶבְרוֹן וְשָׁם אֲחִימַן שֵׁשַׁי וְתַלְמַי יְלִידֵי הָעֲנָק וְחֶבְרוֹן שֶׁבַע שָׁנִים נִבְנְתָה לִפְנֵי צֹעַן מִצְרָיִם: 23 וַיָּבֹאוּ עַד־נַחַל אֶשְׁכֹּל וַיִּכְרְתוּ מִשָּׁם זְמוֹרָה וְאֶשְׁכּוֹל עֲנָבִים אֶחָד וַיִּשָּׂאֻהוּ בַמּוֹט בִּשְׁנָיִם וּמִן־הָרִמֹּנִים וּמִן־הַתְּאֵנִים:

Moses asked them to find out if Job, who lived in the land of Israel, was still alive. He is referred to as a "tree," because his years were as many as those of a tree, and he protected his generation like a tree shields others through its shade (*Babylonian Talmud, Bava Batra* 15a).

22. He came to Hebron. Caleb went there alone and prostrated himself at the graves of the Patriarchs, praying that he not be drawn into his colleagues' scheme (*Rashi, 11th century*).

23. They cut a branch with a cluster of grapes and they carried it on (two) double poles. (They also took) pomegranates and figs. Rabbi Isaac Luria teaches that the commandment of the first fruit offering (see *Deuteronomy* 26:1-16) was given by God to rectify the sin of the spies. The spies had spoken slanderously of the land, so a new commandment was required that would highlight the land's fine qualities.

The *Mishnah* (*Bikkurim* 3:1), in its description of the first fruit selection process, seems to allude to Rabbi Isaac Luria's explanation. Of the seven species with which the land of Israel is blessed, the *Mishnah* uses the example of only three species—grape, pomegranate, and fig—which are precisely the same fruits which the spies brought back with them (*Rabbi Menahem Zemba, 20th century*).

They carried it on (two) double poles. Eight of them took the bunch of grapes, one took a fig and one took a pomegranate. Joshua and Caleb did not take anything, for the whole intention of the others was to speak negatively about the land—that its people, like its fruit, are abnormal (*Rashi, 11th century*).

Joshua and Caleb were men of importance, so it was not appropriate for them to carry a load (*Babylonian Talmud, Sotah* 34a).

> **kabbalah bites**
>
> **13:22** Caleb was a reincarnation of Eliezer, Abraham's loyal servant (see *Genesis* 24:31). Therefore, Caleb now prostrated himself before the grave of his soul-master, Abraham.

numbers 13:17–23 — shelaḥ-lekha

coast until you reach Hamath, which is by) the (Hor) mountain. ¹⁸ See what kind of land it is. Are the people who inhabit it strong or weak? Are there a few of them, or many? ¹⁹ How is the land which they inhabit? Does it have good (springs and wells) or bad (ones)? How are the cities in which they live? Are they in unenclosed cities, or in fortresses? ²⁰ What is the soil like? Is it fertile or barren? Are there any (righteous people) there (who are like) trees (that protect the people), or not? Be courageous and take some of the land's fruit."

It was the season when the first grapes ripen.

[SECOND READING] ²¹ They went up and explored the land, from the desert of Zin (at the southeast corner of the land) until Rehob, at the approach to Hamath.

²² When they went up along the south border, (Caleb) came to Hebron (to pray at the graves of the Patriarchs not to be enticed by the advice of the spies). The giants Ahiman, Sheshai and Talmai were there. Hebron (was the rockiest part of the land of Israel, and yet it was) seven times more cultivated than Zoan (which was the best part of) Egypt.

²³ They came to the valley of Eshcol and they cut a branch with a cluster of grapes and they carried it on (two) double poles. (They also took) pomegranates

---

spelling one of the names of God. This hints to the fact that Moses prayed for him, "May God save you from the advice of the spies!" (*Rashi, 11th century*).

Because the spies enjoyed great public esteem, and knowing that Joshua was an exceptionally humble man, Moses was afraid that Joshua might humbly follow the spies' lead. Therefore he prayed on his behalf, "May God save you from the advice of the spies!" (*Rabbi Moses b. Joseph Schick, 19th century*).

Why did Moses pray more for Joshua than the other spies? Because Joshua was Moses' personal disciple. If Joshua failed, people would think he was following instructions he had received from Moses (*Rabbi Judah Loew b. Bezalel of Prague, 16th century*).

20. Are there any trees? Is there an upright man there who will protect them with his merit? (*Rashi, 11th century*).

After asking if the land was fertile, the question *"Are there any trees?"* seems superfluous. Moses must therefore have been hinting that they find out whether any righteous person lived in the land, whose merit would protect it from conquest (*Rabbi Elijah Mizraḥi, 15th–16th century*).

---

kabbalah bites

13:20 *"Is there a tree there or not?"* Moses was like the face of the sun; Joshua, like the face of the moon (*Babylonian Talmud, Bava Batra 75a*). Moses knew that the land of Israel was associated with *Malkhut* (receptiveness), a quality that is associated with the moon, not the sun. He was concerned that because his own light was too great, he would not enter the land.

Therefore, he asked the spies to ascertain: *"Is there a tree there or not?"* Is the Tree of Life, *Tiferet*—known as the "sun"—there? If it is, then I can enter the land. Otherwise, I cannot.

במדבר יג:כד-ל · שלח לך

24 לַמָּק֣וֹם הַה֗וּא קָרָא֙ נַ֣חַל אֶשְׁכּ֔וֹל עַ֚ל אֹד֣וֹת הָֽאֶשְׁכּ֔וֹל אֲשֶׁר־כָּרְת֥וּ מִשָּׁ֖ם בְּנֵ֥י יִשְׂרָאֵֽל: 25 וַיָּשֻׁ֖בוּ מִתּ֣וּר הָאָ֑רֶץ מִקֵּ֖ץ אַרְבָּעִ֥ים יֽוֹם: 26 וַיֵּלְכ֡וּ וַיָּבֹאוּ֩ אֶל־מֹשֶׁ֨ה וְאֶֽל־אַהֲרֹ֜ן וְאֶל־כָּל־עֲדַ֧ת בְּנֵֽי־יִשְׂרָאֵ֛ל אֶל־מִדְבַּ֥ר פָּארָ֖ן קָדֵ֑שָׁה וַיָּשִׁ֨יבוּ אוֹתָ֤ם דָּבָר֙ וְאֶת־כָּל־הָ֣עֵדָ֔ה וַיַּרְא֖וּם אֶת־פְּרִ֥י הָאָֽרֶץ: 27 וַיְסַפְּרוּ־לוֹ֙ וַיֹּ֣אמְר֔וּ בָּ֕אנוּ אֶל־הָאָ֖רֶץ אֲשֶׁ֣ר שְׁלַחְתָּ֑נוּ וְ֠גַ֠ם זָבַ֨ת חָלָ֥ב וּדְבַ֛שׁ הִ֖וא וְזֶה־פִּרְיָֽהּ: 28 אֶ֚פֶס כִּֽי־עַ֣ז הָעָ֔ם הַיֹּשֵׁ֖ב בָּאָ֑רֶץ וְהֶֽעָרִ֗ים בְּצֻר֤וֹת גְּדֹלֹת֙ מְאֹ֔ד וְגַם־יְלִדֵ֥י הָֽעֲנָ֖ק רָאִ֥ינוּ שָֽׁם: 29 עֲמָלֵ֥ק יוֹשֵׁ֖ב בְּאֶ֣רֶץ הַנֶּ֑גֶב וְ֠הַחִתִּ֨י וְהַיְבוּסִ֤י וְהָֽאֱמֹרִי֙ יוֹשֵׁ֣ב בָּהָ֔ר וְהַֽכְּנַעֲנִי֙ יוֹשֵׁ֣ב עַל־הַיָּ֔ם וְעַ֖ל יַ֥ד הַיַּרְדֵּֽן: 30 וַיַּ֧הַס כָּלֵ֛ב אֶת־הָעָ֖ם אֶל־מֹשֶׁ֑ה וַיֹּ֗אמֶר

Joshua (*Rashi* to 11:28). Hearing this, they could not imagine how, without Moses' leadership, they would be able to conquer the heavily fortified cities that the spies had described. *"Caleb silenced the people,"* telling them that it would be an error to attribute all the great miracles they had witnessed to Moses himself. God performs miracles *for the sake of the Israelites,* so they would be able to conquer the Promised Land even without Moses—*"We will definitely go up! We will take possession of (the land)."*

Caleb, not Joshua, needed to be the bearer of this message. Had Joshua said it, the people—after hearing Eldad and Medad's prophecy—might have suspected Joshua's motives in downplaying Moses' role, because Joshua was Moses' appointed successor (*Rabbi Meir Simhah of Dvinsk, 19th–20th century*).

In Moses' briefing to the spies, he had instructed them first of all to evaluate the power of the enemy (*"Are the people who inhabit it strong or weak? Are there a few of them, or many?"*—v. 18), since conquering the land was their immediate concern. Secondly, Moses told them to collect information about the fertility of the land (*"What is the soil like? Is it fertile or barren?"*—v. 20), so the people would know what their reward would be after the conquest was complete.

But when the spies gave their report they switched the order: First they mentioned the quality of the land (*"It is flowing with milk and honey"*—v. 27), and only then did they progress to discuss the enemy (*"The people who live in the land are (extraordinarily) powerful"*—v. 28).

spiritual vitamin

> The Torah teaches us not to rely on miracles where things can and ought to be approached in natural ways and means. However, while doing so it is necessary to bear in mind that these so-called "natural" ways and means are also miracles ordained by God.

numbers 13:23–30 — shelaḥ-lekha

and figs. ²⁴ They called that place the valley of Eshcol because of the cluster [*eshkol*] the children of Israel cut from there.

The Spies' Report

²⁵ At the end of forty days, they returned from scouting the land.

²⁶ They went (with bad intentions, and their intentions remained bad when) they came to Moses and Aaron and the entire congregation of the children of Israel in Kadesh, in the desert of Paran.

They brought them back a report (to Moses and Aaron), as well as to the entire congregation, and they showed them the land's fruit. ²⁷ They reported to (Moses) and said: "We came to the land to which you sent us. It is flowing with milk and honey, and this is its fruit!"

²⁸ "However… the people who live in the land are (extraordinarily) powerful. The cities are huge and well fortified, and we even saw the children of a giant there! ²⁹ Amalek lives in the south of the land, the Hittites, Jebusites, and Amorites live in the mountains, and the Canaanites live (both) on the coast and alongside the Jordan."

³⁰ Caleb silenced the people to (listen to what he would say about) Moses.

---

27. It is flowing with milk and honey, and this is its fruit! Any lie which does not begin with a bit of truth cannot be sustained in the end (*Rashi, 11th century*).

Their lie was the statement at the end of verse 27, that *"this is its fruit!"* For one of the main purposes of their mission was to evaluate whether the land was fertile and capable of sustaining a nation, as Moses said in his briefing, *"What is the soil like? Is it fertile or barren?"* (v. 20). Thus by claiming, *"This is its fruit,"* while producing a mere offering of grapes, pomegranates and figs, the spies were indicating that the main produce of wheat, barley and oil, which give a person sustenance, was lacking from the land. This was their lie (*Rabbi Samuel Edels, 16th–17th century*).

29. Amalek lives in the south of the land. The spies mentioned Amalek in order to frighten the people, who had been traumatized by Amalek in the past (*Rashi, 11th century*).

30. Caleb silenced the people to (listen to what he would say about) Moses. Why did Caleb speak up and not Joshua? The children of Israel had just heard Eldad and Medad's prediction that Moses would pass away, to be succeeded by

---

kabbalah bites

13:26 *"They went and they came."* Why does the Torah restate the fact of their departure here?

When the spies were appointed they became impregnated with the souls of Jacob's sons as an aid to fulfil their mission (see Genesis 42:9). But as soon as they demurred, choosing to criticize the land, these lofty souls departed from them. *"They went"*—the souls of Jacob's sons departed from them; *"and they (the spies) came to Moses."*

עָלֹה נַעֲלֶה וְיָרַשְׁנוּ אֹתָהּ כִּי־יָכוֹל נוּכַל לָהּ: 31 וְהָאֲנָשִׁים אֲשֶׁר־עָלוּ עִמּוֹ אָמְרוּ לֹא נוּכַל לַעֲלוֹת אֶל־הָעָם כִּי־חָזָק הוּא מִמֶּנּוּ: 32 וַיּוֹצִיאוּ דִּבַּת הָאָרֶץ אֲשֶׁר תָּרוּ אֹתָהּ אֶל־בְּנֵי יִשְׂרָאֵל לֵאמֹר הָאָרֶץ אֲשֶׁר עָבַרְנוּ בָהּ לָתוּר אֹתָהּ אֶרֶץ אֹכֶלֶת יוֹשְׁבֶיהָ הִוא וְכָל־הָעָם אֲשֶׁר־רָאִינוּ בְתוֹכָהּ אַנְשֵׁי מִדּוֹת: 33 וְשָׁם רָאִינוּ אֶת־הַנְּפִילִים בְּנֵי עֲנָק מִן־הַנְּפִלִים וַנְּהִי בְעֵינֵינוּ כַּחֲגָבִים וְכֵן הָיִינוּ בְּעֵינֵיהֶם:

31. We are unable. The sin of the spies was not, as it may first seem, their report that the land of Israel harbored a formidable enemy—*"The people who live in the land are (extraordinarily) powerful. The cities are huge and well fortified"* (13:28). For they were sent by Moses to collect information, and what they reported was true. Rather, their sin was *the conclusion that they added—that God's command to conquer the land was, in their opinion, not possible, "We are unable to go up against the people, for they are stronger than us"* (Rabbi Elijah Mizraḥi, 15th–16th century).

God's promise to enter the land was going to come true, regardless of whether the Jewish people would enjoy a natural or a supernatural victory. The command "not to rely on a miracle" (*Babylonian Talmud, Pesaḥim* 64b) means that the Jewish people were required to make logistical and tactical plans for their war, in case God wished to send them a victory garbed in nature. And this necessitated the sending of spies, to gather information.

The spies' mistake was that *the fulfillment of God's command is not dependent on finding a practical solution.* We must "not rely on a miracle" to exempt us from trying to find a natural means through which God might send salvation. But if no such means can be found, then we must indeed rely on a miracle, because the alternative is that God's command will not be carried out, and that is unacceptable.

This is a fundamental premise upon which our approach to observing all the commandments should be based: *God's command includes an implicit promise that it will be possible to carry out that command* (Rabbi Menaḥem Mendel Schneerson, 20th century).

They are stronger than us. This could also be rendered "they are stronger than *Him.*" They said this in reference to God, so to speak (*Rashi, 11th century*).

32. A land that consumes its inhabitants. In every place, the people were found burying their dead (*Rashi, 11th century*).

The Canaanites had a custom not to bury their dead immediately, waiting instead until a prominent person had died. They would then bury all the dead along with the important person, believing that he would watch over them and take them to heaven. Job died during the spies' mission (*Babylonian Talmud, Sotah* 35a), and many people were buried along with him. When the spies saw so many people being buried, they mistakenly presumed that the death rate was very high in the land (*Rabbi Mordecai ha-Kohen, 17th century*).

33. We appeared like grasshoppers in our eyes, and that's how we were in their eyes. God said to the spies, "I could tolerate you saying, *'We appeared like grasshoppers in our eyes,'* but I take offense at you concluding, *'and that's how we were in their eyes.'* Could you possibly know how I made you appear in their eyes? Who can say that in their eyes you were not like angels? (*Midrash Tanḥuma*).

numbers 13:30–33 — shelaḥ-lekha

Then he said, "We will definitely go up! We will take possession of (the land), for we are certainly capable (of conquering) it!"

³¹ But the men who went up with him said, "We are unable to go up against the people, for they are stronger than us (and our God)."

³² They produced a report about the land which they had explored, telling the children of Israel: "The land we passed through and explored is a land that consumes its inhabitants. All the people we saw in it are enormous men. ³³ We saw Nephilim-giants there, supersized giants (that blocked the sun, descended) from the Nephilim-giants (Shemḥazzai and Azael). We appeared like grasshoppers in our eyes, and that's how we were in their eyes."

From this, Caleb immediately sensed that the spies had corrupted their priorities. Moses had prefaced the effort (conquest) before reward (the land's fruit); but the spies were primarily interested in the rewards, so they stressed that first.

On noticing this, Caleb immediately "silenced the people," for Caleb understood that focusing on the reward would lead them to calculate whether it was worth the effort, which would soon develop into a full-blown rebellion (*Rabbi Menahem Mendel Schneerson, 20th century*).

We will definitely go up! *"We will definitely go up,"* even to heaven. If Moses tells us, "Make ladders and go up there," we will succeed in whatever he says (*Rashi, 11th century*).

The spies had offered some sound arguments, *"the people who live in the land are (extraordinarily) powerful. The cities are huge and well fortified"* (v. 28). Why did Caleb not debate with the other spies or respond to their arguments? All he said was the simple statement, *"We will definitely go up!"*

But this is how our faith ought to be. We shouldn't just believe that God will save us when we can see some viable paths of salvation, but also when we see no way out.

In such dark times it is better *not to look* for natural paths for salvation, because failure to find any may result in a lack of faith. We just need to say: *"Logically* it is true. The people of the land are very strong, and their cities are well fortified—*but still I believe in God, who is above nature.* I believe that He will save us."

That is what Caleb meant with his simple reply, *"We will definitely go up."* If the task seems impossible, then we shouldn't rationalize or theorize about it. Just having faith alone in God's supernatural power will bring our salvation close (*Rabbi Kalonymous Kalman Shapira, 20th century*).

There had been three different intentions in sending the spies. The intentions of *the spies* themselves was self-serving—they ran after honor, and because of this they regressed from one mistake to another until they eventually denied God's power.

The *Jewish people's* intention was to know the truth—whether it was possible to conquer the land or not through natural means. But limiting their faith to the natural was something ugly in the eyes of Moses and God.

God's intention had been that when the spies would report that a military conquest was impossible in the natural order, the Jewish people would strengthen their faith that God would nevertheless help them to win (*Rabbi Isaiah Horowitz, 16th–17th century*).

במדבר יד:א-ט · שלח לך

לֶךְ ‎1 וַתִּשָּׂא כָּל־הָעֵדָה וַיִּתְּנוּ אֶת־קוֹלָם וַיִּבְכּוּ הָעָם בַּלַּיְלָה הַהוּא: ‎2 וַיִּלֹּנוּ עַל־מֹשֶׁה וְעַל־אַהֲרֹן כֹּל בְּנֵי יִשְׂרָאֵל וַיֹּאמְרוּ אֲלֵהֶם כָּל־הָעֵדָה לוּ־מַתְנוּ בְּאֶרֶץ מִצְרַיִם אוֹ בַּמִּדְבָּר הַזֶּה לוּ־מָתְנוּ: ‎3 וְלָמָה יְהֹוָה מֵבִיא אֹתָנוּ אֶל־הָאָרֶץ הַזֹּאת לִנְפֹּל בַּחֶרֶב נָשֵׁינוּ וְטַפֵּנוּ יִהְיוּ לָבַז הֲלוֹא טוֹב לָנוּ שׁוּב מִצְרָיְמָה: ‎4 וַיֹּאמְרוּ אִישׁ אֶל־אָחִיו נִתְּנָה רֹאשׁ וְנָשׁוּבָה מִצְרָיְמָה: ‎5 וַיִּפֹּל מֹשֶׁה וְאַהֲרֹן עַל־פְּנֵיהֶם לִפְנֵי כָּל־קְהַל עֲדַת בְּנֵי יִשְׂרָאֵל: ‎6 וִיהוֹשֻׁעַ בִּן־נוּן וְכָלֵב בֶּן־יְפֻנֶּה מִן־הַתָּרִים אֶת־הָאָרֶץ קָרְעוּ בִּגְדֵיהֶם: ‎7 וַיֹּאמְרוּ אֶל־כָּל־עֲדַת בְּנֵי־יִשְׂרָאֵל לֵאמֹר הָאָרֶץ אֲשֶׁר עָבַרְנוּ בָהּ לָתוּר אֹתָהּ טוֹבָה הָאָרֶץ מְאֹד מְאֹד: ‎8 [THIRD READING] אִם־חָפֵץ בָּנוּ יְהֹוָה וְהֵבִיא אֹתָנוּ אֶל־הָאָרֶץ הַזֹּאת וּנְתָנָהּ לָנוּ אֶרֶץ אֲשֶׁר־הִוא זָבַת חָלָב וּדְבָשׁ: ‎9 אַךְ בַּיהֹוָה אַל־תִּמְרֹדוּ וְאַתֶּם אַל־תִּירְאוּ אֶת־עַם הָאָרֶץ כִּי לַחְמֵנוּ הֵם סָר צִלָּם מֵעֲלֵיהֶם וַיהֹוָה אִתָּנוּ אַל־תִּירָאֻם:

longer produce water, meaning that the people would be forced to seek their sustenance through natural means. Then, the spies argued, they would be helpless. For these miracles had only proven that God could provide assistance by breaking nature; they had no evidence that God's providence would extend *within* nature.

They concluded, it is *"A land that consumes its inhabitants"* (v. 32), as if to say, "When we will be preoccupied with earning a living through natural means, our ability to worship God will be completely consumed!"

Joshua and Caleb responded, *"If God desires us, He will bring us to this land."* God is not bound by any limitation whatsoever. His providence will extend to us within the confines of nature. God will help us every single day, not with earth-shattering miracles, but with "small miracles," that do not overtly break the natural order (*Rabbi Menahem Mendel Schneerson, 20th century*).

9. Do not rebel against God, and then you will not fear the people of that land. Moses and Aaron were telling the people, "If you feel intimidated by *'the people of that land,'*—that *in itself* is an act of rebellion against God."

"God performed miracles for you when we left Egypt, and He has assured you that He will drive them out of the land. Your success has never been dependent purely on your own efforts; faith in God will ensure your success" (*Naḥmanides, 13th century*).

Food for thought

1. Why does complaining feel so good?

2. Are you more inclined to believe negative reports than positive ones?

3. Have you ever betrayed God's kindness?

shelaḥ-lekha

The People Rebel

14 ¹ The whole assembly (of the seventy elders) was stirred and they raised their voices, and the people cried on that night. ² All the children of Israel complained about Moses and Aaron. The whole assembly (of elders) said, "If only we had died in the land of Egypt! Or if only we had died in this desert! ³ Why is God bringing us to this land to fall by the sword? Our wives and small children will be captives! Wouldn't it be better for us to return to Egypt?"

⁴ They said to each other, "Let's appoint a leader and return to Egypt!"

⁵ Moses and Aaron fell on their faces before the entire congregation of the children of Israel.

⁶ Joshua son of Nun and Caleb son of Jephunneh, who were among those who had explored the land, tore their clothes. ⁷ They spoke to the entire congregation of the children of Israel, saying, "The land we passed through to explore is a very, very good land. [THIRD READING] ⁸ If God desires us, He will bring us to this land and give it to us—a land flowing with milk and honey. ⁹ Do not rebel against God, and then you will not fear the people of that land, for (we will eat them up as if) they are our bread. Their (righteous ones, who were their) protection have passed away, and God is with us. Don't be afraid of them!"

14:1 The whole assembly (of the seventy elders) was stirred and they raised their voices, and the people cried on that night. That night was the ninth of the Hebrew month of *Av*. God said to them, "Tonight you are weeping for nothing, for you believed the lies of the spies. But I will establish this night as an occasion for weeping throughout the generations." It was decreed that the first and second Temples would be destroyed on the Ninth of *Av* (*Babylonian Talmud, Ta'anit* 29a).

5-6. Moses and Aaron fell on their faces … Joshua son of Nun and Caleb son of Jephunneh, who were among those who had explored the land, tore their clothes. While Moses and Aaron were praying, Joshua and Caleb tore their garments in mourning, because they knew that the decree had been sealed and that prayer would not be effective.

How could Moses and Aaron, who were certainly greater than Joshua and Caleb, not realize the futility of their actions?

By repeating that Joshua and Caleb were *"among those who had explored the land,"* the Torah answers this question. Joshua and Caleb had been uplifted by setting foot on the Holy Land, and this helped them gain a greater insight than Moses and Aaron, on this occasion (*Rabbi Solomon Kluger, 19th century*).

8. If God desires us, He will bring us to this land and give it to us. The spies suffered from binary logic—they believed in God, and in the power of Divine intervention, but they imagined that life is guided *either* by the laws of nature *or* by God's direct mediation. They could not conceive of the scenario where God's supernatural providence would extend *through* the veil of nature.

When the people would settle in the land of Israel the miracles which had sustained them until now were going to cease. The manna would no longer fall, and Miriam's well would no

במדבר יד:י-כג　　　שלח לך

10 וַיֹּאמְרוּ֙ כָּל־הָ֣עֵדָ֔ה לִרְגּ֥וֹם אֹתָ֖ם בָּאֲבָנִ֑ים וּכְב֣וֹד יְהֹוָ֗ה נִרְאָה֙ בְּאֹ֣הֶל מוֹעֵ֔ד אֶֽל־כָּל־בְּנֵ֖י יִשְׂרָאֵֽל׃ פ 11 וַיֹּ֤אמֶר יְהֹוָה֙ אֶל־מֹשֶׁ֔ה עַד־אָ֥נָה יְנַאֲצֻ֖נִי הָעָ֣ם הַזֶּ֑ה וְעַד־אָ֙נָה֙ לֹא־יַאֲמִ֣ינוּ בִ֔י בְּכֹל֙ הָֽאֹת֔וֹת אֲשֶׁ֥ר עָשִׂ֖יתִי בְּקִרְבּֽוֹ׃ 12 אַכֶּ֥נּוּ בַדֶּ֖בֶר וְאוֹרִשֶׁ֑נּוּ וְאֶֽעֱשֶׂה֙ אֹֽתְךָ֔ לְגוֹי־גָּד֥וֹל וְעָצ֖וּם מִמֶּֽנּוּ׃ 13 וַיֹּ֥אמֶר מֹשֶׁ֖ה אֶל־יְהֹוָ֑ה וְשָׁמְע֣וּ מִצְרַ֔יִם כִּֽי־הֶעֱלִ֧יתָ בְכֹחֲךָ֛ אֶת־הָעָ֥ם הַזֶּ֖ה מִקִּרְבּֽוֹ׃ 14 וְאָמְר֗וּ אֶל־יוֹשֵׁב֮ הָאָ֣רֶץ הַזֹּאת֒ שָֽׁמְעוּ֙ כִּֽי־אַתָּ֣ה יְהֹוָ֔ה בְּקֶ֖רֶב הָעָ֣ם הַזֶּ֑ה אֲשֶׁר־עַ֣יִן בְּעַ֗יִן נִרְאָ֤ה ׀ אַתָּה֙ יְהֹוָ֔ה וַעֲנָֽנְךָ֖ עֹמֵ֣ד עֲלֵהֶ֑ם וּבְעַמֻּ֣ד עָנָ֗ן אַתָּ֨ה הֹלֵ֤ךְ לִפְנֵיהֶם֙ יוֹמָ֔ם וּבְעַמּ֥וּד אֵ֖שׁ לָֽיְלָה׃ 15 וְהֵמַתָּ֛ה אֶת־הָעָ֥ם הַזֶּ֖ה כְּאִ֣ישׁ אֶחָ֑ד וְאָֽמְרוּ֙ הַגּוֹיִ֔ם אֲשֶׁר־שָׁמְע֥וּ אֶֽת־שִׁמְעֲךָ֖ לֵאמֹֽר׃ 16 מִבִּלְתִּ֞י יְכֹ֣לֶת יְהֹוָ֗ה לְהָבִיא֙ אֶת־הָעָ֣ם הַזֶּ֔ה אֶל־הָאָ֖רֶץ אֲשֶׁר־נִשְׁבַּ֣ע לָהֶ֑ם וַיִּשְׁחָטֵ֖ם בַּמִּדְבָּֽר׃ 17 וְעַתָּ֕ה יִגְדַּל־נָ֖א כֹּ֣חַ אֲדֹנָ֑י כַּאֲשֶׁ֥ר דִּבַּ֖רְתָּ לֵאמֹֽר׃ 18 יְהֹוָ֗ה אֶ֤רֶךְ אַפַּ֙יִם֙ וְרַב־חֶ֔סֶד נֹשֵׂ֥א עָוֺ֖ן וָפָ֑שַׁע וְנַקֵּה֙ לֹ֣א יְנַקֶּ֔ה פֹּקֵ֞ד עֲוֺ֤ן אָבוֹת֙ עַל־בָּנִ֔ים עַל־שִׁלֵּשִׁ֖ים וְעַל־רִבֵּעִֽים׃ 19 סְלַֽח־נָ֗א לַעֲוֺ֛ן הָעָ֥ם הַזֶּ֖ה כְּגֹ֣דֶל חַסְדֶּ֑ךָ וְכַאֲשֶׁ֤ר נָשָׂ֙אתָה֙ לָעָ֣ם הַזֶּ֔ה מִמִּצְרַ֖יִם וְעַד־הֵֽנָּה׃ 20 וַיֹּ֣אמֶר יְהֹוָ֔ה סָלַ֖חְתִּי כִּדְבָרֶֽךָ׃ 21 וְאוּלָ֖ם חַי־אָ֑נִי וְיִמָּלֵ֥א כְבוֹד־יְהֹוָ֖ה אֶת־כָּל־הָאָֽרֶץ׃ 22 כִּ֣י כָל־הָאֲנָשִׁ֗ים הָרֹאִ֤ים אֶת־כְּבֹדִי֙ וְאֶת־אֹ֣תֹתַ֔י אֲשֶׁר־עָשִׂ֥יתִי בְמִצְרַ֖יִם וּבַמִּדְבָּ֑ר וַיְנַסּ֣וּ אֹתִ֗י זֶ֚ה עֶ֣שֶׂר פְּעָמִ֔ים וְלֹ֥א שָׁמְע֖וּ בְּקוֹלִֽי׃ 23 אִם־יִרְאוּ֙ אֶת־הָאָ֔רֶץ אֲשֶׁ֥ר נִשְׁבַּ֖עְתִּי לַאֲבֹתָ֑ם וְכָל־מְנַאֲצַ֖י לֹ֥א יִרְאֽוּהָ׃

Rabbi Ḥiyya said, "The spies themselves caused it to be removed from the list. They were liars, and you are always treated in the same way that you behave" (*Zohar*).

19. Please forgive this nation's sin. When asking God for forgiveness, why did Moses not mention the merit of the Patriarchs, as he had done after the sin of the Golden Calf? At that time, his prayer to *"remember Abraham, Isaac and Israel, Your servants"* (*Exodus* 32:13), helped annul God's decree against the children of Israel.

In this case, Moses felt it inappropriate to invoke the merit of the Patriarchs, because the people were currently rejecting the very land chosen by the Patriarchs themselves (*Rabbi Bahya b. Asher, 13ᵗʰ century*).

¹⁰ The entire congregation threatened to pelt (Joshua and Caleb) with stones, but the glory of God which (usually) appeared in the Tent of Meeting (came down there, for) all the children of Israel (to see).

Moses Prays to God

¹¹ God said to Moses, "How long will this people provoke Me? How much longer will they refuse to believe in Me after all the miraculous signs I have performed in their midst? ¹² I'm going to strike them with a plague and eliminate them, and then I'll make from you a greater and stronger nation than them."

¹³ Moses said to God, "And (what will) the Egyptians (think when they) hear that (You killed the Jewish people? They'll say, 'While) You did bring this nation out from among them with great power, ¹⁴ but,' they will say, ('You weren't able to defeat) the inhabitants of this land.' (They will never believe that the people were punished for their sins) because they heard that You, God, are with this people, and that You, God, appeared to them eye to eye, and that Your cloud rests over them (and that) You go before them with a pillar of cloud by day, and with a pillar of fire by night. ¹⁵ So, if You kill this nation (suddenly), like (killing just) one man, the nations who have heard of Your reputation will say: ¹⁶ 'It is because God lacked the ability to bring this nation to the land which He swore to them, that He slaughtered them in the desert.'

¹⁷ "Now, please, let God's power (to forgive the wicked) be amplified, as You (yourself) spoke, when You said, ¹⁸ 'God is slow to anger, abundant in loving kindness, forgiving intentional sin and rebellion, who absolves (those who repent) and does not absolve (those who do not). He visits the sins of parents upon the children, and the grandchildren, to the third and fourth generations.' ¹⁹ Please forgive this nation's sin with your abounding kindness, just as You have carried this people from Egypt until now."

God Forgives / Decree of Forty Years of Wandering

²⁰ God said, "I have forgiven them because of your words (and I will not eliminate them)." ²¹ "However (what I will do is), as surely as I live, and the glory of God fills the earth, ²² (I swear) that all the people who, while seeing My glory and the miraculous signs that I performed in Egypt and in the desert, have tested Me these ten times and not listened to My voice— ²³ they will not see the land that I swore to their fathers. All those who provoked Me will not see it."

18. God is slow to anger, abundant in loving kindness. Why is "truth" missing here from the list of God's attributes?

במדבר יד:כד-לד • שלח לך

24 וְעַבְדִּי כָלֵב עֵקֶב הָיְתָה רוּחַ אַחֶרֶת עִמּוֹ וַיְמַלֵּא אַחֲרָי וַהֲבִיאֹתִיו אֶל־הָאָרֶץ אֲשֶׁר־בָּא שָׁמָּה וְזַרְעוֹ יוֹרִשֶׁנָּה: 25 וְהָעֲמָלֵקִי וְהַכְּנַעֲנִי יוֹשֵׁב בָּעֵמֶק מָחָר פְּנוּ וּסְעוּ לָכֶם הַמִּדְבָּר דֶּרֶךְ יַם־סוּף: פ [FOURTH READING] 26 וַיְדַבֵּר יְהֹוָה אֶל־מֹשֶׁה וְאֶל־אַהֲרֹן לֵאמֹר: 27 עַד־מָתַי לָעֵדָה הָרָעָה הַזֹּאת אֲשֶׁר הֵמָּה מַלִּינִים עָלָי אֶת־תְּלֻנּוֹת בְּנֵי יִשְׂרָאֵל אֲשֶׁר הֵמָּה מַלִּינִים עָלַי שָׁמָעְתִּי: 28 אֱמֹר אֲלֵהֶם חַי־אָנִי נְאֻם־יְהֹוָה אִם־לֹא כַּאֲשֶׁר דִּבַּרְתֶּם בְּאׇזְנָי כֵּן אֶעֱשֶׂה לָכֶם: 29 בַּמִּדְבָּר הַזֶּה יִפְּלוּ פִגְרֵיכֶם וְכׇל־פְּקֻדֵיכֶם לְכׇל־מִסְפַּרְכֶם מִבֶּן עֶשְׂרִים שָׁנָה וָמָעְלָה אֲשֶׁר הֲלִינֹתֶם עָלָי: 30 אִם־אַתֶּם תָּבֹאוּ אֶל־הָאָרֶץ אֲשֶׁר נָשָׂאתִי אֶת־יָדִי לְשַׁכֵּן אֶתְכֶם בָּהּ כִּי אִם־כָּלֵב בֶּן־יְפֻנֶּה וִיהוֹשֻׁעַ בִּן־נוּן: 31 וְטַפְּכֶם אֲשֶׁר אֲמַרְתֶּם לָבַז יִהְיֶה וְהֵבֵיאתִי אֹתָם וְיָדְעוּ אֶת־הָאָרֶץ אֲשֶׁר מְאַסְתֶּם בָּהּ: 32 וּפִגְרֵיכֶם אַתֶּם יִפְּלוּ בַּמִּדְבָּר הַזֶּה: 33 וּבְנֵיכֶם יִהְיוּ רֹעִים בַּמִּדְבָּר אַרְבָּעִים שָׁנָה וְנָשְׂאוּ אֶת־זְנוּתֵיכֶם עַד־תֹּם פִּגְרֵיכֶם בַּמִּדְבָּר: 34 בְּמִסְפַּר הַיָּמִים אֲשֶׁר־תַּרְתֶּם אֶת־הָאָרֶץ אַרְבָּעִים יוֹם יוֹם לַשָּׁנָה יוֹם לַשָּׁנָה תִּשְׂאוּ אֶת־עֲוֺנֹתֵיכֶם אַרְבָּעִים שָׁנָה

The sin of the spies was not that they were too spiritual, but that *they were not spiritual enough*. To be involved with the physical world and remain spiritually attuned demands the highest degree of attachment to God. So when the generation showed that they were lacking this level of dedication, they were given forty more years of unrestricted Divine worship, enabling them to reach the level where they would be ready to engage in the world (*Rabbi Menahem Mendel Schneerson, 20th century*).

spiritual vitamin

> It is a great fault to *sanctify* compromise. None of us can possibly do everything correctly all of the time, but we must resist the temptation to blur the boundary between right and wrong, merely to still our conscience. We need to remember what the Torah demands of us, even if we are currently finding it difficult to comply, so that we at least leave open the possibility of return.

numbers 14:24-34 — shelaḥ-lekha

²⁴ "But as for My servant, Caleb, since (despite his outward appearance of being with the spies) he had a different intention, and he followed Me, so I will bring him to the land to which he came, and his descendants will drive it(s inhabitants) out."

²⁵ "(If the people will go to the land now), the Amalekites and the Canaanites (that) inhabit the valley (will kill you all). Tomorrow, turn, journey back into the desert toward the Reed Sea."

[FOURTH READING] ²⁶ God spoke to Moses and Aaron, saying, ²⁷ "How much longer (must I bear) this evil congregation (of spies) who are provoking (the Jewish people) against Me? I have heard the complaints of the children of Israel whom they provoked against Me (too many times)!"

²⁸ "Say to them, 'As I live,' says God, '(I swear that) I will do to you none other than what you said to My ears (when you said, "If only we had died in this desert.") ²⁹ Your corpses will fall in this desert, (including) all of you who were counted—all those from the age of twenty and up, who were counted—because you complained against Me. ³⁰ You will not come to the land concerning which I raised My hand that you would settle in it, except Caleb son of Jephunneh and Joshua son of Nun. ³¹ As for your small children, of whom you said that they will be captives, I will bring them (there), and they will come to know the land which You despised. ³² But as for you, your corpses will fall in this desert."

³³ "Your children will wander in the desert for forty years and bear your guilt, until the last of your corpses has fallen in the desert. ³⁴ You will bear your sins for forty years, corresponding to the number of days which you explored the land—

---

24. My servant Caleb ... had a different intention. Why does the verse not mention Joshua, as it does Caleb?

Moses had given Joshua a special blessing to be saved from the spies' plan (above, 13:11), but Caleb had managed to avoid becoming ensnared without any help. For this reason, only Caleb is referred to here as *"My servant"* (*Rabbi Ḥayyim ibn Attar, 18th century*).

30. You will not come to the land. Man cannot be expected to suddenly leave a mentality of slavery, from working with bricks and straw, and at the spur of the moment, wage war with giants. It was therefore part of the Divine plan to make the Jewish people wander in the desert until they had developed a good degree of courage, for that is the inevitable effect of a difficult, nomadic existence. Also, a new generation of people would now be born who had not known any slavery (*Maimonides, 12th century*).

God does not issue a punishment to take revenge on the sinner. Rather, the "punishment" is a form of spiritual "medicine" aimed at correcting the spiritual deficiency caused by a sin.

With this in mind, the "punishment" given to the Jewish people here is difficult to understand. Their sin was their unwillingness to enter the land, because they desired to remain in the desert where they could serve God without distraction—and yet, their punishment was to receive what they wanted: to remain in the desert (for forty years)! How would this "correct" their sin of not wanting to enter the land?

במדבר יד:לד - טו:ג
שלח לך

וִידַעְתֶּ֖ם אֶת־תְּנוּאָתִֽי: 35 אֲנִ֣י יְהֹוָה֮ דִּבַּ֒רְתִּי֒ אִם־לֹ֣א ׀ זֹ֣את אֶֽעֱשֶׂ֗ה לְכׇל־הָעֵדָ֤ה הָֽרָעָה֙ הַזֹּ֔את הַנּוֹעָדִ֖ים עָלָ֑י בַּמִּדְבָּ֥ר הַזֶּ֛ה יִתַּ֖מּוּ וְשָׁ֥ם יָמֻֽתוּ: 36 וְהָ֣אֲנָשִׁ֔ים אֲשֶׁר־שָׁלַ֥ח מֹשֶׁ֖ה לָת֣וּר אֶת־הָאָ֑רֶץ וַיָּשֻׁ֗בוּ [וילונו כ׳] וַיַּלִּ֤ינוּ עָלָיו֙ אֶת־כׇּל־הָ֣עֵדָ֔ה לְהוֹצִ֥יא דִבָּ֖ה עַל־הָאָֽרֶץ: 37 וַיָּמֻ֙תוּ֙ הָֽאֲנָשִׁ֔ים מוֹצִאֵ֥י דִבַּת־הָאָ֖רֶץ רָעָ֑ה בַּמַּגֵּפָ֖ה לִפְנֵ֥י יְהֹוָֽה: 38 וִיהוֹשֻׁ֣עַ בִּן־נ֔וּן וְכָלֵ֖ב בֶּן־יְפֻנֶּ֑ה חָיוּ֙ מִן־הָאֲנָשִׁ֣ים הָהֵ֔ם הַהֹלְכִ֖ים לָת֥וּר אֶת־הָאָֽרֶץ: 39 וַיְדַבֵּ֤ר מֹשֶׁה֙ אֶת־הַדְּבָרִ֣ים הָאֵ֔לֶּה אֶֽל־כׇּל־בְּנֵ֖י יִשְׂרָאֵ֑ל וַיִּֽתְאַבְּל֥וּ הָעָ֖ם מְאֹֽד: 40 וַיַּשְׁכִּ֣מוּ בַבֹּ֔קֶר וַיַּֽעֲל֥וּ אֶל־רֹאשׁ־הָהָ֖ר לֵאמֹ֑ר הִנֶּ֗נּוּ וְעָלִ֛ינוּ אֶל־הַמָּק֛וֹם אֲשֶׁר־אָמַ֥ר יְהֹוָ֖ה כִּ֥י חָטָֽאנוּ: 41 וַיֹּ֣אמֶר מֹשֶׁ֔ה לָ֥מָּה זֶּ֛ה אַתֶּ֥ם עֹבְרִ֖ים אֶת־פִּ֣י יְהֹוָ֑ה וְהִ֖וא לֹ֥א תִצְלָֽח: 42 אַֽל־תַּעֲל֔וּ כִּ֛י אֵ֥ין יְהֹוָ֖ה בְּקִרְבְּכֶ֑ם וְלֹא֙ תִּנָּ֣גְפ֔וּ לִפְנֵ֖י אֹיְבֵיכֶֽם: 43 כִּי֩ הָעֲמָלֵקִ֨י וְהַכְּנַעֲנִ֤י שָׁם֙ לִפְנֵיכֶ֔ם וּנְפַלְתֶּ֖ם בֶּחָ֑רֶב כִּֽי־עַל־כֵּ֤ן שַׁבְתֶּם֙ מֵאַחֲרֵ֣י יְהֹוָ֔ה וְלֹא־יִהְיֶ֥ה יְהֹוָ֖ה עִמָּכֶֽם: 44 וַיַּעְפִּ֕לוּ לַעֲל֖וֹת אֶל־רֹ֣אשׁ הָהָ֑ר וַאֲר֤וֹן בְּרִית־יְהֹוָה֙ וּמֹשֶׁ֔ה לֹא־מָ֖שׁוּ מִקֶּ֥רֶב הַֽמַּחֲנֶֽה: 45 וַיֵּ֤רֶד הָעֲמָלֵקִי֙ וְהַֽכְּנַעֲנִ֔י הַיֹּשֵׁ֖ב בָּהָ֣ר הַה֑וּא וַיַּכּ֥וּם וַֽיַּכְּת֖וּם עַד־הַֽחׇרְמָֽה: פ

טו 1 וַיְדַבֵּ֥ר יְהֹוָ֖ה אֶל־מֹשֶׁ֥ה לֵּאמֹֽר: 2 דַּבֵּר֙ אֶל־בְּנֵ֣י יִשְׂרָאֵ֔ל וְאָמַרְתָּ֖ אֲלֵהֶ֑ם כִּ֣י תָבֹ֗אוּ אֶל־אֶ֙רֶץ֙ מֽוֹשְׁבֹ֣תֵיכֶ֔ם אֲשֶׁ֥ר אֲנִ֖י נֹתֵ֥ן לָכֶֽם: 3 וַעֲשִׂיתֶ֨ם אִשֶּׁ֤ה

15:2 When you arrive in the land of your residence. Why is this passage recorded after the account of the spies?

kabbalah bites

14:38 *"Joshua son of Nun and Caleb son of Jephunneh remained alive."* The souls of Jacob's sons, which had been impregnated into the spies at the onset of their mission, departed when they decided to speak badly about the land (see above, 13:26). Here we learn two exceptions to that rule. Joshua and Caleb, who had remained loyal to the mission ("remained alive"). Their impregnated souls continued to enliven them.

forty days, a day for each year. You will then know what it means to be estranged from Me."

³⁵ "I, God, have spoken! (I swear) I will do this to the entire evil congregation who have assembled against me. They will meet their end in this desert, and they will die there."

Death of the Spies

³⁶ But the men whom Moses had sent to explore the land (could not be saved by his prayers because) they returned and caused the entire congregation to complain against him, by producing a report about the land (that constituted a rebellion against Moses). ³⁷ So the men who produced a bad report about the land died (straightaway) in the plague, before God.

³⁸ From the men who went to explore the land, (only) Joshua son of Nun and Caleb son of Jephunneh remained alive.

The Second Rebellion

³⁹ Moses related all these words to the children of Israel, and the people mourned greatly. ⁴⁰ They got up early in the morning and went up (along the route to the land, in the direction of the) mountaintop, saying, "We're ready to go up to the place which God spoke about, for we have sinned!"

⁴¹ Moses said, "Why are you transgressing the word of God? (What you are doing) will not succeed. ⁴² Do not go up, because God is not among you, to prevent you from being beaten by your enemies. ⁴³ The Amalekites and the Canaanites are ahead of you, and you will fall by the sword. For you have turned away from God, and God will not be with you."

⁴⁴ They were adamant and went up (towards the land, in the direction of the) mountaintop, but God's Ark of the Covenant and Moses did not move from the camp. ⁴⁵ The Amalekites and the Canaanites who lived on the mountain came down, thrashed them and thwarted them as far as (a place which was later named) Hormah ("Destruction," due to what happened there).

Meal-Offerings and Wine Libations to Accompany Sacrifices

15 ¹ God spoke to Moses, saying: ² Speak to the children of Israel and say to them: When you arrive in the land of your residence, which I am giving you, ³ and you make a (voluntary) fire-offering to God to make a pleasant

35. They will meet their end in this desert, and they will die there. What was the reason for this irrevocable decree? Why should it matter to God that they rejected a *physical* land, flowing with milk and honey?

It was not merely the earthly things that they rejected. In rejecting the land, they showed that they did not desire to ascend the ladder of spiritual growth, but preferred to go back to Egypt, regressing to an impure land (*Rabbi Isaac b. Moses Arama, 15th century*).

במדבר ט״ו:ג-יד   שלח לך

לַיהוָה עֹלָה אוֹ־זֶבַח לְפַלֵּא־נֶדֶר אוֹ בִנְדָבָה אוֹ בְּמֹעֲדֵיכֶם לַעֲשׂוֹת רֵיחַ נִיחֹחַ לַיהוָה מִן־הַבָּקָר אוֹ מִן־הַצֹּאן: 4 וְהִקְרִיב הַמַּקְרִיב קָרְבָּנוֹ לַיהוָה מִנְחָה סֹלֶת עִשָּׂרוֹן בָּלוּל בִּרְבִעִית הַהִין שָׁמֶן: 5 וְיַיִן לַנֶּסֶךְ רְבִיעִית הַהִין תַּעֲשֶׂה עַל־הָעֹלָה אוֹ לַזָּבַח לַכֶּבֶשׂ הָאֶחָד: 6 אוֹ לָאַיִל תַּעֲשֶׂה מִנְחָה סֹלֶת שְׁנֵי עֶשְׂרֹנִים בְּלוּלָה בַשֶּׁמֶן שְׁלִשִׁית הַהִין: 7 וְיַיִן לַנֶּסֶךְ שְׁלִשִׁית הַהִין תַּקְרִיב רֵיחַ־נִיחֹחַ לַיהוָה:

8 [FIFTH READING] וְכִי־תַעֲשֶׂה בֶן־בָּקָר עֹלָה אוֹ־זָבַח לְפַלֵּא־נֶדֶר אוֹ־שְׁלָמִים לַיהוָה: 9 וְהִקְרִיב עַל־בֶּן־הַבָּקָר מִנְחָה סֹלֶת שְׁלֹשָׁה עֶשְׂרֹנִים בָּלוּל בַּשֶּׁמֶן חֲצִי הַהִין: 10 וְיַיִן תַּקְרִיב לַנֶּסֶךְ חֲצִי הַהִין אִשֵּׁה רֵיחַ־נִיחֹחַ לַיהוָה: 11 כָּכָה יֵעָשֶׂה לַשּׁוֹר הָאֶחָד אוֹ לָאַיִל הָאֶחָד אוֹ־לַשֶּׂה בַכְּבָשִׂים אוֹ בָעִזִּים: 12 כַּמִּסְפָּר אֲשֶׁר תַּעֲשׂוּ כָּכָה תַּעֲשׂוּ לָאֶחָד כְּמִסְפָּרָם: 13 כָּל־הָאֶזְרָח יַעֲשֶׂה־כָּכָה אֶת־אֵלֶּה לְהַקְרִיב אִשֵּׁה רֵיחַ־נִיחֹחַ לַיהוָה: 14 וְכִי־יָגוּר אִתְּכֶם גֵּר אוֹ אֲשֶׁר־בְּתוֹכְכֶם

found in the spiritual worlds, you may eventually reach a state where you simply wish to expire from the world.

The opposite emotion is that instead of feeling the internal desire to soar upwards to higher planes, you are granted *inspiration* from Above, driving you "down to earth"—to engage with the physical world with greater enthusiasm, with the goal of sanctifying mundane existence.

A sacrifice, which is burned on the altar until its blood and fats have *risen* in smoke, represents the mode of expiration. On the other hand, wine libations, which are poured *downwards*, represent the path of inspiration.

After the spies, who excelled in their desire to "expire" from mundane activities and withdraw from physical life, we are told about the libations, representing the need to be inspired back down to action. Both these paths to God are valid, and both are necessary; your daily challenge is to balance the advantages of each approach (*Rabbi Shneur Zalman of Lyady, 18th century*).

13. Every native-born should present (these offerings) in this way, so as to offer up a fire-offering of pleasant aroma to God. At that moment a quarrel broke out between Israelites and converts over the offering. God said to Moses, "Why are they arguing with each other?"

Moses replied, "Master of the Universe! You know, they are quarreling about the words *'every native-born.'*"

God responded, "But didn't I say to you *'One statute applies for the (entire) assembly, (both) for yourselves and for the convert who lives (with you) ... just as it is for you, so shall it be for the convert, before God?'"* (v. 15; *Tanna de-Vei Eliyahu*).

numbers 15:3–14 — shelaḥ-lekha

aroma for God—(be it) a burnt-offering or a (peace-offering) slaughter, (be it) a vow or a voluntary offering or (an offering) on your festivals, (be it) from cattle or from sheep:

⁴ If a person brings his offering (of a lamb) to God:

- ❖ He should present a meal-offering of one-tenth (of an *'ephah* of) fine flour, mixed with a quarter of a *hin* of oil.

- ❖ ⁵ With the burnt-offering or the (peace-offering) slaughter you should offer a quarter of a *hin* of wine as a libation. (All this is) for each lamb.

⁶ Or for a ram:

- ❖ You should present a meal-offering of two-tenths (of an *'ephah* of) fine flour mixed with a third of a *hin* of oil.

- ❖ ⁷ You should offer a third of a *hin* of wine as a libation, a pleasant aroma to God.

[FIFTH READING] ⁸ If you sacrifice a young bull as a burnt-offering or a (peace-offering) slaughter, to fulfil a vow, or for a peace-offering for God:

- ❖ ⁹ With the young bull you should offer up a meal-offering of three-tenths (of an *'ephah* of) fine flour, mixed with half a *hin* of oil.

- ❖ ¹⁰ You should offer half a *hin* of wine as a libation.

(The meal-offering and the oil will be) a fire-offering, a pleasant aroma to God.

¹¹ This is what should be done for each ox or ram, or for each young sheep or young goat. ¹² Corresponding to the number of sacrifices, you should offer the appropriate number of (meal-offerings and wine libations) for each one. ¹³ Every native-born should present (these offerings) in this way, so as to offer up a fire-offering of pleasant aroma to God.

- ❖ ¹⁴ When a convert comes to live with you, or (likewise for the converts already) among you (at any time) throughout the generations, and he offers up a

---

Because when the Jewish people heard God's decree that they must remain in the desert for forty years (14:28-35), they said, "Woe to us! We will never enter the land, for at the end of forty years, if we sin again, God will issue another decree! So there is no end to the matter."

God replied, "After forty years you will most definitely *'arrive in the land'*" (v. 2; *the Tosafists, 12th–14th centuries*).

5. Wine as a libation. There are two methods through which you can come closer to God—*expiration* and *inspiration*.

Expiration is a self-motivated desire to elevate yourself from material existence and merge with a higher reality. If you meditate on the greatness of God and the utter bliss that is to be

במדבר טו:יד-כד ׀ שלח לך

לְדֹרֹתֵיכֶם וְעָשָׂה אִשֵּׁה רֵיחַ־נִיחֹחַ לַיהוָה כַּאֲשֶׁר תַּעֲשׂוּ כֵּן יַעֲשֶׂה: 15 הַקָּהָל חֻקָּה אַחַת לָכֶם וְלַגֵּר הַגָּר חֻקַּת עוֹלָם לְדֹרֹתֵיכֶם כָּכֶם כַּגֵּר יִהְיֶה לִפְנֵי יְהוָה: 16 תּוֹרָה אַחַת וּמִשְׁפָּט אֶחָד יִהְיֶה לָכֶם וְלַגֵּר הַגָּר אִתְּכֶם: פ [SIXTH READING]

17 וַיְדַבֵּר יְהוָה אֶל־מֹשֶׁה לֵּאמֹר: 18 דַּבֵּר אֶל־בְּנֵי יִשְׂרָאֵל וְאָמַרְתָּ אֲלֵהֶם בְּבֹאֲכֶם אֶל־הָאָרֶץ אֲשֶׁר אֲנִי מֵבִיא אֶתְכֶם שָׁמָּה: 19 וְהָיָה בַּאֲכָלְכֶם מִלֶּחֶם הָאָרֶץ תָּרִימוּ תְרוּמָה לַיהוָה: 20 רֵאשִׁית עֲרִסֹתֵכֶם חַלָּה תָּרִימוּ תְרוּמָה כִּתְרוּמַת גֹּרֶן כֵּן תָּרִימוּ אֹתָהּ: 21 מֵרֵאשִׁית עֲרִסֹתֵיכֶם תִּתְּנוּ לַיהוָה תְּרוּמָה לְדֹרֹתֵיכֶם: ס 22 וְכִי תִשְׁגּוּ וְלֹא תַעֲשׂוּ אֵת כָּל־הַמִּצְוֺת הָאֵלֶּה אֲשֶׁר־דִּבֶּר יְהוָה אֶל־מֹשֶׁה: 23 אֵת כָּל־אֲשֶׁר צִוָּה יְהוָה אֲלֵיכֶם בְּיַד־מֹשֶׁה מִן־הַיּוֹם אֲשֶׁר צִוָּה יְהוָה וָהָלְאָה לְדֹרֹתֵיכֶם: 24 וְהָיָה אִם מֵעֵינֵי הָעֵדָה נֶעֶשְׂתָה לִשְׁגָגָה

and whoever does away with the commandment of ḥallah is considered to have perpetuated idol-worship (*Leviticus Rabbah*).

What is the connection between ḥallah and idol-worship? When a person earns his daily bread, it is natural for him to think that market forces control his income, and not God. He may thus "worship" business acumen as a "foreign god," which appears to reap bountiful rewards, the more it is worshiped.

The solution to this problem is, "*You should set aside the first of your dough*" (v. 20), for God. You should meditate on the fact that your income, your "dough," is given directly by God. Going to work merely makes a suitable "receptacle" into which God will pour His bountiful blessings (*Rabbi Samuel Jaffe Ashkenazi, 16th century*).

21. You should give ... from the first of your dough. The commandment of ḥallah brings blessing to your home, "You should give to the priest the first of your dough *that He may cause a blessing to rest on your home*" (*Ezekiel* 44:30).

Following the incident of the spies, the children of Israel were in need of additional blessing, which is why this commandment was instituted here (*Rabbi Obadiah Sforno, 16th century*).

There are two reasons for taking ḥallah. First, since man is dependent on bread for sustenance, God wanted to give him a commandment with bread, so that his daily life would be blessed with a constant holiness. In this way, his dough would provide physical as well as spiritual sustenance.

Second, in order that the priests—the ministers of God—would be supported without having to struggle: A grain offering that the priest receives must be ground into flour before it can be prepared for baking; but the dough is ready to be baked and eaten (*Rabbi Aaron ha-Levi (Ḥinnukh), 13th century*).

numbers 15:14–24 — shelaḥ-lekha

fire-offering of pleasant aroma to God, he should sacrifice it just as you do. ¹⁵ One statute applies for the (entire) assembly, (both) for yourselves and for the convert who lives (with you). One statute applies throughout your generations—just as it is for you, so shall it be for the convert, before God. ¹⁶ There will be one Torah and one law for you and for the convert who lives (with you).

The Dough-Offering

[SIXTH READING] ¹⁷ God spoke to Moses, saying: ¹⁸ Speak to the children of Israel and say to them:

- (Immediately) upon your coming to the land to which I am bringing you, ¹⁹ when you eat from the bread of the land, you should set aside a portion for God.
- ²⁰ (Whenever you knead an *'omer* of dough, or more, before you eat it) you should set aside the first of your dough, a loaf-size portion (for God).
- Just as the *terumah* of the threshing floor (has no fixed minimum), likewise (there is no fixed minimum in this case that) you must separate.
- ²¹ (Nevertheless) you should give to God (enough to be considered) a "gift."
- (You need not give the entire dough, but only a portion) from the first of your dough.
- (Do this) in all your generations.

Offering for Inadvertent Communal Idolatry

²² If you will inadvertently (commit the sin of idolatry—which is equivalent to) not observing all these commandments which God spoke to Moses, ²³ (and denying) everything that God commanded you through Moses, from the day when God (first) commanded and onwards, (including the prophets) of all generations—²⁴ then, if the inadvertent sin was because of (a mistaken ruling of the judges), the "eyes" of the congregation:

19. When you eat bread from the land. Why is the passage concerning *ḥallah* (separating a portion from your dough) recorded next to a passage about idol-worship? To teach you that whoever fulfils the commandment of *ḥallah* is considered to have done away with idol-worship;

spiritual vitamin

> By giving man a set of commandments to carry out in his daily life, God has made it possible for man to attach himself to his Creator and transcend the limitations of a limited human being, living in a limited world.

וְעָשׂוּ כָל־הָעֵדָה פַּר בֶּן־בָּקָר אֶחָד לְעֹלָה לְרֵיחַ נִיחֹחַ לַיהוָה וּמִנְחָתוֹ וְנִסְכּוֹ כַּמִּשְׁפָּט וּשְׂעִיר־עִזִּים אֶחָד לְחַטָּת: 25 וְכִפֶּר הַכֹּהֵן עַל־כָּל־עֲדַת בְּנֵי יִשְׂרָאֵל וְנִסְלַח לָהֶם כִּי־שְׁגָגָה הִוא וְהֵם הֵבִיאוּ אֶת־קָרְבָּנָם אִשֶּׁה לַיהוָה וְחַטָּאתָם לִפְנֵי יְהוָה עַל־שִׁגְגָתָם: 26 וְנִסְלַח לְכָל־עֲדַת בְּנֵי יִשְׂרָאֵל וְלַגֵּר הַגָּר בְּתוֹכָם כִּי לְכָל־הָעָם בִּשְׁגָגָה: ס [SEVENTH READING] 27 וְאִם־נֶפֶשׁ אַחַת תֶּחֱטָא בִשְׁגָגָה וְהִקְרִיבָה עֵז בַּת־שְׁנָתָהּ לְחַטָּאת: 28 וְכִפֶּר הַכֹּהֵן עַל־הַנֶּפֶשׁ הַשֹּׁגֶגֶת בְּחֶטְאָה בִשְׁגָגָה לִפְנֵי יְהוָה לְכַפֵּר עָלָיו וְנִסְלַח לוֹ: 29 הָאֶזְרָח בִּבְנֵי יִשְׂרָאֵל וְלַגֵּר הַגָּר בְּתוֹכָם תּוֹרָה אַחַת יִהְיֶה לָכֶם לָעֹשֶׂה בִּשְׁגָגָה: 30 וְהַנֶּפֶשׁ אֲשֶׁר־תַּעֲשֶׂה | בְּיָד רָמָה מִן־הָאֶזְרָח וּמִן־הַגֵּר אֶת־יְהוָה הוּא מְגַדֵּף וְנִכְרְתָה הַנֶּפֶשׁ הַהִוא מִקֶּרֶב עַמָּהּ: 31 כִּי דְבַר־יְהוָה בָּזָה וְאֶת־מִצְוָתוֹ הֵפַר הִכָּרֵת | תִּכָּרֵת הַנֶּפֶשׁ הַהִוא עֲוֹנָה בָהּ: פ 32 וַיִּהְיוּ בְנֵי־יִשְׂרָאֵל בַּמִּדְבָּר וַיִּמְצְאוּ אִישׁ מְקֹשֵׁשׁ עֵצִים בְּיוֹם הַשַּׁבָּת:

considered to have transgressed any Biblical injunction. The wood gatherer's desired outcome was that people should realize that the commandments were still in force, so he did not in fact desecrate the Sabbath (Biblically).

Why, then, was he punished? Because punishments prescribed by the earthly court must be based on people's actions, which are concrete, and not upon their intentions, which cannot be ascertained objectively (*Rabbi Samuel Edels, 16th–17th century*).

kabbalah bites

15:30-31 *"The fruit of the righteous is a Tree of Life"* (Proverbs 11:30). The union of souls in the upper world produces more fruit than the coupling of bodies in this world. When the souls pair in that world, with their combined desire they generate the souls of future converts to Judaism.

When a person converts, a soul flies from that chamber and enters under the wings of the *Shekhinah* (Divine Presence), and the *Shekhinah* kisses her since she is the fruit of righteous souls.

But if a soul sins on earth it is denied the privilege of coupling in the upper world. *"That soul will be utterly cut off, and his sin ('avonah) is with him"*—the soul forfeited the opportunity for a supernal union ('*onah*) with its mate due to its sin ('*avonah*). (In Hebrew, '*onah* and '*avonah* are spelled with the same consonants.)

- The entire congregation should offer a young bull as a burnt-offering for a pleasant aroma for God, with its prescribed meal-offering and libation, and one young male goat for a sin-offering.

²⁵ The priest will atone on behalf of the entire congregation of the children of Israel, and they will be forgiven, for it was an inadvertent sin, and they have brought their offering as a fire-offering to God, and their sin-offering before God, because of their inadvertent sin. ²⁶ The entire congregation of the children of Israel and the convert who lives with them will be forgiven, for it happened to all the people inadvertently.

Offering for Inadvertent Personal Idolatry

[SEVENTH READING] ²⁷ If one person sins (with idol-worship) inadvertently:

- He should offer a female goat in its first year as a sin-offering.

²⁸ The priest will atone for the erring person who sinned inadvertently before God, atoning on his behalf, and (his act) will be forgiven.

²⁹ A single law will apply to one who sins inadvertently (whether he is) from the native-born of the children of Israel (or he is one of) the converts who lives among them.

³⁰ But if a person sins (with idol-worship) intentionally, whether he is a native-born or a convert, he is expressing contempt for God, and that soul will be cut off from among its people. ³¹ For he has disdained God's word and violated His commandment. That soul will be utterly cut off (if he does not repent) and his sin is (still) with him.

The First Sabbath Desecration

³² When the children of Israel were in the desert (on the second Sabbath that they observed), they found a man gathering sticks on the day of the Sabbath.

---

31. His sin is with him. A person is only cut off spiritually if his sin is still *"with him,"* not if he repents (*Babylonian Talmud, Sanhedrin* 90b).

32. A man gathering sticks. The wood gatherer's intentions were for the sake of heaven. When it was decreed that the people would not enter the land, due to the sin of the spies (14:21*ff.*), the people thought that they were no longer obligated in commandments. So this person took a stance by transgressing the Sabbath, in order that the people should see him be punished for his transgression, from which they would learn that commandments were still obligatory (*The Tosafists, 12ᵗʰ–14ᵗʰ centuries*).

From the words of the Tosafists it follows that the wood gatherer did not really desecrate the Sabbath at all. According to Jewish law, if a person does a forbidden act on the Sabbath, not because he desires the *act itself*, but because of the *outcome* that the act leads to, then he is not

במדבר טו:לג-מא   שלח לך

33 וַיַּקְרִיבוּ אֹתוֹ הַמֹּצְאִים אֹתוֹ מְקֹשֵׁשׁ עֵצִים אֶל־מֹשֶׁה וְאֶל־אַהֲרֹן וְאֶל כָּל־הָעֵדָה: 34 וַיַּנִּיחוּ אֹתוֹ בַּמִּשְׁמָר כִּי לֹא פֹרַשׁ מַה־יֵּעָשֶׂה לוֹ: ס 35 וַיֹּאמֶר יְהֹוָה אֶל־מֹשֶׁה מוֹת יוּמַת הָאִישׁ רָגוֹם אֹתוֹ בָאֲבָנִים כָּל־הָעֵדָה מִחוּץ לַמַּחֲנֶה: 36 וַיֹּצִיאוּ אֹתוֹ כָּל־הָעֵדָה אֶל־מִחוּץ לַמַּחֲנֶה וַיִּרְגְּמוּ אֹתוֹ בָּאֲבָנִים וַיָּמֹת כַּאֲשֶׁר צִוָּה יְהֹוָה אֶת־מֹשֶׁה: פ 37 [MAFTIR] וַיֹּאמֶר יְהֹוָה אֶל־מֹשֶׁה לֵּאמֹר: 38 דַּבֵּר אֶל־בְּנֵי יִשְׂרָאֵל וְאָמַרְתָּ אֲלֵהֶם וְעָשׂוּ לָהֶם צִיצִת עַל־כַּנְפֵי בִגְדֵיהֶם לְדֹרֹתָם וְנָתְנוּ עַל־צִיצִת הַכָּנָף פְּתִיל תְּכֵלֶת: 39 וְהָיָה לָכֶם לְצִיצִת וּרְאִיתֶם אֹתוֹ וּזְכַרְתֶּם אֶת־כָּל־מִצְוֺת יְהֹוָה וַעֲשִׂיתֶם אֹתָם וְלֹא־תָתוּרוּ אַחֲרֵי לְבַבְכֶם וְאַחֲרֵי עֵינֵיכֶם אֲשֶׁר־אַתֶּם זֹנִים אַחֲרֵיהֶם: 40 לְמַעַן תִּזְכְּרוּ וַעֲשִׂיתֶם אֶת־כָּל־מִצְוֺתָי וִהְיִיתֶם קְדֹשִׁים לֵאלֹהֵיכֶם: 41 אֲנִי יְהֹוָה אֱלֹהֵיכֶם אֲשֶׁר הוֹצֵאתִי אֶתְכֶם מֵאֶרֶץ מִצְרַיִם לִהְיוֹת לָכֶם לֵאלֹהִים אֲנִי יְהֹוָה אֱלֹהֵיכֶם: פ פ פ

קי״ט פסוקים, פל״ט סימן.

A thread of turquoise. The turquoise strands of the *tzitzit* allude to "abandoning evil" (negative) and serving God out of fear; the white strands allude to "doing good" (positive) and serving God out of love (*Rabbi Shneur Zalman of Lyady, 18th century*).

In the current era, the turquoise dye (*tekhelet*) is not available to us, leaving all eight strands white. This teaches us that nowadays our emphasis in worshiping God should be on love and positivity (*Rabbi Menahem Mendel Schneerson, 20th century*).

39. When you see it, you will remember all the commandments. Because the numerical value of the word *tzitzit* is six hundred. Add to this the eight threads and five knots, and we have six hundred and thirteen—the number of commandments in the Torah (*Rashi, 11th century*).

numbers 15:33–41   shelaḥ-lekha

³³ Those who found him gathering sticks (warned him not to do so, and when he persisted they) presented him before Moses and Aaron and before the entire congregation. ³⁴ They placed him in custody, since it had not been specified what (type of death penalty) should be meted out to him.

³⁵ God said to Moses, "The man should be put to death (as follows): The entire congregation should pelt him with stones outside the camp."

³⁶ So the entire congregation took him outside the camp, and they pelted him to death with stones, as God had commanded Moses.

The Commandment of *Tzitzit*

[MAFTIR] ³⁷ God spoke to Moses, saying: ³⁸ Speak to the children of Israel and say to them:

- ❖ They should make *tzitzit* (tassels) for themselves on the corners of their garments, throughout their generations.
- ❖ They should place a thread of turquoise (wool) in the *tzitzit* at each corner.

³⁹ These will be your *tzitzit*. When you see it, you will remember all the commandments of God to perform them, and you will not follow after the "spies" (of the evil inclination), your hearts and your eyes, which lead you astray, ⁴⁰ so that you will remember and perform all My commandments and you will be holy to your God.

⁴¹ I am God, your God, who took you out of the land of Egypt to be your God. I am God, your God.

The Haftarah for Shelaḥ-Lekha is on page 1376.

---

38. *Tzitzit*. It is called *tzitzit* because of the threads suspended from it, as in *"He took me by the hair (tzitzit) of my head" (Ezekiel 8:3).*

Another interpretation: It is called *tzitzit* in connection with the requirement to see the *tzitzit*—"When you *see* it" (v. 39), since the word *tzitzit* is similar to *"Peering (metzitz) from the lattices" (Song of Songs 2:9; Rashi, 11th century).*

No pious person would allow himself to become exempt from this precept. You should always wear clothes that need to have *tzitzit* attached so as to observe this commandment.

You should always be meticulous with the commandment of *tzitzit*, since Scripture equates it to all the other commandments of the Torah and makes them dependent on it—as the verse states, "When you see it, you will remember *all the commandments of God*" (*Maimonides, 12th century*).

Although Korah was wicked, he nevertheless **harbored a desire** that is **appropriate** for us to **emulate**—He wanted to be **the High Priest.** His mistake was the **method** of implementation. We can learn from Korah to always desire a **higher spirituality** and work to **achieve that goal.**

KORAḤ
קרח

KORAH'S REBELLION	16:1 – 17:5
AARON SAVES THE PEOPLE	17:6–15
CONFIRMATION OF AARON'S APPOINTMENT	17:16–26
RESPONSIBILITIES OF THE PRIEST AND LEVITES	17:27 – 18:32

NAME
Korah

LINES IN TORAH SCROLL
184

PARASHIYYOT
7 open; 6 closed

VERSES
95

WORDS
1409

LETTERS
5325

DATE
Elul, 2449

LOCATION
Kadesh, desert of Paran, Kadesh-barnea

MITZVOT
5 positive; 4 prohibitions

KEY PEOPLE
Moses, Aaron, Korah, Dathan, Abiram, On son of Peleth, Eleazar, Priests, Levites

MASORETIC FEATURES
17:19 is halfway through the Book of Numbers (in verses)

CHARACTER PROFILE

NAME
Korah ("bald")

FATHER
Izhar

SIBLINGS
Nepheg, Zichri

CHILDREN
Assir, Elkanah, Abiasuph

ACHIEVEMENTS
Was one of those who carried the ark; the richest of all the Israelite nation; overseer of Pharaoh's house and treasury

KNOWN FOR
Leading the rebellion against Moses; took fire-pans to offer incense to God; was swallowed up by the earth together with his family

MOTIVES

Korah was motivated by ego and personal ambition, yet he claimed that he was fighting for justice. Examine your actions honestly during a dispute to see if they are "for the sake of heaven." Ask other people what they think (ch. 16).

JUDGING OTHERS

Although there were many who joined Korah, Moses prayed that "God, who knows everybody's thoughts," should only punish those who were responsible. Never judge externally. Try to imagine how another person's intentions might have been good (16:22).

STANDING GUARD

Although guarding the Sanctuary was extremely important, it was only one job performed by the priests and Levites. You need to guard yourself from negative influences, but that should not take too much of your time and energy. Your main focus should be on doing good, for yourself and others (18:1-7).

קרח

במדבר טז:א-ג

טז 1 וַיִּקַּח קֹרַח בֶּן־יִצְהָר בֶּן־קְהָת בֶּן־לֵוִי וְדָתָן וַאֲבִירָם בְּנֵי אֱלִיאָב וְאוֹן בֶּן־פֶּלֶת בְּנֵי רְאוּבֵן: 2 וַיָּקֻמוּ לִפְנֵי מֹשֶׁה וַאֲנָשִׁים מִבְּנֵי־יִשְׂרָאֵל חֲמִשִּׁים וּמָאתָיִם נְשִׂיאֵי עֵדָה קְרִאֵי מוֹעֵד אַנְשֵׁי־שֵׁם: 3 וַיִּקָּהֲלוּ עַל־מֹשֶׁה וְעַל־אַהֲרֹן וַיֹּאמְרוּ אֲלֵהֶם רַב־לָכֶם כִּי כָל־הָעֵדָה כֻּלָּם קְדֹשִׁים וּבְתוֹכָם יְהוָה וּמַדּוּעַ

authority in the desert. Korah did not challenge Elizaphan's appointment in the month of *Nisan*, because he deemed it to be temporary. Soon, he reasoned, they would enter the Promised Land and Korah—the next in Levi's line of descendents—would replace Elizaphan as tribal leader.

After the incident of the spies, when the children of Israel were sentenced to remain in the desert for forty years, Korah realized that he was not likely to be appointed as leader, so he instigated his rebellion at that point (*Rabbi Saul Lowenstamm, 18th century*).

Korah. It is written in Proverbs, *"The name of the wicked will rot"* (10:7), on which the Talmud comments: *"Let mold grow upon their names, for we do not use their names"* (*Babylonian Talmud, Yoma* 38a).

How, then, could the Torah eternalize the name of Korah, a wicked man who did not repent in his lifetime, by calling an entire Torah portion by his name?

While Korah was indeed wicked in his deeds, he nevertheless harbored a *desire* which is appropriate for every person to emulate: He wanted to be the High Priest. Maimonides describes this as something fitting for all human beings: *"Any type of person whose spirit inspires him, and he resolves in his mind to set himself apart [from worldly pursuits], to stand before God and serve as His minister, to work for Him, and to know God; who [then acts upon his resolution and he] goes in a morally upright manner—following his inherent, God-given disposition, and he discards all the numerous concerns that people are normally preoccupied with—then he will attain the holiness of the Holy of Holies,"* i.e., the spiritual level of the High Priest.

Korah was not corrupt in his *ideology*, but only in his *method of implementation*. His desire to be High Priest was well founded, as Moses confirmed, "I too want this" (*Rashi* to 16:6). His only mistake was attempting to achieve this goal by usurping Moses, rather than following him (*Rabbi Menahem Mendel Schneerson, 20th century*).

2. They confronted Moses. Korah assembled two hundred and fifty men, heads of courts. He dressed them with cloaks made entirely of turquoise wool. They came and stood before Moses and asked him, "Is a cloak made entirely of turquoise wool obligated to have *tzitzit* (fringes), or is it exempt?"

He replied, "It is obligated."

They began laughing at him, saying, "How is it possible that with a cloak of another color, one string of turquoise wool exempts it (see above, 15:38), and yet this one, which is made entirely of turquoise wool, does not exempt itself?" (*Midrash Tanhuma*).

3. Why have you made yourselves elite? Those who dispute righteous men attribute to them traits which are the very opposite of their real personality. The Torah states that Moses was *"extremely humble, more*

Food for thought

1. Are all arguments a form of power-struggle?

2. Are you swayed more by a person's charisma than actual opinion?

3. Moses was set against 250 "men of repute." Do numbers validate a view?

parashat koraḥ

Korah's Rebellion

16 ¹ Korah son of Izhar—the son of Kohath, (who was) the son of Levi—took (issue with Moses. He was joined by) Dathan and Abiram, the sons of Eliab, and On son of Peleth, Reuben's descendants. ² They confronted Moses together with two hundred and fifty men from the children of Israel—leaders of the congregation, representatives of the assembly, men of repute. ³ They ganged up on Moses and Aaron and said to them, "You've made yourselves too important! For the entire congregation are all holy (witnesses to the revelation at Sinai), and God is with them. So why have you made yourselves elite over God's assembly (by appointing Aaron as the priest)?"

16:1 Korah son of Izhar—the son of Kohath, (who was) the son of Levi ... Dathan and Abiram ... Reuben's descendants. Korah was an intelligent man. What did he see to get involved in this foolishness? He saw through a prophetic vision that a line of great men was destined to descend from him, including the prophet Samuel, who was the equal of Moses and Aaron together (*Midrash Tanḥuma*).

Our Sages termed this "the dispute of Korah and all his assembly" because each member of Korah's faction had only himself in mind, even opposing others in *his own group*. Korah, for example, sought the office of High Priest for himself, arguing that this was the right of the tribe of Levi; whereas Dathan and Abiram claimed that the priesthood belonged to the tribe of Reuben, Jacob's firstborn.

All disputes are motivated by personal gain, so there will always be infighting (*Rabbi Meir Loeb Weisser, 19th century*).

Korah ... took. What, exactly, did Korah "take"? He took bad advice for himself. If you chase after something that doesn't belong to you, it will elude you—and you will eventually lose what you already have. Korah chased after something that wasn't his. Therefore, he lost what he had and nobody else profited.

Korah followed the path of arguments. What are arguments? Division. Division of the upper and the lower worlds. Whoever opposes peace takes issue with God's Holy Name, because His Holy Name is "Peace" (*Zohar*).

Korah chose to rebel against Moses and Aaron out of envy for the appointment of Elizaphan whom Moses appointed as chieftain over the sons of Kohath (*Rashi, 11th century*).

If so, why did he not begin his rebellion earlier in the month of *Nisan*, when Elizaphan was appointed? Why did he wait until after the spies returned?

After the children of Israel entered the Promised Land, new leaders were to replace those who had been in

---

kabbalah bites

16:1 Korah's challenge to Moses' authority occurred when Korah was invested with sparks of Cain's soul. Moses himself was a reincarnation of Abel, and the souls of that generation were all derivatives of Abel's soul. Thus Korah, who was spiritually "independent" of Moses, masterminded the rebellion.

Once again, we see that the dispute between Moses and Korah was an example of the primordial tension between Cain and Abel reemerging.

במדבר ט״ז:ג׳-י׳

קרח

תִּתְנַשְּׂא֖וּ עַל־קְהַ֥ל יְהֹוָֽה: 4 וַיִּשְׁמַ֣ע מֹשֶׁ֔ה וַיִּפֹּ֖ל עַל־פָּנָֽיו: 5 וַיְדַבֵּ֨ר אֶל־קֹ֜רַח
וְאֶל־כָּל־עֲדָתוֹ֮ לֵאמֹר֒ בֹּ֠קֶר וְיֹדַ֨ע יְהֹוָ֧ה אֶת־אֲשֶׁר־ל֛וֹ וְאֶת־הַקָּד֖וֹשׁ וְהִקְרִ֣יב
אֵלָ֑יו וְאֵ֛ת אֲשֶׁ֥ר יִבְחַר־בּ֖וֹ יַקְרִ֥יב אֵלָֽיו: 6 זֹ֖את עֲשׂ֑וּ קְחוּ־לָכֶ֣ם מַחְתּ֔וֹת קֹ֖רַח
וְכָל־עֲדָתֽוֹ: 7 וּתְנ֣וּ בָהֵ֣ן ׀ אֵ֗שׁ וְשִׂ֩ימוּ֩ עֲלֵיהֶ֨ן ׀ קְטֹ֜רֶת לִפְנֵ֤י יְהֹוָה֙ מָחָ֔ר וְהָיָ֗ה
הָאִ֛ישׁ אֲשֶׁר־יִבְחַ֥ר יְהֹוָ֖ה ה֣וּא הַקָּד֑וֹשׁ רַב־לָכֶ֖ם בְּנֵ֥י לֵוִֽי: 8 וַיֹּ֥אמֶר מֹשֶׁ֖ה אֶל־
קֹ֑רַח שִׁמְעוּ־נָ֖א בְּנֵ֥י לֵוִֽי: 9 הַמְעַ֣ט מִכֶּ֗ם כִּֽי־הִבְדִּיל֩ אֱלֹהֵ֨י יִשְׂרָאֵ֤ל אֶתְכֶם֙ מֵעֲדַ֣ת
יִשְׂרָאֵ֔ל לְהַקְרִ֥יב אֶתְכֶ֖ם אֵלָ֑יו לַעֲבֹ֗ד אֶת־עֲבֹדַת֙ מִשְׁכַּ֣ן יְהֹוָ֔ה וְלַעֲמֹ֛ד לִפְנֵ֥י
הָעֵדָ֖ה לְשָׁרְתָֽם: 10 וַיַּקְרֵב֙ אֹֽתְךָ֔ וְאֶת־כָּל־אַחֶ֥יךָ בְנֵי־לֵוִ֖י אִתָּ֑ךְ וּבִקַּשְׁתֶּ֖ם גַּם־

What news did Moses hear that caused him to fall on his face? That he was suspected of adultery (*Babylonian Talmud, Sanhedrin* 110a).

Since Moses had separated from his wife to achieve a higher degree of prophetic inspiration, cynics questioned whether his prolonged abstinence was viable (*Rabbi Samuel Edels, 16th–17th century*).

A suspected adulteress (*sotah*) can only be vindicated by a ceremony performed by the priests. Korah argued that Moses had unfairly appointed his own family as priests, and that these appointments had been made to provide Moses with a veil of protection against adulterous behavior (*Rabbi Isaiah Horowitz, 16th–17th century*).

How could such a vile allegation have been leveled against so righteous a person as Moses?

The *Ba'al Shem Tov* taught that, at birth, Moses was utterly wicked in temperament. He later transformed his personality and crushed his bad traits, wrestling with himself only to behave positively.

But since he had *originally* been predisposed to evil, it was possible for people to *imagine* him committing a sin (*Rabbi Moses Ḥayyim Ephraim of Sudylkow, 18th century*).

5. In the morning, God will make known who is His. Why did Moses delay the confirmation of High Priest until the next day?

Because the manna which would fall the next morning would reveal the true nature of each individual. For the righteous, the manna would fall in front of their doors, while ordinary people had to walk a short distance to retrieve their manna. The manna of the wicked, however, fell far away from their homes, and they had to walk a long distance to gather it.

So, when Korah argued that *"the entire congregation are all holy ... why have you made yourself elite"* (v. 3), Moses replied, *"In the morning God will make known"* whom He has chosen—by means of the manna (*Rabbi Eliezer b. Ze'ev Wolf Rosenfeld, 20th century*).

7. Offer incense on them. Moses said, "Take for yourselves the service most dear, the incense, which is more cherished than any other offering—but it also contains deadly poison, by which Nadab and Abihu were burned. The one whom God will choose will survive, and the rest of you will perish" (*Rashi, 11th century*).

numbers 16:4–10 — koraḥ

⁴ When Moses heard (this), he fell on his face.

⁵ He spoke to Korah and to all his company, saying, "In the morning, God will make known who is His (for Levite service), and who is holy (for priesthood), and He will draw them near to Him. He will draw the ones whom He chooses near to Him."

⁶ "Korah and your group! (In order for God's choice to be known) do the following: Take for yourselves fire-pans, ⁷ place fiery (coals) in them and offer incense on them tomorrow, before God. What will happen is, the man whom God chooses (will live, for) he is the holy one (and the others will die). You're taking a very big liability, sons of Levi!"

Moses' Attempts at Reconciliation

⁸ Moses (saw that they were still obstinate) so he said to Korah (in a gentler tone), "Please listen, sons of Levi! ⁹ Isn't it enough that the God of Israel has distinguished you from the congregation of Israel, drawing you near to Him, to perform the service of God's Tabernacle and to stand before the congregation, to be their ministers? ¹⁰ He drew you near, and all your brothers, the sons of Levi with

---

so than any person on the face of the earth" (12:3), but His opponents, wishing to find fault, claimed that Moses was arrogant! (*Rabbi Simḥah Bunem of Przysucha, 18th–19th century*).

Korah's rebellion was prompted by the sin of the spies. The spies had resisted entering the land of Israel because they preferred the exclusively spiritual life of the desert. The spies' downfall sent a powerful message that Judaism prioritizes physical action over spiritual and intellectual pursuits.

It was *this* that prompted Korah to protest to Moses, *"Why have you made yourselves elite over God's assembly?"* "I can appreciate," argued Korah, "that you are a more spiritual and holy person than us. But since we now see that Judaism makes physical action the priority, how are you better than anybody else? Aren't your *actions* the same as ours?"

Korah's mistake was that the Torah does not demand lifeless action, but rather, *deeds that shine with inspiration and spiritual enlightenment*. And in that respect, Moses was far greater than the rest of the people.

The two mistakes of the spies and Korah teach us that a healthy equilibrium is required. You must not shy away from physical life, like the spies. But on the other hand, Judaism's emphasis on action must never lead to a life of meaningless ritual and spiritual bankruptcy; every precept ought to be carried out with the highest levels of spiritual consciousness.

It is relatively easy to be *entirely* spiritual, like the spies, and aloof or *entirely* physical and mundane, like Korah. Our challenge is to harmonize both these qualities in our daily life (*Rabbi Menaḥem Mendel Schneerson, 20th century*).

4. He fell on his face. The verse says, *"he* fell," and not *"they* fell." Only Moses fell on his face and responded, whereas Aaron stood by quietly. Aaron, in his great humility, believed that Korah *was* more worthy than him of becoming High Priest. In fact, Aaron had only accepted the position out of obedience to God's command (*Naḥmanides, 13th century*).

קרח
במדבר ט״ז:י׳-י״ט

11 כִּהֻנָּֽה: לָכֵ֗ן אַתָּה֙ וְכׇל־עֲדָ֣תְךָ֔ הַנֹּעָדִ֖ים עַל־יְהֹוָ֑ה וְאַהֲרֹ֣ן מַה־ה֔וּא כִּ֥י [תלונו כ׳] תַלִּ֖ונוּ עָלָֽיו: 12 וַיִּשְׁלַ֣ח מֹשֶׁ֔ה לִקְרֹ֛א לְדָתָ֥ן וְלַאֲבִירָ֖ם בְּנֵ֣י אֱלִיאָ֑ב וַיֹּאמְר֖וּ לֹ֥א נַעֲלֶֽה: 13 הַמְעַ֗ט כִּ֤י הֶֽעֱלִיתָ֙נוּ֙ מֵאֶ֨רֶץ זָבַ֤ת חָלָב֙ וּדְבַ֔שׁ לַהֲמִיתֵ֖נוּ בַּמִּדְבָּ֑ר כִּֽי־תִשְׂתָּרֵ֥ר עָלֵ֖ינוּ גַּם־הִשְׂתָּרֵֽר: [SECOND READING] 14 אַ֡ף לֹ֣א אֶל־אֶ֩רֶץ֩ זָבַ֨ת חָלָ֤ב וּדְבַשׁ֙ הֲבִ֣יאֹתָ֔נוּ וַתִּ֨תֶּן־לָ֔נוּ נַחֲלַ֖ת שָׂדֶ֣ה וָכָ֑רֶם הַעֵינֵ֞י הָאֲנָשִׁ֥ים הָהֵ֛ם תְּנַקֵּ֖ר לֹ֥א נַעֲלֶֽה: 15 וַיִּ֤חַר לְמֹשֶׁה֙ מְאֹ֔ד וַיֹּ֙אמֶר֙ אֶל־יְהֹוָ֔ה אַל־תֵּ֖פֶן אֶל־מִנְחָתָ֑ם לֹ֠א חֲמ֨וֹר אֶחָ֤ד מֵהֶם֙ נָשָׂ֔אתִי וְלֹ֥א הֲרֵעֹ֖תִי אֶת־אַחַ֥ד מֵהֶֽם: 16 וַיֹּ֤אמֶר מֹשֶׁה֙ אֶל־קֹ֔רַח אַתָּה֙ וְכׇל־עֲדָ֣תְךָ֔ הֱי֖וּ לִפְנֵ֣י יְהֹוָ֑ה אַתָּ֥ה וָהֵ֛ם וְאַהֲרֹ֖ן מָחָֽר: 17 וּקְח֣וּ ׀ אִ֣ישׁ מַחְתָּת֗וֹ וּנְתַתֶּ֤ם עֲלֵיהֶם֙ קְטֹ֔רֶת וְהִקְרַבְתֶּ֞ם לִפְנֵ֤י יְהֹוָה֙ אִ֣ישׁ מַחְתָּת֔וֹ חֲמִשִּׁ֥ים וּמָאתַ֖יִם מַחְתֹּ֑ת וְאַתָּ֥ה וְאַהֲרֹ֖ן אִ֥ישׁ מַחְתָּתֽוֹ: 18 וַיִּקְח֞וּ אִ֣ישׁ מַחְתָּת֗וֹ וַיִּתְּנ֤וּ עֲלֵיהֶם֙ אֵ֔שׁ וַיָּשִׂ֥ימוּ עֲלֵיהֶ֖ם קְטֹ֑רֶת וַיַּֽעַמְד֗וּ פֶּ֛תַח אֹ֥הֶל מוֹעֵ֖ד וּמֹשֶׁ֥ה וְאַהֲרֹֽן: 19 וַיַּקְהֵ֨ל עֲלֵיהֶ֥ם קֹ֨רַח֙ אֶת־כׇּל־הָ֣עֵדָ֔ה אֶל־פֶּ֖תַח אֹ֣הֶל מוֹעֵ֑ד וַיֵּרָ֥א כְבוֹד־יְהֹוָ֖ה אֶל־כׇּל־

The Israelite camp was several miles long. How did Korah manage to singlehandedly gather the *entire* congregation together in one single night? Why was his message so compelling that not one individual refused to come?

Korah must have used a Kabbalistic formula, invoking various names of God, to draw the people to gather together. This is the way the Messiah will eventually cause the ingathering of the exiles, and Korah knew this secret. And we can only marvel at the internal contradictions of a man who, on the one hand, knew the Kabbalistic secrets of the Messiah, and yet on the other, was foolish enough to challenge the authority of Moses (*Rabbi Menahem Mendel of Rymanow, 18th century*).

Korah used cynical rhetoric to woo the crowds: "There is a widow in our neighborhood," he said, "with two orphan girls, and she came to plough her field. Moses said to her, '*You may not plow with an ox and*

kabbalah bites

16:15 The tension between *left* and *right* first arose when God said, "Let the firmament (materialize) between the waters *and let it separate*" (Genesis 1:6).

The conflict of Korah and Aaron was also *left* (Levite) against *right* (priest). Moses said, "I will mediate the conflict between left and right."

When Moses saw that he would not succeed (because Korah was insincere) he became "very angry" *at himself*, at his failure to bring God's glory to the world.

If you get into a quarrel, don't be angry that someone is pitted against you. Be upset that you have failed to heal your opponent.

you, and now you seek the priesthood as well? [11] (When I appointed Aaron as priest, it was upon God's explicit instruction,) therefore you and your entire group are (now) ganging up against God (and not against me). And what (valid reason do you have) to complain about Aaron?"

[12] Moses sent (messengers) to call Dathan and Abiram, the sons of Eliab (in a further attempt to make peace), but they said, "We will not go up (and speak to Moses). [13] Isn't it enough that you have brought us out of a land flowing with milk and honey to kill us in the desert, that you also seek to be a ruler over us? [SECOND READING] [14] Furthermore, you have not brought us to a land flowing with milk and honey, nor have you given us an inheritance of fields and vineyards. Even if you poke out the eyes of those men (who are against Moses), we will not go up (to speak to Moses)."

[15] Moses was extremely upset. He said to God, "Don't turn to their gift-offering. I have not taken a donkey from a single one of them, and I have not wronged a single one of them."

Korah's Demise

[16] Moses said to Korah, "Tomorrow, you and your entire congregation should present yourselves before God—you, them and Aaron. [17] Each person should take his fire-pan and place incense upon it, and each person should bring a fire-pan before God, (a total of) two hundred and fifty fire-pans. Both you and Aaron should each take a fire-pan."

[18] Each person took a fire-pan, put fiery (coals) on it and placed incense on it. They stood at the entrance to the Tent of Meeting with Moses and Aaron. [19] Korah ganged (his) entire congregation against them (by inciting them all night, and they came) to the entrance of the Tent of Meeting. The glory of God appeared before the entire congregation (in a pillar of cloud).

11. (When I appointed Aaron as priest, it was upon God's explicit instruction,) therefore you and your entire congregation are (now) ganging up against God. Moses attempted to explain to Korah how he was, in fact, rebelling against God. Not only was Aaron's appointment by God's command, he had been chosen without any urging or campaigning on Aaron's behalf. When Moses had anointed Aaron with the sanctified oil, Aaron had shuddered with fear that he was not worthy to be High Priest and was, perhaps, violating the sanctity of the oil (*Numbers Rabbah*). This clearly illustrates, Moses said to Korah, that Aaron did not actively seek his position at all (*Rabbi Simḥah Bunem of Przysucha, 18th–19th century*).

19. Korah ganged (his) entire congregation against them. The entire night, Korah went to the tribes and tricked them, saying, "Do you think I care only for myself? I care only for all of you! These men have come and taken all the high positions. Moses took the kingship for himself and the priesthood for his brother." Eventually they were all lured into Korah's rebellion (*Rashi, 11th century*).

הָעֵדָה: ס 20 וַיְדַבֵּר יְהֹוָה אֶל־מֹשֶׁה וְאֶל־אַהֲרֹן לֵאמֹר: 21 הִבָּדְלוּ מִתּוֹךְ הָעֵדָה הַזֹּאת וַאֲכַלֶּה אֹתָם כְּרָגַע: 22 וַיִּפְּלוּ עַל־פְּנֵיהֶם וַיֹּאמְרוּ אֵל אֱלֹהֵי הָרוּחֹת לְכָל־בָּשָׂר הָאִישׁ אֶחָד יֶחֱטָא וְעַל כָּל־הָעֵדָה תִּקְצֹף: 23 וַיְדַבֵּר יְהֹוָה אֶל־מֹשֶׁה לֵּאמֹר: 24 דַּבֵּר אֶל־הָעֵדָה לֵאמֹר הֵעָלוּ מִסָּבִיב לְמִשְׁכַּן־קֹרַח דָּתָן וַאֲבִירָם: 25 וַיָּקָם מֹשֶׁה וַיֵּלֶךְ אֶל־דָּתָן וַאֲבִירָם וַיֵּלְכוּ אַחֲרָיו זִקְנֵי יִשְׂרָאֵל: 26 וַיְדַבֵּר אֶל־הָעֵדָה לֵאמֹר סוּרוּ נָא מֵעַל אָהֳלֵי הָאֲנָשִׁים הָרְשָׁעִים הָאֵלֶּה וְאַל־תִּגְּעוּ בְּכָל־אֲשֶׁר לָהֶם פֶּן־תִּסָּפוּ בְּכָל־חַטֹּאתָם: 27 וַיֵּעָלוּ מֵעַל מִשְׁכַּן־קֹרַח דָּתָן וַאֲבִירָם מִסָּבִיב וְדָתָן וַאֲבִירָם יָצְאוּ נִצָּבִים פֶּתַח אָהֳלֵיהֶם

angry, he punishes them all. But all thoughts are revealed before You, and You know who the sinner is. If one man is the sinner, why should You be angry with the whole congregation?"

God said, "You have spoken well. I know, and I will make known, who sinned and who did not sin" (*Rashi, 11th century*).

Not all of Korah's group were equally guilty. Korah himself was an inciter of rebellion, who used divisive tactics in an active attempt to undermine Moses and Aaron's leadership. The men whom Korah convinced, however, were not essentially rebellious; they were merely lured by the arguments of Korah.

So, argued Moses, a mortal king could be excused for punishing the masses, since he cannot identify the leader of the rebellion (the "sinner"), but, "You know who the sinner is. If one man is the sinner, should You be angry with the whole congregation?"

God replied, "You have spoken well" (*Rabbi Ze'ev Wolf Einhorn, 19th century*).

24. Get away from Korah, Dathan and Abiram's home. On son of Peleth was saved by his wife. She said to him, "What difference does this whole rebellion make to you? What will you gain? Either way, you will remain a disciple. If Moses wins, he will be leader. If Korah wins, he will be leader."

On said, "What should I do? I have already promised Korah that I will join him."

spiritual vitamin

> If the *yetzer ha-ra'* (impulse to evil) would attempt to dissuade you directly from fulfilling your mission, you would not be easily misled. Instead, the *yetzer* tries to discourage you in all sorts of ways, using "pious" arguments which unfortunately can easily prove effective.

numbers 16:20–27 — korah

[THIRD READING] ²⁰ God spoke to Moses and Aaron, saying, ²¹ "Dissociate yourselves from this congregation, and I will destroy them in an instant!"

²² They fell on their faces and said, "O merciful God! God (who knows) everybody's thoughts! (Just because) one man sins, should You be angry with the whole congregation?"

²³ God spoke to Moses, saying, ²⁴ "(You are right. I will punish only the sinners.) Speak to the congregation, saying, 'Get away from Korah, Dathan and Abiram's home!'"

²⁵ Moses set out and went to Dathan and Abiram('s tents). The elders of Israel followed him. ²⁶ He spoke to the congregation saying, "Please get away from the tents of these wicked men and do not touch anything of theirs, so that you don't die because of all their sins."

²⁷ They cleared away from the area of Korah, Dathan, and Abiram's home; but Dathan and Abiram came out and stood (proudly) upright at the entrance of their tents, together with their wives, their children, and their infants.

kabbalah bites

16:27 Dathan and Abiram were reincarnated into the two bulls which were offered on Mount Carmel by Elijah and the prophets of Baal (see *I Kings* 18:25*ff.*). The soul of Abiram, who was less righteous than Dathan, entered the bull offered by the idolatrous Baal prophets. Both cows were burned, just as Dathan and Abiram were utterly consumed here.

---

a donkey together' (*Deuteronomy* 22:10). When she came to plant, he said to her *'You should not sow your field with a mixture of seed'* (*Leviticus* 19:19). When she came to harvest, he told her to leave over produce for the poor. When she came to thresh, he said to her, 'Give me the priestly tithes on this produce.' Since she justified the laws, she gave it all to him.

"What did the poor woman do? She sold the field and bought two sheep so she could dress from their wool and enjoy their offspring.

"When they gave birth, Aaron came and said to her, 'Give me the firstborn, for God has said, *"You must sanctify every firstborn male from your cattle or your flock, to God, your God"* (*Deuteronomy* 15:19). He justified the law to her and she gave him the newborns. When she sheared the sheep, Aaron came and said, 'Give me the first shearings!'

"She said, 'I can't take this man! I'm simply going to slaughter these animals and eat them.'

"When she slaughtered them, Aaron came and said, 'Give me the priestly gifts of the forelimb, the tongue and the stomach!'

"She said, 'Even after I've slaughtered them am I still not spared from your hands? Look, I am simply going to consecrate them all.'

"'Oh,' he said to her, 'if they are consecrated then they are all mine!' and he took them, leaving her to weep over her two daughters" (*Midrash Tehillim*).

22. God (who knows) everybody's thoughts! Moses said, "He who knows man's thoughts! Your attributes are not like those of men of flesh and blood. If part of a country becomes corrupt, a king of flesh and blood does not know who the sinner is, and therefore, when he is

קרח
במדבר טז:כח - יז:ג

28 וַיֹּאמֶר מֹשֶׁה בְּזֹאת תֵּדְעוּן כִּי־יְהֹוָה שְׁלָחַנִי לַעֲשׂוֹת אֵת כָּל־הַמַּעֲשִׂים הָאֵלֶּה כִּי־לֹא מִלִּבִּי: 29 אִם־כְּמוֹת כָּל־הָאָדָם יְמֻתוּן אֵלֶּה וּפְקֻדַּת כָּל־הָאָדָם יִפָּקֵד עֲלֵיהֶם לֹא יְהֹוָה שְׁלָחָנִי: 30 וְאִם־בְּרִיאָה יִבְרָא יְהֹוָה וּפָצְתָה הָאֲדָמָה אֶת־פִּיהָ וּבָלְעָה אֹתָם וְאֶת־כָּל־אֲשֶׁר לָהֶם וְיָרְדוּ חַיִּים שְׁאֹלָה וִידַעְתֶּם כִּי נִאֲצוּ הָאֲנָשִׁים הָאֵלֶּה אֶת־יְהֹוָה: 31 וַיְהִי כְּכַלֹּתוֹ לְדַבֵּר אֵת כָּל־הַדְּבָרִים הָאֵלֶּה וַתִּבָּקַע הָאֲדָמָה אֲשֶׁר תַּחְתֵּיהֶם: 32 וַתִּפְתַּח הָאָרֶץ אֶת־פִּיהָ וַתִּבְלַע אֹתָם וְאֶת־בָּתֵּיהֶם וְאֵת כָּל־הָאָדָם אֲשֶׁר לְקֹרַח וְאֵת כָּל־הָרְכוּשׁ: 33 וַיֵּרְדוּ הֵם וְכָל־אֲשֶׁר לָהֶם חַיִּים שְׁאֹלָה וַתְּכַס עֲלֵיהֶם הָאָרֶץ וַיֹּאבְדוּ מִתּוֹךְ הַקָּהָל: 34 וְכָל־יִשְׂרָאֵל אֲשֶׁר סְבִיבֹתֵיהֶם נָסוּ לְקֹלָם כִּי אָמְרוּ פֶּן־תִּבְלָעֵנוּ הָאָרֶץ: 35 וְאֵשׁ יָצְאָה מֵאֵת יְהֹוָה וַתֹּאכַל אֵת הַחֲמִשִּׁים וּמָאתַיִם אִישׁ מַקְרִיבֵי הַקְּטֹרֶת: ס

יז 1 וַיְדַבֵּר יְהֹוָה אֶל־מֹשֶׁה לֵּאמֹר: 2 אֱמֹר אֶל־אֶלְעָזָר בֶּן־אַהֲרֹן הַכֹּהֵן וְיָרֵם אֶת־הַמַּחְתֹּת מִבֵּין הַשְּׂרֵפָה וְאֶת־הָאֵשׁ זְרֵה־הָלְאָה כִּי קָדֵשׁוּ: 3 אֵת מַחְתּוֹת הַחַטָּאִים הָאֵלֶּה בְּנַפְשֹׁתָם וְעָשׂוּ אֹתָם רִקֻּעֵי פַחִים צִפּוּי לַמִּזְבֵּחַ כִּי־הִקְרִיבֻם לִפְנֵי־יְהֹוָה וַיִּקְדָּשׁוּ וְיִהְיוּ לְאוֹת לִבְנֵי יִשְׂרָאֵל:

overemphasized the spiritual were consumed by fire from above, whereas those who had distorted the importance of physical deeds were swallowed up by the earth from below.

In this vein, the *Mishnah* describes Korah's dispute as "not for the sake of heaven" (*Avot* 5:17). The Hebrew word for "heaven"—*shamayim*—is a composite of the words *'esh* and *mayim*, "fire" and "water" (*Rashi* to Genesis 1:8). This alludes to the fact that Korah's group wished to challenge "heaven," namely, the ability to harmonize the dynamic tension of soul and body, of fire and water (*Rabbi Menahem Mendel Schneerson, 20th century*).

17:3 They have become sanctified because they were brought before God. Even though God commanded that the fire-pans used by Korah and his followers were to be made into a covering for the altar, this does not mean that He was pleased with their offerings. On the contrary, the incense was an abomination to Him. But since these fire-pans had been designated for a holy purpose, they were considered holy *before* the incense was offered in them. They therefore retained their holiness even after Korah's people used them (*Rabbi Ḥayyim ibn Attar, 18th century*).

⁲⁸ Moses said, "Through this you will know that God authorized me to carry out all these acts (of appointing the priests), for it was not my idea: ²⁹ If these men die as all men die and the fate of all men occurs to them, then (Korah is right and) God has not sent me. ³⁰ But if God creates a new form (of death that you have never seen before), and the earth opens its mouth and swallows them along with everything that belongs to them, and they descend alive into the grave—then you will know that these men have provoked God."

³¹ As soon as he finished speaking all these words, the earth beneath them split open. ³² The earth opened its mouth, swallowing them and their houses, all of Korah's people and all of their property. ³³ They descended alive into the grave with everything they possessed. The earth covered them up, and they were lost to the congregation. ³⁴ All the Jewish people who were around them fled from the sound (of the earth swallowing Korah's men), for they said, "Perhaps the earth will swallow us up (too)!"

³⁵ Then a fire came from God and consumed the two hundred and fifty men who had offered up the incense.

A Reminder of Korah

17 ¹ God spoke to Moses, saying: ² "Tell Eleazar son of Aaron the priest to pick up the fire-pans from the burned area because they have become holy, but he should throw the fire (coals) away. ³ Make the fire-pans of those who sinned against their souls into flattened sheets, as a coating for the altar, since they have become sanctified because they were brought before God. They will be a reminder for the children of Israel."

On's wife got her husband drunk, sat outside their tent and uncovered her hair. When Korah's men came to collect him, they saw her sitting at the entrance. Not wanting to approach another man's wife while she was in an immodest state, they turned around and left. In this way, he was saved (*Babylonian Talmud, Sanhedrin* 109b).

30. If God creates a new form (of death that you have never seen before), and the earth opens its mouth and swallows them. At twilight on the eve of the first Sabbath, ten things were created, including the "mouth of the earth" that was to swallow Korah and his assembly (*Mishnah, Avot* 5:6). Did Moses not know this information through his powers of prophecy?

Another of the "ten things" created at that time was Moses' burial spot, the exact location of which is unknown to any man (*Deuteronomy* 34:6). For this reason, God kept from Moses *all* of the "ten things," including the mouth of the earth that swallowed Korah and his assembly (*Rabbi Moses Sofer, 18th–19th century*).

31-35. The earth beneath them split open ... then a fire came. Why were some of Korah's group swallowed up by the earth, whereas others were consumed by fire?

Korah's rebellion was an attempt to upset the healthy equilibrium between the desire for spirituality and the need to be active in the physical world. Those members of the group who

במדבר יז:ד-יט

קרח

4 וַיִּקַּ֞ח אֶלְעָזָ֣ר הַכֹּהֵ֗ן אֵ֚ת מַחְתּ֣וֹת הַנְּחֹ֔שֶׁת אֲשֶׁ֥ר הִקְרִ֖יבוּ הַשְּׂרֻפִ֑ים וַיְרַקְּע֖וּם צִפּ֥וּי לַמִּזְבֵּֽחַ: 5 זִכָּר֞וֹן לִבְנֵ֣י יִשְׂרָאֵ֗ל לְ֠מַעַן אֲשֶׁ֨ר לֹֽא־יִקְרַ֜ב אִ֣ישׁ זָ֗ר אֲ֠שֶׁר לֹ֣א מִזֶּ֤רַע אַהֲרֹן֙ ה֔וּא לְהַקְטִ֥יר קְטֹ֖רֶת לִפְנֵ֣י יְהוָ֑ה וְלֹֽא־יִהְיֶ֤ה כְקֹ֙רַח֙ וְכַ֣עֲדָת֔וֹ כַּאֲשֶׁ֨ר דִּבֶּ֧ר יְהוָ֛ה בְּיַד־מֹשֶׁ֖ה לֽוֹ: פ 6 וַיִּלֹּ֜נוּ כָּל־עֲדַ֤ת בְּנֵֽי־יִשְׂרָאֵל֙ מִֽמָּחֳרָ֔ת עַל־מֹשֶׁ֥ה וְעַֽל־אַהֲרֹ֖ן לֵאמֹ֑ר אַתֶּ֥ם הֲמִתֶּ֖ם אֶת־עַ֥ם יְהוָֽה: 7 וַיְהִ֗י בְּהִקָּהֵ֤ל הָֽעֵדָה֙ עַל־מֹשֶׁ֣ה וְעַֽל־אַהֲרֹ֔ן וַיִּפְנוּ֙ אֶל־אֹ֣הֶל מוֹעֵ֔ד וְהִנֵּ֥ה כִסָּ֖הוּ הֶעָנָ֑ן וַיֵּרָ֖א כְּב֥וֹד יְהוָֽה: 8 וַיָּבֹ֤א מֹשֶׁה֙ וְאַהֲרֹ֔ן אֶל־פְּנֵ֖י אֹ֥הֶל מוֹעֵֽד: ס 9 [FOURTH READING] וַיְדַבֵּ֥ר יְהוָ֖ה אֶל־מֹשֶׁ֥ה לֵּאמֹֽר: 10 הֵרֹ֗מּוּ מִתּוֹךְ֙ הָעֵדָ֣ה הַזֹּ֔את וַאֲכַלֶּ֥ה אֹתָ֖ם כְּרָ֑גַע וַֽיִּפְּל֖וּ עַל־פְּנֵיהֶֽם: 11 וַיֹּ֨אמֶר מֹשֶׁ֜ה אֶֽל־אַהֲרֹ֗ן קַ֣ח אֶת־הַ֠מַּחְתָּה וְתֶן־עָלֶ֨יהָ אֵ֜שׁ מֵעַ֤ל הַמִּזְבֵּ֙חַ֙ וְשִׂ֣ים קְטֹ֔רֶת וְהוֹלֵ֧ךְ מְהֵרָ֛ה אֶל־הָעֵדָ֖ה וְכַפֵּ֣ר עֲלֵיהֶ֑ם כִּֽי־יָצָ֥א הַקֶּ֛צֶף מִלִּפְנֵ֥י יְהוָ֖ה הֵחֵ֥ל הַנָּֽגֶף: 12 וַיִּקַּ֨ח אַהֲרֹ֜ן כַּאֲשֶׁ֣ר | דִּבֶּ֣ר מֹשֶׁ֗ה וַיָּ֙רָץ֙ אֶל־תּ֣וֹךְ הַקָּהָ֔ל וְהִנֵּ֛ה הֵחֵ֥ל הַנֶּ֖גֶף בָּעָ֑ם וַיִּתֵּן֙ אֶֽת־הַקְּטֹ֔רֶת וַיְכַפֵּ֖ר עַל־הָעָֽם: 13 וַיַּעֲמֹ֥ד בֵּֽין־הַמֵּתִ֖ים וּבֵ֣ין הַֽחַיִּ֑ים וַתֵּעָצַ֖ר הַמַּגֵּפָֽה: 14 וַיִּהְי֗וּ הַמֵּתִים֙ בַּמַּגֵּפָ֔ה אַרְבָּעָ֥ה עָשָׂ֛ר אֶ֖לֶף וּשְׁבַ֣ע מֵא֑וֹת מִלְּבַ֥ד הַמֵּתִ֖ים עַל־דְּבַר־קֹֽרַח: 15 וַיָּ֤שָׁב אַהֲרֹן֙ אֶל־מֹשֶׁ֔ה אֶל־פֶּ֖תַח אֹ֣הֶל מוֹעֵ֑ד וְהַמַּגֵּפָ֖ה נֶעֱצָֽרָה: פ 16 [FIFTH READING] וַיְדַבֵּ֥ר יְהוָ֖ה אֶל־מֹשֶׁ֥ה לֵּאמֹֽר: 17 דַּבֵּ֣ר | אֶל־בְּנֵ֣י יִשְׂרָאֵ֗ל וְקַ֣ח מֵֽאִתָּ֡ם מַטֶּ֣ה מַטֶּה֩ לְבֵ֨ית אָ֜ב מֵאֵ֤ת כָּל־נְשִֽׂיאֵהֶם֙ לְבֵ֣ית אֲבֹתָ֔ם שְׁנֵ֥ים עָשָׂ֖ר מַטּ֑וֹת אִ֣ישׁ אֶת־שְׁמ֔וֹ תִּכְתֹּ֖ב עַל־מַטֵּֽהוּ: 18 וְאֵת֙ שֵׁ֣ם אַהֲרֹ֔ן תִּכְתֹּ֖ב עַל־מַטֵּ֣ה לֵוִ֑י כִּ֚י מַטֶּ֣ה אֶחָ֔ד לְרֹ֖אשׁ בֵּ֥ית אֲבוֹתָֽם: 19 וְהִנַּחְתָּ֖ם בְּאֹ֣הֶל מוֹעֵ֑ד לִפְנֵי֙ הָֽעֵד֔וּת אֲשֶׁ֛ר אִוָּעֵ֥ד לָכֶ֖ם שָֽׁמָּה:

---

12. Aaron took it, just as Moses had said. Aaron did not hesitate to carry out Moses' instructions, despite the fact that it involved the transgression of offering incense at an incorrect time and place. Nevertheless, Aaron did so because *"Moses had said,"* and you must follow the words of an acknowledged prophet even when he tells you to transgress a commandment of the Torah (*Rabbi Ḥayyim ibn Attar, 18th century*).

numbers 17:4–19 — koraḥ

⁴ Eleazar the priest took the copper fire-pans which the fire victims had brought, and they flattened them out into a coating for the altar. ⁵ It was a reminder for the children of Israel that no outsider, who is not a descendant of Aaron, should approach (the altar) to burn incense before God, so as not to be like Korah and his company. For it was God who spoke, through Moses, about (Aaron's appointment).

Aaron Saves the People

⁶ The following day, the entire congregation of Israel complained against Moses and Aaron, saying, "You have killed God's people!"

⁷ Then, as the congregation was ganging up against Moses and Aaron, they turned to the Tent of Meeting, and—look!—the cloud had covered it, and the glory of God appeared. ⁸ Moses and Aaron came to the front of the Tent of Meeting. [FOURTH READING] ⁹ God spoke to Moses saying, ¹⁰ Get away from this congregation! I'm going to destroy them in an instant!"

They fell on their faces. ¹¹ Moses said to Aaron, "Take the fire-pan and place fiery (coals) from the top of the altar onto it. Then take it quickly to the congregation and atone for them, for God is very angry, and the plague has begun (but I know that incense stops a plague)."

¹² Aaron took it, just as Moses had said. He ran into the assembly, and—look!—the plague had begun among the people. He placed the incense on (the fire-pan) and atoned for the people. ¹³ He stood between the dead and the living, and the plague ceased.

¹⁴ The number of dead in the plague was fourteen thousand, seven hundred, besides those who died because of the incident with Korah.

¹⁵ Aaron returned to Moses at the entrance of the Tent of Meeting, and the plague had ended.

Confirmation of Aaron's Appointment

[FIFTH READING] ¹⁶ God spoke to Moses, saying: ¹⁷ "Speak to the children of Israel and take from them a staff for each paternal house from all the leaders according to their paternal houses—twelve staffs. Inscribe each man's name on his staff. ¹⁸ Inscribe Aaron's name on Levi's staff, for there is (only) one staff for the head of each paternal house (and the priests are from the tribe of Levi). ¹⁹ Place the staffs in the Tent of Meeting before the (Ark of) the Testimony where I arrange meetings with you."

---

11. Take the fire-pan. Because the children of Israel blamed the death of the two hundred and fifty men on the "deadly" incense, Moses now wanted to demonstrate that incense is far from deadly—it could even save lives (*Rabbi Ḥayyim ibn Attar, 18th century*).

במדבר יז:כ-כח | קרח

20 וְהָיָה הָאִישׁ אֲשֶׁר אֶבְחַר־בּוֹ מַטֵּהוּ יִפְרָח וַהֲשִׁכֹּתִי מֵעָלַי אֶת־תְּלֻנּוֹת בְּנֵי יִשְׂרָאֵל אֲשֶׁר הֵם מַלִּינִם עֲלֵיכֶם: 21 וַיְדַבֵּר מֹשֶׁה אֶל־בְּנֵי יִשְׂרָאֵל וַיִּתְּנוּ אֵלָיו ׀ כָּל־נְשִׂיאֵיהֶם מַטֶּה לְנָשִׂיא אֶחָד מַטֶּה לְנָשִׂיא אֶחָד לְבֵית אֲבֹתָם שְׁנֵים עָשָׂר מַטּוֹת וּמַטֵּה אַהֲרֹן בְּתוֹךְ מַטּוֹתָם: 22 וַיַּנַּח מֹשֶׁה אֶת־הַמַּטֹּת לִפְנֵי יְהֹוָה בְּאֹהֶל הָעֵדֻת: 23 וַיְהִי מִמָּחֳרָת וַיָּבֹא מֹשֶׁה אֶל־אֹהֶל הָעֵדוּת וְהִנֵּה פָּרַח מַטֵּה־אַהֲרֹן לְבֵית לֵוִי וַיֹּצֵא פֶרַח וַיָּצֵץ צִיץ וַיִּגְמֹל שְׁקֵדִים: 24 וַיֹּצֵא מֹשֶׁה אֶת־כָּל־הַמַּטֹּת מִלִּפְנֵי יְהֹוָה אֶל־כָּל־בְּנֵי יִשְׂרָאֵל וַיִּרְאוּ וַיִּקְחוּ אִישׁ מַטֵּהוּ: פ 25 [SIXTH READING] וַיֹּאמֶר יְהֹוָה אֶל־מֹשֶׁה הָשֵׁב אֶת־מַטֵּה אַהֲרֹן לִפְנֵי הָעֵדוּת לְמִשְׁמֶרֶת לְאוֹת לִבְנֵי־מֶרִי וּתְכַל תְּלוּנֹּתָם מֵעָלַי וְלֹא יָמֻתוּ: 26 וַיַּעַשׂ מֹשֶׁה כַּאֲשֶׁר צִוָּה יְהֹוָה אֹתוֹ כֵּן עָשָׂה: פ 27 וַיֹּאמְרוּ בְּנֵי יִשְׂרָאֵל אֶל־מֹשֶׁה לֵאמֹר הֵן גָּוַעְנוּ אָבַדְנוּ כֻּלָּנוּ אָבָדְנוּ: 28 כֹּל הַקָּרֵב ׀ הַקָּרֵב אֶל־מִשְׁכַּן יְהֹוָה יָמוּת הַאִם תַּמְנוּ לִגְוֺעַ: ס

922

The fruit symbolizes our achievements; the blossoms, our effort. Usually most attention is paid to achievements. Aaron's staff, with the blossoms and fruit remaining together, teaches us that when we perform commandments and study Torah, the blossoms—the effort and sweat that we put in—are not forgotten (*Rabbi Moses Feinstein, 20th century*).

24. Moses took out all the staffs ... they saw (what had happened) and each man took his staff (back). Aaron took his rod because it had *"blossomed, started to produce fruit and developed ripe almonds"* (v. 23). But why did the leaders retrieve their rods?

The leaders took their rods to show everyone that they had *not* budded, publicly proclaiming that Aaron was chosen, and not them. This is the way honest and humble people behave (*Rabbi Ḥayyim Meir Jehiel Shapiro of Mogielnica, 19th century*).

spiritual vitamin

> There may always be some individual who might make a joke about your convictions. But when you are sincerely dedicated to your faith, you will only call forth respect and admiration.

numbers 17:20–28   korah

²⁰ "What will happen is, the staff of the man whom I will choose will blossom. I will (thus) rid Myself of the complaints of the children of Israel, which they are directing at you."

²¹ Moses spoke to the children of Israel. All their leaders gave him a staff, one staff per leader according to their paternal houses, (a total of) twelve staffs. Aaron's staff was in the middle of their staffs. ²² Moses placed the staffs before God in the Tent of Testimony.

²³ On the following day Moses came to the Tent of Testimony, and—look!—Aaron's staff, of the house of Levi, had blossomed! It had blossomed, started to produce fruit, and developed ripe almonds.

²⁴ Moses took out all the staffs from before God, to the children of Israel. They saw (what had happened) and each man took his staff (back).

[SIXTH READING] ²⁵ God said to Moses, "Put Aaron's staff back in front of (the Ark of) the Testimony, guarding it as a sign for rebellious people. Then their complaints against Me will end and they will not die."

²⁶ Moses did what God had commanded him. He did it (precisely).

Guarding the Tabernacle

²⁷ The children of Israel spoke to Moses, saying, "(We can't be so careful about not entering the Tent of Meeting.) We're going to die! We will be destroyed! We are all lost! ²⁸ Whoever comes close to the Sanctuary of God dies! Are we doomed to death?"

23. It had blossomed, started to produce fruit and developed ripe almonds. Usually trees do not bear fruit until after the blossoms are long gone, yet here the staff produced fruit while the blossoms were still on it. This miracle hints at the degree to which God cherishes man's effort.

kabbalah bites

17:23 Why did Aaron's staff sprout *almonds*? Because almonds grow quickly, hinting to the idea that a priest's blessing will materialize quickly.

But why should there be quick blessings and slow ones? Surely if God has decided to give us something, shouldn't it happen right away?

Just like we procrastinate and debate an idea before putting it into practice, the spiritual worlds have numerous "judgment points" too. Even after God issues a blessing, it can take a while to come down, or even get completely stuck.

So next time you see one of Aaron's descendants, a *kohen* (priest), get him to bless you, because a priest's blessing has "diplomatic immunity" from all barriers and very quickly becomes "ripe almonds."

במדבר יח:א-ט

יח 1 וַיֹּאמֶר יְהוָה אֶל־אַהֲרֹן אַתָּה וּבָנֶיךָ וּבֵית־אָבִיךָ אִתָּךְ תִּשְׂאוּ אֶת־עֲוֺן הַמִּקְדָּשׁ וְאַתָּה וּבָנֶיךָ אִתָּךְ תִּשְׂאוּ אֶת־עֲוֺן כְּהֻנַּתְכֶם: 2 וְגַם אֶת־אַחֶיךָ מַטֵּה לֵוִי שֵׁבֶט אָבִיךָ הַקְרֵב אִתָּךְ וְיִלָּווּ עָלֶיךָ וִישָׁרְתוּךָ וְאַתָּה וּבָנֶיךָ אִתָּךְ לִפְנֵי אֹהֶל הָעֵדֻת: 3 וְשָׁמְרוּ מִשְׁמַרְתְּךָ וּמִשְׁמֶרֶת כָּל־הָאֹהֶל אַךְ אֶל־כְּלֵי הַקֹּדֶשׁ וְאֶל־הַמִּזְבֵּחַ לֹא יִקְרָבוּ וְלֹא־יָמֻתוּ גַם־הֵם גַּם־אַתֶּם: 4 וְנִלְווּ עָלֶיךָ וְשָׁמְרוּ אֶת־מִשְׁמֶרֶת אֹהֶל מוֹעֵד לְכֹל עֲבֹדַת הָאֹהֶל וְזָר לֹא־יִקְרַב אֲלֵיכֶם: 5 וּשְׁמַרְתֶּם אֵת מִשְׁמֶרֶת הַקֹּדֶשׁ וְאֵת מִשְׁמֶרֶת הַמִּזְבֵּחַ וְלֹא־יִהְיֶה עוֹד קֶצֶף עַל־בְּנֵי יִשְׂרָאֵל: 6 וַאֲנִי הִנֵּה לָקַחְתִּי אֶת־אֲחֵיכֶם הַלְוִיִּם מִתּוֹךְ בְּנֵי יִשְׂרָאֵל לָכֶם מַתָּנָה נְתֻנִים לַיהוָה לַעֲבֹד אֶת־עֲבֹדַת אֹהֶל מוֹעֵד: 7 וְאַתָּה וּבָנֶיךָ אִתְּךָ תִּשְׁמְרוּ אֶת־כְּהֻנַּתְכֶם לְכָל־דְּבַר הַמִּזְבֵּחַ וּלְמִבֵּית לַפָּרֹכֶת וַעֲבַדְתֶּם עֲבֹדַת מַתָּנָה אֶתֵּן אֶת־כְּהֻנַּתְכֶם וְהַזָּר הַקָּרֵב יוּמָת: פ 8 וַיְדַבֵּר יְהוָה אֶל־אַהֲרֹן וַאֲנִי הִנֵּה נָתַתִּי לְךָ אֶת־מִשְׁמֶרֶת תְּרוּמֹתָי לְכָל־קָדְשֵׁי בְנֵי־יִשְׂרָאֵל לְךָ נְתַתִּים לְמָשְׁחָה וּלְבָנֶיךָ לְחָק־עוֹלָם: 9 זֶה יִהְיֶה לְךָ מִקֹּדֶשׁ הַקֳּדָשִׁים מִן־הָאֵשׁ כָּל־קָרְבָּנָם לְכָל־מִנְחָתָם וּלְכָל־חַטָּאתָם וּלְכָל־אֲשָׁמָם אֲשֶׁר יָשִׁיבוּ לִי קֹדֶשׁ

It is a Biblical commandment to guard the Temple. This is so even if there is no fear of enemies or thieves, for the guarding of the Temple is done purely as an act of respect, for a palace with guards is incomparably superior to a palace without guards.

The commandment of guarding the Temple is carried out the entire night.

The guardians are the priests and Levites, as the verse states, *"You along with your sons will be before the Tent of Testimony"* (v. 2), i.e., you should keep watch over it for Me. Also, it is said (v. 4), *"they should safeguard the duties of the Tent of Meeting"* (*Maimonides, 12th century*).

8. My gift (offerings, which you must) guard. Why do the laws of gifts to the priests appear here? This could be compared to a king who gave a field to his friend but did not write a deed or sign anything, and did not record it in court. A person came and disputed the ownership of the field. The king said to him: "Anyone can come and contest your rights. So I will write a deed, sign it for you, and record it in court."

Likewise here, since Korah came and disputed Aaron's rights to the priesthood, the Torah gave him twenty-four priestly gifts as an everlasting covenant (v. 19). Therefore, this passage is placed here, next to the incident with Korah (*Rashi, 11th century*).

numbers 18:1–9 — koraḥ

18

¹ God said to (Moses: Say to) Aaron:

- You, your sons and (the rest of) your paternal house (of Kohath) will (protect the Jewish people by) taking responsibility for sins concerning (touching unauthorized parts of) the Sanctuary (warning them at all times).
- You, along with your sons (the priests), will take responsibility for sins (of the Levites) concerning (unauthorized participation in the duties of) your priesthood.

² You should also draw close your brothers (the descendants of Gershon and Merari) from the tribe of Levi, your father's tribe:

- They should join you (in the above work).
- They should serve as ministers to you (helping you with duties of guarding and administration, so that) you, along with your sons, will be before the Tent of Testimony.
- ³ They should safeguard your duties and the duties of the Tent, but they may not approach the holy vessels or the altar, so that neither they nor you will die. ⁴ They should join you, and they should safeguard the duties of the Tent of Meeting for all the services of the Tent, and (you should make sure that) no outsider should come near you. ⁵ You should safeguard the duties of the Sanctuary and the duties of the altar, so that there will be no more (Divine) anger against the children of Israel (as there has been in the past).

⁶ Look! I have taken your brothers, the Levites, from among the children of Israel, and have given them to you as a gift to help (you with the work of) God, to perform the service in the Tent of Meeting.

⁷ You, along with your sons, should guard your priesthood in all matters concerning the altar, and that which is behind the partition screen, and you should serve. I have given you the service of your priesthood as a gift. Any non-priest who approaches (to participate) will die.

Gifts to the Priests

⁸ God said to Aaron: Look! I have given you My gift (offerings, which you must) guard (from ritual impurity). I have given you all the children of Israel's holy things as a sign of greatness, and to your sons as an eternal portion.

⁹ The following will be yours from the holiest of holies, (after) the fire(-offerings are put on the altar):

18:1 Taking responsibility for sins concerning (touching unauthorized parts of) the Sanctuary. God says: "I impose upon you the punishment for outsiders who sin by using the sacred objects entrusted to you: the Tent, the ark, the table, and the sacred apparatus. You must sit and warn any outsider who attempts to touch them (*Rashi, 11th century*).

במדבר יח:ט-כא   קרח

קָדָשִׁים לְךָ הוּא וּלְבָנֶיךָ: 10 בְּקֹדֶשׁ הַקֳּדָשִׁים תֹּאכְלֶנּוּ כָּל־זָכָר יֹאכַל אֹתוֹ קֹדֶשׁ יִהְיֶה־לָּךְ: 11 וְזֶה־לְּךָ תְּרוּמַת מַתָּנָם לְכָל־תְּנוּפֹת בְּנֵי יִשְׂרָאֵל לְךָ נְתַתִּים וּלְבָנֶיךָ וְלִבְנֹתֶיךָ אִתְּךָ לְחָק־עוֹלָם כָּל־טָהוֹר בְּבֵיתְךָ יֹאכַל אֹתוֹ: 12 כֹּל חֵלֶב יִצְהָר וְכָל־חֵלֶב תִּירוֹשׁ וְדָגָן רֵאשִׁיתָם אֲשֶׁר־יִתְּנוּ לַיהוָה לְךָ נְתַתִּים: 13 בִּכּוּרֵי כָּל־אֲשֶׁר בְּאַרְצָם אֲשֶׁר־יָבִיאוּ לַיהוָה לְךָ יִהְיֶה כָּל־טָהוֹר בְּבֵיתְךָ יֹאכְלֶנּוּ: 14 כָּל־חֵרֶם בְּיִשְׂרָאֵל לְךָ יִהְיֶה: 15 כָּל־פֶּטֶר רֶחֶם לְכָל־בָּשָׂר אֲשֶׁר־יַקְרִיבוּ לַיהוָה בָּאָדָם וּבַבְּהֵמָה יִהְיֶה־לָּךְ אַךְ | פָּדֹה תִפְדֶּה אֵת בְּכוֹר הָאָדָם וְאֵת בְּכוֹר־הַבְּהֵמָה הַטְּמֵאָה תִּפְדֶּה: 16 וּפְדוּיָו מִבֶּן־חֹדֶשׁ תִּפְדֶּה בְּעֶרְכְּךָ כֶּסֶף חֲמֵשֶׁת שְׁקָלִים בְּשֶׁקֶל הַקֹּדֶשׁ עֶשְׂרִים גֵּרָה הוּא: 17 אַךְ בְּכוֹר־שׁוֹר אוֹ־בְכוֹר כֶּשֶׂב אוֹ־בְכוֹר עֵז לֹא תִפְדֶּה קֹדֶשׁ הֵם אֶת־דָּמָם תִּזְרֹק עַל־הַמִּזְבֵּחַ וְאֶת־חֶלְבָּם תַּקְטִיר אִשֶּׁה לְרֵיחַ נִיחֹחַ לַיהוָה: 18 וּבְשָׂרָם יִהְיֶה־לָּךְ כַּחֲזֵה הַתְּנוּפָה וּכְשׁוֹק הַיָּמִין לְךָ יִהְיֶה: 19 כֹּל | תְּרוּמֹת הַקֳּדָשִׁים אֲשֶׁר יָרִימוּ בְנֵי־יִשְׂרָאֵל לַיהוָה נָתַתִּי לְךָ וּלְבָנֶיךָ וְלִבְנֹתֶיךָ אִתְּךָ לְחָק־עוֹלָם בְּרִית מֶלַח עוֹלָם הִוא לִפְנֵי יְהוָה לְךָ וּלְזַרְעֲךָ אִתָּךְ: 20 וַיֹּאמֶר יְהוָה אֶל־אַהֲרֹן בְּאַרְצָם לֹא תִנְחָל וְחֵלֶק לֹא־יִהְיֶה לְךָ בְּתוֹכָם אֲנִי חֶלְקְךָ וְנַחֲלָתְךָ בְּתוֹךְ בְּנֵי יִשְׂרָאֵל: ס [SEVENTH READING]

21 וְלִבְנֵי לֵוִי הִנֵּה נָתַתִּי כָּל־מַעֲשֵׂר בְּיִשְׂרָאֵל לְנַחֲלָה חֵלֶף עֲבֹדָתָם אֲשֶׁר־הֵם

19. An everlasting covenant (as if preserved in) salt. Just as salt preserves meat, preventing it from rotting, God promises that His covenant with the priests will not be canceled by sins (*Rashi, 11th century*).

21. I have given all tithes of Israel to the descendants of Levi. How are the "Gifts to the Levites" (v. 21-24) connected to the rebellion of Korah, the theme of our Torah portion?

At first glance, Korah's rebellion appears to be hypocritical, for while he complained to Moses and Aaron, *"Why have you made yourselves elite over God's assembly?"* (16:3), Korah nevertheless sought to become the High Priest himself.

Korah sought a different kind of priesthood, one in which the priests remain *aloof* and *removed* from the people. "There is nothing wrong with there being a spiritual elite," Korah would argue, "but they should not be 'over God's assembly,' as leaders of the people."

numbers 18:9–21 — korah

- ❖ (A portion of) all the offerings (of the community)—their meal-offerings, their sin-offerings, their guilt-offerings, (and) what they return to Me (from the property of a deceased convert. These gifts) will be holy of holies to you and to your sons.

- ❖ [10] You must eat (these gifts) in the holiest of places, (the Tabernacle courtyard).

- ❖ All male (priests) may eat (these offerings, which) will be holy to you.

[11] The following will be yours:

- ❖ The parts which are set aside as gifts from all the children of Israel's wave-offerings. I have given these to you, along with your sons and your daughters, as an eternal portion. Any ritually pure member of your household may eat it.

- ❖ [12] I have given (*terumah*) to you, (which is) the first portion of the best oil and the best wine which (the Jewish people) give to God.

- ❖ [13] The first fruit of everything that grows in their land, which they will bring to God, will be yours. Any ritually pure member of your household may eat of it.

- ❖ [14] Any segregated (field) in Israel should be yours.

- ❖ [15] Every firstborn of the womb of any creature, which they present to God, either a man or an animal, will be yours. But you must redeem the firstborn of a person (and return him to his father. Likewise,) you must redeem the firstborn of a ritually impure animal. [16] (A person) should be redeemed from the age of one month, at the (prescribed) value of five silver shekels, according to the shekel (system used for) holy (matters), which is twenty *gerah* (per shekel).

- ❖ [17] However, a firstborn ox, a firstborn sheep or a firstborn goat should not be redeemed, for they are holy. Their blood should be sprinkled on the altar, and their fats should be burned as a fire-offering, as a pleasant aroma to God. [18] Their meat will be yours. It will be yours (and may be eaten by you and your family) like the breast of the wave-offering and the right thigh.

[19] I have given to you, and to your sons and daughters along with you, all the gifts of the holy (offerings) which are set aside by the children of Israel for God as an eternal portion. It is an everlasting covenant (as if preserved in) salt before God, for you and your descendants along with you.

[20] God said to Aaron:

- ❖ You will not come to possess their land, nor will you have a portion (of their spoils of war) along with them. I am your inheritance and portion among the children of Israel.

Gifts to the Levites

- ❖ [SEVENTH READING] [21] And I have given all tithes of Israel to the descendants of Levi as an inheritance, in exchange for their service which they perform—the service of the Tent of Meeting.

במדבר יח:כא-לב   קרח

עֹבְדִ֖ים אֶת־עֲבֹדַ֣ת אֹ֣הֶל מוֹעֵֽד: 22 וְלֹא־יִקְרְב֥וּ ע֛וֹד בְּנֵ֥י יִשְׂרָאֵ֖ל אֶל־אֹ֣הֶל מוֹעֵ֑ד לָשֵׂ֥את חֵ֖טְא לָמֽוּת: 23 וְעָבַ֨ד הַלֵּוִ֜י ה֗וּא אֶת־עֲבֹדַת֙ אֹ֣הֶל מוֹעֵ֔ד וְהֵ֖ם יִשְׂא֣וּ עֲוֺנָ֑ם חֻקַּ֤ת עוֹלָם֙ לְדֹרֹ֣תֵיכֶ֔ם וּבְתוֹךְ֙ בְּנֵ֣י יִשְׂרָאֵ֔ל לֹ֥א יִנְחֲל֖וּ נַחֲלָֽה: 24 כִּ֞י אֶת־מַעְשַׂ֣ר בְּנֵֽי־יִשְׂרָאֵ֗ל אֲשֶׁ֨ר יָרִ֤ימוּ לַֽיהֹוָה֙ תְּרוּמָ֔ה נָתַ֖תִּי לַלְוִיִּ֣ם לְנַחֲלָ֑ה עַל־כֵּן֙ אָמַ֣רְתִּי לָהֶ֔ם בְּתוֹךְ֙ בְּנֵ֣י יִשְׂרָאֵ֔ל לֹ֥א יִנְחֲל֖וּ נַחֲלָֽה: פ 25 וַיְדַבֵּ֥ר יְהֹוָ֖ה אֶל־מֹשֶׁ֥ה לֵּאמֹֽר: 26 וְאֶל־הַלְוִיִּ֤ם תְּדַבֵּר֙ וְאָמַרְתָּ֣ אֲלֵהֶ֔ם כִּֽי־תִ֠קְח֠וּ מֵאֵ֨ת בְּנֵֽי־יִשְׂרָאֵ֜ל אֶת־הַֽמַּעֲשֵׂ֗ר אֲשֶׁ֨ר נָתַ֧תִּי לָכֶ֛ם מֵאִתָּ֖ם בְּנַחֲלַתְכֶ֑ם וַהֲרֵמֹתֶ֤ם מִמֶּ֙נּוּ֙ תְּרוּמַ֣ת יְהֹוָ֔ה מַעֲשֵׂ֖ר מִן־הַֽמַּעֲשֵֽׂר: 27 וְנֶחְשַׁ֥ב לָכֶ֖ם תְּרוּמַתְכֶ֑ם כַּדָּגָן֙ מִן־הַגֹּ֔רֶן וְכַֽמְלֵאָ֖ה מִן־הַיָּֽקֶב: 28 כֵּ֣ן תָּרִ֤ימוּ גַם־אַתֶּם֙ תְּרוּמַ֣ת יְהֹוָ֔ה מִכֹּל֙ מַעְשְׂרֹ֣תֵיכֶ֔ם אֲשֶׁ֣ר תִּקְח֔וּ מֵאֵ֖ת בְּנֵ֣י יִשְׂרָאֵ֑ל וּנְתַתֶּ֤ם מִמֶּ֙נּוּ֙ אֶת־תְּרוּמַ֣ת יְהֹוָ֔ה לְאַהֲרֹ֖ן הַכֹּהֵֽן: 29 מִכֹּל֙ מַתְּנֹ֣תֵיכֶ֔ם תָּרִ֕ימוּ אֵ֖ת כׇּל־תְּרוּמַ֣ת יְהֹוָ֑ה מִכׇּ֨ל־חֶלְבּ֔וֹ אֶֽת־מִקְדְּשׁ֖וֹ מִמֶּֽנּוּ: [MAFTIR] 30 וְאָמַרְתָּ֖ אֲלֵהֶ֑ם בַּהֲרִֽימְכֶ֤ם אֶת־חֶלְבּוֹ֙ מִמֶּ֔נּוּ וְנֶחְשַׁב֙ לַלְוִיִּ֔ם כִּתְבוּאַ֥ת גֹּ֖רֶן וְכִתְבוּאַ֥ת יָֽקֶב: 31 וַאֲכַלְתֶּ֤ם אֹתוֹ֙ בְּכׇל־מָק֔וֹם אַתֶּ֖ם וּבֵֽיתְכֶ֑ם כִּֽי־שָׂכָ֥ר ה֛וּא לָכֶ֖ם חֵ֣לֶף עֲבֹֽדַתְכֶ֑ם בְּאֹ֖הֶל מוֹעֵֽד: 32 וְלֹא־תִשְׂא֤וּ עָלָיו֙ חֵ֔טְא בַּהֲרִֽימְכֶ֥ם אֶת־חֶלְבּ֖וֹ מִמֶּ֑נּוּ וְאֶת־קׇדְשֵׁ֧י בְנֵֽי־יִשְׂרָאֵ֛ל לֹ֥א תְחַלְּל֖וּ וְלֹ֥א תָמֽוּתוּ: פ פ פ

צ"ה פסוקים. דניא"ל סימן.

people, and must be returned to the priest (see verses 12-13). So, on a deeper level, the idea that the people's own property is connected with the priests is still lacking.

Therefore the Torah now records the gifts to the Levites, in which the people's *own property* is given away in support of the Levites, demonstrating a much more fundamental connection between the people and their spiritual leaders (*Rabbi Menahem Mendel Schneerson, 20th century*).

27. The *terumah* you set aside shall be reckoned for you like (the *terumah* that the children of Israel set aside from) the grain of the threshing-floor. Giving charitably from money that was hard-earned is a greater act than giving charitably from money received as a gift. It would follow then that the "*terumah* of the tithe," which the Levites set aside for the priests, would be less favorable than the donations (*terumah*) of the Israelites, which was given from the grain that they had grown with great effort and toil. It was therefore necessary for the Torah to ensure the Levites that their *terumah* would be considered as if it had been given from the grain of their own threshing floor (*Rabbi Solomon Kluger, 19th century*).

numbers 18:22–32 — korah

❖ ²² The children of Israel must no longer approach the Tent of Meeting, so that they do not sin and die. ²³ The Levites should perform the service of the Tent of Meeting, and they will take responsibility for (anybody who approaches it). This is an eternal statute for your generations.

❖ (The Levites) will not come to possess (land) together with the children of Israel. ²⁴ For I have given the children of Israel's tithes, which they must set aside for God as a gift, to the Levites as an inheritance. Therefore, I told them that they will not inherit (land) together with the children of Israel.

Levites' Gifts to the Priests

²⁵ God spoke to Moses, saying: ²⁶ Speak to the Levites and tell them:

❖ When you take the tithes from the children of Israel—which I have given to you from them as your inheritance—you should set aside *terumah* from it for God, a tithe of the tithe. ²⁷ The *terumah* you set aside (will have the same laws as the *terumah* of the children of Israel set aside from) the grain of the threshing-floor and (the first ripe grapes), the produce of the vat. ²⁸ Likewise, you too must set aside *terumah* for God from all the tithes you take from the children of Israel, and you should give God's *terumah* to Aaron the priest.

Food for thought

1. Why did the Torah make its elite class dependent on citizens for support?

2. Would you support a group devoted to God's service on your behalf?

3. Would you want to devote your life exclusively to spiritual pursuits?

❖ ²⁹ From all your gifts (that you receive that have not had *terumah* separated) you should (first) set aside (the original owner's obligation of) *terumah* for God, from its choicest portion, that part of it which is to be consecrated (to the priest; and then you must separate your own obligation of *terumah* from the tithe afterwards).

❖ [MAFTIR] ³⁰ Say to them: When you (do this and) separate its choicest part (as *terumah*), it will be considered for the Levites as (totally permissible) produce from the threshing-floor and as (totally permissible) produce from the vat. ³¹ You and your household may eat it anywhere, for it is your wage in exchange for your service in the Tent of Meeting.

³² You will not bear a sin on account of it, if you separate its choicest part from it. Do not violate the sanctity of that which has been made holy by the children of Israel, and you will not die.

Haftarot: Koraḥ—page 1378.   *Erev Rosh Ḥodesh*—page 1415.   *Rosh Ḥodesh*—page 1417.

Maftir: Rosh Ḥodesh—page 1000 (28:9–15).

Therefore, as a direct response to Korah's complaint, the commandment of gifts to the priests was given. For these gifts emphasize how the priests and the people are closely connected with each other, to the extent that the people support the priests with gifts.

However, this still does not represent a total rebuttal of Korah's position. For, ultimately, the priestly gifts are God's property (or the priest's property) which is found in the hands of the

> The word Ḥukkat is a derivative of the Hebrew word ḥakikah, meaning **"engraving."** The **goal** of all your worship is that **love of God** should totally **permeate your heart and mind,** like letters engraved in stone.

ḤUKKAT
חקת

THE RED HEIFER	19:1–22
MIRIAM'S PASSING AND THE WATER CRISIS	20:1–13
ATTEMPT TO PASS THROUGH EDOM	20:14–21
AARON'S PASSING	20:22–29
SECOND ATTACK OF AMALEK	21:1–3
COMPLAINT AND SNAKE ATTACK	21:4–9
JOURNEYS AND WARS	21:10 – 22:1

NAME
Ḥukkat

MEANING
"Supranational command"

LINES IN TORAH SCROLL
160

PARASHIYYOT
6 open; 4 closed

VERSES
87

WORDS
1245

LETTERS
4670

LOCATION
Sinai Desert, desert of Zin, Kadesh, "Double Mountain," Hormah, Oboth, Iye-abarim, Arnon, Jahaz, Amorite cities, Heshbon, Bashan, and Plains of Moab

DATE
Nisan, 2449; Nisan-Elul, 2487; Tishri, 2488

MITZVOT
3 positive

KEY PEOPLE
Moses, Aaron, Miriam, Eleazar, King Sihon of the Amorites, King Og of Bashan

MASORETIC FEATURES
Dot on the resh of the word 'asher (21:30)

NOTES
Often read together with portion of Balak

CHARACTER PROFILE

NAME
Og ("cake"), king of Bashan

OTHER NAME
Palit ("fugitive")

FATHER
Ahijah son of Shemhazzai

SIBLING
Sihon

LIFE SPAN
Over 832 years

ACHIEVEMENTS
Survived the Flood; informed Abraham that Lot had been captured and was blessed with long life; was circumcised

KNOWN FOR
One of the strongest men ever to live; he was a giant, although his body was out of proportion; killed by Moses on his way to attack the Jewish people

OBEDIENCE

The laws of the Red Heifer are not logical and no explanation is given. They highlight an important element of God's worship—observing His commands simply because He commanded us to do so (19:1).

SELFLESS GIVING

Those who prepared the ashes of the Red Heifer became impure, even as those who were impure were purified by those same ashes. Sometimes in life you should lower yourself and become "impure" for the sake of others (19:10).

ETERNAL MERIT OF GOOD DEEDS

Moses worried about the war with Og because Og had merited to aid Abraham and was blessed with long life. Every single deed you do has a positive effect and protects you (21:34).

במדבר יט:א-ד　　　　　　　　　　　　　　חקת

ט 1 וַיְדַבֵּ֣ר יְהֹוָ֔ה אֶל־מֹשֶׁ֥ה וְאֶֽל־אַהֲרֹ֖ן לֵאמֹֽר: 2 זֹ֚את חֻקַּ֣ת הַתּוֹרָ֔ה אֲשֶׁר־צִוָּ֥ה יְהֹוָ֖ה לֵאמֹ֑ר דַּבֵּ֣ר ׀ אֶל־בְּנֵ֣י יִשְׂרָאֵ֗ל וְיִקְח֣וּ אֵלֶ֩יךָ֩ פָרָ֨ה אֲדֻמָּ֜ה תְּמִימָ֗ה אֲשֶׁ֤ר אֵֽין־בָּהּ֙ מ֔וּם אֲשֶׁ֛ר לֹא־עָלָ֥ה עָלֶ֖יהָ עֹֽל: 3 וּנְתַתֶּ֣ם אֹתָ֔הּ אֶל־אֶלְעָזָ֖ר הַכֹּהֵ֑ן וְהוֹצִ֤יא אֹתָהּ֙ אֶל־מִח֣וּץ לַֽמַּחֲנֶ֔ה וְשָׁחַ֥ט אֹתָ֖הּ לְפָנָֽיו: 4 וְלָקַ֞ח אֶלְעָזָ֧ר הַכֹּהֵ֛ן מִדָּמָ֖הּ בְּאֶצְבָּע֑וֹ וְהִזָּ֞ה אֶל־נֹ֨כַח פְּנֵ֧י אֹֽהֶל־מוֹעֵ֛ד מִדָּמָ֖הּ

as the drive to explore and innovate new ideas, never remaining content with your present knowledge. In practical observance, it ensures that you do not stagnate at your present level, but always seek to grow.

But God desires that you find your destiny here, in the lowly, physical world. So while *ratzo'* has a positive effect, in that it lifts your perception and aspirations above the mundane, it must be coupled with *shov*—a sense of responsibility and discipline that causes you to redirect your ambitions back down into this world.

Shov leads you to draw Godliness downwards into the world, through an emphasis on the practical. It is a disciplined commitment to a Torah life motivated by an acceptance of the yoke of the commandments.

The Red Heifer is the suprarational command *"of the Torah,"* a central theme of Torah life, because it exhibits a combination of both *ratzo'* and *shov*. First the heifer is completely burned, representing the passionate ascendancy of *ratzo'*; but then its ash is used to make sprinkling-water, resembling *shov*, since water flows downwards until it settles in a level place.

The lesson: Just as both fire and water are crucial in preparing a Red Heifer, the dynamic tension between *ratzo'* and *shov* is the very essence of our relationship with God, a principle "of the Torah" (*Rabbi Shneur Zalman of Lyady, 18th century*).

They should bring you. To perform a commandment without meditating on what is being accomplished is like having a body without a soul (*Rabbi Isaac Luria, 16th century*). How, then, could a suprarational command, such as the precept of the Red Heifer, be performed properly, if we don't know its meaning?

Moses was the only person to whom God revealed the reason for the Red Heifer (*Midrash Tanhuma*). When the children of Israel would prepare a subsequent Red Heifer, they would simply say, "Let this commandment be infused with whatever intentions Moses had when preparing the first Red Heifer." In this way, the commandment would be complete (*Rabbi Ḥayyim ibn Attar, 18th century*).

Which is devoid of blemish and has never had a yoke placed on it. Those who consider themselves without fault, *"devoid of blemish,"* have never carried the *"yoke"* of heaven. If they had accepted this yoke, they would have realized that they still have many blemishes (*Rabbi Israel Hapstein of Kozienice, 18th century*).

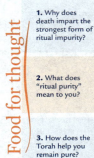

Food for thought

1. Why does death impart the strongest form of ritual impurity?

2. What does "ritual purity" mean to you?

3. How does the Torah help you remain pure?

parashat ḥukkat

The Red Heifer

19 ¹ God spoke to Moses and Aaron, saying: ² This is the suprarational command of the Torah which God commanded, saying: Tell the children of Israel:

- They should bring you a perfectly red heifer, which is devoid of blemish and has never had a yoke placed on it.

- ³ You should give it to Eleazar the priest. He should take it outside (all three) camp(s) and (a non-priest may) slaughter it in his presence.

- ⁴ Eleazar the priest should take some of its blood with his finger, (turn so that he faces) towards the front of the Tent of Meeting, and sprinkle it seven times.

19:2 This is the suprarational command (*ḥok*) ... a perfectly red heifer. Because Satan and the nations of the world cause grief to the Jewish people, saying, "What is this commandment? What purpose does it have?" Therefore, the Torah uses the term *ḥok* (suprarational command). God says, "It is My personal decree. You do not have permission to analyze it" (*Rashi, 11th century*).

The source of derision is the rule that the ritually pure person who performs the process is rendered impure, while the ritually impure person on whom the procedure is performed becomes pure (*Rabbi Ḥayyim b. Bezalel of Prague, 16th century*).

This harmony of opposites can be applied to our daily lives. When our own honor is at stake, we ought to remain humble; but with another person's honor, we must rise to their defense. In this way we use two opposite traits—humility and pride—in our service of God.

We should spend money in the same paradoxical manner, being frugal with other people's money, while at the same time giving charity generously (*Rabbi Moses Feinstein, 20th century*).

The suprarational command of the Torah. Why does the Torah use the expression, "This is the suprarational command *of the Torah*," as if to say that the commandment is representative of the entire Torah?

Because the laws of ritual purity and impurity discussed here bring to light the effect of the Torah as a whole on the Jewish people. By receiving the Torah, the Jewish people became a holy people and therefore they became a "magnet" for spiritual impurity.

An additional explanation: By writing, "This is the suprarational command of the Torah," the verse hints that if a person observes this commandment, he is credited with observing the entire Torah. Observing a commandment which makes no sense at all demonstrates a person's strong faith and commitment to observe all the other commandments too (*Rabbi Ḥayyim ibn Attar, 18th century*).

The spiritual root of all existence is rhythmic, not static. Just as man's heart must continually contract and then relax, and his lungs must always inhale then exhale, so too, the universe's life-force also fluctuates in a constant cycle.

The Kabbalists describe this cycle as *ratzo'* followed by *shov*, which means "running" towards spirituality, and subsequently "returning" to the lower reality.

In your own life, *ratzo'* is the desire for transcendence and, in its most extreme form, the yearning to escape from corporeal existence and merge with Divinity. *Ratzo'* expresses itself

שֶׁבַע פְּעָמִים: 5 וְשָׂרַף אֶת־הַפָּרָה לְעֵינָיו אֶת־עֹרָהּ וְאֶת־בְּשָׂרָהּ וְאֶת־דָּמָהּ עַל־פִּרְשָׁהּ יִשְׂרֹף: 6 וְלָקַח הַכֹּהֵן עֵץ אֶרֶז וְאֵזוֹב וּשְׁנִי תוֹלָעַת וְהִשְׁלִיךְ אֶל־תּוֹךְ שְׂרֵפַת הַפָּרָה: 7 וְכִבֶּס בְּגָדָיו הַכֹּהֵן וְרָחַץ בְּשָׂרוֹ בַּמַּיִם וְאַחַר יָבוֹא אֶל־הַמַּחֲנֶה וְטָמֵא הַכֹּהֵן עַד־הָעָרֶב: 8 וְהַשֹּׂרֵף אֹתָהּ יְכַבֵּס בְּגָדָיו בַּמַּיִם וְרָחַץ בְּשָׂרוֹ בַּמָּיִם וְטָמֵא עַד־הָעָרֶב: 9 וְאָסַף ׀ אִישׁ טָהוֹר אֵת אֵפֶר הַפָּרָה וְהִנִּיחַ מִחוּץ לַמַּחֲנֶה בְּמָקוֹם טָהוֹר וְהָיְתָה לַעֲדַת בְּנֵי־יִשְׂרָאֵל לְמִשְׁמֶרֶת לְמֵי נִדָּה חַטָּאת הִוא: 10 וְכִבֶּס הָאֹסֵף אֶת־אֵפֶר הַפָּרָה אֶת־בְּגָדָיו וְטָמֵא עַד־הָעָרֶב וְהָיְתָה לִבְנֵי יִשְׂרָאֵל וְלַגֵּר הַגָּר בְּתוֹכָם לְחֻקַּת עוֹלָם: 11 הַנֹּגֵעַ בְּמֵת לְכָל־נֶפֶשׁ אָדָם וְטָמֵא שִׁבְעַת יָמִים: 12 הוּא יִתְחַטָּא־בוֹ בַּיּוֹם הַשְּׁלִישִׁי וּבַיּוֹם הַשְּׁבִיעִי

there were seven from Ezra until the destruction of the Temple. The tenth will be made by the King Messiah—May he be speedily revealed! Amen, may this be Your will! (*Maimonides, 12th century*).

11. Anyone touching the corpse of a human being. One of the reasons for this precept is to discourage people from consulting the dead or other spirits, since the corpse is rendered a source of formidable contamination for a person and his possessions (*Rabbi Joseph ben Isaac Bekhor Shor, 12th century*).

Becoming angry at God is like "touching a corpse"—you are trying to get involved in something that has happened already, it is "dead." Do not harbor any complaints or anger in your

kabbalah bites

19:7-8 The ritual of the Red Heifer was peculiar in that the pure person who performed the ritual was rendered impure, whereas the subject, upon whom the ritual was performed, was rendered pure from his prior state of impurity. Why was this the case?

The Red Heifer elicited a disclosure of *Keter* ("crown"), the highest point of the *Sefirotic* tree. This was redeeming for the spiritually impure, and overwhelming—and therefore counterproductive—for the one who was healthy and pure. It was rather like a very strong medicine which heals a sick person but would harm somebody who was already healthy.

The study of Kabbalah contains within it a disclosure of *Keter*. In years gone by, when people were more spiritually healthy, the Kabbalah was not studied, as it might have proved harmful. But now that we are "sick," its waters are rejuvenating and life-enhancing.

- ⁵ The cow should then be burned in his presence. Its hide, its flesh, its blood, and its dung should be burned.
- ⁶ The priest should take a piece of cedar wood, hyssop, and crimson wool, and cast them into the burning cow.
- ⁷ The priest should immerse his garments and wash his body in (the) water (of a ritual-pool). The priest will remain impure until the evening, and then he may enter the (inner) camp(s).
- ⁸ The one who burns (the cow) should immerse his clothes in (the) water (of a ritual-pool) and ritually purify his body in (the) water (of a ritual-pool), and then he will remain ritually impure until the evening.
- ⁹ A ritually pure person should gather the cow's ashes and (divide them into three portions. He should leave one portion in the Temple for the priests working there), place (another on the Mount of Olives) outside the camp in a ritually pure place (for priests preparing the red cow), and (the third portion) should be (placed just outside the wall of the Temple courtyard) as a secure reminder for the congregation of the children of Israel.
- (The ashes are to be added to the) sprinkling-water, (which is used) for ritual purification.
- ¹⁰ The one who gathers the cow's ashes should immerse his clothes (in a ritual-pool), and he will remain ritually impure until the evening.
- This is an everlasting law (both) for the children of Israel and for the convert who lives with them.

Ritual Impurity from a Corpse

- ¹¹ Anyone touching the corpse of a human being will become ritually impure for seven days.
- ¹² On the third and seventh days, he should ritually purify himself with (the ashes of the red cow), in order to become ritually pure. But if he does not sprinkle himself with it on the third and seventh days, he will not become ritually pure.

9. As a secure reminder. The third portion of ashes from the Red Heifer offered by Moses were kept as "a secure reminder for the congregation."

One of the lessons here is that when you dedicate yourself to reaching out and helping others (the "purification" of others), you may come to neglect your own spiritual standing. To prevent such a mistake, the Torah teaches you to keep a portion of the ashes of the Red Heifer as a "secure reminder"—that it is crucial to dedicate some time to yourself as well as to others (*Rabbi Menahem Mendel Schneerson, 20th century*).

Nine Red Heifers were prepared from the time this commandment was given until the destruction of the Second Temple. The first was prepared by Moses, the second by Ezra, and

במדבר יט:יב-כא　　　חקת

יִטְהָר וְאִם־לֹא יִתְחַטָּא בַּיּוֹם הַשְּׁלִישִׁי וּבַיּוֹם הַשְּׁבִיעִי לֹא יִטְהָר: 13 כָּל־הַנֹּגֵעַ בְּמֵת בְּנֶפֶשׁ הָאָדָם אֲשֶׁר־יָמוּת וְלֹא יִתְחַטָּא אֶת־מִשְׁכַּן יְהֹוָה טִמֵּא וְנִכְרְתָה הַנֶּפֶשׁ הַהִוא מִיִּשְׂרָאֵל כִּי מֵי נִדָּה לֹא־זֹרַק עָלָיו טָמֵא יִהְיֶה עוֹד טֻמְאָתוֹ בוֹ:

14 זֹאת הַתּוֹרָה אָדָם כִּי־יָמוּת בְּאֹהֶל כָּל־הַבָּא אֶל־הָאֹהֶל וְכָל־אֲשֶׁר בָּאֹהֶל יִטְמָא שִׁבְעַת יָמִים: 15 וְכֹל כְּלִי פָתוּחַ אֲשֶׁר אֵין־צָמִיד פָּתִיל עָלָיו טָמֵא הוּא: 16 וְכֹל אֲשֶׁר־יִגַּע עַל־פְּנֵי הַשָּׂדֶה בַּחֲלַל־חֶרֶב אוֹ בְמֵת אוֹ־בְעֶצֶם אָדָם אוֹ בְקָבֶר יִטְמָא שִׁבְעַת יָמִים: 17 וְלָקְחוּ לַטָּמֵא מֵעֲפַר שְׂרֵפַת הַחַטָּאת וְנָתַן עָלָיו מַיִם חַיִּים אֶל־כֶּלִי: [SECOND READING] 18 וְלָקַח אֵזוֹב וְטָבַל בַּמַּיִם אִישׁ טָהוֹר וְהִזָּה עַל־הָאֹהֶל וְעַל־כָּל־הַכֵּלִים וְעַל־הַנְּפָשׁוֹת אֲשֶׁר הָיוּ־שָׁם וְעַל־הַנֹּגֵעַ בַּעֶצֶם אוֹ בֶחָלָל אוֹ בַמֵּת אוֹ בַקָּבֶר: 19 וְהִזָּה הַטָּהֹר עַל־הַטָּמֵא בַּיּוֹם הַשְּׁלִישִׁי וּבַיּוֹם הַשְּׁבִיעִי וְחִטְּאוֹ בַּיּוֹם הַשְּׁבִיעִי וְכִבֶּס בְּגָדָיו וְרָחַץ בַּמַּיִם וְטָהֵר בָּעָרֶב: 20 וְאִישׁ אֲשֶׁר־יִטְמָא וְלֹא יִתְחַטָּא וְנִכְרְתָה הַנֶּפֶשׁ הַהִוא מִתּוֹךְ הַקָּהָל כִּי אֶת־מִקְדַּשׁ יְהֹוָה טִמֵּא מֵי נִדָּה לֹא־זֹרַק עָלָיו טָמֵא הוּא: 21 וְהָיְתָה לָּהֶם לְחֻקַּת עוֹלָם

936

He says, "May I have a drink of water, please."

She gives him the water. When he takes the glass from her, he says, "Here is your divorce."

"What have I done wrong?" she asks.

"Get out of my house," he retorts. "You have served me a warm drink."

"It seems," she says, "that you already knew that I was going to serve you a warm drink. You had already prepared a bill of divorce and brought it with you!"

That is what Adam told God. "Master of the Universe! The Torah predated the world by two thousand years, and in the Torah it is written, *'This is the law regarding a man that dies in a tent.'* If You hadn't *already* decreed death for mankind, You wouldn't have written this in the Torah!" (*Midrash Tanhuma*).

spiritual vitamin

" When it comes to any one of the many commandments which God has given us, no man can understand all the reasons for it, because a man's understanding is limited, while God's wisdom is without end. "

numbers 19:13–21 — ḥukkat

- ¹³ Anyone who touches the corpse of a human being that died and does not ritually purify himself (and then enters the Temple courtyard) has made God's Tabernacle ritually impure, so his soul will be cut off from Israel.

- Being that the sprinkling-water was not sprinkled on him, he remained ritually impure, and (even if he immersed in the ritual-pool) his ritual impurity remains with him.

¹⁴ This is the law regarding a man that dies in a tent:

- Anyone entering the tent and anything in the tent will be ritually impure for seven days.

- ¹⁵ Any open vessel which has no seal fastened around it(s cover) becomes ritually impure.

- ¹⁶ Anyone who is in an open field and touches a person who was killed by the sword, or a corpse, or a human bone or a grave will be ritually impure for seven days.

¹⁷ For the ritually impure person:

- They should take some of the ashes of the burned purification offering (of the red heifer), and place them in a vessel (filled) with spring water.

- [SECOND READING] ¹⁸ A ritually pure person should take hyssop, dip it into the water and sprinkle it on the tent, on all the vessels, and on the people who were in it, and on anyone who touched the bone, the killed person, the corpse, or the grave.

- ¹⁹ The ritually pure person should sprinkle (the ash-water) on the ritually impure person on the third day and on the seventh day.

- On the seventh day he will become ritually pure. (But first) he should immerse his clothes and wash (himself) in (the) water (of a ritual-pool), and he will become ritually pure in the evening.

- ²⁰ If a person becomes ritually impure and does not purify himself (and enters the Sanctuary), his soul will be cut off from the congregation, because he has made God's Sanctuary ritually impure. For he remained ritually impure since the sprinkling-waters were not sprinkled upon him.

- ²¹ This will be an eternal suprarational law: One who (carries) the sprinkling-

---

heart about something that has already taken place in this world (*Rabbi Mordecai Joseph Leiner of Izbica, 19th century*).

14. This is the law regarding a man that dies in a tent. God blamed Adam for introducing death into the world, saying, *"On the day you eat from it you will certainly die"* (*Genesis* 2:17). What could you compare this to?

To a man who wished to divorce his wife. Before he goes into his home, he writes out a divorce document and he has it ready in his hand. He then looks for a way to hand it to her.

במדבר יט:כא - כ:ח   חקת

וּמַזֵּה מֵי־הַנִּדָּה יְכַבֵּס בְּגָדָיו וְהַנֹּגֵעַ בְּמֵי הַנִּדָּה יִטְמָא עַד־הָעָרֶב: 22 וְכֹל אֲשֶׁר־יִגַּע־בּוֹ הַטָּמֵא יִטְמָא וְהַנֶּפֶשׁ הַנֹּגַעַת תִּטְמָא עַד־הָעָרֶב: פ

א 1 וַיָּבֹאוּ בְנֵי־יִשְׂרָאֵל כָּל־הָעֵדָה מִדְבַּר־צִן בַּחֹדֶשׁ הָרִאשׁוֹן וַיֵּשֶׁב הָעָם בְּקָדֵשׁ וַתָּמָת שָׁם מִרְיָם וַתִּקָּבֵר שָׁם: 2 וְלֹא־הָיָה מַיִם לָעֵדָה וַיִּקָּהֲלוּ עַל־מֹשֶׁה וְעַל־אַהֲרֹן: 3 וַיָּרֶב הָעָם עִם־מֹשֶׁה וַיֹּאמְרוּ לֵאמֹר וְלוּ גָוַעְנוּ בִּגְוַע אַחֵינוּ לִפְנֵי יְהֹוָה: 4 וְלָמָה הֲבֵאתֶם אֶת־קְהַל יְהֹוָה אֶל־הַמִּדְבָּר הַזֶּה לָמוּת שָׁם אֲנַחְנוּ וּבְעִירֵנוּ: 5 וְלָמָה הֶעֱלִיתֻנוּ מִמִּצְרַיִם לְהָבִיא אֹתָנוּ אֶל־הַמָּקוֹם הָרָע הַזֶּה לֹא | מְקוֹם זֶרַע וּתְאֵנָה וְגֶפֶן וְרִמּוֹן וּמַיִם אַיִן לִשְׁתּוֹת: 6 וַיָּבֹא מֹשֶׁה וְאַהֲרֹן מִפְּנֵי הַקָּהָל אֶל־פֶּתַח אֹהֶל מוֹעֵד וַיִּפְּלוּ עַל־פְּנֵיהֶם וַיֵּרָא כְבוֹד־יְהֹוָה אֲלֵיהֶם: פ 7 [THIRD READING / SECOND WHEN JOINED] וַיְדַבֵּר יְהֹוָה אֶל־מֹשֶׁה לֵּאמֹר: 8 קַח אֶת־הַמַּטֶּה וְהַקְהֵל אֶת־הָעֵדָה אַתָּה וְאַהֲרֹן אָחִיךָ וְדִבַּרְתֶּם אֶל־הַסֶּלַע לְעֵינֵיהֶם

the Torah properly, because the Divine Presence had removed itself from Israel. This was to teach everyone—including the leaders of that generation who had not mourned for her—how righteous she had been. It was due to her merit that the Divine Presence had rested over Israel, and this message soon became very clear to the Sages (*Rabbi Rahamim Shealtiel Jacob Ninio, 19th century*).

1-2. Miriam died ... The congregation had no water. From here we learn that throughout the forty years they had the well in Miriam's merit (*Rashi, 11th century*).

There were three siblings, Moses, Aaron and Miriam. Miriam was the moon, Moses the sun, and Aaron the right arm. At first Miriam died—the moon departed and the well disappeared. Then, the right arm broke. Afterwards, the sun was gathered in and it was darkened. Happy is the generation in which Moses, Aaron, and Miriam existed in the world! (*Zohar*).

A few have the custom to draw water every Saturday night from wells or springs, because the well of Miriam passes through all the wells after the conclusion of each Sabbath. Whoever finds it and drinks from it will be healed from all his illnesses (*Rabbi Shneur Zalman of Lyady, 18th century*).

8. Speak to the rock. When a child is small, his teacher may hit him to teach him, but when he has grown, his teacher will only caution him verbally. God said to Moses, "When this rock was small, you hit it, as the verse states, '*You shall strike into the rock*' (*Exodus* 17:6). But now, you must 'speak to the rock'—recite one chapter over it, and it will produce water" (*Yalkut Shimoni*).

God wanted all those present to be motivated to carry out His will of their own accord; not by coercion, but joyfully. Therefore He told Moses and Aaron to talk to the rock, since when

waters should immerse his clothes (in a ritual-pool), and one who comes into contact with the sprinkling-waters will (only) be ritually impure until the evening.

- ❖ ²² Whatever a ritually impure person touches will become ritually impure. Anyone touching him will be ritually impure until the evening.

Miriam's Passing and the Water Crisis

(The following occurred close to forty years later, when those who were to die in the desert had passed on:)

20 ¹ The entire (next generation of) the congregation of the children of Israel arrived at the desert of Zin in the first month, and the people settled in Kadesh.

Miriam died there and was buried there.

² The congregation had no water, so they ganged up against Moses and Aaron, ³ and the people quarreled with Moses. They spoke up, saying, "If only we had died (in the plague) before God with the (same) death as our brothers (rather than through thirst)! ⁴ Why have you brought God's congregation to this desert so that we should die here, both we and our animals? ⁵ Why have you taken us out of Egypt to bring us to this terrible place? It's not a place fit for agriculture, for fig trees, grapevines, or pomegranate trees. And there's no water to drink!"

⁶ Moses and Aaron went away from the assembly to the entrance of the Tent of Meeting, and they fell on their faces.

Then the glory of God appeared to them. [THIRD READING / SECOND WHEN JOINED] ⁷ God spoke to Moses, saying: ⁸ "Take the staff and, together with your brother Aaron, you should assemble the congregation. In their presence, speak to the rock (that was within

---

20:1 Miriam died there. Why does the story of Miriam's death follow straight after the laws of the Red Heifer? To teach you that just as sacrifices bring atonement, the death of the righteous also brings atonement.

She died through a "kiss" from God's mouth, like the great saints, and not through the angel of death, the way of ordinary people. Why, then, does the verse not state "by God's mouth" as it does with Moses and Aaron? Because it is not respectful to speak of God kissing a woman (*Babylonian Talmud, Mo'ed Katan* 28a).

The leaders of the generation did not feel the need to publicly grieve Miriam's passing at all, or to eulogize her, because she was, after all, a woman. Had any religious instruction emanated from her that there was now a need to make a big deal? Instruction was given to Israel by Moses and Aaron! Even the well that had disappeared when Miriam died would, without doubt, return in the merit of Moses and Aaron.

To counteract this faulty line of reasoning, the Torah makes a point of mourning her passing explicitly, "*Miriam died there.*" In fact, she died through a "Divine kiss," just like her brothers, indicating that she was on par with them spiritually.

And her passing made an immediate impression, "*the congregation had no water*" (v. 2), water being a metaphor for Torah. Suddenly, even the great scholars could not understand

במדבר כ:ח-יג

וְנָתַן מֵימָיו וְהוֹצֵאתָ לָהֶם מַיִם מִן־הַסֶּלַע וְהִשְׁקִיתָ אֶת־הָעֵדָה וְאֶת־בְּעִירָם:
9 וַיִּקַּח מֹשֶׁה אֶת־הַמַּטֶּה מִלִּפְנֵי יְהֹוָה כַּאֲשֶׁר צִוָּהוּ: 10 וַיַּקְהִלוּ מֹשֶׁה וְאַהֲרֹן אֶת־הַקָּהָל אֶל־פְּנֵי הַסָּלַע וַיֹּאמֶר לָהֶם שִׁמְעוּ־נָא הַמֹּרִים הֲמִן־הַסֶּלַע הַזֶּה נוֹצִיא לָכֶם מָיִם: 11 וַיָּרֶם מֹשֶׁה אֶת־יָדוֹ וַיַּךְ אֶת־הַסֶּלַע בְּמַטֵּהוּ פַּעֲמָיִם וַיֵּצְאוּ מַיִם רַבִּים וַתֵּשְׁתְּ הָעֵדָה וּבְעִירָם: ס 12 וַיֹּאמֶר יְהֹוָה אֶל־מֹשֶׁה וְאֶל־אַהֲרֹן יַעַן לֹא־הֶאֱמַנְתֶּם בִּי לְהַקְדִּישֵׁנִי לְעֵינֵי בְּנֵי יִשְׂרָאֵל לָכֵן לֹא תָבִיאוּ אֶת־הַקָּהָל הַזֶּה אֶל־הָאָרֶץ אֲשֶׁר־נָתַתִּי לָהֶם: 13 הֵמָּה מֵי מְרִיבָה אֲשֶׁר־רָבוּ בְנֵי־יִשְׂרָאֵל אֶת־

Therefore, Moses struck the rock, preventing God from having this claim against the people. Moses was so devoted to the children of Israel that he was willing to forfeit his life and entry into the land of Israel in order to protect them (*Rabbi Isaac Meir Alter of Gur, 19th century*).

12. Since you did not believe in Me … you will not bring this congregation into the land. The Torah indicates here that if it were not for this sin *alone*, they would have entered the land of Israel—so that it should not be said about them, "Moses and Aaron's sin was similar to the sin of the generation of the desert who were prevented from entering the land."

But wasn't Moses' question, *"Could enough sheep and cattle possibly be slaughtered for them?"* (11:22) a more serious sin than this?

There he spoke in private, so the Torah spared him from punishment. But here, on the other hand, he spoke in the presence of all Israel (*Rashi, 11th century*).

13. These are the waters of strife. The *"waters of strife"* are the waters that Pharaoh's astrologers saw and erred in interpreting their significance. They saw that the future savior of Israel, Moses, would be smitten through water. So they advised Pharaoh, *"Every boy who is born you shall cast into the Nile"* (*Exodus* 1:22). They did not realize, however, that Moses' downfall through water was not literal, but through the *"waters of strife"*— when Moses struck the rock (*Babylonian Talmud, Sanhedrin* 101b).

kabbalah bites

20:9-10 Do you prefer Torah teachings that are simple, clear and direct? Or do you prefer to study complex passages that constantly argue backwards and forwards?

Most of us would drift to whatever is easier, but studying the complex passages achieves something that simple ones don't. The tremendous mental friction involved in plumbing the complexities of a text purifies you spiritually in a way that the more accessible teachings cannot.

Moses *hit* the rock, and did not merely speak to it, because he wanted the Torah to include also these "frictional" elements. Today these are to be found in the complex dialectics of the Talmud. (Thus he hit the rock twice corresponding to the two Talmuds, Jerusalem and Babylonian.)

Miriam's well, the one that always produced water), and it will produce water. You will produce water for them from the rock, and allow the congregation and their animals to drink."

⁹ Moses took the staff from before God, as He had commanded him. ¹⁰ Moses and Aaron assembled the congregation in front of the rock (but they could not figure out which rock to speak to. The people began to mock) so he said to them, "Listen, you rebels! (How) could we draw water for you from this rock (if it is not the right one)?"

¹¹ (Moses and Aaron spoke to the rock, but it did not produce any water, since it was the wrong rock. Remembering that he had produced water from a rock in Rephidim by hitting it) Moses raised his hand and hit the rock with his staff (and this time he hit the correct rock, but only a small amount of water came out, since God had not told him to hit it, but to speak to it. But when he hit it) a second time a lot of water came out, and the congregation drank, along with their animals.

¹² God said to Moses and Aaron, "Since you did not believe in Me to sanctify Me in the presence of the children of Israel (for you hit the rock and did not speak to it), therefore you will not bring this congregation into the land which I have given them."

¹³ These are the waters (which the Egyptian astrologers had seen would cause) strife (to Moses, and they are the waters) over which the children of Israel contended with God. But (God) was sanctified through them (via the death of Moses and Aaron).

---

things are encouraged verbally the actions which follow are done willingly and joyfully. This is the essence of faith (*Rabbi Judah Loew b. Bezalel of Prague, 16th century*).

10. Listen, you rebels! Moses committed two sins. First, he lost his temper, saying, *"Listen, you rebels!"* Second, he caused the people to think mistakenly that God was angry with them for requesting water (*Maimonides, 12th century*).

Moses and Aaron's sin was saying, "Could *we* draw water for you from this rock," when they should have said, *"God* will get water out of the rock." Perhaps the people would now think that Moses and Aaron had extracted water from the rock through their own powers (*Rabbi Hananel b. Ḥushi'el, 11th century*).

All religious anger, all intolerance for the spiritual shortcomings of others, is rooted in this angry outburst of Moses. When he should have sought reconciliation, he shouted, "Listen, you rebels!" There may be such a thing as righteous indignation, but in practice our highest goals will only be achieved through mutual respect (*Rabbi Abraham Isaac Kook, 20th century*).

11. Moses raised his hand and hit the rock. If Moses had produced water by merely speaking to the rock, God's name would have been sanctified greatly. This, however, would have left an eternal claim against the children of Israel: If an inanimate rock fulfils God's word, then certainly the children of Israel, who have witnessed God's miracles, should heed His command.

חקת
במדבר כ:יג-כד

יְהֹוָה וַיִּקָּדֵשׁ בָּם: ס 14 [FOURTH READING] וַיִּשְׁלַח מֹשֶׁה מַלְאָכִים מִקָּדֵשׁ אֶל־מֶלֶךְ אֱדוֹם כֹּה אָמַר אָחִיךָ יִשְׂרָאֵל אַתָּה יָדַעְתָּ אֵת כָּל־הַתְּלָאָה אֲשֶׁר מְצָאָתְנוּ: 15 וַיֵּרְדוּ אֲבֹתֵינוּ מִצְרַיְמָה וַנֵּשֶׁב בְּמִצְרַיִם יָמִים רַבִּים וַיָּרֵעוּ לָנוּ מִצְרַיִם וְלַאֲבֹתֵינוּ: 16 וַנִּצְעַק אֶל־יְהֹוָה וַיִּשְׁמַע קֹלֵנוּ וַיִּשְׁלַח מַלְאָךְ וַיֹּצִאֵנוּ מִמִּצְרָיִם וְהִנֵּה אֲנַחְנוּ בְקָדֵשׁ עִיר קְצֵה גְבוּלֶךָ: 17 נַעְבְּרָה־נָּא בְאַרְצֶךָ לֹא נַעֲבֹר בְּשָׂדֶה וּבְכֶרֶם וְלֹא נִשְׁתֶּה מֵי בְאֵר דֶּרֶךְ הַמֶּלֶךְ נֵלֵךְ לֹא נִטֶּה יָמִין וּשְׂמֹאול עַד אֲשֶׁר־נַעֲבֹר גְּבֻלֶךָ: 18 וַיֹּאמֶר אֵלָיו אֱדוֹם לֹא תַעֲבֹר בִּי פֶּן־בַּחֶרֶב אֵצֵא לִקְרָאתֶךָ: 19 וַיֹּאמְרוּ אֵלָיו בְּנֵי־יִשְׂרָאֵל בַּמְסִלָּה נַעֲלֶה וְאִם־מֵימֶיךָ נִשְׁתֶּה אֲנִי וּמִקְנַי וְנָתַתִּי מִכְרָם רַק אֵין־דָּבָר בְּרַגְלַי אֶעֱבֹרָה: 20 וַיֹּאמֶר לֹא תַעֲבֹר וַיֵּצֵא אֱדוֹם לִקְרָאתוֹ בְּעַם כָּבֵד וּבְיָד חֲזָקָה: 21 וַיְמָאֵן | אֱדוֹם נְתֹן אֶת־יִשְׂרָאֵל עֲבֹר בִּגְבֻלוֹ וַיֵּט יִשְׂרָאֵל מֵעָלָיו: פ 22 [FIFTH READING THIRD WHEN JOINED] וַיִּסְעוּ מִקָּדֵשׁ וַיָּבֹאוּ בְנֵי־יִשְׂרָאֵל כָּל־הָעֵדָה הֹר הָהָר: 23 וַיֹּאמֶר יְהֹוָה אֶל־מֹשֶׁה וְאֶל־אַהֲרֹן בְּהֹר הָהָר עַל־גְּבוּל אֶרֶץ־אֱדוֹם לֵאמֹר: 24 יֵאָסֵף אַהֲרֹן אֶל־עַמָּיו כִּי לֹא יָבֹא אֶל־הָאָרֶץ אֲשֶׁר נָתַתִּי לִבְנֵי יִשְׂרָאֵל

want them to have any inside knowledge of his roads, fortresses or other areas of strategic significance (*Rabbi Judah Aryeh Leib Alter of Gur, 19th century*).

22. The double mountain. A mountain on top of a mountain, like a small apple on top of a big apple (*Rashi, 11th century*).

One of the lessons that you can learn from the fact that the Torah was given on a mountain is that while, generally speaking, you are supposed to be meek and humble, this should nevertheless not lead you to be easily "walked over." When it comes to defending matters of Torah, you ought to be proud and confident, like a mountain.

That is the case for Torah in general, which was given through Moses. But when it comes to the love and concern for the physical and spiritual needs of others—which was the trait of Aaron, you should have a double measure of determination, a "double mountain" (*Rabbi Menahem Mendel Schneerson, 20th century*).

23. At the border of the land of Edom. This teaches us that because they attempted to forge a relationship with Edom, descendants of the

Food for thought

1. When is it acceptable to complain?

2. What effect does complaining have on you and on those around you?

3. Does complaining always come from the ego?

numbers 20:14–24 — ḥukkat

An Attempt to Pass Through the Land of Edom

[FOURTH READING] ¹⁴ Moses sent messengers from Kadesh to the king of Edom: "This is what your brother Israel said: You know of all the hardship that has befallen us. ¹⁵ Our fathers went down to Egypt. We stayed in Egypt for a long time, and the Egyptians mistreated us, and our Patriarchs (were pained in the grave). ¹⁶ We cried out to God and He heard our voice. He sent an angel (Moses), and he took us out of Egypt.

"Now we are in Kadesh, a city on the edge of your border. ¹⁷ Please let us pass through your land (so we can reach the land of Israel). We will not pass through fields or vineyards. (Even though we have our own supply of water) we will not drink water (from our) well (but we will purchase it from you). We will go along the king's highway, and we will (muzzle our animals so that they) do not turn to the right or to the left (to eat from your fields) until we have passed your border."

¹⁸ Edom replied to him, "You will not pass through My (territory), or I'll go out towards you with the sword!"

¹⁹ The children of Israel said to him, "We will keep to the highway. If either we or our cattle drink your water, we will pay whatever it costs. Nothing will (harm you). We will pass through on foot."

²⁰ But he said, "You will not pass through!" and Edom came out toward them with many men and with the strong hand (of Esau).

²¹ Since Edom refused to allow Israel to cross his border, Israel headed away from him.

Aaron's Passing and Eleazar's Appointment

[FIFTH READING / THIRD WHEN JOINED] ²² They traveled from Kadesh, and the entire (next generation of the) congregation of the children of Israel arrived at the double mountain.

²³ God spoke to Moses and Aaron, at the double mountain, at the border of the land of Edom, saying, ²⁴ "Aaron will (now) be gathered to his people. He will not come to the land which I have given to the children of Israel, because you defied My word at the waters of strife."

---

14. Moses sent messengers from Kadesh to the king of Edom. Moses had just been informed that he could not enter the promised land of Israel. Nevertheless, his spirits did not waver, and he continued to lead his people with confidence and determination. He did not renounce his ties with the people. This is an exceptional and rare virtue for a leader, not to let his personal fate interfere with his leadership responsibilities (*Rabbi Samson Raphael Hirsch, 19th century*).

18. You will not pass through my (territory). Why did the king of Edom refuse to allow the children of Israel to cross his land? Moses had offered to pay him generously, even for any water that they might drink.

The Edomite king knew that the children of Israel would not cause any undue damage by passing through his kingdom, but since he might wage war on them in the future, he did not

במדבר כ:כה - כא:ב | חקת

עַל אֲשֶׁר־מְרִיתֶם אֶת־פִּי לְמֵי מְרִיבָה: 25 קַח אֶת־אַהֲרֹן וְאֶת־אֶלְעָזָר בְּנוֹ וְהַעַל אֹתָם הֹר הָהָר: 26 וְהַפְשֵׁט אֶת־אַהֲרֹן אֶת־בְּגָדָיו וְהִלְבַּשְׁתָּם אֶת־אֶלְעָזָר בְּנוֹ וְאַהֲרֹן יֵאָסֵף וּמֵת שָׁם: 27 וַיַּעַשׂ מֹשֶׁה כַּאֲשֶׁר צִוָּה יְהֹוָה וַיַּעֲלוּ אֶל־הֹר הָהָר לְעֵינֵי כָּל־הָעֵדָה: 28 וַיַּפְשֵׁט מֹשֶׁה אֶת־אַהֲרֹן אֶת־בְּגָדָיו וַיַּלְבֵּשׁ אֹתָם אֶת־אֶלְעָזָר בְּנוֹ וַיָּמָת אַהֲרֹן שָׁם בְּרֹאשׁ הָהָר וַיֵּרֶד מֹשֶׁה וְאֶלְעָזָר מִן־הָהָר: 29 וַיִּרְאוּ כָּל־הָעֵדָה כִּי גָוַע אַהֲרֹן וַיִּבְכּוּ אֶת־אַהֲרֹן שְׁלֹשִׁים יוֹם כֹּל בֵּית יִשְׂרָאֵל: ס

כא

1 וַיִּשְׁמַע הַכְּנַעֲנִי מֶלֶךְ־עֲרָד יֹשֵׁב הַנֶּגֶב כִּי בָּא יִשְׂרָאֵל דֶּרֶךְ הָאֲתָרִים וַיִּלָּחֶם בְּיִשְׂרָאֵל וַיִּשְׁבְּ | מִמֶּנּוּ שֶׁבִי: 2 וַיִּדַּר יִשְׂרָאֵל נֶדֶר לַיהֹוָה

---

an accidental murderer and his family would be *joyful* when the High Priest died. However, when Aaron passed away, *everyone* mourned; not even one family had reason to rejoice in the return of an exiled relative (*Rabbi Meir Simhah of Dvinsk, 19th–20th century*).

21:1 The Canaanite king of Arad ... heard. He heard that Aaron had died and that the clouds of glory had departed (*Rashi, 11th century*).

Three good leaders arose for the Jewish people, namely, Moses, Aaron, and Miriam, and three special gifts were given to the Jewish people through them: the well, the cloud and the manna. The well was in Miriam's merit, the cloud in Aaron's merit and the manna in Moses' merit.

When Miriam died the well ceased. When Aaron died the clouds of glory disappeared. But these two returned in Moses' merit.

When Moses died all of them disappeared, as the verse states: *"I cut off the three shepherds in one month"* (*Zechariah* 11:8). Did they all die in one month? Miriam died in *Nisan*, Aaron in *Av* and Moses in *Adar!* Rather, this teaches you that the three good gifts which were given in their merit all disappeared in one month (*Babylonian Talmud, Ta'anit* 9a).

The Canaanite ... who lived in the south. This was Amalek, as the verse states, *"Amalek lives in the south of the land"* (13:29). But the Torah calls them Canaanites because they changed their language and spoke Canaanite so that the Jewish people would mistakenly pray to God to deliver the Canaanites into their hands, rendering the prayers ineffective (because they were not Canaanites). But the Jewish

> ### kabbalah bites
>
> **20:29-21:1 The clouds of glory departed when Aaron died. What is the connection between the clouds and Aaron?**
>
> A cloud engulfs people indiscriminately. It does not say, "You I will cover, but you I will not." Everyone gets the same treatment.
>
> This is symbolic of the *unconditional love* for which Aaron was famous, directed at everyone equally, regardless of their personal status. (Thus, "the *entire* house of Israel wept for Aaron.")
>
> When you shower unconditional love, not only are people soothed and healed, the unity and good will that result protect us, like clouds of glory.

²⁵ "Persuade Aaron, along with Eleazar his son, to go up the double mountain. ²⁶ Divest Aaron of his (priestly) garments and dress Eleazar his son with them. Then Aaron will be gathered in (to his people) and die there."

²⁷ Moses did what God commanded him. They went up the double mountain in the presence of the entire congregation. ²⁸ Moses divested Aaron of his (priestly) garments and dressed Eleazar his son in them, and Aaron died there on top of the mountain.

(Then) Moses and Eleazar descended from the mountain. ²⁹ The whole congregation saw that Aaron had died, and the entire house of Israel wept for Aaron for thirty days.

The Second Amalekite Attack

21 ¹ The Canaanite king of Arad, who lived in the south, heard that Israel had come by (the south, following) the route of the spies. (Presuming that they were weak) he waged war against Israel, but he took (only) one captive from them.

² Israel made a vow to God and said, "If You deliver this people into my hand, I will consecrate (the plunder of) their cities."

---

wicked Esau, their accomplishments were ruined and they lost this righteous man, Aaron. Similarly, the prophet said to Jehoshaphat, *"Since you joined with Ahaziah, God has ruined your accomplishments"* (*II Chronicles* 20:37; *Rashi, 11ᵗʰ century*).

29. The entire house of Israel wept for Aaron. The *entire* house of Israel wept for Aaron. But for Moses, only men wept, because Moses used to rebuke the people severely. Aaron, on the other hand, never said to a man or woman, "You have acted offensively."

When Aaron was walking in the street and met a wicked person, Aaron would greet him. The next day, when the man wanted to commit a sin, he would say, "Dear me! How will I lift up my eyes afterwards and look at my friend Aaron? I am ashamed, because he greeted me." In this way, the man would refrain from sinning.

When two people quarreled, Aaron went and sat down with one of them and said to him, "My son! Do you know what your friend is saying? His heart is in a turmoil and he is tearing his clothes saying, 'Dear me! How can I lift up my eyes and look at my friend? I am ashamed because I have wronged him.'" Aaron would then sit with him until he had dispelled the grudge from his heart.

Then Aaron would go and sit with the other one, and say to him, "Do you know what your friend is saying? His heart is in a turmoil and he is tearing his clothes saying, 'Dear me! How can I lift up my eyes and look at my friend? I am ashamed because I have wronged him.'" Aaron would then sit with him until he had dispelled the grudge from his heart. When the two of them would then meet, they hugged and kissed each other (*Avot de-Rabbi Nathan*).

By saying "the *entire* house of Israel wept for Aaron" we can deduce that during all the years that the Israelites traveled in the desert, not even one case of manslaughter had occurred.

According to Jewish law, anyone guilty of manslaughter would have been exiled to the Levites' camp; he would be allowed to return home only after the passing of the High Priest. Therefore,

במדבר כא:ב־יא　חקת

3 וַיֹּאמַר אִם־נָתֹן תִּתֵּן אֶת־הָעָם הַזֶּה בְּיָדִי וְהַחֲרַמְתִּי אֶת־עָרֵיהֶם: וַיִּשְׁמַע יְהֹוָה בְּקוֹל יִשְׂרָאֵל וַיִּתֵּן אֶת־הַכְּנַעֲנִי וַיַּחֲרֵם אֶתְהֶם וְאֶת־עָרֵיהֶם וַיִּקְרָא שֵׁם־הַמָּקוֹם חָרְמָה: פ 4 וַיִּסְעוּ מֵהֹר הָהָר דֶּרֶךְ יַם־סוּף לִסְבֹב אֶת־אֶרֶץ אֱדוֹם וַתִּקְצַר נֶפֶשׁ־הָעָם בַּדָּרֶךְ: 5 וַיְדַבֵּר הָעָם בֵּאלֹהִים וּבְמֹשֶׁה לָמָה הֶעֱלִיתֻנוּ מִמִּצְרַיִם לָמוּת בַּמִּדְבָּר כִּי אֵין לֶחֶם וְאֵין מַיִם וְנַפְשֵׁנוּ קָצָה בַּלֶּחֶם הַקְּלֹקֵל: 6 וַיְשַׁלַּח יְהֹוָה בָּעָם אֵת הַנְּחָשִׁים הַשְּׂרָפִים וַיְנַשְּׁכוּ אֶת־הָעָם וַיָּמָת עַם־רָב מִיִּשְׂרָאֵל: 7 וַיָּבֹא הָעָם אֶל־מֹשֶׁה וַיֹּאמְרוּ חָטָאנוּ כִּי־דִבַּרְנוּ בַיהֹוָה וָבָךְ הִתְפַּלֵּל אֶל־יְהֹוָה וְיָסֵר מֵעָלֵינוּ אֶת־הַנָּחָשׁ וַיִּתְפַּלֵּל מֹשֶׁה בְּעַד הָעָם: 8 וַיֹּאמֶר יְהֹוָה אֶל־מֹשֶׁה עֲשֵׂה לְךָ שָׂרָף וְשִׂים אֹתוֹ עַל־נֵס וְהָיָה כָּל־הַנָּשׁוּךְ וְרָאָה אֹתוֹ וָחָי: 9 וַיַּעַשׂ מֹשֶׁה נְחַשׁ נְחֹשֶׁת וַיְשִׂמֵהוּ עַל־הַנֵּס וְהָיָה אִם־נָשַׁךְ הַנָּחָשׁ אֶת־אִישׁ וְהִבִּיט אֶל־נְחַשׁ הַנְּחֹשֶׁת וָחָי: 10 [SIXTH READING] וַיִּסְעוּ בְּנֵי יִשְׂרָאֵל וַיַּחֲנוּ בְּאֹבֹת: 11 וַיִּסְעוּ מֵאֹבֹת וַיַּחֲנוּ בְּעִיֵּי הָעֲבָרִים בַּמִּדְבָּר אֲשֶׁר עַל־פְּנֵי

about what you do in the synagogue. But if you wish to be successful in the business world, forget about avoiding gossip, unfair competition, and collecting interest. You must act like a Canaanite!"

Such a notion is nothing but the enticements of Amalek. Judaism is not merely to be practiced at home and in the synagogue. It is equally as important, if not more so, to be a proud and ethical Jew at work, too. For in this way you make the world—and not just the synagogue—"a home for God below" (*Rabbi Menahem Mendel Schneerson, 20th century*).

7-8. "Pray to God that He should remove the snakes from us!" Moses prayed on behalf of the people. The people erroneously thought that the snakes were the cause of the many deaths. Therefore they begged Moses to pray that God "remove the *snakes.*"

Moses, however, knew that it was their sins, not the snakes that were responsible for all the deaths. Therefore Moses prayed "on behalf of the *people,*" that they should repent (*Rabbi Solomon Kluger, 19th century*).

9. He would stare at the copper snake and he would live. Obviously, the copper snake was not capable of curing people. It was meant to trigger an emotional response from the people, encouraging them to focus heavenward and repent, so that God would let them live (*Rashi, 11th century*).

The reason a serpent was chosen and not some other object was to magnify the miracle. If God had so desired, the need for an object could have been avoided, and the people would

numbers 21:3–11 — ḥukkat

³ God heard Israel's voice and delivered the Canaanite. He destroyed them and (consecrated) their cities. The place was called Hormah.

The People Complain and Are Attacked by Snakes

⁴ They journeyed from the double mountain (retracing their steps) in the direction of the Reed Sea, to circumvent the land of Edom (which had not let them pass through). The people became demoralized because (changing) direction (brought back bad memories of how their parents had been sent back into the desert for thirty-eight years). ⁵ The people criticized God and Moses, "Why have you brought us up out of Egypt to die in the desert? There's no bread and no water, and we're sick of this unwholesome (manna) bread."

⁶ God sent venomous snakes upon the people, and they bit the people. Many people of Israel died.

⁷ The people came to Moses and said, "We have sinned! For we have spoken against God and against you! Pray to God that He should remove the snakes from us!"

Moses prayed on behalf of the people.

⁸ God said to Moses, "Make yourself a venomous (snake) and place it on a pole. What will happen is, whoever has been bitten will look at it and live."

⁹ Moses made a copper snake and placed it on a pole. Whenever a snake bit a man, he would stare at the copper snake and he would live.

Further Journeys / The Miraculous Encampment at Arnon

[SIXTH READING] ¹⁰ The children of Israel traveled, and they camped in Oboth.

¹¹ They traveled from Oboth and camped in Iye-abarim, in the wilderness between Moab (and the land of the Amorites, to the east, where) the sun rises.

---

people saw that they were dressed like Amalekites, although they spoke Canaanite, so they said, "We will pray generally," as the verse states, "If You deliver *this people* into my hand" (v. 2; *Rashi, 11th century*).

Why did Amalek come disguised as Canaanites? Amalek is a particularly dangerous enemy of the Jewish people, because the opposition to the Torah which Amalek represents is subtle and indirect, and thus does not appear to be contrary to Torah. Sympathy with the ideology of Amalek can set you on a "slippery slope," eventually leading you away from the Torah altogether.

In our Torah portion, the Jewish people had completed forty years of isolation in the desert and were about to begin their conquest of the land of Canaan—representing the challenge of maintaining your Judaism in the workplace and the marketplace.

Amalek's aim was to undermine the observance of Torah in a non-Jewish setting (the workplace), so they came disguised as Canaanites. Their message was: "We won't bother you

חקת // במדבר כא:יא-יח

מוֹאָב מִמִּזְרַח הַשָּׁמֶשׁ: 12 מִשָּׁם נָסָעוּ וַיַּחֲנוּ בְּנַחַל זָרֶד: 13 מִשָּׁם נָסָעוּ וַיַּחֲנוּ מֵעֵבֶר אַרְנוֹן אֲשֶׁר בַּמִּדְבָּר הַיֹּצֵא מִגְּבֻל הָאֱמֹרִי כִּי אַרְנוֹן גְּבוּל מוֹאָב בֵּין מוֹאָב וּבֵין הָאֱמֹרִי: 14 עַל־כֵּן יֵאָמַר בְּסֵפֶר מִלְחֲמֹת יְהוָה אֶת־וָהֵב בְּסוּפָה וְאֶת־הַנְּחָלִים אַרְנוֹן: 15 וְאֶשֶׁד הַנְּחָלִים אֲשֶׁר נָטָה לְשֶׁבֶת עָר וְנִשְׁעַן לִגְבוּל מוֹאָב: 16 וּמִשָּׁם בְּאֵרָה הִוא הַבְּאֵר אֲשֶׁר אָמַר יְהוָה לְמֹשֶׁה אֱסֹף אֶת־הָעָם וְאֶתְּנָה לָהֶם מָיִם: ס 17 אָז יָשִׁיר יִשְׂרָאֵל אֶת־הַשִּׁירָה הַזֹּאת עֲלִי בְאֵר עֱנוּ־לָהּ:
18 בְּאֵר חֲפָרוּהָ שָׂרִים כָּרוּהָ נְדִיבֵי הָעָם בִּמְחֹקֵק בְּמִשְׁעֲנֹתָם וּמִמִּדְבָּר

There were caves in the rock on the Moabite side of the valley, and directly opposite the caves there were protrusions on the mountain on the Amorite side. When the Jewish people were about to pass through, the mountain moved toward the mountain of Moab. The protrusions entered the caves, killing the Amorites.

This is the meaning of the words, *"It turned to settle at Ar"* (v. 15)—The mountain veered from its place and moved toward the side of the Moabite border, and attached itself to it. It was thus *"leaning against the border of Moab"* (ibid.).

The Jewish people passed on top of the mountains, and they only became aware of the miracles through the well water that entered the valley, as the Torah continues: *"From there (the blood flowed) to the well"* (v. 16).

How did this occur? God said, "Who will inform My children of these miracles?"—as in the proverb, "If you give a small child bread, inform his mother." So, after they passed through, the mountains returned to their places and the well water went down into the valley. It brought the blood of the people who were killed, their arms, and their limbs, and carried them around the camp. When the Jewish people saw this, they burst into song (verses 17-20; *Rashi, 11th century*).

17. O well, arise! When the Israelites desired water, they would stand over the well and sing, *"O well, arise!* Bring up your water for everyone to drink!"—and they would sing the rest of the song, *"A well dug by ministers, etc."* (v. 18ff.). They spoke words of truth!

From here we learn that whoever wishes to cause an arousal on high, either through deed or through speech, nothing will be aroused if that deed or speech is not performed properly. Everyone goes to the synagogue to arouse something on high, but there are few who know how to arouse the heavens. God is near those who know how to call on Him and arouse Him properly. But if they do not know how to call on Him, He is not near—as the verse states, *"God is near to all those who call upon Him; to all who call upon Him in truth"* (Psalms 145:18). What is "in truth"? If they know how to bring about an arousal with a truthful word, said properly (*Zohar*).

18. A well dug by ministers, carved out by nobles of the people. At the splitting of the Reed Sea, the children of Israel had sung with Moses, but here no mention is made of Moses' participation. Why is this the case?

Because after forty years of studying the Torah and worshiping God, their souls had become one with it. They were no longer spiritually dependent on Moses (*Rabbi Judah Aryeh Leib Alter of Gur, 19th century*).

numbers 21:12–18 — ḥukkat

¹² From there they traveled, and they encamped along the Zered Brook.

¹³ From there they traveled, and they encamped on the other side of the Arnon (Brook), which is in the desert, extending from the Amorite border—for Arnon was the Moabite border between Moab and the Amorites.

¹⁴ About this (miraculous encampment) it will be told when God's wars are recounted:

"He gave a gift (of miracles) at the (Sea of) Reeds and (they were matched by the miracles) at the valleys of Arnon! ¹⁵ The (blood of the Amorites was) spilling into the valleys when (the mountain actually moved, crushing the Amorites, and) it turned to settle at Ar, leaning against the border of Moab. ¹⁶ From there (the blood flowed) to the well (so the Jewish people could see the victory). That is the well about which God said to Moses, 'Gather the people, and I will give them water.'"

¹⁷ Then (when) Israel (saw the remains of the enemy in the well water) they sang this song:

O well, arise (from the valley)! Raise your voices (in song) to it!

¹⁸ A well dug by ministers, carved out by (Moses and Aaron), nobles of the people, through the lawgiver, with their staffs, from the desert, (they received the well as) a gift.

---

have been immediately healed. By using the serpent, the miracle was made more overt, so that they would not say it was mere chance (*Rabbi Joseph b. Isaac Bekhor Shor, 12th century*).

If remembering God brought about the cure for the Jewish people, then why was the copper snake necessary at all? Why did Moses not simply tell them to think about God?

Even the most negative or tragic occurrence in this world has a spiritual root which is entirely good. *"From heaven, no evil is issued forth"* (*Lamentations* 3:18)—it is only that sometimes the physical world is not ready to absorb the good which comes from heaven. The resulting incompatibility presents itself as something negative.

The solution, therefore, is not to eliminate the negative thing, *but to reveal its true inner essence as something good.*

And this was the purpose of the copper snake, erected on a pole, which Moses made. By encouraging the Jewish people to look upwards at the snake, Moses was reminding them that, in their spiritual source above, the snakes which had bitten the Jewish people were rooted in Divine goodness. In this way, the people "reconnected" the snakes with their true source above, revealing their inner good—and that good was then also revealed below (*Rabbi Shneur Zalman of Lyady, 18th century*).

14. About this (miraculous encampment) it will be told. The mountains were high and the valley between them was deep and narrow. The mountains were so close to each other, that a person standing on the mountain on one side of the valley could speak to his friend standing on the mountain on the other side.

The route of the Jewish people passed along the valley. The Amorites said, "When the Jewish people enter the valley to pass through, we'll come out of the caves in the mountains above them and kill them with arrows and catapult stones."

במדבר כא:יח-ל
חקת

מַתָּנָה: 19 וּמִמַּתָּנָה נַחֲלִיאֵל וּמִנַּחֲלִיאֵל בָּמוֹת: 20 וּמִבָּמוֹת הַגַּיְא אֲשֶׁר בִּשְׂדֵה מוֹאָב רֹאשׁ הַפִּסְגָּה וְנִשְׁקָפָה עַל־פְּנֵי הַיְשִׁימֹן: פ

[SEVENTH READING / FOURTH WHEN JOINED] 21 וַיִּשְׁלַח יִשְׂרָאֵל מַלְאָכִים אֶל־סִיחֹן מֶלֶךְ־הָאֱמֹרִי לֵאמֹר: 22 אֶעְבְּרָה בְאַרְצֶךָ לֹא נִטֶּה בְּשָׂדֶה וּבְכֶרֶם לֹא נִשְׁתֶּה מֵי בְאֵר בְּדֶרֶךְ הַמֶּלֶךְ נֵלֵךְ עַד אֲשֶׁר־נַעֲבֹר גְּבֻלֶךָ: 23 וְלֹא־נָתַן סִיחֹן אֶת־יִשְׂרָאֵל עֲבֹר בִּגְבֻלוֹ וַיֶּאֱסֹף סִיחֹן אֶת־כָּל־עַמּוֹ וַיֵּצֵא לִקְרַאת יִשְׂרָאֵל הַמִּדְבָּרָה וַיָּבֹא יָהְצָה וַיִּלָּחֶם בְּיִשְׂרָאֵל: 24 וַיַּכֵּהוּ יִשְׂרָאֵל לְפִי־חָרֶב וַיִּירַשׁ אֶת־אַרְצוֹ מֵאַרְנֹן עַד־יַבֹּק עַד־בְּנֵי עַמּוֹן כִּי עַז גְּבוּל בְּנֵי עַמּוֹן: 25 וַיִּקַּח יִשְׂרָאֵל אֵת כָּל־הֶעָרִים הָאֵלֶּה וַיֵּשֶׁב יִשְׂרָאֵל בְּכָל־עָרֵי הָאֱמֹרִי בְּחֶשְׁבּוֹן וּבְכָל־בְּנֹתֶיהָ: 26 כִּי חֶשְׁבּוֹן עִיר סִיחֹן מֶלֶךְ הָאֱמֹרִי הִוא וְהוּא נִלְחַם בְּמֶלֶךְ מוֹאָב הָרִאשׁוֹן וַיִּקַּח אֶת־כָּל־אַרְצוֹ מִיָּדוֹ עַד־אַרְנֹן: 27 עַל־כֵּן יֹאמְרוּ הַמֹּשְׁלִים בֹּאוּ חֶשְׁבּוֹן תִּבָּנֶה וְתִכּוֹנֵן עִיר סִיחוֹן: 28 כִּי־אֵשׁ יָצְאָה מֵחֶשְׁבּוֹן לֶהָבָה מִקִּרְיַת סִיחֹן אָכְלָה עָר מוֹאָב בַּעֲלֵי בָּמוֹת אַרְנֹן: 29 אוֹי־לְךָ מוֹאָב אָבַדְתָּ עַם־כְּמוֹשׁ נָתַן בָּנָיו פְּלֵיטִם וּבְנֹתָיו בַּשְּׁבִית לְמֶלֶךְ אֱמֹרִי סִיחוֹן: 30 וַנִּירָם אָבַד חֶשְׁבּוֹן עַד־דִּיבֹן וַנַּשִּׁים עַד־נֹפַח אֲשֶׁר עַד־מֵידְבָא:

21. Israel sent messengers to Sihon. Elsewhere, Scripture attributes the sending of the very same messengers *to Moses*—"*I (Moses) sent messengers from the desert of Kedemoth to Sihon*" (*Deuteronomy* 2:26); and, *"Moses sent messengers ... to the king of Edom"* (above, 20:14).

But these verses actually complement one another—one "locks" and the other "opens."

For Moses is Israel, and Israel is Moses.

The leader of the generation is like the entire generation, for the leader is everything (*Rashi, 11th century*).

23. Sihon ... went out to the desert toward Israel. All the Canaanite kings paid him a levy for protecting them against invading armies. Thus, when Israel said to him, *"Let me pass through your land"* (v. 22), he said to them, "My entire aim is only to protect them from you, so how can you say such a thing?" Thus, *"Sihon ... went out ... toward Israel."* Even if Heshbon were full of mosquitoes and not men, nobody would have been able to conquer it, since it was so well fortified. And if Sihon had been in an unfortified village on his own, no man could have defeated him because he was so strong. How much more so were they invincible when Sihon was in

¹⁹ From the (time they received this) gift, (it went down with them) to the streams, and from the streams (it went up with them) to the heights.

²⁰ From the heights to the valley in the field of Moab, at the top of the summit that overlooks the wastelands.

The War with Sihon

[SEVENTH READING / FOURTH WHEN JOINED] ²¹ Israel sent messengers to Sihon the king of the Amorites, saying: ²² "Let me pass through your land. We will not turn to any fields or vineyards, nor drink water from the well. We will walk along the king's highway, until we have passed through your border."

²³ But Sihon did not permit Israel to pass through his borders. Sihon gathered all his people and went out to the desert toward Israel. He came to Jahaz and fought against Israel. ²⁴ Israel struck him with the sword, and took possession of his land—from Arnon to Jabbok, as far as Ammon's descendants, because the border of Ammon's descendants was strong. ²⁵ Israel took all these cities, and the Jewish people settled in all the cities of the Amorites, in Heshbon and all its villages. ²⁶ For Heshbon was the city of Sihon, king of the Amorites, and he had fought against the first king of Moab, seizing all his land from his possession, as far as Arnon.

²⁷ Concerning this (victory) the poets (Balaam and his father) would say:

Come to (conquer) Heshbon! May it be built and established as the city of Sihon! ²⁸ For fire went forth from Heshbon, a flame from the city of Sihon, it consumed Ar of Moab, the masters of the high places of Arnon.

²⁹ Woe is to you, Moab! You are lost, people of Chemosh! He has given his sons over as refugees, and his daughters into captivity to Sihon, king of the Amorites.

³⁰ Their kingdom is destroyed from Heshbon, it has been removed from Dibon. We laid them waste as far as Nophah, which is near Medeba.

spiritual vitamin

> The Torah is called *"The Torah of Light"* (*Proverbs* 6:23), because the essential nature of the Torah is to illuminate man's path in life. And when the path is illuminated in this way, one can see clearly which actions and conduct are good, and which have to be avoided.

במדבר כא:לא - כב:א | חקת

³¹ וַיֵּ֥שֶׁב יִשְׂרָאֵ֖ל בְּאֶ֥רֶץ הָאֱמֹרִֽי: ³² וַיִּשְׁלַ֤ח מֹשֶׁה֙ לְרַגֵּ֣ל אֶת־יַעְזֵ֔ר וַֽיִּלְכְּד֖וּ בְּנֹתֶ֑יהָ [וַיִּ֖ירֶשׁ כ׳] וַיּ֕וֹרֶשׁ אֶת־הָאֱמֹרִ֖י אֲשֶׁר־שָֽׁם: ³³ וַיִּפְנוּ֙ וַֽיַּעֲל֔וּ דֶּ֖רֶךְ הַבָּשָׁ֑ן וַיֵּצֵ֣א עוֹג֩ מֶֽלֶךְ־הַבָּשָׁ֨ן לִקְרָאתָ֜ם ה֧וּא וְכָל־עַמּ֛וֹ לַמִּלְחָמָ֖ה אֶדְרֶֽעִי: ³⁴ [MAFTIR] וַיֹּ֨אמֶר יְהֹוָ֤ה אֶל־מֹשֶׁה֙ אַל־תִּירָ֣א אֹת֔וֹ כִּ֣י בְיָדְךָ֞ נָתַ֧תִּי אֹת֛וֹ וְאֶת־כָּל־עַמּ֖וֹ וְאֶת־אַרְצ֑וֹ וְעָשִׂ֣יתָ לּ֔וֹ כַּאֲשֶׁ֣ר עָשִׂ֗יתָ לְסִיחֹן֙ מֶ֣לֶךְ הָֽאֱמֹרִ֔י אֲשֶׁ֥ר יוֹשֵׁ֖ב בְּחֶשְׁבּֽוֹן: ³⁵ וַיַּכּ֨וּ אֹת֤וֹ וְאֶת־בָּנָיו֙ וְאֶת־כָּל־עַמּ֔וֹ עַד־בִּלְתִּ֥י הִשְׁאִֽיר־ל֖וֹ שָׂרִ֑יד וַיִּֽירְשׁ֖וּ אֶת־אַרְצֽוֹ:

כב ¹ וַיִּסְע֖וּ בְּנֵ֣י יִשְׂרָאֵ֑ל וַיַּחֲנוּ֙ בְּעַֽרְב֣וֹת מוֹאָ֔ב מֵעֵ֖בֶר לְיַרְדֵּ֥ן יְרֵחֽוֹ: ס ס ס

פ"ז פסוקים, למידב"א סימן. ימוא"ל סימן.

In truth, Og's intentions were evil—he wanted Abraham to be killed at war so that he could marry Sarah (*Rashi* to *Genesis* 14:13). Nevertheless, the fact that this led to Lot's rescue was a merit for him. A meritorious act is considered great in the eyes of God, even if the intentions behind it may not be pure (*The Tosafists, 12ᵗʰ–14ᵗʰ centuries*).

kabbalah bites

21:34 Og's soul, while predominantly *kelippah* (evil), also contained a spark of what would later be the soul of Rabbi Shimon (Simeon) ben Nethanel (mentioned in *Avot* 2:8).

Thus Og's kingdom, BaShaN is an acronym of **SH**imon **B**en **N**ethanel.

It was due to the presence of this holy soul that Moses was afraid to kill him.

numbers 21:31 – 22:1 — ḥukkat

The War with King Og of Bashan

³¹ Israel settled in the land of the Amorites. ³² Moses sent men to spy out Jazer and they captured its villages, driving out the Amorites who lived there.

³³ Then they turned and headed north toward the Bashan. Og, the king of Bashan, came out toward them with all his people, to wage war at Edrei.

[MAFTIR] ³⁴ God said to Moses, "Do not fear him, for I have given him into your hand—as well as all his people and his land. You will do the same to him as you did to Sihon, king of the Amorites, who lived in Heshbon."

³⁵ They struck him down, as well as his sons and all his people—no survivors remained—and they took possession of his land.

22 ¹ The children of Israel traveled and camped in the plains of Moab, across the Jordan, near Jericho.

Haftarot: Ḥukkat—page 1381. Erev Rosh Ḥodesh—page 1415. Rosh Ḥodesh—page 1417.
Maftir: Rosh Ḥodesh—page 1000 (28:9–15).

Heshbon. God said, "Why should I trouble My children to besiege every city?" He placed the idea into all the warriors' minds to leave the cities. They all gathered in one place, where they fell in battle. From there Israel proceeded to the cities, where they met with no opposition, since only women and children were left there (*Rashi, 11th century*).

32. They captured its villages. The spies captured it. They said, "We won't be like the first spies! We trust in the power of Moses' prayers to help us fight!" (*Rashi, 11th century*).

34. Do not fear him (ʾoto). The word ʾoto ("him") is related to ʾot ("sign").

Og was an adherent of Abraham, who took on himself the sign (ʾot) of circumcision. When Og saw the Israelites approaching, he said, "I can surpass their merit. With this I will confront them."

At that moment Moses was seized by fear—how could he possibly destroy the sign that Abraham had made?

God said, *"Do not fear him (ʾoto)."* Do not fear the sign which he has, for he defiled his sign, and whoever defiles this sign deserves to be removed from the face of the earth (*Zohar*).

Naming a holy Torah portion after a **wicked man** suggests that **every part of creation,** even the most negative aspects, can be **transformed to good.** That is why the promise of the **Redemption** appears in this portion—because then **we will witness** the complete **transformation** of the world **to good.**

BALAK
בלק

BALAK SEEKS SERVICES OF BALAAM	22:2-20
BALAAM'S JOURNEY	22:21-40
BALAAM'S BLESSINGS	22:41 – 24:25
ZEALOTRY OF PHINEHAS	25:1-9

NAME
Balak

LINES IN TORAH SCROLL
178

PARASHIYYOT
1 open; 1 closed

VERSES
104

WORDS
1455

LETTERS
5357

MITZVOT
none

DATE
2488

LOCATION
Pethor, Kiriath-huzoth, Bamoth-baal, peak of Peor and Shittim

KEY PEOPLE
Balak, Balaam, Moses, Phinehas

NOTES
Often read together with Ḥukkat; this is the only portion that we rely on Moses prophecy to verify, since no Jews were present.

CHARACTER PROFILE

NAME
Balak ("destroy")

ANCESTORS
Lot, Jethro

DESCENDANT
Ruth, the Messiah

CHILD
Eglon

ACHIEVEMENTS
Became king of Moab after Sihon's death; was an accomplished sorcerer

KNOWN FOR
Hatred for the Jewish people; hired Balaam to curse the Jewish people; sent maidens of Moab (including his own daughter) to seduce the Jewish people, resulting in the death of tens of thousands; he was the spiritual counterforce to Aaron

MODESTY

Balaam praised the Jewish tents which were set up to respect privacy. Respecting others' limits and boundaries is the basis of good neighborliness and moral society (24:5).

INNER STRENGTH

The Jewish people are compared to a "crouching lion." Their strength may be dormant, but it is nevertheless present and enables them to rise and overcome challenges (24:9).

DECISIVE ACTION

Even though Moses and Aaron did not take action when Zimri acted immorally, Phinehas did not hesitate. Overcome your powerlessness and ambivalence, to take bold decisive action when necessary (25:7).

במדבר כב:ב-ט

2 וַיַּרְא בָּלָק בֶּן־צִפּוֹר אֵת כָּל־אֲשֶׁר־עָשָׂה יִשְׂרָאֵל לָאֱמֹרִי: 3 וַיָּגָר מוֹאָב מִפְּנֵי הָעָם מְאֹד כִּי רַב־הוּא וַיָּקָץ מוֹאָב מִפְּנֵי בְּנֵי יִשְׂרָאֵל: 4 וַיֹּאמֶר מוֹאָב אֶל־זִקְנֵי מִדְיָן עַתָּה יְלַחֲכוּ הַקָּהָל אֶת־כָּל־סְבִיבֹתֵינוּ כִּלְחֹךְ הַשּׁוֹר אֵת יֶרֶק הַשָּׂדֶה וּבָלָק בֶּן־צִפּוֹר מֶלֶךְ לְמוֹאָב בָּעֵת הַהִוא: 5 וַיִּשְׁלַח מַלְאָכִים אֶל־בִּלְעָם בֶּן־בְּעֹר פְּתוֹרָה אֲשֶׁר עַל־הַנָּהָר אֶרֶץ בְּנֵי־עַמּוֹ לִקְרֹא־לוֹ לֵאמֹר הִנֵּה עַם יָצָא מִמִּצְרַיִם הִנֵּה כִסָּה אֶת־עֵין הָאָרֶץ וְהוּא יֹשֵׁב מִמֻּלִי: 6 וְעַתָּה לְכָה־נָּא אָרָה־לִּי אֶת־הָעָם הַזֶּה כִּי־עָצוּם הוּא מִמֶּנִּי אוּלַי אוּכַל נַכֶּה־בּוֹ וַאֲגָרְשֶׁנּוּ מִן־הָאָרֶץ כִּי יָדַעְתִּי אֵת אֲשֶׁר־תְּבָרֵךְ מְבֹרָךְ וַאֲשֶׁר תָּאֹר יוּאָר: 7 וַיֵּלְכוּ זִקְנֵי מוֹאָב וְזִקְנֵי מִדְיָן וּקְסָמִים בְּיָדָם וַיָּבֹאוּ אֶל־בִּלְעָם וַיְדַבְּרוּ אֵלָיו דִּבְרֵי בָלָק: 8 וַיֹּאמֶר אֲלֵיהֶם לִינוּ פֹה הַלַּיְלָה וַהֲשִׁבֹתִי אֶתְכֶם דָּבָר כַּאֲשֶׁר יְדַבֵּר יְהֹוָה אֵלָי וַיֵּשְׁבוּ שָׂרֵי־מוֹאָב עִם־בִּלְעָם: 9 וַיָּבֹא אֱלֹהִים אֶל־בִּלְעָם וַיֹּאמֶר מִי הָאֲנָשִׁים

22:7 The elders of Moab and the elders of Midian went. Midian and Moab had never shared peace. Why, then, did they suddenly unite?

We can understand it through a parable. Two watchdogs guarding a flock of sheep were fiercely hostile to each other, until one day a wolf attacked one of the dogs. The other dog said to himself, "If I don't help my fellow dog, the wolf will kill him today and come back to kill me tomorrow." So the two dogs joined together and killed the wolf.

In the same way, Moab and Midian set aside their longstanding hostility to unite against a common threat—the Israelites (*Babylonian Talmud, Sanhedrin* 105a).

8. So the Moabite dignitaries stayed with Balaam. The previous verse states that the elders of Midian also came to Balaam. Why, then, does this verse mention only the dignitaries of Moab?

The elders of Midian tested Balaam. If he would go with them straightaway, they would believe in his powers. But if he would stall them, they would know he was not what he claimed to be. When Balaam suggested staying overnight, the elders of Midian said, "We have no hope in him," and they left, leaving only the Moabite delegation (*Rashi, 11th century*).

Alternatively, when Balaam said, *"I will give you an answer when God speaks to me,"* the Midianites responded, "Is there any father who hates his own son?" Obviously not! If Balaam needed permission from

Food for thought

1. What are the causes of anti-Semitism?

2. Should the Jewish community actively target anti-Semitism?

3. What obligations do we have to the non-Jewish world?

parashat balak

Balak Seeks the Assistance of Balaam

² Balak son of Zippor saw everything that Israel had done to the Amorites. ³ Moab became terrified of Israel, because they were numerous. (In fact), because of the children of Israel, Moab became sick (of their own lives).

⁴ Moab said to the elders of Midian, "This community (of Jews) is now going to gnaw away everything around us, just as an ox in the field eats up vegetation!"

Balak son of Zippor (was not fit for sovereignty, but he had just been appointed) king of Moab at that time (as an emergency measure after Sihon's death). ⁵ He sent messengers to Balaam son of Beor—to Pethor, which is by the river of (Balak's own) native land—calling him, saying:

"Look! A nation has come out of Egypt! Look, it has covered the 'eye' of the land (by killing Sihon and Og, who used to protect us)! They are sitting right by me (and are poised to attack). ⁶ So now, please come and curse this people for me, for they are more powerful than me. Perhaps I will (then) be able to strike them and drive them out of the land. For I know that whoever you bless is blessed and whoever you curse is cursed."

⁷ The elders of Moab and the elders of Midian went, with tools of black-magic in their hands (so that Balaam would not complain he did not have the right tools available). They came to Balaam and told him Balak's message.

⁸ He said to them, "Stay here overnight, and I will give you an answer when God speaks to me." So the Moabite dignitaries stayed with Balaam.

⁹ God came to Balaam and said, "Who are these men with you?"

kabbalah bites

22:5 The souls of both Cain and Abel contained a mixture of good and evil. The good in Cain passed to Jethro, and the good in Abel to Moses.

The evil from Abel passed to both Balak and Balaam. (Thus both of their names contain the letters *B* and *L*, from A*B*e*L*, representing the evil, unrectified part of Abel.)

The evil from Cain was passed to Amalek, and from there to Balak and Balaam. (The letters *A, M, L* of Amalek passed to Ba*L*Aa*M*; and the *K* of Amalek to Bala*K*.)

While Balak and Balaam both shared the evils of Cain and Abel, Balak predominantly represented Cain, and Balaam, Abel.

בלק / במדבר כב:ט-יט

הָאֵלֶּה עִמָּךְ: 10 וַיֹּאמֶר בִּלְעָם אֶל־הָאֱלֹהִים בָּלָק בֶּן־צִפֹּר מֶלֶךְ מוֹאָב שָׁלַח אֵלָי: 11 הִנֵּה הָעָם הַיֹּצֵא מִמִּצְרַיִם וַיְכַס אֶת־עֵין הָאָרֶץ עַתָּה לְכָה קָבָה־לִּי אֹתוֹ אוּלַי אוּכַל לְהִלָּחֶם בּוֹ וְגֵרַשְׁתִּיו: 12 וַיֹּאמֶר אֱלֹהִים אֶל־בִּלְעָם לֹא תֵלֵךְ עִמָּהֶם לֹא תָאֹר אֶת־הָעָם כִּי בָרוּךְ הוּא: [SECOND READING FIFTH WHEN JOINED] 13 וַיָּקָם בִּלְעָם בַּבֹּקֶר וַיֹּאמֶר אֶל־שָׂרֵי בָלָק לְכוּ אֶל־אַרְצְכֶם כִּי מֵאֵן יְהֹוָה לְתִתִּי לַהֲלֹךְ עִמָּכֶם: 14 וַיָּקוּמוּ שָׂרֵי מוֹאָב וַיָּבֹאוּ אֶל־בָּלָק וַיֹּאמְרוּ מֵאֵן בִּלְעָם הֲלֹךְ עִמָּנוּ: 15 וַיֹּסֶף עוֹד בָּלָק שְׁלֹחַ שָׂרִים רַבִּים וְנִכְבָּדִים מֵאֵלֶּה: 16 וַיָּבֹאוּ אֶל־בִּלְעָם וַיֹּאמְרוּ לוֹ כֹּה אָמַר בָּלָק בֶּן־צִפּוֹר אַל־נָא תִמָּנַע מֵהֲלֹךְ אֵלָי: 17 כִּי־כַבֵּד אֲכַבֶּדְךָ מְאֹד וְכֹל אֲשֶׁר־תֹּאמַר אֵלַי אֶעֱשֶׂה וּלְכָה־נָּא קָבָה־לִּי אֵת הָעָם הַזֶּה: 18 וַיַּעַן בִּלְעָם וַיֹּאמֶר אֶל־עַבְדֵי בָלָק אִם־יִתֶּן־לִי בָלָק מְלֹא בֵיתוֹ כֶּסֶף וְזָהָב לֹא אוּכַל לַעֲבֹר אֶת־פִּי יְהֹוָה אֱלֹהָי לַעֲשׂוֹת קְטַנָּה אוֹ גְדוֹלָה: 19 וְעַתָּה שְׁבוּ נָא בָזֶה גַּם־אַתֶּם

Why did God prevent Balaam from cursing the children of Israel? And why would his curse have been significant if they had God's blessing in any case?

Balaam's reputation was so great that if he had cursed Israel, the surrounding nations might have gone to war with them on the strength of his curses. But when the nations would hear how God had transformed the curses into blessings, they would lose all desire to fight. So there was a very practical reason why Balaam's efforts needed to be confounded (*Rabbi Isaac Abravanel, 15th century*).

18. Balaam replied, saying to Balak's servants, "Even if Balak would give me his house full of silver and gold…" How do you know that if you honor someone for the sake of money, in the end you will have it taken from you in disgrace? From Balaam who honored Balak for the sake of money, as the verse states, *"Balaam replied, saying to Balak's servants, 'Even if Balak would give me his house full of silver and gold.'"*

How do you know that it was taken from him in disgrace? From the verse, *"Run off home right now! … God has just deprived you of honor"* (24:11; *Avot de-Rabbi Nathan*).

kabbalah bites

22:18 Balaam was also a reincarnation of Laban (who himself was a reincarnation of the evil within Abel's soul). Just as Laban had been very desirous of money, we find this same trait here with Balaam, who said, *"Even if Balak will give me his house full of silver and gold…"*

Later, the same soul would find itself reincarnated as Nabal (see *I Samuel 25*). Thus the Hebrew word LaBaN is an acronym for **L**aban = **B**alaam and **N**abal.

¹⁰ Balaam said to God, "Balak son of Zippor the king of Moab has sent them to me (with this message): ¹¹ 'Look! The nation coming out of Egypt has covered the "eye" of the land. Now come and condemn them for me. Perhaps I will (then) be able to fight with them and drive them away.'"

¹² God said to Balaam, "Don't go with them! (And) don't curse the nation (even without going with them. They don't need your blessing either) because they are blessed."

[SECOND READING / FIFTH WHEN JOINED] ¹³ When Balaam got up in the morning, he said to Balak's dignitaries, "Go back to your country, for God has refused to let me go with you (because you are not sufficiently high-ranking officers)." ¹⁴ So Moab's dignitaries set off.

They returned to Balak and said, "Balaam refuses to come with us (because we're not high-ranking enough)."

¹⁵ Balak sent many more dignitaries, higher in rank than these (previous ones).

¹⁶ They came to Balaam and said to him, "This is what Balak son of Zippor said, 'Please do not refrain from coming to me. ¹⁷ For I will give you tremendous honor (even more than in the past), and whatever you tell me to do I will do. So please come and condemn this people for me.'"

¹⁸ Balaam replied, saying to Balak's servants, "Even if Balak would give me his house full of silver and gold, I cannot transgress the word of God, my God, be it a small or large (transgression). ¹⁹ Now, you should also please remain here overnight, and I will know what God will add when He speaks to me."

God to curse the children of Israel, God, the Father of the Israelites, would never allow this to happen. They despaired and returned home (*Babylonian Talmud, Sanhedrin* 105a).

11. Come and condemn them for me. The term *kavah li*, "condemn for me," used by Balaam here is stronger than *'arah li*, "curse for me," used by Balak in verse 6. "Condemning" suggests a specific and detailed curse.

Balaam wanted to *"Drive them away,"* i.e., to rid them from the world.

Balak said only to *"Drive them out of the land"* (v. 6), as if to say, "I only want to get them away from me." But Balaam hated them more than Balak (*Rashi, 11ᵗʰ century*).

spiritual vitamin

> It is very difficult to be objective in a matter concerning your own self. You might see yourself as a victim of circumstances, when it is not necessarily so in actual fact.

בלק

במדבר כב:יט-כח

הַלַּיְלָה וְאֵדְעָה מַה־יֹּסֵף יְהוָה דַּבֵּר עִמִּי: 20 וַיָּבֹא אֱלֹהִים ׀ אֶל־בִּלְעָם לַיְלָה וַיֹּאמֶר לוֹ אִם־לִקְרֹא לְךָ בָּאוּ הָאֲנָשִׁים קוּם לֵךְ אִתָּם וְאַךְ אֶת־הַדָּבָר אֲשֶׁר־אֲדַבֵּר אֵלֶיךָ אֹתוֹ תַעֲשֶׂה: [THIRD READING] 21 וַיָּקָם בִּלְעָם בַּבֹּקֶר וַיַּחֲבֹשׁ אֶת־אֲתֹנוֹ וַיֵּלֶךְ עִם־שָׂרֵי מוֹאָב: 22 וַיִּחַר־אַף אֱלֹהִים כִּי־הוֹלֵךְ הוּא וַיִּתְיַצֵּב מַלְאַךְ יְהוָה בַּדֶּרֶךְ לְשָׂטָן לוֹ וְהוּא רֹכֵב עַל־אֲתֹנוֹ וּשְׁנֵי נְעָרָיו עִמּוֹ: 23 וַתֵּרֶא הָאָתוֹן אֶת־מַלְאַךְ יְהוָה נִצָּב בַּדֶּרֶךְ וְחַרְבּוֹ שְׁלוּפָה בְּיָדוֹ וַתֵּט הָאָתוֹן מִן־הַדֶּרֶךְ וַתֵּלֶךְ בַּשָּׂדֶה וַיַּךְ בִּלְעָם אֶת־הָאָתוֹן לְהַטֹּתָהּ הַדָּרֶךְ: 24 וַיַּעֲמֹד מַלְאַךְ יְהוָה בְּמִשְׁעוֹל הַכְּרָמִים גָּדֵר מִזֶּה וְגָדֵר מִזֶּה: 25 וַתֵּרֶא הָאָתוֹן אֶת־מַלְאַךְ יְהוָה וַתִּלָּחֵץ אֶל־הַקִּיר וַתִּלְחַץ אֶת־רֶגֶל בִּלְעָם אֶל־הַקִּיר וַיֹּסֶף לְהַכֹּתָהּ: 26 וַיּוֹסֶף מַלְאַךְ־יְהוָה עֲבוֹר וַיַּעֲמֹד בְּמָקוֹם צָר אֲשֶׁר אֵין־דֶּרֶךְ לִנְטוֹת יָמִין וּשְׂמֹאול: 27 וַתֵּרֶא הָאָתוֹן אֶת־מַלְאַךְ יְהוָה וַתִּרְבַּץ תַּחַת בִּלְעָם וַיִּחַר־אַף בִּלְעָם וַיַּךְ אֶת־הָאָתוֹן בַּמַּקֵּל: 28 וַיִּפְתַּח יְהוָה אֶת־פִּי הָאָתוֹן וַתֹּאמֶר לְבִלְעָם מֶה־עָשִׂיתִי לְךָ כִּי הִכִּיתַנִי זֶה שָׁלֹשׁ רְגָלִים:

wise, Balaam's prophetic powers had only been granted for the sake of the Jewish people (*Rabbi Ephraim of Luntshits, 16th–17th century*).

This miracle was intended to make Balaam repent, when he would be reminded that *"the utterances of the tongue come from God"* (Proverbs 16:1; *Rabbi Obadiah Sforno, 16th century*).

Balaam was a sorcerer, so God made a startling miracle to warn him not to use sorcery to curse the Jewish people (*Naḥmanides, 13th century*).

The entire story of Balaam's donkey speaking must have been a *prophetic vision* of Balaam. For otherwise, how would you explain: (1) Why Balaam, who was a prophet, did not see God's angel at first, whereas his donkey did (v. 23); (2) The point of God's sending the angel to deter Balaam from his journey if he was unble to see it; (3) The astonishing miracle of a speaking donkey, which does not appear to have been for any purpose, yet we are taught that God does not make a miracle in vain (*Rabbi Levi b. Gershom, 14th century*)?

The truth is that the donkey *did* speak. If you can fathom the mystery of the angels that appeared to Abraham and Jacob as people, then you will understand the miracle of the donkey. God can cause a man to see angels as people, and He can cause other supernatural occurrences, such as a talking donkey (*Rabbi Abraham ibn Ezra, 12th century*).

Why did God perform this extraordinary miracle that was witnessed by only a select few?

God wanted the nations of the world to respect the Israelites, and to achieve that purpose they would need to hear praise of the children of Israel from someone whom they greatly

numbers 22:20–28 — balak

²⁰ God came to Balaam at night and said to him, "If (you feel) that the offer of these men (will be profitable) for you, get moving and go with them. But you must (only) do whatever I tell you."

Balaam's Journey

[THIRD READING] ²¹ Balaam got up in the morning, saddled his donkey and went with the Moabite dignitaries. ²² God was angry that he was going, and so God's angel was placed on the road to obstruct him. He was riding on his donkey, and his two lads were with him. ²³ The donkey saw God's angel standing on the road, with a sword drawn in its hand, so the donkey turned aside from the road and went into a field. Balaam beat the donkey to get it back onto the road.

²⁴ God's angel stood in a path through the vineyards, with a wall on one side and a wall on the other side. ²⁵ The donkey saw God's angel, and it pushed itself against the wall. It pressed Balaam's leg against the wall, and he beat it again.

²⁶ God's angel went further ahead, and stood in a narrow place where there was no room to turn right or left. ²⁷ The donkey saw God's angel, and it crouched down under Balaam. Balaam became angry, and he beat the donkey with a stick.

²⁸ God opened the donkey's mouth, and it said to Balaam, "What have I done to you that made you hit me these three times?"

---

21. Balaam got up in the morning, saddled his donkey. Motivated by his hatred of the children of Israel and his strong desire to curse them, Balaam gleefully saddled his donkey by himself, though it was a menial chore for someone of his high ranking (*Babylonian Talmud, Sanhedrin* 105b).

God retorted: "You wicked man! Their ancestor, Abraham, has already preceded you," as it is written regarding the binding of Isaac, *"Abraham got up early in the morning (to perform God's command) and he saddled his donkey (personally)"* (*Genesis* 22:3; *Rashi, 11ᵗʰ century*).

How can *Rashi* compare the actions of Balaam, who was so wicked, with those of Abraham, who was saintly?

Balaam saddled his donkey on his way to annihilate the children of Israel and, ironically, Abraham's intended actions would also have resulted in the destruction of the Israelite nation: If Isaac had been sacrificed, we would not have come into being.

God said, "When Abraham rose early and saddled his donkey on his way to 'destroy the Israelite nation,' he did so *out of his great love for Me* and in adherence to My command. Yet I did not allow it to materialize. Certainly then, when you, Balaam, saddle your donkey in preparation to harm the children of Israel—*against* My instructions—I will stop you from fulfilling your wretched plan!" (*Rabbi Menahem Mendel Morgensztern of Kotsk, 19ᵗʰ century*).

22. God's angel. It was an angel of mercy. God wanted to prevent him from sinning, so that he would not die because of his sins (*Rashi, 11ᵗʰ century*).

28. God opened the donkey's mouth. God was suggesting to Balaam that just as it is not a donkey's nature to speak, and it only was able to do so for the sake of the Jewish people, like-

במדבר כב:כט-מא — בלק

29 וַיֹּ֤אמֶר בִּלְעָם֙ לָֽאָת֔וֹן כִּ֥י הִתְעַלַּ֖לְתְּ בִּ֑י ל֤וּ יֶשׁ־חֶ֙רֶב֙ בְּיָדִ֔י כִּ֥י עַתָּ֖ה הֲרַגְתִּֽיךְ: 30 וַתֹּ֨אמֶר הָאָת֜וֹן אֶל־בִּלְעָ֗ם הֲלוֹא֩ אָנֹכִ֨י אֲתֹֽנְךָ֜ אֲשֶׁר־רָכַ֣בְתָּ עָלַ֗י מֵעֽוֹדְךָ֙ עַד־הַיּ֣וֹם הַזֶּ֔ה הַֽהַסְכֵּ֣ן הִסְכַּ֔נְתִּי לַעֲשׂ֥וֹת לְךָ֖ כֹּ֑ה וַיֹּ֖אמֶר לֹֽא: 31 וַיְגַ֣ל יְהוָה֮ אֶת־עֵינֵ֣י בִלְעָם֒ וַיַּ֞רְא אֶת־מַלְאַ֤ךְ יְהוָה֙ נִצָּ֣ב בַּדֶּ֔רֶךְ וְחַרְבּ֥וֹ שְׁלֻפָ֖ה בְּיָד֑וֹ וַיִּקֹּ֥ד וַיִּשְׁתַּ֖חוּ לְאַפָּֽיו: 32 וַיֹּ֤אמֶר אֵלָיו֙ מַלְאַ֣ךְ יְהוָ֔ה עַל־מָ֗ה הִכִּ֙יתָ֙ אֶת־אֲתֹ֣נְךָ֔ זֶ֖ה שָׁל֣וֹשׁ רְגָלִ֑ים הִנֵּ֤ה אָנֹכִי֙ יָצָ֣אתִי לְשָׂטָ֔ן כִּֽי־יָרַ֥ט הַדֶּ֖רֶךְ לְנֶגְדִּֽי: 33 וַתִּרְאַ֙נִי֙ הָֽאָת֔וֹן וַתֵּ֣ט לְפָנַ֔י זֶ֖ה שָׁל֣שׁ רְגָלִ֑ים אוּלַי֙ נָטְתָ֣ה מִפָּנַ֔י כִּ֥י עַתָּ֛ה גַּם־אֹתְכָ֥ה הָרַ֖גְתִּי וְאוֹתָ֥הּ הֶחֱיֵֽיתִי: 34 וַיֹּ֨אמֶר בִּלְעָ֜ם אֶל־מַלְאַ֤ךְ יְהוָה֙ חָטָ֔אתִי כִּ֚י לֹ֣א יָדַ֔עְתִּי כִּ֥י אַתָּ֛ה נִצָּ֥ב לִקְרָאתִ֖י בַּדָּ֑רֶךְ וְעַתָּ֛ה אִם־רַ֥ע בְּעֵינֶ֖יךָ אָשׁ֥וּבָה לִּֽי: 35 וַיֹּאמֶר֩ מַלְאַ֨ךְ יְהוָ֜ה אֶל־בִּלְעָ֗ם לֵ֚ךְ עִם־הָ֣אֲנָשִׁ֔ים וְאֶ֗פֶס אֶת־הַדָּבָ֛ר אֲשֶׁר־אֲדַבֵּ֥ר אֵלֶ֖יךָ אֹת֣וֹ תְדַבֵּ֑ר וַיֵּ֥לֶךְ בִּלְעָ֖ם עִם־שָׂרֵ֥י בָלָֽק: 36 וַיִּשְׁמַ֥ע בָּלָ֖ק כִּ֣י בָ֣א בִלְעָ֑ם וַיֵּצֵ֨א לִקְרָאת֜וֹ אֶל־עִ֣יר מוֹאָ֗ב אֲשֶׁר֙ עַל־גְּב֣וּל אַרְנֹ֔ן אֲשֶׁ֖ר בִּקְצֵ֥ה הַגְּבֽוּל: 37 וַיֹּ֨אמֶר בָּלָ֜ק אֶל־בִּלְעָ֗ם הֲלֹא֩ שָׁלֹ֨חַ שָׁלַ֤חְתִּי אֵלֶ֙יךָ֙ לִקְרֹא־לָ֔ךְ לָ֥מָּה לֹא־הָלַ֖כְתָּ אֵלָ֑י הַֽאֻמְנָ֔ם לֹ֥א אוּכַ֖ל כַּבְּדֶֽךָ: 38 וַיֹּ֨אמֶר בִּלְעָ֜ם אֶל־בָּלָ֗ק הִֽנֵּה־בָ֙אתִי֙ אֵלֶ֔יךָ עַתָּ֕ה הֲיָכֹ֥ל אוּכַ֖ל דַּבֵּ֣ר מְא֑וּמָה הַדָּבָ֗ר אֲשֶׁ֨ר יָשִׂ֧ים אֱלֹהִ֛ים בְּפִ֖י אֹת֥וֹ אֲדַבֵּֽר: [FOURTH READING / SIXTH WHEN JOINED] 39 וַיֵּ֥לֶךְ בִּלְעָ֖ם עִם־בָּלָ֑ק וַיָּבֹ֖אוּ קִרְיַ֥ת חֻצֽוֹת: 40 וַיִּזְבַּ֥ח בָּלָ֖ק בָּקָ֣ר וָצֹ֑אן וַיְשַׁלַּ֣ח לְבִלְעָ֔ם וְלַשָּׂרִ֖ים אֲשֶׁ֥ר אִתּֽוֹ: 41 וַיְהִ֣י בַבֹּ֔קֶר וַיִּקַּ֤ח בָּלָק֙ אֶת־בִּלְעָ֔ם וַֽיַּעֲלֵ֖הוּ בָּמ֣וֹת בָּ֑עַל וַיַּ֥רְא מִשָּׁ֖ם קְצֵ֥ה הָעָֽם:

---

should not say, "This is the one that silenced Balaam with its rebuke, and he could not respond"—for God cares about people's dignity (*Rashi, 11th century*).

34. Balaam said to God's angel, "I have sinned." As soon as Balaam admitted to having acted improperly, the angel refrained from doing him harm.

When a person admits that he has sinned, the angel sent to punish him can no longer touch him (*Rabbi Bahya b. Asher, 13th century*).

I have sinned, for I didn't know that you were standing opposite me on the road. If he didn't know, what sin could there be? The answer is that, sometimes, *ignorance itself* is a sin (*Rabbi Isaiah Horowitz, 16th–17th century*).

numbers 22:29–41 — balak

²⁹ Balaam said to the donkey, "It's because you've embarrassed me. If I had a sword in my hand, I'd kill you right now!"

³⁰ The donkey said to Balaam, "Aren't I your donkey on which you have ridden since you first started, until today? Do I normally do this to you?"

"No," he said.

³¹ God opened Balaam's eyes, and he saw God's angel standing in the road with a sword drawn in its hand. He bowed and prostrated himself on his face. ³² God's angel said to him, "Why have you beaten your donkey these three times? Look, I have come out to obstruct you because you are hurrying on a journey against my (God). ³³ When the donkey saw me, it turned away these three times. Had it not turned away from me, I would have killed you now and spared (the donkey)."

³⁴ Balaam said to God's angel, "I have sinned, for I didn't know that you were standing opposite me on the road. Now, if it displeases you, I'll go back."

³⁵ God's angel said to Balaam, "Go with these men, but you may only speak the words which I will tell you to say." So Balaam went with Balak's dignitaries.

³⁶ Balak heard that Balaam was coming, so he went out towards him to the (largest) city of Moab, which is on the border of Arnon, at the extreme edge of the border (to show Balaam what important cities he needed to protect).

³⁷ Balak said to Balaam, "Didn't I send (messengers) to you to call for you, many times? Why didn't you come to me (straightaway)? Aren't I able to honor you properly?"

³⁸ Balaam said to Balak, "Look, (at least) I've come to you. Do (you think) I have any power to say anything (I want)? I will (only) speak whatever words God puts into my mouth."

[FOURTH READING / SIXTH WHEN JOINED] ³⁹ Balaam went with Balak, and they came to Kiriath-huzoth. ⁴⁰ Balak slaughtered an animal and a sheep and sent them to Balaam and to his dignitaries.

Balaam's First Parable

⁴¹ Then, in the morning, Balak took Balaam and brought him up to Bamoth-baal, and from there he saw part of the people.

---

respected. At that time, Balaam was highly renowned for his great mind. Were he to praise the Israelites, it would have brought them much honor—but there would also have been a suspicion that he had been bribed.

To make it clear that Balaam was, in fact, communicating with God, God now performed a miracle in front of the Moabite dignitaries (*Rabbi Meir Simhah of Dvinsk, 19th–20th century*).

33. I would have killed you now and spared (the donkey). Now however, that it has spoken and rebuked you and you were unable to endure her rebuke, I have killed it, so that people

בלק

במדבר כג:א-יא

כג 1 וַיֹּאמֶר בִּלְעָם אֶל־בָּלָק בְּנֵה־לִי בָזֶה שִׁבְעָה מִזְבְּחֹת וְהָכֵן לִי בָּזֶה שִׁבְעָה פָרִים וְשִׁבְעָה אֵילִים: 2 וַיַּעַשׂ בָּלָק כַּאֲשֶׁר דִּבֶּר בִּלְעָם וַיַּעַל בָּלָק וּבִלְעָם פָּר וָאַיִל בַּמִּזְבֵּחַ: 3 וַיֹּאמֶר בִּלְעָם לְבָלָק הִתְיַצֵּב עַל־עֹלָתֶךָ וְאֵלְכָה אוּלַי יִקָּרֵה יְהֹוָה לִקְרָאתִי וּדְבַר מַה־יַּרְאֵנִי וְהִגַּדְתִּי לָךְ וַיֵּלֶךְ שֶׁפִי: 4 וַיִּקָּר אֱלֹהִים אֶל־בִּלְעָם וַיֹּאמֶר אֵלָיו אֶת־שִׁבְעַת הַמִּזְבְּחֹת עָרַכְתִּי וָאַעַל פָּר וָאַיִל בַּמִּזְבֵּחַ: 5 וַיָּשֶׂם יְהֹוָה דָּבָר בְּפִי בִלְעָם וַיֹּאמֶר שׁוּב אֶל־בָּלָק וְכֹה תְדַבֵּר: 6 וַיָּשָׁב אֵלָיו וְהִנֵּה נִצָּב עַל־עֹלָתוֹ הוּא וְכָל־שָׂרֵי מוֹאָב: 7 וַיִּשָּׂא מְשָׁלוֹ וַיֹּאמַר מִן־אֲרָם יַנְחֵנִי בָלָק מֶלֶךְ־מוֹאָב מֵהַרְרֵי־קֶדֶם לְכָה אָרָה־לִּי יַעֲקֹב וּלְכָה זֹעֲמָה יִשְׂרָאֵל: 8 מָה אֶקֹּב לֹא קַבֹּה אֵל וּמָה אֶזְעֹם לֹא זָעַם יְהֹוָה: 9 כִּי־מֵרֹאשׁ צֻרִים אֶרְאֶנּוּ וּמִגְּבָעוֹת אֲשׁוּרֶנּוּ הֶן־עָם לְבָדָד יִשְׁכֹּן וּבַגּוֹיִם לֹא יִתְחַשָּׁב: 10 מִי מָנָה עֲפַר יַעֲקֹב וּמִסְפָּר אֶת־רֹבַע יִשְׂרָאֵל תָּמֹת נַפְשִׁי מוֹת יְשָׁרִים וּתְהִי אַחֲרִיתִי כָּמֹהוּ: 11 וַיֹּאמֶר בָּלָק אֶל־בִּלְעָם מֶה עָשִׂיתָ לִי לָקֹב

---

a donkey together" (*Deuteronomy* 22:10), "You should not sow your field with a mixture of seeds" (*Leviticus* 19:19), the ashes of the Red Heifer (*Numbers* 19:1ff.), the soil of the *sotah* ("wayward wife"—ibid., 5:17), and others similar to these (*Rashi, 11th century*).

There is an inner connection between *Rashi*'s two interpretations of verse 10, that the verse refers to "infants" or "soil." The highest possible level of observing the commandments is with humility and complete dedication, regardless of understanding. This is alluded to by soil, which is: (a) lowly, representing humility; and, (b) plain, alluding to a pure and simple service of God.

By observing commandments in the manner of "soil," *Rashi*'s second interpretation, you elicit *Rashi*'s first interpretation, that God will look upon you with the inherent love that a father has for his "infant" (*Rabbi Menahem Mendel Schneerson, 20th century*).

May my soul die the death of the upright. Like so many people, Balaam did not wish to live the life of the upright, which is very restrictive—what is wrong, you cannot do and what is not yours, you cannot have. When the time comes to meet their Maker, the wicked beg to *"die the death of the*

---

kabbalah bites

23:7 Balaam was the only one of the prophets throughout history whose level of prophecy approached that of Moses. This is not difficult to appreciate when we consider that both Moses and Balaam shared the same soul-root, that of Abel (see above, 22:5). Their same soul powers endowed them with comparable prophetic abilities.

numbers 23:1–11 — balak

23 ¹ Balaam said to Balak, "Build me seven altars here and prepare seven bulls and seven rams for me." ² Balak did as Balaam had requested. Balak and Balaam offered up a bull and a ram on each altar.

³ Balaam said to Balak, "Stand with your burnt-offering, and I'll go for a walk. Perhaps God will happen to appear to me and show me something that I can tell you." He then went off alone.

⁴ God happened to appear to Balaam. (Balaam) said to Him, "I have set up (seven altars corresponding to) the seven altars (which the Patriarchs built for you), and I have offered up a bull and a ram on each altar."

⁵ God then placed words in Balaam's mouth. He said, "Return to Balak and say as follows…."

⁶ When he returned, Balak was standing next to his burnt-offering. He was with all the Moabite dignitaries. ⁷ (Balaam) launched into his parable and said:

From Aram, Balak has brought me; the king of Moab (has brought me) from the east mountains. (He says,) "Come, curse Jacob for me, come and bring anger against Israel."

⁸ But how can I condemn, one whom God has not condemned? How can I bring anger, if God has not been angered?

⁹ I see them from the head of rocks, I look at them from hills. It is a nation that will dwell alone, and will not be reckoned with the nations.

¹⁰ Who has counted the infants of Jacob? Or the number of (one of) the divisions of Israel? May my soul die the death of the upright, and let my end be like his.

¹¹ Balak said to Balaam, "What have you done to me? I took you to curse my enemies, and you've just blessed them!"

23:1 Build me seven altars. This was to counter the seven altars built by seven righteous men: Adam, Abel, Noah, Abraham, Isaac, Jacob, and Moses (*Rabbi Hezekiah b. Manoah, 13th century*).

5. God then placed words in Balaam's mouth. God wanted the entire world to hear the prophecies of the Messianic Era and of the survival of the children of Israel. He wanted the news spread by an enemy of the Israelites so that everyone would believe in the future fulfillment of his predictions (*Rabbi Ḥayyim ibn Attar, 18th century*).

9. I see them from the head of rocks. I look at the "head" and beginning of their roots, and I see that they are well-founded and powerful, like these mountains and hills, because of their Patriarchs and Matriarchs (*Rashi, 11th century*).

10. Who has counted the infants (ʿafar) of Jacob? ʿAfar refers to the infants of the house of Jacob, about whom it was written, *"I will make your descendants like the soil (ʿafar) of the earth"* (*Targum Onkelos*).

Targum Onkelos renders, "The infants of the house of Jacob."

Another interpretation: ʿAfar yaʿakov means "the *soil* of Jacob," suggesting that the number of commandments they fulfil with soil are innumerable: *"You may not plow with an ox and*

בלק
במדבר כג:יא-כג

אֹיְבַ֖י לְקַחְתִּ֑יךָ וְהִנֵּ֖ה בֵּרַ֥כְתָּ בָרֵֽךְ׃ 12 וַיַּ֖עַן וַיֹּאמַ֑ר הֲלֹ֗א אֵת֩ אֲשֶׁ֨ר יָשִׂ֤ים יְהֹוָה֙ בְּפִ֔י אֹת֖וֹ אֶשְׁמֹ֥ר לְדַבֵּֽר׃ 13 [FIFTH READING] וַיֹּ֨אמֶר אֵלָ֜יו בָּלָ֗ק לְךָ־נָּ֨א אִתִּ֜י אֶל־מָק֤וֹם אַחֵר֙ אֲשֶׁ֣ר תִּרְאֶ֣נּוּ מִשָּׁ֔ם אֶ֥פֶס קָצֵ֖הוּ תִרְאֶ֑ה וְכֻלּ֖וֹ לֹ֣א תִרְאֶ֑ה וְקׇבְנוֹ־לִ֖י מִשָּֽׁם׃ 14 וַיִּקָּחֵ֙הוּ֙ שְׂדֵ֣ה צֹפִ֔ים אֶל־רֹ֖אשׁ הַפִּסְגָּ֑ה וַיִּ֙בֶן֙ שִׁבְעָ֣ה מִזְבְּחֹ֔ת וַיַּ֥עַל פָּ֖ר וָאַ֥יִל בַּמִּזְבֵּֽחַ׃ 15 וַיֹּ֙אמֶר֙ אֶל־בָּלָ֔ק הִתְיַצֵּ֥ב כֹּ֖ה עַל־עֹלָתֶ֑ךָ וְאָנֹכִ֖י אִקָּ֥רֶה כֹּֽה׃ 16 וַיִּקָּ֤ר יְהֹוָה֙ אֶל־בִּלְעָ֔ם וַיָּ֥שֶׂם דָּבָ֖ר בְּפִ֑יו וַיֹּ֛אמֶר שׁ֥וּב אֶל־בָּלָ֖ק וְכֹ֥ה תְדַבֵּֽר׃ 17 וַיָּבֹ֣א אֵלָ֗יו וְהִנּ֤וֹ נִצָּב֙ עַל־עֹ֣לָת֔וֹ וְשָׂרֵ֥י מוֹאָ֖ב אִתּ֑וֹ וַיֹּ֤אמֶר לוֹ֙ בָּלָ֔ק מַה־דִּבֶּ֖ר יְהֹוָֽה׃ 18 וַיִּשָּׂ֥א מְשָׁל֖וֹ וַיֹּאמַ֑ר ק֤וּם בָּלָק֙ וּֽשְׁמָ֔ע הַאֲזִ֥ינָה עָדַ֖י בְּנ֥וֹ צִפֹּֽר׃ 19 לֹ֣א אִ֥ישׁ אֵל֙ וִֽיכַזֵּ֔ב וּבֶן־אָדָ֖ם וְיִתְנֶחָ֑ם הַה֤וּא אָמַר֙ וְלֹ֣א יַעֲשֶׂ֔ה וְדִבֶּ֖ר וְלֹ֥א יְקִימֶֽנָּה׃ 20 הִנֵּ֥ה בָרֵ֖ךְ לָקָ֑חְתִּי וּבֵרֵ֖ךְ וְלֹ֥א אֲשִׁיבֶֽנָּה׃ 21 לֹֽא־הִבִּ֥יט אָ֙וֶן֙ בְּיַעֲקֹ֔ב וְלֹא־רָאָ֥ה עָמָ֖ל בְּיִשְׂרָאֵ֑ל יְהֹוָ֤ה אֱלֹהָיו֙ עִמּ֔וֹ וּתְרוּעַ֥ת מֶ֖לֶךְ בּֽוֹ׃ 22 אֵ֖ל מוֹצִיאָ֣ם מִמִּצְרָ֑יִם כְּתוֹעֲפֹ֥ת רְאֵ֖ם לֽוֹ׃ 23 כִּ֤י לֹא־נַ֙חַשׁ֙ בְּיַעֲקֹ֔ב וְלֹא־קֶ֖סֶם בְּיִשְׂרָאֵ֑ל כָּעֵ֗ת יֵאָמֵ֤ר

Indeed, around the year 4976 (1216) we find a number of sages among the Jewish people who were known for their prophetic insight: Rabbi Samuel b. Kalonymus *ha-Navi* ("The Prophet") or *he-Ḥasid* ("The Pious") of Speyer (12th century); his son Rabbi Judah b. Samuel *he-Ḥasid* ("The Pious") of Regensburg (12th–13th century); Rabbi Eleazar b. Judah of Worms, author of *Sefer ha-Rokeah* (12th–13th century); Naḥmanides (13th century); Rabbi Abraham b. David of Posquières (12th century); and the Tosafist, Rabbi Ezra *ha-Navi* ("The Prophet") of Montcontour (12th–13th century).

spiritual vitamin

> Your happiness is largely up to you, regardless of your circumstances. There are people who, considering their external circumstances, should be happy and content, yet they are not. Then there are those whose external circumstances are just the opposite, yet they are at peace with themselves, are cheerful, and are strong in their confidence that the external circumstances will also change for the good very soon.

numbers 23:12–23   balak

¹² "Am I not careful to say only that which God puts into my mouth?" he replied.

Balaam's Second Parable

[FIFTH READING] ¹³ Balak said to him, "Come with me to another place from where you will see them. (Since you are not able to curse them all, I'll place you where) you will only see a part of them, but not all of them. Curse (at least part of) them for me from there."

¹⁴ He took him to the lookouts' field, to the top of the summit. He built seven altars and offered up a bull and a ram on each altar. ¹⁵ (Balaam) said to Balak, "Stand here next to your burnt-offering, and (God) might happen to appear to me here."

¹⁶ God happened to appear to Balaam. He placed something into his mouth (to coerce it to speak positively about Israel to Balak). He said, "Return to Balak, and say the following…."

¹⁷ When (Balaam) came to (Balak), he was standing next to his burnt-offering. The Moabite dignitaries were with him.

"What did God say?" Balak said to him.

¹⁸ (Balaam) launched into his parable and said:

Get up Balak (onto your feet), and hear (God's words)! Listen closely to me, son of Zippor!

¹⁹ God is not a man that He should lie, nor is He a mortal that will change His mind. Would He say and not do? Speak and not fulfil?

²⁰ I have received (instructions) to bless; He has blessed, and I will not retract it.

²¹ He observed no evil (idolators) among Jacob, and has seen no transgression in Israel. (Even when Jacob rebels), God, his God, is with him; he has the King's affection.

²² God takes them out of Egypt, with His towering strength.

²³ For there is no divination in Jacob, and no sorcery in Israel.

In that (future) time (the angels) will say to Jacob and Israel, "What has God done?" (For Israel will be closer to God than the angels.)

---

upright." To the upright, death does not signify the end, but the beginning of life in the world to come. But in order to die the death of the upright, you have to *live* the life of the upright (*Rabbi Israel Meir Kagan, 19ᵗʰ–20ᵗʰ century*).

23. In that (future) time (the angels) will say. The words *"In that time,"* are a hint that when the world reaches twice its age at the time when Balaam said his parable (2488 years from Creation), then prophecy will return to the Jewish people. There is no doubt that this is a prelude to the Messiah (*Maimonides, 12ᵗʰ century*).

במדבר כג:כד - כד:ב בלק

לְיַעֲקֹב וּלְיִשְׂרָאֵל מַה־פָּעַל אֵל: 24 הֶן־עָם כְּלָבִיא יָקוּם וְכַאֲרִי יִתְנַשָּׂא לֹא יִשְׁכַּב עַד־יֹאכַל טֶרֶף וְדַם־חֲלָלִים יִשְׁתֶּה: 25 וַיֹּאמֶר בָּלָק אֶל־בִּלְעָם גַּם־קֹב לֹא תִקֳּבֶנּוּ גַּם־בָּרֵךְ לֹא תְבָרֲכֶנּוּ: 26 וַיַּעַן בִּלְעָם וַיֹּאמֶר אֶל־בָּלָק הֲלֹא דִּבַּרְתִּי אֵלֶיךָ לֵאמֹר כֹּל אֲשֶׁר־יְדַבֵּר יְהֹוָה אֹתוֹ אֶעֱשֶׂה: 27 [SIXTH READING / SEVENTH WHEN JOINED] וַיֹּאמֶר בָּלָק אֶל־בִּלְעָם לְכָה־נָּא אֶקָּחֲךָ אֶל־מָקוֹם אַחֵר אוּלַי יִישַׁר בְּעֵינֵי הָאֱלֹהִים וְקַבֹּתוֹ לִי מִשָּׁם: 28 וַיִּקַּח בָּלָק אֶת־בִּלְעָם רֹאשׁ הַפְּעוֹר הַנִּשְׁקָף עַל־פְּנֵי הַיְשִׁימֹן: 29 וַיֹּאמֶר בִּלְעָם אֶל־בָּלָק בְּנֵה־לִי בָזֶה שִׁבְעָה מִזְבְּחֹת וְהָכֵן לִי בָּזֶה שִׁבְעָה פָרִים וְשִׁבְעָה אֵילִם: 30 וַיַּעַשׂ בָּלָק כַּאֲשֶׁר אָמַר בִּלְעָם וַיַּעַל פָּר וָאַיִל בַּמִּזְבֵּחַ:

כד 1 וַיַּרְא בִּלְעָם כִּי טוֹב בְּעֵינֵי יְהֹוָה לְבָרֵךְ אֶת־יִשְׂרָאֵל וְלֹא־הָלַךְ כְּפַעַם־בְּפַעַם לִקְרַאת נְחָשִׁים וַיָּשֶׁת אֶל־הַמִּדְבָּר פָּנָיו: 2 וַיִּשָּׂא בִלְעָם אֶת־עֵינָיו וַיַּרְא אֶת־יִשְׂרָאֵל שֹׁכֵן לִשְׁבָטָיו וַתְּהִי עָלָיו רוּחַ אֱלֹהִים:

Also, while most warriors lose their strength as they age, the lion retains its strength. In the same way, says Balaam, the children of Israel will continue to fight off their adversaries without displaying signs of aging and weakening (*Rabbi Ḥayyim ibn Attar, 18th century*).

29. Build me seven altars here. Always busy yourself with Torah and its commandments, even if you have ulterior motives, because eventually you will do so for the sake of heaven.

What is the basis of this principle? King Balak of Moab offered forty-two sacrifices—he set up seven altars in each of three places (23:1, 23:14 and 23:29), and on each altar he offered a bull and a ram. Surely he did not bring these sacrifices for the sake of heaven, but to entice God to allow Balaam to curse Israel! Nevertheless, he merited that Ruth should be his descendant, and Ruth was the ancestor of Solomon, of whom it says *"Solomon offered up a thousand burnt-offerings on that altar"* (*I Kings* 3:4; *Babylonian Talmud, Sotah* 47a).

24:2 Settled (modestly) according to its tribes. He saw that their tent openings were not facing one another, so that they could not peek into each other's tents. Admiring their modesty and decency, Balaam declared, "People such as these deserve to have the Divine Presence rest upon them" (*Rashi, 11th century; Babylonian Talmud, Bava Batra* 60a).

Food for thought

1. Balaam was awed by the Jews' modesty. Why is modesty impressive?

2. How can we cultivate the inner strength that modesty requires?

3. When were you last impressed by someone's modesty?

²⁴ Look! A people that rises like an awesome lion, and raises itself like a lion. It does not lie down until it eats its prey, and drinks the blood of the slain.

²⁵ Balak said to Balaam, "If you're not going to curse them, (at least) don't bless them!"

²⁶ "Didn't I tell you," Balaam replied to Balak, "I will only do whatever God says."

Balaam's Third Parable

[SIXTH READING / SEVENTH WHEN JOINED] ²⁷ Balak said to Balaam, "Come now, I'll take you to a different place. Perhaps it will be right in God's eyes, and you will condemn them for me from there." ²⁸ Balak took Balaam to the peak of Peor, overlooking the wastelands.

²⁹ Balaam said to Balak, "Build me seven altars here and prepare seven bulls and seven rams for me." ³⁰ Balak did what Balaam told him, and offered up a bull and a ram on each altar.

24 ¹ Balaam saw that blessing Israel was good in God's eyes, so he did not go to seek methods of divination (to communicate with God) as he had done the (previous) two times, (as God would surely tell him to bless Israel. Rather,) he focused on (the sins of the Jewish people, such as the Golden Calf in) the desert (hoping that this would discredit the Jews). ² Balaam raised his eyes (hoping to cast the evil eye on them), but when he saw Israel settled (modestly) according to its tribes, he changed his mind to be like God (desired, and did not curse them).

Unfortunately, this era of prophecy did not immediately lead to the Redemption. Nevertheless, years later Rabbi Israel Ba'al Shem Tov (18th century) and his successors openly demonstrated the prophetic spirit once again—and there is no doubt that *this* is a prelude to the Messiah (*Rabbi Menahem Mendel Schneerson, 20th century*).

24. A people that rises like an awesome lion, and raises itself like a lion. When they arise from their sleep in the morning they show the vigor of an awesome lion; and a (regular) lion in grasping commandments—to put on a *tallit* (prayer shawl), recite the *Shema* and put on *tefillin*.

And he *"does not lie down,"* on his bed at night until he consumes and destroys any harmful thing that comes to cause him damage. How is this? He recites the *Shema* on his bed and entrusts his soul to God. If an army or a troop were then to come and attempt to harm them, God protects him, fights his battles and slays the enemy (*Rashi, 11th century*).

Balaam compares the children of Israel to a lion in two ways: the way a young lion *"rises"* up at first and the way it continues to *"raise itself"* in maturity. When soldiers battle for the first time, they usually do not distinguish themselves for bravery, but the lion rises to display courage the first time he faces an enemy.

Balaam attributed this same quality to the children of Israel. Although their history had been one of slavery, the Israelites proved themselves immediately powerful and courageous, as they overcame the great nations of Sihon and Og.

בלק • במדבר כד:ג-י

3 וַיִּשָּׂ֥א מְשָׁל֖וֹ וַיֹּאמַ֑ר נְאֻ֤ם בִּלְעָם֙ בְּנ֣וֹ בְעֹ֔ר וּנְאֻ֥ם הַגֶּ֖בֶר שְׁתֻ֥ם הָעָֽיִן: 4 נְאֻ֕ם שֹׁמֵ֖עַ אִמְרֵי־אֵ֑ל אֲשֶׁ֨ר מַחֲזֵ֤ה שַׁדַּי֙ יֶֽחֱזֶ֔ה נֹפֵ֖ל וּגְל֥וּי עֵינָֽיִם: 5 מַה־טֹּ֥בוּ אֹהָלֶ֖יךָ יַעֲקֹ֑ב מִשְׁכְּנֹתֶ֖יךָ יִשְׂרָאֵֽל: 6 כִּנְחָלִ֣ים נִטָּ֔יוּ כְּגַנֹּ֖ת עֲלֵ֣י נָהָ֑ר כַּאֲהָלִים֙ נָטַ֣ע יְהֹוָ֔ה כַּאֲרָזִ֖ים עֲלֵי־מָֽיִם: 7 יִֽזַּל־מַ֙יִם֙ מִדָּ֣לְיָ֔ו וְזַרְע֖וֹ בְּמַ֣יִם רַבִּ֑ים וְיָרֹ֤ם מֵֽאֲגַג֙ מַלְכּ֔וֹ וְתִנַּשֵּׂ֖א מַלְכֻתֽוֹ: 8 אֵ֚ל מוֹצִיא֣וֹ מִמִּצְרַ֔יִם כְּתוֹעֲפֹ֥ת רְאֵ֖ם ל֑וֹ יֹאכַ֞ל גּוֹיִ֣ם צָרָ֗יו וְעַצְמֹתֵיהֶ֛ם יְגָרֵ֖ם וְחִצָּ֥יו יִמְחָֽץ: 9 כָּרַ֨ע שָׁכַ֤ב כַּאֲרִי֙ וּכְלָבִ֔יא מִ֖י יְקִימֶ֑נּוּ מְבָרֲכֶ֣יךָ בָר֔וּךְ וְאֹרְרֶ֖יךָ אָרֽוּר: 10 וַיִּֽחַר־אַ֤ף בָּלָק֙ אֶל־בִּלְעָ֔ם וַיִּסְפֹּ֖ק אֶת־כַּפָּ֑יו וַיֹּ֨אמֶר בָּלָ֜ק אֶל־בִּלְעָ֗ם לָקֹ֤ב אֹֽיְבַי֙ קְרָאתִ֔יךָ וְהִנֵּה֙ בֵּרַ֣כְתָּ בָרֵ֔ךְ זֶ֖ה שָׁלֹ֥שׁ פְּעָמִֽים:

souls! But if their intentions are for the sake of heaven, then they are certainly deserving that the Divine Presence should rest with them (*Rabbi Dov Baer of Mezhirech, 18th century*).

Balaam refers to two different types of Israelites in this verse. There are those who study Torah sporadically, those in the *"tents of Jacob,"* the temporary structures. Then there are those who make the Torah the foundation of their daily lives. When Balaam referred to this second group of Israelites, he spoke of *"dwellings,"* of permanent homes (*Rabbi Ḥayyim ibn Attar, 18th century*).

6. They spread out like streams, like gardens by the river, like spices which God planted (in Eden), like cedars by the water. Balaam hinted at four different types of righteous people among the children of Israel.

One type, suggested by the words, *"they spread out like streams,"* are like the prophet Samuel, who would journey across the land of Israel teaching Torah. Like streams, they spread out and make it possible for others to enjoy the knowledge of Torah.

Another type of righteous individual is *"like gardens by the river,"* planted firmly in place. These people sit teaching and judging cases. They differ from the first group in the sense that, although anyone can study from them, those who are interested have to put in effort in order to come and seek what is offered.

"Like spices which God planted," refers to those who study Torah seriously, but do not have the talents to teach others. Like plants that grow stronger the longer they remain in the ground, these people become more involved with the Torah and its spirit the longer they study.

Finally, *"like cedars by the water,"* refers to men of means, who support Torah study financially. The tall and majestic cedar tree hints at the respect enjoyed by these men of great stature. Although they do not study Torah much themselves, they, too, draw their strength from the *"water,"* that is to say, Torah (*Babylonian Talmud, Ta'anit* 7a), because they are equal partners in its study (*Rabbi Ḥayyim ibn Attar, 18th century*).

9. He will crouch ... like a lion. The "crouching lion" is a metaphor for the might of the Jewish people lying dormant during the time of exile (*Genesis Rabbah*). But a lion can never be fully tamed, for it is one of the five types of wild animals which are predisposed to cause damage by their very nature, even if they have been tamed. Therefore if one of them causes damage the owner is liable to pay full compensation (*Code of Jewish Law*).

numbers 24:3–10 — balak

³ He launched into his parable and said:

The word of Balaam son of Beor, the word of a man with an open eye. ⁴ The word of the one who hears God's sayings, who sees God's vision lying down, yet with open eyes.

⁵ Your tents are so good, O Jacob! Your dwellings, O Israel!

⁶ They spread out like streams, like gardens by the river, like spices which God planted (in Eden), like cedars by the water.

⁷ Water will flow from his wells, and his seed will have much water.

His king will prevail over Agag, his sovereignty will be uplifted.

⁸ God who brought them out of Egypt with His towering strength, will consume the nations, his enemies, break their bones and dip His arrows (in their blood).

⁹ He will crouch and lie down (in his land) like a lion, an awesome lion; who will dare rouse him?

Those who bless you will be blessed, and those who curse you will be cursed.

¹⁰ Balak became furious at Balaam, and clapped his hands (together). Balak said to Balaam, "I called you to curse my enemies, and you've just now blessed them

5. Your tents are so good, O Jacob! Your dwellings, O Israel! He said this because he saw that the entrances were not opposite each other. *"Your dwellings"* thus refers to "your encampments," as *Targum Onkelos* states.

Another explanation: *"Your Tents are so good"*—The Tabernacle at Shiloh and the eternal Temple are so good when they are inhabited, for sacrifices are offered in them to atone for you.

"Your dwellings" (*mishkenoteykha*)—Even when they are desolate, for they are held as collateral security (*mashkon*) for you, and their destruction atones for your souls, as the verse states, *"God has exhausted His fury"* (*Lamentations* 4:11). And how did He exhaust it? *"He has kindled a fire in Zion"* (ibid.; *Rashi, 11th century*).

Rashi writes that Balaam was inspired by the Jewish tents, "Because he saw that the entrances were not opposite each other." The "arrangement of tents" alludes to scholars convening together to discuss matters of Torah, each one offering his own interpretations. If their "entrances"—meaning their mouths—are "opposite each other," i.e., their intentions are to show that their ideas are superior to those of the others, then woe to them and their

spiritual vitamin

> You might sometimes think that your accomplishments are small, but you are not really in a position to fully estimate your accomplishments and what fruits might come forth from the tiny seeds that you plant.

בלק | במדבר כד:יא-יח

11 וְעַתָּ֖ה בְּרַח־לְךָ֣ אֶל־מְקוֹמֶ֑ךָ אָמַ֙רְתִּי֙ כַּבֵּ֣ד אֲכַבֶּדְךָ֔ וְהִנֵּ֛ה מְנָעֲךָ֥ יְהֹוָ֖ה מִכָּבֽוֹד:
12 וַיֹּ֥אמֶר בִּלְעָ֖ם אֶל־בָּלָ֑ק הֲלֹ֗א גַּ֧ם אֶל־מַלְאָכֶ֛יךָ אֲשֶׁר־שָׁלַ֥חְתָּ אֵלַ֖י דִּבַּ֥רְתִּי לֵאמֹֽר:
13 אִם־יִתֶּן־לִ֨י בָלָ֜ק מְלֹ֣א בֵיתוֹ֮ כֶּ֣סֶף וְזָהָב֒ לֹ֣א אוּכַ֗ל לַֽעֲבֹר֙ אֶת־פִּ֣י יְהֹוָ֔ה לַעֲשׂ֥וֹת טוֹבָ֛ה א֥וֹ רָעָ֖ה מִלִּבִּ֑י אֲשֶׁר־יְדַבֵּ֥ר יְהֹוָ֖ה אֹת֥וֹ אֲדַבֵּֽר:
14 [SEVENTH READING] וְעַתָּ֕ה הִנְנִ֥י הוֹלֵ֖ךְ לְעַמִּ֑י לְכָה֙ אִיעָ֣צְךָ֔ אֲשֶׁ֨ר יַעֲשֶׂ֜ה הָעָ֥ם הַזֶּ֛ה לְעַמְּךָ֖ בְּאַחֲרִ֥ית הַיָּמִֽים:
15 וַיִּשָּׂ֥א מְשָׁל֖וֹ וַיֹּאמַ֑ר נְאֻ֤ם בִּלְעָם֙ בְּנ֣וֹ בְעֹ֔ר וּנְאֻ֥ם הַגֶּ֖בֶר שְׁתֻ֥ם הָעָֽיִן:
16 נְאֻ֗ם שֹׁמֵ֙עַ֙ אִמְרֵי־אֵ֔ל וְיֹדֵ֖עַ דַּ֣עַת עֶלְי֑וֹן מַחֲזֵ֤ה שַׁדַּי֙ יֶֽחֱזֶ֔ה נֹפֵ֖ל וּגְל֥וּי עֵינָֽיִם:
17 אֶרְאֶ֙נּוּ֙ וְלֹ֣א עַתָּ֔ה אֲשׁוּרֶ֖נּוּ וְלֹ֣א קָר֑וֹב דָּרַ֨ךְ כּוֹכָ֜ב מִֽיַּעֲקֹ֗ב וְקָ֥ם שֵׁ֙בֶט֙ מִיִּשְׂרָאֵ֔ל וּמָחַץ֙ פַּאֲתֵ֣י מוֹאָ֔ב וְקַרְקַ֖ר כָּל־בְּנֵי־שֵֽׁת:
18 וְהָיָ֨ה אֱד֜וֹם יְרֵשָׁ֗ה וְהָיָ֧ה יְרֵשָׁ֛ה שֵׂעִ֖יר

act instant when God becomes enraged, and he intended to curse the children of Israel precisely at that moment (*Rashi, 11th century*).

Had Balaam done so, the curse would have been very effective. It is a testament to God's great benevolence that He did not "become enraged" all those days when the wicked Balaam was seeking to curse the Israelites (*Babylonian Talmud, Sanhedrin 105b*).

17-18. A star will shoot forth from Jacob. In the Torah passage of Balaam, he prophesies about two Messiahs—the first Messiah, David, who saved Israel from her oppressors; and the final Messiah, who will arise from his descendants and ultimately save Israel.

There it is written, *"I see him, but not now"*—this refers to David;

"I perceive him, but he is not near" (verses 17-18)—this refers to the King Messiah;

"A star will shoot forth from Jacob"—this refers to David;

"And a staff will arise from Israel"—this refers to the King Messiah;

"He will crush the princes of Moab"—this refers to David, as the verse states, *"He smote Moab and measured them with a line"* (*II Samuel 8:2*);

> **kabbalah bites**
>
> **24:17 Who is the Messiah?**
>
> It's you.
>
> At least that was the conclusion reached by Rabbi Menahem Nahum of Chernobyl (1730-97) in his work *The Light of the Eyes*. Of course Judaism always maintained that there will be a particular Messiah, a man descended from King David who would bring about the political restoration of Biblical Israel. What Rabbi Menahem Nahum added to this idea is that the global change in consciousness necessary to make this possible depends not only upon the Messiah himself but on the individual too. Each one of us, he argued, contains a spark of the Messiah (what the Torah refers to here as a "star"), an inner sanctum of the very purest spirituality which it is our task to "locate" and make an active part of our lives.

three times! ¹¹ Run off home right now! I said I was going to give you tremendous honor, but God has just deprived you of honor."

¹² Balaam said to Balak, "Didn't I even speak to the messengers you sent me, saying, ¹³ 'If Balak gives me his house full of silver and gold, I cannot transgress the word of God to do either good or evil on my own (and) I will (only) say what God says'?"

Balaam Foretells the End of Days

[SEVENTH READING] ¹⁴ "I'm going back to my people now," (said Balaam). "Come, I will advise you (how to bring about Israel's downfall: Just tempt them to immorality with Moabite women....). (Now I will tell you) what this people will do to your people at the end of days." ¹⁵ He launched into his parable and said:

The word of Balaam son of Beor, the word of a man with an open eye. ¹⁶ The word of the one who hears God's sayings, and knows the thoughts of the Supernal One, who sees God's vision lying down, yet with open eyes.

¹⁷ I see him, but not now. I perceive him, but he is not near.

A star will shoot forth from Jacob, and a staff will arise from Israel. He will crush the princes of Moab, he will devastate all the descendants of Seth. ¹⁸ Edom will be possessed, Seir, his enemy, will be possessed, and Israel will grow strong.

Likewise, while the might of the Jewish people may appear to be dormant during the Exile, they nevertheless remain strong like a crouched lion. This takes expression in the power of a Jew to remain loyal to the Torah and its commandments despite all obstacles, for the soul is impervious to the Exile, and grants a Jew the strength to rise above it (*Rabbi Menahem Mendel Schneerson, 20th century*).

Food for thought

1. How close are we to the End of Days?

2. Why is belief in the Messiah so central to Judaism?

3. After frustrated Messianic hope, how can we put our faith in the real Messiah?

13. I cannot transgress the word of God. The forces of evil themselves are not invested in a body that conceals God, *so they are aware of their Master* and do not rebel against Him by performing any rebellious act which is not ordered by the Almighty, God forbid. Representing the forces of evil, Balaam said, *"I cannot transgress the word of God"* (v. 13)—they are unable to transgress the Divine will at all, since they are aware that He is their life-force and sustenance.

It is only because their nourishment and life-force is in "exile" within them that they see themselves as having independent power and deny God's Oneness. But they do not deny God completely, recognizing that their life-force and sustenance is passed down to them from God's will.

Thus, a person who transgresses God's will is very much worse and inferior to the forces of evil, because he denies God completely, whereas they do not (*Rabbi Shneur Zalman of Lyady, 18th century*).

16. The word of the one who ... knows the thoughts of the Supernal One. Balaam was certainly unable to fathom the workings of God's mind. Rather, this means that Balaam knew how to determine the ex-

בלק
במדבר כד:יח – כה:ו

אֹיְבָ֔יו וְיִשְׂרָאֵ֖ל עֹ֥שֶׂה חָֽיִל: 19 וְיֵ֖רְדְּ מִֽיַּעֲקֹ֑ב וְהֶֽאֱבִ֥יד שָׂרִ֖יד מֵעִֽיר: 20 וַיַּרְא֙ אֶת־עֲמָלֵ֔ק וַיִּשָּׂ֥א מְשָׁל֖וֹ וַיֹּאמַ֑ר רֵאשִׁ֤ית גּוֹיִם֙ עֲמָלֵ֔ק וְאַחֲרִית֖וֹ עֲדֵ֥י אֹבֵֽד: 21 וַיַּרְא֙ אֶת־הַקֵּינִ֔י וַיִּשָּׂ֥א מְשָׁל֖וֹ וַיֹּאמַ֑ר אֵיתָן֙ מֽוֹשָׁבֶ֔ךָ וְשִׂ֥ים בַּסֶּ֖לַע קִנֶּֽךָ: 22 כִּ֥י אִם־יִהְיֶ֖ה לְבָ֣עֵֽר קָ֑יִן עַד־מָ֖ה אַשּׁ֥וּר תִּשְׁבֶּֽךָּ: 23 וַיִּשָּׂ֥א מְשָׁל֖וֹ וַיֹּאמַ֑ר א֕וֹי מִ֥י יִחְיֶ֖ה מִשֻּׂמ֥וֹ אֵֽל: 24 וְצִים֙ מִיַּ֣ד כִּתִּ֔ים וְעִנּ֥וּ אַשּׁ֖וּר וְעִנּוּ־עֵ֑בֶר וְגַם־ה֖וּא עֲדֵ֥י אֹבֵֽד: 25 וַיָּ֣קָם בִּלְעָ֔ם וַיֵּ֖לֶךְ וַיָּ֣שָׁב לִמְקֹמ֑וֹ וְגַם־בָּלָ֖ק הָלַ֥ךְ לְדַרְכּֽוֹ: פ

כה 1 וַיֵּ֥שֶׁב יִשְׂרָאֵ֖ל בַּשִּׁטִּ֑ים וַיָּ֤חֶל הָעָם֙ לִזְנ֔וֹת אֶל־בְּנ֖וֹת מוֹאָֽב: 2 וַתִּקְרֶ֣אןָ לָעָ֔ם לְזִבְחֵ֖י אֱלֹֽהֵיהֶ֑ן וַיֹּ֣אכַל הָעָ֔ם וַיִּֽשְׁתַּחֲו֖וּ לֵאלֹֽהֵיהֶֽן: 3 וַיִּצָּ֥מֶד יִשְׂרָאֵ֖ל לְבַ֣עַל פְּע֑וֹר וַיִּֽחַר־אַ֥ף יְהוָ֖ה בְּיִשְׂרָאֵֽל: 4 וַיֹּ֨אמֶר יְהוָ֜ה אֶל־מֹשֶׁ֗ה קַ֚ח אֶת־כָּל־רָאשֵׁ֣י הָעָ֔ם וְהוֹקַ֥ע אוֹתָ֛ם לַיהוָ֖ה נֶ֣גֶד הַשָּׁ֑מֶשׁ וְיָשֹׁ֛ב חֲר֥וֹן אַף־יְהוָ֖ה מִיִּשְׂרָאֵֽל: 5 וַיֹּ֣אמֶר מֹשֶׁ֔ה אֶל־שֹׁפְטֵ֖י יִשְׂרָאֵ֑ל הִרְגוּ֙ אִ֣ישׁ אֲנָשָׁ֔יו הַנִּצְמָדִ֖ים לְבַ֥עַל פְּעֽוֹר: 6 וְהִנֵּ֡ה אִישׁ֩ מִבְּנֵ֨י יִשְׂרָאֵ֜ל בָּ֗א וַיַּקְרֵ֤ב אֶל־אֶחָיו֙ אֶת־

only appointed due to the threat of the Jewish people, and being that Balaam had shown that the Jewish people were peace-loving, Balak's leadership had proven itself unnecessary (*Rabbi Ḥayyim ibn Attar, 18th century*).

25:3 Became attached to the deity Baal-peor. Peor was so named because its worshipers would bare (*po'arin*) their anuses before it and defecate. That was the way they worshiped this idol (*Rashi, 11th century*).

The idol "Baal-peor" was worshiped in an extremely crude fashion, by depositing the body's waste matter before it. Its worshipers made the unimportant, important.

Ḥasidic thought teaches that the angels too have "waste matter." Just like the digestive system gradually sifts out the nutritious elements of the food, eventually leaving nothing but waste, the angels "sift out" the most lofty and pleasurable Divine emanations, which they transfer to the Garden of Eden (Paradise), and allow the "wastage" to fall to earth. The spiritual wastage is the source of all physical pleasures found in this world.

The pursuit of physical pleasures (spiritual "wastage") is thus a subtle form of "Baal-peor." For it is fitting for man, who is made in God's image, to focus primarily on filling his life with more lofty spiritual pleasures (*Rabbi Shneur Zalman of Lyady, 18th century*).

¹⁹ A ruler will come from Jacob, and destroy the remnant of a city.

²⁰ When he saw (the future retribution of) Amalek, he launched into his parable and said: Amalek was the first of the nations (to fight Israel), his end is eternal destruction.

²¹ When he saw (what would happen to) the Kenites, he launched into his parable and said: How firm is your dwelling place! Your nest is set in stone. ²² For even if the Kenite is laid waste (and exiled), how far will Assyria take you captive?

²³ (Pondering the Assyrian Exile), he launched into his parable and said: Oh! Who can survive (God) placing these (things on him)? ²⁴ Ships will come from the Kittites; they will afflict Assyria and afflict the other side (of the river), but he too will perish forever.

²⁵ Balaam got moving. He went off and returned to his home, and Balak also went on his way.

Zealotry of Phinehas Stops the Plague

25 ¹ The Jewish people settled in Shittim, and (as a result of Balaam's plot) the people began to be immoral with Moabite girls. ² (The Moabites) invited the (Jewish) people to feasts (that they made) to their gods, and the (Jewish) people ate and prostrated themselves to (the Moabite) gods. ³ Israel (thus) became attached to (the deity) Baal-peor.

God became furious with Israel (and sent a plague upon them).

⁴ God said to Moses, "Take all the leaders of the people (to judge those who worshiped idols) and hang them before God, in view of the sun (so everyone can see). Then God's fury will withdraw from Israel.

⁵ Moses said to the (eighty-eight thousand six hundred) judges of Israel, "Each of you should kill (two) men who became attached to Baal-peor."

⁶ Then, an Israelite man came and brought (an important) Midianite woman to his brothers (and took her into a tent) in full view of Moses and in full view of the entire congregation of the children of Israel.

"He will devastate all of the descendants of Seth"—this refers to the King Messiah, about whom it is written, *"He will rule from sea to sea"* (Zechariah 9:10);

"Edom will be possessed"—this refers to David, as the verse states, *"Edom became the servants of David, etc."* (II Samuel 8:6; ibid.,14);

"Seir ... will be possessed"—this refers to the Messiah, as the verse states, *"Saviors will ascend Mount Zion to judge Mount Esau"* (Obadiah 1:21; Maimonides, 12ᵗʰ century).

25. Balak also went on his way. Balak did not escort Balaam home. Perhaps the Torah is also suggesting here that Balak ceased to be the king of Moab and "went on his way." For Balak was

בלק · במדבר כה:ו-ט

הַמִּדְיָנִית לְעֵינֵי מֹשֶׁה וּלְעֵינֵי כָּל־עֲדַת בְּנֵי־יִשְׂרָאֵל וְהֵמָּה בֹכִים פֶּתַח אֹהֶל מוֹעֵד: [MAFTIR] 7 וַיַּרְא פִּינְחָס בֶּן־אֶלְעָזָר בֶּן־אַהֲרֹן הַכֹּהֵן וַיָּקָם מִתּוֹךְ הָעֵדָה וַיִּקַּח רֹמַח בְּיָדוֹ: 8 וַיָּבֹא אַחַר אִישׁ־יִשְׂרָאֵל אֶל־הַקֻּבָּה וַיִּדְקֹר אֶת־שְׁנֵיהֶם אֵת אִישׁ יִשְׂרָאֵל וְאֶת־הָאִשָּׁה אֶל־קֳבָתָהּ וַתֵּעָצַר הַמַּגֵּפָה מֵעַל בְּנֵי יִשְׂרָאֵל: 9 וַיִּהְיוּ הַמֵּתִים בַּמַּגֵּפָה אַרְבָּעָה וְעֶשְׂרִים אָלֶף: פ פ פ

ק"ד פסוקים, מנו"ח סימן.

At that moment, Moses forgot the law and all the people burst into tears. With the Golden Calf, Moses had stood up against six hundred thousand people, yet here he seemed helpless! But all this was orchestrated so that Phinehas could come and take the reward that he deserved (*Babylonian Talmud, Sanhedrin* 82a).

In fact, there was an important distinction between the two cases. Moses married Jethro's daughter before the Torah was given, when the children of Israel were permitted to intermarry with non-Israelites. Zimri's actions, on the other hand, took place after receiving the Torah, which forbade such relationships (*Rashi, 11th century*).

7. But Phinehas son of Eleazar saw ... (what happened and remembered the law). After Phinehas saw what was happening and *"remembered the law,"* he consulted with Moses (see *Rashi*). Before we do something, even if it is correct and according to the law, we must first turn to a higher authority for guidance (*Rabbi Isaac Meir Alter of Gur, 19th century*).

(Moses was indecisive because he could not recall what the law was in this case) and they were weeping at the entrance of the Tent of Meeting.

[MAFTIR] ⁷ But Phinehas son of Eleazar son of Aaron the priest saw (what had happened, and remembered the law). He stood up from among the congregation and, taking a spear in his hand, ⁸ he went into the tent after the Israelite man and pierced (the spear through) both of them—the Israelite man, and the woman—right through her (lower) abdomen. The plague then ceased from the children of Israel.

⁹ A total of twenty-four thousand died in the plague.

The Haftarah for Balak (and Ḥukkat–Balak) is on page 1384.

6. They were weeping. Zimri said to Moses, "Is this Midianite woman forbidden or permitted? And if you say she is forbidden, who permitted you to marry Jethro's daughter, Zipporah, when Jethro was a Midianite?"

kabbalah bites

25:7 Phinehas' zealous act against Zimri coincided with his receiving additional soul powers: he was impregnated with the souls of Nadab and Abihu. Later Phinehas himself would be reincarnated as Elijah the prophet.

> Phinehas sets an example for all of us: **whenever it is possible** to further the moral or **spiritual standing** of other people, **do not stand back** and ponder, "Surely there are greater people than myself for this task?" **Rise to the occasion** without hesitation!

PINḤAS
פינחס

PHINEHAS AWARDED THE PRIESTHOOD	25:10–18
MOSES' LAST CENSUS	26:1–65
ZELOPHEHAD'S DAUGHTERS	27:1–11
JOSHUA APPOINTED AS MOSES' SUCCESSOR	27:12–23
COMMUNAL OFFERINGS	28:1 – 30:1

NAME
Pinḥas

MEANING
"Lantern"

LINES IN TORAH SCROLL
280

PARASHIYYOT
10 open; 25 closed

VERSES
168

WORDS
1887

LETTERS
7853

DATE
2488

LOCATION
Plains of Moab

KEY PEOPLE
Moses, Phinehas, Eleazar, Zelophehad's daughters, Joshua, Levites

MITZVOT
6 positive

MASORETIC FEATURES
Vav of Shalom (25:12) is split into two letters: a yod above and a small vav below

NOTE
Read during or immediately before the three weeks of mourning for the Temple

CHARACTER PROFILE

NAME
Phinehas (Pinḥas)

FATHER
Eleazar

GRANDFATHERS
Aaron and Jethro

ACHIEVEMENTS
One of the second set of spies sent by Moses; one of the spies sent by Joshua; captured Balaam during war with Midian; headed a delegation of tribal leaders that settled a dispute between the tribes

KNOWN FOR
Slaying Zimri the tribal leader of Simeon; completed writing the Book of Joshua

REPENTANCE

Korah's sons, although swallowed up by the ground, did not die. They repented completely and later rejoined the Jewish people. Repentance has the power to achieve a complete personal transformation (26:11).

BIAS

After Zelophehad's daughters declared that their father was not one of Korah's supporters, Moses declined to judge their case. The knowledge that Zelophehad had supported his cause may have stopped him from judging without bias (27:1-6).

DAILY DOSE

The daily sacrifices—nowadays replaced by prayer—are a constant reminder of God and our connection to Him (28:3-8).

פינחס / במדבר כה:י-טו

10 וַיְדַבֵּ֥ר יְהֹוָ֖ה אֶל־מֹשֶׁ֥ה לֵּאמֹֽר: 11 פִּֽינְחָ֨ס בֶּן־אֶלְעָזָ֜ר בֶּן־אַהֲרֹ֣ן הַכֹּהֵ֗ן הֵשִׁ֤יב אֶת־חֲמָתִי֙ מֵעַ֣ל בְּנֵֽי־יִשְׂרָאֵ֔ל בְּקַנְא֥וֹ אֶת־קִנְאָתִ֖י בְּתוֹכָ֑ם וְלֹא־כִלִּ֥יתִי אֶת־בְּנֵֽי־יִשְׂרָאֵ֖ל בְּקִנְאָתִֽי: 12 לָכֵ֖ן אֱמֹ֑ר הִנְנִ֨י נֹתֵ֥ן ל֛וֹ אֶת־בְּרִיתִ֖י שָׁלֽוֹם: 13 וְהָ֤יְתָה לּוֹ֙ וּלְזַרְע֣וֹ אַחֲרָ֔יו בְּרִ֖ית כְּהֻנַּ֣ת עוֹלָ֑ם תַּ֗חַת אֲשֶׁ֤ר קִנֵּא֙ לֵֽאלֹהָ֔יו וַיְכַפֵּ֖ר עַל־בְּנֵ֥י יִשְׂרָאֵֽל: 14 וְשֵׁם֩ אִ֨ישׁ יִשְׂרָאֵ֜ל הַמֻּכֶּ֗ה אֲשֶׁ֤ר הֻכָּה֙ אֶת־הַמִּדְיָנִ֔ית זִמְרִ֖י בֶּן־סָל֑וּא נְשִׂ֥יא בֵֽית־אָ֖ב לַשִּׁמְעֹנִֽי: 15 וְשֵׁ֨ם הָֽאִשָּׁ֧ה הַמֻּכָּ֛ה הַמִּדְיָנִ֖ית כָּזְבִּ֣י בַת־צ֑וּר רֹ֣אשׁ אֻמּ֥וֹת בֵּֽית־אָ֖ב

the person who "showed off" with his worship was at least open about his pride and did not attempt to conceal it. The critic, on the other hand, cannot tolerate the truth that he is proud, and he stoops to dishonesty, veiling his pride in a "cloak" of humility and righteous indignation.

The lesson is obvious: It is much wiser to be an activist than a critic. A little pride can make criticism destructive, rather than constructive; but a good deed always remains good, regardless of the intention (*Rabbi Menahem Mendel Schneerson, 20th century*).

Zealously avenging Me in their presence. Phinehas' zealous act caused God's anger to subside because it was performed *"in their presence"*—in public. The people were not guilty of immorality or idol-worship, but they were culpable for witnessing these grave transgressions *"in full view of the entire congregation"* (v. 6), and failing to intervene. Phinehas atoned for this by avenging God's honor in sight of everyone (*Rabbi Obadiah Sforno, 16th century*).

13. Because he was zealous for his God. Often when committing a sin, people excuse themselves by accusing others of the same misdeeds. That is why when God spoke at Mount Sinai, He addressed the children of Israel in the singular (*"I am God, (the) God (of every one) of you"—Exodus 20:2*), indicating that somebody else's behavior is of no relevance.

Phinehas could have pointed out that Moses, Eleazar, and the elders had witnessed Zimri's indiscretion and had taken no action. Instead, Phinehas took the initiative in defending God's honor. That is why the Torah states, "because he was zealous for *his* God"—Phinehas conducted himself as if he *alone* was responsible for God's honor. He did not excuse himself by looking at how others had acted (*Rabbi Menahem Eisenstadter, 19th century*).

15. Cozbi the daughter of Zur, a national leader of a paternal house in Midian. Balaam said to Balak, "The God of these people hates immorality. If you make your daughters available to Israel for immoral purposes, you will be able to rule over them, because their God will be angry with them."

> **kabbalah bites**
>
> **25:10** *"Whoever becomes angry is as if he worships idols"* (Zohar I, 27b). When you become angry, you have lost your faith. If you really believed that what happened to you was God's doing, you would not have become angry at all.
>
> In fact, it is not only "as if" you worshiped idols, but in a higher realm, you actually did.
>
> Rabbi Isaac Luria taught that when you become angry your soul actually departs from your body and is replaced by a substitute, "external soul."

parashat pinḥas

Phinehas is Awarded the Priesthood

¹⁰ God spoke to Moses, saying: ¹¹ "Phinehas son of Eleazar son of Aaron the priest has turned My anger away from the children of Israel by zealously avenging Me in their presence, and I did not destroy the children of Israel because of My zealous anger. ¹² Therefore, say (to him): I am hereby giving him My covenant of peace. ¹³ It will be an eternal covenant of priesthood for him, and for his descendants after him, because he was zealous for his God and atoned for the children of Israel."

¹⁴ The name of the Israelite man that was killed, who was killed along with the Midianite woman, was Zimri son of Salu, the leader of Simeon's paternal house.

¹⁵ The name of the Midianite woman who was killed was Cozbi the daughter of Zur, a national leader of a paternal house in Midian.

25:11 Phinehas son of Eleazar son of Aaron the priest. One usually would associate an act of zealotry with someone who has a fiery, irritable nature. The Torah informs us that this was not the case with Phinehas—he shared the calm, peace-loving nature of his grandfather, Aaron. His act of zealotry was not motivated by his natural tendencies; it was purely a matter of defending God's honor.

It is not enough to fulfil only those commandments to which you are naturally inclined. You must be prepared to go beyond or even against your natural predisposition to do God's will (*Rabbi Tzevi Elimelech of Dynow, 19th century*).

The tribes ridiculed him, saying, "Have you seen the descendant of Puti (Jethro—see *Rashi* to *Exodus* 6:25), whose mother's father fattened calves for idol-worship, and yet he killed a leader of one of the tribes of Israel?" Therefore, Scripture traces his lineage to Aaron (*Rashi, 11th century*).

From where does the desire come to find fault in people who are doing something good? In this case, the tribes appeared to have holy intentions: They were concerned that Phinehas had slighted the honor of Moses by taking the law into his own hands.

Often, a man will find that he has a low tolerance for other people's bad motives. Perhaps it's because he is humble, and he finds the pride of others distasteful?

Probably, the opposite is true—the *critic himself* is proud. *He doesn't like the idea that somebody else accomplished something that he didn't.*

Of course, he will not admit this, even to himself, because his pride is a "ticket" to laziness, and recognizing somebody else's achievements makes it more uncomfortable to remain lazy. So, instead, his arrogance spurs him to put down the other person's good deeds, so that they don't wound his pride or inspire him to be a better person—which would, of course, require some effort.

Even if it's true that somebody's worship does have overtones of haughtiness, *the critic's pride is even more distasteful.* For, ultimately,

---

Food for thought

1. May citizens ever take the law into their own hands?

2. Are you able to take bold action when required?

3. When is anger appropriate and when should it be restrained?

במדבר כה:טו – כו:ח | פינחס

בְּמִדְיָ֖ן הֽוּא׃ פ 16 וַיְדַבֵּ֥ר יְהֹוָ֖ה אֶל־מֹשֶׁ֥ה לֵּאמֹֽר׃ 17 צָר֖וֹר אֶת־הַמִּדְיָנִ֑ים וְהִכִּיתֶ֖ם אוֹתָֽם׃ 18 כִּ֣י צֹרְרִ֥ים הֵם֙ לָכֶ֔ם בְּנִכְלֵיהֶ֛ם אֲשֶׁר־נִכְּל֥וּ לָכֶ֖ם עַל־דְּבַ֣ר פְּע֑וֹר וְעַל־דְּבַ֞ר כׇּזְבִּ֨י בַת־נְשִׂ֤יא מִדְיָן֙ אֲחֹתָ֔ם הַמֻּכָּ֥ה בְיוֹם־הַמַּגֵּפָ֖ה עַל־דְּבַר־פְּעֽוֹר׃

כו 1 וַיְהִ֖י אַחֲרֵ֣י הַמַּגֵּפָ֑ה פ וַיֹּ֤אמֶר יְהֹוָה֙ אֶל־מֹשֶׁ֔ה וְאֶ֧ל אֶלְעָזָ֛ר בֶּן־אַהֲרֹ֥ן הַכֹּהֵ֖ן לֵאמֹֽר׃ 2 שְׂא֞וּ אֶת־רֹ֣אשׁ ׀ כׇּל־עֲדַ֣ת בְּנֵי־יִשְׂרָאֵ֗ל מִבֶּ֨ן עֶשְׂרִ֥ים שָׁנָ֛ה וָמַ֖עְלָה לְבֵ֣ית אֲבֹתָ֑ם כׇּל־יֹצֵ֥א צָבָ֖א בְּיִשְׂרָאֵֽל׃ 3 וַיְדַבֵּ֨ר מֹשֶׁ֜ה וְאֶלְעָזָ֧ר הַכֹּהֵ֛ן אֹתָ֖ם בְּעַֽרְבֹ֣ת מוֹאָ֑ב עַל־יַרְדֵּ֥ן יְרֵח֖וֹ לֵאמֹֽר׃ 4 מִבֶּ֛ן עֶשְׂרִ֥ים שָׁנָ֖ה וָמָ֑עְלָה כַּאֲשֶׁר֩ צִוָּ֨ה יְהֹוָ֤ה אֶת־מֹשֶׁה֙ וּבְנֵ֣י יִשְׂרָאֵ֔ל הַיֹּצְאִ֖ים מֵאֶ֥רֶץ מִצְרָֽיִם׃ [SECOND READING] 5 רְאוּבֵ֖ן בְּכ֣וֹר יִשְׂרָאֵ֑ל בְּנֵ֣י רְאוּבֵ֗ן חֲנוֹךְ֙ מִשְׁפַּ֣חַת הַחֲנֹכִ֔י לְפַלּ֕וּא מִשְׁפַּ֖חַת הַפַּלֻּאִֽי׃ 6 לְחֶצְרֹ֕ן מִשְׁפַּ֥חַת הַחֶצְרוֹנִ֖י לְכַרְמִ֑י מִשְׁפַּ֖חַת הַכַּרְמִֽי׃ 7 אֵ֖לֶּה מִשְׁפְּחֹ֣ת הָרֽאוּבֵנִ֑י וַיִּהְי֣וּ פְקֻדֵיהֶ֗ם שְׁלֹשָׁ֤ה וְאַרְבָּעִים֙ אֶ֔לֶף וּשְׁבַ֥ע מֵא֖וֹת וּשְׁלֹשִֽׁים׃ 8 וּבְנֵ֥י פַלּ֖וּא אֱלִיאָֽב׃

5. The Enochite (*ha-Ḥanokhy*) family, descended from Enoch (*Ḥanokh*). The nations would taunt Israel, saying, "Why do they trace their lineage by tribe? Do they really think that the Egyptians did not have their way with their mothers?"

So God placed His name, spelled *yod-he*, upon them—the letter *he* at one side and the letter *yod* at the other (e.g., Ḥanokh becoming *Ha-ḤanokhY*), as if to say, "I testify that these people are indeed the sons of their fathers" (*Rashi, 11th century*).

The letter *yod* was added to Phinehas' name and the letter *he* was added to Joseph's name (see *Psalms* 81:6) because they were both zealous about the prohibition of cohabiting with a non-Israelite woman—Phinehas killed Zimri and Joseph resisted the persistent attempts of Potiphar's wife (*Zohar*).

The Hebrew words for "man" (*'ish*, spelled: *alef-yod-shin*) and "woman" (*'ishah*, spelled: *alef-shin-he*) only differ in the letters *yod* and *he*, which spell God's name. If a couple is found worthy, the Divine Presence will be with them (*Babylonian Talmud, Sotah* 17a).

spiritual vitamin

> A minor concession today leads to a major one tomorrow, and an evasion of duty towards God leads to an evasion of duty towards man. And who is to say where this downsliding is to stop?

numbers 25:16 – 26:8 — pinḥas

¹⁶ God spoke to Moses, saying: ¹⁷ Be hostile to the Midianites and strike them down! ¹⁸ For they were hostile to you with their schemes which they plotted against you with the Peor affair and the affair of Cozbi their sister, daughter of the Midianite leader, who was killed on the day of the plague (which came) because of the Peor affair.

Moses' Final Census

26 ¹ It was after the plague. God spoke to Moses and to Eleazar son of Aaron the priest, saying: ² "Take the sum of the entire congregation of the children of Israel. (Include in this census all those) from twenty years old and upwards, according to their paternal houses, (i.e.) all who are fit to go out to the army in Israel."

³ Moses and Eleazar the priest spoke with (the people) in the plains of Moab, by the Jordan near Jericho, saying: ⁴ "(You must be counted) from the age of twenty years and upward, as God commanded Moses and the children of Israel when coming out of Egypt."

The Census Results

[SECOND READING] ⁵ Reuben (was) Israel's firstborn. Reuben's descendants were:

— The Enochite family, descended from Enoch;

— The Palluite family, descended from Pallu;

— ⁶ The Hezronite family, descended from Hezron;

— The Carmite family, descended from Carmi.

⁷ These were the Reubenite families. They totaled forty-three thousand, seven hundred and thirty.

— ⁸ The sons of Pallu were: Eliab.

"But will our daughters listen to us?" Balak replied.

"Begin with the daughters of your tribal leaders first," Balaam suggested, "and the others will follow."

That is why the verse states, *"Cozbi the daughter of Zur, a national leader of a paternal house in Midian,"* showing that Cozbi was a Midianite chieftain's daughter (*Jerusalem Talmud, Sanhedrin* 10:2).

26:1-2 It was after the plague ... "Take the sum." This could be compared to a shepherd whose flock was attacked by wolves and some sheep were killed, so he counted them to know how many were left.

Another interpretation: When the people left Egypt and were placed in Moses' charge, they were handed over to him with an account of their number. Now that he was close to death and would soon have to return his flock, he gave them back with an account of their number (*Rashi, 11ᵗʰ century*).

9 וּבְנֵי אֱלִיאָב נְמוּאֵל וְדָתָן וַאֲבִירָם הוּא־דָתָן וַאֲבִירָם [קרואי כ׳] קְרִיאֵי הָעֵדָה אֲשֶׁר הִצּוּ עַל־מֹשֶׁה וְעַל־אַהֲרֹן בַּעֲדַת־קֹרַח בְּהַצֹּתָם עַל־יְהֹוָה: 10 וַתִּפְתַּח הָאָרֶץ אֶת־פִּיהָ וַתִּבְלַע אֹתָם וְאֶת־קֹרַח בְּמוֹת הָעֵדָה בַּאֲכֹל הָאֵשׁ אֵת חֲמִשִּׁים וּמָאתַיִם אִישׁ וַיִּהְיוּ לְנֵס: 11 וּבְנֵי־קֹרַח לֹא־מֵתוּ: ס 12 בְּנֵי שִׁמְעוֹן לְמִשְׁפְּחֹתָם לִנְמוּאֵל מִשְׁפַּחַת הַנְּמוּאֵלִי לְיָמִין מִשְׁפַּחַת הַיָּמִינִי לְיָכִין מִשְׁפַּחַת הַיָּכִינִי: 13 לְזֶרַח מִשְׁפַּחַת הַזַּרְחִי לְשָׁאוּל מִשְׁפַּחַת הַשָּׁאוּלִי: 14 אֵלֶּה מִשְׁפְּחֹת הַשִּׁמְעֹנִי שְׁנַיִם וְעֶשְׂרִים אֶלֶף וּמָאתָיִם: ס 15 בְּנֵי גָד לְמִשְׁפְּחֹתָם לִצְפוֹן מִשְׁפַּחַת הַצְּפוֹנִי לְחַגִּי מִשְׁפַּחַת הַחַגִּי לְשׁוּנִי מִשְׁפַּחַת הַשּׁוּנִי: 16 לְאָזְנִי מִשְׁפַּחַת הָאָזְנִי לְעֵרִי מִשְׁפַּחַת הָעֵרִי: 17 לַאֲרוֹד מִשְׁפַּחַת הָאֲרוֹדִי לְאַרְאֵלִי מִשְׁפַּחַת הָאַרְאֵלִי: 18 אֵלֶּה מִשְׁפְּחֹת בְּנֵי־גָד לִפְקֻדֵיהֶם אַרְבָּעִים אֶלֶף וַחֲמֵשׁ מֵאוֹת: ס 19 בְּנֵי יְהוּדָה עֵר וְאוֹנָן וַיָּמָת עֵר וְאוֹנָן בְּאֶרֶץ כְּנָעַן: 20 וַיִּהְיוּ בְנֵי־יְהוּדָה לְמִשְׁפְּחֹתָם לְשֵׁלָה מִשְׁפַּחַת הַשֵּׁלָנִי לְפֶרֶץ מִשְׁפַּחַת הַפַּרְצִי לְזֶרַח מִשְׁפַּחַת הַזַּרְחִי: 21 וַיִּהְיוּ בְנֵי־פֶרֶץ לְחֶצְרֹן מִשְׁפַּחַת

---

killed in Korah's rebellion? The intimation here is that Dathan and Abiram were not just the leaders in the rebellion, they actually were the instigators.

Korah himself was possibly influenced by Dathan and Abiram. This would explain why *"Moses sent (messengers) to call Dathan and Abiram (in a further attempt to make peace)" (16:12)*—Moses went straight to the root of the controversy, to the two brothers who had instigated the rebellion (*Rabbi Ḥayyim ibn Attar, 18th century*).

11. Korah's sons, however, did not die. Korah's sons originally joined their father in the fight against Moses, but during the rebellion they had thoughts of repentance in their hearts. Therefore, when the earth opened to swallow Korah and his assembly, God provided them a high place in *Gehinnom* (Purgatory) for refuge (*Rashi, 11th century*).

According to the *Midrash*, Korah's sons left their underground shelter, and later went up to the land of Israel and became prophets. Their descendants then merited to chant Psalms in the Temple beginning with the words, *"By the sons of Korah, a psalm"* (*Rabbi Elijah Mizraḥi, 15th–16th century*).

15. Gad's descendants, according to their families: The Zephonite family, descended from Zephon. Gad's son's name was really "Ziphion" (*Genesis* 46:16), but it is written here as "Zephon" which means "hidden." This alludes the fact that Moses was buried in Gad's portion of the land, and it is a site that remains hidden to this day (*Rabbi Jacob b. Asher, 14th century*).

— ⁹ The sons of Eliab were: Nemuel, Dathan and Abiram.

— (These were) the same Dathan and Abiram who were the communal delegates from Korah's group that incited (the people) against Moses and Aaron, (thereby) inciting them against God. ¹⁰ But the earth opened its mouth and swallowed them with Korah, when that group died, (and) when fire destroyed (the other) two hundred and fifty men. Thus they became a sign (of the right of Aaron's descendants to the priesthood). ¹¹ Korah's sons, however, did not die. —

¹² Simeon's descendants, according to their families:

- The Nemuelite family, descended from Nemuel;
- The Jaminite family, descended from Jamin;
- The Jachinite family, descended from Jachin;
- ¹³ The Zerahite family, descended from Zerah;
- The Saulite family, descended from Saul.

¹⁴ (The total of) the Simeonite families (was) twenty-two thousand, two hundred.

¹⁵ Gad's descendants, according to their families:

- The Zephonite family, descended from Zephon;
- The Haggite family, descended from Haggi;
- The Shunite family, descended from Shuni;
- ¹⁶ The Oznite family, descended from Ozni;
- The Erite family, descended from Eri;
- ¹⁷ The Arodite family, descended from Arod;
- The Arelite family, descended from Areli.

¹⁸ These were families of Gad's descendants. Their total number was forty thousand, five hundred.

¹⁹ Judah's (first two) sons were Er and Onan, but Er and Onan died in the land of Canaan.

²⁰ Judah's descendants, according to their families:

- The Shelanite family, descended from Shelah;
- The Perezite family, descended from Perez;
- The Zerahite family, descended from Zerah.

²¹ The descendants of Perez were:

9. The same Dathan and Abiram who … incited (the people) against Moses and Aaron.
Why does the Torah mention only Dathan and Abiram, and not the other individuals who were

במדבר כו:כא-לה • פינחס

הַחֶצְרֹנִי לְחָמוּל מִשְׁפַּחַת הֶחָמוּלִי: 22 אֵלֶּה מִשְׁפְּחֹת יְהוּדָה לִפְקֻדֵיהֶם שִׁשָּׁה וְשִׁבְעִים אֶלֶף וַחֲמֵשׁ מֵאוֹת: ס 23 בְּנֵי יִשָּׂשכָר לְמִשְׁפְּחֹתָם תּוֹלָע מִשְׁפַּחַת הַתּוֹלָעִי לְפֻוָּה מִשְׁפַּחַת הַפּוּנִי: 24 לְיָשׁוּב מִשְׁפַּחַת הַיָּשֻׁבִי לְשִׁמְרֹן מִשְׁפַּחַת הַשִּׁמְרֹנִי: 25 אֵלֶּה מִשְׁפְּחֹת יִשָּׂשכָר לִפְקֻדֵיהֶם אַרְבָּעָה וְשִׁשִּׁים אֶלֶף וּשְׁלֹשׁ מֵאוֹת: ס 26 בְּנֵי זְבוּלֻן לְמִשְׁפְּחֹתָם לְסֶרֶד מִשְׁפַּחַת הַסַּרְדִּי לְאֵלוֹן מִשְׁפַּחַת הָאֵלֹנִי לְיַחְלְאֵל מִשְׁפַּחַת הַיַּחְלְאֵלִי: 27 אֵלֶּה מִשְׁפְּחֹת הַזְּבוּלֹנִי לִפְקֻדֵיהֶם שִׁשִּׁים אֶלֶף וַחֲמֵשׁ מֵאוֹת: ס 28 בְּנֵי יוֹסֵף לְמִשְׁפְּחֹתָם מְנַשֶּׁה וְאֶפְרָיִם: 29 בְּנֵי מְנַשֶּׁה לְמָכִיר מִשְׁפַּחַת הַמָּכִירִי וּמָכִיר הוֹלִיד אֶת־גִּלְעָד לְגִלְעָד מִשְׁפַּחַת הַגִּלְעָדִי: 30 אֵלֶּה בְּנֵי גִלְעָד אִיעֶזֶר מִשְׁפַּחַת הָאִיעֶזְרִי לְחֵלֶק מִשְׁפַּחַת הַחֶלְקִי: 31 וְאַשְׂרִיאֵל מִשְׁפַּחַת הָאַשְׂרִאֵלִי וְשֶׁכֶם מִשְׁפַּחַת הַשִּׁכְמִי: 32 וּשְׁמִידָע מִשְׁפַּחַת הַשְּׁמִידָעִי וְחֵפֶר מִשְׁפַּחַת הַחֶפְרִי: 33 וּצְלָפְחָד בֶּן־חֵפֶר לֹא־הָיוּ לוֹ בָּנִים כִּי אִם־בָּנוֹת וְשֵׁם בְּנוֹת צְלָפְחָד מַחְלָה וְנֹעָה חָגְלָה מִלְכָּה וְתִרְצָה: 34 אֵלֶּה מִשְׁפְּחֹת מְנַשֶּׁה וּפְקֻדֵיהֶם שְׁנַיִם וַחֲמִשִּׁים אֶלֶף וּשְׁבַע מֵאוֹת: ס 35 אֵלֶּה בְנֵי־אֶפְרַיִם לְמִשְׁפְּחֹתָם לְשׁוּתֶלַח מִשְׁפַּחַת הַשֻּׁתַלְחִי

35, 42. These were Ephraim's descendants ... These were Dan's descendants. Ephraim and Dan are the only two tribes whose census is introduced with the word *'eleh*, "these are"—a word that is reminiscent of the Golden Calf, when the people said, *"These are ('eleh) your gods, O Israel, who have brought you up from the land of Egypt"* (Exodus 32:4).

The Torah hints here to the fact that Jeroboam son of Nebat, who was from the tribe of Ephraim, would later set up two golden calves, one of which was in the territory of Dan (see *II Kings* 10:29; *Rabbi Jacob b. Asher, 14th century*).

spiritual vitamin

> After such a large portion of our people has been brutally annihilated in the Holocaust, the obligation of every surviving Jew is so much the greater.

- The Hezronite family, descended from Hezron;
- The Hamulite family, descended from Hamul.

²² These were Judah's families. Their total number was seventy-six thousand, five hundred.

²³ Issachar's descendants, according to their families:

- The Tolaite family, descended from Tola;
- The Punite family, descended from Puvah;
- ²⁴ The Jashubite family, descended from Jashub;
- The Shimronite family, descended from Shimron.

²⁵ These were Issachar's families. Their total number was sixty-four thousand, three hundred.

²⁶ Zebulun's descendants, according to their families:

- The Seredite family, descended from Sered;
- The Elonite family, descended from Elon;
- The Jahleelite family, descended from Jahleel.

²⁷ These were the Zebulunite families. Their total number was sixty thousand, five hundred.

²⁸ The descendants of Joseph according to their families (included) Manasseh and Ephraim.

²⁹ The descendants of Manasseh:

- The Machirite family, descended from Machir; Machir fathered Gilead.
- The Gileadite family, descended from Gilead.

³⁰ These were the families of Gilead's descendants:

- The Iezerite family, descended from Iezer;
- The Helekite family, descended from Helek;
- ³¹ The Asrielite family, descended from Asriel;
- The Shechemite family, descended from Shechem;
- ³² The Shemidaite family, descended from Shemida;
- The Hepherite family, descended from Hepher.
- ³³ Zelophehad son of Hepher did not have sons, but daughters. The names of Zelophehad's daughters were Mahlah, Noah, Hoglah, Milcah and Tirzah.

³⁴ These were Manasseh's families. Their total number was fifty-two thousand, seven hundred.

³⁵ These were Ephraim's descendants, according to their families:

במדבר כו:לה-מח — פינחס

לְבֶ֕כֶר מִשְׁפַּ֖חַת הַבַּכְרִ֑י לְתַ֕חַן מִשְׁפַּ֖חַת הַתַּחֲנִֽי׃ 36 וְאֵ֖לֶּה בְּנֵ֣י שׁוּתָ֑לַח לְעֵרָ֕ן מִשְׁפַּ֖חַת הָעֵרָנִֽי׃ 37 אֵ֣לֶּה מִשְׁפְּחֹ֤ת בְּנֵֽי־אֶפְרַ֙יִם֙ לִפְקֻ֣דֵיהֶ֔ם שְׁנַ֧יִם וּשְׁלֹשִׁ֛ים אֶ֖לֶף וַחֲמֵ֣שׁ מֵא֑וֹת אֵ֥לֶּה בְנֵי־יוֹסֵ֖ף לְמִשְׁפְּחֹתָֽם׃ ס 38 בְּנֵ֣י בִנְיָמִן֮ לְמִשְׁפְּחֹתָם֒ לְבֶ֗לַע מִשְׁפַּ֙חַת֙ הַבַּלְעִ֔י לְאַשְׁבֵּ֕ל מִשְׁפַּ֖חַת הָאַשְׁבֵּלִ֑י לַאֲחִירָ֕ם מִשְׁפַּ֖חַת הָאֲחִירָמִֽי׃ 39 לִשְׁפוּפָ֕ם מִשְׁפַּ֖חַת הַשּׁוּפָמִ֑י לְחוּפָ֕ם מִשְׁפַּ֖חַת הַחוּפָמִֽי׃ 40 וַיִּהְי֥וּ בְנֵי־בֶ֖לַע אַ֣רְדְּ וְנַעֲמָ֑ן מִשְׁפַּ֙חַת֙ הָֽאַרְדִּ֔י לְנַֽעֲמָ֕ן מִשְׁפַּ֖חַת הַֽנַּעֲמִֽי׃ 41 אֵ֣לֶּה בְנֵֽי־בִנְיָמִ֖ן לְמִשְׁפְּחֹתָ֑ם וּפְקֻ֣דֵיהֶ֔ם חֲמִשָּׁ֧ה וְאַרְבָּעִ֛ים אֶ֖לֶף וְשֵׁ֥שׁ מֵאֽוֹת׃ ס 42 אֵ֤לֶּה בְנֵי־דָן֙ לְמִשְׁפְּחֹתָ֔ם לְשׁוּחָ֕ם מִשְׁפַּ֖חַת הַשּׁוּחָמִ֑י אֵ֛לֶּה מִשְׁפְּחֹ֥ת דָּ֖ן לְמִשְׁפְּחֹתָֽם׃ 43 כׇּל־מִשְׁפְּחֹ֥ת הַשּׁוּחָמִ֖י לִפְקֻדֵיהֶ֑ם אַרְבָּעָ֧ה וְשִׁשִּׁ֛ים אֶ֖לֶף וְאַרְבַּ֥ע מֵאֽוֹת׃ ס 44 בְּנֵ֣י אָשֵׁר֮ לְמִשְׁפְּחֹתָם֒ לְיִמְנָ֕ה מִשְׁפַּ֖חַת הַיִּמְנָ֑ה לְיִשְׁוִ֕י מִשְׁפַּ֖חַת הַיִּשְׁוִ֑י לִבְרִיעָ֕ה מִשְׁפַּ֖חַת הַבְּרִיעִֽי׃ 45 לִבְנֵ֣י בְרִיעָ֔ה לְחֶ֕בֶר מִשְׁפַּ֖חַת הַֽחֶבְרִ֑י לְמַ֨לְכִּיאֵ֔ל מִשְׁפַּ֖חַת הַמַּלְכִּֽיאֵלִֽי׃ 46 וְשֵׁ֥ם בַּת־אָשֵׁ֖ר שָֽׂרַח׃ 47 אֵ֣לֶּה מִשְׁפְּחֹ֤ת בְּנֵֽי־אָשֵׁר֙ לִפְקֻ֣דֵיהֶ֔ם שְׁלֹשָׁ֧ה וַחֲמִשִּׁ֛ים אֶ֖לֶף וְאַרְבַּ֥ע מֵאֽוֹת׃ ס 48 בְּנֵ֤י נַפְתָּלִי֙ לְמִשְׁפְּחֹתָ֔ם לְיַ֨חְצְאֵ֔ל מִשְׁפַּ֖חַת הַיַּחְצְאֵלִ֑י לְגוּנִ֕י מִשְׁפַּ֖חַת הַגּוּנִֽי׃

spiritual vitamin

> There is a basic difference between our Jewish tradition and those of other faiths, such as Christianity or Islam. For, whereas in the latter cases, the traditions go back to one individual or a limited number of individuals, our traditions go back to a revelation, which was experienced by a whole people at once, so that at no time did we have to place our trust in the veracity of one, or a few, individuals.

- The Shuthelahite family, descended from Shuthelah;
- The Becherite family, descended from Becher;
- The Tahanite family, descended from Tahan.

³⁶ These were the descendants of Shuthelah: The Eranite family, descended from Eran.

³⁷ These were the families of Ephraim's descendants. Their total number was thirty-two thousand, five hundred. (All) these were Joseph's descendants, according to their families.

³⁸ Benjamin's descendants, according to their families:

- The Belaite family, descended from Bela;
- The Ashbelite family, descended from Ashbel;
- The Ahiramite family, descended from Ahiram (also known as Ehi);
- ³⁹ The Shuphamite family, descended from Shephupham (also known as Muppim);
- The Huphamite family, descended from Hupham.
- ⁴⁰ The sons of Bela were Ard and Naaman:
- The Ardite family;
- The Naamanite family, descended from Naaman.

⁴¹ These were Benjamin's descendants, according to their families. Their total number was forty-five thousand, six hundred.

⁴² These were Dan's descendants, according to their families:

- The Shuhamite family, descended from Shuham (Hushim); These were Dan's families.

⁴³ The total number of all the Shuhamite families was sixty-four thousand, four hundred.

⁴⁴ Asher's descendants, according to their families:

- The Imnite family, descended from Imnah;
- The Ishvite family, descended from Ishvi;
- The Beriite family, descended from Beriah.

⁴⁵ The descendants of Beriah:

- The Heberite family, descended from Heber;
- The Malchielite family, descended from Malchiel.

⁴⁶ The name of Asher's daughter was Serah.

⁴⁷ These were the families of Asher's descendants. Their total was fifty-three thousand, four hundred.

⁴⁸ Naphtali's descendants, according to their families:

פינחס

במדבר כו:מט-סא

49 לְיֵ֙צֶר֙ מִשְׁפַּ֣חַת הַיִּצְרִ֔י לְשִׁלֵּ֖ם מִשְׁפַּ֥חַת הַשִּׁלֵּמִֽי׃ 50 אֵ֛לֶּה מִשְׁפְּחֹ֥ת נַפְתָּלִ֖י לְמִשְׁפְּחֹתָ֑ם וּפְקֻ֣דֵיהֶ֔ם חֲמִשָּׁ֧ה וְאַרְבָּעִ֛ים אֶ֖לֶף וְאַרְבַּ֥ע מֵאֽוֹת׃ 51 אֵ֗לֶּה פְּקוּדֵ֖י בְּנֵ֣י יִשְׂרָאֵ֑ל שֵׁשׁ־מֵא֥וֹת אֶ֖לֶף וָאָ֑לֶף שְׁבַ֥ע מֵא֖וֹת וּשְׁלֹשִֽׁים׃ פ [THIRD READING] 52 וַיְדַבֵּ֥ר יְהֹוָ֖ה אֶל־מֹשֶׁ֥ה לֵּאמֹֽר׃ 53 לָאֵ֗לֶּה תֵּחָלֵ֥ק הָאָ֛רֶץ בְּנַחֲלָ֖ה בְּמִסְפַּ֥ר שֵׁמֽוֹת׃ 54 לָרַ֗ב תַּרְבֶּה֙ נַחֲלָת֔וֹ וְלַמְעַ֕ט תַּמְעִ֖יט נַחֲלָת֑וֹ אִישׁ֙ לְפִ֣י פְקֻדָ֔יו יֻתַּ֖ן נַחֲלָתֽוֹ׃ 55 אַךְ־בְּגוֹרָ֕ל יֵחָלֵ֖ק אֶת־הָאָ֑רֶץ לִשְׁמ֥וֹת מַטּוֹת־אֲבֹתָ֖ם יִנְחָֽלוּ׃ 56 עַל־פִּי֙ הַגּוֹרָ֔ל תֵּחָלֵ֖ק נַחֲלָת֑וֹ בֵּ֥ין רַ֖ב לִמְעָֽט׃ ס 57 וְאֵ֨לֶּה פְקוּדֵ֣י הַלֵּוִי֮ לְמִשְׁפְּחֹתָם֒ לְגֵרְשׁ֗וֹן מִשְׁפַּ֙חַת֙ הַגֵּ֣רְשֻׁנִּ֔י לִקְהָ֕ת מִשְׁפַּ֖חַת הַקְּהָתִ֑י לִמְרָרִ֕י מִשְׁפַּ֖חַת הַמְּרָרִֽי׃ 58 אֵ֣לֶּה ׀ מִשְׁפְּחֹ֣ת לֵוִ֗י מִשְׁפַּ֨חַת הַלִּבְנִ֜י מִשְׁפַּ֤חַת הַֽחֶבְרֹנִי֙ מִשְׁפַּ֣חַת הַמַּחְלִ֔י מִשְׁפַּ֖חַת הַמּוּשִׁ֑י מִשְׁפַּ֖חַת הַקׇּרְחִ֑י וּקְהָ֖ת הוֹלִ֥ד אֶת־עַמְרָֽם׃ 59 וְשֵׁ֣ם ׀ אֵ֣שֶׁת עַמְרָ֗ם יוֹכֶ֙בֶד֙ בַּת־לֵוִ֔י אֲשֶׁ֨ר יָלְדָ֥ה אֹתָ֛הּ לְלֵוִ֖י בְּמִצְרָ֑יִם וַתֵּ֣לֶד לְעַמְרָ֗ם אֶֽת־אַהֲרֹן֙ וְאֶת־מֹשֶׁ֔ה וְאֵ֖ת מִרְיָ֥ם אֲחֹתָֽם׃ 60 וַיִּוָּלֵ֣ד לְאַהֲרֹ֔ן אֶת־נָדָ֖ב וְאֶת־אֲבִיה֑וּא אֶת־אֶלְעָזָ֖ר וְאֶת־אִיתָמָֽר׃ 61 וַיָּ֥מׇת נָדָ֖ב וַאֲבִיה֑וּא בְּהַקְרִיבָ֛ם אֵשׁ־זָרָ֖ה לִפְנֵ֥י יְהֹוָֽה׃

---

of spiritual "lottery"—your primary mission in life has been pre-allotted on high, and you have no choice in the matter! (*Rabbi Shneur Zalman of Lyady, 18th century*).

Your soul has a particular "special commandment" because each soul is a "spark" of the "general soul" which Adam possessed. Your soul's specific path corresponds to its original "location" within Adam's soul. Only when you observe your "special commandment" will you become spiritually fulfilled (*Rabbi Ḥayyim b. Joseph Vital, 16th–17th century*).

How can you discover what your "special commandment" is?

There is no simple solution. But since your mission in life revolves around your special commandment, your "evil impulse" will definitely oppose this commandment strongly, which may give you a clue what it is.

Also, Divine Providence will inevitably lead you to circumstances which are conducive to the observance of your special commandment. So if you are wealthy, for example, your special commandment is quite possibly to give charity.

In addition to all the above, we all have another special commandment *of our generation*, by virtue of the times in which we live. This is the need to awaken to the global flowering of Divine consciousness towards which the world is currently shifting (*Rabbi Menaḥem Mendel Schneerson, 20th century*).

numbers 26:48–61 — pinḥas

- The Jahzeelite family, descended from Jahzeel;
- The Gunite family, descended from Guni;
- ⁴⁹ The Jezerite family, descended from Jezer;
- The Shillemite family, descended from Shillem.

⁵⁰ These were Naphtali's families according to their families. Their total was forty-five thousand, four hundred.

⁵¹ This was the total number of the children of Israel (counted): Six hundred and one thousand, seven hundred and thirty.

Division of the Land

[THIRD READING] ⁵² God spoke to Moses, saying: ⁵³ "You should apportion the land as an inheritance (only) among these names (who were included) in the (above) census. ⁵⁴ To a large (tribe) you should give a larger inheritance and to a small (tribe) you should give a smaller inheritance. Each one should be given an inheritance according to its size. ⁵⁵ You must only apportion the land by means of a lottery. They will inherit it (in portions that are divided) according to the names of their tribal ancestors (that came out of Egypt). ⁵⁶ Whether (a group) is numerous or small, their inheritance of land should be apportioned through the mouth of the (miraculous, talking) lottery.

Census of the Levites

⁵⁷ These were the Levite families included in the census:

- The Gershonite family, descended from Gershon; The Kohathite family, descended from Kohath; The Merarite family, descended from Merari.

⁵⁸ These were the Levite families:

- The Libnite family, the Hebronite family, the Mahlite family, the Mushite family, the Korahite family.
- Kohath fathered Amram. ⁵⁹ The name of Amram's wife was Jochebed, the daughter of Levi, whom (Levi's wife) bore to Levi in Egypt.
- For Amram, (Jochebed) bore Aaron and Moses, and their sister Miriam. ⁶⁰ Nadab, Abihu, Eleazar and Ithamar were born to Aaron. ⁶¹ Nadab and Abihu died when they offered up an extraneous fire before God.

55. You must only apportion the land by means of a lottery. While Jewish law obligates you to observe all the commandments, there is always at least one particular command to which your soul is drawn more strongly (cf. *Babylonian Talmud, Shabbat* 118b). This is a kind

62 וַיִּהְי֣וּ פְקֻדֵיהֶ֗ם שְׁלֹשָׁ֤ה וְעֶשְׂרִים֙ אֶ֔לֶף כָּל־זָכָ֖ר מִבֶּן־חֹ֣דֶשׁ וָמָ֑עְלָה כִּ֣י | לֹ֣א הָתְפָּקְד֗וּ בְּתוֹךְ֙ בְּנֵ֣י יִשְׂרָאֵ֔ל כִּ֠י לֹא־נִתַּ֤ן לָהֶם֙ נַחֲלָ֔ה בְּת֖וֹךְ בְּנֵ֥י יִשְׂרָאֵֽל׃ 63 אֵ֚לֶּה פְּקוּדֵ֣י מֹשֶׁ֔ה וְאֶלְעָזָ֖ר הַכֹּהֵ֑ן אֲשֶׁ֨ר פָּקְד֜וּ אֶת־בְּנֵ֤י יִשְׂרָאֵל֙ בְּעַֽרְבֹ֣ת מוֹאָ֔ב עַ֖ל יַרְדֵּ֥ן יְרֵחֽוֹ׃ 64 וּבְאֵ֨לֶּה֙ לֹא־הָ֣יָה אִ֔ישׁ מִפְּקוּדֵ֣י מֹשֶׁ֔ה וְאַהֲרֹ֖ן הַכֹּהֵ֑ן אֲשֶׁ֥ר פָּקְד֛וּ אֶת־בְּנֵ֥י יִשְׂרָאֵ֖ל בְּמִדְבַּ֥ר סִינָֽי׃ 65 כִּֽי־אָמַ֤ר יְהֹוָה֙ לָהֶ֔ם מ֥וֹת יָמֻ֖תוּ בַּמִּדְבָּ֑ר וְלֹא־נוֹתַ֤ר מֵהֶם֙ אִ֔ישׁ כִּ֚י אִם־כָּלֵ֣ב בֶּן־יְפֻנֶּ֔ה וִיהוֹשֻׁ֖עַ בִּן־נֽוּן׃ ס

כז

1 וַתִּקְרַ֜בְנָה בְּנ֣וֹת צְלׇפְחָ֗ד בֶּן־חֵ֤פֶר בֶּן־גִּלְעָד֙ בֶּן־מָכִ֣יר בֶּן־מְנַשֶּׁ֔ה לְמִשְׁפְּחֹ֖ת מְנַשֶּׁ֣ה בֶן־יוֹסֵ֑ף וְאֵ֙לֶּה֙ שְׁמ֣וֹת בְּנֹתָ֔יו מַחְלָ֣ה נֹעָ֔ה וְחׇגְלָ֥ה וּמִלְכָּ֖ה וְתִרְצָֽה׃ 2 וַֽתַּעֲמֹ֜דְנָה לִפְנֵ֣י מֹשֶׁ֗ה וְלִפְנֵי֙ אֶלְעָזָ֣ר הַכֹּהֵ֔ן וְלִפְנֵ֥י הַנְּשִׂיאִ֖ם וְכׇל־הָעֵדָ֑ה פֶּ֥תַח אֹֽהֶל־מוֹעֵ֖ד לֵאמֹֽר׃ 3 אָבִ֘ינוּ֮ מֵ֣ת בַּמִּדְבָּר֒ וְה֨וּא לֹא־הָיָ֜ה בְּת֣וֹךְ הָעֵדָ֗ה הַנּוֹעָדִ֛ים עַל־יְהֹוָ֖ה בַּעֲדַת־קֹ֑רַח כִּֽי־בְחֶטְא֣וֹ מֵ֔ת וּבָנִ֖ים לֹא־הָ֥יוּ לֽוֹ׃ 4 לָ֣מָּה יִגָּרַ֤ע שֵׁם־אָבִ֙ינוּ֙ מִתּ֣וֹךְ מִשְׁפַּחְתּ֔וֹ כִּ֛י אֵ֥ין ל֖וֹ בֵּ֑ן תְּנָה־לָּ֣נוּ אֲחֻזָּ֔ה בְּת֖וֹךְ אֲחֵ֥י אָבִֽינוּ׃

penalty for rebellion against the king, in which case his possessions are confiscated and given to the king (*Babylonian Talmud, Sanhedrin* 46b).

If Zelophehad had suffered the death penalty because he had tried to enter the land without permission (14:45), or for desecrating the Sabbath by gathering wood (15:33), his possessions would have been permitted to be passed on to his children. Korah and his assembly, on the

kabbalah bites

27:1-5 The tension between Zelophehad's daughters and Moses was a reemergence of the ancient conflict between Cain and Abel. As we have noted before, Moses was a reincarnation of Abel. Zelophehad, on the other hand, possessed a spark of Cain's soul. Therefore Zelophehad's daughters were careful to stress, "*He was not part of… Korah's assembly,*" because Korah and his group had all been incarnations of Cain. Rather, they argued, he was from the good side of Cain.

But since Moses was from Abel's side he could not remain impartial and "*brought their case before God.*"

⁶² The total number counted was twenty-three thousand. (This included) every male aged one month and upward. (The Levites) were not counted with the (other) children of Israel (from the age of twenty), since they did not receive any inheritance (of land) together with the children of Israel.

⁶³ This (concludes) the census of Moses and Eleazar the priest, who counted the children of Israel in the plains of Moab, by the Jordan, near Jericho. ⁶⁴ Among these (who were counted here, there) was not one man who had been included in the census of Moses and Aaron when they counted the children of Israel in the Sinai Desert. ⁶⁵ For God had said to them that they would definitely die in the desert. Not one man remained from them, except for Caleb son of Jephunneh and Joshua son of Nun.

Complaint of Zelophehad's Daughters

27 ¹ The daughters of Zelophehad—the son of Hepher, who was the son of Gilead, who was the son of Machir, who was the son of Manasseh, from the families of Joseph's son Manasseh—came forward. His daughters' names were Mahlah, Noah, Hoglah, Milcah and Tirzah. ² They stood before Moses, Eleazar the priest, the (tribal) leaders and the entire congregation, at the entrance of the Tent of Meeting, saying, ³ "Our father died in the desert. He was not part of the group that rebelled against God (nor was he) in Korah's assembly, but rather, he died due to his own sin. He had no sons. ⁴ Why should our father's name be missed out from his family because he had no son? Give us a portion along with our father's brothers!"

62. They did not receive any inheritance. The entire tribe of Levi is prohibited from taking a share in the apportionment of the land of Canaan.

Why did the tribe of Levi not merit a portion in the land of Israel and its spoils, as their brothers did? Because they have been separated to serve God as His ministers. Therefore they were also separated from worldly matters. They are not required to fight in a war, like other Jewish people, and they do not inherit the land (*Maimonides, 12th century*).

In the future era, the Levites will be given a portion in the land (*Rabbi Moses b. Jacob of Coucy, 13th century*).

64. There was not one man who had been included in the census of Moses and Aaron when they counted the children of Israel in the Sinai Desert. The women were not included in the decree which followed the sin of the spies, for they cherished the land of Israel. The men said, *"Let's appoint a leader and return to Egypt!"* (14:4), but the women said, *"Give us a portion"* in the land of Israel (27:4). That is why the passage of Zelophehad's daughters follows here (*Rashi, 11th century*).

27:3 He was not part of the group that rebelled against God (nor was he) in Korah's assembly. Those who receive the death penalty are permitted to pass their possessions on to their children as an inheritance. An exception to this rule is when a person receives the death

5 וַיַּקְרֵב מֹשֶׁה אֶת־מִשְׁפָּטָן לִפְנֵי יְהוָֹה: פ 6 [FOURTH READING] וַיֹּאמֶר יְהוָֹה אֶל־מֹשֶׁה לֵּאמֹר: 7 כֵּן בְּנוֹת צְלָפְחָד דֹּבְרֹת נָתֹן תִּתֵּן לָהֶם אֲחֻזַּת נַחֲלָה בְּתוֹךְ אֲחֵי אֲבִיהֶם וְהַעֲבַרְתָּ אֶת־נַחֲלַת אֲבִיהֶן לָהֶן: 8 וְאֶל־בְּנֵי יִשְׂרָאֵל תְּדַבֵּר לֵאמֹר אִישׁ כִּי־יָמוּת וּבֵן אֵין לוֹ וְהַעֲבַרְתֶּם אֶת־נַחֲלָתוֹ לְבִתּוֹ: 9 וְאִם־אֵין לוֹ בַּת וּנְתַתֶּם אֶת־נַחֲלָתוֹ לְאֶחָיו: 10 וְאִם־אֵין לוֹ אַחִים וּנְתַתֶּם אֶת־נַחֲלָתוֹ לַאֲחֵי אָבִיו: 11 וְאִם־אֵין אַחִים לְאָבִיו וּנְתַתֶּם אֶת־נַחֲלָתוֹ לִשְׁאֵרוֹ הַקָּרֹב אֵלָיו מִמִּשְׁפַּחְתּוֹ וְיָרַשׁ אֹתָהּ וְהָיְתָה לִבְנֵי יִשְׂרָאֵל לְחֻקַּת מִשְׁפָּט כַּאֲשֶׁר צִוָּה יְהוָֹה אֶת־מֹשֶׁה: פ 12 וַיֹּאמֶר יְהוָֹה אֶל־מֹשֶׁה עֲלֵה אֶל־הַר הָעֲבָרִים הַזֶּה וּרְאֵה אֶת־הָאָרֶץ אֲשֶׁר נָתַתִּי לִבְנֵי יִשְׂרָאֵל: 13 וְרָאִיתָה אֹתָהּ וְנֶאֱסַפְתָּ אֶל־עַמֶּיךָ גַּם־אָתָּה כַּאֲשֶׁר נֶאֱסַף אַהֲרֹן אָחִיךָ: 14 כַּאֲשֶׁר מְרִיתֶם פִּי בְּמִדְבַּר־צִן בִּמְרִיבַת הָעֵדָה לְהַקְדִּישֵׁנִי בַמַּיִם לְעֵינֵיהֶם הֵם מֵי־מְרִיבַת קָדֵשׁ מִדְבַּר־צִן: ס 15 וַיְדַבֵּר מֹשֶׁה אֶל־יְהוָֹה לֵּאמֹר: 16 יִפְקֹד יְהוָֹה אֱלֹהֵי הָרוּחֹת לְכָל־בָּשָׂר אִישׁ עַל־הָעֵדָה: 17 אֲשֶׁר־

had been decreed to remain there for forty years (see *Tosafists* to *Babylonian Talmud, Bava Batra* 119b).

But how is it possible to go about proving a man's intentions?

God can examine the heart of man and know his true intent—so Moses passed their case to God. The reply was, *"Zelophehad's daughters speak well."* Their father's intentions had been purely for the sake of heaven (*Rabbi Menahem Mendel Morgensztern of Kotsk, 19th century*).

When Zelophehad's daughters told Moses that their father was not part of Korah's rebellion (v. 3), Moses could no longer judge their case impartially, knowing that Zelophehad had been one of his own supporters. For this reason, Moses was forced to bring their case directly "before God," to obtain an unbiased verdict (cited by *Rabbi Bahya b. Asher, 13th century*).

16. God must appoint somebody (capable) over the congregation. When Moses was instructed by God to give Zelophehad's inheritance to his daughters, he said, "It's time to ask for my own needs, that my son should inherit my high position."

God said to him, "That thought did not arise in My mind! Joshua deserves to be rewarded for his service, because he *'would not depart from the tent'"* (Exodus 33:11).

This is the meaning of Solomon's saying, *"The one who guards the fig tree eats its fruit"* (Proverbs 27:18; *Rashi, 11th century*).

Moses was actually requesting that the job of leadership should be divided into two. Moses' son would inherit the position of king and military leader, whereas Joshua, who excelled in the area of Torah study, would be appointed as the leader in Torah matters.

numbers 27:5–17 — pinḥas

⁵ Moses (didn't know what to do, so he) brought their case before God. [FOURTH READING] ⁶ God spoke to Moses, saying: ⁷ "Zelophehad's daughters speak well. Give them a double portion of inheritance along with their father's brothers. Transfer their father's inheritance to them."

Laws of Inheritance

⁸ Speak to the children of Israel, saying:

- ❖ If a man dies and has no son, you should transfer his inheritance to his daughter.
- ❖ ⁹ If he has no daughter, you should give his inheritance to his brothers.
- ❖ ¹⁰ If he has no brothers, you should give his inheritance to his father's brothers.
- ❖ ¹¹ If his father has no brothers, you should give his inheritance to the relative who is closest to him in his (father's) family, who will inherit it.

This will be a statutory law for the Jewish people, as God commanded Moses.

Joshua Is Appointed as Moses' Successor

¹² God said to Moses, "Ascend here, up the Abarim mountains, and look at the land which I have given to the children of Israel. ¹³ When you have seen it, you too will be gathered to your people, just as Aaron your brother was gathered, ¹⁴ because you disobeyed My command in the desert of Zin during the communal dispute (when you were supposed) to sanctify Me with the water in their presence. They were the "waters of strife" at Kadesh, in the desert of Zin."

¹⁵ Moses spoke to God, saying: ¹⁶ "O God (who knows) everybody's thoughts! God must appoint somebody (capable) over the congregation, ¹⁷ (somebody) who will

---

other hand, were killed for rebelling against Moses, the leader, which would have excluded their children from an inheritance. Therefore Zelophehad's daughters emphasized that their father was not a part of Korah's uprising, and was eligible to bequeath his possessions (*Rabbi Meir Simḥah of Dvinsk, 19th–20th century*).

5. Moses brought their case before God. According to the Talmud, Zelophehad had been the one who violated the Sabbath by gathering wood (see 15:33). His daughters claimed, however, that his intentions had been sincere: He had given his own life, incurring the death penalty, to prove that the laws of the Sabbath were still binding in the Sinai Desert even after the Israelites

spiritual vitamin

> When you resolve to do a good thing, the One Above immediately opens for you additional channels if necessary, to accomplish it even better than expected.

יֵצֵא לִפְנֵיהֶם וַאֲשֶׁר יָבֹא לִפְנֵיהֶם וַאֲשֶׁר יוֹצִיאֵם וַאֲשֶׁר יְבִיאֵם וְלֹא תִהְיֶה
עֲדַת יְהֹוָה כַּצֹּאן אֲשֶׁר אֵין־לָהֶם רֹעֶה: 18 וַיֹּאמֶר יְהֹוָה אֶל־מֹשֶׁה קַח־לְךָ
אֶת־יְהוֹשֻׁעַ בִּן־נוּן אִישׁ אֲשֶׁר־רוּחַ בּוֹ וְסָמַכְתָּ אֶת־יָדְךָ עָלָיו: 19 וְהַעֲמַדְתָּ
אֹתוֹ לִפְנֵי אֶלְעָזָר הַכֹּהֵן וְלִפְנֵי כָּל־הָעֵדָה וְצִוִּיתָה אֹתוֹ לְעֵינֵיהֶם: 20 וְנָתַתָּה
מֵהוֹדְךָ עָלָיו לְמַעַן יִשְׁמְעוּ כָּל־עֲדַת בְּנֵי יִשְׂרָאֵל: 21 וְלִפְנֵי אֶלְעָזָר הַכֹּהֵן
יַעֲמֹד וְשָׁאַל לוֹ בְּמִשְׁפַּט הָאוּרִים לִפְנֵי יְהֹוָה עַל־פִּיו יֵצְאוּ וְעַל־פִּיו יָבֹאוּ
הוּא וְכָל־בְּנֵי־יִשְׂרָאֵל אִתּוֹ וְכָל־הָעֵדָה: 22 וַיַּעַשׂ מֹשֶׁה כַּאֲשֶׁר צִוָּה יְהֹוָה אֹתוֹ
וַיִּקַּח אֶת־יְהוֹשֻׁעַ וַיַּעֲמִדֵהוּ לִפְנֵי אֶלְעָזָר הַכֹּהֵן וְלִפְנֵי כָּל־הָעֵדָה: 23 וַיִּסְמֹךְ
אֶת־יָדָיו עָלָיו וַיְצַוֵּהוּ כַּאֲשֶׁר דִּבֶּר יְהֹוָה בְּיַד־מֹשֶׁה: פ

23. He laid his hands upon him. God commanded Moses to "lay your *hand* upon him" (v. 18), in the singular, indicating that Moses was to impart only some of his prophetic powers to Joshua. But this verse relates that Moses leaned *both* of his hands upon Joshua, thereby conferring a full measure of his wisdom unto Joshua (*Rashi, 11th century*).

The fact that Moses extended himself beyond God's instructions in favor of Joshua, shows that a teacher is never jealous of his own disciple. In the same way, a father is never jealous of his son, hoping that his son's achievement will be greater than his own (*Babylonian Talmud, Sanhedrin 105b*).

kabbalah bites

27:20 "*Grant him some of your glow (hod).*" Prophecy is derived from the two *Sefirot Netzah* (victory) and *Hod* (glory), which constitute the outward expression of the Divine "personality." These two *Sefirot* are metaphorically termed God's "legs," since they ensure that His message spreads forth (through prophecy), like legs which mobilize a person to be present in different places.

Since Joshua was Moses' direct disciple you would have expected him to receive from *Netzah*, the higher *Sefirah*, symbolized by the stronger right leg, and not *Hod*, the weaker, left one. Why did Moses grant him *Hod*?

Because when Esau's angel attacked Jacob, it succeeded in damaging Jacob's right leg (*Genesis* 32:26), i.e., *Netzah*. Only with the prophet Samuel would this spiritual wound be healed. Until then, post-Mosaic prophecy would only come from the lower *Sefirah, Hod*.

(courageously) go out (to war) ahead of them and return in front of them; (somebody whose merit is sufficient) to lead them out (to war) and bring them back (safely), so that God's congregation will not be like sheep that have no shepherd."

[18] God said to Moses, "Persuade your (own loyal servant) Joshua son of Nun (to accept the leadership, for) he is a strong-willed person. Lay your hand upon him, [19] and present him to Eleazar the priest and the entire congregation. Instruct him in their presence. [20] Grant him some of the glow (that is on your face), so that the entire congregation of the children of Israel will listen (to him, just as they listen to you. [21] When Joshua needs to go to war), he should stand in front of Eleazar the priest and ask him to clarify the law through the Urim, before God. They will go (out to war only by) the word (of Eleazar) and they will come back (from war) by his word—both he together with all Israel, and the entire congregation (of the Sanhedrin)."

[22] Moses did what God had commanded him. He took Joshua and presented him to Eleazar the priest and the entire congregation. [23] He laid his hands upon him and instructed him, in accordance with what God had said to Moses.

God replied that there can only be one leader, in the spirit of the saying that *"two kings cannot wear the same crown"* (*Babylonian Talmud, Ḥullin* 60b; *Rabbi Nathan Nata b. Solomon Spira, 17th century*).

Previously, Moses had assumed that Phinehas would succeed him, but after witnessing Phinehas' zealousness, Moses asks God to *"appoint somebody (capable) over the congregation."* A leader must exhibit exceptional tolerance (*Rabbi Menahem Mendel Morgensztern of Kotsk, 19th century*).

17. Who will (courageously) go out (to war) ahead of them and return in front of them. A leader must *"go out ahead"* of his people and not follow their lead. He must elevate them to his level and not allow himself to descend to theirs. He must have the courage of conviction to do what is right, rather than follow the sentiments of the public (*Rabbi Alexander Zusya Friedman, 20th century*).

To lead them out (to war) and bring them back (safely). A true leader of his people will *"lead them out"* from the depths of sin and *"bring them back"* to the gates of holiness (*Rabbi Isaac Meir Alter of Gur, 19th century*).

So that God's congregation will not be like sheep that have no shepherd. A shepherd herds the flock while thinking of himself first, doing his job in order to receive payment from the flock's owner. He walks *behind* the sheep, so that he will be able to turn and flee in case an armed robber or a dangerous animal should come.

This behavior differs from true leaders, "Israel's shepherds," whose *first* concern is to worry about the needs of the flock.

Moses asked God to replace him with a worthy leader, *"who will go out ahead of them and return in front of them"* (*Rabbi Abraham Samuel Benjamin Sofer, 19th century*).

במדבר כח:א-ה פינחס

כח 1 וַיְדַבֵּר יְהֹוָה אֶל־מֹשֶׁה לֵּאמֹר: 2 צַו אֶת־בְּנֵי יִשְׂרָאֵל [FIFTH READING] וְאָמַרְתָּ אֲלֵהֶם אֶת־קָרְבָּנִי לַחְמִי לְאִשַּׁי רֵיחַ נִיחֹחִי תִּשְׁמְרוּ לְהַקְרִיב לִי בְּמוֹעֲדוֹ: 3 וְאָמַרְתָּ לָהֶם זֶה הָאִשֶּׁה אֲשֶׁר תַּקְרִיבוּ לַיהֹוָה כְּבָשִׂים בְּנֵי־שָׁנָה תְמִימִם שְׁנַיִם לַיּוֹם עֹלָה תָמִיד: 4 אֶת־הַכֶּבֶשׂ אֶחָד תַּעֲשֶׂה בַבֹּקֶר וְאֵת הַכֶּבֶשׂ הַשֵּׁנִי תַּעֲשֶׂה בֵּין הָעַרְבָּיִם: 5 וַעֲשִׂירִית הָאֵיפָה סֹלֶת לְמִנְחָה

Since the prayers were instituted as a direct compensation for the sacrifices (*Babylonian Talmud, Berakhot* 26b), it follows that every one of our daily prayers is of tremendous significance to God, to the extent that He describes them as His very "sustenance" (*Rabbi Shneur Zalman of Lyady, 18th century*).

Through the sacrifices, the *Shekhinah* (Divine Presence) entered the Holy Temple, from which it spread throughout the entire world. It follows, then, that each different type of sacrifice was responsible for a different aspect of Godly revelation, and this was expressed by the nature of the sacrifice and the mode in which it was offered.

The sacrifices which are discussed here in the current passage could be broadly divided into two categories: (a) Continual Offerings—the two offerings which are offered on a daily basis, each morning and afternoon (v. 3-8); and, (b) Occasional Offerings—brought on a special occasion, such as the Sabbath, New Month or the Festivals (v. 8ff.).

The fact that the occasional offerings were bound by a specific time suggests that the spiritual revelation which they brought also possessed a certain limitation. The continual offerings, however, were offered every single day, suggesting that they brought a totally unlimited form of spiritual revelation that could not be "contained" by any particular time or moment (*Rabbi Menahem Mendel Schneerson, 20th century*).

3. This is the fire-offering which you should (ensure is) offered to God. This "fire-offering" represents the fiery enthusiasm we should have while praying to God. It is this passion and intensity that enables our prayers to draw down abundant blessings from on high. We are reminded to ensure that our prayers are offered to God with the appropriate passion and fervor (*Rabbi Menahem Mendel b. Jacob Koppel of Kosov, 18th–19th century*).

Two perfect lambs. Why was a sheep chosen for the daily offering, and not a more expensive offering, such as a bull?

A bull is generally calm but, on occasion, can wreak destruction. It therefore atones for the most difficult of circumstances, a life of extreme dysfunction. A sheep, on the other hand, is a more steady animal. It represents the more consistent temptation of materialism which we need assistance in battling. Therefore, it was chosen for the daily offering of the community, as it represents the general challenge which we all face in our daily lives (*Rabbi Abraham Isaac Kook, 20th century*).

Food for thought

1. What is more important, observance or the intention which accompanies it?

2. Why is it important to observe *mitzvot* (commandments) daily?

3. Why did the Torah require animal sacrifices?

The Communal Offerings

28 [FIFTH READING] ¹ God spoke to: Moses, saying: ² Command the children of Israel. Say to them:

- You should be careful to offer to Me (each communal offering) in its appointed time, including: (The blood of) My offering (and the parts of the animal burnt on the altar as) My food on My fires—a pleasant aroma for Me.

The Continual-Offering

³ Say to the (court): This is the fire-offering which you should (ensure is) offered to God:

- Two perfect (unblemished) lambs in their first year each day, as a daily burnt-offering. ⁴ You should offer one lamb in the morning, and you should offer the other lamb in the afternoon.

- ⁵ (Offer) a tenth of an *'ephah* of fine flour as a meal-offering, mixed with a quarter of a *hin* of crushed (olive) oil.

28:2 Be careful to offer to Me (each communal offering) in its appointed time. Why was this passage, which speaks of the sacrifices, written immediately after the passages discussing Moses' succession?

God said to Moses, "Before charging Me about children (i.e. successors), charge My children not to rebel against Me" (*Sifrei*).

Moses had acquired his prophetic powers in the merit of the sacrifices. Now, shortly before Moses was to pass away, it was important to place additional emphasis on the sacrifices so that prophecy would continue after his death. The sacrifices needed to be strengthened and expanded to compensate for the fact that Israelites were now losing the greatest of all prophets (*Rabbi Isaac Abravanel, 15th century*).

If Moses had taken the Jewish people into the land of Israel, he would have eliminated the impulse for idol-worship. Joshua, on the other hand, did not have the ability to do that. So now, as Joshua was appointed, it was especially pertinent for the Jewish people to find other methods to combat that impulse so that their Torah-worship would be as tangible as possible. Therefore, God commanded that they bring a sacrifice in the morning, when the sun rises, and one at night, when the sun sets, in order to deter them from serving the sun (*Rabbi Meir Loeb Weisser, 19th century*).

My food on My fires. God describes the daily sacrifices as *"My food,"* a metaphor that suggests that the sacrifices actually "sustain" the Almighty, so to speak.

---

kabbalah bites

28:2 *"To offer (le-hakriv) to Me."* The Hebrew term normally used to suggest two entities being brought close together is *le-karev* (to bring close). The term used here, *le-hakriv*, is conjugated in the causative, suggesting that we are inducing an inner closeness and consistency in a *single* entity.

How does this relate to the sacrifices? The Kabbalah teaches that the chaotic, anxiety-inducing qualities of our world are a symptom of God's name being in a state of disrepair. The messianic dream of a New Era is one where God's name will, once again, be unified.

The spiritual effect of the sacrifices is *"le-hakriv,"* to bring an inner unity and healing to God's name, thereby healing the world, too.

במדבר כח:ה-טו • פינחס

בְּלוּלָה בְּשֶׁמֶן כָּתִית רְבִיעִת הַהִין: 6 עֹלַת תָּמִיד הָעֲשֻׂיָה בְּהַר סִינַי לְרֵיחַ נִיחֹחַ אִשֶּׁה לַיהוה: 7 וְנִסְכּוֹ רְבִיעִת הַהִין לַכֶּבֶשׂ הָאֶחָד בַּקֹּדֶשׁ הַסֵּךְ נֶסֶךְ שֵׁכָר לַיהוה: 8 וְאֵת הַכֶּבֶשׂ הַשֵּׁנִי תַּעֲשֶׂה בֵּין הָעַרְבָּיִם כְּמִנְחַת הַבֹּקֶר וּכְנִסְכּוֹ תַּעֲשֶׂה אִשֵּׁה רֵיחַ נִיחֹחַ לַיהוה: פ 9 וּבְיוֹם הַשַּׁבָּת שְׁנֵי־כְבָשִׂים בְּנֵי־שָׁנָה תְּמִימִם וּשְׁנֵי עֶשְׂרֹנִים סֹלֶת מִנְחָה בְּלוּלָה בַשֶּׁמֶן וְנִסְכּוֹ: 10 עֹלַת שַׁבַּת בְּשַׁבַּתּוֹ עַל־עֹלַת הַתָּמִיד וְנִסְכָּהּ: פ 11 וּבְרָאשֵׁי חָדְשֵׁיכֶם תַּקְרִיבוּ עֹלָה לַיהוה פָּרִים בְּנֵי־בָקָר שְׁנַיִם וְאַיִל אֶחָד כְּבָשִׂים בְּנֵי־שָׁנָה שִׁבְעָה תְּמִימִם: 12 וּשְׁלֹשָׁה עֶשְׂרֹנִים סֹלֶת מִנְחָה בְּלוּלָה בַשֶּׁמֶן לַפָּר הָאֶחָד וּשְׁנֵי עֶשְׂרֹנִים סֹלֶת מִנְחָה בְּלוּלָה בַשֶּׁמֶן לָאַיִל הָאֶחָד: 13 וְעִשָּׂרֹן עִשָּׂרוֹן סֹלֶת מִנְחָה בְּלוּלָה בַשֶּׁמֶן לַכֶּבֶשׂ הָאֶחָד עֹלָה רֵיחַ נִיחֹחַ אִשֶּׁה לַיהוה: 14 וְנִסְכֵּיהֶם חֲצִי הַהִין יִהְיֶה לַפָּר וּשְׁלִישִׁת הַהִין לָאַיִל וּרְבִיעִת הַהִין לַכֶּבֶשׂ יָיִן זֹאת עֹלַת חֹדֶשׁ בְּחָדְשׁוֹ לְחָדְשֵׁי הַשָּׁנָה: 15 וּשְׂעִיר עִזִּים אֶחָד לְחַטָּאת לַיהוה עַל־עֹלַת הַתָּמִיד יֵעָשֶׂה וְנִסְכּוֹ: ס

6. (It is) a daily burnt-offering, (like) the one offered up (lit. "that was made") at Mount Sinai—a pleasant aroma (for God). How can a burnt-offering cause a pleasant aroma for God? After all, *"Does God eat the flesh of bulls or drink the blood of goats?"* (*Psalms* 50:13).

The answer lies in this very same verse, *"that was made at Mount Sinai."* There is no Godly pleasure inherent in the sacrifices we offer. Rather, this phenomenon is something that originated at the revelation of Sinai. At that time, God *"made,"* so to speak, that He will derive pleasure from the sacrifices brought in accordance with His instructions.

The same holds true for all commandments. God's enjoyment when we perform the rituals—many of which involve physical objects and activities, like waving a palm branch (*lulav*) on the Festival of Tabernacles—is not because of any tangible benefit that He gains from them. Rather, it is something much deeper and beyond our comprehension—it is His will (*Rabbi Simḥah Bunem of Przysucha, 18th–19th century*).

15. As a sin-offering to God. Why is the goat offered on the New Moon singled out as a "Sin-offering *to God*"? The phrase "to God" is not mentioned in connection with the sacrifices of other festivals.

God said, "Let this goat be an atonement for Me, for making the moon smaller!"

When God created the sun and the moon, they were of equal size. The moon asked, "Is it possible for two kings to wear the same crown?"

"So go and make yourself smaller," God replied.

The moon pleaded, "Why should I make myself smaller just because I made a reasonable suggestion?" God proceeded to console the moon, but when He saw that the moon could not

⁶ (It is) a daily burnt-offering, (like) the one offered up at Mount Sinai—a pleasant aroma (for God), a fire-offering to God.

- ⁷ Its accompanying libation should be a quarter of a *hin* (of wine) for each lamb, to be poured on the holy (altar) as a libation of strong wine to God.

- ⁸ You should offer up the second lamb in the afternoon. You should offer it up with the same meal-offering and libation as the morning (offering. It is) a fire-offering with a pleasant aroma to God.

The Additional-Offering of the Sabbath

⁹ On the day of the Sabbath, (offer):

- Two perfect (unblemished) lambs in their first year.

- Two-tenths (of an *'ephah* of) fine flour as a meal-offering, mixed with oil.

- Its accompanying (wine) libation.

- ¹⁰ The burnt-offering of the Sabbath (may only be offered) on its (appropriate) Sabbath; (it may not be compensated for on a later Sabbath).

- (All of the above is to be offered) in addition to the daily burnt-offering and its accompanying libation.

Communal Offering for the New Moon

¹¹ At the beginning of every month, you should offer:

- A burnt-offering to God: two young bulls, one ram, and seven lambs in their first year, (all) perfect (and unblemished).

- ¹² Three-tenths (of an *'ephah*) of fine flour mixed with oil as a meal-offering for each bull, two-tenths (of an *'ephah*) of fine flour mixed with oil as a meal-offering for each ram, ¹³ and one-tenth (of an *'ephah*) of fine flour mixed with oil as a meal-offering for each lamb.

(It is) a burnt-offering with a pleasant aroma (for God), a fire-offering to God.

- ¹⁴ The accompanying libations are: a half of a *hin* (of wine) for each bull, a third of a *hin* for each ram, and a quarter of a *hin* for each lamb.

- This burnt-offering of each new month (must be offered) on its (appropriate) month throughout the months of the year; (there is no possibility of compensation).

- ¹⁵ One young male goat should be offered up as a sin-offering to God (to atone for your inadvertent ritual contamination of the Temple).

- (All of the above is to be offered) in addition to the daily burnt-offering and its libation.

16 וּבַחֹ֣דֶשׁ הָרִאשׁ֗וֹן בְּאַרְבָּעָ֨ה עָשָׂ֥ר י֛וֹם לַחֹ֖דֶשׁ פֶּ֥סַח לַיהֹוָֽה: [SIXTH READING]
17 וּבַחֲמִשָּׁ֨ה עָשָׂ֥ר י֛וֹם לַחֹ֥דֶשׁ הַזֶּ֖ה חָ֑ג שִׁבְעַ֣ת יָמִ֔ים מַצּ֖וֹת יֵאָכֵֽל: 18 בַּיּ֣וֹם הָרִאשׁ֖וֹן מִקְרָא־קֹ֑דֶשׁ כָּל־מְלֶ֥אכֶת עֲבֹדָ֖ה לֹ֥א תַעֲשֽׂוּ: 19 וְהִקְרַבְתֶּ֨ם אִשֶּׁ֤ה עֹלָה֙ לַֽיהֹוָ֔ה פָּרִ֧ים בְּנֵי־בָקָ֛ר שְׁנַ֖יִם וְאַ֣יִל אֶחָ֑ד וְשִׁבְעָ֤ה כְבָשִׂים֙ בְּנֵ֣י שָׁנָ֔ה תְּמִימִ֖ם יִהְי֥וּ לָכֶֽם: 20 וּמִ֨נְחָתָ֔ם סֹ֖לֶת בְּלוּלָ֣ה בַשָּׁ֑מֶן שְׁלֹשָׁ֨ה עֶשְׂרֹנִ֜ים לַפָּ֗ר וּשְׁנֵ֧י עֶשְׂרֹנִ֛ים לָאַ֖יִל תַּעֲשֽׂוּ: 21 עִשָּׂר֤וֹן עִשָּׂרוֹן֙ תַּעֲשֶׂ֔ה לַכֶּ֖בֶשׂ הָאֶחָ֑ד לְשִׁבְעַ֖ת הַכְּבָשִֽׂים: 22 וּשְׂעִ֥יר חַטָּ֛את אֶחָ֖ד לְכַפֵּ֥ר עֲלֵיכֶֽם: 23 מִלְּבַד֙ עֹלַ֣ת הַבֹּ֔קֶר אֲשֶׁ֖ר לְעֹלַ֣ת הַתָּמִ֑יד תַּעֲשׂ֖וּ אֶת־אֵֽלֶּה: 24 כָּאֵ֜לֶּה תַּעֲשׂ֤וּ לַיּוֹם֙ שִׁבְעַ֣ת יָמִ֔ים לֶ֛חֶם אִשֵּׁ֥ה רֵֽיחַ־נִיחֹ֖חַ לַיהֹוָ֑ה עַל־עוֹלַ֧ת הַתָּמִ֛יד יֵעָשֶׂ֖ה וְנִסְכּֽוֹ: 25 וּבַיּוֹם֙ הַשְּׁבִיעִ֔י מִקְרָא־קֹ֖דֶשׁ יִהְיֶ֣ה לָכֶ֑ם כָּל־מְלֶ֥אכֶת עֲבֹדָ֖ה לֹ֥א תַעֲשֽׂוּ: ס 26 וּבְי֣וֹם הַבִּכּוּרִ֗ים בְּהַקְרִ֨יבְכֶ֜ם מִנְחָ֤ה חֲדָשָׁה֙ לַֽיהֹוָ֔ה בְּשָׁבֻעֹ֖תֵיכֶ֑ם מִקְרָא־קֹ֙דֶשׁ֙ יִהְיֶ֣ה לָכֶ֔ם כָּל־מְלֶ֥אכֶת עֲבֹדָ֖ה לֹ֥א תַעֲשֽׂוּ: 27 וְהִקְרַבְתֶּ֨ם עוֹלָ֜ה לְרֵ֤יחַ נִיחֹ֙חַ֙ לַֽיהֹוָ֔ה פָּרִ֧ים בְּנֵי־בָקָ֛ר שְׁנַ֖יִם אַ֣יִל אֶחָ֑ד שִׁבְעָ֥ה כְבָשִׂ֖ים בְּנֵ֥י שָׁנָֽה: 28 וּמִ֨נְחָתָ֔ם סֹ֖לֶת בְּלוּלָ֣ה בַשָּׁ֑מֶן שְׁלֹשָׁ֤ה עֶשְׂרֹנִים֙ לַפָּ֣ר הָֽאֶחָ֔ד שְׁנֵי֙ עֶשְׂרֹנִ֔ים לָאַ֖יִל הָאֶחָֽד: 29 עִשָּׂר֤וֹן עִשָּׂרוֹן֙ לַכֶּ֣בֶשׂ הָאֶחָ֔ד לְשִׁבְעַ֖ת הַכְּבָשִֽׂים:

spiritual vitamin

> There can be a state of "winter," of apparent unproductivity in the life of a person. But no-one should consider themselves as having terminated their usefulness, even though a long time of fruitlessness has elapsed. Given the proper inspiration and stimulus, the state of "winter" can easily and suddenly be changed into "spring" and blossom time, which eventually will ripen into good fruits for God and man.

numbers 28:16–29 — pinḥas

Communal Offerings for Passover

- ❖ [SIXTH READING] ¹⁶ In the first month, on the fourteenth day of the month, (bring) a Passover-offering to God.

- ❖ ¹⁷ On the fifteenth day of this month, a festival (begins). You must eat unleavened bread for seven days.

¹⁸ The first day is a holy celebration:

- ❖ You may not perform any manual work.

- ❖ ¹⁹ You should offer a fire-offering, a burnt-offering to God: Two young bulls, one ram, and seven lambs in their first year. They should be perfect (and unblemished) for you.

- ❖ ²⁰ Their accompanying meal-offerings (should be from) fine flour mixed with oil. You should offer three-tenths (of an *'ephah* of flour) for each bull, two-tenths for the ram, ²¹ and you should offer one-tenth for each lamb, for all seven lambs.

- ❖ ²² One young male goat (should be brought) as a sin-offering, to atone for your (inadvertent ritual contamination of the Temple).

- ❖ ²³ You should offer these up in addition to the morning burnt-offering which is offered as a daily burnt-offering.

- ❖ ²⁴ You should offer the same as this, every day for seven days.

- ❖ It is a fire-offering, "food" for the altar, a pleasant aroma for God.

- ❖ You should offer all this in addition to the daily burnt-offering and its accompanying libation.

- ❖ ²⁵ The seventh day will be a holy celebration for you. You may not perform any manual work.

Communal Offerings for the Festival of Weeks

²⁶ On your Festival of Weeks, the "Day of the First Fruits," when you offer a meal-offering to God from the new (crop of wheat), you will have a holy celebration:

- ❖ You may not perform any manual work.

- ❖ ²⁷ You should offer a burnt-offering as a pleasant aroma to God: Two young bulls, one ram, and seven lambs in their first year.

- ❖ ²⁸ Their accompanying meal-offerings (should be) fine flour mixed with oil: three-tenths (of an *'ephah*) for each bull, two-tenths for the ram, ²⁹ and one-tenth for each lamb, for all seven lambs.

---

be placated, He said to the children of Israel, "Bring an atonement for Me, for making the moon smaller" (*Babylonian Talmud, Ḥullin* 60b).

פינחס · במדבר כח:ל - כט:יא

30 שְׂעִיר עִזִּים אֶחָד לְכַפֵּר עֲלֵיכֶם: 31 מִלְּבַד עֹלַת הַתָּמִיד וּמִנְחָתוֹ תַּעֲשׂוּ תְּמִימִם יִהְיוּ־לָכֶם וְנִסְכֵּיהֶם: פ

כט

1 וּבַחֹדֶשׁ הַשְּׁבִיעִי בְּאֶחָד לַחֹדֶשׁ מִקְרָא־קֹדֶשׁ יִהְיֶה לָכֶם כָּל־מְלֶאכֶת עֲבֹדָה לֹא תַעֲשׂוּ יוֹם תְּרוּעָה יִהְיֶה לָכֶם: 2 וַעֲשִׂיתֶם עֹלָה לְרֵיחַ נִיחֹחַ לַיהֹוָה פַּר בֶּן־בָּקָר אֶחָד אַיִל אֶחָד כְּבָשִׂים בְּנֵי־שָׁנָה שִׁבְעָה תְּמִימִם: 3 וּמִנְחָתָם סֹלֶת בְּלוּלָה בַשָּׁמֶן שְׁלֹשָׁה עֶשְׂרֹנִים לַפָּר שְׁנֵי עֶשְׂרֹנִים לָאָיִל: 4 וְעִשָּׂרוֹן אֶחָד לַכֶּבֶשׂ הָאֶחָד לְשִׁבְעַת הַכְּבָשִׂים: 5 וּשְׂעִיר־עִזִּים אֶחָד חַטָּאת לְכַפֵּר עֲלֵיכֶם: 6 מִלְּבַד עֹלַת הַחֹדֶשׁ וּמִנְחָתָהּ וְעֹלַת הַתָּמִיד וּמִנְחָתָהּ וְנִסְכֵּיהֶם כְּמִשְׁפָּטָם לְרֵיחַ נִיחֹחַ אִשֶּׁה לַיהֹוָה: ס 7 וּבֶעָשׂוֹר לַחֹדֶשׁ הַשְּׁבִיעִי הַזֶּה מִקְרָא־קֹדֶשׁ יִהְיֶה לָכֶם וְעִנִּיתֶם אֶת־נַפְשֹׁתֵיכֶם כָּל־מְלָאכָה לֹא תַעֲשׂוּ: 8 וְהִקְרַבְתֶּם עֹלָה לַיהֹוָה רֵיחַ נִיחֹחַ פַּר בֶּן־בָּקָר אֶחָד אַיִל אֶחָד כְּבָשִׂים בְּנֵי־שָׁנָה שִׁבְעָה תְּמִימִם יִהְיוּ לָכֶם: 9 וּמִנְחָתָם סֹלֶת בְּלוּלָה בַשָּׁמֶן שְׁלֹשָׁה עֶשְׂרֹנִים לַפָּר שְׁנֵי עֶשְׂרֹנִים לָאַיִל הָאֶחָד: 10 עִשָּׂרוֹן עִשָּׂרוֹן לַכֶּבֶשׂ הָאֶחָד לְשִׁבְעַת הַכְּבָשִׂים: 11 שְׂעִיר־עִזִּים אֶחָד חַטָּאת מִלְּבַד חַטַּאת הַכִּפֻּרִים

his reach—in the so-called "Four Kingdoms"—*domem, tzome'ah, ḥai* and *medabber* (inorganic matter, vegetable, animal, and man).

Significantly, this finds expression in the special commandments which are connected with the beginning of the year, by way of introduction to the entire year—in the festivals of the month of *Tishri*:

The commandment of the *sukkah* (booth), the Jew's dwelling during the seven days of *Sukkot* (Festival of Tabernacles), where the walls of the *sukkah* represent the "inorganic kingdom";

The commandment of the "four kinds"—*etrog, lulav,* myrtle and willow—which come from the "vegetable kingdom";

The commandment of the *shofar* (ram's horn) on *Rosh Ha-Shanah* (Jewish New Year), the *shofar* being a horn of an animal;

And all of these things (by virtue of being Divine commandments) are elevated through the *medabber*, the "speaking" (human) being—the person carrying out these (and all other) commandments, through which he elevates also himself and mankind—both in the realm of doing as well as that of not doing—the latter is represented in the *mitzvah* of the fast on the Holy Day, the Day of Atonement, *Yom Kippur*.

- ❖ ³⁰ (Offer) one young male goat to atone for your (inadvertent ritual contamination of the Temple). ³¹ You should offer this in addition to the daily burnt-offering and its accompanying meal-offering. The (offerings) should be perfect (quality) for you, as well as their libations.

29 Communal Offerings and the Ram's Horn for the New Year

¹ In the seventh month, on the first day, you will have a holy celebration:

- ❖ You may not perform any manual work.
- ❖ It will be a day of sounding (the ram's horn) for you.
- ❖ ² You should bring a burnt-offering as a pleasant aroma to God: one young bull, one ram, and seven lambs in their first year, (all) perfect (and unblemished). ³ Their accompanying meal-offerings (should be) fine flour mixed with oil: three-tenths (of an *ʾephah*) for the bull, two-tenths for the ram, ⁴ and one-tenth for each lamb, for the seven lambs. ⁵ (Offer) one young male goat as a sin-offering to atone for your (inadvertent ritual contamination of the Temple). ⁶ All this is) in addition to the New Moon burnt-offering and its accompanying meal-offering, and (in addition to) the daily burnt-offering and its accompanying meal-offering and libations, as prescribed for them. (It will be) a pleasant aroma, a fire-offering to God.

Communal Offerings for the Day of Atonement

⁷ On the tenth day of this seventh month, you will have a holy celebration:

- ❖ You must afflict yourselves.
- ❖ You may not perform any work.
- ❖ ⁸ You should bring a burnt-offering to God, as a pleasant aroma: one young bull, one ram, and seven lambs in their first year. They should be perfect (and unblemished). ⁹ Their accompanying meal-offering (should be) fine flour mixed with oil: three-tenths (of an *ʾephah*) for the bull, two-tenths for the ram, ¹⁰ and one-tenth for each lamb, for the seven lambs. ¹¹ (Offer) one young male goat for a sin-offering (to atone for your inadvertent ritual contamination of the Temple. All this is) in addition to the atonement sin-offering and the daily burnt-offering, its accompanying meal-offering and libations.

30. One young male goat to atone. With the additional-offering (*musaf*) of all the other festivals, the Torah says "One young male goat *as a sin-offering*" (as in 28:22); but with the Festival of Weeks—the time associated with the giving of the Torah—it does not say "as a sin-offering."

God says to Israel, "Because you have accepted on yourselves the yoke of the Torah, I consider it as if you had never sinned" (*Jerusalem Talmud, Rosh Ha-Shanah* 4:8).

29:1 In the seventh month. Man's mission in life includes also "elevating" the environment in which he lives, in accordance with the Divine intent in the entire creation and in all its particulars, by infusing holiness and Godliness into all the aspects of the physical world within

וְעֹלַת הַתָּמִיד וּמִנְחָתָהּ וְנִסְכֵּיהֶם: ס 12 [SEVENTH READING] וּבַחֲמִשָּׁה עָשָׂר יוֹם לַחֹדֶשׁ הַשְּׁבִיעִי מִקְרָא־קֹדֶשׁ יִהְיֶה לָכֶם כָּל־מְלֶאכֶת עֲבֹדָה לֹא תַעֲשׂוּ וְחַגֹּתֶם חַג לַיהוָה שִׁבְעַת יָמִים: 13 וְהִקְרַבְתֶּם עֹלָה אִשֵּׁה רֵיחַ נִיחֹחַ לַיהוָה פָּרִים בְּנֵי־בָקָר שְׁלֹשָׁה עָשָׂר אֵילִם שְׁנָיִם כְּבָשִׂים בְּנֵי־שָׁנָה אַרְבָּעָה עָשָׂר תְּמִימִם יִהְיוּ: 14 וּמִנְחָתָם סֹלֶת בְּלוּלָה בַשֶּׁמֶן שְׁלֹשָׁה עֶשְׂרֹנִים לַפָּר הָאֶחָד לִשְׁלֹשָׁה עָשָׂר פָּרִים שְׁנֵי עֶשְׂרֹנִים לָאַיִל הָאֶחָד לִשְׁנֵי הָאֵילִם: 15 וְעִשָּׂרוֹן עִשָּׂרוֹן לַכֶּבֶשׂ הָאֶחָד לְאַרְבָּעָה עָשָׂר כְּבָשִׂים: 16 וּשְׂעִיר־עִזִּים אֶחָד חַטָּאת מִלְּבַד עֹלַת הַתָּמִיד מִנְחָתָהּ וְנִסְכָּהּ: ס 17 וּבַיּוֹם הַשֵּׁנִי פָּרִים בְּנֵי־בָקָר שְׁנֵים עָשָׂר אֵילִם שְׁנָיִם כְּבָשִׂים בְּנֵי־שָׁנָה אַרְבָּעָה עָשָׂר תְּמִימִם: 18 וּמִנְחָתָם וְנִסְכֵּיהֶם לַפָּרִים לָאֵילִם וְלַכְּבָשִׂים בְּמִסְפָּרָם כַּמִּשְׁפָּט: 19 וּשְׂעִיר־עִזִּים אֶחָד חַטָּאת מִלְּבַד עֹלַת הַתָּמִיד וּמִנְחָתָהּ וְנִסְכֵּיהֶם: ס 20 וּבַיּוֹם הַשְּׁלִישִׁי פָּרִים עַשְׁתֵּי־עָשָׂר אֵילִם שְׁנָיִם כְּבָשִׂים בְּנֵי־שָׁנָה אַרְבָּעָה עָשָׂר תְּמִימִם: 21 וּמִנְחָתָם וְנִסְכֵּיהֶם לַפָּרִים לָאֵילִם וְלַכְּבָשִׂים בְּמִסְפָּרָם כַּמִּשְׁפָּט: 22 וּשְׂעִיר חַטָּאת אֶחָד מִלְּבַד עֹלַת הַתָּמִיד וּמִנְחָתָהּ וְנִסְכָּהּ: ס 23 וּבַיּוֹם הָרְבִיעִי פָּרִים עֲשָׂרָה אֵילִם שְׁנָיִם כְּבָשִׂים בְּנֵי־שָׁנָה אַרְבָּעָה עָשָׂר תְּמִימִם: 24 מִנְחָתָם וְנִסְכֵּיהֶם לַפָּרִים לָאֵילִם וְלַכְּבָשִׂים בְּמִסְפָּרָם כַּמִּשְׁפָּט: 25 וּשְׂעִיר־עִזִּים אֶחָד חַטָּאת מִלְּבַד עֹלַת הַתָּמִיד מִנְחָתָהּ וְנִסְכָּהּ: ס 26 וּבַיּוֹם הַחֲמִישִׁי פָּרִים תִּשְׁעָה אֵילִם שְׁנָיִם כְּבָשִׂים בְּנֵי־שָׁנָה אַרְבָּעָה עָשָׂר תְּמִימִם: 27 וּמִנְחָתָם וְנִסְכֵּיהֶם

18. For the bulls, for the rams. The seventy bulls of the festival correspond to the seventy nations, which progressively decrease in number, symbolizing the obliteration of their negative influences. In Temple times, the sacrifices of the bulls would protect the nations from punishments. *"The lambs"* correspond to the Jewish people, who are called *"a scattered lamb"* (*Jeremiah* 50:17), but their number remains constant, fourteen lambs per day, totaling ninety-eight over the seven days, in order to eradicate the ninety-eight curses related in *Deuteronomy* (28:15-68; Rashi, 11th century).

numbers 29:12–27 — pinḥas

Communal Offerings for the Festival of Tabernacles

[SEVENTH READING] [12] On the fifteenth day of the seventh month, you will have a holy celebration:

- You may not perform any manual work.
- You will celebrate a festival to God for seven days.
- (On the first day): [13] You should offer a burnt-offering, a fire-offering as a pleasant aroma to God: Thirteen young bulls, two rams, and fourteen lambs in their first year. They should be perfect (and unblemished). [14] Their accompanying meal-offering (should be) fine flour mixed with oil: three-tenths (of an ʾ*ephah*) for each bull, for the thirteen bulls, two-tenths for each ram, for the two rams, [15] and one-tenth for each lamb, for the fourteen lambs. [16] (Offer) one young male goat for a sin-offering (to atone for your inadvertent ritual contamination of the Temple. All this is) in addition to the daily burnt-offering, its accompanying meal-offering and libation.

- [17] On the second day: Twelve young bulls, two rams, and fourteen lambs in their first year, perfect (and unblemished). [18] Their accompanying meal-offerings and their libations, for the bulls, for the rams, and for the lambs, according to their legally required number (stated on the first day). [19] (Offer) one young male goat for a sin-offering (to atone for your inadvertent ritual contamination of the Temple. All this is) in addition to the daily burnt-offering, its accompanying meal-offering and libations.

- [20] On the third day: Eleven bulls, two rams, and fourteen lambs in their first year, perfect (and unblemished). [21] Their accompanying meal-offerings and their libations, for the bulls, for the rams, and for the lambs, according to their legally required number (stated on the first day). [22] (Offer) one young male goat for a sin-offering (to atone for your inadvertent ritual contamination of the Temple. All this is) in addition to the daily burnt-offering, its accompanying meal-offering and libation.

- [23] On the fourth day: Ten bulls, two rams, and fourteen lambs in their first year, perfect (and unblemished). [24] Their accompanying meal-offerings and their libations, for the bulls, for the rams, and for the lambs, according to their legally required number (stated on the first day). [25] (Offer) one young male goat for a sin-offering (to atone for your inadvertent ritual contamination of the Temple. All this is) in addition to the daily burnt-offering, its accompanying meal-offering and libation.

- [26] On the fifth day: Nine bulls, two rams, and fourteen lambs in their first year, perfect (and unblemished). [27] Their accompanying meal-offerings and their libations, for the bulls, for the rams, and for the lambs, according to their legally required

---

Through infusing holiness into all four kingdoms of the physical world and making them into "vessels" (and instruments) of Godliness in carrying out God's command—a Jew elevates them to their true perfection (*Rabbi Menahem Mendel Schneerson, 20th century*).

במדבר כט:כח - ל:א — פינחס

לַפָּרִים לָאֵילִם וְלַכְּבָשִׂים בְּמִסְפָּרָם כַּמִּשְׁפָּט: 28 וּשְׂעִיר חַטָּאת אֶחָד מִלְּבַד עֹלַת הַתָּמִיד וּמִנְחָתָהּ וְנִסְכָּהּ: ס 29 וּבַיּוֹם הַשִּׁשִּׁי פָּרִים שְׁמֹנָה אֵילִם שְׁנָיִם כְּבָשִׂים בְּנֵי־שָׁנָה אַרְבָּעָה עָשָׂר תְּמִימִם: 30 וּמִנְחָתָם וְנִסְכֵּיהֶם לַפָּרִים לָאֵילִם וְלַכְּבָשִׂים בְּמִסְפָּרָם כַּמִּשְׁפָּט: 31 וּשְׂעִיר חַטָּאת אֶחָד מִלְּבַד עֹלַת הַתָּמִיד מִנְחָתָהּ וּנְסָכֶיהָ: ס 32 וּבַיּוֹם הַשְּׁבִיעִי פָּרִים שִׁבְעָה אֵילִם שְׁנָיִם כְּבָשִׂים בְּנֵי־שָׁנָה אַרְבָּעָה עָשָׂר תְּמִימִם: 33 וּמִנְחָתָם וְנִסְכֵּהֶם לַפָּרִים לָאֵילִם וְלַכְּבָשִׂים בְּמִסְפָּרָם כְּמִשְׁפָּטָם: 34 וּשְׂעִיר חַטָּאת אֶחָד מִלְּבַד עֹלַת הַתָּמִיד מִנְחָתָהּ וְנִסְכָּהּ: ס 35 [MAFTIR] בַּיּוֹם הַשְּׁמִינִי עֲצֶרֶת תִּהְיֶה לָכֶם כָּל־מְלֶאכֶת עֲבֹדָה לֹא תַעֲשׂוּ: 36 וְהִקְרַבְתֶּם עֹלָה אִשֵּׁה רֵיחַ נִיחֹחַ לַיהוָה פַּר אֶחָד אַיִל אֶחָד כְּבָשִׂים בְּנֵי־שָׁנָה שִׁבְעָה תְּמִימִם: 37 מִנְחָתָם וְנִסְכֵּיהֶם לַפָּר לָאַיִל וְלַכְּבָשִׂים בְּמִסְפָּרָם כַּמִּשְׁפָּט: 38 וּשְׂעִיר חַטָּאת אֶחָד מִלְּבַד עֹלַת הַתָּמִיד וּמִנְחָתָהּ וְנִסְכָּהּ: 39 אֵלֶּה תַּעֲשׂוּ לַיהוָה בְּמוֹעֲדֵיכֶם לְבַד מִנִּדְרֵיכֶם וְנִדְבֹתֵיכֶם לְעֹלֹתֵיכֶם וּלְמִנְחֹתֵיכֶם וּלְנִסְכֵּיכֶם וּלְשַׁלְמֵיכֶם:

ל 1 וַיֹּאמֶר מֹשֶׁה אֶל־בְּנֵי יִשְׂרָאֵל כְּכֹל אֲשֶׁר־צִוָּה יְהוָה אֶת־מֹשֶׁה: פ פ פ

קס"ח פסוקים, לחל"ק סימן. ואליפלה"ו סימן.

The *Midrashic* interpretation: Being that they brought sacrifices all the days of the Festival of Tabernacles, corresponding to the seventy nations, when they came to leave, God said to them, "Please make Me a small feast, so that I can have some pleasure from you alone" (*Rashi, 11th century*).

spiritual vitamin

> The strength of our people as a whole, and of each individual man and woman, lies in a closer adherence to our ancient spiritual heritage, which contains the secret of harmonious life, hence of a healthy and happy life.

number (stated on the first day). ²⁸ (Offer) one young male goat for a sin-offering (to atone for your inadvertent ritual contamination of the Temple. All this is) in addition to the daily burnt-offering, its accompanying meal-offering and libation.

❖ ²⁹ On the sixth day: Eight bulls, two rams, and fourteen lambs in their first year, perfect (and unblemished). ³⁰ Their accompanying meal-offerings and their libations, for the bulls, for the rams, and for the lambs, according to their legally required number (stated on the first day). ³¹ (Offer) one young male goat for a sin-offering (to atone for your inadvertent ritual contamination of the Temple. All this is) in addition to the daily burnt-offering, its accompanying meal-offering and libations.

❖ ³² On the seventh day: Seven bulls, two rams and fourteen lambs in their first year, perfect (and unblemished). ³³ Their accompanying meal-offerings and their libations, for the bulls, for the rams, and for the lambs, according to the legally required number for them (stated on the first day). ³⁴ (Offer) one young male goat for a sin-offering (to atone for your inadvertent ritual contamination of the Temple. All this is) in addition to the daily burnt-offering, its accompanying meal-offering and libation.

Communal Offerings for Eighth Day (*Shemini Atzeret*)

[MAFTIR] ³⁵ The eighth day will be a time of restriction for you:

❖ You may not perform any manual work.

❖ ³⁶ You should bring a burnt-offering, a fire-offering as a pleasant aroma to God: One bull, one ram, and seven lambs in their first year, perfect (and unblemished). ³⁷ (Offer) their accompanying meal-offerings and their libations, for the bull, for the ram, and for the lambs, according to the legally required number. ³⁸ (Offer) one young male goat for a sin-offering (to atone for your inadvertent ritual contamination of the Temple). (All this is) in addition to the daily burnt-offering, its accompanying meal-offering and libation.

³⁹ All the above is what you should offer to God on your festivals, in addition to (voluntary offerings that) you vowed and (other) voluntary offerings—your burnt-offerings, your meal-offerings, your libations, and your peace-offerings.

30

¹ Moses told the children of Israel everything that God had commanded Moses.

The *Haftarah* for *Pinḥas* is on page 1386. [When *Parashat Pinḥas* coincides with the Three Weeks, the *Haftarah* for *Parashat Mattot* is read—page 1388.]

35. The eighth day will be a time of restriction (*atzeret*). It is restricted from performing manual work. Alternatively: *'Atzeret* means "restrict yourselves from leaving." This indicates that they were required to remain in Jerusalem overnight.

Even now that **your soul has descended** to this world and is **detached** from overt revelation, like **branches** ("*mattot*") cut from a tree, you can still worship God under all circumstances. In this way, your **commitment** will grow stronger, like a **hardened branch**.

MATTOT
מטות

LAWS OF PERSONAL VOWS	30:2–17
WAR AGAINST MIDIAN	31:1–54
REQUEST TO SETTLE THE TRANSJORDAN	32:1–42

NAME
Mattot

MEANING
"Tribes," "branches"

LINES IN TORAH SCROLL
190

PARASHIYYOT
4 open; 5 closed

VERSES
112

WORDS
1484

LETTERS
5652

DATE
Marḥeshvan-Shevat, 2448

LOCATION
Plains of Moab

KEY PEOPLE
Moses, Phinehas, Midianite kings, Balaam, Eleazar, Joshua, tribes of Reuben and Gad

MITZVOT
1 positive; 1 prohibition

NOTES
Often read together with portion of *Mase'ei;* read during the three weeks of mourning over the destruction of the Temple

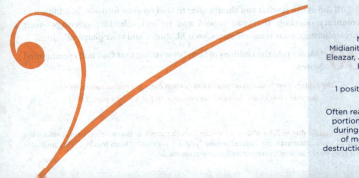

CHARACTER PROFILE

NAME
Balaam ("swallower of a people")

FATHER
Beor

ANCESTOR
Kemuel father of Aram

HOME
Pethor

DEATH
Captured during war with Midian and put to death by the Jewish court

ACHIEVEMENTS
Advised Pharaoh to kill Jewish children and bathe in their blood to heal his skin; achieved prophecy; spoke Hebrew

KNOWN FOR
Born circumcised; was rebuked by his donkey; attempted to curse the Jews for Balak and ended up blessing them instead; advised Balak to send Midianite girls to seduce the Jewish men

POWER OF SPEECH

Your words are not just a way to express yourself. Every time you promise, you are making a binding contract, which should not be violated. Careful thought beforehand is crucial (30:2-17).

RESTRAINT

Vows are a tool for someone whose excessive physical urges interfere with his ability to worship God. You need to evaluate what levels of restraint are needed in your life (30:2-17).

UNITY

The war against Midian was, spiritually speaking, a war against human divisiveness. Is maintaining harmonious relations, at all costs, one of your core spiritual values? (31:48-50)

RESPONSIBILITY

Moses was upset that the tribes of Reuben and Gad wanted to settle on the other side of the Jordan, leaving the rest of the people to conquer the land. Only when they assured him that they would fight, too, did he agree. Always go out of your way to see that your family and colleagues have what they need before worrying about your own needs (ch. 32).

במדבר ל:ב-ה · מטות

2 וַיְדַבֵּ֤ר מֹשֶׁה֙ אֶל־רָאשֵׁ֣י הַמַּטּ֔וֹת לִבְנֵ֥י יִשְׂרָאֵ֖ל לֵאמֹ֑ר זֶ֣ה הַדָּבָ֔ר אֲשֶׁ֥ר צִוָּ֖ה יְהֹוָֽה׃ 3 אִישׁ֩ כִּֽי־יִדֹּ֨ר נֶ֜דֶר לַֽיהֹוָ֗ה אֽוֹ־הִשָּׁ֤בַע שְׁבֻעָה֙ לֶאְסֹ֤ר אִסָּר֙ עַל־נַפְשׁ֔וֹ לֹ֥א יַחֵ֖ל דְּבָר֑וֹ כְּכׇל־הַיֹּצֵ֥א מִפִּ֖יו יַעֲשֶֽׂה׃ 4 וְאִשָּׁ֕ה כִּֽי־תִדֹּ֥ר נֶ֖דֶר לַיהֹוָ֑ה וְאָסְרָ֥ה אִסָּ֛ר בְּבֵ֥ית אָבִ֖יהָ בִּנְעֻרֶֽיהָ׃ 5 וְשָׁמַ֨ע אָבִ֜יהָ אֶת־נִדְרָ֗הּ וֶֽאֱסָרָהּ֙ אֲשֶׁ֣ר אָֽסְרָ֣ה עַל־

3. When a person makes a vow. Vows are a "fence" for abstinence (*Mishnah, Avot* 3:13).

Has the Torah not forbidden you enough that you wish to forbid yourself more things? (*Jerusalem Talmud, Nedarim* 9:1)

The advice of the Jerusalem Talmud, that you should avoid making vows, appears to contradict the Mishnah's teaching that vows are a valuable tool for you to restrain from indulgence.

In truth, however, there is no contradiction, since these two texts are addressing two different types of people. The Mishnah speaks to a person who *cannot restrain himself* from excessive physical indulgence which interferes with his observance of Torah. For him, the only solution is to make a vow of abstinence.

The Jerusalem Talmud, on the other hand, is pitched at someone who is able to harmonize physical pleasures with a life of sanctity and worship. For such a person it would be inadvisable to abstain from these physical things, since the purpose of creation is to sanctify the physical world, so that it becomes a "home" for God below (*Rabbi Shneur Zalman of Lyady, 18th century*).

All your interactions with the physical world should be carried out in order to extract the sparks of holiness that are trapped there. Making vows of abstinence, therefore, to deprive yourself from enjoying the physical world, is really a sin. *Deriving benefit from the physical is as much a part of worshiping God as putting on tefillin and praying.* The important thing is that your actions should be carried out for the sake of heaven, and not for your own personal gratification.

Obviously, most people are far from this level. But even if what you do is not entirely pure, you still achieve a certain amount of elevation of the sparks. It is similar to your prayers and Torah study, which even if carried out without the best intent are still a legitimate form of worship. In the same way, if you eat and drink and your intention is not perfect, you are still considered to be serving God (*Rabbi Menahem Nahum Twersky of Chernobyl, 18th century*).

An oath to prohibit himself.

You might think that even if you took an oath to eat non-kosher foods, the command *"He must act in accordance with whatever he uttered,"* applies to you, and you must eat these forbidden things. Therefore, the verse states, *"to prohibit himself"*—that is, to prohibit from yourself something that was previously permitted (*Rashi, 11th century*).

He must act in accordance with whatever he uttered.

Although *making* a vow is usually done excitedly and emotionally, *keeping* the vow frequently is done with some reluctance. But really, *"He must act in accordance with whatever he uttered"*—fulfillment of the vow should be done with the same enthusiasm with which it was made (*Rabbi Abraham Samuel Benjamin Sofer, 19th century*).

---

kabbalah bites

30:3 You are created in the image of God. Every one of your limbs is a branch from the Tree of Life. *When you open your mouth to speak, you represent the Divine.* Therefore, you may not violate your word and you must act in accordance with whatever you uttered.

parashat mattot

The Laws of Personal Vows

² Moses spoke to the children of Israel's tribal heads, saying: This is what God has commanded: ³ (Concerning the principle that) when a person makes a vow to God or makes an oath to prohibit himself (something which the Torah permits), he may not violate his word (and) he must act in accordance with whatever he uttered. (The following rules apply):

- ⁴ If a woman is in her adolescence (and thus still) under (the jurisdiction) of her father's house, (and) she makes a vow to God, or imposes a ban (on herself):

- ⁵ If her father heard about her vow, or her ban which she forbade to herself, and her father remained silent, then all her vows stand, and any ban that she forbade to herself stands.

30:2 Tribal heads. Moses honored the leaders by teaching them first, and only later the rest of the Jewish people.

How do we know that with other commandments he did the same? From this verse: *"Aaron and all the leaders of the community returned to him, and Moses would speak to them. Afterwards, all the children of Israel would draw near"* (*Exodus* 34:31-32).

Why did Scripture choose to mention this point here?

To indicate that when the annulment of vows is done by an individual, he must be an expert (such as a tribal "leader"). If no individual expert is available, the annulment may be done by three laymen (*Rashi, 11th century*).

This is what God has commanded. All the other prophets prophesied with the words, *"So said God."* But Moses also prophesied with the more precise expression, *"This is what God has commanded"* (*Rashi, 11th century*).

All the prophets looked through "unclear glass," but Moses looked through "clear glass" (*Babylonian Talmud, Yevamot* 49b).

The meaning of the Sages' analogy of "clear glass" is that Moses' prophetic visions were direct and stripped of all physical garb, which is why he was unable to "see" God (see *Exodus* 33:20). Isaiah, however, was able to perceive *"God sitting on a throne, high and exalted"* (*Isaiah* 6:1), because he perceived his visions through a physical veil ("unclear glass"). He was really only able to *imagine* what was behind the veil, just as the form of a person's clothing gives you a picture of what is inside (*Rabbi Judah Loew b. Bezalel of Prague, 16th century*).

2-3. This is what God has commanded ... he may not violate his word. This is the most fundamental of all Torah principles: you may not violate something you have accepted on yourself as a vow or oath. Without this, there would no basis for the entire Torah, which we accepted as a covenant (*Rabbi Moses Sofer, 18th–19th century*).

Food for thought

1. How careful are you with your words?

2. Do you always keep your word—even to your disadvantage?

3. When might a promise be retractable?

במדבר ל:ה-ט״ז מטות

נַפְשָׁהּ וְהֶחֱרִישׁ לָהּ אָבִיהָ וְקָמוּ כָּל־נְדָרֶיהָ וְכָל־אִסָּר אֲשֶׁר־אָסְרָה עַל־נַפְשָׁהּ יָקוּם: 6 וְאִם־הֵנִיא אָבִיהָ אֹתָהּ בְּיוֹם שָׁמְעוֹ כָּל־נְדָרֶיהָ וֶאֱסָרֶיהָ אֲשֶׁר־אָסְרָה עַל־נַפְשָׁהּ לֹא יָקוּם וַיהֹוָה יִסְלַח־לָהּ כִּי־הֵנִיא אָבִיהָ אֹתָהּ: 7 וְאִם־הָיוֹ תִהְיֶה לְאִישׁ וּנְדָרֶיהָ עָלֶיהָ אוֹ מִבְטָא שְׂפָתֶיהָ אֲשֶׁר אָסְרָה עַל־נַפְשָׁהּ: 8 וְשָׁמַע אִישָׁהּ בְּיוֹם שָׁמְעוֹ וְהֶחֱרִישׁ לָהּ וְקָמוּ נְדָרֶיהָ וֶאֱסָרֶהָ אֲשֶׁר־אָסְרָה עַל־נַפְשָׁהּ יָקֻמוּ: 9 וְאִם בְּיוֹם שְׁמֹעַ אִישָׁהּ יָנִיא אוֹתָהּ וְהֵפֵר אֶת־נִדְרָהּ אֲשֶׁר עָלֶיהָ וְאֵת מִבְטָא שְׂפָתֶיהָ אֲשֶׁר אָסְרָה עַל־נַפְשָׁהּ וַיהֹוָה יִסְלַח־לָהּ: 10 וְנֵדֶר אַלְמָנָה וּגְרוּשָׁה כֹּל אֲשֶׁר־אָסְרָה עַל־נַפְשָׁהּ יָקוּם עָלֶיהָ: 11 וְאִם־בֵּית אִישָׁהּ נָדָרָה אוֹ־אָסְרָה אִסָּר עַל־נַפְשָׁהּ בִּשְׁבֻעָה: 12 וְשָׁמַע אִישָׁהּ וְהֶחֱרִשׁ לָהּ לֹא הֵנִיא אֹתָהּ וְקָמוּ כָּל־נְדָרֶיהָ וְכָל־אִסָּר אֲשֶׁר־אָסְרָה עַל־נַפְשָׁהּ יָקוּם: 13 וְאִם־הָפֵר יָפֵר אֹתָם ׀ אִישָׁהּ בְּיוֹם שָׁמְעוֹ כָּל־מוֹצָא שְׂפָתֶיהָ לִנְדָרֶיהָ וּלְאִסַּר נַפְשָׁהּ לֹא יָקוּם אִישָׁהּ הֲפֵרָם וַיהֹוָה יִסְלַח־לָהּ: 14 כָּל־נֵדֶר וְכָל־שְׁבֻעַת אִסָּר לְעַנֹּת נָפֶשׁ אִישָׁהּ יְקִימֶנּוּ וְאִישָׁהּ יְפֵרֶנּוּ: 15 וְאִם־הַחֲרֵשׁ יַחֲרִישׁ לָהּ אִישָׁהּ מִיּוֹם אֶל־יוֹם וְהֵקִים אֶת־כָּל־נְדָרֶיהָ אוֹ אֶת־כָּל־אֱסָרֶיהָ אֲשֶׁר עָלֶיהָ הֵקִים אֹתָם כִּי־הֶחֱרִשׁ לָהּ בְּיוֹם שָׁמְעוֹ: 16 וְאִם־הָפֵר יָפֵר אֹתָם אַחֲרֵי שָׁמְעוֹ וְנָשָׂא אֶת־עֲוֺנָהּ:

spiritual vitamin

" Your Judaism is actually intact deep inside of you, and it is entirely up to you to make it an integral and active ingredient of your daily life. You don't have to look for it elsewhere; all you have to do is brush off those external layers that, for one reason or another, have covered your inner essence. "

- ❖ ⁶ But if, on the day he hears about it, her father vetoes her (vow by annulling her words) then all her vows and her bans that she forbade to herself will not stand.
- ❖ (If she is unaware of her father's veto, and subsequently violated her "vow"), God will forgive her because her father vetoed her (vow, and thus annulled it).
- ❖ ⁷ If she is (betrothed) to a man while her (earlier) vows (are still pending) upon her, (because her father did not hear about the vows, so they were never ratified or annulled); or (she has a pre-existing) verbal obligation which she imposed upon herself (which was not heard by her father):
- ❖ ⁸ (If) the man to whom she is (betrothed) hears about it but remains silent on the day that he hears about it, her vows will stand, and her ban that she forbade to herself will stand (even if her father annuls them).
- ❖ ⁹ But if the man to whom she is (betrothed) vetoes her (vow) on the day he heard about it (as her father did), he revokes the vow (pending) upon her, or the verbal obligation which she forbade to herself (jointly with her father).
- ❖ (If she is unaware of the veto, and subsequently violated her "vow"), God will forgive her (because it was, in fact, annulled).
- ❖ ¹⁰ (Concerning) the vow of a widow or a divorcee: Anything that she forbids to herself will stand for her (as a vow, since she is not under the jurisdiction of her husband or her father).
- ❖ ¹¹ If (a married woman) made a vow or banned something from herself with an oath in her husband's house:
- ❖ ¹² (If) her husband heard about it and remained silent, not vetoing her, all her vows will stand, and every ban that she forbade to herself will stand.
- ❖ ¹³ But if her husband vetoes them on the day he hears about them, then anything she uttered as her vows or personal bans will not stand.
- ❖ (Since) her husband has vetoed them (thus annulling them, if she is unaware of this and subsequently violated her "vow"), God will forgive her (because it was, in fact, annulled).
- ❖ ¹⁴ (However, it is only regarding) a vow or oath of self-affliction (that) her husband (has the right) either to ratify or annul it.
- ❖ ¹⁵ (Concerning the time limit on the husband): If her husband remained silent (during the whole) day until (the next) day (begins, in the evening), then he has ratified all the vows and prohibitions which are (pending) upon her. He has ratified them because he remained silent on the day he heard about it.
- ❖ ¹⁶ If, after having heard about (a vow and ratifying it that day), he then annuls it (later in the day), he will be responsible for her sin.

במדבר ל:יז – לא:ו   מטות

17 אֵ֣לֶּה הַֽחֻקִּ֗ים אֲשֶׁ֨ר צִוָּ֤ה יְהוָה֙ אֶת־מֹשֶׁ֔ה בֵּ֥ין אִ֖ישׁ לְאִשְׁתּ֑וֹ בֵּֽין־אָ֣ב לְבִתּ֔וֹ בִּנְעֻרֶ֖יהָ בֵּ֥ית אָבִֽיהָ: פ

לא 1 וַיְדַבֵּ֥ר יְהוָ֖ה אֶל־מֹשֶׁ֥ה לֵּאמֹֽר: [SECOND READING] 2 נְקֹ֗ם נִקְמַת֙ בְּנֵ֣י יִשְׂרָאֵ֔ל מֵאֵ֖ת הַמִּדְיָנִ֑ים אַחַ֖ר תֵּאָסֵ֥ף אֶל־עַמֶּֽיךָ: 3 וַיְדַבֵּ֤ר מֹשֶׁה֙ אֶל־הָעָ֣ם לֵאמֹ֔ר הֵחָלְצ֧וּ מֵאִתְּכֶ֛ם אֲנָשִׁ֖ים לַצָּבָ֑א וְיִהְיוּ֙ עַל־מִדְיָ֔ן לָתֵ֥ת נִקְמַת־יְהוָ֖ה בְּמִדְיָֽן: 4 אֶ֚לֶף לַמַּטֶּ֔ה אֶ֖לֶף לַמַּטֶּ֑ה לְכֹל֙ מַטּ֣וֹת יִשְׂרָאֵ֔ל תִּשְׁלְח֖וּ לַצָּבָֽא: 5 וַיִּמָּֽסְרוּ֙ מֵאַלְפֵ֣י יִשְׂרָאֵ֔ל אֶ֖לֶף לַמַּטֶּ֑ה שְׁנֵים־עָשָׂ֥ר אֶ֖לֶף חֲלוּצֵ֥י צָבָֽא: 6 וַיִּשְׁלַ֨ח אֹתָ֥ם מֹשֶׁ֛ה אֶ֥לֶף לַמַּטֶּ֖ה לַצָּבָ֑א אֹ֠תָ֠ם וְאֶת־פִּ֨ינְחָ֜ס בֶּן־אֶלְעָזָ֤ר הַכֹּהֵן֙ לַצָּבָ֔א

out God's revenge"—they could overlook their own honor, but God's honor had to be avenged, even if it would hasten Moses' death (*Rabbi Ephraim of Luntshits, 16th–17th century*).

4. All the tribes. This includes the tribe of Levi (*Rashi, 11th century*).

Why did the tribe of Levi not merit a portion in the land of Israel and its spoils, as their brothers did? Because they have been singled out to serve God as His ministers. Therefore they were also separated from worldly matters. They are not required to fight in war, like other Jewish people, and they do not inherit the land (*Maimonides, 12th century*).

The war against the seven Canaanite nations alludes to the "battle" of refining overtly undesirable character traits (which fall into seven broad categories, stemming from the seven emotional faculties of the soul). The war against Midian, on the other hand, involved fighting against a subtle type of evil that can plague even the most dedicated servant of God—a lack of unity and camaraderie between one person and another (*Rabbi Isaac Luria, 16th century*).

All this arises from a sense of overinflated self-importance, which causes one person to be intolerant of others and eventually view them as enemies. Clearly the war against these attributes is very important indeed! (*Rabbi Shalom Dov Baer Schneersohn of Lubavitch, 19th–20th century*).

spiritual vitamin

> Never be discouraged if you find the going hard and sometimes without success, for discouragement is one of the very tricks of the impulse to evil in order to weaken the fighting spirit of the impulse to good. So never become discouraged and never think the battle lost, but keep on fighting; be on guard to overcome a bad habit as soon as it seems to tempt you.

[SUP]17[/SUP] These are the suprarational commands which God commanded Moses concerning a man and his wife, (and) a father and his adolescent daughter who is (under the jurisdiction of) her father's house.

The War Against Midian

31 [SECOND READING] [SUP]1[/SUP] God spoke to Moses, saying, [SUP]2[/SUP] "Take revenge against the Midianites for the children of Israel. After that, you will be gathered to your people."

[SUP]3[/SUP] Moses (immediately) spoke to the people, saying, "From among yourselves, get men armed and ready for combat against Midian, to carry out God's revenge against Midian. [SUP]4[/SUP] You should send for the army a thousand from each tribe; a thousand from each tribe. (This applies to) all the tribes of Israel."

[SUP]5[/SUP] From Israel's population, one thousand (men) were handed over from each tribe, (totaling) twelve thousand armed for combat. [SUP]6[/SUP] Moses sent them, the thousand from each tribe, for the army. (He sent) them with Phinehas son of Eleazar the priest to the army, with the sacred vessels and the signal trumpets entrusted to him.

31:2 Take revenge against the Midianites for the children of Israel. After that you will be gathered to your people. Why was Moses commanded to fight the Midianites before his passing?

If Moses had not fought the Midianites, people would have suspected it was because of his stay in Midian and his marriage to the daughter of Jethro, priest of Midian. God commanded Moses to avenge the children of Israel before his own demise and, in this way, dispel any skepticism from the people (*Rabbi Meir Simḥah of Dvinsk, 19th–20th century*).

3. To carry out God's revenge against Midian. Moses enthusiastically announced God's command to fight Midian, without imposing any delay. This was in full realization that after the war ended he would pass away—*"after that you will be gathered to your people"* (31:2; *Rashi, 11th century*).

What evidence is there that Moses announced God's command with enthusiasm? A hint to this fact lies in a difference between God's command to Moses, and Moses' delivery of that command to the people. God commanded Moses to "take revenge for *the children of Israel*"; but Moses instructed them to "carry out *God's* revenge."

What inspired Moses to change the emphasis here? The Midianites had led the Israelites astray, sending their daughters to seduce the Israelites to act immorally. The Midianites had not only sinned against God, they had also caused the Israelites to be struck by a plague that had wiped out twenty-four thousand people. When conveying the command to Moses, God implied that even if He could overlook the slight against Himself, He could not overlook what the Midianites had done to Israel—*"Take revenge for the children of Israel."*

When Moses received the announcement that he was to die when the war was over, he was afraid that the Israelites would choose not to go to war, overlooking what the Midianites had done to them, in an attempt to postpone his death. So Moses instructed the people to *"carry*

מטות
במדבר לא:ו-יט

וּכְלֵי הַקֹּדֶשׁ וַחֲצֹצְרוֹת הַתְּרוּעָה בְּיָדוֹ: 7 וַיִּצְבְּאוּ עַל־מִדְיָן כַּאֲשֶׁר צִוָּה יְהֹוָה אֶת־מֹשֶׁה וַיַּהַרְגוּ כָּל־זָכָר: 8 וְאֶת־מַלְכֵי מִדְיָן הָרְגוּ עַל־חַלְלֵיהֶם אֶת־אֱוִי וְאֶת־רֶקֶם וְאֶת־צוּר וְאֶת־חוּר וְאֶת־רֶבַע חֲמֵשֶׁת מַלְכֵי מִדְיָן וְאֵת בִּלְעָם בֶּן־בְּעוֹר הָרְגוּ בֶּחָרֶב: 9 וַיִּשְׁבּוּ בְנֵי־יִשְׂרָאֵל אֶת־נְשֵׁי מִדְיָן וְאֶת־טַפָּם וְאֵת כָּל־בְּהֶמְתָּם וְאֶת־כָּל־מִקְנֵהֶם וְאֶת־כָּל־חֵילָם בָּזָזוּ: 10 וְאֵת כָּל־עָרֵיהֶם בְּמוֹשְׁבֹתָם וְאֵת כָּל־טִירֹתָם שָׂרְפוּ בָּאֵשׁ: 11 וַיִּקְחוּ אֶת־כָּל־הַשָּׁלָל וְאֵת כָּל־הַמַּלְקוֹחַ בָּאָדָם וּבַבְּהֵמָה: 12 וַיָּבִאוּ אֶל־מֹשֶׁה וְאֶל־אֶלְעָזָר הַכֹּהֵן וְאֶל־עֲדַת בְּנֵי־יִשְׂרָאֵל אֶת־הַשְּׁבִי וְאֶת־הַמַּלְקוֹחַ וְאֶת־הַשָּׁלָל אֶל־הַמַּחֲנֶה אֶל־עַרְבֹת מוֹאָב אֲשֶׁר עַל־יַרְדֵּן יְרֵחוֹ: ס 13 [THIRD READING SECOND WHEN JOINED] וַיֵּצְאוּ מֹשֶׁה וְאֶלְעָזָר הַכֹּהֵן וְכָל־נְשִׂיאֵי הָעֵדָה לִקְרָאתָם אֶל־מִחוּץ לַמַּחֲנֶה: 14 וַיִּקְצֹף מֹשֶׁה עַל פְּקוּדֵי הֶחָיִל שָׂרֵי הָאֲלָפִים וְשָׂרֵי הַמֵּאוֹת הַבָּאִים מִצְּבָא הַמִּלְחָמָה: 15 וַיֹּאמֶר אֲלֵיהֶם מֹשֶׁה הַחִיִּיתֶם כָּל־נְקֵבָה: 16 הֵן הֵנָּה הָיוּ לִבְנֵי יִשְׂרָאֵל בִּדְבַר בִּלְעָם לִמְסָר־מַעַל בַּיהֹוָה עַל־דְּבַר־פְּעוֹר וַתְּהִי הַמַּגֵּפָה בַּעֲדַת יְהֹוָה: 17 וְעַתָּה הִרְגוּ כָל־זָכָר בַּטָּף וְכָל־אִשָּׁה יֹדַעַת אִישׁ לְמִשְׁכַּב זָכָר הֲרֹגוּ: 18 וְכֹל הַטַּף בַּנָּשִׁים אֲשֶׁר לֹא־יָדְעוּ מִשְׁכַּב זָכָר הַחֲיוּ לָכֶם: 19 וְאַתֶּם חֲנוּ מִחוּץ לַמַּחֲנֶה שִׁבְעַת יָמִים כֹּל הֹרֵג נֶפֶשׁ וְכֹל | נֹגֵעַ בֶּחָלָל תִּתְחַטְּאוּ בַּיּוֹם הַשְּׁלִישִׁי וּבַיּוֹם הַשְּׁבִיעִי

action should be taken, you must do it without waiting for an explicit command (*Rabbi Isaiah Horowitz, 16th–17th century*).

kabbalah bites

31:8 *"They killed Balaam the son of Beor with a sword."* Balaam's sin was the abuse of his mouth, which he used to curse rather than to bless. To achieve *tikkun* (spiritual healing) for this, he was reincarnated into a stone. In Hebrew, inanimate objects are referred to as *domem*, "silent." This silent existence would achieve *tikkun* for his abuse of speech.

numbers 31:7-19 — mattot

⁷ They besieged Midian, as God had commanded Moses, and they killed every male. ⁸ They killed the Midianite kings, (who fell) upon their (own people's) corpses. The five kings of Midian (that they killed were): Evi, Rekem, Zur, Hur, and Reba. They killed Balaam son of Beor with a sword.

⁹ The children of Israel took the Midianite women captive, along with their small children. They plundered all their animals and herds, and all their possessions. ¹⁰ They set fire to all their residential cities and their cloisters.

¹¹ They took all the booty and all the plunder of both man and beast (but kept nothing for themselves). ¹² They brought the captives, the plunder, and the booty to Moses, Eleazar the priest and the entire community of Israel, to the camp at the plains of Moab by the Jordan at Jericho.

[THIRD READING / SECOND WHEN JOINED] ¹³ (When they heard that some youths had gone outside the camp to grab plunder) Moses, Eleazar the priest, and all the leaders of the community went out to meet them outside the camp (to put an end to it).

¹⁴ Moses became angry with the officers of the army, (both) the officers over thousands (of men) and the officers over hundreds (of men), who had returned from the campaign of war. ¹⁵ Moses said to them, "You've allowed all the females to live? ¹⁶ They were the very ones who acted on Balaam's words against the children of Israel to betray God in the Peor affair, resulting in a plague among God's congregation!"

¹⁷ "Now kill every male child! And kill every woman capable of knowing a man, (I mean every one) who could sleep with a male. ¹⁸ But you may keep alive all the young girls who have never experienced sleeping with a man."

Purification, Purging and Immersion Following the War

¹⁹ "You must stay outside the camp for seven days. Whoever killed a person or who touched a corpse should cleanse himself (with the sprinkling water of the Red

8. They killed the Midianite kings ... They killed Balaam son of Beor. What was Balaam doing in Midian when he had already returned home to Aram (24:25)?

He went to Midian to collect a reward for his part in the death of twenty-four thousand Israelites. He had helped caused their demise by advising the Midianite daughters to seduce the Israelites to sin. So Balaam's desire for reward actually led to his own death (*Babylonian Talmud, Sanhedrin* 106a).

14-15. Moses became angry ... "You've allowed all the females to live?" Why was Moses angry with the soldiers for not killing the Midianite women, when he had not given them instructions to do so?

It was obvious that taking revenge against the Midianite women was the proper thing to do. *"They were the very ones who acted on Balaam's words against the children of Israel"* (v. 16) by seducing them to sin, which resulted in a devastating plague. When it stands to reason that an

מטות • במדבר לא:יט-כז

20 אַתֶּ֥ם וּשְׁבִיכֶֽם: וְכָל־בֶּ֧גֶד וְכָל־כְּלִי־ע֛וֹר וְכָל־מַעֲשֵׂ֥ה עִזִּ֖ים וְכָל־כְּלִי־עֵ֑ץ תִּתְחַטָּֽאוּ: ס 21 וַיֹּ֨אמֶר אֶלְעָזָ֤ר הַכֹּהֵן֙ אֶל־אַנְשֵׁ֣י הַצָּבָ֔א הַבָּאִ֖ים לַמִּלְחָמָ֑ה זֹ֚את חֻקַּ֣ת הַתּוֹרָ֔ה אֲשֶׁר־צִוָּ֥ה יְהֹוָ֖ה אֶת־מֹשֶֽׁה: 22 אַ֥ךְ אֶת־הַזָּהָ֖ב וְאֶת־הַכָּ֑סֶף אֶֽת־הַנְּחֹ֔שֶׁת אֶת־הַבַּרְזֶ֕ל אֶֽת־הַבְּדִ֖יל וְאֶת־הָעֹפָֽרֶת: 23 כָּל־דָּבָ֞ר אֲשֶׁר־יָבֹ֣א בָאֵ֗שׁ תַּעֲבִ֤ירוּ בָאֵשׁ֙ וְטָהֵ֔ר אַ֕ךְ בְּמֵ֥י נִדָּ֖ה יִתְחַטָּ֑א וְכֹ֨ל אֲשֶׁ֧ר לֹֽא־יָבֹ֛א בָּאֵ֖שׁ תַּעֲבִ֥ירוּ בַמָּֽיִם: 24 וְכִבַּסְתֶּ֧ם בִּגְדֵיכֶ֛ם בַּיּ֥וֹם הַשְּׁבִיעִ֖י וּטְהַרְתֶּ֑ם וְאַחַ֖ר תָּבֹ֥אוּ אֶל־הַֽמַּחֲנֶֽה: ס 25 וַיֹּ֥אמֶר יְהֹוָ֖ה אֶל־מֹשֶׁ֥ה לֵּאמֹֽר: [FOURTH READING] 26 שָׂ֗א אֵ֣ת רֹ֤אשׁ מַלְק֨וֹחַ֙ הַשְּׁבִ֔י בָּאָדָ֖ם וּבַבְּהֵמָ֑ה אַתָּה֙ וְאֶלְעָזָ֣ר הַכֹּהֵ֔ן וְרָאשֵׁ֖י אֲב֥וֹת הָעֵדָֽה: 27 וְחָצִ֨יתָ֙ אֶת־הַמַּלְק֔וֹחַ בֵּ֚ין תֹּפְשֵׂ֣י הַמִּלְחָמָ֔ה הַיֹּצְאִ֖ים לַצָּבָ֑א וּבֵ֖ין כָּל־הָעֵדָֽה:

(*Babylonian Talmud, Ḥullin* 17a)—and obviously, then, to eat from non-kosher vessels.

But the war with Midian was not part of the conquest of the land of Israel, so, for the first time, the Jewish people were faced with purging the non-kosher vessels. That is why the laws of purging were given at this point (*Naḥmanides, 13th century*).

Naḥmanides explains why the laws of purging were given at this point, but he does not explain why the requirement to immerse vessels in a ritual pool (v. 23) was only given here.

But in truth it is inappropriate to ask why a commandment was given at a particular time and not beforehand, since *the obligation only arises at the time when the Torah deems fit to introduce it*. The case of purging vessels however, appears to be an exception to this principle, since it is a logical extension of the prohibition against eating non-kosher food, *that was already in force*. That is why Naḥmanides was troubled by this question in particular (*Rabbi Tzevi Pesaḥ Frank, 20th century*).

And then it will be purified. The Sages teach us that as a prerequisite to purging, all rust must be removed (*Sifrei*). Rust is symbolic of superfluous material desires, which cover

kabbalah bites

31:27 Plunder, which is acquired violently, is symbolic of *Gevurah*, your soul's power of severity and limitation. The division of the plunder into two halves suggests that your *Gevurah* is active in two key areas: *cognition* (*Binah*) and *articulation* (*Malkhut*).

Cognition is the flip-side of inspiration. We all have wonderful ideas but those ideas are only valuable if their boundaries have been defined into clear and succinct arguments. This requires the limiting force of *Gevurah*.

Gevurah is needed again when you attempt to explain your idea to others. You will only be effective if you choose your words carefully and precisely, exercising your *Gevurah* of articulation.

Of the two *Gevurot*, cognition needs to be stronger, as an error in the conceptual stage will destroy an idea, whereas failing to articulate it properly will not.

Heifer) on the third and seventh day. (And just as) you (require purification because you are members of the covenant, so too,) your captives (will require purification when they enter the covenant). [20] All garments, leather articles, any goat products, and every wooden article must be cleansed (with sprinkling water)."

[21] Eleazar the priest said to the soldiers returning from battle: "This (purification through sprinkling water which was stated above) is the suprarational law of the Torah that God commanded Moses.

- [22] "However, (in addition to ritually purifying the vessels with sprinkling water, Moses taught us that they must be purged from the flavor of the non-kosher food, as follows): The gold, the silver, the copper, the iron, the tin, and the lead, [23] whatever is used in fire, must be passed through fire by you, and then it will be purified.

- "They must, however, (also) be cleansed with sprinkling water (alternatively: with the water of a ritual-pool).

- "Whatever (utensils) are not used in fire (but rather, with cold foods), should be passed through (the) water (of a ritual-pool) by you (straightaway, since they do not need to be purged).

- [24] "You should wash your garments on the seventh day and (they will) become ritually pure. Afterwards, you may enter the camp."

Dividing the Spoils of War

[FOURTH READING] [25] God spoke to Moses, saying, [26] "Calculate the total plunder of the captured people and animals. You (should do this) together with Eleazar the priest and the community's paternal (tribal) leaders. [27] Divide the plunder equally between the soldiers that went out to battle and (the rest of) the entire congregation.

21. Eleazar the priest said to the soldiers. Moses fell into a state of anger (v. 14), so he fell into a state of error, and the laws of purging vessels were concealed from him. Therefore, Eleazar, rather than Moses, clarified these laws.

A similar incident occurred on the eighth day of inauguration: Moses *"became angry with Eleazar and Ithamar"* (*Leviticus* 10:16)—he fell into a state of anger, so he fell into a state of error, criticizing them for burning the sin-offering.

Likewise, when Moses said: *"Listen, you rebels!"* (above, 20:10), *"he hit the rock"* (ibid., v. 11). Through anger, he came to err (*Rashi, 11th century*).

Anger is a sin more serious than all others. When you commit any sin other than becoming angry, your soul still remains in your body. But when angry, *your soul departs from your body* and is replaced by an "external soul." That is why you tend to forget things through becoming angry, due to the departure of the soul (*Rabbi Isaac Luria, 16th century*).

23. Whatever is used in fire, must be passed through fire. In the earlier wars with Sihon and Og the Jewish people had also taken plunder (*Deuteronomy* 2:35), which presumably included non-kosher vessels. Nevertheless, those wars were part of the conquest of the land of Israel, and the Talmud states that during the conquest the people were allowed to eat non-kosher food

במדבר לא:כח-מא | מטות

28 וַהֲרֵמֹתָ֨ מֶ֜כֶס לַֽיהוָ֗ה מֵאֵ֞ת אַנְשֵׁ֤י הַמִּלְחָמָה֙ הַיֹּצְאִ֣ים לַצָּבָ֔א אֶחָ֣ד נֶ֔פֶשׁ מֵחֲמֵ֖שׁ הַמֵּא֑וֹת מִן־הָֽאָדָם֙ וּמִן־הַבָּקָ֔ר וּמִן־הַחֲמֹרִ֖ים וּמִן־הַצֹּֽאן׃ 29 מִֽמַּחֲצִיתָ֖ם תִּקָּ֑חוּ וְנָתַתָּ֛ה לְאֶלְעָזָ֥ר הַכֹּהֵ֖ן תְּרוּמַ֥ת יְהוָֽה׃ 30 וּמִמַּחֲצִ֨ת בְּנֵֽי־יִשְׂרָאֵ֜ל תִּקַּ֣ח ׀ אֶחָ֣ד ׀ אָחֻ֣ז מִן־הַחֲמִשִּׁ֗ים מִן־הָאָדָ֧ם מִן־הַבָּקָ֛ר מִן־הַחֲמֹרִ֖ים וּמִן־הַצֹּ֣אן מִכָּל־הַבְּהֵמָ֑ה וְנָתַתָּ֤ה אֹתָם֙ לַלְוִיִּ֔ם שֹׁמְרֵ֕י מִשְׁמֶ֖רֶת מִשְׁכַּ֥ן יְהוָֽה׃ 31 וַיַּ֣עַשׂ מֹשֶׁ֔ה וְאֶלְעָזָ֖ר הַכֹּהֵ֑ן כַּאֲשֶׁ֛ר צִוָּ֥ה יְהוָ֖ה אֶת־מֹשֶֽׁה׃ 32 וַיְהִי֙ הַמַּלְק֔וֹחַ יֶ֣תֶר הַבָּ֔ז אֲשֶׁ֥ר בָּזְז֖וּ עַ֣ם הַצָּבָ֑א צֹ֗אן שֵׁשׁ־מֵא֥וֹת אֶ֛לֶף וְשִׁבְעִ֥ים אֶ֖לֶף וַחֲמֵֽשֶׁת־אֲלָפִֽים׃ 33 וּבָקָ֕ר שְׁנַ֥יִם וְשִׁבְעִ֖ים אָֽלֶף׃ 34 וַחֲמֹרִ֕ים אֶחָ֥ד וְשִׁשִּׁ֖ים אָֽלֶף׃ 35 וְנֶ֣פֶשׁ אָדָ֔ם מִן־הַ֨נָּשִׁ֔ים אֲשֶׁ֥ר לֹֽא־יָדְע֖וּ מִשְׁכַּ֣ב זָכָ֑ר כָּל־נֶ֕פֶשׁ שְׁנַ֥יִם וּשְׁלֹשִׁ֖ים אָֽלֶף׃ 36 וַתְּהִי֙ הַֽמֶּחֱצָ֔ה חֵ֕לֶק הַיֹּצְאִ֖ים בַּצָּבָ֑א מִסְפַּ֣ר הַצֹּ֗אן שְׁלֹשׁ־מֵא֥וֹת אֶ֛לֶף וּשְׁלֹשִׁ֥ים אֶ֖לֶף וְשִׁבְעַ֥ת אֲלָפִ֖ים וַחֲמֵ֥שׁ מֵאֽוֹת׃ 37 וַיְהִ֛י הַמֶּ֥כֶס לַֽיהוָ֖ה מִן־הַצֹּ֑אן שֵׁ֥שׁ מֵא֖וֹת וְשִׁבְעִֽים׃ 38 וְהַ֨בָּקָ֔ר שִׁשָּׁ֥ה וּשְׁלֹשִׁ֖ים אָ֑לֶף וּמִכְסָ֥ם לַיהוָ֖ה שְׁנַ֥יִם וְשִׁבְעִֽים׃ 39 וַחֲמֹרִ֕ים שְׁלֹשִׁ֥ים אֶ֖לֶף וַחֲמֵ֣שׁ מֵא֑וֹת וּמִכְסָ֥ם לַיהוָ֖ה אֶחָ֥ד וְשִׁשִּֽׁים׃ 40 וְנֶ֣פֶשׁ אָדָ֔ם שִׁשָּׁ֥ה עָשָׂ֖ר אָ֑לֶף וּמִכְסָם֙ לַֽיהוָ֔ה שְׁנַ֥יִם וּשְׁלֹשִׁ֖ים נָֽפֶשׁ׃ 41 וַיִּתֵּ֣ן מֹשֶׁ֗ה אֶת־מֶ֨כֶס֙ תְּרוּמַ֣ת יְהוָ֔ה לְאֶלְעָזָ֖ר הַכֹּהֵ֑ן כַּאֲשֶׁ֛ר צִוָּ֥ה יְהוָ֖ה אֶת־מֹשֶֽׁה׃

give one as the "tax"; or (b) perhaps you take four hundred and ninety-nine and then give one to the "tax"? The details of the plunder's distribution were recorded to indicate that the latter method was God's intention (*Rabbi Ḥayyim ibn Attar, 18th century*).

32-35. The (total) plunder. *"Six hundred and seventy-five thousand sheep"*—in the merit of the daily burnt offering (*tamid*), brought from sheep, which is *"a fire-offering with a pleasant aroma to God"* (above, 28:8). The numerical value of this phrase, if calculated by combining both the letters and the words, is exactly six hundred and seventy five.

"Seventy-two thousand cattle"—in the merit of the *ḥesed* (kindness) of Abraham—the word *ḥesed* having the numerical value of seventy-two—as the verse states, *"Abraham ran to the cattle"* (*Genesis* 18:7).

"Sixty-one thousand donkeys"—also alluding to Abraham, whose donkey had served him for sixty-one years at the time of the binding of Isaac.

"And people ... thirty-two thousand"—corresponding to the thirty-two merits of Keturah (Hagar), Midian's mother (see *Genesis* 25:2), while she was in Abraham's house: the sixteen

⁲⁸ "You should take a tax for God from the soldiers who went out to battle: From the people, from the cattle, donkeys, and sheep, (take) one individual from every five hundred. ²⁹ Take this from their half (of the plunder) and give it to Eleazar the priest as a gift to God.

³⁰ "From the half belonging to the children of Israel, take one fiftieth of the people, cattle, donkeys, sheep, and all the animals, and give them to the Levites, the guardians of God's Tabernacle."

³¹ Moses and Eleazar the priest did what God had commanded Moses.

³² The (total) plunder—in addition to the spoils that the army had taken as spoils (from inanimate objects that were not taxable)—was:

- Six hundred and seventy-five thousand sheep.
- ³³ Seventy-two thousand cattle.
- ³⁴ Sixty-one thousand donkeys.
- ³⁵ And people: The total number of the women who had not experienced sleeping with a man, was thirty-two thousand.

³⁶ (Thus, these were the taxes from) the half that was apportioned to those who went out to battle:

- The number of sheep was three hundred and thirty-seven thousand, five hundred. ³⁷ Thus, the tax to God from the sheep was six hundred and seventy-five.
- ³⁸ Thirty-six thousand cattle, of which the tax to God was seventy-two.
- ³⁹ Thirty thousand, five hundred donkeys, of which the tax to God was sixty-one.
- ⁴⁰ Sixteen thousand people, of which the tax to God was thirty-two people.

⁴¹ Moses gave the tax, which was a gift to God, to Eleazar the priest, as God had commanded Moses.

---

over a man's essence. The first step to self-improvement is to examine that there is no "rust"—excess materialism—that is holding you back from more noble aspirations (*Rabbi Samuel Shmelke Horowitz of Nikolsburg, 18th century*).

32. The (total) plunder, in addition to the spoils. The Torah details the division of the spoils to inform us of a miracle, that from the time the plunder was taken, until the time it was distributed, not one of the animals died (*Nahmanides, 13th century*).

Nahmanides' explanation does not convince me. The fact that no animals were lost in this short period of time does not appear to be a miracle. And why would the Torah list all these details of the plunder just to convey that single point?

Rather, it appears to me that the details of the plunder's distribution were recorded to clarify the meaning of the command to take *"One individual from every five hundred"* (v. 28). For this could have one of two interpretations: (a) Either you count five hundred animals and then

במדבר לא:מב-נד · מטות

42 [FIFTH READING] וּמִמַּחֲצִית בְּנֵי יִשְׂרָאֵל אֲשֶׁר חָצָה מֹשֶׁה מִן־הָאֲנָשִׁים הַצֹּבְאִים: 43 וַתְּהִי מֶחֱצַת הָעֵדָה מִן־הַצֹּאן שְׁלֹשׁ־מֵאוֹת וּשְׁלֹשִׁים אֶלֶף שִׁבְעַת אֲלָפִים וַחֲמֵשׁ מֵאוֹת: 44 וּבָקָר שִׁשָּׁה וּשְׁלֹשִׁים אָלֶף: 45 וַחֲמֹרִים שְׁלֹשִׁים אֶלֶף וַחֲמֵשׁ מֵאוֹת: 46 וְנֶפֶשׁ אָדָם שִׁשָּׁה עָשָׂר אָלֶף: 47 וַיִּקַּח מֹשֶׁה מִמַּחֲצִת בְּנֵי־יִשְׂרָאֵל אֶת־הָאָחֻז אֶחָד מִן־הַחֲמִשִּׁים מִן־הָאָדָם וּמִן־הַבְּהֵמָה וַיִּתֵּן אֹתָם לַלְוִיִּם שֹׁמְרֵי מִשְׁמֶרֶת מִשְׁכַּן יְהֹוָה כַּאֲשֶׁר צִוָּה יְהֹוָה אֶת־מֹשֶׁה: 48 וַיִּקְרְבוּ אֶל־מֹשֶׁה הַפְּקֻדִים אֲשֶׁר לְאַלְפֵי הַצָּבָא שָׂרֵי הָאֲלָפִים וְשָׂרֵי הַמֵּאוֹת: 49 וַיֹּאמְרוּ אֶל־מֹשֶׁה עֲבָדֶיךָ נָשְׂאוּ אֶת־רֹאשׁ אַנְשֵׁי הַמִּלְחָמָה אֲשֶׁר בְּיָדֵנוּ וְלֹא־נִפְקַד מִמֶּנּוּ אִישׁ: 50 וַנַּקְרֵב אֶת־קָרְבַּן יְהֹוָה אִישׁ אֲשֶׁר מָצָא כְלִי־זָהָב אֶצְעָדָה וְצָמִיד טַבַּעַת עָגִיל וְכוּמָז לְכַפֵּר עַל־נַפְשֹׁתֵינוּ לִפְנֵי יְהֹוָה: 51 וַיִּקַּח מֹשֶׁה וְאֶלְעָזָר הַכֹּהֵן אֶת־הַזָּהָב מֵאִתָּם כֹּל כְּלִי מַעֲשֶׂה: 52 וַיְהִי ׀ כָּל־זְהַב הַתְּרוּמָה אֲשֶׁר הֵרִימוּ לַיהֹוָה שִׁשָּׁה עָשָׂר אֶלֶף שְׁבַע־מֵאוֹת וַחֲמִשִּׁים שָׁקֶל מֵאֵת שָׂרֵי הָאֲלָפִים וּמֵאֵת שָׂרֵי הַמֵּאוֹת: 53 אַנְשֵׁי הַצָּבָא בָּזְזוּ אִישׁ לוֹ: 54 וַיִּקַּח מֹשֶׁה וְאֶלְעָזָר הַכֹּהֵן אֶת־הַזָּהָב מֵאֵת שָׂרֵי הָאֲלָפִים וְהַמֵּאוֹת וַיָּבִאוּ אֹתוֹ אֶל־אֹהֶל מוֹעֵד זִכָּרוֹן לִבְנֵי־יִשְׂרָאֵל לִפְנֵי יְהֹוָה: פ

With this in mind you can carry out your mission with joy, knowing that with the proper dedication, you are assured of success (*Rabbi Menahem Mendel Schneerson, 20th century*).

50. To atone for our souls before God (for thoughts about the Midianite women). It would have been more appropriate to bring the offering for atonement immediately upon returning from battle. Why did the officers delay until now?

Throughout the entire Midianite war, not a single soldier engaged in any illicit behavior (*Babylonian Talmud, Shabbat 64a*). It was their understanding, therefore, that no atonement-offering was required. The laws of purging vessels (31:23) subsequently taught them that the Torah was concerned, not only about a non-kosher substance attached to the surface of a vessel, but also the flavor absorbed inside it. So the officers understood that although no immoral act was committed, atonement was still required for the improper thoughts harbored within their minds (*Rabbi Isaac Meir Alter of Gur, 19th century*).

numbers 31:42-54 — mattot

[FIFTH READING] ⁴² (The following was the calculation) from the half allotted to the children of Israel, which Moses had divided from the men who had gone into the army. ⁴³ The community's half (consisted of):

- Three hundred and thirty-seven thousand, five hundred sheep.
- ⁴⁴ Thirty-six thousand cattle.
- ⁴⁵ Thirty-thousand, five hundred donkeys.
- ⁴⁶ Sixteen thousand people.

⁴⁷ Moses took one fiftieth of the children of Israel's half, (from) the people and the animals, and gave them to the Levites, the guardians of God's Tabernacle.

The Officers' Offering

⁴⁸ The officers appointed over the army's thousands (of men)—the commanders of (units of) a thousand (men) and the commanders of (units of) a hundred (men)—approached Moses. ⁴⁹ They said to Moses, "Your servants counted the soldiers who were under us, and not one man is missing from us! ⁵⁰ So we have brought an offering for God: All the gold items which people found—anklets, bracelets, rings, earrings, and body ornaments—to atone for our souls before God (for thoughts about the Midianite women).

⁵¹ Moses and Eleazar the priest took all the finished gold items from them. ⁵² The total of the gift of gold which they dedicated to God was sixteen thousand, seven hundred and fifty shekels, donated by the officers over thousands (of men) and the officers over hundreds (of men).

—⁵³ The soldiers, however, took the spoils (they found) for themselves.—

⁵⁴ Moses and Eleazar the priest took the gold from the officers over thousands (of men) and the officers over hundreds (of men), and brought it to the Tent of Meeting, as a remembrance for the children of Israel before God.

---

years she served him from Ishmael's birth until her eviction, and the sixteen families that she established for him after Sarah's passing (ibid. 2-4; *Rabbi Menahem Azariah da Fano, 16ᵗʰ–17ᵗʰ century*).

49. Not one man is missing from us! Although the Jewish people won numerous victories in the other wars they waged, they always suffered some casualties. In the war against Midian, all the Jewish soldiers returned safely, and the officers declared in astonishment, *"Not one man is missing from us!"* (v. 49).

From the victory of the physical battle against Midian, we can learn a lesson about the ongoing spiritual war against Midian—eradicating conflicts. When you embark on such a war, you are given the assurance that you will return whole in body, soul, and even financially, and you will declare, *"Not one man is missing from us!"*

מטות

במדבר לב:א-טו

לב 1 וּמִקְנֶה | רַב הָיָה לִבְנֵי רְאוּבֵן וְלִבְנֵי־גָד עָצוּם [SIXTH READING THIRD WHEN JOINED]
מְאֹד וַיִּרְאוּ אֶת־אֶרֶץ יַעְזֵר וְאֶת־אֶרֶץ גִּלְעָד וְהִנֵּה הַמָּקוֹם מְקוֹם
מִקְנֶה: 2 וַיָּבֹאוּ בְנֵי־גָד וּבְנֵי רְאוּבֵן וַיֹּאמְרוּ אֶל־מֹשֶׁה וְאֶל־אֶלְעָזָר הַכֹּהֵן
וְאֶל־נְשִׂיאֵי הָעֵדָה לֵאמֹר: 3 עֲטָרוֹת וְדִיבֹן וְיַעְזֵר וְנִמְרָה וְחֶשְׁבּוֹן וְאֶלְעָלֵה
וּשְׂבָם וּנְבוֹ וּבְעֹן: 4 הָאָרֶץ אֲשֶׁר הִכָּה יְהוָה לִפְנֵי עֲדַת יִשְׂרָאֵל אֶרֶץ מִקְנֶה
הִוא וְלַעֲבָדֶיךָ מִקְנֶה: ס 5 וַיֹּאמְרוּ אִם־מָצָאנוּ חֵן בְּעֵינֶיךָ יֻתַּן אֶת־הָאָרֶץ
הַזֹּאת לַעֲבָדֶיךָ לַאֲחֻזָּה אַל־תַּעֲבִרֵנוּ אֶת־הַיַּרְדֵּן: 6 וַיֹּאמֶר מֹשֶׁה לִבְנֵי־גָד
וְלִבְנֵי רְאוּבֵן הַאַחֵיכֶם יָבֹאוּ לַמִּלְחָמָה וְאַתֶּם תֵּשְׁבוּ פֹה: 7 וְלָמָּה [תנואון כ׳]
תְנִיאוּן אֶת־לֵב בְּנֵי יִשְׂרָאֵל מֵעֲבֹר אֶל־הָאָרֶץ אֲשֶׁר־נָתַן לָהֶם יְהוָה: 8 כֹּה
עָשׂוּ אֲבֹתֵיכֶם בְּשָׁלְחִי אֹתָם מִקָּדֵשׁ בַּרְנֵעַ לִרְאוֹת אֶת־הָאָרֶץ: 9 וַיַּעֲלוּ
עַד־נַחַל אֶשְׁכּוֹל וַיִּרְאוּ אֶת־הָאָרֶץ וַיָּנִיאוּ אֶת־לֵב בְּנֵי יִשְׂרָאֵל לְבִלְתִּי־בֹא
אֶל־הָאָרֶץ אֲשֶׁר־נָתַן לָהֶם יְהוָה: 10 וַיִּחַר־אַף יְהוָה בַּיּוֹם הַהוּא וַיִּשָּׁבַע
לֵאמֹר: 11 אִם־יִרְאוּ הָאֲנָשִׁים הָעֹלִים מִמִּצְרַיִם מִבֶּן עֶשְׂרִים שָׁנָה וָמַעְלָה
אֵת הָאֲדָמָה אֲשֶׁר נִשְׁבַּעְתִּי לְאַבְרָהָם לְיִצְחָק וּלְיַעֲקֹב כִּי לֹא־מִלְאוּ אַחֲרָי:
12 בִּלְתִּי כָּלֵב בֶּן־יְפֻנֶּה הַקְּנִזִּי וִיהוֹשֻׁעַ בִּן־נוּן כִּי מִלְאוּ אַחֲרֵי יְהוָה: 13 וַיִּחַר־
אַף יְהוָה בְּיִשְׂרָאֵל וַיְנִעֵם בַּמִּדְבָּר אַרְבָּעִים שָׁנָה עַד־תֹּם כָּל־הַדּוֹר הָעֹשֶׂה
הָרַע בְּעֵינֵי יְהוָה: 14 וְהִנֵּה קַמְתֶּם תַּחַת אֲבֹתֵיכֶם תַּרְבּוּת אֲנָשִׁים חַטָּאִים
לִסְפּוֹת עוֹד עַל חֲרוֹן אַף־יְהוָה אֶל־יִשְׂרָאֵל: 15 כִּי תְשׁוּבֻן מֵאַחֲרָיו וְיָסַף עוֹד

---

people would not understand that this had been their intention. The people would interpret their lack of willingness to fight as plain fear. So Moses argued, *"Why are you discouraging the children of Israel?"* (v. 7; Rabbi Ḥayyim ibn Attar, 18th century).

8. This is exactly what your fathers did. Moses said to them, "The land is the most glorious of lands! How could you treat it with such disdain by choosing not to live in it? Perhaps the Jewish people will think it has something really disgraceful about it, or some hidden defect. You are blaspheming and despising the Holy Land!" (Rabbi Abraham b. Jacob Saba, 15th century).

The Request of Reuben and Gad's Descendants

32 [SIXTH READING / THIRD WHEN JOINED] ¹ Reuben and Gad's descendants had a lot of livestock, an extraordinarily large amount. They saw the land of Jazer and the land of Gilead, and it was clearly a suitable place for livestock. ² Gad's descendants and Reuben's descendants came and spoke to Moses and to Eleazar the priest and to the leaders of the community, saying, ³ "(The lands of) Ataroth, Dibon, Jazer, Nimrah, Heshbon, Elealeh, Sebam, Nebo, and Beon—⁴ the land which God defeated in front of the congregation of Israel—is a land suitable for livestock, and your servants have (a lot of) livestock." ⁵ They said, "If it finds favor in your eyes, let this land be given to your servants as a heritage. Do not take us across the Jordan."

⁶ Moses said to Gad's descendants and Reuben's descendants, "Your brothers should go to war while you stay here? ⁷ Why are you discouraging the children of Israel from crossing over to the land which God has given them? ⁸ This is exactly what your fathers did when I sent them from Kadesh-barnea to explore the land. ⁹ They went up to the valley of Eshcol, saw the land, and then they discouraged the children of Israel from crossing into the land which God has given them. ¹⁰ God became angry on that day, and He made an oath, saying, ¹¹ 'None of the men from the age of twenty years and over who came out of Egypt will see the land that I swore to Abraham, to Isaac, and to Jacob, because they did not follow Me wholeheartedly ¹²—except for Caleb son of Jephunneh the Kenizzite, and Joshua son of Nun, because they followed God wholeheartedly.' ¹³ God became angry with Israel, and He made them wander in the desert for forty years until the entire generation who acted wrongly in God's eyes had passed on.

¹⁴ "You've just now protested in the same way as your fathers. What a group of wicked men, who are further inciting God's anger against Israel! ¹⁵ If you turn

---

32:5 Let this land be given to your servants as a heritage. The tribes of Reuben and Gad had an additional motive when requesting these lands: they thought it would annul the decree against Moses' crossing the Jordan into the land of Israel. If they were given the lands of Sihon and Og as their portion, these lands would acquire the holiness of the land of Israel and the decree against Moses' entering the land would be canceled automatically: Moses would already be standing in the land of Israel! (*Rabbi Isaac Meir Alter of Gur, 19th century*).

Do not take us across the Jordan. Moses suspected that they were scared to fight, like the spies (see above, 13:31), so he accused them of lacking trust in God (v. 6–15). Therefore they responded that they were not at all scared and that they would lead the conquest (v. 16-19; *Naḥmanides, 13th century*).

Reuben and Gad's descendants stressed that since God had defeated so many lands for the Jewish people (v. 4), the conquest of the land of Israel would also be aided by miraculous assistance from God, and their own help would not be required.

Moses replied that, while it was true that God would assist them and that, in essence, the help of Reuben and Gad's descendants was not required, nevertheless, the rest of the Jewish

במדבר לב:טו-כט מטות

לְהַנִּיחוֹ בַּמִּדְבָּר וְשִׁחַתֶּם לְכָל־הָעָם הַזֶּה: ס 16 וַיִּגְּשׁוּ אֵלָיו וַיֹּאמְרוּ גִּדְרֹת צֹאן נִבְנֶה לְמִקְנֵנוּ פֹּה וְעָרִים לְטַפֵּנוּ: 17 וַאֲנַחְנוּ נֵחָלֵץ חֻשִׁים לִפְנֵי בְּנֵי יִשְׂרָאֵל עַד אֲשֶׁר אִם־הֲבִיאֹנֻם אֶל־מְקוֹמָם וְיָשַׁב טַפֵּנוּ בְּעָרֵי הַמִּבְצָר מִפְּנֵי יֹשְׁבֵי הָאָרֶץ: 18 לֹא נָשׁוּב אֶל־בָּתֵּינוּ עַד הִתְנַחֵל בְּנֵי יִשְׂרָאֵל אִישׁ נַחֲלָתוֹ: 19 כִּי לֹא נִנְחַל אִתָּם מֵעֵבֶר לַיַּרְדֵּן וָהָלְאָה כִּי בָאָה נַחֲלָתֵנוּ אֵלֵינוּ מֵעֵבֶר הַיַּרְדֵּן מִזְרָחָה: פ 20 [SEVENTH READING / FOURTH WHEN JOINED] וַיֹּאמֶר אֲלֵיהֶם מֹשֶׁה אִם־תַּעֲשׂוּן אֶת־הַדָּבָר הַזֶּה אִם־תֵּחָלְצוּ לִפְנֵי יְהֹוָה לַמִּלְחָמָה: 21 וְעָבַר לָכֶם כָּל־חָלוּץ אֶת־הַיַּרְדֵּן לִפְנֵי יְהֹוָה עַד הוֹרִישׁוֹ אֶת־אֹיְבָיו מִפָּנָיו: 22 וְנִכְבְּשָׁה הָאָרֶץ לִפְנֵי יְהֹוָה וְאַחַר תָּשֻׁבוּ וִהְיִיתֶם נְקִיִּם מֵיְהֹוָה וּמִיִּשְׂרָאֵל וְהָיְתָה הָאָרֶץ הַזֹּאת לָכֶם לַאֲחֻזָּה לִפְנֵי יְהֹוָה: 23 וְאִם־לֹא תַעֲשׂוּן כֵּן הִנֵּה חֲטָאתֶם לַיהֹוָה וּדְעוּ חַטַּאתְכֶם אֲשֶׁר תִּמְצָא אֶתְכֶם: 24 בְּנוּ־לָכֶם עָרִים לְטַפְּכֶם וּגְדֵרֹת לְצֹנַאֲכֶם וְהַיֹּצֵא מִפִּיכֶם תַּעֲשׂוּ: 25 וַיֹּאמֶר בְּנֵי־גָד וּבְנֵי רְאוּבֵן אֶל־מֹשֶׁה לֵּאמֹר עֲבָדֶיךָ יַעֲשׂוּ כַּאֲשֶׁר אֲדֹנִי מְצַוֶּה: 26 טַפֵּנוּ נָשֵׁינוּ מִקְנֵנוּ וְכָל־בְּהֶמְתֵּנוּ יִהְיוּ־שָׁם בְּעָרֵי הַגִּלְעָד: 27 וַעֲבָדֶיךָ יַעַבְרוּ כָּל־חֲלוּץ צָבָא לִפְנֵי יְהֹוָה לַמִּלְחָמָה כַּאֲשֶׁר אֲדֹנִי דֹּבֵר: 28 וַיְצַו לָהֶם מֹשֶׁה אֵת אֶלְעָזָר הַכֹּהֵן וְאֵת יְהוֹשֻׁעַ בִּן־נוּן וְאֶת־רָאשֵׁי אֲבוֹת הַמַּטּוֹת לִבְנֵי יִשְׂרָאֵל: 29 וַיֹּאמֶר מֹשֶׁה אֲלֵהֶם אִם־יַעַבְרוּ בְנֵי־גָד וּבְנֵי־רְאוּבֵן | אִתְּכֶם אֶת־הַיַּרְדֵּן כָּל־חָלוּץ לַמִּלְחָמָה לִפְנֵי יְהֹוָה וְנִכְבְּשָׁה הָאָרֶץ לִפְנֵיכֶם

world, which means that most Jews need to be engaged in a predominantly physical life. But, they argued, there was a need for a *minority* of the Jewish people to be less involved with physical matters, devoting all their time to Torah study and prayer, to provide support and inspiration for the rest of the people (as is the case to this day). And to make this intention clear, they offered to lead the conquest of the land (v. 17-19), showing that they wished to assist the rest of the people and not remain aloof from them.

Being that Reuben and Gad's descendants did not propose that all the people remain outside the land, and they delineated a role for themselves which was supportive of—and not isolated from—the rest of the Jewish people, Moses agreed to their plan.

away from Him, He will leave you in the desert again, and you'll destroy this entire nation!"

¹⁶ They approached him and said, "We'll build sheep enclosures for our livestock here and cities for our children. ¹⁷ We'll then arm ourselves quickly (and go) ahead of the children of Israel (and fight) until we've brought them to their place. (Meanwhile) our children will live in the fortified cities due to the (threat of) the land's inhabitants. ¹⁸ We'll not return to our homes until each member of the children of Israel has taken possession of his inheritance. ¹⁹ For we will not inherit with them on the other side of the Jordan and beyond, because our inheritance (will have already) come to us on the east side of the Jordan."

[SEVENTH READING / FOURTH WHEN JOINED] ²⁰ Moses said to them, "If you do this thing (that you said), if you arm yourselves for battle before God, ²¹ and your army crosses the Jordan before God until He has driven out His enemies before Him, ²² and the land will be conquered before God—then afterwards you may return. You will be free (of any obligation) to God and Israel, and this land will become your heritage before God.

²³ "But, if you do not do so, then you will have sinned against God, and you should know that your sin will find you. ²⁴ So build yourselves cities for your children and enclosures for your sheep, and do what your mouths have uttered."

²⁵ Gad's descendants and Reuben's descendants spoke to Moses, saying, "Your servants will do as my master commands. ²⁶ Our children and our wives, our livestock and our cattle will remain there, in the cities of Gilead. ²⁷ (We), your servants, who are armed for combat before God, will cross over (the Jordan) to battle, as my master has spoken."

²⁸ Moses gave instructions about them to Eleazar the priest and Joshua son of Nun and, all the paternal heads of the children of Israel's tribes. ²⁹ Moses said to them, "If the descendants of Gad and Reuben cross the Jordan with you before God, and the land is conquered before you, give them the land of Gilead as

---

16. We'll build sheep enclosures for our livestock here and cities for our children. God said to them, "You have shown more affection for your sheep than for your children's souls! Your lives will have no blessing!" About them it is said, *"An inheritance gained hastily in the beginning will not be blessed in the end"* (*Proverbs* 20:21). They cherished their money and settled outside the land of Israel, therefore they were exiled first of all the tribes (*Numbers Rabbah*).

Like the spies, Reuben and Gad's descendants wished to live a spiritual life, detached from worldly affairs. They did not wish to enter the land, which would lead to a demanding life of agriculture, but preferred instead to remain as shepherds, a profession that would leave them much time for Torah study and prayer.

However, unlike the spies, they did not suggest that all the Jewish people follow their example. They were fully aware that the ultimate purpose of creation is to sanctify the physical

וּנְתַתֶּם לָהֶם אֶת־אֶרֶץ הַגִּלְעָד לַאֲחֻזָּה: 30 וְאִם־לֹא יַעַבְרוּ חֲלוּצִים אִתְּכֶם וְנֹאחֲזוּ בְתֹכְכֶם בְּאֶרֶץ כְּנָעַן: 31 וַיַּעֲנוּ בְנֵי־גָד וּבְנֵי רְאוּבֵן לֵאמֹר אֵת אֲשֶׁר דִּבֶּר יְהֹוָה אֶל־עֲבָדֶיךָ כֵּן נַעֲשֶׂה: 32 נַחְנוּ נַעֲבֹר חֲלוּצִים לִפְנֵי יְהֹוָה אֶרֶץ כְּנָעַן וְאִתָּנוּ אֲחֻזַּת נַחֲלָתֵנוּ מֵעֵבֶר לַיַּרְדֵּן: 33 וַיִּתֵּן לָהֶם ׀ מֹשֶׁה לִבְנֵי־גָד וְלִבְנֵי רְאוּבֵן וְלַחֲצִי ׀ שֵׁבֶט ׀ מְנַשֶּׁה בֶן־יוֹסֵף אֶת־מַמְלֶכֶת סִיחֹן מֶלֶךְ הָאֱמֹרִי וְאֶת־מַמְלֶכֶת עוֹג מֶלֶךְ הַבָּשָׁן הָאָרֶץ לְעָרֶיהָ בִּגְבֻלֹת עָרֵי הָאָרֶץ סָבִיב: 34 וַיִּבְנוּ בְנֵי־גָד אֶת־דִּיבֹן וְאֶת־עֲטָרֹת וְאֵת עֲרֹעֵר: 35 וְאֶת־עַטְרֹת שׁוֹפָן וְאֶת־יַעְזֵר וְיָגְבֳּהָה: 36 וְאֶת־בֵּית נִמְרָה וְאֶת־בֵּית הָרָן עָרֵי מִבְצָר וְגִדְרֹת צֹאן: 37 וּבְנֵי רְאוּבֵן בָּנוּ אֶת־חֶשְׁבּוֹן וְאֶת־אֶלְעָלֵא וְאֵת קִרְיָתָיִם: 38 וְאֶת־נְבוֹ וְאֶת־בַּעַל מְעוֹן מוּסַבֹּת שֵׁם וְאֶת־שִׂבְמָה וַיִּקְרְאוּ בְשֵׁמֹת אֶת־שְׁמוֹת הֶעָרִים אֲשֶׁר בָּנוּ: 39 [MAFTIR] וַיֵּלְכוּ בְּנֵי מָכִיר בֶּן־מְנַשֶּׁה גִּלְעָדָה וַיִּלְכְּדֻהָ וַיּוֹרֶשׁ אֶת־הָאֱמֹרִי אֲשֶׁר־בָּהּ: 40 וַיִּתֵּן מֹשֶׁה אֶת־הַגִּלְעָד לְמָכִיר בֶּן־מְנַשֶּׁה וַיֵּשֶׁב בָּהּ: 41 וְיָאִיר בֶּן־מְנַשֶּׁה הָלַךְ וַיִּלְכֹּד אֶת־חַוֹּתֵיהֶם וַיִּקְרָא אֶתְהֶן חַוֹּת יָאִיר: 42 וְנֹבַח הָלַךְ וַיִּלְכֹּד אֶת־קְנָת וְאֶת־בְּנֹתֶיהָ וַיִּקְרָא לָה נֹבַח בִּשְׁמוֹ: פ פ פ

קי"ב פסוקים, בק"י סימן. יק"ב סימן. עיב"ל סימן.

kabbalah bites

32:33 Why did the tribes of Reuben and Gad, and half the tribe of Manasseh inherit territory outside the land of Israel?

Because each of these three groups harbored a spiritual blemish:

When Reuben was conceived, Jacob's mind was on Rachel, and not his partner Leah (see *Genesis 29:21*).

When Gad was conceived, Jacob's mind was on Leah, and not his partner Zilpah (see ibid. 30:9).

Manasseh was only half blemished, from his mother, Asenath, who was the child conceived from the abduction of Dinah by Shechem (ibid. 34:2). But because half of his lineage was pure—through his father, Joseph—half the tribe of Manasseh merited to enter the land.

a heritage. ³⁰ But if they do not cross over with you armed (for battle), they will receive an inheritance with you in the land of Canaan."

³¹ Gad's descendants and Reuben's descendants answered, saying, "We will do what God has said to your servants. ³² We will cross over, armed before God to the land of Canaan (and conquer it). Then we will come to possess our inheritance on this side of the Jordan."

³³ Moses gave Gad's descendants and Reuben's descendants and half the tribe of Manasseh, Joseph's son: the kingdom of King Sihon of the Amorites, and the kingdom of King Og of Bashan. (He gave) the land together with the cities within its borders, and the cities of the surrounding territory.

³⁴ Gad's descendants built (the cities of) Dibon, Ataroth, Aroer, ³⁵ Atroth-shophan, Jazer, Jogbehah, ³⁶ Beth-nimrah and Beth-haran. (They built them all to be) fortified cities with sheep enclosures.

³⁷ The descendants of Reuben built (the cities of): Heshbon, Elealeh, Kiriathaim, ³⁸ Nebo, Baal-meon—changing the names (of these latter two, since they were named after foreign deities)—and Sibmah. They retained the names of the other cities that they built.

[MAFTIR] ³⁹ The children of Machir son of Manasseh went to Gilead and conquered it, driving out the Amorites who were there. ⁴⁰ Moses gave Gilead to Machir son of Manasseh, and he settled in it.

⁴¹ Jair son of Manasseh went and conquered their villages, and called them Havvoth-jair ("Jair's Villages").

⁴² Nobah went and conquered Kenath and its surrounding villages. He called it Nobah, after his own name.

The *Haftarah* for *Mattot* is on page 1388.

However, in the final analysis, while they presented a plan which appeared to harmonize introspection with integration, *their decision not to enter the land reflected a subtle imbalance, away from the Torah's emphasis on integration.* And, as a result of this, many years later they were the first tribes to be exiled, as the Midrash states (*Rabbi Menahem Mendel Schneerson, 20ᵗʰ century*).

33. Half the tribe of Manasseh. They had also petitioned with the descendants of Reuben and Gad, but the Torah did not mention them up to this point because they were only half a tribe (*Rabbi Abraham ibn Ezra, 12ᵗʰ century*).

The half of Manasseh's tribe that settled east of the Jordan did not choose to settle there. Moses commanded them to settle there in order to protect the tribes of Reuben and Gad. It was the merit of Joseph—Manasseh's father—that protected the Jewish people, so Moses wanted Joseph's descendants to live wherever the Jewish people were found (*Rabbi Abraham b. Jacob Saba, 15ᵗʰ century*).

At every stage of **your journey** there will be **obstacles** which, however unpleasant they may seem, have the positive effect of **helping you grow.** Look at obstacles as **transformational tools.** Remember that there are **no shortcuts**—and that **every stage is crucial** to your soul's journey.

MASE'EI
מסעי

THE FORTY-TWO JOURNEYS IN THE DESERT	33:1–49
ENTERING THE LAND	33:50 – 35:5
LAWS OF A MURDERER	35:6–34
PRESERVING TRIBAL DIVISION OF THE LAND	36:1–13

NAME
Mase'ei

MEANING
"Journeys"

LINES IN TORAH SCROLL
189

PARASHIYYOT
6 open; 2 closed

VERSES
132

WORDS
1461

LETTERS
5773

DATE
Marḥeshvan-Shevat, 2488

LOCATION
Plains of Moab

KEY PEOPLE
Moses, Joshua, Eleazar, paternal heads of the tribe of Manasseh, daughters of Zelophehad

MITZVOT
2 positive; 4 prohibitions

MASORETIC FEATURES
A rare cantillation note, karnei parah (קפ), appears in 35:5

NOTE
Read during the three weeks of mourning for the Temples' destruction

CHARACTER PROFILE

NAME
Zelophehad's daughters:
Mahlah, Tirzah, Hoglah,
Milcah and Noah

HUSBANDS
Relatives from the tribe of
Manasseh

GRANDFATHER
Hepher

ACHIEVEMENTS
Zelophehad's daughters
were equal to each other
in wisdom; the youngest
married at forty, yet they all
merited children; the law of
a daughter's inheritance was
written in the Torah through
their merit

KNOWN FOR
Championing the cause of
women; love of the land
of Israel

UNBIASED JUDGMENT

Two witnesses are always necessary, as a safeguard against bias and framed actions. Withhold your judgments until you are aware of all the facts. Never rely on hearsay and circumstantial evidence (35:30).

GOOD COMPANY

An unintentional murderer becomes distant from God through his sin. Living in the Levites' cities will help him reconnect to God, as Levites devote their entire lives to God. Spend time with people who will help you draw closer to God (35:6).

REFUGE

When an unintentional murderer is in one of the cities of refuge, he is completely safe from any harm. Leaving, however, could be dangerous. The words of Torah are a spiritual refuge of absolute safety (35:26-27).

מסעי במדבר לג:א-ט

לג 1 אֵ֜לֶּה מַסְעֵ֣י בְנֵֽי־יִשְׂרָאֵ֗ל אֲשֶׁ֥ר יָצְא֛וּ מֵאֶ֥רֶץ מִצְרַ֖יִם לְצִבְאֹתָ֑ם בְּיַד־מֹשֶׁ֖ה וְאַהֲרֹֽן: 2 וַיִּכְתֹּ֨ב מֹשֶׁ֜ה אֶת־מוֹצָאֵיהֶ֛ם לְמַסְעֵיהֶ֖ם עַל־פִּ֣י יְהוָ֑ה וְאֵ֥לֶּה מַסְעֵיהֶ֖ם לְמוֹצָאֵיהֶֽם: 3 וַיִּסְע֤וּ מֵֽרַעְמְסֵס֙ בַּחֹ֣דֶשׁ הָרִאשׁ֔וֹן בַּחֲמִשָּׁ֥ה עָשָׂ֛ר י֖וֹם לַחֹ֣דֶשׁ הָרִאשׁ֑וֹן מִֽמָּחֳרַ֣ת הַפֶּ֗סַח יָצְא֤וּ בְנֵֽי־יִשְׂרָאֵל֙ בְּיָ֣ד רָמָ֔ה לְעֵינֵ֖י כָּל־מִצְרָֽיִם: 4 וּמִצְרַ֣יִם מְקַבְּרִ֗ים אֵת֩ אֲשֶׁ֨ר הִכָּ֧ה יְהוָ֛ה בָּהֶ֖ם כָּל־בְּכ֑וֹר וּבֵאלֹ֣הֵיהֶ֔ם עָשָׂ֥ה יְהוָ֖ה שְׁפָטִֽים: 5 וַיִּסְע֥וּ בְנֵֽי־יִשְׂרָאֵ֖ל מֵֽרַעְמְסֵ֑ס וַֽיַּחֲנ֖וּ בְּסֻכֹּֽת: 6 וַיִּסְע֖וּ מִסֻּכֹּ֑ת וַיַּחֲנ֣וּ בְאֵתָ֔ם אֲשֶׁ֖ר בִּקְצֵ֥ה הַמִּדְבָּֽר: 7 וַיִּסְעוּ֙ מֵֽאֵתָ֔ם וַיָּ֨שָׁב֙ עַל־פִּ֣י הַֽחִירֹ֔ת אֲשֶׁ֥ר עַל־פְּנֵ֖י בַּ֣עַל צְפ֑וֹן וַֽיַּחֲנ֖וּ לִפְנֵ֥י מִגְדֹּֽל: 8 וַיִּסְעוּ֙ מִפְּנֵ֣י הַֽחִירֹ֔ת וַיַּֽעַבְר֥וּ בְתוֹךְ־הַיָּ֖ם הַמִּדְבָּ֑רָה וַיֵּ֨לְכ֜וּ דֶּ֣רֶךְ שְׁלֹ֤שֶׁת יָמִים֙ בְּמִדְבַּ֣ר אֵתָ֔ם וַֽיַּחֲנ֖וּ בְּמָרָֽה: 9 וַיִּסְעוּ֙ מִמָּרָ֔ה וַיָּבֹ֖אוּ אֵילִ֑מָה וּ֠בְאֵילִם שְׁתֵּ֣ים עֶשְׂרֵ֞ה עֵינֹ֥ת מַ֛יִם

---

until they arrived in Rithmah (v. 18) where the spies were sent. Subtract a further eight encampments which took place after Aaron's death: from Mount Hor to the plains of Moab (verses 37-48), which were all during the fortieth year—and we will find that throughout the thirty-eight years they made only twenty journeys. I found this in the treatise of Rabbi Moses ha-Darshan.

Rabbi Tanḥuma offered a different explanation: The account of the journeys is analogous to a king whose son became sick, and was taken to a distant place to be healed. On their return, the father began to mention all the stages of their journey, saying to him, "This is where we slept. This is where we felt cold. Here you had a headache, etc." (*Rashi, 11th century*).

2. Moses recorded the starting points of their journeys. What was the purpose of detailing each resting place of the journey in the desert?

Miracles are only convincing to those who witness them. One of the greatest miracles described in the Torah is the Israelites' receiving a daily supply of food from heaven during their forty-year sojourn in the desert. However, with the passing of time, this miracle was likely to be downplayed or

---

kabbalah bites

33:1 The Ba'al Shem Tov taught that the forty-two journeys of the Israelite people represent the ups and downs of your life. Sometimes you encamp for many years in a safe haven of financial security and good relationships; on other occasions your passions overwhelm you and you ruin your life. ("*They camped in Kibroth-hattaavah*" (v. 16), where "*they buried the people who craved*"—Numbers 11:34.)

Does that mean that your failures are preordained and out of your control?

Of course not. Each journey is a test from God. When He fires your passions, He also gives you the *hokhmah* (insight) to conquer them. Whether that journey is an "up" or a "down" is for you to choose.

parashat maseʻei

The Forty-Two Journeys of the Jewish People

33 ¹ The following are the journeys of the children of Israel by which they left the land of Egypt, in their regiments, by the hand of Moses and Aaron. ² Moses recorded the starting points of their journeys, (given) by the word of God. The following were their journeys and their starting points.

Journeys 1-12: From the Exodus to Sinai

[1] ³ They journeyed from Rameses in the first month. On the fifteenth day of the first month, the day following the Passover-offering, the children of Israel left triumphantly in the presence of all the Egyptians. ⁴ The Egyptians were (busy) burying (their dead) because God had struck their firstborn and had performed acts of judgment upon their gods.

[2] ⁵ The children of Israel journeyed from Rameses, and camped in Succoth.

[3] ⁶ They journeyed from Succoth, and camped in Etham, at the edge of the desert.

[4] ⁷ They journeyed from Etham, and settled at Pi-hahiroth ("Mouth of the Rocks"), opposite Baal-zephon, and they camped in front of Migdol.

[5] ⁸ They journeyed from "the Rocks," and crossed through the sea to the desert. They walked for three days in the Etham Desert and camped in Marah.

[6] ⁹ They journeyed from Marah, and arrived in Elim. In Elim, there were twelve springs of water and seventy palm trees, and they camped there.

33:1 The following are the journeys of the children of Israel by which they left the land of Egypt. Would it not have been more appropriate to refer to these journeys by their destination—the land of Israel—rather than by their point of departure, *"the land of Egypt"*?

The purpose of the Israelites' lengthy journey through the desert was to rid them of the immoral character traits of the Egyptians, to which they had become so attached. The journeys were therefore *"by which they left the land of Egypt."*

At each stage of their journey the children of Israel ascended higher, distancing themselves further from the impurity of Egypt. The reason why they stopped at each of these locations was not due to physical fatigue, but in order to grow spiritually. Once the goal was achieved, they were given the signal to move on to the next location and to begin lifting themselves once again (*Rabbi Meir Loeb Weisser, 19th century*).

Living in this world, which conceals God's presence, while striving constantly to remain loyal to His will, is a considerable challenge. The eventful journeys of the Jewish people, with all the ups and downs that they endured, allude to the spiritual journeys of life (*Rabbi Israel Baʻal Shem Tov, 18th century*).

Why were these journeys written? To inform us of God's kindness, that although He had decreed that they would wander aimlessly in the desert, we should not imagine that they were wandering from place to place throughout the forty years and had no rest.

For we see that there were only forty-two encampments. Now deduct fourteen of them which all took place in the first year, before the decree, from when they journeyed from Rameses (v. 3)

במדבר לג:ט-לו — מסעי

וְשִׁבְעִים תְּמָרִים וַיַּחֲנוּ־שָׁם: 10 וַיִּסְעוּ מֵאֵילִם וַיַּחֲנוּ עַל־יַם־סוּף: 11 וַיִּסְעוּ מִיַּם־סוּף וַיַּחֲנוּ בְּמִדְבַּר־סִין: 12 וַיִּסְעוּ מִמִּדְבַּר־סִין וַיַּחֲנוּ בְּדָפְקָה: 13 וַיִּסְעוּ מִדָּפְקָה וַיַּחֲנוּ בְּאָלוּשׁ: 14 וַיִּסְעוּ מֵאָלוּשׁ וַיַּחֲנוּ בִּרְפִידִם וְלֹא־הָיָה שָׁם מַיִם לָעָם לִשְׁתּוֹת: 15 וַיִּסְעוּ מֵרְפִידִם וַיַּחֲנוּ בְּמִדְבַּר סִינָי: 16 וַיִּסְעוּ מִמִּדְבַּר סִינָי וַיַּחֲנוּ בְּקִבְרֹת הַתַּאֲוָה: 17 וַיִּסְעוּ מִקִּבְרֹת הַתַּאֲוָה וַיַּחֲנוּ בַּחֲצֵרֹת: 18 וַיִּסְעוּ מֵחֲצֵרֹת וַיַּחֲנוּ בְּרִתְמָה: 19 וַיִּסְעוּ מֵרִתְמָה וַיַּחֲנוּ בְּרִמֹּן פָּרֶץ: 20 וַיִּסְעוּ מֵרִמֹּן פָּרֶץ וַיַּחֲנוּ בְּלִבְנָה: 21 וַיִּסְעוּ מִלִּבְנָה וַיַּחֲנוּ בְּרִסָּה: 22 וַיִּסְעוּ מֵרִסָּה וַיַּחֲנוּ בִּקְהֵלָתָה: 23 וַיִּסְעוּ מִקְּהֵלָתָה וַיַּחֲנוּ בְּהַר־שָׁפֶר: 24 וַיִּסְעוּ מֵהַר־שָׁפֶר וַיַּחֲנוּ בַּחֲרָדָה: 25 וַיִּסְעוּ מֵחֲרָדָה וַיַּחֲנוּ בְּמַקְהֵלֹת: 26 וַיִּסְעוּ מִמַּקְהֵלֹת וַיַּחֲנוּ בְּתָחַת: 27 וַיִּסְעוּ מִתָּחַת וַיַּחֲנוּ בְּתָרַח: 28 וַיִּסְעוּ מִתָּרַח וַיַּחֲנוּ בְּמִתְקָה: 29 וַיִּסְעוּ מִמִּתְקָה וַיַּחֲנוּ בְּחַשְׁמֹנָה: 30 וַיִּסְעוּ מֵחַשְׁמֹנָה וַיַּחֲנוּ בְּמֹסֵרוֹת: 31 וַיִּסְעוּ מִמֹּסֵרוֹת וַיַּחֲנוּ בִּבְנֵי יַעֲקָן: 32 וַיִּסְעוּ מִבְּנֵי יַעֲקָן וַיַּחֲנוּ בְּחֹר הַגִּדְגָּד: 33 וַיִּסְעוּ מֵחֹר הַגִּדְגָּד וַיַּחֲנוּ בְּיָטְבָתָה: 34 וַיִּסְעוּ מִיָּטְבָתָה וַיַּחֲנוּ בְּעַבְרֹנָה: 35 וַיִּסְעוּ מֵעַבְרֹנָה וַיַּחֲנוּ בְּעֶצְיֹן גָּבֶר: 36 וַיִּסְעוּ מֵעֶצְיֹן גָּבֶר וַיַּחֲנוּ בְמִדְבַּר־צִן הִוא קָדֵשׁ:

vegetation from which they were able to sustain themselves? God therefore enumerated all of the stages in the Israelite journey, to make clear that it was a barren desert with no natural means of survival (*Maimonides, 12th century*).

spiritual vitamin

> Angels are called *'omedim*—stationary—for although they fulfil the will of their Maker with awe and fear, and praise God in song and melody, no complete departure and change is involved in their nature, so this cannot be termed perfect "going." Only man is called *mehallekh*, a "walker," for his task is to go ever higher, even if his previous spiritual station is satisfactory.

numbers 33:10–36 — mase'ei

[7] ¹⁰ They journeyed from Elim, and camped by the Reed Sea.

[8] ¹¹ They journeyed from the Reed Sea, and camped in the Sin Desert.

[9] ¹² They journeyed from the Sin Desert, and camped in Dophkah.

[10] ¹³ They journeyed from Dophkah, and camped in Alush.

[11] ¹⁴ They journeyed from Alush, and camped in Rephidim, but there was no water for the people to drink.

[12] ¹⁵ They journeyed from Rephidim, and camped in the Sinai Desert.

Journeys 13-15: Sinai to Kadesh-Barnea

[13] ¹⁶ They journeyed from the Sinai Desert, and camped in Kibroth-hattaavah.

[14] ¹⁷ They journeyed from Kibroth-hattaavah, and camped in Hazeroth.

[15] ¹⁸ They journeyed from Hazeroth, and camped in Rithmah (also known as Kadesh-barnea).

Journeys 16-33: Desert Wanderings

[16] ¹⁹ They journeyed from Rithmah, and camped in Rimmon-perez.

[17] ²⁰ They journeyed from Rimmon-perez, and camped in Libnah.

[18] ²¹ They journeyed from Libnah, and camped in Rissah.

[19] ²² They journeyed from Rissah, and camped in Kehelath.

[20] ²³ They journeyed from Kehelath, and camped in Mount Shepher.

[21] ²⁴ They journeyed from Mount Shepher, and camped in Haradah.

[22] ²⁵ They journeyed from Haradah, and camped in Makheloth.

[23] ²⁶ They journeyed from Makheloth, and camped in Tahath.

[24] ²⁷ They journeyed from Tahath, and camped in Terah.

[25] ²⁸ They journeyed from Terah, and camped in Mithkah.

[26] ²⁹ They journeyed from Mithkah, and camped in Hashmonah.

[27] ³⁰ They journeyed from Hashmonah, and camped in Moseroth.

[28] ³¹ They journeyed from Moseroth, and camped in Bene-jaakan.

[29] ³² They journeyed from Bene-jaakan, and camped in Hor-haggidgad.

[30] ³³ They journeyed from Hor-haggidgad, and camped in Jotbath.

[31] ³⁴ They journeyed from Jotbath, and camped in Abronah.

[32] ³⁵ They journeyed from Abronah, and camped in Ezion-geber.

[33] ³⁶ They journeyed from Ezion-geber, and camped in the Zin Desert, which is Kadesh.

even denied. Perhaps the route taken by the Israelites through the desert was alongside settled land where they were able to purchase food? Or possibly this desert had some form of natural

מסעי

במדבר לג:לז-נד

37 וַיִּסְעוּ מִקָּדֵשׁ וַיַּחֲנוּ בְּהֹר הָהָר בִּקְצֵה אֶרֶץ אֱדוֹם: 38 וַיַּעַל אַהֲרֹן הַכֹּהֵן אֶל־הֹר הָהָר עַל־פִּי יְהוָה וַיָּמָת שָׁם בִּשְׁנַת הָאַרְבָּעִים לְצֵאת בְּנֵי־יִשְׂרָאֵל מֵאֶרֶץ מִצְרַיִם בַּחֹדֶשׁ הַחֲמִישִׁי בְּאֶחָד לַחֹדֶשׁ: 39 וְאַהֲרֹן בֶּן־שָׁלֹשׁ וְעֶשְׂרִים וּמְאַת שָׁנָה בְּמֹתוֹ בְּהֹר הָהָר: ס 40 וַיִּשְׁמַע הַכְּנַעֲנִי מֶלֶךְ עֲרָד וְהוּא־יֹשֵׁב בַּנֶּגֶב בְּאֶרֶץ כְּנָעַן בְּבֹא בְּנֵי יִשְׂרָאֵל: 41 וַיִּסְעוּ מֵהֹר הָהָר וַיַּחֲנוּ בְּצַלְמֹנָה: 42 וַיִּסְעוּ מִצַּלְמֹנָה וַיַּחֲנוּ בְּפוּנֹן: 43 וַיִּסְעוּ מִפּוּנֹן וַיַּחֲנוּ בְּאֹבֹת: 44 וַיִּסְעוּ מֵאֹבֹת וַיַּחֲנוּ בְּעִיֵּי הָעֲבָרִים בִּגְבוּל מוֹאָב: 45 וַיִּסְעוּ מֵעִיִּים וַיַּחֲנוּ בְּדִיבֹן גָּד: 46 וַיִּסְעוּ מִדִּיבֹן גָּד וַיַּחֲנוּ בְּעַלְמֹן דִּבְלָתָיְמָה: 47 וַיִּסְעוּ מֵעַלְמֹן דִּבְלָתָיְמָה וַיַּחֲנוּ בְּהָרֵי הָעֲבָרִים לִפְנֵי נְבוֹ: 48 וַיִּסְעוּ מֵהָרֵי הָעֲבָרִים וַיַּחֲנוּ בְּעַרְבֹת מוֹאָב עַל יַרְדֵּן יְרֵחוֹ: 49 וַיַּחֲנוּ עַל־הַיַּרְדֵּן מִבֵּית הַיְשִׁמֹת עַד אָבֵל הַשִּׁטִּים בְּעַרְבֹת מוֹאָב: ס 50 [SECOND READING] וַיְדַבֵּר יְהוָה אֶל־מֹשֶׁה בְּעַרְבֹת מוֹאָב עַל־יַרְדֵּן יְרֵחוֹ לֵאמֹר: 51 דַּבֵּר אֶל־בְּנֵי יִשְׂרָאֵל וְאָמַרְתָּ אֲלֵהֶם כִּי אַתֶּם עֹבְרִים אֶת־הַיַּרְדֵּן אֶל־אֶרֶץ כְּנָעַן: 52 וְהוֹרַשְׁתֶּם אֶת־כָּל־יֹשְׁבֵי הָאָרֶץ מִפְּנֵיכֶם וְאִבַּדְתֶּם אֵת כָּל־מַשְׂכִּיֹּתָם וְאֵת כָּל־צַלְמֵי מַסֵּכֹתָם תְּאַבֵּדוּ וְאֵת כָּל־בָּמוֹתָם תַּשְׁמִידוּ: 53 וְהוֹרַשְׁתֶּם אֶת־הָאָרֶץ וִישַׁבְתֶּם־בָּהּ כִּי לָכֶם נָתַתִּי אֶת־הָאָרֶץ לָרֶשֶׁת אֹתָהּ: 54 [THIRD READING / FIFTH WHEN JOINED] וְהִתְנַחַלְתֶּם אֶת־הָאָרֶץ בְּגוֹרָל לְמִשְׁפְּחֹתֵיכֶם לָרַב תַּרְבּוּ אֶת־נַחֲלָתוֹ וְלַמְעַט תַּמְעִיט אֶת־נַחֲלָתוֹ אֶל אֲשֶׁר־יֵצֵא לוֹ שָׁמָּה הַגּוֹרָל

53. You should rid the land (of its inhabitants, then) you should settle in it. *"You shall rid the land"*—You should rid it of its inhabitants, and then, *"you should settle in it."* Only then will you be able to survive there; but if not, you will not be able to survive there (*Rashi, 11th century*).

In my opinion, this verse conveys a positive commandment of the Torah to settle in the land of Israel. Thus we find that our Sages greatly praised the precept of living in the land of Israel and the prohibition of leaving it. It is in this verse that the commandment is conveyed (*Naḥmanides, 13th century*).

Maimonides clearly did not agree that it is a commandment from the Torah to live in the land of Israel, as he omitted any mention of it from his *Book of Commandments*. Presumably,

numbers 33:37–54 mase'ei

Journeys 34–42: Journey Towards the Land of Israel

[34] ³⁷ They journeyed from Kadesh, and camped at Mount Hor, at the edge of the land of Edom.

—³⁸ Aaron the priest went up Mount Hor and died there (by a kiss) from God's mouth, on the first day of the fifth month in the fortieth year of the children of Israel's exodus from Egypt. ³⁹ Aaron was one hundred and twenty-three years old when he died at Mount Hor. ⁴⁰ The Canaanite king of Arad, who dwelt in the south in the land of Canaan, heard (that the clouds of glory had departed after Aaron's passing and) the children of Israel had come. (Presuming that they were weak, he attacked them.)—

[35] ⁴¹ They journeyed from Mount Hor, and camped in Zalmonah.

[36] ⁴² They journeyed from Zalmonah, and camped in Punon.

[37] ⁴³ They journeyed from Punon, and camped in Oboth.

[38] ⁴⁴ They journeyed from Oboth, and camped at Iye-abarim, on the Moabite boundary.

[39] ⁴⁵ They journeyed from Iyim, and camped in Dibon-gad.

[40] ⁴⁶ They journeyed from Dibon-gad, and camped in Almon-diblathaim.

[41] ⁴⁷ They journeyed from Almon-diblathaim, and camped in the mountains of Abarim, in front of Mount Nebo.

[42] ⁴⁸ They journeyed from the mountains of Abarim, and camped in the plains of Moab, by the Jordan, near Jericho. ⁴⁹ They camped along the Jordan from Beth-jeshimoth to Abel-shittim, in the plains of Moab.

Entering the Land

[SECOND READING / FIFTH WHEN JOINED] ⁵⁰ God spoke to Moses in the plains of Moab by the Jordan near Jericho, saying: ⁵¹ "Speak to the children of Israel and say to them: 'When you cross the Jordan into the land of Canaan (the waters of the Jordan will split for you. But this is on condition that) ⁵² you drive out all the inhabitants of the land from before you, destroy all their temples, destroy their molten idols, and demolish their high places. ⁵³ You should rid the land (of its inhabitants, then) you should settle in it, for I have given you the land to occupy it.

[THIRD READING] ⁵⁴ "'You should allocate the possession of the land to your families by a lottery. Give a larger inheritance to a large (family), and give a smaller inheritance to a small (family). Wherever the lot falls (for a person) that will be his (portion). You will inherit (a portion) corresponding to (the size) of your paternal tribes (that left Egypt).

---

38. And died there. The Angel of Death did not hold sway over Aaron. He died by a kiss *"from God's mouth"* (*Babylonian Talmud, Bava Batra* 17a).

מסעי　　　　　　　　　　　　　　　　　　　　　　　　　　במדבר לג:נד - לד:ט

לוֹ יִהְיֶה לַמַּטּוֹת אֲבֹתָיו תִּתְנֶחָלוּ: 55 וְאִם־לֹא תוֹרִישׁוּ אֶת־יֹשְׁבֵי הָאָרֶץ מִפְּנֵיכֶם וְהָיָה אֲשֶׁר תּוֹתִירוּ מֵהֶם לְשִׂכִּים בְּעֵינֵיכֶם וְלִצְנִינִם בְּצִדֵּיכֶם וְצָרֲרוּ אֶתְכֶם עַל־הָאָרֶץ אֲשֶׁר אַתֶּם יֹשְׁבִים בָּהּ: 56 וְהָיָה כַּאֲשֶׁר דִּמִּיתִי לַעֲשׂוֹת לָהֶם אֶעֱשֶׂה לָכֶם: פ

לד

1 וַיְדַבֵּר יְהוָה אֶל־מֹשֶׁה לֵּאמֹר: 2 צַו אֶת־בְּנֵי יִשְׂרָאֵל וְאָמַרְתָּ אֲלֵהֶם כִּי־אַתֶּם בָּאִים אֶל־הָאָרֶץ כְּנָעַן זֹאת הָאָרֶץ אֲשֶׁר תִּפֹּל לָכֶם בְּנַחֲלָה אֶרֶץ כְּנַעַן לִגְבֻלֹתֶיהָ: 3 וְהָיָה לָכֶם פְּאַת־נֶגֶב מִמִּדְבַּר־צִן עַל־יְדֵי אֱדוֹם וְהָיָה לָכֶם גְּבוּל נֶגֶב מִקְצֵה יָם־הַמֶּלַח קֵדְמָה: 4 וְנָסַב לָכֶם הַגְּבוּל מִנֶּגֶב לְמַעֲלֵה עַקְרַבִּים וְעָבַר צִנָה [לַהֶהֱצִנָה] וְהָיוּ תּוֹצְאֹתָיו מִנֶּגֶב לְקָדֵשׁ בַּרְנֵעַ וְיָצָא חֲצַר־אַדָּר וְעָבַר עַצְמֹנָה: 5 וְנָסַב הַגְּבוּל מֵעַצְמוֹן נַחְלָה מִצְרַיִם וְהָיוּ תוֹצְאֹתָיו הַיָּמָה: 6 וּגְבוּל יָם וְהָיָה לָכֶם הַיָּם הַגָּדוֹל וּגְבוּל זֶה־יִהְיֶה לָכֶם גְּבוּל יָם: 7 וְזֶה־יִהְיֶה לָכֶם גְּבוּל צָפוֹן מִן־הַיָּם הַגָּדֹל תְּתָאוּ לָכֶם הֹר הָהָר: 8 מֵהֹר הָהָר תְּתָאוּ לְבֹא חֲמָת וְהָיוּ תּוֹצְאֹת הַגְּבֻל צְדָדָה: 9 וְיָצָא הַגְּבֻל זִפְרֹנָה וְהָיוּ תוֹצְאֹתָיו חֲצַר עֵינָן

Since many commandments are practiced in the land of Israel and do not apply outside the land, it was necessary for Scripture to chart the outer limits of its boundaries from all sides,

kabbalah bites

34:2 Why does the land *"fall* to you as an *inheritance"*?

Your soul is pristine. Before you were born, *it* inhabited the heavens and loved God passionately.

The moment you were born on this physical land it "fell." Your body hungers for earthly pleasures, obscuring and silencing your soul's love for God.

Now that it has been "gagged," your soul must shout louder to be heard. It needs to discover a deeper love for God than it has ever known. You have indeed fallen upon this land, but your spirit, the spark of the Divine in you, will lead you to rise up.

⁵⁵ "'But if you do not drive out the inhabitants of the land from before you, then those whom you leave over will be like spikes in your eyes and thorns in your sides. They will harass you in the land in which you settle. ⁵⁶ Then I will do to you what I had intended to do to them.'"

Borders of the Land

34 ¹ God spoke to Moses, saying: ² Command the children of Israel and say to them: When you arrive in the land of Canaan, the following is the land which will fall to you as an inheritance: The land of Canaan according to its borders:

³ Your southern border (from east to west) will be by the desert of Zin, along (the border of) Edom: The southern border will stretch from the edge of the Salt Sea in the east; ⁴ the border then turns south of Maaleh-akrabbim, passing toward Zin, and its edge will be south of Kadesh-barnea; then it will extend to Hazar-addar and continue towards Azmon; ⁵ the border then turns from Azmon to the stream of Egypt (which forms the border with Egypt), and its end will be at the (Mediterranean) Sea.

⁶ Your western border will be through the Great (Mediterranean) Sea (including the islands within) the border. This will be your western border.

⁷ The following will be your northern border: From the Great (Mediterranean) Sea turn yourselves toward Mount Hor; ⁸ from Mount Hor turn towards the route to Hamath; the (northernmost) point of the border will be towards Zedad; ⁹ the border will then extend to Ziphron, and its end will be Hazar-enan. This will be your northern border.

Maimonides maintained that verse 53 was a command to Moses and Joshua which was only in force until the Jewish people were exiled from the land, but not to future generations (*Rabbi Isaac Leon b. Eliezer ibn Tzur, 16th century*).

55. Then those whom you leave over will be like spikes in your eyes and thorns in your sides. The Torah places special emphasis on driving out the inhabitants of Canaan, although throughout history those that waged war against Israel proved to be from other nations such as Philistia, Babylonia, and Rome.

Many nations are open about their hatred of the children of Israel; they pose an obvious danger from which the Israelites know to be watchful. The Canaanites, on the other hand, represent the threat of assimilation, which causes a gradual erosion of religious practices. The Torah cautions us to be especially careful of this (*Rabbi Menahem Mendel of Rymanow, 18th century*).

34:2 The land of Canaan according to its borders. God informed them of the precise parameters of the land, so that they would not conquer too little or too much land (*Rabbi Levi b. Gershom, 14th century*).

מסעי • במדבר לד:ט-כז

זֶה־יִהְיֶה לָכֶם גְּבוּל צָפוֹן: 10 וְהִתְאַוִּיתֶם לָכֶם לִגְבוּל קֵדְמָה מֵחֲצַר עֵינָן שְׁפָמָה: 11 וְיָרַד הַגְּבֻל מִשְּׁפָם הָרִבְלָה מִקֶּדֶם לָעָיִן וְיָרַד הַגְּבֻל וּמָחָה עַל־כֶּתֶף יָם־כִּנֶּרֶת קֵדְמָה: 12 וְיָרַד הַגְּבוּל הַיַּרְדֵּנָה וְהָיוּ תוֹצְאֹתָיו יָם הַמֶּלַח זֹאת תִּהְיֶה לָכֶם הָאָרֶץ לִגְבֻלֹתֶיהָ סָבִיב: 13 וַיְצַו מֹשֶׁה אֶת־בְּנֵי יִשְׂרָאֵל לֵאמֹר זֹאת הָאָרֶץ אֲשֶׁר תִּתְנַחֲלוּ אֹתָהּ בְּגוֹרָל אֲשֶׁר צִוָּה יְהֹוָה לָתֵת לְתִשְׁעַת הַמַּטּוֹת וַחֲצִי הַמַּטֶּה: 14 כִּי לָקְחוּ מַטֵּה בְנֵי הָראוּבֵנִי לְבֵית אֲבֹתָם וּמַטֵּה בְנֵי־הַגָּדִי לְבֵית אֲבֹתָם וַחֲצִי מַטֵּה מְנַשֶּׁה לָקְחוּ נַחֲלָתָם: 15 שְׁנֵי הַמַּטּוֹת וַחֲצִי הַמַּטֶּה לָקְחוּ נַחֲלָתָם מֵעֵבֶר לְיַרְדֵּן יְרֵחוֹ קֵדְמָה מִזְרָחָה: פ 16 [FOURTH READING / SIXTH WHEN JOINED] וַיְדַבֵּר יְהֹוָה אֶל־מֹשֶׁה לֵּאמֹר: 17 אֵלֶּה שְׁמוֹת הָאֲנָשִׁים אֲשֶׁר־יִנְחֲלוּ לָכֶם אֶת־הָאָרֶץ אֶלְעָזָר הַכֹּהֵן וִיהוֹשֻׁעַ בִּן־נוּן: 18 וְנָשִׂיא אֶחָד נָשִׂיא אֶחָד מִמַּטֶּה תִּקְחוּ לִנְחֹל אֶת־הָאָרֶץ: 19 וְאֵלֶּה שְׁמוֹת הָאֲנָשִׁים לְמַטֵּה יְהוּדָה כָּלֵב בֶּן־יְפֻנֶּה: 20 וּלְמַטֵּה בְּנֵי שִׁמְעוֹן שְׁמוּאֵל בֶּן־עַמִּיהוּד: 21 לְמַטֵּה בִנְיָמִן אֱלִידָד בֶּן־כִּסְלוֹן: 22 וּלְמַטֵּה בְנֵי־דָן נָשִׂיא בֻּקִּי בֶּן־יָגְלִי: 23 לִבְנֵי יוֹסֵף לְמַטֵּה בְנֵי־מְנַשֶּׁה נָשִׂיא חַנִּיאֵל בֶּן־אֵפֹד: 24 וּלְמַטֵּה בְנֵי־אֶפְרַיִם נָשִׂיא קְמוּאֵל בֶּן־שִׁפְטָן: 25 וּלְמַטֵּה בְנֵי־זְבוּלֻן נָשִׂיא אֱלִיצָפָן בֶּן־פַּרְנָךְ: 26 וּלְמַטֵּה בְנֵי־יִשָּׂשכָר נָשִׂיא פַּלְטִיאֵל בֶּן־עַזָּן: 27 וּלְמַטֵּה

portion for each one, and whatever they do is binding, as if they had been designated as agents by the members of the tribes (*Rashi, 11th century*).

spiritual vitamin

> The concentration on, and preoccupation with, national and international problems provides a convenient justification for diverting the necessary, vital and utmost attention from the self: from self-searching and the reappraisal of your personal life—precisely those areas where personal resolutions can be effective.

numbers 34:10–27 — mase'ei

¹⁰ You should then turn yourselves toward the eastern border: From Hazar-enan to Shepham; ¹¹ the border then goes down from Shepham towards Riblah, to the east of Ain; the border then goes down and hits the eastern shore of Lake Chinnereth. ¹² The border then continues down along the Jordan, and its end is the Salt Sea.

This will be your land, defined by its surrounding borders.

¹³ Moses commanded the children of Israel, saying, "This (stated above) is the land that God has commanded to give to nine and a half tribes, which you are to apportion as an inheritance through a lottery. ¹⁴ For the tribe of Reuben's descendants, according to their paternal house, and the tribe of Gad's descendants, according to their paternal house, and half the tribe of Manasseh have already received their inheritance. ¹⁵ (These) two and a half tribes have received their inheritance on this side of the Jordan, near Jericho, facing 'forward,' (i.e.) eastward."

Tribal Leaders Appointed to Divide the Land

[FOURTH READING / SIXTH WHEN JOINED] ¹⁶ God spoke to Moses, saying: ¹⁷ These are the names of the men who will inherit the land for you: Eleazar the priest and Joshua son of Nun. ¹⁸ You should take one leader from each tribe; one leader is to acquire the land (on your behalf).

¹⁹ These are the names of the men:

For the tribe of Judah, Caleb son of Jephunneh.

²⁰ For the tribe of Simeon's descendants, Samuel son of Ammihud.

²¹ For the tribe of Benjamin, Elidad son of Chislon.

²² The leader of the tribe of Dan's descendants is Bukki son of Jogli.

²³ For the descendants of Joseph:

The leader for the tribe of Manasseh's descendants is Hanniel son of Ephod.

²⁴ The leader for the tribe of Ephraim's descendants is Kemuel son of Shiphtan.

²⁵ The leader of the tribe of Zebulun's descendants is Elizaphan son of Parnach.

²⁶ The leader of the tribe of Issachar's descendants is Paltiel son of Azzan.

²⁷ The leader of the tribe of Asher's descendants is Ahihud son of Shelomi.

to inform you that the commandments are practiced everywhere within these borders (*Rashi, 11ᵗʰ century*).

17. Who will inherit the land for you. *"For you"*—on your behalf. Each leader is a trustee for his tribe, to divide the tribal inheritance among families and men. He chooses an appropriate

מסעי

במדבר לד:כז - לה:ח

בְּנֵי־אָשֵׁר נָשִׂיא אֲחִיהוּד בֶּן־שְׁלֹמִי: 28 וּלְמַטֵּה בְנֵי־נַפְתָּלִי נָשִׂיא פְּדַהְאֵל בֶּן־עַמִּיהוּד: 29 אֵלֶּה אֲשֶׁר צִוָּה יְהֹוָה לְנַחֵל אֶת־בְּנֵי־יִשְׂרָאֵל בְּאֶרֶץ כְּנָעַן: פ

לה [FIFTH READING]

1 וַיְדַבֵּר יְהֹוָה אֶל־מֹשֶׁה בְּעַרְבֹת מוֹאָב עַל־יַרְדֵּן יְרֵחוֹ לֵאמֹר: 2 צַו אֶת־בְּנֵי יִשְׂרָאֵל וְנָתְנוּ לַלְוִיִּם מִנַּחֲלַת אֲחֻזָּתָם עָרִים לָשָׁבֶת וּמִגְרָשׁ לֶעָרִים סְבִיבֹתֵיהֶם תִּתְּנוּ לַלְוִיִּם: 3 וְהָיוּ הֶעָרִים לָהֶם לָשָׁבֶת וּמִגְרְשֵׁיהֶם יִהְיוּ לִבְהֶמְתָּם וְלִרְכֻשָׁם וּלְכֹל חַיָּתָם: 4 וּמִגְרְשֵׁי הֶעָרִים אֲשֶׁר תִּתְּנוּ לַלְוִיִּם מִקִּיר הָעִיר וָחוּצָה אֶלֶף אַמָּה סָבִיב: 5 וּמַדֹּתֶם מִחוּץ לָעִיר אֶת־פְּאַת־קֵדְמָה אַלְפַּיִם בָּאַמָּה וְאֶת־פְּאַת־נֶגֶב אַלְפַּיִם בָּאַמָּה וְאֶת־פְּאַת־יָם | אַלְפַּיִם בָּאַמָּה וְאֵת פְּאַת צָפוֹן אַלְפַּיִם בָּאַמָּה וְהָעִיר בַּתָּוֶךְ זֶה יִהְיֶה לָהֶם מִגְרְשֵׁי הֶעָרִים: 6 וְאֵת הֶעָרִים אֲשֶׁר תִּתְּנוּ לַלְוִיִּם אֵת שֵׁשׁ־עָרֵי הַמִּקְלָט אֲשֶׁר תִּתְּנוּ לָנֻס שָׁמָּה הָרֹצֵחַ וַעֲלֵיהֶם תִּתְּנוּ אַרְבָּעִים וּשְׁתַּיִם עִיר: 7 כָּל־הֶעָרִים אֲשֶׁר תִּתְּנוּ לַלְוִיִּם אַרְבָּעִים וּשְׁמֹנֶה עִיר אֶתְהֶן וְאֶת־מִגְרְשֵׁיהֶן: 8 וְהֶעָרִים אֲשֶׁר תִּתְּנוּ מֵאֲחֻזַּת בְּנֵי־יִשְׂרָאֵל מֵאֵת הָרַב תַּרְבּוּ וּמֵאֵת הַמְעַט תַּמְעִיטוּ

1044

Practically speaking, this was the result of associating with the Levites, who were full-time ministers of God who devoted their entire lives to the Torah—both commandments between

kabbalah bites

35:6 According to the Kabbalah every sin is a kind of "murder," a metaphorical spilling of blood. The *kelippot* (the demonic forces) have no power of their own; they survive only when we give them energy through our sins, when we "spill blood" into their domain.

We can heal ourselves from a sinful past by rededicating ourselves completely to God, by *surrendering* ourselves to him.

The best time to surrender to God is when reciting the first paragraph of the prayer called *Shema*, especially the first line of that prayer.

This is the esoteric idea that "murder" (sin) is atoned for through six Levite cities and forty-two additional cities: because the *Shema* has six words in its first line, and forty-two words in its first paragraph.

numbers 34:28 – 35:8   mase'ei

²⁸ The leader of the tribe of Naphtali's descendants is Pedahel son of Ammihud.

²⁹ These are the ones whom God commanded to apportion the inheritance of the land of Canaan to the children of Israel.

Cities for the Levites

35 [FIFTH READING] ¹ God spoke to Moses in the plains of Moab, by the Jordan near Jericho, saying: ² Command the children of Israel:

- They should give the Levites cities to live in from their hereditary possession (of land).

- You should give the Levites (non-developed) open spaces around the cities (to enhance their beauty).

- ³ The cities will be theirs to live in, and the open spaces will be for their cattle, their property, and for all their needs.

- ⁴ The areas of open space for the cities which you should give to the Levites (should extend) from the wall of the city outward, one thousand cubits all around (as a non-developed space).

- ⁵ You should measure from outside the city, two thousand cubits on the eastern side, two thousand cubits on the southern side, two thousand cubits on the western side, and two thousand cubits on the northern side, with the city in the middle. This will be your (Levite) cities' (extended) open spaces, (for agriculture).

- ⁶ Among the cities you will give to the Levites, six should be cities of refuge, which you should provide (as places) to which a murderer can flee.

- In addition to this, you should provide forty-two cities. ⁷ Thus, the total number of cities you should give to the Levites will be forty-eight cities, together with their open spaces.

- ⁸ When you give cities from the hereditary land of the children of Israel, you should take more (land) from a larger (inheritance) and less (land) from a smaller one.

35:2 They should give the Levites cities to live in. Even though the tribe of Levi does not have a portion in the land, the Jewish people have already been commanded to give them cities to live in and for open space. These cities are: the six cities of refuge, to which were added forty-two further cities, and the additional cities of refuge in the days of the Messiah. All these are for the Levites (*Maimonides, 12th century*).

It is no coincidence that the cities of refuge were also Levite cities. When Levi was born, his mother said, *"Now this time my husband will be attached (yilLaVeh) to me"* (*Genesis* 29:34), the name Levi denoting reattachment after a period of disconnection. When the accidental murderer becomes "disconnected" from God through his sin, he seeks refuge in a Levite city, so that the association with the Levites will assist in reestablishing and revealing his connection with God.

במדבר ל״ה:ח-כא   מסעי

9 וַיְדַבֵּר [SIXTH READING / SEVENTH WHEN JOINED] אִישׁ כְּפִי נַחֲלָתוֹ אֲשֶׁר יִנְחָלוּ יִתֵּן מֵעָרָיו לַלְוִיִּם: פ
יְהֹוָה אֶל־מֹשֶׁה לֵּאמֹר: 10 דַּבֵּר אֶל־בְּנֵי יִשְׂרָאֵל וְאָמַרְתָּ אֲלֵהֶם כִּי אַתֶּם
עֹבְרִים אֶת־הַיַּרְדֵּן אַרְצָה כְּנָעַן: 11 וְהִקְרִיתֶם לָכֶם עָרִים עָרֵי מִקְלָט תִּהְיֶינָה
לָכֶם וְנָס שָׁמָּה רֹצֵחַ מַכֵּה־נֶפֶשׁ בִּשְׁגָגָה: 12 וְהָיוּ לָכֶם הֶעָרִים לְמִקְלָט מִגֹּאֵל
וְלֹא יָמוּת הָרֹצֵחַ עַד־עָמְדוֹ לִפְנֵי הָעֵדָה לַמִּשְׁפָּט: 13 וְהֶעָרִים אֲשֶׁר תִּתֵּנוּ
שֵׁשׁ־עָרֵי מִקְלָט תִּהְיֶינָה לָכֶם: 14 אֵת | שְׁלֹשׁ הֶעָרִים תִּתְּנוּ מֵעֵבֶר לַיַּרְדֵּן וְאֵת
שְׁלֹשׁ הֶעָרִים תִּתְּנוּ בְּאֶרֶץ כְּנָעַן עָרֵי מִקְלָט תִּהְיֶינָה: 15 לִבְנֵי יִשְׂרָאֵל וְלַגֵּר
וְלַתּוֹשָׁב בְּתוֹכָם תִּהְיֶינָה שֵׁשׁ־הֶעָרִים הָאֵלֶּה לְמִקְלָט לָנוּס שָׁמָּה כָּל־מַכֵּה־
נֶפֶשׁ בִּשְׁגָגָה: 16 וְאִם־בִּכְלִי בַרְזֶל | הִכָּהוּ וַיָּמֹת רֹצֵחַ הוּא מוֹת יוּמַת הָרֹצֵחַ:
17 וְאִם בְּאֶבֶן יָד אֲשֶׁר־יָמוּת בָּהּ הִכָּהוּ וַיָּמֹת רֹצֵחַ הוּא מוֹת יוּמַת הָרֹצֵחַ:
18 אוֹ בִּכְלִי עֵץ־יָד אֲשֶׁר־יָמוּת בּוֹ הִכָּהוּ וַיָּמֹת רֹצֵחַ הוּא מוֹת יוּמַת הָרֹצֵחַ:
19 גֹּאֵל הַדָּם הוּא יָמִית אֶת־הָרֹצֵחַ בְּפִגְעוֹ־בוֹ הוּא יְמִתֶנּוּ: 20 וְאִם־בְּשִׂנְאָה
יֶהְדֳּפֶנּוּ אוֹ־הִשְׁלִיךְ עָלָיו בִּצְדִיָּה וַיָּמֹת: 21 אוֹ בְאֵיבָה הִכָּהוּ בְיָדוֹ וַיָּמֹת מוֹת־

---

human soul. *Mase'ei* is the body, since we read here of the accidental murderer who does not find peace after having separated a soul from its body, its Divinely formed container (*Rabbi Isaiah Horowitz, 16th–17th century*).

16. If a person struck another with an iron instrument and he dies. A very small piece of iron—even a needle—can kill, if it is thrust into a vital organ. Therefore, the Torah prescribed no specific size for an iron weapon (*Babylonian Talmud, Sanhedrin 76b*).

spiritual vitamin

> A feeling of dissatisfaction with yourself is a good sign. It indicates vitality and an urge to rise and improve yourself, which is accomplished in a two-way method: withdrawal from the present state, and turning to a higher level.

Each one should give cities to the Levites, commensurate with (the size of) the inheritance allotted to him.

Cities of Refuge for Unintentional Murder

[SIXTH READING / SEVENTH WHEN JOINED] [9] God spoke to Moses, saying: [10] Speak to the children of Israel and say to them:

- When you cross the Jordan to the land of Canaan, [11] you should prepare (special) cities for yourselves. They will be cities of refuge for you, such that a murderer who killed a person unintentionally can flee there.

- [12] These cities should serve for you as a refuge from an avenger, so that the murderer will not die until he stands in judgment before the congregation.

- [13] The cities that you will provide will serve as six cities of refuge for you: [14] You should provide the three cities in Transjordan and the three cities in the land of Canaan to act as cities of refuge.

- [15] These six cities should be a refuge for the children of Israel, the convert and resident (alien) among them, so that anyone who unintentionally kills a person can flee there.

Laws Pertaining to Intentional Murder

- [16] If a person struck another with an iron instrument and he dies, he is a murderer (no matter how small the instrument was). The murderer must be put to death.

- [17] If a person struck another with a fist-sized stone which is (big enough to be) deadly, and he dies, he is a murderer. The murderer must be put to death. [18] Or (if he strikes) with a fist-sized wooden instrument which is (big enough to be) deadly, and he dies, he is a murderer. The murderer must be put to death.

- [19] An avenger of the blood may kill the (intentional) murderer. He may kill him (even) when he meets him (in a city of refuge).

- [20] If a person pushed another out of hatred, or he threw something at him with premeditation, and he died; [21] or if he maliciously struck him with his hand and he died, the attacker must be put to death. He is (considered to be) an (intentional)

man and God, and those between man and his fellow (*Rabbi Menahem Mendel Schneerson, 20th century*).

11. A murderer who killed a person unintentionally can flee there. One reason for this commandment is that by keeping the unintentional murderer far away in a city of refuge, the painful meeting between him and the family of the victim is deferred, emphasizing the Torah's way of keeping peace and harmony among all (*Rabbi Aaron ha-Levi (Ḥinnukh), 13th century*).

The two Torah portions of *Mattot* and *Mase'ei* speak of soul and body. *Mattot* is the soul, since it speaks of vows, the faculty of speech, which brings to light the unique qualities of the

מסעי   במדבר לה:כא-לב

22 יוּמַ֣ת הַמַּכֶּ֔ה רֹצֵ֖חַ ה֑וּא גֹּאֵ֣ל הַדָּ֗ם יָמִ֛ית אֶת־הָרֹצֵ֖חַ בְּפִגְעוֹ־בֽוֹ: 23 וְאִם־בְּפֶ֜תַע בְּלֹא־אֵיבָ֣ה הֲדָפ֗וֹ אוֹ־הִשְׁלִ֥יךְ עָלָ֛יו כָּל־כְּלִ֖י בְּלֹ֥א צְדִיָּֽה: 24 א֣וֹ בְכָל־אֶ֜בֶן אֲשֶׁר־יָמ֤וּת בָּהּ֙ בְּלֹ֣א רְא֔וֹת וַיַּפֵּ֥ל עָלָ֖יו וַיָּמֹ֑ת וְהוּא֙ לֹא־אוֹיֵ֣ב ל֔וֹ וְלֹ֥א מְבַקֵּ֖שׁ רָעָתֽוֹ: 25 וְשָֽׁפְטוּ֙ הָֽעֵדָ֔ה בֵּ֚ין הַמַּכֶּ֔ה וּבֵ֖ין גֹּאֵ֣ל הַדָּ֑ם עַ֥ל הַמִּשְׁפָּטִ֖ים הָאֵֽלֶּה: 26 וְהִצִּ֨ילוּ הָעֵדָ֜ה אֶת־הָרֹצֵ֗חַ מִיַּד֮ גֹּאֵ֣ל הַדָּם֒ וְהֵשִׁ֤יבוּ אֹתוֹ֙ הָֽעֵדָ֔ה אֶל־עִ֥יר מִקְלָט֖וֹ אֲשֶׁר־נָ֣ס שָׁ֑מָּה וְיָ֣שַׁב בָּ֗הּ עַד־מוֹת֙ הַכֹּהֵ֣ן הַגָּדֹ֔ל אֲשֶׁר־מָשַׁ֥ח אֹת֖וֹ בְּשֶׁ֥מֶן הַקֹּֽדֶשׁ: 27 וְאִם־יָצֹ֥א יֵצֵ֖א הָרֹצֵ֑חַ אֶת־גְּבוּל֙ עִ֣יר מִקְלָט֔וֹ אֲשֶׁ֥ר יָנ֖וּס שָֽׁמָּה: 28 וּמָצָ֤א אֹתוֹ֙ גֹּאֵ֣ל הַדָּ֔ם מִח֕וּץ לִגְב֖וּל עִ֣יר מִקְלָט֑וֹ וְרָצַ֞ח גֹּאֵ֤ל הַדָּם֙ אֶת־הָ֣רֹצֵ֔חַ אֵ֥ין ל֖וֹ דָּֽם: כִּ֣י בְעִ֤יר מִקְלָטוֹ֙ יֵשֵׁ֔ב עַד־מ֖וֹת הַכֹּהֵ֣ן הַגָּדֹ֑ל וְאַֽחֲרֵי֙ מוֹת֙ הַכֹּהֵ֣ן הַגָּדֹ֔ל יָשׁוּב֙ הָרֹצֵ֔חַ אֶל־אֶ֖רֶץ אֲחֻזָּתֽוֹ: 29 וְהָי֨וּ אֵ֧לֶּה לָכֶ֛ם לְחֻקַּ֥ת מִשְׁפָּ֖ט לְדֹרֹֽתֵיכֶ֑ם בְּכֹ֖ל מֽוֹשְׁבֹֽתֵיכֶֽם: 30 כָּל־מַכֵּה־נֶ֔פֶשׁ לְפִ֣י עֵדִ֔ים יִרְצַ֖ח אֶת־הָרֹצֵ֑חַ וְעֵ֣ד אֶחָ֔ד לֹֽא־יַעֲנֶ֥ה בְנֶ֖פֶשׁ לָמֽוּת: 31 וְלֹֽא־תִקְח֥וּ כֹ֨פֶר֙ לְנֶ֣פֶשׁ רֹצֵ֔חַ אֲשֶׁר־ה֥וּא רָשָׁ֖ע לָמ֑וּת כִּי־מ֥וֹת יוּמָֽת: 32 וְלֹֽא־תִקְח֣וּ כֹ֔פֶר לָנ֖וּס אֶל־עִ֣יר מִקְלָט֑וֹ לָשׁוּב֙ לָשֶׁ֣בֶת בָּאָ֔רֶץ

Food for thought

1. How far should we go in protecting the rights of a criminal?

2. Is it ever appropriate to take revenge?

3. Do you listen carefully to all sides of the story before assuming guilt?

Accidental death is not handled in the same manner in all cases. Each situation depends on the motives and particular circumstances of the incident. It would be unjust therefore to set a standard sentence for all cases of manslaughter. Only God, who knows the true degree of culpability for each killer, can determine the length of their punishment. By linking the murderer's release with the death of the High Priest, God can orchestrate events in a way that the duration of each person's term in the city of refuge will be in accordance with his actual level of guilt (*Rabbi Jacob Tzevi Meklenburg, 19th century*).

26. If the murderer goes outside. If a person leaves the boundaries of the city of refuge intentionally, then he is permitting himself to die, and the bereaved relative may avenge the deceased's blood and kill him. If another person kills him, he is not liable for any penalty, since the verse states, *"He has no (liability for the) blood"* (v. 27; *Maimonides, 12th century*).

murderer. The avenger of the blood may kill this murderer (even) when he meets him (in a city of refuge).

Laws Pertaining to Unintentional Murder

²² But if a person pushed another accidentally, without malice, or threw an object at him without premeditation, ²³ or he threw a stone which is deadly down at another without seeing (him) and it killed him, but he was not his enemy and did not want to hurt him, ²⁴ then the congregation should enact justice between the attacker and the avenger of the blood, according to the following laws:

- ²⁵ The congregation should protect the murderer from the avenger of the blood. The congregation should return him to the city of refuge to which he had fled.

- He must remain there until the death of the High Priest, the one who was anointed with the sacred oil.

- ²⁶ But if the murderer goes outside the border of the city of refuge to which he had fled, ²⁷ and the avenger of the blood finds him outside the limits of his city of refuge, and the avenger of the blood kills the murderer, he has no (liability for the) blood (he spilled). ²⁸ For (the accidental murderer) must remain in his city of refuge until the High Priest dies, and only after the High Priest has died may the murderer return to the land which is his possession.

- ²⁹ (The small *Sanhedrin*) will be (a body that issues) laws of justice for you, throughout all your generations, in all the places that you live (even outside the land of Israel, so long as the small *Sanhedrin* exists inside the land, too).

- ³⁰ (When an avenger of the blood) kills a person, the murderer may only be put to death based on the testimony of witnesses (who first warned the murderer).

- A single witness may not testify against a person to put him to death.

- ³¹ Do not accept an atonement fee for the life of a murderer who is condemned to death, because he must be put to death.

- ³² Do not accept an atonement fee for one who has fled to his city of refuge, to allow him to return to live in the land, before the priest has died.

25. He must remain there until the death of the High Priest. Why would a murderer be allowed to leave a city of refuge when the High Priest died? How would that calm the victim's avenger?

When the High Priest passed away, it was a time for the entire nation to take stock and repent for their sins. The avenger, too, would think about his murdered relative. Pondering the fact that even the High Priest eventually passes away, and no man lives forever, the avenger's anger would calm, and he would no longer want to murder the person who accidentally killed his relative (*Rabbi Isaac Abravanel, 15th century*).

במדבר לה:לב - לו:ח

עַד־מֹ֥ות הַכֹּהֵֽן׃ 33 וְלֹא־תַחֲנִ֣יפוּ אֶת־הָאָ֗רֶץ אֲשֶׁ֤ר אַתֶּם֙ בָּ֔הּ כִּ֣י הַדָּ֔ם ה֥וּא יַחֲנִ֖יף אֶת־הָאָ֑רֶץ וְלָאָ֣רֶץ לֹֽא־יְכֻפַּ֗ר לַדָּם֙ אֲשֶׁ֣ר שֻׁפַּךְ־בָּ֔הּ כִּי־אִ֖ם בְּדַ֥ם שֹׁפְכֽוֹ׃ 34 וְלֹ֧א תְטַמֵּ֣א אֶת־הָאָ֗רֶץ אֲשֶׁ֤ר אַתֶּם֙ יֹשְׁבִ֣ים בָּ֔הּ אֲשֶׁ֥ר אֲנִ֖י שֹׁכֵ֣ן בְּתוֹכָ֑הּ כִּ֚י אֲנִ֣י יְהֹוָ֔ה שֹׁכֵ֕ן בְּת֖וֹךְ בְּנֵ֥י יִשְׂרָאֵֽל׃ פ

לו [SEVENTH READING] 1 וַיִּקְרְב֞וּ רָאשֵׁ֣י הָֽאָב֗וֹת לְמִשְׁפַּ֤חַת בְּנֵֽי־גִלְעָד֙ בֶּן־מָכִ֣יר בֶּן־מְנַשֶּׁ֔ה מִֽמִּשְׁפְּחֹ֖ת בְּנֵ֣י יוֹסֵ֑ף וַֽיְדַבְּר֞וּ לִפְנֵ֤י מֹשֶׁה֙ וְלִפְנֵ֣י הַנְּשִׂאִ֔ים רָאשֵׁ֥י אָב֖וֹת לִבְנֵ֥י יִשְׂרָאֵֽל׃ 2 וַיֹּאמְר֗וּ אֶת־אֲדֹנִי֙ צִוָּ֣ה יְהֹוָ֔ה לָתֵ֨ת אֶת־הָאָ֧רֶץ בְּנַחֲלָ֛ה בְּגוֹרָ֖ל לִבְנֵ֣י יִשְׂרָאֵ֑ל וַֽאדֹנִי֙ צֻוָּ֣ה בַֽיהֹוָ֔ה לָתֵ֗ת אֶֽת־נַחֲלַ֛ת צְלׇפְחָ֥ד אָחִ֖ינוּ לִבְנֹתָֽיו׃ 3 וְ֠הָי֠וּ לְאֶחָ֞ד מִבְּנֵ֨י שִׁבְטֵ֥י בְנֵֽי־יִשְׂרָאֵל֮ לְנָשִׁים֒ וְנִגְרְעָ֤ה נַחֲלָתָן֙ מִנַּחֲלַ֣ת אֲבֹתֵ֔ינוּ וְנוֹסַ֕ף עַ֚ל נַחֲלַ֣ת הַמַּטֶּ֔ה אֲשֶׁ֥ר תִּהְיֶ֖ינָה לָהֶ֑ם וּמִגֹּרַ֥ל נַחֲלָתֵ֖נוּ יִגָּרֵֽעַ׃ 4 וְאִם־יִהְיֶ֣ה הַיֹּבֵל֮ לִבְנֵ֣י יִשְׂרָאֵל֒ וְנֽוֹסְפָה֙ נַחֲלָתָ֔ן עַ֚ל נַחֲלַ֣ת הַמַּטֶּ֔ה אֲשֶׁ֥ר תִּהְיֶ֖ינָה לָהֶ֑ם וּמִנַּחֲלַת֙ מַטֵּ֣ה אֲבֹתֵ֔ינוּ יִגָּרַ֖ע נַחֲלָתָֽן׃ 5 וַיְצַ֤ו מֹשֶׁה֙ אֶת־בְּנֵ֣י יִשְׂרָאֵ֔ל עַל־פִּ֥י יְהֹוָ֖ה לֵאמֹ֑ר כֵּ֛ן מַטֵּ֥ה בְנֵֽי־יוֹסֵ֖ף דֹּבְרִֽים׃ 6 זֶ֣ה הַדָּבָ֗ר אֲשֶׁר־צִוָּ֤ה יְהֹוָה֙ לִבְנ֣וֹת צְלׇפְחָד֙ לֵאמֹ֔ר לַטּ֥וֹב בְּעֵינֵיהֶ֖ם תִּֽהְיֶ֣ינָה לְנָשִׁ֑ים אַ֗ךְ לְמִשְׁפַּ֛חַת מַטֵּ֥ה אֲבִיהֶ֖ם תִּהְיֶ֥ינָה לְנָשִֽׁים׃ 7 וְלֹֽא־תִסֹּ֤ב נַחֲלָה֙ לִבְנֵ֣י יִשְׂרָאֵ֔ל מִמַּטֶּ֖ה אֶל־מַטֶּ֑ה כִּ֣י אִ֗ישׁ בְּנַחֲלַת֙ מַטֵּ֣ה אֲבֹתָ֔יו יִדְבְּק֖וּ בְּנֵ֥י יִשְׂרָאֵֽל׃ 8 וְכׇל־בַּ֞ת יֹרֶ֣שֶׁת נַחֲלָ֗ה מִמַּטּוֹת֮ בְּנֵ֣י יִשְׂרָאֵל֒ לְאֶחָ֗ד מִמִּשְׁפַּ֛חַת מַטֵּ֥ה אָבִ֖יהָ תִּהְיֶ֣ה לְאִשָּׁ֑ה לְמַ֨עַן֙ יִֽירְשׁוּ֙ בְּנֵ֣י

---

34. Do not defile the land where you reside, in which I dwell, for I am God who dwells among the children of Israel. The Jewish people are cherished by God. Even when they are impure, the Divine Presence is with them, as the verse states, *"in which I dwell,"* and it also says, *"do not defile the land."*

Rabbi Nathan says: "The Jewish people are cherished by God, for in every place that they were exiled the Divine Presence was with them."

Rabbi Judah ha-Nasi says: "To what could this be compared? To a king who said to his servant, 'If you want me, I am with my son. Any time that you want me, I am with my son.'" Thus, the verse states, *"He dwells with the (Jewish people, despite) their ritual impurity"* (Leviticus 16:16; Sifrei).

³³ Do not corrupt the land in which you live, for the (spilling of) blood corrupts the land, and blood which is shed in the land cannot be atoned for except by the blood of the one who shed it. ³⁴ Do not defile the land where you reside, in which I dwell, for I am God Who dwells among the children of Israel.

Preserving the Tribal Inheritance of Land

36 [SEVENTH READING] ¹ The paternal heads of the family of the descendants of Gilead—the son of Machir, the son of Manasseh, of the families of Joseph's descendants—approached and spoke before Moses and the leaders, the paternal heads of the children of Israel. ² They said, "God commanded my master to give the land as an inheritance via lottery to the children of Israel, and our master was commanded by God to give the inheritance of Zelophehad, our brother, to his daughters. ³ Now, if they marry a member of another tribe of the children of Israel, their inheritance will be deducted from the inheritance of our father, and it will be added to the inheritance of the tribe into which they marry. Thus, it will be deducted from the lot of our inheritance. ⁴ Even when the children of Israel will have a Jubilee year (when hereditary land returns to its owner), their inheritance will be added to the inheritance of the tribe into which they marry, and their inheritance will be deducted from the inheritance of our father's tribe."

⁵ Moses commanded the children of Israel with God's word saying, "The tribe of Joseph's descendants speaks well. ⁶ This is what God has commanded regarding Zelophehad's daughters: Let them marry whom they wish, but they may marry only within the family of their father's tribe. ⁷ Thus, the inheritance of the children of Israel will not be transferred from tribe to tribe, as each person from the children of Israel will remain attached to the inheritance of his father's tribe. ⁸ Every girl from the children of Israel's tribes who inherits property (because her father had no son) should marry a member of her father's tribe, so that each one

---

33. Do not corrupt (*taḥanifu*) the land in which you live. This is a warning against flatterers (*ḥaneifim*) (*Sifrei*).

spiritual vitamin

> To some, the Torah may be a means to gain reward and avoid punishment. To others, the Torah is a guide to good, wholesome living, and an ideal social system. Both views are limited because the Torah, being God-given, is infinite.

בְּמִדְבַּר לו:ח-יג מַסְעֵי

יִשְׂרָאֵ֔ל אִ֖ישׁ נַחֲלַ֥ת אֲבֹתָֽיו: 9 וְלֹֽא־תִסֹּ֤ב נַחֲלָה֙ מִמַּטֶּ֔ה לְמַטֶּ֖ה אַחֵ֑ר כִּי־אִישׁ֙ בְּנַ֣חֲלָת֔וֹ יִדְבְּק֕וּ מַטּ֖וֹת בְּנֵ֥י יִשְׂרָאֵֽל: 10 כַּאֲשֶׁ֛ר צִוָּ֥ה יְהוָ֖ה אֶת־מֹשֶׁ֑ה כֵּ֥ן עָשׂ֖וּ בְּנ֥וֹת צְלָפְחָֽד: [MAFTIR] 11 וַתִּהְיֶ֜ינָה מַחְלָ֣ה תִרְצָ֗ה וְחָגְלָ֧ה וּמִלְכָּ֛ה וְנֹעָ֖ה בְּנ֣וֹת צְלָפְחָ֑ד לִבְנֵ֥י דֹדֵיהֶ֖ן לְנָשִֽׁים: 12 מִֽמִּשְׁפְּחֹ֛ת בְּנֵֽי־מְנַשֶּׁ֥ה בֶן־יוֹסֵ֖ף הָי֣וּ לְנָשִׁ֑ים וַתְּהִי֙ נַחֲלָתָ֔ן עַל־מַטֵּ֖ה מִשְׁפַּ֥חַת אֲבִיהֶֽן: 13 אֵ֣לֶּה הַמִּצְוֺ֞ת וְהַמִּשְׁפָּטִ֗ים אֲשֶׁ֨ר צִוָּ֧ה יְהוָ֛ה בְּיַד־מֹשֶׁ֖ה אֶל־בְּנֵ֣י יִשְׂרָאֵ֑ל בְּעַֽרְבֹ֣ת מוֹאָ֔ב עַ֖ל יַרְדֵּ֥ן יְרֵחֽוֹ:

חֲזַק חֲזַק וְנִתְחַזֵּק

קל"ב פסוקים, מחל"ה חול"ה סימן, סכום פסוקי דספר במדבר אלף ומאתים ושמנים ושמנה אפר"ח סימן. וחציו והנה האיש אשר אבחר בו מטהו יפרח. ופרשיותיו עשרה. י"ד בדד ינחנו סימן. וסדריו ל"ב לך טהור ברא לי אלהים סימן. (ס"א וסדריו כ"ח). ופרקיו ל"ו. לו חכמו ישכילו זאת סימן. מנין הפתוחות שתים ותשעים וסתומות ששים ושש. הכל מאה וחמשים ושמנה פרשיות. אני חלק"ך ונחלתך סימן:

you desire only to escape the world's limitations and join in an ecstatic union with God, nor will you find physical chores a distraction from your calling in life.

This level of seamless integration between spiritual enlightenment and worldly involvement is alluded to by the number *four*, which is a step removed from both *one* and *two*, representing the ability not to be over-influenced by either of these two contradictory worlds. The *four*-type personality is balanced and stable, like a chair possessing four legs which stands firmly on the ground.

All this sheds light on the fact that we finish the fourth book of the Torah in the period of mourning for the destruction of the Temple. For the way to end this long, bitter exile—which is in fact the fourth exile of the Jews—and bring the true and final redemption, is to harmonize our personalities in a *four*-like manner. And then we will enjoy a permanent redemption, because it will be built on steady foundations (*Rabbi Menahem Mendel Schneerson, 20th century*).

of the children of Israel will inherit the property of his fathers. ⁹ No inheritance will be transferred from one tribe to another tribe, for each person of the tribes of the children of Israel will remain bound to his own inheritance." ¹⁰ Zelophehad's daughters did what God had commanded Moses.

[MAFTIR] ¹¹ Mahlah, Tirzah, Hoglah, Milcah and Noah, the daughters of Zelophehad, married their cousins. ¹² They married into the families of the descendants of Manasseh, Joseph's son, and their inheritance remained within the family of their father's tribe.

¹³ These are the commandments and the laws that God commanded the children of Israel through Moses in the plains of Moab, by the Jordan near Jericho.

The congregation, followed by the reader, proclaims:

Be strong! Be strong! And may we be strengthened!

The *Haftarah* for *Maseʻei* (and *Mattot-Maseʻei*) is on page 1390 [It is read even on *Rosh Ḥodesh*].

Maftir: Rosh Ḥodesh—page 1000 (28:9–15).

36:13 These are the commandments. *One* represents *unity*, Godliness and spirituality. *Two* represents the *dichotomy* and *division* of the physical world, which hides God and acts as an obstacle in His worship. *Three* is the reconciliation of *one* and *two*, to saturate the world with the Divine flow, which is the goal and purpose of creation.

But, as we know, this process is fraught with difficulty. In attempting to sanctify the physical world, man is likely either to remain too spiritual and aloof—in which case he will not be effective in bringing his spirituality "down to earth"—or too influenced by the physical world, which would compromise his ability to live in a spirit of true sanctity and purity.

So *three* represents the *incomplete* harmonization of *one* and *two*, because it still remains influenced by, and torn between, both of these worlds.

But if you persist, a perfect balance *can* be achieved; eventually you will lift yourself above both spiritual and physical imbalance. You will no longer have moods of transcendence, when

ספר דברים

THE BOOK *of* DEUTERONOMY

Deuteronomy ("repetition of the law") is a **new book** with a **different approach.** As you rise **each morning** don't view the new day as a repetition; it is **a new page in your life,** requiring a novel approach.

DEVARIM
דברים

MOSES' REBUKE	1:1–46
EFFORTS TO AVERT CONFLICT	2:1–23
SUCCESSFUL MILITARY CAMPAIGNS	2:24 – 3:11
TRANSJORDAN SETTLEMENT	3:12–17
BATTLE ORDERS FOR THE CANAANITE WARS	3:18–22

NAME
Devarim

MEANING
"Words"

LINES IN TORAH SCROLL
197

PARASHIYYOT
1 open; 4 closed

VERSES
105

WORDS
1548

LETTERS
5972

LOCATION
Plains of Moab

DATE
1 *Shevat*, 2488

MASORETIC FEATURES
Rare mid-verse paragraph break (2:8)

MITZVOT
2 prohibitions

NOTES
Read the week before the Ninth of *Av*

CHARACTER PROFILE

NAME
Sihon ("speech," "foal")

OTHER NAMES
Arad ("wild donkey");
Canaan

FATHER
Ahijah son of Shemhazzai,
a fallen angel

BROTHER
King Og of Bashan

ACHIEVEMENTS
King of the Amorites;
protector of entire land of
Canaan

KNOWN FOR
He was an invincible giant;
received tributes from
Canaanite kings to keep
them in power; was paid to
protect entire Canaan from
attack; refused to travel
a day's journey to save his
brother; hired Balaam to
curse the Moabites; attacked
the Jews in response to
a peaceful request for
passage; was killed in
a failed attack on the Jews
at Jahaz

REBUKE

Moses rebuked the Jews with subtle hints. Avoid spelling out an embarrassing fault in another person; instead, allude to it sensitively (1:1).

TRUST

God will fight your battles for you. But to be genuine, you have to put great effort into nurturing your trust (1:8).

JUDGMENT

In judging honestly, you are a partner with God (1:16-17).

BROTHERHOOD

Another person's struggle is also your own. How could you use your strengths and talents to assist your fellow? (1:16-17).

דברים א:א-ג

¹ אֵ֣לֶּה הַדְּבָרִ֗ים אֲשֶׁ֨ר דִּבֶּ֤ר מֹשֶׁה֙ אֶל־כָּל־יִשְׂרָאֵ֔ל בְּעֵ֖בֶר הַיַּרְדֵּ֑ן בַּמִּדְבָּ֡ר בָּֽעֲרָבָה֩ מ֨וֹל ס֜וּף בֵּֽין־פָּארָ֧ן וּבֵֽין־תֹּ֛פֶל וְלָבָ֥ן וַחֲצֵרֹ֖ת וְדִ֥י זָהָֽב: ² אַחַ֨ד עָשָׂ֥ר יוֹם֙ מֵֽחֹרֵ֔ב דֶּ֖רֶךְ הַר־שֵׂעִ֑יר עַ֖ד קָדֵ֥שׁ בַּרְנֵֽעַ: ³ וַיְהִי֙ בְּאַרְבָּעִ֣ים שָׁנָ֔ה בְּעַשְׁתֵּֽי־עָשָׂ֥ר חֹ֖דֶשׁ בְּאֶחָ֣ד לַחֹ֑דֶשׁ דִּבֶּ֤ר מֹשֶׁה֙ אֶל־בְּנֵ֣י יִשְׂרָאֵ֔ל כְּכֹל֩

Thus, the book begins, "These are the words which *Moses spoke*" (*Rabbi Ḥayyim ibn Attar, 18th century*).

The book was nevertheless said with Divine Inspiration (*The Tosafists, 12th–14th centuries*).

The Torah which God gave to the Jewish people contains two "dimensions"—one from God's perspective, the One who gave the Torah, and a second dimension from the perspective of the Jewish people, who received the Torah.

Now, when a person gives a gift to his friend, if they are both on the same level then the gift only has one dimension. But when God, who is far beyond us all, gave the Torah to the Jewish people here on earth, it is impossible for there not to be in it a unique dimension from the Giver's perspective and another dimension suited to the recipient.

The entire Torah, with the exception of the Book of Deuteronomy, the final book, represents the "Giver's dimension," because the needs of the recipient are inevitably catered to last, after the Giver has concluded articulating His words. That is why the Book of Deuteronomy is referred to as *Mishneh Torah* "the repetition of the Torah" [the word "Deuteronomy" (Δευτερονόμιον) is Greek for "second law"] to stress that it was said specifically with the recipient in mind.

Consequently, every word of the first four books of the Torah, despite the fact that they were said by Moses, is nevertheless phrased as if God were speaking—"This is what God decreed" and "this is what God said." God literally put the words in his mouth.

But in the "repetition of the Torah," Moses spoke his own words, like an agent representing the One who sent him.

This explains our Sages' statement that Moses said the Book of Deuteronomy *"of his own initiative"*—God did not put the actual words into his mouth, because the "repetition of the Torah" represents the "recipients' dimension," and to be compatible with the recipient it must be said by somebody who is close to the recipients' level. Therefore, it was said by Moses (*Rabbi Judah Loew b. Bezalel of Prague, 16th century*).

2. From Horeb (where the Torah was given) **to Kadesh-barnea** (where the spies were sent out) **by way of Mount Seir** (normally) **takes eleven days.** Moses was saying to them: "See what you

> **kabbalah bites**
>
> **1:1** The Book of Deuteronomy is a "repetition of the law," a restatement of many of the precepts stated in the first four books of the Torah. What was the point of this exercise?
>
> The first four books of the Torah correspond to the four letters of the Tetragrammaton, God's ineffable name. The current book is a reflection of *Malkhut* (sovereignty), God's projection into this world. So we have here an emanation of the same light—a repetition of the Torah—but in a more worldly articulation. In Deuteronomy we are empowered to take the light of the Torah and deliver it to our daily lives in a practical, relevant way.

deuteronomy 1:1–3 — devarim

parashat devarim

Moses' Subtle Rebuke to the Jewish People

1 ¹ These are the words (of subtle rebuke) which Moses spoke to all the Jewish people in (the plains of Moab, on the east) bank of the Jordan. (He mentioned the places where they rebelled against God): "in the wilderness, in the plain(s of Moab), at the Sea of Reeds, (in the wilderness) of Paran, between Tophel and Laban, at Hazeroth and at Di-zahab."

² "From Horeb (where the Torah was given) to Kadesh-barnea, (where the spies were sent out), by way of Mount Seir (normally) takes eleven days, (but you took just three days, because God was speeding your entry into the land)."

(However, the Jewish people forfeited this blessing, and were delayed in the desert for forty years:)

³ It happened that in the fortieth year, in the eleventh month, on the first of the month, Moses spoke to the children of Israel (shortly before his passing, and

---

1:1 These are the words. These are words of rebuke, since all the places where they angered God are listed here. But, out of respect for the Jewish people, Moses was vague with his words and he only hinted at their sins, by mentioning the *places* where the sins occurred, and not the sins themselves.

"In the wilderness"—he rebuked them for angering God in the desert when they said, *"If only we had died by the hand of God in the land of Egypt"* (*Exodus* 16:3).

"In the plain"—the sin of Baal-peor at Shittim, in the plains of Moab (*Numbers* 25:1-9).

"At the Sea of Reeds"—their rebellion at the Reed Sea (*Exodus* 14:11; *Psalms* 106:7).

"Paran"—what they did in the desert of Paran, through the spies.

"Between Tophel and Laban"—Rabbi Johanan said, "We have searched the entire Torah, but we have found no place named Tophel or Laban!" This means that he rebuked them because of the foolish things—*tafelu*—"that they had said" about the manna, which was—*lavan*—"white," saying *"We're sick of this unwholesome (manna) bread"* (*Numbers* 21:5).

"Hazeroth"—with the rebellion of Korah. Another explanation: He said to them, "You should have learned from what I did to Miriam at Hazeroth because of slander. But you spoke against God."

"Di-zahab" (lit. "enough gold")—He rebuked them for the calf they had made as a result of their abundance of gold (*Rashi, 11th century*).

When rebuking the Jewish people here, Moses did not mention, or even allude to their sins. In order to maintain their dignity, he merely mentioned *the places* where they had sinned.

This teaches us how careful you should be not to cause distress to another person. If, on occasion, it proves necessary to rebuke somebody—even for serious mistakes, such as the ones Moses indicated here—you must do so subtly and gently (*Rabbi Ephraim of Luntshits, 16th–17th century*).

Which Moses spoke. Moses was not commanded by God to say the Book of Deuteronomy. Rather, he said it of his own initiative, as our Sages taught (*Babylonian Talmud, Megillah* 31b).

דברים א:ג-ח

אֲשֶׁר צִוָּה יְהֹוָה אֹתוֹ אֲלֵהֶם: 4 אַחֲרֵי הַכֹּתוֹ אֵת סִיחֹן מֶלֶךְ הָאֱמֹרִי אֲשֶׁר יוֹשֵׁב בְּחֶשְׁבּוֹן וְאֵת עוֹג מֶלֶךְ הַבָּשָׁן אֲשֶׁר־יוֹשֵׁב בְּעַשְׁתָּרֹת בְּאֶדְרֶעִי: 5 בְּעֵבֶר הַיַּרְדֵּן בְּאֶרֶץ מוֹאָב הוֹאִיל מֹשֶׁה בֵּאֵר אֶת־הַתּוֹרָה הַזֹּאת לֵאמֹר: 6 יְהֹוָה אֱלֹהֵינוּ דִּבֶּר אֵלֵינוּ בְּחֹרֵב לֵאמֹר רַב־לָכֶם שֶׁבֶת בָּהָר הַזֶּה: 7 פְּנוּ | וּסְעוּ לָכֶם וּבֹאוּ הַר הָאֱמֹרִי וְאֶל־כָּל־שְׁכֵנָיו בָּעֲרָבָה בָהָר וּבַשְּׁפֵלָה וּבַנֶּגֶב וּבְחוֹף הַיָּם אֶרֶץ הַכְּנַעֲנִי וְהַלְּבָנוֹן עַד־הַנָּהָר הַגָּדֹל נְהַר־פְּרָת: 8 רְאֵה נָתַתִּי לִפְנֵיכֶם אֶת־הָאָרֶץ בֹּאוּ וּרְשׁוּ אֶת־הָאָרֶץ אֲשֶׁר נִשְׁבַּע יְהֹוָה לַאֲבֹתֵיכֶם

all forms of resistance to their religion presented by their surroundings (*Rabbi Isaac Meir Alter of Gur, 19th century*).

Why did Moses bother the Jewish people to listen to the Torah being translated into seventy languages, when surely most of the people were not familiar with the majority of these languages? Moses did this not for the people's sake, but *for the Torah's sake*. For Moses' translation broke the barrier between Hebrew and all the other languages, ensuring that the holiness of the Torah remains even when it is translated into another language (*Rabbi Menahem Mendel Schneerson, 20th century*).

6. You have been living too much (*rav*). This is to be interpreted literally, i.e., too much time. The explanation of the *Midrash Aggadah* is: I have given you much greatness and reward as a result of living at this mountain. You made the Tabernacle, the candelabrum, and the Tabernacle apparatus. You received the Torah. You appointed for yourselves a *Sanhedrin* (Supreme Court), leaders over thousands and leaders over hundreds (*Rashi, 11th century*).

7. The great river, the river Euphrates. The Euphrates actually is the smallest of the four rivers that issues forth from Eden, as we see from the fact that it is mentioned by Scripture

> **kabbalah bites**
>
> **1:5 How many possible interpretations of the Torah are there?**
>
> When you have a truly original idea, a fresh Torah insight, it is ultimately rooted in your soul. The reason why you thought of it and nobody else is because your soul is unique.
>
> But how unique, really, is your soul? The Kabbalah teaches that there are only 600,000 core Jewish souls, of which we are all derivatives. So, in essence, there are only 600,000 possible interpretations of any Torah idea.
>
> And since Moses' soul contained, in microcosm, all those 600,000, we say that "every future insight was already given to Moses at Sinai" (*Babylonian Talmud, Megillah 19b*)—if not consciously, at least in his soul.

deuteronomy 1:3–8 — devarim

rebuked them) about everything that God had commanded him on their behalf. ⁴ (Moses waited to rebuke them until) after he had (proven his military might by) defeating (the powerful) King Sihon of the Amorites, who lived in (the powerful city of) Heshbon, and (the powerful) King Og of the Bashan, who lived in (the powerful city of) Ashtaroth(-karnaim), in (the kingdom of) Edrei.

⁵ On the (east) bank of the Jordan, in the land of Moab, Moses began to explain the Torah (translating it into seventy languages), saying:

⁶ God, our God, spoke to us in Horeb, saying, "You have been living too much (time) by this mountain. ⁷ Redirect yourselves (towards Arad and Hormah) and travel until you come to the Amorite mountain, and through its neighboring territories (Ammon, Moab and Mount Seir), through the (forested) plain, on the mountain (of the king), through the lowlands (of the South), through (Gaza and Ashkelon) in the south and (Caesarea) by the seashore, (conquering) the land of the Canaanites, and the Lebanon, all the way until the great river, the river Euphrates. ⁸ See that I have (already) put the land (into your hands) before you! (All you have to do is) come and take possession of the land which God swore to Abraham, to Isaac, and to Jacob, that He would give (the land to) them and their descendants after them. (Nobody will even oppose you.)"

---

caused! There is no shorter route from Horeb to Kadesh-barnea than by way of Mount Seir, and even that is a journey of eleven days. But you covered it in three days! The Divine Presence exerted itself to such an extent to hasten your arrival at the land of Canaan, but because you ruined things, He made you travel around Mount Seir for forty years!" (*Rashi, 11ᵗʰ century*).

5. In the land of Moab, Moses began to explain the Torah. He translated it into seventy languages (*Rashi, 11ᵗʰ century*).

Moses feared that not every person understood Hebrew (*Rabbi Mordecai b. Abraham Jaffe, 16ᵗʰ century*).

Moses anticipated that the Jewish people would be exiled in the future, and he wanted to ensure that they would be able to study Torah in any language that they might come to speak (*Rabbi Nathan Ashkenazi Shapira of Grodno, 16ᵗʰ century*).

Perhaps people would think that the Torah's laws are applicable only in the wilderness, while dwelling apart from other nations, or in the land of Israel, while enjoying autonomous rule? To repudiate this, Moses translated the Torah into seventy languages while *"in the land of Moab"*—after they had already left the desert but before entering the land of Israel—indicating that Torah laws are always binding, regardless of location or historical time (*Rabbi Abraham Samuel Benjamin Sofer, 19ᵗʰ century*).

In every culture and civilization there are forces that oppose Judaism, posing a different challenge to the study of Torah and observance of its commandments. Knowing that the children of Israel would eventually be exiled and scattered among the nations of the world, Moses translated the Torah into seventy languages, extending the light of Torah to the seventy core nations of the world. Now, the children of Israel were empowered to overcome

דברים א:ח-יז

לְאַבְרָהָ֧ם לְיִצְחָ֛ק וּֽלְיַעֲקֹ֖ב לָתֵ֣ת לָהֶ֑ם וּלְזַרְעָ֖ם אַחֲרֵיהֶֽם: 9 וָאֹמַ֣ר אֲלֵכֶ֔ם בָּעֵ֥ת הַהִ֖וא לֵאמֹ֑ר לֹא־אוּכַ֥ל לְבַדִּ֖י שְׂאֵ֥ת אֶתְכֶֽם: 10 יְהֹוָ֥ה אֱלֹֽהֵיכֶ֖ם הִרְבָּ֣ה אֶתְכֶ֑ם וְהִנְּכֶ֣ם הַיּ֔וֹם כְּכֽוֹכְבֵ֥י הַשָּׁמַ֖יִם לָרֹֽב: 11 יְהֹוָ֞ה אֱלֹהֵ֣י אֲבֽוֹתֵכֶ֗ם יֹסֵ֧ף עֲלֵיכֶ֛ם כָּכֶ֖ם אֶ֣לֶף פְּעָמִ֑ים וִיבָרֵ֣ךְ אֶתְכֶ֔ם כַּאֲשֶׁ֖ר דִּבֶּ֥ר לָכֶֽם: 12 [SECOND READING] אֵיכָ֥ה אֶשָּׂ֖א לְבַדִּ֑י טָרְחֲכֶ֥ם וּמַֽשַּׂאֲכֶ֖ם וְרִֽיבְכֶֽם: 13 הָב֣וּ לָ֠כֶ֠ם אֲנָשִׁ֨ים חֲכָמִ֧ים וּנְבֹנִ֛ים וִֽידֻעִ֖ים לְשִׁבְטֵיכֶ֑ם וַאֲשִׂימֵ֖ם בְּרָאשֵׁיכֶֽם: 14 וַֽתַּעֲנ֖וּ אֹתִ֑י וַתֹּ֣אמְר֔וּ טֽוֹב־הַדָּבָ֥ר אֲשֶׁר־דִּבַּ֖רְתָּ לַעֲשֽׂוֹת: 15 וָאֶקַּ֞ח אֶת־רָאשֵׁ֣י שִׁבְטֵיכֶ֗ם אֲנָשִׁ֤ים חֲכָמִים֙ וִֽידֻעִ֔ים וָאֶתֵּ֥ן אוֹתָ֛ם רָאשִׁ֖ים עֲלֵיכֶ֑ם שָׂרֵ֨י אֲלָפִ֜ים וְשָׂרֵ֣י מֵא֗וֹת וְשָׂרֵ֤י חֲמִשִּׁים֙ וְשָׂרֵ֣י עֲשָׂרֹ֔ת וְשֹׁטְרִ֖ים לְשִׁבְטֵיכֶֽם: 16 וָאֲצַוֶּה֙ אֶת־שֹׁ֣פְטֵיכֶ֔ם בָּעֵ֥ת הַהִ֖וא לֵאמֹ֑ר שָׁמֹ֤עַ בֵּֽין־אֲחֵיכֶם֙ וּשְׁפַטְתֶּ֣ם צֶ֔דֶק בֵּֽין־אִ֥ישׁ וּבֵין־אָחִ֖יו וּבֵ֥ין גֵּרֽוֹ: 17 לֹֽא־תַכִּ֨ירוּ פָנִ֜ים בַּמִּשְׁפָּ֗ט כַּקָּטֹ֤ן כַּגָּדֹל֙ תִּשְׁמָע֔וּן לֹ֤א תָג֨וּרוּ֙ מִפְּנֵי־אִ֔ישׁ כִּ֥י הַמִּשְׁפָּ֖ט לֵאלֹהִ֣ים

obstructing your view of the much greater Torah because they are placed directly in front of your eyes, like a small coin placed on the eyelid that prevents you from seeing objects that are much larger than the coin itself. You need only lift up your head slightly, and the light of the Torah will be readily accessible (*Rabbi Naḥman of Bratslav, 18th century*).

12. How could I bear singlehandedly your (tactical legal) maneuvers (in court, the) burden of your (slander against me), and your disputes (with each other)? Traditionally, this verse is read to the cantillation tune of the Book of Lamentations. The message here is: If you shirk the responsibility of the community's needs, thinking it will make your life easier, you will in the end be alone and isolated—*"How she sits all alone…"* (*Lamentations 1:1; Rabbi Joseph Yozel Hurvitz of Novogrudok, 19th–20th century*).

13. Insightful men. Those who can infer one thing from another. This is what Arius the bishop asked Rabbi Yose: "What is the difference between wise men and insightful *men*?"

Rabbi Yose replied: "A wise man is like a rich money changer. When people bring him coins to look at, he examines them; when they don't bring him anything, he sits and does nothing."

"An insightful man is like an enterprising money changer. When they bring him coins to look at, he examines them. But when they don't bring him any, he goes out and does business with his own money" (*Rashi, 11th century*).

Food for thought

1. Do the heads of your community lead by example?

2. Which leadership figure inspired you most towards commitment to God?

3. Are you tempted to positions of leadership for the right reasons?

deuteronomy 1:9–17 — devarim

Rebuke Concerning the Appointment of Judges

⁹ I said to you at that time—saying (only that which I had been told by God)—"I cannot carry (the burden of judging) you on my own, ¹⁰ (for) God, your God, has made you great. You are (so great that you are everlasting like the sun which shines during) the day, and like (the moon and) the (individual) stars of the heavens, (so you would be an awesome responsibility to judge even if you were few, all the more so that you are) many. ¹¹ (In fact, in the future,) God, the God of your ancestors, will multiply your number a thousand times. He will bless you as He told you (He would, when He took Abraham outside his tent and showed him the stars).

[SECOND READING] ¹² "(If you argue that I should judge you alone, despite the responsibility and risk of punishment, God has forbidden me from doing so. For) how could I bear singlehandedly your (tactical legal) maneuvers (in court, the) burden of your (slander against me), and your disputes (with each other)? ¹³ (So) prepare (righteous), wise and insightful men for yourselves, known among your tribes, and I will appoint them as your leaders."

¹⁴ You answered me (disrespectfully) and said, "The thing which you have proposed to do is good (for us)."

¹⁵ I selected (and persuaded) wise and well known men from the leaders of your tribes, and I made them leaders over you—leaders of thousands, leaders of hundreds, leaders of fifties, leaders of tens, and police officers over your tribes.

¹⁶ On that occasion, I instructed your judges, saying, "Listen (patiently) to your brothers' (claims, even if you have heard a similar case before), and judge righteously between a man and his brother who disputes him. ¹⁷ Do not show favoritism (and appoint judges who are not qualified, who will err) in judgment. You should listen (with equal interest) to (a case involving) a small (amount of money as you do to a case involving) a large amount. Do not fear any man (and show him favoritism, for this is as if one has exacted money from) God, (who

---

last (*Genesis* 2:14). The Torah only refers to it here as "the *great* river" because it is mentioned in connection with the land of Israel—as the saying goes, "Touch one who is anointed with oil, and you will become anointed yourself" (*Rashi, 11ᵗʰ century*).

10. Like the sun which shines during the day. The sun shines equally bright at all times throughout the day, it is just the earth's position with respect to the sun that obstructs the path of sunlight, preventing it from reaching you. The lesson here is that the earth—representing attachment to worldly matters—prevents you from receiving the light of the Torah. You need to rise above the nonsense of this world in order to appreciate the greatness of the Torah.

This may seem like a daunting task, but consider that this world is truly insignificant compared to the greatness of God's holy Torah. The temptations of this world are only capable of

דברים   דברים א:יז-כה

הוּא וְהַדָּבָר֙ אֲשֶׁ֣ר יִקְשֶׁ֣ה מִכֶּ֔ם תַּקְרִב֥וּן אֵלַ֖י וּשְׁמַעְתִּֽיו: 18 וָאֲצַוֶּ֥ה אֶתְכֶ֖ם בָּעֵ֣ת הַהִ֑וא אֵ֥ת כָּל־הַדְּבָרִ֖ים אֲשֶׁ֥ר תַּעֲשֽׂוּן: 19 וַנִּסַּ֣ע מֵחֹרֵ֗ב וַנֵּ֡לֶךְ אֵ֣ת כָּל־הַמִּדְבָּ֣ר הַגָּד֣וֹל וְהַנּוֹרָא֩ הַה֨וּא אֲשֶׁ֤ר רְאִיתֶם֙ דֶּ֚רֶךְ הַ֣ר הָֽאֱמֹרִ֔י כַּאֲשֶׁ֥ר צִוָּ֛ה יְהוָ֥ה אֱלֹהֵ֖ינוּ אֹתָ֑נוּ וַנָּבֹ֕א עַ֖ד קָדֵ֥שׁ בַּרְנֵֽעַ: 20 וָאֹמַ֖ר אֲלֵכֶ֑ם בָּאתֶם֙ עַד־הַ֣ר הָאֱמֹרִ֔י אֲשֶׁר־יְהוָ֥ה אֱלֹהֵ֖ינוּ נֹתֵ֥ן לָֽנוּ: 21 רְ֠אֵה נָתַ֨ן יְהוָ֧ה אֱלֹהֶ֛יךָ לְפָנֶ֖יךָ אֶת־הָאָ֑רֶץ עֲלֵ֣ה רֵ֗שׁ כַּאֲשֶׁר֩ דִּבֶּ֨ר יְהוָ֜ה אֱלֹהֵ֤י אֲבֹתֶ֙יךָ֙ לָ֔ךְ אַל־תִּירָ֖א וְאַל־תֵּחָֽת: 22 **[THIRD READING]** וַתִּקְרְב֣וּן אֵלַי֮ כֻּלְּכֶם֒ וַתֹּאמְר֗וּ נִשְׁלְחָ֤ה אֲנָשִׁים֙ לְפָנֵ֔ינוּ וְיַחְפְּרוּ־לָ֖נוּ אֶת־הָאָ֑רֶץ וְיָשִׁ֤בוּ אֹתָ֙נוּ֙ דָּבָ֔ר אֶת־הַדֶּ֙רֶךְ֙ אֲשֶׁ֣ר נַעֲלֶה־בָּ֔הּ וְאֵת֙ הֶֽעָרִ֔ים אֲשֶׁ֥ר נָבֹ֖א אֲלֵיהֶֽן: 23 וַיִּיטַ֥ב בְּעֵינַ֖י הַדָּבָ֑ר וָאֶקַּ֤ח מִכֶּם֙ שְׁנֵ֣ים עָשָׂ֣ר אֲנָשִׁ֔ים אִ֥ישׁ אֶחָ֖ד לַשָּֽׁבֶט: 24 וַיִּפְנוּ֙ וַיַּעֲל֣וּ הָהָ֔רָה וַיָּבֹ֖אוּ עַד־נַ֣חַל אֶשְׁכֹּ֑ל וַֽיְרַגְּל֖וּ אֹתָֽהּ: 25 וַיִּקְח֤וּ בְיָדָם֙ מִפְּרִ֣י הָאָ֔רֶץ וַיּוֹרִ֖דוּ אֵלֵ֑ינוּ וַיָּשִׁ֨בוּ אֹתָ֤נוּ דָבָר֙ וַיֹּ֣אמְר֔וּ טוֹבָ֥ה הָאָ֖רֶץ

you should reflect upon your actions to see if you may be guilty of a similar offense, albeit in a more subtle way.

The same holds true when a subject in Torah proves *"too difficult,"* you should know that the problem is *"from you"*—because you contain a trace of that very issue with which you find difficulty. After a thorough soul-searching to correct the area of concern, you will deepen your understanding of the Torah (*Rabbi Tzevi Elimelech of Dynow, 19th century*).

23. It seemed like a good idea to me. If Moses had thought that sending spies was a good idea why did he include it here in his words of rebuke?

Moses' complaint was: Not only did you propose something against the will of God, you persisted to such an extent that you even convinced me it was a good idea! (*Rabbi Judah Aryeh Leib Alter of Gur, 19th century*).

spiritual vitamin

> If you make no effort and do not strive hard, to advance to a higher level beyond your habitual routine which has become second nature, you have not yet achieved true freedom.

must correct) the judgment (and restore the money to its rightful owner). If a case is too difficult for you, bring it to me, and I will hear it." ¹⁸ And, on that occasion, I gave you instructions about all the things you should do (in a monetary case and in a capital case).

Rebuke for the Incident with the Spies

¹⁹ We journeyed from Horeb and went through that entire great and fearful desert (filled with the giant snakes and scorpions) that you saw, towards the Amorite mountain as God, our God, commanded us—and we arrived at Kadesh-barnea.

²⁰ I said to you, "You have arrived at the Amorite mountain, which God, our God, is giving us!"

²¹ "Look! God, your God, has put the land (into your hands) before you! (All you have to do is) go and take possession of it, as God, the God of your fathers, has told you! Don't be afraid or demoralized!"

[THIRD READING] ²² But you all approached me (in a rowdy mob) and said, "Let's send men ahead of us who will search out the land for us and bring us back (a report detailing which language the people use to speak their) word(s), which route we should follow, and which cities we should come to (first, to conquer)."

²³ (I claimed that) it seemed like a good idea to me (hoping that this would convince you of the truth of my words, when you would see that I was ready to put them to the test, but you did not retract your demands). So I selected twelve men from (the finest among) you, one man for each tribe. ²⁴ They set off and went up the mountain, until they came to the valley of Eshcol. Then, they spied out (the entire land).

²⁵ They took some of the fruit of the land in their hands and brought it down to us. They brought us back a report and said, "The land that God, our God, is giving us is good!"

17. If a case is too difficult for you, bring it to me, and I will hear it. When you are unsure what to do, try to set aside all your personal bias. Then you will arrive at the truth and proceed in accordance with God's will.

"If a case is too difficult," and you cannot decide what to do, know that this uncertainty is *"from you,"* because of your bias. Therefore, you should *"bring it to me"*—try to detach yourself from it, asking only what is God's will? Then, *"I will hear it"*—God will enlighten you (*Rabbi Israel Ba'al Shem Tov, 18ᵗʰ century*).

If a case is too difficult for you. Whatever you see or hear is a reflection of your current spiritual standing. You need to take note of all your experiences and think how they might be taken as lessons to improve your behavior. If, for example, you were to witness a robbery,

אֲשֶׁר־יְהֹוָה אֱלֹהֵינוּ נֹתֵן לָנוּ: 26 וְלֹא אֲבִיתֶם לַעֲלֹת וַתַּמְרוּ אֶת־פִּי יְהֹוָה אֱלֹהֵיכֶם: 27 וַתֵּרָגְנוּ בְאָהֳלֵיכֶם וַתֹּאמְרוּ בְּשִׂנְאַת יְהֹוָה אֹתָנוּ הוֹצִיאָנוּ מֵאֶרֶץ מִצְרָיִם לָתֵת אֹתָנוּ בְּיַד הָאֱמֹרִי לְהַשְׁמִידֵנוּ: 28 אָנָה | אֲנַחְנוּ עֹלִים אַחֵינוּ הֵמַסּוּ אֶת־לְבָבֵנוּ לֵאמֹר עַם גָּדוֹל וָרָם מִמֶּנּוּ עָרִים גְּדֹלֹת וּבְצוּרֹת בַּשָּׁמָיִם וְגַם־בְּנֵי עֲנָקִים רָאִינוּ שָׁם: 29 וָאֹמַר אֲלֵכֶם לֹא־תַעַרְצוּן וְלֹא־תִירְאוּן מֵהֶם: 30 יְהֹוָה אֱלֹהֵיכֶם הַהֹלֵךְ לִפְנֵיכֶם הוּא יִלָּחֵם לָכֶם כְּכֹל אֲשֶׁר עָשָׂה אִתְּכֶם בְּמִצְרַיִם לְעֵינֵיכֶם: 31 וּבַמִּדְבָּר אֲשֶׁר רָאִיתָ אֲשֶׁר נְשָׂאֲךָ יְהֹוָה אֱלֹהֶיךָ כַּאֲשֶׁר יִשָּׂא־אִישׁ אֶת־בְּנוֹ בְּכָל־הַדֶּרֶךְ אֲשֶׁר הֲלַכְתֶּם עַד־בֹּאֲכֶם עַד־הַמָּקוֹם הַזֶּה: 32 וּבַדָּבָר הַזֶּה אֵינְכֶם מַאֲמִינִם בַּיהֹוָה אֱלֹהֵיכֶם: 33 הַהֹלֵךְ לִפְנֵיכֶם בַּדֶּרֶךְ לָתוּר לָכֶם מָקוֹם לַחֲנֹתְכֶם בָּאֵשׁ | לַיְלָה לַרְאֹתְכֶם בַּדֶּרֶךְ אֲשֶׁר תֵּלְכוּ־בָהּ וּבֶעָנָן יוֹמָם: 34 וַיִּשְׁמַע יְהֹוָה אֶת־קוֹל דִּבְרֵיכֶם וַיִּקְצֹף וַיִּשָּׁבַע לֵאמֹר: 35 אִם־יִרְאֶה אִישׁ בָּאֲנָשִׁים הָאֵלֶּה הַדּוֹר הָרָע הַזֶּה אֵת הָאָרֶץ הַטּוֹבָה אֲשֶׁר נִשְׁבַּעְתִּי לָתֵת לַאֲבֹתֵיכֶם: 36 זוּלָתִי כָּלֵב בֶּן־יְפֻנֶּה הוּא יִרְאֶנָּה וְלוֹ־אֶתֵּן אֶת־הָאָרֶץ אֲשֶׁר דָּרַךְ־בָּהּ וּלְבָנָיו יַעַן אֲשֶׁר מִלֵּא אַחֲרֵי יְהֹוָה: 37 גַּם־בִּי הִתְאַנַּף יְהֹוָה בִּגְלַלְכֶם לֵאמֹר גַּם־אַתָּה לֹא־תָבֹא שָׁם: 38 יְהוֹשֻׁעַ בִּן־נוּן הָעֹמֵד לְפָנֶיךָ הוּא יָבֹא שָׁמָּה אֹתוֹ חַזֵּק כִּי־הוּא יַנְחִלֶנָּה אֶת־יִשְׂרָאֵל: [FOURTH READING] 39 וְטַפְּכֶם אֲשֶׁר אֲמַרְתֶּם לָבַז יִהְיֶה וּבְנֵיכֶם אֲשֶׁר לֹא־יָדְעוּ הַיּוֹם טוֹב וָרָע הֵמָּה יָבֹאוּ שָׁמָּה

---

37. You will not come there either. Why was Moses punished for the sin of the spies when he didn't believe their reports, and when he didn't doubt God's ability to bring the people to the land? Because by *consenting* to send the spies, which God hadn't commanded, Moses was responsible for the sin that resulted.

Nevertheless, since Moses' error was unintentional, and the people's sin was intentional, God did not punish Moses with them.

But when Moses erred with the waters of Meribah, by hitting the rock, God barred him from entering the land. Really, though, the punishment was a result of *both* the sin of the spies and the waters of Meribah (*Rabbi Isaac Abravanel, 15th century*).

deuteronomy 1:26–39   devarim

[26] But you did not want to go up (to the land), and you rebelled against the word of God, your God. [27] You spoke slanderously in your tents. You said, "God took us out of the land of Egypt because He hates us! (He wishes) to deliver us into the hands of the Amorites and destroy us! [28] Where shall we go? Our brothers have demoralized us, saying, '(We saw) a people larger and taller than ourselves and enormous cities, fortified up to the heavens. And we have even seen giants there!'"

[29] I said to you, "Don't (let your spirits) be broken! Don't be afraid of them! [30] God—your God, who goes ahead of you—will fight on your behalf, just as He did everything (on your behalf) in Egypt, before your eyes. [31] And as you have seen how God, your God, has carried you in the desert as a man carries his son, throughout your entire journey, until you arrived here. [32] But you do not believe God, your God, about this statement (that He promised to bring you to the land. [33] Yet you see that God) goes along the route ahead of you, to search out a place for you in which to encamp, and (He provides a pillar of) fire at night, to enable you to see while you travel, and a cloud (of protection) by day!"

[34] God heard the sound of your comments and became angry. He swore, saying, [35] "Not a single man from this evil generation will see the good land, which I swore to give to your forefathers, [36] except for Caleb son of Jephunneh. He will see it, and I will give the land (of Hebron) which he trod upon to him and his children, because he followed God loyally."

—[37] Because of you, God also became angry with me, saying, "You will not come there (to the land) either!"—

[38] "Joshua son of Nun, who stands at your side, will go there. Support him, for he will lead the Jewish people to inherit it."

[FOURTH READING] [39] "(Also,) your small children, about whom you said that they will be taken as captives, and your children, who do not yet know (the difference

27. You spoke slanderously in your tents. When Joshua and Caleb persisted in urging the people to go to war, the other spies met with the Jewish people in their tents to speak slanderously about the land.

These meetings were held secretly in the tents in order to hide what was happening from Moses (*Naḥmanides, 13th century*).

Because He hates us. He loved you, but you hated Him, as in the common saying: "What is in your heart about your beloved is in his heart about you" (*Rashi, 11th century*).

In other words, since the Jewish people hated God, they *imagined* that God hated them too (*Rabbi Shabbetai b. Joseph Bass, 17th–18th century*).

Thus, the "common saying" (*"What is in your heart, etc."*) is not, in fact, applicable to God, for He loved the Jewish people, even though they hated Him (*Rabbi Jacob b. Benjamin Aaron Slonik, 17th century*).

דברים

וְלָהֶם אֶתְּנֶנָּה וְהֵם יִירָשֽׁוּהָ: 40 וְאַתֶּם פְּנוּ לָכֶם וּסְעוּ הַמִּדְבָּרָה דֶּרֶךְ יַם־סֽוּף:
41 וַֽתַּעֲנ֣וּ ׀ וַתֹּאמְר֣וּ אֵלַ֗י חָטָ֘אנוּ֘ לַֽיהֹוָה֒ אֲנַ֣חְנוּ נַעֲלֶ֗ה וְנִלְחַ֕מְנוּ כְּכֹ֥ל אֲשֶׁר־
צִוָּ֖נוּ יְהֹוָ֣ה אֱלֹהֵ֑ינוּ וַֽתַּחְגְּר֗וּ אִ֚ישׁ אֶת־כְּלֵ֣י מִלְחַמְתּ֔וֹ וַתָּהִ֖ינוּ לַעֲלֹ֥ת הָהָֽרָה:
42 וַיֹּ֨אמֶר יְהֹוָ֜ה אֵלַ֗י אֱמֹ֤ר לָהֶם֙ לֹ֤א תַֽעֲלוּ֙ וְלֹא־תִלָּ֣חֲמ֔וּ כִּ֥י אֵינֶ֖נִּי בְּקִרְבְּכֶ֑ם
וְלֹא֙ תִּנָּ֣גְפ֔וּ לִפְנֵ֖י אֹיְבֵיכֶֽם: 43 וָאֲדַבֵּ֥ר אֲלֵיכֶ֖ם וְלֹ֣א שְׁמַעְתֶּ֑ם וַתַּמְרוּ֙ אֶת־פִּ֣י
יְהֹוָ֔ה וַתָּזִ֖דוּ וַתַּעֲל֥וּ הָהָֽרָה: 44 וַיֵּצֵ֨א הָאֱמֹרִ֜י הַיֹּשֵׁ֨ב בָּהָ֤ר הַהוּא֙ לִקְרַאתְכֶ֔ם
וַיִּרְדְּפ֣וּ אֶתְכֶ֔ם כַּאֲשֶׁ֥ר תַּעֲשֶׂ֖ינָה הַדְּבֹרִ֑ים וַֽיַּכְּת֥וּ אֶתְכֶ֛ם בְּשֵׂעִ֖יר עַד־חׇרְמָֽה:
45 וַתָּשֻׁ֥בוּ וַתִּבְכּ֖וּ לִפְנֵ֣י יְהֹוָ֑ה וְלֹא־שָׁמַ֤ע יְהֹוָה֙ בְּקֹ֣לְכֶ֔ם וְלֹ֥א הֶאֱזִ֖ין אֲלֵיכֶֽם:
46 וַתֵּשְׁב֥וּ בְקָדֵ֖שׁ יָמִ֣ים רַבִּ֑ים כַּיָּמִ֖ים אֲשֶׁ֥ר יְשַׁבְתֶּֽם:

ב 1 וַנֵּ֜פֶן וַנִּסַּ֤ע הַמִּדְבָּ֙רָה֙ דֶּ֣רֶךְ יַם־ס֔וּף כַּאֲשֶׁ֛ר דִּבֶּ֥ר יְהֹוָ֖ה אֵלָ֑י וַנָּ֥סׇב אֶת־
הַר־שֵׂעִ֖יר יָמִ֥ים רַבִּֽים: ס [FIFTH READING] 2 וַיֹּ֥אמֶר יְהֹוָ֖ה אֵלַ֥י לֵאמֹֽר: 3 רַב־
לָכֶ֕ם סֹ֖ב אֶת־הָהָ֣ר הַזֶּ֑ה פְּנ֥וּ לָכֶ֖ם צָפֹֽנָה: 4 וְאֶת־הָעָם֮ צַ֣ו לֵאמֹר֒ אַתֶּ֣ם עֹֽבְרִ֗ים
בִּגְבוּל֙ אֲחֵיכֶ֣ם בְּנֵי־עֵשָׂ֔ו הַיֹּשְׁבִ֖ים בְּשֵׂעִ֑יר וְיִֽירְא֣וּ מִכֶּ֔ם וְנִשְׁמַרְתֶּ֖ם מְאֹֽד:
5 אַל־תִּתְגָּר֣וּ בָ֔ם כִּ֠י לֹֽא־אֶתֵּ֤ן לָכֶם֙ מֵֽאַרְצָ֔ם עַ֖ד מִדְרַ֣ךְ כַּף־רָ֑גֶל כִּֽי־יְרֻשָּׁ֣ה
לְעֵשָׂ֔ו נָתַ֖תִּי אֶת־הַ֥ר שֵׂעִֽיר: 6 אֹ֣כֶל תִּשְׁבְּר֧וּ מֵֽאִתָּ֛ם בַּכֶּ֖סֶף וַאֲכַלְתֶּ֑ם וְגַם־מַ֜יִם
תִּכְר֧וּ מֵאִתָּ֛ם בַּכֶּ֖סֶף וּשְׁתִיתֶֽם: 7 כִּי֩ יְהֹוָ֨ה אֱלֹהֶ֜יךָ בֵּֽרַכְךָ֗ בְּכֹל֙ מַעֲשֵׂ֣ה יָדֶ֔ךָ יָדַ֣ע

Moses said: If you had confessed sincerely for the sin of the spies, you certainly would have been forgiven and allowed to enter the land. But you only *"said to me, 'We've sinned against God'"*—you merely *spoke* words of confession. They were only remorseful *"to me,"* but were insufficient before God, who could discern your insincerity (*Rabbi Solomon Kluger, 19th century*).

2:6 You can purchase food from them with money, so you can eat. You can purchase water from them with money, so you can drink. Here the Torah teaches us proper behavior. If you travel to a foreign country and you have food and drink with you, keep it aside and buy what you need from the local shopkeepers, in order to stimulate trade. Moses said to the king of Edom, "We have a well but we won't drink its waters, and we won't eat the manna which we have with us. So you won't be able to say that we're nothing but trouble for you, because you will be doing business!" (*Midrash Tanḥuma*).

between) good and evil—they will come there (to the land) and I will give it to them to inherit."

⁴⁰ "You, (on the other hand), should turn yourselves around (180 degrees) and journey (back) through the desert, towards the Reed Sea (and then circle the south side of Mount Seir)."

⁴¹ You responded and said to me, "We've sinned against God! We will go up and we will fight, in accordance with all the instructions of God, our God."

Each of you then equipped yourself with weapons, and you prepared yourselves to go up to the mountain.

⁴² God said to me, "Say to them, 'Do not go up and do not fight, so you will not be struck down by your enemies, for I am not with you.'"

⁴³ I spoke to you, but you did not listen. You rebelled against God's command. You deliberately (ignored God) and went up to the mountain. ⁴⁴ The Amorites who lived in the mountain came out towards you and pursued you like bees. They struck you down from Seir to Hormah.

⁴⁵ You came back and wept before God, but God would not accept your prayers. He wouldn't (even) listen to you.

⁴⁶ You stayed in Kadesh for a long time, as long as you stayed (in all the other desert encampments put together).

Passing the Land of Edom

2 ¹ We turned ourselves around (180 degrees) and journeyed into the desert towards the Reed Sea, as God told me, and we circled (the south side of) Mount Seir for a long time.

[FIFTH READING] ² God spoke to me, saying, ³ "You have circled this mountain long enough! Turn northward!"

⁴ "Instruct the people, saying, 'You are about to pass by the border of your brothers, the children of Esau who live in Seir, and they will be afraid of you. Be very careful ⁵ not to provoke them, because I will not give you any of their land—not even the right of passage (without their permission)—since I have given Mount Seir to Esau as an inheritance. ⁶ You can purchase food from them with money, so you can eat. You can purchase water from them with money, so you can drink. ⁷ (Don't be afraid to show them you have money, since you should be proud) that God, your God, has blessed you in everything that you do while you were

41. You responded and said to me, "We've sinned against God!" Repentance is only accepted by God when carried out sincerely, since God knows the thoughts of man. A purely outward, verbal exercise of confessing sins is meaningless.

דברים ב:ז-יט

לְכִתְּךָ אֶת־הַמִּדְבָּר הַגָּדֹל הַזֶּה | אַרְבָּעִים שָׁנָה יְהֹוָה אֱלֹהֶיךָ עִמָּךְ לֹא חָסַרְתָּ דָּבָר: 8 וַנַּעֲבֹר מֵאֵת אַחֵינוּ בְנֵי־עֵשָׂו הַיֹּשְׁבִים בְּשֵׂעִיר מִדֶּרֶךְ הָעֲרָבָה מֵאֵילַת וּמֵעֶצְיֹן גָּבֶר ס וַנֵּפֶן וַנַּעֲבֹר דֶּרֶךְ מִדְבַּר מוֹאָב: 9 וַיֹּאמֶר יְהֹוָה אֵלַי אַל־תָּצַר אֶת־מוֹאָב וְאַל־תִּתְגָּר בָּם מִלְחָמָה כִּי לֹא־אֶתֵּן לְךָ מֵאַרְצוֹ יְרֻשָּׁה כִּי לִבְנֵי־לוֹט נָתַתִּי אֶת־עָר יְרֻשָּׁה: 10 הָאֵמִים לְפָנִים יָשְׁבוּ בָהּ עַם גָּדוֹל וְרַב וָרָם כָּעֲנָקִים: 11 רְפָאִים יֵחָשְׁבוּ אַף־הֵם כָּעֲנָקִים וְהַמֹּאָבִים יִקְרְאוּ לָהֶם אֵמִים: 12 וּבְשֵׂעִיר יָשְׁבוּ הַחֹרִים לְפָנִים וּבְנֵי עֵשָׂו יִירָשׁוּם וַיַּשְׁמִידוּם מִפְּנֵיהֶם וַיֵּשְׁבוּ תַחְתָּם כַּאֲשֶׁר עָשָׂה יִשְׂרָאֵל לְאֶרֶץ יְרֻשָּׁתוֹ אֲשֶׁר־נָתַן יְהֹוָה לָהֶם: 13 עַתָּה קֻמוּ וְעִבְרוּ לָכֶם אֶת־נַחַל זָרֶד וַנַּעֲבֹר אֶת־נַחַל זָרֶד: 14 וְהַיָּמִים אֲשֶׁר־הָלַכְנוּ | מִקָּדֵשׁ בַּרְנֵעַ עַד אֲשֶׁר־עָבַרְנוּ אֶת־נַחַל זֶרֶד שְׁלֹשִׁים וּשְׁמֹנֶה שָׁנָה עַד־תֹּם כָּל־הַדּוֹר אַנְשֵׁי הַמִּלְחָמָה מִקֶּרֶב הַמַּחֲנֶה כַּאֲשֶׁר נִשְׁבַּע יְהֹוָה לָהֶם: 15 וְגַם יַד־יְהֹוָה הָיְתָה בָּם לְהֻמָּם מִקֶּרֶב הַמַּחֲנֶה עַד תֻּמָּם: 16 וַיְהִי כַאֲשֶׁר־תַּמּוּ כָּל־אַנְשֵׁי הַמִּלְחָמָה לָמוּת מִקֶּרֶב הָעָם: ס 17 וַיְדַבֵּר יְהֹוָה אֵלַי לֵאמֹר: 18 אַתָּה עֹבֵר הַיּוֹם אֶת־גְּבוּל מוֹאָב אֶת־עָר: 19 וְקָרַבְתָּ מוּל בְּנֵי

9. I will not give you any of their land as an inheritance. At the Covenant of the Parts, Abraham was promised *"the (land of the) Kenites, the Kenizzites, the Kadmonites, the Hittites, the Perizzites, the Rephaim, the Amorites, the Canaanites, the Girgashites and the Jebusites"* (*Genesis* 15:19-21). *Rashi* explains: *"There are ten nations listed here, but He gave them only seven nations. The other three, Edom, Moab, and Ammon, which are the Kenites, the Kenizzites, and the Kadmonites, are destined to be our heritage in the future."*

Here we read that the Jewish people were forced to circumvent these three lands, because, *"I will not give you any of their land as an inheritance"*—in the current era.

The seven lands which the Jewish people have historically possessed correspond to the seven emotional attributes of the soul—kindness, severity, empathy, endurance, humility, bonding and presence—and that the three lands which will be acquired in the future correspond to the three intellectual faculties of the soul—inspiration, cognition and realization.

In the current era, God commands us primarily to "conquer" our emotional attributes—to coerce and ultimately transform our animalistic desires toward the worship of God.

In the future however, when this "conquest" will be complete, our main occupation will be to develop the intellectual bond between man and God—symbolized by the three lands of Edom, Moab, and Ammon (*Rabbi Isaac Luria, 16th century*).

wandering through this great desert for the past forty years. God has been with you, (so) you have lacked nothing.'"

Passing the Land of Moab

⁸ We departed from our brothers, the children of Esau who lived in Seir, by way of the plain which runs from Elath and from Ezion-geber, directing ourselves (northward) and traveling toward the Moab Desert.

⁹ God said to me, "Do not besiege Moab, and do not incite them to war, because I will not give you any of their land as an inheritance, since I have given (the land of Moab, also known as) Ar, to the children of Lot as an inheritance. ¹⁰ Since the Emim—a great and numerous people, tall like giants—lived there previously (before the Moabites, you might be under the impression that this is the land of the Rephaim, which I promised to Abraham, since the Emim are also known as Rephaim. ¹¹ In truth, however, the Emim that lived here are a totally different nation to the one promised to Abraham, and) they are also called Rephaim, because they are giants, but the Moabites call them Emim. ¹² (The Moabites drove out the Emim who lived there previously, and settled in it as their God-given land, just as) the Horites originally lived in Seir, and the children of Esau (gradually) drove them out, eliminated them from their presence, and settled in their place—and just as the Jewish people (will) have done to the land of their inheritance, which God gave them."

End of the Generation that Left Egypt

¹³ "Now get moving and cross the Zered Brook!"

So we crossed the Zered Brook. ¹⁴ The time from when we left Kadesh-barnea until we crossed the Zered Brook was thirty-eight years, (sufficient time) for the entire generation of the men among the camp that were eligible for war to die out, as God had sworn to them. ¹⁵ (So as not to delay the entry into the land of Israel), the hand of God came to eliminate those among the camp (who did not die naturally during this time), until they were all gone.

Passing the Land of Ammon

¹⁶ Then, when all the men among the people who were eligible for war had all died, ¹⁷ God spoke to me, saying, ¹⁸ "Today you are going to cross the border of Moab (which is also known as) Ar. ¹⁹ When you come near the Ammonites, do not besiege them or incite

Food for thought

1. Do you tend to avoid conflict, or confront it?

2. At what cost should we avoid confrontation?

3. How does being in conflict cripple your spirit?

דברים ב:יט-ל

עַמּוֹן אַל־תְּצֻרֵם וְאַל־תִּתְגָּ֣ר בָּ֑ם כִּ֠י לֹֽא־אֶתֵּ֨ן מֵאֶ֤רֶץ בְּנֵֽי־עַמּוֹן֙ לְךָ֣ יְרֻשָּׁ֔ה כִּ֥י לִבְנֵי־ל֖וֹט נְתַתִּ֥יהָ יְרֻשָּֽׁה: 20 אֶֽרֶץ־רְפָאִ֥ים תֵּחָשֵׁ֖ב אַף־הִ֑וא רְפָאִ֤ים יָֽשְׁבוּ־בָהּ֙ לְפָנִ֔ים וְהָֽעַמֹּנִ֔ים יִקְרְא֥וּ לָהֶ֖ם זַמְזֻמִּֽים: 21 עַ֣ם גָּד֥וֹל וְרַ֛ב וָרָ֖ם כָּעֲנָקִ֑ים וַיַּשְׁמִידֵ֤ם יְהֹוָה֙ מִפְּנֵיהֶ֔ם וַיִּירָשֻׁ֖ם וַיֵּשְׁב֥וּ תַחְתָּֽם: 22 כַּאֲשֶׁ֤ר עָשָׂה֙ לִבְנֵ֣י עֵשָׂ֔ו הַיֹּֽשְׁבִ֖ים בְּשֵׂעִ֑יר אֲשֶׁ֨ר הִשְׁמִ֤יד אֶת־הַחֹרִי֙ מִפְּנֵיהֶ֔ם וַיִּֽירָשֻׁם֙ וַיֵּשְׁב֣וּ תַחְתָּ֔ם עַ֖ד הַיּ֥וֹם הַזֶּֽה: 23 וְהָעַוִּ֛ים הַיֹּשְׁבִ֥ים בַּחֲצֵרִ֖ים עַד־עַזָּ֑ה כַּפְתֹּרִים֙ הַיֹּצְאִ֣ים מִכַּפְתֹּ֔ר הִשְׁמִידֻ֖ם וַיֵּשְׁב֥וּ תַחְתָּֽם: 24 ק֣וּמוּ סְּע֗וּ וְעִבְרוּ֮ אֶת־נַ֣חַל אַרְנֹן֒ רְאֵ֣ה נָתַ֣תִּי בְ֠יָדְךָ֠ אֶת־סִיחֹ֨ן מֶֽלֶךְ־חֶשְׁבּ֧וֹן הָאֱמֹרִ֛י וְאֶת־אַרְצ֖וֹ הָחֵ֣ל רָ֑שׁ וְהִתְגָּ֥ר בּ֖וֹ מִלְחָמָֽה: 25 הַיּ֣וֹם הַזֶּ֗ה אָחֵל֙ תֵּ֤ת פַּחְדְּךָ֙ וְיִרְאָ֣תְךָ֔ עַל־פְּנֵי֙ הָֽעַמִּ֔ים תַּ֖חַת כָּל־הַשָּׁמָ֑יִם אֲשֶׁ֤ר יִשְׁמְעוּן֙ שִׁמְעֲךָ֔ וְרָגְז֥וּ וְחָל֖וּ מִפָּנֶֽיךָ: 26 וָאֶשְׁלַ֤ח מַלְאָכִים֙ מִמִּדְבַּ֣ר קְדֵמ֔וֹת אֶל־סִיח֖וֹן מֶ֣לֶךְ חֶשְׁבּ֑וֹן דִּבְרֵ֥י שָׁל֖וֹם לֵאמֹֽר: 27 אֶעְבְּרָ֣ה בְאַרְצֶ֔ךָ בַּדֶּ֥רֶךְ בַּדֶּ֖רֶךְ אֵלֵ֑ךְ לֹ֥א אָס֖וּר יָמִ֥ין וּשְׂמֹֽאול: 28 אֹ֣כֶל בַּכֶּ֤סֶף תַּשְׁבִּרֵ֙נִי֙ וְאָכַ֔לְתִּי וּמַ֛יִם בַּכֶּ֥סֶף תִּתֶּן־לִ֖י וְשָׁתִ֑יתִי רַ֖ק אֶעְבְּרָ֥ה בְרַגְלָֽי: 29 כַּאֲשֶׁ֨ר עָֽשׂוּ־לִ֜י בְּנֵ֣י עֵשָׂ֗ו הַיֹּֽשְׁבִים֙ בְּשֵׂעִ֔יר וְהַמּ֣וֹאָבִ֔ים הַיֹּשְׁבִ֖ים בְּעָ֑ר עַ֤ד אֲשֶֽׁר־אֶעֱבֹר֙ אֶת־הַיַּרְדֵּ֔ן אֶל־הָאָ֕רֶץ אֲשֶׁר־יְהוָ֥ה אֱלֹהֵ֖ינוּ נֹתֵ֥ן לָֽנוּ: 30 וְלֹ֣א אָבָ֗ה סִיחֹן֙ מֶ֣לֶךְ חֶשְׁבּ֔וֹן הַעֲבִרֵ֖נוּ בּ֑וֹ כִּֽי־הִקְשָׁה֩ יְהֹוָ֨ה אֱלֹהֶ֜יךָ אֶת־רוּח֗וֹ וְאִמֵּץ֙ אֶת־לְבָב֔וֹ

it was clear to Him that they would not accept it, nevertheless, He started with them for the sake of peace. So too, I first called to Sihon with words of peace" (*Rashi, 11th century*).

spiritual vitamin

> It is highly significant that the Torah was given in a desert, the Sinai Desert. This emphasizes that the Torah is not conditional upon any particular place, or time, or any "normal" set of conditions.

them, for I will not give you any of the Ammonites' land as an inheritance, since I have given it as an inheritance to the children of Lot."

²⁰ "(Even though) this is also considered the land of the Rephaim (it is not the land of Rephaim that I promised to Abraham, but rather, its name comes from a different group of) Rephaim that lived there before (the Ammonites), whom the Ammonites call Zamzummim. ²¹ (They were) a great, numerous people, tall like giants, but God annihilated them before (the Ammonites), who drove them out and settled in their place—²² just as He did for the children of Esau, who live in Seir, when He destroyed the Horites from before them, and (the children of Esau) drove them out and settled in their place, (where they remain) to this day. ²³ The Avvim, who lived in open cities as far as Gaza (are descended from the Philistines whom the Jewish people are forbidden from conquering. However,) the Caphtorim came from Caphtor and destroyed them, and then settled in their place (so the Jewish people may now conquer this land, as it no longer belongs to the Avvim)."

The War with King Sihon of Heshbon

²⁴ "Get moving and travel, and cross the Arnon Brook!" (said God).

"Look, I have delivered Sihon the Amorite, king of Heshbon, and his land into your hand! Start driving him out, and provoke him to war! ²⁵ Today I begin to make all the nations under the skies fear and dread you. When they hear of your reputation they will tremble and shudder because of you."

²⁶ I sent messengers from the desert of Kedemoth to Sihon, king of Heshbon, with a peaceful message, saying, ²⁷ "Allow me to pass through your land. I will only go along the main route. I will not veer to the right or the left. ²⁸ I will pay for food with money so I can eat, and I will pay for water with money so I can drink. I will only pass through on foot. ²⁹ (Similar terms to this were agreed upon) with me by the children of Esau, who live in Seir, and the Moabites who live in Ar. (I only require to pass through your land) until I cross the Jordan, to the land which God, our God, is giving us."

³⁰ But Sihon, king of Heshbon, did not wish to let us pass through his (land), for God, your God, hardened his spirit and made his heart obstinate, so that He could give (his land) into our hand, as it is today.

26. I sent messengers from the desert of Kedemoth to Sihon, king of Heshbon, with a peaceful message. Why did Moses send a "peaceful message" to Sihon when God said to *"provoke him to war"* (v. 24)?

Moses said, "Even though God had not commanded me to make peace with Sihon, I learned from what happened in the Sinai Desert, with the Torah that preceded the world. When God was about to give the Torah to Israel, He took it to the people of Esau and Ishmael. Although

דברים ב:ל – ג:ז

לְמַעַן תִּתּוֹ בְיָדְךָ כַּיּוֹם הַזֶּה: ס [SIXTH READING] 31 וַיֹּאמֶר יְהֹוָה אֵלַי רְאֵה הַחִלֹּתִי תֵּת לְפָנֶיךָ אֶת־סִיחֹן וְאֶת־אַרְצוֹ הָחֵל רָשׁ לָרֶשֶׁת אֶת־אַרְצוֹ: 32 וַיֵּצֵא סִיחֹן לִקְרָאתֵנוּ הוּא וְכָל־עַמּוֹ לַמִּלְחָמָה יָהְצָה: 33 וַיִּתְּנֵהוּ יְהֹוָה אֱלֹהֵינוּ לְפָנֵינוּ וַנַּךְ אֹתוֹ וְאֶת־בָּנָו וְאֶת־כָּל־עַמּוֹ: 34 וַנִּלְכֹּד אֶת־כָּל־עָרָיו בָּעֵת הַהִוא וַנַּחֲרֵם אֶת־כָּל־עִיר מְתִם וְהַנָּשִׁים וְהַטָּף לֹא הִשְׁאַרְנוּ שָׂרִיד: 35 רַק הַבְּהֵמָה בָּזַזְנוּ לָנוּ וּשְׁלַל הֶעָרִים אֲשֶׁר לָכָדְנוּ: 36 מֵעֲרֹעֵר אֲשֶׁר עַל־שְׂפַת־נַחַל אַרְנֹן וְהָעִיר אֲשֶׁר בַּנַּחַל וְעַד־הַגִּלְעָד לֹא הָיְתָה קִרְיָה אֲשֶׁר שָׂגְבָה מִמֶּנּוּ אֶת־הַכֹּל נָתַן יְהֹוָה אֱלֹהֵינוּ לְפָנֵינוּ: 37 רַק אֶל־אֶרֶץ בְּנֵי־עַמּוֹן לֹא קָרָבְתָּ כָּל־יַד נַחַל יַבֹּק וְעָרֵי הָהָר וְכֹל אֲשֶׁר־צִוָּה יְהֹוָה אֱלֹהֵינוּ:

ג 1 וַנֵּפֶן וַנַּעַל דֶּרֶךְ הַבָּשָׁן וַיֵּצֵא עוֹג מֶלֶךְ־הַבָּשָׁן לִקְרָאתֵנוּ הוּא וְכָל־עַמּוֹ לַמִּלְחָמָה אֶדְרֶעִי: 2 וַיֹּאמֶר יְהֹוָה אֵלַי אַל־תִּירָא אֹתוֹ כִּי בְיָדְךָ נָתַתִּי אֹתוֹ וְאֶת־כָּל־עַמּוֹ וְאֶת־אַרְצוֹ וְעָשִׂיתָ לּוֹ כַּאֲשֶׁר עָשִׂיתָ לְסִיחֹן מֶלֶךְ הָאֱמֹרִי אֲשֶׁר יוֹשֵׁב בְּחֶשְׁבּוֹן: 3 וַיִּתֵּן יְהֹוָה אֱלֹהֵינוּ בְּיָדֵנוּ גַּם אֶת־עוֹג מֶלֶךְ־הַבָּשָׁן וְאֶת־כָּל־עַמּוֹ וַנַּכֵּהוּ עַד־בִּלְתִּי הִשְׁאִיר־לוֹ שָׂרִיד: 4 וַנִּלְכֹּד אֶת־כָּל־עָרָיו בָּעֵת הַהִוא לֹא הָיְתָה קִרְיָה אֲשֶׁר לֹא־לָקַחְנוּ מֵאִתָּם שִׁשִּׁים עִיר כָּל־חֶבֶל אַרְגֹּב מַמְלֶכֶת עוֹג בַּבָּשָׁן: 5 כָּל־אֵלֶּה עָרִים בְּצֻרֹת חוֹמָה גְבֹהָה דְּלָתַיִם וּבְרִיחַ לְבַד מֵעָרֵי הַפְּרָזִי הַרְבֵּה מְאֹד: 6 וַנַּחֲרֵם אוֹתָם כַּאֲשֶׁר עָשִׂינוּ לְסִיחֹן מֶלֶךְ חֶשְׁבּוֹן הַחֲרֵם כָּל־עִיר מְתִם הַנָּשִׁים וְהַטָּף: 7 וְכָל־הַבְּהֵמָה וּשְׁלַל הֶעָרִים בַּזּוֹנוּ לָנוּ:

at war (from a spiritual perspective) was their own "populated cities"—places of communal harmony.

The Torah therefore stresses, *"There was no populated city too strong for us, etc., there was no populated city that we did not take from them"* (2:36, 3:4), for this represented the dismantling of the spiritual—and consequently the physical—strongholds of Sihon and Og (*Rabbi Menahem Mendel Schneerson, 20th century*).

[SIXTH READING] ³¹ God said to me, "Look! I have begun to put (the ministering angel of) Sihon and his land (under) you! Start driving him out, so you can inherit his land!"

³² At Jahaz, Sihon came out towards us to war. He was with all his people. ³³ But God, our God, gave him over to us. We destroyed him, his sons—(one of whom was as strong as him)—and all his people. ³⁴ On that occasion, we conquered all his cities, annihilating (the inhabitants of) each city, the men, women, and the young children. We left no survivors. ³⁵ We only plundered the cattle for ourselves, with the spoils of the cities which we had taken. ³⁶ (Throughout the entire land) from Aroer, which is on the edge of the valley of Arnon, and the city in the valley, to Gilead, there was no populated city too strong for us. God, our God, delivered them all before us.

³⁷ (The) only (places that) you did not approach (were): the Ammonite's land, the entire area bordering the river Jabbok, the cities of the mountain, and everywhere God, our God, commanded us (not to conquer).

The War with King Og of Bashan

3 ¹ We changed direction and went up (northward) toward Bashan. At Edrei, King Og of Bashan came out toward us for war. He was with all his people.

² God said to me, "Do not fear him (even though he has the merit of having helped Abraham), for I have given him, all his people, and his land into your hands. You will do the same to him as you did to King Sihon of the Amorites, who lived in Heshbon."

³ God, our God, also delivered King Og of Bashan and all his people into our hands. We struck his (people) down until no survivors remained. ⁴ On that occasion, we conquered all his cities. There was no populated city that we did not take from them: sixty cities, all the area of the royal palace—the (entire) kingdom of Og in Bashan. ⁵ All these cities were fortified with high walls, double doors, and bolts, in addition to a large number of unwalled cities, ⁶ but we destroyed them, just as we did to (the people of) King Sihon of Heshbon, annihilating the men, women, and young children of every city. ⁷ We (reluctantly) took all the cattle and the spoils of the cities, as plunder for ourselves (since we already had plenty of plunder from the war with Sihon).

---

36. There was no populated city too strong for us. Even the forces of evil become stronger through unity. Thus, we find that the "Generation of Dispersion," who rebelled against God, nevertheless understood the great power of being a totally harmonious community (see commentaries to *Genesis,* ch. 11).

Likewise, Sihon and Og were aware of the great spiritual power in communal harmony, which is why they opposed the Jewish people's entering the land of Israel to become a true community. Sihon and Og knew that their strongest force in opposing the Jewish people

דברים ג:ח-כ

8 וַנִּקַּ֞ח בָּעֵ֤ת הַהִוא֙ אֶת־הָאָ֔רֶץ מִיַּ֗ד שְׁנֵי֙ מַלְכֵ֣י הָאֱמֹרִ֔י אֲשֶׁ֖ר בְּעֵ֣בֶר הַיַּרְדֵּ֑ן מִנַּ֥חַל אַרְנֹ֖ן עַד־הַ֥ר חֶרְמֽוֹן: 9 צִידֹנִ֛ים יִקְרְא֥וּ לְחֶרְמ֖וֹן שִׂרְיֹ֑ן וְהָ֣אֱמֹרִ֔י יִקְרְאוּ־ל֖וֹ שְׂנִֽיר: 10 כֹּ֣ל | עָרֵ֣י הַמִּישֹׁ֗ר וְכָל־הַגִּלְעָד֙ וְכָל־הַבָּשָׁ֔ן עַד־סַלְכָ֖ה וְאֶדְרֶ֑עִי עָרֵ֛י מַמְלֶ֥כֶת ע֖וֹג בַּבָּשָֽׁן: 11 כִּ֣י רַק־ע֞וֹג מֶ֣לֶךְ הַבָּשָׁ֗ן נִשְׁאַר֮ מִיֶּ֣תֶר הָרְפָאִים֒ הִנֵּ֤ה עַרְשׂוֹ֙ עֶ֣רֶשׂ בַּרְזֶ֔ל הֲלֹ֣ה הִ֔וא בְּרַבַּ֖ת בְּנֵ֣י עַמּ֑וֹן תֵּ֧שַׁע אַמּ֣וֹת אָרְכָּ֗הּ וְאַרְבַּ֥ע אַמּ֛וֹת רָחְבָּ֖הּ בְּאַמַּת־אִֽישׁ: 12 וְאֶת־הָאָ֧רֶץ הַזֹּ֛את יָרַ֖שְׁנוּ בָּעֵ֣ת הַהִ֑וא מֵעֲרֹעֵ֞ר אֲשֶׁר־עַל־נַ֣חַל אַרְנֹ֗ן וַחֲצִ֤י הַר־הַגִּלְעָד֙ וְעָרָ֔יו נָתַ֕תִּי לָרֽאוּבֵנִ֖י וְלַגָּדִֽי: 13 וְיֶ֨תֶר הַגִּלְעָ֜ד וְכָל־הַבָּשָׁן֙ מַמְלֶ֣כֶת ע֔וֹג נָתַ֕תִּי לַחֲצִ֖י שֵׁ֣בֶט הַֽמְנַשֶּׁ֑ה כֹּ֣ל חֶ֤בֶל הָֽאַרְגֹּב֙ לְכָל־הַבָּשָׁ֔ן הַה֥וּא יִקָּרֵ֖א אֶ֥רֶץ רְפָאִֽים: 14 יָאִ֣יר בֶּן־מְנַשֶּׁ֗ה לָקַח֙ אֶת־כָּל־חֶ֣בֶל אַרְגֹּ֔ב עַד־גְּב֥וּל הַגְּשׁוּרִ֖י וְהַמַּֽעֲכָתִ֑י וַיִּקְרָא֩ אֹתָ֨ם עַל־שְׁמ֤וֹ אֶת־הַבָּשָׁן֙ חַוֺּ֣ת יָאִ֔יר עַ֖ד הַיּ֥וֹם הַזֶּֽה: [SEVENTH READING] 15 וּלְמָכִ֖יר נָתַ֥תִּי אֶת־הַגִּלְעָֽד: 16 וְלָרֽאוּבֵנִ֨י וְלַגָּדִ֜י נָתַ֣תִּי מִן־הַגִּלְעָ֗ד וְעַד־נַ֤חַל אַרְנֹן֙ תּ֣וֹךְ הַנַּ֣חַל וּגְבֻ֔ל וְעַד֙ יַבֹּ֣ק הַנַּ֔חַל גְּב֖וּל בְּנֵ֥י עַמּֽוֹן: 17 וְהָֽעֲרָבָ֖ה וְהַיַּרְדֵּ֣ן וּגְבֻ֑ל מִכִּנֶּ֗רֶת וְעַ֨ד יָ֤ם הָֽעֲרָבָה֙ יָ֣ם הַמֶּ֔לַח תַּ֛חַת אַשְׁדֹּ֥ת הַפִּסְגָּ֖ה מִזְרָֽחָה: 18 וָֽאֲצַ֣ו אֶתְכֶ֔ם בָּעֵ֥ת הַהִ֖וא לֵאמֹ֑ר יְהֹוָ֣ה אֱלֹֽהֵיכֶ֗ם נָתַ֨ן לָכֶ֜ם אֶת־הָאָ֤רֶץ הַזֹּאת֙ לְרִשְׁתָּ֔הּ חֲלוּצִ֣ים תַּֽעַבְר֗וּ לִפְנֵ֛י אֲחֵיכֶ֥ם בְּנֵֽי־יִשְׂרָאֵ֖ל כָּל־בְּנֵי־חָֽיִל: 19 רַ֠ק נְשֵׁיכֶ֣ם וְטַפְּכֶם֮ וּמִקְנֵכֶם֒ יָדַ֕עְתִּי כִּֽי־מִקְנֶ֥ה רַ֖ב לָכֶ֑ם יֵֽשְׁבוּ֙ בְּעָ֣רֵיכֶ֔ם אֲשֶׁ֥ר נָתַ֖תִּי לָכֶֽם: [MAFTIR] 20 עַ֠ד אֲשֶׁר־יָנִ֨יחַ

spiritual vitamin

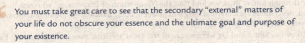

" You must take great care to see that the secondary "external" matters of your life do not obscure your essence and the ultimate goal and purpose of your existence. "

deuteronomy 3:8–20 — devarim

⁸ On that occasion we took over the land from the two Amorite kings who were on that side of the Jordan, from the Arnon Brook to Mount Hermon ⁹—the Sidonians call Hermon, Sirion, and the Amorites call it Senir—¹⁰ all the cities of the plain, all of Gilead, and all of Bashan, up to Salcah and Edrei, cities of Og's kingdom in Bashan. ¹¹ For only King Og of Bashan remained from the rest of the Rephaim (that were killed by Amraphel and his colleagues). His bed was a bed of iron, nine cubits long, and four cubits wide, according to the cubit of a (giant) man. It is found in the Ammonite (city) of Rabbah.

The Lands of Reuben, Gad and Half the Tribe of Manasseh

¹² I gave this land, which we acquired on that occasion—from Aroer, which is by the Arnon Brook, half of Mount Gilead and its cities—to the tribes of Reuben and Gad.

¹³ I gave the remainder of Gilead, and the whole of Bashan—Og's kingdom—to half the tribe of Manasseh. (This included) the whole area of the royal palace and all of Bashan, which is called the land of Rephaim (which God gave to Abraham).

¹⁴ Jair son of Manasseh took the whole area of the royal palace until the Geshurite-Maacathite border, and named (that part of) Bashan after himself: "Jair's Villages," (a name that remains) to this day.

[SEVENTH READING] ¹⁵ I gave Gilead to Machir.

¹⁶ I gave to the tribes of Reuben and Gad: from Gilead to the (area of the) Arnon Brook—(including) the middle of the brook and its bank, right up to the Jabbok Brook on the Ammonite border—¹⁷ the plain, the (width of the) Jordan and the area (beyond) its bank from Chinnereth to the Sea of the Plain, the Sea of Salt, under the waterfalls of Pisgah, eastward.

Instructions for Battle with Canaan

¹⁸ On that occasion, I commanded (the tribes of Reuben and Gad) saying:

"God, your God, has given you this land to take possession of it. (When Israel goes to battle) those of you who are in the army (should) pass over (the land) armed, in front of your brothers, the children of Israel, (for you are the mightiest tribe)."

¹⁹ "Only your wives, your young children, and your cattle—for I know that you have a lot of cattle—may live in your cities, which I have given you, [MAFTIR] ²⁰ until

---

3:18 In front of your brothers. The tribes of Reuben and Gad would go in front of the Jewish people to battle because they were mighty, and the enemies would fall before them, as the verse states, *"He will tear off an arm (of his enemy in one blow, along) with the head"* (Deuteronomy 33:20; Rashi, 11th century).

דברים ג:כ-כב

יְהֹוָה ׀ לַאֲחֵיכֶם֮ כָּכֶם֒ וְיָרְשׁ֣וּ גַם־הֵ֔ם אֶת־הָאָ֕רֶץ אֲשֶׁ֨ר יְהֹוָ֧ה אֱלֹהֵיכֶ֛ם נֹתֵ֥ן לָהֶ֖ם בְּעֵ֣בֶר הַיַּרְדֵּ֑ן וְשַׁבְתֶּ֗ם אִ֚ישׁ לִֽירֻשָּׁת֔וֹ אֲשֶׁ֥ר נָתַ֖תִּי לָכֶֽם: 21 וְאֶת־יְהוֹשׁ֣וּעַ צִוֵּ֔יתִי בָּעֵ֥ת הַהִ֖וא לֵאמֹ֑ר עֵינֶ֣יךָ הָרֹאֹ֗ת אֵת֩ כׇּל־אֲשֶׁ֨ר עָשָׂ֜ה יְהֹוָ֤ה אֱלֹֽהֵיכֶם֙ לִשְׁנֵי֙ הַמְּלָכִ֣ים הָאֵ֔לֶּה כֵּֽן־יַעֲשֶׂ֤ה יְהֹוָה֙ לְכׇל־הַמַּמְלָכ֔וֹת אֲשֶׁ֥ר אַתָּ֖ה עֹבֵ֥ר שָֽׁמָּה: 22 לֹ֖א תִּֽירָא֑וּם כִּ֚י יְהֹוָ֣ה אֱלֹֽהֵיכֶ֔ם ה֖וּא הַנִּלְחָ֥ם לָכֶֽם: ס ס ס

ק"ה פסוקים, מלכ"ה סימן.

deuteronomy 3:20–22 — devarim

God settles your brothers like you. Then they too will possess the land which God, your God, is giving them on the other side of the Jordan. (Only) then may each man return to (settle in) his inherited land, which I have given to you."

²¹ I commanded Joshua at that time (since he would be leading the battle), saying, "Your eyes have seen all that God, your God, has done to these two kings. God will do likewise to all the kingdoms through which you will pass."

²² (To the tribes of Reuben and Gad, I said,) "Do not fear them, for it is God, your God, who is fighting for you."

The *Haftarah* for *Devarim* is on page 1394.

> Moses **prayed 515 times** to enter the land of Israel, **to no avail.** But prayer is not always about receiving **an answer.** Sometimes, it is enough merely to **acknowledge** that you are **in God's hands.**

VA-'ETHANNAN
ואתחנן

MOSES' PLEA TO ENTER CANAAN IS REFUSED	3:23–29
PRINCIPLES OF THE FAITH	4:1–40
MOSES ALLOCATES CITIES OF REFUGE	4:41–43
REPETITION OF THE TEN COMMANDMENTS	4:44 – 5:18
AFTERMATH OF SINAI	5:19 – 6:3
FIRST PARAGRAPH OF THE *SHEMA*	6:4–9
ADMONITION AND GUIDANCE	6:10 – 7:11

NAME
Va-'Ethannan

MEANING
"I requested"

LINES IN TORAH SCROLL
250

PARASHIYYOT
5 open; 16 closed

VERSES
122

WORDS
1878

LETTERS
7343

LOCATION
Plains of Moab

DATE
Shevat–Adar, 2488

MASORETIC FEATURES
Enlarged letters *ayin*, in the word *shema'*, and *dalet*, in *'eḥad* (6:4).

MITZVOT
8 positive; 4 prohibitions

NOTES
Read the week following the Ninth of *Av*

CHARACTER PROFILE

NAME
Baal-peor (Moabite idol)

MEANING
"God of exposure"

LOCATION
Mount of Peor, in Shittim, along the Moabite border

METHOD OF WORSHIP
Exposing the anus in order to defecate before it; worshipers first ate and drank substances that loosen the bowels, such as beets and beer; even some veteran idolators were repulsed by this practice

HISTORY
Moabite and Midianite women seduced Israelite men camping at Shittim, in order to expose them to the worship of Peor. 24,000 Jews were killed by God in a plague, as a result.

REVELATION

Judaism has an unbroken tradition of a mass revelation to millions of men, women, and children (4:32-33).

TRADITION

Institutionalized Torah education cannot replace the spiritual nurturing you need to provide at home (6:7).

TEFILLIN

Tefillin are placed first on the arm and only then on the head, for ultimately, your fulfillment of God's word is even more important to Him than your scholarly comprehension (6:8).

WHOLEHEARTEDNESS

Do not test God, performing a commandment to see whether He will reciprocate as you desire. Act out of true commitment, and trust Him to act out of pure goodness (6:16).

ואתחנן   דברים ג:כג-כח

23 וָאֶתְחַנַּ֖ן אֶל־יְהֹוָ֑ה בָּעֵ֥ת הַהִ֖וא לֵאמֹֽר: 24 אֲדֹנָ֣י יֱהֹוִ֗ה אַתָּ֤ה הַֽחִלּ֙וֹתָ֙ לְהַרְא֣וֹת אֶֽת־עַבְדְּךָ֔ אֶ֨ת־גׇּדְלְךָ֔ וְאֶת־יָדְךָ֖ הַחֲזָקָ֑ה אֲשֶׁ֤ר מִי־אֵל֙ בַּשָּׁמַ֣יִם וּבָאָ֔רֶץ אֲשֶׁר־יַעֲשֶׂ֥ה כְמַעֲשֶׂ֖יךָ וְכִגְבוּרֹתֶֽךָ: 25 אֶעְבְּרָה־נָּ֗א וְאֶרְאֶה֙ אֶת־הָאָ֣רֶץ הַטּוֹבָ֔ה אֲשֶׁ֖ר בְּעֵ֣בֶר הַיַּרְדֵּ֑ן הָהָ֥ר הַטּ֛וֹב הַזֶּ֖ה וְהַלְּבָנֹֽן: 26 וַיִּתְעַבֵּ֨ר יְהֹוָ֥ה בִּי֙ לְמַ֣עַנְכֶ֔ם וְלֹ֥א שָׁמַ֖ע אֵלָ֑י וַיֹּ֨אמֶר יְהֹוָ֤ה אֵלַי֙ רַב־לָ֔ךְ אַל־תּ֗וֹסֶף דַּבֵּ֥ר אֵלַ֛י ע֖וֹד בַּדָּבָ֥ר הַזֶּֽה: 27 עֲלֵ֣ה | רֹ֣אשׁ הַפִּסְגָּ֗ה וְשָׂ֥א עֵינֶ֛יךָ יָ֧מָּה וְצָפֹ֛נָה וְתֵימָ֥נָה וּמִזְרָ֖חָה וּרְאֵ֣ה בְעֵינֶ֑יךָ כִּי־לֹ֥א תַעֲבֹ֖ר אֶת־הַיַּרְדֵּ֥ן הַזֶּֽה: 28 וְצַ֥ו אֶת־יְהוֹשֻׁ֖עַ וְחַזְּקֵ֣הוּ וְאַמְּצֵ֑הוּ

This was an additional prayer: If God would grant his request to enter the land, Moses asked that he should see only "the *good* land," its positive qualities.

Always pray to God that He lead you to see the good in everything (Rabbi Menahem Mendel Morgensztern of Kotsk, 19th century).

Why did Moses want so much to enter the land? Surely it was not the fruit he desired, or the land's other delicacies?

Moses said, "The Jewish people have been given many commandments which can only be observed in the land of Israel. I will enter the land so that all the commandments will be fulfilled through me" (*Babylonian Talmud, Sotah* 14a).

Moses knew that the work of his hands was eternal. If he had led the Jewish people into the land, the Temple would not have been destroyed and the Jewish people would never have been exiled.

Moses did not say, "I will enter the land so *I* can observe all the commandments," because his agenda was not a personal one. He wanted to enter the land so that "the commandments will be fulfilled *through me*"—so that the commandments observed in the land would be everlasting, without interruption or exile, because they would be a function of Moses' leadership (*Rabbi Samuel Bornstein of Sochaczew, 19th century*).

kabbalah bites

3:26 The term *va-yit'abber bi* ("*He became angry with me*"), could also be rendered "He impregnated me": God decreed that Moses' soul would have to endure *'ibbur*, soul impregnation. This is a process where, after death, part of the soul returns to this world and is "impregnated" into an existing soul-body unit to provide additional spiritual potential.

Moses prayed to God that his soul should not have to endure future impregnation, but his request was denied ("*He did not listen to me*"). And this was "*because of you*," because of the sins of the people.

Moses' soul was required to be impregnated every fifty years. Moses prayed so many times not to have to come back in every generation, but his request was denied!

deuteronomy 3:23–28 — va-ʾethannan

parashat va-ʾethannan

Moses' Request to Enter the Land

²³ I requested from God, at that time, saying, ²⁴ "God Almighty (who is merciful in judgment)! You have begun to show Your greatness and Your strong hand to Your servant (with our victory over Sihon and Og)! For who is like God in heaven or on earth who can perform deeds and mighty acts like You? ²⁵ Please let me cross over and see the good land that is on the other side of the Jordan, this good mountain (of Jerusalem) and the Lebanon (i.e. the Holy Temple)."

²⁶ But God became angry with me because of you, and He did not listen to me. God said to me, "Enough of your (requests)! Do not speak to Me any more about this matter. ²⁷ (If you want to see the land), go up to the top of the hill and lift up your eyes westward, northward, southward and eastward, and see (it from there) with your eyes, for you will not cross this (river) Jordan. ²⁸ Command Joshua (about the burdens of leadership). Strengthen him and encourage him (that he will not be punished because of the Jewish people, as you were), because (I assure you that) he will cross over (the Jordan) ahead of the people, and he will bring them to inherit the land which you will see."

3:23 I requested from God, at that time. The Torah states that Moses prayed *"at that time,"* but we are not told what the occasion was. And below the Torah states, *"From there you will seek God"* (4:29), without identifying a specific place. From here you can learn that any time is good for prayer, and every place is good for seeking God (*Rabbi Naphtali Tzevi of Ropczyce, 18ᵗʰ–19ᵗʰ century*).

Va-ʾethannan, "I requested," is a derivative of the word *ḥinnun*, which means the request for an unearned (*ḥinnam*) gift. Even though the righteous could justify their requests based on their good deeds, in their humility they only request "unearned" gifts from God.

Another explanation: This is one of ten terms which denote prayer, listed in *Sifrei* (*Rashi, 11ᵗʰ century*).

Rabbi Johanan said, "There are ten terms which can denote prayer, and they are: *keriʿah, nippul, pillul, taḥanunim, shaveʿah, tzeʿakah, neʿakah, rinnah, pegiʿah,* and *bitzur.* Of all these expressions, Moses only used the approach of *taḥanunim* (an appeal to God's grace). Rabbi Johanan said, "From here you can learn that no creature has any real worth to the Creator, for even Moses only asked God with an expression of grace (*Deuteronomy Rabbah*).

25. Please let me cross over and see the good land. Moses' request to see the land seems unnecessary—if he were to cross over to the land he would obviously get to *see* it.

Food for thought

1. Have you ever been "turned down" by God?

2. Have you ever pleaded with God until He acceded?

3. Why did God decline the heartfelt pleas of his loyal servant Moses?

דברים ג:כח - ד:ה | ואתחנן

כִּי־הוּא יַעֲבֹר לִפְנֵי הָעָם הַזֶּה וְהוּא יַנְחִיל אוֹתָם אֶת־הָאָרֶץ אֲשֶׁר תִּרְאֶה:

29 וַנֵּשֶׁב בַּגָּיְא מוּל בֵּית פְּעוֹר: פ

ד 1 וְעַתָּה יִשְׂרָאֵל שְׁמַע אֶל־הַחֻקִּים וְאֶל־הַמִּשְׁפָּטִים אֲשֶׁר אָנֹכִי מְלַמֵּד אֶתְכֶם לַעֲשׂוֹת לְמַעַן תִּחְיוּ וּבָאתֶם וִירִשְׁתֶּם אֶת־הָאָרֶץ אֲשֶׁר יְהֹוָה אֱלֹהֵי אֲבֹתֵיכֶם נֹתֵן לָכֶם: 2 לֹא תֹסִפוּ עַל־הַדָּבָר אֲשֶׁר אָנֹכִי מְצַוֶּה אֶתְכֶם וְלֹא תִגְרְעוּ מִמֶּנּוּ לִשְׁמֹר אֶת־מִצְוֹת יְהֹוָה אֱלֹהֵיכֶם אֲשֶׁר אָנֹכִי מְצַוֶּה אֶתְכֶם: 3 עֵינֵיכֶם הָרֹאוֹת אֵת אֲשֶׁר־עָשָׂה יְהֹוָה בְּבַעַל פְּעוֹר כִּי כָל־הָאִישׁ אֲשֶׁר הָלַךְ אַחֲרֵי בַעַל־פְּעוֹר הִשְׁמִידוֹ יְהֹוָה אֱלֹהֶיךָ מִקִּרְבֶּךָ: 4 וְאַתֶּם הַדְּבֵקִים בַּיהֹוָה אֱלֹהֵיכֶם חַיִּים כֻּלְּכֶם הַיּוֹם: [SECOND READING:] 5 רְאֵה | לִמַּדְתִּי אֶתְכֶם חֻקִּים וּמִשְׁפָּטִים

But if the High Court of a particular era, in collaboration with a prophet, issues a command in the form of an enactment, instruction or decree, it is not considered to be an addition to the Torah. For they do not claim that *God* commanded the precept of the *'eruv*, or the reading of the *Megillah* in its appropriate time—if they were to say that, it would indeed be an addition (*Maimonides, 12th century*).

A man often would borrow utensils from his neighbor, always returning double of whatever he borrowed—for one plate he returned two plates, for one spoon, two spoons. "It became pregnant and gave birth to another one," the borrower would always explain.

One day the man asked to borrow his neighbor's large silver candelabra for a party he was planning. Without hesitation, the neighbor excitedly agreed, imagining that he would get two in return. When some time had passed and he still had not received his candelabra, the neighbor confronted the borrower.

"Oh, the candelabra contracted a severe illness and died" the borrower explained.

The neighbor protested angrily, "Who ever heard of a candelabra dying?!"

To which the borrower responded, "Who ever heard of a spoon giving birth?" (*Rabbi Jacob Kranz of Dubno, 18th century*).

4. You—who remain attached to God, your God—are all alive today. Regarding the possibility of man's connecting with God, the philosophers adopt various positions. Some maintain that it is only possible *through* angels or other heavenly figures, but not directly with God Himself. Others understand that while it is possible to cleave to God, this can occur only after death, when the soul departs and is liberated from the physical body. Still others propose that an attachment to God can be achieved in this world but only by exceptional individuals.

All of these views are inconsistent with the Torah's position: *"You who remain attached to God, your God"*—who can connect to God? *"Are all"*—everyone; *"alive"*—in this world, while the soul is incarnated in the body; *"today"*—instantly, through a single moment of sincere commitment to follow the Torah and its commandments (*Rabbi Abraham Lichtstein, 18th–19th century*).

deuteronomy 3:29 – 4:5 · va-'ethannan

²⁹ We were living (at that time) in the valley opposite Beth-peor (where you had worshiped idols. Unlike me, you were forgiven by God and He allowed you to enter the land).

Moses Reiterates Principles of the Faith

4 ¹ Now Israel, listen to the suprarational commands and to the rational commands which I am teaching you to perform, in order that you may live. Come and possess the land which God, the God of your forefathers, is giving you.

² Do not add (any additional clauses) to the word(s) of Torah law) which I am commanding you, nor take away (any clauses) from it, in order to preserve the commandments of God, your God, which I am commanding you. ³ Your eyes have seen what God did at Baal-peor, for God, your God, has eliminated every man who went after Baal-peor from among you, ⁴ but you—who remain attached to God, your God—are all alive today.

[SECOND READING] ⁵ Look! As God, my God, commanded me, I have taught you suprarational commands and rational commands to observe within the land which you

---

4:1 Now Israel, listen. If you hear that your country is ruled by a powerful king who is surrounded by ministers that tremble in his presence, then it is likely you will follow the king's orders. But if you actually *see* such a powerful king, you will be affected more profoundly by the experience—for seeing is incomparable to hearing (*Mekhilta*).

Moses' consciousness of the Divine had visual clarity. Therefore, he wanted to be the one to lead the Jewish people into the land of Israel, to lift them to his level, so he said, *"Please let me cross over and see the good land"* (v. 25).

When God refused his request, Moses began to address the Jewish people with the words, "Now Israel, *listen*." Moses now recognized that he would only be able to inspire the Jewish people towards a consciousness of God on the level of "hearing" and not "seeing."

However, with the coming of the Messiah, Moses' request will be finally granted. For the Messiah will bring our consciousness to the level of "seeing" (*Rabbi Shneur Zalman of Lyady, 18th century*).

2. Do not add to the word which I am commanding you, nor take away from it. There are various commandments that were introduced after the giving of the Torah, instituted by the prophets and sages, which were accepted by all Israel, e.g., reading the *Megillah*, Ḥanukkah lights, fasting on the Ninth of *Av*, the various types of *'eruv* which relax the Sabbath laws, and the ritual washing of the hands. We are required to accept and observe all these newly established commandments, as the verse states, *"You must not divert from the words that they (the Sages) tell you"* (*Deuteronomy* 17:11). These are not considered to be an expansion of the body of Torah commandments.

What, then, is the purpose of the Torah's warning, *"Do not add to the word which I am commanding you, nor take away from it"*?

It means that a prophet does not have the right to introduce any new precept, saying God commanded this to be added to the commandments of the Torah; or that we should discontinue one of the six hundred thirteen commandments.

דברים ד:ה-טז | ואתחנן

כַּאֲשֶׁר צִוַּנִי יְהֹוָה אֱלֹהָי לַעֲשׂוֹת כֵּן בְּקֶרֶב הָאָרֶץ אֲשֶׁר אַתֶּם בָּאִים שָׁמָּה לְרִשְׁתָּהּ: 6 וּשְׁמַרְתֶּם וַעֲשִׂיתֶם כִּי הִוא חָכְמַתְכֶם וּבִינַתְכֶם לְעֵינֵי הָעַמִּים אֲשֶׁר יִשְׁמְעוּן אֵת כָּל־הַחֻקִּים הָאֵלֶּה וְאָמְרוּ רַק עַם־חָכָם וְנָבוֹן הַגּוֹי הַגָּדוֹל הַזֶּה: 7 כִּי מִי־גוֹי גָּדוֹל אֲשֶׁר־לוֹ אֱלֹהִים קְרֹבִים אֵלָיו כַּיהֹוָה אֱלֹהֵינוּ בְּכָל־קָרְאֵנוּ אֵלָיו: 8 וּמִי גּוֹי גָּדוֹל אֲשֶׁר־לוֹ חֻקִּים וּמִשְׁפָּטִים צַדִּיקִם כְּכֹל הַתּוֹרָה הַזֹּאת אֲשֶׁר אָנֹכִי נֹתֵן לִפְנֵיכֶם הַיּוֹם: 9 רַק הִשָּׁמֶר לְךָ וּשְׁמֹר נַפְשְׁךָ מְאֹד פֶּן־תִּשְׁכַּח אֶת־הַדְּבָרִים אֲשֶׁר־רָאוּ עֵינֶיךָ וּפֶן־יָסוּרוּ מִלְּבָבְךָ כֹּל יְמֵי חַיֶּיךָ וְהוֹדַעְתָּם לְבָנֶיךָ וְלִבְנֵי בָנֶיךָ: 10 יוֹם אֲשֶׁר עָמַדְתָּ לִפְנֵי יְהֹוָה אֱלֹהֶיךָ בְּחֹרֵב בֶּאֱמֹר יְהֹוָה אֵלַי הַקְהֶל־לִי אֶת־הָעָם וְאַשְׁמִעֵם אֶת־דְּבָרָי אֲשֶׁר יִלְמְדוּן לְיִרְאָה אֹתִי כָּל־הַיָּמִים אֲשֶׁר הֵם חַיִּים עַל־הָאֲדָמָה וְאֶת־בְּנֵיהֶם יְלַמֵּדוּן: 11 וַתִּקְרְבוּן וַתַּעַמְדוּן תַּחַת הָהָר וְהָהָר בֹּעֵר בָּאֵשׁ עַד־לֵב הַשָּׁמַיִם חֹשֶׁךְ עָנָן וַעֲרָפֶל: 12 וַיְדַבֵּר יְהֹוָה אֲלֵיכֶם מִתּוֹךְ הָאֵשׁ קוֹל דְּבָרִים אַתֶּם שֹׁמְעִים וּתְמוּנָה אֵינְכֶם רֹאִים זוּלָתִי קוֹל: 13 וַיַּגֵּד לָכֶם אֶת־בְּרִיתוֹ אֲשֶׁר צִוָּה אֶתְכֶם לַעֲשׂוֹת עֲשֶׂרֶת הַדְּבָרִים וַיִּכְתְּבֵם עַל־שְׁנֵי לֻחוֹת אֲבָנִים: 14 וְאֹתִי צִוָּה יְהֹוָה בָּעֵת הַהִוא לְלַמֵּד אֶתְכֶם חֻקִּים וּמִשְׁפָּטִים לַעֲשֹׂתְכֶם אֹתָם בָּאָרֶץ אֲשֶׁר אַתֶּם עֹבְרִים שָׁמָּה לְרִשְׁתָּהּ: 15 וְנִשְׁמַרְתֶּם מְאֹד לְנַפְשֹׁתֵיכֶם כִּי לֹא רְאִיתֶם כָּל־תְּמוּנָה בְּיוֹם דִּבֶּר יְהֹוָה אֲלֵיכֶם בְּחֹרֵב מִתּוֹךְ הָאֵשׁ: 16 פֶּן־תַּשְׁחִתוּן

remain true to religious observance. They allow the Torah to *"depart from their own heart,"* but at the same time wish to *"inform their children"* about its observance. This is a flawed approach. *"They must learn to fear Me"*—themselves—and only then can they successfully *"teach their children"* (v. 10; Rabbi Solomon ha-Kohen Rabinowich of Radomsko, 19*th* century).

15. Look after yourselves very well. Having a totally healthy body is a key element of worshiping God, for you cannot have an understanding or knowledge of God when you are sick. Therefore, you must distance yourself from things that harm the body.

In fact, it is forbidden for you to cause injury to any person, including yourself. Even withholding food or drink from your body is shunned (Maimonides, 12*th* century).

deuteronomy 4:5–16 va-ʾethannan

are going to enter and possess. ⁶ You should preserve (the laws by studying them) and perform them. For this is your (key to) wisdom and understanding in the eyes of the nations, who will hear all these laws and say, "Only this great nation is a (truly) wise and understanding people." ⁷ Which (other) nation is so great that it has a god so close to it, as God, our God, is (near to us) whenever we call Him? For, whenever we call upon Him (in prayer He answers). ⁸ And which nation is so great that it has suprarational commands and rational commands which are fair, like all (the laws) in this Torah (of ours), which I am presenting before you today?

⁹ Just be careful and keep track of yourself well, so that you do not forget the things that your eyes saw (at Sinai). Do not let these things depart from your heart, all the days of your life. You should inform your children and your children's children about ¹⁰ the day you stood before God, your God, at Horeb (and saw the flames and the sounds. For) God said to me then: "Assemble the people for Me. I will let them hear My words, so that they will learn to fear Me all the days that they live on the earth, and so that they will teach their children (what they heard and saw)." ¹¹ You approached and stood at the foot of the mountain. The mountain was burning with fire up to the heart of the heavens (and there was) darkness, a cloud, and fog. ¹² God spoke to you from the fire. You were hearing the sound of the words, but you did not see any image—only sound.

¹³ He told you His covenant, which He commanded you to observe—the Ten Commandments—and He wrote them on two stone tablets. ¹⁴ On that occasion, God commanded me to teach you (the Oral Torah, which explains the) suprarational commands and rational commands, so that you would observe them in the land to which you are (now) entering, to take possession of it.

¹⁵ Look after yourselves very well (and remember) that you did not see any image on the day God spoke to you at Horeb from the fire, ¹⁶ in order that you will

6. The nations who will hear all these laws and say, "Only this great nation is a wise and understanding people." The term used here for laws—*ḥukkim*—refers specifically to suprarational commands. How could laws which are beyond our understanding evoke praise for Israel as *"a wise and understanding people"*?

If an ordinary person does something eccentric, it is immediately dismissed as foolish. But when a renowned scholar, whose actions are known to reflect deep wisdom, does something strange, people ascribe his bizarre actions to some profound motive that is beyond their comprehension.

Since the nations recognize the great wisdom inherent in all the rational commands of the Torah (v. 8), they conclude that even the laws which are not understood must be rooted in wisdom (*Rabbi Abraham Samuel Benjamin Sofer, 19ᵗʰ century*).

9. Do not let these things depart from your heart ... you should inform your children. Some people are not too bothered themselves about the Torah, but they want their children to

דברים ד:טז-כו | ואתחנן

וַעֲשִׂיתֶם לָכֶם פֶּסֶל תְּמוּנַת כָּל־סָמֶל תַּבְנִית זָכָר אוֹ נְקֵבָה: 17 תַּבְנִית כָּל־בְּהֵמָה אֲשֶׁר בָּאָרֶץ תַּבְנִית כָּל־צִפּוֹר כָּנָף אֲשֶׁר תָּעוּף בַּשָּׁמָיִם: 18 תַּבְנִית כָּל־רֹמֵשׂ בָּאֲדָמָה תַּבְנִית כָּל־דָּגָה אֲשֶׁר בַּמַּיִם מִתַּחַת לָאָרֶץ: 19 וּפֶן־תִּשָּׂא עֵינֶיךָ הַשָּׁמַיְמָה וְרָאִיתָ אֶת־הַשֶּׁמֶשׁ וְאֶת־הַיָּרֵחַ וְאֶת־הַכּוֹכָבִים כֹּל צְבָא הַשָּׁמַיִם וְנִדַּחְתָּ וְהִשְׁתַּחֲוִיתָ לָהֶם וַעֲבַדְתָּם אֲשֶׁר חָלַק יְהֹוָה אֱלֹהֶיךָ אֹתָם לְכֹל הָעַמִּים תַּחַת כָּל־הַשָּׁמָיִם: 20 וְאֶתְכֶם לָקַח יְהֹוָה וַיּוֹצִא אֶתְכֶם מִכּוּר הַבַּרְזֶל מִמִּצְרָיִם לִהְיוֹת לוֹ לְעַם נַחֲלָה כַּיּוֹם הַזֶּה: 21 וַיהֹוָה הִתְאַנַּף־בִּי עַל־דִּבְרֵיכֶם וַיִּשָּׁבַע לְבִלְתִּי עָבְרִי אֶת־הַיַּרְדֵּן וּלְבִלְתִּי־בֹא אֶל־הָאָרֶץ הַטּוֹבָה אֲשֶׁר יְהֹוָה אֱלֹהֶיךָ נֹתֵן לְךָ נַחֲלָה: 22 כִּי אָנֹכִי מֵת בָּאָרֶץ הַזֹּאת אֵינֶנִּי עֹבֵר אֶת־הַיַּרְדֵּן וְאַתֶּם עֹבְרִים וִירִשְׁתֶּם אֶת־הָאָרֶץ הַטּוֹבָה הַזֹּאת: 23 הִשָּׁמְרוּ לָכֶם פֶּן־תִּשְׁכְּחוּ אֶת־בְּרִית יְהֹוָה אֱלֹהֵיכֶם אֲשֶׁר כָּרַת עִמָּכֶם וַעֲשִׂיתֶם לָכֶם פֶּסֶל תְּמוּנַת כֹּל אֲשֶׁר צִוְּךָ יְהֹוָה אֱלֹהֶיךָ: 24 כִּי יְהֹוָה אֱלֹהֶיךָ אֵשׁ אֹכְלָה הוּא אֵל קַנָּא: פ 25 כִּי־תוֹלִיד בָּנִים וּבְנֵי בָנִים וְנוֹשַׁנְתֶּם בָּאָרֶץ וְהִשְׁחַתֶּם וַעֲשִׂיתֶם פֶּסֶל תְּמוּנַת כֹּל וַעֲשִׂיתֶם הָרַע בְּעֵינֵי יְהֹוָה־אֱלֹהֶיךָ לְהַכְעִיסוֹ: 26 הַעִידֹתִי בָכֶם הַיּוֹם אֶת־הַשָּׁמַיִם וְאֶת־הָאָרֶץ כִּי־אָבֹד תֹּאבֵדוּן מַהֵר מֵעַל הָאָרֶץ אֲשֶׁר אַתֶּם עֹבְרִים אֶת־הַיַּרְדֵּן שָׁמָּה לְרִשְׁתָּהּ לֹא־תַאֲרִיכֻן יָמִים עָלֶיהָ כִּי הִשָּׁמֵד

or overcome physical shortcomings. In many cases, even physical treatments, prescriptions and drugs are considerably more effective when accompanied by the patient's strong will and determination to cooperate.

Since physical health depends on spiritual health, if you become ill, God forbid, you should try to identify what shortcoming might have caused the illness.

But this approach should be taken only regarding *your own* lack of physical health. If you see that someone else is sick, never imagine that it was caused by a spiritual shortcoming—*"Do not judge your fellow until you have stood in his place"* (*Mishnah, Avot* 2:4; *Rabbi Menahem Mendel Schneerson, 20th century*).

not lapse and make a statue for yourselves, or an image of any form: the shape of a male or female, ¹⁷ the shape of any animal that is on the earth, the shape of any winged bird that flies in the skies, ¹⁸ the shape of anything that crawls on the ground, the shape of any fish that is in the waters, beneath the earth. ¹⁹ (Be careful if you) lift up your eyes to the skies, and see the sun, the moon, the stars, and all the hosts of the skies—which God, your God, has given (to provide illumination) under the skies for all the nations—not to be drawn astray to bow down to them and worship them. ²⁰ God took you and brought you out of the iron melting pot, from Egypt, to be His heritage nation as (you are) today.

²¹ God was angry with me, because of you(r actions), and He swore that I would not cross the Jordan and that I would not come into the good land that God, your God, is giving you as an inheritance. ²² For I will die in this land (and even my bones) will not cross the Jordan. You, however, will cross, and you will take possession of this good land.

²³ Be careful not to forget the covenant of God, your God, which He made with you, and make for yourselves a statue, an image of anything, which God, your God, has commanded you (not to make). ²⁴ For God, your God, is a consuming fire, a jealous God (who settles His score against idol-worshipers).

²⁵ If you have children and grandchildren, and you grow old in the land, and you lapse and make an idol, an image of anything, and (thereby) do evil in the eyes of God, your God, to provoke His anger, ²⁶ I call the skies and the earth to be witnesses against you today, that you will be eliminated speedily from the land

---

A tiny hole in the body causes a big hole in the soul (*Rabbi Dov Baer of Mezhirech, 18th century*).

So much of physical health depends on spiritual health. Even a small defect spiritually could lead to a grievous defect physically; and the healthier the spirit, the greater its ability to correct

kabbalah bites

4:23 Everyone has an ego, but whose is the hardest to tame? The super-talented, famous speaker and thinker, or good old Mr. Ordinary?

You might think that Mr. Ordinary would have an easier time, but the matter is not so simple. You see, the greater you are, the easier it is for you to realize that most profound principle of life: *It's not about you.* The more intelligent you are, the easier it is for you to understand the idea of "win-win," that the universe is a system to which you have a sacred obligation to contribute, and not to abuse for your own purposes. The ordinary person, on the other hand, may have less pride to crush, but at the same time, he has weaker tools with which to do so.

Reading the Torah, which is implanted with light, helps you to control your ego and render it transparent to a higher purpose.

ואתחנן   דברים ד:כז-לו

27 וְהֵפִ֧יץ יְהֹוָ֛ה אֶתְכֶ֖ם בָּעַמִּ֑ים וְנִשְׁאַרְתֶּם֙ מְתֵ֣י מִסְפָּ֔ר בַּגּוֹיִ֕ם תִּשָּׁמֵדֽוּן׃
אֲשֶׁ֨ר יְנַהֵ֧ג יְהֹוָ֛ה אֶתְכֶ֖ם שָֽׁמָּה׃ 28 וַעֲבַדְתֶּם־שָׁ֣ם אֱלֹהִ֔ים מַעֲשֵׂ֖ה יְדֵ֣י אָדָ֑ם
עֵ֣ץ וָאֶ֔בֶן אֲשֶׁ֤ר לֹֽא־יִרְאוּן֙ וְלֹ֣א יִשְׁמְע֔וּן וְלֹ֥א יֹֽאכְל֖וּן וְלֹ֥א יְרִיחֻֽן׃ 29 וּבִקַּשְׁתֶּ֥ם
מִשָּׁ֛ם אֶת־יְהֹוָ֥ה אֱלֹהֶ֖יךָ וּמָצָ֑אתָ כִּ֣י תִדְרְשֶׁ֔נּוּ בְּכָל־לְבָבְךָ֖ וּבְכָל־נַפְשֶֽׁךָ׃
30 בַּצַּ֣ר לְךָ֔ וּמְצָא֕וּךָ כֹּ֖ל הַדְּבָרִ֣ים הָאֵ֑לֶּה בְּאַחֲרִית֙ הַיָּמִ֔ים וְשַׁבְתָּ֙ עַד־יְהֹוָ֣ה
אֱלֹהֶ֔יךָ וְשָׁמַעְתָּ֖ בְּקֹלֽוֹ׃ 31 כִּ֣י אֵ֤ל רַחוּם֙ יְהֹוָ֣ה אֱלֹהֶ֔יךָ לֹ֥א יַרְפְּךָ֖ וְלֹ֣א יַשְׁחִיתֶ֑ךָ
וְלֹ֣א יִשְׁכַּ֔ח אֶת־בְּרִ֥ית אֲבֹתֶ֖יךָ אֲשֶׁ֥ר נִשְׁבַּ֥ע לָהֶֽם׃ 32 כִּ֣י שְׁאַל־נָא֩ לְיָמִ֨ים
רִֽאשֹׁנִ֜ים אֲשֶׁר־הָי֣וּ לְפָנֶ֗יךָ לְמִן־הַיּוֹם֙ אֲשֶׁר֩ בָּרָ֨א אֱלֹהִ֤ים ׀ אָדָם֙ עַל־הָאָ֔רֶץ
וּלְמִקְצֵ֥ה הַשָּׁמַ֖יִם וְעַד־קְצֵ֣ה הַשָּׁמָ֑יִם הֲנִֽהְיָ֗ה כַּדָּבָ֤ר הַגָּדוֹל֙ הַזֶּ֔ה א֖וֹ הֲנִשְׁמַ֥ע
כָּמֹֽהוּ׃ 33 הֲשָׁ֣מַֽע עָם֩ ק֨וֹל אֱלֹהִ֜ים מְדַבֵּ֧ר מִתּוֹךְ־הָאֵ֛שׁ כַּאֲשֶׁר־שָׁמַ֥עְתָּ אַתָּ֖ה
וַיֶּֽחִי׃ 34 א֣וֹ ׀ הֲנִסָּ֣ה אֱלֹהִ֗ים לָבוֹא֩ לָקַ֨חַת ל֣וֹ גוֹי֮ מִקֶּ֣רֶב גּוֹי֒ בְּמַסֹּת֩ בְּאֹתֹ֨ת
וּבְמוֹפְתִ֜ים וּבְמִלְחָמָ֗ה וּבְיָ֤ד חֲזָקָה֙ וּבִזְר֣וֹעַ נְטוּיָ֔ה וּבְמוֹרָאִ֖ים גְּדֹלִ֑ים כְּ֠כֹ֠ל
אֲשֶׁר־עָשָׂ֨ה לָכֶ֜ם יְהֹוָ֧ה אֱלֹהֵיכֶ֛ם בְּמִצְרַ֖יִם לְעֵינֶֽיךָ׃ 35 אַתָּה֙ הָרְאֵ֣תָ לָדַ֔עַת
כִּ֥י יְהֹוָ֖ה ה֣וּא הָאֱלֹהִ֑ים אֵ֥ין ע֖וֹד מִלְבַדּֽוֹ׃ 36 מִן־הַשָּׁמַ֛יִם הִשְׁמִֽיעֲךָ֥ אֶת־קֹל֖וֹ

---

tual wealth. In truth, however, *"you will find Him ... within your very own heart and soul"* (*Rabbi Simhah Bunem of Przysucha, 18th–19th century*).

In order for any entity to exist at all, God must renew it continually, by enlivening it with a spark of His own existence. Without being connected to God—the True Existence—the entity is unable to exist. Even the forces of evil must contain a Godly spark that enables them to exist.

Why, then, is it possible for the forces of evil to conceal this presence of Godliness within them? The answer is: to make possible the amazing elevation that can be reached through repentance. When a person has regressed to a very low spiritual state, the Torah teaches that *"from there—from amid the forces of evil—you will seek God"* (*Rabbi Shneur Zalman of Lyady, 18th century*).

35. There is none other besides Him. In truth, even the creations do not exist as entities in their own right, as it appears to our eyes. We perceive it that way because we do not see Godly energy. However, from the perspective of the Godly energy which enlivens us, our existence is totally nullified into absolute nothingness, like a ray of light inside the globe of the sun. There is no existence at all outside that of God (*Rabbi Shneur Zalman of Lyady, 18th century*).

which you will (soon be) crossing the Jordan to take possession. You will not live a long time upon it, for you will be utterly destroyed. ²⁷ God will scatter you among the nations, and you will remain few in number among the nations where God will lead you. ²⁸ (Through being subjugated to idol-worshipers) there (it will be as if) you are worshiping (their) gods—man's handiwork, wood and stone, that neither sees, hears, eats, nor smells.

²⁹ From there you will seek God, your God, and you will find Him—if you seek Him with all your heart and with all your soul. ³⁰ At the end of days when you are in distress, and all these things (have) happened to you, then you will return to God, your God, and obey Him. ³¹ For God, your God, is a merciful God. He will not loosen (His connection with) you or destroy you. He will not forget the covenant of your fathers, which He swore to them.

³² (If you want proof of this) inquire now about the earliest times that were before you, from the day that God created man on the earth! (Inquire from the creatures that are found) from one extremity of the skies to the other extremity of the skies! Was there ever such a great thing, or even a rumor like it, ³³ that a people should hear God's voice speaking out of the midst of the fire, as you heard, and survive? ³⁴ Or has any deity performed miracles, coming to a nation and taking it for himself out from another nation, with proofs (of true power), signs (of God's direct involvement), wondrous (plagues), with a war (fought by God Himself), a strong hand, an outstretched arm, and with awesome acts—like everything that God, your God, did for you in Egypt, before your eyes?

³⁵ (When the Torah was given) you were shown (the seven heavens), in order (for you) to know that God is God. There is none other besides Him. ³⁶ From the skies,

---

29. From there you will seek God, your God, and you will find Him—if you seek Him with all your heart. People tend to seek God *"from there"*—in remote areas of supposed vast spiri-

spiritual vitamin

> You have "hidden reserves" of powers to create new possibilities, and inner qualities that give you the ability to overcome obstacles and to shape your life and the life around you to be in harmony with Truth and Goodness. In order to reveal and apply these powers you need to search for and release your potential forces. But you are promised: *"You will find Him—if you seek Him with all your heart and with all your soul"* (v. 29).

דברים ד:לו-מח ואתחנן

לְיַסְּרֶ֑ךָ וְעַל־הָאָ֗רֶץ הֶרְאֲךָ֙ אֶת־אִשּׁ֣וֹ הַגְּדוֹלָ֔ה וּדְבָרָ֥יו שָׁמַ֖עְתָּ מִתּ֥וֹךְ הָאֵֽשׁ: 37 וְתַ֗חַת כִּ֤י אָהַב֙ אֶת־אֲבֹתֶ֔יךָ וַיִּבְחַ֥ר בְּזַרְע֖וֹ אַחֲרָ֑יו וַיּוֹצִֽאֲךָ֧ בְּפָנָ֛יו בְּכֹח֥וֹ הַגָּדֹ֖ל מִמִּצְרָֽיִם: 38 לְהוֹרִ֗ישׁ גּוֹיִ֛ם גְּדֹלִ֧ים וַעֲצֻמִ֛ים מִמְּךָ֖ מִפָּנֶ֑יךָ לַהֲבִֽיאֲךָ֗ לָֽתֶת־לְךָ֧ אֶת־אַרְצָ֛ם נַחֲלָ֖ה כַּיּ֥וֹם הַזֶּֽה: 39 וְיָדַעְתָּ֣ הַיּ֗וֹם וַהֲשֵׁבֹתָ֮ אֶל־לְבָבֶךָ֒ כִּ֤י יְהֹוָה֙ ה֣וּא הָֽאֱלֹהִ֔ים בַּשָּׁמַ֣יִם מִמַּ֔עַל וְעַל־הָאָ֖רֶץ מִתָּ֑חַת אֵ֖ין עֽוֹד: 40 וְשָׁמַרְתָּ֞ אֶת־חֻקָּ֣יו וְאֶת־מִצְוֺתָ֗יו אֲשֶׁ֨ר אָנֹכִ֤י מְצַוְּךָ֙ הַיּ֔וֹם אֲשֶׁר֙ יִיטַ֣ב לְךָ֔ וּלְבָנֶ֖יךָ אַחֲרֶ֑יךָ וּלְמַ֨עַן תַּאֲרִ֤יךְ יָמִים֙ עַל־הָ֣אֲדָמָ֔ה אֲשֶׁ֨ר יְהֹוָ֧ה אֱלֹהֶ֛יךָ נֹתֵ֥ן לְךָ֖ כָּל־הַיָּמִֽים: פ [THIRD READING]

41 אָ֣ז יַבְדִּ֤יל מֹשֶׁה֙ שָׁלֹ֣שׁ עָרִ֔ים בְּעֵ֖בֶר הַיַּרְדֵּ֑ן מִזְרְחָ֖ה שָֽׁמֶשׁ: 42 לָנֻ֨ס שָׁ֜מָּה רוֹצֵ֗חַ אֲשֶׁ֨ר יִרְצַ֤ח אֶת־רֵעֵ֙הוּ֙ בִּבְלִי־דַ֔עַת וְה֛וּא לֹא־שֹׂנֵ֥א ל֖וֹ מִתְּמ֣וֹל שִׁלְשֹׁ֑ם וְנָ֗ס אֶל־אַחַ֛ת מִן־הֶעָרִ֥ים הָאֵ֖ל וָחָֽי: 43 אֶת־בֶּ֧צֶר בַּמִּדְבָּ֛ר בְּאֶ֥רֶץ הַמִּישֹׁ֖ר לָרֽאוּבֵנִ֑י וְאֶת־רָאמֹ֤ת בַּגִּלְעָד֙ לַגָּדִ֔י וְאֶת־גּוֹלָ֥ן בַּבָּשָׁ֖ן לַֽמְנַשִּֽׁי: 44 וְזֹ֖את הַתּוֹרָ֑ה אֲשֶׁר־שָׂ֣ם מֹשֶׁ֔ה לִפְנֵ֖י בְּנֵ֥י יִשְׂרָאֵֽל: 45 אֵ֚לֶּה הָֽעֵדֹ֔ת וְהַֽחֻקִּ֖ים וְהַמִּשְׁפָּטִ֑ים אֲשֶׁ֨ר דִּבֶּ֤ר מֹשֶׁה֙ אֶל־בְּנֵ֣י יִשְׂרָאֵ֔ל בְּצֵאתָ֖ם מִמִּצְרָֽיִם: 46 בְּעֵ֨בֶר הַיַּרְדֵּ֜ן בַּגַּ֗יְא מ֚וּל בֵּ֣ית פְּע֔וֹר בְּאֶ֗רֶץ סִיחֹן֙ מֶ֣לֶךְ הָֽאֱמֹרִ֔י אֲשֶׁ֥ר יוֹשֵׁ֖ב בְּחֶשְׁבּ֑וֹן אֲשֶׁ֨ר הִכָּ֤ה מֹשֶׁה֙ וּבְנֵ֣י יִשְׂרָאֵ֔ל בְּצֵאתָ֖ם מִמִּצְרָֽיִם: 47 וַיִּֽירְשׁ֨וּ אֶת־אַרְצ֜וֹ וְאֶת־אֶ֣רֶץ | ע֣וֹג מֶֽלֶךְ־הַבָּשָׁ֗ן שְׁנֵי֙ מַלְכֵ֣י הָֽאֱמֹרִ֔י אֲשֶׁ֖ר בְּעֵ֣בֶר הַיַּרְדֵּ֑ן מִזְרַ֖ח שָֽׁמֶשׁ: 48 מֵעֲרֹעֵ֡ר

spiritual vitamin

" The essence of the idea of the unity of God, is to know that *"in the heavens above, and on the earth below there is no other"* (v. 39), because God fills all the worlds and transcends all the worlds, and nothing has any reality but the Divine Word that creates everything continuously, every instant. "

He let you hear His voice, to educate you. He showed you His great fire upon the earth, and you heard His words from the fire.

⁳⁷ (He did all of this) because He loved your forefathers, and He chose their children after them. He brought you out of Egypt (like a father who leads his son) ahead of him, with His great strength. ³⁸ (He intended) to clear nations that are greater and stronger than you out of your way, so as to bring you and give you their land as an inheritance—as (you see He is doing) today.

³⁹ Today, you should know and take to your heart, that God is God in the heavens above, and on the earth below. There is no other. ⁴⁰ You should observe His supra-rational commands and His (other) commandments, which I am commanding you today, so that He will be good to you and your children after you. Then you will remain for a long time in the land that God, your God, is giving you eternally.

Separation of Cities of Refuge in Transjordan

[THIRD READING] ⁴¹ At that time, Moses separated three cities on the (east) side of the Jordan where the sun rises, ⁴² so that (at a later time, when the cities would become active) a murderer might flee there. (If a person) murders his fellow unintentionally, provided he did not hate him yesterday or the day before, he may flee to one of these cities and live:

- ⁴³ Bezer in the desert, in the flatlands of (the tribe of) Reuben.
- Ramoth in Gilead, which belongs to (the tribe of) Gad.
- Golan in the Bashan which belongs to (the tribe of) Manasseh.

Review of the Laws of the Torah

⁴⁴ The following is the law which Moses put before the children of Israel. ⁴⁵ These are the (same) testimonies, suprarational commands and rational commands which Moses told the children of Israel when they went out of Egypt, ⁴⁶ (and he repeated them now, while they were) on the (east) side of the Jordan area (in the plains of Moab), in the valley opposite Beth-peor. (It was) the land of King Sihon of the Amorites, who lived in Heshbon, whom Moses and the children of Israel defeated, after they left Egypt. ⁴⁷ They took possession of his land, and the land of King Og of Bashan—the two Amorite kings, who were on the (east) side of the Jordan, where the sun rises—⁴⁸ from Aroer, which is on the edge of the valley of

---

41. Moses separated three cities. The three cities in the Transjordan did not serve as a haven until the three in the land of Canaan were set aside. Why then did Moses set them aside? He said, "Since a commandment has come to my hand, I will do it" (*Maimonides, 12th century*).

דברים ד:מח - ה:ט ואתחנן

אֲשֶׁ֥ר עַל־שְׂפַת־נַ֣חַל אַרְנֹ֑ן וְעַד־הַ֥ר שִׂיאֹ֖ן ה֥וּא חֶרְמֽוֹן: 49 וְכָל־הָ֨עֲרָבָ֜ה עֵ֤בֶר הַיַּרְדֵּן֙ מִזְרָ֔חָה וְעַ֖ד יָ֣ם הָעֲרָבָ֑ה תַּ֖חַת אַשְׁדֹּ֥ת הַפִּסְגָּֽה: פ

ה 1 [FOURTH READING] וַיִּקְרָ֣א מֹשֶׁה֮ אֶל־כָּל־יִשְׂרָאֵל֒ וַיֹּ֣אמֶר אֲלֵהֶ֔ם שְׁמַ֤ע יִשְׂרָאֵל֙ אֶת־הַחֻקִּ֣ים וְאֶת־הַמִּשְׁפָּטִ֔ים אֲשֶׁ֧ר אָנֹכִ֛י דֹּבֵ֥ר בְּאָזְנֵיכֶ֖ם הַיּ֑וֹם וּלְמַדְתֶּ֣ם אֹתָ֔ם וּשְׁמַרְתֶּ֖ם לַעֲשֹׂתָֽם: 2 יְהֹוָ֣ה אֱלֹהֵ֗ינוּ כָּרַ֥ת עִמָּ֛נוּ בְּרִ֖ית בְּחֹרֵֽב: 3 לֹ֣א אֶת־אֲבֹתֵ֔ינוּ כָּרַ֥ת יְהֹוָ֖ה אֶת־הַבְּרִ֣ית הַזֹּ֑את כִּ֣י אִתָּ֗נוּ אֲנַ֨חְנוּ אֵ֧לֶּה פֹ֛ה הַיּ֖וֹם כֻּלָּ֥נוּ חַיִּֽים: 4 פָּנִ֣ים | בְּפָנִ֗ים דִּבֶּ֨ר יְהֹוָ֧ה עִמָּכֶ֛ם בָּהָ֖ר מִתּ֥וֹךְ הָאֵֽשׁ: 5 אָנֹכִ֞י עֹמֵ֨ד בֵּֽין־יְהֹוָ֤ה וּבֵֽינֵיכֶם֙ בָּעֵ֣ת הַהִ֔וא לְהַגִּ֥יד לָכֶ֖ם אֶת־דְּבַ֣ר יְהֹוָ֑ה כִּ֤י יְרֵאתֶם֙ מִפְּנֵ֣י הָאֵ֔שׁ וְלֹֽא־עֲלִיתֶ֥ם בָּהָ֖ר לֵאמֹֽר: ס 6 *אָנֹכִי֙ יְהֹוָ֣ה אֱלֹהֶ֔יךָ אֲשֶׁ֧ר הוֹצֵאתִ֛יךָ מֵאֶ֥רֶץ מִצְרַ֖יִם מִבֵּ֣ית עֲבָדִ֑ים: 7 לֹֽא־יִהְיֶ֥ה לְךָ֛ אֱלֹהִ֥ים אֲחֵרִ֖ים עַל־פָּנָֽי: 8 לֹֽא־תַעֲשֶׂ֨ה לְךָ֥ פֶ֨סֶל֙ כָּל־תְּמוּנָ֔ה אֲשֶׁ֤ר בַּשָּׁמַ֨יִם֙ מִמַּ֔עַל וַאֲשֶׁ֥ר בָּאָ֖רֶץ מִתָּ֑חַת וַאֲשֶׁ֥ר בַּמַּ֖יִם מִתַּ֥חַת לָאָֽרֶץ: 9 לֹֽא־תִשְׁתַּחֲוֶ֥ה לָהֶ֖ם וְלֹ֣א תָעָבְדֵ֑ם כִּ֣י אָנֹכִ֞י

*Cantillation notes for public reading on page 1282.

The answer: from the two accounts of the Ten Commandments written in the Torah. The first account (*Exodus*, ch. 19-20) where God's voice shattered the heavens and the earth, gives us the ability to break through the barriers between spiritual and physical, and saturate the mundane world with Divinity. The repetition of the Ten Commandments here, was said by Moses, and was thus articulated in a more human voice. This gives us the strength to bring Divine revelation to the world harmoniously, respecting the limitations that exist and yet gradually inspiring the world to overcome its limitations and become a "home for God below" (*Rabbi Menahem Mendel Schneerson, 20th century*).

spiritual vitamin

> Our intellect is created, and therefore limited within the boundaries of creation, beyond which it has no access. Consequently, it cannot know the ways and means that lead beyond those bounds. The Torah, on the other hand, is the bond that unites the created with the Creator, as it is written, *"But you—who remain attached to God, your God—are all alive today"* (Deuteronomy 4:4).

deuteronomy 4:48 – 5:9 — va-'ethannan

Arnon, to Mount Sion, which is (Mount) Hermon, ⁴⁹ and all the plain across the Jordan eastward as far as the Sea of the Plain, under the waterfalls of Pisgah.

Repetition of the Ten Commandments

5 [FOURTH READING] ¹ Moses called all Israel and said to them:

Listen, Israel, to the suprarational commands and rational commands which I am speaking in your ears today! Learn them, and be careful to observe them!

² God, our God, made a covenant with us in Horeb. ³ God did not make this covenant (only) with our ancestors, but with us, all of us who are here alive today. ⁴ At the mountain, God spoke with you from the fire face to face. ⁵ On that occasion, I stood between God and you, to tell you the word of God, since you were afraid of the fire, and you did not go up on the mountain.

(God spoke to you,) saying:

❖ ⁶ "I am God, (the) God (of every one) of you, Who took you out of the land of Egypt, out of the house of bondage."

❖ ⁷ "You shall not (possess an idol) of other deities (so long as I exist). ⁸ You shall not make for yourself a sculptured image or any picture of that which is in the heavens above, which is on the earth below, or which is in the water beneath the earth. ⁹ You shall not bow down before them nor worship them, for I, God, your God, am

---

5:5 I stood between God and you. It is the *"I"*—the conscious recognition of self—which stands between man and his Creator.

By taking pride in your accomplishments, you are effectively denying God's true existence, for man is nothing but for the Godly life-force that sustains him.

Recognize your non-existence, and you will be able to approach God (Rabbi Jehiel Mikhel of Zloczow, 18th century).

Saying. God's purpose in creating the world was to enable a fusion of spirit and matter. Since God created the world in a manner that it is predominantly material, our task—generally speaking—is to infuse it with a higher purpose, and to reveal the inner, spiritual core which pulsates within every one of God's creations.

There is, however, a danger in "overdosing" the world with too much spirit, beyond what it can comfortably absorb. We must never forget that the goal is a *unity* of matter and spirit, where the physical world is "at home" with its Creator. We need to invigorate and inspire our world, not burn or blind it with a light that is too intense.

From where do we derive the sensitivity to achieve this difficult balance?

Food for thought

1. Can you name a few contemporary "equivalents" of idolatry?

2. Is anything more important to you than God?

3. What is wrong with making an image of God?

דברים ה:ט-כ ואתחנן

יְהֹוָה אֱלֹהֶ֗יךָ אֵ֣ל קַנָּ֔א פֹּ֠קֵד עֲוֺ֨ן אָב֧וֹת עַל־בָּנִ֛ים וְעַל־שִׁלֵּשִׁ֥ים וְעַל־רִבֵּעִ֖ים לְשֹׂנְאָֽי׃ 10 וְעֹ֥שֶׂה חֶ֖סֶד לַאֲלָפִ֑ים לְאֹהֲבַ֖י וּלְשֹׁמְרֵ֥י [מצותו כ׳] מִצְוֺתָֽי׃ ס 11 לֹ֥א תִשָּׂ֛א אֶת־שֵֽׁם־יְהֹוָ֥ה אֱלֹהֶ֖יךָ לַשָּׁ֑וְא כִּ֣י לֹ֤א יְנַקֶּה֙ יְהֹוָ֔ה אֵ֛ת אֲשֶׁר־יִשָּׂ֥א אֶת־שְׁמ֖וֹ לַשָּֽׁוְא׃ ס 12 שָׁמ֣וֹר אֶת־י֤וֹם הַשַּׁבָּת֙ לְקַדְּשׁ֔וֹ כַּאֲשֶׁ֥ר צִוְּךָ֖ יְהֹוָ֥ה אֱלֹהֶֽיךָ׃ 13 שֵׁ֤שֶׁת יָמִים֙ תַּֽעֲבֹ֔ד וְעָשִׂ֖יתָ כׇּל־מְלַאכְתֶּֽךָ׃ 14 וְי֨וֹם֙ הַשְּׁבִיעִ֔י שַׁבָּ֖ת ׀ לַיהֹוָ֣ה אֱלֹהֶ֑יךָ לֹ֣א תַעֲשֶׂ֣ה כׇל־מְלָאכָ֡ה אַתָּ֣ה וּבִנְךָ־וּ֠בִתֶּ֠ךָ וְעַבְדְּךָֽ־וַ֠אֲמָתֶ֠ךָ וְשׁוֹרְךָ֨ וַחֲמֹרְךָ֜ וְכׇל־בְּהֶמְתֶּ֗ךָ וְגֵֽרְךָ֙ אֲשֶׁ֣ר בִּשְׁעָרֶ֔יךָ לְמַ֗עַן יָנ֛וּחַ עַבְדְּךָ֥ וַאֲמָתְךָ֖ כָּמֽוֹךָ׃ 15 וְזָכַרְתָּ֗ כִּי־עֶ֤בֶד הָיִ֙יתָ֙ בְּאֶ֣רֶץ מִצְרַ֔יִם וַיֹּצִ֨אֲךָ֜ יְהֹוָ֤ה אֱלֹהֶ֙יךָ֙ מִשָּׁ֔ם בְּיָ֥ד חֲזָקָ֖ה וּבִזְרֹ֣עַ נְטוּיָ֑ה עַל־כֵּ֗ן צִוְּךָ֙ יְהֹוָ֣ה אֱלֹהֶ֔יךָ לַעֲשׂ֖וֹת אֶת־י֥וֹם הַשַּׁבָּֽת׃ ס 16 כַּבֵּ֤ד אֶת־אָבִ֙יךָ֙ וְאֶת־אִמֶּ֔ךָ כַּאֲשֶׁ֥ר צִוְּךָ֖ יְהֹוָ֣ה אֱלֹהֶ֑יךָ לְמַ֣עַן ׀ יַאֲרִיכֻ֣ן יָמֶ֗יךָ וּלְמַ֙עַן֙ יִ֣יטַב לָ֔ךְ עַ֚ל הָֽאֲדָמָ֔ה אֲשֶׁר־יְהֹוָ֥ה אֱלֹהֶ֖יךָ נֹתֵ֥ן לָֽךְ׃ ס 17 לֹ֥֖א תִּֿרְצָֽח׃ ס וְלֹ֣֖א תִּֿנְאָֽ֑ף׃ ס וְלֹ֣֖א תִּֿגְנֹֽ֔ב׃ ס וְלֹֽא־תַעֲנֶ֥ה בְרֵעֲךָ֖ עֵ֥ד שָֽׁוְא׃ ס 18 וְלֹ֥א תַחְמֹ֖ד אֵ֣שֶׁת רֵעֶ֑ךָ ס וְלֹ֨א תִתְאַוֶּ֜ה בֵּ֣ית רֵעֶ֗ךָ שָׂדֵ֜הוּ וְעַבְדּ֤וֹ וַאֲמָתוֹ֙ שׁוֹר֣וֹ וַחֲמֹר֔וֹ וְכֹ֖ל אֲשֶׁ֥ר לְרֵעֶֽךָ׃ ס 19 אֶֽת־הַדְּבָרִ֣ים הָאֵ֡לֶּה דִּבֶּר֩ יְהֹוָ֨ה אֶל־כׇּל־קְהַלְכֶ֜ם בָּהָ֗ר מִתּ֤וֹךְ הָאֵשׁ֙ הֶֽעָנָ֣ן וְהָֽעֲרָפֶ֔ל ק֥וֹל גָּד֖וֹל וְלֹ֣א יָסָ֑ף וַֽיִּכְתְּבֵ֗ם עַל־שְׁנֵי֙ לֻחֹ֣ת אֲבָנִ֔ים וַֽיִּתְּנֵ֖ם אֵלָֽי׃ 20 וַיְהִ֗י כְּשׇׁמְעֲכֶ֤ם אֶת־הַקּוֹל֙ מִתּ֣וֹךְ הַחֹ֔שֶׁךְ וְהָהָ֖ר בֹּעֵ֣ר בָּאֵ֑שׁ [FIFTH READING]

kabbalah bites

5:16 While you are related to your parents in body, your souls did not necessarily come from the same spiritual "family." In fact, sometimes an extremely lofty soul will be born to very undeserving parents.

If your soul is unrelated to your parents, why do you have to honor them? Because every soul, no matter how lofty, has a *levush*, a spiritual "garment" or "container" which acts as an interface between soul and body. And that "garment" is *always* related to your parents' souls.

deuteronomy 5:9–20 — va-ʾethannan

a God who is zealous (to exact punishment), who visits the iniquity of the fathers upon the sons, upon the third and the fourth generation of those who (continue in their fathers' ways) hate Me. [10] But I act kindly to those who love Me and to those who keep My commandments for two thousand generations."

❖ [11] "You shall not take the name of God, your God, in vain, for God will not absolve anyone who takes His name in vain."

❖ [12] "Guard the Sabbath day to sanctify it, as God commanded you (at Marah, before the giving of the Torah). [13] Six days you may work and perform all your labor, [14] but the seventh day is a Sabbath to God, your God. You shall perform no labor, neither you, your son, your daughter, your manservant, your maidservant, your ox, your donkey, nor all your (other) animals, and your convert who is within your gates, so that your manservant and maidservant may rest like you. [15] You should remember that you were a slave in the land of Egypt, and that God, your God, took you out from there with a strong hand and an outstretched arm (in order that you serve Him). Therefore, God, your God, has commanded you to make the Sabbath day."

❖ [16] "Honor your father and your mother, as God commanded you (at Marah), in order that your days will be lengthened on the land that God, your God, is giving you."

❖ [17] "You shall not murder."

❖ "You shall not commit adultery."

❖ "You shall not steal (people, i.e., kidnap)."

❖ "You shall not bear false witness against your neighbor."

❖ [18] "You shall not covet your neighbor's wife. You shall not desire your neighbor's house, his field, his manservant, his maidservant, his ox, his donkey, or whatever belongs to your neighbor."

Aftermath of the Revelation at Sinai

[FIFTH READING] [19] God spoke these words to your entire assembly at the mountain from the fire, the cloud, and the fog, with a great voice, which did not stop (for breath). He inscribed them on two stone tablets and gave them to me.

[20] Then, when you heard the voice from the darkness, and the mountain was burning with fire, all the heads of your tribes and your elders approached me

---

19. A great voice, which did not stop. At the giving of the Torah the voice of God had no echo (*Exodus Rabbah*).

An echo can lead you to imagine that there are two people speaking. When God spoke, there was no echo, so that no one would make the mistake that there are two gods (*Rabbi Jacob Moses Hellin, 17th century*).

דברים ה:כ - ו:ג | ואתחנן

וַתִּקְרְב֣וּן אֵלַ֔י כָּל־רָאשֵׁ֥י שִׁבְטֵיכֶ֖ם וְזִקְנֵיכֶ֑ם: 21 וַתֹּאמְר֗וּ הֵ֣ן הֶרְאָ֜נוּ יְהוָ֤ה אֱלֹהֵ֙ינוּ֙ אֶת־כְּבֹד֣וֹ וְאֶת־גָּדְל֔וֹ וְאֶת־קֹל֥וֹ שָׁמַ֖עְנוּ מִתּ֣וֹךְ הָאֵ֑שׁ הַיּ֤וֹם הַזֶּה֙ רָאִ֔ינוּ כִּֽי־יְדַבֵּ֧ר אֱלֹהִ֛ים אֶת־הָֽאָדָ֖ם וָחָֽי: 22 וְעַתָּה֙ לָ֣מָּה נָמ֔וּת כִּ֣י תֹֽאכְלֵ֔נוּ הָאֵ֥שׁ הַגְּדֹלָ֖ה הַזֹּ֑את אִם־יֹסְפִ֣ים | אֲנַ֗חְנוּ לִ֠שְׁמֹ֠עַ אֶת־ק֨וֹל יְהוָ֧ה אֱלֹהֵ֛ינוּ ע֖וֹד וָמָֽתְנוּ: 23 כִּ֣י מִ֣י כָל־בָּשָׂ֡ר אֲשֶׁ֣ר שָׁמַ֣ע קוֹל֩ אֱלֹהִ֨ים חַיִּ֜ים מְדַבֵּ֧ר מִתּוֹךְ־הָאֵ֛שׁ כָּמֹ֖נוּ וַיֶּֽחִי: 24 קְרַ֤ב אַתָּה֙ וּֽשֲׁמָ֔ע אֵ֛ת כָּל־אֲשֶׁ֥ר יֹאמַ֖ר יְהוָ֣ה אֱלֹהֵ֑ינוּ וְאַ֣תְּ | תְּדַבֵּ֣ר אֵלֵ֗ינוּ אֵת֩ כָּל־אֲשֶׁ֨ר יְדַבֵּ֜ר יְהוָ֧ה אֱלֹהֵ֛ינוּ אֵלֶ֖יךָ וְשָׁמַ֥עְנוּ וְעָשִֽׂינוּ: 25 וַיִּשְׁמַ֤ע יְהוָה֙ אֶת־ק֣וֹל דִּבְרֵיכֶ֔ם בְּדַבֶּרְכֶ֖ם אֵלָ֑י וַיֹּ֨אמֶר יְהוָ֜ה אֵלַ֗י שָׁ֠מַ֠עְתִּי אֶת־ק֨וֹל דִּבְרֵ֜י הָעָ֤ם הַזֶּה֙ אֲשֶׁ֣ר דִּבְּר֣וּ אֵלֶ֔יךָ הֵיטִ֖יבוּ כָּל־אֲשֶׁ֥ר דִּבֵּֽרוּ: 26 מִֽי־יִתֵּ֡ן וְהָיָה֩ לְבָבָ֨ם זֶ֜ה לָהֶ֗ם לְיִרְאָ֥ה אֹתִ֛י וְלִשְׁמֹ֥ר אֶת־כָּל־מִצְוֺתַ֖י כָּל־הַיָּמִ֑ים לְמַ֨עַן יִיטַ֥ב לָהֶ֛ם וְלִבְנֵיהֶ֖ם לְעֹלָֽם: 27 לֵ֖ךְ אֱמֹ֣ר לָהֶ֑ם שׁ֥וּבוּ לָכֶ֖ם לְאָהֳלֵיכֶֽם: 28 וְאַתָּ֗ה פֹּה֮ עֲמֹ֣ד עִמָּדִי֒ וַאֲדַבְּרָ֣ה אֵלֶ֗יךָ אֵ֧ת כָּל־הַמִּצְוָ֛ה וְהַחֻקִּ֥ים וְהַמִּשְׁפָּטִ֖ים אֲשֶׁ֣ר תְּלַמְּדֵ֑ם וְעָשׂ֣וּ בָאָ֔רֶץ אֲשֶׁ֧ר אָנֹכִ֛י נֹתֵ֥ן לָהֶ֖ם לְרִשְׁתָּֽהּ: 29 וּשְׁמַרְתֶּ֣ם לַעֲשׂ֔וֹת כַּאֲשֶׁ֥ר צִוָּ֛ה יְהוָ֥ה אֱלֹהֵיכֶ֖ם אֶתְכֶ֑ם לֹ֥א תָסֻ֖רוּ יָמִ֥ין וּשְׂמֹֽאל: 30 בְּכָל־הַדֶּ֗רֶךְ אֲשֶׁ֨ר צִוָּ֜ה יְהוָ֧ה אֱלֹהֵיכֶ֛ם אֶתְכֶ֖ם תֵּלֵ֑כוּ לְמַ֤עַן תִּֽחְיוּן֙ וְט֣וֹב לָכֶ֔ם וְהַאֲרַכְתֶּ֣ם יָמִ֔ים בָּאָ֖רֶץ אֲשֶׁ֥ר תִּֽירָשֽׁוּן:

ו 1 וְזֹ֣את הַמִּצְוָ֗ה הַֽחֻקִּים֙ וְהַמִּשְׁפָּטִ֔ים אֲשֶׁ֥ר צִוָּ֛ה יְהוָ֥ה אֱלֹהֵיכֶ֖ם לְלַמֵּ֣ד אֶתְכֶ֑ם לַעֲשׂ֣וֹת בָּאָ֔רֶץ אֲשֶׁ֥ר אַתֶּ֛ם עֹבְרִ֥ים שָׁ֖מָּה לְרִשְׁתָּֽהּ: 2 לְמַ֨עַן תִּירָ֜א אֶת־יְהוָ֣ה אֱלֹהֶ֗יךָ לִ֠שְׁמֹ֠ר אֶת־כָּל־חֻקֹּתָ֣יו וּמִצְוֺתָיו֮ אֲשֶׁ֣ר אָנֹכִ֣י מְצַוֶּךָ֒ אַתָּה֙ וּבִנְךָ֣ וּבֶן־בִּנְךָ֔ כֹּ֖ל יְמֵ֣י חַיֶּ֑יךָ וּלְמַ֖עַן יַאֲרִכֻ֥ן יָמֶֽיךָ: 3 וְשָׁמַעְתָּ֤ יִשְׂרָאֵל֙ וְשָׁמַרְתָּ֣ לַעֲשׂ֔וֹת אֲשֶׁר֙ יִיטַ֣ב לְךָ֔ וַאֲשֶׁ֥ר תִּרְבּ֖וּן מְאֹ֑ד כַּאֲשֶׁר֩ דִּבֶּ֨ר יְהוָ֜ה אֱלֹהֵ֤י אֲבֹתֶ֙יךָ֙ לָ֔ךְ

deuteronomy 5:21 – 6:3 — va-'ethannan

²¹ and said, "Look! God, our God, has shown us His glory and His greatness, and we heard His voice from the fire. We saw today that God speaks with man, and (yet) he can still live. ²² But why should we now die? For if we continue to hear the voice of God, our God, any longer, this great fire will consume us and we will die! ²³ What (mortal of) flesh (and blood) has heard the voice of the living God speaking from the fire, as we have, and lived? ²⁴ You should approach (God) and listen to everything that God, our God, says, and then you can tell us everything that God, our God, tells you. We will listen and obey."

²⁵ God heard what you said when you spoke to me. God said to me, "I have heard what the people said when they spoke to you. Everything that they said to you is good. ²⁶ If only their hearts would remain like this, fearing Me and keeping all My commandments eternally, so that things would be good for them and their children forever! ²⁷ Go and say to them, 'Return to your tents.' ²⁸ You, however, must remain here with Me, and I will tell you the entire body of commandments, the suprational commands and the rational commands, which you will teach them, so that they can observe them in the land which I am giving them to possess."

²⁹ Be careful about observing them, as God, your God, has commanded you. Do not deviate to the right or to the left. ³⁰ Follow along the complete path which God, your God, has commanded you, so that you will live and prosper, and your days will be lengthened in the land that you will possess.

6 ¹ This is the body of commandments, the suprational commands and the rational commands, that God, your God, commanded (me) to teach you, to be performed in the land which you are about to enter and possess. ² (This is) so that you should fear God, your God, and keep all His suprational commands and His commandments that I am commanding you, all the days of your life—(both) you, your son, and your son's son—in order that your days be lengthened. ³ You should listen, Israel, and be careful to do what is good for you, so that you will increase greatly,

Food for thought

1. How will you impart to your children a love for Torah?

2. How can we overcome the "generation gap" when communicating Torah?

3. How can we make Torah exciting for children exposed to modern culture?

---

27. Go and say to them, "Return to your tents." After the extremely uplifting experience of Sinai, God instructed the people to *"return to your tents."*

While the outpouring of emotion at times of revelation is laudable, the real challenge is to draw upon those moments of awakening and bring them into your home, applying them to the mundane chores of life (*Rabbi Simhah Bunem of Przysucha, 18ᵗʰ–19ᵗʰ century*).

דברים ו:ג-ט · ואתחנן

אֶרֶץ זָבַת חָלָב וּדְבָשׁ: פ 4 [SIXTH READING] שְׁמַע יִשְׂרָאֵל יְהֹוָה אֱלֹהֵינוּ יְהֹוָה | אֶחָד: 6 וְאָהַבְתָּ אֵת יְהֹוָה אֱלֹהֶיךָ בְּכָל־לְבָבְךָ וּבְכָל־נַפְשְׁךָ וּבְכָל־מְאֹדֶךָ: 7 וְהָיוּ הַדְּבָרִים הָאֵלֶּה אֲשֶׁר אָנֹכִי מְצַוְּךָ הַיּוֹם עַל־לְבָבֶךָ: וְשִׁנַּנְתָּם לְבָנֶיךָ וְדִבַּרְתָּ בָּם בְּשִׁבְתְּךָ בְּבֵיתֶךָ וּבְלֶכְתְּךָ בַדֶּרֶךְ וּבְשָׁכְבְּךָ וּבְקוּמֶךָ: 8 וּקְשַׁרְתָּם לְאוֹת עַל־יָדֶךָ וְהָיוּ לְטֹטָפֹת בֵּין עֵינֶיךָ: 9 וּכְתַבְתָּם עַל־מְזֻזוֹת בֵּיתֶךָ וּבִשְׁעָרֶיךָ: ס

To successfully impart a message to others, it is essential for the teacher to be firmly committed to that message. This thought is reflected here: If these words will *"be upon your heart"* (v. 6), then you can *"teach them thoroughly to your sons"* (Rabbi Moses Alshekh, 16th century).

To your sons. These are your students. We find universally that students are termed "sons" (Rashi, 11th century).

8. Totafot. These are the *tefillin* (phylacteries). They are called *"totafot"* because of the number of scrolls contained within them: *tat* in Coptic means "two" and *fot* in Phrygian means "two," making a total of four (Rashi, 11th century).

The commandment of *tefillin* has already been stated in *Exodus* 13:9. It is repeated here to stress that you must *"bind them"*—that *tefillin* must be secured tightly with a knot (Nahmanides, 13th century).

9. Write them on the doorposts of your house. Every person is obligated to be extremely cautious about *mezuzah* since it is a universally binding obligation. Then, every time you enter or leave you will encounter the unity of God—the holy name of God (Maimonides, 12th century).

kabbalah bites

6:4 Before observing a commandment, Kabbalists always say: *"This is for the sake of coupling the Holy One, blessed be He, with His Shekhinah."*

What, exactly, does it mean to "couple" different elements of God? And how does this square with the basic monotheistic idea that God is One?

We are speaking here, not about God Himself, but about His *emanations* and *expressions* which are known by different names. These expressions could broadly be divided into two groups: those which are *compatible* with the world; and those which are *incompatible*. The former we refer to as *Shekhinah*, which means "dwelling" below and taking expression through the world. The incompatible emanations are "Holy," aloof and beyond reach, even if they are actually right under your nose.

By observing a *holy* precept *in this world* we help to heal the rift between these emanations, and "couple" them together.

This is not a mere ritual. You are rendering the infinite finite!

deuteronomy 6:3–9   va-ʾethannan

just as God, the God of your fathers told you (that He would give you) a land flowing with milk and honey.

First Paragraph of the *Shema*

- [SIXTH READING] ⁴ Hear, O Israel! (Right now) God is our God (and the nations have their own gods, but in the future all will realize that) God is one.

- ⁵ Love God, your God, with all your heart, with all your soul, and with all your might. ⁶ (I.e.) these words, which I am commanding you today, shall be upon your heart.

- ⁷ Teach them thoroughly to your (students, who are like your) sons. Speak of them when you sit in your house and when you walk on the way.

- (Recite the *Shema*) when you lie down (at night) and when you get up (in the morning).

- ⁸ Bind them as a sign upon your hand, and they shall be *totafot* (*tefillin*/phylacteries) between your eyes.

- ⁹ Write them on the doorposts of your house and upon your (public) gates.

6:4 Hear, O Israel! God is our God, God is one. Man possesses two apparently contradictory elements, no less incompatible than matter and spirit, the counterpart of which in the physical world is matter and energy—the *yetzer ha-tov* (impulse to goodness) and *yetzer ha-raʿ* (impulse to evil).

But this incompatibility stands out only in the early stages of worship. Advancing in worship leads to a realization of the essential unity in human nature, rather like the advancement of science has led to an appreciation of the underlying unity of nature. *At a certain point, the yetzer ha-tov and yetzer ha-raʿ can become one—through the transformation of the yetzer ha-raʿ by and into the yetzer ha-tov.*

That is the goal of inner peace that we proclaim by saying, *"Hear, O Israel! God is our God, God is one" (Rabbi Menahem Mendel Schneerson, 20ᵗʰ century).*

5. Love God, your God, with all your heart. Do you really love God, or yourself? Perhaps you love Him because you expect some benefit from Him, either in this world or in the next? In that case, it is really yourself that you love, not God (*Rabbi Menahem Mendel Morgensztern of Kotsk, 19ᵗʰ century*).

With all your soul. Even if worshiping him means losing your life, your "soul." You must be prepared to sacrifice your life for the love of God (*Babylonian Talmud, Berakhot 54a*).

And with all your might (*me'odekha*). The Hebrew word *me'odekha* is generally translated as "your might," but it also conveys the meaning of *middah*—"measure" or "dimension." This means that you should love God regardless of the kind of "deal" you think is meted out to you by Divine Providence (*Babylonian Talmud, Berakhot 54a*).

7. Teach them thoroughly. Instead of the usual word for teaching—*ve-limmad'tam*—the term used here—*ve-shinnantam*—implies sharpness, indicating that the words of Torah ought to be "sharp" in your mouth in a way that you can recite them immediately, without hesitation (*Rashi, 11ᵗʰ century*).

דברים ו׃י-כה ואתחנן

10 וְהָיָ֞ה כִּ֥י יְבִיאֲךָ֣ ׀ יְהֹוָ֣ה אֱלֹהֶ֗יךָ אֶל־הָאָ֜רֶץ אֲשֶׁ֨ר נִשְׁבַּ֧ע לַאֲבֹתֶ֛יךָ לְאַבְרָהָ֧ם לְיִצְחָ֖ק וּֽלְיַעֲקֹ֑ב לָ֣תֶת לָ֑ךְ עָרִ֛ים גְּדֹלֹ֥ת וְטֹבֹ֖ת אֲשֶׁ֥ר לֹא־בָנִֽיתָ׃ 11 וּבָ֨תִּ֜ים מְלֵאִ֣ים כׇּל־טוּב֮ אֲשֶׁ֣ר לֹא־מִלֵּ֒אתָ֒ וּבֹרֹ֤ת חֲצוּבִים֙ אֲשֶׁ֣ר לֹא־חָצַ֔בְתָּ כְּרָמִ֥ים וְזֵיתִ֖ים אֲשֶׁ֣ר לֹא־נָטָ֑עְתָּ וְאָכַלְתָּ֖ וְשָׂבָֽעְתָּ׃ 12 הִשָּׁ֣מֶר לְךָ֔ פֶּן־תִּשְׁכַּ֖ח אֶת־יְהֹוָ֑ה אֲשֶׁ֧ר הוֹצִיאֲךָ֛ מֵאֶ֥רֶץ מִצְרַ֖יִם מִבֵּ֥ית עֲבָדִֽים׃ 13 אֶת־יְהֹוָ֧ה אֱלֹהֶ֛יךָ תִּירָ֖א וְאֹת֣וֹ תַעֲבֹ֑ד וּבִשְׁמ֖וֹ תִּשָּׁבֵֽעַ׃ 14 לֹ֣א תֵלְכ֔וּן אַחֲרֵ֖י אֱלֹהִ֣ים אֲחֵרִ֑ים מֵאֱלֹהֵי֙ הָֽעַמִּ֔ים אֲשֶׁ֖ר סְבִיבוֹתֵיכֶֽם׃ 15 כִּ֣י אֵ֥ל קַנָּ֛א יְהֹוָ֥ה אֱלֹהֶ֖יךָ בְּקִרְבֶּ֑ךָ פֶּן־יֶ֠חֱרֶ֠ה אַף־יְהֹוָ֤ה אֱלֹהֶ֙יךָ֙ בָּ֔ךְ וְהִשְׁמִ֣ידְךָ֔ מֵעַ֖ל פְּנֵ֥י הָאֲדָמָֽה׃ ס 16 לֹ֣א תְנַסּ֔וּ אֶת־יְהֹוָ֖ה אֱלֹהֵיכֶ֑ם כַּאֲשֶׁ֥ר נִסִּיתֶ֖ם בַּמַּסָּֽה׃ 17 שָׁמ֣וֹר תִּשְׁמְר֔וּן אֶת־מִצְוֺ֖ת יְהֹוָ֣ה אֱלֹהֵיכֶ֑ם וְעֵדֹתָ֥יו וְחֻקָּ֖יו אֲשֶׁ֥ר צִוָּֽךְ׃ 18 וְעָשִׂ֛יתָ הַיָּשָׁ֥ר וְהַטּ֖וֹב בְּעֵינֵ֣י יְהֹוָ֑ה לְמַ֙עַן֙ יִ֣יטַב לָ֔ךְ וּבָ֗אתָ וְיָרַשְׁתָּ֙ אֶת־הָאָ֣רֶץ הַטֹּבָ֔ה אֲשֶׁר־נִשְׁבַּ֥ע יְהֹוָ֖ה לַאֲבֹתֶֽיךָ׃ 19 לַהֲדֹ֥ף אֶת־כׇּל־אֹיְבֶ֖יךָ מִפָּנֶ֑יךָ כַּאֲשֶׁ֖ר דִּבֶּ֥ר יְהֹוָֽה׃ ס 20 כִּֽי־יִשְׁאָלְךָ֥ בִנְךָ֛ מָחָ֖ר לֵאמֹ֑ר מָ֣ה הָעֵדֹ֗ת וְהַֽחֻקִּים֙ וְהַמִּשְׁפָּטִ֔ים אֲשֶׁ֥ר צִוָּ֛ה יְהֹוָ֥ה אֱלֹהֵ֖ינוּ אֶתְכֶֽם׃ 21 וְאָמַרְתָּ֣ לְבִנְךָ֔ עֲבָדִ֛ים הָיִ֥ינוּ לְפַרְעֹ֖ה בְּמִצְרָ֑יִם וַיֹּצִיאֵ֧נוּ יְהֹוָ֛ה מִמִּצְרַ֖יִם בְּיָ֥ד חֲזָקָֽה׃ 22 וַיִּתֵּ֣ן יְהֹוָ֡ה אוֹתֹ֣ת וּ֠מֹפְתִ֠ים גְּדֹלִ֨ים וְרָעִ֧ים ׀ בְּמִצְרַ֛יִם בְּפַרְעֹ֥ה וּבְכׇל־בֵּית֖וֹ לְעֵינֵֽינוּ׃ 23 וְאוֹתָ֖נוּ הוֹצִ֣יא מִשָּׁ֑ם לְמַ֙עַן֙ הָבִ֣יא אֹתָ֔נוּ לָ֤תֶת לָ֙נוּ֙ אֶת־הָאָ֔רֶץ אֲשֶׁ֥ר נִשְׁבַּ֖ע לַאֲבֹתֵֽינוּ׃ 24 וַיְצַוֵּ֣נוּ יְהֹוָ֗ה לַעֲשׂוֹת֙ אֶת־כׇּל־הַחֻקִּ֣ים הָאֵ֔לֶּה לְיִרְאָ֖ה אֶת־יְהֹוָ֣ה אֱלֹהֵ֑ינוּ לְט֥וֹב לָ֙נוּ֙ כׇּל־הַיָּמִ֔ים לְחַיֹּתֵ֖נוּ כְּהַיּ֥וֹם הַזֶּֽה׃ 25 וּצְדָקָ֖ה תִּֽהְיֶה־לָּ֑נוּ כִּֽי־נִשְׁמֹ֨ר לַעֲשׂ֜וֹת אֶת־כׇּל־הַמִּצְוָ֣ה הַזֹּ֗את לִפְנֵ֛י יְהֹוָ֥ה אֱלֹהֵ֖ינוּ כַּאֲשֶׁ֥ר צִוָּֽנוּ׃ ס

18. You shall do what is proper and good in the eyes of God. This refers to compromise (*Rashi, 11th century*).

Although compromise does not exact real justice, we are taught that it is the preferred method, since it fosters a more peaceful arrangement among all those involved. It may not be perfectly just ("*proper*"), but it is "*good*" (*Rabbi David Pardo, 18th century*).

deuteronomy 6:10–25 — va-ʾethannan

Warning Not to Forget God

¹⁰ When God, your God, will bring you to the land He swore to your fathers—Abraham, Isaac, and Jacob—that He would give you, (you will find) great and good cities that you did not build, ¹¹ houses full of all good things that you did not fill (them with), reservoirs (in the rock) that you did not carve out, vineyards and olive trees that you did not plant—and you will eat and be satisfied. ¹² But beware not to forget God, who brought you out of the land of Egypt, out of the house of slavery.

¹³ You should fear God, your God, worship Him, and (only on this condition may you) swear by His name. ¹⁴ Do not go after other gods, the gods of the nations who are around you, ¹⁵ so that the anger of God, your God, does not become kindled against you, leading Him to destroy you off the face of the earth. For God, your God, who is among you, is a jealous God ¹⁶ Do not test God, your God, as you tested Him in Masah.

¹⁷ You should always be careful to observe the commands of God, your God, His testimonies and His suprarational commands, which He has commanded you. ¹⁸ You shall do what is proper and good in the eyes of God, in order that you prosper, and so that you will come and possess the good land which God swore to your forefathers, ¹⁹ driving out all your enemies from before you, as God has said.

Remembering the Exodus

²⁰ In the future, when your son asks you, saying, "What are the testimonies, the suprarational commands, and the rational commands, which God, our God, has commanded you?"

²¹ You should say to your son, "We were slaves to Pharaoh in Egypt, and God took us out of Egypt with a strong hand. ²² God enacted great and terrifying signs and wonders upon Egypt, Pharaoh, and his entire household, before our eyes. ²³ He brought us out of there, in order that He might bring us to the land which He swore to our fathers, and give it to us. ²⁴ God commanded us to perform all these suprarational commands, to fear God, our God, so (He could) give us good all the time, and keep us alive, as (we are) today. ²⁵ It is a merit for us that we are careful to observe all these commandments before God, our God, as He has commanded us."

spiritual vitamin

> If it were a valid argument to do what others do, or even what the majority does, Jews who are, and always have been, in the minority would have long ago disappeared from the face of the earth.

דברים ז:א–יא ואתחנן

[SEVENTH READING] א כִּ֤י יְבִֽיאֲךָ֙ יְהֹוָ֣ה אֱלֹהֶ֔יךָ אֶל־הָאָ֕רֶץ אֲשֶׁר־אַתָּ֥ה בָא־שָׁ֖מָּה לְרִשְׁתָּ֑הּ וְנָשַׁ֣ל גּוֹיִֽם־רַבִּ֣ים ׀ מִפָּנֶ֡יךָ הַֽחִתִּי֩ וְהַגִּרְגָּשִׁ֨י וְהָאֱמֹרִ֜י וְהַכְּנַעֲנִ֣י וְהַפְּרִזִּ֗י וְהַֽחִוִּי֙ וְהַיְבוּסִ֔י שִׁבְעָ֣ה גוֹיִ֔ם רַבִּ֥ים וַעֲצוּמִ֖ים מִמֶּֽךָּ: ב וּנְתָנָ֞ם יְהֹוָ֧ה אֱלֹהֶ֛יךָ לְפָנֶ֖יךָ וְהִכִּיתָ֑ם הַחֲרֵ֤ם תַּחֲרִים֙ אֹתָ֔ם לֹא־תִכְרֹ֥ת לָהֶ֛ם בְּרִ֖ית וְלֹ֥א תְחָנֵּֽם: ג וְלֹ֥א תִתְחַתֵּ֖ן בָּ֑ם בִּתְּךָ֙ לֹא־תִתֵּ֣ן לִבְנ֔וֹ וּבִתּ֖וֹ לֹא־תִקַּ֥ח לִבְנֶֽךָ: ד כִּֽי־יָסִ֤יר אֶת־בִּנְךָ֙ מֵֽאַחֲרַ֔י וְעָבְד֖וּ אֱלֹהִ֣ים אֲחֵרִ֑ים וְחָרָ֤ה אַף־יְהֹוָה֙ בָּכֶ֔ם וְהִשְׁמִֽידְךָ֖ מַהֵֽר: ה כִּֽי־אִם־כֹּ֤ה תַעֲשׂוּ֙ לָהֶ֔ם מִזְבְּחֹתֵיהֶ֣ם תִּתֹּ֔צוּ וּמַצֵּבֹתָ֖ם תְּשַׁבֵּ֑רוּ וַאֲשֵֽׁירֵהֶם֙ תְּגַדֵּע֔וּן וּפְסִילֵיהֶ֖ם תִּשְׂרְפ֥וּן בָּאֵֽשׁ: ו כִּ֣י עַ֤ם קָדוֹשׁ֙ אַתָּ֔ה לַיהֹוָ֖ה אֱלֹהֶ֑יךָ בְּךָ֞ בָּחַ֣ר ׀ יְהֹוָ֣ה אֱלֹהֶ֗יךָ לִהְי֥וֹת לוֹ֙ לְעַ֣ם סְגֻלָּ֔ה מִכֹּל֙ הָֽעַמִּ֔ים אֲשֶׁ֖ר עַל־פְּנֵ֥י הָאֲדָמָֽה: ז לֹ֣א מֵֽרֻבְּכֶ֞ם מִכׇּל־הָֽעַמִּ֗ים חָשַׁ֧ק יְהֹוָ֛ה בָּכֶ֖ם וַיִּבְחַ֣ר בָּכֶ֑ם כִּֽי־אַתֶּ֥ם הַמְעַ֖ט מִכׇּל־הָעַמִּֽים: ח כִּי֩ מֵאַֽהֲבַ֨ת יְהֹוָ֜ה אֶתְכֶ֗ם וּמִשׇּׁמְר֤וֹ אֶת־הַשְּׁבֻעָה֙ אֲשֶׁ֤ר נִשְׁבַּע֙ לַאֲבֹ֣תֵיכֶ֔ם הוֹצִ֧יא יְהֹוָ֛ה אֶתְכֶ֖ם בְּיָ֣ד חֲזָקָ֑ה וַֽיִּפְדְּךָ֙ מִבֵּ֣ית עֲבָדִ֔ים מִיַּ֖ד פַּרְעֹ֥ה מֶֽלֶךְ־מִצְרָֽיִם: [MAFTIR] ט וְיָ֣דַעְתָּ֔ כִּֽי־יְהֹוָ֥ה אֱלֹהֶ֖יךָ ה֣וּא הָֽאֱלֹהִ֑ים הָאֵל֙ הַנֶּֽאֱמָ֔ן שֹׁמֵ֧ר הַבְּרִ֣ית וְהַחֶ֗סֶד לְאֹהֲבָ֛יו וּלְשֹׁמְרֵ֥י מִצְוֺתָ֖ו לְאֶ֥לֶף דּֽוֹר: י וּמְשַׁלֵּ֧ם לְשֹׂנְאָ֛יו אֶל־פָּנָ֖יו לְהַאֲבִיד֑וֹ לֹ֤א יְאַחֵר֙ לְשֹׂ֣נְא֔וֹ אֶל־פָּנָ֖יו יְשַׁלֶּם־לֽוֹ: יא וְשָׁמַרְתָּ֣ אֶת־הַמִּצְוָ֗ה וְאֶת־הַֽחֻקִּים֙ וְאֶת־הַמִּשְׁפָּטִ֔ים אֲשֶׁ֧ר אָנֹכִ֛י מְצַוְּךָ֥ הַיּ֖וֹם לַעֲשׂתָֽם: פ פ פ

קי"ח פסוקים, עזיא"ל סימן.

(b) The reward comes "miraculously"—the commandment and its reward are not in a "cause and effect" relationship. Rather, the reward must be generated independently, rather like rewards from one human being to another, which are awarded willingly (and not automatically) (*Rabbi Isaiah Horowitz, 16th–17th century*).

The first approach ("a") is the method by which we receive rewards in the current era. Since they come "automatically," they are simply "received" by their recipients. However, the rewards of the future era will not be a natural consequence of our deeds, but rather, like a separate "miracle" that is generated by God. Since the process of reward will be an additional activity by God, it will require an additional act from ourselves, that of "taking" the reward. That is why *Rashi* stresses, "in the world to come, you will *take* the reward for observing them" (*Rabbi Menahem Mendel Schneerson, 20th century*).

deuteronomy 7:1–11   va-'ethannan

Entering the Land

7 [SEVENTH READING] ¹ When God, your God, brings you into the land which you are going to enter and possess, He will drive away many nations from before you: the Hittites, the Girgashites, the Amorites, the Canaanites, the Perizzites, the Hivites, and the Jebusites—seven nations more numerous and powerful than you.

❖ ² God, your God, will deliver them to you, and you will defeat them. You must destroy them completely. Do not make a treaty with them. Do not admire them (in any way).

❖ ³ You must not intermarry with them. You must not give your daughter to their sons, and you must not take their daughters for your son. ⁴ For (one of their sons) will turn away your (grand)son from following Me, and they will worship other gods. Then God's anger will be kindled against you, and He will quickly destroy you.

⁵ This is what you should do to them: You should demolish their altars, smash their monuments, cut down their idolatrous trees, and burn their statues in fire. ⁶ For you are a holy people to God, your God. God, your God, has chosen you from all the peoples upon the face of the earth to be His treasured people. ⁷ God did not desire you and choose you because you are more numerous than all the other nations, for you are (in fact) the smallest of all the nations. ⁸ Rather, God took you out with a strong hand and redeemed you from the house of slavery, from the hand of Pharaoh, the king of Egypt, because of God's love for you, and because He is keeping the oath that He swore to your forefathers.

[MAFTIR] ⁹ You should know that God, your God, is the Almighty God, the faithful God, who upholds the covenant and (rewards acts of) kindness to those who (observe) His (commands out of) love and (those who) keep His commandments (out of fear) for a thousand generations. ¹⁰ He causes (each of) those who hate Him to perish (in the world to come) by paying (him fully in this world) to his face (for any good that he has done). He will not delay (payment to) the one who hates Him. He will repay him to his face.

¹¹ You should keep the body of commandments, the suprarational commands and the rational commands, which I am commanding you to observe today.

The Haftarah for Va-'Ethannan is on page 1396.

7:11 To observe today. For "tomorrow" in the world to come, you will take the reward for observing them (*Rashi, 11ᵗʰ century*).

There are two ways of understanding the mechanism by which rewards are given for observing the commandments: (a) the reward comes "naturally"—God created the universe in a way that the observance of a commandment automatically opens spiritual channels that bring you positive results.

We are at the **heel** (*'ekev*) **of history,** right before the New Era. **Step forward** and leave your footprints as a **trailblazer!** Do something **spectacular;** the moment requires it.

'EKEV
עקב

REWARDS FOR COMMANDMENTS	7:12-16
NOT TO FEAR THE NATIONS	7:17-26
LESSONS FROM THE DESERT JOURNEY	8:1 – 9:6
THE GOLDEN CALF	9:7 – 10:11
DUTIES TO GOD	10:12-22
PAST MIRACULOUS EXPERIENCES	11:1-9
QUALITIES OF THE PROMISED LAND	11:10-12
SECOND PARAGRAPH OF THE *SHEMA*	11:13-21
KEYS TO CONQUEST OF THE LAND	11:22-25

NAME
'Ekev

MEANING
"As a result," "heel"

LINES IN TORAH SCROLL
232

PARASHIYYOT
6 open; 4 closed

VERSES
111

WORDS
1747

LETTERS
6865

MITZVOT
6 positive; 2 prohibitions

DATE
Shevat–Adar, 2488

LOCATION
Plains of Moab

MASORETIC FEATURES
Missing letter *alef* in the word *me-reshit* (11:12)

CHARACTER PROFILE

NAME
Aaron

MEANING
"Mountain," "shining"

PARENTS
Amram and Jochebed

GRANDFATHERS
Levi, Kohath

SIBLINGS
Miriam, Moses

WIFE
Elisheba, sister of Nahshon ben Amminadab

CHILDREN
Nadab, Abihu, Eleazar, Ithamar

LIFE SPAN
123 years

BURIAL PLACE
Mount Hor

ACHIEVEMENTS
Prophesied about the redemption for 80 years before Moses came to Egypt; was Moses' spokesman; was equal to Moses; was the High Priest; did not question God when his sons died; successful marital counselor and arbiter; died through a Divine "kiss"

KNOWN FOR
Initiated three of the Ten Plagues; attempted to stop the creation of the Golden Calf but ended up assisting; clouds of glory were in his merit; mourned by entire house of Israel for thirty days

APPRECIATION

Our everyday blessings are easily overlooked. By thanking God after every meal, you train yourself to remain aware and appreciative of the good things in life (8:10).

BRIBERY

God does not accept bribes. Being good or charitable in one area does not exempt you from fixing those areas of your life and relationships that need repair (10:17).

STRANGERS

We must love the "stranger," finding compassion for the ignored, oppressed, silenced and abused. The notion of empathy for the underprivileged is a central theme running throughout the Torah (10:19).

עקב

דברים ז:יב-יח

12 וְהָיָ֣ה ׀ עֵ֣קֶב תִּשְׁמְע֗וּן אֵ֤ת הַמִּשְׁפָּטִים֙ הָאֵ֔לֶּה וּשְׁמַרְתֶּ֥ם וַעֲשִׂיתֶ֖ם אֹתָ֑ם וְשָׁמַר֩ יְהֹוָ֨ה אֱלֹהֶ֜יךָ לְךָ֗ אֶֽת־הַבְּרִית֙ וְאֶת־הַחֶ֔סֶד אֲשֶׁ֥ר נִשְׁבַּ֖ע לַאֲבֹתֶֽיךָ:
13 וַאֲהֵ֣בְךָ֔ וּבֵרַכְךָ֖ וְהִרְבֶּ֑ךָ וּבֵרַ֣ךְ פְּרִֽי־בִטְנְךָ֣ וּפְרִֽי־אַדְמָתֶ֗ךָ דְּגָנְךָ֤ וְתִירֹֽשְׁךָ֙ וְיִצְהָרֶ֔ךָ שְׁגַר־אֲלָפֶ֖יךָ וְעַשְׁתְּרֹ֣ת צֹאנֶ֑ךָ עַ֚ל הָֽאֲדָמָ֔ה אֲשֶׁר־נִשְׁבַּ֥ע לַאֲבֹתֶ֖יךָ לָ֥תֶת לָֽךְ:
14 בָּר֥וּךְ תִּֽהְיֶ֖ה מִכָּל־הָעַמִּ֑ים לֹא־יִהְיֶ֥ה בְךָ֛ עָקָ֥ר וַעֲקָרָ֖ה וּבִבְהֶמְתֶּֽךָ:
15 וְהֵסִ֧יר יְהֹוָ֛ה מִמְּךָ֖ כָּל־חֹ֑לִי וְכָל־מַדְוֵי֩ מִצְרַ֨יִם הָרָעִ֜ים אֲשֶׁ֣ר יָדַ֗עְתָּ לֹ֤א יְשִׂימָם֙ בָּ֔ךְ וּנְתָנָ֖ם בְּכָל־שֹׂנְאֶֽיךָ:
16 וְאָכַלְתָּ֣ אֶת־כָּל־הָ֣עַמִּ֗ים אֲשֶׁ֨ר יְהֹוָ֤ה אֱלֹהֶ֙יךָ֙ נֹתֵ֣ן לָ֔ךְ לֹא־תָחֹ֥ס עֵֽינְךָ֖ עֲלֵיהֶ֑ם וְלֹ֤א תַעֲבֹד֙ אֶת־אֱלֹ֣הֵיהֶ֔ם כִּֽי־מוֹקֵ֥שׁ ה֖וּא לָֽךְ: ס
17 כִּ֣י תֹאמַ֤ר בִּלְבָֽבְךָ֙ רַבִּ֛ים הַגּוֹיִ֥ם הָאֵ֖לֶּה מִמֶּ֑נִּי אֵיכָ֥ה אוּכַ֖ל לְהֽוֹרִישָֽׁם: 18 לֹ֥א תִירָ֖א מֵהֶ֑ם זָכֹ֣ר תִּזְכֹּ֗ר אֵ֤ת אֲשֶׁר־עָשָׂה֙ יְהֹוָ֣ה אֱלֹהֶ֔יךָ לְפַרְעֹ֖ה וּלְכָל־מִצְרָֽיִם:

Even so, God will not make *you* suffer from all of this. *"He will not give you any of the diseases"* in the first instance. Instead, *"He will give it to all your enemies"*—and seeing *them* suffer will bring about the desired reaction from you (*Rabbi Abraham Samuel Benjamin Sofer, 19th century*).

17. You might say to yourself, '"These nations are more numerous than us! How will we be able to drive them out?" The Torah is addressing a possible concern the people might have when going off to war. Do not be intimidated by the powerful enemy, because the Almighty will fight on your behalf (*Rashi, 11th century*).

This verse could be rendered, *"If you will say to yourself."* If you recognize that you cannot overcome your enemies by your own might alone, then *"do not fear them,"* because God will crush them just as He *"did to Pharaoh and to the whole of Egypt"* (v. 18). But if you believe that these nations are not more numerous than yourselves, that you have superior military intelligence and weaponry than them, then you *do* have cause to fear, for you have relinquished God's assistance (*Rabbi Eliezer b. Elijah Ashkenazi, 16th century*).

kabbalah bites

7:14-15 *"There will be no sterile male or barren female among you."* In the spiritual realm, there are two types of *Sefirot* through which blessings flow: masculine and feminine, "providers" and "recipients." Here we are blessed that both will be brimming with Divine flow.

"Or among your cattle." The flow will be so great that it will overpower even the *sitra' 'aḥara'* (demonic forces), which is the spiritual root of the animals.

"God will keep every sickness away from you." He will remove from *kedushah*, the side of holiness, all the parasitic forces which try to steal energy from it.

parashat ʿekev

Rewards for Observing the Commandments

¹² And what will happen is, as a result of your listening to (even the most neglected of) these laws, and your care in their observance, God, your God, will keep (His promise) to you: the covenant and the kindness that He swore to your fathers. ¹³ He will love you, bless you and multiply you. He will bless the fruit of your womb, the fruit of your soil, your grain, your wine, your oil, your cattle's offspring and the best of your flocks, in the land which He swore to your forefathers to give to you. ¹⁴ You will be blessed above all nations. There will be no sterile male or barren female among you or among your cattle. ¹⁵ God will keep every sickness away from you. He will not give you any of the diseases of Egypt which you experienced, (rather), He will give them to all your enemies.

¹⁶ You should annihilate all the nations which God, your God, delivers to you. Do not let your eye pity them, and do not worship their gods, for this is a tempting trap for you.

Not to Fear the Nations

¹⁷ You might say to yourself, "These nations are more numerous than us! How will we be able to drive them out?" ¹⁸ Do not fear them! You should always

---

7:12 As a result (ʿekev) of your listening. The Hebrew term used here for "as a result of" (ʿekev) can also mean "heel." *Before every step you take, listen*—search your soul to see whether it is for the sake of heaven. If the motive is for personal honor or to satisfy a physical craving, then that step should not be taken (*Rabbi Moses Leib of Sasov, 18th century*).

David said, "Master of the universe! I do not fear the important precepts of the Torah, because they are obviously important. I fear the minor precepts! Perhaps I was lax with them because they are minor, and You said, 'Be careful with a minor precept just like an important one.'"

Thus the verse says: *"In keeping them there is great reward—ʿekev rav"* (*Psalms* 19:12). And it is also written, *"Oh how great—rav—is Your goodness, which You have laid up for those who fear You"* (ibid., 31:20). This is the reward for observing "minor" precepts (*Midrash Tanḥuma*).

15. God will keep every sickness away (alt. "remove every sickness") from you. He will not give you any of the diseases. God will sometimes afflict a man with suffering so that he will mend his ways and re-connect with God, imploring God to remove the ailment.

But the same thing can be achieved by witnessing the suffering of *others*, which can inspire you in sincere prayer to God, that you and your loved ones should not suffer the same fate.

This is what the Torah is telling you here. After enjoying the abundant blessings detailed in the previous verses, it is possible that the recipients will no longer worship God with the same devotion as before, causing God to bring upon them "afflictions of love." Still, they are assured: *"God will remove every sickness."*

דברים ז:יט - ח:ב

19 הַמַּסֹּת הַגְּדֹלֹת אֲשֶׁר־רָאוּ עֵינֶיךָ וְהָאֹתֹת וְהַמֹּפְתִים וְהַיָּד הַחֲזָקָה וְהַזְּרֹעַ הַנְּטוּיָה אֲשֶׁר הוֹצִאֲךָ יְהֹוָה אֱלֹהֶיךָ כֵּן־יַעֲשֶׂה יְהֹוָה אֱלֹהֶיךָ לְכָל־הָעַמִּים אֲשֶׁר־אַתָּה יָרֵא מִפְּנֵיהֶם: 20 וְגַם אֶת־הַצִּרְעָה יְשַׁלַּח יְהֹוָה אֱלֹהֶיךָ בָּם עַד־אֲבֹד הַנִּשְׁאָרִים וְהַנִּסְתָּרִים מִפָּנֶיךָ: 21 לֹא תַעֲרֹץ מִפְּנֵיהֶם כִּי־יְהֹוָה אֱלֹהֶיךָ בְּקִרְבֶּךָ אֵל גָּדוֹל וְנוֹרָא: 22 וְנָשַׁל יְהֹוָה אֱלֹהֶיךָ אֶת־הַגּוֹיִם הָאֵל מִפָּנֶיךָ מְעַט מְעָט לֹא תוּכַל כַּלֹּתָם מַהֵר פֶּן־תִּרְבֶּה עָלֶיךָ חַיַּת הַשָּׂדֶה: 23 וּנְתָנָם יְהֹוָה אֱלֹהֶיךָ לְפָנֶיךָ וְהָמָם מְהוּמָה גְדֹלָה עַד הִשָּׁמְדָם: 24 וְנָתַן מַלְכֵיהֶם בְּיָדֶךָ וְהַאֲבַדְתָּ אֶת־שְׁמָם מִתַּחַת הַשָּׁמָיִם לֹא־יִתְיַצֵּב אִישׁ בְּפָנֶיךָ עַד הִשְׁמִדְךָ אֹתָם: 25 פְּסִילֵי אֱלֹהֵיהֶם תִּשְׂרְפוּן בָּאֵשׁ לֹא־תַחְמֹד כֶּסֶף וְזָהָב עֲלֵיהֶם וְלָקַחְתָּ לָךְ פֶּן תִּוָּקֵשׁ בּוֹ כִּי תוֹעֲבַת יְהֹוָה אֱלֹהֶיךָ הוּא: 26 וְלֹא־תָבִיא תוֹעֵבָה אֶל־בֵּיתֶךָ וְהָיִיתָ חֵרֶם כָּמֹהוּ שַׁקֵּץ ׀ תְּשַׁקְּצֶנּוּ וְתַעֵב ׀ תְּתַעֲבֶנּוּ כִּי־חֵרֶם הוּא: פ

ח 1 כָּל־הַמִּצְוָה אֲשֶׁר אָנֹכִי מְצַוְּךָ הַיּוֹם תִּשְׁמְרוּן לַעֲשׂוֹת לְמַעַן תִּחְיוּן וּרְבִיתֶם וּבָאתֶם וִירִשְׁתֶּם אֶת־הָאָרֶץ אֲשֶׁר־נִשְׁבַּע יְהֹוָה לַאֲבֹתֵיכֶם: 2 וְזָכַרְתָּ אֶת־כָּל־הַדֶּרֶךְ אֲשֶׁר הוֹלִיכֲךָ יְהֹוָה אֱלֹהֶיךָ זֶה אַרְבָּעִים שָׁנָה בַּמִּדְבָּר לְמַעַן עַנֹּתְךָ לְנַסֹּתְךָ לָדַעַת אֶת־אֲשֶׁר בִּלְבָבְךָ הֲתִשְׁמֹר מִצְוֺתָו אִם־לֹא:

spiritual vitamin

" In the case of a human king, one can never be certain that the task he assigns is all for good, or that it can be carried out fully, or that he can fully keep his promise of reward. All this, of course, does not apply in the case of a Divine command. "

remember what God, your God, did to Pharaoh and to the whole of Egypt: [19] the great proofs (of true power) that your eyes saw, the signs (of God's direct involvement), the wondrous (plagues), the mighty hand (of God that brought disease to Egyptian cattle), and the outstretched arm (that killed the firstborn), with which God, your God, brought you out. God, your God, will do likewise to all the nations whom you fear. [20] God, your God, will also send swarms of hornets upon them, until the survivors and those who hide from you are destroyed.

[21] Do not be demoralized by them, because God, your God—a great and awesome God—is among you. [22] Little by little God, your God, will drive away those nations from before you. You will not be able to destroy them quickly, for then there might be too many wild animals for you to contend with.

[23] God, your God, will deliver them to you, and He will drive them crazy until they are destroyed. [24] He will deliver their kings into your hand, and you will eradicate their names from beneath the skies. Nobody will stand up against you, until you have destroyed them.

Eradication of Idolatry

[25] You should burn the statues of their gods in fire.

- ❖ Do not covet the silver or gold that is on them and take it for yourself, so that you are not tempted (to idolatry) by it, for it is an abomination to God, your God.

- ❖ [26] Do not bring any abominable (idol) into your house, for then you will become liable to destruction, like it.

You should utterly detest it, and utterly abhor it, for it is something to be destroyed.

Remembering the Forty Years in the Desert

8 [1] You should safeguard the observance of all the commandment(s) that I am commanding you today, so that you will live, multiply, and come to possess the land that God swore to your forefathers. [2] You should remember the entire path along which God, your God, led you these forty years in the desert, in order to afflict you. It was to test you, to find out what is in your heart: Would you keep

---

8:1 All the commandment(s). If you have started a commandment, finish it, because only the one who completes it is credited with the commandment—as the verse states, *"And they buried the bones of Joseph, which the Jewish people had brought up from Egypt, in Shechem"* (*Joshua* 24:32). Didn't Moses alone fulfil this commandment of taking the bones, and not the Jewish people? However, since he failed to complete it, and the Jewish people did, they received the credit (*Rashi, 11th century*).

דברים ח:ג-יא

3 וַיְעַנְּךָ וַיַּרְעִבֶךָ וַיַּאֲכִלְךָ אֶת־הַמָּן אֲשֶׁר לֹא־יָדַעְתָּ וְלֹא יָדְעוּן אֲבֹתֶיךָ לְמַעַן הוֹדִיעֲךָ כִּי לֹא עַל־הַלֶּחֶם לְבַדּוֹ יִחְיֶה הָאָדָם כִּי עַל־כָּל־מוֹצָא פִי־יְהֹוָה יִחְיֶה הָאָדָם: 4 שִׂמְלָתְךָ לֹא בָלְתָה מֵעָלֶיךָ וְרַגְלְךָ לֹא בָצֵקָה זֶה אַרְבָּעִים שָׁנָה: 5 וְיָדַעְתָּ עִם־לְבָבֶךָ כִּי כַּאֲשֶׁר יְיַסֵּר אִישׁ אֶת־בְּנוֹ יְהֹוָה אֱלֹהֶיךָ מְיַסְּרֶךָּ: 6 וְשָׁמַרְתָּ אֶת־מִצְוֺת יְהֹוָה אֱלֹהֶיךָ לָלֶכֶת בִּדְרָכָיו וּלְיִרְאָה אֹתוֹ: 7 כִּי יְהֹוָה אֱלֹהֶיךָ מְבִיאֲךָ אֶל־אֶרֶץ טוֹבָה אֶרֶץ נַחֲלֵי מָיִם עֲיָנֹת וּתְהֹמֹת יֹצְאִים בַּבִּקְעָה וּבָהָר: 8 אֶרֶץ חִטָּה וּשְׂעֹרָה וְגֶפֶן וּתְאֵנָה וְרִמּוֹן אֶרֶץ־זֵית שֶׁמֶן וּדְבָשׁ: 9 אֶרֶץ אֲשֶׁר לֹא בְמִסְכֵּנֻת תֹּאכַל־בָּהּ לֶחֶם לֹא־תֶחְסַר כֹּל בָּהּ אֶרֶץ אֲשֶׁר אֲבָנֶיהָ בַרְזֶל וּמֵהֲרָרֶיהָ תַּחְצֹב נְחֹשֶׁת: 10 וְאָכַלְתָּ וְשָׂבָעְתָּ וּבֵרַכְתָּ אֶת־יְהֹוָה אֱלֹהֶיךָ עַל־הָאָרֶץ הַטֹּבָה אֲשֶׁר נָתַן־לָךְ: 11 [SECOND READING] הִשָּׁמֶר לְךָ פֶּן־תִּשְׁכַּח אֶת־יְהֹוָה אֱלֹהֶיךָ לְבִלְתִּי שְׁמֹר מִצְוֺתָיו וּמִשְׁפָּטָיו וְחֻקֹּתָיו אֲשֶׁר אָנֹכִי מְצַוְּךָ הַיּוֹם:

"Man does not live by bread alone"—from its physical component, *"but rather, from the utterances of God's mouth"*—from the word of God that created the food and continues to energize it (*Rabbi Isaac Luria, 16th century*).

10. You will eat and be satisfied. You must (then) bless God. God says, "Although the people are obligated to recite Grace After Meals only once they are satisfied, nevertheless they show Me favor by reciting a blessing even after they eat just a small amount. So I, too, will show them favor in return (*Numbers Rabbah*).

You would probably gain more satisfaction from a token gift given to you by a very influential personality, than from a more valuable gift given by an ordinary person. Saying Grace even on a smaller amount of bread shows favor to God, because it demonstrates that even a small gift gives great satisfaction to us, which means that we consider God to be very important. God reciprocates by showing favor to us, attributing value to our limited worship because He appreciates its sincerity (*Rabbi Simḥah Bunem of Przysucha, 18th–19th century*).

kabbalah bites

8:3 *"Man does not live by bread alone, but rather … from all the utterances of God's mouth."* It is not merely the physical energy in the food that keeps you alive; the holy sparks hidden within (*"the utterances of God's mouth"*) fuel your spirit.

But don't you, as a human being, have your own holy sparks? Why are you reliant on the sparks found in the food?

Your sparks are from the tamed, stable world of *tikkun* ("order"). The sparks in the food are remnants from the chaotic, primordial world of *tohu*. So despite your overt superiority over the animal and vegetable kingdoms, a sandwich can actually infuse you with an intensity of spirit not to be found elsewhere.

deuteronomy 8:2–11 — 'ekev

His commandments (without questioning Him) or not? ³ He afflicted you and let you go hungry. He fed you with manna, which you had never experienced, nor had your fathers experienced, to make you realize that man does not live by bread alone, but rather, that man lives from all the utterances of God's mouth. ⁴ For these (past) forty years, your clothing (was kept miraculously and) did not become worn (with age) upon you, (and you always had shoes, so) your feet did not become swollen.

⁵ You should know in your heart that just as a person reprimands his son, so too God, your God, will reprimand you. ⁶ You should keep the commandments of God, your God, to go in His ways, and to fear Him. ⁷ For God, your God, is bringing you to a good land, a land with streams of water, of springs and underground water that flows into valleys and mountains, ⁸ a land of wheat, barley, vines, figs and pomegranates, a land of oil-(producing) olives and honey, ⁹ a land in which you will eat bread without poverty (and) you will lack nothing in it, a land whose stones are (rich in) iron, and from whose mountains you will quarry copper.

❖ ¹⁰ You will eat and be satisfied. You must (then) bless God, your God, for the good land He has given you.

Not to Take the Credit for Prosperity

[SECOND READING] ¹¹ Be careful not to forget God, your God, failing to keep His commandments, rational commands and suprarational commands, which I am

---

3. He fed you with manna. The manna failed to satisfy, and it actually left people hungry.

Being a food permeated with spirituality, manna gave people a taste of the infinite. When consuming "bread from the earth," you eventually become satisfied, since it is impossible to develop an infinite appetite for a limited taste. Manna, on the other hand, cultivated an inner appetite for spirituality which can never be satisfied.

Eating the manna was an appropriate preparation for entering the land, where the Jewish people would be challenged by various constraints—be they the trials of poverty, or (more preferably) the trials of wealth. Because our physical desires limit us; our spiritual desires—like those developed by the manna—liberate us (*Rabbi Menahem Mendel Schneerson, 20th century*).

To make you realize that man does not live by bread alone, but rather, that man lives from all the utterances of God's mouth. How can the physical food we eat provide sustenance for the *soul*?

Food also contains a spiritual component—the Godly life-force that sustains it. For all of creation exists only by God's utterance, *"by the word of God the heavens were made"* (*Psalms* 33:6). When you make a blessing over some food, its spiritual essence is released, nourishing the soul.

Food for thought

1. Are you ever too proud of your successes?

2. Has success made you more or less religious?

3. Are there any greater challenges to your religiosity than pride and success?

12 פֶּן־תֹּאכַל וְשָׂבָעְתָּ וּבָתִּים טֹבִים תִּבְנֶה וְיָשָׁבְתָּ: 13 וּבְקָרְךָ וְצֹאנְךָ יִרְבְּיֻן וְכֶסֶף וְזָהָב יִרְבֶּה־לָּךְ וְכֹל אֲשֶׁר־לְךָ יִרְבֶּה: 14 וְרָם לְבָבֶךָ וְשָׁכַחְתָּ אֶת־יְהֹוָה אֱלֹהֶיךָ הַמּוֹצִיאֲךָ מֵאֶרֶץ מִצְרַיִם מִבֵּית עֲבָדִים: 15 הַמּוֹלִיכְךָ בַּמִּדְבָּר | הַגָּדֹל וְהַנּוֹרָא נָחָשׁ | שָׂרָף וְעַקְרָב וְצִמָּאוֹן אֲשֶׁר אֵין־מָיִם הַמּוֹצִיא לְךָ מַיִם מִצּוּר הַחַלָּמִישׁ: 16 הַמַּאֲכִלְךָ מָן בַּמִּדְבָּר אֲשֶׁר לֹא־יָדְעוּן אֲבֹתֶיךָ לְמַעַן עַנֹּתְךָ וּלְמַעַן נַסֹּתֶךָ לְהֵיטִבְךָ בְּאַחֲרִיתֶךָ: 17 וְאָמַרְתָּ בִּלְבָבֶךָ כֹּחִי וְעֹצֶם יָדִי עָשָׂה לִי אֶת־הַחַיִל הַזֶּה: 18 וְזָכַרְתָּ אֶת־יְהֹוָה אֱלֹהֶיךָ כִּי הוּא הַנֹּתֵן לְךָ כֹּחַ לַעֲשׂוֹת חָיִל לְמַעַן הָקִים אֶת־בְּרִיתוֹ אֲשֶׁר־נִשְׁבַּע לַאֲבֹתֶיךָ כַּיּוֹם הַזֶּה: פ 19 וְהָיָה אִם־שָׁכֹחַ תִּשְׁכַּח אֶת־יְהֹוָה אֱלֹהֶיךָ וְהָלַכְתָּ אַחֲרֵי אֱלֹהִים אֲחֵרִים וַעֲבַדְתָּם וְהִשְׁתַּחֲוִיתָ לָהֶם הַעִדֹתִי בָכֶם הַיּוֹם כִּי אָבֹד תֹּאבֵדוּן: 20 כַּגּוֹיִם אֲשֶׁר יְהֹוָה מַאֲבִיד מִפְּנֵיכֶם כֵּן תֹּאבֵדוּן עֵקֶב לֹא תִשְׁמְעוּן בְּקוֹל יְהֹוָה אֱלֹהֵיכֶם: פ

ט 1 שְׁמַע יִשְׂרָאֵל אַתָּה עֹבֵר הַיּוֹם אֶת־הַיַּרְדֵּן לָבֹא לָרֶשֶׁת גּוֹיִם גְּדֹלִים וַעֲצֻמִים מִמֶּךָּ עָרִים גְּדֹלֹת וּבְצֻרֹת בַּשָּׁמָיִם: 2 עַם־גָּדוֹל וָרָם בְּנֵי עֲנָקִים אֲשֶׁר אַתָּה יָדַעְתָּ וְאַתָּה שָׁמַעְתָּ מִי יִתְיַצֵּב לִפְנֵי בְּנֵי עֲנָק: 3 וְיָדַעְתָּ הַיּוֹם כִּי

19. What will happen is, if you forget God. The expression *ve-hayah*, "What will happen is..." usually introduces a joyful event (*Genesis Rabbah*). Its usage here seems inappropriate, considering that this verse speaks about forgetting God. The Torah also repeats the verb "forget" —*shakho'ah tishkah*—indicating absolute neglect. Surely this passage is no cause for joy?

spiritual vitamin

> Mealtime should not be an opportunity for indulging in ordinary and natural "eating habits," but a hallowed time to serve God, where the table is an "altar" to God.

commanding you today. ¹² You might then eat and be satisfied, build good houses and live in them, ¹³ as your herds and your flocks will increase, your silver and gold accumulate, and everything that you have prospers.¹⁴ As your heart becomes arrogant you (might) forget God, your God, who brought you out of the land of Egypt, out of the house of bondage, ¹⁵ who led you through that great and awesome desert, where there were snakes, serpents and scorpions, and thirst, but no water; who brought you water out of solid rock; ¹⁶ who fed you with manna in the desert, which your forefathers never experienced, in order to afflict you and test you—though it was for your benefit in the end— ¹⁷ and you will say in your heart, "My own ability and the strength of my own hand has accumulated this wealth for me!" ¹⁸ Then you must remember God, your God, for it is He who gives you the ability to make wealth, in order to establish His covenant which He swore to your fathers, to this day.

¹⁹ What will happen is, if you forget God, your God, and follow other gods, and worship them, and prostrate yourself before them, I testify to you today, that you will be destroyed again and again. ²⁰ You will be destroyed just like the nations that God (is now going to) destroy before you, since you did not listen to the calling of God, your God.

Not to Be Self-righteous

9 ¹ Hear, O Israel! Today, you are about to cross the Jordan to come and take control of nations that are (even) greater and stronger than you, great cities fortified up to the skies, ² a great and tall people, the children of giants, whom you know and (about whom) you have heard (it said), "Who can stand against the children of a giant?" ³ You should know today, that God, your God, who is passing

kabbalah bites

8:16 *"To test you."* While you are required to observe all 613 commandments, the Kabbalah teaches there is one "connection ritual" in particular for which your soul was primarily sent to this earth. By observing this "personal" commandment, you will be infused with sufficient enthusiasm to carry out all the others. It represents your own spiritual gate of entry.

How do you know what your "personal" commandment is?

Well, the bad news is you can never really know for certain. But one important clue is that your "gate" will undoubtedly be obstructed by formidable obstacles. The demonic forces have a special interest in distracting you from this one commandment, since they know it is the key to your success.

So next time a commandment seems especially difficult for you, ask yourself: Perhaps this challenge holds the key to my future?

עקב | דברים ט:ג-יד

יְהֹוָה אֱלֹהֶיךָ הוּא־הָעֹבֵר לְפָנֶיךָ אֵשׁ אֹכְלָה הוּא יַשְׁמִידֵם וְהוּא יַכְנִיעֵם לְפָנֶיךָ וְהוֹרַשְׁתָּם וְהַאֲבַדְתָּם מַהֵר כַּאֲשֶׁר דִּבֶּר יְהֹוָה לָךְ: [THIRD READING] 4 אַל־תֹּאמַר בִּלְבָבְךָ בַּהֲדֹף יְהֹוָה אֱלֹהֶיךָ אֹתָם ׀ מִלְּפָנֶיךָ לֵאמֹר בְּצִדְקָתִי הֱבִיאַנִי יְהֹוָה לָרֶשֶׁת אֶת־הָאָרֶץ הַזֹּאת וּבְרִשְׁעַת הַגּוֹיִם הָאֵלֶּה יְהֹוָה מוֹרִישָׁם מִפָּנֶיךָ: 5 לֹא בְצִדְקָתְךָ וּבְיֹשֶׁר לְבָבְךָ אַתָּה בָא לָרֶשֶׁת אֶת־אַרְצָם כִּי בְּרִשְׁעַת ׀ הַגּוֹיִם הָאֵלֶּה יְהֹוָה אֱלֹהֶיךָ מוֹרִישָׁם מִפָּנֶיךָ וּלְמַעַן הָקִים אֶת־הַדָּבָר אֲשֶׁר נִשְׁבַּע יְהֹוָה לַאֲבֹתֶיךָ לְאַבְרָהָם לְיִצְחָק וּלְיַעֲקֹב: 6 וְיָדַעְתָּ כִּי לֹא בְצִדְקָתְךָ יְהֹוָה אֱלֹהֶיךָ נֹתֵן לְךָ אֶת־הָאָרֶץ הַטּוֹבָה הַזֹּאת לְרִשְׁתָּהּ כִּי עַם־קְשֵׁה־עֹרֶף אָתָּה: 7 זְכֹר אַל־תִּשְׁכַּח אֵת אֲשֶׁר־הִקְצַפְתָּ אֶת־יְהֹוָה אֱלֹהֶיךָ בַּמִּדְבָּר לְמִן־הַיּוֹם אֲשֶׁר־יָצָאתָ ׀ מֵאֶרֶץ מִצְרַיִם עַד־בֹּאֲכֶם עַד־הַמָּקוֹם הַזֶּה מַמְרִים הֱיִיתֶם עִם־יְהֹוָה: 8 וּבְחֹרֵב הִקְצַפְתֶּם אֶת־יְהֹוָה וַיִּתְאַנַּף יְהֹוָה בָּכֶם לְהַשְׁמִיד אֶתְכֶם: 9 בַּעֲלֹתִי הָהָרָה לָקַחַת לוּחֹת הָאֲבָנִים לוּחֹת הַבְּרִית אֲשֶׁר־כָּרַת יְהֹוָה עִמָּכֶם וָאֵשֵׁב בָּהָר אַרְבָּעִים יוֹם וְאַרְבָּעִים לַיְלָה לֶחֶם לֹא אָכַלְתִּי וּמַיִם לֹא שָׁתִיתִי: 10 וַיִּתֵּן יְהֹוָה אֵלַי אֶת־שְׁנֵי לוּחֹת הָאֲבָנִים כְּתֻבִים בְּאֶצְבַּע אֱלֹהִים וַעֲלֵיהֶם כְּכָל־הַדְּבָרִים אֲשֶׁר דִּבֶּר יְהֹוָה עִמָּכֶם בָּהָר מִתּוֹךְ הָאֵשׁ בְּיוֹם הַקָּהָל: 11 וַיְהִי מִקֵּץ אַרְבָּעִים יוֹם וְאַרְבָּעִים לָיְלָה נָתַן יְהֹוָה אֵלַי אֶת־שְׁנֵי לֻחֹת הָאֲבָנִים לֻחוֹת הַבְּרִית: 12 וַיֹּאמֶר יְהֹוָה אֵלַי קוּם רֵד מַהֵר מִזֶּה כִּי שִׁחֵת עַמְּךָ אֲשֶׁר הוֹצֵאתָ מִמִּצְרָיִם סָרוּ מַהֵר מִן־הַדֶּרֶךְ אֲשֶׁר צִוִּיתָם עָשׂוּ לָהֶם מַסֵּכָה: 13 וַיֹּאמֶר יְהֹוָה אֵלַי לֵאמֹר רָאִיתִי אֶת־הָעָם הַזֶּה וְהִנֵּה עַם־קְשֵׁה־עֹרֶף הוּא: 14 הֶרֶף מִמֶּנִּי וְאַשְׁמִידֵם וְאֶמְחֶה אֶת־שְׁמָם מִתַּחַת

To avoid neglecting your duties to God you must always remain positive (*Rabbi Israel Friedman of Ruzhin, 19th century*).

(into the land) before you is a consuming fire. He will destroy them, and He will subjugate them before you. You will evict them and destroy them quickly, just as God said to you.

[THIRD READING] ⁴ When God, your God, has driven them from before you, do not say in your heart, "God has brought me to possess this land because of my righteousness," and God (also) drove them out from before you because of the wickedness of these nations. ⁵ It is not because of your righteousness or the integrity of your heart that you are coming to possess their land, but rather, it is because of the wickedness of these nations (alone) that God, your God, is driving them out from before you. (It is also) in order to keep the word which God swore to your fathers, Abraham, Isaac, and Jacob. ⁶ You must realize that God, your God, is not giving you this land as a possession because of your righteousness, for you are a stiff-necked people.

Remembering the Golden Calf

⁷ Remember—do not forget—how you angered God, your God, in the desert. From the day that you went out of the land of Egypt, until you came to this place, you have been rebels against God.

⁸ At Horeb, you angered God, and God was furious with you and wanted to destroy you:

⁹ When I went up the mountain to receive the stone tablets—the Tablets of the Testimony which God made with you—I was delayed on the mountain for forty days and forty nights. I did not eat bread or drink water. ¹⁰ God gave me two stone tablets, written with the finger of God. On them were all the words that God said to you on the mountain, from the fire, on the Day of Assembly.

¹¹ What happened was, at the end of the forty days and forty nights, when God gave me the two stone tablets, the Tablets of the Testimony, ¹² God said to me, "Get moving, and go down quickly from here, for your people, whom you have brought out of Egypt, have become corrupt. They have rapidly abandoned the way which I commanded them. They have made themselves a molten statue!"

¹³ God then spoke to me, saying, "I have observed this people and—look!—they are a stiff-necked people (who do not like being rebuked). ¹⁴ Leave Me, and I will destroy them. I will obliterate their name from beneath the skies, and I will make you into a mightier and more numerous nation than them."

The message here is: *If you forget to be joyous, then you will eventually forget God*. Melancholy is a step away from depression, a state in which you are unable to accomplish anything positive.

דברים ט:יד-כא

15 הַשָּׁמָיִם וְאֶעֱשֶׂה אוֹתְךָ לְגוֹי־עָצוּם וָרָב מִמֶּנּוּ: וָאֵפֶן וָאֵרֵד מִן־הָהָר וְהָהָר בֹּעֵר בָּאֵשׁ וּשְׁנֵי לוּחֹת הַבְּרִית עַל שְׁתֵּי יָדָי: 16 וָאֵרֶא וְהִנֵּה חֲטָאתֶם לַיהוָה אֱלֹהֵיכֶם עֲשִׂיתֶם לָכֶם עֵגֶל מַסֵּכָה סַרְתֶּם מַהֵר מִן־הַדֶּרֶךְ אֲשֶׁר־צִוָּה יְהוָה אֶתְכֶם: 17 וָאֶתְפֹּשׂ בִּשְׁנֵי הַלֻּחֹת וָאַשְׁלִכֵם מֵעַל שְׁתֵּי יָדָי וָאֲשַׁבְּרֵם לְעֵינֵיכֶם: 18 וָאֶתְנַפַּל לִפְנֵי יְהוָה כָּרִאשֹׁנָה אַרְבָּעִים יוֹם וְאַרְבָּעִים לַיְלָה לֶחֶם לֹא אָכַלְתִּי וּמַיִם לֹא שָׁתִיתִי עַל כָּל־חַטַּאתְכֶם אֲשֶׁר חֲטָאתֶם לַעֲשׂוֹת הָרַע בְּעֵינֵי יְהוָה לְהַכְעִיסוֹ: 19 כִּי יָגֹרְתִּי מִפְּנֵי הָאַף וְהַחֵמָה אֲשֶׁר קָצַף יְהוָה עֲלֵיכֶם לְהַשְׁמִיד אֶתְכֶם וַיִּשְׁמַע יְהוָה אֵלַי גַּם בַּפַּעַם הַהִוא: 20 וּבְאַהֲרֹן הִתְאַנַּף יְהוָה מְאֹד לְהַשְׁמִידוֹ וָאֶתְפַּלֵּל גַּם־בְּעַד אַהֲרֹן בָּעֵת הַהִוא: 21 וְאֶת־חַטַּאתְכֶם אֲשֶׁר־עֲשִׂיתֶם אֶת־הָעֵגֶל לָקַחְתִּי וָאֶשְׂרֹף אֹתוֹ | בָּאֵשׁ וָאֶכֹּת אֹתוֹ טָחוֹן הֵיטֵב עַד אֲשֶׁר־דַּק לְעָפָר וָאַשְׁלִךְ אֶת־עֲפָרוֹ אֶל־הַנַּחַל הַיֹּרֵד מִן־הָהָר:

This is precisely what Moses did. When he saw what the Jewish people had done, he took the tablets and broke them. Now he could argue that if the Jewish people had seen the punishment for idol-worship written there, they would not have sinned (*Exodus Rabbah*).

Shattered them before your eyes. *"Before your eyes"* suggests that something miraculous occurred, which drew the attention of the people.

What was the miracle they observed?

The tablets broke, but the letters flew upwards towards the heavens (*Babylonian Talmud, Pesaḥim* 87b).

When God instructed Moses to carve out the second tablets, He said: "I will write on the tablets *'the words that were on the first tablets'*" (*Exodus* 34:1). This is a reference to the very same letters that were on the first tablets, which, as the Talmud states, flew up to heaven. These same letters later set themselves on the second tablets (*Rabbi Ephraim of Luntshits, 16th–17th century*).

Thus the tablets were only shattered *"before their eyes."* To the people it seemed as though the tablets were destroyed. In reality, however, only the stone was shattered. Its essence—the letters and words—was preserved in the second tablets (*Rabbi Ezekiel Landau of Prague, 18th century*).

18. I prayed to God ... for forty days and forty nights, as before. After spending forty days on Mount Sinai, Moses came down from the mountain with the first set of tablets, on the seventeenth of *Tammuz*—and on witnessing the sin of the Golden Calf, he broke them.

The following day, Moses went back up the mountain and spent forty more days and nights in prayer, after which God instructed him to carve out a second set of tablets.

deuteronomy 9:15–21   ʿekev

¹⁵ I turned and came down from the mountain. The mountain was burning with fire and the two Tablets of the Testimony were upon my two hands. ¹⁶ Then I saw—look!—you had sinned against God, your God, you had made yourselves a molten calf. You had rapidly abandoned the way which God had commanded you. ¹⁷ So, I took hold of the two tablets, cast them out of my two hands, and shattered them before your eyes.

¹⁸ I prayed to God about all your sins that you had committed—doing evil in the eyes of God to anger Him—for forty days and forty nights (on the mountain), as before. I did not eat bread or drink water. ¹⁹ For I was frightened of the anger and fury with which God had shown His discontent with you, wanting to destroy you, but God listened to me also on that occasion.

²⁰ God was very angry with Aaron (whom you misled) and wanted to destroy his (children). So I prayed for Aaron too on that occasion (but only two of his children were saved).

²¹ I took your sinful object which you had made—the calf—and I burned it in fire. I crushed it, grinding it well, until it was fine dust, and I cast its dust into the brook that descends from the mountain.

9:17 So, I took hold of the two tablets. Until Moses saw that the Jewish people had sinned, the tablets hovered in the air above his hands (*"upon* my two hands"—v. 15). When he witnessed their sin, the tablets lost their holiness, and he had to "take hold" of them and support them (*Rabbi Ḥayyim ibn Attar, 18th century*).

And shattered them. What can this be compared to? To a nobleman who wished to marry a woman through an agent. The agent went and found that the woman had been promiscuous with another man.

What did the agent—who was totally innocent—do?

He took the marriage document that was given to him by the nobleman, and tore it up. He said, "It is better that this woman be judged as a single woman and not as a married woman!"

spiritual vitamin

> A human being, however perfect he or she may be, is liable to fail occasionally. God has therefore provided the way in which misdeeds can be rectified, namely by way of repentance which, as our Sages declare, was created even before the world. And repentance is effective not only in respect to the future, but also retroactively to a large extent, since God is omnipotent and is not restricted in any way.

דברים ט:כב – י:ו

עקב

22 וּבְתַבְעֵרָה֙ וּבְמַסָּ֔ה וּבְקִבְרֹ֖ת הַֽתַּאֲוָ֑ה מַקְצִפִ֥ים הֱיִיתֶ֖ם אֶת־יְהֹוָֽה: 23 וּבִשְׁלֹ֨חַ יְהֹוָ֜ה אֶתְכֶ֗ם מִקָּדֵ֤שׁ בַּרְנֵ֙עַ֙ לֵאמֹ֔ר עֲלוּ֙ וּרְשׁ֣וּ אֶת־הָאָ֔רֶץ אֲשֶׁ֥ר נָתַ֖תִּי לָכֶ֑ם וַתַּמְר֗וּ אֶת־פִּ֤י יְהֹוָה֙ אֱלֹ֣הֵיכֶ֔ם וְלֹ֤א הֶֽאֱמַנְתֶּם֙ ל֔וֹ וְלֹ֥א שְׁמַעְתֶּ֖ם בְּקֹלֽוֹ: 24 מַמְרִ֥ים הֱיִיתֶ֖ם עִם־יְהֹוָ֑ה מִיּ֖וֹם דַּעְתִּ֥י אֶתְכֶֽם: 25 וָֽאֶתְנַפַּ֞ל לִפְנֵ֣י יְהֹוָ֗ה אֵ֣ת אַרְבָּעִ֥ים הַיּ֛וֹם וְאֶת־אַרְבָּעִ֥ים הַלַּ֖יְלָה אֲשֶׁ֣ר הִתְנַפָּ֑לְתִּי כִּֽי־אָמַ֥ר יְהֹוָ֖ה לְהַשְׁמִ֥יד אֶתְכֶֽם: 26 וָאֶתְפַּלֵּ֣ל אֶל־יְהֹוָה֮ וָֽאֹמַר֒ אֲדֹנָ֣י יֱהֹוִ֗ה אַל־תַּשְׁחֵ֤ת עַמְּךָ֙ וְנַחֲלָ֣תְךָ֔ אֲשֶׁ֥ר פָּדִ֖יתָ בְּגׇדְלֶ֑ךָ אֲשֶׁר־הוֹצֵ֥אתָ מִמִּצְרַ֖יִם בְּיָ֥ד חֲזָקָֽה: 27 זְכֹר֙ לַעֲבָדֶ֔יךָ לְאַבְרָהָ֥ם לְיִצְחָ֖ק וּלְיַעֲקֹ֑ב אַל־תֵּ֗פֶן אֶל־קְשִׁי֙ הָעָ֣ם הַזֶּ֔ה וְאֶל־רִשְׁע֖וֹ וְאֶל־חַטָּאתֽוֹ: 28 פֶּן־יֹאמְר֗וּ הָאָרֶץ֮ אֲשֶׁ֣ר הוֹצֵאתָ֣נוּ מִשָּׁם֒ מִבְּלִ֨י יְכֹ֤לֶת יְהֹוָה֙ לַהֲבִיאָ֔ם אֶל־הָאָ֖רֶץ אֲשֶׁר־דִּבֶּ֣ר לָהֶ֑ם וּמִשִּׂנְאָת֣וֹ אוֹתָ֔ם הוֹצִיאָ֖ם לַהֲמִתָ֥ם בַּמִּדְבָּֽר: 29 וְהֵ֥ם עַמְּךָ֖ וְנַחֲלָתֶ֑ךָ אֲשֶׁ֤ר הוֹצֵ֙אתָ֙ בְּכֹחֲךָ֣ הַגָּדֹ֔ל וּבִֽזְרֹעֲךָ֖ הַנְּטוּיָֽה: פ

[FOURTH READING]

1 בָּעֵ֨ת הַהִ֜וא אָמַ֧ר יְהֹוָ֣ה אֵלַ֗י פְּסׇל־לְךָ֞ שְׁנֵֽי־לוּחֹ֤ת אֲבָנִים֙ כָּרִ֣אשֹׁנִ֔ים וַעֲלֵ֥ה אֵלַ֖י הָהָ֑רָה וְעָשִׂ֥יתָ לְּךָ֖ אֲר֥וֹן עֵֽץ: 2 וְאֶכְתֹּב֙ עַל־הַלֻּחֹ֔ת אֶת־הַדְּבָרִ֔ים אֲשֶׁ֥ר הָי֛וּ עַל־הַלֻּחֹ֥ת הָרִאשֹׁנִ֖ים אֲשֶׁ֣ר שִׁבַּ֑רְתָּ וְשַׂמְתָּ֖ם בָּאָרֽוֹן: 3 וָאַ֤עַשׂ אֲרוֹן֙ עֲצֵ֣י שִׁטִּ֔ים וָאֶפְסֹ֛ל שְׁנֵי־לֻחֹ֥ת אֲבָנִ֖ים כָּרִאשֹׁנִ֑ים וָאַ֣עַל הָהָ֔רָה וּשְׁנֵ֥י הַלֻּחֹ֖ת בְּיָדִֽי: 4 וַיִּכְתֹּ֨ב עַֽל־הַלֻּחֹ֜ת כַּמִּכְתָּ֣ב הָרִאשׁ֗וֹן אֵ֚ת עֲשֶׂ֣רֶת הַדְּבָרִ֔ים אֲשֶׁ֣ר דִּבֶּר֩ יְהֹוָ֨ה אֲלֵיכֶ֥ם בָּהָ֛ר מִתּ֥וֹךְ הָאֵ֖שׁ בְּי֣וֹם הַקָּהָ֑ל וַיִּתְּנֵ֥ם יְהֹוָ֖ה אֵלָֽי: 5 וָאֵ֗פֶן וָֽאֵרֵד֙ מִן־הָהָ֔ר וָֽאָשִׂם֙ אֶת־הַלֻּחֹ֔ת בָּאָר֖וֹן אֲשֶׁ֣ר עָשִׂ֑יתִי וַיִּ֣הְיוּ שָׁ֔ם כַּאֲשֶׁ֥ר צִוַּ֖נִי יְהֹוָֽה: 6 וּבְנֵ֣י יִשְׂרָאֵ֗ל נָֽסְע֛וּ מִבְּאֵרֹ֥ת בְּנֵי־יַעֲקָ֖ן מוֹסֵרָ֑ה שָׁ֣ם מֵ֤ת אַהֲרֹן֙

10:6 Aaron died. Moses said this rebuke about Aaron's passing straight after discussing the breaking of the tablets, even though it occurred forty years later, to indicate that the death of the righteous is as difficult for God as the day the tablets were broken (*Rashi, 11th century*).

deuteronomy 9:22 – 10:6 — 'ekev

— [22] (Since then) you (also) provoked God's anger at Taberah, at Massah, and at Kibroth-hattaavah. [23] (Furthermore), when God sent you from Kadesh-barnea, saying, "Go up and possess the land I have given you," you defied the word of God, your God, and you did not believe Him, nor did you obey Him. [24] You have been rebels against God since the day I became acquainted with you! —

[25] So I prayed before God. I prayed for forty days and forty nights, because God said He would destroy you. [26] In my prayers to God I said, "God Almighty! Do not destroy Your people, Your inheritance which in Your greatness You have redeemed and brought out of Egypt with a mighty hand! [27] Remember Your servants, Abraham, Isaac and Jacob! Do not react to this people's stubbornness, to their wickedness or to their sin, [28] so that the nation from which you brought us out won't say, 'Because of God's inability to bring them to the land which He told them about, and because of His hatred toward them, He took them out to slaughter them in the desert.' [29] They are Your people and Your inheritance, which You brought out with Your great strength and with Your outstretched arm!"

The Second Tablets

10 [FOURTH READING] [1] At that time (after forty days), God (forgave the Jewish people, and) said to me, "Carve for yourself two stone tablets like the first ones, and come up to Me onto the mountain. And make for yourself a wooden ark. [2] On the tablets I will write the words that were on the first tablets, which you broke, and you should place them into the ark."

[3] I made an ark of acacia wood. I carved two stone tablets, like the first ones, and I went up the mountain with the two tablets in my hand. [4] He wrote on the tablets the same thing that was written on the first ones: the Ten Commandments, which God said to you on the mountain, from the fire, on the Day of Assembly. God then gave them to me.

[5] I turned around and came down from the mountain. I placed the tablets in the ark which I had made, and they remained there, as God had commanded me.

Rebellion in the Desert

— [6] (Later on you did another sin which, in my eyes, was as bad as the Golden Calf. It was when forty years later) Aaron died (in Mount Hor) and he was buried there, and Eleazar his son was appointed as priest in his place. (A rebellious

---

He continued praying on behalf of the people for another forty days, which concluded on the Day of Atonement. On that very day God was joyfully reconciled with the Jewish people, and said, *"I have forgiven them in accordance with your word"* (Numbers 14:20). Therefore it was designated as a time of pardon and forgiveness (*Rashi, 11th century*).

דברים י:ו-יא

וַיִּקָּבֵ֣ר שָׁ֔ם וַיְכַהֵ֛ן אֶלְעָזָ֥ר בְּנ֖וֹ תַּחְתָּֽיו: 7 מִשָּׁ֥ם נָסְע֖וּ הַגֻּדְגֹּ֑דָה וּמִן־הַגֻּדְגֹּ֣דָה יָטְבָ֔תָה אֶ֖רֶץ נַ֥חֲלֵי מָֽיִם: 8 בָּעֵ֣ת הַהִ֗וא הִבְדִּ֤יל יְהוָה֙ אֶת־שֵׁ֣בֶט הַלֵּוִ֔י לָשֵׂ֖את אֶת־אֲר֣וֹן בְּרִית־יְהוָ֑ה לַעֲמֹד֩ לִפְנֵ֨י יְהוָ֤ה לְשָֽׁרְתוֹ֙ וּלְבָרֵ֣ךְ בִּשְׁמ֔וֹ עַ֖ד הַיּ֥וֹם הַזֶּֽה: 9 עַל־כֵּ֞ן לֹֽא־הָיָ֧ה לְלֵוִ֛י חֵ֥לֶק וְנַחֲלָ֖ה עִם־אֶחָ֑יו יְהוָה֙ ה֣וּא נַחֲלָת֔וֹ כַּאֲשֶׁ֥ר דִּבֶּ֛ר יְהוָ֥ה אֱלֹהֶ֖יךָ לֽוֹ: 10 וְאָנֹכִ֞י עָמַ֣דְתִּי בָהָ֗ר כַּיָּמִים֙ הָרִ֣אשֹׁנִ֔ים אַרְבָּעִ֣ים י֔וֹם וְאַרְבָּעִ֖ים לָ֑יְלָה וַיִּשְׁמַ֨ע יְהוָ֜ה אֵלַ֗י גַּ֚ם בַּפַּ֣עַם הַהִ֔וא לֹא־אָבָ֥ה יְהוָ֖ה הַשְׁחִיתֶֽךָ: 11 וַיֹּ֤אמֶר יְהוָה֙ אֵלַ֔י ק֥וּם לֵ֛ךְ לְמַסַּ֖ע לִפְנֵ֣י הָעָ֑ם וְיָבֹ֨אוּ֙ וְיִֽירְשׁ֣וּ אֶת־הָאָ֔רֶץ

Therefore, they were separated from worldly matters: They do not join the army as the rest of the Jewish people, they do not inherit, and they cannot acquire things for themselves by a physical act. They are the army of God.

But this is not exclusive to the tribe of Levi. Rather, any type of person from among all the inhabitants of the world, whose spirit inspires him, and he resolves in his mind to set himself apart from worldly pursuits, to stand before God and serve as His minister, to work for Him, and to know God; who goes in a morally upright manner—following his inherent, God-given disposition, and he discards all the numerous concerns that people are normally preoccupied with—*then he will attain the holiness of the Holy of Holies,* and God will be his portion and his inheritance for all eternity. Even in this world, he will merit to receive his material needs, in a similar manner to the priests and Levites, as we see that David [who was not from the tribe of Levi] said (*Psalms 16:5*), *"God is the portion of my inheritance and of my cup. You support my lot!"* (*Maimonides, 12th century*).

10. Like the first days. Just as those days were with God's goodwill, so were these with God's goodwill. But the middle (forty-day period), when I stood there to pray for you, was amid God's anger (*Rashi, 11th century*).

spiritual vitamin

> God does not demand the impossible, and having set forth a program and a goal, He has simultaneously given the full ability and capacity to fulfil them. It is only that He wants everyone to fulfil his purpose in life out of his own free choice, in spite of temptations and difficulties. When you realize that you have it in your power to overcome them, life becomes easier.

group from) the children of Israel (arose, planning to lead the Jewish people back to Egypt). They journeyed (backwards from Mount Hor, where Aaron died,) through the wells of Bene-jaakan to Moserah (at which point a group of Levites, who were chasing them, caught up with them and defeated them. After mourning Aaron's death while they were still) there (in Moserah), ⁷ they journeyed from there (and returned to the camp at Mount Hor, first passing) Gudgod, and from Gudgod to Jotbath, an area with flowing brooks. —

Appointment of the Tribe of Levi

⁸ At that time (after the sin of the Golden Calf), God separated the tribe of Levi (who did not participate in the sin), to carry the Ark of the Testimony of God. (He separated the priests) to stand before God and serve Him, and to (make the priestly) blessing in His name, which continues to this day. ⁹ (Since they were set aside for holy service and would not have time for agriculture) therefore, a (priest, who is from the tribe of) Levi, has no portion or inheritance (in the land) with his brothers. His inheritance (comes directly from) God('s house), as God, your God, told him.

Moses' Third Period on the Mountain

¹⁰ I remained on the mountain forty days and forty nights (when I went to receive the second tablets, and God was appeased) like the first (period of forty) days (when I was on the mountain), for God listened to me also at that time and God did not wish to destroy you.

¹¹ God said to me, "Get going! Lead the people in their journeys to come and take possession of the land I promised their forefathers to give them."

"No righteous man departs from this world before another like him is created, as the verse states, 'The sun goes up and then the sun goes down'" (Ecclesiastes 1:5; *Babylonian Talmud, Yoma* 38a). This is stressed by the Torah here, that after *"Aaron died,"* immediately, *"Eleazar his son was appointed as priest in his place."* Since Aaron was replaced by another righteous person, one would think that this minimized the tragedy of his passing for the Jewish people.

Therefore, *Rashi* stresses that this did not soften the blow and "the death of the righteous is as difficult for God as the day the tablets were broken." Just as the breaking of the first tablets remained a tragedy even after they were replaced by the second tablets, so too, the passing of a righteous person is particularly tragic, even though God sends us other righteous people (*Rabbi David b. Samuel ha-Levi, 17th century*).

8. God separated the tribe of Levi. Because they were singled out to work for God and serve as His ministers, and to teach the public about His morally upright ways and fair laws—as the verse states, *"They will teach Your laws to Jacob and Your Torah to Israel"* (Deuteronomy 33:10).

דברים י:יא-יח

אֲשֶׁר־נִשְׁבַּעְתִּי לַאֲבֹתָם לָתֵת לָהֶם׃ פ 12 **[FIFTH READING]** וְעַתָּה יִשְׂרָאֵל מָה יְהֹוָה אֱלֹהֶיךָ שֹׁאֵל מֵעִמָּךְ כִּי אִם־לְיִרְאָה אֶת־יְהֹוָה אֱלֹהֶיךָ לָלֶכֶת בְּכָל־דְּרָכָיו וּלְאַהֲבָה אֹתוֹ וְלַעֲבֹד אֶת־יְהֹוָה אֱלֹהֶיךָ בְּכָל־לְבָבְךָ וּבְכָל־נַפְשֶׁךָ׃ 13 לִשְׁמֹר אֶת־מִצְוֺת יְהֹוָה וְאֶת־חֻקֹּתָיו אֲשֶׁר אָנֹכִי מְצַוְּךָ הַיּוֹם לְטוֹב לָךְ׃ 14 הֵן לַיהֹוָה אֱלֹהֶיךָ הַשָּׁמַיִם וּשְׁמֵי הַשָּׁמָיִם הָאָרֶץ וְכָל־אֲשֶׁר־בָּהּ׃ 15 רַק בַּאֲבֹתֶיךָ חָשַׁק יְהֹוָה לְאַהֲבָה אוֹתָם וַיִּבְחַר בְּזַרְעָם אַחֲרֵיהֶם בָּכֶם מִכָּל־הָעַמִּים כַּיּוֹם הַזֶּה׃ 16 וּמַלְתֶּם אֵת עָרְלַת לְבַבְכֶם וְעָרְפְּכֶם לֹא תַקְשׁוּ עוֹד׃ 17 כִּי יְהֹוָה אֱלֹהֵיכֶם הוּא אֱלֹהֵי הָאֱלֹהִים וַאֲדֹנֵי הָאֲדֹנִים הָאֵל הַגָּדֹל הַגִּבֹּר וְהַנּוֹרָא אֲשֶׁר לֹא־יִשָּׂא פָנִים וְלֹא יִקַּח שֹׁחַד׃ 18 עֹשֶׂה מִשְׁפַּט יָתוֹם וְאַלְמָנָה וְאֹהֵב גֵּר לָתֶת לוֹ

the free expression of this Godly spark. *"You must 'circumcise' the foreskin of your heart,"* by not surrendering to all of your heart's desires. This will liberate your Godly spark, enabling it to express itself freely throughout your entire being (*Rabbi Shneur Zalman of Lyady, 18th century*).

17. God ... will not accept a bribe. It is written in Your Torah, *"Do not accept a bribe"* (*Exodus* 23:8). But You *do* accept bribes, as the verse states, *"He will take a bribe from a wicked man's bosom to turn the roads of justice"* (*Proverbs* 17:23)?

kabbalah bites

10:12 Did you know that even your soul itself has a soul?

The soul is, in a way, selfish, having its own more subtle sort of "ego" problems. Of course the soul loves God, and it hates all those worldly pleasures that pull you away from God; but, ultimately, the soul's yearnings are coming from its *own* instincts. *It* loves God, *it* wants you to worship Him. So life is still not really about God; it's about how *you* love God.

Your soul, therefore, needs its own soul, something to remind it that we are here to serve *God's* needs, and not the other way around.

Your soul's soul is called the *yehidah*—the "singularity." The *yehidah* understands that nothing exists outside God's orbit, that there is only one "singular" existence: God. He is the only thing that matters, not us. We only matter because we serve His needs.

The *yehidah* is the spark of the Messiah in all of us. As you awaken to your *yehidah*, you will participate in the great collective process of enlightened understanding that will soon redirect the world from its destructive course.

deuteronomy 10:12–18 — 'ekev

Moses Encourages the People to Serve God

[FIFTH READING] ¹² Now, O Israel, (even though you sinned) what does God, your God, demand of you? (Because He still has compassion on you and He still loves you, He does not punish you, but asks you) only to fear God, your God, to follow all His ways, to love Him, to serve God, your God, with all your heart and with all your soul, ¹³ and to keep the commandments of God and His suprarational commands, which I command you today—(and even this) is for your own benefit (because you will receive reward).

¹⁴ God, your God, (has the choice of everything in) the lower and upper skies, the earth and all that is on it. ¹⁵ But God desired only to love your forefathers, and He chose their descendants after them —(i.e.) you—out of all nations, (a choice which) remains until today.

¹⁶ You should "circumcise" the "foreskin" of your heart (which blocks you from serving God), and you should stop being stiff-necked. ¹⁷ For God, your God, is God of gods and the Master of masters, the great, mighty and awesome God, who does not show favor and will not accept a bribe. ¹⁸ (Yet) He (is sensitive) to enact judgment for the orphan and widow. And He loves the convert and gives him bread and clothing.

---

12. What does God demand of you? Only to fear God. The verse seems to imply that fear of God is easily attainable. This begs the question: Is fear of God such a small and easy matter?

Yes, for Moses, who was narrating this verse, it was a small matter (*Babylonian Talmud, Berakhot* 33b).

The Talmud's answer seems inadequate since Moses was addressing the people, "What does God demand *of you*." What difference does it make that the matter was simple for Moses?

In order to develop fear of God you first need to meditate upon His awesome might—that everything exists only at His mercy, and that, at every moment, God freely chooses to continue creating the world. For the awe to be palpable, you need to connect deeply with these thoughts, both mentally and emotionally. *This ability to connect with thoughts of God's greatness is the spiritual legacy of Moses*, who, as Israel's shepherd, was charged with nourishing the people's faith.

Yes, *"for Moses"*—because of the gift of attachment, which was given to us by Moses— *"it is indeed a simple matter,"* to develop a real fear of God by meditating upon His greatness (*Rabbi Shneur Zalman of Lyady, 18th century*).

16. You should "circumcise" the "foreskin" of your heart. In the heart of every Jewish soul there is a Godly spark, which, when left uninhibited, will bring you to a deep-rooted love for God. But following your own desires and indulging in the many delights of this world, even if they are not strictly prohibited, creates a *"foreskin,"* obstructing

---

Food for thought

1. What feelings have you cultivated towards God in the last year?

2. What have you done to demonstrate profound love or respect for God?

3. How can we experience true delight for an unseen and intangible God?

עקב   דברים י:יח - יא:ט

לֶ֥חֶם וְשִׂמְלָֽה׃ 19 וַאֲהַבְתֶּ֖ם אֶת־הַגֵּ֑ר כִּֽי־גֵרִ֥ים הֱיִיתֶ֖ם בְּאֶ֥רֶץ מִצְרָֽיִם׃ 20 אֶת־
יְהֹוָ֧ה אֱלֹהֶ֛יךָ תִּירָ֖א אֹת֣וֹ תַעֲבֹ֑ד וּב֣וֹ תִדְבָּ֔ק וּבִשְׁמ֖וֹ תִּשָּׁבֵֽעַ׃ 21 ה֥וּא תְהִלָּתְךָ֖
וְה֣וּא אֱלֹהֶ֑יךָ אֲשֶׁר־עָשָׂ֣ה אִתְּךָ֗ אֶת־הַגְּדֹלֹ֤ת וְאֶת־הַנּֽוֹרָאֹת֙ הָאֵ֔לֶּה אֲשֶׁ֥ר רָא֖וּ
עֵינֶֽיךָ׃ 22 בְּשִׁבְעִ֣ים נֶ֔פֶשׁ יָרְד֥וּ אֲבֹתֶ֖יךָ מִצְרָ֑יְמָה וְעַתָּ֗ה שָֽׂמְךָ֙ יְהֹוָ֣ה אֱלֹהֶ֔יךָ
כְּכוֹכְבֵ֥י הַשָּׁמַ֖יִם לָרֹֽב׃

יא 1 וְאָ֣הַבְתָּ֔ אֵ֖ת יְהֹוָ֣ה אֱלֹהֶ֑יךָ וְשָׁמַרְתָּ֣ מִשְׁמַרְתּ֗וֹ וְחֻקֹּתָ֧יו וּמִשְׁפָּטָ֛יו
וּמִצְוֺתָ֖יו כָּל־הַיָּמִֽים׃ 2 וִֽידַעְתֶּם֮ הַיּוֹם֒ כִּ֣י ׀ לֹ֣א אֶת־בְּנֵיכֶ֗ם אֲשֶׁ֤ר לֹֽא־
יָדְעוּ֙ וַאֲשֶׁ֣ר לֹא־רָא֔וּ אֶת־מוּסַ֖ר יְהֹוָ֣ה אֱלֹהֵיכֶ֑ם אֶת־גָּדְל֕וֹ אֶת־יָדוֹ֙ הַחֲזָקָ֔ה
וּזְרֹע֖וֹ הַנְּטוּיָֽה׃ 3 וְאֶת־אֹֽתֹתָיו֙ וְאֶֽת־מַעֲשָׂ֔יו אֲשֶׁ֥ר עָשָׂ֖ה בְּת֣וֹךְ מִצְרָ֑יִם לְפַרְעֹ֥ה
מֶֽלֶךְ־מִצְרַ֖יִם וּלְכָל־אַרְצֽוֹ׃ 4 וַאֲשֶׁ֣ר עָשָׂה֩ לְחֵ֨יל מִצְרַ֜יִם לְסוּסָ֣יו וּלְרִכְבּ֗וֹ
אֲשֶׁ֨ר הֵצִ֜יף אֶת־מֵ֤י יַם־סוּף֙ עַל־פְּנֵיהֶ֔ם בְּרָדְפָ֖ם אַחֲרֵיכֶ֑ם וַיְאַבְּדֵ֣ם יְהֹוָ֔ה עַ֖ד
הַיּ֥וֹם הַזֶּֽה׃ 5 וַאֲשֶׁ֥ר עָשָׂ֛ה לָכֶ֖ם בַּמִּדְבָּ֑ר עַד־בֹּאֲכֶ֖ם עַד־הַמָּק֥וֹם הַזֶּֽה׃ 6 וַאֲשֶׁ֨ר
עָשָׂ֜ה לְדָתָ֣ן וְלַאֲבִירָ֗ם בְּנֵ֣י אֱלִיאָב֮ בֶּן־רְאוּבֵן֒ אֲשֶׁ֨ר פָּצְתָ֤ה הָאָ֙רֶץ֙ אֶת־פִּ֔יהָ
וַתִּבְלָעֵ֥ם וְאֶת־בָּתֵּיהֶ֖ם וְאֶת־אׇהֳלֵיהֶ֑ם וְאֵ֤ת כָּל־הַיְקוּם֙ אֲשֶׁ֣ר בְּרַגְלֵיהֶ֔ם
בְּקֶ֖רֶב כָּל־יִשְׂרָאֵֽל׃ 7 כִּ֤י עֵֽינֵיכֶם֙ הָֽרֹאֹ֔ת אֶת־כָּל־מַעֲשֵׂ֥ה יְהֹוָ֖ה הַגָּדֹ֑ל אֲשֶׁ֖ר
עָשָֽׂה׃ 8 וּשְׁמַרְתֶּם֙ אֶת־כָּל־הַמִּצְוָ֔ה אֲשֶׁ֛ר אָנֹכִ֥י מְצַוְּךָ֖ הַיּ֑וֹם לְמַ֣עַן תֶּחֶזְק֗וּ
וּבָאתֶם֙ וִֽירִשְׁתֶּ֣ם אֶת־הָאָ֔רֶץ אֲשֶׁ֥ר אַתֶּ֛ם עֹבְרִ֥ים שָׁ֖מָּה לְרִשְׁתָּֽהּ׃ 9 וּלְמַ֨עַן
תַּאֲרִ֤יכוּ יָמִים֙ עַל־הָ֣אֲדָמָ֔ה אֲשֶׁר֩ נִשְׁבַּ֨ע יְהֹוָ֤ה לַאֲבֹֽתֵיכֶם֙ לָתֵ֣ת לָהֶ֔ם וּלְזַרְעָ֑ם

How could God be associated with monetary bribes? It would seem more appropriate to understand this verse as referring to bribery in terms of His commandments, that God will not accept good deeds as a bribe to overlook sin. Rather, He will reward you for the good deeds and punish you for the bad (*Rabbi Elijah Mizraḥi, 15th–16th century*).

God will not consider charity as atonement for a sin without wholehearted repentance (*Rabbi David b. Samuel ha-Levi, 17th century*).

- ❖ ¹⁹ You should love the convert, because you were aliens in the land of Egypt.
- ❖ ²⁰ You must fear God, your God.
- ❖ You must serve Him.
- ❖ You must cleave to Him.
- ❖ (If you do all the above, then you may) swear by His name.

²¹ He is your praise and He is your God, who did these great and awesome things for you, which your eyes have seen. ²² Your forefathers went down to Egypt with seventy souls, and now God, your God, has made you as numerous as the stars of the skies.

Miracles Witnessed by the Jewish People

11 ¹ So you should love God, your God, keep what He has entrusted to you: His supranational commands, His rational commands, and His commandments, for all time.

² You should now realize (by focusing your heart to take my rebuke), that (I am) not (speaking) with your children, who (could claim that they) did not know and did not see God, your God, reprimand (us).

— (They did not see) His greatness, His mighty hand, His outstretched arm, ³ His signs (of Divine Providence), and His deeds, which He performed within Egypt, to Pharaoh, king of Egypt and to his entire land. ⁴ And what He did to Egypt's army, to its horses and chariots, how He swamped the waters of the Reed Sea upon them when they pursued you. God destroyed them (and they cease to exist) to this day. ⁵ (They did not see) what He did for you in the desert, until you arrived at this place, ⁶ and what He did to Dathan and Abiram, sons of Eliab, Reuben's son, when the earth opened its mouth and swallowed up: them, their households, their tents, and all the possessions (that kept them on) their feet, in the presence of all Israel —

⁷ But your eyes did see all the great acts of God, which He performed. ⁸ Therefore, you should keep all the commandments that I am commanding you today, so that:

- You will be strong to come and take possession of the land, that you are crossing over to acquire.
- ⁹ And in order that you may prolong your days on the land that God swore to give to your forefathers—to them and to their descendants—a land flowing with milk and honey.

What is the "bribe" that God accepts? He accepts repentance and good deeds from the wicked. God says, "My children! So long as the gates of repentance are open, I will accept bribes in this world. But when I sit in judgment in the world to come, I will not accept bribes, as the verse states (ibid., 6:35), *'He will not regard any ransom'*" (*Yalkut Shimoni*).

אֶרֶץ זָבַת חָלָב וּדְבָשׁ: ס 10 כִּי הָאָרֶץ אֲשֶׁר אַתָּה בָא־שָׁמָּה לְרִשְׁתָּהּ [SIXTH READING] לֹא כְאֶרֶץ מִצְרַיִם הִוא אֲשֶׁר יְצָאתֶם מִשָּׁם אֲשֶׁר תִּזְרַע אֶת־זַרְעֲךָ וְהִשְׁקִיתָ בְרַגְלְךָ כְּגַן הַיָּרָק: 11 וְהָאָרֶץ אֲשֶׁר אַתֶּם עֹבְרִים שָׁמָּה לְרִשְׁתָּהּ אֶרֶץ הָרִים וּבְקָעֹת לִמְטַר הַשָּׁמַיִם תִּשְׁתֶּה־מָּיִם: 12 אֶרֶץ אֲשֶׁר־יְהֹוָה אֱלֹהֶיךָ דֹּרֵשׁ אֹתָהּ תָּמִיד עֵינֵי יְהֹוָה אֱלֹהֶיךָ בָּהּ מֵרֵשִׁית הַשָּׁנָה וְעַד אַחֲרִית שָׁנָה: ס 13 וְהָיָה אִם־שָׁמֹעַ תִּשְׁמְעוּ אֶל־מִצְוֺתַי אֲשֶׁר אָנֹכִי מְצַוֶּה אֶתְכֶם הַיּוֹם לְאַהֲבָה אֶת־יְהֹוָה אֱלֹהֵיכֶם וּלְעָבְדוֹ בְּכָל־לְבַבְכֶם וּבְכָל־נַפְשְׁכֶם: 14 וְנָתַתִּי מְטַר־אַרְצְכֶם בְּעִתּוֹ יוֹרֶה וּמַלְקוֹשׁ וְאָסַפְתָּ דְגָנֶךָ וְתִירֹשְׁךָ וְיִצְהָרֶךָ: 15 וְנָתַתִּי עֵשֶׂב בְּשָׂדְךָ לִבְהֶמְתֶּךָ וְאָכַלְתָּ וְשָׂבָעְתָּ: 16 הִשָּׁמְרוּ לָכֶם פֶּן יִפְתֶּה לְבַבְכֶם וְסַרְתֶּם וַעֲבַדְתֶּם אֱלֹהִים אֲחֵרִים וְהִשְׁתַּחֲוִיתֶם לָהֶם: 17 וְחָרָה אַף־יְהֹוָה בָּכֶם וְעָצַר אֶת־הַשָּׁמַיִם וְלֹא־יִהְיֶה מָטָר וְהָאֲדָמָה לֹא תִתֵּן אֶת־יְבוּלָהּ וַאֲבַדְתֶּם מְהֵרָה מֵעַל הָאָרֶץ הַטֹּבָה אֲשֶׁר יְהֹוָה נֹתֵן לָכֶם: 18 וְשַׂמְתֶּם אֶת־דְּבָרַי אֵלֶּה עַל־לְבַבְכֶם וְעַל־נַפְשְׁכֶם וּקְשַׁרְתֶּם אֹתָם לְאוֹת עַל־יֶדְכֶם וְהָיוּ לְטוֹטָפֹת בֵּין

11:13 If you always listen. While the second paragraph of the *Shema* appears to be little more than a repetition of the first paragraph (above, 6:4-9), with various additions and changes, from a metaphysical perspective the two paragraphs are fundamentally different.

kabbalah bites

11:15-16 When you eat, the *sitra' aḥara'* (demonic forces) hover over your table. At this time, you are most susceptible to being *seduced under its lure*. One powerful way to dispel the *sitra' aḥara'* is to recite a *zimmun* ("invitation to grace") at the meal.

Another weapon is to wash the fingertips at the end of the meal (*mayim 'aḥaronim*).

God's sacred name *Ekyeh* has forty-one letters when spelled out in full, ten for each finger, plus one for the thumb. By washing the fingertips at the end of the meal you invoke this holy name on your behalf to banish the *sitra' aḥara'*.

Have this in mind when you perform the ritual and it will be so powerful.

Qualities of the Land of Israel

[SIXTH READING] ¹⁰ For the land to which you are coming to take possession of is not (bad) like the land of Egypt, out of which you came, where you would plant your seed and (then have to) water (it by carrying buckets from the Nile) by foot, like (looking after) a vegetable garden. ¹¹ (No!) The land which you are (soon) crossing over to acquire is a land of (arable) mountains and plains, and it is watered by rains from the skies, ¹² a land which God, your God, cares about. The eyes of God Almighty are continually upon it, from the beginning of the year to the end of the year.

Second Paragraph of the Shema

¹³ What will happen is:
- If you always listen to My commandments that I am commanding you, (regarding them as if you heard them) today.
- (And you keep them, not for personal gain, but rather out of) love for God, your God,
- And you serve Him (in prayer)
- (And, as a community, you serve Him) with all your heart and with all your soul,

¹⁴ then I will grant the early and late rains of your land at their proper time, and you—(not your enemies)—will gather in your grain, wine, and oil. ¹⁵ I will provide grass in your field for your livestock (so you do not have to take them to pasture at a distance. When) you will eat, you will be satisfied.

¹⁶ (But when you are in a state of satisfaction) beware not to let your heart be lured away (from the Torah, causing you to) go astray and worship other (strange) gods, and prostrate yourselves before them. ¹⁷ Then the anger of God will be kindled against you! He will close up the skies, and there will be no rain. The ground will not yield its produce, and you will perish quickly from the good land that God is giving you.

¹⁸ (Even after you go into exile) you should (continue to) place these words of Mine upon your heart and upon your soul. You should bind them as a sign upon

spiritual vitamin

"*Tefillin* is put on the arm facing the heart, and on the head, the seat of reason, thus bringing peace and harmony between the two great forces in human life, emotion and reason."

עֵינֵיכֶם: 19 וְלִמַּדְתֶּם אֹתָם אֶת־בְּנֵיכֶם לְדַבֵּר בָּם בְּשִׁבְתְּךָ בְּבֵיתֶךָ וּבְלֶכְתְּךָ בַדֶּרֶךְ וּבְשָׁכְבְּךָ וּבְקוּמֶךָ: 20 וּכְתַבְתָּם עַל־מְזוּזוֹת בֵּיתֶךָ וּבִשְׁעָרֶיךָ: 21 לְמַעַן יִרְבּוּ יְמֵיכֶם וִימֵי בְנֵיכֶם עַל הָאֲדָמָה אֲשֶׁר נִשְׁבַּע יְהוָה לַאֲבֹתֵיכֶם לָתֵת לָהֶם כִּימֵי הַשָּׁמַיִם עַל־הָאָרֶץ: ס 22 [SEVENTH READING AND MAFTIR] כִּי אִם־שָׁמֹר תִּשְׁמְרוּן אֶת־כָּל־הַמִּצְוָה הַזֹּאת אֲשֶׁר אָנֹכִי מְצַוֶּה אֶתְכֶם לַעֲשֹׂתָהּ לְאַהֲבָה אֶת־יְהוָה אֱלֹהֵיכֶם לָלֶכֶת בְּכָל־דְּרָכָיו וּלְדָבְקָה־בוֹ: 23 וְהוֹרִישׁ יְהוָה אֶת־כָּל־הַגּוֹיִם הָאֵלֶּה מִלִּפְנֵיכֶם וִירִשְׁתֶּם גּוֹיִם גְּדֹלִים וַעֲצֻמִים מִכֶּם: 24 כָּל־הַמָּקוֹם אֲשֶׁר תִּדְרֹךְ כַּף־רַגְלְכֶם בּוֹ לָכֶם יִהְיֶה מִן־הַמִּדְבָּר וְהַלְּבָנוֹן מִן־הַנָּהָר נְהַר־פְּרָת וְעַד הַיָּם הָאַחֲרוֹן יִהְיֶה גְּבֻלְכֶם: 25 לֹא־יִתְיַצֵּב אִישׁ בִּפְנֵיכֶם פַּחְדְּכֶם וּמוֹרַאֲכֶם יִתֵּן | יְהוָה אֱלֹהֵיכֶם עַל־פְּנֵי כָל־הָאָרֶץ אֲשֶׁר תִּדְרְכוּ־בָהּ כַּאֲשֶׁר דִּבֶּר לָכֶם: ס ס ס

קי"א פסוקים, א"ק סימן. יעל"א סימן.

Put on *tefillin* and make *mezuzot*, so that they will not be new and unfamiliar to you when you return—as the verse states, *"Set up markers for yourself"* (*Jeremiah 31:20; Rashi, 11th century*).

During the exile you might think that the people would be exempt from *tefillin* and *mezuzah*. The worries of the exile might exempt the people from *tefillin*, which require total concentration—and, as a wandering nation, the people would not purchase any property that would obligate them in *mezuzah*.

This verse teaches us that during exile you should clear your mind of worry to ensure that you are obligated in *tefillin*, and purchase a house so that you will be obligated in *mezuzah* (*Rabbi Judah Loew b. Bezalel of Prague, 16th century*).

19. You should teach these (words) to your sons. While in times gone by, women and girls were not taught Torah at all, nowadays it is not only permissible to teach women even the deepest parts of the Torah, but it is an absolute necessity to do so. For, in the modern world, women are no longer confined to the home and they are highly exposed to the "marketplace" of secular ideas. If the policy of not teaching women Torah at an advanced level will be upheld, a girl's sophisticated, worldly knowledge—which is likely to harbor many ideas that are antithetical to Torah—will be insubstantially compensated for by her rudimentary Torah knowledge.

And it goes without saying that Ḥasidic wisdom should be taught to women and girls, as this provides us with the tools to *"Know the God of your father, and serve Him with a perfect heart"* (*I Chronicles 28:9*), in which their obligation is identical to men and boys (*Rabbi Menaḥem Mendel Schneerson, 20th century*).

your hand, and they should be *totafot* between your eyes. ¹⁹ (From infancy) you should teach these (words) to your sons to (be accustomed to) speak of them, when you sit in your house and when you walk on the way, when you lie down (at night) and when you get up (in the morning). ²⁰ You shall write them on the doorposts of your house and upon your (public) gates. ²¹ (All this is) in order that your days and your children's days will be prolonged upon the land which God swore to your forefathers to give them, so long as the skies will be above the earth.

Commandments: Key to Conquest of the Land

[SEVENTH READING AND MAFTIR] ²² For if you will always be careful to keep these commandments which I am commanding you to keep, to love God, your God, to follow all His ways, and to cleave to Him, ²³ then God will drive out all these nations from before you, and you will take over nations that are greater and stronger than you. ²⁴ Every place upon which the soles of your feet will tread will be yours. Your boundary will be from the desert and the Lebanon, and from the river, the Euphrates River, until the western sea. ²⁵ No man will stand before you. God, your God, will cast the fear and dread of you upon all the land where you will tread, just as He said to you.

The Haftarah for 'Ekev is on page 1398.

The first paragraph of the Shema is speaking at an expanded level of consciousness, where Godliness is visibly present. The second paragraph speaks to a lower state of mind, where Godly revelation is absent.

Consequently, the first paragraph speaks of loving God, not only *"with all your heart and with all your soul,"* but, *"with all your might"* (6:3), alluding to an unlimited form of love, which is granted to a person by revelation from Above. In the second paragraph, however, we are commanded to serve God only *"with all your heart and with all your soul,"* since no further Divine assistance is available (*Rabbi Shneur Zalman of Lyady, 18th century*).

18. You should bind them. Why is the observance of *tefillin* and *mezuzah* mentioned immediately after the threat of exile in verse 17?

God says: Even after you go into exile, make yourselves distinctive with My commandments.

spiritual vitamin

> Every *mezuzah* is a Divine protection not only for your own home, with everybody and everything in it, but it also adds to the protection of all our people everywhere.

At first, you simply **obey,** fulfilling the Torah's **laws.** Later, you **appreciate,** examining their sacred **wisdom.** Ultimately, you **see** (*re'eh*) the laws as **indispensable** and self-evident blessings: You see **eye-to-eye with God.**

RE'EH
ראה

LAWS UPON ENTERING CANAAN	11:26 – 12:19
EATING NON-SACRIFICIAL MEAT	12:20–31
IDOL-WORSHIP	13:1–19
BODILY SANCTITY	14:1–21
LAWS OF TITHES	14:22–29
LAWS OF LOANS	15:1–11
SEVERANCE GIFTS	15:12–18
LAWS OF THE FIRSTBORN ANIMAL	15:19–23
THE FESTIVALS	16:1–17

NAME
Re'eh

MEANING
"See"

LINES IN TORAH SCROLL
258

PARASHIYYOT
5 open; 15 closed

VERSES
126

WORDS
1932

LETTERS
7442

LOCATION
Plains of Moab

DATE
Shevat–Adar, 2488

MITZVOT
17 positive;
38 prohibitions

CHARACTER PROFILE

NAME
Pig (animal)

OTHER NAMES
Ḥazir; davar aher

STATUS
Currently not kosher; will be kosher in the Messianic Era

CHARACTER
Fortunate in that it eats almost anything; commonly afflicted by disease; similar in taste to the *shibuta* fish, which is kosher; the pig's hooves are split, which is one sign of kosher status, but it does not chew the cud, and is not kosher

SYMBOLISM
The split hooves, which deceptively imply a kosher status, allude to the Romans, who committed violence and robbery under the guise of justice.

DESTINY

At every moment of the day, you are faced with opposing paths of *"blessing and curse."* Regardless of the route you have traveled until this moment, the future direction of your life depends entirely on your decisions today (11:26).

WRONGS

Reminding the Jews of their Egyptian slavemasters, the Torah requires special treatment of slaves. Left unchecked, human nature would have us subconsciously perpetuating the wrongs we have suffered in past interactions with others. Avoid becoming a monster of your past (15:14-15).

PILGRIMAGE

The Jews traveled to Jerusalem three times a year to celebrate their relationship with God. It is not good enough merely to feel love of God in your heart. It needs to be expressed in action (16:16-17).

דברים י״א:כ״ו-ל״ב

26 רְאֵה אָנֹכִי נֹתֵן לִפְנֵיכֶם הַיּוֹם בְּרָכָה וּקְלָלָה: 27 אֶת־הַבְּרָכָה אֲשֶׁר תִּשְׁמְעוּ אֶל־מִצְוֺת יְהֹוָה אֱלֹהֵיכֶם אֲשֶׁר אָנֹכִי מְצַוֶּה אֶתְכֶם הַיּוֹם: 28 וְהַקְּלָלָה אִם־לֹא תִשְׁמְעוּ אֶל־מִצְוֺת יְהֹוָה אֱלֹהֵיכֶם וְסַרְתֶּם מִן־הַדֶּרֶךְ אֲשֶׁר אָנֹכִי מְצַוֶּה אֶתְכֶם הַיּוֹם לָלֶכֶת אַחֲרֵי אֱלֹהִים אֲחֵרִים אֲשֶׁר לֹא־יְדַעְתֶּם: ס 29 וְהָיָה כִּי יְבִיאֲךָ יְהֹוָה אֱלֹהֶיךָ אֶל־הָאָרֶץ אֲשֶׁר־אַתָּה בָא־שָׁמָּה לְרִשְׁתָּהּ וְנָתַתָּה אֶת־הַבְּרָכָה עַל־הַר גְּרִזִים וְאֶת־הַקְּלָלָה עַל־הַר עֵיבָל: 30 הֲלֹא־הֵמָּה בְּעֵבֶר הַיַּרְדֵּן אַחֲרֵי דֶּרֶךְ מְבוֹא הַשֶּׁמֶשׁ בְּאֶרֶץ הַכְּנַעֲנִי הַיֹּשֵׁב בָּעֲרָבָה מוּל הַגִּלְגָּל אֵצֶל אֵלוֹנֵי מֹרֶה: 31 כִּי אַתֶּם עֹבְרִים אֶת־הַיַּרְדֵּן לָבֹא לָרֶשֶׁת אֶת־הָאָרֶץ אֲשֶׁר־יְהֹוָה אֱלֹהֵיכֶם נֹתֵן לָכֶם וִירִשְׁתֶּם אֹתָהּ וִישַׁבְתֶּם־בָּהּ: 32 וּשְׁמַרְתֶּם לַעֲשׂוֹת אֵת כָּל־הַחֻקִּים וְאֶת־הַמִּשְׁפָּטִים אֲשֶׁר אָנֹכִי נֹתֵן לִפְנֵיכֶם הַיּוֹם:

keeping the Torah's precepts, you *see* it. The necessity and positive results of observing the commandments become as clear and self-evident as seeing a physical object with your eyes.

And it is this third level which this Torah portion commands and spiritually empowers us all to reach, with the words: *"See! I am giving to you today a blessing"* (Rabbi Menahem Mendel Schneerson, 20th century).

A blessing and a curse. *"No evil thing is issued from Above"* (Genesis Rabbah). God does not issue curses at all—only blessings are *"issued from Above."* The problem lies "below," in our ability to receive God's blessings. If you are not a fitting receptacle, you will simply be unable to accommodate God's blessings. The result will be that after its downward path through the spiritual worlds, the blessing will be received in a way that appears, to human eyes, as a curse (*Rabbi Isaiah Horowitz, 16th–17th century*).

In the Messianic Era, we will not only forgive God for the sufferings of exile, but we will thank Him (see *Isaiah* 12:1), for then it will be evident how even God's "curses" were in fact blessings in disguise (*Rabbi Ezekiel Landau of Prague, 18th century*).

27. That you will listen to the commandments of God. When describing the cause of a blessing, the verse simply states *"that you will listen to the commandments of God,"* but with the curse, an additional clause is added, *"If you do not listen to the commandments of God ... and go astray"* (v. 28).

This reflects an important distinction between the consequences of good and evil. Thoughts of doing a good deed are considered by God like an actual good deed, but thoughts of sin are not regarded as having actually sinned (*Babylonian Talmud, Kiddushin* 40a). The Torah stresses that blessing will come when *"you will listen to the commandments,"* that is, when you consider doing the commandments, even if you are eventually unable to fulfil them. The curse, on the other hand, will only come once you follow your evil thoughts and actually *"go astray"* (*Rabbi Hayyim of Tchernowitz, 18th century*).

deuteronomy 11:26–32

parashat re'eh

A Blessing and a Curse

²⁶ See! I am giving to you today a blessing and a curse.

— ²⁷ The blessing (is being given) on the basis that you will listen to the commandments of God, your God, which I am commanding you today. ²⁸ And the curse (will come) if you do not listen to the commandments of God, your God, and go astray from the way I am commanding you today, to follow other gods, with which you are unacquainted—

²⁹ What will happen is, when God, your God, will bring you to the land which you are going to come and take possession of, you should place (the people who will recite) the blessing (facing) towards Mount Gerizim, and (when they recite) the curse (they should turn so that they face) towards Mount Ebal.

³⁰ (These mountains) are to be found well beyond the other side of the Jordan, (to the west) where the sun sets, in the land of the Canaanites, who dwell in the plain, far from Gilgal, near (Shechem in) the plains of Moreh.

³¹ When you cross the Jordan (you will see miracles that will be a sign for you that you are going) to come and take possession of the land which God, your God, is giving you. You will take possession of it and settle in it. ³² So be careful about observing all the suprarational commands and rational commands that I am presenting before you today.

---

kabbalah bites

11:26 Why did Moses say "see"? What was there to be seen?

Extremely lofty souls, such as Moses, can actually see spiritual things with their eyes. Moses spoke of the "blessings and curses" in very physical terms, *"See! I am giving to you today…,"* because he could actually envision the spiritual.

And that is why the word *re'eh* ("*See!*") is conjugated in the singular, because Moses was addressing those few individuals who shared his capacity for envisioning the spiritual.

11:26 See! What, exactly, is the Torah demanding, in asking us to "see" God's blessings and curses?

Broadly speaking, worship of God could fall into one of three categories. (a) *Plain obedience*. At this level, you are willing to observe the commandments because you are aware of a Higher Authority. However, your observance is not inspired by an understanding or appreciation of the Torah. You simply "accept the yoke of heaven."

(b) *Intellectual appreciation*. A higher level is where you not only observe the precepts of the Torah out of deference to a Higher Authority, but you also have an intellectual appreciation of the commandments, and you understand the rewards that observance brings.

But even then you have not yet reached perfection. For intellectual conviction alone—while immensely powerful—still leaves room to explore other avenues, so it does not represent an absolute commitment.

Thus, the highest level of observance is: (c) *Vision*. At this level, you do not merely *appreciate* the value of

דברים יב:א-יא

ראה

יב ¹ אֵ֚לֶּה הַֽחֻקִּ֣ים וְהַמִּשְׁפָּטִ֔ים אֲשֶׁ֥ר תִּשְׁמְר֖וּן לַעֲשׂ֑וֹת בָּאָ֕רֶץ אֲשֶׁר֩ נָתַ֨ן יְהֹוָ֜ה אֱלֹהֵ֧י אֲבֹתֶ֛יךָ לְךָ֖ לְרִשְׁתָּ֑הּ כׇּל־הַ֨יָּמִ֔ים אֲשֶׁר־אַתֶּ֥ם חַיִּ֖ים עַל־הָאֲדָמָֽה: ² אַבֵּ֣ד תְּ֠אַבְּד֠וּן אֶֽת־כׇּל־הַמְּקֹמ֞וֹת אֲשֶׁ֧ר עָֽבְדוּ־שָׁ֣ם הַגּוֹיִ֗ם אֲשֶׁ֥ר אַתֶּ֛ם יֹרְשִׁ֥ים אֹתָ֖ם אֶת־אֱלֹהֵיהֶ֑ם עַל־הֶהָרִ֤ים הָֽרָמִים֙ וְעַל־הַגְּבָע֔וֹת וְתַ֖חַת כׇּל־עֵ֥ץ רַעֲנָֽן: ³ וְנִתַּצְתֶּ֣ם אֶת־מִזְבְּחֹתָ֗ם וְשִׁבַּרְתֶּם֙ אֶת־מַצֵּ֣בֹתָ֔ם וַאֲשֵֽׁרֵיהֶם֙ תִּשְׂרְפ֣וּן בָּאֵ֔שׁ וּפְסִילֵ֥י אֱלֹֽהֵיהֶ֖ם תְּגַדֵּע֑וּן וְאִבַּדְתֶּ֣ם אֶת־שְׁמָ֔ם מִן־הַמָּק֖וֹם הַהֽוּא: ⁴ לֹא־תַעֲשׂ֣וּן כֵּ֔ן לַיהֹוָ֖ה אֱלֹהֵיכֶֽם: ⁵ כִּ֠י אִֽם־אֶל־הַמָּק֞וֹם אֲשֶׁר־יִבְחַ֨ר יְהֹוָ֤ה אֱלֹֽהֵיכֶם֙ מִכׇּל־שִׁבְטֵיכֶ֔ם לָשׂ֥וּם אֶת־שְׁמ֖וֹ שָׁ֑ם לְשִׁכְנ֥וֹ תִדְרְשׁ֖וּ וּבָ֥אתָ שָּֽׁמָּה: ⁶ וַהֲבֵאתֶ֣ם שָׁ֗מָּה עֹלֹֽתֵיכֶם֙ וְזִבְחֵיכֶ֔ם וְאֵת֙ מַעְשְׂרֹ֣תֵיכֶ֔ם וְאֵ֖ת תְּרוּמַ֣ת יֶדְכֶ֑ם וְנִדְרֵיכֶם֙ וְנִדְבֹ֣תֵיכֶ֔ם וּבְכֹרֹ֥ת בְּקַרְכֶ֖ם וְצֹאנְכֶֽם: ⁷ וַאֲכַלְתֶּם־שָׁ֗ם לִפְנֵי֙ יְהֹוָ֣ה אֱלֹֽהֵיכֶ֔ם וּשְׂמַחְתֶּ֗ם בְּכֹל֙ מִשְׁלַ֣ח יֶדְכֶ֔ם אַתֶּ֖ם וּבָתֵּיכֶ֑ם אֲשֶׁ֥ר בֵּֽרַכְךָ֖ יְהֹוָ֥ה אֱלֹהֶֽיךָ: ⁸ לֹ֣א תַעֲשׂ֔וּן כְּ֠כֹ֠ל אֲשֶׁ֨ר אֲנַ֧חְנוּ עֹשִׂ֛ים פֹּ֖ה הַיּ֑וֹם אִ֖ישׁ כׇּל־הַיָּשָׁ֥ר בְּעֵינָֽיו: ⁹ כִּ֥י לֹא־בָּאתֶ֖ם עַד־עָ֑תָּה אֶל־הַמְּנוּחָה֙ וְאֶל־הַֽנַּחֲלָ֔ה אֲשֶׁר־יְהֹוָ֥ה אֱלֹהֶ֖יךָ נֹתֵ֥ן לָֽךְ: ¹⁰ וַעֲבַרְתֶּם֮ אֶת־הַיַּרְדֵּן֒ וִֽישַׁבְתֶּ֣ם בָּאָ֔רֶץ אֲשֶׁר־יְהֹוָ֥ה אֱלֹֽהֵיכֶ֖ם מַנְחִ֣יל אֶתְכֶ֑ם וְהֵנִ֨יחַ לָכֶ֧ם מִכׇּל־אֹיְבֵיכֶ֛ם מִסָּבִ֖יב וִֽישַׁבְתֶּם־בֶּֽטַח: ¹¹ [SECOND READING] וְהָיָ֣ה הַמָּק֗וֹם אֲשֶׁר־יִבְחַ֨ר יְהֹוָ֤ה אֱלֹֽהֵיכֶם֙ בּ֔וֹ לְשַׁכֵּ֥ן שְׁמ֖וֹ שָׁ֑ם שָֽׁמָּה

Abraham carried out the binding of Isaac there, and we are taught that Adam offered his sacrifice there. So how could Shiloh be described as *"the site where God, your God, will choose"*?

Rather, I maintain that every reference to God's chosen site here refers to the site of the Holy Temple in Jerusalem (*Rabbi Ephraim of Luntshits, 16ᵗʰ–17ᵗʰ century*).

The Torah mentions only *"the place which God, your God, will choose,"* without making any *explicit reference* that it refers to Jerusalem. This hints to the fact that God "chooses" every place in which you make your personal "offering" of prayer to your Maker. That is why when you pray, you face in the direction of Jerusalem, because spiritually speaking you are found in Jerusalem— *"the place which God, your God, will choose"*—at that very moment (*Rabbi Hayyim b. Bezalel of Prague, 16ᵗʰ century*).

You should seek out His dwelling place and come there. If you will *"seek out His dwelling,"* then you will definitely *"come there."* God will help you (*Rabbi Moses Sofer, 18ᵗʰ–19ᵗʰ century*).

deuteronomy 12:1–11 — re'eh

Commandments to be Observed upon Entering the Land

12 ¹ These are the suprarational commands and rational commands that you should be careful to perform in the land which God, the God of your fathers, is giving you as a possession for all the days that you live on the earth:

❖ ² From all the places where the nations—that you will take over—performed acts of worship, upon the high mountains, the hills, and under every lush tree, you should progressively destroy their gods (until nothing remains of them). ³ You should demolish their altars, smash their monuments, burn their idolatrous trees with fire, cut down the graven images of their gods, and spoil the names (of their gods with ridicule, ensuring they have no respect) from that place.

The Uniqueness of Shiloh and Jerusalem

⁴ You should not do any (act of sacrificial worship) to God, your God, ⁵ other than at the site where God, your God, will choose, to place His name there, from among all your tribes. You should seek out His dwelling (place in the Tabernacle at Shiloh) and come there. ⁶ You should bring there your burnt-offerings, and your (obligatory peace-)offerings, your tithes, (your first fruits—which are) lifted from your hand (by the priests)—your vows, your pledges, and the firstborn of your cattle and of your sheep (which are to be given to the priests. ⁷ It is) there that you should eat (your sacrifices) before God, your God. Then you and your households will rejoice in all the work of your hands. (You should bring offerings according to the means with) which God, your God, blesses you.

⁸ (When you cross the Jordan, for the first fourteen years, before the Tabernacle at Shiloh is established) you should not (erect private altars to) carry out all the (obligatory sacrifices) that we are currently offering (in the Tabernacle. At that time, private altars will be permitted only for) all (the voluntary sacrifices) which each man sees fit (to offer. ⁹ Obligatory sacrifices will be prohibited at that time), for you will not yet have come to the resting place (at Shiloh) or to the eternal abode (in Jerusalem), which God, your God, is giving you.

¹⁰ You should cross the Jordan, (apportion) the land that God, your God, is giving you as an inheritance (and) settle in it. Then (after the conquest and apportionment), He will give you rest from all your enemies surrounding you, and you will dwell securely. [SECOND READING] ¹¹ Then (you will build the Holy Temple) in the place in which God, your God, will choose to make His name rest there.

12:5 The site where God, your God, will choose. This refers to the Tabernacle at Shiloh (*Rashi, 11ᵗʰ century*).

How could the Torah possibly suggest that Shiloh is God's chosen location, when we know that the site of the Temple in Jerusalem has always been revered as God's chosen place?

דברים יב:יא-כ · ראה

תָּבִיאוּ אֵת כָּל־אֲשֶׁר אָנֹכִי מְצַוֶּה אֶתְכֶם עוֹלֹתֵיכֶם וְזִבְחֵיכֶם מַעְשְׂרֹתֵיכֶם וּתְרֻמַת יֶדְכֶם וְכֹל מִבְחַר נִדְרֵיכֶם אֲשֶׁר תִּדְּרוּ לַיהֹוָה: 12 וּשְׂמַחְתֶּם לִפְנֵי יְהֹוָה אֱלֹהֵיכֶם אַתֶּם וּבְנֵיכֶם וּבְנֹתֵיכֶם וְעַבְדֵיכֶם וְאַמְהֹתֵיכֶם וְהַלֵּוִי אֲשֶׁר בְּשַׁעֲרֵיכֶם כִּי אֵין לוֹ חֵלֶק וְנַחֲלָה אִתְּכֶם: 13 הִשָּׁמֶר לְךָ פֶּן־תַּעֲלֶה עֹלֹתֶיךָ בְּכָל־מָקוֹם אֲשֶׁר תִּרְאֶה: 14 כִּי אִם־בַּמָּקוֹם אֲשֶׁר־יִבְחַר יְהֹוָה בְּאַחַד שְׁבָטֶיךָ שָׁם תַּעֲלֶה עֹלֹתֶיךָ וְשָׁם תַּעֲשֶׂה כֹּל אֲשֶׁר אָנֹכִי מְצַוֶּךָּ: 15 רַק בְּכָל־אַוַּת נַפְשְׁךָ תִּזְבַּח ׀ וְאָכַלְתָּ בָשָׂר כְּבִרְכַּת יְהֹוָה אֱלֹהֶיךָ אֲשֶׁר נָתַן־לְךָ בְּכָל־שְׁעָרֶיךָ הַטָּמֵא וְהַטָּהוֹר יֹאכְלֶנּוּ כַּצְּבִי וְכָאַיָּל: 16 רַק הַדָּם לֹא תֹאכֵלוּ עַל־הָאָרֶץ תִּשְׁפְּכֶנּוּ כַּמָּיִם: 17 לֹא־תוּכַל לֶאֱכֹל בִּשְׁעָרֶיךָ מַעְשַׂר דְּגָנְךָ וְתִירֹשְׁךָ וְיִצְהָרֶךָ וּבְכֹרֹת בְּקָרְךָ וְצֹאנֶךָ וְכָל־נְדָרֶיךָ אֲשֶׁר תִּדֹּר וְנִדְבֹתֶיךָ וּתְרוּמַת יָדֶךָ: 18 כִּי אִם־לִפְנֵי יְהֹוָה אֱלֹהֶיךָ תֹּאכְלֶנּוּ בַּמָּקוֹם אֲשֶׁר יִבְחַר יְהֹוָה אֱלֹהֶיךָ בּוֹ אַתָּה וּבִנְךָ וּבִתֶּךָ וְעַבְדְּךָ וַאֲמָתֶךָ וְהַלֵּוִי אֲשֶׁר בִּשְׁעָרֶיךָ וְשָׂמַחְתָּ לִפְנֵי יְהֹוָה אֱלֹהֶיךָ בְּכֹל מִשְׁלַח יָדֶךָ: 19 הִשָּׁמֶר לְךָ פֶּן־תַּעֲזֹב אֶת־הַלֵּוִי כָּל־יָמֶיךָ עַל־אַדְמָתֶךָ: ס 20 כִּי־יַרְחִיב יְהֹוָה אֱלֹהֶיךָ אֶת־גְּבֻלְךָ כַּאֲשֶׁר דִּבֶּר־לָךְ וְאָמַרְתָּ אֹכְלָה בָשָׂר כִּי־תְאַוֶּה נַפְשְׁךָ לֶאֱכֹל בָּשָׂר בְּכָל־אַוַּת נַפְשְׁךָ תֹּאכַל בָּשָׂר:

spiritual vitamin

> When one plans a visit to another country, it often requires a visa, and the "visa" to the Holy Land is in terms of an extra measure of holiness. This applies not only while living there, but also while making preparations to make *aliyah* when still at home. And this is the inner meaning of *aliyah*, meaning "ascendancy," namely, to a higher spiritual level.

deuteronomy 12:11–20 — re'eh

- ❖ (Only) there should you bring everything that I am commanding you: your burnt-offerings, your (obligatory peace-)offerings, your tithes, (your first fruits—which are) lifted from your hand (by the priests)—and all your vow-offerings which you will vow to God (from your) choicest (quality produce).

- ❖ ¹² You should rejoice before God, your God: you, your sons, daughters, servants and maidservants, and the Levite who lives in your town, for he has no portion or inheritance with you.

- ❖ ¹³ Be careful not to offer up your burnt-offerings in any place you see (fit to do so. ¹⁴ This must be done) only in the place God will choose in (the territory of) one of your tribes. (Only) there may you offer up your burnt-offerings, and there you should do everything that I am commanding you.

- ❖ ¹⁵ (If a blemish develops in a holy offering and you) desire with all your soul (to eat its meat):

- ❖ You may slaughter (it in any place) and eat (its) meat in all your cities, for God, your God, is giving it to you as a blessing (but you may not make use of its fleece or milk).

- ❖ (You may) only (redeem it and slaughter it if it is a permanent blemish that will not heal).

- ❖ (Even though the animal was originally a holy offering which may not become ritually impure, after it has been redeemed) a ritually impure person and a ritually pure person may eat it (together on the same plate).

- ❖ (The foreleg, jaw and end-stomach do not need to be given to the priest), as if (you were slaughtering) a deer, or a gazelle.

- ❖ ¹⁶ Even though (the blood of this animal is exempt from being thrown on the altar) you may not eat the blood. You should spill it on the ground like water (and you do not have to cover it).

- ❖ ¹⁷ You may not eat (the following) within your (own) cities: your grain, wine, or oil tithes, the firstborn of your cattle or of your sheep, any of your vow-offerings that you will vow, your pledge-offerings, or (your first fruits—which are) lifted from your hand (by the priests). ¹⁸ Rather, you should eat them before God, your God, in (Jerusalem, which is) the place God, your God, will choose. You (should eat them along with) your son, daughter, servant, maidservant, and the Levite who lives in your town, and you should rejoice before God, your God, in all the work of your hands.

- ❖ ¹⁹ Be careful not to abandon the Levite, all your days upon your land.

Consumption of Non-Sacrificial Meat

- ❖ ²⁰ When God, your God, extends your boundary, as He said to you, and you say, "I want to eat meat," because your soul desires to eat meat, then you may eat as

דברים יב:כא-כח ראה

21 כִּֽי־יִרְחַ֨ק מִמְּךָ֜ הַמָּק֗וֹם אֲשֶׁ֨ר יִבְחַ֜ר יְהֹוָ֣ה אֱלֹהֶ֘יךָ֮ לָשׂ֣וּם שְׁמ֣וֹ שָׁם֒ וְזָבַחְתָּ֞ מִבְּקָרְךָ֣ וּמִצֹּֽאנְךָ֗ אֲשֶׁ֨ר נָתַ֤ן יְהֹוָה֙ לְךָ֔ כַּאֲשֶׁ֖ר צִוִּיתִ֑ךָ וְאָֽכַלְתָּ֙ בִּשְׁעָרֶ֔יךָ בְּכֹ֖ל אַוַּ֥ת נַפְשֶֽׁךָ׃ 22 אַ֗ךְ כַּאֲשֶׁ֨ר יֵאָכֵ֤ל אֶֽת־הַצְּבִי֙ וְאֶת־הָ֣אַיָּ֔ל כֵּ֖ן תֹּאכְלֶ֑נּוּ הַטָּמֵא֙ וְהַטָּה֔וֹר יַחְדָּ֖ו יֹאכְלֶֽנּוּ׃ 23 רַ֣ק חֲזַ֗ק לְבִלְתִּי֙ אֲכֹ֣ל הַדָּ֔ם כִּ֥י הַדָּ֖ם ה֣וּא הַנָּ֑פֶשׁ וְלֹא־תֹאכַ֥ל הַנֶּ֖פֶשׁ עִם־הַבָּשָֽׂר׃ 24 לֹ֖א תֹּאכְלֶ֑נּוּ עַל־הָאָ֥רֶץ תִּשְׁפְּכֶ֖נּוּ כַּמָּֽיִם׃ 25 לֹ֖א תֹּאכְלֶ֑נּוּ לְמַ֨עַן יִיטַ֤ב לְךָ֙ וּלְבָנֶ֣יךָ אַחֲרֶ֔יךָ כִּֽי־תַעֲשֶׂ֥ה הַיָּשָׁ֖ר בְּעֵינֵ֥י יְהֹוָֽה׃ 26 רַ֣ק קָֽדָשֶׁ֧יךָ אֲשֶׁר־יִהְי֛וּ לְךָ֖ וּנְדָרֶ֑יךָ תִּשָּׂ֣א וּבָ֔אתָ אֶל־הַמָּק֖וֹם אֲשֶׁר־יִבְחַ֥ר יְהֹוָֽה׃ 27 וְעָשִׂ֤יתָ עֹלֹתֶ֙יךָ֙ הַבָּשָׂ֣ר וְהַדָּ֔ם עַל־מִזְבַּ֖ח יְהֹוָ֣ה אֱלֹהֶ֑יךָ וְדַם־זְבָחֶ֗יךָ יִשָּׁפֵךְ֙ עַל־מִזְבַּח֙ יְהֹוָ֣ה אֱלֹהֶ֔יךָ וְהַבָּשָׂ֖ר תֹּאכֵֽל׃ 28 שְׁמֹ֣ר וְשָׁמַעְתָּ֗ אֵ֚ת כָּל־הַדְּבָרִ֣ים הָאֵ֔לֶּה אֲשֶׁ֥ר אָנֹכִ֖י מְצַוֶּ֑ךָּ לְמַ֩עַן֩ יִיטַ֨ב לְךָ֜ וּלְבָנֶ֤יךָ אַחֲרֶ֙יךָ֙ עַד־עוֹלָ֔ם כִּ֣י

---

maintained that God would not have empowered the Jewish people to do something which is spiritually "irrelevant." Therefore, he maintained that meat was forbidden.

But Rabbi Akiva maintained that, since eating meat was spiritually "irrelevant" to the Jewish people, the Torah would not have legislated any rules regarding its consumption. Therefore, he argued, it could be eaten freely (*Rabbi Menahem Mendel Schneerson, 20th century*).

23. Be strong not to eat the blood. "From the statement '*be strong*,' you can infer that the people used to eat blood excessively. Therefore, the Torah found it necessary to say, '*be strong*'"—these are the words of Rabbi Judah.

Rabbi Simeon son of Azzai says, "This comes to teach you how much you should strengthen your observance of the commandments. If the Torah needed to 'strengthen' you to observe the prohibition of eating blood—which is easy to guard yourself against, because you have no desire for it—then how much more so must you strengthen yourself to observe all the other commandments!" (*Rashi, 11th century*).

28. Safeguard. This refers to study of the law, which you must guard in your heart, so that it should not be forgotten, as the verse states: *"For it is pleasant that you guard them in your heart"* (Proverbs 22:18; *Rashi, 11th century*).

All these words. This means that a minor commandment should be as precious to you as a major one (*Rashi, 11th century*).

---

kabbalah bites

12:21 *Shehitah* (ritual slaughter), in general, is a process of sweetening harsh forces of judgment and severity.

Also, sometimes human souls are reincarnated into animals to achieve *tikkun* (spiritual healing).

If the animal is slaughtered according to Torah law, the soul will be extricated from its animal incarnation and can re-enter a human body in its next life.

much meat as your soul desires. ²¹ If the place where God, your God, chooses to put His name is far from you (so you cannot bring peace-offerings every day), you may (eat) from your cattle and sheep, which God has given you, (provided that you first) slaughter (them, as) I have commanded you (in the Oral Law). Then, you may eat (meat) in your (own) cities, as much as your soul desires.

- ²² You may eat them just as a deer or a gazelle is eaten, (i.e.) a ritually impure person may eat together with a ritually pure person. However, (unlike in the case of a deer or a gazelle, their sacrificial fats are not permitted).

- ²³ However, be strong not to eat the blood, for the blood is the soul, and you may not eat the soul with the flesh.

- ²⁴ You may not eat (the blood which trickles out of an animal). Spill it on the ground, like water. ²⁵ You should not eat (the blood within internal organs), for your own benefit, and for your children after you, because you will be doing what is proper in the eyes of God.

- ²⁶ (Although I have permitted you to sacrifice non-sacred animals), however, your holy offerings and voluntary offerings which you will have should be carried and brought to (the Holy Temple), the place that God will choose. ²⁷ (If they are) burnt-offerings, the meat and the blood should go upon the altar of God, your God. (If they are peace-)offerings, their blood should be poured upon the altar of God, your God, and you should eat the meat.

²⁸ Safeguard and listen to all these words that I am commanding you, which are for your benefit and that of your children after you, for all time, because (God

21. Slaughter (them, as) I have commanded you. Why was the requirement of ritual slaughter only introduced here, shortly before entering the land of Israel?

Rabbi Ishmael says: "Originally, it was *prohibited* to eat (non-sacrificial) meat. When they entered the land of Israel, meat was permitted to them."

Rabbi Akiva says: "Originally, they were *permitted* to eat meat from an animal that was not ritually slaughtered. When they entered the land, non-ritually slaughtered meat became forbidden to them" (*Babylonian Talmud, Ḥullin* 16b-17a).

When you eat food it becomes incorporated into your body, and is "elevated" from its prior state, be it animal, vegetable or mineral. In the case of meat, which is a material luxury, this spiritual elevation is more difficult, so the special procedure of *sheḥitah* (ritual slaughter) is required.

This helps us understand why the precept of (non-sacrificial) *sheḥitah* was only introduced as the people entered the land of Israel. In the desert, they were removed from worldly matters, and the need to elevate them; but upon entering the land, the Jewish people were charged with the mission to interact with, and spiritually elevate, the material world.

Both Rabbi Ishmael and Rabbi Akiva agreed with this reasoning—that "elevation" of meat was spiritually "irrelevant" to the unworldly mode of Divine service in the desert. Where they differed was regarding the practical implication of this spiritual "irrelevance." Rabbi Ishmael

תַּעֲשֶׂה הַטּוֹב וְהַיָּשָׁר בְּעֵינֵי יְהֹוָה אֱלֹהֶיךָ: ס 29 [THIRD READING] כִּי־יַכְרִית יְהֹוָה אֱלֹהֶיךָ אֶת־הַגּוֹיִם אֲשֶׁר אַתָּה בָא־שָׁמָּה לָרֶשֶׁת אוֹתָם מִפָּנֶיךָ וְיָרַשְׁתָּ אֹתָם וְיָשַׁבְתָּ בְּאַרְצָם: 30 הִשָּׁמֶר לְךָ פֶּן־תִּנָּקֵשׁ אַחֲרֵיהֶם אַחֲרֵי הִשָּׁמְדָם מִפָּנֶיךָ וּפֶן־תִּדְרֹשׁ לֵאלֹהֵיהֶם לֵאמֹר אֵיכָה יַעַבְדוּ הַגּוֹיִם הָאֵלֶּה אֶת־אֱלֹהֵיהֶם וְאֶעֱשֶׂה־כֵּן גַּם־אָנִי: 31 לֹא־תַעֲשֶׂה כֵן לַיהֹוָה אֱלֹהֶיךָ כִּי כָל־תּוֹעֲבַת יְהֹוָה אֲשֶׁר שָׂנֵא עָשׂוּ לֵאלֹהֵיהֶם כִּי גַם אֶת־בְּנֵיהֶם וְאֶת־בְּנֹתֵיהֶם יִשְׂרְפוּ בָאֵשׁ לֵאלֹהֵיהֶם:

יג 1 אֵת כָּל־הַדָּבָר אֲשֶׁר אָנֹכִי מְצַוֶּה אֶתְכֶם אֹתוֹ תִשְׁמְרוּ לַעֲשׂוֹת לֹא־תֹסֵף עָלָיו וְלֹא תִגְרַע מִמֶּנּוּ: פ 2 כִּי־יָקוּם בְּקִרְבְּךָ נָבִיא אוֹ חֹלֵם חֲלוֹם וְנָתַן אֵלֶיךָ אוֹת אוֹ מוֹפֵת: 3 וּבָא הָאוֹת וְהַמּוֹפֵת אֲשֶׁר־דִּבֶּר אֵלֶיךָ לֵאמֹר נֵלְכָה אַחֲרֵי אֱלֹהִים אֲחֵרִים אֲשֶׁר לֹא־יְדַעְתָּם וְנָעָבְדֵם: 4 לֹא תִשְׁמַע אֶל־דִּבְרֵי הַנָּבִיא הַהוּא אוֹ אֶל־חוֹלֵם הַחֲלוֹם הַהוּא כִּי מְנַסֶּה יְהֹוָה אֱלֹהֵיכֶם אֶתְכֶם לָדַעַת הֲיִשְׁכֶם אֹהֲבִים אֶת־יְהֹוָה אֱלֹהֵיכֶם בְּכָל־לְבַבְכֶם וּבְכָל־נַפְשְׁכֶם: 5 אַחֲרֵי יְהֹוָה אֱלֹהֵיכֶם תֵּלֵכוּ וְאֹתוֹ תִירָאוּ וְאֶת־מִצְוֺתָיו תִּשְׁמֹרוּ וּבְקֹלוֹ תִשְׁמָעוּ וְאֹתוֹ תַעֲבֹדוּ וּבוֹ תִדְבָּקוּן: 6 וְהַנָּבִיא הַהוּא אוֹ חֹלֵם הַחֲלוֹם

In the eyes of God. Some people will readily do good deeds when they stand to gain recognition, but if no one is there to witness their piety, they are not so eager. But you must do "what is good *in the eyes of God*"—the commandments ought to be fulfilled as though nobody but God is there to see it. Such good deeds, God assures us, will benefit you and your children forever (*Rabbi Abraham Samuel Benjamin Sofer, 19th century*).

13:1 Do not add to it. Do not detract from it. Why does the Torah state first, "*Do not add to it*," and only afterwards, "*Do not detract from it*"? Surely, detracting from the Torah is the more serious crime, and should have been stated first?

The *yetzer ha-ra'* (impulse to evil) knows that if it will tell you to "detract from the Torah," you will simply not listen. Therefore it encourages you to "add" to Judaism, in the hope that this will begin to corrupt you, eventually leading you to "detract" from observance. So, the Torah warns you of the *yetzer's* ploy, by warning you first of all not to add to the Torah (*Rabbi Menahem Mendel Schneerson, 20th century*).

5. You should follow God. Is it possible for a human being to follow God, who is *"a consuming fire"* (Deuteronomy 4:24)?

benefits you) when you have done what is good in the eyes of God, your God, and proper (in the eyes of man).

[THIRD READING] ²⁹ When God, your God will cut off the nations (from the land) where you are (soon) to come and drive them out from before you, and you (succeed) in driving them out, and settle in their land, ³⁰ be careful not to be lured into following (their ways, especially) after (you witness how) they have been destroyed from before you (for their degenerate behavior). Be careful not to inquire about their gods, saying, "How did these nations serve their gods? I will do likewise!"

³¹ Do not do this to God, your God. For they worshiped their gods with all the abominable methods which God hates. They also burned their sons and daughters in fire to their gods.

Preserving the Precepts of the Torah

13 ¹ Be careful to observe everything which I am commanding you (no matter how trivial it may seem):

- ❖ Do not add to it.
- ❖ Do not detract from it.

The False Prophet

❖ ² If a prophet will arise from among you, or a person who has a vision in his dream, and he indicates to you a sign (in the heavens) or a miracle (upon the earth), ³ and then the sign or the miracle which he told you happens, (and he) says, "Let's go after other gods with which you are unacquainted, and let's worship them!" ⁴ You should not listen to the words of that prophet, or to the person, who had a vision in his dream, for God, your God, is testing you, to know whether you do in fact love God, your God, with all your heart and with all your soul.

⁵ You should follow (only) God, your God, and fear Him. (You should) keep His commandments (that were given through Moses), listen to His voice (through genuine prophets), worship Him (in the Holy Temple), and adhere to His (ways of kindness).

❖ ⁶ That prophet, or that person who had a vision in his dream should be put to death because he spoke falsehood about God, your God—who brought you out of the land of Egypt, who redeemed you

Food for thought

1. Why would God empower false prophets to make wonders and miracles?

2. Has your faith ever been severely tested?

3. What would be a modern equivalent of the false prophet?

דברים יג:ו-טו

הַהוּא יוּמָת כִּי דִבֶּר־סָרָה עַל־יְהֹוָה אֱלֹהֵיכֶם הַמּוֹצִיא אֶתְכֶם | מֵאֶרֶץ מִצְרַיִם וְהַפֹּדְךָ מִבֵּית עֲבָדִים לְהַדִּיחֲךָ מִן־הַדֶּרֶךְ אֲשֶׁר צִוְּךָ יְהֹוָה אֱלֹהֶיךָ לָלֶכֶת בָּהּ וּבִעַרְתָּ הָרָע מִקִּרְבֶּךָ: ס 7 כִּי יְסִיתְךָ אָחִיךָ בֶן־אִמֶּךָ אוֹ־בִנְךָ אוֹ־בִתְּךָ אוֹ | אֵשֶׁת חֵיקֶךָ אוֹ רֵעֲךָ אֲשֶׁר כְּנַפְשְׁךָ בַּסֵּתֶר לֵאמֹר נֵלְכָה וְנַעַבְדָה אֱלֹהִים אֲחֵרִים אֲשֶׁר לֹא יָדַעְתָּ אַתָּה וַאֲבֹתֶיךָ: 8 מֵאֱלֹהֵי הָעַמִּים אֲשֶׁר סְבִיבֹתֵיכֶם הַקְּרֹבִים אֵלֶיךָ אוֹ הָרְחֹקִים מִמֶּךָּ מִקְצֵה הָאָרֶץ וְעַד־קְצֵה הָאָרֶץ: 9 לֹא־תֹאבֶה לוֹ וְלֹא תִשְׁמַע אֵלָיו וְלֹא־תָחוֹס עֵינְךָ עָלָיו וְלֹא־תַחְמֹל וְלֹא־תְכַסֶּה עָלָיו: 10 כִּי הָרֹג תַּהַרְגֶנּוּ יָדְךָ תִּהְיֶה־בּוֹ בָרִאשׁוֹנָה לַהֲמִיתוֹ וְיַד כָּל־הָעָם בָּאַחֲרֹנָה: 11 וּסְקַלְתּוֹ בָאֲבָנִים וָמֵת כִּי בִקֵּשׁ לְהַדִּיחֲךָ מֵעַל יְהֹוָה אֱלֹהֶיךָ הַמּוֹצִיאֲךָ מֵאֶרֶץ מִצְרַיִם מִבֵּית עֲבָדִים: 12 וְכָל־יִשְׂרָאֵל יִשְׁמְעוּ וְיִרָאוּן וְלֹא־יוֹסִפוּ לַעֲשׂוֹת כַּדָּבָר הָרָע הַזֶּה בְּקִרְבֶּךָ: ס 13 כִּי־תִשְׁמַע בְּאַחַת עָרֶיךָ אֲשֶׁר יְהֹוָה אֱלֹהֶיךָ נֹתֵן לְךָ לָשֶׁבֶת שָׁם לֵאמֹר: 14 יָצְאוּ אֲנָשִׁים בְּנֵי־בְלִיַּעַל מִקִּרְבֶּךָ וַיַּדִּיחוּ אֶת־יֹשְׁבֵי עִירָם לֵאמֹר נֵלְכָה וְנַעַבְדָה אֱלֹהִים אֲחֵרִים אֲשֶׁר לֹא־יְדַעְתֶּם: 15 וְדָרַשְׁתָּ וְחָקַרְתָּ וְשָׁאַלְתָּ הֵיטֵב וְהִנֵּה אֱמֶת נָכוֹן הַדָּבָר נֶעֶשְׂתָה הַתּוֹעֵבָה הַזֹּאת בְּקִרְבֶּךָ:

As He visits the sick (God visited Abraham after his circumcision—ibid. 18:1), so should you visit the sick. As He comforts mourners (God comforted Isaac after Abraham's passing—ibid. 25:11), so should you comfort mourners. And as He buries the dead (*"He buried him in the valley"*—Deuteronomy 34:6), you should do the same (*Babylonian Talmud, Sotah* 14a).

spiritual vitamin

> Trusting in God is a vessel and channel to receive God's blessings, apart from the fact that such confidence is good for your health, disposition, and therefore is also a natural means to the desired end.

from the house of bondage—to lead you astray from the path in which God, your God, commanded you to go. (By killing him) you will eliminate the evil from your midst.

Incitement to Idol-Worship

- ⁷ If you are incited in secret by your (paternal) brother, (or) your mother's son, your son or your daughter, your wife who is one with you, your friend, (or your father) who is as (dear to you) as yourself, and are told, "Let us go and worship other gods!"—(gods) with which you are unacquainted and your ancestors, ⁸ from among the gods of the peoples around you, (whether) near to you or far from you, from one end of the earth to the other end of the earth:

- ⁹ You should not feel affection for him.

- You should not listen to him (when he pleads forgiveness for his life).

- You should not pity him (if he is in a life-threatening situation).

- You should not have mercy upon him (to turn justice in his favor).

- You should not withhold evidence (that may lead to) his (conviction).

- ¹⁰ Rather, you should (try his case) repeatedly (until he is sentenced) to be killed.

- (The victim's) own hand should be the first against him, to put him to death, and afterwards the hands of all the people.

- ¹¹ You should pelt him with stones until he dies, because he sought to lead you astray from God, your God, who brought you out of the land of Egypt, out of the house of bondage.

¹² All Israel should hear (of it) and be afraid, so they should no longer do such an evil thing in your midst.

A City of Idol-Worshipers

- ¹³ If, in one of your cities which God, your God, is giving you as a place to live, you hear a report, ¹⁴ "Reckless men, from among you, have gone and led the inhabitants of their city astray, saying, 'Let's go and worship other gods, with which you are unacquainted!'":

- ¹⁵ You should interrogate, probe, and question (the witnesses) thoroughly.

If indeed the matter is confirmed to be true, that this abomination has occurred in your midst:

What this means is that you should emulate God's attributes. As He clothes the naked (*"God made for Adam and his wife skintight garments"—Genesis* 3:21), so should you clothe the naked.

דברים יג:טז - יד:ז

16 הַכֵּה תַכֶּה אֶת־יֹשְׁבֵי הָעִיר הַהִוא לְפִי־חָרֶב הַחֲרֵם אֹתָהּ וְאֶת־כָּל־אֲשֶׁר־בָּהּ וְאֶת־בְּהֶמְתָּהּ לְפִי־חָרֶב: 17 וְאֶת־כָּל־שְׁלָלָהּ תִּקְבֹּץ אֶל־תּוֹךְ רְחֹבָהּ וְשָׂרַפְתָּ בָאֵשׁ אֶת־הָעִיר וְאֶת־כָּל־שְׁלָלָהּ כָּלִיל לַיהוָה אֱלֹהֶיךָ וְהָיְתָה תֵּל עוֹלָם לֹא תִבָּנֶה עוֹד: 18 וְלֹא־יִדְבַּק בְּיָדְךָ מְאוּמָה מִן־הַחֵרֶם לְמַעַן יָשׁוּב יְהוָה מֵחֲרוֹן אַפּוֹ וְנָתַן־לְךָ רַחֲמִים וְרִחַמְךָ וְהִרְבֶּךָ כַּאֲשֶׁר נִשְׁבַּע לַאֲבֹתֶיךָ: 19 כִּי תִשְׁמַע בְּקוֹל יְהוָה אֱלֹהֶיךָ לִשְׁמֹר אֶת־כָּל־מִצְוֹתָיו אֲשֶׁר אָנֹכִי מְצַוְּךָ הַיּוֹם לַעֲשׂוֹת הַיָּשָׁר בְּעֵינֵי יְהוָה אֱלֹהֶיךָ: ס

יד

1 [FOURTH READING] בָּנִים אַתֶּם לַיהוָה אֱלֹהֵיכֶם לֹא תִתְגֹּדְדוּ וְלֹא־תָשִׂימוּ קָרְחָה בֵּין עֵינֵיכֶם לָמֵת: 2 כִּי עַם קָדוֹשׁ אַתָּה לַיהוָה אֱלֹהֶיךָ וּבְךָ בָּחַר יְהוָה לִהְיוֹת לוֹ לְעַם סְגֻלָּה מִכֹּל הָעַמִּים אֲשֶׁר עַל־פְּנֵי הָאֲדָמָה: ס 3 לֹא תֹאכַל כָּל־תּוֹעֵבָה: 4 זֹאת הַבְּהֵמָה אֲשֶׁר תֹּאכֵלוּ שׁוֹר שֵׂה כְשָׂבִים וְשֵׂה עִזִּים: 5 אַיָּל וּצְבִי וְיַחְמוּר וְאַקּוֹ וְדִישֹׁן וּתְאוֹ וָזָמֶר: 6 וְכָל־בְּהֵמָה מַפְרֶסֶת פַּרְסָה וְשֹׁסַעַת שֶׁסַע שְׁתֵּי פְרָסוֹת מַעֲלַת גֵּרָה בַּבְּהֵמָה אֹתָהּ תֹּאכֵלוּ: 7 אַךְ אֶת־זֶה לֹא תֹאכְלוּ מִמַּעֲלֵי הַגֵּרָה וּמִמַּפְרִיסֵי הַפַּרְסָה הַשְּׁסוּעָה אֶת־הַגָּמָל וְאֶת־הָאַרְנֶבֶת וְאֶת־הַשָּׁפָן כִּי־מַעֲלֵה גֵרָה הֵמָּה וּפַרְסָה לֹא הִפְרִיסוּ

---

18. He will have mercy on you. The literal translation of this verse reads, "He will *give* you mercy." God assures you that He will bolster your trait of compassion.

Destroying an apostate city will inevitably foster cruel tendencies in those carrying out the command. The Torah thus assures us that the Merciful One will renew the person's trait of mercy, *"God will give you mercy"* (*Rabbi Ḥayyim ibn Attar, 18th century*).

14:1 You may not gash yourself ... (as a sign of morning) ... You are children of God. Since God is our Father and loves us dearly, He will certainly not bring upon us any misfortune. Therefore, *"you must not gash yourself"* in anguish, for although we may not understand the death of a loved one, we should trust that God's actions are in our best interests (*Rabbi Abraham ibn Ezra, 12th century*).

The soul is God's most precious treasure, and as such, He would certainly never allow it to perish. Instead, at the appropriate time, God brings it back near to Him. To God's children, death does not signify the end, but the beginning of life in the world to come. This is certainly no reason for *excessive* mourning (*Nahmanides, 13th century*).

deuteronomy 13:16 – 14:7 — re'eh

- ❖ ¹⁶ (If possible) you should kill the inhabitants of that city by sword, (but otherwise just) kill (them by any means). Wipe out (the city) together with all that is in it, (killing) its livestock by sword.

- ❖ ¹⁷ You should gather all its spoil into its main square, and burn the city with all its spoil completely with fire, for (the sake of) God, your God. It should remain a heap of destruction forever, never to be rebuilt.

- ❖ ¹⁸ Nothing that is doomed to destruction should remain in your hands.

(The city must be destroyed) in order for God's anger to cease, and (only then) will He have mercy on you. (When) He will have mercy on you He will cause you to multiply, as He swore to your forefathers.

¹⁹ So you should listen to the voice of God, your God, and keep all His commandments which I am commanding you today, so as to do that which is proper in the eyes of God, your God.

14

The Holiness of the Jewish People

[FOURTH READING] ¹ You may not gash yourselves or make any baldness between your eyes (as a sign of mourning) for the dead (as the Amorites do, because) you are children of God, your God, (and thus your appearance should be pleasant).

² For you are a(n inherently) holy people to God, your God, and (furthermore), God has chosen you to be a treasured people for Him, out of all the nations that are upon the earth.

Laws of Forbidden Foods

- ❖ ³ You may not eat any abomination.

- ❖ ⁴ These are the animals that you may eat:

- ❖ ox, sheep, goat, ⁵ gazelle, deer, and *yaḥmur*, ibex, antelope, buffalo, and giraffe.

- ❖ ⁶ You may eat any animal which has a split hoof which is completely split into two hooves, if it chews the cud; (and you may eat the fetus) inside the animal (once the animal is slaughtered).

- ❖ ⁷ But, among those that chew the cud and those that have a cloven hoof, you may not eat these:

- ❖ The dromedary, the camel, the hare, and the hyrax, because they chew the cud, but do not have split hooves. They are impure for you.

Food for thought

1. Why are the vast majority of animals not kosher?

2. How deeply are we affected by the food we eat?

3. Is kosher food better for you physically?

דברים יד:ז-כב

טְמֵאִים הֵם לָכֶם: 8 וְאֶת־הַחֲזִיר כִּי־מַפְרִיס פַּרְסָה הוּא וְלֹא גֵרָה טָמֵא הוּא לָכֶם מִבְּשָׂרָם לֹא תֹאכֵלוּ וּבְנִבְלָתָם לֹא תִגָּעוּ: ס 9 אֶת־זֶה תֹּאכְלוּ מִכֹּל אֲשֶׁר בַּמָּיִם כֹּל אֲשֶׁר־לוֹ סְנַפִּיר וְקַשְׂקֶשֶׂת תֹּאכֵלוּ: 10 וְכֹל אֲשֶׁר אֵין־לוֹ סְנַפִּיר וְקַשְׂקֶשֶׂת לֹא תֹאכֵלוּ טָמֵא הוּא לָכֶם: ס 11 כָּל־צִפּוֹר טְהֹרָה תֹּאכֵלוּ: 12 וְזֶה אֲשֶׁר לֹא־תֹאכְלוּ מֵהֶם הַנֶּשֶׁר וְהַפֶּרֶס וְהָעָזְנִיָּה: 13 וְהָרָאָה וְאֶת־הָאַיָּה וְהַדַּיָּה לְמִינָהּ: 14 וְאֵת כָּל־עֹרֵב לְמִינוֹ: 15 וְאֵת בַּת הַיַּעֲנָה וְאֶת־הַתַּחְמָס וְאֶת־הַשָּׁחַף וְאֶת־הַנֵּץ לְמִינֵהוּ: 16 אֶת־הַכּוֹס וְאֶת־הַיַּנְשׁוּף וְהַתִּנְשָׁמֶת: 17 וְהַקָּאָת וְאֶת־הָרָחָמָה וְאֶת־הַשָּׁלָךְ: 18 וְהַחֲסִידָה וְהָאֲנָפָה לְמִינָהּ וְהַדּוּכִיפַת וְהָעֲטַלֵּף: 19 וְכֹל שֶׁרֶץ הָעוֹף טָמֵא הוּא לָכֶם לֹא יֵאָכֵלוּ: 20 כָּל־עוֹף טָהוֹר תֹּאכֵלוּ: 21 לֹא תֹאכְלוּ כָל־נְבֵלָה לַגֵּר אֲשֶׁר־בִּשְׁעָרֶיךָ תִּתְּנֶנָּה וַאֲכָלָהּ אוֹ מָכֹר לְנָכְרִי כִּי עַם קָדוֹשׁ אַתָּה לַיהוָה אֱלֹהֶיךָ לֹא־תְבַשֵּׁל גְּדִי בַּחֲלֵב אִמּוֹ: פ 22 [FIFTH READING] עַשֵּׂר תְּעַשֵּׂר אֵת כָּל־תְּבוּאַת זַרְעֶךָ הַיֹּצֵא הַשָּׂדֶה

22. You should always take the tithe (*'asser te'asser*). The Hebrew word *'asser*, when read with the left phonetic marking—*sin*—means tithe, but when read with the right marking—*shin*—it means wealth. Thus the term *te'asser, you shall tithe*, is homiletically interpreted as *"you will become wealthy."* If you separate the tithes, giving charitably, you will become wealthy (*Babylonian Talmud, Ta'anit* 9a; *Rabbi Samuel Edels, 16th–17th century*).

kabbalah bites

14:22 The last two letters of the Hebrew word *tzedakah* (charity), are *kof* (ק) and *he* (ה). If you examine the nodal structure of these two letters you will see that they are virtually identical, the only difference being that in the *kof*, the left side is extended further downwards, below the baseline.

The *kof* represents the spirit of Cain (*Kayin*) and the Serpent. Its overextension of the left side tells us that these dark forces wish to "extend" themselves and impose themselves upon us. Our task is to resist this temptation, rendering the left side shortened, like the *he*.

When you give charity, have this in mind.

deuteronomy 14:8–22 — re'eh

- ⁸ The pig, because it has a split hoof, but does not chew the cud. It is impure for you.

- You may not eat their flesh. (When it comes to a festival, you must make yourself ritually pure to come to the Temple, so then) you may not touch their carcasses (which would render you impure).

- ⁹ Among all (the creatures) that are in the water, you may eat these:

- You may eat any (of) those (creatures) in the water that have fins and scales. ¹⁰ But you must not eat any that do not have fins and scales. They are impure for you.

- ¹¹ You may eat every bird from a ritually pure species (even the one which is sent off after the ritual purification of a *tzara'at* sufferer).

- ¹² Among (birds), you may not eat the following:

- The griffon vulture, the bearded vulture, the osprey, ¹³ the buzzard, the kite and the buzzard family, ¹⁴ the entire raven family, ¹⁵ the ostrich, the *taḥmas*, the gull, the hawk family, ¹⁶ the *kos* owl, the *yanshuf* owl, the barn owl, ¹⁷ the *ka'at* owl, the roller, the cormorant, ¹⁸ the stork, the heron family, the hoopoe and the bat.

- ¹⁹ Every flying insect is impure for you. They may not be eaten.

- ²⁰ You may eat any ritually pure species of clean fowl.

- ²¹ You may not eat any carcass. You can give it to the (non-Jewish resident) alien who is in your cities, and he may eat it, or you can sell it to a non-Jew.

- You are a holy people to God, your God, so (you should abstain even from things that are permitted).

- Do not cook a tender young animal in its mother's milk.

The Second Tithe

- [FIFTH READING] ²² You should always take the (second) tithe from all the produce of the seed crop that the field produces.

---

18. The stork. Scripture calls this bird *ḥasidah*, which relates to the word *ḥesed*, "kindness." Why is this bird called *ḥasidah*? Because she performs kindness, sharing her food with other birds of her kind (*Babylonian Talmud, Ḥullin* 63a).

The Jerusalem Talmud also makes reference to "evil mice" who, on seeing a pile of food in the storehouse, call their friends to eat with them (*Jerusalem Talmud, Bava Metzia* 3:5). Why is the stork regarded as *kind* for sharing her food, whereas the mouse is called *evil* for doing the same thing?

The stork feeds from the wild, so when she shares her food with others she is giving from her own portion—that is benevolence. The mouse, on the other hand, takes from the storehouse of others. By calling for its friends to join, it is actually causing more harm.

Kindness must be performed from what is yours, not at the expense of others (*Rabbi Alexander Zusya Friedman, 20th century*).

דברים יד:כב - טו:ב

ראה

שָׁנָה שָׁנָה: 23 וְאָכַלְתָּ לִפְנֵי | יְהוָה אֱלֹהֶיךָ בַּמָּקוֹם אֲשֶׁר־יִבְחַר לְשַׁכֵּן שְׁמוֹ שָׁם מַעְשַׂר דְּגָנְךָ תִּירֹשְׁךָ וְיִצְהָרֶךָ וּבְכֹרֹת בְּקָרְךָ וְצֹאנֶךָ לְמַעַן תִּלְמַד לְיִרְאָה אֶת־יְהוָה אֱלֹהֶיךָ כָּל־הַיָּמִים: 24 וְכִי־יִרְבֶּה מִמְּךָ הַדֶּרֶךְ כִּי לֹא תוּכַל שְׂאֵתוֹ כִּי־יִרְחַק מִמְּךָ הַמָּקוֹם אֲשֶׁר יִבְחַר יְהוָה אֱלֹהֶיךָ לָשׂוּם שְׁמוֹ שָׁם כִּי יְבָרֶכְךָ יְהוָה אֱלֹהֶיךָ: 25 וְנָתַתָּה בַּכָּסֶף וְצַרְתָּ הַכֶּסֶף בְּיָדְךָ וְהָלַכְתָּ אֶל־הַמָּקוֹם אֲשֶׁר יִבְחַר יְהוָה אֱלֹהֶיךָ בּוֹ: 26 וְנָתַתָּה הַכֶּסֶף בְּכֹל אֲשֶׁר־תְּאַוֶּה נַפְשְׁךָ בַּבָּקָר וּבַצֹּאן וּבַיַּיִן וּבַשֵּׁכָר וּבְכֹל אֲשֶׁר תִּשְׁאָלְךָ נַפְשֶׁךָ וְאָכַלְתָּ שָּׁם לִפְנֵי יְהוָה אֱלֹהֶיךָ וְשָׂמַחְתָּ אַתָּה וּבֵיתֶךָ: 27 וְהַלֵּוִי אֲשֶׁר־בִּשְׁעָרֶיךָ לֹא תַעַזְבֶנּוּ כִּי אֵין לוֹ חֵלֶק וְנַחֲלָה עִמָּךְ: ס 28 מִקְצֵה | שָׁלֹשׁ שָׁנִים תּוֹצִיא אֶת־כָּל־מַעְשַׂר תְּבוּאָתְךָ בַּשָּׁנָה הַהִוא וְהִנַּחְתָּ בִּשְׁעָרֶיךָ: 29 וּבָא הַלֵּוִי כִּי אֵין־לוֹ חֵלֶק וְנַחֲלָה עִמָּךְ וְהַגֵּר וְהַיָּתוֹם וְהָאַלְמָנָה אֲשֶׁר בִּשְׁעָרֶיךָ וְאָכְלוּ וְשָׂבֵעוּ לְמַעַן יְבָרֶכְךָ יְהוָה אֱלֹהֶיךָ בְּכָל־מַעֲשֵׂה יָדְךָ אֲשֶׁר תַּעֲשֶׂה: ס

טו 1 מִקֵּץ שֶׁבַע־שָׁנִים תַּעֲשֶׂה שְׁמִטָּה: 2 וְזֶה דְּבַר הַשְּׁמִטָּה [SIXTH READING] שָׁמוֹט כָּל־בַּעַל מַשֵּׁה יָדוֹ אֲשֶׁר יַשֶּׁה בְּרֵעֵהוּ לֹא־יִגֹּשׂ אֶת־רֵעֵהוּ

and go to the place that God will choose" (v. 25)—supplant your craving for wealth with a love for God, and fulfilling His commandments will seem easy (*Rabbi Mordecai ha-Kohen, 17th century*).

26. You should use the money to buy whatever your soul desires. Do not squander your money on the body's desires to indulge in the fleeting delights of this world. Instead, spend it

spiritual vitamin

> If you consider the many benevolent acts that you have done in the past, and will continue to do in the days and years ahead, you will surely realize that there is a great deal of meaning to life.

deuteronomy 14:22 – 15:2 — re'eh

- (Do not separate tithes for this) year from (last) year('s produce).
- ²³ You should eat the (second) tithes of your grain, your wine, and your oil—and the firstborn of your cattle and of your sheep—before God, your God, in (Jerusalem), the place where He will choose to make His name rest. (Do this) in order that you will learn to fear God, your God, for all time.
- ²⁴ If the journey is great for you, because the place which God, your God, will choose to make His name rest there, is too far from you and God has blessed you (with so much produce) that you are unable to carry it, ²⁵ then you should exchange it for money, bind up the money in your hand, and you should go to the place that God, your God, will choose. ²⁶ You should use the money to buy whatever your soul desires—cattle, sheep, wine or beer, or whatever your soul desires—and you should eat there before God, your God, and you should rejoice, (both) you and your household.
- ²⁷ Do not abandon the Levite who lives in your town (by failing to give him the first tithe), for he has no portion or inheritance with you.

Disposal of Undistributed Tithes and Tithe for the Poor

- ²⁸ At the end of three years, you should take out all the (undistributed first and second) tithes from your crop, (before the end) of that year, and put it in a public place.
- ²⁹ The Levite (will come and take the first tithe) because he has no portion or inheritance with you.
- (That year you will not separate the second tithe and take it to Jerusalem. Instead, you will give the poor man's tithe, so that the destitute) converts, orphans, and widows, who are in your cities, will come and eat. (You must give them enough to) be satisfied.

(Do this) in order that God, your God, will bless you in all the work of your hand that you will do.

15 Annulment of Loans

- [SIXTH READING] ¹ At the end of (the) seven-year (cycle) you must annul (all loans). ² These are the terms of the annulment: Every creditor should release from his hand the

---

Alternatively, the word retains its original sense, *"you shall tithe."* The promise for wealth is that you will merit many more opportunities to tithe in the future. *Tithe, and you shall tithe again,* from the extra produce that you will gain (*Rabbi Baḥya b. Asher, 13th century*).

24. If the journey is great for you because the place which God, your God, will choose to make His name rest there, is too far from you. If managing your business is so time-consuming that it leaves no time for Torah study and prayer—this is because *"the Place,"* i.e., the Omnipresent, *"is too far from you,"*—you have distanced yourself from God. *"Bind up the money*

דברים ט״ו:ב-י

3 וְאֶת־אָחִ֖יו כִּֽי־קָרָ֥א שְׁמִטָּ֖ה לַיהוָֽה׃ אֶת־הַנָּכְרִ֖י תִּגֹּ֑שׂ וַאֲשֶׁ֨ר יִהְיֶ֥ה לְךָ֛ אֶת־אָחִ֖יךָ תַּשְׁמֵ֥ט יָדֶֽךָ׃ 4 אֶ֕פֶס כִּ֛י לֹ֥א יִֽהְיֶה־בְּךָ֖ אֶבְי֑וֹן כִּֽי־בָרֵ֤ךְ יְבָרֶכְךָ֙ יְהוָ֔ה בָּאָ֕רֶץ אֲשֶׁר֙ יְהוָ֣ה אֱלֹהֶ֔יךָ נֹֽתֵן־לְךָ֥ נַחֲלָ֖ה לְרִשְׁתָּֽהּ׃ 5 רַ֚ק אִם־שָׁמ֣וֹעַ תִּשְׁמַ֔ע בְּק֖וֹל יְהוָ֣ה אֱלֹהֶ֑יךָ לִשְׁמֹ֤ר לַעֲשׂוֹת֙ אֶת־כָּל־הַמִּצְוָ֣ה הַזֹּ֔את אֲשֶׁ֛ר אָנֹכִ֥י מְצַוְּךָ֖ הַיּֽוֹם׃ 6 כִּֽי־יְהוָ֤ה אֱלֹהֶ֙יךָ֙ בֵּֽרַכְךָ֔ כַּאֲשֶׁ֖ר דִּבֶּר־לָ֑ךְ וְהַֽעֲבַטְתָּ֞ גּוֹיִ֣ם רַבִּ֗ים וְאַתָּה֙ לֹ֣א תַעֲבֹ֔ט וּמָֽשַׁלְתָּ֙ בְּגוֹיִ֣ם רַבִּ֔ים וּבְךָ֖ לֹ֥א יִמְשֹֽׁלוּ׃ ס 7 כִּֽי־יִהְיֶה֩ בְךָ֨ אֶבְי֜וֹן מֵאַחַ֤ד אַחֶ֙יךָ֙ בְּאַחַ֣ד שְׁעָרֶ֔יךָ בְּאַ֨רְצְךָ֔ אֲשֶׁר־יְהוָ֥ה אֱלֹהֶ֖יךָ נֹתֵ֣ן לָ֑ךְ לֹ֧א תְאַמֵּ֣ץ אֶת־לְבָבְךָ֗ וְלֹ֤א תִקְפֹּץ֙ אֶת־יָ֣דְךָ֔ מֵאָחִ֖יךָ הָאֶבְיֽוֹן׃ 8 כִּֽי־פָתֹ֧חַ תִּפְתַּ֛ח אֶת־יָדְךָ֖ ל֑וֹ וְהַעֲבֵט֙ תַּעֲבִיטֶ֔נּוּ דֵּ֚י מַחְסֹר֔וֹ אֲשֶׁ֥ר יֶחְסַ֖ר לֽוֹ׃ 9 הִשָּׁ֣מֶר לְךָ֡ פֶּן־יִהְיֶ֣ה דָבָר֩ עִם־לְבָבְךָ֨ בְלִיַּ֜עַל לֵאמֹ֗ר קָֽרְבָ֣ה שְׁנַֽת־הַשֶּׁ֘בַע֮ שְׁנַ֣ת הַשְּׁמִטָּה֒ וְרָעָ֣ה עֵֽינְךָ֗ בְּאָחִ֙יךָ֙ הָֽאֶבְי֔וֹן וְלֹ֥א תִתֵּ֖ן ל֑וֹ וְקָרָ֤א עָלֶ֙יךָ֙ אֶל־יְהוָ֔ה וְהָיָ֥ה בְךָ֖ חֵֽטְא׃ 10 נָת֤וֹן תִּתֵּן֙ ל֔וֹ וְלֹא־יֵרַ֥ע לְבָבְךָ֖ בְּתִתְּךָ֣ ל֑וֹ כִּ֞י בִּגְלַ֣ל ׀ הַדָּבָ֣ר הַזֶּ֗ה יְבָרֶכְךָ֙ יְהוָ֣ה אֱלֹהֶ֔יךָ בְּכָל־

10. You should give to him repeatedly. There is a distinct advantage in giving lesser amounts of charity numerous times, in contrast to giving an entire sum all at once. While making a large donation is praiseworthy, the repeated act of giving transforms your character to become more generous and giving, for the soul is refined by means of repeated action (*Maimonides, 12th century*).

This is hinted to here: *"You should give to him repeatedly"*—repeat the charitable acts numerous times; then, *"your heart will not feel bad when you give to him."* You will attain a generous character and give joyfully (*Rabbi Isaac b. Moses Arama, 15th century*).

Give to him repeatedly. Charity is the most important of the practical commandments, and surpasses them all. *Through giving charity your mind and heart become refined one thousand times.*

kabbalah bites

15:7-8 According to the Kabbalah you should give charity every day (except the Sabbath) in the morning and afternoon, but not the evening, because at night the forces of *Din* (severity) abound. The purpose of charity, *tzedakah*, is to "sweeten" these harsh forces, but this is only viable during the day, not at night when they are strong.

However, this only applies to charity initiated by the giver, the requirement to *"repeatedly open your hand"* (v. 8). If a person *asks* you for charity, you should give him at any time, even at night: *"you must not harden your heart or shut your hand"* (v. 7).

debt which he can claim from his fellow. He may not demand payment from his friend or his brother, because the time of God's annulment has arrived.

❖ ³ You should demand payment from a gentile (who owes you money), but your hand should release whatever (claim) you have against your (Jewish) brother.

⁴ (So long as you perform the commandments), there will no longer be any destitute people among you, for God will bless you repeatedly in the land God, your God, is giving you as an inheritance and a possession. ⁵ However, (this is only) if you listen to the voice of God, your God, and are careful to observe every commandment, which I am commanding you today. ⁶ For God, your God, has blessed you, as He has told you: You will lend to many nations, and you will not borrow. You will rule over many nations, and they will not rule over you.

Charity and Loans to the Poor

❖ ⁷ If there will be a destitute person—(especially) from among one of your (own paternal) brothers, (or from) one (of the residents) in your (own) town—in the land that God, your God, is giving you, you must not harden your heart or shut your hand from your destitute brother. ⁸ Rather, you must repeatedly open your hand to him, and give him (charity—and if he will not take a gift, then) give him a loan—sufficient to fulfil his requirements that he is lacking.

❖ ⁹ Be careful that a reckless thought should not enter your heart, saying, "The seventh year, the year of cancellation (of loans) is approaching," and you look begrudgingly upon your destitute brother and do not give him—then he might cry out against you to God, and it will be an (even more serious) sin for you. ¹⁰ (Rather) you should give to him repeatedly, and your heart should not feel bad when you

---

wisely on what "your *soul* desires." Give it to charity and acquire an eternal merit for your soul (*Rabbi Elimelech of Lyzhansk, 18th century*).

15:8 You must repeatedly open your hand to him. Once, Rabbi Pappa was climbing a ladder and he slipped on one of the rungs, nearly falling to his death. This incident troubled Rabbi Papa greatly, as he wondered what he might have done to deserve this nearly fatal mishap. Rabbi Ḥiyya son of Rav suggested to him, "Perhaps a pauper came to you and you did not give him charity" (*Babylonian Talmud, Bava Batra* 10a).

The cantillation notes on the words "repeatedly open" are *darga-tevir*. In a cryptic allusion to the above incident from the Talmud, the names of these notes translate as "broken step" (*Rabbi Elijah of Vilna, 18th century*).

Open your hand to him. *"In the morning sow your seed and in the evening do not withhold your hand, for you do not know which will succeed—this one, or that one, or whether both of them will be equally good"* (*Ecclesiastes* 11:6). Rabbi Joshua says: "If a poor man comes to you in the morning, give to him. If he comes again in the evening, give to him. For you do not know on account of which one God will inscribe you for the good—this one, or that one; or if both are 'equally good'" (*Genesis Rabbah*).

רְאֵה　　　　　　　　　　　　　　　　　　　דברים טו:י-כ

מַעֲשֶׂךָ וּבְכֹל מִשְׁלַח יָדֶךָ: 11 כִּי לֹא־יֶחְדַּל אֶבְיוֹן מִקֶּרֶב הָאָרֶץ עַל־כֵּן אָנֹכִי מְצַוְּךָ לֵאמֹר פָּתֹחַ תִּפְתַּח אֶת־יָדְךָ לְאָחִיךָ לַעֲנִיֶּךָ וּלְאֶבְיֹנְךָ בְּאַרְצֶךָ: ס 12 כִּי־יִמָּכֵר לְךָ אָחִיךָ הָעִבְרִי אוֹ הָעִבְרִיָּה וַעֲבָדְךָ שֵׁשׁ שָׁנִים וּבַשָּׁנָה הַשְּׁבִיעִת תְּשַׁלְּחֶנּוּ חָפְשִׁי מֵעִמָּךְ: 13 וְכִי־תְשַׁלְּחֶנּוּ חָפְשִׁי מֵעִמָּךְ לֹא תְשַׁלְּחֶנּוּ רֵיקָם: 14 הַעֲנֵיק תַּעֲנִיק לוֹ מִצֹּאנְךָ וּמִגָּרְנְךָ וּמִיִּקְבֶךָ אֲשֶׁר בֵּרַכְךָ יְהוָה אֱלֹהֶיךָ תִּתֶּן־לוֹ: 15 וְזָכַרְתָּ כִּי עֶבֶד הָיִיתָ בְּאֶרֶץ מִצְרַיִם וַיִּפְדְּךָ יְהוָה אֱלֹהֶיךָ עַל־כֵּן אָנֹכִי מְצַוְּךָ אֶת־הַדָּבָר הַזֶּה הַיּוֹם: 16 וְהָיָה כִּי־יֹאמַר אֵלֶיךָ לֹא אֵצֵא מֵעִמָּךְ כִּי אֲהֵבְךָ וְאֶת־בֵּיתֶךָ כִּי־טוֹב לוֹ עִמָּךְ: 17 וְלָקַחְתָּ אֶת־הַמַּרְצֵעַ וְנָתַתָּה בְאָזְנוֹ וּבַדֶּלֶת וְהָיָה לְךָ עֶבֶד עוֹלָם וְאַף לַאֲמָתְךָ תַּעֲשֶׂה־כֵּן: 18 לֹא־יִקְשֶׁה בְעֵינֶךָ בְּשַׁלֵּחֲךָ אֹתוֹ חָפְשִׁי מֵעִמָּךְ כִּי מִשְׁנֶה שְׂכַר שָׂכִיר עֲבָדְךָ שֵׁשׁ שָׁנִים וּבֵרַכְךָ יְהוָה אֱלֹהֶיךָ בְּכֹל אֲשֶׁר תַּעֲשֶׂה: פ 19 [SEVENTH READING] כָּל־הַבְּכוֹר אֲשֶׁר יִוָּלֵד בִּבְקָרְךָ וּבְצֹאנְךָ הַזָּכָר תַּקְדִּישׁ לַיהוָה אֱלֹהֶיךָ לֹא תַעֲבֹד בִּבְכֹר שׁוֹרֶךָ וְלֹא תָגֹז בְּכוֹר צֹאנֶךָ: 20 לִפְנֵי יְהוָה אֱלֹהֶיךָ תֹאכְלֶנּוּ שָׁנָה בְשָׁנָה בַּמָּקוֹם אֲשֶׁר־יִבְחַר יְהוָה

---

faculties of your vitalizing soul that were immersed in doing the business through which you earned this money. When you give it to charity, your entire vitalizing soul is elevated to God (*Rabbi Shneur Zalman of Lyady, 18th century*).

14. You should give him. The command to give severance gifts was in force only in Temple times. Nevertheless, even today, *"Let the wise man hear and increase in learning"* (*Proverbs 1:5*)—if you hire a Jewish person who serves for a long period of time, or even a short period, that person should be given gifts on dismissal (*Rabbi Aaron ha-Levi (Ḥinnukh), 13th century*).

spiritual vitamin

> Trust in God does not mean relying solely on miracles. The Torah requires us to do everything possible in the natural order of things to earn a living, etc., except that we should at the same time remember that success and blessing come from God. Thus the Torah states, "God will bless you *in all that you do*" (v. 18).

give to him. For God, your God, will bless all your work and everything you do, as a result of (the promises you made to the poor and the money you gave to them). ¹¹ There will never cease to be destitute people within the land, and therefore I am commanding you, as follows: you should repeatedly open your hand to your poor brother and to your destitute (resident) in your land.

Gifts to Jewish Slaves upon their Release

- ¹² If one of your brethren—a Hebrew man or woman—is sold to you (by the courts), he should work for you for six years, and in the seventh year you should send him away, free from you.

- ¹³ When you send him away, free from you, you should not let him go empty-handed.

- ¹⁴ You should give him many gifts from your flock, your threshing floor, or from your wine vat, (or) you should give him from whatever God, your God, has blessed you with.

¹⁵ Remember that you were slaves in the land of Egypt, and that God, your God, redeemed you. Therefore, I am commanding you today to do this thing.

- ¹⁶ In the event that he says to you, "I will not leave you," because he loves you and your household, since it suits him to be with you, ¹⁷ then you should take a pointed tool and put it through his ear and into the door, and he will then be a servant to you permanently (until the Jubilee year).

- You should give the same (adornment of gifts) to a maidservant.

¹⁸ Let it not seem difficult in your eyes when you send him away free from you, for he has served you (day and night) for six years, twice as many (hours) as a salaried worker (who only works by day). God, your God, will bless you in all that you do.

Sanctity of Firstborn Animals

- [SEVENTH READING] ¹⁹ You must sanctify every firstborn male, from your cattle or your flock, to God, your God, (by declaring it sacred as a firstborn).

- You must not work the firstborn of your ox, or shear the firstborn of your flock (or vice-versa).

- ²⁰ In the same year (it is born) you should (give it to the priest who will) eat it before God, your God, in the place God will choose. You, (the priest, should eat it) with your household.

The purpose of all the commandments is to elevate your *vitalizing soul*, which animates the physical body, to God—and you will find no other commandment in which the vitalizing soul is elevated to the same extent as in the commandment of charity. In the case of all other commandments, which require action from just one part of the body, only one aspect of the vitalizing soul becomes involved. But with charity you give away "the toil of your hands"—all the

דברים טו:כ - טז:ז   ראה

21 אַתָּה וּבֵיתֶךָ: וְכִי־יִהְיֶה בוֹ מוּם פִּסֵּחַ אוֹ עִוֵּר כֹּל מוּם רָע לֹא תִזְבָּחֶנּוּ
לַיהוָה אֱלֹהֶיךָ: 22 בִּשְׁעָרֶיךָ תֹּאכְלֶנּוּ הַטָּמֵא וְהַטָּהוֹר יַחְדָּו כַּצְּבִי וְכָאַיָּל:
23 רַק אֶת־דָּמוֹ לֹא תֹאכֵל עַל־הָאָרֶץ תִּשְׁפְּכֶנּוּ כַּמָּיִם: פ

טז

1 שָׁמוֹר אֶת־חֹדֶשׁ הָאָבִיב וְעָשִׂיתָ פֶּסַח לַיהוָה אֱלֹהֶיךָ כִּי בְּחֹדֶשׁ הָאָבִיב הוֹצִיאֲךָ יְהוָה אֱלֹהֶיךָ מִמִּצְרַיִם לָיְלָה: 2 וְזָבַחְתָּ פֶּסַח לַיהוָה אֱלֹהֶיךָ צֹאן וּבָקָר בַּמָּקוֹם אֲשֶׁר־יִבְחַר יְהוָה לְשַׁכֵּן שְׁמוֹ שָׁם: 3 לֹא־תֹאכַל עָלָיו חָמֵץ שִׁבְעַת יָמִים תֹּאכַל־עָלָיו מַצּוֹת לֶחֶם עֹנִי כִּי בְחִפָּזוֹן יָצָאתָ מֵאֶרֶץ מִצְרַיִם לְמַעַן תִּזְכֹּר אֶת־יוֹם צֵאתְךָ מֵאֶרֶץ מִצְרַיִם כֹּל יְמֵי חַיֶּיךָ: 4 וְלֹא־יֵרָאֶה לְךָ שְׂאֹר בְּכָל־גְּבֻלְךָ שִׁבְעַת יָמִים וְלֹא־יָלִין מִן־הַבָּשָׂר אֲשֶׁר תִּזְבַּח בָּעֶרֶב בַּיּוֹם הָרִאשׁוֹן לַבֹּקֶר: 5 לֹא תוּכַל לִזְבֹּחַ אֶת־הַפָּסַח בְּאַחַד שְׁעָרֶיךָ אֲשֶׁר־יְהוָה אֱלֹהֶיךָ נֹתֵן לָךְ: 6 כִּי אִם־אֶל־הַמָּקוֹם אֲשֶׁר־יִבְחַר יְהוָה אֱלֹהֶיךָ לְשַׁכֵּן שְׁמוֹ שָׁם תִּזְבַּח אֶת־הַפֶּסַח בָּעָרֶב כְּבוֹא הַשֶּׁמֶשׁ מוֹעֵד צֵאתְךָ מִמִּצְרָיִם: 7 וּבִשַּׁלְתָּ וְאָכַלְתָּ בַּמָּקוֹם אֲשֶׁר יִבְחַר יְהוָה אֱלֹהֶיךָ בּוֹ

When the Jewish people came out of Egypt, on Passover, the Torah had not yet been given. Therefore, the Torah does not stress the concept of rejoicing. Also, the Jewish people did not see the Egyptians drown until the seventh day of their departure, and it was only at this point that they rejoiced (*Rabbi Abraham b. Jacob Saba, 15th century*).

On Passover, the crops have not yet been harvested, so the Torah does not mention rejoicing at all. By the Festival of Weeks, the harvest has taken place, and the grapes have not yet been made into wine, so rejoicing is mentioned just once (v. 11). But by the Festival of Tabernacles, all the harvest is ready to eat, so the Torah mentions rejoicing twice (v. 14 -15; *Rabbi Jacob b. Asher, 14th century*).

kabbalah bites

16:1-17 Why did the momentous events celebrated by each of the Jewish festivals occur? Obviously, each festival has its own history, but a Kabbalist understands that we are speaking here of different events of *Divine disclosure*.

Each year when we remember and celebrate the festival in the physical world *that very same Divine disclosure occurs once again*. Only, this time it is stronger and more effective than ever before.

Festivals are not only about remembering the events of the past; the most important thing is capturing the freshly disclosed light of the present.

deuteronomy 15:21 – 16:7 — re'eh

- ❖ ²¹ If there is any blemish in it, whether it is lame, blind, or has any defective blemish, you should not offer it to God, your God:

- ❖ ²² You may eat it within your (own) cities.

- ❖ (Even though the animal was originally a holy offering, after it has been redeemed) a ritually impure person and a ritually pure person may eat it (together on the same plate).

- ❖ (The foreleg, jaw and end-stomach do not need to be given to the priest,) as if (you were slaughtering) a deer, or a gazelle.

- ❖ ²³ Only, you may not eat its blood. You should spill it on the ground like water (and you do not have to cover it).

16 The Laws of Passover

- ❖ ¹ Ensure that the month of (*Nisan* occurs in) springtime—(by declaring a leap-year if necessary, so that the produce will have ripened by *Nisan*, allowing the *'omer*-offering to be brought)—and offer the Passover sacrifice (then) to God, your God. For in the month of springtime, God, your God, brought you out of Egypt, at night.

- ❖ ² You must slaughter the Passover-offering to God, your God, (from the) flock, and (the festival sacrifices from the) cattle, in the place where God will choose to place His name.

- ❖ ³ You may not eat leaven with it. (Rather,) because of it, eat unleavened bread for seven days. (This is) a bread (which reminds you of) affliction since you went out of the land of Egypt in haste (and did not have time for the bread to rise. Eat the unleavened bread) in order to remember all the days of your life, the day when you went out of the land of Egypt.

- ❖ ⁴ No leaven may be seen with you within all your borders for seven days.

- ❖ You may not leave over any of the flesh that you slaughtered on the preceding day, in the afternoon, (uneaten) until the morning.

- ❖ ⁵ You may not slaughter the Passover-offering in any of your cities, which God, your God, is giving you, ⁶ except in the place which God, your God, will choose to place His name. You should slaughter the Passover-offering there, in the afternoon (after the sixth hour).

- ❖ (You must eat it after) the sun comes down, (and you must burn any meat that is left uneaten past) the precise time that you went out of Egypt.

- ❖ ⁷ You should cook it (by roasting) and eat it in (Jerusalem), the place which God, your God, will choose.

16:1-8 Offer the Passover sacrifice. Why does the Torah not tell us to rejoice on Passover as it does regarding the Festival of Weeks (v. 11) and Festival of Tabernacles (v. 14-15)?

דברים טז:ז-יז   ראה

וּפָנִ֣יתָ בַבֹּ֔קֶר וְהָלַכְתָּ֖ לְאֹהָלֶֽיךָ: 8 שֵׁ֥שֶׁת יָמִ֖ים תֹּאכַ֣ל מַצּ֑וֹת וּבַיּ֣וֹם הַשְּׁבִיעִ֗י עֲצֶ֙רֶת֙ לַיהֹוָ֣ה אֱלֹהֶ֔יךָ לֹ֥א תַעֲשֶׂ֖ה מְלָאכָֽה: ס 9 שִׁבְעָ֥ה שָׁבֻעֹ֖ת תִּסְפָּר־לָ֑ךְ מֵהָחֵ֤ל חֶרְמֵשׁ֙ בַּקָּמָ֔ה תָּחֵ֣ל לִסְפֹּ֔ר שִׁבְעָ֖ה שָׁבֻעֽוֹת: 10 וְעָשִׂ֜יתָ חַ֤ג שָׁבֻעוֹת֙ לַיהֹוָ֣ה אֱלֹהֶ֔יךָ מִסַּ֛ת נִדְבַ֥ת יָדְךָ֖ אֲשֶׁ֣ר תִּתֵּ֑ן כַּאֲשֶׁ֥ר יְבָרֶכְךָ֖ יְהֹוָ֥ה אֱלֹהֶֽיךָ: 11 וְשָׂמַחְתָּ֞ לִפְנֵ֣י | יְהֹוָ֣ה אֱלֹהֶ֗יךָ אַתָּ֨ה וּבִנְךָ֣ וּבִתֶּךָ֮ וְעַבְדְּךָ֣ וַאֲמָתֶךָ֒ וְהַלֵּוִי֙ אֲשֶׁ֣ר בִּשְׁעָרֶ֔יךָ וְהַגֵּ֛ר וְהַיָּת֥וֹם וְהָאַלְמָנָ֖ה אֲשֶׁ֣ר בְּקִרְבֶּ֑ךָ בַּמָּק֗וֹם אֲשֶׁ֤ר יִבְחַר֙ יְהֹוָ֣ה אֱלֹהֶ֔יךָ לְשַׁכֵּ֥ן שְׁמ֖וֹ שָֽׁם: 12 וְזָ֣כַרְתָּ֔ כִּי־עֶ֥בֶד הָיִ֖יתָ בְּמִצְרָ֑יִם וְשָׁמַרְתָּ֣ וְעָשִׂ֔יתָ אֶת־הַחֻקִּ֖ים הָאֵֽלֶּה: פ [MAFTIR] 13 חַ֧ג הַסֻּכֹּ֛ת תַּעֲשֶׂ֥ה לְךָ֖ שִׁבְעַ֣ת יָמִ֑ים בְּאָ֨סְפְּךָ֔ מִֽגָּרְנְךָ֖ וּמִיִּקְבֶֽךָ: 14 וְשָׂמַחְתָּ֖ בְּחַגֶּ֑ךָ אַתָּ֨ה וּבִנְךָ֤ וּבִתֶּ֙ךָ֙ וְעַבְדְּךָ֣ וַאֲמָתֶ֔ךָ וְהַלֵּוִ֗י וְהַגֵּ֛ר וְהַיָּת֥וֹם וְהָאַלְמָנָ֖ה אֲשֶׁ֥ר בִּשְׁעָרֶֽיךָ: 15 שִׁבְעַ֣ת יָמִ֗ים תָּחֹג֙ לַיהֹוָ֣ה אֱלֹהֶ֔יךָ בַּמָּק֖וֹם אֲשֶׁר־יִבְחַ֣ר יְהֹוָ֑ה כִּ֣י יְבָרֶכְךָ֞ יְהֹוָ֣ה אֱלֹהֶ֗יךָ בְּכֹ֤ל תְּבוּאָֽתְךָ֙ וּבְכֹל֙ מַעֲשֵׂ֣ה יָדֶ֔יךָ וְהָיִ֖יתָ אַ֥ךְ שָׂמֵֽחַ: 16 שָׁל֣וֹשׁ פְּעָמִ֣ים | בַּשָּׁנָ֡ה יֵרָאֶ֨ה כָל־זְכ֜וּרְךָ֗ אֶת־פְּנֵ֣י | יְהֹוָ֣ה אֱלֹהֶ֗יךָ בַּמָּקוֹם֙ אֲשֶׁ֣ר יִבְחָ֔ר בְּחַ֧ג הַמַּצּ֛וֹת וּבְחַ֥ג הַשָּׁבֻע֖וֹת וּבְחַ֣ג הַסֻּכּ֑וֹת וְלֹ֧א יֵרָאֶ֛ה אֶת־פְּנֵ֥י יְהֹוָ֖ה רֵיקָֽם: 17 אִ֖ישׁ כְּמַתְּנַ֣ת יָד֑וֹ כְּבִרְכַּ֛ת יְהֹוָ֥ה אֱלֹהֶ֖יךָ אֲשֶׁ֥ר נָֽתַן־לָֽךְ: ס ס ס

קכ"ו פסוקים, פליא"ה סימן.

14. Rejoice on your festival—you, your son, your daughter. Your children and the members of your household should rejoice on the festivals, as the verse states, *"Rejoice on your festival— you, your son, your daughter."* Everyone should be given whatever pleases them, such as wine for men and new clothes for women (*Babylonian Talmud, Pesaḥim* 109a).

deuteronomy 16:7–17 — re'eh

- ❖ (You must stay in Jerusalem the night following the festival) and in the morning you may depart and go to your homes.

- ❖ ⁸ For you should eat unleavened bread six days, and on the seventh day there should be a holiday to God, your God, when you may not do any manual work.

Counting the 'Omer and the Festival of Weeks

- ❖ ⁹ Count for yourself seven weeks. From when the sickle is first put to the standing crop (and the 'omer is reaped), you should begin to count seven weeks.

- ❖ ¹⁰ And you should make the Festival of Weeks to God, your God. Offer as many gift-offerings (and invite as many guests) as you can afford, according to how God, your God, blesses you.

- ❖ ¹¹ And you should rejoice before God, your God—you, your son, your daughter, your servant, your maidservant, the Levite who lives in your town, the convert, the orphan, and the widow among you—in the place which God, your God, will choose to place His name there.

¹² Remember that you were slaves in Egypt, and (that I took you out in order that) you should be careful to perform these statutes.

The Festival of Tabernacles

- ❖ [MAFTIR] ¹³ When you gather in (the produce) from your threshing floor and your wine vat, make for yourself the Festival of Tabernacles, for a seven-day period,

- ❖ ¹⁴ Rejoice on your festival—you, your son, your daughter, your servant, your maidservant, the Levite, the convert, the orphan, and the widow who lives in your town.

- ❖ ¹⁵ Celebrate the festival to God, your God, for seven days in the place which God will choose, because God, your God, will bless all your produce and all the work of your hands, and you will only be happy.

Pilgrimage to Jerusalem

- ❖ ¹⁶ Every male among you must appear before God, your God, three times in the year, in the place He will choose: on the Festival of Unleavened Bread, on the Festival of Weeks, and on the Festival of Tabernacles.

- ❖ He may not appear before God empty-handed (without animals for the festival offerings). ¹⁷ Each man (must bring sufficient animals to feed the people) that he supports, according to the blessing of God, your God, which He has given you.

Haftarot: Re'eh (even on Erev Rosh Ḥodesh)—page 1401.   Rosh Ḥodesh—page 1417.
Maftir: Rosh Ḥodesh—page 1000 (28:9–15).

What power does a **judge** have without **law enforcement?** It is not enough to have won **your inner battle,** acknowledging what is truthful and just. You must be **your own policeman,** enforcing your ruling in practice.

SHOFETIM
שופטים

JUDICIAL SYSTEM AND LAW ENFORCEMENT	16:18–20
FORBIDDEN STRUCTURES AND OFFERINGS	16:21 – 17:1
PENALTY FOR IDOL-WORSHIP	17:2–7
AUTHORITY AND DIVINE RIGHTS	17:8 – 18:8
FORTUNE-TELLING	18:9–13
PROPHECY	18:14–22
CITIES OF REFUGE	19:1–13
FRAUD AND PERJURY	19:14–21
LAWS OF WARFARE	20:1–20
UNRESOLVED MURDER	21:1–9

NAME
Shofetim

MEANING
"Judges"

LINES IN TORAH SCROLL
192

PARASHIYYOT
3 open; 15 closed

VERSES
97

WORDS
1523

LETTERS
5590

DATE
Shevat–Adar, 2488

LOCATION
Plains of Moab

MITZVOT
14 positive;
27 prohibitions

MASORETIC FEATURES
Extra letter *he* in the word
ve-yashavtah (17:14)

CHARACTER PROFILE

NAME
Molech (idol, 18:10)

MEANING
"Ruler"

CULTURAL ORIGIN
Ammonite

DESCRIPTION
Hollow idol made from brass divided into seven compartments: In one a bird could be placed, in the second a goat, in the third a lamb, in the fourth a calf, in the fifth a cow, in the sixth an ox, and in the seventh a child.

METHOD OF WORSHIP
The idol was heated from the inside to burn its contents; when the child screamed, the priests beat a drum so that the father would not hear.

JUSTICE

The Torah demands, *"Pursue justice, justice"* (16:20). If you forget your Divine Creator, your mind assumes that you are your own creator. That narcissistic psychosis is the root of all injustice.

ENCROACHMENT

Reversing a neighbor's fence deeper into his territory (19:14) is symptomatic of all encroachment. Find a way to expand your business without detracting from someone else. Develop a win-win attitude, and trust God to provide you with an honest livelihood.

NATURAL RESOURCES

When attacking an enemy city, destroy only non-fruit-bearing trees (20:19). Avoid wasting or damaging natural resources.

שופטים   דברים טז:יח - יז:ב

18 שֹׁפְטִ֣ים וְשֹֽׁטְרִ֗ים תִּֽתֶּן־לְךָ֙ בְּכׇל־שְׁעָרֶ֔יךָ אֲשֶׁ֨ר יְהֹוָ֧ה אֱלֹהֶ֛יךָ נֹתֵ֥ן לְךָ֖ לִשְׁבָטֶ֑יךָ וְשָׁפְט֥וּ אֶת־הָעָ֖ם מִשְׁפַּט־צֶֽדֶק: 19 לֹא־תַטֶּ֣ה מִשְׁפָּ֔ט לֹ֥א תַכִּ֖יר פָּנִ֑ים וְלֹא־תִקַּ֣ח שֹׁ֔חַד כִּ֣י הַשֹּׁ֗חַד יְעַוֵּר֙ עֵינֵ֣י חֲכָמִ֔ים וִֽיסַלֵּ֖ף דִּבְרֵ֥י צַדִּיקִֽם: 20 צֶ֥דֶק צֶ֖דֶק תִּרְדֹּ֑ף לְמַ֤עַן תִּֽחְיֶה֙ וְיָרַשְׁתָּ֣ אֶת־הָאָ֔רֶץ אֲשֶׁר־יְהֹוָ֥ה אֱלֹהֶ֖יךָ נֹתֵ֥ן לָֽךְ: ס 21 לֹֽא־תִטַּ֥ע לְךָ֛ אֲשֵׁרָ֖ה כׇּל־עֵ֑ץ אֵ֗צֶל מִזְבַּ֛ח יְהֹוָ֥ה אֱלֹהֶ֖יךָ אֲשֶׁ֥ר תַּעֲשֶׂה־לָּֽךְ: 22 וְלֹֽא־תָקִ֥ים לְךָ֖ מַצֵּבָ֑ה אֲשֶׁ֥ר שָׂנֵ֖א יְהֹוָ֥ה אֱלֹהֶֽיךָ: ס

יז 1 לֹא־תִזְבַּח֩ לַיהֹוָ֨ה אֱלֹהֶ֜יךָ שׁ֣וֹר וָשֶׂ֗ה אֲשֶׁ֨ר יִהְיֶ֥ה ב֛וֹ מ֖וּם כֹּ֣ל דָּבָ֣ר רָ֑ע כִּ֧י תוֹעֲבַ֛ת יְהֹוָ֥ה אֱלֹהֶ֖יךָ הֽוּא: ס 2 כִּֽי־יִמָּצֵ֤א בְקִרְבְּךָ֙ בְּאַחַ֣ד שְׁעָרֶ֔יךָ אֲשֶׁר־יְהֹוָ֥ה אֱלֹהֶ֖יךָ נֹתֵ֣ן לָ֑ךְ אִ֣ישׁ אוֹ־אִשָּׁ֗ה אֲשֶׁ֨ר יַעֲשֶׂ֧ה אֶת־הָרַ֣ע

21. (You should not plant) any tree (or build any house on the Temple Mount). It was common for idol-worshipers to plant beautiful trees beside their houses of worship. Therefore, God prohibited this practice in for His Temple, for He wished to disassociate anything idolatrous from the minds of those coming to serve Him (*Maimonides, 12th century*).

Also, this precept highlights that a holy place should be appreciated for its sacred character, not its external trappings, such as beautiful landscaping or fine architecture. Although it is important to beautify a holy site, we are cautioned against losing sight of its real beauty, that is, its inherent holiness (*Rabbi Alexander Zusya Friedman, 20th century*).

kabbalah bites

16:18 Our three-dimensional universe consists of four horizontal compass points, plus the two vertical directions, totaling six. This alludes to the universe's six spiritual foundations: *Torah, worship, kindness, judgment, truth* and *peace*.

The commandments in this Torah portion fit neatly into these six categories:

Judgment—Laws of judges and court (16:18-20).

Truth—Laws to discern a true prophet (18:9-22).

Peace—Laws minimizing war (20:1-20).

Torah—Laws benefiting Levites, enabling them to teach Torah (18:1-8).

Worship—Laws of prohibited worship (16:21-17:1).

Kindness—True kindnesses enacted for a deceased person who cannot repay you, such as laws of cities of refuge (19:1-13) and laws of Unsolved Murder (21:1-9).

deuteronomy 16:18 – 17:2 — shofetim

parashat shofetim

Appointment of Judges and Police

¹⁸ You should appoint judges and police officers for yourself—for each of your tribes—in all your (city) gates that God, your God, is giving you:

- (Appoint expert judges so that) they should judge the people correctly.
- ¹⁹ Do not pervert justice, do not show favoritism, and do not take a bribe (even to judge correctly), for bribery blinds the eyes of the wise and perverts legitimate words.
- ²⁰ Pursue justice, (by seeking a high quality court of) justice.

(In the merit of appointing judges) you will live and settle upon the land God, your God, is giving you.

Prohibited Structures and Offerings

- ²¹ You should not (even) plant for yourself an idolatrous tree (let alone worship it).
- (You should not plant) any tree (or build any house on the Temple Mount) near the altar of God, your God, which you will make for yourself.
- ²² You should not set up for yourself a monument (consisting of a single stone), which God, your God, hates.

17
- ¹ You should not offer to God, your God, an ox or a sheep that has in it a blemish, or (one that is slaughtered with) any incorrect statement (of intention), for that is an abomination to God, your God.

Punishment for Idol-Worship

² If there is found among you—in one of your cities which God, your God, is giving you—a man or woman who does what is evil in the eyes of God, your God,

---

16:18 Appoint judges … for yourself. People tend to judge others more harshly than they judge themselves. This is the cause of many quarrels, as people fail to see their own misdeeds while at the same time magnifying the faults of their friends. Therefore the Torah teaches, "Appoint judges *for yourself*." Do not be judgmental of others. Reserve your strict scrutiny for yourself (*Rabbi Jacob Joseph of Polonnoye, 18th century*).

In all your (city) gates. The term "gates" here alludes to the "gates" of the body—the two eyes, the two ears, the nose, the mouth, etc. The verse teaches you that you should place "judges" and "police" over all your bodily "gates" to ensure that only positive and kosher influences enter your body (*Rabbi Mordecai ha-Kohen, 17th century*).

20. Pursue justice. The pursuit of justice must also be *with* justice. Unlike the misguided principle that "the ends justify the means," the Torah's approach is that the process for achieving justice must itself be righteous (*Rabbi Simḥah Bunem of Przysucha, 18th–19th century*).

דברים יז:ב-יא שופטים

בְּעֵינֵי יְהֹוָה־אֱלֹהֶיךָ לַעֲבֹר בְּרִיתוֹ: 3 וַיֵּלֶךְ וַיַּעֲבֹד אֱלֹהִים אֲחֵרִים וַיִּשְׁתַּחוּ לָהֶם וְלַשֶּׁמֶשׁ | אוֹ לַיָּרֵחַ אוֹ לְכָל־צְבָא הַשָּׁמַיִם אֲשֶׁר לֹא־צִוִּיתִי: 4 וְהֻגַּד־לְךָ וְשָׁמָעְתָּ וְדָרַשְׁתָּ הֵיטֵב וְהִנֵּה אֱמֶת נָכוֹן הַדָּבָר נֶעֶשְׂתָה הַתּוֹעֵבָה הַזֹּאת בְּיִשְׂרָאֵל: 5 וְהוֹצֵאתָ אֶת־הָאִישׁ הַהוּא אוֹ אֶת־הָאִשָּׁה הַהִוא אֲשֶׁר עָשׂוּ אֶת־הַדָּבָר הָרָע הַזֶּה אֶל־שְׁעָרֶיךָ אֶת־הָאִישׁ אוֹ אֶת־הָאִשָּׁה וּסְקַלְתָּם בָּאֲבָנִים וָמֵתוּ: 6 עַל־פִּי | שְׁנַיִם עֵדִים אוֹ שְׁלֹשָׁה עֵדִים יוּמַת הַמֵּת לֹא יוּמַת עַל־פִּי עֵד אֶחָד: 7 יַד הָעֵדִים תִּהְיֶה־בּוֹ בָרִאשֹׁנָה לַהֲמִיתוֹ וְיַד כָּל־הָעָם בָּאַחֲרֹנָה וּבִעַרְתָּ הָרָע מִקִּרְבֶּךָ: פ 8 כִּי יִפָּלֵא מִמְּךָ דָבָר לַמִּשְׁפָּט בֵּין־דָּם | לְדָם בֵּין־דִּין לְדִין וּבֵין נֶגַע לָנֶגַע דִּבְרֵי רִיבֹת בִּשְׁעָרֶיךָ וְקַמְתָּ וְעָלִיתָ אֶל־הַמָּקוֹם אֲשֶׁר יִבְחַר יְהֹוָה אֱלֹהֶיךָ בּוֹ: 9 וּבָאתָ אֶל־הַכֹּהֲנִים הַלְוִיִּם וְאֶל־הַשֹּׁפֵט אֲשֶׁר יִהְיֶה בַּיָּמִים הָהֵם וְדָרַשְׁתָּ וְהִגִּידוּ לְךָ אֵת דְּבַר הַמִּשְׁפָּט: 10 וְעָשִׂיתָ עַל־פִּי הַדָּבָר אֲשֶׁר יַגִּידוּ לְךָ מִן־הַמָּקוֹם הַהוּא אֲשֶׁר יִבְחַר יְהֹוָה וְשָׁמַרְתָּ לַעֲשׂוֹת כְּכֹל אֲשֶׁר יוֹרוּךָ: 11 עַל־פִּי הַתּוֹרָה אֲשֶׁר יוֹרוּךָ וְעַל־הַמִּשְׁפָּט אֲשֶׁר־יֹאמְרוּ

This scriptural decree is somewhat rational, because a person's soul was not given to him as a personal acquisition; rather, it belongs to God, as the verse states, *"all souls are Mine"* (Ezekiel 18:4). A person's admission will not help to cause damage to something that is not his.

A person's money, however, *does* belong to him. Therefore, in monetary cases we rule that a defendant's admission is equivalent to the testimony of a hundred witnesses (*Babylonian Talmud, Gittin* 40b). Nevertheless, I agree that this is a decree of God which we cannot fully fathom (*Rabbi David b. Solomon ibn Abi Zimra, 16th century*).

9. The judges who exist at that time. Even if they are not like the other judges who preceded them, you must listen to them, for you have only the judges of your time (*Rashi, 11th century*).

The judge in each generation is like Samuel in his generation, and like Moses in his generation (*Babylonian Talmud, Rosh Ha-Shanah* 20b).

Food for thought

1. Is the leadership in your community or organization honest?

2. Why does the Torah discourage Jews from attending a secular court?

3. What makes a good judge? Would you do a good job?

and violates His covenant, ³ by going and worshiping other gods—or the sun, the moon, or any heavenly body which I have not commanded (you to worship)—and he prostrated himself before them. ⁴ Then when you are informed (by witnesses), and you hear (the case), investigating (them) thoroughly, you see that the(ir) statements (of testimony) are consistent and true, and that this abomination has occurred in Israel:

- ⁵ You should bring outside the (city) gates that man or that woman who has committed this evil thing, and you should pelt them—the man or the woman—with stones, and they should die.

- ⁶ The one liable to death should be put to death only by the testimony of two witnesses, or three witnesses. He should not be put to death by the testimony of one witness.

- ⁷ The hands of the witnesses should be against him first to put him to death, and afterwards the hands of all the people—and you will eliminate this evil from among you.

Authority of the High Court

⁸ If a point of law eludes you(r local court)—be it the distinction between (pure) blood and (impure) blood, between a verdict (of innocence) and a verdict (of guilt), or between a (pure) lesion and an (impure) lesion, (resulting in) conflicting rulings (among the sages) in your city:

- You should make the journey up to (the Holy Temple), the place that God, your God, will choose. ⁹ You should come to the priests, (who are from) the (tribe) of Levites, and to the judges who exist at that time. You should question them, and they will tell you words of judgment.

- ¹⁰ You must obey the words that they will tell you—from the place God will choose. You should carefully obey everything they instruct you. ¹¹ You should act in

---

17:6 The one liable to death should be put to death. Literally, this verse reads, *"The dead person should be put to death."* Why does Scripture refer to him as *"the dead person,"* when he is still alive? Because the wicked, even in their lifetime are called "dead" (*Babylonian Talmud, Berakhot* 18b).

All life flows from God, the source of life. When a person sins against God, he severs his "umbilical cord" of sustenance from the living God. Through sinning, his lifeline is re-routed to the demonic forces, the source of "death and evil," and so he is considered to be "dead" (*Rabbi Shneur Zalman of Lyady, 18th century*).

By the testimony of two witnesses. It is a scriptural decree that the court does not execute a person or administer lashes to him through his own admission, but only *"by the testimony of two witnesses"* (*Maimonides, 12th century*).

שופטים   דברים יז:י״א-ט״ז

לְךָ תַּעֲשֶׂה לֹא תָסוּר מִן־הַדָּבָר אֲשֶׁר־יַגִּידוּ לְךָ יָמִין וּשְׂמֹאל: 12 וְהָאִישׁ אֲשֶׁר־יַעֲשֶׂה בְזָדוֹן לְבִלְתִּי שְׁמֹעַ אֶל־הַכֹּהֵן הָעֹמֵד לְשָׁרֶת שָׁם אֶת־יְהֹוָה אֱלֹהֶיךָ אוֹ אֶל־הַשֹּׁפֵט וּמֵת הָאִישׁ הַהוּא וּבִעַרְתָּ הָרָע מִיִּשְׂרָאֵל: 13 וְכָל־הָעָם יִשְׁמְעוּ וְיִרָאוּ וְלֹא יְזִידוּן עוֹד: ס 14 [SECOND READING] כִּי־תָבֹא אֶל־הָאָרֶץ אֲשֶׁר יְהֹוָה אֱלֹהֶיךָ נֹתֵן לָךְ וִירִשְׁתָּהּ וְיָשַׁבְתָּה בָּהּ וְאָמַרְתָּ אָשִׂימָה עָלַי מֶלֶךְ כְּכָל־הַגּוֹיִם אֲשֶׁר סְבִיבֹתָי: 15 שׂוֹם תָּשִׂים עָלֶיךָ מֶלֶךְ אֲשֶׁר יִבְחַר יְהֹוָה אֱלֹהֶיךָ בּוֹ מִקֶּרֶב אַחֶיךָ תָּשִׂים עָלֶיךָ מֶלֶךְ לֹא תוּכַל לָתֵת עָלֶיךָ אִישׁ נָכְרִי אֲשֶׁר לֹא־אָחִיךָ הוּא: 16 רַק לֹא־יַרְבֶּה־לּוֹ סוּסִים וְלֹא־יָשִׁיב אֶת־הָעָם מִצְרַיְמָה לְמַעַן הַרְבּוֹת סוּס וַיהֹוָה אָמַר לָכֶם לֹא תֹסִפוּן לָשׁוּב בַּדֶּרֶךְ הַזֶּה עוֹד:

Even if you are correct in your reasoning and the food in question should actually be forbidden, the very same Torah that issued this prohibition gave the Rabbis the authority, using a given set of rules, to determine what is included in that prohibition. If they rule that it is permissible, then the Torah itself permits consumption.

And what may seem to be an incorrect ruling is surely a misapprehension on your part, for God directs His righteous servants, ensuring that they reach the correct decision. Therefore, *"You must not divert from the words they tell you"* (Naḥmanides, 13th century).

15. You should always set a king over you. The commentators wonder why Samuel was displeased with Israel's request to *"appoint for us a king to judge us like all the nations"* (I Samuel 8:4-6), considering that the Torah commands us here to appoint a king.

Israel's request contained a short clause that does not appear in this verse, namely, *"to judge us like all the nations."* Rather than implementing Torah's laws, they wanted a king who would rule in accordance with secular law.

If the people would have openly stated their wishes, Samuel would have been able to show them their error and encourage them to repent. But they masked their intentions through ambiguous wording, making it impossible for him to admonish them. (Their request could be read, *"appoint for us a king to judge us, like all the nations,"*—"we just want a king like everybody else"; but what they meant was, *"appoint for us a king, to judge us like all the nations"*—"we want to be judged by the standards of secular law, like the nations.") This is what angered Samuel.

The lesson here is relevant to us all: *You can improve your behavior only if you are willing to recognize what you did wrong* (Rabbi David Solomon Eybeschuetz, 18th century).

You should always set a king over you. The king is the heart of the entire congregation of Israel (*Maimonides, 12th century*).

Like a heart which moves constantly in the service of the other limbs, a king is utterly devoted to the people and involved with their needs (*Rabbi Baḥya b. Asher, 13th century*).

deuteronomy 17:11-16 — shofetim

accordance with the teachings that they instruct you, and according to the judgments they issue to you.

- You must not divert from the words they tell you, (even if they tell you that) right (is left) and left (is right).

- ¹² (If) any man intentionally disobeys and fails to listen to the priest who is standing and officiating there before God, your God, or to the judge, that man must die. Thus you will eliminate this evil from Israel.

- ¹³ (They should wait until the next festival to execute him, so that) all the people will hear (of it) and be afraid, so they will no longer disobey intentionally.

Appointment of a King

[SECOND READING] ¹⁴ When you come to the land God, your God, is giving you, and you take possession of it and settle in it, you will (eventually) say, "I will set a king over myself, like all the nations around me":

- ¹⁵ You should always set a king over you, one whom God, your God, chooses.

- The king that you appoint over yourselves must be from among your (Jewish) brothers.

- You may not appoint a gentile over yourselves, one who is not your brother.

- ¹⁶ However, he may not acquire many horses for himself (more than he needs for his chariot).

- (This is) so that he will not bring the people back to Egypt, in order to get more horses, for God said to you: "You should never return on that road again!"

11. (Even if they tell you that) right (is left) and left (is right). Although you may be absolutely certain that the judges are mistaken, and the matter is as obvious to you as the difference between right and left, you still must follow their ruling.

If, for example, according to your understanding the Rabbis erroneously ruled that a certain food is permissible, do not say to yourself, "How can I eat something forbidden by the Torah?"

spiritual vitamin

> However wise you may be, it is not always wise to rely entirely on your own judgment, especially in a case where you are personally and deeply involved, since the wisest person may sometimes make a mistake.

שופטים — דברים יז:יז - יח:ו

17 וְלֹא יַרְבֶּה־לּוֹ נָשִׁים וְלֹא יָסוּר לְבָבוֹ וְכֶסֶף וְזָהָב לֹא יַרְבֶּה־לּוֹ מְאֹד: 18 וְהָיָה כְשִׁבְתּוֹ עַל כִּסֵּא מַמְלַכְתּוֹ וְכָתַב לוֹ אֶת־מִשְׁנֵה הַתּוֹרָה הַזֹּאת עַל־סֵפֶר מִלִּפְנֵי הַכֹּהֲנִים הַלְוִיִּם: 19 וְהָיְתָה עִמּוֹ וְקָרָא בוֹ כָּל־יְמֵי חַיָּיו לְמַעַן יִלְמַד לְיִרְאָה אֶת־יְהֹוָה אֱלֹהָיו לִשְׁמֹר אֶת־כָּל־דִּבְרֵי הַתּוֹרָה הַזֹּאת וְאֶת־הַחֻקִּים הָאֵלֶּה לַעֲשֹׂתָם: 20 לְבִלְתִּי רוּם־לְבָבוֹ מֵאֶחָיו וּלְבִלְתִּי סוּר מִן־הַמִּצְוָה יָמִין וּשְׂמֹאול לְמַעַן יַאֲרִיךְ יָמִים עַל־מַמְלַכְתּוֹ הוּא וּבָנָיו בְּקֶרֶב יִשְׂרָאֵל: ס

יח 1 [THIRD READING] לֹא־יִהְיֶה לַכֹּהֲנִים הַלְוִיִּם כָּל־שֵׁבֶט לֵוִי חֵלֶק וְנַחֲלָה עִם־יִשְׂרָאֵל אִשֵּׁי יְהֹוָה וְנַחֲלָתוֹ יֹאכֵלוּן: 2 וְנַחֲלָה לֹא־יִהְיֶה־לּוֹ בְּקֶרֶב אֶחָיו יְהֹוָה הוּא נַחֲלָתוֹ כַּאֲשֶׁר דִּבֶּר־לוֹ: ס 3 וְזֶה יִהְיֶה מִשְׁפַּט הַכֹּהֲנִים מֵאֵת הָעָם מֵאֵת זֹבְחֵי הַזֶּבַח אִם־שׁוֹר אִם־שֶׂה וְנָתַן לַכֹּהֵן הַזְּרֹעַ וְהַלְּחָיַיִם וְהַקֵּבָה: 4 רֵאשִׁית דְּגָנְךָ תִּירֹשְׁךָ וְיִצְהָרֶךָ וְרֵאשִׁית גֵּז צֹאנְךָ תִּתֶּן־לּוֹ: 5 כִּי בוֹ בָּחַר יְהֹוָה אֱלֹהֶיךָ מִכָּל־שְׁבָטֶיךָ לַעֲמֹד לְשָׁרֵת בְּשֵׁם־יְהֹוָה הוּא וּבָנָיו כָּל־הַיָּמִים: ס 6 [FOURTH READING] וְכִי־יָבֹא הַלֵּוִי מֵאַחַד שְׁעָרֶיךָ מִכָּל־יִשְׂרָאֵל אֲשֶׁר־הוּא גָּר שָׁם וּבָא

---

20. He and his sons. Once a king is anointed, he and his descendants are granted the monarchy forever, since the monarchy is transferred by means of inheritance. Not only the monarchy, but all other positions of authority and appointments in Israel are transferred to the children and grandchildren forever, provided the son's wisdom and fear of God equal that of the father.

Once David was anointed, he earned the rights to the "Crown of Kingship." The monarchy belongs to him and his male descendants forever. However, this right was only transferred to his righteous descendants. Nevertheless, God promised him that the monarchy would never cease from his descendants (*Maimonides, 12th century*).

18:2 God is his inheritance. In addition to the gifts of food and shearings promised to the priests for their service in the Temple, they also received a spiritual reward as an inheritance— the opportunity to concentrate fully on their devotion to God without being distracted by the difficulties of earning a livelihood (*Rabbi Isaac Abravanel, 15th century*).

This applies not just to the Levites, but anyone who dedicates his heart and mind to the service of God is sanctified with the highest degree of holiness and merits that *"God is his inheritance,"* for all eternity. In this world, too, he is assured that he will be able to earn a livelihood with minimal effort so that he can focus properly on strengthening his bond with the Almighty (*Maimonides, 12th century*).

deuteronomy 17:17 – 18:6 — shofetim

- ¹⁷ He should not take too many wives for himself, so his heart will not be led astray.
- He should not acquire an abundance of silver and gold for himself.
- ¹⁸ After he is already sitting upon his royal throne, he should write two copies of this Torah scroll for himself, in the presence of the priests, the sons of Levi.
- ¹⁹ (One copy should be placed in his treasury, and the other) should remain with him, and he should read from it all the days of his life, so that he may learn to fear God, his God, to carefully guard the observance of all the words of this Torah, and its suprarational commands. ²⁰ (This is) so that his heart will not be arrogant over his brothers, and he will not veer away from (even) the (smallest) commandment, either to the right or to the left, in order that he will reign for a long time over his kingdom—he and his sons—among Israel.

18 Rights of the Priests and Levites

- [THIRD READING] ¹ The priests (who are from) the (tribe of the) Levites shall have no portion (from the spoils of war).
- Nor (shall they have any) inheritance (of the land) with the (rest of) the Jewish people.
- (This applies to) all (the priests who are from) the tribe of Levi (regardless of whether they are fit to serve in the Temple, or not).
- (Rather, the priest and Levite) will eat God's fire-offerings (*terumah* and tithes) that He bequeathed (to them).
- ² But (the priest) will have no (territorial) inheritance among his brothers. God is his inheritance, as He told (Aaron).

³ These are the priests' rights from the people:

- When any ox or sheep is slaughtered, the priest should be given the foreleg, the jaw (with the tongue), and the end-stomach.
- ⁴ You should give him (*terumah*, which is) the first portion of your grain, your wine, and your oil.
- You should give him the first (shearings) of the fleece of your sheep.

⁵ For God, your God, has chosen him out of all your tribes, to stand and serve in the name of God—he and his sons—for all time.

- [FOURTH READING] ⁶ If a (priest, a member of the) Levite (tribe), comes from any one of your cities through-

Food for thought

1. Is your Rabbi honored sufficiently?

2. Is your Rabbi overworked?

3. Is your Rabbi given a fair salary?

שופטים
דברים יח:ו-טז

בְּכָל־אַוַּ֣ת נַפְשׁ֔וֹ אֶל־הַמָּק֖וֹם אֲשֶׁר־יִבְחַ֥ר יְהֹוָֽה: 7 וְשֵׁרֵ֕ת בְּשֵׁ֖ם יְהֹוָ֣ה אֱלֹהָ֑יו כְּכָל־אֶחָיו֙ הַלְוִיִּ֔ם הָעֹמְדִ֥ים שָׁ֖ם לִפְנֵ֥י יְהֹוָֽה: 8 חֵ֥לֶק כְּחֵ֖לֶק יֹאכֵ֑לוּ לְבַ֥ד מִמְכָּרָ֖יו עַל־הָאָבֽוֹת: ס 9 כִּ֤י אַתָּה֙ בָּ֣א אֶל־הָאָ֔רֶץ אֲשֶׁר־יְהֹוָ֥ה אֱלֹהֶ֖יךָ נֹתֵ֣ן לָ֑ךְ לֹֽא־תִלְמַ֣ד לַעֲשׂ֔וֹת כְּתוֹעֲבֹ֖ת הַגּוֹיִ֥ם הָהֵֽם: 10 לֹֽא־יִמָּצֵ֣א בְךָ֔ מַעֲבִ֥יר בְּנֽוֹ־וּבִתּ֖וֹ בָּאֵ֑שׁ קֹסֵ֣ם קְסָמִ֔ים מְעוֹנֵ֥ן וּמְנַחֵ֖שׁ וּמְכַשֵּֽׁף: 11 וְחֹבֵ֖ר חָ֑בֶר וְשֹׁאֵ֥ל אוֹב֙ וְיִדְּעֹנִ֔י וְדֹרֵ֖שׁ אֶל־הַמֵּתִֽים: 12 כִּֽי־תוֹעֲבַ֥ת יְהֹוָ֖ה כָּל־עֹ֣שֵׂה אֵ֑לֶּה וּבִגְלַל֙ הַתּוֹעֵבֹ֣ת הָאֵ֔לֶּה יְהֹוָ֣ה אֱלֹהֶ֔יךָ מוֹרִ֥ישׁ אוֹתָ֖ם מִפָּנֶֽיךָ: 13 תָּמִ֣ים תִּֽהְיֶ֔ה עִ֖ם יְהֹוָ֥ה אֱלֹהֶֽיךָ: [FIFTH READING] 14 כִּ֣י ׀ הַגּוֹיִ֣ם הָאֵ֗לֶּה אֲשֶׁ֤ר אַתָּה֙ יוֹרֵ֣שׁ אוֹתָ֔ם אֶל־מְעֹנְנִ֥ים וְאֶל־קֹסְמִ֖ים יִשְׁמָ֑עוּ וְאַתָּ֕ה לֹ֣א כֵ֔ן נָ֥תַן לְךָ֖ יְהֹוָ֥ה אֱלֹהֶֽיךָ: 15 נָבִ֨יא מִקִּרְבְּךָ֤ מֵאַחֶ֙יךָ֙ כָּמֹ֔נִי יָקִ֥ים לְךָ֖ יְהֹוָ֣ה אֱלֹהֶ֑יךָ אֵלָ֖יו תִּשְׁמָעֽוּן: 16 כְּכֹ֨ל אֲשֶׁר־שָׁאַ֜לְתָּ מֵעִ֨ם יְהֹוָ֤ה אֱלֹהֶ֙יךָ֙ בְּחֹרֵ֔ב בְּי֥וֹם הַקָּהָ֖ל לֵאמֹ֑ר

---

13. Be simple-hearted (tamim) with God, your God. The Torah uses the expression *tamim*, meaning that you should walk with Him simple-heartedly (*bitmimut*) and look forward to what He has in store. Do not probe the future, but rather accept whatever happens to you simple-heartedly (*Rashi, 11th century*).

This verse can also be translated *"be complete together with God"*—just as God is "perfect," you must also be "perfect." How can we demand perfection from a mortal? By being *"with God"*—by shedding your ego, you become unified with God, attaining some of God's perfection (*Rabbi Samuel Shmelke Horowitz of Nikolsburg, 18th century*).

15. Establish a prophet. Torah is superior to prophecy in that Torah is an eternal code and the core of the Jewish existence. Prophecy is a "means to an end," to encourage people to observe the Torah (*Maimonides, 12th century*).

spiritual vitamin

> Don't try to make forecasts about future events. We are commanded in the Torah, *"be simple-hearted with God, your God"* (v. 13). This means that we should wholeheartedly put our faith in God, following His commandments without question or speculation, and enjoy a complete sense of security in the faith and conviction that God's benevolent Providence extends to every one individually.

deuteronomy 18:6–16 — shofetim

out Israel where he lives, he may come whenever his soul desires, to the place God will choose, ⁷ and he may minister in the name of God, his God, just like all his (priestly) brothers, (from) the (tribe of the) Levites, who stand there before God.

- ⁸ They should eat equal portions (of the hides and meat of the festival offerings), except for (the continual-offering, the additional-offering of the Sabbath and voluntary offerings, for which the priests) were (divided into "watches," whose rights were) sold by their ancestors.

Prohibitions against Fortune-Telling

⁹ When you come to the land God, your God, is giving you, you must not learn to do the abominable practices of those nations. ¹⁰ There must not be found anyone among you who:

- Passes his son or daughter (between two) fires (to Molech),
- Practices stick divination,
- Acts on the basis of fortuitous times,
- Divines (on the basis of strange occurrences),
- Practices sorcery,
- ¹¹ Divines with animals,
- Turns to (the sorcery of) *'ov* or *yidde'oni*,
- (Raises and) consults with (spirits of) the dead.

¹² For whoever does these things is an abomination to God, and it is because of these abominations that God, your God, is driving out these (nations) before you.

- ¹³ (Do not probe into the future, but) be simple-hearted with God, your God.

Food for thought

1. Why do we desire to know and control the future?

2. Why is this inappropriate?

3. Isn't prophecy a kind of fortune telling?

True and False Prophecy

[FIFTH READING] ¹⁴ While these nations, which you are about to take possession of, listen to diviners of fortuitous times and stick diviners, in your case however, God, your God, has not given you things like these (but rather, genuine prophets and the Urim and Thummim).

- ¹⁵ God, your God, will establish a prophet like me, from among you, from your brothers, and you must listen to him.

¹⁶ This is what you asked from God, your God, at Horeb, on the Day of Assembly, saying, "I don't want to hear the voice of God, my God, any more, or see this great fire, so that I will not die!"

דברים יח:טז - יט:ה · שופטים

לֹא אֹסֵף לִשְׁמֹעַ אֶת־קוֹל יְהֹוָה אֱלֹהָי וְאֶת־הָאֵשׁ הַגְּדֹלָה הַזֹּאת לֹא־אֶרְאֶה עוֹד וְלֹא אָמוּת: 17 וַיֹּאמֶר יְהֹוָה אֵלָי הֵיטִיבוּ אֲשֶׁר דִּבֵּרוּ: 18 נָבִיא אָקִים לָהֶם מִקֶּרֶב אֲחֵיהֶם כָּמוֹךָ וְנָתַתִּי דְבָרַי בְּפִיו וְדִבֶּר אֲלֵיהֶם אֵת כָּל־אֲשֶׁר אֲצַוֶּנּוּ: 19 וְהָיָה הָאִישׁ אֲשֶׁר לֹא־יִשְׁמַע אֶל־דְּבָרַי אֲשֶׁר יְדַבֵּר בִּשְׁמִי אָנֹכִי אֶדְרֹשׁ מֵעִמּוֹ: 20 אַךְ הַנָּבִיא אֲשֶׁר יָזִיד לְדַבֵּר דָּבָר בִּשְׁמִי אֵת אֲשֶׁר לֹא־צִוִּיתִיו לְדַבֵּר וַאֲשֶׁר יְדַבֵּר בְּשֵׁם אֱלֹהִים אֲחֵרִים וּמֵת הַנָּבִיא הַהוּא: 21 וְכִי תֹאמַר בִּלְבָבֶךָ אֵיכָה נֵדַע אֶת־הַדָּבָר אֲשֶׁר לֹא־דִבְּרוֹ יְהֹוָה: 22 אֲשֶׁר יְדַבֵּר הַנָּבִיא בְּשֵׁם יְהֹוָה וְלֹא־יִהְיֶה הַדָּבָר וְלֹא יָבוֹא הוּא הַדָּבָר אֲשֶׁר לֹא־דִבְּרוֹ יְהֹוָה בְּזָדוֹן דִּבְּרוֹ הַנָּבִיא לֹא תָגוּר מִמֶּנּוּ: ס

יט 1 כִּי־יַכְרִית יְהֹוָה אֱלֹהֶיךָ אֶת־הַגּוֹיִם אֲשֶׁר יְהֹוָה אֱלֹהֶיךָ נֹתֵן לְךָ אֶת־אַרְצָם וִירִשְׁתָּם וְיָשַׁבְתָּ בְעָרֵיהֶם וּבְבָתֵּיהֶם: 2 שָׁלוֹשׁ עָרִים תַּבְדִּיל לָךְ בְּתוֹךְ אַרְצְךָ אֲשֶׁר יְהֹוָה אֱלֹהֶיךָ נֹתֵן לְךָ לְרִשְׁתָּהּ: 3 תָּכִין לְךָ הַדֶּרֶךְ וְשִׁלַּשְׁתָּ אֶת־גְּבוּל אַרְצְךָ אֲשֶׁר יַנְחִילְךָ יְהֹוָה אֱלֹהֶיךָ וְהָיָה לָנוּס שָׁמָּה כָּל־רֹצֵחַ: 4 וְזֶה דְּבַר הָרֹצֵחַ אֲשֶׁר־יָנוּס שָׁמָּה וָחָי אֲשֶׁר יַכֶּה אֶת־רֵעֵהוּ בִּבְלִי־דַעַת וְהוּא לֹא־שֹׂנֵא לוֹ מִתְּמֹל שִׁלְשֹׁם: 5 וַאֲשֶׁר יָבֹא אֶת־רֵעֵהוּ בַיַּעַר לַחְטֹב

However, a sin is only like *accidental* murder, since the true intention of every Jew is—as Maimonides testifies—*"to fulfil all the commandments and to avoid any sins."* The act of sin is considered to have been done "unintentionally," for *"a person does not commit a sin unless he is possessed by a spirit of folly"* (*Babylonian Talmud, Sotah* 3a).

The atonement for this is to study Torah, which is analogous to the escape to a city of refuge—because, *"the words of Torah protect"* (*Babylonian Talmud, Makkot* 10a). Just as a city of refuge is a haven to protect accidental murderers from "avengers of the blood" (relatives of the deceased who seek revenge), the Torah is a refuge from your personal "avenger of the blood," the impulse to evil (*Babylonian Talmud, Bava Batra* 16a).

Torah study is effective in achieving atonement for the "spilled blood," since your energies become re-devoted to holiness and Torah, which is described as the "Torah of life" (*Rabbi Menahem Mendel Schneerson, 20th century*).

deuteronomy 18:17 – 19:5 — shofetim

¹⁷ God said to me, "They have spoken well! ¹⁸ I will establish for them a prophet like you from among their brothers. I will put My words into his mouth, and he will tell them everything that I command him. ¹⁹ And then, if anybody does not listen to My words that he speaks in My name, I will punish him (with death from heaven)."

- ²⁰ But if a prophet intentionally utters a word in My name, which I did not command him to say, or he speaks in the name of other gods, that prophet must be (put to) death.

²¹ If you will say to yourself, "How will we know if a declaration was not said by God?" (The answer is):

- ²² If the prophet (claims to) speak in the name of God, and the thing does not occur and (you see that it will) never come about, then it is a declaration which God did not say. The prophet has spoken it (to deceive you) intentionally. Do not be afraid of him.

Cities of Refuge

19 ¹ When God, your God, cuts off the nations, whose land God, your God, is giving you, and you inherit them, and settle in their cities and in their houses:

- ² You should separate three cities for yourself within your land, which God, your God, is giving you as a possession.

- ³ Prepare (signs to indicate) for yourself the route (to these cities), and (position the) three (cities so that they) are equally spaced across the expanse of your land, which God, your God, is giving you as an inheritance. They will be (available) for every (accidental) murderer to flee there.

⁴ These are the terms upon which the murderer may flee there in order to live:

- Whoever gives a (fatal) blow to his fellow unintentionally, provided he did not hate him yesterday or the day before; ⁵ or if a man goes with his fellow into the

---

18. I will establish for them a prophet. God only allows His Presence to rest on a person who is strong, wealthy, wise and humble. All of these requirements are derived from Moses (*Babylonian Talmud, Nedarim* 38a).

It is one of the principles of faith to know that God communicates to man via prophecy. In order to receive prophecy a person must be extremely wise, a master of his emotions, and unperturbed by his evil inclination in worldly matters. He must constantly control his evil impulse with his mind, and he must have an extremely broad and fine mind (*Maimonides, 12th century*).

19:4 The murderer may flee there in order to live. Any sin is a kind of "murder," since the abuse of energy for the purposes of evil is like the spilling of blood (*Rabbi Shneur Zalman of Lyady, 18th century*).

דברים יט:ה-טו · שופטים

עֵצִים֒ וְנִדְּחָ֨ה יָד֤וֹ בַגַּרְזֶן֙ לִכְרֹ֣ת הָעֵ֔ץ וְנָשַׁ֤ל הַבַּרְזֶל֙ מִן־הָעֵ֔ץ וּמָצָ֥א אֶת־רֵעֵ֖הוּ וָמֵ֑ת ה֗וּא יָנ֛וּס אֶל־אַחַ֥ת הֶעָרִים־הָאֵ֖לֶּה וָחָֽי: 6 פֶּן־יִרְדֹּף֩ גֹּאֵ֨ל הַדָּ֜ם אַחֲרֵ֣י הָרֹצֵ֗חַ כִּי־יֵחַם֮ לְבָבוֹ֒ וְהִשִּׂיג֛וֹ כִּֽי־יִרְבֶּ֥ה הַדֶּ֖רֶךְ וְהִכָּ֣הוּ נָ֑פֶשׁ וְלוֹ֙ אֵ֣ין מִשְׁפַּט־מָ֔וֶת כִּ֠י לֹ֣א שֹׂנֵ֥א ה֛וּא ל֖וֹ מִתְּמ֥וֹל שִׁלְשֽׁוֹם: 7 עַל־כֵּ֛ן אָנֹכִ֥י מְצַוְּךָ֖ לֵאמֹ֑ר שָׁלֹ֥שׁ עָרִ֖ים תַּבְדִּ֥יל לָֽךְ: 8 וְאִם־יַרְחִ֞יב יְהֹוָ֤ה אֱלֹהֶ֙יךָ֙ אֶת־גְּבֻ֣לְךָ֔ כַּאֲשֶׁ֥ר נִשְׁבַּ֖ע לַאֲבֹתֶ֑יךָ וְנָ֤תַן לְךָ֙ אֶת־כָּל־הָאָ֔רֶץ אֲשֶׁ֥ר דִּבֶּ֖ר לָתֵ֥ת לַאֲבֹתֶֽיךָ: 9 כִּֽי־תִשְׁמֹ֣ר אֶת־כָּל־הַמִּצְוָ֣ה הַזֹּאת֮ לַעֲשֹׂתָהּ֒ אֲשֶׁ֨ר אָנֹכִ֤י מְצַוְּךָ֙ הַיּ֔וֹם לְאַהֲבָ֞ה אֶת־יְהֹוָ֧ה אֱלֹהֶ֛יךָ וְלָלֶ֥כֶת בִּדְרָכָ֖יו כָּל־הַיָּמִ֑ים וְיָסַפְתָּ֨ לְךָ֥ עוֹד֙ שָׁלֹ֣שׁ עָרִ֔ים עַ֖ל הַשָּׁלֹ֥שׁ הָאֵֽלֶּה: 10 וְלֹ֤א יִשָּׁפֵךְ֙ דָּ֣ם נָקִ֔י בְּקֶ֣רֶב אַרְצְךָ֔ אֲשֶׁר֙ יְהֹוָ֣ה אֱלֹהֶ֔יךָ נֹתֵ֥ן לְךָ֖ נַחֲלָ֑ה וְהָיָ֥ה עָלֶ֖יךָ דָּמִֽים: פ 11 וְכִֽי־יִהְיֶ֥ה אִישׁ֙ שֹׂנֵ֣א לְרֵעֵ֔הוּ וְאָ֤רַב לוֹ֙ וְקָ֣ם עָלָ֔יו וְהִכָּ֥הוּ נֶ֖פֶשׁ וָמֵ֑ת וְנָ֕ס אֶל־אַחַ֖ת הֶעָרִ֥ים הָאֵֽל: 12 וְשָֽׁלְחוּ֙ זִקְנֵ֣י עִיר֔וֹ וְלָקְח֥וּ אֹת֖וֹ מִשָּׁ֑ם וְנָתְנ֣וּ אֹת֗וֹ בְּיַ֛ד גֹּאֵ֥ל הַדָּ֖ם וָמֵֽת: 13 לֹא־תָח֥וֹס עֵֽינְךָ֖ עָלָ֑יו וּבִֽעַרְתָּ֧ דַֽם־הַנָּקִ֛י מִיִּשְׂרָאֵ֖ל וְט֥וֹב לָֽךְ: ס [SIXTH READING] 14 לֹ֤א תַסִּיג֙ גְּב֣וּל רֵֽעֲךָ֔ אֲשֶׁ֥ר גָּבְל֖וּ רִאשֹׁנִ֑ים בְּנַחֲלָֽתְךָ֙ אֲשֶׁ֣ר תִּנְחַ֔ל בָּאָ֕רֶץ אֲשֶׁר֙ יְהֹוָ֣ה אֱלֹהֶ֔יךָ נֹתֵ֥ן לְךָ֖ לְרִשְׁתָּֽהּ: ס 15 לֹֽא־יָק֩וּם עֵ֨ד אֶחָ֜ד בְּאִ֗ישׁ לְכָל־עָוֺן֙ וּלְכָל־חַטָּ֔את בְּכָל־חֵ֖טְא אֲשֶׁ֣ר יֶֽחֱטָ֑א

9. You should add for yourself three more cities. In the days of the Messianic king, three additional cities of refuge will be added (*Maimonides, 12th century*).

This is a scriptural decree. Logically there will not be a need for cities of refuge in the future, as then there will be only peace, truth and good (*Rabbi Joseph b. Moses Babad, 19th century*).

The cities might be used to provide refuge for acts committed *before* the Redemption (*Rabbi Moses Alshekh, 16th century*).

15. A single witness cannot incriminate another person. A judgment is never issued based on the testimony of a single witness, neither in financial nor capital cases. The Oral Tradition teaches that a single witness is sufficient to obligate another person to take an oath.

The Torah accepts the testimony of one witness in two instances: In the case of a *sotah* ("suspected wife"), so she does not drink the bitter waters (see *Numbers*, ch. 5); and in the case of a calf whose neck is to be broken (below, ch. 21), to prevent its neck from being broken (*Maimonides, 12th century*).

deuteronomy 19:5–15 — shofetim

forest to chop wood, and his hand swings with the ax to cut down the tree, and the iron flies off the handle, and it happens (to hit) his fellow, and he dies—he should flee to one of these cities in order to live.

- ❖ ⁶ (I instructed you to signpost these cities clearly and place them at equal distances) in case an avenger of the blood pursues the killer, while his heart is hot, and he (manages) to catch up with him, because of the long road, and he strikes him to death. (For) being that (the murderer) had not hated (the victim) yesterday or the day before, he did not deserve (to be punished) with death. ⁷ Therefore, I am commanding you, saying, "You should separate three cities for yourself."

⁸ When God, your God, will expand your borders, as He swore to your forefathers, and He gives you the entire land which He told your forefathers He would give, ⁹ as a result of your safeguarding and observing all these commandments which I am commanding you today—to love God, your God, and to walk in His ways for all time:

- ❖ You should add for yourself three more cities, in addition to these three, ¹⁰ so that innocent blood will not be shed within your land which God, your God, is giving you for an inheritance, and you will be responsible for his blood.

¹¹ However, if a man hates his fellow, lies in wait for him, rises up against him, and issues him a fatal blow and he dies, and then (the murderer) flees to one of these cities:

- ❖ ¹² The elders of his city should send (representatives) and take him from there, and allow him to die at the hands of the avenger of the blood.

- ❖ ¹³ Do not have pity on him. You should eliminate from Israel (one who sheds) innocent blood, and you will benefit from it.

Territorial Fraud and Laws Relating to Witnesses

- ❖ [SIXTH READING] ¹⁴ You should not move back your neighbor's boundary (marker) that the initial (settlers) will fix as borders in your inherited (land), which you will inherit in the land that God, your God, is giving you as a possession.

- ❖ ¹⁵ A single witness cannot incriminate another person for any sin (for which

spiritual vitamin

> Disappointment, which usually is a negative factor, being closely linked with discouragement, can be converted into a positive force, to redouble your efforts in the right direction. It can be made into a springboard for an even greater accomplishment.

דברים יט:טו - כ:ב ‎ ‎שופטים

עַל־פִּ֣י ׀ שְׁנֵ֣י עֵדִ֗ים א֛וֹ עַל־פִּ֥י שְׁלֹשָֽׁה־עֵדִ֖ים יָק֥וּם דָּבָֽר׃ 16 כִּֽי־יָק֥וּם עֵד־חָמָ֖ס בְּאִ֑ישׁ לַעֲנ֥וֹת בּ֖וֹ סָרָֽה׃ 17 וְעָמְד֧וּ שְׁנֵֽי־הָאֲנָשִׁ֛ים אֲשֶׁר־לָהֶ֥ם הָרִ֖יב לִפְנֵ֣י יְהֹוָ֑ה לִפְנֵ֤י הַכֹּֽהֲנִים֙ וְהַשֹּׁ֣פְטִ֔ים אֲשֶׁ֥ר יִהְי֖וּ בַּיָּמִ֥ים הָהֵֽם׃ 18 וְדָרְשׁ֥וּ הַשֹּׁפְטִ֖ים הֵיטֵ֑ב וְהִנֵּ֤ה עֵֽד־שֶׁ֙קֶר֙ הָעֵ֔ד שֶׁ֖קֶר עָנָ֥ה בְאָחִֽיו׃ 19 וַעֲשִׂ֣יתֶם ל֔וֹ כַּאֲשֶׁ֥ר זָמַ֖ם לַעֲשׂ֣וֹת לְאָחִ֑יו וּבִֽעַרְתָּ֥ הָרָ֖ע מִקִּרְבֶּֽךָ׃ 20 וְהַנִּשְׁאָרִ֖ים יִשְׁמְע֣וּ וְיִרָ֑אוּ וְלֹֽא־יֹסִ֨פוּ לַעֲשׂ֜וֹת ע֗וֹד כַּדָּבָ֥ר הָרָ֛ע הַזֶּ֖ה בְּקִרְבֶּֽךָ׃ 21 וְלֹ֥א תָח֖וֹס עֵינֶ֑ךָ נֶ֣פֶשׁ בְּנֶ֗פֶשׁ עַ֤יִן בְּעַ֙יִן֙ שֵׁ֣ן בְּשֵׁ֔ן יָ֥ד בְּיָ֖ד רֶ֥גֶל בְּרָֽגֶל׃ ס

1 כִּֽי־תֵצֵ֨א לַמִּלְחָמָ֜ה עַל־אֹיְבֶ֗ךָ וְֽרָאִ֜יתָ ס֤וּס וָרֶ֙כֶב֙ עַ֚ם רַ֣ב מִמְּךָ֔ לֹ֥א תִירָ֖א מֵהֶ֑ם כִּֽי־יְהֹוָ֤ה אֱלֹהֶ֙יךָ֙ עִמָּ֔ךְ הַמַּֽעַלְךָ֖ מֵאֶ֥רֶץ מִצְרָֽיִם׃ 2 וְהָיָ֕ה כְּקָרׇבְכֶ֖ם

This is compounded further by *"a people more numerous than you"*—the negative forces created by passed misdeeds, which now stand against you in this battle, making it even more difficult for you to overcome temptation.

Despite all these difficulties, *"You should not be afraid ... for God is with you."* If you were alone, it would be a losing battle for you, but God is here to assist you.

kabbalah bites

19:15 How does God sustain the world? Through concealing Himself? Or by revealing His presence?

It's actually a bit of both. God must reveal Himself in order to sustain the world, as it is the spark of the Divine within every created being that makes its existence possible. But He must also conceal Himself so as not to overwhelm us with too much light.

This careful balance between Divine restraint and disclosure is mapped out by the first two letters of God's name (the Tetragrammaton), *yod* and *he*. The *yod* is a tiny point (י) suggesting an extreme of restraint to the bare minimum. Any less ink and there would be no letter at all!

The *he* (ה), on the other hand, extends to the full median width and height of the font, suggesting a disclosure and revelation in all directions.

These two letters are God's "witnesses" which testify to the secret of creation. Two witnesses are necessary and not just one, because the world exists through the equilibrium of two opposing metaphysical forces: disclosure and restraint.

a person is liable for lashes or death) or for any type of fraud. An allegation must be confirmed by the verbal testimony of two witnesses, or three witnesses.

¹⁶ If a false witness attempts to incriminate a person (who has given testimony in court), by claiming that he was not present (to witness the act that he testified he had seen):

- ❖ ¹⁷ The two men should stand before God, before the priests and the judges who will exist in those days, together with (the litigants) who have the (original) dispute.

- ❖ ¹⁸ The judges should cross-examine him thoroughly, and if the witness is (proven to be) a false witness who has testified falsely against his brother, ¹⁹ then you should do to him as he plotted to do to his brother. You will thus eliminate this evil from among you.

- ❖ ²⁰ (The court should announce the verdict publicly so that) those who remain will hear (what happened) and be afraid, and they will never commit any such evil thing in your midst again.

- ❖ ²¹ You should not have pity (on the false witness). He must (pay with his) life for (attempting to end a) life. (Or he must pay the value of) an eye for (a false testimony about) an eye, (the value of) a tooth for (false testimony about) a tooth, (the value of) a hand for (false testimony about) a hand, (and the value of) a foot for (false testimony about) a foot.

20 Preparation for a War

- ❖ ¹ If you go out to war against your enemies, and see a horse and chariot, a people (which appears to be) more numerous than you—you should not be afraid of them! For God, your God, who brought you out of the land of Egypt is with you.

- ❖ ² Then, when you (have left your land and) are close to the battle, the (specially

Confirmed by the verbal testimony of two witnesses, or three witnesses. As it appears in the Torah scroll, the first line of the *Shema* contains two enlarged letters, *ayin* and *dalet*, which, when combined, form the word *'ed*, "witness." By reciting the *Shema*, we attest to the unity of God, *"God is one"* (Deuteronomy 6:4). We are commanded to proclaim this verbal testimony twice daily, once in the morning and once in the evening, and it is proper to recite it again before retiring for the night. The *"verbal testimony"* in our verse alludes to the recitation of the *Shema* two or three times daily—*"two witnesses or three witnesses."* Through this, the oneness of God as the only true and independent existence is *"confirmed"* to all of creation (*Rabbi Moses Ḥayyim Ephraim of Sudylkow, 18ᵗʰ century*).

20:1 If you go out to war against your enemies, and see a horse and chariot, a people more numerous than you. This alludes to the war waged by the "evil impulse." In this battle, you face a number of distinct disadvantages. First, you are not trained to fight this form of internal struggle, whereas the evil impulse stands as *"a horse,"* ready for battle. Furthermore, your very makeup—the word *"chariot"* (*rekhev*) implying *"composition"* (*harkavah*)—is naturally inclined to the urgings of your evil impulse, to lie, cheat and follow your heart's desires, whereas the Torah remains an external voice.

דברים כ:ב-יא שופטים

אֶל־הַמִּלְחָמָה וְנִגַּשׁ הַכֹּהֵן וְדִבֶּר אֶל־הָעָם: ג וְאָמַר אֲלֵהֶם שְׁמַע יִשְׂרָאֵל אַתֶּם קְרֵבִים הַיּוֹם לַמִּלְחָמָה עַל־אֹיְבֵיכֶם אַל־יֵרַךְ לְבַבְכֶם אַל־תִּירְאוּ וְאַל־תַּחְפְּזוּ וְאַל־תַּעַרְצוּ מִפְּנֵיהֶם: ד כִּי יְהֹוָה אֱלֹהֵיכֶם הַהֹלֵךְ עִמָּכֶם לְהִלָּחֵם לָכֶם עִם־אֹיְבֵיכֶם לְהוֹשִׁיעַ אֶתְכֶם: ה וְדִבְּרוּ הַשֹּׁטְרִים אֶל־הָעָם לֵאמֹר מִי־הָאִישׁ אֲשֶׁר בָּנָה בַיִת־חָדָשׁ וְלֹא חֲנָכוֹ יֵלֵךְ וְיָשֹׁב לְבֵיתוֹ פֶּן־יָמוּת בַּמִּלְחָמָה וְאִישׁ אַחֵר יַחְנְכֶנּוּ: ו וּמִי־הָאִישׁ אֲשֶׁר נָטַע כֶּרֶם וְלֹא חִלְּלוֹ יֵלֵךְ וְיָשֹׁב לְבֵיתוֹ פֶּן־יָמוּת בַּמִּלְחָמָה וְאִישׁ אַחֵר יְחַלְּלֶנּוּ: ז וּמִי־הָאִישׁ אֲשֶׁר אֵרַשׂ אִשָּׁה וְלֹא לְקָחָהּ יֵלֵךְ וְיָשֹׁב לְבֵיתוֹ פֶּן־יָמוּת בַּמִּלְחָמָה וְאִישׁ אַחֵר יִקָּחֶנָּה: ח וְיָסְפוּ הַשֹּׁטְרִים לְדַבֵּר אֶל־הָעָם וְאָמְרוּ מִי־הָאִישׁ הַיָּרֵא וְרַךְ הַלֵּבָב יֵלֵךְ וְיָשֹׁב לְבֵיתוֹ וְלֹא יִמַּס אֶת־לְבַב אֶחָיו כִּלְבָבוֹ: ט וְהָיָה כְּכַלֹּת הַשֹּׁטְרִים לְדַבֵּר אֶל־הָעָם וּפָקְדוּ שָׂרֵי צְבָאוֹת בְּרֹאשׁ הָעָם: ס 10 [SEVENTH READING] כִּי־תִקְרַב אֶל־עִיר לְהִלָּחֵם עָלֶיהָ וְקָרָאתָ אֵלֶיהָ לְשָׁלוֹם: יא וְהָיָה אִם־שָׁלוֹם תַּעַנְךָ וּפָתְחָה לָךְ וְהָיָה כָּל־הָעָם

all strength is the Almighty's. Those that recite the *Shema* twice daily have internalized this belief and are assured that they will see it fulfilled in war. Therefore they have nothing to fear (*Rabbi Judah Loew b. Bezalel of Prague, 16th century*).

8. Fearful or fainthearted. Rabbi Akiva says, "This is to be taken literally, that he cannot stand at the front line of battle and look upon a drawn sword."

Rabbi Yose ha-Galili says: "It refers to a person who is afraid to go to war because of his sins. Therefore, the Torah gives him the pretext of returning home because of his house, vineyard, or wife (v. 5-7). Anyone seeing such a person would say, 'Perhaps he has built a house, or planted a vineyard, or betrothed a woman'" (*Babylonian Talmud, Sotah* 44a).

Why did Rabbi Akiva reject the view of Rabbi Yose ha-Galili, that the "fearful or fainthearted" of our verse refers to those afraid to go to war because of their sins?

Because Rabbi Akiva "consistently judged the Jewish people favorably" (*Rashi to Babylonian Talmud, Sanhedrin* 110b), he felt that the very fact that a person is "afraid because of his sins" *was a sign that he truly regretted sinning.* Even if he had not yet changed his behavior, he had already started the repentance process—sufficiently at least, to ensure that God would not punish him for his sins during battle. Having started to repent, this person would have nothing to fear from his former sins (*Rabbi Menahem Mendel Schneerson, 20th century*).

10-13. If you approach a city. When seeking to attain mastery over your body and its urges, which the *Zohar* refers to as winning control over a "small city," there are two possible approaches—the *peaceful* and the *combative*.

deuteronomy 20:2–11 — shofetim

anointed) priest should approach and speak to the people (in Hebrew). ³ He should say to them:

"Hear, O Israel! Today you are coming close to the battle against your enemies. Do not let your hearts become faint (from the noise of their horses)! Do not be afraid (when they bang their shields together)! Do not panic (when they sound their trumpets), and do not be terrified of them (when you hear them shout)! ⁴ For (the Holy Ark of) God, your God, is going with you, to fight your enemies for you, (and) to save you!"

⁵ Then the officers should speak to the people and say:

"Is there any man who has built a new house and did not begin to live in it? Let him go back home, in case he dies at war and another man will begin to live in it!

⁶ "Is there any man who has planted a vineyard, and has not yet rendered it fit for ordinary use? Let him go back home, in case he dies at war, and another man will render it fit for use!

⁷ "Is there any man who has betrothed a woman and has not yet taken her? Let him go back home, in case he dies at war, and another man will take her!"

⁸ The officers should speak to the people further and say:

"Is there any man who is fearful or fainthearted? Let him go back home, so he will not cause his brothers' hearts to melt, like his heart (has melted)!"

⁹ Then, when the officials finish speaking to the people, they should appoint disciplinary officers for the troops at (both) ends of the people, (to ensure that nobody flees).

Making a Peaceful Proposal

[SEVENTH READING] ¹⁰ If you approach a city to wage (a non-obligatory) war against it:

❖ You should (first) make a peaceful proposal to it.

¹¹ What will then happen is:

What better illustration could there be than the exodus from Egypt, as the verse continues, *"Who brought you out of the land of Egypt."* God liberated the Israelites from the spiritually negative forces of Egypt, and He will do the same for you now (*Rabbi Ḥayyim ibn Attar, 18th century*).

3. Hear, O Israel! Why does the priest begin his address to those going off to war with this particular phrase?

These words are the opening words of the *Shema* (*Deuteronomy* 4:6). God says to Israel, "Even if you have no other merits than the reciting of the *Shema*, you will not be delivered into your enemies' hands" (*Babylonian Talmud, Sotah* 42a).

The *Shema* is a declaration of God's unity—*"God is One."* Despite outward appearances to the contrary, nothing exists independently of God; the seemingly powerful are, in fact, futile, for

שופטים   דברים כ:יא-יט

הַנִּמְצָא־בָהּ יִהְיוּ לְךָ לָמַס וַעֲבָדוּךָ: 12 וְאִם־לֹא תַשְׁלִים עִמָּךְ וְעָשְׂתָה עִמְּךָ
מִלְחָמָה וְצַרְתָּ עָלֶיהָ: 13 וּנְתָנָהּ יְהֹוָה אֱלֹהֶיךָ בְּיָדֶךָ וְהִכִּיתָ אֶת־כָּל־זְכוּרָהּ
לְפִי־חָרֶב: 14 רַק הַנָּשִׁים וְהַטַּף וְהַבְּהֵמָה וְכֹל אֲשֶׁר יִהְיֶה בָעִיר כָּל־שְׁלָלָהּ
תָּבֹז לָךְ וְאָכַלְתָּ אֶת־שְׁלַל אֹיְבֶיךָ אֲשֶׁר נָתַן יְהֹוָה אֱלֹהֶיךָ לָךְ: 15 כֵּן תַּעֲשֶׂה
לְכָל־הֶעָרִים הָרְחֹקֹת מִמְּךָ מְאֹד אֲשֶׁר לֹא־מֵעָרֵי הַגּוֹיִם־הָאֵלֶּה הֵנָּה: 16 רַק
מֵעָרֵי הָעַמִּים הָאֵלֶּה אֲשֶׁר יְהֹוָה אֱלֹהֶיךָ נֹתֵן לְךָ נַחֲלָה לֹא תְחַיֶּה כָּל־נְשָׁמָה:
17 כִּי־הַחֲרֵם תַּחֲרִימֵם הַחִתִּי וְהָאֱמֹרִי הַכְּנַעֲנִי וְהַפְּרִזִּי הַחִוִּי וְהַיְבוּסִי כַּאֲשֶׁר
צִוְּךָ יְהֹוָה אֱלֹהֶיךָ: 18 לְמַעַן אֲשֶׁר לֹא־יְלַמְּדוּ אֶתְכֶם לַעֲשׂוֹת כְּכֹל תּוֹעֲבֹתָם
אֲשֶׁר עָשׂוּ לֵאלֹהֵיהֶם וַחֲטָאתֶם לַיהֹוָה אֱלֹהֵיכֶם: ס 19 כִּי־תָצוּר אֶל־עִיר
יָמִים רַבִּים לְהִלָּחֵם עָלֶיהָ לְתָפְשָׂהּ לֹא־תַשְׁחִית אֶת־עֵצָהּ לִנְדֹּחַ עָלָיו גַּרְזֶן
כִּי מִמֶּנּוּ תֹאכֵל וְאֹתוֹ לֹא תִכְרֹת כִּי הָאָדָם עֵץ הַשָּׂדֶה לָבֹא מִפָּנֶיךָ בַּמָּצוֹר:

by denying yourself even things which are normally permitted. This will serve to weaken the power of the evil urge, and *"God will deliver it"*—your evil impulse—*"into your hands"* (v. 13; *Rabbi Ḥayyim ibn Attar, 18th century*).

19. You should not destroy its trees. When an army realizes that it will not be victorious and will have to retreat, it endeavors to destroy whatever resources it can from enemy territory in order to inflict as much damage as possible. But if the army is certain that it will conquer the land, then it is careful to preserve enemy property so that it might benefit after the conquest.

The Torah instructs the Israelite soldiers, *"You should not destroy its trees,"* because, *"you may eat from them."* God has assured you that you will *definitely* conquer the land, and you will eventually eat from its fruit. So it is in your best interest not to destroy the country's vegetation (*Rabbi Obadiah Sforno, 16th century*).

Is the tree of the field a man? The "tree" in you is that part of your make-up which is: (a) the most deeply rooted in the soul; and consequently, (b) it is the most powerful. And that is: *your character and emotions*.

Intellect has no fixed roots. You are able to be intellectually involved in all sorts of matters with which you have no personal connection. That's why changing your mind is relatively easy, whereas changing your personality—from miserly to generous, or from evil to good—is no easier than uprooting a tree and planting it somewhere else.

Nevertheless, the Torah wants you to do exactly that: to change your character and emotional traits for the good. Then you will bring perfection to even the innermost aspects of the soul, where the "roots" of your emotions reach (*Rabbi Menahem Mendel Schneerson, 20th century*).

deuteronomy 20:11-19

shofetim

- If it responds to you peacefully, and it opens (its gates) up to you, then all the people found in it should give you a (monetary) tribute, and serve you.

- ¹² But if it does not make peace with you, it will (eventually) wage war against you. So you should besiege it, ¹³ and God, your God, will (eventually) deliver it into your hands.

- You should strike down all its males by the sword, ¹⁴ but you may take for yourself the women, the children, the livestock, and everything that is in the city, all its spoils. You should eat the spoils of your enemies, which God, your God, has given you.

¹⁵ That is what you should do to all the cities that are very far from you, which are not among the cities of these (local) nations.

¹⁶ But from these (local) peoples' cities, which God, your God, is giving you as an inheritance:

- You may not allow any soul to live. ¹⁷ Rather, you should utterly destroy them—the Hittites, the Amorites, the Canaanites, and the Perizzites, the Hivites, and the Jebusites—as God, your God, has commanded you, ¹⁸ so that they will not teach you to copy all their abominable acts that they have performed for their gods, causing you to sin against God, your God.

¹⁹ If you besiege a city for many days in order to wage (a non-obligatory) war against it, to capture it:

- You should not destroy its trees by wielding an ax against them. You may eat from them, but you may not cut them down.

—(For why should you need to destroy it?) Is the tree of the field a man, that you should include it in the siege (and destroy it)? —

Natural human tendencies are not inherently evil. So long as you do not engage in sinful pursuits, you may engage the body in *"a peaceful proposal."* Initially, you need not lay siege to the city, depriving the body of its needs. On the contrary, there can be a peaceful relationship where the soul harnesses the body's energy for the worship of God. Eventually, you are assured, *"all the people found in it should ... serve you"* (v. 11)—your whole body will be at peace with the desires of your soul.

"But if it does not make peace with you" (v. 12), if you abuse your body for sinful pursuits, then you must *"wage war"* against it. *"You should besiege it,"* that is, you must exercise self-control

spiritual vitamin

" Man is like a tree. Your purpose in life is to grow and develop and produce "fruits" to be enjoyed not only by yourself, but also by others. "

דברים כ:כ – כא:ט שופטים

20 רַק עֵץ אֲשֶׁר־תֵּדַ֞ע כִּֽי־לֹא־עֵ֤ץ מַֽאֲכָל֙ ה֔וּא אֹת֥וֹ תַשְׁחִ֖ית וְכָרָ֑תָּ וּבָנִ֣יתָ מָצ֗וֹר עַל־הָעִיר֙ אֲשֶׁר־הִ֨וא עֹשָׂ֧ה עִמְּךָ֛ מִלְחָמָ֖ה עַ֥ד רִדְתָּֽהּ׃ פ

כא 1 כִּֽי־יִמָּצֵ֣א חָלָ֗ל בָּֽאֲדָמָה֙ אֲשֶׁר֩ יְהֹוָ֨ה אֱלֹהֶ֜יךָ נֹתֵ֤ן לְךָ֙ לְרִשְׁתָּ֔הּ נֹפֵ֖ל בַּשָּׂדֶ֑ה לֹ֥א נוֹדַ֖ע מִ֥י הִכָּֽהוּ׃ 2 וְיָצְא֥וּ זְקֵנֶ֖יךָ וְשֹֽׁפְטֶ֑יךָ וּמָדְדוּ֙ אֶל־הֶ֣עָרִ֔ים אֲשֶׁ֖ר סְבִיבֹ֥ת הֶחָלָֽל׃ 3 וְהָיָ֣ה הָעִ֔יר הַקְּרֹבָ֖ה אֶל־הֶחָלָ֑ל וְלָ֨קְח֜וּ זִקְנֵ֨י הָעִ֤יר הַהִוא֙ עֶגְלַ֣ת בָּקָ֔ר אֲשֶׁ֤ר לֹֽא־עֻבַּד֙ בָּ֔הּ אֲשֶׁ֥ר לֹא־מָשְׁכָ֖ה בְּעֹֽל׃ 4 וְהוֹרִ֡דוּ זִקְנֵי֩ הָעִ֨יר הַהִ֤וא אֶת־הָֽעֶגְלָה֙ אֶל־נַ֣חַל אֵיתָ֔ן אֲשֶׁ֛ר לֹא־יֵֽעָבֵ֥ד בּ֖וֹ וְלֹ֣א יִזָּרֵ֑עַ וְעָֽרְפוּ־שָׁ֥ם אֶת־הָעֶגְלָ֖ה בַּנָּֽחַל׃ 5 וְנִגְּשׁ֣וּ הַכֹּהֲנִים֮ בְּנֵ֣י לֵוִי֒ כִּ֣י בָ֗ם בָּחַ֞ר יְהֹוָ֤ה אֱלֹהֶ֨יךָ֙ לְשָׁ֣רְת֔וֹ וּלְבָרֵ֖ךְ בְּשֵׁ֣ם יְהֹוָ֑ה וְעַל־פִּיהֶ֥ם יִהְיֶ֖ה כׇּל־רִ֥יב וְכׇל־נָֽגַע׃ 6 וְכֹ֗ל זִקְנֵי֙ הָעִ֣יר הַהִ֔וא הַקְּרֹבִ֖ים אֶל־הֶֽחָלָ֑ל יִרְחֲצוּ֙ אֶת־יְדֵיהֶ֔ם עַל־הָעֶגְלָ֖ה הָעֲרוּפָ֥ה בַנָּֽחַל׃ [MAFTIR] 7 וְעָנ֖וּ וְאָמְר֑וּ יָדֵ֗ינוּ לֹ֤א [שפכה כ׳] שָֽׁפְכוּ֙ אֶת־הַדָּ֣ם הַזֶּ֔ה וְעֵינֵ֖ינוּ לֹ֥א רָאֽוּ׃ 8 כַּפֵּר֩ לְעַמְּךָ֨ יִשְׂרָאֵ֤ל אֲשֶׁר־פָּדִ֨יתָ֙ יְהֹוָ֔ה וְאַל־תִּתֵּן֙ דָּ֣ם נָקִ֔י בְּקֶ֖רֶב עַמְּךָ֣ יִשְׂרָאֵ֑ל וְנִכַּפֵּ֥ר לָהֶ֖ם הַדָּֽם׃ 9 וְאַתָּ֗ה תְּבַעֵ֛ר הַדָּ֥ם הַנָּקִ֖י מִקִּרְבֶּ֑ךָ כִּֽי־תַעֲשֶׂ֥ה הַיָּשָׁ֖ר בְּעֵינֵ֥י יְהֹוָֽה׃ ס ס ס

צ"ז פסוקים, סלו"א סימן.

measuring and the taking of the calf, become the subject of much talk, and by making the event public, the murderer might be discovered (*Maimonides, 12th century*).

This commandment, together with the scapegoat of the Day of Atonement and the Red Heifer, are suprarational decrees of Scripture (*Naḥmanides, 13th century*).

8. Atone for Your people Israel. The entire nation is not responsible for this man's murder, as the elders have declared, *"Our hands did not (do anything that might have indirectly caused) cause this bloodshed"* (v. 7). Why, then, is it necessary to seek atonement for the entire nation?

We see from here that all of us are responsible for one other. Although you yourself may be on high moral ground, completely removed from the possibility of committing such heinous crimes, nevertheless you still bear responsibility for the misdeeds of your brother; much like a guarantor is responsible for money that he did not borrow. You may not sit back in contentment with your own piety while your brother sinks further and further into the evil abyss. We are all in this together (*Rabbi Jacob b. Asher, 14th century*).

❖ ²⁰ However, if you know it is a (type of) tree which is not a fruit tree, you may destroy it by cutting it down. (Use it to) build a barricade against the city that is waging war with you, until it is conquered.

Unsolved Murder

21 ¹ If a murder victim is found lying in the field in the land which God, your God, is giving you as a possession, (and) it is not known who killed him:

❖ ² Your senior judges should go out, and they should measure (the distance from where the corpse is lying) to the cities around the corpse (in each direction).

³ What will happen is, that (from) the city closest to the corpse:

❖ The elders of that city should take a female calf which has never been used for work, one that has never drawn a yoke.

❖ ⁴ The elders of that city should bring the calf down to a rock-hard valley, which was never tilled or sown, and there in the valley, they should break the calf's neck.

❖ ⁵ The priests, the sons of Levi, should then draw near—for God, your God, has chosen them to serve Him, to issue blessings in the name of God, and to pass judgment on every controversy and lesion.

❖ ⁶ All the elders of that city, which is closest to the corpse, should wash their hands over the calf that was decapitated in the valley. [MAFTIR] ⁷ They should announce and proclaim, "Our hands did not (do anything that might have indirectly caused) this bloodshed, nor did our eyes see (this crime)."

❖ ⁸ (The priests then say): "Atone for Your people Israel, whom You have redeemed, O God! Do not place (the liability of) innocent blood among Your people, Israel." The blood will thus be atoned for them.

❖ ⁹ (If the murderer is found) you should (execute him and) eliminate the (shedding of) innocent blood from among you, and you will thus do what is proper in the eyes of God.

The *Haftarah* for *Shofetim* is on page 1402.

21:2 They should measure ... the cities around the corpse. Even if the corpse is found adjacent to a city such that it is clear that this city is the closest, it is nevertheless our duty to measure (*Maimonides, 12th century*).

4. They should break the (back of the) calf's neck. He breaks its neck with a hatchet. God says: "A calf which is in its first year, which has not yielded any fruit, should come and be decapitated in a place that does not yield fruit, to atone for the murder of this man, whom they did not allow to yield fruit" (*Rashi, 11th century*).

The city that is nearest to the victim brings the calf, and in most cases the murderer comes from that place. Generally speaking, the investigation, the procession of the elders, the

From your soul's heavenly abode, **"you go out** *(ki tetze')* **to war,"** entering a body that struggles with **powerful urges.** But your soul never forgets—it retains its **strength** and **sense of mission.** Meditate on this truth, and **you will be victorious.**

KI TETZE'
כי תצא

VARIOUS SOCIAL AND MARITAL LAWS | 21:10 – 25:19

NAME
Ki Tetze'

MEANING
"If you go out"

LINES IN TORAH SCROLL
213

PARASHIYYOT
2 open; 42 closed

VERSES
110

WORDS
1582

LETTERS
5856

LOCATION
Plains of Moab

DATE
Shevat–Adar, 2488

MITZVOT
27 positive;
47 prohibitions

MASORETIC FEATURES
Thirteen instances of the word *na'ara(h)* missing the letter *he* (22:15-29)

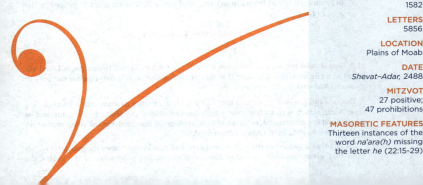

CHARACTER PROFILE

NAME
Amalekites ("nation of blood-suckers")

DESCENDANT
Haman

ANCESTOR
Amalek, grandson of Esau

LOCATION
Southern Canaan

ACHIEVEMENTS
First enemy that Israel encountered after crossing the Sea of Reeds

KNOWN FOR
The irreconcilable enemy of Israel which is wholly dedicated to their destruction; battled Israel at Rephidim; battled with Saul; God is at war with the Amalekites through all ages; they were fully conscious of the greatness of God but acted intentionally and irrationally against His will (*chutzpah* of *kelipah*)

RESPECT FOR THE DEAD

A corpse must not remain unburied (21:33). The body, which acts as a temple for the Divine throughout a person's lifetime, remains sacred even after its soul has departed.

SAFETY

If you own a flat roof with access, you must install a fence to prevent an accidental fall (22:8). Your sacred responsibility is to ensure that the home and workplace are kept safe and free of any potential hazard.

COMPASSION

A donkey may not be yoked with an ox; eggs may not be removed from a nest in sight of the bird that laid them. The Torah teaches us to extend compassion to all of God's creations (22:6-7, 10).

דברים כא:י-יח　　　　כי תצא

10 כִּי־תֵצֵא לַמִּלְחָמָה עַל־אֹיְבֶיךָ וּנְתָנוֹ יְהֹוָה אֱלֹהֶיךָ בְּיָדֶךָ וְשָׁבִיתָ שִׁבְיוֹ:
11 וְרָאִיתָ בַּשִּׁבְיָה אֵשֶׁת יְפַת־תֹּאַר וְחָשַׁקְתָּ בָהּ וְלָקַחְתָּ לְךָ לְאִשָּׁה:
12 וַהֲבֵאתָהּ אֶל־תּוֹךְ בֵּיתֶךָ וְגִלְּחָה אֶת־רֹאשָׁהּ וְעָשְׂתָה אֶת־צִפָּרְנֶיהָ:
13 וְהֵסִירָה אֶת־שִׂמְלַת שִׁבְיָהּ מֵעָלֶיהָ וְיָשְׁבָה בְּבֵיתֶךָ וּבָכְתָה אֶת־אָבִיהָ וְאֶת־אִמָּהּ יֶרַח יָמִים וְאַחַר כֵּן תָּבוֹא אֵלֶיהָ וּבְעַלְתָּהּ וְהָיְתָה לְךָ לְאִשָּׁה:
14 וְהָיָה אִם־לֹא חָפַצְתָּ בָּהּ וְשִׁלַּחְתָּהּ לְנַפְשָׁהּ וּמָכֹר לֹא־תִמְכְּרֶנָּה בַּכָּסֶף לֹא־תִתְעַמֵּר בָּהּ תַּחַת אֲשֶׁר עִנִּיתָהּ: ס 15 כִּי־תִהְיֶיןָ לְאִישׁ שְׁתֵּי נָשִׁים הָאַחַת אֲהוּבָה וְהָאַחַת שְׂנוּאָה וְיָלְדוּ־לוֹ בָנִים הָאֲהוּבָה וְהַשְּׂנוּאָה וְהָיָה הַבֵּן הַבְּכוֹר לַשְּׂנִיאָה: 16 וְהָיָה בְּיוֹם הַנְחִילוֹ אֶת־בָּנָיו אֵת אֲשֶׁר־יִהְיֶה לוֹ לֹא יוּכַל לְבַכֵּר אֶת־בֶּן־הָאֲהוּבָה עַל־פְּנֵי בֶן־הַשְּׂנוּאָה הַבְּכֹר: 17 כִּי אֶת־הַבְּכֹר בֶּן־הַשְּׂנוּאָה יַכִּיר לָתֶת לוֹ פִּי שְׁנַיִם בְּכֹל אֲשֶׁר־יִמָּצֵא לוֹ כִּי־הוּא רֵאשִׁית אֹנוֹ לוֹ מִשְׁפַּט הַבְּכֹרָה: ס 18 כִּי־יִהְיֶה לְאִישׁ בֵּן סוֹרֵר וּמוֹרֶה אֵינֶנּוּ שֹׁמֵעַ בְּקוֹל

God will see the plight of the mistreated wife and grant her the first offspring to ease her pain, just as Leah had children before the more favored Rachel (*Genesis* 29:31). God always cares for the brokenhearted (*Rabbi Ḥayyim ibn Attar, 18th century*).

17. A double share. The Torah stipulates that the firstborn son receives a double share of inheritance. The Hebrew letters of the word "*firstborn*" (*bekhor*, spelled: *bet-kaf-resh*) demonstrates this: in the word *bekhor*, the value of each Hebrew letter is double the value of the letter that precedes it in the alphabet. The numeric value of *bet* is two, preceded in the alphabet by *alef*—one; *kaf* has the value of twenty, and is preceded by *yod*—ten; *resh* has the value of two hundred, and is preceded by *kof*—one hundred (*Rabbi Jacob b. Asher, 14th century*).

He must acknowledge the firstborn. God's initial choice for the appointment of priesthood, to serve as His ministers in the Holy Temple, were the firstborn. But when the firstborn sinned with the Golden Calf, God chose His priests instead from among the tribe of Levites who had not worshiped the calf (*Numbers Rabbah*).

18. If a man has a deviant and rebellious son. The section of the rebellious son follows the section dealing with the rights of the firstborn, since they both highlight the importance of *beginnings*.

Food for thought

1. To what extent does Judaism espouse pacifism?

2. How can we eliminate war?

3. How has the world changed since the end of the Cold War?

parashat ki tetze'

Female Captives of War

¹⁰ If you go out to (wage a non-obligatory) war upon your enemies, and God, your God, delivers them into your hand, and you seize their captives, ¹¹ and you see among the captives a beautiful woman, and you desire her:

- ❖ You may take her for yourself as a wife (even if she is married).
- ❖ ¹² You should bring her into your home. She should shave her head and let her nails grow (to make her repulsive), ¹³ and she should remove from herself the (attractive) clothing in which she was captured.
- ❖ She should stay in your house (so you see her at her worst), and weep for her father and her mother for a full month.
- ❖ After that, you may come to her and be intimate with her, and she will be your wife.
- ❖ ¹⁴ What will happen is, if you do not desire her, then you should send her away to do as she wishes. But you should not sell her for money, or keep her as a slave, because you have afflicted her.

Rights of the Firstborn Son

¹⁵ If a man has two wives, one whom he loves and the other whom he hates, and both the one whom he loves and the one whom he hates bear him sons, and the firstborn son is from the one whom he hates, ¹⁶ what will happen is:

- ❖ On the day (the father) bequeaths his property to his sons, he will not be able to give the son of the one whom he loves birthright precedence over the son of the one whom he hates, the firstborn son.
- ❖ ¹⁷ Rather, he must acknowledge the firstborn, the son of the one whom he hates, and give him a double share in all that he possesses, because he was (conceived) in his prime. He has the firstborn rights.

The Rebellious Son

¹⁸ If a man has a deviant and rebellious son, who (steals, eats meat and drinks excessively and) does not listen to his father and mother's voice—and when they reprimand him (legally) he does not listen to them:

21:13 Weep … for a full month. The current month of repentance (*Elul*) is alluded to in our Torah portion. The "beautiful woman" of verse 11 alludes to the soul, and her capture from the enemy (v. 10-11) alludes to the release of the soul from the desires of the body (the "enemy"), at the outset of the month of *Elul* (*Rabbi Isaac Luria, 16ᵗʰ century*).

15. The firstborn son is from the one whom he hates. The Torah does not state this as a mere possibility, but with certainty, that the firstborn son will be from the neglected wife (*Sifrei*).

דברים כא:יח - כב:ב — כי תצא

אָבִיו וּבְקוֹל אִמּוֹ וְיִסְּרוּ אֹתוֹ וְלֹא יִשְׁמַע אֲלֵיהֶם: 19 וְתָפְשׂוּ בוֹ אָבִיו וְאִמּוֹ וְהוֹצִיאוּ אֹתוֹ אֶל־זִקְנֵי עִירוֹ וְאֶל־שַׁעַר מְקֹמוֹ: 20 וְאָמְרוּ אֶל־זִקְנֵי עִירוֹ בְּנֵנוּ זֶה סוֹרֵר וּמֹרֶה אֵינֶנּוּ שֹׁמֵעַ בְּקֹלֵנוּ זוֹלֵל וְסֹבֵא: 21 וּרְגָמֻהוּ כָּל־אַנְשֵׁי עִירוֹ בָאֲבָנִים וָמֵת וּבִעַרְתָּ הָרָע מִקִּרְבֶּךָ וְכָל־יִשְׂרָאֵל יִשְׁמְעוּ וְיִרָאוּ: ס [SECOND READING]

22 וְכִי־יִהְיֶה בְאִישׁ חֵטְא מִשְׁפַּט־מָוֶת וְהוּמָת וְתָלִיתָ אֹתוֹ עַל־עֵץ: 23 לֹא־תָלִין נִבְלָתוֹ עַל־הָעֵץ כִּי־קָבוֹר תִּקְבְּרֶנּוּ בַּיּוֹם הַהוּא כִּי־קִלְלַת אֱלֹהִים תָּלוּי וְלֹא תְטַמֵּא אֶת־אַדְמָתְךָ אֲשֶׁר יְהוָה אֱלֹהֶיךָ נֹתֵן לְךָ נַחֲלָה: ס

כב 1 לֹא־תִרְאֶה אֶת־שׁוֹר אָחִיךָ אוֹ אֶת־שֵׂיוֹ נִדָּחִים וְהִתְעַלַּמְתָּ מֵהֶם הָשֵׁב תְּשִׁיבֵם לְאָחִיךָ: 2 וְאִם־לֹא קָרוֹב אָחִיךָ אֵלֶיךָ וְלֹא יְדַעְתּוֹ וַאֲסַפְתּוֹ אֶל־תּוֹךְ בֵּיתֶךָ וְהָיָה עִמְּךָ עַד דְּרשׁ אָחִיךָ אֹתוֹ וַהֲשֵׁבֹתוֹ לוֹ:

The message, then, is to be especially meticulous of your conduct at the beginning of a fresh phase in your life: when becoming a *bar* or *bat mitzvah*, when beginning a new life together in marriage, at the start of a new year or even a new day. A good start will carry you through (*Rabbi Samuel Bornstein of Sochaczew, 20th century*).

20. He does not listen to our voice. The precept of the "rebellious son" applies only if his father and mother speak in the same voice (*Babylonian Talmud, Sanhedrin* 71a). Both parents must take an active role in educating their children, and they must speak to him in the same voice. That is, they must relate to the child with an equal sense of seriousness, and most importantly, both parents must convey to him the same message and value system.

Only if the parents have met these criteria are they not to blame if their child becomes rebellious. But if the parents have not worked together harmoniously in bringing up their child, then the fact that the child has become unruly may not reflect his innate depravity, but rather a dysfunctional upbringing. If these factors would change, the child might improve (*Rabbi Samson Raphael Hirsch, 19th century*).

22. If a man commits a sin for which he is sentenced to death, and he is put to death, you should hang him on a gallows. Rabbi Isaac Luria used this verse to eulogize Rabbi Moses Cordovero. *"If a man commits a sin, etc."*—Literally, the verse reads, "when a man has a sin for which he is sentenced to death and he is put to death." However since the word for "sin"—*het*—can also mean "deficiency," Rabbi Isaac Luria expounded: "When a man is lacking any cause to be sentenced to death, then why is he put to death?"

kabbalah bites

21:23 Adam's body was formed from earth taken from all parts of the world. That is the inner reason why people end up buried in different countries: we are all derived from different parts of Adam's body and we must return to our original source in God's earth.

- 19 His father and his mother should take hold of him and bring him out to the elders of his city, to the gates (of justice) in his locality.
- 20 They should say to the elders of his city, "This son of ours is deviant and rebellious! He does not listen to our voice! He is a binger and a boozer!"
- 21 All the people of his city should pelt him to death with stones, and you will eliminate the evil from among you.
- (The court should publicize what has happened so that) all Israel will hear (what happened) and be afraid.

Hanging and Burial

- [SECOND READING] 22 If a man commits a sin for which he is sentenced to death (by stoning), and he is put to death, you should hang him on a gallows (afterwards).
- 23 You should not leave his body on the gallows overnight.
- Rather, you should bury him on that very day, for a hanging (corpse) is offensive to God (who created man in His image). Then you will not defile your land, which God, your God, is giving you as an inheritance.

22 Care for Another's Property

- 1 You should not watch your brother's ox or sheep straying, and turn a blind eye. You should return them to your brother.
- 2 But if your brother is not near to you, or if you do not know him, you should bring it into your house and it should remain with you until your brother seeks it out. (If he proves to be the genuine owner) you should return it to him.

The firstborn son has special status, because, in many ways, he is like the head of the family, setting the tone for the children that come after him.

The rebellious son also stresses the significance of a child's early development. A child is only classified as a *"rebellious son"* in the first few months after becoming a *bar mitzvah*. He is dealt with severely because, if he has followed an extreme path at such an impressionable point in his life, he will inevitably commit heinous crimes later on.

spiritual vitamin

> The Torah is not a burden which you should force yourself to carry. It is something you should willingly and eagerly do, for this is the road to real happiness not only spiritually, but also materially, and in this life, too.

דברים כב:ג-ח | כי תצא

3 וְכֵן תַּעֲשֶׂה לַחֲמֹרוֹ וְכֵן תַּעֲשֶׂה לְשִׂמְלָתוֹ וְכֵן תַּעֲשֶׂה לְכָל־אֲבֵדַת אָחִיךָ אֲשֶׁר־תֹּאבַד מִמֶּנּוּ וּמְצָאתָהּ לֹא תוּכַל לְהִתְעַלֵּם: ס 4 לֹא־תִרְאֶה אֶת־חֲמוֹר אָחִיךָ אוֹ שׁוֹרוֹ נֹפְלִים בַּדֶּרֶךְ וְהִתְעַלַּמְתָּ מֵהֶם הָקֵם תָּקִים עִמּוֹ: ס 5 לֹא־יִהְיֶה כְלִי־גֶבֶר עַל־אִשָּׁה וְלֹא־יִלְבַּשׁ גֶּבֶר שִׂמְלַת אִשָּׁה כִּי תוֹעֲבַת יְהֹוָה אֱלֹהֶיךָ כָּל־עֹשֵׂה אֵלֶּה: פ 6 כִּי יִקָּרֵא קַן־צִפּוֹר ׀ לְפָנֶיךָ בַּדֶּרֶךְ בְּכָל־עֵץ ׀ אוֹ עַל־הָאָרֶץ אֶפְרֹחִים אוֹ בֵיצִים וְהָאֵם רֹבֶצֶת עַל־הָאֶפְרֹחִים אוֹ עַל־הַבֵּיצִים לֹא־תִקַּח הָאֵם עַל־הַבָּנִים: 7 שַׁלֵּחַ תְּשַׁלַּח אֶת־הָאֵם וְאֶת־הַבָּנִים תִּקַּח־לָךְ לְמַעַן יִיטַב לָךְ וְהַאֲרַכְתָּ יָמִים: ס 8 [THIRD READING] כִּי תִבְנֶה בַּיִת חָדָשׁ וְעָשִׂיתָ מַעֲקֶה לְגַגֶּךָ

1190

7. You should always send away the mother. Taking both the mother bird and the chicks before they have a chance to grow up and procreate is symbolic of exterminating an entire species. Although God permits the consumption of animals for the benefit of man, He wants us to consider the myriad species that He has preserved by Divine Providence since the beginning of creation. That is why the reward for fulfilling this precept is the assurance of your own continuity, *"you will live a long time"* and merit progeny, as hinted in the words, *"the young for yourself"* (Midrash Tanḥuma; Rabbi Aaron ha-Levi (Ḥinnukh), 13th century).

When the mother bird is sent away she is extremely pained and worried about the destruction of her nest and the fate of her offspring, so much so that she wishes to take her own life. Seeing her unbearable anguish, God's mercy is aroused and He showers her, along with anyone else that might be suffering, with compassion and benevolence. Thus, fulfillment of this precept is *"for your own benefit,"* for it serves to arouse God's mercy on all of creation (Rabbi Baḥya b. Asher, 13th century).

You will live a long time. If in the case of such an easy commandment, which involves no financial loss, the Torah states, *"(This will be) for your own benefit and you will live a long time"*—how much more so will you be rewarded for commandments that are more difficult to observe (Rashi, 11th century).

8. Make a guardrail for your roof. A roof, being the highest part of any structure, alludes to the ego, which gives you an elevated impression

kabbalah bites

22:3 A soul can return to this earth in one of two ways. It can be *impregnated* into an existing body/soul unit for a limited period to provide an additional, subconscious soul-power to complete a certain mission. Or it can be *reincarnated* completely, joining a body consciously for the entire period of its life on earth. Of the two, *impregnation* is the lighter, less painful experience for a soul.

"You should not turn a blind eye to it." If a person fails to return a piece of lost property, his soul will have to endure conscious *reincarnation*. Subconscious *impregnation* alone will not suffice. The soul's re-entry cannot be concealed.

deuteronomy 22:3–8 — ki tetze'

- ³ You should do the same with his donkey, you should do the same with his clothes, and you should do the same with any lost property of your brother which he has lost and you have found. You should not turn a blind eye to it.

- ⁴ You should not watch your brother's donkey or his ox fallen (under its load) on the road and turn a blind eye to him.

- (Rather,) you should pick up (the load) with him.

Cross-Dressing

- ⁵ An article of men's clothing may not be worn by a woman,

- A man may not wear an article of women's clothing.

For whoever does these (things) is an abomination to God, your God.

Sending Away the Mother Bird

- ⁶ If you encounter a bird's nest in the street—on any tree, or on the ground—containing chicks or eggs, and the mother is sitting upon the chicks or upon the eggs:

- You should not take the mother from upon the young.

- ⁷ You should always send away the mother, and then you may take the young for yourself.

(This will be) for your own benefit, and you will live a long time.

Constructing Guardrails

- [THIRD READING] ⁸ When you build a new house, you must make a guardrail for your roof.

"You should hang him on a gallows"—The term "hang"—*ve-talita*—can also be translated as "blame," while *'etz*, the term for gallows here literally means "tree." When a person devoid of sin, such as Rabbi Moses Cordovero, passes away: "you should blame it on the tree," i.e., not on his own sins, which are lacking, but to Adam's sin with the Tree of Knowledge (*etz ha-da'at*), which caused death to be decreed upon the world (*Rabbi Jonathan Eybeschuetz, 18th century*).

22:4 You should not watch your brother's donkey, etc. The obligation to assist your fellow with his overloaded donkey also appears earlier in the Torah (*Exodus* 23:5). There, however, the person in need of assistance is referred to as *"your enemy"* (*"If you see your enemy's donkey"*), whereas in this verse he is called *"your brother."*

If previously he was your enemy, he should now become your friend. Forget your hatred of him and help him out, like you would your own brother (*Rabbi Bahya b. Asher, 13th century*).

You should pick up (the load) with him. The verse uses a double expression for *"pick up"* (*hakem takim*). Bearing your friend's burden along with him will not bog you down or stunt your spiritual development. On the contrary, you, too, will benefit. You will merit even greater heights than you could possibly have achieved by focusing only on improving your personal situation. You will experience the *"pick up,"* along *"with him"* (*Rabbi Judah Aryeh Leib Alter of Gur, 19th century*).

דברים כב:ח-יז   כי תצא

וְלֹא־תָשִׂים דָּמִים בְּבֵיתֶךָ כִּי־יִפֹּל הַנֹּפֵל מִמֶּנּוּ: 9 לֹא־תִזְרַע כַּרְמְךָ כִּלְאָיִם פֶּן־תִּקְדַּשׁ הַמְלֵאָה הַזֶּרַע אֲשֶׁר תִּזְרָע וּתְבוּאַת הַכָּרֶם: ס 10 לֹא־תַחֲרֹשׁ בְּשׁוֹר־וּבַחֲמֹר יַחְדָּו: 11 לֹא תִלְבַּשׁ שַׁעַטְנֵז צֶמֶר וּפִשְׁתִּים יַחְדָּו: ס 12 גְּדִלִים תַּעֲשֶׂה־לָּךְ עַל־אַרְבַּע כַּנְפוֹת כְּסוּתְךָ אֲשֶׁר תְּכַסֶּה־בָּהּ: ס 13 כִּי־יִקַּח אִישׁ אִשָּׁה וּבָא אֵלֶיהָ וּשְׂנֵאָהּ: 14 וְשָׂם לָהּ עֲלִילֹת דְּבָרִים וְהוֹצִא עָלֶיהָ שֵׁם רָע וְאָמַר אֶת־הָאִשָּׁה הַזֹּאת לָקַחְתִּי וָאֶקְרַב אֵלֶיהָ וְלֹא־מָצָאתִי לָהּ בְּתוּלִים: 15 וְלָקַח אֲבִי הַנַּעֲרָ וְאִמָּהּ וְהוֹצִיאוּ אֶת־בְּתוּלֵי הַנַּעֲרָ אֶל־זִקְנֵי הָעִיר הַשָּׁעְרָה: 16 וְאָמַר אֲבִי הַנַּעֲרָ אֶל־הַזְּקֵנִים אֶת־בִּתִּי נָתַתִּי לָאִישׁ הַזֶּה לְאִשָּׁה וַיִּשְׂנָאֶהָ: 17 וְהִנֵּה־הוּא שָׂם עֲלִילֹת דְּבָרִים לֵאמֹר לֹא־מָצָאתִי לְבִתְּךָ בְּתוּלִים וְאֵלֶּה

with conflicting personalities work together on a project, as this would lead to much frustration (*Rabbi Aaron ha-Levi (Ḥinnukh), 13th century*).

Plowing with an ox and a donkey together is forbidden because it would lead to the further prohibition of crossbreeding species (*Leviticus* 19:19). The farmer will house the ox and the donkey together, and they will breed with each other (*Naḥmanides, 13th century*).

16. I gave my daughter to this man. Why was this concept recorded here, amid the laws of defamation? Defamation is an allusion to exile, as we find that the spies brought about the first "exile" through defaming the land of Israel. So the Torah recorded the law of child betrothal

kabbalah bites

22:8 The metaphysical universe is, essentially, a three-story construction: the worlds of *Asiyyah* (action), *Yetzirah* (formation), and *Beriah* (creation). Above this is the realm of God's immediate light, the world of *Atzilut* (emanation).

According to the Kabbalah, we must construct a "guardrail" on the "roof" of this three-story metaphysical building to prevent the lights of *Atzilut* from "falling down" and "dying."

How does a spiritual light die?

It's rather like a brilliant idea which you try to convey to others but, when words elude you, people glare at you stony-faced. What happened was you "killed" the idea by letting it "fall down" too fast. It needed a guardrail to hold it back until it could descend gracefully, articulately and compellingly.

Don't let your bright ideas "fall" and "die." Hold back your brilliance until you have found a way to communicate it effectively.

deuteronomy 22:8–17   ki tetze'

- Do not allow blood (to be spilled) in your house, when one (who is destined) to fall falls from (your unprotected roof).

Forbidden Mixtures

- ⁹ You may not sow your vineyard with a mixture of seeds, for then the (seeds') growth and even the seed that you planted together with the (fruit) yield of the vineyard will become forbidden.
- ¹⁰ You may not plow with an ox and a donkey together.
- ¹¹ You may not wear *sha'atnez*, (which is) wool and linen together.
- ¹² You should make yourself twisted threads (*tzitzit*) on the four corners of your garment with which you cover yourself (even from a mixture of wool and linen).

Defamation of a Married Woman

¹³ If a man takes a wife, is intimate with her and hates her, ¹⁴ and he makes scandalous accusations against her and defames her name, saying, "I took this woman, and when I came to her, I did not find proof of her virginity." ¹⁵ Then the girl's father and her mother should take proof of the girl's virginity, and bring it out to the elders of the city, at the gate(s of justice):

- ¹⁶ The girl's father should say to the elders, "I gave my daughter to this man as a wife, and he hated her. ¹⁷ He has now made scandalous accusations, saying, 'I did not find proof of your daughter's virginity.' But here is the evidence of my daughter's virginity!"

Food for thought

1. Are there rational reasons for all the commandments?

2. What do you do if the stated reason does not resonate with you?

3. Do you get a greater "thrill" from observing a small *mitzvah* or a big one?

---

of yourself. In order to prevent you from "falling off your roof," allowing your feelings of overstated self-esteem to degenerate into selfishness, you are warned to "make a guardrail for your roof"—to carefully control and temper the ego with "guardrails"! (*Rabbi Isaiah Horowitz, 16ᵗʰ–17ᵗʰ century*).

10. You may not plow with an ox and a donkey together. This is to prevent causing pain to animals. Since the donkey is considerably weaker than the ox, it would have to exert itself far more in order to keep up, therefore it is forbidden to have both kinds plow together (*Rabbi Abraham ibn Ezra, 12ᵗʰ century*).

The ox chews its cud while the donkey does not. If they were bound together, it would seem to the donkey as though the ox is constantly being fed while she receives nothing, causing her undue distress (*Rabbi Asher b. Jehiel, 13ᵗʰ–14ᵗʰ century*).

Generally, animals prefer to cling to their own kind. Bringing different animals together and having them work together in tandem would cause them much anxiety, just as it would be wrong to have people

דברים כב:יז-כח | כי תצא

בְּתוּלֵ֣י בִתִּ֑י וּפָֽרְשׂוּ֙ הַשִּׂמְלָ֔ה לִפְנֵ֖י זִקְנֵ֥י הָעִֽיר: 18 וְלָ֥קְח֛וּ זִקְנֵ֥י הָֽעִיר־הַהִ֖וא אֶת־הָאִ֑ישׁ וְיִסְּר֖וּ אֹתֽוֹ: 19 וְעָנְשׁ֨וּ אֹת֜וֹ מֵ֣אָה כֶ֗סֶף וְנָֽתְנוּ֙ לַֽאֲבִ֣י הַנַּֽעֲרָ֔ה כִּ֤י הוֹצִיא֙ שֵׁ֣ם רָ֔ע עַ֖ל בְּתוּלַ֣ת יִשְׂרָאֵ֑ל וְלוֹ־תִֽהְיֶ֣ה לְאִשָּׁ֔ה לֹֽא־יוּכַ֥ל לְשַׁלְּחָ֖הּ כָּל־יָמָֽיו: ס 20 וְאִם־אֱמֶ֣ת הָיָ֔ה הַדָּבָ֖ר הַזֶּ֑ה לֹֽא־נִמְצְא֥וּ בְתוּלִ֖ים לַֽנַּֽעֲרָֽ: 21 וְהוֹצִ֨יאוּ אֶת־הַֽנַּֽעֲרָ֜ה אֶל־פֶּ֣תַח בֵּית־אָבִ֗יהָ וּסְקָל֩וּהָ֩ אַנְשֵׁ֨י עִירָ֤הּ בָּֽאֲבָנִים֙ וָמֵ֔תָה כִּי־עָשְׂתָ֤ה נְבָלָה֙ בְּיִשְׂרָאֵ֔ל לִזְנ֖וֹת בֵּ֣ית אָבִ֑יהָ וּבִֽעַרְתָּ֥ הָרָ֖ע מִקִּרְבֶּֽךָ: ס 22 כִּֽי־יִמָּצֵ֨א אִ֜ישׁ שֹׁכֵ֣ב | עִם־אִשָּׁ֣ה בְעֻֽלַת־בַּ֗עַל וּמֵ֨תוּ֙ גַּם־שְׁנֵיהֶ֔ם הָאִ֛ישׁ הַשֹּׁכֵ֥ב עִם־הָֽאִשָּׁ֖ה וְהָֽאִשָּׁ֑ה וּבִֽעַרְתָּ֥ הָרָ֖ע מִיִּשְׂרָאֵֽל: ס 23 כִּ֤י יִֽהְיֶה֙ נַֽעֲרָ֣ה בְתוּלָ֔ה מְאֹֽרָשָׂ֖ה לְאִ֑ישׁ וּמְצָאָ֥הּ אִ֛ישׁ בָּעִ֖יר וְשָׁכַ֥ב עִמָּֽהּ: 24 וְהֽוֹצֵאתֶ֨ם אֶת־שְׁנֵיהֶ֜ם אֶל־שַׁ֣עַר | הָעִ֣יר הַהִ֗וא וּסְקַלְתֶּ֨ם אֹתָ֤ם בָּֽאֲבָנִים֙ וָמֵ֔תוּ אֶת־הַֽנַּֽעֲרָ֗ה עַל־דְּבַ֞ר אֲשֶׁ֤ר לֹֽא־צָֽעֲקָה֙ בָעִ֔יר וְאֶ֨ת־הָאִ֔ישׁ עַל־דְּבַ֥ר אֲשֶׁר־עִנָּ֖ה אֶת־אֵ֣שֶׁת רֵעֵ֑הוּ וּבִֽעַרְתָּ֥ הָרָ֖ע מִקִּרְבֶּֽךָ: ס 25 וְאִם־בַּשָּׂדֶ֞ה יִמְצָ֣א הָאִ֗ישׁ אֶת־הַֽנַּֽעֲרָ֣ה הַֽמְאֹ֣רָשָׂ֔ה וְהֶֽחֱזִֽיק־בָּ֥הּ הָאִ֖ישׁ וְשָׁכַ֣ב עִמָּ֑הּ וּמֵ֗ת הָאִ֛ישׁ אֲשֶׁר־שָׁכַ֥ב עִמָּ֖הּ לְבַדּֽוֹ: 26 וְלַֽנַּֽעֲרָ֙ לֹֽא־תַֽעֲשֶׂ֣ה דָבָ֔ר אֵ֥ין לַֽנַּֽעֲרָ֖ה חֵ֣טְא מָ֑וֶת כִּ֡י כַּֽאֲשֶׁר֩ יָק֨וּם אִ֤ישׁ עַל־רֵעֵ֙הוּ֙ וּרְצָח֣וֹ נֶ֔פֶשׁ כֵּ֖ן הַדָּבָ֥ר הַזֶּֽה: 27 כִּ֥י בַשָּׂדֶ֖ה מְצָאָ֑הּ צָֽעֲקָ֗ה הַֽנַּֽעֲרָ֙ה הַֽמְאֹ֣רָשָׂ֔ה וְאֵ֥ין מוֹשִׁ֖יעַ לָֽהּ: ס 28 כִּֽי־יִמְצָ֣א אִ֗ישׁ נַֽעֲרָ֤ה בְתוּלָה֙ אֲשֶׁ֣ר לֹא־אֹרָ֔שָׂה וּתְפָשָׂ֖הּ וְשָׁכַ֣ב עִמָּ֑הּ

will be heard, as God will redeem Israel and slay the evil spirit (*Rabbi Abraham Mordecai Alter of Gur, 20th century*).

spiritual vitamin

" If circumstances prevent you from carrying out a Divine commandment, but this itself causes you distress to the core of your soul, you will achieve a very close attachment to God. Not only are you guiltless for not having fulfilled the commandment, you will be rewarded for your intense desire to fulfil it. "

deuteronomy 22:17–28 — ki tetze'

(If the facts are as clear) before the elders of the city, (like a) garment (which is) spread out:

- ❖ [18] The elders of the city should take the man and reprimand him (with lashes).
- ❖ [19] They should fine him one hundred silver (shekels), because he defamed the name of a Jewish virgin, and give it to the girl's father.
- ❖ She must remain as his wife. He may not send her away all the days of his life.

[20] But if these words (of the husband) were true, and it was proven that the girl was not a virgin (and she had committed adultery after she was betrothed):

- ❖ [21] They should take the girl out to the entrance of her father's house, and the people of her city should pelt her to death with stones—because she did a disgraceful act in Israel, committing adultery (in) her father's house—and you will eliminate the evil from among you.

Violations of Intimacy

- ❖ [22] If a man is found lying with a married woman, both of them must die—the man lying with the woman, and the woman. Thus you will eliminate the evil from Israel.
- ❖ [23] If there is a virgin girl betrothed to a man, and (another) man finds her (lurking) in the city, and lies with her, [24] you should take them both out to the gate of that city, and you should pelt them both to death with stones—the girl, because she did not cry out in the city, and the man, because he violated his fellow's wife. Thus you will eliminate the evil from Israel.
- ❖ [25] But if a man finds the betrothed girl in a field, and the man overpowers her and lies with her, then only the man who lay with her should die. [26] To the girl, you should do nothing. The girl did not commit a sin deserving of death, for in this case (the girl was forcibly coerced) like a man who assaults his fellow and murders him, [27] and since he found her in a field, there was nobody to save the betrothed girl when she cried out.

[28] If a man finds a virgin girl who was not betrothed, takes hold of her and lies with her, and they are found:

---

here, to teach us that even amid the darkest moments of exile, God remains loyally betrothed to the Jewish people—and from this love the Redemption will blossom (*Rabbi Levi Isaac Schneersohn of Yekaterinoslav, 20th century*).

25. If a man finds the betrothed girl in a field. The *"betrothed girl"* alludes to Israel, who is said to be "betrothed" to the Torah (*Babylonian Talmud, Pesaḥim* 49b). The *"man in the field"* is the spirit of Esau, *"a man of the field"* (*Genesis* 25:27). The helpless victim must use any means necessary to subdue her attacker, even at the expense of her pursuer's life (*ibid., Sanhedrin* 73a).

Israel employs her most reliable defense, *"The voice is the voice of Jacob"* (*Genesis* 27:22)— *"she cries out"* (v. 27) to her Father in Heaven by means of Torah and prayer. Although now, in the time of exile, it may seem as though *"there was nobody to save her"* (v. 27), ultimately, her voice

כי תצא

דברים כב:כח - כג:יא

וְנִמְצָאוּ: 29 וְנָתַן הָאִישׁ הַשֹּׁכֵב עִמָּהּ לַאֲבִי הַנַּעֲרָ חֲמִשִּׁים כָּסֶף וְלוֹ־תִהְיֶה לְאִשָּׁה תַּחַת אֲשֶׁר עִנָּהּ לֹא־יוּכַל שַׁלְּחָהּ כָּל־יָמָיו: ס

כג 1 לֹא־יִקַּח אִישׁ אֶת־אֵשֶׁת אָבִיו וְלֹא יְגַלֶּה כְּנַף אָבִיו: ס 2 לֹא־יָבֹא פְצוּעַ־דַּכָּא וּכְרוּת שָׁפְכָה בִּקְהַל יְהֹוָה: ס 3 לֹא־יָבֹא מַמְזֵר בִּקְהַל יְהֹוָה גַּם דּוֹר עֲשִׂירִי לֹא־יָבֹא לוֹ בִּקְהַל יְהֹוָה: ס 4 לֹא־יָבֹא עַמּוֹנִי וּמוֹאָבִי בִּקְהַל יְהֹוָה גַּם דּוֹר עֲשִׂירִי לֹא־יָבֹא לָהֶם בִּקְהַל יְהֹוָה עַד־עוֹלָם: 5 עַל־דְּבַר אֲשֶׁר לֹא־קִדְּמוּ אֶתְכֶם בַּלֶּחֶם וּבַמַּיִם בַּדֶּרֶךְ בְּצֵאתְכֶם מִמִּצְרָיִם וַאֲשֶׁר שָׂכַר עָלֶיךָ אֶת־בִּלְעָם בֶּן־בְּעוֹר מִפְּתוֹר אֲרַם נַהֲרַיִם לְקַלְלֶךָּ: 6 וְלֹא־אָבָה יְהֹוָה אֱלֹהֶיךָ לִשְׁמֹעַ אֶל־בִּלְעָם וַיַּהֲפֹךְ יְהֹוָה אֱלֹהֶיךָ לְּךָ אֶת־הַקְּלָלָה לִבְרָכָה כִּי אֲהֵבְךָ יְהֹוָה אֱלֹהֶיךָ: 7 לֹא־תִדְרֹשׁ שְׁלֹמָם וְטֹבָתָם כָּל־יָמֶיךָ לְעוֹלָם: ס

[FOURTH READING] 8 לֹא־תְתַעֵב אֲדֹמִי כִּי אָחִיךָ הוּא לֹא־תְתַעֵב מִצְרִי כִּי־גֵר הָיִיתָ בְאַרְצוֹ: 9 בָּנִים אֲשֶׁר־יִוָּלְדוּ לָהֶם דּוֹר שְׁלִישִׁי יָבֹא לָהֶם בִּקְהַל יְהֹוָה: ס

10 כִּי־תֵצֵא מַחֲנֶה עַל־אֹיְבֶיךָ וְנִשְׁמַרְתָּ מִכֹּל דָּבָר רָע: 11 כִּי־יִהְיֶה בְךָ אִישׁ אֲשֶׁר לֹא־יִהְיֶה טָהוֹר מִקְּרֵה־לָיְלָה וְיָצָא אֶל־מִחוּץ לַמַּחֲנֶה לֹא יָבֹא אֶל־

and mixed them together, exiling them from their homelands. Those "Egyptians" who now inhabit Egypt are different people, and likewise the "Edomites" in the area of Edom.

Now that these four forbidden nations have become mixed with all the other nations of the world from whom it is permissible to marry their converts, every convert has become permitted. This is because when one of them separates himself out from the others by converting, we presume that he belongs to the majority of permitted nations.

Nowadays, wherever a convert converts, regardless of whether he is an Edomite, Egyptian, Ammonite, Moabite, Kushite, or of another nationality, whether male or female—that person is permitted to "enter the congregation" immediately (*Maimonides, 12th century*).

6. God transformed the curse into a blessing for you. Whoever blesses the Jewish people will themselves be blessed (*Babylonian Talmud, Sotah* 38b). You might think that since Balaam's curse was transformed into blessing, he, too, is qualified to be blessed. To refute this notion, the verse states, "God transformed the curse into a blessing *for you*." Only for "*you*," God's beloved children, was the curse transformed into a blessing, but as far as Balaam is concerned, he was hired "*to curse you*" (v. 5). Therefore, "*You must never seek anything good with them*" (v. 7; *Rabbi Moses Ḥayyim Ephraim of Sudylkow, 18th century*).

deuteronomy 22:29 – 23:11 — ki tetze'

- ²⁹ The man who lay with her must give fifty (shekels of) silver to the girl's father, because he violated her.
- She must become his wife.
- He may not send her away all the days of his life.

23 Prohibited Marriages

- ¹ A man may not marry his father's wife.
- One may not uncover the clothing of (a woman destined for) his father (in Levirate marriage).
- ² (A man) with damaged testicles or whose phallus is severed may not (marry a Jewish woman and) enter the congregation of God.
- ³ A *mamzer* may not (marry a Jewish woman and) enter the congregation of God. Even his tenth generation may not enter the congregation of God.

⁴ An Ammonite or Moabite may not (convert and marry a Jewish woman and) enter the congregation of God. Even their tenth generation may not enter the congregation of God, ⁵ because of the (persuasive) talk (of the Moabite women that led you to sin, and because) they did not greet you with bread and water on the road when you were (exhausted after) leaving Egypt, and because (the people of Moab) hired Balaam—the son of Beor, from Pethor in Aram-naharaim—against you, to curse you. ⁶ But God, your God, did not want to listen to Balaam, and God, your God, transformed the curse into a blessing for you, because God, your God, loves you.

- ⁷ You must never seek peace or anything good with them all your days.
- [FOURTH READING] ⁸ You should not (completely) despise an Edomite, for he is your brother, and you should not (completely) despise an Egyptian, for you were residents in his land. ⁹ Children who are born to them in the third generation may (convert and marry a Jewish woman and) enter the congregation of God.

Sanctity of the Camp

¹⁰ When you go out as a camp against your enemies, you should be careful to avoid anything evil (because, at a time of danger, prosecutions of the Heavenly Court are more severe).

¹¹ If there is a man among you who is ritually impure, (e.g.,) due to a nocturnal emission:

- He should go outside the camp.

23:4-8 An Ammonite or Moabite may not (convert and marry a Jewish woman and) enter the congregation of God … You should not (completely) despise an Edomite … an Egyptian. When King Sennacherib of Assyria rose to power, he confused the identity of all the nations

דברים כג:יא-כ ‏ כי תצא

תּוֹךְ הַמַּחֲנֶה: 12 וְהָיָה לִפְנוֹת־עֶרֶב יִרְחַץ בַּמָּיִם וּכְבֹא הַשֶּׁמֶשׁ יָבֹא אֶל־תּוֹךְ הַמַּחֲנֶה: 13 וְיָד תִּהְיֶה לְךָ מִחוּץ לַמַּחֲנֶה וְיָצָאתָ שָׁמָּה חוּץ: 14 וְיָתֵד תִּהְיֶה לְךָ עַל־אֲזֵנֶךָ וְהָיָה בְּשִׁבְתְּךָ חוּץ וְחָפַרְתָּה בָהּ וְשַׁבְתָּ וְכִסִּיתָ אֶת־צֵאָתֶךָ: 15 כִּי יְהֹוָה אֱלֹהֶיךָ מִתְהַלֵּךְ ׀ בְּקֶרֶב מַחֲנֶךָ לְהַצִּילְךָ וְלָתֵת אֹיְבֶיךָ לְפָנֶיךָ וְהָיָה מַחֲנֶיךָ קָדוֹשׁ וְלֹא־יִרְאֶה בְךָ עֶרְוַת דָּבָר וְשָׁב מֵאַחֲרֶיךָ: ס 16 לֹא־תַסְגִּיר עֶבֶד אֶל־אֲדֹנָיו אֲשֶׁר־יִנָּצֵל אֵלֶיךָ מֵעִם אֲדֹנָיו: 17 עִמְּךָ יֵשֵׁב בְּקִרְבְּךָ בַּמָּקוֹם אֲשֶׁר־יִבְחַר בְּאַחַד שְׁעָרֶיךָ בַּטּוֹב לוֹ לֹא תּוֹנֶנּוּ: ס 18 לֹא־תִהְיֶה קְדֵשָׁה מִבְּנוֹת יִשְׂרָאֵל וְלֹא־יִהְיֶה קָדֵשׁ מִבְּנֵי יִשְׂרָאֵל: 19 לֹא־תָבִיא אֶתְנַן זוֹנָה וּמְחִיר כֶּלֶב בֵּית יְהֹוָה אֱלֹהֶיךָ לְכָל־נֶדֶר כִּי תוֹעֲבַת יְהֹוָה אֱלֹהֶיךָ גַּם־שְׁנֵיהֶם: ס 20 לֹא־תַשִּׁיךְ לְאָחִיךָ נֶשֶׁךְ כֶּסֶף נֶשֶׁךְ אֹכֶל נֶשֶׁךְ כָּל־דָּבָר אֲשֶׁר יִשָּׁךְ:

14. In addition to your weapons, you should keep a shovel (alt. "spike"). There is a warning here to avoid listening to inappropriate speech. The term *"your weapons"* ('*azenekha*), using different vowel markings, also can be read "your ears" (*'aznekha*). If you hear gossip or vulgar speech, you should use your fingers, the tips of which are tapered like *"a spike"* to close up your ears (*Babylonian Talmud, Ketubbot* 5a).

Alternatively, to avoid listening to such speech, *"you can go out,"* (v. 13), that is, simply leave the room (*Rabbi Jacob b. Asher, 14th century*).

19. Exchanged for a dog. Some people raise vicious dogs for sport or as watchdogs. These ferocious dogs often attack *people* or destroy *property*. If these dog breeders were allowed to bring their dogs' exchange as an offering to God, then their deplorable practice would only be reinforced, for they would believe that they can easily achieve atonement by using the dogs' exchange for a noble cause (*Naḥmanides, 13th century*).

---

kabbalah bites

23:20 Have you ever wondered why your shirt ended up as *your* shirt and not somebody else's?

The Kabbalah teaches that all your property—the food you eat, the clothes you wear, the objects you own, even the money you possess—contains holy sparks which you elevate by using your property for a good or holy purpose.

But it goes further than that: the sparks in your property are *personalized*. They were meant for you to elevate. They come from the same spiritual "flavor" as your soul.

So when the Torah says that you may not charge interest, it is simply giving you a guide to identify which sparks belong to whom. Don't ask your friend for interest; the sparks in his money belong to him and not to you.

deuteronomy 23:11–20   ki tetze'

- He should not come within the (Levite) camp.
- ¹² Then, towards evening he should immerse in (the) water (of a ritual-pool), and when the sun sets, he may come into the camp.
- ¹³ You should have a designated place outside (the cloud surrounding) the camp, so that you can go out there (to use it as a toilet).
- ¹⁴ In addition to your weapons, you should keep a shovel. Then, when you sit down outside (to relieve yourself), you should (first) dig a hole with it, and then you may sit down, (and afterwards) cover your excrement.

¹⁵ Since God, your God, is accompanying your camp, to save you and to place your enemies before you, your camp should be holy. Then He will not see any immorality in you and turn away from you.

Providing Refuge for Fleeing Slaves

- ¹⁶ You should not hand over a slave to his master if he seeks refuge with you (in the land of Israel) from his master. ¹⁷ He should (be allowed to) reside among you wherever he chooses, in one of your cities where it is good for him.
- You should not oppress him.

Modesty

- ¹⁸ No Jewish girl may be promiscuous.
- No Jewish man may be promiscuous.
- ¹⁹ You should not bring an (animal that was used to) pay a harlot, or (an animal that) was exchanged for a dog, to the House of God, your God, to fulfil any (sacrificial) vow, because both (the animal and anything it is exchanged for) are an abomination to God, your God.

Interest

- ²⁰ You may not cause your brother to pay interest—interest on money, interest on food or interest on any other item for which interest may be taken.

spiritual vitamin

> Everything in this world is derived from the supernal worlds. All things in this world, even the most material and corporeal, are directly related to their spiritual sources in the higher order of things and derive their existence and their being through a series of channels and vessels of purity and holiness.

דברים כג:כא - כד:ג — כי תצא

21 לַנָּכְרִ֣י תַשִּׁ֔יךְ וּלְאָחִ֖יךָ לֹ֣א תַשִּׁ֑יךְ לְמַ֨עַן יְבָרֶכְךָ֜ יְהֹוָ֣ה אֱלֹהֶ֗יךָ בְּכֹל֙ מִשְׁלַ֣ח יָדֶ֔ךָ עַל־הָאָ֕רֶץ אֲשֶׁר־אַתָּ֥ה בָא־שָׁ֖מָּה לְרִשְׁתָּֽהּ׃ ס 22 כִּֽי־תִדֹּ֥ר נֶ֨דֶר֙ לַיהֹוָ֣ה אֱלֹהֶ֔יךָ לֹ֥א תְאַחֵ֖ר לְשַׁלְּמ֑וֹ כִּֽי־דָרֹ֨שׁ יִדְרְשֶׁ֜נּוּ יְהֹוָ֤ה אֱלֹהֶ֨יךָ֙ מֵֽעִמָּ֔ךְ וְהָיָ֥ה בְךָ֖ חֵֽטְא׃ 23 וְכִ֥י תֶחְדַּ֖ל לִנְדֹּ֑ר לֹֽא־יִהְיֶ֥ה בְךָ֖ חֵֽטְא׃ 24 מוֹצָ֥א שְׂפָתֶ֖יךָ תִּשְׁמֹ֣ר וְעָשִׂ֑יתָ כַּאֲשֶׁ֨ר נָדַ֜רְתָּ לַיהֹוָ֤ה אֱלֹהֶ֨יךָ֙ נְדָבָ֔ה אֲשֶׁ֥ר דִּבַּ֖רְתָּ בְּפִֽיךָ׃ ס [FIFTH READING] 25 כִּ֤י תָבֹא֙ בְּכֶ֣רֶם רֵעֶ֔ךָ וְאָכַלְתָּ֧ עֲנָבִ֛ים כְּנַפְשְׁךָ֖ שָׂבְעֶ֑ךָ וְאֶֽל־כֶּלְיְךָ֖ לֹ֥א תִתֵּֽן׃ ס 26 כִּ֤י תָבֹא֙ בְּקָמַ֣ת רֵעֶ֔ךָ וְקָטַפְתָּ֥ מְלִילֹ֖ת בְּיָדֶ֑ךָ וְחֶרְמֵשׁ֙ לֹ֣א תָנִ֔יף עַ֖ל קָמַ֥ת רֵעֶֽךָ׃ ס

1 כִּֽי־יִקַּ֥ח אִ֛ישׁ אִשָּׁ֖ה וּבְעָלָ֑הּ וְהָיָ֞ה אִם־לֹ֧א תִמְצָא־חֵ֣ן בְּעֵינָ֗יו כִּי־מָ֤צָא בָהּ֙ עֶרְוַ֣ת דָּבָ֔ר וְכָ֨תַב לָ֜הּ סֵ֤פֶר כְּרִיתֻת֙ וְנָתַ֣ן בְּיָדָ֔הּ וְשִׁלְּחָ֖הּ מִבֵּיתֽוֹ׃ 2 וְיָצְאָ֖ה מִבֵּית֑וֹ וְהָלְכָ֖ה וְהָיְתָ֥ה לְאִישׁ־אַחֵֽר׃ 3 וּשְׂנֵאָהּ֮

25. When you come (to work during the harvest season) in your fellow's vineyard. The Torah states, *"When you come into your fellow's vineyard … When you come into your fellow's standing grain."* Oral Tradition teaches us that Scripture is referring specifically to an employee. If he was not hired as an employee, how could he be allowed to come into his fellow's vineyard or standing grain without permission? Rather, the verse means: When you come with the permission of the owner to work, you may eat (*Maimonides, 12th century*).

25-26. You may eat as many grapes as you desire … You may pluck ears with your hand. Grapes are an expensive commodity, whereas grain is relatively cheap. After reading that a person may eat his employer's grapes, is it not obvious that he would be allowed to eat his employer's less valuable grain? Surely the Torah should have stated the more obvious case first?

Grapes are a sweet and tasty food eaten for pleasure, whereas grain is eaten as a necessary, staple food. If you worship God in the way of "grain" then you see the commandments as a necessary chore, and you fulfil the minimum requirement out of a sense of obligation. On the other hand, if you worship God in the way of "grapes," then you see the *commandments* as a delight and a pleasure.

When our Supernal "Employer" provides us with comfortable "working conditions" in this world, so we can perform the task of observing His commandments, it is more obvious that He will provide for those who work in His "vineyard," serving Him with the joy and delight characterized by grapes. Being that this is the more obvious case, the Torah recorded it first (*Rabbi Menahem Mendel Schneerson, 20th century*).

Food for thought

1. When is divorce necessary?

2. What can we do to lessen the prevalence of divorce?

3. Should a couple stay married for the sake of their children?

deuteronomy 23:21 – 24:3 — ki tetze'

- ²¹ You should charge a gentile interest, but to your brother you may not pay interest, in order that God, your God, will bless all the work of your hands upon the land which you are coming to take possession.

Fulfilling Pledges

- ²² When you make a vow to God, your God, you should not delay in paying it (beyond three festivals), since God, your God, will be sure to exact it from you, and you will have sinned.

- ²³ It is not considered sinful for you to refrain from making vows.

- ²⁴ Be careful to carry out what is uttered by your lips—whatever you have pledged to God, your God, as a donation, which you have spoken with your mouth.

An Employee's Rights

- [FIFTH READING] ²⁵ When you come (to work during the harvest season) in your fellow's vineyard, you may eat as many grapes as you desire until you are satisfied, but you may not put any into your container.

- ²⁶ When you come (to work) in your fellow's (field of) standing grain, you may pluck ears with your hand (to eat them), but you may not lift a sickle on your fellow's standing grain.

Divorce

24 ¹ If a man takes a wife and is intimate with her, and it happens that she does not find favor in his eyes because he has found something immoral about her:

- He must write a bill of divorce for her, place it into her hand, and send her away from his house.

- ² If she leaves his house and goes and marries another man, ³ and the latter husband hates her and writes her a bill of divorce, places it into her hand and sends

---

21. You should charge a gentile interest. There is nothing inherently unjust about lending with interest, for it is done with the knowledge and consent of both parties. Rather, lending money interest-free is a special kindness that the Torah demands of us to extend to our Jewish brethren, *"to your brother you may not pay interest."* That is, it is only improper to charge interest because he is *"your brother,"* but we are not required to extend such kindness to everyone. We are only expected to deal with them honestly and fairly (*Naḥmanides, 13ᵗʰ century*).

22. God will be sure to exact it from you and you will have sinned. A person might delay paying his pledge because he does not wish to part with his money. In response to this the Torah says, *"God will exact it from you"*—He will cause you to lose that exact sum on another unforeseen expenditure. You will not gain anything by not paying. And your soul will become blemished for *"you will have sinned."* You are better off paying, so that you don't lose on both ends (*Rabbi Ephraim of Luntshits, 16ᵗʰ–17ᵗʰ century*).

דברים כד:ג-יג · כי תצא

הָאִישׁ הָאַחֲרוֹן וְכָתַב לָהּ סֵפֶר כְּרִיתֻת וְנָתַן בְּיָדָהּ וְשִׁלְּחָהּ מִבֵּיתוֹ אוֹ כִי יָמוּת הָאִישׁ הָאַחֲרוֹן אֲשֶׁר־לְקָחָהּ לוֹ לְאִשָּׁה: 4 לֹא־יוּכַל בַּעְלָהּ הָרִאשׁוֹן אֲשֶׁר־שִׁלְּחָהּ לָשׁוּב לְקַחְתָּהּ לִהְיוֹת לוֹ לְאִשָּׁה אַחֲרֵי אֲשֶׁר הֻטַּמָּאָה כִּי־תוֹעֵבָה הִוא לִפְנֵי יְהֹוָה וְלֹא תַחֲטִיא אֶת־הָאָרֶץ אֲשֶׁר יְהֹוָה אֱלֹהֶיךָ נֹתֵן לְךָ נַחֲלָה: ס [SIXTH READING] 5 כִּי־יִקַּח אִישׁ אִשָּׁה חֲדָשָׁה לֹא יֵצֵא בַּצָּבָא וְלֹא־יַעֲבֹר עָלָיו לְכָל־דָּבָר נָקִי יִהְיֶה לְבֵיתוֹ שָׁנָה אֶחָת וְשִׂמַּח אֶת־אִשְׁתּוֹ אֲשֶׁר־לָקָח: 6 לֹא־יַחֲבֹל רֵחַיִם וָרָכֶב כִּי־נֶפֶשׁ הוּא חֹבֵל: ס 7 כִּי־יִמָּצֵא אִישׁ גֹּנֵב נֶפֶשׁ מֵאֶחָיו מִבְּנֵי יִשְׂרָאֵל וְהִתְעַמֶּר־בּוֹ וּמְכָרוֹ וּמֵת הַגַּנָּב הַהוּא וּבִעַרְתָּ הָרָע מִקִּרְבֶּךָ: ס 8 הִשָּׁמֶר בְּנֶגַע־הַצָּרַעַת לִשְׁמֹר מְאֹד וְלַעֲשׂוֹת כְּכֹל אֲשֶׁר־יוֹרוּ אֶתְכֶם הַכֹּהֲנִים הַלְוִיִּם כַּאֲשֶׁר צִוִּיתִם תִּשְׁמְרוּ לַעֲשׂוֹת: 9 זָכוֹר אֵת אֲשֶׁר־עָשָׂה יְהֹוָה אֱלֹהֶיךָ לְמִרְיָם בַּדֶּרֶךְ בְּצֵאתְכֶם מִמִּצְרָיִם: ס 10 כִּי־תַשֶּׁה בְרֵעֲךָ מַשַּׁאת מְאוּמָה לֹא־תָבֹא אֶל־בֵּיתוֹ לַעֲבֹט עֲבֹטוֹ: 11 בַּחוּץ תַּעֲמֹד וְהָאִישׁ אֲשֶׁר אַתָּה נֹשֶׁה בוֹ יוֹצִיא אֵלֶיךָ אֶת־הָעֲבוֹט הַחוּצָה: 12 וְאִם־אִישׁ עָנִי הוּא לֹא תִשְׁכַּב בַּעֲבֹטוֹ: 13 הָשֵׁב תָּשִׁיב לוֹ אֶת־הַעֲבוֹט כְּבוֹא הַשֶּׁמֶשׁ וְשָׁכַב

8. Be careful (not to interfere with) *tzara'at* lesions. You may not cut away the *tzara'at* lesions in order to remove evidence of the affliction (*Babylonian Talmud, Shabbat* 132b).

spiritual vitamin

> *"Increasing knowledge increases pain"* (*Ecclesiastes* 1:18). When you strive to increase your knowledge of Judaism you will find that, with the increase of this knowledge, comes an increased longing and thirst for more and more and an impatience and dissatisfaction with yourself, etc. These are the natural "growing pains" of spiritual advancement.

Newlyweds

- [SIXTH READING] ⁵ When a man takes a wife who is new (to him), he must not go out (to war) in the army, and no (military) duty may be imposed upon him.

- He must remain free for his (own) house for one year and make his wife whom he has taken happy.

Debt Collection

- ⁶ One may not take (things used to prepare food, such as) a lower or upper millstone, as security (for a loan), because that is taking a life-(sustaining entity) as security.

Kidnapping a Jewish Person

- ⁷ If a man is witnessed kidnapping any person from among his brothers, the children of Israel, and then he treats him as a slave and sells him—that kidnapper must die, and you will eliminate the evil from among you.

Caution with *Tzara'at* Lesions

- ⁸ Be careful (not to interfere with) *tzara'at* lesions, and be very cautious about carrying out all the instructions of the priests, (who are from the tribe of) the Levites. Be careful to observe what I have commanded them.

- ⁹ Remember what God, your God, did to Miriam on your journey out of Egypt.

Security for Loans

- ¹⁰ When you hold any sort of debt against your fellow, you may not enter his home to take any of his property as security. ¹¹ You must stand outside, and the man to whom you are lending should bring the security to you, outside.

- ¹² If he is a poor man, you may not go to sleep while holding his security. ¹³ You must return the security to him by sunset, so that he can go to sleep in his garment,

---

24:4 Her first husband, who had sent her away may not take her again as his wife. Were it not for this prohibition, people might come to exchange wives with one another, divorcing so that they could be with someone else for a short time, only to remarry afterwards and continue living together as husband and wife. This would make a total mockery of the sanctity of marriage and *"bring sin to the land"* (*Naḥmanides, 13ᵗʰ century*).

דברים כד:יג-כב | כי תצא

בִּשְׂלְמָת֔וֹ וּבֵרֲכֶ֑ךָּ וּלְךָ֙ תִּהְיֶ֣ה צְדָקָ֔ה לִפְנֵ֖י יְהֹוָ֥ה אֱלֹהֶֽיךָ׃ ס 14 [SEVENTH READING] לֹא־תַעֲשֹׁ֥ק שָׂכִ֖יר עָנִ֣י וְאֶבְי֑וֹן מֵאַחֶ֕יךָ א֧וֹ מִגֵּרְךָ֛ אֲשֶׁ֥ר בְּאַרְצְךָ֖ בִּשְׁעָרֶֽיךָ׃ 15 בְּיוֹמוֹ֩ תִתֵּ֨ן שְׂכָר֜וֹ וְלֹא־תָב֧וֹא עָלָ֣יו הַשֶּׁ֗מֶשׁ כִּ֤י עָנִי֙ ה֔וּא וְאֵלָ֕יו ה֥וּא נֹשֵׂ֖א אֶת־נַפְשׁ֑וֹ וְלֹֽא־יִקְרָ֤א עָלֶ֙יךָ֙ אֶל־יְהֹוָ֔ה וְהָיָ֥ה בְךָ֖ חֵֽטְא׃ ס 16 לֹֽא־יוּמְת֤וּ אָבוֹת֙ עַל־בָּנִ֔ים וּבָנִ֖ים לֹא־יוּמְת֣וּ עַל־אָב֑וֹת אִ֥ישׁ בְּחֶטְא֖וֹ יוּמָֽתוּ׃ ס 17 לֹ֣א תַטֶּ֔ה מִשְׁפַּ֖ט גֵּ֣ר יָת֑וֹם וְלֹ֣א תַחֲבֹ֔ל בֶּ֖גֶד אַלְמָנָֽה׃ 18 וְזָכַרְתָּ֗ כִּ֣י עֶ֤בֶד הָיִ֙יתָ֙ בְּמִצְרַ֔יִם וַֽיִּפְדְּךָ֛ יְהֹוָ֥ה אֱלֹהֶ֖יךָ מִשָּׁ֑ם עַל־כֵּ֞ן אָנֹכִ֤י מְצַוְּךָ֙ לַעֲשׂ֔וֹת אֶת־הַדָּבָ֖ר הַזֶּֽה׃ ס 19 כִּ֣י תִקְצֹר֩ קְצִֽירְךָ֨ בְשָׂדֶ֜ךָ וְשָֽׁכַחְתָּ֧ עֹ֣מֶר בַּשָּׂדֶ֗ה לֹ֤א תָשׁוּב֙ לְקַחְתּ֔וֹ לַגֵּ֛ר לַיָּת֥וֹם וְלָאַלְמָנָ֖ה יִהְיֶ֑ה לְמַ֤עַן יְבָרֶכְךָ֙ יְהֹוָ֣ה אֱלֹהֶ֔יךָ בְּכֹ֖ל מַעֲשֵׂ֥ה יָדֶֽיךָ׃ ס 20 כִּ֤י תַחְבֹּט֙ זֵֽיתְךָ֔ לֹ֥א תְפָאֵ֖ר אַחֲרֶ֑יךָ לַגֵּ֛ר לַיָּת֥וֹם וְלָאַלְמָנָ֖ה יִהְיֶֽה׃ 21 כִּ֤י תִבְצֹר֙ כַּרְמְךָ֔ לֹ֥א תְעוֹלֵ֖ל אַחֲרֶ֑יךָ לַגֵּ֛ר לַיָּת֥וֹם וְלָאַלְמָנָ֖ה יִהְיֶֽה׃ 22 וְזָ֣כַרְתָּ֔ כִּי־עֶ֥בֶד הָיִ֖יתָ בְּאֶ֣רֶץ מִצְרָ֑יִם עַל־כֵּ֞ן אָנֹכִ֤י מְצַוְּךָ֙ לַעֲשׂ֔וֹת אֶת־הַדָּבָ֖ר הַזֶּֽה׃ ס

13. A righteous act for you, before God. There is no foolproof method to protect your wealth. Many factors beyond your control could lead to the loss of an entire fortune. Only the *"righteous act"* of charity is stored in a most secure place, *"before God,"* beneath His Throne of Glory. The reward for your charitable acts will be reserved *"for you"* to enjoy. It will never be lost or destroyed (*Rabbi Ephraim of Luntshits, 16th–17th century*).

17. You may not (come and) take a widow's garment as security. The Torah warns, *"You may not take a widow's garment as security,"* even in reference to a widow who is wealthy (*Maimonides, 12th century*).

Now, it could be the case that the lender does not intend to pain the widow at all by taking her garment as security, and since she is wealthy it is extremely unlikely that she will become upset. And by failing to take any security, the lender is actually endangering his own assets. Nevertheless, he *"may not take a widow's garment as security,"* for there is a remote possibility that, for a widow, this may be a distressing experience.

From this we can learn that even in a situation where: (a) it appears unlikely that somebody will be hurt by your actions; (b) there is no intention to hurt another's feelings; and (c) you suffer a personal loss—nevertheless, there remains an obligation to *"love your fellow like (you love) yourself"* (*Rabbi Menahem Mendel Schneerson, 20th century*).

19. And forget a (single) bundle. If you dropped a coin, and a poor man found it and was sustained by it, then you will be blessed on its account (*Rashi, 11th century*).

and he will bless you. (Even if he does not bless you), it will be considered as a righteous act for you, before God, your God.

Paying Wages on Time

- [SEVENTH READING] ¹⁴ You must not withhold the wages of a poor or destitute hired worker, (regardless of whether he is) one of your brothers, one of your converts in your land, (or a resident alien) within your cities. ¹⁵ You must give him his wage on the day it is due, and not let the sun set upon him, for he is poor, and he endangers his life (to work for you). Do not cause him to cry out to God against you, for then (the punishment for) this sin will be upon you (more quickly).

Testimony of Relatives

- ¹⁶ Fathers may not be put to death by (the testimony) of sons, nor may sons be put to death by (the testimony) of fathers. A man should be put to death (only) for his own sin.

The Convert, Widow and Orphan

- ¹⁷ You must not pervert the judgment of a convert or an orphan,
- You may not (come and) take a widow's garment as security (for a pre-existing loan).

¹⁸ Remember that you were once a slave in Egypt, and that God, your God, redeemed you from there (to observe his laws, even if they cause you to lose money). Therefore, I am commanding you to do this thing.

- ¹⁹ When you reap your harvest in your field and forget a (single) bundle (behind you) in the field, you may not go back to take it.
- It must be left for the convert, the orphan, and the widow, so that God, your God, will bless you in everything you do.
- ²⁰ When you beat your olive tree (to shake off the olives), do not remove (all of) its best produce. This should remain for the convert, the orphan and the widow.
- ²¹ When you pick the grapes of your vineyard, do not harvest the young grapes. They should remain for the convert, the orphan and the widow.

²² Remember that you were once a slave in the land of Egypt. Therefore, I am commanding you to do this thing.

The cause of *tzara'at* is speaking derogatorily of others. Rather than merely cutting away the symptom, the lesion, you need to eliminate the *cause* of the disease by rehabilitating the character flaw that brought it about in the first place (*Rabbi Ḥayyim ibn Attar, 18ᵗʰ century*).

דברים כה:א-ט · כי תצא

כה ‏1 כִּי־יִהְיֶ֥ה רִיב֙ בֵּ֣ין אֲנָשִׁ֔ים וְנִגְּשׁ֥וּ אֶל־הַמִּשְׁפָּ֖ט וּשְׁפָט֑וּם וְהִצְדִּ֙יקוּ֙ אֶת־הַצַּדִּ֔יק וְהִרְשִׁ֖יעוּ אֶת־הָרָשָֽׁע׃ 2 וְהָיָ֛ה אִם־בִּ֥ן הַכּ֖וֹת הָרָשָׁ֑ע וְהִפִּיל֤וֹ הַשֹּׁפֵט֙ וְהִכָּ֣הוּ לְפָנָ֔יו כְּדֵ֥י רִשְׁעָת֖וֹ בְּמִסְפָּֽר׃ 3 אַרְבָּעִ֥ים יַכֶּ֖נּוּ לֹ֣א יֹסִ֑יף פֶּן־יֹסִ֨יף לְהַכֹּת֤וֹ עַל־אֵ֙לֶּה֙ מַכָּ֣ה רַבָּ֔ה וְנִקְלָ֥ה אָחִ֖יךָ לְעֵינֶֽיךָ׃ 4 לֹא־תַחְסֹ֥ם שׁ֖וֹר בְּדִישֽׁוֹ׃ ס 5 כִּֽי־יֵשְׁב֨וּ אַחִ֜ים יַחְדָּ֗ו וּמֵ֨ת אַחַ֤ד מֵהֶם֙ וּבֵ֣ן אֵֽין־ל֔וֹ לֹֽא־תִהְיֶ֧ה אֵֽשֶׁת־הַמֵּ֛ת הַח֖וּצָה לְאִ֣ישׁ זָ֑ר יְבָמָהּ֙ יָבֹ֣א עָלֶ֔יהָ וּלְקָחָ֥הּ ל֛וֹ לְאִשָּׁ֖ה וְיִבְּמָֽהּ׃ 6 וְהָיָ֗ה הַבְּכוֹר֙ אֲשֶׁ֣ר תֵּלֵ֔ד יָק֕וּם עַל־שֵׁ֥ם אָחִ֖יו הַמֵּ֑ת וְלֹֽא־יִמָּחֶ֥ה שְׁמ֖וֹ מִיִּשְׂרָאֵֽל׃ 7 וְאִם־לֹ֤א יַחְפֹּץ֙ הָאִ֔ישׁ לָקַ֖חַת אֶת־יְבִמְתּ֑וֹ וְעָלְתָה֩ יְבִמְתּ֨וֹ הַשַּׁ֜עְרָה אֶל־הַזְּקֵנִ֗ים וְאָֽמְרָה֙ מֵאֵ֨ן יְבָמִ֜י לְהָקִ֨ים לְאָחִ֥יו שֵׁם֙ בְּיִשְׂרָאֵ֔ל לֹ֥א אָבָ֖ה יַבְּמִֽי׃ 8 וְקָרְאוּ־ל֥וֹ זִקְנֵי־עִיר֖וֹ וְדִבְּר֣וּ אֵלָ֑יו וְעָמַ֣ד וְאָמַ֔ר לֹ֥א חָפַ֖צְתִּי לְקַחְתָּֽהּ׃ 9 וְנִגְּשָׁ֨ה יְבִמְתּ֣וֹ אֵלָיו֮ לְעֵינֵ֣י הַזְּקֵנִים֒ וְחָלְצָ֤ה נַעֲלוֹ֙ מֵעַ֣ל רַגְל֔וֹ וְיָרְקָ֖ה בְּפָנָ֑יו וְעָֽנְתָה֙ וְאָ֣מְרָ֔ה כָּ֚כָה יֵעָשֶׂ֣ה לָאִ֔ישׁ אֲשֶׁ֥ר לֹא־יִבְנֶ֖ה אֶת־בֵּ֥ית אָחִֽיו׃

1206

with worms and maggots; and that you will be required to give an accounting of your deeds before God (*Mishnah, Avot* 3:1). This man is now liable for lashes because he sinned, ignoring these three considerations. Of the three, one is a reflection on the period *before* you were born and two refer to *after* you will pass away. This is hinted to by the fact that the lashes are administered one part on the front and two parts on the back (*Rabbi Ephraim of Luntshits, 16ᵗʰ–17ᵗʰ century*).

3. Flog him with (almost) forty (lashes). Once the *"guilty person"* (v. 2) accepted upon himself the court's judgment and received lashes, he regains his upright status and is once again called *"your brother"* (v. 3; *Maimonides, 12ᵗʰ century*).

A man might become comfortable thinking that he has completely wiped away his sin and is now absolutely *righteous*. Therefore they *"flog him with (almost) forty lashes;"* the Torah says forty, but he receives one less.

Although you should not allow past sins to bog you down and prevent you from moving forward, you must nevertheless not be content. *"My sin is constantly before me"* (Psalms 51:5), King David said. As you mature, you need to carry out a more profound level of repentance (*Rabbi Ezekiel Shraga Halberstam of Sieniawa, 19ᵗʰ century*).

> **kabbalah bites**
>
> **25:5-10** Like a river that flows constantly, God does not desire that a soul's lineage should cease from this world. Therefore, if a man dies without having children he must be reincarnated to ensure continuity for his soul. If, however, levirate marriage is carried out by his brother then his name is not "lost from Israel," and the soul is spared an especially painful reincarnation.

deuteronomy 25:1–9

ki tetze'

Administering Lashes

25 ¹ If there is a quarrel between (two) men who come to court to be judged, the innocent one will be acquitted and the guilty one will be condemned.

- ² If the guilty person (from a court case) is liable for lashes, the judge should make him bend over, and flog him with (one third of) the (total) number (of thirty-nine lashes) he deserves on his front (and two thirds on his back).

- ³ He should flog him with (almost) forty (lashes), but he must not give more, for if he gives him many more lashes than this, your brother will be degraded before your eyes.

- ⁴ Do not muzzle an ox (or another animal) while it is threshing (or doing other agricultural work).

Levirate Marriage

⁵ If brothers (from the same father) live together (in the world at the same time) and one of them dies having no child (or grandchild):

- The wife of the deceased may not marry outside (the family) to a strange man. Her husband's brother must come to her, taking her as a wife for himself in Levirate marriage.

- ⁶ What should happen is that the eldest brother (will perform the Levirate marriage with her), provided she can bear (children), standing in the place of his deceased brother, so that his name should not be lost from Israel.

⁷ But if the man does not wish to take his brother's wife:

- The brother's wife should go up to the gates (of justice), to the elders, and say: "My brother-in-law has refused to perpetuate his brother's name in Israel. He does not wish to perform a Levirate marriage with me."

- ⁸ The elders of his city should call him and speak to him. He should stand up and say (in Hebrew), "I do not wish to take her."

- ⁹ His brother's wife should approach him, in the presence of the elders, and remove his shoe from his foot. She should spit before him (on the ground). She should respond to him, and say (in Hebrew), "That is what should be done to the man who will not build his brother's household!"

25:1 If there is a quarrel. "If there is a quarrel," they will eventually go to court. We learn from this that *a quarrel will not end in peace*. What caused Lot to leave the righteous Abraham? It was a quarrel (see *Genesis 13:7-12; Rashi, 11ᵗʰ century*).

2. (One third of) the (total) number (of thirty-nine lashes) he deserves on his front (and two thirds on his back). Our Sages teach that you should bear in mind three things to avoid sin: that you originate from a putrid drop; that your flesh will, one day, become infested

דברים כה:י-יט — כי תצא

10 וְנִקְרָא שְׁמוֹ בְּיִשְׂרָאֵל בֵּית חֲלוּץ הַנָּעַל: ס 11 כִּי־יִנָּצוּ אֲנָשִׁים יַחְדָּו אִישׁ וְאָחִיו וְקָרְבָה אֵשֶׁת הָאֶחָד לְהַצִּיל אֶת־אִישָׁהּ מִיַּד מַכֵּהוּ וְשָׁלְחָה יָדָהּ וְהֶחֱזִיקָה בִּמְבֻשָׁיו: 12 וְקַצֹּתָה אֶת־כַּפָּהּ לֹא תָחוֹס עֵינֶךָ: ס 13 לֹא־יִהְיֶה לְךָ בְּכִיסְךָ אֶבֶן וָאָבֶן גְּדוֹלָה וּקְטַנָּה: 14 לֹא־יִהְיֶה לְךָ בְּבֵיתְךָ אֵיפָה וְאֵיפָה גְּדוֹלָה וּקְטַנָּה: 15 אֶבֶן שְׁלֵמָה וָצֶדֶק יִהְיֶה־לָּךְ אֵיפָה שְׁלֵמָה וָצֶדֶק יִהְיֶה־לָּךְ לְמַעַן יַאֲרִיכוּ יָמֶיךָ עַל הָאֲדָמָה אֲשֶׁר־יְהֹוָה אֱלֹהֶיךָ נֹתֵן לָךְ: 16 כִּי תוֹעֲבַת יְהֹוָה אֱלֹהֶיךָ כָּל־עֹשֵׂה אֵלֶּה כֹּל עֹשֵׂה עָוֶל: פ 17 [MAFTIR] זָכוֹר אֵת אֲשֶׁר־עָשָׂה לְךָ עֲמָלֵק בַּדֶּרֶךְ בְּצֵאתְכֶם מִמִּצְרָיִם: 18 אֲשֶׁר קָרְךָ בַּדֶּרֶךְ וַיְזַנֵּב בְּךָ כָּל־הַנֶּחֱשָׁלִים אַחֲרֶיךָ וְאַתָּה עָיֵף וְיָגֵעַ וְלֹא יָרֵא אֱלֹהִים: 19 וְהָיָה בְּהָנִיחַ יְהֹוָה אֱלֹהֶיךָ | לְךָ מִכָּל־אֹיְבֶיךָ מִסָּבִיב בָּאָרֶץ אֲשֶׁר יְהֹוָה־אֱלֹהֶיךָ נֹתֵן לְךָ נַחֲלָה לְרִשְׁתָּהּ תִּמְחֶה אֶת־זֵכֶר עֲמָלֵק מִתַּחַת הַשָּׁמָיִם לֹא תִּשְׁכָּח: פ פ פ

ק"י פסוקים, על"י סימן.

19. Erase any reminder of Amalek. What, precisely, is the subtle evil of Amalek which is so dangerous? Our Sages explained: *"He knows his Master, and yet intentionally rebels against Him."* We are not speaking here of a heretical belief which denies the existence of God (for Amalek "knows his Master"). If Amalek simply denied the existence of God, or advocated idol-worship, any believing Jew would find the matter easy to reject. It is precisely because the Amalekite philosophy recognizes the existence of God ("knows his Master") that it poses a danger for a Jewish person, who may easily become sympathetic to this outlook, eventually leading him to rebel against God, Heaven forbid. Due to its seemingly acceptable "front," extra vigilance is required to ensure that a person does not sympathize with the Amalekite ideology in any way whatsoever (*Rabbi Menahem Mendel Schneerson, 20th century*).

spiritual vitamin

> A person should always consider his positive and negative deeds as equally balanced, and so too the whole world. If one does an additional good deed, he places himself, as well as the whole world, in the scale of merit, outweighing the negative side.

- [10] His name in Israel will be called, "The household of the one whose shoe was removed."

Penalty for Embarrassment

- [11] If (two) men, a man and his brother, are fighting together, and the wife of one of them comes close to rescue her husband from his assailant, and she stretches forth her hand and grabs hold of (the assailant's) private parts, [12] you should decide (an appropriate penalty for her, for the embarrassment that she caused with) her hand. You should not look (upon her with) pity.

Correct Weights and Measures

- [13] You must not keep in your pocket (two apparently identical) weights (and yet) one is a bigger weight and one is smaller.

- [14] You must not keep in your house (two apparently identical) dry-measures, (and yet) one is a bigger dry-measure and one is smaller.

- [15] You must have (only) perfect and correct weights, perfect and correct dry-measures, in order that your days will be prolonged on the land which God, your God, is giving you.

[16] For anybody who does these things—anybody who acts dishonestly (with weights and measures)—is an abomination to God, your God.

Remembering Amalek

- [MAFTIR] [17] Remember what Amalek did to you on your journey out of Egypt; [18] how they surprised you on the road and cut off all the weak people at your rear, when you were parched and weary (from the journey), and they did not fear (retribution from) God (for hurting you).

- [19] Consequently, when God, your God, gives you relief from all your surrounding enemies, in the land which God, your God, is giving to you as an inheritance to keep as a possession—you must (destroy every man, woman, child and animal belonging to Amalek, so that you) erase any reminder of Amalek from beneath the skies.

- Do not forget (what they did to you)!

The Haftarah for Ki Tetze' is on page 1404.

---

17. Remember what Amalek did to you. It is a positive command to constantly remember their evil deeds and ambush, to arouse hatred for them, as the verse states, *"Remember what Amalek did to you."* According to Oral Tradition we are taught: *"'Remember'*—with your mouths; *'Do not forget'* (v. 19)—in your hearts," for it is forbidden to forget the hatred we have for them (*Maimonides, 12th century*).

> "When you **enter** (*ki tavo'*) a **duty,** an **opportunity,** or a **relationship,** enter it in the same way your soul enters your body: **fill it with vibrancy and life.**

KI TAVO'
כי תבוא

FIRST FRUITS	26:1-11
TITHE DECLARATION	26:12-15
ISRAELITE STATUS	26:16-19
COMMANDS UPON CROSSING THE JORDAN	27:1-10
BLESSINGS AND CURSES AT GERIZIM AND EBAL	27:11-26
TORAH OBSERVANCE	28:1-69
OPENING OF MOSES' FINAL ADDRESS	29:1-8

NAME
Ki Tavo'

MEANING
"When you enter"

LINES IN TORAH SCROLL
233

PARAGRAPHS
5 open; 16 closed

VERSES
122

WORDS
1747

LETTERS
6811

MITZVOT
3 positive; 3 prohibitions

DATE
Shevat-Adar, 2488

LOCATION
Plains of Moab

MASORETIC FEATURES
Missing letter *alef* in the word *ha-yotzet* (28:57)

CHARACTER PROFILE

NAME
Laban the Aramean (26:5)

MEANING
"White"—he "shone" with wickedness

OTHER NAMES
Kemuel

FATHER
Bethuel

SISTER
Rebekah

CHILDREN
Rachel, Leah

HOME
Paddan-aram, Mesopotamia

ACHIEVEMENTS
Participated in negotiations for Rebekah's betrothal to Isaac; provided haven for Jacob's escape from Esau

KNOWN FOR
Greediness and craftiness; impudence (he negotiated in his father's presence); not paying correct wages; practiced sorcery, consulting *terafim* (idols) for advice

PROVIDENCE

Bringing the first fruits to ripen each year to the Holy Temple reinforced the recognition of Divine Providence (26:10). Count your blessings every day and thank God.

BLESSINGS

The Torah's way is one of pleasantness and peace. Rather than judging the people in your life, bless them all with love (28:1-14).

GOD'S WAYS

Walk in God's ways: compassion, kindness, charity, righteousness and justice. It is not demanded that you attain perfection, like God; but you do need to be actively "walking" in that direction (28:9).

EXILE

As a farmer scatters seeds across his furrows in order to produce a field of produce, God scattered us around the world. Upon completion of our global mission, the sheaves of blessing will become apparent to us all (28:64).

דברים כו:א-ח | כי תבוא

כו 1 וְהָיָה כִּי־תָבוֹא אֶל־הָאָרֶץ אֲשֶׁר יְהֹוָה אֱלֹהֶיךָ נֹתֵן לְךָ נַחֲלָה וִירִשְׁתָּהּ וְיָשַׁבְתָּ בָּהּ: 2 וְלָקַחְתָּ מֵרֵאשִׁית | כָּל־פְּרִי הָאֲדָמָה אֲשֶׁר תָּבִיא מֵאַרְצְךָ אֲשֶׁר יְהֹוָה אֱלֹהֶיךָ נֹתֵן לָךְ וְשַׂמְתָּ בַטֶּנֶא וְהָלַכְתָּ אֶל־הַמָּקוֹם אֲשֶׁר יִבְחַר יְהֹוָה אֱלֹהֶיךָ לְשַׁכֵּן שְׁמוֹ שָׁם: 3 וּבָאתָ אֶל־הַכֹּהֵן אֲשֶׁר יִהְיֶה בַּיָּמִים הָהֵם וְאָמַרְתָּ אֵלָיו הִגַּדְתִּי הַיּוֹם לַיהֹוָה אֱלֹהֶיךָ כִּי־בָאתִי אֶל־הָאָרֶץ אֲשֶׁר נִשְׁבַּע יְהֹוָה לַאֲבֹתֵינוּ לָתֶת לָנוּ: 4 וְלָקַח הַכֹּהֵן הַטֶּנֶא מִיָּדֶךָ וְהִנִּיחוֹ לִפְנֵי מִזְבַּח יְהֹוָה אֱלֹהֶיךָ: 5 וְעָנִיתָ וְאָמַרְתָּ לִפְנֵי | יְהֹוָה אֱלֹהֶיךָ אֲרַמִּי אֹבֵד אָבִי וַיֵּרֶד מִצְרַיְמָה וַיָּגָר שָׁם בִּמְתֵי מְעָט וַיְהִי־שָׁם לְגוֹי גָּדוֹל עָצוּם וָרָב: 6 וַיָּרֵעוּ אֹתָנוּ הַמִּצְרִים וַיְעַנּוּנוּ וַיִּתְּנוּ עָלֵינוּ עֲבֹדָה קָשָׁה: 7 וַנִּצְעַק אֶל־יְהֹוָה אֱלֹהֵי אֲבֹתֵינוּ וַיִּשְׁמַע יְהֹוָה אֶת־קֹלֵנוּ וַיַּרְא אֶת־עָנְיֵנוּ וְאֶת־עֲמָלֵנוּ וְאֶת־לַחֲצֵנוּ: 8 וַיּוֹצִאֵנוּ יְהֹוָה מִמִּצְרַיִם בְּיָד חֲזָקָה וּבִזְרֹעַ נְטוּיָה וּבְמֹרָא גָּדֹל וּבְאֹתוֹת וּבְמֹפְתִים:

---

yourself to the matter at hand with devotion and concentration. You need to surrender yourself and not allow any personal bias to interfere with the purity of this act.

Even though you have many "layers" through which you interface with the world and cope with day-to-day life, it is possible for you to "peel away" these layers and forge a direct soul-connection with what you are doing. If you succeed in doing so, then you will merge fully with the activity.

And that is the lesson from this Torah portion: You should "enter" into every precept that you perform, and every act with which you serve God (*Rabbi Menahem Mendel Schneerson, 20th century*).

5. (Laban the) Aramean (wanted to) destroy my father. *"Aramean"* also means swindler. This verse hints to the primordial sin wherein the *"cunning"* serpent (*Genesis* 3:1) tricked Adam (*"my father"*) into eating from the Tree of Knowledge. As a result of this, all souls became contaminated with a spiritual pollutant, the elements themselves became defiled, and death was decreed on all of creation ("The Aramean wanted to *destroy* my father"). Because of the corruption of the elements, man is inclined naturally toward the urges of his evil impulse, making it difficult to resist temptation.

Therefore the Torah advises that *we cry out to God* (v. 7) in prayer: *"May the evil impulse not have mastery over us!"* (*Liturgy, The Morning Blessings*). Although God created the evil impulse in order to facilitate free choice, by your praying to God, He will help you to overcome it (*Rabbi Ḥayyim ibn Attar, 18th century*).

Food for thought

1. When did you last contemplate the source of your blessings?

2. How often do you thank God?

3. How do you feel when you are sincerely thanked?

deuteronomy 26:1–8 — ki tavo'

parashat ki tavo'

Conquest and Settlement of the Land

26 ¹ What will happen is, when you enter the land which God, your God, is giving you as an inheritance, you should take possession of it and settle in it.

First Fruits

- ² Then (when the land is fully settled) you should take some of the first (to ripen) from every fruit of the ground, which you gather in from your land, that God, your God, is giving you.

- You should put it into a basket and go to the place which God, your God, will choose to make His name rest there.

- ³ You should come to the priest who is present in (your times, whatever caliber he may be), and say to him:

    "I am declaring today to God, your God, that I have come to the land which God swore to our fathers to give us."

- ⁴ The priest will take the basket from your hand (and wave it together with you). He will then place it before the altar of God, your God.

- ⁵ You should (hold the basket and) say out loud before God, your God:

    "(Laban the) Aramean (wanted to) destroy my father (Jacob. And his sorrows did not stop there, because) he went down to Egypt and lived there in a small (family) group (of seventy souls). But he became a great, powerful, and populous nation there. ⁶ The Egyptians treated us cruelly and afflicted us, and they imposed hard labor on us.

    ⁷ "We cried out to God, God of our fathers, and God heard our voice and saw our affliction, our toil, and our oppression. ⁸ God brought us out from Egypt with a strong hand and with an outstretched arm, with great awe, and with signs and wonders.

26:1 When you enter. *The Talmud teaches, "Partial entry is not considered entry" (Babylonian Talmud, Hullin 33b). Likewise, Rashi explains at the beginning of our Torah portion that "when you enter the land" refers to the time of complete entry when "they conquered the land and divided it."*

This teaches us a powerful lesson in daily life: You should "enter" yourself totally and wholeheartedly into everything that you do for God.

When you become fully immersed in what you are doing, there is not merely a quantitative improvement in your actions (how much you are involved), but a qualitative change, which radically affects the way in which you are involved. In order to reach a state of total immersion ("entering"), you need to temporarily relinquish any other cares or concerns, and dedicate

דברים כו:ט-יד | כי תבוא

9 וַיְבִאֵנוּ אֶל־הַמָּקוֹם הַזֶּה וַיִּתֶּן־לָנוּ אֶת־הָאָרֶץ הַזֹּאת אֶרֶץ זָבַת חָלָב וּדְבָשׁ: 10 וְעַתָּה הִנֵּה הֵבֵאתִי אֶת־רֵאשִׁית פְּרִי הָאֲדָמָה אֲשֶׁר־נָתַתָּה לִּי יְהֹוָה וְהִנַּחְתּוֹ לִפְנֵי יְהֹוָה אֱלֹהֶיךָ וְהִשְׁתַּחֲוִיתָ לִפְנֵי יְהֹוָה אֱלֹהֶיךָ: 11 וְשָׂמַחְתָּ בְכָל־הַטּוֹב אֲשֶׁר נָתַן־לְךָ יְהֹוָה אֱלֹהֶיךָ וּלְבֵיתֶךָ אַתָּה וְהַלֵּוִי וְהַגֵּר אֲשֶׁר בְּקִרְבֶּךָ: ס

[SECOND READING] 12 כִּי תְכַלֶּה לַעְשֵׂר אֶת־כָּל־מַעְשַׂר תְּבוּאָתְךָ בַּשָּׁנָה הַשְּׁלִישִׁת שְׁנַת הַמַּעֲשֵׂר וְנָתַתָּה לַלֵּוִי לַגֵּר לַיָּתוֹם וְלָאַלְמָנָה וְאָכְלוּ בִשְׁעָרֶיךָ וְשָׂבֵעוּ: 13 וְאָמַרְתָּ לִפְנֵי יְהֹוָה אֱלֹהֶיךָ בִּעַרְתִּי הַקֹּדֶשׁ מִן־הַבַּיִת וְגַם נְתַתִּיו לַלֵּוִי וְלַגֵּר לַיָּתוֹם וְלָאַלְמָנָה כְּכָל־מִצְוָתְךָ אֲשֶׁר צִוִּיתָנִי לֹא־עָבַרְתִּי מִמִּצְוֹתֶיךָ וְלֹא שָׁכָחְתִּי: 14 לֹא־אָכַלְתִּי בְאֹנִי מִמֶּנּוּ וְלֹא־בִעַרְתִּי מִמֶּנּוּ בְּטָמֵא וְלֹא־נָתַתִּי מִמֶּנּוּ לְמֵת שָׁמַעְתִּי בְּקוֹל יְהֹוָה אֱלֹהָי עָשִׂיתִי כְּכֹל אֲשֶׁר צִוִּיתָנִי:

God's kindness, they managed to take possession of the land of Israel. For this reason, a person bringing first fruits to the Temple describes how from the moment Jacob left his father's house, Jacob was unsettled and in a position of strategic weakness which continued throughout the Egyptian exile. And, nevertheless, God's kindness ensured that the Jewish people came to possess the land, despite all odds (*Rabbi Baruch Epstein, 19th–20th century*).

10. Look! I have now brought. *"Now"* implies without delay, *"Look!"* implies with joy, and *"I have brought"* indicates from that which is mine (*Sifrei*).

These are the three essential principles for observing any commandment. First, you should not postpone it; it should be done, "now," without delay. Second, it should be performed with great joy and enthusiasm. And third, you should be prepared to use your personal resources to fulfil a commandment (*Rabbi Ḥayyim b. Mordecai Ephraim Fischel Sofer, 19th century*).

11. Rejoice with all the good that God ... has granted you. When you receive a gift from an important person, you are excited, not so much about the gift's actual value, but more about the fact that it was given to you by a great person. Therefore, the Torah says, *"You will rejoice with all the good,"* not just because it is good, but primarily in the thought that it is God who has granted it to you (*Rabbi Solomon ha-Kohen Rabinowich of Radomsko, 19th century*).

14. I did not give any ... for the dead. Love and awe of God are the wings that enable the Torah and commandments to ascend heavenward (*Zohar*). When you learn Torah or perform

> **kabbalah bites**
>
> **26:11** When the opportunity for you to perform a rare *mitzvah* comes along, God permits a now departed soul that was never able to fulfil that *mitzvah* to join your soul, enabling her to participate in this great act. This is the *"ger* (lit. stranger) who is among you"* mentioned here.

deuteronomy 26:9–14 — ki tavo'

⁹ "He brought us to this site (of the Holy Temple), and He gave us this land, a land flowing with milk and honey.

¹⁰ "Look! I have now brought here the first fruit of the ground which you, God, have given to me."

- You should (wave the basket once again, and) place it before God, your God.
- Then prostrate yourself before God, your God.
- ¹¹ Then you will rejoice with all the good that God, your God, has granted you and your household—(both) you, the Levite, and the convert who is among you.

The Tithe Declaration

[SECOND READING] ¹² When you have reached (the day before Passover of the fourth year of the tithing cycle, which is) the end (of the period when you may) separate all the tithes of your produce for the third year—the year when (only) the (first) tithe (is separated which) you give to the Levite. (And instead of separating the second tithe, which is eaten in Jerusalem, you shall separate the tithe for the poor, which you shall give) to the convert, the orphan, and the widow, so that they can eat to their satisfaction in your cities—

- ¹³ Then you should say before God, your God, (the following declaration):

    "I have removed the holy (second tithe and fourth-year fruits) from the house.

    "I have also (separated *terumah* and first fruits).

    "(I have) given (the first tithe) to the Levite.

    "(I have given the tithe for the poor to) the convert, the orphan, and the widow.

    "(I did all this) in accordance with Your command which You have commanded me (about the precise order of separation).

    "I have not transgressed Your commands (about cross-separation).

    "I have not forgotten (to bless You).

    ¹⁴ "I did not eat any (second tithe) while I was in a state of mourning.

    "I did not consume any of it while in a state of ritual impurity.

    "I did not give any of it (for making a coffin or shrouds) for the dead.

    "I listened to the voice of God, my God, (and brought these offerings to the Temple).

    "I did everything that You commanded me. (I rejoiced and brought joy to others.)

9. He brought us to this site. You bring first fruits to thank God for His kindness in giving the land of Israel to the Jewish people. Normally, a nation can only acquire a land when they themselves are settled, and in a position of strength. The Jewish people, however, were lacking any strength at all, spending all their time wandering from place to place, and yet thanks to

דברים כו:טו-יט ‏ כי תבוא

15 הַשְׁקִיפָה מִמְּעוֹן קָדְשְׁךָ מִן־הַשָּׁמַיִם וּבָרֵךְ אֶת־עַמְּךָ אֶת־יִשְׂרָאֵל וְאֵת הָאֲדָמָה אֲשֶׁר נָתַתָּה לָנוּ כַּאֲשֶׁר נִשְׁבַּעְתָּ לַאֲבֹתֵינוּ אֶרֶץ זָבַת חָלָב וּדְבָשׁ: ס

16 [THIRD READING] הַיּוֹם הַזֶּה יְהֹוָה אֱלֹהֶיךָ מְצַוְּךָ לַעֲשׂוֹת אֶת־הַחֻקִּים הָאֵלֶּה וְאֶת־הַמִּשְׁפָּטִים וְשָׁמַרְתָּ וְעָשִׂיתָ אוֹתָם בְּכָל־לְבָבְךָ וּבְכָל־נַפְשֶׁךָ: 17 אֶת־יְהֹוָה הֶאֱמַרְתָּ הַיּוֹם לִהְיוֹת לְךָ לֵאלֹהִים וְלָלֶכֶת בִּדְרָכָיו וְלִשְׁמֹר חֻקָּיו וּמִצְוֹתָיו וּמִשְׁפָּטָיו וְלִשְׁמֹעַ בְּקֹלוֹ: 18 וַיהֹוָה הֶאֱמִירְךָ הַיּוֹם לִהְיוֹת לוֹ לְעַם סְגֻלָּה כַּאֲשֶׁר דִּבֶּר־לָךְ וְלִשְׁמֹר כָּל־מִצְוֹתָיו: 19 וּלְתִתְּךָ עֶלְיוֹן עַל כָּל־הַגּוֹיִם אֲשֶׁר עָשָׂה לִתְהִלָּה וּלְשֵׁם וּלְתִפְאָרֶת וְלִהְיֹתְךָ עַם־קָדֹשׁ לַיהֹוָה אֱלֹהֶיךָ כַּאֲשֶׁר דִּבֵּר: פ

---

study is superior, this is only because it leads to practical observance. Our verse places "Your people," the observant Jew, before "Israel," the scholar, *to emphasize that, overall, observance is more important.*

However, while the Talmud appears to stress that practical observance is more important, it nevertheless employs the expression, "Torah is greater." So why are "Your people" placed before "Israel," suggesting that observance is *unequivocally* superior?

The answer lies in a comment of the Jerusalem Talmud on our verse: *"Come and behold the greatness of those who observe the commandments! For every time the term 'look down' is mentioned in the Torah, it refers to a curse, but here it refers to a blessing"* (*Jerusalem Talmud, Ma'aser Sheni* 5:5). The unique quality of practical observance is brought to light by the fact that it transforms curses into blessings. And since this is the message conveyed by our verse, "Your people" is placed first (*Rabbi Joseph Isaac Schneersohn of Lubavitch, 20th century*).

16. Today, God, your God, is commanding you. Every day they shall be new in your eyes, as though you have been commanded them today (*Rashi, 11th century*).

17-18. Selected ... selected. There is no conclusive proof in Scripture as to what the Hebrew terms *he'emarta* and *he'emirekha* mean, and it appears to me that they mean "separation" and "distinction." The meaning here is: You have separated God for yourself from all the foreign gods to be your God, and He distinguished you for Himself from all the nations on earth to be His treasured people.

Alternatively these words could be understood as being similar to the term for "glory" (*tif'eret*), as in the verse "all workers of violence glorify themselves (*yit'ammeru*)" (*Psalms* 94:4; *Rashi, 11th century*).

He'emarta means "exalted." Rabbi Judah Halevi understood it as meaning "speech": "Today, you have caused God to say that He is your God ... And today God has caused you to say that you are His treasured people" (*Rabbi Abraham ibn Ezra, 12th century*).

deuteronomy 26:15–19 — ki tavo'

¹⁵ "(We have done what is incumbent upon us. Now do what You promised and) look down from Your holy abode in heaven, and bless Your people Israel and the land which You have given to us—as (You fulfilled the oath that) You swore to our fathers (and gave us) a land flowing with milk and honey."

Conclusion of Moses' Address

[THIRD READING] ¹⁶ (It should always appear in your eyes that) today God, your God, is commanding you to fulfil these suprarational commands and rational commands (for the first time). Be careful to observe them, with all your heart and all your soul.

¹⁷ (It should always appear in your eyes that) today you have selected God (from all the foreign gods), to be your God (for the first time)—to go in His ways, and to observe His suprarational commands, His (other) commandments and His rational commands, and to listen to His voice.

¹⁸ And (it should always appear in your eyes that) today God has selected you (from all the nations of the earth) to be His treasured people (for the first time)—as He told you—and to observe all His commandments, ¹⁹ and to make you elite above all the nations that He made, in acclaim, renown and splendor, being that you are a holy people to God, your God, as He said.

---

commandments for the wrong reasons, such as personal honor, these improper motives cause the good deeds to become trapped among the demonic forces.

You need to declare, *"I did not give any of it for the dead"*—I did not give my good deeds to the demonic forces, which are called "dead," by performing commandments for ulterior motives. They were performed for the sake of heaven, to connect to God through His Torah and commandments (*Rabbi Solomon ha-Kohen Rabinowich of Radomsko, 19th century*).

15. Look down from Your holy abode in heaven, and bless your people Israel. Why does the verse use the repetitive phrase, "Your people Israel"? Surely "Your people" and "Israel" are one and the same? And why are "Your people" mentioned before "Israel"?

"Israel" refers to Torah scholars, and "Your people" to ordinary Jews, who observe the commandments loyally. In the Talmud, a debate is recorded whether Torah study or practical observance is greater, and the conclusion is that *"Torah study is greater, since it leads to practical observance"* (*Babylonian Talmud, Kiddushin* 40b). Even according to the opinion that Torah

spiritual vitamin

> Even one single good deed creates an everlasting bond and communion with God.

דברים כז:א-טו

כז

[FOURTH READING] 1 וַיְצַו מֹשֶׁה וְזִקְנֵי יִשְׂרָאֵל אֶת־הָעָם לֵאמֹר שָׁמֹר אֶת־כָּל־הַמִּצְוָה אֲשֶׁר אָנֹכִי מְצַוֶּה אֶתְכֶם הַיּוֹם: 2 וְהָיָה בַּיּוֹם אֲשֶׁר תַּעַבְרוּ אֶת־הַיַּרְדֵּן אֶל־הָאָרֶץ אֲשֶׁר־יְהֹוָה אֱלֹהֶיךָ נֹתֵן לָךְ וַהֲקֵמֹתָ לְךָ אֲבָנִים גְּדֹלוֹת וְשַׂדְתָּ אֹתָם בַּשִּׂיד: 3 וְכָתַבְתָּ עֲלֵיהֶן אֶת־כָּל־דִּבְרֵי הַתּוֹרָה הַזֹּאת בְּעָבְרֶךָ לְמַעַן אֲשֶׁר תָּבֹא אֶל־הָאָרֶץ אֲשֶׁר־יְהֹוָה אֱלֹהֶיךָ | נֹתֵן לְךָ אֶרֶץ זָבַת חָלָב וּדְבַשׁ כַּאֲשֶׁר דִּבֶּר יְהֹוָה אֱלֹהֵי־אֲבֹתֶיךָ לָךְ: 4 וְהָיָה בְּעָבְרְכֶם אֶת־הַיַּרְדֵּן תָּקִימוּ אֶת־הָאֲבָנִים הָאֵלֶּה אֲשֶׁר אָנֹכִי מְצַוֶּה אֶתְכֶם הַיּוֹם בְּהַר עֵיבָל וְשַׂדְתָּ אוֹתָם בַּשִּׂיד: 5 וּבָנִיתָ שָּׁם מִזְבֵּחַ לַיהֹוָה אֱלֹהֶיךָ מִזְבַּח אֲבָנִים לֹא־תָנִיף עֲלֵיהֶם בַּרְזֶל: 6 אֲבָנִים שְׁלֵמוֹת תִּבְנֶה אֶת־מִזְבַּח יְהֹוָה אֱלֹהֶיךָ וְהַעֲלִיתָ עָלָיו עוֹלֹת לַיהֹוָה אֱלֹהֶיךָ: 7 וְזָבַחְתָּ שְׁלָמִים וְאָכַלְתָּ שָּׁם וְשָׂמַחְתָּ לִפְנֵי יְהֹוָה אֱלֹהֶיךָ: 8 וְכָתַבְתָּ עַל־הָאֲבָנִים אֶת־כָּל־דִּבְרֵי הַתּוֹרָה הַזֹּאת בַּאֵר הֵיטֵב: ס 9 וַיְדַבֵּר מֹשֶׁה וְהַכֹּהֲנִים הַלְוִיִּם אֶל־כָּל־יִשְׂרָאֵל לֵאמֹר הַסְכֵּת | וּשְׁמַע יִשְׂרָאֵל הַיּוֹם הַזֶּה נִהְיֵיתָ לְעָם לַיהֹוָה אֱלֹהֶיךָ: 10 וְשָׁמַעְתָּ בְּקוֹל יְהֹוָה אֱלֹהֶיךָ וְעָשִׂיתָ אֶת־מִצְוֺתָו וְאֶת־חֻקָּיו אֲשֶׁר אָנֹכִי מְצַוְּךָ הַיּוֹם: ס **[FIFTH READING]** 11 וַיְצַו מֹשֶׁה אֶת־הָעָם בַּיּוֹם הַהוּא לֵאמֹר: 12 אֵלֶּה יַעַמְדוּ לְבָרֵךְ אֶת־הָעָם עַל־הַר גְּרִזִּים בְּעָבְרְכֶם אֶת־הַיַּרְדֵּן שִׁמְעוֹן וְלֵוִי וִיהוּדָה וְיִשָּׂשכָר וְיוֹסֵף וּבִנְיָמִן: 13 וְאֵלֶּה יַעַמְדוּ עַל־הַקְּלָלָה בְּהַר עֵיבָל רְאוּבֵן גָּד וְאָשֵׁר וּזְבוּלֻן דָּן וְנַפְתָּלִי: 14 וְעָנוּ הַלְוִיִּם וְאָמְרוּ אֶל־כָּל־אִישׁ יִשְׂרָאֵל קוֹל רָם: ס 15 אָרוּר הָאִישׁ אֲשֶׁר יַעֲשֶׂה פֶסֶל וּמַסֵּכָה תּוֹעֲבַת יְהֹוָה מַעֲשֵׂה יְדֵי חָרָשׁ וְשָׂם בַּסָּתֶר וְעָנוּ כָל־הָעָם וְאָמְרוּ אָמֵן: ס

15-25. Cursed. I saw in the treatise of Rabbi Moses ha-Darshan that there are eleven curses here, corresponding to eleven of the twelve tribes. But in connection with Simeon, Moses did not write "Cursed be the man, etc.," because he did not have it in his heart to bless Simeon before his passing, when he blessed the other tribes. Therefore, he did not wish to curse him (*Rashi, 11th century*).

deuteronomy 27:1–15 — ki tavo'

Instructions upon Crossing the Jordan

27 [FOURTH READING] ¹ Moses and the elders of Israel commanded the people, saying, "You are to keep all of the commandment(s) that I am commanding you today!"

² "What will happen is, on the day that you cross the Jordan to the land God, your God, is giving you, you should set up (at the Jordan) huge stones for yourself, and plaster them with lime. ³ When you cross over, you should write on them all the words of this Torah, so that you may come into the land which God, your God, is giving you, a land flowing with milk and honey, as God, the God of your forefathers, has told you.

⁴ "Then, when you cross the Jordan, you should set up (a further set of) these stones, which I am commanding you about today, on Mount Ebal, and you should plaster them with lime. ⁵ You should build there an altar to God, your God, (by making these stones into) an altar of stones. You should not use any iron (tool) on them. ⁶ You should build the altar of God, your God, out of whole stones, and you should offer up burnt-offerings on it to God, your God. ⁷ You should slaughter peace-offerings, and eat there, rejoicing before God, your God. ⁸ You should write upon the stones all the words of this Torah, very clearly (rendered into seventy languages)."

⁹ Moses and the priests (from the tribe of) Levi spoke to all of Israel, saying, "Pay attention and listen, O Israel! (It should always be in your eyes as if) today, you have become a people to God, your God (for the first time). ¹⁰ Listen to the voice of God, your God. Perform His commandments and His suprarational commands, which I am commanding you today."

Blessings and Curses at Mount Gerizim and Mount Ebal

[FIFTH READING] ¹¹ Moses commanded the people on that day, saying, ¹² "When you cross the Jordan, the following should stand on Mount Gerizim (where the priests and Levites will face) to bless the people: Simeon, Levi, Judah, Issachar, Joseph, and Benjamin. ¹³ The following should stand on Mount Ebal (where the priests and Levites will face) for the curse: Reuben, Gad, Asher, Zebulun, Dan, and Naphtali.

¹⁴ The Levites should speak up, saying to every Jewish person, in a loud voice:

» ¹⁵ "Cursed be the man who makes a graven or molten image—an abomination to God—the handiwork of a craftsman, and sets it up in secret!" Then all the people should respond, and say, "Amen!"

27:9 Today, you have become a people. *"Today,"* when you take the oath to observe the Torah, even before entering the land of Israel, *"you have become a people."* The children of Israel achieve nationhood not by virtue of acquiring their own land, for political sovereignty is transient; empires rise and fall. Rather, the nation of Israel is based on an unwavering commitment to the Torah, and the Torah is eternal (*Rabbi Samson Raphael Hirsch, 19th century*).

דברים כז:טז – כח:ד | כי תבוא

16 אָר֗וּר מַקְלֶ֛ה אָבִ֥יו וְאִמּ֖וֹ וְאָמַ֥ר כׇּל־הָעָ֖ם אָמֵֽן׃ ס 17 אָר֕וּר מַסִּ֖יג גְּב֣וּל רֵעֵ֑הוּ וְאָמַ֥ר כׇּל־הָעָ֖ם אָמֵֽן׃ ס 18 אָר֕וּר מַשְׁגֶּ֥ה עִוֵּ֖ר בַּדָּ֑רֶךְ וְאָמַ֥ר כׇּל־הָעָ֖ם אָמֵֽן׃ ס 19 אָר֗וּר מַטֶּ֛ה מִשְׁפַּ֥ט גֵּר־יָת֖וֹם וְאַלְמָנָ֑ה וְאָמַ֥ר כׇּל־הָעָ֖ם אָמֵֽן׃ ס 20 אָרוּר שֹׁכֵב֙ עִם־אֵ֣שֶׁת אָבִ֔יו כִּ֥י גִלָּ֖ה כְּנַ֣ף אָבִ֑יו וְאָמַ֥ר כׇּל־הָעָ֖ם אָמֵֽן׃ ס 21 אָר֕וּר שֹׁכֵ֖ב עִם־כׇּל־בְּהֵמָ֑ה וְאָמַ֥ר כׇּל־הָעָ֖ם אָמֵֽן׃ ס 22 אָר֗וּר שֹׁכֵב֙ עִם־אֲחֹת֔וֹ בַּת־אָבִ֖יו א֣וֹ בַת־אִמּ֑וֹ וְאָמַ֥ר כׇּל־הָעָ֖ם אָמֵֽן׃ ס 23 אָר֕וּר שֹׁכֵ֖ב עִם־חֹתַנְתּ֑וֹ וְאָמַ֥ר כׇּל־הָעָ֖ם אָמֵֽן׃ ס 24 אָר֕וּר מַכֵּ֥ה רֵעֵ֖הוּ בַּסָּ֑תֶר וְאָמַ֥ר כׇּל־הָעָ֖ם אָמֵֽן׃ ס 25 אָרוּר֙ לֹקֵ֣חַ שֹׁ֔חַד לְהַכּ֥וֹת נֶ֖פֶשׁ דָּ֣ם נָקִ֑י וְאָמַ֥ר כׇּל־הָעָ֖ם אָמֵֽן׃ ס 26 אָר֗וּר אֲשֶׁ֧ר לֹא־יָקִ֛ים אֶת־דִּבְרֵ֥י הַתּוֹרָֽה־הַזֹּ֖את לַעֲשׂ֣וֹת אוֹתָ֑ם וְאָמַ֥ר כׇּל־הָעָ֖ם אָמֵֽן׃ פ

כח 1 וְהָיָ֗ה אִם־שָׁמ֤וֹעַ תִּשְׁמַע֙ בְּקוֹל֙ יְהֹוָ֣ה אֱלֹהֶ֔יךָ לִשְׁמֹ֣ר לַעֲשׂ֔וֹת אֶת־כׇּל־מִצְוֺתָ֔יו אֲשֶׁ֛ר אָנֹכִ֥י מְצַוְּךָ֖ הַיּ֑וֹם וּנְתָ֨נְךָ֜ יְהֹוָ֤ה אֱלֹהֶ֙יךָ֙ עֶלְי֔וֹן עַ֖ל כׇּל־גּוֹיֵ֥י הָאָֽרֶץ׃ 2 וּבָ֧אוּ עָלֶ֛יךָ כׇּל־הַבְּרָכ֥וֹת הָאֵ֖לֶּה וְהִשִּׂיגֻ֑ךָ כִּ֣י תִשְׁמַ֔ע בְּק֖וֹל יְהֹוָ֥ה אֱלֹהֶֽיךָ׃ 3 בָּר֥וּךְ אַתָּ֖ה בָּעִ֑יר וּבָר֥וּךְ אַתָּ֖ה בַּשָּׂדֶֽה׃ 4 בָּר֛וּךְ

a blessing. Therefore it is sometimes necessary for the blessings to chase after you, *"and overtake you"* (*Rabbi Ḥayyim Aryeh Leib of Jedwabne, 19th century*).

3. You will be blessed in the city. This refers to the reward for the commandments that you observe in the city (*Deuteronomy Rabbah*).

Do not be concerned only with your own piety. Have a positive influence on your surroundings, those *"in the city."* Then, *"you will be blessed"* (*Rabbi Ḥayyim b. Mordecai Ephraim Fischel Sofer, 19th century*).

spiritual vitamin

> While both the intellect and the emotions need to fully participate in your religious experience, the intellect has its natural limitations, while the emotions go deeper and farther. Joy and enthusiasm break through barriers and inspire you to accomplish things that would otherwise be unattainable.

» ¹⁶ "Cursed be the one who disgraces his father and mother!" Then all the people should say, "Amen!"

» ¹⁷ "Cursed be the one who moves his neighbor's landmark!" Then all the people should say, "Amen!"

» ¹⁸ "Cursed be the one who misdirects the path of a person who is blind (to a certain matter)!" Then all the people should say, "Amen!"

» ¹⁹ "Cursed be the one who perverts the judgment of the convert, the orphan, or the widow!" Then all the people should say, "Amen!"

» ²⁰ "Cursed be the one who lies with his father's wife, uncovering the robe of his father!" Then all the people should say, "Amen!"

» ²¹ "Cursed be the one who lies with any animal!" Then all the people should say, "Amen!"

» ²² "Cursed be the one who lies with his sister, his father's daughter or his mother's daughter!" Then all the people should say, "Amen!"

» ²³ "Cursed be the one who lies with his mother-in-law!" Then all the people should say, "Amen!"

» ²⁴ "Cursed be the one who hurts his fellow (by maligning him) in secret!" Then all the people should say, "Amen!"

» ²⁵ "Cursed be the one who takes a bribe to put an innocent person to death!" Then all the people should say, "Amen!"

» ²⁶ "Cursed be the one who does not uphold the words of this Torah and observe them!" Then all the people should say, "Amen!"

Blessings for Observing the Commandments

28 ¹ What will happen is, if you always listen to the voice of God, your God, and are careful to observe all His commandments which I am commanding you today, then God, your God, will make you an elite (nation), above all the nations of the earth. ² All the following blessings will come upon you and overtake you, if you listen to the voice of God, your God:

³ You will be blessed in the city, and blessed in the field. ⁴ The fruit of your womb,

28:2 All the following blessings will come upon you and overtake you. Often you will run away from something beneficial because you are unaware or cannot recognize the good that will come from it. To you it might seem like something harmful, but God knows that it is

דברים כח:ד-יג · כי תבוא

פְּרִי־בִטְנְךָ וּפְרִי אַדְמָתְךָ וּפְרִי בְהֶמְתֶּךָ שְׁגַר אֲלָפֶיךָ וְעַשְׁתְּרוֹת צֹאנֶךָ: 5 בָּרוּךְ טַנְאֲךָ וּמִשְׁאַרְתֶּךָ: 6 בָּרוּךְ אַתָּה בְּבֹאֶךָ וּבָרוּךְ אַתָּה בְּצֵאתֶךָ: [SIXTH READING] 7 יִתֵּן יְהֹוָה אֶת־אֹיְבֶיךָ הַקָּמִים עָלֶיךָ נִגָּפִים לְפָנֶיךָ בְּדֶרֶךְ אֶחָד יֵצְאוּ אֵלֶיךָ וּבְשִׁבְעָה דְרָכִים יָנוּסוּ לְפָנֶיךָ: 8 יְצַו יְהֹוָה אִתְּךָ אֶת־הַבְּרָכָה בַּאֲסָמֶיךָ וּבְכֹל מִשְׁלַח יָדֶךָ וּבֵרַכְךָ בָּאָרֶץ אֲשֶׁר־יְהֹוָה אֱלֹהֶיךָ נֹתֵן לָךְ: 9 יְקִימְךָ יְהֹוָה לוֹ לְעַם קָדוֹשׁ כַּאֲשֶׁר נִשְׁבַּע־לָךְ כִּי תִשְׁמֹר אֶת־מִצְוֹת יְהֹוָה אֱלֹהֶיךָ וְהָלַכְתָּ בִּדְרָכָיו: 10 וְרָאוּ כָּל־עַמֵּי הָאָרֶץ כִּי שֵׁם יְהֹוָה נִקְרָא עָלֶיךָ וְיָרְאוּ מִמֶּךָּ: 11 וְהוֹתִרְךָ יְהֹוָה לְטוֹבָה בִּפְרִי בִטְנְךָ וּבִפְרִי בְהֶמְתְּךָ וּבִפְרִי אַדְמָתֶךָ עַל הָאֲדָמָה אֲשֶׁר נִשְׁבַּע יְהֹוָה לַאֲבֹתֶיךָ לָתֶת לָךְ: 12 יִפְתַּח יְהֹוָה ׀ לְךָ אֶת־אוֹצָרוֹ הַטּוֹב אֶת־הַשָּׁמַיִם לָתֵת מְטַר־אַרְצְךָ בְּעִתּוֹ וּלְבָרֵךְ אֵת כָּל־מַעֲשֵׂה יָדֶךָ וְהִלְוִיתָ גּוֹיִם רַבִּים וְאַתָּה לֹא תִלְוֶה: 13 וּנְתָנְךָ יְהֹוָה לְרֹאשׁ וְלֹא לְזָנָב וְהָיִיתָ רַק לְמַעְלָה וְלֹא תִהְיֶה לְמָטָּה כִּי־תִשְׁמַע אֶל־מִצְוֺת ׀ יְהֹוָה אֱלֹהֶיךָ אֲשֶׁר אָנֹכִי מְצַוְּךָ

11. God will grant you a good surplus in the fruit of your womb. Maimonides writes that man is better off concluding his business in this world quickly so that his soul can sooner begin its delight in the world to come. However, that is only as far as the individual is concerned, but when he has a family that is reliant on him for care and guidance, the longer he is with them the greater the influence he will have.

This verse could be expounded in the same vein: *"God will grant you a good surplus"*—more years than you personally might require—for the benefit of your family, *"the fruit of your womb"* (*Rabbi Moses Sofer, 18th–19th century*).

13. You will be only at the top, and not at the bottom. Doesn't being "on top" automatically preclude being "on bottom"? Why is it necessary to state both, "You will be only at the top, *and not at the bottom*"?

The world to come is "inverted"—those that are "on top" in this world (people who are highly regarded in this world for their material achievements), are lowly in the next world, and *vice versa* (*Babylonian Talmud, Pesaḥim* 50a). The Torah promises you that through listening to the commandments of God, *"You will only be on top"*—you will be highly regarded in the next world—but you also will *"not be at the bottom,"* in this world either. You will find success in both worlds (*Rabbi Eleazar b. Aryeh Leib Loew, 18th century*).

deuteronomy 28:4–13 — ki tavo'

the fruit of your soil, the fruit of your livestock, the offspring of your cattle, and the flocks of your sheep will be blessed.

⁵ Your fruits and your dough will be blessed. ⁶ (Just as) you were blessed (and without sin) when you arrived (in this world, so too), you will be blessed (and without sin) when you depart.

[SIXTH READING] ⁷ God will cause your enemies who rise up against you to be beaten before you. They will come out against you in one direction, and flee from you (in a panic) in seven directions.

⁸ God will direct (His) blessing to be with you in your granaries, and with everything to which you put your hand. He will bless you in the land which God, your God, is giving you.

⁹ God will establish you as His holy people, as He swore to you, if you observe the commandments of God, your God, and walk in His ways. ¹⁰ Then all the nations of the earth will see that the name of God is upon you, and they will fear you.

¹¹ God will grant you a good surplus in the fruit of your womb, the fruit of your livestock, and the fruit of your soil, on the land which God swore to your forefathers to give you. ¹² God will open up for you His good treasury, the skies, to give your land its rain in the (right) time, and to bless everything you put your hand to. You will lend to many nations, but you will not (need to) borrow.

¹³ God will put you at the head, and not at the tail. You will be only at the top, and not at the bottom.

9. Walk in His ways. We are commanded to emulate the Almighty as much as possible, as the verse states "walk in His ways." Just as God is gracious, you are to be gracious. Just as He is compassionate, you are to be compassionate. Just as He is benevolent, you are to be benevolent (*Maimonides, 12th century*).

When you act in a manner of graciousness, compassion or benevolence, it should not be merely out of an ethical imperative, or for the general benefit of society, but rather, in an attempt to resemble God. *Just as God is … you are to be.*

Practically speaking, this will ensure that you will not allow yourself to become emotionally "carried away" to an extreme. For in attempting to emulate God, you will always be conscious of the need to balance your attributes—like God, whose qualities of kindness and severity are in perfect harmony (*Rabbi Menahem Mendel Schneerson, 20th century*).

10. Then all the nations of the earth will see that the name of God is upon you, and they will fear you. *"They will fear you,"* could be read as "they will fear God *because of you.*" When *"the nations of the earth will see that the name of God is upon you,"* by observing your devout commitment to God, this will influence them to revere God (*Rabbi Baruch of Medzibezh, 18th century*).

דברים כח:יג-כה • כי תבוא

הַיּוֹם לִשְׁמֹר וְלַעֲשׂוֹת: 14 וְלֹא תָסוּר מִכָּל־הַדְּבָרִים אֲשֶׁר אָנֹכִי מְצַוֶּה אֶתְכֶם הַיּוֹם יָמִין וּשְׂמֹאול לָלֶכֶת אַחֲרֵי אֱלֹהִים אֲחֵרִים לְעָבְדָם: פ 15 וְהָיָה אִם־לֹא תִשְׁמַע בְּקוֹל יְהֹוָה אֱלֹהֶיךָ לִשְׁמֹר לַעֲשׂוֹת אֶת־כָּל־מִצְוֺתָיו וְחֻקֹּתָיו אֲשֶׁר אָנֹכִי מְצַוְּךָ הַיּוֹם וּבָאוּ עָלֶיךָ כָּל־הַקְּלָלוֹת הָאֵלֶּה וְהִשִּׂיגוּךָ: 16 אָרוּר אַתָּה בָּעִיר וְאָרוּר אַתָּה בַּשָּׂדֶה: 17 אָרוּר טַנְאֲךָ וּמִשְׁאַרְתֶּךָ: 18 אָרוּר פְּרִי־בִטְנְךָ וּפְרִי אַדְמָתֶךָ שְׁגַר אֲלָפֶיךָ וְעַשְׁתְּרֹת צֹאנֶךָ: 19 אָרוּר אַתָּה בְּבֹאֶךָ וְאָרוּר אַתָּה בְּצֵאתֶךָ: 20 יְשַׁלַּח יְהֹוָה | בְּךָ אֶת־הַמְּאֵרָה אֶת־הַמְּהוּמָה וְאֶת־הַמִּגְעֶרֶת בְּכָל־מִשְׁלַח יָדְךָ אֲשֶׁר תַּעֲשֶׂה עַד הִשָּׁמֶדְךָ וְעַד־אֲבָדְךָ מַהֵר מִפְּנֵי רֹעַ מַעֲלָלֶיךָ אֲשֶׁר עֲזַבְתָּנִי: 21 יַדְבֵּק יְהֹוָה בְּךָ אֶת־הַדָּבֶר עַד כַּלֹּתוֹ אֹתְךָ מֵעַל הָאֲדָמָה אֲשֶׁר־אַתָּה בָא־שָׁמָּה לְרִשְׁתָּהּ: 22 יַכְּכָה יְהֹוָה בַּשַּׁחֶפֶת וּבַקַּדַּחַת וּבַדַּלֶּקֶת וּבַחַרְחֻר וּבַחֶרֶב וּבַשִּׁדָּפוֹן וּבַיֵּרָקוֹן וּרְדָפוּךָ עַד אָבְדֶךָ: 23 וְהָיוּ שָׁמֶיךָ אֲשֶׁר עַל־רֹאשְׁךָ נְחֹשֶׁת וְהָאָרֶץ אֲשֶׁר־תַּחְתֶּיךָ בַּרְזֶל: 24 יִתֵּן יְהֹוָה אֶת־מְטַר אַרְצְךָ אָבָק וְעָפָר מִן־הַשָּׁמַיִם יֵרֵד עָלֶיךָ עַד הִשָּׁמְדָךְ: 25 יִתֶּנְךָ יְהֹוָה | נִגָּף לִפְנֵי אֹיְבֶיךָ בְּדֶרֶךְ אֶחָד תֵּצֵא אֵלָיו וּבְשִׁבְעָה

The word *daver*, "plague," could also be read as *davar*, "word," alluding to words of prayer. The message here is: If you "cling" to God earnestly with words of prayer, then you will be "consumed"—you will be lifted to a higher plane of consciousness and lose any sensation of self or ego (*Rabbi Kalonymous Kalman Epstein of Cracow, 18th–19th century*).

spiritual vitamin

> Any sad interlude in Jewish life is only transitory, and is based on the principle of "descent for the purpose of ascent." In other words, any and all sad events in our history which are commemorated on the few sad days on our calendar are backwards steps which are necessary for a greater forward leap.

deuteronomy 28:13–25 — ki tavo'

(All this is) if you listen to the commandments of God, your God, which I am commanding you today, being careful to observe (them). [14] You must not deviate, right or left, from all of the words I am commanding you today, to follow other gods and worship them.

Consequences of Failing to Observe the Commandments

[15] What will happen is, if you do not listen to God, your God, to be careful to observe all His commandments and suprarational commands which I am commanding you this day, then the following curses will come upon you and overtake you:

[16] You will be cursed in the city, and cursed in the field. [17] Your fruits and your dough will be cursed. [18] The fruit of your womb, the fruit of your soil, and the fruit of your livestock—those born from your cattle and the flock of your sheep—will be cursed. [19] You will be cursed when you arrive, and cursed when you depart.

[20] God will send you shortages, confusion, and turmoil in everything you put your hand to, until you are destroyed and quickly vanish, because of your evil deeds in forsaking Me. [21] God will make a plague cleave to you until it has consumed you from upon the land of which you are coming to take possession. [22] God will strike you with inflammation, illnesses, burning fevers, unquenchable thirst, with the sword (of invading armies), with blasting and withering (of the crops), and this will pursue you until you perish. [23] Your skies above you will (not rain, but merely exude moisture like) copper, and the earth below you (will be dry like) iron. [24] God will make the rain of your land (insufficient, causing the wind that follows to blow) dust and dirt (onto your sprouting crops). It will come down upon you from the skies until you are destroyed. [25] God will cause you to be struck down before your enemy. You will come out against them in one direction, but you will flee from them (in panic) in seven directions. You will become a (cause of) dread to all the kingdoms on earth (when they hear what has happened

---

15. The following curses will come upon you. This section of reproof is read in the synagogues before the Jewish New Year (*Rosh Ha-Shanah*). The reason for arranging the Torah reading schedule in this manner is so that the year will end along with its curses (*Babylonian Talmud, Megillah* 31b).

If there is a negative decree from heaven, we attempt to fulfil it through the verbal recitation of the curses, following the principle that words can sometimes substitute for events—"*We will offer the words of our lips instead of calves*" (*Hosea* 14:3). May God consider the reading of these curses instead of their actual infliction, and let us begin to receive only blessings! (*Rabbi Solomon ha-Kohen Rabinowich of Radomsko, 19th century*).

21. God will make a plague cling to you until it has consumed you. All the curses are really veiled blessings. What blessing is hinted to here?

דברים כח:כה-מד

כי תבוא

דְרָכִים֙ תֵּצֵ֣א אֵלָ֔יו וְהָיִ֣יתָ לְזַעֲוָ֔ה לְכֹ֖ל מַמְלְכ֥וֹת הָאָֽרֶץ: 26 וְהָיְתָ֤ה נִבְלָֽתְךָ֙ לְמַאֲכָ֔ל לְכָל־ע֥וֹף הַשָּׁמַ֖יִם וּלְבֶהֱמַ֣ת הָאָ֑רֶץ וְאֵ֖ין מַחֲרִֽיד: 27 יַכְּכָ֨ה יְהֹוָ֜ה בִּשְׁחִ֤ין מִצְרַ֨יִם֙ [ובעפלים כ׳] וּבַטְּחֹרִ֔ים וּבַגָּרָ֖ב וּבֶחָ֑רֶס אֲשֶׁ֥ר לֹא־תוּכַ֖ל לְהֵרָפֵֽא: 28 יַכְּכָ֣ה יְהֹוָ֔ה בְּשִׁגָּע֖וֹן וּבְעִוָּר֑וֹן וּבְתִמְה֖וֹן לֵבָֽב: 29 וְהָיִ֜יתָ מְמַשֵּׁ֣שׁ בַּֽצׇּהֳרַ֗יִם כַּאֲשֶׁר֩ יְמַשֵּׁ֨שׁ הָעִוֵּ֜ר בָּאֲפֵלָ֗ה וְלֹ֥א תַצְלִ֖יחַ אֶת־דְּרָכֶ֑יךָ וְהָיִ֜יתָ אַ֣ךְ עָשׁ֧וּק וְגָז֛וּל כׇּל־הַיָּמִ֖ים וְאֵ֥ין מוֹשִֽׁיעַ: 30 אִשָּׁ֣ה תְאָרֵ֗שׂ וְאִ֤ישׁ אַחֵר֙ [ישגלנה כ׳] יִשְׁכָּבֶ֔נָּה בַּ֥יִת תִּבְנֶ֖ה וְלֹא־תֵשֵׁ֣ב בּ֑וֹ כֶּ֥רֶם תִּטַּ֖ע וְלֹ֥א תְחַלְּלֶֽנּוּ: 31 שׁוֹרְךָ֞ טָב֣וּחַ לְעֵינֶ֗יךָ וְלֹ֣א תֹאכַל֮ מִמֶּ֒נּוּ֒ חֲמֹֽרְךָ֙ גָּז֣וּל מִלְּפָנֶ֔יךָ וְלֹ֥א יָשׁ֖וּב לָ֑ךְ צֹֽאנְךָ֙ נְתֻנ֣וֹת לְאֹיְבֶ֔יךָ וְאֵ֥ין לְךָ֖ מוֹשִֽׁיעַ: 32 בָּנֶ֨יךָ וּבְנֹתֶ֜יךָ נְתֻנִ֨ים לְעַ֤ם אַחֵר֙ וְעֵינֶ֣יךָ רֹא֔וֹת וְכָל֥וֹת אֲלֵיהֶ֖ם כׇּל־הַיּ֑וֹם וְאֵ֥ין לְאֵ֖ל יָדֶֽךָ: 33 פְּרִ֤י אַדְמָֽתְךָ֙ וְכׇל־יְגִ֣יעֲךָ֔ יֹאכַ֥ל עַ֖ם אֲשֶׁ֣ר לֹא־יָדָ֑עְתָּ וְהָיִ֗יתָ רַ֛ק עָשׁ֥וּק וְרָצ֖וּץ כׇּל־הַיָּמִֽים: 34 וְהָיִ֖יתָ מְשֻׁגָּ֑ע מִמַּרְאֵ֥ה עֵינֶ֖יךָ אֲשֶׁ֥ר תִּרְאֶֽה: 35 יַכְּכָ֨ה יְהֹוָ֜ה בִּשְׁחִ֣ין רָ֗ע עַל־הַבִּרְכַּ֙יִם֙ וְעַל־הַשֹּׁקַ֔יִם אֲשֶׁ֥ר לֹא־תוּכַ֖ל לְהֵרָפֵ֑א מִכַּ֥ף רַגְלְךָ֖ וְעַ֥ד קׇדְקֳדֶֽךָ: 36 יוֹלֵ֨ךְ יְהֹוָ֜ה אֹֽתְךָ֗ וְאֶֽת־מַלְכְּךָ֙ אֲשֶׁ֣ר תָּקִ֣ים עָלֶ֔יךָ אֶל־גּ֕וֹי אֲשֶׁ֥ר לֹא־יָדַ֖עְתָּ אַתָּ֣ה וַאֲבֹתֶ֑יךָ וְעָבַ֥דְתָּ שָּׁ֛ם אֱלֹהִ֥ים אֲחֵרִ֖ים עֵ֥ץ וָאָֽבֶן: 37 וְהָיִ֣יתָ לְשַׁמָּ֔ה לְמָשָׁ֖ל וְלִשְׁנִינָ֑ה בְּכֹל֙ הָֽעַמִּ֔ים אֲשֶׁר־יְנַהֶגְךָ֥ יְהֹוָ֖ה שָֽׁמָּה: 38 זֶ֥רַע רַ֖ב תּוֹצִ֣יא הַשָּׂדֶ֑ה וּמְעַ֣ט תֶּאֱסֹ֔ף כִּ֥י יַחְסְלֶ֖נּוּ הָאַרְבֶּֽה: 39 כְּרָמִ֥ים תִּטַּ֖ע וְעָבָ֑דְתָּ וְיַ֤יִן לֹֽא־תִשְׁתֶּה֙ וְלֹ֣א תֶאֱגֹ֔ר כִּ֥י תֹאכְלֶ֖נּוּ הַתֹּלָֽעַת: 40 זֵיתִ֛ים יִהְי֥וּ לְךָ֖ בְּכׇל־גְּבוּלֶ֑ךָ וְשֶׁ֙מֶן֙ לֹ֣א תָס֔וּךְ כִּ֥י יִשַּׁ֖ל זֵיתֶֽךָ: 41 בָּנִ֥ים וּבָנ֖וֹת תּוֹלִ֑יד וְלֹא־יִהְי֣וּ לָ֔ךְ כִּ֥י יֵלְכ֖וּ בַּשֶּֽׁבִי: 42 כׇּל־עֵצְךָ֖ וּפְרִ֣י אַדְמָתֶ֑ךָ יְיָרֵ֖שׁ הַצְּלָצַֽל: 43 הַגֵּר֙ אֲשֶׁ֣ר בְּקִרְבְּךָ֔ יַעֲלֶ֥ה עָלֶ֖יךָ מַ֣עְלָה מָּ֑עְלָה וְאַתָּ֥ה תֵרֵ֖ד מַ֥טָּה מָּֽטָּה: 44 ה֣וּא יַלְוְךָ֔ וְאַתָּ֖ה לֹ֣א תַלְוֶ֑נּוּ ה֚וּא יִהְיֶ֣ה לְרֹ֔אשׁ וְאַתָּ֖ה תִּהְיֶ֥ה לְזָנָֽב:

to you). ²⁶ Your corpses will be food for every bird of the skies and for the beasts of the earth, and no one will frighten them (away). ²⁷ God will strike you with the boils of Egypt, with hemorrhoids, with oozing sores, and with dry lesions, from which you will not be able to be cured. ²⁸ God will strike you with insanity, with blindness, and with bewilderment. ²⁹ You will grope around at midday, as the blind man gropes in the dark, and you will be unsuccessful in your ways. You will be nothing but oppressed and robbed all the time, and no one will save you. ³⁰ You will betroth a woman, but another man will lie with her. You will build a house, but you will not live in it. You will plant a vineyard, but you will not render it fit (for use). ³¹ Your ox will be slaughtered before your eyes, but you will not eat from it. Your donkey will be robbed right in front of you, and it will never come back to you. Your flocks will be given over to your enemies, and you will have no savior. ³² Your sons and daughters will be given over to another people, and your eyes will see (what happened), and yearn for them all day long, but you will be powerless. ³³ The fruit of your soil and all your hard work will be eaten up by a people unknown to you. You will be nothing but wronged and downtrodden all the time. ³⁴ You will go insane from the things that your eyes will see. ³⁵ God will strike you on the knees and on the legs with severe boils from which you will not be able to be cured, (spreading out) from the sole of your foot to the top of your head. ³⁶ God will lead you, and your king whom you will have appointed over you, to a nation unknown to you or your fathers, and there you will serve other gods of wood and stone. ³⁷ Among all the nations to whom God will lead you, you will become a (source of) astonishment, an example (of persecution), and a topic of discussion. ³⁸ You will take a lot of seed out to the field, but you will gather in little, for the locusts will consume it. ³⁹ You will plant vineyards and work them, but you will neither drink their wine, nor gather their grapes, because the worms will devour them. ⁴⁰ You will have olive trees throughout all your borders, but you will not anoint with their oil, because your olive trees will shed (their fruit). ⁴¹ You will bear sons and daughters, but they will not be yours, because they will go into captivity. ⁴² The locusts will deplete all your trees and all the fruit of your soil. ⁴³ The foreigner who is among you will arise above you, higher and higher, while you will descend lower and lower. ⁴⁴ He will lend to you, but you will not lend to him. He will be at the head, while you will be at the tail.

38. You will take a lot of seed out of the field, but you will gather in little. When you study Torah, never look at how much you have already mastered; consider how much there is still left to absorb! This attitude is encapsulated here in our verse: *"You will take a lot of seed out of the field"*—even when you have acquired "a lot" of wisdom; *"you will gather in little"*—look upon your achievements as something little, compared to how much you have left to learn (*Rabbi Meir Horowitz of Dzieckowitz, 19ᵗʰ century*).

דברים כח:מה-נט   כי תבוא

45 וּבָ֨אוּ עָלֶ֜יךָ כָּל־הַקְּלָל֣וֹת הָאֵ֗לֶּה וּרְדָפ֙וּךָ֙ וְהִשִּׂיג֔וּךָ עַ֖ד הִשָּֽׁמְדָ֑ךְ כִּי־לֹ֣א שָׁמַ֗עְתָּ בְּקוֹל֙ יְהֹוָ֣ה אֱלֹהֶ֔יךָ לִשְׁמֹ֛ר מִצְוֺתָ֥יו וְחֻקֹּתָ֖יו אֲשֶׁ֥ר צִוָּֽךְ: 46 וְהָי֣וּ בְךָ֔ לְא֖וֹת וּלְמוֹפֵ֑ת וּֽבְזַרְעֲךָ֖ עַד־עוֹלָֽם: 47 תַּ֗חַת אֲשֶׁ֤ר לֹא־עָבַ֙דְתָּ֙ אֶת־יְהֹוָ֣ה אֱלֹהֶ֔יךָ בְּשִׂמְחָ֖ה וּבְט֣וּב לֵבָ֑ב מֵרֹ֖ב כֹּֽל: 48 וְעָבַדְתָּ֣ אֶת־אֹיְבֶ֗יךָ אֲשֶׁ֨ר יְשַׁלְּחֶ֤נּוּ יְהֹוָה֙ בָּ֔ךְ בְּרָעָ֧ב וּבְצָמָ֛א וּבְעֵירֹ֖ם וּבְחֹ֣סֶר כֹּ֑ל וְנָתַ֞ן עֹ֤ל בַּרְזֶל֙ עַל־צַוָּארֶ֔ךָ עַ֥ד הִשְׁמִיד֖וֹ אֹתָֽךְ: 49 יִשָּׂ֣א יְהֹוָה֩ עָלֶ֨יךָ גּ֤וֹי מֵרָחֹק֙ מִקְצֵ֣ה הָאָ֔רֶץ כַּאֲשֶׁ֥ר יִדְאֶ֖ה הַנָּ֑שֶׁר גּ֕וֹי אֲשֶׁ֥ר לֹא־תִשְׁמַ֖ע לְשֹׁנֽוֹ: 50 גּ֖וֹי עַ֣ז פָּנִ֑ים אֲשֶׁ֨ר לֹא־יִשָּׂ֤א פָנִים֙ לְזָקֵ֔ן וְנַ֖עַר לֹ֥א יָחֹֽן: 51 וְ֠אָכַ֠ל פְּרִ֨י בְהֶמְתְּךָ֥ וּפְרִֽי־אַדְמָתְךָ֮ עַ֣ד הִשָּֽׁמְדָךְ֒ אֲשֶׁ֣ר לֹא־יַשְׁאִ֣יר לְךָ֗ דָּגָן֙ תִּיר֣וֹשׁ וְיִצְהָ֔ר שְׁגַ֥ר אֲלָפֶ֖יךָ וְעַשְׁתְּרֹ֣ת צֹאנֶ֑ךָ עַ֥ד הַאֲבִיד֖וֹ אֹתָֽךְ: 52 וְהֵצַ֨ר לְךָ֜ בְּכָל־שְׁעָרֶ֗יךָ עַ֣ד רֶ֤דֶת חֹמֹתֶ֙יךָ֙ הַגְּבֹהֹ֣ת וְהַבְּצֻר֔וֹת אֲשֶׁ֥ר אַתָּ֛ה בֹּטֵ֥חַ בָּהֵ֖ן בְּכָל־אַרְצֶ֑ךָ וְהֵצַ֤ר לְךָ֙ בְּכָל־שְׁעָרֶ֔יךָ בְּכָ֨ל־אַרְצְךָ֔ אֲשֶׁ֥ר נָתַ֛ן יְהֹוָ֥ה אֱלֹהֶ֖יךָ לָֽךְ: 53 וְאָכַלְתָּ֣ פְרִֽי־בִטְנְךָ֗ בְּשַׂ֤ר בָּנֶ֙יךָ֙ וּבְנֹתֶ֔יךָ אֲשֶׁ֥ר נָֽתַן־לְךָ֖ יְהֹוָ֣ה אֱלֹהֶ֑יךָ בְּמָצוֹר֙ וּבְמָצ֔וֹק אֲשֶׁר־יָצִ֥יק לְךָ֖ אֹיְבֶֽךָ: 54 הָאִישׁ֙ הָרַ֣ךְ בְּךָ֔ וְהֶעָנֹ֖ג מְאֹ֑ד תֵּרַ֨ע עֵינ֤וֹ בְאָחִיו֙ וּבְאֵ֣שֶׁת חֵיק֔וֹ וּבְיֶ֥תֶר בָּנָ֖יו אֲשֶׁ֥ר יוֹתִֽיר: 55 מִתֵּ֣ת ׀ לְאַחַ֣ד מֵהֶ֗ם מִבְּשַׂ֤ר בָּנָיו֙ אֲשֶׁ֣ר יֹאכֵ֔ל מִבְּלִ֥י הִשְׁאִֽיר־ל֖וֹ כֹּ֑ל בְּמָצוֹר֙ וּבְמָצ֔וֹק אֲשֶׁ֨ר יָצִ֥יק לְךָ֛ אֹיִבְךָ֖ בְּכָל־שְׁעָרֶֽיךָ: 56 הָרַכָּ֨ה בְךָ֜ וְהָעֲנֻגָּ֗ה אֲשֶׁ֨ר לֹא־נִסְּתָ֤ה כַף־רַגְלָהּ֙ הַצֵּ֣ג עַל־הָאָ֔רֶץ מֵהִתְעַנֵּ֖ג וּמֵרֹ֑ךְ תֵּרַ֤ע עֵינָהּ֙ בְּאִ֣ישׁ חֵיקָ֔הּ וּבִבְנָ֖הּ וּבְבִתָּֽהּ: 57 וּֽבְשִׁלְיָתָ֞הּ הַיּוֹצֵ֣ת ׀ מִבֵּ֣ין רַגְלֶ֗יהָ וּבְבָנֶ֙יהָ֙ אֲשֶׁ֣ר תֵּלֵ֔ד כִּֽי־תֹאכְלֵ֥ם בְּחֹֽסֶר־כֹּ֖ל בַּסָּ֑תֶר בְּמָצוֹר֙ וּבְמָצ֔וֹק אֲשֶׁ֨ר יָצִ֥יק לְךָ֛ אֹיִבְךָ֖ בִּשְׁעָרֶֽיךָ: 58 אִם־לֹ֨א תִשְׁמֹ֜ר לַעֲשׂ֗וֹת אֶת־כָּל־דִּבְרֵי֙ הַתּוֹרָ֣ה הַזֹּ֔את הַכְּתֻבִ֖ים בַּסֵּ֣פֶר הַזֶּ֑ה לְ֠יִרְאָ֠ה אֶת־הַשֵּׁ֞ם הַנִּכְבָּ֤ד וְהַנּוֹרָא֙ הַזֶּ֔ה אֵ֖ת יְהֹוָ֥ה אֱלֹהֶֽיךָ: 59 וְהִפְלָ֤א יְהֹוָה֙ אֶת־מַכֹּ֣תְךָ֔

Because you did not serve God, your God, with joy and with gladness of heart, when (you had an) abundance of everything. Worshiping God should mean more to you than

deuteronomy 28:45–59 — ki tavo'

⁴⁵ All these curses will befall you, pursuing you, overtaking you until they destroy you because you did not listen to God, your God, and observe His commandments and suprarational commands which He commanded you. ⁴⁶ They will be as a sign and a wonder, upon you and your children forever, ⁴⁷ because you did not serve God, your God, with joy and with gladness of heart, when (you had an) abundance of everything.

⁴⁸ Therefore, you will serve your enemies, whom God will send against you, amid hunger, thirst, nakedness and total destitution. He will place an iron yoke on your neck, until He has destroyed you. ⁴⁹ God will bring upon you a nation from afar, from the end of the earth, (suddenly) as the eagle swoops down—a nation whose language you will not recognize, ⁵⁰ an arrogant nation, which will not respect the elderly, or be kind to the young. ⁵¹ They will devour the fruit of your livestock and the fruit of your soil, destroying you. They will not leave over anything for you from the grain, the wine, the oil, the offspring of your cattle or the flocks of your sheep, until they destroy you. ⁵² They will besiege you in all your cities, until your tall and fortified walls in which you trust are conquered, throughout your entire land. They will besiege you in all your cities throughout your entire land, which God, your God, has given you. ⁵³ During the siege and the distress which your enemies will bring upon you, (you will be so hungry that) you will eat the fruit of your womb, the flesh of your sons and daughters, whom God, your God, has given you. ⁵⁴ The most sensitive and squeamish man among you (will be so hungry for his own children's flesh that he) will be selfish to his own brother, his darling wife and the rest of his children whom he has allowed to remain ⁵⁵ (refusing) to give any one of them of his children's flesh that he is eating. For not a thing will remain for him in the siege and distress which your enemies will bring upon you, in all your cities. ⁵⁶ (Even) the most sensitive and squeamish woman among you, who had never dared to place her foot upon the ground because of (her) sensitivity and squeamishness, will begrudge (giving flesh to) her darling husband, her (adult) sons and daughters, ⁵⁷ the infants who came from between her legs, and her own children whom she will bear—for she will (slaughter them and) eat them in secret, in destitution, amid the siege and distress which your enemies will inflict upon you in your cities.

⁵⁸ If you are not careful to observe all the words of this Torah, which are written in this scroll, to fear this glorious and awesome name of God, your God, ⁵⁹ then God will distinguish your plagues and your children's plagues, (to be) powerful

---

45-47. All these curses will befall you ... because you did not serve God, your God, with joy. Merely because they did not serve joyously, should they deserve all these curses? Rather, the verse means that not only did they fail to serve God, they *enjoyed* that fact that they were not serving Him (*Rabbi Menahem Mendel Morgensztern of Kotsk, 19ᵗʰ century*).

דברים כח:נט-סח — כי תבוא

וְאֵת מַכּוֹת זַרְעֶךָ מַכּוֹת גְּדֹלֹת וְנֶאֱמָנוֹת וָחֳלָיִם רָעִים וְנֶאֱמָנִים: 60 וְהֵשִׁיב בְּךָ אֵת כָּל־מַדְוֵה מִצְרַיִם אֲשֶׁר יָגֹרְתָּ מִפְּנֵיהֶם וְדָבְקוּ בָּךְ: 61 גַּם כָּל־חֳלִי וְכָל־מַכָּה אֲשֶׁר לֹא כָתוּב בְּסֵפֶר הַתּוֹרָה הַזֹּאת יַעְלֵם יְהֹוָה עָלֶיךָ עַד הִשָּׁמְדָךְ: 62 וְנִשְׁאַרְתֶּם בִּמְתֵי מְעָט תַּחַת אֲשֶׁר הֱיִיתֶם כְּכוֹכְבֵי הַשָּׁמַיִם לָרֹב כִּי־לֹא שָׁמַעְתָּ בְּקוֹל יְהֹוָה אֱלֹהֶיךָ: 63 וְהָיָה כַּאֲשֶׁר־שָׂשׂ יְהֹוָה עֲלֵיכֶם לְהֵיטִיב אֶתְכֶם וּלְהַרְבּוֹת אֶתְכֶם כֵּן יָשִׂישׂ יְהֹוָה עֲלֵיכֶם לְהַאֲבִיד אֶתְכֶם וּלְהַשְׁמִיד אֶתְכֶם וְנִסַּחְתֶּם מֵעַל הָאֲדָמָה אֲשֶׁר־אַתָּה בָא־שָׁמָּה לְרִשְׁתָּהּ: 64 וֶהֱפִיצְךָ יְהֹוָה בְּכָל־הָעַמִּים מִקְצֵה הָאָרֶץ וְעַד־קְצֵה הָאָרֶץ וְעָבַדְתָּ שָּׁם אֱלֹהִים אֲחֵרִים אֲשֶׁר לֹא־יָדַעְתָּ אַתָּה וַאֲבֹתֶיךָ עֵץ וָאָבֶן: 65 וּבַגּוֹיִם הָהֵם לֹא תַרְגִּיעַ וְלֹא־יִהְיֶה מָנוֹחַ לְכַף־רַגְלֶךָ וְנָתַן יְהֹוָה לְךָ שָׁם לֵב רַגָּז וְכִלְיוֹן עֵינַיִם וְדַאֲבוֹן נָפֶשׁ: 66 וְהָיוּ חַיֶּיךָ תְּלֻאִים לְךָ מִנֶּגֶד וּפָחַדְתָּ לַיְלָה וְיוֹמָם וְלֹא תַאֲמִין בְּחַיֶּיךָ: 67 בַּבֹּקֶר תֹּאמַר מִי־יִתֵּן עֶרֶב וּבָעֶרֶב תֹּאמַר מִי־יִתֵּן בֹּקֶר מִפַּחַד לְבָבְךָ אֲשֶׁר תִּפְחָד וּמִמַּרְאֵה עֵינֶיךָ אֲשֶׁר תִּרְאֶה: 68 וֶהֱשִׁיבְךָ יְהֹוָה | מִצְרַיִם בָּאֳנִיּוֹת בַּדֶּרֶךְ אֲשֶׁר אָמַרְתִּי

---

return. This is alluded to in the concluding curse, *"God will return you to Egypt."* To explain the unique quality of repentance, the verse continues:

"There, you will offer yourselves for sale to your enemies"—through observing the commandments, you can only sanctify and spiritually elevate those parts of the physical world which the Torah permits you to interact with. In contrast, the penitent elevates all his prior *forbidden* interactions with the world, and his *"intentional sins are transformed to merits"* (Babylonian Talmud, Yoma 86b). This is alluded to by the verse: *"There*—in the realms of the forbidden; *you will offer yourselves for sale to*—spiritually elevate; *your enemies*—the forbidden entities that the *penitent* interacted with."

"As slaves and handmaids"—in addition to elevating the parts of the physical world with which he came into contact, the penitent also enjoys a substantial spiritual elevation himself, as a result of conquering his strong desires. Being a master of self-control, the penitent is compared to a "slave," who does not initially find his allotted tasks easy, but does them nonetheless with utmost dedication.

Food for thought

1. Is a natural disaster any easier to bear than suffering inflicted by humans?

2. Why has God allowed such great suffering to happen to the people He loves?

3. When is a "curse" a blessing in disguise?

deuteronomy 28:59-68 — ki tavo'

and effective plagues, with sicknesses that are nasty and effective. ⁶⁰ He will bring back upon you all the diseases of Egypt of which you were terrified (when you saw the Egyptians suffer from them), and they will cling to you. ⁶¹ God will also bring upon you every disease and plague that is not written in this Torah scroll, to destroy you.

⁶² You will remain few in number, instead of being as numerous as the stars of the heavens as you once were, because you did not listen to God, your God. ⁶³ Then, just as God rejoiced over you to do good for you and to increase you, God will likewise make (your enemies) rejoice over you, annihilating you and destroying you. You will be uprooted from the land of which you are now entering to take possession. ⁶⁴ God will scatter you among all the nations, from one end of the earth to the other, and there you(r taxes) will (be used to) serve other gods unknown to you or your fathers, (gods of) wood and stone. ⁶⁵ You will not be at ease among those nations, nor will your foot find rest. There, God will give you a trembling heart, dashed hopes, and a suffering soul. ⁶⁶ Your life will hang in suspense before you. You will be frightened night and day, and you will not be certain of your life. ⁶⁷ (Things will constantly get worse, so) in the morning, you will say, "If only it were (yesterday) evening!" and in the evening, you will say, "If only it were (this) morning!"—because of the fear in your heart which you will experience and because of the things that you will see. ⁶⁸ God will return you to

"an abundance of everything," more than immense wealth and all the pleasures of this world (*Rabbi Isaac Luria, 16th century*).

kabbalah bites

28:1-69 While both parents must discipline their child, the mother will inevitably have more compassion and will not strike her child as hard as the father.

The first four books of the Torah derive from God's "masculine side." The fifth book, Deuteronomy, emanates from God's "feminine side." Thus, the "masculine" curses in Leviticus, while shorter in length, are more harsh than those found here in the "feminine" book of Deuteronomy.

The challenge of wealth poses a greater threat to religious and spiritual life than the challenge of poverty. Only by adopting the attitude of Rabbi Isaac Luria, that worshiping God means more to you than the pleasures and fortunes of this world, can you be assured to withstand the challenge of wealth (*Rabbi Judah Aryeh Leib Alter of Gur, 19th century*).

66. Your life will hang in suspense before you. You will be frightened night and day. Our life force, the energy which sustains our very existence, comes from God—specifically from His exalted four-lettered name, the Tetragrammaton.

"Your life will hang in suspense before you"—you should always envision the Tetragrammaton ("your life") before you; and then, *"you will be frightened"*—you will fear God, *"night and day"* (*Rabbi Moses Ḥayyim Ephraim of Sudylkow, 18th century*).

68. God will return you. The ultimate purpose of the admonition is to lead the Jewish people to repentance—

דברים כח:סח - כט:ח   כי תבוא

לְךָ לֹא־תֹסִיף עוֹד לִרְאֹתָהּ וְהִתְמַכַּרְתֶּם שָׁם לְאֹיְבֶיךָ לַעֲבָדִים וְלִשְׁפָחוֹת וְאֵין קֹנֶה: ס 69 אֵלֶּה דִבְרֵי הַבְּרִית אֲשֶׁר־צִוָּה יְהֹוָה אֶת־מֹשֶׁה לִכְרֹת אֶת־בְּנֵי יִשְׂרָאֵל בְּאֶרֶץ מוֹאָב מִלְּבַד הַבְּרִית אֲשֶׁר־כָּרַת אִתָּם בְּחֹרֵב: פ

כט 1 [SEVENTH READING] וַיִּקְרָא מֹשֶׁה אֶל־כָּל־יִשְׂרָאֵל וַיֹּאמֶר אֲלֵהֶם אַתֶּם רְאִיתֶם אֵת כָּל־אֲשֶׁר עָשָׂה יְהֹוָה לְעֵינֵיכֶם בְּאֶרֶץ מִצְרַיִם לְפַרְעֹה וּלְכָל־עֲבָדָיו וּלְכָל־אַרְצוֹ: 2 הַמַּסּוֹת הַגְּדֹלֹת אֲשֶׁר רָאוּ עֵינֶיךָ הָאֹתֹת וְהַמֹּפְתִים הַגְּדֹלִים הָהֵם: 3 וְלֹא־נָתַן יְהֹוָה לָכֶם לֵב לָדַעַת וְעֵינַיִם לִרְאוֹת וְאָזְנַיִם לִשְׁמֹעַ עַד הַיּוֹם הַזֶּה: 4 וָאוֹלֵךְ אֶתְכֶם אַרְבָּעִים שָׁנָה בַּמִּדְבָּר לֹא־בָלוּ שַׂלְמֹתֵיכֶם מֵעֲלֵיכֶם וְנַעַלְךָ לֹא־בָלְתָה מֵעַל רַגְלֶךָ: 5 לֶחֶם לֹא אֲכַלְתֶּם וְיַיִן וְשֵׁכָר לֹא שְׁתִיתֶם לְמַעַן תֵּדְעוּ כִּי אֲנִי יְהֹוָה אֱלֹהֵיכֶם: [MAFTIR] 6 וַתָּבֹאוּ אֶל־הַמָּקוֹם הַזֶּה וַיֵּצֵא סִיחֹן מֶלֶךְ־חֶשְׁבּוֹן וְעוֹג מֶלֶךְ־הַבָּשָׁן לִקְרָאתֵנוּ לַמִּלְחָמָה וַנַּכֵּם: 7 וַנִּקַּח אֶת־אַרְצָם וַנִּתְּנָהּ לְנַחֲלָה לָראוּבֵנִי וְלַגָּדִי וְלַחֲצִי שֵׁבֶט הַמְנַשִּׁי: 8 וּשְׁמַרְתֶּם אֶת־דִּבְרֵי הַבְּרִית הַזֹּאת וַעֲשִׂיתֶם אֹתָם לְמַעַן תַּשְׂכִּילוּ אֵת כָּל־אֲשֶׁר תַּעֲשׂוּן: פ פ פ

קכ״ב פסוקים, לעבדיי״ו סימן.

1232

spiritual vitamin

> Remember that you have the inner capacity and actual ability to transform yourself, in a short time, from one extreme to the other.

Egypt (in captivity) in ships, through the route about which I had said to you, "You will never see it again." There, you will offer yourselves for sale to your enemies as slaves and handmaids, but there will be no buyer.

⁶⁹ These are the words of the covenant, which God commanded Moses to make with the children of Israel in the land of Moab, besides the covenant of (curses) which He made with them in Horeb.

Moses' Final Address

29 [SEVENTH READING] ¹ Moses called all of Israel and said to them, "You have seen all that God did before your eyes in the land of Egypt, to Pharaoh, to all his servants, and to all his land, ² the great tests (of faith) which your eyes saw and those great signs (of God's direct involvement) and wondrous (plagues).

³ Until this day, God has not yet given you a heart to recognize (His true kindness), eyes to see (it) or ears to hear (it). ⁴ I led you through the desert for forty years, but your garments did not wear out from your (using them), nor did your shoes wear out from (being used by) your feet. ⁵ You did not eat bread, nor drink new wine or old wine, in order that you would know that I am God, your God.

[MAFTIR] ⁶ When you arrived at this place, King Sihon of Heshbon and King Og of Bashan came out towards us in battle, and we annihilated them. ⁷ We took their land, and we gave it as an inheritance to the tribes of Reuben and Gad, and to half the tribe of Manasseh.

⁸ (Since you have witnessed God's greatness), guard the words of this covenant and observe them, in order that you succeed in everything that you do.

The Haftarah for Ki Tavo' is on page 1405.

"But there will be no buyer"—Rashi explains: *"Because they will decree death and expiration upon you."* The penitent manages to "kill" his obsession with the pleasures of the world, and instead he yearns to "expire"—to become free from the shackles of physical existence and be one with God (*Rabbi Menahem Mendel Schneerson, 20th century*).

29:3 Until this day, God has not yet given you a heart to recognize. No person can appreciate the depths of his teacher's mind or the profundity of his teachings before forty years. Thus, the Omnipresent was not strict with you until this day, but from now on, He will be strict with you. Therefore, *"guard the words of this covenant, etc."* (v. 8; *Rashi, 11th century*).

We are **diverse** in so many ways, with our own **strengths** and **weaknesses;** but we are **equal at our core,** *"standing firmly (nitzavim) all of you together before God."* Discover the power of that **unified essence.**

NITZAVIM
נצבים

THE NATION ENTERS GOD'S COVENANT	29:9–28
INGATHERING OF THE EXILES FORETOLD	30:1–10
ACCESSIBILITY OF THE TORAH	30:11–14
CHARGE TO "CHOOSE LIFE"	30:15–20

NAME
Nitzavim

MEANING
"Standing firmly"

LINES IN TORAH SCROLL
72

PARASHIYYOT
1 open; 3 closed

VERSES
40

WORDS
657

LETTERS
2575

DATE
7 *Adar*, 2488

LOCATION
Plains of Moab

MITZVOT
None

MASORETIC FEATURES
Oversized *lamed* in the word *va-yashlikhem* (29:27). Eleven dots above the phrase *lanu u-le-vanenu 'ad* (29:28).

NOTE
Read the week before *Rosh Ha-Shanah*

CHARACTER PROFILE

NAME
Sodomites (29:22)

LOCATION
Jordan Valley, east of Bethel

ACHIEVEMENTS
Their country was totally independent, not relying on any imported goods; Abraham pleaded on their behalf to be saved from God's wrath; their sins caused the Divine Presence to depart to the Sixth Heaven; their sins came about due to inherent, bad character traits, not a heretical theology

KNOWN FOR
Punished by God, through Angel Gabriel, for their grievous sins of inhospitable behavior; a corrupt legal system; intolerance of charity; violent crime; extreme arrogance and autonomy. They were spiritually rooted in the realm of *tohu* (chaos), which is why they could not achieve *tikkun* (civilization)

ETERNAL BOND

God entered into an eternal bond with us all (29:12). Your road to self-discovery will inevitably lead to God.

RETURN

In the End of Days, all of us will return to God with heart and soul, and we will be gathered in from our worldwide dispersion. We will experience Divine guidance and success as a nation, and the Torah will be implemented as God originally intended (30:1-10).

A FEASIBLE TORAH

Since the Torah was given by the Creator of the universe, the world cannot present a true obstacle to its implementation. When you face a challenge, appeal to the Creator, forge ahead with determination—and you will succeed (30:11-14).

CHOOSE LIFE

Everything material fades, disintegrates, and dies. Only, God is the Source of all life. "Choosing life" means seeing the soul in each person, object and event, and basing your interaction on its spiritual potential (30:19-20).

נצבים | דברים כט:ט-יז

9 אַתֶּ֨ם נִצָּבִ֤ים הַיּוֹם֙ כֻּלְּכֶ֔ם לִפְנֵ֖י יְהֹוָ֣ה אֱלֹהֵיכֶ֑ם רָאשֵׁיכֶ֣ם שִׁבְטֵיכֶ֗ם זִקְנֵיכֶם֙ וְשֹׁ֣טְרֵיכֶ֔ם כֹּ֖ל אִ֥ישׁ יִשְׂרָאֵֽל: 10 טַפְּכֶ֣ם נְשֵׁיכֶ֔ם וְגֵ֣רְךָ֔ אֲשֶׁ֖ר בְּקֶ֣רֶב מַחֲנֶ֑יךָ מֵחֹטֵ֣ב עֵצֶ֔יךָ עַ֖ד שֹׁאֵ֥ב מֵימֶֽיךָ: 11 לְעָבְרְךָ֗ בִּבְרִ֛ית יְהֹוָ֥ה אֱלֹהֶ֖יךָ וּבְאָלָת֑וֹ אֲשֶׁר֙ יְהֹוָ֣ה אֱלֹהֶ֔יךָ כֹּרֵ֥ת עִמְּךָ֖ הַיּֽוֹם: [SECOND READING] 12 לְמַ֣עַן הָקִֽים־אֹתְךָ֩ הַיּ֨וֹם ׀ ל֜וֹ לְעָ֗ם וְה֤וּא יִֽהְיֶה־לְּךָ֙ לֵֽאלֹהִ֔ים כַּאֲשֶׁ֖ר דִּבֶּר־לָ֑ךְ וְכַאֲשֶׁ֤ר נִשְׁבַּע֙ לַאֲבֹתֶ֔יךָ לְאַבְרָהָ֥ם לְיִצְחָ֖ק וּֽלְיַעֲקֹֽב: 13 וְלֹ֥א אִתְּכֶ֖ם לְבַדְּכֶ֑ם אָנֹכִ֗י כֹּרֵת֙ אֶת־הַבְּרִ֣ית הַזֹּ֔את וְאֶת־הָאָלָ֖ה הַזֹּֽאת: 14 כִּי֩ אֶת־אֲשֶׁ֨ר יֶשְׁנ֜וֹ פֹּ֗ה עִמָּ֨נוּ֙ עֹמֵ֣ד הַיּ֔וֹם לִפְנֵ֖י יְהֹוָ֣ה אֱלֹהֵ֑ינוּ וְאֵ֨ת אֲשֶׁ֥ר אֵינֶ֛נּוּ פֹּ֖ה עִמָּ֥נוּ הַיּֽוֹם: [THIRD READING] 15 כִּֽי־אַתֶּ֣ם יְדַעְתֶּ֔ם אֵ֥ת אֲשֶׁר־יָשַׁ֖בְנוּ בְּאֶ֣רֶץ מִצְרָ֑יִם וְאֵ֧ת אֲשֶׁר־עָבַ֛רְנוּ בְּקֶ֥רֶב הַגּוֹיִ֖ם אֲשֶׁ֥ר עֲבַרְתֶּֽם: 16 וַתִּרְאוּ֙ אֶת־שִׁקּ֣וּצֵיהֶ֔ם וְאֵ֖ת גִּלֻּלֵיהֶ֑ם עֵ֣ץ וָאֶ֔בֶן כֶּ֥סֶף וְזָהָ֖ב אֲשֶׁ֥ר עִמָּהֶֽם: 17 פֶּן־יֵ֣שׁ בָּ֠כֶ֠ם אִ֣ישׁ אוֹ־אִשָּׁ֞ה א֧וֹ מִשְׁפָּחָ֣ה אוֹ־שֵׁ֗בֶט אֲשֶׁר֩ לְבָב֨וֹ פֹנֶ֤ה הַיּוֹם֙ מֵעִם֙ יְהֹוָ֣ה אֱלֹהֵ֔ינוּ לָלֶ֣כֶת לַעֲבֹ֔ד אֶת־אֱלֹהֵ֖י הַגּוֹיִ֣ם הָהֵ֑ם פֶּן־יֵ֣שׁ בָּכֶ֗ם

"You are standing firmly today"—you have angered God many times, but He has not destroyed you. And you see that you continue to exist before Him, *"today"*—just as this day exists.

Another explanation: Since the Jewish people were now passing from leader to leader, from Moses to Joshua, Moses brought them to a standing assembly, in order to encourage them (*Rashi, 11th century*).

The *"standing"* of the Jewish people follows the order of *"today,"* i.e., the day of Genesis, *"It became evening and it became morning—one day"* (*Genesis 1:5*). Just as in the Hebrew calendar the night precedes the day, so it is with the Jewish people. First there is persecution and exile, and then we will come to merit redemption and salvation (*Rabbi Eliezer Horowitz of Tarnogrod, 18th century*).

9-10. All of you together, the heads of your tribes ... to your water-drawers. At first glance, this declaration appears to harbor a contradiction: It begins by saying, *"You are standing firmly ... all of you together"* (without distinction); yet, it proceeds immediately to divide the people into various and separate categories, *"the heads of your tribes ... to your water-*

kabbalah bites

29:9 Rabbi Isaac Luria taught: "Any person who does not cry on Rosh Ha-Shanah and Yom Kippur has an imperfect soul." This, of course, does not refer to tears of sadness and depression, but tears of joy at the immense spiritual disclosure which occurs on these holy days—like Rabbi Akiva, who shed tears when secrets of the Torah were revealed to him by his teacher, Rabbi Eliezer.

parashat nitzavim

The Eternal Covenant with God

⁹ You are standing firmly today, all of you together, before God, your God—the heads of your tribes, your elders, your police officers (standing in front of) every Jewish person: ¹⁰ your young children, your women, and the converts within your camp (who were assigned positions ranging) from your woodcutters to your water-drawers— ¹¹ in order to bring you into the covenant of God, your God, and His oath which God, your God, is making with you today.

[SECOND READING] ¹² (This is) in order to establish you today as His people, that He will be your God, as He told you, and as He swore to your forefathers, to Abraham, Isaac, and Jacob (that He would never swap you for another nation).

¹³ I am not only making this covenant and this oath with you, ¹⁴ but with (both) those standing here with us today before God, our God, and with those (in future generations) who are not here with us today.

[THIRD READING] ¹⁵ For you know how we lived in the land of Egypt, and how we went among the nations, (and) as you went on your way, ¹⁶ you saw their disgusting and repugnant (idols of) wood and stone (in their streets, and their idols of) silver and gold which were (hidden in their houses) with them. ¹⁷ So perhaps there is among you a man, a woman, a family, or a tribe, whose heart is straying today from God, our God, (and does not want to enter into the covenant with Him, but would rather) go and worship the gods of those nations. Perhaps there is among you (a person growing in wickedness like) a root that is sprouting (bitter herbs, like)

29:9 You are standing firmly today. This teaches us that on the day he died, Moses assembled the Jewish people before God, to bring them into a covenant.

The Midrashic explanation is as follows: Why is this Torah portion juxtaposed with the admonition (the curses in the previous section)? Because when the Jewish people heard these ninety-eight curses, besides the forty-nine curses in Leviticus (26:14-39), their faces turned pale, and they said, "Who could withstand all these?" So Moses began to appease them, saying,

spiritual vitamin

> The ultimate purpose of Torah is not to increase our knowledge per se, but to instruct us to conduct our lives to the fullest advantage of both ourselves and the community at large. As a matter of course, it provides all the knowledge necessary for the attainment of this ultimate purpose.

דברים כט:יז-כז — נצבים

שֹׁ֣רֶשׁ פֹּרֶ֥ה רֹ֖אשׁ וְלַעֲנָֽה׃ 18 וְהָיָ֡ה בְּשָׁמְעוֹ֩ אֶת־דִּבְרֵ֨י הָאָלָ֜ה הַזֹּ֗את וְהִתְבָּרֵ֨ךְ בִּלְבָב֤וֹ לֵאמֹר֙ שָׁל֣וֹם יִֽהְיֶה־לִּ֔י כִּ֛י בִּשְׁרִר֥וּת לִבִּ֖י אֵלֵ֑ךְ לְמַ֛עַן סְפ֥וֹת הָרָוָ֖ה אֶת־הַצְּמֵאָֽה׃ 19 לֹא־יֹאבֶ֣ה יְהֹוָה֮ סְלֹ֣חַֽ לוֹ֒ כִּ֣י אָ֠ז יֶעְשַׁ֨ן אַף־יְהֹוָ֤ה וְקִנְאָתוֹ֙ בָּאִ֣ישׁ הַה֔וּא וְרָ֤בְצָה בּוֹ֙ כָּל־הָ֣אָלָ֔ה הַכְּתוּבָ֖ה בַּסֵּ֣פֶר הַזֶּ֑ה וּמָחָ֤ה יְהֹוָה֙ אֶת־שְׁמ֔וֹ מִתַּ֖חַת הַשָּׁמָֽיִם׃ 20 וְהִבְדִּיל֤וֹ יְהֹוָה֙ לְרָעָ֔ה מִכֹּ֖ל שִׁבְטֵ֣י יִשְׂרָאֵ֑ל כְּכֹל֙ אָל֣וֹת הַבְּרִ֔ית הַכְּתוּבָ֕ה בְּסֵ֥פֶר הַתּוֹרָ֖ה הַזֶּֽה׃ 21 וְאָמַ֞ר הַדּ֣וֹר הָאַחֲר֗וֹן בְּנֵיכֶם֙ אֲשֶׁ֤ר יָק֙וּמוּ֙ מֵאַ֣חֲרֵיכֶ֔ם וְהַ֨נָּכְרִ֔י אֲשֶׁ֥ר יָבֹ֖א מֵאֶ֣רֶץ רְחוֹקָ֑ה וְרָא֞וּ אֶת־מַכּ֤וֹת הָאָ֣רֶץ הַהִ֔וא וְאֶת־תַּחֲלֻאֶ֔יהָ אֲשֶׁר־חִלָּ֥ה יְהֹוָ֖ה בָּֽהּ׃ 22 גׇּפְרִ֣ית וָמֶ֘לַח֮ שְׂרֵפָ֣ה כׇל־אַרְצָהּ֒ לֹ֤א תִזָּרַע֙ וְלֹ֣א תַצְמִ֔חַ וְלֹא־יַעֲלֶ֥ה בָ֖הּ כׇּל־עֵ֑שֶׂב כְּמַהְפֵּכַ֞ת סְדֹ֤ם וַעֲמֹרָה֙ אַדְמָ֣ה [וּצְבֹיִ֔ם] וצביים כ׳ אֲשֶׁר֙ הָפַ֣ךְ יְהֹוָ֔ה בְּאַפּ֖וֹ וּבַחֲמָתֽוֹ׃ 23 וְאָֽמְרוּ֙ כׇּל־הַגּוֹיִ֔ם עַל־מֶ֨ה עָשָׂ֧ה יְהֹוָ֛ה כָּ֖כָה לָאָ֣רֶץ הַזֹּ֑את מֶ֥ה חֳרִ֛י הָאַ֥ף הַגָּד֖וֹל הַזֶּֽה׃ 24 וְאָ֣מְר֔וּ עַ֚ל אֲשֶׁ֣ר עָֽזְב֔וּ אֶת־בְּרִ֥ית יְהֹוָ֖ה אֱלֹהֵ֣י אֲבֹתָ֑ם אֲשֶׁר֙ כָּרַ֣ת עִמָּ֔ם בְּהוֹצִיא֥וֹ אֹתָ֖ם מֵאֶ֥רֶץ מִצְרָֽיִם׃ 25 וַיֵּלְכ֗וּ וַיַּֽעַבְדוּ֙ אֱלֹהִ֣ים אֲחֵרִ֔ים וַיִּֽשְׁתַּחֲו֖וּ לָהֶ֑ם אֱלֹהִים֙ אֲשֶׁ֣ר לֹֽא־יְדָע֔וּם וְלֹ֥א חָלַ֖ק לָהֶֽם׃ 26 וַיִּֽחַר־אַ֥ף יְהֹוָ֖ה בָּאָ֣רֶץ הַהִ֑וא לְהָבִ֤יא עָלֶ֙יהָ֙ אֶת־כׇּל־הַקְּלָלָ֔ה הַכְּתוּבָ֖ה בַּסֵּ֥פֶר הַזֶּֽה׃ 27 וַיִּתְּשֵׁ֤ם יְהֹוָה֙ מֵעַ֣ל אַדְמָתָ֔ם בְּאַ֥ף וּבְחֵמָ֖ה וּבְקֶ֣צֶף גָּד֑וֹל וַיַּשְׁלִכֵ֛ם אֶל־אֶ֥רֶץ אַחֶ֖רֶת כַּיּ֥וֹם הַזֶּֽה׃

23-27. All the nations will say, "Why did God do such a thing to this land?" It was God's goodwill that led Him to take out His anger on the land, its trees and stones, rather than on the people. Otherwise, the people might have been wiped out as a result of their sins.

This is the meaning of our passage: The nations will view the utter destruction of the land described in the previous verses (21 and 22) and they will wonder, *"Why did God do such a thing to the land? It is because they abandoned the covenant of God"* (v. 24). The people sinned against God, and they were deserving of annihilation. But God did not want to destroy His people, so He let out His wrath upon the land, *"God's fury raged against the land"* (v. 26). The people, therefore, survived *"to this day"* (v. 27; *Rabbi Eleazar b. Aryeh Leib Loew, 18th century*).

hemlock and wormwood, ¹⁸ such that when he hears the words of this oath, (he will think that they do not apply to him) and he will convince himself in his heart, saying, "I will be okay, even if I follow my heart's desires." (To such a person) I will add (to the punishment for his sins which were done inadvertently, as if) in a drunken stupor, (a further punishment for his sins done intentionally, out of a conscious) thirsting. ¹⁹ God will not be willing to forgive him! Rather, God's fury and His zeal will then fume against that man, and the entire curse written in this book will come down upon him, and God will obliterate his name from beneath the skies. ²⁰ God will single him out him from all the tribes of Israel for severe treatment, according to all the curses of the covenant, written in this Book of the Torah.

²¹ The later generation— your descendants, who will come after you, along with the foreigner who comes from a distant land—will say upon seeing the plagues of that land and the diseases with which God afflicted it: ²² Sulfur and salt have burned up their entire land! It cannot be sown. It is infertile, and not even grass will sprout upon it. It is like the overturning of Sodom, Gomorrah, Admah and Zeboiim, (the cities) which God overturned in His fury and rage. ²³ All the nations will say, "Why did God do such a thing to this land? What caused this great rage of fury? ²⁴ Then they will say, "It is because they abandoned the covenant of God, the God of their fathers, which He made with them when He took them out of the land of Egypt, ²⁵ For they went and served other gods, prostrating themselves to them—gods which they knew were devoid (of Divine power), and which He had not apportioned to them. ²⁶ God's fury raged against that land, bringing upon it the entire curse written in this book. ²⁷ God uprooted them from upon their land, with fury, anger and great wrath, and He cast them to another land, (where they are) to this day."

drawers." Besides, what is the purpose of enumerating the various classes of Jews, from the highest to the lowest, after they had already been all included in the general term *"all of you"*?

But here we find a basic rule, namely, that both go together: (a) *"all of you,"* all as one, and yet (b) at the same time, each individual, man or woman, has his or her specific contribution (*Rabbi Shneur Zalman of Lyady, 18ᵗʰ century*).

21. The foreigner who comes from a distant land. This is an allusion to Nero Caesar, who came from the distant land of Rome to destroy Jerusalem. The Talmud relates that upon reaching Jerusalem, Nero recognized that it is God who orchestrates all worldly affairs, and he fled, later converting to Judaism. Subsequently, the great Talmudic sage Rabbi Meir descended from him (*Babylonian Talmud, Gittin* 56a). To hint to this point, the first letters of the phrase *"who comes from a distant land"* (*'asher yavo' me-eretz rehokah*), combine to spell the name Meir [*m-a-y-r*] (*Rabbi Isaac Luria, 16ᵗʰ century*).

דברים כט:כח - ל:ה

28 הַנִּסְתָּרֹת לַיהוָה אֱלֹהֵינוּ וְהַנִּגְלֹת לָנוּ וּלְבָנֵינוּ עַד־עוֹלָם לַעֲשׂוֹת אֶת־כָּל־דִּבְרֵי הַתּוֹרָה הַזֹּאת: ס

ל [FOURTH READING / SECOND WHEN JOINED] 1 וְהָיָה כִי־יָבֹאוּ עָלֶיךָ כָּל־הַדְּבָרִים הָאֵלֶּה הַבְּרָכָה וְהַקְּלָלָה אֲשֶׁר נָתַתִּי לְפָנֶיךָ וַהֲשֵׁבֹתָ אֶל־לְבָבֶךָ בְּכָל־הַגּוֹיִם אֲשֶׁר הִדִּיחֲךָ יְהוָה אֱלֹהֶיךָ שָׁמָּה: 2 וְשַׁבְתָּ עַד־יְהוָה אֱלֹהֶיךָ וְשָׁמַעְתָּ בְקֹלוֹ כְּכֹל אֲשֶׁר־אָנֹכִי מְצַוְּךָ הַיּוֹם אַתָּה וּבָנֶיךָ בְּכָל־לְבָבְךָ וּבְכָל־נַפְשֶׁךָ: 3 וְשָׁב יְהוָה אֱלֹהֶיךָ אֶת־שְׁבוּתְךָ וְרִחֲמֶךָ וְשָׁב וְקִבֶּצְךָ מִכָּל־הָעַמִּים אֲשֶׁר הֱפִיצְךָ יְהוָה אֱלֹהֶיךָ שָׁמָּה: 4 אִם־יִהְיֶה נִדַּחֲךָ בִּקְצֵה הַשָּׁמָיִם מִשָּׁם יְקַבֶּצְךָ יְהוָה אֱלֹהֶיךָ וּמִשָּׁם יִקָּחֶךָ: 5 וֶהֱבִיאֲךָ יְהוָה אֱלֹהֶיךָ אֶל־הָאָרֶץ אֲשֶׁר־יָרְשׁוּ אֲבֹתֶיךָ

the Jewish people to survive despite so much persecution at the hands of many powerful oppressors. How could one solitary nation survive the nations of the world that wish to destroy her? This is a great display of God's awesomeness! (*Babylonian Talmud, Yoma* 69b).

When you reflect on this astonishing phenomenon, that the curse carries within it blessing, that even during the dark exile God's mercy is apparent as He ensures Israel's survival from the countless attempts at her annihilation—this will inevitably inspire you to *"return to God"* (v. 2; *Rabbi Abraham Samuel Benjamin Sofer, 19th century*).

So long as the Jewish people had not sinned, they did not attribute their blessings to observing the commandments; they only began to recognize the source of their blessings after they sinned and were punished. In order to return to God, you need to contemplate both *"the blessing and the curse which I have set before you"* (*Rabbi Ḥayyim ibn Attar, 18th century*).

kabbalah bites

30:2 We are at the dawn of a New Era of a flowering global consciousness and the *eradication of dysfunctional cognitive constraints*. As the dissonance of our minds dissolves, the *tikkun* (spiritual healing) of the world will be complete and God's presence will once again be felt on earth.

In previous generations, a mistake in one lifetime could always be corrected by reincarnation in a subsequent lifetime. But as we find ourselves at the end of history, there is simply no time for any more seventy-year incarnations. We desperately need to get it right this time around.

deuteronomy 29:28 – 30:5   nitzavim

[28] (If you will say, "Since this punishment will come on us even if an individual is harboring thoughts of idolatry, what hope is there for us?" My response is:) the hidden things (in a person's mind) are for God, our God, (to deal with privately), but the revealed things (where people's sins are known) are for us and for our children forever (to deal with, and enact justice), to fulfil all the words of this Torah.

Ingathering of the Exiles

30 [FOURTH READING / SECOND WHEN JOINED] [1] What will happen is, when all these things come upon you (while you are) among all the nations where God, your God, has banished you—the blessing and the curse which I have set before you—you will take it to your heart, [2] and you will return to God, your God, with all your heart and with all your soul. You will listen to His voice, to everything that I am commanding you today, you and your children. [3] Then, God, your God, will return your captives (from exile), and He will have mercy upon you. He will gather you again from all the nations, where God, your God, had dispersed you.

[4] Even if your exiles will be (on mountains reaching) the extremities of the skies, God, your God, will gather you from there, and He will take you from there.

[5] God, your God, will bring you to the land which your forefathers possessed, and you will take possession of it. He will be good to you, and He will make you more numerous than your forefathers.

---

28. The hidden things are for God, but the revealed things are for us. When will *"this day"* (v. 27) come? When will the darkness of this bitter exile pass, to be replaced by the light of the redemption?

This is not revealed to anyone—*"the hidden things are for God."*

What is revealed *"for us and for our children,"* is how to bring about this special time. And that is when we *"fulfil all the words of this Torah"* (*Rabbi Eleazar b. Aryeh Leib Loew, 18th century*).

30:1 When all these things come upon you ... the blessing and the curse ... you will take it to your heart. It is actually during a curse, when Jews are plagued by their oppressors, that a blessing is most apparent. God's blessing is His special care and providence that has enabled

spiritual vitamin

> It is impossible to describe the joys of the life of the soul in the world to come, for even in this world, while the soul is connected to the body, its life is on an infinitely higher plane than the body—how much more so when the soul is no longer enmeshed in the body!

נצבים | דברים ל:ה-יד

וִירִשְׁתָּהּ וְהֵיטִבְךָ וְהִרְבְּךָ מֵאֲבֹתֶיךָ: 6 וּמָל יְהֹוָה אֱלֹהֶיךָ אֶת־לְבָבְךָ וְאֶת־לְבַב זַרְעֶךָ לְאַהֲבָה אֶת־יְהֹוָה אֱלֹהֶיךָ בְּכָל־לְבָבְךָ וּבְכָל־נַפְשְׁךָ לְמַעַן חַיֶּיךָ: 7 [FIFTH READING / THIRD WHEN JOINED] וְנָתַן יְהֹוָה אֱלֹהֶיךָ אֵת כָּל־הָאָלוֹת הָאֵלֶּה עַל־אֹיְבֶיךָ וְעַל־שֹׂנְאֶיךָ אֲשֶׁר רְדָפוּךָ: 8 וְאַתָּה תָשׁוּב וְשָׁמַעְתָּ בְּקוֹל יְהֹוָה וְעָשִׂיתָ אֶת־כָּל־מִצְוֺתָיו אֲשֶׁר אָנֹכִי מְצַוְּךָ הַיּוֹם: 9 וְהוֹתִירְךָ יְהֹוָה אֱלֹהֶיךָ בְּכֹל | מַעֲשֵׂה יָדֶךָ בִּפְרִי בִטְנְךָ וּבִפְרִי בְהֶמְתְּךָ וּבִפְרִי אַדְמָתְךָ לְטוֹבָה כִּי | יָשׁוּב יְהֹוָה לָשׂוּשׂ עָלֶיךָ לְטוֹב כַּאֲשֶׁר־שָׂשׂ עַל־אֲבֹתֶיךָ: 10 כִּי תִשְׁמַע בְּקוֹל יְהֹוָה אֱלֹהֶיךָ לִשְׁמֹר מִצְוֺתָיו וְחֻקֹּתָיו הַכְּתוּבָה בְּסֵפֶר הַתּוֹרָה הַזֶּה כִּי תָשׁוּב אֶל־יְהֹוָה אֱלֹהֶיךָ בְּכָל־לְבָבְךָ וּבְכָל־נַפְשֶׁךָ: ס 11 [SIXTH READING] כִּי הַמִּצְוָה הַזֹּאת אֲשֶׁר אָנֹכִי מְצַוְּךָ הַיּוֹם לֹא־נִפְלֵאת הִוא מִמְּךָ וְלֹא־רְחֹקָה הִוא: 12 לֹא בַשָּׁמַיִם הִוא לֵאמֹר מִי יַעֲלֶה־לָּנוּ הַשָּׁמַיְמָה וְיִקָּחֶהָ לָּנוּ וְיַשְׁמִעֵנוּ אֹתָהּ וְנַעֲשֶׂנָּה: 13 וְלֹא־מֵעֵבֶר לַיָּם הִוא לֵאמֹר מִי יַעֲבָר־לָנוּ אֶל־עֵבֶר הַיָּם וְיִקָּחֶהָ לָּנוּ וְיַשְׁמִעֵנוּ אֹתָהּ וְנַעֲשֶׂנָּה: 14 כִּי־קָרוֹב אֵלֶיךָ הַדָּבָר מְאֹד בְּפִיךָ וּבִלְבָבְךָ לַעֲשֹׂתוֹ: ס

14. This thing is very near to you. A fisherman attempted to justify his disregard for Torah study to the prophet Elijah by claiming that God had not endowed him with sufficient intellectual ability. Elijah said to him, "Hasn't God given you enough intelligence to gather flax, weave nets and catch fish? Why shouldn't you have enough intelligence to understand the Torah about which it is written, *'This thing is very near to you'*? (*Tanna de-Vei Eliyahu*).

The fisherman claimed that he had never been shown the path to God and His Torah, so how could he be expected to reach there on his own? Elijah explained to him that although he was not born a fisherman, the need to earn a livelihood had forced him to learn the trade. In the same way, if he would feel the intense necessity for Torah study in order to provide a "livelihood" for his soul, he would apply himself and succeed (*Rabbi Menahem Mendel Morgensztern of Kotsk, 19th century*).

The statement that *"this thing is very near to you … in your heart,"* seems contrary to our experience, that it is simply *not* a "very near thing" to transform your heart's desires from wanting worldly pleasures

Food for thought

1. What does it mean that the Torah is "very near"?

2. Why did God entrust mortals with determining religious law?

3. Do you find it empowering that God entrusted His law in our hands?

deuteronomy 30:6–14 — nitzavim

⁶ God, your God, will "circumcise" your heart and the heart of your children, (enabling you) to love God, your God, with all your heart and with all your soul, for the sake of your life.

[FIFTH READING / THIRD WHEN JOINED] ⁷ God, your God, will place all these curses upon your enemies and upon those who hate you, who have pursued you. ⁸ You will return and listen to the voice of God, and fulfil all His commandments, which I am commanding you today. ⁹ God, your God, will give you prosperity in all the work of your hands, the fruit of your womb, the fruit of your livestock, and the fruit of your soil—for God will, once again, rejoice over you, being good (to you), as He rejoiced over (being good to) your fathers. ¹⁰ For then you will listen to the voice of God, your God, to observe His commandments and His suprarational commands written in this Torah scroll, (and) you will then return to God, your God, with all your heart and with all your soul.

Accessibility of the Torah

[SIXTH READING] ¹¹ For this (body of) commandment(s) which I am commanding you this day, is not concealed from you, nor is it far away. ¹² It is not in the skies, that you should say, "Who will go up to the skies for us and take it for us, to tell it to us, so that we can keep it?" ¹³ Nor is it across the sea, that you should say, "Who will cross the other side of the sea for us and fetch it for us, to tell it to us, so that we can keep it?" ¹⁴ Rather, this thing is very near to you, in your mouth and in your heart, to observe it.

---

6. God, your God, will "circumcise" your heart. God will empower the Jewish people to serve Him, not only out of fear, but out of love, as the verse stresses, *"God, your God, will circumcise your heart and the heart of your children, to love God, your God, with all your heart and with all your soul."* Since you can only serve God out of love and joy when not threatened by your enemies, the Torah continues, *"God, your God, will place all these curses upon your enemies and upon those that hate you, who have pursued you"* (v. 7; *Rabbi Ephraim of Luntshits, 16ᵗʰ–17ᵗʰ century*).

In the future era, to which this verse refers, God will totally eliminate the existence of impurity and evil, and consequently, the evil impulse will cease to exist. This is the meaning of the statement, *"God will circumcise your heart"* (*Naḥmanides, 13ᵗʰ century*).

Your heart and the heart, etc. The first letters of the words *"your heart and the heart"* (*'et levavekha ve-'et levav*) are *alef-lamed-vav-lamed*, which spell the word *Elul*, the final month of the Jewish calendar during which we rise early in the morning to recite *seliḥot* (penitential prayers). From this it follows that the predominant theme of the month of *Elul* is repentance (*Rabbi Jacob b. Asher, 14ᵗʰ century*).

12. It is not in the skies. The Torah is not to be found with those who think that they have reached the highest of the heavens (*Babylonian Talmud, Eruvin 55a*).

It is clearly explained in the Torah that its commandments are eternal and cannot be changed. The verse, *"It is not in the skies,"* teaches us that it is no longer the prerogative of any prophet to introduce a new part of the Torah (*Maimonides, 12ᵗʰ century*).

נצבים / דברים ל:טו-כ

15 רְאֵה נָתַתִּי לְפָנֶיךָ הַיּוֹם אֶת־הַחַיִּים וְאֶת־הַטּוֹב [SEVENTH READING AND MAFTIR / FOURTH WHEN JOINED] וְאֶת־הַמָּוֶת וְאֶת־הָרָע: 16 אֲשֶׁר אָנֹכִי מְצַוְּךָ הַיּוֹם לְאַהֲבָה אֶת־יְהֹוָה אֱלֹהֶיךָ לָלֶכֶת בִּדְרָכָיו וְלִשְׁמֹר מִצְוֹתָיו וְחֻקֹּתָיו וּמִשְׁפָּטָיו וְחָיִיתָ וְרָבִיתָ וּבֵרַכְךָ יְהֹוָה אֱלֹהֶיךָ בָּאָרֶץ אֲשֶׁר־אַתָּה בָא־שָׁמָּה לְרִשְׁתָּהּ: 17 וְאִם־יִפְנֶה לְבָבְךָ וְלֹא תִשְׁמָע וְנִדַּחְתָּ וְהִשְׁתַּחֲוִיתָ לֵאלֹהִים אֲחֵרִים וַעֲבַדְתָּם: 18 הִגַּדְתִּי לָכֶם הַיּוֹם כִּי אָבֹד תֹּאבֵדוּן לֹא־תַאֲרִיכֻן יָמִים עַל־הָאֲדָמָה אֲשֶׁר אַתָּה עֹבֵר אֶת־הַיַּרְדֵּן לָבוֹא שָׁמָּה לְרִשְׁתָּהּ: 19 הַעִדֹתִי בָכֶם הַיּוֹם אֶת־הַשָּׁמַיִם וְאֶת־הָאָרֶץ הַחַיִּים וְהַמָּוֶת נָתַתִּי לְפָנֶיךָ הַבְּרָכָה וְהַקְּלָלָה וּבָחַרְתָּ בַּחַיִּים לְמַעַן תִּחְיֶה אַתָּה וְזַרְעֶךָ: 20 לְאַהֲבָה אֶת־יְהֹוָה אֱלֹהֶיךָ לִשְׁמֹעַ בְּקֹלוֹ וּלְדָבְקָה־בוֹ כִּי הוּא חַיֶּיךָ וְאֹרֶךְ יָמֶיךָ לָשֶׁבֶת עַל־הָאֲדָמָה אֲשֶׁר נִשְׁבַּע יְהֹוָה לַאֲבֹתֶיךָ לְאַבְרָהָם לְיִצְחָק וּלְיַעֲקֹב לָתֵת לָהֶם: פ פ פ

מ' פסוקים, לבב"ו סימן.

much to be desired, then you should turn over a new leaf today. And if you led a virtuous life until today, that will not automatically make you a good person tomorrow. Each new day brings new choices. Each day places you at a crossroads, and each day you must endeavor to *"choose life"* (v. 19; *Rabbi Moses Feinstein, 20th century*).

19-20. Choose life! ... to listen to His voice, and to cleave to Him. These two verses are connected: Choose life *so that you will be able to worship God*. Unlike those who live life only for personal indulgence, the purpose of your life should be to worship God (*Rabbi Eleazar b. Aryeh Leib Loew, 18th century*).

spiritual vitamin

> The Torah that we have and cherish is God-given, and it contains not only our way of life, but also the key to our existence for all times, since it is eternal, as its Giver. It is not a book of theory, philosophy and speculation, but a practical guide for our daily life, valid in all places and at all times, including 21st century America.

deuteronomy 30:15–20 — nitzavim

Choosing Good

[SEVENTH READING AND MAFTIR / FOURTH WHEN JOINED] **15** See! I have given you today (a choice of) life and good, or death and evil! **16** For I am commanding you today to love God, your God, to walk in His ways, and to observe His commandments, His suprarational commands, and His rational commands, so that you will live and prosper. God, your God, will then bless you in the land to which you are coming to take possession.

17 But if your heart strays and you do not listen, and you turn away and prostrate yourself to other gods and serve them, **18** I am declaring to you today, that you will definitely perish! You will not live a long time on the land, which you are crossing via the Jordan, to come and take possession.

19 I am calling upon the heaven and the earth (which are eternal) as witnesses against you! I have set before you (a choice of) life or death, blessing or curse. Choose life! Then you and your children will live, **20** to love God, your God, to listen to His voice, and to cleave to Him—for He is your life and the length of your days—to live on the land which God swore to your fathers to Abraham, Isaac, and Jacob, to give to them.

The *Haftarah* for *Nitzavim* is on page 1407.

---

kabbalah bites

30:19 Free choice is granted to us from the Tetragrammaton (*HaVaYaH*), God's four-letter ineffable name, and not from the name *Elokim*. When God follows the laws of metaphysics that He has made, we call Him *Elokim*. When He breaks those rules, *Havayah* is at play.

According to the laws of metaphysics, no created being may have free choice because we are all governed by the network of higher spiritual forces in which we are enmeshed. So when God broke that rule, empowering us with the ability to makes choices that are utterly free and independent from external forces, He was expressing himself through His ineffable, "essential" name.

And this is the inner reason why we speak of the Torah, which challenges us to exercise our choice of good over evil, as the "four cubits of law" (*Babylonian Talmud, Berakhot* 8a). Because our ability to choose to observe the law is empowered by God's four-lettered name.

---

to a sincere love of God. Yet we believe the Torah is eternally relevant.

The answer is that the words *"to observe it"* at the end of the verse qualify what is written at the beginning of the verse: *We are speaking here only of a love sufficient to bring about the practical observance of the commandments.*

This really is "very near" and easy for any person who has a brain inside his skull. Your mind *is* under your control, and you are free to think about whatever you please, on any subject. So when you will use your mind to think about the greatness of God, you will inevitably generate—in your mind, at least—a love of God, sufficient to make you want to connect to Him through the performance of His commandments and the study of His Torah (*Rabbi Shneur Zalman of Lyady, 18th century*).

15. I have given you today (a choice of) life and good. Why must this choice be given "today"? If, in the past, your life left

Va-Yelekh means "he went," indicating **movement,** the **hallmark of vitality** and life. Be firm in **your principles,** but always seek to grow. **Hold to truth** without compromise, but **always seek to expand.**

VA-YELEKH

וילך

MOSES CONCLUDES HIS FINAL MESSAGE	31:1–8
MOSES WRITES A TORAH SCROLL	31:9
LAWS OF *HAKHEL*	31:10–13
GOD'S TESTIMONY FOR THE FUTURE	31:14–23
MOSES' SCROLL IS PLACED WITH THE HOLY ARK	31:24–27
ELDERS GATHER TO HEAR *SONG OF HA'AZINU*	31:28–30

NAME
Va-Yelekh

MEANING
"He went"

LINES IN TORAH SCROLL
72

PARASHIYYOT
2 open; 1 closed

VERSES
30

WORDS
553

LETTERS
2123

DATE
7 Adar, 2488

LOCATION
Plains of Moab

KEY PEOPLE
Moses, Joshua, the Levites, the tribal elders and officers

MITZVOT
2 positive

NOTE
Read the week before *Rosh Ha-Shanah* together with the portion of *Nitzavim,* or alone, after *Rosh Ha-Shanah*

CHARACTER PROFILE

NAME
Joshua ("May God save you"); formerly, Hoshea

FATHER
Nun (tribe of Ephraim)

WIFE
Rahab

CHILDREN
Daughters; no sons

DEATH
Aged 110

ACHIEVEMENTS
Accompanied Moses part of the way up Mount Sinai; commander at battle against Amalek; successor to Moses; one of the twelve spies who was not corrupted; led the Israelite tribes in the conquest of Canaan and allocated land to the tribes; authored Book of Joshua

KNOWN FOR
Loyal discipleship; manna fell on his body, and he would eat it; circumcised the Israelites in Egypt; said six things that displeased Moses

COURAGEOUS LEADERSHIP

God urges Moses' successor, Joshua, to be a courageous leader, with a strong backbone. Joshua was appointed because of his enthusiasm, loyalty and faith (31:1-8).

MESSAGE FOR EVERYONE

Every seven years, the entire nation would gather in Jerusalem to hear the king read from a Torah scroll. Men, women, and children participated (31:10-13). The Torah has a message for every person, regardless of age or circumstance.

DIVINE ECLIPSE

When God "hides His face" (31:16-18), it is to spur us to strengthen our bond with Him. When that goal is reached, great revelation follows.

TORAH SCROLL

The charge to write a Torah scroll applies to all Jews. God's message is not the property of an elite or initiated segment, but the heritage of each member of our nation (31:19).

דברים לא:א-ח

וילך

א 1 וַיֵּלֶךְ מֹשֶׁה וַיְדַבֵּר אֶת־הַדְּבָרִים הָאֵלֶּה אֶל־כָּל־יִשְׂרָאֵל: 2 וַיֹּאמֶר אֲלֵהֶם בֶּן־מֵאָה וְעֶשְׂרִים שָׁנָה אָנֹכִי הַיּוֹם לֹא־אוּכַל עוֹד לָצֵאת וְלָבוֹא וַיהֹוָה אָמַר אֵלַי לֹא תַעֲבֹר אֶת־הַיַּרְדֵּן הַזֶּה: 3 יְהֹוָה אֱלֹהֶיךָ הוּא | עֹבֵר לְפָנֶיךָ הוּא־יַשְׁמִיד אֶת־הַגּוֹיִם הָאֵלֶּה מִלְּפָנֶיךָ וִירִשְׁתָּם יְהוֹשֻׁעַ הוּא עֹבֵר לְפָנֶיךָ כַּאֲשֶׁר דִּבֶּר יְהֹוָה: 4 [SECOND READING] וְעָשָׂה יְהֹוָה לָהֶם כַּאֲשֶׁר עָשָׂה לְסִיחוֹן וּלְעוֹג מַלְכֵי הָאֱמֹרִי וּלְאַרְצָם אֲשֶׁר הִשְׁמִיד אֹתָם: 5 וּנְתָנָם יְהֹוָה לִפְנֵיכֶם וַעֲשִׂיתֶם לָהֶם כְּכָל־הַמִּצְוָה אֲשֶׁר צִוִּיתִי אֶתְכֶם: 6 חִזְקוּ וְאִמְצוּ אַל־תִּירְאוּ וְאַל־תַּעַרְצוּ מִפְּנֵיהֶם כִּי | יְהֹוָה אֱלֹהֶיךָ הוּא הַהֹלֵךְ עִמָּךְ לֹא יַרְפְּךָ וְלֹא יַעַזְבֶךָּ: ס 7 [THIRD READING / FIFTH WHEN JOINED] וַיִּקְרָא מֹשֶׁה לִיהוֹשֻׁעַ וַיֹּאמֶר אֵלָיו לְעֵינֵי כָל־יִשְׂרָאֵל חֲזַק וֶאֱמָץ כִּי אַתָּה תָּבוֹא אֶת־הָעָם הַזֶּה אֶל־הָאָרֶץ אֲשֶׁר נִשְׁבַּע יְהֹוָה לַאֲבֹתָם לָתֵת לָהֶם וְאַתָּה תַּנְחִילֶנָּה אוֹתָם: 8 וַיהֹוָה הוּא | הַהֹלֵךְ

---

leadership, the conquest would have been instant and miraculous. Under Joshua, however, the Jewish people were required to conquer the land within the confines of nature, with the tremendous courage and self-sacrifice which that involves.

Nevertheless, this was not in fact a disadvantage, but to the contrary, it was for the overall good. The purpose of creation is to make "a home for God in the lowest realms" by human effort *within an everyday setting*. Miracles are generally counterproductive to this goal, as they serve to *impose* spirituality on the world, rather than letting the "lowest realms" develop a spiritual sensitivity *for themselves*.

So, ultimately, the non-miraculous entry into the land via Joshua fulfilled the purpose of creation to a greater extent (*Rabbi Dov Baer Schneuri of Lubavitch, 19th century*).

7. Moses called Joshua and said to him in the presence of all Israel, "Be strong and courageous!" The cantillation marks for this verse link the phrase "in the presence of all Israel" with "Be strong and courageous!" This implies: "Be strong and courageous while

kabbalah bites

31:2 Literally, Moses said, "*I can no more go out and come in.*" To pass from one level of spiritual maturity and insight to a truly superior one requires a paradigm shift, a fundamental change in outlook. You first "go out" of your current paradigm, and only then is it possible to "come into" a new one.

At the end of his life Moses exclaimed, "*I can no more go out and come in.*" I have reached the limits of human perception. I have ascended the forty-nine gates of wisdom. If I reached the fiftieth I would know the mind of God, and that is impossible.

deuteronomy 31:1–8 — va-yelekh

parashat va-yelekh

The Appointment of Joshua

31 [1] Moses went, and he spoke the following words to all Israel. [2] He said to them, "Today I am one hundred and twenty years old. I am no longer (permitted by God) to lead (you) out (to war) and bring (you) back (safely again, even though I am physically capable of doing so, because) God said to me, "You may not cross this (river) Jordan."

[3] It is God, your God, who will take you across the Jordan. He will destroy these nations before you so that you will take possession of their (lands. And) it is Joshua who will lead you across, as God has said. [SECOND READING] [4] God will do to them what He did to the Amorite kings, Sihon and Og, and to their land when He destroyed them. [5] God will deliver them to you, and you should do to them in accordance with all the commandment(s) that I have instructed you.

[6] Be strong and courageous! Do not be afraid or dismayed because of them! For God, your God, is the One who is going with you. He will not loosen (his hold on) you and forsake you!"

[THIRD READING / FIFTH WHEN JOINED] [7] Moses called Joshua and said to him in the presence of all Israel, "Be strong and courageous! For you will come with this people to the land which God swore to their fathers to give them, and you will apportion it to them as an inheritance. [8] It is God who will lead you forward. He will be with you. He will not loosen (His hold on) you and forsake you. Do not be afraid or dismayed."

31:1 Moses went. Moses went quickly throughout the entire Jewish camp to prove that his leadership was not ending due to physical weakness, but because he had not been granted permission by God to continue (*Rabbi Ephraim of Luntshits, 16th–17th century*).

Before a person passes away, his spirit leaves him. The verse implies that "the spirit of Moses went" (*Rabbi Ḥayyim ibn Attar, 18th century*).

"Moses went" to Abraham, Isaac and Jacob, who are mentioned in the previous verse, to inform them that God was fulfilling His promise to bring the Jewish people to the land of Israel (*Rabbi Jacob b. Asher, 14th century*).

Moses went, and he spoke the following words to all Israel. Each of us has a spark of Moses' spirit that awakens us to connect to God in a palpable way. The sowing of this "spark" is hinted to here: *"Moses went ... to all Israel"*—Moses imparted a portion of his own spirit into every soul of Israel. Perhaps this is why *"no person knows the place of his burial"* (below, 34:6), because, in fact, Moses is enshrined within all of our hearts (*Rabbi Alexander Zusya Friedman, 20th century*).

3. It is Joshua who will lead you across. At first glance, the transfer of leadership from Moses to Joshua represented a weakening of the strength of the Jewish people, as our Sages taught: *"Moses' face was like that of the sun. Joshua's face was like that of the moon"* (*Babylonian Talmud, Bava Batra* 75a). If the people had merited to enter the land of Israel under Moses'

דברים לא:ח-טו

לְפָנֶ֔יךָ ה֚וּא יִהְיֶ֣ה עִמָּ֔ךְ לֹ֥א יַרְפְּךָ֖ וְלֹ֣א יַעַזְבֶ֑ךָּ לֹ֥א תִירָ֖א וְלֹ֥א תֵחָֽת׃ 9 וַיִּכְתֹּ֣ב מֹשֶׁ֘ה אֶת־הַתּוֹרָ֣ה הַזֹּאת֒ וַֽיִּתְּנָ֗הּ אֶל־הַכֹּהֲנִים֙ בְּנֵ֣י לֵוִ֔י הַנֹּ֣שְׂאִ֔ים אֶת־אֲר֖וֹן בְּרִ֣ית יְהֹוָ֑ה וְאֶל־כׇּל־זִקְנֵ֖י יִשְׂרָאֵֽל׃ 10 [FOURTH READING] וַיְצַ֥ו מֹשֶׁ֖ה אוֹתָ֣ם לֵאמֹ֑ר מִקֵּ֣ץ ׀ שֶׁ֣בַע שָׁנִ֗ים בְּמֹעֵ֛ד שְׁנַ֥ת הַשְּׁמִטָּ֖ה בְּחַ֥ג הַסֻּכּֽוֹת׃ 11 בְּב֣וֹא כׇל־יִשְׂרָאֵ֗ל לֵרָאוֹת֙ אֶת־פְּנֵי֙ יְהֹוָ֣ה אֱלֹהֶ֔יךָ בַּמָּק֖וֹם אֲשֶׁ֣ר יִבְחָ֑ר תִּקְרָ֞א אֶת־הַתּוֹרָ֥ה הַזֹּ֛את נֶ֥גֶד כׇּל־יִשְׂרָאֵ֖ל בְּאׇזְנֵיהֶֽם׃ 12 הַקְהֵ֣ל אֶת־הָעָ֗ם הָֽאֲנָשִׁ֤ים וְהַנָּשִׁים֙ וְהַטַּ֔ף וְגֵרְךָ֖ אֲשֶׁ֣ר בִּשְׁעָרֶ֑יךָ לְמַ֨עַן יִשְׁמְע֜וּ וּלְמַ֣עַן יִלְמְד֗וּ וְיָֽרְאוּ֙ אֶת־יְהֹוָ֣ה אֱלֹֽהֵיכֶ֔ם וְשָֽׁמְר֣וּ לַעֲשׂ֔וֹת אֶת־כׇּל־דִּבְרֵ֖י הַתּוֹרָ֥ה הַזֹּֽאת׃ 13 וּבְנֵיהֶ֞ם אֲשֶׁ֣ר לֹֽא־יָדְע֗וּ יִשְׁמְעוּ֙ וְלָ֣מְד֔וּ לְיִרְאָ֖ה אֶת־יְהֹוָ֣ה אֱלֹהֵיכֶ֑ם כׇּל־הַיָּמִ֗ים אֲשֶׁ֨ר אַתֶּ֤ם חַיִּים֙ עַל־הָ֣אֲדָמָ֔ה אֲשֶׁ֨ר אַתֶּ֜ם עֹבְרִ֧ים אֶת־הַיַּרְדֵּ֛ן שָׁ֖מָּה לְרִשְׁתָּֽהּ׃ פ 14 [FIFTH READING / SIXTH WHEN JOINED] וַיֹּ֨אמֶר יְהֹוָ֜ה אֶל־מֹשֶׁ֗ה הֵ֣ן קָרְב֣וּ יָמֶ֘יךָ֮ לָמוּת֒ קְרָ֣א אֶת־יְהוֹשֻׁ֗עַ וְהִֽתְיַצְּב֛וּ בְּאֹ֥הֶל מוֹעֵ֖ד וַאֲצַוֶּ֑נּוּ וַיֵּ֤לֶךְ מֹשֶׁה֙ וִיהוֹשֻׁ֔עַ וַיִּֽתְיַצְּב֖וּ בְּאֹ֥הֶל מוֹעֵֽד׃ 15 וַיֵּרָ֧א יְהֹוָ֛ה בָּאֹ֖הֶל

וילך

12. Assemble the people—the men, the women, and the minors. Why do the small children come when they are still too young to listen and learn? In order to reward those who bring them (*Babylonian Talmud, Ḥagigah* 3a).

This serves as the basis for the practice of bringing young children to the synagogue (*The Tosafists, 12th–14th centuries*).

Going to the trouble of bringing even young children to synagogue demonstrates the parents' sincere aspirations for their children to become imbued with the Torah's spirit and remain committed to Judaism. As a result, God will reward them with success in their efforts, and they will merit to reap much joy and satisfaction from their children's Jewish upbringing (*Rabbi Judah Aryeh Leib Alter of Gur, 19th century*).

When Rabbi Joshua was informed of this teaching, about bringing small children to the *Hakhel* gathering, he remarked "You had such a precious gem in your hands and you wished to withhold it from me!" (*Babylonian Talmud, Ḥagigah* 3a).

When Rabbi Joshua was an infant, his mother would bring him to the study hall in his bassinet so that his ears would absorb the Torah (*Jerusalem Talmud, Yevamot* 1:6). Since Rabbi Joshua himself was greatly influenced by this early form of education, the "osmosis" of Torah as a young child, it is no wonder why this particular teaching was so dear to him (*Rabbi Meir Simhah of Dvinsk, 19th–20th century*).

deuteronomy 31:9–15 — va-yelekh

⁹ Then Moses wrote down this (entire) Torah, and gave it to the priests, (on behalf of) the descendants of Levi, who carry the Ark of God's Covenant, and to all the elders of the Jewish people (on behalf of the Jewish people).

The Command to Assemble the Nation [Hakhel]

[FOURTH READING] ¹⁰ Moses commanded them, saying: "At the end of seven years (in the year following) the sabbatical year, during the holiday on the Festival of Tabernacles, ¹¹ when all Israel comes to appear before God, your God, in the place that He will choose:

- ❖ (The king) should read this Torah before all of Israel, in their ears.
- ❖ ¹² Assemble the people—the men, the women, and the minors, and the convert in your cities—in order that they will hear, and in order that they will learn and fear God, your God, and be careful to observe all the words of this Torah. ¹³ Their children, who do not understand, will hear and learn to fear God, your God, all the days that you live on the land, of which you are crossing the Jordan to take possession.

Moses is Informed of the Events after his Passing

[FIFTH READING / SIXTH WHEN JOINED] ¹⁴ God said to Moses, "The time is now approaching for you to die. Call Joshua and stand in the Tent of Meeting, and I will encourage him."

Moses and Joshua went, and stood in the Tent of Meeting. ¹⁵ God appeared in the Tent, in a pillar of cloud, and the pillar of cloud stood at the entrance to the Tent.

---

in the presence of all Israel!" When others look to you for guidance, you need to display an aura of strength and courage (*Rabbi Samuel Bornstein of Sochaczew, 20th century*).

spiritual vitamin

> The common denominator that binds all Jews together, and serves as the basis for Jewish survival, cannot be considered in terms of territory, language or other cultural and social factors, since all these have changed over the course of history. The only things that have not changed in Jewish life are Sabbath observance, kosher food, *tefillin*, and all the other commandments of the Torah, both the Written Torah and the Oral Torah. The more your daily life and conduct adheres to this pattern of Jewish living, the more you are attached to the Jewish people.

דברים לא:טו-כב · וילך

בְּעַמּוּד עָנָן וַיַּעֲמֹד עַמּוּד הֶעָנָן עַל־פֶּתַח הָאֹהֶל: 16 וַיֹּאמֶר יְהֹוָה אֶל־מֹשֶׁה הִנְּךָ שֹׁכֵב עִם־אֲבֹתֶיךָ וְקָם הָעָם הַזֶּה וְזָנָה ׀ אַחֲרֵי ׀ אֱלֹהֵי נֵכַר־הָאָרֶץ אֲשֶׁר הוּא בָא־שָׁמָּה בְּקִרְבּוֹ וַעֲזָבַנִי וְהֵפֵר אֶת־בְּרִיתִי אֲשֶׁר כָּרַתִּי אִתּוֹ: 17 וְחָרָה אַפִּי בוֹ בַיּוֹם־הַהוּא וַעֲזַבְתִּים וְהִסְתַּרְתִּי פָנַי מֵהֶם וְהָיָה לֶאֱכֹל וּמְצָאֻהוּ רָעוֹת רַבּוֹת וְצָרוֹת וְאָמַר בַּיּוֹם הַהוּא הֲלֹא עַל כִּי־אֵין אֱלֹהַי בְּקִרְבִּי מְצָאוּנִי הָרָעוֹת הָאֵלֶּה: 18 וְאָנֹכִי הַסְתֵּר אַסְתִּיר פָּנַי בַּיּוֹם הַהוּא עַל כָּל־הָרָעָה אֲשֶׁר עָשָׂה כִּי פָנָה אֶל־אֱלֹהִים אֲחֵרִים: 19 וְעַתָּה כִּתְבוּ לָכֶם אֶת־הַשִּׁירָה הַזֹּאת וְלַמְּדָהּ אֶת־בְּנֵי־יִשְׂרָאֵל שִׂימָהּ בְּפִיהֶם לְמַעַן תִּהְיֶה־לִּי הַשִּׁירָה הַזֹּאת לְעֵד בִּבְנֵי יִשְׂרָאֵל: 20 [SIXTH READING / SEVENTH WHEN JOINED] כִּי־אֲבִיאֶנּוּ אֶל־הָאֲדָמָה ׀ אֲשֶׁר־נִשְׁבַּעְתִּי לַאֲבֹתָיו זָבַת חָלָב וּדְבַשׁ וְאָכַל וְשָׂבַע וְדָשֵׁן וּפָנָה אֶל־אֱלֹהִים אֲחֵרִים וַעֲבָדוּם וְנִאֲצוּנִי וְהֵפֵר אֶת־בְּרִיתִי: 21 וְהָיָה כִּי־תִמְצֶאןָ אֹתוֹ רָעוֹת רַבּוֹת וְצָרוֹת וְעָנְתָה הַשִּׁירָה הַזֹּאת לְפָנָיו לְעֵד כִּי לֹא תִשָּׁכַח מִפִּי זַרְעוֹ כִּי יָדַעְתִּי אֶת־יִצְרוֹ אֲשֶׁר הוּא עֹשֶׂה הַיּוֹם בְּטֶרֶם אֲבִיאֶנּוּ אֶל־הָאָרֶץ אֲשֶׁר נִשְׁבָּעְתִּי: 22 וַיִּכְתֹּב מֹשֶׁה אֶת־הַשִּׁירָה הַזֹּאת בַּיּוֹם הַהוּא וַיְלַמְּדָהּ אֶת־בְּנֵי יִשְׂרָאֵל:

19. Now, write for yourselves this song. It is a positive command for every Jewish man to write a Torah scroll for himself, as the verse states, *"Now, write for yourselves this song,"* meaning to say, "write for yourselves a Torah which contains this song," for a Torah consisting of separate scrolls is invalid. If a person writes one with his own hand, it is as if he received the Torah scroll from Mount Sinai (*Maimonides, 12th century*).

Since the theme of this precept is to facilitate Torah study—*"teach it to the children of Israel; place it into their mouths"*—therefore, for future generations, this commandment also includes the purchase of texts of the Oral Law, such as the Mishnah and Talmud (*Rabbi Asher b. Jehiel, 13th–14th century*).

Write for yourselves. This Torah portion contains two commandments: (1) *Hakhel*—Gathering the entire people in Jerusalem after the Sabbatical year to hear the king read from the Torah (verses 10-13); and, (2) the commandment of writing a Torah scroll (v. 19).

What is the significance of the fact that these last two commandments in the Torah were both transmitted by Moses on the day of his passing?

As long as the Jewish people were in the desert, memories of the experience at Sinai remained fresh. Even those members of the next generation who had not seen the giving of the Torah

deuteronomy 31:16–22 — va-yelekh

[16] God said to Moses, "You are soon to lie with your fathers. This nation will rise up and desire to follow the gods of the people of the land into which they are coming. They will forsake Me and violate My covenant which I made with them. [17] On that day, I will become very angry with them. I will forsake them and hide My face from them, (appearing as if I do not see their distress). They will be consumed, and many misfortunes and traumas will happen to them. On that day, they will say, 'It is surely because our God is no longer among us, that these evils have befallen us.' [18] I will surely hide My face on that day, because of all the evil they have committed, when they turned to other gods."

God's Testimony for the Future

❖ [19] "Now, write for yourselves this song (in *Parashat Ha'azinu*), and teach it to the Children of Israel."

"Place it into their mouths, so that this song will be for Me as a witness to the children of Israel."

[SIXTH READING / SEVENTH WHEN JOINED] [20] "When I bring them to the land which I have sworn to their forefathers, a land flowing with milk and honey, they will eat, be satisfied, and become fat. Then they will turn to other gods and serve them, angering Me and violating My covenant.

[21] "What will happen is, when numerous misfortunes and traumas will happen to them, this song (which warns them of the consequences of their actions) will speak out to them as a witness, for it will not be forgotten from the mouths of their children; for I know their inclination that they (are planning) to do today, (even) before I bring them into the land which I swore (to give them)."

[22] On that day, Moses wrote down this song, and taught it to the children of Israel.

17. It is surely because God is no longer among us that these evils have befallen us. By admitting that these misfortunes have come upon them because *"God is no longer among us,"* the people expressed remorse for their wrongdoing. Why, then, are they still deserving of punishment, *"I will surely hide My face"* (v. 18)?

Although the recognition that misfortune befalls man as a result of sin is well founded, nevertheless, the sentiment that *"God is no longer among us"* is itself sinful. God is always among us, even at a time of terrible misfortune. It is just that His *face*, His loving countenance, is hidden (*Rabbi Simḥah Bunem of Przysucha, 18th–19th century*).

18. I will surely hide My face. Scripture uses a double expression for "hide" (*haster 'astir*), alluding to an extremely pitiful state of the children of Israel. *Not only will Godliness be concealed, but the fact that it is hidden also will elude them.* They will say, "God is no longer among us" (v. 17). When a young child knows that his parents are present, even if he cannot see them he is comforted. If he believes that they are gone, it is devastating (*Rabbi Meir b. Jacob Schiff, 17th century*).

דברים לא:כג-ל וילך

23 וַיְצַו אֶת־יְהוֹשֻׁעַ בִּן־נוּן וַיֹּאמֶר חֲזַק וֶאֱמָץ כִּי אַתָּה תָּבִיא אֶת־בְּנֵי יִשְׂרָאֵל אֶל־הָאָרֶץ אֲשֶׁר־נִשְׁבַּעְתִּי לָהֶם וְאָנֹכִי אֶהְיֶה עִמָּךְ: 24 וַיְהִי ׀ כְּכַלּוֹת מֹשֶׁה לִכְתֹּב אֶת־דִּבְרֵי הַתּוֹרָה־הַזֹּאת עַל־סֵפֶר עַד תֻּמָּם: 25 וַיְצַו מֹשֶׁה [SEVENTH READING] אֶת־הַלְוִיִּם נֹשְׂאֵי אֲרוֹן בְּרִית־יְהֹוָה לֵאמֹר: 26 לָקֹחַ אֵת סֵפֶר הַתּוֹרָה הַזֶּה וְשַׂמְתֶּם אֹתוֹ מִצַּד אֲרוֹן בְּרִית־יְהֹוָה אֱלֹהֵיכֶם וְהָיָה־שָׁם בְּךָ לְעֵד: 27 כִּי אָנֹכִי יָדַעְתִּי אֶת־מֶרְיְךָ וְאֶת־עָרְפְּךָ הַקָּשֶׁה הֵן בְּעוֹדֶנִּי חַי עִמָּכֶם הַיּוֹם מַמְרִים הֱיִתֶם עִם־יְהֹוָה וְאַף כִּי־אַחֲרֵי מוֹתִי: 28 [MAFTIR] הַקְהִילוּ אֵלַי אֶת־כָּל־זִקְנֵי שִׁבְטֵיכֶם וְשֹׁטְרֵיכֶם וַאֲדַבְּרָה בְאָזְנֵיהֶם אֵת הַדְּבָרִים הָאֵלֶּה וְאָעִידָה בָּם אֶת־הַשָּׁמַיִם וְאֶת־הָאָרֶץ: 29 כִּי יָדַעְתִּי אַחֲרֵי מוֹתִי כִּי־הַשְׁחֵת תַּשְׁחִתוּן וְסַרְתֶּם מִן־הַדֶּרֶךְ אֲשֶׁר צִוִּיתִי אֶתְכֶם וְקָרָאת אֶתְכֶם הָרָעָה בְּאַחֲרִית הַיָּמִים כִּי־תַעֲשׂוּ אֶת־הָרַע בְּעֵינֵי יְהֹוָה לְהַכְעִיסוֹ בְּמַעֲשֵׂה יְדֵיכֶם: 30 וַיְדַבֵּר מֹשֶׁה בְּאָזְנֵי כָּל־קְהַל יִשְׂרָאֵל אֶת־דִּבְרֵי הַשִּׁירָה הַזֹּאת עַד תֻּמָּם: פ פ פ

ע' פסוקים, אדנ"י ה סימן.

Almighty, for the king is an agent to make the words of God heard" (*Maimonides*).

However, this only recreates the *national* experience of being commanded by God to observe the commandments. In order to re-enact the *personal* experience of being given the Torah by God to study, a further commandment was given—to write a Torah scroll. For when "a person writes one with his own hand, it is as if he received it from Mount Sinai" (*ibid.; Rabbi Menahem Mendel Schneerson, 20th century*).

27. You have been rebels against God. Literally, this verse reads, "You have been rebels *with* God"—even when you are rebels, you still are with God (*Rabbi Zadok ha-Kohen Rabinowitz of Lublin, 19th century*).

Man's Divine soul believes in God and remains faithful to Him even at the time when the sin is committed. However, it is in a form of "exile" within the animal soul that caused the body to sin (*Rabbi Shneur Zalman of Lyady, 18th century*).

Food for thought

1. What emotion does the sight of a Torah Scroll evoke in you?

2. Would you like to own an authentic Torah Scroll?

3. Did you ever have a letter written in a Torah Scroll on your behalf?

deuteronomy 31:23–30 — va-yelekh

²³ (God) commanded Joshua son of Nun and said:

"Be strong and courageous! For you will bring the children of Israel to the land that I have sworn to them, and I will be with you."

Moses' Torah Scroll is Placed with the Ark

²⁴ Then, when Moses finished writing the words of this Torah, until its very end, in a scroll, [SEVENTH READING] ²⁵ Moses commanded the Levites, who carried the Ark of God's Covenant, saying: ²⁶ "Take this Torah scroll and place it beside the Ark of the Covenant of God, your God, and it will be there as a witness. ²⁷ For I know your rebellious spirit and your stubbornness. Look!—even while I am alive with you today you have been rebels against God, surely (you will be) after my death (too)!"

Gathering of the Elders to Hear the Song of Ha'azinu

[MAFTIR] ²⁸ "Gather to me all the elders of your tribes and your police officers, and I will speak these words (of the song of Ha'azinu) into their ears. I will call upon the heavens and the earth as witnesses against them, ²⁹ for I know that long after my (disciple Joshua's) death you will surely become corrupted (with idol-worship), and depart from the way which I commanded you. Misfortune will inevitably come upon you in the end, because you did evil in the eyes of God, to provoke His anger through your actions."

³⁰ Then Moses spoke the words of the following song, into the ears of the entire assembly of Israel, until their completion.

Haftarot: Nitzavim–Va-Yelekh—page 1407.   Shabbat Shuvah—page 1409.

---

kabbalah bites

31:30 Spiritual teachers can sometimes speak to us in spiritual ways that fail to make a significant impact on our concrete, empirical outlook on life. To be an effective communicator of spiritual truth you must make sure, as Moses did here, that your words enter *"into the ears … until their completion."* Do not make the mistake of just speaking to your disciple's soul. You must speak to his body too.

---

with their eyes, had nevertheless grown up in a spiritual oasis where the effects of Sinai were still palpable. But at this junction in time, the Jewish people were leaving that oasis and embarking on the formidable challenge of living a life dominated by earning physical needs—and this was to be without the leadership of Moses. To help overcome these hurdles, the Jewish people were given two commandments whose purpose was to enable them *to recreate the experience of Sinai in their new setting.*

At a *Hakhel* gathering: "They must prepare their hearts and alert their ears to listen with dread and awe and with trembling joy, like the day it was given on Sinai … as though the Torah was being commanded to him now, and he was hearing it from the mouth of the

> *"Listen (ha'azinu), O heavens ... Let the earth hear!"*
> In **your preoccupation** with matters of the earth, **do not forget the heavens.**

HA'AZINU
האזינו

THE SONG OF *HA'AZINU*	32:1 – 32:44
MOSES' CONCLUDING WORDS	32:45–47
MOSES IS TOLD TO ASCEND MOUNT NEBO	32:48–52

NAME
Ha'azinu

MEANING
"Listen"

LINES IN TORAH SCROLL
92

PARASHIYYOT
3 open; 0 closed

VERSES
52

WORDS
614

LETTERS
2326

DATE
7 *Adar*, 2488

LOCATION
Plains of Moab

MASORETIC FEATURES
Enlarged, detached *he* (32:6); extra *vav* in *bama(v)te* (32:13); and small *yod* in *teshi* (32:18)

NOTE
Read the week before or after *Yom Kippur*

MITZVOT
None

CHARACTER PROFILE

NAME
Ketev Meriri (a demon—32:24)

MEANING
"Bitter destruction"

APPEARANCE
His head is like a calf, with a horn emerging from the center of his forehead. He is covered with scales and is hairy all over. His body is full of eyes, but he sees from one giant eye in his chest. He rolls around like a ball.

KNOWN FOR
Found in the shade, near the sun; active in the three weeks between 17 *Tammuz* and 9 *Av*; targets schoolchildren, especially between 10am and 4pm, during which time one should avoid hitting children; active in uninhabited areas

ACHIEVEMENTS
His gaze brings instant death; killed Hezekiah; gave Rabbi Phinehas leprosy

PRAISING GOD

Moses called upon the Jews to ascribe greatness when they hear mention of God's name (32:3). Since the earliest times, Jewish conversation began and ended with, *"Thank God!" "With God's help!"* Make God part of your daily thought and speech.

DIVINE JUSTICE

As Moses was about to die, his dreams of entering Canaan crushed, he proclaimed: God's every decision is righteous—whether or not it agrees with our limited mortal sensibilities (32:4).

HISTORY

Moses calls for a review of history in order to make better use of the present and future (32:7).

SUCCESS

Success and victory come from God (32:27-31). Acknowledge the source of your achievements; strengthen your connection with Him and enjoy even greater success.

האזינו
דברים לב:א-ד

לב ۱ הַאֲזִינוּ הַשָּׁמַיִם וַאֲדַבֵּרָה וְתִשְׁמַע הָאָרֶץ אִמְרֵי־פִי: ۲ יַעֲרֹף כַּמָּטָר לִקְחִי תִּזַּל כַּטַּל אִמְרָתִי כִּשְׂעִירִם עֲלֵי־דֶשֶׁא וְכִרְבִיבִים עֲלֵי־עֵשֶׂב: ۳ כִּי שֵׁם יְהֹוָה אֶקְרָא הָבוּ גֹדֶל לֵאלֹהֵינוּ: ۴ הַצּוּר תָּמִים פָּעֳלוֹ כִּי כָל־דְּרָכָיו מִשְׁפָּט

The soul is literally a part of God. So the feeling of being "close to the heavens" is not something that needs to be acquired, but merely *uncovered*. In some way, it is relatively easy and natural for you to feel "close to the heavens and distant from the earth," because your soul, which sustains your very life, is truly "distant from the earth."

But nevertheless, after being born into a body, you are firmly rooted in this world too, enabling you to bring your natural affinity with "the heavens" down to the earth—making "a home for God below" (*Rabbi Menahem Mendel Schneerson, 20th century*).

2. Let my words flow like dew. In the *Song of Ha'azinu*, Torah is described as both "rain" and "dew." Physically, rain and dew are both sources of nourishment, but the causes which bring them about differ. Rain is formed from water which is lost to the atmosphere as vapor from the earth, and then precipitates back—as the verse states: *"(God caused) a mist to ascend from the earth (moistening the clouds in order to) soak the entire surface of the ground"* (Genesis 2:6). Dew, by contrast, "never ceases" (*Babylonian Talmud, Ta'anit* 3b), and appears spontaneously, regardless of the amount of water which is being evaporated from the earth.

Rain represents the influx of Divine revelation which is bestowed in *direct response* to man's efforts (on earth). Dew, on the other hand, alludes to what God bestows *unconditionally*, disproportionately to man's efforts.

So, since "rain" and "dew" in this verse both refer to Torah, it follows that "rain" represents the parts of Torah which are dependent on human mastery—namely, the extensive legal discussions of the Torah. The comparatively effortless "dew" alludes to the mystical parts of the Torah which transcend the limitation of the human mind, since they "flow" directly from their Divine source, as the verse states, *"Let my words flow like dew"* (*Rabbi Shneur Zalman of Lyady, 18th century*).

3. Ascribe greatness to our God. From where do we derive the principle that you answer "Amen" after a blessing is made? From the words, *"Ascribe greatness to our God"* (*Sifrei*).

4. His acts are perfect. These acts refer to the previously mentioned heavens and earth (v. 1). Only acts performed by God could be said to be perfectly complete. When a man builds a house, for example, he simply is combining or changing the form of other preexisting materials such as stone and wood to form a desired structure. God, on the other hand, created this magnificent world from absolute nothingness—a *"perfect"* and complete *"act"* of creation (*Rabbi Hezekiah b. Manoah, 13th century*).

kabbalah bites

32:4 Adam was God's "deed" in that he was created by the hand of God. When Adam sinned, incurring the penalty of expulsion from the Garden of Eden, it was the Sabbath eve. But God allowed him to stay in the Garden for the Sabbath, at which time he composed Psalm 92.

Later Adam was reincarnated as King David, who recorded the Psalm, but the text nevertheless hints to Adam's authorship: "For I rejoiced, O God, in *Your deed*" (v. 5).

parashat ha'azinu

The Song of *Ha'azinu*

32 ¹ Listen, O heavens (and be my witness), for I will speak! Let the earth hear (and witness) the (following) words of my mouth!

² Let my (Torah) teaching drip like rain (and give life to the world). Let my words flow like dew, like storm winds (that bring rain) on vegetation (to make them grow), and like raindrops on grass.

³ When I call out (and mention) the name of God, (respond and) ascribe greatness to our God.

⁴ (Though He is powerful, like a) rock, His acts (of retribution) are perfect(ly balanced), for all His ways are just. God is faithful (to reward his righteous ones,

32:1 Listen, O heavens. Reciting the *Song of Ha'azinu* and knowing it by heart (with its cantillation notes) purifies the mind and heart. It also leads to longevity and success in business (*Rabbi Judah Loew of Prague 16th century*).

Listen, O heavens (and be my witness), for I will speak! Let the earth hear (and witness) the (following) words of my mouth! Man's body and soul each seem to have an excellent pretext to excuse themselves from judgment. The body can say, "Since my soul departed I am like a stone in the grave unable to sin," shifting the blame to the soul; and the soul can say, "since I have departed from the body I am like a bird flying in the wind," shifting the blame to the body.

But the argument is easily refuted with a parable. A king once stationed two people to guard his beautiful orchard, one lame and the other blind. The lame one said to the blind one, "I see delicious figs in the orchard. Mount me on your shoulders and we will reach the figs together and eat them." And that is what they did.

When the owner of the orchard noticed the missing figs he confronted the guards, but they each excused themselves—the lame one claiming that he could not have possibly walked to the figs, and the blind one saying that he could not have seen them. *So the king mounted the lame one on top of the blind one and judged them together* (*Babylonian Talmud, Sanhedrin* 91a).

In the opening line of our Torah portion, *"heavens"* refers to the soul, and *"earth"* corresponds to the body. Moses addressed both the body and soul *together*, for the rebuke of one without the other would be meaningless (*Rabbi Simḥah Bunem Sofer, 19th century*).

Listen O heavens ... Let the earth hear. Moses was "close to the heavens," so he told them to "listen"—a term which suggests a closeness between speaker and listener. But since he was "distant from the earth," he told it to "hear," from afar (*Sifrei*).

You have a "spark" of Moses within your soul, which enables you to attain, to some small extent, the spiritual greatness of Moses. So it *is* relevant to you—sometimes, at least—to appreciate that spiritual matters are more important than physical things, to be "close to the heavens and distant from the earth."

How is it possible for an ordinary person, who lives a normal, bodily existence, to feel "close to the heavens and distant from the earth"? And are we not taught that the ultimate purpose of creation is to be found here on earth by making a *"home for God, below"* (*Midrash Tanḥuma*)? What is to be gained, then, from feeling "distant from the earth"?

דברים לב:ד-יג | האזינו

אֵ֥ל אֱמוּנָ֛ה וְאֵ֥ין עָ֖וֶל צַדִּ֥יק וְיָשָׁ֖ר הֽוּא׃ 5 שִׁחֵ֥ת ל֛וֹ לֹ֖א בָּנָ֣יו מוּמָ֑ם דּ֥וֹר עִקֵּ֖שׁ וּפְתַלְתֹּֽל׃ 6 הַ֤־לַיהֹוָה֙ תִּגְמְלוּ־זֹ֔את עַ֥ם נָבָ֖ל וְלֹ֣א חָכָ֑ם הֲלוֹא־הוּא֙ אָבִ֣יךָ קָּנֶ֔ךָ ה֥וּא עָֽשְׂךָ֖ וַֽיְכֹנְנֶֽךָ׃ [SECOND READING] 7 זְכֹר֙ יְמ֣וֹת עוֹלָ֔ם בִּ֖ינוּ שְׁנ֣וֹת דֹּר־וָדֹ֑ר שְׁאַ֤ל אָבִ֙יךָ֙ וְיַגֵּ֔דְךָ זְקֵנֶ֖יךָ וְיֹ֥אמְרוּ לָֽךְ׃ 8 בְּהַנְחֵ֤ל עֶלְיוֹן֙ גּוֹיִ֔ם בְּהַפְרִיד֖וֹ בְּנֵ֣י אָדָ֑ם יַצֵּב֙ גְּבֻלֹ֣ת עַמִּ֔ים לְמִסְפַּ֖ר בְּנֵ֥י יִשְׂרָאֵֽל׃ 9 כִּ֛י חֵ֥לֶק יְהֹוָ֖ה עַמּ֑וֹ יַעֲקֹ֖ב חֶ֥בֶל נַחֲלָתֽוֹ׃ 10 יִמְצָאֵ֙הוּ֙ בְּאֶ֣רֶץ מִדְבָּ֔ר וּבְתֹ֖הוּ יְלֵ֣ל יְשִׁמֹ֑ן יְסֹֽבְבֶ֙נְהוּ֙ יְב֣וֹנְנֵ֔הוּ יִצְּרֶ֖נְהוּ כְּאִישׁ֥וֹן עֵינֽוֹ׃ 11 כְּנֶ֙שֶׁר֙ יָעִ֣יר קִנּ֔וֹ עַל־גּוֹזָלָ֖יו יְרַחֵ֑ף יִפְרֹ֤שׂ כְּנָפָיו֙ יִקָּחֵ֔הוּ יִשָּׂאֵ֖הוּ עַל־אֶבְרָתֽוֹ׃ 12 יְהֹוָ֖ה בָּדָ֣ד יַנְחֶ֑נּוּ וְאֵ֥ין עִמּ֖וֹ אֵ֥ל נֵכָֽר׃ [THIRD READING] 13 יַרְכִּבֵ֙הוּ֙ עַל־[במותי כ׳] בָּ֣מֳתֵי אָ֔רֶץ וַיֹּאכַ֖ל תְּנוּבֹ֣ת שָׂדָ֑י וַיֵּנִקֵ֤הֽוּ דְבַשׁ֙ מִסֶּ֔לַע וְשֶׁ֖מֶן

1260

7. Remember the days gone by (when God punished the wicked). Reflect upon the years of one generation and another. *"Remember the days gone by"*—what God did to past generations who provoked Him to anger. *"Reflect upon the years of one generation and another"*—the generation of Enosh, upon which He inundated the waters of the ocean, and the generation of the Flood, which He washed away (*Rashi, 11th century*).

Ask your father and he will tell you (about days gone by. Ask) your elders, and they will inform you. If you did not *"remember the days gone by,"* and set your attention to the past, then, *"reflect upon the years of one generation and another."* Recognize the future: that He has the power to bestow good upon you and to give you the days of the Messiah and the world to come, as an inheritance. *"Ask your father"*—these are the prophets, who are called "fathers," as Scripture states regarding Elijah, *"My father, my father, the chariot of Israel!"* (II Kings 2:12). *"Your elders"*—these are the Sages (*Rashi, 11th century*).

9. Jacob ... a rope. The soul is like a rope, with its upper end attached to God and its lower end to the body. This rope is comprised of six hundred and thirteen thin strands, each corresponding to a specific precept of the Torah. If a person violates one of these commands, one strand is severed, weakening his connection with God (*Rabbi Shneur Zalman of Lyady, 18th century*).

11. Carrying them (safely) on its upper side. Unlike other species of bird that carry their young with their feet, for fear that a different bird might fly above them and snatch their children from their back, the eagle has no such fear; it soars higher than all other birds. Its only fear is that an arrow could be shot from below, so she carries her young on her upper side saying, "Let the arrow pierce me rather than my children."

kabbalah bites

32:5 *"A crooked and twisted generation."* Here Moses hints to the secret of reincarnation. If a person is "crooked" and sinful in his lifetime he must be reincarnated ("twisted") into another generation.

deuteronomy 32:4–13 — ha'azinu

He even rewards the wicked) without injustice. (All acknowledge that) He is righteous and upright (in judgment).

⁵ Corruption (is theirs), not His! It is His children's defect, a crooked and twisted generation!

⁶ Is this how you repay God, you disgraceful, unwise people? Is He not your Father, your Master? He has made you (a special nation), and established you (to be self-sufficient).

[SECOND READING] ⁷ Remember the days gone by (when God punished the wicked). Reflect upon the years of one generation and another. Ask your father, and he will tell you (about days gone by, ask) your elders, and they will inform you (what the early generations did).

⁸ When the Supernal One gave nations their lot (with the Flood), when He separated the sons of man (after the Tower of Babel), He (allowed them to exist by) establishing (seventy) distinct nations, (for the sake of) the children of Israel (who would later arise, and) number (seventy souls).

⁹ (He saved all the nations) because of God's portion, His people, (hidden among them). Jacob (and his sons were) His inheritance, (for Jacob's merit was threefold, like the strands of) a rope.

¹⁰ He found them (faithful to Him, accepting the Torah) in a desert land, (following Moses) into a desolate, howling wasteland. He encompassed them (with clouds), and bestowed understanding upon them (through the Torah). He protected them (from snakes and scorpions) like the pupil of His eye.

¹¹ (He guided them with compassion) like an eagle (that) wakens its nest (gently), hovering over its young (without touching them); it spreads its wings, taking them, carrying them (safely) on its upper side. ¹² God alone guided them, and there was no strange god (able to attack) them.

[THIRD READING] ¹³ He settled them on (the land of Israel), the peak of the earth, so they could eat (its fast-growing) produce of the field. He let them suck honey from (its figs, which grow) from a rock(y, hard crust), and oil from the (olives that grow at

spiritual vitamin

> The Babylonians and the Romans were able to destroy only the Sanctuaries of wood and stone, of gold and silver, but they could not harm the inner "Sanctuary" in the heart of every one of us, for it is eternal.

דברים לב:יג-כד　　　　האזינו

מֵחַלְמִישׁ צוּר: 14 חֶמְאַת בָּקָר וַחֲלֵב צֹאן עִם־חֵלֶב כָּרִים וְאֵילִים בְּנֵי־בָשָׁן
וְעַתּוּדִים עִם־חֵלֶב כִּלְיוֹת חִטָּה וְדַם־עֵנָב תִּשְׁתֶּה־חָמֶר: 15 וַיִּשְׁמַן יְשֻׁרוּן
וַיִּבְעָט שָׁמַנְתָּ עָבִיתָ כָּשִׂיתָ וַיִּטֹּשׁ אֱלוֹהַּ עָשָׂהוּ וַיְנַבֵּל צוּר יְשֻׁעָתוֹ: 16 יַקְנִאֻהוּ
בְּזָרִים בְּתוֹעֵבֹת יַכְעִיסֻהוּ: 17 יִזְבְּחוּ לַשֵּׁדִים לֹא אֱלֹהַּ אֱלֹהִים לֹא יְדָעוּם
חֲדָשִׁים מִקָּרֹב בָּאוּ לֹא שְׂעָרוּם אֲבֹתֵיכֶם: 18 צוּר יְלָדְךָ תֶּשִׁי וַתִּשְׁכַּח אֵל
מְחֹלְלֶךָ: 19 [FOURTH READING] וַיַּרְא יְהוָה וַיִּנְאָץ מִכַּעַס בָּנָיו וּבְנֹתָיו: 20 וַיֹּאמֶר אַסְתִּירָה
פָנַי מֵהֶם אֶרְאֶה מָה אַחֲרִיתָם כִּי דוֹר תַּהְפֻּכֹת הֵמָּה בָּנִים לֹא־אֵמֻן בָּם:
21 הֵם קִנְאוּנִי בְלֹא־אֵל כִּעֲסוּנִי בְּהַבְלֵיהֶם וַאֲנִי אַקְנִיאֵם בְּלֹא־עָם בְּגוֹי נָבָל
אַכְעִיסֵם: 22 כִּי־אֵשׁ קָדְחָה בְאַפִּי וַתִּיקַד עַד־שְׁאוֹל תַּחְתִּית וַתֹּאכַל אֶרֶץ
וִיבֻלָהּ וַתְּלַהֵט מוֹסְדֵי הָרִים: 23 אַסְפֶּה עָלֵימוֹ רָעוֹת חִצַּי אֲכַלֶּה־בָּם: 24 מְזֵי
רָעָב וּלְחֻמֵי רֶשֶׁף וְקֶטֶב מְרִירִי וְשֶׁן־בְּהֵמֹת אֲשַׁלַּח־בָּם עִם־חֲמַת זֹחֲלֵי עָפָר:

---

collect he should jump around and make strange noises. This would lead the creditors to believe that he has lost his mind and there would be no reason for further contact. The idea seemed to work, and the creditors ceased to harass him.

Some time later he borrowed money from this friend who had advised him regarding the creditors. When the loan was due he began to play the same trick, acting insane. His friend shouted angrily, "You scoundrel! I was the one who gave you this advice to save you from your other creditors, and now you are attempting to use my own advice against me?"

In a similar way, God created man with the ability to forget, for his own benefit, so that he would be distracted from pain and suffering and be able to move forward with life. But man abuses this ability in order to forget God!

This is the message of our verse. You were born with the ability to forget, but you abused this trait and instead, *"You forgot the God who delivered you"* (*Rabbi Jacob Kranz of Dubno, 18th century*).

---

kabbalah bites

32:18 *"You forgot the Rock who gave birth to you."* Literally, the word *teshi* ("forgot"), means "weakened."

How could you possibly "weaken" God?

Obviously, you can't, but you could make Him *look* weak. A poor craftsman fails to fashion his object correctly at the first attempt and has to remodel it a number of times. If we sin in this lifetime and the next, requiring multiple reincarnations, it makes it look as if God can't get it right the first time. So we "weaken" Him, so to speak.

deuteronomy 32:13–24 — ha'azinu

the) hard, rock(y ground of Gush Ḥalav). ¹⁴ The cream of cattle and the milk of sheep, with the fat of lambs, fattened rams from Bashan and he-goats, with fat kernels of wheat. You will drink the blood of grapes, delicious (wine).

¹⁵ But Jeshurun became fat and rebelled. You grew fat, rotund and obese. (Israel) forsook the God who made them, and disgraced the Rock of their salvation.

¹⁶ They made him furious with alien (worship), they made Him angry with abominable acts. ¹⁷ They sacrificed to demons, which have no power, deities with which they were not acquainted, new (idols) that just arrived (and were not even known by idolators themselves), which your fathers did not fear. ¹⁸ You forgot the Rock who gave birth to you. You forgot the God who delivered you (from the womb).

[FOURTH READING] ¹⁹ God saw this and became angry, provoked by His sons and daughters. ²⁰ He said: I will hide My face from them; I will see what their end will be. For they are a generation that changes (My goodwill into anger), children that have no (signs of My good) upbringing.

²¹ They have made Me furious with something that is not a god, provoked My anger with their nonsense. So I will make them furious by a nation devoid (of a name), I will provoke their anger with a vile (heretical) nation. ²² For a fire burned in My nostrils, and it will blaze (in you) to the lowest depths (of your foundations). It will consume (your) land and its produce, setting aflame (Jerusalem which is), founded upon mountains.

²³ I will heap misfortunes upon them. I will use up My arrows on them. ²⁴ They will sprout hair from famine, be attacked by flying (demons), and be cut down by (the demon) Meriri. I will send animal's teeth upon them, with the venom of those (snakes) that slither in the dust.

In the same way, when the children of Israel left Egypt they were pursued by the Egyptians, who began shooting arrows at them, and a protective cloud came between the two camps to absorb the arrows (*Rashi, 11th century*).

17. New (idols) that just arrived (and were not even known by idolators themselves), which your fathers did not fear. Parents are always concerned that their children should maintain their parent's value system without slipping because of the new generation's shift in culture. In the past, the slip of religious conviction was within a "normal" range; children were not as devout as their parents but generally reflected their parents' ideals. In recent times, though, the generation gap has become so wide that the young generation hardly resemble their parents at all—they are a *"new"* entity *"that just arrived,"* suddenly. This phenomenon is something *"which your fathers did not fear,"* something of which your parents could not even have conceived (*Rabbi Moses Sofer, 18th–19th century*).

18. You forgot the Rock who gave birth to you. You forgot the God who delivered you. A man, beleaguered with debt, once asked his friend for advice how to find relief from his creditors' constant pestering. The friend advised him that whenever the creditors come to

האזינו
דברים לב:כה-לו

25 מִחוּץ תְּשַׁכֶּל־חֶרֶב וּמֵחֲדָרִים אֵימָה גַּם־בָּחוּר גַּם־בְּתוּלָה יוֹנֵק עִם־אִישׁ שֵׂיבָה: 26 אָמַרְתִּי אַפְאֵיהֶם אַשְׁבִּיתָה מֵאֱנוֹשׁ זִכְרָם: 27 לוּלֵי כַּעַס אוֹיֵב אָגוּר פֶּן־יְנַכְּרוּ צָרֵימוֹ פֶּן־יֹאמְרוּ יָדֵנוּ רָמָה וְלֹא יְהֹוָה פָּעַל כָּל־זֹאת: 28 כִּי־גוֹי אֹבַד עֵצוֹת הֵמָּה וְאֵין בָּהֶם תְּבוּנָה: [FIFTH READING] 29 לוּ חָכְמוּ יַשְׂכִּילוּ זֹאת יָבִינוּ לְאַחֲרִיתָם: 30 אֵיכָה יִרְדֹּף אֶחָד אֶלֶף וּשְׁנַיִם יָנִיסוּ רְבָבָה אִם־לֹא כִּי־צוּרָם מְכָרָם וַיהוָה הִסְגִּירָם: 31 כִּי לֹא כְצוּרֵנוּ צוּרָם וְאֹיְבֵינוּ פְּלִילִים: 32 כִּי־מִגֶּפֶן סְדֹם גַּפְנָם וּמִשַּׁדְמֹת עֲמֹרָה עֲנָבֵמוֹ עִנְּבֵי־רוֹשׁ אַשְׁכְּלֹת מְרֹרֹת לָמוֹ: 33 חֲמַת תַּנִּינִם יֵינָם וְרֹאשׁ פְּתָנִים אַכְזָר: 34 הֲלֹא־הוּא כָּמֻס עִמָּדִי חָתֻם בְּאוֹצְרֹתָי: 35 לִי נָקָם וְשִׁלֵּם לְעֵת תָּמוּט רַגְלָם כִּי קָרוֹב יוֹם אֵידָם וְחָשׁ עֲתִדֹת לָמוֹ: 36 כִּי־יָדִין יְהֹוָה עַמּוֹ וְעַל־עֲבָדָיו יִתְנֶחָם כִּי יִרְאֶה כִּי־אָזְלַת יָד

Even though Abner had strayed far from the path of observance, his name was nevertheless recorded in the Torah with his title, *Rabbi* Abner, indicating his status as a fully observant Jew, *after* he had returned—for this was indeed his true essence (*Rabbi Menahem Mendel Schneerson, 20th century*).

30. How can one (of us) pursue a thousand. When speaking of God's "measure of retribution" (the enemy chasing away the Jewish people), there is a ratio of 1:1000, *"How can one (of us) pursue a thousand (of Israel)."* Yet, when speaking of God's corresponding "measure of benevolence," the Torah states, *"Five of you will be able to chase away a hundred"* (Leviticus 26:8), a ratio of just 1:20. How is this to be reconciled with the principle that God's measure of benevolence always exceeds His measure of retribution?

In truth, however, you cannot compare these two cases. For the verse in Leviticus refers to the annihilation of the enemy, *"Five of you(r weakest men) will be able to chase away a hundred ... They will fall (dead) by the(ir own) sword(s) before you,"* whereas the verse here speaks only of being chased away by the enemy. Therefore, it would be unreasonable to compare the two cases (*The Tosafists, 12th–14th centuries*).

spiritual vitamin

> Always consider yourself as a mountain climber, in the process of ascending a steep mountain. You must continue to climb or slide back, because you cannot remain stationary. And remember: the rate of a falling object accelerates.

deuteronomy 32:25–36 — ha'azinu

²⁵ From outside (the city), the sword (of invading armies) will bereave (them), and terror (will destroy) the chambers (of the heart of even) young men and maidens, suckling babes with old men.

²⁶ I said (in My heart) that I would scatter them, causing their memory to cease from mankind. ²⁷ If it were not for the enemy's anger heaped up (against them), lest their adversaries attribute (their power) to a foreign (power); lest they claim, "Our hand was triumphant!" and, "It was not God who did all of this!"

²⁸ For (the enemy of Israel) is a nation devoid of good advice, and they have no understanding (to see that their victory would come from God). [FIFTH READING] ²⁹ If they were wise, they would understand this; they would reflect upon (Israel's) demise. ³⁰ (They would have thought): How can one (of us) pursue a thousand (of Israel), and two put ten thousand to flight, unless their Rock has sold them out, and God has delivered them (into our hands)?

³¹ For their rock is not (a true power) like our Rock. (If) our enemies judge (and defeat us it is because our Rock has decreed so).

³² (God says: I wish to scatter Israel) because their vine is of the vine of Sodom, and of the (grain) fields of Gomorrah. Their grapes are grapes of bitterness, they (deserve) clusters (with) bitter juice. ³³ Their (cup of punishing) wine (will be like) the bitter venom of serpents, and the cruel poison of cobras.

³⁴ Is not (the evidence of all their wicked actions) stored away with Me, sealed up in My treasuries? ³⁵ Within Me vengeance is (prepared), and it will repay, at the moment their foothold (of merit of their fathers) falters. (As soon as I decide to punish them) the day of their reckoning (will be) close, and what is destined for them will happen quickly.

³⁶ When God will judge His people (and bring these sufferings upon them), He will (then) change His mind about His servants; when He sees that the power (of the enemy) is increasing, and no one (among Israel has a source of) salvation or help.

26. I said (in My heart) that I would scatter them, causing their memory to cease from mankind. Naḥmanides once confronted his former student, Abner, and asked him why he had strayed from the path of observant Judaism.

Abner replied that Naḥmanides had once taught that "everything is to be found in the *Song of Ha'azinu*," and Abner found the idea so utterly preposterous that it led him to lose faith. When Naḥmanides stated that he still held by his assertion, Abner challenged him, "If so, where is my name to be found in the Song?"

Naḥmanides turned to the wall, praying to God, and it soon occurred to him that the third letter of each word in verse 26 spelled Abner's name—"R. Abner": *'amaRti* (*resh*) *'af'Ehem* (*alef*) *'ashBita* (*bet*) *me-'eNosh* (*nun*) *zikhRam* (*resh*). On hearing this, Abner repented and mended his ways (*Rabbi Yeḥiel Heilprin, 18th century*).

וְאֶ֖פֶס עָצ֥וּר וְעָזֽוּב׃ 37 וְאָמַ֖ר אֵ֣י אֱלֹהֵ֑ימוֹ צ֖וּר חָסָ֥יוּ בֽוֹ׃ 38 אֲשֶׁ֨ר חֵ֤לֶב זְבָחֵ֙ימוֹ֙ יֹאכֵ֔לוּ יִשְׁתּ֖וּ יֵ֣ין נְסִיכָ֑ם יָק֙וּמוּ֙ וְיַעְזְרֻכֶ֔ם יְהִ֥י עֲלֵיכֶ֖ם סִתְרָֽה׃ 39 רְא֣וּ ׀ עַתָּ֗ה כִּ֣י אֲנִ֤י אֲנִי֙ ה֔וּא וְאֵ֥ין אֱלֹהִ֖ים עִמָּדִ֑י אֲנִ֧י אָמִ֣ית וַאֲחַיֶּ֗ה מָחַ֙צְתִּי֙ וַאֲנִ֣י אֶרְפָּ֔א וְאֵ֥ין מִיָּדִ֖י מַצִּֽיל׃ [SIXTH READING] 40 כִּֽי־אֶשָּׂ֥א אֶל־שָׁמַ֖יִם יָדִ֑י וְאָמַ֕רְתִּי חַ֥י אָנֹכִ֖י לְעֹלָֽם׃ 41 אִם־שַׁנּוֹתִי֙ בְּרַ֣ק חַרְבִּ֔י וְתֹאחֵ֥ז בְּמִשְׁפָּ֖ט יָדִ֑י אָשִׁ֤יב נָקָם֙ לְצָרָ֔י וְלִמְשַׂנְאַ֖י אֲשַׁלֵּֽם׃ 42 אַשְׁכִּ֤יר חִצַּי֙ מִדָּ֔ם וְחַרְבִּ֖י תֹּ֣אכַל בָּשָׂ֑ר מִדַּ֤ם חָלָל֙ וְשִׁבְיָ֔ה מֵרֹ֖אשׁ פַּרְע֥וֹת אוֹיֵֽב׃ 43 הַרְנִ֤ינוּ גוֹיִם֙ עַמּ֔וֹ כִּ֥י דַם־עֲבָדָ֖יו יִקּ֑וֹם וְנָקָם֙ יָשִׁ֣יב לְצָרָ֔יו וְכִפֶּ֥ר אַדְמָת֖וֹ עַמּֽוֹ׃ פ [SEVENTH READING] 44 וַיָּבֹ֣א מֹשֶׁ֗ה וַיְדַבֵּ֛ר אֶת־כָּל־דִּבְרֵ֥י הַשִּׁירָֽה־הַזֹּ֖את בְּאָזְנֵ֣י הָעָ֑ם ה֖וּא וְהוֹשֵׁ֥עַ בִּן־נֽוּן׃ 45 וַיְכַ֣ל מֹשֶׁ֗ה לְדַבֵּ֛ר אֶת־כָּל־הַדְּבָרִ֥ים הָאֵ֖לֶּה אֶל־כָּל־יִשְׂרָאֵֽל׃ 46 וַיֹּ֤אמֶר אֲלֵהֶם֙ שִׂ֣ימוּ לְבַבְכֶ֔ם לְכָל־הַדְּבָרִ֔ים אֲשֶׁ֧ר אָנֹכִ֛י מֵעִ֥יד בָּכֶ֖ם הַיּ֑וֹם אֲשֶׁ֤ר תְּצַוֻּם֙ אֶת־בְּנֵיכֶ֔ם לִשְׁמֹ֣ר לַעֲשׂ֔וֹת אֶת־כָּל־דִּבְרֵ֥י

44. Hosea son of Nun. Why does Scripture call Joshua with his prior name, "Hosea"?

To indicate that Joshua did not become arrogant. Although he was given high status, he humbled himself to be like he was at the beginning, when he was still called Hosea (*Rashi, 11th century*).

The Jerusalem Talmud relates that when Sarai's name was changed to Sarah, the letter (*yod*)—that was removed in order to accommodate a new letter (*he*)—complained because it did not wish to be removed from the name of such a righteous woman. God appeased the letter, saying that it would later be added to the righteous leader Joshua. (The difference between "Hosea" and "Joshua" in Hebrew, is just the addition of a letter *yod*) (*Jerusalem Talmud, Sanhedrin* 2:6).

When Sarah's name was changed she was eighty-nine years old, and she passed away at the age of one hundred and twenty-seven. That leaves thirty-eight years for which the letter (*yod*) had a grievance. Remarkably, from the time Joshua's name was changed until this point where it returns to Hosea, there were also thirty-eight years: Joshua's name was changed in the second year from the exodus from Egypt, and Moses passed away after the fortieth year (*Rabbi Aryeh Judah Leib, 18th century*).

He and Hosea. It was a rulership of two pairs, two leaders each with their own spokesman through whom they lectured. For complete authority had been taken from one and given to be shared with the other. Moses appointed a spokesman for Joshua in Moses' lifetime, so that the Jewish people would not say, "During your teacher's lifetime you did not dare to raise your head!" (*Rashi, 11th century*).

deuteronomy 32:37–46 — ha'azinu

³⁷ Then He will say: Where is their deity (that they worshiped), the rock in which they trusted, ³⁸ which ate the fat of their sacrifices, and drank the wine of their libations? Let them stand up and help you! Let them be your shelter!

³⁹ See now that it is Me! I am the One! There is no god (to stand against) Me. I cause death and I bring to life. I injure and I heal. And no one can rescue from My hand (those who sin against Me)!

[SIXTH READING] ⁴⁰ For (when the Jewish people repent, I will turn My anger upon the nations!) I (will) raise up My hand to (Myself in) heaven, and say: Just as I live forever, ⁴¹ (I swear that) when I sharpen the blade of My sword, and My hand grasps judgment (to punish the enemies of Israel), I will bring vengeance upon (them, for they are) My enemies (too). I will repay those who hate Me.

⁴² I will make My arrows drunk with (enemy) blood, and My sword will consume (their) flesh, on account of the blood of the slain (of Israel) and the captives (seized), from (even) the first attacks of the enemy.

⁴³ (At that time) the nations will sing praises for His people! When (they see how) He will avenge the blood of His servants (that they spilled), inflict revenge upon His enemies (for the robberies and losses they caused), and appease His land (and) His people (for their distress).

[SEVENTH READING] ⁴⁴ Moses came and spoke all the words of this song into the ears of the people, he and Hosea son of Nun.

Moses' Concluding Words

⁴⁵ When Moses finished speaking all these words to all of Israel, ⁴⁶ he said to them, "Turn your hearts to all of the words which I am bearing witness for you today, so that you will command your children to be careful to observe all the

---

39. I cause death and I bring to life. I injure and I heal. Rava noted an inconsistency: The verse states, *"I cause death and I bring to life,"* and then it continues, *"I injure and I heal."* If He can bring about life, doesn't it go without saying that He can heal?

What God is saying is: "To the same person that I bring death, I will bring life, just as I heal the same person that I injure."

The Sages taught: When the verse states, *"I cause death and I bring to life,"* you might think that it is speaking of the natural phenomenon that one person dies and another comes to life. Therefore, the verse states, *"I strike and I injure,"* to teach you that just as one person is injured and then healed, so too, this same person who dies is brought to life. *From here we have a proof from the Torah that the dead will be revived* (Babylonian Talmud, Pesaḥim 68a).

43. The nations will sing praises. At that time, the nations will praise Israel, saying: See how praiseworthy this nation is, that they remained attached to God throughout all the hardships that they suffered and they did not forsake Him! (*Rashi, 11ᵗʰ century*).

דברים לב:מו-נב האזינו

הַתּוֹרָה הַזֹּאת: 47 כִּי לֹא־דָבָר רֵק הוּא מִכֶּם כִּי־הוּא חַיֵּיכֶם וּבַדָּבָר הַזֶּה תַּאֲרִיכוּ יָמִים עַל־הָאֲדָמָה אֲשֶׁר אַתֶּם עֹבְרִים אֶת־הַיַּרְדֵּן שָׁמָּה לְרִשְׁתָּהּ: פ
48 [MAFTIR] וַיְדַבֵּר יְהֹוָה אֶל־מֹשֶׁה בְּעֶצֶם הַיּוֹם הַזֶּה לֵאמֹר: 49 עֲלֵה אֶל־הַר הָעֲבָרִים הַזֶּה הַר־נְבוֹ אֲשֶׁר בְּאֶרֶץ מוֹאָב אֲשֶׁר עַל־פְּנֵי יְרֵחוֹ וּרְאֵה אֶת־אֶרֶץ כְּנַעַן אֲשֶׁר אֲנִי נֹתֵן לִבְנֵי יִשְׂרָאֵל לַאֲחֻזָּה: 50 וּמֻת בָּהָר אֲשֶׁר אַתָּה עֹלֶה שָׁמָּה וְהֵאָסֵף אֶל־עַמֶּיךָ כַּאֲשֶׁר־מֵת אַהֲרֹן אָחִיךָ בְּהֹר הָהָר וַיֵּאָסֶף אֶל־עַמָּיו: 51 עַל אֲשֶׁר מְעַלְתֶּם בִּי בְּתוֹךְ בְּנֵי יִשְׂרָאֵל בְּמֵי־מְרִיבַת קָדֵשׁ מִדְבַּר־צִן עַל אֲשֶׁר לֹא־קִדַּשְׁתֶּם אוֹתִי בְּתוֹךְ בְּנֵי יִשְׂרָאֵל: 52 כִּי מִנֶּגֶד תִּרְאֶה אֶת־הָאָרֶץ וְשָׁמָּה לֹא תָבוֹא אֶל־הָאָרֶץ אֲשֶׁר־אֲנִי נֹתֵן לִבְנֵי יִשְׂרָאֵל: פ פ פ

נ״ב פסוקים, כל״ב סימן.

If a person helps you, there is a Torah obligation not to be ungrateful to that person. Moses had helped the Jewish people in so many ways: *"He is the man who brought us out of Egypt! He split the Reed Sea for us! He brought the manna down for us! He made flocks of quails fly over to us! He brought up the well for us! And he gave us the Torah!"* So when Moses heard a decree of death, the people were obliged to help him, by restraining him from going on the mountain where the decree was to be enacted.

There were actually two conflicting obligations here: *Moses* was obligated to ascend the mountain, but *the people* were obligated to ensure that Moses did not ascend the mountain!

As far as the people were concerned, they had one single obligation resting upon them which they were required to carry out: to save Moses. And the fact that God had put it within the control of the Jewish people to nullify the decree was taken as a hint by them from God that they should do everything in their power to keep Moses alive (*Rabbi Menahem Mendel Schneerson, 20th century*).

50. Just as your brother Aaron died. Aaron's death occurred in a particularly gracious manner. Moses removed Aaron's priestly garments and put them on Eleazar, Aaron's son, so that Aaron would see his son in his glory. Then Moses said to Aaron: "My brother, go up onto the bed," and he went up; "Stretch out your arms," and he stretched them out; "Stretch out your legs," and he stretched them out; "Close your eyes," and he closed them; "Close your mouth," and he closed it. Then his soul departed peacefully.

Moses longed for such a death saying, "Fortunate is he who dies in this manner."

Now, God informed Moses that his wish would be granted (*Rashi, 11th century*).

Food for thought

1. What are your feelings about Moses' not entering the Promised Land?

2. Why is failing God in public so serious an offense?

3. Have you ever committed a public disgrace?

deuteronomy 32:46–52 — ha'azinu

words of this Torah. ⁴⁷ For it is not an empty thing for you (for which you will not be rewarded). Rather, it is your life! Through this thing, you will lengthen your days upon the land of which you are crossing over the Jordan, to take possession."

Moses is Told to Ascend Mount Nebo

[MAFTIR] ⁴⁸ God spoke to Moses on that very day, saying, ⁴⁹ "Climb up the Abarite mountains here, (at) Mount Nebo—which is in the land of Moab that is facing Jericho—and see the land of Canaan, which I am giving to the children of Israel as a possession. ⁵⁰ Then die on the mountain upon which you are climbing and be gathered to your people, just as your brother Aaron died on the double mountain and was gathered to his people. ⁵¹ For, in the presence of the children of Israel, you (caused people to) betray Me at the waters of Meribath-kadesh, in the desert of Zin, for you did not (allow) My (name) to be sanctified in the presence of the children of Israel. ⁵² While you will see the land from afar, you will not come there, to the land I am giving to the children of Israel."

Haftarot: Ha'azinu—page 1412.   Shabbat Shuvah—page 1409.

kabbalah bites

32:49 "Abarite" means "dissension." What was the dissension over Moses' burial place?

Desolate places such as desert plains are ruled by the *sitra' 'aḥara'* (demonic forces). During their forty years in the desert, the Israelites failed to break the fierce power of the *sitra' 'aḥara'*. Instead, it overpowered them: they sinned, and were buried there.

The spiritual control of the Abarite Mountains was dissented between the forces of *kedushah* (holiness) and the *sitra' 'aḥara'*.

Moses, who did not sin, was not buried in the desert plains. Instead, his burial won over the "disputed" mountains to the side of holiness.

Nevertheless, God planted the people's shepherd near them, so that they will all rise together at the End of Days.

48. On that very day. The Jewish people were saying, "We swear, that if we notice Moses is going to die, we will not let him! He is the man who brought us out of Egypt! He split the Reed Sea for us! He brought the manna down for us! He made flocks of quails fly over to us! He brought up the well for us! And he gave us the Torah! We will not let him die!"

But God said, "I will take him in broad daylight!" (*Rashi, 11ᵗʰ century*).

Life and death are in the hands of God and cannot be decided by man. How could the Jewish people have possibly "not let" Moses die?

The Jewish people wished to avert Moses' death by preventing him from relocating to another place, namely, to Mount Nebo. God had said, *"Climb up the Abarite mountains here, (at) Mount Nebo ... Then die on the mountain"* (v. 49-50), indicating that Moses' death was to be the result of a Divine decree (not from natural causes), after ascending the mountain. So the people figured: If Moses does not "climb up Mount Nebo," then the decree will not take effect, and he will not die.

However, this leaves us with another question: How could a righteous generation attempt to defy God's will and prevent Moses from dying by Divine decree?

The Torah **never ends.** We read it every year in a cycle, but really it is a **spiral** that forever **ascends heavenward.** Having read the entire Torah, how **have you changed?** What **have you learned?** What **blessings** have you discovered **in your life?**

VE-ZO'T HA-BERAKHAH
וזאת הברכה

MOSES PRAISES GOD	33:1–5
MOSES BLESSES EACH TRIBE INDIVIDUALLY	33:6–24
MOSES BLESSES ALL ISRAEL	33:25–29
MOSES' PASSING	34:1–12

NAME
Ve-Zo't Ha-Berakhah

MEANING
"This is the blessing"

LINES IN TORAH SCROLL
189

PARASHIYYOT
8 open; 2 closed

VERSES
41

WORDS
512

LETTERS
1969

DATE
7 *Adar*, 2488

LOCATION
Plains of Moab,
Mount Nebo

KEY PEOPLE
Moses, Joshua

MASORETIC FEATURES
The words 'esh dot are joined—'eshdot (33:2)

NOTE
Read on *Simḥat Torah* (*Shemini Atzeret* in the land of Israel)

MITZVOT
None

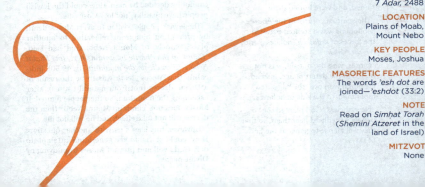

CHARACTER PROFILE

NAME
You

GRANDFATHERS
Abraham, Isaac and Jacob

GRANDMOTHERS
Sarah, Rebekah, Rachel and Leah

ACHIEVEMENTS
Entered into a covenant with God at Sinai; loves all of mankind; strives to be a better person; never judges or blames others; loves and pursues peace; has an attitude of abundance

KNOWN FOR
Unique contribution to the history of mankind; soul is a "piece" of God; never gives up hope; believes more in the limitlessness of God than the limitations of the world

GOD'S MESSENGER

The hero, redeemer, lawgiver, and prophet of God—Moses is not made into an icon of worship, nor does his grave become a shrine. He passes away alone, his burial place unknown (34:1-6). We believe in God's messengers, but we worship only God.

MAN OF GOD

Moses is described as a "man of God" (33:1). Your body protests that you are only human, while your soul insists that you are part of God. The Torah provides you with the means for a synthesis—to become a "man of God."

HERITAGE

As a Jew, the Torah is your heritage (33:4), a rich and wonderful heritage spanning thousands of years.

PROVIDENCE

Fortunate is the people for whom the Omnipresent, who transcends and pervades all heaven and earth, shows overt involvement in their lives and concern for their destiny! (33:26).

דברים לג:א-ט | וזאת הברכה

לג ׀ וְזֹאת הַבְּרָכָה אֲשֶׁר בֵּרַךְ מֹשֶׁה אִישׁ הָאֱלֹהִים אֶת־בְּנֵי יִשְׂרָאֵל
לִפְנֵי מוֹתוֹ: 2 וַיֹּאמַר יְהֹוָה מִסִּינַי בָּא וְזָרַח מִשֵּׂעִיר לָמוֹ הוֹפִיעַ מֵהַר
פָּארָן וְאָתָה מֵרִבְבֹת קֹדֶשׁ מִימִינוֹ [אשדת כ׳] אֵשׁ דָּת לָמוֹ: 3 אַף חֹבֵב עַמִּים כָּל־
קְדֹשָׁיו בְּיָדֶךָ וְהֵם תֻּכּוּ לְרַגְלֶךָ יִשָּׂא מִדַּבְּרֹתֶיךָ: 4 תּוֹרָה צִוָּה־לָנוּ מֹשֶׁה מוֹרָשָׁה
קְהִלַּת יַעֲקֹב: 5 וַיְהִי בִישֻׁרוּן מֶלֶךְ בְּהִתְאַסֵּף רָאשֵׁי עָם יַחַד שִׁבְטֵי יִשְׂרָאֵל:
6 יְחִי רְאוּבֵן וְאַל־יָמֹת וִיהִי מְתָיו מִסְפָּר: ס 7 וְזֹאת לִיהוּדָה וַיֹּאמַר שְׁמַע
יְהֹוָה קוֹל יְהוּדָה וְאֶל־עַמּוֹ תְּבִיאֶנּוּ יָדָיו רָב לוֹ וְעֵזֶר מִצָּרָיו תִּהְיֶה: פ [SECOND READING]
8 וּלְלֵוִי אָמַר תֻּמֶּיךָ וְאוּרֶיךָ לְאִישׁ חֲסִידֶךָ אֲשֶׁר נִסִּיתוֹ בְּמַסָּה תְּרִיבֵהוּ עַל־
מֵי מְרִיבָה: 9 הָאֹמֵר לְאָבִיו וּלְאִמּוֹ לֹא רְאִיתִיו וְאֶת־אֶחָיו לֹא הִכִּיר וְאֶת־בָּנָו

1272

The previous Torah portion concludes, *"You will not come there, to the land I am giving to the children of Israel"* (32:52). The decree preventing Moses from entering the land of Israel resulted from the Israelites' behavior, as the verse states, *"God became angry with me because of you"* (3:26). You might imagine, then, that Moses would bear at least some degree of animosity toward a people that prevented him from achieving his lifelong dream.

But Moses, faithful shepherd of Israel, disregarded his personal aspirations and concerned himself only with the needs of his precious flock. Out of great love for his people, Moses overlooked their iniquity and blessed them.

And it is due to this extraordinary expression of selflessness and forgiveness that Moses is called *"a man of God"* (*Rabbi Abraham b. Jacob Saba, 15th century*).

This is the blessing. A *"man of God,"* who spends much of his time in study and prayer, is often too preoccupied with his own spiritual advancement and cannot relate to the ordinary person. Moses, however, was blessed with a unique quality, *"This is the blessing which Moses (was blessed with)"*—He was *"a man of God,"* achieving the highest degree of spiritual perfection, and yet at the same time he *"gave to the children of Israel,"* because he was attuned to the needs of the people (*Rabbi Meir b. Aaron Leib of Peremyshlyany, 19th century*).

spiritual vitamin

> The festival of rejoicing with the Torah is an inspiring demonstration of our love and loyalty to God, showing that we accept the Torah not as a compulsorily imposed code, but as God's greatest gift to man, which we accept with joy.

deuteronomy 33:1–9 — ve-zo't ha-berakhah

parashat ve-zo't ha-berakhah

Moses' Final Blessings

33 ¹ And this is the blessing which Moses, a man of God, gave to the children of Israel, (shortly) before his death.

² He (first) said (words of praise about God): "God came (out) from Sinai (to meet the Jewish people), and He shined His glory on them (after coming) from Seir (where the children of Esau had declined to accept the Torah). He appeared (to them after coming) from Mount Paran (where the children of Ishmael had declined to accept the Torah). He came (to the Jewish people along) with some of the holy myriads. (Then He gave) them a fiery Law, (written with) His right hand.

³ He also showed affection for the (tribes, who are all) nations (unto themselves). All the holy (souls of the righteous) are in Your hand (a privilege which they deserve), for they let themselves be placed at Your feet (at Mount Sinai), bearing (the yoke of) Your utterances (and decrees with joy).

⁴ The Torah (which) Moses commanded us is an inheritance for the congregation of Jacob, (which will never be abandoned).

⁵ Whenever the people gathered as a numerous group, with the tribes of Israel together, (they always accepted God's rulership), so He was King in Jeshurun (and He wished to bless them).

Moses Blesses the Tribes

⁶ "May Reuben live (in this world), and (when he reaches the world to come, may he) not 'die' (because of the incident with Bilhah). May his people be counted in the (official) number (of the tribes, and not be punished for his sin by being excluded)."

⁷ The following was (said) about Judah. He said, "Listen, God, to Judah's voice (when he prays to You), and bring him (in peace) to his people (back from war). May his hands do battle for him (successfully), and may You be a help against his enemies."

[SECOND READING] ⁸ About Levi he said: "(God!) Your Thummim and Urim belong to Your pious man, (Levi), who (remained faithful when) you tested him at Massah, (and when) you tried him at the waters of Meribah. ⁹ He said about his (non-Levite grand-)father (from) his mother('s side, who was guilty of perpetrating the sin of

---

33:1 This is the blessing which Moses, a man of God, gave to the children of Israel. In this verse Moses is referred to as *"a man of God,"* a unique title which he is not awarded elsewhere in the Torah, because here Moses exhibited exceptional virtues.

דברים לג:ט-יט | וזאת הברכה

לֹא יְדָעוֹ כִּי שָׁמְרוּ אִמְרָתֶךָ וּבְרִיתְךָ יִנְצֹרוּ: 10 יוֹרוּ מִשְׁפָּטֶיךָ לְיַעֲקֹב וְתוֹרָתְךָ לְיִשְׂרָאֵל יָשִׂימוּ קְטוֹרָה בְּאַפֶּךָ וְכָלִיל עַל־מִזְבְּחֶךָ: 11 בָּרֵךְ יְהֹוָה חֵילוֹ וּפֹעַל יָדָיו תִּרְצֶה מְחַץ מָתְנַיִם קָמָיו וּמְשַׂנְאָיו מִן־יְקוּמוּן: ס 12 לְבִנְיָמִן אָמַר יְדִיד יְהֹוָה יִשְׁכֹּן לָבֶטַח עָלָיו חֹפֵף עָלָיו כָּל־הַיּוֹם וּבֵין כְּתֵפָיו שָׁכֵן: ס [THIRD READING]

13 וּלְיוֹסֵף אָמַר מְבֹרֶכֶת יְהֹוָה אַרְצוֹ מִמֶּגֶד שָׁמַיִם מִטָּל וּמִתְּהוֹם רֹבֶצֶת תָּחַת: 14 וּמִמֶּגֶד תְּבוּאֹת שָׁמֶשׁ וּמִמֶּגֶד גֶּרֶשׁ יְרָחִים: 15 וּמֵרֹאשׁ הַרְרֵי־קֶדֶם וּמִמֶּגֶד גִּבְעוֹת עוֹלָם: 16 וּמִמֶּגֶד אֶרֶץ וּמְלֹאָהּ וּרְצוֹן שֹׁכְנִי סְנֶה תָּבוֹאתָה לְרֹאשׁ יוֹסֵף וּלְקָדְקֹד נְזִיר אֶחָיו: 17 בְּכוֹר שׁוֹרוֹ הָדָר לוֹ וְקַרְנֵי רְאֵם קַרְנָיו בָּהֶם עַמִּים יְנַגַּח יַחְדָּו אַפְסֵי־אָרֶץ וְהֵם רִבְבוֹת אֶפְרַיִם וְהֵם אַלְפֵי מְנַשֶּׁה: ס

18 וְלִזְבוּלֻן אָמַר שְׂמַח זְבוּלֻן בְּצֵאתֶךָ וְיִשָּׂשכָר בְּאֹהָלֶיךָ: 19 עַמִּים הַר־יִקְרָאוּ שָׁם יִזְבְּחוּ זִבְחֵי־צֶדֶק כִּי שֶׁפַע יַמִּים יִינָקוּ וּשְׂפוּנֵי טְמוּנֵי חוֹל: ס [FOURTH READING]

1274

The fact that the Temple site, even after its destruction, still elicits a sense of awe and reverence by all who visit it, is evidence that the King will one day return to His palace (*Rabbi Ḥayyim Aryeh Leib of Jedwabne, 19th century*).

18. Succeed, Zebulun ... and Issachar. Zebulun and Issachar entered into a partnership: *"Zebulun will live by the sea coast" (Genesis 49:13)*, and go out in ships to trade. He would make a profit and feed Issachar's mouth, while they would sit and occupy themselves with Torah. Therefore, Moses mentioned Zebulun before Issachar, even though the latter was older, because Issachar's Torah was supported by Zebulun (*Rashi, 11th century*).

The purpose of creation, according to *Midrash Tanḥuma*, is that man should make *"a home for God below,"* in this physical world. While the fulltime Torah scholar (Issachar) achieves this goal through his devoted study and observance of commandments, he nevertheless remains somewhat withdrawn from interaction with the world, and so he only transforms a relatively small part of this world into "a home for God." On the other hand, the businessman (Zebulun) sanctifies his *entire* working environment, through observing the laws of business ethics, being attuned to acts of Divine Providence that he witnesses, and donating generously to charity. That is why the Torah mentions Zebulun before Issachar—*because Zebulun furthers the goal of creation to a greater extent*.

In fact, that is the inner reason why God made the world in such a way that most people are businessmen, and not Torah scholars (*Rabbi Menahem Mendel Schneerson, 20th century*).

Succeed (lit. "rejoice"), Zebulun, when you go out (to work), and Issachar, in your tents (of Torah). When a businessman departs on a trip he is usually tense and nervous, for he does not know if he will be successful. Only after returning home after making a lucrative deal is he relaxed and able to rejoice.

deuteronomy 33:9–19 — ve-zo't ha-berakhah

the Golden Calf), 'I do not see him (as my grandfather any more),' neither did he recognize his (guilty, non-Levite half-)brothers, nor did he know his (guilty non-Levite grand-)children, (and he loyally followed God's orders to kill them. But none of the Levites were guilty), because they kept Your word (never worshiping idols) and kept Your covenant (of circumcision, when others lapsed). [10] They will teach Your laws to Jacob, and Your Torah to Israel (because they are fit to do so). They will place incense before You, and burnt-offerings upon Your altar. [11] May God bless him with his possessions, and may You favor the work of his hands. May You smash the loins of his foes and his enemies, so that they will never recover."

[12] About Benjamin he said, "May God's beloved dwell securely with Him, (when the Holy Temple will be built in Benjamin's portion. May the Divine Presence) cover him (and protect him) forever, and dwell among (the high places of Benjamin's territory, which are likened to) his shoulders."

[THIRD READING] [13] About Joseph he said: "May his land be blessed by God, with delicacies (nourished by rains) from the skies, from dew, and (from underground waters that rise) from the depths that lie below. [14] (May it be blessed with) the delicacies of produce (sweetened by) the sun, and with delicacies from crops (ripened) by moon(light. [15] May it be blessed) with crops (that ripen) early (on its) mountains, and with delicacies from its hills, all year round. [16] (May it be blessed) with the abundant delicacies of the (low)lands, through the goodwill (of God, who was first revealed to Me) dwelling in the thorn-bush. May (all this) come upon Joseph's head, upon the crown of the one (who was) separated from his brothers (when they sold him. [17] Joshua, a descendant of Joseph, is like) his firstborn ox (for he is to be a powerful king, and) glory will be (given to) him. His horns are (beautiful like) horns of an oryx. With them, he will gore (thirty-one) nations together, (as far as) the ends of the land (of Israel). These (nations will number) tens of thousands (all killed by Joshua, a descendant) of Ephraim, (besides) the thousands (to be killed in Midian by Gideon, a descendent) of Manasseh."

[FOURTH READING] [18] About Zebulun he said: "Succeed, Zebulun, when you go out (to work), and Issachar, in your tents (of Torah, where you will establish the calendar. [19] Then, when the festivals arrive), they will call (all the Jewish) people to Mount (Moriah, and) there, they will slaughter offerings of righteousness. For (Zebulun —and Issachar, whom they support)—will be nourished by the abundance of the seas, and by the valuable things hidden in the sand."

---

12. (May the Divine Presence) cover him (and protect him) forever. This verse discusses the Holy Temple that was to be built in Benjamin's territory. When a king is forced into exile, his palace remains nothing more than a historic site; the awe and reverence that would fall upon his subjects at the palace is gone. But when the king leaves on a short trip, his presence can still be felt in the palace.

דברים לג:כ - לד:א | וזאת הברכה

20 וּלְגָד אָמַר בָּרוּךְ מַרְחִיב גָּד כְּלָבִיא שָׁכֵן וְטָרַף זְרוֹעַ אַף־קָדְקֹד: 21 וַיַּרְא רֵאשִׁית לוֹ כִּי־שָׁם חֶלְקַת מְחֹקֵק סָפוּן וַיֵּתֵא רָאשֵׁי עָם צִדְקַת יְהֹוָה עָשָׂה וּמִשְׁפָּטָיו עִם־יִשְׂרָאֵל: ס [FIFTH READING] 22 וּלְדָן אָמַר דָּן גּוּר אַרְיֵה יְזַנֵּק מִן־הַבָּשָׁן: 23 וּלְנַפְתָּלִי אָמַר נַפְתָּלִי שְׂבַע רָצוֹן וּמָלֵא בִּרְכַּת יְהֹוָה יָם וְדָרוֹם יְרָשָׁה: ס 24 וּלְאָשֵׁר אָמַר בָּרוּךְ מִבָּנִים אָשֵׁר יְהִי רְצוּי אֶחָיו וְטֹבֵל בַּשֶּׁמֶן רַגְלוֹ: 25 בַּרְזֶל וּנְחֹשֶׁת מִנְעָלֶךָ וּכְיָמֶיךָ דָּבְאֶךָ: 26 אֵין כָּאֵל יְשֻׁרוּן רֹכֵב שָׁמַיִם בְּעֶזְרֶךָ וּבְגַאֲוָתוֹ שְׁחָקִים: [SIXTH READING] 27 מְעֹנָה אֱלֹהֵי קֶדֶם וּמִתַּחַת זְרֹעֹת עוֹלָם וַיְגָרֶשׁ מִפָּנֶיךָ אוֹיֵב וַיֹּאמֶר הַשְׁמֵד: 28 וַיִּשְׁכֹּן יִשְׂרָאֵל בֶּטַח בָּדָד עֵין יַעֲקֹב אֶל־אֶרֶץ דָּגָן וְתִירוֹשׁ אַף־שָׁמָיו יַעַרְפוּ־טָל: 29 אַשְׁרֶיךָ יִשְׂרָאֵל מִי כָמוֹךָ עַם נוֹשַׁע בַּיהֹוָה מָגֵן עֶזְרֶךָ וַאֲשֶׁר־חֶרֶב גַּאֲוָתֶךָ וְיִכָּחֲשׁוּ אֹיְבֶיךָ לָךְ וְאַתָּה עַל־בָּמוֹתֵימוֹ תִדְרֹךְ: ס

לד [SEVENTH READING] 1 וַיַּעַל מֹשֶׁה מֵעַרְבֹת מוֹאָב אֶל־הַר נְבוֹ רֹאשׁ הַפִּסְגָּה אֲשֶׁר עַל־פְּנֵי יְרֵחוֹ וַיַּרְאֵהוּ יְהֹוָה אֶת־כָּל־הָאָרֶץ אֶת־הַגִּלְעָד עַד־דָּן:

20. He will tear off an arm (of his enemy in one blow, along) with the head. It would have been sufficient to simply state that the tribe of Gad will become mighty warriors. What is the significance of this particular feat?

Making an interruption between donning the hand-*tefillin* (phylacteries) and the head-*tefillin* is regarded as a transgression for which a Jewish soldier must return home from his deployment, because of the fear that he will no longer be protected in battle (*Babylonian Talmud, Menahot* 36a). The Torah attests to the exceptional righteousness of the tribe of Gad in that not one member of the entire tribe ever violated even this minor infraction, *"They will troop back in their own tracks (and not one man will be missing from them)"* (Genesis 49:19). Therefore, measure for measure, they exhibited this remarkable ability to tear off the enemy soldier's head and arm in one blow, without any pause (*Rabbi Elijah of Vilna, 18th century*).

25. May your locks … iron and copper. May the days of your old age be like the days of your youth. When you harness your youthful energy with *"locks of iron and copper,"* and guard yourself from immoral behavior, you will be blessed with strength and vitality in your old age (*Rabbi Isaac Meir Alter of Gur, 19th century*).

34:1 Moses went up… to mount Nebo. Our Sages taught: "The world was created with fifty gates of understanding, and they were all given to Moses except for the fiftieth, as the verse

deuteronomy 33:20 – 34:1 — ve-zo't ha-berakhah

²⁰ About Gad he said: "Blessed is He who grants an expanding (territory) to Gad, who lives (in a territorial stronghold) like a lion. He will tear off an arm (of his enemy in one blow, along) with the head. ²¹ He saw (fit to take) the first portion (of the land that was conquered) for himself (in the territory of Sihon and Og), because there the (burial) plot of (Moses) the lawgiver is hidden. (Gad) came (out to war) at the head of the people (even after he had acquired his own portion), doing what was right for God, and what is lawful with Israel."

[FIFTH READING] ²² About Dan he said: "Dan is a young lion (for he, too, has a territorial stronghold. His land drinks from a) stream that runs from Bashan."

²³ About Naphtali he said: "Naphtali('s land brings) satisfaction (to its inhabitants) and is filled with God's blessing. Take possession of (part of) the south of the (Chinnereth) Sea (to spread your fishing nets)."

²⁴ About Asher he said: "May Asher be blessed with sons. He will be pleasing to his brothers (through producing special oils), and he will (have so much) oil (that he will be able to) immerse his foot."

Moses Blesses All Israel

²⁵ "May your locks (on your border towns) be (strong like) iron and copper. May the days of your old age be like the days of your youth.

²⁶ "Jeshurun, there is none like God! (God), who rides the heavens is at your assistance! (He rides) the heavens in His majesty!"

[SIXTH READING] ²⁷ "(The heavens) are the abode for God, who precedes all. The mighty ones of the world are found (only) below. He expelled the enemy from before you, and said, 'Destroy!' ²⁸ Israel will live safely and (it will be safe for each person to live) alone—as Jacob (blessed them)—in a land of grain and wine, with skies that drip dew, (as Isaac blessed them).

²⁹ Fortunate are you, O Israel! Who is like you, O people saved by God, the Shield who helps you, your majestic Sword! Your enemies will lie to you, but you will trample upon their exalted ones."

Moses' Passing

34 [SEVENTH READING] ¹ Moses went up from the plains of Moab to Mount Nebo, (to the) top of the summit facing Jericho. God showed him the land (and visions of what was to happen there in the future): The (events at) Gilead as far as

---

This is not true for the "Zebulun" businessman who supports Torah institutions. "Rejoice Zebulun when you *go out*"—his mind is at ease from the moment he sets off. He is confident that God will help him be successful, because *"Issachar, in your tents (of Torah)."* The merit of the Torah study he supports will stand him in good stead (*Rabbi Ḥayyim ibn Attar, 18th century*).

דברים לד:ב-ט | וזאת הברכה

2 וְאֵת כָּל־נַפְתָּלִי וְאֶת־אֶרֶץ אֶפְרַיִם וּמְנַשֶּׁה וְאֵת כָּל־אֶרֶץ יְהוּדָה עַד הַיָּם הָאַחֲרוֹן: 3 וְאֶת־הַנֶּגֶב וְאֶת־הַכִּכָּר בִּקְעַת יְרֵחוֹ עִיר הַתְּמָרִים עַד־צֹעַר: 4 וַיֹּאמֶר יְהֹוָה אֵלָיו זֹאת הָאָרֶץ אֲשֶׁר נִשְׁבַּעְתִּי לְאַבְרָהָם לְיִצְחָק וּלְיַעֲקֹב לֵאמֹר לְזַרְעֲךָ אֶתְּנֶנָּה הֶרְאִיתִיךָ בְעֵינֶיךָ וְשָׁמָּה לֹא תַעֲבֹר: 5 וַיָּמָת שָׁם מֹשֶׁה עֶבֶד־יְהֹוָה בְּאֶרֶץ מוֹאָב עַל־פִּי יְהֹוָה: 6 וַיִּקְבֹּר אֹתוֹ בַגַּי בְּאֶרֶץ מוֹאָב מוּל בֵּית פְּעוֹר וְלֹא־יָדַע אִישׁ אֶת־קְבֻרָתוֹ עַד הַיּוֹם הַזֶּה: 7 וּמֹשֶׁה בֶּן־מֵאָה וְעֶשְׂרִים שָׁנָה בְּמֹתוֹ לֹא־כָהֲתָה עֵינוֹ וְלֹא־נָס לֵחֹה: 8 וַיִּבְכּוּ בְנֵי־יִשְׂרָאֵל אֶת־מֹשֶׁה בְּעַרְבֹת מוֹאָב שְׁלֹשִׁים יוֹם וַיִּתְּמוּ יְמֵי בְכִי אֵבֶל מֹשֶׁה: 9 וִיהוֹשֻׁעַ בִּן־נוּן מָלֵא רוּחַ חָכְמָה כִּי־סָמַךְ מֹשֶׁה אֶת־יָדָיו עָלָיו וַיִּשְׁמְעוּ אֵלָיו בְּנֵי־יִשְׂרָאֵל

beg and demand from God that Moses lead us into the land of Israel!" and the decree would subsequently be annulled.

But when something is written in the Torah surely it *must* happen? By writing *"Moses … died there,"* wasn't he guaranteeing his own death?

The answer is that Moses hoped that the prayers of the Jewish people would transform the decree of his actual death to an allegorical equivalent (*Rabbi Menahem Mendel Schneerson, 20th century*).

8. The men of Israel wept for Moses. Here Moses was only mourned by the men. But about Aaron, the Torah states, *"The entire house of Israel"* wept for him (*Numbers* 20:29), meaning both men and women. This is because he used to pursue and bring peace between a man and his fellow, and between man and wife (*Rashi, 11th century*).

Since the current passage relates the passing of Moses, we would expect the Torah to stress Moses' own greatness. Why did *Rashi* choose an interpretation which indicates *Aaron's superiority* over Moses?

spiritual vitamin

> When a person makes a far-reaching discovery, or reaches an important resolution, he or she can in effect put "ages" into minutes. On the other hand, time allowed to go by without proper content, has no reality at all, however long it may last.

deuteronomy 34:1–9 — ve-zo't ha-berakhah

Dan, ² all (the land of) Naphtali, the land of Ephraim and Manasseh, all the land of Judah until the western sea, ³ the Negev, and the plain, (including) the valley of Jericho, and the city of palm trees as far as Zoar. ⁴ God said to him, "This is the land I swore to Abraham, to Isaac, and to Jacob, saying, 'I will give it to your offspring.' I have let you see it with your eyes, but you should not cross over there."

⁵ Moses, the servant of God, died there, in the land of Moab, by (a kiss from) the mouth of God. ⁶ (God) buried him in the valley, in the land of Moab, opposite Beth-peor. No person knows the place of his burial, to this day.

⁷ Moses was one hundred and twenty years old when he died. His eye never dimmed, nor did moisture leave his (body, even after he died).

⁸ The men of Israel wept for Moses in the plains of Moab for thirty days, and then the days of weeping over the mourning for Moses came to an end.

⁹ Joshua son of Nun was filled with a spirit of wisdom, because Moses had laid his hands upon him. The children of Israel obeyed him, and they did as God had commanded Moses.

---

states, *'You have made him slightly less than the angels'* (*Psalms* 8:6; *Babylonian Talmud, Rosh Ha-Shanah* 21b).

But on the very last day of his life, Moses *was* granted access to the elusive "fiftieth gate." This is hinted to by the verse, *"Moses went up … to Mount Nebo,"* since the word Nebo (spelled: *nun-bet-vav*) can be read *nun bo'*, meaning, "the fiftieth is in him" (*Rabbi Dov Baer of Mezhirech, 18th century*).

5. Moses, the servant of God, died. Is it possible that Moses died, and then wrote, *"Moses … died there"*? Rather, Moses wrote up to this point, and Joshua wrote from here on.

Rabbi Meir says: "Is it possible that the Torah Scroll which Moses gave to the Levites (*Deuteronomy* 31:26) would be lacking something? Rather, God said this section, and Moses wrote it with tears" (*Rashi, 11th century*).

According to Rabbi Meir, what was the purpose in God's commanding Moses to write about his own passing?

Moses did not write these words with tears of resignation, as it may at first seem, but amid a spirit of determination and optimism. He was using these last moments in a further, practical attempt to avert the looming decree of his death, by motivating the Jewish people to beseech God on his behalf. Moses knew that when the Jewish people would read of his death written down in black and white, it would provoke an uproar. The people were sure to respond: "We will not allow this to happen! We will pray,

kabbalah bites

34:4 Your consciousness is your only real address. If you stand in London but your mind is in New York, then you are in New York. You are not in London at all.

דברים לד:ט-יב — וזאת הברכה

וַיַּעֲשׂוּ כַּאֲשֶׁר צִוָּה יְהֹוָה אֶת־מֹשֶׁה: 10 וְלֹא־קָם נָבִיא עוֹד בְּיִשְׂרָאֵל כְּמֹשֶׁה אֲשֶׁר יְדָעוֹ יְהֹוָה פָּנִים אֶל־פָּנִים: 11 לְכָל־הָאֹתֹת וְהַמּוֹפְתִים אֲשֶׁר שְׁלָחוֹ יְהֹוָה לַעֲשׂוֹת בְּאֶרֶץ מִצְרָיִם לְפַרְעֹה וּלְכָל־עֲבָדָיו וּלְכָל־אַרְצוֹ: 12 וּלְכֹל הַיָּד הַחֲזָקָה וּלְכֹל הַמּוֹרָא הַגָּדוֹל אֲשֶׁר עָשָׂה מֹשֶׁה לְעֵינֵי כָּל־יִשְׂרָאֵל:

חֲזַק חֲזַק וְנִתְחַזֵּק

מ"א פסוקים, גאוא"ל סימן. אל"י סימן. סכום פסוקים של ספר דברים תשע מאות וחמשים וחמשה הנ"ך סימן. וחציו ועשית על פי הדבר אשר יגידו לך. ופרשיותיו י"א, אסרה ח"ג בעבותים סימן. וסדריו כ"ז, יפיח אמונה יגי"ד צדק סימן. ופרקיו ל"ד, אודה ה' בכל לב"ב סימן. מנין הפתוחות ל"ד. והסתומות קכ"ד. סך הכל קנ"ח פרשיות, וכסא כבוד ינחיל"ם סימן.

סדרי תורה נ"ד, למען יזמרך כבוד ולא יד"ם סימן. מנין הפרשיות הפתוחות של כל התורה ר"ץ, יבא דודי לגנו ויאכל פר"י מגדיו סימן. והסתומות שע"ט, או אסרה אסר על נפשה בשבע"ה סימן. נמצאו מנין כל הפרשיות פתוחות וסתומות תרס"ט, לא תחסר כל בה סימן.

סכום הפסוקים של כל התורה ה' אלפים תמ"ה, ואור החמ"ה יהיה שבעתיים סימן. וחציו וישם עליו את החשן ויתן אל החשן את האורים ואת התומים.

מנין תיבות של כל התורה ע"ט אלף ותתקע"ו, עט סופר מהיר יפיפית מבני אדם סימן. מנין אותיות של כל התורה ד"ש אלף ות"ה, וסימנו ארצה בו ואכבדה אמר ה' גדול יהיה כבוד הבית הזה האחרון מן הראשון. שיבנה במהרה בימינו אמן כן יהי רצון.

---

be in "breach of contract" for worshiping the calf (see *Rashi* to *Exodus* 34:1). So there *is* a positive message here: that when faced with a dilemma between saving the holy tablets of Torah fashioned by God, and saving the Jewish people from being liable for breach of contract, Moses chose the latter.

This, however, seems to reflect negatively on the Torah itself. When faced with a choice between protecting the Torah and protecting the Jewish people, Moses chose not to protect the Torah!

We can glean the answer to this problem from the following Midrash: *There are two things in the world and I love them totally with all my heart: the Torah and the Jewish people. But I do not know which comes first? People say that the Torah comes first … but since the Torah states, "Command the children of Israel. Speak to the children of Israel," I say that the Jewish people come first"* (*Tanna de-Vei Eliyahu*).

When Moses broke the tablets he was making a very similar statement—the Jewish people come first. And this is a fitting conclusion for the Torah; the message is that *the purpose of the Torah is to bring the greatness of the Jewish people to light* (*Rabbi Menahem Mendel Schneerson, 20th century*).

deuteronomy 34:10–12 — ve-zo't ha-berakhah

¹⁰ No other prophet ever arose in Israel like Moses, whom God knew face to face, ¹¹ as manifested by all the signs and wonders, which God had sent him to perform in the land of Egypt, to Pharaoh and all his servants, and to all his land, ¹² and all the strength (he needed to receive the Torah with his) hand, and all the (miracles that occurred in the) great, awe(some, wilderness), which Moses performed before the eyes of all Israel.

The congregation, followed by the reader, proclaims:

Be strong! Be strong! And may we be strengthened!

The *Haftarah* for *Ve-Zo't Ha-Berakhah* (*Simḥat Torah*) is on page 1476.

Moses personified the quality of truth (*Babylonian Talmud, Sanhedrin* 111a). Therefore, while he would certainly have made great efforts to "pursue peace and bring peace" during his lifetime, Moses found himself unable to go to the same lengths as Aaron in the pursuit of peace.

Aaron followed the principle, *"It is permissible to modify the facts for the sake of peace"* (ibid., *Yevamot* 65b). He would bring quarreling parties together by "modifying the facts," claiming that the opposing party really wished to make peace. Moses, however, was unable to do so—not because he disagreed with the principle that "it is permissible to modify," since, after all, this was part of the Torah which Moses himself had taught the Jewish people. Rather, Moses could simply not take advantage of this "permission" to "modify the facts" even for the sake of peace, since he embodied truth.

Nevertheless, on the last day of his life, Moses was able to reflect on his life's work (something he would have been far too busy to do before), and, at this point, *he came to appreciate the additional advantage of Aaron's approach,* which succeeded in reaching more people than Moses.

Therefore, in an act of true love for his fellow Jews, Moses recorded the events of his own passing in a way that brought to light Aaron's greatness, which Moses only attained at this point in his life (*Rabbi Menahem Mendel Schneerson, 20th century*).

12. Moses performed before the eyes of all Israel. This refers to when his heart inspired him to smash the tablets before their eyes, as the verse states, *"I shattered them before your eyes"* (*Deuteronomy* 9:17). God gave His approval, saying "Well done for breaking them!" (*Rashi, 11th century*).

How can *Rashi* conclude his commentary to the Torah with a reference to Moses' breaking of the tablets, in contradiction, it would seem, to the traditional emphasis of always ending on a positive note?

Moses' breaking of the tablets was like tearing up a contract, to ensure that the Jewish people would not

---

kabbalah bites

34:10 *"No other prophet ever arose in Israel like Moses,"* but there has arisen one like him among the nations of the world. Who is this? Balaam son of Beor (*Sifrei*).

Moses and Balaam were both reincarnations of Abel. When Abel sinned—through gazing at the Divine Presence, after God accepted his offering (*Tikkunei Zohar*)—evil became mixed into his soul.

Moses later received the good within Abel's soul, and Balaam the bad; but since they came from the same soul root, they were capable of achieving comparable levels of prophecy.

עשרת הדברות בטעם העליון לקריאה בציבור
THE TEN COMMANDMENTS WITH NOTES USED BY THE READER FOR PUBLIC TORAH READING

PARASHAT YITRO

אָנֹכִ֨י יְהֹוָ֣ה אֱלֹהֶ֔יךָ אֲשֶׁ֧ר הוֹצֵאתִ֛יךָ מֵאֶ֥רֶץ מִצְרַ֖יִם מִבֵּ֣ית עֲבָדִֽ֑ים לֹ֣א יִהְיֶֽה־לְךָ֩ אֱלֹהִ֨ים אֲחֵרִ֜ים עַל־פָּנַ֗י לֹֽא־תַֽעֲשֶׂ֨ה לְךָ֥ פֶ֣סֶל ׀ וְכָל־תְּמוּנָ֡ה אֲשֶׁ֣ר בַּשָּׁמַ֣יִם ׀ מִמַּ֡עַל וַֽאֲשֶׁ֣ר בָּאָ֣רֶץ מִתַּ֗חַת וַֽאֲשֶׁ֣ר בַּמַּ֣יִם ׀ מִתַּ֣חַת לָאָ֑רֶץ לֹֽא־תִשְׁתַּחֲוֶ֥ה לָהֶ֖ם וְלֹ֣א תָֽעָבְדֵ֑ם כִּ֣י אָֽנֹכִ֞י יְהֹוָ֤ה אֱלֹהֶ֨יךָ֙ אֵ֣ל קַנָּ֔א פֹּ֠קֵ֠ד עֲוֺ֨ן אָבֹ֧ת עַל־בָּנִ֛ים עַל־שִׁלֵּשִׁ֥ים וְעַל־רִבֵּעִ֖ים לְשֹׂנְאָ֑י וְעֹ֤שֶׂה חֶ֨סֶד֙ לַֽאֲלָפִ֔ים לְאֹהֲבַ֖י וּלְשֹׁמְרֵ֥י מִצְוֺתָֽי׃ ס לֹ֥א תִשָּׂ֛א אֶת־שֵֽׁם־יְהֹוָ֥ה אֱלֹהֶ֖יךָ לַשָּׁ֑וְא כִּ֣י לֹ֤א יְנַקֶּה֙ יְהֹוָ֔ה אֵ֛ת אֲשֶׁר־יִשָּׂ֥א אֶת־שְׁמ֖וֹ לַשָּֽׁוְא׃ פ זָכ֛וֹר֩ אֶת־י֥֨וֹם הַשַּׁבָּ֖֜ת לְקַדְּשֽׁ֗וֹ שֵׁ֤֣שֶׁת יָמִ֣ים֙ תַּֽעֲבֹ֔ד וְעָשִׂ֖֣יתָ כָּל־מְלַאכְתֶּֽךָ֒ ׀ וְיוֹם֙ הַשְּׁבִיעִ֔֜י שַׁבָּ֖֣ת ׀ לַיהֹוָ֣֖ה אֱלֹהֶ֑֗יךָ לֹֽ֣א־תַֽעֲשֶׂ֣ה כָל־מְלָאכָ֡ה אַתָּ֣ה ׀ וּבִנְךָ֣־וּ֠בִתֶּ֠ךָ עַבְדְּךָ֨ וַֽאֲמָֽתְךָ֜ וּבְהֶמְתֶּ֗ךָ וְגֵֽרְךָ֙ אֲשֶׁ֣ר בִּשְׁעָרֶ֔יךָ כִּ֣י שֵֽׁשֶׁת־יָמִים֩ עָשָׂ֨ה יְהֹוָ֜ה אֶת־הַשָּׁמַ֣יִם וְאֶת־הָאָ֗רֶץ אֶת־הַיָּם֙ וְאֶת־כָּל־אֲשֶׁר־בָּ֔ם וַיָּ֖נַח בַּיּ֣וֹם הַשְּׁבִיעִ֑י עַל־כֵּ֗ן בֵּרַ֧ךְ יְהֹוָ֛ה אֶת־י֥וֹם הַשַּׁבָּ֖ת וַֽיְקַדְּשֵֽׁהוּ׃ ס כַּבֵּ֥ד אֶת־אָבִ֖יךָ וְאֶת־אִמֶּ֑ךָ לְמַ֨עַן֙ יַֽאֲרִכ֣וּן יָמֶ֔יךָ עַ֚ל הָֽאֲדָמָ֔ה אֲשֶׁר־יְהֹוָ֥ה אֱלֹהֶ֖יךָ נֹתֵ֥ן לָֽךְ׃ ס לֹ֥א תִרְצָֽ֖ח׃ ס לֹ֣א תִנְאָֽ֑ף׃ ס לֹ֣א תִגְנֹֽ֔ב׃ ס לֹֽא־תַֽעֲנֶ֥ה בְרֵֽעֲךָ֖ עֵ֥ד שָֽׁקֶר׃ ס לֹ֥א תַחְמֹ֖ד בֵּ֣ית רֵעֶ֑ךָ ס לֹֽא־תַחְמֹ֞ד אֵ֣שֶׁת רֵעֶ֗ךָ וְעַבְדּ֤וֹ וַֽאֲמָתוֹ֙ וְשׁוֹר֣וֹ וַֽחֲמֹר֔וֹ וְכֹ֖ל אֲשֶׁ֥ר לְרֵעֶֽךָ׃

PARASHAT VA-ETHANAN

אָֽנֹכִ֖י֙ יְהֹוָ֣ה אֱלֹהֶ֑֔יךָ אֲשֶׁ֧ר הוֹצֵאתִ֛יךָ מֵאֶ֥רֶץ מִצְרַ֖יִם מִבֵּ֥֣ית עֲבָדִֽ֑ים לֹ֣א יִהְיֶ֥ה־לְךָ֛֩ אֱלֹהִ֥֨ים אֲחֵרִ֖ים עַל־פָּנַ֗י לֹֽא־תַֽעֲשֶׂ֨ה־לְךָ֥֣ פֶ֣֗סֶל ׀ כָּל־תְּמוּנָ֡֔ה אֲשֶׁ֤֣ר בַּשָּׁמַ֣֨יִם ׀ מִמַּ֔֡עַל וַֽאֲשֶׁ֥ר בָּאָ֖֨רֶץ מִתָּ֑֜חַת וַֽאֲשֶׁ֥ר בַּמַּ֣֣יִם ׀ מִתַּ֖֣חַת לָאָֽ֑רֶץ לֹֽא־תִשְׁתַּחֲוֶ֥֣ה לָהֶ֖ם֮ וְלֹ֣א תָֽעָבְדֵ֑ם֒ כִּ֣י אָֽנֹכִ֞י יְהֹוָ֤ה אֱלֹהֶ֨יךָ֙ אֵ֣ל קַנָּ֔א פֹּ֠קֵד עֲוֺ֨ן אָב֧וֹת עַל־בָּנִ֛ים וְעַל־שִׁלֵּשִׁ֥ים וְעַל־רִבֵּעִ֖ים לְשֹׂנְאָ֑י וְעֹ֧שֶׂה חֶ֛סֶד לַֽאֲלָפִ֖ים לְאֹהֲבַ֥י וּלְשֹׁמְרֵ֛י [מצותו כ׳] מִצְוֺתָֽי׃ ס לֹ֥א תִשָּׂ֛א אֶת־שֵֽׁם־יְהֹוָ֥ה אֱלֹהֶ֖יךָ לַשָּׁ֑וְא כִּ֣י לֹ֤א יְנַקֶּה֙ יְהֹוָ֔ה אֵ֛ת אֲשֶׁר־יִשָּׂ֥א אֶת־שְׁמ֖וֹ לַשָּֽׁוְא׃ ס שָׁמ֣֛וֹר אֶת־י֥וֹם֩ הַשַּׁבָּ֖֨ת לְקַדְּשׁ֑֜וֹ כַּֽאֲשֶׁ֥֣ר צִוְּךָ֖֣ ׀ יְהֹוָ֥֣ה אֱלֹהֶ֑֗יךָ שֵׁ֤֣שֶׁת יָמִ֣ים֙ תַּֽעֲבֹ֔ד וְעָשִׂ֖֣יתָ כָּל־מְלַאכְתֶּֽךָ֒ ׀ וְיוֹם֙ הַשְּׁבִיעִ֔֜י שַׁבָּ֖֣ת ׀ לַיהֹוָ֣֖ה אֱלֹהֶ֑֗יךָ לֹ֣א תַֽעֲשֶׂ֣ה כָל־מְלָאכָ֡ה אַתָּ֣ה וּבִנְךָֽ־וּבִתֶּ֣ךָ וְעַבְדְּךָֽ־וַ֠אֲמָתֶ֠ךָ וְשֽׁוֹרְךָ֨ וַחֲמֹֽרְךָ֜ וְכָל־בְּהֶמְתֶּ֗ךָ וְגֵֽרְךָ֙ אֲשֶׁ֣ר בִּשְׁעָרֶ֔יךָ לְמַ֗עַן יָנ֛וּחַ עַבְדְּךָ֥ וַֽאֲמָֽתְךָ֖ כָּמ֑וֹךָ וְזָֽכַרְתָּ֞֗ כִּ֣י־עֶ֤֥בֶד הָיִ֣֨יתָ ׀ בְּאֶ֣רֶץ מִצְרַ֔֗יִם וַיֹּצִ֨אֲךָ֜֩ יְהֹוָ֤֨ה אֱלֹהֶ֤֨יךָ֙ מִשָּׁ֔ם בְּיָ֤֥ד חֲזָקָ֖ה֙ וּבִזְרֹ֣עַ נְטוּיָ֑֔ה עַל־כֵּ֗ן צִוְּךָ֙ יְהֹוָ֣ה אֱלֹהֶ֔יךָ לַעֲשׂ֖וֹת אֶת־י֥וֹם הַשַּׁבָּֽת׃ ס כַּבֵּ֤ד אֶת־אָבִ֨יךָ֙ וְאֶת־אִמֶּ֔ךָ כַּֽאֲשֶׁ֥ר צִוְּךָ֖ יְהֹוָ֣ה אֱלֹהֶ֑יךָ לְמַ֣עַן ׀ יַֽאֲרִיכֻ֣ן יָמֶ֗יךָ וּלְמַ֨עַן֙ יִ֣יטַב לָ֔ךְ עַ֚ל הָֽאֲדָמָ֔ה אֲשֶׁר־יְהֹוָ֥ה אֱלֹהֶ֖יךָ נֹתֵ֥ן לָֽךְ׃ ס לֹ֥א תִרְצָֽח׃ ס וְלֹ֣א תִנְאָֽף׃ ס וְלֹ֣א תִגְנֹֽב׃ ס וְלֹֽא־תַעֲנֶ֥ה בְרֵֽעֲךָ֖ עֵ֥ד שָֽׁוְא׃ ס וְלֹ֥א תַחְמֹ֖ד אֵ֣שֶׁת רֵעֶ֑ךָ ס וְלֹ֨א תִתְאַוֶּ֜ה בֵּ֣ית רֵעֶ֗ךָ שָׂדֵ֜הוּ וְעַבְדּ֤וֹ וַֽאֲמָתוֹ֙ שׁוֹר֣וֹ וַֽחֲמֹר֔וֹ וְכֹ֖ל אֲשֶׁ֥ר לְרֵעֶֽךָ׃ ס

הפטרות

HAFTAROT

ברכות ההפטרה
BLESSINGS ON READING *the* HAFTARAH

The person who was called up for Maftir says the following before reading the Haftarah:

בָּרוּךְ אַתָּה יְהֹוָה אֱלֹהֵינוּ מֶלֶךְ הָעוֹלָם אֲשֶׁר בָּחַר בִּנְבִיאִים טוֹבִים וְרָצָה בְדִבְרֵיהֶם הַנֶּאֱמָרִים בֶּאֱמֶת, בָּרוּךְ אַתָּה יְהֹוָה הַבּוֹחֵר בַּתּוֹרָה וּבְמֹשֶׁה עַבְדּוֹ וּבְיִשְׂרָאֵל עַמּוֹ וּבִנְבִיאֵי הָאֱמֶת וָצֶדֶק:

After the Haftarah the following blessings are recited:

בָּרוּךְ אַתָּה יְיָ אֱלֹהֵינוּ מֶלֶךְ הָעוֹלָם, צוּר כָּל הָעוֹלָמִים, צַדִּיק בְּכָל הַדּוֹרוֹת, הָאֵל הַנֶּאֱמָן הָאוֹמֵר וְעוֹשֶׂה, הַמְדַבֵּר וּמְקַיֵּם, שֶׁכָּל דְּבָרָיו אֱמֶת וָצֶדֶק:

נֶאֱמָן אַתָּה הוּא יְיָ אֱלֹהֵינוּ, וְנֶאֱמָנִים דְּבָרֶיךָ, וְדָבָר אֶחָד מִדְּבָרֶיךָ אָחוֹר לֹא יָשׁוּב רֵיקָם, כִּי אֵל מֶלֶךְ נֶאֱמָן וְרַחֲמָן אָתָּה. בָּרוּךְ אַתָּה יְיָ, הָאֵל הַנֶּאֱמָן בְּכָל דְּבָרָיו:

רַחֵם עַל צִיּוֹן כִּי הִיא בֵּית חַיֵּינוּ, וְלַעֲלוּבַת נֶפֶשׁ תּוֹשִׁיעַ וּתְשַׂמַּח בִּמְהֵרָה בְיָמֵינוּ. בָּרוּךְ אַתָּה יְיָ, מְשַׂמֵּחַ צִיּוֹן בְּבָנֶיהָ:

שַׂמְּחֵנוּ, יְיָ אֱלֹהֵינוּ, בְּאֵלִיָּהוּ הַנָּבִיא עַבְדֶּךָ, וּבְמַלְכוּת בֵּית דָּוִד מְשִׁיחֶךָ, בִּמְהֵרָה יָבֹא וְיָגֵל לִבֵּנוּ, עַל כִּסְאוֹ לֹא יֵשֵׁב זָר, וְלֹא יִנְחֲלוּ עוֹד אֲחֵרִים אֶת כְּבוֹדוֹ, כִּי בְשֵׁם קָדְשְׁךָ נִשְׁבַּעְתָּ לּוֹ, שֶׁלֹּא יִכְבֶּה נֵרוֹ לְעוֹלָם וָעֶד. בָּרוּךְ אַתָּה יְיָ, מָגֵן דָּוִד:

On fast days end here. On Shabbat (including intermediate Shabbat of festivals) continue:

עַל הַתּוֹרָה וְעַל הָעֲבוֹדָה וְעַל הַנְּבִיאִים וְעַל יוֹם הַשַּׁבָּת הַזֶּה,
שֶׁנָּתַתָּ לָּנוּ יְיָ אֱלֹהֵינוּ לִקְדֻשָּׁה וְלִמְנוּחָה, לְכָבוֹד וּלְתִפְאָרֶת:

עַל הַכֹּל, יְיָ אֱלֹהֵינוּ, אֲנַחְנוּ מוֹדִים לָךְ, וּמְבָרְכִים אוֹתָךְ, יִתְבָּרַךְ
שִׁמְךָ בְּפִי כָּל חַי תָּמִיד לְעוֹלָם וָעֶד. בָּרוּךְ אַתָּה יְיָ, מְקַדֵּשׁ הַשַּׁבָּת
(On intermediate Shabbat of Sukkot add – וְיִשְׂרָאֵל וְהַזְּמַנִּים):

On a festival, and *Shabbat* that coincides with a festival, continue here:

עַל הַתּוֹרָה וְעַל הָעֲבוֹדָה וְעַל הַנְּבִיאִים (On Shabbat – וְעַל יוֹם הַשַּׁבָּת הַזֶּה) וְעַל יוֹם

| *Pesah* | *Shavuot* | *Sukkot* | *Shemini Atzeret / Simhat Torah* |
| חַג הַמַּצּוֹת | חַג הַשָּׁבוּעוֹת | חַג הַסֻּכּוֹת | שְׁמִינִי עֲצֶרֶת הַחַג |

הַזֶּה, וְעַל יוֹם טוֹב מִקְרָא קֹדֶשׁ הַזֶּה, שֶׁנָּתַתָּ לָּנוּ יְיָ אֱלֹהֵינוּ (On Shabbat – לִקְדֻשָּׁה וְלִמְנוּחָה)
לְשָׂשׂוֹן וּלְשִׂמְחָה, לְכָבוֹד וּלְתִפְאָרֶת. עַל הַכֹּל, יְיָ אֱלֹהֵינוּ, אֲנַחְנוּ מוֹדִים לָךְ וּמְבָרְכִים אוֹתָךְ,
יִתְבָּרַךְ שִׁמְךָ בְּפִי כָּל חַי תָּמִיד לְעוֹלָם וָעֶד. בָּרוּךְ אַתָּה יְיָ, מְקַדֵּשׁ (On Shabbat – הַשַּׁבָּת וְ)
יִשְׂרָאֵל וְהַזְּמַנִּים:

On *Rosh Ha-Shanah* continue here:

עַל הַתּוֹרָה וְעַל הָעֲבוֹדָה וְעַל הַנְּבִיאִים (On Shabbat – וְעַל יוֹם הַשַּׁבָּת הַזֶּה) וְעַל יוֹם הַזִּכָּרוֹן הַזֶּה,
וְעַל יוֹם טוֹב מִקְרָא קֹדֶשׁ הַזֶּה, שֶׁנָּתַתָּ לָּנוּ יְיָ אֱלֹהֵינוּ (On Shabbat – לִקְדֻשָּׁה וְלִמְנוּחָה) לְכָבוֹד
וּלְתִפְאָרֶת. עַל הַכֹּל, יְיָ אֱלֹהֵינוּ, אֲנַחְנוּ מוֹדִים לָךְ וּמְבָרְכִים אוֹתָךְ, יִתְבָּרַךְ שִׁמְךָ בְּפִי כָּל חַי
תָּמִיד לְעוֹלָם וָעֶד, וּדְבָרְךָ מַלְכֵּנוּ אֱמֶת וְקַיָּם לָעַד. בָּרוּךְ אַתָּה יְיָ, מֶלֶךְ עַל כָּל הָאָרֶץ, מְקַדֵּשׁ
(On Shabbat – הַשַּׁבָּת וְ)יִשְׂרָאֵל וְיוֹם הַזִּכָּרוֹן:

On *Yom Kippur* continue here:

עַל הַתּוֹרָה וְעַל הָעֲבוֹדָה וְעַל הַנְּבִיאִים (On Shabbat – וְעַל יוֹם הַשַּׁבָּת הַזֶּה) וְעַל יוֹם הַכִּפּוּרִים הַזֶּה,
וְעַל יוֹם סְלִיחַת הֶעָוֹן הַזֶּה, וְעַל יוֹם מִקְרָא קֹדֶשׁ הַזֶּה, שֶׁנָּתַתָּ לָּנוּ יְיָ אֱלֹהֵינוּ (On Shabbat – לִקְדֻשָּׁה
וְלִמְנוּחָה) לִסְלִיחָה וְלִמְחִילָה וּלְכַפָּרָה, לְכָבוֹד וּלְתִפְאָרֶת. עַל הַכֹּל, יְיָ אֱלֹהֵינוּ, אֲנַחְנוּ מוֹדִים
לָךְ וּמְבָרְכִים אוֹתָךְ. יִתְבָּרַךְ שִׁמְךָ בְּפִי כָּל חַי תָּמִיד לְעוֹלָם וָעֶד, וּדְבָרְךָ מַלְכֵּנוּ אֱמֶת וְקַיָּם לָעַד.
בָּרוּךְ אַתָּה יְיָ, מֶלֶךְ מוֹחֵל וְסוֹלֵחַ לַעֲוֹנוֹתֵינוּ, וְלַעֲוֹנוֹת עַמּוֹ בֵּית יִשְׂרָאֵל, וּמַעֲבִיר אַשְׁמוֹתֵינוּ בְּכָל
שָׁנָה וְשָׁנָה, מֶלֶךְ עַל כָּל הָאָרֶץ, מְקַדֵּשׁ (On Shabbat – הַשַּׁבָּת וְ)יִשְׂרָאֵל וְיוֹם הַכִּפּוּרִים:

haftarat bere'shit

הפטרת בראשית

ASHKENAZIM—ISAIAH 42:5 – 43:10
SEPHARDIM AND HABAD—ISAIAH 42:5-21

> **SYNOPSIS:** This *Haftarah*—similar to the *Parashah*, which describes the creation of heaven and earth by God—praises God as Creator of heaven and earth.
> The *Haftarah* opens with a description of how God will liberate the Jewish people from exile, and how the entire world will praise God after the final redemption arrives (42:5-12). God promises to destroy the nations that have persecuted the Jewish people and lead the people to their land (13-17). He criticizes the Jewish people for being metaphorically "blind" and "deaf" to the Torah and its commandments (18-21) and laments over their sorry state during exile (22-25). Finally, the prophet repeats God's promise to redeem them, just as He redeemed them from Egypt (43:1-10).

42 [5] This was said by the Almighty God, who created the heavens and stretched them out like a tent, who laid out the earth and made all types of vegetation grow from it, who gives a soul to the people upon it, and a spirit to the other creatures who walk upon it:

[6] "I am God. What I have said about you, O Messiah, through the prophets, is true and everlasting! I will hold your hand to help you overcome every obstacle. I will guard you, and give you the might to bring the covenant of Torah to My people, in order to enlighten the eyes of the nations about God, [7] to open eyes that have blinded themselves not to see the work of God, to release the Jewish people—who are prisoners—from their captivity, and release those who dwell in darkness from their imprisonment.

[8] "I am God—that is My name. I will no longer allow the nations to diminish My honor by worshiping other gods, as they have done until now! No longer will graven images be given My praise."

[9] The first prophecies which I prophesied about Sennacherib have already occurred. I will tell you new ones about the final redemption. I will now let you hear what is going to happen before these events unfold:

[10] When the final redemption comes, they will sing a new song to God, and His praise will be heard from the ends of the earth. Those who navigate the sea, and the creatures that live in it, will praise God. Even the islands themselves and their inhabitants will praise God. [11] The whole desert, together with its cities and villages which are inhabited by the people of Kedar, will raise their voices in song. Those who live on stone peaks will sing—shouts of joy will be heard from the mountaintops. [12] With their mouths they will ascribe glory to God, and they will tell of His praises in the islands.

מב [5] כֹּה־אָמַ֞ר הָאֵ֣ל ׀ יְהֹוָ֗ה בּוֹרֵ֤א הַשָּׁמַ֙יִם֙ וְנ֣וֹטֵיהֶ֔ם רֹקַ֥ע הָאָ֖רֶץ וְצֶאֱצָאֶ֑יהָ נֹתֵ֤ן נְשָׁמָה֙ לָעָ֣ם עָלֶ֔יהָ וְר֖וּחַ לַהֹלְכִ֥ים בָּֽהּ: [6] אֲנִ֧י יְהֹוָ֛ה קְרָאתִ֥יךָֽ בְצֶ֖דֶק וְאַחְזֵ֣ק בְּיָדֶ֑ךָ וְאֶצָּרְךָ֗ וְאֶתֶּנְךָ֛ לִבְרִ֥ית עָ֖ם לְא֥וֹר גּוֹיִֽם: [7] לִפְקֹ֖חַ עֵינַ֣יִם עִוְר֑וֹת לְהוֹצִ֤יא מִמַּסְגֵּר֙ אַסִּ֔יר מִבֵּ֥ית כֶּ֖לֶא יֹ֥שְׁבֵי חֹֽשֶׁךְ: [8] אֲנִ֥י יְהֹוָ֖ה ה֣וּא שְׁמִ֑י וּכְבוֹדִי֙ לְאַחֵ֣ר לֹֽא־אֶתֵּ֔ן וּתְהִלָּתִ֖י לַפְּסִילִֽים: [9] הָרִֽאשֹׁנ֖וֹת הִנֵּה־בָ֑אוּ וַֽחֲדָשׁוֹת֙ אֲנִ֣י מַגִּ֔יד בְּטֶ֥רֶם תִּצְמַ֖חְנָה אַשְׁמִ֥יעַ אֶתְכֶֽם: [10] שִׁ֤ירוּ לַֽיהֹוָה֙ שִׁ֣יר חָדָ֔שׁ תְּהִלָּת֖וֹ מִקְצֵ֣ה הָאָ֑רֶץ יֽוֹרְדֵ֤י הַיָּם֙ וּמְלֹא֔וֹ אִיִּ֖ים וְיֹֽשְׁבֵיהֶֽם: [11] יִשְׂא֤וּ מִדְבָּר֙ וְעָרָ֔יו חֲצֵרִ֖ים תֵּשֵׁ֣ב קֵדָ֑ר יָרֹ֙נּוּ֙ יֹ֣שְׁבֵי סֶ֔לַע מֵרֹ֥אשׁ הָרִ֖ים יִצְוָֽחוּ: [12] יָשִׂ֥ימוּ לַֽיהֹוָ֖ה כָּב֑וֹד

haftarat bere'shit

¹³ God will go out to rescue the Jewish people, aroused with zeal for His people like a man of war. He will shout and cry out against His enemies, and He will overcome them.

¹⁴ Says God, "I have kept quiet for all this time that the nations have persecuted My people. I have been silent and I have restrained Myself. But now I will scream like a woman in childbirth to destroy them. I will obliterate them and swallow them up all together. ¹⁵ I will destroy mountains and valleys, and I will dry out all their grass. I will make rivers into dry and desolate islands, and I will dry up their bodies of water.

¹⁶ "I will walk the Jewish people to their land on a way that they did not know, as if they were blind. I will lead them on a path they did not know. I will turn the darkness of an unknown path into light before them. I will make crooked paths straight for them. I have already done such things previously, when they came out of Egypt, so I will surely not forsake them in the future.

¹⁷ "Then those who trust in graven images will turn backwards, being embarrassed with great shame. That will be the fate of those who say to the molten idols: 'you are our god.'

¹⁸ "You, O Israel, who are deaf towards My words and blind towards My commandments, now listen and look to see the goodness that is awaiting you! ¹⁹ I call all of you blind, even the righteous ones who serve Me, for who is really blind if not one who serves Me, and who knows how corrupt people are, yet he does not attempt to correct them? Who is deaf if not the one whom I grace with wisdom and send to teach the people, and yet he pretends not to hear their evil actions, failing to correct them? Who is as blind as a person who is perfect in himself but does not reprimand others? Who is as blind as a servant of God who turns a blind eye to his people? ²⁰ Such people have seen much wisdom, yet you do not guard others from evil ways, so they deserve to be called 'blind.' They have open ears to understand the commandments, yet act as if they do not hear when it comes to guiding others, so they deserve to be called 'deaf.' ²¹ The main reason why God wants such people is not for their own merits, but in order for them to make another person righteous, and in order for him to increase and strengthen the Torah knowledge of others."

Ḥabad and *Sephardic* communities conclude here. *Ashkenazic* communities continue:

²² This people is looted and trampled. All their young men are dejected and hidden in prisons. They are prey with no one to rescue them from being looted; trampled with no one to say, "Return them so they will be trampled no more."

²³ Who among you will pay attention to this, listen, and hear from now on what will establish him in the end?

וּתְהִלָּתוֹ בָּאִיִּים יַגִּידוּ: 13 יְהֹוָה כַּגִּבּוֹר יֵצֵא כְּאִישׁ מִלְחָמוֹת יָעִיר קִנְאָה יָרִיעַ אַף־יַצְרִיחַ עַל־אֹיְבָיו יִתְגַּבָּר: 14 הֶחֱשֵׁיתִי מֵעוֹלָם אַחֲרִישׁ אֶתְאַפָּק כַּיּוֹלֵדָה אֶפְעֶה אֶשֹּׁם וְאֶשְׁאַף יָחַד: 15 אַחֲרִיב הָרִים וּגְבָעוֹת וְכָל־עֶשְׂבָּם אוֹבִישׁ וְשַׂמְתִּי נְהָרוֹת לָאִיִּים וַאֲגַמִּים אוֹבִישׁ: 16 וְהוֹלַכְתִּי עִוְרִים בְּדֶרֶךְ לֹא יָדָעוּ בִּנְתִיבוֹת לֹא־יָדְעוּ אַדְרִיכֵם אָשִׂים מַחְשָׁךְ לִפְנֵיהֶם לָאוֹר וּמַעֲקַשִּׁים לְמִישׁוֹר אֵלֶּה הַדְּבָרִים עֲשִׂיתִם וְלֹא עֲזַבְתִּים: 17 נָסֹגוּ אָחוֹר יֵבֹשׁוּ בֹשֶׁת הַבֹּטְחִים בַּפָּסֶל הָאֹמְרִים לְמַסֵּכָה אַתֶּם אֱלֹהֵינוּ: 18 הַחֵרְשִׁים שְׁמָעוּ וְהַעִוְרִים הַבִּיטוּ לִרְאוֹת: 19 מִי עִוֵּר כִּי אִם־עַבְדִּי וְחֵרֵשׁ כְּמַלְאָכִי אֶשְׁלָח מִי עִוֵּר כִּמְשֻׁלָּם וְעִוֵּר כְּעֶבֶד יְהֹוָה: 20 [ראית כ'] רָאוֹת רַבּוֹת וְלֹא תִשְׁמֹר פָּקוֹחַ אָזְנַיִם וְלֹא יִשְׁמָע: 21 יְהֹוָה חָפֵץ לְמַעַן צִדְקוֹ יַגְדִּיל תּוֹרָה וְיַאְדִּיר:

22 וְהוּא עַם־בָּזוּז וְשָׁסוּי הָפֵחַ בַּחוּרִים כֻּלָּם וּבְבָתֵּי כְלָאִים הָחְבָּאוּ הָיוּ לָבַז וְאֵין מַצִּיל מְשִׁסָּה וְאֵין־אֹמֵר הָשַׁב: 23 מִי בָכֶם יַאֲזִין זֹאת

הפטרת בראשית

24 מִי־נָתַן [למשוסה כ״י] לִמְשִׁסָּה יַעֲקֹב וְיִשְׂרָאֵל לְבֹזְזִים הֲלוֹא יְהֹוָה זוּ חָטָאנוּ לוֹ וְלֹא־אָבוּ בִדְרָכָיו הָלוֹךְ וְלֹא שָׁמְעוּ בְּתוֹרָתוֹ: 25 וַיִּשְׁפֹּךְ עָלָיו חֵמָה אַפּוֹ וֶעֱזוּז מִלְחָמָה וַתְּלַהֲטֵהוּ מִסָּבִיב וְלֹא יָדָע וַתִּבְעַר־בּוֹ וְלֹא־יָשִׂים עַל־לֵב:

מג 1 וְעַתָּה כֹּה־אָמַר יְהֹוָה בֹּרַאֲךָ יַעֲקֹב וְיֹצֶרְךָ יִשְׂרָאֵל אַל־תִּירָא כִּי גְאַלְתִּיךָ קָרָאתִי בְשִׁמְךָ לִי־אָתָּה: 2 כִּי־תַעֲבֹר בַּמַּיִם אִתְּךָ־אָנִי וּבַנְּהָרוֹת לֹא יִשְׁטְפוּךָ כִּי־תֵלֵךְ בְּמוֹ־אֵשׁ לֹא תִכָּוֶה וְלֶהָבָה לֹא תִבְעַר־בָּךְ: 3 כִּי אֲנִי יְהֹוָה אֱלֹהֶיךָ קְדוֹשׁ יִשְׂרָאֵל מוֹשִׁיעֶךָ נָתַתִּי כָפְרְךָ מִצְרַיִם כּוּשׁ וּסְבָא תַּחְתֶּיךָ: 4 מֵאֲשֶׁר יָקַרְתָּ בְעֵינַי נִכְבַּדְתָּ וַאֲנִי אֲהַבְתִּיךָ וְאֶתֵּן אָדָם תַּחְתֶּיךָ וּלְאֻמִּים תַּחַת נַפְשֶׁךָ: 5 אַל־תִּירָא כִּי אִתְּךָ־אָנִי מִמִּזְרָח אָבִיא זַרְעֶךָ וּמִמַּעֲרָב אֲקַבְּצֶךָּ: 6 אֹמַר לַצָּפוֹן תֵּנִי וּלְתֵימָן אַל־תִּכְלָאִי הָבִיאִי בָנַי מֵרָחוֹק וּבְנוֹתַי מִקְצֵה הָאָרֶץ: 7 כֹּל הַנִּקְרָא בִשְׁמִי וְלִכְבוֹדִי בְּרָאתִיו יְצַרְתִּיו אַף־עֲשִׂיתִיו: 8 הוֹצִיא עַם־עִוֵּר וְעֵינַיִם יֵשׁ וְחֵרְשִׁים וְאָזְנַיִם לָמוֹ: 9 כׇּל־הַגּוֹיִם נִקְבְּצוּ יַחְדָּו וְיֵאָסְפוּ לְאֻמִּים מִי בָהֶם יַגִּיד זֹאת וְרִאשֹׁנוֹת יַשְׁמִיעֻנוּ יִתְּנוּ עֵדֵיהֶם וְיִצְדָּקוּ וְיִשְׁמְעוּ וְיֹאמְרוּ אֱמֶת: 10 אַתֶּם עֵדַי נְאֻם־יְהֹוָה וְעַבְדִּי אֲשֶׁר בָּחָרְתִּי לְמַעַן תֵּדְעוּ וְתַאֲמִינוּ לִי וְתָבִינוּ כִּי־אֲנִי הוּא לְפָנַי לֹא־נוֹצַר אֵל וְאַחֲרַי לֹא יִהְיֶה:

---

²⁴ Who handed Jacob over to be trampled and Israel to looters? Was it not God, against whom we have sinned? For the Jewish people did not desire His ways or obey His Torah, ²⁵ so He poured out His anger, His wrath, and the might of war upon them. It blazed around them, but they paid no attention to the fact that it was caused by God, and even after it burned them they did not take it to heart as Divine intervention.

43 ¹ But despite all this, God—who created you, O Jacob, and formed you, O Israel—nevertheless says: "Do not fear, for I redeemed you from Egypt and I called you My own. ² When you pass through water and nearly drown, I am with you; even powerful rivers will not sweep you away; when you walk through the inferno of life's difficulties, you will not be burnt, and the flame will not consume you, ³ for I am God, your God, the Holy One of Israel, your Savior. Didn't I make Egypt your ransom and save you, even though you did not deserve it? Didn't I send Ethiopia and Seba to be destroyed by Sennacherib instead of you? ⁴ Because you are precious to Me and honored, I loved you! So I will give men in exchange for you and nations to be destroyed in place of you.

⁵ "Do not fear, for I am with you. I will bring your children from the east and gather you from the west. ⁶ I will say to the north: 'Give Me the Jewish people who are scattered there,' and to the south, 'Don't hold them back!' Bring My sons from afar and My daughters from the ends of the earth, ⁷ all the Jewish people who bear My name, who were made for My glory. I have already created, fashioned and made all that is necessary for their redemption in order to ⁸ free the exiled people—who are blind though they have eyes, and deaf though they have ears.

⁹ "Even if all the nations gathered together and all the peoples assembled, who among them could declare future events like this, or announce to us that they had predicted past events? If so, let them produce their witnesses and be proven correct, such that those who hear them will say that it is true.

¹⁰ "You are My witnesses," says God, "My servant whom I have chosen, that you may know and believe in Me, and understand that I am He before whom no god was created, and after whom none will exist."

haftarat noaḥ

haftarat noaḥ

ASHKENAZIM—ISAIAH 54:1 – 55:5
SEPHARDIM AND HABAD—ISAIAH 54:1–10

> **SYNOPSIS:** This *Haftarah* mentions God's promise to Noah not to bring another flood that will destroy the world (v.9). In general, the *Haftarah* describes the rebuilding of Jerusalem with the final redemption, and the universal knowledge of Torah that will be attained by the Jewish people.
>
> The *Haftarah* opens with a description of how Jerusalem will be repopulated with the Redemption (54:1-3), followed with a promise that the present exile is only temporary (4–10). The prophet then describes how God will rebuild Jerusalem with gems (11-12) and how the Jewish people will master the study of Torah and be righteous, thus averting any threat from potential enemies (13-17). The prophet then lauds the virtues of Torah study (55:1-3) and describes the respect that the nations will have for Israel in the Messianic Era (4-5).

54 ¹ Says God: "O Jerusalem! During exile times, you were like a barren woman who never gave birth, since you were a city devoid of people. But now, in the times of the redemption, you can sing! O Jerusalem! Open your mouth and sing loudly, for you were a woman who never had labor pains. Now, the inhabitants of Jerusalem—which previously lay desolate—are more numerous than the inhabitants of the built up cities of Edom.

² "O Jerusalem! Extend the area of your tent to include all your children. Stretch the curtains that mark the edge of your dwellings so that they spread out far—do not hold them back. Lengthen your ropes of your tents, expanding your borders, and strengthen your fastening-pegs so that your borders remain enlarged forever. ³ For you will break through, spilling into the territory to the right and to the left. Your descendants will inherit nations and they will multiply so much that they will inhabit desolate cities."

⁴ "Do not fear another exile after the Redemption. Do not be ashamed or embarrassed to proudly display your greatness, for fear that you may be exiled again, for you will not be disgraced with another exile. You will forget the shame of the exile of your youth, and you will no longer remember the disgrace of your widowhood when you were a people without a king. ⁵ For the name of your Husband, who made you great, is the God of Hosts—so who could possibly oppose you? Isn't your Redeemer none other than the Holy One of Israel, who will then be called 'God of the entire Earth' by all, so why be afraid?

⁶ "For God has called you to return to Him like a husband who calls to his forsaken and dejected wife; like a man who was briefly disgusted by the wife of his youth but soon forgives her," says your God. ⁷ "When I abandoned you it was only for a short moment compared to the time when I will gather you, which will

נד ׀ רָנִּ֣י עֲקָרָ֔ה לֹ֖א יָלָ֑דָה פִּצְחִ֨י רִנָּ֤ה וְצַהֲלִי֙ לֹא־חָ֔לָה כִּֽי־רַבִּ֧ים בְּנֵֽי־שׁוֹמֵמָ֛ה מִבְּנֵ֥י בְעוּלָ֖ה אָמַ֥ר יְהֹוָֽה: 2 הַרְחִ֣יבִי ׀ מְק֣וֹם אָהֳלֵ֗ךְ וִֽירִיע֧וֹת מִשְׁכְּנוֹתַ֛יִךְ יַטּ֖וּ אַל־תַּחְשֹׂ֑כִי הַאֲרִ֨יכִי֙ מֵֽיתָרַ֔יִךְ וִיתֵדֹתַ֖יִךְ חַזֵּֽקִי: 3 כִּי־יָמִ֥ין וּשְׂמֹ֖אול תִּפְרֹ֑צִי וְזַרְעֵךְ֙ גּוֹיִ֣ם יִירָ֔שׁ וְעָרִ֥ים נְשַׁמּ֖וֹת יוֹשִֽׁיבוּ: 4 אַל־תִּֽירְאִי֙ כִּי־לֹ֣א תֵב֔וֹשִׁי וְאַל־תִּכָּֽלְמִ֖י כִּ֣י לֹ֣א תַחְפִּ֑ירִי כִּ֣י בֹ֤שֶׁת עֲלוּמַ֙יִךְ֙ תִּשְׁכָּ֔חִי וְחֶרְפַּ֥ת אַלְמְנוּתַ֖יִךְ לֹ֥א תִזְכְּרִי־עֽוֹד: 5 כִּ֤י בֹֽעֲלַ֙יִךְ֙ עֹשַׂ֔יִךְ יְהֹוָ֥ה צְבָא֖וֹת שְׁמ֑וֹ וְגֹֽאֲלֵךְ֙ קְד֣וֹשׁ יִשְׂרָאֵ֔ל אֱלֹהֵ֥י כָל־הָאָ֖רֶץ יִקָּרֵֽא: 6 כִּֽי־כְאִשָּׁ֧ה עֲזוּבָ֛ה וַעֲצ֥וּבַת ר֖וּחַ קְרָאָ֣ךְ יְהֹוָ֑ה וְאֵ֧שֶׁת נְעוּרִ֛ים כִּ֥י תִמָּאֵ֖ס אָמַ֥ר אֱלֹהָֽיִךְ: 7 בְּרֶ֥גַע קָטֹ֖ן עֲזַבְתִּ֑יךְ וּבְרַחֲמִ֥ים גְּדֹלִ֖ים

הפטרת נח

last forever, due to My great mercy. ⁸ Compared to the everlasting kindness with which I will have mercy upon you, I hid My face from you for just a moment, and I was only a little angry," says God, your Redeemer.

⁹ "This anger was for Me like the waters of Noah. Just as I swore never to allow the waters of Noah to pass again over the earth, so too, I swore not to be angry at you or rebuke you.

¹⁰ "For the mountains may move away and the hills might collapse in an earthquake, but My kindness will not leave you, nor will My covenant of peace collapse," says God, who is merciful to you.

אֶקְבְּצֵךְ: 8 בְּשֶׁצֶף קֶצֶף הִסְתַּרְתִּי פָנַי רֶגַע מִמֵּךְ וּבְחֶסֶד עוֹלָם רִחַמְתִּיךְ אָמַר גֹּאֲלֵךְ יְהֹוָה: 9 כִּי־מֵי נֹחַ זֹאת לִי אֲשֶׁר נִשְׁבַּעְתִּי מֵעֲבֹר מֵי־נֹחַ עוֹד עַל־הָאָרֶץ כֵּן נִשְׁבַּעְתִּי מִקְּצֹף עָלַיִךְ וּמִגְּעָר־בָּךְ: 10 כִּי הֶהָרִים יָמוּשׁוּ וְהַגְּבָעוֹת תְּמוּטֶנָה וְחַסְדִּי מֵאִתֵּךְ לֹא־יָמוּשׁ וּבְרִית שְׁלוֹמִי לֹא תָמוּט אָמַר מְרַחֲמֵךְ יְהֹוָה:

Ḥabad and Sephardic communities conclude here. Ashkenazic communities continue:

¹¹ "O Jerusalem! You afflicted, storm-tossed one, who has not been comforted! I will lay your floor stones upon antimony instead of sapphires. ¹² I will make your window panes from emeralds, your gates from carbuncle stones, and the floor-stones of all your borders will become desirable gems.

¹³ "All your children will be extremely wise, as if they were disciples of God, and your children will have much peace.

¹⁴ "Through your righteousness, you will be fit for all this. You will distance yourself from fraudsters who have no fear of Me at all, and from terror, for it will not come near you. ¹⁵ Indeed, people will fear no one but Me. Whoever attacks you will fall into your power. ¹⁶ Behold, it was I who created the smith to fan coal fires and make the tools of his trade, and it was I who created the destroying enemy to destroy itself. ¹⁷ Every weapon engineered against you will not succeed, and every tongue raised against you in judgment you will have condemned. This is the inheritance of God's servants and their just reward from Me," says God.

11 עֲנִיָּה סֹעֲרָה לֹא נֻחָמָה הִנֵּה אָנֹכִי מַרְבִּיץ בַּפּוּךְ אֲבָנַיִךְ וִיסַדְתִּיךְ בַּסַּפִּירִים: 12 וְשַׂמְתִּי כַּדְכֹד שִׁמְשֹׁתַיִךְ וּשְׁעָרַיִךְ לְאַבְנֵי אֶקְדָּח וְכָל־גְּבוּלֵךְ לְאַבְנֵי־חֵפֶץ: 13 וְכָל־בָּנַיִךְ לִמּוּדֵי יְהֹוָה וְרַב שְׁלוֹם בָּנָיִךְ: 14 בִּצְדָקָה תִּכּוֹנָנִי רַחֲקִי מֵעֹשֶׁק כִּי־לֹא תִירָאִי וּמִמְּחִתָּה כִּי לֹא־תִקְרַב אֵלָיִךְ: 15 הֵן גּוֹר יָגוּר אֶפֶס מֵאוֹתִי מִי־גָר אִתָּךְ עָלַיִךְ יִפּוֹל: 16 [הן כ׳] הִנֵּה אָנֹכִי בָּרָאתִי חָרָשׁ נֹפֵחַ בְּאֵשׁ פֶּחָם וּמוֹצִיא כְלִי לְמַעֲשֵׂהוּ וְאָנֹכִי בָּרָאתִי מַשְׁחִית לְחַבֵּל: 17 כָּל־כְּלִי יוּצַר עָלַיִךְ לֹא יִצְלָח וְכָל־לָשׁוֹן תָּקוּם־אִתָּךְ לַמִּשְׁפָּט תַּרְשִׁיעִי זֹאת נַחֲלַת עַבְדֵי יְהֹוָה וְצִדְקָתָם מֵאִתִּי נְאֻם־יְהֹוָה:

55

¹ "Oh! Everyone who is thirsty for God's word, go to the prophet and drink his 'water'! Even those who have no money, go and eat! Come and take wine and milk without payment, without charge, for the prophet's wisdom is free! ² Why do you 'pay money' and invest your energies in non-Jewish wisdom without getting any real substance or 'bread'? Why do you labor in something that cannot give satisfaction? Listen to Me! Learn Torah and you will 'eat' well and satisfy your souls with 'rich foods'!

נה

1 הוֹי כָּל־צָמֵא לְכוּ לַמַּיִם וַאֲשֶׁר אֵין־לוֹ כֶּסֶף לְכוּ שִׁבְרוּ וֶאֱכֹלוּ וּלְכוּ שִׁבְרוּ בְּלוֹא־כֶסֶף וּבְלוֹא מְחִיר יַיִן וְחָלָב: 2 לָמָּה תִשְׁקְלוּ־כֶסֶף בְּלוֹא־לֶחֶם וִיגִיעֲכֶם בְּלוֹא לְשָׂבְעָה שִׁמְעוּ

haftarat lekh lekha

³ "Incline your ears and come to Me to hear My words! Listen, and you will merit to live again, with the revival of the dead! I will make an eternal covenant with you, as enduring as My loyalty to David. ⁴ Indeed, I have made his enduring dynasty as a proof to the nations that My word always endures, and the Messiah, his descendant, will be a ruler and leader of the nations. ⁵ Likewise My promises to you will be fulfilled. Indeed, nations that you do not know will call upon you to serve you, and nations which never knew you will run to you to follow your orders. But they will not do this due to your own power, but for the sake of the God, your God, the Holy One of Israel, who dwells among you and who has glorified you."

שָׁמוֹעַ אֵלַי וְאִכְלוּ־טוֹב וְתִתְעַנַּג בַּדֶּשֶׁן נַפְשְׁכֶם: 3 הַטּוּ אָזְנְכֶם וּלְכוּ אֵלַי שִׁמְעוּ וּתְחִי נַפְשְׁכֶם וְאֶכְרְתָה לָכֶם בְּרִית עוֹלָם חַסְדֵי דָוִד הַנֶּאֱמָנִים: 4 הֵן עֵד לְאוּמִּים נְתַתִּיו נָגִיד וּמְצַוֵּה לְאֻמִּים: 5 הֵן גּוֹי לֹא־תֵדַע תִּקְרָא וְגוֹי לֹא־יְדָעוּךָ אֵלֶיךָ יָרוּצוּ לְמַעַן יְהֹוָה אֱלֹהֶיךָ וְלִקְדוֹשׁ יִשְׂרָאֵל כִּי פֵאֲרָךְ:

haftarat lekh lekha

ALL COMMUNITIES—ISAIAH 40:27 – 41:16

> **SYNOPSIS:** This *Haftarah* alludes to Abraham's victory over the four kings (41:2-3) which is chronicled in *Parashat Lekh Lekha* (14:13-16). The *Haftarah* also recounts how God caused Abraham to leave his homeland and settle in the land of Israel, where he taught the world about God.
>
> The first part of the *Haftarah* contains words of comfort to the Jewish people, that they will survive the sufferings of exile (40:27–41:1).
>
> The prophet then explains to us the messages from Abraham's life (2–8), and this is followed by more words of encouragement for the Jewish people in exile (9–16).

40 ²⁷ Jacob, why do you say—and Israel, why do you declare—"My way of serving God has been hidden from and ignored by God, and my judgment passes unrewarded from my God"?

²⁸ Don't you know from your own mind, even if you have not heard from your teachers, that God is an everlasting God, the Creator of the entire world from end to end? He does not become tired or weary and fluctuate in His performance. So your reward will definitely come, but there is no comprehension of His wisdom as to why He delays it.

²⁹ The time will come when He gives strength to the weary people of Israel, and increases power to those without strength. ³⁰ The nations of the world, who are now strong like young men, will become tired and weary, and their young bachelors will repeatedly stumble. ³¹ But those who place their hope in God will regain their strength, and grow wings like eagles. They will run to their land and not become weary. They will walk and not get tired.

27 לָמָּה תֹאמַר יַעֲקֹב וּתְדַבֵּר יִשְׂרָאֵל נִסְתְּרָה דַרְכִּי מֵיְהֹוָה וּמֵאֱלֹהַי מִשְׁפָּטִי יַעֲבוֹר: 28 הֲלוֹא יָדַעְתָּ אִם־לֹא שָׁמַעְתָּ אֱלֹהֵי עוֹלָם ׀ יְהֹוָה בּוֹרֵא קְצוֹת הָאָרֶץ לֹא יִיעַף וְלֹא יִיגָע אֵין חֵקֶר לִתְבוּנָתוֹ: 29 נֹתֵן לַיָּעֵף כֹּחַ וּלְאֵין אוֹנִים עָצְמָה יַרְבֶּה: 30 וְיִעֲפוּ נְעָרִים וְיִגָעוּ וּבַחוּרִים כָּשׁוֹל יִכָּשֵׁלוּ: 31 וְקוֹיֵ יְהֹוָה יַחֲלִיפוּ כֹחַ יַעֲלוּ אֵבֶר כַּנְּשָׁרִים יָרוּצוּ וְלֹא יִיגָעוּ יֵלְכוּ וְלֹא יִיעָפוּ:

הפטרת לך לך

41

¹ You, who live in islands, be silent and listen to Me! Let the nations muster their strength to defend themselves before Me. First let them come and listen to My prosecution, and then they can speak if they indeed have anything to say in their defense. Then, the nations and I will debate together, to judge their claims that I am unable to save My people.

² Who awakened Abraham, when he was in the East to leave his home and despise idolatry? Everywhere that he trod, he preached righteousness, demanding that people abandon their idols and believe in God. Who is the One who placed nations before him, and enabled him to dominate four mighty kings? Those killed by his sword were as numerous as the dust, and his bow killed many people like piles of beaten straw. ³ He pursued them, and passed through in peace, though it was a path where his feet had never trodden.

⁴ Who caused and orchestrated this for him? The One who calls and designates the time and place of each generation, from before they are born. I, God, am the first One before all the generations, and I am the same One who remains with the last generations.

⁵ The inhabitants of the distant islands saw the miracles that I performed for Abraham and became frightened. Even the ones who live at the ends of the earth became terrified. They drew near and came to Abraham, not to wage war, but merely to beg for their captives.

⁶ Yet, despite all the miracles that the nations saw God make for Abraham, each man carried on helping his friend to make idols. Each person would encourage his brother, saying "Be strong! Keep on sculpting idols!" ⁷ When a carpenter would make an idol he would rush the goldsmith to finish off the idol's coating quickly. The one who smooths the idol with the small mallet would hurry the blacksmith who did the initial metalwork, beating very hard with the large hammer. The one who glued the idol together would say with glee about the glue: "It's good!" and he would fasten the metal coating onto the idol with nails, so that it should not fall off.

מא ¹ הַחֲרִישׁוּ אֵלַי אִיִּים וּלְאֻמִּים יַחֲלִיפוּ כֹחַ יִגְּשׁוּ אָז יְדַבֵּרוּ יַחְדָּו לַמִּשְׁפָּט נִקְרָבָה: ² מִי הֵעִיר מִמִּזְרָח צֶדֶק יִקְרָאֵהוּ לְרַגְלוֹ יִתֵּן לְפָנָיו גּוֹיִם וּמְלָכִים יַרְדְּ יִתֵּן כֶּעָפָר חַרְבּוֹ כְּקַשׁ נִדָּף קַשְׁתּוֹ: ³ יִרְדְּפֵם יַעֲבוֹר שָׁלוֹם אֹרַח בְּרַגְלָיו לֹא יָבוֹא: ⁴ מִי־פָעַל וְעָשָׂה קֹרֵא הַדֹּרוֹת מֵרֹאשׁ אֲנִי יְהֹוָה רִאשׁוֹן וְאֶת־אַחֲרֹנִים אֲנִי־הוּא: ⁵ רָאוּ אִיִּים וְיִירָאוּ קְצוֹת הָאָרֶץ יֶחֱרָדוּ קָרְבוּ וַיֶּאֱתָיוּן: ⁶ אִישׁ אֶת־רֵעֵהוּ יַעְזֹרוּ וּלְאָחִיו יֹאמַר חֲזָק: ⁷ וַיְחַזֵּק חָרָשׁ אֶת־צֹרֵף מַחֲלִיק פַּטִּישׁ אֶת־הוֹלֶם פָּעַם אֹמֵר לַדֶּבֶק טוֹב הוּא וַיְחַזְּקֵהוּ בְמַסְמְרִים לֹא יִמּוֹט: ⁸ וְאַתָּה יִשְׂרָאֵל עַבְדִּי יַעֲקֹב אֲשֶׁר בְּחַרְתִּיךָ זֶרַע אַבְרָהָם אֹהֲבִי: ⁹ אֲשֶׁר הֶחֱזַקְתִּיךָ מִקְצוֹת הָאָרֶץ וּמֵאֲצִילֶיהָ קְרָאתִיךָ וָאֹמַר לְךָ עַבְדִּי־אַתָּה בְּחַרְתִּיךָ וְלֹא מְאַסְתִּיךָ: ¹⁰ אַל־תִּירָא כִּי עִמְּךָ־אָנִי אַל־תִּשְׁתָּע כִּי־אֲנִי אֱלֹהֶיךָ אִמַּצְתִּיךָ אַף־עֲזַרְתִּיךָ אַף־תְּמַכְתִּיךָ בִּימִין צִדְקִי: ¹¹ הֵן יֵבֹשׁוּ וְיִכָּלְמוּ כֹּל הַנֶּחֱרִים בָּךְ יִהְיוּ כְאַיִן וְיֹאבְדוּ אַנְשֵׁי רִיבֶךָ:

⁸ But you, Israel, are not like them because you are My servants! Children of Jacob! I chose you to be My people because you are the descendants of Abraham, who loved Me and separated you from idol-worship. ⁹ In the future I will grasp you from the corners of the earth, and call to release you from the control of its powerful people. I told you, "You are My servant," from the time that I have chosen you, and I have not despised you.

¹⁰ Do not be afraid, for I am with you. Do not turn away thinking that I have abandoned you, because I am your God, as I have always been. I strengthened you with positive words of comfort, I helped you from the very beginning. When you were in the hands of the enemy I supported you with My righteous right hand.

¹¹ Indeed, all those who were angry with you will eventually be shamed and embarrassed. Those who

haftarat va-yera'

quarrel with you will be like nothing and perish. ¹² Even if you will seek them, you will not find the men who fight with you. The men who wage war with you will be null and void. ¹³ For I am God, your God, who takes hold of your right hand, and says to you, "Don't fear, I will help you," so you can rely on My word. ¹⁴ Do not fear, children of Jacob, people of Israel, who are as weak as a worm whose only strength is in its mouth. I have helped you in the past, says God, and I, the Holy One of Israel, will be your Redeemer in the future.

¹⁵ I have made you into a new grooved threshing-hammer with sharp edges. You will thresh kings mighty as mountains and crush them fine, and make hills like chaff. ¹⁶ You will scatter them. The wind will carry them away, and a storm will scatter them. You will rejoice with God, and praise yourself for trusting in the Holy One of Israel.

12 תְּבַקְשֵׁם וְלֹא תִמְצָאֵם אַנְשֵׁי מַצֻּתֶךָ יִהְיוּ כְאַיִן וּכְאֶפֶס אַנְשֵׁי מִלְחַמְתֶּךָ: 13 כִּי אֲנִי יְהֹוָה אֱלֹהֶיךָ מַחֲזִיק יְמִינֶךָ הָאֹמֵר לְךָ אַל־תִּירָא אֲנִי עֲזַרְתִּיךָ: 14 אַל־תִּירְאִי תּוֹלַעַת יַעֲקֹב מְתֵי יִשְׂרָאֵל אֲנִי עֲזַרְתִּיךְ נְאֻם־יְהֹוָה וְגֹאֲלֵךְ קְדוֹשׁ יִשְׂרָאֵל: 15 הִנֵּה שַׂמְתִּיךְ לְמוֹרַג חָרוּץ חָדָשׁ בַּעַל פִּיפִיּוֹת תָּדוּשׁ הָרִים וְתָדֹק וּגְבָעוֹת כַּמֹּץ תָּשִׂים: 16 תִּזְרֵם וְרוּחַ תִּשָּׂאֵם וּסְעָרָה תָּפִיץ אֹתָם וְאַתָּה תָּגִיל בַּיהֹוָה בִּקְדוֹשׁ יִשְׂרָאֵל תִּתְהַלָּל:

haftarat va-yera'

SEPHARDIM—II KINGS 4:1–23
ASHKENAZIM AND HABAD—II KINGS 4:1–37

SYNOPSIS: This *Haftarah* mentions Elisha's prophecy that the Shunammite woman would bear a child (v.16), resembling the angel's promise that Sarah would bear a child in *Parashat Va-yera'* (18:10).

The *Haftarah* relates two of the miraculous incidents performed by Elisha, a prophet, mentor and guardian of the Jewish people. The first story is of Obadiah's widow and her container of oil that continued to pour oil until she had enough money to pay off all her debts. The second is a story about the Shunammite woman, who was unable to have children. With Elisha's help, she is blessed with a son—according to one view, that son was Habakkuk the prophet—but the child dies tragically. However, Elisha miraculously restores the boy to life.

4 ¹ A certain woman, one of the wives of the disciples of the prophets, cried out to Elisha, saying, "Your servant, my husband, has died. You are aware that your servant feared God. Now, Jehoram son of Ahab the creditor has come to take my two children as slaves for himself!"

² Elisha said to her, "What can I do for you? Tell me what you have in the house upon which a blessing can reside?"

She said, "Your maidservant does not have anything in the house, except a jug of oil used for anointing."

³ He said, "Go and borrow containers from those who are outside your house, namely from all your neighbors—

ד 1 וְאִשָּׁה אַחַת מִנְּשֵׁי בְנֵי־הַנְּבִיאִים צָעֲקָה אֶל־אֱלִישָׁע לֵאמֹר עַבְדְּךָ אִישִׁי מֵת וְאַתָּה יָדַעְתָּ כִּי עַבְדְּךָ הָיָה יָרֵא אֶת־יְהֹוָה וְהַנֹּשֶׁה בָּא לָקַחַת אֶת־שְׁנֵי יְלָדַי לוֹ לַעֲבָדִים: 2 וַיֹּאמֶר אֵלֶיהָ אֱלִישָׁע מָה אֶעֱשֶׂה־לָּךְ הַגִּידִי לִי מַה־יֶּשׁ־ [לכי כ׳] לָךְ בַּבָּיִת וַתֹּאמֶר אֵין לְשִׁפְחָתְךָ כֹל בַּבַּיִת כִּי אִם־אָסוּךְ שָׁמֶן: 3 וַיֹּאמֶר לְכִי שַׁאֲלִי־לָךְ כֵּלִים

הפטרת וירא

מִן־הַח֔וּץ מֵאֵ֖ת כָּל־ [שכניכי כ׳] שְׁכֵנָ֑יִךְ כֵּלִ֣ים רֵקִ֔ים אַל־תַּמְעִֽיטִי: 4 וּבָ֗את וְסָגַ֤רְתְּ הַדֶּ֙לֶת֙ בַּעֲדֵ֣ךְ וּבְעַד־בָּנַ֔יִךְ וְיָצַ֕קְתְּ עַ֥ל כָּל־הַכֵּלִ֖ים הָאֵ֑לֶּה וְהַמָּלֵ֖א תַּסִּֽיעִי: 5 וַתֵּ֣לֶךְ מֵֽאִתּ֔וֹ וַתִּסְגֹּ֣ר הַדֶּ֔לֶת בַּעֲדָ֖הּ וּבְעַ֣ד בָּנֶ֑יהָ הֵ֛ם מַגִּשִׁ֥ים אֵלֶ֖יהָ וְהִ֥יא [מיצקת כ׳] מוֹצָֽקֶת: 6 וַיְהִ֣י ׀ כִּמְלֹ֣את הַכֵּלִ֗ים וַתֹּ֤אמֶר אֶל־בְּנָהּ֙ הַגִּ֤ישָׁה אֵלַי֙ עוֹד֙ כֶּ֔לִי וַיֹּ֣אמֶר אֵלֶ֔יהָ אֵ֥ין ע֖וֹד כֶּ֑לִי וַֽיַּעֲמֹ֖ד הַשָּֽׁמֶן: 7 וַתָּבֹ֗א וַתַּגֵּד֙ לְאִ֣ישׁ הָאֱלֹהִ֔ים וַיֹּ֗אמֶר לְכִי֙ מִכְרִ֣י אֶת־הַשֶּׁ֔מֶן וְשַׁלְּמִ֖י אֶת־ [נשיכי כ׳] נִשְׁיֵ֑ךְ וְאַ֣תְּ [בניכי כ׳] וּבָנַ֔יִךְ תִּֽחְיִ֖י בַּנּוֹתָֽר: 8 וַיְהִ֨י הַיּ֜וֹם וַיַּעֲבֹ֧ר אֱלִישָׁ֣ע אֶל־שׁוּנֵ֗ם וְשָׁם֙ אִשָּׁ֣ה גְדוֹלָ֔ה וַתַּחֲזֶק־בּ֖וֹ לֶֽאֱכָל־לָ֑חֶם וַֽיְהִי֙ מִדֵּ֣י עָבְר֔וֹ יָסֻ֥ר שָׁ֖מָּה לֶֽאֱכָל־לָֽחֶם: 9 וַתֹּ֙אמֶר֙ אֶל־אִישָׁ֔הּ הִנֵּה־נָ֣א יָדַ֔עְתִּי כִּ֛י אִ֥ישׁ אֱלֹהִ֖ים קָד֣וֹשׁ ה֑וּא עֹבֵ֥ר עָלֵ֖ינוּ תָּמִֽיד: 10 נַעֲשֶׂה־נָּ֤א עֲלִיַּת־קִיר֙ קְטַנָּ֔ה וְנָשִׂ֨ים ל֥וֹ שָׁ֛ם מִטָּ֥ה וְשֻׁלְחָ֖ן וְכִסֵּ֣א וּמְנוֹרָ֑ה וְהָיָ֛ה בְּבֹא֥וֹ אֵלֵ֖ינוּ יָס֥וּר שָֽׁמָּה: 11 וַיְהִ֥י הַיּ֖וֹם וַיָּ֣בֹא שָׁ֑מָּה וַיָּ֥סַר אֶל־הָעֲלִיָּ֖ה וַיִּשְׁכַּב־שָֽׁמָּה: 12 וַיֹּ֙אמֶר֙ אֶל־גֵּחֲזִ֣י נַעֲר֔וֹ קְרָ֖א לַשּׁוּנַמִּ֣ית הַזֹּ֑את וַיִּקְרָא־לָ֔הּ וַֽתַּעֲמֹ֖ד לְפָנָֽיו: 13 וַיֹּ֣אמֶר ל֗וֹ אֱמָר־נָ֣א אֵלֶיהָ֮ הִנֵּ֣ה חָרַ֣דְתְּ ׀ אֵלֵינוּ֮ אֶת־כָּל־הַחֲרָדָ֣ה הַזֹּאת֒ מֶ֚ה לַעֲשׂ֣וֹת לָ֔ךְ הֲיֵ֤שׁ לְדַבֶּר־לָךְ֙ אֶל־הַמֶּ֔לֶךְ א֖וֹ אֶל־שַׂ֣ר הַצָּבָ֑א וַתֹּ֕אמֶר בְּת֥וֹךְ עַמִּ֖י אָנֹכִ֥י יֹשָֽׁבֶת: 14 וַיֹּ֕אמֶר וּמֶ֖ה לַעֲשׂ֣וֹת לָ֑הּ וַיֹּ֣אמֶר גֵּיחֲזִ֗י אֲבָ֛ל בֵּ֥ן אֵֽין־לָ֖הּ וְאִישָׁ֥הּ זָקֵֽן: 15 וַיֹּ֖אמֶר קְרָא־לָ֑הּ וַיִּקְרָא־לָ֔הּ וַֽתַּעֲמֹ֖ד בַּפָּֽתַח: 16 וַיֹּ֗אמֶר לַמּוֹעֵ֤ד הַזֶּה֙ כָּעֵ֣ת חַיָּ֔ה [אתי כ׳] אַ֥תְּ חֹבֶ֣קֶת בֵּ֑ן וַתֹּ֗אמֶר אַל־אֲדֹנִי֙ אִ֣ישׁ

---

empty containers. Don't ask for just a few. [4] Then enter your home and shut the door behind you and your sons, and pour the oil into all these containers. Once they are full, remove the filled ones and replace them with empty ones, because the jug will be like a fountain."

[5] She left him and closed the door behind her and her sons. They would bring the empty containers to her so she would not have to move, and she would pour. [6] When the borrowed containers were all full she said to her son, "Bring me another container."

"There aren't any more containers," he said to her. Then the oil stopped flowing.

[7] She came and told the Godly man what had happened. He said, "Go and sell the oil and pay your debts. You and your sons will live off the remaining money."

[8] One day, Elisha passed through Shunem. A distinguished lady who lived there insisted that he eat a meal in her house. From then on, whenever he passed by, he would go there to eat bread.

[9] She said to her husband, "I realize that the person who comes regularly to us is a holy man of God, so it's not right that he live in the same quarters as us. [10] Let's make a small room in the attic, and put a bed, table, chair, and lamp there for him. When he comes to us, he will stay there in privacy."

[11] After they built the room in the attic the day came when Elisha arrived there. He stayed in the attic and slept there.

[12] He said to Gehazi, his servant, "Call this Shunammite woman over here." He called her and she stood before him.

[13] He said to Gehazi, "Please say to her, 'You have gone to all this effort for us, what can I do for you to repay you? Is there any matter about which you want me to speak to the king or army commander on your behalf?'"

She said, "It's fine, I live peacefully with my family."

[14] After she left, he said to Gehazi, "So what is there to do for her?"

Gehazi said, "Actually there is something we can do. She doesn't have a son, and her husband is too old to father a child."

[15] "Call her," Elisha said. Gehazi called her and she stood modestly at the doorway.

[16] Elisha said, "At the next occasion for you to give birth (in nine months) you will be embracing a son!"

haftarat va-yera'

She said, "Please sir, man of God, do not delude your maidservant with false hopes."

¹⁷ The woman became pregnant and gave birth to a boy, at the earliest possible time, just as Elisha said.

¹⁸ The child grew up. One day, he went out to his father, who was supervising the reaping of the harvests, ¹⁹ and he said to his father, "My head hurts! My head hurts!"

His father said to the lad who was working there, "Carry him to his mother."

²⁰ The lad carried him and brought him to his mother. The child sat on her knees until midday, and he died. ²¹ She went upstairs and laid him down on the bed of the Godly man, closed the door behind him and left. ²² She called to her husband and said, "Send me one of the lads and one of the donkeys. I will rush to the Godly man and come back."

²³ He said, "Why are you going to him today? It's not the New Moon or the Sabbath, when you usually see him."

She said, "All is well," because she thought it would be better if it happened in secret.

הָאֱלֹהִ֖ים אַל־תְּכַזֵּ֥ב בְּשִׁפְחָתֶֽךָ: 17 וַתַּ֥הַר הָאִשָּׁ֖ה וַתֵּ֣לֶד בֵּ֑ן לַמּוֹעֵ֤ד הַזֶּה֙ כָּעֵ֣ת חַיָּ֔ה אֲשֶׁר־דִּבֶּ֥ר אֵלֶ֖יהָ אֱלִישָֽׁע: 18 וַיִּגְדַּ֖ל הַיָּ֑לֶד וַיְהִ֣י הַיּ֔וֹם וַיֵּצֵ֥א אֶל־אָבִ֖יו אֶל־הַקֹּצְרִֽים: 19 וַיֹּ֥אמֶר אֶל־אָבִ֖יו רֹאשִׁ֣י ׀ רֹאשִׁ֑י וַיֹּ֙אמֶר֙ אֶל־הַנַּ֔עַר שָׂאֵ֖הוּ אֶל־אִמּֽוֹ: 20 וַיִּשָּׂאֵ֔הוּ וַיְבִיאֵ֖הוּ אֶל־אִמּ֑וֹ וַיֵּ֧שֶׁב עַל־בִּרְכֶּ֛יהָ עַד־הַֽצָּהֳרַ֖יִם וַיָּמֹֽת: 21 וַתַּ֗עַל וַתַּשְׁכִּבֵ֙הוּ֙ עַל־מִטַּ֖ת אִ֣ישׁ הָאֱלֹהִ֑ים וַתִּסְגֹּ֥ר בַּעֲד֖וֹ וַתֵּצֵֽא: 22 וַתִּקְרָא֮ אֶל־אִישָׁהּ֒ וַתֹּ֗אמֶר שִׁלְחָ֨ה נָ֥א לִי֙ אֶחָ֣ד מִן־הַנְּעָרִ֔ים וְאַחַ֖ת הָאֲתֹנ֑וֹת וְאָר֛וּצָה עַד־אִ֥ישׁ הָאֱלֹהִ֖ים וְאָשֽׁוּבָה: 23 וַיֹּ֗אמֶר מַ֠דּוּעַ אַתִּי [אַ֣תְּ כ׳] [הֹלַ֤כְתִּי כ׳] הֹלֶ֙כֶת֙ אֵלָיו֙ הַיּ֔וֹם לֹא־חֹ֖דֶשׁ וְלֹ֣א שַׁבָּ֑ת וַתֹּ֖אמֶר שָׁלֽוֹם:

Sephardic communities conclude here. Ḥabad and Ashkenazic communities continue:

---

²⁴ She saddled the donkey and said to her lad, "Get going! Don't go slowly because of me, unless I tell you."

²⁵ She traveled and came to the Godly man at Mount Carmel. When the Godly man saw her from afar, he said to Gehazi, his servant, "The Shunammite woman is here! ²⁶ Now, please run towards her, and say to her, 'Are you well? Is your husband alright? Is the child well?'"

She said, "Everything is well," for she wanted to conceal the matter even from Gehazi.

²⁷ She came to the Godly man, who was on the mountain, and grabbed hold of his feet. Gehazi came over to push her away, but the Godly man said, "Leave her, for her soul is bitter. God has hidden the problem from me and has not told it to me."

²⁸ She said, "Was it I who asked for a son from my master? Didn't I say, 'Don't mislead me'?"

²⁹ He said to Gehazi, "Fasten your belt so you can travel fast, take my staff in your hand, and go. If you meet someone, do not greet him. If someone greets

24 וַֽתַּחֲבֹשׁ֙ הָֽאָת֔וֹן וַתֹּ֥אמֶר אֶֽל־נַעֲרָ֖הּ נְהַ֣ג וָלֵ֑ךְ אַל־תַּעֲצָר־לִ֣י לִרְכֹּ֔ב כִּ֖י אִם־אָמַ֥רְתִּי לָֽךְ: 25 וַתֵּ֗לֶךְ וַתָּב֛וֹא אֶל־אִ֥ישׁ הָאֱלֹהִ֖ים אֶל־הַ֣ר הַכַּרְמֶ֑ל וַ֠יְהִ֠י כִּרְא֨וֹת אִישׁ־הָאֱלֹהִ֤ים אֹתָהּ֙ מִנֶּ֔גֶד וַיֹּ֙אמֶר֙ אֶל־גֵּיחֲזִ֣י נַעֲר֔וֹ הִנֵּ֖ה הַשּׁוּנַמִּ֥ית הַלָּֽז: 26 עַתָּה֮ רֽוּץ־נָ֣א לִקְרָאתָהּ֒ וֶאֱמָר־לָ֗הּ הֲשָׁל֥וֹם לָ֛ךְ הֲשָׁל֥וֹם לְאִישֵׁ֖ךְ הֲשָׁל֣וֹם לַיָּ֑לֶד וַתֹּ֖אמֶר שָׁלֽוֹם: 27 וַתָּבֹ֞א אֶל־אִ֤ישׁ הָֽאֱלֹהִים֙ אֶל־הָהָ֔ר וַֽתַּחֲזֵ֖ק בְּרַגְלָ֑יו וַיִּגַּ֨שׁ גֵּיחֲזִ֜י לְהָדְפָ֗הּ וַיֹּ֩אמֶר֩ אִ֨ישׁ הָאֱלֹהִ֤ים הַרְפֵּֽה־לָהּ֙ כִּֽי־נַפְשָׁ֣הּ מָֽרָה־לָ֔הּ וַֽיהֹוָה֙ הֶעְלִ֣ים מִמֶּ֔נִּי וְלֹ֥א הִגִּ֖יד לִֽי: 28 וַתֹּ֕אמֶר הֲשָׁאַ֥לְתִּי בֵ֖ן מֵאֵ֣ת אֲדֹנִ֑י הֲלֹ֣א אָמַ֔רְתִּי לֹ֥א תַשְׁלֶ֖ה אֹתִֽי: 29 וַיֹּ֨אמֶר לְגֵיחֲזִ֜י חֲגֹ֣ר מָתְנֶ֗יךָ וְקַ֨ח מִשְׁעַנְתִּ֥י בְיָדְךָ֮ וָלֵךְ֒ כִּֽי־

you, do not reply to him so as not to delay your mission. You should place my staff on the boy's face in order to revive him."

³⁰ The boy's mother said, "I swear by the fact that God lives, and by your life, that I will not leave you alone if you don't come along!" So he got up and followed behind her.

³¹ Gehazi had gone ahead of them and placed the staff on the boy's face, but there was neither a sound nor a response, because Gehazi had not followed orders and he had stopped to jest and tell people of his mission. He returned to Elisha and informed him, saying, "The boy did not wake up."

³² When Elisha arrived at the house, the boy was dead, lying on his bed. ³³ He came inside and closed the door behind both of them, and prayed to God. ³⁴ He climbed up onto the bed and lay on the child. He placed his mouth on the boy's mouth, his eyes on his eyes, his palms on his palms. He spread himself out over him, and the child's flesh became warm.

³⁵ He went back down off the bed and walked backwards and forwards in the house. Then he climbed back onto the bed and spread himself over the body, and repeated these movements seven times. The boy sneezed seven times, and then he opened his eyes.

³⁶ Elisha called to Gehazi, and said, "Call the Shunammite woman!" He called her. When she came to him, he said, "Pick up your child!"

³⁷ She fell down at his feet and prostrated herself. Then she gathered up her son and left.

haftarat ḥayyei sarah

ALL COMMUNITIES—I KINGS 1:1–31

SYNOPSIS: The opening of this *Haftarah*, which describes King David's advanced years, resembles the statement in *Parashat Ḥayyei Sarah* that Abraham had advanced in years (24:1).

The *Haftarah* describes King David's last days before his passing (1–4), during which time his son Adonijah begins to celebrate his succession to the monarchy (5–10). Bathsheba, Solomon's mother, is thus advised to go to the king and reiterate his promise that Solomon would become king (11–14). She does so, and Nathan joins the audience with the king to confirm the reports of Adonijah's behavior (15–27). King David responds by instructing that Solomon should be anointed as king immediately, in his own lifetime (28–31).

haftarat ḥayyei sarah

1 ¹ King David was old. The signs of old age were not premature but came in the right time. They covered him with clothes, but he did not become warm.

² His servants said to him, "Let a virgin girl be sought for my master the king. Let her stand ready before the king and provide warmth for him. She will lie in your bosom, so that my master the king will be warm."

³ They looked for a beautiful girl throughout the entire territory of Israel. They found Abishag the Shunammite and brought her before the king. ⁴ The girl was extremely beautiful. She acted as a "warmer" for the king and served him, but the king did not know her in an intimate way.

⁵ Meanwhile, Adonijah, son of David and Haggith, was acting haughtily like a king, as if he were actually saying, "I will reign." He prepared a chariot and horsemen for himself and fifty men running before him. ⁶ Since his father had never reprimanded him, saying, "Why have you done this?" he presumed that he had his father's approval. He also thought that he was fit to be king because he was very good-looking and he was born right after Absalom who had died, leaving Adonijah the eldest. ⁷ He consulted with Joab son of Zeruiah, and Abiathar the priest. They supported Adonijah because they knew that he was disliked by David. ⁸ But Zadok the priest; Benaiah son of Jehoiada; Nathan the prophet; Shimei; Rei; and David's strongmen Eleazar, Adino, and Shamma were not with Adonijah, for they remained loyal to David.

⁹ Adonijah offered sheep, cattle, and fat oxen at the Zoheleth stone near the fountain En-rogel, and he invited those that supported him from among all his brothers, the king's sons, and all the people of Judah, the king's servants. ¹⁰ But he did not invite Nathan the prophet, Benaiah and the strongmen, nor his brother Solomon.

¹¹ Nathan spoke to Bathsheba, Solomon's mother, saying, "Haven't you heard that Adonijah son of Haggith has plans to become king? Our master David doesn't know about it. ¹² Now, please let me advise you, so that you will save your life and that of your son Solomon, for Adonijah will surely kill you both if he becomes king.

¹³ "Go, and enter before King David, and say to him, 'My master the king! Didn't you swear to your maidservant, saying, "Solomon your son will reign after me, and he will sit on my throne"? So why has Adonijah become king?'

¹⁴ "Then, while you are still talking there with the king, I will enter after you and confirm your words."

א וְהַמֶּ֚לֶךְ דָּוִד֙ זָקֵ֔ן בָּ֖א בַּיָּמִ֑ים וַיְכַסֻּ֙הוּ֙ בַּבְּגָדִ֔ים וְלֹ֥א יִחַ֖ם לֽוֹ: ² וַיֹּ֧אמְרוּ ל֣וֹ עֲבָדָ֗יו יְבַקְשׁ֞וּ לַאדֹנִ֤י הַמֶּ֙לֶךְ֙ נַעֲרָ֣ה בְתוּלָ֔ה וְעָֽמְדָה֙ לִפְנֵ֣י הַמֶּ֔לֶךְ וּתְהִי־ל֖וֹ סֹכֶ֑נֶת וְשָׁכְבָ֣ה בְחֵיקֶ֔ךָ וְחַ֖ם לַאדֹנִ֥י הַמֶּֽלֶךְ: ³ וַיְבַקְשׁוּ֙ נַעֲרָ֣ה יָפָ֔ה בְּכֹ֖ל גְּב֣וּל יִשְׂרָאֵ֑ל וַֽיִּמְצְא֗וּ אֶת־אֲבִישַׁג֙ הַשּׁ֣וּנַמִּ֔ית וַיָּבִ֥אוּ אֹתָ֖הּ לַמֶּֽלֶךְ: ⁴ וְהַֽנַּעֲרָ֖ה יָפָ֣ה עַד־מְאֹ֑ד וַתְּהִ֨י לַמֶּ֚לֶךְ סֹכֶ֙נֶת֙ וַתְּשָׁ֣רְתֵ֔הוּ וְהַמֶּ֖לֶךְ לֹ֥א יְדָעָֽהּ: ⁵ וַאֲדֹנִיָּ֧ה בֶן־חַגִּ֛ית מִתְנַשֵּׂ֥א לֵאמֹ֖ר אֲנִ֣י אֶמְלֹ֑ךְ וַיַּ֣עַשׂ ל֗וֹ רֶ֚כֶב וּפָ֣רָשִׁ֔ים וַחֲמִשִּׁ֥ים אִ֖ישׁ רָצִ֥ים לְפָנָֽיו: ⁶ וְלֹֽא־עֲצָב֨וֹ אָבִ֚יו מִיָּמָיו֙ לֵאמֹ֔ר מַדּ֖וּעַ כָּ֣כָה עָשִׂ֑יתָ וְגַם־ה֚וּא טֽוֹב־תֹּ֙אַר֙ מְאֹ֔ד וְאֹת֥וֹ יָלְדָ֖ה אַחֲרֵ֥י אַבְשָׁלֽוֹם: ⁷ וַיִּהְי֣וּ דְבָרָ֔יו עִ֚ם יוֹאָב֙ בֶּן־צְרוּיָ֔ה וְעִ֖ם אֶבְיָתָ֣ר הַכֹּהֵ֑ן וַֽיַּעְזְר֔וּ אַחֲרֵ֖י אֲדֹנִיָּֽה: ⁸ וְצָד֣וֹק הַ֠כֹּהֵן וּבְנָיָ֨הוּ בֶן־יְהוֹיָדָ֜ע וְנָתָ֣ן הַנָּבִ֗יא וְשִׁמְעִי֙ וְרֵעִ֔י וְהַגִּבּוֹרִ֖ים אֲשֶׁ֣ר לְדָוִ֑ד לֹ֥א הָי֖וּ עִם־אֲדֹנִיָּֽהוּ: ⁹ וַיִּזְבַּ֣ח אֲדֹנִיָּ֗הוּ צֹ֚אן וּבָקָר֙ וּמְרִ֔יא עִ֚ם אֶ֣בֶן הַזֹּחֶ֔לֶת אֲשֶׁר־אֵ֖צֶל עֵ֣ין רֹגֵ֑ל וַיִּקְרָ֗א אֶת־כָּל־אֶחָיו֙ בְּנֵ֣י הַמֶּ֔לֶךְ וּלְכָל־אַנְשֵׁ֥י יְהוּדָ֖ה עַבְדֵ֥י הַמֶּֽלֶךְ: ¹⁰ וְֽאֶת־נָתָן֩ הַנָּבִ֨יא וּבְנָיָ֜הוּ וְאֶת־הַגִּבּוֹרִ֛ים וְאֶת־שְׁלֹמֹ֥ה אָחִ֖יו לֹ֥א קָרָֽא: ¹¹ וַיֹּ֣אמֶר נָתָ֗ן אֶל־בַּת־שֶׁ֤בַע אֵם־שְׁלֹמֹה֙ לֵאמֹ֔ר הֲל֣וֹא שָׁמַ֔עַתְּ כִּ֥י מָלַ֖ךְ אֲדֹנִיָּ֣הוּ בֶן־חַגִּ֑ית וַאֲדֹנֵ֖ינוּ דָוִ֥ד לֹ֥א יָדָֽע: ¹² וְעַתָּ֕ה לְכִ֛י אִיעָצֵ֥ךְ נָ֖א עֵצָ֑ה וּמַלְּטִי֙ אֶת־נַפְשֵׁ֔ךְ וְאֶת־נֶ֥פֶשׁ בְּנֵ֖ךְ שְׁלֹמֹֽה: ¹³ לְכִ֞י וּבֹ֣אִי | אֶל־הַמֶּ֣לֶךְ דָּוִ֗ד וְאָמַ֤רְתְּ אֵלָיו֙ הֲלֹֽא־אַתָּ֞ה אֲדֹנִ֣י הַמֶּ֗לֶךְ נִשְׁבַּ֤עְתָּ לַאֲמָֽתְךָ֙ לֵאמֹ֔ר כִּֽי־שְׁלֹמֹ֤ה בְנֵךְ֙ יִמְלֹ֣ךְ אַחֲרַ֔י וְה֖וּא יֵשֵׁ֣ב עַל־כִּסְאִ֑י וּמַדּ֖וּעַ מָלַ֥ךְ אֲדֹנִיָּֽהוּ: ¹⁴ הִנֵּ֗ה עוֹדָ֛ךְ מְדַבֶּ֥רֶת שָׁ֖ם

הפטרת חיי שרה

עִם־הַמֶּלֶךְ וַאֲנִי אָבוֹא אַחֲרַיִךְ וּמִלֵּאתִי אֶת־דְּבָרָיִךְ: 15 וַתָּבֹא בַת־שֶׁבַע אֶל־הַמֶּלֶךְ הַחַדְרָה וְהַמֶּלֶךְ זָקֵן מְאֹד וַאֲבִישַׁג הַשּׁוּנַמִּית מְשָׁרַת אֶת־הַמֶּלֶךְ: 16 וַתִּקֹּד בַּת־שֶׁבַע וַתִּשְׁתַּחוּ לַמֶּלֶךְ וַיֹּאמֶר הַמֶּלֶךְ מַה־לָּךְ: 17 וַתֹּאמֶר לוֹ אֲדֹנִי אַתָּה נִשְׁבַּעְתָּ בַּיהוָה אֱלֹהֶיךָ לַאֲמָתֶךָ כִּי־שְׁלֹמֹה בְנֵךְ יִמְלֹךְ אַחֲרָי וְהוּא יֵשֵׁב עַל־כִּסְאִי: 18 וְעַתָּה הִנֵּה אֲדֹנִיָּה מָלָךְ וְעַתָּה אֲדֹנִי הַמֶּלֶךְ לֹא יָדָעְתָּ: 19 וַיִּזְבַּח שׁוֹר וּמְרִיא־וְצֹאן לָרֹב וַיִּקְרָא לְכָל־בְּנֵי הַמֶּלֶךְ וּלְאֶבְיָתָר הַכֹּהֵן וּלְיֹאָב שַׂר הַצָּבָא וְלִשְׁלֹמֹה עַבְדְּךָ לֹא קָרָא: 20 וְאַתָּה אֲדֹנִי הַמֶּלֶךְ עֵינֵי כָל־יִשְׂרָאֵל עָלֶיךָ לְהַגִּיד לָהֶם מִי יֵשֵׁב עַל־כִּסֵּא אֲדֹנִי־הַמֶּלֶךְ אַחֲרָיו: 21 וְהָיָה כִּשְׁכַב אֲדֹנִי־הַמֶּלֶךְ עִם־אֲבֹתָיו וְהָיִיתִי אֲנִי וּבְנִי שְׁלֹמֹה חַטָּאִים: 22 וְהִנֵּה עוֹדֶנָּה מְדַבֶּרֶת עִם־הַמֶּלֶךְ וְנָתָן הַנָּבִיא בָּא: 23 וַיַּגִּידוּ לַמֶּלֶךְ לֵאמֹר הִנֵּה נָתָן הַנָּבִיא וַיָּבֹא לִפְנֵי הַמֶּלֶךְ וַיִּשְׁתַּחוּ לַמֶּלֶךְ עַל־אַפָּיו אָרְצָה: 24 וַיֹּאמֶר נָתָן אֲדֹנִי הַמֶּלֶךְ אַתָּה אָמַרְתָּ אֲדֹנִיָּהוּ יִמְלֹךְ אַחֲרָי וְהוּא יֵשֵׁב עַל־כִּסְאִי: 25 כִּי ׀ יָרַד הַיּוֹם וַיִּזְבַּח שׁוֹר וּמְרִיא־וְצֹאן לָרֹב וַיִּקְרָא לְכָל־בְּנֵי הַמֶּלֶךְ וּלְשָׂרֵי הַצָּבָא וּלְאֶבְיָתָר הַכֹּהֵן וְהִנָּם אֹכְלִים וְשֹׁתִים לְפָנָיו וַיֹּאמְרוּ יְחִי הַמֶּלֶךְ אֲדֹנִיָּהוּ: 26 וְלִי אֲנִי־עַבְדֶּךָ וּלְצָדֹק הַכֹּהֵן וְלִבְנָיָהוּ בֶן־יְהוֹיָדָע וְלִשְׁלֹמֹה עַבְדְּךָ לֹא קָרָא: 27 אִם מֵאֵת אֲדֹנִי הַמֶּלֶךְ נִהְיָה הַדָּבָר הַזֶּה וְלֹא הוֹדַעְתָּ אֶת־[עבדך כ׳] עַבְדְּךָ מִי יֵשֵׁב עַל־כִּסֵּא אֲדֹנִי־הַמֶּלֶךְ אַחֲרָיו: 28 וַיַּעַן הַמֶּלֶךְ דָּוִד וַיֹּאמֶר קִרְאוּ־לִי לְבַת־שָׁבַע וַתָּבֹא לִפְנֵי הַמֶּלֶךְ וַתַּעֲמֹד לִפְנֵי הַמֶּלֶךְ: 29 וַיִּשָּׁבַע הַמֶּלֶךְ וַיֹּאמַר חַי־יְהוָה אֲשֶׁר־פָּדָה אֶת־נַפְשִׁי מִכָּל־צָרָה: 30 כִּי כַּאֲשֶׁר

---

15 Bathsheba came to the king, into his bedroom. The king was very old and Abishag the Shunammite was serving the king. 16 Bathsheba bowed down and prostrated herself before the king. "What do you want?" the king said.

17 She said to him, "My master! You swore to your maidservant in the name of God Almighty, 'Solomon, your son, will reign after me and he will sit on my throne.' 18 But now—look!—Adonijah has become king, and you—my master the king—did not know. 19 Proof of the matter is that he made a feast where he sacrificed many cattle, fattened oxen, and sheep. He invited all the king's sons, Abiathar the priest, and Joab the army general, but he did not invite the heir Solomon, your servant. 20 Don't think it was the people that chose Adonijah, for the eyes of all Israel are upon you, my master the king, to tell them who should sit on the throne of my master the king after him. 21 However, if you do not do so, when my master the king passes on and lies with his fathers, I and my son Solomon will be deprived of our lives."

22 Then, while she was still talking to the king, Nathan the prophet arrived in the king's quarters. 23 They announced to the king, saying, "Nathan the prophet is here." He entered the king's presence and he prostrated himself on the ground, on his face.

24 Nathan said, "My master the king! Did you say, 'Adonijah should reign after me and he will sit on my throne'? 25 Because today he went down and sacrificed many cattle, fattened oxen, and sheep, and he invited all the king's sons, the army generals, and Abiathar the priest to what could only be a coronation feast. They are eating and drinking in his presence and they will surely have said, 'Long live King Adonijah!' 26 And he did not invite me, Zadok the priest, Benaiah son of Jehoiada, nor Solomon, your servant. 27 If this matter has come from my master the king, I wonder why you have not previously informed your servant, who should sit on the throne of *my master the king* after him."

28 King David replied and said, "Call Bathsheba for me." She came before the king and stood before the king. 29 The king took an oath, saying, "By the life of God, who has delivered my soul from all suffering! 30 Just as I swore to you in the name of the Almighty

haftarat toledot

God of Israel, saying, 'Solomon, your son, will reign after me, and he will sit on my throne,' so too I will swear today that Solomon will become king immediately, during my lifetime!"

[31] Bathsheba bowed with her face to the ground and prostrated herself to the king. She said, "May my master King David live forever!"

נִשְׁבַּעְתִּי לָךְ בַּיהוָה אֱלֹהֵי יִשְׂרָאֵל לֵאמֹר כִּי־שְׁלֹמֹה בְנֵךְ יִמְלֹךְ אַחֲרַי וְהוּא יֵשֵׁב עַל־כִּסְאִי תַּחְתָּי כִּי כֵּן אֶעֱשֶׂה הַיּוֹם הַזֶּה: 31 וַתִּקֹּד בַּת־שֶׁבַע אַפַּיִם אֶרֶץ וַתִּשְׁתַּחוּ לַמֶּלֶךְ וַתֹּאמֶר יְחִי אֲדֹנִי הַמֶּלֶךְ דָּוִד לְעֹלָם:

haftarat toledot

ALL COMMUNITIES—MALACHI 1:1 – 2:7

SYNOPSIS: The opening of this *Haftarah*, which discusses God's love and preference for Jacob over Esau (1:2-5), acknowledges Jacob's rightful claim to the blessings which he received in the *Parashah* (chapter 27).

The *Haftarah* was addressed to the Jewish people by the prophet Malachi, shortly after their return from their Babylonian exile (approx. 520 B.C.E.). Its predominant theme is an admonition for a lack of respect for the Holy Temple and its offerings. The *Haftarah* opens with a statement of God's love for Israel and a promise of downfall and destruction for Israel's hated enemy, Esau (1:1-5). The prophet then laments Israel's betrayal of God, particularly in the area of sacrificial service (6-10), claiming that Israel honors God less than the idol-worshiping nations (11). Further criticisms include the slandering of the altar (12), and the offering of low-quality animals to the Holy Temple (13-14). God finally threatens to transform the priestly blessings into curses, due to negligence in sacrificial procedure (2:1-3), which has betrayed the true, exalted nature of the priesthood (4-7).

1 [1] The prophecy—the word of God—to Israel, transmitted by Malachi, is as follows:

[2] "I loved you," said God. "But if you say, 'In what way did You show Your love for us personally, and not merely due to the merit of the Patriarchs and Matriarchs?' I will reply to you: 'Was Esau not Jacob's brother who shared the same ancestry as Jacob?'" said God, "Yet I loved Jacob, [3] and I hated Esau despite his ancestors. I laid his mountains desolate, and his inheritance a home for the serpents of the desert. So clearly, when I loved you, it was not only in the merit of your ancestors.

[4] "If Edom, Esau's descendants that destroyed the Holy Temple, say, 'We are now poor, but we will return and rebuild the desolate places,' then the God of Hosts says: 'They will build, and I will destroy!' The destruction will be so awesome that people will call it a wicked place which clearly merited destruction by God, and they will be called a people with

א 1 מַשָּׂא דְבַר־יְהוָה אֶל־יִשְׂרָאֵל בְּיַד מַלְאָכִי: 2 אָהַבְתִּי אֶתְכֶם אָמַר יְהוָה וַאֲמַרְתֶּם בַּמָּה אֲהַבְתָּנוּ הֲלוֹא־אָח עֵשָׂו לְיַעֲקֹב נְאֻם־יְהוָה וָאֹהַב אֶת־יַעֲקֹב: 3 וְאֶת־עֵשָׂו שָׂנֵאתִי וָאָשִׂים אֶת־הָרָיו שְׁמָמָה וְאֶת־נַחֲלָתוֹ לְתַנּוֹת מִדְבָּר: 4 כִּי־תֹאמַר אֱדוֹם רֻשַּׁשְׁנוּ וְנָשׁוּב וְנִבְנֶה חֳרָבוֹת כֹּה אָמַר יְהוָה צְבָאוֹת הֵמָּה יִבְנוּ וַאֲנִי אֶהֱרוֹס וְקָרְאוּ לָהֶם גְּבוּל רִשְׁעָה וְהָעָם אֲשֶׁר־זָעַם יְהוָה עַד־עוֹלָם:

הפטרת תולדות

5 וְעֵינֵיכֶם תִּרְאֶינָה וְאַתֶּם תֹּאמְרוּ יִגְדַּל יְהֹוָה מֵעַל לִגְבוּל יִשְׂרָאֵל: 6 בֵּן יְכַבֵּד אָב וְעֶבֶד אֲדֹנָיו וְאִם־אָב אָנִי אַיֵּה כְבוֹדִי וְאִם־אֲדוֹנִים אָנִי אַיֵּה מוֹרָאִי אָמַר | יְהֹוָה צְבָאוֹת לָכֶם הַכֹּהֲנִים בּוֹזֵי שְׁמִי וַאֲמַרְתֶּם בַּמֶּה בָזִינוּ אֶת־שְׁמֶךָ: 7 מַגִּישִׁים עַל־מִזְבְּחִי לֶחֶם מְגֹאָל וַאֲמַרְתֶּם בַּמֶּה גֵאַלְנוּךָ בֶּאֱמָרְכֶם שֻׁלְחַן יְהֹוָה נִבְזֶה הוּא: 8 וְכִי־תַגִּשׁוּן עִוֵּר לִזְבֹּחַ אֵין רָע וְכִי תַגִּישׁוּ פִּסֵּחַ וְחֹלֶה אֵין רָע הַקְרִיבֵהוּ נָא לְפֶחָתֶךָ הֲיִרְצְךָ אוֹ הֲיִשָּׂא פָנֶיךָ אָמַר יְהֹוָה צְבָאוֹת: 9 וְעַתָּה חַלּוּ־נָא פְנֵי־אֵל וִיחָנֵּנוּ מִיֶּדְכֶם הָיְתָה זֹּאת הֲיִשָּׂא מִכֶּם פָּנִים אָמַר יְהֹוָה צְבָאוֹת: 10 מִי גַם־בָּכֶם וְיִסְגֹּר דְּלָתַיִם וְלֹא־תָאִירוּ מִזְבְּחִי חִנָּם אֵין־לִי חֵפֶץ בָּכֶם אָמַר יְהֹוָה צְבָאוֹת וּמִנְחָה לֹא־אֶרְצֶה מִיֶּדְכֶם: 11 כִּי מִמִּזְרַח־שֶׁמֶשׁ וְעַד־מְבוֹאוֹ גָּדוֹל שְׁמִי בַּגּוֹיִם וּבְכָל־מָקוֹם מֻקְטָר מֻגָּשׁ לִשְׁמִי וּמִנְחָה טְהוֹרָה כִּי־גָדוֹל שְׁמִי בַּגּוֹיִם אָמַר יְהֹוָה צְבָאוֹת: 12 וְאַתֶּם מְחַלְּלִים אוֹתוֹ בֶּאֱמָרְכֶם שֻׁלְחַן אֲדֹנָי מְגֹאָל הוּא וְנִיבוֹ נִבְזֶה אָכְלוֹ: 13 וַאֲמַרְתֶּם הִנֵּה מַתְּלָאָה וְהִפַּחְתֶּם אוֹתוֹ אָמַר יְהֹוָה צְבָאוֹת וַהֲבֵאתֶם גָּזוּל וְאֶת־הַפִּסֵּחַ וְאֶת־הַחוֹלֶה וַהֲבֵאתֶם אֶת־הַמִּנְחָה הַאֶרְצֶה אוֹתָהּ מִיֶּדְכֶם אָמַר יְהֹוָה: 14 וְאָרוּר נוֹכֵל וְיֵשׁ בְּעֶדְרוֹ זָכָר וְנֹדֵר וְזֹבֵחַ מָשְׁחָת לַאדֹנָי כִּי מֶלֶךְ גָּדוֹל אָנִי אָמַר יְהֹוָה צְבָאוֹת וּשְׁמִי נוֹרָא בַגּוֹיִם:

whom God is forever angry.' ⁵ When you return to your territory, with the redemption, your eyes will see the extent of Edom's destruction, and you will say about the territory of Israel, 'God is great, for He performs wonders.'

⁶ "I love you for your own merits! You are not merely a son who naturally honors his father or a servant who naturally honors his master. 'And, if I am a father to you, then where is My proper honor? If I am a master, then where is My fear?' says the God of Hosts to you, the priests who disgrace My name. If you will say, 'How have we disgraced Your name?' ⁷ the answer is: 'You offer on My altar repulsive bread!' And if you still say, 'How have our sacrifices disgraced You?' the answer is: 'By saying that God's table is repulsive, since blood and fats are offered on it.' ⁸ Furthermore when you offer a blind animal to be sacrificed, you do not see it as bad! When you offer a lame or sick animal, you do not see it as bad because the altar is disgusting in your eyes! Try offering such an animal now as a gift to your governor! Would he be pleased, or receive you kindly?" says the God of Hosts. ⁹ If you, the priests, now pray before God that He should be gracious to us, the Jewish people, will He listen? This misfortune that will occur will occur because of you, so how can you expect that He will receive you favorably?" says the God of Hosts.

¹⁰ "If only there was someone among you to close the doors of the Temple so that you do not kindle fire on My altar in vain. Because I have no desire for your appearances in the Temple," says the God of Hosts, "and I do not desire a gift-offering from your hands.

¹¹ "For My name is great among the nations, from the place where the sun rises to the place where it sets. In all places offerings are brought and burned by the nations to their gods; but they know that the Primary Cause of all existence is My name, so their offerings are pure in their eyes. For My name is great among the nations," says the God of Hosts. ¹² "But you are profaning it when you say, 'the table of God is despicable,' and by saying that its food is repulsive.

¹³ "When you bring a lean, skinny animal you say, 'This is so burdensome!', pretending that you are tired from carrying such a heavy animal, when really it could be blown over with a breath," says the God of Hosts. "You also bring stolen animals, lame and sick ones, and you bring them as gift-offerings. Should I accept this from your hands?" says God.

¹⁴ "Cursed is the one who deceives Me, claiming that he has funds only for a poor offering! He has in his flock better male animals and yet he vows and then sacrifices abandoned animals to God. For I am a great King," says the God of Hosts, "and My name is feared among the nations."

haftarat va-yetze'

2 ¹ "And now, this commandment not to accept a poor sacrifice is given to you, the priests. ² If you do not listen, and if you do not take it to heart to honor My name," says the God of Hosts, "then I will release a curse upon you and I will make your erstwhile blessings into curses. Indeed, you are already suffering from being cursed by Me, for you do not take it to heart to be careful about My honor. ³ Look! Because of you I will suppress the seeds so that they will not grow. I will blow dung in your faces like the dung of your festival sacrifices, with which you disgraced Me. Your sin will cause you to be disgraced like this.

⁴ "You should know that I sent you this commandment of honoring My sacrifices in order for you to be rewarded from My covenant with Aaron, the head of the tribe of Levi," says the God of Hosts. ⁵ "My covenant was with him and it brought him life and peace. I gave these commandments to him because of the fear in his heart before Me. He was in awe of My name. ⁶ The Torah of Truth was being taught by his mouth, and no wrong was found on his lips. For the sake of My commandments he walked with Me, guiding others in peace and in righteousness. Through his rebukes he turned many people away from their plans to sin. ⁷ All this applies to every priest, for the lips of a priest are fit to guard knowledge, and it is fitting that people should seek the Torah from his mouth that he should teach them. For a priest is an emissary of the God of Hosts."

ב ¹ וְעַתָּה אֲלֵיכֶם הַמִּצְוָה הַזֹּאת הַכֹּהֲנִים: ² אִם־לֹא תִשְׁמְעוּ וְאִם־לֹא תָשִׂימוּ עַל־לֵב לָתֵת כָּבוֹד לִשְׁמִי אָמַר יְהֹוָה צְבָאוֹת וְשִׁלַּחְתִּי בָכֶם אֶת־הַמְּאֵרָה וְאָרוֹתִי אֶת־בִּרְכוֹתֵיכֶם וְגַם אָרוֹתִיהָ כִּי אֵינְכֶם שָׂמִים עַל־לֵב: ³ הִנְנִי גֹעֵר לָכֶם אֶת־הַזֶּרַע וְזֵרִיתִי פֶרֶשׁ עַל־פְּנֵיכֶם פֶּרֶשׁ חַגֵּיכֶם וְנָשָׂא אֶתְכֶם אֵלָיו: ⁴ וִידַעְתֶּם כִּי שִׁלַּחְתִּי אֲלֵיכֶם אֵת הַמִּצְוָה הַזֹּאת לִהְיוֹת בְּרִיתִי אֶת־לֵוִי אָמַר יְהֹוָה צְבָאוֹת: ⁵ בְּרִיתִי ׀ הָיְתָה אִתּוֹ הַחַיִּים וְהַשָּׁלוֹם וָאֶתְּנֵם־לוֹ מוֹרָא וַיִּירָאֵנִי וּמִפְּנֵי שְׁמִי נִחַת הוּא: ⁶ תּוֹרַת אֱמֶת הָיְתָה בְּפִיהוּ וְעַוְלָה לֹא־נִמְצָא בִשְׂפָתָיו בְּשָׁלוֹם וּבְמִישׁוֹר הָלַךְ אִתִּי וְרַבִּים הֵשִׁיב מֵעָוֹן: ⁷ כִּי־שִׂפְתֵי כֹהֵן יִשְׁמְרוּ־דַעַת וְתוֹרָה יְבַקְשׁוּ מִפִּיהוּ כִּי מַלְאַךְ יְהֹוָה־צְבָאוֹת הוּא:

haftarat va-yetze'

Habad—Hosea 11:7 – 12:14
Sephardim—Hosea 11:7 – 13:5
Ashkenazim—Hosea 12:13 – 14:10

SYNOPSIS: This *Haftarah* describes the sins of "Ephraim," the northern tribes of the land of Israel (among whom Hosea lived), comparing the sins to events in Jacob's life. Most notably, the *Haftarah* mentions Jacob's flight to Aram and life there (12:13), which is chronicled in the course of *Parashat Va-Yetze'*.

The *Haftarah* opens with rebuke, that the Jewish people are reluctant to repent for their sins; nevertheless, they will not be abandoned by God (11:7-9). After pausing to touch upon Hosea's vision of the Messianic Era (10-11), the prophet returns to the mode of rebuke, criticizing the current deceit of Ephraim (12:1-2) and the future deceit of Judah (3). Jacob's story is briefly retold (4-5), and his descendants are begged to return to God (6-7). This is followed by further accusations of deceit (8-9), despite constant Divine assistance (10-12), further historical references to Jacob's life and the exodus from Egypt (13-14), and repeated promises of retribution (15).

הפטרת ויצא

> The *Haftarah* then turns to discuss the sin of Jeroboam, the idol-worship he incited, and the subsequent punishments (13:1–5). The message of guilt and doom is reiterated more vividly and forcefully (13:6–14:1).
>
> Hosea then makes an impassioned plea for repentance and sincere confession (14:2–4), with the promise of subsequent Divine pardon and love (5–9), urging the people to heed these words of wisdom (10).

Ḥabad and *Sephardic* communities begin here. *Ashkenazic* communities begin below, page 1305.

11 ⁷ "My people waver about taking the first step in returning to Me. Even though the prophets call to the people to rise up and take the initiative to return to the One Above, nevertheless they are united in that nobody rises up!

⁸ "Nevertheless, I still have mercy on you, for how can I give you, Ephraim, over to the nations, and deliver you into their hands? How can I let you be overturned like Admah, or make you desolate like Zeboiim? Even though I am angry with you My heart has turned inside Me to be kind to you. All My attributes of mercy have been aroused all at once. ⁹ I will not act with My fierce anger. I will not return to destroy Ephraim, for I am God and not a man who makes rash decisions. Once again the holiness of My presence will rest among you, and I will not enter another city to join the nations instead of you.

¹⁰ "In the times of the Messiah they will follow behind God into their land. Just as animals follow the roar of the lion, their king, so too He will roar like a lion and gather them. For He will arouse their hearts, as if they are being called by a lion's roar, and His children the Jewish people will hurry from the west. ¹¹ They will hurry from Egypt like a bird, and from Assyria like a dove. I will settle them securely in their homes," says God.

12 ¹ The kingdom of Ephraim has surrounded Me pretending to return to Me, but it has been with lies, for they are not genuine, and the house of Israel has treated me with deceit. But Judah is still ruling the *people*, and persuading them to be with God, and he is faithful to the holy God, to carry out His word. ² Ephraim is a shepherd of empty things like the wind, and pursues the easterly wind. All day he speaks much deceit, and extortion. They make a treaty with Assyria to help them, and oil is brought by them as a bribe to Egypt, to unite with Judah against the enemy.

³ But afterwards, Judah too will offend God and God will have a quarrel with Judah. He will remember the bad ways of the children of Jacob, and will repay them according to their deeds.

יא ⁷ וְעַמִּי תְלוּאִים לִמְשׁוּבָתִי וְאֶל־עַל יִקְרָאֻהוּ יַחַד לֹא יְרוֹמֵם: ⁸ אֵיךְ אֶתֶּנְךָ אֶפְרַיִם אֲמַגֶּנְךָ יִשְׂרָאֵל אֵיךְ אֶתֶּנְךָ כְאַדְמָה אֲשִׂימְךָ כִּצְבֹאיִם נֶהְפַּךְ עָלַי לִבִּי יַחַד נִכְמְרוּ נִחוּמָי: ⁹ לֹא אֶעֱשֶׂה חֲרוֹן אַפִּי לֹא אָשׁוּב לְשַׁחֵת אֶפְרָיִם כִּי אֵל אָנֹכִי וְלֹא־אִישׁ בְּקִרְבְּךָ קָדוֹשׁ וְלֹא אָבוֹא בְּעִיר: ¹⁰ אַחֲרֵי יְהֹוָה יֵלְכוּ כְּאַרְיֵה יִשְׁאָג כִּי־הוּא יִשְׁאַג וְיֶחֶרְדוּ בָנִים מִיָּם: ¹¹ יֶחֶרְדוּ כְצִפּוֹר מִמִּצְרַיִם וּכְיוֹנָה מֵאֶרֶץ אַשּׁוּר וְהוֹשַׁבְתִּים עַל־בָּתֵּיהֶם נְאֻם־יְהֹוָה:

יב ¹ סְבָבֻנִי בְכַחַשׁ אֶפְרַיִם וּבְמִרְמָה בֵּית יִשְׂרָאֵל וִיהוּדָה עֹד רָד עִם־אֵל וְעִם־קְדוֹשִׁים נֶאֱמָן: ² אֶפְרַיִם רֹעֶה רוּחַ וְרֹדֵף קָדִים כָּל־הַיּוֹם כָּזָב וָשֹׁד יַרְבֶּה וּבְרִית עִם־אַשּׁוּר יִכְרֹתוּ וְשֶׁמֶן לְמִצְרַיִם יוּבָל: ³ וְרִיב לַיהֹוָה עִם־יְהוּדָה וְלִפְקֹד עַל־יַעֲקֹב כִּדְרָכָיו כְּמַעֲלָלָיו יָשִׁיב לוֹ:

haftarat va-yetze'

⁴ While Jacob, their father, was in the womb he grabbed his brother's heel, and with strength he fought with God's angel, the ministering angel of Esau. ⁵ When he defeated the angel and ruled over him, the angel cried and begged Jacob to allow him to leave, saying, "God will find us together again in Bethel, and will speak with us there and then I will bless you"—so why is Jacob now so weak?

⁶ God is the omnipotent God of all the Hosts! Almighty God is His name! ⁷ Turn to your God in peace. Only be careful to be kind and just, then you can constantly trust in your God that He will grant your wishes.

⁸ But you are like a merchant who has deceitful scales in his hand, who loves to oppress others rather than acting kindly and justly. ⁹ Ephraim said, "Surely the reason that I have become wealthy is that I have found strength for myself and it is not from God. Furthermore the Almighty will not find in all my business dealings and efforts any sinful wrongdoings for God isn't aware."

¹⁰ But am I not God, your God! Since the time of your redemption from the land of Egypt I have looked after you. At a future time I will again settle you in tents, as in those days. ¹¹ I have spoken about you to the prophets and given them many visions. I have given parables through the prophets so you should understand them and be satisfied that I am carefully looking and taking care of you. ¹² If a misfortune befell Gilead it was not by chance, but because they were false. In Gilgal they sacrificed cattle to idols. Their altars for idol-worship are also as numerous as mounds in the furrows of the field.

4 בַּבֶּטֶן עָקַב אֶת־אָחִיו וּבְאוֹנוֹ שָׂרָה אֶת־אֱלֹהִים: 5 וַיָּשַׂר אֶל־מַלְאָךְ וַיֻּכָל בָּכָה וַיִּתְחַנֶּן־לוֹ בֵּית־אֵל יִמְצָאֶנּוּ וְשָׁם יְדַבֵּר עִמָּנוּ: 6 וַיהוָה אֱלֹהֵי הַצְּבָאוֹת יְהוָה זִכְרוֹ: 7 וְאַתָּה בֵּאלֹהֶיךָ תָשׁוּב חֶסֶד וּמִשְׁפָּט שְׁמֹר וְקַוֵּה אֶל־אֱלֹהֶיךָ תָּמִיד: 8 כְּנַעַן בְּיָדוֹ מֹאזְנֵי מִרְמָה לַעֲשֹׁק אָהֵב: 9 וַיֹּאמֶר אֶפְרַיִם אַךְ עָשַׁרְתִּי מָצָאתִי אוֹן לִי כָּל־יְגִיעַי לֹא יִמְצְאוּ־לִי עָוֹן אֲשֶׁר־חֵטְא: 10 וְאָנֹכִי יְהוָה אֱלֹהֶיךָ מֵאֶרֶץ מִצְרָיִם עֹד אוֹשִׁיבְךָ בָאֳהָלִים כִּימֵי מוֹעֵד: 11 וְדִבַּרְתִּי עַל־הַנְּבִיאִים וְאָנֹכִי חָזוֹן הִרְבֵּיתִי וּבְיַד הַנְּבִיאִים אֲדַמֶּה: 12 אִם־גִּלְעָד אָוֶן אַךְ־שָׁוְא הָיוּ בַּגִּלְגָּל שְׁוָרִים זִבֵּחוּ גַּם מִזְבְּחוֹתָם כְּגַלִּים עַל תַּלְמֵי שָׂדָי:

Most Sephardic communities conclude the Haftarah here. Some continue until 13:5.
Ashkenazic communities begin here. Ḥabad communities continue:

¹³ Jacob fled to the field of Aram. Israel worked there for a wife, and for a wife he tended sheep, and left a wealthy man through My blessings. ¹⁴ By means of a prophet God brought Israel up from Egypt, and through a prophet they were guarded on the way.

13 וַיִּבְרַח יַעֲקֹב שְׂדֵה אֲרָם וַיַּעֲבֹד יִשְׂרָאֵל בְּאִשָּׁה וּבְאִשָּׁה שָׁמָר: 14 וּבְנָבִיא הֶעֱלָה יְהוָה אֶת־יִשְׂרָאֵל מִמִּצְרָיִם וּבְנָבִיא נִשְׁמָר:

Ḥabad communities conclude here. Ashkenazic communities continue:

¹⁵ Ephraim bitterly angered God with his evil acts. Revenge for his acts of bloodshed will reach him and be upon him. His Master will repay him for his act of disgrace of worshiping idols.

13 ¹ When Jeroboam, a descendent of Ephraim, spoke strong words with trembling to rebuke King Solomon, he was exalted in Israel by becoming their king. But later, when he was guilty of worshiping the deity Baal, he died. ² Now this generation sinned further. In

15 הִכְעִיס אֶפְרַיִם תַּמְרוּרִים וְדָמָיו עָלָיו יִטּוֹשׁ וְחֶרְפָּתוֹ יָשִׁיב לוֹ אֲדֹנָיו:

יג 1 כְּדַבֵּר אֶפְרַיִם רְתֵת נָשָׂא הוּא בְּיִשְׂרָאֵל וַיֶּאְשַׁם בַּבַּעַל וַיָּמֹת: 2 וְעַתָּה | יוֹסִפוּ לַחֲטֹא וַיַּעֲשׂוּ לָהֶם מַסֵּכָה מִכַּסְפָּם כִּתְבוּנָם עֲצַבִּים מַעֲשֵׂה

הפטרת ויצא

addition to Jeroboam's golden calf, every person has made for themselves molten images in their own houses—cast images from their own silver, of their own design, idols all made by craftsmen. Because they say, "One who kisses the calf is as if he brought a human sacrifice!" Everybody wanted their own idol at home so they could kiss it frequently.

³ Therefore, they will be destroyed like the morning cloud which departs swiftly, and they will disappear early like the dew; like chaff blown away from the threshing floor, like smoke from the chimney. ⁴ They deserve this punishment, because I have been God, your God, since I took you out of the land of Egypt and you accepted me as your God. Do not consider any other than Me to be God, for I am the only Redeemer. ⁵ I took care of you in the wilderness, in a thirsty land, so you deserve destruction for abandoning Me.

Sephardic communities conclude here. *Ashkenazic* communities continue:

⁶ "When they came to pasture in the land of Israel, they were content. When they were content, they became arrogant. This is why they forgot Me. ⁷ Therefore I have become like a lion to them, like a leopard lurking by the road for its prey. ⁸ I confront them like a killer bear and tear them open right down to their hearts hidden below the chest. When I find them I devour them there like an awesome lion, rupture them like the beasts of the field. ⁹ Israel! You harmed yourself by ignoring Me when I was your Helper. ¹⁰ I am still here, but where is your mortal king now? Let him come and save you in all your cities! And where are your rulers of whom you said, 'Give us a king and ministers!'? ¹¹ In My anger I gave you a king, but I took him away in My wrath because your request was not appropriate.

¹² "I have not forgotten Ephraim's sin! It is bound up well; his transgression is stored away. ¹³ The pains of a woman in labor will come upon him. He is an unwise son, as otherwise he would not have delayed a moment in the womb, for he should have realized that his punishment was soon to come. ¹⁴ I would have redeemed him from Sheol, I would have delivered him from death. But now, I will utter death upon you; I will decree Sheol upon you. Reconciliation will be hidden from my eyes."

¹⁵ Originally, Ephraim bore fruit among his brothers and was greater than *them*. *But now he* has sinned with the calves, God will cause an easterly wind to come from the desert so that Ephraim's fountain will be dried up, and his wellspring parched. It will render the treasures of whatever is precious, as plunder.

14 ¹ Let Samaria be annihilated, for she has rebelled against her God. They will fall by the sword. Their

חֲרָשִׁים כֻּלֹּה לָהֶם הֵם אֹמְרִים זֹבְחֵי אָדָם עֲגָלִים יִשָּׁקוּן: 3 לָכֵן יִהְיוּ כַּעֲנַן־בֹּקֶר וְכַטַּל מַשְׁכִּים הֹלֵךְ כְּמֹץ יְסֹעֵר מִגֹּרֶן וּכְעָשָׁן מֵאֲרֻבָּה: 4 וְאָנֹכִי יְהֹוָה אֱלֹהֶיךָ מֵאֶרֶץ מִצְרָיִם וֵאלֹהִים זוּלָתִי לֹא תֵדָע וּמוֹשִׁיעַ אַיִן בִּלְתִּי: 5 אֲנִי יְדַעְתִּיךָ בַּמִּדְבָּר בְּאֶרֶץ תַּלְאֻבוֹת:

6 כְּמַרְעִיתָם וַיִּשְׂבָּעוּ שָׂבְעוּ וַיָּרָם לִבָּם עַל־כֵּן שְׁכֵחוּנִי: 7 וָאֱהִי לָהֶם כְּמוֹ־שָׁחַל כְּנָמֵר עַל־דֶּרֶךְ אָשׁוּר: 8 אֶפְגְּשֵׁם כְּדֹב שַׁכּוּל וְאֶקְרַע סְגוֹר לִבָּם וְאֹכְלֵם שָׁם כְּלָבִיא חַיַּת הַשָּׂדֶה תְּבַקְּעֵם: 9 שִׁחֶתְךָ יִשְׂרָאֵל כִּי־בִי בְעֶזְרֶךָ: 10 אֱהִי מַלְכְּךָ אֵפוֹא וְיוֹשִׁיעֲךָ בְּכָל־עָרֶיךָ וְשֹׁפְטֶיךָ אֲשֶׁר אָמַרְתָּ תְּנָה־לִּי מֶלֶךְ וְשָׂרִים: 11 אֶתֶּן־לְךָ מֶלֶךְ בְּאַפִּי וְאֶקַּח בְּעֶבְרָתִי: 12 צָרוּר עֲוֺן אֶפְרָיִם צְפוּנָה חַטָּאתוֹ: 13 חֶבְלֵי יוֹלֵדָה יָבֹאוּ לוֹ הוּא־בֵן לֹא חָכָם כִּי־עֵת לֹא־יַעֲמֹד בְּמִשְׁבַּר בָּנִים: 14 מִיַּד שְׁאוֹל אֶפְדֵּם מִמָּוֶת אֶגְאָלֵם אֱהִי דְבָרֶיךָ מָוֶת אֱהִי קָטָבְךָ שְׁאוֹל נֹחַם יִסָּתֵר מֵעֵינָי: 15 כִּי הוּא בֵּין אַחִים יַפְרִיא יָבוֹא קָדִים רוּחַ יְהֹוָה מִמִּדְבָּר עֹלֶה וְיֵבוֹשׁ מְקוֹרוֹ וְיֶחֱרַב מַעְיָנוֹ הוּא יִשְׁסֶה אוֹצַר כָּל־כְּלִי חֶמְדָּה:

יד 1 תֶּאְשַׁם שֹׁמְרוֹן כִּי מָרְתָה בֵּאלֹהֶיהָ בַּחֶרֶב יִפֹּלוּ עֹלְלֵיהֶם

haftarat va-yishlaḥ

infants will be split into pieces and their pregnant women ripped open.

² Israel, return to God, your God, for you have stumbled on account of your sins. ³ You do not need to take sacrifices. Just take words of confession with you and return to God. Say to Him: "Lift away all sin and accept our promises for good behavior in the future. Let the confession of our lips be in place of the sacrificing of bullocks.

⁴ "We will no longer ask to be saved by Assyria, and we will not put our trust in riding powerful horses into battle. We will never again call the idol made by our hands, 'our god,' because we know that the orphan finds compassion through You alone. ⁵ Then after they confess I will forgive them for their rebelliousness. I will love them deeply, because My anger will have turned away from them. ⁶ My love for Israel will be perpetual like dew. He will blossom like a rose, and his roots will spread like the roots of a cedar from Lebanon. ⁷ His young leaves will spread out, he will be beautiful like an olive tree, and he will have the aroma of Lebanon.

⁸ "Those who sat in His shade will be peaceful. They will be peacefully self-sufficient like grain sustains life, and they will blossom like the vine. Their fame will be like that of the wine of Lebanon. ⁹ When Ephraim asks, "What do I need idolaters for anymore?" I will answer all his requests and look over and supervise his needs. I will attend to him like a fresh cypress tree which bends its head over its roots. The fruit of your success comes from Me."

¹⁰ Whoever is wise will understand these words. The discerning will recognize them. For the ways of God are straight and the righteous will walk in them, but the wicked will stumble in them.

יְרֻטָּ֔שׁוּ וְהָרִיּוֹתָ֖יו יְבֻקָּֽעוּ: 2 שׁ֚וּבָה יִשְׂרָאֵ֔ל עַ֖ד יְהֹוָ֣ה אֱלֹהֶ֑יךָ כִּ֥י כָשַׁ֖לְתָּ בַּעֲוֺנֶֽךָ: 3 קְח֤וּ עִמָּכֶם֙ דְּבָרִ֔ים וְשׁ֖וּבוּ אֶל־יְהֹוָ֑ה אִמְר֣וּ אֵלָ֗יו כָּל־תִּשָּׂ֤א עָוֺן֙ וְקַח־ט֔וֹב וּֽנְשַׁלְּמָ֥ה פָרִ֖ים שְׂפָתֵֽינוּ: 4 אַשּׁ֣וּר ׀ לֹ֣א יוֹשִׁיעֵ֗נוּ עַל־סוּס֙ לֹ֣א נִרְכָּ֔ב וְלֹא־נֹ֥אמַר ע֛וֹד אֱלֹהֵ֖ינוּ לְמַעֲשֵׂ֣ה יָדֵ֑ינוּ אֲשֶׁר־בְּךָ֖ יְרֻחַ֥ם יָתֽוֹם: 5 אֶרְפָּא֙ מְשׁ֣וּבָתָ֔ם אֹהֲבֵ֖ם נְדָבָ֑ה כִּ֛י שָׁ֥ב אַפִּ֖י מִמֶּֽנּוּ: 6 אֶהְיֶ֤ה כַטַּל֙ לְיִשְׂרָאֵ֔ל יִפְרַ֖ח כַּשּֽׁוֹשַׁנָּ֑ה וְיַ֥ךְ שָׁרָשָׁ֖יו כַּלְּבָנֽוֹן: 7 יֵֽלְכוּ֙ יֹ֣נְקוֹתָ֔יו וִיהִ֥י כַזַּ֖יִת הוֹד֑וֹ וְרֵ֥יחַ ל֖וֹ כַּלְּבָנֽוֹן: 8 יָשֻׁ֨בוּ֙ יֹשְׁבֵ֣י בְצִלּ֔וֹ יְחַיּ֥וּ דָגָ֖ן וְיִפְרְח֣וּ כַגָּ֑פֶן זִכְר֖וֹ כְּיֵ֥ין לְבָנֽוֹן: 9 אֶפְרַ֕יִם מַה־לִּ֥י ע֖וֹד לָֽעֲצַבִּ֑ים אֲנִ֧י עָנִ֣יתִי וַאֲשׁוּרֶ֗נּוּ אֲנִי֙ כִּבְר֣וֹשׁ רַֽעֲנָ֔ן מִמֶּ֖נִּי פֶּרְיְךָ֥ נִמְצָֽא: 10 מִ֤י חָכָם֙ וְיָ֣בֵֽן אֵ֔לֶּה נָב֖וֹן וְיֵֽדָעֵ֑ם כִּֽי־יְשָׁרִ֞ים דַּרְכֵ֣י יְהֹוָ֗ה וְצַדִּקִים֙ יֵ֣לְכוּ בָ֔ם וּפֹשְׁעִ֖ים יִכָּ֥שְׁלוּ בָֽם:

Some communities add the last two verses of *Haftarat Shabbat Shuvah* (Joel 2:26–27)—page 1411.

haftarat va-yishlaḥ

ALL COMMUNITIES—OBADIAH 1:1–21

> **SYNOPSIS:** This *Haftarah* speaks about the revenge of the nation of Edom, who are descendants of Esau, concluding the national conflict between Israel and Edom which has its beginnings in the *Parashah*.
>
> Obadiah, the prophet of Edom's downfall, was himself an Edomite convert, an irony which led the *Babylonian Talmud* to remark, *"From the forest itself comes the handle of the axe which fells it"* (Sanhedrin 39b).
>
> The *Haftarah* opens with an invitation to the nations to go to war against Edom (1), as a punishment for her arrogance (2–4), promising total destruction with no help from her allies (5–7).

הפטרת וישלח

A brief image of the destruction is then painted (8–9), which is parenthetically interrupted to attribute blame to Edom for persecuting the Jewish people and rejoicing at their suffering (10–15), before the narrative of doom and destruction concludes (16–18). The *Haftarah* ends with a description of how Edom's lands will be possessed and settled through the judgment of the King Messiah (19–21).

All Ḥabad, Sephardic and most Ashkenazic communities read the following *Haftarah*.
[some *Ashkenazic* communities read Hosea 11:7-12:12, printed above as *Haftarah* for *Va-Yetze*'—page 1303]

1 ¹ The vision of Obadiah. This is what Almighty God said about Edom: "We the prophets have heard a message from God, and a messenger has been sent among the nations, saying: 'Get up! Let's wage war against her!'

² "Look, initially I made you small among the nations and you were greatly despised. ³ But now that your kingdom is great, the wickedness of your heart has enticed you to be overly proud. You are like one who dwells in the sheltered clefts of a rock, as secure as one whose dwelling is lofty, who says to himself: 'Who can lower me from my lofty position, and bring me down towards earth?' ⁴ But even if you lift yourself high like an eagle, and even if you place your nest between the stars, I will bring you down from there to be conquered by the nations!" says God.

⁵ "If thieves came upon you, or robbers at night, they would not totally clean you out, so how have you been totally wiped out? Don't they only steal what they require? If grape-gatherers came upon you, do they not at least leave some gleanings? Yet you, Edom, will be totally wiped out.

⁶ "How have the houses of Esau been searched and all their belongings removed? How have his hidden places been sought out? ⁷ All your allies accompanied you only to the border but then turned back, and left you to fight alone. Those who are at peace with you induced you to go to war and prevailed over you. Those who eat your bread have schemed against you, and have thereby made a wound in your place. Edom has no understanding to realize that this is happening to *him*.

⁸ "Surely, on that day when the punishment will arrive," says God, "I will cause the wise men from Edom and wisdom from the mountain of Esau to perish, for they will not have the tactics at hand to save their lives. ⁹ And you who live in the south, since you too are from Edom, your mighty men will be broken, so that the slaughter will wipe out every last man from the mountain of Esau.

haftarat va-yishlaḥ

10 "Because you oppressed your brother Jacob, you will be covered in shame, and you will be cut off forever. **11** Yes, you oppressed your brother when you stood aside on the day that strangers confiscated his possessions, and foreigners entered into his gates and cast lots over dividing Jerusalem between themselves. You too are like one of them, since you did nothing to help. **12** You should not have looked on at your brother's anguish, on the day of his estrangement from his land, and all the more so you should not have rejoiced at the children of Judah when they were destroyed. Nor should you have spoken proudly on the day of his distress and since you did these things, I consider them acts of oppression against your brother. **13** You should not have entered the gates of My people to conquer their lands on the day of their calamity when the Temple was destroyed. Nor should you have gazed at his misfortune on the day of his downfall. You should not have stretched your hand out over his possessions and looted them on the day of his calamity. **14** You should not have stood at the dispersion to cut off his refugees, and you should not have arrested his survivors throughout the days of his distress. **15** Because you should have realized that the day of God's reckoning on all the nations is near. As you have done, so will be done to you. Your recompense will come back on your head.

16 "For just as you, Judah, have drunk on My Holy Mount, so too all the nations will constantly drink from the cup of turmoil. They will drink and become confounded, and they will be destroyed as if they never were. **17** But on the Mount of Zion there will still be a remnant, and it will be holy. The House of Jacob will inherit those nations who inherited them previously."

18 The House of Jacob will be a consuming fire, the House of Joseph a consuming flame, and the House of Esau will be like straw. They will set them alight and consume them, and there will be no survivors from the House of Esau—for God has spoken. **19** They will inherit the south, the mountain of Esau, and the lowlands, the land of the Philistines. And they will inherit the field of Ephraim and the field of Samaria. Benjamin will inherit the land of Gilead.

20 The exiled army of the children of Israel, who lived with the Canaanites until Zarephath, and the exiles of Jerusalem until Sepharad, will inherit the cities of the south. **21** And when the Messiah and his ministers, the saviors of Mount Zion, will ascend Mount Seir to judge the children of Esau for all their wrongdoings to Israel, God will be King—all nations will recognize His sole authority.

מֵחֲמַ֨ס אָחִ֧יךָ יַעֲקֹ֛ב תְּכַסְּךָ֥ בוּשָׁ֖ה וְנִכְרַ֥תָּ לְעוֹלָֽם: **11** בְּיוֹם֙ עֲמָֽדְךָ֣ מִנֶּ֔גֶד בְּי֛וֹם שְׁב֥וֹת זָרִ֖ים חֵיל֑וֹ וְנָכְרִ֞ים בָּ֣אוּ שְׁעָרָ֗ו וְעַל־יְרוּשָׁלִַ֙ם֙ יַדּ֣וּ גוֹרָ֔ל גַּם־אַתָּ֖ה כְּאַחַ֥ד מֵהֶֽם: **12** וְאַל־תֵּ֤רֶא בְיוֹם־אָחִ֙יךָ֙ בְּי֣וֹם נָכְר֔וֹ וְאַל־תִּשְׂמַ֥ח לִבְנֵֽי־יְהוּדָ֖ה בְּי֣וֹם אָבְדָ֑ם וְאַל־תַּגְדֵּ֥ל פִּ֖יךָ בְּי֥וֹם צָרָֽה: **13** אַל־תָּב֤וֹא בְשַֽׁעַר־עַמִּי֙ בְּי֣וֹם אֵידָ֔ם אַל־תֵּ֧רֶא גַם־אַתָּ֛ה בְּרָעָת֖וֹ בְּי֣וֹם אֵיד֑וֹ וְאַל־תִּשְׁלַ֥חְנָה בְחֵיל֖וֹ בְּי֥וֹם אֵידֽוֹ: **14** וְאַֽל־תַּעֲמֹד֙ עַל־הַפֶּ֔רֶק לְהַכְרִ֖ית אֶת־פְּלִיטָ֑יו וְאַל־תַּסְגֵּ֥ר שְׂרִידָ֖יו בְּי֥וֹם צָרָֽה: **15** כִּֽי־קָר֥וֹב יוֹם־יְהֹוָ֖ה עַל־כָּל־הַגּוֹיִ֑ם כַּאֲשֶׁ֤ר עָשִׂ֙יתָ֙ יֵעָ֣שֶׂה לָּ֔ךְ גְּמֻלְךָ֖ יָשׁ֥וּב בְּרֹאשֶֽׁךָ: **16** כִּ֗י כַּֽאֲשֶׁ֤ר שְׁתִיתֶם֙ עַל־הַ֣ר קָדְשִׁ֔י יִשְׁתּ֥וּ כָֽל־הַגּוֹיִ֖ם תָּמִ֑יד וְשָׁת֣וּ וְלָע֔וּ וְהָי֖וּ כְּל֥וֹא הָיֽוּ: **17** וּבְהַ֥ר צִיּ֛וֹן תִּהְיֶ֥ה פְלֵיטָ֖ה וְהָ֣יָה קֹ֑דֶשׁ וְיָֽרְשׁוּ֙ בֵּ֣ית יַֽעֲקֹ֔ב אֵ֖ת מוֹרָֽשֵׁיהֶֽם: **18** וְהָיָה֩ בֵית־יַעֲקֹ֨ב אֵ֜שׁ וּבֵ֧ית יוֹסֵ֣ף לֶהָבָ֗ה וּבֵ֤ית עֵשָׂו֙ לְקַ֔שׁ וְדָלְק֥וּ בָהֶ֖ם וַאֲכָל֑וּם וְלֹֽא־יִֽהְיֶ֤ה שָׂרִיד֙ לְבֵ֣ית עֵשָׂ֔ו כִּ֥י יְהֹוָ֖ה דִּבֵּֽר: **19** וְיָרְשׁ֨וּ הַנֶּ֜גֶב אֶת־הַ֣ר עֵשָׂ֗ו וְהַשְּׁפֵלָה֙ אֶת־פְּלִשְׁתִּ֔ים וְיָרְשׁוּ֙ אֶת־שְׂדֵ֣ה אֶפְרַ֔יִם וְאֵ֖ת שְׂדֵ֣ה שֹׁמְר֑וֹן וּבִנְיָמִ֖ן אֶת־הַגִּלְעָֽד: **20** וְגָלֻ֣ת הַֽחֵל־הַ֠זֶּה לִבְנֵ֨י יִשְׂרָאֵ֤ל אֲשֶֽׁר־כְּנַעֲנִים֙ עַד־צָ֣רְפַ֔ת וְגָלֻ֥ת יְרוּשָׁלִַ֖ם אֲשֶׁ֣ר בִּסְפָרַ֑ד יִֽרְשׁ֕וּ אֵ֖ת עָרֵ֥י הַנֶּֽגֶב: **21** וְעָל֤וּ מֽוֹשִׁעִים֙ בְּהַ֣ר צִיּ֔וֹן לִשְׁפֹּ֖ט אֶת־הַ֣ר עֵשָׂ֑ו וְהָיְתָ֥ה לַֽיהֹוָ֖ה הַמְּלוּכָֽה:

haftarat va-yeshev

ALL COMMUNITIES—AMOS 2:6 – 3:8

> **SYNOPSIS:** This *Haftarah* alludes to the sale of Joseph, who was sold for silver by his brothers (v.6). The *Haftarah* is a harsh rebuke by the prophet Amos for the sins of the Jewish people during the reign of King Jeroboam II (8th century B.C.E.).
>
> After opening with a forceful criticism of the corrupt judicial system (2:6-8), the *Haftarah* muses over God's kindness to Israel from the times of the Exodus, lamenting how God's gift of righteous prophets and nazirites was abused (9-11). This is followed by a startling promise of terror, from which even the most mighty will flee (13-16).
>
> The prophet opens chapter three with a statement that God's punishments are enacted only out of a profound sense of love for the Jewish people (1-2). A series of rhetorical questions are then posed that gradually impress upon the reader how every effect has its cause, rendering the concluding statement—that all calamities are orchestrated by God as a consequence of man's actions—all the more powerful (3-6). This, then, is a great incentive to heed the words of the prophet (7-8).

When *Shabbat Parashat Va-Yeshev* coincides with Ḥanukkah,
the *Haftarah* of Ḥanukkah (first *Shabbat*) is read—page 1420.

2 ⁶ This is what God said: "For the three sins I could forgive Israel, but for four I will not forgive, because they perverted justice and traded the fair judgment of a righteous man for bribes of silver, and cheat the poor for a mere pair of shoes. ⁷ These corrupt judges intend that the dust of the earth be thrust upon the heads of the poor by their guards, if they fail to heed the judges' words. They cause the humble people to divert their route from the main roads, to avoid the guards. Father and son will go together unashamedly to defile a betrothed young woman as if they were going specifically to desecrate My holy name. ⁸ The corrupt judges recline beside every altar of idolatry on garments taken as security from poor people that they judged unfairly, and drink the wine purchased from extorting their condemned victims in the house of their god.

⁹ "I destroyed before them even the nations that do not know Me, such as the Amorites, who were as tall as cedars and as strong as trees. I destroyed them completely: their fruit from above and their roots from below.

ב ⁶ כֹּה אָמַר יְהֹוָה עַל־שְׁלֹשָׁה פִּשְׁעֵי יִשְׂרָאֵל וְעַל־אַרְבָּעָה לֹא אֲשִׁיבֶנּוּ עַל־מִכְרָם בַּכֶּסֶף צַדִּיק וְאֶבְיוֹן בַּעֲבוּר נַעֲלָיִם: ⁷ הַשֹּׁאֲפִים עַל־עֲפַר־אֶרֶץ בְּרֹאשׁ דַּלִּים וְדֶרֶךְ עֲנָוִים יַטּוּ וְאִישׁ וְאָבִיו יֵלְכוּ אֶל־הַנַּעֲרָה לְמַעַן חַלֵּל אֶת־שֵׁם קָדְשִׁי: ⁸ וְעַל־בְּגָדִים חֲבֻלִים יַטּוּ אֵצֶל כָּל־מִזְבֵּחַ וְיֵין עֲנוּשִׁים יִשְׁתּוּ בֵּית אֱלֹהֵיהֶם: ⁹ וְאָנֹכִי הִשְׁמַדְתִּי אֶת־הָאֱמֹרִי מִפְּנֵיהֶם אֲשֶׁר כְּגֹבַהּ אֲרָזִים גָּבְהוֹ וְחָסֹן הוּא כָּאַלּוֹנִים וָאַשְׁמִיד פִּרְיוֹ מִמַּעַל וְשָׁרָשָׁיו מִתָּחַת: ¹⁰ וְאָנֹכִי הֶעֱלֵיתִי אֶתְכֶם מֵאֶרֶץ מִצְרָיִם וָאוֹלֵךְ אֶתְכֶם בַּמִּדְבָּר אַרְבָּעִים שָׁנָה לָרֶשֶׁת אֶת־אֶרֶץ הָאֱמֹרִי: ¹¹ וָאָקִים מִבְּנֵיכֶם לִנְבִיאִים וּמִבַּחוּרֵיכֶם לִנְזִרִים הַאַף אֵין־זֹאת בְּנֵי יִשְׂרָאֵל נְאֻם־יְהֹוָה: ¹² וַתַּשְׁקוּ אֶת־הַנְּזִרִים

¹⁰ "But you know Me, because I brought you up from the land of Egypt and led you through the wilderness for forty years and provided all your needs so you could come and possess the land of the Amorites. ¹¹ Throughout the generations, I raised prophets from among your sons so that My Divine Presence should dwell among you and I inspired many nazirites from among your young men. Would you, Israel, deny this?" says God. ¹² "But you persuaded the nazirites

haftarat mikketz

to drink wine and commanded the prophets, 'Do not prophesy.'

[13] "Watch, I will surely afflict you, who were ungrateful to Me! You will not escape Me, for I will afflict you in your own places, as a full load of sheaves weighs down and afflicts a wagon. [14] The swift will not escape because the enemy will be everywhere. The strong will not muster his strength to win a war, and the warrior will not save his life. [15] The archer will not stand his ground, for he will flee out of fear. Even the lightfooted will not escape, and the horse rider will not save his life by fleeing. [16] On that day, even the most courageous of the warriors will run away disarmed so he can run faster," says God.

3 [1] "Listen to this word that God has spoken concerning you, O Israel, concerning the entire people that I brought up from the land of Egypt. [2] Of all the nations of the earth, I loved only you, yet you sinned against Me. That is why I will punish you for all your transgressions."

[3] Do two people walk together without having arranged it beforehand? [4] Does a lion roar in the forest and find no prey? Does a lion cub cry out from its den without having trapped anything? [5] Does a bird fall into a trap on the ground if there is no snare? Does a trap spring up from the ground if it hasn't caught anything? [6] If a ram's horn is sounded in the city to announce that the enemy is approaching, can the inhabitants fail to be terrified? So too, if there is a calamity in the city, can it not be God's doing? [7] For Almighty God does not do anything without first revealing His secret to His servants, the prophets. [8] When the lion roars, who does not fear? So too when Almighty God speaks to His prophets, who could withhold God's words and not prophesy?

יַיִן וְעַל־הַנְּבִיאִים צִוִּיתֶם לֵאמֹר לֹא תִּנָּבְאוּ׃ 13 הִנֵּה אָנֹכִי מֵעִיק תַּחְתֵּיכֶם כַּאֲשֶׁר תָּעִיק הָעֲגָלָה הַמְלֵאָה לָהּ עָמִיר׃ 14 וְאָבַד מָנוֹס מִקָּל וְחָזָק לֹא־יְאַמֵּץ כֹּחוֹ וְגִבּוֹר לֹא־יְמַלֵּט נַפְשׁוֹ׃ 15 וְתֹפֵשׂ הַקֶּשֶׁת לֹא יַעֲמֹד וְקַל בְּרַגְלָיו לֹא יְמַלֵּט וְרֹכֵב הַסּוּס לֹא יְמַלֵּט נַפְשׁוֹ׃ 16 וְאַמִּיץ לִבּוֹ בַּגִּבּוֹרִים עָרוֹם יָנוּס בַּיּוֹם־הַהוּא נְאֻם־יְהוָה׃

ג 1 שִׁמְעוּ אֶת־הַדָּבָר הַזֶּה אֲשֶׁר דִּבֶּר יְהוָה עֲלֵיכֶם בְּנֵי יִשְׂרָאֵל עַל כָּל־הַמִּשְׁפָּחָה אֲשֶׁר הֶעֱלֵיתִי מֵאֶרֶץ מִצְרַיִם לֵאמֹר׃ 2 רַק אֶתְכֶם יָדַעְתִּי מִכֹּל מִשְׁפְּחוֹת הָאֲדָמָה עַל־כֵּן אֶפְקֹד עֲלֵיכֶם אֵת כָּל־עֲוֺנֹתֵיכֶם׃ 3 הֲיֵלְכוּ שְׁנַיִם יַחְדָּו בִּלְתִּי אִם־נוֹעָדוּ׃ 4 הֲיִשְׁאַג אַרְיֵה בַּיַּעַר וְטֶרֶף אֵין לוֹ הֲיִתֵּן כְּפִיר קוֹלוֹ מִמְּעֹנָתוֹ בִּלְתִּי אִם־לָכָד׃ 5 הֲתִפֹּל צִפּוֹר עַל־פַּח הָאָרֶץ וּמוֹקֵשׁ אֵין לָהּ הֲיַעֲלֶה־פַּח מִן־הָאֲדָמָה וְלָכוֹד לֹא יִלְכּוֹד׃ 6 אִם־יִתָּקַע שׁוֹפָר בְּעִיר וְעָם לֹא יֶחֱרָדוּ אִם־תִּהְיֶה רָעָה בְּעִיר וַיהוָה לֹא עָשָׂה׃ 7 כִּי לֹא יַעֲשֶׂה אֲדֹנָי יְהוִה דָּבָר כִּי אִם־גָּלָה סוֹדוֹ אֶל־עֲבָדָיו הַנְּבִיאִים׃ 8 אַרְיֵה שָׁאָג מִי לֹא יִירָא אֲדֹנָי יְהוִה דִּבֶּר מִי לֹא יִנָּבֵא׃

haftarat mikketz

ALL COMMUNITIES—I KINGS 3:15 – 4:1

SYNOPSIS: This *Haftarah*—similar to the beginning of *Parashat Mikketz*, which describes Pharaoh awakening from his dreams—begins abruptly with the awakening of Solomon from a dream.

The preceding narrative, before the *Haftarah* begins, describes how God revealed Himself to Solomon in a dream at Gibeon and offered to grant any request. God is

הפטרת מקץ

pleased when Solomon asks, not for his personal needs, but for wisdom to lead the nation properly. The *Haftarah* then describes an example of how Solomon utilized this Divine gift, after returning to Jerusalem (v.15), in adjudicating a difficult case.

Two harlots appear before Solomon. Both share the same house and both had given birth within a period of a few days. Both concur that one of the children was smothered in the night and that the other harlot had switched the babies so as to have the live one for herself—and both claim that the guilty party is the *other* harlot (16–22).

Having no witnesses to verify either claim, the king employs his wisdom in a tactical maneuver. After summing up the pleas of both parties (23), the king instructs that the living child be severed in two, and that half be given to each of the claimants (24–25).

Inevitably, the true mother could not bear to see her child killed and pleaded to the king that the baby be given to the other woman so as to spare its life. The other woman, however, was willing to accept the king's proposition as a "fair solution" (24–26). Thus, the ploy was successful and Solomon was able to return the child to its true mother (27).

News of Solomon's ingenious solution spread fast, further asserting the authority of his leadership (3:28–4:1).

When *Shabbat Parashat Mikketz* coincides with Ḥanukkah, the *Haftarah* of Ḥanukkah is read—page 1420 (first *Shabbat*) or 1423 (second *Shabbat*).

3 ¹⁵ Solomon awoke and only then he realized it was a dream. He then came to Jerusalem and stood before the Ark of the Covenant of God. He offered burnt-offerings and peace-offerings and made a feast for all his servants.

¹⁶ Then two harlots came to the king and stood before him. ¹⁷ One of the women said, "Please, my master, listen to me! I and this woman live in one house. I gave birth in the house, ¹⁸ and on the third day after I gave birth this woman too gave birth, and we were together. There was nobody else in the house that could see what was going on. Just the two of us were in the house."

¹⁹ "This woman's son then died during the night because she laid upon him and crushed him. ²⁰ She then got up in the middle of the night and took my son from beside me while your maidservant was still asleep, and laid *him* down in her bosom, *and she* put her dead son into my bosom."

²¹ "I got up in the morning to nurse my son and—look!—he was dead. I then examined him in the morning and—look!—he was not the son to whom I had given birth."

ג ¹⁵ וַיִּקַ֣ץ שְׁלֹמֹ֔ה וְהִנֵּ֖ה חֲל֑וֹם וַיָּב֣וֹא יְרוּשָׁלִַ֡ם וַֽיַּעֲמֹ֣ד ׀ לִפְנֵ֣י ׀ אֲר֣וֹן בְּרִית־אֲדֹנָ֗י וַיַּ֤עַל עֹלוֹת֙ וַיַּ֣עַשׂ שְׁלָמִ֔ים וַיַּ֥עַשׂ מִשְׁתֶּ֖ה לְכָל־עֲבָדָֽיו׃

¹⁶ אָ֣ז תָּבֹ֗אנָה שְׁתַּ֛יִם נָשִׁ֥ים זֹנ֖וֹת אֶל־הַמֶּ֑לֶךְ וַֽתַּעֲמֹ֖דְנָה לְפָנָֽיו׃ ¹⁷ וַתֹּ֜אמֶר הָאִשָּׁ֣ה הָאַחַת֮ בִּ֣י אֲדֹנִי֒ אֲנִ֣י וְהָאִשָּׁ֣ה הַזֹּ֗את יֹשְׁבֹ֛ת בְּבַ֥יִת אֶחָ֖ד וָאֵלֵ֥ד עִמָּ֖הּ בַּבָּֽיִת׃ ¹⁸ וַיְהִ֞י בַּיּ֤וֹם הַשְּׁלִישִׁי֙ לְלִדְתִּ֔י וַתֵּ֖לֶד גַּם־הָאִשָּׁ֣ה הַזֹּ֑את וַאֲנַ֣חְנוּ יַחְדָּ֗ו אֵֽין־זָ֤ר אִתָּ֙נוּ֙ בַּבַּ֔יִת זוּלָתִ֥י שְׁתַּֽיִם־אֲנַ֖חְנוּ בַּבָּֽיִת׃

¹⁹ וַיָּ֛מָת בֶּן־הָאִשָּׁ֥ה הַזֹּ֖את לָ֑יְלָה אֲשֶׁ֥ר שָׁכְבָ֖ה עָלָֽיו׃ ²⁰ וַתָּ֩קָם֩ בְּת֨וֹךְ הַלַּ֜יְלָה וַתִּקַּ֧ח אֶת־בְּנִ֣י מֵֽאֶצְלִ֗י וַאֲמָֽתְךָ֙ יְשֵׁנָ֔ה וַתַּשְׁכִּיבֵ֖הוּ בְּחֵיקָ֑הּ וְאֶת־בְּנָ֥הּ הַמֵּ֖ת הִשְׁכִּ֥יבָה בְחֵיקִֽי׃ ²¹ וָאָקֻ֥ם בַּבֹּ֛קֶר לְהֵינִ֥יק אֶת־בְּנִ֖י וְהִנֵּה־מֵ֑ת וָאֶתְבּוֹנֵ֤ן אֵלָיו֙ בַּבֹּ֔קֶר וְהִנֵּ֛ה לֹא־הָיָ֥ה בְנִ֖י אֲשֶׁ֥ר יָלָֽדְתִּי׃

haftarat va-yiggash

22 The other woman said, "No! My son is the living one, and your son is the dead one!" The first woman said, "No! My son is the living one, and your son is the dead one!" and they argued before the king.

23 The king then said, "This one says, 'This, my son, is the living one and your son is the dead one,' and the other one says, 'No! Your son is the dead one, and my son is the living one.'"

24 So the king said, "Bring me a sword," and they brought a sword before the king. 25 The king said, "Cut the living child in two and give half to one woman and the other half to the other woman."

26 The woman whose son was really the living one said to the king, "Please, my master! Give her the living child, but do not kill him!" for her compassion was roused for her son. But the other one said, "Let him be neither mine nor yours. Cut him!" 27 The king then responded and said, "Give the living child to the first woman and do not kill him. She is the mother."

28 All of Israel heard about the case that the king had judged and they were in awe of the king, for they saw that the wisdom of God was with him to carry out true justice.

4 1 Then King Solomon reigned over all Israel, for all the people willingly accepted his sovereignty.

22 וַתֹּאמֶר הָאִשָּׁה הָאַחֶרֶת לֹא כִי בְּנִי הַחַי וּבְנֵךְ הַמֵּת וְזֹאת אֹמֶרֶת לֹא כִי בְּנֵךְ הַמֵּת וּבְנִי הֶחָי וַתְּדַבֵּרְנָה לִפְנֵי הַמֶּלֶךְ: 23 וַיֹּאמֶר הַמֶּלֶךְ זֹאת אֹמֶרֶת זֶה־בְּנִי הַחַי וּבְנֵךְ הַמֵּת וְזֹאת אֹמֶרֶת לֹא כִי בְּנֵךְ הַמֵּת וּבְנִי הֶחָי: 24 וַיֹּאמֶר הַמֶּלֶךְ קְחוּ לִי־חָרֶב וַיָּבִאוּ הַחֶרֶב לִפְנֵי הַמֶּלֶךְ: 25 וַיֹּאמֶר הַמֶּלֶךְ גִּזְרוּ אֶת־הַיֶּלֶד הַחַי לִשְׁנָיִם וּתְנוּ אֶת־הַחֲצִי לְאַחַת וְאֶת־הַחֲצִי לְאֶחָת: 26 וַתֹּאמֶר הָאִשָּׁה אֲשֶׁר־בְּנָהּ הַחַי אֶל־הַמֶּלֶךְ כִּי־נִכְמְרוּ רַחֲמֶיהָ עַל־בְּנָהּ וַתֹּאמֶר ׀ בִּי אֲדֹנִי תְּנוּ־לָהּ אֶת־הַיָּלוּד הַחַי וְהָמֵת אַל־תְּמִיתֻהוּ וְזֹאת אֹמֶרֶת גַּם־לִי גַם־לָךְ לֹא יִהְיֶה גְּזֹרוּ: 27 וַיַּעַן הַמֶּלֶךְ וַיֹּאמֶר תְּנוּ־לָהּ אֶת־הַיָּלוּד הַחַי וְהָמֵת לֹא תְמִיתֻהוּ הִיא אִמּוֹ: 28 וַיִּשְׁמְעוּ כָל־יִשְׂרָאֵל אֶת־הַמִּשְׁפָּט אֲשֶׁר שָׁפַט הַמֶּלֶךְ וַיִּרְאוּ מִפְּנֵי הַמֶּלֶךְ כִּי רָאוּ כִּי־חָכְמַת אֱלֹהִים בְּקִרְבּוֹ לַעֲשׂוֹת מִשְׁפָּט:

ד 1 וַיְהִי הַמֶּלֶךְ שְׁלֹמֹה מֶלֶךְ עַל־כָּל־יִשְׂרָאֵל:

haftarat va-yiggash

ALL COMMUNITIES—Ezekiel 37:15–28

SYNOPSIS: This *Haftarah* depicts a fusion of the kingdom of Judah with the kingdom of Joseph that will occur in the Messianic Redemption, the historical conclusion of the conflict between Judah and Joseph at the opening of *Parashat Va-Yiggash*.

The *Haftarah* opens with a command to Ezekiel the prophet to take two sticks, one representing the Southern Kingdom of Judah and the other the Northern Kingdom of Joseph, and to join them together (37:15-17). The symbolism is then clarified: The joining of the sticks represents the unification of the two kingdoms at the time of the Redemption, under the leadership of the Messiah who is from the tribe of Judah (18-25). The *Haftarah* concludes with an idyllic picture of the Messianic utopia when the Divine Presence will rest among Israel (26-28).

הפטרת ויגש

37

15 Then God's word came to me, saying: **16** "And you, son of man, take a piece of wood and write on it, 'For Judah and his fellow Israelites,' and take another stick and write on it, 'For Joseph —a stick for his son Ephraim and the other tribes the whole House of Israel with him.'

17 "Bring them close to one another, so they resemble one stick and they will miraculously join in your hands to be one.

18 "When your people say to you, 'Tell us what these mean to you,' **19** say to them, 'Almighty God says, "Observe! I am taking the stick of Joseph which is in Ephraim's hand, and the tribes of Israel with him, and I am placing the stick of Judah on it. I will make them one stick, and they will join in My hand."' **20** The sticks on which you have written should be in your hands before their eyes.

21 "While you are holding the sticks tell them, 'This is what Almighty God said: "I will take the Jews from among the nations where they have gone. I will gather them from all around and bring them to their land. **22** I will make them one nation in the land, in the hills of Israel, and all of them will have one king. They will no longer be two nations of Judah and Israel, and they will no longer be divided into two kingdoms. **23** They will no longer be defiled by their idols, their abominations and all their sins. I will save them from where they are lost in all the communities where they sinned, and I will purify them from their sins. They will be My people who believe in Me and observe My commandments, and I will be their God to save them and help them.

24 "My servant the Messiah, a descendant of David, will be king over them and they will all have one shepherd. They will follow My laws and guard My statutes in their hearts, and fulfil them. **25** They will settle in the land that I gave to My servant Jacob, the land where their ancestors lived. They and their children and their grandchildren will live there forever, *and* David my servant will be their leader forever.

26 "I will make a covenant of peace with them, and it will be an eternal covenant with them. I will establish them there forever and cause them to multiply, and I will place My Sanctuary among

---

לז 15 וַיְהִי דְבַר־יְהֹוָה אֵלַי לֵאמֹר: 16 וְאַתָּה בֶן־אָדָם קַח־לְךָ עֵץ אֶחָד וּכְתֹב עָלָיו לִיהוּדָה וְלִבְנֵי יִשְׂרָאֵל חֲבֵרָו וּלְקַח עֵץ אֶחָד וּכְתוֹב עָלָיו לְיוֹסֵף עֵץ אֶפְרַיִם וְכָל־בֵּית יִשְׂרָאֵל חֲבֵרָו: 17 וְקָרַב אֹתָם אֶחָד אֶל־אֶחָד לְךָ לְעֵץ אֶחָד וְהָיוּ לַאֲחָדִים בְּיָדֶךָ: 18 וְכַאֲשֶׁר יֹאמְרוּ אֵלֶיךָ בְּנֵי עַמְּךָ לֵאמֹר הֲלוֹא־תַגִּיד לָנוּ מָה־אֵלֶּה לָּךְ: 19 דַּבֵּר אֲלֵהֶם כֹּה־אָמַר אֲדֹנָי יֱהֹוִה הִנֵּה אֲנִי לֹקֵחַ אֶת־עֵץ יוֹסֵף אֲשֶׁר בְּיַד־אֶפְרַיִם וְשִׁבְטֵי יִשְׂרָאֵל חֲבֵרָו וְנָתַתִּי אוֹתָם עָלָיו אֶת־עֵץ יְהוּדָה וַעֲשִׂיתִם לְעֵץ אֶחָד וְהָיוּ אֶחָד בְּיָדִי: 20 וְהָיוּ הָעֵצִים אֲשֶׁר־תִּכְתֹּב עֲלֵיהֶם בְּיָדְךָ לְעֵינֵיהֶם: 21 וְדַבֵּר אֲלֵיהֶם כֹּה־אָמַר אֲדֹנָי יֱהֹוִה הִנֵּה אֲנִי לֹקֵחַ אֶת־בְּנֵי יִשְׂרָאֵל מִבֵּין הַגּוֹיִם אֲשֶׁר הָלְכוּ־שָׁם וְקִבַּצְתִּי אֹתָם מִסָּבִיב וְהֵבֵאתִי אוֹתָם אֶל־אַדְמָתָם: 22 וְעָשִׂיתִי אֹתָם לְגוֹי אֶחָד בָּאָרֶץ בְּהָרֵי יִשְׂרָאֵל וּמֶלֶךְ אֶחָד יִהְיֶה לְכֻלָּם לְמֶלֶךְ וְלֹא [יהיה כ׳] יִהְיוּ־עוֹד לִשְׁנֵי גוֹיִם וְלֹא יֵחָצוּ עוֹד לִשְׁתֵּי מַמְלָכוֹת עוֹד: 23 וְלֹא יִטַּמְּאוּ עוֹד בְּגִלּוּלֵיהֶם וּבְשִׁקּוּצֵיהֶם וּבְכֹל פִּשְׁעֵיהֶם וְהוֹשַׁעְתִּי אֹתָם מִכֹּל מוֹשְׁבֹתֵיהֶם אֲשֶׁר חָטְאוּ בָהֶם וְטִהַרְתִּי אוֹתָם וְהָיוּ־לִי לְעָם וַאֲנִי אֶהְיֶה לָהֶם לֵאלֹהִים: 24 וְעַבְדִּי דָוִד מֶלֶךְ עֲלֵיהֶם וְרוֹעֶה אֶחָד יִהְיֶה לְכֻלָּם וּבְמִשְׁפָּטַי יֵלֵכוּ וְחֻקּוֹתַי יִשְׁמְרוּ וְעָשׂוּ אוֹתָם: 25 וְיָשְׁבוּ עַל־הָאָרֶץ אֲשֶׁר נָתַתִּי לְעַבְדִּי לְיַעֲקֹב אֲשֶׁר יָשְׁבוּ־בָהּ אֲבוֹתֵיכֶם וְיָשְׁבוּ עָלֶיהָ הֵמָּה וּבְנֵיהֶם וּבְנֵי בְנֵיהֶם עַד־עוֹלָם וְדָוִד עַבְדִּי נָשִׂיא לָהֶם לְעוֹלָם: 26 וְכָרַתִּי לָהֶם בְּרִית שָׁלוֹם בְּרִית עוֹלָם יִהְיֶה אוֹתָם וּנְתַתִּים וְהִרְבֵּיתִי

haftarat va-yeḥi

them so it stands forever. ²⁷ My Divine Presence will be among them. I will be their God to help them and save them, and they will be My people to believe in Me and keep My commandments.

²⁸ "The nations will know that I am God, who sanctifies Israel, since My Sanctuary will be among them forever."

אוֹתָם וְנָתַתִּי אֶת־מִקְדָּשִׁי בְּתוֹכָם לְעוֹלָם: 27 וְהָיָה מִשְׁכָּנִי עֲלֵיהֶם וְהָיִיתִי לָהֶם לֵאלֹהִים וְהֵמָּה יִהְיוּ־לִי לְעָם: 28 וְיָדְעוּ הַגּוֹיִם כִּי אֲנִי יְהֹוָה מְקַדֵּשׁ אֶת־יִשְׂרָאֵל בִּהְיוֹת מִקְדָּשִׁי בְּתוֹכָם לְעוֹלָם:

haftarat va-yeḥi

ALL COMMUNITIES—I KINGS 2:1–12

SYNOPSIS: This *Haftarah* describes the time before David's passing and his instructions to Solomon, his son, similar to the account of Jacob's words to his children shortly before his passing, in *Parashat Va-Yeḥi*.

The *Haftarah* opens with King David on his deathbed, addressing his last wishes to his son Solomon, who was twelve years old at the time. He charges him to keep the Torah (1–4) and offers political advice concerning certain trouble-making personalities that need to be eliminated (5–9).

The *Haftarah* concludes by chronicling David's death and Solomon's succession.

2 ¹ The time of David's death drew near. He instructed his son Solomon, saying, ² "I am going the way of all mortals. Be strong and though you are young, be mature like a man, for I will no longer be here to guide you. ³ Look after the things that God, your God, said to safeguard, so as to follow His ways of mercy and kindness, to keep His supranational laws, His rational commandments of conduct between man and God, His laws of conduct between man and his fellow, and testimonial laws that commemorate various events, as is written in the Torah of Moses. Then you will become wise in whatever aspect of Divine service you do and wherever you turn. ⁴ Do this in order that God may fulfil His word that He spoke about me, saying, 'If your sons are careful in their ways to go before Me truthfully, with all their hearts and all their souls, then,' said God, 'You will never cease to have one of your descendants upon the throne of Israel.'

⁵ "You are also aware of what Joab son of Zeruiah did to me—what he did to the two army generals of Israel, Abner son of Ner and

ב 1 וַיִּקְרְבוּ יְמֵי־דָוִד לָמוּת וַיְצַו אֶת־ שְׁלֹמֹה בְנוֹ לֵאמֹר: 2 אָנֹכִי הֹלֵךְ בְּדֶרֶךְ כָּל־הָאָרֶץ וְחָזַקְתָּ וְהָיִיתָ לְאִישׁ: 3 וְשָׁמַרְתָּ אֶת־מִשְׁמֶרֶת ׀ יְהֹוָה אֱלֹהֶיךָ לָלֶכֶת בִּדְרָכָיו לִשְׁמֹר חֻקֹּתָיו מִצְוֺתָיו וּמִשְׁפָּטָיו וְעֵדְוֺתָיו כַּכָּתוּב בְּתוֹרַת מֹשֶׁה לְמַעַן תַּשְׂכִּיל אֵת כָּל־אֲשֶׁר תַּעֲשֶׂה וְאֵת כָּל־אֲשֶׁר תִּפְנֶה שָׁם: 4 לְמַעַן יָקִים יְהֹוָה אֶת־דְּבָרוֹ אֲשֶׁר דִּבֶּר עָלַי לֵאמֹר אִם־יִשְׁמְרוּ בָנֶיךָ אֶת־דַּרְכָּם לָלֶכֶת לְפָנַי בֶּאֱמֶת בְּכָל־לְבָבָם וּבְכָל־נַפְשָׁם לֵאמֹר לֹא־יִכָּרֵת לְךָ אִישׁ מֵעַל כִּסֵּא יִשְׂרָאֵל: 5 וְגַם אַתָּה יָדַעְתָּ אֵת אֲשֶׁר־עָשָׂה לִי יוֹאָב בֶּן־צְרוּיָה אֲשֶׁר עָשָׂה לִשְׁנֵי־שָׂרֵי צִבְאוֹת יִשְׂרָאֵל לְאַבְנֵר בֶּן־נֵר וְלַעֲמָשָׂא בֶן־יֶתֶר וַיַּהַרְגֵם וַיָּשֶׂם דְּמֵי־ מִלְחָמָה בְּשָׁלֹם וַיִּתֵּן דְּמֵי מִלְחָמָה בַּחֲגֹרָתוֹ

Amasa son of Jether, to whom I guaranteed safety. He killed them and shed the blood of war in times of peace. He put the blood of war in the belt around his loins and the shoes on his feet. ⁶ You must act according to your wisdom, but don't let him have honor for his old age, and see to it that he does not go down to the grave with a peaceful death.

⁷ "Act kindly to the sons of Barzillai the Gileadite, aside from letting them be among those who eat at your table, for that is precisely how they assisted me when I was fleeing from your brother Absalom.

⁸ "Now Shimei son of Gera—of the tribe of Benjamin, from Bahurim, who taught you Torah—cursed me bitterly on the day I went to Mahanaim when I was fleeing from Absalom. But later he came down to meet me at the Jordan and appeased me, so I swore to him in God's name, saying, 'I will not kill you with the sword,' so I can't take revenge against him personally. ⁹ However, now you are not obligated by this oath, so do not free him from punishment, as you're a wise man and you know what to do to him. But don't let him have honor for his old age, and see to it that he goes down to the grave with a bloody death."

¹⁰ David then lay with his fathers, and he was buried in the City of David. ¹¹ David reigned over Israel for a total of forty years. In Hebron he reigned for seven years, in Jerusalem he reigned for thirty-three years.

¹² Solomon then sat on the throne of his father, David, and his sovereignty was firmly established.

haftarat shemot

SEPHARDIM—Jeremiah 1:1 – 2:3
ASHKENAZIM AND HABAD—Isaiah 27:6 – 28:13; 29:22–23

SYNOPSIS: The *Haftarah* is taken from the beginning of a portion of Isaiah which depicts punishments that are due to the Northern Kingdom ("Ephraim") and Southern Kingdom ("Jerusalem"). Throughout the *Haftarah*, the prophet vacillates between promises of hope and redemption on the one hand, and warnings of impending punishment on the other.

The *Haftarah* opens on a positive note, depicting the day when Israel will "take root" and "blossom" (27:6). The mood then shifts to a discussion of iniquity and punishment for Israel's sins of idol-worship (7–11), before returning to the theme of Redemption and the sounding of the "great shofar" (12–13).

haftarat shemot

The following passage of rebuke criticizes the arrogance of Ephraim, depicting a gloomy vision of devastating storms and smothering by the enemy (28:1–4). After a brief glimpse of the future glory of Judah and Benjamin (5–6) is offered, their present sad state of drunkenness and irreverence is then depicted (7–13). The *Haftarah* concludes with a Messianic vision where God's name is sanctified by all the Jewish people (29:22–23).

***Ḥabad* and *Ashkenazic* communities read the following *Haftarah*.**
[*Sephardic* communities read the *Haftarah* for *Parashat Mattot* on page 1388]

27 ⁶ In the coming days, Jacob will take root, Israel will bud and blossom, filling the face of the earth like the produce of the field.

⁷ Even in the days that God struck Israel, did He strike him as He struck those that struck him? Did He slay him as He slew those that slew him, as He struck and slew the Egyptians? ⁸ Only according to their measure of sin did He bring retribution and contend against her fields and gardens but not take the lives of her inhabitants. He removed the fruit with a rough wind, on the day the strong east wind blows mightily. ⁹ Because My mercy is upon them, it will be easy for them to atone for their sins. Only by this small thing shall Jacob's sin be atoned, this will be his fruit of removing his sin: When he makes all the stones of the altar as chalk stones crushed to pieces, the idol-trees and the sun images shall rise no more. ¹⁰ Then the great city will be lonely, its dwelling place will be empty from its inhabitants, forlorn like the desert. In its place a calf will graze, and there it will rest and consume the tree branches that grow there. ¹¹ When Edom's measure of sin has reached its limit, they will have their downfall, a nation of feminine weakness will come and destroy it. For it is not an understanding nation to know that God is the One who gave them any power in the first place. Therefore its Maker will not have mercy upon it and its Creator will not find favor in it.

¹² It will be on that day that God will remove the produce—Israel—from the husks, the nations from Assyria which lie beside the Euphrates River until the land of Egypt, and you will be gathered one by one, children of Israel. ¹³ And it will be on that day, as though a great ram's horn will be blown to call everyone to gather, and those who are lost in the land of Assyria and those who are cast away in the land of Egypt will come and bow down to God upon the holy mountain in Jerusalem.

כז 6 הַבָּאִים יַשְׁרֵשׁ יַעֲקֹב יָצִיץ וּפָרַח יִשְׂרָאֵל וּמָלְאוּ פְנֵי־תֵבֵל תְּנוּבָה: 7 הַכְּמַכַּת מַכֵּהוּ הִכָּהוּ אִם־כְּהֶרֶג הֲרֻגָיו הֹרָג: 8 בְּסַאסְּאָה בְּשַׁלְחָהּ תְּרִיבֶנָּה הָגָה בְּרוּחוֹ הַקָּשָׁה בְּיוֹם קָדִים: 9 לָכֵן בְּזֹאת יְכֻפַּר עֲוֺן־יַעֲקֹב וְזֶה כָּל־פְּרִי הָסִר חַטָּאתוֹ בְּשׂוּמוֹ ׀ כָּל־אַבְנֵי מִזְבֵּחַ כְּאַבְנֵי־גִר מְנֻפָּצוֹת לֹא־יָקֻמוּ אֲשֵׁרִים וְחַמָּנִים: 10 כִּי עִיר בְּצוּרָה בָּדָד נָוֶה מְשֻׁלָּח וְנֶעֱזָב כַּמִּדְבָּר שָׁם יִרְעֶה עֵגֶל וְשָׁם יִרְבָּץ וְכִלָּה סְעִפֶיהָ: 11 בִּיבֹשׁ קְצִירָהּ תִּשָּׁבַרְנָה נָשִׁים בָּאוֹת מְאִירוֹת אוֹתָהּ כִּי לֹא עַם־בִּינוֹת הוּא עַל־כֵּן לֹא־יְרַחֲמֶנּוּ עֹשֵׂהוּ וְיֹצְרוֹ לֹא יְחֻנֶּנּוּ: 12 וְהָיָה בַּיּוֹם הַהוּא יַחְבֹּט יְהֹוָה מִשִּׁבֹּלֶת הַנָּהָר עַד־נַחַל מִצְרָיִם וְאַתֶּם תְּלֻקְּטוּ לְאַחַד אֶחָד בְּנֵי יִשְׂרָאֵל: 13 וְהָיָה ׀ בַּיּוֹם הַהוּא יִתָּקַע בְּשׁוֹפָר גָּדוֹל וּבָאוּ הָאֹבְדִים בְּאֶרֶץ אַשּׁוּר וְהַנִּדָּחִים בְּאֶרֶץ מִצְרָיִם וְהִשְׁתַּחֲווּ לַיהֹוָה בְּהַר הַקֹּדֶשׁ בִּירוּשָׁלָ͏ִם:

הפטרת שמות

28 ¹ Woe to the crown of arrogance that is upon Ephraim's drunkards, it will quickly be destroyed, as fast as a withering blossom. So shall befall the glory of his splendor, the head so pampered, it is as full of oil as a valley of oil. So shall befall those who were battered from wine who became so drunk that they fell and hurt themselves. ² Behold! God's wind is strong and powerful, as the hail that breaks the trees, like a devastating storm which causes destruction, as the speeding flow of mighty water shall the mighty wind hurl their crown of arrogance and throw it upon the ground with a mighty hand. ³ By the feet of the enemy shall they be smothered, the crown of arrogance of the drunkards of Ephraim. ⁴ The glory of their splendor which is similar to a withering blossom, which is like a crown upon the head which is like a valley of oil, will be like a fig which has prematurely ripened before summer, so one who sees it will immediately swallow it, while it is still in his hand so quickly will the enemy cast down their arrogance.

⁵ On that day, God, the Master of Legions, will be the crown of glory, a diadem of beauty for the remnant of His people, the tribes of Judah and Benjamin. ⁶ He will be a spirit of inspiration to justice to Hezekiah, who presides upon the seat of judgment, and for strength to those of Judah who go to war. They will not need to fight, because God will fight for them, and they will be able to return from the place of battle to fortify the gate of the city.

⁷ Though they too have erred through being drunk of wine, and stagger through strong drink. The priest and the false prophet erred because of strong drink; mistaken about what they saw, they stumble in judgment. ⁸ For all the tables they eat at are full of vomit and filth, so that there is no place clean. ⁹ Because the adults have turned to insobriety, to whom shall the prophet teach knowledge? And who shall understand what the prophet has heard from God? To those who are just weaned from the milk and removed from their mothers' breasts?

¹⁰ Because of their indulgence they are so distant from God's commandments that they require precautionary laws one law on top of another, one law on top of another. As the measuring tool of a builder keeps each row of bricks in place, the prophet must give a measuring line for a measuring line, a measuring line for a measuring line. A little there, very little there—even where Torah is learned, very few study it, as it is considered a burden.

¹¹ For with unintelligible speech and another language do the prophet's words appear to this people.

¹² Although he speaks for their benefit, and he tells them, "This is how you will find tranquility: leave the weary alone and do not rob them, that is how you will find satisfaction." But they did not desire to listen.

¹³ To them, the word of God was a law to a law, a law to a law, a measuring line to a measuring line,

haftarat va-ʾeraʾ

a measuring line to a measuring line—it appeared as a precaution of a precaution, not as something important. A little there, very little there—even where Torah is studied, it has minute significance. Therefore, because they did not listen to the Torah, when they go on a path they will stumble, fall backward, be broken, trapped, and captured.

29 ²² Therefore, this is what God, who redeemed Abraham from the furnace of Ur of the Chaldeans, says to the House of Jacob: "Jacob shall no longer be shamed when his children return, nor shall his face now become pale. ²³ Because when he sees his children, the work of My hands, in his midst, they shall sanctify My name, and sanctify the Holy One of Jacob, and shall praise the God of Israel."

יְהוָה צַו לָצָו צַו לָצָו קַו לָקָו קַו לָקָו זְעֵיר שָׁם זְעֵיר שָׁם לְמַעַן יֵלְכוּ וְכָשְׁלוּ אָחוֹר וְנִשְׁבָּרוּ וְנוֹקְשׁוּ וְנִלְכָּדוּ׃

כט 22 לָכֵן כֹּה־אָמַר יְהוָה אֶל־בֵּית יַעֲקֹב אֲשֶׁר פָּדָה אֶת־אַבְרָהָם לֹא־עַתָּה יֵבוֹשׁ יַעֲקֹב וְלֹא עַתָּה פָּנָיו יֶחֱוָרוּ׃ 23 כִּי בִרְאֹתוֹ יְלָדָיו מַעֲשֵׂה יָדַי בְּקִרְבּוֹ יַקְדִּישׁוּ שְׁמִי וְהִקְדִּישׁוּ אֶת־קְדוֹשׁ יַעֲקֹב וְאֶת־אֱלֹהֵי יִשְׂרָאֵל יַעֲרִיצוּ׃

haftarat va-ʾeraʾ

ALL COMMUNITIES—Ezekiel 28:25 – 29:21

SYNOPSIS: This *Haftarah* describes the complete downfall of Egypt, a process which begins in the *Parashah* with the Ten Plagues.

The *Haftarah* is excerpted from a lengthy section of prophecies concerning the downfall of Egypt, which spans three chapters of the book of Ezekiel. At that time, Jerusalem had been surrounded by Babylonians for close to a year, and the Jewish people were hoping to receive assistance from the Egyptians. Ezekiel thus warns the Jewish people that Egypt is a wicked nation that will suffer impending punishment and should therefore not be perceived as a source of salvation. The prophecy was initially a source of conflict among the Jewish population of Babylon, but when the prophecy later materialized Ezekiel was greatly revered.

The *Haftarah* opens with brief words of comfort for the Jewish nation, describing her future ingathering and resettlement (28:25-26), before progressing swiftly to the main theme of Egypt's forty-year period of desolation which is soon to come (1–12). Subsequently, Egypt's glory will remain diminished, never again to be a source of possible salvation for Israel, or any other nation (13–16).

In a second, apparently unrelated prophecy, Ezekiel predicts that the plunder of Egypt will be won by Babylon as a reward for their thirteen-year siege (586–573 B.C.E.) of Tyre (17–20; see Ezekiel 26:7-9).

The concluding words of the *Haftarah* briefly allude to the glory of Israel after Egypt's forty-year period of desolation (21).

28 ²⁵ This is what God, Almighty God, said: "When I have gathered the House of Israel from the people among whom they are scattered, and I will be

כח 25 כֹּה־אָמַר אֲדֹנָי יְהוִה בְּקַבְּצִי ׀ אֶת־בֵּית יִשְׂרָאֵל

הפטרת וארא

sanctified through all the miracles I will perform for them in the sight of the nations, then shall they dwell in their land that I have given to my servant Jacob. [26] They shall dwell safely in it, and shall build houses, and plant vineyards, and they shall dwell securely, when I have executed judgments upon all those around them who despise them—and they will know that I am God, their God."

29

[1] In the tenth year of the kingdom of Zedekiah, in the tenth month, in the twelfth day of the month, the word of God came to me, saying, [2] "Son of man, set your face against Pharaoh, king of Egypt, and prophesy against him, and against all Egypt. [3] Speak, and say, 'This is what God, Almighty God, says, "Behold, I am going to war against you, Pharaoh, king of Egypt, who is compared to a great snake-like fish that lies in the midst of his streams, since he has said, 'My river is my own, and I have made it for myself.' [4] I will put hooks into your jaws, and I will cause the fish of your streams to stick to your scales, and I will bring you up from the midst of your streams, and all the fish of your streams shall stick to your scales. [5] I will cast you into the desert, you and all the fish of your rivers. Your corpse shall fall upon the open fields. You shall not be brought together, nor gathered. I have given you for food to the beasts of the field and to the birds of the sky. [6] Then, all the inhabitants of Egypt shall know that I am God, who bestows reward and punishment." This will befall them because they have been a staff of reed, a weak support that easily breaks, to the House of Israel. [7] When they took hold of you by your hand, you broke, and tore all their shoulders. When they leaned upon you, you broke, and thus you made them stand on their own feet. [8] Therefore, this is what God, Almighty God, says: "Behold, I will bring a sword upon you and cut off man and beast from you. [9] The land of Egypt shall be desolate and waste, and they shall know that I am God. This will happen *because* he has said, 'The river is mine, and I alone have made myself great.' [10] Behold, therefore I am going to attack you and your streams, and I will make the land of Egypt completely dry to the extent that it is utterly waste and desolate, from Migdol

מִן־הָעַמִּים אֲשֶׁר נָפֹצוּ בָם וְנִקְדַּשְׁתִּי בָם לְעֵינֵי הַגּוֹיִם וְיָשְׁבוּ עַל־אַדְמָתָם אֲשֶׁר נָתַתִּי לְעַבְדִּי לְיַעֲקֹב: [26] וְיָשְׁבוּ עָלֶיהָ לָבֶטַח וּבָנוּ בָתִּים וְנָטְעוּ כְרָמִים וְיָשְׁבוּ לָבֶטַח בַּעֲשׂוֹתִי שְׁפָטִים בְּכֹל הַשָּׁאטִים אֹתָם מִסְּבִיבוֹתָם וְיָדְעוּ כִּי אֲנִי יְהֹוָה אֱלֹהֵיהֶם:

כט

[1] בַּשָּׁנָה הָעֲשִׂרִית בָּעֲשִׂרִי בִּשְׁנֵים עָשָׂר לַחֹדֶשׁ הָיָה דְבַר־יְהֹוָה אֵלַי לֵאמֹר: [2] בֶּן־אָדָם שִׂים פָּנֶיךָ עַל־פַּרְעֹה מֶלֶךְ מִצְרָיִם וְהִנָּבֵא עָלָיו וְעַל־מִצְרַיִם כֻּלָּהּ: [3] דַּבֵּר וְאָמַרְתָּ כֹּה־אָמַר | אֲדֹנָי יֱהֹוִה הִנְנִי עָלֶיךָ פַּרְעֹה מֶלֶךְ־מִצְרַיִם הַתַּנִּים הַגָּדוֹל הָרֹבֵץ בְּתוֹךְ יְאֹרָיו אֲשֶׁר אָמַר לִי יְאֹרִי וַאֲנִי עֲשִׂיתִנִי: [4] וְנָתַתִּי [חחיים כ׳] חַחִים בִּלְחָיֶיךָ וְהִדְבַּקְתִּי דְגַת־יְאֹרֶיךָ בְּקַשְׂקְשֹׂתֶיךָ וְהַעֲלִיתִיךָ מִתּוֹךְ יְאֹרֶיךָ וְאֵת כָּל־דְּגַת יְאֹרֶיךָ בְּקַשְׂקְשֹׂתֶיךָ תִּדְבָּק: [5] וּנְטַשְׁתִּיךָ הַמִּדְבָּרָה אוֹתְךָ וְאֵת כָּל־דְּגַת יְאֹרֶיךָ עַל־פְּנֵי הַשָּׂדֶה תִּפּוֹל לֹא תֵאָסֵף וְלֹא תִקָּבֵץ לְחַיַּת הָאָרֶץ וּלְעוֹף הַשָּׁמַיִם נְתַתִּיךָ לְאָכְלָה: [6] וְיָדְעוּ כָּל־יֹשְׁבֵי מִצְרַיִם כִּי אֲנִי יְהֹוָה יַעַן הֱיוֹתָם מִשְׁעֶנֶת קָנֶה לְבֵית יִשְׂרָאֵל: [7] בְּתָפְשָׂם בְּךָ [בכפך כ׳] בַכַּף תֵּרוֹץ וּבָקַעְתָּ לָהֶם כָּל־כָּתֵף וּבְהִשָּׁעֲנָם עָלֶיךָ תִּשָּׁבֵר וְהַעֲמַדְתָּ לָהֶם כָּל־מָתְנָיִם: [8] לָכֵן כֹּה אָמַר אֲדֹנָי יֱהֹוִה הִנְנִי מֵבִיא עָלַיִךְ חָרֶב וְהִכְרַתִּי מִמֵּךְ אָדָם וּבְהֵמָה: [9] וְהָיְתָה אֶרֶץ־מִצְרַיִם לִשְׁמָמָה וְחָרְבָּה וְיָדְעוּ כִּי־אֲנִי יְהֹוָה יַעַן אָמַר יְאֹר לִי וַאֲנִי עָשִׂיתִי: [10] לָכֵן הִנְנִי אֵלֶיךָ וְאֶל־יְאֹרֶיךָ

haftarat va-'era'

to Syene as far as the border of Cush. ¹¹ No foot of man shall pass through it, nor foot of beast shall pass through it, nor shall it be inhabited for forty years. ¹² I will make the land of Egypt desolate in the midst of the countries that are desolate, and her cities among the cities that are laid waste shall be desolate for forty years. I will scatter the Egyptians among the nations, and will disperse them through the lands."

¹³ "'For this is what God, Almighty God, says: "At the end of forty years and not earlier I will gather the Egyptians from the people among whom they were scattered. ¹⁴ I will bring back the captivity of Egypt, and will cause them to return to the land of Pathros, to the land of their origin, and they shall be there a lowly kingdom. ¹⁵ It shall be the most lowly of the kingdoms, and nevermore shall it exalt itself above the nations, for I will so diminish them so that they shall never again rule over the nations. ¹⁶ Never again shall it be the reliance of the House of Israel, recalling their iniquity when they shall turn to them. Then they shall know that I am God, Almighty God."

¹⁷ It was in the twenty-seventh year of the kingdom of Nebuchadrezzar, in the first month, in the first day of the month, the word of God came to me, saying, ¹⁸ "Son of man, King Nebuchadrezzar of Babylon made his army labor hard to set siege against Tyre. Every head was made bald, and every shoulder was sore from the effort of carrying stones on their heads and shoulders. Yet neither he nor his army had any reward for conquering Tyre, on My behalf." ¹⁹ Therefore this is what God, Almighty God, says, "Behold, I will give the land of Egypt to King Nebuchadrezzar of Babylon, and he shall take her multitude, and take her booty, and take her plunder, and it shall be the wages for his army. ²⁰ As a reward for his action which he carried out against Tyre, I have given him the land of Egypt; punishment for what the Egyptians did against Me," says God, Almighty God.

²¹ "On that day at the end of forty years I will cause the glory of Israel to reemerge and I will give you credibility among them because they will have seen your prophecies fulfilled, and they will know that I am God."

וְנָתַתִּ֤י אֶת־אֶ֙רֶץ֙ מִצְרַ֔יִם לְחָרְב֖וֹת חֹ֑רֶב שְׁמָמָ֔ה מִמִּגְדֹּ֥ל סְוֵנֵ֖ה וְעַד־גְּב֥וּל כּֽוּשׁ׃ 11 לֹ֤א תַעֲבָר־בָּהּ֙ רֶ֣גֶל אָדָ֔ם וְרֶ֥גֶל בְּהֵמָ֖ה לֹ֣א תַעֲבָר־בָּ֑הּ וְלֹ֥א תֵשֵׁ֖ב אַרְבָּעִ֥ים שָׁנָֽה׃ 12 וְנָתַתִּ֤י אֶת־אֶ֣רֶץ מִצְרַ֘יִם֮ שְׁמָמָה֒ בְּת֣וֹךְ ׀ אֲרָצ֣וֹת נְשַׁמּ֗וֹת וְעָרֶ֙יהָ֙ בְּת֣וֹךְ עָרִ֣ים מׇֽחֳרָב֔וֹת תִּֽהְיֶ֣יןָ שְׁמָמָ֔ה אַרְבָּעִ֖ים שָׁנָ֑ה וַהֲפִצֹתִ֤י אֶת־מִצְרַ֙יִם֙ בַּגּוֹיִ֔ם וְזֵרִיתִ֖ים בָּאֲרָצֽוֹת׃ 13 כִּ֛י כֹּ֥ה אָמַ֖ר אֲדֹנָ֣י יֱהֹוִ֑ה מִקֵּ֞ץ אַרְבָּעִ֤ים שָׁנָה֙ אֲקַבֵּ֣ץ אֶת־מִצְרַ֔יִם מִן־הָעַמִּ֖ים אֲשֶׁר־נָפֹ֥צוּ שָֽׁמָּה׃ 14 וְשַׁבְתִּי֙ אֶת־שְׁב֣וּת מִצְרַ֔יִם וַהֲשִׁבֹתִ֤י אֹתָם֙ אֶ֣רֶץ פַּתְר֔וֹס עַל־אֶ֖רֶץ מְכוּרָתָ֑ם וְהָ֥יוּ שָׁ֖ם מַמְלָכָ֥ה שְׁפָלָֽה׃ 15 מִן־הַמַּמְלָכוֹת֙ תִּֽהְיֶ֣ה שְׁפָלָ֔ה וְלֹא־תִתְנַשֵּׂ֥א ע֖וֹד עַל־הַגּוֹיִ֑ם וְהִ֨מְעַטְתִּ֔ים לְבִלְתִּ֖י רְד֥וֹת בַּגּוֹיִֽם׃ 16 וְלֹ֣א יִֽהְיֶה־ע֞וֹד לְבֵ֣ית יִשְׂרָאֵ֗ל לְמִבְטָח֙ מַזְכִּ֣יר עָוֺ֔ן בִּפְנוֹתָ֖ם אַחֲרֵיהֶ֑ם וְיָ֣דְע֔וּ כִּ֥י אֲנִ֖י אֲדֹנָ֥י יֱהֹוִֽה׃ 17 וַיְהִ֗י בְּעֶשְׂרִ֤ים וָשֶׁ֙בַע֙ שָׁנָ֔ה בָּרִאשׁ֖וֹן בְּאֶחָ֣ד לַחֹ֑דֶשׁ הָיָ֥ה דְבַר־יְהֹוָ֖ה אֵלַ֥י לֵאמֹֽר׃ 18 בֶּן־אָדָ֗ם נְבוּכַדְרֶאצַּ֣ר מֶֽלֶךְ־בָּ֠בֶ֠ל הֶעֱבִ֨יד אֶת־חֵיל֜וֹ עֲבֹדָ֤ה גְדוֹלָה֙ אֶל־צֹ֔ר כׇּל־רֹ֣אשׁ מֻקְרָ֔ח וְכׇל־כָּתֵ֖ף מְרוּטָ֑ה וְ֠שָׂכָ֠ר לֹא־הָ֨יָה ל֤וֹ וּלְחֵילוֹ֙ מִצֹּ֔ר עַל־הָעֲבֹדָ֖ה אֲשֶׁר־עָבַ֥ד עָלֶֽיהָ׃ 19 לָכֵ֗ן כֹּ֤ה אָמַר֙ אֲדֹנָ֣י יֱהֹוִ֔ה הִנְנִ֥י נֹתֵ֛ן לִנְבוּכַדְרֶאצַּ֥ר מֶֽלֶךְ־בָּבֶ֖ל אֶת־אֶ֣רֶץ מִצְרָ֑יִם וְנָשָׂ֤א הֲמֹנָהּ֙ וְשָׁלַ֣ל שְׁלָלָ֔הּ וּבָזַ֣ז בִּזָּ֔הּ וְהָיְתָ֥ה שָׂכָ֖ר לְחֵילֽוֹ׃ 20 פְּעֻלָּתוֹ֙ אֲשֶׁר־עָ֣בַד בָּ֔הּ נָתַ֥תִּי ל֖וֹ אֶת־אֶ֣רֶץ מִצְרָ֑יִם אֲשֶׁר֙ עָ֣שׂוּ לִ֔י נְאֻ֖ם אֲדֹנָ֥י יֱהֹוִֽה׃ 21 בַּיּ֣וֹם הַה֗וּא אַצְמִ֤יחַ קֶ֙רֶן֙ לְבֵ֣ית יִשְׂרָאֵ֔ל וּלְךָ֛ אֶתֵּ֥ן פִּתְחֽוֹן־פֶּ֖ה בְּתוֹכָ֑ם וְיָדְע֖וּ כִּֽי־אֲנִ֥י יְהֹוָֽה׃

הפטרת בא

haftarat bo'

ALL COMMUNITIES—JEREMIAH 46:13–28

> **SYNOPSIS:** This *Haftarah* describes the destruction of the nation of Egypt in the times of Nebuchadnezzar, similar to the plagues brought upon Egypt during the times of Moses, described in the *Parashah*. The *Haftarah* opens with a proclamation that Nebuchadrezzar (Nebuchadnezzar) and his army will destroy Egypt, and various impressions of the news of impending terror are given (46:13–19). The imagery of Egyptian annihilation is depicted (20–26), but the *Haftarah* concludes with a message of hope and support for Israel, that they will return to their homeland (27–28).

46 [13] The word that God spoke to Jeremiah the prophet, how King Nebuchadrezzar of Babylon would come and strike the land of Egypt. [14] "Announce in Egypt, proclaim in Migdol, and report in Noph and in Tahpanhes! Say to Pharaoh: Stand fast, and prepare, for the sword around you shall devour you. [15] Why are your brave men swept away? None of them stood, because God thrust them down. [16] He caused many to stumble, indeed, one foreign soldier fell upon another, and they said, "Arise, and let us go again to our own people and to the land of our birth, let us flee Egypt and escape, from the oppressing sword of Nebuchadrezzar." [17] They announced in the Babylonian army barracks, Pharaoh, king of Egypt, has arrogantly made such a noise about his strength. He has passed the time appointed for war. He did not come to war because he is terrified.

[18] "As I live," said the King, whose name is the God of Hosts, "surely as Mount Tabor is firmly established among the mountains, and as Mount Carmel is by the sea and immoveable, so shall he come. [19] O you daughter of Egypt who currently dwells in security! Furnish yourself with the baggage of exile, a jug to drink from, and a container to knead dough, for Noph shall be waste and desolate without an inhabitant.

[20] "Egypt was a very beautiful calf-like country. However, Nebuchadnezzar the destroyer will certainly come from the north, from Babylonia. [21] Also her great ministers in her midst are like fattened bulls for slaughter, for they also turned back, and have fled altogether; they did not stand and fight the war, because the day of their death came upon them, their time to be recalled for retribution. [22] Egypt's voice will be heard from a distance as that of a serpent, for they shall march with a great army, and come against her with axes, like woodcutters. [23] They

מו [13] הַדָּבָר֙ אֲשֶׁ֣ר דִּבֶּ֣ר יְהֹוָ֔ה אֶֽל־יִרְמְיָ֖הוּ הַנָּבִ֑יא לָב֗וֹא נְבֽוּכַדְרֶאצַּר֙ מֶ֣לֶךְ בָּבֶ֔ל לְהַכּ֖וֹת אֶת־אֶ֥רֶץ מִצְרָֽיִם: [14] הַגִּ֤ידוּ בְמִצְרַ֙יִם֙ וְהַשְׁמִ֣יעוּ בְמִגְדּ֔וֹל וְהַשְׁמִ֥יעוּ בְנֹ֖ף וּבְתַחְפַּנְחֵ֑ס אִמְר֗וּ הִתְיַצֵּב֙ וְהָכֵ֣ן לָ֔ךְ כִּי־אָכְלָ֥ה חֶ֖רֶב סְבִיבֶֽיךָ: [15] מַדּ֖וּעַ נִסְחַ֣ף אַבִּירֶ֑יךָ לֹ֣א עָמַ֔ד כִּ֥י יְהֹוָ֖ה הֲדָפֽוֹ: [16] הִרְבָּ֖ה כּוֹשֵׁ֑ל גַּם־נָפַ֞ל אִ֣ישׁ אֶל־רֵעֵ֗הוּ וַיֹּֽאמְרוּ֙ ק֣וּמָה ׀ וְנָשֻׁ֣בָה אֶל־עַמֵּ֗נוּ וְאֶל־אֶ֙רֶץ֙ מֽוֹלַדְתֵּ֔נוּ מִפְּנֵ֖י חֶ֥רֶב הַיּוֹנָֽה: [17] קָרְא֖וּ שָׁ֑ם פַּרְעֹ֤ה מֶֽלֶךְ־מִצְרַ֙יִם֙ שָׁא֔וֹן הֶעֱבִ֖יר הַמּוֹעֵֽד: [18] חַי־אָ֙נִי֙ נְאֻם־הַמֶּ֔לֶךְ יְהֹוָ֥ה צְבָא֖וֹת שְׁמ֑וֹ כִּ֚י כְּתָב֣וֹר בֶּהָרִ֔ים וּכְכַרְמֶ֖ל בַּיָּ֥ם יָבֽוֹא: [19] כְּלֵ֤י גוֹלָה֙ עֲשִׂ֣י לָ֔ךְ יוֹשֶׁ֖בֶת בַּת־מִצְרָ֑יִם כִּי־נֹף֙ לְשַׁמָּ֣ה תִֽהְיֶ֔ה וְנִצְּתָ֖ה מֵאֵ֥ין יוֹשֵֽׁב: [20] עֶגְלָ֥ה יְפֵה־פִיָּ֖ה מִצְרָ֑יִם קֶ֥רֶץ מִצָּפ֖וֹן בָּ֥א בָֽא: [21] גַּם־שְׂכִרֶ֤יהָ בְקִרְבָּהּ֙ כְּעֶגְלֵ֣י מַרְבֵּ֔ק כִּֽי־גַם־הֵ֧מָּה הִפְנ֛וּ נָ֥סוּ יַחְדָּ֖יו לֹ֣א עָמָ֑דוּ כִּ֣י י֥וֹם אֵידָ֛ם בָּ֥א עֲלֵיהֶ֖ם עֵ֥ת פְּקֻדָּתָֽם: [22] קוֹלָ֖הּ כַּנָּחָ֣שׁ יֵלֵ֑ךְ כִּי־בְחַ֣יִל יֵלֵ֔כוּ וּבְקַרְדֻּמּוֹת֙ בָּ֣אוּ לָ֔הּ כְּחֹטְבֵ֖י עֵצִֽים: [23] כָּרְת֤וּ יַעְרָהּ֙ נְאֻם־יְהֹוָ֔ה

haftarat be-shallaḥ

shall cut down her forest," says God. The vast number of the Babylonian forces cannot be estimated, because they are more numerous than locusts, and are without number. ²⁴ The daughter of Egypt shall be disgraced. She shall be delivered to the hand of the people of the north."

²⁵ The God of Hosts, the God of Israel, said, "Behold, I will punish the multitude of No, Pharaoh, and Egypt, with their gods, their kings, and just as I will punish Pharaoh, so too I will punish all those who trust in him.

²⁶ "I will deliver them to the hand of those who seek their lives, to the hand of King Nebuchadrezzar of Babylon, and to the hand of his servants; and after forty years it shall be inhabited, in the days of old," says God.

²⁷ "But do not fear, O My servant Jacob, after seeing Egypt return so quickly from being exiled to a nearby country, and be not dismayed, O Israel, for behold, I will save you from your place of exile, though it is far away, and your descendants from the land of their captivity. Jacob shall return, and be in rest and at ease, and none shall make him afraid.

²⁸ "Do not fear, O My servant Jacob," says God, "for I am with you. For I will make a full end of all the nations where I have driven you, but I will not make an end of you—I will punish you with suspended justice, but I will not wipe you out and remove you from the world."

כִּי לֹא יֵחָקֵר כִּי רַבּוּ מֵאַרְבֶּה וְאֵין לָהֶם מִסְפָּר: 24 הֹבִישָׁה בַּת־מִצְרָיִם נִתְּנָה בְּיַד עַם־צָפוֹן: 25 אָמַר יְהֹוָה צְבָאוֹת אֱלֹהֵי יִשְׂרָאֵל הִנְנִי פוֹקֵד אֶל־אָמוֹן מִנֹּא וְעַל־פַּרְעֹה וְעַל־מִצְרַיִם וְעַל־אֱלֹהֶיהָ וְעַל־מְלָכֶיהָ וְעַל־פַּרְעֹה וְעַל הַבֹּטְחִים בּוֹ: 26 וּנְתַתִּים בְּיַד מְבַקְשֵׁי נַפְשָׁם וּבְיַד נְבוּכַדְרֶאצַּר מֶלֶךְ־בָּבֶל וּבְיַד עֲבָדָיו וְאַחֲרֵי־כֵן תִּשְׁכֹּן כִּימֵי־קֶדֶם נְאֻם־יְהֹוָה: 27 וְאַתָּה אַל־תִּירָא עַבְדִּי יַעֲקֹב וְאַל־תֵּחַת יִשְׂרָאֵל כִּי הִנְנִי מוֹשִׁעֲךָ מֵרָחוֹק וְאֶת־זַרְעֲךָ מֵאֶרֶץ שִׁבְיָם וְשָׁב יַעֲקֹב וְשָׁקַט וְשַׁאֲנַן וְאֵין מַחֲרִיד: 28 אַתָּה אַל־תִּירָא עַבְדִּי יַעֲקֹב נְאֻם־יְהֹוָה כִּי אִתְּךָ אָנִי כִּי אֶעֱשֶׂה כָלָה בְּכָל־הַגּוֹיִם | אֲשֶׁר הִדַּחְתִּיךָ שָּׁמָּה וְאֹתְךָ לֹא־אֶעֱשֶׂה כָלָה וְיִסַּרְתִּיךָ לַמִּשְׁפָּט וְנַקֵּה לֹא אֲנַקֶּךָּ:

haftarat be-shallaḥ

Sephardim—Judges 5:1–31
Ashkenazim and Habad—Judges 4:4–5:31

SYNOPSIS: This *Haftarah* is divided into two distinct portions: part prose—which depicts the battle between a group of northern tribes with Canaan to liberate the land of Israel (thus completing the conquest by Joshua, c.12th century B.C.E.)—and part poetry, the "Song of Deborah" chanted over the victory (paralleling the "Song at the Sea" sung by Moses and the Jewish people in the *Parashah*).

At the opening of the *Haftarah*, Deborah, prophetess and judge of the Kingdom of Ephraim, summons the commander Barak and urges the tribes to war, citing a Divine approbation (4:4-7). Barak makes his involvement conditional on Deborah's assistance, but her consent is accompanied by the warning that the victory will be "by the hand of a woman" (8-9). They then head to battle together, and the enemy is defeated, with "not a man left" (10-16). However, General Sisera himself survives and flees to the tent of Heber, an erstwhile ally, but before Barak arrives, Heber's wife Jael

הפטרת בשלח

fools Sisera with a sense of security and kills him in his sleep (17–22). The narrative concludes by briefly mentioning that the subsequent war efforts were successful in defeating the Canaanites (23–24).

Deborah's Song (5:1–31) contains a variety of reflections and themes, including: memories of Moses' war against Sihon and Og and of Mount Sinai (4–5), the difficult times that preceded Deborah's leadership (6–8), and her subsequent positive influence (9–12); rich praises for the victorious armies (13–23) and a poetic portrait of Jael's killing of Sisera (24–30). The Song concludes with prayers for the demise of all enemies of God, and strength for His loyal adherents (31). A final note states that forty years of peace were to follow (31).

Ḥabad and Ashkenazic communities begin here; Sephardic communities begin on page 1326.

4 ⁴ Deborah, a prophetess, a woman of fiery enthusiasm, judged Israel at that time. ⁵ She would sit under the Palm Tree of Deborah between Ramah and Bethel in Mount Ephraim. The people of Israel would come up to her for judgment.

⁶ She sent and called Barak son of Abinoam from Kedesh-naphtali, and said to him, "Has not God, Almighty God of Israel, commanded, saying, 'Go and gather your men to Mount Tabor, and take with you ten thousand men of the sons of Naphtali and of the sons of Zebulun'? ⁷ I will draw Sisera to you, by planting the idea to go to the river Kishon in the heart of Sisera, the captain of Jabin's army, with his chariots and his multitude, and I will deliver him into your hand."

⁸ Barak said to her, "If you go with me, then I will go. But if you do not go with me, then I will not go."

⁹ She said, "I will surely go with you. However, the journey that you take will not be for your honor, as God will deliver Sisera by the hand of a woman."

Deborah got going, and went with Barak to Kedesh. ¹⁰ Barak called Zebulun and Naphtali to Kedesh and went up with ten thousand men at his feet. Deborah *went up* with him.

¹¹ Heber the Kenite, who was from the descendants of Hobab, the father-in-law of Moses, had separated himself from the Kenites and pitched his tent near the plains of Zaanannim, which

ד 4 וּדְבוֹרָה֙ אִשָּׁ֣ה נְבִיאָ֔ה אֵ֖שֶׁת לַפִּיד֑וֹת הִ֛יא שֹׁפְטָ֥ה אֶת־יִשְׂרָאֵ֖ל בָּעֵ֥ת הַהִֽיא: 5 וְ֠הִיא יוֹשֶׁ֨בֶת תַּֽחַת־תֹּ֜מֶר דְּבוֹרָ֗ה בֵּ֧ין הָרָמָ֛ה וּבֵ֥ין בֵּֽית־אֵ֖ל בְּהַ֣ר אֶפְרָ֑יִם וַיַּֽעֲל֥וּ אֵלֶ֛יהָ בְּנֵ֥י יִשְׂרָאֵ֖ל לַמִּשְׁפָּֽט: 6 וַתִּשְׁלַ֗ח וַתִּקְרָא֙ לְבָרָ֣ק בֶּן־אֲבִינֹ֔עַם מִקֶּ֖דֶשׁ נַפְתָּלִ֑י וַתֹּ֨אמֶר אֵלָ֜יו הֲלֹ֥א צִוָּ֣ה | יְהֹוָ֣ה אֱלֹהֵֽי־יִשְׂרָאֵ֗ל לֵ֤ךְ וּמָֽשַׁכְתָּ֙ בְּהַ֣ר תָּב֔וֹר וְלָֽקַחְתָּ֣ עִמְּךָ֗ עֲשֶׂ֤רֶת אֲלָפִים֙ אִ֔ישׁ מִבְּנֵ֥י נַפְתָּלִ֖י וּמִבְּנֵ֥י זְבֻלֽוּן: 7 וּמָֽשַׁכְתִּ֨י אֵלֶ֜יךָ אֶל־ נַ֣חַל קִישׁ֗וֹן אֶת־סִיסְרָא֙ שַׂר־צְבָ֣א יָבִ֔ין וְאֶת־ רִכְבּ֖וֹ וְאֶת־הֲמוֹנ֑וֹ וּנְתַתִּ֖יהוּ בְּיָדֶֽךָ: 8 וַיֹּ֤אמֶר אֵלֶ֨יהָ֙ בָּרָ֔ק אִם־תֵּֽלְכִ֥י עִמִּ֖י וְהָלָ֑כְתִּי וְאִם־לֹ֥א תֵֽלְכִ֥י עִמִּ֖י לֹ֥א אֵלֵֽךְ: 9 וַתֹּ֜אמֶר הָלֹ֧ךְ אֵלֵ֣ךְ עִמָּ֗ךְ אֶ֚פֶס כִּי֩ לֹ֨א תִֽהְיֶ֜ה תִּֽפְאַרְתְּךָ֗ עַל־הַדֶּ֨רֶךְ֙ אֲשֶׁ֣ר אַתָּ֣ה הוֹלֵ֔ךְ כִּ֣י בְיַד־אִשָּׁ֔ה יִמְכֹּ֥ר יְהֹוָ֖ה אֶת־סִֽיסְרָ֑א וַתָּ֧קָם דְּבוֹרָ֛ה וַתֵּ֥לֶךְ עִם־בָּרָ֖ק קֶֽדְשָׁה: 10 וַיַּזְעֵ֨ק בָּרָ֜ק אֶת־זְבוּלֻ֤ן וְאֶת־נַפְתָּלִי֙ קֶ֔דְשָׁה וַיַּ֣עַל בְּרַגְלָ֔יו עֲשֶׂ֥רֶת אַלְפֵ֖י אִ֑ישׁ וַתַּ֥עַל עִמּ֖וֹ דְּבוֹרָֽה: 11 וְחֶ֤בֶר הַקֵּינִי֙ נִפְרָ֣ד מִקַּ֔יִן מִבְּנֵ֥י חֹבָ֖ב חֹתֵ֣ן מֹשֶׁ֑ה וַיֵּ֣ט אָֽהֳל֔וֹ עַד־אֵל֥וֹן [בצעננים כ׳]

haftarat be-shallaḥ

is by Kedesh. [12] They told Sisera that Barak son of Abinoam had gone up to Mount Tabor to wage war.

[13] Sisera gathered together all his chariots, nine hundred chariots of iron, and all the people who were with him, from Harosheth-goiim to the river of Kishon.

[14] Deborah said to Barak, "Arise! Do not hesitate, for this is the day destined for victory. This is the day in which God has delivered Sisera into your hand. Has not God gone out before you?"

So Barak went down from Mount Tabor, with ten thousand men after him.

[15] God confounded Sisera, all his chariots, and all his army to be killed, with the edge of the sword before Barak. Sisera went down from his chariot and fled on foot.

[16] Barak pursued the chariots and the army to Harosheth-goiim. All the army of Sisera fell upon the edge of the sword, and there was not a man left.

[17] Sisera fled on foot to the tent of Jael the wife of Heber the Kenite, for there was peace between King Jabin of Hazor and the House of Heber the Kenite.

[18] Jael went out to meet Sisera and said to him, "Turn in, my lord! Turn in to me! Fear not!" When he had turned in to her, into the tent, she covered him with a mantle.

[19] He said to her, "Give me, I beg you, a little water to drink, for I am thirsty."

She opened a skin of milk and gave him a drink, and covered him.

[20] He said to her, "Stand in the door of the tent, and it shall be, when any man comes and inquires of you and says, 'Is there any man here?', you shall say, 'No.'"

[21] Jael, Heber's wife, took a peg of the tent and took a hammer in her hand, and went softly to him, and struck the peg into his temples and fastened it into the ground, for he was fast asleep and weary. So, he died.

[22] Now, as Barak pursued Sisera, Jael came out to meet him and said to him, "Come, and I will show you the man whom you seek."

בְּצַעֲנַנִּ֖ים אֲשֶׁ֥ר אֶת־קֶֽדֶשׁ׃ 12 וַיַּגִּ֖דוּ לְסִ֣יסְרָ֑א כִּ֥י עָלָ֛ה בָּרָ֥ק בֶּן־אֲבִינֹ֖עַם הַר־תָּבֽוֹר׃ 13 וַיַּזְעֵ֨ק סִֽיסְרָ֜א אֶת־כָּל־רִכְבּ֗וֹ תְּשַׁ֤ע מֵאוֹת֙ רֶ֣כֶב בַּרְזֶ֔ל וְאֶת־כָּל־הָעָ֖ם אֲשֶׁ֣ר אִתּ֑וֹ מֵחֲרֹ֥שֶׁת הַגּוֹיִ֖ם אֶל־נַ֥חַל קִישֽׁוֹן׃ 14 וַתֹּ֩אמֶר֩ דְּבֹרָ֨ה אֶל־בָּרָ֜ק ק֗וּם כִּ֣י זֶ֤ה הַיּוֹם֙ אֲשֶׁר֩ נָתַ֨ן יְהֹוָ֤ה אֶת־סִֽיסְרָא֙ בְּיָדֶ֔ךָ הֲלֹ֥א יְהֹוָ֖ה יָצָ֣א לְפָנֶ֑יךָ וַיֵּ֤רֶד בָּרָק֙ מֵהַ֣ר תָּב֔וֹר וַעֲשֶׂ֧רֶת אֲלָפִ֛ים אִ֖ישׁ אַחֲרָֽיו׃ 15 וַיָּ֣הׇם יְ֠הֹוָ֠ה אֶת־סִֽיסְרָ֨א וְאֶת־כָּל־הָרֶ֧כֶב וְאֶת־כָּל־הַֽמַּחֲנֶ֛ה לְפִי־חֶ֖רֶב לִפְנֵ֣י בָרָ֑ק וַיֵּ֧רֶד סִֽיסְרָ֛א מֵעַ֥ל הַמֶּרְכָּבָ֖ה וַיָּ֥נׇס בְּרַגְלָֽיו׃ 16 וּבָרָ֗ק רָדַ֞ף אַחֲרֵ֤י הָרֶ֙כֶב֙ וְאַחֲרֵ֣י הַֽמַּחֲנֶ֔ה עַ֖ד חֲרֹ֣שֶׁת הַגּוֹיִ֑ם וַיִּפֹּ֞ל כׇּל־מַחֲנֵ֤ה סִֽיסְרָא֙ לְפִי־חֶ֔רֶב לֹ֥א נִשְׁאַ֖ר עַד־אֶחָֽד׃ 17 וְסִ֣יסְרָ֔א נָ֥ס בְּרַגְלָ֖יו אֶל־אֹ֑הֶל יָעֵ֕ל אֵ֖שֶׁת חֶ֣בֶר הַקֵּינִ֑י כִּ֣י שָׁל֗וֹם בֵּ֚ין יָבִ֣ין מֶֽלֶךְ־חָצ֔וֹר וּבֵ֕ין בֵּ֖ית חֶ֥בֶר הַקֵּינִֽי׃ 18 וַתֵּצֵ֣א יָעֵל֮ לִקְרַ֣את סִֽיסְרָא֒ וַתֹּ֣אמֶר אֵלָ֗יו סוּרָ֧ה אֲדֹנִ֛י סוּרָ֥ה אֵלַ֖י אַל־תִּירָ֑א וַיָּ֤סַר אֵלֶ֙יהָ֙ הָאֹ֔הֱלָה וַתְּכַסֵּ֖הוּ בַּשְּׂמִיכָֽה׃ 19 וַיֹּ֧אמֶר אֵלֶ֛יהָ הַשְׁקִינִי־נָ֥א מְעַט־מַ֖יִם כִּ֣י צָמֵ֑אתִי וַתִּפְתַּ֞ח אֶת־נֹ֧אוד הֶחָלָ֛ב וַתַּשְׁקֵ֖הוּ וַתְּכַסֵּֽהוּ׃ 20 וַיֹּ֣אמֶר אֵלֶ֔יהָ עֲמֹ֖ד פֶּ֣תַח הָאֹ֑הֶל וְהָיָה֩ אִם־אִ֨ישׁ יָב֜וֹא וּשְׁאֵלֵ֗ךְ וְאָמַ֛ר הֲיֵֽשׁ־פֹּ֥ה אִ֖ישׁ וְאָמַ֥רְתְּ אָֽיִן׃ 21 וַתִּקַּ֣ח יָעֵ֣ל אֵֽשֶׁת־חֶ֠בֶר אֶת־יְתַ֨ד הָאֹ֜הֶל וַתָּ֧שֶׂם אֶת־הַמַּקֶּ֣בֶת בְּיָדָ֗הּ וַתָּב֤וֹא אֵלָיו֙ בַּלָּ֔אט וַתִּתְקַ֤ע אֶת־הַיָּתֵד֙ בְּרַקָּת֔וֹ וַתִּצְנַ֖ח בָּאָ֑רֶץ וְהֽוּא־נִרְדָּ֥ם וַיָּ֖עַף וַיָּמֹֽת׃ 22 וְהִנֵּ֣ה בָרָק֮ רֹדֵ֣ף אֶת־סִֽיסְרָא֒ וַתֵּצֵ֤א יָעֵל֙ לִקְרָאת֔וֹ וַתֹּ֣אמֶר ל֔וֹ לֵ֣ךְ וְאַרְאֶ֔ךָּ אֶת־הָאִ֖ישׁ אֲשֶׁר־אַתָּ֣ה מְבַקֵּ֑שׁ וַיָּבֹ֣א אֵלֶ֔יהָ וְהִנֵּ֤ה סִֽיסְרָא֙ נֹפֵ֣ל מֵ֔ת וְהַיָּתֵ֖ד בְּרַקָּתֽוֹ׃

הפטרת בשלח

When he came into her tent, behold, Sisera lay dead, and the peg was in his temples.

²³ On that day God subdued King Jabin of Canaan before the people of Israel.

²⁴ The hand of the people of Israel prospered and prevailed against King Jabin of Canaan, until they had destroyed King Jabin of Canaan.

23 וַיַּכְנַ֣ע אֱלֹהִ֗ים בַּיּ֤וֹם הַהוּא֙ אֵ֣ת יָבִ֣ין מֶֽלֶךְ־כְּנָ֑עַן לִפְנֵ֖י בְּנֵ֥י יִשְׂרָאֵֽל: 24 וַתֵּ֜לֶךְ יַ֤ד בְּנֵֽי־יִשְׂרָאֵל֙ הָל֣וֹךְ וְקָשָׁ֔ה עַ֖ל יָבִ֣ין מֶֽלֶךְ־כְּנָ֑עַן עַ֚ד אֲשֶׁ֣ר הִכְרִ֔יתוּ אֵ֖ת יָבִ֥ין מֶֽלֶךְ־כְּנָֽעַן:

Sephardic communities begin here. All others continue:

5 ¹ Then Deborah and Barak son of Abinoam sang on that day, saying:

² "Praise God for the avenging of Israel for making it appear that their strength accomplished the victory, for the people willingly offered themselves against overwhelming odds. ³ Hear, O you kings; give ear, O you princes; I believe in God and He is my portion, therefore I will sing to God because of the salvation He has brought; I will sing praise to God, Almighty God of Israel. ⁴ O God, when the Jewish people passed Mount Seir on the way to Israel, You warred against Sihon and Og, when You marched out of the field of Edom all nations of the world trembled in fear, the angels representing the nations of the world sweated in fear, the clouds also dropped water to frighten the enemy nations with the tremendous downpour. ⁵ The mountains perspired from fear of God, just as Sinai feared God, Almighty God of Israel.

⁶ "However, in the days of Shamgar son of Anath, in the days of Jael, the main roads ceased, and travelers walked through crooked back roads to shake off the enemy who stopped fearing the Jews. ⁷ The inhabitants of the unprotected villages ceased, they ceased only in Israel, until I, Deborah, arose, a mother in Israel. ⁸ For when they chose new gods, there was then war in the cities; however, was there a shield or spear seen among forty thousand in Israel in the days of Joshua? ⁹ My heart goes out toward the dignitaries of Israel, who offered themselves willingly among the people. Bless You, God. ¹⁰ Speak, you who ride on white female donkeys, you who sit in judgment, and you who walk on the road. ¹¹ Instead of the sounds of archers in the places of drawing water, now they recite the righteous acts of God, the righteous acts toward His open cities in Israel; when the people of God go back down to the gates. ¹² Awake, awake, Deborah! Awake, awake, utter a song! Arise, Barak, and lead away your captives, O son of Abinoam.

¹³ "Then the remnant of the Jewish people will have dominion over the mighty gentile nations; God made me

ה 1 וַתָּ֣שַׁר דְּבוֹרָ֔ה וּבָרָ֖ק בֶּן־אֲבִינֹ֑עַם בַּיּ֥וֹם הַה֖וּא לֵאמֹֽר: 2 בִּפְרֹ֤עַ פְּרָעוֹת֙ בְּיִשְׂרָאֵ֔ל בְּהִתְנַדֵּ֖ב עָ֑ם בָּרְכ֖וּ יְהוָֽה: 3 שִׁמְע֣וּ מְלָכִ֔ים הַאֲזִ֖ינוּ רֹֽזְנִ֑ים אָֽנֹכִ֗י לַֽיהוָה֙ אָנֹכִ֣י אָשִׁ֔ירָה אֲזַמֵּ֕ר לַיהוָ֖ה אֱלֹהֵ֥י יִשְׂרָאֵֽל: 4 יְהוָ֗ה בְּצֵאתְךָ֤ מִשֵּׂעִיר֙ בְּצַעְדְּךָ֙ מִשְּׂדֵ֣ה אֱד֔וֹם אֶ֣רֶץ רָעָ֔שָׁה גַּם־שָׁמַ֖יִם נָטָ֑פוּ גַּם־עָבִ֖ים נָ֥טְפוּ מָֽיִם: 5 הָרִ֥ים נָזְל֖וּ מִפְּנֵ֣י יְהוָ֑ה זֶ֣ה סִינַ֔י מִפְּנֵ֕י יְהוָ֖ה אֱלֹהֵ֥י יִשְׂרָאֵֽל: 6 בִּימֵ֞י שַׁמְגַּ֤ר בֶּן־עֲנָת֙ בִּימֵ֣י יָעֵ֔ל חָדְל֖וּ אֳרָח֑וֹת וְהֹלְכֵ֣י נְתִיב֔וֹת יֵלְכ֕וּ אֳרָח֖וֹת עֲקַלְקַלּֽוֹת: 7 חָדְל֧וּ פְרָז֛וֹן בְּיִשְׂרָאֵ֖ל חָדֵ֑לּוּ עַ֤ד שַׁקַּ֙מְתִּי֙ דְּבוֹרָ֔ה שַׁקַּ֖מְתִּי אֵ֥ם בְּיִשְׂרָאֵֽל: 8 יִבְחַר֙ אֱלֹהִ֣ים חֲדָשִׁ֔ים אָ֖ז לָחֶ֣ם שְׁעָרִ֑ים מָגֵ֤ן אִם־יֵֽרָאֶה֙ וָרֹ֔מַח בְּאַרְבָּעִ֥ים אֶ֖לֶף בְּיִשְׂרָאֵֽל: 9 לִבִּי֙ לְחֽוֹקְקֵ֣י יִשְׂרָאֵ֔ל הַמִּֽתְנַדְּבִ֖ים בָּעָ֑ם בָּרְכ֖וּ יְהוָֽה: 10 רֹכְבֵי֩ אֲתֹנ֨וֹת צְחֹר֜וֹת יֹשְׁבֵ֧י עַל־מִדִּ֛ין וְהֹלְכֵ֥י עַל־דֶּ֖רֶךְ שִֽׂיחוּ: 11 מִקּ֣וֹל מְחַֽצְצִ֗ים בֵּ֚ין מַשְׁאַבִּ֔ים שָׁ֤ם יְתַנּוּ֙ צִדְק֣וֹת יְהוָ֔ה צִדְקֹ֥ת פִּרְזֹנ֖וֹ בְּיִשְׂרָאֵ֑ל אָ֛ז יָרְד֥וּ לַשְּׁעָרִ֖ים עַם־יְהוָֽה: 12 עוּרִ֤י עוּרִי֙ דְּבוֹרָ֔ה ע֥וּרִי ע֖וּרִי דַּבְּרִי־שִׁ֑יר ק֥וּם בָּרָ֛ק וּֽשֲׁבֵ֥ה שֶׁבְיְךָ֖ בֶּן־אֲבִינֹֽעַם: 13 אָ֚ז יְרַ֣ד שָׂרִ֔יד לְאַדִּירִ֖ים עָ֑ם יְהוָ֕ה יְרַד־

haftarat be-shallaḥ

have dominion over the mighty. ¹⁴ Joshua who came out of the tribe of Ephraim, out of their root, fought against Amalek. After you, a descendant of Benjamin slew a vast multitude of Amalek with your tribes. Noblemen came down to do battle, leaders came down from Machir, the whole tribe of Zebulun came, even the scribes who draw the pen. ¹⁵ And the scholars of Issachar were with Deborah despite the fact that they were inexperienced in battle—Issachar also joined Barak's forces. Into the valley they rushed forth, at his feet, at the same pace. The fact that Reuben separated himself from his brethren and did not fight there is much to ponder. ¹⁶ If you were afraid, then why did you settle across the border of the Jordan, near enemy territory? Did you think that all you would have to do is to pasture your sheep and hear the bleating of the flocks? For the separation of Reuben there is much to investigate. ¹⁷ Gilead dwells beyond the Jordan; and why did Dan, who lived much closer to the battlefield, remain by the ships of his merchandise and escape from his duty to defend? Asher, however, lives at the seashore and correctly remained by its country's exposed points to protect them. ¹⁸ Zebulun is a people who risked their lives to the death, and Naphtali likewise, on the high places of the field. ¹⁹ The other tribes did not come to defend; however, the kings of other nations came to Sisera's aid and fought; then the kings of Canaan in Taanach by the waters of Megiddo fought together with Sisera. They took no gain of silver, so why didn't Reuben come to help his brethren? ²⁰ Sisera's effort was for naught, because it was as if they fought from heaven. The stars in their courses fought against Sisera. ²¹ The brook of Kishon swept them away, that ancient brook which never overflowed before, the brook Kishon. My soul would march on in strength. ²² Then, upon seeing the flood, the horse hooves beat as the soldiers tried to escape, but the hooves broke off, from the frantic galloping of his mighty ones. ²³ You shall curse the place of Meroz, said the angel of God, curse bitterly its inhabitants, because they did not come to the help of God, to the help of God against the mighty men of Sisera.

²⁴ "Blessed among women shall be Jael the wife of Heber the Kenite, blessed she shall be among the modest, righteous women in the tent. ²⁵ He asked for water, and she gave him milk to make him sleepy. She brought cream in a fancy dish so Sisera should not believe that she disrespected him. ²⁶ She put her hand to the tent peg, and her right hand to the workmen's hammer, and with the hammer she struck Sisera. She struck through his head. She crushed and pierced his temple. ²⁷ At her feet he bent, he fell, he lay down—at her feet he bent, he fell. Where he bowed, there he fell down, bereft of life.

לִי בַּגִּבּוֹרִים: 14 מִנִּי אֶפְרַיִם שָׁרְשָׁם בַּעֲמָלֵק אַחֲרֶיךָ בִנְיָמִין בַּעֲמָמֶיךָ מִנִּי מָכִיר יָרְדוּ מְחֹקְקִים וּמִזְּבוּלֻן מֹשְׁכִים בְּשֵׁבֶט סֹפֵר: 15 וְשָׂרַי בְּיִשָּׂשכָר עִם־ דְּבֹרָה וְיִשָּׂשכָר כֵּן בָּרָק בָּעֵמֶק שֻׁלַּח בְּרַגְלָיו בִּפְלַגּוֹת רְאוּבֵן גְּדֹלִים חִקְקֵי־ לֵב: 16 לָמָּה יָשַׁבְתָּ בֵּין הַמִּשְׁפְּתַיִם לִשְׁמֹעַ שְׁרִקוֹת עֲדָרִים לִפְלַגּוֹת רְאוּבֵן גְּדוֹלִים חִקְרֵי־לֵב: 17 גִּלְעָד בְּעֵבֶר הַיַּרְדֵּן שָׁכֵן וְדָן לָמָּה יָגוּר אֳנִיּוֹת אָשֵׁר יָשַׁב לְחוֹף יַמִּים וְעַל מִפְרָצָיו יִשְׁכּוֹן: 18 זְבֻלוּן עַם חֵרֵף נַפְשׁוֹ לָמוּת וְנַפְתָּלִי עַל מְרוֹמֵי שָׂדֶה: 19 בָּאוּ מְלָכִים נִלְחָמוּ אָז נִלְחֲמוּ מַלְכֵי כְנַעַן בְּתַעְנַךְ עַל־מֵי מְגִדּוֹ בֶּצַע כֶּסֶף לֹא לָקָחוּ: 20 מִן־שָׁמַיִם נִלְחָמוּ הַכּוֹכָבִים מִמְּסִלּוֹתָם נִלְחֲמוּ עִם־סִיסְרָא: 21 נַחַל קִישׁוֹן גְּרָפָם נַחַל קְדוּמִים נַחַל קִישׁוֹן תִּדְרְכִי נַפְשִׁי עֹז: 22 אָז הָלְמוּ עִקְּבֵי־ סוּס מִדַּהֲרוֹת דַּהֲרוֹת אַבִּירָיו: 23 אוֹרוּ מֵרוֹז אָמַר מַלְאַךְ יְהֹוָה אֹרוּ אָרוֹר יֹשְׁבֶיהָ כִּי לֹא־בָאוּ לְעֶזְרַת יְהֹוָה לְעֶזְרַת יְהֹוָה בַּגִּבּוֹרִים: 24 תְּבֹרַךְ מִנָּשִׁים יָעֵל אֵשֶׁת חֶבֶר הַקֵּינִי מִנָּשִׁים בָּאֹהֶל תְּבֹרָךְ: 25 מַיִם שָׁאַל חָלָב נָתָנָה בְּסֵפֶל אַדִּירִים הִקְרִיבָה חֶמְאָה: 26 יָדָהּ לַיָּתֵד תִּשְׁלַחְנָה וִימִינָהּ לְהַלְמוּת עֲמֵלִים וְהָלְמָה סִיסְרָא מָחֲקָה רֹאשׁוֹ וּמָחֲצָה וְחָלְפָה רַקָּתוֹ: 27 בֵּין רַגְלֶיהָ כָּרַע נָפַל

הפטרת יתרו

²⁸ "The mother of Sisera looked out the window and cried through the lattice, 'Why is his chariot so long in coming? Why do the hoofbeats of his chariots tarry?' ²⁹ Her wise ladies answered her, she even answered herself to comfort her, they told her: ³⁰ 'Haven't they been delayed by finding booty? Have they not divided the plunder? To every man a maiden or two; to Sisera a booty of diverse colors, a plunder of multicolored needlework, dyed double-worked garments for the necks of those who take the plunder.'

³¹ "So may all Your enemies perish, O God, but those who love Him should go from strength to strength like the sun when it goes forth in its might towards the afternoon."

And the land had rest for forty years.

שָׁכַב בֵּין רַגְלֶיהָ כָּרַע נָפַל בַּאֲשֶׁר כָּרַע שָׁם נָפַל שָׁדוּד: 28 בְּעַד הַחַלּוֹן נִשְׁקְפָה וַתְּיַבֵּב אֵם סִיסְרָא בְּעַד הָאֶשְׁנָב מַדּוּעַ בֹּשֵׁשׁ רִכְבּוֹ לָבוֹא מַדּוּעַ אֶחֱרוּ פַּעֲמֵי מַרְכְּבוֹתָיו: 29 חַכְמוֹת שָׂרוֹתֶיהָ תַּעֲנֶינָּה אַף־הִיא תָּשִׁיב אֲמָרֶיהָ לָהּ: 30 הֲלֹא יִמְצְאוּ יְחַלְּקוּ שָׁלָל רַחַם רַחֲמָתַיִם לְרֹאשׁ גֶּבֶר שְׁלַל צְבָעִים לְסִיסְרָא שְׁלַל צְבָעִים רִקְמָה צֶבַע רִקְמָתַיִם לְצַוְּארֵי שָׁלָל: 31 כֵּן יֹאבְדוּ כָל־אוֹיְבֶיךָ יְהֹוָה וְאֹהֲבָיו כְּצֵאת הַשֶּׁמֶשׁ בִּגְבֻרָתוֹ וַתִּשְׁקֹט הָאָרֶץ אַרְבָּעִים שָׁנָה:

haftarat yitro

ASHKENAZIM—Isaiah 6:1 – 7:6; 9:5–6
SEPHARDIM AND HABAD—Isaiah 6:1–13

SYNOPSIS: This *Haftarah* describes the revelation of God's glory seen by Isaiah the prophet, similar to the Divine revelation perceived by the Jewish people at the giving of the Torah, in the *Parashah*. The *Haftarah* opens with a vision of God "sitting on a throne," surrounded by angels (seraphim) who sing His praise (6:1-4). Isaiah's immediate reaction is that he is unworthy of such a vision (5), and he is promptly "purged" from sin by a seraph bearing a coal from the altar (6-7).

Upon hearing a request from God to the angels that a messenger be found, Isaiah enthusiastically volunteers (8). God instructs him to rebuke the people for failing to take the prophet's words and God's miracles to heart, and depicts the punishments of destruction that are looming (9-13).

According to Ashkenazic tradition, the *Haftarah* continues to document the failed siege of Jerusalem by the kings of Aram and Israel (7:1). The *Haftarah* then turns backwards to the period immediately before the war, relating how King Ahaz, who ruled Judah at the time, was informed prophetically by Isaiah that he would be victorious (2-6). The concluding passage, taken from a later chapter of Isaiah, announces the birth of Hezekiah, royal heir to the throne of David (9:5-6).

6 ¹ In the year that King Uzziah became afflicted with leprosy, a disease so severe that it is considered like death, I saw God sitting upon a throne, high and exalted, and His feet filled the Temple. ² Above, with Him in Heaven, stood the seraph-angels, to serve Him. Each one had six wings. With two he covered his face so as not to gaze upon the

ו 1 בִּשְׁנַת־מוֹת הַמֶּלֶךְ עֻזִּיָּהוּ וָאֶרְאֶה אֶת־אֲדֹנָי יֹשֵׁב עַל־כִּסֵּא רָם וְנִשָּׂא וְשׁוּלָיו מְלֵאִים אֶת־הַהֵיכָל: 2 שְׂרָפִים עֹמְדִים מִמַּעַל לוֹ שֵׁשׁ כְּנָפַיִם שֵׁשׁ כְּנָפַיִם לְאֶחָד בִּשְׁתַּיִם ׀ יְכַסֶּה פָנָיו וּבִשְׁתַּיִם יְכַסֶּה רַגְלָיו

haftarat yitro

Divine Presence, and with two he covered his feet because of modesty in God's presence, and with two he flew to do God's mission.

³ They called to each other to begin praying together, and all together they said, "Holy, holy, holy, is the God of Hosts, above the world of the angels, above the planets, and this lowly world! The whole earth is full of His glory." ⁴ The posts of the door moved many feet at the voice of he who cried, and the house was as if it was filled with smoke.

⁵ Then I said, "Woe is me! For I am lost; because I am a man of unclean lips, and I dwell in the midst of a people of unclean lips; for my eyes have seen the King, the God of Hosts; I am surely unworthy to do so."

⁶ Then one of the seraphim flew to me, having in his hand a live coal that he had taken with the tongs off from the altar. ⁷ He laid it upon my mouth, and said, "Behold, this has touched your lips, and your iniquity is taken away, and your sin of defaming the Jewish people purged."

⁸ I heard the voice of God consulting the angels, saying, "Whom shall I send to speak to the Jewish people, and who will go for us?"

I said, "Here am I! Send me!"

⁹ He said, "Go, and tell this people: Although you hear the prophet's words, you do not understand. Although you see My miracles, you do not recognize them. ¹⁰ The evil inclination makes the heart of this people fat and makes their ears heavy, and shuts their eyes; lest they see with their eyes, and hear with their ears, and understand with their hearts, and return, and be healed."

¹¹ I said, "God, how long will their hearts be insensitive?"

He said, "Until the cities are destroyed without inhabitants, and the houses without man, and the land is completely desolate, ¹² and God has exiled men far away, and there is a great forsaking in the midst of the land. ¹³ Another ten kings will rule in it before this destruction takes place, then it shall be consumed; but like a terebinth tree, or like an oak, whose stump remains, when they cast their leaves, so the holy seed shall be its stump."

וּבִשְׁתַּ֖יִם יְעוֹפֵֽף׃ ג וְקָרָ֨א זֶ֤ה אֶל־זֶה֙ וְאָמַ֔ר קָד֧וֹשׁ ׀ קָד֛וֹשׁ קָד֖וֹשׁ יְהֹוָ֣ה צְבָא֑וֹת מְלֹ֥א כָל־הָאָ֖רֶץ כְּבוֹדֽוֹ׃ ד וַיָּנֻ֨עוּ֙ אַמּ֣וֹת הַסִּפִּ֔ים מִקּ֖וֹל הַקּוֹרֵ֑א וְהַבַּ֖יִת יִמָּלֵ֥א עָשָֽׁן׃ ה וָאֹמַ֞ר אֽוֹי־לִ֣י כִֽי־נִדְמֵ֗יתִי כִּ֣י אִ֣ישׁ טְמֵֽא־שְׂפָתַ֘יִם֮ אָנֹכִי֒ וּבְתוֹךְ֙ עַם־טְמֵ֣א שְׂפָתַ֔יִם אָנֹכִ֖י יוֹשֵׁ֑ב כִּ֗י אֶת־הַמֶּ֛לֶךְ יְהֹוָ֥ה צְבָא֖וֹת רָא֥וּ עֵינָֽי׃ ו וַיָּ֣עָף אֵלַ֗י אֶחָד֙ מִן־הַשְּׂרָפִ֔ים וּבְיָד֖וֹ רִצְפָּ֑ה בְּמֶ֨לְקָחַ֔יִם לָקַ֖ח מֵעַ֥ל הַמִּזְבֵּֽחַ׃ ז וַיַּגַּ֣ע עַל־פִּ֗י וַיֹּ֙אמֶר֙ הִנֵּ֛ה נָגַ֥ע זֶ֖ה עַל־שְׂפָתֶ֑יךָ וְסָ֣ר עֲוֺנֶ֔ךָ וְחַטָּֽאתְךָ֖ תְּכֻפָּֽר׃ ח וָאֶשְׁמַ֞ע אֶת־ק֤וֹל אֲדֹנָי֙ אֹמֵ֔ר אֶת־מִ֥י אֶשְׁלַ֖ח וּמִ֣י יֵֽלֶךְ־לָ֑נוּ וָאֹמַ֖ר הִנְנִ֥י שְׁלָחֵֽנִי׃ ט וַיֹּ֕אמֶר לֵ֥ךְ וְאָמַרְתָּ֖ לָעָ֣ם הַזֶּ֑ה שִׁמְע֤וּ שָׁמ֙וֹעַ֙ וְאַל־תָּבִ֔ינוּ וּרְא֥וּ רָא֖וֹ וְאַל־תֵּדָֽעוּ׃ י הַשְׁמֵן֙ לֵב־הָעָ֣ם הַזֶּ֔ה וְאָזְנָ֥יו הַכְבֵּ֖ד וְעֵינָ֣יו הָשַׁ֑ע פֶּן־יִרְאֶ֨ה בְעֵינָ֜יו וּבְאָזְנָ֣יו יִשְׁמָ֗ע וּלְבָב֥וֹ יָבִ֛ין וָשָׁ֖ב וְרָ֥פָא לֽוֹ׃ יא וָאֹמַ֖ר עַד־מָתַ֣י אֲדֹנָ֑י וַיֹּ֡אמֶר עַ֣ד אֲשֶׁר֩ אִם־שָׁא֨וּ עָרִ֜ים מֵאֵ֣ין יוֹשֵׁ֗ב וּבָתִּים֙ מֵאֵ֣ין אָדָ֔ם וְהָאֲדָמָ֖ה תִּשָּׁאֶ֥ה שְׁמָמָֽה׃ יב וְרִחַ֥ק יְהֹוָ֖ה אֶת־הָאָדָ֑ם וְרַבָּ֥ה הָעֲזוּבָ֖ה בְּקֶ֥רֶב הָאָֽרֶץ׃ יג וְע֥וֹד בָּהּ֙ עֲשִׂ֣רִיָּ֔ה וְשָׁ֖בָה וְהָיְתָ֣ה לְבָעֵ֑ר כָּאֵלָ֣ה וְכָאַלּ֗וֹן אֲשֶׁ֤ר בְּשַׁלֶּ֙כֶת֙ מַצֶּ֣בֶת בָּ֔ם זֶ֥רַע קֹ֖דֶשׁ מַצַּבְתָּֽהּ׃

Ḥabad and *Sephardic* communities conclude here. *Ashkenazic* communities continue:

7 ¹ It was in the days of Ahaz son of Jotham son of Uzziah, king of Judah, that King Rezin of Aram and King Pekah son of Remaliah of Israel went up to Jerusalem to wage war, but they could not conquer it.

ז א וַיְהִ֡י בִּימֵ֣י אָ֠חָ֠ז בֶּן־יוֹתָ֨ם בֶּן־עֻזִּיָּ֜הוּ מֶ֣לֶךְ יְהוּדָ֗ה עָלָ֣ה רְצִ֣ין מֶֽלֶךְ־אֲ֠רָ֠ם וּפֶ֣קַח בֶּן־רְמַלְיָ֤הוּ מֶֽלֶךְ־יִשְׂרָאֵל֙ יְר֣וּשָׁלַ֔͏ִם לַמִּלְחָמָ֖ה

הפטרת משפטים

² Before the war, the House of David was informed, "Aram has set camp with Ephraim." The king's heart and the heart of his people trembled like the trees of the forest shaking from the wind. ³ God said to Isaiah: "Go out to Ahaz, you and your son Shear-jashub, at the edge of the ditch by the upper reservoir, at the road near the launderer's field. ⁴ Say to him, "Be careful, but be calm. Don't be frightened. Don't become disheartened because of these two firebrands that have no power to burn and are just smoking in anger—Rezin and the Arameans, and the son of Remaliah. ⁵ Since Aram, Ephraim, and the son of Remaliah have plotted evil against you, saying, ⁶ 'Let's go up against Judah, besiege it to repulse them so they will open the gates and we can break into it and take it for ourselves. Let's appoint the son of Tabeel as king.'"

9 ⁵ For a boy—Hezekiah—has been born to us, a son has been given to us, and he will allow the authority of Torah to rest on his shoulders. He will be called "Prince of Peace," by the Wondrous Advisor, God Almighty, Eternal Father. ⁶ His name signifies much authority and peace without end on the throne of David and over his kingdom, to establish it and support it with justice and righteousness, now and forever. God's zeal will accomplish this.

עָלֶיהָ וְלֹא יָכֹל לְהִלָּחֵם עָלֶיהָ: 2 וַיֻּגַּד לְבֵית דָּוִד לֵאמֹר נָחָה אֲרָם עַל־אֶפְרָיִם וַיָּנַע לְבָבוֹ וּלְבַב עַמּוֹ כְּנוֹעַ עֲצֵי־יַעַר מִפְּנֵי־רוּחַ: 3 וַיֹּאמֶר יְהֹוָה אֶל־יְשַׁעְיָהוּ צֵא־נָא לִקְרַאת אָחָז אַתָּה וּשְׁאָר יָשׁוּב בְּנֶךָ אֶל־קְצֵה תְּעָלַת הַבְּרֵכָה הָעֶלְיוֹנָה אֶל־מְסִלַּת שְׂדֵה כוֹבֵס: 4 וְאָמַרְתָּ אֵלָיו הִשָּׁמֵר וְהַשְׁקֵט אַל־תִּירָא וּלְבָבְךָ אַל־יֵרַךְ מִשְּׁנֵי זַנְבוֹת הָאוּדִים הָעֲשֵׁנִים הָאֵלֶּה בָּחֳרִי־אַף רְצִין וַאֲרָם וּבֶן־רְמַלְיָהוּ: 5 יַעַן כִּי־יָעַץ עָלֶיךָ אֲרָם רָעָה אֶפְרַיִם וּבֶן־רְמַלְיָהוּ לֵאמֹר: 6 נַעֲלֶה בִיהוּדָה וּנְקִיצֶנָּה וְנַבְקִעֶנָּה אֵלֵינוּ וְנַמְלִיךְ מֶלֶךְ בְּתוֹכָהּ אֵת בֶּן־טָבְאַל:

ט 5 כִּי־יֶלֶד יֻלַּד־לָנוּ בֵּן נִתַּן־לָנוּ וַתְּהִי הַמִּשְׂרָה עַל־שִׁכְמוֹ וַיִּקְרָא שְׁמוֹ פֶּלֶא יוֹעֵץ אֵל גִּבּוֹר אֲבִי־עַד שַׂר־שָׁלוֹם: 6 [למרבה כ׳] לְםַרְבֵּה הַמִּשְׂרָה וּלְשָׁלוֹם אֵין־קֵץ עַל־כִּסֵּא דָוִד וְעַל־מַמְלַכְתּוֹ לְהָכִין אֹתָהּ וּלְסַעֲדָהּ בְּמִשְׁפָּט וּבִצְדָקָה מֵעַתָּה וְעַד־עוֹלָם קִנְאַת יְהֹוָה צְבָאוֹת תַּעֲשֶׂה־זֹּאת:

haftarat mishpatim
ALL COMMUNITIES—JEREMIAH 34:8–22; 33:25–26

SYNOPSIS: This *Haftarah* mentions the laws of release of Hebrew slaves, which were introduced in the *Parashah*.

The *Haftarah* opens by recalling the proclamation of King Zedekiah, that all Hebrew slaves should be freed. The prophet Jeremiah then laments that, after initial acceptance of the decree, the people soon began to ignore it (34:8-11). Jeremiah recalls how an identical sequence of events occurred after Sinai (12-16). God then proclaims His punishment, that He will "declare freedom" from protecting the Jewish people and that Jerusalem will be destroyed (17-22). In order to conclude on a positive note, the *Haftarah* cites two verses from Chapter 33 of Jeremiah, in which God swears never to eliminate the Jewish people completely.

haftarat mishpatim

34

[8] The word that came to Jeremiah from God, after the King Zedekiah had made a covenant with all the people who were in Jerusalem, to proclaim liberty to the slaves [9] that every man should let his Hebrew slave, and every man his Hebrew slave-woman, go free. No person should enslave his brother Jew after he has worked for six years.

[10] When all the nobles, and all the people, who had entered into the covenant heard that everyone should let his slave, and everyone his slave-woman, go free, that none should enslave them any more, they accepted and let them go. [11] But afterward they regretted their decision, and caused the slaves and the slave-women, whom they had let go free, to return, and brought them into subjection as slaves and slave-women.

[12] The word of God came to Jeremiah from God, saying: [13] This is what God, the God of Israel says: "I made a covenant with your fathers on the day that I brought them forth out of the land of Egypt, out of the house of slaves and gave them the Torah, saying, [14] 'At the end of seven years, each of you shall release his Hebrew brother, who has been sold to you, and when he has served you six years, you shall set him free from you.' But your fathers did not listen to Me to observe this command, nor did they pay attention to it. [15] Now, you repented, and have done right in My sight, by each man proclaiming freedom for his Jewish slave, and you have made a covenant before Me in the house which is called by My name. [16] But you then regretted it and desecrated My name, and each of you brought back your slave or slave-woman, whom you had set free for themselves, and you subjugated them again to be your slaves and slave-women."

[17] Therefore this is what God says: "Since you have not listened to Me, to proclaim freedom, each man for his brother, and each man for his neighbor, therefore I am going to proclaim freedom for you from My protection," says God, "abandoning you to the sword, the pestilence, and the famine. I will make you terrified of all the kingdoms of the earth. [18] I will give the men who have transgressed My covenant, who have

לד [8] הַדָּבָר אֲשֶׁר־הָיָה אֶל־יִרְמְיָהוּ מֵאֵת יְהֹוָה אַחֲרֵי כְּרֹת הַמֶּלֶךְ צִדְקִיָּהוּ בְּרִית אֶת־כָּל־הָעָם אֲשֶׁר בִּירוּשָׁלַם לִקְרֹא לָהֶם דְּרוֹר: [9] לְשַׁלַּח אִישׁ אֶת־עַבְדּוֹ וְאִישׁ אֶת־שִׁפְחָתוֹ הָעִבְרִי וְהָעִבְרִיָּה חָפְשִׁים לְבִלְתִּי עֲבָד־בָּם בִּיהוּדִי אָחִיהוּ אִישׁ: [10] וַיִּשְׁמְעוּ כָל־ הַשָּׂרִים וְכָל־הָעָם אֲשֶׁר־בָּאוּ בַבְּרִית לְשַׁלַּח אִישׁ אֶת־עַבְדּוֹ וְאִישׁ אֶת־שִׁפְחָתוֹ חָפְשִׁים לְבִלְתִּי עֲבָד־בָּם עוֹד וַיִּשְׁמְעוּ וַיְשַׁלֵּחוּ:
[11] וַיָּשׁוּבוּ אַחֲרֵי־כֵן וַיָּשִׁבוּ אֶת־הָעֲבָדִים וְאֶת־הַשְּׁפָחוֹת אֲשֶׁר שִׁלְּחוּ חָפְשִׁים [ויכבישום כ׳] וַיִּכְבְּשׁוּם לַעֲבָדִים וְלִשְׁפָחוֹת: [12] וַיְהִי דְבַר־ יְהֹוָה אֶל־יִרְמְיָהוּ מֵאֵת יְהֹוָה לֵאמֹר: [13] כֹּה־ אָמַר יְהֹוָה אֱלֹהֵי יִשְׂרָאֵל אָנֹכִי כָּרַתִּי בְרִית אֶת־אֲבוֹתֵיכֶם בְּיוֹם הוֹצִאִי אוֹתָם מֵאֶרֶץ מִצְרַיִם מִבֵּית עֲבָדִים לֵאמֹר: [14] מִקֵּץ שֶׁבַע שָׁנִים תְּשַׁלְּחוּ אִישׁ אֶת־אָחִיו הָעִבְרִי אֲשֶׁר־ יִמָּכֵר לְךָ וַעֲבָדְךָ שֵׁשׁ שָׁנִים וְשִׁלַּחְתּוֹ חָפְשִׁי מֵעִמָּךְ וְלֹא־שָׁמְעוּ אֲבוֹתֵיכֶם אֵלַי וְלֹא הִטּוּ אֶת־אָזְנָם: [15] וַתָּשֻׁבוּ אַתֶּם הַיּוֹם וַתַּעֲשׂוּ אֶת־ הַיָּשָׁר בְּעֵינַי לִקְרֹא דְרוֹר אִישׁ לְרֵעֵהוּ וַתִּכְרְתוּ בְרִית לְפָנַי בַּבַּיִת אֲשֶׁר־נִקְרָא שְׁמִי עָלָיו: [16] וַתָּשֻׁבוּ וַתְּחַלְּלוּ אֶת־שְׁמִי וַתָּשִׁבוּ אִישׁ אֶת־עַבְדּוֹ וְאִישׁ אֶת־שִׁפְחָתוֹ אֲשֶׁר־שִׁלַּחְתֶּם חָפְשִׁים לְנַפְשָׁם וַתִּכְבְּשׁוּ אֹתָם לִהְיוֹת לָכֶם לַעֲבָדִים וְלִשְׁפָחוֹת: [17] לָכֵן כֹּה־אָמַר יְהֹוָה אַתֶּם לֹא־שְׁמַעְתֶּם אֵלַי לִקְרֹא דְרוֹר אִישׁ לְאָחִיו וְאִישׁ לְרֵעֵהוּ הִנְנִי קֹרֵא לָכֶם דְּרוֹר נְאֻם־יְהֹוָה אֶל־הַחֶרֶב אֶל־הַדֶּבֶר וְאֶל־הָרָעָב וְנָתַתִּי אֶתְכֶם [לזועה כ׳] לְזַעֲוָה לְכֹל מַמְלְכוֹת הָאָרֶץ: [18] וְנָתַתִּי אֶת־הָאֲנָשִׁים הָעֹבְרִים אֶת־

הפטרת תרומה

not kept the words of the covenant which they had renewed before Me, when they cut the calf in two, and passed between its parts—¹⁹ the nobles of Judah, and the nobles of Jerusalem, the officers, and the priests, and all the people of the land, who passed between the parts of the calf. ²⁰ I will give them into the hand of their enemies and those who seek to kill them. Their carcasses will be so abundant, that they will not be buried, so they will be food for the birds of the heaven and for the beasts of the earth. ²¹ I will give King Zedekiah of Judah and his nobles into the hand of their enemies and those who seek to kill them, and into the hand of the army of the king of Babel, which is now retreating from you. ²² Now, I will arouse them," says God, "and cause them to return to this city; and they shall fight against it, and take it, and burn it with fire; and I will make the cities of Judah a desolation without inhabitants."

בְּרִיתִ֔י אֲשֶׁ֥ר לֹֽא־הֵקִ֖ימוּ אֶת־דִּבְרֵ֣י הַבְּרִ֑ית אֲשֶׁ֤ר כָּֽרְתוּ֙ לְפָנַ֔י הָעֵ֕גֶל אֲשֶׁ֥ר כָּרְת֖וּ לִשְׁנַ֑יִם וַיַּעַבְר֖וּ בֵּ֥ין בְּתָרָֽיו׃ 19 שָׂרֵ֨י יְהוּדָ֜ה וְשָׂרֵ֣י יְרוּשָׁלַ֗͏ִם הַסָּֽרִסִים֙ וְהַכֹּ֣הֲנִ֔ים וְכֹ֖ל עַ֣ם הָאָ֑רֶץ הָעֹ֣בְרִ֔ים בֵּ֖ין בִּתְרֵ֥י הָעֵֽגֶל׃ 20 וְנָתַתִּ֤י אוֹתָם֙ בְּיַ֣ד אֹֽיְבֵיהֶ֔ם וּבְיַ֖ד מְבַקְשֵׁ֣י נַפְשָׁ֑ם וְהָֽיְתָ֤ה נִבְלָתָם֙ לְמַֽאֲכָ֔ל לְע֥וֹף הַשָּׁמַ֖יִם וּלְבֶֽהֱמַ֥ת הָאָֽרֶץ׃ 21 וְאֶת־צִדְקִיָּ֨הוּ מֶֽלֶךְ־יְהוּדָ֜ה וְאֶת־שָׂרָ֗יו אֶתֵּן֙ בְּיַ֣ד אֹֽיְבֵיהֶ֔ם וּבְיַ֖ד מְבַקְשֵׁ֣י נַפְשָׁ֑ם וּבְיַ֗ד חֵ֚יל מֶ֣לֶךְ בָּבֶ֔ל הָעֹלִ֖ים מֵעֲלֵיכֶֽם׃ 22 הִנְנִ֨י מְצַוֶּ֜ה נְאֻם־יְהֹוָ֗ה וַהֲשִֽׁבֹתִים֙ אֶל־הָעִ֣יר הַזֹּ֔את וְנִלְחֲמ֥וּ עָלֶ֛יהָ וּלְכָד֖וּהָ וּשְׂרָפֻ֣הָ בָאֵ֑שׁ וְאֶת־עָרֵ֧י יְהוּדָ֛ה אֶתֵּ֥ן שְׁמָמָ֖ה מֵאֵ֥ין יֹשֵֽׁב׃

33 ²⁵ This is what God says, "Just as I would not cancel My covenant with day and night, and I would not cancel the laws of heaven and earth, ²⁶ so too I will not cast away the descendants of Jacob, and David My servant, from taking of their descendants to be rulers over the descendants of Abraham, Isaac, and Jacob, for I will return their captivity to their land, and have mercy on them."

לג 25 כֹּ֚ה אָמַ֣ר יְהֹוָ֔ה אִם־לֹ֥א בְרִיתִ֖י יוֹמָ֣ם וָלָ֑יְלָה חֻקּ֛וֹת שָׁמַ֥יִם וָאָ֖רֶץ לֹא־שָֽׂמְתִּי׃ 26 גַּם־זֶ֨רַע יַעֲק֜וֹב וְדָוִ֣ד עַבְדִּ֗י אֶמְאַס֙ מִקַּ֣חַת מִזַּרְע֔וֹ מֹֽשְׁלִ֔ים אֶל־זֶ֥רַע אַבְרָהָ֖ם יִשְׂחָ֣ק וְיַעֲקֹ֑ב כִּי־[אשיב כ׳] אָשִׁ֥יב אֶת־שְׁבוּתָ֖ם וְרִחַמְתִּֽים׃

haftarat terumah

All communities—I Kings 5:26 – 6:13

> **SYNOPSIS:** This *Haftarah* describes the beginning of the construction of the First Temple, built by King Solomon, paralleling the description of the Tabernacle which is detailed in the *Parashah*.
>
> The *Haftarah* opens by a brief reference to the treaty between Solomon and King Hiram of Tyre, through which cedar and cypress trees were obtained for the construction of the *Temple* (5:26). The main body of the *Haftarah* is then divided into two distinct parts. The remainder of chapter 5 describes the forced labor which was imposed by Solomon to quarry the necessary stone for the Temple's construction. Chapter 6 then relates various details of the actual building of the Temple, including the date when construction began (6:1), and the dimensions of the Temple and its hall (2-3) and its exterior (4-10). The *Haftarah* concludes with God's promise to Solomon never to forsake Israel so long as they observe the commandments (11-13).

haftarat terumah

5 ²⁶ God gave Solomon wisdom, as He had promised him. This brought about peace between Hiram and Solomon, and the two made a covenant together.

²⁷ King Solomon raised a levy from all Israel that able-bodied men should cut timber in collaboration with Hiram's workers. The levy was thirty thousand men. ²⁸ He sent them to Lebanon, ten thousand a month by turns. They were a month in Lebanon, and two months at home. Adoniram was in charge of the levy.

²⁹ Solomon had seventy thousand men who carried loads, and eighty thousand stone cutters in the mountains, ³⁰ besides the three thousand and three hundred of Solomon's officers who supervised the work and who ruled over the people who did the work.

³¹ The king commanded, and they quarried great stones, heavy stones, to lay the foundation of the House with hewn stones. ³² Solomon's builders, Hiram's builders, and the Gebalites, who were highly skilled craftsmen, cut them, and they prepared timber and stones to build the House.

6 ¹ It was in the four hundred and eightieth year after the people of Israel came out of the land of Egypt, in the fourth year of Solomon's reign over Israel, in the month Ziv, which is the second month, that he began to build the House of God.

² The House which King Solomon built for God was sixty cubits in its length, twenty cubits in its width, and thirty cubits in its height.

³ The hall that was in front of the temple of the House was twenty cubits in its length, along the width of the House, and its width before the House was ten cubits.

⁴ He made windows for the House, wide on the outside and narrow on the inside.

⁵ Against the wall of the House he built an annex around the walls of the House, both of the temple and of the sanctuary, and he made side chambers all around. ⁶ The lowest chamber was five cubits wide, and the middle was six cubits wide, and the third was seven cubits wide, for outside around the wall of the House he made recesses in the walls around, so that the beams should not be fastened into the walls of the House.

ה 26 וַיהוָה נָתַן חָכְמָה לִשְׁלֹמֹה כַּאֲשֶׁר דִּבֶּר־לוֹ וַיְהִי שָׁלֹם בֵּין חִירָם וּבֵין שְׁלֹמֹה וַיִּכְרְתוּ בְרִית שְׁנֵיהֶם: 27 וַיַּעַל הַמֶּלֶךְ שְׁלֹמֹה מַס מִכָּל־יִשְׂרָאֵל וַיְהִי הַמַּס שְׁלֹשִׁים אֶלֶף אִישׁ: 28 וַיִּשְׁלָחֵם לְבָנוֹנָה עֲשֶׂרֶת אֲלָפִים בַּחֹדֶשׁ חֲלִיפוֹת חֹדֶשׁ יִהְיוּ בַלְּבָנוֹן שְׁנַיִם חֳדָשִׁים בְּבֵיתוֹ וַאֲדֹנִירָם עַל־הַמַּס: 29 וַיְהִי לִשְׁלֹמֹה שִׁבְעִים אֶלֶף נֹשֵׂא סַבָּל וּשְׁמֹנִים אֶלֶף חֹצֵב בָּהָר: 30 לְבַד מִשָּׂרֵי הַנִּצָּבִים לִשְׁלֹמֹה אֲשֶׁר עַל־הַמְּלָאכָה שְׁלֹשֶׁת אֲלָפִים וּשְׁלֹשׁ מֵאוֹת הָרֹדִים בָּעָם הָעֹשִׂים בַּמְּלָאכָה: 31 וַיְצַו הַמֶּלֶךְ וַיַּסִּעוּ אֲבָנִים גְּדֹלוֹת אֲבָנִים יְקָרוֹת לְיַסֵּד הַבָּיִת אַבְנֵי גָזִית: 32 וַיִּפְסְלוּ בֹּנֵי שְׁלֹמֹה וּבֹנֵי חִירוֹם וְהַגִּבְלִים וַיָּכִינוּ הָעֵצִים וְהָאֲבָנִים לִבְנוֹת הַבָּיִת:

ו 1 וַיְהִי בִשְׁמוֹנִים שָׁנָה וְאַרְבַּע מֵאוֹת שָׁנָה לְצֵאת בְּנֵי־יִשְׂרָאֵל מֵאֶרֶץ־מִצְרַיִם בַּשָּׁנָה הָרְבִיעִית בְּחֹדֶשׁ זִו הוּא הַחֹדֶשׁ הַשֵּׁנִי לִמְלֹךְ שְׁלֹמֹה עַל־יִשְׂרָאֵל וַיִּבֶן הַבַּיִת לַיהוָה: 2 וְהַבַּיִת אֲשֶׁר בָּנָה הַמֶּלֶךְ שְׁלֹמֹה לַיהוָה שִׁשִּׁים־אַמָּה אָרְכּוֹ וְעֶשְׂרִים רָחְבּוֹ וּשְׁלֹשִׁים אַמָּה קוֹמָתוֹ: 3 וְהָאוּלָם עַל־פְּנֵי הֵיכַל הַבַּיִת עֶשְׂרִים אַמָּה אָרְכּוֹ עַל־פְּנֵי רֹחַב הַבָּיִת עֶשֶׂר בָּאַמָּה רָחְבּוֹ עַל־פְּנֵי הַבָּיִת: 4 וַיַּעַשׂ לַבָּיִת חַלּוֹנֵי שְׁקֻפִים אֲטֻמִים: 5 וַיִּבֶן עַל־קִיר הַבַּיִת [יָצוּעַ כ׳] יָצִיעַ סָבִיב אֶת־קִירוֹת הַבַּיִת סָבִיב לַהֵיכָל וְלַדְּבִיר וַיַּעַשׂ צְלָעוֹת סָבִיב: 6 [הַיְּצוּעַ כ׳] הַיָּצִיעַ הַתַּחְתֹּנָה חָמֵשׁ בָּאַמָּה רָחְבָּהּ וְהַתִּיכֹנָה שֵׁשׁ בָּאַמָּה רָחְבָּהּ וְהַשְּׁלִישִׁית שֶׁבַע בָּאַמָּה רָחְבָּהּ כִּי מִגְרָעוֹת נָתַן לַבַּיִת סָבִיב חוּצָה לְבִלְתִּי אֲחֹז בְּקִירוֹת הַבָּיִת:

הפטרת תצוה

⁷ The House, when it was being built, was built of stone, prepared before it was brought there, so that there was neither hammer nor axe nor any tool of iron heard in the House while it was being built.

⁸ The door for the middle chamber was in the right side of the House. They went up with winding stairs into the middle chamber, and out of the middle into the third.

⁹ He built the walls of the House and finished it. He covered the House with beams and boards of cedar.

¹⁰ He built the annex structure along the entire House, five cubits high, and they rested on the House with beams of cedar.

¹¹ The word of God came to Solomon, saying, ¹² "Concerning this House which you are building, if you will walk in My statutes, and execute My judgments, and keep all My commandments to walk in them—then with you I will fulfil My word, that I spoke to David your father. ¹³ I will dwell among the people of Israel, and will not forsake my people Israel."

⁷ וְהַבַּ֨יִת בְּהִבָּנֹת֜וֹ אֶֽבֶן־שְׁלֵמָ֧ה מַסָּ֛ע נִבְנָ֖ה וּמַקָּב֤וֹת וְהַגַּרְזֶן֙ כָּל־כְּלִ֣י בַרְזֶ֔ל לֹֽא־נִשְׁמַ֥ע בַּבַּ֖יִת בְּהִבָּנֹתֽוֹ: ⁸ פֶּ֗תַח הַצֵּלָע֙ הַתִּ֣יכֹנָ֔ה אֶל־כֶּ֖תֶף הַבַּ֣יִת הַיְמָנִ֑ית וּבְלוּלִּ֗ים יַֽעֲלוּ֙ עַל־הַתִּ֣יכֹנָ֔ה וּמִן־הַתִּֽיכֹנָ֖ה אֶל־הַשְּׁלִשִֽׁים: ⁹ וַיִּ֥בֶן אֶת־הַבַּ֖יִת וַיְכַלֵּ֑הוּ וַיִּסְפֹּ֤ן אֶת־הַבַּ֙יִת֙ גֵּבִ֔ים וּשְׂדֵרֹ֖ת בָּאֲרָזִֽים: ¹⁰ וַיִּ֤בֶן אֶת־[הַיָּצוּעַ כ׳] הַיָּצִ֙יעַ֙ עַל־כָּל־הַבַּ֔יִת חָמֵ֥שׁ אַמּ֖וֹת קֽוֹמָת֑וֹ וַיֶּֽאֱחֹ֥ז אֶת־הַבַּ֖יִת בַּעֲצֵ֥י אֲרָזִֽים: ¹¹ וַֽיְהִי֙ דְּבַר־יְהֹוָ֔ה אֶל־שְׁלֹמֹ֖ה לֵאמֹֽר: ¹² הַבַּ֨יִת הַזֶּ֜ה אֲשֶׁר־אַתָּ֣ה בֹנֶ֗ה אִם־תֵּלֵ֤ךְ בְּחֻקֹּתַי֙ וְאֶת־מִשְׁפָּטַ֣י תַּֽעֲשֶׂ֔ה וְשָֽׁמַרְתָּ֥ אֶת־כָּל־מִצְוֹתַ֖י לָלֶ֣כֶת בָּהֶ֑ם וַהֲקִֽמֹתִ֤י אֶת־דְּבָרִי֙ אִתָּ֔ךְ אֲשֶׁ֥ר דִּבַּ֖רְתִּי אֶל־דָּוִ֥ד אָבִֽיךָ: ¹³ וְשָׁ֣כַנְתִּ֔י בְּת֖וֹךְ בְּנֵ֣י יִשְׂרָאֵ֑ל וְלֹ֥א אֶעֱזֹ֖ב אֶת־עַמִּ֥י יִשְׂרָאֵֽל:

haftarat tetzavveh

ALL COMMUNITIES—Ezekiel 43:10–27

> **SYNOPSIS:** This *Haftarah* describes the construction of the altar and dedication of the priests in the Third Temple, similar to the description of the desert altar, in the *Parashah*. The *Haftarah*, taken from the latter section of the Book of Ezekiel (ch. 40–48), is a vision of the Divine presence returning to Israel with the future Redemption which Ezekiel received in Babylon, shortly after the destruction of Jerusalem in 586 B.C.E. (The *Haftarot* of *Parashat 'Emor* and *Parashat Ha-Hodesh* are also taken from this section of Ezekiel.)
>
> The *Haftarah* opens at the conclusion of Ezekiel's vision of the Third Temple (ch. 40–43:9), as God instructs the prophet to describe the future Temple to the public, so that they will be ashamed of their sins which had just caused the First Temple to be destroyed (10–12).
>
> The main body of the *Haftarah* consists of two passages, one describing the dimensions of the altar (13–17), and the second, the sacrificial inauguration of the altar (18–27).

43 ¹⁰ You, son of man, describe the House which you saw in a vision to the House of Israel, so that they will be reminded of the Temple

מג ¹⁰ אַתָּ֣ה בֶן־אָדָ֗ם הַגֵּ֤ד אֶת־בֵּֽית־יִשְׂרָאֵל֙ אֶת־הַבַּ֔יִת וְיִכָּלְמ֖וּ

haftarat tetzavveh

that was destroyed and they will be ashamed of their iniquities which caused its destruction. Let them think in their hearts the dimensions of the future House which is ready to be built.

¹¹ If they are ashamed of all that they have done which caused the destruction of the Temple, describe to them the general form of the House, its detailed layout, its exits and its entrances, its dimensions of each room, its laws regarding the use of each room, all its sculptured decorations, all its regulations regarding where the priests and the people may stand. Write all this for them to see, so that they may remember its whole form, and all its regulations, so that they will merit to be resurrected in the future and fulfil them.

¹² This is the law of the House: On the top of the mountain, its entire border around it shall be most holy. Behold, this is the law of the House. ¹³ These are the measurements of the altar in cubits. The holy cubit used in Temple measurements is a regular cubit of five handbreadths plus an extra handbreadth making a total of six: The height of the base shall be a regular cubit, and the width a regular cubit, and each of its border horns all around shall be a handbreadth from its center to its edge. The regular cubit shall also be used to measure the side of the golden altar. ¹⁴ From the base on the ground to the top of the lower block shall be two cubits, and then a width of one cubit. From the top of the small block to the top of the large block shall be four cubits, and then a width of one cubit. ¹⁵ The upper part of the altar shall be four cubits high. From the upper part of the altar upwards there shall be four horns.

¹⁶ The burning area at the top of the altar hearth shall be twelve cubits long by twelve wide, perfectly square on its sides. ¹⁷ The entire block shall be fourteen cubits long by fourteen wide, on its four sides. The horns around its edges shall be half a cubit. Its base shall be a cubit around. Its ramp shall be arranged so that a person ascending it faces the east.

¹⁸ He said to me: "Son of man, this is what God, Almighty God, says: These are the laws of inaugurating the altar on the day when they shall finish making it, to make it fit to offer burnt-offerings on it, and to sprinkle blood on it. ¹⁹ You will be resurrected, and you shall give to the priests, who are from the tribe of Levi, who are the descendants of Zadok, who come near Me to minister to Me," says God, Almighty God, "a young bull for a sin-offering. ²⁰ You shall take some

11 וְאִם־מֵעֲוֺנוֹתֵיהֶם וּמָדְדוּ אֶת־תָּכְנִֽית: נִכְלְמ֞וּ מִכֹּ֣ל אֲשֶׁר־עָשׂ֗וּ צוּרַ֣ת הַבַּ֡יִת וּתְכוּנָת֣וֹ וּמוֹצָאָ֣יו וּמוֹבָאָ֡יו וְֽכָל־צֽוּרֹתָ֡ו וְאֵ֣ת כָּל־חֻקֹּתָיו֩ וְכָל־צורתו [צ֨וּרֹתָ֤יו] וְכָל־תּֽוֹרֹתָו֙ הוֹדַ֣ע אוֹתָ֔ם וּכְתֹ֖ב לְעֵֽינֵיהֶ֑ם וְיִשְׁמְר֞וּ אֶת־כָּל־צוּרָת֛וֹ וְאֶת־כָּל־חֻקֹּתָ֖יו וְעָשׂ֥וּ אוֹתָֽם: 12 זֹ֖את תּוֹרַ֣ת הַבָּ֑יִת עַל־רֹ֣אשׁ הָ֠הָר כָּל־גְּבֻל֞וֹ סָבִ֤יב ׀ סָבִיב֙ קֹ֣דֶשׁ קָֽדָשִׁ֔ים הִנֵּה־זֹ֖את תּוֹרַ֥ת הַבָּֽיִת: 13 וְאֵ֨לֶּה מִדּ֤וֹת הַמִּזְבֵּ֙חַ֙ בָּֽאַמּ֔וֹת אַמָּ֥ה אַמָּ֖ה וָטֹ֑פַח וְחֵ֨יק הָאַמָּ֜ה וְאַמָּה־רֹ֗חַב וּגְבוּלָ֨הּ אֶל־שְׂפָתָ֤הּ סָבִיב֙ זֶ֣רֶת הָאֶחָ֔ד וְזֶ֖ה גַּ֥ב הַמִּזְבֵּֽחַ: 14 וּמֵחֵ֨יק הָאָ֜רֶץ עַד־הָֽעֲזָרָ֤ה הַתַּחְתּוֹנָה֙ שְׁתַּ֣יִם אַמּ֔וֹת וְרֹ֖חַב אַמָּ֣ה אֶחָ֑ת וּמֵהֳעֲזָרָ֨ה הַקְּטַנָּ֜ה עַד־הָֽעֲזָרָ֤ה הַגְּדוֹלָה֙ אַרְבַּ֣ע אַמּ֔וֹת וְרֹ֖חַב הָאַמָּֽה: 15 וְהַֽהַרְאֵ֖ל אַרְבַּ֣ע אַמּ֑וֹת וּמֵהָֽאֲרִאֵ֣יל וּלְמַ֔עְלָה הַקְּרָנ֖וֹת אַרְבַּֽע: 16 וְהָאֲרִאֵ֗יל שְׁתֵּ֤ים עֶשְׂרֵה֙ אֹ֔רֶךְ בִּשְׁתֵּ֥ים עֶשְׂרֵ֖ה רֹ֑חַב רָב֕וּעַ אֶ֖ל אַרְבַּ֥עַת רְבָעָֽיו: 17 וְהָעֲזָרָ֞ה אַרְבַּ֧ע עֶשְׂרֵ֣ה אֹ֗רֶךְ בְּאַרְבַּ֤ע עֶשְׂרֵה֙ רֹ֔חַב אֶ֖ל אַרְבַּ֣עַת רְבָעֶ֑יהָ וְהַגְּבוּל סָבִ֨יב אוֹתָ֜הּ חֲצִ֣י הָאַמָּ֗ה וְהַֽחֵיק־לָ֤הּ אַמָּה֙ סָבִ֔יב וּמַעֲלֹתֵ֖הוּ פְּנ֥וֹת קָדִֽים: 18 וַיֹּ֣אמֶר אֵלַ֗י בֶּן־אָדָם֙ כֹּ֤ה אָמַר֙ אֲדֹנָ֣י יֱהֹוִ֔ה אֵ֚לֶּה חֻקּ֣וֹת הַמִּזְבֵּ֔חַ בְּי֖וֹם הֵעָֽשׂוֹת֑וֹ לְהַעֲל֤וֹת עָלָיו֙ עוֹלָ֔ה וְלִזְרֹ֥ק עָלָ֖יו דָּֽם: 19 וְנָתַתָּ֣ה אֶל־הַכֹּהֲנִ֣ים הַלְוִיִּ֗ם אֲשֶׁ֨ר הֵ֜ם מִזֶּ֤רַע צָדוֹק֙ הַקְּרֹבִ֣ים אֵלַ֔י נְאֻ֖ם אֲדֹנָ֣י יֱהֹוִ֑ה לְשָׁרְתֵ֑נִי פַּ֥ר בֶּן־בָּקָ֖ר לְחַטָּֽאת: 20 וְלָקַחְתָּ֣ מִדָּמ֗וֹ וְנָ֨תַתָּ֜ה עַל־אַרְבַּ֤ע קַרְנֹתָיו֙ וְאֶל־אַרְבַּע֙ פִּנּ֣וֹת הָעֲזָרָ֔ה וְאֶל־הַגְּב֖וּל

הפטרת כי תשא

of its blood and put it on the altar's four horns, and on the four corners of the top block and on the surrounding base. With this act you will cleanse and purge it of its prior non-holy identity. [21] You also shall take the bull of the sin-offering, and it shall be burned by someone at the extremity of the House, outside the Sanctuary.

[22] "On the second day you shall offer a male goat without blemish for a sin-offering. They shall cleanse the altar by sprinkling blood, as they cleansed it with the blood of the bull. [23] When you have finished cleansing it with the goat's blood, you shall offer a young bull without blemish and a ram from the flock without blemish. [24] You shall offer them before God, and the priests shall cast salt upon them, and they shall offer them up for a burnt-offering to God.

[25] "For seven days you shall prepare every day a goat for a sin-offering as you did on the second day. They shall also prepare a young bull and a ram from the flock, without blemish. [26] For seven days shall they make atonement for the altar and purify it. Thus, they shall consecrate it. [27] They shall complete these seven days, and then

סָבִיב וְחִטֵּאתָ אוֹתוֹ וְכִפַּרְתָּהוּ: [21] וְלָקַחְתָּ אֵת הַפָּר הַחַטָּאת וּשְׂרָפוֹ בְּמִפְקַד הַבַּיִת מִחוּץ לַמִּקְדָּשׁ: [22] וּבַיּוֹם הַשֵּׁנִי תַּקְרִיב שְׂעִיר־עִזִּים תָּמִים לְחַטָּאת וְחִטְּאוּ אֶת־הַמִּזְבֵּחַ כַּאֲשֶׁר חִטְּאוּ בַּפָּר: [23] בְּכַלּוֹתְךָ מֵחַטֵּא תַּקְרִיב פַּר בֶּן־בָּקָר תָּמִים וְאַיִל מִן־הַצֹּאן תָּמִים: [24] וְהִקְרַבְתָּם לִפְנֵי יְהֹוָה וְהִשְׁלִיכוּ הַכֹּהֲנִים עֲלֵיהֶם מֶלַח וְהֶעֱלוּ אוֹתָם עֹלָה לַיהֹוָה: [25] שִׁבְעַת יָמִים תַּעֲשֶׂה שְׂעִיר־חַטָּאת לַיּוֹם וּפַר בֶּן־בָּקָר וְאַיִל מִן־הַצֹּאן תְּמִימִים יַעֲשׂוּ: [26] שִׁבְעַת יָמִים יְכַפְּרוּ אֶת־הַמִּזְבֵּחַ וְטִהֲרוּ אֹתוֹ וּמִלְאוּ יָדָו: [27] וִיכַלּוּ אֶת־הַיָּמִים וְהָיָה בַיּוֹם הַשְּׁמִינִי וָהָלְאָה יַעֲשׂוּ הַכֹּהֲנִים עַל־הַמִּזְבֵּחַ אֶת־עוֹלוֹתֵיכֶם וְאֶת־שַׁלְמֵיכֶם וְרָצִאתִי אֶתְכֶם נְאֻם אֲדֹנָי יְהוִה:

from the eighth day onwards, the priests shall offer upon the altar your burnt-offerings and your peace-offerings, and I will be pleased with you," said God, Almighty God.

haftarat ki tissa

Ashkenazim—I Kings 18:1–39
Sephardim and Habad—I Kings 18:20–39

SYNOPSIS: This *Haftarah* describes Elijah's admonition of the Jewish people for worshiping the idols of Baal, similar to Moses' efforts in the *Parashah*, after the worship of the Golden Calf.

The historical setting of the *Haftarah* traces itself back to the collapse of King Solomon's empire when the kingdom split between Judah and the Ten Tribes. Both countries suffered greatly in the years that followed, especially from the attack of King Shishak of Egypt, but it was the Ten Tribes whose infrastructure deteriorated much faster.

A few generations later, the country was forced to withstand another blow, an internal war between generals Zimri, Omri and Tibni. Omri eventually succeeded in controlling the kingdom, but it was his son, Ahab, who brought military and economic stability through an alliance with Sidon. To cement this alliance, Ahab married Jezebel, the King of Sidon's daughter.

haftarat ki tissa'

Tragically, Ahab's political and economic success led to the religious corruption of his country. For, under Jezebel's influence, idol-worship became officially sanctioned, and true prophets were eliminated.

Our *Haftarah* describes the efforts of Elijah the prophet to reverse the influence of Jezebel. His initial campaign (related immediately prior to the *Haftarah*) was to orchestrate a drought upon the land, thus sending the message that prosperity comes from God.

The *Haftarah* begins (according to Ashkenazic custom) in the third year of the drought, as God appears to Elijah and sends him to King Ahab with the message that rain is soon to come (18:1). After digressing to describe the support for Elijah given by Obadiah the prophet (3–6)—despite some initial resistance (7–15)—Elijah confronts Ahab (16). Ahab accuses Elijah of terrorizing Israel, and Elijah blames the matter on Ahab's sanction of Baal-worship (17–18). Elijah then challenges Ahab, and his 450 prophets of Baal, to a confrontation on Mount Carmel (19). Ahab accepts the challenge, and gathers the people and Baal prophets on Mount Carmel (v. 20; the beginning of the *Haftarah* according to Ḥabad and Sephardic custom). Elijah pleads that the people should put an end to their ambivalence about Divine worship and Baal-worship, but they do not respond (21).

A "showdown" between the 450 prophets of Baal against the lone prophet Elijah then begins. The terms, suggested by Elijah, are agreed upon: each side will sacrifice a bull and place it on a fireless altar; the prophets of Baal will appeal to their god, and Elijah to his God, to "answer with fire" (22–24).

The prophets go first, but their sustained efforts into the afternoon bring no results (28–29). Elijah then builds his altar from twelve stones, representing the tribes of Israel, and he douses it with water to magnify the impending miracle (30–35). *"Answer me, O God!"* he cries, and *"the fire of God came down"* (38). Stunned by what they had just witnessed, the people once again proclaim their allegiance to God (38–39).

Ashkenazic communities begin here. *Ḥabad* and *Sephardic* communities begin on page 1339.

18 ¹ It was after many days, God's word came to Elijah in the third year of the drought, "Go and appear before Ahab, and I will send rain upon the earth."

² Elijah went to appear before Ahab while the famine was severe in Samaria.

³ Ahab summoned Obadiah, who was in charge of the king's house. Obadiah was very God-fearing. ⁴ For, when Jezebel wanted to kill God's prophets, Obadiah took a hundred prophets, hid fifty in a cave and fifty in another, and supplied them with food and drink. ⁵ Ahab told Obadiah, "Go through the land to all the water sources and the streams; perhaps we can find some grass to

יח 1 וַיְהִי יָמִים רַבִּים וּדְבַר־יְהֹוָה הָיָה אֶל־אֵלִיָּהוּ בַּשָּׁנָה הַשְּׁלִישִׁית לֵאמֹר לֵךְ הֵרָאֵה אֶל־אַחְאָב וְאֶתְּנָה מָטָר עַל־פְּנֵי הָאֲדָמָה: 2 וַיֵּלֶךְ אֵלִיָּהוּ לְהֵרָאוֹת אֶל־אַחְאָב וְהָרָעָב חָזָק בְּשֹׁמְרוֹן: 3 וַיִּקְרָא אַחְאָב אֶל־עֹבַדְיָהוּ אֲשֶׁר עַל־הַבָּיִת וְעֹבַדְיָהוּ הָיָה יָרֵא אֶת־יְהֹוָה מְאֹד: 4 וַיְהִי בְּהַכְרִית אִיזֶבֶל אֵת נְבִיאֵי יְהֹוָה וַיִּקַּח עֹבַדְיָהוּ מֵאָה נְבִיאִים וַיַּחְבִּיאֵם חֲמִשִּׁים אִישׁ בַּמְּעָרָה וְכִלְכְּלָם לֶחֶם וָמָיִם: 5 וַיֹּאמֶר אַחְאָב אֶל־עֹבַדְיָהוּ לֵךְ

הפטרת כי תשא

keep the horses and mules alive, so we will not lose the animals." **6** They divided the land between themselves to pass through it. Ahab went by himself in one direction, and Obadiah went by himself in the other.

7 Obadiah was going on his way, and he saw Elijah coming to greet him. He prostrated himself and said: "Is that you, my master Elijah?"

8 "It's me," he said. "Go and tell your master Ahab that Elijah is here."

9 "In what way have I sinned," Obadiah said, "that you want to deliver your servant to Ahab's hand, so that he will kill me? **10** I swear as God, your God, lives, there is no nation or kingdom where my master did not send messengers there to look for you. When they said, 'He is not here,' he made that kingdom or that nation swear that they couldn't find you. **11** Now you are saying: 'Go and tell your master Elijah is here'? **12** When I leave you, God's spirit will carry you to a place which I do not know, and when I come and tell Ahab that you are here and then he doesn't find you, he will kill me! Your servant has been a God-fearing man since my childhood. **13** Has my master not been told what I did when Jezebel wanted to kill God's prophets? I hid one hundred of God's prophets, fifty in a cave and fifty in another, and I supplied them with food and drink. **14** And now you say: 'Go, tell your master: "Elijah is here!"'; he'll kill me and there will be nobody to protect the prophets!"

15 Elijah said, "I swear by the life of the God of Hosts, before whom I stand, I will appear before him today!"

16 Obadiah went to greet Ahab and told him what had happened, and Ahab went to greet Elijah. **17** When Ahab saw Elijah, Ahab said to him, "Is that you, terrorist of Israel, who withheld the rain from them?"

18 He said, "It is not I who have terrorized Israel, but rather you and your father's *house*, by abandoning God's commandments and following after the deities of Baal.

19 "Now, if you want rain, send messengers and summon all Israel to me at Mount Carmel, along with the four hundred and fifty prophets of Baal and the four hundred prophets of the Asherah who eat at Jezebel's table.

בָּאָ֗רֶץ אֶל־כָּל־מַעְיְנֵ֤י הַמַּ֨יִם֙ וְאֶ֣ל כָּל־הַנְּחָלִ֔ים אוּלַ֣י ׀ נִמְצָ֤א חָצִיר֙ וּנְחַיֶּ֣ה ס֣וּס וָפֶ֔רֶד וְל֥וֹא נַכְרִ֖ית מֵהַבְּהֵמָֽה׃ 6 וַיְחַלְּק֥וּ לָהֶ֛ם אֶת־הָאָ֖רֶץ לַֽעֲבָר־בָּ֑הּ אַחְאָ֞ב הָלַ֨ךְ בְּדֶ֤רֶךְ אֶחָד֙ לְבַדּ֔וֹ וְעֹֽבַדְיָ֛הוּ הָלַ֥ךְ בְּדֶרֶךְ־אֶחָ֖ד לְבַדּֽוֹ׃ 7 וַיְהִ֤י עֹֽבַדְיָ֨הוּ֙ בַּדֶּ֔רֶךְ וְהִנֵּ֥ה אֵלִיָּ֖הוּ לִקְרָאת֑וֹ וַיַּכִּרֵ֨הוּ֙ וַיִּפֹּ֣ל עַל־פָּנָ֔יו וַיֹּ֕אמֶר הַאַתָּ֥ה זֶ֖ה אֲדֹנִ֥י אֵלִיָּֽהוּ׃ 8 וַיֹּ֥אמֶר ל֖וֹ אָ֑נִי לֵ֥ךְ אֱמֹ֛ר לַֽאדֹנֶ֖יךָ הִנֵּ֥ה אֵלִיָּֽהוּ׃ 9 וַיֹּ֖אמֶר מֶ֣ה חָטָ֑אתִי כִּֽי־אַתָּ֞ה נֹתֵ֧ן אֶת־עַבְדְּךָ֛ בְּיַד־אַחְאָ֖ב לַֽהֲמִיתֵֽנִי׃ 10 חַ֣י ׀ יְהֹוָ֣ה אֱלֹהֶ֗יךָ אִם־יֶשׁ־גּ֤וֹי וּמַמְלָכָה֙ אֲשֶׁ֨ר לֹֽא־שָׁלַ֜ח אֲדֹנִ֥י שָׁ֨ם לְבַקֶּשְׁךָ֮ וְאָמְר֣וּ אָ֑יִן וְהִשְׁבִּ֤יעַ אֶת־הַמַּמְלָכָה֙ וְאֶת־הַגּ֔וֹי כִּ֖י לֹ֥א יִמְצָאֶֽכָּה׃ 11 וְעַתָּ֖ה אַתָּ֣ה אֹמֵ֑ר לֵ֛ךְ אֱמֹ֥ר לַֽאדֹנֶ֖יךָ הִנֵּ֥ה אֵלִיָּֽהוּ׃ 12 וְהָיָ֞ה אֲנִ֣י ׀ אֵלֵ֣ךְ מֵֽאִתָּ֗ךְ וְר֣וּחַ יְהֹוָ֣ה ׀ יִֽשָּׂאֲךָ֘ עַ֣ל אֲשֶׁ֣ר לֹֽא־אֵדָע֒ וּבָ֨אתִי לְהַגִּ֧יד לְאַחְאָ֛ב וְלֹ֥א יִמְצָֽאֲךָ֖ וַֽהֲרָגָ֑נִי וְעַבְדְּךָ֛ יָרֵ֥א אֶת־יְהֹוָ֖ה מִנְּעֻרָֽי׃ 13 הֲלֹֽא־הֻגַּ֤ד לַֽאדֹנִי֙ אֵ֣ת אֲשֶׁר־עָשִׂ֔יתִי בַּֽהֲרֹ֣ג אִיזֶ֔בֶל אֵ֖ת נְבִיאֵ֣י יְהֹוָ֑ה וָֽאַחְבִּא֩ מִנְּבִיאֵ֨י יְהֹוָ֜ה מֵ֣אָה אִ֗ישׁ חֲמִשִּׁ֨ים חֲמִשִּׁ֥ים אִישׁ֙ בַּמְּעָרָ֔ה וָֽאֲכַלְכְּלֵ֖ם לֶ֥חֶם וָמָֽיִם׃ 14 וְעַתָּה֙ אַתָּ֣ה אֹמֵ֔ר לֵ֛ךְ אֱמֹ֥ר לַֽאדֹנֶ֖יךָ הִנֵּ֥ה אֵלִיָּ֖הוּ וַֽהֲרָגָֽנִי׃ 15 וַיֹּ֨אמֶר֙ אֵֽלִיָּ֔הוּ חַ֚י יְהֹוָ֣ה צְבָא֔וֹת אֲשֶׁ֥ר עָמַ֖דְתִּי לְפָנָ֑יו כִּ֥י הַיּ֖וֹם אֵרָאֶ֥ה אֵלָֽיו׃ 16 וַיֵּ֧לֶךְ עֹֽבַדְיָ֛הוּ לִקְרַ֥את אַחְאָ֖ב וַיַּגֶּד־ל֑וֹ וַיֵּ֥לֶךְ אַחְאָ֖ב לִקְרַ֥את אֵלִיָּֽהוּ׃ 17 וַיְהִ֛י כִּרְא֥וֹת אַחְאָ֖ב אֶת־אֵלִיָּ֑הוּ וַיֹּ֤אמֶר אַחְאָב֙ אֵלָ֔יו הַאַתָּ֥ה זֶ֖ה עֹכֵ֥ר יִשְׂרָאֵֽל׃ 18 וַיֹּ֗אמֶר לֹ֤א עָכַ֨רְתִּי֙ אֶת־יִשְׂרָאֵ֔ל כִּ֥י אִם־אַתָּ֖ה וּבֵ֣ית אָבִ֑יךָ בַּֽעֲזׇבְכֶם֙ אֶת־מִצְוֺ֣ת יְהֹוָ֔ה וַתֵּ֖לֶךְ אַֽחֲרֵ֥י הַבְּעָלִֽים׃ 19 וְעַתָּ֗ה שְׁלַ֨ח קְבֹ֥ץ אֵלַ֛י אֶת־כׇּל־יִשְׂרָאֵ֖ל אֶל־הַ֣ר הַכַּרְמֶ֑ל וְאֶת־נְבִיאֵ֨י הַבַּ֜עַל אַרְבַּ֧ע מֵא֣וֹת וַֽחֲמִשִּׁ֗ים וּנְבִיאֵ֤י הָֽאֲשֵׁרָה֙ אַרְבַּ֣ע מֵא֔וֹת אֹֽכְלֵ֖י שֻׁלְחַ֥ן אִיזָֽבֶל׃

haftarat ki tissa'

***Ḥabad* and *Sephardic* communities begin here. Others continue:**

²⁰ Ahab sent an order to all the people of Israel, and he gathered the prophets of Baal together in Mount Carmel.

²¹ Elijah approached all the people and said, "How long will you waver between two opinions? If God is the God who rules the world, follow Him. If it is Baal, then follow him." The people did not answer him anything.

²² Elijah said to the people, "I am the sole remaining prophet of God, but Baal's prophets are four hundred and fifty men. ²³ Let them give us two bulls, and let them choose one of the bulls for themselves, and cut it into pieces, and lay it on wood, but put no fire to it. I will prepare the other bull and lay it on wood, but put no fire to it. ²⁴ You call on the name of your gods, and I will call on the name of God. The God who answers by fire, He is God."

All the people answered and said, "The matter is good."

²⁵ Elijah said to the prophets of Baal, "Choose one bull for yourselves and prepare it first, for you are the majority. Call upon the names of your gods, but put no fire to it."

²⁶ They took the bull which was handed to them by Elijah, and they prepared it. They called on the name of Baal from morning until noon, saying, "O Baal, hear us!" But there was no voice, nor any who answered. They jumped on the altar which was made in worship.

²⁷ It was at noon that Elijah ridiculed them. He said, "Cry louder! For you say he is a god. Maybe he is talking to others, or deep in thought, or on a journey? Or maybe he is sleeping and will be awakened by your cries."

²⁸ They cried aloud, and scored themselves with knives and lances, as was their custom, until blood gushed out upon them. ²⁹ Then, when midday was past, they pretended to prophesy until the time of the offering of the afternoon sacrifice. But there was no sound, no one answered for there was no listener.

³⁰ Elijah said to all the people, "Come near to me so you can see that no trickery is taking place," and all the people came near to him.

He repaired the altar of God that was broken.

20 וַיִּשְׁלַ֥ח אַחְאָ֖ב בְּכׇל־בְּנֵ֣י יִשְׂרָאֵ֑ל וַיִּקְבֹּ֥ץ אֶת־הַנְּבִיאִ֖ים אֶל־הַ֥ר הַכַּרְמֶֽל׃ 21 וַיִּגַּ֨שׁ אֵלִיָּ֜הוּ אֶל־כׇּל־הָעָ֗ם וַיֹּ֙אמֶר֙ עַד־מָתַ֞י אַתֶּ֣ם פֹּסְחִים֮ עַל־שְׁתֵּ֣י הַסְּעִפִּים֒ אִם־יְהֹוָ֤ה הָֽאֱלֹהִים֙ לְכ֣וּ אַחֲרָ֔יו וְאִם־הַבַּ֖עַל לְכ֣וּ אַחֲרָ֑יו וְלֹא־עָנ֥וּ הָעָ֛ם אֹת֖וֹ דָּבָֽר׃ 22 וַיֹּ֤אמֶר אֵלִיָּ֙הוּ֙ אֶל־הָעָ֔ם אֲנִ֞י נוֹתַ֧רְתִּי נָבִ֛יא לַיהֹוָ֖ה לְבַדִּ֑י וּנְבִיאֵ֣י הַבַּ֔עַל אַרְבַּע־מֵא֥וֹת וַחֲמִשִּׁ֖ים אִֽישׁ׃ 23 וְיִתְּנוּ־לָ֜נוּ שְׁנַ֣יִם פָּרִ֗ים וְיִבְחֲר֣וּ לָהֶם֩ הַפָּ֨ר הָאֶחָ֜ד וִֽינַתְּחֻ֗הוּ וְיָשִׂ֙ימוּ֙ עַל־הָ֣עֵצִ֔ים וְאֵ֖שׁ לֹ֣א יָשִׂ֑ימוּ וַאֲנִ֞י אֶעֱשֶׂ֣ה ׀ אֶת־הַפָּ֣ר הָאֶחָ֗ד וְנָֽתַתִּי֙ עַל־הָ֣עֵצִ֔ים וְאֵ֖שׁ לֹ֥א אָשִֽׂים׃ 24 וּקְרָאתֶ֞ם בְּשֵׁ֣ם אֱלֹהֵיכֶ֗ם וַֽאֲנִי֙ אֶקְרָ֣א בְשֵׁם־יְהֹוָ֔ה וְהָיָ֧ה הָאֱלֹהִ֛ים אֲשֶׁר־יַעֲנֶ֥ה בָאֵ֖שׁ ה֣וּא הָאֱלֹהִ֑ים וַיַּ֧עַן כׇּל־הָעָ֛ם וַיֹּאמְר֖וּ ט֥וֹב הַדָּבָֽר׃ 25 וַיֹּ֨אמֶר אֵלִיָּ֜הוּ לִנְבִיאֵ֣י הַבַּ֗עַל בַּחֲר֨וּ לָכֶ֜ם הַפָּ֤ר הָֽאֶחָד֙ וַעֲשׂ֣וּ רִאשֹׁנָ֔ה כִּ֥י אַתֶּ֖ם הָרַבִּ֑ים וְקִרְאוּ֙ בְּשֵׁ֣ם אֱלֹהֵיכֶ֔ם וְאֵ֖שׁ לֹ֥א תָשִֽׂימוּ׃ 26 וַ֠יִּקְח֠וּ אֶת־הַפָּ֨ר אֲשֶׁר־נָתַ֣ן לָהֶם֮ וַֽיַּעֲשׂוּ֒ וַיִּקְרְא֣וּ בְשֵׁם־הַ֠בַּ֠עַל מֵהַבֹּ֨קֶר וְעַד־הַצׇּהֳרַ֤יִם לֵאמֹר֙ הַבַּ֣עַל עֲנֵ֔נוּ וְאֵ֥ין ק֖וֹל וְאֵ֣ין עֹנֶ֑ה וַֽיְפַסְּח֔וּ עַל־הַמִּזְבֵּ֖חַ אֲשֶׁ֥ר עָשָֽׂה׃ 27 וַיְהִ֣י בַֽצׇּהֳרַ֗יִם וַיְהַתֵּ֣ל בָּהֶ֤ם אֵלִיָּ֙הוּ֙ וַיֹּ֙אמֶר֙ קִרְא֤וּ בְקוֹל־גָּדוֹל֙ כִּֽי־אֱלֹהִ֣ים ה֔וּא כִּ֣י שִׂ֧יחַ וְכִי־שִׂ֛יג ל֖וֹ וְכִי־דֶ֣רֶךְ ל֑וֹ אוּלַ֛י יָשֵׁ֥ן ה֖וּא וְיִקָֽץ׃ 28 וַֽיִּקְרְאוּ֙ בְּק֣וֹל גָּד֔וֹל וַיִּתְגֹּֽדְדוּ֙ כְּמִשְׁפָּטָ֔ם בַּחֲרָב֖וֹת וּבָרְמָחִ֑ים עַד־שְׁפׇךְ־דָּ֖ם עֲלֵיהֶֽם׃ 29 וַֽיְהִי֙ כַּעֲבֹ֣ר הַֽצׇּהֳרַ֔יִם וַיִּֽתְנַבְּא֔וּ עַ֖ד לַעֲל֣וֹת הַמִּנְחָ֑ה וְאֵֽין־ק֥וֹל וְאֵין־עֹנֶ֖ה וְאֵ֥ין קָֽשֶׁב׃ 30 וַיֹּ֨אמֶר אֵלִיָּ֜הוּ לְכׇל־הָעָ֗ם גְּשׁ֣וּ אֵלַי֒ וַיִּגְּשׁ֥וּ כׇל־הָעָ֖ם אֵלָ֑יו וַיְרַפֵּ֛א אֶת־מִזְבַּ֥ח יְהֹוָ֖ה הֶהָרֽוּס׃

הפטרת ויקהל

³¹ וַיִּקַּח אֵלִיָּהוּ שְׁתֵּים עֶשְׂרֵה אֲבָנִים כְּמִסְפַּר שִׁבְטֵי בְנֵי־יַעֲקֹב אֲשֶׁר הָיָה דְבַר־יְהֹוָה אֵלָיו לֵאמֹר יִשְׂרָאֵל יִהְיֶה שְׁמֶךָ: ³² וַיִּבְנֶה אֶת־הָאֲבָנִים מִזְבֵּחַ בְּשֵׁם יְהֹוָה וַיַּעַשׂ תְּעָלָה כְּבֵית סָאתַיִם זֶרַע סָבִיב לַמִּזְבֵּחַ: ³³ וַיַּעֲרֹךְ אֶת־הָעֵצִים וַיְנַתַּח אֶת־הַפָּר וַיָּשֶׂם עַל־הָעֵצִים: ³⁴ וַיֹּאמֶר מִלְאוּ אַרְבָּעָה כַדִּים מַיִם וְיִצְקוּ עַל־הָעֹלָה וְעַל־הָעֵצִים וַיֹּאמֶר שְׁנוּ וַיִּשְׁנוּ וַיֹּאמֶר שַׁלֵּשׁוּ וַיְשַׁלֵּשׁוּ: ³⁵ וַיֵּלְכוּ הַמַּיִם סָבִיב לַמִּזְבֵּחַ וְגַם אֶת־הַתְּעָלָה מִלֵּא־מָיִם: ³⁶ וַיְהִי | בַּעֲלוֹת הַמִּנְחָה וַיִּגַּשׁ אֵלִיָּהוּ הַנָּבִיא וַיֹּאמַר יְהֹוָה אֱלֹהֵי אַבְרָהָם יִצְחָק וְיִשְׂרָאֵל הַיּוֹם יִוָּדַע כִּי־אַתָּה אֱלֹהִים בְּיִשְׂרָאֵל וַאֲנִי עַבְדֶּךָ [ובדברך כ׳] וּבִדְבָרְךָ עָשִׂיתִי אֵת כָּל־הַדְּבָרִים הָאֵלֶּה: ³⁷ עֲנֵנִי יְהֹוָה עֲנֵנִי וְיֵדְעוּ הָעָם הַזֶּה כִּי־אַתָּה יְהֹוָה הָאֱלֹהִים וְאַתָּה הֲסִבֹּתָ אֶת־לִבָּם אֲחֹרַנִּית: ³⁸ וַתִּפֹּל אֵשׁ־יְהֹוָה וַתֹּאכַל אֶת־הָעֹלָה וְאֶת־הָעֵצִים וְאֶת־הָאֲבָנִים וְאֶת־הֶעָפָר וְאֶת־הַמַּיִם אֲשֶׁר־בַּתְּעָלָה לִחֵכָה: ³⁹ וַיַּרְא כָּל־הָעָם וַיִּפְּלוּ עַל־פְּנֵיהֶם וַיֹּאמְרוּ יְהֹוָה הוּא הָאֱלֹהִים יְהֹוָה הוּא הָאֱלֹהִים:

³¹ Elijah took twelve stones, according to the number of the tribes of the sons of Jacob, to whom the word of God came, saying, "Israel shall be your name." ³² With the stones, he built an altar in the name of God. He made a ditch around the altar, large enough to contain two *seah* of seed to hold the water which he poured, to magnify the miracle. ³³ He arranged the wood, cut the bull in pieces, and laid it on the wood. ³⁴ He said, "Fill four jars with water, and pour it on the burnt-offering, and on the wood." He said, "Do it a second time," and they did it the second time. He said, "Do it a third time," and they did it the third time. ³⁵ The water ran around the altar. He also filled the ditch with water.

³⁶ Then, at the time of the offering of the afternoon sacrifice, Elijah the prophet approached God in prayer and said, "God! God of Abraham, Isaac, and of Israel, let it be known this day that You are God whose Presence dwells in Israel, and that I am Your servant, and that I have done all these things by Your Word. ³⁷ Answer me, O God, answer me with fire, so that this people may know that You are God, Almighty God, and so You will have turned their hearts back again to You."

³⁸ Then the fire of God came down, and consumed the offering, and the wood pile, and the stones, and the dust, and licked up the water that was in the ditch.

³⁹ When all the people saw it, they fell upon their faces, and they said, "God is the Almighty God! God is the Almighty God!"

haftarat va-yakhel

ASHKENAZIM—I KINGS 7:40–50
SEPHARDIM AND HABAD—I KINGS 7:13–26

SYNOPSIS: This *Haftarah* describes work done by Hiram the craftsman for Solomon's Temple, similar to the work of Bezalel which was done on Moses' Tabernacle, as described in the *Parashah*.

The *Haftarah* opens with a brief description of Hiram, his lineage, and his credentials (7:13–14). We then read extensive details about two major aspects of his work in constructing the Temple: a) the two pillars of copper, named "Jachin" and "Boaz," which stood at the entrance to the sanctuary's hall; b) A giant copper water tank (the "Sea of Solomon"), and its base of twelve cast copper oxen (23–26).

haftarat va-yakhel

***Ḥabad* and *Sephardic* communities read the following:**
[*Ashkenazic* communities read the *Haftarah* for *Ḥanukkah* (second *Shabbat*) on page 1423.]

7

13 King Solomon sent and brought Hiram the craftsman from Tyre. **14** He was the son of a widow of the tribe of Naphtali, and his father was a resident of Tyre, a coppersmith. Hiram was filled with wisdom and understanding, and skilled in doing any work in copper. He came to King Solomon and did all his work.

15 He sculptured molds for two pillars of copper. Each were eighteen cubits high, and twelve cubits in circumference.

16 He made two spheres cast out of copper, to put on the tops of the pillars. The height of one sphere was five cubits, including a two-cubit base, and the height of the second sphere was five cubits, including a two-cubit base.

17 He made nets resembling interwoven branches, and wreaths of chainwork, for the spheres which were upon the top of the pillars—seven for one sphere, and seven for the second sphere.

18 Having completed the molds he made the pillars.

He made two rows of copper pomegranates tied together around the nets, to cover the sphere that was on the top of the first pillar. He did likewise for the second sphere.

19 The spheres that were on the top of the pillars were made with a rose-like design on the top four cubits.

20 The spheres were not merely on the edge of the two pillars, but they also covered the hollow in the middle of the pillars, behind the net.

There were a total of two hundred pomegranates in two rows all around, and so too on the second sphere.

21 He erected the pillars in the entrance hall to the sanctuary. He erected the right pillar, and called its name Jachin. He erected the left pillar, and called its name Boaz. **22** After the pillars were erected the rose-like design was affixed to the top of the pillars. The crafting of the pillars was then finished.

23 He made a tank of cast metal, for the priests to immerse in, ten cubits from rim to rim. It was circular all around, and its height was five cubits.

ז 13 וַיִּשְׁלַח הַמֶּלֶךְ שְׁלֹמֹה וַיִּקַּח אֶת־חִירָם מִצֹּר: 14 בֶּן־אִשָּׁה אַלְמָנָה הוּא מִמַּטֵּה נַפְתָּלִי וְאָבִיו אִישׁ־צֹרִי חֹרֵשׁ נְחֹשֶׁת וַיִּמָּלֵא אֶת־הַחָכְמָה וְאֶת־הַתְּבוּנָה וְאֶת־הַדַּעַת לַעֲשׂוֹת כָּל־מְלָאכָה בַּנְּחֹשֶׁת וַיָּבוֹא אֶל־הַמֶּלֶךְ שְׁלֹמֹה וַיַּעַשׂ אֶת־כָּל־מְלַאכְתּוֹ: 15 וַיָּצַר אֶת־שְׁנֵי הָעַמּוּדִים נְחֹשֶׁת שְׁמֹנֶה עֶשְׂרֵה אַמָּה קוֹמַת הָעַמּוּד הָאֶחָד וְחוּט שְׁתֵּים־עֶשְׂרֵה אַמָּה יָסֹב אֶת־הָעַמּוּד הַשֵּׁנִי: 16 וּשְׁתֵּי כֹתָרֹת עָשָׂה לָתֵת עַל־רָאשֵׁי הָעַמּוּדִים מֻצַק נְחֹשֶׁת חָמֵשׁ אַמּוֹת קוֹמַת הַכֹּתֶרֶת הָאֶחָת וְחָמֵשׁ אַמּוֹת קוֹמַת הַכֹּתֶרֶת הַשֵּׁנִית: 17 שְׂבָכִים מַעֲשֵׂה שְׂבָכָה גְּדִלִים מַעֲשֵׂה שַׁרְשְׁרוֹת לַכֹּתָרֹת אֲשֶׁר עַל־רֹאשׁ הָעַמּוּדִים שִׁבְעָה לַכֹּתֶרֶת הָאֶחָת וְשִׁבְעָה לַכֹּתֶרֶת הַשֵּׁנִית: 18 וַיַּעַשׂ אֶת־הָעַמּוּדִים וּשְׁנֵי טוּרִים סָבִיב עַל־הַשְּׂבָכָה הָאֶחָת לְכַסּוֹת אֶת־הַכֹּתָרֹת אֲשֶׁר עַל־רֹאשׁ הָרִמֹּנִים וְכֵן עָשָׂה לַכֹּתֶרֶת הַשֵּׁנִית: 19 וְכֹתָרֹת אֲשֶׁר עַל־רֹאשׁ הָעַמּוּדִים מַעֲשֵׂה שׁוּשַׁן בָּאוּלָם אַרְבַּע אַמּוֹת: 20 וְכֹתָרֹת עַל־שְׁנֵי הָעַמּוּדִים גַּם־מִמַּעַל מִלְּעֻמַּת הַבֶּטֶן אֲשֶׁר לְעֵבֶר [שבכה כ'] הַשְּׂבָכָה וְהָרִמּוֹנִים מָאתַיִם טֻרִים סָבִיב עַל הַכֹּתֶרֶת הַשֵּׁנִית: 21 וַיָּקֶם אֶת־הָעַמֻּדִים לְאֻלָם הַהֵיכָל וַיָּקֶם אֶת־הָעַמּוּד הַיְמָנִי וַיִּקְרָא אֶת־שְׁמוֹ יָכִין וַיָּקֶם אֶת־הָעַמּוּד הַשְּׂמָאלִי וַיִּקְרָא אֶת־שְׁמוֹ בֹּעַז: 22 וְעַל רֹאשׁ הָעַמּוּדִים מַעֲשֵׂה שׁוֹשָׁן וַתִּתֹּם מְלֶאכֶת הָעַמּוּדִים: 23 וַיַּעַשׂ אֶת־הַיָּם מוּצָק עֶשֶׂר בָּאַמָּה מִשְּׂפָתוֹ עַד־שְׂפָתוֹ עָגֹל | סָבִיב וְחָמֵשׁ בָּאַמָּה קוֹמָתוֹ [וקוה כ'] וְקָו

הפטרת פקודי

שְׁלֹשִׁים בָּאַמָּה יָסֹב אֹתוֹ סָבִיב: 24 וּפְקָעִים מִתַּחַת לִשְׂפָתוֹ ׀ סָבִיב סֹבְבִים אֹתוֹ עֶשֶׂר בָּאַמָּה מַקִּפִים אֶת־הַיָּם סָבִיב שְׁנֵי טוּרִים הַפְּקָעִים יְצֻקִים בִּיצֻקָתוֹ: 25 עֹמֵד עַל־שְׁנֵי עָשָׂר בָּקָר שְׁלֹשָׁה פֹנִים ׀ צָפוֹנָה וּשְׁלֹשָׁה פֹנִים ׀ יָמָּה וּשְׁלֹשָׁה ׀ פֹּנִים נֶגְבָּה וּשְׁלֹשָׁה פֹּנִים מִזְרָחָה וְהַיָּם עֲלֵיהֶם מִלְמָעְלָה וְכָל־אֲחֹרֵיהֶם בָּיְתָה: 26 וְעָבְיוֹ טֶפַח וּשְׂפָתוֹ כְּמַעֲשֵׂה שְׂפַת־כּוֹס פֶּרַח שׁוֹשָׁן אַלְפַּיִם בַּת יָכִיל:

It was thirty cubits in circumference. ²⁴ Under its rim all around there were egg-shapes engraved with the face of an ox surrounding it, ten in a cubit, surrounding the tank around. The egg-shapes were cast in two rows. They were cast together with the tank when it was cast.

²⁵ The tank stood upon twelve copper oxen: three looking toward the north, three looking toward the west, three looking toward the south, and three looking toward the east. The pool was set above upon them, and all their hindparts faced inward.

²⁶ The walls and rim of the tank were a handbreadth thick, but its rim was thin, like the rim of a cup, decorated with rose-flower designs. It contained two thousand *bat* measures.

haftarat pekudei

SEPHARDIM—I KINGS 7:40–50
ASHKENAZIM and ḤABAD—I KINGS 7:51 – 8:21

SYNOPSIS: This *Haftarah* describes the completion of the First Temple, similar to the completion of the Tabernacle described in the *Parashah*.

The *Haftarah* begins with an announcement that King Solomon's Temple was complete and that the items which had been consecrated by King David were transferred to the Temple treasury (7:51). Upon Solomon's instructions to the elders, the ark and the holy vessels are then transferred from the City of David, amid a glorious procession, and installed in the Temple (8:1-9). All this meets Divine approval when, as the priests are departing the Holy of Holies after installing the ark, the Divine Presence manifests itself in the form of a cloud (10–11), a sign which is instantly recognized by Solomon (12–13). The king then addresses the crowd, declaring that God has fulfilled His promise made to his father David, to make a permanent "house" for God (14–21).

Ḥabad and *Ashkenazic* communities read the following.

[*Sephardic* communities read the *Haftarah* for Ḥanukkah (second *Shabbat*) on page 1423.]

ז ⁵¹ All the work that King Solomon made for the House of God was finished. Solomon brought in the things which David his father had dedicated. He put the silver, and the gold, and the utensils in the treasuries of the House of God.

ח ¹ Then Solomon assembled the elders of Israel—and all the heads of the tribes who are the chiefs of the ancestral houses of the people of Israel—before King Solomon in Jerusalem, to bring

ז 51 וַתִּשְׁלַם כָּל־הַמְּלָאכָה אֲשֶׁר עָשָׂה הַמֶּלֶךְ שְׁלֹמֹה בֵּית יְהֹוָה וַיָּבֵא שְׁלֹמֹה אֶת־קָדְשֵׁי ׀ דָּוִד אָבִיו אֶת־הַכֶּסֶף וְאֶת־הַזָּהָב וְאֶת־הַכֵּלִים נָתַן בְּאֹצְרוֹת בֵּית יְהֹוָה:

ח 1 אָז יַקְהֵל שְׁלֹמֹה אֶת־זִקְנֵי יִשְׂרָאֵל אֶת־כָּל־רָאשֵׁי הַמַּטּוֹת נְשִׂיאֵי הָאָבוֹת

haftarat pekudei

up the Ark of the Covenant of God from the city of David, which is Zion.

² All the men of Israel assembled before King Solomon at the feast in the month of Ethanim, which is the seventh month. ³ All the elders of Israel came, and the priests took up the ark. ⁴ They brought up the Ark of God, the Tent of Meeting, and all the holy utensils that were in the Tent. The priests and the Levites brought them up.

⁵ King Solomon, and all the congregation of Israel who were assembled before him, were with him before the ark, sacrificing sheep and oxen in such abundance that they could not be counted or numbered.

⁶ The priests brought in the Ark of the Covenant of God to its place, to the Sanctuary of the House, to the most holy place, under the wings of the cherubim. ⁷ For the cherubim spread out their two wings over the place of the ark, and the cherubim covered the ark and its poles above.

⁸ The poles extended so far, that the ends of the poles were seen protruding into the curtain from the sanctuary facing the inner sanctuary, but the poles themselves were not seen outside. They remain there to this day. ⁹ There was nothing in the ark except the two tablets of stone, which Moses put there at Horeb, where God made a covenant with the people of Israel, when they came out of the land of Egypt.

¹⁰ Then, when the priests came out of the holy place, having installed the ark, the smoky cloud filled the House of God, ¹¹ the priests could not stand to perform their service because of the cloud, for the glory of God had filled the House of God.

¹² Then when he saw the cloud, Solomon said, "I know that the Divine Presence is here because God said that He would dwell in the thick cloud. ¹³ Since the Divine Presence has descended, I am sure that I have indeed built You a House to dwell in, a settled place for You to abide in forever."

¹⁴ The king turned his face around towards the people and blessed all the congregation of Israel. All the congregation of Israel stood. ¹⁵ He said, "Blessed be God, Almighty God of Israel, who spoke with His mouth to David my father, and has fulfilled it with His hand, saying, ¹⁶ 'Since the day when I brought My people Israel out of Egypt, I chose no city from

לִבְנֵי יִשְׂרָאֵל אֶל־הַמֶּלֶךְ שְׁלֹמֹה יְרוּשָׁלִַם לְהַעֲלוֹת אֶת־אֲרוֹן בְּרִית־יְהֹוָה מֵעִיר דָּוִד הִיא צִיּוֹן: 2 וַיִּקָּהֲלוּ אֶל־הַמֶּלֶךְ שְׁלֹמֹה כָּל־אִישׁ יִשְׂרָאֵל בְּיֶרַח הָאֵתָנִים בֶּחָג הוּא הַחֹדֶשׁ הַשְּׁבִיעִי: 3 וַיָּבֹאוּ כֹּל זִקְנֵי יִשְׂרָאֵל וַיִּשְׂאוּ הַכֹּהֲנִים אֶת־הָאָרוֹן: 4 וַיַּעֲלוּ אֶת־אֲרוֹן יְהֹוָה וְאֶת־אֹהֶל מוֹעֵד וְאֶת־כָּל־כְּלֵי הַקֹּדֶשׁ אֲשֶׁר בָּאֹהֶל וַיַּעֲלוּ אֹתָם הַכֹּהֲנִים וְהַלְוִיִּם: 5 וְהַמֶּלֶךְ שְׁלֹמֹה וְכָל־עֲדַת יִשְׂרָאֵל הַנּוֹעָדִים עָלָיו אִתּוֹ לִפְנֵי הָאָרוֹן מְזַבְּחִים צֹאן וּבָקָר אֲשֶׁר לֹא־יִסָּפְרוּ וְלֹא יִמָּנוּ מֵרֹב: 6 וַיָּבִאוּ הַכֹּהֲנִים אֶת־אֲרוֹן בְּרִית־יְהֹוָה אֶל־מְקוֹמוֹ אֶל־דְּבִיר הַבַּיִת אֶל־קֹדֶשׁ הַקֳּדָשִׁים אֶל־תַּחַת כַּנְפֵי הַכְּרוּבִים: 7 כִּי הַכְּרוּבִים פֹּרְשִׂים כְּנָפַיִם אֶל־מְקוֹם הָאָרוֹן וַיָּסֹכּוּ הַכְּרֻבִים עַל־הָאָרוֹן וְעַל־בַּדָּיו מִלְמָעְלָה: 8 וַיַּאֲרִכוּ הַבַּדִּים וַיֵּרָאוּ רָאשֵׁי הַבַּדִּים מִן־הַקֹּדֶשׁ עַל־פְּנֵי הַדְּבִיר וְלֹא יֵרָאוּ הַחוּצָה וַיִּהְיוּ שָׁם עַד הַיּוֹם הַזֶּה: 9 אֵין בָּאָרוֹן רַק שְׁנֵי לֻחוֹת הָאֲבָנִים אֲשֶׁר הִנִּחַ שָׁם מֹשֶׁה בְּחֹרֵב אֲשֶׁר כָּרַת יְהֹוָה עִם־בְּנֵי יִשְׂרָאֵל בְּצֵאתָם מֵאֶרֶץ מִצְרָיִם: 10 וַיְהִי בְּצֵאת הַכֹּהֲנִים מִן־הַקֹּדֶשׁ וְהֶעָנָן מָלֵא אֶת־בֵּית יְהֹוָה: 11 וְלֹא־יָכְלוּ הַכֹּהֲנִים לַעֲמֹד לְשָׁרֵת מִפְּנֵי הֶעָנָן כִּי־מָלֵא כְבוֹד־יְהֹוָה אֶת־בֵּית יְהֹוָה: 12 אָז אָמַר שְׁלֹמֹה יְהֹוָה אָמַר לִשְׁכֹּן בָּעֲרָפֶל: 13 בָּנֹה בָנִיתִי בֵּית זְבֻל לָךְ מָכוֹן לְשִׁבְתְּךָ עוֹלָמִים: 14 וַיַּסֵּב הַמֶּלֶךְ אֶת־פָּנָיו וַיְבָרֶךְ אֵת כָּל־קְהַל יִשְׂרָאֵל וְכָל־קְהַל יִשְׂרָאֵל עֹמֵד: 15 וַיֹּאמֶר בָּרוּךְ יְהֹוָה אֱלֹהֵי יִשְׂרָאֵל אֲשֶׁר דִּבֶּר בְּפִיו אֵת דָּוִד אָבִי וּבְיָדוֹ מִלֵּא לֵאמֹר: 16 מִן־הַיּוֹם אֲשֶׁר הוֹצֵאתִי אֶת־עַמִּי אֶת־יִשְׂרָאֵל מִמִּצְרַיִם לֹא־

הפטרת ויקרא

בָּחַרְתִּי בְעִיר מִכֹּל שִׁבְטֵי יִשְׂרָאֵל לִבְנוֹת בַּיִת לִהְיוֹת שְׁמִי שָׁם וָאֶבְחַר בְּדָוִד לִהְיוֹת עַל־עַמִּי יִשְׂרָאֵל: 17 וַיְהִי עִם־לְבַב דָּוִד אָבִי לִבְנוֹת בַּיִת לְשֵׁם יְהֹוָה אֱלֹהֵי יִשְׂרָאֵל: 18 וַיֹּאמֶר יְהֹוָה אֶל־דָּוִד אָבִי יַעַן אֲשֶׁר הָיָה עִם־לְבָבְךָ לִבְנוֹת בַּיִת לִשְׁמִי הֱטִיבֹתָ כִּי הָיָה עִם־לְבָבֶךָ: 19 רַק אַתָּה לֹא תִבְנֶה הַבָּיִת כִּי אִם־בִּנְךָ הַיֹּצֵא מֵחֲלָצֶיךָ הוּא־יִבְנֶה הַבַּיִת לִשְׁמִי: 20 וַיָּקֶם יְהֹוָה אֶת־דְּבָרוֹ אֲשֶׁר דִּבֵּר וָאָקֻם תַּחַת דָּוִד אָבִי וָאֵשֵׁב ׀ עַל־כִּסֵּא יִשְׂרָאֵל כַּאֲשֶׁר דִּבֶּר יְהֹוָה וָאֶבְנֶה הַבַּיִת לְשֵׁם יְהֹוָה אֱלֹהֵי יִשְׂרָאֵל: 21 וָאָשִׂם שָׁם מָקוֹם לָאָרוֹן אֲשֶׁר־שָׁם בְּרִית יְהֹוָה אֲשֶׁר כָּרַת עִם־אֲבֹתֵינוּ בְּהוֹצִיאוֹ אֹתָם מֵאֶרֶץ מִצְרָיִם:

all the tribes of Israel in which to build a House that My name might be in there, but I chose David to be over my people, Israel.'

[17] "It was the intention of David my father to build a House for the sake of God, Almighty God of Israel. [18] God said to David my father, 'Since it was your intention to build a House for My sake, you have done well by so wishing since the preparations will be in your merit. [19] Nevertheless, you shall not build the House, but your son who shall come forth from your loins, he shall build the House for My sake.'

[20] "God has performed His word that He spoke, and I have risen in place of David my father, and I sit on the throne of Israel, as God promised, and I have built a House for the sake of God, Almighty God of Israel. [21] I have set there a place for the ark, where the Covenant of God is, which He made with our fathers, when He brought them out of the land of Egypt."

haftarat va-yikra'

ALL COMMUNITIES—ISAIAH 43:21 – 44:23

SYNOPSIS: Both the *Parashah* and the *Haftarah* speak of sacrificial worship. The *Parashah* introduces a number of basic sacrificial rites, whereas the *Haftarah* criticizes the Jewish people for their abandonment of sacrificial worship.

The *Haftarah* turns to rebuke the Jewish people for their sins and improper worship (43:22–28). Nevertheless, a glimpse of a brighter future is offered, when God will bestow abundant blessings (44:1–5). God declares His own unique greatness (6–7), and the vanity of all other gods (8–11). To reinforce this message, the prophet mocks the absurd notion that man can manufacture his own god, with a satirical description of how various craftsmen construct an idol (9–20). The *Haftarah* concludes with a warning to Israel not to follow after idols, a call for repentance and promises of forgiveness and redemption (21–22).

43

מג 21 עַם־זוּ יָצַרְתִּי לִי תְּהִלָּתִי יְסַפֵּרוּ: 22 וְלֹא־אֹתִי קָרָאתָ יַעֲקֹב כִּי־יָגַעְתָּ בִּי יִשְׂרָאֵל: 23 לֹא־הֵבֵיאתָ לִּי שֵׂה עֹלֹתֶיךָ

[21] I formed this nation for Myself. They will declare My praise.

[22] But you, children of Jacob, did not call upon Me, and rather, you followed other gods. You tired of serving Me, O Israel, and ceased. [23] You did not bring Me sheep for your burnt-offerings nor honor Me with your other sacrifices. I did not burden you with meal-offerings, for only a three-finger fistful is offered on the altar, nor did I weary you tremendously to bring a large amount of frankincense.

haftarat va-yikra'

24 I did not require you to buy herbs with your money to offer on the altar for Me, since it grew in Jerusalem. But you did not satisfy Me with the fat of your sacrifices, because you did not bring any. Instead you burdened Me with your sins and wearied Me with your iniquities.

25 It is I who wiped away your transgressions and I who will wipe them away now—not for your righteousness, but for My sake. I will erase them completely so that I will have no remembrance of your sins. **26** Perhaps I need to be reminded about some favor that I owe you, so remind Me of your merits and let us judge together. Even if you state your case first you will not win.

27 Your first father Adam sinned even though He was formed by My hands, and your spokesmen, the best in each generation, on whom you rely to defend you, also transgressed against Me. **28** Therefore, I will profane your holy nobles. I will give the people of Jacob to utter destruction and Israel to disgrace by their enemies.

44 [1] Now listen, My servant Jacob, Israel whom I have chosen, about the good that is to come! [2] This is what was said by God, your Maker, your Creator, who helped you since birth:

"Fear not, My servant Jacob, the upright people whom I have chosen! [3] Just as I pour water on the thirsty land and liquid on the parched earth, so too I will pour My goodwill on your children and My blessing on your offspring. [4] They will sprout like grass, like willows by streams of water. [5] The righteous among them will say: "I am for God"; the children of the wicked will call themselves by Jacob's name so as not to follow in their fathers' footsteps; the penitents will oblige themselves to return to God as if, 'I am for God' is written by their hand as a binding contract; and the righteous converts will call themselves by the name of Israel."

וּבְזָבֶחֶיךָ לֹא כִבַּדְתָּנִי לֹא הֶעֱבַדְתִּיךָ בְּמִנְחָה וְלֹא הוֹגַעְתִּיךָ בִּלְבוֹנָה: 24 לֹא־קָנִיתָ לִּי בַכֶּסֶף קָנֶה וְחֵלֶב זְבָחֶיךָ לֹא הִרְוִיתָנִי אַךְ הֶעֱבַדְתַּנִי בְּחַטֹּאותֶיךָ הוֹגַעְתַּנִי בַּעֲוֹנֹתֶיךָ: 25 אָנֹכִי אָנֹכִי הוּא מֹחֶה פְשָׁעֶיךָ לְמַעֲנִי וְחַטֹּאתֶיךָ לֹא אֶזְכֹּר: 26 הַזְכִּירֵנִי נִשָּׁפְטָה יָחַד סַפֵּר אַתָּה לְמַעַן תִּצְדָּק: 27 אָבִיךָ הָרִאשׁוֹן חָטָא וּמְלִיצֶיךָ פָּשְׁעוּ בִי: 28 וַאֲחַלֵּל שָׂרֵי קֹדֶשׁ וְאֶתְּנָה לַחֵרֶם יַעֲקֹב וְיִשְׂרָאֵל לְגִדּוּפִים:

מד 1 וְעַתָּה שְׁמַע יַעֲקֹב עַבְדִּי וְיִשְׂרָאֵל בָּחַרְתִּי בוֹ: 2 כֹּה־אָמַר יְהֹוָה עֹשֶׂךָ וְיֹצֶרְךָ מִבֶּטֶן יַעְזְרֶךָּ אַל־תִּירָא עַבְדִּי יַעֲקֹב וִישֻׁרוּן בָּחַרְתִּי בוֹ: 3 כִּי אֶצָּק־מַיִם עַל־צָמֵא וְנֹזְלִים עַל־יַבָּשָׁה אֶצֹּק רוּחִי עַל־זַרְעֶךָ וּבִרְכָתִי עַל־צֶאֱצָאֶיךָ: 4 וְצָמְחוּ בְּבֵין חָצִיר כַּעֲרָבִים עַל־יִבְלֵי־מָיִם: 5 זֶה יֹאמַר לַיהֹוָה אָנִי וְזֶה יִקְרָא בְשֵׁם־יַעֲקֹב וְזֶה יִכְתֹּב יָדוֹ לַיהֹוָה וּבְשֵׁם יִשְׂרָאֵל יְכַנֶּה: 6 כֹּה־אָמַר יְהֹוָה מֶלֶךְ־יִשְׂרָאֵל וְגֹאֲלוֹ יְהֹוָה צְבָאוֹת אֲנִי רִאשׁוֹן וַאֲנִי אַחֲרוֹן וּמִבַּלְעָדַי אֵין אֱלֹהִים: 7 וּמִי־כָמוֹנִי יִקְרָא וְיַגִּידֶהָ וְיַעְרְכֶהָ לִי מִשּׂוּמִי עַם־עוֹלָם וְאֹתִיּוֹת וַאֲשֶׁר תָּבֹאנָה יַגִּידוּ לָמוֹ: 8 אַל־תִּפְחֲדוּ וְאַל־תִּרְהוּ הֲלֹא מֵאָז הִשְׁמַעְתִּיךָ וְהִגַּדְתִּי וְאַתֶּם עֵדָי הֲיֵשׁ אֱלוֹהַּ מִבַּלְעָדַי וְאֵין

[6] This is what was said by God, the King of Israel and its Redeemer, the God of Hosts:

I am the first preceding the world and the last who will continue after the world has ended. There is no god besides Me!

[7] Who can declare and say that he is like Me? Who can relate and specify before Me all that happened since I placed the people of the world upon the earth, until now? Let them tell the things which are soon to come, and the things which are to come in the distant future to prove their words.

[8] Do not fear other gods, and do not be frightened! Did I not tell you and relate to you back then at Mount Sinai that there is no other god besides Me? You are My witnesses to this fact, as I opened up the

הפטרת ויקרא

צוּר בַּל־יָדָעְתִּי: 9 יֹצְרֵי־פֶסֶל כֻּלָּם תֹּהוּ וַחֲמוּדֵיהֶם בַּל־יוֹעִילוּ וְעֵדֵיהֶם הֵמָּה בַּל־יִרְאוּ וּבַל־יֵדְעוּ לְמַעַן יֵבֹשׁוּ: 10 מִי־יָצַר אֵל וּפֶסֶל נָסָךְ לְבִלְתִּי הוֹעִיל: 11 הֵן כָּל־חֲבֵרָיו יֵבֹשׁוּ וְחָרָשִׁים הֵמָּה מֵאָדָם יִתְקַבְּצוּ כֻלָּם יַעֲמֹדוּ יִפְחֲדוּ יֵבֹשׁוּ יָחַד: 12 חָרַשׁ בַּרְזֶל מַעֲצָד וּפָעַל בַּפֶּחָם וּבַמַּקָּבוֹת יִצְּרֵהוּ וַיִּפְעָלֵהוּ בִּזְרוֹעַ כֹּחוֹ גַּם־רָעֵב וְאֵין כֹּחַ לֹא־שָׁתָה מַיִם וַיִּיעָף: 13 חָרַשׁ עֵצִים נָטָה קָו יְתָאֳרֵהוּ בַשֶּׂרֶד יַעֲשֵׂהוּ בַּמַּקְצֻעוֹת וּבַמְּחוּגָה יְתָאֳרֵהוּ וַיַּעֲשֵׂהוּ כְּתַבְנִית אִישׁ כְּתִפְאֶרֶת אָדָם לָשֶׁבֶת בָּיִת: 14 לִכְרָת־לוֹ אֲרָזִים וַיִּקַּח תִּרְזָה וְאַלּוֹן וַיְאַמֶּץ־לוֹ בַּעֲצֵי־יָעַר נָטַע אֹרֶן וְגֶשֶׁם יְגַדֵּל: 15 וְהָיָה לְאָדָם לְבָעֵר וַיִּקַּח מֵהֶם וַיָּחָם אַף־יַשִּׂיק וְאָפָה לָחֶם אַף־יִפְעַל־אֵל וַיִּשְׁתָּחוּ עָשָׂהוּ פֶסֶל וַיִּסְגָּד־לָמוֹ: 16 חֶצְיוֹ שָׂרַף בְּמוֹ־אֵשׁ עַל־חֶצְיוֹ בָּשָׂר יֹאכֵל יִצְלֶה צָלִי וְיִשְׂבָּע אַף־יָחֹם וְיֹאמַר הֶאָח חַמּוֹתִי רָאִיתִי אוּר: 17 וּשְׁאֵרִיתוֹ לְאֵל עָשָׂה לְפִסְלוֹ [סגולו כ׳] יִסְגָּד־לוֹ וְיִשְׁתַּחוּ וְיִתְפַּלֵּל אֵלָיו וְיֹאמַר הַצִּילֵנִי כִּי אֵלִי אָתָּה: 18 לֹא יָדְעוּ וְלֹא יָבִינוּ כִּי טַח מֵרְאוֹת עֵינֵיהֶם מֵהַשְׂכִּיל לִבֹּתָם: 19 וְלֹא־יָשִׁיב אֶל־לִבּוֹ וְלֹא דַעַת וְלֹא־תְבוּנָה לֵאמֹר חֶצְיוֹ שָׂרַפְתִּי בְמוֹ־אֵשׁ וְאַף אָפִיתִי עַל־

---

seven heavens and showed you that there is no other god. Is there any god beside Me? There is no power without My knowledge, because all power comes from Me!

⁹ The craftsmen who make idols are worthless since their work is worthless, and the idols that they treasure have no purpose. The idols themselves bear witness to their own uselessness, since they do not see or think, so how could they help others? Their testimony will cause those who make them to be ashamed.

¹⁰ Who in his stupidity makes a god, or casts a statue that has no benefit? ¹¹ Indeed, all their followers will be ashamed, for the craftsmen who made the idols are mere men, so how could they possibly make a god? The craftsmen and idol-worshipers will all assemble and attempt to fathom what they have done and they will all be frightened of God, and ashamed of what they did.

¹² The ironsmith makes a saw. He makes it with coals and forms it with a hammer. He makes it with all the strength in his arms. Even if he is hungry and weak, even if he has not drunk water and is weary, he does not abandon his work, since he desires it so much.

¹³ Then the woodworker measures his wood with a ruler, marks it with ink, then cuts what he measured and shapes it nicely with a plane. He draws designs on it with a compass and shapes it like a man. It has man's beauty surpassing that of all animals. Yet it stays at home and cannot move.

¹⁴ Another person goes out to the forest and cuts cedars for himself to make the idol. Others use pines and oaks which have more beauty, but since they are not as strong as cedars he strengthens them with stronger wood.

Some go even further, planting firs especially to make idols, and then wait until the rain makes them grow—yet even those firs get rain from God, who will hold the idol sculptors accountable. ¹⁵ Some of the wood is burned by the man as fuel; some of it he takes to warm himself; some of it to light the ovens and bake bread; and with some of it he fashions an idol and bows down to it, and worships it. ¹⁶ He burns part of the wood in the fire, and with part of it he eats meat. He makes a roast and is satisfied. He warms himself and says, "Ah, I have warmed myself! And I have enjoyed looking at the glow of the fire!" ¹⁷ Then, with the rest of the wood he makes a god, an idol for himself! He worships it, bows down to it, and prays to it. He says, "Save me, for you are my god!"

¹⁸ They do not realize or understand, for the evil inclination has closed their eyes from seeing, and their hearts from understanding. ¹⁹ The idol-worshiper does not contemplate what he is doing. He does not have the wisdom and understanding to say, "I burned part in the fire, and I baked bread on its coals.

haftarat tzav

I roasted meat and ate. Shall I make an abomination to God from what is left, and bow down to a piece of wood?" [20] His deluded heart led him astray to accept as his leader something that eventually becomes ashes. Neither does the craftsmen who formed an idol save his soul and say to himself, "What I made with my right hand is a fake god, because I made it myself!"

[21] Even if the nations will worship idols, remember these words, O Jacob, and do not follow after them, for you are My servant, O Israel! I created you to be My servant, therefore you, Israel, do not forget Me!

[22] I have wiped away your sins like a cloud and your transgressions like mist. Return to Me, for I have redeemed you! [23] Sing, O heavens, for God has done what He is destined to do, to redeem Israel! Shout, depths of the earth! Mountains, burst out in song, forests and all your trees! For God has redeemed Jacob, and by Israel's redemption He will be glorified by all.

גְּחָלָיו לֶחֶם אָצְלָה בָּשָׂר וְאֹכֵל וְיִתְרוֹ לְתוֹעֵבָה עָשָׂה לְבוּל עֵץ אֶסְגּוֹד: 20 רֹעֶה אֵפֶר לֵב הוּתַל הִטָּהוּ וְלֹא־יַצִּיל אֶת־נַפְשׁוֹ וְלֹא יֹאמַר הֲלוֹא שֶׁקֶר בִּימִינִי: 21 זְכָר־אֵלֶּה יַעֲקֹב וְיִשְׂרָאֵל כִּי עַבְדִּי־אָתָּה יְצַרְתִּיךָ עֶבֶד־לִי אַתָּה יִשְׂרָאֵל לֹא תִנָּשֵׁנִי: 22 מָחִיתִי כָעָב פְּשָׁעֶיךָ וְכֶעָנָן חַטֹּאותֶיךָ שׁוּבָה אֵלַי כִּי גְאַלְתִּיךָ: 23 רָנּוּ שָׁמַיִם כִּי־עָשָׂה יְהֹוָה הָרִיעוּ תַּחְתִּיּוֹת אָרֶץ פִּצְחוּ הָרִים רִנָּה יַעַר וְכָל־עֵץ בּוֹ כִּי־גָאַל יְהֹוָה יַעֲקֹב וּבְיִשְׂרָאֵל יִתְפָּאָר:

haftarat tzav

Habad—Jeremiah 7:21–28; 9:22–23
Sephardim and Ashkenazim—Jeremiah 7:21 – 8:3; 9:22–23

SYNOPSIS: In continuation of the laws of sacrifices detailed in the *Parashah*, this *Haftarah* contains a rebuke to the Jewish people for abusing the privileges of sacrificial worship (7:21-22). A harsh criticism follows, in which the Jewish people are chastised for being disobedient (23-28). In the following section (omitted by Habad communities), the nation is warned of impending doom for their sins of placing abominations in the Temple, child sacrifices, and worshiping heavenly bodies (7:29-8:3). The concluding passage is a call for true Divine worship (9:22-23).

7 [21] The God of Hosts, Almighty God of Israel, says: "Instead of making completely burnt-offerings, add to your other sacrifices from which you are able to eat the meat, because the burnt-offerings are not pleasing God in any case, so why lose the meat? [22] For I did not speak to your ancestors and command them about burnt-offerings and other sacrifices when I took them out of the land of Egypt, so this is clearly not the main reason why I took them out.

[23] "Rather, this is what I commanded them, saying, 'Listen to My voice and obey Me! I will be your God and you will be My people. Follow the path I commanded you, so things will go well for you.'

ז 21 כֹּה אָמַר יְהֹוָה צְבָאוֹת אֱלֹהֵי יִשְׂרָאֵל עֹלוֹתֵיכֶם סְפוּ עַל־זִבְחֵיכֶם וְאִכְלוּ בָשָׂר: 22 כִּי לֹא־דִבַּרְתִּי אֶת־אֲבוֹתֵיכֶם וְלֹא צִוִּיתִים בְּיוֹם [הוציא כ׳] הוֹצִיאִי אוֹתָם מֵאֶרֶץ מִצְרָיִם עַל־דִּבְרֵי עוֹלָה וָזָבַח: 23 כִּי אִם־אֶת־הַדָּבָר הַזֶּה צִוִּיתִי אוֹתָם לֵאמֹר שִׁמְעוּ בְקוֹלִי וְהָיִיתִי לָכֶם לֵאלֹהִים וְאַתֶּם תִּהְיוּ־לִי לְעָם וַהֲלַכְתֶּם בְּכָל־הַדֶּרֶךְ אֲשֶׁר אֲצַוֶּה

הפטרת צו

²⁴ "But they did not listen or pay attention. Rather, they acted upon their own desires, whatever their evil hearts saw fit. Every day, they went backwards, not forwards, in their Divine service, ²⁵ from the day your ancestors left the land of Egypt, to this day. I sent them all My servants, the prophets—every day I would prepare early and send. ²⁶ But they did not listen to Me or pay attention. They stiffened their necks and acted worse than their ancestors.

²⁷ "You will speak all these words to them, but they will not listen to you. When you call out to them, they will not answer you. ²⁸ Then you will say to them, 'It is as if this is a nation which did not hear the voice of God, your Almighty God, at Mount Sinai, and as if it never learned a lesson. Faith in God is lost from their hearts, cut off from their mouths.'

אֶתְכֶ֖ם לְמַ֣עַן יִיטַ֣ב לָכֶֽם: 24 וְלֹ֤א שָֽׁמְעוּ֙ וְלֹֽא־הִטּ֣וּ אֶת־אָזְנָ֔ם וַיֵּֽלְכוּ֙ בְּמֹ֣עֵצ֔וֹת בִּשְׁרִר֖וּת לִבָּ֣ם הָרָ֑ע וַיִּהְי֥וּ לְאָח֖וֹר וְלֹ֥א לְפָנִֽים: 25 לְמִן־הַיּ֗וֹם אֲשֶׁ֨ר יָֽצְא֤וּ אֲבֽוֹתֵיכֶם֙ מֵאֶ֣רֶץ מִצְרַ֔יִם עַ֖ד הַיּ֣וֹם הַזֶּ֑ה וָאֶשְׁלַ֤ח אֲלֵיכֶם֙ אֶת־כָּל־עֲבָדַ֣י הַנְּבִיאִ֔ים י֖וֹם הַשְׁכֵּ֥ם וְשָׁלֹֽחַ: 26 וְל֤וֹא שָֽׁמְעוּ֙ אֵלַ֔י וְלֹ֥א הִטּ֖וּ אֶת־אָזְנָ֑ם וַיַּקְשׁוּ֙ אֶת־עָרְפָּ֔ם הֵרֵ֖עוּ מֵאֲבוֹתָֽם:

27 וְדִבַּרְתָּ֤ אֲלֵיהֶם֙ אֶת־כָּל־הַדְּבָרִ֣ים הָאֵ֔לֶּה וְלֹ֥א יִשְׁמְע֖וּ אֵלֶ֑יךָ וְקָרָ֥אתָ אֲלֵיהֶ֖ם וְלֹ֥א יַֽעֲנֽוּכָה: 28 וְאָֽמַרְתָּ֣ אֲלֵיהֶ֗ם זֶ֤ה הַגּוֹי֙ אֲשֶׁ֣ר לוֹא־שָֽׁמְע֗וּ בְּקוֹל֙ יְהֹוָ֣ה אֱלֹהָ֔יו וְלֹ֥א לָֽקְח֖וּ מוּסָ֑ר אָֽבְדָה֙ הָאֱמוּנָ֔ה וְנִכְרְתָ֖ה מִפִּיהֶֽם:

Ḥabad communities omit the following and continue on page 1349:

²⁹ "Tear out your hair and throw it away! Raise your voice in a lament on the high places, for God has become disgusted and He has abandoned the generation that angered Him. ³⁰ For the men of Judah have done what is evil in My eyes," says God. "They have put their abominations in this House which bears My name, to defile it. ³¹ They have built 'drumming' altars in the Ben-hinnom Valley to burn their sons and daughters in fire, while the drums are sounded to drown out the child's last cries. I never commanded this activity in My worship, and it never occurred to Me to ask for such a thing.

³² "Therefore, days are coming," says God, "when people will not speak of 'drumming altars' or the Ben-hinnom Valley, but of the Slaughter Valley. People will be buried at the 'drumming altars' until no room is left. ³³ The carcasses of this people for whom there is no room to bury will be food for the birds of the sky and the beasts on earth, and no one will scare them away. ³⁴ I will banish the voice of rejoicing and the voice of joy, the voice of the brides and grooms from the cities of Judah and the streets of Jerusalem, for the land will be desolate.

8 ¹ "At that time," says God, "the bones of the kings of Judah, the bones of its nobles, the

29 גָּזִּ֤י נִזְרֵךְ֙ וְֽהַשְׁלִ֔יכִי וּשְׂאִ֥י עַל־שְׁפָיִ֖ם קִינָ֑ה כִּ֚י מָאַ֣ס יְהֹוָ֔ה וַיִּטֹּ֖שׁ אֶת־דּ֥וֹר עֶבְרָתֽוֹ: 30 כִּֽי־עָשׂ֨וּ בְנֵֽי־יְהוּדָ֥ה הָרַ֛ע בְּעֵינַ֖י נְאֻם־יְהֹוָ֑ה שָׂ֣מוּ שִׁקּֽוּצֵיהֶ֗ם בַּבַּ֛יִת אֲשֶׁר־נִקְרָֽא־שְׁמִ֥י עָלָ֖יו לְטַמְּאֽוֹ: 31 וּבָנ֞וּ בָּמ֣וֹת הַתֹּ֗פֶת אֲשֶׁר֙ בְּגֵ֣יא בֶן־הִנֹּ֔ם לִשְׂרֹ֛ף אֶת־בְּנֵיהֶ֥ם וְאֶת־בְּנֹֽתֵיהֶ֖ם בָּאֵ֑שׁ אֲשֶׁר֙ לֹ֣א צִוִּ֔יתִי וְלֹ֥א עָֽלְתָ֖ה עַל־לִבִּֽי: 32 לָכֵ֞ן הִנֵּֽה־יָמִ֤ים בָּאִים֙ נְאֻם־יְהֹוָ֔ה וְלֹא־יֵֽאָמֵ֨ר ע֤וֹד הַתֹּ֨פֶת֙ וְגֵ֣יא בֶן־הִנֹּ֔ם כִּ֖י אִם־גֵּ֣יא הַֽהֲרֵגָ֑ה וְקָֽבְר֥וּ בְתֹ֖פֶת מֵאֵ֥ין מָקֽוֹם: 33 וְֽהָ֨יְתָ֜ה נִבְלַ֣ת הָעָ֤ם הַזֶּה֙ לְמַֽאֲכָ֔ל לְע֥וֹף הַשָּׁמַ֖יִם וּלְבֶֽהֱמַ֣ת הָאָ֑רֶץ וְאֵ֖ין מַֽחֲרִֽיד: 34 וְהִשְׁבַּתִּ֣י | מֵעָרֵ֣י יְהוּדָ֗ה וּמֵֽחֻצוֹת֙ יְר֣וּשָׁלַ֔ם ק֤וֹל שָׂשׂוֹן֙ וְק֣וֹל שִׂמְחָ֔ה ק֥וֹל חָתָ֖ן וְק֣וֹל כַּלָּ֑ה כִּ֥י לְחָרְבָּ֖ה תִּֽהְיֶ֥ה הָאָֽרֶץ:

ח 1 בָּעֵ֣ת הַהִ֣יא נְאֻם־יְהֹוָ֡ה [ויוציאו כ׳] יוֹצִ֣יאוּ אֶת־עַצְמ֣וֹת מַלְכֵֽי־יְהוּדָ֣ה וְאֶת־עַצְמ֣וֹת שָׂרָיו֩ וְאֶת־עַצְמ֨וֹת הַכֹּֽהֲנִ֜ים וְאֵ֣ת | עַצְמ֣וֹת הַנְּבִיאִ֗ים וְאֵ֛ת עַצְמ֥וֹת יֽוֹשְׁבֵֽי־יְרֽוּשָׁלָ֖ם

haftarat shemini

bones of its idol-worshiping priests, the bones of its false prophets, and bones of the other inhabitants of Jerusalem will be exhumed from their graves by their enemies, as they search for plunder. ² The bones will be spread out under the sun, the moon, and the entire constellation of the skies, which they loved as gods, which they worshiped, which they followed after, which they sought out, and to which they prostrated themselves. The bones will not be gathered back into the grave, they will not be buried. They will be like dung on the earth.

מִקִּבְרֵיהֶֽם: ² וּשְׁטָחוּם֩ לַשֶּׁ֨מֶשׁ וְלַיָּרֵ֜חַ וּלְכֹ֣ל | צְבָ֣א הַשָּׁמַ֗יִם אֲשֶׁ֤ר אֲהֵבוּם֙ וַאֲשֶׁ֣ר עֲבָד֔וּם וַאֲשֶׁר֙ הָלְכ֣וּ אַחֲרֵיהֶ֔ם וַאֲשֶׁ֥ר דְּרָשׁ֖וּם וַאֲשֶׁ֣ר הִשְׁתַּחֲו֣וּ לָהֶ֑ם לֹ֤א יֵאָֽסְפוּ֙ וְלֹ֣א יִקָּבֵ֔רוּ לְדֹ֛מֶן עַל־פְּנֵ֥י הָאֲדָמָ֖ה יִהְיֽוּ: ³ וְנִבְחַ֤ר מָ֨וֶת֙ מֵֽחַיִּ֔ים לְכֹ֗ל הַשְּׁאֵרִית֙ הַנִּשְׁאָרִ֔ים מִן־הַמִּשְׁפָּחָ֥ה הָרָעָ֖ה הַזֹּ֑את בְּכָל־הַמְּקֹמ֤וֹת הַנִּשְׁאָרִים֙ אֲשֶׁ֣ר הִדַּחְתִּ֣ים שָׁ֔ם נְאֻ֖ם יְהֹוָ֥ה צְבָאֽוֹת:

³ "For whoever is left of this evil clan, death will be preferable to life in all the places that they remain; from wherever I have cast them their exile will be excruciating," says the God of Hosts.

All communities conclude with the following:

9 ²² God says, "The wise man should not praise himself because of his wisdom, the strong man because of his strength, nor the rich man because of his money, for it would not save or benefit any of them. ²³ Rather, if a person wishes to praise himself, let it be with this: through understanding and knowing Me, that I am God and there is none besides Me; that I am the One who acts kindly to those who keep my commandments, justly to punish the wicked, and

ט ²² כֹּ֣ה | אָמַ֣ר יְהֹוָ֗ה אַל־יִתְהַלֵּ֤ל חָכָם֙ בְּחָכְמָת֔וֹ וְאַל־יִתְהַלֵּ֥ל הַגִּבּ֖וֹר בִּגְבֽוּרָת֑וֹ אַל־יִתְהַלֵּ֥ל עָשִׁ֖יר בְּעָשְׁרֽוֹ: ²³ כִּ֣י אִם־בְּזֹ֞את יִתְהַלֵּ֣ל הַמִּתְהַלֵּ֗ל הַשְׂכֵּל֘ וְיָדֹ֣עַ אוֹתִי֒ כִּ֚י אֲנִ֣י יְהֹוָ֔ה עֹ֥שֶׂה חֶ֛סֶד מִשְׁפָּ֥ט וּצְדָקָ֖ה בָּאָ֑רֶץ כִּֽי־בְאֵ֥לֶּה חָפַ֖צְתִּי נְאֻם־יְהֹוָֽה:

righteously on earth to accept penitents, and wipe away their due punishments—for I desire to do all these things to give people what they deserve," says God.

haftarat shemini

ASHKENAZIM—II SAMUEL 6:1 – 7:17
SEPHARDIM AND HABAD—II SAMUEL 6:1–19

> **SYNOPSIS:** This *Haftarah* relates the untimely passing of Uzzah which occurred during the transportation of the ark to Jerusalem, similar to the passing of Nadab and Abihu in the *Parashah*, that occurred during the dedication of the Tabernacle.
>
> The *Haftarah* relates events that occurred after King David's coronation, conquest of Jerusalem and victory against the Philistines (*I Samuel* ch. 5). David now perceived it as the opportune moment to bring up the Holy Ark to Jerusalem from Beth-abinadab, where it had been safeguarded since the times of Samuel.
>
> The initial procession is tragically interrupted by the death of Uzzah, who attempted to grab the ark when he feared it was going to fall, forgetting that God's ark did not need such assistance. David took personal responsibility for what had occurred, and was no longer willing to continue the procession (6:1–11). After three months, the

הפטרת שמיני

transportation of the ark is resumed, and this time the destination is reached successfully, amid national celebration (12–19).

According to Ashkenazic custom, the *Haftarah* then continues to relate a criticism leveled by Saul's daughter, Michal, against David for dancing in a fervent manner which, she felt, was not befitting the King. David brushes her words aside, arguing that he was not ashamed of dancing in God's honor, and that she should remember that it was David who was appointed as king, and not Saul, her father! As a punishment, Michal remains barren all her days (20–23).

This is followed by a further chapter, in which David desires to make a permanent home for the ark, a request which is denied by God, and postponed instead for one of David's sons (7:1–17).

6 ¹ David gathered thirty thousand selected men of Israel, in addition to those who had gathered to him after his appointment as king. ² He proceeded with all his troops from Baalim of Judah where they had gathered to bring up from there the Ark of God, which was called by a special name. It was called, "The Name of the God of Hosts, Enthroned on the Cherubim."

³ They placed the Ark of God on a new wagon and the cattle which pulled the wagon carried it from Beth-abinadab in Gibeah. Abinadab's sons, Uzzah and Ahio, led the cattle which drove the new wagon. ⁴ The wagon carried the Ark of God from Beth-abinadab in Gibeah. Ahio walked in front of the ark and Uzzah to the side of the ark.

⁵ David and all Israel played before the Ark of God on all sorts of cypress-wood instruments: lyres, harps, drums, castanets, and cymbals.

⁶ When they arrived at the threshing floor of Nacon, Uzzah reached out to the Ark of God and grabbed it, because being on the side, he noticed that the oxen had slipped and he thought that the ark would fall off the wagon.

⁷ God became angry at Uzzah for his lack of faith in thinking that the ark would fall, and God struck him for inadvertently forgetting that it was God's ark and he died there, next to the Ark of God.

⁸ David *was upset with himself* because of God's outburst against Uzzah, and he called the place Perez-uzzah, "the Breach of Uzzah," as it is known to this day. ⁹ David feared God's ark that day, and he said to himself, "How can God's ark come safely with me since it is so holy? How can I possibly look after it properly?" ¹⁰ So David did not want to bring the Ark of God to his place in the City of David, and he made a detour to the house of Obed-edom the Gittite.

ו 1 וַיֹּ֨סֶף ע֥וֹד דָּוִ֛ד אֶת־כָּל־בָּח֖וּר בְּיִשְׂרָאֵ֑ל שְׁלֹשִׁ֖ים אָֽלֶף: 2 וַיָּ֣קָם ׀ וַיֵּ֣לֶךְ דָּוִ֗ד וְכָל־הָעָם֙ אֲשֶׁ֣ר אִתּ֔וֹ מִֽבַּעֲלֵ֖י יְהוּדָ֑ה לְהַעֲל֣וֹת מִשָּׁ֗ם אֵ֚ת אֲר֣וֹן הָאֱלֹהִ֔ים אֲשֶׁר־נִקְרָ֣א שֵׁ֗ם שֵׁ֣ם יְהוָ֧ה צְבָא֛וֹת יֹשֵׁ֥ב הַכְּרֻבִ֖ים עָלָֽיו: 3 וַיַּרְכִּ֜בוּ אֶת־אֲר֤וֹן הָֽאֱלֹהִים֙ אֶל־עֲגָלָ֣ה חֲדָשָׁ֔ה וַיִּשָּׂאֻ֔הוּ מִבֵּ֥ית אֲבִֽינָדָ֖ב אֲשֶׁ֣ר בַּגִּבְעָ֑ה וְעֻזָּ֣א וְאַחְי֗וֹ בְּנֵי֙ אֲבִ֣ינָדָ֔ב נֹהֲגִ֖ים אֶת־הָעֲגָלָ֥ה חֲדָשָֽׁה: 4 וַיִּשָּׂאֻ֗הוּ מִבֵּ֤ית אֲבִֽינָדָב֙ אֲשֶׁ֣ר בַּגִּבְעָ֔ה עִ֖ם אֲר֣וֹן הָאֱלֹהִ֑ים וְאַחְי֕וֹ הֹלֵ֖ךְ לִפְנֵ֥י הָאָרֽוֹן: 5 וְדָוִ֣ד ׀ וְכָל־בֵּ֣ית יִשְׂרָאֵ֗ל מְשַֽׂחֲקִים֙ לִפְנֵ֣י יְהוָ֔ה בְּכֹ֖ל עֲצֵ֣י בְרוֹשִׁ֑ים וּבְכִנֹּר֤וֹת וּבִנְבָלִים֙ וּבְתֻפִּ֔ים וּבִמְנַעַנְעִ֖ים וּֽבְצֶלְצֶלִֽים: 6 וַיָּבֹ֖אוּ עַד־גֹּ֣רֶן נָכ֑וֹן וַיִּשְׁלַ֨ח עֻזָּ֜א אֶל־אֲר֤וֹן הָֽאֱלֹהִים֙ וַיֹּ֣אחֶז בּ֔וֹ כִּ֥י שָׁמְט֖וּ הַבָּקָֽר: 7 וַיִּֽחַר־אַ֤ף יְהוָה֙ בְּעֻזָּ֔ה וַיַּכֵּ֥הוּ שָׁ֛ם הָאֱלֹהִ֖ים עַל־הַשַּׁ֑ל וַיָּ֣מָת שָׁ֔ם עִ֖ם אֲר֥וֹן הָאֱלֹהִֽים: 8 וַיִּ֣חַר לְדָוִ֔ד עַל֩ אֲשֶׁ֨ר פָּרַ֧ץ יְהוָ֛ה פֶּ֖רֶץ בְּעֻזָּ֑ה וַיִּקְרָ֞א לַמָּק֤וֹם הַהוּא֙ פֶּ֣רֶץ עֻזָּ֔ה עַ֖ד הַיּ֥וֹם הַזֶּֽה: 9 וַיִּרָ֥א דָוִ֛ד אֶת־יְהוָ֖ה בַּיּ֣וֹם הַה֑וּא וַיֹּ֕אמֶר אֵ֛יךְ יָב֥וֹא אֵלַ֖י אֲר֥וֹן יְהוָֽה: 10 וְלֹֽא־אָבָ֣ה דָוִ֗ד לְהָסִ֥יר אֵלָ֛יו

haftarat shemini

[11] The Ark of God was delayed there for three months, and God blessed Obed-edom and his entire household.

[12] Then King David was informed, "God has blessed the household of Obed-edom and everything he owns in an unprecedented manner because of the Ark of God which is in his house." Then, David proceeded joyfully from the house of Obed-edom with the Ark of God, towards the City of David.

[13] Each time the men carrying the Ark of God took six paces, he sacrificed an ox and a fattened ox. [14] David danced joyfully with all his strength before God, dressed in a linen apron. [15] He proceeded with bringing up the Ark of God, along with the entire House of Israel, with horn blasts and the sound of the ram's horn.

[16] When the Ark of God arrived at the City of David, Saul's daughter, Michal, was gazing out the window. She saw her husband King David leaping and dancing before God; she looked upon him with contempt because she felt that it was not appropriate for the king to dance, and certainly not in front of the ark.

[17] They brought the Ark of God and set it in its place in the tent which David had pitched. Then David offered burnt-offerings and peace-offerings before God.

[18] When David finished bringing the burnt-offerings and peace-offerings, he blessed the people in the name of the God of Hosts. [19] He distributed to all the people, to the whole crowd of Israel, men and women: a loaf of bread, a generous portion of good meat, and a bottle of wine, after which everyone went home.

אֶת־אֲרוֹן יְהֹוָה עַל־עִיר דָּוִד וַיַּטֵּהוּ דָוִד בֵּית עֹבֵד־אֱדֹם הַגִּתִּי: 11 וַיֵּשֶׁב אֲרוֹן יְהֹוָה בֵּית עֹבֵד אֱדֹם הַגִּתִּי שְׁלֹשָׁה חֳדָשִׁים וַיְבָרֶךְ יְהֹוָה אֶת־עֹבֵד אֱדֹם וְאֶת־כָּל־בֵּיתוֹ: 12 וַיֻּגַּד לַמֶּלֶךְ דָּוִד לֵאמֹר בֵּרַךְ יְהֹוָה אֶת־בֵּית עֹבֵד אֱדֹם וְאֶת־כָּל־אֲשֶׁר־לוֹ בַּעֲבוּר אֲרוֹן הָאֱלֹהִים וַיֵּלֶךְ דָּוִד וַיַּעַל אֶת־אֲרוֹן הָאֱלֹהִים מִבֵּית עֹבֵד אֱדֹם עִיר דָּוִד בְּשִׂמְחָה: 13 וַיְהִי כִּי צָעֲדוּ נֹשְׂאֵי אֲרוֹן־יְהֹוָה שִׁשָּׁה צְעָדִים וַיִּזְבַּח שׁוֹר וּמְרִיא: 14 וְדָוִד מְכַרְכֵּר בְּכָל־עֹז לִפְנֵי יְהֹוָה וְדָוִד חָגוּר אֵפוֹד בָּד: 15 וְדָוִד וְכָל־בֵּית יִשְׂרָאֵל מַעֲלִים אֶת־אֲרוֹן יְהֹוָה בִּתְרוּעָה וּבְקוֹל שׁוֹפָר: 16 וְהָיָה אֲרוֹן יְהֹוָה בָּא עִיר דָּוִד וּמִיכַל בַּת־שָׁאוּל נִשְׁקְפָה | בְּעַד הַחַלּוֹן וַתֵּרֶא אֶת־הַמֶּלֶךְ דָּוִד מְפַזֵּז וּמְכַרְכֵּר לִפְנֵי יְהֹוָה וַתִּבֶז לוֹ בְּלִבָּהּ: 17 וַיָּבִאוּ אֶת־אֲרוֹן יְהֹוָה וַיַּצִּגוּ אֹתוֹ בִּמְקוֹמוֹ בְּתוֹךְ הָאֹהֶל אֲשֶׁר נָטָה־לוֹ דָּוִד וַיַּעַל דָּוִד עֹלוֹת לִפְנֵי יְהֹוָה וּשְׁלָמִים: 18 וַיְכַל דָּוִד מֵהַעֲלוֹת הָעוֹלָה וְהַשְּׁלָמִים וַיְבָרֶךְ אֶת־הָעָם בְּשֵׁם יְהֹוָה צְבָאוֹת: 19 וַיְחַלֵּק לְכָל־הָעָם לְכָל־הֲמוֹן יִשְׂרָאֵל לְמֵאִישׁ וְעַד־אִשָּׁה לְאִישׁ חַלַּת לֶחֶם אַחַת וְאֶשְׁפָּר אֶחָד וַאֲשִׁישָׁה אֶחָת וַיֵּלֶךְ כָּל־הָעָם אִישׁ לְבֵיתוֹ:

Ḥabad and *Sephardic* communities conclude here. *Ashkenazic* communities continue:

[20] David then returned to bless his household, and Saul's daughter Michal went out to meet him. "What an honorable day it was," she said cynically, "when the king of Israel exposed some of his body while dancing in the sight of his servants' maids, just like a simpleton."

[21] "We were dancing before God," David said to Michal, "Who chose me over your father and his entire house to appoint me as ruler over God's people Israel. Therefore I will rejoice before God!

20 וַיָּשָׁב דָּוִד לְבָרֵךְ אֶת־בֵּיתוֹ וַתֵּצֵא מִיכַל בַּת־שָׁאוּל לִקְרַאת דָּוִד וַתֹּאמֶר מַה־נִּכְבַּד הַיּוֹם מֶלֶךְ יִשְׂרָאֵל אֲשֶׁר נִגְלָה הַיּוֹם לְעֵינֵי אַמְהוֹת עֲבָדָיו כְּהִגָּלוֹת נִגְלוֹת אַחַד הָרֵקִים: 21 וַיֹּאמֶר דָּוִד אֶל־מִיכַל לִפְנֵי יְהֹוָה אֲשֶׁר בָּחַר־בִּי מֵאָבִיךְ וּמִכָּל־בֵּיתוֹ לְצַוֹּת אֹתִי נָגִיד עַל־עַם יְהֹוָה עַל־יִשְׂרָאֵל וְשִׂחַקְתִּי לִפְנֵי יְהֹוָה:

הפטרת שמיני

22 וּנְקַלֹּתִי עוֹד מִזֹּאת וְהָיִיתִי שָׁפָל בְּעֵינָי וְעִם־הָאֲמָהוֹת אֲשֶׁר אָמַרְתְּ עִמָּם אִכָּבֵדָה:
23 וּלְמִיכַל בַּת־שָׁאוּל לֹא־הָיָה לָהּ יָלֶד עַד יוֹם מוֹתָהּ:

1 וַיְהִי כִּי־יָשַׁב הַמֶּלֶךְ בְּבֵיתוֹ וַיהֹוָה הֵנִיחַ־לוֹ מִסָּבִיב מִכָּל־אֹיְבָיו: **2** וַיֹּאמֶר הַמֶּלֶךְ אֶל־נָתָן הַנָּבִיא רְאֵה נָא אָנֹכִי יוֹשֵׁב בְּבֵית אֲרָזִים וַאֲרוֹן הָאֱלֹהִים יֹשֵׁב בְּתוֹךְ הַיְרִיעָה: **3** וַיֹּאמֶר נָתָן אֶל־הַמֶּלֶךְ כֹּל אֲשֶׁר בִּלְבָבְךָ לֵךְ עֲשֵׂה כִּי יְהֹוָה עִמָּךְ: **4** וַיְהִי בַּלַּיְלָה הַהוּא וַיְהִי דְּבַר־יְהֹוָה אֶל־נָתָן לֵאמֹר: **5** לֵךְ וְאָמַרְתָּ אֶל־עַבְדִּי אֶל־דָּוִד כֹּה אָמַר יְהֹוָה הַאַתָּה תִּבְנֶה־לִּי בַיִת לְשִׁבְתִּי: **6** כִּי לֹא יָשַׁבְתִּי בְּבַיִת לְמִיּוֹם הַעֲלֹתִי אֶת־בְּנֵי יִשְׂרָאֵל מִמִּצְרַיִם וְעַד הַיּוֹם הַזֶּה וָאֶהְיֶה מִתְהַלֵּךְ בְּאֹהֶל וּבְמִשְׁכָּן: **7** בְּכֹל אֲשֶׁר־הִתְהַלַּכְתִּי בְּכָל־בְּנֵי יִשְׂרָאֵל הֲדָבָר דִּבַּרְתִּי אֶת־אַחַד שִׁבְטֵי יִשְׂרָאֵל אֲשֶׁר צִוִּיתִי לִרְעוֹת אֶת־עַמִּי אֶת־יִשְׂרָאֵל לֵאמֹר לָמָּה לֹא־בְנִיתֶם לִי בֵּית אֲרָזִים: **8** וְעַתָּה כֹּה־תֹאמַר לְעַבְדִּי לְדָוִד כֹּה אָמַר יְהֹוָה צְבָאוֹת אֲנִי לְקַחְתִּיךָ מִן־הַנָּוֶה מֵאַחַר הַצֹּאן לִהְיוֹת נָגִיד עַל־עַמִּי עַל־יִשְׂרָאֵל: **9** וָאֶהְיֶה עִמְּךָ בְּכֹל אֲשֶׁר הָלַכְתָּ וָאַכְרִתָה אֶת־כָּל־אֹיְבֶיךָ מִפָּנֶיךָ וְעָשִׂתִי לְךָ שֵׁם גָּדוֹל כְּשֵׁם הַגְּדֹלִים אֲשֶׁר בָּאָרֶץ: **10** וְשַׂמְתִּי מָקוֹם לְעַמִּי לְיִשְׂרָאֵל וּנְטַעְתִּיו וְשָׁכַן תַּחְתָּיו וְלֹא יִרְגַּז עוֹד וְלֹא־יֹסִיפוּ בְנֵי־עַוְלָה לְעַנּוֹתוֹ כַּאֲשֶׁר בָּרִאשׁוֹנָה: **11** וּלְמִן־הַיּוֹם אֲשֶׁר צִוִּיתִי שֹׁפְטִים עַל־עַמִּי יִשְׂרָאֵל וַהֲנִיחֹתִי לְךָ מִכָּל־אֹיְבֶיךָ וְהִגִּיד לְךָ יְהֹוָה כִּי־בַיִת יַעֲשֶׂה־לְּךָ יְהֹוָה: **12** כִּי יִמְלְאוּ יָמֶיךָ וְשָׁכַבְתָּ אֶת־אֲבֹתֶיךָ וַהֲקִימֹתִי אֶת־זַרְעֲךָ אַחֲרֶיךָ אֲשֶׁר

---

22 If I would have lowered myself even further, and become humble in my own eyes to dispense with my honor, then I would be even more honored among the maids which you mentioned."

23 For the sin of insulting King David, Michal, Saul's daughter, had no child to the day of her death.

7

1 What happened was, as the king was sitting in his palace after God had given him peace from all his enemies surrounding him, **2** the king said to Nathan the prophet: "See now! I live in a cedar palace fit for my honor, but God's ark is sitting in a mere tent!"

3 Nathan said to the king, "Go and do whatever you have in your heart, for God is with you."

4 That night, God's word came to Nathan, saying, **5** "Go and inform My servant David, 'This is what God says, "Are you not happy with all the good I have done for you that you want to build Me a house to live in? **6** I have not resided in a house from the day I brought the children of Israel out of Egypt to this day, and I have moved around in a Tent and a Tabernacle, and you want to change that? **7** In all my travels among all the Jewish people, have I ever spoken to any of the judges of Israel whom I commanded to look after My people Israel, saying, 'Why have you not built Me a house of cedar?'

8 "Now say this to My servant David, 'This is what the God of Hosts says, "Have I not done enough for you already? I have taken you from the sheep pen, from following after the sheep, to be leader over My people Israel. **9** I was with you wherever you went and I eliminated all your enemies before you. I made your name great, like the name of the greatest men on earth. **10** In your days I will make a place for My people Israel, and I will plant them firmly. They will remain secure and will not be disturbed any more. Evil people will no longer oppress them, as they did initially, **11** before the day I commanded the judges about My people Israel. I gave you peace from all your enemies and God told you that He would establish a royal house for you and your descendants—and you are still not satisfied!

12 "When your days are complete and you lie with your fathers, I will raise up your descendants

haftarat tzaria'

that follow you, one who comes from your loins, and I will establish his kingdom. [13] He will build a house for My name, and I will establish his royal throne forever. [14] I will be like a father to him, and he will be like a son to Me, in that I will rebuke him with the rod of men and the plagues of mortals when he sins.

[15] "But My kindness will not depart from him as I withdrew it from Saul, whom I removed before you due to his sins. [16] Your house and your sovereignty will remain before you forever; your throne will be firmly established forever."

[17] Nathan told all these words and all this vision to David.

יֵצֵ֣א מִמֵּעֶ֔יךָ וַהֲכִינֹתִ֖י אֶת־מַמְלַכְתּֽוֹ: [13] ה֗וּא יִבְנֶה־בַּ֖יִת לִשְׁמִ֑י וְכֹנַנְתִּ֛י אֶת־כִּסֵּ֥א מַמְלַכְתּ֖וֹ עַד־עוֹלָֽם: [14] אֲנִי֙ אֶֽהְיֶה־לּ֣וֹ לְאָ֔ב וְה֖וּא יִֽהְיֶה־לִּ֣י לְבֵ֑ן אֲשֶׁר֙ בְּהַ֣עֲו‍ֹת֔וֹ וְהֹֽכַחְתִּיו֙ בְּשֵׁ֣בֶט אֲנָשִׁ֔ים וּבְנִגְעֵ֖י בְּנֵ֥י אָדָֽם: [15] וְחַסְדִּ֖י לֹא־יָס֣וּר מִמֶּ֑נּוּ כַּאֲשֶׁ֤ר הֲסִרֹ֙תִי֙ מֵעִ֣ם שָׁא֔וּל אֲשֶׁ֥ר הֲסִרֹ֖תִי מִלְּפָנֶֽיךָ: [16] וְנֶאְמַ֨ן בֵּיתְךָ֧ וּמַֽמְלַכְתְּךָ֛ עַד־עוֹלָ֖ם לְפָנֶ֑יךָ כִּסְאֲךָ֕ יִהְיֶ֥ה נָכ֖וֹן עַד־עוֹלָֽם: [17] כְּכֹל֙ הַדְּבָרִ֣ים הָאֵ֔לֶּה וּכְכֹ֖ל הַחִזָּי֣וֹן הַזֶּ֑ה כֵּ֣ן דִּבֶּ֥ר נָתָ֖ן אֶל־דָּוִֽד:

haftarat tzaria'

All communities—II Kings 4:42 – 5:19

SYNOPSIS: This *Haftarah* relates the miraculous healing of Naaman's *tzara'at*, in connection with the laws of *tzara'at* delineated in the *Parashah*.

The *Haftarah* relates two miracles performed by Elisha, a prophet living in the northern kingdom during the reign of King Jehoram (9th century B.C.E.). In the first miracle, Elisha is offered a sack of twenty bread-rolls, but he declines, saying that it should be offered to the crowd of one hundred men. While the suggestion appears ludicrous, as there does not appear to be enough food, Elisha's word is nevertheless fulfilled and, miraculously, there is even food left over (4:42–44).

The second miracle centers around Naaman, the commander of Aram's army, a *tzara'at* sufferer who receives news of Elisha's healing powers (5:1-3). Naaman approaches the King of Israel with a formal letter from the King of Aram, but the move is misunderstood—the King of Israel presumes that this is the pretense of an imminent attack, and he rents his clothes (4-7). Elisha hears of this and offers his services, and Naaman soon arrives (8-9). However, Elisha does not even come to the door to greet Naaman, and merely sends a message that he should bathe in the Jordan (10). Although initially outraged, Naaman is pressured by his servants to listen to Elisha's advice, and he is cured (11-14). Naaman returns to Elisha offering gifts, but Elisha declines (15-16). Finally, Naaman seeks Elisha's advice in spiritual matters, pledging allegiance to monotheism (17-19).

4 [42] A man came from Baal-shalishah and he brought bread from the first harvest to Elisha the man of God—twenty loaves of barley bread and fresh grain still in its husks, in a sack.

ד [42] וְאִ֨ישׁ בָּ֜א מִבַּ֣עַל שָׁלִ֗שָׁה וַיָּבֵא֩ לְאִ֨ישׁ הָאֱלֹהִ֜ים לֶ֤חֶם בִּכּוּרִים֙ עֶשְׂרִֽים־לֶ֣חֶם שְׂעֹרִ֔ים וְכַרְמֶ֖ל בְּצִקְלֹנ֑וֹ וַיֹּ֕אמֶר תֵּ֥ן לָעָ֖ם

הפטרת תזריע

Elisha said, "Give it to the people to eat."

⁴³ His servant asked, "How can I give this to a hundred men? It's simply not enough."

Elisha said, "Give it to the people to eat, for God said, 'They will eat and have food left over!'"

⁴⁴ He placed the food before them and they ate. There was food left over, just as God had said.

5 ¹ Naaman, commander of the king of Aram's army, was respected by his master and greatly honored by the people, for God had granted victory to Aram through him. He was strong and was willing to fight at any time, but he was unable to do so because he was a *tzara'at* sufferer.

² When the Arameans had gone out in raiding parties, they had captured a young girl from the land of Israel, who became Naaman's wife's servant. ³ She told her mistress, "If my master's request will be brought before the prophet in Samaria, then he will cure him of his *tzara'at*."

⁴ He went and told his master the king, saying, "The girl from the land of Israel told me this...."

⁵ The king of Aram replied, "Go and approach the prophet. I will send a letter to the king of Israel telling him to instruct the prophet to cure you."

Naaman left, taking ten talents of silver, six thousand gold shekels, and ten items of clothing with him as a gift for the prophet.

⁶ He brought the letter to the king of Israel, which read, "When this letter reaches you, know that I have sent my servant Naaman to you, that you should heal him of his *tzara'at*," thinking that the king would understand for himself that he should instruct the prophet to heal Naaman. ⁷ But when the king of Israel read the letter, approaching the prophet did not even enter his mind, since he did not really believe in the prophet and thought that the king of Aram was asking him to heal Naaman himself. He rent his clothes in fright and said: "Am I God who can kill or restore to life, that he sends someone to me to cure him of his *tzara'at*? He is obviously seeking a pretext to come and fight against me!"

⁸ When Elisha, the man of God, heard that the king of Israel had rent his clothes, he sent a messenger to the king, saying: "Why have you rent your clothes? Let Naaman come to me, and he will know that there is a prophet in Israel!"

וְיֹאכֵלוּ: 43 וַיֹּאמֶר מְשָׁרְתוֹ מָה אֶתֵּן זֶה לִפְנֵי מֵאָה אִישׁ וַיֹּאמֶר תֵּן לָעָם וְיֹאכֵלוּ כִּי כֹה אָמַר יְהֹוָה אָכֹל וְהוֹתֵר: 44 וַיִּתֵּן לִפְנֵיהֶם וַיֹּאכְלוּ וַיּוֹתִרוּ כִּדְבַר יְהֹוָה:

ה 1 וְנַעֲמָן שַׂר־צְבָא מֶלֶךְ־אֲרָם הָיָה אִישׁ גָּדוֹל לִפְנֵי אֲדֹנָיו וּנְשֻׂא פָנִים כִּי־בוֹ נָתַן־יְהֹוָה תְּשׁוּעָה לַאֲרָם וְהָאִישׁ הָיָה גִּבּוֹר חַיִל מְצֹרָע: 2 וַאֲרָם יָצְאוּ גְדוּדִים וַיִּשְׁבּוּ מֵאֶרֶץ יִשְׂרָאֵל נַעֲרָה קְטַנָּה וַתְּהִי לִפְנֵי אֵשֶׁת נַעֲמָן: 3 וַתֹּאמֶר אֶל־גְּבִרְתָּהּ אַחֲלֵי אֲדֹנִי לִפְנֵי הַנָּבִיא אֲשֶׁר בְּשֹׁמְרוֹן אָז יֶאֱסֹף אֹתוֹ מִצָּרַעְתּוֹ: 4 וַיָּבֹא וַיַּגֵּד לַאדֹנָיו לֵאמֹר כָּזֹאת וְכָזֹאת דִּבְּרָה הַנַּעֲרָה אֲשֶׁר מֵאֶרֶץ יִשְׂרָאֵל: 5 וַיֹּאמֶר מֶלֶךְ־אֲרָם לֶךְ־בֹּא וְאֶשְׁלְחָה סֵפֶר אֶל־מֶלֶךְ יִשְׂרָאֵל וַיֵּלֶךְ וַיִּקַּח בְּיָדוֹ עֶשֶׂר כִּכְּרֵי־כֶסֶף וְשֵׁשֶׁת אֲלָפִים זָהָב וְעֶשֶׂר חֲלִיפוֹת בְּגָדִים: 6 וַיָּבֵא הַסֵּפֶר אֶל־מֶלֶךְ יִשְׂרָאֵל לֵאמֹר וְעַתָּה כְּבוֹא הַסֵּפֶר הַזֶּה אֵלֶיךָ הִנֵּה שָׁלַחְתִּי אֵלֶיךָ אֶת־נַעֲמָן עַבְדִּי וַאֲסַפְתּוֹ מִצָּרַעְתּוֹ: 7 וַיְהִי כִּקְרֹא מֶלֶךְ־יִשְׂרָאֵל אֶת־הַסֵּפֶר וַיִּקְרַע בְּגָדָיו וַיֹּאמֶר הַאֱלֹהִים אָנִי לְהָמִית וּלְהַחֲיוֹת כִּי־זֶה שֹׁלֵחַ אֵלַי לֶאֱסֹף אִישׁ מִצָּרַעְתּוֹ כִּי אַךְ־דְּעוּ־נָא וּרְאוּ כִּי־מִתְאַנֶּה הוּא לִי: 8 וַיְהִי כִּשְׁמֹעַ ׀ אֱלִישָׁע אִישׁ־הָאֱלֹהִים כִּי־קָרַע מֶלֶךְ־יִשְׂרָאֵל אֶת־בְּגָדָיו וַיִּשְׁלַח אֶל־הַמֶּלֶךְ לֵאמֹר לָמָּה קָרַעְתָּ בְּגָדֶיךָ יָבֹא־

haftarat tazria‛

⁹ Naaman came with his horses and chariots and stood at the door of Elisha's house. ¹⁰ Elisha sent a messenger to tell him, "Go and wash in the Jordan seven times, and your healthy skin will be restored to you, and you will be ritually pure."

¹¹ Naaman became angry and walked off. "Here I was thinking that he'll come out in my honor, stand before me respectfully, and in order to cure me he'll call out in the name of God, his God, and he'll wave his hand towards the afflicted area and I, the *tzara'at* sufferer, would miraculously be healed! ¹² Aren't Amanah and Pharpar, the rivers of Damascus, better than all the waters of Israel? I am always washing there, and yet am I pure of *tzara'at*?" He turned away and left in anger.

¹³ His servants approached him and spoke to him. They said, "Sir, if the prophet had told you to do something difficult, wouldn't you have done it? All the more so when he tells you an easy thing, 'Wash and become pure,' you should listen."

¹⁴ Naaman went and immersed himself seven times in the Jordan, as the man of God had told him. His skin returned to be like the skin of a young child, and he was pure of *tzara'at*.

¹⁵ Naaman returned to the man of God—both he and all his entourage—and came and stood before him. Naaman said, "Now I know that there is no God in the whole world other than in Israel. Now, please accept a gift from your servant."

¹⁶ Elisha replied, "By the living God, before whom I regularly stand in prayer, I cannot accept any gift!"

Naaman begged Elisha to take something, but he refused. ¹⁷ Naaman said, "At least let your servant be given two mule-loads of earth from the Holy Land, to build an altar, for your servant will no longer offer burnt-offerings or sacrifices to other gods, but only to God!"

¹⁸ "May your servant please ask God to forgive me though for this one thing: When my master the King goes to the temple of Rimmon to bow down there, his bowing coerces me to bow down too in the temple of Rimmon. May God please forgive your servant for this, for bowing down in the temple of Rimmon."

¹⁹ Elisha told him, "Go in peace," and Naaman traveled away from him some distance.

9 וַיָּבֹא נַעֲמָן בְּסוּסָיו וּבְרִכְבּוֹ וַיַּעֲמֹד פֶּתַח־הַבַּיִת לֶאֱלִישָׁע: 10 וַיִּשְׁלַח אֵלָיו אֱלִישָׁע מַלְאָךְ לֵאמֹר הָלוֹךְ וְרָחַצְתָּ שֶׁבַע־פְּעָמִים בַּיַּרְדֵּן וְיָשֹׁב בְּשָׂרְךָ לְךָ וּטְהָר: 11 וַיִּקְצֹף נַעֲמָן וַיֵּלַךְ וַיֹּאמֶר הִנֵּה אָמַרְתִּי אֵלַי ׀ יֵצֵא יָצוֹא וְעָמַד וְקָרָא בְּשֵׁם־יְהֹוָה אֱלֹהָיו וְהֵנִיף יָדוֹ אֶל־הַמָּקוֹם וְאָסַף הַמְּצֹרָע: 12 הֲלֹא טוֹב [אבנה כ׳] אֲמָנָה וּפַרְפַּר נַהֲרוֹת דַּמֶּשֶׂק מִכֹּל מֵימֵי יִשְׂרָאֵל הֲלֹא־אֶרְחַץ בָּהֶם וְטָהָרְתִּי וַיִּפֶן וַיֵּלֶךְ בְּחֵמָה: 13 וַיִּגְּשׁוּ עֲבָדָיו וַיְדַבְּרוּ אֵלָיו וַיֹּאמְרוּ אָבִי דָּבָר גָּדוֹל הַנָּבִיא דִּבֶּר אֵלֶיךָ הֲלוֹא תַעֲשֶׂה וְאַף כִּי־אָמַר אֵלֶיךָ רְחַץ וּטְהָר: 14 וַיֵּרֶד וַיִּטְבֹּל בַּיַּרְדֵּן שֶׁבַע פְּעָמִים כִּדְבַר אִישׁ הָאֱלֹהִים וַיָּשָׁב בְּשָׂרוֹ כִּבְשַׂר נַעַר קָטֹן וַיִּטְהָר: 15 וַיָּשָׁב אֶל־אִישׁ הָאֱלֹהִים הוּא וְכׇל־מַחֲנֵהוּ וַיָּבֹא וַיַּעֲמֹד לְפָנָיו וַיֹּאמֶר הִנֵּה־נָא יָדַעְתִּי כִּי אֵין אֱלֹהִים בְּכׇל־הָאָרֶץ כִּי אִם־בְּיִשְׂרָאֵל וְעַתָּה קַח־נָא בְרָכָה מֵאֵת עַבְדֶּךָ: 16 וַיֹּאמֶר חַי־יְהֹוָה אֲשֶׁר־עָמַדְתִּי לְפָנָיו אִם־אֶקָּח וַיִּפְצַר־בּוֹ לָקַחַת וַיְמָאֵן: 17 וַיֹּאמֶר נַעֲמָן וָלֹא יֻתַּן־נָא לְעַבְדְּךָ מַשָּׂא צֶמֶד־פְּרָדִים אֲדָמָה כִּי לוֹא־יַעֲשֶׂה עוֹד עַבְדְּךָ עֹלָה וָזֶבַח לֵאלֹהִים אֲחֵרִים כִּי אִם־לַיהֹוָה: 18 לַדָּבָר הַזֶּה יִסְלַח יְהֹוָה לְעַבְדֶּךָ בְּבוֹא אֲדֹנִי בֵית־רִמּוֹן לְהִשְׁתַּחֲוֺת שָׁמָּה וְהוּא ׀ נִשְׁעָן עַל־יָדִי וְהִשְׁתַּחֲוֵיתִי בֵּית רִמֹּן בְּהִשְׁתַּחֲוָיָתִי בֵּית רִמֹּן [יסלח־נא כ׳] יִסְלַח־יְהֹוָה לְעַבְדְּךָ בַּדָּבָר הַזֶּה: 19 וַיֹּאמֶר לוֹ לֵךְ לְשָׁלוֹם וַיֵּלֶךְ מֵאִתּוֹ כִּבְרַת־אָרֶץ:

הפטרת מצורע

haftarat metzora'
and tazria'–metzora'

ALL COMMUNITIES—II KINGS 7:3–20

> **SYNOPSIS:** This *Haftarah* relates the account of "four *tzara'at* sufferers," in connection with the *Parashah* which discusses the purification from *tzara'at*.
>
> The *Haftarah* takes place during the siege of Samaria by King Ben-Hadad of Aram, which caused a terrible famine, even driving people to cannibalism (*II Kings* 6:24–29). The king blames Elisha, who in the past had averted famine with his prayers, but Elisha states calmly—to the disbelief of the king's messenger—that food will be freely available "at this time tomorrow" (6:30–7:3).
>
> Against this backdrop, the *Haftarah* begins. We read of four starving *tzara'at* sufferers quarantined outside the city, who defect to the Aramean camp. To their immense surprise, they find the Aramean camp deserted, *"(because) God had caused the Aramean camp to (imagine that they) heard … the sound of a great army … and fled"* (7:3–7). The *tzara'at* sufferers seize the moment to rejoice, looting silver and gold (8), but realizing the consequences of hiding this good news from the king, they return to the city and inform the palace of what had happened (9–11). The king, however, perceives the whole affair as a conspiracy, thinking that the Arameans would surely ambush the Jewish people when they came out to the "deserted" camp, so he sends two horsemen to investigate (12–14). The report is soon confirmed, and Elisha's astonishing prediction thus corroborated (15–16). As a final twist to the story, the king's messenger who initially dismissed Elisha's prediction is trampled to death, fulfilling the prophet's words, *"You will see it with your eyes, but you will not eat any of it"* (17–20).

7 ³ There were four men, *tzara'at* sufferers, sitting at the city gate.

They said to each other, "Why are we sitting here until we die of hunger? ⁴ If we decide, 'Let's go into the city,' we'll die there, with the famine in town. And if we sit here, we'll certainly die! So let's turn to the Aramean camp. If they let us live, we'll live, and if they kill us, we won't lose because we'll die here in any case!" ⁵ So they set out in the evening for the Aramean camp.

When they came to the edge of the Aramean camp, there was no one there, ⁶ because God had caused the Aramean camp to imagine that they heard the sound of chariots and horses, the sound of a great army. The Arameans said to each other, "Look! The king of Israel has hired the Hittite kings and the Egyptian kings to attack us and it is their sound we are hearing!" ⁷ They got going and fled in the evening, abandoning their tents, horses, and donkeys. They left the camp as it was and fled for their lives.

ז ³ וְאַרְבָּעָה אֲנָשִׁים הָיוּ מְצֹרָעִים פֶּתַח הַשָּׁעַר וַיֹּאמְרוּ אִישׁ אֶל־רֵעֵהוּ מָה אֲנַחְנוּ יֹשְׁבִים פֹּה עַד־מָתְנוּ: ⁴ אִם־אָמַרְנוּ נָבוֹא הָעִיר וְהָרָעָב בָּעִיר וָמַתְנוּ שָׁם וְאִם־יָשַׁבְנוּ פֹה וָמָתְנוּ לְכוּ וְנִפְּלָה אֶל־מַחֲנֵה אֲרָם אִם־יְחַיֻּנוּ נִחְיֶה וְאִם־יְמִיתֻנוּ וָמָתְנוּ: ⁵ וַיָּקֻמוּ בַנֶּשֶׁף לָבוֹא אֶל־מַחֲנֵה אֲרָם וַיָּבֹאוּ עַד־קְצֵה מַחֲנֵה אֲרָם וְהִנֵּה אֵין־שָׁם אִישׁ: ⁶ וַאדֹנָי הִשְׁמִיעַ | אֶת־מַחֲנֵה אֲרָם קוֹל רֶכֶב קוֹל סוּס קוֹל חַיִל גָּדוֹל וַיֹּאמְרוּ אִישׁ אֶל־אָחִיו הִנֵּה שָׂכַר־עָלֵינוּ מֶלֶךְ יִשְׂרָאֵל אֶת־מַלְכֵי הַחִתִּים וְאֶת־מַלְכֵי מִצְרַיִם לָבוֹא עָלֵינוּ: ⁷ וַיָּקוּמוּ וַיָּנוּסוּ בַנֶּשֶׁף וַיַּעַזְבוּ אֶת־אָהֳלֵיהֶם וְאֶת־סוּסֵיהֶם וְאֶת־חֲמֹרֵיהֶם הַמַּחֲנֶה כַּאֲשֶׁר

haftarat metzora‘

⁸ When these *tzara'at* sufferers came to the edge of the camp, they entered one of the tents. They ate and drank, and carried away silver, gold, and clothing from there. Then they went and hid it, came back, entered another tent, carried away its contents from there, and hid it again.

⁹ They said to each other, "We're not doing the right thing! Today is a day of good news, and we're being silent. If we wait until daybreak, the king will find out about it through other sources and we'll be guilty in his eyes of withholding good news. Let's go and inform the king's palace."

¹⁰ When they arrived they called out to the city's gatekeeper and told him, "We entered the Aramean camp and—look!—there was not a person or a sound there; only horses tied up, donkeys tied up, and tents, just as they were."

¹¹ The city gatekeepers called the gatekeepers of the king's palace who informed the king's household within.

¹² The king got up in the night and said to his servants, "Now I'll tell you what Aram is plotting to do to us. They know that we're starving, so they've left their camp and hidden in the fields, saying, 'When the Jews will leave the town looking for food, we'll take them alive and enter the town.'"

¹³ One of his servants responded, saying, "Let us take five of the horses which are still here to investigate. Their rider's lives are in danger, anyway, like the masses of Jewish people who remain here, and even if they die a bit sooner they will be like the masses of Jewish people who have already perished. So let us send the riders and see what happens."

¹⁴ Because of the danger they took only two horsemen. The king sent them out to the Aramean camp, saying, "Go and investigate." ¹⁵ They followed the Arameans to the Jordan, and—look!—the whole road was filled with clothing and utensils which the Arameans had thrown away in their haste so they could flee quickly.

The messengers returned and reported back to the king, ¹⁶ and the people went out and plundered the Aramean camp.

Then—as Elisha, the man of God had predicted—a *seah* of fine flour went for a shekel, and two *seah* of barley also went for a shekel.

¹⁷ The king put the official, on whom he had relied, in charge of the gate. The people trampled him to

8 וַיָּבֹאוּ הַמְצֹרָעִים הָאֵלֶּה עַד־קְצֵה הַמַּחֲנֶה וַיָּבֹאוּ אֶל־אֹהֶל אֶחָד וַיֹּאכְלוּ וַיִּשְׁתּוּ וַיִּשְׂאוּ מִשָּׁם כֶּסֶף וְזָהָב וּבְגָדִים וַיֵּלְכוּ וַיַּטְמִנוּ וַיָּשֻׁבוּ וַיָּבֹאוּ אֶל־אֹהֶל אַחֵר וַיִּשְׂאוּ מִשָּׁם וַיֵּלְכוּ וַיַּטְמִנוּ: 9 וַיֹּאמְרוּ אִישׁ אֶל־רֵעֵהוּ לֹא־כֵן ׀ אֲנַחְנוּ עֹשִׂים הַיּוֹם הַזֶּה יוֹם־בְּשֹׂרָה הוּא וַאֲנַחְנוּ מַחְשִׁים וְחִכִּינוּ עַד־אוֹר הַבֹּקֶר וּמְצָאָנוּ עָווֹן וְעַתָּה לְכוּ וְנָבֹאָה וְנַגִּידָה בֵּית הַמֶּלֶךְ: 10 וַיָּבֹאוּ וַיִּקְרְאוּ אֶל־שֹׁעֵר הָעִיר וַיַּגִּידוּ לָהֶם לֵאמֹר בָּאנוּ אֶל־מַחֲנֵה אֲרָם וְהִנֵּה אֵין־שָׁם אִישׁ וְקוֹל אָדָם כִּי אִם־הַסּוּס אָסוּר וְהַחֲמוֹר אָסוּר וְאֹהָלִים כַּאֲשֶׁר־הֵמָּה: 11 וַיִּקְרָא הַשֹּׁעֲרִים וַיַּגִּידוּ בֵּית הַמֶּלֶךְ פְּנִימָה: 12 וַיָּקָם הַמֶּלֶךְ לַיְלָה וַיֹּאמֶר אֶל־עֲבָדָיו אַגִּידָה־נָּא לָכֶם אֵת אֲשֶׁר־עָשׂוּ לָנוּ אֲרָם יָדְעוּ כִּי־רְעֵבִים אֲנַחְנוּ וַיֵּצְאוּ מִן־הַמַּחֲנֶה לְהֵחָבֵה [בהשדה כ׳] בַשָּׂדֶה לֵאמֹר כִּי־יֵצְאוּ מִן־הָעִיר וְנִתְפְּשֵׂם חַיִּים וְאֶל־הָעִיר נָבֹא: 13 וַיַּעַן אֶחָד מֵעֲבָדָיו וַיֹּאמֶר וְיִקְחוּ־נָא חֲמִשָּׁה מִן־הַסּוּסִים הַנִּשְׁאָרִים אֲשֶׁר נִשְׁאֲרוּ־בָהּ הִנָּם כְּכָל־[ההמון כ׳] הֲמוֹן יִשְׂרָאֵל אֲשֶׁר נִשְׁאֲרוּ־בָהּ הִנָּם כְּכָל־הֲמוֹן יִשְׂרָאֵל אֲשֶׁר־תָּמּוּ וְנִשְׁלְחָה וְנִרְאֶה: 14 וַיִּקְחוּ שְׁנֵי רֶכֶב סוּסִים וַיִּשְׁלַח הַמֶּלֶךְ אַחֲרֵי מַחֲנֵה־אֲרָם לֵאמֹר לְכוּ וּרְאוּ: 15 וַיֵּלְכוּ אַחֲרֵיהֶם עַד־הַיַּרְדֵּן וְהִנֵּה כָל־הַדֶּרֶךְ מְלֵאָה בְגָדִים וְכֵלִים אֲשֶׁר־הִשְׁלִיכוּ אֲרָם [בהחפזם כ׳] בְּחָפְזָם וַיָּשֻׁבוּ הַמַּלְאָכִים וַיַּגִּדוּ לַמֶּלֶךְ: 16 וַיֵּצֵא הָעָם וַיָּבֹזּוּ אֵת מַחֲנֵה אֲרָם וַיְהִי סְאָה־סֹלֶת בְּשֶׁקֶל וְסָאתַיִם שְׂעֹרִים בְּשֶׁקֶל כִּדְבַר יְהוָה: 17 וְהַמֶּלֶךְ הִפְקִיד אֶת־הַשָּׁלִישׁ אֲשֶׁר־נִשְׁעָן עַל־יָדוֹ עַל־הַשַּׁעַר וַיִּרְמְסֻהוּ הָעָם בַּשַּׁעַר

הפטרת אחרי מות

death at the gate, just as Elisha the man of God had said when the king came to him and Elisha spoke with the official.

¹⁸ For when the man of God told the king, "Two *seah* of barley will go for a shekel, and a *seah* of fine flour will go for a shekel tomorrow at the gate of Samaria," ¹⁹ the official answered the man of God, "Even if God made windows in the sky, could such a thing happen?" and Elisha responded, "You will see it with your eyes, but you will not eat any of it."

²⁰ And so it happened to him as Elisha, the man of God had said: the people trampled him at the gate, and he died.

וַיְמָת כַּאֲשֶׁר דִּבֶּר אִישׁ הָאֱלֹהִים אֲשֶׁר דִּבֶּר בְּרֶדֶת הַמֶּלֶךְ אֵלָיו: 18 וַיְהִי כְּדַבֵּר אִישׁ הָאֱלֹהִים אֶל־הַמֶּלֶךְ לֵאמֹר סָאתַיִם שְׂעֹרִים בְּשֶׁקֶל וּסְאָה־סֹלֶת בְּשֶׁקֶל יִהְיֶה כָּעֵת מָחָר בְּשַׁעַר שֹׁמְרוֹן: 19 וַיַּעַן הַשָּׁלִישׁ אֶת־אִישׁ הָאֱלֹהִים וַיֹּאמַר וְהִנֵּה יְהוָֹה עֹשֶׂה אֲרֻבּוֹת בַּשָּׁמַיִם הֲיִהְיֶה כַּדָּבָר הַזֶּה וַיֹּאמֶר הִנְּךָ רֹאֶה בְּעֵינֶיךָ וּמִשָּׁם לֹא תֹאכֵל: 20 וַיְהִי־לוֹ כֵּן וַיִּרְמְסוּ אֹתוֹ הָעָם בַּשַּׁעַר וַיָּמֹת:

haftarat 'aḥarei mot
and *'aḥarei mot–kedoshim**

SEPHARDIM—EZEKIEL 22:1–16
ASHKENAZIM AND HABAD—AMOS 9:7–15

SYNOPSIS: This *Haftarah* contains God's rebuke to the Jewish people for acting like the non-Jewish nations, similar to that found in the *Parashah* (18:3; 28).

Amos, the author of the *Haftarah*, lived in the mid-eighth century B.C.E. in Tekoa, five miles to the south of Bethlehem. The predominant theme of his prophecies is morality and Divine justice. He was killed by King Uzziah, who struck him on the forehead with a glowing iron. (The *Haftarah* of *Parashat Va-Yeshev* is also taken from Amos.) The *Haftarah*, taken from the concluding chapter of the Book of Amos, contains a message of comfort. After a brief introduction in which the prophet criticizes the Jewish people for their sins, and threatens Divine retribution (7–8), the mood shifts swiftly to one of hope and promise. We are consoled that God will not wipe out the Jewish people entirely (8–10), that the Davidic monarchy will be reestablished (11–12), and that the remnant will return and the land will yield abundantly (13–15).

Habad and *Ashkenazic* communities read the following *Haftarah*:
[*Sephardic* communities read the *Ashkenazic Haftarah* of *Kedoshim*, page 1362.]

ט ⁷ "O children of Israel," says God, "you are to Me like the loyal children of Cush who serve their masters for life. For I only took Israel out from Egypt to serve Me, but I did not take the Philistines from Caphtor, nor Aram from Kir.

⁸ "But since you sinned, the eyes of God Almighty are upon the sinful kingdom of Ephraim, and I will

ט 7 הֲלוֹא כִבְנֵי כֻשִׁיִּים אַתֶּם לִי בְּנֵי יִשְׂרָאֵל נְאֻם־יְהוָֹה הֲלוֹא אֶת־יִשְׂרָאֵל הֶעֱלֵיתִי מֵאֶרֶץ מִצְרַיִם וּפְלִשְׁתִּיִּים מִכַּפְתּוֹר וַאֲרָם מִקִּיר: 8 הִנֵּה עֵינֵי | אֲדֹנָי יְהֹוִה בַּמַּמְלָכָה הַחַטָּאָה וְהִשְׁמַדְתִּי אֹתָהּ מֵעַל

---

* When *'Aharei Mot* and *Kedoshim* are combined, *Sephardic* communities read the *Haftarah* for *Kedoshim*—page 1359.

haftarat kedoshim

wipe it off the face of the earth! But I will not completely destroy the House of Jacob," says God, "I will only destroy the monarchy of Ephraim." ⁹ For I shall issue a command, and I will exile the House of Israel among all the nations! But the righteous will persevere just as a pebble shakes back and forth in a sieve but does not fall to the ground. ¹⁰ All the sinners of My people who say, 'No evil will approach or come to us quickly,' because they deny the principle of reward and punishment, will die at the sword of the nations, but the righteous will persevere.

¹¹ "On that day when the wicked are punished, I will erect David's fallen booth. I will build its broken walls caused by the split into two kingdoms, erect its ruined status during exile, and rebuild it as it was in former times. ¹² The monarchy will be such that the Jewish people, who are called by My name 'the people of God,' will inherit the remaining peoples of Edom and all the other nations to be their servants," says God, who will carry out this promise.

¹³ "Look! Days are coming," says God, "when the plowman will be so busy with the large amount of crops that he continues plowing up to the time of reaping, so that he meets up with the reaper. The treader of grapes will be so busy with the large volume of grapes, that he meets with the seed carrier who is going to plant the new crop. So many grapes will grow on the mountains that wine will drip from the mountains and there will be such an abundance of food that it will appear as if the hills have melted forming oil and milk.

פְּנֵי הָאֲדָמָה אָפֶס כִּי לֹא הַשְׁמֵיד אַשְׁמִיד אֶת־בֵּית יַעֲקֹב נְאֻם־יְהוָה: ⁹ כִּי־הִנֵּה אָנֹכִי מְצַוֶּה וַהֲנִעוֹתִי בְכָל־הַגּוֹיִם אֶת־בֵּית יִשְׂרָאֵל כַּאֲשֶׁר יִנּוֹעַ בַּכְּבָרָה וְלֹא־יִפּוֹל צְרוֹר אָרֶץ: ¹⁰ בַּחֶרֶב יָמוּתוּ כֹּל חַטָּאֵי עַמִּי הָאֹמְרִים לֹא־תַגִּישׁ וְתַקְדִּים בַּעֲדֵינוּ הָרָעָה: ¹¹ בַּיּוֹם הַהוּא אָקִים אֶת־סֻכַּת דָּוִיד הַנֹּפֶלֶת וְגָדַרְתִּי אֶת־פִּרְצֵיהֶן וַהֲרִסֹתָיו אָקִים וּבְנִיתִיהָ כִּימֵי עוֹלָם: ¹² לְמַעַן יִירְשׁוּ אֶת־שְׁאֵרִית אֱדוֹם וְכָל־הַגּוֹיִם אֲשֶׁר־נִקְרָא שְׁמִי עֲלֵיהֶם נְאֻם־יְהוָה עֹשֶׂה זֹּאת: ¹³ הִנֵּה יָמִים בָּאִים נְאֻם־יְהוָה וְנִגַּשׁ חוֹרֵשׁ בַּקֹּצֵר וְדֹרֵךְ עֲנָבִים בְּמֹשֵׁךְ הַזָּרַע וְהִטִּיפוּ הֶהָרִים עָסִיס וְכָל־הַגְּבָעוֹת תִּתְמוֹגַגְנָה: ¹⁴ וְשַׁבְתִּי אֶת־שְׁבוּת עַמִּי יִשְׂרָאֵל וּבָנוּ עָרִים נְשַׁמּוֹת וְיָשָׁבוּ וְנָטְעוּ כְרָמִים וְשָׁתוּ אֶת־יֵינָם וְעָשׂוּ גַנּוֹת וְאָכְלוּ אֶת־פְּרִיהֶם: ¹⁵ וּנְטַעְתִּים עַל־אַדְמָתָם וְלֹא יִנָּתְשׁוּ עוֹד מֵעַל אַדְמָתָם אֲשֶׁר נָתַתִּי לָהֶם אָמַר יְהוָה אֱלֹהֶיךָ:

¹⁴ "I will then pacify the exiles of Israel, My people. They will rebuild the cities that were destroyed during the exile and inhabit them forever. They will plant vineyards and they alone will drink their wine. They will cultivate gardens and eat their fruits. ¹⁵ I will plant them on their land with firm roots, like a tree, and they will never again be uprooted from the land that I have given them," says God, your God.

haftarat kedoshim

ASHKENAZIM—EZEKIEL 22:1–16
SEPHARDIM AND HABAD—EZEKIEL 20:2–20

SYNOPSIS: The *Haftarah* and the *Parashah* both stress the theme of observing the law (*Leviticus* 20:8; *Ezekiel* 20:19), and doing so "in order to live" (*Leviticus* 18:5; *Ezekiel* 20:11,13).

The *Haftarah* is a historical review of Israel's sinful past, spanning a number of different time periods. Each unit concludes that God preserved the Jewish people only so

הפטרת קדושים

that His name would not be profaned among the nations. Initially, the Jewish people in Egypt are condemned for clinging to idolatry (2–9), and this is followed by a rebuke to the same generation for abandoning God's commands after reaching the desert (10–14). They are then criticized for the sin of the spies (15–17). Finally, the second desert generation are warned not to follow in their parents' ways (18). The *Haftarah* concludes with a call to observe the commandments and keep the Sabbath (19–20).

Ḥabad and *Sephardic* communities read the following;
Ashkenazic communities read the *Haftarah* on page 1362.

[*Sephardic* communities read this *Haftarah* when *Aḥarei Mot* and *Kedoshim* are combined.]

20

² The word of God came to me, saying, ³ "Son of Man, speak to the elders of Israel and say to them, 'This is what God Almighty says: "Have you come to petition Me in prayer, to save Jerusalem? As I live," says God Almighty, "I will not let you petition Me!"'

⁴ "If you need to debate with them to prove that I am the One who passes judgment on man, then inform them of their ancestors' abominations in addition to their own sins! ⁵ Say to them: This is what God Almighty says: When I chose Israel at the time they were in Egypt, I raised My hand and took an oath to the descendants of Jacob's house, and I revealed Myself to them in the land of Egypt by bringing the Divine Presence upon Aaron. I raised My hand and swore to them, saying, 'I am God, your God, who guides you personally.' ⁶ On that day I also lifted My hand and swore to take them out of the land of Egypt to a land which I had sought out for them—a land flowing with milk and honey, the most beautiful of all lands.

⁷ "I said to them through Aaron, 'Let each man discard the detestable things which your eyes attract you to! Do not contaminate yourselves by following after the idols of Egypt. If I am God, your God, how could you trade Me for idols?'

⁸ "But even while they were in Egypt they rebelled against Me and did not want to listen to Me. They did not discard the detestable things that they saw, nor did they abandon the idols of Egypt. So I intended to *pour out My fury upon them and release all of My anger against them in the land of Egypt.*

⁹ "However, I acted for the sake of My name, so it would not be profaned in the eyes of the nations

כ

2 וַיְהִ֥י דְבַר־יְהֹוָ֖ה אֵלַ֥י לֵאמֹֽר: 3 בֶּן־אָדָ֗ם דַּבֵּ֞ר אֶת־זִקְנֵ֤י יִשְׂרָאֵל֙ וְאָמַרְתָּ֣ אֲלֵהֶ֔ם כֹּ֤ה אָמַר֙ אֲדֹנָ֣י יֱהֹוִ֔ה הֲלִדְרֹ֥שׁ אֹתִ֖י אַתֶּ֣ם בָּאִ֑ים חַי־אָ֜נִי אִם־אִדָּרֵ֤שׁ לָכֶם֙ נְאֻ֖ם אֲדֹנָ֥י יֱהֹוִֽה: 4 הֲתִשְׁפֹּ֥ט אֹתָ֖ם הֲתִשְׁפּ֣וֹט בֶּן־אָדָ֑ם אֶת־תּוֹעֲבֹ֥ת אֲבוֹתָ֖ם הֽוֹדִיעֵֽם: 5 וְאָֽמַרְתָּ֣ אֲלֵיהֶ֗ם כֹּה־אָמַר֮ אֲדֹנָ֣י יֱהֹוִה֒ בְּיוֹם֙ בָּחֳרִ֣י בְיִשְׂרָאֵ֔ל וָאֶשָּׂ֣א יָדִ֗י לְזֶ֨רַע֙ בֵּ֣ית יַֽעֲקֹ֔ב וָֽאִוָּדַ֥ע לָהֶ֖ם בְּאֶ֣רֶץ מִצְרָ֑יִם וָֽאֶשָּׂ֨א יָדִ֤י לָהֶם֙ לֵאמֹ֔ר אֲנִ֖י יְהֹוָ֥ה אֱלֹֽהֵיכֶֽם: 6 בַּיּ֣וֹם הַה֗וּא נָשָׂ֤אתִי יָדִי֙ לָהֶ֔ם לְהֽוֹצִיאָ֖ם מֵאֶ֣רֶץ מִצְרָ֑יִם אֶל־אֶ֜רֶץ אֲשֶׁר־תַּ֣רְתִּי לָהֶ֗ם זָבַ֤ת חָלָב֙ וּדְבַ֔שׁ צְבִ֥י הִ֖יא לְכָל־הָֽאֲרָצֽוֹת: 7 וָאֹמַ֣ר אֲלֵהֶ֗ם אִ֚ישׁ שִׁקּוּצֵ֣י עֵינָ֔יו הַשְׁלִ֕יכוּ וּבְגִלּוּלֵ֥י מִצְרַ֖יִם אַל־תִּטַּמָּ֑אוּ אֲנִ֖י יְהֹוָ֥ה אֱלֹֽהֵיכֶֽם: 8 וַיַּמְרוּ־בִ֗י וְלֹ֤א אָבוּ֙ לִשְׁמֹ֣עַ אֵלַ֔י אִ֚ישׁ אֶת־שִׁקּוּצֵ֤י עֵֽינֵיהֶם֙ לֹ֣א הִשְׁלִ֔יכוּ וְאֶת־גִּלּוּלֵ֥י מִצְרַ֖יִם לֹ֣א עָזָ֑בוּ וָֽאֹמַ֞ר לִשְׁפֹּ֧ךְ חֲמָתִ֣י עֲלֵיהֶ֗ם לְכַלּ֤וֹת אַפִּי֙ בָּהֶ֔ם בְּת֖וֹךְ אֶ֥רֶץ מִצְרָֽיִם: 9 וָאַ֨עַשׂ֙ לְמַ֣עַן שְׁמִ֔י לְבִלְתִּ֥י

haftarat kedoshim

among whom they lived. For I had revealed Myself to the Jewish people through Aaron in the presence of the nations, promising to take them out of the land of Egypt, so I did not want the Egyptians to think I was incapable of doing so.

¹⁰ "I took them out of the land of Egypt and brought them to the desert. ¹¹ I gave them My suprarational commands and informed them of My rational commands, which a man should do in order to help a person live in this world and the next. ¹² I also gave them My Sabbaths as a sign between Myself and them, so that they should know that I am God, who sanctifies them to be My people.

¹³ "But the House of Israel rebelled against Me in the desert! They did not follow My suprarational commands and they spurned My rational commands, even though a man follows them for his own benefit, in order to help him live in this world and the next. And they greatly profaned My Sabbaths, transgressing on the very first occasion. So I intended to pour out My fury upon them in the desert, and destroy them.

¹⁴ "However, I acted for the sake of My name, so it would not be profaned in the eyes of the nations who watched Me take them out, for they might think that I was unable to bring the Jewish people to the land of Canaan.

¹⁵ "And, after the sin of the spies, I also lifted My hand and swore to them in the desert that I would not bring them to the land which I had given them, the one flowing with milk and honey, the most beautiful of all lands. ¹⁶ This is because they had spurned My rational laws, had not followed My suprarational commands and profaned My Sabbaths, for their hearts followed their idols which they had worshiped in Egypt.

¹⁷ "Even though they deserved to be destroyed, I had pity on them, so I did not wipe them out in the desert.

¹⁸ "I said to their children, the next generation, in the desert, 'Do not follow the statutes of your parents, and do not keep their laws which God has not commanded. Do not defile yourselves with their idols.

¹⁹ "I am God, your God. So listen to Me and follow My suprarational commands; guard your hearts and observe My rational commands. ²⁰ Keep My Sabbaths holy, in order that they should be a sign between Me and you, to know that I am God, your God.'"

הַחֵל לְעֵינֵי הַגּוֹיִם אֲשֶׁר־הֵמָּה בְתוֹכָם אֲשֶׁר נוֹדַעְתִּי אֲלֵיהֶם לְעֵינֵיהֶם לְהוֹצִיאָם מֵאֶרֶץ מִצְרָיִם: 10 וָאוֹצִיאֵם מֵאֶרֶץ מִצְרַיִם וָאֲבִאֵם אֶל־הַמִּדְבָּר: 11 וָאֶתֵּן לָהֶם אֶת־חֻקּוֹתַי וְאֶת־מִשְׁפָּטַי הוֹדַעְתִּי אוֹתָם אֲשֶׁר יַעֲשֶׂה אוֹתָם הָאָדָם וָחַי בָּהֶם: 12 וְגַם אֶת־שַׁבְּתוֹתַי נָתַתִּי לָהֶם לִהְיוֹת לְאוֹת בֵּינִי וּבֵינֵיהֶם לָדַעַת כִּי אֲנִי יְהֹוָה מְקַדְּשָׁם: 13 וַיַּמְרוּ־בִי בֵית־יִשְׂרָאֵל בַּמִּדְבָּר בְּחֻקּוֹתַי לֹא־הָלָכוּ וְאֶת־מִשְׁפָּטַי מָאָסוּ אֲשֶׁר יַעֲשֶׂה אוֹתָם הָאָדָם וָחַי בָּהֶם וְאֶת־שַׁבְּתֹתַי חִלְּלוּ מְאֹד וָאֹמַר לִשְׁפֹּךְ חֲמָתִי עֲלֵיהֶם בַּמִּדְבָּר לְכַלּוֹתָם: 14 וָאֶעֱשֶׂה לְמַעַן שְׁמִי לְבִלְתִּי הֵחֵל לְעֵינֵי הַגּוֹיִם אֲשֶׁר הוֹצֵאתִים לְעֵינֵיהֶם: 15 וְגַם־אֲנִי נָשָׂאתִי יָדִי לָהֶם בַּמִּדְבָּר לְבִלְתִּי הָבִיא אוֹתָם אֶל־הָאָרֶץ אֲשֶׁר־נָתַתִּי זָבַת חָלָב וּדְבַשׁ צְבִי הִיא לְכָל־הָאֲרָצוֹת: 16 יַעַן בְּמִשְׁפָּטַי מָאָסוּ וְאֶת־חֻקּוֹתַי לֹא־הָלְכוּ בָהֶם וְאֶת־שַׁבְּתוֹתַי חִלֵּלוּ כִּי אַחֲרֵי גִלּוּלֵיהֶם לִבָּם הֹלֵךְ: 17 וַתָּחָס עֵינִי עֲלֵיהֶם מִשַּׁחֲתָם וְלֹא־עָשִׂיתִי אוֹתָם כָּלָה בַּמִּדְבָּר: 18 וָאֹמַר אֶל־בְּנֵיהֶם בַּמִּדְבָּר בְּחוּקֵּי אֲבוֹתֵיכֶם אַל־תֵּלֵכוּ וְאֶת־מִשְׁפְּטֵיהֶם אַל־תִּשְׁמֹרוּ וּבְגִלּוּלֵיהֶם אַל־תִּטַּמָּאוּ: 19 אֲנִי יְהֹוָה אֱלֹהֵיכֶם בְּחֻקּוֹתַי לֵכוּ וְאֶת־מִשְׁפָּטַי שִׁמְרוּ וַעֲשׂוּ אוֹתָם: 20 וְאֶת־שַׁבְּתוֹתַי קַדֵּשׁוּ וְהָיוּ לְאוֹת בֵּינִי וּבֵינֵיכֶם לָדַעַת כִּי אֲנִי יְהֹוָה אֱלֹהֵיכֶם:

הפטרת קדושים

***Haftarah* of *Kedoshim* read by Ashkenazic communities:**

> **SYNOPSIS:** In this *Haftarah*, the Jewish people are admonished for abominations that they were warned about in the *Parashah*.
>
> The *Haftarah* is an elaborate criticism of the city of Jerusalem, detailing its many sins and "abominations," delivered by the prophet Ezekiel some time before the destruction of Jerusalem in 586 B.C.E.
>
> The *Haftarah* is divided into three units. In the first (22:1–5), God instructs Ezekiel to condemn Jerusalem for its moral and religious crimes. The following section specifies these sins in graphic detail (6–12), and this is followed by a declaration of impending punishment and destruction so that *"you will know that I am God"* (13–16).

22 ¹ God's word came to me, saying, ² "And you, son of man, will you contest? Will you contest with the people of the city who spill innocent blood, and declare to her all her abominations? ³ You should say to them: This is what God Almighty says, 'To a city in which blood is shed, its time of retribution will come. The city is also guilty of making idols with which to defile itself. ⁴ You are guilty because of the blood you shed, and you have become defiled by the idols which you made! You have brought near the days of your retribution, and caused your years to end. Therefore, I have made you an object of shame for the nations, a mockery for all the lands. ⁵ Those near and far from you will mock you, Israel, you who have a defiled name, and who are of great turmoil.'

⁶ "Look, leaders of Israel! Each one of you used his strength to shed blood. ⁷ Fathers and mothers have been disgraced by you, the convert has been oppressed by you, the orphan and widow have been cheated through you. ⁸ You desecrated My holy things and profaned My Sabbaths. ⁹ Gossipers were among you whose goal was that blood be shed. Through you, they ate the remains of idol-worship on the mountains, and performed disgraceful acts in your midst. ¹⁰ Through you, they revealed the nakedness of their fathers' wives; through you they violated women who were in a state of ritual impurity. ¹¹ Through you, a man would perform abominations with his friend's wife; another man would defile his daughter-in-law in lust; another would violate his sister, his father's daughter. ¹² They took bribes to pervert justice and shed innocent blood in your midst. You took cash-interest and goods-interest,

כב ¹ וַיְהִי דְבַר־יְהֹוָה אֵלַי לֵאמֹר: ² וְאַתָּה בֶן־אָדָם הֲתִשְׁפֹּט הֲתִשְׁפֹּט אֶת־עִיר הַדָּמִים וְהוֹדַעְתָּהּ אֵת כָּל־תּוֹעֲבוֹתֶיהָ: ³ וְאָמַרְתָּ כֹּה אָמַר אֲדֹנָי יֱהֹוִה עִיר שֹׁפֶכֶת דָּם בְּתוֹכָהּ לָבוֹא עִתָּהּ וְעָשְׂתָה גִלּוּלִים עָלֶיהָ לְטָמְאָה: ⁴ בְּדָמֵךְ אֲשֶׁר־שָׁפַכְתְּ אָשַׁמְתְּ וּבְגִלּוּלַיִךְ אֲשֶׁר־עָשִׂית טָמֵאת וַתַּקְרִיבִי יָמַיִךְ וַתָּבוֹא עַד־שְׁנוֹתָיִךְ עַל־כֵּן נְתַתִּיךְ חֶרְפָּה לַגּוֹיִם וְקַלָּסָה לְכָל־הָאֲרָצוֹת: ⁵ הַקְּרֹבוֹת וְהָרְחֹקוֹת מִמֵּךְ יִתְקַלְּסוּ־בָךְ טְמֵאַת הַשֵּׁם רַבַּת הַמְּהוּמָה:

⁶ הִנֵּה נְשִׂיאֵי יִשְׂרָאֵל אִישׁ לִזְרֹעוֹ הָיוּ בָךְ לְמַעַן שְׁפָךְ־דָּם: ⁷ אָב וָאֵם הֵקַלּוּ בָךְ לַגֵּר עָשׂוּ בַעֹשֶׁק בְּתוֹכֵךְ יָתוֹם וְאַלְמָנָה הוֹנוּ בָךְ: ⁸ קָדָשַׁי בָּזִית וְאֶת־שַׁבְּתֹתַי חִלָּלְתְּ: ⁹ אַנְשֵׁי רָכִיל הָיוּ בָךְ לְמַעַן שְׁפָךְ־דָּם וְאֶל־הֶהָרִים אָכְלוּ בָךְ זִמָּה עָשׂוּ בְתוֹכֵךְ: ¹⁰ עֶרְוַת־אָב גִּלָּה־בָךְ טְמֵאַת הַנִּדָּה עִנּוּ־בָךְ: ¹¹ וְאִישׁ ׀ אֶת־אֵשֶׁת רֵעֵהוּ עָשָׂה תּוֹעֵבָה וְאִישׁ אֶת־כַּלָּתוֹ טִמֵּא בְזִמָּה וְאִישׁ אֶת־אֲחֹתוֹ בַת־אָבִיו עִנָּה־בָךְ: ¹² שֹׁחַד לָקְחוּ־בָךְ לְמַעַן שְׁפָךְ־דָּם נֶשֶׁךְ וְתַרְבִּית לָקַחַתְּ וַתְּבַצְּעִי

haftarat 'emor

and made your idol-worshiping friends rich through fraud, but you forgot Me," says God Almighty.

¹³ "I clapped My hands in distress over the fraud you have committed and over the innocent blood spilled in your midst. ¹⁴ Will your heart endure and your hands remain strong to fight in the days of recompense which I am preparing for you? I, God, have spoken, and I will act! ¹⁵ I will scatter you among the nations and disperse you among the lands, and I will eliminate your impurity from you. ¹⁶ You will be profaned in the eyes of the nations, and you will know that I am God."

רֵעַיִךְ בַּעֹשֶׁק וְאֹתִי שָׁכַחַתְּ נְאֻם אֲדֹנָי יֱהֹוִה: 13 וְהִנֵּה הִכֵּיתִי כַפִּי אֶל־בִּצְעֵךְ אֲשֶׁר עָשִׂית וְעַל־דָּמֵךְ אֲשֶׁר הָיוּ בְּתוֹכֵךְ: 14 הֲיַעֲמֹד לִבֵּךְ אִם־תֶּחֱזַקְנָה יָדַיִךְ לַיָּמִים אֲשֶׁר אֲנִי עֹשֶׂה אוֹתָךְ אֲנִי יְהֹוָה דִּבַּרְתִּי וְעָשִׂיתִי: 15 וַהֲפִיצוֹתִי אוֹתָךְ בַּגּוֹיִם וְזֵרִיתִיךְ בָּאֲרָצוֹת וַהֲתִמֹּתִי טֻמְאָתֵךְ מִמֵּךְ: 16 וְנִחַלְתְּ בָּךְ לְעֵינֵי גוֹיִם וְיָדַעַתְּ כִּי־אֲנִי יְהֹוָה:

haftarat 'emor

All communities—Ezekiel 44:15–31

> **SYNOPSIS:** This *Haftarah*, like the *Parashah*, mentions many laws which relate to priests. The *Haftarah* opens by delegitimizing all priests who are not descendants of Zadok, due to past offenses (44:15-16). We then read various details of the priestly rites: Day of Atonement attire (17-19), hairstyles (20), not to drink wine (21), marriage laws (23), communal responsibilities (23-24), rules of ritual purity (25-26), inaugural sacrifices (27), land-related rights (28-30), and the prohibition of eating carcasses (31).

44 ¹⁵ "The priests who are from the tribe of Levi—the descendants of Zadok who kept the watch of My Sanctuary in the times of Solomon even when the Jewish people strayed from Me—they will draw near to Me to serve Me, and they will stand before Me to offer Me fat and blood," says God Almighty. ¹⁶ "They will enter My Sanctuary and draw near to My table to serve Me by arranging the multi-surface bread, and they will observe My precautions regarding all the other forms of service.

¹⁷ "On the Day of Atonement, when the High Priest enters the gates of the Inner Courtyard standing before the Holy of Holies, he must wear linen garments. His regular garments that contain wool should not be on him when he serves inside the gates of the Inner Court and further inward.

¹⁸ "Linen turbans should be on the priests' heads, and linen pants should be on their hips. They should not tie their belts where they perspire.

¹⁹ "When the priests go out from the Temple Courtyard to the outer court where the people stand,

מה 15 וְהַכֹּהֲנִים הַלְוִיִּם בְּנֵי צָדוֹק אֲשֶׁר שָׁמְרוּ אֶת־מִשְׁמֶרֶת מִקְדָּשִׁי בִּתְעוֹת בְּנֵי־יִשְׂרָאֵל מֵעָלַי הֵמָּה יִקְרְבוּ אֵלַי לְשָׁרְתֵנִי וְעָמְדוּ לְפָנַי לְהַקְרִיב לִי חֵלֶב וָדָם נְאֻם אֲדֹנָי יֱהֹוִה: 16 הֵמָּה יָבֹאוּ אֶל־מִקְדָּשִׁי וְהֵמָּה יִקְרְבוּ אֶל־שֻׁלְחָנִי לְשָׁרְתֵנִי וְשָׁמְרוּ אֶת־מִשְׁמַרְתִּי: 17 וְהָיָה בְּבוֹאָם אֶל־שַׁעֲרֵי הֶחָצֵר הַפְּנִימִית בִּגְדֵי פִשְׁתִּים יִלְבָּשׁוּ וְלֹא־יַעֲלֶה עֲלֵיהֶם צֶמֶר בְּשָׁרְתָם בְּשַׁעֲרֵי הֶחָצֵר הַפְּנִימִית וָבָיְתָה: 18 פַּאֲרֵי פִשְׁתִּים יִהְיוּ עַל־רֹאשָׁם וּמִכְנְסֵי פִשְׁתִּים יִהְיוּ עַל־מָתְנֵיהֶם לֹא יַחְגְּרוּ בַּיָּזַע: 19 וּבְצֵאתָם אֶל־הֶחָצֵר הַחִיצוֹנָה אֶל־הֶחָצֵר הַחִיצוֹנָה אֶל־הָעָם יִפְשְׁטוּ

הפטרת אמור

אֶת־בִּגְדֵיהֶם אֲשֶׁר־הֵמָּה מְשָׁרְתִם בָּם וְהִנִּיחוּ אוֹתָם בְּלִשְׁכֹת הַקֹּדֶשׁ וְלָבְשׁוּ בְּגָדִים אֲחֵרִים וְלֹא־יְקַדְּשׁוּ אֶת־הָעָם בְּבִגְדֵיהֶם: 20 וְרֹאשָׁם לֹא יְגַלֵּחוּ וּפֶרַע לֹא יְשַׁלֵּחוּ כָּסוֹם יִכְסְמוּ אֶת־רָאשֵׁיהֶם: 21 וְיַיִן לֹא־יִשְׁתּוּ כָּל־כֹּהֵן בְּבוֹאָם אֶל־הֶחָצֵר הַפְּנִימִית: 22 וְאַלְמָנָה וּגְרוּשָׁה לֹא־יִקְחוּ לָהֶם לְנָשִׁים כִּי אִם־בְּתוּלֹת מִזֶּרַע בֵּית יִשְׂרָאֵל וְהָאַלְמָנָה אֲשֶׁר תִּהְיֶה אַלְמָנָה מִכֹּהֵן יִקָּחוּ: 23 וְאֶת־עַמִּי יוֹרוּ בֵּין קֹדֶשׁ לְחֹל וּבֵין־טָמֵא לְטָהוֹר יוֹדִיעֻם: 24 וְעַל־רִיב הֵמָּה יַעַמְדוּ [לשפט כ׳] לְמִשְׁפָּט בְּמִשְׁפָּטַי יִשְׁפְּטֻהוּ [ושפטהו כ׳] וְאֶת־תּוֹרֹתַי וְאֶת־חֻקֹּתַי בְּכָל־מוֹעֲדַי יִשְׁמֹרוּ וְאֶת־שַׁבְּתוֹתַי יְקַדֵּשׁוּ: 25 וְאֶל־מֵת אָדָם לֹא יָבוֹא לְטָמְאָה כִּי אִם־לְאָב וּלְאֵם וּלְבֵן וּלְבַת לְאָח וּלְאָחוֹת אֲשֶׁר־לֹא־הָיְתָה לְאִישׁ יִטַּמָּאוּ: 26 וְאַחֲרֵי טָהֳרָתוֹ שִׁבְעַת יָמִים יִסְפְּרוּ־לוֹ: 27 וּבְיוֹם בֹּאוֹ אֶל־הַקֹּדֶשׁ אֶל־הֶחָצֵר הַפְּנִימִית לְשָׁרֵת בַּקֹּדֶשׁ יַקְרִיב חַטָּאתוֹ נְאֻם אֲדֹנָי יֱהֹוִה: 28 וְהָיְתָה לָהֶם לְנַחֲלָה אֲנִי נַחֲלָתָם וַאֲחֻזָּה לֹא־תִתְּנוּ לָהֶם בְּיִשְׂרָאֵל אֲנִי אֲחֻזָּתָם: 29 הַמִּנְחָה וְהַחַטָּאת וְהָאָשָׁם הֵמָּה יֹאכְלוּם וְכָל־חֵרֶם בְּיִשְׂרָאֵל לָהֶם יִהְיֶה: 30 וְרֵאשִׁית כָּל־בִּכּוּרֵי כֹל וְכָל־תְּרוּמַת כֹּל מִכֹּל תְּרוּמוֹתֵיכֶם לַכֹּהֲנִים יִהְיֶה וְרֵאשִׁית עֲרִיסוֹתֵיכֶם תִּתְּנוּ לַכֹּהֵן לְהָנִיחַ בְּרָכָה אֶל־בֵּיתֶךָ: 31 כָּל־נְבֵלָה וּטְרֵפָה מִן־הָעוֹף וּמִן־הַבְּהֵמָה לֹא יֹאכְלוּ הַכֹּהֲנִים:

they should remove the priestly garments in which they serve, and leave them in the holy chambers. They should put on other non-holy clothes and not make the people appear holy by allowing them to come in contact with their vestments.

20 "They may never shave their heads, nor let their hair grow longer than thirty days. The High Priests must keep their heads trimmed.

21 "All priests and High Priests may not drink wine when they enter the Inner Court.

22 "The High Priests may not take widows or divorcees as wives, but only virgins of Jewish lineage. A widow who is a widow that did not need to perform a release from a levirate tie (*halitzah*) may be taken as a wife by a priest, but not a High Priest.

23 "The priests should teach My people about the differences between holy and mundane. They should make the differences between ritual impurity and purity known to them.

24 "They will act as judges in financial disputes, and they will judge according to My laws and not their own views. They should observe My teachings and My statutes pertaining to My holy days, and they should sanctify My Sabbaths with the appropriate sacrifices.

25 "The priests may not come in contact with a human corpse and become ritually impure. They may make themselves impure only for a father, a mother, a son, a daughter, a brother, or a sister who has not married. 26 After he is ready for purification, having separated from the corpse, they must count seven days for him and then he will be ritually pure.

27 "On the day that a priest begins his holy service in the Inner Court by the altar, to serve in the Sanctuary, he must offer his sin-offering," says God Almighty.

28 "Do not give them possession of the land of Israel, for the priesthood is their full-time inheritance. I am their inheritance so they shall have leftovers of My sacrifices. I am their possession and so are My sacrifices. 29 They will eat the leftovers of the meal-offering, the sin-offering, and the guilt-offering; what Israel sanctifies will be theirs. 30 All the first fruits of every kind, and every kind of *terumah* from all the *terumah* that you are required to give will go to the priests, and you should give the first portion of your dough to the priest. By doing all this a blessing will rest upon your house.

31 "The priests shall not eat from any carcass or mauled animal, of any type of bird or animal."

haftarat be-har

HABAD—JEREMIAH 32:6–22
SEPHARDIM AND ASHKENAZIM—JEREMIAH 32:6–27

SYNOPSIS: This *Haftarah* mentions the concept of buying and redeeming fields, mentioned in the *Parashah*.

The *Haftarah* was said by the prophet Jeremiah in the royal compound of King Zedekiah, in which he had been confined for predicting the downfall of Jerusalem into the hands of the Babylonians, which was now occurring (587 B.C.E.). In order to underscore hopes for a future restoration of the Jewish homeland, Jeremiah purchases the field of his cousin Hanamel.

The *Haftarah* opens with God's instructions to purchase the field, which were promptly followed according to all the requirements of the law (6–12). On Divine instruction, the deed was stored in an earthenware jar as a statement of confidence in the future restoration of the land (13–15). The prophet then turns to God in prayer, thanking the Almighty for His kindness and for the miracles of the past (16–22). According to Habad tradition the *Haftarah* ends here. Other communities read the continuation of Jeremiah's prayer, in which he attributes the current tragedy to a failure to follow God, and briefly describes the horrors of the Babylonian siege (23–24). He concludes by referring to the field he had just purchased as a symbol of hope, which God immediately confirms (25–26).

32

⁶ Jeremiah said: God's word came to me, saying, ⁷ "Hanamel, the son of your uncle Shallum, will come to you and say, 'Buy my field in Anathoth, for you have the right to redeem it by purchasing it.'"

⁸ My cousin Hanamel came to me, to the prison courtyard, as God said. He said to me, "Please buy my field in Anathoth, which is in the land of Benjamin, for you are my closest relative who will have the right to take possession of it. So you might as well redeem it now, rather than have to redeem it from another person, to whom I am forced to sell it. Buy it for yourself."

I knew that this was God's word, ⁹ so I bought the field in Anathoth from my cousin Hanamel. I weighed out the money for him: seven silver shekels and ten silver *sela'*, ¹⁰ I instructed that the transaction be recorded in a deed of sale, and I instructed the vendor to sign his name. I summoned witnesses who watched me weigh the silver on a balance.

¹¹ Then I took the signed deed of sale which had been made in accordance with the laws and statutes of those times with the deed of public endorsement. ¹² I gave the deed of sale and the deed of public endorsement to Baruch son of Neriah who was the son of Mahseiah, in the presence of my uncle('s son), Hanamel, for they were the witnesses who signed the deeds. This was also done

לב ⁶ וַיְהִי דְבַר־יְהֹוָה אֵלַי לֵאמֹר: ⁷ הִנֵּה חֲנַמְאֵל בֶּן־שַׁלֻּם דֹּדְךָ בָּא אֵלֶיךָ לֵאמֹר קְנֵה לְךָ אֶת־שָׂדִי אֲשֶׁר בַּעֲנָתוֹת כִּי לְךָ מִשְׁפַּט הַגְּאֻלָּה לִקְנוֹת: ⁸ וַיָּבֹא אֵלַי חֲנַמְאֵל בֶּן־דֹּדִי כִּדְבַר יְהֹוָה אֶל־חֲצַר הַמַּטָּרָה וַיֹּאמֶר אֵלַי קְנֵה נָא אֶת־שָׂדִי אֲשֶׁר־בַּעֲנָתוֹת אֲשֶׁר | בְּאֶרֶץ בִּנְיָמִין כִּי־לְךָ מִשְׁפַּט הַיְרֻשָּׁה וּלְךָ הַגְּאֻלָּה קְנֵה־לָךְ וָאֵדַע כִּי דְבַר־יְהֹוָה הוּא: ⁹ וָאֶקְנֶה אֶת־הַשָּׂדֶה מֵאֵת חֲנַמְאֵל בֶּן־דֹּדִי אֲשֶׁר בַּעֲנָתוֹת וָאֶשְׁקֲלָה־לּוֹ אֶת־הַכֶּסֶף שִׁבְעָה שְׁקָלִים וַעֲשָׂרָה הַכָּסֶף: ¹⁰ וָאֶכְתֹּב בַּסֵּפֶר וָאֶחְתֹּם וָאָעֵד עֵדִים וָאֶשְׁקֹל הַכֶּסֶף בְּמֹאזְנָיִם:

¹¹ וָאֶקַּח אֶת־סֵפֶר הַמִּקְנָה אֶת־הֶחָתוּם הַמִּצְוָה וְהַחֻקִּים וְאֶת־הַגָּלוּי: ¹² וָאֶתֵּן אֶת־הַסֵּפֶר הַמִּקְנָה אֶל־בָּרוּךְ בֶּן־נֵרִיָּה

הפטרת בהר

בֶּן־מַחְסֵיָה֙ לְעֵינֵ֣י חֲנַמְאֵ֔ל דֹּדִ֕י וּלְעֵינֵי֙ הָעֵדִ֔ים הַכֹּתְבִ֖ים בְּסֵ֣פֶר הַמִּקְנָ֑ה לְעֵינֵי֙ כׇּל־הַיְּהוּדִ֔ים הַיֹּשְׁבִ֖ים בַּחֲצַ֥ר הַמַּטָּרָֽה׃ 13 וָֽאֲצַוֶּה֙ אֶת־בָּר֔וּךְ לְעֵינֵיהֶ֖ם לֵאמֹֽר׃ 14 כֹּֽה־אָמַר֩ יְהֹוָ֨ה צְבָא֜וֹת אֱלֹהֵ֣י יִשְׂרָאֵ֗ל לָק֣וֹחַ אֶת־הַסְּפָרִ֣ים הָאֵ֡לֶּה אֵ֣ת סֵ֩פֶר֩ הַמִּקְנָ֨ה הַזֶּ֜ה וְאֵ֣ת הֶחָת֗וּם וְאֵ֨ת סֵ֤פֶר הַגָּלוּי֙ הַזֶּ֔ה וּנְתַתָּ֖ם בִּכְלִי־חָ֑רֶשׂ לְמַ֥עַן יַעַמְד֖וּ יָמִ֥ים רַבִּֽים׃ 15 כִּ֣י כֹ֥ה אָמַ֛ר יְהֹוָ֥ה צְבָא֖וֹת אֱלֹהֵ֣י יִשְׂרָאֵ֑ל ע֣וֹד יִקָּנ֥וּ בָתִּ֛ים וְשָׂד֥וֹת וּכְרָמִ֖ים בָּאָ֥רֶץ הַזֹּֽאת׃ 16 וָאֶתְפַּלֵּ֖ל אֶל־יְהֹוָ֑ה אַחֲרֵ֣י תִתִּ֗י אֶת־סֵ֙פֶר֙ הַמִּקְנָ֔ה אֶל־בָּר֥וּךְ בֶּן־נֵרִיָּ֖ה לֵאמֹֽר׃ 17 אֲהָהּ֙ אֲדֹנָ֣י יְהֹוִ֔ה הִנֵּ֣ה ׀ אַתָּ֣ה עָשִׂ֗יתָ אֶת־הַשָּׁמַ֙יִם֙ וְאֶת־הָאָ֔רֶץ בְּכֹֽחֲךָ֙ הַגָּד֔וֹל וּבִֽזְרֹעֲךָ֖ הַנְּטוּיָ֑ה לֹֽא־יִפָּלֵ֥א מִמְּךָ֖ כׇּל־דָּבָֽר׃ 18 עֹ֤שֶׂה חֶ֙סֶד֙ לַֽאֲלָפִ֔ים וּמְשַׁלֵּם֙ עֲוֺ֣ן אָב֔וֹת אֶל־חֵ֥יק בְּנֵיהֶ֖ם אַחֲרֵיהֶ֑ם הָאֵ֤ל הַגָּדוֹל֙ הַגִּבּ֔וֹר יְהֹוָ֥ה צְבָא֖וֹת שְׁמֽוֹ׃ 19 גְּדֹל֙ הָעֵצָ֔ה וְרַ֖ב הָעֲלִֽילִיָּ֑ה אֲשֶׁר־עֵינֶ֣יךָ פְקֻח֗וֹת עַל־כׇּל־דַּרְכֵי֙ בְּנֵ֣י אָדָ֔ם לָתֵ֤ת לְאִישׁ֙ כִּדְרָכָ֔יו וְכִפְרִ֖י מַעֲלָלָֽיו׃ 20 אֲשֶׁר־שַׂ֠מְתָּ אֹת֨וֹת וּמֹפְתִ֤ים בְּאֶֽרֶץ־מִצְרַ֙יִם֙ עַד־הַיּ֣וֹם הַזֶּ֔ה וּבְיִשְׂרָאֵ֖ל וּבָאָדָ֑ם וַתַּעֲשֶׂה־לְּךָ֥ שֵׁ֖ם כַּיּ֥וֹם הַזֶּֽה׃ 21 וַתֹּצֵ֛א אֶת־עַמְּךָ֥ אֶת־יִשְׂרָאֵ֖ל מֵאֶ֣רֶץ מִצְרָ֑יִם בְּאֹת֣וֹת וּבְמ֣וֹפְתִ֗ים וּבְיָ֤ד חֲזָקָה֙ וּבְאֶזְר֣וֹעַ נְטוּיָ֔ה וּבְמוֹרָ֖א גָּדֽוֹל׃ 22 וַתִּתֵּ֤ן לָהֶם֙ אֶת־הָאָ֣רֶץ הַזֹּ֔את אֲשֶׁר־נִשְׁבַּ֥עְתָּ לַאֲבוֹתָ֖ם לָתֵ֣ת לָהֶ֑ם אֶ֛רֶץ זָבַ֥ת חָלָ֖ב וּדְבָֽשׁ׃

in the presence of all the Jews who were sitting in the prison courtyard.

13 In their presence, I instructed Baruch, saying, 14 "This is what the God of Hosts, God of Israel, says: 'Take these deeds—the signed deed of sale and the deed of public endorsement—and put them into an earthenware jar, so they should be preserved for a long time.'

15 "Do not think that all this is being done in vain, because the fact that the God of Hosts, God of Israel, said that I should buy Hanamel's field is a hint that the time will come when houses, fields, and vineyards will again be purchased in this land."

16 After I gave the deed of sale and the deed of public endorsement to Baruch son of Neriah, I prayed to God, saying, 17 "Ah! If only I knew the true reason why You told me to buy this field! God Almighty! You have made heaven and earth with Your great might and Your outstretched arm, so nothing is concealed from You. 18 You show kindness to a righteous man's descendants for a thousand generations, and You punish children for the sins of their ancestors—O great and mighty God, who is called the God of Hosts! 19 Great in counsel, mighty in the ability to do any deeds You choose, Your eyes are open to oversee all the ways of men, to repay each man according to his ways and even according to his unintentional deeds.

20 "You performed signs and wonders in the land of Egypt, which people remember to this day—both miracles to help Israel and miracles to hinder other men who were our enemies. You made a great name for Yourself that lives on to this day. 21 You took Your people Israel out of the land of Egypt with signs and wonders, with a mighty hand and an outstretched arm, placing great terror upon the Egyptians, 22 and You gave them this land which You swore to their ancestors that You would give them—a land flowing with milk from its animals who enjoy its good pasture and dates dripping with honey.

Habad communities conclude here. All others continue:

23 וַיָּבֹ֙אוּ֙ וַיִּ֣רְשׁ֣וּ אֹתָ֔הּ וְלֹֽא־שָׁמְע֖וּ בְקוֹלֶ֑ךָ [וּבְתֹרוֹתְךָ֣ כ'] וּבְתוֹרָֽתְךָ֙ לֹא־הָלָ֔כוּ אֵת֩ כׇּל־אֲשֶׁ֨ר

23 "They came and took possession of it, but they did not listen to Your voice, they did not follow Your Torah. They did not do everything that You

haftarat be-ḥukkotai

commanded them, so You caused all this tragedy to befall them.

²⁴ "The enemies have already climbed the mounds which are piled up at the city so they are ready to conquer it. It is as if the city has already been handed over to the Chaldeans who are attacking it because the people are weak and will soon die by the sword, through hunger or plague. Whatever disaster You said might happen will occur, and You will see it.

²⁵ "But You, God Almighty, said to me, 'Buy for yourself this field with money and call witnesses,' though the city is in the hands of the Chaldeans!"

²⁶ God's word came to Jeremiah, saying, ²⁷ "Look! I am God, the God of all flesh! Is anything too difficult for Me that I cannot return the field later?"

צִוִּיתָה לָהֶם לַעֲשׂוֹת לֹא עָשׂוּ וַתַּקְרֵא אֹתָם אֵת כָּל־הָרָעָה הַזֹּאת: 24 הִנֵּה הַסֹּלְלוֹת בָּאוּ הָעִיר לְלָכְדָהּ וְהָעִיר נִתְּנָה בְּיַד הַכַּשְׂדִּים הַנִּלְחָמִים עָלֶיהָ מִפְּנֵי הַחֶרֶב וְהָרָעָב וְהַדָּבֶר וַאֲשֶׁר דִּבַּרְתָּ הָיָה וְהִנְּךָ רֹאֶה: 25 וְאַתָּה אָמַרְתָּ אֵלַי אֲדֹנָי יֱהֹוִה קְנֵה־לְךָ הַשָּׂדֶה בַּכֶּסֶף וְהָעֵד עֵדִים וְהָעִיר נִתְּנָה בְּיַד הַכַּשְׂדִּים: 26 וַיְהִי דְבַר־יְהֹוָה אֶל־יִרְמְיָהוּ לֵאמֹר: 27 הִנֵּה אֲנִי יְהֹוָה אֱלֹהֵי כָּל־בָּשָׂר הֲמִמֶּנִּי יִפָּלֵא כָּל־דָּבָר:

haftarat be-ḥukkotai
and be-har – be-ḥukkotai

ALL COMMUNITIES—JEREMIAH 16:19 – 17:14

> **SYNOPSIS:** This *Haftarah* mentions calamities that were forewarned by the "curses" issued in the *Parashah*.
>
> The *Haftarah* was said by the prophet Jeremiah in the Kingdom of Judah, close to the turn of the sixth century B.C.E.
>
> Despite its overall theme of punishment and retribution, the *Haftarah* opens on a positive note, as Jeremiah affirms his trust in God and the fallacy of idol-worship (16:19-21). This is contrasted with sins of idol-worship committed by the Kingdom of Jeremiah (1–4), and those fools who trust in man and not in God (5–8). The prophet then describes how God probes the heart of man, and treats him accordingly (9–11). In a final plea for obedience, Jeremiah mentions the Temple as a symbol of God's encouragement to man, and reaffirms his absolute trust in Divine providence (12–14).

16 ¹⁹ God! My strength and stronghold! My refuge in times of trouble! One day, nations will come to You from the ends of the earth, and they will say, "Our ancestors inherited idols as gods, but they are false—futility that has no purpose. ²⁰ Could a man possibly make a god, when he himself is not a god?"

²¹ So this time I will let them know My might and power, and they will know that My name is God!

טז 19 יְהֹוָה עֻזִּי וּמָעֻזִּי וּמְנוּסִי בְּיוֹם צָרָה אֵלֶיךָ גּוֹיִם יָבֹאוּ מֵאַפְסֵי־אָרֶץ וְיֹאמְרוּ אַךְ־שֶׁקֶר נָחֲלוּ אֲבוֹתֵינוּ הֶבֶל וְאֵין בָּם מוֹעִיל: 20 הֲיַעֲשֶׂה־לּוֹ אָדָם אֱלֹהִים וְהֵמָּה לֹא אֱלֹהִים: 21 לָכֵן הִנְנִי מוֹדִיעָם בַּפַּעַם הַזֹּאת אוֹדִיעֵם אֶת־יָדִי וְאֶת־גְּבוּרָתִי וְיָדְעוּ כִּי־שְׁמִי יְהֹוָה:

הפטרת בחקתי

17 ¹ Judah's sin is kept in their hearts as if it were inscribed with an iron pen, with a steel nail. It is engraved on the walls of their hearts and on the horns of their altars. ² As frequently as they remember their children, they also remember their altars and their idol-worship trees, near the leafy trees and on the high hills. ³ O Judah, who serves idols which stand on mountains in the plain! I will hand over your wealth, all your treasures as booty, because of your private altars made in sin throughout your boundaries. ⁴ You will be forced to withdraw from your inheritance which I have given you, since you did not observe the Sabbatical year, and I will make you serve your enemies in a land which you do not know. For you have kindled a fire of anger in My nostrils, which will burn for a long time.

⁵ God says: You will not escape My anger with mortal help, for cursed is the man who turns his thoughts away from God and puts his trust in man, relying on mortal flesh for his strength. ⁶ A person who trusts in man alone will be like a tree in the desert, which does not witness the good when it comes, for when it rains everywhere else, it does not rain in the desert. He will dwell in scorched places in the wilderness, in a salt-sodden soil that is not inhabitable.

⁷ Blessed is the man who trusts in God, and to whom God will be his trust. ⁸ He will be devoid of problems like a tree planted by water, which sends its roots out into a stream, so it is not affected by the coming of the heat and its leaves remain fresh. It does not worry in a year of drought, and it never stops producing fruit. Likewise the person who trusts in God will be devoid of problems, and never lack anything.

⁹ But the heart of man is the most crooked of all his limbs, and it is warped. It says: "Who will know if I really trust in God or not?"

¹⁰ So I, God, probe the heart and test the kidneys to see where each person really holds, repaying each man according to the ways of his heart and the product of his thoughts, which are the deeds of the heart.

¹¹ One who amasses wealth unjustly is like a cuckoo which hatches eggs that it did not lay and it is only a matter of time until the chicks realize that this is not their mother, and run away. Likewise, the wealth will leave him during his life, and ultimately he will be exposed as a scoundrel.

¹² Just like Your Throne of Glory is exalted since the beginning of time, so too the Divine Presence dwells down here in our Holy Temple. ¹³ Since God has placed His Presence among us, Israel's hope should be only with Him. Anyone who abandons You, O God, and trusts in man, deserves to be ashamed.

יז ¹ חַטַּאת יְהוּדָה כְּתוּבָה בְּעֵט בַּרְזֶל בְּצִפֹּרֶן שָׁמִיר חֲרוּשָׁה עַל־לוּחַ לִבָּם וּלְקַרְנוֹת מִזְבְּחוֹתֵיכֶם: ² כִּזְכֹּר בְּנֵיהֶם מִזְבְּחוֹתָם וַאֲשֵׁרֵיהֶם עַל־עֵץ רַעֲנָן עַל גְּבָעוֹת הַגְּבֹהוֹת: ³ הֲרָרִי בַּשָּׂדֶה חֵילְךָ כָל־אוֹצְרוֹתֶיךָ לָבַז אֶתֵּן בָּמֹתֶיךָ בְּחַטָּאת בְּכָל־גְּבוּלֶיךָ: ⁴ וְשָׁמַטְתָּה וּבְךָ מִנַּחֲלָתְךָ אֲשֶׁר נָתַתִּי לָךְ וְהַעֲבַדְתִּיךָ אֶת־אֹיְבֶיךָ בָּאָרֶץ אֲשֶׁר לֹא־יָדָעְתָּ כִּי־אֵשׁ קְדַחְתֶּם בְּאַפִּי עַד־עוֹלָם תּוּקָד:

⁵ כֹּה | אָמַר יְהֹוָה אָרוּר הַגֶּבֶר אֲשֶׁר יִבְטַח בָּאָדָם וְשָׂם בָּשָׂר זְרֹעוֹ וּמִן־יְהֹוָה יָסוּר לִבּוֹ: ⁶ וְהָיָה כְּעַרְעָר בָּעֲרָבָה וְלֹא יִרְאֶה כִּי־יָבוֹא טוֹב וְשָׁכַן חֲרֵרִים בַּמִּדְבָּר אֶרֶץ מְלֵחָה וְלֹא תֵשֵׁב: ⁷ בָּרוּךְ הַגֶּבֶר אֲשֶׁר יִבְטַח בַּיהֹוָה וְהָיָה יְהֹוָה מִבְטַחוֹ: ⁸ וְהָיָה כְּעֵץ | שָׁתוּל עַל־מַיִם וְעַל־יוּבַל יְשַׁלַּח שָׁרָשָׁיו וְלֹא [ירא כ׳] יִרְאֶה כִּי־יָבֹא חֹם וְהָיָה עָלֵהוּ רַעֲנָן וּבִשְׁנַת בַּצֹּרֶת לֹא יִדְאָג וְלֹא יָמִישׁ מֵעֲשׂוֹת פֶּרִי: ⁹ עָקֹב הַלֵּב מִכֹּל וְאָנֻשׁ הוּא מִי יֵדָעֶנּוּ: ¹⁰ אֲנִי יְהֹוָה חֹקֵר לֵב בֹּחֵן כְּלָיוֹת וְלָתֵת לְאִישׁ כִּדְרָכָו כִּפְרִי מַעֲלָלָיו: ¹¹ קֹרֵא דָגַר וְלֹא יָלָד עֹשֶׂה עֹשֶׁר וְלֹא בְמִשְׁפָּט בַּחֲצִי יָמָו יַעַזְבֶנּוּ וּבְאַחֲרִיתוֹ יִהְיֶה נָבָל: ¹² כִּסֵּא כָבוֹד מָרוֹם מֵרִאשׁוֹן מְקוֹם מִקְדָּשֵׁנוּ: ¹³ מִקְוֵה יִשְׂרָאֵל יְהֹוָה כָּל־עֹזְבֶיךָ יֵבֹשׁוּ [וסורי כ׳] וְסוּרַי בָּאָרֶץ יִכָּתֵבוּ כִּי עָזְבוּ מְקוֹר מַיִם־חַיִּים אֶת־יְהֹוָה:

haftarat be-midbar

God says, "Those who turn away from Me will be inscribed in a book, signifying that they will descend into the depths of the earth," for they have abandoned God, the Source of living waters.

14 רְפָאֵ֤נִי יְהֹוָה֙ וְאֵ֣רָפֵ֔א הוֹשִׁיעֵ֖נִי וְאִוָּשֵׁ֑עָה כִּ֥י תְהִלָּתִ֖י אָֽתָּה׃

[14] Only when you heal me, O God, will I be healed. Only when You save me from those that rise against me will I be saved. I praise myself in saying that You are my God, who saves me.

haftarat be-midbar

ALL COMMUNITIES—HOSEA 2:1–22

> **SYNOPSIS:** This *Haftarah* mentions *"the number of the children of Israel"* (v.1), similar to the census described in the *Parashah*. The *Haftarah* was said by Hosea the prophet in the eighth century B.C.E.
>
> The *Haftarah* opens with a vision of the future Redemption, when the kingdoms of Judah and Israel will come under the unified leadership of the Messiah (2:1-3). The children of Israel are instructed to reprimand their "mother" Israel, the nation who has gone astray after her "lovers" (false gods). She abandons her first Husband (God), imagining that her "lovers" will supply her with all her needs (4-7). The threat of punishment thus looms (8-15). But God will restore His intimate relationship with the Jewish people and renew His covenant with them (16-25).

2 [1] In the time of the Redemption the number of the children of Israel will be like the sand of the seashore, which can neither be measured nor counted. Instead of being called "You are not My people," they will be called "children of the living God."

[2] The children of Judah and the children of Israel will be gathered together, and they will appoint for themselves the Messiah as their one head. They will go up from the land of their exile to their own land, for great is the day when God's scattered people will be gathered. [3] Say to your brothers from the ten lost tribes, "My people!" and to your lost sisters, "Object of pity!"

[4] But until the Redemption, O righteous ones, reprimand your congregation which is compared to a "mother." Reprimand her for her bad ways, for she is no longer My "wife," since she has betrayed Me, and I am no longer her Husband. Let her remove her make-up from her face which she used as an enticement for harlotry, and her perfume from between her breasts which she used as an enticement for adultery. [5] Or else, I will strip her naked to embarrass her and leave her standing like the day she was born. I will make

ב [1] וְֽהָיָ֞ה מִסְפַּ֣ר בְּנֵֽי־יִשְׂרָאֵ֗ל כְּח֤וֹל הַיָּם֙ אֲשֶׁ֣ר לֹא־יִמַּ֔ד וְלֹ֖א יִסָּפֵ֑ר וְֽ֠הָיָ֠ה בִּמְק֞וֹם אֲשֶׁר־יֵאָמֵ֤ר לָהֶם֙ לֹֽא־עַמִּ֣י אַתֶּ֔ם יֵאָמֵ֥ר לָהֶ֖ם בְּנֵ֥י אֵֽל־חָֽי׃ [2] וְ֠נִקְבְּצ֠וּ בְּנֵֽי־יְהוּדָ֤ה וּבְנֵֽי־יִשְׂרָאֵל֙ יַחְדָּ֔ו וְשָׂמ֥וּ לָהֶ֛ם רֹ֥אשׁ אֶחָ֖ד וְעָל֣וּ מִן־הָאָ֑רֶץ כִּ֥י גָד֖וֹל י֥וֹם יִזְרְעֶֽאל׃ [3] אִמְר֥וּ לַאֲחֵיכֶ֖ם עַמִּ֑י וְלַאֲחֽוֹתֵיכֶ֖ם רֻחָֽמָה׃ [4] רִ֤יבוּ בְאִמְּכֶם֙ רִ֔יבוּ כִּֽי־הִיא֙ לֹ֣א אִשְׁתִּ֔י וְאָנֹכִ֖י לֹ֣א אִישָׁ֑הּ וְתָסֵ֤ר זְנוּנֶ֙יהָ֙ מִפָּנֶ֔יהָ וְנַאֲפוּפֶ֖יהָ מִבֵּ֥ין שָׁדֶֽיהָ׃ [5] פֶּן־אַפְשִׁיטֶ֣נָּה עֲרֻמָּ֔ה וְהִ֨צַּגְתִּ֔יהָ כְּי֖וֹם הִוָּלְדָ֑הּ וְשַׂמְתִּ֣יהָ כַמִּדְבָּ֗ר וְשַׁתִּ֙הָ֙ כְּאֶ֣רֶץ צִיָּ֔ה וַהֲמִתִּ֖יהָ

הפטרת במדבר

בַּצָּמָא: ⁶ וְאֶת־בָּנֶיהָ לֹא אֲרַחֵם כִּי־בְנֵי זְנוּנִים הֵמָּה: ⁷ כִּי זָנְתָה אִמָּם הֹבִישָׁה הוֹרָתָם כִּי אָמְרָה אֵלְכָה אַחֲרֵי מְאַהֲבַי נֹתְנֵי לַחְמִי וּמֵימַי צַמְרִי וּפִשְׁתִּי שַׁמְנִי וְשִׁקּוּיָי: ⁸ לָכֵן הִנְנִי־שָׂךְ אֶת־דַּרְכֵּךְ בַּסִּירִים וְגָדַרְתִּי אֶת־גְּדֵרָהּ וּנְתִיבוֹתֶיהָ לֹא תִמְצָא: ⁹ וְרִדְּפָה אֶת־מְאַהֲבֶיהָ וְלֹא־תַשִּׂיג אֹתָם וּבִקְשָׁתַם וְלֹא תִמְצָא וְאָמְרָה אֵלְכָה וְאָשׁוּבָה אֶל־אִישִׁי הָרִאשׁוֹן כִּי טוֹב לִי אָז מֵעָתָּה: ¹⁰ וְהִיא לֹא יָדְעָה כִּי אָנֹכִי נָתַתִּי לָהּ הַדָּגָן וְהַתִּירוֹשׁ וְהַיִּצְהָר וְכֶסֶף הִרְבֵּיתִי לָהּ וְזָהָב עָשׂוּ לַבָּעַל: ¹¹ לָכֵן אָשׁוּב וְלָקַחְתִּי דְגָנִי בְּעִתּוֹ וְתִירוֹשִׁי בְּמוֹעֲדוֹ וְהִצַּלְתִּי צַמְרִי וּפִשְׁתִּי לְכַסּוֹת אֶת־עֶרְוָתָהּ: ¹² וְעַתָּה אֲגַלֶּה אֶת־נַבְלֻתָהּ לְעֵינֵי מְאַהֲבֶיהָ וְאִישׁ לֹא־יַצִּילֶנָּה מִיָּדִי: ¹³ וְהִשְׁבַּתִּי כָּל־מְשׂוֹשָׂהּ חַגָּהּ חָדְשָׁהּ וְשַׁבַּתָּהּ וְכֹל מוֹעֲדָהּ: ¹⁴ וַהֲשִׁמֹּתִי גַּפְנָהּ וּתְאֵנָתָהּ אֲשֶׁר אָמְרָה אֶתְנָה הֵמָּה לִי אֲשֶׁר נָתְנוּ־לִי מְאַהֲבָי וְשַׂמְתִּים לְיַעַר וַאֲכָלָתַם חַיַּת הַשָּׂדֶה: ¹⁵ וּפָקַדְתִּי עָלֶיהָ אֶת־יְמֵי הַבְּעָלִים אֲשֶׁר תַּקְטִיר לָהֶם וַתַּעַד נִזְמָהּ וְחֶלְיָתָהּ וַתֵּלֶךְ אַחֲרֵי מְאַהֲבֶיהָ וְאֹתִי שָׁכְחָה נְאֻם־יְהוָה: ¹⁶ לָכֵן הִנֵּה אָנֹכִי מְפַתֶּיהָ וְהֹלַכְתִּיהָ הַמִּדְבָּר וְדִבַּרְתִּי עַל־לִבָּהּ: ¹⁷ וְנָתַתִּי לָהּ אֶת־כְּרָמֶיהָ מִשָּׁם וְאֶת־עֵמֶק עָכוֹר לְפֶתַח תִּקְוָה וְעָנְתָה

her public property like a desert, and I will make her public like an arid land, and cause her to die of thirst.

⁶ And I will not pity her "children," the righteous ones of the congregation, for they are "children of harlots" who tolerated the sins of Israel.⁷ For their "mother" the people of Israel was a harlot; she who conceived them behaved shamefully. For the Jewish people placed their trust in the stars, believing that this would be a source of sustenance, like a woman who says, "I will go after my lovers, those who give my bread and my water, my wool and my flax, my oil and my drinks."

⁸ Therefore, behold, I will close off her route of sustenance with thorns, and I make a fence against her so she has no sustenance from the stars, and she will not find her paths of sustenance.⁹ Though she will pursue her "lovers," offering incense to the stars, she will not come close to them to receive anything from them; she will seek them and not find them.

Then she will say, "I will go and return to my First Husband, to God, for it was better for me then, than now."¹⁰ For she did not realize that to begin with it was I who gave her the corn, the wine, and the oil. It was I who gave her much silver and gold, but they used it for the deity Baal.

¹¹ Therefore, I will return and take My corn at its ripening time and My wine in its appointed season! I will cause the sheep to die and thus take away My wool and My flax which I gave her to cover her nakedness and she will have nothing to wear. ¹² And now that she will have no wool or flax her disgrace will be revealed to the eyes of her "lovers," the stars who fail to support her, and no manmade deity will save her from My hand.

¹³ I will put an end to all her rejoicing—her Festival, her New Moon, her Sabbath, and all her High Holidays. ¹⁴ I will turn to wasteland her vine and her fig tree, about which she said, "They are my harlotry fees, which my lovers have given me." I will make her private orchards into a public forest and the beasts of the field will devour them.

¹⁵ I will remind her of the days of worshiping the deities of Baal, to whom she burned incense. It was as if she adorned herself with her earrings and her jewelry, and went after her lovers. Yet she forgot to worship Me!— says God.

¹⁶ Therefore, behold, I will charm her and lead her into the desert where no other men are found, and I will speak to her heart to bring her back to serve Me. ¹⁷ Then, out of her love that she reawakens for Me there, I will give her back her vineyards, and her desolate valley will become a charming gate where

haftarat naso'

people hope to gather. She will sing out loud there, as in the days of her youth before the Exile, just as she sang on the day of her coming out from the land of Egypt. ¹⁸ What will happen on that day—says God—is that you will call Me *'Ishi*, "my Man," and you will no longer call Me *Ba'li*, "my Husband." ¹⁹ I will remove the names of the Baal deities from their mouth, and they will no longer be mentioned by their proper names but rather, by derogatory names.

²⁰ On that day, I will make a covenant for them with the beasts of the field, the birds of the sky and the creeping things of the earth no longer to destroy. I will banish the bow, the sword, and war from the earth, and I will let them lie safely. ²¹ I will betroth you to Me forever and never despise you again. I will betroth you to Me as a reward for your righteousness and justice, lovingkindness and mercy. ²² I will betroth you to Me with your faith in Me, and you will know God.

שָׁמָּה כִּימֵי נְעוּרֶיהָ וּכְיוֹם עֲלוֹתָהּ מֵאֶרֶץ־מִצְרָיִם: 18 וְהָיָה בַיּוֹם־הַהוּא נְאֻם־יְהֹוָה תִּקְרְאִי אִישִׁי וְלֹא־תִקְרְאִי־לִי עוֹד בַּעְלִי: 19 וַהֲסִרֹתִי אֶת־שְׁמוֹת הַבְּעָלִים מִפִּיהָ וְלֹא־יִזָּכְרוּ עוֹד בִּשְׁמָם: 20 וְכָרַתִּי לָהֶם בְּרִית בַּיּוֹם הַהוּא עִם־חַיַּת הַשָּׂדֶה וְעִם־עוֹף הַשָּׁמַיִם וְרֶמֶשׂ הָאֲדָמָה וְקֶשֶׁת וְחֶרֶב וּמִלְחָמָה אֶשְׁבּוֹר מִן־הָאָרֶץ וְהִשְׁכַּבְתִּים לָבֶטַח: 21 וְאֵרַשְׂתִּיךְ לִי לְעוֹלָם וְאֵרַשְׂתִּיךְ לִי בְּצֶדֶק וּבְמִשְׁפָּט וּבְחֶסֶד וּבְרַחֲמִים: 22 וְאֵרַשְׂתִּיךְ לִי בֶּאֱמוּנָה וְיָדַעַתְּ אֶת־יְהֹוָה:

haftarat naso'

ALL COMMUNITIES—JUDGES 13:2–25

SYNOPSIS: This *Haftarah* mentions the nazirite vow made by Samson's parents, similar to the laws of a nazirite described in the *Parashah*.

The *Haftarah* relates the events surrounding the birth of Samson, a warrior of the Jewish people who utilized his extraordinary strength to combat the Philistine oppression of Israel and perform heroic feats. At the opening of the *Haftarah,* an angel of God appears to the barren wife of Manoah, promising her a child so unique that she must observe the laws of naziriteship even during pregnancy (13:2–5). She informs her husband, who promptly prays to God for a further revelation (6–8). The angel appears again, this time speaking to both Manoah and his wife, and offers further encouragement. He declines an offer of food and refuses to give his name (9–18). The angel then ascends back to heaven in the flames of Manoah's sacrifice (19–20). Finally realizing that they had in fact seen an angel of God (and not merely a prophet), Manoah fears that he is destined to die, but his wife comforts him, citing the acceptance of his sacrifice as a sign of Divine approval (21–23). The *Haftarah* concludes by briefly recording Samson's birth and growth to a man of strength in the camp of Dan (24–25).

13 ² There was a man from Zorah, from the tribal family of Dan, whose name was Manoah. His wife was barren and had never given birth.

³ An angel of God appeared to the woman, and said

יג 2 וַיְהִי אִישׁ אֶחָד מִצָּרְעָה מִמִּשְׁפַּחַת הַדָּנִי וּשְׁמוֹ מָנוֹחַ וְאִשְׁתּוֹ עֲקָרָה וְלֹא יָלָדָה: 3 וַיֵּרָא מַלְאַךְ־

הפטרת נשא

to her, "Look! Now, you are barren and have not given birth, but you will conceive and bear a son. [4] So now, be careful not to do anything forbidden to a nazirite: to drink wine or mature wine, or to eat anything that is ritually impure, [5] because you will conceive and bear a son, and a razor must not come upon his head, for the lad will be a nazirite to God from the womb. He will begin to save Israel from the Philistines.

[6] The woman, thinking that she had seen a prophet, came and spoke to her husband, saying, "A man of God came to me, and his appearance looked like an angel of God, his face was very awesome. I did not ask him where he was from, for when I asked his name, he didn't tell me. [7] He said to me, 'You are about to conceive and bear a son. Now, do not drink wine or mature wine, and do not eat anything that is ritually impure, for the lad will be a nazirite to God from the womb until the day of his death.'"

[8] Manoah prayed to God and said, "Please, my Master! Let the man of God whom You sent come now again to us and teach us more about what we should do to the lad that will be born."

[9] God listened to Manoah's request, and the angel of God came again to the woman. She was sitting in the field. Manoah her husband was not with her. [10] The woman hurried and ran, and told her husband.

"Look!" She said to him. "The man that came to me that day has appeared to me!" [11] Manoah stood up and followed his wife.

He came to the man and said to him, "Are you the man that spoke to my wife?"

"I am," he said.

[12] Manoah said, "At first I was uncertain about this, but now I see you have returned I am sure your words will materialize! Please tell me what rules should be followed with the lad, and what must he do?"

[13] The angel of God said to Manoah, "Be careful of everything that I said to your wife. [14] She must not eat anything that comes from the grapevine. She must not drink any wine or mature wine. She must not eat anything that is ritually impure. Be careful about everything that I commanded her."

[15] "Please stay awhile," Manoah said to the angel of God, "and we'll prepare a goat for you."

יְהוָה אֶל־הָאִשָּׁה וַיֹּאמֶר אֵלֶיהָ הִנֵּה־נָא אַתְּ־עֲקָרָה וְלֹא יָלַדְתְּ וְהָרִית וְיָלַדְתְּ בֵּן: [4] וְעַתָּה הִשָּׁמְרִי נָא וְאַל־תִּשְׁתִּי יַיִן וְשֵׁכָר וְאַל־תֹּאכְלִי כָּל־טָמֵא: [5] כִּי הִנָּךְ הָרָה וְיֹלַדְתְּ בֵּן וּמוֹרָה לֹא־יַעֲלֶה עַל־רֹאשׁוֹ כִּי־נְזִיר אֱלֹהִים יִהְיֶה הַנַּעַר מִן־הַבָּטֶן וְהוּא יָחֵל לְהוֹשִׁיעַ אֶת־יִשְׂרָאֵל מִיַּד פְּלִשְׁתִּים: [6] וַתָּבֹא הָאִשָּׁה וַתֹּאמֶר לְאִישָׁהּ לֵאמֹר אִישׁ הָאֱלֹהִים בָּא אֵלַי וּמַרְאֵהוּ כְּמַרְאֵה מַלְאַךְ הָאֱלֹהִים נוֹרָא מְאֹד וְלֹא שְׁאִלְתִּיהוּ אֵי־מִזֶּה הוּא וְאֶת־שְׁמוֹ לֹא־הִגִּיד לִי: [7] וַיֹּאמֶר לִי הִנָּךְ הָרָה וְיֹלַדְתְּ בֵּן וְעַתָּה אַל־תִּשְׁתִּי ׀ יַיִן וְשֵׁכָר וְאַל־תֹּאכְלִי כָּל־טֻמְאָה כִּי־נְזִיר אֱלֹהִים יִהְיֶה הַנַּעַר מִן־הַבֶּטֶן עַד־יוֹם מוֹתוֹ: [8] וַיֶּעְתַּר מָנוֹחַ אֶל־יְהוָה וַיֹּאמַר בִּי אֲדוֹנָי אִישׁ הָאֱלֹהִים אֲשֶׁר שָׁלַחְתָּ יָבוֹא־נָא עוֹד אֵלֵינוּ וְיוֹרֵנוּ מַה־נַּעֲשֶׂה לַנַּעַר הַיּוּלָּד: [9] וַיִּשְׁמַע הָאֱלֹהִים בְּקוֹל מָנוֹחַ וַיָּבֹא מַלְאַךְ הָאֱלֹהִים עוֹד אֶל־הָאִשָּׁה וְהִיא יוֹשֶׁבֶת בַּשָּׂדֶה וּמָנוֹחַ אִישָׁהּ אֵין עִמָּהּ: [10] וַתְּמַהֵר הָאִשָּׁה וַתָּרָץ וַתַּגֵּד לְאִישָׁהּ וַתֹּאמֶר אֵלָיו הִנֵּה נִרְאָה אֵלַי הָאִישׁ אֲשֶׁר־בָּא בַיּוֹם אֵלָי: [11] וַיָּקָם וַיֵּלֶךְ מָנוֹחַ אַחֲרֵי אִשְׁתּוֹ וַיָּבֹא אֶל־הָאִישׁ וַיֹּאמֶר לוֹ הַאַתָּה הָאִישׁ אֲשֶׁר־דִּבַּרְתָּ אֶל־הָאִשָּׁה וַיֹּאמֶר אָנִי: [12] וַיֹּאמֶר מָנוֹחַ עַתָּה יָבֹא דְבָרֶיךָ מַה־יִּהְיֶה מִשְׁפַּט־הַנַּעַר וּמַעֲשֵׂהוּ: [13] וַיֹּאמֶר מַלְאַךְ יְהוָה אֶל־מָנוֹחַ מִכֹּל אֲשֶׁר־אָמַרְתִּי אֶל־הָאִשָּׁה תִּשָּׁמֵר: [14] מִכֹּל אֲשֶׁר־יֵצֵא מִגֶּפֶן הַיַּיִן לֹא תֹאכַל וְיַיִן וְשֵׁכָר אַל־תֵּשְׁתְּ וְכָל־טֻמְאָה אַל־תֹּאכַל כֹּל אֲשֶׁר־צִוִּיתִיהָ תִּשְׁמֹר: [15] וַיֹּאמֶר מָנוֹחַ אֶל־מַלְאַךְ יְהוָה

haftarat be-ha'alotekha

16 The angel of God said to Manoah, "If you want me to stay to feed me the goat, I will not eat your meal. And if you want to prepare the goat as a burnt-offering, you must offer it to God, so why keep me?"

—Obviously, Manoah did not know that the man was an angel of God, otherwise he would not have offered him food.—

17 "What's your name?" Manoah said to the angel of God. "As when your words will materialize we will want to honor you."

18 The angel of God said to him, "I don't want honor, so why do you ask for my name? It's actually a secret."

19 Manoah took the goat and the meal-offering, and offered it upon the rock as a burnt-offering to God. The angel wondrously produced fire from the rock, and Manoah and his wife looked on. 20 Then as the flame went up from the altar towards heaven, the angel of God went up in the altar's flame. Manoah and his wife looked on, and they fell on their faces to the ground.

21 After going up in the flame, the angel of God did not reappear to Manoah and his wife, and then after seeing all this, Manoah realized that it was an angel of God. 22 Manoah said to his wife, "We're going to die, because we have seen an angel of God!"

23 "If God wanted to kill us," his wife said to him, "He would not have accepted a burnt-offering and a meal-offering from us, and He would not have shown us all these things. If it was time for us to die, He would not let us merit to hear something like this."

24 The woman gave birth to a son and called him Samson. The lad grew, and God blessed him. 25 A spirit of strength from God began to move him to the camp of Dan to show acts of strength and wonder. The camp of Dan was between Zorah and Eshtaol.

נַעְצְרָה־נָּא אוֹתָךְ וְנַעֲשֶׂה לְפָנֶיךָ גְּדִי עִזִּים: 16 וַיֹּאמֶר מַלְאַךְ יְהֹוָה אֶל־מָנוֹחַ אִם־תַּעְצְרֵנִי לֹא־אֹכַל בְּלַחְמֶךָ וְאִם־תַּעֲשֶׂה עֹלָה לַיהֹוָה תַּעֲלֶנָּה כִּי לֹא־יָדַע מָנוֹחַ כִּי־מַלְאַךְ יְהֹוָה הוּא: 17 וַיֹּאמֶר מָנוֹחַ אֶל־מַלְאַךְ יְהֹוָה מִי שְׁמֶךָ כִּי־יָבֹא [דבריך כ׳] דְבָרְךָ וְכִבַּדְנוּךָ: 18 וַיֹּאמֶר לוֹ מַלְאַךְ יְהֹוָה לָמָּה זֶּה תִּשְׁאַל לִשְׁמִי וְהוּא־פֶלִאי: 19 וַיִּקַּח מָנוֹחַ אֶת־גְּדִי הָעִזִּים וְאֶת־הַמִּנְחָה וַיַּעַל עַל־הַצּוּר לַיהֹוָה וּמַפְלִא לַעֲשׂוֹת וּמָנוֹחַ וְאִשְׁתּוֹ רֹאִים: 20 וַיְהִי בַעֲלוֹת הַלַּהַב מֵעַל הַמִּזְבֵּחַ הַשָּׁמַיְמָה וַיַּעַל מַלְאַךְ־יְהֹוָה בְּלַהַב הַמִּזְבֵּחַ וּמָנוֹחַ וְאִשְׁתּוֹ רֹאִים וַיִּפְּלוּ עַל־פְּנֵיהֶם אָרְצָה: 21 וְלֹא־יָסַף עוֹד מַלְאַךְ יְהֹוָה לְהֵרָאֹה אֶל־מָנוֹחַ וְאֶל־אִשְׁתּוֹ אָז יָדַע מָנוֹחַ כִּי־מַלְאַךְ יְהֹוָה הוּא: 22 וַיֹּאמֶר מָנוֹחַ אֶל־אִשְׁתּוֹ מוֹת נָמוּת כִּי אֱלֹהִים רָאִינוּ: 23 וַתֹּאמֶר לוֹ אִשְׁתּוֹ לוּ חָפֵץ יְהֹוָה לַהֲמִיתֵנוּ לֹא־לָקַח מִיָּדֵנוּ עֹלָה וּמִנְחָה וְלֹא הֶרְאָנוּ אֶת־כָּל־אֵלֶּה וְכָעֵת לֹא הִשְׁמִיעָנוּ כָּזֹאת: 24 וַתֵּלֶד הָאִשָּׁה בֵּן וַתִּקְרָא אֶת־שְׁמוֹ שִׁמְשׁוֹן וַיִּגְדַּל הַנַּעַר וַיְבָרְכֵהוּ יְהֹוָה: 25 וַתָּחֶל רוּחַ יְהֹוָה לְפַעֲמוֹ בְּמַחֲנֵה־דָן בֵּין צָרְעָה וּבֵין אֶשְׁתָּאֹל:

haftarat be-ha'alotekha

ALL COMMUNITIES—
ZECHARIAH 2:14 – 4:7

> **SYNOPSIS:** This *Haftarah* describes the candelabrum (4:2), which is also depicted at the beginning of the *Parashah*. The *Haftarah* was said by Zechariah around 520 B.C.E. as part of the prophet's efforts to encourage the Jewish people returning from Babylonian captivity to rebuild the Temple.

הפטרת בהעלותך

> This *Haftarah* is also read on the first Sabbath of *Hanukkah*, primarily due to its reference to the candelabrum.
>
> The *Haftarah* opens with words of comfort about the return of the Divine presence and restoration of the land (2:14–17). We then read the first of two visions depicted in the *Haftarah*, that of the "High Priest in soiled garments" who is condemned for his children's sins by the Satan, but vindicated by God's angel (3:1–5). This is followed by promises of a restored Temple and the coming of the Messiah (6–10). In the second vision, Zechariah sees the gold candelabrum, a metaphor for the Messiah's Divine spirit through which he will effortlessly subdue nations (4:1–7).

2 ¹⁴ "Sing and rejoice, daughter of Zion, for I am coming to Jerusalem and I will dwell in your midst," says God. ¹⁵ "Many nations will attach themselves to God on that day, and they will become My people too and believe in Me, but nevertheless I will dwell only in your midst." Then you will know that the God of Hosts sent me only to you.

¹⁶ God will let Judah take possession of his position in the Holy Land, never to be exiled again, and God will once again choose Jerusalem to have His Presence dwell there. ¹⁷ Be silent before God, all you nations! Never again speak badly of the Jewish people, for then He will be roused from His holy abode to exact retribution on the nations.

3 ¹ In the prophetic vision He then showed me Joshua the High Priest standing before God's angel, with Satan standing at Joshua's right to incriminate him for failing to rebuke his children when they married non-Jewish women.

² An angel of God said to Satan, "God will reprimand you, O Satan! He who chooses Jerusalem will reprimand you! Why, this Joshua was miraculously saved like a brand rescued from fire, so how can you prosecute him?"

³ Now, Joshua was wearing "soiled clothes" while standing before the angel. ⁴ The angel spoke up loudly and said to the other angels standing before him, "Remove the *'soiled clothes'*—the non-Jewish women from his sons!"

He said to him, "See, I have taken away your past sins from you and when your current sins will cease you will see that I am clothing you in beautiful clothes."

⁵ Then I prayed for Joshua, saying, "Let them place a pure priestly turban on his head signifying that his descendants would inherit the priesthood." My prayer was immediately answered and they placed the pure turban on his head and clothed him in garments, while God's angel stood by.

haftarat be-ha'alotekha

[6] Afterwards, God's angel warned Joshua, saying, [7] "This is what the God of Hosts said: 'If your children will walk in My paths and keep the things I told them to keep, then your children will be appointed to take charge of My house forever and guard My courtyard. So too in the spiritual world, I will reward you and your children and permit you to walk among those angels who stand there.'

[8] Now listen Joshua, the High Priest! You and also your companions who were saved from a fiery furnace who sit before you, for they are people worthy of miracles. Look! I will bring My servant Zemah—the Messiah.'"

[9] "Here is the foundation stone of the Third Temple that I will place before Joshua's descendant, the High Priest, for him to place. There will be seven eyes guarding a single stone of the Temple, from Above. I will participate in the construction of the Temple by engraving inscriptions on its stones," says the God of Hosts, "and I will remove the sin of that land in one day. [10] On that day," says the God of Hosts, "you will invite each other to come and take shade under the vines and under the fig trees to enjoy the bountiful goodness which will then exist."

4 [1] Then, the angel that spoke with me returned and roused me, like a man woken from his sleep.

[2] "What do you see in your prophetic vision?" he asked me.

I said, "I see a candelabrum made entirely of gold, with a bowl on its top containing oil. It has seven lamps, and each of these lamps that are on its top has seven pipes to carry the oil from the bowl. [3] Near it are two olive trees, one to the right of the bowl and one to its left."

[4] Then I spoke up and asked the angel that spoke with me, "My master, what are these alluding to?"

[5] "Don't you know what they are?" replied the angel that spoke with me.

"No, my master!" I said.

[6] Then he answered me as follows, "This is the word of God about the Messiah, a descendant of Zerubbabel: 'Not by his might, nor by his power will the nations become subservient to the Messiah, but rather it will be effortless, like the kindling of a candelabrum, through My spirit by which I will subdue the nations,' says the God of Hosts.

[7] 'Who are you, Gog and Magog, to appear as a great mountain in Zerubbabel's path, when in truth you will

עַל־רֹאשׁוֹ וַיַּלְבִּשֻׁהוּ בְּגָדִים וּמַלְאַךְ יְהֹוָה עֹמֵד: 6 וַיָּעַד מַלְאַךְ יְהֹוָה בִּיהוֹשֻׁעַ לֵאמֹר: 7 כֹּה־אָמַר יְהֹוָה צְבָאוֹת אִם־בִּדְרָכַי תֵּלֵךְ וְאִם אֶת־מִשְׁמַרְתִּי תִשְׁמֹר וְגַם־אַתָּה תָּדִין אֶת־בֵּיתִי וְגַם תִּשְׁמֹר אֶת־חֲצֵרָי וְנָתַתִּי לְךָ מַהְלְכִים בֵּין הָעֹמְדִים הָאֵלֶּה: 8 שְׁמַע־נָא יְהוֹשֻׁעַ ׀ הַכֹּהֵן הַגָּדוֹל אַתָּה וְרֵעֶיךָ הַיֹּשְׁבִים לְפָנֶיךָ כִּי־אַנְשֵׁי מוֹפֵת הֵמָּה כִּי־הִנְנִי מֵבִיא אֶת־עַבְדִּי צֶמַח: 9 כִּי ׀ הִנֵּה הָאֶבֶן אֲשֶׁר נָתַתִּי לִפְנֵי יְהוֹשֻׁעַ עַל־אֶבֶן אַחַת שִׁבְעָה עֵינָיִם הִנְנִי מְפַתֵּחַ פִּתֻּחָהּ נְאֻם יְהֹוָה צְבָאוֹת וּמַשְׁתִּי אֶת־עֲוֺן הָאָרֶץ־הַהִיא בְּיוֹם אֶחָד: 10 בַּיּוֹם הַהוּא נְאֻם יְהֹוָה צְבָאוֹת תִּקְרְאוּ אִישׁ לְרֵעֵהוּ אֶל־תַּחַת גֶּפֶן וְאֶל־תַּחַת תְּאֵנָה:

ד 1 וַיָּשָׁב הַמַּלְאָךְ הַדֹּבֵר בִּי וַיְעִירֵנִי כְּאִישׁ אֲשֶׁר־יֵעוֹר מִשְּׁנָתוֹ: 2 וַיֹּאמֶר אֵלַי מָה אַתָּה רֹאֶה [ויאמר כ׳] וָאֹמַר רָאִיתִי ׀ וְהִנֵּה מְנוֹרַת זָהָב כֻּלָּהּ וְגֻלָּהּ עַל־רֹאשָׁהּ וְשִׁבְעָה נֵרֹתֶיהָ עָלֶיהָ שִׁבְעָה וְשִׁבְעָה מוּצָקוֹת לַנֵּרוֹת אֲשֶׁר עַל־רֹאשָׁהּ: 3 וּשְׁנַיִם זֵיתִים עָלֶיהָ אֶחָד מִימִין הַגֻּלָּה וְאֶחָד עַל־שְׂמֹאלָהּ: 4 וָאַעַן וָאֹמַר אֶל־הַמַּלְאָךְ הַדֹּבֵר בִּי לֵאמֹר מָה־אֵלֶּה אֲדֹנִי: 5 וַיַּעַן הַמַּלְאָךְ הַדֹּבֵר בִּי וַיֹּאמֶר אֵלַי הֲלוֹא יָדַעְתָּ מָה־הֵמָּה אֵלֶּה וָאֹמַר לֹא אֲדֹנִי: 6 וַיַּעַן וַיֹּאמֶר אֵלַי לֵאמֹר זֶה דְּבַר־יְהֹוָה אֶל־זְרֻבָּבֶל לֵאמֹר לֹא בְחַיִל וְלֹא בְכֹחַ כִּי אִם־בְּרוּחִי אָמַר יְהֹוָה צְבָאוֹת: 7 מִי־אַתָּה הַר־הַגָּדוֹל לִפְנֵי

be easily flattened? The Messiah will produce the precious stone, the foundation of the Temple, amid cheers of "Beautiful stone! Beautiful stone!"'"

זְרֻבָּבֶל לְמֵישֹׁר וְהוֹצִיא אֶת־הָאֶבֶן הָרֹאשָׁה תְּשֻׁאוֹת חֵן חֵן לָהּ:

haftarat shelaḥ-lekha All communities—Joshua 2:1–24

SYNOPSIS: This *Haftarah* relates the story of the delegation of spies which Joshua sent to scout the land of Canaan shortly before its conquest, similar to the story of Moses' spies which is related in the *Parashah*.

The *Haftarah* opens as the two spies are commissioned and sent by Joshua and, on arriving in Canaan, seek refuge in the house of a lady named Rahab (2:1). When news reaches the king, he demands that Rahab release the men, but she claims that they have already left the city, while in truth they are hidden on the roof (2–6). The king's men leave the city in pursuit, and the city gate is locked (7). Rahab relates to the men how the Canaanite people were still terrified of the Jewish people due to their miraculous assistance from God, and she strikes a deal that her family will be saved when the conquest of Canaan takes place (8–21). After hiding on a mountain for three days, the men return and report to Joshua that *"the land's inhabitants melted (in fear) of us"* (22–24).

2 ¹ Joshua son of Nun sent two men from Shittim to spy out the mindset of the land's inhabitants, saying, "Go and see the land and Jericho."

They went, and came to the house of a lady named Rahab who sold food, and they slept there.

² A messenger informed the king of Jericho, saying, "Behold! Men from the children of Israel have come here tonight to search the land!"

³ The king of Jericho sent a message to Rahab, saying, "Release the men who have come to you and have entered your house, for they have come to search the entire land!"

⁴ The woman had taken the two men and had hidden each one separately. She said, "Yes, the men came to me. I didn't know where they were from. ⁵ When it was time to close the city gate at night, the men went off. I don't know where they went. It wasn't long ago, so if you chase after them quickly you'll catch them."

⁶ She had taken them up to the roof, and hidden them well in the flax stalks that were arranged upon the roof.

⁷ The king's men pursued them in the direction

ב ¹ וַיִּשְׁלַח יְהוֹשֻׁעַ־בִּן־נוּן מִן־הַשִּׁטִּים שְׁנַיִם־אֲנָשִׁים מְרַגְּלִים חֶרֶשׁ לֵאמֹר לְכוּ רְאוּ אֶת־הָאָרֶץ וְאֶת־יְרִיחוֹ וַיֵּלְכוּ וַיָּבֹאוּ בֵּית־אִשָּׁה זוֹנָה וּשְׁמָהּ רָחָב וַיִּשְׁכְּבוּ־שָׁמָּה: ² וַיֵּאָמַר לְמֶלֶךְ יְרִיחוֹ לֵאמֹר הִנֵּה אֲנָשִׁים בָּאוּ הֵנָּה הַלַּיְלָה מִבְּנֵי יִשְׂרָאֵל לַחְפֹּר אֶת־הָאָרֶץ: ³ וַיִּשְׁלַח מֶלֶךְ יְרִיחוֹ אֶל־רָחָב לֵאמֹר הוֹצִיאִי הָאֲנָשִׁים הַבָּאִים אֵלַיִךְ אֲשֶׁר־בָּאוּ לְבֵיתֵךְ כִּי לַחְפֹּר אֶת־כָּל־הָאָרֶץ בָּאוּ: ⁴ וַתִּקַּח הָאִשָּׁה אֶת־שְׁנֵי הָאֲנָשִׁים וַתִּצְפְּנוֹ וַתֹּאמֶר כֵּן בָּאוּ אֵלַי הָאֲנָשִׁים וְלֹא יָדַעְתִּי מֵאַיִן הֵמָּה: ⁵ וַיְהִי הַשַּׁעַר לִסְגּוֹר בַּחֹשֶׁךְ וְהָאֲנָשִׁים יָצָאוּ לֹא יָדַעְתִּי אָנָה הָלְכוּ הָאֲנָשִׁים רִדְפוּ מַהֵר אַחֲרֵיהֶם כִּי תַשִּׂיגוּם: ⁶ וְהִיא הֶעֱלָתַם הַגָּגָה וַתִּטְמְנֵם בְּפִשְׁתֵּי הָעֵץ הָעֲרֻכוֹת לָהּ עַל־הַגָּג: ⁷ וְהָאֲנָשִׁים רָדְפוּ אַחֲרֵיהֶם דֶּרֶךְ

haftarat shelaḥ-lekha

of the Jordan, until the river-crossings. As soon as the pursuers had gone out, the gate was shut.

⁸ Before the spies were asleep, she came up to them on the roof. ⁹ She said to the men, "I know that God has given you the land, and that dread of you has fallen upon us. All the inhabitants of the land have melted away because of you.

¹⁰ "For we have heard how God dried up the water of the Reed Sea for you when you came out of Egypt; and what you did to the two kings of the Amorites that were on the other side of the Jordan, Sihon and Og, whom you completely destroyed.

¹¹ "And as soon as we heard, our hearts melted. Because of you, everybody was downhearted, for God, your Almighty God, is Almighty in heaven above and on the earth below."

¹² "Now, I beg, swear to me by God, since I have shown you kindness, that you will also show kindness to my father's house, and give me a true sign so that we will not be harmed, ¹³ and so you will keep alive my father and my mother, and my brothers and my sisters, and preserve all that they have. Deliver our lives from death!"

¹⁴ The men said to her, "We pledge our lives to defend yours from death, if you will not tell anybody about this discussion of ours. Then, what will happen is, when God gives us the land, we will deal with you kindly and truly."

¹⁵ She let them down by a rope through the window out of the town, for her house was in the town wall and she dwelt in the wall. ¹⁶ She said to them, "Go to the mountain in case the pursuers catch you. Hide yourselves there for three days until the pursuers return, and afterwards go on your way."

¹⁷ The men said to her, "We want to be blameless of not fulfilling your oath which you made us swear so we will make ourselves clear. ¹⁸ When we come into the land, bind this line of scarlet thread in the window by which you let us down, and bring your father and your mother, and your brothers and your entire father's household home to you. ¹⁹ Then if anyone goes out of the doors of your house outside, his blood will be upon his head, and we will be blameless. But whoever will be with you in the house, his blood will be upon

הַיַּרְדֵּן עַל הַמַּעְבְּרוֹת וְהַשַּׁעַר סָגָרוּ אַחֲרֵי כַּאֲשֶׁר יָצְאוּ הָרֹדְפִים אַחֲרֵיהֶם: ח וְהֵמָּה טֶרֶם יִשְׁכָּבוּן וְהִיא עָלְתָה עֲלֵיהֶם עַל־הַגָּג: ט וַתֹּאמֶר אֶל־הָאֲנָשִׁים יָדַעְתִּי כִּי־נָתַן יְהֹוָה לָכֶם אֶת־הָאָרֶץ וְכִי־נָפְלָה אֵימַתְכֶם עָלֵינוּ וְכִי נָמֹגוּ כָּל־יֹשְׁבֵי הָאָרֶץ מִפְּנֵיכֶם: י כִּי שָׁמַעְנוּ אֵת אֲשֶׁר־הוֹבִישׁ יְהֹוָה אֶת־מֵי יַם־סוּף מִפְּנֵיכֶם בְּצֵאתְכֶם מִמִּצְרָיִם וַאֲשֶׁר עֲשִׂיתֶם לִשְׁנֵי מַלְכֵי הָאֱמֹרִי אֲשֶׁר בְּעֵבֶר הַיַּרְדֵּן לְסִיחֹן וּלְעוֹג אֲשֶׁר הֶחֱרַמְתֶּם אוֹתָם: יא וַנִּשְׁמַע וַיִּמַּס לְבָבֵנוּ וְלֹא־קָמָה עוֹד רוּחַ בְּאִישׁ מִפְּנֵיכֶם כִּי יְהֹוָה אֱלֹהֵיכֶם הוּא אֱלֹהִים בַּשָּׁמַיִם מִמַּעַל וְעַל־הָאָרֶץ מִתָּחַת: יב וְעַתָּה הִשָּׁבְעוּ־נָא לִי בַּיהֹוָה כִּי־עָשִׂיתִי עִמָּכֶם חָסֶד וַעֲשִׂיתֶם גַּם־אַתֶּם עִם־בֵּית אָבִי חֶסֶד וּנְתַתֶּם לִי אוֹת אֱמֶת: יג וְהַחֲיִתֶם אֶת־אָבִי וְאֶת־אִמִּי וְאֶת־אַחַי וְאֶת־[אחותי כ׳] אַחְיוֹתַי וְאֵת כָּל־אֲשֶׁר לָהֶם וְהִצַּלְתֶּם אֶת־נַפְשֹׁתֵינוּ מִמָּוֶת: יד וַיֹּאמְרוּ לָהּ הָאֲנָשִׁים נַפְשֵׁנוּ תַחְתֵּיכֶם לָמוּת אִם לֹא תַגִּידוּ אֶת־דְּבָרֵנוּ זֶה וְהָיָה בְּתֵת־יְהֹוָה לָנוּ אֶת־הָאָרֶץ וְעָשִׂינוּ עִמָּךְ חֶסֶד וֶאֱמֶת: טו וַתּוֹרִדֵם בַּחֶבֶל בְּעַד הַחַלּוֹן כִּי בֵיתָהּ בְּקִיר הַחוֹמָה וּבַחוֹמָה הִיא יוֹשָׁבֶת: טז וַתֹּאמֶר לָהֶם הָהָרָה לֵּכוּ פֶּן־יִפְגְּעוּ בָכֶם הָרֹדְפִים וְנַחְבֵּתֶם שָׁמָּה שְׁלֹשֶׁת יָמִים עַד שׁוֹב הָרֹדְפִים וְאַחַר תֵּלְכוּ לְדַרְכְּכֶם: יז וַיֹּאמְרוּ אֵלֶיהָ הָאֲנָשִׁים נְקִיִּם אֲנַחְנוּ מִשְּׁבֻעָתֵךְ הַזֶּה אֲשֶׁר הִשְׁבַּעְתָּנוּ: יח הִנֵּה אֲנַחְנוּ בָאִים בָּאָרֶץ אֶת־תִּקְוַת חוּט הַשָּׁנִי הַזֶּה תִּקְשְׁרִי בַּחַלּוֹן אֲשֶׁר הוֹרַדְתֵּנוּ בוֹ וְאֶת־אָבִיךְ וְאֶת־אִמֵּךְ וְאֶת־אַחַיִךְ וְאֵת כָּל־בֵּית אָבִיךְ תַּאַסְפִי אֵלַיִךְ הַבָּיְתָה: יט וְהָיָה כֹּל אֲשֶׁר־יֵצֵא מִדַּלְתֵי בֵיתֵךְ | הַחוּצָה דָּמוֹ בְרֹאשׁוֹ

הפטרת קרח

our head if a hand is laid upon him. ²⁰ And if you tell anyone of this discussion of ours, then we will be blameless of your oath which you have made us swear."

²¹ She said, "It will be as you say." She sent them off, and they left. And later, when the Jewish army invaded, she bound the scarlet line in the window.

²² They went, and came to the mountain, and stayed there three days until the pursuers returned. The pursuers chased them all the way, but they did not find them.

²³ The two men returned and came down from the mountain. They crossed over and came to Joshua son of Nun, and told him all that had happened to them. ²⁴ They said to Joshua, "God has delivered all the land into our hands. Also, all the land's inhabitants melted in fear of us."

וַאֲנַחְנוּ נְקִיִּם מִשְּׁבֻעָתֵךְ הַזֶּה אֲשֶׁר הִשְׁבַּעְתָּנוּ: וְכֹל אֲשֶׁר יִהְיֶה אִתָּךְ בַּבַּיִת דָּמוֹ בְרֹאשֵׁנוּ אִם־יָד תִּהְיֶה־בּוֹ: 20 וְאִם־תַּגִּידִי אֶת־דְּבָרֵנוּ זֶה וְהָיִינוּ נְקִיִּם מִשְּׁבֻעָתֵךְ אֲשֶׁר הִשְׁבַּעְתָּנוּ: 21 וַתֹּאמֶר כְּדִבְרֵיכֶם כֶּן־הוּא וַתְּשַׁלְּחֵם וַיֵּלֵכוּ וַתִּקְשֹׁר אֶת־תִּקְוַת הַשָּׁנִי בַּחַלּוֹן: 22 וַיֵּלְכוּ וַיָּבֹאוּ הָהָרָה וַיֵּשְׁבוּ שָׁם שְׁלֹשֶׁת יָמִים עַד־שָׁבוּ הָרֹדְפִים וַיְבַקְשׁוּ הָרֹדְפִים בְּכָל־הַדֶּרֶךְ וְלֹא מָצָאוּ: 23 וַיָּשֻׁבוּ שְׁנֵי הָאֲנָשִׁים וַיֵּרְדוּ מֵהָהָר וַיַּעַבְרוּ וַיָּבֹאוּ אֶל־יְהוֹשֻׁעַ בִּן־נוּן וַיְסַפְּרוּ־לוֹ אֵת כָּל־הַמֹּצְאוֹת אוֹתָם: 24 וַיֹּאמְרוּ אֶל־יְהוֹשֻׁעַ כִּי־נָתַן יְהֹוָה בְּיָדֵנוּ אֶת־כָּל־הָאָרֶץ וְגַם־נָמֹגוּ כָּל־יֹשְׁבֵי הָאָרֶץ מִפָּנֵינוּ:

haftarat koraḥ

ALL COMMUNITIES—I SAMUEL 11:14 – 12:22

SYNOPSIS: This *Haftarah* speaks of Samuel, a descendant of Korah, including his declaration of innocence (12:3), which is similar to that of Moses in the *Parashah* (16:15).

The *Haftarah* opens as Samuel gathers the nation at Gilgal in order to establish Saul as king of Israel, after a long period of regional leadership under the Judges. At an earlier gathering in Mizpah, Saul had already been appointed king, but the first ceremony lacked the required consensus. Now, however, after Saul had demonstrated his military prowess by saving the Gilead from Amorite hostility, Samuel gathers the people once again to re-establish Saul's monarchy. This time, the gathering is a resounding success (11:14-15).

The main body of the *Haftarah* consists of a speech by Samuel, the outgoing leader, in which he expresses his reservations about the newly formed monarchy. (Initially, Samuel had been opposed to the people's request to appoint a king, and acquiesced only due to a Divine command.)

After opening words in which Samuel stresses his own honest leadership—which is promptly attested to by the people (12:1–5)—he traces Jewish history from the times of the Exodus, demonstrating how a king was never necessary because God is the King (6–12). He thus warns the people how important it is to continue to recognize the supreme authority of God now that a king has been appointed (13–15). To demonstrate that God's acceptance of the people's demands for a king is no proof of the appropriateness of the request, Samuel announces that He will now pray to God for rain, which is extremely damaging at the time of the wheat harvest, and that God will

haftarat koraḥ

respond, despite the destructiveness of the request (16–17). When the rains swiftly follow, the people beg Samuel to pray for the rains to end, and his point is thus made emphatically (18–19). Samuel uses the opportunity to stress, once again, the paramount importance of obedience to God (20–22).

11 [14] Samuel said to the people, "Let's go to Gilgal, and renew the monarchy there." [15] All the people went to Gilgal. They all willingly confirmed Saul as king there, before God in Gilgal, and they slaughtered peace-offerings there before God. Saul and all the people rejoiced greatly.

12 [1] Samuel said to all Israel, "Look! I have listened to your request about everything which you said to me, and I have appointed a king to reign over you. [2] Now, look! The new king is walking before you! I have become old and aged. My sons are supporting the king here with you. I have walked before you from my youth and until this day.

[3] "Here I am! Testify against me before God and before His anointed king: Have I taken anybody's ox? Have I taken anybody's donkey? Have I robbed anybody? Have I oppressed anybody? Did I take a payment from anyone's hand that caused me to hide my eyes about his wrongdoing and not punish him properly? Tell me while I can respond to you!"

[4] They said, "You did not rob us or oppress us, nor did you take anything from anyone's hand."

[5] He said to them, "God is your witness, and His anointed king is witness this day, that you have not found anything inappropriate in my hand."

"God and His anointed are our witness," they said.

[6] Samuel said to the people, "God made miracles through Moses and Aaron, and brought your fathers up from the land of Egypt. [7] Now, stand and I will debate with you before God, concerning all the righteous acts which He did to you and to your forefathers.

[8] "When Jacob came to Egypt, and your fathers cried out to God, and God sent Moses and

יא 14 וַיֹּאמֶר שְׁמוּאֵל אֶל־הָעָם לְכוּ וְנֵלְכָה הַגִּלְגָּל וּנְחַדֵּשׁ שָׁם הַמְּלוּכָה: 15 וַיֵּלְכוּ כָל־הָעָם הַגִּלְגָּל וַיַּמְלִכוּ שָׁם אֶת־שָׁאוּל לִפְנֵי יְהֹוָה בַּגִּלְגָּל וַיִּזְבְּחוּ־שָׁם זְבָחִים שְׁלָמִים לִפְנֵי יְהֹוָה וַיִּשְׂמַח שָׁם שָׁאוּל וְכָל־אַנְשֵׁי יִשְׂרָאֵל עַד־מְאֹד:

יב 1 וַיֹּאמֶר שְׁמוּאֵל אֶל־כָּל־יִשְׂרָאֵל הִנֵּה שָׁמַעְתִּי בְקֹלְכֶם לְכֹל אֲשֶׁר־אֲמַרְתֶּם לִי וָאַמְלִיךְ עֲלֵיכֶם מֶלֶךְ: 2 וְעַתָּה הִנֵּה הַמֶּלֶךְ | מִתְהַלֵּךְ לִפְנֵיכֶם וַאֲנִי זָקַנְתִּי וָשַׂבְתִּי וּבָנַי הִנָּם אִתְּכֶם וַאֲנִי הִתְהַלַּכְתִּי לִפְנֵיכֶם מִנְּעֻרַי עַד־הַיּוֹם הַזֶּה: 3 הִנְנִי עֲנוּ בִי נֶגֶד יְהֹוָה וְנֶגֶד מְשִׁיחוֹ אֶת־שׁוֹר | מִי לָקַחְתִּי וַחֲמוֹר מִי לָקַחְתִּי וְאֶת־מִי עָשַׁקְתִּי אֶת־מִי רַצּוֹתִי וּמִיַּד־מִי לָקַחְתִּי כֹפֶר וְאַעְלִים עֵינַי בּוֹ וְאָשִׁיב לָכֶם: 4 וַיֹּאמְרוּ לֹא עֲשַׁקְתָּנוּ וְלֹא רַצּוֹתָנוּ וְלֹא־לָקַחְתָּ מִיַּד־אִישׁ מְאוּמָה: 5 וַיֹּאמֶר אֲלֵיהֶם עֵד יְהֹוָה בָּכֶם וְעֵד מְשִׁיחוֹ הַיּוֹם הַזֶּה כִּי לֹא מְצָאתֶם בְּיָדִי מְאוּמָה וַיֹּאמֶר עֵד: 6 וַיֹּאמֶר שְׁמוּאֵל אֶל־הָעָם יְהֹוָה אֲשֶׁר עָשָׂה אֶת־מֹשֶׁה וְאֶת־אַהֲרֹן וַאֲשֶׁר הֶעֱלָה אֶת־אֲבוֹתֵיכֶם מֵאֶרֶץ מִצְרָיִם: 7 וְעַתָּה הִתְיַצְּבוּ וְאִשָּׁפְטָה אִתְּכֶם לִפְנֵי יְהֹוָה אֵת כָּל־צִדְקוֹת יְהֹוָה אֲשֶׁר־עָשָׂה אִתְּכֶם וְאֶת־אֲבוֹתֵיכֶם: 8 כַּאֲשֶׁר־בָּא יַעֲקֹב מִצְרָיִם וַיִּזְעֲקוּ אֲבוֹתֵיכֶם אֶל־יְהֹוָה וַיִּשְׁלַח יְהֹוָה אֶת־מֹשֶׁה וְאֶת־אַהֲרֹן וַיּוֹצִיאוּ אֶת־אֲבוֹתֵיכֶם מִמִּצְרַיִם

הפטרת קרח

וַיֵּשְׁבוּ בַּמָּקוֹם הַזֶּה: 9 וַיִּשְׁכְּחוּ אֶת־יְהֹוָה אֱלֹהֵיהֶם וַיִּמְכֹּר אֹתָם בְּיַד סִיסְרָא שַׂר־צְבָא חָצוֹר וּבְיַד־פְּלִשְׁתִּים וּבְיַד מֶלֶךְ מוֹאָב וַיִּלָּחֲמוּ בָּם: 10 וַיִּזְעֲקוּ אֶל־יְהֹוָה [ויאמר כ׳] וַיֹּאמְרוּ חָטָאנוּ כִּי עָזַבְנוּ אֶת־יְהֹוָה וַנַּעֲבֹד אֶת־הַבְּעָלִים וְאֶת־הָעַשְׁתָּרוֹת וְעַתָּה הַצִּילֵנוּ מִיַּד אֹיְבֵינוּ וְנַעַבְדֶךָּ: 11 וַיִּשְׁלַח יְהֹוָה אֶת־יְרֻבַּעַל וְאֶת־בְּדָן וְאֶת־יִפְתָּח וְאֶת־שְׁמוּאֵל וַיַּצֵּל אֶתְכֶם מִיַּד אֹיְבֵיכֶם מִסָּבִיב וַתֵּשְׁבוּ בֶּטַח: 12 וַתִּרְאוּ כִּי נָחָשׁ מֶלֶךְ בְּנֵי־עַמּוֹן בָּא עֲלֵיכֶם וַתֹּאמְרוּ לִי לֹא כִּי־מֶלֶךְ יִמְלֹךְ עָלֵינוּ וַיהֹוָה אֱלֹהֵיכֶם מַלְכְּכֶם: 13 וְעַתָּה הִנֵּה הַמֶּלֶךְ אֲשֶׁר בְּחַרְתֶּם אֲשֶׁר שְׁאֶלְתֶּם וְהִנֵּה נָתַן יְהֹוָה עֲלֵיכֶם מֶלֶךְ: 14 אִם־תִּירְאוּ אֶת־יְהֹוָה וַעֲבַדְתֶּם אֹתוֹ וּשְׁמַעְתֶּם בְּקוֹלוֹ וְלֹא תַמְרוּ אֶת־פִּי יְהֹוָה וִהְיִתֶם גַּם־אַתֶּם וְגַם־הַמֶּלֶךְ אֲשֶׁר מָלַךְ עֲלֵיכֶם אַחַר יְהֹוָה אֱלֹהֵיכֶם: 15 וְאִם־לֹא תִשְׁמְעוּ בְּקוֹל יְהֹוָה וּמְרִיתֶם אֶת־פִּי יְהֹוָה וְהָיְתָה יַד־יְהֹוָה בָּכֶם וּבַאֲבֹתֵיכֶם: 16 גַּם־עַתָּה הִתְיַצְּבוּ וּרְאוּ אֶת־הַדָּבָר הַגָּדוֹל הַזֶּה אֲשֶׁר יְהֹוָה עֹשֶׂה לְעֵינֵיכֶם: 17 הֲלוֹא קְצִיר־חִטִּים הַיּוֹם אֶקְרָא אֶל־יְהֹוָה וְיִתֵּן קֹלוֹת וּמָטָר וּדְעוּ וּרְאוּ כִּי־רָעַתְכֶם רַבָּה אֲשֶׁר עֲשִׂיתֶם בְּעֵינֵי יְהֹוָה לִשְׁאוֹל לָכֶם מֶלֶךְ: 18 וַיִּקְרָא שְׁמוּאֵל אֶל־יְהֹוָה וַיִּתֵּן יְהֹוָה קֹלֹת וּמָטָר בַּיּוֹם הַהוּא וַיִּירָא כָל־הָעָם מְאֹד אֶת־יְהֹוָה וְאֶת־שְׁמוּאֵל: 19 וַיֹּאמְרוּ כָל־הָעָם אֶל־שְׁמוּאֵל הִתְפַּלֵּל בְּעַד־עֲבָדֶיךָ אֶל־יְהֹוָה אֱלֹהֶיךָ וְאַל־נָמוּת כִּי־יָסַפְנוּ עַל־כָּל־חַטֹּאתֵינוּ רָעָה לִשְׁאֹל לָנוּ מֶלֶךְ:

Aaron, they brought your fathers out of Egypt, and they settled them in this place—without a king.

⁹ "But they forgot God, their God, and He delivered them into the hand of Sisera—the commander of the army of Hazor—into the hand of the Philistines, and into the hand of the king of Moab, who waged war with them without a king.

¹⁰ "They cried out to God and said, 'We have sinned, for we have abandoned God, and have served the deities of Baal and Ashtaroth! Now, save us from the hand of our enemies, and we will serve You!' ¹¹ And God sent Jerubbaal, Bedan, Jephthah, and Samuel, and He saved you without a king from the hand of your surrounding enemies, and you lived in safety.

¹² "When you saw that Nahash, the king of the Ammonite nation, came upon you, you said to me, 'We don't want the judge to lead us to war, as in the days of our fathers, but we want the king that rules over us to lead us to war.' But you were foolish, because God, your God, is your King and He is the One who saves you at war, not the judge or human king.

¹³ "But now you have the king whom you have chosen, whom you have requested, and God has now consented for him to be appointed as a king over you. ¹⁴ If you will fear God, and serve Him, and listen to His voice, and do not rebel against God's commandments, both you and the king who reigns over you, then you will follow behind God, your God, when He leads you at war. ¹⁵ But, if you will not listen to God's voice, and you rebel against God's commandments, God's hand will be against you and against your kings, who are like your 'fathers.'"

¹⁶ "Now if you are wondering why God agreed to appoint a king over you, being that it was an inappropriate request, stand and see this great thing that God will do before your eyes which will prove that God grants people's requests even if they are inappropriate. ¹⁷ Is it not the wheat harvest today when rain is destructive? I will nevertheless call to God, and He will send thunder and rain! Then you will know and see that what you did—to ask for a king over yourselves—was likewise very bad in the eyes of God even though He granted your request."

¹⁸ Samuel called to God, and God sent thunder and rain on that day, and all the people feared God and Samuel greatly.

¹⁹ All the people said to Samuel, "Pray for your servants to God, your God, and let us not die! For we

haftarat ḥukkat

have added evil to all our sins by asking for a king for ourselves."

²⁰ "Do not fear," Samuel said to the people, "You have already done all this evil, but do not turn away from following God. Serve God with all your heart and your sin will be forgiven. ²¹ Do not turn away from God, for then you would be following after empty things which cannot help or save you, since they are empty. ²² For God will not abandon His people for the sake of His great name, since it would be a desecration of His name if He abandoned you, because everyone knows that God desired to make you a people for Himself."

20 וַיֹּאמֶר שְׁמוּאֵל אֶל־הָעָם אַל־תִּירָאוּ אַתֶּם עֲשִׂיתֶם אֵת כָּל־הָרָעָה הַזֹּאת אַךְ אַל־תָּסוּרוּ מֵאַחֲרֵי יְהֹוָה וַעֲבַדְתֶּם אֶת־יְהֹוָה בְּכָל־לְבַבְכֶם: 21 וְלֹא תָּסוּרוּ כִּי ׀ אַחֲרֵי הַתֹּהוּ אֲשֶׁר לֹא־יוֹעִילוּ וְלֹא יַצִּילוּ כִּי־תֹהוּ הֵמָּה: 22 כִּי לֹא־יִטֹּשׁ יְהֹוָה אֶת־עַמּוֹ בַּעֲבוּר שְׁמוֹ הַגָּדוֹל כִּי הוֹאִיל יְהֹוָה לַעֲשׂוֹת אֶתְכֶם לוֹ לְעָם:

haftarat ḥukkat

ALL COMMUNITIES—JUDGES 11:1–33

SYNOPSIS: This *Haftarah* discusses the conquest of Sihon and Og, mentioned in the *Parashah*.

The *Haftarah* takes place in the eleventh century B.C.E., when the nation is beginning to repent for years of idol-worship which had brought about Philistine and Ammonite oppression. As the people remove their alien gods, the Ammonites launch a further attack on Israel, prompting the military officers to offer the prize role of army chief to whoever is first to fight the Ammonites and defeat them. The *Haftarah* describes the diplomatic process by which the mighty warrior Jephthah is lured to this challenge, in which he is ultimately triumphant.

The *Haftarah* opens with a brief account of Jephthah's sad life, how he was born to a harlot and expelled from his home by his half-brothers and subsequently mixed with undignified company (11:1-3). The current story then begins, as the elders of Gilead invite Jephthah to the challenge of fighting the Ammonites, offering the prize of military leadership if he succeeds (4-6). After some negotiation, Jephthah accepts on the condition that he is made the leader immediately (7-11). A communication then follows between Jephthah and the king of Ammon, in an attempt to make peace, but it fails (12-28). Vowing to return all the booty to God, Jephthah leads Israel's army to battle and is victorious (29-33).

11

¹ Jephthah the son of Gilead was a mighty warrior. He was the son of a harlot but it was nevertheless certain that Gilead had fathered Jephthah.

² Afterwards, Gilead's wife bore him sons. His wife's sons grew up and drove Jephthah out. They said to him, "You will not inherit in our father's house because you are the son of another woman."

³ Jephthah fled from his brothers and he settled in

יא 1 וְיִפְתָּח הַגִּלְעָדִי הָיָה גִּבּוֹר חַיִל וְהוּא בֶּן־אִשָּׁה זוֹנָה וַיּוֹלֶד גִּלְעָד אֶת־יִפְתָּח: 2 וַתֵּלֶד אֵשֶׁת־גִּלְעָד לוֹ בָּנִים וַיִּגְדְּלוּ בְנֵי־הָאִשָּׁה וַיְגָרְשׁוּ אֶת־יִפְתָּח וַיֹּאמְרוּ לוֹ לֹא־תִנְחַל בְּבֵית־אָבִינוּ כִּי בֶּן־אִשָּׁה אַחֶרֶת אָתָּה: 3 וַיִּבְרַח יִפְתָּח מִפְּנֵי

הפטרת חקת

אֶחָיו וַיֵּשֶׁב בְּאֶרֶץ טוֹב וַיִּתְלַקְּטוּ אֶל־יִפְתָּח אֲנָשִׁים רֵיקִים וַיֵּצְאוּ עִמּוֹ: 4 וַיְהִי מִיָּמִים וַיִּלָּחֲמוּ בְנֵי־עַמּוֹן עִם־יִשְׂרָאֵל: 5 וַיְהִי כַּאֲשֶׁר־נִלְחֲמוּ בְנֵי־עַמּוֹן עִם־יִשְׂרָאֵל וַיֵּלְכוּ זִקְנֵי גִלְעָד לָקַחַת אֶת־יִפְתָּח מֵאֶרֶץ טוֹב: 6 וַיֹּאמְרוּ לְיִפְתָּח לְכָה וְהָיִיתָה לָּנוּ לְקָצִין וְנִלָּחֲמָה בִּבְנֵי עַמּוֹן: 7 וַיֹּאמֶר יִפְתָּח לְזִקְנֵי גִלְעָד הֲלֹא אַתֶּם שְׂנֵאתֶם אוֹתִי וַתְּגָרְשׁוּנִי מִבֵּית אָבִי וּמַדּוּעַ בָּאתֶם אֵלַי עַתָּה כַּאֲשֶׁר צַר לָכֶם: 8 וַיֹּאמְרוּ זִקְנֵי גִלְעָד אֶל־יִפְתָּח לָכֵן עַתָּה שַׁבְנוּ אֵלֶיךָ וְהָלַכְתָּ עִמָּנוּ וְנִלְחַמְתָּ בִּבְנֵי עַמּוֹן וְהָיִיתָ לָּנוּ לְרֹאשׁ לְכֹל יֹשְׁבֵי גִלְעָד: 9 וַיֹּאמֶר יִפְתָּח אֶל־זִקְנֵי גִלְעָד אִם־מְשִׁיבִים אַתֶּם אוֹתִי לְהִלָּחֵם בִּבְנֵי עַמּוֹן וְנָתַן יְהֹוָה אוֹתָם לְפָנָי אָנֹכִי אֶהְיֶה לָכֶם לְרֹאשׁ: 10 וַיֹּאמְרוּ זִקְנֵי־גִלְעָד אֶל־יִפְתָּח יְהֹוָה יִהְיֶה שֹׁמֵעַ בֵּינוֹתֵינוּ אִם־לֹא כִדְבָרְךָ כֵּן נַעֲשֶׂה: 11 וַיֵּלֶךְ יִפְתָּח עִם־זִקְנֵי גִלְעָד וַיָּשִׂימוּ הָעָם אוֹתוֹ עֲלֵיהֶם לְרֹאשׁ וּלְקָצִין וַיְדַבֵּר יִפְתָּח אֶת־כָּל־דְּבָרָיו לִפְנֵי יְהֹוָה בַּמִּצְפָּה: 12 וַיִּשְׁלַח יִפְתָּח מַלְאָכִים אֶל־מֶלֶךְ בְּנֵי־עַמּוֹן לֵאמֹר מַה־לִּי וָלָךְ כִּי־בָאתָ אֵלַי לְהִלָּחֵם בְּאַרְצִי: 13 וַיֹּאמֶר מֶלֶךְ בְּנֵי־עַמּוֹן אֶל־מַלְאֲכֵי יִפְתָּח כִּי־לָקַח יִשְׂרָאֵל אֶת־אַרְצִי בַּעֲלוֹתוֹ מִמִּצְרַיִם מֵאַרְנוֹן וְעַד־הַיַּבֹּק וְעַד־הַיַּרְדֵּן וְעַתָּה הָשִׁיבָה אֶתְהֶן בְּשָׁלוֹם: 14 וַיּוֹסֶף עוֹד יִפְתָּח וַיִּשְׁלַח מַלְאָכִים אֶל־מֶלֶךְ בְּנֵי עַמּוֹן: 15 וַיֹּאמֶר לוֹ כֹּה אָמַר יִפְתָּח לֹא־לָקַח יִשְׂרָאֵל אֶת־אֶרֶץ מוֹאָב וְאֶת־אֶרֶץ בְּנֵי עַמּוֹן: 16 כִּי בַּעֲלוֹתָם מִמִּצְרָיִם וַיֵּלֶךְ יִשְׂרָאֵל בַּמִּדְבָּר עַד־יַם־סוּף וַיָּבֹא קָדֵשָׁה: 17 וַיִּשְׁלַח יִשְׂרָאֵל מַלְאָכִים | אֶל־מֶלֶךְ אֱדוֹם | לֵאמֹר אֶעְבְּרָה־נָּא בְאַרְצֶךָ

---

the land of Tob. Low-class men gathered around Jephthah, and they went around with him.

⁴ A long time later, the people of Ammon went to war with Israel. ⁵ What happened was, when the people of Ammon were fighting with Israel, the elders of Gilead went to take Jephthah from the land of Tob back to Gilead. ⁶ They said to Jephthah, "Come and become our leader, and we'll fight with the people of Ammon."

⁷ "But didn't you despise me," said Jephthah to the elders of Gilead, "and help my brothers drive me from my father's house? If you sincerely regretted what you did, why have you only come to me now when you're in trouble and not before?"

⁸ "Not at all!" the elders of Gilead said to Jephthah. "We hold you in great esteem and therefore we've come in person to you now and did not just send a messenger. Go with us, and fight with the people of Ammon, and you will become our leader, over all the inhabitants of Gilead!"

⁹ Jephthah said to the elders of Gilead, "That's not what I call an expression of great esteem. If you bring me back to fight with the people of Ammon, and God delivers them before me, I will obviously be entitled to be your head. If you want to show me esteem appoint me as your leader now!"

¹⁰ "God will bear witness between us if we do not do as you say," the elders of Gilead said to Jephthah.

¹¹ Jephthah went with the elders of Gilead, and the people appointed him immediately as a leader and ruler over them. And Jephthah recited all his words of prayer before God in Mizpah.

¹² Jephthah sent messengers to the king of Ammon, saying, "What hatred is there between me and you, that you have come to me to fight in my land?"

¹³ The king of Ammon said to Jephthah's messengers, "Because Israel took away my land, when they came out of Egypt, from Arnon and up to the Jabbok, and up to the Jordan. Now please restore them peacefully."

¹⁴ Jephthah sent messengers again to the king of Ammon ¹⁵ and said to him, "This is what Jephthah says: Israel did not take the land of Moab and the land of Ammon from you! ¹⁶ What happened was, when they came up from Egypt, and Israel went through the wilderness up to the Reed Sea, they came to Kadesh. ¹⁷ Israel sent messengers to the

haftarat ḥukkat

king of Edom, saying, 'Let me pass now through your land,' but the king of Edom did not listen. He also sent messengers to the king of Moab, and he was also unwilling. So Israel stayed in Kadesh. ¹⁸ Then they went through the desert, and went around the land of Edom and the land of Moab. They came to the east of the land of Moab, and encamped on the other side of the Arnon, but they did not come within the border of Moab, for the Arnon was the border of Moab.

¹⁹ "Then Israel sent messengers to King Sihon of the Amorites, the King of Heshbon. Israel said to him, 'Please let us pass through your land, up to my place, the land of Canaan, which God has given me.' ²⁰ But Sihon did not trust Israel to pass through his border. Sihon gathered all his people, they encamped in Jahaz, and he fought with Israel. ²¹ And God, the God of Israel, delivered Sihon and all his people into the hand of Israel. They defeated them, and Israel took possession of all the land of the Amorites, the inhabitants of that land. ²² They took possession of the entire border of the Amorites, from the Arnon up to the Jabbok, and from the desert up to the Jordan.

²³ "Now God, the God of Israel, has driven out the Amorites from before His people Israel, and you want to possess it? ²⁴ Surely that which Chemosh, your god, gives you to possess, you may possess; and all that which God, our God, has driven out from before us, we will possess.

²⁵ "Now, are you any better than Balak son of Zippor, King of Moab? Did he ever strive with Israel, or did he ever fight against them? ²⁶ When Israel lived in Heshbon and its towns, and in Aroer and its towns, and in all the cities that are along Arnon, for three hundred years, why did you not recover them from us during that time? ²⁷ I have not sinned against you, and you are wronging me by fighting against me. May God, the Judge, decide this day between the children of Israel and between the children of Ammon."

²⁸ The king of Ammon did not listen to the words of Jephthah which he had sent him.

²⁹ Jephthah had a spirit of bravery from God. He went through Gilead and Manasseh, he went through Mizpeh of Gilead, and from Mizpeh of Gilead he went to fight with the people of Ammon in their territory.

וְלֹא שָׁמַע מֶלֶךְ אֱדוֹם וְגַם אֶל־מֶלֶךְ מוֹאָב שָׁלַח וְלֹא אָבָה וַיֵּשֶׁב יִשְׂרָאֵל בְּקָדֵשׁ: 18 וַיֵּלֶךְ בַּמִּדְבָּר וַיָּסָב אֶת־אֶרֶץ אֱדוֹם וְאֶת־אֶרֶץ מוֹאָב וַיָּבֹא מִמִּזְרַח־שֶׁמֶשׁ לְאֶרֶץ מוֹאָב וַיַּחֲנוּן בְּעֵבֶר אַרְנוֹן וְלֹא־בָאוּ בִּגְבוּל מוֹאָב כִּי אַרְנוֹן גְּבוּל מוֹאָב: 19 וַיִּשְׁלַח יִשְׂרָאֵל מַלְאָכִים אֶל־סִיחוֹן מֶלֶךְ־הָאֱמֹרִי מֶלֶךְ חֶשְׁבּוֹן וַיֹּאמֶר לוֹ יִשְׂרָאֵל נַעְבְּרָה־נָּא בְאַרְצְךָ עַד־מְקוֹמִי: 20 וְלֹא־הֶאֱמִין סִיחוֹן אֶת־יִשְׂרָאֵל עֲבֹר בִּגְבֻלוֹ וַיֶּאֱסֹף סִיחוֹן אֶת־כָּל־עַמּוֹ וַיַּחֲנוּ בְּיָהְצָה וַיִּלָּחֶם עִם־יִשְׂרָאֵל: 21 וַיִּתֵּן יְהוָה אֱלֹהֵי־יִשְׂרָאֵל אֶת־סִיחוֹן וְאֶת־כָּל־עַמּוֹ בְּיַד יִשְׂרָאֵל וַיַּכּוּם וַיִּירַשׁ יִשְׂרָאֵל אֵת כָּל־אֶרֶץ הָאֱמֹרִי יוֹשֵׁב הָאָרֶץ הַהִיא: 22 וַיִּירְשׁוּ אֵת כָּל־גְּבוּל הָאֱמֹרִי מֵאַרְנוֹן וְעַד־הַיַּבֹּק וּמִן־הַמִּדְבָּר וְעַד־הַיַּרְדֵּן: 23 וְעַתָּה יְהוָה | אֱלֹהֵי יִשְׂרָאֵל הוֹרִישׁ אֶת־הָאֱמֹרִי מִפְּנֵי עַמּוֹ יִשְׂרָאֵל וְאַתָּה תִּירָשֶׁנּוּ: 24 הֲלֹא אֵת אֲשֶׁר יוֹרִישְׁךָ כְּמוֹשׁ אֱלֹהֶיךָ אוֹתוֹ תִירָשׁ וְאֵת כָּל־אֲשֶׁר הוֹרִישׁ יְהוָה אֱלֹהֵינוּ מִפָּנֵינוּ אוֹתוֹ נִירָשׁ: 25 וְעַתָּה הֲטוֹב טוֹב אַתָּה מִבָּלָק בֶּן־צִפּוֹר מֶלֶךְ מוֹאָב הֲרוֹב רָב עִם־יִשְׂרָאֵל אִם־נִלְחֹם נִלְחַם בָּם: 26 בְּשֶׁבֶת יִשְׂרָאֵל בְּחֶשְׁבּוֹן וּבִבְנוֹתֶיהָ וּבְעַרְעוֹר וּבִבְנוֹתֶיהָ וּבְכָל־הֶעָרִים אֲשֶׁר עַל־יְדֵי אַרְנוֹן שְׁלֹשׁ מֵאוֹת שָׁנָה וּמַדּוּעַ לֹא־הִצַּלְתֶּם בָּעֵת הַהִיא: 27 וְאָנֹכִי לֹא־חָטָאתִי לָךְ וְאַתָּה עֹשֶׂה אִתִּי רָעָה לְהִלָּחֶם בִּי יִשְׁפֹּט יְהוָה הַשֹּׁפֵט הַיּוֹם בֵּין בְּנֵי יִשְׂרָאֵל וּבֵין בְּנֵי עַמּוֹן: 28 וְלֹא שָׁמַע מֶלֶךְ בְּנֵי עַמּוֹן אֶל־דִּבְרֵי יִפְתָּח אֲשֶׁר שָׁלַח אֵלָיו: 29 וַתְּהִי עַל־יִפְתָּח רוּחַ יְהוָה וַיַּעֲבֹר אֶת־הַגִּלְעָד וְאֶת־מְנַשֶּׁה וַיַּעֲבֹר אֶת־מִצְפֵּה

הפטרת בלק

גִּלְעָד וּמִמִּצְפֵּה גִלְעָד עָבַר בְּנֵי עַמּוֹן: 30 וַיִּדַּר יִפְתָּח נֶדֶר לַיהוָה וַיֹּאמַר אִם־נָתוֹן תִּתֵּן אֶת־בְּנֵי עַמּוֹן בְּיָדִי: 31 וְהָיָה הַיּוֹצֵא אֲשֶׁר יֵצֵא מִדַּלְתֵי בֵיתִי לִקְרָאתִי בְּשׁוּבִי בְשָׁלוֹם מִבְּנֵי עַמּוֹן וְהָיָה לַיהוָה וְהַעֲלִיתִיהוּ עוֹלָה: 32 וַיַּעֲבֹר יִפְתָּח אֶל־בְּנֵי עַמּוֹן לְהִלָּחֶם בָּם וַיִּתְּנֵם יְהוָה בְּיָדוֹ: 33 וַיַּכֵּם מֵעֲרוֹעֵר וְעַד־בֹּאֲךָ מִנִּית עֶשְׂרִים עִיר וְעַד אָבֵל כְּרָמִים מַכָּה גְּדוֹלָה מְאֹד וַיִּכָּנְעוּ בְּנֵי עַמּוֹן מִפְּנֵי בְּנֵי יִשְׂרָאֵל:

[30] Jephthah made a vow to God and said, "If You will deliver the people of Ammon into my hand, [31] then whatever comes forth, that comes out of the doors of my house towards me, when I return in peace from the people of Ammon, will be for God, and I will offer it up for a burnt-offering if it is fit for a sacrifice."

[32] Jephthah went over to the people of Ammon to fight against them, and God delivered them into his hand. [33] He defeated them from Aroer until you come to Minith, twenty cities, and up to Abel-cheramim, a very great defeat. The children of Ammon were then subordinated to the children of Israel.

haftarat balak
and hukkat–balak

ALL COMMUNITIES—Micah 5:6 – 6:8

SYNOPSIS: This *Haftarah* mentions how God confounded the plot of Balak (6:5), described in the *Parashah*. The *Haftarah* was said by the prophet Micah, a contemporary of Isaiah, in the eighth century B.C.E. Both prophets spoke at length about the fate of Jerusalem during a period of increasing Assyrian power, though Isaiah focused more on political and military events, whereas Micah's emphasis lay on social issues, such as the corrupt influences of the wealthy elite.

The *Haftarah* opens with a forecast of the time immediately preceding the future Redemption, when only a remnant of Israel remains, but they are strong due to their trust in God (5:6-8). When the day of Redemption arrives, God will destroy Israel's weapons and fortresses, for God Himself will provide all necessary protection, and all idolatry will be eliminated (9-13). He will also take vengeance on the wicked nations (14).

We then begin a new chapter, in which God calls upon the prophet to rouse the people to a spiritual reckoning (6:1-2). They are to remember all the acts of Divine kindness—the Exodus, salvation from Balak's plot and safe arrival in the Land (3-5). Micah then questions what the people must do to repent, perhaps some form of elaborate sacrificial worship? God, however, dismisses this suggestion with a simple response, *"Simply to do justice, love kindness, and walk humbly with your God"* (6:8).

5 [6] The remnant of Jacob will be among Gog and his many nations, like dew sent by God in reward for their trust in Him; like heavy rain upon vegetation that does not hope for any man and does not wait for the sons of men.

ה 6 וְהָיָה | שְׁאֵרִית יַעֲקֹב בְּקֶרֶב עַמִּים רַבִּים כְּטַל מֵאֵת יְהוָה כִּרְבִיבִים עֲלֵי־עֵשֶׂב אֲשֶׁר לֹא־יְקַוֶּה לְאִישׁ וְלֹא יְיַחֵל לִבְנֵי

haftarat balak

7 The remnant of Jacob will be among the nations, amid many peoples, but due to their trust in God they will be like a lion among the animals of the forest, like a young lion among the flocks of sheep, which, if it passes through, tramples and tears into pieces, and no one can save anything. **8** Then your hand will be raised above your oppressors, and all your enemies will be destroyed.

9 Then, on that day—says God—I will eliminate your reliance on horses from you and I will destroy your chariots, for you will rely only on God. **10** I will eliminate the need for walled cities of your land, and I will break down all your fortresses. **11** I will eliminate sorcery from your hand since you will see My Providence so clearly, and you will have no soothsayers. **12** I will eliminate your graven images and your monuments from among you, for everybody will recognize the One God, and you will no longer prostrate yourselves to idols that you made by hand. **13** I will uproot your idolatrous trees from among you, and I will destroy your enemies. **14** In anger and fury I will take vengeance upon the nations as will never have been heard of before.

6 ¹ Listen now to what God says: "Raise your voice, O prophet, and debate with Israel so that your voice competes with the mountains, and the hills hear My voice. ² Listen, O mountains, to God's dispute, and you mighty ones, the foundations of the earth! For God has a dispute with His people, and with Israel He will contend.

³ "My people! Remember all the good that I have done for you. How have I wearied you to accept My yoke? Testify against Me! ⁴ For I brought you up out of the land of Egypt, I redeemed you from the house of your slavery, and I sent you great leaders, Moses, Aaron, and Miriam. ⁵ My people! Remember now what King Balak of Moab devised, and what Balaam son of Beor answered him. From Shittim where you sinned with Baal-peor, I nevertheless took you into the land of Israel to Gilgal on the other side of the Jordan, so that you may recognize the righteous deeds of God."

⁶ But the people will say; "With what will I come before God to reply and bow before the Supernal God? Will I come before Him with burnt-offerings, with yearling calves? ⁷ Will God be pleased with thousands of rams as sacrifices, or with myriad streams of oil poured on meal-offerings? Will I give my firstborn for my transgression, the fruit of my body for the sin of my soul?"

אָדָם: ⁷ וְהָיָה שְׁאֵרִית יַעֲקֹב בַּגּוֹיִם בְּקֶרֶב עַמִּים רַבִּים כְּאַרְיֵה בְּבַהֲמוֹת יַעַר כִּכְפִיר בְּעֶדְרֵי־צֹאן אֲשֶׁר אִם־עָבַר וְרָמַס וְטָרַף וְאֵין מַצִּיל: ⁸ תָּרֹם יָדְךָ עַל־צָרֶיךָ וְכָל־אֹיְבֶיךָ יִכָּרֵתוּ: ⁹ וְהָיָה בַיּוֹם הַהוּא נְאֻם־יְהֹוָה וְהִכְרַתִּי סוּסֶיךָ מִקִּרְבֶּךָ וְהַאֲבַדְתִּי מַרְכְּבֹתֶיךָ: ¹⁰ וְהִכְרַתִּי עָרֵי אַרְצֶךָ וְהָרַסְתִּי כָּל־מִבְצָרֶיךָ: ¹¹ וְהִכְרַתִּי כְשָׁפִים מִיָּדֶךָ וּמְעוֹנְנִים לֹא יִהְיוּ־לָךְ: ¹² וְהִכְרַתִּי פְסִילֶיךָ וּמַצֵּבוֹתֶיךָ מִקִּרְבֶּךָ וְלֹא־תִשְׁתַּחֲוֶה עוֹד לְמַעֲשֵׂה יָדֶיךָ: ¹³ וְנָתַשְׁתִּי אֲשֵׁירֶיךָ מִקִּרְבֶּךָ וְהִשְׁמַדְתִּי עָרֶיךָ: ¹⁴ וְעָשִׂיתִי בְּאַף וּבְחֵמָה נָקָם אֶת־הַגּוֹיִם אֲשֶׁר לֹא שָׁמֵעוּ:

ו ¹ שִׁמְעוּ־נָא אֵת אֲשֶׁר־יְהֹוָה אֹמֵר קוּם רִיב אֶת־הֶהָרִים וְתִשְׁמַעְנָה הַגְּבָעוֹת קוֹלֶךָ: ² שִׁמְעוּ הָרִים אֶת־רִיב יְהֹוָה וְהָאֵתָנִים מוֹסְדֵי אָרֶץ כִּי רִיב לַיהֹוָה עִם־עַמּוֹ וְעִם־יִשְׂרָאֵל יִתְוַכָּח: ³ עַמִּי מֶה־עָשִׂיתִי לְךָ וּמָה הֶלְאֵתִיךָ עֲנֵה בִי: ⁴ כִּי הֶעֱלִתִיךָ מֵאֶרֶץ מִצְרַיִם וּמִבֵּית עֲבָדִים פְּדִיתִיךָ וָאֶשְׁלַח לְפָנֶיךָ אֶת־מֹשֶׁה אַהֲרֹן וּמִרְיָם: ⁵ עַמִּי זְכָר־נָא מַה־יָּעַץ בָּלָק מֶלֶךְ מוֹאָב וּמֶה־עָנָה אֹתוֹ בִּלְעָם בֶּן־בְּעוֹר מִן־הַשִּׁטִּים עַד־הַגִּלְגָּל לְמַעַן דַּעַת צִדְקוֹת יְהֹוָה: ⁶ בַּמָּה אֲקַדֵּם יְהֹוָה אִכַּף לֵאלֹהֵי מָרוֹם הַאֲקַדְּמֶנּוּ בְעוֹלוֹת בַּעֲגָלִים בְּנֵי שָׁנָה: ⁷ הֲיִרְצֶה יְהֹוָה בְּאַלְפֵי אֵילִים בְּרִבְבוֹת נַחֲלֵי־שָׁמֶן הַאֶתֵּן בְּכוֹרִי פִּשְׁעִי פְּרִי בִטְנִי חַטַּאת נַפְשִׁי:

8. "He has told you, O man, what is good, and what God demands of you:

"Simply to do justice, love kindness, and walk humbly with your God when observing His commands."

8 הִגִּיד לְךָ אָדָם מַה־טּוֹב וּמָה־יְהֹוָה
דּוֹרֵשׁ מִמְּךָ כִּי אִם־עֲשׂוֹת מִשְׁפָּט
וְאַהֲבַת חֶסֶד וְהַצְנֵעַ לֶכֶת עִם־אֱלֹהֶיךָ׃

haftarat pinḥas

ALL COMMUNITIES—I KINGS 18:46 – 19:21

SYNOPSIS: This *Haftarah* speaks of Elijah, who shared the same soul as Phinehas and zealously avenged God, like Phinehas.

The events in the *Haftarah* occurred shortly after the victory over the prophets of Baal at Mount Carmel (chronicled in the *Haftarah* of *Parashat Ki Tissa'*), who were subsequently executed by Elijah at the Kishon Brook. Elijah then informed King Ahab that the prolonged drought is about to end, advising him to run away quickly from the impending storm. As the *Haftarah* begins, Elijah too is fleeing from the storm, and passes Ahab's chariot (18:46). When Ahab's wife, Jezebel, is informed that the Baal prophets were slaughtered, she sends a death threat to Elijah, who promptly flees for his life (19:1-3). He reaches the desert and, in a moment of exasperation, asks God to end his life (4). An angel appears, offering food and drink which miraculously provide sufficient energy for the next forty days. Elijah camps at Mount Sinai, in the same cave where Moses had stood (5-9). God speaks to Elijah and a series of astonishing angelic revelations follow, culminating with a "subtle silent voice," heralding the Divine Presence itself (9–12). God then instructs Elijah to return and make a number of sovereign appointments, and God names Elisha as Elijah's successor. These allies will assist Elijah in the war against Baal (13-18). The *Haftarah* concludes as Elijah meets Elisha and recruits him as his servant (19-21).

If *Parashat Pinhas* falls in the Three Weeks,
the *Haftarah* for *Parashat Mattot* is read instead—page 1388.

18 ⁴⁶ God's hand was with Elijah, granting him strength. He fastened his belt in order to run faster and ran in front of Ahab's chariot until he reached Jezreel.

19 ¹ Ahab told Jezebel everything that Elijah had done bringing down fire and rain, how he had killed all of the prophets of Baal by the sword. ² Jezebel sent a messenger to Elijah saying, "May the gods of Baal *do* the same to you as you did to their prophets and may they do more so. At this time tomorrow, I will do to you what you did to them!"

³ He saw that he was in danger, so he got going and fled for his life.

He came to Beer-sheba, which was under the rule of Judah and not Ahab, and he left his servant there.

יח 46 וְיַד־יְהֹוָה הָיְתָה אֶל־אֵלִיָּהוּ
וַיְשַׁנֵּס מָתְנָיו וַיָּרָץ לִפְנֵי אַחְאָב
עַד־בֹּאֲכָה יִזְרְעֶאלָה׃

יט 1 וַיַּגֵּד אַחְאָב לְאִיזֶבֶל אֵת כָּל־
אֲשֶׁר עָשָׂה אֵלִיָּהוּ וְאֵת כָּל־אֲשֶׁר
הָרַג אֶת־כָּל־הַנְּבִיאִים בֶּחָרֶב׃ 2 וַתִּשְׁלַח
אִיזֶבֶל מַלְאָךְ אֶל־אֵלִיָּהוּ לֵאמֹר כֹּה־יַעֲשׂוּן
אֱלֹהִים וְכֹה יוֹסִפוּן כִּי־כָעֵת מָחָר אָשִׂים
אֶת־נַפְשְׁךָ כְּנֶפֶשׁ אַחַד מֵהֶם׃ 3 וַיַּרְא וַיָּקָם
וַיֵּלֶךְ אֶל־נַפְשׁוֹ וַיָּבֹא בְּאֵר שֶׁבַע אֲשֶׁר

haftarat pinḥas

⁴ He then went into the desert, a distance of one day's travel. He came and sat under a retem bush for shade, and he wanted to die. He said, "God, a life of pain like I'm in now is too much! Take my soul, as I am no better than my fathers."

⁵ He lay down and slept underneath the retem bush. Suddenly, an angel touched him to wake him up and said to him, "Get up and eat!" ⁶ He gazed around, and—look!—by his head there was a grilled cake, and a flask of water. He ate and drank, and then lay back down.

⁷ The angel of God came back to him again. It touched him and said, "Get up and eat, as the journey you wish to undertake is too far for you to go without food."

⁸ He got up, ate and drank. Then miraculously, with the energy from this meal, he went forty days and forty nights without any more food, up to the mountain of God in Horeb. ⁹ He came there to the same cave where Moses had stood, and he slept over there.

Suddenly, the word of God came to him. "Why are you here, Elijah?" God said to him.

¹⁰ He said, "I have zealously avenged God, the God of Hosts, and killed the prophets of Baal. For the children of Israel have abandoned Your covenant, torn down Your altars and killed Your prophets by the sword. I'm the only one left, and they want to take my life."

¹¹ God said, "Go out of the cave and stand at the mountain, before God. God's presence is going to pass." There was a great and strong host of angels of wind, splitting mountains and shattering boulders before God. "God does not come with angels of wind," thought Elijah.

After the angels of wind came angels of thunder. "God does not come with angels of thunder," thought Elijah.

¹² After the angels of thunder came angels of fire. "God does not come with angels of fire," thought Elijah.

After the angels of fire came a subtle, silent voice. ¹³ What happened was, when Elijah heard this silent voice, he covered his face with his cloak because he realized the Divine Presence was there.

Then he went out of the cave and stood at the entrance to the cave. A voice came to him and said, "What are you still doing here, Elijah?"

¹⁴ He said, "I have zealously avenged God, the God of Hosts, and killed the prophets of Baal. Please help me for Your sake! For the children of Israel have abandoned Your covenant, torn down Your altars and

4 וְהוּא־הָלַ֤ךְ לִיהוּדָה֙ וַיַּנַּ֣ח אֶֽת־נַעֲר֔וֹ שָׁ֑ם בַּמִּדְבָּר֙ דֶּ֣רֶךְ י֔וֹם וַיָּבֹ֕א וַיֵּ֕שֶׁב תַּ֖חַת רֹ֣תֶם [אחת כ׳] אֶחָ֑ד וַיִּשְׁאַ֤ל אֶת־נַפְשׁוֹ֙ לָמ֔וּת וַיֹּ֣אמֶר ׀ רַ֗ב עַתָּ֤ה יְהֹוָה֙ קַ֣ח נַפְשִׁ֔י כִּֽי־לֹא־ ט֥וֹב אָנֹכִ֖י מֵאֲבֹתָֽי: 5 וַיִּשְׁכַּ֤ב וַיִּישַׁן֙ תַּ֣חַת רֹ֣תֶם אֶחָ֑ד וְהִנֵּה־זֶ֤ה מַלְאָךְ֙ נֹגֵ֣עַ בּ֔וֹ וַיֹּ֥אמֶר ל֖וֹ ק֥וּם אֱכֽוֹל: 6 וַיַּבֵּ֕ט וְהִנֵּ֧ה מְרַֽאֲשֹׁתָ֛יו עֻגַ֥ת רְצָפִ֖ים וְצַפַּ֣חַת מָ֑יִם וַיֹּ֥אכַל וַיֵּ֖שְׁתְּ וַיָּ֥שָׁב וַיִּשְׁכָּֽב: 7 וַיָּ֩שָׁב֩ מַלְאַ֨ךְ יְהֹוָ֥ה ׀ שֵׁנִית֙ וַיִּגַּע־בּ֔וֹ וַיֹּ֕אמֶר ק֣וּם אֱכֹ֑ל כִּ֛י רַ֥ב מִמְּךָ֖ הַדָּֽרֶךְ: 8 וַיָּ֖קׇם וַיֹּ֣אכַל וַיִּשְׁתֶּ֑ה וַיֵּ֜לֶךְ בְּכֹ֣חַ ׀ הָאֲכִילָ֣ה הַהִ֗יא אַרְבָּעִ֥ים יוֹם֙ וְאַרְבָּעִ֣ים לַ֔יְלָה עַ֛ד הַ֥ר הָאֱלֹהִ֖ים חֹרֵֽב: 9 וַיָּבֹא־שָׁ֥ם אֶל־הַמְּעָרָ֖ה וַיָּ֣לֶן שָׁ֑ם וְהִנֵּ֤ה דְבַר־יְהֹוָה֙ אֵלָ֔יו וַיֹּ֣אמֶר ל֔וֹ מַה־לְּךָ֥ פֹ֖ה אֵלִיָּֽהוּ: 10 וַיֹּ֩אמֶר֩ קַנֹּ֨א קִנֵּ֜אתִי לַיהֹוָ֣ה ׀ אֱלֹהֵ֣י צְבָא֗וֹת כִּֽי־עָזְב֤וּ בְרִֽיתְךָ֙ בְּנֵ֣י יִשְׂרָאֵ֔ל אֶת־מִזְבְּחֹתֶ֣יךָ הָרָ֔סוּ וְאֶת־נְבִיאֶ֖יךָ הָרְג֣וּ בֶחָ֑רֶב וָאִוָּתֵ֤ר אֲנִי֙ לְבַדִּ֔י וַיְבַקְשׁ֥וּ אֶת־נַפְשִׁ֖י לְקַחְתָּֽהּ: 11 וַיֹּ֗אמֶר צֵ֣א וְעָמַדְתָּ֣ בָהָר֮ לִפְנֵ֣י יְהֹוָה֒ וְהִנֵּ֧ה יְהֹוָ֣ה עֹבֵ֗ר וְר֣וּחַ גְּדוֹלָ֡ה וְחָזָ֞ק מְפָרֵק֩ הָרִ֨ים וּמְשַׁבֵּ֤ר סְלָעִים֙ לִפְנֵ֣י יְהֹוָ֔ה לֹ֥א בָר֖וּחַ יְהֹוָ֑ה וְאַחַ֤ר הָר֨וּחַ רַ֔עַשׁ לֹ֥א בָרַ֖עַשׁ יְהֹוָֽה: 12 וְאַחַ֤ר הָרַ֨עַשׁ֙ אֵ֔שׁ לֹ֥א בָאֵ֖שׁ יְהֹוָ֑ה וְאַחַ֣ר הָאֵ֔שׁ ק֖וֹל דְּמָמָ֥ה דַקָּֽה: 13 וַיְהִ֣י ׀ כִּשְׁמֹ֣עַ אֵלִיָּ֗הוּ וַיָּ֤לֶט פָּנָיו֙ בְּאַדַּרְתּ֔וֹ וַיֵּצֵ֕א וַֽיַּעֲמֹ֖ד פֶּ֣תַח הַמְּעָרָ֑ה וְהִנֵּ֤ה אֵלָיו֙ ק֔וֹל וַיֹּ֕אמֶר מַה־לְּךָ֥ פֹ֖ה אֵלִיָּֽהוּ: 14 וַיֹּ֗אמֶר קַנֹּ֤א קִנֵּ֨אתִי֙ לַיהֹוָ֣ה ׀

הפטרת מטות

killed Your prophets by the sword. I'm the only one left, and they want to take my life."

¹⁵ God said to him, "Go back on your way to the Damascus desert through which you came. When you come there, appoint Hazael as king of Aram, ¹⁶ appoint Jehu son of Nimshi as king of Israel, and appoint Elisha son of Shaphat from Abel-meholah to be prophet in your place after you depart this world. ¹⁷ What will happen is, they will be your agents to avenge the worshipers of Baal on your behalf: Jehu will kill those who escape the sword of Hazael, and Elisha will kill those who escape the sword of Jehu. ¹⁸ I will leave over only seven thousand in Israel—all the knees that did not kneel to the Baal and every mouth that did not kiss it."

¹⁹ He left there, and found Elisha son of Shaphat as he was plowing. Twelve pairs of oxen were ahead of him and he was with the twelfth. Elijah went over to him and threw part of his cloak over him to hint that he was to become a prophet.

²⁰ Elisha left the oxen, ran after Elijah and said, "Let me, please, kiss my father and my mother, and I will follow you."

"Go back and kiss your parents, as you wish," he said to him. "But make sure you come back, for if you come with me you too will perform great miracles as I have done."

²¹ Elisha went away from him. He took the pairs of oxen and slaughtered them. Using the wood from the ox's plows as fuel, he cooked the meat and gave it to the people who were working for him, and they ate. He got going, went with Elijah and became his servant.

אֱלֹהֵי צְבָאוֹת כִּי־עָזְבוּ בְרִיתְךָ בְּנֵי יִשְׂרָאֵל אֶת־מִזְבְּחֹתֶיךָ הָרָסוּ וְאֶת־נְבִיאֶיךָ הָרְגוּ בֶחָרֶב וָאִוָּתֵר אֲנִי לְבַדִּי וַיְבַקְשׁוּ אֶת־נַפְשִׁי לְקַחְתָּהּ: 15 וַיֹּאמֶר יְהֹוָה אֵלָיו לֵךְ שׁוּב לְדַרְכְּךָ מִדְבַּרָה דַמָּשֶׂק וּבָאתָ וּמָשַׁחְתָּ אֶת־חֲזָאֵל לְמֶלֶךְ עַל־אֲרָם: 16 וְאֵת יֵהוּא בֶן־נִמְשִׁי תִּמְשַׁח לְמֶלֶךְ עַל־יִשְׂרָאֵל וְאֶת־אֱלִישָׁע בֶּן־שָׁפָט מֵאָבֵל מְחוֹלָה תִּמְשַׁח לְנָבִיא תַּחְתֶּיךָ: 17 וְהָיָה הַנִּמְלָט מֵחֶרֶב חֲזָאֵל יָמִית יֵהוּא וְהַנִּמְלָט מֵחֶרֶב יֵהוּא יָמִית אֱלִישָׁע: 18 וְהִשְׁאַרְתִּי בְיִשְׂרָאֵל שִׁבְעַת אֲלָפִים כָּל־הַבִּרְכַּיִם אֲשֶׁר לֹא־כָרְעוּ לַבַּעַל וְכָל־הַפֶּה אֲשֶׁר לֹא־נָשַׁק לוֹ: 19 וַיֵּלֶךְ מִשָּׁם וַיִּמְצָא אֶת־אֱלִישָׁע בֶּן־שָׁפָט וְהוּא חֹרֵשׁ שְׁנֵים־עָשָׂר צְמָדִים לְפָנָיו וְהוּא בִּשְׁנֵים הֶעָשָׂר וַיַּעֲבֹר אֵלִיָּהוּ אֵלָיו וַיַּשְׁלֵךְ אַדַּרְתּוֹ אֵלָיו: 20 וַיַּעֲזֹב אֶת־הַבָּקָר וַיָּרָץ אַחֲרֵי אֵלִיָּהוּ וַיֹּאמֶר אֶשְּׁקָה־נָּא לְאָבִי וּלְאִמִּי וְאֵלְכָה אַחֲרֶיךָ וַיֹּאמֶר לוֹ לֵךְ שׁוּב כִּי מֶה־עָשִׂיתִי לָךְ: 21 וַיָּשָׁב מֵאַחֲרָיו וַיִּקַּח אֶת־צֶמֶד הַבָּקָר וַיִּזְבָּחֵהוּ וּבִכְלִי הַבָּקָר בִּשְּׁלָם הַבָּשָׂר וַיִּתֵּן לָעָם וַיֹּאכֵלוּ וַיָּקָם וַיֵּלֶךְ אַחֲרֵי אֵלִיָּהוּ וַיְשָׁרְתֵהוּ:

haftarat mattot

ALL COMMUNITIES—JEREMIAH 1:1 – 2:3

> **SYNOPSIS:** This is the first of three *"Haftarot* of punishment" which are read between 17 *Tammuz* and 9 *Av*, when we mourn the destruction of the Holy Temple. The *Haftarah*, taken from the beginning of the book of Jeremiah, describes his inauguration as a prophet by God and his first prophecy of doom.
>
> The *Haftarah* begins with personal details about the prophet, and the dates during which he served (1:1-3). We then read God's first words to Jeremiah, informing him of his role as a prophet, to which Jeremiah initially expresses his misgivings (4-10).

haftarat mattot

In his first vision, God shows Jeremiah an almond tree, as a sign that God's words will speedily be put into action (11–12). The second vision is of a boiling pot, a sign of impending doom for the people of Babylon (13–16), which the prophet is instructed to relay immediately to the people (17–19). The *Haftarah* concludes with introductory verses from the second chapter of the book, which stress God's love for Israel (2:1–3).

1 ¹ These are the words of Jeremiah son of Hilkiah, one of the priests who lived in Anathoth in the territory of Benjamin, ² to whom the word of God first came in the days of King Josiah son of Amon of Judah, in the thirteenth year of his reign. ³ He continued to receive prophecy during the days of Josiah's successor, King Jehoiakim son of Josiah of Judah. His prophecy continued up to the end of eleven years of the rule of Jehoiakim's successor, King Zedekiah son of Josiah of Judah—until the exile of Jerusalem which was in the fifth month.

⁴ The word of God came to me, saying, ⁵ "Before I had formed you in the womb, I knew that you would be fit to be a prophet, and before you emerged from the womb, I had sanctified you; I had appointed you as a prophet to the nations."

⁶ I said, "Woe! God Almighty! I really don't know how to speak, as I am young."

⁷ God said to me, "Don't say, 'I'm young,' because that is not a problem, for you will go wherever I send you, you will only have to speak whatever I command you. ⁸ Do not be afraid that you might mislead the people to whom you will speak prophecy, for I am with you to save you," says God.

⁹ In my prophetic vision I saw God stretch out His hand and touch my mouth. God said to me, "Now I have placed My words into your mouth. ¹⁰ See, I have appointed you this day over the nations and over the kingdoms, to uproot and to crush, and to destroy and to demolish, to build and to plant."

¹¹ The word of God came to me, saying, "What do you see, Jeremiah, in your vision?"

"I see a stick from an almond tree," I said.

¹² "You have seen well," God said to me. "The almond, which grows quickly, is a sign that I will put My word into action speedily."

¹³ The word of God came to me a second time, saying, "What do you see?"

א 1 דִּבְרֵי יִרְמְיָהוּ בֶּן־חִלְקִיָּהוּ מִן־הַכֹּהֲנִים אֲשֶׁר בַּעֲנָתוֹת בְּאֶרֶץ בִּנְיָמִן: 2 אֲשֶׁר הָיָה דְבַר־יְהֹוָה אֵלָיו בִּימֵי יֹאשִׁיָּהוּ בֶן־אָמוֹן מֶלֶךְ יְהוּדָה בִּשְׁלֹשׁ־עֶשְׂרֵה שָׁנָה לְמׇלְכֽוֹ: 3 וַיְהִי בִּימֵי יְהוֹיָקִים בֶּן־יֹאשִׁיָּהוּ מֶלֶךְ יְהוּדָה עַד־תֹּם עַשְׁתֵּי־עֶשְׂרֵה שָׁנָה לְצִדְקִיָּהוּ בֶן־יֹאשִׁיָּהוּ מֶלֶךְ יְהוּדָה עַד־גְּלוֹת יְרוּשָׁלַ͏ִם בַּחֹדֶשׁ הַחֲמִישִֽׁי: 4 וַיְהִי דְבַר־יְהֹוָה אֵלַי לֵאמֹֽר: 5 בְּטֶ֖רֶם [אצורך כ׳] אֶצּוֹרְךָ בַבֶּטֶן יְדַעְתִּיךָ וּבְטֶרֶם תֵּצֵא מֵרֶחֶם הִקְדַּשְׁתִּיךָ נָבִיא לַגּוֹיִם נְתַתִּֽיךָ: 6 וָאֹמַר אֲהָהּ אֲדֹנָי יֱהֹוִה הִנֵּה לֹא־יָדַעְתִּי דַּבֵּר כִּי־נַעַר אָנֹֽכִי: 7 וַיֹּאמֶר יְהֹוָה אֵלַי אַל־תֹּאמַר נַעַר אָנֹכִי כִּי עַל־כׇּל־אֲשֶׁר אֶשְׁלָחֲךָ תֵּלֵךְ וְאֵת כׇּל־אֲשֶׁר אֲצַוְּךָ תְּדַבֵּֽר: 8 אַל־תִּירָא מִפְּנֵיהֶם כִּי־אִתְּךָ אֲנִי לְהַצִּלֶךָ נְאֻם־יְהֹוָֽה: 9 וַיִּשְׁלַח יְהֹוָה אֶת־יָדוֹ וַיַּגַּע עַל־פִּי וַיֹּאמֶר יְהֹוָה אֵלַי הִנֵּה נָתַתִּי דְבָרַי בְּפִֽיךָ: 10 רְאֵה הִפְקַדְתִּיךָ | הַיּוֹם הַזֶּה עַל־הַגּוֹיִם וְעַל־הַמַּמְלָכוֹת לִנְתוֹשׁ וְלִנְתוֹץ וּלְהַאֲבִיד וְלַהֲרוֹס לִבְנוֹת וְלִנְטֽוֹעַ: 11 וַיְהִי דְבַר־יְהֹוָה אֵלַי לֵאמֹר מָה־אַתָּה רֹאֶה יִרְמְיָהוּ וָאֹמַר מַקֵּל שָׁקֵד אֲנִי רֹאֶֽה: 12 וַיֹּאמֶר יְהֹוָה אֵלַי הֵיטַבְתָּ לִרְאוֹת כִּי־שֹׁקֵד אֲנִי עַל־דְּבָרִי לַעֲשֹׂתֽוֹ: 13 וַיְהִי דְבַר־יְהֹוָה | אֵלַי שֵׁנִית לֵאמֹר מָה אַתָּה רֹאֶה וָאֹמַר סִיר נָפוּחַ

הפטרת מסעי

וַיֹּאמֶר אֵלַי מַה־אַתָּה רֹאֶה וָאֹמַר סִיר נָפוּחַ אֲנִי רֹאֶה וּפָנָיו מִפְּנֵי צָפוֹנָה: 14 וַיֹּאמֶר יְהֹוָה אֵלָי מִצָּפוֹן תִּפָּתַח הָרָעָה עַל כָּל־יֹשְׁבֵי הָאָרֶץ: 15 כִּי ׀ הִנְנִי קֹרֵא לְכָל־מִשְׁפְּחוֹת מַמְלְכוֹת צָפוֹנָה נְאֻם־יְהֹוָה וּבָאוּ וְנָתְנוּ אִישׁ כִּסְאוֹ פֶּתַח ׀ שַׁעֲרֵי יְרוּשָׁלַ͏ִם וְעַל כָּל־חוֹמֹתֶיהָ סָבִיב וְעַל כָּל־עָרֵי יְהוּדָה: 16 וְדִבַּרְתִּי מִשְׁפָּטַי אוֹתָם עַל כָּל־רָעָתָם אֲשֶׁר עֲזָבוּנִי וַיְקַטְּרוּ לֵאלֹהִים אֲחֵרִים וַיִּשְׁתַּחֲווּ לְמַעֲשֵׂי יְדֵיהֶם: 17 וְאַתָּה תֶּאְזֹר מָתְנֶיךָ וְקַמְתָּ וְדִבַּרְתָּ אֲלֵיהֶם אֵת כָּל־אֲשֶׁר אָנֹכִי אֲצַוֶּךָּ אַל־תֵּחַת מִפְּנֵיהֶם פֶּן־אֲחִתְּךָ לִפְנֵיהֶם: 18 וַאֲנִי הִנֵּה נְתַתִּיךָ הַיּוֹם לְעִיר מִבְצָר וּלְעַמּוּד בַּרְזֶל וּלְחֹמוֹת נְחֹשֶׁת עַל־כָּל־הָאָרֶץ לְמַלְכֵי יְהוּדָה לְשָׂרֶיהָ לְכֹהֲנֶיהָ וּלְעַם הָאָרֶץ: 19 וְנִלְחֲמוּ אֵלֶיךָ וְלֹא־יוּכְלוּ לָךְ כִּי־אִתְּךָ אֲנִי נְאֻם־יְהֹוָה לְהַצִּילֶךָ:

ב 1 וַיְהִי דְבַר־יְהֹוָה אֵלַי לֵאמֹר: 2 הָלֹךְ וְקָרָאתָ בְאָזְנֵי יְרוּשָׁלַ͏ִם לֵאמֹר כֹּה אָמַר יְהֹוָה זָכַרְתִּי לָךְ חֶסֶד נְעוּרַיִךְ אַהֲבַת כְּלוּלֹתָיִךְ לֶכְתֵּךְ אַחֲרַי בַּמִּדְבָּר בְּאֶרֶץ לֹא זְרוּעָה: 3 קֹדֶשׁ יִשְׂרָאֵל לַיהֹוָה רֵאשִׁית תְּבוּאָתֹה כָּל־אֹכְלָיו יֶאְשָׁמוּ רָעָה תָּבֹא אֲלֵיהֶם נְאֻם־יְהֹוָה:

"I see a boiling pot," I said. "It's bubbling toward the north."

¹⁴ God said to me, "From Babylon, which is in the north, trouble will break forth upon all the inhabitants of the land and they will gather in Jerusalem for protection, like pieces of meat in a pot, only to be boiled by the enemy. ¹⁵ For, behold, I am calling to the hearts of all the families of the kingdoms of the north to come to Jerusalem," says God. "They will come, and each person will place his chair at the entrance gates of Jerusalem and against all its walls around and against all the cities of Judah. ¹⁶ Then, I will utter My judgments against them for all their evil, that they left Me and offered up burnt-offerings to other gods and that they prostrated themselves to the work of their hands.

¹⁷ "You should hurry up, fasten your belt and get going. Repeat to them everything that I command you. Don't fear them and withhold any prophecy, for then I will break you, making you vulnerable for them to hurt you.

¹⁸ I have hereby made you strong today like a fortified city and an iron pillar, like copper walls against the entire land, against the kings of Judah, its princes, its priests, and all the people of the land. ¹⁹ They will fight against you but they will not prevail against you, for I am with you," says God, "to save you."

2 ¹ The word of God came to me, saying, ² "Go and call out into the ears of Jerusalem, saying, 'This is what God said, "I remember, for your sake, the act of lovingkindness that you did for Me in your youth when I chose you as My people; the love you had for Me in the days when you were a bride at Mount Sinai. I remember your faith, when you followed Me into the desert, to an infertile land. ³ Even in exile Israel is holy to God, the choicest of His grain. Anyone who devours him will be guilty, evil will befall them," says God.

haftarat maseʻei
and mattot–maseʻei

ASHKENAZIM—JEREMIAH 2:4–28; 3:4
SEPHARDIM AND HABAD—JEREMIAH 2:4–28; 4:1–2

> **SYNOPSIS:** This is the second of three "*Haftarot* of Punishment" which are read between 17 *Tammuz* and 9 *Av*, when we mourn the destruction of the Holy Temple.

haftarat maseʿei

> The entire *Haftarah* is a harsh critique of Israel by the prophet Jeremiah. The first passage is a historical review, condemning the Jews in Egypt, priests, kings and false prophets (2:4–9). The present generation is then admonished as being worse than the idol-worshiping nations (10–13), thus bringing judgments upon themselves (14–19), and they are rebuked for disloyalty (20–28). Ashkenazic tradition concludes with a hint of forthcoming repentance (3:4), whereas Ḥabad and Sephardic tradition conclude with a more explicit expression of return and Divine pardon (4:1–2).

Most communities, including _Ḥabad_, read this _Haftarah_ even if Rosh Ḥodesh occurs on _Shabbat_.

2 ⁴ Listen to the word of God, O House of Jacob, and all the families of the House of Israel. ⁵ This is what God says:

"What wrong did your fathers find in Me, that they distanced themselves from Me, and they went after gods of emptiness, and became empty themselves? ⁶ They did not repent and say, 'Where is God, who brought us up from the land of Egypt, who led us in the desert, providing all our needs, in a desolate land of pits, in a land of waste and gloom, in a land where no man had passed and where no man had settled?' ⁷ Didn't I bring you to a vegetative land to eat of its produce and its goodness? But you came and contaminated My land, and made My heritage an abomination.

⁸ "The priests who were supposed to teach truth did not teach the people to say, 'Where is God? Why have you abandoned Him?' Those who hold onto the Torah did not want to know Me, and the kings who are shepherds of the people rebelled against Me, and the prophets prophesied in the name of the deity Baal and followed futility. ⁹ Therefore, I will still dispute with you," says God, "and I will contend with your children's children.

¹⁰ "Go to the isles of the Kittim and see! Send messengers to Kedar and ponder deeply! Observe the idolaters there to see if there was ever anything like this, ¹¹ where a nation exchanged a god for another—and their gods are not even real gods! Yet My nation exchanged My glory for futility.

¹² "Oh heavens, be devastated about this and storm; become very desolate," says God. ¹³ "For My people have committed two evils: they have forsaken Me, the Spring of living waters, and furthermore this was only to dig for themselves wells, broken cisterns that do not hold water.

¹⁴ "Is Israel left uncared for like a slave? Is he ignored

הפטרת מסעי

יָלִיד בַּיִת הוּא מַדּוּעַ הָיָה לָבַז: 15 עָלָיו יִשְׁאֲגוּ כְפִרִים נָתְנוּ קוֹלָם וַיָּשִׁיתוּ אַרְצוֹ לְשַׁמָּה עָרָיו [נצתה כ׳] נִצְּתָה מִבְּלִי יֹשֵׁב: 16 גַּם־בְּנֵי־נֹף [ותחפנס כ׳] וְתַחְפַּנְחֵס יִרְעוּךְ קָדְקֹד: 17 הֲלוֹא־זֹאת תַּעֲשֶׂה־לָּךְ עָזְבֵךְ אֶת־יְהֹוָה אֱלֹהַיִךְ בְּעֵת מוֹלִכֵךְ בַּדָּרֶךְ: 18 וְעַתָּה מַה־לָּךְ לְדֶרֶךְ מִצְרַיִם לִשְׁתּוֹת מֵי שִׁחוֹר וּמַה־לָּךְ לְדֶרֶךְ אַשּׁוּר לִשְׁתּוֹת מֵי נָהָר: 19 תְּיַסְּרֵךְ רָעָתֵךְ וּמְשֻׁבוֹתַיִךְ תּוֹכִחֻךְ וּדְעִי וּרְאִי כִּי־רַע וָמָר עָזְבֵךְ אֶת־יְהֹוָה אֱלֹהָיִךְ וְלֹא פַחְדָּתִי אֵלַיִךְ נְאֻם־אֲדֹנָי יֱהֹוִה צְבָאוֹת: 20 כִּי מֵעוֹלָם שָׁבַרְתִּי עֻלֵּךְ נִתַּקְתִּי מוֹסְרוֹתַיִךְ וַתֹּאמְרִי לֹא [אעבוד כ׳] אֶעֱבוֹר כִּי עַל־כָּל־גִּבְעָה גְבֹהָה וְתַחַת כָּל־עֵץ רַעֲנָן אַתְּ צֹעָה זֹנָה: 21 וְאָנֹכִי נְטַעְתִּיךְ שׂוֹרֵק כֻּלֹּה זֶרַע אֱמֶת וְאֵיךְ נֶהְפַּכְתְּ לִי סוּרֵי הַגֶּפֶן נָכְרִיָּה: 22 כִּי אִם־תְּכַבְּסִי בַּנֶּתֶר וְתַרְבִּי־לָךְ בֹּרִית נִכְתָּם עֲוֺנֵךְ לְפָנַי נְאֻם אֲדֹנָי יֱהֹוִה: 23 אֵיךְ תֹּאמְרִי לֹא נִטְמֵאתִי אַחֲרֵי הַבְּעָלִים לֹא הָלַכְתִּי רְאִי דַרְכֵּךְ בַּגַּיְא דְּעִי מֶה עָשִׂית בִּכְרָה קַלָּה מְשָׂרֶכֶת דְּרָכֶיהָ: 24 פֶּרֶה | לִמֻּד מִדְבָּר בְּאַוַּת [נפשו כ׳] נַפְשָׁהּ שָׁאֲפָה רוּחַ תַּאֲנָתָהּ מִי יְשִׁיבֶנָּה כָּל־מְבַקְשֶׁיהָ לֹא יִיעָפוּ בְּחָדְשָׁהּ יִמְצָאוּנְהָ: 25 מִנְעִי רַגְלֵךְ מִיָּחֵף [וגורנך כ׳] וּגְרוֹנֵךְ מִצִּמְאָה וַתֹּאמְרִי נוֹאָשׁ לוֹא כִּי־אָהַבְתִּי זָרִים וְאַחֲרֵיהֶם אֵלֵךְ: 26 כְּבֹשֶׁת גַּנָּב כִּי יִמָּצֵא כֵּן הֹבִישׁוּ בֵּית

like a home-born slave? So why has he become a prey? [15] Young lions roar over him, they have raised their voices. They have made his land desolate; his cities were wiped out without an inhabitant. [16] Even descendants of Noph and Tahpanhes, whom you trust, will break the crown of your head.

[17] "Is this not brought upon you by abandoning God, your God, at the time He was leading you on the right path? [18] Now, why are you taking the path of relying on Egyptian assistance, drinking the water of the Sihor? Why do you follow the path of Assyrian assistance, drinking the water of the river Euphrates, when the only source of true assistance is God? [19] Your evil will chastise you, and you will be rebuked for following the thoughts of your heart. You will know and see that abandoning God, your God, is evil and bitter. Fear of Me was not upon you," says the Almighty God of Hosts.

[20] "For I have helped you since long ago. I broke off the yoke of the nations that was on you and severed your bonds. You said, 'I will not transgress,' but on every lofty hill and under every leafy tree, you wander disloyally like a harlot. [21] I planted you a good vine stock—Abraham, Isaac and Jacob who were all true seed—so how have you turned yourself into a foreign vine to Me? [22] Even if you wash with carbonate of soda and use much soap by giving charity publicly, your private sin is still a stain before Me," says God Almighty.

[23] "How could you possibly say, 'I have not been defiled; I have not gone after the deities of Baal'? Look at what you have done in the valley when you worshiped Baal! Think about what you have done, you swift young she-camel, clinging to her ways. [24] You are like a wild donkey accustomed to the desert, that runs around whenever she wants, drawing the wind into her mouth as she runs fast; like a donkey that seems pained to stay in one place, can anybody make her go back again? All who seek to catch her will not grow weary; in her last month of pregnancy, she will move slowly and they will find her. Likewise, the Jewish people are heavy with sins, and are easily caught by their enemies.

[25] "You thought of correcting your deeds to prevent your foot from going barefoot and your throat from thirst in the exile. But you said, 'I give up hope of serving God. No, for I love strange gods, and I will follow them.'

[26] "The House of Israel—the common folk, their kings, their princes, their priests of idol-worship, and their prophets of the deity Baal—have been ashamed before the nations with the shame of a thief when

haftarat mase'ei

he is caught, for after being established as servants of God, they went and worshiped idols. **27** They say to the wood, 'You are my father,' and to the stone, 'You gave birth to us,' for they turned their back to me and not their face. Then, at the time of their misfortune they say, 'Come and save us!' **28** Where, then, are your gods that you have made for yourself? Let them come, if they are able, to save you at the time of your misfortune! For you had as many gods as cities, O Judah, so can't any of them help you?

יִשְׂרָאֵל הֵמָּה מְלָכֵיהֶם שָׂרֵיהֶם וְכֹהֲנֵיהֶם וּנְבִיאֵיהֶם: 27 אֹמְרִים לָעֵץ אָבִי אַתָּה וְלָאֶבֶן אַתְּ [ילדתני כ׳] יְלִדְתָּנוּ כִּי־פָנוּ אֵלַי עֹרֶף וְלֹא פָנִים וּבְעֵת רָעָתָם יֹאמְרוּ קוּמָה וְהוֹשִׁיעֵנוּ: 28 וְאַיֵּה אֱלֹהֶיךָ אֲשֶׁר עָשִׂיתָ לָּךְ יָקוּמוּ אִם־יוֹשִׁיעוּךָ בְּעֵת רָעָתֶךָ כִּי מִסְפַּר עָרֶיךָ הָיוּ אֱלֹהֶיךָ יְהוּדָה:

The following verse is read by *Ashkenazic* communities only:

3 **4** Will you not from now call to Me, "My Father! You are the Master of my youth!

ג 4 הֲלוֹא מֵעַתָּה [קראתי כ׳] קָרָאת לִי אָבִי אַלּוּף נְעֻרַי אָתָּה:

Ḥabad and *Sephardic* communities continue here:

4 **1** "If you return, O Israel, and confess your sins," says God, "then you will have returned to me. If you remove your detestable things from My Presence in Jerusalem, you will not wander in exile. **2** If you will swear, 'As God lives,' when promising to do truth and justice and righteousness and not swear with My name to do falsehood, as you do now, then nations will bless themselves by wishing others that they should be like you, and they will praise themselves, when they are successful, that they are like you."

ד 1 אִם־תָּשׁוּב יִשְׂרָאֵל | נְאֻם־יְהֹוָה אֵלַי תָּשׁוּב וְאִם־תָּסִיר שִׁקּוּצֶיךָ מִפָּנַי וְלֹא תָנוּד: 2 וְנִשְׁבַּעְתָּ חַי־יְהֹוָה בֶּאֱמֶת בְּמִשְׁפָּט וּבִצְדָקָה וְהִתְבָּרְכוּ בוֹ גּוֹיִם וּבוֹ יִתְהַלָּלוּ:

On *Rosh Ḥodesh Av*, many commmunities, including *Ḥabad*, add the following (*Isaiah* 66:1, 23-24, 23):

66 **1** This is what God said: "The heaven is My throne, and the earth is My footstool, so what House could you build worthy for Me, and what place is worthy for My Presence to rest?

23 "It shall come to pass, that every first of the new month, and every Sabbath, all flesh, even non-Jews, shall come to worship before Me in the holy Temple," says God. **24** The non-Jews shall go out of Jerusalem, to the valley of Jehoshaphat, and look upon the corpses of the men of Gog and Magog who have rebelled against Me, for the worms that eat them will not die, and the fire that burns them shall not be extinguished. They shall be a symbol of disgrace to all flesh—non-Jews, who come to the Holy Temple.

23 "It shall come to pass, that every first of the new month, and every Sabbath, all flesh, even non-Jews, shall come to worship before Me in the holy Temple," says God.

סו 1 כֹּה אָמַר יְהֹוָה הַשָּׁמַיִם כִּסְאִי וְהָאָרֶץ הֲדֹם רַגְלָי אֵי־זֶה בַיִת אֲשֶׁר תִּבְנוּ־לִי וְאֵי־זֶה מָקוֹם מְנוּחָתִי: 23 וְהָיָה מִדֵּי־חֹדֶשׁ בְּחָדְשׁוֹ וּמִדֵּי שַׁבָּת בְּשַׁבַּתּוֹ יָבוֹא כָל־בָּשָׂר לְהִשְׁתַּחֲוֺת לְפָנַי אָמַר יְהֹוָה: 24 וְיָצְאוּ וְרָאוּ בְּפִגְרֵי הָאֲנָשִׁים הַפֹּשְׁעִים בִּי כִּי תוֹלַעְתָּם לֹא תָמוּת וְאִשָּׁם לֹא תִכְבֶּה וְהָיוּ דֵרָאוֹן לְכָל־בָּשָׂר: 23 וְהָיָה מִדֵּי־חֹדֶשׁ בְּחָדְשׁוֹ וּמִדֵּי שַׁבָּת בְּשַׁבַּתּוֹ יָבוֹא כָל־בָּשָׂר לְהִשְׁתַּחֲוֺת לְפָנַי אָמַר יְהֹוָה:

haftarat devarim

הפטרת דברים

ALL COMMUNITIES—ISAIAH 1:1–27

> **SYNOPSIS:** This is the third of three "*Haftarot* of punishment" which are read between 17 *Tammuz* and 9 *Av*, when we mourn the destruction of the Holy Temple. The *Haftarah* is taken from the opening of the Book of Isaiah, though it is unclear whether this was in fact his first prophecy.
>
> After the *Haftarah's* opening words which introduce Isaiah as a prophet (1:1), he laments the sinfulness and rebelliousness of the Jewish people and their consequent punishments (2–9). He rebukes them for insincere confession when bringing sacrifices (10–15), because God desires ethical behavior and repentance (16–20). In his final lament, the prophet grieves over the corrupt state of Jerusalem (21–25), and envisions a future time of restoration (26–27).

1 ¹ This is the prophetic vision of Isaiah son of Amoz.

The following was prophesied about Judah and Jerusalem in the days of Uzziah, Jotham, Ahaz, and Hezekiah, kings of Judah.

² Hear, O heavens, and listen, O earth, for it is God and not I who has spoken these words:

"I have reared and raised My children above all the nations, and they have rebelled against Me! ³ Even an ox recognizes its owner and a donkey its master's trough, but Israel does not want to know Me! My people whom I have helped do not try to understand what is good for them!"

⁴ Oh you sinful nation! A people who were once holy and are now heavy with sin! Holy offspring who became wicked! Corrupt children! They have abandoned God, disgraced the Holy One of Israel, and separated themselves from Him! ⁵ Why do you allow yourselves to commit the same sins repeatedly, continuing to turn astray and be stricken again and again? From being stricken so many times every head is heavy and every heart is pained. ⁶ From the sole of the foot to the head nothing is sound—only wounds, bruises, and open sores, untreated, unbandaged, not softened with oil, yet you continue to sin, and incur yet more lashes.

⁷ Therefore your land is waste, your cities burned down. Strangers eat your farmland before your eyes. It is desolate, as if destroyed by foreign enemies, from afar. ⁸ The city of Zion is left uninhabited like an obsolete hut in a vineyard, like an abandoned night-hut in a cucumber field, like a besieged city. ⁹ If the God of Hosts had not left us a small remnant in His kindness, we would be destroyed like Sodom and like Gomorrah!

א 1 חֲזוֹן֙ יְשַֽׁעְיָ֣הוּ בֶן־אָמ֔וֹץ אֲשֶׁ֣ר חָזָ֔ה עַל־יְהוּדָ֖ה וִירוּשָׁלִָ֑ם בִּימֵ֨י עֻזִּיָּ֧הוּ יוֹתָ֛ם אָחָ֥ז יְחִזְקִיָּ֖הוּ מַלְכֵ֥י יְהוּדָֽה: 2 שִׁמְע֤וּ שָׁמַ֨יִם֙ וְהַאֲזִ֣ינִי אֶ֔רֶץ כִּ֥י יְהֹוָ֖ה דִּבֵּ֑ר בָּנִים֙ גִּדַּ֣לְתִּי וְרוֹמַ֔מְתִּי וְהֵ֖ם פָּ֥שְׁעוּ בִֽי: 3 יָדַ֥ע שׁוֹר֙ קֹנֵ֔הוּ וַחֲמ֖וֹר אֵב֣וּס בְּעָלָ֑יו יִשְׂרָאֵל֙ לֹ֣א יָדַ֔ע עַמִּ֖י לֹ֥א הִתְבּוֹנָֽן: 4 ה֣וֹי ׀ גּ֣וֹי חֹטֵ֗א עַ֚ם כֶּ֣בֶד עָוֹ֔ן זֶ֣רַע מְרֵעִ֔ים בָּנִ֖ים מַשְׁחִיתִ֑ים עָזְב֣וּ אֶת־יְהֹוָ֗ה נִֽאֲצ֛וּ אֶת־קְד֥וֹשׁ יִשְׂרָאֵ֖ל נָזֹ֥רוּ אָחֽוֹר: 5 עַ֣ל מֶ֥ה תֻכּ֛וּ ע֖וֹד תּוֹסִ֣יפוּ סָרָ֑ה כָּל־רֹ֣אשׁ לָֽחֳלִ֔י וְכָל־לֵבָ֖ב דַּוָּֽי: 6 מִכַּף־רֶ֤גֶל וְעַד־רֹאשׁ֙ אֵֽין־בּ֣וֹ מְתֹ֔ם פֶּ֥צַע וְחַבּוּרָ֖ה וּמַכָּ֣ה טְרִיָּ֑ה לֹא־זֹ֨רוּ֙ וְלֹ֣א חֻבָּ֔שׁוּ וְלֹ֥א רֻכְּכָ֖ה בַּשָּֽׁמֶן: 7 אַרְצְכֶ֣ם שְׁמָמָ֔ה עָרֵיכֶ֖ם שְׂרֻפ֣וֹת אֵ֑שׁ אַדְמַתְכֶ֗ם לְנֶגְדְּכֶם֙ זָרִים֙ אֹכְלִ֣ים אֹתָ֔הּ וּשְׁמָמָ֖ה כְּמַהְפֵּכַ֥ת זָרִֽים: 8 וְנֽוֹתְרָ֥ה בַת־צִיּ֖וֹן כְּסֻכָּ֣ה בְכָ֑רֶם כִּמְלוּנָ֥ה בְמִקְשָׁ֖ה כְּעִ֥יר נְצוּרָֽה: 9 לוּלֵי֙ יְהֹוָ֣ה צְבָא֔וֹת הוֹתִ֥יר לָ֛נוּ שָׂרִ֖יד כִּמְעָ֑ט כִּסְדֹ֣ם הָיִ֔ינוּ לַֽעֲמֹרָ֖ה דָּמִֽינוּ:

haftarat devarim

[10] Hear God's word, you who resemble the nobles of Sodom! Listen to the teachings of our God, you who resemble the people of Gomorrah!

[11] "Why do I need all your numerous sacrifices when your accompanying confessions are insincere?" says God. "I had enough of your burnt-offering of \rams and fattened cattle, and I do not desire the blood of cattle, sheep, and goats, since they do not bring you to repent. [12] When you appear before Me at a festival, I will say, 'Who asked you to do this, trampling My Temple courtyards?' [13] Do not bring any more meal-offerings, for they will be in vain, for the three-finger fistful that is burned on the altar is offensive to Me! When groups of you bring the sacrifices of the New Moon, the Sabbath, and the festivals, I cannot bear the falsehood in your hearts! [14] I hate your New Moon and festival offerings. They are like a burden to Me, and I cannot bear them! [15] When you spread your hands in prayer, I will turn My eyes away from you. As much as you pray, I will not listen, because your hands are full of blood!

[16] "Cleanse and purify yourselves by repenting. Remove your evil deeds from My sight, and refrain from doing evil. [17] Learn to do good, seek justice, and support the oppressed. Demand justice for the orphan and plead the cause of the widow!

[18] "Come, now, and let us clarify who has offended whom," says God. "If your sins are like scarlet thread and you return to Me, they will become white like snow. If they are as red as crimson, they will become like wool.

[19] "If you desire to listen, you will eat the best of the land. [20] But if you refuse and rebel, you will be eaten by the sword," for God has spoken.

[21] How the faithful city of Jerusalem has become unfaithful like a harlot! Once it was full of justice, and righteousness was always there, but now it has become a city of murderers! [22] In your business dealings your silver has become dross and your strong drinks diluted with water. [23] Your rulers are corrupt and are friendly with thieves. They all love bribes and run after favors. They do not judge the orphan, and the widow's case does not reach them.

[24] Therefore, the Master of Israel, the God of Hosts, says: "Oh! I will appease Myself of anger against My rivals and take revenge on My enemies! [25] I will pass My hand over you to strike you with one blow after another. I will smelt your impurities as if cleansing them with soap, and I will remove all your impurities of tin.

10 שִׁמְעוּ דְבַר־יְהֹוָה קְצִינֵי סְדֹם הַאֲזִינוּ תּוֹרַת אֱלֹהֵינוּ עַם עֲמֹרָה: 11 לָמָּה־לִּי רֹב־זִבְחֵיכֶם יֹאמַר יְהֹוָה שָׂבַעְתִּי עֹלוֹת אֵילִים וְחֵלֶב מְרִיאִים וְדַם פָּרִים וּכְבָשִׂים וְעַתּוּדִים לֹא חָפָצְתִּי: 12 כִּי תָבֹאוּ לֵרָאוֹת פָּנָי מִי־בִקֵּשׁ זֹאת מִיֶּדְכֶם רְמֹס חֲצֵרָי: 13 לֹא תוֹסִיפוּ הָבִיא מִנְחַת־שָׁוְא קְטֹרֶת תּוֹעֵבָה הִיא לִי חֹדֶשׁ וְשַׁבָּת קְרֹא מִקְרָא לֹא־אוּכַל אָוֶן וַעֲצָרָה: 14 חָדְשֵׁיכֶם וּמוֹעֲדֵיכֶם שָׂנְאָה נַפְשִׁי הָיוּ עָלַי לָטֹרַח נִלְאֵיתִי נְשֹׂא: 15 וּבְפָרִשְׂכֶם כַּפֵּיכֶם אַעְלִים עֵינַי מִכֶּם גַּם כִּי־תַרְבּוּ תְפִלָּה אֵינֶנִּי שֹׁמֵעַ יְדֵיכֶם דָּמִים מָלֵאוּ: 16 רַחֲצוּ הִזַּכּוּ הָסִירוּ רֹעַ מַעַלְלֵיכֶם מִנֶּגֶד עֵינָי חִדְלוּ הָרֵעַ: 17 לִמְדוּ הֵיטֵב דִּרְשׁוּ מִשְׁפָּט אַשְּׁרוּ חָמוֹץ שִׁפְטוּ יָתוֹם רִיבוּ אַלְמָנָה: 18 לְכוּ־נָא וְנִוָּכְחָה יֹאמַר יְהֹוָה אִם־יִהְיוּ חֲטָאֵיכֶם כַּשָּׁנִים כַּשֶּׁלֶג יַלְבִּינוּ אִם־יַאְדִּימוּ כַתּוֹלָע כַּצֶּמֶר יִהְיוּ: 19 אִם־תֹּאבוּ וּשְׁמַעְתֶּם טוּב הָאָרֶץ תֹּאכֵלוּ: 20 וְאִם־תְּמָאֲנוּ וּמְרִיתֶם חֶרֶב תְּאֻכְּלוּ כִּי פִּי יְהֹוָה דִּבֵּר: 21 אֵיכָה הָיְתָה לְזוֹנָה קִרְיָה נֶאֱמָנָה מְלֵאֲתִי מִשְׁפָּט צֶדֶק יָלִין בָּהּ וְעַתָּה מְרַצְּחִים: 22 כַּסְפֵּךְ הָיָה לְסִיגִים סָבְאֵךְ מָהוּל בַּמָּיִם: 23 שָׂרַיִךְ סוֹרְרִים וְחַבְרֵי גַּנָּבִים כֻּלּוֹ אֹהֵב שֹׁחַד וְרֹדֵף שַׁלְמֹנִים יָתוֹם לֹא יִשְׁפֹּטוּ וְרִיב אַלְמָנָה לֹא־יָבוֹא אֲלֵיהֶם: 24 לָכֵן נְאֻם הָאָדוֹן יְהֹוָה צְבָאוֹת אֲבִיר יִשְׂרָאֵל הוֹי אֶנָּחֵם מִצָּרַי וְאִנָּקְמָה מֵאוֹיְבָי: 25 וְאָשִׁיבָה יָדִי עָלַיִךְ וְאֶצְרֹף כַּבֹּר סִיגָיִךְ

הפטרת ואתחנן

²⁶ "I will restore your judges to be righteous as they were at first, and your advisers as they were in the beginning. Afterwards you will be called 'city of righteousness—faithful city.'"

²⁷ The city of Zion will be redeemed through the observance of law, and those who return there will come due to their acts of righteousness.

26 וְאָשִׁיבָה שֹׁפְטַיִךְ כְּבָרִאשֹׁנָה וְיֹעֲצַיִךְ כְּבַתְּחִלָּה אַחֲרֵי־כֵן יִקָּרֵא לָךְ עִיר הַצֶּדֶק קִרְיָה נֶאֱמָנָה: 27 צִיּוֹן בְּמִשְׁפָּט תִּפָּדֶה וְשָׁבֶיהָ בִּצְדָקָה:

haftarat va-'ethannan

ALL COMMUNITIES—ISAIAH 40:1–26

> **SYNOPSIS:** This is the first of a series of "Seven *Haftarot* of Comfort" which are read between the Ninth of *Av* and the Jewish New Year (*Rosh Ha-Shanah*). The Sabbath when this *Haftarah* is read is commonly known as *Shabbat Nahamu* ("The Sabbath of Comfort"). The *Haftarah* was addressed by the prophet Isaiah to the Jewish people in Babylon after the exile at the end of the 6th century B.C.E., and to the ruins of Jerusalem.
>
> The *Haftarah* opens with a message of comfort and images of redemption (40:1-5). We read how the enemies of Jerusalem will ultimately wither like grass (6-8), and how the prophets will herald redemption from the mountaintops (9–11). The latter section of the *Haftarah* praises the greatness of God, His omnipotence, and the fallacy of idol-worship (12–26).

40 ¹ God will say to the prophets, "Comfort, oh comfort, My people! ² Speak in a way that will enter the heart of Jerusalem and announce to her that her period of exile has been fulfilled and that her sins have been forgiven, for she has already been punished for all her sins twice by God with two exiles."

³ It is as if a voice is calling out: "Clear a path in the desert for God to return the exiles! Make a straight road in the wilderness for our God to go ahead of them! ⁴ Every valley will be raised. Every mountain and hill will be lowered. The crooked paths will be made straight, and the high places will become a plain."

⁵ Then God's glory will be revealed and together all flesh will see that God has spoken words of comfort.

⁶ *A voice says to the prophet:* "Announce in public!"

"What shall I announce?" asks the prophet.

"Announce the following," says the voice, "All the people who will come with Gog to Jerusalem to war will wither like grass. Even their good people will wither like the flowers of the field, ⁷ for grass withers and flowers fade when God's breath blows over it. Indeed, the people of Gog will

1 נַחֲמוּ נַחֲמוּ עַמִּי יֹאמַר אֱלֹהֵיכֶם: 2 דַּבְּרוּ עַל־לֵב יְרוּשָׁלַ͏ִם וְקִרְאוּ אֵלֶיהָ כִּי מָלְאָה צְבָאָהּ כִּי נִרְצָה עֲוֺנָהּ כִּי לָקְחָה מִיַּד יְהֹוָה כִּפְלַיִם בְּכָל־חַטֹּאתֶיהָ: 3 קוֹל קוֹרֵא בַּמִּדְבָּר פַּנּוּ דֶּרֶךְ יְהֹוָה יַשְּׁרוּ בָּעֲרָבָה מְסִלָּה לֵאלֹהֵינוּ: 4 כָּל־גֶּיא יִנָּשֵׂא וְכָל־הַר וְגִבְעָה יִשְׁפָּלוּ וְהָיָה הֶעָקֹב לְמִישׁוֹר וְהָרְכָסִים לְבִקְעָה: 5 וְנִגְלָה כְּבוֹד יְהֹוָה וְרָאוּ כָל־בָּשָׂר יַחְדָּו כִּי פִּי יְהֹוָה דִּבֵּר: 6 קוֹל אֹמֵר קְרָא וְאָמַר מָה אֶקְרָא כָּל־הַבָּשָׂר חָצִיר וְכָל־חַסְדּוֹ כְּצִיץ הַשָּׂדֶה: 7 יָבֵשׁ חָצִיר נָבֵל צִיץ כִּי רוּחַ יְהֹוָה נָשְׁבָה

haftarat va-ʾethannan

be like grass!⁸ They are like grass that withers and flowers that fade, but the word of our God will endure forever!"

⁹ You prophets who bring news of redemption to Zion, go up on a high mountain so your voices can be heard from afar! You prophets who bring news of redemption to Jerusalem, raise your voice powerfully! Raise it, do not be afraid that somebody will deny it! Declare to the cities of Judah, "God is coming to redeem you!" ¹⁰ Look! God Almighty is coming with power, and His arm will rule for Him without any help. His reward for every person is ready with Him! His payment for good deeds is ready before Him! ¹¹ God will lead you out of exile like a shepherd pasturing his flock, who gathers the lambs with his arm and not his stick and carries them in his bosom, leading the nurslings carefully.

¹² Who is like God, who knows the depth of the waters as if He measured them with His fist, and He knows the length of the skies as if He measured them with a ruler? He knows the amount of earth on the ground as if He measured it. He knows the weight of the mountains and the hills as if He had used a scale and a balance. ¹³ Who could influence God's will to accord with his own will? What man is His advisor that informs Him? ¹⁴ Whom did He consult and who taught Him? Who instructed Him in the way of justice, taught Him knowledge, or guided Him in the path of wisdom?

¹⁵ The strength of the nations is like a drop which runs down the back of a bucket and becomes bitter from the mold on the bucket. They are like moldy dust on a copper balance which can easily be blown away. He casts away the islands as if they were dust, so surely He can save the Jewish people from the nations? ¹⁶ All the wood of Lebanon is not enough to burn on His altar, and its animals do not provide sufficient burnt-offerings before Him. ¹⁷ All the nations are like nothing to Him. He considers them void and empty.

¹⁸ To whom can you compare God? What image is of any value compared to Him? ¹⁹ Could you possibly compare Him to idols cast by a smith and plated with gold by a goldsmith, with cast silver chains to pull it along, because it cannot move on its own? ²⁰ A poor person sets aside large amounts of money for his idol, as if he were rich. He pays a professional to choose a wood which will not rot, and he seeks an expert to prepare an idol which will not fall apart and shame him for worshiping it.

²¹ Don't you know who the Master of the world is by working it out by yourself? Haven't you heard from somebody else that worked it out? Haven't you been told about God from ancient tradition? Haven't you understood that the earth is not resting on any foundations, for it is a globe surrounded by sky, so God must be decreeing it to stand?

בּוֹ אָכֵן חָצִיר הָעָם: 8 יָבֵשׁ חָצִיר נָבֵל צִיץ וּדְבַר־אֱלֹהֵינוּ יָקוּם לְעוֹלָם: 9 עַל הַר־גָּבֹהַּ עֲלִי־לָךְ מְבַשֶּׂרֶת צִיּוֹן הָרִימִי בַכֹּחַ קוֹלֵךְ מְבַשֶּׂרֶת יְרוּשָׁלָ͏ִם הָרִימִי אַל־תִּירָאִי אִמְרִי לְעָרֵי יְהוּדָה הִנֵּה אֱלֹהֵיכֶם: 10 הִנֵּה אֲדֹנָי יֱהֹוִה בְּחָזָק יָבוֹא וּזְרֹעוֹ מֹשְׁלָה לוֹ הִנֵּה שְׂכָרוֹ אִתּוֹ וּפְעֻלָּתוֹ לְפָנָיו: 11 כְּרֹעֶה עֶדְרוֹ יִרְעֶה בִּזְרֹעוֹ יְקַבֵּץ טְלָאִים וּבְחֵיקוֹ יִשָּׂא עָלוֹת יְנַהֵל: 12 מִי־מָדַד בְּשָׁעֳלוֹ מַיִם וְשָׁמַיִם בַּזֶּרֶת תִּכֵּן וְכָל בַּשָּׁלִשׁ עֲפַר הָאָרֶץ וְשָׁקַל בַּפֶּלֶס הָרִים וּגְבָעוֹת בְּמֹאזְנָיִם: 13 מִי־תִכֵּן אֶת־רוּחַ יְהֹוָה וְאִישׁ עֲצָתוֹ יוֹדִיעֶנּוּ: 14 אֶת־מִי נוֹעָץ וַיְבִינֵהוּ וַיְלַמְּדֵהוּ בְּאֹרַח מִשְׁפָּט וַיְלַמְּדֵהוּ דַעַת וְדֶרֶךְ תְּבוּנוֹת יוֹדִיעֶנּוּ: 15 הֵן גּוֹיִם כְּמַר מִדְּלִי וּכְשַׁחַק מֹאזְנַיִם נֶחְשָׁבוּ הֵן אִיִּים כַּדַּק יִטּוֹל: 16 וּלְבָנוֹן אֵין דֵּי בָּעֵר וְחַיָּתוֹ אֵין דֵּי עוֹלָה: 17 כָּל־הַגּוֹיִם כְּאַיִן נֶגְדּוֹ מֵאֶפֶס וָתֹהוּ נֶחְשְׁבוּ־לוֹ: 18 וְאֶל־מִי תְּדַמְּיוּן אֵל וּמַה־דְּמוּת תַּעַרְכוּ־לוֹ: 19 הַפֶּסֶל נָסַךְ חָרָשׁ וְצֹרֵף בַּזָּהָב יְרַקְּעֶנּוּ וּרְתֻקוֹת כֶּסֶף צוֹרֵף: 20 הַמְסֻכָּן תְּרוּמָה עֵץ לֹא־יִרְקַב יִבְחָר חָרָשׁ חָכָם יְבַקֶּשׁ־לוֹ לְהָכִין פֶּסֶל לֹא יִמּוֹט: 21 הֲלוֹא תֵדְעוּ הֲלוֹא תִשְׁמָעוּ הֲלוֹא הֻגַּד מֵרֹאשׁ לָכֶם הֲלוֹא הֲבִינוֹתֶם

²² God sits above the skies that encompass the earth, and those who live on it seem like grasshoppers. He stretches out the skies like a sheet and spreads them like a tent for dwelling. ²³ He makes princes into nothing and turns rulers of the land to worthlessness. ²⁴ They are as if they were never planted or never sown, as if they never even took root in the earth. Even by blowing at them with an ordinary breath they dry up, and the storm carries them away like straw blowing in the wind.

²⁵ "So to whom can you liken Me? To whom can you compare Me?" asks the Holy One. ²⁶ Lift up your eyes to the heavens and see who created these stars! He brings out their hosts by number, calling each star by name. Because of His great might and tremendous strength, not one star is lost because He made them exist permanently.

מוֹסְדוֹת הָאָֽרֶץ: 22 הַיֹּשֵׁב עַל־חוּג הָאָרֶץ וְיֹשְׁבֶיהָ כַּחֲגָבִים הַנּוֹטֶה כַדֹּק שָׁמַיִם וַיִּמְתָּחֵם כָּאֹהֶל לָשָֽׁבֶת: 23 הַנּוֹתֵן רוֹזְנִים לְאָיִן שֹֽׁפְטֵי אֶרֶץ כַּתֹּהוּ עָשָׂה: 24 אַף בַּל־נִטָּעוּ אַף בַּל־זֹרָעוּ אַף בַּל־שֹׁרֵשׁ בָּאָרֶץ גִּזְעָם וְגַם־נָשַׁף בָּהֶם וַיִּבָשׁוּ וּסְעָרָה כַּקַּשׁ תִּשָּׂאֵם: 25 וְאֶל־מִי תְדַמְּיוּנִי וְאֶשְׁוֶה יֹאמַר קָדוֹשׁ: 26 שְׂאוּ־מָרוֹם עֵינֵיכֶם וּרְאוּ מִי־בָרָא אֵלֶּה הַמּוֹצִיא בְמִסְפָּר צְבָאָם לְכֻלָּם בְּשֵׁם יִקְרָא מֵרֹב אוֹנִים וְאַמִּיץ כֹּחַ אִישׁ לֹא נֶעְדָּֽר:

haftarat ʿekev

ALL COMMUNITIES—Isaiah 49:14 – 51:3

> **SYNOPSIS:** This is the second of a series of "Seven *Haftarot* of Comfort" which are read between the Ninth of *Av* and the Jewish New Year (*Rosh Ha-Shanah*). The *Haftarah* was addressed by the prophet Isaiah to the Jewish people in Babylon after the exile at the end of the 6th century B.C.E.
>
> The *Haftarah* opens with God's consolation to Zion that she will not be abandoned, and promises of restoration (49:14–21). In a second declaration, God reaffirms the ingathering of the exiles and punishment of the nations with more vivid imagery (22–26). In the following chapter, the mood shifts from consolation to criticism. Exile ("divorce") has come, not due to a weakness on God's part, but because of Israel's sins (50:1–3). On a personal note, the prophet declares his own loyalty to God, and his determination to deliver God's word regardless of any opposition (4–9). The only solution, therefore, is to listen to the prophet and trust in God (10–11). The conclusion of the *Haftarah*, from yet another chapter, sees the tone return to conciliation. The Jewish people are advised to find hope in the story of Abraham and Sarah, that God will soon comfort all the ruins of Zion (51:1–3).

49 ¹⁴ Zion will want to say, "God has abandoned me! My God has forgotten me." ¹⁵ But this cannot be the case, for could a woman forget her baby, or not have compassion on the child of her womb? Even if it is conceivable that she would forget her children, nevertheless, I will not forget you! ¹⁶ Indeed, My memory of you is so vivid, it is as if I have engraved you on

מט 14 וַתֹּאמֶר צִיּוֹן עֲזָבַנִי יְהֹוָה וַאדֹנָי שְׁכֵחָֽנִי: 15 הֲתִשְׁכַּח אִשָּׁה עוּלָהּ מֵרַחֵם בֶּן־בִּטְנָהּ גַּם־אֵלֶּה תִשְׁכַּחְנָה וְאָנֹכִי לֹא אֶשְׁכָּחֵֽךְ: 16 הֵן עַל־כַּפַּיִם חַקֹּתִיךְ חֽוֹמֹתַיִךְ נֶגְדִּי תָּמִיד:

haftarat 'ekev

My palms, and your ruined walls are always a reminder before Me that I must rebuild them. [17] In fact it is your children, and not I, who quickly forgot about their land! It was the wicked ones that came from you, and not I, who destroyed you and laid waste to you, O Zion. [18] Lift up your eyes and see how your children have all gathered and come to you. "As I live," says God, "you will be proud of them all like one who wears jewels, and you will tie them to yourself like silk adornments of a bride."

[19] For your worries about your ruins, desolate places, and destroyed land will end, as your land will now be swarming with inhabitants, and your destroyers will be distant from you. [20] Your ears will hear that your children from whom you thought you were bereaved are saying to each other: "This place is too crowded for me. Make room for me to settle too!"

[21] Then you will say in your heart, "Who gave birth to all these people for me? I was bereft and alone for so long, with my children exiled and wandering from me. Who raised them? For I was by myself—where have these people come from?"

[22] This is what God Almighty says: "Look! I will lift up My hand to the nations and hoist My banner to the peoples to arouse their hearts. They will bring your sons in their corners of their garments and carry your daughters on their shoulders.

[23] "Kings will be your child-minders and their princesses your wetnurses. They will bow down to you and lick the dust of your feet, and you will know that I am God who is all-powerful, so that those who trust in Me will not be ashamed."

[24] Can spoil be taken away from the mighty Esau? Or the captive of Jacob the righteous be saved? [25] But God says: "Captives can be freed from the mighty and spoil taken back from tyrants, for I will fight your enemies and save your children. [26] I will feed the flesh of those who verbally abused you to wild animals, and birds will become drunk on their blood as if it were wine. Then all flesh will know that I am God, your Savior and your Redeemer, the Mighty One of Jacob!"

50

[1] God says, "What is the reason for the bill of divorce with which I sent away your mother, the congregation of Israel? To which of My creditors did I sell you to pay back My loan? You were sold because of your sins, and your mother was sent away because of your transgressions, so all this will end when you repent.

[2] "Why was no one there when I came to you, no

17 מִהֲר֖וּ בָּנָ֑יִךְ מְהָֽרְסַ֥יִךְ וּמַחֲרִבַ֖יִךְ מִמֵּ֥ךְ יֵצֵֽאוּ׃ 18 שְׂאִֽי־סָבִ֤יב עֵינַ֙יִךְ֙ וּרְאִ֔י כֻּלָּ֖ם נִקְבְּצ֣וּ בָֽאוּ־לָ֑ךְ חַי־אָ֣נִי נְאֻם־יְהֹוָ֗ה כִּ֤י כֻלָּם֙ כָּעֲדִ֣י תִלְבָּ֔שִׁי וּֽתְקַשְּׁרִ֖ים כַּכַּלָּֽה׃ 19 כִּ֤י חׇרְבֹתַ֙יִךְ֙ וְשֹׁ֣מְמֹתַ֔יִךְ וְאֶ֖רֶץ הֲרִֽסֻתֵ֑ךְ כִּ֤י עַתָּה֙ תֵּצְרִ֣י מִיּוֹשֵׁ֔ב וְרָחֲק֖וּ מְבַלְּעָֽיִךְ׃ 20 ע֚וֹד יֹאמְר֣וּ בְאׇזְנַ֔יִךְ בְּנֵ֖י שִׁכֻּלָ֑יִךְ צַר־לִ֥י הַמָּק֖וֹם גְּשָׁה־לִּ֥י וְאֵשֵֽׁבָה׃ 21 וְאָמַ֣רְתְּ בִּלְבָבֵ֗ךְ מִ֤י יָֽלַד־לִי֙ אֶת־אֵ֔לֶּה וַאֲנִ֥י שְׁכוּלָ֖ה וְגַלְמוּדָ֑ה גֹּלָ֣ה ׀ וְסוּרָ֗ה וְאֵ֙לֶּה֙ מִ֣י גִדֵּ֔ל הֵ֤ן אֲנִי֙ נִשְׁאַ֣רְתִּי לְבַדִּ֔י אֵ֖לֶּה אֵיפֹ֥ה הֵֽם׃ 22 כֹּֽה־אָמַ֞ר אֲדֹנָ֣י יֱהֹוִ֗ה הִנֵּ֨ה אֶשָּׂ֤א אֶל־גּוֹיִם֙ יָדִ֔י וְאֶל־עַמִּ֖ים אָרִ֣ים נִסִּ֑י וְהֵבִ֤יאוּ בָנַ֙יִךְ֙ בְּחֹ֔צֶן וּבְנֹתַ֖יִךְ עַל־כָּתֵ֥ף תִּנָּשֶֽׂאנָה׃ 23 וְהָי֨וּ מְלָכִ֜ים אֹֽמְנַ֗יִךְ וְשָׂרֽוֹתֵיהֶם֙ מֵינִ֣יקֹתַ֔יִךְ אַפַּ֗יִם אֶ֚רֶץ יִשְׁתַּ֣חֲווּ לָ֔ךְ וַעֲפַ֥ר רַגְלַ֖יִךְ יְלַחֵ֑כוּ וְיָדַ֙עַתְּ֙ כִּי־אֲנִ֣י יְהֹוָ֔ה אֲשֶׁ֥ר לֹֽא־יֵבֹ֖שׁוּ קוָֹֽי׃ 24 הֲיֻקַּ֥ח מִגִּבּ֖וֹר מַלְק֑וֹחַ וְאִם־שְׁבִ֥י צַדִּ֖יק יִמָּלֵֽט׃ 25 כִּי־כֹ֣ה ׀ אָמַ֣ר יְהֹוָ֗ה גַּם־שְׁבִ֤י גִבּוֹר֙ יֻקָּ֔ח וּמַלְק֥וֹחַ עָרִ֖יץ יִמָּלֵ֑ט וְאֶת־יְרִיבֵךְ֙ אָנֹכִ֣י אָרִ֔יב וְאֶת־בָּנַ֖יִךְ אָנֹכִ֥י אוֹשִֽׁיעַ׃ 26 וְהַאֲכַלְתִּ֤י אֶת־מוֹנַ֙יִךְ֙ אֶת־בְּשָׂרָ֔ם וְכֶעָסִ֖יס דָּמָ֣ם יִשְׁכָּר֑וּן וְיָדְע֣וּ כׇל־בָּשָׂ֗ר כִּ֣י אֲנִ֤י יְהֹוָה֙ מֽוֹשִׁיעֵ֔ךְ וְגֹאֲלֵ֖ךְ אֲבִ֥יר יַעֲקֹֽב׃

נ 1 כֹּ֣ה ׀ אָמַ֣ר יְהֹוָ֗ה אֵ֣י זֶ֠ה סֵ֣פֶר כְּרִית֤וּת אִמְּכֶם֙ אֲשֶׁ֣ר שִׁלַּחְתִּ֔יהָ א֚וֹ מִ֣י מִנּוֹשַׁ֔י אֲשֶׁר־מָכַ֥רְתִּי אֶתְכֶ֖ם ל֑וֹ הֵ֤ן בַּעֲוֺנֹֽתֵיכֶם֙ נִמְכַּרְתֶּ֔ם וּבְפִשְׁעֵיכֶ֖ם שֻׁלְּחָ֥ה אִמְּכֶֽם׃ 2 מַדּ֨וּעַ בָּ֜אתִי וְאֵ֣ין אִ֗ישׁ קָרָ֙אתִי֙ וְאֵ֣ין עוֹנֶ֔ה הֲקָצ֨וֹר קָצְרָ֤ה יָדִי֙ מִפְּד֔וּת וְאִם־

הפטרת עקב

one to answer when I called? Is My hand too short to redeem? Do I lack strength to save? Indeed, I can dry up a sea of idol-worshipers with My roar and make the rivers of them into a desert, so their fish stink from lack of water and die of thirst. ³ I can clothe the heavens in darkness and cover them with sackcloth."

⁴ The prophet says: God Almighty has given me a tongue for teaching, so I should know how to teach those who thirst for God's word, the right thing at the right time. He wakes me every morning and rouses my ears to hear prophecy, so I will be able to listen like a disciple.

⁵ God Almighty opened my ears, and I did not hold myself back or retreat. ⁶ Even if there was a fear that I would be hurt, I went nonetheless and I gave over my body to floggers and my cheeks to those who tore out my hair. I did not hide my face from the fear of insult and spitting. ⁷ Despite all odds, God Almighty helped me and so I was not ashamed. I saw God was helping me, so I have made my face like hard rock that would deflect any insult, and I know that I will not be ashamed.

⁸ God, who is my defender, is near to me! So who wants to fight me? God and I will stand together! Whoever wishes to be my adversary, let him approach me! ⁹ Indeed, God Almighty will help me, so who could declare me guilty? My opponents will all be worn out like old clothing and consumed by moths.

¹⁰ Who among you fears God and listens to the voice of His servant the prophet? Even he who walked in darkness of suffering, without any light of hope for salvation, should trust in God's name that salvation will indeed come, and rely on his God. ¹¹ But in truth nearly all of you cause the fire of God's anger to blaze and fan the flames. Consequently, you will walk in the light of your fire and the flame you lit! This is no accident! It has come to you from My hand, so that when you lie down to die you will have had only sadness.

51 ¹ Listen to Me, you who pursue justice and seek God! Look to Abraham, the rock from which you were hewn, and to Sarah, the quarry from which you were dug. ² Look to your father Abraham, and to Sarah, *who gave birth to you*. For he was alone without any family when I called him, but I blessed him and caused him to multiply, and likewise, I will make the Jewish people, who are now a minority, multiply greatly.

³ For God will comfort Zion, He will comfort all her ruins. He will make her wilderness like Eden, and her desert like God's garden. Joy and gladness will be found there, thanksgiving and the sound of music.

אֵין־בִּי כֹחַ לְהַצִּיל הֵן בְּגַעֲרָתִי אַחֲרִיב יָם אָשִׂים נְהָרוֹת מִדְבָּר תִּבְאַשׁ דְּגָתָם מֵאֵין מַיִם וְתָמֹת בַּצָּמָא: ³ אַלְבִּישׁ שָׁמַיִם קַדְרוּת וְשַׂק אָשִׂים כְּסוּתָם: ⁴ אֲדֹנָי יֱהֹוִה נָתַן לִי לְשׁוֹן לִמּוּדִים לָדַעַת לָעוּת אֶת־יָעֵף דָּבָר יָעִיר | בַּבֹּקֶר בַּבֹּקֶר יָעִיר לִי אֹזֶן לִשְׁמֹעַ כַּלִּמּוּדִים: ⁵ אֲדֹנָי יֱהֹוִה פָּתַח־לִי אֹזֶן וְאָנֹכִי לֹא מָרִיתִי אָחוֹר לֹא נְסוּגֹתִי: ⁶ גֵּוִי נָתַתִּי לְמַכִּים וּלְחָיַי לְמֹרְטִים פָּנַי לֹא הִסְתַּרְתִּי מִכְּלִמּוֹת וָרֹק: ⁷ וַאדֹנָי יֱהֹוִה יַעֲזָר־לִי עַל־כֵּן לֹא נִכְלָמְתִּי עַל־כֵּן שַׂמְתִּי פָנַי כַּחַלָּמִישׁ וָאֵדַע כִּי־לֹא אֵבוֹשׁ: ⁸ קָרוֹב מַצְדִּיקִי מִי־יָרִיב אִתִּי נַעַמְדָה יָּחַד מִי־בַעַל מִשְׁפָּטִי יִגַּשׁ אֵלָי: ⁹ הֵן אֲדֹנָי יֱהֹוִה יַעֲזָר־לִי מִי־הוּא יַרְשִׁיעֵנִי הֵן כֻּלָּם כַּבֶּגֶד יִבְלוּ עָשׁ יֹאכְלֵם: ¹⁰ מִי בָכֶם יְרֵא יְהֹוָה שֹׁמֵעַ בְּקוֹל עַבְדּוֹ אֲשֶׁר | הָלַךְ חֲשֵׁכִים וְאֵין נֹגַהּ לוֹ יִבְטַח בְּשֵׁם יְהֹוָה וְיִשָּׁעֵן בֵּאלֹהָיו: ¹¹ הֵן כֻּלְּכֶם קֹדְחֵי אֵשׁ מְאַזְּרֵי זִיקוֹת לְכוּ | בְּאוּר אֶשְׁכֶם וּבְזִיקוֹת בִּעַרְתֶּם מִיָּדִי הָיְתָה־זֹּאת לָכֶם לְמַעֲצֵבָה תִּשְׁכָּבוּן:

נא ¹ שִׁמְעוּ אֵלַי רֹדְפֵי צֶדֶק מְבַקְשֵׁי יְהֹוָה הַבִּיטוּ אֶל־צוּר חֻצַּבְתֶּם וְאֶל־מַקֶּבֶת בּוֹר נֻקַּרְתֶּם: ² הַבִּיטוּ אֶל־אַבְרָהָם אֲבִיכֶם וְאֶל־שָׂרָה תְּחוֹלֶלְכֶם כִּי־אֶחָד קְרָאתִיו וַאֲבָרְכֵהוּ וְאַרְבֵּהוּ: ³ כִּי־נִחַם יְהֹוָה צִיּוֹן נִחַם כָּל־חָרְבֹתֶיהָ וַיָּשֶׂם מִדְבָּרָהּ כְּעֵדֶן וְעַרְבָתָהּ כְּגַן־יְהֹוָה שָׂשׂוֹן וְשִׂמְחָה יִמָּצֵא בָהּ תּוֹדָה וְקוֹל זִמְרָה:

haftarat re'eh

ALL COMMUNITIES—ISAIAH 54:11 – 55:5

> **SYNOPSIS:** This is the third of a series of "Seven *Haftarot* of Comfort" which are read between the Ninth of *Av* and the Jewish New Year (*Rosh Ha-Shanah*). The *Haftarah* was addressed by the prophet Isaiah to the Jewish people in Babylon after the exile at the end of the 6th century B.C.E.
>
> The *Haftarah* describes the magnificent rebuilding of Jerusalem (54:11-12), and the peace which will then prevail (13–17). In the following chapter, the people are urged to study Torah, and not secular wisdom (55:1-3), and are promised an everlasting covenant (3–5).

54 ¹¹ "O Jerusalem! You afflicted, storm-tossed one, who has not been comforted! I will lay your floor stones upon antimony instead of sand, and lay your foundations with sapphires. ¹² I will make your windowpanes from emeralds, your gates from carbuncle stones, and the floor-stones of all your borders will become desirable gems.

¹³ "All your children will be extremely wise, as if they were disciples of God, and your children will have much peace.

¹⁴ "Through your righteousness you will be fit for all this. You will distance yourself from crooks who have no fear of Me at all, and from terror, for it will not come near you. ¹⁵ Indeed, people will fear no one but Me. Whoever attacks you will fall into your power. ¹⁶ Behold, it was I who created the smith to fan coal fires and make the tools of his trade, and it was I who created the destroying enemy to destroy itself. ¹⁷ Every weapon engineered against you will not succeed, and every tongue raised against you in judgment you will have condemned. This is the inheritance of God's servants and their just reward from Me," says God.

55 ¹ "Come! All who are thirsty for God's word, go to the prophet and drink his 'water'! Even those who have no money, go and 'eat'! Come and take wine and milk without paying, without charge, for the prophet's wisdom is free! ² Why do you 'pay money' and invest your energies in non-Jewish wisdom without getting any real substance or 'bread'? Why do you labor in something that cannot give satisfaction? Listen to me! Learn Torah and you will 'eat' well and satisfy your souls with rich foods!

³ "Incline your ears and come to Me to hear My

נד 11 עֲנִיָּה סֹעֲרָה לֹא נֻחָמָה הִנֵּה אָנֹכִי מַרְבִּיץ בַּפּוּךְ אֲבָנַיִךְ וִיסַדְתִּיךְ בַּסַּפִּירִים: 12 וְשַׂמְתִּי כַּדְכֹד שִׁמְשֹׁתַיִךְ וּשְׁעָרַיִךְ לְאַבְנֵי אֶקְדָּח וְכָל־גְּבוּלֵךְ לְאַבְנֵי־חֵפֶץ: 13 וְכָל־בָּנַיִךְ לִמּוּדֵי יְהֹוָה וְרַב שְׁלוֹם בָּנָיִךְ: 14 בִּצְדָקָה תִּכּוֹנָנִי רַחֲקִי מֵעֹשֶׁק כִּי־לֹא תִירָאִי וּמִמְּחִתָּה כִּי לֹא־תִקְרַב אֵלָיִךְ: 15 הֵן גּוֹר יָגוּר אֶפֶס מֵאוֹתִי מִי־גָר אִתָּךְ עָלַיִךְ יִפּוֹל: 16 [הן כ׳] הִנֵּה אָנֹכִי בָּרָאתִי חָרָשׁ נֹפֵחַ בְּאֵשׁ פֶּחָם וּמוֹצִיא כְלִי לְמַעֲשֵׂהוּ וְאָנֹכִי בָּרָאתִי מַשְׁחִית לְחַבֵּל: 17 כָּל־כְּלִי יוּצַר עָלַיִךְ לֹא יִצְלָח וְכָל־לָשׁוֹן תָּקוּם־אִתָּךְ לַמִּשְׁפָּט תַּרְשִׁיעִי זֹאת נַחֲלַת עַבְדֵי יְהֹוָה וְצִדְקָתָם מֵאִתִּי נְאֻם־יְהֹוָה:

נה 1 הוֹי כָּל־צָמֵא לְכוּ לַמַּיִם וַאֲשֶׁר אֵין־לוֹ כָּסֶף לְכוּ שִׁבְרוּ וֶאֱכֹלוּ וּלְכוּ שִׁבְרוּ בְּלוֹא־כֶסֶף וּבְלוֹא מְחִיר יַיִן וְחָלָב: 2 לָמָּה תִשְׁקְלוּ־כֶסֶף בְּלוֹא־לֶחֶם וִיגִיעֲכֶם בְּלוֹא לְשָׂבְעָה שִׁמְעוּ שָׁמוֹעַ אֵלַי וְאִכְלוּ־טוֹב וְתִתְעַנַּג בַּדֶּשֶׁן נַפְשְׁכֶם: 3 הַטּוּ אָזְנְכֶם וּלְכוּ

הפטרת שופטים

words! Listen, and you will merit to live again, with the revival of the dead! I will make an eternal covenant with you, as enduring as My loyalty to David. [4] Indeed, I have made his enduring dynasty as a proof to the nations that My word always endures, and the Messiah, his descendant, will be a ruler and leader of the nations. [5] Likewise My promises to you will be fulfilled. Indeed, nations that you do not know will call upon you to serve you, and nations which never knew you will run to you to follow your orders. But they will not do this due to your own power, but for the sake of the God, your God, the Holy One of Israel, who dwells among you and who has glorified you."

אֵלַי שִׁמְעוּ וּתְחִי נַפְשְׁכֶם וְאֶכְרְתָה לָכֶם בְּרִית עוֹלָם חַסְדֵי דָוִד הַנֶּאֱמָנִים: [4] הֵן עֵד לְאוּמִּים נְתַתִּיו נָגִיד וּמְצַוֵּה לְאֻמִּים: [5] הֵן גּוֹי לֹא־תֵדַע תִּקְרָא וְגוֹי לֹא־יְדָעוּךָ אֵלֶיךָ יָרוּצוּ לְמַעַן יְהֹוָה אֱלֹהֶיךָ וְלִקְדוֹשׁ יִשְׂרָאֵל כִּי פֵאֲרָךְ:

If Sunday is *Rosh Ḥodesh*, Ḥabad communities add (*I Samuel* 20:18, 42):

20 [18] Jonathan said to him, "Tomorrow is the first of the new month. You shall be missed, because your seat will be empty."

[42] Jonathan said to David, "Go in peace, as both of us have sworn in the name of God, saying, 'God be a witness between me and you, and between my descendants and your descendants forever.'"

כ [18] וַיֹּאמֶר־לוֹ יְהוֹנָתָן מָחָר חֹדֶשׁ וְנִפְקַדְתָּ כִּי יִפָּקֵד מוֹשָׁבֶךָ: [42] וַיֹּאמֶר יְהוֹנָתָן לְדָוִד לֵךְ לְשָׁלוֹם אֲשֶׁר נִשְׁבַּעְנוּ שְׁנֵינוּ אֲנַחְנוּ בְּשֵׁם יְהֹוָה לֵאמֹר יְהֹוָה יִהְיֶה ׀ בֵּינִי וּבֵינֶךָ וּבֵין זַרְעִי וּבֵין זַרְעֲךָ עַד־עוֹלָם:

haftarat shofetim

All communities—Isaiah 51:12 – 52:12

> **SYNOPSIS:** This is the fourth of a series of "Seven *Haftarot* of Comfort" which are read between the Ninth of *Av* and the Jewish New Year (*Rosh Ha-Shanah*). The *Haftarah* was addressed by the prophet Isaiah to the Jewish people in Babylon, after the Exile, at the end of the 6th century B.C.E.
>
> As the *Haftarah* opens, God announces Himself as the comforter of the Jewish people and urges them not to fear the enemies who are just mortal men (51:12-16). God urges Jerusalem to "rise" from her pitiful state, because all the suffering has now come to an end (17-22). In a second awakening call, Jerusalem is told to prepare for imminent redemption, because God hates the Exile when His name *"is disgraced constantly, all day"* (52:1-5). The day of redemption is then depicted, with universal recognition of God amid song and rejoicing (6-10). The conclusion of the *Haftarah* backtracks to the time preceding Redemption, as the Jewish people are urged to leave the Exile without delay (11-12).

51 [12] It is I, yes I, who comforts you. Why do you, who have so many merits, fear mortal man, human beings who are put into the world like grass? [13] You have forgotten the influence of God, who

נא [12] אָנֹכִי אָנֹכִי הוּא מְנַחֶמְכֶם מִי־אַתְּ וַתִּירְאִי מֵאֱנוֹשׁ יָמוּת וּמִבֶּן־אָדָם חָצִיר יִנָּתֵן: [13] וַתִּשְׁכַּח יְהֹוָה עֹשֶׂךָ

haftarat shofetim

made you, who stretched out the heavens and laid the foundations of the earth. You are constantly afraid, all day, from the anger of the enemy that is preparing to destroy you. But where is the enemy's anger?

¹⁴ The wanderer in exile will be freed quickly. Even while in exile he did not die and he was not destroyed, and his bread did not fail.

¹⁵ For I am God, your God, who calms the sea if He wants, or makes its waves roar. His name is the God of Hosts.

¹⁶ I have put My words of Torah into your mouth, and in the Torah's merit, I sheltered you with the shadow of My hand from the enemy, planting you in your land like the stars of the skies, and establishing you to be as widespread as the earth. All the nations will say to Zion: "God is saying to you, You are My people!"

¹⁷ Wake up! Wake up! Rise, O Jerusalem, you who have been drinking until now the cup of wrath from God's hand to cleanse your sins! You drank and sucked the cup of poison to the dregs so there are no punishments left for you. ¹⁸ Of all the children to whom she gave birth, there is no one to guide her, no one to hold her hand from all the children she raised. ¹⁹ Double suffering has happened to you, but who will even nod his head to comfort you when everybody is your enemy? From the double suffering of robbery and starvation, famine and the sword, who will be able to comfort you? ²⁰ Your children have passed out from the lack of food and drink. They lie unburied at the head of every street, like a bison caught in a trap, filled with the effects of God's fury, the rebuke of your God.

²¹ Therefore, hear this, O afflicted one, who is like a drunk from suffering, and not from wine! ²² This is what your Master, your Almighty God, who fights for His people, says: "I have taken the cup of poison from your hand and the dregs from the cup of My wrath. You will never drink from it again. ²³ I will place it in the hands of your persecutors, who said to you: "Bow down, and we will walk over you, and make your body like the ground, like the street for passersby."

52 ¹ Wake up from your slumber of suffering! Wake up! Clothe yourself with your strength of old, O Zion! Put on your beautiful clothes, O Jerusalem, holy city, for the uncircumcised and unclean will no longer enter you to rule over you!
² Jerusalem, shake off the dust of mourning! Arise and sit on your throne! Release the bonds from your

נוֹטֶה שָׁמַיִם וְיֹסֵד אָרֶץ וַתְּפַחֵד תָּמִיד כָּל־הַיּוֹם מִפְּנֵי חֲמַת הַמֵּצִיק כַּאֲשֶׁר כּוֹנֵן לְהַשְׁחִית וְאַיֵּה חֲמַת הַמֵּצִיק: 14 מִהַר צֹעֶה לְהִפָּתֵחַ וְלֹא־יָמוּת לַשַּׁחַת וְלֹא יֶחְסַר לַחְמוֹ: 15 וְאָנֹכִי יְהֹוָה אֱלֹהֶיךָ רֹגַע הַיָּם וַיֶּהֱמוּ גַּלָּיו יְהֹוָה צְבָאוֹת שְׁמוֹ: 16 וָאָשִׂים דְּבָרַי בְּפִיךָ וּבְצֵל יָדִי כִּסִּיתִיךָ לִנְטֹעַ שָׁמַיִם וְלִיסֹד אָרֶץ וְלֵאמֹר לְצִיּוֹן עַמִּי־אָתָּה: 17 הִתְעוֹרְרִי הִתְעוֹרְרִי קוּמִי יְרוּשָׁלַםִ אֲשֶׁר שָׁתִית מִיַּד יְהֹוָה אֶת־כּוֹס חֲמָתוֹ אֶת־קֻבַּעַת כּוֹס הַתַּרְעֵלָה שָׁתִית מָצִית: 18 אֵין־מְנַהֵל לָהּ מִכָּל־בָּנִים יָלָדָה וְאֵין מַחֲזִיק בְּיָדָהּ מִכָּל־בָּנִים גִּדֵּלָה: 19 שְׁתַּיִם הֵנָּה קֹרְאֹתַיִךְ מִי יָנוּד לָךְ הַשֹּׁד וְהַשֶּׁבֶר וְהָרָעָב וְהַחֶרֶב מִי אֲנַחֲמֵךְ: 20 בָּנַיִךְ עֻלְּפוּ שָׁכְבוּ בְּרֹאשׁ כָּל־חוּצוֹת כְּתוֹא מִכְמָר הַמְלֵאִים חֲמַת־יְהֹוָה גַּעֲרַת אֱלֹהָיִךְ: 21 לָכֵן שִׁמְעִי־נָא זֹאת עֲנִיָּה וּשְׁכֻרַת וְלֹא מִיָּיִן: 22 כֹּה־אָמַר אֲדֹנַיִךְ יְהֹוָה וֵאלֹהַיִךְ יָרִיב עַמּוֹ הִנֵּה לָקַחְתִּי מִיָּדֵךְ אֶת־כּוֹס הַתַּרְעֵלָה אֶת־קֻבַּעַת כּוֹס חֲמָתִי לֹא־תוֹסִיפִי לִשְׁתּוֹתָהּ עוֹד: 23 וְשַׂמְתִּיהָ בְּיַד־מוֹגַיִךְ אֲשֶׁר־אָמְרוּ לְנַפְשֵׁךְ שְׁחִי וְנַעֲבֹרָה וַתָּשִׂימִי כָאָרֶץ גֵּוֵךְ וְכַחוּץ לַעֹבְרִים:

נב 1 עוּרִי עוּרִי לִבְשִׁי עֻזֵּךְ צִיּוֹן לִבְשִׁי | בִּגְדֵי תִפְאַרְתֵּךְ יְרוּשָׁלַםִ עִיר הַקֹּדֶשׁ כִּי לֹא יוֹסִיף יָבֹא־בָךְ עוֹד עָרֵל וְטָמֵא: 2 הִתְנַעֲרִי מֵעָפָר קוּמִי שְּׁבִי יְרוּשָׁלָםִ [התפתחו כ׳] הִתְפַּתְּחִי מוֹסְרֵי

neck, O daughter of Zion, captured in Babylon! ³ For this is what God says: "You were sold for nothing, so you will be redeemed without payment." ⁴ This is what God Almighty says: "My people originally went down to Egypt long ago to live there temporarily, and King Sennacherib of Assyria oppressed them for no reason. ⁵ So why should I leave my people in exile here now?" says God. "For My people were taken captive free of charge, and its oppressors are boasting of their success," says God. "My name is disgraced constantly, all day!

⁶ "Therefore, when My people are redeemed they will recognize My name. Therefore, on that day, they will know that I, who promised redemption, am here having fulfilled My word!" ⁷ How beautiful it will be when the feet of one who announces the redemption goes up upon the mountains to make his voice heard from afar, announcing peace, announcing good, and announcing salvation! He will declare to Zion: "Your God is King over the whole world!" ⁸ Your town-watchmen, who announce visitors with their voices, will raise their voices together and sing, for God's return to Zion will be seen eye to eye! ⁹ Burst forth in song together, O ruins of Jerusalem, for God has comforted His people and redeemed Jerusalem from the control of idolaters. ¹⁰ God has bared His holy arm before the eyes of all the nations when He punished the enemy. All those who live at the ends of the earth will see the salvation of our God.

¹¹ Go out! Go out! Leave that place of exile quickly! Do not touch anything unclean! Go out from the city of your exile! Keep pure, you who carry God's weapons! ¹² But you will not leave too quickly in a panic or depart in flight, since God is going before you, and the God of Israel is your rear guard.

haftarat ki tetze'

ALL COMMUNITIES—Isaiah 54:1–10

The *Haftarah* for *Parashat Noah* ("*O Jerusalem!*"—רָנִּי עֲקָרָה) is read, page 1291.

When *Shabbat Parashat Ki Tetze'* occurs on 14 *Elul*, Ḥabad communities add the section beginning "*Says God*"—עֲנִיָּה סֹעֲרָה [printed above as the Ashkenazic communities' addition to the *Haftarah* for *Parashat Noah*, page 1292].

haftarat ki tavo'

haftarat ki tavo'

ALL COMMUNITIES—ISAIAH 60:1–22

> **SYNOPSIS:** This is the sixth of a series of "Seven *Haftarot* of Comfort" which are read between the Ninth of *Av* and the Jewish New Year (*Rosh Ha-Shanah*). The *Haftarah* was addressed by the prophet Isaiah to the Jewish people in Babylon, after the exile, at the end of the 6th century B.C.E.
>
> The *Haftarah* opens in a wondrous, redemptive mood. A new light is shining on Jerusalem and the exiles are returning (60:1–9). The city is fully restored with the finest wood and precious metals, its gates are opened and a new era of prosperity begins (10–18), Divine light is the only source of illumination (19–20), and the expanding nation is completely righteous (21–22).

60 ¹ Arise, shine and rejoice, O Jerusalem! For your light has arrived, and God's glory has shone upon you. ² Darkness and suffering will cover the earth and thick clouds will cover the nations, but God will shine the light of salvation on you, and His glory will be seen on you. ³ Nations will follow your guiding light, and kings your shining brilliance.

⁴ O Jerusalem, raise your eyes! Look around and see how everybody has gathered together and are coming to you! Your sons will come from afar, and your daughters will be reared by kings. ⁵ When you see this, you will glow with joy. Your heart will throb and swell, for the many possessions of the people who live in the west will be turned over to you, and the wealth of nations will come to you. ⁶ You will be covered by hordes of camels, young camels from Midian and Ephah brought as gifts. They will all come from Sheba, carrying gifts to God of gold and incense, and they will declare God's praises. ⁷ All the sheep of Kedar will be gathered up and brought to you, and the rams of Nebaioth will serve all your needs. They will be accepted favorably on My altar, and I will glorify the House of My splendor by causing the nations to come with gifts of gold and silver.

⁸ People will ask: Who are these exiled people that are returning so quickly like soaring clouds, and like doves to their coop-windows? ⁹ For the people of the islands are gathering with the ships which cross the Sea of Tarshish in the lead, to bring your sons from afar, along with their silver and gold as a gift for God. All this will happen for the sake of the name of God, your God, the Holy One of Israel, who glorifies you.

¹⁰ Foreigners will rebuild the walls of your cities, and their kings will serve you. For I struck you in My anger,

ס ‎1 קוּמִי אוֹרִי כִּי בָא אוֹרֵךְ וּכְבוֹד יְהֹוָה עָלַיִךְ זָרָח: ‎2 כִּי־הִנֵּה הַחֹשֶׁךְ יְכַסֶּה־אֶרֶץ וַעֲרָפֶל לְאֻמִּים וְעָלַיִךְ יִזְרַח יְהֹוָה וּכְבוֹדוֹ עָלַיִךְ יֵרָאֶה: ‎3 וְהָלְכוּ גוֹיִם לְאוֹרֵךְ וּמְלָכִים לְנֹגַהּ זַרְחֵךְ: ‎4 שְׂאִי־סָבִיב עֵינַיִךְ וּרְאִי כֻּלָּם נִקְבְּצוּ בָאוּ־לָךְ בָּנַיִךְ מֵרָחוֹק יָבֹאוּ וּבְנוֹתַיִךְ עַל־צַד תֵּאָמַנָה: ‎5 אָז תִּרְאִי וְנָהַרְתְּ וּפָחַד וְרָחַב לְבָבֵךְ כִּי־יֵהָפֵךְ עָלַיִךְ הֲמוֹן יָם חֵיל גּוֹיִם יָבֹאוּ לָךְ: ‎6 שִׁפְעַת גְּמַלִּים תְּכַסֵּךְ בִּכְרֵי מִדְיָן וְעֵיפָה כֻּלָּם מִשְּׁבָא יָבֹאוּ זָהָב וּלְבוֹנָה יִשָּׂאוּ וּתְהִלֹּת יְהֹוָה יְבַשֵּׂרוּ: ‎7 כָּל־צֹאן קֵדָר יִקָּבְצוּ לָךְ אֵילֵי נְבָיוֹת יְשָׁרְתוּנֶךְ יַעֲלוּ עַל־רָצוֹן מִזְבְּחִי וּבֵית תִּפְאַרְתִּי אֲפָאֵר: ‎8 מִי־אֵלֶּה כָּעָב תְּעוּפֶינָה וְכַיּוֹנִים אֶל־אֲרֻבֹּתֵיהֶם: ‎9 כִּי־לִי | אִיִּים יְקַוּוּ וָאֳנִיּוֹת תַּרְשִׁישׁ בָּרִאשֹׁנָה לְהָבִיא בָנַיִךְ מֵרָחוֹק כַּסְפָּם וּזְהָבָם אִתָּם לְשֵׁם יְהֹוָה אֱלֹהָיִךְ וְלִקְדוֹשׁ יִשְׂרָאֵל כִּי פֵאֲרָךְ: ‎10 וּבָנוּ בְנֵי־נֵכָר חֹמֹתַיִךְ וּמַלְכֵיהֶם יְשָׁרְתוּנֶךְ כִּי בְקִצְפִּי הִכִּיתִיךְ וּבִרְצוֹנִי רִחַמְתִּיךְ:

הפטרת כי תבוא

but in My grace I had mercy on you. ¹¹ Your gates will always be open; they will not close by day or night, so the wealth of nations may be brought in to you, with their kings in procession. ¹² For whatever nation or kingdom does not serve you will perish, and those people will be utterly destroyed.

¹³ The glorious trees of Lebanon will be brought to you together—cypresses, fir, and box trees—to glorify the site of My Sanctuary. I will use them to honor the site of My "footstool," the Holy Temple.

¹⁴ The children of your oppressors will come to you stooped, and all those who disgraced you will prostrate themselves at the soles of your feet. They will call you "Zion, City of God, the Holy One of Israel." ¹⁵ Instead of being abandoned and hated, with no one passing through, I will make you an eternal prodigy, a joy for all generations. ¹⁶ You will suckle the milk of nations and nurse from the breast of kings.

Then you will know that I am God, your Savior, your Redeemer, the Mighty One of Jacob.

¹⁷ In the place of the bronze which the nations took from you, I will bring gold, and in the place of the iron, I will bring silver. In the place of the wood I will bring bronze, and in the place of the stone I will bring iron. In the place of your aggressive, tax-collecting government, I will make a peaceful, friendly one, and in the place of your debt-collectors, I will place people that come to perform justice. ¹⁸ Corruption will no longer be heard of in your land, nor robbery and ruin in your borders. You will call your walls "Salvation of God," and your gates "Glory of God."

¹⁹ You will no longer need the sun for daylight, nor the moon to shine at night. God will always be your light, and your God will be your glory. ²⁰ Your sun will never set and your moon will not be eclipsed by another nation, for God will always be your light and source of power. Your days of mourning will come to an end.

²¹ Your people will be righteous, since the wicked will have perished. They will inherit the land forever, never to be exiled again. They are the shoot I planted, My handiwork in which I take pride.

²² The smallest tribe will become a thousand times the size, and the youngest tribe, a mighty nation. Since I am the all-powerful God, I will hasten the smallest tribe to expand in the time of the redemption!

11 וּפִתְּח֧וּ שְׁעָרַ֛יִךְ תָּמִ֖יד יוֹמָ֣ם וָלָ֑יְלָה לֹ֣א יִסָּגֵ֑רוּ לְהָבִ֤יא אֵלַ֙יִךְ֙ חֵ֣יל גּוֹיִ֔ם וּמַלְכֵיהֶ֖ם נְהוּגִֽים: 12 כִּֽי־הַגּ֧וֹי וְהַמַּמְלָכָ֛ה אֲשֶׁ֥ר לֹא־יַעַבְד֖וּךְ יֹאבֵ֑דוּ וְהַגּוֹיִ֖ם חָרֹ֥ב יֶחֱרָֽבוּ: 13 כְּב֤וֹד הַלְּבָנוֹן֙ אֵלַ֣יִךְ יָב֔וֹא בְּר֛וֹשׁ תִּדְהָ֥ר וּתְאַשּׁ֖וּר יַחְדָּ֑ו לְפָאֵר֙ מְק֣וֹם מִקְדָּשִׁ֔י וּמְק֥וֹם רַגְלַ֖י אֲכַבֵּֽד: 14 וְהָלְכ֨וּ אֵלַ֤יִךְ שְׁח֙וֹחַ֙ בְּנֵ֣י מְעַנַּ֔יִךְ וְהִֽשְׁתַּחֲו֛וּ עַל־כַּפּ֥וֹת רַגְלַ֖יִךְ כָּל־מְנַֽאֲצָ֑יִךְ וְקָ֤רְאוּ לָךְ֙ עִ֣יר יְהֹוָ֔ה צִיּ֖וֹן קְד֥וֹשׁ יִשְׂרָאֵֽל: 15 תַּ֧חַת הֱיוֹתֵ֛ךְ עֲזוּבָ֥ה וּשְׂנוּאָ֖ה וְאֵ֣ין עוֹבֵ֑ר וְשַׂמְתִּיךְ֙ לִגְא֣וֹן עוֹלָ֔ם מְשׂ֖וֹשׂ דּ֥וֹר וָדֽוֹר: 16 וְיָנַ֙קְתְּ֙ חֲלֵ֣ב גּוֹיִ֔ם וְשֹׁ֥ד מְלָכִ֖ים תִּינָ֑קִי וְיָדַ֗עַתְּ כִּ֣י אֲנִ֤י יְהֹוָה֙ מֽוֹשִׁיעֵ֔ךְ וְגֹֽאֲלֵ֖ךְ אֲבִ֥יר יַעֲקֹֽב: 17 תַּ֣חַת הַנְּחֹ֜שֶׁת אָבִ֣יא זָהָ֗ב וְתַ֤חַת הַבַּרְזֶל֙ אָ֣בִיא כֶ֔סֶף וְתַ֤חַת הָֽעֵצִים֙ נְחֹ֔שֶׁת וְתַ֥חַת הָאֲבָנִ֖ים בַּרְזֶ֑ל וְשַׂמְתִּ֤י פְקֻדָּתֵךְ֙ שָׁל֔וֹם וְנֹגְשַׂ֖יִךְ צְדָקָֽה: 18 לֹֽא־יִשָּׁמַ֨ע ע֤וֹד חָמָס֙ בְּאַרְצֵ֔ךְ שֹׁ֥ד וָשֶׁ֖בֶר בִּגְבוּלָ֑יִךְ וְקָרָ֤את יְשׁוּעָה֙ חֽוֹמֹתַ֔יִךְ וּשְׁעָרַ֖יִךְ תְּהִלָּֽה: 19 לֹא־יִֽהְיֶה־לָּ֨ךְ ע֤וֹד הַשֶּׁ֙מֶשׁ֙ לְא֣וֹר יוֹמָ֔ם וּלְנֹ֕גַהּ הַיָּרֵ֖חַ לֹא־יָאִ֣יר לָ֑ךְ וְהָיָה־לָ֤ךְ יְהֹוָה֙ לְא֣וֹר עוֹלָ֔ם וֵֽאלֹהַ֖יִךְ לְתִפְאַרְתֵּֽךְ: 20 לֹא־יָב֥וֹא עוֹד֙ שִׁמְשֵׁ֔ךְ וִירֵחֵ֖ךְ לֹ֣א יֵאָסֵ֑ף כִּ֣י יְהֹוָ֗ה יִֽהְיֶה־לָּךְ֙ לְא֣וֹר עוֹלָ֔ם וְשָׁלְמ֖וּ יְמֵ֥י אֶבְלֵֽךְ: 21 וְעַמֵּךְ֙ כֻּלָּ֣ם צַדִּיקִ֔ים לְעוֹלָ֖ם יִ֣ירְשׁוּ אָ֑רֶץ נֵ֧צֶר [מַטָּעַ כ׳] מַטָּעַ֛י מַעֲשֵׂ֥ה יָדַ֖י לְהִתְפָּאֵֽר: 22 הַקָּטֹן֙ יִֽהְיֶ֣ה לָאֶ֔לֶף וְהַצָּעִ֖יר לְג֣וֹי עָצ֑וּם אֲנִ֥י יְהֹוָ֖ה בְּעִתָּ֥הּ אֲחִישֶֽׁנָּה:

haftarat nitzavim

haftarat nitzavim
and nitzavim–va-yelekh

ALL COMMUNITIES—ISAIAH 61:10 – 63:9

SYNOPSIS: This is the last in a series of "Seven *Haftarot* of Comfort" which are read between the Ninth of *Av* and the Jewish New Year (*Rosh Ha-Shanah*). The *Haftarah* was addressed by the prophet Isaiah to the Jewish people in Babylon after the exile at the end of the 6th century B.C.E. This *Haftarah* is always read on the Sabbath preceding *Rosh Ha-Shanah*.

As the *Haftarah* opens, Zion rejoices in her redemption, as God clothes her in "garments of salvation" (61:10-11). God promises to protect Zion and she will consequently be known by more positive names than in the past (62:1-7). God then reinforces His words with an oath (8-9). In a tone of exultation, the prophet declares that the roads should be smoothed for the ingathering of the Jewish people, because God is now going to pay His "wages" to the Jewish people and redeem them (10-12). In the following chapter, the prophet depicts God as wearing bloodstained garments after wreaking vengeance on the wicked nations (63:1-6). The *Haftarah* concludes by praising God's kindness, His love for Israel, and His sympathy for their distress (7-9).

61 ¹⁰ I will rejoice greatly in God's salvation. My soul will be glad with my God, for He has clothed me in garments of salvation and wrapped me in a robe of righteousness; like a bridegroom who wears majestic clothing, and a bride who adorns herself with her jewelry. ¹¹ For just like the earth brings forth its growth, and a garden makes its seeds grow, so too will God Almighty cause the righteousness and praise of Israel to sprout before all the nations.

62 ¹ For Zion's sake I will not be silent, and for Jerusalem's sake I will not be still, until her righteousness emerges like shining light, and her salvation like a burning torch. ² Nations will see the righteousness which I will do for you, and all the kings, your glory. You will be called a new name, pronounced by the mouth of God.

³ You will be protected like a crown of beauty in God's hand, a royal coronet in the palm of your God. ⁴ You will no longer be called "Abandoned by God," and your land will no longer be called "Desolation." Rather, you will be called "I desire her" and your land "inhabited," for God will desire you, and your land will be inhabited. ⁵ As a young man marries

סא ¹⁰ שׂוֹשׂ אָשִׂישׂ בַּיהוָה תָּגֵל נַפְשִׁי בֵּאלֹהַי כִּי הִלְבִּישַׁנִי בִּגְדֵי־יֶשַׁע מְעִיל צְדָקָה יְעָטָנִי כֶּחָתָן יְכַהֵן פְּאֵר וְכַכַּלָּה תַּעְדֶּה כֵלֶיהָ: ¹¹ כִּי כָאָרֶץ תּוֹצִיא צִמְחָהּ וּכְגַנָּה זֵרוּעֶיהָ תַצְמִיחַ כֵּן | אֲדֹנָי יֱהֹוִה יַצְמִיחַ צְדָקָה וּתְהִלָּה נֶגֶד כָּל־הַגּוֹיִם:

סב ¹ לְמַעַן צִיּוֹן לֹא אֶחֱשֶׁה וּלְמַעַן יְרוּשָׁלִַם לֹא אֶשְׁקוֹט עַד־יֵצֵא כַנֹּגַהּ צִדְקָהּ וִישׁוּעָתָהּ כְּלַפִּיד יִבְעָר: ² וְרָאוּ גוֹיִם צִדְקֵךְ וְכָל־מְלָכִים כְּבוֹדֵךְ וְקֹרָא לָךְ שֵׁם חָדָשׁ אֲשֶׁר פִּי יְהוָה יִקֳּבֶנּוּ: ³ וְהָיִית עֲטֶרֶת תִּפְאֶרֶת בְּיַד־יְהוָה [וּצְנִיף כ׳] מְלוּכָה בְּכַף־אֱלֹהָיִךְ: ⁴ לֹא־יֵאָמֵר לָךְ עוֹד עֲזוּבָה וּלְאַרְצֵךְ לֹא־יֵאָמֵר עוֹד שְׁמָמָה כִּי לָךְ יִקָּרֵא חֶפְצִי־בָהּ וּלְאַרְצֵךְ בְּעוּלָה כִּי־חָפֵץ יְהוָה בָּךְ וְאַרְצֵךְ תִּבָּעֵל: ⁵ כִּי־יִבְעַל בָּחוּר

הפטרת נצבים

a maiden and settles with her, so will your children settle you, and your God will rejoice over you as a bridegroom rejoices over his bride. [6] Over your walls, O Jerusalem, I have appointed the stones as watchmen. They will never be silent from crying and mourning, day or night. Do not be silent, you stones who speak of God! [7] Do not let Him be idle and free from complaint until He restores Jerusalem and establishes it in glory amid the earth!

[8] God has sworn by His right hand and His mighty arm: "I will never again give your grain as food to your enemies or let foreigners drink the wine for which you labored. [9] Rather, those who harvest the grain will eat it and praise God in thanks, and those who gathered the grapes will drink wine in their homes, in My holy courts of Jerusalem."

[10] Go through the gates, you nations, go through the gates of your cities, in order to raise and smooth the road for the people. Clear away stones that obstruct the way. Raise a banner for the nations telling them to bring the Jewish people home.

[11] Look! God has proclaimed to the ends of the earth: "Say to the daughter of Zion: Your salvation is coming! Look! His reward which is due to the Jewish people is with Him, and His wages which he owes to the Jewish people are ready before Him!" [12] They will be called a holy people, God's redeemed. You, Zion, will be called "sought after, a city not forsaken."

63

[1] When God wreaks vengeance on Edom, people will say, "Who is this coming from Edom, from Bozrah, with bloodstained clothing? This one who used to be dressed majestically and ordered people from place to place with his great power!"

Says God, "It is I, who say and fulfil My promises of justice for the Jewish people and I who am mighty to save."

[2] People will say, "Why is your clothing red, and your garments like those of one who treads in a winepress?"

[3] Says God, "I trod the winepress of blood in My righteousness alone, not in the merit of the Jewish people. Not one person from the nations was able to stand against Me. I trod them in My anger and trampled them in My rage. The blood of their strength splashed on My garments and stained all My clothing.

[4] "For I have been planning a day of vengeance against the nations for a long time, and the year of redemption for My people has now come. [5] I looked around for a merit with which the Jewish people might be redeemed, but there was no merit to help. I was amazed that there was

בְּתוּלָה יִבְעָל֖וּךְ בָּנָ֑יִךְ וּמְשׂ֤וֹשׂ חָתָן֙ עַל־כַּלָּ֔ה יָשִׂ֥ישׂ עָלַ֖יִךְ אֱלֹהָֽיִךְ: 6 עַל־חוֹמֹתַ֣יִךְ יְרוּשָׁלִַ֗ם הִפְקַ֙דְתִּי֙ שֹֽׁמְרִ֔ים כָּל־הַיּ֧וֹם וְכָל־הַלַּ֛יְלָה תָּמִ֖יד לֹ֣א יֶחֱשׁ֑וּ הַמַּזְכִּרִים֙ אֶת־יְהֹוָ֔ה אַל־דֳּמִ֖י לָכֶֽם: 7 וְאַל־תִּתְּנ֥וּ דֳמִ֖י ל֑וֹ עַד־יְכוֹנֵ֞ן וְעַד־יָשִׂ֧ים אֶת־יְרֽוּשָׁלִַ֛ם תְּהִלָּ֖ה בָּאָֽרֶץ: 8 נִשְׁבַּ֧ע יְהֹוָ֛ה בִּֽימִינ֖וֹ וּבִזְר֣וֹעַ עֻזּ֑וֹ אִם־אֶתֵּן֩ אֶת־דְּגָנֵ֨ךְ ע֤וֹד מַֽאֲכָל֙ לְאֹ֣יְבַ֔יִךְ וְאִם־יִשְׁתּ֤וּ בְנֵֽי־נֵכָר֙ תִּֽירוֹשֵׁ֔ךְ אֲשֶׁ֥ר יָגַ֖עַתְּ בּֽוֹ: 9 כִּ֤י מְאַסְפָיו֙ יֹאכְלֻ֔הוּ וְהִֽלְל֖וּ אֶת־יְהֹוָ֑ה וּֽמְקַבְּצָ֥יו יִשְׁתֻּ֖הוּ בְּחַצְר֥וֹת קָדְשִֽׁי: 10 עִבְר֤וּ עִבְרוּ֙ בַּשְּׁעָרִ֔ים פַּנּ֖וּ דֶּ֣רֶךְ הָעָ֑ם סֹ֣לּוּ סֹ֤לּוּ הַֽמְסִלָּה֙ סַקְּל֣וּ מֵאֶ֔בֶן הָרִ֥ימוּ נֵ֖ס עַל־הָֽעַמִּֽים: 11 הִנֵּ֣ה יְהֹוָ֗ה הִשְׁמִ֙יעַ֙ אֶל־קְצֵ֣ה הָאָ֔רֶץ אִמְרוּ֙ לְבַת־צִיּ֔וֹן הִנֵּ֥ה יִשְׁעֵ֖ךְ בָּ֑א הִנֵּ֤ה שְׂכָרוֹ֙ אִתּ֔וֹ וּפְעֻלָּת֖וֹ לְפָנָֽיו: 12 וְקָֽרְא֥וּ לָהֶ֛ם עַם־הַקֹּ֖דֶשׁ גְּאוּלֵ֣י יְהֹוָ֑ה וְלָךְ֙ יִקָּרֵ֣א דְרוּשָׁ֔ה עִ֖יר לֹ֥א נֶֽעֱזָֽבָה:

סג

1 מִי־זֶ֣ה ׀ בָּ֣א מֵאֱד֗וֹם חֲמ֤וּץ בְּגָדִים֙ מִבָּצְרָ֔ה זֶ֚ה הָד֣וּר בִּלְבוּשׁ֔וֹ צֹעֶ֖ה בְּרֹ֣ב כֹּח֑וֹ אֲנִ֛י מְדַבֵּ֥ר בִּצְדָקָ֖ה רַ֥ב לְהוֹשִֽׁיעַ: 2 מַדּ֥וּעַ אָדֹ֖ם לִלְבוּשֶׁ֑ךָ וּבְגָדֶ֖יךָ כְּדֹרֵ֥ךְ בְּגַֽת: 3 פּוּרָ֣ה ׀ דָּרַ֣כְתִּי לְבַדִּ֗י וּמֵֽעַמִּים֙ אֵֽין־אִ֣ישׁ אִתִּ֔י וְאֶדְרְכֵ֣ם בְּאַפִּ֔י וְאֶרְמְסֵ֖ם בַּֽחֲמָתִ֑י וְיֵ֤ז נִצְחָם֙ עַל־בְּגָדַ֔י וְכָל־מַלְבּוּשַׁ֖י אֶגְאָֽלְתִּי: 4 כִּ֛י י֥וֹם נָקָ֖ם בְּלִבִּ֑י וּשְׁנַ֥ת גְּאוּלַ֖י בָּֽאָה: 5 וְאַבִּיט֙ וְאֵ֣ין עֹזֵ֔ר וְאֶשְׁתּוֹמֵ֖ם וְאֵ֣ין סוֹמֵ֑ךְ וַתּ֤וֹשַֽׁע לִי֙

haftarat shabbat shuvah

no merit to be of help in redeeming them. So My arm wrought their salvation for Me and not their own merit, and My anger against the nations supported Me in wreaking vengeance upon them. ⁶ I trampled peoples in My wrath and made them drunk with the cup of My rage. I cast the blood of their strength down to the ground."

⁷ The prophet says, "Israel will relate God's kind deeds and His praise for everything He has done for us —all the good He has granted to the House of Israel in His mercy and great kindness." ⁸ When God took them out of Egypt, He said, "Indeed, they alone are My people, children who were not unfaithful and did not forsake Me," and He became their Savior.

⁹ All their sufferings caused Him pain and the angel who stands before Him saved them. Likewise, out of His love and mercy He redeemed them. He will bear them and carry them forever.

זַרְעִי וַחֲמָתִי הִיא סְמָכָתְנִי: 6 וְאָבוּס עַמִּים בְּאַפִּי וַאֲשַׁכְּרֵם בַּחֲמָתִי וְאוֹרִיד לָאָרֶץ נִצְחָם: 7 חַסְדֵי יְהֹוָה ׀ אַזְכִּיר תְּהִלֹּת יְהֹוָה כְּעַל כֹּל אֲשֶׁר־גְּמָלָנוּ יְהֹוָה וְרַב־טוּב לְבֵית יִשְׂרָאֵל אֲשֶׁר־גְּמָלָם כְּרַחֲמָיו וּכְרֹב חֲסָדָיו: 8 וַיֹּאמֶר אַךְ־עַמִּי הֵמָּה בָּנִים לֹא יְשַׁקֵּרוּ וַיְהִי לָהֶם לְמוֹשִׁיעַ: 9 בְּכָל־צָרָתָם ׀ [לֹא כ'] לוֹ צָר וּמַלְאַךְ פָּנָיו הוֹשִׁיעָם בְּאַהֲבָתוֹ וּבְחֶמְלָתוֹ הוּא גְאָלָם וַיְנַטְּלֵם וַיְנַשְּׂאֵם כָּל־יְמֵי עוֹלָם:

haftarat shabbat shuvah

Ashkenazim—Hosea 14:2–10; Joel 2:11–27; Micah 7:18–20
Sephardim and Habad—Hosea 14:2–10; Micah 7:18–20

SYNOPSIS: The Sabbath preceding the Day of Atonement (*Yom Kippur*) is known as *Shabbat Shuvah* ("The Sabbath of Return"), after its special *Haftarah* that stresses the need for repentance by man, and God's forgiveness.

In the opening passage of the *Haftarah*, the prophet Hosea (7th century B.C.E.) urges the people to sincere verbal confession (14:2-3) and to trust in God (4). God will then forgive Israel and love them forever (5-9). The passage concludes with a plea to take the prophet's words to heart (10). In the following section, from Joel (read only by Ashkenazim), the prophet inspires the people towards repentance in order to avert an imminent day of locust destruction (2:11-14). A public fast is declared, and the priests are advised to cry out to God (15-17). In response, God will bring ample sustenance and safety from the enemy, and a spirit of joy will consequently prevail (18-27). A final passage from Micah, read by all communities, stresses God's attributes of forgiveness, kindness, and compassion.

14 ² Israel, return to God, your God, for you have stumbled on account of your sins. ³ You do not need to take sacrifices. Just take words of confession with you and return to God. Say to Him: "Lift away all sin and accept our promises for good behavior in the future. Let

יד 2 שׁוּבָה יִשְׂרָאֵל עַד יְהֹוָה אֱלֹהֶיךָ כִּי כָשַׁלְתָּ בַּעֲוֺנֶךָ: 3 קְחוּ עִמָּכֶם דְּבָרִים וְשׁוּבוּ אֶל־יְהֹוָה אִמְרוּ אֵלָיו כָּל־תִּשָּׂא עָוֺן וְקַח־

הפטרת שבת שובה

the confession of our lips be in place of the sacrificing of bullocks.

⁴ "We will no longer ask to be saved by Assyria, and we will not put our trust in riding powerful horses into battle. We will never again call the idol made by our hands, 'our god,' because we know that the orphan finds compassion through You alone." ⁵ Then after they confess, I will forgive them for their rebelliousness. I will love them deeply, because My anger will have turned away from them. ⁶ My love for Israel will be perpetual like dew. He will blossom like a rose, and his roots will spread like the roots of a cedar from Lebanon. ⁷ His young leaves will spread out, he will be beautiful like an olive tree, and he will have the aroma of Lebanon. ⁸ Those who sat in His shade will be peaceful. They will be peacefully self-sufficient like grain which sustains life, and they will blossom like the vine. Their fame will be like that of the wine of Lebanon.

טוֹב וּנְשַׁלְּמָה פָרִים שְׂפָתֵינוּ: 4 אַשּׁוּר ׀ לֹא יוֹשִׁיעֵנוּ עַל־סוּס לֹא נִרְכָּב וְלֹא־נֹאמַר עוֹד אֱלֹהֵינוּ לְמַעֲשֵׂה יָדֵינוּ אֲשֶׁר־בְּךָ יְרֻחַם יָתוֹם: 5 אֶרְפָּא מְשׁוּבָתָם אֹהֲבֵם נְדָבָה כִּי שָׁב אַפִּי מִמֶּנּוּ: 6 אֶהְיֶה כַטַּל לְיִשְׂרָאֵל יִפְרַח כַּשּׁוֹשַׁנָּה וְיַךְ שָׁרָשָׁיו כַּלְּבָנוֹן: 7 יֵלְכוּ יוֹנְקוֹתָיו וִיהִי כַזַּיִת הוֹדוֹ וְרֵיחַ לוֹ כַּלְּבָנוֹן: 8 יָשֻׁבוּ יֹשְׁבֵי בְצִלּוֹ יְחַיּוּ דָגָן וְיִפְרְחוּ כַגָּפֶן זִכְרוֹ כְּיֵין לְבָנוֹן: 9 אֶפְרַיִם מַה־לִּי עוֹד לָעֲצַבִּים אֲנִי עָנִיתִי וַאֲשׁוּרֶנּוּ אֲנִי כִּבְרוֹשׁ רַעֲנָן מִמֶּנִּי פֶּרְיְךָ נִמְצָא: 10 מִי חָכָם וְיָבֵן אֵלֶּה נָבוֹן וְיֵדָעֵם כִּי־יְשָׁרִים דַּרְכֵי יְהֹוָה וְצַדִּקִים יֵלְכוּ בָם וּפֹשְׁעִים יִכָּשְׁלוּ בָם:

⁹ When Ephraim asks, "What do I need idolaters for anymore?" I will answer all his requests and look over and supervise his needs. I will attend to him like a fresh cypress tree which bends its head over its roots. The fruit of your success comes from Me. ¹⁰ Whoever is wise will understand these words. The discerning will recognize them. For the ways of God are straight and the righteous will walk in them, but the wicked will stumble in them.

Ḥabad and Sephardic communities omit the following (Joel 2:11–27), and continue on page 1412.

2 ¹¹ God makes His voice heard through the prophets before His army of locusts arrive. His camp is extremely large, and those who carry out His word on a mission of destruction are awesome. The day of destruction from God is great and very formidable. Who could endure it?

¹² Yet even now—says God—return to Me with all your heart, with fasting, weeping, and lamenting. ¹³ Rend your hearts, not your garments, and return to God, your God. For He is merciful and compassionate, slow to anger, very kind and renounces bad decrees. ¹⁴ Let anyone who knows what sin he has done repent and regret. Then, when the locusts come they will not destroy, but rather leave behind a blessing from which to bring a meal-offering and a wine libation to God, your God.

ב 11 וַיהֹוָה נָתַן קוֹלוֹ לִפְנֵי חֵילוֹ כִּי רַב מְאֹד מַחֲנֵהוּ כִּי עָצוּם עֹשֵׂה דְבָרוֹ כִּי־גָדוֹל יוֹם־יְהֹוָה וְנוֹרָא מְאֹד וּמִי יְכִילֶנּוּ: 12 וְגַם־עַתָּה נְאֻם־יְהֹוָה שֻׁבוּ עָדַי בְּכָל־לְבַבְכֶם וּבְצוֹם וּבִבְכִי וּבְמִסְפֵּד: 13 וְקִרְעוּ לְבַבְכֶם וְאַל־בִּגְדֵיכֶם וְשׁוּבוּ אֶל־יְהֹוָה אֱלֹהֵיכֶם כִּי־חַנּוּן וְרַחוּם הוּא אֶרֶךְ אַפַּיִם וְרַב־חֶסֶד וְנִחָם עַל־הָרָעָה: 14 מִי יוֹדֵעַ יָשׁוּב וְנִחָם וְהִשְׁאִיר אַחֲרָיו בְּרָכָה מִנְחָה וָנֶסֶךְ לַיהֹוָה אֱלֹהֵיכֶם: 15 תִּקְעוּ שׁוֹפָר בְּצִיּוֹן קַדְּשׁוּ־צוֹם קִרְאוּ עֲצָרָה: 16 אִסְפוּ־עָם קַדְּשׁוּ קָהָל קִבְצוּ זְקֵנִים

¹⁵ Sound the ram's horn in Zion to awaken the people to repent, announce a fast, call an assembly. ¹⁶ Gather the people, instruct the congregation to fast,

haftarat shabbat shuvah

bring together the elders, gather the children and the nursing babies. The groom should leave his room and the bride her canopy to participate; they should not rejoice.

¹⁷ Let the priests, the ministers of God, cry out between the Hall and the altar. Let them say, "God! Have pity on Your people! Do not allow Your inheritance, Your people, to be shamed by letting nations rule over them when they come to beg for food after the locusts destroy everything they have. Why should the nations say, 'Where is their God?'"

¹⁸ Then, when you repent, God will become jealous for His land and have pity on His people. ¹⁹ God will respond and say to His people, "From now on, I will send you grain, wine, and oil, and it will satisfy you. I will no longer let you be shamed among the nations. ²⁰ I will distance from you the locusts that come from the north and drive them to their death in a barren and desolate land. I will send the first locusts that come to the Salt Sea in the east, and the last locusts to the Western Sea. The stench of the dead locusts will go up and its odor will rise, for there were many locusts ready to do harm.

²¹ Do not be afraid, land of Israel, that the locusts may return. Rather, be glad and rejoice, because God has decided from now on to do many great things. ²² Do not be afraid, animals of the field, that pasture may be lacking, because the pastures in the wilderness have sprouted. Even trees which need much more rain than pasture have borne their fruit, and the fig tree and vine have produced their yield.

²³ Rejoice and be happy with God, your God, O children of Zion, because He has given you the early rain as charity and not according to what you deserve. He caused the early and late rain to fall in the first part of the season. ²⁴ The granaries will be filled with grain and the vats will ring with the noise of flowing wine and oil. ²⁵ I will repay you for your losses in the years that were consumed by the different species of locust, known as *'arbeh, yelek, ḥasil* and *gazam*, My mighty army which I sent against you. ²⁶ Then, you will eat and be satisfied, and praise the name of God, your God, who performed such wondrous acts. My people will never be shamed again by being forced to live in other lands due to lack of food. ²⁷ Then you will know that I am in Israel's midst, that I am God, your God, and there is no other. My people will never be shamed again.

אִסְפוּ עוֹלָלִים וְיֹנְקֵי שָׁדָיִם יֵצֵא חָתָן מֵחֶדְרוֹ וְכַלָּה מֵחֻפָּתָהּ: 17 בֵּין הָאוּלָם וְלַמִּזְבֵּחַ יִבְכּוּ הַכֹּהֲנִים מְשָׁרְתֵי יְהוָה וְיֹאמְרוּ חוּסָה יְהוָה עַל־עַמֶּךָ וְאַל־תִּתֵּן נַחֲלָתְךָ לְחֶרְפָּה לִמְשָׁל־בָּם גּוֹיִם לָמָּה יֹאמְרוּ בָעַמִּים אַיֵּה אֱלֹהֵיהֶם: 18 וַיְקַנֵּא יְהוָה לְאַרְצוֹ וַיַּחְמֹל עַל־עַמּוֹ: 19 וַיַּעַן יְהוָה וַיֹּאמֶר לְעַמּוֹ הִנְנִי שֹׁלֵחַ לָכֶם אֶת־הַדָּגָן וְהַתִּירוֹשׁ וְהַיִּצְהָר וּשְׂבַעְתֶּם אֹתוֹ וְלֹא־אֶתֵּן אֶתְכֶם עוֹד חֶרְפָּה בַּגּוֹיִם: 20 וְאֶת־הַצְּפוֹנִי אַרְחִיק מֵעֲלֵיכֶם וְהִדַּחְתִּיו אֶל־אֶרֶץ צִיָּה וּשְׁמָמָה אֶת־פָּנָיו אֶל־הַיָּם הַקַּדְמֹנִי וְסֹפוֹ אֶל־הַיָּם הָאַחֲרוֹן וְעָלָה בָאְשׁוֹ וְתַעַל צַחֲנָתוֹ כִּי הִגְדִּיל לַעֲשׂוֹת: 21 אַל־תִּירְאִי אֲדָמָה גִּילִי וּשְׂמָחִי כִּי־הִגְדִּיל יְהוָה לַעֲשׂוֹת: 22 אַל־תִּירְאוּ בַּהֲמוֹת שָׂדַי כִּי דָשְׁאוּ נְאוֹת מִדְבָּר כִּי־עֵץ נָשָׂא פִרְיוֹ תְּאֵנָה וָגֶפֶן נָתְנוּ חֵילָם: 23 וּבְנֵי צִיּוֹן גִּילוּ וְשִׂמְחוּ בַּיהוָה אֱלֹהֵיכֶם כִּי־נָתַן לָכֶם אֶת־הַמּוֹרֶה לִצְדָקָה וַיּוֹרֶד לָכֶם גֶּשֶׁם מוֹרֶה וּמַלְקוֹשׁ בָּרִאשׁוֹן: 24 וּמָלְאוּ הַגֳּרָנוֹת בָּר וְהֵשִׁיקוּ הַיְקָבִים תִּירוֹשׁ וְיִצְהָר: 25 וְשִׁלַּמְתִּי לָכֶם אֶת־הַשָּׁנִים אֲשֶׁר אָכַל הָאַרְבֶּה הַיֶּלֶק וְהֶחָסִיל וְהַגָּזָם חֵילִי הַגָּדוֹל אֲשֶׁר שִׁלַּחְתִּי בָּכֶם: 26 וַאֲכַלְתֶּם אָכוֹל וְשָׂבוֹעַ וְהִלַּלְתֶּם אֶת־שֵׁם יְהוָה אֱלֹהֵיכֶם אֲשֶׁר־עָשָׂה עִמָּכֶם לְהַפְלִיא וְלֹא־יֵבֹשׁוּ עַמִּי לְעוֹלָם: 27 וִידַעְתֶּם כִּי בְקֶרֶב יִשְׂרָאֵל אָנִי וַאֲנִי יְהוָה אֱלֹהֵיכֶם וְאֵין עוֹד וְלֹא־יֵבֹשׁוּ עַמִּי לְעוֹלָם:

All communities conclude with the following (*Micah 7:18–20*):

7 ¹⁸ Who is like You, O God, forgiving iniquity and overlooking transgression for those who remain of His heritage after the birth pangs of the Messiah? Even when He does become angry, He does not maintain His anger forever, because He is a lover of kindness. ¹⁹ He will once again have mercy on us. He will grasp our iniquities, preventing them from being held against us, and cast all our sins into the depths of the sea. ²⁰ Give to us the fulfillment of the true words that You spoke to Jacob, and the words of lovingkindness that You spoke to Abraham, which you promised our fathers long ago.

ז 18 מִי־אֵל כָּמוֹךָ נֹשֵׂא עָוֺן וְעֹבֵר עַל־פֶּשַׁע לִשְׁאֵרִית נַחֲלָתוֹ לֹא־הֶחֱזִיק לָעַד אַפּוֹ כִּי־חָפֵץ חֶסֶד הוּא: 19 יָשׁוּב יְרַחֲמֵנוּ יִכְבֹּשׁ עֲוֺנֹתֵינוּ וְתַשְׁלִיךְ בִּמְצֻלוֹת יָם כָּל־חַטֹּאתָם: 20 תִּתֵּן אֱמֶת לְיַעֲקֹב חֶסֶד לְאַבְרָהָם אֲשֶׁר־נִשְׁבַּעְתָּ לַאֲבֹתֵינוּ מִימֵי קֶדֶם:

haftarat ha'azinu

ALL COMMUNITIES—II SAMUEL 22:1–51

SYNOPSIS: This *Haftarah* relates the Song of David, similar to the Song of *Ha'azinu* sung by Moses in the *Parashah*. The *Haftarah* is also read on the seventh day of Passover.

The Song was recited by David in his old age in gratitude to God, who *"saved him from all of his enemies and from Saul"* (22:1). David praises God as a "Rock" and personal Savior who responded in times of emergency (2–7), and God's methods of deliverance are depicted with rich imagery (8–20). David then attests to his own loyalty to God (21–24) and hopes for just reward (25–28). The theme of personal gratitude is then redeveloped, as David depicts God's involvement in his victories at length (29–46). In his closing words, David reiterates and intensifies His praises (47–48), promises to publicize God's acts among the nations (50), and prays that God should continue to bestow kindness on his descendants forever (51).

When *Parashat Ha'azinu* occurs between *Rosh Ha-Shanah* and *Yom Kippur*, the *Haftarah* for *Shabbat Shuvah* is read (page 1409).

22 ¹ Then David, in his old age, chanted the words of this song to God on the day God saved him from all of his enemies and from Saul. ² He said:

God is my Rock and my Fortress, who saves me. ³ God! My Rock in whom I trust! My shield! My saving power! My support and my refuge! My Savior! Save me from men of corruption! ⁴ When I call out God's praises I am saved from my enemies.

⁵ When the pains of death engulfed me, and the sicknesses brought by treacherous men frightened

כב 1 וַיְדַבֵּר דָּוִד לַיהֹוָה אֶת־דִּבְרֵי הַשִּׁירָה הַזֹּאת בְּיוֹם הִצִּיל יְהֹוָה אֹתוֹ מִכַּף כָּל־אֹיְבָיו וּמִכַּף שָׁאוּל: 2 וַיֹּאמַר יְהֹוָה סַלְעִי וּמְצֻדָתִי וּמְפַלְטִי־לִי: 3 אֱלֹהֵי צוּרִי אֶחֱסֶה־בּוֹ מָגִנִּי וְקֶרֶן יִשְׁעִי מִשְׂגַּבִּי וּמְנוּסִי מֹשִׁעִי מֵחָמָס תֹּשִׁעֵנִי: 4 מְהֻלָּל אֶקְרָא יְהֹוָה וּמֵאֹיְבַי אִוָּשֵׁעַ: 5 כִּי

haftarat ha'azinu

me; ⁶ when the pains of the grave surrounded me, and the snares of death came before me; ⁷ when I am pained by all these things, I call on God! I call out to my God! He hears my voice from His Temple, and my plea reaches His ears.

⁸ The earth shook and trembled, the foundations of heaven shuddered; they shake because He is angry. ⁹ Smoke rises in His nostrils, fire from His mouth devours those that rise against Him when live coals blaze forth from Him to consume them. ¹⁰ He bent the heavens and descended to reach the enemy, with a thick cloud under His feet with which to punish them. ¹¹ He mounted a cherub and flew off. He appeared on the wings of the wind. ¹² He surrounded Himself with a canopy of darkness ready to punish the enemy, from clouds of water bound together under the heavens. ¹³ From the brightness before Him which he shone to save me blazed fiery coals against those who stood against me. ¹⁴ God thundered from heaven. The Supreme One sent forth His voice. ¹⁵ He shot arrows and scattered the enemy. He sent lightning and He confused them. ¹⁶ With God's roar and the blast of His nostrils, the depths of the sea were visible and the earth split, revealing the world's foundations.

¹⁷ He sent His salvation from on high and took me. He drew me from deep waters. ¹⁸ He saved me from my powerful enemy, from those who hated me, when they were stronger than me. ¹⁹ They took advantage of me by attacking me on the day of my calamity, but God was a support for me. ²⁰ He brought me out to a wide place. He delivered me from the straits, because He wants me.

²¹ May God reward me according to my righteousness. May He repay me according to the purity of my hands. ²² For I have kept God's ways, and I have not acted wickedly before my God. ²³ For all His laws are in my mind before me, and I have not turned away from any one of His suprarational commands. ²⁴ I was wholehearted with Him, and I guarded myself from my sin. ²⁵ So may God pay me according to my righteousness, according to my purity in His eyes. ²⁶ With the kind man You deal kindly, with the wholehearted man, wholeheartedly, ²⁷ with the pure, in purity, with the crooked, You act with guile. ²⁸ You save a humble nation but You look down on the haughty.

אֲפָפֻ֖נִי מִשְׁבְּרֵי־מָ֑וֶת נַחֲלֵ֥י בְלִיַּ֖עַל יְבַעֲתֻֽנִי׃
⁶ חֶבְלֵ֥י שְׁא֖וֹל סַבֻּ֑נִי קִדְּמֻ֖נִי מֹ֥קְשֵׁי־מָֽוֶת׃
⁷ בַּצַּר־לִי֙ אֶקְרָ֣א יְהֹוָ֔ה וְאֶל־אֱלֹהַ֖י אֶקְרָ֑א וַיִּשְׁמַ֤ע מֵהֵֽיכָלוֹ֙ קוֹלִ֔י וְשַׁוְעָתִ֖י בְּאׇזְנָֽיו׃
⁸ [וַתִּגְעַשׁ כ׳] וַיִּתְגָּעַ֤שׁ וַתִּרְעַשׁ֙ הָאָ֔רֶץ מוֹסְד֥וֹת הַשָּׁמַ֖יִם יִרְגָּ֑זוּ וַיִּֽתְגָּעֲשׁ֖וּ כִּי־חָ֥רָה לֽוֹ׃ ⁹ עָלָ֤ה עָשָׁן֙ בְּאַפּ֔וֹ וְאֵ֥שׁ מִפִּ֖יו תֹּאכֵ֑ל גֶּחָלִ֖ים בָּעֲר֥וּ מִמֶּֽנּוּ׃ ¹⁰ וַיֵּ֥ט שָׁמַ֖יִם וַיֵּרַ֑ד וַעֲרָפֶ֖ל תַּ֥חַת רַגְלָֽיו׃ ¹¹ וַיִּרְכַּ֥ב עַל־כְּר֖וּב וַיָּעֹ֑ף וַיֵּרָ֖א עַל־כַּנְפֵי־רֽוּחַ׃ ¹² וַיָּ֥שֶׁת חֹ֛שֶׁךְ סְבִיבֹתָ֖יו סֻכּ֑וֹת חַֽשְׁרַת־מַ֖יִם עָבֵ֥י שְׁחָקִֽים׃ ¹³ מִנֹּ֖גַהּ נֶגְדּ֑וֹ בָּעֲר֖וּ גַּֽחֲלֵי־אֵֽשׁ׃ ¹⁴ יַרְעֵ֥ם מִן־שָׁמַ֖יִם יְהֹוָ֑ה וְעֶלְי֖וֹן יִתֵּ֥ן קוֹלֽוֹ׃ ¹⁵ וַיִּשְׁלַ֥ח חִצִּ֖ים וַיְפִיצֵ֑ם בָּרָ֖ק [וַיְהֻמֵּם כ׳] וַיָּהֹֽם׃ ¹⁶ וַיֵּֽרָאוּ֙ אֲפִ֣קֵי יָ֔ם יִגָּל֖וּ מֹסְד֣וֹת תֵּבֵ֑ל בְּגַעֲרַ֣ת יְהֹוָ֔ה מִנִּשְׁמַ֖ת ר֥וּחַ אַפּֽוֹ׃ ¹⁷ יִשְׁלַ֥ח מִמָּר֖וֹם יִקָּחֵ֑נִי יַֽמְשֵׁ֖נִי מִמַּ֥יִם רַבִּֽים׃ ¹⁸ יַצִּילֵ֕נִי מֵאֹיְבִ֖י עָ֑ז מִשֹּׂ֣נְאַ֔י כִּ֥י אָמְצ֖וּ מִמֶּֽנִּי׃ ¹⁹ יְקַדְּמֻ֖נִי בְּי֣וֹם אֵידִ֑י וַיְהִ֧י יְהֹוָ֛ה מִשְׁעָ֖ן לִֽי׃ ²⁰ וַיֹּצֵ֥א לַמֶּרְחָ֖ב אֹתִ֑י יְחַלְּצֵ֖נִי כִּי־חָ֥פֵֽץ בִּֽי׃ ²¹ יִגְמְלֵ֥נִי יְהֹוָ֖ה כְּצִדְקָתִ֑י כְּבֹ֥ר יָדַ֖י יָשִׁ֥יב לִֽי׃ ²² כִּ֥י שָׁמַ֖רְתִּי דַּרְכֵ֣י יְהֹוָ֑ה וְלֹ֥א רָשַׁ֖עְתִּי מֵאֱלֹהָֽי׃ ²³ כִּ֥י כׇל־מִשְׁפָּטָ֖ו לְנֶגְדִּ֑י וְחֻקֹּתָ֖יו לֹא־אָס֥וּר מִמֶּֽנָּה׃ ²⁴ וָאֶהְיֶ֥ה תָמִ֖ים ל֑וֹ וָאֶשְׁתַּמְּרָ֖ה מֵעֲוֺנִֽי׃ ²⁵ וַיָּ֧שֶׁב יְהֹוָ֛ה לִ֖י כְּצִדְקָתִ֑י כְּבֹרִ֖י לְנֶ֥גֶד עֵינָֽיו׃ ²⁶ עִם־חָסִ֖יד תִּתְחַסָּ֑ד עִם־גִּבּ֥וֹר תָּמִ֖ים תִּתַּמָּֽם׃ ²⁷ עִם־נָבָ֖ר תִּתָּבָ֑ר וְעִם־עִקֵּ֖שׁ תִּתַּפָּֽל׃ ²⁸ וְאֶת־עַ֥ם

הפטרת האזינו

עָנִי תּוֹשִׁיעַ וְעֵינֶיךָ עַל־רָמִים תַּשְׁפִּיל: 29 כִּי־אַתָּה נֵירִי יְהֹוָה וַיהֹוָה יַגִּיהַּ חָשְׁכִּי: 30 כִּי בְכָה אָרוּץ גְּדוּד בֵּאלֹהַי אֲדַלֶּג־שׁוּר: 31 הָאֵל תָּמִים דַּרְכּוֹ אִמְרַת יְהֹוָה צְרוּפָה מָגֵן הוּא לְכֹל הַחֹסִים בּוֹ: 32 כִּי מִי־אֵל מִבַּלְעֲדֵי יְהֹוָה וּמִי צוּר מִבַּלְעֲדֵי אֱלֹהֵינוּ: 33 הָאֵל מָעוּזִּי חָיִל וַיַּתֵּר תָּמִים [דרכו כ׳] דַּרְכִּי: 34 מְשַׁוֶּה [רגליו כ׳] רַגְלַי כָּאַיָּלוֹת וְעַל־בָּמֹתַי יַעֲמִדֵנִי: 35 מְלַמֵּד יָדַי לַמִּלְחָמָה וְנִחַת קֶשֶׁת־נְחוּשָׁה זְרֹעֹתָי: 36 וַתִּתֶּן־לִי מָגֵן יִשְׁעֶךָ וַעֲנֹתְךָ תַּרְבֵּנִי: 37 תַּרְחִיב צַעֲדִי תַּחְתֵּנִי וְלֹא מָעֲדוּ קַרְסֻלָּי: 38 אֶרְדְּפָה אֹיְבַי וָאַשְׁמִידֵם וְלֹא אָשׁוּב עַד־כַּלּוֹתָם: 39 וָאֲכַלֵּם וָאֶמְחָצֵם וְלֹא יְקוּמוּן וַיִּפְּלוּ תַּחַת רַגְלָי: 40 וַתַּזְרֵנִי חַיִל לַמִּלְחָמָה תַּכְרִיעַ קָמַי תַּחְתֵּנִי: 41 וְאֹיְבַי תַּתָּה לִּי עֹרֶף מְשַׂנְאַי וָאַצְמִיתֵם: 42 יִשְׁעוּ וְאֵין מֹשִׁיעַ אֶל־יְהֹוָה וְלֹא עָנָם: 43 וְאֶשְׁחָקֵם כַּעֲפַר־אָרֶץ כְּטִיט־חוּצוֹת אֲדִקֵּם אֶרְקָעֵם: 44 וַתְּפַלְּטֵנִי מֵרִיבֵי עַמִּי תִּשְׁמְרֵנִי לְרֹאשׁ גּוֹיִם עַם לֹא־יָדַעְתִּי יַעַבְדֻנִי: 45 בְּנֵי נֵכָר יִתְכַּחֲשׁוּ־לִי לִשְׁמוֹעַ אֹזֶן יִשָּׁמְעוּ לִי: 46 בְּנֵי נֵכָר יִבֹּלוּ וְיַחְגְּרוּ מִמִּסְגְּרוֹתָם: 47 חַי־יְהֹוָה וּבָרוּךְ צוּרִי וְיָרֻם אֱלֹהֵי צוּר יִשְׁעִי: 48 הָאֵל הַנֹּתֵן נְקָמֹת לִי וּמוֹרִיד עַמִּים תַּחְתֵּנִי: 49 וּמוֹצִיאִי מֵאֹיְבָי וּמִקָּמַי תְּרוֹמְמֵנִי מֵאִישׁ חֲמָסִים תַּצִּילֵנִי: 50 עַל־כֵּן אוֹדְךָ יְהֹוָה בַּגּוֹיִם וּלְשִׁמְךָ אֲזַמֵּר: 51 [מגדיל כ׳] מִגְדּוֹל יְשׁוּעוֹת מַלְכּוֹ וְעֹשֶׂה־חֶסֶד לִמְשִׁיחוֹ לְדָוִד וּלְזַרְעוֹ עַד־עוֹלָם:

---

²⁹ You are my lamp, O God! God lights my darkness! ³⁰ For with your help I can run through a troop of the enemy. With my God I can jump on a wall to conquer cities. ³¹ God's way of justice is perfect. God's word is refined, He is a shield to all who trust in Him. ³² For who has any power against God to stop Him carrying out His word? Who is a rock but our God? ³³ God is my strength and power. He springs me onto my path of perfection. ³⁴ He makes my legs straight like a doe's, He stands me on the high places. ³⁵ He teaches my hands to fight, and He gives my arms the strength to break a copper bow. ³⁶ You grant me the shield of Your protection, and Your humility in caring for me made me powerful like a large number of people. ³⁷ You have broadened my step, so my feet have not slipped. ³⁸ I pursue my enemies and destroy them, not turning back until I annihilate them. ³⁹ I annihilate them and strike them so they rise no more, and they fall beneath my feet. ⁴⁰ You gird me with strength for battle, and cause my attackers to fall before me. ⁴¹ You made my enemies and foes turn around before me, but I still chased them and destroyed them. ⁴² They turned for help, but there was no one to save them. They turned to God, but He did not answer.

⁴³ I ground them like dust of the earth, I pulverized and crushed them like the mud of the streets. ⁴⁴ You saved me from the enemy from among my own people, You protected me from among them all until I became the head of nations, and now even a people unfamiliar to me serves me. ⁴⁵ Foreigners desperately lie to me out of fear, but because of what they heard about me, they listened to me. ⁴⁶ Foreigners wither, and become lame from their confinement that I decree on them.

⁴⁷ God lives! May my Rock be blessed! My exalted God is the Rock of my salvation. ⁴⁸ The God, who avenges on my behalf, who subdues nations before me, ⁴⁹ who saves me from my enemies, who lifts me above my attackers, who rescues me from corrupt men! ⁵⁰ Therefore, for these acts of kindness I will *thank God and publicize His acts among the nations* and sing to Your name. ⁵¹ He granted His king great victories, and He has acted kindly to His anointed one. As He did to David, so may He do to his descendants forever!

haftarat shabbat erev rosh ḥodesh

haftarat shabbat erev rosh ḥodesh

ALL COMMUNITIES—I SAMUEL 20:18–42

> **SYNOPSIS:** This *Haftarah* mentions the eve of *Rosh Ḥodesh*: "Tomorrow is the (first of the) new month" (20:18).
>
> The *Haftarah* describes a climactic moment in the rift between David and Saul, which arose from David's successful military career. Saul, who was king at the time, perceives David as a rebel who needs to be eliminated. Fearing for his life, David seeks the assistance of Jonathan, the king's son, who was David's passionate admirer, but Jonathan finds the conspiracy theory difficult to believe. In order to verify his suspicions, David suggests a plan: he will disappear for three days to test the king's reaction, which would then be reported to David by Jonathan with a secret sign.
>
> The *Haftarah* opens as Jonathan reviews David's plan and confirms a secret sign to be enacted by shooting arrows and instructing certain phrases to his servant (20:18–23). Initially, the king appears indifferent to David's absence (24–28), but on the second day he becomes furious with Jonathan and states that David "deserves death" (29–34). So, the next morning, Jonathan goes out to the field, communicates their pre-arranged sign by shooting arrows, and sends his servant home (35–40). David then comes out of hiding, and they part amid tears, swearing an oath *"between my descendants and your descendants forever"* (41–42).

20 [18] Jonathan said to David, "Tomorrow is the first of the new month. You shall be missed, because your seat will be empty. [19] For three days you should go down and hide yourself well. Come to the place where you hid on the day of the incident when the king swore to me not to kill you, and sit by the traveler's marker stone.

[20] "I will shoot three arrows to the side, as though I shot at a target. [21] Then I will send a lad saying to him, 'Go, find the arrows.' If I say to the lad, 'Look!—the arrows are on this side of you,' then you should take them and return, for it is safe for you, and there is no dangerous thing looming. I swear this as God lives.

[22] "But if I say this to the young man, 'Behold, the arrows are beyond you,' then go, because God has sent you.

[23] "This matter of which you and I have spoken, behold!—God is a witness between me and you forever."

[24] David hid himself in the field. When the first

18 וַיֹּאמֶר־לוֹ יְהוֹנָתָן מָחָר חֹדֶשׁ וְנִפְקַדְתָּ כִּי יִפָּקֵד מוֹשָׁבֶךָ: 19 וְשִׁלַּשְׁתָּ תֵּרֵד מְאֹד וּבָאתָ אֶל־הַמָּקוֹם אֲשֶׁר־נִסְתַּרְתָּ שָּׁם בְּיוֹם הַמַּעֲשֶׂה וְיָשַׁבְתָּ אֵצֶל הָאֶבֶן הָאָזֶל: 20 וַאֲנִי שְׁלֹשֶׁת הַחִצִּים צִדָּה אוֹרֶה לְשַׁלַּח־לִי לְמַטָּרָה: 21 וְהִנֵּה אֶשְׁלַח אֶת־הַנַּעַר לֵךְ מְצָא אֶת־הַחִצִּים אִם־אָמֹר אֹמַר לַנַּעַר הִנֵּה הַחִצִּים | מִמְּךָ וָהֵנָּה קָחֶנּוּ | וָבֹאָה כִּי־שָׁלוֹם לְךָ וְאֵין דָּבָר חַי־יְהֹוָה: 22 וְאִם־כֹּה אֹמַר לָעֶלֶם הִנֵּה הַחִצִּים מִמְּךָ וָהָלְאָה לֵךְ כִּי שִׁלַּחֲךָ יְהֹוָה: 23 וְהַדָּבָר אֲשֶׁר דִּבַּרְנוּ אֲנִי וָאָתָּה הִנֵּה יְהֹוָה בֵּינִי וּבֵינְךָ עַד־עוֹלָם: 24 וַיִּסָּתֵר דָּוִד

הפטרת שבת ערב ראש חודש

בַּשָּׂדֶה וַיְהִי הַחֹדֶשׁ וַיֵּשֶׁב הַמֶּלֶךְ [על כ׳] אֶל־הַלֶּחֶם לֶאֱכוֹל: 25 וַיֵּשֶׁב הַמֶּלֶךְ עַל־מוֹשָׁבוֹ כְּפַעַם ׀ בְּפַעַם אֶל־מוֹשַׁב הַקִּיר וַיָּקָם יְהוֹנָתָן וַיֵּשֶׁב אַבְנֵר מִצַּד שָׁאוּל וַיִּפָּקֵד מְקוֹם דָּוִד: 26 וְלֹא־דִבֶּר שָׁאוּל מְאוּמָה בַּיּוֹם הַהוּא כִּי אָמַר מִקְרֶה הוּא בִּלְתִּי טָהוֹר הוּא כִּי־לֹא טָהוֹר: 27 וַיְהִי מִמָּחֳרַת הַחֹדֶשׁ הַשֵּׁנִי וַיִּפָּקֵד מְקוֹם דָּוִד וַיֹּאמֶר שָׁאוּל אֶל־יְהוֹנָתָן בְּנוֹ מַדּוּעַ לֹא־בָא בֶן־יִשַׁי גַּם־תְּמוֹל גַּם־הַיּוֹם אֶל־הַלָּחֶם: 28 וַיַּעַן יְהוֹנָתָן אֶת־שָׁאוּל נִשְׁאֹל נִשְׁאַל דָּוִד מֵעִמָּדִי עַד־בֵּית לָחֶם: 29 וַיֹּאמֶר שַׁלְּחֵנִי נָא כִּי זֶבַח מִשְׁפָּחָה לָנוּ בָּעִיר וְהוּא צִוָּה־לִי אָחִי וְעַתָּה אִם־מָצָאתִי חֵן בְּעֵינֶיךָ אִמָּלְטָה נָּא וְאֶרְאֶה אֶת־אֶחָי עַל־כֵּן לֹא־בָא אֶל־שֻׁלְחַן הַמֶּלֶךְ: 30 וַיִּחַר־אַף שָׁאוּל בִּיהוֹנָתָן וַיֹּאמֶר לוֹ בֶּן־נַעֲוַת הַמַּרְדּוּת הֲלוֹא יָדַעְתִּי כִּי־בֹחֵר אַתָּה לְבֶן־יִשַׁי לְבָשְׁתְּךָ וּלְבֹשֶׁת עֶרְוַת אִמֶּךָ: 31 כִּי כָל־הַיָּמִים אֲשֶׁר בֶּן־יִשַׁי חַי עַל־הָאֲדָמָה לֹא תִכּוֹן אַתָּה וּמַלְכוּתֶךָ וְעַתָּה שְׁלַח וְקַח אֹתוֹ אֵלַי כִּי בֶן־מָוֶת הוּא: 32 וַיַּעַן יְהוֹנָתָן אֶת־שָׁאוּל אָבִיו וַיֹּאמֶר אֵלָיו לָמָּה יוּמַת מֶה עָשָׂה: 33 וַיָּטֶל שָׁאוּל אֶת־הַחֲנִית עָלָיו לְהַכֹּתוֹ וַיֵּדַע יְהוֹנָתָן כִּי־כָלָה הִיא מֵעִם אָבִיו לְהָמִית אֶת־דָּוִד: 34 וַיָּקָם יְהוֹנָתָן מֵעִם הַשֻּׁלְחָן בָּחֳרִי־אָף וְלֹא־אָכַל בְּיוֹם־הַחֹדֶשׁ הַשֵּׁנִי לֶחֶם כִּי נֶעְצַב אֶל־דָּוִד כִּי הִכְלִמוֹ אָבִיו: 35 וַיְהִי בַבֹּקֶר וַיֵּצֵא יְהוֹנָתָן הַשָּׂדֶה לְמוֹעֵד דָּוִד וְנַעַר קָטֹן עִמּוֹ: 36 וַיֹּאמֶר לְנַעֲרוֹ רֻץ מְצָא־נָא אֶת־הַחִצִּים אֲשֶׁר אָנֹכִי מוֹרֶה הַנַּעַר רָץ וְהוּא־יָרָה הַחֵצִי לְהַעֲבִרוֹ: 37 וַיָּבֹא הַנַּעַר עַד־מְקוֹם הַחֵצִי אֲשֶׁר יָרָה יְהוֹנָתָן

---

of the new month came, the king sat down to eat the meal. [25] The king sat at his seat, as usual, on a seat by the wall. Jonathan stood up so that Abner could sit at Saul's side. David's place was empty. [26] Nevertheless Saul said nothing on that day, for he thought, "He had a nocturnal accident. He is not ritually pure. He didn't come because he has not been ritually purified."

[27] It came to pass on the next day, which was the second day of the month, that David's place was empty. Saul said to his son Jonathan, "Why didn't the son of Jesse come to the meal, neither yesterday, nor today?"

[28] Jonathan answered Saul, "David asked me permission to go to Bethlehem. [29] He said, 'Please let me go, because our family is offering sacrifices today in the city and my oldest brother Eliab has instructed me to be there. Now, if I have found favor in your eyes, please excuse me from the king's duties to see my brothers.' Therefore he has not come to the king's table."

[30] Saul became furious with Jonathan, and he said to him, "You are the son of a sinful and rebellious woman! Do I not know that you have chosen the son of Jesse for the monarchy to your own shame, and to the shame of your mother's nakedness, for the fact that you prefer that my enemy will lead people to suspect that you are not my son? [31] For as long as the son of Jesse lives on the earth, you shall not be established, nor your kingdom. Now since you sent him away, send for him and fetch him to me, for he deserves death."

[32] Jonathan answered Saul, his father, and said to him, "Why should he be killed? What has he done?"

[33] Saul raised a spear to strike him. Jonathan realized that his father was determined to slay David.

[34] Jonathan rose from the table in fierce anger. He ate no food on the second day of the new moon, for he was upset for David, and his father had put him to shame by insulting and threatening him.

[35] In the morning, Jonathan went out to the field to the appointed place that he had arranged with David, and a young lad was with him. [36] He said to his lad, "Run! Find now the arrows which I shoot." As the lad ran for the first arrow, he shot an arrow beyond him.

[37] When the lad came to the place of the first arrow which Jonathan had shot, Jonathan called

haftarat shabbat rosh ḥodesh

out after the lad and said, "Isn't the last arrow beyond you?"

³⁸ Jonathan called out after the lad, "Go quickly! Hurry after the second arrow. Don't stay by the first!"

Jonathan's lad gathered up both the arrows, and came to his master. ³⁹ The lad knew nothing about the sign. Only Jonathan and David knew the matter.

⁴⁰ Jonathan gave his bow and arrows to his lad, and said to him, "Go and carry them to the city." ⁴¹ As soon as the lad had gone towards the city, David understood that it was safe and stood up from near the south side of the stone. He fell on his face to the ground, and prostrated himself three times. They kissed one another, and wept with one another, until David wept greatly more than Jonathan.

⁴² Jonathan said to David, "Go in peace, as both of us have sworn in the name of God, saying, 'God be a witness between me and you, and between my descendants and your descendants forever.'"

וַיִּקְרָא יְהוֹנָתָן אַחֲרֵי הַנַּעַר וַיֹּאמֶר הֲלוֹא הַחֵצִי מִמְּךָ וָהָלְאָה: 38 וַיִּקְרָא יְהוֹנָתָן אַחֲרֵי הַנַּעַר מְהֵרָה חוּשָׁה אַל־תַּעֲמֹד וַיְלַקֵּט נַעַר יְהוֹנָתָן אֶת־[החצי כ'] הַחִצִּים וַיָּבֹא אֶל־אֲדֹנָיו: 39 וְהַנַּעַר לֹא־יָדַע מְאוּמָה אַךְ יְהוֹנָתָן וְדָוִד יָדְעוּ אֶת־הַדָּבָר: 40 וַיִּתֵּן יְהוֹנָתָן אֶת־כֵּלָיו אֶל־הַנַּעַר אֲשֶׁר־לוֹ וַיֹּאמֶר לוֹ לֵךְ הָבֵיא הָעִיר: 41 הַנַּעַר בָּא וְדָוִד קָם מֵאֵצֶל הַנֶּגֶב וַיִּפֹּל לְאַפָּיו אַרְצָה וַיִּשְׁתַּחוּ שָׁלֹשׁ פְּעָמִים וַיִּשְּׁקוּ ׀ אִישׁ אֶת־רֵעֵהוּ וַיִּבְכּוּ אִישׁ אֶת־רֵעֵהוּ עַד־דָּוִד הִגְדִּיל: 42 וַיֹּאמֶר יְהוֹנָתָן לְדָוִד לֵךְ לְשָׁלוֹם אֲשֶׁר נִשְׁבַּעְנוּ שְׁנֵינוּ אֲנַחְנוּ בְּשֵׁם יְהֹוָה לֵאמֹר יְהֹוָה יִהְיֶה ׀ בֵּינִי וּבֵינֶךָ וּבֵין זַרְעִי וּבֵין זַרְעֲךָ עַד־עוֹלָם:

haftarat shabbat rosh ḥodesh

Maftir—Numbers 28:9–15 (p. 1000)

ALL COMMUNITIES—Isaiah 66:1–24; 23

SYNOPSIS: This *Haftarah* mentions the sacrificial worship that will occur every new month (*Rosh Ḥodesh*) after the ingathering of the exiles. The *Haftarah* was addressed by the prophet Isaiah to the Jewish people in Babylon after the exile, at the end of the 6th century B.C.E.

The *Haftarah* opens with God's proclamation of omnipresence and the insufficiency of one House to contain Him (66:1). God will turn His attention to those who fear Him (2), and all types of insincere worship are abhorred by Him (3–4). Those who fear God will ultimately be joyous, but those who hate and ostracize God's servants will be chastised by a "voice from the Temple" (5–6). Zion's deliverance is compared to that of a mother who gives birth without pain (7–9), and the rejoicing at Jerusalem's rebuilding is depicted (10–14). All enemies and idol-worshipers will be punished (15–18) and the nations that remain will come to Zion, bringing the Jewish people along with them (19–20). New priests will be appointed, and all mankind will worship God (21–23). The rebels' corpses will remain in the valley of Jehoshaphat as an ominous reminder to all mankind (24; verse 23 is then repeated so as to finish on a positive note).

הפטרת שבת ראש חודש

סו ¹ כֹּה אָמַר יְהֹוָה הַשָּׁמַיִם כִּסְאִ֔י וְהָאָ֖רֶץ הֲדֹ֣ם רַגְלָ֑י אֵי־זֶ֥ה בַ֙יִת֙ אֲשֶׁ֣ר תִּבְנוּ־לִ֔י וְאֵי־זֶ֥ה מָק֖וֹם מְנוּחָתִֽי: ² וְאֶת־כָּל־אֵ֙לֶּה֙ יָדִ֣י עָשָׂ֔תָה וַיִּהְי֥וּ כָל־אֵ֖לֶּה נְאֻם־יְהֹוָ֑ה וְאֶל־זֶ֣ה אַבִּ֔יט אֶל־עָנִי֙ וּנְכֵה־ר֔וּחַ וְחָרֵ֖ד עַל־דְּבָרִֽי: ³ שׁוֹחֵ֨ט הַשּׁ֜וֹר מַכֵּה־אִ֗ישׁ זוֹבֵ֤חַ הַשֶּׂה֙ עֹ֣רֵֽף כֶּ֔לֶב מַעֲלֵ֤ה מִנְחָה֙ דַּם־חֲזִ֔יר מַזְכִּ֥יר לְבֹנָ֖ה מְבָ֣רֵֽךְ אָ֑וֶן גַּם־הֵ֗מָּה בָּֽחֲרוּ֙ בְּדַרְכֵיהֶ֔ם וּבְשִׁקּוּצֵיהֶ֖ם נַפְשָׁ֥ם חָפֵֽצָה: ⁴ גַּם־אֲנִ֞י אֶבְחַ֣ר בְּתַעֲלֻֽלֵיהֶ֗ם וּמְגֽוּרֹתָם֙ אָבִ֣יא לָהֶ֔ם יַ֤עַן קָרָ֙אתִי֙ וְאֵ֣ין עוֹנֶ֔ה דִּבַּ֖רְתִּי וְלֹ֣א שָׁמֵ֑עוּ וַיַּעֲשׂ֤וּ הָרַע֙ בְּעֵינַ֔י וּבַאֲשֶׁ֥ר לֹֽא־חָפַ֖צְתִּי בָּחָֽרוּ: ⁵ שִׁמְעוּ֙ דְּבַר־יְהֹוָ֔ה הַחֲרֵדִ֖ים אֶל־דְּבָר֑וֹ אָמְרוּ֩ אֲחֵיכֶ֨ם שֹׂנְאֵיכֶ֜ם מְנַדֵּיכֶ֗ם לְמַ֤עַן שְׁמִי֙ יִכְבַּ֣ד יְהֹוָ֔ה וְנִרְאֶ֥ה בְשִׂמְחַתְכֶ֖ם וְהֵ֥ם יֵבֹֽשׁוּ: ⁶ ק֤וֹל שָׁאוֹן֙ מֵעִ֔יר ק֖וֹל מֵֽהֵיכָ֑ל ק֣וֹל יְהֹוָ֔ה מְשַׁלֵּ֥ם גְּמ֖וּל לְאֹיְבָֽיו: ⁷ בְּטֶ֥רֶם תָּחִ֖יל יָלָ֑דָה בְּטֶ֨רֶם יָב֥וֹא חֵ֛בֶל לָ֖הּ וְהִמְלִ֥יטָה זָכָֽר: ⁸ מִֽי־שָׁמַ֣ע כָּזֹ֗את מִ֤י רָאָה֙ כָּאֵ֔לֶּה הֲי֤וּחַל אֶ֙רֶץ֙ בְּי֣וֹם אֶחָ֔ד אִם־יִוָּ֥לֵֽד גּ֖וֹי פַּ֣עַם אֶחָ֑ת כִּֽי־חָ֛לָה גַּם־יָלְדָ֥ה צִיּ֖וֹן אֶת־בָּנֶֽיהָ: ⁹ הַאֲנִ֥י אַשְׁבִּ֛יר וְלֹ֥א אוֹלִ֖יד יֹאמַ֣ר יְהֹוָ֑ה אִם־אֲנִ֧י הַמּוֹלִ֛יד וְעָצַ֖רְתִּי אָמַ֥ר אֱלֹהָֽיִךְ: ¹⁰ שִׂמְח֧וּ אֶת־יְרוּשָׁלִַ֛ם וְגִ֥ילוּ בָ֖הּ כָּל־אֹהֲבֶ֑יהָ שִׂ֤ישׂוּ אִתָּהּ֙ מָשׂ֔וֹשׂ כָּל־הַמִּֽתְאַבְּלִ֖ים עָלֶֽיהָ: ¹¹ לְמַ֤עַן תִּֽינְקוּ֙ וּשְׂבַעְתֶּ֔ם מִשֹּׁ֖ד תַּנְחֻמֶ֑יהָ לְמַ֧עַן תָּמֹ֛צּוּ וְהִתְעַנַּגְתֶּ֖ם מִזִּ֥יז כְּבוֹדָֽהּ: ¹² כִּי־כֹ֣ה ׀ אָמַ֣ר יְהֹוָ֗ה הִנְנִ֥י נֹטֶֽה־אֵ֠לֶ֠יהָ כְּנָהָ֨ר שָׁל֜וֹם וּכְנַ֧חַל שׁוֹטֵ֛ף כְּב֥וֹד גּוֹיִ֖ם וִֽינַקְתֶּ֑ם עַל־צַ֣ד

66 ¹ This is what God said: "The heaven is My throne, and the earth is My footstool, so what house could you build worthy for Me, and what place is worthy for My Presence to rest? ² My hand has made all these things, and therefore all these things came into being," says God. "But even though I am so exalted, to this I will pay attention: to he who is poor and of a contrite spirit, and trembles at My word. ³ "However, he who kills an ox, offering his sacrifice without trembling at My word, it is as if he slew a man. He who sacrifices a lamb without trembling, is as if he cut off a dog's neck. He who offers a meal-offering without trembling is as if he offered swine's blood. He who burns incense without trembling is as if he blessed an idol. He who offers up frankincense without trembling is as if he offered an inappropriate gift. They have chosen their own ways, and their soul delights in their abominations. ⁴ So too will I choose to mock them, and will bring their fears upon them, because when I called to them through the prophets, none answered. When I spoke, they did not listen. They did evil before My eyes, and chose what I did not desire.

⁵ "Hear the word of God, you who tremble at His word! Your wicked brothers who hate you and who ostracize you say, 'I am so great that God is glorified because of my name!' But in truth we shall see your joy and they shall be shamed. ⁶ Then there will be a voice of rumbling from the city of Zion, a voice from the Temple, the voice of God rendering recompense to his enemies Gog and Magog.

⁷ "Before she feels labor pains, she will give birth. Before her labor pain will come, she will be delivered a son. ⁸ Who has heard such a thing? Who has seen such a thing? Has a land gone through its labor in one day? Has a nation been born all at once, for Zion labored and gave birth to her children? ⁹ Shall I bring to the birthstool, and not cause her to give birth?" says God. "Shall I, who cause birth, hold back?" says your God.

¹⁰ Rejoice with Jerusalem, and be glad with her, all you who love her to see her rebuilt. Rejoice for joy with her, all you who mourn for her in her destruction, ¹¹ so that you may be rewarded to nurse, and be satisfied with the breasts of her consolations. That you may drink deeply, and be delighted with the abundance of her glory. ¹² For this is what God says: "Behold, I will extend peace to her like a river, and the wealth of the nations will rush to her like a flowing stream. You who mourned for her shall be rewarded

haftarat shabbat rosh ḥodesh

to draw effortlessly from the wealth of the nations. You shall be honored by the nations, like a baby who is carried on its mother's sides, and dandled on her knees. ¹³ Like one whom his mother comforts, so will I comfort you, and you shall be comforted in Jerusalem for your suffering. ¹⁴ When you see Jerusalem rebuilt, your heart will rejoice, and the health of your bones will be strengthened like flourishing grass. The mighty hand of God will be known to His servants, and His anger toward His enemies.

¹⁵ "For, behold, God will come with fire to destroy the armies of Gog and Magog, and with His chariots like a storm to repay His enemies with fury. His rebuke will be with flames of fire. ¹⁶ For by fire God will execute judgment, and by His sword upon all flesh. The slain by God will be many.

¹⁷ "Those who prepare and purify themselves to go to the gardens of idolatry, one group after another to worship the idol in the center of the garden; those who eat swine's flesh, abominable creatures, and mice — they will all perish together," says God. ¹⁸ "I know their works and their thoughts. The time has come, that I will gather all nations and tongues, and they shall come and see My glory. ¹⁹ I will scar them, but from them I will let survivors escape to the nations, to Tarshish, Pul, and Lud, the archers, to Tubal, and Javan, to far-off islands, that have not heard My fame, nor have they seen My glory. They shall declare My glory among the nations. ²⁰ They will then bring all your brothers from all nations as an offering to God, on horses, in chariots, in covered wagons, on mules and with songs and dances to My holy mountain in Jerusalem," says God, "just as respectfully as the people of Israel bring an offering in a pure utensil to the House of God.

²¹ "From them too I will take to be priests and Levites even though they will have forgotten their lineage," says God. ²² "For just as the new heavens and the new earth, which I will make in those days, shall remain before Me," says God, "so shall your descendants and your name remain forever."

²³ "It will then be, that every first of the new month, and every Sabbath, all mankind shall come to worship before Me in the Holy Temple," says God. ²⁴ "The non-Jews shall go out of Jerusalem, to the valley of Jehoshaphat, and look upon the corpses of the men of Gog and Magog who have rebelled against Me, for

תִּנָּשֵׂאוּ וְעַל־בִּרְכַּיִם תְּשָׁעֳשָׁעוּ: 13 כְּאִישׁ אֲשֶׁר אִמּוֹ תְּנַחֲמֶנּוּ כֵּן אָנֹכִי אֲנַחֶמְכֶם וּבִירוּשָׁלַ͏ִם תְּנֻחָמוּ: 14 וּרְאִיתֶם וְשָׂשׂ לִבְּכֶם וְעַצְמוֹתֵיכֶם כַּדֶּשֶׁא תִפְרַחְנָה וְנוֹדְעָה יַד־יְהֹוָה אֶת־עֲבָדָיו וְזָעַם אֶת־אֹיְבָיו: 15 כִּי־הִנֵּה יְהֹוָה בָּאֵשׁ יָבוֹא וְכַסּוּפָה מַרְכְּבֹתָיו לְהָשִׁיב בְּחֵמָה אַפּוֹ וְגַעֲרָתוֹ בְּלַהֲבֵי־אֵשׁ: 16 כִּי בָאֵשׁ יְהֹוָה נִשְׁפָּט וּבְחַרְבּוֹ אֶת־כָּל־בָּשָׂר וְרַבּוּ חַלְלֵי יְהֹוָה: 17 הַמִּתְקַדְּשִׁים וְהַמִּטַּהֲרִים אֶל־הַגַּנּוֹת אַחַר [אחד כ׳] אַחַת בַּתָּוֶךְ אֹכְלֵי בְּשַׂר הַחֲזִיר וְהַשֶּׁקֶץ וְהָעַכְבָּר יַחְדָּו יָסֻפוּ נְאֻם־יְהֹוָה: 18 וְאָנֹכִי מַעֲשֵׂיהֶם וּמַחְשְׁבֹתֵיהֶם בָּאָה לְקַבֵּץ אֶת־כָּל־הַגּוֹיִם וְהַלְּשֹׁנוֹת וּבָאוּ וְרָאוּ אֶת־כְּבוֹדִי: 19 וְשַׂמְתִּי בָהֶם אוֹת וְשִׁלַּחְתִּי מֵהֶם ׀ פְּלֵיטִים אֶל־הַגּוֹיִם תַּרְשִׁישׁ פּוּל וְלוּד מֹשְׁכֵי קֶשֶׁת תֻּבַל וְיָוָן הָאִיִּים הָרְחֹקִים אֲשֶׁר לֹא־שָׁמְעוּ אֶת־שִׁמְעִי וְלֹא־רָאוּ אֶת־כְּבוֹדִי וְהִגִּידוּ אֶת־כְּבוֹדִי בַּגּוֹיִם: 20 וְהֵבִיאוּ אֶת־כָּל־אֲחֵיכֶם ׀ מִכָּל־הַגּוֹיִם ׀ מִנְחָה ׀ לַיהֹוָה בַּסּוּסִים וּבָרֶכֶב וּבַצַּבִּים וּבַפְּרָדִים וּבַכִּרְכָּרוֹת עַל הַר קָדְשִׁי יְרוּשָׁלַ͏ִם אָמַר יְהֹוָה כַּאֲשֶׁר יָבִיאוּ בְנֵי יִשְׂרָאֵל אֶת־הַמִּנְחָה בִּכְלִי טָהוֹר בֵּית יְהֹוָה: 21 וְגַם־מֵהֶם אֶקַּח לַכֹּהֲנִים לַלְוִיִּם אָמַר יְהֹוָה: 22 כִּי כַאֲשֶׁר הַשָּׁמַיִם הַחֲדָשִׁים וְהָאָרֶץ הַחֲדָשָׁה אֲשֶׁר אֲנִי עֹשֶׂה עֹמְדִים לְפָנַי נְאֻם־יְהֹוָה כֵּן יַעֲמֹד זַרְעֲכֶם וְשִׁמְכֶם: 23 וְהָיָה מִדֵּי־חֹדֶשׁ בְּחָדְשׁוֹ וּמִדֵּי שַׁבָּת בְּשַׁבַּתּוֹ יָבוֹא כָל־בָּשָׂר לְהִשְׁתַּחֲוֺת לְפָנַי אָמַר יְהֹוָה: 24 וְיָצְאוּ וְרָאוּ בְּפִגְרֵי הָאֲנָשִׁים הַפֹּשְׁעִים בִּי כִּי תוֹלַעְתָּם לֹא

הפטרת שבת חנוכה (א)

the worms that eat them will not die, and the fire that burns them shall not be extinguished. They shall be a symbol of disgrace to all mankind.

²³ "It will then be, that every first of the new month, and every Sabbath, all mankind shall come to worship before Me in the Holy Temple," says God.

תָמוּתוּ וְאִשָּׁם לֹא תִכְבֶּה וְהָיוּ דֵרָאוֹן לְכָל־בָּשָׂר: 23 וְהָיָה מִדֵּי־חֹדֶשׁ בְּחָדְשׁוֹ וּמִדֵּי שַׁבָּת בְּשַׁבַּתּוֹ יָבוֹא כָל־בָּשָׂר לְהִשְׁתַּחֲוֹת לְפָנַי אָמַר יְהוָה:

If Sunday is *Rosh Ḥodesh*, Ḥabad communities add (*I Samuel* 20:18, 42):

20 ¹⁸ Jonathan said to him, "Tomorrow is the first of the new month. You shall be missed, because your seat will be empty."

⁴² Jonathan said to David, "Go in peace, as both of us have sworn in the name of God, saying, 'God be a witness between me and you, and between my descendants and your descendants forever.'"

כ 18 וַיֹּאמֶר־לוֹ יְהוֹנָתָן מָחָר חֹדֶשׁ וְנִפְקַדְתָּ כִּי יִפָּקֵד מוֹשָׁבֶךָ: 42 וַיֹּאמֶר יְהוֹנָתָן לְדָוִד לֵךְ לְשָׁלוֹם אֲשֶׁר נִשְׁבַּעְנוּ שְׁנֵינוּ אֲנַחְנוּ בְּשֵׁם יְהוָה לֵאמֹר יְהוָה יִהְיֶה ׀ בֵּינִי וּבֵינֶךָ וּבֵין זַרְעִי וּבֵין זַרְעֲךָ עַד־עוֹלָם:

haftarat ḥanukkah
first shabbat

ALL COMMUNITIES—ZECHARIAH 2:14 – 4:7

> **SYNOPSIS:** This *Haftarah* is read on the first Sabbath of *Hanukkah*, primarily due to its reference to the candelabrum.
>
> The *Haftarah* opens with words of comfort about the return of the Divine presence and restoration of the land (2:14–17). We then read the first of two visions depicted in the *Haftarah*, that of the "High Priest in soiled garments" who is condemned for his children's sins by the Satan, but vindicated by God's angel (3:1–5). This is followed by promises of a restored Temple and the coming of the Messiah (6–10). In the second vision, Zechariah sees the gold candelabrum, a metaphor for the Messiah's Divine spirit through which he will effortlessly subdue nations (4:1–7).

Maftir Readings for *Shabbat Ḥanukkah*: Day One—*Numbers* 7:1–17 (p. 840); Day Two—ibid. 18–23 (p. 844); Day Three—ibid. 24–29 (p. 844); Day Four—ibid. 30–35 (p. 844); Day Six—six *aliyyot* are read from the weekly *Parashah*, seventh *aliyah* is read from *Numbers* 28:9-15 (p. 1000) and *Maftir* is ibid. 7:42–47 (p. 846); Day Seven—ibid. 48–53 (p. 846).

2 ¹⁴ "Sing and rejoice, daughter of Zion, for I am coming to Jerusalem and I will dwell in your midst," says God. ¹⁵ "Many nations will attach themselves to God on that day, and they will become My people too and believe in Me, but nevertheless I will dwell only in your midst." Then you will know that the God of Hosts sent me only to you.

¹⁶ God will let Judah take possession of his position in the Holy Land, never to be exiled again, and

ב 14 רָנִּי וְשִׂמְחִי בַּת־צִיּוֹן כִּי הִנְנִי־בָא וְשָׁכַנְתִּי בְתוֹכֵךְ נְאֻם־יְהוָה: 15 וְנִלְווּ גוֹיִם רַבִּים אֶל־יְהוָה בַּיּוֹם הַהוּא וְהָיוּ לִי לְעָם וְשָׁכַנְתִּי בְתוֹכֵךְ וְיָדַעַתְּ כִּי־יְהוָה צְבָאוֹת שְׁלָחַנִי אֵלָיִךְ: 16 וְנָחַל יְהוָה אֶת־יְהוּדָה חֶלְקוֹ עַל אַדְמַת הַקֹּדֶשׁ וּבָחַר עוֹד

haftarat ḥanukkah (first shabbat)

God will once again choose Jerusalem to have His Presence dwell there. [17] Be silent before God, all you nations! Never again speak badly of the Jewish people, for then He will be roused from His holy abode to exact retribution on the nations.

3 [1] In the prophetic vision He then showed me Joshua the High Priest standing before God's angel, with Satan standing at Joshua's right to incriminate him for failing to rebuke his children when they married non-Jewish women.

[2] An angel of God said to Satan, "God will reprimand you, O Satan! He who chooses Jerusalem will reprimand you! Why, this Joshua was miraculously saved like a brand rescued from fire, so how can you prosecute him?"

[3] Now, Joshua was wearing "soiled clothes" while standing before the angel. [4] The angel spoke up loudly and said to the other angels standing before him, "Remove the 'soiled clothes'—the non-Jewish women—from his sons!"

He said to him, "See, I have taken away your past sins from you and when your current sins will cease you will see that I am clothing you in beautiful clothes."

[5] Then I prayed for Joshua, saying, "Let them place a pure priestly turban on his head signifying that his descendants would inherit the priesthood." My prayer was immediately answered and they placed the pure turban on his head and clothed him in garments, while God's angel stood by.

[6] Afterwards, God's angel warned Joshua, saying, [7] "This is what the God of Hosts said: 'If your children will walk in My paths and keep the things I told them to keep, then your children will be appointed to take charge of My house forever and guard My courtyard. So too in the spiritual world, I will reward you and your children and permit you to walk among those angels who stand there.'

[8] "Now listen Joshua, the High Priest! You and also your companions were saved from a fiery furnace who sit before you, for they are people worthy of miracles. Look! I will bring My servant Zemah—the Messiah.'

[9] "Here is the foundation stone of the Third Temple that I will place before Joshua's descendant, the High Priest, for him to place. There will be seven eyes guarding a single stone of the Temple, from Above. I will participate in the construction of the Temple by engraving inscriptions on its stones," says the God of Hosts, "and I will remove the sin of that land in one day. [10] On that day," says the God of Hosts, "you will

בִּירוּשָׁלָ͏ִם: 17 הַס כָּל־בָּשָׂר מִפְּנֵי יְהֹוָה כִּי נֵעוֹר מִמְּעוֹן קָדְשׁוֹ:

ג 1 וַיַּרְאֵנִי אֶת־יְהוֹשֻׁעַ הַכֹּהֵן הַגָּדוֹל עֹמֵד לִפְנֵי מַלְאַךְ יְהֹוָה וְהַשָּׂטָן עֹמֵד עַל־יְמִינוֹ לְשִׂטְנוֹ: 2 וַיֹּאמֶר יְהֹוָה אֶל־הַשָּׂטָן יִגְעַר יְהֹוָה בְּךָ הַשָּׂטָן וְיִגְעַר יְהֹוָה בְּךָ הַבֹּחֵר בִּירוּשָׁלָ͏ִם הֲלוֹא זֶה אוּד מֻצָּל מֵאֵשׁ: 3 וִיהוֹשֻׁעַ הָיָה לָבֻשׁ בְּגָדִים צוֹאִים וְעֹמֵד לִפְנֵי הַמַּלְאָךְ: 4 וַיַּעַן וַיֹּאמֶר אֶל־הָעֹמְדִים לְפָנָיו לֵאמֹר הָסִירוּ הַבְּגָדִים הַצֹּאִים מֵעָלָיו וַיֹּאמֶר אֵלָיו רְאֵה הֶעֱבַרְתִּי מֵעָלֶיךָ עֲוֹנֶךָ וְהַלְבֵּשׁ אֹתְךָ מַחֲלָצוֹת: 5 וָאֹמַר יָשִׂימוּ צָנִיף טָהוֹר עַל־רֹאשׁוֹ וַיָּשִׂימוּ הַצָּנִיף הַטָּהוֹר עַל־רֹאשׁוֹ וַיַּלְבִּשֻׁהוּ בְּגָדִים וּמַלְאַךְ יְהֹוָה עֹמֵד: 6 וַיָּעַד מַלְאַךְ יְהֹוָה בִּיהוֹשֻׁעַ לֵאמֹר: 7 כֹּה־אָמַר יְהֹוָה צְבָאוֹת אִם־בִּדְרָכַי תֵּלֵךְ וְאִם אֶת־מִשְׁמַרְתִּי תִשְׁמֹר וְגַם־אַתָּה תָּדִין אֶת־בֵּיתִי וְגַם תִּשְׁמֹר אֶת־חֲצֵרָי וְנָתַתִּי לְךָ מַהְלְכִים בֵּין הָעֹמְדִים הָאֵלֶּה: 8 שְׁמַע־נָא יְהוֹשֻׁעַ | הַכֹּהֵן הַגָּדוֹל אַתָּה וְרֵעֶיךָ הַיֹּשְׁבִים לְפָנֶיךָ כִּי־אַנְשֵׁי מוֹפֵת הֵמָּה כִּי־הִנְנִי מֵבִיא אֶת־עַבְדִּי צֶמַח: 9 כִּי | הִנֵּה הָאֶבֶן אֲשֶׁר נָתַתִּי לִפְנֵי יְהוֹשֻׁעַ עַל־אֶבֶן אַחַת שִׁבְעָה עֵינָיִם הִנְנִי מְפַתֵּחַ פִּתֻּחָהּ נְאֻם יְהֹוָה צְבָאוֹת וּמַשְׁתִּי אֶת־עֲוֹן הָאָרֶץ־הַהִיא בְּיוֹם אֶחָד: 10 בַּיּוֹם הַהוּא נְאֻם יְהֹוָה

הפטרת שבת חנוכה (א)

invite each other to come and take shade under the vines and under the fig trees to enjoy the bountiful goodness which will then exist."

4 [1] Then, the angel that spoke with me returned and roused me, like a man woken from his sleep.

[2] "What do you see in your prophetic vision?" he asked me.

I said, "I see a candelabrum made entirely of gold, with a bowl on its top containing oil. It has seven lamps, and each of these lamps that are on its top has seven pipes to carry the oil from the bowl. [3] Near it are two olive trees, one to the right of the bowl and one to its left."

[4] Then I spoke up and asked the angel that spoke with me, "My master, what are these alluding to?"

[5] "Don't you know what they are?" replied the angel that spoke with me.

"No, my master!" I said.

[6] Then he answered me as follows, "This is the word of God about the Messiah, a descendant of Zerubbabel: 'Not by his might, nor by his power will the nations become subservient to the Messiah, but rather it will be effortless, like the kindling of a candelabrum, through My spirit by which I will subdue the nations,' says the God of Hosts.

[7] "Who are you Gog and Magog to appear as a great mountain in Zerubbabel's path, when in truth you will be easily flattened. The Messiah will produce the precious stone, the foundation of the Temple, amid cheers of 'Beautiful stone! Beautiful stone!'"

צְבָאוֹת תִּקְרְאוּ אִישׁ לְרֵעֵהוּ אֶל־תַּחַת גֶּפֶן וְאֶל־תַּחַת תְּאֵנָה:

ד [1] וַיָּשָׁב הַמַּלְאָךְ הַדֹּבֵר בִּי וַיְעִירֵנִי כְּאִישׁ אֲשֶׁר־יֵעוֹר מִשְּׁנָתוֹ: [2] וַיֹּאמֶר אֵלַי מָה אַתָּה רֹאֶה [ויאמר כ׳] וָאֹמַר רָאִיתִי וְהִנֵּה מְנוֹרַת זָהָב כֻּלָּהּ וְגֻלָּהּ עַל־רֹאשָׁהּ וְשִׁבְעָה נֵרֹתֶיהָ עָלֶיהָ שִׁבְעָה וְשִׁבְעָה מוּצָקוֹת לַנֵּרוֹת אֲשֶׁר עַל־רֹאשָׁהּ: [3] וּשְׁנַיִם זֵיתִים עָלֶיהָ אֶחָד מִימִין הַגֻּלָּה וְאֶחָד עַל־שְׂמֹאלָהּ: [4] וָאַעַן וָאֹמַר אֶל־הַמַּלְאָךְ הַדֹּבֵר בִּי לֵאמֹר מָה־אֵלֶּה אֲדֹנִי: [5] וַיַּעַן הַמַּלְאָךְ הַדֹּבֵר בִּי וַיֹּאמֶר אֵלַי הֲלוֹא יָדַעְתָּ מָה־הֵמָּה אֵלֶּה וָאֹמַר לֹא אֲדֹנִי: [6] וַיַּעַן וַיֹּאמֶר אֵלַי לֵאמֹר זֶה דְּבַר־יְהֹוָה אֶל־זְרֻבָּבֶל לֵאמֹר לֹא בְחַיִל וְלֹא בְכֹחַ כִּי אִם־בְּרוּחִי אָמַר יְהֹוָה צְבָאוֹת: [7] מִי־אַתָּה הַר־הַגָּדוֹל לִפְנֵי זְרֻבָּבֶל לְמִישֹׁר וְהוֹצִיא אֶת־הָאֶבֶן הָרֹאשָׁה תְּשֻׁאוֹת חֵן חֵן לָהּ:

If Shabbat is Rosh Hodesh, Habad communities add the following (Isaiah 66:1, 23-24, 23; I Samuel 20:18; ibid. 42):

66 [1] This is what God said: "The heaven is My throne, and the earth is My footstool, so what house could you build worthy for Me, and what place is worthy for My Presence to rest? [23] It will then be, that every first of the new month, and every Sabbath, all mankind shall come to worship before Me in the Holy Temple," says God. [24] "The non-Jews shall go out of Jerusalem, to the valley of Jehoshaphat, and look upon the corpses of the men of Gog and Magog who have rebelled against Me, for the worms that eat them shall not die, and the fire that burns them shall not be extinguished. They shall be a symbol of disgrace to all mankind. [23] It will then be, that every first of the new month, and every Sabbath, all flesh shall come to worship before Me," says God.

סו [1] כֹּה אָמַר יְהֹוָה הַשָּׁמַיִם כִּסְאִי וְהָאָרֶץ הֲדֹם רַגְלָי אֵי־זֶה בַיִת אֲשֶׁר תִּבְנוּ־לִי וְאֵי־זֶה מָקוֹם מְנוּחָתִי: [23] וְהָיָה מִדֵּי־חֹדֶשׁ בְּחָדְשׁוֹ וּמִדֵּי שַׁבָּת בְּשַׁבַּתּוֹ יָבוֹא כָל־בָּשָׂר לְהִשְׁתַּחֲוֹת לְפָנַי אָמַר יְהֹוָה: [24] וְיָצְאוּ וְרָאוּ בְּפִגְרֵי הָאֲנָשִׁים הַפֹּשְׁעִים בִּי כִּי תוֹלַעְתָּם לֹא תָמוּת וְאִשָּׁם לֹא תִכְבֶּה וְהָיוּ דֵרָאוֹן לְכָל־בָּשָׂר: [23] וְהָיָה מִדֵּי־חֹדֶשׁ בְּחָדְשׁוֹ וּמִדֵּי שַׁבָּת בְּשַׁבַּתּוֹ יָבוֹא כָל־בָּשָׂר לְהִשְׁתַּחֲוֹת לְפָנַי אָמַר יְהֹוָה:

haftarat ḥanukkah (second shabbat)

20 ⁱ⁸ Jonathan said to David, "Tomorrow is the first of the new month. You shall be missed, because your seat will be empty." ⁴² Jonathan said to David, "Go in peace, as both of us have sworn in the name of God, saying, 'God be a witness between me and you, and between my descendants and your descendants forever.'"

כ 18 וַיֹּאמֶר־לוֹ יְהוֹנָתָן מָחָר חֹדֶשׁ וְנִפְקַדְתָּ כִּי יִפָּקֵד מוֹשָׁבֶךָ: 42 וַיֹּאמֶר יְהוֹנָתָן לְדָוִד לֵךְ לְשָׁלוֹם אֲשֶׁר נִשְׁבַּעְנוּ שְׁנֵינוּ אֲנַחְנוּ בְּשֵׁם יְהוָה לֵאמֹר יְהוָה יִהְיֶה | בֵּינִי וּבֵינֶךָ וּבֵין זַרְעִי וּבֵין זַרְעֲךָ עַד־עוֹלָם:

haftarat ḥanukkah
second shabbat

Maftir—Numbers 7:54–8:4 (p. 846)
ALL COMMUNITIES—I KINGS 7:40–50

> **SYNOPSIS:** This *Haftarah* summarizes the copper work completed by Hiram, the master craftsman of Solomon's Temple (see *Haftarah* for *Parashat Va-Yakhel*, page 1340), including small utensils, columns and their fixtures, and the vat (40–47). The concluding section describes the golden vessels which were made by Solomon himself: the altar, table, supplementary candelabra—hence the connection to *Hanukkah*—musical instruments, small utensils, and the keys to the Inner House (48–49).

7 ⁴⁰ Hiram then made the pots, shovels, and basins. Hiram completed all the work that he had done on behalf of King Solomon for the House of God:

⁴¹ The two columns, the two bowls of the spheres which were on top of the columns, and the two nets to cover the two bowls of the spheres which were on top of the columns.

⁴² The four hundred pomegranates for the two nets: two rows of one hundred pomegranates for each net to cover the two bowls of the spheres, which were on top of the columns.

⁴³ The ten bases, and the ten basins set upon the bases.

⁴⁴ The one vat, with the twelve copper oxen under the vat.

⁴⁵ The pots, shovels, and basins.

All these utensils which Hiram made on behalf of King Solomon for the House of God were of refined copper. ⁴⁶ The king had them cast in earthen molds in the plain of the Jordan, between Succoth and Zarethan.

ז 40 וַיַּעַשׂ חִירוֹם אֶת־הַכִּיֹּרוֹת וְאֶת־הַיָּעִים וְאֶת־הַמִּזְרָקוֹת וַיְכַל חִירָם לַעֲשׂוֹת אֶת־כָּל־הַמְּלָאכָה אֲשֶׁר עָשָׂה לַמֶּלֶךְ שְׁלֹמֹה בֵּית יְהוָה: 41 עַמֻּדִים שְׁנַיִם וְגֻלֹּת הַכֹּתָרֹת אֲשֶׁר־עַל־רֹאשׁ הָעַמּוּדִים שְׁתָּיִם וְהַשְּׂבָכוֹת שְׁתַּיִם לְכַסּוֹת אֶת־שְׁתֵּי גֻּלֹּת הַכֹּתָרֹת אֲשֶׁר עַל־רֹאשׁ הָעַמּוּדִים: 42 וְאֶת־הָרִמֹּנִים אַרְבַּע מֵאוֹת לִשְׁתֵּי הַשְּׂבָכוֹת שְׁנֵי־טוּרִים רִמֹּנִים לַשְּׂבָכָה הָאֶחָת לְכַסּוֹת אֶת־שְׁתֵּי גֻּלֹּת הַכֹּתָרֹת אֲשֶׁר עַל־פְּנֵי הָעַמּוּדִים: 43 וְאֶת־הַמְּכֹנוֹת עָשֶׂר וְאֶת־הַכִּיֹּרֹת עֲשָׂרָה עַל־הַמְּכֹנוֹת: 44 וְאֶת־הַיָּם הָאֶחָד וְאֶת־הַבָּקָר שְׁנֵים־עָשָׂר תַּחַת הַיָּם: 45 וְאֶת־הַסִּירוֹת וְאֶת־הַיָּעִים וְאֶת־הַמִּזְרָקוֹת וְאֵת כָּל־הַכֵּלִים [האהל כ׳] הָאֵלֶּה אֲשֶׁר עָשָׂה חִירָם לַמֶּלֶךְ שְׁלֹמֹה בֵּית יְהוָה נְחֹשֶׁת מְמֹרָט: 46 בְּכִכַּר הַיַּרְדֵּן

הפטרת פרשת שקלים

יְצָקָם הַמֶּלֶךְ בְּמַעֲבֵה הָאֲדָמָה בֵּין סֻכּוֹת וּבֵין צָרְתָן: 47 וַיַּנַּח שְׁלֹמֹה אֶת־כָּל־הַכֵּלִים מֵרֹב מְאֹד מְאֹד לֹא נֶחְקַר מִשְׁקַל הַנְּחֹשֶׁת: 48 וַיַּעַשׂ שְׁלֹמֹה אֵת כָּל־הַכֵּלִים אֲשֶׁר בֵּית יְהֹוָה אֵת מִזְבַּח הַזָּהָב וְאֶת־הַשֻּׁלְחָן אֲשֶׁר עָלָיו לֶחֶם הַפָּנִים זָהָב: 49 וְאֶת־הַמְּנֹרוֹת חָמֵשׁ מִיָּמִין וְחָמֵשׁ מִשְּׂמֹאול לִפְנֵי הַדְּבִיר זָהָב סָגוּר וְהַפֶּרַח וְהַנֵּרֹת וְהַמֶּלְקַחַיִם זָהָב: 50 וְהַסִּפּוֹת וְהַמְזַמְּרוֹת וְהַמִּזְרָקוֹת וְהַכַּפּוֹת וְהַמַּחְתּוֹת זָהָב סָגוּר וְהַפֹּתוֹת לְדַלְתוֹת הַבַּיִת הַפְּנִימִי לְקֹדֶשׁ הַקֳּדָשִׁים לְדַלְתֵי הַבַּיִת לַהֵיכָל זָהָב:

47 Solomon left all the copper utensils unweighed because there were so very many, so the weight of the copper was not investigated.

48 Solomon made all the vessels which were for the House of God:

The golden altar, and the golden table, on which the showbread was placed, 49 and the supplementary candelabra of precious gold, in addition to the candelabrum made by Moses: five on its right and five on its left, in front of the inner sanctuary. Their flowers, lamps, and tongs were made of gold; 50 the hand-drums, the various musical instruments, the basins, spoons and firepans were of precious gold; and the keys to the doors of the Inner House, which is the Holy of Holies, and to the doors of the House, which is the Sanctuary, were made of gold.

haftarat parashat shekalim

Maftir—Exodus 30:11–16 (p. 520)

ASHKENAZIM—II KINGS 12:1–17
SEPHARDIM AND HABAD—II KINGS 11:17 – 12:17

SYNOPSIS: *Parashat Shekalim* (*Exodus* 30:11-16) is a supplementary reading for the Sabbath which falls on, or precedes, the New Moon (*Rosh Hodesh*) of the month of *Adar*. Its purpose is to remind the community of their mandatory annual donation to the Temple of a half-shekel per head, and is continued in the current era so as not to forget this obligation.

The *Haftarah* chosen to reflect this reading recounts the efforts of King Jehoash (9th century B.C.E.) to use donations to the Temple for a repair fund (see 12:5). The Temple had been in disrepair for a number of years, since King Jehoshaphat of Judah (c. 735–711 B.C.E.) formed a military alliance with King Ahab (of Israel—see introduction to *Haftarah* to *Parashat Ki Tissa*), and allowed his son Jehoram to marry Ahab's daughter Athaliah, bringing Baal-worship to the Kingdom of Judah under Ahab's influence. This state of affairs lasted for many years, throughout Jehoram's reign (711–706 B.C.E.) and the first year of his son Ahaziah's reign. When Jehoram and Ahaziah were then murdered by Jehu, the King of Israel, Athaliah executed the remainder of the royal family so as to establish herself as queen, but Ahaziah's baby son Jehoash was saved secretly by Jehosheba, Athaliah's sister. Six years later (699 B.C.E.), Athaliah was assassinated in a revolt led by Jehoiada the High Priest, leaving the seven-year-old Jehoash as king.

At this point the *Haftarah* begins. We read how the covenant with God was restored, the sites of Baal-worship destroyed, and Temple appointments reinstated after a long period of neglect (11:17-19). It was thus a time of national celebration (20). The following chapter (where Ashkenazim begin the *Haftarah*), opens with a brief account of Jehoash's reign (12:1-4), before the central theme of the Temple repair begins.

haftarat parashat shekalim

> King Jehoash enacts that the half-shekel and other donations may be kept by the priests if they will repair the House in return (5–6). But after twenty-three years of reign the repairs have still not been carried out, so the king amends his instructions, requesting that future donations should be placed in a special building fund (7–10). Any accumulated funds would be carefully audited and used to pay workers (11–12). No funds were used to manufacture gold or silver vessels until the construction work was complete (14). The contractors were not audited, since they were trusted implicitly (15–16). The *Haftarah* concludes by noting that surplus funds from guilt- and sin-offerings were not used for construction but given to the priests (17).

Ḥabad and *Sephardic* communities begin here. *Ashkenazic* communities begin below:

20 ¹⁷ Jehoiada made anew the covenant between God, and the king and the people, that they and the king should be God's people. He also made a covenant between the king and the people that the king should wage wars for the people, and that the people should show allegiance to the king.

¹⁸ All the people of the land went to the temple of Baal and broke it down. They broke its altars and its images thoroughly into pieces, and killed Mattan the priest of Baal in front of the altars.

Jehoiada the priest appointed officers over the House of God, since the worship of Baal had caused these appointments to be neglected. ¹⁹ He took the officers of hundreds, the leaders, and the runners, and all the people of the land, and they brought down the king from the House of God, and entered by the way of the Runner's Gate to the king's house. He sat on the throne of the kings.

²⁰ All the people of the land rejoiced, and the city was quiet, for they had killed Athaliah with the sword in the king's house and there was no one else capable of starting a war.

Ashkenazic communities begin here. All others continue:

12 ¹ Jehoash was seven years old when he became king. ² Jehoash became king in the seventh year of Jehu's reign. He reigned for forty years in Jerusalem. His mother's name was Zibiah of Beer-sheba. ³ Jehoash did that which was right in the eyes of God his entire lifetime, so long as Jehoiada the priest instructed him. ⁴ However, the unauthorized private altars were not taken away. The people still sacrificed and burned incense on the high altars.

⁵ Jehoash said to the priests, "All the money of the consecrated things that is brought to the

יא 17 וַיִּכְרֹת יְהוֹיָדָע אֶת־הַבְּרִית בֵּין יְהוָה וּבֵין הַמֶּלֶךְ וּבֵין הָעָם לִהְיוֹת לְעָם לַיהוָה וּבֵין הַמֶּלֶךְ וּבֵין הָעָם: 18 וַיָּבֹאוּ כָל־עַם הָאָרֶץ בֵּית־הַבַּעַל וַיִּתְּצֻהוּ אֶת־מִזְבְּחֹתָו וְאֶת־ צְלָמָיו שִׁבְּרוּ הֵיטֵב וְאֵת מַתָּן כֹּהֵן הַבַּעַל הָרְגוּ לִפְנֵי הַמִּזְבְּחוֹת וַיָּשֶׂם הַכֹּהֵן פְּקֻדֹּת עַל־בֵּית יְהוָה: 19 וַיִּקַּח אֶת־שָׂרֵי הַמֵּאוֹת וְאֶת־הַכָּרִי וְאֶת־הָרָצִים וְאֵת | כָּל־עַם הָאָרֶץ וַיֹּרִידוּ אֶת־ הַמֶּלֶךְ מִבֵּית יְהוָה וַיָּבוֹאוּ דֶּרֶךְ־שַׁעַר הָרָצִים בֵּית הַמֶּלֶךְ וַיֵּשֶׁב עַל־כִּסֵּא הַמְּלָכִים: 20 וַיִּשְׂמַח כָּל־עַם־הָאָרֶץ וְהָעִיר שָׁקָטָה וְאֶת־עֲתַלְיָהוּ הֵמִיתוּ בַחֶרֶב בֵּית [מלך כ׳] הַמֶּלֶךְ:

יב 1 בֶּן־שֶׁבַע שָׁנִים יְהוֹאָשׁ בְּמָלְכוֹ: 2 בִּשְׁנַת־שֶׁבַע לְיֵהוּא מָלַךְ יְהוֹאָשׁ וְאַרְבָּעִים שָׁנָה מָלַךְ בִּירוּשָׁלָםִ וְשֵׁם אִמּוֹ צִבְיָה מִבְּאֵר שָׁבַע: 3 וַיַּעַשׂ יְהוֹאָשׁ הַיָּשָׁר בְּעֵינֵי יְהוָה כָּל־יָמָיו אֲשֶׁר הוֹרָהוּ יְהוֹיָדָע הַכֹּהֵן: 4 רַק הַבָּמוֹת לֹא־סָרוּ עוֹד הָעָם מְזַבְּחִים וּמְקַטְּרִים בַּבָּמוֹת: 5 וַיֹּאמֶר יְהוֹאָשׁ אֶל־הַכֹּהֲנִים כֹּל כֶּסֶף הַקֳּדָשִׁים אֲשֶׁר יוּבָא

הפטרת פרשת שקלים

בֵּית־יְהֹוָה כֶּסֶף עוֹבֵר אִישׁ כֶּסֶף נַפְשׁוֹת עֶרְכּוֹ כָּל־כֶּסֶף אֲשֶׁר יַעֲלֶה עַל לֶב־אִישׁ לְהָבִיא בֵּית יְהֹוָה: 6 יִקְחוּ לָהֶם הַכֹּהֲנִים אִישׁ מֵאֵת מַכָּרוֹ וְהֵם יְחַזְּקוּ אֶת־בֶּדֶק הַבַּיִת לְכֹל אֲשֶׁר־יִמָּצֵא שָׁם בָּדֶק: 7 וַיְהִי בִּשְׁנַת עֶשְׂרִים וְשָׁלֹשׁ שָׁנָה לַמֶּלֶךְ יְהוֹאָשׁ לֹא־חִזְּקוּ הַכֹּהֲנִים אֶת־בֶּדֶק הַבָּיִת: 8 וַיִּקְרָא הַמֶּלֶךְ יְהוֹאָשׁ לִיהוֹיָדָע הַכֹּהֵן וְלַכֹּהֲנִים וַיֹּאמֶר אֲלֵהֶם מַדּוּעַ אֵינְכֶם מְחַזְּקִים אֶת־בֶּדֶק הַבָּיִת וְעַתָּה אַל־תִּקְחוּ־כֶסֶף מֵאֵת מַכָּרֵיכֶם כִּי־לְבֶדֶק הַבַּיִת תִּתְּנֻהוּ: 9 וַיֵּאֹתוּ הַכֹּהֲנִים לְבִלְתִּי קְחַת־כֶּסֶף מֵאֵת הָעָם וּלְבִלְתִּי חַזֵּק אֶת־בֶּדֶק הַבָּיִת: 10 וַיִּקַּח יְהוֹיָדָע הַכֹּהֵן אֲרוֹן אֶחָד וַיִּקֹּב חֹר בְּדַלְתּוֹ וַיִּתֵּן אֹתוֹ אֵצֶל הַמִּזְבֵּחַ [בימין כ׳] מַיָּמִין בְּבוֹא־אִישׁ בֵּית יְהֹוָה וְנָתְנוּ־שָׁמָּה הַכֹּהֲנִים שֹׁמְרֵי הַסַּף אֶת־כָּל־הַכֶּסֶף הַמּוּבָא בֵית־יְהֹוָה: 11 וַיְהִי כִּרְאוֹתָם כִּי־רַב הַכֶּסֶף בָּאָרוֹן וַיַּעַל סֹפֵר הַמֶּלֶךְ וְהַכֹּהֵן הַגָּדוֹל וַיָּצֻרוּ וַיִּמְנוּ אֶת־הַכֶּסֶף הַנִּמְצָא בֵית־יְהֹוָה: 12 וְנָתְנוּ אֶת־הַכֶּסֶף הַמְתֻכָּן עַל־יְדֵי [ידי כ׳] עֹשֵׂי הַמְּלָאכָה הַמֻּפְקָדִים [הפקדים כ׳] בֵּית יְהֹוָה וַיּוֹצִיאֻהוּ לְחָרָשֵׁי הָעֵץ וְלַבֹּנִים הָעֹשִׂים בֵּית יְהֹוָה: 13 וְלַגֹּדְרִים וּלְחֹצְבֵי הָאֶבֶן וְלִקְנוֹת עֵצִים וְאַבְנֵי מַחְצֵב לְחַזֵּק אֶת־בֶּדֶק בֵּית־יְהֹוָה וּלְכֹל אֲשֶׁר־יֵצֵא עַל־הַבַּיִת לְחָזְקָה: 14 אַךְ לֹא יֵעָשֶׂה בֵּית יְהֹוָה סִפּוֹת כֶּסֶף מְזַמְּרוֹת מִזְרָקוֹת חֲצֹצְרוֹת כָּל־כְּלִי זָהָב וּכְלִי־כָסֶף מִן־הַכֶּסֶף הַמּוּבָא בֵית־יְהֹוָה: 15 כִּי־לְעֹשֵׂי הַמְּלָאכָה יִתְּנֻהוּ וְחִזְּקוּ־בוֹ אֶת־בֵּית יְהֹוָה: 16 וְלֹא יְחַשְּׁבוּ אֶת־הָאֲנָשִׁים אֲשֶׁר יִתְּנוּ אֶת־הַכֶּסֶף עַל־יָדָם לָתֵת לְעֹשֵׂי

House of God, the census money and the money which a person vows to donate according to the value of his life, and the money that any man is prompted by his heart to bring to the House of God— [6] let the priests take it for themselves, each man from his acquaintance, and in return let them repair the cracks of the House, wherever any crack shall be found, with their own money.

[7] But by the twenty-third year of the reign of King Jehoash, the priests had not repaired the cracks of the House. [8] King Jehoash called for Jehoiada the priest and the other priests, and said to them, "Why are you not repairing the cracks of the House? From now on, do not take any more money from your acquaintances for yourself, but give it to a special fund for repairing the cracks of the House."

[9] The priests agreed not to receive money from the people for themselves, and not to repair the cracks of the House from their own money.

[10] Jehoiada the priest took a chest, bored a hole in its lid, and set it beside the altar, on the right side as one comes into the House of God. The priests who guarded the door put into it all the money immediately, as it was brought to the House of God.

[11] Whenever they saw that there was much money in the chest, the king's scribe and a representative of the High Priest would come up. They would mint the silver coins which had no stamp and count the money that was found in the House of God. [12] They would give the money that was counted into the hands of the treasurers who were in charge of the skilled craftsmen in the House of God. They paid it out to the wood sculptors and carpenters who worked in the House of God, [13] to the builders and the masons, to buy timber and additional quarried stones to repair the cracks of the House of God, and for all other expenses that were spent on the House to repair it. [14] However, so long as the construction work had not been completed, silver jugs, musical instruments, sacrificial basins, trumpets, any utensils of gold or utensils of silver, were not made from the money that was brought to the House of God. [15] Rather, they would give it to the workmen, and the workmen repaired the House of God with it. [16] They did not ask for an accounting from the men into whose hands they delivered the money to be paid to the workmen, for they had a reputation for dealing honestly.

haftarat parashat zakhor

17 The surplus money of guilt-offerings and the surplus money of sin-offerings were not brought to repair the House of God. It was delivered to the priests.

כֶּסֶף אָשָׁם וְכֶסֶף חַטָּאוֹת לֹא יוּבָא בֵּית יְהֹוָה לַכֹּהֲנִים יִהְיוּ׃

If Shabbat is Rosh Ḥodesh, Ḥabad communities add the following (Isaiah 66:1, 23-24; ibid. 23):

66 **1** This is what God said: "The heaven is My throne, and the earth is My footstool, so what house could you build worthy for Me, and what place is worthy for My Presence to rest? **23** It will then be, that every first of the new month, and every Sabbath, all mankind shall come to worship before Me in the Holy Temple," says God. **24** The non-Jews shall go out of Jerusalem, to the valley of Jehoshaphat, and look upon the corpses of the men of Gog and Magog who have rebelled against Me, for the worms that eat them will not die, and the fire that burns them shall not be extinguished. They shall be a symbol of disgrace to all mankind. **23** "It will then be, that every first of the new month, and every Sabbath, all flesh shall come to worship before Me," says God.

סו 1 כֹּה אָמַר יְהֹוָה הַשָּׁמַיִם כִּסְאִי וְהָאָרֶץ הֲדֹם רַגְלָי אֵי־זֶה בַיִת אֲשֶׁר תִּבְנוּ־לִי וְאֵי־זֶה מָקוֹם מְנוּחָתִי׃ 23 וְהָיָה מִדֵּי־חֹדֶשׁ בְּחָדְשׁוֹ וּמִדֵּי שַׁבָּת בְּשַׁבַּתּוֹ יָבוֹא כָל־בָּשָׂר לְהִשְׁתַּחֲוֺת לְפָנַי אָמַר יְהֹוָה׃ 24 וְיָצְאוּ וְרָאוּ בְּפִגְרֵי הָאֲנָשִׁים הַפֹּשְׁעִים בִּי כִּי תוֹלַעְתָּם לֹא תָמוּת וְאִשָּׁם לֹא תִכְבֶּה וְהָיוּ דֵרָאוֹן לְכָל־בָּשָׂר׃ 23 וְהָיָה מִדֵּי־חֹדֶשׁ בְּחָדְשׁוֹ וּמִדֵּי שַׁבָּת בְּשַׁבַּתּוֹ יָבֹא כָל־בָּשָׂר לְהִשְׁתַּחֲוֺת לְפָנַי אָמַר יְהֹוָה׃

If Sunday is Rosh Ḥodesh, Ḥabad communities add the following (I Samuel 20:18; ibid. 42):

20 **18** Jonathan said to David, "Tomorrow is the first of the new month. You shall be missed, because your seat will be empty." **42** Jonathan said to David, "Go in peace, as both of us have sworn in the name of God, saying, 'God be a witness between me and you, and between my descendants and your descendants forever.'"

כ 18 וַיֹּאמֶר־לוֹ יְהוֹנָתָן מָחָר חֹדֶשׁ וְנִפְקַדְתָּ כִּי יִפָּקֵד מוֹשָׁבֶךָ׃ 42 וַיֹּאמֶר יְהוֹנָתָן לְדָוִד לֵךְ לְשָׁלוֹם אֲשֶׁר נִשְׁבַּעְנוּ שְׁנֵינוּ אֲנַחְנוּ בְּשֵׁם יְהֹוָה לֵאמֹר יְהֹוָה יִהְיֶה ׀ בֵּינִי וּבֵינֶךָ וּבֵין זַרְעִי וּבֵין זַרְעֲךָ עַד־עוֹלָם׃

haftarat parashat zakhor

Maftir—Deuteronomy 25:17–19 (p. 1208)

SOME COMMUNITIES—I SAMUEL 15:1–34
ASHKENAZIM AND ḤABAD—I SAMUEL 15:2–34

SYNOPSIS: *Parashat Zakhor* (*Deuteronomy* 25:17-19) is a supplementary reading for the Sabbath before the festival of *Purim*, dealing with the obligation to remember the evil nation of Amalek (being that Haman, whose downfall was on *Purim*, was a descendant of Amalek).

The *Haftarah* describes King Saul's victory over the nation of Amalek and his subsequent rejection as king by God for failing to obliterate the nation completely—a

הפטרת פרשת זכור

command which we read at the opening of the *Haftarah* (15:1–3). We are informed briefly of the preparations for battle, Amalek's defeat, and the sparing of Jethro's descendants, the Kenites (4–7). All the Amalekite people are executed, but their King Agag is spared, along with all the choice livestock, because Saul and the people "took pity" on them (8–9). God soon makes His disapproval known to the prophet Samuel, who is profoundly distressed and prays all night (10). He confronts the king and cautiously offers the criticism he has heard from God (11–19). Saul defends his actions, claiming that the animals had been spared for a holy purpose, to offer sacrifices (20–21). When Samuel retorts that these sacrifices represent the defiance of God's will and are thus tantamount to idolatry (22–23), Saul finally breaks down, admits his guilt, and pleads with Samuel to ask God for forgiveness (24–25). Samuel rejects the king's request and turns around to walk off, but Saul grabs his cloak and it tears (27). That, concludes Samuel, is a sign that the kingdom has been "torn away" from Saul and given to David (29). Realizing that his cause is lost, the king begs that at least he should not be publicly humiliated (30).

They return to the people together. Saul prostrates himself before God, and Agag is executed by Samuel (31–33). The *Haftarah* concludes with a note that Samuel and Saul then parted company and returned to their respective homes (34).

Some *Sephardic* communities begin here:

15 [1] Samuel said to Saul, "God sent me to anoint you as king over Israel, His people. Now listen to God's voice!"

טו 1 וַיֹּאמֶר שְׁמוּאֵל אֶל־שָׁאוּל אֹתִי שָׁלַח יְהֹוָה לִמְשָׁחֲךָ לְמֶלֶךְ עַל־עַמּוֹ עַל־יִשְׂרָאֵל וְעַתָּה שְׁמַע לְקוֹל דִּבְרֵי יְהֹוָה:

Habad and *Ashkenazic* communities begin here:

[2] This is what the God of Hosts said, "I remember what Amalek did to Israel, how they set an ambush for them on the way, when they were coming up from Egypt. [3] Now, go and strike Amalek, and completely destroy all that they have! Do not have compassion on them. Slay both man and woman, children and babies, oxen and sheep, camels and donkeys."

[4] Saul called the people together, and counted them in the place called Telaim. There were two hundred thousand men on foot, and ten thousand men of Judah.

[5] *Saul came to the city of Amalek, and fought them in the valley.*

[6] Saul said to the Kenites who were descended from Jethro, "Go, depart, descend from among the Amalekites, lest we destroy you accidentally with them, for your father Jethro showed kindness to all the people of Israel, when they came out of Egypt helping them to appoint judges." The Kenites departed from among the Amalekites.

2 כֹּה אָמַר יְהֹוָה צְבָאוֹת פָּקַדְתִּי אֵת אֲשֶׁר־עָשָׂה עֲמָלֵק לְיִשְׂרָאֵל אֲשֶׁר־שָׂם לוֹ בַּדֶּרֶךְ בַּעֲלֹתוֹ מִמִּצְרָיִם: 3 עַתָּה לֵךְ וְהִכִּיתָה אֶת־עֲמָלֵק וְהַחֲרַמְתֶּם אֶת־כָּל־אֲשֶׁר־לוֹ וְלֹא תַחְמֹל עָלָיו וְהֵמַתָּה מֵאִישׁ עַד־אִשָּׁה מֵעֹלֵל וְעַד־יוֹנֵק מִשּׁוֹר וְעַד־שֶׂה מִגָּמָל וְעַד־חֲמוֹר: 4 וַיְשַׁמַּע שָׁאוּל אֶת־הָעָם וַיִּפְקְדֵם בַּטְּלָאִים מָאתַיִם אֶלֶף רַגְלִי וַעֲשֶׂרֶת אֲלָפִים אֶת־אִישׁ יְהוּדָה: 5 וַיָּבֹא שָׁאוּל עַד־עִיר עֲמָלֵק וַיָּרֶב בַּנָּחַל: 6 וַיֹּאמֶר שָׁאוּל אֶל־הַקֵּינִי לְכוּ סֻּרוּ רְדוּ מִתּוֹךְ

haftarat parashat zakhor

[7] Saul defeated the Amalekites from Havilah to the approach to Shur, which faces Egypt. [8] He took King Agag of the Amalekites alive, and completely destroyed all the people with the edge of the sword.

[9] Saul and the people took pity on Agag, and the best of the sheep, the oxen, the fat cattle, the fat lambs, and all that was good, and would not completely destroy them. The cattle that were of low quality or slaughtered, they destroyed.

[10] The word of God came to Samuel, saying, [11] "I regret that I have appointed Saul to be king. For he has turned away from Me and has not performed My word." It upset Samuel and he prayed to God all night on Saul's behalf.

[12] Samuel rose early to go and meet Saul in the morning. Samuel was told as follows, "Saul came to Carmel, and behold, he was setting up a place for himself there to distribute the spoils, and then he turned around and continued traveling to Gilgal."

[13] When he arrived in Gilgal, Samuel came to Saul. Saul said to him, "May God bless you because, through you I have been able to perform God's command to me!"

[14] Samuel said, "But if you have fulfilled God's command, then what is the sound of sheep in my ears, and the sound of the cattle which I hear? Are they from Amalek?"

[15] Saul said, "They have indeed brought them from the Amalekites. The people only spared the best of the sheep and of the oxen not for themselves, but for the service of God: to sacrifice to God, your God, how could I rebuke them? The rest which were not fit to be sacrificed we have completely destroyed."

[16] Samuel said to Saul, "Retract your words! I will tell you what God has said to me last night."

He said to him, "Speak."

[17] Samuel said, "Even if you are little in your own eyes, you are nevertheless the chief of the tribes of Israel, and furthermore God anointed you king over Israel, so why did you not exert your authority and rebuke them? [18] God sent you on a mission, and said, 'Go and completely destroy the sinners, the Amalekites, and fight against them until they are annihilated.' [19] Why then did you not obey the voice of God to destroy them completely? Through failing to rebuke the people it is as if you yourself rushed to grab the booty and did evil in the eyes of God!"

עֲמָלֵקִי פֶּן־אֹסִפְךָ עִמּוֹ וְאַתָּה עָשִׂיתָה חֶסֶד עִם־כָּל־בְּנֵי יִשְׂרָאֵל בַּעֲלוֹתָם מִמִּצְרָיִם וַיָּסַר קֵינִי מִתּוֹךְ עֲמָלֵק: [7] וַיַּךְ שָׁאוּל אֶת־עֲמָלֵק מֵחֲוִילָה בּוֹאֲךָ שׁוּר אֲשֶׁר עַל־פְּנֵי מִצְרָיִם: [8] וַיִּתְפֹּשׂ אֶת־אֲגַג מֶלֶךְ־עֲמָלֵק חָי וְאֶת־כָּל־הָעָם הֶחֱרִים לְפִי־חָרֶב: [9] וַיַּחְמֹל שָׁאוּל וְהָעָם עַל־אֲגָג וְעַל־מֵיטַב הַצֹּאן וְהַבָּקָר וְהַמִּשְׁנִים וְעַל־הַכָּרִים וְעַל־כָּל־הַטּוֹב וְלֹא אָבוּ הַחֲרִימָם וְכָל־הַמְּלָאכָה נְמִבְזָה וְנָמֵס אֹתָהּ הֶחֱרִימוּ: [10] וַיְהִי דְּבַר־יְהֹוָה אֶל־שְׁמוּאֵל לֵאמֹר: [11] נִחַמְתִּי כִּי־הִמְלַכְתִּי אֶת־שָׁאוּל לְמֶלֶךְ כִּי־שָׁב מֵאַחֲרַי וְאֶת־דְּבָרַי לֹא הֵקִים וַיִּחַר לִשְׁמוּאֵל וַיִּזְעַק אֶל־יְהֹוָה כָּל־הַלָּיְלָה: [12] וַיַּשְׁכֵּם שְׁמוּאֵל לִקְרַאת שָׁאוּל בַּבֹּקֶר וַיֻּגַּד לִשְׁמוּאֵל לֵאמֹר בָּא־שָׁאוּל הַכַּרְמֶלָה וְהִנֵּה מַצִּיב לוֹ יָד וַיִּסֹּב וַיַּעֲבֹר וַיֵּרֶד הַגִּלְגָּל: [13] וַיָּבֹא שְׁמוּאֵל אֶל־שָׁאוּל וַיֹּאמֶר לוֹ שָׁאוּל בָּרוּךְ אַתָּה לַיהוָה הֲקִימֹתִי אֶת־דְּבַר יְהֹוָה: [14] וַיֹּאמֶר שְׁמוּאֵל וּמֶה קוֹל־הַצֹּאן הַזֶּה בְּאָזְנָי וְקוֹל הַבָּקָר אֲשֶׁר אָנֹכִי שֹׁמֵעַ: [15] וַיֹּאמֶר שָׁאוּל מֵעֲמָלֵקִי הֱבִיאוּם אֲשֶׁר חָמַל הָעָם עַל־מֵיטַב הַצֹּאן וְהַבָּקָר לְמַעַן זְבֹחַ לַיהוָה אֱלֹהֶיךָ וְאֶת־הַיּוֹתֵר הֶחֱרַמְנוּ: [16] וַיֹּאמֶר שְׁמוּאֵל אֶל־שָׁאוּל הֶרֶף וְאַגִּידָה לְּךָ אֵת אֲשֶׁר דִּבֶּר יְהֹוָה אֵלַי הַלָּיְלָה [ויאמרו כ׳] וַיֹּאמֶר לוֹ דַּבֵּר: [17] וַיֹּאמֶר שְׁמוּאֵל הֲלוֹא אִם־קָטֹן אַתָּה בְּעֵינֶיךָ רֹאשׁ שִׁבְטֵי יִשְׂרָאֵל אָתָּה וַיִּמְשָׁחֲךָ יְהֹוָה לְמֶלֶךְ עַל־יִשְׂרָאֵל: [18] וַיִּשְׁלָחֲךָ יְהֹוָה בְּדָרֶךְ וַיֹּאמֶר לֵךְ וְהַחֲרַמְתָּה אֶת־הַחַטָּאִים אֶת־עֲמָלֵק וְנִלְחַמְתָּ בוֹ עַד־כַּלּוֹתָם אֹתָם: [19] וְלָמָּה לֹא־שָׁמַעְתָּ בְּקוֹל יְהֹוָה וַתַּעַט אֶל־הַשָּׁלָל וַתַּעַשׂ

הפטרת פרשת זכור

20 וַיֹּאמֶר שָׁאוּל אֶל־שְׁמוּאֵל אֲשֶׁר שָׁמַעְתִּי בְּקוֹל יְהֹוָה וָאֵלֵךְ בַּדֶּרֶךְ אֲשֶׁר־שְׁלָחַנִי יְהֹוָה וָאָבִיא אֶת־אֲגַג מֶלֶךְ עֲמָלֵק וְאֶת־עֲמָלֵק הֶחֱרַמְתִּי: 21 וַיִּקַּח הָעָם מֵהַשָּׁלָל צֹאן וּבָקָר רֵאשִׁית הַחֵרֶם לִזְבֹּחַ לַיהֹוָה אֱלֹהֶיךָ בַּגִּלְגָּל: 22 וַיֹּאמֶר שְׁמוּאֵל הַחֵפֶץ לַיהֹוָה בְּעֹלוֹת וּזְבָחִים כִּשְׁמֹעַ בְּקוֹל יְהֹוָה הִנֵּה שְׁמֹעַ מִזֶּבַח טוֹב לְהַקְשִׁיב מֵחֵלֶב אֵילִים: 23 כִּי חַטַּאת־קֶסֶם מֶרִי וְאָוֶן וּתְרָפִים הַפְצַר יַעַן מָאַסְתָּ אֶת־דְּבַר יְהֹוָה וַיִּמְאָסְךָ מִמֶּלֶךְ: 24 וַיֹּאמֶר שָׁאוּל אֶל־שְׁמוּאֵל חָטָאתִי כִּי־עָבַרְתִּי אֶת־פִּי־יְהֹוָה וְאֶת־דְּבָרֶיךָ כִּי יָרֵאתִי אֶת־הָעָם וָאֶשְׁמַע בְּקוֹלָם: 25 וְעַתָּה שָׂא נָא אֶת־חַטָּאתִי וְשׁוּב עִמִּי וְאֶשְׁתַּחֲוֶה לַיהֹוָה: 26 וַיֹּאמֶר שְׁמוּאֵל אֶל־שָׁאוּל לֹא אָשׁוּב עִמָּךְ כִּי מָאַסְתָּה אֶת־דְּבַר יְהֹוָה וַיִּמְאָסְךָ יְהֹוָה מִהְיוֹת מֶלֶךְ עַל־יִשְׂרָאֵל: 27 וַיִּסֹּב שְׁמוּאֵל לָלֶכֶת וַיַּחֲזֵק בִּכְנַף־מְעִילוֹ וַיִּקָּרַע: 28 וַיֹּאמֶר אֵלָיו שְׁמוּאֵל קָרַע יְהֹוָה אֶת־מַמְלְכוּת יִשְׂרָאֵל מֵעָלֶיךָ הַיּוֹם וּנְתָנָהּ לְרֵעֲךָ הַטּוֹב מִמֶּךָּ: 29 וְגַם נֵצַח יִשְׂרָאֵל לֹא יְשַׁקֵּר וְלֹא יִנָּחֵם כִּי לֹא אָדָם הוּא לְהִנָּחֵם: 30 וַיֹּאמֶר חָטָאתִי עַתָּה כַּבְּדֵנִי נָא נֶגֶד זִקְנֵי־עַמִּי וְנֶגֶד יִשְׂרָאֵל וְשׁוּב עִמִּי וְהִשְׁתַּחֲוֵיתִי לַיהֹוָה אֱלֹהֶיךָ: 31 וַיָּשָׁב שְׁמוּאֵל אַחֲרֵי שָׁאוּל וַיִּשְׁתַּחוּ שָׁאוּל לַיהֹוָה: 32 וַיֹּאמֶר שְׁמוּאֵל הַגִּישׁוּ אֵלַי אֶת־אֲגַג מֶלֶךְ עֲמָלֵק וַיֵּלֶךְ אֵלָיו אֲגַג מַעֲדַנֹּת וַיֹּאמֶר אֲגָג אָכֵן סָר מַר־הַמָּוֶת: 33 וַיֹּאמֶר שְׁמוּאֵל כַּאֲשֶׁר שִׁכְּלָה נָשִׁים חַרְבֶּךָ כֵּן־תִּשְׁכַּל מִנָּשִׁים

[1430]

20 Saul said to Samuel, "Actually, I have obeyed the voice of God and have followed the way which God sent me. I have detained King Agag of Amalek, and I have completely destroyed the Amalekites. 21 I, personally, have taken nothing and the people took from the booty sheep and oxen—the best of what was to be destroyed—for a holy purpose, to sacrifice to God, your God, in Gilgal."

22 Samuel said, "Does God have as great a delight in burnt-offerings and sacrifices, as in obeying the voice of God? Indeed, to obey God is better than a sacrifice to Him, and to listen to Him better than the fat of rams offered from a sacrifice. 23 For disobedience is like the sin of sorcery, since both sinners believe in man more than God, and adding to a prophet's words is like serving false gods and idols. Because you have rejected the word of God, He has also rejected you from being king."

24 Saul said to Samuel, "I have sinned, for I have transgressed the command of God and added to your words, because I feared the people and obeyed their voice. 25 But now, please forgive my sin against you. Return with me, and I will prostrate myself before God!"

26 Samuel said to Saul, "I will not return with you, for you have rejected the word of God, and God has rejected you from being king over Israel."

27 Samuel turned about to go away, and Saul grabbed the hem of his cloak to prevent him from going, and it ripped.

28 Samuel said to him, "This is a sign that God has torn the kingdom of Israel from you this day, and has given it to a peer of yours, David, who is better than you. 29 Furthermore, the Powerful One of Israel has already given the monarchy to somebody else, and He will not lie or change His mind, for He is not a man that He should change His mind."

30 Saul said, "Even though I have sinned, please honor me in the presence of the elders of my people, and before Israel, and return with me, and I will prostrate myself before God, your God." 31 Samuel returned, following after Saul, and Saul prostrated himself before God.

32 Samuel said, "Bring King Agag of the Amalekites to me." Agag came to him in chains.

Agag said, "Surely, the bitterness of death is turned to me!"

33 Samuel said, "Just as your sword has made

haftarat parashat parah

women widowed and childless, so shall your mother be childless among women!"

Samuel cut Agag in pieces before God in Gilgal.

³⁴ Samuel went to Ramah. Saul went up to his house at Saul's Hill.

אֵמֶּךְ וַיְשַׁסֵּף שְׁמוּאֵל אֶת־אֲגָג לִפְנֵי יְהֹוָה בַּגִּלְגָּל׃ 34 וַיֵּלֶךְ שְׁמוּאֵל הָרָמָתָה וְשָׁאוּל עָלָה אֶל־בֵּיתוֹ גִּבְעַת שָׁאוּל׃

haftarat parashat parah

Maftir—Numbers 19:1–22 (p. 932)

ASHKENAZIM—Ezekiel 36:16–38
SEPHARDIM AND HABAD—Ezekiel 36:16–36

SYNOPSIS: *Parashat Parah* (*Numbers* 19:1–22) is a supplementary reading for the Sabbath read in the weeks preceding the festival of Passover. The reading discusses the ritual purification process through the Red Heifer that is required as a preparation for offering the Passover sacrifice, and the theme of ritual purity is likewise stressed by the *Haftarah*, "Then I will sprinkle clean water upon you" (v. 25).

The *Haftarah* is a prophecy of hope and comfort addressed by the prophet Ezekiel to the Jewish community in Babylon (6th century B.C.E.). The opening words of the *Haftarah* constitute a sharp criticism of the people for defiling the land, which was the cause of the subsequent exile (36:16–21). The ingathering will ultimately occur so as not to profane God's holy name (22–24), and only then will the Jewish people be purified and given a new spirit (25–28). Israel will live in comfort and will be ashamed of her past sins (29–32). Finally, God promises to repopulate the land extensively (33–38).

36 ¹⁶ The word of God came to me, saying, ¹⁷ "Son of man, when the House of Israel dwelt in their own land, they defiled it by their way and by their doings. Their way was before Me like the uncleanliness of a menstruating woman which causes a woman to distance herself from her husband. ¹⁸ Therefore I poured My fury upon them for the blood that they had shed upon the land, and for their idols with which they had defiled it. ¹⁹ I scattered them among the nations, and they were dispersed through the countries, according to their way and according to their doings I judged them. ²⁰ They came to the nations where they were exiled, and they profaned My holy name, because it was said of them, 'These are the people of God, and yet God could not help them and they have gone out from His land!' ²¹ But I had concern for My holy name, which the House of Israel had profaned among the nations where they were exiled."

²² Therefore say to the House of Israel, This is what God, Almighty God, says: "I do not do this for your

16 וַיְהִי דְבַר־יְהֹוָה אֵלַי לֵאמֹר׃ 17 בֶּן־אָדָם בֵּית יִשְׂרָאֵל יֹשְׁבִים עַל־אַדְמָתָם וַיְטַמְּאוּ אוֹתָהּ בְּדַרְכָּם וּבַעֲלִילוֹתָם כְּטֻמְאַת הַנִּדָּה הָיְתָה דַרְכָּם לְפָנָי׃ 18 וָאֶשְׁפֹּךְ חֲמָתִי עֲלֵיהֶם עַל־הַדָּם אֲשֶׁר־שָׁפְכוּ עַל־הָאָרֶץ וּבְגִלּוּלֵיהֶם טִמְּאוּהָ׃ 19 וָאָפִיץ אֹתָם בַּגּוֹיִם וַיִּזָּרוּ בָּאֲרָצוֹת כְּדַרְכָּם וְכַעֲלִילוֹתָם שְׁפַטְתִּים׃ 20 וַיָּבוֹא אֶל־הַגּוֹיִם אֲשֶׁר־בָּאוּ שָׁם וַיְחַלְּלוּ אֶת־שֵׁם קָדְשִׁי בֶּאֱמֹר לָהֶם עַם־יְהֹוָה אֵלֶּה וּמֵאַרְצוֹ יָצָאוּ׃ 21 וָאֶחְמֹל עַל־שֵׁם קָדְשִׁי אֲשֶׁר חִלְּלֻהוּ בֵּית יִשְׂרָאֵל בַּגּוֹיִם אֲשֶׁר־בָּאוּ שָׁמָּה׃ 22 לָכֵן אֱמֹר

הפטרת פרשת פרה

לְבֵית־יִשְׂרָאֵל כֹּה אָמַר אֲדֹנָי יֱהֹוִה לֹא לְמַעַנְכֶם אֲנִי עֹשֶׂה בֵּית יִשְׂרָאֵל כִּי אִם־לְשֵׁם־קׇדְשִׁי אֲשֶׁר חִלַּלְתֶּם בַּגּוֹיִם אֲשֶׁר־בָּאתֶם שָׁם: 23 וְקִדַּשְׁתִּי אֶת־שְׁמִי הַגָּדוֹל הַמְחֻלָּל בַּגּוֹיִם אֲשֶׁר חִלַּלְתֶּם בְּתוֹכָם וְיָדְעוּ הַגּוֹיִם כִּי־אֲנִי יְהֹוָה נְאֻם אֲדֹנָי יֱהֹוִה בְּהִקָּדְשִׁי בָכֶם לְעֵינֵיהֶם: 24 וְלָקַחְתִּי אֶתְכֶם מִן־הַגּוֹיִם וְקִבַּצְתִּי אֶתְכֶם מִכׇּל־הָאֲרָצוֹת וְהֵבֵאתִי אֶתְכֶם אֶל־אַדְמַתְכֶם: 25 וְזָרַקְתִּי עֲלֵיכֶם מַיִם טְהוֹרִים וּטְהַרְתֶּם מִכֹּל טֻמְאוֹתֵיכֶם וּמִכׇּל־גִּלּוּלֵיכֶם אֲטַהֵר אֶתְכֶם: 26 וְנָתַתִּי לָכֶם לֵב חָדָשׁ וְרוּחַ חֲדָשָׁה אֶתֵּן בְּקִרְבְּכֶם וַהֲסִרֹתִי אֶת־לֵב הָאֶבֶן מִבְּשַׂרְכֶם וְנָתַתִּי לָכֶם לֵב בָּשָׂר: 27 וְאֶת־רוּחִי אֶתֵּן בְּקִרְבְּכֶם וְעָשִׂיתִי אֵת אֲשֶׁר־בְּחֻקַּי תֵּלֵכוּ וּמִשְׁפָּטַי תִּשְׁמְרוּ וַעֲשִׂיתֶם: 28 וִישַׁבְתֶּם בָּאָרֶץ אֲשֶׁר נָתַתִּי לַאֲבֹתֵיכֶם וִהְיִיתֶם לִי לְעָם וְאָנֹכִי אֶהְיֶה לָכֶם לֵאלֹהִים: 29 וְהוֹשַׁעְתִּי אֶתְכֶם מִכֹּל טֻמְאוֹתֵיכֶם וְקָרָאתִי אֶל־הַדָּגָן וְהִרְבֵּיתִי אֹתוֹ וְלֹא־אֶתֵּן עֲלֵיכֶם רָעָב: 30 וְהִרְבֵּיתִי אֶת־פְּרִי הָעֵץ וּתְנוּבַת הַשָּׂדֶה לְמַעַן אֲשֶׁר לֹא תִקְחוּ עוֹד חֶרְפַּת רָעָב בַּגּוֹיִם: 31 וּזְכַרְתֶּם אֶת־דַּרְכֵיכֶם הָרָעִים וּמַעַלְלֵיכֶם אֲשֶׁר לֹא־טוֹבִים וּנְקֹטֹתֶם בִּפְנֵיכֶם עַל עֲוֺנֹתֵיכֶם וְעַל תּוֹעֲבוֹתֵיכֶם: 32 לֹא לְמַעַנְכֶם אֲנִי־עֹשֶׂה נְאֻם אֲדֹנָי יֱהֹוִה יִוָּדַע לָכֶם בּוֹשׁוּ וְהִכָּלְמוּ מִדַּרְכֵיכֶם בֵּית יִשְׂרָאֵל: 33 כֹּה אָמַר אֲדֹנָי יֱהֹוִה בְּיוֹם טַהֲרִי אֶתְכֶם מִכֹּל עֲוֺנוֹתֵיכֶם וְהוֹשַׁבְתִּי אֶת־הֶעָרִים וְנִבְנוּ הֶחֳרָבוֹת: 34 וְהָאָרֶץ הַנְּשַׁמָּה תֵּעָבֵד תַּחַת אֲשֶׁר הָיְתָה שְׁמָמָה לְעֵינֵי כׇּל־עוֹבֵר: 35 וְאָמְרוּ הָאָרֶץ הַלֵּזוּ הַנְּשַׁמָּה הָיְתָה כְּגַן־עֵדֶן וְהֶעָרִים הֶחֳרֵבוֹת וְהַנְשַׁמּוֹת

---

sakes, O House of Israel, but for My holy name's sake, which you have profaned among the nations where you were exiled. 23 I will sanctify My great name, which was profaned among the nations, which you have profaned in their midst, and the nations shall know that I am God," says God, Almighty God, "when I shall be sanctified through you, before their eyes. 24 For I will take you from among the nations, and gather you from all countries, and will bring you into your own land.

25 "Then I will sprinkle clean water upon you from the ashes of the red heifer, and you shall be clean from all your filth, and from all your idols I will cleanse you. 26 I will also give you a new upright heart, and a new spirit I will put inside you. I will take away the stubborn heart of stone from your flesh, and I will give you a soft heart of flesh. 27 I will put My spirit inside you so that you will become prophets, and cause you to follow My statutes, and you shall keep My judgments, and do them.

28 "You shall dwell in the land that I gave to your fathers; and you shall be My people, and I will be your God.

29 "I will save you from all the sinful uncleanliness to which you were accustomed for I will arouse your heart to be aware of it. I will command My blessing upon the grain that it should increase, and lay no famine upon you. 30 I will multiply the fruit of the tree, and the produce of the field, so that you shall never suffer the disgrace of famine among the nations. 31 Then you will remember your evil ways, and your doings that were not good, and will feel cut off due to your former sins and your former abominations.

32 "Not for your sake will I make this redemption," says God, Almighty God, "Let it be known to you, be ashamed and confounded from your bad ways which were insufficient to bring the redemption, O House of Israel!"

33 This is what *God, Almighty God*, says: "On the day when I will have cleansed you from all your iniquities I will populate cities, and the ruins shall be rebuilt fit for human habitation. 34 The land which is desolate will now be tilled, instead of being the desolation that was in view of all who passed by. 35 Passersby will be shocked, and they will say, 'This land that was desolate has become like the garden

haftarat parashat ha-ḥodesh

of Eden! The waste and desolate and ruined cities have become fortified, and are inhabited!' ³⁶ Thus, the nations who remain around you shall know that I, God, have rebuilt the ruined places, and have replanted that which was desolate. I, God, have said it will happen, and I am the One who will do it."

וְהַנֶּהֱרָסוֹת בְּצוּרוֹת יָשָׁבוּ: 36 וְיָדְעוּ הַגּוֹיִם אֲשֶׁר יִשָּׁאֲרוּ סְבִיבוֹתֵיכֶם כִּי | אֲנִי יְהֹוָה בָּנִיתִי הַנֶּהֱרָסוֹת נָטַעְתִּי הַנְּשַׁמָּה אֲנִי יְהֹוָה דִּבַּרְתִּי וְעָשִׂיתִי:

Ḥabad and *Sephardic* communities conclude here. *Ashkenazic* communities continue:

³⁷ This is what God Almighty says: I will be sought by the House of Israel to do one more thing for them, I will make them multiply, men like sheep. ³⁸ Like holy sheep, like the sheep brought to Jerusalem for sacrifices on its holidays, the ruined cities will be filled with flocks of men, and they will know that I am God, faithful to My word!

37 כֹּה אָמַר אֲדֹנָי יֱהֹוִה עוֹד זֹאת אִדָּרֵשׁ לְבֵית־יִשְׂרָאֵל לַעֲשׂוֹת לָהֶם אַרְבֶּה אֹתָם כַּצֹּאן אָדָם: 38 כְּצֹאן קֳדָשִׁים כְּצֹאן יְרוּשָׁלַםִ בְּמוֹעֲדֶיהָ כֵּן תִּהְיֶינָה הֶעָרִים הֶחֳרֵבוֹת מְלֵאוֹת צֹאן אָדָם וְיָדְעוּ כִּי־אֲנִי יְהֹוָה:

haftarat parashat ha-ḥodesh

Maftir—Exodus 12:1–20 (p. 392)
ASHKENAZIM—EZEKIEL 45:16 – 46:18
SEPHARDIM AND ḤABAD—ISAIAH 45:18 – 46:15

SYNOPSIS: *Parashat Ha-Ḥodesh* (*Exodus* 12:1-20) is a supplementary reading for the Sabbath which deals with the special status of the month of *Nisan* and the Passover-offering, offered on the fourteenth of the month. *Parashat Ha-Hodesh* is read on the last Sabbath of the month of *Adar*, unless *Rosh Ḥodesh Nisan* falls on the Sabbath. Its *Haftarah*, which forms part of Ezekiel's vision of the future Temple (6th century B.C.E), describes various laws of sacrificial procedure, including that of the Passover offering.

The *Haftarah* opens with regulations pertaining to communal donations to the Temple, and the responsibilities of the leader to provide offerings for the festivals, new months, and Sabbaths (45:16-17). The next passage, where Ḥabad communities begin the *Haftarah*, details laws pertaining to the inauguration of the Temple (18–20) and the Passover offerings (21–25). We also read various rules pertaining to gate regulations (46:1-3) and details of the regular sacrificial offerings (4-15). Habad and Sephardic communities end here, but Ashkenazic communities add a brief codification of inheritance laws for the leader and his family (16–18).

Many communities begin here. *Ḥabad* and some *Sephardic* communities begin below page 1434:

45 ¹⁶ All the people of the land should join in giving this contribution, including the leader in Israel. ¹⁷ In addition to the contribution, the leader will bear responsibility for the burnt-offerings, the meal-offerings and the wine libation of the festivals, new moons, and Sabbaths, all the gatherings of the Jewish people. He will provide

מה 16 כֹּל הָעָם הָאָרֶץ יִהְיוּ אֶל־הַתְּרוּמָה הַזֹּאת לַנָּשִׂיא בְּיִשְׂרָאֵל: 17 וְעַל־הַנָּשִׂיא יִהְיֶה הָעוֹלוֹת וְהַמִּנְחָה וְהַנֶּסֶךְ בַּחַגִּים וּבֶחֳדָשִׁים וּבַשַּׁבָּתוֹת בְּכָל־מוֹעֲדֵי בֵּית יִשְׂרָאֵל הוּא־יַעֲשֶׂה אֶת־

the sin-offering, the meal-offering, the burnt-offering and the peace-offerings from his personal property to atone for the House of Israel.

הַחַטָּאת וְאֶת־הַמִּנְחָה וְאֶת־הָעוֹלָה וְאֶת־הַשְּׁלָמִים לְכַפֵּר בְּעַד בֵּית־יִשְׂרָאֵל׃

Ḥabad and some Sephardic communities begin here:

18 This is what God, Almighty God, says: "In the first month, on the first day of the month, you shall take a young bull without blemish for a sin-offering, and with it you shall cleanse the Sanctuary, thus inaugurating it. **19** The priest shall take of the blood of the sin-offering, and put it upon the doorposts of the Sanctuary, and upon the four corners of the ledge of the altar, and upon the doorposts of the Men's Courtyard. **20** So you shall do every day until the seventh day of the month to inaugurate the Temple. These sacrifices will atone for the House from those who err and the fools who enter the Temple without permission.

21 In the first month, on the fourteenth day of the month, you shall bring the Passover sacrifice. During the festival of seven days unleavened bread shall be eaten. **22** On that day, the fourteenth of *Nisan*, the leader shall bring a bull for a sin-offering from his own property, for all the people of the land. **23** He shall prepare a burnt-offering to God from his own property for seven days of the festival: seven bulls and seven rams without blemish daily for seven days, and a kid of the goats daily for a sin-offering. **24** He shall prepare a meal-offering of an *'ephah* for a bull, and an *'ephah* for a ram, and a *hin* of oil for an *'ephah*.

25 In the seventh month, on the fifteenth day of the month, he shall do the same on the festival of seven days, like the above-mentioned sin-offering, like the burnt-offering, like the meal-offering, and like the oil.

46 **1** This is what God, Almighty God, says: "The gate of the Men's Courtyard that faces the east shall be closed for the six working days since people do not come during the week, but on the Sabbath it shall be opened, and on the first day of the month it shall be opened.

2 "The leader shall enter by way of the outer porch of that gate from outside, and he shall stand by the post of the gate. While he stands there the priests shall prepare his burnt-offering and his peace-offerings, and he shall bow down at the threshold of the gate. Then he shall go out, but the gate shall not be closed

18 כֹּה־אָמַר אֲדֹנָי יֱהֹוִה בָּרִאשׁוֹן בְּאֶחָד לַחֹדֶשׁ תִּקַּח פַּר־בֶּן־בָּקָר תָּמִים וְחִטֵּאתָ אֶת־הַמִּקְדָּשׁ׃ 19 וְלָקַח הַכֹּהֵן מִדַּם הַחַטָּאת וְנָתַן אֶל־מְזוּזַת הַבַּיִת וְאֶל־אַרְבַּע פִּנּוֹת הָעֲזָרָה לַמִּזְבֵּחַ וְעַל־מְזוּזַת שַׁעַר הֶחָצֵר הַפְּנִימִית׃ 20 וְכֵן תַּעֲשֶׂה בְּשִׁבְעָה בַחֹדֶשׁ מֵאִישׁ שֹׁגֶה וּמִפֶּתִי וְכִפַּרְתֶּם אֶת־הַבָּיִת׃ 21 בָּרִאשׁוֹן בְּאַרְבָּעָה עָשָׂר יוֹם לַחֹדֶשׁ יִהְיֶה לָכֶם הַפָּסַח חָג שְׁבֻעוֹת יָמִים מַצּוֹת יֵאָכֵל׃ 22 וְעָשָׂה הַנָּשִׂיא בַּיּוֹם הַהוּא בַּעֲדוֹ וּבְעַד כָּל־עַם הָאָרֶץ פַּר חַטָּאת׃ 23 וְשִׁבְעַת יְמֵי־הֶחָג יַעֲשֶׂה עוֹלָה לַיהֹוָה שִׁבְעַת פָּרִים וְשִׁבְעַת אֵילִים תְּמִימִם לַיּוֹם שִׁבְעַת הַיָּמִים וְחַטָּאת שְׂעִיר עִזִּים לַיּוֹם׃ 24 וּמִנְחָה אֵיפָה לַפָּר וְאֵיפָה לָאַיִל יַעֲשֶׂה וְשֶׁמֶן הִין לָאֵיפָה׃ 25 בַּשְּׁבִיעִי בַּחֲמִשָּׁה עָשָׂר יוֹם לַחֹדֶשׁ בֶּחָג יַעֲשֶׂה כָאֵלֶּה שִׁבְעַת הַיָּמִים כַּחַטָּאת כָּעֹלָה וְכַמִּנְחָה וְכַשָּׁמֶן׃

מו 1 כֹּה־אָמַר אֲדֹנָי יֱהֹוִה שַׁעַר הֶחָצֵר הַפְּנִימִית הַפֹּנֶה קָדִים יִהְיֶה סָגוּר שֵׁשֶׁת יְמֵי הַמַּעֲשֶׂה וּבְיוֹם הַשַּׁבָּת יִפָּתֵחַ וּבְיוֹם הַחֹדֶשׁ יִפָּתֵחַ׃ 2 וּבָא הַנָּשִׂיא דֶּרֶךְ אוּלָם הַשַּׁעַר מִחוּץ וְעָמַד עַל־מְזוּזַת הַשַּׁעַר וְעָשׂוּ הַכֹּהֲנִים אֶת־עוֹלָתוֹ וְאֶת־שְׁלָמָיו וְהִשְׁתַּחֲוָה עַל־מִפְתַּן הַשַּׁעַר וְיָצָא וְהַשַּׁעַר לֹא־יִסָּגֵר עַד־הָעָרֶב׃

haftarat parashat ha-ḥodesh

until the evening because ³ the people of the land shall bow down at the door of this gate before God on the Sabbath and the first day of the month.

⁴ The burnt-offering that the leader shall offer to God on the Sabbath day for the inauguration shall be six lambs without blemish, and a ram without blemish. ⁵ The meal-offering shall be an *'ephah* for a ram. The meal-offering for the lambs should be whatever he is capable of bringing, and a *hin* of oil to an *'ephah*.

⁶ On the first day of the month it shall be a young bull without blemish, and six lambs, and a ram. They shall be without blemish. ⁷ He shall prepare a meal-offering, an *'ephah* for a bull, and an *'ephah* for a ram, and for the lambs according to his means, and a *hin* of oil to an *'ephah*.

⁸ When the leader shall enter to watch the sacrifices being offered, he shall go in by way of the outer porch of that gate, and he shall go out by the same way. ⁹ But when the people of the land shall come before God on the festivals to offer their obligatory sacrifices, he who enters by way of the north gate to bow down shall go out by way of the south gate, and he who enters by way of the south gate shall go out by way of the north gate. He shall not return by way of the gate by which he came in, but shall go out straight ahead. ¹⁰ The leader among them shall join them. When they go in, he shall go in with them, and when they go out, he shall go out with them.

¹¹ On the festivals, the meal-offering shall be an *'ephah* for a bull, and an *'ephah* for a ram, and for the lambs whatever he is capable of bringing, and a *hin* of oil to an *'ephah*.

¹² During the six working days, when the leader shall prepare a voluntary burnt-offering or peace-offering to God, the gate facing east shall be opened for him, and the priest shall bring his burnt-offering and his peace-offerings, as he does on the Sabbath day. Then he shall go out. After he goes out, the gate shall be closed, since people are working and cannot come to the Temple.

¹³ In addition to the above inaugural sacrifices you shall prepare a burnt-offering to God of a year-old lamb without blemish. You shall prepare it every morning. ¹⁴ You shall prepare a meal-offering for it every morning, the sixth part of an *'ephah*, and the third part of a *hin* of oil, to moisten the fine flour—a meal-offering continually by an everlasting ordinance to God.

הפטרת פרשת החדש

¹⁵ In addition to the above they shall continue to prepare the usual lamb, meal-offering and oil, required by the Torah every morning for a continual burnt-offering.

מִנְחָה לַיהוָה חֻקּוֹת עוֹלָם תָּמִיד: 15 [ועש״כ] יַעֲשׂוּ אֶת־הַכֶּבֶשׂ וְאֶת־הַמִּנְחָה וְאֶת־הַשֶּׁמֶן בַּבֹּקֶר בַּבֹּקֶר עוֹלַת תָּמִיד:

Ḥabad and *Sephardic* communities conclude here. *Ashkenazic* communities continue:

¹⁶ This is what God Almighty says, "If during his lifetime the leader gives one of his sons a gift, since it is his rightful property, it will belong to his sons, and it will be their possession by inheritance. ¹⁷ If he gives one of his servants a gift from his property, it shall be the servant's possession only until the Jubilee. It then returns to the leader's possession, and it remains as an inheritance for his descendants. ¹⁸ The leader may not take land from the people's portion and defraud them of their property. He may give his sons an inheritance only from his own property, in order that My people not be scattered, each man from his property.

16 כֹּה־אָמַר אֲדֹנָי יֱהוִֹה כִּי־יִתֵּן הַנָּשִׂיא מַתָּנָה לְאִישׁ מִבָּנָיו נַחֲלָתוֹ הִיא לְבָנָיו תִּהְיֶה אֲחֻזָּתָם הִיא בְּנַחֲלָה: 17 וְכִי־יִתֵּן מַתָּנָה מִנַּחֲלָתוֹ לְאַחַד מֵעֲבָדָיו וְהָיְתָה לּוֹ עַד־שְׁנַת הַדְּרוֹר וְשָׁבַת לַנָּשִׂיא אַךְ נַחֲלָתוֹ בָּנָיו לָהֶם תִּהְיֶה: 18 וְלֹא־יִקַּח הַנָּשִׂיא מִנַּחֲלַת הָעָם לְהוֹנֹתָם מֵאֲחֻזָּתָם מֵאֲחֻזָּתוֹ יַנְחִל אֶת־בָּנָיו לְמַעַן אֲשֶׁר לֹא־יָפֻצוּ עַמִּי אִישׁ מֵאֲחֻזָּתוֹ:

If Shabbat is Rosh Ḥodesh, Ḥabad communities add the following (Isaiah 66:1, 23-24; ibid. 23):

66 ¹ This is what God said: "The heaven is My throne, and the earth is My footstool, so what house could you build worthy for Me, and what place is worthy for My Presence to rest? ²³ It will then be, that every first of the new month, and every Sabbath, all mankind shall come to worship before Me in the Holy Temple," says God. ²⁴ The non-Jews shall go out of Jerusalem, to the valley of Jehoshaphat, and look upon the corpses of the men of Gog and Magog who have rebelled against Me, for the worms that eat them will not die, and the fire that burns them shall not be extinguished. They shall be a symbol of disgrace to all mankind. ²³ It will then be, that every first of the new month, and every Sabbath, all flesh shall come to worship before Me," says God.

סו 1 כֹּה אָמַר יְהוָה הַשָּׁמַיִם כִּסְאִי וְהָאָרֶץ הֲדֹם רַגְלָי אֵי־זֶה בַיִת אֲשֶׁר תִּבְנוּ־לִי וְאֵי־זֶה מָקוֹם מְנוּחָתִי: 23 וְהָיָה מִדֵּי־חֹדֶשׁ בְּחָדְשׁוֹ וּמִדֵּי שַׁבָּת בְּשַׁבַּתּוֹ יָבוֹא כָל־בָּשָׂר לְהִשְׁתַּחֲוֹת לְפָנַי אָמַר יְהוָה: 24 וְיָצְאוּ וְרָאוּ בְּפִגְרֵי הָאֲנָשִׁים הַפֹּשְׁעִים בִּי כִּי תוֹלַעְתָּם לֹא תָמוּת וְאִשָּׁם לֹא תִכְבֶּה וְהָיוּ דֵרָאוֹן לְכָל־בָּשָׂר: 23 וְהָיָה מִדֵּי־חֹדֶשׁ בְּחָדְשׁוֹ וּמִדֵּי שַׁבָּת בְּשַׁבַּתּוֹ יָבוֹא כָל־בָּשָׂר לְהִשְׁתַּחֲוֹת לְפָנַי אָמַר יְהוָה:

If Sunday is Rosh Ḥodesh, Ḥabad communities add the following (I Samuel 20:18; ibid. 42):

20 ¹⁸ Jonathan said to David, "Tomorrow is the first of the new month. You shall be missed, because your seat will be empty. ⁴² Jonathan said to David, "Go in peace, as both of us have sworn in the name of God, saying, 'God be a witness between me and you, and between my descendants and your descendants forever.'"

כ 18 וַיֹּאמֶר־לוֹ יְהוֹנָתָן מָחָר חֹדֶשׁ וְנִפְקַדְתָּ כִּי יִפָּקֵד מוֹשָׁבֶךָ: 42 וַיֹּאמֶר יְהוֹנָתָן לְדָוִד לֵךְ לְשָׁלוֹם אֲשֶׁר נִשְׁבַּעְנוּ שְׁנֵינוּ אֲנַחְנוּ בְּשֵׁם יְהוָה לֵאמֹר יְהוָה יִהְיֶה | בֵּינִי וּבֵינֶךָ וּבֵין זַרְעִי וּבֵין זַרְעֲךָ עַד־עוֹלָם:

haftarat shabbat ha-gadol

haftarat shabbat ha-gadol

ALL COMMUNITIES—MALACHI 3:4–24; 3:23

> **SYNOPSIS:** Many communities, including Habad, have the custom to recite this *Haftarah* only when *Shabbat Ha-Gadol* (the Sabbath prior to the festival of Passover) falls out on the eve of the festival (*Erev Pesah*). This is because the *Haftarah* alludes to the precept of removing tithes from one's possession—*"bring all the tithes to the storehouse"* (v.10)—which, according to Jewish law, must be completed by *Erev Pesah* (see *Deuteronomy* 26:12ff.). Others have the custom to read the *Haftarah* every *Shabbat Ha-Gadol*, because it mentions Elijah, the harbinger of redemption, *"I will send you the prophet Elijah before the arrival of God's great and awesome day"* (v.23), and the miracles of *Shabbat Ha-Gadol*—when the Egyptian firstborn fought a war against their own people—are somewhat reminiscent of the future Redemption.
>
> The *Haftarah*, said by the prophet Malachi shortly after the rebuilding of the Temple, opens with a brief glimpse of the "sweet" sacrifices of the future era (3:4), before passing swiftly to discuss the punishments of the Judgment Day (5–6). A lengthy substantiation of these punishments follows. God criticizes the people for failing to observe the commandments and for acting nonchalantly before Him (7–17). We are warned that the Day of Judgment is coming and only those who fear God will be saved (18–22). Nevertheless, Elijah the prophet will come beforehand and *"bring back the hearts of parents with their children"* (23–24).

According to Ḥabad custom, this *Haftarah* is read only when *Shabbat Ha-Gadol* coincides with *Erev Pesah*.

3 ⁴ "The offerings of Judah and Jerusalem will be sweet to God in the time of the future Redemption as in the early days of Moses and the former years of Solomon, and fire will once again descend on the altar."

⁵ "Then I will approach you in judgment. I will not delay judgment in order to examine witnesses, for I will act as the sole witness and enact judgment quickly upon sorcerers, adulterers, those who swear falsely, those who cheat their salaried workers, those who cheat a widow or an orphan, or pervert the justice of a proselyte," says the God of Hosts.

⁶ "For I, God, have not changed My mind—I still hate evil. And you, the children of Jacob, have not reached the end of your judgment, for many wicked people have died without retribution, and I will only punish them when they are resurrected."

⁷ "Ever since the days of your fathers, you have turned away from My laws and did not keep them. Return to Me and keep My commandments," says the God of Hosts, "and I will return to you and treat you well, as in the past."

ג 4 וְעָרְבָה לַיהֹוָה מִנְחַת יְהוּדָה וִירוּשָׁלָ͏ִם כִּימֵי עוֹלָם וּכְשָׁנִים קַדְמֹנִיּוֹת: 5 וְקָרַבְתִּי אֲלֵיכֶם לַמִּשְׁפָּט וְהָיִיתִי | עֵד מְמַהֵר בַּמְכַשְּׁפִים וּבַמְנָאֲפִים וּבַנִּשְׁבָּעִים לַשָּׁקֶר וּבְעֹשְׁקֵי שְׂכַר־שָׂכִיר אַלְמָנָה וְיָתוֹם וּמַטֵּי־גֵר וְלֹא יְרֵאוּנִי אָמַר יְהֹוָה צְבָאוֹת: 6 כִּי אֲנִי יְהֹוָה לֹא שָׁנִיתִי וְאַתֶּם בְּנֵי־יַעֲקֹב לֹא כְלִיתֶם: 7 לְמִימֵי אֲבֹתֵיכֶם סַרְתֶּם מֵחֻקַּי וְלֹא שְׁמַרְתֶּם שׁוּבוּ אֵלַי וְאָשׁוּבָה

הפטרת שבת הגדול

"But you have the nerve to say, 'What sins have we done for which we need to repent?'

⁸ "So I reply to you, 'Is it right that a human being should steal from God, because you steal from Me?'

"And if you will say, 'What did we steal from You?' My reply is that you stole the tithes and the *terumah* which you failed to give to the priests and the Levites. ⁹ Because of this you are under a curse, causing the land to be infertile. Yet you—the entire people, without a single exception—go on stealing from Me.

¹⁰ "So now, bring all the tithes to the storehouse in the Holy Temple, so that there should be food for the priests and Levites in My House. Please, test Me with the observance of this commandment," says the God of Hosts, "and see if I do not open up the apertures of the skies and pour down such blessings upon you that your crops cannot be contained in your storehouses. ¹¹ I will also destroy all the locusts for you, so that they do not destroy the land's produce or make the vines of the field lose their fruit," says the God of Hosts. ¹² "Then, all the nations will praise you, for you will be in a land which satisfies its inhabitants," says the God of Hosts.

¹³ "Your words distressed Me," says God.

"If you say, 'What did we say against You?' the answer is that ¹⁴ you said, 'It's worthless to serve God! What have we gained by keeping the laws which He told us to keep, and by walking humbly before the God of Hosts? ¹⁵ Now we see there's no value to the commandments, let us praise the intentional transgressors who were not so foolish as to observe the Torah! The wicked have established themselves: they have tested God to see if He enacts punishment and have survived!'"

¹⁶ The response to these people is: Then while the wicked were sinning, the God-fearing people discussed among themselves that God is indeed just. God listened and heard their words. A scroll of remembrance was then written at His command, mentioning those who fear God and contemplate the greatness of His name, so that they may be rewarded in the future.

¹⁷ "Their names will be kept with Me," says the God of Hosts, "until the day when I will take stock and pay reward. I will have compassion on them as a man has compassion on his son who serves him carefully.

¹⁸ "Even before the wicked are punished and while the righteous still suffer, you will return and see the difference between the righteous and the wicked, between the one who serves God and the one who does not serve Him.

¹⁹ "For behold, the day of judgment is coming, burning like an oven. The evildoers and all the wicked will

אֲלֵיכֶם אָמַר יְהוָה צְבָאוֹת וַאֲמַרְתֶּם בַּמֶּה נָשׁוּב: ח הֲיִקְבַּע אָדָם אֱלֹהִים כִּי אַתֶּם קֹבְעִים אֹתִי וַאֲמַרְתֶּם בַּמֶּה קְבַעֲנוּךָ הַמַּעֲשֵׂר וְהַתְּרוּמָה: ט בַּמְּאֵרָה אַתֶּם נֵאָרִים וְאֹתִי אַתֶּם קֹבְעִים הַגּוֹי כֻּלּוֹ: י הָבִיאוּ אֶת־כָּל־הַמַּעֲשֵׂר אֶל־בֵּית הָאוֹצָר וִיהִי טֶרֶף בְּבֵיתִי וּבְחָנוּנִי נָא בָּזֹאת אָמַר יְהוָה צְבָאוֹת אִם־לֹא אֶפְתַּח לָכֶם אֵת אֲרֻבּוֹת הַשָּׁמַיִם וַהֲרִיקֹתִי לָכֶם בְּרָכָה עַד־בְּלִי־דָי: יא וְגָעַרְתִּי לָכֶם בָּאֹכֵל וְלֹא־יַשְׁחִת לָכֶם אֶת־פְּרִי הָאֲדָמָה וְלֹא־תְשַׁכֵּל לָכֶם הַגֶּפֶן בַּשָּׂדֶה אָמַר יְהוָה צְבָאוֹת: יב וְאִשְּׁרוּ אֶתְכֶם כָּל־הַגּוֹיִם כִּי־תִהְיוּ אַתֶּם אֶרֶץ חֵפֶץ אָמַר יְהוָה צְבָאוֹת: יג חָזְקוּ עָלַי דִּבְרֵיכֶם אָמַר יְהוָה וַאֲמַרְתֶּם מַה־נִּדְבַּרְנוּ עָלֶיךָ: יד אֲמַרְתֶּם שָׁוְא עֲבֹד אֱלֹהִים וּמַה־בֶּצַע כִּי שָׁמַרְנוּ מִשְׁמַרְתּוֹ וְכִי הָלַכְנוּ קְדֹרַנִּית מִפְּנֵי יְהוָה צְבָאוֹת: טו וְעַתָּה אֲנַחְנוּ מְאַשְּׁרִים זֵדִים גַּם־נִבְנוּ עֹשֵׂי רִשְׁעָה גַּם בָּחֲנוּ אֱלֹהִים וַיִּמָּלֵטוּ: טז אָז נִדְבְּרוּ יִרְאֵי יְהוָה אִישׁ אֶל־רֵעֵהוּ וַיַּקְשֵׁב יְהוָה וַיִּשְׁמָע וַיִּכָּתֵב סֵפֶר זִכָּרוֹן לְפָנָיו לְיִרְאֵי יְהוָה וּלְחֹשְׁבֵי שְׁמוֹ: יז וְהָיוּ לִי אָמַר יְהוָה צְבָאוֹת לַיּוֹם אֲשֶׁר אֲנִי עֹשֶׂה סְגֻלָּה וְחָמַלְתִּי עֲלֵיהֶם כַּאֲשֶׁר יַחְמֹל אִישׁ עַל־בְּנוֹ הָעֹבֵד אֹתוֹ: יח וְשַׁבְתֶּם וּרְאִיתֶם בֵּין צַדִּיק לְרָשָׁע בֵּין עֹבֵד אֱלֹהִים לַאֲשֶׁר לֹא עֲבָדוֹ: יט כִּי־הִנֵּה הַיּוֹם בָּא בֹּעֵר כַּתַּנּוּר וְהָיוּ כָל־

haftarat pesaḥ (first day)

be like straw, and the day of judgment will come and set them alight," says the God of Hosts. "It will leave them totally obliterated without root or branch.

²⁰ "But for those of you who fear My name, your observance of the precept of charity will shine for you like the sun. Its rays will spread like wings over the earth and will heal. Wherever you go, you will be abundantly satisfied, becoming fat like calves that are fed in their stalls. ²¹ You will crush the wicked, for they will be like dust under the soles of your feet on the day of judgment that I am promising to bring," says the God of Hosts.

²² "You will be well rewarded if you remember the Torah of My servant Moses, whom I commanded directly at Horeb with rules and laws for all Israel.

²³ "Behold, in the merit of observing the Torah, I will send you the prophet Elijah before the arrival of God's great and awesome day of judgment. ²⁴ He will bring back the hearts of parents with their children, and the hearts of children with their parents, for without this I would appear on the day of judgment and strike all the inhabitants of the land a devastating blow.

²³ "Behold, in the merit of observing the Torah, I will send you the prophet Elijah before the arrival of God's great and awesome day of judgment."

זֵדִים וְכָל־עֹשֵׂה רִשְׁעָה קַשׁ וְלִהַט אֹתָם הַיּוֹם הַבָּא אָמַר יְהוָה צְבָאוֹת אֲשֶׁר לֹא־יַעֲזֹב לָהֶם שֹׁרֶשׁ וְעָנָף: 20 וְזָרְחָה לָכֶם יִרְאֵי שְׁמִי שֶׁמֶשׁ צְדָקָה וּמַרְפֵּא בִּכְנָפֶיהָ וִיצָאתֶם וּפִשְׁתֶּם כְּעֶגְלֵי מַרְבֵּק: 21 וְעַסּוֹתֶם רְשָׁעִים כִּי־יִהְיוּ אֵפֶר תַּחַת כַּפּוֹת רַגְלֵיכֶם בַּיּוֹם אֲשֶׁר אֲנִי עֹשֶׂה אָמַר יְהוָה צְבָאוֹת: 22 זִכְרוּ תּוֹרַת מֹשֶׁה עַבְדִּי אֲשֶׁר צִוִּיתִי אוֹתוֹ בְחֹרֵב עַל־כָּל־יִשְׂרָאֵל חֻקִּים וּמִשְׁפָּטִים: 23 הִנֵּה אָנֹכִי שֹׁלֵחַ לָכֶם אֵת אֵלִיָּה הַנָּבִיא לִפְנֵי בּוֹא יוֹם יְהוָה הַגָּדוֹל וְהַנּוֹרָא: 24 וְהֵשִׁיב לֵב־אָבוֹת עַל־בָּנִים וְלֵב בָּנִים עַל־אֲבוֹתָם פֶּן־אָבוֹא וְהִכֵּיתִי אֶת־הָאָרֶץ חֵרֶם: 23 הִנֵּה אָנֹכִי שֹׁלֵחַ לָכֶם אֶת אֵלִיָּה הַנָּבִיא לִפְנֵי בּוֹא יוֹם יְהוָה הַגָּדוֹל וְהַנּוֹרָא:

haftarat pesaḥ
first day

Torah Reading—Exodus 12:21–51 (p. 396)
Maftir—Numbers 28:16–25 (p. 1002)

ALL COMMUNITIES—JOSHUA 3:5–7; 5:2 – 6:1; 27

SYNOPSIS: This *Haftarah* describes the first Passover offering in the land of Israel, brought in the times of Joshua, after a long period in the desert when it had not been possible to bring the offering (see commentaries to *Numbers* 9:1).

The *Haftarah* opens with a brief passage from chapter 3 (verses 5–7), as Joshua promises the people that wonders are to follow. The *Haftarah* resumes in chapter 5, after the Jordan has been crossed. The people are circumcised singlehandedly by Joshua, the only person capable of performing this precept, in preparation to offer the Passover sacrifice (5:2–9). The sacrifice is offered in its correct time (10), and the *ʿomer*-offering was brought (see *Leviticus* 23:9ff.), enabling the people to eat from the produce of the land (11). This signified the end of the era of manna (12). We then read a mystical account of how Joshua receives a revelation of the angel who is "*the commander of God's army*" (14–15). The *Haftarah* concludes by noting Jericho's fear at Joshua's approach (6:1), and skips to the end of the chapter, after the victory was complete, when it became clear to all that "God was with Joshua" (27).

הפטרת פסח יום א'

ג ⁵ Joshua said to the people, "Purify yourselves, because tomorrow God will perform wonders in your presence."

⁶ Joshua spoke to the priests, saying, "Raise the Ark of the Covenant, and pass ahead of the people." So they raised the Ark of the Covenant and went ahead of the people.

⁷ God said to Joshua, "Today I will begin to make you great in the eyes of all Israel, so they will know that just as I was with Moses so will I be with you."

5 ² At that time, God said to Joshua, "Make sharp blades and circumcise the children of Israel again, a second time." ³ So Joshua made sharp blades, and he circumcised the children of Israel at the place which was subsequently named Gibeath-haaraloth, "Mound of Foreskins."

⁴ And this is the reason why Joshua single-handedly circumcised all the people who had left Egypt: All the males fit for war from among those who had left Egypt, who were capable of performing a circumcision, had died in the desert on the way out of Egypt. ⁵ For while all the people who had left Egypt had been circumcised, none of those born in the desert on the way out of Egypt had been circumcised. ⁶ The children of Israel had then wandered in the desert for forty years, until all the people fit for war who had left Egypt died because they did not obey God, so there was nobody left capable of performing a circumcision. Because of their disobedience, God swore that He would not show them the land which He had sworn to their forefathers to give us, a land flowing with milk and honey, ⁷ but He raised their children in their place, and Joshua circumcised them, since they had not been circumcised on the way.

⁸ After all the people had been circumcised they remained where they were in the camp, until they were healed. ⁹ God said to Joshua, "Today through the circumcision I have removed (*GALloti*) the shame of Egypt from you." He called the place Gilgal, as it is known to this day.

¹⁰ The children of Israel camped in Gilgal, and they performed the Passover sacrifice on the fourteenth day of the month, in the afternoon, in the plains of Jericho.

ג ⁵ וַיֹּאמֶר יְהוֹשֻׁעַ אֶל־הָעָם הִתְקַדָּשׁוּ כִּי מָחָר יַעֲשֶׂה יְהֹוָה בְּקִרְבְּכֶם נִפְלָאוֹת: ⁶ וַיֹּאמֶר יְהוֹשֻׁעַ אֶל־הַכֹּהֲנִים לֵאמֹר שְׂאוּ אֶת־אֲרוֹן הַבְּרִית וְעִבְרוּ לִפְנֵי הָעָם וַיִּשְׂאוּ אֶת־אֲרוֹן הַבְּרִית וַיֵּלְכוּ לִפְנֵי הָעָם: ⁷ וַיֹּאמֶר יְהֹוָה אֶל־יְהוֹשֻׁעַ הַיּוֹם הַזֶּה אָחֵל גַּדֶּלְךָ בְּעֵינֵי כָּל־יִשְׂרָאֵל אֲשֶׁר יֵדְעוּן כִּי כַּאֲשֶׁר הָיִיתִי עִם־מֹשֶׁה אֶהְיֶה עִמָּךְ:

ה ² בָּעֵת הַהִיא אָמַר יְהֹוָה אֶל־יְהוֹשֻׁעַ עֲשֵׂה לְךָ חַרְבוֹת צֻרִים וְשׁוּב מֹל אֶת־בְּנֵי־יִשְׂרָאֵל שֵׁנִית: ³ וַיַּעַשׂ־לוֹ יְהוֹשֻׁעַ חַרְבוֹת צֻרִים וַיָּמָל אֶת־בְּנֵי יִשְׂרָאֵל אֶל־גִּבְעַת הָעֲרָלוֹת: ⁴ וְזֶה הַדָּבָר אֲשֶׁר־מָל יְהוֹשֻׁעַ כָּל־הָעָם הַיֹּצֵא מִמִּצְרַיִם הַזְּכָרִים כֹּל ׀ אַנְשֵׁי הַמִּלְחָמָה מֵתוּ בַמִּדְבָּר בַּדֶּרֶךְ בְּצֵאתָם מִמִּצְרָיִם: ⁵ כִּי־מֻלִים הָיוּ כָּל־הָעָם הַיֹּצְאִים וְכָל־הָעָם הַיִּלֹּדִים בַּמִּדְבָּר בַּדֶּרֶךְ בְּצֵאתָם מִמִּצְרַיִם לֹא־מָלוּ: ⁶ כִּי ׀ אַרְבָּעִים שָׁנָה הָלְכוּ בְנֵי־יִשְׂרָאֵל בַּמִּדְבָּר עַד־תֹּם כָּל־הַגּוֹי אַנְשֵׁי הַמִּלְחָמָה הַיֹּצְאִים מִמִּצְרַיִם אֲשֶׁר לֹא־שָׁמְעוּ בְּקוֹל יְהֹוָה אֲשֶׁר נִשְׁבַּע יְהֹוָה לָהֶם לְבִלְתִּי הַרְאוֹתָם אֶת־הָאָרֶץ אֲשֶׁר נִשְׁבַּע יְהֹוָה לַאֲבוֹתָם לָתֶת לָנוּ אֶרֶץ זָבַת חָלָב וּדְבָשׁ: ⁷ וְאֶת־בְּנֵיהֶם הֵקִים תַּחְתָּם אֹתָם מָל יְהוֹשֻׁעַ כִּי־עֲרֵלִים הָיוּ כִּי לֹא־מָלוּ אוֹתָם בַּדָּרֶךְ: ⁸ וַיְהִי כַּאֲשֶׁר־תַּמּוּ כָל־הַגּוֹי לְהִמּוֹל וַיֵּשְׁבוּ תַחְתָּם בַּמַּחֲנֶה עַד חֲיוֹתָם: ⁹ וַיֹּאמֶר יְהֹוָה אֶל־יְהוֹשֻׁעַ הַיּוֹם גַּלּוֹתִי אֶת־חֶרְפַּת מִצְרַיִם מֵעֲלֵיכֶם וַיִּקְרָא שֵׁם הַמָּקוֹם הַהוּא גִּלְגָּל עַד הַיּוֹם הַזֶּה: ¹⁰ וַיַּחֲנוּ בְנֵי־יִשְׂרָאֵל בַּגִּלְגָּל

haftarat pesaḥ (second day)

¹¹ On the intermediate day following the first day of Passover, they brought the *'omer*-offering and ate from the produce of the land—unleavened bread and roasted grain—during daytime.

¹² The remaining stores of manna were depleted the next day, once they began to eat from the land's produce. The children of Israel no longer had manna, and so they began to eat from the crops of the land of Canaan that year.

¹³ When Joshua was in Jericho he lifted his eyes and noticed a man standing right before him, with his sword unsheathed in his hand. Joshua went over to him and said, "Do you come to help us or our enemies?"

¹⁴ "No," he said, "I am the commander of God's army. Only now I have come to you."

Joshua threw himself to the ground, prostrated himself and said to him "What does my master have to say to his servant?"

¹⁵ The commander of God's army said to Joshua, "Remove your shoes from your feet, for the place on which you stand is holy!" Joshua did so.

6 ¹ Jericho's closed doors were re-enforced against the children of Israel. Nobody was allowed to leave or enter.

²⁷ God was with Joshua, and his reputation spread throughout the land.

וַיַּעֲשׂוּ אֶת־הַפֶּסַח בְּאַרְבָּעָה עָשָׂר יוֹם לַחֹדֶשׁ בָּעֶרֶב בְּעַרְבוֹת יְרִיחוֹ: 11 וַיֹּאכְלוּ מֵעֲבוּר הָאָרֶץ מִמָּחֳרַת הַפֶּסַח מַצּוֹת וְקָלוּי בְּעֶצֶם הַיּוֹם הַזֶּה: 12 וַיִּשְׁבֹּת הַמָּן מִמָּחֳרָת בְּאָכְלָם מֵעֲבוּר הָאָרֶץ וְלֹא־הָיָה עוֹד לִבְנֵי יִשְׂרָאֵל מָן וַיֹּאכְלוּ מִתְּבוּאַת אֶרֶץ כְּנַעַן בַּשָּׁנָה הַהִיא: 13 וַיְהִי בִּהְיוֹת יְהוֹשֻׁעַ בִּירִיחוֹ וַיִּשָּׂא עֵינָיו וַיַּרְא וְהִנֵּה־אִישׁ עֹמֵד לְנֶגְדּוֹ וְחַרְבּוֹ שְׁלוּפָה בְּיָדוֹ וַיֵּלֶךְ יְהוֹשֻׁעַ אֵלָיו וַיֹּאמֶר לוֹ הֲלָנוּ אַתָּה אִם־לְצָרֵינוּ: 14 וַיֹּאמֶר | לֹא כִּי אֲנִי שַׂר־צְבָא־יְהוָה עַתָּה בָאתִי וַיִּפֹּל יְהוֹשֻׁעַ אֶל־פָּנָיו אַרְצָה וַיִּשְׁתָּחוּ וַיֹּאמֶר לוֹ מָה אֲדֹנִי מְדַבֵּר אֶל־עַבְדּוֹ: 15 וַיֹּאמֶר שַׂר־צְבָא יְהוָה אֶל־יְהוֹשֻׁעַ שַׁל־נַעַלְךָ מֵעַל רַגְלֶךָ כִּי הַמָּקוֹם אֲשֶׁר אַתָּה עֹמֵד עָלָיו קֹדֶשׁ הוּא וַיַּעַשׂ יְהוֹשֻׁעַ כֵּן:

ו וִירִיחוֹ סֹגֶרֶת וּמְסֻגֶּרֶת מִפְּנֵי בְּנֵי יִשְׂרָאֵל אֵין יוֹצֵא וְאֵין בָּא: 27 וַיְהִי יְהוָה אֶת־יְהוֹשֻׁעַ וַיְהִי שָׁמְעוֹ בְּכָל־הָאָרֶץ:

haftarat pesaḥ
second day

Torah Reading—Leviticus 22:26–23:44 (p. 744)
Maftir—Numbers 28:16–25 (p. 1002)
ALL COMMUNITIES—II KINGS 23:1–9; 21–25

SYNOPSIS: This *Haftarah* describes the Passover sacrifice offered in the days of King Josiah (7th century B.C.E.), a leader of extraordinary importance who orchestrated an ambitious program of religious and national restoration, curbing of idolatrous worship, centralizing worship in the Temple, and attempting reunification of the northern and southern kingdoms. Josiah himself was raised in an atmosphere of idol-worship, and it was only in the eighteenth year of his reign that his desire to serve God was sparked by the finding of an original Torah scroll written by Moses, during the maintenance work on the Temple carried out by Hilkiah the High Priest.

The *Haftarah* describes the beginning of Josiah's campaign, the public reading of the scroll, at which time the king renewed the covenant of Torah which had been

הפטרת פסח יום ב'

neglected (23:1–3). All items associated with idol-worship were immediately removed from the Temple (4–7), and the private altars around the country were destroyed (8). Priests who had officiated in idolatrous ceremonies were banned from serving in the Temple (9). The *Haftarah* then skips further details of Josiah's campaign (in verses 10–20) and concludes with a description of the unique Passover offering made by the king (21–23). The final verses attest to the success and utter uniqueness of Josiah's leadership (24–25).

23 ¹ The king issued a call and all the elders of Judah and Jerusalem assembled before him. ² The king then went up to God's Temple, along with all the men of Judah and the inhabitants of Jerusalem, the priests, the prophets, and all the people, young and old. He read to them all the curses written in the Book of the Covenant which was to be found in God's Temple.

³ As the king stood on his dais, and made the covenant before God—to follow after God; be careful to keep His commandments, testimonies, and statutes with all his heart and soul; and to fulfil the words of this covenant written in this scroll—the entire people stood by the covenant.

⁴ The king instructed the High Priest Hilkiah, the priests of second rank, and the gatekeepers, to remove from God's Sanctuary all the vessels which had been made for idol-worship such as Baal, Asherah, and all the celestial bodies. He burned them outside Jerusalem on the plain near the river of Kidron and brought the ashes to Bethel.

⁵ He dismissed the priests of idol-worship who had been appointed by the kings of Judah to offer incense on private altars in the towns of Judah and the suburbs of Jerusalem, as well as those who had offered incense to Baal, the sun and moon, the constellations, and all the celestial bodies.

⁶ He took the Asherah from God's Temple and brought it outside Jerusalem near the Kidron River. He burned it at the Kidron River until it was dust and then scattered the dust over the graves of the people who had worshiped idols in their lifetime.

⁷ He destroyed the parochial chambers in God's Temple, where the women wove tapestries for the Asherah.

⁸ He brought all the priests from the towns of

כג ¹ וַיִּשְׁלַ֖ח הַמֶּ֑לֶךְ וַיַּאַסְפ֣וּ אֵלָ֔יו כׇּל־זִקְנֵ֥י יְהוּדָ֖ה וִירוּשָׁלָֽ͏ִם׃ ² וַיַּ֣עַל הַמֶּ֣לֶךְ בֵּית־יְהֹוָ֡ה וְכׇל־אִ֣ישׁ יְהוּדָה֩ וְכׇל־יֹשְׁבֵ֨י יְרוּשָׁלַ֜͏ִם אִתּ֗וֹ וְהַכֹּֽהֲנִים֙ וְהַנְּבִיאִ֔ים וְכׇל־הָעָ֖ם לְמִקָּטֹ֣ן וְעַד־גָּד֑וֹל וַיִּקְרָ֣א בְאׇזְנֵיהֶ֗ם אֶת־כׇּל־דִּבְרֵי֙ סֵ֣פֶר הַבְּרִ֔ית הַנִּמְצָ֖א בְּבֵ֥ית יְהֹוָֽה׃ ³ וַיַּעֲמֹ֣ד הַמֶּ֣לֶךְ עַֽל־הָעַמּ֡וּד וַיִּכְרֹ֣ת אֶֽת־הַבְּרִ֣ית ׀ לִפְנֵ֣י יְהֹוָ֡ה לָלֶ֩כֶת֩ אַחַ֨ר יְהֹוָ֜ה וְלִשְׁמֹ֧ר מִצְוֺתָ֣יו וְאֶת־עֵדְוֺתָ֣יו וְאֶת־חֻקֹּתָ֗יו בְּכׇל־לֵב֙ וּבְכׇל־נֶ֔פֶשׁ לְהָקִ֗ים אֶת־דִּבְרֵי֙ הַבְּרִ֣ית הַזֹּ֔את הַכְּתֻבִ֖ים עַל־הַסֵּ֣פֶר הַזֶּ֑ה וַיַּעֲמֹ֥ד כׇּל־הָעָ֖ם בַּבְּרִֽית׃ ⁴ וַיְצַ֣ו הַמֶּ֡לֶךְ אֶת־חִלְקִיָּ֩הוּ֩ הַכֹּהֵ֨ן הַגָּד֜וֹל וְאֶת־כֹּהֲנֵ֣י הַמִּשְׁנֶה֮ וְאֶת־שֹׁמְרֵ֣י הַסַּף֒ לְהוֹצִיא֙ מֵהֵיכַ֣ל יְהֹוָ֔ה אֵ֣ת כׇּל־הַכֵּלִ֗ים הָֽעֲשׂוּיִם֙ לַבַּ֣עַל וְלָֽאֲשֵׁרָ֔ה וּלְכֹ֖ל צְבָ֣א הַשָּׁמָ֑יִם וַֽיִּשְׂרְפֵ֞ם מִח֤וּץ לִירֽוּשָׁלַ֙͏ִם֙ בְּשַׁדְמ֣וֹת קִדְר֔וֹן וְנָשָׂ֥א אֶת־עֲפָרָ֖ם בֵּֽית־אֵֽל׃ ⁵ וְהִשְׁבִּ֣ית אֶת־הַכְּמָרִ֗ים אֲשֶׁ֤ר נָֽתְנוּ֙ מַלְכֵ֣י יְהוּדָ֔ה וַיְקַטֵּ֤ר בַּבָּמוֹת֙ בְּעָרֵ֣י יְהוּדָ֔ה וּמְסִבֵּ֖י יְרוּשָׁלָ֑͏ִם וְאֶת־הַֽמְקַטְּרִ֣ים לַבַּ֗עַל לַשֶּׁ֤מֶשׁ וְלַיָּרֵ֙חַ֙ וְלַמַּזָּל֔וֹת וּלְכֹ֖ל צְבָ֥א הַשָּׁמָֽיִם׃ ⁶ וַיֹּצֵ֣א אֶת־הָאֲשֵׁרָה֩ מִבֵּ֨ית יְהֹוָ֜ה מִח֤וּץ לִירוּשָׁלַ֙͏ִם֙ אֶל־נַ֣חַל קִדְר֔וֹן וַיִּשְׂרֹ֥ף אֹתָ֛הּ בְּנַ֥חַל קִדְר֖וֹן וַיָּ֣דֶק לְעָפָ֑ר וַיַּשְׁלֵךְ֙ אֶת־עֲפָרָ֔הּ עַל־קֶ֖בֶר בְּנֵ֥י הָעָֽם׃ ⁷ וַיִּתֹּץ֙ אֶת־בָּתֵּ֣י הַקְּדֵשִׁ֔ים אֲשֶׁ֖ר בְּבֵ֣ית יְהֹוָ֑ה אֲשֶׁ֤ר הַנָּשִׁים֙ אֹרְג֣וֹת שָׁ֔ם בָּתִּ֖ים לָאֲשֵׁרָֽה׃ ⁸ וַיָּבֵ֤א אֶת־כׇּל־

haftarat pesaḥ (intermediate shabbat)

Judah and defiled the private altars upon which the priests had offered incense, from Geba to Beer-sheba. He destroyed the private altars near the gates, near the entrance of the Gate of Joshua, governor of the city, which is on a man's left when entering the city gate.

⁹ The priests of the private altars were not permitted to ascend the altar of God in Jerusalem even after they repented. They nevertheless were allowed to eat unleavened bread from the sacrifices with their brothers.

²¹ The king commanded all the people, saying, "Bring the Passover-offering to God, your God, as is written in this Book of the Covenant." ²² For no Passover-offering had been offered in a state of purity like this during the times of the judges who ruled Israel or during the times of the kings of Israel and Judah. ²³ Only in the eighteenth year of King Josiah was such a Passover-offering offered to God in Jerusalem.

²⁴ Josiah did away with the mediums, oracles, statues, filthy idols, and abominations which had been seen in the land of Judah and Jerusalem, so as to fulfil the words of the Torah written in the scroll which the priest Hilkiah had found in God's Temple.

²⁵ There was no other king like him before or afterwards, who returned to God with all his heart and soul and might, abiding with all of Moses' Torah.

הַכֹּהֲנִים מֵעָרֵי יְהוּדָה וַיְטַמֵּא אֶת־הַבָּמוֹת אֲשֶׁר קִטְּרוּ־שָׁמָּה הַכֹּהֲנִים מִגֶּבַע עַד־בְּאֵר שָׁבַע וְנָתַץ אֶת־בָּמוֹת הַשְּׁעָרִים אֲשֶׁר־פֶּתַח שַׁעַר יְהוֹשֻׁעַ שַׂר־הָעִיר אֲשֶׁר־עַל־שְׂמֹאול אִישׁ בְּשַׁעַר הָעִיר: 9 אַךְ לֹא יַעֲלוּ כֹּהֲנֵי הַבָּמוֹת אֶל־מִזְבַּח יְהֹוָה בִּירוּשָׁלָ͏ִם כִּי אִם־אָכְלוּ מַצּוֹת בְּתוֹךְ אֲחֵיהֶם: 21 וַיְצַו הַמֶּלֶךְ אֶת־כָּל־הָעָם לֵאמֹר עֲשׂוּ פֶסַח לַיהֹוָה אֱלֹהֵיכֶם כַּכָּתוּב עַל סֵפֶר הַבְּרִית הַזֶּה: 22 כִּי לֹא נַעֲשָׂה כַּפֶּסַח הַזֶּה מִימֵי הַשֹּׁפְטִים אֲשֶׁר שָׁפְטוּ אֶת־יִשְׂרָאֵל וְכֹל יְמֵי מַלְכֵי יִשְׂרָאֵל וּמַלְכֵי יְהוּדָה: 23 כִּי אִם־ בִּשְׁמֹנֶה עֶשְׂרֵה שָׁנָה לַמֶּלֶךְ יֹאשִׁיָּהוּ נַעֲשָׂה הַפֶּסַח הַזֶּה לַיהֹוָה בִּירוּשָׁלָ͏ִם: 24 וְגַם אֶת־ הָאֹבוֹת וְאֶת־הַיִּדְּעֹנִים וְאֶת־הַתְּרָפִים וְאֶת־ הַגִּלֻּלִים וְאֵת כָּל־הַשִּׁקֻּצִים אֲשֶׁר נִרְאוּ בְּאֶרֶץ יְהוּדָה וּבִירוּשָׁלַ͏ִם בִּעֵר יֹאשִׁיָּהוּ לְמַעַן הָקִים אֶת־דִּבְרֵי הַתּוֹרָה הַכְּתֻבִים עַל־הַסֵּפֶר אֲשֶׁר מָצָא חִלְקִיָּהוּ הַכֹּהֵן בֵּית יְהֹוָה: 25 וְכָמֹהוּ לֹא־הָיָה לְפָנָיו מֶלֶךְ אֲשֶׁר־שָׁב אֶל־יְהֹוָה בְּכָל־ לְבָבוֹ וּבְכָל־נַפְשׁוֹ וּבְכָל־מְאֹדוֹ כְּכֹל תּוֹרַת מֹשֶׁה וְאַחֲרָיו לֹא־קָם כָּמֹהוּ:

haftarat pesaḥ
intermediate shabbat

Torah Reading—Exodus 33:12–34:26 (p. 540)
Maftir—Numbers 28:19–25 (p. 1002)
ALL COMMUNITIES—Ezekiel 37:1–14

SYNOPSIS: This *Haftarah* is the account of Ezekiel's resurrection of "dry bones" in the valley. According to tradition, these were the bones of a group from the tribe of Ephraim who attempted to leave Egypt thirty-eight years before the Exodus and were killed by the Philistines—hence the connection with Passover.

A further connection between the *Haftarah* and the festival is a link to the theme of resurrection in general. Rabbi Hai b. Sherira Gaon (10th–11th century) testified to an oral tradition that the final resurrection of the dead will occur in the month of *Nisan*, the month when Passover occurs.

הפטרת פסח שבת חול המועד

As the *Haftarah* begins, the prophet Ezekiel is placed, against his will, in a valley of dry bones (37:1–2). God instructs Ezekiel to "prophesy over the bones" and they will come to life (3–6). The bones rattle, join together, are garbed with flesh and skin, and the spirit of life enters them (7–10). God then explains the message behind what has occurred. The bones represent the Jewish people's spirits in Exile which are exasperated and "dried out." The resurrection which has occurred is a sign that God will once again invigorate His people and restore them to their land (11–14).

37 ¹ God's prophetic power came upon me. God removed me from my place, against my will, but according to His will, and placed me in the valley, which was full of bones. ² He passed me near and all around them. I saw that there were very many of them on the surface of the valley, and I saw that they were very dry.

³ He said to me, "Son of man, can these bones live again?"

I said, "God Almighty, this depends on Your will, and only You know Your will."

⁴ He said to me, "Prophesy over these bones. Say to them, 'O dry bones, hear the word of God!' ⁵ This is what God Almighty says to these bones, 'I will cause a wind to pass through you, and you will be thereby blown together in your correct positions, so that you can take shape and begin to come alive. ⁶ I will place sinews upon you to attach the bones to each other, bring flesh upon you, and cover you with skin. Then I will cause a spirit to enter you and you will come alive—and you will know that I am God.'"

⁷ I prophesied as I was commanded. As I prophesied, there was a sudden noise of gushing wind, and the bones rattled and came together, cleaving to one another. ⁸ I saw sinews and flesh had grown on them, and they were encompassed in skin from above, but there was no spirit in them. ⁹ God said to me, "Prophesy to the spirit! Prophesy, son of man, and say to the spirit that *God Almighty* says, 'Let the spirit come from the four directions to where their souls departed and breathe into these slain ones, and they will live.'"

¹⁰ I prophesied as I was commanded and the spirit entered them, they came to life and they stood on their feet. There was a very great multitude.

¹¹ Then He said to me, "Son of Man! These bones represent the entire House of Israel that have passed away in exile. They are now saying, 'Until the Redemption comes our bones are dried out! Our hope for

לז ¹ הָיְתָ֣ה עָלַי֮ יַד־יְהוָה֒ וַיּוֹצִאֵ֤נִי בְר֙וּחַ֙ יְהוָ֔ה וַיְנִיחֵ֖נִי בְּת֣וֹךְ הַבִּקְעָ֑ה וְהִ֖יא מְלֵאָ֥ה עֲצָמֽוֹת: ² וְהֶעֱבִירַ֥נִי עֲלֵיהֶ֖ם סָבִ֣יב ׀ סָבִ֑יב וְהִנֵּ֨ה רַבּ֤וֹת מְאֹד֙ עַל־פְּנֵ֣י הַבִּקְעָ֔ה וְהִנֵּ֖ה יְבֵשׁ֥וֹת מְאֹֽד: ³ וַיֹּ֣אמֶר אֵלַ֔י בֶּן־אָדָ֕ם הֲתִחְיֶ֖ינָה הָעֲצָמ֣וֹת הָאֵ֑לֶּה וָאֹמַ֕ר אֲדֹנָ֥י יְהוִ֖ה אַתָּ֥ה יָדָֽעְתָּ: ⁴ וַיֹּ֣אמֶר אֵלַ֔י הִנָּבֵ֖א עַל־הָעֲצָמ֣וֹת הָאֵ֑לֶּה וְאָמַרְתָּ֣ אֲלֵיהֶ֔ם הָעֲצָמוֹת֙ הַיְבֵשׁ֔וֹת שִׁמְע֖וּ דְּבַר־יְהוָֽה: ⁵ כֹּ֤ה אָמַר֙ אֲדֹנָ֣י יְהוִ֔ה לָעֲצָמ֖וֹת הָאֵ֑לֶּה הִנֵּ֨ה אֲנִ֜י מֵבִ֥יא בָכֶ֛ם ר֖וּחַ וִחְיִיתֶֽם: ⁶ וְנָתַתִּי֩ עֲלֵיכֶ֨ם גִּדִ֜ים וְהַֽעֲלֵתִ֧י עֲלֵיכֶ֣ם בָּשָׂ֗ר וְקָרַמְתִּ֤י עֲלֵיכֶם֙ ע֔וֹר וְנָתַתִּ֥י בָכֶ֛ם ר֖וּחַ וִחְיִיתֶ֑ם וִידַעְתֶּ֖ם כִּֽי־אֲנִ֥י יְהוָֽה: ⁷ וְנִבֵּ֖אתִי כַּאֲשֶׁ֣ר צֻוֵּ֑יתִי וַֽיְהִי־ק֤וֹל כְּהִנָּֽבְאִי֙ וְהִנֵּה־רַ֔עַשׁ וַתִּקְרְב֣וּ עֲצָמ֔וֹת עֶ֖צֶם אֶל־עַצְמֽוֹ: ⁸ וְרָאִ֜יתִי וְהִנֵּֽה־עֲלֵיהֶ֤ם גִּדִים֙ וּבָשָׂ֣ר עָלָ֔ה וַיִּקְרַ֧ם עֲלֵיהֶ֛ם ע֖וֹר מִלְמָ֑עְלָה וְר֖וּחַ אֵ֥ין בָּהֶֽם: ⁹ וַיֹּ֣אמֶר אֵלַ֔י הִנָּבֵ֖א אֶל־הָר֑וּחַ הִנָּבֵ֣א בֶן־אָ֠דָם וְאָמַרְתָּ֨ אֶל־הָר֜וּחַ כֹּֽה־אָמַ֣ר ׀ אֲדֹנָ֣י יְהוִ֗ה מֵאַרְבַּ֤ע רוּחוֹת֙ בֹּ֣אִי הָר֔וּחַ וּפְחִ֛י בַּהֲרוּגִ֥ים הָאֵ֖לֶּה וְיִֽחְיֽוּ: ¹⁰ וְהִנַּבֵּ֖אתִי כַּאֲשֶׁ֣ר צִוָּ֑נִי וַתָּבוֹא֩ בָהֶ֨ם הָר֜וּחַ וַיִּֽחְי֗וּ וַיַּֽעַמְדוּ֙ עַל־רַגְלֵיהֶ֔ם חַ֖יִל גָּד֥וֹל מְאֹד־מְאֹֽד: ¹¹ וַיֹּאמֶר֮ אֵלַי֒ בֶּן־אָדָ֕ם הָעֲצָמ֣וֹת הָאֵ֔לֶּה כָּל־בֵּ֥ית יִשְׂרָאֵ֖ל הֵ֑מָּה הִנֵּ֣ה אֹמְרִ֗ים

haftarat pesaḥ (last day)

the Redemption is lost, because we are cut off from the living who will witness the Redemption.' [12] "So prophesy and say to them, 'God Almighty says, "These people who were resurrected today are a sign for all that when the redemption comes I am going to open your graves. I will take you out of your graves, My people, and bring you to the land of Israel so you too will witness the Redemption. [13] My people! You will know that I am God who keeps My word when I open your graves and take you out of them. [14] I will cause My spirit to enter you, and you will come to life. I will place you on your soil, and you will know that I, God, have spoken and acted," says God."'

יָבְשׁוּ עַצְמוֹתֵינוּ וְאָבְדָה תִקְוָתֵנוּ נִגְזַרְנוּ לָנוּ: [12] לָכֵן הִנָּבֵא וְאָמַרְתָּ אֲלֵיהֶם כֹּה־אָמַר אֲדֹנָי יְהוִה הִנֵּה אֲנִי פֹתֵחַ אֶת־קִבְרוֹתֵיכֶם וְהַעֲלֵיתִי אֶתְכֶם מִקִּבְרוֹתֵיכֶם עַמִּי וְהֵבֵאתִי אֶתְכֶם אֶל־אַדְמַת יִשְׂרָאֵל: [13] וִידַעְתֶּם כִּי־אֲנִי יְהוָה בְּפִתְחִי אֶת־קִבְרוֹתֵיכֶם וּבְהַעֲלוֹתִי אֶתְכֶם מִקִּבְרוֹתֵיכֶם עַמִּי: [14] וְנָתַתִּי רוּחִי בָכֶם וִחְיִיתֶם וְהִנַּחְתִּי אֶתְכֶם עַל־אַדְמַתְכֶם וִידַעְתֶּם כִּי אֲנִי יְהוָה דִּבַּרְתִּי וְעָשִׂיתִי נְאֻם־יְהוָה:

haftarat pesaḥ
seventh day

Torah Reading—Exodus 13:17–15:26 (p. 408)
Maftir—Numbers 28:19–25 (p. 1002)
ALL COMMUNITIES—II SAMUEL 22:1–51

The *Haftarah* for *Parashat Ha'azinu* ("Then David, in his old age, chanted"—וַיְדַבֵּר דָּוִד) is read, page 1412.

haftarat pesaḥ
last day

Torah Reading—Deut. 15:19–16:17 (p. 1154). On Shabbat:
Deut. 14:22–16:17 (p. 1148). Maftir—Num. 28:19–25 (p. 1002)
ALL COMMUNITIES—ISAIAH 10:32 – 12:6

SYNOPSIS: This *Haftarah* is read during Passover because it opens with a prophecy about the downfall of Sennacherib (king of Assyria, 705-681 B.C.E.; oppressor of Jerusalem in the times of King Hezekiah) whose downfall took place on the first night of Passover.

10 [32] "Today Assyria will stand at Nob," boasted the king of Assyria, as his army marched towards Jerusalem, "and wave their hands mockingly at the mount of the daughter of Zion, the hill of Jerusalem which we will conquer with great ease!"

[33] But the Master, God of Hosts, will send an angel to destroy them, to cut down with an ax their arrogance, which is as high as the tree branches. The tall strong ones will be felled and die and the lofty ones lowered. [34] The army who is like intertwined branches of the forest will be cut down with iron, and Lebanon will fall by an angel as mighty as bronze.

[32] עוֹד הַיּוֹם בְּנֹב לַעֲמֹד יְנֹפֵף יָדוֹ הַר [בֵּית] בַּת־צִיּוֹן גִּבְעַת יְרוּשָׁלָ͏ִם: [33] הִנֵּה הָאָדוֹן יְהוָה צְבָאוֹת מְסָעֵף פֻּארָה בְּמַעֲרָצָה וְרָמֵי הַקּוֹמָה גְּדוּעִים וְהַגְּבֹהִים יִשְׁפָּלוּ: [34] וְנִקַּף סִבְכֵי הַיַּעַר בַּבַּרְזֶל וְהַלְּבָנוֹן בְּאַדִּיר יִפּוֹל:

הפטרת אחרון של פסח

11 ¹ Do not be surprised by this wonder, for a time will come when God will do something even more wondrous, when a staff will come out from the shoots of Jesse; a branch will sprout from his roots and become the King Messiah. ² The spirit of prophecy from God will rest upon him—a spirit of wisdom and understanding, a spirit of counsel and courage, a spirit of knowledge and fear of God. ³ He will be able to "smell" whether people are good or evil, due to his tremendous fear of God; he will not need to judge by appearance or decide what he hears, for he will know the answer in his heart. ⁴ He will judge the poor justly, uninfluenced by the power of the rich, and he will rebuke fairly for the cause of the lowly of the land. He will strike down the wicked of the land with the curse of his mouth, sharp like a rod, and he will slay evildoers with the utterance of his lips. ⁵ Justice will be the belt on his loins, and faith the belt on his waist.

⁶ The wolf will live peacefully with the lamb and the leopard will lie down with the goat. The calf, the lion, and the fattened ox will graze together, and a young boy will lead them without being harmed. ⁷ The cow and the bear will graze together, and their young will lie down together. The lion will eat straw, like an ox. ⁸ A baby will play at a viper's hole, and an infant will stretch his hand over an adder's den. ⁹ These snakes will do no damage or harm anywhere in My holy mount, for the earth will be filled with knowledge of God, as water covers the seabed.

¹⁰ On that day, the Messiah, who will arise from the root of Jesse, will stand as a banner for the nations, and all the people will seek him. His peaceful approach will earn him respect.

¹¹ On that day, God will again show His strength to retake the remnant of His people—those remaining in Assyria, Egypt, Pathros, Ethiopia, Elam, Shinar, Hamath, and the sea islands. ¹² It will be as if He will signal to the nations for He will inspire them to release their Jewish inhabitants. Thus, He will assemble the exiles of Israel, and gather the dispersed of Judah from the four corners of the earth.

¹³ Ephraim's historic jealousy for the throne of Israel will cease, and their antagonism to Judah will be eliminated. The Messiah son of Joseph, a descendant of Ephraim, will not envy the Messiah son of David, a descendant of Judah, and likewise Judah's Messiah will not trouble Ephraim's. ¹⁴ Together they will swiftly

יא ¹ וְיָצָא חֹטֶר מִגֵּזַע יִשָׁי וְנֵצֶר מִשָּׁרָשָׁיו יִפְרֶה: ² וְנָחָה עָלָיו רוּחַ יְהֹוָה רוּחַ חׇכְמָה וּבִינָה רוּחַ עֵצָה וּגְבוּרָה רוּחַ דַּעַת וְיִרְאַת יְהֹוָה: ³ וַהֲרִיחוֹ בְּיִרְאַת יְהֹוָה וְלֹא־לְמַרְאֵה עֵינָיו יִשְׁפּוֹט וְלֹא־לְמִשְׁמַע אׇזְנָיו יוֹכִיחַ: ⁴ וְשָׁפַט בְּצֶדֶק דַּלִּים וְהוֹכִיחַ בְּמִישׁוֹר לְעַנְוֵי־אָרֶץ וְהִכָּה־אֶרֶץ בְּשֵׁבֶט פִּיו וּבְרוּחַ שְׂפָתָיו יָמִית רָשָׁע: ⁵ וְהָיָה צֶדֶק אֵזוֹר מׇתְנָיו וְהָאֱמוּנָה אֵזוֹר חֲלָצָיו: ⁶ וְגָר זְאֵב עִם־כֶּבֶשׂ וְנָמֵר עִם־גְּדִי יִרְבָּץ וְעֵגֶל וּכְפִיר וּמְרִיא יַחְדָּו וְנַעַר קָטֹן נֹהֵג בָּם: ⁷ וּפָרָה וָדֹב תִּרְעֶינָה יַחְדָּו יִרְבְּצוּ יַלְדֵיהֶן וְאַרְיֵה כַּבָּקָר יֹאכַל־תֶּבֶן: ⁸ וְשִׁעֲשַׁע יוֹנֵק עַל־חֻר פָּתֶן וְעַל מְאוּרַת צִפְעוֹנִי גָּמוּל יָדוֹ הָדָה: ⁹ לֹא־יָרֵעוּ וְלֹא־יַשְׁחִיתוּ בְּכׇל־הַר קׇדְשִׁי כִּי־מָלְאָה הָאָרֶץ דֵּעָה אֶת־יְהֹוָה כַּמַּיִם לַיָּם מְכַסִּים: ¹⁰ וְהָיָה בַּיּוֹם הַהוּא שֹׁרֶשׁ יִשַׁי אֲשֶׁר עֹמֵד לְנֵס עַמִּים אֵלָיו גּוֹיִם יִדְרֹשׁוּ וְהָיְתָה מְנֻחָתוֹ כָּבוֹד: ¹¹ וְהָיָה ׀ בַּיּוֹם הַהוּא יוֹסִיף אֲדֹנָי ׀ שֵׁנִית יָדוֹ לִקְנוֹת אֶת־שְׁאָר עַמּוֹ אֲשֶׁר יִשָּׁאֵר מֵאַשּׁוּר וּמִמִּצְרַיִם וּמִפַּתְרוֹס וּמִכּוּשׁ וּמֵעֵילָם וּמִשִּׁנְעָר וּמֵחֲמָת וּמֵאִיֵּי הַיָּם: ¹² וְנָשָׂא נֵס לַגּוֹיִם וְאָסַף נִדְחֵי יִשְׂרָאֵל וּנְפֻצוֹת יְהוּדָה יְקַבֵּץ מֵאַרְבַּע כַּנְפוֹת הָאָרֶץ: ¹³ וְסָרָה קִנְאַת אֶפְרַיִם וְצֹרְרֵי יְהוּדָה יִכָּרֵתוּ אֶפְרַיִם לֹא־יְקַנֵּא אֶת־יְהוּדָה וִיהוּדָה לֹא־יָצֹר אֶת־אֶפְרָיִם: ¹⁴ וְעָפוּ בְכָתֵף פְּלִשְׁתִּים יָמָּה יַחְדָּו יָבֹזּוּ אֶת־בְּנֵי־קֶדֶם אֱדוֹם וּמוֹאָב מִשְׁלוֹחַ יָדָם

haftarat shavuot (first day)

attack the Philistines to the west and plunder the men of the east. Their hand will be extended over Edom and Moab, and the Ammonites will be subordinate to them. ¹⁵ God will dry up the Nile, the "tongue" of the Egyptian Sea. He will raise His hand over the Euphrates River with His powerful wind and He will split the river into seven streams, so that it can be trodden with shoes. ¹⁶ It will become a highway for the remnant of His people who will remain from Assyria, just as there was for Israel on the day they came up from the land of Egypt.

12 ¹ And you will say on that day, "I thank You, God, for You were angry with me, but now let Your wrath calm down and comfort me. ² Since the God of my salvation is with me, I will be secure, and not fear. My salvation came from my attesting to the might of God and singing His praise."

³ You will draw water endlessly with joy from the springs of salvation. ⁴ On that day you will encourage and say, "Give thanks to God! Call out His name! Make His deeds known among the nations! Remind each other that His name is exalted! ⁵ Sing to God, for He has done a great thing! Let this be known throughout the earth! ⁶ Raise your voice in joy, you who live in Zion, for the Holy One of Israel is great due to the wonders He has performed among you!"

וּבְנֵי עַמּוֹן מִשְׁמַעְתָּם: 15 וְהֶחֱרִים יְהֹוָה אֵת לְשׁוֹן יָם־מִצְרַיִם וְהֵנִיף יָדוֹ עַל־הַנָּהָר בַּעְיָם רוּחוֹ וְהִכָּהוּ לְשִׁבְעָה נְחָלִים וְהִדְרִיךְ בַּנְּעָלִים: 16 וְהָיְתָה מְסִלָּה לִשְׁאָר עַמּוֹ אֲשֶׁר יִשָּׁאֵר מֵאַשּׁוּר כַּאֲשֶׁר הָיְתָה לְיִשְׂרָאֵל בְּיוֹם עֲלֹתוֹ מֵאֶרֶץ מִצְרָיִם:

יב 1 וְאָמַרְתָּ בַּיּוֹם הַהוּא אוֹדְךָ יְהֹוָה כִּי אָנַפְתָּ בִּי יָשֹׁב אַפְּךָ וּתְנַחֲמֵנִי: 2 הִנֵּה אֵל יְשׁוּעָתִי אֶבְטַח וְלֹא אֶפְחָד כִּי־עָזִּי וְזִמְרָת יָהּ יְהֹוָה וַיְהִי־לִי לִישׁוּעָה: 3 וּשְׁאַבְתֶּם־מַיִם בְּשָׂשׂוֹן מִמַּעַיְנֵי הַיְשׁוּעָה: 4 וַאֲמַרְתֶּם בַּיּוֹם הַהוּא הוֹדוּ לַיהֹוָה קִרְאוּ בִשְׁמוֹ הוֹדִיעוּ בָעַמִּים עֲלִילֹתָיו הַזְכִּירוּ כִּי נִשְׂגָּב שְׁמוֹ: 5 זַמְּרוּ יְהֹוָה כִּי גֵאוּת עָשָׂה [מידעת כ׳] מוּדַעַת זֹאת בְּכָל־הָאָרֶץ: 6 צַהֲלִי וָרֹנִּי יוֹשֶׁבֶת צִיּוֹן כִּי־גָדוֹל בְּקִרְבֵּךְ קְדוֹשׁ יִשְׂרָאֵל:

haftarat shavuot
first day

Torah Reading—Exodus 19:1–20:23 (p. 440)
Maftir—Numbers 28:26–31 (p. 1002)
ALL COMMUNITIES—Ezekiel 1:1 – 28; 3:12

SYNOPSIS: This *Haftarah* describes Ezekiel's mystical vision of the Divine glory which he received by the Chebar River in Babylon, in 593 B.C.E. It is read on the Festival of *Shavuot*, when we celebrate the revelation at Sinai, at which time the entire nation saw the content of Ezekiel's vision with their own eyes.

1 ¹ It was in the thirtieth year of the last fifty-year Jubilee cycle during the Babylonian exile, on the fifth day of the fourth month. I was among the exiles by the Chebar River, when the heavens opened, and I saw visions of God.

² On the fifth of the month, during the fifth year of

א 1 וַיְהִי | בִּשְׁלֹשִׁים שָׁנָה בָּרְבִיעִי בַּחֲמִשָּׁה לַחֹדֶשׁ וַאֲנִי בְתוֹךְ־הַגּוֹלָה עַל־נְהַר־כְּבָר נִפְתְּחוּ הַשָּׁמַיִם וָאֶרְאֶה מַרְאוֹת אֱלֹהִים: 2 בַּחֲמִשָּׁה לַחֹדֶשׁ הִיא

הפטרת שבועות יום א'

3 הַשָּׁנָה הַחֲמִישִׁית לְגָלוּת הַמֶּלֶךְ יוֹיָכִין: הָיֹה הָיָה דְבַר־יְהֹוָה אֶל־יְחֶזְקֵאל בֶּן־בּוּזִי הַכֹּהֵן בְּאֶרֶץ כַּשְׂדִּים עַל־נְהַר־כְּבָר וַתְּהִי עָלָיו שָׁם יַד־יְהֹוָה: 4 וָאֵרֶא וְהִנֵּה רוּחַ סְעָרָה בָּאָה מִן־הַצָּפוֹן עָנָן גָּדוֹל וְאֵשׁ מִתְלַקַּחַת וְנֹגַהּ לוֹ סָבִיב וּמִתּוֹכָהּ כְּעֵין הַחַשְׁמַל מִתּוֹךְ הָאֵשׁ: 5 וּמִתּוֹכָהּ דְּמוּת אַרְבַּע חַיּוֹת וְזֶה מַרְאֵיהֶן דְּמוּת אָדָם לָהֵנָּה: 6 וְאַרְבָּעָה פָנִים לְאֶחָת וְאַרְבַּע כְּנָפַיִם לְאַחַת לָהֶם: 7 וְרַגְלֵיהֶם רֶגֶל יְשָׁרָה וְכַף רַגְלֵיהֶם כְּכַף רֶגֶל עֵגֶל וְנֹצְצִים כְּעֵין נְחֹשֶׁת קָלָל: 8 [וִידֵי כ׳] וְיִדֵי אָדָם מִתַּחַת כַּנְפֵיהֶם עַל אַרְבַּעַת רִבְעֵיהֶם וּפְנֵיהֶם וְכַנְפֵיהֶם לְאַרְבַּעְתָּם: 9 חֹבְרֹת אִשָּׁה אֶל־אֲחוֹתָהּ כַּנְפֵיהֶם לֹא־יִסַּבּוּ בְלֶכְתָּן אִישׁ אֶל־עֵבֶר פָּנָיו יֵלֵכוּ: 10 וּדְמוּת פְּנֵיהֶם פְּנֵי אָדָם וּפְנֵי אַרְיֵה אֶל־הַיָּמִין לְאַרְבַּעְתָּם וּפְנֵי־שׁוֹר מֵהַשְּׂמֹאול לְאַרְבַּעְתָּן וּפְנֵי־נֶשֶׁר לְאַרְבַּעְתָּן: 11 וּפְנֵיהֶם וְכַנְפֵיהֶם פְּרֻדוֹת מִלְמָעְלָה לְאִישׁ שְׁתַּיִם חֹבְרוֹת אִישׁ וּשְׁתַּיִם מְכַסּוֹת אֵת גְּוִיֹּתֵיהֶנָה: 12 וְאִישׁ אֶל־עֵבֶר פָּנָיו יֵלֵכוּ אֶל אֲשֶׁר יִהְיֶה־שָּׁמָּה הָרוּחַ לָלֶכֶת יֵלֵכוּ לֹא יִסַּבּוּ בְּלֶכְתָּן: 13 וּדְמוּת הַחַיּוֹת מַרְאֵיהֶם כְּגַחֲלֵי־אֵשׁ בֹּעֲרוֹת כְּמַרְאֵה הַלַּפִּדִים הִיא מִתְהַלֶּכֶת בֵּין הַחַיּוֹת וְנֹגַהּ לָאֵשׁ וּמִן־הָאֵשׁ יוֹצֵא בָרָק: 14 וְהַחַיּוֹת רָצוֹא וָשׁוֹב כְּמַרְאֵה הַבָּזָק: 15 וָאֵרֶא הַחַיּוֹת וְהִנֵּה אוֹפַן אֶחָד בָּאָרֶץ אֵצֶל הַחַיּוֹת לְאַרְבַּעַת פָּנָיו: 16 מַרְאֵה הָאוֹפַנִּים וּמַעֲשֵׂיהֶם כְּעֵין תַּרְשִׁישׁ וּדְמוּת אֶחָד לְאַרְבַּעְתָּן וּמַרְאֵיהֶם וּמַעֲשֵׂיהֶם כַּאֲשֶׁר יִהְיֶה הָאוֹפַן בְּתוֹךְ הָאוֹפָן: 17 עַל־אַרְבַּעַת רִבְעֵיהֶן

the exile of King Jehoiachin, [3] God's word came to Ezekiel son of Buzi the priest in the land of Chaldeans, by the Chebar River. God's prophetic power came upon him there.

[4] I looked and saw a stormy wind coming from the north, referring to the Babylonian and Chaldean kings, a great cloud and flashing fire alluding to the destruction of the Temple, surrounded by a radiance, the salvation which is to follow. Inside, within the fire, was the appearance of a pristine glow. [5] Within the radiance was the image of four creatures. Their bodily appearance was in the figure of a person. [6] Each had four faces—human, lion, ox, and eagle, and each face had four wings. [7] Their legs were straight legs without joints, and the soles of their feet were like the bottom of a calf's hoof, sparkling like pure bronze. [8] They had human hands under their wings on their four sides, and their faces and wings were alike on the four of them. [9] Their wings touched each other so that the faces could be hidden. They did not need to turn when they moved, as each moved in the direction of any of its four faces. [10] Their faces had the following appearance: a man's face; and to its right, on each of the four creatures, a lion's face; to the left of the man's face, an ox's face, on each of the four creatures; and to its rear, an eagle's face, on each of the four creatures. [11] Their wings were spread upwards over their faces. Each face had two wings that met each another, concealing it, and two wings covering their bodies. [12] Each moved in the direction of its faces. It went wherever it wanted to move because it had four faces, each in another of the four directions, so it did not have to turn as it moved.

[13] As for the composition of the creatures, they looked like burning coals of fire. The fiery appearance was shared by the creatures. There was additional radiance to the fire, and lightning came out of the fire. [14] The creatures went to and fro, like lightning.

[15] I looked harder at the creatures, and noticed a wheel on the earth near each of the creatures, one wheel for all four faces. [16] The appearance of the wheels and their composition was like topaz. All four wheels had the same shape, and their appearance and composition was like that of a wheel within a wheel facing north-south and east-west. [17] Thus, their movement could occur on their four sides,

haftarat shavuot (first day)

without turning as they moved. **18** The rims of the wheels and their backs were frightening, full of many colors around all four of them.

19 As the creatures moved, the wheels moved with them, and when the creatures lifted themselves above the ground, the wheels were lifted with them. **20** They went wherever the will of God, their Rider, led them to go, because their own will was to go there as well. The wheels were lifted up with them, for the will of the creature was also in the wheels. **21** As the creatures moved, the wheels moved, and when they stopped, the wheels stopped. As they were lifted up above the ground, the wheels were lifted up with them, because the will of the creatures was also in the wheels.

22 There was an image above the heads of each creature, an expanse like ice, awe-inspiring, spread above their heads. **23** Under the expanse, their wings were aligned, one facing the other. Each had two wings covering their bodies here, and two covering them there. **24** I heard the sound of their wings as they moved, like the sound of mighty waters, like the sound of God at Sinai. The sound of the uproar was like the sound of a large camp of people. When they stood, their wings were quiet. **25** When there was a sound of God's voice from the expanse above their heads, they stood and their wings were softened and quiet.

26 On top of the expanse above their heads was something which shined like sapphire stone, the image of a throne. Above, on the image of the throne, was an image that looked like a man. **27** From what appeared to be his waist and above, I saw something like a pristine glow that seemed to have a fiery frame housed around it. But from what appeared to be its waist and below, I saw something that looked like fire with a radiance around it. **28** The radiance around it looked the way a rainbow looks in a cloud on a rainy day. It was the appearance of a semblance of the glory of God! I saw and fell on my face, and I heard a voice speaking.

3 12 Then the spirit carried me up, and I heard a great roaring sound behind me: "Blessed is the glory of God, even after it has moved from its place in the Holy of Holies!"

בְּלֶכְתָּם וְגָבְהֵן וְגֹבַהּ 18 וְגַבֵּיהֶן לָהֶם וְיִרְאָה לָהֶם וְגַבֹּתָם מְלֵאֹת עֵינַיִם סָבִיב לְאַרְבַּעְתָּן: 19 וּבְלֶכֶת הַחַיּוֹת יֵלְכוּ הָאוֹפַנִּים אֶצְלָם וּבְהִנָּשֵׂא הַחַיּוֹת מֵעַל הָאָרֶץ יִנָּשְׂאוּ הָאוֹפַנִּים: 20 עַל אֲשֶׁר יִהְיֶה־שָּׁם הָרוּחַ לָלֶכֶת יֵלֵכוּ שָׁמָּה הָרוּחַ לָלֶכֶת וְהָאוֹפַנִּים יִנָּשְׂאוּ לְעֻמָּתָם כִּי רוּחַ הַחַיָּה בָּאוֹפַנִּים: 21 בְּלֶכְתָּם יֵלֵכוּ וּבְעָמְדָם יַעֲמֹדוּ וּבְהִנָּשְׂאָם מֵעַל הָאָרֶץ יִנָּשְׂאוּ הָאוֹפַנִּים לְעֻמָּתָם כִּי רוּחַ הַחַיָּה בָּאוֹפַנִּים: 22 וּדְמוּת עַל־רָאשֵׁי הַחַיָּה רָקִיעַ כְּעֵין הַקֶּרַח הַנּוֹרָא נָטוּי עַל־רָאשֵׁיהֶם מִלְמָעְלָה: 23 וְתַחַת הָרָקִיעַ כַּנְפֵיהֶם יְשָׁרוֹת אִשָּׁה אֶל־אֲחוֹתָהּ לְאִישׁ שְׁתַּיִם מְכַסּוֹת לָהֵנָּה וּלְאִישׁ שְׁתַּיִם מְכַסּוֹת לָהֵנָּה אֵת גְּוִיֹּתֵיהֶם: 24 וָאֶשְׁמַע אֶת־קוֹל כַּנְפֵיהֶם כְּקוֹל מַיִם רַבִּים כְּקוֹל־שַׁדַּי בְּלֶכְתָּם קוֹל הֲמֻלָּה כְּקוֹל מַחֲנֶה בְּעָמְדָם תְּרַפֶּינָה כַנְפֵיהֶן: 25 וַיְהִי־קוֹל מֵעַל לָרָקִיעַ אֲשֶׁר עַל־רֹאשָׁם בְּעָמְדָם תְּרַפֶּינָה כַנְפֵיהֶן: 26 וּמִמַּעַל לָרָקִיעַ אֲשֶׁר עַל־רֹאשָׁם כְּמַרְאֵה אֶבֶן־סַפִּיר דְּמוּת כִּסֵּא וְעַל דְּמוּת הַכִּסֵּא דְּמוּת כְּמַרְאֵה אָדָם עָלָיו מִלְמָעְלָה: 27 וָאֵרֶא | כְּעֵין חַשְׁמַל כְּמַרְאֵה־אֵשׁ בֵּית־לָהּ סָבִיב מִמַּרְאֵה מָתְנָיו וּלְמָעְלָה וּמִמַּרְאֵה מָתְנָיו וּלְמַטָּה רָאִיתִי כְּמַרְאֵה־אֵשׁ וְנֹגַהּ לוֹ סָבִיב: 28 כְּמַרְאֵה הַקֶּשֶׁת אֲשֶׁר יִהְיֶה בֶעָנָן בְּיוֹם הַגֶּשֶׁם כֵּן מַרְאֵה הַנֹּגַהּ סָבִיב הוּא מַרְאֵה דְּמוּת כְּבוֹד־יְהֹוָה וָאֶרְאֶה וָאֶפֹּל עַל־פָּנַי וָאֶשְׁמַע קוֹל מְדַבֵּר:

ג 12 וַתִּשָּׂאֵנִי רוּחַ וָאֶשְׁמַע אַחֲרַי קוֹל רַעַשׁ גָּדוֹל בָּרוּךְ כְּבוֹד־יְהֹוָה מִמְּקוֹמוֹ:

haftarat shavuot
second day

הפטרת שבועות יום ב'

Torah Reading—Deut. 15:19–16:17 (p. 1154). On Shabbat: Deut. 14:22–16:17 (p. 1148). Maftir—Num. 28:26–31 (p. 1002)

ALL COMMUNITIES—HABAKKUK 2:20 – 3:19

> **SYNOPSIS:** This *Haftarah* is read on Shavuot because verse 3, *"God came through Teman"* alludes to the giving of the Torah. The verse is also expounded in connection with the giving of the Torah: *"This teaches us that God offered the Torah to every nation and every tongue, but none accepted it, until He came to the Jewish people, who accepted it"* (*Avodah Zarah* 2b).
>
> Like the *Haftarah* of the first day of *Shavuot*, this reading centers around a heavenly vision seen by the prophet Habakkuk (3:3–15). It is preceded by a statement that *"God is in His heavenly abode"* (2:20), and a short prayer by the prophet (3:1). The conclusion of the *Haftarah* records Habakkuk's reaction to the revelation he had just witnessed (16–19).

2 ²⁰ God, although He may not be seen, for He is in His holy heavenly abode, nevertheless the entire earth is silent in trepidation before Him, for He rules over it.

3 ¹ The prophet Habakkuk's prayer for having inadvertently erred:

² O God, I heard your message of the long exile and I became terrified! O God, during these years sustain the nation who is Your handiwork, make it known during those years, that even in anger, You will remember to be merciful to them.

³ God came to the Jewish people after they passed through Teman. Indeed, the Holy One came when they passed through Mount Paran, which is close to Edom. Then, when the Jewish people defeated Sihon and Og, God's splendor covered the heavens, and His acclaim filled the earth. ⁴ The glow of the pillar of fire which accompanied the Jewish people at night was as light as day; they were empowered with the might of His hand, and there, with them, were the tablets which had been previously concealed on High, and were inside the ark of His Strength. ⁵ In front of the ark, pestilence loomed, to destroy the Canaanites and when the ark came, fiery coals came out to annihilate them. ⁶ When the ark would stop, the land was conquered, later to be measured out to the tribes. The ark "looked" at the land,

ב 20 וַיהוָה בְּהֵיכַל קָדְשׁוֹ הַס מִפָּנָיו כָּל־הָאָרֶץ:

ג 1 תְּפִלָּה לַחֲבַקּוּק הַנָּבִיא עַל שִׁגְיֹנוֹת: 2 יְהוָה שָׁמַעְתִּי שִׁמְעֲךָ יָרֵאתִי יְהוָה פָּעָלְךָ בְּקֶרֶב שָׁנִים חַיֵּיהוּ בְּקֶרֶב שָׁנִים תּוֹדִיעַ בְּרֹגֶז רַחֵם תִּזְכּוֹר: 3 אֱלוֹהַּ מִתֵּימָן יָבוֹא וְקָדוֹשׁ מֵהַר־פָּארָן סֶלָה כִּסָּה שָׁמַיִם הוֹדוֹ וּתְהִלָּתוֹ מָלְאָה הָאָרֶץ: 4 וְנֹגַהּ כָּאוֹר תִּהְיֶה קַרְנַיִם מִיָּדוֹ לוֹ וְשָׁם חֶבְיוֹן עֻזֹּה: 5 לְפָנָיו יֵלֶךְ דָּבֶר וְיֵצֵא רֶשֶׁף לְרַגְלָיו: 6 עָמַד ׀ וַיְמֹדֶד אֶרֶץ רָאָה וַיַּתֵּר גּוֹיִם וַיִּתְפֹּצְצוּ הַרְרֵי־עַד שַׁחוּ גִּבְעוֹת עוֹלָם הֲלִיכוֹת עוֹלָם לוֹ: 7 תַּחַת אָוֶן רָאִיתִי אָהֳלֵי כוּשָׁן יִרְגְּזוּן

and the nations were displaced. The ancient "mountains" of Canaanite aristocracy were shattered; eternal "hills" were humbled—because those that run the ways of the world belong to God.

⁷ I saw that God did not intervene on Israel's behalf when they came under the rule of the tents of King Cushan, not because He was lacking in strength, but due to the inappropriate behavior of Israel. For when Israel did repent in the days of Gideon, God caused the coverings of Midian's royal tents to tremble in terror.

haftarat shavuot (second day)

⁸ Were You angry with the river Jordan when You split it, O God? Were You furious at the river? Were you incensed at the Reed Sea when you split it? No! You split the waters so that You could ride Your horses with Your chariot of salvation, to redeem the Jewish people!

⁹ Your bow was fully unsheathed to fight against the Canaanites, to fulfil the promise You made to the Patriarchs, to give the land of Israel to the tribes! Thus, in the desert, you split the earth open into rivers so that the Jewish people would have water to live, enabling them to reach the land.

¹⁰ The mountains shook when they saw You and moved together to crush the enemy. A stream of water went by from the well, to bring up the remains of the enemy so that the people could see the victory, and the deep well cried aloud, to announce the miracle. On that day, God's powerful hands were exalted and esteemed, for everybody recognized His miracles.

¹¹ In the days of Joshua, the sun and moon stood still in their place, and Israel went to victory in the light of Your arrows, in the glow of Your spearheads. ¹² In anger, You paced the earth and trampled nations in rage.

¹³ In the days of King Hezekiah, You came out to deliver Your people, to deliver Your anointed one. Through Your angel You crushed the heads of the wicked House of Sennacherib, baring the foundation of their power, even to its core which is in the neck, so that it will never arise again.

¹⁴ With Sennacherib's own spear, you pierced the heads of his senior officials in his open cities. They had stormed towards us, intending to scatter us, but we instead scattered them. Their planned joy was turned on their heads, like that of the Egyptians who wanted to devour their victim in secret in the desert, but ¹⁵ Your clouds, which were like horses, trampled them in the sea, together with piles of mighty waters.

¹⁶ I heard something that caused my heart within my abdomen to tremble. My lips quivered at the news, decay entered my bones, and I shuddered wherever I stood. I heard that when I will come to the land of Israel, which was supposed to be during a time of rest, it will turn to a day of affliction, to come up against a people of troops. ¹⁷ At that time, Israel's military might will still be like a fig tree that has not blossomed with no fruit growth on the vines, like a lean olive produce, like fields that produce no harvest. In the wake of the Babylonian exile, Israel will still be small in number, like flocks cut off from the pen, with no cattle in the stalls, so how will they stand against mighty Gog? ¹⁸ Yet I will rejoice that God will help; I will be joyful at the power of the God of my salvation. ¹⁹ While we are small, God Almighty will be for us like a giant army. He will make our feet swift like the deer's and lead us upon hilltops to catch the enemy.

This song should be given to the Levite conductor of Temple music, who should play it with my designated melody.

יְרִיעוֹת אֶרֶץ מִדְיָן: 8 הֲבִנְהָרִים חָרָה יְהֹוָה אִם בַּנְּהָרִים אַפֶּךָ אִם־בַּיָּם עֶבְרָתֶךָ כִּי תִרְכַּב עַל־סוּסֶיךָ מַרְכְּבוֹתֶיךָ יְשׁוּעָה: 9 עֶרְיָה תֵעוֹר קַשְׁתֶּךָ שְׁבֻעוֹת מַטּוֹת אֹמֶר סֶלָה נְהָרוֹת תְּבַקַּע־אָרֶץ: 10 רָאוּךָ יָחִילוּ הָרִים זֶרֶם מַיִם עָבָר נָתַן תְּהוֹם קוֹלוֹ רוֹם יָדֵיהוּ נָשָׂא: 11 שֶׁמֶשׁ יָרֵחַ עָמַד זְבֻלָה לְאוֹר חִצֶּיךָ יְהַלֵּכוּ לְנֹגַהּ בְּרַק חֲנִיתֶךָ: 12 בְּזַעַם תִּצְעַד־אָרֶץ בְּאַף תָּדוּשׁ גּוֹיִם: 13 יָצָאתָ לְיֵשַׁע עַמֶּךָ לְיֵשַׁע אֶת־מְשִׁיחֶךָ מָחַצְתָּ רֹּאשׁ מִבֵּית רָשָׁע עָרוֹת יְסוֹד עַד־צַוָּאר סֶלָה: 14 נָקַבְתָּ בְמַטָּיו רֹאשׁ פְּרָזָו יִסְעֲרוּ לַהֲפִיצֵנִי עֲלִיצֻתָם כְּמוֹ־לֶאֱכֹל עָנִי בַּמִּסְתָּר: 15 דָּרַכְתָּ בַיָּם סוּסֶיךָ חֹמֶר מַיִם רַבִּים: 16 שָׁמַעְתִּי ׀ וַתִּרְגַּז בִּטְנִי לְקוֹל צָלְלוּ שְׂפָתַי יָבוֹא רָקָב בַּעֲצָמַי וְתַחְתַּי אֶרְגָּז אֲשֶׁר אָנוּחַ לְיוֹם צָרָה לַעֲלוֹת לְעַם יְגוּדֶנּוּ: 17 כִּי־תְאֵנָה לֹא־תִפְרָח וְאֵין יְבוּל בַּגְּפָנִים כִּחֵשׁ מַעֲשֵׂה־זַיִת וּשְׁדֵמוֹת לֹא־עָשָׂה אֹכֶל גָּזַר מִמִּכְלָה צֹאן וְאֵין בָּקָר בָּרְפָתִים: 18 וַאֲנִי בַּיהֹוָה אֶעְלוֹזָה אָגִילָה בֵּאלֹהֵי יִשְׁעִי: 19 יְהֹוִה אֲדֹנָי חֵילִי וַיָּשֶׂם רַגְלַי כָּאַיָּלוֹת וְעַל־בָּמוֹתַי יַדְרִכֵנִי לַמְנַצֵּחַ בִּנְגִינוֹתָי:

הפטרת תשעה באב שחרית

ninth of av
morning service

Torah Reading—Deuteronomy 4:25–40 (p. 1088)
ALL COMMUNITIES—JEREMIAH 8:13 – 9:23

SYNOPSIS: In keeping with the somber mood of the Ninth of *Av*, when the holy Temple was destroyed, the *Haftarah* is taken from a passage of Jeremiah, in which the prophet urges the people to lament and conveys a message of gloom and destruction. After an opening which depicts the inevitable doom that is to come (8:13–17), the *Haftarah* relates heartfelt expressions of the prophet's own grief (18–23). The following chapter is a harsh critique of Israel's sins (9:1–5), and their due punishments (6–15). The people are encouraged to compose dirges in anticipation of what is to come (16-21). The *Haftarah* concludes with words of advice, not to trust in human wisdom or power, and to seek only the knowledge of God and the observance of His commands (22–23).

8 ¹³ "I will eradicate them from the world," says God. "There will be no grapes left on the vine and no figs on the fig tree. The leaves will be obliterated, and I will give them enemies who will remove them from the world. ¹⁴ When the enemy comes, the people of the fields will say, 'Why are we sitting around like bait for our enemies? Let's gather together, and come to the fortified cities, though even there we will probably be destroyed, for God, our God, has destroyed us. He has made us drink bitter hemlock, for we have sinned against God.' ¹⁵ They hope for peace, but nothing is good. They hope for a time of relief, but instead there is terror.

¹⁶ "The snorting of horses will already be heard from Dan when the enemy reaches there. The whole land will shake from the noise of their warriors. They come and devour the land and its manmade contents, cities and their inhabitants. ¹⁷ For behold, I will incite against you enemies that are like serpents, snakes which cannot be charmed, and they will bite you," says God.

¹⁸ "I tried to overcome my grief, but my heart is sick *within me*, ¹⁹ *and* how can it not be, when in my eyes, the exile has already begun and it is as if I hear the voice of my people crying from a distant land. All this could have been avoided through prayer, for is God not in Zion to listen to your prayers? Isn't the Jewish people's King in her midst waiting to respond to her prayers? Why instead of praying to Me do they continue to anger Me with their graven idols, their foreign vanities?

ח ¹³ אָסֹף אֲסִיפֵם נְאֻם־יְהֹוָה אֵין עֲנָבִים בַּגֶּפֶן וְאֵין תְּאֵנִים בַּתְּאֵנָה וְהֶעָלֶה נָבֵל וָאֶתֵּן לָהֶם יַעַבְרוּם: ¹⁴ עַל־מָה אֲנַחְנוּ יֹשְׁבִים הֵאָסְפוּ וְנָבוֹא אֶל־עָרֵי הַמִּבְצָר וְנִדְּמָה־שָּׁם כִּי יְהֹוָה אֱלֹהֵינוּ הֲדִמָּנוּ וַיַּשְׁקֵנוּ מֵי־רֹאשׁ כִּי חָטָאנוּ לַיהֹוָה: ¹⁵ קַוֵּה לְשָׁלוֹם וְאֵין טוֹב לְעֵת מַרְפֵּה וְהִנֵּה בְעָתָה: ¹⁶ מִדָּן נִשְׁמַע נַחְרַת סוּסָיו מִקּוֹל מִצְהֲלוֹת אַבִּירָיו רָעֲשָׁה כָּל־הָאָרֶץ וַיָּבוֹאוּ וַיֹּאכְלוּ אֶרֶץ וּמְלוֹאָהּ עִיר וְיֹשְׁבֵי בָהּ: ¹⁷ כִּי הִנְנִי מְשַׁלֵּחַ בָּכֶם נְחָשִׁים צִפְעֹנִים אֲשֶׁר אֵין־לָהֶם לָחַשׁ וְנִשְּׁכוּ אֶתְכֶם נְאֻם־יְהֹוָה: ¹⁸ מַבְלִיגִיתִי עֲלֵי יָגוֹן עָלַי לִבִּי דַוָּי: ¹⁹ הִנֵּה־קוֹל שַׁוְעַת בַּת־עַמִּי מֵאֶרֶץ מַרְחַקִּים הַיהֹוָה אֵין בְּצִיּוֹן אִם־מַלְכָּהּ אֵין בָּהּ מַדּוּעַ הִכְעִסוּנִי

haftarat ninth of av (morning service)

20 "We await salvation, but the harvest has passed and summer is over, and we have not been saved.

21 "I am broken because I have seen how in the future my people will be broken. I am dulled, and desolation has taken hold of me.

22 "Is there no study of Torah or observance of commandments among the Jewish people to save them like the healing balm from Gilead? Is there no sage, no spiritual 'doctor' there? Why have my people not been 'healed' and redeemed?

23 "If only my head were water and my eyes fountains of tears so I could cry day and night over the slain of my people!

9 **1** "If only I were in the desert, at a traveler's inn, so I could abandon my people and go away from them. For they are all adulterers, a bunch of traitors! **2** They bend their tongues like bows to speak falsehood and hurt others.

"Those who grow powerful in the land do not do so to promote faith. For they go from evil to evil, and they do not know Me," says God.

3 "Let each person beware of his friend not to tell him your secrets. Don't trust any brother, for every brother acts crookedly and every friend goes around gossiping. **4** Each man mocks another. They do not speak the truth. They have trained their tongues to speak falsehood, and they strive to be dishonest. **5** You live amid deceit. In their deceit, they refuse to know Me," says God. **6** Therefore, the God of Hosts says, "I will refine them and test them with suffering, for what I can do to My people? I cannot leave them to destroy themselves through their own sins.

7 "Their tongue is a drawn arrow, which speaks deception. Openly a person speaks peacefully to his friend, but inside he plans to attack him.

8 "Shall I not watch them and punish them for this?" says God. "Shall My soul not take vengeance on a nation like this?

9 "I will weep a chant over the mountains and a lament over the pastures in the desert, for they have been laid waste so that no man passes by, and no sound of cattle is heard. The birds of the sky and the beasts have moved and left. **10** I will turn Jerusalem into rubble, into a den for snakes. I will make the cities of Judah desolate, void of inhabitants.

בְּפִסְלֵיהֶ֖ם בְּהַבְלֵ֥י נֵכָֽר: 20 עָבַ֥ר קָצִ֖יר כָּ֣לָה קָ֑יִץ וַאֲנַ֖חְנוּ ל֥וֹא נוֹשָֽׁעְנוּ: 21 עַל־שֶׁ֥בֶר בַּת־עַמִּ֖י הָשְׁבָּ֑רְתִּי קָדַ֕רְתִּי שַׁמָּ֖ה הֶחֱזִקָֽתְנִי: 22 הַצֳרִי֙ אֵ֣ין בְּגִלְעָ֔ד אִם־רֹפֵ֖א אֵ֣ין שָׁ֑ם כִּ֗י מַדּ֙וּעַ֙ לֹ֣א עָֽלְתָ֔ה אֲרֻכַ֖ת בַּת־עַמִּֽי: 23 מִֽי־יִתֵּ֤ן רֹאשִׁי֙ מַ֔יִם וְעֵינִ֖י מְק֣וֹר דִּמְעָ֑ה וְאֶבְכֶּה֙ יוֹמָ֣ם וָלַ֔יְלָה אֵ֖ת חַֽלְלֵ֥י בַת־עַמִּֽי:

ט 1 מִֽי־יִתְּנֵ֣נִי בַמִּדְבָּ֗ר מְלוֹן֙ אֹֽרְחִ֔ים וְאֶֽעֶזְבָה֙ אֶת־עַמִּ֔י וְאֵלְכָ֖ה מֵֽאִתָּ֑ם כִּ֤י כֻלָּם֙ מְנָ֣אֲפִ֔ים עֲצֶ֖רֶת בֹּֽגְדִֽים: 2 וַֽיַּדְרְכ֤וּ אֶת־לְשׁוֹנָם֙ קַשְׁתָּ֣ם שֶׁ֔קֶר וְלֹ֥א לֶאֱמוּנָ֖ה גָּבְר֣וּ בָאָ֑רֶץ כִּי֩ מֵרָעָ֨ה אֶל־רָעָ֧ה ׀ יָצָ֛אוּ וְאֹתִ֥י לֹֽא־יָדָ֖עוּ נְאֻם־יְהֹוָֽה: 3 אִ֤ישׁ מֵרֵעֵ֙הוּ֙ הִשָּׁמֵ֔רוּ וְעַל־כָּל־אָ֖ח אַל־תִּבְטָ֑חוּ כִּ֤י כָל־אָח֙ עָק֣וֹב יַעְקֹ֔ב וְכָל־רֵ֖עַ רָכִ֥יל יַהֲלֹֽךְ: 4 וְאִ֤ישׁ בְּרֵעֵ֙הוּ֙ יְהָתֵ֔לּוּ וֶאֱמֶ֖ת לֹ֣א יְדַבֵּ֑רוּ לִמְּד֧וּ לְשׁוֹנָ֛ם דַּבֶּר־שֶׁ֖קֶר הַעֲוֵ֥ה נִלְאֽוּ: 5 שִׁבְתְּךָ֖ בְּת֣וֹךְ מִרְמָ֑ה בְּמִרְמָ֛ה מֵאֲנ֥וּ דַֽעַת־אוֹתִ֖י נְאֻם־יְהֹוָֽה: 6 לָכֵ֗ן כֹּ֤ה אָמַר֙ יְהֹוָ֣ה צְבָא֔וֹת הִנְנִ֥י צֽוֹרְפָ֖ם וּבְחַנְתִּ֑ים כִּי־אֵ֣יךְ אֶעֱשֶׂ֔ה מִפְּנֵ֖י בַּת־עַמִּֽי: 7 חֵ֥ץ [שוחט כ׳] שָׁח֛וּט לְשׁוֹנָ֖ם מִרְמָ֣ה דִבֵּ֑ר בְּפִ֗יו שָׁל֤וֹם אֶת־רֵעֵ֙הוּ֙ יְדַבֵּ֔ר וּבְקִרְבּ֖וֹ יָשִׂ֥ים אָרְבּֽוֹ: 8 הַעַל־אֵ֥לֶּה לֹֽא־אֶפְקָד־בָּ֖ם נְאֻם־יְהֹוָ֑ה אִ֚ם בְּג֣וֹי אֲשֶׁר־כָּזֶ֔ה לֹ֥א תִתְנַקֵּ֖ם נַפְשִֽׁי: 9 עַל־הֶ֨הָרִ֜ים אֶשָּׂ֧א בְכִ֣י וָנֶ֗הִי וְעַל־נְא֤וֹת מִדְבָּר֙ קִינָ֔ה כִּ֤י נִצְּתוּ֙ מִבְּלִי־אִ֣ישׁ עֹבֵ֔ר וְלֹ֥א שָׁמְע֖וּ ק֣וֹל מִקְנֶ֑ה מֵע֤וֹף הַשָּׁמַ֙יִם֙ וְעַד־בְּהֵמָ֔ה נָדְד֖וּ הָלָֽכוּ: 10 וְנָתַתִּ֧י אֶת־יְרוּשָׁלַ֛͏ִם לְגַלִּ֖ים מְע֣וֹן תַּנִּ֑ים וְאֶת־עָרֵ֤י

הפטרת תשעה באב שחרית

11 "Whoever is wise will understand the following, and whoever God has spoken to can interpret this: Why has the land been destroyed and laid waste like a desert, with no one passing through? 12 God says, 'It is because they abandoned the study of My Torah, which I have given before them and therefore they did not obey Me and did not follow it. 13 They followed the fancies of their hearts and the Baal idols, as their fathers taught them.'"

14 "Therefore, this is what the God of Hosts, the God of Israel, says: I will feed this people wormwood and make them drink hemlock water. 15 I will scatter them among nations which neither they nor their ancestors knew, and there I will send the sword after them until I have destroyed them."

16 This is what the God of Hosts says, "Contemplate this impending misfortune! Call the dirge-singers and have them come. Send for the skilled women who compose verses of doom and have them come. 17 Let them hurry and start lamenting for us, so our eyes will run with tears and our eyelids will drip with water. 18 For the sound of wailing is heard from Zion, 'How we are ruined! We are greatly ashamed, for we have abandoned our land and have been thrown out of our dwellings.' 19 O women! Listen to God's words of impending punishment. Let your ears take heed of the word of His mouth! Teach your daughters how to wail, and each woman teach dirges to her friend. 20 For even if we shut our doors, death will enter our windows and come into our palaces, cutting off babies outside and young men in the streets.

21 "Say this to the Jewish people," says God. "That men's carcasses will fall, numerous like dung on the fields, like sheaves behind the reaper, with no one to gather them up for burial, for they will be afraid to leave their homes themselves."

22 This is what God says, "The wise man should not be proud of his wisdom, the warrior should not be proud of his heroism, and the rich should not be *proud of his riches, for none of them will be able to* save themselves. 23 Rather, it is only with this that a person may be proud of himself—knowing and understanding Me. For I am God, who performs kindness, justice, and righteousness on earth, since these are the things that I desire," says God.

11 מִי־הָאִישׁ הֶחָכָם וְיָבֵן אֶת־זֹאת וַאֲשֶׁר דִּבֶּר פִּי־יְהֹוָה אֵלָיו וְיַגִּדָהּ עַל־מָה אָבְדָה הָאָרֶץ נִצְּתָה כַמִּדְבָּר מִבְּלִי עֹבֵר: 12 וַיֹּאמֶר יְהֹוָה עַל־עׇזְבָם אֶת־תּוֹרָתִי אֲשֶׁר נָתַתִּי לִפְנֵיהֶם וְלֹא־שָׁמְעוּ בְקוֹלִי וְלֹא־הָלְכוּ בָהּ: 13 וַיֵּלְכוּ אַחֲרֵי שְׁרִרוּת לִבָּם וְאַחֲרֵי הַבְּעָלִים אֲשֶׁר לִמְּדוּם אֲבוֹתָם: 14 לָכֵן כֹּה־אָמַר יְהֹוָה צְבָאוֹת אֱלֹהֵי יִשְׂרָאֵל הִנְנִי מַאֲכִילָם אֶת־הָעָם הַזֶּה לַעֲנָה וְהִשְׁקִיתִים מֵי־רֹאשׁ: 15 וַהֲפִצוֹתִים בַּגּוֹיִם אֲשֶׁר לֹא יָדְעוּ הֵמָּה וַאֲבוֹתָם וְשִׁלַּחְתִּי אַחֲרֵיהֶם אֶת־הַחֶרֶב עַד כַּלּוֹתִי אוֹתָם: 16 כֹּה אָמַר יְהֹוָה צְבָאוֹת הִתְבּוֹנְנוּ וְקִרְאוּ לַמְקוֹנְנוֹת וּתְבוֹאֶינָה וְאֶל־הַחֲכָמוֹת שִׁלְחוּ וְתָבוֹאנָה: 17 וּתְמַהֵרְנָה וְתִשֶּׂנָה עָלֵינוּ נֶהִי וְתֵרַדְנָה עֵינֵינוּ דִּמְעָה וְעַפְעַפֵּינוּ יִזְּלוּ־מָיִם: 18 כִּי קוֹל נְהִי נִשְׁמַע מִצִּיּוֹן אֵיךְ שֻׁדָּדְנוּ בֹּשְׁנוּ מְאֹד כִּי־עָזַבְנוּ אָרֶץ כִּי הִשְׁלִיכוּ מִשְׁכְּנוֹתֵינוּ: 19 כִּי־שְׁמַעְנָה נָשִׁים דְּבַר־יְהֹוָה וְתִקַּח אׇזְנְכֶם דְּבַר־פִּיו וְלַמֵּדְנָה בְנוֹתֵיכֶם נֶהִי וְאִשָּׁה רְעוּתָהּ קִינָה: 20 כִּי־עָלָה מָוֶת בְּחַלּוֹנֵינוּ בָּא בְּאַרְמְנוֹתֵינוּ לְהַכְרִית עוֹלָל מִחוּץ בַּחוּרִים מֵרְחֹבוֹת: 21 דַּבֵּר כֹּה נְאֻם־יְהֹוָה וְנָפְלָה נִבְלַת הָאָדָם כְּדֹמֶן עַל־פְּנֵי הַשָּׂדֶה וּכְעָמִיר מֵאַחֲרֵי הַקֹּצֵר וְאֵין מְאַסֵּף: 22 כֹּה | אָמַר יְהֹוָה אַל־יִתְהַלֵּל חָכָם בְּחׇכְמָתוֹ וְאַל־יִתְהַלֵּל הַגִּבּוֹר בִּגְבוּרָתוֹ אַל־יִתְהַלֵּל עָשִׁיר בְּעׇשְׁרוֹ: 23 כִּי אִם־בְּזֹאת יִתְהַלֵּל הַמִּתְהַלֵּל הַשְׂכֵּל וְיָדֹעַ אוֹתִי כִּי אֲנִי יְהֹוָה עֹשֶׂה חֶסֶד מִשְׁפָּט וּצְדָקָה בָּאָרֶץ כִּי־בְאֵלֶּה חָפַצְתִּי נְאֻם־יְהֹוָה:

haftarat public fast day (afternoon service)

public fast day
afternoon service

Torah Reading—Exodus 32:11-14; 34:1-10 (p. 530)

ALL COMMUNITIES—ISAIAH 55:6 – 56:8

> **SYNOPSIS:** The *Babylonian Talmud* teaches that the merit of a fast day lies in the charity dispensed in the late afternoon to poor people who are fasting, in order that they should have food to eat when the fast ends. For this reason a *Haftarah* which mentions charity was instituted for the fast day ("*Guard My law and act charitably (to your fellow)*"—56:1), and it is read, contrary to the usual practice, in the afternoon service, so that this merit should be mentioned *after* the charity has already been distributed. Consequently, it is customary to give charity before the afternoon service, giving the value of the food usually consumed in one day, i.e., two or three meals.
>
> The *Haftarah*, said by the prophet Isaiah, opens with a call to the people to return to God (55:6-7), and God's forgiveness is depicted with the use of various metaphors (6-11). The first chapter concludes with a brief description of the Redemption (12-13). The next chapter begins by stressing that the Redemption will only come through observance of the law (56:1). Those who observe the Sabbath are promised happiness in this world and a place in the future Temple (3-5), and righteous converts, too, will have a role in the Redemption (6-8).

At afternoon services of the Ninth of Av, Sephardic communities read the Haftarah of Shabbat Shuvah—page 1409.

55 ⁶ Seek God while He may still be found among you, before you are exiled from your land, and call upon Him while He is still near. ⁷ The wicked person should abandon his wicked ways and the sinner his thoughts. He should return to God, who will have mercy on him; let the sinner return to our God and there is hope for him, for He is very forgiving.

⁸ "You might consider a person to be beyond hope," says God, "but My thoughts of forgiveness are not as your thoughts, and your ways are not My ways, since I can accept repentance and do not need to punish. ⁹ For as high as the skies are above the earth, so are My ways of forgiveness higher than your mortal ways, and My thoughts higher than your thoughts. ¹⁰ Just as the rain and snow fall from the skies, and do not return there through evaporation caused by the sun before they have nourished the earth, making it germinate and then sprout, providing seed for sowing elsewhere and bread to eat— ¹¹ so will be the case with My word which comes from My mouth: It will not return to Me unfulfilled. Rather, it will accomplish what I want and succeed in the task to which I sent it."

נה ⁶ דִּרְשׁוּ יְהֹוָה בְּהִמָּצְאוֹ קְרָאֻהוּ בִּהְיוֹתוֹ קָרוֹב: ⁷ יַעֲזֹב רָשָׁע דַּרְכּוֹ וְאִישׁ אָוֶן מַחְשְׁבֹתָיו וְיָשֹׁב אֶל־יְהֹוָה וִירַחֲמֵהוּ וְאֶל־אֱלֹהֵינוּ כִּי־יַרְבֶּה לִסְלוֹחַ: ⁸ כִּי לֹא מַחְשְׁבוֹתַי מַחְשְׁבוֹתֵיכֶם וְלֹא דַרְכֵיכֶם דְּרָכָי נְאֻם יְהֹוָה: ⁹ כִּי־גָבְהוּ שָׁמַיִם מֵאָרֶץ כֵּן גָּבְהוּ דְרָכַי מִדַּרְכֵיכֶם וּמַחְשְׁבֹתַי מִמַּחְשְׁבֹתֵיכֶם: ¹⁰ כִּי כַּאֲשֶׁר יֵרֵד הַגֶּשֶׁם וְהַשֶּׁלֶג מִן־הַשָּׁמַיִם וְשָׁמָּה לֹא יָשׁוּב כִּי אִם־הִרְוָה אֶת־הָאָרֶץ וְהוֹלִידָהּ וְהִצְמִיחָהּ וְנָתַן זֶרַע לַזֹּרֵעַ וְלֶחֶם לָאֹכֵל: ¹¹ כֵּן יִהְיֶה דְבָרִי אֲשֶׁר יֵצֵא מִפִּי לֹא־יָשׁוּב אֵלַי רֵיקָם

הפטרת תענית צבור מנחה

[English column:]

[12] Thus you have the promise that you will go out of exile with joy and you will be brought back in peace. It will seem as if the mountains and the hills will be bursting out in song before you, and all the trees of the field will be clapping their hands. [13] Instead of "thorn-bushes" of gentile rulership, "cypress trees" of Jewish rulership will shoot up; instead of nettles, myrtles will spring up. And this will establish a powerful reputation for God, a sign that this will be the state of affairs forever and it will never cease.

56 [1] This is what God says: "Guard My Torah law and act charitably to your fellow! For in this way My salvation will arrive soon and My charity towards you will be revealed for all to see."

[2] Whoever does the following will be a happy man, any person who holds onto it tightly: Let him be careful not to profane the Sabbath, thereby proclaiming his belief in God, and he will surely guard his hand from doing any evil. [3] The foreigner who contemplates conversion because he attaches himself to God should not say, "God will separate me from His people when He rewards them, so why should I be righteous and convert?" The infertile should not say, "Look, I am a withered tree that cannot produce fruit, so why should I be good if there is nobody to remember me?" [4] For this is what God says: "As for the infertile who keep My Sabbaths, who choose what I desire and hold fast to My covenant, [5] I will give them a place and name in My Temple and in My walls, which will be a better memory than sons and daughters. I will give them an everlasting memorial, which will not be destroyed. [6] And as for the foreigners who attach themselves to God to fulfil His duties, to love God's name and to be His servants—they should know that I promise everyone who is careful not to profane the Sabbath, and holds fast to My covenant of Torah, [7] that I will bring them to My holy mount and let them rejoice in My house of prayer. Their burnt-offerings and other sacrifices will be *accepted favorably on My altar*, for My Temple will be called a house of prayer for all the nations." [8] God Almighty, who gathers the dispersed of Israel, says, "I will gather still more converts, aside from those already gathered."

[Hebrew column:]

כִּי אִם־עָשֹׂה אֶת־אֲשֶׁר חָפַצְתִּי וְהִצְלִיחַ אֲשֶׁר שְׁלַחְתִּיו: [12] כִּי־בְשִׂמְחָה תֵצֵאוּ וּבְשָׁלוֹם תּוּבָלוּן הֶהָרִים וְהַגְּבָעוֹת יִפְצְחוּ לִפְנֵיכֶם רִנָּה וְכָל־עֲצֵי הַשָּׂדֶה יִמְחֲאוּ־כָף: [13] תַּחַת הַנַּעֲצוּץ יַעֲלֶה בְרוֹשׁ [תחת כ׳] וְתַחַת הַסִּרְפַּד יַעֲלֶה הֲדַס וְהָיָה לַיהֹוָה לְשֵׁם לְאוֹת עוֹלָם לֹא יִכָּרֵת:

נו [1] כֹּה אָמַר יְהֹוָה שִׁמְרוּ מִשְׁפָּט וַעֲשׂוּ צְדָקָה כִּי־קְרוֹבָה יְשׁוּעָתִי לָבוֹא וְצִדְקָתִי לְהִגָּלוֹת: [2] אַשְׁרֵי אֱנוֹשׁ יַעֲשֶׂה־זֹּאת וּבֶן־אָדָם יַחֲזִיק בָּהּ שֹׁמֵר שַׁבָּת מֵחַלְּלוֹ וְשֹׁמֵר יָדוֹ מֵעֲשׂוֹת כָּל־רָע: [3] וְאַל־יֹאמַר בֶּן־הַנֵּכָר הַנִּלְוָה אֶל־יְהֹוָה לֵאמֹר הַבְדֵּל יַבְדִּילַנִי יְהֹוָה מֵעַל עַמּוֹ וְאַל־יֹאמַר הַסָּרִיס הֵן אֲנִי עֵץ יָבֵשׁ: [4] כִּי־כֹה | אָמַר יְהֹוָה לַסָּרִיסִים אֲשֶׁר יִשְׁמְרוּ אֶת־שַׁבְּתוֹתַי וּבָחֲרוּ בַּאֲשֶׁר חָפָצְתִּי וּמַחֲזִיקִים בִּבְרִיתִי: [5] וְנָתַתִּי לָהֶם בְּבֵיתִי וּבְחוֹמֹתַי יָד וָשֵׁם טוֹב מִבָּנִים וּמִבָּנוֹת שֵׁם עוֹלָם אֶתֶּן־לוֹ אֲשֶׁר לֹא יִכָּרֵת: [6] וּבְנֵי הַנֵּכָר הַנִּלְוִים עַל־יְהֹוָה לְשָׁרְתוֹ וּלְאַהֲבָה אֶת־שֵׁם יְהֹוָה לִהְיוֹת לוֹ לַעֲבָדִים כָּל־שֹׁמֵר שַׁבָּת מֵחַלְּלוֹ וּמַחֲזִיקִים בִּבְרִיתִי: [7] וַהֲבִיאוֹתִים אֶל־הַר קָדְשִׁי וְשִׂמַּחְתִּים בְּבֵית תְּפִלָּתִי עוֹלֹתֵיהֶם וְזִבְחֵיהֶם לְרָצוֹן עַל־מִזְבְּחִי כִּי בֵיתִי בֵּית־תְּפִלָּה יִקָּרֵא לְכָל־הָעַמִּים: [8] נְאֻם אֲדֹנָי יֱהֹוִה מְקַבֵּץ נִדְחֵי יִשְׂרָאֵל עוֹד אֲקַבֵּץ עָלָיו לְנִקְבָּצָיו:

haftarat rosh ha-shanah (first day)

rosh ha-shanah
first day

Torah Reading—Genesis 21:1–34 (p. 106)
Maftir—Numbers 29:1–6 (p. 1004)

ALL COMMUNITIES—I SAMUEL 1:1 – 2:10

SYNOPSIS: This *Haftarah* is read on the first day of *Rosh Ha-Shanah* because, according to tradition, Hannah was "remembered" by God (v.19) on *Rosh Ha-Shanah*. Hannah's being "remembered" also parallels the theme of this festival which is known as "The Day of Remembrance."

The *Haftarah*, excerpted from the beginning of the Book of Samuel, describes the events leading to the prophet's birth and his subsequent "dedication to God." After introducing Elkanah (Samuel's father) (1:1), we read that he had two wives, Peninnah, who had borne children, and Hannah, who had not (2). The rivalry between the two wives is depicted against the annual family trip to the Sanctuary at Shiloh. Elkanah gives Hannah a superior portion of the sacrifices, which elicits contempt from Peninnah (3–6). Hannah is so upset that she is barely able to eat (7–8).

On one of the annual visits, Hannah decides to visit the Sanctuary herself and pour out her troubles in prayer to G-d (9–10). She vows that if God will grant her a son she will dedicate him to Divine worship and rear him as a nazirite (11). Hannah's impassioned prayer catches the attention of Eli, the High Priest. Rather peculiarly, her lips are moving but no words are to be heard (12–13). Eli presumes that she is drunk and rebukes her (13–14), but when Hannah makes her position clear, Eli blesses her that her prayers should be fulfilled (15–18). The experience has an immediate beneficial effect on Hannah, who is now able to eat properly (18), and the family returns home (19).

Hannah conceives and gives birth to Samuel (20). When the family is scheduled to return to Shiloh the following year, Hannah declines to participate, waiting until Samuel is weaned before dedicating him to a life of Divine worship in the Sanctuary (21–23). When she does arrive with Samuel, laden with offerings to God, she shows the boy to Eli, who promptly prostrates himself before God (24–28).

Hannah then bursts into a song of praise to God, stressing the theme of Divine providence and omnipotence (2:1–9), before concluding with prayers for Samuel's success in life (10).

1 ¹ There was a certain man from Ramathaim-zophim, in the peaks of Ephraim, whose name was Elkanah son of Jeroham son of Elihu son of Tohu son of Zuph who lived in the hills of Ephraim. ² He had two wives: one was named Hannah, and the other named Peninnah. Peninnah had children, but Hannah did not.

³ Every year the man Elkanah would go up from his town to prostrate himself and slaughter sacrifices to the God of Hosts in Shiloh. Eli's two sons, Hophni and

א ¹ וַיְהִי אִישׁ אֶחָד מִן־הָרָמָתַיִם צוֹפִים מֵהַר אֶפְרָיִם וּשְׁמוֹ אֶלְקָנָה בֶּן־יְרֹחָם בֶּן־אֱלִיהוּא בֶּן־תֹּחוּ בֶן־צוּף אֶפְרָתִי: ² וְלוֹ שְׁתֵּי נָשִׁים שֵׁם אַחַת חַנָּה וְשֵׁם הַשֵּׁנִית פְּנִנָּה וַיְהִי לִפְנִנָּה יְלָדִים וּלְחַנָּה אֵין יְלָדִים: ³ וְעָלָה הָאִישׁ הַהוּא מֵעִירוֹ מִיָּמִים ׀ יָמִימָה לְהִשְׁתַּחֲוֺת

הפטרת ראש השנה יום א׳

וְלִזְבֹּחַ לַיהֹוָה צְבָאוֹת בְּשִׁלֹה וְשָׁם שְׁנֵי בְנֵי־עֵלִי חָפְנִי וּפִינְחָס כֹּהֲנִים לַיהֹוָה: 4 וַיְהִי הַיּוֹם וַיִּזְבַּח אֶלְקָנָה וְנָתַן לִפְנִנָּה אִשְׁתּוֹ וּלְכׇל־בָּנֶיהָ וּבְנוֹתֶיהָ מָנוֹת: 5 וּלְחַנָּה יִתֵּן מָנָה אַחַת אַפָּיִם כִּי אֶת־חַנָּה אָהֵב וַיהֹוָה סָגַר רַחְמָהּ: 6 וְכִעֲסַתָּה צָרָתָהּ גַּם־כַּעַס בַּעֲבוּר הַרְּעִמָהּ כִּי־סָגַר יְהֹוָה בְּעַד רַחְמָהּ: 7 וְכֵן יַעֲשֶׂה שָׁנָה בְשָׁנָה מִדֵּי עֲלֹתָהּ בְּבֵית יְהֹוָה כֵּן תַּכְעִסֶנָּה וַתִּבְכֶּה וְלֹא תֹאכַל: 8 וַיֹּאמֶר לָהּ אֶלְקָנָה אִישָׁהּ חַנָּה לָמֶה תִבְכִּי וְלָמֶה לֹא תֹאכְלִי וְלָמֶה יֵרַע לְבָבֵךְ הֲלוֹא אָנֹכִי טוֹב לָךְ מֵעֲשָׂרָה בָּנִים: 9 וַתָּקׇם חַנָּה אַחֲרֵי אׇכְלָה בְשִׁלֹה וְאַחֲרֵי שָׁתֹה וְעֵלִי הַכֹּהֵן יֹשֵׁב עַל־הַכִּסֵּא עַל־מְזוּזַת הֵיכַל יְהֹוָה: 10 וְהִיא מָרַת נָפֶשׁ וַתִּתְפַּלֵּל עַל־יְהֹוָה וּבָכֹה תִבְכֶּה: 11 וַתִּדֹּר נֶדֶר וַתֹּאמַר יְהֹוָה צְבָאוֹת אִם־רָאֹה תִרְאֶה | בׇּעֳנִי אֲמָתֶךָ וּזְכַרְתַּנִי וְלֹא־תִשְׁכַּח אֶת־אֲמָתֶךָ וְנָתַתָּה לַאֲמָתְךָ זֶרַע אֲנָשִׁים וּנְתַתִּיו לַיהֹוָה כׇּל־יְמֵי חַיָּיו וּמוֹרָה לֹא־יַעֲלֶה עַל־רֹאשׁוֹ: 12 וְהָיָה כִּי הִרְבְּתָה לְהִתְפַּלֵּל לִפְנֵי יְהֹוָה וְעֵלִי שֹׁמֵר אֶת־פִּיהָ: 13 וְחַנָּה הִיא מְדַבֶּרֶת עַל־לִבָּהּ רַק שְׂפָתֶיהָ נָּעוֹת וְקוֹלָהּ לֹא יִשָּׁמֵעַ וַיַּחְשְׁבֶהָ עֵלִי לְשִׁכֹּרָה: 14 וַיֹּאמֶר אֵלֶיהָ עֵלִי עַד־מָתַי תִּשְׁתַּכָּרִין הָסִירִי אֶת־יֵינֵךְ מֵעָלָיִךְ: 15 וַתַּעַן חַנָּה וַתֹּאמֶר לֹא אֲדֹנִי אִשָּׁה קְשַׁת־רוּחַ אָנֹכִי וְיַיִן וְשֵׁכָר לֹא שָׁתִיתִי וָאֶשְׁפֹּךְ אֶת־נַפְשִׁי לִפְנֵי יְהֹוָה: 16 אַל־תִּתֵּן אֶת־אֲמָתְךָ לִפְנֵי בַּת־בְּלִיָּעַל כִּי־מֵרֹב שִׂיחִי וְכַעְסִי דִּבַּרְתִּי עַד־הֵנָּה: 17 וַיַּעַן עֵלִי וַיֹּאמֶר לְכִי לְשָׁלוֹם וֵאלֹהֵי יִשְׂרָאֵל יִתֵּן אֶת־שֵׁלָתֵךְ אֲשֶׁר שָׁאַלְתְּ מֵעִמּוֹ: 18 וַתֹּאמֶר תִּמְצָא שִׁפְחָתְךָ חֵן בְּעֵינֶיךָ וַתֵּלֶךְ הָאִשָּׁה לְדַרְכָּהּ

Phinehas, served there as priests of God. **4** When that day came each year, Elkanah would slaughter a peace-offering and give portions to his wife Peninnah, and to all her sons and daughters. **5** To Hannah, he would give an especially nice portion, because he wanted to show extra affection to Hannah, who was pained that God had closed her womb.

6 Her competitor Peninnah would anger her all the time with rude remarks in order to upset her about the fact that God had closed her womb. **7** Elkanah would do the same thing year in and year out, showing preferential treatment to Hannah when she went up to God's Temple. Likewise, Peninnah would upset her and she would cry so much that she could not eat more than a morsel. **8** Her husband Elkanah would say to her, "Hannah, why are you crying? Why don't you eat? Why are you so upset? Doesn't my love mean more to you than ten sons?"

9 One year, after eating and drinking at Shiloh, Hannah went off back to the Sanctuary. Eli the priest was sitting on the chair at the doorpost of God's Sanctuary. **10** She was in a sorrowful mood when she came. She prayed to God, weeping profusely.

11 She made a vow, saying, "O God of Hosts! If You will look upon the grief of Your maidservant and remember me—if You will not put Your maidservant out of mind—give your maidservant a son, and I will ensure that He is devoted to God all his life. He will be a nazirite and a razor will never touch his head."

12 While she was praying at length before God, Eli watched her mouth, trying to hear what she was saying. **13** But Hannah whispered, as if she spoke to her heart. Only her lips moved, but her voice could not be heard.

He presumed she was drunk. **14** Eli said to her, "Enough of this drunken behavior of yours! If you drank a lot it's time for you to sober up."

15 "It's not true, my master," Hannah replied. She said, "I am a tormented woman. I drank no wine or beer. I'm pouring out my soul to God. **16** Don't think that your maidservant is an irresponsible woman. I've been praying the whole time due to my immense grief and frustration."

17 "Go in peace," Eli answered. He said, "May the God of Israel grant the request you made of Him."

18 "I am glad your maidservant has found favor in your eyes," she said.

haftarat rosh ha-shanah (first day)

Then she went on her way and was able to eat normally with her family; she was no longer frustrated.

[19] Elkanah and his family got up early, prostrated themselves before God, and returned home to Ramah.

Elkanah knew his wife Hannah and God remembered her. [20] Hannah conceived, and at the end of the pregnancy she gave birth to a son. She named him Samuel, saying, "For I requested him of God."

[21] The following year, Hannah's husband Elkanah and his entire household went up to slaughter their yearly sacrifice and whatever else he vowed to God that year. [22] But Hannah did not go.

She said to her husband, "I will bring the boy up to Shiloh when he is weaned, and when he appears before God, he will remain there indefinitely as Eli's assistant.

[23] Her husband Elkanah said to her, "Do as you see fit. Stay until you wean him. I hope God fulfils what you said about him, that he will remain there forever."

And so the woman stayed home and nursed her son until she weaned him. [24] When she had weaned him, she brought him up with an offering of three oxen, an *'ephah* of flour, and a flask of wine. Even though the boy was still very young she still brought him to God's Temple at Shiloh. [25] As soon as the first ox was slaughtered, she brought the boy to Eli to show him that his prayer had been answered. [26] "Please, my master!" she said, "Will my master swear by his life that he will look after this boy? I am the woman who stood with you here, praying to God. [27] It was this boy I prayed for and God granted me the request that I made of Him. [28] At the time that I prayed I dedicated him to God. All his life he shall be dedicated to God." When Eli heard this, he prostrated himself there to God.

2 [1] Hannah decided to pray to God, but first she said words of praise. "My heart rejoices in God's salvation! My triumph over persecution from Peninnah is from God! I can now speak before my enemies, for I rejoice in Your salvation! [2] None is as holy as God, for there is none besides You. There is no Rock like our God. [3] O Peninnah! You will no longer boast on and on. Let no arrogance pass your lips, for the God is an all-knowing God, and deeds are counted by Him. [4] Therefore, the bows of the mighty

וַתֹּאכַ֔ל וּפָנֶ֖יהָ לֹא־הָ֥יוּ־לָ֖הּ עֽוֹד׃ 19 וַיַּשְׁכִּ֣מוּ בַבֹּ֗קֶר וַיִּֽשְׁתַּחֲווּ֙ לִפְנֵ֣י יְהוָ֔ה וַיָּשֻׁ֥בוּ וַיָּבֹ֖אוּ אֶל־בֵּיתָ֣ם הָרָמָ֑תָה וַיֵּ֤דַע אֶלְקָנָה֙ אֶת־חַנָּ֣ה אִשְׁתּ֔וֹ וַיִּֽזְכְּרֶ֖הָ יְהוָֽה׃ 20 וַיְהִי֙ לִתְקֻפ֣וֹת הַיָּמִ֔ים וַתַּ֥הַר חַנָּ֖ה וַתֵּ֣לֶד בֵּ֑ן וַתִּקְרָ֤א אֶת־שְׁמוֹ֙ שְׁמוּאֵ֔ל כִּ֥י מֵיְהוָ֖ה שְׁאִלְתִּֽיו׃ 21 וַיַּ֛עַל הָאִ֥ישׁ אֶלְקָנָ֖ה וְכָל־בֵּית֑וֹ לִזְבֹּ֧חַ לַיהוָ֛ה אֶת־זֶ֥בַח הַיָּמִ֖ים וְאֶת־נִדְרֽוֹ׃ 22 וְחַנָּ֖ה לֹ֣א עָלָ֑תָה כִּֽי־אָמְרָ֣ה לְאִישָׁ֗הּ עַ֣ד יִגָּמֵ֤ל הַנַּ֙עַר֙ וַהֲבִאֹתִ֔יו וְנִרְאָה֙ אֶת־פְּנֵ֣י יְהוָ֔ה וְיָ֥שַׁב שָׁ֖ם עַד־עוֹלָֽם׃ 23 וַיֹּ֣אמֶר לָהּ֩ אֶלְקָנָ֨ה אִישָׁ֜הּ עֲשִׂ֧י הַטּ֣וֹב בְּעֵינַ֗יִךְ שְׁבִי֙ עַד־גָּמְלֵ֣ךְ אֹת֔וֹ אַ֛ךְ יָקֵ֥ם יְהוָ֖ה אֶת־דְּבָר֑וֹ וַתֵּ֤שֶׁב הָֽאִשָּׁה֙ וַתֵּ֣ינֶק אֶת־בְּנָ֔הּ עַד־גָּמְלָ֖הּ אֹתֽוֹ׃ 24 וַתַּעֲלֵ֙הוּ עִמָּ֜הּ כַּאֲשֶׁ֣ר גְּמָלַ֗תּוּ בְּפָרִ֤ים שְׁלֹשָׁה֙ וְאֵיפָ֨ה אַחַ֥ת קֶ֙מַח֙ וְנֵ֣בֶל יַ֔יִן וַתְּבִאֵ֥הוּ בֵית־יְהוָ֖ה שִׁל֑וֹ וְהַנַּ֖עַר נָֽעַר׃ 25 וַֽיִּשְׁחֲט֖וּ אֶת־הַפָּ֑ר וַיָּבִ֥אוּ אֶת־הַנַּ֖עַר אֶל־עֵלִֽי׃ 26 וַתֹּ֙אמֶר֙ בִּ֣י אֲדֹנִ֔י חֵ֥י נַפְשְׁךָ֖ אֲדֹנִ֑י אֲנִ֣י הָאִשָּׁ֗ה הַנִּצֶּ֤בֶת עִמְּכָה֙ בָּזֶ֔ה לְהִתְפַּלֵּ֖ל אֶל־יְהוָֽה׃ 27 אֶל־הַנַּ֥עַר הַזֶּ֖ה הִתְפַּלָּ֑לְתִּי וַיִּתֵּ֨ן יְהוָ֥ה לִי֙ אֶת־שְׁאֵ֣לָתִ֔י אֲשֶׁ֥ר שָׁאַ֖לְתִּי מֵעִמּֽוֹ׃ 28 וְגַ֣ם אָנֹכִ֗י הִשְׁאִלְתִּ֙הוּ֙ לַֽיהוָ֔ה כָּל־הַיָּמִים֙ אֲשֶׁ֣ר הָיָ֔ה ה֥וּא שָׁא֖וּל לַֽיהוָ֑ה וַיִּשְׁתַּ֥חוּ שָׁ֖ם לַֽיהוָֽה׃

ב 1 וַתִּתְפַּלֵּ֤ל חַנָּה֙ וַתֹּאמַ֔ר עָלַ֥ץ לִבִּ֖י בַּֽיהוָ֑ה רָ֤מָה קַרְנִי֙ בַּֽיהוָ֔ה רָ֥חַב פִּ֖י עַל־אוֹיְבַ֔י כִּ֥י שָׂמַ֖חְתִּי בִּישׁוּעָתֶֽךָ׃ 2 אֵין־קָד֥וֹשׁ כַּיהוָ֖ה כִּ֣י אֵ֣ין בִּלְתֶּ֑ךָ וְאֵ֥ין צ֖וּר כֵּאלֹהֵֽינוּ׃ 3 אַל־תַּרְבּ֤וּ תְדַבְּרוּ֙ גְּבֹהָ֣ה גְבֹהָ֔ה יֵצֵ֥א עָתָ֖ק מִפִּיכֶ֑ם כִּ֣י אֵ֤ל דֵּעוֹת֙ יְהוָ֔ה [ולא כ׳] וְל֥וֹ נִתְכְּנ֖וּ עֲלִלֽוֹת׃ 4 קֶ֥שֶׁת גִּבֹּרִ֖ים חַתִּ֑ים וְנִכְשָׁלִ֖ים

הפטרת ראש השנה יום ב'

are broken, and the stumbling are suddenly clothed in strength. [5] Those who were once fed to satisfaction become laborers, and those once hungry retired from work. The barren woman bears seven, but the woman with many children becomes bereft. [6] Because it is God who takes life and gives life. He casts down to the grave and He raises up. [7] God makes poor and makes rich; He humbles and He elevates. [8] He raises the poor from the dust, the impoverished from the dung heaps, to seat them with nobles, giving them the seat of honor. For the foundations of the earth are God's, and He set the lands on them. [9] He guards the steps of His pious ones, but the wicked are cut off in darkness, for a man does not prevail because of his own strength.

[10] "O God! May those that oppose Him be shattered. May He thunder over them in heaven. O God! May He be a judge over the earth to its furthest parts! May God grant power to His king, and raise the strength of His anointed one."

אֲזֻ֥רוּ חָֽיִל׃ [5] שְׂבֵעִ֤ים בַּלֶּ֙חֶם֙ נִשְׂכָּ֔רוּ וּרְעֵבִ֖ים חָדֵ֑לּוּ עַד־עֲקָרָה֙ יָלְדָ֣ה שִׁבְעָ֔ה וְרַבַּ֥ת בָּנִ֖ים אֻמְלָֽלָה׃ [6] יְהוָ֖ה מֵמִ֣ית וּמְחַיֶּ֑ה מוֹרִ֥יד שְׁא֖וֹל וַיָּֽעַל׃ [7] יְהוָ֖ה מוֹרִ֣ישׁ וּמַעֲשִׁ֑יר מַשְׁפִּ֖יל אַף־מְרוֹמֵֽם׃ [8] מֵקִ֨ים מֵעָפָ֜ר דָּ֗ל מֵֽאַשְׁפֹּת֙ יָרִ֣ים אֶבְי֔וֹן לְהוֹשִׁיב֙ עִם־נְדִיבִ֔ים וְכִסֵּ֥א כָב֖וֹד יַנְחִלֵ֑ם כִּ֤י לַֽיהוָה֙ מְצֻ֣קֵי אֶ֔רֶץ וַיָּ֥שֶׁת עֲלֵיהֶ֖ם תֵּבֵֽל׃ [9] רַגְלֵ֤י חֲסִידָיו֙ יִשְׁמֹ֔ר וּרְשָׁעִ֖ים בַּחֹ֣שֶׁךְ יִדָּ֑מּוּ כִּי־לֹ֥א בְכֹ֖חַ יִגְבַּר־אִֽישׁ׃ [10] יְהוָ֞ה יֵחַ֣תּוּ מְרִיבָ֗יו עָלָיו֙ בַּשָּׁמַ֣יִם יַרְעֵ֔ם יְהוָ֖ה יָדִ֣ין אַפְסֵי־אָ֑רֶץ וְיִתֶּן־עֹ֣ז לְמַלְכּ֔וֹ וְיָרֵ֖ם קֶ֥רֶן מְשִׁיחֽוֹ׃

rosh ha-shanah
second day

Torah Reading—Genesis 22:1–24 (p. 112)
Maftir—Numbers 29:1–6 (p. 1004)

ALL COMMUNITIES—JEREMIAH 31:1–19

SYNOPSIS: This *Haftarah* is recited on the Second Day of *Rosh Ha-Shanah* since its conclusion alludes to the themes of Divine remembrance and mercy for Israel. The final verse (19) is also included in the Additional (*Musaf*) prayer of *Rosh Ha-Shanah* as one of the ten "Verses of Remembrance."

The *Haftarah* stresses God's love for Israel, His ongoing promises of restoration and redemption (31:1–5), and the joyous ingathering of the exiles amid jubilant proclamations to the nations (7–13). In a poignant passage which follows, the pain of the Exile is depicted through Rachel's laments which are heard in heaven, prompting words of consolation from God (14–16). The *Haftarah* concludes with an illustration of how God hears the repentance and prayers of His people and, out of deep fatherly love, promises to redeem them (17–19).

31 [1] This is what God said: The nation who survived terror of Egypt by the sword found favor with Me when they went faithfully into the desert. Therefore Israel was led to settle in their land in tranquility."

[2] A long way back, God revealed Himself to Moses

לא [1] כֹּ֚ה אָמַ֣ר יְהוָ֔ה מָצָ֥א חֵ֖ן בַּמִּדְבָּ֑ר עַ֖ם שְׂרִ֣ידֵי חָ֑רֶב הָל֥וֹךְ לְהַרְגִּיע֖וֹ יִשְׂרָאֵֽל׃ [2] מֵרָח֕וֹק יְהוָ֖ה נִרְאָ֣ה לִ֑י וְאַהֲבַ֤ת עוֹלָם֙ אֲהַבְתִּ֔יךְ עַל־

haftarat rosh ha-shanah (second day)

and Aaron, who were prophets like me, saying, "I have loved you, O Israel, with an everlasting love, and therefore I constantly extend kindness to you. ³ I will build your Temple again, and being the work of God and not of man it will remain built forever.

"O Israel! You are cherished to me like a virgin to her newlywed husband. You will again decorate your tambourines and go out in a merry dance. ⁴ You will again plant vineyards in the desolate mountains of Samaria. Planters will plant, and there will be such an abundance of fruit that they will not be able to carry it to Jerusalem in the fourth year, so they will redeem it for money on site.

⁵ "For the day of the final redemption will come when the watchmen posted on the mountain of Ephraim will call out, 'Let's go! Let's go up to the Divine Presence which has returned to Zion, to God, our God!'

⁶ For this is what God has said to Jacob's people: "Sing praises with joy! Shout jubilantly at the high-points of the lands of the nations so your voice is heard by all! Make your voice heard, give praise, and say, 'O God! You have saved Your people, the remnant of Israel!'

⁷ "I am then going to bring those exiled in Babylon back from the northern land, and gather the ten lost tribes from the ends of the earth; among them even the blind and lame, pregnant women and mothers of newborn, all together. They will return here in a great crowd. ⁸ They will come in tears of repentance; I will bring them here because of their prayers.

"I will lead them past streams of water to quench their thirst, on a straight road on which they will not stumble, for I became like a father to Israel, and Ephraim is dear to Me like a firstborn.

⁹ "O Nations, listen to the word of God! Tell it in the distant islands, and say, 'He who scattered Israel will gather them together, and guard them like a shepherd does his flock—¹⁰ for God redeemed Jacob's people, and delivered them from a power that is stronger than themselves.'

¹¹ "They will then come and sing praises from Mount Zion, and converge to receive God's goodness—the grain, the wine, and the oil, and the young of flocks and cattle. Their soul will be satiated like an irrigated garden, and they will never again experience grief.

¹² "Then, young girls will rejoice in dance, and young and old men will dance vigorously together. I will turn their former mourning into joy, and comfort them and make them happier, more than the degree of their previous sorrow. ¹³ And I will satiate the priests with fat meat, and My people will become satisfied with My goodness," says God.

14 This is what God said: "A voice has been heard on High, of wailing and bitter weeping. Rachel is weeping for her children, refusing to be consoled about her children, for they are no longer in their land."

15 This is what God said to Rachel: "Restrain your voice from weeping, and your eyes from tears, for there is reward for your action," says God, "and your children will return from the land of their enemies. **16** There is hope for your children's final destiny," says God. "Your children will return to their border.

17 "I heard the kingdom of Ephraim moaning again and again. 'You chastised me, and I accepted chastisement, though initially with difficulty like an untrained calf. Now inspire my heart so that I may return to You, since You are God, my God. **18** For after departing from my wicked ways, I regret them; after I was made aware of what I did, I slapped my thighs. I am ashamed and even embarrassed, for I bear the disgrace of my youth.'

19 "Is Ephraim not a precious son to Me, a delightful child?" says God. "For whenever I speak of him I don't want to stop thinking about him and I remember him again and again. Therefore, My innards melt for him.

"I will always have mercy upon him," says God.

נְאֻם־יְהֹוָה: 14 כֹּה ׀ אָמַר יְהֹוָה קוֹל בְּרָמָה נִשְׁמָע נְהִי בְּכִי תַמְרוּרִים רָחֵל מְבַכָּה עַל־בָּנֶיהָ מֵאֲנָה לְהִנָּחֵם עַל־בָּנֶיהָ כִּי אֵינֶנּוּ: 15 כֹּה ׀ אָמַר יְהֹוָה מִנְעִי קוֹלֵךְ מִבֶּכִי וְעֵינַיִךְ מִדִּמְעָה כִּי יֵשׁ שָׂכָר לִפְעֻלָּתֵךְ נְאֻם־יְהֹוָה וְשָׁבוּ מֵאֶרֶץ אוֹיֵב: 16 וְיֵשׁ־תִּקְוָה לְאַחֲרִיתֵךְ נְאֻם־יְהֹוָה וְשָׁבוּ בָנִים לִגְבוּלָם: 17 שָׁמוֹעַ שָׁמַעְתִּי אֶפְרַיִם מִתְנוֹדֵד יִסַּרְתַּנִי וָאִוָּסֵר כְּעֵגֶל לֹא לֻמָּד הֲשִׁיבֵנִי וְאָשׁוּבָה כִּי אַתָּה יְהֹוָה אֱלֹהָי: 18 כִּי־אַחֲרֵי שׁוּבִי נִחַמְתִּי וְאַחֲרֵי הִוָּדְעִי סָפַקְתִּי עַל־יָרֵךְ בֹּשְׁתִּי וְגַם־נִכְלַמְתִּי כִּי נָשָׂאתִי חֶרְפַּת נְעוּרָי: 19 הֲבֵן יַקִּיר לִי אֶפְרַיִם אִם יֶלֶד שַׁעֲשֻׁעִים כִּי־מִדֵּי דַבְּרִי בּוֹ זָכֹר אֶזְכְּרֶנּוּ עוֹד עַל־כֵּן הָמוּ מֵעַי לוֹ רַחֵם אֲרַחֲמֶנּוּ נְאֻם־יְהֹוָה:

yom kippur
morning service

Torah Reading—Leviticus 16:1–34 (p. 698)
Maftir—Numbers 29:7–11 (p. 1004)

ALL COMMUNITIES—ISAIAH 57:14 – 58:14

SYNOPSIS: This *Haftarah* was chosen for *Yom Kippur* since it speaks of repentance (54:18-21) and the appropriate manner in which a fast should be carried out (58:6-7).

The *Haftarah* opens with a statement of God's compassion for the sinner who repents contritely and sincerely (57:14-19) and resentment for those who do not repent (20-21). The prophet is called upon to rebuke the nation for its transgressions (58:1), for insincere worship in general (2) and making a mockery of fasting (3-5). After stating the correct approach to a fast day (6-7), God promises success to all those who follow in this path (8-12). The concluding passage praises the importance of Sabbath observance, and the rewards that it reaps (13-14).

57 **14** He said, "Make a path! Make a path! Clear the way! Remove all obstacles from My people's way."
15 For this is what the High and Exalted One says, He who dwells forever and whose His name is Holy:

נז 14 וְאָמַר סֹלּוּ־סֹלּוּ פַּנּוּ־דָרֶךְ הָרִימוּ מִכְשׁוֹל מִדֶּרֶךְ עַמִּי: 15 כִּי כֹה אָמַר רָם וְנִשָּׂא שֹׁכֵן עַד

haftarat yom kippur (morning service)

"I dwell on High in holiness, yet I am with the broken-hearted and humble-spirited, reviving the spirits of the humble and reviving the hearts of the broken. ¹⁶ But I will not contend with the sinner forever, nor be angry and punish him eternally, for the spirit which comes into the bodily wrapping is from Me, and it is I, after all, who made the souls, so I will have mercy on them.

¹⁷ "It was for his sin of theft that I was angry with him and struck him and not for no reason. I hid My face from him so as not to see his pain and showed anger to him so he should suffer even more. But while My face was hidden he disobediently followed the ways of his heart and I punished him even more.

¹⁸ "But when I observed his repentant ways, I healed him from his suffering. I am guiding him on a straight path and I will compensate and console him, and those who grieved for him, for all their suffering. ¹⁹ Unlike in the past when he was rebuked by all, I will make a new speech of the lips so that people praise him, 'Peace, peace unto you!' regardless of whether those who are speaking are far from him or close—says God—and I will heal him.

²⁰ "But the wicked who refuse to repent are suffering constantly like the turbulent sea which is unable to calm down; its waters cast up mud and dirt. ²¹ There is no peace for the wicked"—says my God.

58 ¹ "Call out in full voice! Don't hold back! Raise your voice like a ram's horn! Tell My people their transgression, and the House of Jacob, their sin. ² Acting as if they were like a nation that performed righteous deeds and had not abandoned God's laws, they seek Me every day in prayer and act as if they desire to know My ways. So as to appear as if they desire to draw close to God, they ask Me about the laws of justice. ³ They ask, 'Why is it we fasted but You have not seen to it that we are cared for? We afflicted ourselves, but You made Yourself unaware?'

"To this I say: You just entertain yourself on your fast day to relieve the difficulty of fasting, and you fail to repent! You push away all your distress by having fun. ⁴ Your fast just leads you to quarrels and arguments with the other congregants whom you hate, striking each other with a wicked fist. You do not fast properly on this day, praying intently to let your voices be heard on High. ⁵ Is the fast I desire merely a day when a person afflicts himself? Do I merely desire that he bend his head over like a bulrush, or spread out a mattress of sackcloth with ashes? Is this what you call a fast, and a desirable day for God?

הפטרת יום כפור מנחה

6 הֲלוֹא זֶה צוֹם אֶבְחָרֵהוּ פַּתֵּחַ חַרְצֻבּוֹת רֶשַׁע הַתֵּר אֲגֻדּוֹת מוֹטָה וְשַׁלַּח רְצוּצִים חָפְשִׁים וְכָל־מוֹטָה תְּנַתֵּקוּ: 7 הֲלוֹא פָרֹס לָרָעֵב לַחְמֶךָ וַעֲנִיִּים מְרוּדִים תָּבִיא בָיִת כִּי־תִרְאֶה עָרֹם וְכִסִּיתוֹ וּמִבְּשָׂרְךָ לֹא תִתְעַלָּם: 8 אָז יִבָּקַע כַּשַּׁחַר אוֹרֶךָ וַאֲרֻכָתְךָ מְהֵרָה תִצְמָח וְהָלַךְ לְפָנֶיךָ צִדְקֶךָ כְּבוֹד יְהֹוָה יַאַסְפֶךָ: 9 אָז תִּקְרָא וַיהֹוָה יַעֲנֶה תְּשַׁוַּע וְיֹאמַר הִנֵּנִי אִם־ תָּסִיר מִתּוֹכְךָ מוֹטָה שְׁלַח אֶצְבַּע וְדַבֶּר־אָוֶן: 10 וְתָפֵק לָרָעֵב נַפְשֶׁךָ וְנֶפֶשׁ נַעֲנָה תַּשְׂבִּיעַ וְזָרַח בַּחֹשֶׁךְ אוֹרֶךָ וַאֲפֵלָתְךָ כַּצָּהֳרָיִם: 11 וְנָחֲךָ יְהֹוָה תָּמִיד וְהִשְׂבִּיעַ בְּצַחְצָחוֹת נַפְשֶׁךָ וְעַצְמֹתֶיךָ יַחֲלִיץ וְהָיִיתָ כְּגַן רָוֶה וּכְמוֹצָא מַיִם אֲשֶׁר לֹא־יְכַזְּבוּ מֵימָיו: 12 וּבָנוּ מִמְּךָ חָרְבוֹת עוֹלָם מוֹסְדֵי דוֹר־וָדוֹר תְּקוֹמֵם וְקֹרָא לְךָ גֹּדֵר פֶּרֶץ מְשֹׁבֵב נְתִיבוֹת לָשָׁבֶת: 13 אִם־תָּשִׁיב מִשַּׁבָּת רַגְלֶךָ עֲשׂוֹת חֲפָצֶיךָ בְּיוֹם קָדְשִׁי וְקָרָאתָ לַשַּׁבָּת עֹנֶג לִקְדוֹשׁ יְהֹוָה מְכֻבָּד וְכִבַּדְתּוֹ מֵעֲשׂוֹת דְּרָכֶיךָ מִמְּצוֹא חֶפְצְךָ וְדַבֵּר דָּבָר: 14 אָז תִּתְעַנַּג עַל־יְהֹוָה וְהִרְכַּבְתִּיךָ עַל־ [במותי כ׳] בָּמֳתֵי אָרֶץ וְהַאֲכַלְתִּיךָ נַחֲלַת יַעֲקֹב אָבִיךָ כִּי פִּי יְהֹוָה דִּבֵּר:

6 "No, this is the fast I desire: loosening the bonds of wickedness, unlocking the fetters of injustice to the poor, setting the oppressed free, and breaking off every yoke from your slaves. 7 Surely you should divide your bread for the hungry on this day, and bring the moaning poor into your house. When you see a naked person you should clothe him, and do not ignore your own kin."

8 "Then if you will do this, the light of your success will break through like the dawn, and your healing will speedily sprout. Your acts of righteousness will go before you and lead you to eternal bliss; the glory of God will gather you to the resting place of the righteous. 9 Then, you will call out in prayer and God will answer; you will cry out to Him and He will say, "I am here to fulfil your request.

But this is only if you remove from among you the yoke you have placed on the poor, the pointing-finger, and corrupt speech. 10 If you open your heart to the hungry, and satiate the afflicted person, then your light will shine in the darkness, and your deepest gloom will turn into bright daylight. 11 God will always guide you, satisfy your needs in times of drought, and strengthen your bones. You will become like a well-watered garden, and like a water spring whose waters never cease.

12 "Ancient ruins will be rebuilt through your good deeds; you will reestablish the foundations of past generations. You will be called Repairer of the Breach, and Restorer of Civilized Behavior.

13 "If you restrain your foot because it is the Sabbath and do not walk outside the city limits; and refrain from carrying out the prohibited labors you desire on My holy day; and you declare the Sabbath as a time for pleasure, a holy day of honor for God when no work is done; and you actually honor it by not carrying out your regular activities, not pursuing your desired labors, and not speaking about financial things— 14 then you will be rewarded and will find pleasure with God. I will raise you to the high places of the earth, and give you the land of Israel, the heritage of Jacob, your father, for the mouth of God has spoken."

yom kippur
afternoon service

Torah Reading—Leviticus 18:1–30 (p. 710)

ALL COMMUNITIES—JONAH 1:1 – 4:11; MICAH 7:18-20

SYNOPSIS: The Book of Jonah was chosen as the *Haftarah* for the Afternoon service of *Yom Kippur* since it stresses that: a) you can never run away from God, as Jonah at-

haftarat yom kippur (afternoon service)

tempted; and, b) God forgives penitents, as we find the wicked inhabitants of Nineveh were spared destruction due to their sincere repentance.

The *Haftarah* takes place in the year 640 B.C.E., during the reign of Jeroboam II, some fifty years before the rise of the Assyrian Empire. At the opening of the *Haftarah*, God commands Jonah to go to Nineveh, the capital of Assyria, and rebuke them (1:1–2). Jonah attempts to escape God's mission by fleeing to a place where he can no longer receive prophecy (3–4), but the ship he boards is caught in a violent storm that threatens its destruction (4–6). Jonah's sin is identified as the cause of the storm and, with his consent, he is thrown overboard to save the others (7–15). Jonah is swallowed by a giant fish (2:1), from which he praises God for saving him (2–10) and is subsequently released (11). This time, he carries out his mission (3:1–4). The people of Nineveh respond with drastic measures and repent (5–9), bringing about their salvation (10). But Jonah is troubled, feeling that the people were worthy of destruction (4:1–3). God responds with a "sign." A castor tree miraculously sprouts to offer shade to Jonah, pleasing him immensely, but the next day it is destroyed (5–8). The message is then made clear by God: If Jonah was upset at the loss of a tree which he did not create, then God should certainly be concerned for Nineveh, which was made by His hand (9–10). A final passage from Micah (7:18–20) alludes to God's Thirteen Attributes of Mercy.

1

¹ God's word came to Jonah the son of Amittai, saying, ² "Get going and travel to the great city of Nineveh and reprimand them, because their wickedness has risen before Me." ³ But instead Jonah got going and fled to Tarshish, a place outside the land of Israel, where no further prophecy could be received to clarify his mission, and he would thus be away from God. He went down to Joppa and found a ship going to Tarshish. He paid the ship's full fare and boarded it to go with them to Tarshish, to be away from God.

⁴ But God brought a powerful wind upon the sea. There was a great storm in the sea, and it seemed that the ship would be broken to pieces. ⁵ The sailors were afraid, and each one cried out to his god. They threw all the items that were on the ship into the sea, to lighten their load. But Jonah went down to the ship's hold, lay down and fell fast asleep. ⁶ The ship's captain approached him and said to him, "What are you doing sleeping? Get up and pray to your God! Maybe God will bear us in mind and we will not perish."

⁷ The men said to each other, "Come, let's cast lots to find out who has brought this disaster on us." They cast many lots and every lot fell upon Jonah.

א

א וַיְהִי דְּבַר־יְהֹוָה אֶל־יוֹנָה בֶן־אֲמִתַּי לֵאמֹר: 2 קוּם לֵךְ אֶל־נִינְוֵה הָעִיר הַגְּדוֹלָה וּקְרָא עָלֶיהָ כִּי־עָלְתָה רָעָתָם לְפָנָי: 3 וַיָּקָם יוֹנָה לִבְרֹחַ תַּרְשִׁישָׁה מִלִּפְנֵי יְהֹוָה וַיֵּרֶד יָפוֹ וַיִּמְצָא אֳנִיָּה | בָּאָה תַרְשִׁישׁ וַיִּתֵּן שְׂכָרָהּ וַיֵּרֶד בָּהּ לָבוֹא עִמָּהֶם תַּרְשִׁישָׁה מִלִּפְנֵי יְהֹוָה: 4 וַיהֹוָה הֵטִיל רוּחַ־גְּדוֹלָה אֶל־הַיָּם וַיְהִי סַעַר־גָּדוֹל בַּיָּם וְהָאֳנִיָּה חִשְּׁבָה לְהִשָּׁבֵר: 5 וַיִּירְאוּ הַמַּלָּחִים וַיִּזְעֲקוּ אִישׁ אֶל־אֱלֹהָיו וַיָּטִלוּ אֶת־הַכֵּלִים אֲשֶׁר בָּאֳנִיָּה אֶל־הַיָּם לְהָקֵל מֵעֲלֵיהֶם וְיוֹנָה יָרַד אֶל־יַרְכְּתֵי הַסְּפִינָה וַיִּשְׁכַּב וַיֵּרָדַם: 6 וַיִּקְרַב אֵלָיו רַב הַחֹבֵל וַיֹּאמֶר לוֹ מַה־לְּךָ נִרְדָּם קוּם קְרָא אֶל־אֱלֹהֶיךָ אוּלַי יִתְעַשֵּׁת הָאֱלֹהִים לָנוּ וְלֹא נֹאבֵד: 7 וַיֹּאמְרוּ אִישׁ אֶל־רֵעֵהוּ לְכוּ וְנַפִּילָה גוֹרָלוֹת וְנֵדְעָה בְּשֶׁלְּמִי הָרָעָה הַזֹּאת לָנוּ וַיַּפִּלוּ גּוֹרָלוֹת וַיִּפֹּל הַגּוֹרָל עַל־

הפטרת יום כפור מנחה

יוֹנָה: 8 וַיֹּאמְר֣וּ אֵלָ֔יו הַגִּֽידָה־נָּ֣א לָ֔נוּ בַּאֲשֶׁ֛ר לְמִי־הָרָעָ֥ה הַזֹּ֖את לָ֑נוּ מַה־מְּלַאכְתְּךָ֙ וּמֵאַ֣יִן תָּב֔וֹא מָ֣ה אַרְצֶ֔ךָ וְאֵֽי־מִזֶּ֥ה עַ֖ם אָֽתָּה: 9 וַיֹּ֥אמֶר אֲלֵיהֶ֖ם עִבְרִ֣י אָנֹ֑כִי וְאֶת־יְהֹוָ֞ה אֱלֹהֵ֤י הַשָּׁמַ֙יִם֙ אֲנִ֣י יָרֵ֔א אֲשֶׁר־עָשָׂ֥ה אֶת־הַיָּ֖ם וְאֶת־הַיַּבָּשָֽׁה: 10 וַיִּֽירְא֤וּ הָֽאֲנָשִׁים֙ יִרְאָ֣ה גְדוֹלָ֔ה וַיֹּאמְר֥וּ אֵלָ֖יו מַה־זֹּ֣את עָשִׂ֑יתָ כִּֽי־יָדְע֣וּ הָאֲנָשִׁ֗ים כִּֽי־מִלִּפְנֵ֤י יְהֹוָה֙ ה֣וּא בֹרֵ֔חַ כִּ֥י הִגִּ֖יד לָהֶֽם: 11 וַיֹּאמְר֤וּ אֵלָיו֙ מַה־נַּ֣עֲשֶׂה לָּ֔ךְ וְיִשְׁתֹּ֥ק הַיָּ֖ם מֵֽעָלֵ֑ינוּ כִּ֥י הַיָּ֖ם הוֹלֵ֥ךְ וְסֹעֵֽר: 12 וַיֹּ֣אמֶר אֲלֵיהֶ֗ם שָׂא֙וּנִי֙ וַהֲטִילֻ֣נִי אֶל־הַיָּ֔ם וְיִשְׁתֹּ֥ק הַיָּ֖ם מֵֽעֲלֵיכֶ֑ם כִּ֚י יוֹדֵ֣עַ אָ֔נִי כִּ֣י בְשֶׁלִּ֔י הַסַּ֧עַר הַגָּד֛וֹל הַזֶּ֖ה עֲלֵיכֶֽם: 13 וַיַּחְתְּר֣וּ הָאֲנָשִׁ֗ים לְהָשִׁ֛יב אֶל־הַיַּבָּשָׁ֖ה וְלֹ֣א יָכֹ֑לוּ כִּ֣י הַיָּ֔ם הוֹלֵ֥ךְ וְסֹעֵ֖ר עֲלֵיהֶֽם: 14 וַיִּקְרְא֨וּ אֶל־יְהֹוָ֜ה וַיֹּאמְר֗וּ אָנָּ֤ה יְהֹוָה֙ אַל־נָ֣א נֹאבְדָ֗ה בְּנֶ֙פֶשׁ֙ הָאִ֣ישׁ הַזֶּ֔ה וְאַל־תִּתֵּ֥ן עָלֵ֖ינוּ דָּ֣ם נָקִ֑יא כִּֽי־אַתָּ֣ה יְהֹוָ֔ה כַּאֲשֶׁ֥ר חָפַ֖צְתָּ עָשִֽׂיתָ: 15 וַיִּשְׂאוּ֙ אֶת־יוֹנָ֔ה וַיְטִלֻ֖הוּ אֶל־הַיָּ֑ם וַיַּעֲמֹ֥ד הַיָּ֖ם מִזַּעְפּֽוֹ: 16 וַיִּֽירְא֧וּ הָאֲנָשִׁ֛ים יִרְאָ֥ה גְדוֹלָ֖ה אֶת־יְהֹוָ֑ה וַיִּֽזְבְּחוּ־זֶ֙בַח֙ לַֽיהֹוָ֔ה וַֽיִּדְּר֖וּ נְדָרִֽים:

ב 1 וַיְמַ֤ן יְהֹוָה֙ דָּ֣ג גָּד֔וֹל לִבְלֹ֖עַ אֶת־יוֹנָ֑ה וַיְהִ֤י יוֹנָה֙ בִּמְעֵ֣י הַדָּ֔ג שְׁלֹשָׁ֥ה יָמִ֖ים וּשְׁלֹשָׁ֥ה לֵילֽוֹת: 2 וַיִּתְפַּלֵּ֣ל יוֹנָ֔ה אֶל־יְהֹוָ֖ה אֱלֹהָ֑יו מִמְּעֵ֖י הַדָּגָֽה: 3 וַיֹּ֗אמֶר קָרָ֩אתִי֩ מִצָּ֨רָה לִ֤י אֶל־יְהֹוָה֙ וַֽיַּעֲנֵ֔נִי מִבֶּ֧טֶן שְׁא֛וֹל שִׁוַּ֖עְתִּי שָׁמַ֥עְתָּ קוֹלִֽי: 4 וַתַּשְׁלִיכֵ֤נִי מְצוּלָה֙ בִּלְבַ֣ב יַמִּ֔ים וְנָהָ֖ר יְסֹבְבֵ֑נִי כָּל־מִשְׁבָּרֶ֥יךָ וְגַלֶּ֖יךָ עָלַ֥י עָבָֽרוּ: 5 וַאֲנִ֣י אָמַ֔רְתִּי נִגְרַ֖שְׁתִּי מִנֶּ֣גֶד עֵינֶ֑יךָ אַ֚ךְ אוֹסִ֣יף לְהַבִּ֔יט אֶל־

---

[8] "Please tell us," they said to him, "who was the victim of your sin that has brought this disaster upon us? Perhaps you did something that could be corrected? What's your business? Perhaps you cheated somebody? Where do you come from? Perhaps you wronged someone there? What is your nationality? Perhaps you did something inappropriate in that land? And with which god are you? Perhaps you offended him?"

[9] "I am a Hebrew," he answered them. "I have wronged nobody. I fear God, the God of the Heavens, and my sin is only against Him. He made the sea and the dry land, and I see now that He can reach me even here."

[10] The men were terribly afraid, and said to him, "Why did you do such a thing?" for the men had realized that he was fleeing from God, since he had effectively told them this with his reply.

[11] "What must we do to you so that the sea will calm down for us?" they said to him, for the sea was becoming increasingly stormy.

[12] "Pick me up and throw me into the sea," he said to them, "and the sea will calm down for you, because I know that this great storm that you're experiencing is due to me."

[13] The men rowed hard to return to shore but they were unsuccessful, because the sea around them was becoming increasingly turbulent.

[14] They then cried out to God and said, "Please, God! Do not let us perish for taking the life of this man, and do not attribute innocent bloodshed to us, for You are God, and You obviously desired that he should die through us, and You have done as You wished."

[15] They then picked up Jonah and threw him into the sea, and the sea stopped raging. [16] The men feared God tremendously. They promised to slaughter sacrifices to God and made vows to charity.

2 [1] God summoned a big fish to swallow Jonah straightaway, so that he should not drown. Jonah was inside the fish's belly for three days and three nights. [2] Jonah prayed to God, his God, from the fish's belly. [3] He said, "In my distress, I called out to God and He answered me. From this abdominal tomb I cried out and You heard my voice.

[4] "You cast me into the depths, into the mighty seas, and a river engulfed me. All your breakers and waves swept over me. [5] I thought I had been driven from Your sight, but now I realize I will again gaze upon Your

haftarat yom kippur (afternoon service)

holy Sanctuary. [6] Water surrounded me until my soul almost departed. The depths whirled around me; seaweed wrapped around my head. [7] I sank to the bottom of the seabed; I thought that the earth was barred from me forever. But You, God, my God, will raise me up from this tomb to life. [8] When my soul was enshrouded with misery, I remembered God, and my prayer went up to You, to Your Holy Sanctuary. [9] Those sailors in the boat who worship vanities will forsake their kind promises that they made to you in a moment of despair, [10] but I, with loud thanksgiving, will offer sacrifices to You. What I vowed for God's salvation I will fulfil."

[11] God uttered a decree upon the fish, and it spewed up Jonah onto the shore.

3 [1] God's word came to Jonah a further time, saying, [2] "Get going and travel to the great city of Nineveh and reprimand them with the proclamation that I will tell you." [3] So Jonah got going and traveled to Nineveh, following God's word.

Nineveh was a very large city for God, that took three days to walk across. [4] Jonah began making his way into the city, a day's walking distance. He then proclaimed and said, "In another forty days Nineveh will be overturned!"

[5] The people of Nineveh believed that this was a message from God. They declared a fast, and old and young alike put on sackcloth. [6] When the news reached the king of Nineveh, he got up from his throne, removed his robes, covered himself with sackcloth and sat on ashes. [7] He gave instructions to make a declaration in Nineveh by order of the king and his senior officers, saying, "Neither people nor animals, cattle, and flocks may taste anything. They may not graze, or drink water. [8] Both man and beast should put on sackcloth, and cry out fervently to God. Each person must repent from his evil ways, and from the corruption in his hands. [9] Whoever knows how, must repent. Then God will reconsider and revoke his vehement anger, and we will not perish."

[10] God saw what they did, that they repented from their evil ways, and God reconsidered the harm He said he would bring upon them, and He did not do it.

הֵיכַל קָדְשֶׁךָ: 6 אֲפָפוּנִי מַיִם עַד־נֶפֶשׁ תְּהוֹם יְסֹבְבֵנִי סוּף חָבוּשׁ לְרֹאשִׁי: 7 לְקִצְבֵי הָרִים יָרַדְתִּי הָאָרֶץ בְּרִחֶיהָ בַעֲדִי לְעוֹלָם וַתַּעַל מִשַּׁחַת חַיַּי יְהוָה אֱלֹהָי: 8 בְּהִתְעַטֵּף עָלַי נַפְשִׁי אֶת־יְהוָה זָכָרְתִּי וַתָּבוֹא אֵלֶיךָ תְּפִלָּתִי אֶל־הֵיכַל קָדְשֶׁךָ: 9 מְשַׁמְּרִים הַבְלֵי־שָׁוְא חַסְדָּם יַעֲזֹבוּ: 10 וַאֲנִי בְּקוֹל תּוֹדָה אֶזְבְּחָה־לָּךְ אֲשֶׁר נָדַרְתִּי אֲשַׁלֵּמָה יְשׁוּעָתָה לַיהוָה: 11 וַיֹּאמֶר יְהוָה לַדָּג וַיָּקֵא אֶת־יוֹנָה אֶל־הַיַּבָּשָׁה:

ג 1 וַיְהִי דְבַר־יְהוָה אֶל־יוֹנָה שֵׁנִית לֵאמֹר: 2 קוּם לֵךְ אֶל־נִינְוֵה הָעִיר הַגְּדוֹלָה וּקְרָא אֵלֶיהָ אֶת־הַקְּרִיאָה אֲשֶׁר אָנֹכִי דֹּבֵר אֵלֶיךָ: 3 וַיָּקָם יוֹנָה וַיֵּלֶךְ אֶל־נִינְוֵה כִּדְבַר יְהוָה וְנִינְוֵה הָיְתָה עִיר־גְּדוֹלָה לֵאלֹהִים מַהֲלַךְ שְׁלֹשֶׁת יָמִים: 4 וַיָּחֶל יוֹנָה לָבוֹא בָעִיר מַהֲלַךְ יוֹם אֶחָד וַיִּקְרָא וַיֹּאמַר עוֹד אַרְבָּעִים יוֹם וְנִינְוֵה נֶהְפָּכֶת: 5 וַיַּאֲמִינוּ אַנְשֵׁי נִינְוֵה בֵּאלֹהִים וַיִּקְרְאוּ־צוֹם וַיִּלְבְּשׁוּ שַׂקִּים מִגְּדוֹלָם וְעַד־קְטַנָּם: 6 וַיִּגַּע הַדָּבָר אֶל־מֶלֶךְ נִינְוֵה וַיָּקָם מִכִּסְאוֹ וַיַּעֲבֵר אַדַּרְתּוֹ מֵעָלָיו וַיְכַס שַׂק וַיֵּשֶׁב עַל־הָאֵפֶר: 7 וַיַּזְעֵק וַיֹּאמֶר בְּנִינְוֵה מִטַּעַם הַמֶּלֶךְ וּגְדֹלָיו לֵאמֹר הָאָדָם וְהַבְּהֵמָה הַבָּקָר וְהַצֹּאן אַל־יִטְעֲמוּ מְאוּמָה אַל־יִרְעוּ וּמַיִם אַל־יִשְׁתּוּ: 8 וְיִתְכַּסּוּ שַׂקִּים הָאָדָם וְהַבְּהֵמָה וְיִקְרְאוּ אֶל־אֱלֹהִים בְּחָזְקָה וְיָשֻׁבוּ אִישׁ מִדַּרְכּוֹ הָרָעָה וּמִן־הֶחָמָס אֲשֶׁר בְּכַפֵּיהֶם: 9 מִי־יוֹדֵעַ יָשׁוּב וְנִחַם הָאֱלֹהִים וְשָׁב מֵחֲרוֹן אַפּוֹ וְלֹא נֹאבֵד: 10 וַיַּרְא הָאֱלֹהִים אֶת־מַעֲשֵׂיהֶם כִּי־שָׁבוּ מִדַּרְכָּם הָרָעָה וַיִּנָּחֶם הָאֱלֹהִים עַל־הָרָעָה אֲשֶׁר־דִּבֶּר לַעֲשׂוֹת־לָהֶם וְלֹא עָשָׂה:

הפטרת יום כפור מנחה

4 ¹ This displeased Jonah greatly, and he was perturbed. ² He prayed to God, saying, "O God! Isn't this what I said would happen when I was still in my land? That's why I took the initiative and fled to Tarshish, hoping to avoid a clear command from You to warn Nineveh of imminent destruction. For I knew that You are a kind and merciful God, slow to anger and abundant in kindness, and that You reconsider harsh decrees, and that I wanted the people of Nineveh to miss the chance to repent and be destroyed for their sins because they persecute the Jewish people. ³ So now, God, please take my soul from me, for I would rather die than live."

⁴ "Does it really bother you so much?" God replied, rhetorically. "I will soon show you a sign that you have no reason to be upset."

⁵ Jonah left the city, and settled to the east side of the city. He made for himself a shade-hut there, and sat underneath it in the shade, waiting to see what would happen in the city. ⁶ When the foliage that was providing the shade dried up, God Almighty summoned a castor tree to grow up above Jonah to act as a shade over his head, to save him from his discomfort. Jonah rejoiced over the castor tree and was tremendously happy, since he now had permanent shade.

⁷ The following morning, God summoned a worm. It severed the roots of the castor tree and it withered. ⁸ When the sun rose, God summoned a deafening east wind. The sun beat down upon Jonah's head and he felt weak. He wished death on himself, saying, "I'd rather die than live, for my pain is too much to bear."

⁹ "Does it really bother you so much about the castor tree?" God asked Jonah.

"I will be genuinely upset until I die," he replied,

¹⁰ God said, "You were concerned for the castor tree, for which you made no effort, and which you did not grow; one night it was there, and the next night it was gone. ¹¹ So should I not be concerned for the great city Nineveh, which I made, that has many more than one hundred and twenty thousand child citizens who do not know their right hand from their left, as well as many *animals*, who are all innocent?"

7 ¹⁸ Who is like You, O God, forgiving iniquity and overlooking transgression for those who remain of His heritage after the birth pangs of the Messiah? Even when He does become angry He does not maintain His anger forever, because He is a lover of kindness. ¹⁹ He will once again have mercy on us. He will

ד ¹ וַיֵּרַע אֶל־יוֹנָה רָעָה גְדוֹלָה וַיִּחַר לוֹ: ² וַיִּתְפַּלֵּל אֶל־יְהֹוָה וַיֹּאמַר אָנָּה יְהֹוָה הֲלוֹא־זֶה דְבָרִי עַד־הֱיוֹתִי עַל־אַדְמָתִי עַל־כֵּן קִדַּמְתִּי לִבְרֹחַ תַּרְשִׁישָׁה כִּי יָדַעְתִּי כִּי אַתָּה אֵל־חַנּוּן וְרַחוּם אֶרֶךְ אַפַּיִם וְרַב־חֶסֶד וְנִחָם עַל־הָרָעָה: ³ וְעַתָּה יְהֹוָה קַח־נָא אֶת־נַפְשִׁי מִמֶּנִּי כִּי טוֹב מוֹתִי מֵחַיָּי: ⁴ וַיֹּאמֶר יְהֹוָה הַהֵיטֵב חָרָה לָךְ: ⁵ וַיֵּצֵא יוֹנָה מִן־הָעִיר וַיֵּשֶׁב מִקֶּדֶם לָעִיר וַיַּעַשׂ לוֹ שָׁם סֻכָּה וַיֵּשֶׁב תַּחְתֶּיהָ בַּצֵּל עַד אֲשֶׁר יִרְאֶה מַה־יִּהְיֶה בָּעִיר: ⁶ וַיְמַן יְהֹוָה־אֱלֹהִים קִיקָיוֹן וַיַּעַל | מֵעַל לְיוֹנָה לִהְיוֹת צֵל עַל־רֹאשׁוֹ לְהַצִּיל לוֹ מֵרָעָתוֹ וַיִּשְׂמַח יוֹנָה עַל־הַקִּיקָיוֹן שִׂמְחָה גְדוֹלָה: ⁷ וַיְמַן הָאֱלֹהִים תּוֹלַעַת בַּעֲלוֹת הַשַּׁחַר לַמָּחֳרָת וַתַּךְ אֶת־הַקִּיקָיוֹן וַיִּיבָשׁ: ⁸ וַיְהִי | כִּזְרֹחַ הַשֶּׁמֶשׁ וַיְמַן אֱלֹהִים רוּחַ קָדִים חֲרִישִׁית וַתַּךְ הַשֶּׁמֶשׁ עַל־רֹאשׁ יוֹנָה וַיִּתְעַלָּף וַיִּשְׁאַל אֶת־נַפְשׁוֹ לָמוּת וַיֹּאמֶר טוֹב מוֹתִי מֵחַיָּי: ⁹ וַיֹּאמֶר אֱלֹהִים אֶל־יוֹנָה הַהֵיטֵב חָרָה־לְךָ עַל־הַקִּיקָיוֹן וַיֹּאמֶר הֵיטֵב חָרָה־לִי עַד־מָוֶת: ¹⁰ וַיֹּאמֶר יְהֹוָה אַתָּה חַסְתָּ עַל־הַקִּיקָיוֹן אֲשֶׁר לֹא־עָמַלְתָּ בּוֹ וְלֹא גִדַּלְתּוֹ שֶׁבִּן־לַיְלָה הָיָה וּבִן־לַיְלָה אָבָד: ¹¹ וַאֲנִי לֹא אָחוּס עַל־נִינְוֵה הָעִיר הַגְּדוֹלָה אֲשֶׁר יֶשׁ־בָּהּ הַרְבֵּה מִשְׁתֵּים־עֶשְׂרֵה רִבּוֹ אָדָם אֲשֶׁר לֹא־יָדַע בֵּין־יְמִינוֹ לִשְׂמֹאלוֹ וּבְהֵמָה רַבָּה:

ז ¹⁸ מִי־אֵל כָּמוֹךָ נֹשֵׂא עָוֺן וְעֹבֵר עַל־פֶּשַׁע לִשְׁאֵרִית נַחֲלָתוֹ לֹא־הֶחֱזִיק לָעַד אַפּוֹ כִּי־חָפֵץ חֶסֶד הוּא: ¹⁹ יָשׁוּב

haftarat sukkot (first day)

grasp our iniquities, preventing them from being held against us, and cast all our sins into the depths of the sea. [20] Give to us the fulfillment of the true words that You spoke to Jacob, and the words of lovingkindness that You spoke to Abraham, which you promised our fathers long ago, at the Binding of Isaac.

יְרַחֲמֵנוּ יִכְבֹּשׁ עֲוֹנֹתֵינוּ וְתַשְׁלִיךְ בִּמְצֻלוֹת יָם כָּל־חַטֹּאתָם: [20] תִּתֵּן אֱמֶת לְיַעֲקֹב חֶסֶד לְאַבְרָהָם אֲשֶׁר־נִשְׁבַּעְתָּ לַאֲבֹתֵינוּ מִימֵי קֶדֶם:

haftarat sukkot
first day

Torah Reading—Leviticus 22:26–23:44 (p. 744)
Maftir—Numbers 29:12–16 (p. 1006)

ALL COMMUNITIES—ZECHARIAH 14:1–21

> **SYNOPSIS:** This *Haftarah* is read on *Sukkot* since it contains the verse *"to celebrate the Festival of Sukkot"* (v. 16).
>
> The *Haftarah* forms the conclusion of the Book of Zechariah, a series of inspirational prophecies which were delivered during a period of national low morale, seventeen years after permission to rebuild the Temple had been given, when construction had ceased at the command of King Ahasuerus.
>
> The *Haftarah* commences with a description of the wars fought against the nations over Jerusalem prior to the Redemption (14:1-5). An image of the marvelous events of the day of Redemption then follows, including the resolution of uncertainty (6-7), a new flow of fresh, running water (8), a global acceptance of God (9), flattening of the earth (10-11), and an elimination of the enemy by plague (12-15). The remnant of the oppressive nations will make an annual pilgrimage to Jerusalem on the festival of *Sukkot* (16-19). The concluding passage speaks of the ritual purity of Jerusalem in the future era (20-21).

14 [1] Behold, an awaited day of God is coming when the spoils which have been captured from you throughout the generations will be apportioned back among you.

[2] How will this come to pass? I will first gather all the peoples of Gog and Magog to Jerusalem for a war. The city will be captured, the houses crushed, the women violated, and half the city will go into exile. But the remaining half of the population will not be displaced from the city.

[3] God will then come forth and fight against those nations like the day He fought against Egypt on the day of battle at the Sea of Reeds. [4] On that day, His feet will stand on the Mount of Olives, which faces Jerusalem from the east, and the Mount of Olives will crack in the middle from east to west, forming a huge gaping valley. Half the mountain will shift to the north and half of it to the south. [5] You will then flee from

יד [1] הִנֵּה יוֹם־בָּא לַיהוָֹה וְחֻלַּק שְׁלָלֵךְ בְּקִרְבֵּךְ: [2] וְאָסַפְתִּי אֶת־כָּל־הַגּוֹיִם ׀ אֶל־יְרוּשָׁלַםִ לַמִּלְחָמָה וְנִלְכְּדָה הָעִיר וְנָשַׁסּוּ הַבָּתִּים וְהַנָּשִׁים [תשגלנה כ׳] תִּשָּׁכַבְנָה וְיָצָא חֲצִי הָעִיר בַּגּוֹלָה וְיֶתֶר הָעָם לֹא יִכָּרֵת מִן־הָעִיר: [3] וְיָצָא יְהוָֹה וְנִלְחַם בַּגּוֹיִם הָהֵם כְּיוֹם הִלָּחֲמוֹ בְּיוֹם קְרָב: [4] וְעָמְדוּ רַגְלָיו בַּיּוֹם־הַהוּא עַל־הַר הַזֵּיתִים אֲשֶׁר עַל־פְּנֵי יְרוּשָׁלַםִ מִקֶּדֶם וְנִבְקַע הַר הַזֵּיתִים מֵחֶצְיוֹ מִזְרָחָה וָיָמָּה גֵּיא גְּדוֹלָה מְאֹד וּמָשׁ חֲצִי הָהָר צָפוֹנָה וְחֶצְיוֹ־נֶגְבָּה: [5] וְנַסְתֶּם גֵּיא־הָרַי כִּי־

הפטרת סוקות יום א'

יַגִּיעַ גֵּי־הָרִים אֶל־אָצַל וְנַסְתֶּם כַּאֲשֶׁר נַסְתֶּם מִפְּנֵי הָרַעַשׁ בִּימֵי עֻזִּיָּה מֶלֶךְ־יְהוּדָה וּבָא יְהֹוָה אֱלֹהַי כָּל־קְדֹשִׁים עִמָּךְ: 6 וְהָיָה בַּיּוֹם הַהוּא לֹא־יִהְיֶה אוֹר יְקָרוֹת [יקפאון כ׳] וְקִפָּאוֹן: 7 וְהָיָה יוֹם־אֶחָד הוּא יִוָּדַע לַיהֹוָה לֹא־יוֹם וְלֹא־לָיְלָה וְהָיָה לְעֵת־עֶרֶב יִהְיֶה־אוֹר: 8 וְהָיָה | בַּיּוֹם הַהוּא יֵצְאוּ מַיִם־חַיִּים מִירוּשָׁלַ͏ִם חֶצְיָם אֶל־הַיָּם הַקַּדְמוֹנִי וְחֶצְיָם אֶל־הַיָּם הָאַחֲרוֹן בַּקַּיִץ וּבָחֹרֶף יִהְיֶה: 9 וְהָיָה יְהֹוָה לְמֶלֶךְ עַל־כָּל־הָאָרֶץ בַּיּוֹם הַהוּא יִהְיֶה יְהֹוָה אֶחָד וּשְׁמוֹ אֶחָד: 10 יִסּוֹב כָּל־הָאָרֶץ כָּעֲרָבָה מִגֶּבַע לְרִמּוֹן נֶגֶב יְרוּשָׁלָ͏ִם וְרָאֲמָה וְיָשְׁבָה תַחְתֶּיהָ לְמִשַּׁעַר בִּנְיָמִן עַד־מְקוֹם שַׁעַר הָרִאשׁוֹן עַד־שַׁעַר הַפִּנִּים וּמִגְדַּל חֲנַנְאֵל עַד יִקְבֵי הַמֶּלֶךְ: 11 וְיָשְׁבוּ בָהּ וְחֵרֶם לֹא יִהְיֶה־עוֹד וְיָשְׁבָה יְרוּשָׁלַ͏ִם לָבֶטַח: 12 וְזֹאת | תִּהְיֶה הַמַּגֵּפָה אֲשֶׁר יִגֹּף יְהֹוָה אֶת־כָּל־הָעַמִּים אֲשֶׁר צָבְאוּ עַל־יְרוּשָׁלָ͏ִם הָמֵק | בְּשָׂרוֹ וְהוּא עֹמֵד עַל־רַגְלָיו וְעֵינָיו תִּמַּקְנָה בְחֹרֵיהֶן וּלְשׁוֹנוֹ תִּמַּק בְּפִיהֶם: 13 וְהָיָה בַּיּוֹם הַהוּא תִּהְיֶה מְהוּמַת־יְהֹוָה רַבָּה בָּהֶם וְהֶחֱזִיקוּ אִישׁ יַד רֵעֵהוּ וְעָלְתָה יָדוֹ עַל־יַד רֵעֵהוּ: 14 וְגַם־יְהוּדָה תִּלָּחֵם בִּירוּשָׁלָ͏ִם וְאֻסַּף חֵיל כָּל־הַגּוֹיִם סָבִיב זָהָב וָכֶסֶף וּבְגָדִים לָרֹב מְאֹד: 15 וְכֵן תִּהְיֶה מַגֵּפַת הַסּוּס הַפֶּרֶד הַגָּמָל וְהַחֲמוֹר וְכָל־הַבְּהֵמָה אֲשֶׁר

---

your captors through the valley formed between My mountains, for the valley of the mountains will reach to Azal. You will flee in haste as your ancestors fled from the earthquake during the days of King Uzziah of Judah. And God, my God, will come with you, together with all the holy angels, to help you, in the battle against Gog.

⁶ On that day there will be such uncertainty that there will not be a bright light indicating salvation or thick darkness signaling pending destruction. ⁷ It will be one day—only God knows when—of neither "day" nor "night." But towards the evening, there will be light.

⁸ On that day, running spring water will flow from Jerusalem throughout the entire world, half of it to the eastern sea and half to the western sea; it will remain flowing in both summer and winter. ⁹ And God will be accepted as King over all the nations of the earth. On that day, God will be the only one worshiped by all the nations, and His name will be the only one mentioned.

¹⁰ All the land will be transformed to be flat like a plain, from Geba to Rimmon, which is south of Jerusalem. But Jerusalem will be higher, once the rest of the land is flattened, and stay in its original place, from the Gate of Benjamin to the site of the First Gate, up to the Corner Gate; and from Tower of Hananel to the winery of the king. ¹¹ They will live in it forever, and there will be no more destruction. Jerusalem will dwell securely.

¹² The following will be the method of plague with which God will attack all the nations that besieged Jerusalem: Their flesh will dissolve even as they stand on their feet without becoming sick. Their eyes will melt away in their sockets and their tongues will dissolve in their mouths. ¹³ On that day, there will be a great confusion from God among them: each man will grab hold of his friend's hand to help him, but his friend will mistakenly think that the other is attacking him, and he will in return raise his hand in attack against his friend's hand. ¹⁴ Judah, too, will battle against Jerusalem with the enemy, thus adding to their confusion later on, as they will not be able to identify who is on their side. The wealth of all the surrounding nations who had joined the enemy will be *gathered in*—very large amounts of gold, silver, and clothes.

¹⁵ Likewise, will be the plague of the horses, mules, camels, and donkeys, along with all the other animals found in those encampments. It will be just like this above-mentioned destruction.

haftarat sukkot (second day)

¹⁶ Whoever survives of all those nations who come to attack Jerusalem will come up to Jerusalem every year to bow down to the King, the God of Hosts, and to celebrate the Festival of Tabernacles by offering sacrifices, to commemorate the destruction of their people that occurred on this date. ¹⁷ And if there are from the people of the land some who fail to go up to Jerusalem to bow down to the King, the God of Hosts, rain will not fall for them, for it is on the Festival of Tabernacles that God decides the year's rainfall.

¹⁸ And if the Egyptian people do not go up and do not come to Jerusalem—since they do not need rain to fall upon them, since their crops are irrigated by the Nile—their punishment will be instead through the plague with which God will strike the people who fail to go up to Jerusalem to celebrate the Festival of Tabernacles.

¹⁹ All this melting of the flesh will be the punishment of Egypt and the punishment of all the peoples that fail to go up to Jerusalem to celebrate the Festival of Tabernacles.

²⁰ On that day of destruction, it will be as if the horses' bells had written on them "Sanctified to God" because their death in the plague will be an eternal reminder. The gold from the bells will be used to make cooking pots inside God's House. They will be solid gold like the sacrificial bowls before the altar.

²¹ From the vast number of sacrifices brought to the Temple, every pot in Jerusalem and Judah will be needed in the Temple, where they will be sanctified to the God of Hosts. And all those who bring sacrifices will come and take indiscriminately from the golden pots to cook in them, without even asking which ones may be used, because they will know that all the pots are being used for sacrificial purposes.

On that day, there will no longer be Canaanite woodchoppers and water-drawers working in the House of the God of Hosts, because even the most aristocratic of gentiles will be volunteering their own services.

יְהָיָה בַּמַּחֲנוֹת הָהֵמָּה כַּמַּגֵּפָה הַזֹּאת: 16 וְהָיָה כָּל־הַנּוֹתָר מִכָּל־הַגּוֹיִם הַבָּאִים עַל־יְרוּשָׁלָ͏ִם וְעָלוּ מִדֵּי שָׁנָה בְשָׁנָה לְהִשְׁתַּחֲוֺת לְמֶלֶךְ יְהֹוָה צְבָאוֹת וְלָחֹג אֶת־חַג הַסֻּכּוֹת: 17 וְהָיָה אֲשֶׁר לֹא־יַעֲלֶה מֵאֵת מִשְׁפְּחוֹת הָאָרֶץ אֶל־יְרוּשָׁלַ͏ִם לְהִשְׁתַּחֲוֺת לְמֶלֶךְ יְהֹוָה צְבָאוֹת וְלֹא עֲלֵיהֶם יִהְיֶה הַגָּשֶׁם: 18 וְאִם־מִשְׁפַּחַת מִצְרַיִם לֹא־תַעֲלֶה וְלֹא בָאָה וְלֹא עֲלֵיהֶם תִּהְיֶה הַמַּגֵּפָה אֲשֶׁר יִגֹּף יְהֹוָה אֶת־הַגּוֹיִם אֲשֶׁר לֹא יַעֲלוּ לָחֹג אֶת־חַג הַסֻּכּוֹת: 19 זֹאת תִּהְיֶה חַטַּאת מִצְרָיִם וְחַטַּאת כָּל־הַגּוֹיִם אֲשֶׁר לֹא יַעֲלוּ לָחֹג אֶת־חַג הַסֻּכּוֹת: 20 בַּיּוֹם הַהוּא יִהְיֶה עַל־מְצִלּוֹת הַסּוּס קֹדֶשׁ לַיהֹוָה וְהָיָה הַסִּירוֹת בְּבֵית יְהֹוָה כַּמִּזְרָקִים לִפְנֵי הַמִּזְבֵּחַ: 21 וְהָיָה כָּל־סִיר בִּירוּשָׁלַ͏ִם וּבִיהוּדָה קֹדֶשׁ לַיהֹוָה צְבָאוֹת וּבָאוּ כָּל־הַזֹּבְחִים וְלָקְחוּ מֵהֶם וּבִשְּׁלוּ בָהֶם וְלֹא־יִהְיֶה כְנַעֲנִי עוֹד בְּבֵית־יְהֹוָה צְבָאוֹת בַּיּוֹם הַהוּא:

haftarat sukkot
second day

Torah Reading—Leviticus 22:26–23:44 (p. 744)
Maftir—Numbers 29:12–16 (p. 1006)
ALL COMMUNITIES—I KINGS 8:2–21

The *Haftarah* for the second day of *Sukkot* is the same as the *Haftarah* for *Parashat Pekudei* (page 1342), except that it begins two verses later, in chapter 8, verse 2 (*"All the men of Israel"*—וַיִּקָּהֲלוּ אֶל־הַמֶּלֶךְ), page 1343.

haftarat sukkot
intermediate shabbat

הפטרת סוכות שבת חול המועד

Torah Reading—Exodus 33:12–34:26 (p. 540)
Maftir—Numbers 29:17–34 *

ALL COMMUNITIES—Ezekiel 38:18 – 39:16

> **SYNOPSIS:** This *Haftarah* does not mention the festival of *Sukkot* explicitly, but the war spoken of here is identical with that discussed in Zechariah ch. 14, the *Haftarah* of the first day of *Sukkot*, and that *Haftarah* refers to the nations' observance of *Sukkot* in the future.
>
> A further connection between the *Haftarah* and the festival is a link to the timing of the war of Gog and Magog which is depicted here. Rabbi Hai ben Sherira Gaon (10th–11th century) testified to an oral tradition that the war will occur in the month of *Tishri*, the month during which the festival of *Sukkot* occurs.
>
> The reading, taken from chapters 38–39 of the Book of Ezekiel, follows a series of prophecies of hope for national restoration (ch. 36–37), and precedes Ezekiel's lengthy vision of the future Temple (ch. 40–48). The events of the *Haftarah*—the war against Israel of King Gog of the land of Magog—are thus depicted as the final event which precipitates the Redemption.
>
> The identity of Magog and its allies has been given various interpretations. The *Midrash* associates Magog with "Germania," a northern area of ancient Europe largely included in modern Germany (*Genesis Rabbah* 37:1). The *Babylonian Talmud* states that Magog is "Candia" (*Yoma* 10a), which possibly refers to the Caucasian region between the Black and Caspian seas in the southwestern part of Russia.
>
> The timing of the war of Gog and Magog is shrouded with uncertainty. Rabbi Samuel Bornstein of Sochaczew (20th century) testifies to a Hasidic tradition that we have been exempted from the war of Gog and Magog because the current exile has already been so long and protracted.
>
> The *Haftarah* opens with a description of God's rage at Gog for setting foot in the land of Israel, and God's intention to eliminate him (38:18-23). The following chapter contains a more detailed prophecy of Gog's demise, which will sanctify God's name (39:1-7). The Jewish people will burn Gog's weapons, which will provide them with fuel for seven years, and it will take seven months to bury the enemy (9–13). Officials will then be appointed to scout the land so as to remove any further corpses, ensuring that the land remains pure (14–18).

38 ¹⁸ "On that day, when Gog comes upon the soil of Israel," says God Almighty, "My blazing anger will flare. ¹⁹ I have declared in My blazing anger due to My zeal, I swear that on that day there will be a great earthquake upon the land of Israel. ²⁰ The fish of the sea, the birds of the skies, the beasts of the field, all the creeping things that creep on the ground, and every man on the face of the earth will tremble before Me.

לח 18 וְהָיָה | בַּיּוֹם הַהוּא בְּיוֹם בּוֹא גּוֹג עַל־אַדְמַת יִשְׂרָאֵל נְאֻם אֲדֹנָי יֱהֹוִה תַּעֲלֶה חֲמָתִי בְּאַפִּי: 19 וּבְקִנְאָתִי בְאֵשׁ־עֶבְרָתִי דִּבַּרְתִּי אִם־לֹא | בַּיּוֹם הַהוּא יִהְיֶה רַעַשׁ גָּדוֹל עַל אַדְמַת יִשְׂרָאֵל: 20 וְרָעֲשׁוּ מִפָּנַי דְּגֵי הַיָּם וְעוֹף הַשָּׁמַיִם וְחַיַּת הַשָּׂדֶה

---

* *Maftir* Readings for intermediate *Shabbat* of *Sukkot*: Day One—*Numbers* 29:17–22 (p. 1006); Day Three—ibid. 23–28 (p. 1006); Day Four—ibid. 26–31 (p. 1006).

haftarat sukkot (intermediate shabbat)

Mountains will be destroyed, stairways will collapse, and every wall will fall to the ground.

[21] "I will summon Gog to take the sword against all My mountains," says God Almighty. "Amid the confusion, men will turn their swords against their brothers. [22] I will do justice and therefore punish them with plague and blood, torrential rain and hailstones. I will pour down fire and brimstone upon them, their divisions, and the many people that are with them. [23] Then I will be magnified and sanctified, and I will make Myself known to many nations. They will know that I am God.

39 [1] "Now, son of man, prophesy against Gog! You shall say that God Almighty says, 'See! I am against you, O Gog, chief prince of Meshech and Tubal. [2] I will lead you astray and subvert you. I will bring you up from the most distant parts of the north, and I will bring you to the mountains of Israel. [3] I will knock the bow out of your left hand and strike the arrows from your right hand. [4] You will fall on the mountains of Israel, you, all your divisions, and the people who are with you. I will leave you as food for all the birds of prey and the beasts of the field.

[5] "You will not fall at war, but in the open field, for I have spoken and I will fulfil My word!" says God Almighty. [6] "I will set aflame Magog and those who dwell securely on the islands, and they will know that I am God. [7] I will make My holy name known among My people Israel. I will no longer allow My holy name to be profaned. The nations will know that I am the Holy God, who dwells among Israel.'"

[8] "Behold! The time is coming and it will be a time of salvation," says God Almighty. "It is the day of which I spoke. [9] The inhabitants of Israel's cities will go out and kindle and set fire to the weapons—the shields and buckles, bows and arrows, staffs and spears. They will fuel fires with them for seven years. [10] They will not need to carry wood from the field or chop it in the forests, because the weapons will fuel their fires. They will take spoils from those who plundered them and plunder those who looted them," says God Almighty.

[11] "On that day I will give Gog's people a burial site there in Israel—the Valley of the Travelers,

וְכָל־הָרֶמֶשׂ הָרֹמֵשׂ עַל־הָאֲדָמָה וְכֹל הָאָדָם אֲשֶׁר עַל־פְּנֵי הָאֲדָמָה וְנֶהֶרְסוּ הֶהָרִים וְנָפְלוּ הַמַּדְרֵגוֹת וְכָל־חוֹמָה לָאָרֶץ תִּפּוֹל: 21 וְקָרָאתִי עָלָיו לְכָל־הָרַי חֶרֶב נְאֻם אֲדֹנָי יֱהֹוִה חֶרֶב אִישׁ בְּאָחִיו תִּהְיֶה: 22 וְנִשְׁפַּטְתִּי אִתּוֹ בְּדֶבֶר וּבְדָם וְגֶשֶׁם שׁוֹטֵף וְאַבְנֵי אֶלְגָּבִישׁ אֵשׁ וְגָפְרִית אַמְטִיר עָלָיו וְעַל־אֲגַפָּיו וְעַל־עַמִּים רַבִּים אֲשֶׁר אִתּוֹ: 23 וְהִתְגַּדִּלְתִּי וְהִתְקַדִּשְׁתִּי וְנוֹדַעְתִּי לְעֵינֵי גּוֹיִם רַבִּים וְיָדְעוּ כִּי־אֲנִי יְהֹוָה:

לט 1 וְאַתָּה בֶן־אָדָם הִנָּבֵא עַל־גּוֹג וְאָמַרְתָּ כֹּה אָמַר אֲדֹנָי יֱהֹוִה הִנְנִי אֵלֶיךָ גּוֹג נְשִׂיא רֹאשׁ מֶשֶׁךְ וְתֻבָל: 2 וְשֹׁבַבְתִּיךָ וְשִׁשֵּׁאתִיךָ וְהַעֲלִיתִיךָ מִיַּרְכְּתֵי צָפוֹן וַהֲבִאוֹתִךָ עַל־הָרֵי יִשְׂרָאֵל: 3 וְהִכֵּיתִי קַשְׁתְּךָ מִיַּד שְׂמֹאולֶךָ וְחִצֶּיךָ מִיַּד יְמִינְךָ אַפִּיל: 4 עַל־הָרֵי יִשְׂרָאֵל תִּפּוֹל אַתָּה וְכָל־אֲגַפֶּיךָ וְעַמִּים אֲשֶׁר אִתָּךְ לְעֵיט צִפּוֹר כָּל־כָּנָף וְחַיַּת הַשָּׂדֶה נְתַתִּיךָ לְאָכְלָה: 5 עַל־פְּנֵי הַשָּׂדֶה תִּפּוֹל כִּי אֲנִי דִבַּרְתִּי נְאֻם אֲדֹנָי יֱהֹוִה: 6 וְשִׁלַּחְתִּי־אֵשׁ בְּמָגוֹג וּבְיֹשְׁבֵי הָאִיִּים לָבֶטַח וְיָדְעוּ כִּי־אֲנִי יְהֹוָה: 7 וְאֶת־שֵׁם קָדְשִׁי אוֹדִיעַ בְּתוֹךְ עַמִּי יִשְׂרָאֵל וְלֹא־אַחֵל אֶת־שֵׁם־קָדְשִׁי עוֹד וְיָדְעוּ הַגּוֹיִם כִּי־אֲנִי יְהֹוָה קָדוֹשׁ בְּיִשְׂרָאֵל: 8 הִנֵּה בָאָה וְנִהְיָתָה נְאֻם אֲדֹנָי יֱהֹוִה הוּא הַיּוֹם אֲשֶׁר דִּבַּרְתִּי: 9 וְיָצְאוּ יֹשְׁבֵי | עָרֵי יִשְׂרָאֵל וּבִעֲרוּ וְהִשִּׂיקוּ בְּנֶשֶׁק וּמָגֵן וְצִנָּה בְּקֶשֶׁת וּבְחִצִּים וּבְמַקֵּל יָד וּבְרֹמַח וּבִעֲרוּ בָהֶם אֵשׁ שֶׁבַע שָׁנִים: 10 וְלֹא־יִשְׂאוּ עֵצִים מִן־הַשָּׂדֶה וְלֹא יַחְטְבוּ מִן־הַיְּעָרִים כִּי בַנֶּשֶׁק יְבַעֲרוּ־אֵשׁ וְשָׁלְלוּ אֶת־שֹׁלְלֵיהֶם וּבָזְזוּ אֶת־בֹּזְזֵיהֶם נְאֻם אֲדֹנָי יֱהֹוִה: 11 וְהָיָה בַיּוֹם הַהוּא אֶתֵּן לְגוֹג |

הפטרת שמיני עצרת

east of the sea. It will block the path of the travelers, because Gog and all his multitudes will be buried there. It will be called the Valley of Gog's Multitude.

[12] "The House of Israel will bury them not out of respect, but merely to purify the land, and there will be so many of them, the burial will last for seven months. [13] All the people of the land will bury them, and the fact that so many people took so long to bury the dead will cause renown. It will be a day when I am honored," says God Almighty.

[14] Afterwards, permanent officials will be set aside to pass through the land and bury, with the help of the passersby, those bodies that still remain on the surface of the ground, so as to purify it. They will begin to search only after the main burial of seven months. [15] What will happen is, if when a traveler is passing through the land and he sees a human bone, he will place a marker near it so the permanent officials will spot it as they roam, and the marker will remain there until the buriers have buried it in the Valley of Gog's Multitude.

[16] In addition to the valley, the town, too, will be called Gog's Multitudes.

The land will thus be purified.

מְקוֹם־שָׁם קֶבֶר בְּיִשְׂרָאֵל גֵּי הָעֹבְרִים קִדְמַת הַיָּם וְחֹסֶמֶת הִיא אֶת־הָעֹבְרִים וְקָבְרוּ שָׁם אֶת־גּוֹג וְאֶת־כָּל־הֲמוֹנֹה וְקָרְאוּ גֵּיא הֲמוֹן גּוֹג: [12] וּקְבָרוּם בֵּית יִשְׂרָאֵל לְמַעַן טַהֵר אֶת־הָאָרֶץ שִׁבְעָה חֳדָשִׁים: [13] וְקָבְרוּ כָּל־עַם הָאָרֶץ וְהָיָה לָהֶם לְשֵׁם יוֹם הִכָּבְדִי נְאֻם אֲדֹנָי יֱהֹוִה: [14] וְאַנְשֵׁי תָמִיד יַבְדִּילוּ עֹבְרִים בָּאָרֶץ מְקַבְּרִים אֶת־הָעֹבְרִים אֶת־הַנּוֹתָרִים עַל־פְּנֵי הָאָרֶץ לְטַהֲרָהּ מִקְצֵה שִׁבְעָה־חֳדָשִׁים יַחְקֹרוּ: [15] וְעָבְרוּ הָעֹבְרִים בָּאָרֶץ וְרָאָה עֶצֶם אָדָם וּבָנָה אֶצְלוֹ צִיּוּן עַד קָבְרוּ אֹתוֹ הַמְקַבְּרִים אֶל־גֵּיא הֲמוֹן גּוֹג: [16] וְגַם שֶׁם־עִיר הֲמוֹנָה וְטִהֲרוּ הָאָרֶץ:

---

haftarat shemini atzeret

Torah Reading—Deuteronomy 14:22–16:17 (p. 1148)
Maftir—Numbers 29:35–30:1 (p. 1008)

HABAD—I KINGS 8:54–66
SEPHARDIM AND ASHKENAZIM—I KINGS 8:54 – 9:1

> **SYNOPSIS:** This *Haftarah* is read on *Shemini Atzeret* ("rest of the eighth day"), because of the verse, *"On the eighth day, he sent the people off"* (8:66).
>
> The *Haftarah* begins after Solomon has just completed his great prayer at the dedication of the Temple, and he begins to bless the people (8:54-55). In the blessing, he acknowledges the fulfillment of God's promises (56), and prays that God will be with the people, helping them with their spiritual and physical needs (57-61). A very large number of sacrifices is then offered to dedicate the Temple (62-64). A fourteen-day festival follows, after which the people return home in good spirits (65-66). Sephardic and Ashkenazic communities add the first verse from the following chapter, which states that Solomon had finished *"doing everything he desired to do"* (9:1).

8 [54] When Solomon finished offering this prayer and supplication to God, he stood up from his kneeling position before God's altar, his

ח [54] וַיְהִי | כְּכַלּוֹת שְׁלֹמֹה לְהִתְפַּלֵּל אֶל־יְהֹוָה אֵת כָּל־הַתְּפִלָּה וְהַתְּחִנָּה הַזֹּאת

haftarat shemini atzeret

hands were spread out to the heavens. 55 He stood and blessed the entire congregation of Israel in a loud voice, saying:

56 "Blessed is God, who has given peace to His people Israel, in accordance with everything that He said. Not a single word of all the good promises which He made through His servant Moses has failed!

57 "May God, our God, be with us, as He was with our ancestors. May He never abandon us or forsake us! 58 To turn our hearts towards Him, that we may follow all His ways and be careful to keep His commandments, statutes, and laws, which he commanded our ancestors.

59 "May these words of mine which I have entreated before God be close to God, our God, day and night. May He grant the needs of His servant and the needs of His people Israel, according to the requirements of each day. 60 So that all the peoples of the earth will know that God is God, and there is no other.

61 "All these blessings will only come when you will be wholehearted with God, our God, follow His statutes and keep His commandments, as you do this day."

62 The king, and all Israel along with him, offered sacrifices before God. 63 Solomon offered up the peace-offering, sacrificing twenty-two thousand oxen and one hundred and twenty thousand sheep to God. The king and all the children of Israel thus dedicated God's Temple.

64 On that day, the king sanctified the floor of the court in front of God's Temple, for there He offered burnt-offerings, meal-offerings, and the fat of peace-offerings on the new stone altar which replaced the bronze altar built by Moses, because the bronze altar built by Moses before God was too small for the volume of burnt-offerings, the meal-offerings, and the fat of the peace-offerings in the Holy Temple.

65 On that occasion, Solomon made a celebratory festival—along with all Israel, a huge group, from the approach to Hamath to the river of Egypt—before God, our God, for seven days of inauguration and another seven days of celebration, fourteen days in all.

66 On the eighth day, he sent the people off. They blessed the king and returned home, happy

קָם מִלִּפְנֵי מִזְבַּח יְהוָה מִכְּרֹעַ עַל־בִּרְכָּיו וְכַפָּיו פְּרֻשׂוֹת הַשָּׁמָיִם: 55 וַיַּעֲמֹד וַיְבָרֶךְ אֵת כָּל־קְהַל יִשְׂרָאֵל קוֹל גָּדוֹל לֵאמֹר: 56 בָּרוּךְ יְהוָה אֲשֶׁר נָתַן מְנוּחָה לְעַמּוֹ יִשְׂרָאֵל כְּכֹל אֲשֶׁר דִּבֵּר לֹא־נָפַל דָּבָר אֶחָד מִכֹּל דְּבָרוֹ הַטּוֹב אֲשֶׁר דִּבֶּר בְּיַד מֹשֶׁה עַבְדּוֹ: 57 יְהִי יְהוָה אֱלֹהֵינוּ עִמָּנוּ כַּאֲשֶׁר הָיָה עִם־אֲבֹתֵינוּ אַל־יַעַזְבֵנוּ וְאַל־יִטְּשֵׁנוּ: 58 לְהַטּוֹת לְבָבֵנוּ אֵלָיו לָלֶכֶת בְּכָל־דְּרָכָיו וְלִשְׁמֹר מִצְוֹתָיו וְחֻקָּיו וּמִשְׁפָּטָיו אֲשֶׁר צִוָּה אֶת־אֲבֹתֵינוּ: 59 וְיִהְיוּ דְבָרַי אֵלֶּה אֲשֶׁר הִתְחַנַּנְתִּי לִפְנֵי יְהוָה קְרֹבִים אֶל־יְהוָה אֱלֹהֵינוּ יוֹמָם וָלָיְלָה לַעֲשׂוֹת | מִשְׁפַּט עַבְדּוֹ וּמִשְׁפַּט עַמּוֹ יִשְׂרָאֵל דְּבַר־יוֹם בְּיוֹמוֹ: 60 לְמַעַן דַּעַת כָּל־עַמֵּי הָאָרֶץ כִּי יְהוָה הוּא הָאֱלֹהִים אֵין עוֹד: 61 וְהָיָה לְבַבְכֶם שָׁלֵם עִם יְהוָה אֱלֹהֵינוּ לָלֶכֶת בְּחֻקָּיו וְלִשְׁמֹר מִצְוֹתָיו כַּיּוֹם הַזֶּה: 62 וְהַמֶּלֶךְ וְכָל־יִשְׂרָאֵל עִמּוֹ זֹבְחִים זֶבַח לִפְנֵי יְהוָה: 63 וַיִּזְבַּח שְׁלֹמֹה אֵת זֶבַח הַשְּׁלָמִים אֲשֶׁר זָבַח לַיהוָה בָּקָר עֶשְׂרִים וּשְׁנַיִם אֶלֶף וְצֹאן מֵאָה וְעֶשְׂרִים אָלֶף וַיַּחְנְכוּ אֶת־בֵּית יְהוָה הַמֶּלֶךְ וְכָל־בְּנֵי יִשְׂרָאֵל: 64 בַּיּוֹם הַהוּא קִדַּשׁ הַמֶּלֶךְ אֶת־תּוֹךְ הֶחָצֵר אֲשֶׁר לִפְנֵי בֵית־יְהוָה כִּי־עָשָׂה שָׁם אֶת־הָעֹלָה וְאֶת־הַמִּנְחָה וְאֵת חֶלְבֵי הַשְּׁלָמִים כִּי־מִזְבַּח הַנְּחֹשֶׁת אֲשֶׁר לִפְנֵי יְהוָה קָטֹן מֵהָכִיל אֶת־הָעֹלָה וְאֶת־הַמִּנְחָה וְאֵת חֶלְבֵי הַשְּׁלָמִים: 65 וַיַּעַשׂ שְׁלֹמֹה בָעֵת־הַהִיא | אֶת־הֶחָג וְכָל־יִשְׂרָאֵל עִמּוֹ קָהָל גָּדוֹל מִלְּבוֹא חֲמָת | עַד־נַחַל מִצְרַיִם לִפְנֵי יְהוָה אֱלֹהֵינוּ שִׁבְעַת יָמִים וְשִׁבְעַת יָמִים אַרְבָּעָה עָשָׂר יוֹם: 66 בַּיּוֹם הַשְּׁמִינִי שִׁלַּח אֶת־הָעָם

and good-hearted over all the good which God had done for His servant David, by fulfilling His word that his son Solomon would build the Temple, and His people Israel.

וַיְבָרְכוּ אֶת־הַמֶּלֶךְ וַיֵּלְכוּ לְאָהֳלֵיהֶם שְׂמֵחִים וְטוֹבֵי לֵב עַל כָּל־הַטּוֹבָה אֲשֶׁר עָשָׂה יְהֹוָה לְדָוִד עַבְדּוֹ וּלְיִשְׂרָאֵל עַמּוֹ:

Ḥabad communities conclude here. Other communities continue:

9¹ Now Solomon had finished building God's Temple and the royal palace and doing everything he desired to do.

ט ¹ וַיְהִי כְּכַלּוֹת שְׁלֹמֹה לִבְנוֹת אֶת־בֵּית־יְהֹוָה וְאֶת־בֵּית הַמֶּלֶךְ וְאֵת כָּל־חֵשֶׁק שְׁלֹמֹה אֲשֶׁר חָפֵץ לַעֲשׂוֹת:

haftarat simḥat torah

Torah Reading—Deut. 33:1–34:12 (p. 1272); Gen. 1:1–2:3 (p. 4)
Maftir—Num. 29:35–30:1 (p. 1008)

SEPHARDIM—JOSHUA 1:1–9
ASHKENAZIM AND ḤABAD—JOSHUA 1:1–18

> **SYNOPSIS:** This *Haftarah* mentions the passing of Moses, which is related in the Torah portion for *Simḥat Torah*. The *Haftarah* opens with God's communication to Joshua after Moses' passing, instructing him to lead the conquest of the land (1:1-4). God promises to assist Joshua, encourages him to be "strong and firm," and warns him that he must observe the Torah (5-9). Joshua immediately instructs the people to prepare for war (10-11). He reminds the tribes of Reuben and Gad and the half-tribe of Manasseh of their promise to lead the battle before returning to settle in the Transjordan (12-15), and they wholeheartedly consent (16-18).

1¹ It was after the death of Moses, God's servant, that God said to Moses' attendant, Joshua son of Nun:

² "My servant Moses is dead. Now, set off and cross this river Jordan now—both you and this entire people—to the land which I am giving the children of Israel. ³ I will give you every place on which the soles of your feet tread, as I said to Moses: ⁴ Your borders will be from the desert and Lebanon here, to the Great River, the Euphrates River—all the land of the Hittites, to the *Great Sea, to the direction where the sun sets.*

⁵ "No one will stand against you all the days of your life. I will be with you, as I was with Moses. I will not weaken My support of you and I will not abandon you.

א ¹ וַיְהִי אַחֲרֵי מוֹת מֹשֶׁה עֶבֶד יְהֹוָה וַיֹּאמֶר יְהֹוָה אֶל־יְהוֹשֻׁעַ בִּן־נוּן מְשָׁרֵת מֹשֶׁה לֵאמֹר: ² מֹשֶׁה עַבְדִּי מֵת וְעַתָּה קוּם עֲבֹר אֶת־הַיַּרְדֵּן הַזֶּה אַתָּה וְכָל־הָעָם הַזֶּה אֶל־הָאָרֶץ אֲשֶׁר אָנֹכִי נֹתֵן לָהֶם לִבְנֵי יִשְׂרָאֵל: ³ כָּל־מָקוֹם אֲשֶׁר תִּדְרֹךְ כַּף־רַגְלְכֶם בּוֹ לָכֶם נְתַתִּיו כַּאֲשֶׁר דִּבַּרְתִּי אֶל־מֹשֶׁה: ⁴ מֵהַמִּדְבָּר וְהַלְּבָנוֹן הַזֶּה וְעַד־הַנָּהָר הַגָּדוֹל נְהַר־פְּרָת כֹּל אֶרֶץ הַחִתִּים וְעַד־הַיָּם הַגָּדוֹל מְבוֹא הַשָּׁמֶשׁ יִהְיֶה גְּבוּלְכֶם: ⁵ לֹא־יִתְיַצֵּב אִישׁ לְפָנֶיךָ כֹּל יְמֵי חַיֶּיךָ כַּאֲשֶׁר הָיִיתִי עִם־מֹשֶׁה אֶהְיֶה עִמָּךְ לֹא אַרְפְּךָ וְלֹא אֶעֶזְבֶךָּ:

haftarat simḥat torah

6 "Be strong and firm, for you will bring this people to take possession of the land which I swore to their fathers to give them.

7 "But you must be very strong and firm to be careful to observe the entire Torah which My servant Moses commanded you. Do not turn aside from it to the right or the left, so that you succeed wherever you go. 8 This Book of the Torah must not depart from your mouth. You must pore over it day and night, so you will be careful to observe everything written in it. Only then will you prosper in all your ways and be successful. 9 Have I not commanded you: Be strong and firm! Do not be anxious or afraid, for God, your God, is with you wherever you go."

6 חֲזַ֣ק וֶאֱמָ֑ץ כִּ֣י אַתָּ֗ה תַּנְחִיל֙ אֶת־הָעָ֣ם הַזֶּ֔ה אֶת־הָאָ֕רֶץ אֲשֶׁר־נִשְׁבַּ֥עְתִּי לַאֲבוֹתָ֖ם לָתֵ֥ת לָהֶֽם׃ 7 רַק֩ חֲזַ֨ק וֶֽאֱמַ֜ץ מְאֹ֗ד לִשְׁמֹ֤ר לַעֲשׂוֹת֙ כְּכׇל־הַתּוֹרָ֗ה אֲשֶׁ֤ר צִוְּךָ֙ מֹשֶׁ֣ה עַבְדִּ֔י אַל־תָּס֥וּר מִמֶּ֖נּוּ יָמִ֣ין וּשְׂמֹ֑אול לְמַ֣עַן תַּשְׂכִּ֔יל בְּכֹ֖ל אֲשֶׁ֥ר תֵּלֵֽךְ׃ 8 לֹֽא־יָמ֡וּשׁ סֵ֩פֶר֩ הַתּוֹרָ֨ה הַזֶּ֜ה מִפִּ֗יךָ וְהָגִ֤יתָ בּוֹ֙ יוֹמָ֣ם וָלַ֔יְלָה לְמַ֙עַן֙ תִּשְׁמֹ֣ר לַעֲשׂ֔וֹת כְּכׇל־הַכָּת֖וּב בּ֑וֹ כִּי־אָ֛ז תַּצְלִ֥יחַ אֶת־דְּרָכֶ֖ךָ וְאָ֥ז תַּשְׂכִּֽיל׃ 9 הֲל֤וֹא צִוִּיתִ֙יךָ֙ חֲזַ֣ק וֶאֱמָ֔ץ אַֽל־תַּעֲרֹ֖ץ וְאַל־תֵּחָ֑ת כִּ֤י עִמְּךָ֙ יְהֹוָ֣ה אֱלֹהֶ֔יךָ בְּכֹ֖ל אֲשֶׁ֥ר תֵּלֵֽךְ׃

Sephardic communities conclude here. *Ashkenazic* and *Ḥabad* communities continue:

10 Joshua then commanded the officers of the people: 11 "Go through the camp and instruct the people, saying, 'Prepare provisions for yourselves, for in another three days you will cross this river Jordan to enter and take possession of the land which God, your God, is giving you as an inheritance.'"

12 Joshua then told the tribes of Reuben, Gad, and half the tribe of Manasseh, saying: 13 "Remember the words which Moses, God's servant, commanded you, saying: 'God, your God, is granting you a place to settle, and He has given you land on this side of the Jordan.' 14 Your wives, children, and flocks can settle in this land which Moses has assigned you across the Jordan from the land of Israel, but all of you—all your mighty warriors—must pass armed ahead of your brothers and help them, 15 until God grants your brothers a place to settle as you already have, and they take possession of the land which God, your God, has given them. Then you will return to the land of your inheritance which Moses, God's servant, gave you on the east side of the Jordan, where the sun rises, and take possession of it."

16 They answered Joshua: "Everything you have commanded us, we will do, and wherever you send us, we will go! 17 Just as we listen to everything Moses said, so will we listen to you,

10 וַיְצַ֣ו יְהוֹשֻׁ֔עַ אֶת־שֹׁטְרֵ֥י הָעָ֖ם לֵאמֹֽר׃ 11 עִבְר֣וּ ׀ בְּקֶ֣רֶב הַֽמַּחֲנֶ֗ה וְצַוּ֤וּ אֶת־הָעָם֙ לֵאמֹ֔ר הָכִ֥ינוּ לָכֶ֖ם צֵידָ֑ה כִּ֞י בְּע֣וֹד ׀ שְׁלֹ֣שֶׁת יָמִ֗ים אַתֶּם֙ עֹֽבְרִים֙ אֶת־הַיַּרְדֵּ֣ן הַזֶּ֔ה לָבוֹא֙ לָרֶ֣שֶׁת אֶת־הָאָ֔רֶץ אֲשֶׁר֙ יְהֹוָ֣ה אֱלֹֽהֵיכֶ֔ם נֹתֵ֥ן לָכֶ֖ם לְרִשְׁתָּֽהּ׃ 12 וְלָרֽאוּבֵנִי֙ וְלַגָּדִ֔י וְלַחֲצִ֖י שֵׁ֣בֶט הַֽמְנַשֶּׁ֑ה אָמַ֥ר יְהוֹשֻׁ֖עַ לֵאמֹֽר׃ 13 זָכוֹר֙ אֶת־הַדָּבָ֔ר אֲשֶׁ֨ר צִוָּ֥ה אֶתְכֶ֛ם מֹשֶׁ֥ה עֶֽבֶד־יְהֹוָ֖ה לֵאמֹ֑ר יְהֹוָ֤ה אֱלֹֽהֵיכֶם֙ מֵנִ֣יחַ לָכֶ֔ם וְנָתַ֥ן לָכֶ֖ם אֶת־הָאָ֥רֶץ הַזֹּֽאת׃ 14 נְשֵׁיכֶ֣ם טַפְּכֶם֮ וּמִקְנֵיכֶם֒ יֵשְׁב֕וּ בָּאָ֕רֶץ אֲשֶׁ֨ר נָתַ֥ן לָכֶ֛ם מֹשֶׁ֖ה בְּעֵ֣בֶר הַיַּרְדֵּ֑ן וְאַתֶּם֩ תַּעַבְר֨וּ חֲמֻשִׁ֜ים לִפְנֵ֣י אֲחֵיכֶ֗ם כֹּ֚ל גִּבּוֹרֵ֣י הַחַ֔יִל וַעֲזַרְתֶּ֖ם אוֹתָֽם׃ 15 עַ֠ד אֲשֶׁר־יָנִ֨יחַ יְהֹוָ֥ה ׀ לַאֲחֵיכֶם֮ כָּכֶם֒ וְיָרְשׁ֣וּ גַם־הֵ֔מָּה אֶת־הָאָ֕רֶץ אֲשֶׁר־יְהֹוָ֥ה אֱלֹהֵיכֶ֖ם נֹתֵ֣ן לָהֶ֑ם וְשַׁבְתֶּ֞ם לְאֶ֤רֶץ יְרֻשַּׁתְכֶם֙ וִֽירִשְׁתֶּ֣ם אוֹתָ֔הּ אֲשֶׁ֣ר ׀ נָתַ֣ן לָכֶ֗ם מֹשֶׁה֙ עֶ֣בֶד יְהֹוָ֔ה בְּעֵ֥בֶר הַיַּרְדֵּ֖ן מִזְרַ֥ח הַשָּֽׁמֶשׁ׃ 16 וַֽיַּעֲנ֔וּ אֶת־יְהוֹשֻׁ֖עַ לֵאמֹ֑ר כֹּ֤ל אֲשֶׁר־צִוִּיתָ֙נוּ֙ נַֽעֲשֶׂ֔ה וְאֶֽל־כׇּל־אֲשֶׁ֥ר תִּשְׁלָחֵ֖נוּ נֵלֵֽךְ׃ 17 כְּכֹ֤ל אֲשֶׁר־שָׁמַ֙עְנוּ֙ אֶל־מֹשֶׁ֔ה כֵּ֖ן נִשְׁמַ֣ע

הפטרת שמחת תורה

so long as God, your God, is with you, as He was with Moses. ¹⁸ Any man who rebels against you and does not listen to your words concerning anything you command us will be put to death. Just be strong and firm to punish them, and do not forgo your honor!"

אֵלֶיךָ רַק יִהְיֶה יְהֹוָה אֱלֹהֶיךָ עִמָּךְ כַּאֲשֶׁר הָיָה עִם־מֹשֶׁה: 18 כָּל־אִישׁ אֲשֶׁר־יַמְרֶה אֶת־פִּיךָ וְלֹא־יִשְׁמַע אֶת־דְּבָרֶיךָ לְכֹל אֲשֶׁר־תְּצַוֶּנּוּ יוּמָת רַק חֲזַק וֶאֱמָץ:

REFERENCES*

Book of Genesis

1:1 In the beginning. Maimonides' *Commentary to the Mishneh, Sanhedrin*, ch. 10, principle 4; *Moreh Nevukhim*, 2:13, 30. **In the beginning.** *Al ha-Torah* by Mordecai ben Ḥanokh ha-Kohen (Jerusalem, 1957), p. 13. *Teshu'ot Ḥen, Shelaḥ-Lekha*. **2. Astoundingly desolate.** *Tanḥuma, Naso'*, 16; *Yakar Mipaz* (Warsaw, 1932), p. 3. **God's breath.** *Genesis Rabbah* 2:4; *To'afot Re'em*, ch. 1 (p. 49 in ed. Jerusalem, 2004). **Hovered.** *Likkutei Torah* (Vital), *Bere'shit* (p. 2b). **4. God separated.** *Gur Aryeh*, 1:14. *Oholei Ya'akov* (Israel, 196?), p. 333. **6. Let the firmament.** *Tanya, Sha'ar ha-Yiḥud ve-ha-Emunah*, ch. 1. **26. Let us make.** *Kol Simḥah*, p. 5. *Amarot Tehorot, Em Kol Ḥai* 2:33. **Let us make.** *Yeshu'ot Ya'akov, Oraḥ Ḥayyim*, ch. 46, par. 5. **God said, "Let us make man."** *Genesis Rabbah*, 8:5. *Mi-Peninei ha-Rav*, Hershel Shachter, ed. (Jerusalem, 2005), p. 338. **28. Be fruitful and multiply.** *Sefer ha-Siḥot* 5751, vol. 1, pp. 85ff.

2:2 God completed. *Likkutei Siḥot*, vol. 5, pp. 33-35. **He rested.** *Zohar* II, 88b. *Keter Shem Tov ha-Shalem*, pp. 248-249. **3. God blessed.** *She'elot u-Teshuvot ha-Rashba*, vol. 3, Responsa 290. **6. A mist.** *Rashi* to 2:5. **7. He blew into his nostrils.** *Torah Or*, pp. 3d-4a. **He blew into his nostrils.** *The Lonely Man of Faith*, Doubleday (New York, 1992), pp. 10ff. **8. God planted.** *Perush Radak al ha-Torah*, 2:15. **18. It is not good.** Letter of the Lubavitcher Rebbe. **19. Whatever the man called.** *Shenei Luḥot ha-Berit, Toledot Adam, Bayit Aḥaron* (vol. 1, p. 10d, in ed. Warsaw, 1863). *Likkutei Torah, Naso'*, p. 26b.

3:1 Did God perhaps say? *Siaḥ Sarfei Kodesh*, vol. 1, p. 86, par. 472. **4. Your eyes will be opened.** *Ohel Elimelekh*, p. 55a, par. 272. **13. The serpent misled me, and I ate.** *Tzavva'at ha-Ribash*, p. 71, par. 141. **14. You shall eat soil.** *Matzmi'aḥ Yeshu'ot* (Cracow, 1910), p. 27a. **18. Thorns and thistles.** *Ḥiddushei Maharsha, Pesaḥim* 118a.

4:3-4 At the end of days. *Siaḥ Sarfei Kodesh*, vol. 2, p. 106, par. 397. **Of his flocks.** *Midrash Rabbenu Baḥya*, 4:12. **Their fattest ones.** *Laws of Things Prohibited for the Altar*, 7:11. **6. Why is your face dejected?** *Parpera'ot la-Torah* (Baker, Jerusalem, 1983-1986), vol. 1, p. 31. **7. Sin is crouching.** *Ketav Sofer, Bere'shit*, 10a. **9. Where is Abel your brother?** *Siaḥ Sarfei Kodesh*, vol. 1, p. 119, par. 619. **13. Is my sin too great to bear?** *Genesis Rabbah*, 22:12-13. *Likkutei Siḥot*, vol. 35, pp. 7-9. **26. Then (God's name) became profaned.** *Laws of Idolatry*, 1:1-2. **Calling humans and idols.** *Tanya, Sha'ar ha-Yiḥud ve-ha-Emunah*, ch. 1, 3-4, 6.

5:1 Adam's offspring. *Likkutei Siḥot*, vol. 35, pp. 7ff. **24. Enoch followed God.** *Ketav Sofer, Bere'shit*, 10b.

6:6 God was consoled. *Siftei Tzaddik* (Justman, Jerusalem, 1956), *Bere'shit*, p. 22, par. 56. **8. But Noah found favor.** Ibid., p. 26, par. 9. **9. Noah was a righteous man.** *Or la-Yesharim* (Ze'evi, Izmir, 1763), *Noaḥ*, p. 2c. **He was perfect.** *Zohar* I, 67b-68a. *Likkutei Siḥot*, vol. 25, pp. 19ff. and vol. 15, pp. 40-41. **10. Noah fathered three sons.** *Be'erot ha-Mayim*, p. 8b. **13. The earth has become full of robbery.** *Sefat Emet, Noaḥ*, 5656. **14. A light for the ark.** *Toledot Ya'akov Yosef, Noaḥ* (p. 10c-d).

7:11 All the wellsprings. *Zohar* I, 117a. See Ashlag's *Ha-Sulam* commentary to *Zohar* (London, 1975), *Hilufei Girsa'ot*. **12. Forty days and forty nights.** *Torah Or, Noaḥ*, p. 8c-d.

8:11 A torn olive leaf. *Genesis Rabbah*, 33:6. **16. Go out of the ark.** *Tanḥuma, Noaḥ*, par. 8. **21. For the imagination of man's heart.** *Moreh Nevukhim*, 3:22. **22. There will not cease.** *Tanḥuma, Bere'shit*, 12.

9:14 When I (will consider) causing clouds. *Midrash Rabbenu Baḥya*, 9:13. **16. Everlasting covenant.** *Sefer ha-Siḥot* 5751, pp. 75ff.; *Likkutei Siḥot*, vol. 15, pp. 51ff. **21. He drank of the wine.** *Gilgulei Neshamot*, p. 29b, par. 156. **23. They did not see their father's nakedness.** *Me'or Einayim, Ḥukkat* (p. 88c); *Likkutei Siḥot*, vol. 10, p. 24.

11:3 The bricks were like stones. *Pirkei de-Rabbi Eliezer*, ch. 24. **4. So we do not become scattered.** *Torat Ḥayyim, Noaḥ*, pp. 63cff. **8. God dispersed them.** *Rashi*, 11:9. **9. God confused the language.** *Me'or Einayim, Noaḥ* (p. 9c). **28. Haran died during the lifetime of his father.** *Genesis Rabbah*, 38:13; *Etz Yosef*, ibid.

12:1 Go ... from your land. *Kedushat Yom Tov* (Teitelbaum), p. 7c-d. **Go, etc.** *Zohar* I, 77b. *Sefer ha-Ma'amarim 5666*, p. 67. **4. Abram left.** *Pirkei de-Rabbi Eliezer*, chs. 26-31. **10. Abram went down to Egypt.** *Genesis Rabbah*, 40:6. **Abram went down.** *Me'or Einayim, Lekh Lekha* (pp. 13c-14a). **13. Please say that you are my sister.** *Zohar* III,

---

* NOTE: The works from which the insights in this book were drawn are cited in the Bibliography (page 1495). Some of these works were composed as actual running commentaries on the Torah, while others are in a variety of different formats (philosophical treatises, legal compendiums, letters, Ḥasidic discourses, etc.). For the sake of brevity, if an insight in this book was adapted from a running commentary which, in its original source, is to be found on the very same verse that it appears here, **it was not included in this list**. The reader should simply identify the source in the Bibliography, and will find the original text on the appropriate verse.

מקורות

52a. **16. (Abram) had flocks, cattle.** *Asarah Ma'amarot, Em Kol Ḥai*, 1:6.

13:14 God said to Abram, after Lot had parted. *Sefer ha-Siḥot 5750*, pp. 101-102.

14:18 King Melchizedek of Salem. *Tanḥuma, Noaḥ*, 9. *Asarah Ma'amarot, Ḥikkur ha-Din*, 4:18. **24. Except for what the lads (my servants who went with me) ate.** *Ḥafetz Ḥayyim al ha-Torah*.

15:5 Please look heavenward and count the stars. *Imrei Da'at. Divrei Sha'ul*, p. 14b. **13. They will enslave them and oppress them.** *Laws of Repentance*, 6:5. **14. I will also pronounce judgment on the nation they will serve.** *Ha-Emunoth ve-ha-De'ot, Ma'amar* 8 (pp. 118-119). **They will leave with substantial wealth.** *Zohar I*, 196a. **19. The land of the Kenites.** *Likkutei Torah* (Vital), *Lekh Lekha* (p. 50b).

16:6-9. Sarai mistreated her. *Perush Abravanel al ha-Torah, Lekh Lekha*, ch. 16 (pp. 217b-218a).

17:1 Come close to Me in worship. *Sefat Emet, Lekh Lekha*, 5637. **10. Every male among you should be circumcised.** *Avodat Yisrael, Lekh Lekha*, 12a. **26. On that very day, Abraham was circumcised.** *Genesis Rabbah*, 47:9. *Imrei Yosher*, vol. 2, 140:3.

18:1 God appeared. *Sefer ha-Siḥot 5750*, vol. 1, pp. 112-113. **God appeared.** *Zohar I*, 98b; *Me'or Einayim, Va-Yera'* (pp. 17c-17d). **2. Three (angels, in the form of) men.** *Moreh Nevukhim*, 2:6. **6. Abraham rushed to Sarah's tent.** *Mayanah Shel Torah*. **8. Cream, milk and the calves.** *Da'at Zekeinim. Me-Am Lo'ez, Mishpatim, Laws of Meat and Milk* (vol. 4, p. 894 in ed. Jerusalem, 1967). *Zohar I, Sitrei Torah*, 97b; *Menaḥem Tziyyon*, pp. 88a. **As they (pretended) to eat.** *Toledot Ya'akov Yosef, Ve-Zo't Ha-Berakhah*, p. 58d. *Kuntres Or Yisrael*, p. 3, par. 1. **11. Abraham and Sarah were old.** *Zohar I*, 129a, 224a. **12. Sarah laughed.** *Rashi*, 17:17. **13. Is it really true?** *Me'or Einayim, Toledot* (p. 27c). **21. I will descend now and see.** *Menaḥem Tziyyon, Yalkut Menaḥem*, p. 135. **23. Abraham approached.** *Likkutei Siḥot*, vol. 10, pp. 58-59. **24. Perhaps there are fifty righteous men.** *Shem mi-Shemu'el, Tetzavveh*, 5673 (p. 125a). **27. I would be dust and ashes.** *Asarah Ma'amarot, Ḥikkur ha-Din*, 3:17. *Si'aḥ Sarfei Kodesh*, vol. 1, p. 50, par. 233; see also *Yismaḥ Yisrael* (Lodz, 1911), *Zakhor*, p. 79.

19:14 He seemed like a comedian. *Shem mi-Shemu'el, Va-Yera'*, 5680 (p. 200a). **25. God turned over these four cities.** *Genesis Rabbah*, 50:10. *Shenei Luḥot ha-Berit, Lekh Lekha, Kedushat ha-Aretz* (vol. 3, p. 12a). *Ma'amarei Admor ha-Zaken* 5567, p. 405; *Ma'amarei Admor ha-Zaken al Nevi'im*, p. 66. **31-32. There is no man on earth.** *Asarah Ma'amarot, Ḥikkur ha-Din*, 19. **33. He wasn't aware of her lying down or of her getting up.** *Zohar I*, 110b. *Or Yakar to Zohar* (Jerusalem, 1967), vol. 4, p. 201a-b.

20:8 The men were very frightened. *Genesis Rabbah*, 52:9. **16. I have given a thousand pieces of silver.** *Degel Maḥaneh Efrayim, Va-Yera'* (p. 10a).

21:1 God remembered. *Etz Yosef to Ein Yaakov, Bava Kamma* 92a. **17. God has heard the boy's cry.** *Genesis Rabbah*, 53:11. *Asarah Ma'amarot, Ḥikkur ha-Din*, 2:23. **30. As proof that I dug this well.** *Zohar III*, 284b; *Likkutei Siḥot*, vol. 15, pp. 118ff. **33. Abraham planted an orchard.** *Midrash Tehillim*, 37:1. *Kol Eliyahu*.

22:1 God tested Abraham. *Sefer ha-Ma'amarim 5678*, p. 283. **4. On the third day.** *She'erit Menaḥem* (Rubenstein) vols. 3-4, p. 117; *Mo'adei Kodesh—Rosh Ha-Shanah* (Adler) p. 371, par. 86. **12. Now I know that you are a God-fearing man.** *Sefat Emet, Va-Yera'*, 5641. *Me'or Einayim, Toledot* (p. 26d). **15. A second time.** *Naḥmanides*, 22:16.

23:1 One hundred years, twenty years and seven years. *Genesis Rabbah*, 58:1. *Siḥot Kodesh* 5726, *Ḥayyei Sarah*, pp. 66ff. **2. Sarah died.** *Esh Kodesh, Ḥayyei Sarah*, 5700. **5. The people of Het answered.** *Pirkei de-Rabbi Eliezer*, ch. 36.

24:1 God had blessed Abraham with everything. *Ma'aseh Adonai, Ḥayyei Sarah*, ch. 24 (p. 107c). **6. Be insistent not to take my son back there.** *Keli Yakar*, 24:3. **10. In his hand was all his master's belongings.** *Siḥot Kodesh* 5730, vol. 1, *Ḥayyei Sarah*, pp. 209–210. **15. He had not yet finished speaking.** *Midrash Sekhel Tov*, 24:15. **18. She said, "I will also draw water for your camels."** *Mi-Peninei ha-Rav* (Shachter, Jerusalem, 2005), pp. 349-350. **57. Let us call the girl and ask her.** *Torat Moshe*, 24:55. **67. Isaac was comforted.** *Genesis Rabbah*, 60:16. *Likkutei Siḥot*, vol. 15, pp. 168ff.

25:19 And these are the descendants of Isaac. *Me'or Einayim, Toledot* (p. 28c). **22. The children struggled inside her.** *Likkutei Siḥot*, vol. 20, pp. 108ff. **She went to ask God.** *Ḥedvat Simḥah, Toledot*, p. 28c, par. 4. **23. Two esteemed individuals are in your womb.** *Me'or Einayim, Toledot* (p. 30d). **27. A man who knew how to trap.** *Shem mi-Shemu'el, Toledot*, 5671 (pp. 260a-261b). **Jacob was ... dwelling in tents.** *Ma'amar Tzive'ot Hashem*, 1:28.

26:15. The Philistines stopped up all the wells. *No'am Elimelekh*, 26:12 (p. 13b). **19. A well of living waters.** *Sefat Emet, Toledot*, 5632. **21. They dug another well.** *Naḥmanides*. *Likkutei Siḥot*, vol. 30, pp. 116ff.

27:1 He summoned Esau. *Esh Kodesh, Toledot*, 5700. **5. Rebekah was listening as Isaac spoke.** *Naḥmanides*, 27:4. **19. I am... Esau your firstborn.** *Zohar III*, 55b; *Asarah Ma'amarot, Ḥikkur ha-Din*, 3:18. **21. Come closer, so that I may feel you.** *Genesis Rabbah*, 65:19. *Torah Or*, p. 20b-c. **27. The fragrance of my son is like the fragrance of a field.** *Pirkei de-Rabbi Eliezer*, ch. 24. **28. May the Almighty give you.** *Shem mi-Shemu'el, Toledot*, 5672 (p. 266b). *Esh Kodesh, Toledot*, 5700. **From the dew of the skies and from the fatness of the earth.** *Zohar I*, 143b. **33. Isaac was extremely bewildered.** *Rashi*, 27:36.

28:1 Isaac called Jacob and blessed him. *He-Ḥafetz Ḥayyim Ḥayyav u-Fo'alo* (Tel Aviv, 1961), vol. 3, p. 1114. **9. In addition to his other wives.** *Likkutei Siḥot*, vol. 35, pp. 116-118. **10. Jacob left Beer-sheba.** *Ilana de-Ḥayyei*. **Beer-sheba.** *Genesis Rabbah*, 68:7; 54:4. *Mattenot Kehunnah*, ibid. **And went towards Haran.** *Genesis Rabbah*, 68:13; *Etz Yosef*. ibid. **11. He came across the place.** *Menaḥem Tziyyon*, pp. 26b-27a. **He took some of the stones of the place.** *Me'or Einayim, Va-Yetze'* (p. 33a-b). **12-13. He dreamt.** *Zohar I*, 149b. *Shem mi-Shemu'el, Va-Yetze'*, 5672

references

(pp. 319b-320b). **A ladder was wedged in the ground.** *Sefer Ba'al Shem Tov, Va-Yetze'*, p. 240, par. 3. *Me'or Einayim, Va-Yetze'* (p. 34c). **God was standing over him.** *Esh Kodesh, Va-Yetze'*, 5700. **20. Jacob made a vow.** *Pa'neaḥ Raza, Va-Yetze'*, p. 64b.

29:2 Look!—a well was in the field. *Torat Levi Yitzḥak*, p. 174. **There was a huge rock.** *Sefat Emet, Va-Yetze'*, 5644. **7. It's still the middle of the day.** *Divrei Gedolim, Shevil ha-Yashar*, p. 11 par. 20. **17. Rachel had beautiful facial features.** *Tzidkat ha-Tzaddik*, p. 28a-b, par. 164. **19. Laban said, "It's better for me to give her to you."** *Kol Simḥah*, p. 12. **Therefore, (God) named him Levi.** *Likkutei Siḥot*, vol. 10, pp. 96-98.

30:9 She took her maid Zilpah. *Asarah Ma'amarot, Ḥikkur ha-Din*, 3:18. **19. She gave birth.** *Midrash Tadshe* cited in *Midrash Rabbenu Baḥya, Exodus* 1:6; *Yalkut Shimoni, Exodus* 162. **27. God has blessed me because of you.** *Zohar I*, 161a. **39. The flocks became stimulated.** *To'aliyyot ha-Ralbag*, p. 29, par. 135. *Or ha-Ḥayyim*, 31:8.

31:10 Ringed, spotted and striped. *Etz Ḥayyim, Heikhal Adam Kadmon, Sha'ar ha-Akuddim*, ch. 1.; ibid., *Heikhal Nekudim, Sha'ar Derushei Nekudot*, ch. 1.; ibid., *Sha'ar ha-Tikkun*, ch. 4. **19. Rachel stole her father's idols.** *Tanḥuma, Va-Yetze'*, 12. *Pirkei de-Rabbi Eliezer*, ch. 36. **23. And pursued him.** *Me'or Einayim, Va-Yetze'* (p. 32b-d). *Likkutei Siḥot*, vol. 15, pp. 260ff. **52. Nor are you to pass.** *Sefer ha-Siḥot* 5748, vol. 2, pp. 437-438, fn. 88.

32:5 I have been living with Laban. *Sefer ha-Siḥot* 5751, vol. 1, pp. 167ff.; *Sefer ha-Siḥot*, vol. 1, pp. 137ff. **7. The angels returned to Jacob.** *Al ha-Torah* by Mordecai ben Ḥanokh ha-Kohen (Jerusalem, 5717), p. 98; *Otzar Agudat ha-Ḥasidim*, vol. 10 (Gutman, Jerusalem, 1976), *Torati Al Ta'azovu*, p. 309. **9. If Esau comes to one camp and strikes it down.** *Ḥanukkat ha-Torah*. 11. **(My merits) have become small.** *Tanya, Iggeret ha-Kodesh*, ch. 2. *Peri Etz Ḥayyim, Sha'ar ha-Tefillin*, ch. 10. **25. (Esau's guardian angel, appearing as) a man.** *Shem mi-Shemu'el, Va-Yishlaḥ*, 5673 (p. 15a). **26. He touched the joint of his hip.** *Likkutei Siḥot*, vol. 25, p. 174; *Sefer ha-Siḥot* 5751, vol. 1, pp. 262-263. **27. I will not let you go unless you bless me.** *Esh Kodesh, Va-Yishlaḥ*, 5700. **29. Your name will no longer be called Jacob.** *Perush Ralbag al ha-Torah* (p. 42a). *Sefat Emet, Va-Yishlaḥ*, 5636. **You have fought with (an angel) of God.** *Esh Kodesh, Va-Yishlaḥ*, 5700. *Laws of the Foundations of the Law*, 2:7. *Midrash Rabbenu Baḥya*, 32:29. **32. He was limping on his thigh.** *Tosefet Berakhah*. **33. Consequently, to this day.** *Me'or Einayim, Va-Yishlaḥ* (p. 41d).

33:14 Until I come (and meet) my master. *Genesis Rabbah*, 78:14.

34:1 Dinah, Leah's daughter. *Likkutei Siḥot*, vol. 35, pp. 154-155. **25. They killed every male.** *Code of Maimonides, Laws of Kings and Their Wars*, 9:14. Nahmanides, 34:13. *Perush ha-Radbaz* to *Code of Maimonides*, ibid.

35:10 Israel shall be your name. *Likkutei Torah*, pp. 70c-72b. **21. Israel journeyed.** *Ruth Rabbah*, 2:7.

36:6 He went to (find another) land. Rashi, 36:7. *Perush Abravanel al ha-Torah*, 36:1. **8. Esau settled in Mount Seir.** *Likkutei Siḥot*, vol. 10, p. 114.

37:1 Jacob settled. Rashi, 37:2. **2. These are Jacob's descendants, Joseph.** *Menaḥem Tziyyon, Yalkut Menaḥem*, p. 146. **4. They hated him.** *Ma'amar Me'ah Kesitah*, ch. 95. *Tiferet Yehonatan*. **10. He then told it to his father.** *Hadar Zekeinim*, 37:8. **21. When Reuben heard (their plan).** *Sefat Emet, Va-Yeshev*, 5637. **22. In order to save Joseph from their hands.** *Or ha-Ḥayyim*, 37:21. **24. The pit was empty. There was no water in it.** *Zohar I*, 185a-b. *Siḥot Kodesh* 5736, vol. 1, pp. 290, 295-297. **25. They sat down to eat a meal.** *Menaḥem Tziyyon, Yalkut Menaḥem*, pp. 146-147. **28. They sold Joseph.** *Zohar I*, 184a.

38:1 It was at that time that Judah went down. *Genesis Rabbah*, 85:1; *Mattenot Kehunnah*, ibid. **14. She sat down at the crossroads.** *Genesis Rabbah*, 85:7. **24. Take her out and let her be burned.** *Zohar III*, 72a; *Likkutei Torah, Numbers*, p. 2c.

39:2 God was with Joseph. *Va-Yedabber Moshe*, p. 60b. **8-9. He refused.** *Sefat Emet, Va-Yeshev*, 5633. **12. She grabbed him by his clothes.** *Me'or Einayim, Mikketz* (p. 43b).

40:7 Why do your faces (look) so down today. *Siḥot Kodesh* 5734, vol. 1, pp. 211ff.

41:1 Pharaoh was dreaming. *Torat Moshe*, 41:33. *Torah Or*, p. 28c-d. *Likkutei Siḥot*, vol. 3, p. 820. **2. They pastured in the marshland.** *Me'or Einayim, Mikketz* (p. 44b). **4. The ugly looking, thin cows devoured.** *Sefat Emet, Mikketz*, 5631. **6. Seven thin ears of grain ... were growing up after them.** *Perush ha-Tur al ha-Torah*. **8. But no one interpreted them (satisfactorily).** *Genesis Rabbah*, 89:6. **15. You listen to a dream.** *Tzidkat ha-Tzaddik*, p. 41a, par. 203. **38. Would we find like this?** *Ḥedvat Simḥah, Mikketz*, p. 39c, par. 4. **50. Two sons were born to Joseph before the year that the famine set in.** Babylonian Talmud, *Ta'anit* 11a, s.v. *'assur*. **55. Do whatever he will tell you.** *Etz Yosef* to *Tanḥuma, Mikketz*, par. 7.

42:1 Jacob saw that there was grain. *Me'or Einayim, Mikketz* (p. 45b-c). **Why are you showing off?** *Ḥiddushei Maharsha* to Babylonian Talmud, *Ta'anit* 10b, s.v. *lo'*. *Keli Yakar, Deuteronomy* 2:3. **8. They did not recognize him.** *Torat Ḥayyim, Va-Yeḥi*, pp. 104bff. **12. You have come to survey the land's weak points!** *Keli Yakar*, 42:14. **21. We are guilty for our brother.** *To'aliyyot ha-Ralbag*, p. 41, par. 12. Seforno, 42:21-22. **22. Reuben responded.** *Genesis Rabbah*, 84:19.

43:14 May God Almighty grant you mercy. *Genesis Rabbah*, 5:8. *Esh Kodesh, Mikketz*, 5700. *Hitva'aduyyot* 5748, pp. 982-984.

44:18 Judah approached him. *Sefat Emet, Va-Yiggash*, 5637. *Sefer ha-Siḥot* 5751, vol. 1, pp. 206ff. **Judah approached Joseph and said.** *Torat Moshe, Va-Yiggash*, 44:16-18. **19. My master interrogated his servants.** *Likkutei Tzevi* (Tel Aviv, 1981), p. 31.

45:1 No one stood with Joseph when he revealed himself. *Shem mi-Shemu'el, Va-Yiggash*, 5672 (pp. 271b-272a). **3. Is my father still

מקורות

alive? *Perush Abravanel al ha-Torah, Va-Yiggash*, 45:1 (p. 414). *Tiferet Yehonatan. Hiddushei u-Ferushei ha-Maharik*. **4. Please come closer to me.** *Tanya, Likkutei Amarim*, ch. 12. **I am your brother Joseph.** *Sefat Emet, Va-Yiggash*, 5636. **14. Joseph fell on his brother Benjamin's neck.** *Likkutei Sihot*, vol. 10, pp. 148-149. **26. His heart denied it.** *Avot de-Rabbi Nathan*, 31:4. **27. The spirit of their father Jacob was revived.** *Avot de-Rabbi Nathan*, 31:4. **28. Israel said, "(I have) a lot (to look forward to now)."** *Menahem Tziyyon, Yalkut Menahem*, p. 149.

46:3 I will make you into a great nation. *Likkutei Sihot*, vol. 30, pp. 234-235.

47:2 Joseph took five men. *Genesis Rabbah*, 95:4. **27. They acquired property.** *Midrash Tadshe*, ch. 17. **28. Jacob lived in the land of Egypt for seventeen years.** *Sefat Emet, Va-Yehi*, 5631. **Jacob lived in the land of Egypt for seventeen years.** *Zohar I*, 216b; *Midrash Rabbenu Bahya, Introduction to Parashat Va-Yehi*. *Ketav Sofer*, p. 76b. **31. Swear to me.** *Likkutei Sihot*, vol. 25, pp. 272-273.

48:20 May God make you like Ephraim and Manasseh. *Igra de-Kallah, Va-Yehi*, p. 160b.

49:1 Gather round and I will tell you. *Al ha-Torah* by Mordecai ben Hanokh ha-Kohen (Jerusalem, 1957), p. 138. *Sefat Emet, Va-Yehi*, 5637. **3-4. Reuben ... you will not be privileged.** *Perush Abravanel al ha-Torah, Va-Yehi*, 49:1 (p. 431b). **9. You withdrew yourself.** *Likkutei Sihot*, vol. 15, pp. 441ff. **13. Zebulun will live (in his territory).** *Tanhuma, Naso*, 16. **16. Dan will enact vengeance.** *Rashi, Numbers* 10:25. **27. Benjamin is a wolf.** *Zohar I*, 153b.

50:15 Joseph's brothers saw their father had died. *Sefer ha-Sihot* 5749, vol. 1, pp. 170-173.

Book of Exodus

1:14 They embittered their lives with hard labor. *Zohar III*, 153a. *Me'or Einayim, Shemot* (p. 47a).

2:2 She saw that he was good. *Exodus Rabbah*, 2:4. **5. She sent her maidservant.** *Emet ve-Emunah*,

p. 95, par. 636. **11. He went out to his brothers.** *Sefat Emet, Shemot*, 5643. **12. He turned this way and that way.** *Zohar II*, 12b. **19. An Egyptian man rescued us.** *Zohar II*, 14a.

3:1 Moses was pasturing the flocks. *Exodus Rabbah*, 2:2. **2. The thornbush was not being consumed.** *Sefer ha-Sihot* 5702 (Brooklyn, 1986), p. 47. **5. Take your shoes off your feet.** *Olelot Efrayim*, sec. 2, *Amud* 36, *Ma'amar* 248. **22. Each woman shall request from her neighbor.** Cited in *Midrash Rabbenu Bahya*, 3:22.

4:8-9 If they do not believe you. *Exodus Rabbah*, 3:13; *Shem mi-Shemu'el, Shemot*, 5673 (p. 17b). **10. For I am heavy of mouth.** *Derashot ha-Ran, Derush* 5.

5:7 Let them go and gather straws. *Ohel Yitzchak*, p 18b.

6:2 God (*Elokim*) spoke to Moses and said to him, "I am God (*Havayah*)." *Me'or Einayim, Va-'Era'* (p. 53a). **With My (true) name.** *Likkutei Sihot*, vol. 3, pp. 854ff. **6. I will take you out from under the burdens.** *Sefat Emet, Va-'Era'*, 5631. **12. If the children of Israel did not listen.** *Ha-Derash ve-ha-Iyyun, Exodus*, 50. *Sefat Emet, Va-'Era'*, 5659. **14-16. The sons of Reuben.** *Numbers Rabbah*, 13:8. *Meshekh Hokhmah, Exodus* 6:13. **16. These are the names of Levi's sons.** *Shenei Luhot ha-Berit, Va-'Era', Derekh Hayyim Tokhehot Musar* (vol. 3, p. 35c-d). **26. Aaron and Moses.** *Divrei Emet*, pp. 17d-18a.

7:3 I will harden Pharaoh's heart. *Code of Maimonides, Laws of Repentance*, 6:3, 5. *Tosefot Yom Tov* to *Mishneh, Avot*, 2:6. **5. The Egyptians shall know that I am God.** *Likkutei Sihot*, vol. 25, pp. 189-192; ibid., vol. 23, pp. 177-178. **9. Take your staff, and cast it in front of Pharaoh.** *Imrei Da'at*. **12. Aaron's staff swallowed their staffs.** *Likkutei Sihot*, vol. 26, pp. 57-58. **19. Take your staff and extend your hand.** *Exodus Rabbah*, 20:1. **24. The Egyptians dug.** *Exodus Rabbah*, 9:10. *Likkutei Sihot*, vol. 11, pp. 31-32; ibid., vol. 31, pp. 36-37; *Hitva'aduyyot* 5747, vol. 2, p. 342.

8:2 The frog came up. *Birkhat Peretz*. **18. I will set apart the land of** **Goshen.** *Keli Yakar*, 7:17. **19. I will bring about salvation.** *Aderet Eliyahu*.

9:10 Boils broke out into blisters. *Midrash Rabbenu Bahya* to *Exodus* 9:8. *Nahmanides* to *Exodus* 9:9. *Hizzekuni* to *Exodus* 9:8. **17. I am going to rain down.** *Zohar II*, 31b.

10:1 Come to Pharaoh. *Shem mi-Shemu'el, Bo'*, 5671 (p. 117b). *Zohar II*, 34a. **I have hardened his heart.** *Seforno* to *Exodus* 9:35. **In order that I may put these miracles.** *Peri Etz Hayyim, Sha'ar Hag ha-Matzot*, ch. 6. **14. The swarm of locusts went up.** *Tanna de-Vei Eliyahu*, ch. 7. **22. There was thick darkness.** *Likkutei Sihot*, vol. 11, pp. 2ff. **23. No person could see his brother.** *Ramatayim Tzofim* (Warsaw, 1881), *Eliyahu Zuta*, p. 50, par. 4. **The children of Israel had light.** *Exodus Rabbah*, 14:3. *Asarah Ma'amarot, Hikur Din*, 3:21. **26. We do not know how much worship.** *Ketav Sofer*, p. 95b.

11:1 When he sends you out. *Sefat Emet, Bo'*, 5637, 5645. **2. Please speak in the ears of the people.** *Mei ha-Yam*, p. 66, par. 20. *Sha'ar Bat Rabbim, Parashat Bo'*, p. 27c. *Menahem Tziyyon*, pp. 28b-29b. **4. At the dividing point.** *Keter Shem Tov*, p. 12, par. 14. **9. Pharaoh will not listen.** *Ahavat Torah*, sec. 2, *Bo'*, p. 18.

12:2 This month shall be the head of the months. *Ibn Ezra, Introduction to Commentary on Bible*. **13. The blood will be for you as a sign.** *Perush Abravanel al ha-Torah, Bo'*, 12:3 (p. 98a). **22. You shall take a bunch of hyssop.** *Likkutei Sihot*, vol. 3, pp. 864ff. **34. Their leftovers.** *Mekhilta, Bo'*, par. 13. **38. A great mixed multitude.** *Zohar II*, 191a; ibid., p. 45b. **This is the law.** *Exodus Rabbah*, 19:2. **46. You must not break.** *Sefer ha-Hinnukh*, Commandment 16.

13:16 It shall be for a sign upon your arm. *Zohar I*, 14a. **18-19. The children of Israel were armed.** *Manot ha-Levi, Introduction*, p. 18a. **Moses took Joseph's bones.** *Likkutei Sihot*, vol. 26, pp. 86ff.

14:14 God will fight for you. *Mekhilta (de-Rabbi Yishmael), Be-Shallah*, sec. 2. **16. You should lift your hand.** *Tanhuma, Be-Shallah*, 10. **29. The children of Israel went on dry land.**

1484

references

No'am Elimelekh, Likkutei Shoshanah, p. 110a.

15:1 Moses (led) the children of Israel in this song. *Mekhilta (de-Rabbi Yishmael), Be-Shallah, Parashat ha-Shirah,* sec. 1. *Ma'amarei Admor ha-Zaken al Ma'amarei Razal,* pp. 414-415; *Seder Tefillot mi-Kol ha-Shanah,* p. 67b-c. **17. A foundation for Your dwelling place.** *Zohar III,* 221a. **25. God instructed him about a (type of) wood.** *Zohar II,* 60a; *Mekhilta (de-Rabbi Yishmael), Be-Shallah, Parashat Va-Yassa,* sec. 1; *Likkutei Sihot,* vol. 6, p. 393. **26. All the sicknesses that I have placed.** *Or Yesharim* (Jerusalem, 1958), *Torat Moshe,* p. 74.

16:8 God will give you meat to eat in the evening. *Likkutei Sihot,* vol. 16, pp. 168-172. **35. The children of Israel ate the manna for (almost) forty years.** *Haggadah Shel Pesach im Midrash be-Hiddush* (Bene Berak, 1965), *Imrei Kodesh,* p. 126.

17:7-8 Amalek came. *Sefer ha-Sihot 5696-5700,* p.128. **12. (Aaron and Hur) took a stone.** *She'iltot, Ha'azinu,* par. 163.

18:6 Your wife and her two sons. *Amarot Tehorot, Hikur Din* 2:17; *Yad Yehuda,* ibid. **11. Now I know that God is greater.** *Zohar II,* 67b; 68a. *Sihot Kodesh* 5725, vol. 1, pp. 356-357. **18. The matter is too heavy.** *Likkutei Sihot,* vol. 16, pp. 203- 210. **26. They would bring any difficult case to Moses.** *Korban he-Ani, Yitro,* p. 31a.

19:1 On the third month. *Midrash* cited in *Torah Shelemah.* See also *Avodat Yisrael* (Hapstein). *Pesikta de-Rav Kahana* 12 (p. 107a). **2. Israel encamped there.** *Yalkut Sinai* (Jerusalem, 1964), p. 29. **3. You should say the following to the House of Jacob.** *Imrei Shefer,* p. 120c. **8. All the people replied in unison.** *Maggid Meisharim, Yitro,* p. 62b. **13. When the ram's horn sounds.** *Mekhilta, Yitro, Ba-Hodesh,* par. 3. **22. The (firstborn) priests.** *Mekhilta, Yitro, Ba-Hodesh,* par. 4.

20:1 God spoke. *Heikhal ha-Berakhah, Deuteronomy* 5:19; ibid., *Exodus,* 15:26. **2. I am God.** *Or Yesha* (Przemysl, 1899), p. 7a. **I am God, (the) God of (every one) of you.** *Zohar III,* 73a. *Iggerot Kodesh, Rayyatz,* vol. 3, pp. 533-535. **5. You shall not bow down before them.** *Sefer ha-Ma'amarim* 5657, pp. 56ff. *Torah Or,* p. 61a. **9-10. Six days you may work.** *Sefer ha-Likkutim, Be-Har; Ta'amei ha-Mitzvot,* ibid. **12. Honor your father and your mother.** *Sefer ha-Hinnukh,* Commandment 33. *Derekh Mitzvotekha,* 6b; *Or ha-Torah, Shemot,* vol. 8, p. 3003. **13. You shall not murder.** *Zohar II,* 90a. Ibid., 93b. **14. You shall not covet.** *Torat ha-Maggid mi-Zlatchuv,* p. 55. **15. All the people could see the sounds.** *Sefat Emet, Yitro,* 5639. *The People saw and they trembled. Emet ve-Emunah,* p. 54, par. 385. **16. You speak to us, and we will listen.** *Me'or Einayim, Yitro* (61c). *Degel Mahaneh Efrayim, Yitro* (42a). **20-21. You should not make for yourselves gods of silver.** *Likkutei Sihot,* vol. 2, p. 564.

21:1 These are the laws that you should set. *Kol Simhah,* p. 45. **2. If you buy a Hebrew slave.** *Zohar II,* 96b; *Code of Maimonides, Laws of Slaves,* 4:11; *Likkutei Sihot,* vol. 26, pp. 371ff. **6. Standing (the slave) next to a door.** *Keli Yakar,* 21:5. **16. If a person kidnaps.** Cited in *Ibn Ezra.* **19. He must (pay all) his medical (fees).** See *Rashi,* s.v. *nitnah,* and, *Tosefot,* s.v. *she-nitenah,* to *Babylonian Talmud, Bava Kamma* 85a.

22:3 If the stolen article is found in his possession. *Moreh Nevukhim,* 3:41. **6-14. If a person gives his friend money.** *Shenei Luhot ha-Berit, Pesahim, Matzah Ashirah* (vol. 1, p. 11a). **21. You shall not oppress.** *Ibn Ezra,* 22:20. **30. If you will be holy men.** *Sefat Emet, Mishpatim,* 5632.

23:2 By the majority. *Commentary to the Mishneh, Introduction.* **5. If you see your enemy's donkey.** *Ha-Yom Yom,* 28 Shevat. **12. On the seventh day you must rest.** *Torah Temimah.* **14. Three times you shall celebrate for Me.** *Likkutei Sihot,* vol. 36, pp. 82ff. **19. Do not cook a tender young animal.** Nahmanides to *Deuteronomy* 14:21. *Otzar Midrashim* (New York, 1915), vol. 2, p. 491. *Shenei Luhot ha-Berit, Mishpatim, Torah she-bi-Khetav* (vol. 3, p. 43a).

24:6 Two basins. *Hizzekuni* 24:7. **18. Within the cloud.** *Likkutei Sihot,* vol. 16, pp. 280-283. **Moses was upon the mountain forty days and forty nights.** *Exodus Rabbah,* 41:6. *Sefer ha-Ikkarim,* 3:23.

25:1 Have them (dedicate). *Likkutei Sihot,* vol. 16, pp. 284ff. **18. Two golden cherubim.** *Nahal Kedumim.* **20. The cherubim should have their wings spread upwards.** *Tzeror ha-Mor,* 25:18. **22. I will arrange My meetings with you there.** *Moreh Nevukhim,* 2:45. **23. Make a table.** *Tosefot ha-Shalem,* 25:3, par. 10. **32. Six branches.** *Likkutei Sihot,* vol. 21, pp. 168ff. **33. Three decorated cups.** *Midrash Rabbenu Bahya,* 25:31.

26:15 Make the beams of the Tabernacle. *Tanhuma, Terumah,* 10. *Likkutei Torah, Torat Shemu'el,* 5630, p. 94.

27:1-2 Make the altar of acacia wood. *Tanhuma, Terumah,* 11. **20. Clear olive oil, crushed for lighting.** *Exodus Rabbah,* 36:1.

28:15 You should make a breastplate of judgment. *Akedat Yitzhak, Tetzavveh,* 51. **35. Its sound should be heard.** *Ha-Derash ve-ha-Iyyun, Exodus,* 242. **39. A sash.** *Code of Maimonides, Laws of Vessels of the Sanctuary,* 8:19. *Likkutei Sihot,* vol. 36, pp. 155, 159.

29:20 Put it on the cartilage of Aaron's right ear. *Kol Yehudah* to *Kuzari,* 3:5. **25. A pleasurable fragrance before God.** *Ibn Ezra,* 29:25, according to understanding of A. Weiser in ed. Mossad Harav Kook (Jerusalem, 1977). **33. They should eat those things.** *Sefer ha-Hinnukh,* Commandment 102. **39. One lamb you should offer up in the morning.** *Ha-Derash ve-ha-Iyyun, Exodus,* 248. **45. I will dwell in the midst of the children of Israel.** *No'am Megadim, Tetzavveh,* 40a.

30:1 Make an altar for bringing incense. *Torat Hayyim, Terumah,* 306a. **12. When you take the sum.** *Tanhuma, Ki Tissa',* 4. **13. This is what they should give.** *Tanhuma, Ki Tissa',* 9; *Tosefot, Hullin* 42a, s.v. *zo't. Ohel Torah. No'am Elimelekh,* p. 52c. **18. An urn of copper.** *Tanhuma, Naso',* 16; *Likkutei Torah, Torat Shemu'el* 5632, pp. 96ff.

מקורות

31:4 To do master weaving. *Kanfei Nesharim, Mahazeh Avraham*, 31:3-4. **13. But keep My Sabbath.** *Mizrahi* to *Leviticus* 19:30. *Zohar II*, 88b; *Me'or Einayim, Ki Tissa'* (65c). **14. Keep the Sabbath.** *Moreh Nevukhim*, 2:31. **It is a sacred thing for you.** *Zohar III*, 94a. *Esh Kodesh, Va-Yakhel*, 5700. **18. When He had finished.** *Me'or Einayim, Ki Tissa'* (p. 67d). **He gave Moses the two tablets.** *She'elot u-Teshuvot Ḥatan Sofer, Ma'aneh Simḥah*, p. 18a.

32:3 All the people stripped themselves of the golden earrings. *Tanhuma, Ki Tissa'*, 19. **4. A molten calf.** Saadiah ben Joseph Gaon, cited in *Ibn Ezra, Exodus* 32:1. *Ibn Ezra*, ibid.; *Kuzari*, 1:97. *Nahmanides*, ibid. *Da'at Zekenim*, 32:26. **7. Go down.** *Hitva'aduyyot 5748*, vol. 2, p. 453. **11. Why, O God, should Your anger be kindled?** *Exodus Rabbah*, 43:7. **14. God changed His mind.** *Emet mi-Kotzk Titzmaḥ*, p. 48. **19. He threw the tablets from his hands.** *Moshav Zekenim. Midrash Rabbenu Baḥya* 32:16. *Sefat Emet, Ki Tissa'*, 5637. **And shattered them.** *Exodus Rabbah*, 46:1. *Likkutei Siḥot*, vol. 26, pp. 250-252. **They have made themselves a god of gold.** *Laws of Repentance*, 2:3.

33:11 God would speak to Moses face to face. *Sefat Emet, Ki Tissa'*, 5643.

34:1 Two stone tablets like the first ones. *Sefat Emet, Ki Tissa'*, 5639.

35:1 Moses caused the whole community. *Numbers Rabbah*, 13;2; 12:6. *Sefer ha-Siḥot 5749*, vol. 1, pp. 293ff. **2. For six days work may be done.** *Torat Moshe, Ki Tissa'*, 85b. **5. Collect from among yourselves.** *Exodus Rabbah*, 48;6; *Yefeh To'ar*, ibid. **26. All the women whose heart inspired them.** *Likkutei Siḥot*, vol. 16, p. 452. **30. Bezalel son of Uri son of Hur.** *Exodus Rabbah*, 48:2; *Likkutei Torah* (Vital), *Va-Yakhel*. **31. He has filled him with the spirit of God.** *Meshekh Ḥokhmah*, 35:30. **34. Oholiab.** *Likkutei Siḥot*, vol. 31, pp. 216-217.

36:6 Moses issued a command. *Menahem Tziyyon, Yalkut Menahem*, p. 178. **8. Then every wisehearted.** *Perush Abravanel al ha-Torah, Va-Yakhel* (p. 355a). *Or ha-Ḥayyim*, 36:11.

37:6 He made a lid. *Mei ha-Shiloaḥ, Tetzavveh*, p. 57a-b.

38:21 These are the accounts. *Ha-Torah ve-ha-Mitzvah*, 38:22-23. **The Tabernacle of the Testimony.** *Sefat Emet, Pekudei*, 5657. **At Moses' command.** *Tanhuma, Naso'*, 18; *Zohar II*, 240a; *Ben Porat Yosef, Introduction*, pp. 8d-9a. **27. One hundred sockets.** *Ḥiddushei ha-Rim al ha-Torah, Mo'adim ve-Likkutim*.

39:25-30 Bells of pure gold. *Exodus Rabbah*, 51:6; *Keli Yakar*, 38:21.

40:2 You should set up the Tabernacle, the Tent of Meeting. *Siḥot Kodesh*, 5730, vol. 1, pp. 556, 562-563. **17. The Tabernacle was set up.** *Imrei Emet*, 18. **Moses set up.** *Shem mi-Shemu'el, Pekudei*, 5675 (pp. 339b-340a).

Book of Leviticus

1:1 He called. *Pa'neaḥ Raza, Va-Yikra'*, p. 135a. *Yalkut Shimoni, Pinḥas*, 776. *Siḥot Kodesh*, 5741, vol. 2, pp. 615ff. **2. When a man from (among) you brings a (voluntary) offering to God.** *Likkutei Torah, Va-Yikra'*, p. 2b. *Ibn Ezra*, 1:1. *Nahmanides*, 1-9. *Kuzari* 2:26; *Akedat Yitzḥak, Va-Yikra'*, 57 (pp. 4d-5a). *Midrash Rabbenu Baḥya*, 1:9. **9. A burnt-offering.** *Shulḥan Arukh [ha-Rav], Laws of Torah Study*, 2:11.

2:1 If a (poor) soul. *Shem mi-Shemu'el, Tzav*, 5675 (p. 75b). **13. You should offer salt.** *Or ha-Torah, Va-Yikra'*, vol. 1, Addendum, pp. 226-227.

3:1 A peace-offering. *Zohar III*, 11a. **5. A pleasant aroma.** *Ma'asei Adonai, Ma'asei Bere'shit*, ch. 27.

4:2 Unintentionally. *Tanya, Iggeret ha-Kodesh*, ch. 28; *Likkutei Amarim*, ch. 13. **3. If it is the anointed.** *Tosefot Berakhah*, 21. **Burn it.** *Moreh Nevukhim*, 3:46. **27. If an individual.** *Tiferet Shemu'el, Va-Yikra'*, 7 (p. 5d).

5:1-2 If a person sins. *Sefer ha-Ḥinnukh*, Commandment 123. **5. He should confess.** *Zohar III*, 63a. **8. He should cut its head.** *Sefer ha-Ḥinnukh*, Commandment 124. **17. If a person is uncertain.** *Rabbenu Yonah*, commentary to *Alfasi (Rif), Berakhot* 1b, s.v. *ve-ha'*. **23. He should return the article.** *Rabbenu Noah*, 4.

6:2 Command. *Sefat Emet, Tzav*, 5658. **This is the law of the burnt-offering.** *Ma'amarei Admor ha-Zaken*, 5572, p. 148. **3. Shovel out.** *Ta'amei ha-Mitzvot*, Commandment 59. **5-6. It must not go out.** *Laws of the Daily Offerings and the Additional Offerings*, 3:13. **13. The offering of Aaron and his sons.** *Sefer ha-Ḥinnukh*, Commandment 136. **18. The sin-offering should be slaughtered.** *Torat Moshe*, 6:23. **21. If it is cooked in a copper vessel.** *Zohar III, Ra'aya Meheimna*, 224b.

7:1 This is the law of the guilt-offering. *Atzei Levanon*, vol. 2, p. 114. **12. The thanksgiving-offering.** *Tosefot* to Babylonian Talmud, *Berakhot* 54b, s.v. *'arba'ah*. *Sefer ha-Ma'amarim* 5737, pp. 284-285. **17. Whatever is left over.** *Sefer ha-Ḥinnukh*, Commandment 143. **18. Remission.** *Arba'ah Turim, Oraḥ Ḥayyim*, ch. 98. **19. Burned in fire.** *Hitva'aduyyot 5746*, vol. 1, p. 104. **26. You should not eat any blood.** *Nahmanides*, 17:11.

8:11 He sprinkled. *Siḥot Kodesh*, 5735, vol. 1, p. 529. **33, 35. You should not leave.** *Nahmanides* to *Exodus* 40:2.

9:3 Take a he-goat as a sin-offering. *Yalkut Shimoni, Shemini*, 521. **7. Approach the altar.** *Likkutei Torah* (Vital).

10:2 Fire came out. *Leviticus Rabbah*, 12:1. *Ma'amarei Admor ha-Zaken, Ethallekh, Liozna*, pp. 33-34.

11:4-7 The camel. *Leviticus Rabbah*, 13:5; *Mattenot Kehunnah*, ibid. **14. The buzzard.** *Oznayim la-Torah, Deuteronomy* 14:13. **19. The stork.** *Ḥiddushei ha-Rim al ha-Torah, Mo'adim ve-Likkutim*. **24-40. Ritually impure.** *Laws of the Uncleanness of Foodstuffs*, 16:8-12. **33. If any of these (dead creatures).** *Ohel Torah*, ibid. **44. Sanctify yourselves.** *Ḥiddushei Maharsha* to *Yoma* 39a; *Iyyun Ya'akov*, ibid.

12:2 She will be ritually impure. *Leviticus Rabbah*, 14:1. *Tanya, Likkutei Amarim*, ch. 29; ibid., ch. 24. **5. If she gives birth to a female.** *Ḥiddushei Maharsha* to *Niddah* 31b.

13:2 He should be brought to Aaron. *Leviticus Rabbah*, 17:4. *Shema Shelomo, Yashresh Ya'akov*, p. 30. **Tzara'at on the skin of his body.** *Torat Moshe*, beginning of *Parashat Tazria'*. *Likkutei Torah, Tazria'*, p. 22b. **13. Tzara'at has covered all of his body.** *Midrash*

references

Rabbenu Bahya, Numbers 19:2, s.v. *be'er*. *Perush ha-Tur al ha-Torah*, 13:12. **14. On the day that healthy(-looking).** *Likkutei Sihot*, vol. 37, pp. 39-40.

20. The priest should examine. *Beit ha-Behirah*, Avot 1:7. **40. If a man loses the hair.** Nahmanides, 13:29-30. **45. Call out, "(I'm) ritually impure!"** *Sefer ha-Mitzvot*, Positive Commandment 112. **46. He should remain isolated.** *Laws of the Uncleanness of Leprosy*, 16:10.

14:2 The law of the *tzara'at* sufferer. *Akedat Yitzhak, Metzora'*, 62. *Likkutei Sihot*, vol. 7, pp. 103-104; ibid., vol. 22, pp. 76-77; *Sefer ha-Sihot* 5751, vol. 2, pp. 491ff.; see also *Likkutei Sihot*, vol. 37, pp. 33ff. **6. The (remaining) live bird.** Rashi to Arakhin 15b, s.v. *deva'ei*; Hiddushei Maharsha, ibid., p. 16b, s.v. *she-'amerah*. **11. The person who is to be ritually purified.** *Torat Moshe*, beginning of *Parashat Metzora'*; ibid., 14:7. **21. If he is poor.** *Laws of Those Whose Atonement Is Not Complete*, 5:11. *Likkutei Sihot*, vol. 27, pp. 104-106. **35. There appears to me.** *Tosefot Yom Tov, Nega'im*, 12:5. **54. Sprinkle.** *Sifra, Parashat Metzora'*, 5:14. **54. Garments and houses.** *Leviticus Rabbah*, 17:4. *Or ha-Hayyim*, 14:34.

15:2 Discharge. *Likkutei Sihot*, vol. 37, pp. 42ff. **13. Immerse his flesh.** *Sefer ha-Hinnukh*, Commandment 173, 175. **31. Ensure that the children of Israel are dissociated.** *Zohar III*, 55a.

16:1 They came near. *Sefer ha-Ma'amarim* 5649, pp. 256-257. *Likkutei Sihot*, vol. 3, pp. 991-992. **4. Linen tunic.** *Likkutei Sihot*, vol. 22, p. 95. **13. Place the incense.** *Zohar Hadash, Shir ha-Shirim*, p. 67d; *Zohar II*, 218b. *Likkutei Sihot*, vol. 14, pp. 128-131. **21. All the sins.** *Laws of Repentance*, 1:2-3. **30. On this day.** *Laws of Repentance*, 1:3. *Likkutei Torah, 'Aharei Mot*, p. 26c.

17:12 None of you should eat blood. *Moreh Nevukhim*, 3:46. **13. He should cover (the blood).** Nahmanides, 17:11-12. *Likkutei Sihot*, vol. 37, pp. 52-53.

18:3 Do not follow the practices. *Sefat Emet, 'Aharei Mot*, 5635. **5. You will live by them.** *Or ha-Torah, Devarim*, vol. 2, p. 656; *Ha-Yom Yom*, 10 Shevat.

19:2 I, God, your God, am holy. *Sifra, Kedoshim*, 1:1. **3. Every person should fear.** *Hiddushei Maharsha* to *Kiddushin* 30b. **11,13. You should not steal.** *Laws of Theft*, 1:3; *Laws of Robbery and Lost Property*, 1:13. **You should not steal.** *Ha-Yom Yom*, 3 Iyyar. **16. You should not stand.** *Likkutei Sihot*, vol. 32, pp. 125-126. **18. You should love.** *Ha-Yom Yom*, 12 Menahem-Av. *Tanya, Likkutei Amarim*, ch. 32. **31. You should not turn.** *Devash ve-Halav*. **36. You should have accurate scales.** *Laws of Theft*, 7:12. *Maggid Mishneh*, ibid.

20:2 In (worship of the pagan deity). *Hamishah Homshei Torah im Perush Shimshon ben Refa'el Hirsh*, Exodus 20:2; 18:21. **7. You should sanctify yourselves.** *Torah Or*, p. 61a; *Seder Tefillot mi-Kol ha-Shanah*, p. 56d. **17. If a man takes his sister.** *Me'or Einayim, Mikketz* (p. 45c). **22. You should guard.** Rashi, 19:19. *Laws of Sacrificial Exchanges*, 4:13; *Laws of Misappropriation*, 8:8; *Moreh Nevukhim*, 3:26. *Likkutei Sihot*, vol. 32, pp. 174ff. **My supranational commands.** Rashi, 20:26. *Shemonah Perakim*, ch. 6. *Likkutei Torah, Va-'Ethannan*, p. 9d.

21:1 Speak to the priests. *Bayit Hadash to Arba'ah Turim, Yoreh De'ah*, ch. 373. **Let no (priest) become ritually impure.** *Maggid Devarav le-Ya'akov*, par. 23. **8. You should (force him) to be holy.** *Ketav Sofer, 'Emor*, p. 180b.

22:1 Speak to Aaron. *No'am Elimelekh*, p. 63b-c. **21. It should be perfect.** *Sefer ha-Hinnukh*, Commandment 286. **It should not have any blemish.** *Laws of Things Prohibited for the Altar*, 3:1. **28. You should not slaughter.** *Moreh Nevukhim*, 3:48. **29. Accepted for you.** *Ketav Sofer, 'Emor*, p. 181b. **32. My name should be sanctified.** *Laws of the Foundations of the Law*, 5:4. *Sha'arei Orah, Sha'ar Hanukkah*, pp. 8aff.

23:4 Festivals of God. *Midrash Rabbenu Bahya*, Exodus 23:17. **6. Festival of Unleavened Bread.** *Kedushat Levi, Bo'*, p. 45b-c. **15. Count for yourself.** *Maggid Devarav le-Ya'akov*, Addendum, par. 10. **17. They should be baked leavened.** *Torat Shemu'el* 5631, vol. 1, p. 274. **21. Proclaim this very day.** *Keli Yakar*, 23:16. **24. In the seventh month.** *Shenei Luhot ha-Berit, Shemini* (vol. 3, p. 57b). **40. Fruit of the (citron) tree.** *Leviticus Rabbah*, 30:12. **You should rejoice.** *Laws of the Ram's Horn, the Booth, and the Palm Branch*, 8:12-14. **43. Know that I caused the children of Israel.** *Moreh Nevukhim*, 3:43.

24:4 Arrange the lamps. *Hamishah Homshei Torah im Perush Shimshon ben Refa'el Hirsh*, 24:8. **8. On each Sabbath day.** *Laws of the Daily Offerings and the Additional Sacrifices*, 5:3. *Zohar II*, 63b.

25:1 At Mount Sinai. *Sifra, Be-Har*, 1:1. **2. When you come to the land.** *Maharam Shik al Massekhet Avot*, 5:9. **11. (Just like during a Sabbatical year).** *Tzeror ha-Mor*, 25:20-21. **14. You should not cheat.** *Si'ah Sarfei Kodesh*, vol. 3, p. 5, par. 1; *Kol Mevasser*, vol. 2, p. 243. **17. You must fear your God.** *Melo ha-Omer al ha-Torah*. **18. (The Jewish people) will live on the land securely.** *Ketav Sofer, Be-Har*, p. 185a. **20-21. "What will we eat?"** *Likkutei Sihot*, vol. 27, p. 190. **29. When a man sells a residential house.** *Lamentations Rabbah*, 4:14. **35. You should support him.** *Laws of Gifts to the Poor*, 10:7. **42. They should not be sold as slaves.** *Sifra, Be-Har*, 6:1. **53. Harsh labor.** *Darash Moshe*, 25:55.

26:1 You should not make idols for yourselves. *Ha-Torah ve-ha-Mitzvah, Parashat Be-Har*, par. 106. *Sihot Kodesh* 5725, vol. 2, p. 114. **3-4. Pursue (the study of) My laws.** *Laws of Repentance*, 9:1; *Keli Yakar*, 26:12. *Ibn Ezra, Deuteronomy*, 32:39. *Keli Yakar*, ibid. *Kuzari*, 1:104-106; *Keli Yakar*, ibid. *Sefer ha-Ikkarim*, 4:40. **Panic, inflammation.** *Likkutei Torah, Be-Hukkotai*, p. 48a-b. **24. Then I, too, will be offhand.** *Laws of Fast Day*, 1:3; *Iggerot u-Teshuvot* (Jerusalem 1954), *Iggerot Shonot*, p. 25. **26. Ten woman will bake bread.** *Likkutei Torah, Be-Hukkotai*, p. 48b-c. **40. They will confess their sins.** *Hizzekuni*, 26:41. **42. My covenant with Isaac.** *Sifra, Be-Hukkotai*, 8:7.

27:2 Value of an (adult or child's) life. *Imrei Da'at*. **6. The amount for a male.** *Siftei Kohen*, 27:6; ibid., 27:2. **14. If a man consecrates his house.** *Laws of Valuations and Things Votive*, 8:12-13. **26. A firstborn animal.** *Hamishah Homshei Torah im Perush Shimshon ben Refa'el Hirsh*, 27:33. **33. Nor should he

מקורות

offer a substitute. *Laws of Sacrificial Exchanges*, 4:13. *Likkutei Siḥot*, vol. 17, pp. 527-528.

Book of Numbers

1:1 In the Sinai Desert. *Ohel Torah. Numbers Rabbah*, 1:7. *Shem mi-Shemu'el, Be-Midbar*, 5675 (p. 35a). *Imrei Da'at. Midrash Tehillim*, 68:9. *No'am Elimelekh*, p. 68b. **2. Take the sum.** *Rashi*, 1:1. *Likkutei Siḥot*, vol. 8, pp. 3ff. **Take the sum of the entire congregation.** *Shenei Luḥot ha-Berit, Torah she-bi-Khetav, Sheloshah Maḥanot* (vol. 3, p. 62a-d). **A head count.** *Me'or Einayim, Be-Midbar* (p. 83a). **20-43. Second Tribal Sequence.** *Ibn Ezra*, 1:19. **44. These were the numbers.** *Naḥmanides*, 1:45. **49. Do not count the tribe of Levi.** *Laws of the Sabbatical Year and the Year of the Jubilee*, 13:12; *Likkutei Siḥot*, vol. 33, pp. 6ff. **52. Each man should be in his own division.** *Sha'ar ha-Kavvanot, Derush Aleinu le-Shabbe'aḥ* (p. 74c); *Shenei Luḥot ha-Berit, Torah she-bi-Khetav, Sheloshah Maḥanot* (vol. 3, p. 66b).

3:6 Draw the tribe of Levi. *Numbers Rabbah*, 3:1. *Tzavva'at ha-Ribash*, par. 125. **39. The total head-count.** *Exodus Rabbah*, 5:16; *Naḥmanides*, 3:14. *Meshekh Ḥokhmah, 3:39. 47. (From each firstborn).** *Rashi*, 3:46.

4:2 Single out. *Numbers Rabbah*, 6:1. **6. They should place a covering.** *Ma'amar Tzive'ot Adonai*, 2:16. **22. Gershon's descendants.** *Numbers Rabbah*, 6:1. **29. Count Merari's descendants.** *Numbers Rabbah*, 6:4. *Likkutei Torah, Naso'*, pp. 20a-21b.

5:4 The children of Israel did so. *Binah le-Ittim*, p. 261b. **6. If a man or woman commits.** *Numbers Rabbah*, 8:2. **7. They should confess.** *Laws of Repentance*, 1:1, 2:2-3. *Sefer ha-Ḥinnukh*, Commandment 364. *Sefat Emet, Naso'*, 5631. **10. A person's holy gifts.** *Binah le-Ittim*, p. 262a-b. **12. If any man's wife goes astray.** *Tanya, Likkutei Amarim*, chs. 24-25. **17. The priest should take holy water.** *Keter Shem Tov*, par. 249, p. 149. **18. He should uncover.** *Zohar III*, 126a. **23. Erase it.** *Iyyun Ya'akov, Sotah* 17a.

6:2 To abstain. *Laws of Ethical Behavior*, 3:1. *Torat ha-Olah*, 3:71 (p. 73a). **23. Speak to Aaron and his sons.** *Ketav Sofer, Naso'*, p. 199a-b. **24. May God bless you.** *Tanna de-Vei Eliyahu*, chs. 25, 31. *Sifrei, Naso'*, par. 40. **25. Favor you.** *Ibid.*, par. 41.

7:3 Six covered wagons. *Numbers Rabbah*, 12:17. **10. The leaders presented.** *Likkutei Siḥot*, vol. 8, pp. 47-8. **11. One leader each day.** *Numbers Rabbah*, 13:14ff. **13-17.** *Rashi*, 7:19-23. **18-19. Nethanel son of Zuar.** *Naḥmanides* to 7:2. *Si'aḥ Sarfei Kodesh*, vol.1, p. 10. **84. On the day it was anointed.** *Numbers Rabbah*, 14:13. *Likkutei Siḥot*, vol. 23, pp. 53-55. **89. He would hear the voice.** *Laws of the Foundations of the Law*, 7:6.

8:2 When you fire up. *Likkutei Siḥot*, vol. 2, pp. 316-320. **3. Aaron did so.** *Sefat Emet, Be-Ha'alotekha*, 5635. *Si'aḥ Sarfei Kodesh*, vol. 1, p. 10, par. 7. **4. This is the construction method.** *Tanḥuma, Be-Ha'alotekha*, par. 3. **6. Persuade the Levites.** *Numbers Rabbah*, 15:3. **19. I have given the Levites.** *Sefat Emet, Be-Ha'alotekha*, 5636.

9:7 Why should we be the losers? *Tiferet Shelomo al ha-Zemanim ve-ha-Mo'adim*, p. 155d. **11. They should make it.** *Sefer ha-Siḥot* 5701, p. 115. **They should eat it with unleavened.** *Rashi*, 9:10. *Likkutei Siḥot*, vol. 18, pp. 121-125. **18. The children of Israel traveled.** *Shenei Luḥot ha-Berit, Torah she-bi-Khetav, Sheloshah Maḥanot* (vol. 3, p. 67c). **20. Sometimes.** *Perush Abravanel al ha-Torah, Be-Ha'alotekha*, 9:15 (pp. 22b, 39a-b). **22. Whether it was for two days.** *Sefer ha-Siḥot* 5701, p. 162.

10:9 If you go to war. *Shenei Luḥot ha-Berit, Torah she-bi-Khetav, Sheloshah Maḥanot* (vol. 3, p. 65c). **Blow a long blast.** *Moreh Nevukhim*, 3:36.

11:11-14 Moses said to God. *Reflections of the Rav*, vol. 1, pp. 150ff. **17. I will magnify.** *Likkutei Torah, Be-Ha'alotekha*, 33b; *Ma'amarei Admor ha-Zaken* 5562, p. 535. **21. A people of six hundred thousand.** *Ma'amarei Admor ha-Zaken* 5565, p. 711. **24. He assembled.** *Rashi*, 11:26. **One was called Eldad.** *Tanḥuma, Be-Ha'alotekha*, 2; *Etz Yosef*, ibid.

29. Moses said to him. *Akedat Yitzḥak, Be-Ha'alotekha*, 75 (p. 33b). **34. He named that place Kibroth-hattaavah.** *Binah le-Ittim*, vol. 1, p. 60.

12:1 For he had married a woman of renowned beauty. *Ibn Ezra*, 12:1-2. *Divrei ha-Yamim Shel Moshe Rabbenu* (p. 6). **3. The man, Moses.** *Torah Temimah, Commentary to the Mishneh, Avot* 4:4. *Ma'amarei Admor ha-Zaken* 5562, p. 51. *Sefer ha-Ma'amarim* 5665, p. 219. **7. This is not the case.** *Laws of the Foundations of the Law*, 7:6. **13. Please God!** *Iggeret Kodesh, Rayyatz*, vol. 4, p. 352.

13:2 Send out men. *Yalkut Shimoni, Pinḥas*, 773. **4. These were their names.** *Ma'amar Me'ah Kesitah*, ch. 72. **16. Moses called Hosea.** *Maharam Shik al ha-Torah, Shelaḥ-lekha*, p. 60b. **23. They cut a branch.** *Ḥiddushei ha-Geramaz*, vol. 1, p. 117. **27. It is flowing.** *Ḥiddushei Maharsha to Sotah* 35a, s.v. *va-yesapperu*. **30. We will definitely.** *Esh Kodesh, Shelaḥ-lekha*, 5700. *Shenei Luḥot ha-Berit, Shelaḥ-lekha, Torah she-bi-Khetav* (vol. 3, p. 65b, in ed. Warsaw, 1863). **31. We are unable.** *Mizraḥi*, 13:2. *Likkutei Siḥot*, vol. 13, pp. 39ff. **33. We appeared like grasshoppers.** *Tanḥuma, Shelaḥ-lekha*, 7.

14:8 If God desires us. *Likkutei Siḥot*, vol. 4, pp. 1041ff.; vol. 28, pp. 91-92. **18. God is slow to anger.** *Zohar III*, 161b. **19. Please forgive.** *Midrash Rabbenu Baḥya*, 14:17. **30. You will not come.** *Perush Nevukhim*, 3:32. **35. They will meet their end.** *Akedat Yitzḥak, Shelaḥ-lekha*, 77 (p. 47b).

15:2 When you arrive in the land. *Hadar Zekeinim*, 15. **5. Wine as a libation.** *Likkutei Torah, Shelaḥ-lekha*, pp. 40aff. **13. Every native-born.** *Tanna de-Vei Eliyahu* (Warsaw, 1876), ch. 29; *Yeshu'ot Ya'akov*, ibid. **19. When you eat bread.** *Leviticus Rabbah*, 15:6. *Yefeh Toar*, ibid. **21. You should give.** *Seforno*, 15:20. **The first of your dough.** *Sefer ha-Ḥinnukh*, Commandment 385. **32. A man gathering sticks.** *Tosefot to Bava Batra* 119b, s.v. *'aflu*. *Ḥiddushei Maharsha to Bava Batra* 119a, s.v. *u-re'uyah*. **38. Tzitzit.** *Laws of Fringes*, 3:11-12. **A thread of turquoise.** *Likkutei Torah, Shelaḥ-lekha*, p. 44a-b.

references

16:1 Korah son of Izhar. *Tanhuma, Korah,* 5. **Korah ... took.** *Zohar III,* 176a-b. **Korah.** *Sefer ha-Sihot* 5750, vol. 2, pp. 528-531. **2. They confronted Moses.** *Tanhuma, Korah,* 2. **3. Why have you made yourselves elite?** *Si'ah Sarfei Kodesh,* vol. 3, p. 54, par. 145. *Likkutei Siḥot,* vol. 4, pp. 1048*ff.*; vol. 8, p. 108*ff.* **4. He fell on his face.** *Ḥiddushei Maharsha* to *Sanhedrin* 110a, s.v. *va-yishma'. Shenei Luḥot ha-Berit, Korah, Torah she-bi-Khetav* (vol. 3, p. 69c). *Degel Mahaneh Efrayim, Ki Tissa',* 34:35 (p. 49c-d). **7. Offer incense.** *Rashi,* 16:6. **11. (When I appointed).** *Numbers Rabbah,* 18:9. *Kol Simḥah,* 16:7. **19. Korah ganged.** *Mevaser Tov* (Podgorze, 1900), 16:7. *Midrash Tehillim,* 1:15. **22. God (who knows).** *Perush Maharzu, Numbers Rabbah,* 18:11. **31-35. The earth beneath them.** *Sihot Kodesh* 5734, vol. 2, pp. 134-135.

17:24 Moses took out all the staffs. *Sippurei Ḥasidim* (Zevin, Jerusalem, 2002), vol. 2, p. 141.

18:1 Taking responsibility. *Laws of the Temple,* 8:1-2. **21. I have given all tithes.** *Likkutei Sihot,* vol. 18, pp. 218*ff.*

19:2 The suprarational command. *Likkutei Torah, Ḥukkat,* p. 56*aff.* **They should bring.** *Likkutei Torah* (Vital), *'Ekev* 8:1. *Tanḥuma, Ḥukkat,* par. 8. **Which is devoid of blemish.** *Avodat Yisrael,* p. 72a. **9. As a secure reminder.** *Laws of the Red Heifer,* 3:4. **11. Anyone touching.** *Perush le-Ḥamishah Ḥomshei Torah Me'et Rabbi Yosef Bekhor Shor, Ḥukkat* 19:2. *Mei ha-Shiloaḥ,* p. 101a. **14. This is the law.** *Tanhuma, Va-Yeshev,* 4.

20:1 Miriam died there. *Ḥen ve-Khavod,* Sermon 55, p. 198. **1-2. Miriam died there.** *Zohar III,* 181b. *Shulḥan Arukh [ha-Rav], Oraḥ Ḥayyim,* 299:20. **8. Speak to the rock.** *Yalkut Shimoni, Ḥukkat,* 763. *Gur Aryeh, Numbers* 20:12, s.v. *she-'illu.* **10. Listen, you rebels!** *Shemonah Perakim,* ch. 4. *Rabbenu Ḥananel* cited in *Naḥmanides* to *Numbers* 20:8. *Orot HaKodesh,* vol. 4, p. 500. **11. Moses raised his hand.** *Si'ah Sarfei Kodesh,* vol. 1, p. 58, par. 172. **18. You will not pass.** *Si'ah Sarfei Kodesh,* vol. 1, p. 61, par. 219. **29. The entire house of Israel.** *Avot de-Rabbi Nathan,* 12:3-4.

21:9 He would stare. *Rashi,* 21:8. *Perush le-Ḥamishah Ḥomshei Torah Me'et Rabbi Yosef Bekhor Shor, Ḥukkat* 21:8. *Likkutei Torah, Ḥukkat,* pp. 61d-62b. **14. About this.** *Rashi,* 21:15-16. **17. O well, arise!** *Zohar III,* 183b. **18. A well dug by ministers.** *Sefat Emet, Ḥukkat,* 5659; ibid., 5653. **34. Do not fear him.** *Zohar III,* 184a. *Da'at Zekenim.*

22:8 So the Moabite dignitaries. *Rashi,* 22:7. **11. Come and condemn.** *Perush Abravanel al ha-Torah,* 22:7. **18. Balaam replied.** *Avot de-Rabbi Nathan,* 29:4. **21. Balaam got up.** *Ohel Torah.* **28. God opened.** *Naḥmanides,* 22:23. *Perush Ralbag al ha-Torah,* beginning of *Parashat Balak.* **God opened.** *Meshekh Ḥokhmah,* 22:20-22. **34. I have sinned.** *Shenei Luḥot ha-Berit, Balak, Torah she-bi-Khetav* (vol. 3, p. 75b).

23:10 Who has counted. *Likkutei Siḥot,* vol. 38, pp. 96-98. **23. In that (future) time.** *Iggerot u-Teshuvot* (Jerusalem, 1954), *Iggeret Teiman,* p. 30. *Likkutei Siḥot,* vol. 2, pp. 588-589.

24:5 Your tents are so good. *Maggid Devarav le-Ya'akov, Rimzei Torah,* p. 49a-b. **9. He will crouch.** *Genesis Rabbah,* 98:7; *Shulḥan Arukh, Ḥoshen Mishpat,* 389:8. **13. I cannot transgress.** *Tanya, Likkutei Amarim,* ch. 24. **17-18. A star will shoot forth.** *Laws of Kings and Their Wars,* 11:1.

25:3 Became attached. *Ma'amarei Admor ha-Zaken, Ethaliekh, Liozna,* pp. 258*ff.* **6. They were weeping.** *Rashi* to *Sanhedrin* 82a, s.v. *bat Yitro.* **11. Phineas son of Eleazar.** *Likkutei Siḥot,* vol. 8, pp. 167-169.

26:5 The Enochite. *Zohar III,* 213b. **55. You must only apportion.** *Tanya, Iggeret ha-Kodesh,* ch. 7. *Etz Ḥayyim, Sha'ar Kelippat Nogah,* ch. 5; ibid., *Introduction to Sha'ar ha-Hakdomot,* p. 3a. *Likkutei Siḥot,* vol. 2, pp. 346*ff. Sefer ha-Siḥot* 5752, vol. 1, p. 97. **62. They did not receive.** *Laws of the Sabbatical Year and the Year of the Jubilee,* 13:10, 12.

27:5 Moses brought their case. *Ohel Torah.* **16. God must appoint.** *Megallah Amukkot,* ch. 1. *Ohel Torah.* **17. Who will (courageously) go out.** *Mayanah Shel Torah* (Avnei Ezel). **To lead them out.** *Imrei Emet, Be-Midbar,*

p. 28. **So that God's congregation.** *Ketav Sofer, Pinḥas,* p. 227a.

28:2 Be careful to offer. *Sifrei, Pinhas,* par. 11. *Perush Abravanel al ha-Torah, Deuteronomy* 32:48. *Ha-Torah ve-ha-Mitzvah,* 28:1. **My food on My fires.** *Sefer ha-Ma'amarim* 5571, pp. 198, 210. *Likkutei Siḥot,* vol. 28, pp. 189-190. **3. Two perfect lambs.** *Seder Tefillah Im Perush Olat Re'iyah,* vol. 1, p. 13. **6. A daily burnt-offering.** *Ramatayim Tzofim,* p. 130, par. 18.

30:2 This is what God has commanded. *Maharal mi-Prag le-Aggadot ha-Shas, Nazarof* 49b. **2-3. This is what God has commanded.** *Torat Moshe.* **3. When a person makes a vow.** *Me'or Einayim, Mattot* (p. 92a). **He must act in accordance.** *Ketav Sofer, Mattot,* p. 229b. **4. All the tribes.** *Laws of the Sabbatical Year and the Year of the Jubilee,* 13:12. *Likkutei Torah* (Vital), end of *Parashat Shelaḥ-Lekha;* ibid., beginning of *Parashat Yitro. Sefer ha-Ma'amarim* 5659, p. 56. **14-15. Moses became angry.** *Shenei Luḥot ha-Berit, Mattot, Derekh Ḥayyim Tokheḥot Musar* (vol. 3, p. 77b). **21. Eleazar the priest.** *Sha'ar Ma'amarei Rashbi u-Ma'amarei Razal, Avot* 2:10. **23. And then it will be purified.** *Sifrei Zuta* 31:22; *Divrei Shemu'el,* p. 139. **32. The (total) plunder.** *Naḥmanides* 31:36. **32-35. The (total) plunder.** *Ma'amar Me'ah Kesitah,* ch. 89. **50. To atone for our souls.** *Ḥiddushei ha-Rim al ha-Torah,* 31:49-50.

32:5 Let this land be given. *Ḥiddushei ha-Rim al ha-Torah,* 32:1. **Do not take us across.** *Naḥmanides,* 32:1-2. **Or ha-Ḥayyim,* 32:3. **8. This is exactly what your fathers did.** *Tzeror ha-Mor,* 32:6. **16. We'll build sheep enclosures.** *Numbers Rabbah,* 22:9, 7. *Likkutei Siḥot,* vol. 8, pp. 189-191. **33. Half the tribe of Manasseh.** *Ibn Ezra,* 32:32.

33:1 The following are the journeys. *Degel Mahaneh Efrayim, Mase'ei* (p. 80a). **2. Moses recorded.** *Moreh Nevukhim,* 3:50. **53. You should rid the land.** *Megillat Ester,* commentary to Maimonides' *Sefer ha-Mitzvot, List of Omissions.* **55. Then those whom you leave.** *Menahem Tziyyon, Yalkut Menahem,* pp. 209-210.

מקורות

34:2 The land of Canaan. *Perush Ralbag al ha-Torah,* p. 204c.

35:2 They should give the Levites. *Laws of the Sabbatical Year and the Year of the Jubilee,* 13:1. *Likkutei Sihot,* vol. 25, pp. 97-98. **11. A murderer.** *Sefer ha-Ḥinnukh,* Commandment 410. *Shenei Luḥot ha-Berit, Mattot, Torah Ohr; Mase'ei, Torah Or* (vol. 3, p. 76c-d). **25. He must remain there.** *Perush Abravanel al ha-Torah, Mase'ei,* p. 164b. **26. If the murderer goes outside.** *Laws concerning Murder and the Preservation of Life,* 5:10. **33. Do not corrupt.** *Sifrei, Mase'ei,* par. 3. **34. Do not defile.** *Sifrei, Mase'ei,* par. 3.

36:13 These are the commandments. *Sefer ha-Siḥot* 5751, vol. 2, pp. 709ff.

Book of Deuteronomy

1:1 Which Moses spoke. *Babylonian Talmud, Megillah* 31b, s.v. *Moshe. Tiferet Yisrael,* ch. 43. **5. In the land of Moab.** *Imrei Shefer, Deuteronomy* 27:8. *Sefat Emet, Devarim,* 5631. **7. The great river.** *Rashi, Genesis* 15:18. **10. Like the sun.** *Likkutei Moharan,* ch. 133. **12. How could I bear?** *Itturei Torah* (Bene Berak, 1976). **17. If a case is too difficult.** *Keter Shem Tov,* p. 8, par. 6. **If a case is too difficult.** *Igra de-Kallah, Devarim,* p. 166. **23. It seemed like a good idea.** *Sefat Emet, Devarim,* 5635. **27. You spoke slanderously.** *Naḥmanides,* 1:25. **37. You will not come there.** *Perush Abravanel al ha-Torah, Devarim,* p. 24a-b.

2:6 You can purchase food. *Tanḥuma, Ḥukkat,* 12. **9. I will not give you.** *Likkutei Torah* (Vital), *Lekh Lekha;* ibid. *Devarim.*

3:23 I requested from God. *Zera Kodesh, Va-'Etḥannan,* p. 110. *Deuteronomy Rabbah,* 2:1. **25. Please let me cross over.** *Ohel Torah. Shem mi-Shemu'el, Va-'Etḥannan,* 5675.

4:1 Now Israel, listen. *Mekhilta, Yitro, Ba-Ḥodesh,* par. 2 *Ma'amarei Admor ha-Zaken* 5564, pp. 201-202. **2. Do not add.** *Hakdamat ha-Rambam,* end of *Minyan ha-Mitzvot. Ohel Ya'akov, Va-'Etḥannan,* 9d. **15. Look after yourselves.** *Laws of Ethical Behavior,* 4:1; ibid., 3:1; *Laws of Wounding and Damaging,* 5:1. *Ha-Tamim,* 7:28. **29. From there you will seek God.**

Ramatayim Tzofim, p. 92. *Tanya, Sha'ar ha-Yiḥud ve-ha-Emunah,* ch. 1; *Likkutei Torah, Re'eh,* p. 32b-c. **35. There is none other besides Him.** *Tanya, Sha'ar ha-Yiḥud ve-ha-Emunah,* ch. 1. **41. Moses separated three cities.** *Laws of Murder and the Preservation of Life,* 8:3.

5:5 I stood between God and you. *Ma'or va-Shemesh, Exodus,* p. 62. **Saying.** *Sefer ha-Siḥot,* vol. 2, pp. 334ff. **19. A great voice.** *Exodus Rabbah,* 28:6. *Yedei Moshe,* ibid. **27. Go and say to them.** *Si'ah Sarfei Kodesh,* vol. 1, p. 114.

6:5 Love God. *Kokhav ha-Shaḥar,* ch. 6. **9. Write them on the doorposts.** *Law of Tefillin, Mezuzah, and the Torah Scroll,* 6:13. **18. You shall do what is proper.** *Maskil le-David,* 12:28.

7:11 To observe today. *Shenei Luḥot ha-Berit, Bayit Aharon* (vol. 1, pp. 9bff.). *Likkutei Siḥot,* vol. 29, pp. 46-47. **12. As a result of your listening.** *Or Tzaddikim,* 8b. **As a result.** *Tanḥuma, 'Ekev,* 1. **17. You might say.** *Ma'asei Adonai, Ma'asei Torah, 'Ekev,* p. 83b.

8:3 To make you realize. *Likkutei Torah, 'Ekev,* p. 246a-b. **10. You will eat and be satisfied.** *Numbers Rabbah,* 11:7. *Kol Simḥah, Naso',* p. 52. **19. What will happen is.** *Irin Kedishin, Ki Tavo'.*

9:17 And shattered them. *Exodus Rabbah,* 43:1. **Shattered them before your eyes.** *Keli Yakar, Exodus* 20:15. *Sefer Tzelaḥ, Pesaḥim* 87b.

10:6 Aaron died. *Rashi,* 10:7. *Divrei David,* ibid. **8. God separated.** *Laws of the Sabbatical Year and the Year of the Jubilee,* 13:12-13. **12. What does God demand?** *Tanya, Likkutei Amarim,* ch. 42. **16. You should "circumcise."** *Tanya, Iggeret ha-Kodesh,* ch. 4. **17. God ... will not accept.** *Yalkut Shimoni, Psalms,* 670.

11:13 If you always listen. *Likkutei Torah, Va-'Etḥannan,* p. 13b. **19. You should teach.** *Siḥot Kodesh,* vol. 2, pp. 809ff; *Sefer ha-Siḥot,* vol. 2, p. 455. **26. See!** *Hitva'aduyyot* 5743, vol. 4, p. 1934. **A blessing and a curse.** *Genesis Rabbah,* 51:3; *Shenei Luḥot ha-Berit, Re'eh* (vol. 3, p. 82d). *Sefer Tzelaḥ, Pesaḥim,* p. 50a. **27. That you will listen.** *Be'er Mayim Ḥayyim,* 11:28.

12:5 The site. *Keli Yakar,* 12:4. *Sefer ha-Ḥayyim, Sefer Ge'ulah ve-Yeshu'ah,*

end of ch. 1. **You should seek out.** *Torat Moshe* (Jerusalem, 2004).

21. Slaughter. *Likkutei Siḥot,* vol. 4, pp. 1108ff.

13:1 Do not add. *Hitva'aduyyot* 5742, vol. 3, p. 1715.

14:22 You should always take the tithe. *Ḥiddushei Maharsha, Ta'anit* 9a, s.v. *'amar leih. Midrash Rabbenu Baḥya,* 14:23. **26. You should use the money.** *No'am Elimelekh, Re'eh,* 14:24 (p. 93a).

15:8 You must repeatedly. *Bikkurei Aviv, Binah ba-Mikra.* **Open your hand.** *Genesis Rabbah,* 61:3. **10. You should give.** Commentary to the Mishneh, *Avot,* 3:18. *Akedat Yitzḥak, Re'eh,* ch. 94 (pp. 41d-42a). **You should give.** *Tanya, Iggeret ha-Kodesh,* ch. 21. **14. You should give.** *Minḥat Ḥinnukh,* Commandment 482.

16:1-8 Offer the Passover. *Tzeror ha-Mor,* 16:11. *Ba'al ha-Turim,* ibid. **18. Appoint judges.** *Toledot Ya'akov Yosef, Shofetim,* p. 42b. **20. Pursue justice.** *Sefat Emet, Shofetim,* 5631. **21. (You should not plant).** *Sefer ha-Mitzvot,* Prohibition 13. *Mayanah Shel Torah* (Avnei Ezel).

17:6 The one liable to death. *Tanya, Iggeret ha-Teshuvah,* ch. 7. **By the testimony.** *Laws of the Sanhedrin,* 18:6. *Perush ha-Radbaz,* ibid. **15. You should always set a king.** *Arvei Naḥal, Shofetim,* p. 80d. **You should always set.** *Laws of Kings and Their Wars,* 3:6. *Midrash Rabbenu Baḥya,* Introduction to *Parashat Be-Shallaḥ.* **20. He and his sons.** *Laws of Kings and Their Wars,* 1:7.

18:2 God is his inheritance. *Perush Abravanel al ha-Torah,* 18:1. *Laws of the Sabbatical Year and the Year of the Jubilee,* 13:13. **13. Be simple-hearted.** *Divrei Shemu'el,* p. 81. **15. Establish a prophet.** *Laws of the Foundations of the Law,* 9:1-2. **18. I will establish for them a prophet.** *Laws of the Foundations of the Law,* 7:1.

19:4 The murderer may flee. *Likkutei Torah, Be-Midbar,* p. 13c. *Sefer ha-Siḥot* 5751, vol. 2, pp. 575-576. **9. You should add.** *Laws of Murder and the Preservation of Life,* 8:4. *Minḥat Ḥinnukh,* Commandment 520, par. 1. **15. A single witness.** *Laws of Evidence,* 5:1-2.

1490

references

20:3 Hear, O Israel! *Maharal mi-Prag le-Aggadot ha-Shas, Sotah* 42a.
8. Fearful or fainthearted. *Likkutei Sihot*, vol. 9, pp. 128-129. **10-13. If you approach a city.** *Zohar Ḥadash, Ruth*, p. 80c.

21:2 They should measure. *Laws of Murder and the Preservation of Life*, 9:1. **4. They should break.** *Moreh Nevukhim*, 3:40. *Nahmanides*, 21:5.
13. Weep. *Likkutei Torah* (Vital), *Ki Tetze'*. **15. The firstborn son.** *Sifrei, Ki Tetze'*, par. 5. **17. He must acknowledge.** *Numbers Rabbah*, 6:2.
18. If a man has a deviant. *Shem mi-Shemu'el, Ki Tetze'*, 5671 (p. 137a).
22. If a man commits. *Ya'arot Devash*, vol. 2, p. 126c.

22:4 You should pick up. *Sefat Emet, Ki Tetze'*, 5636. **7. You should always send away.** *Tanhuma, Ki Tetze'*, 2. *Sefer ha-Ḥinnukh*, Commandment 545.
8. Make a guardrail. *Shenei Luhot ha-Berit, Ki Seitzei, Derekh Ḥayyim Tokhehot Musar* (vol. 3, p. 89d). **10. You may not plow.** *Sefer ha-Ḥinnukh*, Commandment 550. **16. I gave my daughter.** *Likkutei Levi Yitzchak, Ha'arot le-Zohar, Exodus–Deuteronomy*, p. 339. **25. If a man finds the betrothed girl.** *Imrei Emet, Ki Tetze'*, 22:27.

23:4-8 An Ammonite. *Laws Concerning Forbidden Intercourse*, 12:25. **25. When you come.** *Laws of Hiring*, 12:1. **25-26. You may eat as many grapes.** *Likkutei Sihot*, vol. 34, pp. 133-134.

24:17 You may not (come and) take. *Sefer ha-Mitzvot*, Prohibition 241. *Sefer ha-Sihot* 5747, vol. 1, p. 183.

25:3 Flog him. *Laws of the Sanhedrin*, 17:7. *Si'aḥ Sarfei Kodesh*, vol. 4, p. 126, par. 238. **17. Remember what Amalek did.** *Laws of Kings and Their Wars*, 5:5.
19. Erase any reminder of Amalek. *Likkutei Sihot*, vol. 21, pp. 193-196.

26:1 When you enter. *Likkutei Sihot*, vol. 19, pp. 245-247; *Sihot Kodesh* 5733, vol. 2, p. 366. **5. (Laban the) Aramean.** *Or ha-Ḥayyim*, 26:5, 6, 9. **He brought us to this site.** *Torah Temimah*, 26:5, fn. 27. **10. Land I have now brought.** *Sifrei, Ki Tavo'*, par. 5. **14. I did not give.** *Tikkunei Zohar, Tikkun* 10; *Tiferet Shelomo, Likkutim*, p. 338, s.v. *vi'arti*.
15. Look down from your holy abode. *Sefer ha-Ma'amarim* 5700, pp. 155, 160.

28:3 You will be blessed. *Deuteronomy Rabbah*, 7:5. **9. Walk in His ways.** *Sefer ha-Mitzvot*, Commandment 8. *Likkutei Sihot*, vol. 34, pp. 153ff. **15. The following curses.** *Tiferet Shelomo al ha-Torah, Ki Tavo'*, p. 135c. **38. You will take a lot of seed.** *Imrei No'am, Ki Tavo'*, p. 80c. **45-47. All these curses.** *Ohel Torah*. **Because you did not serve.** *Sha'ar Ru'aḥ ha-Kodesh, Derush* 2 (p. 33b). *Sefat Emet, Ki Tavo'*, 5643.
68. God will return. *Likkutei Sihot*, vol. 19, pp. 239-242.

29:3 Until this day. *Rashi*, 29:6. **9. You are standing firmly.** *Rashi*, 29:9, 12. *No'am Megadim*, p. 143d. **9-10. All of you together.** *Likkutei Torah, Nitzavim*, 44a. **21. The foreigner.** *Etz ha-Da'at Tov, Nitzavim*, 23c. **23-27. All the nations.** *Yavin Shemu'ah, Nitzavim*, par. 479. **28. The hidden things.** Ibid.

30:1 When all these things come. *Ketav Sofer, Nitzavim*, p. 266a.
12. It is not in the skies. *Laws of the Foundations of the Law*, 9:1. **14. This thing is very near.** *Tanna de-Vei Eliyahu Zuta*, ch. 14. *Ohel Torah*. **This thing is very near.** *Tanya, Likkutei Amarim*, ch. 17.

31:1 Moses went. *Mayanah Shel Torah*. **3. It is Joshua.** *Sha'arei Teshuvah*, vol. 2, *Hinnukh*, ch. 5. **7. Moses called Joshua.** *Shem mi-Shemu'el, Nitzavim*, 5672. **12. Assemble the people.** *Tosefot to Ḥagigah* 3a, s.v. *kedei*. *Sefat Emet, Va-Yelekh*, 5634. **17. It is surely because God.** *Sefat Emet, Nitzavim*, 5732. **18. I will surely hide.** *Ha-Even ha-Roshah* (Piotrkow, 1928), p. 54.
19. Now, write for yourselves. *Law of Tefillin, Mezuzah, and the Torah Scroll*, 7:1. *Tur, Yoreh De'ah*, ch. 270. *Laws of the Festal Offerings*, 3:6. *Likkutei Sihot*, vol. 34, pp. 189-193. **27. You have been rebels.** *Divrei Soferim, Likkutei Amarim*, 88a. *Tanya, Likkutei Amarim*, ch. 24.

32:1 Listen O heavens. *Sefer ha-Zikhronot*, vol. 1, ch. 29. **Listen O heavens.** *Sifrei, Ha'azinu*, par. 1. *Sefer ha-Sihot* 5750, vol. 1, pp. 21-22.
2. Let my words flow. *Likkutei Torah, Ha'azinu*, p. 73b-c, *Shir ha-Shirim*, pp. 22bff.; *Ma'amarei Admor ha-Zaken* 5567, pp. 355ff. **3. Ascribe greatness.** *Sifrei, Ha'azinu*, par. 1; See *Yalkut Shimoni, Ha'azinu*, 942. **9. Jacob ... a rope.** *Tanya, Iggeret ha-Kodesh*, ch. 5. **18. You forgot the Rock.** *Mishlei Ya'akov*. **26. I said (in My heart).** *Seder ha-Dorot*, p. 356. *Hitva'aduyyot* 5742, vol. 1, p. 110. **30. How can one?** *Tosefot to Sotah* 11a, s.v. *u-le'olam*.

33:18 Succeed, Zebulun. *Likkutei Sihot*, vol. 30, pp. 134ff. **20. He will tear off an arm.** *Kol Eliyahu, Ve-Zo't Ha-Berakhah*, par. 132.
25. May your locks. *Sefat Emet, Ve-Zo't Ha-Berakhah*, 5653.

34:1 Moses went up. *Likkutei Torah, Be-Midbar*, p. 12a. **5. Moses, the servant of God.** *Sefer ha-Sihot* 5749, vol. 1, pp. 8-9. **12. Moses performed.** *Tanna de-Vei Eliyahu Rabbah*, ch. 14. *Likkutei Sihot*, vol. 34, pp. 217ff.

KABBALAH BITES

Book of Genesis

1:1 *Ecclesiastes Rabbah*, 3:13; *Torah Or*, p. 51d.
2:6 *Sefer Hama'amarim Melukat*, vol. 4, pp. 254-255.
2:22 *Zohar III*, 7b; *Ta'amei ha-Mitzvot, Bere'shit*; *Sefer ha-Sihot*, 5751, p. 84.
2:23 *Likkutei Torah, Bere'shit*.
3:7 *Babylonian Talmud, Shabbat* 146a; *Zohar I*, 52b, 54a.
4:1-2 *Sha'ar ha-Gilgulim*, ch. 36.
4:15 *Sha'ar ha-Gilgulim*, ch. 36.
4:25 *Sha'ar ha-Gilgulim*, ch. 29.
4:26 *Likkutei Torah, Noah*.
5:3 *Babylonian Talmud, Eruvin* 18b; *Zohar I*, 19b; ibid. III, 76b; *Sha'ar ha-Pesukim, Exodus* 1:8.
6:9 *Sha'ar ha-Pesukim, Genesis* 6:3.
6:12 *Sha'ar ha-Pesukim, Exodus* 1:8.
7:23 *Sha'ar ha-Pesukim, Genesis* 6:3.
11:5 *Sha'ar ha-Pesukim, Exodus* 1:8.
11:27 *Sha'ar ha-Gilgulim*, ch. 33; *Zohar, Ra'aya Meheimna, Be-Har* 111b.
11:30 *Zohar III*, 168a.
12:1-2 *Maggid Meisharim*.
12:12 *Maggid Meisharim*.
13:8-9 *Sha'ar ha-Gilgulim*, ch. 36.
13:13 *Sha'ar ha-Pesukim, Exodus* 1:8.
15:15 *Sha'ar ha-Pesukim*.
16:6 *Sha'ar ha-Gilgulim*, Introduction, par. 20.
17:5 *Or ha-Torah, Genesis*, fol. 714a.

מקורות

18:2 *Sefer ha-Likkutim.*
18:27 *Sefer ha-Likkutim.*
21:3 *Likkutei Torah.*
21:9 *Sefer ha-Likkutim, Toledot;* see *Zohar III,* 111b.
22:7 *Sefer ha-Likkutim, Toledot;* see *Zohar III,* 111b.
23:9 *Zohar II,* 128a; *Likkutei Sihot,* vol. 10, p. 64.
24:24 *Hitva'aduyyot,* 5742, vol. 1, p. 403.
24:31 *Genesis Rabbah* 60:7; *Zohar III,* 103a; *Sha'ar ha-Gilgulim,* ch. 36.
25:8 *Babylonian Talmud, Bava Metzia* 87a, according to *Maharsha; Or ha-Torah, Genesis,* p. 1556.
25:22-23 *Sefer ha-Likkutim.*
25:26 *Sha'ar Ha-Gilgulim,* ch. 36.
27:4 *Sefer ha-Likkutim.*
27:13 *Sefer ha-Likkutim.*
27:27 *Zohar I,* 36b; *Sefer ha-Likkutim, Bere'shit* 3:21.
28:12 *Zohar II,* 69a.
28:15 *Sha'ar ha-Gilgulim,* ch. 36.
29:18 *Sha'ar ha-Gilgulim,* ch. 36.
29:21 *Zohar I,* 155a; *Sha'ar ha-Pesukim, Numbers* 32:5; *Benei Aharon* to *Sha'ar ha-Gilgulim,* ch. 33.
30:18 *Sha'ar ha-Gilgulim,* ch. 33; ibid., ch. 36.
32:4 *Torah Or,* pp. 24aff.; *Sefer ha-Sihot,* 5751, p. 474; ibid., 5752, pp. 172-3.
32:25 *Or ha-Torah, Genesis,* p. 1749ff.
32:33 *Me'or Einayim.*
34:8 *Likkutei Torah.*
35:18 *Zohar II,* 99b; *Etz Ḥayyim* 39:8; *Sha'ar ha-Pesukim, Genesis* 21:2.
36:12 *Sha'ar ha-Pesukim, Numbers* 12:1.
36:31 *Ma'amarei Admor ha-Zaken* 5568, p. 48.
37:2 *Sha'ar ha-Gilgulim,* ch. 31.
38:16 *Or Yakar* to *Zohar,* vol. 4, p. 201a-b.
39:6 *Sha'ar ha-Gilgulim,* ch. 31.
41:2-3 *Me'or Einayim.*
41:33 *Maggid Meisharim.*
41:44 *Sha'ar ha-Gilgulim,* ch. 31.
41:55 *Sha'ar ha-Pesukim, Exodus* 1:8.
42:9 *Sha'ar ha-Gilgulim,* ch. 36.
44:1 *Me'or Einayim.*
45:3 *Or ha-Torah, Genesis,* pp. 1974ff.
46:3 *Or ha-Torah, Genesis,* fol. 1111a.
46:29 *Or ha-Torah, Genesis,* fol. 1113a.
46:29-30 *Sihot Kodesh* 5725, p. 201.

47:9 *Sha'ar ha-Pesukim, Genesis* 47:9.
47:31 *Shenei Luhot ha-Berit.*
48:14 *Pirkei de-Rabbi Eliezer* 38; *Sefer ha-Likkutim, Mattot.*
49:1 *Sha'ar ha-Gilgulim,* ch. 36.
49:5 *Zohar I,* 236a.
49:8 *Or ha-Torah, Genesis,* pp. 2277ff.

Book of Exodus

2:2 *Likkutei Sihot,* vol. 6, p. 33.
2:10 *Hitva'aduyyot* 5751, vol. 3, pp. 126-127.
4:1 *Sefat Emet, Shemot,* 5637.
4:10 *Sefer ha-Sihot* 5752, vol. 1, pp. 285-286.
6:2 *Be-Sha'ah she-Hikdimu,* p. 831.
7:1 *Torat Menahem, Sefer ha-Ma'amarim* 5715, pp. 59ff.
7:7 *Sha'ar ha-Pesukim, Exodus* 1:8.
7:14 *Likkutei Sihot,* vol. 31, p. 31.
7:28 *Likkutei Sihot,* vol. 1, p. 121.
8:15 *Or Yakar* to *Sefer Yetzirah* 1:3; *Sihot Kodesh* 5734, vol. 2, p. 292.
10:1 *Mikdash Melekh* to *Zohar II,* 34b; *Or ha-Torah, Exodus,* p. 2611.
10:2 *Maggid Meisharim.*
10:8-11 *Maggid Meisharim.*
10:23 *Or ha-Torah, Exodus,* p. 250.
12:2 *Or ha-Torah, Exodus,* p. 262.
12:38 *Sha'ar ha-Pesukim, Exodus* 1:8.
13:17 *Sefer ha-Sihot* 5752, pp. 302-4.
14:21 *Ner Mitzvah ve-Torah Or, Sha'ar ha-Emunah,* p. 64-6.
15:1-19 *Ḥayyim va-Ḥesed* (Jerusalem, 1975), pp. 38-9.
15:23 *Zohar III,* 47b.
15:25 *Sha'ar ha-Pesukim, Exodus* 1:8.
17:14 *Sefer ha-Sihot* 5752, p. 310, fn. 31.
18:1 *Sha'ar ha-Gilgulim,* ch. 36; *Likkutei Torah, Genesis* 4:22.
18:14 *Sha'ar ha-Pesukim, Exodus* 1:8.
18:21 *Sha'ar ha-Pesukim, Exodus* 1:8.
20:1 *Likkutei Torah* (Rabbi Shneur Zalman of Lyady), p. 57c; *Likkutei Sihot,* vol. 1, p. 148.
20:18 *Likkutei Moharan,* par. 115.
21:1 *Torat Menaḥem, Hitva'aduyyot* 5721, vol. 2, p. 113.
21:24 *Recanati.*
21:37 *Sha'ar ha-Pesukim, Exodus* 1:8.
23:19 *Likkutei Sihot,* vol. 16, p. 242; ibid., vol. 32, p. 179.

24:17 *Likkutei Sihot,* vol. 16, p. 281.
25:13 *Likkutei Sihot,* vol. 6, pp. 152ff.
25:10 *Sefer ha-Hakirah,* p. 68.
25:31 *Recanati.*
26:1 *Zohar II,* 164b.
26:19 *Or ha-Torah, Exodus,* pp. 1508aff.
28:1 *Recanati.*
28:17 *Recanati.*
28:28 *Degel Mahaneh Efrayim.*
29:1 *Tzeror ha-Mor.*
29:10,16,20 *Recanati.*
30:13 *Alshekh.*
30:19 *Sefer Yetzirah; Recanati.*
32:1 *Sha'ar ha-Gilgulim,* ch. 33.
32:4 *Sha'ar ha-Gilgulim, Introduction,* par. 20.
33:13 *Sha'ar ha-Gilgulim,* ch. 29.
34:6-7 *Tomer Devorah,* ch. 1.
35:1 *Maggid Meisharim.*
35:30 *Babylonian Talmud, Berakhot* 55a, with *Rashi.*

Book of Leviticus

1:1 *Zohar I,* 239a; *Or ha-Torah, Leviticus,* vol. 3, p. 725.
Ch. 2 *Ta'amei ha-Mitzvot.*
2:11 *Recanati.*
3:16 *Sefer ha-Ma'amarim* 5696, p. 132.
4:2 *Yalkut Shimoni, Ezekiel,* 358; *Sefer ha-Ma'amarim* 5709, p. 187.
6:6 *Likkutei Sihot,* vol. 1, p. 217.
7:15 *Recanati.*
8:6 *Shenei Luhot ha-Berit; Tzeror ha-Mor.*
9:6 *Zohar III,* 53b; *Likkutei Sihot,* vol. 7, p. 298.
10:6 *Sha'ar ha-Gilgulim,* ch. 33.
11:1-23 *Recanati.*
12:1 *Zohar III,* 43b.
13:2 *Sefer ha-Likkutim.*
13:14 *Maggid Meisharim.*
14:8 *Ḥesed le-Avraham, Ma'ayan* 2, *Nahar* 59.
14:34 *Likkutei Sihot,* vol. 27, p. 107; *Torat Menahem, Tiferet Levi Yitzhak, Leviticus,* pp. 136ff.
15:19 *Recanati.*
16:2 *Zohar III,* 58a; and Glosses by Rabbi Hayyim Vital in Vilna 1895, Romm ed.
16:12-13 *Shenei Luhot ha-Berit; Sefer Ha-ma'amarim Melukat,* vol. 1, p. 248.
17:13-14 *Recanati.*

references

18:6-20 *Sefer ha-Likkutim, Toledot; Torat Menaḥem, Hitva'aduyyot 5721*, pp. 262-4.
19:4 *Ta'amei ha-Mitzvot.*
19:13 *Ta'amei ha-Mitzvot.*
19:27 *Sha'ar ha-Mitzvot.*
21:1 *Likkutei Siḥot*, vol. 27, p. 165.
22:27 *Kuntres ha-Tefillah*, p. 20.
23:15 See *Ha-Yom Yom, 11 Iyyar—Maggid.*
24:16 *Imrei Binah, Sha'ar Keriat Shema*, ch. 1.
25:1-2 *Likkutei Siḥot*, vol. 1, p. 273.
25:10 *Likkutei Siḥot*, vol. 7, p. 173.
26:4 *Likkutei Dibburim*, vol. 1, p. 115.
26:13 *Likkutei Siḥot*, vol. 7, pp. 198*ff.*

Book of Numbers

1:1 *Zohar III*, 117a-b.
1:50 *Recanati.*
2:3-31 *Recanati.*
3:2 *Sha'ar ha-Gilgulim*, ch. 33.
4:21 *Shenei Luḥot ha-Berit.*
5:23 *Zohar III*, 124b.
6:3-5 *Recanati.*
6:22-26 *Recanati.*
7:12 *Or ha-Torah, Numbers*, p. 279.
8:2 *Me'or Einayim.*
9:7 *Sha'ar ha-Pesukim.*
10:3-7 *Recanati.*
11:15 *Sefer ha-Likkutim.*
13:20 *Sha'ar ha-Pesukim*, end of *Be-Ha'alotekha.*
13:22 *Sha'ar ha-Gilgulim*, ch. 36.
13:26 *Sha'ar ha-Gilgulim*, ch. 36.
14:38 *Sha'ar ha-Gilgulim*, ch. 36.
15:30-31 *Zohar III*, 167b; *Likkutei Torah.*
16:1 *Sha'ar ha-Gilgulim*, ch. 33; ibid., ch. 36.
16:15 *Zohar I*, 17b; *Sefer ha-Likkutim.*
16:27 *Likkutei Torah.*
17:23 *Sefer ha-Ma'amarim 5733*, pp. 436*ff.*
19:7-8 *Or ha-Torah, Numbers*, p. 777.
20:9-10 *Sefer ha-Likkutim.*
20:29-21:1 *Torat Menaḥem, Hitva'aduyyot 5713*, vol. 3, p. 45.

21:34 *Sha'ar ha-Gilgulim*, ch. 36.
22:5 *Sha'ar ha-Pesukim.*
22:18 *Sha'ar ha-Gilgulim*, ch. 36; *Sefer ha-Likkutim, Va-Yetze'*, ch. 31.
23:7 *Numbers Rabbah*, 14:34; *Sha'ar ha-Pesukim.*
24:17 *Me'or Einayim*, end of *Parashat Pinḥas*; *Sefer ha-Siḥot 5751*, vol. 1, p. 190, fn. 120.
25:7 *Sha'ar ha-Gilgulim*, ch. 33.
25:10 *Tanya, Iggeret ha-Kodesh*, ch. 25; *Sha'ar ha-Yiḥudim* at end; see *Likkutei Torah* (Shneur Zalman of Lyady), *Pinḥas*, p. 80d; *Torat Menaḥem, Hitva'aduyyot 5713*, vol. 3, p. 120.
27:1-5 *Megallah Amukkot al ha-Torah.*
27:20 *Zohar I*, 21b.
28:2 *Recanati.*
30:3 *Recanati.*
31:8 *Sha'ar ha-Gilgulim*, ch. 29.
31:27 *Sha'ar ha-Pesukim.*
32:33 *Pirkei de-Rabbi Eliezer 38*; *Sefer ha-Likkutim, Mattot.*
33:1 *Degel Mahaneh Efrayim*; *Likkutei Siḥot*, vol. 4, p. 1083.
34:2 *Likkutei Siḥot*, vol. 13, pp. 126-7.
35:6 *Ohev Yisrael*, 35:6.

Book of Deuteronomy

1:1 *Maggid Meisharim.*
1:5 *Sha'ar ha-Gilgulim*, ch. 17; *Torat Menaḥem, Hitva'aduyyot 5719*, vol. 2, p. 112.
3:26 *Likkutei Torah.*
4:23 *Torat Menaḥem, Hitva'aduyyot 5719*, vol. 1, p. 213.
5:16 *Likkutei Torah, Va-Yera'*; *Torat Menaḥem, Hitva'aduyyot 5710*, p. 127, fn. 4.
6:4 *Peri Etz Ḥayyim, Sha'ar ha-Zemirot*, ch. 5; *Torat Menaḥem, Sefer ha-Ma'amarim 5718*, pp. 300*ff.*
7:14-15 *Maggid Meisharim.*
8:3 *Likkutei Torah*; *Torat Menaḥem, Sefer ha-Ma'amarim 5711*, pp. 100*ff.*
8:16 *Sha'ar ha-Gilgulim*, ch. 16; *Torat Menaḥem, Sefer ha-Ma'amarim 5729*, pp. 65*ff.*

10:12 *Torat Menaḥem, Sefer ha-Ma'amarim 5719*, pp. 73*ff.*
11:15-16 *Sha'ar ha-Mitzvot.*
11:26 *Maggid Meisharim.*
12:21 *Ta'amei ha-Mitzvot.*
14:22 *Peri Etz Ḥayyim, Sha'ar Minḥah u-Ma'ariv*, ch. 2.
15:7-8 *Peri Etz Ḥayyim, Sha'ar Minḥah u-Ma'ariv*, ch. 1-2; *Torat Menaḥem, Hitva'aduyyot 5716*, vol. 1, p. 48.
16:1 Rabbi Isaac Luria cited in *Lev David*, ch. 29; Rabbi Moses Zacuto in *Sefer Tikkun Shovavim*; *Likkutei Siḥot*, vol. 9, p. 337.
16:18 *Shenei Luḥot ha-Berit.*
19:15 *Or ha-Torah, Deuteronomy*, p. 997.
21:23 *Sha'ar Ma'amarei Rashbi u-Ma'amarei Razal, Sukkah 53a.*
22:3 *Sha'ar ha-Mitzvot.*
22:8 *Sha'ar ha-Mitzvot.*
23:20 *Keter Shem Tov*, par. 218; *Likkutei Siḥot*, vol. 12, p. 118.
25:5-10 *Nishmat Ḥayyim*, 4:7.
26:11 *Or ha-Ḥayyim* based on *Zohar III*, 217a.
28:1-69 *Maggid Meisharim.*
29:9 *Peri Etz Ḥayyim, Sha'ar ha-Shofar*, ch. 5; *Zohar, Midrash ha-Ne'elam, Va-Yera'* 98b; *Torat Menaḥem, Hitva'aduyyot 5711*, vol. 2, p. 349.
30:2 *Torat Menaḥem, Hitva'aduyyot*, 5716, vol. 2, pp. 258-9; ibid., 5742, vol. 1, p. 356.
30:19 *Peri Etz Ḥayyim, Sha'ar ha-Zemirot*, ch. 4; *Torat Menaḥem, Hitva'aduyyot 5716*, vol. 1, p. 77*ff.*
31:2 *Me'or Einayim.*
31:30 *Recanati*; *Likkutei Siḥot*, vol. 19, p. 305.
32:4 *Likkutei Torah.*
32:5 *Likkutei Torah.*
32:18 *Likkutei Torah.*
32:49 *Zohar, II* 157a.
34:4 *Keter Shem Tov*, par. 275; *Likkutei Dibburim*, vol. 1, 113b; see *Jerusalem Talmud, Berakhot*, end of ch. 6.
34:10 *Tikkunei Zohar*, par. 69; *Sha'ar ha-Pesukim, Exodus* 1:8.

BIBLIOGRAPHY

Aaron ha-Levi, *Sefer ha-Ḥinnukh* (Jerusalem, 1984).

Abi Zimra, David ben Solomon ibn, *Migdal David* (Lvov, 1883).

——*Perush ha-Radbaz*, commentary to *Code of Maimonides*, ed. Frankel (Jerusalem–Bene Berak, 2005).

Abraham Joshua Heschel of Apta, *Ohev Yisrael* (Zhitomir, 1863).

Abraham Joshua Heschel of Cracow, *Ḥanukkat ha-Torah*, compiled by E. Ersohn (Piotrkow, 1900).

Abraham Mordecai Alter of Gur, *Imrei Emet* (Bene Berak, 1980).

Abravanel, Isaac, *Perush Abravanel al ha-Torah* (Jerusalem, 1979).

Adeni, Solomon bar Joshua, *Melekhet Shelomo*, commentary to Mishnah, ed. Vilna.

Adler, Benjamin ben Moses, *Mo'adei Kodesh—Rosh Ha-Shanah* (Jerusalem, 1988).

Adret, Solomon ben Abraham, *She'elot u-Teshuvot ha-Rashba*, ed. Makhon Yerushalayim (Jerusalem, 1997-2005).

Agassi, Simeon Aaron, *Benei Aharon*, commentary to *Sha'ar ha-Gilgulim* (Baghdad, 1908).

Aḥai Gaon of Shabha, *She'iltot* (Jerusalem, 1960-1977).

Albo, Joseph, *Sefer ha-Ikkarim* (Warsaw, 1930).

Alexander Zusya ha-Kohen, *Yakar Mipaz* (Warsaw, 1932).

Al-Ḥakam, Joseph Ḥayyim ben Elijah of Baghdad, *Ben Yehoyada* (Jerusalem, 1898-1904).

Alkabetz, Solomon ha-Levi, *Manot ha-Levi* (Lvov, 1911).

Alshekh, Moses, *Torat Moshe*, ed. Vagshal (Jerusalem, 1990).

Arama, Isaac ben Moses, *Akedat Yitzḥak* (Gen., Ex., Lev., Deut.—Warsaw, 1883-1884; Num.—Lvov, 1868).

Arik, Meir ben Aaron Judah, *Imrei Yosher* (Mukachevo, 1913-1925).

Aryeh Judah Leib, *Livyat Ḥen ve-Or Yikarot* (Venice, 1742).

Asher ben Jehiel, *Hadar Zekenim* (Jerusalem, 1944).

Asher Isaiah of Ropczyce, *Or Yesha* (Przemysl, 1899).

Ashkenazi, Eliezer ben Elijah, *Ma'asei Adonai* (Warsaw, 1871-1933).

Ashkenazi, Samuel Jaffe, *Yefeh To'ar*, commentary to *Midrash Rabbah* (Genesis—Fuerth, 1692; Exodus—Venice, 1657; Leviticus—Wilherms, 1714).

Ashkenazi, Tzevi Hirsch, *Shevil ha-Yashar*, compiled by T. E. Michelson and printed in *Divrei Gedolim* (Piotrkow, 1933).

Attar, Ḥayyim ibn, *Or ha-Ḥayyim*, printed in std. eds. of *Mikra'ot Gedolot*.

Azikri, Eleazar ben Moses, *Sefer Ḥaredim* (Jerusalem, 1990).

Azulai, Abraham ben Mordecai, *Ḥesed le-Avraham* (Vilna, 1877).

Azulai, Ḥayyim Joseph David, *Lev David* (Berlin, 1924).

——*Naḥal Kedumim* (Jerusalem, 2003).

Ba'al Shem Tov, Israel, *Keter Shem Tov (ha-Shalem)*, compiled by Aaron of Opatow (Brooklyn, 2004).

——*Tzavva'at ha-Ribash*, compiled by Isaiah of Janow (Brooklyn, 1998).

——*Sefer Ba'al Shem Tov*, compiled by S. M. M. Wodnik (Jerusalem, 1962).

Babad, Joseph ben Moses, *Minḥat Ḥinnukh*, ed. Makhon Yerushalayim (Jerusalem, 1988-1991).

Bacharach, Naphtali ben Jacob Elhanan, *Emek ha-Melekh* (Amsterdam, 1648).

Bahya ben Asher, *Midrash Rabbenu Baḥya* (Warsaw, 1879).

Baker, Menahem, *Parpera'ot la-Torah* (Jerusalem, 1983-1986).

Baruch of Medzibezh, *Butzina di-Nehora*, compiled by L. Altchideiver (New York, 1956).

Bass, Shabbetai ben Joseph, *Siftei Ḥakhamim*, printed in std. eds. of *Mikra'ot Gedolot*.

Bekhor Shor, Joseph ben Isaac, *Perush le-Ḥamishah Ḥomshei Torah* (Jerusalem, 1978).

Berlin, Naphtali Tzevi Judah, *Ha'amek Davar* (Vilna, 1879-1880).

Bertinoro, Obadiah ben Abraham di, *Commentary to the Mishnah*, printed in std. eds. of Mishnah.

——*Amar Neke* (Czernowitz, 1857).

Besdin, Abraham R., *Reflections of the Rav* (Ketav Publishing, Hoboken, New Jersey, 1993).

Bick, Abraham ben Jacob, *Bikkurei Aviv* (Lvov, 1873).

Bornstein, Samuel of Sochaczew, *Shem mi-Shemu'el* (Jerusalem, 1992).

Broida, Simḥah Zissel of Kelme, *Ḥokhmah u-Musar* (New York, 1957-1964).

Bukarat, Abraham ben Solomon ha-Levi, *Sefer ha-Zikkaron* (Livorno, 1845).

רשימת ספרים

Buzaglo, Shalom ben Moses, *Mikdash Melekh ha-Shalem* (Jerusalem, 1995-2000).

Caro, Isaac ben Joseph, *Toledot Yitzhak* (Warsaw, 1878).

Caro, Joseph ben Ephraim, *Maggid Meisharim* (Jerusalem, 1960).

——*Shulhan Arukh*, ed. Vagshal (Jerusalem, 1994).

Colon, Joseph ben Solomon, *Hiddushei u-Ferushei ha-Maharik*, ed. Makhon Yerushalayim (Jerusalem, 1984).

Cordovero, Moses ben Jacob, *Elimah Rabbati* (Brody, 1881).

——*Or Yakar*, commentary to *Sefer Yetzirah* (Jerusalem, 1989).

——*Or Yakar*, commentary to *Zohar* (Jerusalem, 1962-1983).

——*Pardes Rimmonim* (Mukachevo, 1906).

——*Tomer Devorah* (Jerusalem, 1977).

Culi, Jacob, *Me-Am Lo'ez* (Jerusalem, 1967).

Danon, Meir Benjamin Menahem, *Be'er ba-Sadeh* (Jerusalem, 1846).

Danziger, Jerahmeel Israel Isaac of Aleksandrow, *Yismah Yisrael* (Lodz, 1911).

Danziger, Samuel Tzevi of Aleksandrow, *Tiferet Shemu'el* (Lodz, 1925-1930).

David ben Samuel ha-Levi, *Divrei David* (Svaliava, 1912).

Diskin, Moses Joshua Leib, *Likkut Omarim* (Jerusalem, 1922-1935).

——*Torat Ohel Moshe* (Jerusalem, 1902).

Dov Baer of Mezhirech, *Maggid Devarav le-Ya'akov* (Brooklyn, 2005).

Edels, Samuel, *Hiddushei Maharsha*, printed in the Romm ed. of the Babylonian Talmud.

Ehrenfeld, Samuel, *Hatan Sofer, Hiddushim al ha-Torah u-Mo'adim* (New York, 2001).

——*She'elot u-Teshuvot Hatan Sofer* (Paks, 1912).

Ehrenfeld, Simhah Bunim, *Ma'aneh Simhah* (Jerusalem, 1969).

Einhorn, Ze'ev Wolf, *Perush Maharzu*, commentary to *Midrash Rabbah*, ed. Wagshal.

Eisenstadter, Meir, *Imrei Esh* (Mukachevo, 1901).

Eisenstadter, Menahem, *Homat Esh* (Paks, 1906).

Elijah of Vilna, *Aderet Eliyahu* (Warsaw, 1887).

——*Kol Eliyahu* (Piotrkow, 1905).

Elimelech of Lyzhansk, *No'am Elimelekh* (Cracow, 1896).

——*Ohel Elimelekh*, compiled by A. H. S. B. Michelson (Przemysl, 1910).

Ephraim ben Isaac of Regensburg, see Gellis, Jacob.

Ephraim of Luntshits, *Keli Yakar*, printed in std. eds. of *Mikra'ot Gedolot*.

——*Olelot Efrayim* (Vilna, 1877).

Epstein, Baruch, *Torah Temimah* (Vilna, 1904).

——*Tosefet Berakhah* (Tel Aviv, 1999).

Epstein, Kalonymous Kalman of Cracow, *Ma'or va-Shemesh* (Breslau, 1842 / Jerusalem, 1994).

Ergas, Joseph ben Emanuel, *Shomer Emunim* (Jerusalem, 1965).

Eybeschuetz, David Solomon, *Arvei Nahal* (Warsaw, 1905).

Eybeschuetz, Jonathan, *Tiferet Yehonatan* (Jozefow, 1873).

——*Ya'arot Devash* (Warsaw, 1889).

Fano, Menahem Azariah da, *Amarot Tehorot* (Frankfort, 1698).

——*Asarah Ma'amarot* (Lvov, 1858 / Jerusalem, 2000).

——*Gilgulei Neshamot* (Lublin, 1907).

——*Ma'amar Me'ah Kesitah* (Mukachevo, 1982).

——*Ma'amar Tzive'ot Adonai* (Berditchev, 1814).

Feinstein, Moses, *Darash Moshe* (Bene Berak, 1988).

Figo, Azariah, *Binah le-Ittim* (Bene Berak, 1994).

Frank, Tzevi Pesah, *Har Tzevi al ha-Torah* (Jerusalem, 1996).

Friedman, Alexander Zusya, *Mayanah Shel Torah* (Tel Aviv, 1956).

Friedman, Israel of Ruzhin, *Irin Kedishin* (Warsaw, 1885).

Friedman, Jacob ben Isaac, *Oholei Ya'akov* (Israel, 196?).

Gellis, Jacob, *Tosefot ha-Shalem* (Jerusalem, 1982-2003).

Gentili, Moses ben Gershom, *Melekhet Mahashevet* (Warsaw, 1914).

Gerondi, Jonah ben Abraham, *Rabbenu Yonah*, commentary to Alfasi (*Rif*), printed in the Romm ed. of tractate *Berakhot* of the Babylonian Talmud.

Gerondi, Nissim ben Reuben, *Derashot ha-Ran* (Jerusalem, 1996).

——*Rabbenu Nissim*, commentary to Alfasi (*Rif*), printed in the Romm ed. of the Babylonian Talmud.

Ginsburg, Judah Leib, *Yalkut Yehudah* (Dvinsk [Daugavpils], 1931-1935).

Greenberg, Aaron Jacob, *Itturei Torah* (Bene Berak, 1976).

Grünwald, Moses of Huszt, *Arugot ha-Bosem al ha-Torah* (Khust, 1913).

Hager, Israel of Vizhnitz, *Ahavat Yisrael* (Oradea Mare, 1943).

——*Kuntres Or Yisrael*, compiled by M. A. Horowitz (Oradea Mare, 1943).

Halberstam, Ezekiel Shraga of Sieniawa, *Divrei Yehezkel* (Cracow, 1922).

Halberstam, Hayyim ben Leibush of Zanz, *Divrei Hayyim* (Svaliava, 1913).

Hananel ben Hushi'el, *Rabbenu Hananel*, printed in the Romm ed. of the Babylonian Talmud.

Hanokh Zundel ben Joseph of Bialystok, *Etz Yosef*, commentary to *Ein Yaakov*, ed. Vilna (1923).

——*Etz Yosef*, commentary to *Midrash Rabbah*, ed. Wagshal (Jerusalem, 2001).

Hapstein, Israel of Kozienice, *Avodat Yisrael* (Jerusalem, 1955-1956).

Hayyim Aryeh Leib of Jedwabne, *Sha'ar Bat Rabbim* (Warsaw, 1890-1902, and Piotrkow, 1920).

Hayyim ben Bezalel of Prague, *Be'er Mayim Hayyim* (London, 1964-1969).

bibliography

Ḥayyim of Tchernowitz, *Be'er Mayim Ḥayyim* (Warsaw, 1910).

Heilprin, Jehiel ben Solomon, *Seder ha-Dorot* (Bene Berak, 2003).

Heller, Yom Tov Lipmann, *Tosefot Yom Tov*, printed in the Romm ed. of the Mishnah.

Hellin, Jacob Moses, *Yedei Moshe*, printed in the Wagshal ed. of *Midrash Rabbah*.

Hezekiah ben Manoah, *Ḥizzekuni* (Vilna, 1880).

Hirsch, Samson Raphael, *Hamishah Homshei Torah im Perush Shimshon ben Refa'el Hirsh* (Jerusalem, 2001).

Horowitz, Eliezer of Tarnogrod, *No'am Megadim* (Mukachevo, 1905).

Horowitz, Isaiah, *Shenei Luḥot ha-Berit* (Warsaw, 1863).

Horowitz, Jacob Isaac ha-Levi, *Divrei Emet* (Mukachevo, 1913).

Horowitz, Meir of Dzieckowitz, *Imrei No'am* (Jaroslaw, 1907).

Horowitz, Phinehas Zalman, *Ahavat Torah* (Podgorze, 1905).

Horowitz, Samuel Shmelke of Nikolsburg, *Divrei Shemu'el* (Jerusalem, 1974).

Horowitz, Shabbetai Sheftel ben Akiva, *Shefa Tal* (Jerusalem, 2007).

Ibn Ezra, Abraham, *Commentary on the Pentateuch*, printed in std. eds. of *Mikra'ot Gedolot*.

Isaac ben Judah ha-Levi, *Pane'aḥ Raza* (Warsaw, 1932).

Isaac ben Mordecai of Neskhiz, *Toledot Yitzḥak* (Warsaw, 1868).

Isaac Meir Alter of Gur, *Ḥiddushei ha-Rim al ha-Torah*, compiled by J.L. Levin (Jerusalem, 1992).

Issachar Berman ben Naphtali ha-Kohen, *Mattenot Kehunnah*, commentary to *Midrash Rabbah*, printed in std. eds.

Isserlein, Israel ben Pethahiah, *Bi'urei Maharai* (Marghita, 1937).

Isserles, Moses ben Israel, *Torat ha-Olah* (Lvov, 1858).

Israel ben Tzevi ha-Kohen, *Tzevi Yisra'el* (Vilna, 1897).

Jacob ben Asher, *Arba'ah Turim* (Warsaw, 1861-1868).

——*Ba'al ha-Turim*, printed in std. eds. of *Mikra'ot Gedolot*.

——*Perush ha-Tur [ha-Arokh] al ha-Torah* (Warsaw, 1881).

Jacob Isaac ha-Hozeh of Lublin, *Divrei Emet* (Lvov, 1864).

——*Zikaron Zot* (Mukachevo, 1942).

——*Zot Zikaron* (Warsaw, 1883).

Jacob Joseph of Polonnoye, *Ben Porat Yosef* (Piotrokow, 1884).

——*Toledot Ya'akov Yosef* (Medzibezh, 1817).

Jaffe, Mordecai b. Abraham, *Levush ha-Orah* (New York, 1965).

Jehiel Mikhel of Zloczow, *Torat ha-Maggid mi-Zlatchuv*, compiled by E.E. Horowitz (Jerusalem, 1999).

Joseph Grunwald of Puppa, *Va-Yehi Yosef al ha-Torah* (New York, 2005).

Judah Aryeh Leib Alter of Gur, *Sefat Emet* (Piotrkow, 1905-1908).

Judah ben Eliezer, *Riva*, printed in *Rabbotenu Ba'alei ha-Tosefot al Ḥamishah Homshei Torah* (New York, 1944).

Judah Halevi, *Sefer ha-Kuzari* (Vilna, 1905).

Judah Loew ben Bezalel of Prague, *Gur Aryeh* (Israel, 1980).

——*Sefer Perushei Maharal mi-Prag le-Aggadot ha-Shas* (Jerusalem, 1958-1960).

——*Tiferet Yisrael*, ed. Pardes (Tel Aviv, 1985).

Justman, Phinehas Menahem Eleazar, *Siftei Tzaddik* (Jerusalem, 1956).

Kagan, Israel Meir, *Ḥafetz Ḥayyim al ha-Torah*, compiled by S. Greiniman (Bene Berak, 1957).

Kamelhar, Gershon ben Isaac, *Mevasser Tov* (Podgorze, 1900).

Kanievsky, Jacob Israel, *Birkhat Peretz* (Bene Berak, 1990).

Kattina, Jacob, *Korban he-Ani* (Lvov, 1882).

Kayyara, Simeon, *Halakhot Gedolot*, ed. Makhon Yerushalayim (Jerusalem, 1992).

Kimḥi, David, *Perush Radak al ha-Torah* (Bratislava, 1842).

Kleinbaum, Jacob Moses, *Yashresh Ya'akov*, commentary to *Shema Shelomo* (Jerusalem, 1885).

Kleinman, Moses Ḥayyim, *Or Yesharim* (Jerusalem, 1958).

Kluger, Solomon, *Imrei Shefer* (Lvov, 1895).

Kook, Abraham Isaac, *Orot ha-Kodesh* (Jerusalem, 1938-1950).

——*Seder Tefillah Im Perush Olat Re'iyah* (Jerusalem, 1939-1949).

Koppel, Menahem Mendel ben Jacob of Kosov, *Ahavat Shalom* (Chernovtsy, 1883).

Kranz, Jacob of Dubno, *Mishlei Ya'akov*, compiled by Moses Nussbaum (Przemysl, 1875).

——*Ohel Ya'akov* (Warsaw, 1903).

Krengel, Menahem Mendel, *Devash ve-Ḥalav* (Cracow, 1911).

Landau, Ezekiel of Prague, *Ahavat Tziyyon* (Warsaw, 1913).

——*Sefer Tziyyun le-Nefesh Ḥayyah*, or *Sefer Tzelaḥ* (Jerusalem, 1995).

Leiner, Mordecai Joseph of Izbica, *Mei ha-Shiloah*, compiled by G. Leiner (Jerusalem, 1956).

Levi ben Gershom, *Perush Ralbag al ha-Torah* (Venice, 1547).

——*To'aliyyot ha-Ralbag* (Lublin, 1814).

Levi Isaac of Berdichev, *Kedushat Levi* (Jerusalem, 1958).

Lewin, Aaron of Rzeszow, *Ha-Derash ve-ha-Iyyun* (Bilgoraj, 1928-1939).

Lichtstein, Abraham, *Kanfei Nesharim* (Vilna, 1913).

Lifschits, Jehiel Meir of Gostynin, *Mei ha-Yam* (Lodz, 1922).

Lits-Rosenbaum, Moses Aryeh Leib, *To'afot Re'em* (Jerusalem, 2004).

Loew, Eleazar ben Aryeh Leib, *Yavin Shemu'ah* (Cracow, 1904).

Lowenstamm, Saul, *Binyan Ari'el* (Lvov, 1885).

Lunietz, Gedaliah ben Isaac of, *Teshu'ot Ḥen* (Jerusalem, 1965).

Maimonides, see Moses ben Maimon.

Manasseh Ben Israel, *Nishmat Ḥayyim* (Jerusalem, 1995).

Margoloit, Moses ben Simeon, *Mareh ha-Panim*, commentary to Jerusalem Talmud, ed. Vilna.

——*Penei Moshe*, commentary to Jerusalem Talmud, ed. Vilna.

רשימת ספרים

Meir of Peremyshlyany, *Divrei Me'ir* (Bardejov, 1909).

Meir Simhah of Dvinsk, *Meshekh Ḥokhmah* (Jerusalem, 2002).

Meiri, Menahem ben Solomon, *Beit ha-Beḥirah* (Jerusalem, 1947-1977).

——*Perush Rabbenu Menahem Me'iri al ha-Torah* (London, 1957).

Meklenburg, Jacob Tzevi, *Ha-Ketav ve-ha-Kabbalah* (Nuremberg, 1924).

Menahem ben Moses ha-Bavli, *Ta'amei Mitzvot* (Przemysl, 1888).

Menahem Mendel of Vitebsk, *Peri ha-Aretz* (Zhitomir, 1868).

Mizraḥi, Elijah, *Sefer Eliyyah Mizraḥi* on the Pentateuch (Amsterdam, 1718).

Mordecai ben Ḥanokh Ḥayyim ha-Kohen, *Al ha-Torah* (Jerusalem, 1957).

Mordecai ha-Kohen, *Siftei Kohen [Shakh] al ha-Torah* (Warsaw, 1884).

Morgensztern, Menahem Mendel of Kotsk, *Emet mi-Kotzk Titzmaḥ*, compiled by M. Shenfeld (Bene Berak, 1961).

——*Emet ve-Emunah*, compiled by I.J. Arten (Jerusalem, 1940).

——*Ohel Torah*, compiled by E. Tzigelman (Lublin, 1909).

Moses ben Jacob of Coucy, *Sefer Mitzvot Gadol*, ed. Makhon Yerushalayim (Jerusalem, 2003).

Moses ben Maimon, *Commentary to the Mishneh*, ed. Kook (Jerusalem, 1963-1968).

——*Mishneh Torah*, ed. Frankel (Jerusalem–Bene Berak, 2001-2007).

——*Moreh Nevukhim*, ed. Kook (Jerusalem, 1977).

——*Responsa*, printed as *Iggerot u-Teshuvot*, ed. Levin-Epstein (Jerusalem, 1954).

——*Sefer ha-Mitzvot*, ed. Kook (1971).

Moses ben Naḥman, *Commentary on the Pentateuch*, printed in std. eds. of *Mikra'ot Gedolot*.

Moses Ḥayyim Ephraim of Sudylkow, *Degel Maḥaneh Efrayim* (Seini, 1942).

Moses Leib of Sasov, quoted by the anonymous Ḥasidic compiler of *Or Tzaddikim* (Kolomyya, 1886).

Muscato, Judah ben Joseph, *Kol Yehudah*, commentary to *Kuzari*, printed in ed. Vilna (1905).

Naḥman of Bratslav, *Likkutei Moharan* (Jerusalem, 1995).

Naḥmanides, *see* Moses ben Naḥman.

Naphtali Tzevi of Ropczyce, *Zera Kodesh* (Lvov, 1868).

Nathanson, Joseph Saul, *Divrei Sha'ul* (Lvov, 1875-1876).

Neuman, Simeon Bezalel, *Peninim Yekarim* (Warsaw, 1924).

Peninim Yekarim ha-Ḥadash (Cracow, 1925).

Ninio, Rahamim Shealtiel Jacob, *Ḥen ve-Khavod* (Jerusalem, 1884).

Ornstein, Jacob Meshullam of Lvov, *Yeshu'ot Ya'akov, Oraḥ Ḥayyim* (Zholkva, 1809-1811).

Padwa, Isaac Mordecai, *Ilana de-Ḥayyei* (Piotrkow, 1908).

Paquda, Bahya ben Joseph ibn, *Ḥovot ha-Levavot* (Jerusalem, 1984).

Pardo, David, *Maskil le-David* (Venice, 1761).

Patsanovski, Joseph, *Pardes Yosef* (Piotrkow, 1930-1939).

Polier, Moses of Kobrin, *Amarot Tehorot* (Warsaw, 1910); *see also* Kleinman, M.Ḥ.

Pollak, Moses ha-Levi, *Va-Yedabber Moshe* (Bratislava, 1894).

Poppers, Meir, *Sefer ha-Likkutim* (Jerusalem, 1997).

Prisco, Moses, *Yadav Shel Moshe*, quoted in *Yalkut Sinai* (Jerusalem, 1964).

Rabinowich, Solomon ha-Kohen of Radomsko, *Tiferet Shelomo al ha-Torah* (Piotrkow, 1890).

——*Tiferet Shelomo al ha-Zemanim ve-ha-Mo'adim* (Bedzin, 1910).

Rabinowitz, Zadok ha-Kohen of Lublin, *Divrei Soferim* (Bene Berak, 1956).

——*Peri Tzaddik* (Lublin, 1901-1934).

——*Tzidkat ha-Tzaddik* (Lublin, 1913).

Rakatz, Yoetz Kim Kadish, *Si'aḥ Sarfei Kodesh* (Piotrkow, 1923 / Warsaw, 1923-1931).

Rapa, Abraham Menahem of Porto, *Minḥah Belulah* (Bene Berak, 1989).

Rashi, *see* Solomon ben Isaac.

Ravitzki, Menahem Mendel, *Matzmi'aḥ Yeshu'ot* (Cracow, 1910).

Recanati, Menahem ben Benjamin, *Perush ha-Rekanati al ha-Torah* (Jerusalem, 2003).

Reischer, Jacob, *Iyyun Ya'akov* (Wilhermsdorf, 1729).

Reitbard, Isaac, *Beit Yitzḥak al ha-Torah* (Jerusalem, 1910).

——*Kehillat Yitzḥak* (Vilna, 1899).

Rosenfeld, Eliezer ben Ze'ev Wolf, *Ḥemdah Genuzah* (Podgorze, 1903).

Rozin, Joseph of Rogachov, *Tzafenat Pane'aḥ al ha-Torah* (New York, 1960-1965).

Rubin, Joseph David, *Atzei Levanon* (Lvov and New York, 1928-1967).

Rubenstein, Samuel Jacob, *She'erit Menaḥem* (Paris, 1954).

Rymanower, Menahem Mendel, *see* Kamelhar, Gershon.

——*Menaḥem Tziyyon*, compiled by Ezekiel Panet (Jerusalem, 2007).

——*Yalkut Menaḥem*, compiled by M. M. Weisbaum (Jerusalem, 2007).

Rymanower, Tzevi Hirsch, *see* Kamelhar, Gershon.

——*Be'erot ha-Mayim* (London, 1957).

Saadiah ben Joseph Gaon, *Sefer ha-Emunot ve-ha-De'ot* (Berlin, 1928).

Saba, Abraham ben Jacob, *Tzeror ha-Mor ha-Shalem* (Bene Berak, 1990).

Safrin, Isaac Judah Jehiel of Komarno, *Heikhal ha-Berakhah*, printed in the Lvov, 1864-1874, ed. of the Pentateuch.

bibliography

Samuel ben Meir, *Perush ha-Torah—Rashbam*, printed in std. eds. of *Mikra'ot Gedolot*.

Samuel of Sieniawa, *Ramatayim Tzofim* (Warsaw, 1908).

Schick, Moses b. Joseph, *Maharam Shik al ha-Torah* (Jerusalem, 1990).

——*Maharam Shik al Massekhet Avot* (Seini, 1929).

Schneersohn, Joseph Isaac of Lubavitch, *Iggerot Kodesh [Rayyatz]* (Brooklyn, 1982-1998).

——*Likkutei Dibburim* (Brooklyn, 2003).

——*Sefer ha-Ma'amarim* (Brooklyn, 1982-2007).

——*Sefer ha-Sihot* (Brooklyn, 1986-2004).

——*Sefer ha-Zikhronot* (Brooklyn, 1955).

Schneersohn, Levi Isaac of Yekaterinoslav, *Likkutei Levi Yitzhak* (Brooklyn, 2004).

——*Torat Levi Yitzhak* (Brooklyn, 2004).

Schneersohn, Menahem Mendel of Lubavitch (*Tzemah Tzedek*), *Derekh Mitzvotekha* (Brooklyn, 2002).

——Glosses to *Likkutei Torah* (Brooklyn, 2002).

——*Or ha-Torah* (Brooklyn, 1951-1983).

——*Sefer ha-Hakirah* (Brooklyn, 2003).

Schneersohn, Samuel of Lubavitch, *Likkutei Torah, Torat Shem'uel* (Kefar Habad, 1951-2006).

Schneersohn, Shalom Dov Baer of Lubavitch, *Be-Sha'ah she-Hikdimu [Hemshekh Ayin Bet]* (Brooklyn, 1977 / 2001-2004).

——*Kuntres ha-Tefillah* (Kefar Habad, 1993).

——*Kuntres u-Mayan* (Kefar Habad, 1993).

——*Sefer ha-Ma'amarim* (Brooklyn, 1984-2009).

Schneerson, Menahem Mendel, *Ha-Yom Yom* (Brooklyn, 2003).

——*Hitva'aduyyot* (Brooklyn, 1990-1994).

——*Iggerot Kodesh* (Brooklyn, 1980-2008).

——*Letters From The Rebbe* (Brooklyn, 1997-2005).

——*Likkutei Sihot* (Brooklyn, 1962-2001).

——*Sefer ha-Ma'amarim* (Brooklyn, 1982-2004).

——*Sefer ha-Ma'amarim Melukat* (Brooklyn, 1997-2002).

——*Sefer ha-Sihot* (Brooklyn, 2003).

——*Sihot Kodesh* (Brooklyn, 1985-1993).

——*Torat Menahem, Hitva'aduyyot*, Hebrew, annotated (Brooklyn, 1995-2010).

——*Torat Menahem, Sefer ha-Ma'amarim* (Brooklyn, 2001-2007).

——*Torat Menahem, Tiferet Levi Yitzhak*, commentary to *Likkutei Levi Yitzhak* on *Zohar* (Brooklyn, 1991-2003).

Schneuri, Dov Baer of Lubavitch, *Imrei Binah* (Brooklyn, 2009).

——*Ma'amarei Admor ha-Emtza'i* (Brooklyn, 1985-2005).

——*Ner Mitzvah ve-Torah Or* (Brooklyn, 2003).

——*Sha'arei Orah* (Brooklyn, 1986).

——*Sha'arei Teshuvah* (Brooklyn, 1984).

——*Torat Hayyim* (Brooklyn, 1974, 2003).

Sforno, Obadiah, *Seforno, Commentary on the Pentateuch*, printed in std. eds. of *Mikra'ot Gedolot*.

Shapira, Kalonymous Kalman, *Esh Kodesh* (Jerusalem, 1960).

Shapira, Meir of Lublin, *Imrei Da'at*, compiled by D. A. Mendelbaum (Bene Berak, 1998).

Shapira, Nathan Ashkenazi of Grodno, *Imrei Shefer* (Lublin, 1591-1597).

Shapiro, Phinehas of Korets, *Imrei Pinhas* (Bene Berak, 2003).

Shik, Abraham ben Aryeh Judah Leib, *Eshed ha-Nehalim*, commentary to *Midrash Rabbah* (Vilna, 1843-1845).

Shneur Zalman of Lyady, *Likkutei Torah* (Brooklyn, 2002).

——*Ma'amarei Admor ha-Zaken* (Brooklyn, 1958-2008).

——*Seder Tefillot mi-Kol ha-Shanah* (Brooklyn, 2002).

——*Shulhan Arukh [ha-Rav]* (Brooklyn, 2005-2006).

——*Tanya* (Kefar Habad, 1997).

——*Torah Or* (Brooklyn, 1990).

Simhah Bunem of Przysucha, *Hedvat Simhah*, compiled by J. Eybeschuetz (Warsaw, 1930).

——*Kol Mevasser*, compiled by J.M. Boem (Bene Berak, 1995).

——*Kol Simhah*, compiled by A. Volden (Piotrkow, 1903).

Sirkes, Joel, *Bayit Hadash*, commentary to *Arba'ah Turim* (Warsaw, 1861-1868).

Slonik, Jacob ben Benjamin Aaron, *Nahalat Ya'akov* (Jerusalem, 1993-1998).

Sofer, Abraham Samuel Benjamin, *Ketav Sofer* (Bratislava, 1883).

Sofer, Hayyim ben Mordecai Ephraim Fischel, *Divrei Sha'arei Hayyim* (Mukachevo, 1887).

Sofer, Moses, *Hatam Sofer al ha-Torah* (Jerusalem, 2007).

——*Torat Moshe* (Jerusalem, 2005).

——*Torat Moshe ha-Shalem* (Jerusalem, 2004).

Sofer, Simhah Bunem, *Sha'arei Simhah* (Vienna, 1923).

Solomon ben Isaac, *Commentary on the Pentateuch*, printed in std. eds. of *Mikra'ot Gedolot*.

Solomon ben Meir of Karlin, *Shema Shelomo*, compiled by J.M. Kleinbaum (Jerusalem, 1956).

Soloveitchik, Joseph B., *Mi-Peninei ha-Rav*, compiled by Hershel Schachter (Jerusalem, 2005).

——*The Lonely Man of Faith*, published by Doubleday (New York, 1992).

——*see* Besdin, Abraham.

Soloveichik, Joseph Baer of Volozhin, *Beit ha-Levi* (Jerusalem, 1985).

Sorotzkin, Zalman ben Ben-Zion, *Oznayim la-Torah* (Jerusalem, 1951-1960).

Spira, Nathan Nata ben Solomon, *Megallah Amukkot* (Fuerth, 1691).

——*Megallah Amukkot al ha-Torah* (Lublin, 1901).

רשימת ספרים

Tarab, Ezra ben Elijah, *Va-Yomer Ezra* (Jerusalem, 1914).

Taub, Ezekiel of Kazimierz, *Nehmad mi-Zahav* (Piotrkow, 1909).

Teitelbaum, Hananiah Yom Tov Lipa, *Kedushat Yom Tov* (Sighet, 1905).

Trunk, Isaac Judah, *Mikra Meforash* (Piotrkow, 1936).

Twersky, Menahem Nahum of Chernobyl, *Me'or Einayim* (Slavita, 1798).

Tzevi Elimelech of Dynow, *Benei Yissakhar* (New York, 1946).

——*Igra de-Kallah* (Przemysl, 1910).

Tzevi Hirsch ha-Kohen, *Likkutei Tzevi* (Tel Aviv, 1981).

Tzur, Isaac Leon ben Eliezer ibn, *Megillat Ester*, commentary to Maimonides' *Sefer ha-Mitzvot*, ed. Frankel (Jerusalem, 2002).

Uceda, Samuel ben Isaac, *Midrash Shemu'el al Massekhet Avot* (Bene Berak, 1989).

Valle, Moses David, *Shivtei Kah* (Jerusalem, 1993).

Vidal, Yom Tov of Tolosa, *Maggid Mishneh*, printed in std. eds. of *Code of Maimonides*.

Vidas, Elijah ben Moses de, *Reshit Hokhmah* (Mukachevo, 1942-1943).

Vital, Hayyim ben Joseph, *Etz ha-Da'at Tov* (Zloczow, 1871).

——*Etz Hayyim* (Jerusalem, 1910).

——*Likkutei Torah*, of Rabbi Isaac Luria (Tel Aviv, 1973).

——*Peri Etz Hayyim* (Jerusalem, 1987).

——*Sha'ar ha-Hakdamot* (Jerusalem, 1865).

——*Sefer ha-Gilgulim* (Vilna, 1886).

——*Sha'ar ha-Gilgulim* (Jerusalem, 1984).

——*Sha'ar ha-Kavvanot* (Salonika, 1952).

——*Sha'ar ha-Mitzvot* (Jerusalem, 1987).

——*Sha'ar ha-Pesukim* (Jerusalem, 1987).

——*Sha'ar Ma'amarei Rashbi u-Ma'amarei Razal* (Jerusalem, 1898).

——*Sha'ar Ru'ah ha-Kodesh* (Jerusalem, 1888).

——*Ta'amei ha-Mitzvot*, printed with *Likkutei Torah* (Tel Aviv, 1973).

Walden, Moses Menahem, *Ohel Yitzhak* (Piotrkow, 1914).

Weisser, Meir Loeb, *Ha-Torah ve-ha-Mitzvah* (Jerusalem, 1957).

Yosher, Moses Meir, *He-Hafetz Hayyim Hayyav u-Fo'alo* (Tel Aviv, 1958-1961).

Zacuto, Moses ben Mordecai, *Sefer Tikkun Shovavim* (Mantua, 1674).

Ze'evi, Abraham Israel ben Benjamin, *Or la-Yesharim* (Izmir, 1763).

Zemba, Menahem, *Hiddushei ha-Geramaz*, compiled by D. A. Mendelbaum (Bene Berak, 1980-1999).

Zevin, Solomon Joseph, *Sippurei Hasidim* (Jerusalem, 2002).

Zuenz, Aryeh Leib of Plotsk, *Melo ha-Omer al ha-Torah* (New York, 1971).

Zusya of Hanipoli, *Menorat ha-Zahav*, compiled by Nathan Neta ha-Kohen (Piotrkow, 1928).

לזכות

הרה"ח **מאיר** שיחי' הכהן **גוטניק**

זוגתו שינדל טעמא תחי'
ויוצאי חלציהם

הרה"ת שמואל מרדכי זאב הכהן וזוגתו פייגע דינה
וילדיהם שיינא אסתר שפרה, דוד ארי'ה הכהן חי' מושקא, וסימא ליבא

חנה ובעלה הרה"ת צבי אלימלך שפירא
וילדיהם חי' מושקא, מנחם מענדל, דוד ארי'ה, וליפמאן

מנוחה רחל ובעלה הרה"ת יוסף יצחק בארבער
וילדיהם איטא, חי' מושקא ובתיה

זעלדא ובעלה הרה"ת מיכאל אלעזר לערנער
וילדיהם חי' מושקא, שבתי ואברהם דוד אריה

מנחם מענדל הכהן וזוגתו רייזל
ובנם שמואל מרדכי זאב הכהן

סימא אסתר ובעלה הרה"ת מנחם מענדל הכהן כהן
שפרינצא לאה, יוסף יצחק הכהן, אברהם שלמה הכהן, חיה בתיה, ודוד
אריה הכהן שיחיו

לעילוי נשמות

החסיד ר' אברהם וזוגתו זעלדא פייגלין
הרה"ג הרה"ח ר' מרדכי זאב הכהן גוטניק
הרה"ג הרה"ח ר' אשר וזוגתו חי'ה בתי'ה אברמסאן
הרה"ג הרה"ח ר' דוד ארי'ה הכהן יארמוש
זכרונם לברכה
תהיינה נשמותיהם צרורות בצרור החיים

∞

ולזכות
הרה"ג הרה"ת ר' שלום דובער שיחי' הכהן גוטניק
ראב"ד דק"ק מעלבורן יע"א
וזוגתו מרת דבורה תחי'

∞

מרת שרה נחמה תחי' יארמוש

∞

לזכות

דוד שיחי׳ סלאגער

זוגתו לארא תחי׳

ויוצאי חלציהם

חנה ושרה מלכה

שיחיו